INTELLECTUAL PROPERTY LAW

BPP Professional Education
32-34 Colmore Circus
Birmingham B4 6BN
Phone: 0121 345 9843

INTELLECTUAL PROPERTY LAW

Fifth Edition

L. BENTLY, B. SHERMAN, D. GANGJEE,
AND
P. JOHNSON

OXFORD
UNIVERSITY PRESS

OXFORD

UNIVERSITY PRESS

Great Clarendon Street, Oxford, OX2 6DP,
United Kingdom

Oxford University Press is a department of the University of Oxford.
It furthers the University's objective of excellence in research, scholarship,
and education by publishing worldwide. Oxford is a registered trade mark of
Oxford University Press in the UK and in certain other countries

Second edition 2004
Third edition 2008
Fourth edition 2014

Impression: 1

Published in the United States of America by Oxford University Press
198 Madison Avenue, New York, NY 10016, United States of America

British Library Cataloguing in Publication Data

Data available

Library of Congress Control Number: 2018934545

ISBN 978-0-19-876995-8

Printed in Italy by L.E.G.O. S.p.A.

In memory of
Helen Joy Bently
(13 May 1929–8 December 2016)

ACKNOWLEDGEMENTS

In writing the fifth edition, we have accumulated a number of debts. In particular, we would like to thank Anna Kretowicz and Hamish MacDonald for their valuable research assistance. We are also indebted to Christina Angelopoulos, Carol Ballard, Graeme Dinwoodie, and Jonathan Griffiths for their generous assistance and input. We would like to thank the staff at Oxford University Press (particularly Tom Young) for their help and forbearance, and Fiona Tatham for her excellent copy-editing. We would like to express gratitude to Mark Hashemi, Gaenor Moore, Peter O'Byrne, Hamish Porter, and John Swarbrick, for either granting permission, or helping us locate or obtain permission, to use various images. Finally, we would like to pay tribute to Allison Fish, Johanna Gibson, Clair Milligan, and Nikita Sud for their patience, tolerance, and ongoing support.

NEW TO THIS EDITION

- The latest analysis of the implications of Brexit for intellectual property law
- New UK case law on TV formats, fair dealing for reporting current events, along with the Supreme Court decisions of *Actavis v. Eli Lilly*, *Starbucks*, and *Trunki*
- Takes account of latest CJEU case law, in particular on communication to the public (*GS Media, Filmspeler*, and *Pirate Bay*), especially with respect to intermediaries
- Includes treatment of new EU legislation on portability and implementation of the Marrakesh Treaty
- Incorporates important recent legislative changes including the European trade marks regime, the consolidated EU Trade Mark Regulation, the Trade Secrets Directive, and the Intellectual Property (Unjustified Threats) Act 2017
- An update on recent developments in relation to the proposed Unitary Patent and the Unified Patent Court
- Outlines proposed changes in EU Copyright Package, including proposed new defences, press publisher right, and responsibilities of online platforms
- A new chapter on the misuse of private information

CONTENTS

PART I   COPYRIGHT

PART II PATENTS

PART III LEGAL REGULATION OF DESIGNS

PART IV TRADE MARKS AND PASSING OFF

PART V CONFIDENTIAL INFORMATION

PART VI LITIGATION AND REMEDIES

DETAILED CONTENTS

PART I COPYRIGHT

PART II PATENTS

PART III LEGAL REGULATION OF DESIGNS

PART IV TRADE MARKS AND PASSING OFF

LIST OF ABBREVIATIONS

AALR	*Anglo-American Law Review*
AC	*Appeal Cases*
ACS	Artists Collecting Society
ACTA	Anti-Counterfeiting Trade Agreement
ADR	alternative dispute resolution
AG	Advocate-General
AIDA	*Association Internationale de Droit des Assurances*
AIPJ	*Australian Intellectual Property Journal*
AIPLA QJ	*American Intellectual Property Law Association Quarterly Journal*
AIPPI	*Association Internationale pour la Protection de la Propriété Intellectuelle* (International Association for the Protection of Intellectual Property)
AJL & Soc	*Australian Journal of Law & Society*
ALCS	Authors' Licensing and Collecting Society
ALJR	*Australian Law Journal Reports*
All ER	*All England Reports*
All ER (D)	*All England Reports (Digest)*
ALR	*Australian Law Reports*
AM	*Auteurs en Mediarecht (Copyright and Media Law)*
Am Econ Rev	*American Economic Review*
Am J Comp L	*American Journal of Comparative Law*
Am U Int'l L Rev	*American University International Law Review*
Annand and Norman (1994)	R. Annand and H. Norman, *Blackstone's Guide to the Trade Marks Act 1994* (London: Blackstone, 1994)
Annand and Norman (1998)	R. Annand and H. Norman, *Blackstone's Guide to the Community Trade Mark* (London: Blackstone, 1998)
Anthro Forum	*Anthropological Forum*
AOC	*appellation d'origine controlée* (protected designation of origin)
AP	Appointed Person
Aplin	T. F. Aplin, *Copyright Law in the Digital Society: The Challenges of Multimedia* (Oxford: Hart, 2005)
App Cas	*Appeal Cases*
APRA	Australasian Performing Right Association

Ariz L Rev	*Arizona Law Review*
ARR Regs	Artist's Resale Right Regulations 2006 (SI 2006/346)
ASA	Advertising Standards Authority
ASCAP	American Society of Composers, Authors and Publishers
BBC	British Broadcasting Corporation
BCAP Code	Committee on Advertising Practice (CAP), *UK Code of Broadcast Advertising* (2010)
BCC	British Copyright Council
BCLT	Berkeley Center for Law & Technology
Beav	*Beavan's Reports*
BECS	British Equity Collecting Society
Beier and Shricker	F. K. Beir and G. Shricker (eds), *From GATT to TRIPS* (Weinheim: IIC/VCH, 1996)
Bently and Sherman (2001)	L. Bently and B. Sherman, *Intellectual Property Law* (1st edn, Oxford: OUP, 2001)
Bently and Sherman (2004)	L. Bently and B. Sherman, *Intellectual Property Law* (2nd edn, Oxford: OUP, 2004)
Bently and Sherman (2008)	L. Bently and B. Sherman, *Intellectual Property Law* (3rd edn, Oxford: OUP, 2008)
Bently and Sherman (2014)	L. Bently and B. Sherman, *Intellectual Property Law* (4th edn, Oxford: OUP, 2014)
Bently, Davis, and Ginsburg	L. Bently, J. Davis, and J. Ginsburg (eds), *Trade Marks and Brands: An Interdisciplinary Critique* (Cambridge: CUP, 2008)
Berkeley J Emp & Lab L	*Berkeley Journal of Employment and Labor Law*
Berne	Berne Convention for the Protection of Literary and Artistic Works of 9 September 1886
BERR	Department for Business, Enterprise and Regulatory Reform
BGH	*Bundesgerichtshof* (German Federal Court of Justice)
Bing NC	*Bingham, New Cases*
BiOS	Biological Innovation for Open Society agreement
Bioscience L Rev	*Bioscience Law Review*
Biotech. Dir.	Directive 98/44/EC of 6 July 1998 on the legal protection of biotechnological inventions [1998] *OJ L* 213/13 (the 'Biotechnology Directive')
BIS	Department for Business, Innovation and Skills
BMA	British Medical Association
BMI	Broadcast Music, Inc.
BMR	Regulation (EU) No. 608/2013 of 12 June 2013 concerning customs enforcement of intellectual property rights and repealing Council Regulation (EC) 1383/2003 [2013] *OJ L* 181/15 (the 'Border Measures Regulation')
BoA	Board of Appeals (formerly OHIM; now EUIPO)

Boston U L Rev	*Boston University Law Review*
BPI	British Phonogram Industry
Brook L Rev	*Brooklyn Law Review*
Brown's Parl Cases	*Brown's Parliamentary Cases*
Brussels	Brussels Convention on Jurisdiction and Enforcement of Judgments in Civil and Commercial Matters 1968
Brussels Reg.	EC Regulation 44/2001 of 22 December 2000 on jurisdiction and the recognition and enforcement of judgments in civil and commercial matters [2001] *OJ L* 12/1 (the 'Brussels Regulation')
BTLJ	*Berkeley Technology Law Journal*
Burr	*Burrow's English King's Bench Reports*
CA	Court of Appeal
CA 1911	Copyright Act 1911
CA 1956	Copyright Act 1956
Calboli and Senftleben (2018)	I. Calboli and M. Senftleben (eds), *The Protection of Non-Traditional Marks: Critical Perspectives* (2018)
Cal L Rev	*California Law Review*
Can BR	*Canadian Bar Review*
Can J L Juris	*Canadian Journal of Law and Jurisprudence*
CANZ	Court of Appeal of New Zealand
CAP Code	Committee on Advertising Practice (CAP), *UK Code of Non-Broadcast Advertising, Sales Promotion and Direct Marketing* (12th edn, 2010)
Cardozo AELJ	*Cardozo Arts & Entertainment Law Journal*
Cardozo L Rev	*Cardozo Law Review*
Case W Res L Rev	*Case Western Reserve Law Review*
CBD	Convention on Biological Diversity (5 June 1992)
CB (NS)	*Common Bench Reports (New Series)*
CC BY	Creative Commons Attribution licence
CC BY-NC	Creative Commons Attribution-Non Commercial licence
CC BY-NC-ND	Creative Commons Attribution-Non Commercial-No Derivs licence
CC BY-ND	Creative Commons Attribution-NoDerivs licence
CC BY-SA	Creative Commons Attribution-Share Alike licence
CCPA	US Court of Customs and Patent Appeals
CDIR	Commission Regulation (EC) No. 2245/2002 of 21 October 2002 implementing Council Regulation (EC) No. 6/2002 on Community designs [2002] *OJ L* 341/28 (the 'Community Design Implementing Regulation')
CDPA 1988	Copyright, Designs and Patents Act 1988

CDR	Council Regulation (EC) No. 6/2002 of 12 December 2001 on Community designs [2002] *OJ L* 3/1 (5 January 2002) (the 'Community Design Regulation')
CFI	Court of First Instance (*now* General Court)
Ch	*Chancery*
Ch App	*Chancery Appeal*
Ch D	*Chancery Division*
Ch LR	*Chancery Law Reports*
Chi-Kent L Rev	*Chicago-Kent Law Review*
Chip Dir.	Council Directive 87/54/EEC of 16 December 1986 on the legal protection of semiconductor products [1986] *OJ L* 24/36 (the 'Chip Directive')
CIPA	Chartered Institute of Patent Attorneys
CIPA	*Chartered Institute of Patent Attorneys' Guide to the Patents Act 1977* (8th edn, London: Sweet & Maxwell, 2016)
CIPAJ	*Journal of the Chartered Institute of Patent Attorneys*
CITMA	Chartered Institute of Trade Mark Agents (formerly ITMA)
CJEU	Court of Justice of the European Union
CJJA 1982	Civil Jurisdiction and Judgments Act 1982
CLA	Copyright Licensing Agency
CLJ	*Cambridge Law Journal*
CLP	*Current Legal Problems*
CLR	*Commonwealth Law Reports*
CLSR	*Computer Law and Security Report*
CMA	Competition and Markets Authority
CMLR	*Commonwealth Market Law Reports*
Colum JL & Arts	*Columbia Journal of Law & the Arts*
Colum L Rev	*Columbia Law Review*
Computer-Implemented Inventions Dir.	European Commission, *Proposal for a Directive on the Patentability of Computer-implemented Inventions* (2002) COM (2002) 92 final
Copinger	K. Garnett, G. Davies, and G. Harbottle (eds), *Copinger and Skone James on Copyright* (17th edn, London: Sweet & Maxwell, 2016)
Copyright and Duration Regs	Copyright and Duration of Rights in Performances Regulations 2013 (SI 2013/1782)
Co Rep	*Coke's Reports*
Cornell L Rev	*Cornell Law Review*
Cowp	*Cowper's King's Bench Reports*
CPA 1998	Civil Procedure Act 1998
CPC	Community Patent Convention
CPR	*Canadian Patent Reporter*
CPR	Civil Procedure Rules 1998 (SI 1998/3132)

CPS	Crown Prosecution Service
CPVO	Community Plant Variety Office
CPVO BA	Community Plant Variety Office Board of Appeal
CPVR	Regulation (EC) No. 2100/94 of 27 July 1994 on Community plant varieties [1994] *OJ L* 227/1 (the 'Community Plant Varieties Regulation')
Cr App R	*Criminal Appeal Reports*
Crim LR	*Criminal Law Review*
CRM Dir.	Directive 2014/26/EU of 26 February 2014 on collective management of copyright and related rights and multi-territorial licensing of rights in musical works for online use in the internal market [2014] *OJ L* 84/72 (the 'Collective Rights Management Directive')
Cro Jac	*Croke Jacob Reports*
CSOH	Scottish Court of Session Outer House
CTLR	*Computer and Telecommunications Law Review*
CTM	Community trade mark
CTMIR	Regulation (EC) No. 2868/95 of 13 December 1995 implementing Council Regulation (EC) No. 40/94 on the Community trade mark [1995] *OJ L* 303/1 (the 'Community Trade Mark Implementing Regulation')
CTMR	Regulation (EC) No. 207/2009 of 26 February 2009 on the Community trade mark, replacing Council Regulation (EC) No. 40/94 of 20 December 1993 on the Community trade mark [2009] *OJ L* 78/1 (the 'Community Trade Mark Regulation')
DACS	Design and Artistic Copyright Society
DARDNI	Department of Agriculture and Rural Development for Northern Ireland
Database Dir.	Directive 96/9/EC of 11 March 1996 on the legal protection of databases [1996] *OJ L* 77/20 (the 'Database Directive')
Database Regs	Copyright and Rights in Database Regulations 1997 (SI 1997/3032)
Davison	M. Davison, *The Legal Protection of Databases* (Cambridge: CUP, 2003)
DCMS	Department for Culture, Media and Sport
Dean	R. Dean, *Law of Trade Secrets and Personal Secrets* (North Ryde, NSW: Law Books Co., 2002)
Defra	Department for Environment, Food and Rural Affairs
De G & Sm	*De Gex & Smale's Chancery Reports (England)*
DePaul L Rev	*DePaul Law Review*
Derclaye	E. Derclaye, *The Legal Protection of Databases: A Comparative Analysis* (Cheltenham: Edward Elgar, 2008)

Designs Dir.	Directive 98/71/EC of 13 October 1998 on the legal protection of designs [1998] *OJ L* 289/28 (the 'Designs Directive')
Dinwoodie and Janis (2008)	G. B. Dinwoodie and M. D. Janis (eds), *Trademark Law and Theory: A Handbook of Contemporary Research* (Cheltenham: Edward Elgar, 2008)
DMCA 1998	Digital Millennium Copyright Act of 1998 (US)
DNA	deoxyribonucleic acid
DOOR	Database of Origin Register
Dreyfuss and Ginsburg (2014)	R. C. Dreyfuss and J. C. Ginsburg (eds), *Intellectual Property at the Edge: The Contested Contours of IP* (Cambridge: CUP, 2014)
Dreyfuss and Pila (2018)	R. C. Dreyfuss and J. Pila (eds), *The Oxford Handbook of Intellectual Property Law* (Oxford: OUP, 2018)
DTI	Department of Trade and Industry (defunct; *see now* BERR *and* BIS)
Duke LJ	*Duke Law Journal*
Duration Regs	Duration of Copyright and Rights in Performances Regulations 1995 (SI 1995/3297)
DUS	distinct, uniform, and stable
EBA	Enlarged Board of Appeal
e-Commerce Dir.	Directive 2000/31/EC of 8 June 2000 on certain legal aspects of information society services, in particular electronic commerce in the Internal Market [2000] *OJ L* 178/1 (the 'e-Commerce Directive')
e-Commerce Regs	Electronic Commerce (EC Directive) Regulations 2002 (SI 2002/2013)
EC	Treaty establishing the European Community (or EC Treaty)
ECDR	*European Copyright and Design Reports*
ECHR	European Convention on Human Rights
ECJ	European Court of Justice
ECLR	*European Competition Law Review*
Econ Hist Rev	*Economic History Review*
ECR	*European Court Reports*
ECtHR	European Court of Human Rights
Edin L Rev	*Edinburgh Law Review*
EEA	European Economic Area
EEC	European Economic Community
EHRLR	*European Human Rights Law Review*
EHRR	*European Human Rights Reports*
EFTA	European Free Trade Association
EFTA Ct Rep	*EFTA Court Reports*
EGE	European Commission's European Group on Ethics in Science and New Technologies

EIPR	*European Intellectual Property Review*
ELR	*European Law Review*
EMLR	*Entertainment and Media Law Reports*
Emory LJ	*Emory Law Journal*
Enforcement Dir.	Directive 2004/48/EC of 29 April 2004 on the enforcement of intellectual property rights [2004] *OJ L* 195/16 (the 'Enforcement Directive')
Ent L Rev	*Entertainment Law Review*
EPC 1973	Convention on the Grant of European Patents, Munich, 5 October 1973
EPC 1973 Regs	Implementing Regulations to the Convention on the Grant of European Patents (introduced by [1999] *OJ EPO* 437)
EPC 2000	European Patent Convention 2000
EPC 2000 Regs	Implementing Regulations to the Convention on the Grant of European Patents (2006)
EPC Revision Act	Act Revising the Convention on the Grant of European Patents (EPC), (29 November 2000) MR/3/00 Rev. 1e
EPO	European Patent Office
EPOR	*European Patent Office Reports*
ERA	Educational Recording Agency
ERA 1986	Employment Rights Act 1986
ER	*English Reports*
ERR 2013	Enterprise and Regulatory Reform Act 2013
ETMR	*European Trade Mark Reports*
ETSI	European Telecommunication Standardization Institute
EU	European Union
EUConst	*European Constitutional Law Review*
EUIPO	European Union Intellectual Property Office
EUIPO *Examination Guidelines*	EUIPO, *Guidelines for Examination of European Union Trade Marks and Registered Community Designs at the EUIPO* (1 October 2017).
Eur J L Econ	*European Journal of Law and Economics*
EUTM	European Union Trade Mark (formerly Community Trade Mark or CTM)
EUTMDR	Commission Delegated Regulation (EU) 2018/625 of 5 March 2018 supplementing Regulation (EU) 2017/1001 of the European Parliament and of the Council on the European Union trade mark, and repealing Delegated Regulation (EU) 2017/1430 [2018] *OJ L* 104/1
EUTMIR	Commission Implementing Regulation (EU) 2018/626 of 5 March 2018 laying down detailed rules for implementing certain provisions of Regulation (EU) 2017/1001 of the European Parliament and of the Council on the European Union trade mark, and repealing Implementing Regulation (EU) 2017/1431 [2018] *OJ L* 104/37

EUTMR	Regulation (EU) 2017/1001 of the European Parliament and of the Council of 14 June 2017 on the European Union trade mark [2017] *OJ L* 154/1
EWCA Civ	England and Wales Court of Appeal (Civil Division) Decisions
EWHC	High Court of Justice of England and Wales
EWPCC	Patents County Court of England and Wales
FACT	Federation against Copyright Theft
FAST	Federation against Software Theft
Fawcett and Torremans	J. Fawcett and P. Torremans, *Intellectual Property and Private International Law* (2nd edn, Oxford: Clarendon Press, 2010)
FCA	Federal Court of Australia
FCAFC	Federal Court of Australia Full Court
FCTD	Federal Court Trial Division (Canada)
Fellner	C. Fellner, *Industrial Design Law* (London: Sweet & Maxwell, 1995)
FFII	Association for the Promotion of Free Information Infrastructure
Ficsor	M. Ficsor, *The Law of Copyright and the Internet* (Oxford: OUP, 2002)
FLA St U L Rev	*Florida State University Law Review*
Fordham L Rev	*Fordham Law Review*
FRAND	fair, reasonable and non-discriminatory
Franzosi	M. Franzosi (ed.), *European Design Protection: Commentary to Directive and Regulation Proposals* (The Hague: Kluwer, 1996)
FSR	*Fleet Street Reports*
Gangjee (2012)	D. Gangjee, *Relocating the Law of Geographical Indications* (Cambridge: CUP, 2012).
Gangjee (2016)	D. Gangjee (ed.), *Research Handbook on Intellectual Property and Geographical Indications* (Cheltenham: Edward Elgar, 2016).
GATT	General Agreement on Tariffs and Trade
GBoA	Grand Board of Appeals (formerly OHIM; now EUIPO)
GEMA	*Gesellschaft für musikalische Aufführungs- und mechanische Vervielfältigungsrechte* (Society for Musical Performing and Mechanical Reproduction Rights)
Geo Mason L Rev	*George Mason Law Review*
Geo Wash L Rev	*George Washington Law Review*
Georgetown LJ	*Georgetown Law Journal*
Gervais	D. Gervais, *The TRIPS Agreement* (4th edn, London: Sweet & Maxwell, 2012)

GI Reg. 1992	Regulation (EC) No. 2081/92 of 14 July 1992 on the protection of geographical indications and designations of origin for agricultural products and foodstuffs [1992] *OJ L* 208/1 (the '1992 GI Regulation')
GI Reg. 2006	Regulation (EC) No. 509/2006 of 20 March 2006 on agricultural products and foodstuffs as traditional specialities guaranteed [2006] *OJ L* 93/1 (the '2006 GI Regulation')
Godb R	*Godbolt's Reports*
Gowers Review	*Gowers Review of Intellectual Property* (London: HMSO, 2006)
GPL	General Public License
Gregory Committee	*Report of the Gregory Committee* (London: HMSO, Cmnd. 8662, 1952)
GRUR	*Gewerblicher Rechtsschutz und Urheberrecht*
Gurry (1984)	F. Gurry, *Breach of Confidence* (Oxford: Clarendon Press, 1984)
Gurry (2012)	T. Aplin, L. Bently, P. Johnson, and S. Malynicz, *Gurry on Breach of Confidence: The Protection of Confidential Information* (Oxford: OUP, 2012)
GURTs	genetic use restriction technologies
Hague Agreement	Geneva Act of the Hague Agreement Concerning the International Deposit of Industrial Designs 1999
H & Tw	*Hall and Twell's Chancery Reports*
Hansard	Hansard's Parliamentary Debates
Hargreaves Review	*Digital Opportunity: A Review of Intellectual Property and Growth. An Independent Report by Professor Ian Hargreaves* (London: UK IPO, 2011)
Harv JL & Pub Pol'y	*Harvard Journal of Law and Public Policy*
Harv JL & Tech	*Harvard Journal of Law and Technology*
Harv L Rev	*Harvard Law Review*
HBV	hepatitis B virus
HCA	High Court of Australia
HCJ	High Court of Justiciary (Scotland)
HEFCE	Higher Education Funding Council for England
Henning-Bodewig (2013)	F. Henning-Bodewig (ed.), *International Handbook on Unfair Competition* (Munich/Oxford: Beck/Hart, 2013)
Hert LJ	*Hertfordshire Law Journal*
HKCFA	Hong Kong Court of Final Appeal
HL	House of Lords
HLC	*House of Lords Cases*
HMRC	HM Revenue & Customs

Hooper Report   R. Hooper and R. Lynch, *Copyright Works: Streamlining Copyright Licensing for the Digital Age—An Independent Report* (London: UK IPO, July 2012)

Hous L Rev   *Houston Law Review*

HPC   *Hayward's Patent Cases*

IAP   Internet access provider

ICANN   Internet Corporation for Assigned Names and Numbers

ICJ   International Court of Justice

ICR   *Industrial Court Reports*

IDA   international depository authority

IDEA   *Intellectual Property Law Review*

IEHC   *High Court of Ireland Law Reports*

IGR   Regulation (EC) No. 1383/2003 of 12 June 2013 concerning customs action against goods suspected of infringing certain intellectual property rights and the measures to be taken against goods found to have infringed such rights [2003] *OJ L* 181/15 (the 'Infringing Goods Regulation')

IIC   *International Review of Intellectual Property and Competition Law* (formerly the *International Review of Industrial Property and Copyright Law*)

IJSL   *International Journal for the Semiotics of Law*

ILJ   *Industrial Law Journal*

Indiana LJ   *Indiana Law Journal*

Info. Soc. Dir.   Directive 2001/29/EC of 22 May 2001 on the harmonization of certain aspects of copyright and related rights in the information society [2001] *OJ L* 167/10 (the 'Information Society Directive')

Info TLR   *Information Technology Law Reports*

Int J Comm   *International Journal of Communication*

Int J Comm L & Pol'y   *International Journal of Commercial Law & Policy*

Int J Sociol L   *International Journal of the Sociology of Law*

Iowa L Rev   *Iowa Law Review*

IP Act 2014   Intellectual Property Act 2014

IPC   International Patent Classification

IPD   *Intellectual Property Decisions*

IPEA   international preliminary examining authority

IPEC   Intellectual Property Enterprise Court

IPI   Intellectual Property Institute (formerly Common Law Institute of Intellectual Property)

IPJ   *Intellectual Property Journal*

IPO   UK Intellectual Property Office

IPQ   *Intellectual Property Quarterly*

IPR   *Intellectual Property Reports*

IPReg	Intellectual Property Regulation Board
IRLR	*Industrial Relations Law Reports*
ISA	international search authority
ISP	Internet service provider
ITMA	Institute of Trade Mark Attorneys
IViR	*Instituut voor Informatierecht* (Institute for Information Law, University of Amsterdam)
J Bus L	*Journal of Business Law*
JC	*Justiciary Cases (Scotland)*
J Copyright Soc'y USA	*Journal of the Copyright Society of the USA*
J Ec Hist	*Journal of Economic History*
JILT	*Journal of Information, Law and Technology*
JIPITEC	*Journal of Intellectual Property, Information Technology & E-Commerce Law*
JIPL	*Journal of Intellectual Property Law*
JIPLP	*Journal of Intellectual Property Law & Practice*
J L & Econ	*Journal of Law & Economics*
J Legal Hist	*Journal of Legal History*
J Liber Sts	*Journal of Libertarian Studies*
JLS	*Journal of Legal Studies*
J Media L	*Journal of Media Law*
JP	*Justice of the Peace Reports*
JPO	Japanese Patents Office
JPTOS	*Journal of the Patent and Trademark Office Society*
JRMA	*Journal of the Royal Musical Association*
JSPTL	*Journal of the Society for the Public Teachers of Law*
Jur (NS)	*Jurist (New Series)*
Jurimetrics J	*Jurimetrics Journal*
JWIP	*Journal of World Intellectual Property*
Kamina (2000)	P. Kamina, *Film Copyright in the European Union* (Cambridge: CUP, 2000)
Kamina (2016)	P. Kamina, *Film Copyright in the European Union* (Cambridge, CUP, 2016)
KB	*King's Bench*
Kerly	Kerly J. Mellor, D. Llewelyn, T. Moody-Stuart, D. Keeling, and I. Berkeley (eds), Kerly's Law of Trade Marks and Trade Names (16th edn, London: Sweet & Maxwell, 2017)
King's LJ	*King's Law Journal*
Know-How BER	Regulation (EEC) No. 556/89 of 30 November 1988 on the application of Article 85(3) of the Treaty to certain categories of know-how licensing [1988] *OJ L* 61/1 (the 'Know-How Block Exemption Regulation')

L & CP	*Law and Contemporary Problems*
La L Rev	*Louisiana Law Review*
Laddie et al.	M. Vitoria, A. Speck, L. Lane, et al., *Laddie, Prescott, and Vitoria: The Modern Law of Copyright* (4th edn, London: Butterworths, 2011)
LCLR	*Lewis and Clark Law Review*
LEAD	*Law, Environment and Development Journal*
LJ Ch	*Law Journal, Chancery*
LJ (NS) Ch	*Law Journal (New Series), Chancery*
Lloyds LR	*Lloyd's Law Reports*
LMCLQ	*Lloyd's Maritime and Commercial Law Quarterly*
Loyola LA L Rev	*Loyola of Los Angeles Law Review*
LQR	*Law Quarterly Review*
LR	*Law Reports*
LR Eq	*Law Reports (Equity)*
LTOS	*Law Times Reports (Old Series)*
LTR	*Law Times Reports*
Lugano	Lugano Convention of 16 September 1988 on jurisdiction and the enforcement of judgments in civil and commercial matters
Mac & G	*MacNaghten and Gordon's Reports*
MacG CC	*MacGillivray's Copyright Cases*
Macph	*Macpherson's Session Cases*
Madrid	Madrid Agreement Concerning the International Registration of Marks of 14 April 1891
Madrid Prot.	Protocol Relating to the Madrid Agreement, adopted at Madrid on 27 June 1989
MAFF	Ministry for Agriculture, Fisheries and Food (defunct; see now Defra)
Managing IP	*Managing Intellectual Property*
Manag Sci	*Management Science*
MCAD	Directive 2006/114/EC of 12 December 2006 concerning misleading and comparative advertising (repealing Directive 97/55/EC) [2006] *OJ L* 376/21 (the 'Misleading and Comparative Advertising Directive')
MCC	Monopoly and Mergers Commission
MCPS	Mechanical-Copyright Protection Society
Media & Arts L Rev	*Media & Arts Law Review*
Med L Int	*Medical Law International*
Med L Rev	*Medical Law Review*
Melb U L Rev	*Melbourne University Law Review*
Mich L Rev	*Michigan Law Review*
Minn L Rev	*University of Minnesota Law Review*

MLR	*Modern Law Review*
Monash U L Rev	*Monash University Law Review*
MoU	memorandum of understanding
Musker	D. Musker, *Community Design Law: Principles and Practice* (London: Sweet & Maxwell, 2002)
My & Cr	*Mylne & Craig's Chancery Reports*
NAF	National Arbitration Forum
NC L Rev	*North Carolina Law Review*
Neb L Rev	*Nebraska Law Review*
NIAB	National Institute of Agricultural Botany
NILQ	*Northern Ireland Legal Quarterly*
NIQB	Northern Ireland Queen's Bench
NLA	Newspaper Licensing Agency
Notre Dame L Rev	*Notre Dame Law Review*
Nw J Intl L & Bus	*Northwestern Journal of International Law and Business*
Nw J Tech & Intell Prop	*Northwestern Journal of Technology and Intellectual Property*
Nw U L Rev	*Northwestern University Law Review*
NYU JILP	*NYU Journal of International Law and Politics*
NYU L Rev	*New York University Law Review*
NZLR	*New Zealand Law Reports*
OECD	Organisation for Economic Co-operation and Development
OFT	Office of Fair Trading
OHIM	Office of Harmonization in the Internal Market
Ohio St LJ	*Ohio State Law Journal*
OJ C	*Official Journal of the European Union (C Series)*
OJ EPO	*Official Journal of the European Patent Office*
OJ L	*Official Journal of the European Union (L Series)*
OJLS	*Oxford Journal of Legal Studies*
OJ OHIM	*Official Journal of the Office of Harmonization in the Internal Market*
OJ Sp Ed	*Official Journal of the European Union (Special Edition)*
OWD	Directive 2012/28/EU of 25 October 2012 on certain permitted uses of orphan works [2012] *OJ L* 299/5 (the 'Orphan Works Directive')
PA 1949	Patents Act 1949
PA 1977	Patents Act 1977
PAC	Practice Amendment Circular
PACE 1984	Police and Criminal Evidence Act 1984
PAN	Practice Amendment Notice
Paris	Paris Convention for the Protection of Industrial Property of March 1883 (latest revision, Stockholm 1967, with 1979 amendments)

PA Rules	Patent Rules 2007 (SI 2007/3291)
Patents Regs 2000	Patents Regulations 2000 (SI 2000/2037)
Paterson	G. Paterson, The European Patent System: The Law and Practice of the EPC (2nd edn, London: Sweet & Maxwell, 2001)
PC	Privy Council
PCC	Patents County Court (now IPEC)
PCT	Patent Cooperation Treaty 1970
PCT Regs	Regulations under the Patent Cooperation Treaty (7 December 2006)
PDO	protected designation of origin
PGI	protected geographical indication
Philos Public Aff	*Philosophy & Public Affairs*
PLR	public lending right
PLS	Publishers Licensing Society
PLT	WIPO Patent Treaty Law 2000
PP	*Parliamentary Papers*
PPL	Phonographic Performance Ltd
PRCA	Public Relations Consultants Association
Protocol on Jurisdiction	Protocol on Jurisdiction and the Recognition of Decisions in respect to the Right to the Grant of a European Patent 1973
Protocol on Litigation	Protocol on the Settlement of Litigation Concerning the Infringement and Validity of Community Patents 1989
PRS	Performing Right Society
Pub L	*Public Law*
Pub L Rev	*Public Law Review*
PVA 1997	Plant Varieties Act 1997
PVR	plant variety right
QB	*Queens Bench*
QBD	*Queens Bench Division*
Qd R	*Queensland Reports*
QMJIP	*Queen Mary Journal of Intellectual Property*
R&DBER	Regulation (EC) No. 2659/2000 of 29 November 2000 on the application of Article 81(3) of the Treaty to categories of research and development agreements [2000] *OJ L* 304/3 (the 'R&D Block Exemption Regulation')
RAM	random-access memory
RCD	registered Community design
RCUK	Research Councils UK
RDA 1949	Registered Designs Act 1949
RDAT	Registered Designs Appeal Tribunal
RDR	Registered Design Rules

Recasting Copyright	IViR, *Recasting Copyright for the Knowledge Economy* (2006)
Reinbothe and von Lewinski (2002)	J. Reinbothe and S. von Lewinski, *The WIPO Copyright Treaties* (London: Butterworths, 2002)
Rel. Rights Dir.	Directive 2006/115/EC of 12 December 2006 on rental right and lending right and on certain rights related to copyright in the field of intellectual property (codified version) (replacing Council Directive 92/100/EEC of 19 November 1992 on rental and lending right and on certain rights related to copyright in the field of intellectual property) [2006] *OJ L* 376/28 (the 'Related Rights Directive')
Rel. Rights Regs	Copyright and Related Rights Regulations 1996 (SI 1996/2967)
Resale Rights Dir.	Directive 2001/83/EC of 27 September 2001 on the resale right for the benefit of the author of an original work of art [2001] *OJ L* 83/1 (the 'Resale Rights Directive')
Restitution L Rev	*Restitution Law Review*
Ricketson (1987)	S. Ricketson, The Berne Convention for the Protection of Literary and Artistic Works (London: Kluwer & QMW, 1987)
Ricketson (2015)	S. Ricketson, *The Paris Convention for the Protec tion of Industrial Property: A Commentary* (Oxford: OUP, 2015)
Ricketson and Ginsburg	S. Ricketson and J. C. Ginsburg, International Copyright and Neighbouring Rights: The Berne Convention and Beyond (2nd edn, Oxford: OUP, 2006)
RIDA	*Revue international du droit d'auteur*
Rome	International Convention for the Protection of Performers, Producers of Phonograms, and Broadcasting Organizations, Rome, 26 October 1961
Rome II	Regulation (EC) No. 864/2007 of 11 July 2007 on the law applicable to non-contractual obligations [2007] *OJ L* 199/40
Roughton, Johnson, and Cook	Roughton, Johnson, and Cook, *Modern Law Patents* (3rd edn, Lexisnexis, 2014).
RPC	*Report of Patent Cases*
Russ	Russell's English Chancery Reports
Rutgers Comput Technol LJ	*Rutgers Computer and Technology Law Journal*
S & LS	*Social & Legal Studies*
SABAM	Société d'Auteurs Belge—Belgische Auteurs Maatschappij (Society of Belgian Authors—Belgian Authors Society)
SABER	Regulation (EU) No. 1218/2010 of 14 December 2010 on the application of Article 101(3) of the Treaty on the Functioning of the European Union to certain categories of specialisation agreements [2010] *OJ L* 335/43 (the 'Specialization Agreements Block Exemption Regulation')
SACEM	Société des Auteurs, Compositeurs et Editeurs de musique (Society of Authors, Composers and Editors of Music)

Santa Clara High Tech LJ	*Santa Clara High Technology Law Journal*
SASA	Scottish Agricultural Science Agency
Satellite Dir.	Directive 93/83/EEC of 27 September 1993 on the coordination of certain rules concerning copyright and rights related to copyright applicable to satellite broadcasting and cable retransmission [1993] *OJ L* 248/15 (the 'Satellite Directive')
S Cal L Rev	*Southern California Law Review*
SC	Supreme Court
SCC	Supreme Court of Canada
SCMS	Serial Copy Management System
SCOTUS	Supreme Court of the United States
SCP	WIPO Standing Committee on the Law of Patents
SDLR	*San Diego Law Review*
SGCA	Singapore Court of Appeal
Sherman and Bently	B. Sherman and L. Bently, *The Making of Modern Intellectual Property Law* (Cambridge: CUP, 1999)
Sherman and Strowel	B. Sherman and A. Strowel (eds), *Of Authors and Origins: Essays on Copyright Law* (Oxford: Clarendon Press, 1994)
Sing JLS	*Singapore Journal of Legal Studies*
Singer and Stauder	R. Singer, *The European Patent Convention: A Commentary* (3rd edn, Cologne: Heymann, 2003)
SLT	*Scots Law Times*
SMEs	small and medium-sized enterprises
Soc Probs	*Social Problems*
Soc Res	*Social Research*
Software Dir.	Directive 2009/24/EC of 23 April 2009 on the legal protection of computer programs (codifying Council Directive 91/250/EEC of 14 May 1991) [2009] *OJ L* 111/16 (the 'Software Directive')
Software Regs	Copyright (Computer Programs) Regulations 1992 (SI 1992/3233)
SPC	supplementary protection certificate
SPC (MP) Reg.	Regulation (EEC) No. 1768/92 of 18 June 1992 concerning the creation of a supplementary protection certificate for medicinal products [1992] *OJ L* 182/1 ('SPC Medicinal Products Regulation')
SPC (PM) Reg.	Regulation (EC) No. 469/2009 of 6 May 2009 concerning the creation of a supplementary protection certificate for medicinal products [2009] *OJ L* 152/1 ('SPC Protection for Medicinal Products Regulation')
SPC (PPP) Reg.	Regulation (EC) No. 1610/96 of 23 July 1996 concerning the creation of a supplementary protection certificate for plant protection products [1986] *OJ L* 198/30 ('SPC Plant Protection Products Regulation')

SSS	Social Studies of Science
Stamatoudi	I. Stamatoudi, *Copyright and Multimedia Works* (Cambridge: CUP, 2002)
Stanford L Rev	*Stanford Law Review*
Stone (2016)	D. Stone, *European Union Design Law* (2nd edn, Oxford: OUP, 2016)
Stothers	C. Stothers, *Parallel Trade in Europe: Intellectual Property, Competition and Regulatory Law* (Oxford: Hart, 2007)
Strasbourg	Strasbourg Convention on the Unification of Certain Points of Substantive Law on Patents for Inventions 1963
Suthersanen	U. Suthersanen, *Design Law in Europe* (London: Sweet & Maxwell, 2000)
Sydney L Rev	*Sydney Law Review*
TBA	Technical Board of Appeal
TCE	traditional cultural expression
Technol & Cult	*Technology & Culture*
Term Dir.	Directive 2006/116/EC of 12 December 2006 on the term of protection of copyright and certain related rights (codified version) (repealing and replacing Council Directive 93/98/EEC of 29 October 1993 harmonizing the term of protection of copyright and certain related rights) [2006] *OJ L* 372/12 (the 'Term Directive')
TEU	Treaty establishing the European Union
Texas L Rev	*Texas Law Review*
TFEU	Treaty on the Functioning of the European Union
TIL	*Theoretical Inquiries in Law*
TLR	*Times Law Reports*
TMA 1875	Trade Marks Act 1875
TMA 1938	Trade Marks Act 1938
TMA 1994	Trade Marks Act 1994
TMD 1989	First Council Directive 89/104/EEC of 21 December 1988 to approximate the laws of the Member States relating to trade marks [1989] *OJ L* 40/1
TMD 2008	Directive No. 2008/95/EC of 22 October 2008 to approximate the laws of the member states relating to trade marks, replacing Council Directive 89/104 of 21 December 1988 to approximate the laws of member states relating to trade marks [2008] *OJ L* 299/25 (the 'Trade Marks Directive')
TMD 2015	Directive (EU) 2015/2436 of the European Parliament and of the Council of 16 December 2015 to approximate the laws of the Member States relating to trade marks [2015] *OJ L* 336/1
TMDN	Trade Mark and Design Network
TMR	Trade Mark Rules 2008 (SI 2008/1797)
TM Rep	*Trademark Reporter*

TPN	*Tribunal Practice Notice*
Translation Reg.	Regulation (EU) No. 1260/2012 of 17 December 2012 implementing enhanced cooperation in the area of the creation of unitary patent protection with regard to the applicable translation arrangements [2012] *OJ L* 361/89 (the 'Translation Regulation')
TRIPS	Agreement on Trade Related Aspects of Intellectual Property Rights 1994
Tritton (2007)	G. Tritton (ed.), *Intellectual Property in Europe* (3rd edn, London: Sweet & Maxwell, 2007)
Tritton (2016)	G. Tritton (ed.), *Intellectual Property in Europe* (4th edn, London: Sweet & Maxwell, 2016)
TSG	traditional speciality guaranteed
TTBER 2004	Regulation (EC) No. 772/2004 of 27 April 2004 on the application of Article 81(3) of the Treaty to categories of technology transfer agreements [2004] *OJ L* 123/11 (the '2004 Technology Transfer Block Exemption Regulation')
TTBER 2014	Regulation No. 316/2014 of 21 March 2014 on the application of Article 101(3) of the Treaty on the Functioning of the European Union to categories of technology transfer agreements [2014] *OJ L* 93/17 (the '2014 Technology Transfer Block Exemption Regulation')
TTR	Regulation (EC) No. 240/96 of 31 January 1996 on the application of Article 85(3) of the Treaty to certain categories of technology transfer agreements [1996] *OJ L* 31/2 (the 'Technology Transfer Regulation')
Tul L Rev	*Tulane Law Review*
U Balt IPJ	*University of Baltimore Intellectual Property Journal*
U Balt L Rev	*University of Baltimore Law Review*
U Cal Davis L Rev	*University of California Davis Law Review*
U Chi L Rev	*University of Chicago Law Review*
UCLA L Rev	*UCLA Law Review*
UDR	unregistered design right
UDRP	Uniform Domain Name Dispute Resolution Policy
UK	United Kingdom
UKSC	UK Supreme Court Decisions
Unitary Patent Reg.	Regulation (EU) No. 1257/2012 of 17 December 2012 implementing enhanced cooperation in the area of the creation of unitary patent protection [2012] *OJ L* 361/1 (the 'Unitary Patent Regulation')
UNSWLJ	*University of New South Wales Law Journal*
UPC	Unified Patent Court
UPC Agreement	Agreement on a Unified Patent Court [2013] OJ C 175/1 (20 June 2013)

U Penn J Int L	*University of Pennsylvania Journal of International Law*
UPOV	International Convention for the Protection of New Varieties of Plants of 2 December 1961 (latest revision 19 March 1991)
USC	US Code
USPTO	US Patent and Trademark Office
UTLJ	*University of Toronto Law Journal*
UWA L Rev	*University of Western Australia Law Review*
Vand L Rev	*Vanderbilt Law Review*
VLR	*Virginia Law Review*
VPL	Video Performance Ltd
VR	*Victorian Reports*
VRR	Regulation (EC) No. 2790/99 of 22 December 1999 on the application of Article 81(3) of the Treaty of categories of vertical agreements and concerted practices [1999] *OJ L* 336/21 (the 'Vertical Restraints Regulation')
VRR Guidelines	European Commission, Guidelines on Vertical Restraints [2010] *OJ C* 130/1 (19 May 2010)
Wadlow (1998)	C. Wadlow, *Enforcement of Intellectual Property in European and International Law* (London: Sweet & Maxwell, 1998)
Wadlow (2004)	C. Wadlow, *The Law of Passing off* (3rd edn, London: Sweet & Maxwell, 2004)
Wadlow (2011)	C. Wadlow, *The Law of Passing off* (4th edn, London: Sweet & Maxwell, 2011)
Wadlow (2016)	C. Wadlow, *The Law of Passing off* (5th edn, London: Sweet & Maxwell, 2016)
Walter and von Lewinski	M. Walter and S. von Lewinski, *European Copyright Law* (Oxford: OUP, 2010)
Wash L Rev	*Washington Law Review*
WCT	WIPO Copyright Treaty adopted by the Diplomatic Conference on 20 December 1996
Whitford Committee	Whitford Committee, *Report of the Committee on Copyright and Designs Law* (Cmnd. 6732, London: HMSO, 1977)
WIPO	World Intellectual Property Organization
WIPOJ	*WIPO Journal*
WLR	*Weekly Law Reports*
WMLR	*William & Mary Law Review*
WPC	*Webster's Patent Cases*
WPPT	WIPO Performances and Phonograms Treaty adopted by the Diplomatic Conference on 20 December 1996
WR	*Weekly Reporter*
WTLR	*Wills and Trusts Law Report*
WTO	World Trade Organization

Yale JL & Human	*Yale Journal of Law & the Humanities*
Yale LJ	*Yale Law Journal*
YC & ML	*Yearbook of Copyright and Media Law*

LIST OF USEFUL WEBSITES

	http://www.
Advertising Standards Authority	**asa.org.uk**
Chartered Institute of Patent Agents	**cipa.org.uk**
Community Plant Variety Office	**cpvo.fr**
Competition and Markets Authority	**gov.uk/government/organisations/ competition-and-markets-authority**
Copyright Hub	**copyrighthub.org**
Copyright Licensing Agency	**cla.co.uk**
Court of Justice of the European Union	**curia.europa.eu**
CREATe	**create.ac.uk**
Educational Recording Agency Ltd	**era.org.uk**
European Commission	**ec.europa.eu**
European Free Trade Association	**efta.int**
European Patent Office	**epo.org**
European Union Intellectual Property Office	**euipo.europa.eu**
Her Majesty's Revenue and Customs	**hmrc.gov.uk**
Institute of Trade Mark Attorneys	**itma.org.uk**
Intellectual Property Office (UK)	**ipo.gov.uk**
IP Kat	**ipkitten.blogspot.co.uk/**
Kluwer Copyright Blog	**kluwercopyrightblog.com**
Office of Public Sector Information	**opsi.gov.uk**
Parliamentary Debates	**hansard.millbanksystems.com**
	parliament.uk/business/publications/ hansard/
Performing Right Society	**prsformusic.com**
Plant Varieties Office	**defra.gov.uk.planth/pvs**
Public Lending Right	**plr.uk.com**
Supreme Court (UK)	**supremecourt.uk**
UK Courts	**courtservice.gov.uk**
UK Government	**direct.gov.uk**
US Patent Office	**uspto.gov**
World Intellectual Property Organization	**wipo.org**
World Trade Organization	**wto.org**
1709 Blog	**the1709blog.blogspot.co.uk**

LIST OF FIGURES

LIST OF TABLES

TABLE OF CASES

TABLE OF UK LEGISLATION

TABLE OF EU LEGISLATION

TABLE OF FOREIGN STATUTES

TABLE OF INTERNATIONAL TREATIES

1

INTRODUCTION

1 INTRODUCTION

Intellectual property law creates exclusive rights in a wide and diverse range of things, from novels, computer programs, paintings, films, television broadcasts, and performances, through to dress designs, pharmaceuticals, and genetically modified animals and plants. Intellectual property law also creates rights in the various insignia that are applied to goods and services, from FUJITSU for computers, to 'I CAN'T BELIEVE IT'S SO GOOD FOR EVERYTHING' (formerly 'I CAN'T BELIEVE IT'S NOT BUTTER') for margarine. We are surrounded by and constantly interact with the subject matter of intellectual property law. For example, you are reading a copyright work bearing the Oxford University Press trade mark. You are probably sitting on a chair which might be (or have once been) protected by design right (of some sort) and marking the book with a pen the mechanism for which has, at some stage, been patented. Alternatively, you may be typing notes into a computer, which no doubt has parts (such as the mouse) that are protected by patents and design right (in the shape of the product, as well as the semiconductor chip topographies inside).

Perhaps not surprisingly, given the wide range of subject matter with which it is concerned, intellectual property law is not a single homogeneous body of law; rather, the term is usually used to describe a number of areas of law, typically including copyright law, patent law, and trade mark law, each of which has its own characteristics. The adjective 'intellectual' is regarded as descriptive of the character of some of the material that this area of law regulates—namely, the products of the human mind or 'intellect'. The designation 'property' is said to describe the form of regulation—that is, primarily the grant of individual exclusive rights that operate in a manner similar to private property rights over tangibles. Neither component is uncontroversial. Certainly, not everything that this field of the law protects can be described as 'intellectual'. Moreover, there are those who question whether, whatever the legislators may say, these rights can really be called 'property rights' as opposed to 'monopolies' or 'rights to exclude'. Others worry that, by referring to these rights as 'property', particular attitudes are engendered that lead to their expansion.[1]

---

[1] Y. Benkler, 'Free as the Air to Common Use: First Amendment Constraints on Enclosure of the Public Domain' (1999) 74 *NYU L Rev* 354; R. Burrell and A. Coleman, *Copyright Exceptions: The Digital Impact* (2005), 180–7, 200, 225–6, 239; M. Lemley, 'The Modern Lanham Act and the Death of Common Sense' (1999) 108 *Yale LJ* 1687, 1697; N. Netanel, 'Why Has Copyright Expanded? Analysis and Critique', in F. MacMillan (ed.), *New Directions in Copyright Law* (2008), 1, 11–15.

Although it is possible to trace usage of the term 'intellectual property' back for almost 150 years to refer to the general area of law that encompasses copyright, patents, designs, and trade marks,[2] it has been commonly used in this way for only the last 30 or 40 years.[3] Nevertheless, in that relatively brief period, it has become part of the basic legal vocabulary. Legal commentators write books about 'intellectual property';[4] students study courses on 'intellectual property'; publishers publish journals on 'intellectual property';[5] agencies (such as the United Kingdom's 'Intellectual Property Office', or UK IPO) and organizations gather under the banner of 'intellectual property'.[6] Perhaps more significantly, intergovernmental meetings agree treaties relating to 'intellectual property',[7] the European Parliament and Council adopts directives concerning intellectual property,[8] and national legislators utilize the term in drafting legislation.[9] This move has led to the transformation of 'intellectual property' from a category *of* laws to a category *in* law. Article 17 of the European Charter of Rights and Freedoms even declares that 'intellectual property shall be protected'.[10]

Although widely deployed, there is little agreement on the precise coverage of the term 'intellectual property'. Most definitions have the character of lists—sometimes exhaustive,[11] sometimes open-ended.[12] Nearly all definitions include 'copyright' and 'patents', and most include 'trade marks'. But matters become more difficult when the question becomes, for example, whether the protection granted over confidential information (including personal information) counts as 'intellectual property'.[13] Indeed, when asked to decide whether confidential information fell within the term 'intellectual property' as used in the Senior Courts Act 1981,[14] the Supreme Court in *Phillips v. Mulcaire* indicated that the term lacked 'potency'—that is, it intrinsically does not possess (for the moment at

---

[2] See Sherman and Bently, 95–100.

[3] A key factor in the widespread adoption of the term 'intellectual property' to refer to a broader range of rights has been the establishment of the World Intellectual Property Organization by the WIPO Convention (1967).

[4] In the United Kingdom, Bill Cornish wrote the first contemporary textbook, published in 1981.

[5] The *European Intellectual Property Review* was first published in October 1978.

[6] The Patent Office adopted the trading name 'Intellectual Property Office' in 2006 following the Gowers Review.

[7] Most significantly, the Treaty on Trade Related Aspects of Intellectual Property Rights (TRIPS), an annex to the World Trade Organization Agreement (1994).

[8] See Enforcement Dir., discussed in Chapter 49.

[9] See Intellectual Property Act 2014.

[10] Charter of Fundamental Rights of the European Union [2000] *OJ C* 364. C. Geiger, 'Intellectual Property Shall Be Protected: Art. 17(2) of the Charter of Fundamental Rights of the EU—A Mysterious Provision with an Unclear Scope' [2009] *EIPR* 113. See further, C. Geiger, 'Intellectual "property" after the Treaty of Lisbon: Towards a Different Approach in the New European Legal Order?' [2010] *EIPR* 255; S. Peers, T. Hervey, J. Kenner, and A. Ward (eds), *The EU Charter of Fundamental Rights: A Commentary* (2014).

[11] BMR, Art. 2.

[12] WIPO Convention (1967), Art. 2(viii); EC Statement 2005/295/EC on the Enforcement Directive 2004/48/EC.

[13] Other difficult cases include the non-assignable 'moral' rights given to authors to be named as such on their works (see Chapter 10, section 1, pp. 285–7) or the protection given to devices or technologies that provide access to data only on prescribed conditions (see Chapter 13, section 4, pp. 374–83), or those rights granted to certain producers to use geographically descriptive names of products associated with particular locations (e.g. 'Parma ham', 'parmesan cheese', and so on) (see Chapter 43).

[14] Senior Courts Act 1981, s. 72. The provision creates an exception to the rule against self-incrimination, such that a person is not excused from answering questions put in proceedings or complying with an order on the basis that doing so would tend to expose that person to proceedings for a related offence if proceedings are civil proceedings 'for infringement of rights pertaining to any intellectual property or passing off'. Under s. 72(5), 'intellectual property' is defined as 'any patent, trade mark, copyright, design right, registered design, technical or commercial information or other intellectual property'.

least) the power to define the boundaries of the field.[15] Instead, whenever the term 'intellectual property' appears as a legal concept, its meaning must be determined by reference to the specific legislative context.[16]

While there are a number of important differences between the various forms of intellectual property,[17] one factor that they share in common is that they establish property protection over intangible entities such as ideas, inventions, signs, and information. While there is a close relationship between intangible property and the tangible objects in which they are embodied, intellectual property rights are distinct and separate from property rights in tangible goods. For example, when a person posts a letter to someone, the personal property in the ink and parchment is transferred to the recipient. If the recipient is pleased with the letter, they can frame it and hang it on the wall; if they are unhappy with the letter, they can burn it; if it is a love letter, they might store it away, in which case it will pass under the recipient's will when they die. Despite the recipient having personal property rights in the letter as a physical object, the sender (as author) retains intellectual property rights in the letter. The author will be the first owner of copyright in the letter, which will enable them to stop the recipient (or anyone else) from copying the letter or from posting it on the Internet.

For many, the fact that intellectual property rights are separate from the physical objects in which they are embodied may be counterintuitive. For example, if someone owns a recipe book, why should they not be able to photograph a couple of recipes to email to a relative? Similarly, if someone owns an animal or plant, should they not be able to buy and sell seeds from the plant, or offspring of the animals? Or if someone purchases bottles of perfume in Singapore, should they not be able to sell them in the United Kingdom? One of the consequences of intellectual property rights being separate from property rights is that the legal answer to these questions might well be 'no'. As rights over intangibles, intellectual property rights limit what the owners of personal property are able to do with the things that they own.

While the law has long granted property rights in intangibles, the law did not accept 'intellectual property' as a distinct and form of property until late in the eighteenth century. In granting property status to intangibles, the question arose as to how and where the boundary lines of the intangible property were to be determined. That is, once it was accepted that the law should grant property rights over intangibles, the question arose: how was the object of the property to be identified and its limits defined? While in real and personal property law, questions of this nature are answered by reference to the boundary posts and physical markers of the objects in question, one of the defining features of intangible property is that these reference points do not exist. As a result, each area of intellectual property law has developed its own techniques to define the parameters of the intangible property. These include schemes of deposit and registration, techniques of representation (such as the patent specification and claims), statutory rules and legal concepts such as the requirement of sufficiency of disclosure (in patent law),[18] and the originality requirement (in copyright law).[19]

---

[15] *Phillips v. Mulcaire* [2012] *UKSC* 28; [2013] 1 *AC* 1. But cf. *Vestergaard Frandsens A/s v. Bestnet Europe Ltd* [2013] *UKSC* 31, [2013] 1 *WLR* 1556 [44] (Lord Neuberger) (referring to 'the protection of intellectual property, including trade secrets').

[16] L. Bently, 'What Is Intellectual Property?' (2012) 71 *CLJ* 501; L. Bently, 'Trade Secrets: Intellectual Property but not Property?', in R. Howe and J. Griffiths (eds), *Concepts of Property in Intellectual Property Law* (2013), ch. 3.

[17] See W. R. Cornish, *Intellectual Property: Omnipresent, Distracting, Irrelevant?* (2004), 2–5.

[18] Which effectively means that the property claimed must correspond to the invented subject matter: see Chapter 20.

[19] See Sherman and Bently, 25, 153–5, 185–93; O. Bracha, *Owning Ideas: The Intellectual Origins of American Intellectual Property, 1790-1909* (2016).

One fact that will become apparent as we look at the various forms of intellectual property law is that they share a similar image of what it means to 'create' (or produce), for example, a book, a design for a car, or a new type of pharmaceutical. More specifically, it is commonly assumed that it is an individual, rather than a god, a machine, a force of nature, or a muse, who creates ideas, information, and technical principles. It is also assumed that the act of creation occurs when an individual exercises their mental labour to manipulate the underlying raw material.

Another fact that will become clear as we progress through the book is that intellectual property law is highly politicized. On the one hand, there are groups who represent existing (or putative) right holders, which have tended to argue that the existing laws provide inadequate protection—that, for example, that copyright protection should be extended to give publishers' their own rights to control reuse of press publications, that the term of patent protection be increased, or that the rights of trade mark owners be extended to encompass the use of trade marks to generate advertising on the Internet, and so on. At the other extreme, there are a range of groups who oppose stronger intellectual property protection—whether they be representatives of the developing world, consumers and users of intellectual property (such as digital samplers, appropriation artists, users of peer-to-peer sharing systems, and librarians), defenders of free speech, classical liberal economic theorists, competition lawyers, post-modern theorists, ecologists, or religious groups.[20] While there is a tendency to caricature such debates about intellectual property as battles between 'good' and 'evil', there are many shades of opinion between these extremes that deploy a diversity of more nuanced arguments.

The remainder of this chapter provides an introduction to some topics that impinge upon all areas of intellectual property law. After looking at some of the justifications that have been given for the grant of intellectual property rights, we explain the key international and regional structures that are central to an understanding of British intellectual property law.

2 JUSTIFICATIONS FOR INTELLECTUAL PROPERTY

Legal and political philosophers have often debated the status and legitimacy of intellectual property.[21] In so doing, philosophers have typically asked 'why should we grant intellectual property rights?' For philosophers, it is important that (and how) this question is answered, since we have a choice as to whether we should grant such rights.[22] It is also important because the decision to grant property rights in intangibles impinges on traders, the press and media, and the public.[23] (Indeed, as the work by Danish art group

[20] M. Boldrin and D. Levine, *Against Intellectual Monopoly* (2005), available online at http://www.dklevine.com/general/intellectual/against.htm (describing 'intellectual property' as a 'cancer').
[21] For useful collections, see A. Moore (ed.), *Intellectual Property: Moral, Legal and International Dilemmas* (1997); A. Gosseries, A Marciano, and A. Strowel (eds), *Intellectual Property and Theories of Justice* (2008); A. Lever (ed.), *New Frontiers in the Philosophy of Intellectual Property* (2012).
[22] For the, perhaps surprising, view that these 'high level' arguments are less important than mid-level principles (such as proportionality, efficiency, dignity, and non-removal from the public domain), see R. P. Merges, *Justifying Intellectual Property* (2011).
[23] For emphasis on free speech, see P. Drahos, 'Decentring Communication: The Dark Side of Intellectual Property', in T. Campbell and W. Sidurski (eds), *Freedom of Communication* (1994); J. Waldron, 'From Authors to Copiers: Individual Rights and Social Values in Intellectual Property' (1993) 68 *Chi-Kent L Rev* 841. For emphasis on the relationship between intellectual properties, identity, and alterity, see R. Coombe, *The Cultural Life of Intellectual Properties: Authorship, Appropriation and the Law* (1998).

Superflex on the cover to this textbook suggests, 'copying' can be regarded as much a part of contemporary conceptions of being human as shopping.[24]) Moreover, because the conventional arguments that justify the grant of private property rights in land and tangible resources are often premised on the scarcity or limited availability of such resources, and the impossibility of sharing, it seems especially important to justify the grant of exclusive rights over resources—ideas and information—that are not scarce and can be replicated without any direct detriment to the original possessor of the intangible (who continues to be able to use the idea or information). As we will see, philosophers have not always found intellectual property rights to be justified,[25] and there are now many commentators who doubt that all intellectual property rights are justified in the form they currently take.[26]

The justifications that have been given for intellectual property tend to fall into one of two general categories. First, commentators often call upon ethical and moral arguments to justify intellectual property rights. For example, it is often said that copyright is justified because the law recognizes authors' natural or human rights over the products of their labour.[27] Similarly, trade mark protection is justified insofar as it prevents third parties from becoming unjustly enriched by 'reaping where they have not sown'.

Alternatively, commentators often rely upon instrumental justifications that focus on the fact that intellectual property induces or encourages desirable activities.[28] For example, the patent system is sometimes justified on the basis that it provides inventors with an incentive to invest in research and development of new products,[29] or an incentive to disclose valuable technical information to the public, which would otherwise have remained secret. Similarly, the trade mark system is justified because it encourages traders to

---

[24] The Superflex image is a riff on an earlier work by the feminist artist, Barbara Kruger, that featured the same photographic representation of a hand holding a card stating 'I shop, therefore I am'. On the latter, see online at https://www.moma.org/collection/works/64897 for Kruger's image.

[25] A. Plant, 'The Economics of Copyright' (1934) *Economica* 167; S. Breyer, 'The Uneasy Case for Copyright: A Study of Copyright in Books, Photocopies and Computer Programs' (1970) 84 *Harv L Rev* 281; R. Brown, 'Advertising and the Public Interest: The Legal Protection of Trade Symbols' (1948) 57 *Yale LJ* 1165 (on trade marks); N. Kinsella, 'Against Intellectual Property' (2002) 15 *J Liber Sts* 1; D. Boldrin and M. Levine, *Against Intellectual Monopoly* (2005). Different theories may work better for different intellectual property rights: L. Paine, 'Trade Secrets and the Justifications of Intellectual Property: A Comment on Hettinger' (1990) 19 *Philos Public Aff* 247.

[26] J. Silbey, *The Eureka Myth: Creators, Innovators and Everyday Intellectual Property* (2015) (an important empirical exploration that 'begins to dismantle the stunningly persistent and monolithic explanation of intellectual property protection in the United States: that IP is necessary to facilitate robust production and dissemination of art and science': p. 7).

[27] Universal Declaration of Human Rights, Art. 27(2); Charter of Fundamental Rights of the European Union (7 December 2000), Art. 17. For a critical assessment of such claims, see P. Drahos, 'Intellectual Property and Human Rights' [1999] *IPQ* 349. On the theoretical basis of these claims, see H. Breakey, *Intellectual Liberty: Natural Rights and Intellectual Liberty* (2012) (highlighting the natural rights constraints on intellectual property rights); J. Hughes, 'The Philosophy of Intellectual Property' (1988) 77 *Georgetown LJ* 287 (exploring application of Locke and Hegel); A. Moore, *Intellectual Property and Information Control: Philosophical Foundations and Contemporary Issues* (2001) (rejecting utilitarian argument and favouring a version of Lockean theory); W. Gordon, 'Property Right in Self Expression' (1993) 102 *Yale LJ* 1533. On desert, see L. Becker, 'Deserving to Own Intellectual Property' (1993) 68 *Chi-Kent L Rev* 609.

[28] For an overview, see E. Hettinger, 'Justifying Intellectual Property Rights' (1989) 18 *Philos Public Aff* 31; F. Machlup and E. Penrose, 'The Patent Controversy in the Nineteenth Century' (1950) *J Ec Hist* 1, 10ff; T. Palmer, 'Are Patents and Copyrights Morally Justified?' (1990) 13 *Harv JL & Pub Pol'y* 817.

[29] See, e.g., W. Landes and R. Posner, 'An Economic Analysis of Copyright Law' (1989) 18 *JLS* 325. See N. Elkin-Koren and E. M. Salzberger, *The Law and Economics of Intellectual Property in the Digital Age: The Limits of Analysis* (2013), ch. 3. For the view that incentive theories are no longer supportable, see E. E. Johnson, 'Intellectual Property and the Incentive Fallacy' (2011) 39 *FLA St U L Rev* 623.

manufacture and sell high-quality products. It also encourages them to provide information to the public about the attributes of those products.[30] Instrumental arguments are typically premised on the position that, without intellectual property protection, there would be under-production of intellectual products. This is because while such products might be costly to create, once made available to the public, they can often be readily copied. This means that (in the absence of rights giving exclusivity) a creator is likely to be undercut by competitors who have not incurred the costs of creation. The inability of the market to guarantee that an investor in research could recoup its investment is sometimes called 'market failure'.

A related, but distinct, economic theory argues that by transforming potentially valuable intangible artefacts into property rights, those artefacts are more likely to be exploited to their optimal extent.[31] Such a theory (in contrast with theories of intellectual property rights as incentives to create or disclose) is not concerned with how the intangibles came into existence and tends towards the protection of a broader range of subject matter, potentially in perpetuity. This 'neoliberal' economic theory would draw the limit of intellectual property protection at the point at which it begins to inhibit efficient uses (that is, the point at which the costs of transacting with a property holder start to prevent uses to which parties would agree were there no such costs).[32]

These justifications are examined in more detail in the introductory sections dealing with copyright, patents, and trade marks.[33]

3 INTERNATIONAL INFLUENCES

One of the primary characteristics of intellectual property rights is that they are national or territorial in nature—that is, they do not ordinarily operate outside the national territory in which they are granted.[34] The territorial nature of intellectual property rights has long been a problem to rights holders whose works, inventions, and brands are the subject of transnational trade. Throughout the nineteenth century, a number of countries that saw themselves as net exporters of intellectual property began to explore ways of protecting their authors, designers, inventors, and trade mark owners in other jurisdictions. Initially, this was done by way of bilateral treaties, whereby two nations agreed to allow nationals of the other country to claim the protection of their respective laws. Towards the end of the nineteenth century, a number of (largely European) countries entered into two multilateral arrangements: the Paris Convention for the Protection of Industrial Property of 1883; and the Berne Convention for the Protection of Literary and Artistic Works of 1886. While the detail of these treaties

---

[30] See, e.g., W. Landes and R. Posner, 'The Economics of Trademark Law' (1988) 78 *TM Rep* 267.

[31] N. Elkin-Koren and E. M. Salzberger, *The Law and Economics of Intellectual Property in the Digital Age: The Limits of Analysis* (2013), ch. 4.

[32] Classic texts include: W. Landes and R. Posner, *The Economic Structure of Intellectual Property* (2003); E. Kitch, 'The Nature and Function of the Patent System' (1977) 20 *J L & Econ* 265; W. Gordon, 'Fair Use as Market Failure: A Structural and Economic Analysis of the Betamax Case and Its Predecessors' (1982) 82 *Colum L Rev* 1600. For a general discussion, see W. Gordon and R. Watt (eds), *The Economics of Copyright: Developments in Research and Analysis* (2003).

[33] See Chapter 2, Chapter 14, and Part IV, respectively.

[34] On the ability of UK courts to decide issues of infringement of foreign intellectual property rights, see Chapter 48.

is left for later chapters, it is worth observing here that both treaties adopted as their central criterion for protection the principle of 'national treatment'. This provides that a member state of the Paris and Berne Union ('country A') must offer the same protection to the nationals of another member state (say, 'country B') as country A gives to its own nationals. Thus, the principle of national treatment is a rule of non-discrimination. The beauty of the principle of national treatment is that it allows countries the autonomy to develop and enforce their own laws,[35] while meeting the demands for international protection. Effectively, national treatment is a mechanism of international protection without harmonization.

While the principle of national treatment provides rights owners with some protection in other jurisdictions, it offers only a partial solution. One problem that national treatment fails to address is that, where country A requires registration as a prerequisite for protection, the right holder in country B must endure the time and cost of registration to protect its creations in country A. Since the end of the nineteenth century, one of the goals of international intellectual property law has been to reduce the inconvenience caused by registration. In the copyright field, this was achieved by requiring members of the Berne Union to grant copyright protection without the need for formalities (such as registration). In the field of trade marks, a mechanism was developed under which a national trade mark owner could make an 'international registration', which would take effect almost automatically in designated countries.[36] A similar procedure for international application for patents was not developed until 1970.[37]

The expansion of international arrangements for the protection of intellectual property continued through the twentieth century and into the twenty-first. Over this time, the Paris and Berne Conventions have been revised on a number of occasions, their membership has expanded (particularly as former colonies achieved independence), and a number of new treaties have been formulated. Most of these treaties have been developed and are supervised by the World Intellectual Property Organization (WIPO), which has its headquarters in Geneva.[38] It continues to be the main forum for the development of new intellectual property initiatives at an international level.

Early intellectual property treaties were largely established between countries with a shared interest in recognizing such rights (even if arrangements often implicated colonies that had quite different interests). For a long time, countries such as the United States, the Soviet Union, and the People's Republic of China remained outside the treaty arrangements, often believing that, as 'net consumers' of intellectual property, recognition of the rights of foreigners would work against their national economic interests. The persistent refusal of the United States to protect British copyright owners in the nineteenth century was a cause of great annoyance. While more acceptable arrangements were made in the twentieth century, the United States did not join the Berne Convention until 1 March 1989.

By the 1980s, the United States had realized that it was a net producer of intellectual property-based goods and, along with the European Economic Community and Japan, began to

---

[35] Although this is usual, it is not a necessary consequence of national treatment: see Chapter 48.

[36] The Madrid Agreement concerning the International Registration of Marks 1891. The United Kingdom did not adhere.

[37] The Patent Cooperation Treaty (PCT): see Chapter 14, section 4.6.1, pp. 416–17.

[38] WIPO, a specialized agency of the United Nations, was established by a treaty signed in Stockholm on 14 July 1967. See C. May, *WIPO: Resurgence and Development* (2007).

advocate for higher levels of intellectual property protection on a global basis. Frustrated by the difficulties encountered under the traditional treaty arrangements,[39] the developed countries began to employ tactics that were much more aggressive than had hitherto operated at WIPO.[40] More specifically, in the 1980s, the US government started to take advantage of its trading power to threaten trade sanctions against countries that did not offer sufficient protection to American intellectual property rights owners.[41] Frustrated by the experience of WIPO-controlled treaty negotiations, the United States also sought to bring intellectual property protection within the General Agreement on Tariffs and Trade (GATT) system.[42]

The GATT was formed after the Second World War with a view to stabilizing and liberalizing trade conditions on a worldwide basis. In 1986, a new round of negotiations began, which included 'Trade-Related Aspects of Intellectual Property Rights' (TRIPS) on the agenda.[43] The negotiations concluded in 1993[44] and became part of the World Trade Organization (WTO) Agreement signed in Marrakesh in April 1994. There are now 164 parties to the Agreement.[45]

The TRIPS Agreement is the first significant agreement to adopt the concept of 'intellectual property' to define its remit (and it has played a critical role in placing the concept of 'intellectual property' at the forefront of policymaking). TRIPS defines 'intellectual property' by reference to the rights specifically mentioned or implicitly included via the clauses that require members of the WTO to recognize the existing standards of protection within the Berne and Paris Conventions.[46] It demands substantive protection for 'neighbouring rights' to copyright,[47] trade marks,[48] geographical indications,[49] designs,[50] patents,[51] topographies of integrated circuits,[52] and undisclosed information.[53] Apart from orienting legal thinking around the concept of intellectual property, the most important practical difference between TRIPS and the existing treaties is in the detailed provisions on enforcement of intellectual property rights in Part III. Prior to

---

[39] The frustrations of the developed world can be traced back to 1967, with the Stockholm Protocol to the Berne Convention: H. Sacks, 'Crisis in International Copyright: The Protocol Regarding Developing Countries' (1969) *J Bus L* 26. This was compounded by the failure to revise the Paris Convention between 1980 and 1984: K. Beier, 'One Hundred Years of International Cooperation: The Role of the Paris Convention in the Past, Present and Future' (1994) 15 *IIC* 1; *Opinion 1/94* (1994) *ECR* I–5267, 5294. See also K. Beier and G. Schricker (eds), *GATT or WIPO?* (1996).

[40] See E. Uphoff, *Intellectual Property and US Relations with Indonesia, Malaysia, Singapore and Thailand* (1991).

[41] Most notoriously, under 'Special 301' of the Omnibus Trade and Competitiveness Act of 1988, *Pub L*, No. 100–418, 102 *Stat* 1176–9, the US Trade Representative conducts an annual audit, placing countries that fail to give adequate and effective protection on a 'watch list', followed by sanctions (the withdrawal of trade privileges). For annual reports and current watch lists, see http://www.ustr.gov. See M. Kennedy, *WTO Dispute Settlement and the TRIPs Agreement* (2016) 16–17.

[42] L. Helfer, 'Regime Shifting' (2004) 29 *Yale Journal of International Law* 29.

[43] See C. Wadlow, 'Including Trade in Counterfeit Goods: The Origins of TRIPS as a GATT Anticounterfeiting Code' [2007] *IPQ* 350.

[44] S. Sell, *Private Power, Public Law: The Globalization of Intellectual Property Rights* (2003); P. Drahos, 'Global Property Rights in Information: The Story of TRIPS at the GATT' (1995) 13 *Prometheus* 6.

[45] (As of May 2018). China became a party in December 2001.

[46] TRIPS, Arts 2(1), 9. For a conclusion that TRIPS covers trade names, although they are not specifically referred to, see *EC v. US*, WT/DS 176/AR. Parallel reasoning would suggest that the prohibition on unfair competition in Art. 10*bis* of Paris constitutes a TRIPS obligation.

[47] TRIPS, Art. 14.   [48] TRIPS, Arts 15–21.   [49] TRIPS, Arts 22–4.   [50] TRIPS, Arts 25–6.
[51] TRIPS, Arts 27–34.   [52] TRIPS, Arts 35–8.   [53] TRIPS, Art. 39.

TRIPS, matters of procedure, remedies, and criminal sanctions had largely been left to national law.[54]

TRIPS has had an important impact on the general development of intellectual property law since it came into force on 1 January 1995.[55] As the procedures of enforcement through the International Court of Justice (ICJ) are cumbersome, little could be done in instances in which a country ratified, but did not comply with, an intellectual property treaty. However, as a result of TRIPS being part of the WTO Agreement, if a country fails to bring its laws into line with TRIPS, another member may complain to the WTO and set in motion a so-called 'dispute resolution procedure'.[56] This involves initial consultations between the parties, followed by the establishment of a panel of three experts, which produces a report that the parties either accept or appeal. Where a successful complaint has been made against a nation, it is usually required that the relevant laws are amended so as to comply with the TRIPS Agreement,[57] although the possibility exists for the parties to the dispute to reach an alternative arrangement.[58] At the time of writing, the consultation procedures have been invoked more than 34 times (in 24 disputes), and—perhaps surprisingly—most of the disputes have arisen between developed countries,[59] rather than between developed and less-developed countries.[60] A number of actions have even been brought by developing countries against developed countries.[61] To date, there have been a limited number of panel reports,[62] with even fewer appeals.[63] Although such panel reports are not 'definitive interpretations', and their status very much depends on how subsequent panels and states respond,[64] an important body of jurisprudence has

---

[54] See F.-K. Beier and G. Schricker (eds), *GATT or WIPO?* (1996); D. Gervais, *The TRIPS Agreement: Drafting History and Analysis* (4th edn, 2012); C. Arup, *The New WTO Agreements: Globalizing Law through Services and Intellectual Property* (2002); J. Malbon and C. Lawson, *Interpreting the TRIPS Agreement: Is It Fair?* (2014); H. Ullrich et al., *TRIPS plus 20: From Trade Rules to Market Principles* (2016); H. Grosse Ruse-Khan, *The Protection of Intellectual Property in International Law* (2016).

[55] Developed countries were granted a transitional period of one year; developing countries, five years. Although TRIPS has had little direct impact on UK law, in general because the standards embodied in the Agreement reflect pre-existing European standards, it has been frequently referred to in cases interpreting UK (and European) legislation: see, e.g., *IBM/Computer program product* T-1173/97 [1999] *OJ EPO* 609 (referring to TRIPS, Art. 27); *S. v. Havering Borough Council* (20 November 2002), [11]; *Libertel Groep BV v. Benelux MerkenBureau*, Case C-104/01 [2004] *FSR* (4) 65 (ECJ); *Nova Productions v. Mazooma Games* [2007] *EWCA Civ* 219.

[56] TRIPS, Arts 63–4; Understanding on Rules and Procedures Governing the Settlement of Disputes.

[57] Procedures exist for determining a timescale, if necessary by way of arbitration.

[58] As occurred in *EC v. US*, WT/DS 160 (in which, following a Panel Report that the United States violated TRIPS, Art. 13, the EC accepted compensation in lieu of change in US law).

[59] See, e.g., *US v. Japan*, WT/DS 28; *EC v. Japan*, WT/DS 42; *US v. Portugal*, WT/DS 37; *US v. Ireland*, WT/DS 82; *US v. EC/Denmark*, WT/DS 83/1; *US v. Sweden*, WT/DS 86/1; *EC v. Canada*, WT/DS 114; *US v. EC/Greece*, WT/DS 124/1; *US v. EC/Greece*, WT/DS 125/1; *Canada v. EC*, WT/DS 153; *EC v. US*, WT/DS 160; *US v. EC*, WT/DS 174; *Australia v. EC*, WT/DS 290; *EC v. US*, WT/DS 176; *US v. Canada*, WT/DS 179.

[60] *US v. Pakistan*, WT/DS 36; *US v. India*, WT/DS 50; *EC v. India*, WT/DS 79; *US v. Argentina*, WT/DS 171; *US v. Argentina*, WT/DS 196; *US v. Brazil*, WT/DS 199; *Brazil v. US*, WT/DS 224.

[61] *Honduras v. Australia,* DS 435 (plain packaging of tobacco products); *Dominican Republic v. Australia,* DS 441 (plain packaging); *Cuba v. Australia,* DS 458; *Indonesia v. Australia,* DS467; *Brazil v. EU,* DS 409; *India v. EU,* DS 408 (seizure of goods in transit).

[62] See, e.g., *Brazil v. US*, WT/DS 224 (re US Patents Code); *Australia v. EC*, WT/DS 290; *US v. EC*, WT/DS 174 (geographical indications); *US v. India*, WT/DS 50; *EC v. India*, WT/DS 79/1; *EC v. Canada*, WT/DS 114; *US v. Canada*, WT/DS 170; *EC v. US*, WT/DS 160; *US v. China*, WT/DS362/R. The Panel Report in the four plain packaging cases was promised in the final quarter of 2017, but is still awaited.

[63] *US v. India*, WT/DS 50; *US v. Canada*, WT/DS 170; *EC v. US*, WT/DS 176.

[64] C. Correa, *Trade Related Aspects of Intellectual Property Rights: A Commentary on the TRIPS Agreement* (2007), 151 ('panel interpretations lack precedential value in the WTO system').

been developing. Although there are aspects of the process that might be thought to need improvement,[65] so far the enforcement machinery has been effective without any need to resort to trade sanctions.[66]

Although TRIPS is the single most important development in international intellectual property law of the last 30 years,[67] it does not appear to have permanently eclipsed the role of WIPO. Indeed, new intellectual property treaties formulated and agreed through WIPO include the 1996 WIPO Copyright Treaty;[68] and the 1996 WIPO Performances and Phonograms Treaty,[69] the Beijing Treaty on Audiovisual Performances, signed in 2012;[70] the Marrakesh Treaty for the Visually Impaired, signed in 2013;[71] and the revised Lisbon Treaty on Appellations of Origin (2015).[72] Other WIPO initiatives, particularly in relation to traditional knowledge and standardization of patent law, will continue to play a significant role in international intellectual property law (albeit now in tandem with the WTO).

Although the intellectual property instruments that have been developed at the international level have occasionally recognized the peculiar needs of the developing and least-developed countries (most notably in terms of transitional periods),[73] the globalization of intellectual property standards has largely been a process whereby the wish-lists of various developed-world lobby groups are inscribed into public international law.[74] One notable exception to this is found in the 1992 Convention on Biological Diversity (CBD), which recognizes the rights of the (indigenous) peoples who preserve biological resources to share in the benefits arising from the commercial exploitation thereof.[75] This has prompted further calls for greater protection for traditional intellectual resources of the developing world—notably, plant culture, medicinal products, and indigenous folklore.[76] Recent years have also witnessed growing resistance to the wholesale imposition of intellectual property standards on the developing world.[77] Most importantly, the Ministerial Declaration at the Doha Review of TRIPS in December 2001 acknowledged the primacy of the right to life and health over the protection of intellectual property

---

[65] One problem is the possibility of successive actions by different complainants over identical issues, as occurred in *US v. India*, WT/DS50, and *EC v. India*, WT/DS 79.

[66] On three occasions, members of the WTO have been permitted to retaliate for breaches of other aspects of the WTO Agreement by withholding privileges under TRIPS. See, e.g., *Antigua and Bermuda v. US*, WT/DS/285.

[67] For important appraisals, see G. Dinwoodie and R. Dreyfuss, *A Neo-Federalist Vision of TRIPS* (2012); A. Kur (ed.), *Intellectual Property Rights in a Fair World Trade System* (2011); H. Grosse Ruse-Khan, *The Protection of Intellectual Property in International Law* (2016) (the first comprehensive examination of intersections, overlaps, and conflicts with other areas of international law, including trade, investment, environmental, and human rights laws) and various essays in C. Geiger (ed.), *The Intellectual Property System in a Time of Change* (2016) 220–316.

[68] For analysis of the WCT in terms of shifts in language (to rhetoric of balance) and process, see G. Dinwoodie, 'The WIPO Copyright Treaty: A Transition to the Future of International Copyright Lawmaking?' (2007) 57 *Case W Res L Rev* 751.

[69] Chapter 2, section 6.5, pp. 48–9.   [70] Chapter 2, section 6.7, pp. 50–1.

[71] See Chapter 2, section 6.6, pp. 49–50; Chapter 9, section 12.3, pp. 261–2 (EU implementation).

[72] See Chapter 43, section 1.2.3, pp. 1188–9.

[73] TRIPS, Arts 65–7. On 11 June 2013, the TRIPS Council extended the transition period for least developed countries to 1 July 2021 (or whenever the country ceases to be least developed, if that occurs earlier).

[74] P. Gerhart, 'Why Lawmaking for Global Intellectual Property is Unbalanced' [2000] *EIPR* 309.

[75] Chapter 14, section 4.6.3, pp. 48–9.

[76] See V. Shiva, *Protecting Our Biological and Intellectual Heritage in the Age of Bio-piracy* (1996).

[77] See, e.g., V. Shiva, *Protect or Plunder? Understanding Intellectual Property Rights* (2001).

rights.[78] A third important exception is the so-called 'Development Agenda' at WIPO, established in 2007.[79]

While the acknowledgement of the different positions and interests of developing countries is a welcome development, a number of commentators have observed a parallel trend for the further 'ratcheting up' of standards through bilateral trade negotiations (particularly between the United States/European Union and developing-world countries).[80] One of the notable developments in recent years is the gradual shift away from multilateral treaties as the sole domain in which the aims of the standardization and harmonization of intellectual property are pursued.[81] The progressive geographical extension of higher standards for intellectual property rights through such trade arrangements raises the spectre of further norm-setting in the multilateral arena.[82]

These bilateral arrangements also include 'investment treaties,' under which countries agree to guarantee investments made by foreign investors, which are often stated to include 'intellectual property.'[83] Such regimes are often coupled with arbitration systems,[84] where such investments are alleged to have been appropriated or investors have not been granted so-called 'fair and equitable treatment.' In recent years, these have been used by international companies in an attempt to influence the substantive intellectual property norms of the 'host' state. Actions have proceeded against Canada alleging that judicial development of its patent law placed it in breach of NAFTA,[85] against Australia on the basis that its plain packaging for tobacco rules misappropriated investments made by Phillip Morris (Asia) Ltd,[86] and against the Republic of Panama on the basis that a trade mark licensee was denied benefits of its investment.[87] This is a new, startling, and fast-developing dimension of contemporary intellectual property.[88]

---

[78] WTO, *Declaration on the TRIPS Agreement and Public Health* (20 November 2001) WT/MIN(01)/DEC/2. The declaration came into force on 23 January 2017. See Chapter 14, Section 4.6.2, pp. 417–19.

[79] N. Netanel, *The Development Agenda: Global Intellectual Property and Developing Countries* (2009). See also Commission on Intellectual Property Rights, *Integrating Intellectual Property Rights and Development Policy* (2002); Royal Society, *Keeping Science Open: The Effects of Intellectual Property Policy on the Conduct of Science* (2003); C. May, 'Why IPRs are a Global Political Issue' [2003] *EIPR* 1.

[80] See, e.g., Commission, op. cit., 162–4. See, e.g., Ch. 17 of the US–Chile Trade Agreement, requiring implementation in Chile of standards well above those in TRIPS. An EU–Chile Agreement, while less ambitious, also contains TRIPS-plus obligations: see Council Decision of 18 November 2002, [2002] *OJ L* 352/1, esp. Art. 170.

[81] For a proposed set of principles, see H. Grosse Ruse-Khan, (2013) 44 *IIC* 873; [2014] *EIPR* 207.

[82] Despite the failure of the Anti-Counterfeiting Trade Agreement to be ratified, negotiations continued with the Trans Pacific Partnership (between a host of Pacific Rim countries), the Regional Comprehensive Economic Partnership (in the Asia-Pacific region), and the Transatlantic Trade and Investment Partnership (between the European Union and United States). However, the Trump Presidency has altered the agenda in unpredictable ways.

[83] R. Okediji, 'Is Intellectual Property Investment?' (2014) 35 *University of Pennsylvania Journal of International Law* 1121; R. Dreyfuss and S. Frankel, 'From Incentive to Commodity to Asset' (2015) *Michegan Journal of International Law* 557; P. Yu, 'The Investment-Related Aspects of Intellectual Property Rights' (2017) 66 *American University Law Review* 829.

[84] Often referred to as 'ISDS'—investor-state dispute settlement.

[85] *Eli Lilly & Co v. Government of Canada*, Case No UNCT/14/2, available online at https://www.italaw.com/sites/default/files/case-documents/italaw8546.pdf.

[86] *Phillip Morris Asia Ltd v. Commonwealth of Australia*, PCA Case No. 2012–12 (17 December 2015) available online at https://pcacases.com/web/sendAttach/1711.

[87] *Bridgestone Licensing Services, Inc. v. Republic of Panama*, ICSID No. ARB/16/34 (13 December 2017).

[88] H. Grosse Ruse-Khan, *The Protection of Intellectual Property in International Law* (2016), ch. 7 (on investment law), ch. 10 (on trade agreements); Special Issue on Intellectual Property and Investment Protection (2016) 19(1) *Journal of International Economic Law*.

There have also been moves towards subtler forms of harmonization,[89] particularly in the standards applied in the different intellectual property offices throughout the world.[90] As well as the standardization of examination practice (such as is being developed between the 'IP5', that is, the Chinese, Korean, US, European, and Japanese patent offices), the fact that the US Patent and Trademark Office (USPTO) has outsourced some of its patent examination work to patent offices in Australia and South Korea is likely to have a subtle, but nonetheless important, impact on patent standards.[91]

4 REGIONAL INFLUENCES

If an understanding of some of the basic aspects of international intellectual property is important for students of UK intellectual property law, familiarity with EU law is essential. This is because the majority of developments in UK intellectual property law over the last 30 years have had their origin in the European Union.[92] While the likely departure of the United Kingdom from the European Union in 2019 means that the influence of the Union will probably diminish, EU norm-setting will likely continue to have a dominating influence over British intellectual property law.[93]

Since the Lisbon Reform Treaty (which came into force on 1 December 2009),[94] the powers of the European Union are now embodied in a consolidated version of the Treaty establishing the European Union (TEU) and Treaty on the Functioning of the European Union (TFEU) (formerly the 'EC Treaty', or simply EC). In its early years, European intervention in British intellectual property law came largely through two avenues. First, the judicial interpretation of the Treaty of Rome produced various doctrines that limited the operation of national intellectual property laws in the European Union. In addition, the Commission also played a role in policing various competition law aspects of the Treaty that had an impact on intellectual property law. However, for the last 25 years or so, most of the important interventions have been legislative in nature.[95] In particular, there have been moves to centralize the administration of intellectual property rights and to harmonize national laws. As a result, it is not possible to describe British intellectual property law in any sensible way without constant reference to various European Council and Parliament directives and regulations, to the decisions of the Court of Justice and the

---

[89] Three 'soft law' instruments are worth mentioning: the Joint Recommendations of the Paris Union and WIPO on Use of Trade Marks on the Internet (2001), on Trademark Licenses (2000), and on Well-Known Trade Marks (1999).

[90] In relation to trade marks, the Trademark Law Treaty (1994) (in force from 1996) and the Singapore Treaty on the Law of Trade Marks (2006) (in force from 2009, and in the United Kingdom from 2012) are the most prescriptive.

[91] P. Drahos, *Global Governance of Knowledge: Patent Offices and Their Clients* (2010).

[92] See C. Geiger (ed.), *Constructing European Intellectual Property: Achievements and New Perspectives* (2012); A. Ohly and J. Pila (eds), *The Europeanisation of Intellectual Property Law* (2013); C. Seville, *EU Intellectual Property Law and Policy* (2nd edn, 2016); T. Cook, *EU Intellectual Property Law* (2010).

[93] R. Arnold, L. Bently, E. Derclaye, and G. Dinwoodie, 'IP Law after Brexit' (2017) 101 *Judicature* 65; M. Mimler, *The Effect of Brexit on Trademarks, Designs and other Europeanized areas of Intellectual Property in the United Kingdom* (Centre for International Governance Innovation; BICL Working Paper, 2017).

[94] [2007] *OJ C* 306, signed 13 December 2007, in force from 1 December 2009.

[95] The impetus to legislate flowed in large measure from the adoption in the Single European Act of 1986 of new legislative procedures (based on what is now Art. 114 TFEU), which required only a 'qualified majority' of votes in Council, rather than unanimity: TEU, Art. 16(3), (4) (defining 'qualified majority' from 1 November 2014).

General Court (interpreting the various directives and regulations),[96] and to the decisions of the various intellectual property-granting offices, such as the European Union Intellectual Property Office (EUIPO) and the Community Plant Variety Office (CPVO).[97]

4.1 FREE MOVEMENT OF GOODS AND THE INTERNAL MARKET

In the 1970s and 1980s, much of the influence of EU law on British intellectual property law was a consequence of the interpretation of Articles 34 and 36 TFEU.[98] These two provisions reflect the desire to establish an 'internal market'—that is, a single European market with no internal frontiers or national barriers to trade. To this end, Article 34 TFEU prohibits 'quantitative restrictions' on trade and provisions 'having equivalent effect'.[99] While the use of intellectual property rights to prevent the importing of goods from one EU country into another would be a 'quantitative restriction', Article 36 TFEU permits such restrictions where they are necessary to protect industrial and commercial property. This is conditional on the fact that such restrictions do not 'constitute a means of arbitrary discrimination or a disguised restriction on trade between member states'.[100]

While Articles 34 and 36 TFEU appear to be contradictory, the two provisions were reconciled by permitting the maintenance and use of different national intellectual property laws while simultaneously limiting the negative effects of the territorial nature of such rights through the so-called 'doctrine of exhaustion'.[101]

4.1.1 Exhaustion within the European Union

In a nutshell, the doctrine of exhaustion prohibits an intellectual property right owner from utilizing their rights to control the resale, import, or export of any goods that have been placed on the market in the European Union by or with their consent. For example, if A, who has acquired a patent in France and the United Kingdom over a particular machine, sells a machine in France, they cannot use their UK patent rights to prevent importing of the machine into the United Kingdom. This is based on the idea that the 'first sale' gives the intellectual property owner the reward that constitutes the 'specific subject matter'[102] of the right. It is irrelevant that the patentee expressly prohibited the

---

[96] The Court of Justice has jurisdiction to give preliminary rulings concerning the interpretation of the Treaty. Where any question arises before a court or tribunal of a member state, then it may refer the question to the Court under Art. 267 TFEU. If the court or tribunal is one against whose decision there is no judicial remedy under national law, that court or tribunal must refer the matter to the Court of Justice.

[97] The EUIPO was, until 23 March 2016, known as the Office of Harmonization in the Internal Market (OHIM). Although one high-profile judicial figure asked, in 2001, whether national intellectual property rights have become 'a moribund anachronism' (H. Laddie, 'National IPRS: A Moribund Anachronism in a Federal Europe?' [2001] *EIPR* 402, 407), it seems that British political sentiment means that UK rights are again to become a more central part of the IP landscape.

[98] Formerly Arts 28 and 30 EC, and, before that, Arts 30 and 36 of the Treaty of Rome.

[99] Article 56 TFEU (ex Art. 49 EC and Art. 59 of the Treaty) makes similar prohibition on restrictions on freedom to provide services.

[100] Note also Art. 345 (ex Art. 295 EC and Art. 222 of the Treaty).

[101] In this context, the national and territorial nature of the rights refers to the essential separateness of each right—e.g. the idea that a copyright owner in France and the United Kingdom has two separate French and UK copyrights. It was thought to follow from this that consent to distribution in France could in no way affect the exercise of the separate UK copyright. The doctrine of exhaustion does not change the distinctness of the two national rights (so, for example, each might be assigned separately to different persons); rather, it limits the scope of each national law where the rights are in common control.

[102] *Centrafarm BV v. Sterling Drug*, Case C-15/74 [1974] *ECR* 1147 (defining the specific subject matter of patents and trade marks).

purchaser from reselling the machine or exporting it. This is because it is the consent to first sale that is important.[103] Because the doctrine of exhaustion facilitates the 'parallel importation' of goods within the European Union, it operates to minimize price differentials for identical goods between countries in the European Union.[104]

The doctrine of exhaustion of rights applies only to the right to control distribution (resale, export, or import); it does not apply to the right to rent, perform, or show a (copyright) work in public where the 'specific subject matter' of the right allows the owner to control each and every use (for it is through charging for each use that the essential function of the right is achieved).[105] The case law of the Court of Justice has elaborated this general principle in a range of subsequent cases. Rather than rehearse the detailed reasoning, the resulting principles can be summarized as follows.

(i)   The principle of exhaustion applies to all types of intellectual property.[106]

(ii) Consent by the intellectual property right owner includes the consent of a person or persons legally or economically dependent on the proprietor (for example a licensee or subsidiary).[107]

(iii) Consent by the intellectual property right owner does *not* include the consent of a person who is an independent assignee of the right (or who happens to be the holder of a right that once had a 'common origin'). For example, the owner of copyright in countries A and B may assign the copyright in a particular work in country B. If the new owner of the right places works on the market in country B, the owner of copyright in country A (being independent) has not exhausted their rights in country A.[108] Although assignments of this nature will often be void as illegitimate agreements to divide up the market (and contrary to Article 101 TFEU),[109] where the assignments are valid, the exception to the principle of exhaustion leaves open the possibility that intellectual property rights might restrict the free movement of goods. This can be rectified only by harmonized regimes (such as the European Union trade mark), which forbid separate assignments of national rights.

(iv) National intellectual property rights may be used to prevent the further circulation of pirated, counterfeit, and other illicitly manufactured goods, which by definition have not been placed on the market in the European Union with the right holder's consent.

---

[103] *Dansk Supermarked A/S v. Imerco A/S*, Case C-58/80 [1981] *ECR* 181.

[104] *Deutsche Grammophon GmbH v. Metro GmbH*, Case C-78/70 [1971] *ECR* 487.

[105] *Warner Bros v. Christiansen*, Case C-158/86 [1988] *ECR* 2605 (rental); *Coditel SA v. Cine Vog Films SA (No. 1)*, Case C-62/79 [1980] *ECR* 881 (public performance). On the status of *Coditel*, see Chapter 12, section 3.4.1, pp. 340–3.

[106] See, e.g., *Deutsche Grammophon GmbH v. Metro GmbH*, Case C-78/70 [1971] *ECR* 487; *Music Vertrieb Membran GmbH and K-tel International v. GEMA*, Joined Cases C-55/80 and C-57/80 [1981] *ECR* 147; *EMI Electrola GmbH v. Patricia Im-und Export*, Case C-341/87 [1989] *ECR* 79.

[107] *Deutsche Grammophon GmbH v. Metro GmbH*, Case C-78/70 [1971] *ECR* 487 (subsidiary); *Keurkoop BV v. Nancy Kean Gifts BV*, Case C-144/81 [1982] *ECR* 2853.

[108] *IHT International Heiztechnik v. Ideal-Standard*, Case C-9/93 [1994] *ECR* I–2789. This reversed *Sirena*, Case C-40/70 [1971] *ECR* 3711, and *Hag I*, Case C-192/73 [1974] *ECR* 731.

[109] Whether the agreement is treated as market sharing will depend on the context, the commitments, the intention of the parties, and the consideration provided: see *Etablissements Consten SARL and Grundig-Verkaufs-GmbH v. EEC Commission*, Case C-58/64 [1966] *ECR* 299 (assignment void); cf. *IHT International Heiztechnik v. Ideal-Standard*, Case C-9/93 [1994] *ECR* I–2789 (assignment had been prompted by the assignor's financial difficulties); *GSK Services Unlimited v. Commission*, Case T–168/01 [2006] *ECR* II–2969.

(v)   Where intellectual property rights subsist in country A, but not in country B (where A and B are both in the European Union), and goods are legitimately placed on the market by parties unconnected with the right holder in country B, the right owner has not consented to the marketing of those goods and, as such, will not have exhausted their rights. The right holder can therefore prevent import into and distribution of the goods in country A.[110]

(vi) Where intellectual property rights subsist in country A, but not in country B (where A and B are both in the European Union), and goods are legitimately placed on the market by the right holder (or parties connected with the right holder) in country B, the right owner will have been taken to have consented to the marketing of those goods and so have exhausted their rights.[111]

(vii) Where intellectual property rights subsist in country A, but are subject to a compulsory licence (that is, any person may exploit the intellectual property right on payment of a fee), the rights are *not* exhausted when goods are manufactured under such a licence. Here, the intellectual property right owner will be able to use national laws to prevent imports into country B.[112]

(viii) Where goods have been marketed in the European Union by the intellectual property right holder (or with their consent), the right of the owner of the goods to resell might permit behaviour (such as advertising) that overrides other aspects of the proprietor's intellectual property rights.[113]

(ix) Where goods have been marketed in the European Union by the intellectual property right holder (or with their consent), but the goods have subsequently been altered, a series of specific rules have been developed that define when a resale is legitimate. These are considered later, in the context of trade marks.[114]

Although the doctrine of exhaustion of rights has reduced some of the disruption that national intellectual property laws pose to the internal market, it has not provided a complete solution. This is because the national intellectual property laws of the member states can vary significantly. Since the principle of exhaustion comes into effect when the right owner consents to goods being placed on the market, that consent will not exist where a third party makes and distributes goods in a country in which the right does not exist or has lapsed.[115] It is largely for this reason that the Commission set about to harmonize intellectual property laws in Europe.

4.1.2 Exhaustion and countries outside the European Union

Where goods have been marketed *outside* the European Union by the intellectual property right holder (or with their consent), the principle of exhaustion has no application.

---

[110] *EMI Electrola GmbH v. Patricia Im-und Export*, Case C-341/87 [1989] *ECR* 79. For the limits of this, see *Commission v. French Republic*, Case C-23/99 [2000] *ECR* I–7653.

[111] *Merck & Co. v. Stephar BV & Exler*, Case C-187/80 [1981] *ECR* 2063; *Merck & Co. v. Primecrown*, Joined Cases C-267/95 and C-268/95 [1996] *ECR* I–6285.

[112] *Pharmon v. Hoechst*, Case C-19/84 [1985] *ECR* 2281; *Music Vertrieb Membran GmbH and K-tel International v. GEMA*, Joined Cases C-55/80 and C-57/80 [1981] *ECR* 147.

[113] *Parfums Christian Dior SA v. Evora BV*, Case C-337/95 [1997] *ECR* I–6013; *Norwegian Government v. Astra Norge SA*, E1–98 [1999] 1 *CMLR* 860.

[114] See Chapter 41, section 8.3, pp. 1151–8. Note also the discussion in relation to copyright in Chapter 6, section 3.4, pp. 153–4 and patents in Chapter 22, section 2.2.1, pp. 640–3.

[115] *Bassett v. SACEM*, Case C-402/85 [1987] *ECR* 1747; *EMI Electrola GmbH v. Patricia Im-und Export*, Case C-341/87 [1989] *ECR* 79.

In the absence of harmonization, it is for member states to determine the effects of such marketing.[116] Where there is harmonization, it is on a EU-wide basis only, so the intellectual property right holder will normally be able to prevent importation into the Union.[117]

4.2 COMPETITION RULES

The second way in which European initiatives have exerted an influence over British intellectual property law is through the rules on competition contained in Articles 101 and 102 TFEU (formerly Articles 81 and 82 EC and, prior to that, Articles 85 and 86 of the Treaty). These provisions are designed to prevent anti-competitive agreements and practices, as well as abusive conduct by monopolies. These provisions impact on intellectual property law in a number of ways. Articles 101 and 102 EC are both couched as prohibitions and thus automatically render void arrangements between 'undertakings' that meet the specified criteria (or, in the case of Article 101, those that are not exempted by Article 101(3)).[118] In certain cases, they also provide the basis for an action for damages,[119] a ground for applying to the Commission for a compulsory licence to exploit an intellectual property right,[120] and a defence (a so-called 'Euro-defence') to an action for infringement of intellectual property rights.[121] Articles 101 and 102 EC are both enforced by the European Commission and, from May 2004, by national competition authorities (in the United Kingdom, the Competition and Markets Authority, and on appeal from a finding of infringement or rejecting a complaint, the Competition Appeal Tribunal).[122] If an undertaking is found to have been acting anti-competitively, the European Commission has the ability to impose serious fines, whether the behaviour was intentional or negligent.[123]

Article 101 prohibits 'all agreements between undertakings . . . and concerted practices which may affect trade between member states and which have as their object or effect

---

[116] *EMI Records v. CBS United Kingdom*, Case C-51/75 [1976] *ECR* 811 (stopping import of copyright works from the United States).

[117] See Chapter 6, section 3.5, pp. 154–5 (copyright) and Chapter 41, section 8.5, pp. 1151–6 (trade marks).

[118] TFEU, Art. 101.

[119] In the United Kingdom, either before a court, or the Competition Appeal Tribunal: Competition Act 1998, s. 47A (introduced by the Enterprise Act 2002, s. 18).

[120] *RTE and ITP v. EC Commission*, Joined Cases C-241/91 and C-242/91 [1995] *ECR* 808.

[121] *Sirena v. Eda*, Case 40/70, EU:C;1971:18 (nexus test); *Oracle v. M-Tech Data* [2012] *UKSC* 27, [2012] 1*WLR* 2026, [7] (Euro-defence should be scrutinized with some care) (Lord Sumption); *FAPL v. Luxton* [2016] *EWCA Civ* 1097, [2017] *ECDR* (7) 126 (rejecting defence). Whether, and if so, when abuse can be used as a defence is a controversial issue: see *Chiron Corp. v. Organon Teknika* [1993] *FSR* 324; [1994] *FSR* 202; *Intel v. Via Technologies* [2003] *FSR* (33) 574, [115]; *Sportswear Spa v. Stonestyle* [2007] *FSR* (2) 33. Two other penalties are available in serious cases: criminal penalties as regards dishonest 'horizontal agreements' (Enterprise Act 2002, Pt 6) and disqualification of directors (Enterprise Act 2002, s. 204).

[122] Council Regulation (EC) No. 1/2003 of 16 December 2002 on the implementation of the rules on competition laid down in Arts 81 and 82 of the Treaty [2003] *OJ L* 1/1, Art. 5. This Regulation sees a 'modernization' and decentralization of the enforcement of European competition law, with the European Commission operating as part of a 'European Competition Network' of national authorities. In general, the European Commission will enforce cases involving practices or agreements that affect at least three member states.

[123] Council Regulation No. 17/62 of 6 February 1962: First Regulation Implementing Arts 85 and 86 of the Treaty [1962] *OJ Sp Ed* 204/62, 87, reg. 15(2) (fines of up to €1 million or 10 per cent of turnover in the preceding business year); Council Regulation No. 1/2003, Arts 7 (empowering the Commission to impose behavioural or structural remedies that are 'proportionate' and necessary to bring the infringement to an end), 23(2) (fines of up to 10 per cent of turnover in the preceding business year), and 24 (periodic penalties of up to 5 per cent of average daily turnover per day); Competition Act 1998 (giving the CMA power to impose penalties of up to 10 per cent of turnover for up to three years).

the prevention, restriction or distortion of competition'. Because the term 'undertakings' has been interpreted liberally, Article 101 potentially applies to agreements concerning the licensing and assignment of intellectual property rights,[124] whether between competitors or parties at different levels of distribution (for example exclusive distribution agreements). Article 101 goes on to outline certain practices, such as price fixing and market sharing, which will normally be prohibited. In other cases, a conclusion that the agreement has an anti-competitive effect depends on the actual conditions in which the agreement would function, including the economic contexts, the products covered by the agreement, and the structure of the market.[125]

Even though the Treaty is not meant to prejudice the rules in member states governing the system of property ownership,[126] the European Commission and the Court of Justice of the European Union have had little hesitation in applying Article 101(1) to agreements involving intellectual property rights. According to the Court, interference with intellectual property rights is justified on the basis that it 'does not affect the grant of those rights but only limits their exercise to the extent necessary to give effect to the prohibition under [Article 101]'.[127] Article 101 also applies to institutions and arrangements for the collective administration of rights—a common feature of copyright exploitation.[128]

Given the potential breadth of Article 101, it is important to note that Article 101(3) allows for Article 101(1) to be 'declared inapplicable' in a number of circumstances.[129] Such exemptions must 'contribute to improving the production or distribution of goods or to promoting technical or economic progress, while allowing consumers a fair share of the resulting benefit'.[130] The European Commission has issued a number of such 'block exemptions' in the form of Commission regulations; the most important relate to 'technology transfer agreements',[131] 'research and development agreements',[132] and 'vertical agreements'.[133] These block exemptions enable operators to be confident that their agreements are exempt (although the benefit of a block exemption may be withdrawn as regards an individual agreement) and may also be treated as 'guidelines'

[124] For example, *Etablissements Consten SARL and Grundig-Verkaufs-GmbH v. EEC Commission*, Case C-583/64 [1966] *ECR* 299. Minor agreements are excluded: Commission Notice on agreements of minor importance which do not fall within the meaning of Art. 81(1) EC [2001] *OJ C* 368/13 (agreements between firms that are not competitors as falling outside of Art. 101(1) TFEU if the market share held by each of the parties does not exceed 15 per cent of any of the relevant markets affected by the agreement). See generally, Stothers, ch. 3.

[125] *European Night Services v. Commission*, T-374/94 [1998] *ECR* II–3141.

[126] Article 345 TFEU (ex Art. 295 EC and Art. 222 of the Treaty).

[127] *Etablissements Consten SARL and Grundig-Verkaufs-GmbH v. EEC Commission*, Case C-58/64 [1966] *ECR* 299; cf. *Panayiotou v. Sony Music Entertainment* [1994] *EMLR* 229.

[128] See Chapter 11, section 9, pp. 318–23, and Chapter 12, section 7, pp. 350–5.

[129] Regulation No. 19/65/EEC.   [130] TFEU, Art. 101(3).

[131] Council Regulation No. 316/2014 of 21 March 2014 on the application of Article 101(3) of the Treaty on the Functioning of the European Union to categories of technology transfer agreements [2014] *OJ L* 93/17 (28 March 2014) (the 'Technology Transfer Block Exemption Regulation 2014', or TTBER 2014); see Chapter 23, section 3.3ff, pp. 683–4.

[132] Commission Regulation (EC) No. 2659/2000 of 29 November 2000 on the application of Article 81(3) of the Treaty to categories of research and development agreements [2000] *OJ L* 304/3 (5 December 2000) (the 'R&D Block Exemption Regulation', or R&DBER; see Chapter 23, section 3.3, p. 683.

[133] Commission Regulation (EU) No. 330/2010 of 20 April 2010 on the application of Article 101(3) of the Treaty on the Functioning of the European Union of categories of vertical agreements and concerted practices [2010] *OJ L* 102/1 (23 April 2010) (the 'Vertical Restraints Regulation', or VRR); see Chapter 42, section 4.1, pp. 1175–7.

even for agreements that fall outside the scope of the block exemption. In other situations, operators will have to form their own judgements as to whether agreements are exempt.[134]

Article 102 TFEU prohibits an undertaking from abusing a dominant position. This prohibition has primarily affected intellectual property law in two ways. First, it provides a basis for regulating collective organizations that administer intellectual property rights on behalf of owners and which occupy a dominant position in the market. To prevent abuse, organizations in a dominant position are able to impose only those obligations and restrictions that are necessary to achieve their legitimate aims.[135] Second, Article 102 provides a remedy for misuse or abuse of intellectual property rights. On one reading of Article 102, it is possible to argue that, because intellectual property rights confer monopoly rights, they necessarily place owners in a dominant position for the market covered by the intellectual property right. On this basis, all activities carried on by intellectual property right holders would need to be scrutinized to ensure that they were not abusive. However, the Court of Justice has declined to use Article 102 in this way; instead, the Court has made it clear that ownership of an intellectual property right does not of itself confer dominance in a market. As a consequence, a refusal to license an intellectual property right constitutes an abuse of a dominant position only in exceptional circumstances.[136]

4.3 CENTRALIZATION AND HARMONIZATION

While the doctrine of exhaustion has reduced the impact of national intellectual property rights on the functioning of the internal market, it has been unable to guarantee that barriers to trade will not arise where national laws differ in terms of substance or duration. Consequently, it soon became apparent that, to achieve the holy grail of an internal market, some level of harmonization would be necessary.

4.3.1 The basis for legislation

Although there are three relevant ways in which the European Union is able to harmonize national laws, the primary mechanism (in our field) has been by way of directives under Article 114 TFEU. This provides for the adoption of measures for the approximation of the provisions laid down by law in member states that have as their object the establishment and functioning of the internal market.[137] This occurs under what is now called the 'ordinary legislative procedure', a process that begins with a Commission proposal, which must be approved by the Council and the European Parliament. Because only a qualified majority of the Council must support the proposal, it is not necessary to have

---

[134] A system of prior notification that was formerly in operation became unworkable and has now been abolished. From 1 May 2004, Art. 101(3) TFEU is directly applicable by the courts of member states: Council Regulation No. 1/2003, Arts 1(2) and 6, Recital 4. The Commission may still produce block exemptions, may make decisions withdrawing the benefit of such exemptions in individual cases (Art. 29), or may find that Arts 101 or 102 TFEU are inapplicable to individual cases (Art. 10).

[135] These are discussed in Chapter 12, section 7, pp. 350–5. See *Re GEMA (No. 1)* [1971] *CMLR* D35; *Belgische Radio en Televise (BRT) v. SABAM*, Case C-127/73 [1974] *ECR* 313.

[136] *RTE and ITP v. EC Commission*, Joined Cases C-241/91 and C-242/91 [1995] *ECR* 808 (the 'Magill' case). See Chapter 12, section 3, pp. 334–8.

[137] Article 114 TFEU (ex Art. 95 EC and Art. 100A of the Treaty). See A. Ramalho, *The Competence of the European Union in Copyright Lawmaking* (2016); S Halpern and P Johnson, *Harmonising Copyright Law and Dealing with Dissonance* (2014), Ch 4.

the unanimous approval of all of the member states.[138] In addition, a residual power in the TFEU relating to the internal market has been used to justify most of the regulations hitherto adopted that establish unitary rights operative in the European Union (relating to the Community trade mark, designs, and plant breeders' rights).[139] Finally, Article 118 TFEU provides for the adoption of legislation relating to the creation of European intellectual property rights with unitary effect throughout the Union.[140] As this power was introduced into the Treaty only in 2009, it has been used for the first time in relation to the establishment of the unitary patent.[141]

4.3.2 An overview of the progress of harmonization

European Union involvement with intellectual property can be divided into five stages.

(i) Patents from the 1960s In the 1960s, the focus of attention was on the establishment of a Community patent system—that is, a system in which a single patent would be granted for the whole of the Community, enforceable in Community patent courts. To this end, in 1975, the Community Patent Convention was agreed to at an intergovernmental level between the (then nine) member states. However, the political will to introduce the scheme never materialized.[142] In part, this was because, in 1973, a separate instrument for the granting of patents, the European Patent Convention (EPC), had been agreed to between states (a number of which were then outside the European Community). As such, there was little urgency to implement the distinct (although linked) Community patent. Despite attempts to revive the Treaty through a 1989 Protocol in Luxembourg,[143] it is only in recent years that a real will for a single European patent regime has emerged. The existence of the EPC has limited the ability of the EU to harmonize national patent laws. The reason for this is that all member states are parties to, and therefore bound by, the EPC; at the same time, they cannot amend the Convention without the assent of the

---

[138] In addition, under TFEU, Art. 115 (ex Art. 94 EC), the Council can issue directives for the approximation of the laws of member states 'as directly affect the establishing and function of the common market'. Under this process, the Commission issues a proposal and then consults with the European Parliament and Economic and Social Committee. To be passed, a proposal must be approved unanimously by the Council.

[139] Article 352 TFEU (ex Art. 308 EC and Art. 235 of the Treaty), which provides that if action by the Union is 'necessary to attain, in the course of the operation of the common market, one of the objectives of the Union and this Treaty has not provided the necessary powers, the Council shall, acting unanimously on a proposal from the Commission after consulting the European Parliament, take the appropriate measures'. See, e.g., CTMR, Recital 4. In these cases, the legislature is not harmonizing, but creating new rights: see *Opinion 1/94* [1994] *ECR* I–5267, [59]; *Netherlands v. European Parliament and Council*, Case C-377/98 [2001] *ECR* I–7079, [35].

[140] Article 118 TFEU mandating action establishing uniform intellectual property rights under the 'ordinary procedure'. Under the TEU, the possibility exists for further forms of action at Community level, e.g. in the field of criminal law. The 'third' pillar of the TEU (Maastricht) covers 'justice and home affairs'. But see *Commission v. Council*, Case C-176/03 [2005] *ECR* I–7879 (striking down a 'framework decision' under the TEU because its object was environmental protection, a matter under the EC Treaty). This decision suggests that the EU can adopt criminal provisions under Art. 114 TFEU. See *Proposal for a European Parliament and Council Directive on criminal measures aimed at ensuring the enforcement of intellectual property rights* {SEC(2005)848}/*COM/2005/0276 final COD 2005/0127*/(referring to Art. 95).

The TEU is important for intellectual property rights partly because of its provisions recognizing fundamental rights as guaranteed by the European Convention for the Protection of Human Rights and Fundamental Freedoms (ECHR) (Art. 6 TEU) and on police and judicial cooperation in criminal matters (Arts 29–30 TEU, ex Art. K.1).

[141] Regulation 1257/2012 of 17 December 2012 (under the ordinary legislative procedure) and Regulation 1260/2012 (on translations, adopted under the special legislative procedure).

[142] [1976] *OJ L* 17/43.

[143] Luxembourg Agreement of 15 December 1989 relating to Community Patents [1989] *OJ L* 401/1.

non-EU participants. In the two fields in which EU action has taken place, the proposals have been made to appear as if they leave the EPC untouched. The two Regulations on Supplementary Protection Certificates (SPC Regulations) are worded so as to avoid appearing to be extensions of the patent term.[144] Similarly, Directive 98/44/EC of the European Parliament and Council on the Legal Protection of Biotechnological Inventions (the Biotech Directive), which attempts to harmonize patent law for biological inventions, is presented as a directive to harmonize the 'interpretation' of existing provisions of the EPC, rather than to amend or modify those provisions.

(ii) Trade marks from the 1980s In the 1980s, attention turned to the harmonization of trade mark law. The first part of a two-pronged strategy was to approximate national trade mark laws. This was eventually completed by way of a directive.[145] The second prong saw the establishment of a single office that granted Community (now EU) trade marks enforceable in the courts of member states designated as Community trade mark courts. The Community trade mark was introduced by way of a Council regulation and, in 1996, the Office of Harmonization in the Internal Market (OHIM) (now known as the European Union Intellectual Property Office (EUIPO)) was established in Alicante, Spain.[146] As the substantive rules of the Regulation are virtually identical to those of the Directive, appeals of decisions of EUIPO to its Boards of Appeal, to the General Court (formerly the Court of First Instance), and the Court of Justice offer valuable guidance to national authorities. Following a series of amendments, the Directive and Regulation were codified in 2008 and 2009 and further reforms have led to a new 2015 Directive and a codified Regulation in 2017.[147]

(iii) Copyright in the 1990s At the end of the 1980s, the third wave of harmonization began when the Commission set out to harmonize a number of aspects of copyright law.[148] The need for action arose because the different levels of copyright protection in different member states was seen to constitute a potential barrier to trade.[149] In contrast with the approach taken to trade marks, the EU passed a series of seven directives, each harmonizing particular aspects of copyright law (especially relating to areas of technological change). In so doing, the Commission also aimed to set the standard of protection to be given to creators at a 'high level'.[150]

Further reform of copyright has become increasingly difficult (because the whole field has become increasingly politicized). The European Commission has therefore turned to different modes of regulation, including soft law recommendations, and has also sponsored agreements (so-called 'memoranda of understanding', or MoUs) between industry

---

[144] SPC (PM) Reg.; SPC (PPP) Reg; [1992] *OJ EPO* 1.

[145] First Council Directive 89/104 of 21 December 1988 to approximate the laws of Member States Relating to Trade Marks, [1989] *OJ L* 140/1.

[146] See Chapter 31, section 4.3, pp. 861–2 and Chapter 35, section 1, p. 928 section 3, pp. 945 ff.

[147] See Chapter 31, section 4.3, p. 861; Chapter 35, section 1.1, pp. 929–30. Directive (EU) 2015/2436 of the European Parliament and of the Council of 16 December 2015 to approximate the laws of the Member States relating to trade marks must be implemented by 14 January 2019, and Directive 2008/95/EC is repealed with effect from 15 January 2019. Regulation (EU) 2017/1001 of the European Parliament and of the Council of 14 June 2017 on the European Union trade mark is effective from 1 October 2017 and codifies Council Regulation (EC) 207/2009 to take account of Regulation (EU) 2015/2424. In at least one case, the Commission has sought to sponsor agreement through a memorandum of understanding. See *Memorandum of Understanding on the Sale of Counterfeit Goods via the Internet*, 4 May 2011 (Brussels).

[148] See Chapter 2, section 7, pp. 51–4.

[149] It was also motivated by the prompting of the Court of Justice, e.g. in *EMI Electrola GmbH v. Patricia Im-und Export*, Case C-341/87 [1989] *ECR* 79.

[150] For example, Term Dir., Recital 10.

participants.[151] Nevertheless, latterly there has been further piecemeal legislation: in 2011, a directive was adopted amending the Term Directive (increasing the term of copyright in sound recordings from 50 to 70 years);[152] in 2012, a directive was adopted on so-called 'orphan works';[153] in 2014, a directive was agreed relating to the governance of organizations that manage copyright (so-called 'collecting societies');[154] in 2017, a directive and regulation have been adopted to implement the Marrakesh Treaty,[155] and a regulation on the portability of online services.[156] A proposal for a directive that deals with a selection of problems entered the legislative machinery in September 2016,[157] alongside a proposed regulation on online transmissions.[158]

(iv) Plants and designs from the 1990s The 1990s also witnessed Community intervention in relation to a number of the so-called *sui generis* intellectual property rights. A Community Plant Variety Regulation (CPVR) established a Community Office in Angers, France. In contrast to the strategy in relation to trade marks, no harmonization directive was passed regulating national law.[159] A directive was also passed relating to the harmonization of the law relating to designs, which was followed by a Regulation introducing a Community registered design (to be administered by EUIPO), and a Community unregistered design right.[160] The latter, available since April 2002, is the first Europe-wide, unitary right to be granted automatically, rather than after application to an office.

(v) The unified patent in the new millennium As we will see later,[161] over the last few years there have been renewed efforts to introduce a centralized single patent and a centralized patent court in Europe. This represents the latest efforts to harmonize intellectual property in Europe. The so-called 'unitary patent package', which highlights many of the structural problems with efforts to reform patent law in Europe, consists of a mixture of two new European Union Regulations[162] (which were adopted by means of the little-used 'enhanced cooperation mechanism'[163] and entered into force in January 2013) and the

---

[151] *Access to copyright works for people with print disabilities: Memorandum of Understanding (between European Blind Union and European Federation of Publishers)* and *Memorandum of Understanding on Key Principles on the Digitization and Making Available of Out-of-Commerce Work* (between library organizations and representatives for writers, visual artists and publishers).

[152] Directive 2011/77/EU. See Chapter 7, section 1, pp. 181–4.

[153] Directive 2012/28/EU. See Chapter 12, section 5, pp. 346–7.

[154] Directive 2014/26/EU. See Chapter 12, section 7, pp. 352, 353.

[155] Regulation (EU) 2017/1563 and Directive (EU) 2017/1564, both dated September 13, 2017. See Chapter 2, section 6.6, pp. 49–50 and Chapter 9, section 12.3, pp. 261–2.

[156] Regulation 2017/1128 of June 14, 2017. See Chapter 12, section 6, pp. 349–50.

[157] Proposal for a Directive of the European Parliament and of the Council on Copyright in the Digital Single Market—COM(2016) 593. See: Chapter 6, section 6.7, p. 177; Chapter 9, section 6, pp. 244–5, section 13.7, p. 267, section 14.3, p. 270; Chapter 12, section 2.5, pp. 333–4; and Chapter 13, section 8, pp. 389–90; and Chapter 48, section 3.5.5, pp. 1293–6.

[158] Proposal for a Regulation of the European Parliament and of the Council laying down rules on the exercise of copyright and related rights applicable to certain online transmissions of broadcasting organizations and retransmissions of television and radio programmes, 2016, discussed further in Chapter 6, section 6.5.2, p. 174–5.   [159] See Chapter 24, section 2, p. 699.

[160] See Part III, Introduction, section 4, pp. 721–4.   [161] See Chapter 14, section 4.5.1, pp. 409–16.

[162] Council Regulation (EU) No. 1260/2012 of 17 December 2012 implementing enhanced cooperation in the area of the creation of unitary patent protection with regard to the applicable translation arrangements [2012] *OJ L* 361/89; Council Regulation (EU) No. 1257/2012 of 17 December 2012 implementing enhanced cooperation in the area of the creation of unitary patent protection [2012] *OJ L* 361/1.

[163] The general arrangements for enhanced cooperation are laid down by the TEU, Title IV. This allows member states to move forward at different speeds and/or towards different goals. It does not allow extension of the powers as laid down by the Treaties, nor may it be applied to areas that fall within the exclusive competence of the Union. Enhanced cooperation may be undertaken only as a last resort, when it has been established within the Council that the objectives of such cooperation cannot be attained within a reasonable period by the Union as a whole.

Agreement on a Unified Patent Court, signed on 19 February 2013 (which, following the Court of Justice's ruling that a proposal to establish a unified patent was incompatible with EU law, is an intergovernmental treaty formed outside of the Union). While 25 countries have expressed an interest in implementing the unitary patent, Spain and Poland have decided not to join. The United Kingdom ratified the Agreement in April 2018, so that only Germany need do so for it to come into force.

4.3.3 Challenges

Given the breadth of European intervention in intellectual property law, it is not surprising that a number of challenges have been made to particular European initiatives. In most cases, such challenges must be brought by national governments before the Court of Justice. National courts do not have the power to declare acts of the Community institutions to be invalid.[164] If past experiences are much to go on, it seems that attempts to set aside European Union legislation are unlikely to be successful.[165]

4.3.4 Implementation

In the United Kingdom, directives have been implemented through the introduction of new statutes (as with the Trade Marks Act 1994) or, more commonly, by amending existing statutes by way of statutory instrument.[166] When implementing directives, the UK government has tended to rewrite the (often abstract) provisions used in the directives into the language that is more commonly found in British statutes. Unfortunately, such rewriting can make interpretation doubly difficult, and a number of UK judges have made adverse comments about this practice.[167] Unlike the case with directives, regulations do not need to be implemented into national law to be effective.[168] However, where national procedures need to be established (as with the SPC Regulations), some action must necessarily follow.

   If a government fails to implement a directive, or implements it only partially or tardily, the Commission may commence an action against that member state before the Court of Justice.[169] Moreover, pending implementation, a number of consequences may follow automatically. First, in accordance with general principles of European law, the provision has a direct effect 'vertically' on state bodies, including rights-granting bodies such as the UK Intellectual Property Office. This direct effect applies only where the provision is clear and unconditional. Second, the national courts must interpret existing national law in line with the unimplemented provisions of a directive—a consequence sometimes referred to as 'indirect effect'.[170] Where this is not possible, individuals are not able to rely

---

[164] *Foto-Frost*, Case C-314/85 [1987] *ECR* 4199.

[165] *Spain v. The Council of the European Union*, Case C-350/92 [1995] *ECR* I–1985; *Metronome Music v. Music Point Hokamp GmbH*, Case C-200/96 [1998] *ECR* I–1953; *Netherlands v. European Parliament and Council*, Case C-377/98 [2001] *ECR* I–7079.

[166] European Communities Act 1972, s. 1(2).

[167] It is now common practice to refer straight to the text of the Directive: *SAS Institute v. World Programming Ltd* [2010] *EWHC* 1829 (Ch), [291]; *Newspaper Licensing Agency Ltd v. Public Relations Consultants Association* [2013] *UKSC* 18, [5].

[168] Article 288 TFEU. Consequently, regulations have immediate effect and operate to confer rights on individuals that the national courts have a duty to protect: *Bureau national interprofessionnel du Cognac v. Gust. Ranin Oy*, Joined Cases C-4/10 and C-27/10 , EU:C:2011:484 (ECJ) (considering impact of Regulation (EC) No. 110/2008 on the protection of geographical indications of spirit drink).

[169] See, e.g., *Commission v. United Kingdom*, Case C-30/90 [1992] *ECR* I–829 (UK compulsory licence provisions incompatible with Treaty).

[170] *Marleasing v. La Comercial Internacional de Alimentacion*, Case C-106/89 [1990] *ECR* I–4135.

on the unimplemented provisions to bring an action against other private bodies—that is, there is no 'horizontal' direct effect.[171] While, in these circumstances, private individuals may not get the remedy to which they would have been entitled had the directive been implemented, they are not left without a course of action. This is because if a private individual has suffered damage as a result of a government's failure to implement a directive, the member state may be required to compensate the individual. For this to occur, the claimant must show that the object of the directive was to create rights, that the scope of rights is identifiable, and that failure to introduce such rights caused the damage.[172]

4.3.5 Interpretation

Unless provisions in EU legislation make reference to national law (or expressly leave interpretation to national law), the Court has indicated that terms contained in EU law should be given an 'autonomous interpretation'. In many cases, this means that the Court of Justice is free to interpret—and thus harmonize—many fundamental concepts that the legislators may not have foreseen as being harmonized. In interpreting EU legislation, the Court tends to focus, as one would expect, on the wording, but will also give close consideration to the context and purpose.[173] That systemic and teleological approach has, on occasions, allowed the Court to interpret a word as meaning its apparent opposite, as in the case of trade marks, when 'dissimilar' was taken to mean 'dis-similar, similar or identical'.[174] It also has allowed the Court to offer interpretations that respond to technological changes.[175] While the text of the directive remains critical, particular attention should be given to the recitals at the front of the directive, since these often provide specific examples explaining what a clause is intended to cover.[176] In addition, attention is often paid to the European *travaux préparatoires*, such as Commission proposals, explanatory memoranda, and perhaps statements made adopting a common position.[177] In exceptional cases, it may be helpful to refer to the so-called 'agreed statements'—that is, to the minutes of what was agreed between the Commission and the Council.[178] Two other sources

[171] *Ochranný svaz autorský pro práva k dílům hudebním, o.s. (OSA) v. Léčebné lázně Mariánské Lázně a. s.*, Case C-351/12 EU:C:2014:110 (ECJ), [43]–[48]; *Football Association Premier League v. QC Leisure* [2012] *FSR* (12) 366 (Kitchin LJ), affirmed [2012] *EWCA Civ* 1708, [2013] *FSR* (20) 392 (concerning CDPA 1988, s. 72). However, for the possible disapplication of provisions, see *Google Inc v. Vidall-Hall* [2015] *EWCA Civ* 311, [90]–[105] (disapplying provision of Data Protection Act, but not on the basis of *Marleasing* but conflict with the EU Charter).

[172] *Francovich v. Italian Republic*, Joined Cases C-6 and 9/90 [1991] *ECR* I–5357, [31]–[45].

[173] E.g. *Louis Vuitton v. Google France*, Cases 236/08–238/08 [2010] *ECR* I–2417 (ECJ, Grand Chamber), [48].

[174] *Davidoff*, Case C-292/00 [2003] *ECR* I–389, [24]–[30].

[175] *VOB v. Stichting Leenrecht*, Case C-174/15, EU:C:2016:459, [2016] *ECDR* (24) 399, [AG27]–[AG32] (AG Szpunar).

[176] *SAS Institute Inc. v. World Programming Ltd* [2010] *EWHC* 1829 (Ch), [166] (Arnold J). But note the caveats expressed by AG Sharpston in *VG Wort v. KYOCERA Document Solutions Deutschland GmbH*, Joined Cases C-457/11, C-458/11, C-459/11, and 460/11 EU:C:2013:34, [AG28], [AG29], [AG32].

[177] For some examples, see *Gerolsteiner*, Case C-100/02 [2004] *ECR* I–691 (ECJ), [14]–[15], [AG40] (referring to earlier versions of proposed TMD 1989 to draw inferences as to the scope of TMD 1989, Art. 6(1)(b)); *VG Wort*, Joined Cases C-457/11, C 458/11, C-459/11, and C-460/11, EU:C:2013:426, [28] (referring to Commission proposal when interpreting Info. Soc. Dir., Art. 10(2)), [69] (referring to Explanatory Memorandum); EU:C:2013:34, [AG 69] (using *travaux* to confirm interpretation of Info. Soc. Dir. Art. 5(2) (a)). But for situations in which the *travaux* have been ignored where they contradict the wording, see *VG Wort* [AG97] (declining to rely on Common Position when interpreting the scope of 'any medium' in Art. 5(2) of the Info. Soc. Dir.).

[178] In relation to the TMD 1989, see *Libertel Groep BV v. Benelux MerkenBureau*, Case C-104/01 [2004] *FSR* (4) 65 (ECJ), [25] (noting that the minutes specifically acknowledge that they should not be used in interpretation); *Leno Merken*, Case C-149/11, EU:C:2012:816 (ECJ), esp. [45]–[47].

also have a strong influence on the interpretation of legislation by the Court of Justice: the first comprises any international agreements to which the EU is a party, including, importantly, the TRIPS Agreement;[179] the second is the Charter of Fundamental Rights of the European Union, proclaimed on 7 December 2000,[180] in particular its reference to the principle that 'intellectual property shall be protected'.[181] The Court has also relied on human rights reasoning as an aid to interpretation of the directives, including the case law on transferability of copyright, the meaning of communication to the public, as well as that relating to copyright exceptions.[182] The Court also requires that the Charter be considered in fashioning remedies for infringement of intellectual property, a context in which rights of privacy, free speech, and freedom to conduct a business. Frequently, the Court of Justice has suggested that where conflicting rights are engaged a 'fair balance' must be sought.[183]

Ultimately, the question of the way in which a directive (or regulation) is to be interpreted is decided by the Court of Justice. The Court is assisted by one of the eleven Advocates-General, who make reasoned submissions in order to assist the Court. The Advocate-General's opinion may be a useful interpretative tool to resolve doubts over a decision of the Court. In some situations, particularly in relation to appeals from the Boards of Appeal of the EUIPO, hearings are initially to the General Court (from whence appeals can be heard by the Court of Justice). That case law is voluminous.

4.4 EXTERNAL RELATIONS

Another way in which the European Union is involved in intellectual property law is through the role that it plays in negotiating and signing treaties. The EU's treaty powers are now set out in Article 207 TFEU (formerly Article 133 EC and Article 113 of the Treaty).[184] The question of whether the EU has 'exclusive competence' or 'shared competence' in such matters has frequently proved controversial. It has been held that TRIPS and the Singapore Free Trade Agreement (which includes a Chapter on IP) fall

---

[179] See, e.g., *Heidelberger Bauchemie*, Case C-49/02 [2004] *ECR* 1–6129, [19]–[21]; *Art & AllPosters*, Case C-409/13, EU:C:2015: 27 (ECJ), [39] (relying on agreed statement in WCT); *VOB v. Stichting Leenrecht*, Case C-174/15, EU:C:2016:856, [2017] *ECDR* (3) 81, [33]–[34].

[180] The Charter of Fundamental Rights has the same legal value as other Treaty provisions: see Art. 6 TEU. See J. Griffiths and L. McDonagh, 'Fundamental Rights and European Intellectual Property Law: The Case of Art. 17(2) of the EU Charter', in C. Geiger (ed.), *Constructing European Intellectual Property: Achievements and New Perspectives* (2012), ch. 4; J. Griffiths, 'Constitutionalising or Harmonising? The Court of Justice, the Right to Property and European Copyright Law' (2013) 38 *ELR* 65.

[181] See *Scarlet Extended v. SABAM*, Case C-70/10, [2011] *ECR* I–11959 (ECJ, Third Chamber), [43]; *SABAM v. Netlog NV*, Case C-360/10, EU:C:2012:85 (ECJ), [41] (this does not suggest that the right is inviolable and must be absolutely protected); *UPC Telekabel Wien GmbH v. Constantin Film Verleih GmbH, Wega Filmproduktionsgesellschaft mbH*, Case C-314/12, EU:C:2014:192 (ECJ), [47], [61].

[182] *Martin Luksan v. Petrus van der Let*, Case C-277/10, EU:C:2012:65, [68]–[71] (presumed transfer of rights from director to producer contrary to Art 17) discussed in Chapter 5, section 4, p. 140; *GS Media BV v. Sanoma Media Netherlands BV*, Case C-160/15, EU:C:2016:644, [45]–[46] (concept of communication to the public needed to allow for freedom of expression under Art. 11), discussed in Chapter 6, section 6.2.3, pp. 169–71; *J. Deckmyn v. H. Vandersteen*, Case C-201/13, EU:C:2014:2132, [27], [30] (on parody and freedom of expression), discussed in Chapter 9, section 8, pp. 249–52.

[183] For commentary, see J. Griffiths, 'Constitutionalising or Harmonising? The Court of Justice, the Right to Property and European Copyright Law' [2013] *ELR* 65.

[184] The TRIPS Agreement was entered into by the Community (under implied powers) and member states: *Opinion 1/94* [1994] *ECR* I–5267.

within the exclusive competence of the EU as they relate to 'commercial aspects of IP' and thus 'common commercial policy'.[185] What is required is a 'specific link' to trade.[186] However, even where there is no such link (a matter determined by looking at the institutional framework, the aims, and context of the treaty in question), as with the Marrakesh Treaty, [187] the European Union may nevertheless have exclusive competence under Article 3(2) of the TFEU if the proposed treaty would affect 'common rules or alter their scope'.[188]

To date, the European Union has entered into a number of intellectual property-related treaties. For example, the European Union is now a party to TRIPS (which itself refers to the Berne and Paris Conventions), the Madrid Protocol on international registration of trade marks,[189] the WIPO Copyright Treaty and WIPO Performances and Phonograms Treaty (which refers to the Rome Convention),[190] and the Hague Agreement on designs; [191] having adopted relevant legislation, a Council Decision on ratification of the Marrakesh Treaty seems likely to follow very soon.[192] Under Article 216(2) TFEU, '[a]greements concluded by the Union are binding upon the institutions of the Union and on its Member States'. While the Court of Justice has been willing to interpret EU legislation in the light of its treaty obligation,[193] it has yet to hold that any provisions in international treaties

[185] *Daiichi Sankyo Co. Ltd, Sanofi-Aventis Deutschland GmbH v. Demo Anonimos Viomikhaniki kai Emporiki Etairia Farmakon*, Case C-414/11, EU:C:2013:520, [53] (ECJ, Grand Chamber) (holding that the whole of TRIPS falls within 'common commercial policy' of Art. 207 TFEU); Opinion 2/15 (*EU-Singapore Free Trade Agreement*) of 16 May 2017, EU:C:2017:376 (ECJ, Grand Chamber), [121]–[130].

[186] Case C-414/11, EU:C:2013:520, [52]; Opinion 2/15, EU:C:2017:376, [31]–[32]. Moreover, at [129], the Court found there may be such a link at a general level, even if certain specific indirect commitments cover non-trade-related matters, such as moral rights. For the view that the Lisbon Agreement on Appellations Falls within the notion of common commercial policy/commercial aspects of intellectual property, see *European Commission v. Council of the European Union*, Case C-389/15, EU:C:2017;604 (AG Bot).

[187] Opinion 3/15, EU:C:2017:114 (ECJ, Grand Chamber). On the Treaty, see Chapter 2, section 6.6, pp. 49–50. The Court, [61]–[101], noted particularly the humanitarian goals of the Treaty, as well as the fact that the rules on import and export of accessible format copies were limited to transactions involving not-for-profit 'authorized entities.'

[188] Opinion 3/15, EU:C:2017:114, [102]–[130] (ECJ, Grand Chamber) (noting that InfoSoc Dir, Art 5(3)(b) offers a highly constrained freedom to Member States to derogate from the harmonized rights of reproduction, communication, and distribution, and Marrakesh implementation would affect this); *European Commission v. Council of the European Union*, Case C-114/12, EU:C:2014:2151 (European Union has exclusive competence in the field of broadcasters' rights).

[189] Council Decision 2000/278 of 16 April 2000 [2000] *OJ L* 89/6; Council Decision of 27 October 2003 approving accession of the European Community to the Protocol relating to the Madrid Agreement Concerning the International Registration of Marks [2003] *OJ L* 296/1.

[190] *Società Consortile Fonografici (SCF) v. Marco Del Corso*, Case C-135/10, EU:C:2012:140 (ECJ, Third Chamber), [50] (stating that the Rome Convention has indirect effects within the European Union).

[191] Council Decision of 18 December 2006 approving accession to the Geneva Act of the Hague Agreement Concerning the International Registration of Industrial Designs [2006] *OJ L* 386/28 (29 December 2006).

[192] A Proposal for a Council Decision on the conclusion, on behalf of the European Union, of the Marrakesh Treaty to Facilitate Access to Published Works for Persons who are Blind, Visually Impaired, or Otherwise Print Disabled, COM/2014/0638 final, was initially rejected by the Council pending adoption of the relevant legislation and clarification of the legal basis. Now those matters are resolved, the matter is in Council but, as of May 2018, has not yet been resolved.

[193] *Bezpečnostní softwarová asociace—Svaz softwarové ochrany v. Ministerstvo kultury*, Case 393/09 [2010] *ECR* I–13971 (ECJ) (interpreting Software Dir. in light of TRIPS, Art. 10); *Bericap Záródástechnikai bt v. Plastinnova 2000 kft*, C-180/11, EU:C:2012:717 (ECJ) (interpreting Enforcement Dir., Arts 2(1) and 3(2), in light of Art. 2(1) Paris and Art. 41(1) and (2) TRIPS); *Hermes*, Case C-53/96 [1998] *ECR* I–3603 (interpreting Art. 50(6) TRIPS to assist the national court to determine its own obligations and 'to forestall future differences of interpretation').

have direct effect.[194] Before it will do so, the provisions must 'as regards their content, be unconditional and sufficiently precise' and, as regards their nature and broad logic, must not preclude their being so relied on.

4.5 EUROPEAN ECONOMIC AREA

To understand intellectual property law in the United Kingdom, it is important to be familiar with the European Economic Area (EEA). This is an initiative entered into between the European Union and certain satellite countries, which are members of the European Free Trade Area (EFTA). In 1994, the majority of the countries then in EFTA decided to enter into a joint EU–EFTA initiative and form the EEA.[195] The countries that joined the EEA from EFTA undertook to implement a raft of EU directives (including those on trade marks and copyright).[196] These provisions are enforced by the 'EFTA Surveillance Authority' and the 'EFTA Court'.[197] In return, the EU agreed to extend its provisions to the EEA countries. As a result, where the terms 'European Union', 'Community', or 'internal market' are used in provisions falling within the EEA Agreement, they refer to the territories of the contracting parties.[198] Moreover, the doctrine of exhaustion and the jurisprudence of the Court of Justice on Article 34 TFEU explicitly apply to goods placed on the market in the EEA.[199]

4.5.1 'Europe agreements'

Increasingly, 'European' intellectual property law is having an ever-expanding significance outside the Union. In part, this is because of the expansion of the Union to 28 states.[200] In addition, the European Union has entered into 'Europe agreements' with so-called 'candidate countries'.[201] The agreements, which aim to establish a free-trade area, contain a number of provisions in relation to intellectual property.

---

[194] *Parfums Christian Dior SA v. Tuk Consultancy BV*, Cases C-300/98 and C-392/98 [2000] *ECR* I–11307 (refusing to treat Art. 50 TRIPS as having 'direct effect'); *Develey Holding v. OHIM*, Case C-238/06P [2007] *ECR* I–9375 (ECJ) (refusing to treat Art. 6*quinquies* of Paris as of direct applicability because the European Union is not a party to the Convention; holding that it was not indirectly applicable via Art. 2 TRIPS, because TRIPS is not itself to be regarded as directly applicable); *Merck Genericos v. Merck & Co.*, Case C-431/05 [2007] *ECR* I–7001 (holding that patent term, a subject dealt with in Art. 33 TRIPS was primarily a matter of national competence, because of the limited harmonization in the patent field to date). Note Council Decision 94/800/EC of 22 December 1994 [1994] *OJ L* 336/1 (23 December 1994), Recital 11 ('whereas, by its nature, the Agreement Establishing the WTO, including the Annexes thereto, is not susceptible to being directly invoked in Community [now EU] or Member State courts').

[195] EFTA countries that are parties to the EEA are: Iceland, Norway, and Liechtenstein. Switzerland refused to join the EEA.

[196] Agreement on the European Economic Area [1994] *OJ L* 1/572 (3 January 1994), see esp. Arts 11, 13, 53, 54. Subsequent instruments have updated the content of the obligations.

[197] See http://www.efta.int. There have been few decisions of the EFTA Court of interest in intellectual property: *Mag Instrument v. California Trading Co.*, E2–97 [1998] 1 *CMLR* 331, now reversed by *L'Oreal Norge SA v. Smart Club Norge SA*, E-9/07 and E-10/07 [2008] *EFTA Ct Rep* 259; *Norwegian Govt v. Astra Norge A/S*, E-1/98 (24 November 1998) (on copyright and free movement of medicines); *Paranova v. Merck*, E–3/02 [2003] *EFTA Ct Rep* 101; Case E-5/16, *Municipality of Oslo* [2017] *EFTA Ct Rep* 52.

[198] Paragraph 8 of Protocol 1 to the EEA Agreement on horizontal adaptation.

[199] Protocol 28 on intellectual property, Art. 2.

[200] Cyprus, the Czech Republic, Estonia, Hungary, Latvia, Lithuania, Malta, Poland, the Slovak Republic, and Slovenia joined in 2004; Bulgaria and Romania joined on 1 January 2008; Croatia joined on 1 July 2013.

[201] Turkey, Iceland, Montenegro, Serbia, and the former Yugoslav Republic of Macedonia (with potential candidates being Bosnia and Herzegovina, Albania, and Kosovo).

The Union also operates a number of initiatives and has agreements with many satellite countries.[202] It has also entered into 'Euro-Med association agreements' with countries of the South and East Mediterranean,[203] 'partnership and co-operation agreements' with countries in Eastern Europe and Central Asia,[204] and 'stabilization and association agreements' with Balkan states (such as Albania, although most of these are also candidate or potential candidate countries).[205]

Typically, these agreements include prohibitions on 'quantitative restriction on imports and measures having equivalent effect', as well as competition provisions similar to Articles 101 and 102 TFEU. The agreements usually also require the contracting party to apply to become a party to (or if already a party, to affirm its commitment to) various intellectual property treaties, such as the European Patent Convention, the Union for the Protection of Plant Varieties, the Rome Convention, the Madrid Protocol, the Berne and Paris Conventions, the Madrid Agreement, and the Patent Cooperation Treaty. They also require states to implement the EU *acquis* (that is, the accumulated body of legislation, legal acts, and court decisions that constitutes EU law) so as to approximate their laws on intellectual property with those of the European Union.

The European Union also enters into bilateral agreements with countries outside of the region, such as the Central American Association Agreement of 2012,[206] and the Comprehensive Economic and Trade Agreement (CETA) between the European Union and Canada was agreed in principle towards the end of 2013.[207]

4.6 NON-EU REGIONAL INITIATIVES

Finally, it is important to note that there are a number of European initiatives that are independent of the European Union that relate to intellectual property law. One of the most important is the 1973 European Patent Convention (EPC). The EPC established a single central office for the granting of bundles of national patents in Munich. The EPC is a treaty independent of the European Union, and includes all of its member states and the EEA states, as well as a number of non-EEA countries, such as Switzerland and Turkey.[208]

The Council of Europe, a political organization founded in 1949 comprising 47 European countries, has also had an impact on intellectual property. While the Council of Europe is largely concerned with the promotion of democracy and human rights, it has undertaken a number of initiatives in the field of intellectual property. The

---

[202] As part of the so-called 'neighbourhood policy'. See, e.g., *Communication from the Commission to the European Council and Parliament on Strengthening the Neighbourhood Policy*, COM(2006) 726 final.

[203] For example, Tunisia, Morocco, Israel, Jordan, Egypt, and Syria. The Agreement with Egypt came into force on 1 June 2004. Article 37 and Annex VI relate to intellectual property rights, obliging the parties mostly in relation to the international treaties.

[204] These include Armenia (partnership and cooperation, 1999), and Russia (partnership and cooperation, 1997), and Georgia (association agreement, 2014, in force 2016) and Moldova (association agreement, 2014, in force 2016) and the Ukraine (association agreement, in force September 2017).

[205] EC–Albania Stabilization and Association Agreement (22 May 2006), esp. Arts 70 and 73, and Annex V, and most recently with Serbia [2013] *OJ L* 278 (18 October 2014), Art. 75 and Annex VII.

[206] [2012] *OJ L* 346/3, Title VI (Arts 228 *ff*) (an elaborate list of undertakings).

[207] The CETA negotiations, which began in 2009, concluded in August 2014. The text can be found *OJ L* 11, 23–1079 (14 January 2017), Chapter 20 deals with intellectual property. As a result of Council Decision (EU) 2017/37 of 28 October 2016, CETA entered into force provisionally on 21 September 2017, and will do so fully once it has been ratified by the 28 member states.

[208] See Chapter 14, section 4, pp. 400–3.

Council supervises certain treaties, including treaties on patents (relating to formalities required for patents, international classification of patents, and the 1963 Strasbourg Convention on the Unification of Certain Points of Substantive Law on Patents for Inventions) and copyright (in particular requiring recognition of the rights of broadcasting organizations), and the protection of those authors whose works are broadcast across frontiers.[209]

The European Convention on Human Rights and Fundamental Freedoms (ECHR), a treaty signed in 1950 under the aegis of the Council of Europe, requires contracting parties to recognize certain rights such as fair trial (Article 6), privacy (Article 8), freedom of expression (Article 10), and property (Article 1 of the First Protocol). Alleged failures to comply with the Convention are justiciable before the European Court of Human Rights (ECtHR) (Article 19). Until recently, the impact of the Convention on British intellectual property law was limited to cases of breach of confidence and remedies.[210] However, with the coming into force of the Human Rights Act 1998 in October 2000, arguments based on the Convention have become more frequent and the jurisprudence of the Court more relevant.[211] The Convention has, however, had some impact on the law of countries with more expansive intellectual property rights than those of the United Kingdom, particularly countries with broad laws against 'unfair' competition,[212] and the Court has now given decisions in a number of cases in which copyright enforcement was alleged to amount to a violation of Article 10 ECHR.[213]

---

[209] For example, the Convention on the Unification of Certain Points of Substantive Law on Patents for Inventions (1963) ETS No. 47 (the United Kingdom ratified the Convention, which came into force in 1980); European Agreement on the Protection of Television Broadcasts (1960) ETS No. 34 and Protocol (1965) ETS No. 54, Additional Protocol (1974) ETS No. 81, and Additional Protocol (1985) ETS No. 113 (the United Kingdom ratified this treaty in 1965); European Convention on Transfrontier Broadcasting (1989) ETS No. 132 (which the United Kingdom ratified in 1993) (defining, e.g., the act of broadcasting). With the stalling of the proposed WIPO Broadcasting Treaty, attention turned in 2008 to the possibility of formulating a treaty within this forum, though it seems that this is no longer being pursued: *European Commission v. Council of the European Union*, Case C-114/12, EU:C:2014:2151 (European Union has exclusive competence in the field of broadcasters' rights).

[210] The European Convention on Human Rights informs, but is not identical to, the EU Charter. According to EU Charter, Art. 52(3) the interpretation of corresponding provisions is to be 'the same as those laid down by the said Convention', though the EU can provide 'more extensive protection'. There had been an intention that the European Union would join the Convention but the likelihood of such adherence has been much reduced as a result of the Judgment of 18 December 2014, Opinion 2/13, Re Accession of European Union to the Convention for the Protection of Human Rights and Fundamental Freedoms, EU:C:2014:2454.

[211] For arguments based on Art. 6(2) ECHR (presumption of innocence), see the discussion of criminal liability for trade mark infringement in *R v. Johnstone* [2003] *FSR* (42) 748. For arguments based on Art. 10 ECHR (free expression), see e.g *Confetti Records v. Warner Music UK* [2003] *EMLR* (35) 790, [161] (rejecting argument that Art. 10 requires a narrow reading of moral rights); *FCUK Trade Mark* [2007] *RPC* (1) 1 (Arnold QC) (relevance of Art. 10 in assessment of the 'morality' objection to trade mark registration).

[212] *Hertel v. Switzerland*, Case 25181/94 (1999) 28 *EHRR* 534 (application of Swiss unfair competition law to publication of research on health impact of microwaves breached Art. 10 ECHR); *Krone Verlag GmbH & Co. Kg v. Austria*, Case 39069/97 (2006) 42 *EHRR* (28) 578 (application of Austrian unfair competition law against comparative advertiser breached Art. 10).

[213] *Ashby Donald and ors v. France*, Case 36769/08 [2013] *ECHR* 28 (ECtHR, 5th section) (finding no breach of Art. 10 where photographers were found liable for infringing French copyright in fashion designs, recognizing that Art. 10 was implicated, but, at [41], finding that nations had a wide margin of appreciation because the case involved commercial speech and balancing of Art. 10 with Art. 1 of the First Protocol); *Neij and Kolmisoppi (The Pirate Bay) v. Sweden*, Case 40397/12 [2013] *ECDR* (7) 213 (ECtHR, 5th section) (criminal sanctions of website used to facilitate copyright infringements was interference with Art. 10, but justified). For commentary, see J. Jones, 'Internet Pirates Walk the Plank with Article 10 Kept at Bay: Neij and Sunde Kolmisoppi v. Sweden' [2013] *EIPR* 695.

One development is likely to prove particularly significant: in *Anheuser-Busch Inc. v. Portugal*,[214] the Grand Chamber of the ECtHR held that a trade mark application was a 'possession' for the purposes of Article 1 of the First Protocol. The question was whether the Convention had been breached when the Portuguese Supreme Court held that Anheuser-Busch's trade mark application for BUDWEISER, made in 1981, was invalid on the basis of a bilateral treaty entered between Portugal and the Czech Republic in 1986—that is, five years *after* the trade mark application had been made. Having held that the application was a 'possession',[215] the majority found there was no undue deprivation, because the Supreme Court had been applying domestic law between parties in circumstances in which the precise intent of the domestic law was in issue. This was not something that the Court felt it to be its place to judge. A much clearer and persuasive dissent (from Judges Caflisch and Cabral Barreto) carries the majority holding that a trade mark application is a possession to its logical conclusion: the 1986 bilateral treaty, found to be retrospective, deprived Anheuser-Busch of its property and was not undertaken in the public interest or with compensation.[216] Because the status of intellectual property rights as protected property is confirmed,[217] policymakers will at the very least need to acquaint themselves with ECHR jurisprudence on when a 'deprivation' occurs and in what circumstances such a taking is legitimate.[218] At the same time, the recognition of intellectual property as protected within Article 1 of the First Protocol effectively limits the significance of the Convention. This is because, when faced with arguments concerning violation of Article 10, the ECHR will give a wide margin of appreciation where such violation is justified in order to protect intellectual property.[219]

5 BREXIT

The outcome of the Referendum on June 2016,[220] and the UK government's subsequent decision to trigger Article 50 of the Treaty on the European in March 2017,[221] mean that it is difficult to be confident about the future direction of the protection of Intellectual Property in the United Kingdom. As should be clear from this chapter, much of the detail of policymaking in this field has, since the late 1980s, come from the European Union and the Court of Justice. The British legislature has tended to implement carefully and on time, and the UK courts have been assiduous in making references and applying EU law, even if they have not always been happy with the substance or indeed the quality of reasoning.

---

[214] Case 73049/01, [2007] *EHRR* (36) 830, [2007] *ETMR* (24) 343. L. R. Helfer, 'The New Innovation Frontier? Intellectual Property and the European Court of Human Rights' (2008) 49 *Harvard International Law Journal* 1.

[215] [2007] *EHRR* (36) 830, [78], [2007] *ETMR* (24) 343, 364–5.

[216] [2007] *ETMR* (24) 343, 369–71.

[217] *Neij and Kolmisoppi (The Pirate Bay) v. Sweden*, Case 40397/12, [2013] *ECDR* (7) 213 (ECtHR, 5th section), [35] ('the Court would stress that intellectual property benefits from the protection afforded by Art.1 of Protocol No. 1 to the Convention').

[218] In general, a 'deprivation' must be lawful, in the public interest, and strike a fair balance between the needs of the state and the rights of an individual. The latter balance, in all but exceptional cases, is achieved only by the payment of compensation.

[219] *Ashby Donald and ors v. France*, Case 36769/08, [2013] *ECHR* 28 (ECtHR, 5th section), [40]; *Neij and Kolmisoppi (The Pirate Bay) v. Sweden*, Case 40397/12, [2013] *ECDR* (7) 213 (ECtHR, 5th section), [35].

[220] The referendum was carried out under the European Union Referendum Act 2015.

[221] Prime Minister to President Tusk, 29 March 2017, made under the European Union (Notification of Withdrawal) Act 2017.

5.1 THE IMMEDIATE TRANSITION

The government is taking steps to implement the transition. The so-called 'Great Repeal Act' will, in fact, be precisely the opposite: laws that apply the day before the United Kingdom departs from the European Union will become part of UK law, and thus apply after departure.[222] For Directives (e.g. the Trade Mark and Designs Directives, the swathe of copyright directives, and the Enforcement Directive) that have been implemented into UK law (particularly under the European Communities Act 1972) this should be straightforward.[223] For regulations that have not been translated into domestic law (because they are directly applicable), the effect is that they will come to be treated as UK law.[224] Interpretations of EU legislation offered by the CJEU before 'exit day' remain binding (on all but the Court of Appeal and Supreme Court),[225] but those issued thereafter do not (and, obviously, no references may be made after that date).[226] However, a UK court may choose to have regard to decisions made after 'exit day' by the CJEU 'so far as it is relevant to any matter before the court or tribunal'.[227]

A number of transitional issues will need to be dealt with.[228] One set of such issues concerns unitary EU rights: the Community Designs regime, Community Plant Variety Right and EU Trade Marks, as well as Geographical Indications. These currently confer rights over acts that occur in the European Union,[229] and, after Brexit, in the absence of some transitional rule, the rights would no longer be actionable in the United Kingdom because evidently it will no longer be in the Union. Under the proposed transitional arrangements, such EU rights will automatically be transformed, in respect of the United Kingdom, after Brexit, into equivalent national rights.[230]

For most unregistered rights (copyright, unregistered design right,[231] trade secrets), the principle of national treatment means that no changes should be necessary: EU entities will automatically be protected under UK law. However, as we will see (in Chapter 13), this is not the case for the special (so-called 'sui generis') right granted under the Database Directive.[232] The negotiations seem likely to require the United Kingdom to undertake to continue to protect databases that prior to exit were created by EU nationals, residents, and businesses, and EU countries will do the same.[233]

The transitional arrangement will also deal with exhaustion.[234] Objects marketed before the day of exit in the United Kingdom or European Union will continue to circulate freely. The United Kingdom will need to decide on the rules it applies thereafter, but (unless the United Kingdom joins the EEA), the European Union will not treat rights in goods placed on the market in the United Kingdom as having been exhausted for EU purposes.

---

[222] European Union (Withdrawal) Act 2018, s. 2(1).

[223] Ibid., s. 2 ('EU-derived legislation').   [224] Ibid., s. 3(2)(a) (defining 'direct EU legislation').

[225] Ibid., s. 6(4)(a).   [226] Ibid., s. 6(1). 'Retained EU case law' is defined in s. 6(7).

[227] Ibid., s. 6(2).

[228] TF50(2017)11—Commission to EU 27 (6 September 2017), Position Paper to EU 27 on Intellectual Property Rights (including Geographical Indications). Forwarded to UK on 20 September 2017; Draft Agreement on the withdrawal of the United Kingdom of Great Britain and Northern Ireland from the European Union (19 March 2018), TFSO (2018) 35 – Commission to EU27 ('Draft Transitional Agreement').

[229] Regulation 2017/1001, Art. 1 (EU trade mark has effect throughout the Union).

[230] Draft Transitional Agreement, Art. 50 (continued protection in the UK of registered or granted rights).

[231] These are explicitly dealt with in Draft Transitional Agreement, Art. 53.

[232] SI 1997/3032, reg. 18. In fact this will need to modified to ensure that UK citizens (etc) qualify for database right, since they will no longer be EEA citizens.

[233] Draft Transitional Agreement, Art. 54.   [234] Draft Transitional Agreement, Art. 57.

Although not yet flagged, the European Union has been developing rules that give privileges or immunities to persons in one EU country on the basis of status or actions in another. The Orphan Works Directive, for example, confers orphan status on a work in all Member States based on an appropriate search carried out in the member state of first publication. Post-Brexit, will EU countries continue to apply the exceptions in Article 6 where the orphan work status was established in the United Kingdom? Likewise, will the United Kingdom continue to apply exemptions for orphan works under CDPA s. 76A, Sch. ZA1 based on entry in the EUIPO database?

It seems highly unlikely that the United Kingdom will be able to remain, post-Brexit in the Unified Patent Court Agreement, despite the government continuing to put in place appropriate subordinate legislation. The commitments to EU law involved seem inconsistent with the Great Repeal Bill.

5.2 THE LONGER TERM

It is much more difficult to have any confidence as to the direction of intellectual property in the United Kingdom in the longer term. Questions have been raised, such as whether copyright term might be shortened, supplementary protection certificates, *droit de suite* or database right abolished, the trade mark functions jurisprudence rejected, rights conferred on trade marks with a reputation slimmed (perhaps to permit non-damaging free-riding by third parties), the copyright/designs interface be reformed or fair use introduced for copyright. It is therefore important to recognize immediately constraints on policy freedom.

First, any post-Brexit trade agreement with the European Union is likely to include a chapter on intellectual property and may well require the United Kingdom to maintain the same standards at it currently has. Experience with existing EU external agreements gives strong indications about what the EU will try to secure (or retain). For example, the EU-Korea Free Trade Agreement requires cumulation between the copyright and registered design laws;[235] the EU-Moldova Association agreement requires operation of a *droit de suite*;[236] the EU Korea Agreement requires recognition of unregistered design right;[237] the EU Georgia Agreement requires the operation of a supplementary protection certificate system (SPC).[238]

Second, the United Kingdom will remain a party to the European Convention on Human Rights. There will therefore be a limit on the actions it might take because Article 1 of the First Protocol restricts the taking of vested property rights.

[235] EU-Korea FTA [2011] *OJ L* 127/1: Art 10.32. On the current EU law, see Chapter 29, section 4, pp. 815–16.

[236] EU-Moldova Association Agreement [2004] *OJ L* 260/4, Art. 290. *On droit de suite*, see Chapter 13, section 7, pp. 386–9.

[237] Art. 10.29. On unregistered design right, see Chapter 30, pp. 809–31.

[238] EU-Georgia Association Agreement [2014] *OJ L 261*, Art. 186. On SPCS, see Chapter 24, Section 3, pp. 708–15.

PART I
COPYRIGHT

2

INTRODUCTION TO COPYRIGHT

1 INTRODUCTION

In British legal parlance, 'copyright' is the term used to describe the area of intellectual property law that regulates the creation and use made of a range of cultural goods such as books, songs, films, and computer programs.[1] British law describes the various objects that are protected by copyright law as 'works'. The intangible property protected by copyright law is distinctive in that it arises automatically and usually for the benefit of the author.[2] Various rights are conferred on the owner of copyright, including the right to copy the work and the right to communicate the work to the public.[3] The rights vested in the owner are limited, notably in that they are not infringed when another person copies or communicates to the public a work that they have created themselves. The rights given to a copyright owner last for a considerable time: in many cases, for 70 years after the death of the author of the work.[4] The basic framework of British copyright law is largely to be found in the Copyright, Designs and Patents Act 1988 (CDPA 1988),[5] although this has now been amended significantly.

This chapter provides an outline of certain background matters that will make the next chapters easier to follow. We begin by looking at some of the concepts that we will encounter in the coming chapters. We then turn to look at the history and functions of copyright law, as well as international and European influences on British copyright law.

2 'COPYRIGHT' AND *DROIT D'AUTEUR*

Many factors shape the way in which we view British copyright law. To some, it may appear to be an unnecessary restriction on their ability to express themselves; for others,

---

[1] For an analysis of various other perspectives on copyright, see P. Goldstein, 'Copyright' (1990–91) 38 *J Copyright Soc'y USA* 109.

[2] See Chapter 5.   [3] See Chapter 6.   [4] See Chapter 7.

[5] Certain related rights, such as the 'publication right' and the 'database right', are found in statutory instruments. On these rights, see Chapter 13.

copyright law provides the means to protect significant investment and labour. More generally, the image that we have of British copyright law is shaped by the way in which we think it relates to other legal regimes. Most famously, UK copyright (and that of many other 'common law' countries) is said to be distinct from and in many ways in opposition to the civil law *droit d'auteur* system (such as that of France). While there is now a growing body of literature that questions the accuracy of these portrayals,[6] nonetheless these caricatures have had and undoubtedly will continue to have an impact on the way in which the law develops.

The common law copyright model is said to be primarily concerned with encouraging the production of new works.[7] This is reflected in copyright law's emphasis on economic rights, such as the right to produce copies. Another factor that is held to typify the copyright model is its relative indifference to authors. This is said to be reflected in the fact that British law presumes that an employer is the first owner of works made by an employee,[8] the paucity of legal restrictions on alienability,[9] and the limited and half-hearted recognition of so-called 'moral rights'.[10] In contrast, the civil law *droit d'auteur* model is said to be more concerned with the natural rights of authors in their creations. This is reflected in the fact that the civil law model not only aims to secure the author's economic interests, but also aims to protect works against uses that are prejudicial to an author's spiritual interests (in particular through moral rights).

3　AUTHOR'S RIGHTS AND NEIGHBOURING RIGHTS

While British copyright law abandoned the formal distinction between different categories of work with the passage of the 1988 Act, nonetheless an informal distinction is still drawn between two general categories of subject matter: 'authorial works' and 'entrepreneurial works'.[11] This reflects the distinction drawn in many legal systems between 'author's rights' and 'neighbouring rights'. 'Author's rights' refer to works created by 'authors', such as books, plays, music, art, and films. In contrast, 'neighbouring rights' (which are sometimes called 'related rights' or *droits voisins*) refer to 'works' created by 'entrepreneurs', such as sound recordings, broadcasts, and the typographical format of published editions. The rationale for differentiating between these two categories of subject matter lies in the facts that neighbouring (or entrepreneurial) rights are typically derivative, in the sense that they use or develop existing authorial works, that they are a product of technical and organizational skill rather than authorial skill, and that the rights are initially given not to the human creator, but to the body or person that was financially and organizationally responsible for the production of the material.[12]

---

[6] G. Davies, *Copyright and the Public Interest* (1994; 2nd edn, 2002); J. Ginsburg, 'A Tale of Two Copyrights: Literary Property in Revolutionary France and America', in Sherman and Strowel; A. Strowel, '*Droit d'auteur* and Copyright: Between History and Nature', in Sherman and Strowel.

[7] For a typical statement, see T. Cook (ed.), *Sterling on World Copyright Law* (4th edn, 2015), [16.09].

[8] See Chapter 5, section 3, pp. 133–7.　　　[9] See Chapter 12, section 2, pp. 333–4.　　　[10] See Chapter 10.

[11] In fact, as we will see, the process of European harmonization has reinforced the relevance of the distinction: see, e.g., section 7, pp. 52–3.

[12] For a general discussion, see W. Grosheide, 'Paradigms in Copyright Law', in Sherman and Strowel, 223.

4 HISTORY

The history of copyright is a complex, subtle, and rich subject. Depending on one's interest, it is possible to highlight many different themes and trends. For example, a history of copyright could look at the gradual expansion of the subject matter and the rights granted to owners, the role that copyright law plays in shaping the notion of authorship, or the impact that copyright has on particular cultural practices. Most histories of British copyright law tend to focus on the origins of copyright, which are usually traced back to the 1709/10 Statute of Anne, or occasionally to the practices developed in the sixteenth century to regulate the book trade.[13] In this section, we limit ourselves to a brief chronological account of some of the more important political and legal events that frame and shape the current law.

While aspects of copyright law have a long history, copyright law did not take on its modern meaning as a discrete area of law that grants rights in works of literature and art until at least the mid-nineteenth century.[14] Moreover, it was not until the passage of the Copyright Act 1911 that copyright law in Great Britain was rationalized and codified into the type of modern, abstract, and forward-looking statute that concerns us here.[15] The 1911 Act was also important insofar as it abolished the rights in unpublished works (often called 'copyright') that had been recognized at common law (and also repealed the plethora of subject-specific statutes that existed at the time). In their place, the 1911 Act established a single code that conferred copyright protection on a number of works (whether published or not, and including many previously unprotectable works, such as works of architecture, sound recordings, and films). In most cases, protection lasted for 50 years after the death of the author of the work. At the same time, the 1911 Act abandoned all requirements concerning formalities (in particular the need for registration with the Stationers' Company). Infringement was also expanded to include translations and adaptation, as well as reproductions 'in a material form'.[16]

Following a review in 1952, the 1911 Act was replaced by the Copyright Act 1956.[17] This extended the scope of copyright to encompass sound and television broadcasts, as well as

---

[13] Primary sources and commentaries are available online at http://www.copyrighthistory.org. For secondary accounts, see B. Kaplan, *An Unhurried View of Copyright* (1967), 1–25; L. R. Patterson, *Copyright in Historical Perspective* (1968); D. Saunders, *Authorship and Copyright* (1992); M. Rose, *Authors and Owners* (1993); C. Seville, *Literary Copyright Reform in Early Victorian England* (1999); R. Deazley, *On the Origin of the Right to Copy: Charting the Movement of Copyright Law in Britain throughout the Eighteenth Century (1695-1775)* (2004); C. Seville, *Internationalisation of Copyright: Books, Buccaneers and the Black Flag* (2006); R. Deazley, *Rethinking Copyright: History, Theory, Language* (2006); R. Deazley, L. Bently, and M. Kretschmer (eds), *Privilege and Property: Essays on the History of Copyright Law* (2010); I. J. Alexander, *Copyright Law and the Public Interest in the Nineteenth Century* (2010); R. Spoo, *Without Copyrights: Piracy, Publishing and the Public Domain* (2013); M. Rose, *Authors in Court* (2016); O. Bracha, *Owning Ideas: The Intellectual Origins of American Intellectual Property, 1790-1909* (2016); E. Cooper and R. Deazley, 'Interrogating Copyright History' [2016] *EIPR* 467; I. Alexander and T. Gómez-Arostegui, *Research Handbook on the History of Copyright Law* (2016); E. Cooper, *Art and Modern Copyright: The Contested Image* (2018). For a historiography, see K. Bowrey, 'Who's Painting Copyright's History?', in D. McClean and K. Schubert, *Dear Images: Art, Culture and Copyright* (2002), 257.

[14] See Sherman and Bently, 111–28; B. Sherman, 'Remembering and Forgetting: The Birth of Modern Copyright Law' (1995) 10 *IPJ* 1.

[15] For historical accounts, see C. Seville, *The Internationalisation of Copyright* (2006), 139–45; R. Burrell, 'Copyright Reform in the Early Twentieth Century: The View from Australia' (2006) 27 *J Legal Hist* 239.

[16] CA 1911, s. 1(2).

[17] *Report of the Copyright Committee* (Cmnd. 8662, 1951–2) (Gregory Committee).

typographical formats of published editions.[18] The 1956 Act was amended on a number of occasions, primarily to take account of new technologies such as cable television and computer software.[19] A further periodic review in 1977 proposed a general revision of the 1956 Act.[20] After further negotiations and refinement, these proposals led to the passage of the Copyright, Designs and Patents Act 1988.[21]

The 1988 Act expanded significantly the rights given to copyright owners (notably by introducing a distribution right and a rental right).[22] At the same time, the Copyright Tribunal was established to ensure that copyright owners did not exercise their rights in an anti-competitive manner.[23] The 1988 Act also introduced a new category of rights, called 'moral rights', conferred on authors as such and not assignable.[24] Performers' rights, which were formerly dealt with under special Acts, were also included within the 1988 Act (where they are protected separately under Part II).[25]

Although the 1988 Act forms the basis of contemporary copyright law, it has been amended on a number of occasions since it came into force in August 1989. In most cases, these amendments were made to give effect to obligations imposed by EU directives. As we will see, while the European Union has stopped short of a wholesale approximation of copyright law, a series of specific interventions has altered the contents of the 1988 Act to such an extent that a recodification of national law would be desirable.

More significantly, however, the Court of Justice has set out to fill the gaps in the partial harmonization effected by legislation. In a remarkable series of decisions beginning with *Infopaq*,[26] the Court has ruled on the concept of originality,[27] the notion of the work,[28] authorship,[29] and the public,[30] as well as the copyright/design law interface—all matters that it had been thought remained unharmonized.[31] Moreover, the Court has started to interpret harmonizing legislation that appeared to afford member states flexibility as to its implementation, in ways that increasingly deprive member states of that freedom. In short, the Court has been reworking and developing the so-called *acquis communitaire*, with a view to harmonizing as much as it reasonably can.[32]

Alongside the shift over the last two decades in the sources of British copyright law, the law has inevitably had to respond to the challenges and opportunities raised by digitization, and particularly the Internet. Some of the responses occurred at EU level (such as

---

[18] CA 1956, ss 12–16.

[19] Cable and Broadcasting Act 1984 (adding cable programmes to protected subject matter); Copyright (Computer Software) Act 1985 (establishing copyright protection for computer programs). The Design Copyright Act 1968 sought to remedy certain problems in relation to copyright protection for designs.

[20] *Report of the Committee on Copyright and Designs Law* (Cmnd. 6732, 1977) (the 'Whitford Committee').

[21] See Green Paper, *Reform of the Law relating to Copyright, Designs and Performers' Protection* (Cmnd. 8302, 1981); Green Paper, *Intellectual Property Rights and Innovation* (Cmnd. 9117, 1983); White Paper, *Intellectual Property and Innovation* (Cmnd. 9712, 1986).

[22] See Chapter 6, section 3, pp. 149–56.   [23] See Chapter 12, section 7.3.2, pp. 353–4.

[24] See Chapter 10.   [25] See Chapter 13, section 2, pp. 356–65.

[26] *Infopaq Int v. Danske Dagblades Forening*, Case C-5/08 [2009] ECR I–6569 (ECJ), [37]. See Chapter 4, section 3.4, pp. 98–9; M. van Eechoud, 'Along the Road to Uniformity: Diverse Readings of the Court of Justice Judgments on Copyright Work' (2012) 1 *JIPITEC* 60.

[27] See Chapter 4, Section 3.4, pp. 98–9.

[28] *Bezpečnostní softwarová asociace*, Case C-393/09 [2010] ECR I–13,972 (ECJ), [45]–[46] (graphic user interface treated as a work). See further Chapter 3, Section 1, pp. 59–62.

[29] *Martin Luksan v. Petrus van der Let*, Case C-277/10, EU:C:2012:65 (ECJ). See Chapter 5, section 4, p. 140.

[30] *Socieded General de Autores y Editores de Espana (SGAE) v. Rafael Hotels SL*, Case C-306/05 [2006] ECR I–11,519. See Chapter 6, section 6.5, pp. 165–7.

[31] *Commission Staff Working Paper on the Review of the EC Legal Framework in the field of copyright*, SEC(2004)995, 14–15 ('originality' and 'the public' are unharmonized concepts).

[32] See also J. Griffiths, 'Constitutionalising or Harmonising?' (2013) 38 *ELR* 65.

the introduction of the making available right), and some fundamental issues—such as whether browsing and hyperlinking are permissible—have only recently been considered by the Court of Justice.[33]

Following a review of intellectual property and growth conducted by Professor Ian Hargreaves,[34] provisions on orphan works,[35] alongside significant reform of the exceptions to copyright, were effected in 2014.[36]

5 JUSTIFICATIONS

The existence of copyright in a particular work restricts the uses that can be made of the work. For example, a person who buys a protected CD cannot legally rip the recordings from that CD for a friend to use on that friend's mp3 player. As well as being inconvenient and/or expensive, copyright has the potential to inhibit the public's ability to communicate, to develop ideas, and to produce new works. For example, it seems that a blogger who creates a link to material on the Internet that happens to be there without the authority of the rightholder needs permission to do so, at least if the blog is commercial. Given that in the digital environment, just about any interaction with expressive material involves copying, it is understandable that the Danish art group, Superflex, has parodied Descartes famous aphorism, 'I think, therefore I am', with an alternative 'I copy, therefore I am' (which we reproduce on the cover of this textbook).

Because copyright law prohibits the unauthorized use of 'copies', it has the potential to inhibit the way in which people interact with and use cultural objects. It is therefore important that we constantly reassess its legitimacy. More specifically, we need to ask whether (and why) copyright is desirable. In this context, it is important to note that not everyone thinks that copyright is a good thing.[37] In fact, with the advent of the Internet, there are many who think that copyright unjustifiably stifles our ability to make the most of the new environment or that it impinges upon the public domain.[38] Others consider that while some aspects of copyright are justifiable, others are not. Typically, the argument is that copyright law has gone too far.[39] In response to these copyright sceptics or critics, six basic arguments are used to support the recognition (and further extension) of copyright: (i) natural rights arguments; (ii) reward arguments; (iii) arguments based on speech right; (iv) incentive arguments; (v) neoliberal economics; and (vi) arguments from democracy.[40]

---

[33] See Chapter 6, section 2, pp. 144–5, section 6.2.3, pp. 169–71, and Chapter 9, section 3, pp. 237–9.

[34] Prof. I. Hargreaves, *Digital Opportunity: A Review of Intellectual Property and Growth* (2011) (the 'Hargreaves Review'), available online at https://www.gov.uk/government/uploads/system/uploads/attachment_data/file/32563/ipreview-finalreport.pdf.

[35] See Chapter 12, section 5, pp. 346–8.

[36] See Chapter 9, section 1, p. 226.

[37] Criticism of copyright has come from the 'Pirate Party', which has famously won seats in the European, Czech, and Icelandic parliaments. Anti-copyright sentiment has also given rise to a religion, 'the missionary church of kopimism'. Initiatives to expand the role of copyright in the Internet context have produced a wave of popular antipathy towards it. For a review, see M. A. Carrier, 'SOPA, PIPA, ACTA, TPP: An Alphabet Soup of Innovation-Stifling Copyright Legislation and Agreements' (2013) 11 *Nw J Tech & Intell Prop* 21.

[38] For a general discussion of the public domain, see (2003) 66 *L & CP* (Special edition on the public domain); B. Hugenholtz and L. Guibault (eds), *The Future of the Public Domain: Identifying the Commons in Information Law* (2006).

[39] S. Trosow, 'The Illusive Search for Justificatory Theories: Copyright, Commodification and Capital' (2003) 16 *Can J L Juris* 217.

[40] For an overview, see M. Spence, 'Justifying Copyright', in D. McClean and K. Schubert (eds), *Dear Images: Art, Culture and Copyright* (2002), 388.

5.1 NATURAL RIGHTS

According to natural rights theorists, the reason why copyright protection is granted is not that we think that the public will benefit from copyright; rather, copyright protection is granted because it is right and proper to do so. More specifically, it is right to recognize a property right in intellectual productions *because* such productions emanate from the mind of an individual author. For example, a poem is seen as the product of a poet's mind, of their intellectual effort and inspiration. As such, it should be seen as their property, and copying as equivalent to theft. Copyright is the positive law's realization of this self-evident, ethical precept. However, at this point, natural rights theorists divide as to exactly what it is about origination that entitles an author to protection. Some, particularly those associated with the continental European traditions, explain that works should be protected because (and insofar as) they are the expressions of each particular author's personality.[41] On the assumption that a work created by an individual reflects the unique nature of them as an individual, the natural rights arguments require that we allow the creator to protect the work (from misattribution, modification, or unauthorized exploitation) because it is an extension of the persona of its creator. A second version of natural right theory, strongly represented in the US literature, has tended to found itself on labour. Drawing on Locke's idea that a person has a natural right over the products of their labour, it is argued that an author has a natural right over the productions of their intellectual labour.[42]

Critics of natural rights theories of copyright take a number of different positions. Some simply reject the idea of 'natural rights'; others criticize the assumptions within the theory, for example that a natural right in labour justifies a natural right in the product of mixing labour and unowned resources. Some criticize the extension of natural rights theories to copyright, challenging the idea of individual creation of ideas, emphasizing the social (or 'intertextual') nature of writing and painting.[43] If works are seen less as the products of individual labour or personality and more as reworkings of previous ideas and texts, the claim to ownership seems weaker. Another critique questions why it is that a natural right in the products of one's labour should justify recognition of anything more than a right over the manuscript or immediate creation. A final argument criticizes natural rights theory on the ground that it provides no normative guidance as to the specific form of copyright law.[44]

5.2 REWARD

According to reward arguments, copyright protection is granted because we think it is fair to reward an author for the effort expended in creating a work and giving it to the public. Copyright is a legal expression of gratitude to an author for doing more than

[41] For personality theory based on Hegel, see J. Hughes, The Philosophy of Intellectual Property' (1988) 77 *Georgetown LJ* 287.

[42] On Locke and labour, see Hughes, ibid.; A. Yen, 'Restoring the Natural Law: Copyright as Labour and Possession' (1990) 51 *Ohio St LJ* 517; W. Gordon, 'A Property Right in Self-Expression: Equality and Individualism in the Natural Law of Intellectual Property' (1993) 102 *Yale LJ* 1533. Note, too, H. Breakey, *Intellectual Liberty: Natural Rights and Intellectual Liberty* (2012) (highlighting the natural rights constraints on intellectual property rights).

[43] S. Shiffrin, 'Lockean Arguments for Private Intellectual Property', in S. Munzer (ed.), *New Essays in the Legal and Political Theory of Property* (2001); P. Drahos, *The Philosophy of Intellectual Property* (1996), ch. 3; L. Zemer, *The Idea of Authorship in Copyright* (2006).

[44] J. O. Garon, 'Normative Copyright: A Conceptual Framework for Copyright Philosophy and Ethics' (2003) 88 *Cornell L Rev* 1278, 1299–306.

society expects or feels that they are obliged to do. In a sense, the grant of copyright is similar to the repayment of a debt. (Although the language of reward often appears when discussing the 'incentive' theory of copyright, it differs from incentive theory: in reward theory proper, the reward is an end in itself; in incentive theory, the reward is a means to an end.)

Critiques of reward theory tend to pose two questions. First, they ask: do the circumstances in which copyright protection is granted correspond to the circumstances in which people deserve rewards? One answer is that a reward is deserved only where someone has done something that they felt was unpleasant and which they would not otherwise have done. If this is the case, copyright does seem to give far too many rewards. As we will see, copyright's threshold is set at a very low level and thus catches works that are created for their own sake, such as letters, holiday photographs, and amateur paintings. Another account sees the reward as being deserved where the person invested labour (irrespective of their ulterior motives or the pleasure or pain of labouring).

The second criticism questions the nature of the reward: why should a person be granted an exclusive right? There are other systems of reward (such as the MAN Booker Prize) that have fewer social and economic costs. The usual answer is that copyright allows the general public to determine who should be rewarded and the size of that reward: the more copies of a book that are purchased or the more times a record is played on the radio, the greater the financial reward that accrues to the copyright owner. Consequently, a property right is often the best way in which to ensure that the reward is proportional to the public's appreciation of the work.

5.3 ARGUMENTS BASED ON SPEECH

There is a growing group of scholars who emphasize the relationship between copyright and communication, figuring copyright either as a vehicle to protect the 'expressive autonomy' of authors or as an unwarranted constraint upon such autonomy.[45] Drawing on philosophical foundations that can be traced to the German philosopher, Immanuel Kant, it has been eloquently argued that copyright law serves as the legal mechanism to ensure that only persons authorized by the author 'speak' in the name of the author.[46] If unauthorized persons publish or communicate works without authorization, in effect, they compel the author to speak, thereby harming the author's autonomy. This wrong seems all the worse if such publishers alter the work.

If this theory seems to confer strong rights on authors, it is important to note the inherent limits: one author's rights should give way where another author needs to copy parts of an earlier work to express themselves effectively.

5.4 INCENTIVE-BASED THEORIES

In contrast to the natural rights and reward theories, the third argument for copyright is not based on ideas of what is right or fair to an author or creator; rather, it is based

---

[45] See A. Drassinower, 'Copyright Infringement as Compelled Speech', in A. Lever (ed.), *New Frontiers in the Philosophy of Intellectual Property* (2012), ch. 8; L. Biron, 'Public Reason, Communication and Intellectual Property', in Lever, op. cit., ch. 9; A. Barron, 'Kant, Copyright and Communicative Freedom' (2012) 31(1) *Law and Philosophy* 1.

[46] The best account is A. Drassinower, *What's Wrong with Copying?* (2015), who argues that this principle is already embodied in Canadian (and British) copyright law.

on an idea of what is good for society or the public in general. The incentive argument presupposes that the production and public dissemination of cultural objects such as books, music, art, and films is an important and valuable activity. It also presupposes that, without copyright protection, the production and dissemination of cultural objects would not take place at an optimal level. The reason for this is that while works are often very costly to produce, once published they can readily be copied. For example, while this textbook took a considerable amount of time and energy to write, once published it can be reproduced easily and cheaply. Consequently, in the absence of copyright protection, a competitor could reproduce Bently, Sherman, Gangjee, and Johnson's *Intellectual Property Law* without having to recoup the expense of its initial production. In so doing, they could undercut Oxford University Press. According to the incentive argument, if Bently, Sherman, Gangjee, and Johnson, and Oxford University Press were not given any legal protection, *Intellectual Property Law* would never have been written or published—and the world would have been a commensurably poorer place. The legal protection given by copyright is intended to rectify this 'market failure' by providing incentives that encourage the production and dissemination of works. In short, copyright provides a legal means by which those who invest time and labour in producing cultural and informational goods can not only recoup that investment, but also reap a profit proportional to the popularity of their work.[47]

Utilitarian arguments for copyright are commonly met with three criticisms. Some question whether an incentive is really necessary for much production, and certainly there are plenty of examples of practices of creation and dissemination of works that do not depend on the existence of copyright.[48] Others, admitting the need for an artificial incentive to rectify the market failure, question whether the grant of an exclusive property is the appropriate incentive.[49] After all, exclusive properties impose costs on people who wish to use the work, costs of policing rights and enforcement on owners, and transaction costs on those who seek permissions.[50] In some cases, in fact, exclusive rights are replaced by payments from general taxation (as with the public lending right discussed in Chapter 13), thus ensuring that authors are provided with an incentive, but that the costs associated with exclusive rights are minimized. Even if we accept that exclusive rights are the optimal form of incentive, the third problem with the utilitarian approach is deciding exactly what incentive is optimal: what should a copyright owner be able to prevent another person from doing and for how long?

---

[47] W. Landes and R. Posner, 'An Economic Analysis of Copyright Law' (1989) 18 *JLS* 325; W. Gordon, 'An Inquiry into the Merits of Copyright: The Challenges of Consistency, Consent and Encouragement Theory' (1989) 41 *Stanford L Rev* 1343. For recent endorsement at international level, see Marrakesh Treaty, Recital 3 ('emphasizing the importance of copyright protection as an incentive and reward for literary and artistic creations').

[48] S. Breyer, 'The Uneasy Case for Copyright: A Study of Copyright in Books, Photocopies and Computer Programs' (1970) 84 *Harv L Rev* 281 (emphasizing, in particular, the incentives provided by lead time and possible use of contractual methods such as subscription); D. Zimmerman, 'Copyright as Incentives: Did We Just Imagine That?' (2011) 12 *TIL* 29; K. Darling and A. Perzanowski (eds), *Creativity Without Law: Challenging the assumptions of Intellectual Property* (2017). For suggestions that copyright rules be modified to reflect the workings of different incentives, see L. Loren, 'The Pope's Copyright? Aligning Incentives with Reality by Using Creative Motivation to Shape Copyright Protection' (2008) 69 *LA L Rev* 1 (suggesting that works not motivated by monetary incentive should receive less protection); S. Balganesh, 'Foreseeability and Copyright Incentives' (2009) 122 *Harv L Rev* 1569.

[49] R. Hurt and R. Schuchman, 'The Economic Rationale for Copyright' (1966) 56 *Am Econ Rev* 421 (suggesting private patronage and government support).

[50] See *Eldred v. Ashcroft* (2003) 537 US 186, 242 *ff*, 123 *S Ct* 769, 804 *ff* (Breyer J).

5.5 NEOLIBERAL ECONOMICS

If economic theory that sees copyright as an incentive to create or publish implies a rather narrow right, an alternative economic theory, associated with neoliberal economics, would justify protection of virtually all 'value'.[51] According to this school of thought, private ownership of resources is the juridical arrangement most conducive to optimal exploitation. In contrast, common ownership or non-ownership is likely to lead to over-exploitation (the so-called 'tragedy of the commons'). For example, it has been argued that failure to protect sound recordings by copyright would lead to their overuse, so that the public interest in the recordings would tire, and their value, diminish.[52] Accordingly, copyright protection should be limited only where the transaction costs involved in locating and negotiating licence agreements would prevent the conclusion of optimal agreements. These theoretical positions have not only featured in the arguments of scholars and treatise writers, and in the lobbying process, but have also even been adopted by some US courts.[53] However, the idea that copyright should be unlimited in coverage, scope, and duration because this will promote optimal use of intellectual resources seems to neglect a fundamental characteristic of intellectual products—namely, their 'non-rival nature'.[54] Fears about overexploitation of physical resources, which (might) make private ownership the most satisfactory allocative model, simply do not apply to cultural resources: the more people who can get access to the works of Shakespeare, Mozart, and even Jeremy Bentham, the better.

5.6 DEMOCRATIC AND REPUBLICAN ARGUMENTS

In an important intervention in 1996, Neil Netanel has tried to justify copyright by reference to the 'democratic paradigm'.[55] Netanel sees copyright as 'fortifying our democratic institutions by promoting public education, self-reliant authorship, and robust debate. More precisely, this democratic paradigm views copyright law as a 'state measure designed to enhance the independent and pluralist character of civil society'.[56] Copyright encourages greater production, but also 'is designed to secure the qualitative condition for creative autonomy and expressive diversity'.[57]

5.7 THE PLACE OF JUSTIFICATIONS

There is a large body of literature criticizing, developing, and refining these six justifications. There is not room here to recount and assess this literature further. Nevertheless, it is worth noting a number of points about the ways in which these theories are marshalled in support of legal arguments relating to copyright. It is often said that a natural

---

[51] For a concise, if unsympathetic, explanation, see N. W. Netanel, 'Copyright and a Democratic Civil Society' (1996) 106 *Yale LJ* 283, 290, 306–7, 308–36.

[52] W. Landes and R. Posner, 'Indefinitely Renewable Copyright' (2003) 70 *U Chi LR* 471. For discussion of the empirical evidence refuting this, see Chapter 7, section 7, pp. 190–2.

[53] *Harper & Row Publishers Inc v. Nation Enterprises*, 471 US 539 (1985).

[54] For a compelling critique, see M. Lemley, 'Ex Ante versus Ex Post Justifications for Intellectual Property' (2004) 71 *U Chi L Rev* 129.

[55] N. W. Netanel, 'Copyright and a Democratic Civil Society' (1996) 106 *Yale LJ* 283, 291. For an argument that copyright diminishes diversity, see G. Pessach, 'Copyright Law as a Silencing Restriction on Non-Infringing Materials: Unveiling the Scope of Copyright's Diversity Externalities' (2003) 76 *S Cal L Rev* 1067.

[56] Netanel, op. cit., 291.

rights-based justification for copyright inevitably produces a different conception of copyright from that which results from an incentive argument. More specifically, it is argued that a natural rights conception of copyright leads to longer and stronger protection for authors (and copyright owners) than an incentive-based conception. This is because a natural rights argument for copyright is assumed to result in a form of property that is perpetual and unqualified.[58] In contrast, an incentive-based argument justifies the grant of only the minimum level of protection necessary to induce the right holder to create and release the work.

Although the various theories have relatively distinct philosophical pedigrees, when they have been employed in support of various claims, little, if any, attention has been given to such niceties. Instead, the six arguments are typically deployed side by side. In fact, in most cases in which a claim is made for the legal protection of works not previously protected (such as television formats or special rights for newspapers) or for the expansion of the rights conferred by the law in respect of such works, one can reasonably anticipate that all six types of justification will be used. While it is understandable that lobby groups use (or abuse) the various justifications to further their ends, more problems arise when people begin to believe the rhetoric, and assume that copyright law is determined and shaped by these philosophical ideals.[59]

6 INTERNATIONAL INFLUENCES

One of the constant themes in the history of British copyright law is that it has been influenced by foreign and international trends and developments. While the sources may have changed, contemporary law is no different. There are a number of international treaties that impact upon British copyright law.[60] Here, we will limit ourselves to the seven most significant treaties:[61] the Berne Convention; the Rome Convention; the Agreement on Trade Related Aspects of Intellectual Property Rights (TRIPS); the World Intellectual Property Organization (WIPO) Copyright Treaty; the WIPO Performances and Phonograms Treaty; the Beijing Treaty on Audiovisual Performances; and the Marrakesh Treaty for the Visually Impaired.[62]

---

[57] Ibid., 339.

[58] See *Millar v. Taylor* (1769) 4 *Burr* 2303, 98 *ER* 201, 218–22 (Aston J), 252 (Mansfield CJ). However, if the processes of authorship are perceived as processes of a combination of existing texts, of *bricolage* and collocation, a natural rights approach might justify only a short-term and highly qualified 'property' in the resulting work.

[59] J. Litman, *Digital Copyright* (2001), 77 ('normative arguments ... typically, change nobody's mind'); G. Austin, 'Copyright's Modest Ontology: Theory and Pragmatism in *Eldred v. Ashcroft*' (2003) 16 *Can J L Juris* 163 ('there are few instances where theory dictates ... positive law'). For the suggestion that when real policy is negotiated the philosophical arguments are abandoned in favour of 'mid-level principles', see R. Merges, *Justifying Intellectual Property* (2011).

[60] Also important are the Universal Copyright Conventions (last revised at Paris in 1971), the Geneva Convention on Phonograms of 1971, and the Convention Relating to the Distribution of Programme-Carrying Signals Transmitted by Satellite (Brussels, 21 May 1974).

[61] The leading texts are S. Ricketson and J. Ginsburg, *International Copyright and Neighbouring Rights: The Berne Convention and Beyond* (2nd edn, 2006); P. Goldstein and B. Hugenholtz, *International Copyright; Principles, Law and Practice* (3rd edn, 2012); S. von Lewinski, *International Copyright Law and Policy* (2008).

[62] The Marrakesh Treaty to Facilitate Access to Published Works for Persons who are Blind, Visually Impaired or Otherwise Print Disabled (2013).

6.1 BERNE CONVENTION (1886–1971)

The most important international influence on the development of UK copyright has been the Berne Convention on the Protection of Literary and Artistic Works. The Berne Convention was drawn up in 1886 as a small treaty allowing for mutual recognition of rights amongst a few largely European countries. Since then, the Treaty has been revised on a number of occasions[63] and the membership of the so-called 'Berne Union' has expanded to 175 states.[64]

In its earliest form, there were two key provisions of the Berne Convention. The first was the adoption of the principle of 'national treatment'. This meant that, with certain exceptions, a country of the Union should not discriminate between its own nationals and those of other countries of the Union.[65] For example, under the principle of national treatment, French law was obliged to confer the same rights on a British author as it conferred on French authors. In addition to the principle of national treatment, the Berne Convention has long required that the 'enjoyment and exercise' of copyright in the works of the Convention should not be 'subject to any formality'. This means that registration or notices cannot be made prerequisites for protection.[66] Because international protection is to be automatic, there is no need for international bureaucratic regimes to simplify registration processes.

Over time, the Berne Convention has come to demand that members of the Union provide certain minimum standards of protection to copyright owners and authors. These include the rights to reproduce the work,[67] to perform the work publicly,[68] to translate the work,[69] to adapt the work,[70] and to broadcast the work.[71] Such protection is to last at least for the life of the author, plus 50 years thereafter.[72] In recognition of the need for the public to be able to utilize works without payment, there is a mandatory exception for fair quotation and limited scope for members of the Union to create other exceptions.[73] In relation to the reproduction right, the permissible exceptions must satisfy the so-called 'three-step test'. This requires that any such exceptions must be limited to certain special cases, must not conflict with a normal exploitation of the work, and must not unreasonably prejudice the legitimate interests of the author.[74] Members of the Union are also to give authors (rather than copyright owners) the moral rights of attribution and integrity.[75]

---

[63] The last revision was at Paris on 24 July 1971 and the last amendment on 28 September 1979.

[64] As of 1 January 2018. The Convention applies to all works in which copyright has not expired at the time of accession to the Convention: Berne, Art. 18.

[65] Berne, Art. 5(1). These are to be enjoyed by authors who are nationals of one of the countries of the Union for their works, whether published or not, and authors who are not nationals of one of the countries of the Union for their works first published in one of those countries: Berne, Art. 3. The exceptions to national treatment relate to: (i) copyright terms that exceed the Berne minimum (Art. 7(8)); (ii) copyright in applied art; and (iii) *droit de suite* (Art. 14*ter* (2)).   [66] Berne, Art. 5(2).

[67] Berne, Art. 9 ('in any manner or form'). Art. 9(3) specifically states that a sound or visual recording is to be considered a reproduction.   [68] Berne, Arts 11, 11*ter*.

[69] Berne, Arts 8 and 11(2) (translation).

[70] Berne, Arts 12 (authorizing adaptations, arrangements, and other alterations of their works) and 14 (cinematographic adaptation).

[71] Berne, Art. 11*bis*.   [72] Berne, Art. 7.

[73] Minor exceptions are permitted in accordance with the understandings expressed at various conferences, but these must be *de minimis*: see WTO Panel Report, WT/DS/16OR (June 2000). Compulsory licences are permitted under Arts 11*bis* (2) and 13 (mechanical copying).

[74] Berne, Art. 9(2). Note also Art. 10(2) (use by way of illustration in publications for teaching) and 10*bis* (use for reporting current events). The character of the 'three-step test' has become much debated. Recital 10 of the Marrakesh Treaty 2013 reaffirms 'the importance and flexibility' of the test.

[75] Berne, Art. 6*bis*. See Chapter 10.

6.2 ROME CONVENTION (1961)

The coverage of the Berne Convention is limited to literary and artistic works, which includes cinematographic works.[76] International recognition of the rights of phonogram producers, performers, and broadcasters is, however, offered under a separate instrument. In 1961, an international agreement on these 'neighbouring rights' was reached at the Rome Convention[77] (which, at time of writing, has 93 signatories).[78] Like the Berne Convention, the central principle of the Rome Convention is national treatment. National treatment must be provided to: performances that take place in a contracting state, or which are embodied on protected sound recordings, or carried by a protected broadcast; sound recordings produced by nationals of a contracting state, fixed in a contracting state, or first published in a contracting state; and broadcasts where the broadcasting organization is situated in a contracting state or the broadcast is transmitted from a contracting state.[79]

The Rome Convention also requires that phonogram producers, performers, and broadcasters be granted certain substantive rights. For performers, these are relatively limited, being largely restricted to matters relating to 'bootlegging' (that is, the fixation of their unfixed performances without their consent), the broadcasting of their unfixed performances without their consent, and the duplication of any such recordings that have been made illicitly.[80] Notably, contracting states are not required to give performers rights to control the reproduction, distribution, or public communication of legitimately made recordings of their performances. (As a result, there is no requirement, for example, that performers be paid when films are shown at a cinema.) The protection that is given is to last for 20 years from the first fixation of the performance, or if it has not been fixed, 20 years from the date on which the performance took place.

Producers of phonograms and broadcasting organizations received better treatment. Producers of phonograms are to be granted the right to prevent the reproduction of those recordings for 20 years.[81] Broadcasting organizations are to be given exclusive rights, for a minimum of 20 years from when a broadcast took place, to authorize or prohibit the rebroadcasting of their broadcasts, the fixation of their broadcasts, and the reproduction of fixations of their broadcasts. Broadcasters were also given the right to control the showing of television broadcasts in places accessible to the public (against payment of an entrance fee).[82]

The three divergent interests that coexist in the Rome Convention gave rise to one further and important compromise: that contracting states are to confer a right to a *single* equitable remuneration when phonograms are broadcast or played in public.[83] This right to remuneration must be provided either to the performers whose performances are embodied on phonograms or to the producers of phonograms, or both. This means that broadcasters, nightclubs, restaurants, etc., must pay a single fee to play sound recordings. It is left to the contracting states whether the beneficiary of the right is to be the performer or the phonogram producer, or both.

---

[76] Berne, Art. 14*bis*.

[77] International Convention for the Protection of Performers, Producers of Phonograms and Broadcasting Organizations.

[78] As at 1 January 2018. The United States is not a party, as a result of its refusal to give broadcasting organizations copyright.

[79] Rome, Arts 4 (performers), 5 (phonograms), and 6 (broadcasts). National treatment is defined in Rome, Art. 2.   [80] Rome, Art. 7. Note also Art. 19.

[81] Rome, Art. 10. If formalities are required, they are complied with by using the 'P' symbol: Rome, Art. 11.

[82] Rome, Arts 13, 14.   [83] Rome, Art. 12. This can be excluded under Art. 16.

Contracting states are permitted to make these rights subject to defences as regards private use, news reporting, ephemeral recordings, and teaching and scientific research,[84] as well as the same kind of limitations as are provided for literary and artistic works under the Berne Convention.[85]

6.3 TRIPS (1994)

The third important international development that impacts upon British copyright law is TRIPS.[86] There are a number of provisions in TRIPS that relate to copyright. The most significant of these is that members must implement Articles 1–21 of the Berne Convention (but not Article 6*bis* dealing with moral rights).[87] One of the consequences of this is that disputes over compliance with Berne can now be considered by the World Trade Organization (WTO).[88] While the TRIPS Agreement does not require member states to adhere to the Rome Convention, Article 14 of TRIPS contains substantively similar provisions to those of Rome (although the term of protection in such cases is substantially longer under TRIPS).[89]

In addition, the TRIPS Agreement contains certain 'Berne-plus' features, as regards various aspects of copyright. Some of these were responses to new technologies that have given rise to new sorts of work and new modes of distribution. For example, under TRIPS, protection must be given to computer programs, as literary works within the Berne Convention,[90] and to compilations of data or other material that, by reason of the selection or arrangement of their contents, 'constitute intellectual creations'.[91] Reflecting the growing concern that existed in the 1980s with new modes of distribution, members must (in most cases) give copyright owners the right to authorize rental of computer programs, cinematographic works, and phonograms.[92] Other provisions flow from more general concerns as to the nature of copyright protection. In particular, copyright is defined generally as covering 'expressions' and *not* ideas or methods.[93] Moreover, TRIPS requires that *all* non-mandatory limitations or exceptions (rather than merely those limiting the right of reproduction) must satisfy the three-step test.[94]

6.4 WIPO COPYRIGHT TREATY (1996)

In December 1996, two treaties were agreed at Geneva: the WIPO Copyright Treaty (WCT); and the WIPO Performances and Phonograms Treaty.[95] Both treaties are intended to supplement the existing conventions to reflect, in particular, technological changes and changes in practice.[96]

---

[84] Rome, Art. 15(1).   [85] Rome, Art. 15(2).

[86] See Chapter 1, section 3, pp. 8–10.   [87] TRIPS, Art. 9(1).

[88] As has occurred in the WTO Dispute Panel Report on US limitations on the public performance right: WT/DS160/R (15 June 2000). According to TRIPS, Art. 14(6), the provisions on neighbouring rights in performances and phonograms apply to existing works. The WTO dispute resolution procedure was used to induce Japan to comply with this requirement: WT/DS22 and WT/DS 48.

[89] TRIPS, Art. 14.   [90] TRIPS, Art. 10(1); see also WCT, Art. 4.

[91] TRIPS, Art. 10(2). In what turned out to be a rather short-lived phenomenon, the 1990s saw the emergence of 'video-rental', with most town high streets in the UK hosting a 'Blockbuster'.

[92] TRIPS, Arts 11, 14(4).   [93] TRIPS, Art. 9(2).   [94] TRIPS, Art. 13.

[95] Reinbothe and von Lewinski, *The WIPO Treaties on Copyright* (2nd edn, 2015); M. Ficsor, *Copyright and the Internet* (2002).

[96] WCT, Art. 1, defines the Treaty as a 'special agreement' within Berne, Art. 20.

For the most part, the WCT, which came into force in 2002,[97] repeats many of the extensions in the TRIPS Agreement,[98] although importantly the WCT places them back under the supervision of the WIPO. Some of these are extended: for example, contracting parties must provide copyright owners with the exclusive right to distribute fixed copies that can be put into circulation as tangible objects.[99]

The WCT also embodies three provisions that reflect the so-called 'digital agenda'. (In essence, these were responses to the concerns then raised by copyright owners about new digital communication technologies.) First, as part of the 'communication right', contracting parties must provide copyright owners with the exclusive rights to make their works available to the public in such a way that members may access the work from a place and at a time individually chosen by them.[100] In 1996, this was intended to cover the placing of a work on a website that can be accessed by the public (though 20 years later some argue that the language is broad enough to cover acts such as aggregation of hyperlinks). Second, contracting parties must provide adequate legal protection against the circumvention of 'effective technological measures' used by authors to protect their rights.[101] Third, contracting parties must provide adequate remedies to those who tamper with 'rights management information'—that is, information used to facilitate the identification or exploitation of those works.[102]

6.5 WIPO PERFORMANCES AND PHONOGRAMS TREATY (1996)

Although the WIPO Performances and Phonograms Treaty (WPPT) was intended to supplement the Rome Convention, it contains provisions relating only to rights of performers and phonogram producers, and *not* to those of broadcasters.[103] The WPPT upgraded the position of performers whose performances are embodied on phonograms. Under the WPPT, contracting parties must confer on all performers rights against bootlegging equivalent to those in the Rome Convention. This is an improvement for performers from 'the possibility of preventing' to an exclusive right.[104] Performers in the music industry (whose performances have been 'fixed in phonograms') are to be given three extra rights. First, they are to be given rights to control various acts in relation to fixations of their performances—that is, the reproduction, distribution, rental, and making available of copies of such fixations.[105] Second, where there is public performance or broadcasting of such fixations, contracting states are to ensure that performers receive a share in the remuneration that is paid.[106] Third, contracting states are to confer moral rights of attribution and integrity on the performers of 'live aural performances or performances fixed in phonograms'.[107]

---

[97] As of 1 January 2018, there are 96 contracting parties. The United Kingdom ratified the Treaty in 2009 and it came into operation on 14 March 2010.

[98] WCT, Art. 2, is on a par with TRIPS, Art. 9(2); WCT, Art. 4, is on a par with TRIPS, Art. 10(1); WCT, Art. 5, is on a par with TRIPS, Art. 10(2); WCT, Art. 10, is on a par with TRIPS, Art. 13; WCT, Art. 14, is on a par with TRIPS, Art. 41.

[99] WCT, Art. 6; 'Agreed Statement' concerning Arts 6 and 7. In addition, contracting parties must provide copyright owners whose works are embodied in phonograms (not only those in computer programs or cinematographic works) with the exclusive right to authorize the commercial rentals of those fixed copies: WCT, Art. 7. Note the qualifications in Art. 7(2)–(3).

[100] WCT, Art. 8.　　　[101] WCT, Art. 11.　　　[102] WCT, Art. 12.

[103] The WPPT entered into force on 20 May 2002. As of 1 January 2018, there are 96 contracting parties to the WPPT.　　　　　　　　　　　　　　　　　　　　　　　　　[104] WPPT, Art. 6.

[105] WPPT, Arts 7–10.　　　[106] WPPT, Art. 15.

[107] WPPT, Art. 5. See Chapter 13, section 2.4, pp. 361–2.

The WPPT also extends the rights given to producers of phonograms. Contracting states are to confer on the producers of phonograms not only the right to control reproduction, but also the exclusive right to control the distribution, rental, and making available of copies of phonograms.[108] The WPPT also requires certain action for the benefit of *both* performers and phonogram producers. In particular, the WPPT replicates the three provisions of the WCT on the digital agenda—that is, the 'making available' right, the requirements relating to technological measures of protection, and the provisions on rights management information. The Treaty also provides that contracting states may create exceptions and limitations to the rights of performers or phonogram producers only if those limitations pass the three-step test.[109]

6.6 MARRAKESH TREATY FOR THE VISUALLY IMPAIRED (2013)

Significant concern has been expressed about the potential impact of copyright law on the ability of peoples with disabilities to access cultural materials: copyright, by preventing the making of reproductions and adaptations, as well as their communication and distribution, has the potential to deter the making of Braille copies or large-print editions. A particular problem is that the markets are small (often with the largest numbers in the developing world) and that national exceptions, if they exist, are formulated in different ways. These differences make the task of providing resources on an international level particularly difficult. It is thought that this has contributed to the so-called 'book famine'—that is, that only a small percentage of the world's literature (between 1 and 7 per cent) is accessible to the blind, visually impaired, and print disabled. Moreover, technological locks designed to protect copyright works may prevent deployment of 'read-aloud' mechanisms that allow printed materials to be automatically converted into the spoken word.

Following the lead of a 2006 UN Convention,[110] the WIPO has nurtured the development of a treaty specifically targeted at the protection of the blind, visually impaired, and print disabled.[111] At the heart of the Marrakesh Treaty for the Visually Impaired, signed in 2013,[112] is an *obligation* on contracting parties to provide in their national copyright laws for a limitation or exception to copyright to facilitate the availability of works in 'accessible format copies' to the blind and print disabled.[113] The Treaty provides that the goal can be achieved by permitting 'authorized entities', which essentially are government-recognized, not-for-profit operators (such as the Royal National Institute for Blind People) to make, acquire, or supply such 'accessible-format copies'. Moreover, acknowledging the difficulty with small markets, permitted acts can include importation

---

[108] WPPT, Arts 11–14.

[109] WPPT, Art. 16.

[110] UN Convention on the Rights of Persons with Disabilities (2006), Art. 30(3). The UNCRPD requires parties to the Convention to take all appropriate steps, in accordance with international law, to ensure that laws protecting intellectual property rights do not constitute an unreasonable or discriminatory barrier to access by persons with disabilities to cultural materials. The United Kingdom is a signatory and ratified the Convention in 2009.

[111] The Marrakesh Treaty to Facilitate Access to Published Works for Persons who are Blind, Visually Impaired or Otherwise Print Disabled (2013).

[112] L. R. Helfer, M. Land, R Okediji, and J. Reichman, *World Blind Union Guide to the Marrakesh Treaty: Facilitating Access to Books for Print-Disabled Individuals* (2017); Reinbothe and von Lewinski (2015), ch. 18.

[113] The beneficiaries are defined in Art. 3, while the notion of 'accessible format copies' is explained in Art. 2 (as a copy of a work in an alternative manner or form that gives a beneficiary person access to the work).

of accessible-format copies.[114] Parties must also 'take appropriate measures' to ensure that the legal protection of technological measures 'does not prevent beneficiary persons from enjoying the limitations and exceptions' required by the Treaty. The Treaty, which came into force on 30 September 2016, has been welcomed by the World Blind Union as a first step towards ending the 'book famine'.[115] Although the Treaty states in express terms that it does not affect the scope of obligations under the Berne or WIPO treaties,[116] it is an important development symbolically, in that it recognizes the benefits of international minimum standardization not merely of exclusive rights, but also of limitations (or user rights). As such, it may pave the way for the formulation of other more balanced international instruments. The 31 parties to the Treaty do not, as yet, include the United Kingdom.[117] The EU has, however, now adopted a Regulation and Directive that, once implemented, will enable the ratification of the Treaty.[118]

6.7 BEIJING TREATY ON AUDIOVISUAL PERFORMANCES (2012)

The Beijing Treaty on Audiovisual Performances (if it comes into force) will require contracting parties to confer rights upon actors to parallel those required to be granted to musical performers under the WPPT.[119] This topic was largely excluded from the 1996 WIPO treaties because of opposition from US-based interests, and a diplomatic conference that was held in Geneva in December 2000 concluded without agreement.[120] However, in June 2012 at Beijing, the stumbling block (which related to the transfer of rights) was overcome.[121] Whereas, at the earlier conference, delegates battled over a single regime governing transfers, in the Beijing Treaty, contracting parties are given considerable freedom to determine the effect of agreements by performers allowing fixation of their performances.[122] Thus contracting parties have the option (as the United States wants) to treat such consent as effective to transfer the economic rights of the performer in the fixation to the film producer, or to require express signed contracts ('with respect to audiovisual fixations produced under its national law') before such rights pass, or to require that performers receive royalties or equitable remuneration for such uses irrespective of the terms of the contract. The 2000 draft included a provision that would have identified the relevant national law applicable to any such agreement, but the Beijing Treaty does not do so (although it does imply that national rules on formalities may not be applied to films produced elsewhere). In other respects, the text is the same as that which had been agreed in 2000.

In many respects, the Treaty will confer on actors similar rights to those offered to performers in relation to sound recordings under the WPPT. Thus audiovisual performers who are nationals in one contracting party are to be offered, without being subjected to any formalities, national treatment by other contracting countries (subject to some

---

[114] Marrakesh Treaty, Arts 5–6.

[115] World Blind Union, *The Marrakesh Treaty Explained*, available online at http://www.worldblindunion.org/english/news/Pages/The-Treaty-of-Marrakesh.aspx (stating that the WBU is 'happy, by and large').

[116] See Marrakesh Treaty, Art. 1, Recital 10.   [117] As of 1 January 2018.

[118] Regulation (EU) 2017/1563, *OJ L* 242/1 (20 September 2017) (in force from 12 October 2018); Directive (EU) 2017/1564, *OJ L* 242/6 (20 September 2017). Although in many respects these replicate the Marrakesh Treaty, the EU Directive controversially permits Member States to make the exemption granted to authorized entities (but not individual beneficiaries) subject to a compensation scheme: Art. 3(6), Recital 14.

[119] Reinbothe and von Lewinski (2015), ch. 9. As of 1 January 2018, 19 countries have ratified the Convention. 30 ratifications are required for it to come into force.

[120] Impetus came not just from the United States and European Union, but also India and Mexico.

[121] Beijing Treaty, Art. 12.   [122] Beijing Treaty, Art. 4. The exceptions relate to Art. 11.

limited exceptions),[123] and are to be granted moral rights of attribution and integrity,[124] rights to control the fixation, broadcasting, and other public communication of their unfixed performances (such as secretly filming or televising the performance of a play),[125] rights to control the reproduction, distribution, and making available of fixations of performances,[126] and all for a minimum term of 50 years from the year in which the performance was fixed. Performers are also to be afforded protection for any technological protection measures that they deploy or rights management information that they use. The chief difference relates to the provision on transfers, but there are other differences as to the scope of the moral right of integrity,[127] the right of rental of fixations,[128] and the right to control the broadcasting or communication to the public of fixations. There are also notable differences between the WPPT provision on transitional measures and those in the Beijing Treaty, but both offer flexibility for countries that do not wish to apply the treaty standards to pre-existing fixations of performances. The Beijing Treaty will come into force once 30 countries have ratified it. Despite there being 74 signatories (in 2012/2013), as of July 2017, there were 18 ratifications.

7 EUROPEAN INFLUENCES

In the last 30 years or so, European initiatives have had an important and growing impact on British copyright law. This is because various European instruments (mostly directives) now prescribe in some detail when and in what manner member states must (and sometimes may) recognize intellectual property rights in this field. As we saw in Chapter 1, the need for harmonizing legislation initially arose because, despite the efforts of the Court of Justice (notably through the doctrine of exhaustion),[129] differences in national laws relating to copyright and related rights operate to produce barriers to trade within the internal market.[130] Consequently, the European Commission decided that if the plan for an internal market free from barriers were to be made good, then certain aspects of copyright would have to be harmonized. The first step in the harmonization programme was the publication of the Green Paper, *Copyright and the Challenge of Technology*,[131] which was followed by a White Paper in 1990.[132] Given that it was widely believed that national copyright traditions were very different, it was decided that the wholesale approximation of copyright law was impossible. Instead, it was decided to harmonize specific areas of copyright, particularly those relating to new technologies.

The subsequent decade witnessed the formulation and passage of a series of directives on software, cable and satellite broadcasting, rental and lending rights and 'neighbouring rights', the duration of copyright, databases, the resale royalty right, and copyright in the 'information society'. While each of these directives concerned itself primarily with a specific aspect of copyright (that is, a specific type of subject matter or a specific right), the Directive on Copyright in the Information Society concerned a series of

---

[123] Beijing Treaty, Art. 5. But note Agreed Statement.   [124] Beijing Treaty, Art. 6.
[125] Beijing Treaty, Arts 7, 8, 10.   [126] Beijing Treaty, Agreed Statement to Art. 5.
[127] Beijing Treaty, Art. 9.   [128] Beijing Treaty, Art. 11.
[129] Chapter 1, Section 4.1, pp. 13 *ff*; *Deutsche Grammophon v. Metro*, Case C-78/70 [1971] *ECR* 487.
[130] Perhaps the clearest example of this was in the decision in *EMI Electrola GmbH v. Patricia Im-und Export*, Case C-341/87 [1989] *ECR* 79 (highlighting how differences in calculating the term of protection for sound recordings in different member states led to barriers to trade).
[131] *Copyright and the Challenge of Technology* (June 1988), COM(88) 172 final.
[132] *Follow Up to the Green Paper* (17 January 1991), COM(90) 584 final.

rights and exceptions applicable to virtually all copyright works.[133] The Directive was intended to implement the two WIPO treaties agreed in Geneva in 1996, but the Directive harmonizes the reproduction, communication, and distribution rights, and limits the number and scope of the exceptions (or defences) that a national regime can operate.[134] Consequently, the Directive is widely regarded as heralding a shift from 'vertical' harmonization to 'horizontal' harmonization.[135] In parallel with the Information Society Directive, the European legislature adopted the 'e-Commerce' Directive which required the creation of certain safe harbours for Internet intermediaries.[136]

If the 2001 Information Society Directive seemed to some to be the first step on the road towards an EU copyright law, those persons will be disappointed by the relative lack of progress since. No further legislative intervention specifically directed at copyright occurred for a decade, and since 2011 the interventions have been 'problem-focused', that is, rather narrow and focused on particular topics that have been understood as pressing problems. Thus, there have been new instruments dealing with the duration of copyright in sound recordings (2011), 'orphan works' (2012), collective management (2014), cross-border portability (2017), and the rights of visually impaired persons (2017). The latter two follow the initiation of the so-called 'digital single market' strategy of 2015, designed to ensure that Europe remains 'a world leader in the digital economy'.[137] Further proposals aimed to help achieve that goal, on so-called 'geo-blocking' (initiated in May 2016),[138] and more ambitiously, a proposed directive on copyright in the digital single market (initiated in September 2016) are making progress through the EU legislative organs.[139]

While we look at these directives at appropriate points in the following chapters, here we wish merely to note a few thematic elements.[140]

The first notable feature is that the directives consistently distinguish between two categories of work: 'authorial works', falling under the Berne Convention; and 'related rights' (specifically not 'neighbouring rights'), which refer to various rights of performers, phonogram producers, the producers of the first fixations of films, and broadcasting organizations. The related rights given to producers of the first fixations of 'films' by various

---

[133] This Directive has its origin in the Green Paper *Copyright in the Information Society* (27 July 1995), COM(95) 382 final and the 1996 White Paper that followed it, *Follow Up to the Green Paper on Copyright in the Information Society* (20 November 1996), COM(96) 568 final. See M. Hart, 'The Copyright in the Information Society Directive: An Overview' [2002] *EIPR* 58; B. Hugenholtz, 'Why the Copyright Directive is Unimportant and Possibly Invalid' [2000] *EIPR* 499.

[134] See Chapter 6, sections 2, 3 and, 6, pp. 144, 160, 176 and Chapter 9, pp. 227-9.

[135] As the title of the Directive makes clear, its remit was only to harmonize 'certain aspects' of copyright. The sloppy use of the shorthand 'Copyright Directive' by the Court can be traced to the Opinions of Advocate-General Sharpston in *Laserdisken ApS v. Kulturministeriet*, Case C-479/04 [2006] *ECR* I–8089 and *SGAE v. Rafael Hotels SL*, Case C-306/05 [2006] *ECR* I–11,519. The Court, for the most part, has resisted the shorthand.

[136] See Chapter 48, section 3.5, pp. 1289–96.

[137] Commission Communication, *A Digital Single Market Strategy for Europe* (6 May 2015), COM(2015) 192 final (promising a legislative programme on copyright by the end of 2015, 'to reduce the differences between national copyright regimes and allow for wider online access to works by users across the EU, including through further harmonisation measures'). In July 2014, the new President of the Commission, Jean-Claude Juncker, issued his 'Political Guidelines for the next European Commission—A New Start for Europe: My Agenda for Jobs, Growth, Fairness and Democratic Change (15 July 2014), indicating that to 'make much better use of the great opportunities offered by digital technologies, which know no borders . . . we will need to have the courage to break down national silos in . . . copyright . . . legislation.'

[138] See Chapter 12, section 3.4.1, pp. 342–3 (adopted in Regulation (EU) 2018/302).

[139] On this, see Chapter 6, section 6.7, p. 177, Chapter 9, section 6, p. 245, section 13.7, p. 267, section 14.3, p. 270, Chapter 12, section 2.6, pp. 333–4, and Chapter 13, section 8, pp. 389–90.

[140] For a detailed treatment, see M. Walter and S. von Lewinski, *European Copyright Law* (2010).

directives are important in that they are not confined to audiovisual or cinematographic works, but also extend to other moving images (such as films of sporting events).

The second notable aspect of the directives concerns the way in which they manage the (supposed) differences between the different legal regimes (copyright and *droit d'auteur*). Given that the directives are largely the result of lobbying and horse-trading between interest groups and member states, it is not surprising that the end results are a hybrid mix of concepts taken from both the *droit d'auteur* and copyright law. For example, there is recognition of an unwaivable right to 'equitable remuneration' for the authors of works that are the subject of rental and lending.[141] This corresponds to similar (although more general) provisions in French and German law guaranteeing authors proportionate remuneration.[142] On the other hand (and much to the disappointment of some French commentators), computer programs are recognized as literary works.[143] In addition, where a computer program is made by an employee in the course of employment, the economic rights are given to the employer rather than to the employee.[144] One Advocate-General has referred to the Information Society Directive as a 'compromise . . . which takes into account the differing legal traditions of Member States'.[145]

A third characteristic that is apparent is that the European legislature aims at a 'high' standard of protection. The most obvious example of this was the decision to increase the term of copyright to the term of life plus 70 years, which existed in Germany, rather than to ask that the German term be reduced to life plus 50 years (which was the term then used by many member states). While the strengthening of protection has sometimes been explained in terms of legislative convenience, it also suggests that it is at least an implicit agenda that aims to maximize copyright protection. This can be detected in Recital 10 to the Term Directive, which says that 'these rights are fundamental to intellectual creation . . . their protection ensures the maintenance and development of creativity in the interests of authors, cultural industries, consumers and society as a whole'.

Another example of the strengthening of the position of right holders has been the progressive restriction of the defences or exceptions that member states are able to use in their laws.[146] This is particularly noticeable in the Database Directive, in which the option of a 'private use' defence is excluded when the database is in an electronic form and in which use in scientific research is confined to uses for 'non-commercial purposes'.[147] However, it should be acknowledged that the Orphan Works Directive,[148] the Regulation on Content-Portability,[149] the Directive and Regulation on providing access to works for persons with print disabilities all add new exceptions or modifications for the benefit of 'users',[150] and some of the proposals in the Proposed Directive on Copyright in the Digital Single Market also relate to new exceptions.[151] One significant trend here is the shift away from the traditional conception of 'territoriality'.

---

[141] Rel. Rights Dir., Art. 5. See Chapter 12, section 2.4, p. 333.

[142] Further proposals in this vein are contained in the Proposal for a Directive on Copyright in the Digital Single Market, Art. 15 of which would require member states to confer on authors a right to have contractual terms varied where they are, or turn out to be, 'disproportionately low'. See Chapter 12, section 2.5, pp. 333–4.

[143] Software Dir., Art. 1. See Chapter 3, section 2.4, pp. 65–6.   [144] Software Dir., Art. 2(3).

[145] *Padawan SL v. SGAE*, Case C-467/08 [2010] *ECR* I–10,555, [AG43] (AG Trstenjak). See also *Amazon. com International Sales Inc v. Austro-Mechana Gesellschaft zur Wahrnehmung mechanisch-musikalischer Urheberrechte Gesellschaft mbH*, Case C-521/11, EU:2013:145, [AG2] (AG Mengozzi).

[146] Rel. Rights Dir., Art. 10(1).   [147] Database. Dir., Art. 6(2)(a).

[148] See Chapter 12, section 5, pp. 346–7.   [149] See Chapter 12, section 6, pp. 349–50.

[150] See Chapter 9, section 12.3, pp. 261–2.

[151] See Chapter 9, section 6, p. 244–5, section 13.7, p. 267.

A fourth notable trend is that at least some parts of the directives adopted in the name of harmonization have only a very limited harmonizing effect. In fact, there are many situations in which the directives tolerate a level of difference between the laws of member states. [152] For example, in relation to subject matter, member states are expressly permitted to protect non-original photographs and critical and scientific publications of works that have fallen into the public domain.[153] Although there is some degree of prescription, member states have flexibility as regards specifying who are the co-authors of cinematographic works.[154] Member states are sometimes permitted to confer greater rights on right holders than those specified in the directives[155] and occasionally (as with the lending right) to derogate from the standards set by the directives.[156] There are also permissive clauses in relation to defences,[157] presumed transfer of rights,[158] and the kinds of collective licensing regime required.[159] The details of 'transitional provisions' are also left largely to member states.[160] Moreover, as the case law on transitional provisions in the Term Directive and that on the concept of 'equitable remuneration' make clear, the harmonizing directives often offer loose, open-textured concepts around which member states must formulate specific rules, within certain limited parameters.

As already observed, the Court has started to build on the framework, reasoning from one directive to another, to offer up some harmonized norms.[161] The most notable example of this trend relates to the notion of originality, which we discuss in Chapter 4. The legislature harmonized the originality requirement in an identical manner for computer programs, photographs, and databases, and the Court has gone on to adopt the same standard for all authorial works—namely, that works should be protected only where they are their author's 'own intellectual creations'.[162] However, not all areas are amenable to judicial harmonization, and it is notable that at least one Advocate-General has specifically urged the legislature to pursue 'a much greater level of harmonization'. [163]

---

[152] *VG Wort v. KYOCERA Document Solutions Deutschland GmbH*, Joined Cases C-457/11, C-458/11, C-459/11 and 460/11, EU:2013:34, [AG30] ('far from pursuing uniformity or harmonisation, [InfoSoc Dir., Art. 5] seems practically to amount to a renunciation of those goals').

[153] Term Dir., Arts 5 and 6.

[154] Rel. Rights Dir., Art. 2(2); Term Dir., Art. 2(1). As well as designating 'legal persons' as rights holders: Software Dir., Art. 2(1); Database Dir., Art. 4(1).

[155] Satellite Dir., Art. 6 (expressly permitting member states to provide more far-reaching broadcasting and communication rights than those mandated by Rel. Rights Dir., Art. 8).

[156] Rel. Rights Dir., Art. 6.

[157] Rel. Rights Dir., Art. 10, and the more restricted Database Dir., Art. 6(2), and Info. Soc. Dir., Art. 5(2), (3).

[158] Rel. Rights Dir., Art. 2(6), (7).

[159] Rel. Rights Dir., Arts 8(2) (conditions as to sharing remuneration for broadcasting and public performance between performers and the producers of phonograms) and 13(9) (level of remuneration for rental); Satellite Dir., Arts 3(2), 9(3), 13.

[160] Rel. Rights Dir., Art. 13(3)–(8); Satellite Dir., Art. 7; Term Dir., Art. 10(3), which was considered by the ECJ in *Butterfly Music Srl v. Carosello Edizioni Musicali e Discografiche Srl*, Case C-60/98 [1999] *ECDR* 1; *Flos SpA v. Semararo Case e Famiglia SpA*, Case C-168/09, [2011] *ECR* I–181 (ECJ).

[161] J. Griffiths, 'The Role of the CJEU in the Development of EU Copyright Law,' in I. Stamatoudi and P. Torremans (eds), *EU Copyright Law: A Commentary* (2014) 1098.

[162] Software Dir., Art. 1(3); Term Dir., Art. 6, Recital 17; Database Dir., Art. 3(1); *Infopaq Int v. Danske Dagblades Forening*, Case C-5/08 [2009] *ECR* I–6569 (ECJ), [37] ('copyright within the meaning of Article 2(a) of Directive 2001/29 is liable to apply only in relation to a subject-matter which is original in the sense that it is its author's own intellectual creation'). But cf. IViR, *Recasting Copyright* (2006), 36–7, (suggesting that the test differs for photographs).

[163] *Amazon.com International Sales Inc v. Austro-Mechana Gesellschaft zur Wahrnehmung mechanisch-musikalischer Urheberrechte Gesellschaft mbH*, Case C-521/11, EU:C:2013:145, [AG6] (AG Mengozzi). Note also *VG Wort v. KYOCERA Document Solutions Deutschland GmbH*, Joined Cases C-457/11, C-458/11, C-459/11 and 460/11, EU:C:2013:34, [AG31] ('there comes a point at which only the legislature is competent to ensure … evolution').

8 THE FUTURE

8.1 INTERNATIONAL CHANGES

After recent successes in developing international norms in the Beijing and Marrakesh treaties, emphasis has turned toward bringing other WIPO projects to fruition.[164]

The first area in which the WIPO is active is in relation to broadcasting organizations.[165] This has been under consideration for over twenty years and various versions of a possible treaty text are in circulation. As with the two 1996 WIPO treaties, the initiative was prompted by a desire to update international copyright standards to bring them into line with the 'information age'. Even though much of the content of the proposed treaty echoes that which was adopted for copyright, sound recordings, and performers in the two 1996 treaties, in the subsequent years opposition to copyright has grown. One recurring issue has been the best way in which to deal with Internet services, which are similar to broadcasting.[166] There had been some hope for a diplomatic conference in 2014,[167] but nothing materialized. According to the 2017 report of the Director-General: '[t]he [Standing Committee on Copyright] is approaching the stage where it will need to decide if it will be able to recommend to the 2018 Assemblies the convening of a diplomatic conference for the conclusion of a treaty.'

Second, the Standing Committee has been considering some sort of instrument on exceptions to copyright. This began with exceptions for libraries and archives and educational institutions. Once again, this is being achieved through commissioning studies,[168] as well as discussion of proposed texts (on preservation, deposit, lending, and so forth), although the nature of any instrument (a model law, a joint recommendation, a treaty, or something else) remains unsettled. It is clear that representatives of many rights owners, particularly educational publishers, are unenthusiastic.[169]

Third, the WIPO has long been involved examining possible systems of protection for so-called 'traditional cultural expressions' (TCEs).[170] In reflection of the fact that many indigenous cultures do not draw a rigid line between art and science in the way that Western cultures often do, WIPO's activities extend beyond copyright to include patents, trade marks, and other related rights. The work is conducted by the Intergovernmental Committee on Intellectual Property and Genetic Resources, Traditional Knowledge and Folklore, which has now completed its 34th session. The IGC has recommended to the General Assembly that it be allowed to continue its work over the 2018–19 period.[171] Clearly, the IGC is some way from a final text.

---

[164] See Ficsor, 74–6, 702–4.

[165] Current discussions are based on a draft treaty text, SCCR/24/10 Corr., which was proposed at the 24th session of the WIPO Standing Committee on Copyright and Related Rights in 2012.

[166] There is also a parallel initiative in the Council of Europe. For discussion, see *European Commission v. Council of the European Union*, Case C-114/12 EU:C:2014:2151 (ECJ, Grand Chamber); EU:C:2014:224, [AG2]–[AG8], [AG122]–[AG139] (AG Sharpston).

[167] The latest working document is SCCR/26/3 from December 2013.

[168] D. Seng's mammoth *Study on Copyright Limitations and Exceptions for Educational Activities* (2016) SCCR/33/6; K. Crews, *Copyright Limitations and Exceptions for Libraries and Archives* (2015) SCCR/30/3.

[169] It is said that educational publishing comprises 60 per cent of the publishing market worldwide.

[170] The latest draft provisions on TCEs are contained in WIPO/GRTKF/IC/34/8 (June 2017).

[171] Decisions of the 34th session (WIPO/GRTKF/IC/34/DECISIONS).

8.2 EUROPEAN INITIATIVES

As mentioned, following a broad consultation in 2014, the European Commission adopted a strategy for a 'Digital Single Market' that included significant levels of copyright reform.[172] Some of this has now been achieved,[173] but some is still in progress. The most important is the proposed Directive on Copyright in the Digital Single Market, published by the Commission in September 2016,[174] which has been working its way through the EU legislature, particularly the Council Working Party and the various Parliamentary committees. This deals with five important topics: exceptions to copyright (in particular as regards data mining, teaching, and preservation of cultural heritage—but not, as many had sought so-called 'freedom of panorama');[175] treatment by extended collective licensing of 'out of commerce' works;[176] regulation of the treatment of copyright material by Internet hosting services;[177] regulation of authors' contracts;[178] and a press publishers right.[179] Although the proposals will be referred to in a little more detail in the relevant chapters, it is worth noting that they have been extremely controversial.[180]

There have now been murmurings for some time about the possible codification of European copyright law. In its study for the European Commission, entitled *Recasting Copyright for the Knowledge Economy*, the Instituut voor Informatierecht [Institute for Information Law, University of Amsterdam] (IViR) has made a tentative proposal that long-term consideration be given to creation of a European Copyright Code, conferring a single, Europe-wide, indivisible copyright (and pre-empting any corresponding national rights).[181] The proposed right would be created by an EU regulation, and would draw on the existing directives and the jurisprudence of the Court of Justice. It would also fill in many of the gaps, but would not cover aspects of copyright that do not affect the operation of the internal market or which reflect national cultural policy. The study thus suggests that moral rights, authorship, ownership, and supervision of collective administration would remain aspects of national law. In addition, lest such a code introduce undue inflexibility, the study suggests that national legislatures be provided with some flexibility to introduce new exceptions or limitations. Subsequently, a group of academics

---

[172] Commission Communication, *A Digital Single Market Strategy for Europe* (6 May 2015), COM(2015) 192 final. See section 7, p. 52.

[173] The most important achievements relate to cross-border portability and the rights of the visually-impaired: see Chapter 12, section 6, pp. 349–50 and Chapter 9, section 12.3, pp. 261–2.

[174] European Commission, *Proposal for a Directive of the European Parliament and of the Council on Copyright in the Digital Single Market*, COM(2016) 593.

[175] Proposed Arts 3–6, discussed further in See Chapter 9, section 6, pp. 244–5, section 13.7, p. 267.

[176] Proposed Art. 7–9, discussed further in Chapter 12, section 5.3, pp. 348–9.

[177] Proposed Art. 13. Discussed further in Chapter 6, section 6.7, p. 177, and Chapter 48, section 3.5.5, pp. 1279–82.

[178] Proposed Arts 14–16, discussed further in Chapter 12, section 2.5, pp. 333–4.

[179] Proposal, Art. 11, discussed further in Chapter 13, section 8, pp. 389–90.

[180] For commentary, see European Copyright Society, General Opinion on the EU Copyright Reform Package, available online at https://europeancopyrightsocietydotorg.files.wordpress.com/2015/12/ecs-opinion-on-eu-copyright-reform-def.pdf.

[181] T. Dreier, 'The Wittem Project of a European Copyright Code', in C. Geiger (ed.), *Constructing European Intellectual Property: Achievements and New Perspectives* (2012), ch. 13; T.-E. Synodinou, *Codification of European Copyright Law: Challenges and Perspectives* (2012); E. Rosati, 'The Wittem Group and the European Copyright Code' [2010] *JIPLP* 862; J. Ginsburg, 'European Copyright Code: Back to First Principles (with Some Additional Detail)' (2011) 58 *J Copyright Soc'y USA* 265; T. Cook and E. Derclaye, 'An EU Copyright Code: What and How, if Ever?' [2011] *IPQ* 255.

have published a draft code, called the 'Wittem Code', which builds on the existing rules ('the *acquis*') and offers a template of substantive norms in key areas. It has received a somewhat mixed reception.[182]

The potential advantages of such a change are self-evident. A code would be simpler, insofar as it consists of a single law, rather than a series of national laws. If drafted correctly, it would remove inconsistencies between the existing directives. Such a code would also be more user-friendly, insofar as it enabled rights to be enforced in a single action across Europe. Despite these attractions, however, it is unlikely that it will be introduced, at least in the near future. While the Commission has so far shown little enthusiasm, the Court of Justice seems intent on deepening copyright law through case law (and the developing jurisprudence may alleviate some of the immediate difficulties caused by the fragmented legislative approach). In the longer term, however, the idea of a code deserves further exploration and it is referred to in the current consultation. Having explained the idea, the consultation asked: 'Should this be the next step in the development of copyright in the EU? Does the current level of difference among the Member State legislation mean that this is a longer term project?'[183]

The digital single market strategy of 2015 promised 'a more harmonised copyright regime which provides incentives to create and invest while allowing transmission and consumption of content across borders, building on our rich cultural diversity'. However, it adopted a 'problem oriented' approach, focusing on particular issues. Nevertheless, it recognized the importance of a long-term vision of a European copyright law, towards which these initiatives constituted incremental steps.[184] It looks increasingly as if that vision will be realized without the input, or involvement, of the United Kingdom.

8.3 POST BREXIT COPYRIGHT IN THE UK

If, as seems likely, the United Kingdom leaves the European Union, the question will arise as to what course its laws will take. One possibility would be towards alignment with other common law countries such as the United States, for example by introducing an open-ended 'fair use' exception,[185] or abolishing the *droit de suite* (that UK-based art auctioneers especially detest).[186] Some have suggested that the former approach to originality might be revived,[187] and the 'sui generis' database right done away with.[188] Whatever substantive changes are adopted, if any, it is to be hoped, although not expected, that parliamentary time will be made available for the passage of a Copyright Act that codifies the law so that it is more comprehensible.[189]

---

[182] European Commission, *A Single Market for IPRS* (2011), COM(2011) 287 final.

[183] European Commission, *Public Consultation on the Review of the EU Copyright Rules* (2013), 36, Q79.

[184] Commission Communication, *Toward a modern, more European copyright framework* (9 December 2015) COM(2015) 626 final, p. 12. For the positions taken by different categories of respondents in response to the EC consultation, see D. G. Internal Market, *Report on the Response to the Public Consultation on the Review of the EU Copyright Rules* (July 2014) 98*ff*, available online at http://ec.europa.eu/internal_market/consultations/2013/copyright-rules/docs/contributions/consultation-report_en.pdf.

[185] See Chapter 9, section 22, pp. 283–4.   [186] See Chapter 13, section 7, pp. 386–9.

[187] See Chapter 4, section 3.3, pp. 96–8.   [188] See Chapter 13, section 4, pp. 365–74.

[189] R. Arnold, 'The Need for a New Copyright Act: A Case Study in Law Reform' (2015) *QMJIP* 110–31.

3

SUBJECT MATTER

1 INTRODUCTION

This chapter examines the subject matter protected by copyright law. In formal terms, the Copyright, Designs and Patents Act 1988 (CDPA 1988) provides a detailed and exhaustive list of the types of creation protected by copyright law. In order for a creation to be protected by copyright, the Act stipulates that it must fall within one of the following eight categories of work: (i) literary works; (ii) dramatic works; (iii) musical works; (iv) artistic works; (v) films; (vi) sound recordings; (vii) broadcasts; and (viii) published editions (or typographical works). The definitions of these categories of work are elaborated in greater detail in the case law and through the jurisprudence of the Court of Justice.

Before looking at the categories of subject matter in more detail, it is necessary to make three preliminary points. First, it should also be noted that the legal categories do not necessarily correspond to the objects commonly associated with copyright law. Instead, individual tangible objects may embody a number of different copyright works. For example, a book or newspaper might contain a literary work, an artistic work, and a typographical arrangement;[1] an artistic work (such as that by Superflex on the cover of this textbook) may embody literary as well as visual components; a song may consist of literary and musical works (the lyrics being a literary work); and a CD might contain a sound recording, a musical work, and a literary work. While the legal categories do not necessarily correspond to the objects protected by copyright, in most cases there have been few problems in matching a particular creative act to one of the protected categories.

Second, all types of subject matter that are protected by British copyright law are called 'works'. This is in marked contrast to the position in civil law systems, such as in France, which distinguish between 'author's rights' (or *droits d'auteur*) and 'neighbouring rights' or entrepreneurial works (*droits voisins*). Author's rights typically cover literary, dramatic, musical, and artistic work, whereas neighbouring rights are afforded to sound recordings, broadcasts, and performers.[2] This distinction is also reflected in the international conventions, with the 1886 Berne Convention protecting 'author's rights' and the 1961 Rome Convention protecting 'neighbouring rights'. Under EU law, 'neighbouring rights' are

---

[1] *Newspaper Licensing Agency v. Marks and Spencer* [2003] 1 *AC* 551, 557, [4].

[2] The division of subject matter into 'authorial' and 'entrepreneurial' works is based upon a belief that copyright for authors is the pure form and should not be conflated or equated with rights given in return for investment. See Chapter 2, section 3, p. 36.

Fig. 3.1 The album cover of Oasis's *Be Here Now*
Source: Big Brother Recordings

usually classed as 'related rights'. As we will see, the distinction (never fully abandoned in the details of UK law), has started to take on renewed importance, as the Court of Justice develops principles that are applicable to authors rights.

The third and most problematic issue is whether the list of eight works is to be regarded as an exhaustive list. Until recently, the list was understood to be closed. This meant that there was little opportunity for the courts to recognize new forms of subject matter, other than through the creative interpretation of the existing categories. Thus some 'works' that would be protected in countries operating a non-exhaustive system have been regarded as unprotected under the 1988 Act. This was graphically illustrated in the case of *Creation Records*.[3] Here, as preparation in the production of the cover for Oasis's album *Be Here Now* (see Fig. 3.1), Noel Gallagher arranged for a series of objects (a Rolls Royce, a motor bike, a clock) to be placed around a swimming pool. This collection of 'artistically' distributed objects was then photographed by the claimant and the photograph used as the album cover. However, a photographer from the defendant newspaper was present and also took a photograph of the scene. When the newspaper published this photograph and offered to sell posters of the scene, the record company sought an interim injunction alleging infringement of its copyright. The claim based on copyright failed because the scene did not fall within the meaning of any of the (then) nine (now eight) categories of protected work; in particular, it was neither an artistic work nor a dramatic work.[4]

However, the assumption that the list is closed is under challenge.[5] The source of the change is the interpretation of the various EU directives by the Court of Justice. Although

---

[3] *Creation Records v. News Group* [1997] *EMLR* 444.

[4] Interim relief, however, was granted on the basis of breach of confidence: see Chapters 44–46.

[5] For discussion of the merits (and disadvantages) of a closed list, see T. Aplin, 'Subject Matter,' in E. Derclaye (ed.), *Research Handbook on the Future of EU Copyright* (2009) 49–76.

the directives say very little about what constitutes a work, the Court has taken the view that harmonization of the concept of a work is implicit within the directives. Drawing on the terms used to define when works are 'original' in three directives, the Court has suggested that 'literary and artistic works' should be protected by member states where they constitute 'intellectual creations'. Thus the Court has said that a 'graphic user interface' should be protected, but that a football match would not be.[6] At the same time, the Court seems to have recognized the existence of works that do not fall within any conventional category. In *Nintendo v. PC Box*,[7] before addressing the questions that had been referred to it by the national court, the Court of Justice went out of its way to confirm that a video game, which contained a computer program, as well as visual and sonic material, was a work. It explained:

> [V]ideogames . . . constitute complex matter comprising not only a computer program but also graphic and sound elements, which, although encrypted in computer language, have a unique creative value which cannot be reduced to that encryption. In so far as the parts of a videogame, in this case, the graphic and sound elements, are part of its originality, they are protected, together with the entire work, by copyright in the context of the system established by Directive 2001/29.[8]

Three consequences of this development should be observed.[9]

First, existing British case law that purports to define the limits of the different categories of protected works will need to be revisited. Following general principles of European law, the terms of the UK statute must now be read (as far as possible) to reflect the EU principle that anything that constitutes an 'intellectual creation' should be protected. At least one court has recognized this, stating that the fact that a work does not fall within the definitions adopted for the existing categories does not necessarily mean that such a work is not protected.[10]

Second, and in turn, the supposed benefits of having an exhaustive list of copyright works have necessarily been abandoned: whatever a literal reading of any of the categories might now be, henceforth they should be offered a broad reading so as to ensure protection of anything that constitutes an intellectual creation. Thus one might doubt whether the outcome in *Creation Records* would remain justified (though there may well be certain 'intellectual creations', such as perfumes, which simply cannot be fitted within the UK's legislative scheme, no matter how flexibly it is interpreted).[11]

---

[6] *Bezpečnostní softwarová asociace* [2010] *ECR* I–13971 (ECJ), [45]–[46]; *Football Association Premier League v. QC Leisure*, Case C-403/08 and *Karen Murphy v. Media Protection Services*, Case C-429/08 [2011] *ECR* I–9083 (ECJ, Grand Chamber), [97]. See also *Flos v. Semararo Case e Famiglia*, Case C-168/09 [2011] *ECR* I–181 (ECJ), [34].　　　　　　　　　　　　　　[7] Case C-355/12, EU:C:2014:25 (ECJ).

[8] Ibid., [23]. For an analysis of videogames, see Y. H. Lee, 'Play Again? Revisiting the Case for Copyright Protection of Gameplay in Videogames' [2012] *EIPR* 865. For further thoughts on videogames, see Daithí Mac Síthigh, 'The Game's the Thing', in M. Richardson and S. Ricketson, *Intellectual Property in Media and Entertainment* (2017), ch. 13.

[9] M. van Eechoud, 'Along the Road to Uniformity: Diverse Readings of the Court of Justice Judgments on Copyright Work' (2012) 1 *JIPITEC* 60; C. Handig, 'The "Sweat of the Brow" is not Enough! More than a Blueprint of the European Copyright Term "Work"' [2013] *EIPR* 334; C. Handig, 'Infopaq: Is the Term "Work" in the CDPA in Line with the European Directive?' [2010] *EIPR* 53; C. Handig, 'The Copyright Term "Work": European Harmonization at an Unknown Level' (2009) 40 *IIC* 665.

[10] *SAS Institute v. World Programming* [2013] *EWHC* 69 (Ch), [27]. For consideration of how far magic tricks might be protected, see A. Struthers, 'Copyright Protection for Magic Tricks: A Danger Lurking in the Shadows?' [2017] *EIPR* 136, esp. 141.

[11] Some European countries have even protected perfumes by copyright: *Lancôme Parfums v. Kecofa* [2006] *ECDR* (26) 363 (Dutch Supreme Court); cf. *Bsiri-Barbir v. Haarmann & Reimer* [2006] *ECDR* (28) 380 (French *Cour de Cassation*). See C. Seville, 'Copyright in Perfume: Smelling a Rat' (2007) 66 *CLJ* 49; H. Cohen Jehoram [2006] *EIPR* 629. Even with EU obligations, it is difficult to see how this could be possible under UK law.

Third, the approach of the Court of Justice raises doubts about the significance of the various categories of work.[12] Hitherto, UK law has used the categories to provide for different conditions and consequences (for example in defining when a work must be recorded in material form in order to be protected or what counts as a reproduction). Questions have thus been asked as to whether the same creative effort can be protected under more than one category.[13] At least where rights (and exceptions thereto) are harmonized, such differentiation may no longer be appropriate or meaningful. The way in which a work is initially perceived or understood should be irrelevant as to the scope of protection of 'authorial works'.

Given the implications of the Court's case law for the United Kingdom, it is vital to understand precisely what criteria the Court of Justice considers applicable in deciding whether an intellectual product must be protected. At first glance, it looks as if the Court has eliminated any subject matter requirement, collapsing the question of whether an intellectual production is protected into an assessment of its originality. However, in *SAS Institute v. World Programming*,[14] Arnold J rejected that reading. Called upon to decide whether a computer language might be protected, he said that it was not enough that the subject be an 'intellectual creation'; rather, 'it remains clear that the putative copyright work must be a literary or artistic work within the meaning of Article 2(1) of the Berne Convention'.[15] A 'scientific theory', Arnold J explained, might be an intellectual creation, but would not in itself be a work. Consequently, he stated that his provisional view was that a computer 'language' (as opposed to, say, the collection of instances in a dictionary), being 'a system of rules for the generation and recognition of meaningful statements', is not a work.[16]

Further clarification may be provided when the Court of Justice gives judgment in response to the reference from the Netherlands in *Levola Hengelo BV v. Smilde Foods BV*.[17] In this case, a person claimed to have created an original taste for a cream cheese, and to be entitled as a result to rely on copyright to prevent the defendant from selling cheese with the same taste. The Dutch Court (Gerechtshof Arnhem-Leeuwarden) has asked the CJEU whether EU law precludes such protection, and, if so, whether this is because copyright is limited to intellectual creations appreciated via the senses of sight and hearing, because of the unstable and subjective quality of 'taste', or for some other reason. The Court, then, will be given an opportunity to clearly specify the depth of EU harmonization on the question of the subject matter of copyright.[18]

With these general points in mind, we now turn to look at the eight types of work recognized by copyright law. Until the full implications of the Court of Justice's jurisprudence are made clear, these categories remain the starting point for any claim to

---

[12] That said, European copyright law does not avoid categories completely. First, the directives require distinct regimes of protection for 'computer programs' and 'databases' (with different rules on ownership, exceptions, secondary infringement, and 'para-copyright' for 'computer programs'). Second, computer programs must be protected as 'literary works': Software Dir., Art. 1(1). Special rules also apply in relation to authorship of 'cinematographic works' under Term Dir., Art. 2(1), and the term of copyright for 'musical compositions with lyrics' under Directive 2011/77/EU See Yin Harn Lee, 'The Persistence of the Text,' [2018] *IPQ* 22 and 107, 135.

[13] Compare *Electronic Technique v. Critchley* [1997] *FSR* 401 (arguing against protection as both literary and artistic work) with *Anacon Corp. v. Environmental Research Technology* [1994] *FSR* 659 (Jacob J suggesting that a circuit diagram is both a literary and artistic work) and *Sandman v. Panasonic UK* [1998] *FSR* 651 (Pumfrey J indicating that a poem could be both).

[14] [2013] *EWHC* 69 (Ch).   [15] Ibid., [27].   [16] Ibid., [33].   [17] Case C-310/17 (pending).

[18] For an argument that 'subject matter' questions are best left to the legislature, see R. A. Reese, 'What Should Copyright Protect?' in R. Giblin and K. Weatherall, *What If We Could Re-imagine Copyright?* (2016), ch. 4.

copyright. Even if it comes to be accepted, as Arnold J suggests, that there is an obligation to protect all 'intellectual creations', in the first instance this will be done through
interpreting the existing statutory language. In any case, even if some 'intellectual
creations' that fall outside the existing categories must be protected, the categories
continue to play a role in four situations: where they reflect European differentiations
between authors rights and related rights (sound recordings, broadcasts, fixations,
of films); where they reflect European differentiations within authors rights (as with
computer programs, databases, photographs, cinematographic/audiovisual works,
artistic works, works of applied art, and buildings);[19] where they determine matters
that have not been harmonized (most obviously questions of ownership of copyright
and moral rights); and, finally, where they underpin implementation in the United
Kingdom of European standards (reflecting the basic principle that an EU directive is
binding as regards the end to be achieved, but is designed to allow for different means
of implementation).

2 LITERARY WORKS

Literary works have been protected from unauthorized reproduction since at least 1710.[20]
Literary works are defined in section 3(1) of the CDPA 1988 to mean:

> ... any work, other than a dramatic or musical work, which is written, spoken or sung,
> and accordingly includes (a) a table or compilation (other than a database), (b) a computer
> program, (c) preparatory design material for a computer program, and (d) a database.

Literary works are also a category of authorial works expressly referred to in the Software
Directive.[21]

It is important to note that literary works are not limited to works of literature, but
include all works expressed in print or writing (other than dramatic or musical works).[22]
'Writing' includes symbols and numerals. A literary work will be protected irrespective
of the quality or style of the creation in question: copyright law does not pass judgment
on the standard of the work. As a result, the types of thing that will be protected as a literary work include novels, poems, and song lyrics, as well as advertising slogans, railway
timetables, and examination papers.[23] The fact that literary works include works that are
spoken means that spontaneous conversations, interviews, and the like may also be protected (although, as we shall see, copyright does not subsist in a spoken work unless it is
recorded).

Where problems have arisen in deciding what is meant by a literary work, the courts
have tended to rely on the test in *Hollinrake v. Truswell*[24] that, to qualify as a 'book' under
the Literary Copyright Act 1842, the creation must afford 'either information and instruction, or pleasure, in the form of literary enjoyment'.

---

[19] See, e.g., Software Dir. (special rules for computer programs); Database Dir. (special rules for databases); Term Dir., Arts 2, 6 (special rules for photographs, cinematographic, and audiovisual works); Rel.
Rights Dir., Art. 3(2) (exclusion of 'buildings' and 'applied art'); Info. Soc. Dir., Art. 5(3)(j) (permissible
exception for 'artistic work') and 5(3)(m) (permissible exception for 'building').

[20] The Statute of Anne 1710 and the Literary Copyright Act 1842 used the term 'book'. However, since
1911, the statutes have referred to literary works.

[21] Software Dir., Art. 1(1) (referring to Berne). See also Term Dir., Art. 1(1).

[22] *University of London Press v. University Tutorial Press* [1916] 2 *Ch* 601.

[23] Ibid.   [24] (1894) 3 *Ch* 420, 428 (Davey LJ).

HERE'S HOW TO WIN THE

PRIZE OF A LIFETIME

♦ THIS is your bonus chance to win £1 million. Just match your personal cash code on your card against the single line grid, from left to right IN ORDER. IF you have the perfect match you are in with a chance for that magical million.

Fig. 3.2 The grids in *Express Newspapers v. Liverpool Daily Post*
Source: Express Newspapers

Most of the cases in which the meaning of literary work has arisen have been concerned with works that afford 'information' or 'instruction.' These cases have made it clear that, for a work to provide information or instruction, it must be capable of conveying an intelligible meaning.[25] This is a low threshold. For example, in one case, it was accepted that sequences of letters set out in grids published in a newspaper provided 'information' as to whether a reader had won or lost a bingo game and, as such, were literary works (see Fig. 3.2).[26] In order for a work to 'convey an intelligible meaning', it is not necessary that the work be understood by the general public; it is sufficient that the work is understood by a limited group with special knowledge. Thus a telegraphic code has been held to be a literary work, even though the words of the code were meaningless in themselves.[27] It has also been held that ciphers, mathematical tables, systems of shorthand, and Braille catalogues convey meaning, and as such qualify as literary works.[28] One of the few situations in which works have been held not to provide information or instruction is where the work is meaningless or gibberish.[29] Another situation in which a work fails to provide information is where it is an invented name. For example, it was held that the word 'exxon', which had been created to act as a company name, conveyed no information and hence was not protected as a literary work (although, as we will see, there may have been other grounds for this decision).[30]

---

[25] Ibid., 521.   [26] *Express Newspapers v. Liverpool Daily Post* [1985] 3 *All ER* 680.
[27] *D. P. Anderson v. Lieber Code Company* [1917] 2 *KB* 469.
[28] *Apple Computer v. Computer Edge* [1984] *FSR* 481 (FCA), 521.
[29] Ibid., 495 ('meaningless rubbish would plainly be excluded').
[30] *Exxon Corp. v. Exxon Insurance* [1982] *RPC* 69, 90.

The test of 'literary work' provided in *Hollinrake v. Truswell* suggests that the term also includes works that 'provide pleasure in the form of literary enjoyment'. The requirement of 'literary enjoyment' seems to suggest a qualitative test: if so, it would run counter to the widely accepted principle that the quality of the literary work is not to be taken into account when deciding whether a work should be protected.

With these general points in mind, we now turn to look in more detail at the types of thing that are protected as literary works. After looking at names and invented words (which are not protected), we turn to look at titles, tables and compilations, computer programs, preparatory material for computer programs, and databases.

2.1 NAMES AND INVENTED WORDS

Despite the fact that names and titles are expressions in writing or print (and are often traded for substantial amounts of money), the United Kingdom (like most countries) refuses to protect them as literary works.[31] Thus invented words such as EXXON, which had been invented by Esso Petroleum as a trade name, have been held not to be protected by copyright as literary works.[32] This is because although such names are in writing, they do not afford 'information, instruction or pleasure of a literary kind'.[33] The Court of Justice, likewise, has stated that words 'considered in isolation, are not as such an intellectual creation of the author who employs them'.[34]

There are a number of policy reasons why names may be excluded from protection as literary works by copyright law. Perhaps the main reason for not protecting names and titles relates to the general inconvenience that would arise if someone were able to control the way in which certain words and phrases were used. It would be inconvenient—indeed absurd—if business commentators and political activists could not refer (for example in broadcasts, newspapers, or campaign literature) to the oil conglomerate by using the term EXXON without gaining permission in advance. Another reason for refusing protection to names and titles as literary works under copyright law is that it is unnecessary to do so, given that they are adequately protected by passing off, trade mark law,[35] and artistic copyright.[36]

2.2 TITLES AND HEADLINES

A similar approach used to be taken to titles. Thus courts have refused protection to the name of game shows such as *Opportunity Knocks*[37] or song titles such as 'The Man Who Broke the Bank at Monte Carlo'.[38] In the latter case, the Privy Council indicated that it did not regard a title as sufficiently 'substantial enough' to warrant protection

---

[31] See R. Stone, 'Copyright Protection for Titles, Character Names and Catch-phrases in the Film and Television Industry' [1996] *Ent L Rev* 178, [1997] *Ent L Rev* 34.

[32] *Exxon Corp. v. Exxon Insurance* [1982] *RPC* 69.   [33] Ibid.

[34] *Infopaq International v. Danske Dagblades Forening*, Case C-5/08 [2009] *ECR* I–6569 (ECJ), [45].

[35] The corollary of this is that while a person is usually free (as far as copyright is concerned) to appropriate names and short titles, care must be taken to ensure that the use of such a title cannot be seen as passing off or a trade mark infringement: see Chapters 32–34.

[36] 'Karo Step' Trade Mark [1977] *RPC* 255 (a pictorial mark may be an artistic work); *Hutchinson Personal Communications v. Hook Advertising* [1996] *FSR* 549; *News Group v. Mirror Group* [1989] *FSR* 126.

[37] *Green v. Broadcasting Corp. of New Zealand* [1989] *RPC* 469 (CANZ), 472, 475, 490.

[38] *Francis Day and Hunter v. 20th Century Fox* [1940] *AC* 112 (copyright in the song 'The Man Who Broke the Bank at Monte Carlo' was not infringed by the performance of a motion picture of the same title). See also *Dick v. Yates* [1881] *Ch* 6 (no copyright in 'Splendid Misery').

in its own right.[39] This approach leaves room for the possibility that some creative titles might still qualify for copyright protection.[40] The standard of 'originality' is reviewed in Chapter 4.

2.3 TABLES AND COMPILATIONS (OTHER THAN DATABASES)

Section 3(1)(a) of the CDPA 1988 specifically states that literary work includes 'tables or compilations (other than a database)'. Implementing the EU Database Directive, 'databases' are a separate type of literary work,[41] subject to a distinct requirement of originality. As we will see, a database is defined in very wide terms. As a result, there is little that will fall within the category of 'tables and compilations'.

2.4 COMPUTER PROGRAMS

After considerable debate at both national and international levels over whether computer programs should be regulated by copyright law, patent law, or by a *sui generis* regime, it was decided in the 1980s that computer programs ought to be protected as literary works.[42] This position is now well entrenched in European and international intellectual property law.[43] In line with these trends, the 1988 Act protects computer programs as literary works.[44] While the Act does not define what is meant by a 'computer program',[45] it is clear that it includes source code,[46] assembly code, and object code. It is also clear that 'computer program' is not synonymous with software. On this basis, the definition of computer program includes instructions permanently wired into an integrated circuit (that is, firmware).[47]

In a decision in which it held that a 'graphic user interface' (GUI) is not a computer program (although it may be some other type of work), the Court of Justice has articulated the defining characteristics of a computer program. The 'object of the protection', the Court of Justice said, 'is the expression in any form of a computer program *which permits reproduction in different computer languages,* such as the source code and the object code.'[48] Because the key characteristic of a program is that it enables the reproduction of

---

[39] *Rose v. Information Services* [1987] *FSR* 254 (Hoffmann J) (there was too slight a degree of skill and labour in *The Lawyer's Diary*). In *Sinanide v. La Maison Kosmeo* (1928) 139 *LTR* 365 (CA), protection was refused to the advertising slogan 'Youthful appearances are social necessities, not luxuries' by reference to the principle *de minimis non curat lex* ('the law does not concern itself with trifles').

[40] In *Francis Day and Hunter v. 20th Century Fox* [1940] *AC* 112, the Privy Council indicated that if a title were extensive and important enough, it might be possible to protect it. For cases of protection, see *Lamb v. Evans* [1893] 1 *Ch* 218 (headings in trade directory protected) and *Shetland Times v. Dr Jonathan Wills* [1997] *FSR* 604 (arguable that newspaper headline of eight or so words—'Bid to save centre after council funding cock-up'—was protected because it was designedly put together for the purpose of imparting information).

[41] CDPA 1988, s. 3(1)(d).

[42] *Gates v. Swift* [1982] *RPC* 339; *Sega Enterprises v. Richards* [1983] *FSR* 73; *Thrustcode v. WW Computing* [1983] *FSR* 502. [43] Software Dir., Art. 1(1); TRIPS, Art. 10(1); WCT, Art. 4.

[44] CDPA 1988, s. 3(1)(b). The Copyright (Computer Software) Act 1985 had declared only that computer programs were to be *considered* as literary works.

[45] But cf. the WIPO *Model Provisions on Protection of Computer Software* (1978); Green Paper, *Copyright and the Challenge of Technology* (June 1988), COM(88) 172 final, 170; Copyright Act 1976, 17 USC §101 (all offering definitions). [46] *Ibcos Computers v. Barclays Mercantile Highland Finance* [1994] *FSR* 275.

[47] Software Dir., Recital 7.

[48] *Bezpečnostní softwarová asociace*, Case C-393/09 [2010] *ECR* I-13971 (ECJ), [28]-[42] (emphasis added). See also *SAS Institute v. World Programming*, Case C-406/10 [2012] 3 *CMLR* (4) 55 (ECJ, Grand Chamber), [35]-[37].

the computer program itself, so that the computer can perform its task, it does not include a GUI.[49] This is because a GUI merely enables communication between the computer program and the user, and so does not enable the reproduction of the computer program. The Court said that a GUI 'merely constitutes one element of that program' by means of which users make use of the features of that program.[50]

2.5 PREPARATORY DESIGN MATERIAL FOR COMPUTER PROGRAMS

To bring British law into conformity with the Software Directive, preparatory design material for computer programs is now included within the general definition of literary works. It has been suggested that this is an inappropriate way of implementing the Directive and that preparatory design material should be treated as part of a computer program.[51]

2.6 DATABASES

As we mentioned earlier, in order to comply with the Database Directive, the definition of literary works was amended from 1 January 1998 to introduce 'databases' as a distinct class of literary works. Section 3(1)(d) of the CDPA 1988, corresponding to Article 1(2) of the Directive, defines a database very broadly as 'a collection of independent works, data or other materials which (a) are arranged in a systematic or methodical way, and (b) are individually accessible by electronic or other means'. It seems that the definition is broad enough to cover most, if not all, of the material previously protected as tables and compilations.[52]

The Court of Justice explained some aspects of the definition of a database in *Fixtures Marketing v. Organismos Prognostikon Agonon Podosfairou AE (OPAP)*.[53] The case concerned a claim that English football fixtures were databases (and protected by database right).[54] The defendant organization, which used the fixtures in its betting games, asserted that the fixtures lists were not 'databases'. The Court of Justice considered that the notion of 'database' was intended to have 'a wide scope, unencumbered by considerations of a formal, technical or material nature'.[55] Consequently, there was no reason why a collection of sporting information should not be a 'database'. As regards the prerequisite of 'independence', the Court said that this required the constituent material to be 'separable from one another without their informative ... or other value being affected',[56] and the

---

[49] Case C-393/09, [38].

[50] Interpreted literally, one might form the view that the Court was saying that a GUI is 'part' of a program. But if that were the case, it would be protected, and clearly the Court thought that it was not protected under the Software Directive.

[51] Software Regs, reg. 3; *Bezpečnostní softwarová asociace*, Case C-393/09 [2010] *ECR* I–13971 (ECJ), [36]–[37]. For commentary, see S. Chalton, 'Implementation of the Software Directive in the UK' [1993] *EIPR* 138, 140.

[52] Cf. *Football Association Premier League v. Panini UK* [2004] *FSR* (1) 1, [25], [29] (suggesting that an album for stickers of football players—the stickers being artistic works—is a compilation, but it is probably a database).

[53] Case C-444/02 [2005] 1 *CMLR* (16) 367.   [54] On this right, see Chapter 13.

[55] *Fixtures Marketing v. OPAP*, Case C-444/02 [2005] 1 *CMLR* (16) 367, [20]. See also *Ryanair*, C-30/14, EU:C:2015:10, [33]; *Freistaat Bayern*, Case C-490/14, EU:C:2015:735, [12], (ECJ).

[56] *Fixtures Marketing v. OPAP*, Case C-444/02 [2005] 1 *CMLR* (16) 367, [29]. See also E. Derclaye, 'Do Sections 3 and 3A of the CDPA Violate the Database Directive? A Closer Look at the Definition of a Database in the UK and its Compatibility with European Law' [2002] *EIPR* 466, 469 ('"independent" means that an element makes sense by itself'); Davison, 72.

Court intimated that this was true of individual fixtures, each of which had 'autonomous informative value' by providing 'interested third parties with relevant information'.[57] The Court also commented on the requirement that the materials be arranged in a 'systematic or methodical' manner so as to be individually accessible, and stated that this required either that there be technical means for searching or other means, such as an index, table of contents, plan, or classification, to allow retrieval.[58] The fixture lists, being organized chronologically and, within the chronology, alphabetically, constituted just such an arrangement.

Applying these definitions, the poems in a book of poems by the same poet would most likely be regarded as 'independent' and 'individually accessible', and thus would constitute a database. Each poem has value on its own, and each can be read separately.[59] While one might have questioned whether the data on a map would be considered to be 'independent', because the meaning and value of the information typically depends on its relationship to other information on the map, the CJEU has now confirmed that it usually will be (and thus that in most, if not all cases, a map is a 'database').[60] Importantly, the Court pointed out that the 'unit' of data which is collected in a database could comprise combinations of information (for example, an item, such as a church, and its geographic location), so that it was irrelevant that the item, taken by itself, would have no value.[61] However, the Court went on to offer a different way of determining whether data was 'independent.' While one might have assumed that the question was whether each datum was 'independent' before its collection into a 'database,' the Court instead considered the question 'ex post', asking whether the information would continue to have some value if extracted from the collection. Observing that mere diminution in the value was not such as to lead to a conclusion that each item did not have 'autonomous informative value',[62] the Court considered this from the perspective of 'each third party interested by the extracted material' (rather than the 'typical user').[63] As long as extracted information could be of some value to some third parties, the Court concluded, it could be regarded as 'independent' for the purposes of the definition.[64]

A database does not include a computer program used in the making or operation of databases accessible by electronic means.[65] It should be noted that a computer program might itself be or include a compilation of information and hence be a database as well. Insofar as a computer program incorporates parts that fall within the definition of a database, it seems that these components may be independently protected as databases (whether under copyright or the *sui generis* database right).

One question that has arisen in this context is the extent to which a multimedia work as a whole (as distinct from the sound, pictures, text, and moving images of which it is made up) can be protected as a database.[66] Given that a database is defined, seemingly without

---

[57] *Fixtures Marketing v. OPAP*, Case C-444/02, [2005] 1 *CMLR* (16) 367, [33].   [58] Ibid., [30].

[59] Information displayed on a 'pdf' might be 'individually accessible': *Technomed v. Bluecrest Health Screening* [2017] *EWHC* 2142 (Ch) (Judge D Stone), [69] ('the contents of the pdf can be accessed, either through electronic conversion, through digital character recognition, or old-fashioned reading or re-typing'). See, to the same effect, *Freistaat Bayern*, Case C-490/14, EU:C:2015:735, [15] (ECJ, Second Chamber) (analogue nature of maps, which required they be subject to process of OCR before each element could be searched electronically, did not mean those elements were not individually accessible).

[60] *Freistaat Bayern v. Verlag Esterbauer GmbH*, Case C-490/14, EU:C:2015:735, [29]. The conclusion is likely more important for database right, as most maps are unlikely to be original.

[61] Ibid., [21].   [62] Ibid., [24].   [63] Ibid., [27].   [64] Ibid., [28].

[65] Database Dir., Art. 1(3).

restriction to the type of material, as a collection of 'works data or other materials', there seems no reason why a multimedia work should not be a database. While it may seem odd that a compilation of artistic works or sound recordings is protected as a literary work,[67] this conclusion now seems unavoidable.

3 DRAMATIC WORKS

The CDPA 1988 does not define what a 'dramatic work' is, except to state that it includes a work of dance or mime.[68] However, it is relatively clear that dramatic work includes the scenario or script for films, plays (written for the theatre, cinema, television, or radio),[69] and choreographic works.[70]

For a creation to qualify as a 'dramatic work', it must be a 'work of action' that is 'capable of being performed'.[71] While the courts have not yet fully explored what is meant by a 'work of action', it is clear that it does not include static objects, sets, scenery, or costumes,[72] although these might be protected as artistic works.[73] It has been said that a film will usually be a dramatic work where there is 'cinematographic work' on the film.[74] In some limited circumstances, a work of action might include sports, such as gymnastics or synchronized swimming.[75]

The requirement that, to be a dramatic work, the subject matter must be 'capable of being performed' initially operated in a restrictive manner. In the *Hughie Green* case,[76] Green was the originator and producer of a talent show called *Opportunity Knocks*—a programme that followed a particular format: certain catchphrases were used; sponsors introduced contestants; and a 'clapometer' was used to measure audience reaction. Beyond this, the content of the show varied from show to show. The Broadcasting Corporation of

---

[66] See Stamatoudi, ch. 5.; Aplin, ch. 3; S. Beutler, 'The Protection of Multimedia Products through the European Community's Directive on the Legal Protection of Databases' [1997] *Ent L Rev* 317.

[67] See *Football Association Premier League v. Panini UK* [2004] *FSR* (1) 1, [32] (Mummery LJ) (giving examples of compilations made up of artistic works). One effect could be that a compilation of sound recordings would achieve much longer protection under copyright as a database than as a single sound recording.

[68] CDPA 1988, s. 3(1).   [69] *Green v. Broadcasting Corp. of New Zealand* [1989] *RPC* 469, 493.

[70] The fixation of such a work can be in writing 'or otherwise' and may accordingly be, for instance, on film. Where a dramatic work is recorded on a film, the film must contain the whole of the dramatic work in an unmodified state: *Norowzian v. Arks (No. 2)* [2000] *EMLR* 67 (dance recorded on film held unprotected because the film had been drastically edited and so was no longer a recording of the dance).

[71] *Norowzian v. Arks (No. 2)* [2000] *EMLR* 67 (CA), 73.

[72] *Creation Records* [1997] *EMLR* 444 (finding no arguable case that a photo shoot is dramatic work, since scene was inherently static, having no movement, story, or action).

[73] *Shelley Films v. Rex Features* [1994] *EMLR* 134; cf. *Creation Records* [1997] *EMLR* 444.

[74] *Norowzian v. Arks (No. 2)* [2000] *EMLR* 67. In the view of Buxton LJ, such a construction went some way towards ensuring compliance with Berne, Art. 14*bis*, which specifies that a cinematographic work must be protected 'as an original work' and that the owner of copyright therein 'shall enjoy the same rights as the author of an original work'. Nourse LJ said that he reached his conclusion without reference to the Convention.

[75] Although a film of a sporting event may be a work of action, it is probably not an 'original' dramatic work, being a mere recording of actions.

[76] *Green v. Broadcasting Corp. of New Zealand* [1989] *RPC* 469 (CANZ), 477 (scripts could not constitute dramatic works because they could not be acted or performed, which is the essence of drama); on appeal [1989] 2 *All ER* 1056 (Privy Council).

New Zealand broadcast a television talent quest that was similar to *Opportunity Knocks* in that the title and catchphrases were the same. It also used a clapometer, as well as the idea of using sponsors to introduce contestants.[77] Green's action for copyright infringement against the Broadcasting Corporation of New Zealand failed, primarily because he was unable to show that the programme was a dramatic work. In part, this was because, when looked at as a whole, the show lacked the specificity or detail for it to be performed. In particular, the Privy Council said that the scripts provided only a general idea or concept of a talent quest, which was not capable of being protected. The Privy Council also held that the features of the programme that were repeated in each show (namely, the format or style of the show) were not dramatic works. The reason for this was that a dramatic work must have sufficient unity for it to be capable of being performed.[78] On the facts, it was held that the particular features that were repeated from show to show (the format) were unrelated to each other except as accessories to be used in the presentation of some other dramatic performance.[79]

The requirement of 'unity' means that interactive video games are not 'dramatic works', since the sequence of images will not be the same from one play to another. Thus, in *Nova Productions v. Mazooma Games*,[80] Kitchin J held that a computer game simulating billiards involved artistic works and literary works, but not a dramatic work. Moreover, it has been held these requirements precluded the protection of an elaborated idea of having a group of musicians, dressed in formal attire, playing music not written for the ukulele on that instrument, could not be considered a dramatic 'work'. The judge explained that the supposed 'work' lacked certainty, for example, as to the number of musicians, the precise nature of their formal attire, the particular music played, etc. Moreover, the 'work' lacked the necessary 'unity', because, if protected, a vast array of alternative performances would infringe.[81]

The failure of the Privy Council to protect television formats in the *Hughie Green* case prompted a number of (unsuccessful) attempts to have formats recognized by British law.[82] The proponents of format rights appealed to the usual moral and economic arguments to support their cases. In particular, it was argued that formats require creative input similar to that involved in existing copyright works. It was also argued that failure to protect formats is not only unjust, but also fails to provide sufficient incentives to television producers. Those opposed to format rights noted the problems of

---

[77] Ibid. [1989] *RPC* 469, 478, 480, 493.

[78] Cf. *Ladbroke v. William Hill* [1964] 1 *All ER* 465 (copyright held to exist in pools coupons even though the matches changed each week).

[79] *Green v. Broadcasting Corp. of New Zealand* [1989] *RPC* 469, 477, on appeal [1988] 2 *NZLR* 490 (CANZ), 497; cf. *Television New Zealand v. Newsmonitor Services* [1994] 2 *NZLR* 91 (High Court of Auckland) (television news programme made up of unscripted and unchoreographed interviews and discussions was not a dramatic work).

[80] [2006] *RPC* (14) 379, [116]–[119].

[81] *The Ukulele Orchestra of Great Britain v. Clausen* [2015] *EWHC* 177 (IPEC), [104] (Judge Hacon).

[82] See 'Programme Formats: A Further Consultative Document' [1996] *Ent L Rev* 216; R. McD. Bridge and S. Lane, 'Programme Formats: The Write-In Vote' [1996] *Ent L Rev* 212; U. Klement, 'Protecting Television Show Formats under Copyright Law: New Developments in Common Law and Civil Law Countries' [2007] *EIPR* 52; M. Kretschmer and S. Singh, 'Exploiting *Idols*: A Case Study of International TV Formats Trading in the Absence of Intellectual Property Protection', available online at https://cemp.ac.uk/tvformats/Downloads/Exploiting_Idols.pdf; K. Bowrey and M. Handler, 'Instituting Copyright', in K. Bowrey and M. Handler (eds), *Law and Creativity in the Age of the Entertainment Franchise* (2014), 140.

defining what a format is, the anti-competitive effects, and the costs of such rights, as well as the potential for nuisance litigation.[83] The opponents of format rights favour leaving the developers of formats to the remedies offered by passing off[84] and breach of confidence.[85]

While formats are not protected to the extent that some would like, the need for *sui generis* format protection is less pressing as a result of the Court of Appeal decision in *Norowzian v. Arks*.[86] This is because, in this case, the Court liberally interpreted the requirement that a dramatic work must be 'capable of being performed' to include performances by artificial means, such as the playing of a film.[87] Consequently, a cartoon may be a dramatic work. In this decision, the Court of Appeal was called upon to decide whether a Guinness advertisement (which featured an actor dancing while a pint of Guinness was being poured) had infringed copyright in an earlier film *Joy* (which the advertisement copied). To answer this question, it was necessary to determine whether *Joy* was a dramatic work.[88] One of the notable features of *Joy* was that it utilized a particular editing technique known as 'jump-cutting' (that is, cutting segments out of the film to produce a series of artificial effects). One of the consequences of this was that the finished film contained a series of movements that could not be performed by an actor.[89] At first instance, it was held that because the (artificial) dance shown on the edited film could not be performed, the film did not embody a dramatic work. (If the film had shown all of the movements of the actor, it would have been protected.) However, on appeal, it was held that the film itself was a dramatic work. The Court said that, because it was possible for the film to be played, it was therefore 'capable of being performed'.

One might wonder whether, in the light of European developments, the question of the protection of formats needs to be revisited. If a format comprises more than 'ideas' and amounts to an 'intellectual creation', existing Court of Justice case law suggests that it should receive protection from various acts, including reproduction. The language of dramatic work is open-textured and certainly can be interpreted more broadly than occurred in the *Hughie Green* case. Overall, that case is increasingly likely to be seen as denying copyright to formats where they fail to meet certain standards of identity and repeatability.[90] In *Banner Universal*,[91] Snowden J took the view that it was 'at least arguable' that the format of a television game show or quiz could be a dramatic work. Without seeking to establish 'precise conditions', the Court indicated that there must be clearly identified features which, together, distinguish the format from other

---

[83] Mr Mellor, Standing Committee F, IV Hansard, 8 March 1990, cols 1293–4.

[84] *Green v. Broadcasting Corp. of New Zealand* [1989] *RPC* 469, 474, 480–1, 488–9 (passing off claim failed because the British show had never been broadcast in New Zealand, so there was no goodwill).

[85] Lord Sanderson of Bowden, 521 Hansard (HL), 26 July 1990, cols 1718–19. See Chapter 44, section 4, p. 1211, and Chapter 46, section 2.2.1, p. 1240.

[86] *Norowzian v. Arks (No. 2)* [2000] *EMLR* 67, 73.   [87] Ibid.

[88] Note that the argument on appeal was not that there was copyright in the dance as a dramatic work (recorded on film), but that the film was not merely a 'record' of a dramatic work, but was itself a dramatic work: ibid.

[89] That is, the finished film owed as much to the editing technique as to the dance that was filmed.

[90] *Meakin v. BBC* [2010] *EWHC* 2065 (Ch) (Arnold J), [30] (distinguishing *Green*); *The Ukulele Orchestra of Great Britain v. Clausen* [2015] *EWHC* 177 (IPEC), [104] (Judge Hacon) (not impossible to claim copyright in a TV format); L. Golding, 'Opportunity Knocks for Dramatic Copyright in Television Formats', in M. Richardson and S. Ricketson, *Intellectual Property in Media and Entertainment* (2017), ch. 14, 380 (proposition that TV formats are unprotected 'seems incorrect now as a general statement').

[91] *Banner Universal Motion Pictures v. Friday TV AB* [2017] *EWHC* 2600 (Ch).

shows; and those distinguishing features must be 'a coherent framework that can be repeatedly applied.'[92]

4 MUSICAL WORKS

The CDPA 1988 also protects musical works. A 'musical work' is defined to mean 'a work consisting of music exclusive of any words or action intended to be sung, spoken or performed with the music'.[93] Thus the words and the music of songs and similar works are treated as the subject matter of distinct copyrights. A song therefore consists of both a musical work and a literary work: the tune and lyrics, respectively.

The meaning of 'music' was discussed in *Sawkins v. Hyperion Records*.[94] This case concerned the efforts of Sawkins in producing what are termed 'performing editions' of four of the works of the seventeenth-century composer Michel-Richard de Lalande. Sawkins' efforts included 'figuring of the bass', adding 'ornamentation', and performance directions. Hyperion, which made recordings of performances of the works of Lalande by musicians using Sawkins' scores, denied that, by so doing, it infringed copyright, arguing that Sawkins' contribution had not created an original *musical* work. One question was whether Sawkins' contributions could count as contributions to the music in circumstances under which they did not involve alteration of the notes or melody. The Court of Appeal held that they could. Mummery LJ explained that the:

> . . . essence of music is combining sounds for listening to. Music is not the same as mere noise. The sound of music is intended to produce effects of some kind on the listener's emotions and intellect. The sounds may be produced by an organised performance on instruments played from a musical score, though that is not essential for the existence of the music or of copyright in it.[95]

The defendant's argument mistakenly assumed that the *actual notes* were the only matter covered by musical copyright; according to the Court of Appeal, other elements that contributed to the sound as performed, such as tempo and performance practice indicators, were equally music.

Although the Court of Appeal explicitly excluded 'noise' from the scope of 'music', it said nothing about the controversial question of whether 'silence' can be music.[96] According to newspaper reports, a dispute over just such a work of 'silence' resulted in a settlement—and a six-figure payment for the rights to use the work! The work in question was by the avant-garde composer John Cage, who, in the 1950s, wrote a piece entitled *4' 33'*, a work of silence. Apparently, the basis for the claim was that classical–pop fusion group The Planets included 60 seconds of silence on its recording. A member of the group claimed that this was an improvement on Cage's effort—because they had achieved in 60

---

[92] Ibid., [44]. The Court gave summary judgment to the defendant, finding that the claimed 'format' for a television show 'Minute Winner' comprised features that were 'commonplace and indistinguishable' from other game shows [46], and, moreover, (at [52]) that the defendant's show 'Minute to Win It' was 'different in every material respect'.

[93] CDPA 1988, s. 3(1). Sheet music was held to be covered by the term 'book' in the Statute of Anne: see *Bach v. Longman* (1777) 2 *Cowp* 623.

[94] *Sawkins v. Hyperion Records* [2005] 1 *WLR* 3281.   [95] Ibid., 3295, [53].

[96] C. L. Saw, 'Protecting the Sound of Silence in *4' 33'*" [2005] *EIPR* 467; Copinger, [3–100], ('it is doubtful that a passage of silence by itself is capable of being a musical work, even if claimed by the author or critics to be such').

seconds what he accomplished in 273! The payment to Cage's publisher suggests, however, that the legal advisers to The Planets (and the group's record company) feared that a court would treat Cage's work as protected.[97]

5 ARTISTIC WORKS

The fourth category of works protected by copyright is artistic works.[98] Section 4(1) of the CDPA 1988 contains a detailed list of the types of subject matter that are protectable as 'artistic works'. These are divided into the following three categories:

(i)   irrespective of artistic quality, a graphic work (including a painting, drawing, diagram, map, chart or plan, engraving, etching, lithograph, woodcut, or similar work), a photograph (excluding a film), a sculpture, or a collage;

(ii) a work of architecture, being a building or fixed structure or a model thereof; or

(iii) a work of artistic craftsmanship.[99]

5.1 GRAPHIC WORKS, PHOTOGRAPHS, SCULPTURES, AND COLLAGES

The first subcategory of artistic works, set out in section 4(1)(a), includes graphic works, photographs, sculptures, and collages. It is important to note that the material contained in section 4(1)(a) is protected irrespective of artistic quality. This ensures that, once a creation falls within a particular category of works, copyright protection is not contingent on the work reaching a certain aesthetic standard. As a result, the task of having to decide what is good or bad art and all of the associated problems are thus avoided.[100] More controversially, the decision that copyright law should not concern itself with the artistic quality of these types of work has been used to expand the *types* of subject matter (as distinct from the *quality* of subject matter) protected as artistic works. While few would have problems with Marcel Duchamp's 'readymades' (for example his famous urinal) being protected as an artistic work, more problems arise when objects exclusively used for industrial purposes to achieve commercial ends are protected as artistic works. For a period of time, a fear of making aesthetic judgements (when combined with a degree of formalism) led the courts to provide such protection. In recent years, however, the courts have been more willing to use a general sense of what is meant by 'art' to limit the scope of protectable works.

5.1.1 Paintings

Graphic works are specifically defined in section 4(1)(a) to include 'paintings'. For the most part, there have been few problems in determining whether something is a 'painting' and thus whether it qualifies as an artistic work. One of the few situations in which

---

[97] (22 June 2002) *The Independent*.

[98] See S. Stokes, *Art and Copyright* (2nd edn, 2012); A. Barron, 'Copyright, Art and Objecthood', in D. McClean and K. Schubert (eds), *Dear Images: Art, Copyright and Culture* (2002), 277 ('copyright law's conception of the artistic work now faces a crisis of credibility').   [99] CDPA 1988, s. 4(1).

[100] In *Burge v. Swarbrick* [2007] *HCA* 17, (2007) 234 *ALR* 204, 81 *ALJR* 950, [63], the Australian High Court referred to 'the supposed terrors for judicial assessment of matters involving aesthetics'.

Fig. 3.3 The defendant's poster in *Merchandising Corp. v. Harpbond* (created by Mr Langford)
Source: Merchandising Corporation of America v. Harpbond [1983] 3 *FSR* 32

this was not the case was *Merchandising Corp. v. Harpbond*,[101] in which it was argued that the facial make-up of the pop star Adam Ant was a painting and thus protected by copyright. The Court of Appeal rejected this submission, Lawton LJ remarking that it was fantastic to suggest that make-up on anyone's face could possibly be a painting. He held that a painting required a surface and that Adam Ant's face did not qualify as such, noting that '[a] painting is not an *idea*: it is an object; and paint without a surface is not a painting' (see Fig. 3.3).[102]

The reasoning of Lawton LJ seems odd, for it is difficult to see why Adam Ant's face is less of a surface than a piece of canvas. The decision could, however, be justified on the ground that a painting must be intended to be permanent. If so, a tattoo would be protected, but dramatic or cosmetic make-up would not.[103] Equally, since the make-up in question consisted of two broad red lines round a light-blue line running from nose to jaw, it is arguable that the work did not satisfy the criteria of originality. Alternatively, the decision could be seen as a case of merger of idea and expression (for which no protection is granted).[104] In light of European developments,[105] it is suggested that the courts should revisit the unconvincing reasoning in the Adam Ant case. If a work made out of face paint or a tattoo constitutes its author's own intellectual creation, then, under European law, it should be protected. The most obvious way to do so under British law is to treat such works as paintings.

---

[101] [1983] *FSR* 32.   [102] Ibid., 46.

[103] *J. & S. Davis (Holdings) v. Wright Health Group* [1988] *RPC* 403 may lend support to such a view; cf. *Metix v. Maughan* [1997] *FSR* 718, 721. For discussion in the US context, see A. Perzanowski, 'Owning the Body: Creative Norms in the Tattoo Industry', in K. Darling and A. Perzanowski (eds), *Creativity Without Law: Challenging the assumptions of Intellectual Property* (2017), ch 4.

[104] E. Derclaye, 'Debunking Some of UK Copyright Law's Longstanding Myths and Misunderstandings' [2013] *IPQ* 1; cf. *Ibcos Computers v. Barclays Mercantile Highland Finance* [1994] *FSR* 275.

[105] See earlier, section 1, pp. 59–62.

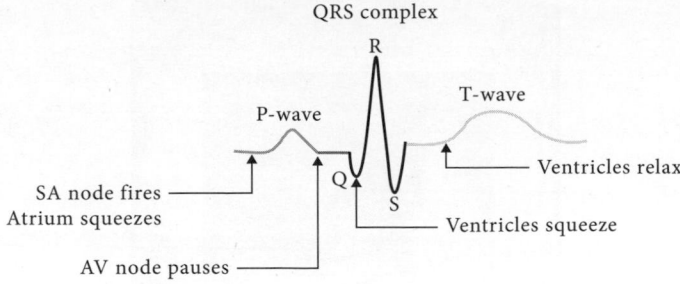

Fig. 3.4 Wave diagram in *Technomed v. Bluecrest Health Screening*
Source: Courtesy of Technomed Ltd

5.1.2 Drawings and Diagrams

The next type of subject protected as an artistic work under section 4(1)(a) is 'drawings'. In addition to sketches of people and landscapes that we expect to be classified as drawings, protection has been granted to the drawing of a hand on a 'how to vote' card,[106] type-face design,[107] architects' plans (as distinct from actual buildings), and sketches for dress designs.[108] Because protection is granted 'irrespective of artistic quality', copyright in drawings has been widely used to protect industrial designs.[109] Thus drawings of exhaust pipes, boxes for storing kiwi fruit, and the like have been protected.[110] Importantly, such protection has frequently prevented the copying of the (three-dimensional) designed artefact itself. As we will see later, section 51 of the CDPA 1988 has reduced the significance of copyright in drawings for three-dimensional designs, other than in designs for artistic works.[111]

Section 4 of the CDPA 1988 also defines graphic work as including 'diagrams'. In *Technomed Bluecrest Health Screening*,[112] the High Court held that a simple line diagram, called the 'wave diagram', was an artistic work (and protected as original); see Fig. 3.4.

5.1.3 Engravings

Engravings were first protected by copyright in 1735. For the most part, the way in which the law has developed since then has provided few surprises, protection being granted to etchings, aquatints, woodcuts, lithographs, and the like. In the last 40 years, however, a range of somewhat surprising objects have been protected as engravings. For example, in *Wham-O Manufacturing v. Lincoln Industries*,[113] the New Zealand Court of Appeal held that both the mould from which a frisbee was pressed and the frisbee itself were protected, because the mould was made by cutting onto a surface and so was an engraving, and the frisbee itself was a print from the engraving (see Fig. 3.5).

---

[106] *Kenrick v. Lawrence* (1890) 25 *QBD* 99.

[107] *Stephenson Blake & Co. v. Grant, Legros & Co.* (1916) 33 *RPC* 406.

[108] *Bernstein v. Murray* [1981] *RPC* 303.

[109] D. Booton, 'Framing Pictures: Defining Art in UK Copyright Law' [2003] *IPQ* 38 (arguing that circuit diagrams, architects' plans, and engineering drawings are not artistic, but literary).

[110] *British Leyland v. Armstrong* [1986] *RPC* 279; *Plix Products v. Frank Winstone* [1986] *FSR* 92 (NZ).

[111] See Chapter 29, section 3, pp. 811–15.   [112] [2017] *EWHC* 2142 (Ch), [133] (Judge D Stone).

[113] [1985] *RPC* 127. See also *James Arnold v. Miafern* [1980] *RPC* 397 (articles made from a block and also the block itself); *Martin v. Polyplas* [1969] *NZLR* 1046 (coin is an engraving).

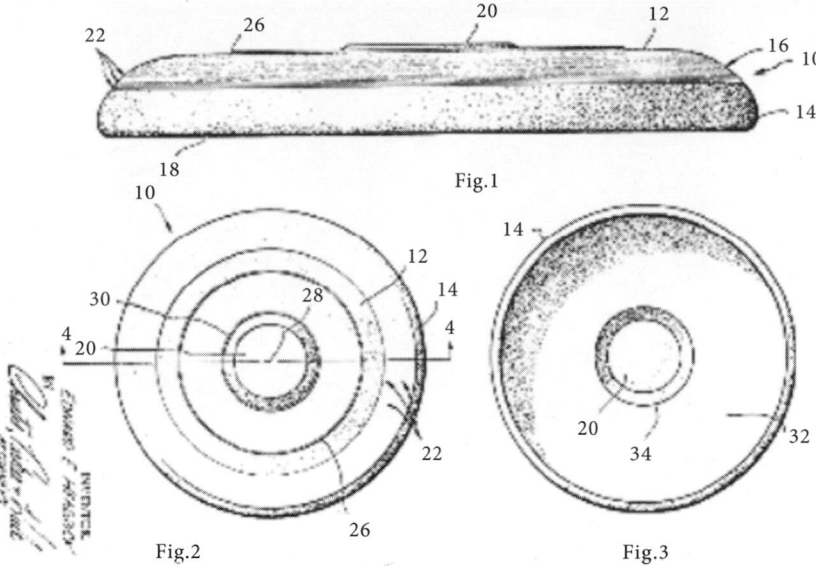

Fig. 3.5 Headrick's flying saucer

Source: Wham-O Manufacturing v. Lincoln Industries [1982] RPC 281, 296

In *Hi-Tech Autoparts v. Towergate Two*,[114] Judge Christopher Floyd QC held that copies of the claimant's rubber floor mats for cars could not be sold by the defendant on the grounds that the moulds used in the production of the mats, and the mats themselves, were 'engravings.' The moulds had been made by cutting a series of concentric circles, to a depth of 1/16th of an inch and a bevel angle of 45°, into flat plates. In so holding, the judge placed particular emphasis on the fact that the statute requires engravings to be protected 'irrespective of their artistic quality'.

5.1.4 Photographs

Although photographs were protected by copyright shortly after photography was invented in the 1840s,[115] copyright law has never been completely comfortable with photographs, primarily because they seem to be ill-suited to the paradigm of the 'original' and the 'copy'.[116] Photographs are defined in the 1988 Act as 'a recording of light or other radiation on any medium on which an image is produced or from which an image may by any means be produced, and which is not part of a film'.[117] The definition is broad enough to include digital photographs (where there is no film). Individual frames from a film are not treated as photographs.[118]

---

[114] *Hi-Tech Autoparts v. Towergate Two* [2002] *FSR* (15) 254 (plates); *Hi-Tech Autoparts v. Towergate Two (No. 2)* [2002] *FSR* (16) 270 (mats). [115] Fine Art Copyright Act 1862.

[116] K. Bowrey, 'Copyright, Photography and Computer Works: The Fiction of an Original Expression' (1995) 18 *UNSWLJ* 278.

[117] CDPA 1988, s. 4(2). Whether something is a photograph may also be important because of CDPA 1988, ss 30(2) and 62.

[118] *Spelling Goldberg Productions v. BPC Publishing* [1981] *RPC* 283, 288, 297, 298, 300 (single frames from *Starsky and Hutch* were not photographs, but part of a film under CA 1956). See Kamina, 92–4.

Fig. 3.6 Stormtrooper helmet design
Source: *Lucasfilm v. Ainsworth* [2009] *FSR* (2) 103

5.1.5 Other graphic works

The examples elaborated of 'graphic works' are non-exhaustive, so non-itemized works may also be protected as artistic works. In *Abraham Moon & Sons v. Thornber*, the Patents County Court (now the IPEC)—held that the instructions for generating fabric designs were graphic works, because they had visual significance for experts.[119] Moreover the subcategory 'graphic work' has also been held to protect computer screen icons and graphic user interfaces.[120] However, the dynamic effect created by a series of drawings is not protected as an artistic work.[121]

5.1.6 Sculpture

The protection of 'sculpture' by copyright has required the courts to make some difficult determinations. Most notoriously, in *Wham-O Manufacturing v. Lincoln*, the New Zealand Court of Appeal held that the wooden model that was used as a mould to make the frisbees was 'a sculpture';[122] in *Lucasfilm v. Ainsworth*, however, Mann J 'respectfully disagreed' with that conclusion.[123] The UK courts have adopted a more restrictive interpretation of the term 'sculpture'.

Lucasfilm v. Ainsworth, which concerned the question of whether a plastic version of a 'stormtrooper' helmet was a 'sculpture', went to the Supreme Court, which approved the approach taken by Mann J and his conclusion that the helmet was not a 'sculpture' (see Fig. 3.6).[124] While acknowledging that the assessment of whether an object was a sculpture was one in which 'subjective considerations are likely to intrude', Mann J identified a number of guidelines.[125] His articulation of the guidance is worth consulting directly, but here we will note only the emphasis that the legal meaning should not stray too far

---

[119] [2012] *EWPCC* 37, [100]–[107] (leaving undecided whether the fabric designs themselves were graphic works).

[120] *Navitaire v. EasyJet Airline Co. & Bulletproof Technologies* [2006] *RPC* 111, 153, [98]; *Nova Productions v. Mazooma Games* [2006] *RPC* (14) 379, [100].

[121] *Nova Productions v. Mazooma Games* [2007] *EWCA Civ* 219, [16].

[122] *Wham-O v. Lincoln Industries* [1985] *RPC* 127, 157. See also *Breville Europe v. Thorn EMI* [1995] *FSR* 77, 94 (Falconer J) (scallop-shaped moulds that were used in toasted-sandwich makers were sculptures).

[123] [2009] *FSR* (2) 103, 153, [118].   [124] [2011] *UKSC* 39, [2012] 1 *AC* 208, [37], [48].

[125] [2008] *EWHC* 1878 (Ch), [2009] *FSR* (2), [118]; [2009] *EWCA Civ* 1328, [2010] *Ch* 503, [54], [71].

from the 'normal' understanding of what was a sculpture. Thus Mann J noted that while something could be a 'sculpture' even though one would not expect to find it in an art gallery, 'some regard' has to be had to the normal use of the word 'sculpture' and care should be taken to avoid straying too far from what would normally be regarded as such. At the same time, it was stated that no judgement is to be made about artistic worth. Mann J's guidelines go on to focus on the structural nature, mode of fabrication, and—probably most importantly—the purpose of the object. As to its nature, Mann J is clear that while it is a necessary requirement that a sculpture be a 'three-dimensional representation of a concept,' not every three-dimensional construction would be a sculpture. Likewise, the process of fabrication, such as whether the representation is carved and the material used (for example, wood or stone), might be another relevant factor—although not a determinative one: not everything carved in wood is a sculpture.[126] Ultimately, the determinative factor seems to be the purpose of the process. A purely functional item, not intended to be at all decorative, would not be a sculpture. It is:

> . . . of the essence of a sculpture that it should have, as part of its purpose, a visual appeal in the sense that it might be enjoyed for that purpose alone, whether or not it might have another purpose as well. The purpose is that of the creator . . . An artist (in the realm of the visual arts) creates something because it has visual appeal which he wishes to be enjoyed as such. He may fail, but that does not matter (no judgments are to be made about artistic merit). It is the underlying purpose that is important.[127]

The fact that the object has some other use does not necessarily disqualify it from being a sculpture, but it still has to have the intrinsic quality of being intended to be enjoyed as a visual thing.

Applying these guidelines to the material before him, Mann J held that none of the articles were sculpture. His reasons are surprising, so are probably worth quoting in full:

> The purpose of the helmet was that it was to be worn as an item of costume in a film, to identify a character, but in addition to portray something about that character—its allegiance, force, menace, purpose and, to some extent, probably its anonymity. It was a mixture of costume and prop. But its primary function is utilitarian. While it was intended to express something, that was for utilitarian purposes. While it has an interest as an object, and while it was intended to express an idea, it was not conceived, or created, with the intention that it should do so other than as part of character portrayal in the film . . . Not everything which has design appeal is necessarily a sculpture. I think that the ordinary perception of what is a sculpture would be over-stretched by including this helmet within it . . . It is not that it lacks artistic merit; it lacks artistic purpose.[128]

This seems to give undue emphasis to one conception of the purpose of the costumes and mistakenly to undervalue the importance of appearance in the designs. His explanation for holding that the toys were not sculptures was equally surprising:

> These are, as already described, articulated models which are sold as toys and which are intended for the purposes of play. Play is their primary, if not sole, purpose. While their appearance is obviously highly important (if they did not look like the original, the child would not be so interested) they are not made for the purposes of their visual appearance as such. While there is no accounting for taste, it is highly unlikely that they would be placed on display and periodically admired as such. The child is intended to use them in

---

[126] *Lucasfilm v. Ainsworth* [2009] *FSR* (2) 103, 153, [118].   [127] Ibid., 153, [118], point (vi).
[128] Ibid., 154 [121].

a (literally) hands-on way, in a form of delegated role play, and that is doubtless how they are actually used. That means, in my view, they are not sculptures.[129]

Nevertheless, the Court of Appeal and Supreme Court affirmed the decision. In a speech composed jointly by Lords Walker and Collins, the Supreme Court agreed that the term 'sculpture' should be given its ordinary meaning,[130] and approved Laddie J's definition in *Metix v. Maughan* that 'sculpture' refers to a 'three-dimensional work made by an artist's hand'.[131] The Court said that Mann J's multifactor approach was consistent with that test. It went on to note that there were good policy reasons for differentiating between copyright and designs law, so that the definition of sculpture should not be permitted to 'creep outwards'.[132] Because the question was one of fact, on which the judge had heard evidence, the assessment was one that a higher court should respect. In the view of the Supreme Court, the assessment by Mann J that the helmet was utilitarian in the sense that it was an element in the process of producing the film was not 'obviously untenable'.[133] Consequently, the first-instance decision was affirmed.

While the legal understanding of 'sculpture' is by no means confined to the works of those who exhibit in art galleries, not all three-dimensional works exhibited in art galleries and attributed to artists will necessarily qualify as sculptures. In *Creation Records* (the Oasis record cover case—see Fig. 3.1), Lloyd J held that the collection of a series of objects around a swimming pool was not itself a sculpture.[134] He explained that he could not see how:

... the process of assembling these disparate objects together with the members of the group can be regarded as having anything in common with sculpture . . . No element in the composition has been carved, modelled or made in any of the other ways in which sculpture is made . . .[135]

This conclusion leaves unclear the position in relation to so-called *objets trouvés* and other situations in which artists 'create' artistic works from found material, famous examples being Duchamp's urinal, Carl André's bricks, Damien Hirst's shark, or Tracy Emin's bed. Although it seems that these are unlikely to fall within Laddie J's definition of sculpture as a three-dimensional work *made by an artist's hand*, Mann J's multifactor test, which stresses the 'purpose' of the object, seems better able to accommodate such practices.[136]

All of this concern with what counts as a 'sculpture' may, however, be of limited significance in terms of determining whether a work is protected.[137] If the Court of Justice continues the trend of harmonizing EU copyright law, then it seems that the key question is less whether the object is a 'sculpture' than it is whether it is an 'intellectual creation'. In reaching that conclusion, the question of the quality or purpose of the work may be assumed to be irrelevant except insofar as they limit the potential creative choices of the creator. Moreover, the fact that there is another regime that protects three-dimensional

---

[129] Ibid., 154 [123].   [130] [2012] 1 *AC* 208, [29].

[131] *Metix v. Maughan* [1997] *FSR* 718, 722 (moulds for making functional cartridges in the shape of double-barrelled syringes are not sculptures). The Supreme Court said that this definition had 'not attracted adverse comment from any quarter': [2012] 1 *AC* 208, [34]. It seems that the Court overlooked *Hi-Tech Autoparts v. Towergate Two* [2002] *FSR* (15) 254, [48].

[132] [2012] 1 *AC* 208, [48].   [133] Ibid., [44], [46].

[134] *Creation Records v. News Group* [1997] *EMLR* 444.   [135] Ibid., 449.

[136] In *Creation Records*, Lloyd J distinguished Gallagher's assemblage from Carl André's bricks by reference to the 'ephemerality of the former'. In *Lucasfilm v. Ainsworth* [2009] *FSR* (2) 103, 153, [118], Mann J agreed that André's bricks would be a sculpture, emphasizing that it was its 'artistic purpose' that was key.

[137] However, at least for the moment, it retains significance particularly when examining whether the defence provided by CDPA 1988, s. 51, is in play. See further Chapter 29, section 3.1.2*ff*, p. 805.

artefacts—namely, the law of designs, which was considered relevant by the Supreme Court—seems likely to be regarded as irrelevant by the Court of Justice. If the question were to arise today of whether a stormtrooper helmet is a work protected by copyright, there is some possibility that a different answer would be reached.

5.2 WORKS OF ARCHITECTURE

The second subcategory of artistic works listed in section 4(1)(b) of the CDPA 1988 is 'works of architecture'. A 'work of architecture' is defined as a building or a model for a building.[138] In turn, a 'building' is defined as including 'any fixed structure, and a part of a building or fixed structure'. It should be noted that copyright also exists in the architect's plans as drawings.

One question that has arisen is whether buildings include things such as greenhouses, portable cabins, and swimming pools that are built off-site. The main obstacle to protection is that a building is defined as a *fixed* structure.[139] While this was apparently intended to prevent ships from being protected as works of architecture, the status of articles that are not fixed when they are created, but which are intended to be subsequently fixed or permanently placed, is unclear. In an Australian case, the Supreme Court of the Northern Territory held that a plug and mould used for manufacture of pre-cast fibreglass swimming pools were protected by copyright.[140] Explaining that there was no single test for what is a building, Mildren J said that a number of factors needed to be considered, including the size of the structure, its proposed use, whether it is fixed or portable, and its degree of permanence. As a result, he concluded that while neither the plug nor the mould was a building, the pools were. This was despite the fact that the pools were manufactured off-site and were capable of being removed.

In contrast to other types of artistic work, there is no requirement that architectural works should be protected 'irrespective of artistic quality'. This might imply that, when deciding whether subject matter qualifies as an architectural work, we should consider whether the work is a work of architecture, and if so, whether it is sufficiently artistic. However, the legislative history points to a contrary conclusion: a requirement of 'artistic quality' existed under the 1911 Act, but was removed in 1956. Therefore it seems that the legislature intended there to be no need for a work of architecture to be 'artistic' for it to be protected. This would be in line with the current trend of jurisprudence from the Court of Justice.

5.3 WORKS OF ARTISTIC CRAFTSMANSHIP

The final category of artistic works listed in section 4(1)(c) of the CDPA 1988 is 'works of artistic craftsmanship'. The legislative origins of this category of work, which first appeared in the Copyright Act 1911, are obscure.[141] Works of artistic craftsmanship cover creations such as handcrafted jewellery, tiles, pots, stained-glass windows, wrought-iron gates, hand-knitted jumpers, and crocheted doilies. In order for a work to fall within this category, it is necessary to show that the work is 'artistic' and that it is a work of 'craftsmanship'. We will deal with each in turn.

---

[138] CDPA 1988, s. 4(1)(b). Copyright protection for works of architecture was first introduced under the 1911 Act to give effect to the Berlin Revision of the Berne Convention.

[139] CDPA 1988, s. 4(2) (but note that the provision says 'building' *includes* 'any fixed structure').

[140] *Darwin Fibreglass v. Kruhse Enterprises* (1998) 41 *IPR* 649.

[141] *George Hensher v. Restawile Upholstery (Lancs)* [1976] *AC* 64 (Lord Simon).

5.3.1 Requirement of 'artistic quality'

A work will qualify as a work of artistic craftsmanship only if it is 'artistic'—that is, if it has an element of real artistic or aesthetic quality.[142] This approach is unusual in copyright law because it requires the courts to consider whether the work satisfies the qualitative threshold of being artistic. The question of what is meant by a work of *artistic* craftsmanship was discussed by the House of Lords in *Hensher v. Restawile Upholstery*.[143] Because the defendants conceded that the claimant's prototype of a mass-market upholstered chair was a work of craftsmanship, the only question to be determined was whether the chair was a work of *artistic* craftsmanship. While all of their Lordships agreed that the chair was not artistic, they differed in their explanations as to why.

- Lord Reid said that an object could be said to be artistic if a person gets 'pleasure or satisfaction ... from contemplating it'.[144] As a result, his Lordship said that the test to decide whether a work was artistic was whether 'any substantial section of the public genuinely admires and values a thing for its appearance and gets pleasure or satisfaction, whether emotional or intellectual, from looking at it'.[145] Lord Reid noted that 'looking nice appears to me to fall short of having artistic appeal'.[146] While the author's intention that the resulting product is artistic might be important, Lord Reid indicated it was neither 'necessary [n]or conclusive'. Since there was no evidence that anyone regarded the furniture in issue as artistic, Lord Reid concluded that the prototype was not protected by copyright.

- Lord Morris said that, in this context, the word 'artistic' required no interpretation. However, he acknowledged that, because the question of whether a particular artefact was artistic was a matter of personal judgement, courts might be faced with differences of opinion. Because of this, Lord Morris said that a court should look to see if there was a general consensus of opinion 'among those whose views command respect'.[147] The views of the artist and the person acquiring the object might act as pointers as to whether something is artistic. However, the question was ultimately one for the courts, guided by evidence (particularly of specialists). Since the most favourable thing that had been said about the prototype chair was that it was distinctive, Lord Morris was content to conclude that it was not artistic.

- Lord Kilbrandon said that the question of whether something was a work of art depended on whether it had come into existence as the product of an author who was consciously concerned to produce a work of art.[148] For Lord Kilbrandon, this must be judged from the work itself and the circumstances of its creation. A work did not become a work of art as a result of the opinions of critics or the public at large. As a consequence, expert evidence was irrelevant. Instead, it was for the judge to determine whether the author had the 'desire to produce a thing of beauty which would have an artistic justification for its own existence'.[149] Since, in the case in hand, the objective was to produce a commercially successful chair, it was not a work of artistic craftsmanship.

- In deciding whether a craftwork was artistic, Viscount Dilhorne explained that this was really a question of fact for the court to answer. As such, he declined to elaborate much further on the meaning of artistic.[150] He did say, however, that a work would

---

[142] *Cuisenaire v. Reed* [1963] *VR* 719, 730; *Hensher v. Restawile Upholstery (Lancs)* [1976] *AC* 64, 77, 78, 81, 85, 86, 96; *Merlet v. Mothercare plc* [1986] *RPC* 115; *Bonz Group v. Cooke* [1994] 3 *NZLR* 216, 222.

[143] *George Hensher v. Restawile Upholstery (Lancs)* [1976] *AC* 64.   [144] Ibid., 78E.

[145] Ibid., 78G.   [146] Ibid., 79C–D.   [147] Ibid., 81D.   [148] Ibid., 96G.   [149] Ibid., 98C.

[150] Ibid., 86G–87A.

not be artistic merely because there was originality of design, but that it could be artistic even if it were functional. While Viscount Dilhorne said that expert evidence and public opinion would be relevant,[151] in the end it seems that he preferred to act on his own intuition as to what was a 'work of art'. However, since no witness had described the chair as a work of art, he said that this was not even a borderline case: the prototype was not protected by copyright.[152]

- Lord Simon took a rather different approach from his colleagues, insofar as he emphasized that it was the craftsmanship rather than the work that must be artistic. Lord Simon also said that the fact that the work 'appeals to the eye of the beholder, giving him visual pleasure' was irrelevant.[153] Examples of 'artistic crafts-men' included hand-painters of tiles, and makers of stained-glass windows and wrought-iron gates, but not 'plumbers'. Lord Simon said that many craftsmen fell into an intermediate category, some of their products being the result of artistic craftsmanship, while others were the product of craftsmanship. In making the decision as to whether a particular object was created by a person who was an 'artist craftsman', Lord Simon took the view that 'the most cogent evidence is likely to be either from those who are themselves acknowledged artistic-craftsmen or from those who are concerned with the training of artist-craftsmen—in other words, expert evidence'.[154] Lord Simon added, however, that the crucial question was 'the intent of the creator and its result'.[155] Like the other Law Lords, he found the application of his test to the facts relatively easy: none of the experts had regarded the settee as exhibiting anything more than originality of design and appeal to the eye. The settee was an ordinary piece of furniture and not an example of artistic craftsmanship.

Given the 'different and apparently irreconcilable' tests employed in *Hensher*, it is not surprising to find that there has been little consistency in subsequent case law as to the approach to be taken when assessing 'artistry'.

In *Merlet v. Mothercare*,[156] in which a baby's cape made by Madame Merlet was held not to be a work of artistic craftsmanship, Walton J concluded that, in the first instance, the question is whether the artist-craftsman *intended* to create a work of art.[157] If the intention was present and the creator had not 'manifestly failed' in this regard, then the work was a work of art. Because Madame Merlet had not set out to create a work of art, but instead had utilitarian considerations in mind (she hoped that the cape would shield her son from the rigours of the climate when visiting her mother in the Scottish Highlands), Walton J concluded that the baby cape was not a work of artistic craftsmanship. In contrast, in *Vermaat v. Boncrest*,[158] Evans-Lombe J adopted a different test, requiring not merely intention but actual evidence of creativity. The case concerned the design of a patchwork bedspread and whether this was a work of artistic craftsmanship. Evans-Lombe J held that the finished work must have some artistic quality, in the sense of being produced by someone with creative ability and having aesthetic appeal.[159] Applying that test of artistry to the facts, the judge held that though the designs were 'pleasing to the eye', they did not exhibit the necessary requirement of creativity.

---

[151] Ibid., 87C–D.   [152] Ibid., 87E–F.   [153] Ibid., 93C.   [154] Ibid., 94H.

[155] Ibid., 95B–C.

[156] *Merlet v. Mothercare* [1986] *RPC* 115. The Court of Appeal (at 129 *ff*) considered only issues relating to infringement of copyright in Mme Merlet's drawings.

[157] Ibid., 125–6, citing Viscount Dilhorne, Lord Simon, and Lord Kilbrandon.

[158] [2001] *FSR* (5) 49.   [159] *Bonz Group v. Cooke* [1994] 3 *NZLR* 216.

Yet more confusion has been created by the rather incoherent judgment of Rimer J in *Guild v. Eskandar*.[160] In this case, the question was whether the claimant's wide, square-shaped designs for a cardigan and sweater were works of artistic craftsmanship.

Initially, Rimer J purported to follow *Merlet* and found that there was no evidence that the claimant regarded herself as an artist or intended to create a work of art; she chose the design because it appealed to her and she therefore believed that it would appeal to others. If he had been rigorously following *Merlet*, that should have put an end to the investigation; instead, Rimer J went on to consider whether the garment 'can fairly be regarded as satisfying the aesthetic emotions of a substantial section of the public'.[161] (He may have done so purely out of deference to Lord Reid in *Hensher* or just in case a different criterion was applied on appeal, but the case is unsatisfactory for failing to explain the reasons for this examination.) The judge took account of the conflicting expert evidence, but ultimately concluded that the garments were not works of art. This was in spite of the fact they had been displayed in the Victoria & Albert Museum, Rimer J explaining that they were exhibited as examples of developments in fashion rather than because anyone regards them as works of art.

Clearly, the decisions in *Vermaat* and *Guild* have done little to clarify when a work of craftsmanship is to be treated as artistic.[162] Further guidance from a higher court would be welcome indeed.

5.3.2 Requirement of 'craftsmanship'

As well as showing that the work is artistic, it is also necessary to show that it is a work of 'craftsmanship'. In *Hensher v. Restawile*, Lord Simon defined a work of craftsmanship as presupposing 'special training, skill and knowledge' for its production.[163] He also said that it implied 'a manifestation of pride in sound workmanship'. A rather different definition was provided by Lord Reid, who referred to a work of craftmanship as 'a durable, useful handmade object'.[164] Lord Reid seemed to suggest that if the defendant had not conceded that the prototype was a work of craftsmanship, he would not have been inclined to that view. This was because the prototype, which was a flimsy, temporary, knock-up that had subsequently been destroyed, was better described as a 'step in a commercial operation' with no value of its own rather than as a work of craftsmanship.[165] While wooden rods (used to teach addition and subtraction to children) have been held not to be products of craftsmanship,[166] knitting and tapestry-making have been held to be a craft,[167] and the baby's cape in *Merlet v. Mothercare* was said to be 'very much on the borderline'.[168]

One problem with the courts' failure to provide a helpful definition of craftsmanship is that it is unclear whether the work needs to be handmade to be protected. In *Hensher v. Restawile*, Lord Reid and Viscount Dilhorne suggested that craftsmanship implied that the work was handmade.[169] In contrast, Lord Simon said that 'craftsmanship' could

---

[160]   *Guild v. Eskandar* [2001] *FSR* (38) 645.   [161]   Ibid., 700.

[162]   Note also *Lucasfilm v. Ainsworth* [2008] *EWHC* 1878 (Ch) (Mann J holding that the stormtrooper helmets in *Star Wars IV* were not works of 'artistic craftsmanship' because '[t]heir purpose was not to appeal to the aesthetic at all. It was to give a particular impression in a film'; not discussed on appeal).

[163]   *George Hensher v. Restawile Upholstery (Lancs)* [1976] *AC* 64, 91.

[164]   Ibid., 77.   [165]   Ibid., 77.

[166]   *Cuisenaire v. Reed* [1963] *VR* 719 (Supreme Court of Victoria); *Komesaroff v. Mickle* [1988] *RPC* 204 (Supreme Court of Victoria), 210.

[167]   *Bonz Group v. Cooke* [1994] 3 *NZLR* 216 (High Court of New Zealand), a case approved by the High Court of England and Wales in *Vermaat* [2001] *FSR* (5) 49.   [168]   [1986] *RPC* 115, 122.

[169]   *George Hensher v. Restawile Upholstery (Lancs)* [1976] *AC* 64, 77 (Lord Reid), 84 (Viscount Dilhorne) (made by hand and not mass-produced).

not be limited to handicrafts, nor was the word 'artistic' incompatible with machine pro-duction.[170] The approach of Lord Simon was followed by the Federal Court of Australia in *Coogi Australia v. Hysport International*.[171] In that case, Drummond J held that the stitch structure of a fabric made up of different yarns (used to make jumpers), which was constructed in such a way as to produce a mixture of textured surfaces (some flat, some rolled, some protruding), was a work of artistic craftsmanship. Drummond J said that the way in which the designer had used the stitch structures and colour to pro-duce an unusual textured and multicoloured fabric meant that the design was artis-tic. This was so even though the design was mass-produced and had been formulated on a computer, rather than using traditional craft techniques. As regards the issue of mass-production, Drummond J reviewed the authorities and found that he preferred Lord Simon's approach in *Hensher v. Restawile*. To hold otherwise, he said, would be to import a Luddite philosophy into copyright legislation, which was enacted against a background of modern industrial organization and was intended to regulate rights of value to persons in the area of activity.[172] Because Drummond J's approach presents a realistic and workable approach to this issue, hopefully it will be followed in the United Kingdom.[173]

Another aspect of the notion of artistic craftsmanship that has proved to be problem-atic is whether the requirements of artistic quality and craftsmanship must emanate from the same person. In *Burke v. Spicer's Dress Designs*,[174] Clauson J suggested as much when he said that a woman's dress was not a work of artistic craftsmanship because the artistic element (the sketch of the dress) did not originate from the person who made the dress (the dressmaker).[175] However, in *Bonz Group v. Cooke*,[176] the New Zealand High Court held that hand-knitted woollen sweaters depicting dancing lambs and golfing kiwis were a work of artistic craftsmanship, the hand-knitters being craftspeople and the designer an artist. Tipping J observed that it was not essential that the same person both conceive and execute the work.[177]

5.3.3 Australian escape route

It is clear that the English courts have struggled with the interpretation of the notion of artistic craftsmanship. An indication as to how the problems can be avoided has been pro-vided by the unanimous decision of Australia's highest court, the High Court, in *Burge v. Swarbrick*.[178] The question in that case was whether Swarbrick's design for a yacht, the JS9000 (see Fig. 3.7)—in particular, the hull and deck mouldings—were works of artistic craftsmanship.

---

[170] Ibid., 90.

[171] (1998) 157 *ALR* 247 (FCA). See also *Burge v. Swarbrick* [2007] *HCA* 17, (2007) 234 *ALR* 204, 81 *AJLR* 950, [60] (noting that something such as a 'plug' for a mass-produced boat could be a work of artistic craftsmanship).

[172] *Coogi Australia v. Hysport International* (1999) 157 *ALR* 247, 258–9.

[173] The fact that a design is created without using traditional 'craftsmanship techniques', or is intended to be mass-produced, may be a factor. See, e.g., *Guild v. Eskander* [2001] *FSR* (38) 645, 700, not considered on appeal at [2003] *FSR* (3) 23.   [174] [1936] 1 *Ch* 400, 408.

[175] This approach is consistent with the views of Lord Simon in *George Hensher v. Restawile Upholstery (Lancs)* [1976] *AC* 64 to the effect that a work of artistic craftsmanship is the work of a person who is an 'artist-craftsman'.

[176] *Bonz Group v. Cooke* [1994] 3 *NZLR* 216 (High Court of New Zealand). See also *Spyrou v. Radley* [1975] *FSR* 455; *Bernstein v. Sydney Murray* [1981] *RPC* 303; *Merlet v. Mothercare* [1986] *RPC* 115, 123–4.

[177] *Bonz Group v. Cooke* [1994] 3 *NZLR* 216 (High Court of New Zealand), 224; *Vermaat v. Boncrest* [2001] *FSR* 49.   [178] [2007] *HCA* 17, (2007) 234 *ALR* 204, 81 *ALJR* 950.

Fig. 3.7 JS9000 yacht
Source: Mr John Swarbrick

While refusing to provide 'any exhaustive and fully predictive identification of what can and cannot amount to a "work of artistic craftsmanship"', the High Court concluded that the key factor that separates protected works of artistic craftsmanship from mere industrial designs is the significance of functional constraints.[179] With works of artistic craftsmanship, there is considerable 'freedom of design choice' and thus scope for 'real or substantial artistic effort'. The intention of the designer could cast some light on this and, in his evidence, Swarbrick had acknowledged that he sought to produce a 'well mannered, easily balanced boat that was fast'. However, in most cases, the crucial evidence would be the views of experts, and here this confirmed that speed was the overriding consideration in the design of 'sports boats'.[180] Designing the JS 9000 therefore involved the application of principles of mathematics, physics, and engineering, rather than making something visually or aesthetically appealing. Thus the plug and mouldings were not works of artistic craftsmanship.

Although the decision in *Burge v. Swarbrick* is based on legislation that now differs substantially from that operating in the United Kingdom, there is much to be said for the clarity that it brings to the notion of a work of artistic craftsmanship. Had the 'design freedom' test been applied in *Guild v. Eskander* or *Vermaat v. Boncrest*, one could imagine that a different result might well have been reached: both look like cases in which the creator possessed and utilized the freedom available in creating the design of clothes and bedspreads. Of course, other cases, such as *Hensher* itself or *Merlet v. Mothercare*, would require the courts to face up to the difficult question as to how much design freedom would suffice to render a work one of artistic craftsmanship. The High Court was willing to say only that this was a question of 'fact and degree'.

5.3.4 European escape route

An alternative way out of the problem of defining works of artistic craftsmanship—at least for the purposes of subject matter—is to question what role quality determinations can have in a harmonized system of EU copyright law. It is not simply that the EU law requires the United Kingdom to protect intellectual creations, but also that it appears to prohibit

---

[179] Ibid., [82]–[84].

[180] See ibid., [63]–[65], noting the problems with such evidence, in particular that 'few alleged authors of works of artistic craftsmanship [will] be heard readily to admit the absence of any aesthetic element in their endeavours'.

the use of qualitative criteria.[181] Recital 8 of the Software Directive states that originality is the only criterion for protection and that 'no *tests as to the qualitative or aesthetic merits* of the program should be applied',[182] while the Term Directive indicates that 'no other *criteria such as merit or purpose*' should be used when assessing the originality of photographs,[183] and the Database Directive directs that 'no *aesthetic or qualitative criteria*' may be used when determining the eligibility of a database for copyright.[184] Assuming, as the Court of Justice has been willing to do, that the logic expressed in these directives applies to all 'works', then no qualitative criteria could be applied when deciding on the eligibility of 'works of artistic craftsmanship' for protection. Applying this logic, 'artistic' could not be understood as having the same meaning as it has for 'artistic works' in copyright law generally (that is, referring to something that is perceived visually). Applying such a criterion, if a work of craftsmanship is original, in the sense described in Chapter 4 (that is, the result of creative, as opposed to functionally constrained, choices), then it should be protectable.

6 FILMS

Copyright law has struggled to find a convenient way to treat 'films' or 'motion pictures'. One reason for this is that such productions can be the product both of significant investment, and creativity (particularly the creative vision of the director). Another reason is that films are often the result of a large number of inputs—screenplays, music, set-design, costumes, performance (and direction), cinematography, and so forth. A third is that some of these contributions can receive separate protection, but the film as a whole may be more than 'the sum of its parts'.[185]

Under the CDPA 1988, UK law recognizes a distinct category of work, 'film'. This term is defined as a recording on any medium from which a moving image may be produced by any means.[186] This broad definition encompasses celluloid films and video recordings or disks, as long as they produce 'moving images'. Multimedia products may sometimes be protected as films.[187]

In contrast, the EU's Term and Related Rights Directives distinguish between two distinct subject matters of protection for motion pictures: on the one hand, 'cinematographic and audiovisual works'; and on the other, related rights in fixations of moving images, so-called 'films', or 'videograms'.[188] The former are conceived as authorial works (like literary or artistic works) and thus would be subject to a requirement of originality, and

---

[181] S. Van Gompel and E. Lavik, 'Quality, Merit, Aesthetics and Purpose: An Inquiry into EU Copyright Law's Eschewal of other Criteria than Originality' (2013) 236 *RIDA* 100.

[182] Emphasis added. [183] Term Dir., Recital 16 (emphasis added).

[184] Database Dir., Recital 16 (emphasis added).

[185] E. Derclaye, 'Debunking Some of UK Copyright Law's Longstanding Myths and Misunderstandings' [2013] *IPQ* 1 (highlighting the problems involved in using the term 'film' both colloquially and in its legal sense).

[186] CDPA 1988, s. 5B(1); cf. CA 1956, s. 13(10), and *Spelling Goldberg v. BPC Publishing* [1981] *RPC* 283 (stating that film has three characteristics: a sequence of images, recorded on material, capable of being shown as a moving picture).

[187] Aplin, ch. 3; T. Aplin, 'Not in Our Galaxy: Why Film Won't Rescue Multimedia' [1999] *EIPR* 633; Stamatoudi, ch. 6, esp. 126–51. Despite these criticisms, the biggest problem with relying on film copyright to protect multimedia works derives from the narrow scope of protection given by film copyright.

[188] Term Dir., Art. 3(3), defining film, as 'a cinematographic or audiovisual work *or moving images, whether or not accompanied by sound*' (emphasis added).

protection lasts for 70 years from the death of the principal director or author of the screenplay, dialogue, or music.[189] Rights in fixations, in contrast, vest in the 'producer' and last for 50 years.[190]

Unfortunately, although the United Kingdom has attempted to implement those Directives, no corresponding adjustment has been made to the structure of UK law. As a result, the 1988 Act continues expressly to acknowledge only one copyright work, a 'film', which appears primarily as a 'related right' (although modified, as to authorship and term, to comply with the Directives).[191] However, the courts have gone some way to alleviating the legislative deficit by recognizing that original 'cinematographic works' under the Berne Convention are also 'dramatic works' under UK copyright law.[192] Nevertheless, in various respects, the UK approach can be said to fail to implement the various Directives.[193]

The soundtrack accompanying a film is treated as part of the film. As we will see, there is no reason why such a soundtrack would not also qualify as a sound recording. This leads to a potential problem of overlap. Section 5B(3)(a) and (b) of the CDPA 1988 clarifies the position by stating that references to the showing of a film include playing the film soundtrack to accompany the film, and references to playing a sound recording do not include playing the film soundtrack to accompany the film. Consequently, if a cinema were to wish to show a film that included a soundtrack, the cinema would need to obtain rights clearances only from the owner of copyright in the film.[194] In contrast, where the soundtrack is played without the moving images, for example on a jukebox in a pub, it is necessary to obtain the consent only of the right holder in the sound recording of the soundtrack.[195]

7 SOUND RECORDINGS

Under the CDPA 1988, section 5A(1), sound recordings are defined to mean either:

(a) a recording of sounds, from which the sounds may be reproduced, or

(b) a recording of the whole or any part of a literary, dramatic or musical work, from which sounds reproducing the work or part may be produced,

regardless of the medium on which the recording is made or the method by which the sounds are reproduced or produced.

The definition thus covers vinyl records, tapes, compact discs, digital audiotapes, and mp3s, which embody recordings. The definition also seems to encompass digital instructions embodied in electronic form that produce sounds. In a different legal context (that of licensing places of entertainment), it has been held that 'recorded sounds' can include CD-ROM embodiments of Musical Interface Digital Interface (MIDI) instructions

---

[189] Term Dir., Art. 2. See Chapter 7, section 3, pp. 186–7.

[190] Rel. Rights Dir., Art. 3(1)(d), 9(1)(c), Info. Soc. Dir., Art. 2(d), 3(2)(c) (conferring rights of rental, distribution, reproduction and making available on the producer); Term Dir., Art. 3(3).

[191] CDPA 1988, s. 13B(9). For an argument that this fails to implement the directives, see P. Kamina, 'British Film Copyright and the Incorrect Implementation of the EC Copyright Directives' [1998] *Ent L Rev* 109.

[192] *Norowzian v. Arks (No. 2)* [2000] *EMLR* 67. For criticism, see T. Rivers, '*Norowzian* Revisited' [2000] *EIPR* 389.   [193] P. Kamina, *Film Copyright in the European Union* (2nd edn, 1999), 134–5.

[194] See also P. Kamina, 'The Protection of Film Soundtracks under British Copyright after the Copyright Regulations 1995 and 1996' [1998] *Ent L Rev* 153.   [195] CDPA 1988, s. 5B(2)–(3).

(rather than data in wave form) that cause a sound module or synthesizer to generate sounds.[196]

As the definition of sound recording requires that there be 'sounds', it appears to exclude a single sound from protection (even though a considerable amount of production work may go into its recording). Interesting questions have also arisen as to how the limits of a sound recording are to be determined. We review these issues when we look at copyright infringement.[197] Because sound recordings exist irrespective of the medium on which the sounds are recorded, a soundtrack of a film is a sound recording. However, the soundtrack of a film will also be treated as part of the film insofar as the soundtrack 'accompanies' the film.[198] The effect of this is that the public showing of a film and its soundtrack requires the consent of only the owner of copyright in the film.[199] In contrast, where the soundtrack is played without the moving images,[200] this would require the consent of only the holder of rights in the sound recording.

8 BROADCASTS

Broadcasts, whether of sounds or images, were first included as copyright works in the Copyright Act 1956. Subsequently, they were deemed to be suitable subject matter for protection by neighbouring rights at the 1961 Rome Convention.[201] The decision to extend copyright protection to broadcasts marked an important change in copyright law. In contrast with art, literature, films, and recordings, a broadcast is essentially the provision of a service that involves a communication; it is not the creation of a thing, but an action. This is because broadcasts are not fixed or embodied (although they can be); rather, they are ephemeral acts of communication. This means that a broadcast does not protect any fixed entity per se. Instead, what is protected are the signals that are transmitted. In a sense, copyright law recognizes the value in the act of communication itself as distinct from the content of what is being communicated.[202]

A 'broadcast' is defined as:

. . . an electronic transmission of visual images, sounds, or other information which—
(a) is transmitted for simultaneous reception by members of the public and is capable of being lawfully received by them, or
(b) is transmitted at a time determined solely by the person making the transmission for presentation to members of the public . . .[203]

This definition merely requires that the transmission be 'electronic',[204] being indifferent otherwise as to the means of transmission, the route taken, or the form of the signals.[205]

---

[196] *Sean Toye v. London Borough of Southwark* (2002) 166 JP 389.

[197] See Chapter 8, esp. section 2.3.3, pp. 210–12.   [198] Term Dir., Art. 3.

[199] CDPA 1988, s. 5B (3)(a).   [200] CDPA 1988, s. 5B(3)(b).

[201] Rome, Arts 3(f), 6, 13, 14, 16(1)(b); TRIPS, Art. 14(3).

[202] On the question of what amounts to a 'work' in this context, see the Australian High Court decision in *TCN Channel Nine v. Network Ten* [2004] HCA 14, in which the majority held that, in the case of a broadcast, the work is the individual programme transmitted.   [203] CDPA 1988, s. 6(1) (as amended).

[204] Defined in CDPA 1988, s. 178, as 'actuated by electric, magnetic, electro-magnetic, electro-chemical or electro-mechanical energy'.

[205] The Copyright Directorate refers to this as a 'technologically neutral definition': *Consultation on UK Implementation of Directive 2001/29/EC on Copyright and Related Rights in the Information Society: An Analysis of Responses and Government Conclusions* (2003), [3.6].

The definition therefore covers transmissions both by wire ('cable television') and wireless (such as 'free-to-air' broadcasts), terrestrial and satellite transmission, and analogue and digital broadcasts. By referring to the transmission of 'visual images, sound, or other information', the definition is also broad enough to cover systems that transmit different forms of content, such as radio, television, and other broadcasts (for example teletext). It also takes into account the forms of broadcasting that may be directly received by individuals or may be received by subscribers who obtain a decoder.[206]

While the basic definition of 'broadcast' is deliberately broad, two alternative criteria provide important limits: to constitute a broadcast, the transmission must be 'for simultaneous reception by members of the public' (and capable of being lawfully received) or be made 'at a time determined solely by the person making the transmission for presentation to members of the public'. Moreover, section 6(1A) excludes from broadcasts 'any Internet transmission', although with three (not insubstantial) exceptions.

The limitation of broadcasts to transmissions *for* simultaneous reception 'by members of the public' excludes from protection transmissions between individuals, such as telephone calls, faxes, or emails, as well as transmissions on private networks (such as company 'intranets'): these are not for reception by members of the public. The requirement that the transmission be 'capable of lawful reception' reinforces the exclusion of private communications from the definition of broadcast, because the interception of such a transmission would be illegal under the Regulation of Investigatory Powers Act 2000.[207] The requirement for 'simultaneous reception', too, excludes transmissions for which the individual recipient decides the time of the transmission, as with on-demand services, or interactive database services (such as *Lexis Library* or *Westlaw*). The alternative criterion—that the transmission be at a time determined solely by the person making the transmission 'for presentation to members of the public'—is designed to cover transmission for playing or showing, such as when a football game is beamed back to the away team's stadium.[208] It also covers what is frequently referred to as 'narrow-casting', such as transmission to shops for presentation to the public.

The scope of the definition of broadcast is confined further by excluding 'any Internet transmission', but this exclusion is subject to three exceptions of its own. No definition is provided for an 'Internet transmission', but the better view is that the Internet is not confined to the 'world wide web'. Emails to news groups therefore are generally excluded from protection as 'broadcasts' (although they might be protected as literary or artistic works).[209]

As an exclusion from broadcasts of 'any Internet transmission' would be unfathomably broad, the Act seeks to keep broadcast protection for 'Internet transmissions of a

---

[206] That is, any encrypted broadcast, whether terrestrial or by satellite relay, is 'lawfully' received if decoding equipment has been made available through the person transmitting it in encrypted form: CDPA 1988, s. 6(2).

[207] Rather surprisingly, this might mean that foreign encrypted broadcasts, such as satellite broadcasts, for which there is no authorized distribution of decoders in the United Kingdom are unprotected because they are not capable of lawful reception in the United Kingdom. This would be a breach of Rome, Art. 6(1)(b), and is best avoided by treating the definition as covering broadcasts that are capable of lawful reception in the country at which the signals are primarily targeted.

[208] Copyright Directorate, *Consultation on UK Implementation of Directive 2001/29/EC*, [3.9] (explaining requirement that timing be determined by the person making the transmission as designed to exclude on-demand services from the definition of broadcast).

[209] Ibid., [3.10] (explaining the exclusion as a response to concerns that websites would be protected and that exceptions, such as research and private study, at the time limited to use of works of specified types, would therefore be unavailable). In this respect, the decision in *Shetland Times v. Dr Jonathan Wills* [1997] *FSR* 604 that a website is protected (then, as items included in a cable programme service) is no longer good law.

conventional broadcast character' by means of three exceptions to the exclusion. First, section 6(1A)(a) clarifies that the exclusion of 'Internet transmissions' does not encompass 'a transmission taking place simultaneously on the Internet and by other means'. This means that websites that transmit sounds and images simultaneously with broadcasts—all of the BBC radio stations, for example, are accessible from the BBC's website—remain protected broadcasts.

A second provision in section 6(1A)(b) allows for broadcasts to include an Internet transmission that is a 'concurrent transmission of a live event'. The term 'concurrent' implies that the Internet transmission must occur at the same time as the 'live event', so would seem to cover Internet transmission of a cricket match or sounds of a pop concert. The provision refers to transmission *of* a live event and so would not treat as a broadcast a transmission of *commentary* on a live event. Newsgroup emails of progress at the latest international copyright convention would not be a broadcast therefore, nor would the commentary on a football match (unless the commentary itself were to be treated as an event). Whether the courts will interpret 'live event' to cover transmissions of the *Big Brother* house (even where these were not being broadcast on television) remains to be seen; an approach that refuses to discriminate will end up treating all live web-cam feeds into websites as broadcasts.

A third exception in section 6(1A)(c) indicates that an Internet transmission is not excluded from the definition of broadcast if it is 'a transmission of recorded moving images or sounds forming part of a programme service offered by the person responsible for making the transmission, being a service in which programmes are transmitted at scheduled times determined by that person'. This means that a person who wishes to set up a conventional style of broadcast service, solely utilizing the Internet to distribute the programme service, does gain protection for the broadcasts.

9 PUBLISHED EDITIONS

The final category of works that are protected by copyright is 'typographical arrangements of published editions'. This category of works was first introduced in the United Kingdom in 1956 and remains largely a peculiarity of the British, and British-influenced, copyright systems (having no corresponding international regime).[210] A 'published edition' means 'a published edition of the whole or any part of one or more literary, dramatic or musical works'.[211] In *Newspaper Licensing Agency v. Marks & Spencer*, Lord Hoffmann stated that 'the "edition" is the product, generally between covers, which the publisher offers to the public'.[212] In this context, the copyright in the published edition protects the typographical arrangement—that is, the overall appearance of the page or pages. This protects the publisher's skill and investment in typesetting, as well as the processes of design and selection that are reflected in the appearance of the text.[213] There is no requirement that

---

[210] CA 1956, s. 15. See *Report of the Copyright Committee* (Cmd. 8662, October 1952), [306]–[310].

[211] CDPA 1988, s. 8(1).

[212] *Newspaper Licensing Agency v. Marks and Spencer* [2003] 1 *AC* 551, 558, [2001] 3 *WLR* 390 (Lord Hoffmann) (holding that the whole newspaper was the 'edition').

[213] Ibid., [23]: It is not the choice of a particular typeface, the precise number or width of the columns, the breadth of margins and the relationship of headlines and strap-lines to the other text, the number of articles on a page and the distribution of photographs and advertisements but the combination of all of these into pages which give the newspaper as a whole its distinctive appearance ... The particular fonts, columns, margins and so forth are only, so to speak, the typographical vocabulary in which the arrangement is expressed.

the published edition must be a previously unpublished work. It therefore covers modern editions of works in the public domain (such as the complete works of Shakespeare) and prohibits the reproduction of the layout (but not the work itself). It should be noted that the concept of reproduction of a typographical arrangement is extremely narrow, being restricted to facsimile reprography. Consequently, the reproduction of the material contained in a published work will not infringe this limited copyright where a different layout is employed.

4

CRITERIA FOR PROTECTION

1 INTRODUCTION

In order for a work to be protected by copyright, it is necessary to show that, as well as being the sort of work protected by the Copyright, Designs and Patents Act 1988 (CDPA 1988), the work also satisfies the particular requirements that are imposed on it. As we will see, the requirements vary, sometimes considerably, between different categories of work.

(i) The *first* requirement is that the work must be recorded in a material form. As we will see, this applies only to literary, dramatic, and musical works.

(ii) The *second* requirement is that the work must be 'original'. It should be noted that this applies only to literary, dramatic, musical, and artistic works. In contrast, there is no need for entrepreneurial works (sound recordings, films, broadcasts, and typographical arrangements) to be 'original'. Instead, the 1988 Act declares that copyright subsists only to the extent that such works are not copied from previous works of the same sort.[1]

(iii) The *third* requirement, which applies to all works, is the work is sufficiently connected to the United Kingdom to qualify for protection under UK law.

(iv) The *fourth* requirement is that the work is not excluded from protection on public policy grounds.

We will deal with each of these requirements in turn.

2 RECORDED IN MATERIAL FORM

There is no requirement that a work be registered for copyright protection to arise;[2] copyright arises automatically. However, the CDPA 1988 provides that copyright does not subsist in literary, dramatic, or musical works 'unless and until' the works are 'recorded

---

[1] CDPA 1988, ss 5(2), 6(6), 7(6), 8(2).

[2] Registration requirements for published literary works and some artistic works existed until 1912. Over the last decade, there has been a revival of interest in an 'opt-in' copyright regime. For an extensive treatment, see S. van Gompel, *Formalities in Copyright* (2012), and the *BTLJ*/BCLT Symposium: The Next Great Copyright Act (2014) 29 *BTLJ*.

in writing or otherwise'.[3] This is usually referred to as the 'requirement that the work be recorded in a material form'. Writing is defined to include any form of notation or code 'regardless of the method by which, or medium in or on which, it is recorded'.[4] Thus it seems that any digital embodiment of a work will suffice.[5]

There is no requirement of recording in the case of artistic works,[6] sound recordings, films, and published editions. In the case of sound recording and films, 'recording' is implicit in the statutory definition of subject matter. In the case of artistic works, material form will often be present: for example, we have already noted that the Court of Appeal has said that a painting requires a 'surface',[7] and it has been stated that an ice sculpture, although not permanent, is protected as a sculpture.[8] But what about, for example, a display of coloured lights? It could be argued that since fixation is not specifically required by the 1988 Act for artistic works, such a display could be protected.[9] If so, live televising of the display would infringe. The point remains to be decided by the courts. An Australian authority suggests that a work of kinetic art will not be protected.[10]

There is no requirement that broadcasts be fixed or embodied in any particular form. Thus broadcasts are protected whether or not the broadcasting organization makes a permanent version of them.

The requirement that literary, dramatic, and musical works be recorded is rarely a serious impediment to copyright protection.[11] The reason for this is that the fixation requirement will be satisfied even if the recording is carried out by someone other than the creator (with or without their permission),[12] whether the recorded form is in the claimant's hands or has subsequently been destroyed.[13] Given that when someone infringes copyright, they will normally have reproduced the work, and that parties unconnected with the creator can carry out the requisite recording, this means that in most cases the work will in fact have been recorded.

---

[3] CDPA 1988, s. 3. This is deemed to be the time when the work is 'made': CDPA 1988, s. 3(2). One commentator has suggested that this requirement may no longer be appropriate in the light of European harmonization of the 'work' concept, which requires member states to protect 'intellectual creations' and says nothing about fixation: see C. Handig, 'The Copyright Term "Work": European Harmonisation at an Unknown Level' (2009) 40 *IIC* 665, 673.   [4] CDPA 1988, s. 178.

[5] Written in the pre-digital era, the CDPA 1988 here seems to assume that using notation ensures that is a material version of a work. Digitization, of course, creates the possibility that there could be highly unstable or ephemeral versions that are 'in writing'. Consider, for example, a student's essay that is written before the computer crashes and cannot be recovered: it seems that this was 'in writing', but it would be strange to say that it was 'recorded' until a version was saved either automatically or by the author.

[6] But cf. *Komesaroff v. Mickle* [1988] *RPC* 204 (a device consisting of a mixture of sand, liquid, and bubble-producing substance did not qualify as a work of artistic craftsmanship).

[7] See *Merchandising Corporation v. Harpbond* [1983] *FSR* 32, 46 (Lawton LJ), discussed in Chapter 3, section 5.1, pp. 72–3.   [8] *Metix v. Maughan* [1997] *FSR* 718, 721.

[9] Such a work does not fall easily within any of the designations of artistic work in CDPA 1988, s. 4. But EU law may require that it be protected nonetheless. See Chapter 3, section 1, pp. 58–62.

[10] *Komesaroff v. Mickle* [1988] *RPC* 204, 210 (King J) (definition of the work of artistic craftsmanship on which she bases her action can be done only by a reference to a static aspect).

[11] For a rare example, see *McCormack Training v. Goldmark Training Services* [2015] *EWHC* 41 (IPEC), [89] (Judge Hacon) (on assumption that a physical restraint technique is a dramatic work, a single photograph of the technique in operation is not a recording of that technique as a dramatic work).

[12] CDPA 1988, s. 3(3).

[13] *Lucas v. Williams & Sons* [1892] 2 *QB* 113, 116; *Wham-O Manufacturing Co. v. Lincoln Industries* [1985] *RPC* 127 (CANZ), 142–5; *J & S Davis (Holdings) v. Wright Health Group* [1988] *RPC* 403, 409.

3 ORIGINALITY: LITERARY, DRAMATIC, MUSICAL, AND ARTISTIC WORKS

Perhaps the most important requirement that must be satisfied for copyright protection to arise is that the work must be 'original'. It should be noted that this applies only to literary, dramatic, musical, and artistic works (authorial works).[14] In contrast, there is no need for entrepreneurial works (sound recordings, films, broadcasts, and typographical arrangements) to be original for them to qualify for protection.[15]

While the originality requirement has been a general statutory requirement since 1911,[16] it is very difficult to state with any precision what copyright law means when it demands that works be 'original'.[17] Perhaps the most common account is that the work must be the result of 'labour, skill and judgement'.[18] This uncertainty has been exacerbated by the fact that, as part of the harmonization of copyright law in Europe, a new concept—that of the *author's own intellectual creation*—determines the originality not only of databases, computer programs, and photographs, but also of all literary, dramatic, musical, and artistic works. In what follows, therefore, we need to examine the difference between the traditional British conception of originality and the European one.

3.1 COMMON CHARACTERISTICS OF ORIGINALITY

While we will explore the differences between the traditional British and European conceptions of originality below, both conceptions share a number of characteristics. First, in both traditional British and European conceptions, 'originality' is concerned with the relationship between an author or creator and the work—that is, originality is not concerned with whether the work is inventive, novel, or unique.[19] While the novelty requirement in patent law focuses on the relationship between the invention and the 'state of the art',[20] the originality examination is primarily concerned with the relationship between the creator and the work. When copyright says that a work must be original, this means that the author must have exercised the requisite intellectual qualities (in the British version, 'labour, skill, or effort'; in the European, 'intellectual creation') in producing the work.[21] More specifically, in determining whether a work is original, copyright law focuses on the input that the author contributed to the resulting work. Consequently, a person who writes a film script based on an original story recounted by Homer in *The Odyssey* produces an 'original' work even though the story and characters have been widely known for thousands of years.[22]

---

[14] CDPA 1988, s. 1(1).   [15] See section 4, pp. 118–19.

[16] Although the requirement was introduced for paintings, drawings, and photographs by the Fine Art Copyright Act 1862.

[17] E. Judge and D. Gervais, 'Of Silos and Constellations: Comparing Notions of Originality in Copyright Law' (2009) 27 *Cardozo AELJ* 375 (identifying and contrasting four conceptions of originality: 'personal intellectual creation', associated with civil law and Europe; 'minimal creativity', associated with the United States after *Feist Publications v. Rural Telephone Service Co.*, 499 *US* 340 (1991); 'skill and judgement', the Canadian test after *CCH Canadian v. Law Society of Upper Canada* [2004] *SCC* 13, [16]; and 'labour, skill and judgement', the traditional British test). But, as we will see, there is no single 'civil law' approach and the traditional British test has more uncertainties than this suggests.

[18] See the case law described in section 3.3, pp. 97–8.

[19] *University of London Press v. University Tutorial Press* [1916] 2 *Ch* 601; *Sawkins v. Hyperion* [2005] 1 *WLR* 3281, 3288, [3] (Mummery LJ).   [20] See Chapter 18, section 1, pp. 551–2.

[21] *Ladbroke v. William Hill* [1964] 1 *All ER* 465, 469 (Lord Reid).

[22] *Christoffer v. Poseidon Film Distributors* [2000] *ECDR* 487.

Second, the test of originality in the traditional and European conception is concerned with the manner in which the work is *expressed*—in the way in which the paint is applied, the words are chosen and ordered, ideas are executed, or the clay moulded. That is, in assessing originality, copyright law is concerned with the originality of expression rather than ideas.[23]

Third, whether we are concerned with the traditional UK approach or the new EU test, it is clear that 'derivative works' can be original.[24] 'Derivative works' are works that were derived from or based upon existing works (whether or not they are protected by copyright). Obvious examples of such works are new editions, translations, arrangements of music, and engravings, as well as anthologies. To be protected, the derivative work must also be 'original' in itself (although as we will see, precisely what this requires in this context may vary from country to country).

It is worth reiterating that, in such cases, copyright may subsist in a derivative work even though it might infringe copyright in the existing work[25]—that is, a derivative work may be both original and infringing. In such a situation, any copyright that is acquired in a derivative work will be distinct from and subordinate to the copyright in any prior original work that is incorporated into it. Provided that the original work is still apparent in the new version, both the maker of the new version and any third-party copier will need the licence of the owner of copyright in the original.

The fourth point to note is that the originality threshold has been set at a very low level.[26] English courts have accepted as original such things as railway timetables and exam papers (which were drawn from the stock of knowledge common to mathematicians, produced quickly, and included questions similar to ones that had previously been asked by other examiners), while (as we will see) the Court of Justice has implied that 11 words might amount to an original work.[27] One of the consequences of the originality standard being set at a low level is that there have been relatively few instances in which subject matter has been excluded on the basis that it was non-original. Most of the problems that have arisen have been in relation to informational works, derivative works, and industrial designs.

Fifth, when considering the relevance of previous cases, it is worth bearing in mind that, whatever test is applied, the question of whether a work is original inevitably depends on the particular cultural, social, and political context in which the judgment is made. In part, this is because originality turns on the way in which the inputs into the work are perceived by the courts. One of the consequences of this is that what is seen as original may change over time. A good example of this is provided by photography. When invented in the 1840s, photography was seen as a non-creative (and non-original) mechanical process whereby images were produced by exposing chemically sensitive materials to light. In the late nineteenth century, however, photography came to be seen as an artistic activity. As a result, photographs came to be seen as creative and thus potentially original works.[28]

[23] *University of London Press v. University Tutorial Press* [1916] 2 *Ch* 601, 608 (Peterson J); *SAS Institute v. World Programming*, Case C-406/10 [2012] 3 *CMLR* (4) 55, 68, [AG44] (AG Bot).

[24] This is specifically required by Berne, Art. 2(3) ('Translations, adaptations, arrangements of music and other alterations of a literary or artistic work shall be protected as original works without prejudice to the copyright in the original work').

[25] *Redwood Music v. Chappell* [1982] *RPC* 109, 120; *ZYX Music GmbH v. King* [1995] 3 *All ER* 1, 9–11.

[26] *Technomed v Bluecrest Health Screening* [2017] *EWHC* 2142 (Ch) (Judge D Stone), [89] (calling *Infopaq* a 'low hurdle'). Cf. *Football Dataco v. Yahoo! UK*, Case C-604/10 [2012] 2 *CMLR* (24) 703, [AG41] (AG Mengozzi).   [27] *University of London Press v. University Tutorial Press* [1916] 2 *Ch* 601.

[28] B. Edelman, *Ownership of the Image: Elements for a Marxist Theory of Law* (1979); J. Gaines, *Contested Culture: The Image, The Voice and the Law* (1992).

Recent developments in technology may, however, have rendered some photographs that were creative in 1900 distinctly mundane in today's terms.[29] Similar changes recently occurred in relation to the artistic works of Aboriginal Australians, which were once assumed to be 'non-original' on the basis that the works reflected traditional themes and imagery, but are now recognized as not merely original, but also artistic (in the sense of being of such quality as to merit inclusion in art galleries).[30]

3.2 PURPOSE OF THE ORIGINALITY REQUIREMENT

Before going into detail, it is worth pausing for a moment and considering the 'function' of the originality requirement. The originality requirement sets a threshold that determines when material falling within the definition of literary, dramatic, musical, or artistic work is protected by copyright law. Nevertheless, the policy basis for the threshold requirement has never been made clear.[31]

From one natural rights perspective, the requirement of originality merely reflects the premise that copyright ought to protect the personality of authors as expressed in their works: absent such 'originality'—that is, indicia or traces of personality—there is no justification for protection. Consequently, works that do not reflect their author's personality—works of labour or investment, works that different creators would come up with independently, as well as 'objective' features of works (facts, many ideas, functions)—would not warrant protection.[32] Moreover, no protection should be afforded to those features of works that are necessary for others to exercise their natural rights—in this respect, their creative or expressive freedom.[33] In contrast, from a reward perspective, where effort has been made in creating a work, the creator may be said to deserve some protection from the exploitation of that effort by another (who would be unjustly enriched). This strand of thinking points towards making protection readily available for anyone who invests labour or capital in producing a work (at least where other forms of legal protection, such as unfair competition law, are unavailable).

From a utilitarian perspective, the 'originality' threshold might have been expected to sit at a different, often more taxing, level to ensure that copyright protects only those works that would not have been produced but for the incentive provided by copyright.[34] While such an approach might also justify protection of works of investment or industrious collection (even though they do not reflect the individuality of their creator),[35] it ought to mean that trivial and insubstantial works are unprotected (and that there is no need to offer copyright protection to works that are subject to other incentive mechanisms, such as patents or design rights). In addition, a utilitarian approach to originality

---

[29] R. Deazley, 'Photographing Paintings in the Public Domain: A Response to Garnett' [2001] *EIPR* 179, 181.

[30] See B. Sherman, 'From the Non-original to the Aboriginal', in Sherman and Strowel.

[31] T. Dreier and G. Karnell, 'Originality of the Copyrighted Work: A European Perspective' (1991–92) 39 *J Copyright Soc'y USA* 289, 294.

[32] But cf. J. Hughes, 'Created Facts and the Flawed Ontology of Copyright Law' (2007) 83 *Notre Dame L Rev* 43 (pointing out that many 'facts' are created).

[33] *Irene A*** v. K*** GmbH*, Case 4 Ob 162/08i (Austrian Supreme Court, 14 October 2008), [2010] *ECC* (12) 186, 191 ('To afford copyright protection to all works, including those that are mundane or banal, would intolerably hamper the creative freedom of others').

[34] J. Wiley, 'Copyright at the School of Patent' (1991) 58 *U Chi L Rev* 119; J. S. Miller, 'Hoisting Originality' (2009) 31 *Cardozo L Rev* 451.

[35] P. Jaszi, 'On the Author Effect: Contemporary Copyright and Collective Creativity' (1992) 10 *Cardozo AELJ* 293, 300–1.

might be expected to ensure that no exclusivity is conferred on matters that are essential components with which others can create or express themselves (for example facts, functions, ideas, names, and titles).[36] Thus 'originality' can be seen as a key threshold in defining the 'public domain'.[37]

While the natural rights and utilitarian perspectives do seem to have influenced the development of the 'originality' requirement, it will be unsurprising to discover that the legal tests do not reflect with precision any particular theoretical perspective. In part, this is because the legal system does not comprise philosophers, nor is it primarily concerned with philosophical consistency (natural rights, reward theories, and incentive rationales often being merged). Moreover, the legal system inevitably takes into account other matters, such as procedural economy and the desire for certainty. This leads courts to shy away from adopting or developing tests that are difficult to apply, towards ones that are simple and objective. In traditional British case law on originality, this has tended to lead courts to dilute the originality standard so as to protect works that have not been copied.[38] In civil law systems, originality is often assumed, particularly in relation to the productions of well-known artists.[39]

In addition to operating as a threshold, originality may be important in establishing whether a person has infringed copyright. This is because a person will not infringe copyright if they merely copy elements that are not original in the claimant's work.[40] That is, deciding what is original in a claimant's work plays an important role in ascertaining whether a 'part' of a work has been taken by the defendant. (However, it should be noted that the fact that a person creates an original work does not mean that they are not infringing copyright in work on which they have drawn.[41] This is because, as we see in Chapter 8, infringement depends on what a person has taken from a copyright work; the effort that such a person adds is irrelevant.)

3.3 BRITISH CONCEPTION OF ORIGINALITY

It would be foolish to claim that the case law developed since 1912 (or carried over from earlier jurisprudence) has defined clearly the circumstances in which a literary, dramatic, musical, or artistic work will be treated as original. Much of the case law seems inconsistent and, according to one commentator 'the dividing line between original . . . works, and unoriginal . . . works, remains an uncertain and shifting one'.[42] In part, these difficulties arise because originality 'must depend largely on the facts of the case and must in each case be very much a question of degree'.[43] As a result, it is very difficult to explain the traditional British approach to originality in terms of any overarching principles or rules. Nevertheless, two characterizations have tended to be deployed. First, in the words

---

[36] One need only think of a whole host of products and services—from bibliographies to listings magazines—that would be placed in an uncomfortable legal position if the protection of the names and titles of books, films, etc., were to be regarded as the norm. See *Fairfax Media v. Reed International Books* [2010] *FCA* 984; *Francis Day and Hunter v. 20th Century Fox* [1940] *AC* 112 (PC), 123.

[37] *CCH Canadian v. Law Society of Upper Canada* [2004] *SCC* 13, [23].

[38] *University of London Press v. University Tutorial Press* [1916] 2 *Ch* 601.

[39] P. Kamina, 'France', in L. Bently (ed.), *International Copyright: Law and Practice* (2017), FRA-21–3.

[40] *Infopaq Int. v. Danske Dagblades Forening*, Case C-5/08 [2009] *ECR* I–6569 (ECJ).

[41] See *Wood v. Boosey* (1868) *LR* 3 *QB* 223, 229; *Redwood Music v. Chappell* [1982] *RPC* 109, 120; *ZYX Music GmbH v. King* [1995] 3 *All ER* 1, 9–11; cf. *Ashmore v. Douglas Home* [1987] *FSR* 553.

[42] S. Ricketson, 'The Concept of Originality in Anglo-Australian Copyright Law' (1991) 9(2) *Copyright Reporter* 1 and (1991–92) 39 *J Copyright Soc'y USA* 265.

[43] *Macmillan v. Cooper* (1923) 93 *LJPC* 113 (Lord Atkinson).

of Peterson J in *University of London Press*, works are original if they originate with the author and are not copied.[44] While this highlights the fact that 'originality' is linked to 'origination', it unfortunately tells the reader very little about when we can say that a work originates with an author. Hence a second characterization has tended to be found to be more valuable: a work is original if an author has exercised the requisite *labour, skill, or judgement* in producing the work. This characterization of the originality standard was adopted at the highest level in *Ladbroke v. William Hill*,[45] a case in which the House of Lords treated football pools coupons (tables of football matches arranged such that customers could gamble on the results in a certain number of matches) as original compilations because of the labour, skill, and judgement that had gone into devising the betting system that informed the coupon.

While the phrase 'labour, skill, or judgement' may be a useful label by which to describe the traditional British test of originality, it should be noted that it is a form of words that has not been deployed with great precision (and thus should not be viewed as if it were a statutory phrase). Sometimes, the courts have used the phrase disjunctively, referring to labour, skill, *or* judgement;[46] sometimes cumulatively, as labour, skill, *and* judgement.[47] On other occasions, the words 'work', 'capital', 'effort', 'industry', 'time', 'knowledge', 'taste', 'ingenuity', 'experience', or 'investment' are used.[48] If 'labour, skill, and judgement' have been the defining characteristics of the British concept of originality, it is worth noting that the accumulation of case law had added a series of additional requirements.

First, the amount of 'labour, skill, and judgement' must be 'substantial'—or at least not trivial.[49] British law has always declined to recognize originality where the labour is trivial or insignificant and the result is trivial or insignificant. A possible example is the case of *Merchandising Corporation v. Harpbond*,[50] in which face paint was held to be unprotected by copyright. While, as we saw in Chapter 3, protection was refused on the rather unsatisfactory basis that the work was not a painting, the decision was justifiable on the basis that the work was a trivial outcome of an insignificant amount of labour. Yet other examples can be found in the case law on titles and advertising slogans: titles, such as *The Lawyer's Diary*, involve too trivial an amount of labour to be regarded as original.[51]

Second, as Lord Oliver said in the Privy Council in *Interlego v. Tyco*, 'only certain kinds of skill, labour and judgement confer originality'.[52] Consequently, a person may exercise a considerable amount of labour, yet the resulting work will not be original if the labour is of the wrong kind. This would be the case, for example, where there is a direct or slavish copy of another work.[53] While the tracing or copying of drawings, especially technical drawings, requires patience, skill, and labour, as Lord Oliver said in *Interlego*, 'copying per se, however much skill or labour may be devoted to the process, cannot make a work original'.[54] More specifically, he said that a 'well-executed tracing is the result of much

---

[44] *University of London Press v. University Tutorial Press* [1916] 2 *Ch* 601, 609.

[45] [1964] 1 *All ER* 465, 469 (Lord Reid).　　[46] Ibid., 469 (Lord Reid).

[47] Ibid., 473f (Lord Evershed); *Interlego v. Tyco* [1988] *RPC* 343, 371.

[48] *Ladbroke v. William Hill* [1964] 1 *All ER* 465, 475 (Lord Hodson: 'work, labour and skill'), 478 (Lord Devlin: 'skill, industry, or experience'), and 480 (Lord Pearce: 'labour or skill or ingenuity or expense').

[49] Ibid., 478 (Lord Devlin), 476 (Lord Hodson).　　　　　　　[50] [1983] *FSR* 32.

[51] *Rose v. Information Services* [1987] *FSR* 254; *Sinanide v. La Maison Kosmeo* (1928) 139 *LTR* 365.

[52] *Interlego AG v. Tyco Industries* [1989] *AC* 217, 268.

[53] *British Northrop v. Texteam (Blackburn)* [1974] *RPC* 57, 68 (a drawing that is simply traced from another drawing is not an original artistic work); *Rexnold v. Ancon* [1983] *FSR* 662, 664 (improbable that copyright would be given to a mere tracing); *Davis (Holdings) v. Wright Health Group* [1988] *RPC* 403, 409 (casts made from models are not original) and 412 (tracing not original).

[54] *Interlego AG v. Tyco Industries* [1989] *AC* 217, 263.

labour and skill but remains what it is, a tracing'.[55] It is clear that the reason why tracing and photocopying do not produce original works is not that there is no labour; rather, it is that it is not the right type of labour.[56]

3.4 EUROPEAN ORIGINALITY

Although, as we noted in Chapter 2, a process of partial harmonization of copyright law has been inaugurated by the legislature in Europe, the Court of Justice has begun a more thoroughgoing harmonization of 'originality'.[57] While the Software and Database Directives require that a computer program or database can be protected by copyright only where the program or database is original in the sense that it is the 'author's own intellectual creation'[58] (and a similar test was also introduced for photographs in the Term Directive),[59] the Court of Justice has held that this standard is applicable to all works of authorship.

The key case was *Infopaq*.[60] In this case, a Danish court had to decide whether an electronic news-clippings service infringed copyright when it reproduced 11-word snippets comprising the eight words either side of a search term. The Court of Justice was asked whether this comprised a 'part' of an article protected by copyright. The Court took the view that to decide whether 11 words were a 'part' required an investigation of the conditions of protection for a work. Reviewing the Berne Convention and the Community *acquis* on copyright (the Software, Database, and Term Directives), the Court of Justice concluded that there was a generalized standard of originality—namely, the 'author's own intellectual creation'.[61] Whether the 11 words were a 'part' depended on whether they were themselves intellectual creations, which the Court indicated was a matter to be assessed by the national court.

As a matter of strict precedent, the *Infopaq* case might have been regarded as limited in its application to matters of infringement rather than subsistence,[62] but it soon came to be applied to issues of subsistence. In *Bezpečnostní softwarová asociace* (or *BSA*)[63] (as we noted in Chapter 3), the Court indicated that a graphic user interface would be protected under the Information Society Directive were it 'its author's own intellectual creation', while in *Football Association Premier League*,[64] the Court stated that football matches were not protected, because they lacked the relevant originality. There thus seems little doubt that, going forward, as far as 'authorial works' are concerned, it is necessary to apply the European standard of originality.[65]

The adoption of a generalized 'originality' test has a number of obvious advantages. For one, it makes the European copyright regime more coherent than it would otherwise

---

[55] Ibid., 262.   [56] *The Reject Shop v. Robert Manners* [1995] *FSR* 870, 876.

[57] See E. Rosati, *Originality in EU Copyright: Full Harmonization through Case Law* (2013); E Rosati, 'Towards an EU-Wide Copyright? (Judicial) Pride and (Legislative) Prejudice' [2013] *IPQ* 47; A Rahmatian, 'Originality in UK Copyright Law: The Old "Skill and Labour" Doctrine under Pressure' (2013) 44 *IIC* 4.

[58] Software Dir., Art. 1(3); Database Dir., Art. 3(1).

[59] Term Dir., Art. 6, states that photographs that are original in the sense that they are the author's own intellectual creation shall be protected in accordance with Art. 1.

[60] *Infopaq Int v. Danske Dagblades Forening*, Case C-5/08 [2009] *ECR* I–6569 (ECJ).   [61] Ibid., [37].

[62] T. Hoppner, 'Reproduction in Part of Online Articles in the Aftermath of *Infopaq*' [2011] *EIPR* 331, 332.

[63] *Bezpečnostní softwarová asociace–Svaz softwarové ochrany v. Ministerstvo kultury*, Case C-393/09 [2011] *ECR* I–13,971 (ECJ), [49]. See also *Nintendo Co. v. PC Box Srl*, Case C-355/12 (23 January 2014) (ECJ), [21].

[64] *Football Association Premier League v. QC Leisure* and *Karen Murphy v. Media Protection Services*, Joined Cases C-403/08 and C-429/08 [2011] *ECR* I–9083 (ECJ, Grand Chamber).

[65] In relation to copyright protection of designs, see Chapter 29.

have been—both horizontally (treating different works according to a single standard) and vertically (in creating a coherent relationship between standards of infringement and subsistence). Moreover, the adoption of a single standard removes some of the difficulties that arise from the failure to harmonize the work concept: for example, if the standard of originality applicable to databases is the same as that applicable to 'database-like' entities (in UK law, 'tables and compilations other than databases'), legal skirmishes over the precise meaning of a database are less likely to be warranted.[66] Nevertheless, whatever its benefits, commentators have questioned whether deepening harmonization in this way is legitimate from a constitutional perspective and have highlighted the considerable uncertainties to which such judicial activism gives rise. In addition, the choice of a single standard for all works removes flexibility that a number of member states employed to modulate the criterion in relation to different types of work (the most notorious example of which was the German level of creativity doctrine—*Schöpfungshöhe*—according to which a higher threshold of originality was required for works of applied art).

The new standard, in principle, applies to computer programs after 1 January 1993, photographs after 1 July 1995,[67] and databases after 11 March 1996,[68] and all other authorial works (including, possibly, designs) after 22 December 2002 (when the Information Society Directive came into force). In implementing the Database Directive, the UK Database Regulations 1997[69] explicitly amended the originality requirement of the CDPA 1988 in relation to databases to include the new criterion of the 'author's own intellectual creation'.[70] In particular, section 3A(2) says that 'a literary work consisting of a database is original if, and only if, by reason of the selection or arrangement of the contents of the database the database constitutes the author's own intellectual creation'. Although the British legislature has, as yet, not responded to the emerging jurisprudence (either by extending section 3A(2) generally, or by repealing the specific reference that might otherwise be taken to imply a different standard is applicable to works other than databases) and the courts have been slow to adapt their language,[71] there can be little doubt that UK law has to be interpreted in line with the case law of the Court of Justice.

That said, any works that were protected prior to the relevant dates under UK law according to the traditional standard should remain protected, because all of the directives indicate that their operation should be without prejudice to 'acquired rights'.[72] For this reason, the 'traditional' British jurisprudence will continue to be important *at least* in determining the subsistence of older works for many decades to come.

3.4.1 Personality and creative choices

What, then, does the requirement that a work be its 'author's own intellectual creation' involve? The legislation offers very little guidance. Perhaps most notoriously, a recital in the Term Directive hints at its content when it refers to the need for a photograph to 'reflect its author's personality'.[73] The clear suggestion is that the test to be employed is

---

[66] *Forensic Telecommunications Services v. West Yorkshire Police* [2011] *EWHC* 2893 (Ch).
[67] Council Directive 93/98/EEC, Art. 13(1).   [68] Database Dir, Arts 14(2), 16(1).
[69] The Copyright and Rights in Database Regulations 1997 (SI 1997/3032).
[70] CDPA 1988, s. 3A(2), introduced by Database Regs 1997, r. 6.
[71] *Newspaper Licensing Agency v. Meltwater and the PRCA* [2011] *EWCA Civ* 890, [19]–[20] (Morritt C said that he did not understand the decision of the Court of Justice in *Infopaq* 'to have qualified the long standing test'). Even in cases that accept *Infopaq* as authoritative, such as *Temple Island v. New English Teas* [2012] *UKPCC* 1, there is still a tendency, e.g. at [27], to treat 'skill and labour' as interchangeable with 'intellectual creation'.   [72] Software Dir., Art. 9(2); Term Dir., Art. 10(1); Database Dir., Art. 14(2), (4).
[73] Term Dir., Recital 16.

something similar to that operative in some civil law *droit d'auteur* regimes, in which reference has frequently been made to the need for a work to bear the 'imprint' of the personality of its author.[74] The Court of Justice has thus felt it necessary to give further content to the concept, referring to the need for the exercise of 'creative choices'. Thus, in *Infopaq* itself, the Court explained that:

> [W]ords . . . considered in isolation, are not as such an intellectual creation of the author who employs them. It is only through the choice, sequence and combination of those words that the author may express his creativity in an original manner and achieve a result which is an intellectual creation.[75]

In the *Painer* case,[76] the Court considered a portrait photograph of a young girl and indicated that this would be an 'intellectual creation' if the photographer had been able to stamp the work with their 'personal touch'. Similarly, in *Football Dataco*,[77] in which the Court was asked to advise on whether the creation of football fixture lists was an act of 'intellectual creation', the Court observed:

> As regards the setting up of a database, that criterion of originality is satisfied when, through the selection or arrangement of the data which it contains, its author expresses his creative ability in an original manner by making free and creative choices . . . and thus stamps his 'personal touch'.[78]

3.4.2 Non-functional

The Court has also sought to indicate when originality will not be present by indicating that where expression is 'dictated by function', then it is not original. In *BSA*,[79] the Court considered when a 'graphic user interface' would fall to be protected as an ordinary work (as opposed to a computer program). The Court indicated that there was no originality where 'the expression of [the] components is dictated by their technical function', explaining that 'the criterion of originality is not met since the different methods of implementing an idea are so limited that the idea and the expression become indissociable'. In *Football Association Premier League*,[80] the Court used equivalent reasoning to explain why sporting events cannot be regarded as intellectual creations: '[F]ootball matches, which are subject to rules of the game, leaving no room for creative freedom for the purposes of copyright.' While no doubt, to anyone who plays or watches football, the claim that there is no 'creative freedom' because of the constraints provided by the 'rules of the game' may seem misguided (so that the absence of copyright in football matches may need to be explained in some other way), the Court is making the important point that where creative choice is highly constrained by rules or functional considerations, the resulting 'work' is unlikely to be original. This point was reiterated by the Court in *SAS Institute v. World Programming*.[81]

---

[74] In *Football Dataco v. Yahoo! UK*, Case C-604/10 [2012] 2 *CMLR* (24) 703, [AG41], Advocate-General Mengozzi stated that the European legislature had preferred the 'more "rigorous"' paradigm of the countries of the continental tradition' to the 'common law standard'.

[75] *Infopaq Int. v. Danske Dagblades Forening*, Case C-5/08 [2009] *ECR* I–6569 (ECJ), [45].

[76] *Eva-Maria Painer v. Standard VerlagsGmbH*, Case C-145/10 [2012] *ECDR* (6) 89 (ECJ), [87]–[93].

[77] *Football Dataco v. Yahoo! UK*, Case C-604/10 [2012] 2 *CMLR* (24) 703 (ECJ).

[78] Ibid., 724–5, [38].

[79] *Bezpečnostní softwarová asociace*, Case C-393/09 [2011] *ECR* I–13,971, [49].

[80] *Football Association Premier League v. QC Leisure* and *Karen Murphy v. Media Protection Services*, Joined Cases C-403/08 and C-429/08 [2011] *ECR* I–9083 (ECJ, Grand Chamber), [98].

[81] Case C-406/10 [2012] 3 *CMLR* (4) 55, 68, [AG44] (AG Bot).

3.4.3 Clarifying the concept

The Court has talked about 'creative choice' and it is clear that decisions that are limited by functional constraints or 'rules' are not to be regarded as 'creative choices', in part because there is no—or very little—choice. But when is a choice 'creative'? It seems clear that choices can be creative even though they are not 'artistic': the scope of copyright in Europe certainly includes such matters as computer programs, technical manuals, and so on, which could hardly be so if the choices required by copyright were to be 'artistic' in nature. The Court has referred instead to choices that focus on the form of the work: the choice, combination, and ordering of words, for example. One academic has gone further and argued that:

> [A] creative choice is one made by the author that is not dictated by the function of the work, the method or technique used, or by applicable standards or relevant 'good practice'. Conversely, purely arbitrary or insignificant selection is insufficient. A conscious, human choice must have been made, even though it may be irrational.[82]

Does the requirement of 'intellectual creation' relate to the process or the outcome? Does 'creation' merely imply that the work has been through a process ('creation'), or that the result has certain distinctive features? As far as the jurisprudence goes, it seems that there must be both components for the work to be protected, although usually the existence of creative freedom will mean that the outcome is an 'intellectual creation'. Thus Advocate-General Bot has said that:

> [P]rotection for a computer program is conceivable only from the point at which the selection and compilation of those elements are indicative of the creativity and skill of the author and *thus* set his work apart from that of other authors.[83]

In our view, it is implicit *both* that there must have been actual choices *and* that the resulting work must as a consequence be individualized.[84] The distinction would become important in a situation in which there was a high level of creative freedom, but the work was produced either by making the obvious choices or by applying an arbitrary rule. In the former case, one could say there was creative freedom and that has been taken, but the resulting work does not reflect any 'personal touch'; in the latter, the application of an arbitrary rule (or indeed random selection) may give rise to an individualized work, but that could not properly be said to be the outcome of choices.

Must there be a certain 'quantity' of effort or decision making before a work is 'original'? Recital 19 of the Database Directive states that the compilation of several recordings of musical performances on a CD does not meet the conditions for copyright protection.[85]

---

[82] D. Gervais, 'Feist Goes Global: A Comparative Analysis of the Notion of Originality in Copyright Law' (2002) *Jo Copyright Soc'y USA* 949, 976–7; E. Derclaye and D. Gervais, 'The Scope of Computer Program Protection after SAS: Are We Closer to Answers?' [2012] *EIPR* 565, 567 ('creative choices are those that one can isolate by asking whether two authors in similar situations (tools, direction, budget etc) would likely have produced essentially the same thing'); J. Hughes, 'The Personality Interest' (1998) 16 *Cardozo AELJ* 81, 114 (choices are 'creative' where they are neither mechanical nor random).

[83] *SAS Institute v. World Programming*, Case C-406/10 [2012] 3 *CMLR* (4) 55, 68, [AG48], emphasis added.

[84] B. Hugenholtz, 'Works of Literature, Science and Art', in B. Hugenholtz, A. Quaedvlieg, and D. Visser (eds), *A Century of Dutch Copyright Law: Auteurswet 1912–2012* (2012), 33, 43 ('Whether the originality requirement is met depends on whether the author has had enough "creative space"—and used it so that the work shows sufficient subjective characteristics').

[85] For a discussion of whether the reasoning extends to 'playlists', prompted by (settled) litigation between the Ministry of Sound and Spotify, see T. Iverson, 'Can Copyright Subsist in a Music Compilation or Playlist?' [2014] *Ent L Rev* 145.

This has been read, at least by one British court, as implying that there might be a quantitative dimension to the requirement that a work be its author's own intellectual creation.[86] However, outside the domain of databases, the indications are that the Court of Justice envisages that even some rather small works can be 'intellectual creations'. Thus, in *Infopaq* itself, the Court seemed to envision the possibility that 11 words from a newspaper article might be an intellectual creation, because it said that this was a matter for the national court to decide.[87] Perhaps the better view is that a quantitative threshold is not required so long as there is such an accumulation of creative decisions as to give the product the character of an intellectual creation. This may derive from a mass of decisions of limited creativity,[88] or from a smaller number of highly personal decisions, such as with the composition of an 11-word haiku.

3.5 DIFFERENCES BETWEEN THE EUROPEAN AND BRITISH STANDARDS

Although the new EU standard is higher in some respects than the previous British standard of originality,[89] for the most part the new standard probably will not lead to different results.[90] Most novels, plays, poems, paintings, engravings, or sculptures that were protected under the traditional UK standard would also satisfy the requirement of 'author's own intellectual creation'. However, we can identify some circumstances in which the rules do differ. These relate to six situations: where the work is a product of mere labour; where creativity is involved in the creation of data; where the work is a product of mere skill; where the creative contribution to the work is at the 'pre-expressive stage'; where the creative contribution is regarded as being 'of the wrong kind'; and where the creative contribution is trivial. It might be noted that while the European standard may be said to be 'higher', it is probably preferable to say it is different. This is because while, in the first four examples, some works that would qualify under the 'labour, skill, and judgement' standard will not reach the European threshold, in the latter two categories it may be that efforts disregarded under traditional British law will be relevant under the EU standard.

3.5.1 Mere labour

The most obvious area in which the new definition may lead to a change is where originality arises through the mere exercise of routine labour. Although the British position

---

[86] *British Horseracing Board v. William Hill* [2001] *ECDR* 257, 269 (Laddie J). For discussion of a claim by the Ministry of Sound to copyright in its compilation albums, see V. Barnet et al., 'Compilation Album Copyright' [2014] *Ent L Rev* 1 (the dispute described there was settled).

[87] One example before the Court was 'a forthcoming sale of the telecommunications group TDC which is expected to be bought': *Infopaq Int. v. Danske Dagblades Forening*, Case C-5/08 [2009] *ECR* I–6569 (ECJ), [21].

[88] For example, choosing the 1,000 'most important' poems: *Gedichttitelliste* [*Poem Title List*] (2008) 39 *IIC* 985 (German Supreme Court).

[89] *SAS Institute v. World Programming* [2013] *EWCA Civ* 1482, [37] (Lewison LJ) ('raised rather than lowered the hurdle'); *Football Dataco v. Yahoo! UK*, Case C-604/10 [2012] 2 *CMLR* (24) 703, [AG41] (AG Mengozzi); Davison, 15–16. Cf. W. Blocher and M. Walter, 'Computer Program Directive', in M. Walter and S. von Lewinski (eds), *European Copyright Law* (2010), 94, [5.1.11] (suggesting test in Software Dir. corresponds to UK and Irish standard); M. Walter, 'Term Directive', in M. Walter and S. von Lewinski, op. cit., 587, [8.6.10] (suggesting standard in Term Dir. 'is a compromise'); E. Judge and D. Gervais, 'Of Silos and Constellations: Comparing Notions of Originality in Copyright Law' (2009) 27 *Cardozo AELJ* 375, 386–7 (suggesting standard is close to that of the United Kingdom).

[90] Judge and Gervais, op. cit., at 404; E. Derclaye and D. Gervais, 'The Scope of Computer Program Protection after SAS: Are We Closer to Answers?' [2012] *EIPR* 565, 567; *Action Storage Systems v G-Force*

was never completely clear, some of the case law suggests that where a work resulted from a great quantity of labour, it might fall to be protected. In certain situations, the British courts had accepted that the mere exercise of a substantial amount of routine labour may give rise to an original work.[91] For example, where a compiler had spent a considerable amount of time and effort creating a chronological list of television programmes or an alphabetically ordered list of lawyers,[92] the resulting work was treated as original. That is, even though, in creating the table or compilation, the author might not have exercised any 'skill or judgement', nonetheless the work might still have been treated as original if the process of compilation involved a sufficient amount of (mundane) labour. However, this would be the case only if the amount of labour was substantial. For example, where the process of compilation involves little effort or judgement and the effect is commonplace, the work will not be treated as original; thus the selection of seven tables at the front of a diary, consisting of things such as days and dates of the year, tables of weights and measures, and postal information,[93] was held by the House of Lords to be non-original. Similarly, in another case involving a local timetable showing a selection of trains to and from a particular town that was prepared from official railway timetables, the compilation was held to be non-original.[94] In these sorts of cases, the difficult question was predicting how much labour was required for the resulting work to be original.

Insofar as these were good decisions under British law,[95] it seems clear that they would have to be decided differently under the EU standard: mere mechanical or routine labour, even if quantitatively significant, will never render a work 'original' in the European sense. Where all that an author has done is to exert a considerable amount of effort in the creation of a work, it is difficult to see how this, on its own, could be seen as an 'intellectual creation', especially one that reflects the author's personality. Anyone exerting the same effort would produce the same result.[96]

3.5.2 Creation of data, ideas, or functions

The second area in which traditional British notions of originality have been displaced is in relation to the creativity that goes into the creation of data. Although UK copyright law did not protect data as such, the courts seemed to recognize that 'labour, skill, and effort' in the creation of data could itself contribute to the originality of expression of the resulting work. Thus, prior to harmonization, it was assumed that television listings would be regarded as 'original' because of the skill and effort that went into devising

Europe.com [2016] *EWHC* 3151 (IPEC), [2017] *FSR* (18) 418, [22] (HHJ Hacon) (in context of unregistered design right, distinction between UK and EU tests made no difference).

[91] *Ladbroke v. William Hill* [1964] 1 *All ER* 465, 478 (Lord Devlin).

[92] *BBC v. Wireless League Gazette Publishing Co.* [1926] *Ch* 433; *Independent Television Publications v. Time Out* [1984] *FSR* 64; *Waterlow Directories v. Reed Information Services* [1992] *FSR* 409; *Dun & Bradstreet v. Typesetting Facilities* [1992] *FSR* 320; *Football League v. Littlewoods Pools* [1959] 1 *Ch* 637, 656–7 (Upjohn J).

[93] *Cramp v. Smythson* [1944] *AC* 329.   [94] *Leslie v. Young* [1894] *AC* 335.

[95] *Ice TV Pty v. Nine Network Australia Pty* [2009] *HCA* 14 (the Australian High Court—Gummow, Hayne and Heydon JJ—suggested that cases in which routine labour had been held sufficient to give rise to copyright should be treated with caution). See K. Bowrey, 'On Clarifying the Role of Originality and Fair Use in Nineteenth Century UK Jurisprudence', in C. W. Ng, L. Bently, and G. D'Agostino (eds), *The Common Law of Intellectual Property* (2010), ch. 3.

[96] Cf. *Technomed v Bluecrest Health Screening* [2017] *EWHC* 2142 (Ch), [122] (Judge D Stone) (claiming that there was no difference between how the EU and old UK originality standard might apply, and concluding that 'sufficient, non-negligible intellectual effort was expended' in each patient definition to give rise to protection. This would hardly seem likely to meet the CJEU's threshold).

what shows to broadcast, as well at what days and times were best suited for the programmes (for example to avoid children seeing adult content, but also to maximize audience figures).

The new criterion does not appear to permit a court to take account of the *creation* of information included in the database. This was made clear by the Court of Justice in its decision in *Football Dataco*.[97] In this case, the question was whether the skill and effort that went into compiling football fixture lists constituted them as original databases. The Court held that any creativity that went into the generation of data (the dates and times of the football fixtures) was irrelevant to the originality of the database.[98]

Although the reasoning of the Court in *Football Dataco* was grounded in special rules relating to databases,[99] it seems clear that the Court regards the input into the creation of basic facts, ideas, and functions as irrelevant to the assessment of whether the ultimate production based upon those facts, ideas, and function is an 'intellectual creation'. In the *SAS* decision, when considering whether and when a user manual might be an original literary work, the Court of Justice was explicit in stating that 'keywords, syntax, commands and combinations of commands, options, defaults and iterations' used in creating software are unprotected because they consist of 'words, figures or mathematical concepts', which are not intellectual creations of the author of the computer program.[100] However, the Court accepted that the 'choice, sequence and combination' of these elements might be such that the author expresses his or her creativity and creates an 'intellectual creation'.[101] Although it is not stated in so many words, it seems clear that the Court means that originality can arise only from the 'choice, sequence, and combination' of these elements, and that the skill (etc.) in creating each of them is not considered in that assessment.

Difficult questions, of course, remain as to what activity relates to the 'creation' of data and what to its selection or arrangement into a database (or other work). The Court of Appeal in *Football Dataco* had assumed that the data in football fixture lists was the games that would be played and that determining the chronology of the games (that is, when each team played each other) was creative effort expended on pre-existing data. The Court of Justice disagreed: on these facts, the finalization of dates and times took place at 'the data creation stage'.[102]

3.5.3 Mere skill

A third way in which the new European test may differ from the old British test is in terms of the relevance of 'skill'. Whatever may have been the position in relation to mere labour, it is clear that the British test of originality took account of the skill involved in producing a work. Nowhere was this clearer than in *Walter v. Lane*, in which various members of the House of Lords expressly recognized the copyright in newspaper reports of speeches because the skill involved in reducing to writing the words of a person who spoke quickly was an art requiring considerable training.[103]

The mere existence of skill has been said to be irrelevant to the assessment of whether there is 'intellectual creation'. In *SAS Institute*, Advocate-General Bot said that:

---

[97] Case C-604/10 [2012] 2 *CMLR* (24) 703 (ECJ).   [98] Ibid., 723–4, [32]–[33], [37].

[99] Ibid., 723, [31].

[100] *SAS Institute v. World Programming*, Case C-406/10 [2012] 3 *CMLR* (4) 55, [66].   [101] Ibid., [67].

[102] Case C-604/10 [2012] 2 *CMLR* (24) 703, [AG29].

[103] *Walter v. Lane* [1900] *AC* 539, 551–2 (Lord Davey), 554 (Lord James of Hereford).

[I]n order to determine whether a computer program is eligible for legal protection under copyright, account should be taken not of the time and work devoted to devising the program nor of the level of skill of its author but of the degree of originality of its writing.[104]

Likewise, in *Football Dataco*, the Court indicated that 'skill' was not itself sufficient to render a work original in the European sense.[105] It stated that:

[T]he fact that the setting up of the database required . . . significant labour and skill of its author . . . cannot as such justify the protection of copyright . . ., if that labour and that skill do not express any originality in the selection and arrangement of that data.[106]

Skill of itself does not give rise to an author's own intellectual creation; what is required is an 'original expression of the creative freedom of its author'.[107]

3.5.4 Pre-expressive contributions

A fourth way in which the traditional British test and the European notion of originality *may* differ (the position is not completely clear) is in the treatment of 'pre-expressive' contributions. Traditionally, the UK courts have accepted that the originality of a work may arise in the steps preceding the production of the work (that is, in the *pre-expressive* stage). So, for example, in relation to the labour that confers originality with respect to literary compilations, the courts would consider the footwork involved in discovering the information,[108] or the selection or choice of the materials that are later embodied in the work. This was made clear in *Ladbroke v. William Hill*, in which the question arose as to whether football pools coupons (which listed matches to be played and offered a variety of bets arranged into 16 categories) were original compilations.[109] On the basis that the expressive form of the coupons inevitably followed from the preceding commercial decisions as to the bets that should be offered, the appellants argued that the coupons were not original. The House of Lords rejected these claims.[110] According to Lord Reid, it was artificial to divide the inquiry up into, on the one hand, the commercial decisions about which bets to offer and, on the other, the form and arrangement of the table. The selection of wagers and their presentation was so interconnected as to be inseparable. Consequently, when considering originality, it is inappropriate to dissect the labour, skill, and judgement into pre-expressive and expressive stages; both elements should be taken into account to determine whether the threshold had been reached.[111]

Preparatory work has been recognized as relevant to determining 'originality' under the European standard, but it seems unlikely that pre-expressive work will be relevant. In *SAS Institute*, Advocate-General Bot pointed to a stage in the production of a computer program, between defining the tasks to be performed and developing the code, from

---

[104] *SAS Institute v. World Programming*, Case C-406/10 [2012] 3 *CMLR* (4) 55, 71, [AG66]. But cf. at 68–9, [AG 48] (referring to the 'creativity *and skill* of the author').

[105] Case C-604/10 [2012] 2 *CMLR* (24) 703, [AG35].   [106] Ibid., 725, [42].

[107] Ibid., 725, [45].   [108] *Kelly v. Morris* (1866) *LR* 1 *Eq* 697.

[109] [1964] 1 *All ER* 465, 469 (Lord Reid), 477 (Lord Hodson), 479 (Lord Devlin), and 481 (Lord Pearce). See also *Football League v. Littlewoods* [1959] *Ch* 637, 656; *Bookmakers' Afternoon v. Gilbert* [1994] *FSR* 723.

[110] Note, however, *Ladbroke v. William Hill* [1964] 1 *All ER* 465, 472 (Lord Evershed, who considered the task of expressing the wagers a distinct one involving 'considerable skill, labour and judgement').

[111] Even under the traditional British test, pre-expressive work was relevant only where (i) it was causally relevant to the expression and (ii) was undertaken with expression as its object: *Purefoy Engineering v. Sykes Boxall & Co.* (1955) 72 *RPC* 89; *Sawkins v. Hyperion* [2005] 1 *WLR* 3280, 3291, [43]; *Ladbroke v. William Hill* [1964] 1 *All ER* 465, 477 (Lord Hodson), 479 (Lord Devlin), and 481 (Lord Pearce).

which the selection and compilation of elements could contribute towards the originality of the program.[112] In the case of a photograph, the Court has indicated that 'pre-expressive' choices will be relevant at least insofar as the 'preparation stage' is concerned—that is, choosing 'the background, the subject's pose and the lighting'.[113] In the case of data-bases, it is quite clear that the 'intellectual creation' must be the result of 'selection' and/ or 'arrangement' of the data.[114] But it seems that the sort of commercial decisions that were considered relevant 'pre-expressive' work in the *Ladbroke* case would no longer be relevant; rather, the European standard seems focused on contributions and choices that are directly relevant to the structuring of the expression of the work.

3.5.5 Creativity of the wrong kind

Although, in most respects, the European test of 'author's own intellectual creation' is regarded as a 'higher' standard than the former British standard, it is worth observing that this is not necessarily the case with respect to every aspect of the originality assess-ment. In particular, because of the traditional 'box' approach to copyright categories, the British courts have sometimes held that contributions to derivative works are to be ignored because they are of the 'wrong kind'. In *Interlego v. Tyco Industries*,[115] the Privy Council was called upon to decide whether there was copyright in drawings for the chil-dren's building blocks known as Lego bricks. The particular drawings had been produced in 1973, but were based upon earlier drawings, so the question arose as to whether the alterations made in 1973 were sufficient to produce an original artistic work. The major differences between the drawings concerned the sharpening of the outer edges of the tubes in the brick, changes in tolerances, and increase in the radii on the outer edges of the knobs on the brick from 0.2 mm to 0.3 mm. Of the changes made, only the first was shown pictorially; the others, by letters and figures. While the Privy Council recognized that the alterations were technically important, they were not sufficient to render the work original because, in the case of artistic works, the change must be *visually significant*— that is, to confer copyright, the skill and labour must produce a change that is relevant to the category of work in question. On the facts, it was held that because the changes made to the drawings were primarily to the written specifications, this was not an alteration of visual significance.[116] As such, the drawings were not original.

The reasoning employed by the Privy Council looks suspect in the light of the European jurisprudence. The Court of Justice has not been willing to differentiate between different categories of 'creation' or types of creativity. From the logic of the decisions, the Court would simply ask whether the addition of the text to the traced drawings of the bricks involved creativity, not whether that creativity was literary or artistic. Nevertheless, on the facts, the same outcome could be justified under the new European originality stand-ard. Although the Privy Council found that the act of tracing involved 'skill', but that the skill was of the wrong kind, under European case law 'originality' is no longer to be con-ceived in terms of skill, but instead of creative freedom—and there is clearly no creative freedom in tracing. Moreover, while the decisions as to the dimensions of various aspects of the modified bricks would not be disregarded because they were 'literary' rather than 'artistic', those decisions would not have been regarded as creative, because they were heavily constrained by function and left little formative freedom to the designer.

---

[112] *SAS Institute v. World Programming*, Case C-406/10 [2012] 3 *CMLR* (4) 55, 68–9, [AG47]–[AG48] (AG Bot).

[113] *Eva-Maria Painer v. Standard VerlagsGmbH*, Case C-145/10 [2012] *ECDR* (6) 89, 106, [91] (ECJ).

[114] Database Dir., Art. 3(1).   [115] [1989] *AC* 217.   [116] Ibid., 268 (Lord Oliver).

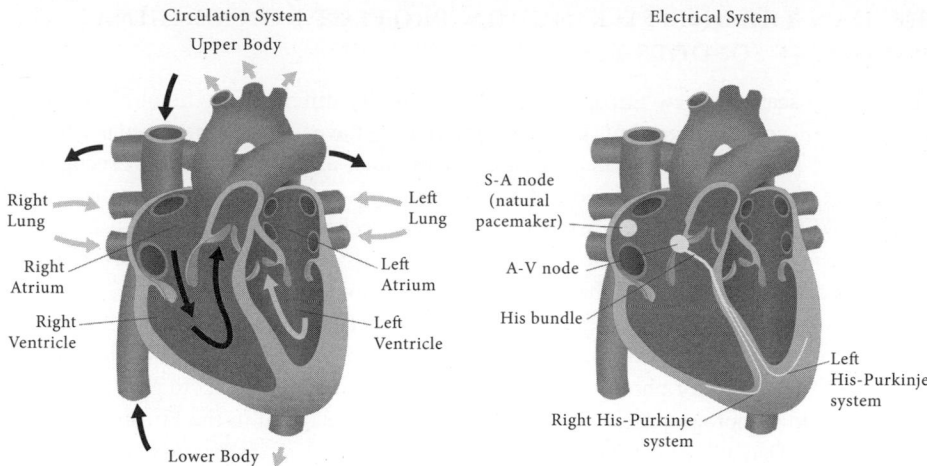

Fig. 4.1 Heart images in *Technomed v. Bluecrest Health Screening*
Source: Courtesy of Technomed Ltd

In *Technomed v. Bluecrest Health Screening*,[117] the High Court treated relatively trivial visual and literary changes to a drawing of a heart (see Fig. 4.1) as being sufficient to create an original work.[118] The claimant argued it had copyright in two images of the human heart. To develop these, two of the claimant's employees had begun with a stock diagram of a heart (that had been licensed) and then, having copied it (to create two hearts next to each other), they labelled the left one 'circulation system' and the right one 'electrical system'. To the left one, they simply added eight labels indicating where the blood was coming from or going. As to the right, they deleted 14 arrows which represented blood flow, and added two nodes and two lines in yellow, representing the electric system, along with five labels.[119] According to the judge, the standard of originality was low, and the changes, including the words, were sufficient to create 'a new, original work'. While we think the Court was correct to consider the changes as a whole and not to divide the work into literary and visual elements, we are surprised at some of the reasoning and the result: at no point did the court reflect on the nature of the choices made by the two authors, whether they amounted to mere skill or to creative choices. Surely, this was a good example of a situation where the change in the test would have made a difference?

3.5.6 Trivial and insubstantial contributions

As already observed, British law traditionally refused to protect trivial and insubstantial efforts, or labour, skill, and judgement with trivial or insubstantial effects. This can be seen in the case law on titles, which ruled out protection on the basis that titles were typically 'too insubstantial'.[120] So far, it is unclear whether there is any requirement of substance before a work will be protected under European Union law. Outside the environment of databases, the sole test seems to be that the work is the author's own intellectual creation. Consequently, there may well be works that would not have been protected under UK law that might qualify for protection under the European standard.

---

[117] [2017] *EWHC* 2142 (Ch) (Judge D Stone).   [118] See also the wave diagram in Chapter 3, Fig. 3.4, p. 74.
[119] [29].   [120] See Chapter 3, sections 2.1–2.2, pp. 64–5.

3.6 CAN THE UNITED KINGDOM PROTECT NON-ORIGINAL WORKS? IF SO, DOES IT?

As we have seen, the new European test of originality differs from the old UK test of 'labour, skill, and/or judgement'. One question that we have not yet considered is whether the United Kingdom—and other member states, such as Germany, which recognizes *kleine Münze* (so-called protection of 'small change')—are permitted to protect 'non-original writings' (for example instruction manuals, recipes, knitting patterns), and if so, whether they are entitled to do so by copyright. The answer to this very important question is (except in respect of databases) unfortunately, not yet clear.[121]

The first point to observe is that various directives clearly envisage the possibility of some protection being offered to non-original works. The Term Directive, which harmonizes the 'originality' standard for photographs, expressly allows member states to give protection to non-original photographs (that is, those that are non-original in the European sense). Similarly, the Database Directive requires protection by *sui generis* right for databases even though they do not meet the originality standard.[122] In addition, the latter Directive preserved the system of protection afforded to non-original catalogues in the Nordic countries. Other directives have said little (in part, no doubt, because the legislature gave no explicit consideration to the question of originality outside the Software, Database, and Term Directives). However, the Software, Database, and Information Society Directives leave unaffected the operation of 'unfair competition law'.[123]

If the United Kingdom (and other member states) are free to give protection to non-original works, the question arises whether they are free to do so by 'copyright' or whether they must do so only by way of some sort of 'related right' or by 'unfair competition'. As regards databases, the Court of Justice, in its decision in *Football Dataco*,[124] has made it clear that no other *copyright* protection is to be available for databases. The Court inferred this not merely from the harmonizing intent, but from the specific transitional provisions in the Directive (which would have made no sense if member states had been able to continue to offer protection through different standards).[125] The answer is less clear as regards software and photographs, but is probably the same. The Software Directive, when referring to the originality standard, states in Article 1(3) that 'no other criteria shall be applied to determine its eligibility for protection' and it seems, from the context, that the term 'protection' means 'protection by *copyright*'. Thus member states may not offer copyright protection to non-original programs (although they may protect any effort or investment from unfair competition). The position is even more murky in other areas, particularly as to photographs. Here, Article 6 of the Term Directive states that 'Member States may provide for the protection of other photographs' and says nothing about the term or scope of such protection—implying that it might be equivalent to copyright. However, because Article 6 indicates that no criteria other than that of 'the author's own intellectual creation' can be applied to determining protection of photographs falling within 'Article 1', which relates to works within the Berne Convention, the better view is that the 'other protection' must be by means of a 'related right' rather than

---

[121] The Dutch regarded the issue as clear enough to abolish the protection of 'non-original writings': P. B. Hugenholtz, 'Goodbye, Geschriftenbescherming!', Kluwer Copyright Blog, 6 March, 2013, available online at http://copyrightblog.kluweriplaw.com/2013/03/06/goodbye-geschriftenbescherming/.

[122] See Chapter 13.

[123] Software Dir., Art. 9(1); Database Dir., Art. 13; Info. Soc. Dir., Art. 9. The Term Dir. has no such saving, but in any case it explicitly leaves open the possibility of protecting non-original photographs.

[124] Case C-604/10 [2012] 2 *CMLR* (24) 703.

[125] Ibid., 716, [AG51]; 726, [49]–[52]. See E. Derclaye, '*Football Dataco*: Skill and Labour is Dead!' (1 March 2012), Kluwer Copyright Blog (protection via unfair competition is also precluded).

Fig. 4.2 The image produced by Mr Fielder for Temple Island Collection and used on various souvenirs

Source: *Temple Island Collection v. New English Teas* [2011] *EWPCC* 21

'copyright'.[126] The answer must be regarded as a more open one in relation to works falling within the general remit of the Information Society Directive and the *Infopaq* ruling.

If member states are free to protect non-original works, has the United Kingdom elected to do so? The difficulty with interpreting the British law lies in the fact that the legislature said nothing about this issue when implementing the directives. So, for example, after 1 January 1996, UK law protects 'original' photographs, but it is unclear whether by that it means 'original' in the British sense or 'original' in the European sense. The same is true of British inaction since *Infopaq*. As things stand, the most obvious way in which to interpret the originality requirement in the CDPA 1988 so that it complies with the directives and jurisprudence is to treat the word 'original' as referring to the European standard—that is, as requiring all 'original literary, dramatic, musical and artistic works' to be an author's own intellectual creation reflecting their personality. This was the assumption on which Judge Colin Birss QC operated in *Temple Island Collections v. New English Teas*[127] (Figs 4.2 and 4.3), in which it was held that an image of a London double-decker bus crossing Westminster Bridge, albeit modified so that the bus was in colour and the background in black and white, was original in the European sense (and infringed by the defendant's similar image).

However, it is still just about possible to argue that—databases apart—the United Kingdom continues to protect by copyright works that are merely 'original' in the old UK understanding. One basis for such an argument is the recognition that the low UK

---

[126] D. Visser, 'Directive 93/98/EEC', in T. Dreier and B. Hugenholtz (eds), *Concise European Copyright Law* (2013), 299; C. Angelopoulos, 'Directive 2006/116/EC', in T. Dreier and B. Hugenholtz (eds), *Concise European Copyright Law* (2nd edn, 2016), 364; cf. M. Walter in M. Walter and S. von Lewinski (eds), *European Copyright Law* (2010), [8.6.12], 588 (suggesting extending copyright protection to non-original photographs might be compliant). [127] [2012] *EWPCC* 1, [20] (common ground).

Fig. 4.3 The defendant's proposed image, a photograph taken by Mr Houghton and manipulated by Sphere Design, which New English Teas wished to use on packets of tea
Source: Temple Island Collection v. New English Teas [2011] *EWPCC* 21

threshold of originality *functioned* as a form of 'unfair competition' law,[128] which could be preserved even in areas of European harmonization. While it might then be objected that the United Kingdom wrongly protects the works from unfair competition by means of 'copyright', it could be answered that the form of protection is British copyright (rather than as required under EU law) and that the general nature of directives leaves the freedom as to the technique of implementation to member states. The British legislature has, in effect, chosen to implement the various directives and their originality standard by incorporating them within a broader regime (which also protects works from unfair competition using identical property rights). This view is further supported by the absence of any transitional provisions, a fact that might suggest that the legislature intended the courts to continue to apply the traditional British standard.

3.7 EXAMPLES

While, as we noted earlier, the different tests will frequently not produce different results, the best way in which to understand what is at stake is to consider some of the difficult situations that have already come before the courts.

3.7.1 Spontaneous conversations

We have already observed that UK law will, since 1989, protect 'spoken works' where they have been recorded. But when will a spoken work be 'original'? Does a person create an 'original work' when they order tickets by telephone (the request being taped)? Is a conversation between a television presenter and a celebrity on a chat show sufficiently original? British courts have not, as yet, been asked to rule on this issue (whether under the traditional

---

[128] *Ladbroke v. William Hill* [1964] 1 *All ER* 465, 478 (Lord Devlin); S. Ricketson, 'The Concept of Originality in Anglo-Australian Copyright Law' (1991–92) 39 *J Copyright Soc'y USA* 265, 269.

test or under the new European standard), but the issue did arise in the Netherlands. In the *Endstra Tapes* case,[129] the question arose whether the contents of an interview by the police with an informant, William Endstra, were protected. Endstra had subsequently been murdered and his family wished to prevent publication of the transcripts by a newspaper to which the tapes had been leaked. The Court of Appeal of Amsterdam denied that these were works of authorship because they had not been conceived as a coherent creation, but the Dutch Supreme Court reversed this decision on appeal. Although it stated that, under Dutch law the form of the work must be a result of human creative choices and must be neither banal nor trivial, Endstra's conversations met those standards. To require the claimant to show that the author was consciously creating a work would be unfairly burdensome. There is no reason to think that any different result would have occurred from applying the European standard of 'author's own intellectual creation'.

3.7.2 Insubstantial creations: words, titles, etc.

Traditionally, British courts had been reluctant to protect titles, slogans, and short phrases. As a result of *Infopaq*, however, that attitude seems to be changing. In that case, the Court indicated that 11 words of a newspaper article might be original in the European sense of an 'intellectual creation'. In the light of that holding, in *Newspaper Licensing Agency v. Meltwater and the PRCA*,[130] the High Court and Court of Appeal have held that 'policy considerations' that may once have informed the United Kingdom's reluctance to protect titles are now irrelevant. In that case, the Newspaper Licensing Agency (NLA), which represents publishers of newspapers, brought an action against Meltwater and the Public Relations Consultants Association (PRCA), claiming that members of the latter association needed NLA's permission to receive electronic mailshots containing links to newspaper articles publicly available on the Internet. The links were accompanied by the title of the newspaper articles and a couple of sentences of text surrounding the search term. The issue before the Court was whether to award a declaration that the PRCA were infringers when they received these services. The NLA did not claim that *all* headlines were protected, but rather that (in order for the Court to give the declaration) the Court need be persuaded only that *some* would be protected. Proudman J, whose judgment was affirmed by the Court of Appeal, found that at least some of the titles would constitute original literary works. She adopted a definition of originality articulated in the *Infopaq* decision and concluded that the evidence established that headlines involve 'considerable skill in devising and they are specifically designed to entice by informing the reader of the content of the article in an entertaining manner'.[131] The Court of Appeal affirmed. The Chancellor concluded that the finding that newspaper headlines *are capable of being* original literary works is 'plainly correct', so that the lower court's conclusion was 'unassailable'.[132]

The ruling in *Meltwater* provides little guidance on when an individual title will be protected, apart from that this depends on whether it is original in the European sense. This seems to depend in part on length (the longer the title, the more opportunity to impose one's personal touch), but mostly on quality—that is, whether the title describes the book, and whether the language chosen is alliterative or has other individual qualities. There seems little doubt that short descriptive titles, such as *The Lawyer's Diary*, remain unprotected.[133] There is simply

---

[129] *Zonen Endstra v. Nieuw Amsterdam* [2008] *EIPR* N73 (Netherlands Supreme Court, 30 May 2008), described in B. Hugenholtz, 'Works of Literature, Science and Art', in B. Hugenholtz, A. Quaedvlieg, and D. Visser (eds), *A Century of Dutch Copyright Law: Auteurswet 1912–2012* (2012), 33, at 52–3.

[130] [2010] *EWHC* 3099, [67]–[72]; [2011] *EWCA Civ* 890, [19]–[22].   [131] [2010] *EWHC* 3099, [70].

[132] [2011] *EWCA Civ* 890, [22]. For a critical appraisal, see D. Liu, '*Meltwater* Melts not Water but Principle! The Danger of the Court Adjudicating an Issue outwith the Ambit of Referral' [2013] *EIPR* 327.

[133] *Rose v. Information Services* [1987] *FSR* 254.

too little creative freedom involved in coming up with the name of a diary targeted at lawyers (and, insofar as there is freedom, in that case the claimant took the most obvious of routes). Moreover, in many cases, where titles allude to or parody existing well-known public domain titles, such as 'A Tale of Two Council Houses' or 'Trunks are Too Tight to Mention' (both examples before the courts in the *Meltwater* case), one might doubt that the creative input in substituting one or two words in *A Tale of Two Cities* or 'Money's Too Tight To Mention' would give rise to copyright.[134] More difficulty attends the determination of whether the nine-word combination 'The Man Who Broke the Bank At Monte Carlo' might be thought sufficiently creative,[135] although Monte Carlo is primarily known for gambling and the phrase 'to break the bank' is a very commonly used description of winning heavily in gambling institutions.[136] Our view is that it would not do so.

On the assumption that *Meltwater* is right and that the protection of titles is governed by European law (and the *Infopaq* standard), it might have been hoped or anticipated that some guidance as to where the line is to be drawn could be elicited from case law in countries that have been applying similar criteria to those now embraced by the Court of Justice.[137] However, different countries seem to draw distinctions in different places—the French being perhaps the most generous and the Germans, the most parsimonious.[138] Moreover, even within those jurisdictions, there seems to be very little consistency.[139]

As we have noted, the English Court of Appeal declined to find copyright in the single word EXXON, on the basis that it was not a literary work.[140] That basis for the decision may no longer be sustainable in Europe, given the Court of Justice's implicit harmonization of the 'work' concept. But could a single word be original in the relevant European sense? Although the French courts have occasionally gone so far as to protect titles comprising single words,[141] such an approach must now be doubtful as a matter of European law. In *Infopaq*, the Court indicated that the components of the 11-word phrases 'consist of words which, considered in isolation, are not as such an intellectual creation of the author who employs them', so that such 'words as such do not . . . constitute elements covered by the protection'.[142] Similarly, in *SAS Institute*, the Court was explicit in stating that 'keywords, syntax, commands' were unprotected because they consist of 'words, figures or mathematical concepts', which are not intellectual creations of the author of the computer program.[143]

3.7.3 Snapshots and non-creative photographs

No judicial guidance had been provided by British courts as to whether pointing a camera and pressing the button was sufficient 'labour, skill, and effort' to justify protection. It was possible to claim that, in such circumstances, the photograph 'originated with the author'

---

[134] Cf. the Belgian decision rejecting copyright in the reworking of a proverb 'So many men, so many minds' into 'So many people, so many shoes': [2002] *AM* 414 (Brussels, 21 September 2001), note F. Brison and A. Coppieters.   [135] *Francis Day and Hunter v. 20th Century Fox* [1940] *AC* 112 (PC).

[136] Ibid., 123.

[137] J. Klink, 'Titles in Europe: Trade Names, Copyright Works or Title Marks?' [2004] *EIPR* 291 (comparing Germany, France, and the United Kingdom).

[138] M. Gruenberger, 'Germany', in L. Bently (ed.), *International Copyright: Law and Practice* (2017), GER-52–53.   [139] P. Kamina, 'France', in Bently, op. cit., FRA-36–7.

[140] *Exxon Corp. v. Exxon Insurance* [1982] *RPC* 69.

[141] For example, the Lyon Court of Appeal protected 'Clochemerle' (the name of a satirical novel written by Gabriel Chevallier and published in 1934 about installing a urinal in a French village square): Cour d'appel Lyon, 5 July 1979.

[142] *Infopaq Int. v. Danske Dagblades Forening*, Case C-5/08 [2009] *ECR* I–6569 (ECJ), [45]–[46].

[143] *SAS Institute v. World Programming*, Case C-406/10 [2012] 3 *CMLR* (4) 55, [66].

and so should be treated as original. Elsewhere in Europe, simple snapshots have often been refused copyright, as have paparazzi photographs.[144]

The European standard, as described in *Painer*, allows for protection of simple portraits, as long as there is sufficient creative freedom.[145] Thus a portrait photographer had creative freedom because:

> In the preparation phase, the photographer can choose the background, the subject's pose and the lighting. When taking a portrait photograph, he can choose the framing, the angle of view and the atmosphere created. Finally, when selecting the snapshot, the photographer may choose from a variety of developing techniques the one he wishes to adopt or, where appropriate, use computer software.[146]

Applying a similar standard (albeit a few years prior to *Painer*)—namely, that the photographer's personality is reflected in the arrangements (motif, angle, lighting, etc.)—the Supreme Court of Austria held that a photograph of some grapes was original and added that 'a lot of amateur photographers, who take pictures of everyday scenes in the form of photos of landscapes, persons and holiday pictures' might also be protected.[147] Subsequently to *Painer*, the Patents County Court referred to the Austrian decision approvingly, Judge Birss QC saying that he did not think that the UK law was any different.[148]

3.7.4 Derivative works

British courts have long recognized the possibility of protecting 'derivative works'—that is, those based on pre-existing materials. Thus the courts have protected new editions,[149] compilations, anthologies, translations,[150] and adaptations of existing materials,[151] as well as arrangements of music[152] and engravings. Importantly, the courts have indicated that, to be protected, not only need there be skill, labour, and judgement, but also the derivative work must have 'some quality or character which the raw material did not possess, and which differentiates the product from the raw material'.[153] It was for this reason that, in *Interlego v. Tyco*,[154] the technically significant alterations to the drawing, which were the result of considerable labour and expertise, were insufficient to render the later drawings original. The mere fact that the drawing took skill and labour to produce did not necessarily mean that it was therefore an original drawing. As Lord Oliver explained:

---

[144] A. and G. Bercovitz, 'Spain', in Bently, op. cit., SPA-96, (referring to decision of Audiencia Provincial (Court of Appeal) Madrid (Section 28), 28 November 2016, Aranzadi Civil 2016, no. 2152 (holding that a photograph of Spanish Prince leaving a cinema was not an original work)); M. Pavis, 'Paparazzi and copyright', IPKat, May 31, 2018.

[145] *Eva-Maria Painer v. Standard VerlagsGmbH*, Case C-145/10 [2012] *ECDR* (6) 89 (ECJ), [87]–[93].

[146] Ibid., [91].

[147] *Peter O**** v. F**** KG* [2006] *ECDR* (9) 77 (Austrian Supreme Court, 16 December 2003), 79, [2.1]. See also *Decision of the Supreme Court*, 20 June 2006, Case No. 4 Ob 47/06z, (2007) 38 *IIC* 622, 624, [4] (photographs of famous sports personalities); C. Handig, 'The Copyright Term "Work": European Harmonisation at an Unknown Level' (2009) 50 *IIC* 665, 674–5. But cf. Audiencia Provincial (Court of Appeal) Pontevedra (Section 1), 3 May 2013, Westlaw JURisprudencia 2013, no. 206,951, cited in A. and G. Bercovitz, in Bently, op. cit., SPA-19, (Spanish court declining to treat as an original work a photograph of a live butterfly, even though this required a great deal of patience). [148] *Temple Island v. New English Teas* [2012] *EWPCC* 1, [20].

[149] *Black v. Murray* (1870) 9 *Macph* 341, 355.

[150] *Byrne v. Statist Co.* [1914] 1 *KB* 622; *Cummins v. Bond* [1927] 1 *Ch* 167.

[151] *Warwick Films v. Eisinger* [1969] 1 *Ch* 508.

[152] *ZYX Music GmbH v. King* [1995] 3 *All ER* 1.

[153] *Macmillan v. Cooper* (1924) 40 *TLR* 186, 188 (a passage described in *Interlego* as 'perhaps the most useful exegesis' on the issue of originality).

[154] [1989] *AC* 217. But a gloss was added in *LA Gear Inc. v. Hi-Tech Sports plc* [1992] *FSR* 121 (each successive drawing made during design process by single designer was original).

'There must in addition be some element of material alteration or embellishment which suffices to make the totality of the work an original work.'[155]

To date, the Court of Justice has not offered any views on 'derivative works'. The practice in member states varies: some merely require that the added or altered material constitutes a personal intellectual creation; others seem to require something more (as the United Kingdom did in *Interlego*). The Italian law, for example, refers to 'additions constituting a substantial recasting of the original work'.[156] There may be much to be said for excluding slight variations to existing material. Certainly, the Privy Council in *Interlego* was concerned about the effects of allowing 'evergreening' of the copyright drawings.[157] Whatever the precise test for originality of derivative works, it is unlikely that copyright will protect 'appropriation art'—that is, where artists copy existing works, but by so doing attempt to give it a different meaning rather than altering the appearance of the work itself.[158]

3.7.5 Reporters' copyright

In the famous case of *Walter v. Lane*,[159] the House of Lords held that a newspaper report of an oral speech given by Lord Rosebery, transcribed by a reporter from the talk, was protected by copyright (see Fig. 4.3). This was because, as we have noted, the reporter exercised considerable labour, skill, and judgement in producing a verbatim transcript of the speech.

How would such a case be decided under the European standard? It might be argued that while the reporter's skill in using shorthand is no longer relevant, the choices that the reporter made in deciding what to include (for example audience reaction), how to describe those reactions (for example 'laughter'), and how to punctuate the text were 'creative'. Certainly, it could be said there was some limited freedom here in deciding the way in which the report 'expressed' or reported the speech. In our view, however, these choices would not be treated as being sufficient. The reason for this is that the amount of freedom is too limited: choices over how to punctuate exist, but are limited by rules of grammar and syntax; the choices over whether and how to report the audience reaction leave only a very few options. The reports would therefore no longer be protected by copyright (in the European sense).

While newspapers today tend to provide summaries and added matter to reports of speeches (thus creating original works), the conclusion that verbatim reports are no longer protected must have potentially significant consequences for reporting services such as law reporters (such as Martin Walsh Cherer) and parliamentary reporters (such as Hansard). Whether the removal of copyright will render such services unsustainable will depend on the business models that these services operate: it may be that exclusive rights in the reports are less important than other attributes of the service, such as speed, and reputation for accuracy.

---

[155] *Interlego v. Tyco Industries* [1989] *AC* 217, 268. This leads to the rather bizarre conclusion that good reproductions are denied copyright, but poor ones have sufficient visually significant variation. This was explicitly stated by Lord Oliver, ibid. For further discussion, see Laddie et al., 228–30, [4.42].

[156] Italian Copyright Law 1941, art. 4, cited in V. Falce, 'Italy', in Bently, op. cit., ITA-19.

[157] *Interlego v. Tyco Industries* [1989] *AC* 217, 256.

[158] *Irene A*** v. K*** GmbH*, Case 4 Ob 162/08i [2010] *ECC* (12) 186 (Austrian Supreme Court, 14 October 2008) (copy of standard ladies shoe in chocolate, even though the idea was that of a well-known artist, was not original). For discussion, see B. Sherman, 'Appropriating the Postmodern: Copyright and the Challenge of the New' (1995) 4 *S & LS* 31; D. McClean and K. Schubert (eds), *Dear Images: Art, Copyright and Culture* (2002), 405.

[159] [1900] *AC* 539, treated as being good law in *Sawkins v. Hyperion* [2005] 1 *WLR* 3280, 3288, [33] (Mummery LJ), [79] (Jacob LJ). For a creative interpretation, see E. Derclaye, 'Debunking Some of UK Copyright Law's Longstanding Myths and Misunderstandings' [2013] *IPQ* 1 (claiming that the reporter has copyright in the report as a sound recording), and a persuasive response from N. P. Gravells, 'Reporter's Copyright and Sound Recordings: A Reply to Professor Derclaye' [2013] *IPQ* 91.

THE TIMES, FRIDAY, JUNE 26, 1896.

LORD ROSEBERY ON FREE LIBRARIES.

Yesterday afternoon the Earl of Rosebery opened a new free public library, named after its munificent donor, the Passmore Edwards Library, and erected as a memorial of Leigh Hunt and Charles Keene, at Uxbridge-road, near Shepherd's-bush-green, W. The special feature of this building is the complete supervision throughout all the departments from the librarian's counter, and to insure this advantage the several public rooms are divided by glazed screens. Ample light is provided everywhere, and the interior is bright and cheerful. The exterior has been designed in accordance with the English Renaissance style with bold cornices and handsome mullioned windows. The central gable is sculptured with a life-size group representing the "Shepherd in the Bush," suggested by the name of the district in which the library has been built. The librarian's house is on the first floor of the front buildings, and above are large storage rooms in connexion with the library. The architect was Mr. Maurice B. Adams, F.R.I.B.A., of Bedford-park, Chiswick. The cost of the building, exclusive of the site, has been rather more than £6,000. Lord Rosebery and Mr. Passmore Edwards were received on their arrival by the Library Commissioners, and conducted to the central room, where the chair was taken by Prebendary Snowden, chairman of the commissioners.

The CHAIRMAN, in opening the proceedings, explained that the site, which was peculiarly well adapted for the purpose of a public library, and which was very valuable, having an excellent building frontage, was a benefaction from the copyholders and the Ecclesiastical Commissioners, and when, after the refusal of the ratepayers to increase the library rate, those in favour of the library were almost in despair as to raising the necessary funds, Mr. Passmore Edwards came forward to their relief. (Cheers.) With noble, but not unaccustomed, generosity, he had erected that beautiful building, which was complete in all its arrangements as far as experience and skill could make it so. The chairman also made a reference to Lord Rosebery's literary achievements, and expressed the hope that he would present the library with a volume of his life of Pitt, inscribed with the author's autograph.

LORD ROSEBERY, who was received with loud cheers on rising to speak, said:—Mr. Chairman, Ladies, and Gentlemen,—I have much pleasure in declaring this library open. (Cheers.) I do that at the beginning and not at the end of what I have to say because I have observed almost invariably that public speakers whenever they have a formal duty to discharge and attempt to discharge it at the end of their speech forget to do so. (Laughter.) Now, Mr. Chairman, you have been very kind in the remarks that you have made. I shall cherish your reference to my little book which I had great pleasure in seeing on your shelves, but I will not accept your invitation to present the book to your library. In the first place, you already have a copy of it, which I do not think was at all worn out. (Laughter.) And in the second place, as it is sold I believe—although I have never bought a copy myself—at the ridiculously inadequate sum of 1s. 10d. (laughter), it is not at all a suitable offering for me to make to this library. I trust to find a more valuable book that I may leave as a memento of my visit here to-day. (Cheers.)

MR. PASSMORE EDWARDS.

But I have another duty to perform besides declaring this library open, it is that of proposing a vote of thanks to the generous donor of the building. (Cheers.) You have expressed a wish that I may have a long time before me to devote to literary pursuits. (Hear, hear.) I thought my neighbour on my right expressed a particularly fervent and enthusiastic assent to that sentiment. (Laughter.) I for my part have nothing to say in contravention of it. "Sweet are the uses of adversity," or what is called adversity, and it is difficult for those who are intrusted with the government of the country to come and open public libraries or perform functions of that kind; and therefore you have reason to thank her Majesty's Opposition for their existence when it comes to any question of a function of this kind. But I am bound to say that even when I was in office, and when I was subject to the responsibilities and censures of office, I found time in the very first beginning of that period to go and open another library, founded of course, and given of course, by Mr. Passmore Edwards. (Cheers.) Now there is something about the permanence of pursuits in individuals which gives one a sense of the nothingness of time. We must all have known in our younger days some venerable ancestress or female relative who was occupied in some interminable piece of worsted work. (Laughter.) We went to school, we went on our travels, and we returned again and found that piece of worsted was still progressing (laughter), and I had something of the same feeling when I came here to-day and found Mr. Passmore Edwards still giving public libraries. (Cheers.) I do not know whether you remember the old story of the gambler who lost an enormous sum at Crockford's in the old days, and came out of that haunt with a generally vicious feeling against himself and the whole human race which he did not know how to vent. Looking opposite at White's Club-house he saw a gentleman kneeling against the stairs and tying his shoe lace. The gambler saw in him an object on which to vent his feeling, and, rushing up to the gentleman, he kicked him, and cried, "Bless you"—he did not say "Bless you," but in the presence of the chairman I will not quote the exact word he did use (laughter)—but he said, "Bless you, you are always tying up your shoe lace." (Laughter.) Well, I feel inclined to approach Mr. Passmore Edwards, not to kick him, but to say, "Bless you, you are always doing good." (Cheers.) Another word about Mr. Passmore Edwards. I am given to understand by those who are accustomed to commendation that it is not pleasant to be praised, in public at any rate, and therefore I think I shall best suit his feelings if I say nothing more on a subject which I could not adorn by eloquence, and which certainly does not need eloquence to recommend it.

OUTDOOR SPORTS IN ENGLAND.

But I think those who watch the growth of the free libraries system in this country, in spite of the almost persistent opposition of the ratepayers, have some cause to inquire, What object is it that these free libraries answer in our modern commonwealth? I confess I have formed a very clear conviction on that head. I think no one can watch the progress of our nation without seeing the enormous predominance that is given everywhere to-day to outdoor sports. I welcome that tendency. I think it is a healthy and rational tendency, but of course it may be carried too far. What we do see in the tendency to outdoor sport at this time is that it weans the race from occupations that might be objectionable, and it is rearing a noble and muscular set of human beings; and it subserves other objects which are not so immediately apparent. For instance, I take it the connexion between Australia and the mother country has been rendered closer than it would have been otherwise by the cricket contests which take place between the two countries; and I am given to understand, though I

Fig. 4.4 One of the newspaper reports considered protected by copyright in *Walter v. Lane*
Source: The Times, Friday 26 June 1896, p. 12

3.7.6 Restoration and reconstruction

In *Sawkins v. Hyperion*,[160] the question was whether 'performing editions' of musical works first composed in the seventeenth and eighteenth centuries were original musical works. It was argued by Hyperion that the reconstructed and edited scores were not

[160] [2005] 1 *WLR* 3280.

original musical works, because Lionel Sawkins had added no new music over and above that in the original. While he had laboured to reconstruct the manuscripts and make them more user-friendly to today's performers, that did not involve labour, skill, or judgement of a musical sort. Mummery LJ agreed that some aspects of Sawkins' efforts, 'such as time and labour spent on discovery or retrieval of the original scores and in their layout on the page', were irrelevant.[161] However, labour, skill, and judgement in adding information that could potentially affect the totality of sounds produced by musicians were pertinent. On the facts, the additions to work had sufficient aural and musical significance to attract copyright protection.

How would *Sawkins* fair under the European standard? Certainly, the analysis would have to change: Lionel Sawkins' skills as an expert would no longer be relevant and his application of standardized rules to convert old formats so as to make them understandable today (for example by so-called 'figuring the bass') also might be regarded as insufficient to amount to 'intellectual creation', in the sense of the exercise of creative choices. But it is notable that, in parallel proceedings in France,[162] which has traditionally applied a standard akin to that now adopted by the Court of Justice,[163] Sawkins also succeeded. The French Court observed that:

> Given the state of the sources, the defendants have not proven a degree of strict faithfulness of the restored work to [the composer's] intention that would be capable of denying any personal character in the restoration and composition work such that it became a mere act of transcription.[164]

Had the case been one of pure 'reconstruction', without adding the missing notes and musical phrases, it seems difficult to imagine that either court could now describe the work as an 'intellectual creation' bearing the 'personal touch' of its author.

3.7.7 Photographs of artistic works

For art galleries, the revenues generated through *claiming* copyright in photographs of paintings and other art works that they hold can be substantial. In the United Kingdom, claims to such rights have depended on the interpretation of *Graves' Case*,[165] in which Blackburn J held that a photograph of an engraving of a painting was an 'original photograph' and therefore protected under the Fine Art Copyright Act 1862. However, even prior to EU harmonization, doubts had been raised as to the usefulness of this case as an authority, given that the technological apparatus for taking photographs is now so much more developed (and thus the act of taking photograph so much easier),[166] as well as because of developments in jurisprudence.[167] Nevertheless, in *Antiquesportfolio. com v. Rodney Fitch*,[168] it was held that copyright subsists in simple photographs of

---

[161] Ibid., 3291, [43].   [162] *Sawkins v. Harmonia Mundi* (2006) 37 *IIC* 116.

[163] See (2006) 37 *IIC* 116, 119 (a work must bear the intellectual and personal stamp of author).

[164] *Sawkins v. Harmonia Mundi* (2006) 37 *IIC* 116, 119.

[165] *Graves' Case* (1869) *LR* 4 *QB* 715. See R. Deazley, 'Photography, Copyright and the South Kensington Experiment' [2010] *IPQ* 293.

[166] R. Deazley, 'Photographing Paintings in the Public Domain: A Response to Garnett' [2001] *EIPR* 179, 181.

[167] See, e.g., K. Garnett, 'Copyright in Photographs' [2000] *EIPR* 229; cf. Deazley, op. cit. (arguing that *Graves' Case* is inapplicable in the light of *Interlego*); S. Stokes, '*Graves' Case* revisited in the USA: The *Bridgeman Art Library v. The Corel Corporation*' [2000] *Ent L Rev* 104; S. Stokes, 'Photographing Paintings in the Public Domain: A Response to Garnett' [2001] *EIPR* 354 (arguing for copyright in such works to protect the labour and skill of the photographer); R. Deazley, 'Copyright; Originality; Photographs; Works of Art' [2001] *EIPR* 601 (responding to Stokes); S. Stokes, '*Graves' Case* and Copyright in Photographs: *Bridgman v. Corel*', in D. McClean and K. Schubert (eds), *Dear Images: Art, Copyright and Culture* (2002), 109.

[168] [2001] *FSR* 345, [2001] *ECDR* 51.

three-dimensional objects because the taking of such photographs involves judgement—that is, the positioning of the object, the angle from which the picture is taken, the lighting, and the focus.

The position after the Term Directive appears to be different. As we have seen, intellectual creation involves more than the exercise of technical skill. Instead, there must be 'formative freedom'—that is, the possibility of choices that result in an individualized outcome reflecting the author's personal touch. This may be present in portrait photography, for example in the lighting, camera angle, choice of pose, the capturing of a particular expression, etc., but it is difficult to see that any such creativity might be present in the case of technically excellent photographic reproductions of artistic works. Indeed, it is notable that such protection had been denied to such photographs in the jurisprudence of countries applying a civilian standard of 'creative choices' or 'imprint of the personality'.[169]

If galleries wish to have the protection for photographs taken after 1996, they should seek legislative reform to introduce a related right. Such related rights are recognized in a number of member states, including Germany and Italy.[170]

3.7.8 Computer-generated works

Although in the 1980s there were probably very few genuine 'computer-generated works', the 1988 Act provides that a literary, dramatic, musical, or artistic work attracts copyright protection even where it has been generated by computer in circumstances under which there was no human author.[171] By 2018, artificial intelligence systems produce outputs that appear as, and can function as works: from automated translations to paintings based on Rembrandt's oeuvre. While the Act clearly envisages that products generated by a computer could be classified as works, it said nothing about how the originality of such works was to be determined. The particular problem that arises with computer-generated works is that it is difficult to see how the existing criterion of originality, which focuses on the relationship between the author and the work, can be applied to computer-generated works, which, by definition, have no readily identifiable author.

Given that computer-generated works are protected where there is no human author, the question arises: what test for originality should be applied to such works? One possible test would have been to ask whether the work was produced as a result of the independent acts of the computer—that is, whether the work is original in the sense that it was 'not copied'. Alternatively, a court might have said that originality exists where the computer has produced a work that is different from previous works (that is, it is novel). It has also been suggested that the courts ought to ask the hypothetical question: if the same work had been generated by a human author, would it have required the exercise of a substantial amount of skill, labour, and effort? If so, then the computer-generated work would be original.[172]

---

[169] *SOFAM v. Galerij Montevideo* [1999] *AM* 355 (Brussels Cour de Cassation, 10 December 1998) (suggesting some aesthetic requirement where photograph merely copies a work of art), cited in A. Strowel and N. Ide, 'Belgium', in Y. Gendreau, A. Nordemann, and R. Oesch, *Copyright and Photographs: An International Survey* (1999), 83; *Pretura of Saluzzo* [1995] *AIDA* 311 (13 October 1993), 453, cited in L. C. Ubertazzi, 'Italy' in Gendreau et al., op. cit., 165–6 ('Rarely … does the photographic reproduction of works of figurative art and, in particular, works of architecture … involve creativity'); Court of Appeal, Warsaw, 5 July 1995, cited by J. Barta and R. Markiewicz, 'Poland', in L. Bently (ed.), *International Copyright: Law and Practice* (2017), POL-11.

[170] German Copyright Act 1965, art. 72; Italian Copyright Law 1941, art. 87; Swedish Copyright Act 1960, art. 49a.

[171] CDPA 1988, s. 9(3), 178. See A Ramalho, 'Will Robots Rule the (Artistic) World?' (2017) 21 *Journal of Internet Law* 12; J. McCutcheon, 'Curing the Authorless Void?' (2013) 37 *Melb ULR* 46.

[172] Laddie et al., [36.44].

Because the European standard now applies to all works, it must be doubted whether copyright protection (in a European sense) should be regarded as available at all to 'computer-generated' works. Advocate-General Trstenjak remarked, in her opinion in the *Painer* case, that 'only human creations are . . . protected', although these can 'include those for which the person employs a technical aid, such as a camera'.[173] It seems to follow that no computer-generated work can be protected by copyright in accordance with European law. As we have noted, there is no reason why such productions could not be protected by related rights or unfair competition law. It might be said that, given the special provisions on authorship and term that are applicable to computer-generated works,[174] this is in fact what the UK law in substance achieves. If so, the standard of 'originality' applicable is a matter for UK law alone.

4 ENTREPRENEURIAL WORKS: 'NOT COPIED'

Unlike the case with literary, dramatic, musical, and artistic works (authorial works), there is no requirement that films, sound recordings, broadcasts, or published editions be original. Instead, the CDPA 1988 provides that copyright does not subsist in a sound recording, a film, or a published edition to the extent that it is itself copied from a previous work of the same kind.[175] In relation to broadcasts, the Act provides that copyright does not subsist to the extent that it infringes copyright in another broadcast.[176] One of the consequences of this is that entrepreneurial works will be protected irrespective of whether or not the author exerted mental skill, labour, or effort in the creation of the work. This means that if a video recorder or tape recorder is turned on and left on a table, the resulting film or sound recording will be protected.

It has been suggested that the reason why a lower standard is applied to entrepreneurial works than to authorial works relates to the nature of the rights that are granted.[177] In relation to authorial works, copyright protects 'the content', not merely 'the signal'.[178] As a result, it is more important that the law monitors the types of authorial work that are protected. Conversely, in the case of entrepreneurial works for which protection is thin, there is less need to monitor the subject matter protected. This does not mean, however, that it is not necessary to regulate the types of subject matter protected as entrepreneurial works. In particular, to have allowed such works to be protected with no threshold requirement would have created the undesirable position that rights in entrepreneurial works could have continued in perpetuity. The reason for this is that, in the absence of some limitation, every time someone copied an entrepreneurial work, they would have obtained a fresh copyright in the 'new' work. This problem is avoided in the 1988 Act by ensuring that entrepreneurial works are protected only to the extent that they are not copied.

For the most part, these provisions are relatively straightforward. However, three issues remain unsettled. The first is whether a compilation of parts of sound recordings (such as a 'megamix') would be protected as a separate sound recording.[179] On one view, if the megamix is compiled from existing recordings, then nothing is protectable. The reason for this is that each existing element is excluded on the basis that it is copied from another sound

---

[173] *Eva-Maria Painer v. Standard VerlagsGmbH*, Case C-145/10 [2011] *ECDR* (13) 297, 324, [AG121].
[174] CDPA 1988, ss 9(3), 12(7).   [175] CDPA 1988, ss 5A(2), 5B(4), 8(2).
[176] CDPA 1988, s. 6(6).   [177] Laddie et al., 392–3, [6.15].
[178] See Chapter 6, section 2.1, pp. 145–8.
[179] P. Theberge, 'Technology, Economy and Copyright Reform in Canada', in S. Frith (ed.), *Music and Copyright* (1993), 53.

recording. However, if such an approach were to be followed, it would lead to the bizarre result that the absence of a notion of originality in respect of entrepreneurial works means that the threshold of protection is higher than with respect to authorial works (where collections of materials are protected as databases, tables, and compilations).[180] Perhaps the better view is that a compilation of sound recordings ought to be protected as a sound recording, on the basis that the compilation is more than the sum of its parts.[181]

The second question is whether, in the process of digitally remastering an old work, the resulting work would be protected. Where no change is made to the contents of the work, it is difficult to see how the digital version of the work could be protected by copyright, since the recording is copied from existing recording of sounds. Would the position be any different if, in the process of remastering an old recording, it were to be cleaned of unnecessary noise and interfering sound? It seems that the way in which this question will be answered depends on the way in which the phrase 'to the extent that' is construed.[182]

5 IS THE WORK 'QUALIFIED'?

In order for a work to be protected in the United Kingdom, it is necessary to show that the work is suitably 'qualified'[183]—that is, it is necessary to show that the work is sufficiently connected to the United Kingdom to qualify for protection under UK law. UK law withholds protection from works that fail to establish a sufficient connection to the United Kingdom. In essence, the requirement that the work be qualified helps to balance the protection offered to British authors in other jurisdictions against the protection given to foreign authors in the United Kingdom. Once a work qualifies, in general, British law applies the principle of national treatment—that is, UK copyright law generally treats foreign works as it does those of British authors.[184]

5.1 CONNECTING FACTORS

The benefits of British copyright law have been extended to cover a vast array of works created by foreign authors or published in foreign countries. Nevertheless, the task of determining whether a particular work is protected under British copyright law is remarkably complex. While, in some situations, this task may be avoided through the use of statutory presumptions,[185] in most situations it needs to be undertaken. Given that British law effectively provides universal protection, some regard the complexity of the task as unnecessary.[186]

There are three connecting factors that enable works to qualify for copyright protection (sections 154–6). These are by reference to: (i) authorship; (ii) country of first publication;

---

[180] It might be the case that a 'megamix' would indirectly create an original musical work or that the process of digitization creates an original literary work.

[181] *Football Association Premier League v. QC Leisure* [2008] *EWHC* 1411, [2008] *FSR* (32) 789, [224].

[182] Laddie et al., 392–3, [6.15] (sound recording) and 422–3, [7.31] (films); Kamina (2nd edn), 106–7 (noting that the film producers' copyright required under the Rel. Rights Dir. and Term Dir. refers to the *first* fixation).   [183] For further details, see Copinger (17th edn), [3–279] *ff.*

[184] But see Chapter 7, section 1, p. 181 for an exception to this concerning duration (applying shorter term in country of origin). Note also that the Order specifying to which countries that Act 'applies' may specify that the rights granted are limited in particular respects: CDPA, s 159(4); Copyright and Performances (Application to Other Countries) Order (SI 2016/1219).

[185] See *Microsoft Corp. v. Electro-wide* [1997] *FSR* 580, 594.

[186] Laddie et al., 275, 382–3, [5.10], [5.154]–[5.158].

and (iii) place of transmission. A work qualifies if it satisfies *any* of these three factors. Once a work qualifies for copyright protection, British copyright law does not usually discriminate between it and a work created by an author from or first published in the United Kingdom.[187]

5.1.1 Qualification via authorship

Section 154(1) of the CDPA 1988 provides that a work qualifies for copyright protection if, at the 'material time', the author of the work was a 'qualifying person'.[188]

In order for a work to qualify for protection, it is necessary that the author be connected to a relevant country at the 'material time'.[189] For unpublished literary, dramatic, musical, and artistic works, the 'material time' is the date on which the work was made. Where the work has been published, it is the author's status at the date of first publication that is decisive, or if the author died before publication, their status at the date of death.[190] By contrast, the material time for other types of copyright work does not change; qualification depends on the personal status of the 'author' of a sound recording or film at the time of its making or, for the organization broadcasting a transmission, at the date of transmission, and for typographical format, it is the publisher at publication that is relevant.[191] Since a work may take a considerable time to make, section 154(4)(a) provides that, in the case of an unpublished literary, dramatic, musical, or artistic work, the 'material time' is 'a substantial part of that period'. Rather oddly, no such provision exists for films.

To qualify under section 154, it is necessary to show that the author was a 'qualifying person'. There are three ways in which this can be achieved. First, a person will be a 'qualifying person' if they can show that they are: a British citizen, national, or subject; a national of an EEA state; a person within certain categories of the British Nationality Act 1981; or a person domiciled or resident in, or a body incorporated in, part of the United Kingdom or the EEA.[192] The concepts of 'domicile' and 'residence' are not defined in the Act. It seems, however, that 'domicile' refers to the country in which a person makes their permanent home. In contrast, the concept of 'residence' is more flexible, simply demanding some degree of continuous association with the country in question. A person can be a resident of more than one country, although a person will not be a resident if they are a casual visitor.[193]

Second, a person will qualify if they can show that they are an individual domiciled or resident in, or a body incorporated under the law of, a country to which the law has been 'extended'.[194] In this context, it should be noted that 'extension' refers to the fact that Her Majesty, by Order in Council, is given the power to extend the 1988 Act to other territories, including the Isle of Man, the Channel Islands, and any colony.[195] Along with the power of 'application' (discussed later), 'extension' is a technique that is used to protect works that originate from outside the United Kingdom. While only a few Orders have been made under the 1988 Act,[196] some Orders made under the equivalent section of the

[187] But note the special rule on duration: see Chapter 7, section 1, p. 181.
[188] This may make determination of authorship important: see *Century Communications v. Mayfair Entertainment* [1993] *EMLR* 335.   [189] CDPA 1988, s. 154(4).
[190] CDPA 1988, s. 154(4).   [191] CDPA 1988, s. 154(4), s. 154(5).
[192] CDPA 1988, s. 154(1)(a). The references to the EEA were added by the Intellectual Property Act 2014, s. 22 (though, if Brexit proceeds, this may need to be reviewed).
[193] Laddie et al., 312–14, [5.62]–[5.63].   [194] CDPA 1988, s. 154(1)(b); British Nationality Act 1981, s. 51.
[195] CDPA 1988, s. 157.
[196] Copyright (Cayman Islands) Order 2015 (SI 2015/795), as amended by Copyright (Cayman Islands) (Amendment) Order 2016 (SI 2016/370).

Copyright Act 1956 continue to operate,[197] for example in the Falkland Islands.[198] The effect of such Orders is not simply to provide protection in the United Kingdom for categories of work with a relevant connection to those countries; protection is also afforded in those countries to works protected in the United Kingdom.[199] Because the power to extend the 1988 Act permits the extension to be 'subject to such exceptions and modifications as may be specified', each Order needs to be considered individually.

Third, a person will qualify if they can show that they are a citizen or subject of, and an individual domiciled or resident in, or a body incorporated under a law of, a country to which the Act has been 'applied'.[200] Section 159 both contains generic provisions indicating when the Act will apply to works with relevant links to Convention countries,[201] and empowers Her Majesty, by Order in Council, to 'apply' the copyright sections of the 1988 Act to other countries.[202] This is done so as to allow either authors connected to such countries, works first published in such countries, or broadcasts sent from such countries to qualify for protection in the United Kingdom. Moreover, such 'applications' may be subjected to such exceptions and modifications as are specified or confined to certain classes of cases specified in the Order, and in this respect, care must be taken, particularly in relation to sound recordings and broadcasts.[203] The power to make such Orders is restricted to countries that give adequate protection to the owners of copyright in respect of the class of works to which the Order relates.[204] The latest version of the Order is the Copyright and Performances (Application to Other Countries) Order 2016.[205]

Where a work has been jointly authored, the work qualifies for copyright protection if any of the joint authors is qualified. However, the non-qualifying author is ignored when considering issues of first ownership[206] and duration.[207] Consequently, if one joint author qualifies and another does not, the qualifying owner alone will be first owner.[208] Similarly, copyright in a co-written literary work expires 70 years after the death of the last qualifying co-author.[209]

5.1.2 Qualification by first publication

A work may also qualify for protection if it is first published in the United Kingdom or in another country to which the Act has been 'extended' or 'applied'.[210] (These concepts were discussed earlier.) A work is published when copies of the work are issued to the public,[211] or, in the case of literary, dramatic, musical, and artistic works, when the work is made available to the public through an electronic retrieval system.[212] It does not include:

---

[197] They continue to operate because of CDPA 1988, Sch. 1, para. 36.

[198] *Copyright (Falkland Islands) Order 1963* (SI 1963/1037) and (SI 1987/2200).

[199] Laddie et al., 331–2, [5.85].   [200] CDPA 1988, s. 154(1)(c).

[201] CDPA 1988, s. 159(1) (Berne Convention and WTO Countries, for literary, dramatic, musical and artistic works, films and typographical arrangements), s. 159(2) (Rome Convention, for sounds and broadcasts), s. 159(3) (WPPT, for sound recordings). This was added by the Intellectual Property Act 2014, s. 22, with effect from 1 December 2016.   [202] CDPA, s. 159(4).

[203] For sound recordings, the Order differentiates between connections to WTO countries, WPPT countries, Rome signatories and miscellaneous countries, offering different levels of protection to each: SI 2016/1219, Regs 3–5.

[204] CDPA, s. 159(6). Under CDPA 1988, s. 160, the Order may limit protection by virtue of first publication in respect of works from a country that does not adequately protect British works.

[205] SI 2016/1219 (in force from 6 April 2017.)   [206] Under CDPA 1988, s. 11.

[207] Under CDPA 1988, s. 12.

[208] But the non-qualifying author, it seems, can claim moral rights and therefore should be named on the work, and the work should not be subjected to any derogatory treatment without their consent.

[209] CDPA 1988, s. 154(3).   [210] CDPA 1988, s. 155(1).   [211] CDPA 1988, s. 175.

[212] CDPA 1988, s. 175(1).

performing a literary, dramatic, or musical work; exhibiting an artistic work; issuing specified types of copies of such works;[213] playing or publicly showing a sound recording or film; or communicating to the public any work.[214]

If a work is to qualify for protection by publication, the publication must be 'authorized' (typically by the author).[215] The 1988 Act provides that publication does not include merely colourable publications, which are not intended to satisfy the reasonable requirements of the public.[216] The threshold for protection is very low. At a minimum, if a work attracts no interest, the mere fact that a few copies have been made available for sale will suffice.[217] Publication takes place wherever the publisher invites the public to acquire copies[218] and may take the form of gift, hire, or sale.[219] Since publication consists in offering reproductions to the public, it has been suggested that anything that amounts to a reproduction will suffice (although commentators have raised doubts about this view).[220]

To qualify for protection, the work must be published *first* in the United Kingdom or in another country to which the Act has been 'extended' or 'applied'. The fact that publication first occurs in a non-qualifying country will not matter, so long as that work is published within 30 days in the United Kingdom or in another country to which the Act has been 'extended' or 'applied'.[221] It should also be noted that films that have been released commercially under conditions of restricted distribution may well not have been published, since copies will not have been made available to the public.[222]

5.1.3 Qualification by place of transmission: broadcasts

A broadcast qualifies for protection if it is made or sent from a place in the United Kingdom, or a country to which the Act 'extends' or 'applies'.[223] In the case of satellite broadcasts, the broadcast is made where the signals are introduced.[224]

6 EXCLUDED SUBJECT MATTER

Although a work may be recorded in material form, may be original, and may be sufficiently connected to the United Kingdom, in some circumstances the courts may nonetheless refuse to recognize copyright for policy reasons. It appears that copyright protection will not be granted for obscene, blasphemous, or immoral works. This can

---

[213] CDPA 1988, s. 175(4)(a)–(b). Publication of an artistic work does not include issuing copies of a film depicting such a work, nor copies of graphic works or photographs representing a sculpture, a work of artistic craftsmanship, or a work of architecture. However, the construction of a building is the equivalent of publishing the architectural work that it embodies: CDPA 1988, s. 175(3).

[214] CDPA 1988, s. 175(4). But an electronic retrieval system may still serve to publish literary, dramatic, musical, or artistic works even if it operates by way of broadcasting: CDPA 1988, s. 175(4)(a)(ii), (b)(iv).

[215] CDPA 1988, ss. 175(6) (no account shall be taken of any unauthorized act), 178.

[216] CDPA 1988, s. 175(5).

[217] *Francis Day & Hunter v. Feldman* [1914] 2 *Ch* 728; cf. *Bodley Head v. Flegon* [1972] 1 *WLR* 680.

[218] *British Northrop v. Texteam* [1974] *RPC* 57.   [219] Ibid.

[220] *Merchant Adventurers v. Grew* [1973] *RPC* 1; *British Northrop v. Texteam* [1974] *RPC* 57, doubted in Laddie et al., 287–91, [5.31]–[5.34].   [221] CDPA 1988, s. 155(3).

[222] Cf. *Bodley Head v. Flegon* [1972] 1 *WLR* 680.

[223] The Copyright and Performances (Application to Other Countries) Order 2016 (SI 2016/1219) specifies the countries to which the Act applies with respect to broadcasts in Regs 6–8. In respect of wireless broadcasts, these regulations differentiate between, on the one hand, those made by persons or entities appropriately connected to Rome countries, which receive 'full protection' and, on the other, those by parties thus connected to WTO countries, which benefit from a more modest regime of rights.

[224] CDPA 1988, s. 156(1).

be seen from *Glyn v. Weston Film Feature*,[225] in which Younger J refused to grant an injunction for infringement of copyright in the claimant's dramatic work, *Three Weeks*, which he described as a 'sensual adulterous intrigue' and condemned on the ground that it advocated 'free love'. Younger J said: '[I]t is clear that copyright cannot subsist in a work of a tendency so grossly immoral as this.'[226]

For some time, it had been thought that *Glyn* and the other cases in which copyright had been denied to obscene, blasphemous, libellous, irreligious, or misleading works[227] were the products of less enlightened times and, as such, would no longer be followed.[228] However, in *A-G v. Guardian (No. 2)*,[229] the House of Lords cited *Glyn* with approval. In that case, Peter Wright, a former security services agent, had written a book (*Spycatcher*) about the various operations of the service. Importantly, in writing the book, Wright breached the duty of confidence that he owed to the Crown. The House of Lords held that Wright would not be able to bring a copyright infringement action because of the 'disgraceful circumstances' in which the book was written. As well as citing *Glyn* with approval, the Lords extended the scope of the immorality exclusion beyond the content of the work to include the circumstances in which the work was created.

While the House of Lords affirmed the continued existence of the public policy exclusion, there is still some doubt as to the exact effect of immorality. It is unclear whether it means that there is no copyright in the work at all or that equity will not enforce the copyright.[230] The way in which this question is answered might be important given that if there were no copyright, presumably all contracts that purported to deal with the copyright would be vulnerable.

The scope of the exclusion is also unclear. Although hitherto it has been concerned with matters such as sexual morality, the exclusion may also be a basis for declining to protect so-called 'malware'—that is, software designed to appropriate sensitive information from a user's infected personal computer.

The effect of the public policy exclusions is somewhat paradoxical. Because the denial of copyright to obscene works effectively places them in the public domain, this might increase the speed and breadth of circulation. If dissemination is deemed to be undesirable, the denial of copyright seems to be counter-productive.[231] (It may also stimulate public interest in the work.) Presumably, other reasons have motivated the courts. The approach taken by the courts is consistent with the view that the primary concern of copyright is to encourage creation rather than to control dissemination. Denying copyright will (supposedly) remove the incentive to produce obscene works.

As we have seen, a derivative work that infringes copyright in the work on which it is based can be original. In such circumstances, the question arises as to whether an original, but infringing, work should be denied protection on grounds of public policy. With

---

[225] [1916] 1 *Ch* 261.   [226] Ibid., 269.

[227] One difficulty with the *Glyn* decision is that it is by no means clear when a work is immoral. Generally, the criminal law restricts circulation of obscene works—works that are likely to deprave and corrupt. Immorality appears to be a wider test. It is certainly difficult to believe that a work that 'advocated free love' would today be denied copyright. In *Stephens v. Avery* [1988] *Ch* 449, in the context of breach of confidence, Browne-Wilkinson V-C stated that he thought the *Glyn* exception should not apply in the absence of public consensus that the work in question was immoral. In *Fraserside Holdings v. Venus* [2005] *FMCA* 997, the Federal Magistrates' Court of Australia was prepared to enforce copyright in 'adult films', explaining that the Court should look at the attitudes taken towards the work both in Australia and overseas.

[228] *Chaplin v. Frewin* (1966) 1 *Ch* 71.   [229] [1990] 1 *AC* 109.

[230] Copinger (17th edn), [3–432] (copyright subsists, but will not be enforced); also, generally, A. Sims, 'The Denial of Copyright on Public Policy Grounds' [2008] *EIPR* 189.

[231] See *Fraserside v. Venus* [2005] *FMCA* 997, [39]–[42].

one or two exceptions,[232] the courts have generally been willing to enforce copyright in derivative works even though they infringe.[233] This has been explained on the basis that if protection were to be denied to such works, it would lead to a substantial injustice. As Goff J said:

> It is understandable that the owner of copyright should be entitled to restrain publication of an infringing work; but the idea that he should be entitled to reap the benefit of another's original work, by exploiting it, however extensive such work might be, however innocently it might have been made, offends against justice and common sense.[234]

---

[232] For example, *Ashmore v. Douglas Home* [1987] *FSR* 553.

[233] See *Wood v. Boosey* (1868) *LR* 3 QB 223, 229; *Chappell v. Redwood Music* [1982] *RPC* 109, 120; *ZYX Music, GmbH v. King* [1995] 3 *All ER* 1, 9–11; *Ludlow Music Inc. v. Williams* [2002] *FSR* (57) 868, 886, [39]–[40]. Cf. Indian Copyright Act 1957, s. 13(3) (denying copyright to films or sound recordings which infringe copyright).   [234] *Chappell v. Redwood Music* [1982] *RPC* 109, 120.

5

AUTHORSHIP AND FIRST OWNERSHIP

1 INTRODUCTION

A considerable amount has been written about authorship and the role that it plays in copyright law. It has become clear from these discussions that the concept of authorship that operates in copyright law is not the same as that used in many other fields.[1] One explanation for this relates to the particular role that the author plays in copyright law. More specifically, it is because, in copyright law, the author acts as a focal point around which many of the rules and concepts are organized. For example, as we have just seen, the status of the author helps to determine whether a work qualifies for protection. Where relevant, the contribution that an author makes will also influence whether the resulting work is original. In other situations, the duration of many types of work is determined by reference to the lifespan of the author. Similarly, the moral rights that are recognized in the United Kingdom attach to the author of the work in question.

In this chapter, we explore two closely related themes. First, we look at the concept of authorship, as it is understood in copyright law. In turn, we look at one of the most important consequences that flow from being identified as author of a work—namely, first ownership of copyright and the various exceptions to this general rule.

2 AUTHORSHIP

The author of a work is defined in the Copyright, Designs and Patents Act 1988 (CDPA 1988) as the person who creates the work.[2] Special provisions deal with the situation in which more than one person is involved in the creation of a work.[3] While to describe the

---

[1] Frequently, it is more expansive, treating as legal authors those whose effort might not reach the creative levels of literary authorship. See, e.g., *Walter v. Lane* [1900] *AC* 539. But at other times 'social' conceptions of authorship are more plural. For the example of 'scientific authorship', see M. Biagioli, 'Rights or Rewards? Changing Frameworks of Scientific Authorship', in M. Biagioli and P. Galison (eds), *Scientific Authorship: Credit and Intellectual Property in Science* (2003), 253–80. For thoughts on the legal implications, see D. Simone, 'Recalibrating the Joint Authorship Test: Insights from Scientific Collaborations' (2013) 26 *IPJ* 111; L. Bently and L. Biron, 'Legal and Social Conceptions of Authorship: What, if anything, is to be done?', in M. van Eechoud, *The Work of Authorship* (2015), 237 *ff*. For an overview, see C. Fisk, 'Credit Where It's Due: The Law and Norms of Attribution' (2007) 95 *Georgetown LJ* 49.

[2] CDPA 1988, s. 9(1). For comparative analysis, see J. Ginsburg, 'The Many Faces of Authorship: Legal and Interdisciplinary Perspectives' (2003) 52 *DePaul L Rev* 1063.   [3] See section 2.3, pp. 130–3.

creator of a painting or a sculpture as an 'author' may jar, few problems arise in ascertaining who is the author of most literary, dramatic, musical, and artistic works.[4] This is because, in relation to the traditional categories of literary, dramatic, musical, and artistic work, there is a general consensus as to which of the various people involved in the production of a work is to be treated as the creator or author of it.

More problems arise, however, in relation to entrepreneurial works and computer-generated works. In part, this is because the concept of authorship does not sit comfortably with the way in which we tend to think about such works—that is, we do not normally think of a sound recording, a typographical arrangement, or a broadcast as having an author, even in the broad sense in which it is used in copyright law. In these circumstances, it is important to appreciate that the 'author' is an artificial construct, a legal fiction, which is used to allocate rights. This can be seen in the fact that, in relation to sound recordings, broadcasts, and typographical arrangements, the 'author' is (effectively) defined as the person who made the work possible (as distinct from the creator). In the case of a literary, dramatic, musical, or artistic work that is computer-generated (which by definition has no author), the 'author' is 'the person by whom the arrangements necessary for the creation of the work are undertaken'.[5]

The task of determining who is the author of a work is made easier because the 1988 Act sets out a series of statutory presumptions as to who is the author of a work. Section 104 provides that the name that appears on a literary, dramatic, musical, and artistic work as published, or on the work when it is made, shall be presumed to be the author. Section 105 establishes similar presumptions with respect to sound recordings, films, and computer programs.[6] The upshot of these presumptions, which operate only in civil matters, is that the burden of proof is placed on the person claiming that someone other than the 'named' author is the true creator of the work in question.

2.1 AUTHORSHIP OF LITERARY, DRAMATIC, MUSICAL, AND ARTISTIC WORKS

The author of literary, dramatic, musical, or artistic work is the person who creates it.[7] No further guidance is given in the 1988 Act as to what this means. The only exception to this is to be found in section 3(2), which indicates that the author need not necessarily be the person who fixes or records the work (although this will usually be the case).[8] The lack of statutory guidance as to the way in which the author is to be construed in this context does not matter that much given that there are few problems in identifying who is the author of a literary, dramatic, musical, or artistic work.

Having said that, problems have occasionally arisen in determining whether a person involved in the production of a literary, dramatic, musical, or artistic work is to be regarded as an author (or creator). The way in which this question is answered is similar to the way in which the originality of a work is determined. Basically, in order for someone to be classified as an author, it is necessary for them to be able to show that their contribution to the work is of the *type and amount* that is protected by copyright—that is, that the

---

[4] For consideration of the question of whether an amanuensis is an author, see *Donoghue v. Allied Newspapers* [1938] 1 *Ch* 106. But note that a medium who transcribed messages from the spiritual world was the author of the work: *Cummins v. Bond* [1927] 1 *Ch* 167 (Eve J held that the medium 'had exercised sufficient skill, labour and effort to justify being treated as author').

[5] CDPA 1988, ss 9(4), 178.   [6] CDPA 1988, s. 105.   [7] CDPA 1988, s. 9(1).

[8] CDPA 1988, s. 3(2).

contribution would be sufficient to confer originality on the relevant work.[9] Hitherto, this has tended to be expressed by saying that they must contribute 'skill and labour of the right kind' (reflecting the traditional British test of originality). However, as the United Kingdom adjusts to the new European standard of originality explained in Chapter 4, one would expect a shift in the terminology, so that a person will be regarded as an author only where they contribute towards the 'intellectual creation'.

Whatever concepts are deployed, it is unlikely that a stenographer, an amanuensis, or a person who merely photocopies or traces a work would ever be considered an author.[10] This is either because the skill and labour is of the wrong kind, or because the contribution does not involve 'creative choices' regarding the expressive form of the work (in 'Euro-copyright speak'). However, if the person makes creative choices in producing the work, even if only a very small amount, it is more likely that they will be treated as an author. This can be seen, for example, in *Cummins v. Bond*,[11] in which it was held that a spiritualist who produced 'automatic writing' dictated to her from beyond the grave at a séance was the author of the resulting work. Because the spiritualist exercised great speed in writing down the messages and used great skill in translating the spiritual communication given in an 'unknown tongue' into 'archaic English', it was held that she had exercised sufficient 'skill, labour, and effort' (the relevant test of originality at that time) to justify her being treated as author.

Where the contribution made by someone is at an abstract level, such as the idea for a play, or a book, or a structure of a computer program, they are unlikely to be treated as an author of the resulting work. Thus, for example, the telling of a person's experiences to form the basis of a 'ghostwritten' book is (without more) unlikely to render the narrator of the tales an author of the resulting book; rather, the ghostwriter who determines the way in which the stories are expressed will be regarded in law as the author.[12] The more specific the contribution, however, the more likely it is that the person in question will be treated as an author. Thus, at the opposite extreme to that of the ghostwriter, in the case of a person who dictates text and punctuation to another who merely follows the instructions, UK law would regard the dictator rather than the amanuensis as the author.[13] In between the two extremes lies a host of possibilities. In one case, it was held that a person who developed an idea for a house design that he had explained in detail (both verbally and through sketches) to a technical draftsman was joint author of the plans that the draftsman subsequently produced.[14] Similarly, a political figure who dictated his memoirs to a friend, then read every word and altered parts of the manuscript, was held to be joint author of the resulting book.[15]

As we saw in relation to the originality requirement, the mere fact that a person expended labour in the creation of a work will not necessarily mean that the resulting work is original (or that the person is an author) if it is the 'wrong type' of labour. In the case of a book, for example, while the copy-editor plays an important role in giving shape to the final product, they will not normally be treated as author of the resulting literary

---

[9] Because the type of labour that confers originality is the same as that which enables someone to be classified as an author, reference should be made to the earlier discussions on this topic: see Chapter 4, section 3, pp. 93 *ff*.   [10] *Donoghue v. Allied Newspapers* [1938] 1 *Ch* 106.

[11] [1927] 1 *Ch* 167. See also *Leah v. Two Worlds Publishing* [1951] 1 *Ch* 393.

[12] *Donoghue v. Allied Newspapers* [1938] 1 *Ch* 106 (reporter was author of stories about jockey Steve Donoghue's life); *Celebrity Pictures v. B. Hannah* [2012] *EWPCC* 32, [8] (providing a 'general' brief to a photographer as to the types of pose that the party commissioning the photographs wanted did not make that party a joint author); *Martin v. Kogan* [2017] *EWHC* 2927 (IPEC), [54] (contributions to editing not sufficient).   [13] *Donoghue v. Allied Newspapers* [1938] 1 *Ch* 106, 109–10.

[14] *Cala Homes (South) v. Alfred McAlpine Homes East* [1995] *FSR* 818.

[15] *Heptulla v. Orient Longman* [1989] *FSR* 598 (Indian High Court).

work.[16] Similarly, while copyright law has few problems in categorizing the person who wrote a play as the author of the play, in one case it was held that a person who had suggested the title, the leading characters, a few catchwords, and the scenic effects for the play had not contributed sufficiently to the play to justify being treated as a joint author.[17] In *Brighton v. Jones*,[18] Park J held that the suggestions made by a director to a playwright, prompted by problems with the script encountered during rehearsals, were not of the right kind to justify the director's claim to co-authorship. He said that the director had failed to establish 'that the contributions which she made were contributions to the creation of the dramatic work rather than contributions to the interpretation and theatrical presentation of the dramatic work'.[19]

2.1.1 Computer-generated works

In the case of literary, dramatic, musical, or artistic works that have been computer-generated, the creator is 'the person by whom the arrangements necessary for the creation of the work are undertaken'.[20] While the identification of the relevant person will depend on the facts, it seems that in an appropriate case it might include the person who operates the computer, the person who provides inputs for the computer system or even the programmer.[21]

2.1.2 Unknown authorship

In certain situations, it may not be possible to ascertain who is the author of a literary, dramatic, musical, or artistic work. This may be because the name of the author is not attached to the work and it is not possible to ascertain authorship by other means. In other cases, an author may wish that their works be published anonymously, under a false name or a pseudonym. Because the author acts as the focal point around which many of the rules of copyright are organized, this creates a number of potential problems. To remedy this, the CDPA 1988 includes the notion of 'unknown authorship'. A work is a work of unknown authorship if the identity of the author is unknown and it is not possible for a person to ascertain the author's identity by reasonable inquiry.[22] While, in this situation, the author remains the first copyright owner, since it is impossible to know when the author of such a work died, the duration of copyright is limited to 70 years from the date on which the work was first made available to the public (or 70 years from the date on which the work is made, if it is not made available before the expiry of that period).[23]

2.2 ENTREPRENEURIAL WORKS: STATUTORY AUTHORS

As we mentioned earlier, authorship does not sit comfortably with the way in which we tend to think about entrepreneurial works. Any potential difficulties in having to identify

---

[16] A technician expending skill and labour in testing software, detecting bugs, and providing information towards debugging was likened to a proofreader and therefore was not a joint author, since he did not contribute to the authorship of the software as such: *Fylde Microsystems v. Key Radio Systems* [1998] *FSR* 449. See L. Bently and L. Biron, 'Discontinuities between Legal Conceptions of Authorship and Social Practices: What, If Anything, Is to Be Done?', in M. Van Eechoud (ed.), *The Work of Authorship* (2014) (exploring conceptual art and editing).   [17] *Tate v. Thomas* [1921] 1 *Ch* 503.

[18] [2005] *FSR* (16) 288.   [19] Ibid., [56].

[20] CDPA 1988, s. 178 (where a work is created by a computer in circumstances such that there is no human author of the work). For discussion of the problem of defining 'originality' for such works, see Chapter 4, section 3.7.8, pp. 117–18, where we suggest that such works might be regarded under EU law as productions protected by the United Kingdom as related rights.

[21] *Nova Productions v. Mazooma Games* [2006] *EWHC* 24 (Ch), [105]–[106] (author of computer-generated videogame was author of graphics and software, rather than player of the game). See Chapter 3, Fig. 3.2, p. 63.

[22] CDPA 1988, s. 9(4), (5).   [23] CDPA 1988, s. 12(3).

who is the author of, say, a broadcast or a sound recording are resolved by section 9(2) of the CDPA 1988, which defines who is the author of each of the different entrepreneurial works.

2.2.1 Sound recordings: the producer

Section 9(2)(aa) provides that the author of a sound recording is the 'producer'.[24] In turn, the 'producer' is defined as the 'person by whom the arrangements necessary for the making of the sound recording are undertaken'. In most cases, the 'producer' of a sound recording will be the record company. This may change, however, where a sound recording is produced cooperatively, or where non-traditional modes of distribution (such as the Internet) are used. The question of what is meant by 'the producer' is discussed in more detail in the next section.

2.2.2 Films: the producer and the principal director

When the 1988 Act was enacted,[25] for the purposes of determining authorship, films were treated in a similar fashion to sound recordings: the author was defined as 'the person by whom the arrangements necessary for the making of the film are undertaken'. In order to bring UK law into line with the Term Directive, the 1988 Act was amended so that the authors of a film made on or after 1 July 1994 are the producer *and the principal director* of the film. The principal director and producer are treated as joint authors, except where they are the same person.[26] The recognition of the principal director as author of the film marks an important change in the way in which films are regarded by British copyright law, from being treated as a type of entrepreneurial work to being treated as a hybrid of entrepreneurial and authorial works.

The 'principal director' is not defined in the 1988 Act. In *Slater v. Wimmer*, Judge Birss QC held that the director was 'the person who had creative control of the making of the film' and, in the case of a small-scale film about sky-diving on Everest, that person was the cameraman.[27] In more expensive productions, the director will rarely operate the cameras, but will likely be more involved in instructing the actors. Problems with identifying authorship are often resolved through industry practice, which carefully controls who is to be designated as an author.[28] In turn, the CDPA 1988 states that where a film bears a statement that a particular person was the director (or principal director) of the film, this shall be presumed to be correct until the contrary is proved.[29] Section 105(6) adds that, where a person is named as the director of a film, this shall be presumed to mean that they are the principal director.

The 'producer' of a film is defined as 'the person by whom the arrangements necessary for the making of the film are undertaken'.[30] This is the same definition as is used to describe the producer of a sound recording. The question of whether a person is a 'producer' of a film or a sound recording is a question of fact.[31] For the most part, there will be few problems in determining who is the producer of a film or a sound recording. Most questions regarding the allocation of ownership of copyright will be dealt with contractually. Problems may arise, however, because the production of sound

---

[24] CDPA 1988, s. 9(2)(aa).   [25] CDPA 1988, s. 9(2)(ab).   [26] CDPA 1988, ss 9(2)(ab) and 10(1A).
[27] [2012] *EWPCC* 7, [13].
[28] For a discussion of credit practices in the US film industry, see C. Fisk, 'The Role of Private Intellectual Property Rights in Markets for Labor and Ideas: Screen Credit and the Writers Guild of America, 1938–2000' (2011) 32 *Berkeley J Emp & Lab L* 215.   [29] CDPA 1988, s. 105(5).
[30] CDPA 1988, s. 178. It is unclear whether the term 'principal director' will be treated as narrower than the term 'director' when used in relation to moral rights.
[31] *Beggars Banquet Records v. Carlton Television* [1993] *EMLR* 349, 361; *A & M Records v. Video Collection* [1995] *EMLR* 25, 29.

recordings and films frequently involves the input of a range of different people, many of whom may lay claim to having helped to organize and facilitate the making of the sound recording or the film. Although the term 'producer' is used to define who is the creator, it should be noted that the courts have emphasized that there is a distinction between someone who 'makes' a recording and someone who 'makes the arrangements for the production of a recording': it is the latter who is the author, rather than the person who actually records or makes the sound recording or film (the person who operates the recording system).[32]

The notion of the 'producer' presupposes that, at the core of the production process, there is a person (or more often a company) that coordinates, controls, and organizes the production of the work.[33] It seems that, to be a 'producer', a person must exercise some degree of direct (organizational) control over the process of production.[34] If a person operates at the periphery of the process, such as the person who merely commissions the making of the recording, or merely provides the finance for a film or a sound recording, that person will not be regarded as a producer. If this were not the case, banks and other lending institutions would qualify as authors. However, provision of finance may be one of the organizational matters that, in combination with others, amount to a 'necessary arrangement'.[35]

2.2.3 Broadcasts

In the case of sound and television broadcasts, the author is the person who makes the broadcast.[36] Where a person receives and immediately retransmits a broadcast, the author is the maker of the original broadcast rather than the person who relays it.

2.2.4 Typographical arrangements

The author of a typographical arrangement of a published edition of a work is the publisher.[37]

2.3 JOINT AUTHORSHIP

Collaborative research and creation is often a fruitful and productive way for authors to work.[38] Copyright recognizes this mode of creation through the notion of joint

[32] *Adventure Films v. Tully* [1993] *EMLR* 376; *A & M Records v. Video Collection* [1995] *EMLR* 25; *Bamgboye v. Reed* [2004] *EMLR* (5) 61, 84, [77]; *Slater v. Wimmer* [2012] *EWPCC* 7, [85].

[33] See also *Century Communications v. Mayfair Entertainment* [1993] *EMLR* 335 (film made under restrictive conditions in China was produced by organizer outside China).

[34] *Adventure Films v. Tully* [1993] *EMLR* 376.

[35] Ibid., 378–9. See also *Beggars Banquet Records v. Carlton Television* [1993] *EMLR* 349 (arguable claim that person who provided finance and arranged access to venue where event was filmed was a person who made arrangements); *Century Communications v. Mayfair Entertainment* [1993] *EMLR* 335 (person had undertaken the arrangements necessary for the production of the film when it initiated the making of the film, organized the activity necessary for making it, and paid for it).   [36] CDPA 1988, s. 9(2)(b).

[37] CDPA 1988, s. 9(2)(d).

[38] R. Dreyfuss, 'Collaborative Research: Conflicts on Authorship, Ownership and Accountability' (2000) 53 *Vand L Rev* 1159. For consideration of the issues raised by mass collaboration, such as Wikipedia, see D. Simone, 'Copyright or Copyleft: Wikipedia as a Turning Point for Authorship' (2014) 25 *Kings LJ* 102. For a discussion of legal issues surrounding a historical precursor, see E. Cooper, 'Copyright and Mass Social Authorship: A Case Study on the Making of the Oxford English Dictionary' (2015) 24(4) *S & LS* 509.

authorship.[39] A number of important consequences, such as the way in which the work can be exploited, flow from a work being jointly authored.[40] While joint authorship is normally associated with literary, dramatic, musical, and artistic works, it is possible for any work to be jointly authored. As we saw earlier, the 1988 Act specifically provides that films are treated as works of joint authorship between the principal director and the producer, unless those are the same person.[41] The 1988 Act also extends the concept of joint authorship to a broadcast 'where more than one person is taken as making the broadcast'—namely, those 'providing' or taking 'responsibility' for the contents of the programme, and those making the 'arrangements necessary for its transmission'.[42] No special definition of joint authorship is applied to sound recordings or to published editions.

In cases other than those special circumstances under which joint authorship is deemed, a general principle applies: a work is a work of joint authorship if it is 'a work produced by the collaboration of two or more authors in which the contribution of each author is not distinct from that of the other author or authors'.[43] A work is one of joint authorship if it satisfies three conditions.

(i)   First, it is necessary to show that each of the authors *contributed to the making of the work*. In order to render a person a joint author, the contribution must be 'significant' and 'original'.[44] The requirement of originality is easily satisfied: this merely requires that the claimant's contribution consist of 'creative choices' (formerly 'skill and effort').[45] The requirement that the contribution be 'significant' has proved more problematic.[46] The better view is that 'significant' here means 'substantial', or 'considerable', or 'non-trivial', rather than 'aesthetically important'.[47]

---

[39]   Contrast the notion of a 'work of co-authorship', i.e. 'a work produced by collaboration of the author of a musical work and the author of a literary work where the two works are created in order to be used together', in CDPA 1988, s. 10A, introduced with effect from 1 November 2013 by the Copyright and Duration of Rights in Performances Regulations 2013 (SI 2013/1782), reg. 4, to implement Directive 2011/77/EU. See Chapter 7, section 2, pp. 184–6.

[40]   A joint owner (or other co-owner of copyright) can sue an infringer independently and can also bring an action against another co-owner.

[41]   CDPA 1988, ss 9(2)(ab) and 10(1A). Note, however, that the general scheme applies to determine authorship, or co-authorship, of the 'dramatic work': on which, see Kamina (2nd edn), 155–65.

[42]   CDPA 1988, s. 10(2), cross-referenced to s. 6(3).

[43]   For valuable comparative work, see M. Perry and T. Margoni, 'Ownership in Complex Authorship: A Comparative Study of Joint Works' [2012] *EIPR* 22; E Cooper, 'Joint Authorship in Comparative Perspective,' (2015) 62 *J Copyright Soc'y USA* 245.

[44]   *Godfrey v. Lees* [1995] *EMLR* 307, 325–8; *Hadley v. Kemp* [1999] *EMLR* 589; *Brighton v. Jones* [2005] *FSR* (16) 288, [34]. See also *Fylde Microsystems v. Key Radio Systems* [1998] *FSR* 449 (suggestions not sufficient); *Robin Ray v. Classic FM* [1998] *FSR* 622.

[45]   *Martin v. Kogan* [2017] *EWHC* 2927 (IPEC), [43]; *Locksley Brown v. Mcasso Music Production* [2005] *FSR* (40) 846, [42].

[46]   One can contrast the decision of *Godfrey v. Lees* [1995] *EMLR* 307 (classically trained musician who acted as orchestral arranger for a rock band was held to be joint author of a number of arrangements that included orchestral passages linking the verses and choruses) with *Hadley v. Kemp* [1999] *EMLR* 589 (contribution of saxophonist, singer, and drummer insufficient to render them co-authors because contributions were simply what one would have expected). See A. Barron, 'Introduction: Harmony or Dissonance? Copyright Concepts and Musical Practice' (2006) 15 *S & LS* 25; L. Bently, 'Authorship of Popular Music in UK Copyright Law' (2009) 12(2) *Information, Communication and Society* (Special issue) 179.

[47]   *Fisher v. Brooker and Onward Music* [2007] *FSR* (12) 255, [46] (Blackburne J preferred to ask whether the claimant's contribution was 'non-trivial').

While, to be a joint author, it is necessary for an author to have made a significant and original contribution to the work, joint authorship does not require that the respective contributions be in equal proportions.[48] However, it does require the contribution to be of the 'right kind': a contribution to the words of a song will normally give rise to joint authorship of the literary work, but not of the music; and a contribution to the 'performance' of a piece of music will not render the performer a co-author of the musical work.[49] Equally, a contribution to 'interpretation and theatrical presentation' is not to be regarded as a contribution to the creation of a dramatic work.[50]

(ii) The second requirement that must be satisfied for a work to be one of joint authorship is that the work must have been produced through a process of *collaboration* between the authors. This means that, when setting out to create a work, there must have been some common design, cooperation, or plan that united the authors (even if only in a very loose sense).[51] So long as the authors have a shared plan of some sort, there is no need for them to be in close proximity for them to collaborate. Indeed, it is possible for the collaboration to take place over long distances (a practice made much easier because of email).[52] There is no additional requirement that the parties must have intended to create a work of joint authorship.[53] The upshot of this second requirement is that, although two people may work on the same project, unless there is a shared goal, they will not be classified as joint authors. This means, for example, that where one person writes a poem and another person translates it into another language, the author of the original poem will not be a joint author of the translation. Similarly, where a musician arranges an existing musical work, the author of the original musical piece will not be able to claim joint authorship over the subsequent work; instead, there will be separate copyrights in the two pieces.[54]

(iii) Third, for a work to be jointly authored, the respective contributions must not be *distinct* or *separate* from each other. In more positive terms, this means that the contributions must merge to form an integrated whole (rather than a series of

---

[48] Joint authorship will usually be presumed to lead to equal shares, but this may be varied either by the court, where it feels comfortable evaluating the contributions—as in *Bamgboye v. Reed* [2004] *EMLR* (5) 61, 86, [85], and *Fisher v. Brooker and Onward Music* [2007] *FSR* (12) 255 (Fisher, author of the organ solo for 'A Whiter Shade of Pale', was awarded a 40 per cent share)—or according to the agreement of the parties: *Beckingham v. Hodgens* [2003] *FSR* (14) 238, 249 (equal shares); *Minder Music v. Sharples* [2015] *EWHC* 1454 (IPEC), [73], [84]–[90] (A. Michaels) (a producer who added string elements to song by The Fall was entitled to 20 per cent share in music copyright); *Peter Hayes v. Phonogram* [2003] *ECDR* (11) 110, 123 *ff* (agreement as to size of share).
[49] *Peter Hayes v. Phonogram* [2003] *ECDR* (11) 110, 128; *Hadley v. Kemp* [1999] *EMLR* 589, 643. See R. Arnold, 'Are Performers Authors?' [1999] *EIPR* 464. Expert evidence may need to be employed to assist the court in distinguishing between what is the work and what is performance: *Barrett v. Universal Island Records* [2006] *EWHC* 1009, [356].   [50] *Brighton v. Jones* [2005] *FSR* (16) 288, [56].
[51] *Levy v. Rutley* (1871) LR 6 CP 583; *Cala Homes (South) v. Alfred McAlpine Homes East* [1995] *FSR* 818, 835; *Martin v. Kogan* [2017] *EWHC* 2927 (IPEC), [25].
[52] *Cala Homes (South) v. Alfred McAlpine Homes East* [1995] *FSR* 818, 835.
[53] *Beckingham v. Hodgens* [2003] *FSR* (14) 238, 249.
[54] *Chappell v. Redwood Music* [1981] *RPC* 337. Cf. *Godfrey v. Lees* [1995] *EMLR* 307 (claimant who provided orchestral arrangements of existing songs was treated as a co-author); *Beckingham v. Hodgens* [2003] *FSR* 238 (session musician who added an introduction to a song was held to own 50 per cent of the copyright in the new arrangement). It seems that, where the author of a song collaborates in a new arrangement thereof, they acquire co-ownership of the arrangement even where they contribute nothing new.

distinct works).[55] For example, if the contributions of two authors were to merge in such a way that no single author were able to point to a substantial part of the work and say 'that is mine', the authors would be joint authors. If, however, one author were to write the first four chapters of a book and the other author, the remaining six chapters, instead of the resulting book being a joint work, the respective authors would have copyright in the particular chapters that they wrote.[56] Similarly, a song that comprises music and lyrics is not a work of joint authorship if one author writes the lyrics, while the other composes the music: the music and lyrics are distinct works, each of which has a single author.[57] In relation to a more difficult set of facts, it has been held that where one person added an introduction to the music of a song, this introduction was not 'distinct' because it was 'heavily dependent' on the rest of the tune and because, by itself, it would 'sound odd and lose meaning'.[58]

3 FIRST OWNERSHIP

Authorship and ownership have long been closely intertwined in copyright law. Indeed, one of the notable features of the 1709/10 Statute of Anne was that it recognized authors as first owners of the literary property that they created. This basic formula is repeated in the CDPA 1988, which declares that the author of a work is the first owner of copyright.[59] The rule that copyright initially vests in the author is, however, subject to a number of exceptions. The first and most important concerns works made by employees.[60] Exceptions also exist in relation to Crown copyright, parliamentary copyright, and works created by officers of international organizations.[61] Judicially originated exceptions also exist where a work is created in breach of a fiduciary duty or in breach of confidence.

Before looking at these in more detail, it is important to note that, although the author is usually the first owner, it is possible for an author to assign their copyright to third parties. This means that the question of who is the copyright owner at any particular point of time will depend upon what has happened to the copyright since it was first created. Since valid agreements can be made in relation to the transfer of future copyright, it may be that, when copyright arises, the first owner of copyright under the statutory scheme is immediately divested of their rights in favour of an assignee. It is also important to note that, while the law recognizes that a person other than the author may be first owner, the question of who is the author remains a distinct one (and an important one). A work made by an employee author, for example, has a duration dependent on the life of the author (that is, the employee) even if first ownership vests in the employer. Equally, issues of qualification and moral rights are determined by reference to authorship (not first ownership).

---

[55] In some legal systems, most notably France, there is no such 'integration' requirement at all. Article L. 113–2 of the French Intellectual Property Code of 1992 defines a 'collaborative work' as one 'to the creation of which several natural persons have contributed together', implying collaboration and contribution, but not necessarily integration: P. Kamina, 'France', in L. Bently (ed.), *International Copyright: Law and Practice* (2017), FRA 48–50. Belgian copyright law explicitly distinguishes between two types of collaborative work—referred to as 'divisible' and 'indivisible'—each category having particular rules as to whose consent is required to exploit the contribution: see further M. Perry and T. Margoni, 'Ownership in Complex Authorship' [2012] *EIPR* 22.   [56] CDPA 1988, s. 10(1).

[57] But this will count as a work of 'co-authorship', a designation with implications in terms of term of protection, but not the rights of the contributors: CDPA 1988, ss 10A, 12(8).

[58] *Beckingham v. Hodgens* [2003] *FSR* 238, 248. In any case, the introductory fiddle music was repeated a number of times elsewhere in the arrangement. Cf. *Hadley v. Kemp* [1999] *EMLR* 589, in which Park J suggested that a saxophone solo in the middle of Spandau Ballet's 'Gold' might be a distinct work.

[59] CDPA 1988, s. 11(1).   [60] CDPA 1988, s. 11(2).   [61] CDPA 1988, s. 11(3).

3.1 WORKS CREATED BY EMPLOYEES

Section 11(2) of the 1988 Act provides that, in the absence of an agreement to the contrary, where a literary, dramatic, musical, or artistic work, or a film is made in the course of employment, the employer is the first owner of any copyright in the work.[62] While employees retain moral rights in the works that they create, these are subject to a number of limitations.[63]

Critics have suggested that, by granting first ownership of works made by employees to employers, British law fails to provide creators with sufficient additional incentives to create.[64] It is also said that British law also fails to acknowledge the natural rights that employee-authors have in their creations. In so doing, it is suggested that British law fails to follow the underlying rationales for copyright. In response to arguments of this sort, it is argued that, while employers might not create works, they provide the facilities and materials that enable the act of creation to take place. In so doing, they make an important contribution to the production of new works. It is argued that granting first ownership to employers encourages employers to invest in the infrastructure that supports creators. Because employers are often in a better position than employees to exploit the copyright in a work, it is also suggested that it makes more sense to give copyright to employers than to employees. Another argument in favour of giving ownership to employers is that, in the absence of a provision that formally granted first ownership to employers, employers would require employees to assign their copyright to them. As section 11(2) achieves what would otherwise happen in practice, it thus serves to reduce transaction costs. In response to the argument that, in granting first ownership to employers, employees are not properly rewarded for their creative efforts, it is suggested that employees are rewarded through other means, such as pay, continued employment, and promotion.[65]

However problematic may be the arguments in favour of granting first ownership of employee works to employers, they have dominated UK policy in this area. In particular, while, under the Copyright Act 1956, employee journalists presumptively shared copyright with the newspapers, this 'anomaly' was removed in the 1988 Act.[66] As a result, under the current law, copyright in all works made in the course of employment belongs to the employer (unless there is an agreement to the contrary).

For an employer to be first owner of copyright, it is necessary to show that:

(i)   the literary, dramatic, musical, artistic work, or film was made by an employee;

(ii) the work was made in the course of employment; and

(iii) there is no agreement to the contrary.[67]

We will deal with each of these in turn.

---

[62] In the United States, related, but distinct, principles operate in relation to so-called 'works made for hire'. On the history, see C. Fisk, 'Authors at Work: The Origins of the Work for Hire Doctrine' (2003) 15 *Yale JL & Human* 1.   [63] CDPA 1988, ss 79(3) and 82.

[64] For a useful review, see M. Birnhack, 'Working Authors', *Tel Aviv University Law Faculty Working Papers No. 97* (2008).

[65] The Whitford Committee considered whether a scheme should be implemented, such as that which exists under the Patents Act 1977, providing for extra reward for particularly successful works: Cmnd 6732 (1977), [555]–[575]. The idea was quickly abandoned: *Reform of the Law relating to Copyright, Designs and Performers' Protection* (Cmnd. 8302, 1981) (pointing to practical difficulties).

[66] More specifically, under the previous law, copyright in a work made by an author in the course of employment by the daily or periodical press presumptively vested in the employer for purposes of its publication in the newspaper or periodical: CA 1956. s. 4(2).

[67] While the CDPA 1988 introduced changes on point, effective from 1 August 1989, the initial ownership of copyright continues generally to be determined by the law in effect when the materials in question were made: CDPA 1988, Sch. 1, para. 11.

3.1.1 Who is an employee?

An 'employee' is defined in the 1988 Act as a person who is employed under a contract of service or apprenticeship.[68] A contract of service is frequently distinguished from a contract *for* services. In general, it is easy to determine whether someone is an employee or not. However, there are many different sorts of work relationship, some of which are less easy to designate as employment relations. In such situations there is no simple way in which to tell whether the contract is an employment contract. At various times, courts have emphasized different elements, such as the degree of control that one party exercised over another or whether one party was part of the 'organization' of the other. *Chitty on Contracts* suggests the following eight factors:

(1) the degree of control exercised by the employer;

(2) whether the worker's interest in the relationship involved any prospect of profit or risk of loss;

(3) whether the worker was properly regarded as part of the employer's organisation;

(4) whether the worker was carrying on business on his own account or carrying on the business of the employer;

(5) the provision of equipment;

(6) the incidence of tax and national insurance;

(7) the parties' own view of their relationship;

(8) the structure of the trade or profession concerned and the arrangements within it.[69]

3.1.2 Was the work made in the course of employment?

In order for an employer to be first owner of copyright, it is also necessary to show that the work was made in 'the course of the employment'. Even though an author is an employee, if the work was not created in the course of employment, the author retains ownership of copyright. The question whether a work has been made in the course of employment will depend on the particular circumstances of the case in hand.

An important factor that has influenced the courts when determining whether a work has been made in the course of employment is whether the making of the work falls within the types of activity that an employer could reasonably expect or demand from an employer. In turn, this depends on the scope of the employee's duties. This can be seen, for example, in *Stevenson Jordan v. MacDonald & Evans*,[70] in which the question arose as to whether an accountant or his employer (a firm of management consultants) owned copyright in a series of public lectures that the accountant had given about the budgetary control of businesses. Morris LJ noted that the employer had paid the expenses of the lecturers, that the employee-accountant could have prepared the lectures in the company's time, used its library, and had the lectures typed up by company secretaries, and that the lectures were a useful accessory to his contracted work.[71] Nonetheless, Morris LJ found

---

[68] CDPA 1988, s. 178.   [69] H. G. Beale (ed.), *Chitty on Contracts* (32nd edn, 2015), [40–010].

[70] (1952) 69 *RPC* 10, 10 *TLR* 101. However, a journalist who wrote a confidential memorandum to colleagues about a possible article was acting in the course of her employment: *Beloff v. Pressdram* [1973] 1 *All ER* 241. For background to this holding, see J. Bellido, 'The Failure of a Copyright Action: Confidences in the Papers of Nora Beloff' (2013) 3 *Media & Arts L Rev* 249.

[71] In *Byrne v. Statist* [1914] 1 *KB* 622, a journalist made a translation to be used in the newspaper in his own time; this was held not to be in the course of his employment.

that, since it was not shown that the accountant could have been *ordered* to write and deliver the lectures, they were not created in the course of his employment. As such, the copyright belonged to the employee rather than to the employer.

Similar reasoning was also applied in *Noah v. Shuba*.[72] This was a copyright infringement action in relation to a book called *A Guide to Hygienic Skin Piercing*, written by the claimant, Dr Noah. During the proceedings, it was argued that, when Dr Noah wrote the guide, he was employed as a consultant epidemiologist at the Public Health Laboratory Service; as such, the copyright vested in his employer. While there was no doubt that Dr Noah was an employee of the Public Health Laboratory, it was less clear as to whether the guide had been written in the course of his employment. Dr Noah discussed his work with colleagues, made use of the services of the Public Health Laboratory Service library, and had the manuscript typed up by his secretary. In addition, the guide was published by the Public Health Laboratory Service at its own expense. Nonetheless, Mummery J held that the guide had not been written in the course of Noah's employment. One factor that influenced this decision was that Dr Noah had written the draft at home in the evenings and at weekends. Another was that Noah's contract required him to publish articles, but did not require him to write books.

It should be pointed out that the mere facts that a work is made at home or that the employee makes use of their personal resources do not necessarily mean that it will fall outside the scope of the employee's duties. Ultimately, the question of whether a work is made within the scope of employment depends upon the contract of employment. This can be seen in *Missing Link Software v. Magee*,[73] in which the question arose as to whether software written by an employee outside work time and on his own equipment was created in the course of his employment and thus copyright in it owned by his employer. The claimant company argued that, since it had employed the defendant to write programs of the kind in dispute, similar programs, even if written in his spare time, were created in the course of his employment. The Court held that although the employee had written the software in his own time and on his own equipment, nonetheless it was not unarguable that, because it fell within the scope of the tasks that he was employed to carry out, the computer programs were created within the course of his employment.

3.1.3 Agreements to the contrary

Finally, it should be noted that the copyright in works made in the course of employment will not be treated as belonging to the employer where there is an agreement to the contrary. Such an agreement may be written or oral, express, or implied.[74]

In some cases, such agreements have been implied from custom. For example, in *Noah v. Shuba*, Mummery J said that if the skin-piercing guide had been written in the course of Dr Noah's employment, he would nonetheless have implied a term into Dr Noah's contract that the copyright remained with the employee.[75] The reason for this was the Public Health Laboratory Service's long-standing practice of allowing its employees to act as if they owned copyright in their works: it allowed employees to assign copyright

---

[72] [1991] *FSR* 14.   [73] [1989] *FSR* 361.

[74] As we will see, there is a general requirement that assignments of copyright be in writing. However, such formality is unnecessary with respect to the agreement reversing the presumption of initial ownership, which can be oral or implied. But to refer to a relationship as not being one of employment was not an implied agreement that copyright was to vest in the employee: *Robin Ray v. Classic FM* [1998] *FSR* 622.

[75] *Noah v. Shuba* [1991] *FSR* 14, 26–7.

to publishers, to claim royalties, and (with respect to the case itself) did not assert that it owned copyright. This decision has important ramifications where employers allow employees to act as if they own copyright.

3.2 CROWN COPYRIGHT

Another exception to the general rule that the author is the first owner relates to works governed by Crown copyright. Where a work is made by an officer or servant of the Crown in the course of their duties,[76] copyright in the work belongs to the Crown and not to the author of the work.[77]

3.3 PARLIAMENTARY COPYRIGHT

Where a work is made under the direction or control of the House of Commons or the House of Lords, the respective House owns copyright therein.[78] Such parliamentary copyright lasts for 50 years from the year in which the work was made. All Bills introduced into Parliament attract parliamentary copyright, but this ceases on royal assent, withdrawal, or rejection of the Bill.[79]

3.4 INTERNATIONAL ORGANIZATIONS

Where a literary, dramatic, musical, or artistic work is made by an officer or employee of an 'international organization',[80] the organization is the first owner of the resulting copyright.[81]

3.5 COMMISSIONED WORKS AND EQUITABLE ASSIGNMENT

Another exception to the general rule that the author is first owner arises, in limited circumstances, where a person commissions someone to make a work. Under the CDPA 1988, copyright in a commissioned work belongs to the author of the commissioned work.[82] However, in certain circumstances, the courts may infer that an independent contractor is subject to an implied obligation to assign the copyright to the commissioner. This may give rise to a trust with respect to the copyright in the commissioned work and render the commissioner the equitable owner. A good example is provided by *R. Griggs*

---

[76] CDPA 1988, ss 163, 164.

[77] CDPA 1988, s. 163. It lasts for 125 years from when the work is made or 50 years from its commercial publication. Crown copyright also exists in all Acts of Parliament and Measures of the General Synod of the Church of England.

[78] CDPA 1988, s. 164. The Government of Wales Act 1998, Sch. 12, has added to this list 'any sound recording, film, or live broadcast of the National Assembly for Wales which is made by or under the direction or control of the Assembly'. [79] CDPA 1988, ss 165–7.

[80] This means an organization the members of which include one or more states: CDPA 1988, s. 178.

[81] CDPA 1988, s. 168.

[82] Under the Copyright Act 1956, a party commissioning a photograph, portrait, or engraving for value presumptively acquired copyright in that work: CA 1956, s. 4(3), Sch. 8, para. 1(a). When this position was changed in the 1988 Act, commissioners of photographers and films for private and domestic purposes were 'compensated' with the so-called 'moral' right of 'privacy': CDPA 1988, s. 85. The right covers issuing of copies of the work to the public, its exhibition in public, and its communication to the public.

Group v. Evans,[83] in which Griggs, distributors of DR MARTEN'S AIRWAIR, commissioned the advertising agency, Jordan, in 1988 to produce a logo for it. Evans, who did freelance work for Jordan, produced the logo and was paid at his standard rate of £15 an hour. Nothing was said about copyright in the logo. In 2002, Evans purported to assign copyright in the artistic work to Raben Footwear, an Australian competitor of Griggs. In response, Griggs brought an action seeking a declaration that it was beneficial owner of copyright and an assignment of legal title. Peter Prescott QC, sitting as deputy High Court judge, granted the relief sought. He held that while Evans was the author and first owner of the legal title, an agreement that copyright was to belong to Griggs was to be implied. Such an agreement was necessary to give business efficacy to the arrangement, under which it was clearly contemplated that Griggs would be able to use the logo and stop others from using it.[84] This could be achieved only if the implied agreement was to assign the copyright or give a perpetual exclusive licence (and the latter solution would be less convenient for Evans). The Court of Appeal affirmed.

Implied agreements to assign have also been found where a choreographer undertook to arrange certain dances for the Russian ballet,[85] a design of a trade mark was produced,[86] a person upgraded a previous version of a computer program,[87] a person arranged for the making of a sound recording,[88] and a person developed a prototype of a mask based on an artist's sketches.[89] These decisions amount to judicial variations of a clear legislative scheme.[90] Clearly, the judges are looking at transactions after the event and are motivated by gut feelings of justice to prevent opportunistic behaviour by creators. However, the impact of the decisions is to undermine a clear scheme that is designed both to achieve certainty in transactions and to protect authors.[91] It does so by requiring parties to allocate ownership through written assignments and, in so doing, requires those acquiring rights to specify what they want, thus giving authors an opportunity to reflect upon whether they wish to transfer all of those rights.[92] Under that scheme, the penalty for

---

[83] [2004] *FSR* (31) 673, [2005] *FSR* (31) 706 (CA). This decision is remarkable in two respects. First, the implied assignment is in favour of a third party, Griggs, rather than the design company, Jordan. The more orthodox (if artificial) view would be that there are two implied agreements: one between Jordan and Evans; and another between Griggs and Jordan. The distinction would have been important if, for example, Jordan had decided that the logo supplied by Evans was unsuitable. Second, the agreement to assign is implied in this case even though Evans did not know of the use intended by Griggs, Evans thinking the use was for point-of-sale only. The judge seems to have ignored this on the ground that Evans was 'indifferent' to the use and, had he known, he would have accepted the more extensive use without charging a different fee.

[84] [2004] *FSR* (31) 673, [57].

[85] *Massine v. De Basil* [1936–45] *MacG CC* 223. See also *Brighton v. Jones* [2005] *FSR* (16) 288, [57]–[58] (contributions of director to play were made on behalf of theatre and so director was unable to claim copyright therein).

[86] *Auvi Trade Mark* [1995] *FSR* 288; *R. Griggs Group v. Evans* [2003] *EWHC* 2914.

[87] *Flanders v. Richardson* [1993] *FSR* 497, 516–19 (Ferris J held that where a computer program was improved, in circumstances under which there was an acceptance or understanding that the plaintiff owned all of the rights in the program, the court would hold the plaintiff to be the copyright owner, relying on *Massine v. De Basil* [1936–45] *MacG CC* 223).

[88] *A & M Records v. Video Collection* [1995] *EMLR* 25.

[89] *Lucasfilm v. Ainsworth* [2010] *Ch* 502 (CA), 556–7.

[90] *Clearsprings Management v. Businesslinx* [2006] *FSR* (3) 21, [9] (Floyd J).

[91] *Effects Associates, Inc. v. Cohen*, 908 *F.2d* 555 (9th Cir. 1990). But cf. D. Booton, 'Informal Dealings with Copyright' [2011] *IPQ* 28.

[92] In *Effects Associates, Inc. v. Larry Cohen; Larco Productions, Inc. & New World Entertainment*, 908 *F.2d* 555, 15 *USPQ.2d* 1559 (9th Cir. 1990), Judge Alex Kozinski explained §204A of 17 *USC* thus: 'Section 204 ensures that the creator of a work will not give away his copyright inadvertently and forces a party who wants to use the copyrighted work to negotiate with the creator to determine precisely what rights are being transferred and at what price . . .'

those commissioners who fail to organize their legal rights properly is that they risk having to bargain for them later. The courts, by repeatedly responding to their sense that rights should follow money, remove this 'penalty' and, with it, undermine the goals that the statutory scheme aims to achieve. The better view is that these cases should be confined to their specific facts[93] and implied assignments found only in exceptional cases.[94]

3.6 BREACH OF CONFIDENCE

It also seems that copyright in works that are created in breach of a fiduciary duty or in breach of confidence will be held on constructive trust for the person to whom the duty was owed.[95] The same may be true of works made 'in circumstances involving the invasion of legal or equitable rights of the [claimant] or breach of the obligation of the maker to the [claimant]'.[96]

4 HARMONIZATION

Questions of authorship and the position of employed authors are matters on which there has been little harmonization. As we have already noted, the issue was tackled, but only partially, in relation to films, by stating that the director is to be regarded as one of the authors of a cinematographic work. The only other harmonization has been in respect of the position of authors who create computer programs while employed: the Software Directive requires that the employer exclusively shall be entitled to exercise all economic rights in programs so created.[97] Although differences in the rules operated by member states may lead to different conclusions as to who is an author or owner of a particular copyright work, it seems unlikely that the European Commission will attempt harmonization in the near future. This is because these rules raise thorny political issues that go well beyond the field of copyright, in particular touching on national traditions as regards labour relations.[98]

Whether the Court of Justice will be active is more difficult to predict. The various directives require member states to confer harmonized rights on 'authors'.[99] Insofar as there is no reference to national law, it might well be the case that the Court will treat the

---

[93] For example, *Saphena Computing v. Allied Collection Agencies* [1995] *FSR* 616, distinguishing *Warner v. Gestetner* [1988] *EIPR* D–89.

[94] There are, in fact, many cases in which claims to equitable assignments have failed: *Tate v. Thomas* [1921] 1 *Ch* 503; *Robin Ray v. Classic FM* [1998] FSR 622; *Clearsprings Management v. Businesslinx* [2006] *FSR* (3) 21; *Slater v. Wimmer* [2012] *UKPCC* 7.

[95] *A-G v. Guardian (No. 2)* [1990] *AC* 109, 263, 276. Insofar as the constructive trust analysis is adopted, there is no obvious reason why the analysis should be restricted to cases of breach of duties owed to the Crown: see *Ultraframe UK v. Clayton (No. 2)* [2003] *EWCA Civ* 1805 (director held unregistered design rights on trust for company). See Chapter 30, section 3, pp. 825–6.

[96] *Australian Broadcasting Corp. v. Lenah Game Meats Pty* (2001) 208 *CLR* 199, [101]–[102] (Gummow and Hayne JJ), and [309] (Callinan J).

[97] Software Dir., Art. 2(3). See also Council Directive 87/54/EEC of 16 December 1986 on the legal protection of topographies of semiconductor products [1986] *OJ L* 24/36, Art. 3(2)(a).

[98] A. Quaedvlieg, 'Authorship and Ownership,' in T. Synodinou (ed.), *Codification of European Copyright Law* (2012) 197.

[99] Rel. Rights Dir., Art. 3(1)(a); Info. Soc. Dir., Arts 2(1), 3(a), 4(1) (rights to be conferred on 'authors').

term 'author' as an autonomous concept of European law.[100] If it does so, it seems likely that it will insist that an author must be a human being, rather than a legal entity. The most obvious definition would be the natural person who is the source of the intellectual creation. Of course, those rights could be assigned, and it seems that there would be no objection to presumptions of transfer. However, if the logic of *Luksan* is followed,[101] there would be no room for a reallocation that was more than presumptive.[102] Whether it will go as far as developing rules on joint authorship is more difficult to predict.

---

[100] But cf. Database Dir., Art 4(1) ('The author of a database shall be the natural person or group of natural persons who created the base *or, where the legislation of the Member States so permits, the legal person designated as the rightholder by that legislation*', emphasis added). Recital 29 indicates that the arrangements applicable to databases created by employees are left to the discretion of the member states. The various provisions requiring that the principal director be recognized as one of the authors of a cinematograph, but which permit member states to recognize 'other authors'—Rel. Rights Dir., Art. 2(2); Term Dir., Art. 2(1)— might lend weight to the notion that this matter is, overall, one for member states.

[101] *Martin Luksan v. Petrus van der Let*, Case C-277/10, EU:C:2012:65 (ECJ), [67] (holding that Austrian law vesting exploitation rights in film in the producer, rather than the director, was incompatible with the Directive—although, at [87], a rule of presumptive transfer would be acceptable).

[102] The rules in CDPA 1988, ss 163 (Crown copyright), 165 (parliamentary copyright), and 168 (international organizations), which are not presumptive/subject to agreement to the contrary, may be objectionable.

6

NATURE OF THE RIGHTS

1 INTRODUCTION

This chapter is concerned with the rights that the law confers on the copyright owner. The scope of these rights determines the types of activity that, unless done with the copyright owner's consent, amount to an infringement of copyright.

One of the most consistent themes in the history of copyright law is that the types of activity that have fallen within the copyright owner's control have steadily expanded. While the 1709/10 Statute of Anne conferred on authors and proprietors of books the limited right to 'print and reprint' those books, subsequently, the copyright owner's monopoly was extended to cover the public representation of the work,[1] the 'adaptation' of a work (such as translation and conversion into dramatic forms of literary works),[2] broadcasting, and more recently rights to distribute, rent, and lend copies of the work.[3] While the copyright owner is able to control the use that can be made of the work in many circumstances, there are still some that do not fall within the owner's control. If we take the case of the rights in a literary work, for example, the copyright owner is not able, at least yet, to control reading, browsing, private lending, or resale of a book containing the work that has been sold with their consent.

For the most part, the rights have developed in a piecemeal way in response to external pressures, most obviously to technological change.[4] As well as producing a complicated regime, the cumulative way in which the rights have developed has also led to a degree of overlap between them.[5] The expansion of the rights granted to the copyright owner has continued with the implementation of the Information Society Directive,[6] which harmonizes the rights of reproduction, communication to the public, and distribution.

---

[1] Dramatic Literary Property Act, 1833, 3 & 4 Will.IV, c.15 (representation at places of dramatic entertainment); Copyright Law Amendment Act, 1842, 5 & 6 Vict., c.45, s 20 (giving right to copyright holders in musical works).

[2] Copyright Act 1911. For background, see L. Bently, 'Copyright, Translations, and Relations Between Britain and India in the Nineteenth and Early Twentieth Centuries' (2007) 82(3) *Chi-Kent L Rev* 1181–1240.

[3] CDPA 1988, s. 18 (as enacted, but substantially amended to implement Rel. Rights Dir.).

[4] B. Sherman and L. Wiseman, *Copyright and the Challenge of the New* (2012); N. Netanel, 'Why Has Copyright Expanded? Analysis and Critique', in F. MacMillan (ed.), *New Directions in Copyright Law* (2007), vol. 6, ch. 1; L. Bently, 'R v. The Author: From the Death Penalty to Community Service' (2008) 32 *Colum JL & Arts* 1.

[5] For example, between the right of reproduction and the right of adaptation. This overlap is all the more problematic because the reproduction right is harmonized under EU law, whereas the adaptation right is not.

[6] Copyright and Related Rights Regulations 2003 (SI 2003/2498).

Table 6.1 Harmonization of the copyright owner's rights in the European Union

	Computer programs	Related rights	Databases	Authorial works
Reproduction	Software Dir., Art. 4(a)	Info. Soc. Dir., Art. 2(b)–(d)	Database Dir., Art. 5(a)	Info. Soc. Dir., Art. 2
Fixation	n/a	Rel. Rights Dir., Art. 7	n/a	n/a
Distribution	Software Dir., Art. 4(c)	Rel. Rights Dir., Art. 9	Database Dir., Art. 5(c)	Info. Soc. Dir., Art. 4(1)
Rental	Software Dir., Art. 4(c) Rel. Rights Dir., Art. 5(2)	Rel. Rights Dir., Art. 3(1)(b)–(d)	Rel. Rights Dir., Art. 3; Database Dir., Recital 24	Rel. Rights Dir., Art. 3(1)(a)
Public performance	Not referred to	Unharmonized	Database Dir., Art. 5(d)	Unharmonized
Communication	Info. Soc. Dir., Art. 3(1)[10]	Rel. Rights Dir., Art. 8	Database Dir., Art. 5(d)	Info. Soc. Dir., Art. 3(1)
Making available	Info. Soc. Dir., Art. 3(1)[11]	Info. Soc. Dir., Art. 3(2)(a)-(d)		Info. Soc. Dir., Art. 3(1)
Adaptation	Software Dir., Art. 4(b)	Unharmonized	Database Dir., Art. 5(b)	Unharmonized

Significantly, the public performance right has not been harmonized,[7] nor has the adaptation right (other than in relation to computer programs and databases) (see Table 6.1). This has at least three important implications. First, it means that, with respect to the harmonized rights, the detailed provisions of the Copyright, Designs and Patents Act 1988 (CDPA 1988)—for example section 17(3) on what counts as reproduction of an artistic work or section 18 on the 'issuing right'—need to be treated with some caution, because they must be interpreted to give effect to the relevant directives. Second, and relatedly, in relation to the harmonized provisions, the Court of Justice is the key forum in which the scope of these rights is elucidated (at least until the United Kingdom leaves the European Union, if that in fact occurs). Third, because EU law 'harmonizes' these rights, it creates *upper*, as well as lower, limits.[8] This raises interesting questions (particularly for civil law jurisdictions) about what precisely is covered (and the relationship with other rights and doctrines).[9]

The primary rights that are currently granted to copyright owners are set out in sections 16–21 of the 1988 Act. Anyone who carries out any of these activities, or who authorizes

---

[7] *Circul Globus Bucureşti v. Uniunea Compozitorilor şi Muzicologilor din România*, Case C-283/10 [2011] *ECR* I–12031 (ECJ).

[8] In a few contexts, the EU prescribes only minimum standards: Satellite Dir., Art. 6(1); Rel. Rights Dir, Art 8(3).

[9] Consider, for example, a 'public exhibition' right (a right not known to UK law, but recognized in some member states): is this unharmonized (and thus left to national law), or no longer permitted because it falls outside the scope of the distribution right?

[10] M. Walter, 'Information Society Directive', in Walter and von Lewinski, 958, [11.1.20].

[11] Ibid., [11.3.36].

someone else to carry out these activities, is liable for primary infringement (unless the defendant has the permission of the copyright owner or can show that the activity falls within one of the defences available to them.) While the nature of the rights that are granted varies according to the type of work in question, these include the exclusive right to:

(i) copy the work (a reproduction right);

(ii) issue copies of the work to the public (a distribution right);

(iii) rent or lend the work to the public (a rental or lending right);

(iv) perform, show, or play the work in public (a public performance right);

(v) communicate the work to the public;

(vi) make an adaptation of the work, or do any of the above acts in relation to an adaptation (a right of adaptation); or

(vii) authorize others to carry out any of these activities.

It should be noted that the particular rights that are granted to copyright owners vary depending on the type of work that is protected. In particular, while the right of reproduction and the right to issue copies of the work to the public exist in relation to all types of work, the other rights apply only to certain of them. For example, the performing right applies to all works except artistic works and typographical arrangements; the right to communicate the work to the public applies to all works except typographical arrangements; the right to make an adaptation of a work applies only to literary, dramatic, or musical works. Care must be taken to check which rights a copyright owner is given by the 1988 Act (see Table 6.2).

Traditionally, it has been understood that the restricted activities found in sections 16–21 are based on a notion of strict liability. This means that the state of mind of the defendant is not normally relevant when determining whether an infringement has taken

Table 6.2 Rights under the CDPA 1988

Works	To copy the work (s. 17)	To issue copies of the work to the public (s. 18)	To rent or lend the work (s. 18A)	To perform or show the work in public (s. 19)	To communicate the work to the public (s. 20)	To make an adaptation (s. 21)
Literary, dramatic, and musical	✓	✓	✓	✓	✓	✓
Artistic	✓	✓	(but not buildings/ applied art)	×	✓	×
Film	✓	✓	✓	✓	✓	×
Sound recordings	✓	✓	✓	✓	✓	×
Broadcasts	✓	✓	×	✓	✓	×
Typographical	✓	✓	×	×	×	×

place.[12] As such, it does not matter if a defendant knew that the work was protected by copyright or that the claimant owned the work. All that matters, at least in relation to primary infringement, is that the defendant carried out one of the acts reserved to the copyright holder with the claimant's work (or a part of it).[13]

In addition to the primary rights set out in sections 16–21, it is also worth noting that there are regimes of accessory and secondary liability. Accessory liability is based on common law principles of joint tortfeasance (and is discussed in Chapter 48). Secondary liability, which is set out in sections 22–6 of the CDPA largely concerns the commercial exploitation of copies where the defendant knew or had reason to believe that the copies were or would be infringements when made.[14] We deal with secondary infringement in Chapter 8.[15] For now, however, it is perhaps worth making one point about the place of 'accessory' and 'secondary infringement' in EU copyright law. While these matters hardly feature in the harmonized copyright *acquis*,[16] it would, however, be a mistake to assume this is an area in which there is very little harmonization. In fact, some of the jurisprudence of the Court of Justice seems to be interpreting the scope of the primary rights so broadly that accessory and secondary liability would have little, if any, place in a European copyright regime.

2 THE REPRODUCTION RIGHT

The oldest right given to copyright owners is the right to copy the work (section 17).[17] The right has been the subject of harmonization at an EU level specifically with respect to computer programs[18] and databases,[19] and more generally with respect to other works. Article 2 of the Information Society Directive requires member states to confer on authors, film producers, phonogram producers, and broadcasters 'the exclusive right to authorise or prohibit direct or indirect, temporary or permanent reproduction by any means and in any form, in whole or in part'.

While the precise understanding of what counts as a 'reproduction' varies (particularly as between authorial works and related rights, or what Mr Justice Arnold calls 'signal' and 'content' copyright),[20] one factor that is common to all works is that infringement takes place whether the copy is permanent, transient, temporary, or even incidental to some other use of the work.[21] This means a person will infringe (absent a defence) when they store a work (or other subject matter) on a USB,[22] when they take material from one

---

[12] But see the case law of the Court of Justice described in section 3, p. 150 and section 6, p. 165, where the CJEU treats such knowledge as relevant in cases of distribution and communication to the public.

[13] A defendant's innocence may be relevant when damages are being determined: CDPA 1988, s. 97(1). See Chapter 49, section 5, pp. 1340–7, and section 6, p. 1334. For reflections, see P. Gould, 'Is Copyright Infringement a Strict Liability Tort?' (2015) 30 *BTLJ* 305.   [14] CDPA 1988, ss 22–4, 27.

[15] See Chapter 8, section 3, pp. 222–5.   [16] The main example is Software Dir., Art. 7.

[17] *VG Wort v. KYOCERA Document Solutions Deutschland GmbH*, Joined Cases C-457/11, C-458/11, C-459/11, and 460/11, EU:C:2013:34, [AG33] (AG Sharpston, referring to reproduction as the 'fundamental' right); cf. J. Litman, *Digital Copyright* (2001), 180 *ff* (proposing instead a general right to control commercial exploitation).   [18] Software Dir., Art. 4(a).

[19] Database Dir., Art. 5(a).

[20] R. Arnold, 'Content Copyrights and Signal Copyrights: The Case for a Rational Scheme of Protection' (2011) 1 *QMJIP* 272; *England & Wales Cricket Board v. Tixdaq* [2016] *EWHC* 575 (Ch), [60].

[21] CDPA 1988, s. 17(6); Info. Soc. Dir., Art. 2. But note CDPA 1988, s. 28A and Info. Soc. Dir., Art. 5(1) discussed in Chapter 9, section 3, pp. 235–9.

[22] *Technische Universität Darnstadt v. Eugen Ulmer KG*, Case C-117/13, EU:C:2014:2196, [52] (ECJ).

website and place it on another, when they upload on to sites, or when they download through peer-to-peer systems (such as Newzbin and The Pirate Bay).[23] More startling, a person will reproduce material when they access material from a computer (at which point, a temporary copy is made in the 'memory' of a computer),[24] or when they run a satellite box, because the buffer system of the decoder generates a temporary technical copy,[25] or when they access an Internet stream.[26] Moreover, the image created on a computer screen, or television screen,[27] is also regarded as a copy (albeit a temporary one).

It is also worth noting that, under the current approach, reproduction occurs irrespective of whether the user values the work for its expressive or communicative content.[28] For example, a person might digitize a work in order to conduct a search (e.g. to detect plagiarism), or to allow others to search the text (by creating indices for search engines).[29] In such cases, the text is not valued as an expression or communication, but only as a set of relationships to be examined (usually by a non-human means), or as Borghi and Karapapa have said, 'as data'.[30] These non-expressive uses are currently caught by the reproduction right, and their legality therefore turns on the availability of a defence or exception.[31] There are a growing number of commentators who argue that this approach is unjustified, and copyright should only protect a work *as* a communication.[32]

2.1 LITERARY, DRAMATIC, MUSICAL, AND ARTISTIC WORKS

In relation to literary, dramatic, musical, and artistic works, copying means 'reproducing the work in any material form'.[33] European law also refers to reproduction as covering reproduction by 'any means and in any form'.[34] Thus reproduction is not limited to replicating a work in the same manner as it was originally produced, for example repainting a painting or reprinting a book; reproduction also includes reproduction in other forms. Thus it is clear that a photocopy or electronic scan of a printed book,[35] an engraving of a painting, a painting of a photograph, and a sound recording of a song are (potentially) reproductions.[36] The conversion of a work into digital form—from symbols perceptible

---

[23] All these examples involve a proliferation of instances of the work, even if temporary. But the CJEU has suggested that 'reproduction' does not require multiplication, but can occur where material from one object is relocated on a different object: *Art & Allposters v. Pictoright*, Case C-419/13, EU:C:2015;27, [43]–[46] (ECJ) (removing image from poster and reapplying it to canvas involved 'reproduction'). Cf. *Théberge v. Galerie d'Art du Petit Champlain Inc.*, 2002 SCC 34, [2002] 2 *SCR* 336 (Supreme Court of Canada) (on similar facts finding no reproduction absent multiplication).   [24] *R v. Higgs* [2008] *EWCA Civ* 1324, [9].

[25] *Football Association Premier League Ltd and ors v. QC Leisure and ors* and *Karen Murphy v. Media Protection Services Ltd* ('*FAPL*'), Joined Cases C-403/08 and C-429/08 [2011] *ECR* I-9083 (ECJ, Grand Chamber); *ITV Broadcasting Ltd v. TV Catchup Ltd* [2011] *EWHC* 1874 (Pat).

[26] *FAPL v. British Communications* [2017] EWHC 480 (Ch), [31] (Arnold J).

[27] *FAPL*, Joined Cases C-403/08 and C-429/08 [2011] *ECR* I-9083, [159].

[28] See e.g. J. Litman, 'Festischizing Copies', in R. Okediji (ed.), *Copyright in An Age of Limitations and Exceptions* (2017).

[29] *Technische Universität Darnstadt v. Eugen Ulmer KG*, Case C-117/13, EU:C:2014:2196, [37] (ECJ) (digitization is an act of reproduction).

[30] M. Borghi and S. Karapapa, 'Non-Display Uses of Copyright Works' (2011) 1 *QMJIP* 21.

[31] On Art. 5(1) of the Info. Soc. Dir., see Chapter 9, section 3, pp. 235–9.

[32] A. Drassinower, *What's Wrong with Copying?* (2015), ch. 3 (arguing that copyright does not cover non-communicative uses); A. Strowel and A. Ohly in B. Hugenholtz (ed), *Copyright Reconstructed: Rethinking Copyright's Econonmic Rights* (2018), chs. 3 and 7.   [33] CDPA 1988, s. 17(2).

[34] Info. Soc. Dir., Art. 2; Software Dir., Art. 4(a); Database Dir., Art. 5(a).

[35] *Norowzian v. Arks* [1998] *FSR* 394, 398; *Technische Universität Darnstadt v. Eugen Ulmer KG*, Case C-117/13, EU:C:2014:2196, [52] (ECJ) (copy on USB drive).   [36] *Bauman v. Fussell* [1978] *RPC* 485.

and understandable to the senses into a series of ones and zeros—will likewise be treated as a reproduction.[37] Moreover, the CDPA 1988 specifies in relation to artistic works that a person will reproduce a work if there is a change of dimensions, so that, for example, photographing a sculpture and making a car exhaust pipe from a design drawing involve reproduction.[38] One would expect the same result under the harmonized law (although it is not obvious that the limitation to artistic works can still be justified).[39]

Are there limits on the extent to which a work can be changed and still constitute a reproduction? In the nineteenth century, British law encountered difficulty with treating an act as transformative as a translation as a reproduction and as a result introduced a distinct category of exclusive right, the right of adaptation. This suggests that there are limits to the concept of reproduction, even if it can be 'in any form'. In particular, British courts have stated that, in order to infringe, the derived form must be 'objectively similar' to the copyright work.[40] The requirement of objective similarity means that, to infringe, the relevant part of the defendant's work must be a copy or representation of the whole or part of the original work.[41]

In interpreting the concept of 'reproduction' under EU law, it is worth noting that, except in the field of databases and computer programs, there has been no harmonization of the right to make an adaptation of a work (see Table 6.1), so that if a protected work is transformed such that it is no longer a reproduction, the question of liability falls to national law.[42] The Court of Justice has yet to determine the limits of the concept of reproduction.[43]

Two interesting questions as to the limits of 'reproduction' arose in British case law from the pre-harmonization era. The first is whether the copyright in a work that consists of *instructions* how to make something is infringed by making the thing as instructed. Case law indicated that the answer was 'no': a person will not infringe the literary copyright in a recipe if they follow the instructions and bake a cake to the recipe, for example.[44]

---

[37] *Technische Universität Darnstadt v. Eugen Ulmer KG*, Case C-117/13, EU:C:2014:2196, [37] (ECJ); *Pinckney*, Case C-170/12, EU:C:2013:400, [AG29] (AG Jääskinen); *Autospin (Oil Seals) v. Beehive Spinning (A Firm)* [1995] *RPC* 683, 698.   [38] CDPA 1988, s. 17(3).

[39] CDPA 1988, s. 17(3), is best understood as an example. No negative inference as to the scope of copyright in literary works should be drawn from it. Cf. *Moon v. Thornber* [2012] *EWPCC* 37, [98]–[99] (Birss J resisting the invitation to so hold), discussed in Yin Harn Lee, 'The Persistence of the Text' [2018] *IPQ* 22 and 107, 129-30.

[40] *Francis Day Hunter v. Bron* [1963] *Ch* 587, 623.

[41] *Brigid Foley v. Ellot* [1982] *RPC* 433 (Megarry VC).

[42] Some inferences might be drawn from the materials surrounding the implementation of the Marrakesh Treaty. As will be seen, the EU has introduced a Directive providing for a derogation from the reproduction right that will allow for accessible format copies to be made. As the most obvious form of 'accessible format copies' would be braille documents, one might think of the conversion as involving 'adaptation' rather than 'reproduction'. In turn, one could infer that the EU legislature conceives of the reproduction right as very broad. Moreover, it is interesting that in putting the case that the Marrakesh Treaty was a matter of joint rather than exclusive EU competence, nowhere does there appear the argument that making accessible format copies is (unharmonized) adaptation, rather than reproduction: Opinion 3/15, EU:C:2017:114 (ECJ, Grand Chamber).

[43] *Eva-Maria Painer v. Standard VerlagsGmbH*, Case C-145/10 [2012] *ECDR* (6) 89 (ECJ), [AG129]; *SAS Institute v. World Programming*, Case C-406/10 [2012] 3 *CMLR* (4) 55, [77], (use of a computer manual, a literary work, as a basis for constructing a program, might be a reproduction of part of the manual if the part reproduced were to constitute a part that was its own intellectual creation). Cf. *Infopaq Int. v. Danske Dagblades Forening*, Case C-302/10, EU:C:2012:16 (Order) (ECJ), [44]–[45] (making of an abstract summarizing a newspaper article would not amount to an infringement under EU law, perhaps because the transformation was so extensive that it cannot be treated as a reproduction, but possibly also because all that was reproduced was unprotected 'facts').

[44] *Davis (J & S) Holdings v. Wright Health Group* [1988] *RPC* 403, 414; *Autospin (Oil Seals) v. Beehive Spinning* [1995] *RPC* 683, 698; *Lambretta Clothing v. Teddy Smith* [2003] RPC (41) 728, [78]-[79]; *Abraham Moon & Sons v. Thornber* [2013] *FSR* (17) 312, [99].

This is because what is protected is the intellectual creation of the recipe as a literary work and not the creation of the cake per se. Similarly, a person who knits clothes according to a knitting guide does not infringe copyright in the guide.[45] We would expect the same result under harmonized EU law.

The second issue concerned whether there is infringement where a copyright work *describes* something and the thing is made to the description. If a novel describes a scene, would copyright be infringed by someone painting the scene so described? As with instructional works, the key issue here is: when is a description 'reproduced'? The issue is not merely theoretical: with developments in computer-aided design, computer code now commonly represents the three-dimensional article.[46] In *Sandman v. Panasonic*,[47] the Court indicated that, in certain circumstances, a two-dimensional literary work that describes something (in this case, circuit diagrams) could be reproduced in a three-dimensional form (the circuits that were incorporated into amplifiers and CD players). Pumfrey J explained that 'the circuit itself is a reproduction because it still contains all the literary content of the literary work, albeit in a form which would require analysis for it to be extracted'.[48] Nevertheless, it is unlikely that the copyright in a novel that describes a particular scene will ever be infringed when someone draws it.[49] This may be because the description is unlikely to be sufficiently detailed.[50]

2.2 SOUND RECORDINGS AND FILMS

The definition of 'reproduction' used in relation to films and sound recordings is narrower than that used in relation to literary, dramatic, musical, and artistic works. These are what Arnold J has referred to, writing extrajudicially, as 'signal' copyrights.[51] As we saw earlier, entrepreneurial works (or, in EU parlance, 'related rights'), which are seen as the product more of investment than of creativity, are given a 'thinner' protection than is given to authorial works.[52] This is reflected in the fact that the scope of the reproduction right is inextricably linked to the way in which the particular work is defined.[53] Sound recordings are defined as the 'recording of sounds from which the sounds may be reproduced',[54] Consequently, what is protected in relation to sound recordings is not the content per se—the song, storyline, plot, or language—or the music or lyrics (which are protected, if at all, as authorial works). Instead, copyright protects the 'signal'—that is, the recording of these sounds. Similarly, because a film is defined as a recording on a medium from which a moving image may be produced, the courts have held that film copyright protects the recording of the image (rather than the image itself).[55] Although the Court of Justice has yet to confirm this, there is no reason to suspect that it would come to any other conclusion.

---

[45] *Brigid Foley v. Ellot* [1982] *RPC* 433; *Autospin (Oil Seals) v. Beehive Spinning* [1995] *RPC* 683, 701.

[46] *Autospin (Oil Seals) v. Beehive Spinning* [1995] *RPC* 683, 698.   [47] [1998] *FSR* 651.

[48] Ibid., [10]. Cf *Moon v. Thornber* [2012] *EWPCC* 37, [98]–[99].

[49] Laddie et al., [3.152]–[3.153]. See the German litigation over 'Pippi Longstocking': BGH (Federal Court of Justice), 17 July 2013—*Pippi-Langstrumpf-Kostüm* (Pippi-Longstocking-Costume) [2014] *GRUR* 258, (2014) 45 *IIC* 467; B. Clark, '"Freckles on her nose, diddle diddle dee": copyright protection of a literary figure' (2013) 8(3) *JIPLP* 817.

[50] *Autospin (Oil Seals) v. Beehive Spinning* [1995] *RPC* 683, 701.

[51] R. Arnold, 'Content Copyrights and Signal Copyrights: The Case for a Rational Scheme of Protection' (2011) 1 *QMJIP* 272.   [52] The protection is limited to the 'signal' rather than 'content'.

[53] This is not the case with photographs, where the copyright extends to the content or arrangement, not only the 'recording': *Creation Records v. News Group Newspapers* [1997] *EMLR* 444, 450.

[54] CDPA 1988, s. 5A(1)(a).   [55] CDPA 1988, s. 5B(1); *Norowzian v. Arks (No. 1)* [1998] *FSR* 394.

One of the consequences of reproduction being defined very narrowly is that copyright in a sound recording of a speech is not infringed where a person transcribes the speech; and copyright in a film (in EU parlance, a fixation) is not infringed when somebody writes a description of the film, or stages a play replicating events in the film. Likewise, the reshooting of a film sequence (in which not a single frame of the copyright film had been included) was held not to be a copy for the purpose of the CDPA 1988.[56] Similarly, copyright in a sound recording is not infringed where a person remakes (or 'covers') the same song or records the same song performed in a similar style (also known as a 'sound-alike').[57] However, it should be noted that while an entrepreneurial copyright will not be infringed where a new recording of identical or similar sounds or images is made, this might infringe copyright in an underlying work such as the music, lyrics, or screenplay,[58] or violate some other intellectual property right.[59]

Having observed that the reproduction right in relation to films (i.e fixations) and sound recordings is confined to the reproduction of the recording, it should be noted that the recording will be treated as having being reproduced even though the recording medium has changed (as long as the particular sounds or images embodied on the claimant's recording are replicated). For example, a reproduction occurs where a person records a film that is being screened in a cinema on a digital camcorder, or uploads or downloads a sound recording from the Internet. Even though the Act does not specify that copying of a film or sound recording includes storing it by electronic means, there is no room for doubt that it does.

2.3 BROADCASTS

The 1988 Act provides little guidance as to what it means to 'copy' a broadcast. However, it is clear that the making of an audio-recording of a radio broadcast or a video-recording of any image forming part of a television broadcast would amount to a reproduction of the broadcast (as well as the contents of the broadcast, be they sound recordings, films, or other works). In contrast with some jurisdictions, UK law does not differentiate between the first fixation and other reproductions of broadcasts.[60] Following the logic of entrepreneurial copyright, it seems that the reproduction of a broadcast protects only the information, sound, and images sent through particular signals. Thus a person would not infringe if they were to summarize a broadcast, or describe its contents. Similarly, the right to copy the broadcast would not be infringed if someone were to broadcast exactly the same sound recordings in the same order as had been used by another broadcaster.

2.4 TYPOGRAPHICAL ARRANGEMENTS

The scope of the reproduction right in relation to typographical arrangements is very narrow. This is because copying of a typographical arrangement means making a facsimile copy of the arrangement.[61] Although 'facsimile' is defined to include enlargements and reductions,[62] it seems to be confined to reproduction by way of reprography, photocopies,

---

[56] *Norowzian v. Arks (No. 1)* [1998] *FSR* 394, 400. This is the case even if the second film closely resembles and imitates the claimant's copyright film, or reproduces the essential features of that film.

[57] Ibid., 394; *CBS Records v. Telemark* (1988) 79 *ALR* 604, (1987) 9 *IPR* 440.

[58] *Norowzian v. Arks (No. 1)* [1998] *FSR* 394.

[59] For example, by passing the recording off as the recording of the claimant; cf. *Sim v. Heinz* [1959] 1 *WLR* 313, [1959] *RPC* 75 (CA).   [60] Cf. Rel. Rights Dir., Arts 6 (fixation), 7 (reproduction of fixations).

[61] CDPA 1988, s. 17(5).   [62] CDPA 1988, s. 178.

digital scanning, faxing, and little more. Retyping a work in a different font is a sure way of avoiding infringement of copyright in the typographical arrangement.

3 THE DISTRIBUTION RIGHT

The owner of copyright in all categories of work is given the right to issue copies of the work to the public under section 18 of the CDPA 1988. This is commonly known as the 'distribution right'.[63] The provision is understood to implement various provisions of European copyright law,[64] the most important of which is Article 4 of the Information Society Directive.

The distribution right is given in respect of the issuing of each and every copy (including the original).[65] As such, it needs to be distinguished from a right to make the works available to the public for the first time (that is, a 'publication' or 'divulgation' right of the kind previously recognized in UK law).[66] Essentially, the distribution right is a right to put each tangible copy (which has not previously been circulated) into commercial circulation.[67] Once particular copies are in circulation (at least where the first circulation was consensual), the right no longer operates in relation to those objects. Because the right of distribution does not include 'any subsequent distribution',[68] copyright owners cannot control resale.[69]

3.1 DISTRIBUTION

Although section 18 refers to 'issuing' copies to the public, the Directives use the term 'distribution'.[70] Recent case law of the Court of Justice exhibits a tendency to define the concept very broadly.

In *Peek & Cloppenburg*,[71] the Court was asked whether distribution 'by sale *or otherwise*' (the words of Article 4(1) of the Information Society Directive) could be interpreted to encompass display in a shop of an article for use by customers as well as display in a shop window. The Court rejected such a broad interpretation of distribution, taking the view that distribution is primarily defined as an act involving transfer of ownership, and the phrase 'or otherwise' was limited to situations in which ownership of the goods was transferred.[72]

---

[63] The 1988 Act has been amended twice in this regard to implement the Software Dir., Art. 4(c), and the original Rel. Rights Dir., Art. 9.

[64] Software Dir., Art. 4(c); Rel. Rights Dir., Art. 9; Database Dir., Art. 5(c); Info. Soc. Dir., Art. 4 (which, in turn, implements WCT, Art. 6). [65] CDPA 1988, s. 18(4).

[66] For example, through so-called 'common law copyright' in unpublished works before 1912.

[67] Info. Soc. Dir., Art. 4(1), refers to distribution 'by sale or otherwise', whereas CDPA 1988, s. 18, refers to 'putting into circulation'. Info. Soc. Dir., Recital 28, indicates that distribution relates to distribution in the form of a 'tangible article'.

[68] CDPA 1988, s. 18(3)(a). Rel. Rights Dir., Art. 9(2), and the Software Dir., Art. 4(c), refer to exhaustion on 'first sale', whereas Info. Soc. Dir., Art. 4(2), allows for exhaustion in cases of 'first sale or other transfer of ownership in the Community'.

[69] This corresponds with the idea of exhaustion of rights. Note, however, the resale royalty right: see Chapter 13, section 6, pp. 386–9.

[70] Info. Soc. Dir., Art. 4 (distribution to the public 'by sale or otherwise'); Database Dir., Art. 5(c) ('any form of distribution to the public'); Rel. Rights Dir., Art. 9 ('right to make available to the public, by sale or otherwise'); Software Dir., Art. 4(c) ('any form of distribution to the public, including the rental').

[71] *Peek & Cloppenburg SA v. Cassina SpA*, Case C-456/06 [2008] *ECR* I–2731(ECJ).

[72] Or its functional equivalent. Thus it seems an act will be seen as transferring ownership even if it is 'dressed up' as an indefinite loan: *UsedSoft GmbH v. Oracle*, Case C-128/11, EU:C:2012:407 (ECJ, Grand Chamber).

Despite the conclusion in *Peek & Cloppenburg*, in the *Donner* and *Dimensione Direct* cases,[73] the Court indicated that 'distribution' can encompass a series of acts: advertising,[74] agreement to sell, sale, and subsequent delivery.[75] Moreover, a distribution occurs with each of these acts. Thus if a sale transaction occurred in one member state in which a work is unprotected, but delivery occurs in a second member state in which the work is protected, there may be infringing distribution in the latter member state (even if there is none in the former).

At first sight, the *Donner and Dimensione Direct* cases are in tension with *Peek & Cloppenburg*; the latter focused on the act of 'transfer of ownership', whereas the former appears to envision other acts that do not involve transfer of ownership (advertising, agreement to sell, delivery). However, the key to their reconciliation is that *Peek* is to be understood now as limited to display of goods other than for sale.[76]

Under conventional principles, a person is only primarily liable for their own acts. Therefore, it is also worth noting that in *Donner* the Court stated that a trader 'bears responsibility' for any act carried out by him or on his behalf giving rise to a 'distribution to the public'. The acts of the third party are 'attributed to him', where the trader specifically targeted the public of the state of destination and must have been aware of the actions of that third party.[77] In doing so, the Court used language that comes very close to 'accessory' liability (in English terms, joint tortfeasance).[78] There has been no legislative harmonization of the concepts and the Court, in the trade mark context, has acknowledged this.[79] The Court in *Donner* showed no such scruples.[80]

3.2 TO THE PUBLIC

What is to be understood by the limitation of the right to distribution 'to the public'? On its face, it would exclude from liability the distribution of infringing copies within a small personal network, such as a family network, or within a firm (including between subsidiaries). However, a transfer of a copy between two individual entities at arm's length—say, a retailer to a wholesaler—would seem to be a distribution to 'the public'. Further sale, from the wholesaler to the consumer, would not require further permission.

---

[73] *Donner,* Case C-5/11, EU:C:2012:370, [26]–[30].

[74] *Dimensione Direct Sales Srl, Michele Labianca v. Knoll International SpA,* Case C-516/13, EU:C:2015:315, [2015] *ECDR* (12) 223, [25]–[32] (ECJ) (holding that there is distribution if an advertisement 'invites consumers of the Member State in which that work is protected by copyright to purchase it', even if no-one does).

[75] Note the analogous reasoning in relation to 'communication to the public' in *Football Dataco Ltd v. Sportradar GmbH,* Case C-173/11 [2013] 1 *CMLR* (29) 903 (ECJ). See section 6.4, pp. 173–4.

[76] Copinger rightly observes, [7–140], CDPA s. 18 fails to cover many of the acts that EU law now treats as 'distribution'.

[77] *Football Dataco Ltd v. Sportradar GmbH,* Case C-173/11 [2013] 1 *CMLR* (29) 903 (ECJ), [27].

[78] See Chapter 48, section 3.4, pp. 1287–9. UK copyright law has its own, narrow version, that is 'authorization'. R. Arnold and P. Davies, 'Accessory Liability for Intellectual Property Infringement: The Case of Authorisation, (2017) 133 *LQR* 442.

[79] See Chapter 48, section 3.4, pp. 1287–9, and *Google France,* Cases 236/08–238/08 [2010] *ECR* I–2417, [57], [AG114]–[AG125] (AG Poiares Maduro); *L'Oréal SA v. eBay International AG,* Case C-324/09 [2011] *ECR* I–6011, EU:C:2011:474 (ECJ, Grand Chamber), [104], [AG55]–[AG56]; *Frisdranken Industrie Winters BV v. Red Bull GmbH,* Case C-119/10 [2011] *ECR* I–13179, [35].

[80] Note also section 6.3, pp. 169–73, where the CJEU has extended the notion of 'communication' into the zone of what would, traditionally, have been thought of as accessory liability.

3.3 EXHAUSTION

The distribution right applies to the first issuing of a copy; thereafter, the copy can be resold. This is the principle of 'exhaustion', first recognized in the context of trade between member states, but extended by the Directives into the definition of the right and thus equally applicable to transactions within member states.[81] The Directives make clear that for there to be exhaustion, the act of sale or transfer must be by the rights holder or with their consent and must occur within 'the Community' (though, in fact, the principle extends to copies placed on the market anywhere in the European Economic Area). Moreover, the legislation makes clear that exhaustion occurs in relation to the distribution right and that there will only be exhaustion of that right (and not, in particular, of the rental right).

It is suggested that, despite the variations in language between the Directives, there is nothing special about 'sales', and the distribution right is exhausted by each and every act of distribution (as understood in *Peek & Cloppenburg*)—that is, transfer of ownership. This certainly is what the United Kingdom does in section 18 of the CDPA 1988, through the notion of 'issue'. Moreover, extending exhaustion beyond 'sale' reflects the idea that, by transferring ownership, the transferor confers on the transferee the normal incidents of ownership of personal property, which include the capacity to resell. From a pragmatic perspective, too, the question of whether an initial act of transfer had been made by way of a 'sale' is a matter that would often be difficult to investigate.[82]

It had been widely assumed that the distribution right applied only to the distribution of tangible copies.[83] One consequence of this was that there would be no exhaustion where digital copies were made available electronically to consumers.[84] This view was supported by reference to Recitals 28 and 29 of the Information Society Directive: the former refers to the right of distribution as a right to control distribution of 'tangible articles' and to exhausting the right to control resale of 'that object'; while the latter states that 'the question of exhaustion' does not arise in the case of services and 'online services in particular' even 'with regards to a material copy . . . made by a user of such a service'. Moreover, the different characteristics of 'electronic copies' could justify treating them differently from tangible ones: in contrast with physical copies, which deteriorate to such an extent that the market for new and second-hand copies (of books, records, or DVDs) are relatively distinct, in the case of electronic copies, no such deterioration occurs. From an economic perspective, second-hand copies of digital goods are actually 'as good as new'.

---

[81] Software Dir., Art. 4(c); Database Dir., Art. 5(c); Info. Soc. Dir., Art. 4(2); Rel. Rights Dir., Art. 9(2). The various directives define the scope of exhaustion in different terms. The Software and Database Directives refer to 'the first sale . . . of a copy', the Info. Soc. Dir. to the 'first sale or other transfer of ownership . . . of that object', and the Rel. Rights Dir. to 'the first sale . . . of that object'.

[82] See Chapter 41, section 8.2, pp. 1140–1. But cf, *Aleksandrs Ranks v. Finanšu un ekonomisko noziegumu izmeklēšanas prokoratūra, Microsoft Corp.*, Case C-166/15, EU:C:2016:762, [43]–[44] (ECJ) (in relation to exhaustion of electronic copies, differentiating between 'back up' copies made by the transferee, in relation to which there is no exhaustion, and copies received directly from the copyright-holder).

[83] A. Ohly, 'Economic Rights', in E. Derclaye (ed.), *Research Handbook on the Future of EU Copyright Law* (2009), 237–8.

[84] Cf. A. Perzanowski and J. Schultz, 'Digital Exhaustion' (2011) 58 *UCLA L Rev* 889 (reviewing benefits of US concept of exhaustion and articulating a continued need in the digital context).

However, the Court of Justice has rejected such an interpretation (at least) in the context of the Software Directive. In *UsedSoft GmbH v. Oracle*,[85] the Court held that the exhaustion doctrine applies to computer programs made available electronically where the substance of the arrangement is to transfer the copy to the user for an indefinite period (and thus is functionally the same as a sale of a copy on a CD-ROM). Nevertheless, there are special features of such electronic copies which mean that further transfer is subject to a number of conditions, including a requirement that the reseller themselves destroy their own copy.[86] A later decision clarified that there is no exhaustion of lawfully made 'back-up' copies. [87]

The Court acknowledged that there were good reasons to treat other works in the same way as computer programs, but also left room in its decision for a different interpretation of the different provisions of the Software Directive and the Information Society Directive. In particular, Recital 28 of the latter Directive and the Agreed Statement relating to the distribution right in the WIPO Copyright Treaty refer to tangible articles (and Recital 29 states that 'the question of exhaustion does not arise in the case of services and on-line services', even with respect 'to a material copy of a work or other subject-matter made by a user of such a service with the consent of the rightholder').[88] A further decision will be necessary before we can be confident about the application of the exhaustion principle in relation to intangible copies of works other than computer programs.[89]

Moreover, even with respect to computer programs, the decision in *UsedSoft* seems likely to generate further questions: is a licence that permits use of a program for 100 years, but no longer, a sale? If not, can copyright holders avoid the implications of the Court's decision by means of this simple drafting device? Or will the Court insist that the matter be one of substance, so that there is a sale whenever permission to use extends for as long as the predicted life of the program?

---

[85] Case C-128/11, EU:C:2012:407 (Grand Chamber), [47], [49], [58], and [61]. The case has spawned a host of commentary: B. Batchelor and D. Keohane, 'UsedSoft—Where To Now for Software Vendors?' [2012] *ECLR* 545; C. Stothers, 'When is Copyright Exhausted by a Software Licence?: UsedSoft v. Oracle' [2012] *EIPR* 787; R. Hilty and K. Koklu, 'Software Agreements: Stocktaking and Outlook—Lessons from the *Oracle v. UsedSoft* Case from a Comparative Law Perspective' (2013) 44 *IIC* 263; L. Longdin and P. H. Lim, 'Inexhaustible Distribution Rights for Copyright Owners and the Foreclosure of Secondary Markets for Software' (2013) 44(5) *IIC* 541 (comparing the position on resale of digitally distributed software in the European Union, United States, and New Zealand); O-A Rognstad, 'Legally Flawed but Politically Sound' (2014) *Oslo Law Review* 1; K. Moon, 'Resale of Digital Content: *UsedSoft* v *ReDigi*' [2013] *EIPR* 193; E. F. Schulze, 'Resale of Digital Content such as Music, Films or eBooks under European Law' [2014] 3 *EIPR* 9; M. Savic, 'The Legality of Resale of Digital Content after UsedSoft in Subsequent German and CJEU Case Law' [2015] *EIPR* 414–29; G Mazziotti, 'Is Geo-Blocking a Real Cause for Concern in Europe?' [2016] *EIPR* 365, 368.   [86] *UsedSoft GmbH v. Oracle*, Case C-128/11, EU:C:2012:407, [78], [87].
[87] *Aleksandrs Ranks v. Finanšu un ekonomisko noziegumu izmeklēšanas prokoratūra, Microsoft Corp.*, Case C-166/15, EU:C:2016:762, [43]–[44] (ECJ) (this was so even where the recipient had damaged, destroyed, or lost the original material medium: [53]).
[88] Info. Soc. Dir., Recital 29.
[89] Some regard *Art & Allposters*, Case C-419/13, EU:C:2015;27 (ECJ) as indicating that exhaustion relates only to the marketing of tangible articles: see, e.g., E. Rosati, 'Online exhaustion' [2015] 10 *JIPLP* 673. However, we doubt the Court was attempting to address an issue of such economic significance as this one in a tangential observation in a case concerned with very different facts: *Vereniging Openbare Bibliotheken v. Stichting Leenrecht*, Case C-174/15, EU:C:2016:459, [AG54] (AG Szpunar) (case 'in no way touched' issue of digital exhaustion). A reference has been made by the Court of the Hague, in a case concerning the resale of ebooks by the Dutch business 'Tom Kabinet': *Nederlands Uitgeversbond*, Case C-263/18 (pending).

3.4 LEGITIMATE REASONS TO OPPOSE FURTHER COMMERCIALIZATION

In general, then, a copyright owner cannot prevent resale of works placed on the market in the European Economic Area (EEA). Copyright law stands thus in contrast with trade mark law, which explicitly allows the trade mark holder to prevent further commercialization of goods bearing its mark, even though they have been placed on the market, if there are 'legitimate reasons' to do so.[90] Nevertheless, a similar qualification might apply in relation to copyright. In *Art & Allposters International BV v. Stichting Pictoright*,[91] the Court of Justice was asked to consider the limits to the exhaustion principle in relation to a practice of taking lawfully marketed posters of famous artworks and transferring the image onto canvas for resale. The claimant was Pictoright, a Dutch collecting society, which represents the interests of artists, and they argued that the distribution right is infringed by this practice. The Court agreed, though it offered three inter-related reasons for its conclusion. First, at a textual level, it noted that the exhaustion principle applied only in relation to the 'object' transferred or sold: as a result of the process, the defendant presented the claimant's picture on a different object, and could not claim exhaustion in relation to that 'object'.[92] Second, the Court suggested that the process of transfer of the image itself involved reproduction, and therefore the sale by the defendant was of a copy that had not previously been marketed with the right holder's consent.[93] Third, and finally, the Court noted that the market for the object sold by the claimant, and that of the defendant were different, and in particular that there were significant differences as to what consumers were willing to pay.[94] Quite which of these reasons can be said to be the true *ratio* of the case is difficult to say. We have doubts, in particular, about the Court's assumption that there was a 'reproduction'; if this were regarded as the *ratio*, it would seem that a copyright owner would not be able to prevent circulation of modified copies, as had occurred in a Dutch case in which pictures from a Christmas calendar, in which rights had been exhausted, were removed from the calendar and sold as entities in their own right.[95] We also feel uncomfortable with making the answer dependent on a level of divergence in the conditions of the markets for the object (which would seem to require a judgement to be made about when there are 'significant' differences of value between two markets), though we acknowledge that this is likely to affect a copyright owner's inclination to intervene.

Ultimately, then, the most convincing of the three reasons offered is that which relates to the transformation of the 'object'.[96] If this is the true *ratio*, questions will arise as to

---

[90] See Chapter 41, section 8.3, pp. 1143–8.   [91] Case C-419/13, EU:C:2015:27 (ECJ).

[92] *Art & Allposters*, Case C-419/13, EU:C:2015;27 (ECJ) [35], [39].

[93] Ibid., [43]–[46]. This reflected the French submissions and had attracted the Advocate-General, though he had sought to answer the questions put in their own terms (i.e. the distribution right): EU:C:2014: 2215, [AG53], [AG73]–[AG74]. It may be that the key to understanding the Court's 'reproduction' analysis lies in the fact that the image was being applied to the same sort of article as the original, so that the defendant transformed a copy in the form of derivative work, an image *of* a painting on a poster, to 'a copy' in the sense of *another painting*.

[94] *Art & Allposters*, Case C-419/13, EU:C:2015;27 (ECJ), [48].

[95] *Poortvliet v. Hovener* (19 September 1979) (Supreme Court of the Netherlands), discussed in F. Verkade, '"First Sale" or Exhaustion Doctrine in the Netherlands', in P. B. Hugenholtz, A. Quaedvlieg, and D. Visser (eds), *A Century of Dutch Copyright* (2013), 304, who argues that 'a physical transformation of a physical copy prevents exhaustion'.

[96] This seemed to be the primary reason offered by the Advocate-General, at [AG76]–[AG77], who declined to try and offer an abstract rule as to when a change in the object would be 'sufficiently significant', that there was no exhaustion.

when two objects are the same: presumably a mounted and/or framed poster is not a different object from a poster; but is a collection of monthly issues of a journal a different object once it has been sent for binding? And is a work of architecture, dismantled piece by piece and reassembled in a different location 'a different object'? Moreover, as is clear from *UsedSoft*,[97] a digital copy is not to be regarded as a different object from the copy originally purchased (at least where that copy has been destroyed). One test for a change in the identity of the object for these purposes might be whether the object has a new and different function, but as the case itself shows, this cannot be the only manner in which the 'nature' of the object is determined (as the image on paper has the same function as the image on canvas). In addition, focusing on the transformation of the 'object' leaves unclear the answer to the question whether the right owner might object where the *object* remains the same, but the *work* has been transformed. Can the owner of copyright in a painting, for example, complain about its resale where *the image* has been altered? Can a photographer complain where an artist creates a collage that includes a published photograph by the photographer?[98] As we will see (in Chapter 10), this is the province in part of authors' 'moral right of integrity', as well as the adaptation right (in international law),[99] though, in the absence of full copyright harmonization in the European Union, one could imagine the rules on exhaustion being adapted to protect author right holders from such acts.

3.5 IMPORTATION

The distribution right is exhausted by distribution in the EEA.[100] Consequently, if a copy is legitimately put on the marketplace in the Netherlands, and then imported into the United Kingdom and sold, the importation and sale in the latter state does not infringe the issuing right (or constitute secondary infringement). The corollary of Union-wide exhaustion is that there is no 'international exhaustion' and that the distribution right should be usable to prevent importation of copies into the EEA from outside.[101] This was confirmed (as a matter of EU law) by the Court of Justice in *Laserdisken ApS v. Kulturministeriet*.[102] The UK implementation is achieved by means of somewhat convoluted drafting.[103]

But is 'importation' itself distribution? While importation need not involve a change in ownership, so falls outside the definition of 'distribution' offered in *Peek & Cloppenburg*,[104] the Court has subsequently held that, where distribution in the recipient state would be illegal, the importation of the goods is illegal. *Blomqvist v. Rolex SA*[105] concerned a counterfeit Rolex watch (apparently the subject matter of some sort of copyright), which a consumer purchased from a Chinese vendor through an Internet site and which was in the process of being sent to the customer. The Danish customs authorities confiscated the watch and proposed to destroy it, an act to which the customer objected. Drawing on the *Donner* decision (rather than concerning itself with any niceties of ownership),[106] the

[97] *UsedSoft GmbH v. Oracle*, Case C-128/11, EU:C:2012:407.

[98] This was the example that the United Kingdom gave in its intervention: see [AG32]. See further, S. Stokes, 'Copyright and Artistic Practice' [2016] *Ent LR* 172.

[99] [AG55]–[AG60] (discussing, in particular, Berne, Art. 12).   [100] CDPA 1988, s. 18(3).

[101] Info. Soc. Dir., Recital 28.   [102] Case C-479/04 [2006] *ECR* I–8089 (ECJ).

[103] CDPA 1988, s. 18(3)(b), subject to the proviso that refers back to s. 18(2)(a).

[104] In contrast to the TMD 2015, Art. 10(3)(c), (which defines use of a trade mark as including importation of goods under the sign), there is no explicit mention of importation in the Info. Soc. Dir.

[105] Case C-98/13, EU:C:2014:55 (ECJ), [28]. See also *Independiente Ltd v. Music Trading On-Line (HK) Ltd* [2007] *EWHC* 533 (Ch), [2007] *FSR* 525; *KK Sony Computer Entertainment v. Pacific Game Technology Ltd* [2006] *EWHC* 2509 (Pat).   [106] *Donner*, Case C-5/11, EU:C:2012:370.

Court of Justice held that the Danish authority was entitled to prevent the importation of the watch.

4 THE RENTAL AND LENDING RIGHTS

While subsequent distribution of copies of the work is not generally within the control of the copyright owner, an owner of copyright in literary, dramatic, or musical works, artistic works (other than works of architecture or applied art),[107] sound recordings, and films is granted an exclusive right to rent and lend copies of such works to the public (CDPA 1988, section 18A).

Rental and lending both involve the making of the original or a copy of a work available for use on terms that it will or may be returned.[108] The distinction between 'rental' and 'lending' is that the act of rental involves making the work available 'for direct or indirect economic or commercial advantage', whereas lending occurs where there is no such advantage.[109] It has been suggested that rental might include the situation in which DVDs are loaned to hotel guests.[110]

Lending means 'making a copy of the work available for use, on terms that it will or may be returned, otherwise than for direct or indirect economic or commercial advantage, through an establishment which is accessible to the public'.[111] The right does not cover loans between private individuals. This is because lending is only prohibited when it is made 'through an establishment which is accessible to the public'. Lending does not become a rental, at least as regards loans between establishments accessible to the public, where payment does not go beyond what is necessary to cover the operating costs of the establishment.[112]

When the Rental Directive was adopted, rental of tangible copies of films was particularly common, with retail outlets such as Blockbuster stores featuring on every high street. It was easy to understand that owners of copyright in films regarded such uses as interfering with their returns from public playing at cinemas and broadcasting. However,

---

[107] Rel. Rights Dir., Art. 2(3). Apparently, these were excluded because it was thought that the rental right would then cover rental of housing, cars, etc.

[108] CDPA 1988, ss 18A(2), 18A(6), 182C(2) (performers); cf. the terms of Rel. Rights Dir., Art. 1 ('making available for use, for a limited period of time'). The Rel. Rights Dir., and the 1988 Act both contain a number of limitations to the rental and lending rights: first, neither covers the making available of a copy for public performance, playing or showing in public, or broadcast for example, where a cinema owner rents a film from a film distributor; second, neither rental nor lending covers situations in which a work, such as a painting, is made available for the purposes of exhibition in public; third, the rental and lending rights do not cover situations in which a work is made available for on-the-spot reference, for example, magazines are made available in waiting rooms; and fourth, 'lending' does not cover the making available of a work between establishments that are accessible to the public, making permissible 'inter-library loans'. See J. Griffiths, 'Copyright and Public Lending in the United Kingdom' [1997] *EIPR* 499, 500. All these points, however, are thrown into question by some of the broadest visions of the 'communication right'.

[109] Cf. Software Dir., Recital 16 ('rental' is the making available of a computer program for use, for a limited time, and for 'profit-making purposes').

[110] Although strangely—and we think certainly erroneously—the Court of Justice has treated some such acts as 'communication to the public': *Phonographic Performance (Ireland) Ltd v. Ireland*, Case C-162/10 [2012] 2 *CMLR* (29) 859 (ECJ), [62]–[63].

[111] CDPA 1988, s. 18A(2)(b). For exemptions for educational establishments and libraries, see Chapter 9, section 13, p. 266, and section 14, p. 268; for the 'public lending right' compensation scheme, see Chapter 13, section 6, pp. 385–6.

[112] CDPA 1988, s. 18A(5), reflecting the Rel. Rights Dir., Recital 14.

in the quarter of a century since the adoption of the Directive, video rental has collapsed, and it has become much more common to offer temporary access to works in electronic form. Is such activity (so-called 'e-lending') also within the scope of this right? In *VOB*,[113] the Court differentiated between rental and lending, concluding that lending included the temporary making available of a digital copy,[114] but that rental did not.[115] The differential treatment was justified by reference to international law: Article 7 of the 1996 WIPO Copyright Treaty required recognition of a rental right,[116] but not a lending right, and for the former indicates that in that context the concept of 'originals' and 'copies' is limited to fixed copies.[117]

While we are sympathetic to the idea that rental and lending must be interpreted to include what, in a different technological environment, are functional equivalents,[118] we are surprised about the attempt to distinguish between rental and lending in this respect. First, we observe that the Directive introducing the rental and lending right was adopted in 1992, several years before the diplomatic conference in 1996 which agreed the WIPO Copyright Treaty. It is odd that the meaning of 'rental' should be dictated by subsequent adherence to that Treaty.[119] Second, the WIPO Copyright Treaty establishes minimum standards: its terms do not prevent a contracting party from extending rental to digital rental. It is hard to see that there would be any 'conflict' between it and EU law even were rental to include 'digital rental'.[120] Third, in so far as 'digital rental' would count as 'communication to the public' under Article 8 of the WIPO Copyright Treaty, we do not see that this obligation could not be fulfilled in the European Union by way of the rental right (for example, if the European Union took the view that something that amounted to rental or lending was not, for that reason, communication to the public under EU law.)[121] As the question of electronic rental was not, in fact, in issue in *VOB*, we think that the statements to the effect that such rental is not encompassed by the rental right cannot be regarded as having conclusively settled the matter (in common law terms, they were 'obiter dicta'). If electronic rental were regarded as falling within the scope of the 'rental right', it might be that 'video on demand' would be regarded as rental,[122] and that authors and performers would be entitled to an unwaivable right to equitable remuneration from such exploitation.[123]

[113] *Vereniging Openbare Bibliotheken (VOB) v. Stichting Leenrecht*, Case C-174/15, EU:C:2016:856. For an intelligent commentary, see V. Breemen, 'E-Lending according to the ECJ: Focus on Functions and Similar Characteristics in *VOB v. Stichting Leenrecht*' [2017] *EIPR* 249.

[114] *Vereniging Openbare Bibliotheken (VOB) v. Stichting Leenrecht*, Case C-174/15, EU:C:2016:856, [54].

[115] Ibid., [34]–[35].   [116] Ibid., [30]–[34], [39].

[117] WCT, Agreed Statement concerning Arts 6 and 7; *Vereniging Openbare Bibliotheken (VOB) v. Stichting Leenrecht*, Case C-174/15, EU:C:2016:856, [34].

[118] Ibid., [45], [53]. See also EU:C:2016:459, [AG30]–[AG31], [AG73].

[119] The Court in *Vereniging Openbare Bibliotheken (VOB) v. Stichting Leenrecht*, Case C-174/15, EU:C:2016:856, [31], relies on Recital 7 of Dir. 2006/115, but as Advocate-General Szpunar recognizes at EU:C:2016:459 [AG24], that Directive merely codified Directive 92/100, where Recital 10 was in precisely the same terms.   [120] Rel. Rights Dir., Recital 7.

[121] Compare Advocate-General Szpunar's treatment of the supposed overlap between 'lending' and 'communication to the public' at EU:C:2016:459, [AG55], [AG65].

[122] Downloading for a limited time (e.g. from the BBC iPlayer) would certainly be equivalent, though most video on-demand depends on streaming, a practice that has distinct features (in that a copy of the whole work is not in the control of the user at any given time).

[123] On the equitable remuneration right, see Chapter 12, section 2.4, p. 333 and Chapter 13, section 2.3.3, pp. 360–1. Indeed, similar reasoning was thought to justify interpreting lending to cover electronic lending: EU:C:2016:459, [AG34]–[AG36].

5 THE PUBLIC PERFORMANCE RIGHT

The fourth right conferred on a copyright owner is the right to perform the work in public (CDPA 1988, section 19).[124] This right, which is usually known as the 'performing right', was first introduced by statute in 1833 to protect owners of copyright in dramatic works.[125] This was because, since the primary way in which dramatic works are exploited is by way of performance, if the protection given to dramatic works were to be limited to the reproduction right, this would have been inadequate. In order to be consistent, the performing right was also extended to musical works and literary works in general. Today, section 19(1) of the 1988 Act provides that performance of a work in public is an act restricted by the copyright in a literary, dramatic, or musical work; section 19(3) states that the playing or showing of the work in public is an act restricted by the copyright in a sound recording, film, or broadcast. There is no performing right for artistic works (and hence no right to authorize the public exhibition of the work)[126] or for typographical arrangements (see Table 6.2).

5.1 EUROPEAN DIVISION BETWEEN PERFORMANCE AND COMMUNICATION

As already observed, there has been harmonization of the 'communication to the public right', but not the 'public performance right' (see Table 6.1). Unfortunately, the European categories do not map onto the division in UK law between section 19 and section 20 of the 1988 Act. But quite what division the EU categories require is more difficult to say. The answer matters, insofar as the tests adopted by the Court of Justice (for example the test of 'the public') differ from the tests adopted in domestic law.

Under UK law, the term 'performance' is defined in section 19 as including the 'delivery' of lectures, addresses, speeches, and sermons, as well as 'any mode of visual or acoustic presentation of a work', such as by means of a sound recording, film, or broadcast. Performance is distinguished from communication to the public in that, in the case of performance, the public must be present at the place where the performance occurs, the recording is played, or the film or broadcast shown.

Importantly, in this latter respect, the British performance right covers some of the ground of the European 'communication to the public' right, which has been held to cover cases in which the public is not present where the communication *originated* (rather than where the showing occurred). Thus, in *Football Association Premier League v. QC Leisure*, the Court of Justice held that the showing of a broadcast of a football match on a screen in a public house was a communication to the public, whereas it would fall squarely within section 19(3) of the 1988 Act.[127] Subsequently, the Court also held that there was a communication to the public when a cafe played to its customers songs broadcast by a radio broadcasting station, by means of a radio apparatus connected to loudspeakers and/or amplifiers.[128] In contrast, in *Circul*

---

[124] M. F. Makeen, 'Rationalising Performance "in Public" under U.K. Copyright Law' [2016] *IPQ* 117.

[125] See *Russell v. Smith* (1848) 12 QB 217, 236.

[126] But see moral right of attribution, discussed in Chapter 10, section 2.2.2, p. 291.

[127] *FAPL*, Joined Cases C-403/08 and C-429/08 [2011] *ECR* I–9083 (ECJ, Grand Chamber), [200]–[203]; cf. the opinion of Advocate-General Kokott at [AG144]. Subsequently, Kitchin J. confirmed that there is indeed overlap, and that showing a broadcast in a pub infringes both CDPA s. 19 and s. 20: *FAPL v. QC Leisure* [2012] *EWHC* 108 (Ch), [63].

[128] *Sociedade Portuguesa de Autores CRL v. Ministério Público* et al., Case C-151/15, EU:C:2015:468 (ECJ) (Order). Note also *Technische Universität Darnstadt v. Eugen Ulmer KG*, Case C-117/13, EU:C:2014:2196, [42] (ECJ) (making available scan of book on dedicated terminal in library was communication to the public).

Globus Bucureşti, the Court affirmed that the playing of live music before a circus audience constituted public performance, rather than communication to the public, and that, because 'public performance' is unharmonized, it is not a matter regulated by European law.[129]

Quite whether showing a film or playing a jukebox (clearly covered in UK law under section 19(2)(b) and (3)) is to be understood in European terms as a 'public performance' or 'communication to the public' has yet to be conclusively determined.[130] Given the Court's inclination to deepen harmonization, we think that the interpretation the Court is most likely to adopt is that the unharmonized public performance right relates only to live performances.[131] However, even this conclusion creates its own anomalies.[132]

5.2 LOCATION

It has been held that a performance of a musical work (or a sound recording, if this still falls within the domestic performance right) takes place where it can be heard.[133] Presumably, a performance of a film (if there can be such a thing) takes place where it can be seen. Where the performance is live, it should be fairly obvious who is responsible for the performance. Where an apparatus is used, it is the person who operates the mechanism.[134]

5.3 'IN PUBLIC' (UNDER DOMESTIC JURISPRUDENCE)

In order to infringe, the performance must be carried on 'in public'. There are many situations in which it is clear that a performance is in public: a performance at the Brixton Academy, the Royal Albert Hall, a West End theatre, or in a public house would normally all be to the public. Beyond these examples, however, what is meant by 'in public' is less clear.[135] Over time, three different conceptions of the 'public' have been used in the case law.

---

[129] *Circul Globus Bucureşti (Circ & Variete Globus Bucureşti) v. Uniunea Compozitorilor şi Muzicologilor din România*, Case C-283/10 [2011] *ECR* I–12031 (ECJ).

[130] It may be implicit from *Phonographic Performance (Ireland) Ltd v. Ireland*, Case C-162/10 [2012] 2 *CMLR* (29) 859 (ECJ), [62]–[63], that playing sound recordings counts as 'communication to the public'. *Technische Universität Darmstadt v. Eugen Ulmer KG*, Case C-117/13, EU:C:2014:2196, [42] (ECJ) (seems also to support the view that any mediated representation is to be regarded as communication). In its reasoning in *FAPL*, Cases C-403/08 and C-429/08 [2011] *ECR* I–9083, [188], the Court of Justice sought to interpret Art. 3 of the Info. Soc. Dir. and Art. 8 of the Rel. Rights Dir. in the light of the international treaties. However, on this question, the international treaties offer different answers for films and sound recordings. Article 14(1)(ii) of the Berne Convention might support the view that showing a cinematographic work is a 'public performance', whereas Article 2 of the WIPO Performances and Phonograms Treaty (WPPT) points towards a different conclusion in relation to sound recordings. But surely direct representation of a film and sound recording must be treated in the same way by European law?   [131] Ibid., [193].

[132] Public karaoke would thus involve public performance of the lyrics and communication to the public of the sound recording; so the performance of compositions of the scores of twentieth-century avant-gardist composer K.-H. Stockhausen's *Kurzwellen*, which includes instructions to play radio, would equally involve public performance and communication to the public, possibly by the very same act. The complexity that these sort of situations generate suggests that: (i) in the short term, when defining what constitutes 'the public' in relation to the performance right, national courts should realign national case law with Court of Justice case law on the meaning of the 'public' under the right of communication to the public; and (ii) in the longer term, the whole regime of rights, and indeed the whole of copyright, would benefit from full harmonization (on which, see Chapter 2, section 8.2, pp. 56–7).   [133] *PRS v. Camelo* [1936] 3 *All ER* 557.

[134] *PRS v. Hammond's Bradford Brewery Co.* [1934] 1 *Ch* 21; *Messager v. BBC* [1927] 2 *KB* 543, 548.

[135] *Jennings v. Stephens* [1936] 1 *Ch* 469, 476, 481; *Harms v. Martans* [1927] 1 *Ch* 526, 530.

In some cases, the concept of the public is understood according to the 'character of the audience'.[136] In this context, a distinction is drawn between a section of the general public (which has no unifying theme other than the desire to see the performance) and a group of people who share a private or domestic link.[137] Using a test of this sort, a performance in a shop,[138] before members of a club,[139] or in a hotel lounge[140] would be a performance to a 'section of the general public' (so long as anyone could enter the shop, join the club, or enter the hotel lounge), but a performance at a dinner party,[141] or to students at a boarding school,[142] would be treated as a performance to a 'section of the general public'.

Another test that has occasionally been employed to determine whether a performance is in public focuses on whether the performance is motivated by financial considerations.[143] If the performance is run for profit, it is likely to be 'in public'.[144]

A third test has focused upon the copyright owner's monopoly. Under this approach, a performance is 'in public' if it is made to or before 'the copyright owner's public'. This test, which first emerged in the 1930s, later came to be quite widely adopted. In *Jennings v. Stephens*,[145] the performance of a play *The Rest Cure* by the members of a women's institute without charge and without guests was held to be a performance in public. Greene LJ said:

> [T]he expression 'in public' must be considered in relation to the owner of the copyright. If the audience considered in relation to the owner of the copyright may properly be described as the owner's 'public' or part of his 'public', then in performing the work before that audience he would in my opinion be exercising the statutory right conferred upon him.[146]

This test has been used to hold that the playing of the BBC's music broadcasts to 600 workers in a factory infringed the performing right.[147] This test seems prone to manipulation, since it is surely the case that most copyright owners would want to extend their monopoly as widely as possible and would therefore claim that all performances were before their 'public'?[148]

While uncertainties exist over the relationship between the three tests, it should be clear that, historically, the notion of public has been defined increasingly expansively, so as to favour the copyright owner. It is clear that performances in places that are open to the public (from hairdressers' salons to hotel lounges) are performances in public; as are performances before substantial numbers of people not connected by family or domestic ties. The consequences of the different approaches to defining 'the public' now remain to be felt only in marginal cases (such as the case of a band, including the bride's brother, performing at a wedding reception).

---

[136] *Jennings v. Stephens* [1936] 1 *Ch* 469, 476, 479; *PRS v. Harlequin* [1979] 2 *All ER* 828, 833.

[137] *Duck v. Bates*, (1884) 13 *QBD* 843 (CA) (no infringement through performance of play by an amateur dramatic club at Guy's Hospital for the entertainment of the nurses, the event being regarded as 'domestic').

[138] *PRS v. Harlequin* [1979] 2 *All ER* 828.

[139] *Harms v. Martans* [1927] 1 *Ch* 526, 537 (emphasizing that there was an invitation to the general public to become members of the club). [140] *PRS v. Hawthorns Hotel (Bournemouth)* [1933] *Ch* 855.

[141] *Jennings v. Stephens* [1936] 1 *Ch* 469, 481. [142] Ibid., 483.

[143] *Harms v. Martans* [1927] 1 *Ch* 526, 532–3 (CA) (treating as infringing a performance of a musical work to an audience of 150 members of a club and 50 guests, since the members paid a substantial subscription and an entrance fee and the club paid the orchestra). [144] Ibid.

[145] [1936] 1 *Ch* 469. [146] Ibid., 485.

[147] *Ernest Turner Electrical Instruments v. PRS* [1943] 1 *Ch* 167 (Lord Greene MR). This would now count as 'communication to the public', so the EU test would govern the outcome.

[148] See *PRS v. Harlequin Record Shops* [1979] 2 *All ER* 828, 834.

With regard to the infringement of the performing right, it is important to bear in mind that there are a number of related acts of secondary infringement. These are considered in Chapter 8.

6 THE COMMUNICATION RIGHT

Section 20 of the CDPA 1988 confers on the owners of copyright in literary, dramatic, musical, artistic works, films, sound recordings and broadcasts,[149] a right to communicate the work to the public, which includes the right to broadcast it and the right to make it available.[150] The right is often referred to as 'the communication' right. The communication right has taken on pre-eminent importance over the last century, first with the rise of radio and television broadcasting, cable and satellite, and more recently as a consequence of the Internet. Perhaps because of the importance of the right in a rapidly changing technological and business environment, the right is attended with significant uncertainty. In turn, the Court of Justice has been faced with a large number of references and has struggled to offer a consistent interpretation.[151] Matters are exacerbated by the fact that the regional norms differentiate between authors' rights on the one hand[152] and related rights on the other,[153] which, in turn, are informed by provisions in international law.[154] In what follows, we begin by discussing the concepts of 'communication', and the

---

[149] But note that a broadcasting organization's right to prevent communication to the public of its broadcasts is subject only to 'minimal harmonization under EU law': Rel. Rights Dir., Recital 16 allows 'more far-reaching protection': *C More Entertainment AB v. Linus Sandberg*, Case C-279/13, EU:C:2015:199 (ECJ). See, further, *ITV Broadcasting v. TV CatchUp Ltd* [2011] *EWHC* 1874 (Pat), [79] (Floyd J) (holding amendment to CDPA s 20(1)(c), effected under the European Communities Act 1972, creating a general communication right even for broadcasting organizations not to have been *ultra vires*).

[150] *ITV Studios Ltd v. TV Catch Up Ltd* [2010] *EWHC* 3063 (Ch) (Kitchin J) (rejecting view that, in UK implementation, communication comprised two rights, broadcasting and making available, and nothing more).

[151] See, in particular, the Advocate General's Opinion in *Renckhoff*, Case C-161/17, EU:C:2018:279. Cf. *Reha Training Gesellschaft für Sport- und Unfallrehabilitation mbH v. Gesellschaft für musikalische Aufführungs- und mechanische Vervielfältigungsrechte eV (GEMA)*, Case C-117/15, EU:C:2016:109, [AG43] (describing the case-law as 'abundant and consistent').

[152] Under Art. 3(1) of the Info. Soc. Dir., member states are to confer on authors the exclusive right of communicating a work to the public, which 'includes' the making available of that work in such a way that members of the public may access the work from a place and at a time individually chosen by them. This is over and above the right to communicate the work by satellite, which was harmonized in Art. 2 of the Satellite Dir. and which is left intact by the Info. Soc. Dir.

[153] As regards related rights, the right to control broadcasting and communication to the public were harmonized in the Rel. Rights Dir. of 1992 (which was amended by the Satellite Dir. to clarify that broadcasting included communication to the public by satellite). The Info. Soc. Dir. added the right of making available as a stand-alone right: Info. Soc. Dir., Art. 3(2). In this context, then, 'broadcasting' and 'communication to the public' are also distinguished. In the case of performers and owners of copyright in sound recordings, the right of communication and broadcasting is couched as a right to remuneration; Rel. Rights Dir., Art. 8(2) (conferring right to remuneration). For broadcasting organizations, also, communication (which has a particular definition) and making available are two distinct rights. Info. Soc. Dir., Art. 3(2) (making available); Rel. Rights Dir., Art. 8(3) (communication right).

[154] First, the Berne Convention lacks an overarching concept of communication to the public, offering specific rights for specific works. It was only with the WCT that a new generalized right was recognized for authorial works. Second, as regards the case of performers and owners of copyright in sound recordings, the Rome Convention envisaged a shared right to equitable remuneration where a sound recording was communicated or broadcast: Rome, Art. 10. In 1996, the WPPT conferred on each an exclusive right of making available: WPPT, Art. 10.

notion of 'the public', before examining 'broadcasting' and 'making available', which now appear to be treated as sub-categories of 'communication to the public' to which special rules apply.

6.1 COMMUNICATING

Under CDPA 1988, section 20, a right to communicate a work to the public arises with respect to literary, dramatic, musical, and artistic works, sound recordings, films, and broadcasts.[155] The right was introduced in this form to implement the Information Society Directive.[156]

There is no doubt that many important activities fall clearly within the scope of 'communication'. A core example of a 'communication' is an electronic transmission of a work, such as Internet 'streaming'.[157] In addition, it would clearly cover the emailing of digital material to those on email lists.[158] However, the concept of communication to the public has generated considerable case law, and not inconsiderable confusion, as the Court of Justice has interpreted it to embrace a disparate range of activities (from installation of TVs in hotel rooms to playing the radio at a rehabilitation centre, and from posting a hyperlink to supplying TV set-top boxes).[159] Justifying its approach, the Court of Justice has explained, that it is required to afford a 'high level of protection' and to interpret the concept 'broadly'.[160] More enigmatically, the Court states that when deciding whether a particular act is communication to the public 'individual assessment' is required and this will involve consideration of several complementary, but interdependent, considerations.[161]

Not surprisingly, then, it is difficult to identify the boundaries of what counts as 'communication' with much clarity. Nevertheless, at present, a communication requires five elements: (i) an intervention to give access to or experience of works or other subject matter (the 'intervention' condition); (ii) going beyond the mere provision of physical facilities; (iii) to a public that is not present at the place where the work or subject matter originate; (iv) when it would not otherwise have had such access (the 'indispensability' condition); and (v) which is a deliberate act, carried out by a person with full knowledge of 'the consequences' (the 'intention' requirement). We look at each element in turn.

---

[155] CDPA 1988, s. 20.

[156] Info. Soc. Dir., Art. 3, itself implementing WCT, Art. 8; Rel. Rights Dir., Art. 8(3), Recital 16.

[157] *FAPL v. British Communications* [2017] *EWHC* 480 (Ch), [33] (Arnold J). In terms of economic importance to the music industry, streaming (e.g. by services such as Spotify and Deezer) is rapidly outstripping the making available of copies through download (e.g. by iTunes). The same is true of the film industry where DVD sales have fallen quickly as new streaming services such as Netflix became available. See M. Sweeney, 'Film and TV Streaming and Download Overtake DVD Sales for the First Time', *The Guardian*, 5 January 2017.

[158] This would not be a broadcast, because reception is not simultaneous.

[159] C. Angelopoulos, *European Intermediary Liability in Copyright: A Tort-Based Analysis* (2017), 56–64; J. Groom, I. Silverman, and B. Clark, 'Still Lost in the Labyrinth?' [2017] *EIPR* 591.

[160] Referring to Info. Soc. Dir, Recitals 9, 10, 23: *Stichting Brein v. Ziggo BV and XS4All Internet BV*, Case C-610/15, EU:C:2017:456, [22] (ECJ) (high level); *Verwertungsgesellschaft Rundfunk GmbH v. Hettegger Hotel Edelweiss GmbH*, Case 641/15, EU:C:2016:795, [AG14] (AG Szpunar) (a 'very broad right') (AG Szpunar); *Reha Training Gesellschaft für Sport- und Unfallrehabilitation mbH v Gesellschaft für musikalische Aufführungs- und mechanische Vervielfältigungsrechte eV (GEMA)*, Case C-117/15, EU:C:2016:379, [36] (ECJ, Grand Chamber) (interpret broadly).

[161] *Phonographic Performance (Ireland) Ltd v. Ireland*, Case C-162/10 [2012] 2 *CMLR* (29) 859 (ECJ), [29]–[30]; *Reha Training*, Case C-117/15, EU:C:2016:379, [35] (ECJ); *GS Media BV v. Sanoma Media Netherlands BV* et al, Case C-160/15, EU:C:2016:644, [33]-[34] (ECJ); *Wullems*, Case C-527/16, EU:C:2017:300 (ECJ), [30]; *Stichting Brein v. Ziggo BV*, Case C-610/17, EU:C:2017:456 (ECJ).

(i) The Intervention Condition Although some CJEU case law has equated 'communication' with 'transmission',[162] most jurisprudence applies a lower threshold. Instead it is said that 'first and foremost' amongst the factors that determine whether there is 'communication' is the indispensable role of the user *whose intervention gives access to a work* that recipients would not otherwise enjoy.[163] In doing so, the Court has felt the need to define 'communication' in such a way that the specific right of 'making available' fits within it.[164] The test of 'intervening . . . to give access' focuses on protecting right holders against particular effects, and disregards the means by which those effects are produced.[165] As a result the 'intervention' test is significantly broader than 'transmitting' the work.[166]

Applying this test, the Court has indicated that there is an act of communication where a broadcast of sound recordings is played (as the playing gives the listener 'access' to the sounds on the phonograms), and also where a person creates a hyperlink to material freely available elsewhere on the Internet.[167] The Court has also found that there is 'communication' where a person sells a multimedia device loaded with links to streaming services,[168] where a platform created an index for and classifies files in order to facilitate peer-to-peer file sharing,[169] and perhaps most dubiously of all, where a hotel makes available a CD player and CDs in hotel rooms.[170] On the other hand, the Court has held that 'communication' does not cover the mere provision of television in hotel rooms.[171]

---

[162] The Grand Chamber of the Court of Justice in *FAPL*, Joined Cases C-403/08 and C-429/08 [2011] *ECR* I–9083, [193], stated that 'the concept of communication must be construed broadly, as referring to any transmission of the protected works, irrespective of the technical means or process used'. See also *Sociedad General de Autores y Editores de Espana (SGAE) v. Rafael Hotels SL*, Case C-306/05 [2006] *ECR* I–11519, [AG37]; *Circul Globus Bucureşti*, C-283/10, EU:C:2011:772, [40] (ECJ); *ITV Broadcasting v. TV CatchUp*, Case C-607/11 [2013] 3 *CMLR* (1) 1 (ECJ), [23]; *SBS Belgium NV v. SABAM*, Case C-325/14, EU:C:2015:764, [2016] *ECDR* (3) 74 (ECJ), [16]; *Reha Training*, Case C-117/15, EU:C:2016:379, [38]. Recital 23 says that the 'right should cover any such transmission or retransmission of a work to the public by wire or wireless means, including broadcasting', but should not cover any other acts. See also WPPT, Art. 2(g); *The Basic Proposal for the Treaty*, [10.15]–[10.16].

[163] *Phonographic Performance (Ireland) v. Ireland*, Case C-162/10 [2012] 2 *CMLR* (29) 859, [31] (ECJ); *SGAE*, Case C-306/05 [2006] *ECR* I–11519, [42] (ECJ).

[164] *Technische Universität Darmstadt v. Eugen Ulmer KG*, Case C-117/13, EU:C:2014:2196, [42] (ECJ) (making available is 'therefore' a communication). Indeed, if communication is defined this broadly, one might wonder why the legislature bothered with the 'making available' right (apart from in relation to related rights).

[165] As Advocate-General Szpunar explained in *Stichting Brein v. Ziggo BV and XS4All Internet BV*, Case C-610/15, EU:C:2017:99, [AG25], 'one should look for . . . the legal substance of certain acts, irrespective of the technical background to those acts'.

[166] Cf. CDPA, s. 20 (defining 'communication' as involving electronic transmission).

[167] *Svensson and ors v. Retriever Sverige AB*, Case C-466/12, EU:C:2014:76 (ECJ), [18]–[20]. For domestic application, see *Mackie v. Maxi Construction* [2017] SC LIV 11 (link to photograph was communication to public).

[168] *Stichting Brein v. Jack Frederik Wullems*, Case C-527/15, EU:C:2017:300 (ECJ), [39]–[42].

[169] *Stichting Brein v. Ziggo BV and XS4All Internet BV*, Case C-610/15, EU:C:2017:456 (ECJ), [35]; *EMI Records Ltd v. British Sky Broadcasting Ltd* [2013] EWHC 379 (Ch), [45]–[46] (website indexing BitTorrent files so as to enable users to access those files was 'communication to the public').

[170] *Phonographic Performance (Ireland)*, Case C-162/10 [2012] 2 *CMLR* (29) 859 (ECJ).

[171] *SGAE*, Case C–306/05 [2006] *ECR* I–11519, [AG27]; BGH (Federal Court of Justice) (17 December 2015)—*Königshof*, [2016] *Zeitschrift für Urheber- und Medienrecht* (Journal for Copyright and Media Law) 652 (holding that supplying hotel rooms with TV sets picking up the broadcasting signal with an indoor aerial is as such not an act of communication).

While we understand some of the motivation of the Court,[172] we think that the 'intervention' threshold is much too low: if communication really is that broad, then lending libraries, video rentals, bookshops (which permit browsing), retailers who have works of applied art on display, and even art galleries may be involved in communicating to the public.[173] Some of these acts are indeed within the copyright owner's rights, but under specific, carefully defined laws.[174] Moreover, the breadth of definition of 'communication' might interfere with fundamental rights.[175] It might be advisable for the CJEU to revisit the initial decision to define the 'intervention' that constitutes a communication quite so capaciously.[176]

(ii) More than Mere Physical Facilities Second, to communicate a work, a person must do more than provide 'mere physical facilities' that enable access to the work. This limitation on what counts as communication derives from Recital 27 (and in turn, the WIPO Copyright Treaty). Merely supplying television sets to a hotel is, of itself, therefore not 'communication'. However, it is hard to say what the Court regards as the trigger that changes provision of 'physical facilities', into something more, but it does not seem that a person need do much in order to go beyond 'mere' provision. For example, distributing signals collected from a central antenna to such televisions is enough to constitute communication.[177] Moreover, in *Stichting Brein v. Wullems*, the pre-installation of a structured menu of hyperlinks onto a multimedia player which enable users to have direct access to (unauthorized) streams went beyond the 'mere' provision of a physical facility.[178] Equally, in the *Ziggo* case,[179] which concerned the notorious torrent site, The Pirate Bay, the Court indicated that The Pirate Bay could not claim to have been engaged in 'mere provision' because the various acts of indexing and classifying of the torrent files made them readily accessible to users.[180] It seems that any act that involves the content being made accessible (as opposed to the mere technical infrastructure that can supply content) is sufficient to take an intervention beyond the 'mere provision' of physical facilities.

(iii) Public Not Present at Origination Third, for an act to count as communication, the act must give the public access to the work. We discuss the notion of 'the public' in more detail later, but for the moment it is important to note that, in the case of the communication right, the 'public' should not be 'present at the place where the communication originates'. This is because, if the public is present at the place where the communication originates, the act concerns the (unharmonized) public performance right (section

---

[172] One explanation is the unharmonized state of accessory liability—in English parlance, 'joint tortfeasance' (on which, see Chapter 48, section 3.4, pp. 1287–9). Reluctant to leave each member state to its own devices, the Court has chosen to include within 'communication' acts of 'knowing facilitating of communication'. This has in turn led the Court to invent vague and unpredictable knowledge criteria.

[173] *Phonographic Performance (Ireland)*, Case C-162/10 [2012] 2 *CMLR* (29) 859 (ECJ), [62]–[63]. Cf. the memorandum accompanying the Commission Proposal for what became the Info. Soc. Dir., COM(97) 628 final, 25, which stated: 'The expression "communication to the public" of a work covers any means or process other than the distribution of physical copies'.

[174] *Vereniging Openbare Bibliotheken (VOB) v. Stichting Leenrecht*, Case C-174/15, EU:C:2016:459, [AG55], [AG65].

[175] *GS Media BV v. Sanoma Media Netherlands BV* et al., Case C-160/15, EU:C:2016:644, [31].

[176] P. B. Hugenholtz and S. C. van Velze, 'Communication to a New Public? Three Reasons why EU Copyright Law Can Do Without a "New Public"', (2016) 47 *IIC* 796, 813.

[177] *SGAE*, Case C-306/05 [2006] ECR I-11519 EU:C:2006:764, [45] *ff* (ECJ).

[178] *Wullems*, Case C-527/15, EU:C:2017:300 (ECJ). Apparently, over one million such 'illegal streaming devices', often called KODI players (though KODI is itself legitimate software application until configured to access illegal streams), were sold in the United Kingdom 'over the last couple of years': FACT, *Cracking Down on Digital Piracy* (September 2017), 4.   [179] *Ziggo BV*, Case C-610/15, EU:C:2017:456, [38] (ECJ).

[180] Ibid., [38].

19).[181] Thus, for example, converting sounds into electronic signals and 'streaming' them is a communication (rather than a public performance); in contrast, live performance is not.[182] Significantly, the CJEU does not regard a communication as necessarily 'originating' in the place where it 'occurs', so a person who plays a radio broadcast in a dental surgery is regarded as communicating, because the communication originates at the place of broadcast, not the place where the radio is operated.[183]

(iv) The Indispensability Condition Fourth, the CJEU has said that the action of the user must be 'indispensable' or 'essential' to enable the public to access the work (or subject matter).[184] In many cases it has been suggested that this means the public in question would not have access but for the intervention: without the act, the public would be 'unable' to see or hear the work.[185] In the *GS Media* case, the Advocate-General presented this as a reason why hyperlinking to publicly accessible material should not normally be regarded as communicating that material to the public: the hyperlink is only 'indispensable' if it gives access to material that is not otherwise accessible (for example, because it is behind a paywall).[186] However, the Court did not appear to follow that reasoning,[187] and commenced the elaboration of a less exacting standard.[188] In particular, in the recent decision concerning The Pirate Bay, where the Court found that The Pirate Bay communicated the works made accessible by its users to the public, the Court did not require that the intervention render 'possible' access to the work that is otherwise 'impossible', but only that the intervention makes access 'less difficult' (or even 'less complex').[189] Because indexing and classifying made accessing the works much easier for users of the system, The Pirate Bay's intervention amounted to communication. If this standard is adhered to, a wide range of acts of facilitation may be regarded as communications.[190]

---

[181] Info. Soc. Dir., Recital 23.   [182] See section 5.1, pp. 157–8.

[183] *Società Consortile Fonografici (SCF) v. Marco Del Corso*, Case C-135/10, EU:C:2011:431, [AG125] ('the place where the communication originates . . . is . . . the place where the original performance or representation was recorded on the phonograms') (AG Trstenjak). The implication is that a film 'originates' on the film-set or in the editorial suite, and so is 'communicated' where it is shown. But, if so, does a painting not 'originate' in an artist's studio, and thus is communicated when displayed on an art gallery wall? The implications are worrying. See further P. Mysoor, 'Unpacking the Right of Communication to the Public' [2013] *IPQ* 166, 172–4.

[184] *SCF*, Case C-135/10, EU:C:2012:140, [82] (ECJ); *Ziggo BV*, Case C-610/15, EU:C:2017:456, [26] (ECJ).

[185] *SGAE*, Case C–306/05 [2006] *ECR* I–11519, [42] ('In the absence of that intervention, its customers, . . . would not, in principle, be able to enjoy the broadcast work'); *FAPL*, Joined Cases C-403/08 and C-429/08 [2011] *ECR* I–9083, [195] ('Without his intervention the customers cannot enjoy the works broadcast'); *SCF*, Case C-135/10, EU:C:2012:140, [82] (ECJ) (same); *Reha Training*, Case C-117/15, EU:C:2016:379, [46] ('otherwise would not be able to enjoy').

[186] *GS Media BV*, Case C-160/15, EU:C:2016:221 [AG54] (AG Wathelet) (hyperlinks which lead, even directly, to protected works do not *'make available'* those works to a public where the works are already freely accessible on another website, but merely facilitate the finding of those works).

[187] While (as we will see) the Court did not reach the same conclusion, it is not entirely clear that the Court rejected the analysis: see *GS Media*, Case C-160/15, EU:C:2016:644, [48], where the Court observed that: 'where the work in question was already available with unrestricted access on the website to which the hyperlink provides access, all internet users could, in principle, already have access to it even the absence of that intervention.'

[188] *GS Media*, Case C-160/15, EU:C:2016:644, [35] (citing existing tests but adding 'in particular', so that giving access where it would otherwise be unavailable is transformed into an example of a deliberate intervention to give access).

[189] *Ziggo BV*, Case C-610/15, EU:C:2017:456, [26]—[36], (ECJ); [AG50] ('less efficient') (AG Szpunar).

[190] See also *Wullems*, Case C-527/15, EU:C:2017:300 (ECJ), [31], [41] ('without which the purchasers would find it difficult to benefit from those protected works').

(v) The 'Intention' Requirement[191] Fifth, and finally, according to a series of Court of Justice cases, an act of communication to the public must be intentional, or deliberate, in the sense of the actor understanding the *consequences* of their acts.[192] In *Sociedad General de Autores y Editores de Espana (SGAE) v. Rafael Hotels SL*, the Court referred to the fact that the defendant hotel proprietor communicated signals that it received and relayed to hotel rooms 'to the public', because it 'is the organisation which intervenes, *in full knowledge of the consequences* of its action, to give access to the protected work to its customers'.[193] Similarly, in *FAPL*, in which the Court treated the showing of broadcasts of football matches in public houses as communication to the public, the Court stated that 'the proprietor of a public house *intentionally* gives the customers present in that establishment access to a broadcast containing protected works via a television screen and speakers'.[194]

The Court has yet to explain precisely what is meant by this, in particular the relevance of knowledge of the *illegal* (or *unauthorized*) status of the works being made accessible. In *Stichting Brein v. Ziggo*, Advocate-General Szpunar thought such knowledge was necessary for there to be liability (in the factual circumstances in front of him),[195] but the Court, while generally following his lead, did not expressly state such a condition, rather treating knowledge of the illegal nature of the material as relevant to whether it was made available to a 'new public'.[196] In other cases the notion of intentional intervention is contrasted with persons being 'caught by chance'.[197]

6.2 'TO THE PUBLIC'

In a series of cases, the Court of Justice has treated the definition of the public as a matter of European law and sought to elaborate what 'the public' entails.[198] Despite some initial indications to the contrary, the Court has held that the meaning of 'the public' is the same

---

[191] This requirement is surprising because, hitherto, UK law has operated on the basis that infringement of 'primary rights' is a matter of strict liability, the actor being liable for any volitional act falling within the scope of the rights (knowledge of the status of the material being relevant to 'secondary infringement'). Its inclusion seems to be a necessary corollary to the expansive interpretation of 'communication' to encompass accessory liability by facilitating infringement.

[192] *Stichting Brein v. Ziggo BV and XS4All Internet BV*, Case C-610/15, EU:C:2017:456, [34], (ECJ) ('full knowledge of the relevant facts', begging the question 'which facts are relevant?'). Later in the judgment, at [46], the Court develops the requirement of dealing with knowledge of illegality, but it seems this is a distinct, and additional requirement.

[193] Case C-306/05 [2006] *ECR* I–11519, [42] (emphasis added). See also *Societa Consortile Fonografica v. Marco Del Corso*, Case C-135/10 (ECJ), [82].

[194] Joined Cases C-403/08 and C-429/08 [2011] *ECR* I–9083 (ECJ, Grand Chamber), [195] (emphasis added). See also *Ochranný svaz autorský pro práva k dílům hudebnim, o.s. (OSA) v. Léčebné lázně Mariánské Lázně a. s.*, Case C-351/12, EU:C:2014:110 (ECJ), [26], [33].

[195] *Stichting Brein v. Ziggo BV*, Case C-610/15, EU:C:2017:99, [AG51]–[AG52] (requiring actual knowledge of illegal nature).

[196] *Stichting Brein v. Ziggo BV*, Case C-610/17, EU:C:2017:456, [45] (operators could not be unaware platform was used to provide access to material made available without the consent of the right holders), (ECJ).

[197] *SCF*, Case C-135/10, EU:C:2012:140, [91] (though here the comment is made in the context of the relevance of 'profit-making'), [98] ('They have access to certain phonograms by chance and without any active choice on their part, according to the time of their arrival at the practice and the length of time they wait and the nature of the treatment they undergo'); *Reha Training*, Case C-117/15, [48] (in the context of the 'new public').

[198] *SGAE v. Rafael Hotels SL*, Case C-306/05 [2006] *ECR* I–11519 (ECJ).

under the Related Rights Directive and the Information Society Directive; therefore, the concept must be assessed according to the same criteria.[199]

6.2.1 'The public'

Although the legislation simply refers to communication to 'the public', the jurisprudence developed by the Court of Justice differentiates two issues: first, whether the work or subject matter is made accessible to a 'public', and second, whether it is a 'new' public.

It will usually be simple to answer the first question. If a film is streamed over the Internet or a film of a football match is shown in a public house, the communication is 'to the public'. However, as with the question of when a performance is 'in public' there will be some tricky borderline cases. The CJEU has referred to three inter-related criteria that define a 'public':

(i) the size of the group. If the group is 'fairly large', it will likely comprise the public (though the 'group' need not be in the same place at the same time, or even in the same place at all).[200]

(ii) the character of the group. The Court has suggested that the public comprises 'an indeterminate number of potential' listeners or viewers, as opposed to 'a private group';[201] and

(iii) the character of the communication. The Court has emphasized that it is relevant whether the communication is made with a view to making a profit, and whether the consumers were targeted or present by chance.[202]

Applying these criteria, the Court has held that communicating films and sound recordings to hotel guests (albeit in the privacy of their rooms), to residents at a health spa,[203] and individual subscribers to a remote recording system,[204] all constitute communication to 'the public', but—perhaps surprisingly—that playing a radio broadcast of sound recordings to patients attending a dental surgery does not.[205] In the latter instance, the Court explained that the number of patients was small, and apparently a stable, relatively determined group, and the activity was neither profit-making nor a technique for

---

[199] *Reha Training Gesellschaft für Sport- und Unfallrehabilitation mbH v. Gesellschaft für musikalische Aufführungs- und mechanische Vervielfältigungsrechte eV (GEMA)*, Case C-117/15, EU:C:2016:379, [31]–[34]. For commentary, see J. Koo, 'Walking Forward with Backward Facing Feet: The CJEU Decision in Reha Training and the Development of the Communication to the Public Right' (2016) 11 *JIPLP* 732.

[200] *SCF*, Case C-135/10, EU:C:2012:140, [84] (fairly large number), [86]; *VCAST v. RTI SpA*, Case C-265/16, EU:C:2017:913, [47] (ECJ) (communicating to individual subscribers the recordings they had requested be made of television programmes was communication to 'the public' given 'the sum of the persons targeted').

[201] *SGAE*, Case C-306/05 [2006] *ECR* I-11519 [37], [38]; *SCF*, Case C-135/10, EU:C:2012:140, [84]–[85]; *SBS*, Case C-325/14, EU:C:2015:764, [21]; *Zurs*, Case C-138/16, EU:C:2017:218 [24]; *Wullems*, Case C-527/15, EU:C:2017:300, [3]. In *ITV Broadcasting v. TV CatchUp*, Case C-607/11 [2013] 3 *CMLR* (1) 1 (ECJ), [33]–[36], the Court indicated that a large number of individual transmissions to individuals could be to an indeterminate number and therefore was to a public.

[202] *Societa Consortile Fonografica v. Marco Del Corso*, Case C-135/10 [2012] *ECDR* (16) 276, [88], [90]–[91]. The 'profit-making' quality of a transmission is relevant, but not essential to whether it is 'to the public': *ITV Broadcasting v. TV CatchUp*, Case C-607/11 [2013] 3 *CMLR* (1) 1 (ECJ), [42].

[203] *OSA*, Case C-351/12, EU:C:2014:110 (ECJ); *Reha Training*, Case C-117/15, EU:C:2016:379 (patients in a rehabilitation centre).

[204] *VCAST v. RTI SpA*, Case C-265/16, EU:C:2017:913, [47] (ECJ).

[205] *Societa Consortile*, Case C-135/10 [2012] *ECDR* (16) 276 (ECJ).

attracting business.[206] In contrast, in a parallel case concerning music in hotel rooms, the number of guests was 'fairly large', their character was 'indeterminate' ('persons in general'), and the facility was offered as part of a package to attract visitors to a profit-making enterprise.[207] One Advocate-General has suggested that the dentist surgery decision be confined 'to the specific factual circumstances which gave rise to the judgment'.[208]

6.2.2 A 'new public'

Although a communication may be to a public, the Court has indicated that this will not necessarily lead to a finding of liability if the communication is of material that has already been communicated with the right holder's consent. In cases in which there has been an 'initial communication', a retransmission or communication of that initial communication will fall within the right only if it is a communication to a new public.[209] The notion of the 'new public', which Graeme Dinwoodie has described as 'an (at best) enigmatic concept',[210] was first deployed in *SGAE*.[211] There, the Court considered how, if the author had licensed the broadcast, they could be entitled to object to its retransmission to hotel rooms. The Court observed that this was a public that was distinct from that which the 'author' had in mind when it licensed the broadcast. Drawing on the *WIPO Guide to the Berne Convention*, the Court adopted the concept of a 'new public' as being critical in cases in which there is some sort of public retransmission of a work that has already been communicated.[212] Moreover, the Court observed that the provision of access to broadcasts was 'an additional service' provided by the hotel and 'profit-making'.[213] Consequently, the distribution of signals by cable to customers staying in its rooms was a 'communication to the public'. The requirement that there be a 'new public' has been reiterated in a number of subsequent cases.[214]

What constitutes a new public? The test offered by the Court of Justice purports to require an examination of the expectations of the author when the initial communication was made.[215] If the author hoped, or expected, the work to be received by a particular group, then merely doing an act that assists that aim does not make the work available to a new public. Thus if a broadcaster is given permission to broadcast a work and, in addition

---

[206] In *SCF,* the Court said, at [95], that a group of dental patients was a 'determinate' number, a consistent group, and not the public in general. No evidence was referred to in the judgment as to the character of the provision of dental services in Italy. The Court said, at [96], that, even viewed sequentially, the number of patients was not large; indeed, it was 'insignificant'. Details of the actual number were not provided. The Court indicated, at [97]–[99], that the playing of music was not profit-making and did not attract patients.

[207] *Phonographic Performance (Ireland)*, Case C-162/10 [2012] 2 *CMLR* (29) 859 (ECJ), [41]–[43].

[208] *Reha Training*, Case C-117/15, EU:C:2016:109, [AG55] (AG Bot).

[209] For persuasive criticism of the 'new public' criterion, see P. B. Hugenholtz and S. C. van Velze, 'Communication to a New Public? Three Reasons Why EU Copyright Law Can Do Without a "New Public"' (2016) 47 *IIC* 797; S. Karapapa, 'The Requirement for a "New Public" in EU Copyright Law' [2017] *ELR* 63. However, before the 'new public' component is abandoned, the policy concerns that have motivated the Court would need to be reflected in other doctrines: for example, a more limited concept of 'communication' coupled with a tailored notion of accessory liability (and possibly an unfair competition norm).

[210] G. B. Dinwoodie, 'A Comparative Analysis of Secondary Liability of Online Service Providers', in Dinwoodie (ed.), *Secondary Liability of Online Service Providers* (2017), 14.

[211] Case C-306/05 [2006] *ECR* I-11519.   [212] Ibid., [40]–[41].   [213] Ibid., [44].

[214] Ibid., [42]; *Airfield NV*, Joined Cases C-431/09 and C-432/09 [2011] *ECR* I-9363 (ECJ), [77]; *FAPL*, Joined Cases C-403/08 and C-429/08 [2011] *ECR* I-9083 (ECJ, Grand Chamber), [197]; *ITV Broadcasting v. TV CatchUp*, Case C-607/11 [2013] 3 *CMLR* (1) 1 (ECJ), [39]; *Svensson v. Retriever Sverige AB*, Case C-466/12 EU:C:2014:76 (ECJ), [24]; *OSA*, Case C-351/12, EU:C:2014:110 (ECJ), [31]; *Reha Training*, Case C-117/15, EU:C:2016:379, [45].

[215] *Airfield NV*, Joined Cases C-431/09 and C-432/09 [2011] *ECR* I-9363, [76].

to the initial broadcast, uses 'booster' aerials to ensure that the same signal gets to its audience, then the use of the boosters would not involve broadcasting to a new public.[216]

However, if the author is found to have contemplated a specific public and a user transmits the work to a further public, then that act requires authorization from the right holder. In the hotel room cases, the Court found that the expectation of right holders who permitted broadcasts was that they would be received by the owners of domestic television sets and their families; thus further transmission to others, for example hotel guests, was to a new public.[217] The same would be true of playing a radio or television in a cafe.[218]

Moreover, if a user utilizes 'new technical means' to retransmit a work, then the Court of Justice has suggested this is per se a transmission to a new public (or that the 'new public' requirement does not apply). Thus, in *ITV Broadcasting v. TV CatchUp*,[219] there was a communication to the public when an Internet-based service captured television signals and retransmitted them at an individual subscriber's request to that individual. The individual recipients were confined to those who would have been entitled to receive the signals from the free-to-air broadcasts (that is, holders of television licences resident in the United Kingdom). TV CatchUp added advertising before sending the signals. The Court rejected the defendant's argument that, because the public was already entitled to view the programmes/broadcasts, there was no communication to a 'new' public. Instead, it found that 'each transmission or retransmission of a work which uses a specific technical means must, as a rule, be individually authorized by the author of the work in question'.[220] Because the defendant streamed the broadcast 'under specific technical conditions, using a different means of transmission for the protected works', it did not matter that, in principle, the recipients were part of the public targeted by the initial communication.[221] While the result in the *TV CatchUp* case seems consistent with those in the hotel transmission cases, the reasoning is different. Indeed, those cases could have been resolved more readily on the basis that transmission to the television sets was a 'new technical means'.

The doctrine established in *TV CatchUp* was both acknowledged and then ignored in *AKM v. Zürs.net Betriebs GmbH*.[222] The case related to an action brought by a collecting society seeking information from a cable network operator which transmitted broadcasts including those of the national broadcaster. Having referred both to Art. 11*bis*(1)(ii) of the Berne Convention, which requires that authors be granted a right to control communication to the public by wire or rebroadcasting of a broadcast of a work whenever the communication is made by an organization other than the original one,[223] and to the established jurisprudence that every transmission or retransmission which uses a specific technical means must, as a rule, be individually authorized by the author,[224] the conclusion ought to have been relatively straightforward. Indeed, the Court observed that Zürs.net used a technical means different from that of the broadcaster.[225] However, the Court

---

[216] *FAPL*, Joined Cases C-403/08 and C-429/08 [2011] *ECR* I–9083 (ECJ, Grand Chamber), [194]; *Airfield NV*, Joined Cases C-431/09 and C-432/09 [2011] *ECR* I–9363, [74], [79]; *ITV Broadcasting v. TV CatchUp*, Case C-607/11 [2013] 3 *CMLR* (1) 1 (ECJ), [28].

[217] *SGAE*, Case C–306/05 [2006] *ECR* I–11519, [41]; *FAPL*, Joined Cases C-403/08 and C-429/08 [2011] *ECR* I–9083, [198].   [218] Ibid., [199].

[219] *ITV Broadcasting v. TV CatchUp*, Case C-607/11 [2013] 3 *CMLR* (1) 1 (ECJ).

[220] Ibid., [24]. The proposition has been repeated in *Wullems*, Case C-527/15, EU:C:2017:300, [33]; *Ziggo BV*, Case C-610/15, EU:C:2017:456, [28] (ECJ).

[221] *ITV Broadcasting v. TV CatchUp*, Case C-607/11 [2013] 3 *CMLR* (1) 1 (ECJ), [39].

[222] Case C-138/16, EU:C:2017:218 (ECJ). The three judge Chamber was chaired by Judge Malenovský, who along with Safjan had sat in Case C-607/11, which Malenovský had also chaired.

[223] Ibid., [21].   [224] Ibid., [23].   [225] Ibid., [26].

determined that there was no communication to the public because there was no 'new public'. At least as regards the transmission of the broadcast by ORF, the copyright owners would have been 'aware that the broadcasts made by the national corporation may be received by all persons within the national territory'.[226] In so far as Zürs.net was distributing the signal within the national territory, the public that received the signals was not a 'new public'.[227] This conclusion takes the 'new public' analysis further than hitherto, and seems on its face inconsistent with a number of previous decisions, including many of the hotel cases (in so far as the hotels were relaying signals from national broadcasters). It seems likely that the case will be quickly recognized as an aberration or reversed by legislation.

6.2.3 Hyperlinking

The Court of Justice has used the 'new public' concept to regulate the legitimacy of hyperlinks. As already observed, the Court found in the *Svensson* case that creating a hyperlink involved 'communicating' the work to which the link led.[228] However, it did not suggest that every hyperlink would infringe; rather, the Court differentiated between linking to material that was generally available (with the consent of the right owner), and linking to material to which access had been limited. Linking to the former material involved no new technical means and was not a communication to a 'new public', and was thus non-infringing.[229] Linking to material that was secured behind technical measures (such as a paywall) would, in contrast, communicate it to a new public.[230]

In a subsequent decision, the Court applied its reasoning to 'framing' (or 'transclusion'), according to which the subject matter to which the link is made appears within the hyperlinker's frame, rather than giving the impression to the user of moving to the site where the material has already been made accessible. The Court found that the specific mode of linking used was irrelevant if the subject matter was not being communicated to a 'new public'.[231] Some commentators have been critical of this step, taking the view that a hyperlinker is involved in some form of misrepresentation when they utilize 'framing' rather than simple hyperlinking.[232] It might also be argued that if the licence granted by the copyright owner to the original site is remunerated by advertising, such transclusion, if permitted, might undermine that business model.

In a third case, *GS Media*,[233] the Court clarified that the new public principle was qualified where the work or subject matter had been made available on the Internet without the permission of the right holder. The case concerned the potential liability of a popular Dutch blog which had linked to nude pictures that had been illegitimately made available on an Australian website. The Court indicated that if a copyright work is freely available on the Internet but has been posted without the consent of the right holder, then *prima facie* the link communicates the work to a new public because the author had not contemplated making the work available to *any* public.[234] However, recognizing that such a conclusion might affect the free speech of many Internet users, who would not be able to know whether the material to which they are linking is authorized or not,[235] the Court

---

[226] Ibid., [28]. See *VCAST v. RTI SpA*, Case C-265/16, EU:C:2017:649, [AG52]-[AG53].   [227] Ibid., [29].

[228] *Svensson v. Retriever Sverige AB*, Case C-466/12, EU:C:2014:76 (ECJ), [24].

[229] Ibid., [24]-[30].

[230] See, e.g., the facts of *C More Entertainment AB v. Linus Sandberg*, Case C-279/13, EU:C:2015:199 (ECJ) (where defendant offered access to a service of streamed sports events that the claimant operates behind a paywall).   [231] *Bestwater International GmbH v. Mebes*, C-348/13, EU:C:2014:2315 (ECJ).

[232] M. Leistner, 'Closing the Book on Hyperlinks' [2017] *EIPR* 327.

[233] *GS Media BV v. Sanoma Media Netherlands BV* et al., Case C-160/15, EU:C:2016:644 (ECJ).

[234] Ibid., [39]-[43].   [235] Ibid., [44]-[46].

introduced a 'knowledge' component into the analysis. More specifically, it stated that whether a provider of a clickable link makes a communication to a new public depends on *whether they knew* or could not reasonably have not known the work was posted without the consent of the right holder.[236] If the provider of the link did not know, or could not reasonably have known, then there is no communication to the public.[237] But when the linker knows, there is a communication to the public.[238] Moreover, the Court added that if a linker is motivated by profit-making,[239] this gives rise to a rebuttable presumption of knowledge because 'when the posting of hyperlinks is carried out for profit, it can be expected that the person who posted such a link carries out the necessary checks to ensure that the work concerned is not illegally published on the website to which those hyperlinks lead'.[240] On the facts of the case, the Court suggested that as GS Media was operating for profit, and indeed knew that the photographs had been made available illegally, the posting of the hyperlink counted as a communication to the public.

The case generates both logical and practical questions. First, at a logical level, it is not at all obvious how, if a work is already very widely accessible on the Internet, so that no new audience is generated by adding a hyperlink, the unauthorized status of the material renders the act of creating the link a communication to a 'new public'. Nor is it obvious how a hyperlinker's absence of knowledge can transform an act of communication 'to the public' into an act of communication that is not 'to the public': the same people, after all, gain access to the subject matter irrespective of the knowledge of the linker.

Even if we overlook the absence of logic and just treat the judgment as establishing a series of positive rules, four practical questions arise as to the meaning of those rules. First, when is a hyperlinker to be regarded as profit-making? How close must the nexus be between the 'posting' of the link, and the profit? Second, how easily can the presumption be rebutted? Will it be sufficient to show that the links were created by an automatic system?[241] Third, when will a non-profit making hyperlink provider be regarded as having been in a position where they ought to have appreciated that the subject matter was uploaded without authorization? Fourth, if a person links to subject matter that they know was uploaded without authorization, but which they believe was lawfully uploaded (under an exception, for example, for purposes of reporting current events), will they escape liability?[242]

There is not room here to explore all these questions. One circumstance where the answers would seem to be really quite significant concerns search engines. If these are regarded, as seems likely, as profit-making entities, there is a danger they will be presumed to appreciate that the material they link to is unauthorized, and therefore to be regarded as 'communicating' that material to the public. That would be catastrophic for the Internet. Realistically, search engines cannot reasonably be expected to acquire such knowledge other than through some form of formal de-listing request.[243] Perhaps, the answer is that such search engines are not caught by *Svensson* and *GS Media*, as those

---

[236] Ibid., [47]–[49].   [237] Ibid., [47]–[48].

[238] Ibid., [49] ('knew or ought to have known that the hyperlink he posted provides access to a work illegally placed on the Internet').

[239] Ibid., [51] ('when the posting of hyperlinks is carried out for profit'); cf. ibid., [47] ('when the posting of a hyperlink is carried out by a person who, in so doing, does not pursue a profit').   [240] Ibid., [51].

[241] See especially the discussion in M. Leistner, 'Closing the Book on Hyperlinks' [2017] *EIPR* 327, 330.

[242] The Court, at [51], recognizes two elements: first whether the work/subject matter is protected; and, second, whether there is consent. It says nothing about where the work is protected but that no authorization is needed because the making available of the work is justified by an exception or limitation. However, at [53], the Court recognizes this as another reason why material might already be accessible.

[243] Indeed, the German Supreme Court has held that Google is not subject to the *GS Media* doctrine with respect to its image search: 1ZR 11/16—*Preview III* (21 September 2017).

authorities are limited to cases of 'posting' hyperlinks, rather than including links in individual search returns. Despite cases such as *VCAST* holding the transmission of individual subscriber-requested video recordings to be communications to 'the public', it is still possible that a link created in response to an individual search might not be treated as a communication 'to the public', as it is an automated process providing a link only accessible to a private individual (the searcher).

The *Svensson, Bestwater*, and *GS Media* cases seek to facilitate different legal responses to the range of different purposes to which hyperlinks are put. On the one hand, they recognize the fundamental role hyperlinks play in the operation of the Internet, and their regular use by the public in general. On the other, the Court is conscious that hyperlinking is a means of drawing attention to and spreading access to the vast quantities of illegal material on the Internet. This result might have been achieved better by differentiating between primary and accessory liability, excluding hyperlinking from the notion of 'communication' and instead regulating hyperlinking that facilitates piracy through accessorial liability. This was not the chosen course, and already the Court has found itself adding a knowledge element that seems quite distinct from the knowledge requirement that it has elaborated when determining whether there is a 'communication' at all.

6.3 WHO MAKES A COMMUNICATION?

Mostly, it will be clear who is responsible for making a communication or 'making available': the person who uploads the material onto the website, or who streams the material in question. However, occasionally, while it will be clear that there has been a communication of a work to the public, it will be less obvious *who* is responsible for the act. Take, for example, the vexed question of whether video-sharing platforms (such as 'You Tube', 'Daily Motion', 'Vimeo', or 'Vine') or social networking sites (such as 'Facebook', 'Twitter', 'Instagram', 'Snapchat'), are 'communicating' material which their users upload to the sites. The providers of this 'infrastructure' would argue that it is not they who communicate the works (indeed, they have no idea what is being uploaded), rather the users who upload the material. However, when one adds in features such as 'Auto-play' (on You Tube), such that an end-user of a video-sharing is presented automatically with a succession of automatically selected videos, the end-user experience starts to feel very similar to that of a person who has turned on a radio or television set. The operators of such sites would no doubt say that this is merely a structural feature, and does not transform them into persons who communicate. Rights holder groups, however, maintain that, even without such features, these actors are involved in 'communicating'. Who is right?

Traditionally, UK law has distinguished between primary liability and accessory liability (which we discuss in Chapter 48). For an accessory to be liable, they must have procured or induced an act, or it must have been the result of their common design.[244] In *Twentieth Century Fox v. Sky UK*, Birss J drew the distinction between communication to the public and accessory liability when considering the operator of a website, 'Popcorn Time', which was central to an arrangement that allowed peer-to-peer users to watch unauthorized streams of films.[245] The website allowed users to download, for free, an open-source application which enabled them to obtain content using the BitTorrent protocol. The copying took place between the 'peers', and the indexing and classification of the material that could be downloaded came from a different site (the SUI site, standing for 'source of update information'). Birss J found that 'Popcorn Time' was not communicating the films to the public, but merely providing a tool that would facilitate access to

---

[244] The same act could be both an act of primary liability and give rise to accessory liability for the acts of others: *Twentieth Century Fox Film v. Newzbin* [2010] *EWHC* 608 (Ch) (Kitchin J).

[245] [2015] *EWHC* 1082 (Ch), [17]–[24] for a full description of how 'Popcorn Time' operates.

the streams. Birss J found, likewise, that the SUI site was not communicating the works. Rather, taking into account the perspective of the users, it was the application (on their computers) that was the source of the communication.[246] Nevertheless, the judge did hold that the providers of the 'Popcorn Time' application were liable as accessories, jointly with the operators of the host websites. The application procured the user to access the host website and thereby to make the unauthorized communication.[247]

While a UK court can distinguish different forms of responsibility, unfortunately (in terms of legal coherence), only 'primary' liability has been harmonized within the European Union. Therefore, the Court of Justice is unable to utilize to the same effect the distinction between 'primary' and 'accessory' liability: for the CJEU to deem an act to involve 'accessory' rather than 'primary liability' would require it to decline to offer an answer to the question referred, and to leave the issue without a common, harmonized, answer. The Court has therefore tended to expand the concept of 'communication' rather than to address questions of responsibility.[248] Indeed, the implication is that many people involved in very different ways in a communication, might all be 'communicating' the work. This can perhaps be seen best in *Stichting Brein v. Ziggo BV*,[249] a case which concerned potential remedies against Internet access providers who gave subscribers access to the website The Pirate Bay. The question before the Court was whether The Pirate Bay had made a 'communication to the public'. As the facts revealed, no works are stored on the site, those works being made available by its users.[250] However, the Pirate Bay website did provide the software, the indexing, and classification of the material available. While Advocate-General Szpunar asked whether The Pirate Bay's involvement made them *jointly* responsible with the users for the acts of communication (finding that there was a simultaneous and joint act with the users),[251] the Court did not try to characterize the nature of the relationship between the act of the platform and that of each of its users. Rather, the Court found that the operators of the site *also* communicated the works to the public, because its acts of indexing, categorizing, and deleting defunct files, made access by their users to the works easier. The broad definition of communication had the necessary consequence that multiple actors in a chain could *all*, separately and distinctly, be regarded as legally responsible.

In many respects, this decision seems unsurprising. Given the name of the site, 'The Pirate Bay', and its notorious role in facilitating infringement of copyright, the Court would have found it difficult to resist offering an answer applicable throughout the European Union. Moreover, similar conclusions had already been reached by the High Court of England and Wales, first in the *Newzbin* case,[252] but more regularly in cases concerning so-called 'blocking injunctions'.[253] However, the *Ziggo* decision offers no clear guidance on

---

[246] Ibid., [40]–[42].   [247] Ibid., [55].

[248] G. B. Dinwoodie, 'A Comparative Analysis of Secondary Liability of Online Service Providers', in Dinwoodie (ed.), *Secondary Liability of Online Service Providers* (2017).

[249] Case C-610/15, EU:C:2017:456 (ECJ, Second Chamber).   [250] Ibid., [36].

[251] *Stichting Brein v. Ziggo BV and XS4All Internet BV*, Case C-610/15, EU:C:2017:99, [AG53].

[252] *Twentieth Century Fox Film v. Newzbin* [2010] *EWHC* 608 (Ch) (Kitchin J).

[253] *EMI Records v. British Sky Broadcasting* [2013] *EWHC* 379 (Ch), [2013] *ECDR* (8) 224 ('The Pirate Bay'), [46] (communication involves both operators of website and users); *Football Association Premier League v. British Sky Broadcasting* [2013] *EWHC* 2058 (Ch), [2013] *ECDR* (14) 377, [39]–[42] (raising question of responsibility of 'FirstRow' website but concluding that its role in aggregating streams, indexing them and offering a simple link for users to access, was such that it was 'responsible for the communication'); *Paramount Home Entertainment International v. British Sky Broadcasting* [2013] *EWHC* 3479 (Ch) (Arnold J) ('SolarMovie'), [12] (setting out 18 features of 'communication to the public'), [32] (finding communication because of intervention in a highly material way); *Paramount Home Entertainment International v. British Sky Broadcasting* [2014] *EWHC* 937 (Ch) (Henderson J)) ('Viooz' website); *FAPL v. British Communications* [2017] *EWHC* 480 (Ch) (Arnold J).

the question of whether a video-sharing platform that hosts infringing content uploaded by its users is 'communicating' that content.

6.4 LOCATION OF ACT

Neither the Related Rights nor Information Society Directives, nor the British implementation, explains *where* the act of 'communication' takes place. In the simple case of a British person who subscribes to a British service provider utilizing peer-to-peer software, it seems clear that deploying the software so that others can access files will amount to making available in the United Kingdom (even if those who access the files are, in many cases, outside the United Kingdom).[254] A more difficult case is that of a person in the United States creating a video using copyright-protected material, then uploading that material to a video-sharing platform, so that it can be accessed in the United Kingdom. Whether there is an infringement of UK copyright law may well depend on which acts are regarded as communicating or making the work available and where those acts are understood to occur. One candidate is the place where the individual uploads the work to a website, so that, in this example, there would be no infringement in the United Kingdom (although there might be in the United States). A second possibility is that the act of making available occurs wherever the server that permits access is located: this may, or may not, be the United Kingdom. A third possibility is that the act occurs in the place, or places, from which it can be accessed. This would mean that video-sharing platforms would be making available all over the world. The fourth possibility is that the work is made available in the territory where the public at which the work is targeted is located. In a number of decisions, the Court of Justice appears to have indicated that its preferred approach is to focus on targeting.[255]

In *Football Dataco v. Sportradar*,[256] the question arose as to where a wrongful act of 'reutilization' occurred for the purposes of determining whether so-called *sui generis* rights in a database had been infringed.[257] The defendant uploaded a collection of sports results in Germany onto a server in the Netherlands, from which the results were accessible in the United Kingdom. An action was brought in the English court, relying on the fact that the wrongful act occurred in England.[258] The Court of Justice ruled that the wrongful act takes place in a member state when the person performing the act intends to target members of the public in that member state.[259] Importantly, it rejected the idea that the wrongful act occurred in any territory from which the material could be accessed. Subsequent English case law has adopted the targeting approach to determine whether a communication to the public occurs in the United Kingdom.[260] In determining whether a territory is targeted, obvious considerations would be the language of the site and the top-level domain name, as well as the context (so, for example, it could be assumed that football data relating to the English Premier League would most likely to be of interest to English residents).[261] However, in *Sportradar*, the Court did not rule out the possibility that the act might also

---

[254] *Polydor Ltd v. Brown* [2005] *EWHC* 3191 (Ch).   [255] See Chapter 40, section 8, pp. 1106–7.

[256] *Football Dataco Ltd v. Sportradar GmbH*, Case C-173/11 [2013] 1 *CMLR* (29) 903 (ECJ).

[257] On which, see Chapter 13, section 3.3, pp. 369–71.

[258] On issues of jurisdiction, see Chapter 48, section 10, pp. 1312–21.

[259] *Football Dataco v. Sportradar*, Case C-173/11 [2013] 1 *CMLR* (29) 903 (ECJ).

[260] See *Lilley v. Chartered Institute of Management Accountants* [2013] *EWHC* 1354 (Ch), [25]–[26] (Roth J); *Football Association Premier League v. BSB* [2013] *EWHC* 2058 (Ch), [42].

[261] *EMI Records Ltd v. British Sky Broadcasting Ltd* [2013] *EWHC* 379 (Ch), [50]–[51] (Arnold J) (outlining some factors).

occur elsewhere, for example in the territory where the material was uploaded.[262] At least one English authority has accepted that communication also occurs at the point of introduction of the information.[263]

6.5 BROADCASTING

Section 20 of the CDPA 1988 states that the right of the copyright owner to communicate the work to the public includes the right to broadcast it.[264] As we saw in Chapter 3, a 'broadcast' is defined as an electronic transmission of visual images, sounds, or other information for simultaneous reception by the public, or which is made for presentation to the public, but excludes 'Internet transmissions'.[265] As we have already observed, this covers digital, analogue, terrestrial, and satellite transmissions, but not the placing of a work on a website. The relaying of a broadcast by reception and immediate retransmission constitutes a separate act of communication (retransmission).[266]

For the most part, broadcast are treated just like other 'communication to the public'. However, some special rules apply, especially to satellite broadcasts that may be directly received by individuals as well as those which may be received by subscribers who obtain a decoder.[267]

6.5.1 Who makes a broadcast?

Section 6 of the CDPA specifies that the person who makes a broadcast is *either* the person transmitting an item, such as a programme, where that person has responsibility for its contents, *or* the person providing the item for transmission who 'makes with the person transmitting it the arrangements necessary for its transmission'.[268] In a controversial decision (said to reverse business practice), the CJEU has held that where transmission of programme-carrying signals is made by so-called 'direct injection', according to which a person (A) transmits point-to-point by direct line to a distributor (B) who in turn sends signals to its subscribers, there is a communication by the distributor (B), rather than (A),[269] unless B's role is purely technical. As the distributor's role is rarely merely technical, the decision seems to absolve A of needing to obtain permission, at least for the making of its transmission to B.

6.5.2 Where does a broadcast occur?

Because of the potential transnational nature of broadcasting, it has long been acknowledged that it is important to ascertain where a particular broadcast takes place.[270] A person wishing to make a broadcast needs to obtain consents from copyright holders of

---

[262] *Football Dataco*, Case C-173/11, [47] (stating that reutilization was 'at least' in the country targeted).

[263] *EMI Records v. British Sky Broadcasting* [2013] *EWHC* 379 (Ch), [35]–[38] (Arnold J) (holding that an act of communication can also be said to occur in the place from which the communication originates).

[264] The exclusive right to broadcast a work has been recognized in UK law since 1956. See B. Sherman, 'Public Ownership of Private Spectacles', in B. Sherman and L. Wiseman, *When Old Technologies Were New* (2013), ch. 9.　　　　　　　　　　[265] CDPA 1988, s. 6(1). See Chapter 3, section 8, pp. 87–9.

[266] CDPA 1988, s. 6(5)(a). However, special rules apply to retransmissions of broadcasts from another EEA member state: CDPA 1988, s. 144A.

[267] That is, any encrypted broadcast, whether terrestrial or by satellite relay, is 'lawfully' received if decoding equipment has been made available through the person transmitting it in encrypted form: CDPA 1988, s. 6(2).　　　　　　　　　　　　　　　[268] CDPA 1988, s. 6(3).

[269] *SBS Belgium NV v. SABAM*, Case C-325/14, EU:C:2015:764, [2016] *ECDR* (3) 74 (ECJ), commented on by S. van Leeuwen, 'CJEU: "Direct Injection" Broadcasting not an act of communication to the public' [2016] *EIPR* 458.　　　　　　　　[270] See M. F. Makeen, *Copyright in a Global Information Society* (2000), ch. 4.

works included in the broadcast, but only as regards those copyrights that are operative in the territory in which the broadcast occurs. However, when a signal is sent or uplinked to a satellite (from place A) and is then beamed back to earth over a large reception area or 'footprint' (places A, B, and C), there are at least two possible territories where the act of broadcasting might be thought to take place. On the one hand, it could be said that the broadcast occurs from the place where the signal was sent (the 'emission', or 'introduction', theory). Alternatively, it might be thought that the broadcast occurs in the places where it is received (the 'reception', or 'communication', theory). In the face of conflicting national decisions on this issue, it became clear in the late 1980s that it was necessary to harmonize the law in this area. Two contrary concerns dominated the decision as to the choice of the place of broadcast. On the one hand, the simplest answer and the one that facilitated satellite broadcasting was that the country of broadcast was the country of uplink. However, it was feared that this would lead to satellite uplink facilities migrating to countries in which copyright protection was weak and that copyright owners would thus be best protected if consent was required in all countries where the signal could be received. In the end, a compromise was reached: the country of introduction is treated as the relevant place only where the standard of copyright protection is satisfactory. Accordingly, section 6 of the 1988 Act defines the place of wireless broadcasting as the place where the broadcaster introduces programme-carrying signals into an uninterrupted chain of communication, including any satellite relay.[271] In a case in which signals were transmitted to a satellite from France, back to earth, and then sent to the French public from a receiver situated in Germany, the Court of Justice held that a transmission occurred in Germany.[272] The Directive did not apply because the satellite was inessential for the transmission and the signal was interrupted—by its interception in Germany—before reaching the public.

The European legislature is also considering extending the 'country of origin' principle currently applicable to satellite broadcasts to other related services associated with any broadcast (most obviously, simulcasting, catch-up TV, but not on-demand services not associated with a broadcast).[273] As a consequence, the broadcaster would only need to obtain the permission for these services in one member state (though levels of remuneration would come to be agreed on that basis).[274] It should be noted that there is no need for the broadcast to be by satellite. Under the proposal, acts of reproduction and communication to the public would be deemed to occur only in the country of the principal establishment of the broadcasting organization.[275]

[271] CDPA 1988, s. 6(4). This is subject to the safeguard rules in CDPA 1988, s. 6A, which operate in cases of transmissions from places outside the EEA. The issue as to how the EU countries apply these rules to broadcasts that start from the United Kingdom will be an important matter post-Brexit, and one that UK policymakers have already identified as requiring attention (not least because the Satellite Dir., Art 1(2)(d) and Recital 24, are deeply ambiguous).

[272] *Lagardère Active Broadcast v. Société pour la perception de la remuneration equitable (SPRE)*, Case C-192/04 [2005] *ECR* I–7199 (ECJ).

[273] Proposal for a regulation laying down rules on the exercise of copyright and related rights applicable to certain online transmissions of broadcasting organizations and retransmissions (14 September 2016) COM(2016) 594. In the Proposal, these are called 'ancillary online services'. This is defined as 'an online service consisting in the provision to the public, by or under the control and responsibility of a broadcasting organization, of radio or television programmes simultaneously with or for a defined period of time after their broadcast by the broadcasting organization as well as of any material produced by or for the broadcasting organization which is ancillary to such broadcast': ibid., Proposed Art. 1(a).

[274] Ibid., Proposed Art. 2(2). Hence the transitional term might be quite lengthy: Art 5.

[275] Ibid., Proposed Art. 2(1).

6.6 MAKING THE WORK AVAILABLE

Section 20 of the CDPA 1988 also recognizes that copyright owners have the exclusive right to make the work 'available to the public . . . by electronic transmission in such a way that members of the public may access it from a place and at a time individually chosen by them'. In contrast to the broadcasting right, which is premised on the idea of simultaneous reception, 'making available' encompasses *individual* communications to persons who are members of 'the public'. A recital to the Information Society Directive explains that the right will cover interactive on-demand transmissions,[276] such as 'video-on-demand' services.

A special provision was regarded as necessary (in Article 8 of the WCT, and in turn in Article 3(1) and (2) of the Information Society Directive) because it was assumed the 'communication to the public' rubric was insufficient. At the time it was thought that a communication requires an act of transmission from source to a group of recipients (the public), whereas a making available involves transmission of a work to a place (typically, the Internet) from which it can be accessed individually at will. Conceived in this way, a making available falls short of an act of communication. However, the use of the term 'includes' in Article 3 (and Article 8 of the WCT, on which it is based) has led the Court of Justice to interpret 'communication' so broadly that any 'making available' is necessarily a 'communication'.[277] Nevertheless, the 'making available' notion retains some importance in its own right, at least in the context of related rights. This is because, under international rules, Contracting parties to the Rome Convention were not obliged to grant the holders of rights in sound recordings and performers an exclusive right of communication to the public of published phonograms, but only a right to a 'single equitable remuneration', and this has been translated into EU law in Article 8(2) of the Related Rights Directive. However, under the WIPO Performers and Phonograms Treaty of 1996, Contracting Parties are obliged to grant performers and phonogram producers each their own 'making available right'. The distinction between the two rights, then, becomes important.

So what is covered by the making available right? In addition to 'on-demand' transactions, it includes Internet transmissions where a person places a work on a website in such a way that members of the public can access the work 'from a place' (their terminal, whether it be in their office, home, or on their mobile telephone) and 'at a time' chosen by them.[278] Uploading material onto the (publicly accessible) 'web' is making available,[279] as is installing peer-to-peer software that allows third parties to access works from the installer's computer.[280] However, live-streaming of an event would not amount to 'making available', because the stream is only available for a limited time.[281]

---

[276] Info. Soc. Dir., Recital 25.

[277] *Svensson v. Retriever Sverige AB*, Case C-466/12, EU:C:2014:76 (ECJ), [20].

[278] *UPC Telekabel Wien GmbH v. Constantin Film Verleih GmbH*, C-314/12 EU:C:2014:192, [25] (an act of making protected subject-matter available to the public on a website without the right holders' consent infringes). But rather strangely, in *Technische Universität Darnstadt v. Eugen Ulmer KG*, Case C-117/13, EU:C:2014:2196, [42], giving access to a work on dedicated terminals in a public library is categorized as 'making available'—though the user can hardly be said to choose the place from which they access the work. On the background, see Reinbothe and von Lewinski (2002), 108–11.

[279] *Public Relations Consultants Association v. NLA*, Case C-360/13, EU:C:2014:1195, [57].

[280] *Dramatico Entertainment v. British Sky Broadcasting* [2012] *EWHC* 268 (Ch), [2012] *RPC* (27) 665, [69] (Arnold J); *Stichting Brein v. Ziggo BV and XS4All Internet BV*, Case C-610/15, EU:C:2017:99, [AG49], [AG53].

[281] *C More Entertainment AB v. Linus Sandberg*, Case C-279/13, EU:C:2015:199, [27] (ECJ). As the Court goes on to explain, this act might be covered by the communication right, if a Member State has granted such a right to broadcasting organizations that goes beyond the minimum right in Rel. Rights Dir., Art. 8(3).

6.7 REFORM

Of all the harmonized rights, the communication to the public right seems to be the most controversial, and the related jurisprudence the most incoherent. In an ideal world, the European Commission would have taken the opportunity provided by its proposal for a Directive on Copyright in the Digital Single Market to clarify the law. Perhaps fearing the ferocity of the inevitable lobbying, the Commission chose not do so—or at least not in an open and systematic way. Instead, it merely decided to reference 'communication to the public' in Recital 38. This states:

> Where information society service providers store and provide access to the public to copyright protected works or other subject-matter uploaded by their users, thereby going beyond the mere provision of physical facilities and performing an act of communication to the public, they are obliged to conclude licensing agreements with right-holders . . .

Subsequently, Council and European Parliament are intent on amending the proposal to make the matter explicit. Although yet to be finalized, each proposes to introduce a special definition of 'communication to the public' applicable to 'online content sharing service providers' (OCSSPs), who in turn are defined in a manner similar to that in Recital 38 of the original proposal. Such OCSSPs will be deemed to be communicating to the public any works that appear on their services unless they have taken relevant steps. The details of the steps that must be taken are still being negotiated, but, for some OCSSPs, they may include the installation of filters.

7 RIGHT TO MAKE AN ADAPTATION OF THE WORK

Section 21 confers on the owner of copyright in literary, dramatic, or musical work the exclusive right to make an adaptation of the work.[282] The right is not granted to the owner of copyright in artistic works, sound recordings, and films. The adaptation right is restrictively defined and is not to be confused with a general right to control all derivative works, such as that recognized by copyright law in the United States.[283] The adaptation right includes the right to do any of the other restricted acts in relation to an adaptation, including the right to make an 'adaptation of an adaptation'.[284] Consequently, it is a restricted act not only to make an adaptation, but also to reproduce an adaptation in any material form, to issue copies of it to the public, to perform it in public, or to broadcast it. Because it is not possible to draw a clear line between an adaptation and a reproduction, in many cases the same act might be both a reproduction and an adaptation.[285]

---

[282] Implementing, for the most part, Berne, Arts 8 and 11(2) (translation), 12 (adaptations, arrangements, and other alterations), and 11*ter*(2) (communication of translation).

[283] And in this respect seems narrower than Berne, Art. 12. See P. Goold, 'Why the UK Adaptation Right is Superior to the US Derivative Work Right' (2014) 92 *Neb L Rev* 843.   [284] CDPA 1988, s. 21(2).

[285] CDPA 1988, s. 21(6). For consideration of the relationship between the reproduction right and the adaptation right, see *Hodgson v. Isaac* [2010] *EWPCC* 37, [2012] *ECC* (4) 47, [21] (Judge Birss QC referring to the 'unclear dividing line' between the two rights); for discussion of the relationship in EU harmonization, see D. Jongsma, 'Parody *after Deckmyn*' (2017) 48(6) *IIC* 652, 666–70.

7.1 MEANING OF ADAPTATION

'Adaptation' is defined differently for literary works, dramatic works, computer programs, databases, and musical works. We must deal with each in turn.

In relation to literary or dramatic works, an adaptation means a translation (such as a translation into French, but also translations between technical languages),[286] or a dramatization of a non-dramatic work (such as where a novel is turned into a screenplay or ballet or, after *Norowzian v. Arks*,[287] a film). The adaptation right in a literary or dramatic work will also be infringed where the story or action is conveyed wholly or mainly by means of pictures (such as a comic strip). As regards dramatic works, an adaptation means a version of a dramatic work that is converted into a non-dramatic work (such as the conversion of a film into a novel). In relation to musical works, an adaptation is defined as an arrangement or transcription of the work.[288]

The adaptation right also applies to computer programs and databases. In relation to computer programs, an adaptation means an arrangement, or altered version of the program, or a translation of it.[289] In these circumstances, translation includes the conversion into or out of a computer language, or from a computer language into a different computer language or code.[290] In relation to databases, adaptation means an arrangement or altered version of the database or a translation of it.[291]

8 THE AUTHORIZATION RIGHT

As well as being given the right to carry out the restricted activities, the copyright owner is also given the right to authorize others to do any of the restricted acts.[292] It has been said that 'to authorize' meant to sanction, countenance, or approve,[293] or, alternatively, to grant or purport to grant to a third person the right to do an act.[294] The latter formulation received the approval of the House of Lords in *CBS v. Amstrad*.[295] In order to amount to authorization, the person to whom 'authority' has illegitimately been granted must in fact commit an infringing act.[296] However, the person giving the authorization (in contrast with the person to whom authority is given) need not be located in the United Kingdom.[297]

The concept of authorization has been applied in two distinct ways. First, it has been used to expand the network of potential liability beyond vicarious liability,[298] for example, those who book performers who infringe copyright: hirers have been held liable for 'authorizing' infringing where the hirer was aware of the songs that the band would

---

[286] *Moon v. Thornber* [2012] *EWPCC* 37, [92].   [287] [2000] *FSR* 363.

[288] *Francis Day & Hunter v. Bron* [1963] 1 *Ch* 587, 611 (adaptation and translation must be deliberate).

[289] CDPA 1988, s. 21(3)(ab).   [290] CDPA 1988, s. 21(4); Software Dir., Art. 4(b).

[291] CDPA 1988, s. 21(3)(ac); Database Dir., Art. 5(b).

[292] CDPA 1988, s. 16(2). Y. Gendreau, 'Authorization Revisited' (2001) 48 *J Copyright Soc'y USA* 341. The 'authorization' right needs to be compared with the general principles of joint tortfeasance described in Chapter 48, section 3.4. See R. Arnold and P. Davies, 'Accessory Liability for Intellectual Property Infringement: The Case of Authorisation' (2017) 133 *LQR* 442.

[293] *Falcon v. Famous Players* [1926] 2 *KB* 474, 491.   [294] Ibid.   [295] [1988] AC 1013.

[296] *Nelson v. Rye and Cocteau Records* [1996] *FSR* 313, 337.

[297] CDPA 1988, s. 16(2), is not explicitly confined to 'acts' of authorization within the United Kingdom: *ABKCO Music & Records v. Music Collection International* [1995] *RPC* 657.

[298] *PRS v. Mitchell & Booker (Palais de Danse)* [1924] 1 *KB* 762 (applying a 'control' test); *PRS v. Kwik-Fit Group Ltd* [2008] *ECDR* (2) 13 (OH CS).

perform or did nothing to control the repertoire performed;[299] but not where a warning was given to the performers and the infringements were by way of spontaneous encores of which the hirer had no prior knowledge.[300]

The concept of authorization has also been applied where a person manufactures or supplies equipment or other means that enable or facilitate infringement. In these circumstances, copyright owners have argued that where a person makes facilities available in the knowledge that they will probably be used to infringe, this is equivalent to 'authorizing' infringement. Thus it has been asserted that a person who supplies films to a cinema, who sells blank tapes to the public when renting out records,[301] who makes photocopying equipment available in a library,[302] or who manufactures tape-to-tape machines should be treated as having authorized the resulting infringements. Today, the same kind of arguments are being used in relation to the activities of so-called 'peer-to-peer' operators such as The Pirate Bay, Kickass Torrentz (and in previous years, Grokster or KaZaA),[303] who make available file-sharing software (particularly the bit-torrent protocol),[304] as well as others who provide hyperlinks to infringing material,[305] or provide the Internet locations of infringing material, for example, on aggregation sites or through search engines.

The leading authority in the United Kingdom is *CBS Songs v. Amstrad*,[306] in which the House of Lords defined the term 'authorize' restrictively. Amstrad manufactured and marketed a double-speed twin-tape recorder, which was sold by Dixons. The advertisement, which Lord Templeman described as 'hypocritical and disingenuous', boasted that the model 'now features hi-speed dubbing enabling you to make duplicate recordings from one cassette to another, record direct from any source and then make a copy and you can even make a copy of your favourite cassette'. An asterisk drew attention to a footnote warning that the recording and playback of certain material was possible only with permission. It also referred the user to the relevant legislation. The British Phonogram Industry (BPI), which represents various owners of copyright in musical and literary works and in sound recordings, claimed that Amstrad had authorized infringement of copyright in BPI's sound recordings.

The House of Lords held that neither the sale of the equipment nor the advertisement thereof amounted to an authorization. Lord Templeman said that an authorization means

---

[299] *PRS v. Bradford Corporation* [1917–23] *MacG CC* 309, 312–13, 314. If the hirer were to specify that particular songs were to be performed and those performances were to infringe on copyright, the case would be even stronger. see *Stunden Engineering v. Spalding & Sons* [1984] *FSR* 554; *Pensher v. Sunderland CC* [2000] *RPC* 249, 278–9 (commissioner specifying infringing design). See also *PPL v. CGK Trading* [2016] *EWHC* 2642 (Ch), [60] (Master Clark) (holding that manager of nightclub who booked DJs was liable for authorizing infringing performances even though she did not select or approve the recordings that were played, reasoning that she authorized the DJ to play 'whatever music they select').

[300] *PRS v. Bradford Corporation* [1917–23] *MacG CC* 309, 314. See also *PRS v. Ciryl Theatrical Syndicate* [1924] 1 *KB* 1 (managing director not liable for authorizing the infringing performance of a band as director had taken no interest in the content of the performance and was out of the country when it took place).

[301] *CBS Inc v. Ames Records and Tapes* [1981] 2 *All ER* 812 (not authorization).

[302] *Moorhouse v. UNSW* [1976] *RPC* 151, 159 (High Court of Australia) (authorization); cf. *CCH Canadian Ltd v. Law Society of Upper Canada* [2004] *SCC* 13.

[303] Grokster ceased to operate in 2005, following the decision of the US Supreme Court that it had 'induced' infringements under US law; KaZaA was no longer operating unlicensed from 2006, when it reportedly entered a settlement with the record companies worth $100 million, and it continued as a licensed service until 2012.

[304] As of 2017, levels of infringement through peer-to-peer file sharing are about half as significant as infringement through unauthorized streaming.

[305] For case law in Australia, see *Universal Music Australia v. Cooper* [2006] *FCAFC* 187 (authorization by provision of hyperlinks to infringing material).   [306] [1988] *AC* 1013.

a grant or purported grant, express or implied, of the right to do the act complained of.[307] The House of Lords held that while the machinery enabled a person to copy lawfully or unlawfully, this did not constitute an authorization.[308] Lord Templeman said that it was crucial that the footnote had warned that certain types of copying required permission and that Amstrad did not have the authority to grant that permission.[309] In short, the Lords held that there was no authorization because it was up to the operator whether to infringe or not; Amstrad in no way purported to possess the authority to give permission to copy records.

The leading case applying the 'authorization' standard to those who facilitate infringement on the Internet is *Twentieth Century Fox v. Newzbin*.[310] The case concerned material, particularly films, that third parties had uploaded to Usenet sites without the licence of the relevant copyright holder(s). Newzbin employed editors to index these sites and offered a paid service to access the index. By so doing, Newzbin enabled users to download the infringing files from Usenet bulletin boards (uploaded by third parties), especially using NZB files, which collect together all components of a work for downloading. Many of the Newzbin subcategories were 'obviously' infringing materials and the judge took the view that the defendant knew this.[311] Although Newzbin had instructed its editors not to index unlawful material and operated a delisting facility, these safeguards were found by the judge to be cosmetic.[312]

Kitchin J explained that while authorization required a 'grant' or 'purported grant' of the freedom to do the relevant act, this could be implied from all of the relevant circumstances. The circumstances might include the nature of the relationship between the alleged authorizer and the primary infringer, whether the equipment or other material supplied constitutes the means used to infringe, whether it is inevitable that it will be used to infringe, the degree of control that the supplier retains, and whether it has taken any steps to prevent infringement.[313] In the circumstances, the judge found that the Newzbin facility provided the means for infringement, that it had been created by the defendant, and that was entirely within the defendant's control. Moreover, the defendant did nothing to hinder infringement: there was no filtering and other preventative mechanisms amounted merely to 'window dressing'. Kitchin J said that he was 'entirely satisfied that a reasonable member would deduce from the defendant's activities that it purports to possess the authority to grant any required permission to copy any film that a member may choose from the Movies category on Newzbin'.[314]

The *Newzbin* decision has become a key case in the legal strategy of content owners who are seeking to reduce levels of peer-to-peer copying and unauthorized streaming. Typically, the software providers who operate the peer-to-peer systems, or the operators of the streaming site, are located out of the jurisdiction. It has become common, however, to seek orders blocking user access to such sites. The basis for many such orders is sometimes that the operators communicate the subject matter in the United Kingdom, but also often that they 'authorize' the infringements (making available or reproduction) of the users.[315]

---

[307] Ibid., 1054C.   [308] Ibid., 1053A, E.   [309] Ibid., 1053 C, E.

[310] [2010] *EWHC* 608 (Ch). A similar result was achieved in the United States by means of its tortious notion of 'inducement': see *Metro-Goldwyn-Mayer Studios Inc v. Grokster*, 545 *US* 913, 125 *S. Ct.* 2764 (2005).

[311] [2010] *EWHC* 608 (Ch), [46], [78].   [312] Ibid., [41]–[45].   [313] Ibid., [90].

[314] Ibid., [102].

[315] *Dramatico Entertainment v. British Sky Broadcasting* [2012] *EWHC* 268 (Ch), [73]–[81]; *EMI Records v. British Sky Broadcasting* [2013] *EWHC* 379 (Ch), [52]–[70]. See Chapter 48, section 3.6, pp. 1296–7.

7

DURATION OF COPYRIGHT

1 INTRODUCTION

The question of the appropriate period of protection that ought to be granted to copyright works has long captured the attention of policymakers, legislatures, judges, and commentators. For example, the central question of the literary property debate of the eighteenth century was whether common law literary property protection should be perpetual.[1] Similar debates have arisen at many other times during the history of copyright law. While these debates have always been shaped by the particular circumstances under discussion, they are similar in that they have attempted to mediate between the private interests of owners and the interests of the public in ensuring access to creative works[2]—that is, they have attempted to coordinate and balance the various interests that coexist in copyright law. Another common feature of these debates is that, whenever the question of duration has arisen, the length of protection has typically increased rather than decreased.[3] For example, under the 1710 Statute of Anne, books were protected for 14 years from publication and for a further 14 years if the author was alive when the first term lapsed. This was increased in 1814 to 28 years, or the life of the author. After great debate, the Literary Copyright Act 1842 extended the term of copyright in books to 42 years, or the author's life plus seven years.[4] In 1911, this was increased once again to life plus a 50-year term. As a result of the EU Term Directive, in 1996 the term of protection for 'authorial works' (including cinematographic works) was extended to the life of the author plus 70 years,[5] while in 2011 the term of protection for sound recordings rose from 50 to 70 years.

Before looking at duration in more detail, it is important to note a number of things. The first is that the period of protection changes depending on the type of work in question.

---

[1] That is, the debates surrounding *Millar v. Taylor* (1769) 4 *Burr* 2303, 98 *ER* 201, and *Donaldson v. Beckett* (1774) 2 *Brown's Parl Cases* 129, 1 *ER* 837; *Cobbett's Parliamentary History of England for the Years 1771–1774, Vol. XVII* (1813), 953. See M. Rose, *Authors and Owners* (1993); R. Deazley, *On the Origin of the Right to Copy* (2004); Sherman and Bently, ch. 1.

[2] See further C. Seville, 'Copyright's Bargain: Defining Our Terms' [2003] *IPQ* 312. In recent years, it has become common to articulate the object of the public interest as 'the public domain'.

[3] L. Bently, 'R v. The Author: From the Death Penalty to Community Service' (2008) 32 *Colum JL & Arts* 1.

[4] C. Seville, *Literary Copyright Reform in Early Victorian England* (1999).

[5] Term Dir. On this, see N. Dawson, 'Copyright in the European Union: Plundering the Public Domain' (1994) 45 *NILQ* 193.

This is a reflection of the fact that different interests and policy issues arise with different categories of work. The way in which the term of protection is calculated also differs depending on the type of work in question. In relation to most literary, dramatic, musical, and artistic works, copyright subsists throughout the life of the author and for a fixed term (currently 70 years) calculated from when the author dies (*post mortem*). In the case of entrepreneurial works and certain types of authorial work (such as those of unknown authorship), the protection is a fixed term that is calculated from when the work is either *made, published, or communicated to the public*. The term is calculated from the end of the year in which a particular event occurs.[6]

Second, the question of term of copyright is almost completely harmonized. As a result of the EU Term Directive, the length of protection for literary, dramatic, musical, and artistic works in the United Kingdom was set at the life of the author plus 70 years.[7] The term of protection offered to films also changed as a result of the Directive. Under the Copyright, Designs and Patents Act 1988 (CDPA 1988), as enacted, where films were treated as entrepreneurial works, films were given a fixed term of protection. As a result of harmonization, protection is required both for 'cinematographic works' both as authorial works and 'fixations' on film as 'related rights'.[8] The UK legislature appears not to have fully comprehended the logic underlying the Directive. It has amended the 1988 Act to make the term of 'films' under section 5 (that is, fixations) depend on the life of the principal director, author of the screenplay, author of the dialogue, and the composer of music specifically created for use in the work. No changes needed to be made to the term for broadcasts,[9] and there has been no harmonization at all in relation to rights in typographical arrangements.

In implementing the Term Directive, member states were required to apply the new terms to all works and subject matter that were protected in at least one member state on 1 July 1995.[10] As it turned out, this meant not only that the copyright in many works was extended, but also that the copyright in some works that had previously expired had to be revived.[11] For example, the UK copyright in a work by a British author who died in 1944 and which had first been published in the United Kingdom would have lapsed on 1 January 1995, but would have been revived from 1 January 1996, since the work would have been protected in Germany (which already operated a life-plus-70 term) on 1 July 1995.[12] The Directive also obliged member states when implementing the reforms 'to adopt the necessary provisions to protect in particular acquired rights of third parties'.[13] Acts done pursuant to arrangements made before 1 July 1995 at a time when copyright did not subsist in the work are treated as not infringing any revived copyright in a work.[14] Initially, the revived copyrights were treated as 'licensed by the copyright owner, subject

---

[6] CDPA 1988, s. 12(2); Term Dir., Art. 8.

[7] Duration of Copyright and Rights in Performances Regulations 1995 (SI 1995/3297). The length of protection is greater than that which is required in WCT, Art. 1(4), and TRIPS, Art. 9.

[8] Duration Dir., Art. 3(3) (the rights of the producer of first fixation of a film are to last 50 years after fixation or after the fixation was lawfully published). These are distinct from the rights of the owner of copyright in a cinematographic or audiovisual work.   [9] Term Dir., Art. 3(4).

[10] *Montis Design BV v. Goossens Meubelen* BV, Case C-169/15, EU:C:2016:790, [34]–[35] (new terms did not apply where work had fallen into the public domain in a member state before 1 July 1995, and the work was not protected in the territory of any another member state, even though the work had fallen into the public domain because the rightholder had failed to comply with a formality).

[11] Duration Regs, especially reg. 17.

[12] *Land Hessen v. G. Ricordi & Co.*, Case C-360/00 [2002] *ECR* I–5089.

[13] Term Dir., Art. 10. See also Recitals 26 and 27.

[14] Duration Regs; *Sweeney v. Macmillan Publishers* [2002] *RPC* (35) 651.

only to the payment of such reasonable royalty or other remuneration as was to be be agreed or determined in default of agreement by the Copyright Tribunal'.[15]

As well as extending the period of protection given to many works, as of 1 January 1996 the Term Directive also changed the way in which duration is calculated for works originating from outside the European Economic Area (EEA). Prior to the introduction of the Directive, British law provided the same level of protection to works published outside the United Kingdom as those published within. This principle changed, however, under the Term Directive, which requires only that the extended period of protection be offered to works originating from within the EEA. The period of protection given to works of non-EEA origin—that is, to works not originating in the EEA or without an EEA author—is the same as that which the work would receive in the country of origin.[16] The Term Directive is therefore based on a notion of 'comparison of terms' rather than national treatment.[17] This means that, where a work is first published in Canada[18] and the author is not a national of an EEA state, the work is protected in Europe for only 50 years after the death of the author (because that is the duration of Canadian copyright law).[19]

However, it has been observed that the implementation of the 'comparison of terms' rule in the United Kingdom may be more far-reaching than the Directive was generally thought to have intended.[20] This is because section 12(6), like sections 13A(4), 13B(7), and 14(3), refers to the duration of copyright as being 'that to which the work is entitled' in the country of origin. A literal interpretation requires reference therefore not only to duration in the country of origin, but also to whether copyright subsists at all in that country: after all, if there is no copyright in the work in its country of origin, it is difficult to say that the work is 'entitled' to copyright for any length of time. The impact would be to deny copyright to works that were unprotected in the country of origin, for example, because they fell outside any list of subject matter or failed to reach that country's originality threshold. The Directive, in contrast, states that copyright 'shall expire on the date of expiry of the protection granted in the country of origin'.[21] The use of the term 'expiry' suggests that the rule is not directed at conditions of subsistence. The preferable view is that section 12(6) should be read as dealing only with expiry of term; in cases in which works are not protected in the country of origin, but would meet British requirements for subsistence, the section should be understood as requiring British law to give such works protection until such time as protection of a work *of that sort* would expire in the country of origin.

The Term Directive was amended by the Information Society Directive, codified in 2006[22] and again amended in 2011.[23] The latter amendments followed a period of sustained lobbying by the record industry and allied interests, particularly performers,

---

[15] Duration Regs, regs 23, 24. Regulation 24 was repealed (with effect from 6 April 2017) by the Copyright (Amendment) Regulations 2016 (SI 2016/2010) as it was incompatible with the ECJ rulings in *Butterfly Music Srl v. Carosello Edizioni Musicali e Discografiche Srl*, Case C-60/98 [1999] *ECR* I-3939 and *Flos SpA v. Semeraro Casa e Famiglia*, Case C-168/09 [2011] *ECR* I-181 (ECJ), [53]–[56], in particular that transitional provisions must not generally prevent 'new rules from applying to the future consequences of situations which arose under the earlier rules'; and be temporary and 'not have the effect of deferring for a substantial period the application of the new rules'. As observed in previous editions, a rule that all revived copyrights are subject to compulsory licensing appeared to breach these rules.

[16] On what is a country of origin, see CDPA 1988, s. 15A.   [17] Term Dir., Recital 22, Art. 7.
[18] CDPA 1988, s. 15A(2).   [19] CDPA 1988, s. 12 (6); Canadian Copyright Act, s. 6.
[20] As observed by Mustafa Safiyuddin, of Legasis Partners, Mumbai.   [21] Term Dir., Art. 7.
[22] Directive 2006/116/EC.   [23] Directive 2011/77/EU.

which were concerned about the imminent lapse of sound recording copyright in material from the late 1950s and early 1960s, the heyday of rock 'n' roll and the early years of pop. It was argued that it would be unfair if performers, such as Sir Cliff Richard (or the French performer Johnny Halliday), were no longer able to gain income from their recordings during their lifetime. Despite arguments against such extension from the Gowers Committee[24] and academics,[25] all of which emphasized how increasing copyright term imposed costs on consumers (and welfare generally by increasing so-called 'deadweight loss'),[26] the European legislature decided that an increase in the term of protection for sound recordings and performers from 50 to 70 years was appropriate.

2 LITERARY, DRAMATIC, MUSICAL, AND ARTISTIC WORKS

Subject to the exceptions listed later in this chapter, copyright in a literary, dramatic, musical, or artistic work expires 70 years from the year in which the author of the work dies.[27] Thus, if an author of a book were to have died in 1990, the copyright in the book would expire at the end of 2060. In general, if a literary, dramatic, musical, or artistic work is jointly authored, the 70-year *post-mortem* term of copyright is calculated from the year in which the longest surviving author dies.[28] However, in the case of 'songs', a special rule applies (following from the 2011 Directive). Where, as a result of collaboration, both a literary work and a musical work were 'created in order to be used together',[29] the works are treated as a work of 'co-authorship' (a statutory designation distinct from joint authorship). For the purposes of duration of copyright, co-authored songs are treated in the same way as jointly authored works—that is, copyright continues to subsist until 70 years from the death of the last of the co-authors to die.[30] Thus the Hammerstein lyrics of Rodgers and Hammerstein songs, such as those in the songs in *South Pacific*, continue to be protected beyond 2030 (70 years from Oscar Hammerstein II's death) to the end of 2049—that is, 70 years from the death of the musical composer Richard Rodgers.[31] But

---

[24] *Gowers Review of Intellectual Property* (December 2006), Recommendation 3, [4.20]–[4.47], 48–57.

[25] Centre for Intellectual Property and Information Law, *Review of the Economic Evidence Relating to the Extension of the Term of Copyright in Sound Recordings* (2006); IViR, *Recasting Copyright for the Knowledge Economy* (2006), ch. 3. See also N. Helberger, N. Dufft, S. van Gompel, and B. Hugenholtz, 'Never Forever: Why Extending the Term of Protection for Sound Recordings is a Bad Idea' [2008] *EIPR* 174; M. Kretschmer et al., 'Creativity Stifled? A Joint Academic Statement on the Proposed Copyright Term Extension for Sound Recordings' [2008] 30 *EIPR* 341; C. Geiger, 'The Extension of the Term of Copyright and Certain Neighbouring Rights: A Never Ending Story?' (2009) 40 *IIC* 78.

[26] The 'deadweight loss' is the loss caused to those who would have bought a record at the price for which it would sell in a competitive market (without copyright), but who are not willing to pay the price established by the copyright owner and thus do not make the relevant purchase.   [27] CDPA 1988, s. 12(2).

[28] CDPA 1988, ss 3(1), 12(4).

[29] CDPA 1988, s. 10A (introduced with effect from 1 November 2013) by the Copyright and Duration of Rights in Performances Regulations 2013 (SI 2013/1782), reg. 4, to implement Directive 2011/77/EU of the European Parliament and of the Council of 27 September 2011, Art 1(1), amending Directive 2006/116/EC on the term of protection of copyright and related rights by adding Art. 1(7).

[30] CDPA 1988, s. 12(8) (as amended). The new mechanism for calculating term applies to existing songs where either the musical or literary work was protected on 1 November 2013 in the United Kingdom or any member state of the EEA: Copyright and Duration Regs, reg. 14(d), (e). The Regulations contain specific provisions dealing with the effects of extension to existing copyrights and revival.

[31] Copyright and Duration Regs, reg. 14 (detailing application to existing works). For background, see IViR, *Recasting Copyright*, ch. 4.

the provision does not apply where words are written for pre-existing music (as might be the case with a parody of an existing song), or where a literary work, such as a poem, is later used as the lyrics of a song; in both of these situations, where the music and lyrics were not 'specifically created for the . . . musical composition with words', the normal rules apply.

2.1 EXCEPTIONS TO THE TERM OF LIFE PLUS 70 YEARS

The general rule that the duration of literary, dramatic, musical, and artistic works is life plus 70 years is subject to a number of exceptions.[32]

2.1.1 Computer-generated works

Where a literary, dramatic, musical, or artistic work is computer-generated, the duration of protection lasts for 50 years from the end of the year in which the work was made.[33]

2.1.2 Crown copyright

Crown copyright in a literary, dramatic, musical, or artistic work lasts for 125 years from the year in which the work was made. If the work is published commercially within 75 years from the year in which it was made, then copyright lasts for 50 years from the date on which it was commercially published.[34]

2.1.3 Parliamentary copyright and international organizations

Parliamentary copyright lasts for 50 years from the year in which the work was made.[35] Where an international organization is the first owner, copyright also lasts for 50 years from when the work was made.

2.1.4 Artistic works used in designs

Until recently, copyright in artistic works that have been used in designs of industrially produced articles lasted in effect for 25 years from the year in which such articles were first legitimately marketed. This limitation on term, which took the form of a defence (CDPA 1988, s. 52), was removed by the Enterprise and Regulatory Reform Act 2013 (EER 2013) with effect from 28 July 2016.[36] The practical effect of repeal of the defence is to restore the full term to all works protected in any Member State of the EEA on 1 July 1995.

---

[32] Prior, perpetual copyrights under past law end in 2040. Contrast, however, the curious exception for J. M. Barrie's *Peter Pan*: CDPA 1988, Sch. 1, para. 13, and Sch. 6, respectively. The Peter Pan provision entitles the trustees of the Hospital for Sick Children to a royalty (to be used for the purposes of the hospital) in respect of any public performance, commercial publication, or communication to the public of the whole or any substantial part of the work or an adaptation of the play *Peter Pan* by Sir James Matthew Barrie. Barrie died in 1937, so copyright was about to lapse when the Bill that led to the CDPA 1988 was going through Parliament. Lord Callaghan of Cardiff introduced the provision into the House of Lords as an amendment to the Bill: see 494 Hansard (HL) 494, cols 836–47 (10 March 1988). For an extensive treatment, see C. Seville, 'Peter Pan's rights: "To Die Will Be An Awfully Big Adventure"' (2003) 51 *J Copyright Soc'y USA* 1.

[33] CDPA 1988, s. 12(7). Were this regarded as an 'authorial right', doubts might exist as to compatibility with various requirements of European law. These concerns diminish if the protection is conceived as a 'related right', which has not been the subject of harmonization.

[34] CDPA 1988, ss. 163(3), 164, 165(3), 166(5). International organizations initially acquiring copyright in a work may enjoy it for 50 years from the making or longer if specified by order: CDPA 1988, s. 168(3).

[35] CDPA 1988, s. 165(3).

[36] ERR 2013, s. 74. See B. Lauriat, 'Copyright for Art's Sake' [2014] *EIPR* 275.

Complex transitional provisions allowed for copies created before 28 October 2015 to be sold off before 28 January 2017.[37]

2.1.5 Works of unknown authorship

As we saw earlier, in certain situations it may not be possible to identify the author of a particular work. Given that, with works of unknown authorship, there is no identifiable author whose death can help to set the duration of protection, copyright law is forced to use other trigger points to calculate duration. In these circumstances, the 1988 Act provides that copyright in a literary, dramatic, musical, or artistic work of unknown authorship lasts for 70 years calculated either from the year of creation, or if, during that period, the work is made available to the public, from the year in which it was made available.[38] If the author's name is disclosed before the 70-year term lapses and before the author's death, this disclosure will have the effect of extending the term of copyright to the author's life plus 70 years.[39]

2.1.6 Unpublished works not in the public domain

Section 17 of the Copyright Act 1911 conferred protection on unpublished literary, dramatic, and musical works, and engravings, for 50 years from the date of publication. This meant that, so long as the works remained unpublished, the copyright term was unlimited. The 1988 Act removed this possibility by specifying that copyright in works that were unpublished at the author's death and remained so until 1 August 1989 was to last for a fixed period of 50 years from 1 January 1990—that is, until 31 December 2039.[40] The Minister now has power to reduce the period of copyright in unpublished works.[41]

3 FILMS

Under the Copyright Act 1956 and CDPA 1988 (as enacted), where 'films' were treated as types of entrepreneurial work, protection was limited to 50 years, normally calculated from the year of release.[42] The Term Directive required recognition of copyright in both

---

[37] Enterprise and Regulatory Reform Act 2013 (Commencement No. 10 and Savings Provisions) Order 2016 (SI 2016/593); CDPA 1988, Sched. 1, para. 6A, introduced by Copyright (Amendment) Regulations 2016 (2016/1210), Reg. 2(3) (qualifying CDPA 1988, Sched. 1, para. 6, which had preserved the public domain status of artistic works excluded from copyright under Copyright Act 1911, s. 22, where such works were capable of registration and designs).

[38] CDPA 1988, s. 12(3). For the definition of 'making available', see CDPA 1988, s. 12(5).

[39] CDPA 1988, s. 12(4).

[40] CDPA 1988, Sch. 1, para. 12(4). A work published after the author's death, but before 1 August 1989, obtained a term of 50 years from publication: CDPA 1988, Sch. 1, para. 12(2). Under the 1956 Act, a work unpublished at the author's death continued in copyright until 50 years after first publication: CA 1956, ss 2(3), 3(4). In some cases, certain acts, such as performance in public, had the same effect as publication. For some works unpublished on 1 August 1989, the relevant copyright will have been extended by the recent increase in the term of copyright. For example, if an author died in 1988 leaving unpublished manuscripts (which remained unpublished in 1990), the effect of the changes made in 1988 was that copyright lasted until 31 December 2039. However, as a result of the increase in the duration of copyright to life plus 70 years, copyright will be extended to 31 December 2058.

[41] ERR 2013, s. 76. However, following consultation, a decision was taken not to use this power in the immediate future. See United Kingdom Intellectual Property Office, *Government Response to the Consultation on Reducing the Duration of Copyright in Certain Unpublished Works* (2015).

[42] CDPA 1988, s. 13 (as enacted).

the first fixation of a film, for 50 years, and the 'cinematographic or audiovisual work', for which the term was to be 70 years from the year of the latest death among four categories of person: the principal director; the author of the screenplay; the author of the dialogue; or the composer of music specially created for and used in the cinematographic or audio-visual work.[43] Subsequent British attempts at implementation rather unwisely ignored the distinction, preferring to extend the copyright in 'film'—the section 5B copyright—to 70 years from the death of these four persons.[44] Where the identity of these four people is unknown, the term of protection is 70 years from the year in which the film was made.[45] Alternatively, if, during that period, the film is made available to the public, copyright expires 70 years from the end of the year in which the film was first made available.[46] Foreseeing potential problems in identifying when such copyright expires, the Duration of Copyright and Rights in Performances Regulations 1995[47] also introduced a new exception into the 1988 Act to allow a film to be copied at a time when it is reasonable to assume that copyright has expired.[48]

Not long after this attempted implementation, the Court of Appeal recognized that cinematographic works benefit from copyright not merely through fixation as films, but also as dramatic works.[49] While this decision moved British law some way towards compliance with international and regional obligations, it also exposed further the oddness of the British attempt to give effect to the Term Directive. This is because the term of copyright in the cinematographic work as a dramatic work is left to be determined by reference to the life of the 'author'. In British law, this might well include the director and authors of scripts for the film (as long as they do not exist before the film-making process) and possibly the editors or director of cinematography, but it is highly unlikely to include the composer of music. If normal principles were to be applied, the term of protection would be unlikely to be that required by Article 2(2). If the legislation is not amended, it is not unlikely that a court will be faced with the choice of applying these normal principles and acknowledging failed implementation, or reading the term 'author' in this context as being open-textured enough to take its meaning from the Directive. Moreover, once a *post mortem* term is acknowledged to exist in relation to the cinematographic work as a dramatic work, the wrong-headedness of extending the term of the section 5B film copyright is apparent. If the section 5B copyright is to reflect the Directive's demands in relation to related rights in the first fixation of a film, the period should be confined to 50 years from the making of the fixation.[50]

4 ENTREPRENEURIAL WORKS

Because entrepreneurial works need not necessarily have human authors, the period of protection is calculated using different trigger points.

---

[43] Term Dir., Art. 2(2).

[44] CDPA 1988, s. 13B(2). Each category may include more than one member, but unidentified members do not count: CDPA 1988, s. 13B(3), (10).   [45] CDPA 1988, s. 13B (4)(a), (10).

[46] CDPA 1988, s. 13B(4)(b), (10). The requisite 'making available to the public' includes showing in public or communicating to the public, if authorized: CDPA 1988, s. 13B(6).

[47] SI 1995/3297.   [48] CDPA 1988, s. 66A.   [49] *Norowzian v. Arks (No. 2)* [2000] *FSR* 363.

[50] Term Dir., Art. 3(3). See Kamina, 134.

4.1 SOUND RECORDINGS

For sound recordings, copyright expires 50 years from the end of the year in which the recording was made.[51] If, during that period, the sound recording was published, copyright expires 70 years from the year of such publication. If, during the 70 years from making, the work is not published, but is made available to the public by being played in public or communicated to the public, copyright expires 70 years from the year of communication or playing in public.[52] Thus if a sound recording was made in 1964 (for example unreleased Beatles recordings), but first published in 2013, then copyright might last until the end of 2083—giving a total period of 119 years.

The term of protection for sound recordings is, however, subject to one important—and conceptually quite innovative—qualification. Once 50 years has run from publication (or if there has not been publication, communication to the public),[53] the copyright in the sound recording might be determined by a performer whose performance is embodied on the sound recording if the sound recording is not being exploited.[54] This has been referred to as the 'use it or lose it' provision.[55] The effect of such action is that rights in the phonogram as such expire, leaving the performers with rights in the fixation of the performance embodied therein.[56] However interesting the device may be, its practical effects are likely to be minimal. This is because the conditions in which a performer can terminate the assignment are strictly defined.[57] In particular the right to terminate does not exist if the recording is accessible over the Internet.[58]

4.2 BROADCASTS

The duration of broadcasts is 50 years from when the broadcast was first made.[59] Where the author of a broadcast is not a national of an EEA state, the duration of copyright is that to which the broadcast is entitled in the country of which the author is a national (provided that the period of protection does not exceed 50 years).[60]

4.3 TYPOGRAPHICAL ARRANGEMENTS

For typographical arrangements of published editions, copyright expires 25 years from the year of first publication.[61] This right should be distinguished from the publication right conferred on the publisher of a previously unpublished work in which copyright has expired, which also lasts for 25 years from publication.[62]

---

[51] CDPA 1988, s 13(b) and (c) (introduced with effect from 1 November 2013) by the Copyright and Duration Regs, reg. 6, to implement Directive 2011/77/EU.

[52] CDPA 1988, s. 13A(2) (as amended by SI 2003/2498, with transitional provisions in regs 30–2, 36–9), implementing Term Dir., Art. 3(2) (as amended by Info. Soc. Dir.); and re-amended by the Copyright and Duration Regs (implementing Directive 2011/77/EC). Note that an original collection of recordings would constitute a database and therefore be protected as a literary work.

[53] The eighth recital explains that these are situations in which, 'but for' the term extension, the phonogram would be in the public domain.

[54] CDPA 1988, s. 191HA(3); Directive 2011/77/EU, Art. 1(2)(c), introducing new Art. 3(2a) into Directive 2006/116. Often, there will be multiple performers. Each is entitled to terminate, but all will need to act collectively to exploit the fixation of the performance.

[55] IPO, *Directive 2011/77/EU: A Users Guide to the Directive* (August 2013), 5.

[56] CDPA 1988, s. 191HA(4); Directive 2011/77/EU, Recital 8.

[57] CDPA 1988. s. 191HA(4) (introduced with effect from 1 November 2013 by the Copyright and Duration Regs, reg. 9).   [58] CDPA 1988, s. 191HA(2)(b).

[59] CDPA 1988, s. 14(2).   [60] CDPA 1988, s. 14(3).   [61] CDPA 1988, s. 15.

[62] Rel. Rights Regs, reg. 16(6). See section 6, pp. 189–90.

5 MORAL RIGHTS

In the United Kingdom, moral rights of integrity and attribution subsist as long as copyright subsists.[63] The right to object to false attribution is less extensive, lasting for only 20 years after the author's death. In some other countries, moral rights are capable of operating in perpetuity. The Term Directive made no attempt to harmonize the duration of moral rights and was expressed to be without prejudice to them.[64]

6 PUBLICATION RIGHT IN WORKS IN WHICH COPYRIGHT HAS LAPSED

In order to give effect to Article 4 of the Term Directive, a new property right equivalent to copyright, called a 'publication right', was introduced in the United Kingdom.[65] The right is granted without formality to any person who, after the expiry of copyright protection, publishes for the first time a previously unpublished literary, dramatic, musical, or artistic work, or film. This new right lasts for 25 years from the end of the year in which the work was first published.

In order to have the right, a publisher must publish a 'public domain' literary, dramatic, musical, or artistic work, or a film for the first time.[66] The right is acquired only where the work is previously unpublished. It should be noted that 'publication' in this context has a special meaning.[67] When determining whether the work is previously unpublished, no account is to be taken of any unauthorized act done at a time when there is no copyright in the work. An 'unauthorized act' means an act done without the consent of the owner of the physical medium in which the work is embodied or on which it is recorded.

The publication right that vests in the publisher is available only 'after the expiry' of copyright protection.[68] This means that the publication right is unlikely to be of great significance in the United Kingdom for some time. This is because of the dual effect of the changes made as regards unpublished works in the 1988 Act and the other changes made to the copyright term introduced to give effect to the Term Directive. The effect of these transitional provisions is that the publication right is currently restricted to unpublished artistic works other than engravings.[69]

Another consequence of limiting the availability of the publication right to cases in which copyright has expired is that it may exclude works in which copyright has never subsisted. Since the majority of existing unpublished works received statutory copyright protection in 1911, it will normally be possible to resolve the question of whether a work ever enjoyed copyright protection without too much difficulty (although problems exist in relation to artistic works). It seems that no statutory copyright existed in unpublished paintings, drawings, and photographs created before 1862 by an artist who died before 1855, nor in unpublished sculptures created prior to 1 July 1862.

---

[63] See Chapter 10.   [64] Term Dir., Art. 9.   [65] Rel. Rights Regs, reg. 16.

[66] The publication right does not arise from the publication of a work in which Crown copyright or parliamentary copyright subsisted: Rel. Rights Regs, reg. 16(5).

[67] It includes any making available to the public and, in particular, includes the issue of copies to the public, making the work available by means of an electronic retrieval system, the rental or lending of copies of the work to the public, the performance, exhibition, or showing of the work in public, or communicating the work to the public: Rel. Rights Regs, reg. 16 (as amended).

[68] Rel. Rights Regs, reg. 16 (as amended).

[69] For an elaboration of the reasoning that leads to this conclusion, see Copinger, [17–29]–[17–32].

While the publication right may supplement existing rights given to publishers in their typographical arrangement of published editions, it differs from these rights in three regards. First, the publication right is available only for the first publication of a previously unpublished work. Second, while the new publication right may apply where the publication relates to an artistic work, the typographical arrangement right is not relevant in such circumstances. This is because the right in typographical arrangement is confined to 'a published edition of the whole or any part of one or more literary, dramatic or musical works'.[70] Third, the publication right is much more extensive than the right to prevent facsimile copying of a typographical arrangement.

A work qualifies for a publication right[71] only if the first publication occurs in the EEA and the publisher of the work at the time of first publication is a national of an EEA state.[72] Publication has a more extended meaning than that discussed in relation to copyright. Where two or more people jointly publish a work, it is sufficient if any of them is a national of an EEA state. No provision is made for the extension of the publication right so as to recognize equivalent rights for foreign publishers, where the country of publication provides reciprocal rights to publishers in the EEA.[73]

7 OPTIMAL TERM

There is now an extensive literature debating the optimal term of copyright protection.[74] The arguments divide, in the first place, over understandings of the very nature and purpose of copyright. An initial distinction can be drawn between the 'natural rights' thinkers and those who regard copyright as an 'instrument' by which to achieve specific policy aims.

Natural rights approaches can be divided into two types: 'personality'-based thinking; and 'labour'-based thinking. For those who see copyright as the legal reflection of the 'natural right' of an author to protect their 'personality', a term equivalent at the very least to the lifetime of the author seems appropriate.[75] This, after all, is the period for which the law of defamation protects the reputation of individuals. For those who see copyright as a natural right in the product of one's labour, it is common to claim that the term of copyright should be indefinite.[76] Others counter that this may fail to recognize that works are rarely, if ever, the products of a single author and that there are important competing natural rights (for example to education).[77] Thus some who accept the argument that copyright law is justified as reflecting natural rights in the products of one's labour nevertheless take the view that such protection is justified for only a limited period in time.

For those who view copyright as a legal device that gives effect to public policy, the optimal term depends on a number of matters. First is the starting point: is copyright an incentive to create (or to invest in creation) that is to be accepted only insofar as it is necessary to achieve those ends? Such a view might suggest a very short term, similar to that

---

[70] CDPA 1988, s. 8(1).

[71] For general analysis of concepts relevant to protecting foreign claims, see Chapter 4, section 5, pp. 119–22.

[72] Rel. Rights Regs, reg. 16(4).   [73] Rel. Rights Regs, reg. 16(4).

[74] For an overview, see S. Ricketson, 'The Copyright Term' (1992) 23 *IIC* 753.

[75] In some countries, such as France, the moral rights of authors are perpetual, being exercised after the author's death by heirs and by the state.

[76] This was the basis of much of the argument for perpetual copyright at common law.

[77] H. Breakey, 'User's Rights and the Public Domain' (2010) 3 *IPQ* 312; H. Breakey, *Intellectual Liberty* (2012).

conferred by patent law, and certainly much shorter than those recognized at present by copyright. Or, alternatively, is private ownership of intellectual goods generally desirable as securing the optimal use of those goods, and the 'public domain' necessary only where the value of such goods is so low that the costs of transacting itself prevents the optimal use of such goods? Such a view might support a system of perpetual copyright, subject perhaps to requirements of registration[78] or compulsory licensing to ensure that transaction costs are kept to a minimum.

Second is the question of empirical evidence: what evidence is there that increasing term in fact increases the quantity of creative activity? What evidence is there as to the social costs associated with longer terms? Is the idea that intellectual goods will not be optimally exploited unless they are privately owned borne out by evidence as to the exploitation of public domain materials?

The arguments as to the effect of increasing term were extensively ventilated in the US literature surrounding the Supreme Court case of *Eldred* et al. *v. Ashcroft*.[79] One important point that was made was that no incentive to create is conferred by extending copyright protection for works that are already in existence.[80] Thus some alternative justification needs to be offered for any such legislative changes. Another important insight offered by economists was that increasing term will not necessarily increase incentives. This is because increasing term leads to potential payments in the distant future, and when a present value is calculated for such returns, it is likely to be much reduced. A sum of £10,000 received in 100 years' time is not worth £10,000 today: depending on how one does the calculation (in particular the 'discount rate'), it might be worth very little indeed. In fact, if the discount rate is 7 per cent, the present-day value of £10,000 in 100 years' time is a mere £12.[81] While present-day incentives might thus be minimal, considerable debate surrounds the social costs of increasing copyright term. Those campaigning for increased terms have often argued that the price of 'public domain' works does not differ from the price of copyright-protected works and thus that there are no real 'social costs'. In a remarkable study, however, Paul Heald showed that copyright protection often simply means that protected works are unavailable.[82] Heald randomly sampled fiction works on Amazon, identifying the publication dates and from that determined their copyright status (in the United States). The evidence shows that copyright works tend to be unavailable from a short time after publication and that they only really become available again once copyright lapses. For example, he found that more than twice as many new books originally published in the 1890s are for sale by Amazon than books from the 1950s, even though, in quantitative terms, far fewer books were published in the 1890s. This suggests that copyright protection has a considerable social cost, in that it impedes exploitation without offering returns to anyone.

Heald also studied the counterclaims that, in the absence of private ownership, intellectual goods will not be used 'optimally', but will also either be underexploited or overused.

---

[78] See W. Landes and R. Posner, 'Indefinitely Renewable Copyright' (2003) 70 *U Chi L Rev* 471. For a compelling critique, see M. Lemley, '*Ex Ante* versus *Ex Post* Justifications for Intellectual Property' (2004) 71 *U Chi L Rev* 129.

[79] [2003] 123 *S Ct* 769 (in which the US Supreme Court, Stevens J and Breyer J dissenting, held Congress's extension of copyright for extant works to life plus 70 years to be constitutional).

[80] See especially the amicus brief from Akerlof et al., available online at https://cyber.law.harvard.edu/openlaw/eldredvashcroft/supct/amici/economists.pdf.

[81] A standard way in which to calculate present value is FV ÷ (1 + DR)n.

[82] P. Heald, 'How Copyright Keeps Works Disappeared' (2013) Illinois Public Law Research Paper No. 13–54, available online at http://papers.ssrn.com/sol3/papers.cfm?abstract_id=2290181.

In one study, he compared works published between 1913 and 1922 (which fell into the public domain in the United States from 1988 to 1998—essentially meaning that they had a 75-year term) with those published between 1923 and 1932 (which will be in copyright until at least 2018).[83] The study shows that a higher proportion of the works in the public domain were in print and that, while the average prices of works in and out of the public domain were the same, for a sample of the most-popular works, the price of the public domain editions was substantially lower. In a further study, Heald analysed the use of popular songs from the same period, 1913–32, in films.[84] This study confirmed the finding of the previous study that a work's status as a public domain work did not in fact lead to its 'underexploitation'; public domain songs were no less likely to be in a film than those that were still in copyright. These studies thus flatly contradict the empirical premise of the neoliberal arguments that perpetual copyright is desirable to avoid under-exploitation of works.

[83] P. Heald, 'Property Rights and the Efficient Exploitation of Copyrighted Works: An Empirical Analysis of Public Domain and Copyrighted Fiction Bestsellers' (2008) 92 *Minn L Rev* 1031.

[84] P. Heald, 'Testing the Over- and Under-Exploitation Hypotheses: Bestselling Musical Compositions (1913–32) and Their Use in Cinema (1968–2007)' (2009) 60 *Case W Res L Rev* 1. See also P. Heald and C. Buccafusco, 'Do Bad Things Happen When Works Enter the Public Domain? Empirical Tests of Copyright Term Extension' (2012) 28 *BTLJ* 1 (examining the fate of 334 bestselling books from 1913 to 1932 and whether public domain status—171—was correlated with the availability of professionally recorded audio versions).

8

INFRINGEMENT

1 INTRODUCTION

This chapter examines when copyright is infringed. We begin by discussing 'primary' infringement—that is, the activities of those involved in infringing the copyright owner's exclusive rights (which we described in Chapter 6). We then discuss the statutory provisions that render accessories—whether before or after the act of primary infringement—liable for assisting in the making or distribution of infringing copies or the giving of infringing performances. These liabilities are referred to as 'secondary infringements'.

Before examining 'primary' infringement in detail, it is worth observing that, while there has been a great deal of norm-setting in relation to the rights of the copyright owner, the question of what amounts to copyright infringement has not generally been the subject of international attention and has only recently been regarded as a matter that has been the subject of regional harmonization. The relevant tests for infringement have largely been developed locally and, for the most part, by the judiciary. Having acknowledged that British law on infringement has taken its own course, it is worth noting two recent developments. First, the rule that copyright does not protect ideas has found its way into both regional and international arrangements, and has been interpreted as establishing an outer limit to the scope of protection that any state may grant through copyright.[1] Second, regional harmonization initiatives seem to require that copyright infringement be found to occur where 'any part'—as opposed to any 'substantial part'—of a work is reproduced.[2] This second development is already transforming the fundamental principles by which infringement is analysed.[3] While it should be anticipated that the Court of Justice will elaborate further guidance on infringement of copyright under the various directives after the UK leaves the EU, how far such rulings will be regarded as relevant to the interpretation of UK law is impossible to predict.

---

[1] TRIPS, Art. 9(2) (copyright protection shall extend to expressions and not to ideas, procedures, methods of operation, or mathematical conceptions as such); WCT, Art. 2; *Nova Productions v. Mazooma* [2007] *EWCA Civ* 219, [2007] *RPC* 589, 602, [38]; Software Dir., Art. 1(1).

[2] Database Dir., Art. 5; Software Dir., Art. 4(a); Info. Soc. Dir., Art. 2(1).

[3] *Infopaq International AS v. Danske Dagblades Forening*, Case C-5/08 [2009] *ECR* I–6569 (ECJ, Fourth Chamber).

2 PRIMARY INFRINGEMENT

In an action for primary infringement, the onus falls upon the claimant to show on the balance of probabilities that:

(i) the defendant carried out one of the activities that falls within the copyright owner's control;

(ii) the defendant's work was *derived* from the copyright work (a 'causal connection'); and

(iii) the restricted act was carried out in relation to the *work* or a *substantial part* thereof.[4]

2.1 RESTRICTED ACTIVITIES

The first question that needs to be asked in considering whether copyright in a work has been infringed is whether the defendant carried out one of the activities that falls within the copyright owner's rights. This topic was discussed in Chapter 6.

2.2 A 'CAUSAL CONNECTION'

The second matter that needs to be proved in order to establish infringement is that the defendant's work was *derived* from the claimant's work[5]—that is, it is necessary to show that there is a causal link between the work used (that is, reproduced, issued, rented, performed, communicated, or adapted) by the defendant and the copyright work. This means that, unlike patent law, copyright law does not protect a copyright owner against independent creation. It is important to note that it is not necessary for the defendant's work to be derived directly from the original of the work;[6] it is possible for a defendant to infringe where they base their work on a copy of the work. It is also important to note that it does not matter if the intermediate reproduction is itself a legitimate or a pirated copy.[7] This means, for example, that where a person photographs a three-dimensional object (such as a sculpture), they may infringe the copyright in the drawings on which the sculpture was based, even though they have never seen those drawings.[8]

Whether a defendant's material was derived from a claimant's copyright work is a matter of fact, and it is for the claimant to persuade the tribunal that this has occurred.[9] In order to do so, the claimant may use different forms of evidence. First, and most convincing, is direct evidence that the defendant utilized the claimant's work in producing their own. For example, an ex-employee may be able to give evidence that they were asked by their employer to produce something similar to the claimant's work, or a third party may have witnessed the appropriation. Indeed, a defendant may, in some circumstances, admit that they drew upon the claimant's work.[10]

---

[4] CDPA 1988, s. 16(3). For an overview, see *John Kaldor Fabricmaker U.K. v. Lee Ann Fashions* [2014] *EWHC* 379 (IPEC), [10]–[22] (Judge Hacon).

[5] See, e.g., *Autospin (Oil Seals) v. Beehive Spinning* [1995] *RPC* 683 (failure to show a causal chain); *Sawkins v. Hyperion* [2005] 1 *WLR* 3281, 3288, [30]. As we saw in Chapter 6, section 1, pp. 143–4, the knowledge of the defendant is not important in determining whether an act of primary infringement has taken place, but see also Chapter 6, section 6.1, p. 165.

[6] CDPA 1988, s. 16(3)(b).   [7] CDPA 1988, s. 16(3).

[8] *British Leyland v. Armstong* [1986] *AC* 577 (production of replacement exhaust pipes for claimant's cars indirectly copied the claimant's original drawings).   [9] *BBC v. Mitchell* [2011] *EWPCC* 42, [25].

[10] *SAS Institute v. World Programming* [2010] *EWHC* 1829 (Ch), [70], [2013] *EWCA Civ* 1482, [17].

However, such direct evidence is often unavailable.[11] In these circumstances, the courts have sometimes been willing to infer derivation.[12] In order to persuade a court to infer copying, a claimant will typically rely on similarities between the works, coupled with evidence that the defendant had access and opportunity to copy the copyright work. A court is likely to accept that there is a causal connection between the two works if the similarities are very numerous, or so individual,[13] that the possibility of their having been independently conceived by the defendant is remote.[14] Even if the shared elements are less individual or numerous, an inference of derivation may be drawn where a claimant can positively demonstrate the defendant's familiarity with the copyright work.[15] Where such an inference of copying has been established by a claimant, the onus then shifts onto the defendant to prove that they created the work independently.[16] In order to do so, a defendant may claim that the similarities between the two works can be explained by factors other than copying. For example, a defendant may attempt to show that the similarities are attributable to the fact that the two works were inspired by the same source,[17] to the fact that both works were constrained by the functions that they perform,[18] or, less plausibly, to chance.[19] Such claims are likely to be undermined by evidence that the defendant has been engaged in similar acts of copying on previous occasions.

This process of inference can be well illustrated by the House of Lords' decision in *Designers Guild v. Russell Williams*.[20] The claimant had produced its fabric design, named 'Ixia', in 1994. The design was impressionistic in style, made up of roughly drawn pink and yellow stripes, with flowers scattered haphazardly across them (see Fig. 8.1).

The fabric was made available in shops from September 1995. A year later, the claimant discovered that the defendant was selling fabric with a design called 'Marguerite', also based on vertical stripes in alternating colours, with flowers and associated stalks and leaves scattered across the stripes (see Fig. 8.2).

There were, however, several differences between the two designs, and the defendant denied that 'Marguerite' had been copied from 'Ixia', asserting that its designer had developed it from her own 'Cherry Blossom' design. Nevertheless, Judge Lawrence Collins QC inferred from the evidence that 'Marguerite' in fact had been derived from 'Ixia',[21] a finding that the House of Lords approved. First, the judge found that there were seven similarities between the two designs:[22] both designs were based on stripes with scattered flowers; both were in an impressionistic style, showing brushwork; in both, the stripes had rough edges; in both, the petals were executed in a similar way; in both, the stripes showed

[11] *John Kaldor Fabricmaker U.K. v. Lee Ann Fashions* [2014] *EWHC* 379 (IPEC), [11] ('Spies who were at the defendant's elbow during the relevant time are seldom available').

[12] *IPC Media v. Highbury Leisure* [2005] *FSR* (20) 434, 443.

[13] *Billhöfer Maschinenfabrik GmbH v. Dixon & Co.* [1990] *FSR* 105, 123 (Hoffmann J) (observing the paradox that it is 'the resemblances of inessentials, the small, redundant, even mistaken elements of the copyright work which carry the greatest weight' in proving derivation). See also *L. B. (Plastics) v. Swish Products* [1979] *FSR* 145, 159 (Lord Hailsham); *Ibcos Computers v. Barclays Mercantile Highland Finance* [1994] *FSR* 275, 298.

[14] *Designers Guild v. Russell Williams* [2000] 1 *WLR* 2416, 2425 (Lord Millett).

[15] *Francis Day & Hunter v. Bron* [1963] *Ch* 587 (on facts, derivation not established).

[16] *Designers Guild v. Russell Williams* [2000] 1 *WLR* 2416, 2425 (Lord Millett); *Ibcos Computers v. Barclays Mercantile Highland Finance* [1994] *FSR* 275, 297; *Stoddard International v. William Lomas Carpets* [2001] *FSR* 848, 857–8; *Mitchell v. BBC* [2011] *EWPCC* 42, [25].

[17] *Harman Pictures v. Osborne* [1967] 1 *WLR* 723, 728; *IPC Media v. Highbury Leisure* [2005] *FSR* (20) 434, 443, [10] (Laddie J); *Ogunkoya v Harding* [2017] *EWHC* 470 (IPEC) (A. Michaels).

[18] *Catnic Components v. Hill and Smith* [1982] *RPC* 183 (CA, affirming Whitford J), 222; *Kleeneze v. DRG (UK)* [1984] *FSR* 399, 401.   [19] *Francis Day v. Bron* [1963] *Ch* 587, 615–6 (Willmer LJ).

[20] [2000] 1 *WLR* 2416.   [21] *Designers Guild v. Russell Williams* [1998] *FSR* 803.   [22] Ibid., 815.

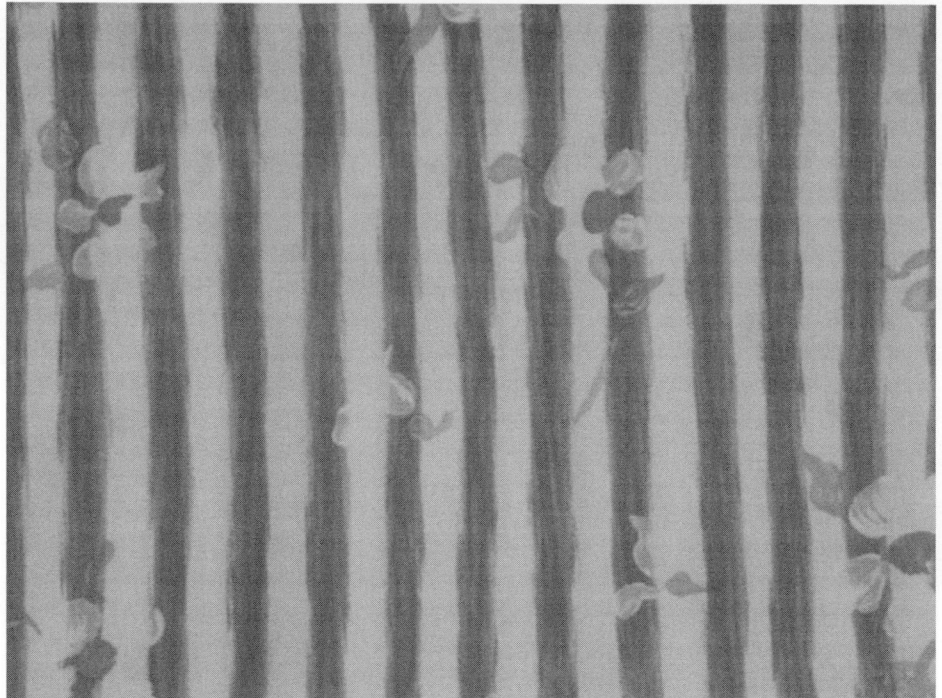

Fig. 8.1 The claimant's 'Ixia' design, created by Helen Burke
Source: Designer's Guild

Fig. 8.2 The defendant's 'Marguerite' design, created by Jane Ibbotson
Source: Designer's Guild

through some of the petals; in each, the flower heads comprised a 'strong blob'; and in each, the leaves were in two shades of green. The judge concluded that these similarities went 'far beyond the similarities which would be expected simply from both being based on an impressionistic style or from both being based on a combination of stripes and scattered flowers and leaves'.[23] Second, the judge found that the designer of 'Marguerite' had had an opportunity to copy 'Ixia', since she was at a trade fair in 1995 at which the 'Ixia' design was exhibited. Third, the judge rejected the defendant's own account of how she came to produce the 'Marguerite' design, finding her story unconvincing. Consequently, he found that the defendant's design was derived from the claimant's.

Designers Guild can be contrasted with *Mitchell v. BBC*,[24] in which a claim that the defendant's television cartoon had copied the claimant's characters (as artistic works) was rejected. The claimant's characters, named 'The Bounce Bunch', were a group of five student eco-rangers (see Fig. 8.3). The claimant had sent details to the defendant, who later produced its own cartoon characters, a group involved in a futuristic race, known as 'Kerwhizz' (see Fig. 8.4), which the claimant argued were so similar as to give rise to an inference of copying.

Judge Birss QC, sitting in what was then the Patents County Court (now known as the IPEC), rejected the claim. Although he found that there were sufficient similarities between the characters—namely, the characters' attire (a form of armour with helmets and microphones), the colour scheme used, and the characters' ethnic mixture, as well as the blonde quiff of the blue character (Charlie/Twist)—to place the onus on the BBC to prove independent creation, the BBC was able to do so. Evidence from the creators of Kerwhizz established that they had begun work (in 2006) before The Bounce Bunch were accessible (they were on Mitchell's website from 2007) and had already developed a series of characters that wore racing gear, with microphones attached to their helmets. While the design of some of the other features, such as chunky body armour and geometric shapes, had been added after 'The Bounce Bunch' was accessible, they were explained as having been inspired by shared sources—that is, Japanese anime and manga characters. The Court also heard evidence that made it highly unlikely that the design team for Kerwhizz had seen Mitchell's proposal for The Bounce Bunch.

One factor that has been useful in proving derivation is the fact that the infringing work contains the same mistakes that occur in the original work. In these circumstances, it is assumed that the reason why the same mistakes appear in the two works is that they are copies of each other. If works involve low levels of innate individuality, in order to assist in the task of proving derivation, copyright owners sometimes place incorrect or meaningless information in their works. Where this incorrect or meaningless information appears in a defendant's work, it is very difficult for them to argue that they created the work independently of the copyright work.[25]

In most cases, the process of copying will be a conscious act. In some cases, however, the courts have been willing to accept that the process of derivation may occur at a subconscious level.[26] While a defendant may honestly not recall having seen or

---

[23] Ibid.   [24] [2011] *EWPCC* 42.

[25] *Waterlow Directories v. Reed Information* [1992] FSR 409; *Waterlow Publishers v. Rose* [1995] FSR 207.

[26] *Francis Day v. Bron* [1963] *Ch* 587. According to Willmer LJ, at 614, to establish subconscious copying, it must be shown that the composer of the offending work was familiar with the work alleged to have been copied; cf. Upjohn LJ, at 621–2 (leaving undecided the issue of whether a different test applied for subconscious copying). In this case, there was not sufficient material from which such an inference could be drawn. See also *Sinanide v. La Maison Kosmeo* (1927) TLR 371; *John Richardson v. Flanders* [1993] FSR 497; *Jones v. London Borough of Tower Hamlets* [2001] RPC (23) 407, 432 [89]–[93].

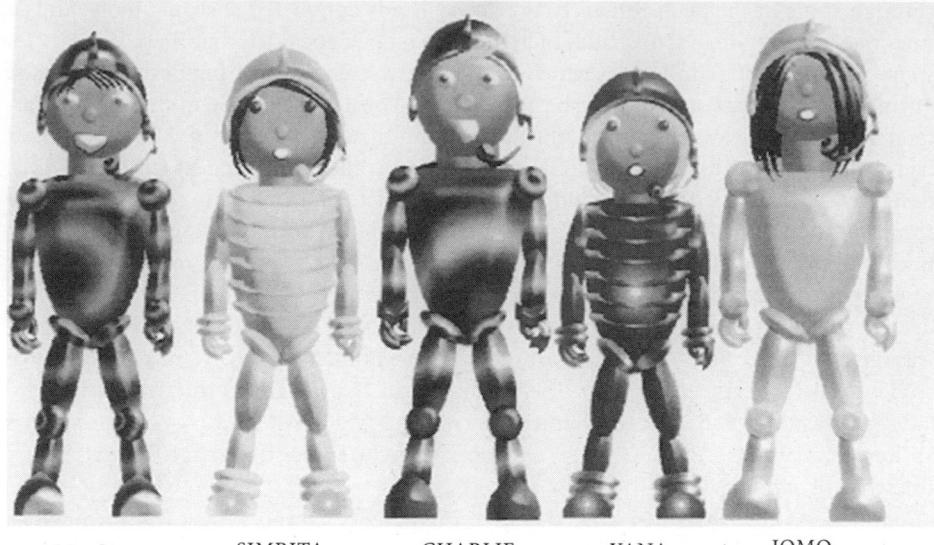

FENG   SIMRITA   CHARLIE   YANA   JOMO

Fig. 8.3 The Bounce Bunch
Source: Mr Mike Mitchell

NINKI   POOP   TWIST   SNOUT   KIT   CABOODLE

Fig. 8.4 Kerwhizz
Source: Mitchell v. BBC [2011] *EWPCC* 42

heard the copyright work, the courts seem open to the argument that the defendant subconsciously copied from the copyright work. This is particularly the case in relation to songs, where catchy—annoying even—tunes embed themselves in the subconscious. The acceptance of subconscious copying provides the courts with a way of reconciling the implausibility of independent creation with the conflicting evidence of a defendant who claims that they cannot remember having any contact with the work.[27] As with drawing inferences of deliberate copying, the court will consider the degree of

---

[27] *Francis Day v. Bron* [1963] *Ch* 587, 619 (Upjohn LJ). The decision of Wilberforce J at first instance is called 'a wise judgment' by Mummery LJ in *Baigent v. Random House* [2007] *EWCA Civ* 247, [2007] *FSR* 579, [122]. See also *Jones v. Tower Hamlets* [2001] *RPC* (23) 407, 432, [89]–[93]; *Elanco Products v. Mandops* [1980] *RPC* 213 (CA), 227.

familiarity that the defendant had with the claimant's work, the character of the work, and the degree of objective similarity between them.[28] However, it is worth noting that there is an important distinction between evidence that leads to a shift in the onus of proof and evidence that established a case of subconscious copying. As Judge Birss QC explained in *Mitchell v. BBC*,[29] while similarity combined with access may shift the onus of proof on to the defendant, the notion of subconscious copying is not concerned with the onus of proof, but depends 'on the evidence as a whole'. After all, the only way in which to rebut an inference of subconscious copying would be to demonstrate that it is impossible for the defendant to have ever come across the claimant's work, whether directly or indirectly. Consequently, the evidence that would be necessary to support an inference of subconscious copying is likely to be a good deal more substantial than the evidence needed simply to shift the onus onto a defendant in a copyright case. Even though, as noted earlier, Judge Birss found sufficient similarities between The Bounce Bunch (Fig. 8.3) and Kerwhizz (Fig. 8.4) to shift the onus onto the BBC, that was a long way from requiring a conclusion that there had been subconscious copying. Having found no evidence of familiarity on the part of the designers of Kerwhizz with The Bounce Bunch, that The Bounce Bunch characters were simple, generic, and unmemorable,[30] and that the similarities were at a rather abstract conceptual level that could readily be explained by reference to common influences, the judge concluded that the two sets of characters were a result of independent creative work and thus rejected the claim that there had been subconscious copying.

2.3 WHOLE WORK OR A (SUBSTANTIAL) PART THEREOF?

The third and final question that needs to be asked in an infringement action is whether the restricted act has been carried out in relation to the *work* or a *substantial part* thereof. Identical copying (that is, copying the totality of the claimant's work in an identical form—sometimes referred to as 'piracy') raises no analytical problems and thus, in the absence of an exception (on which, see Chapter 9), a finding of infringement follows inevitably. Copyright law, however, has long recognized that protection ought not to be limited to situations in which the defendant makes an exact copy of the work. One reason for this is that if copyright protection were limited to situations in which identical copies of the work are used, plagiarists would be able to escape infringement simply by making minor variations to the copied work.[31] Since 1911, UK copyright law has therefore provided protection not only where the whole work has been copied, but also where a defendant has used a substantial part of the protected aspects of the work.[32] In extending protection from identical copying to copying of 'any substantial part' of a work, the law enables a copyright owner to control situations in which a defendant takes *part of a work* (such as where half of a book is photocopied or a sample of a sound recording is copied) and those in which the defendant *changes the form of the work* (such as where a play is converted into a film).[33] This move from protecting only against identical copying to also protecting

---

[28] *Mitchell v. BBC* [2011] *EWPCC* 42, [121].   [29] Ibid., [39].   [30] Ibid., [126], [143]–[146].

[31] As should be clear, the circumstances in which someone infringes copyright are different from the circumstances in which someone might be regarded as a 'plagiarist'. For discussions of the distinction, see I. Alexander, 'Inspiration or Infringement: The Plagiarist in Court', in L. Bently, J. Davis, and J. Ginsburg (eds), *Copyright and Piracy: an Interdisciplinary Critique* (2010).

[32] CDPA 1988, s. 16(3).

[33] These two situations are sometimes referred to as cases of 'literal copying' and 'altered copying'. See, e.g., *Designers Guild v. Williams* [2000] 1 *WLR* 2416, 2431 (Lord Scott).

Table 8.1 How UK and EU law govern the definition of partial copying

	Authorial works	Computer Programs	Databases	Sound recordings	Films (fixations)	Broadcasts	Typographical Arrangements
Reproduction	EU test (*Infopaq*)			EU test (to be developed)			UK substantial part test
Distribution	EU test (*Infopaq*)			EU test (to be developed)			UK substantial part test
Communication	EU test (*Infopaq*)			EU test (to be developed)			N/A
Performance	UK substantial part test	EU test		EU test (to be developed)			N/A
Adaptation	UK substantial part test	EU test		N/A	N/A	N/A	N/A

partial copies or copies of the substance of a work has inevitably required the courts to make difficult value judgements.

It is in relation to the question of partial (and non-literal) copying that we face difficult questions as to the state of British law in the light of European harmonization (see Table 8.1). In particular, it has become clear that there is now a European test for assessing infringement of the reproduction right for authorial works protected under the Information Society Directive: the question is whether the defendant has reproduced 'a part' of the work. There are, as yet, only a few cases applying the latter standard, which may—or may not—turn out to produce different results from those that would arise under the British test. At present, it appears that some of the flexibility—some might say incoherence—inherent in the British approach may have been lost. In order to understand the current state of affairs, we deal initially with cases in which there has been an act in relation to a discrete part of the protected work (as opposed to the situation in which there has been 'non-literal' copying).[34] In relation to acts in relation to discrete parts, we consider in turn:

(i) the British position in relation to what counts as a substantial taking of a literary, dramatic, musical, or artistic works (which remains relevant at the very least to the unharmonized right of public performance and adaptation);[35]

(ii) the European law as to what counts as 'a part' of an authorial work; and

(iii) what counts as a substantial part of a film, sound recording, broadcast, or typographical arrangement.

There is as yet no CJEU case law on what amounts to reproduction of a 'part' of the subject matter of related rights (sound recordings, fixation of films, or broadcasts).

2.3.1 The 'British' approach

The 'British' approach (by which we mean the approach that had been developed prior to harmonization) was set out by Lord Millett in *Designers Guild*:

---

[34] This is an artificial distinction, because rarely will there be cases of pure partial copying or non-literal copying; most cases involve taking some literal fragments and some aspects of structure, organization, plot, theme, or idea. Nevertheless, the structure of EU law may imply such a distinction, and it will make the test relatively manageable.

[35] *England & Wales Cricket Board & Sky UK v. Tixdaq & Fanatix* [2016] *EWHC* 575 (Ch) [67]; J. Griffiths, 'Dematerialization, Pragmatism and the European Copyright Revolution' (2013) 33(4) *OJLS* 767, 784 ('part' test in Info. Soc. Dir., Art. 2, applies also to Arts 3 and 4).

Once the judge has found that the defendants' design incorporates features taken from the copyright work, the question is whether what has been taken constitutes all or a substantial part of the copyright work. This is a matter of impression, for whether the part taken is substantial must be determined by its quality rather than its quantity. It depends upon its importance to the copyright work. It does not depend upon its importance to the defendants' work . . . The pirated part is considered on its own . . . and its importance to the copyright work assessed. There is no need to look at the infringing work for this purpose.[36]

In principle, in order to answer this question, it is necessary to ask two subsidiary questions, as follows.

(i)   What is the claimant's work?

(ii) Has the defendant utilized the whole of the claimant's work or a substantial part thereof?

(i) What is the work for the purposes of infringement?

Logically, the first task that arises when determining whether the defendant has utilized the whole or a substantial part of the copyright work is ascertaining the limits of the copyright work. To determine what the work is, it is necessary first to determine the parameters of the work and then to distinguish the protected from non-protected elements of the work. We will deal with each of these in turn.[37]

(a) The parameters of the work In many situations, the parameters of the work will not be in dispute. However, where a work is divisible into smaller elements, the question may arise as to whether the 'parts' should be treated as separate and distinct works. If we take the case of a book, for example, while it is clear that the book as a whole is a copyright work, what of the chapters, pages, paragraphs, sentences, or words that are included in the book? The decision as to the size of the copyright work may have an important bearing on the outcome of an infringement action. The reason for this is that the question of whether something is 'the whole or a substantial part' of something else depends on what it is being judged against. In this case, that something else is the copyright work.

The question of how the parameters of the work are to be determined was considered by Judge Laddie QC in *Hyperion Records v. Warner Music*.[38] This was an application for summary judgment brought by Hyperion Records, which owned copyright in a sound recording of the medieval chant, 'O Euchari'. The chant, which was 5 minutes 18 seconds long, appeared on the album *A Feather on the Breath of God*. Hyperion Records alleged that its copyright had been infringed when the electro-pop band, The Beloved, copied (or sampled) eight notes from 'O Euchari' and incorporated them into its record 'Happiness'.

While it was clear that the song 'O Euchari' was a work, Hyperion Records argued that the eight notes sampled by The Beloved also formed a distinct copyright work in their own right. If this were accepted, it would clearly have been an infringement, because 100 per cent of the 'work' would have been taken. Judge Laddie QC rejected the argument, saying: 'I do not accept that all copyright works can be considered as a package of copyright

---

[36] *Designers Guild v. Williams* [2000] 1 *WLR* 2426, 2426.

[37] The task of identifying the work is made easier because the claimants will specify in their statement of case the parameters of the work, as well as the parts of the work that they believe have been infringed. While not definitive, this provides a useful starting point for demarcating the scope of the work.

[38] (1991, unreported). See also *IPC Media v. Highbury-Leisure Publishing* [2005] *EWHC* 2985 (Ch), [2005] *FSR* (20) 434, [22] (Laddie J) (copyright is not a legal millefeuille with layers of different artistic copyrights); *Spelling Goldberg Productions v. BPC Publishing* [1981] *RPC* 283 (Buckley LJ); *Merchandising Corporation v. Harpbond* [1983] *FSR* 32, 39; *Coffey v. Warner/Chappell* [2005] *FSR* (34) 747.

works, consisting of the copyright in the whole and an infinite number of subdivisions of it.'[39] He added that 'if the copyright owner is entitled to redefine his copyright work so as to match the size of the alleged infringement, there would never be a requirement for substantiality'.[40] More specifically, Judge Laddie did not accept that it was legitimate 'to arbitrarily cut out of a large work that portion which has been allegedly copied and then to call that the copyright work'.[41] The eight notes sampled by The Beloved were not a work in their own right, because a work has a discrete, natural, or non-artificial shape. Thus a day's footage on a film that is 'a discrete product of the film-maker's art' may be treated as a distinct work. Presumably, the results of a recording session, as distinct from the final product, would also attract separate copyright protection.

Judge Laddie's judgment provides us with some useful assistance in undertaking the (much neglected) task of defining the parameters of the work. In addition to focusing on whether a particular item can be seen as 'natural' or 'non-artificial', it seems that other relevant considerations would include the intention of the creator, the level of interdependence or independence of the units concerned, and the commercial form in which the work is to be published or made available. Given that one consequence of recognizing small units as discrete copyright works is potentially to increase the level of protection, a useful starting point should be that, where a work has been published, the form in which the work is first issued is presumed to determine the parameters of the work.

(b) Distinguishing the protected parts from the non-protected parts Once the 'work' has been identified, the question arises as to what aspects of the work are protected. In most cases, there will be certain parts of a work that are not protected (which form part of what is sometimes called the 'public domain'). When deciding whether a copyright work has been infringed, copyright law is concerned only with the protected parts of the work—that is, those that are original.[42]

A person will infringe only if they appropriate a part of the work that is original.[43] This means that the copying of an unoriginal part of the work is not an infringement.[44] As an example, we might consider the situation if a person were to compile a list of the names of Arsenal supporters living in Australia. If the originality of the compilation were to lie in the way in which the information was arranged, third parties would not be able to make use of that arrangement. They would, however, be able to make use of the information (if, for example, they were to scramble the list). Alternatively, if the originality of the compilation were to stem from the selection of the material (but not its arrangement), third parties would not be able to make use of the information (although they would not be prevented from independently compiling the list themselves).

A great deal of care needs to be taken when distinguishing between original and non-original aspects of a work. Although, in some situations, the work as a whole can be dissected and non-original aspects ignored for the purposes of the infringement analysis, such

---

[39] *Hyperion Records v. Warner Music* (1991, unreported).   [40] Ibid.

[41] Ibid. It is not always in the copyright owner's interests to define the work in this way. Where a defendant has taken small helpings from a number of separate publications, there may be benefits from asserting that the separate publications were, in fact, one. See, e.g., *PCR v. Dow Jones Telerate* [1998] *FSR* 170, 183; *Electronic Techniques (Anglia) v. Critchley Components* [1997] *FSR* 401.

[42] *Ladbroke (Football) v. William Hill (Football)* [1964] 1 *WLR* 273, 293 (Lord Pearce); *Warwick Film v. Eisenger* [1969] 1 *Ch* 508.

[43] *Designers Guild v. Williams* [2000] 1 *WLR* 2416, 2431 (Lord Scott); *Cantor Fitzgerald International v. Tradition (UK)* [2000] *RPC* 95, 131; *Autospin (Oil Seals) v. Beehive Spinning* [1995] *RPC* 683, 697; *Ibcos Computers v. Barclays Mercantile Highland Finance* [1994] *FSR* 275.

[44] *Ladbroke (Football) v. William Hill (Football)* [1964] 1 *WLR* 273, 293 (Lord Pearce); *Bowater Windows v. Aspen Windows* [1999] *FSR* 759, 781–2.

'dissection' carries with it a potential danger. This danger arises from the fact that original-ity can be provided not merely from labour and skill (or, in European parlance, the 'creative choices') in the creation of new, original, material, but also from the collation or collection of existing, non-original, material. A process of dissection can cause a tribunal to overlook the creativity involved in such collation or arrangement. In other words, dissection may cause a tribunal to treat the whole incorrectly as merely the sum of its parts. However, if a defendant takes a number of elements from the claimant's work, each of which might indi-vidually be non-original, there may well nevertheless be a taking of a substantial part of the labour and skill (or intellectual creativity) involved in collating the material.[45]

(ii) Has the defendant taken the whole or a substantial part of the copyright work?

Once the protected elements of the work have been identified, it is then possible to con-sider what the defendant has taken from the copyright work and to ask whether the defendant has used the whole or a substantial part of the claimant's work.[46]

The term 'substantial' is one with a 'wide range of meanings' and the courts have pre-ferred those at the lower end of the range.[47] This is not the place for a historical review of the case law, but it can be said that there has been a discernible shift towards allowing a copyright owner to control ever-smaller uses and reuses of their works. In the not-too-distant past, the courts often took the view that a person would infringe only where the part taken was an essential, vital, or important part of the work.[48] In recent years, how-ever, tribunals have being willing to find infringement as long as the defendant's use is not of an 'insignificant' part or *de minimis*.[49]

Although the answer to the question of whether a restricted act has been carried out in relation to a 'substantial part' of a work always depends on the facts of the case, in essence the fate of a defendant depends on the relative *importance* of the part that is taken.[50]

It is for the court to decide whether the part taken is important.[51] Although the focus of the tribunal should be on whether the part taken was important to the copyright work, in reach-ing a determination a court will inevitably be influenced by the surrounding circumstances, including: the way in which the claimant's work was created; the nature of the work, for exam-ple whether it is a work of information or fiction; the relationship between the parties, in par-ticular whether they are in competition; the conduct of the parties, in particular whether the defendant has copied merely to save itself effort; the reason why the part was taken, for exam-ple whether it has been used for the purposes of parody; and whether the use is degrading.[52]

---

[45] *Designers' Guild v. Williams* [2000] 1 *WLR* 2416, 2421 (Lord Hoffmann), 2424 (Lord Scott). See also *Baigent v. Random House* [2007] *EWCA Civ* 247, [2007] *FSR* 579, [127]–[129] (Mummery LJ).

[46] *Designers Guild v. Williams* [2000] 1 *WLR* 2416, 2425 (Lord Millett).

[47] *Newspaper Licensing Agency v. Marks & Spencer plc* [2001] *Ch* 257, 268 (Peter Gibson LJ), 286–7 (Mance LJ).

[48] *Hawkes & Sons v. Paramount Film Service* [1934] 1 *Ch D* 593, 606 (Slesser LJ) (defendant's broadcast of part of the claimant's song, while not prolonged, was held to be 'a substantial, vital and essential part').

[49] *Designers Guild v. Williams* [2000] 1 *WLR* 2416, 2418 (Lord Bingham). See also *Newspaper Licensing Agency v. Marks & Spencer plc* [2001] *Ch* 257, 268 (Peter Gibson LJ), 287 (Mance LJ).

[50] *Sillitoe v. McGraw-Hill Book Co. (UK)* [1983] *FSR* 545, 549–50; *Hawkes & Sons v. Paramount Film Service* [1934] 1 *Ch D* 593 (CA), 605–6.

[51] In cases involving technical or esoteric subject matter, the court might rely on expert evidence from computer programmers, musicologists, choreographers, and other specialists as to the relative importance of the part: *Ibcos Computers v. Barclays Mercantile Highland Finance* [1994] *FSR* 275, 302; *Cantor Fitzgerald International v. Tradition (UK)* [2000] *RPC* 95; *The Newspaper Licensing Agency v. Marks and Spencer plc* [2003] *AC* 551, [21].

[52] But note the emphatic statements of Lloyd LJ in *Baigent v. Random House* [2007] *EWCA Civ* 247, [2007] *FSR* 579, 620, [95], [97], that the intention of the copier is 'irrelevant as a matter of law' and 'a red herring in modern English copyright law that … should not be invoked in the future'.

(a) Importance to claimant's work The importance of the part taken is judged in terms of its importance to the copyright work and not the defendant's work.[53] The reason for this is that the test imposed by the statute is whether the part used by the defendant is a substantial part of the *claimant's* copyright work, not whether it is a substantial part of the *defendant's* work.[54] This has two consequences. First, it means that it does not matter that the part taken forms an unimportant part of the defendant's work, nor that the defendant has expended considerable labour, skill, and effort themselves. The contributions of the defendant in transforming a copyright work have been regarded as largely irrelevant, the courts preferring merely to attend to what the defendant has taken. Translations and abridgements, however valuable, have for more than a century been regarded as infringements.[55] Equally, in the case of copying elements of an artistic work (as with that of 'Ixia' by 'Marguerite' in *Designer's Guild*[56]—see Figs 8.1 and 8.2), it is a matter of no relevance to a finding of substantial taking that the defendant's work gives off an overall different impression from that of the claimant. For the same reason, (most) parodic uses of copyright works are regarded as infringements, irrespective of the parodist's skill or the social value accorded to parody.[57] The second consequence of focusing on whether the part is important to the claimant's work is that if it is not, then, in principle, it does not matter whether the part is used repeatedly in the defendant's work (as often happens with the digital sampling of musical works).

(b) Substantiality: a qualitative criterion While the use of the term 'substantial' suggests that importance should be judged in terms of the amount taken, the inquiry is as much concerned with the *quality* as the *quantity* of the part taken.[58] Indeed, in two significant decisions, Lord Hoffmann went further, saying that the question of substantiality is a matter of quality *rather than* quantity.[59] So long as a part is qualitatively an important part of the work as a whole, even a very small part of a work may be a substantial part.

(c) Assessing quality To say that the issue is one of quality leaves open how quality is to be determined. In *The Newspaper Licensing Agency v. Marks and Spencer*, Lord Hoffmann provided some guidance when he stated that the qualitatively important parts of a work were to be identified 'by reference to the reason why the work is given copyright protection'.[60] He explained that, in the case of literary copyright, copyright is conferred (irrespective of literary merit) upon an original literary work, and it followed that the quality relevant for the purposes of substantiality is the 'literary originality' of that which has

---

[53] *Designers Guild v. Williams* [2000] 1 *WLR* 2416, 2420, 2426.

[54] *Warwick Films v. Eisinger* [1969] 1 *Ch* 508; *Hyperion Records v. Warner Music* (17 May 1991, unreported).

[55] D. Vaver, 'Abridgments and Abstracts: Copyright Implications' [1995] *EIPR* 225; R. Burrell, 'Reining in Copyright Law: Is Fair Use the Answer?' [2001] *IPQ* 361, 365 *ff*.

[56] *Designers Guild v. Williams* [2000] 1 *WLR* 2416.

[57] *Williamson Music v. Pearson* [1987] *FSR* 97, 107; *Schweppes v. Wellington* [1984] *FSR* 210; cf. *Glyn v. Weston Feature Film* [1916] 1 *Ch* 261 and *Joy Music v. Sunday Pictorial Newspapers* [1960] 2 *QB* 60 (both suggesting that the defendant's effort is relevant, and if sufficient, parodies are non-infringing). On the new fair dealing defence for parody, see Chapter 9, section 8, pp. 248–52.

[58] *Ladbroke (Football) v. William Hill (Football)* [1964] 1 *WLR* 273, 276 (Lord Reid), 283 (Lord Evershed) (not only physical amount, but also substantial significance).

[59] *The Newspaper Licensing Agency v. Marks and Spencer* [2003] 1 *AC* 551, 559, [19]; *Designers Guild v. Williams* [2000] 1 *WLR* 2416, 2422, 2426 (Lord Millett); *Ladbroke (Football) v. William Hill (Football)* [1964] 1 *WLR* 273, 288 (Lord Hodson); *L. B. (Plastics) v. Swish Products* [1979] *FSR* 145, 152 (Lord Wilberforce), 159 (Lord Hailsham).

[60] *The Newspaper Licensing Agency v. Marks and Spencer* [2003] 1 *AC* 551, 559. Ascertaining parliamentary intention was relatively easy in relation to 'typographical arrangements', but may be less easy in relation to other works.

been copied.[61] In the case of an artistic work, Lord Hoffmann said, it is the 'artistic origi-nality' of that which has been copied—which primarily relates to the visual significance of what has been copied.[62] However, it is not always easy to determine exactly which types of labour and skill are 'relevant'. This is because each category of works accommodates a whole variety of different genres—'literary works' include not only novels and poems, but also databases and computer programs; 'artistic works' include realist and abstract paint-ings and drawings, as well as engineering drawings and maps, and so on—and in turn there is potentially a wide variety of types of relevant skill and labour.[63]

(d) *Importance to audience* It is sometimes said that the importance of the part is judged from the point of view of the person to whom the work is addressed.[64] For example, in dealing with an infringement action brought in 1934 in relation to the copying of 28 bars from the well-known military march 'Colonel Bogey', the Court of Appeal concluded that the part was substantial because anyone hearing the part taken would recognize it.[65] It was also the part by which the march was chiefly known and the cause of its popularity.

This approach to the determination of the importance of a part may be misleading because the audience to whom the work is addressed might be interested in parts of the works that involve little *relevant* labour, skill, or investment. The key inquiry is that stated by Lord Hoffmann: the importance of a part of a work is to be judged in terms of criteria that are relevant to the type of work in question. In contrast, the mere fact that part of a work becomes commercially significant or that there is a market for it should not matter when deciding whether the part is substantial.

(e) *Functional importance* A similar difficulty has arisen in relation to determining the importance of parts of functional works. Here, the courts have held that while a part may be important to the functioning of the work, if it is not also significant in terms of the originality of the work, it will not be substantial.[66] The issue has arisen where a small part of a computer program is copied. Although the program will not function, or will not function properly, without the part,[67] this does not mean that every part, however small, should be treated as a 'substantial part' of the program.[68]

(f) *The part must itself be capable of being protected* In some cases, the courts have sug-gested that a part will not be substantial if the amount that is taken would not itself attract copyright.[69] This can be seen in *Francis Day & Hunter v. 20th Century Fox*,[70] in which the owners of copyright in the song 'The Man Who Broke the Bank at Monte Carlo' brought

---

[61] At times, the courts come dangerously close to analysing quality in aesthetic terms and thus breaching the principle of 'non-discrimination', which they attempt to apply in the context of determining subsistence: cf. *Chappell v. D.C. Thompson* [1928–35] *MacG CC* 467 with *Kipling v. Genatosan* [1917–23] *MacG CC* 203.

[62] *Billhöfer Maschinenfabrik v. T. H. Dixon & Co.* [1990] *FSR* 105 (Hoffmann J).

[63] *Baigent v. Random House* [2007] *EWCA Civ* 247, [2007] *FSR* (24) 579. [145] (Mummery LJ).

[64] *Billhöfer Maschinenfabrik v. T. H. Dixon & Co.* [1990] *FSR* 105; *Francis Day & Hunter v. Bron* [1963] *Ch* 587, 623.

[65] *Hawkes & Sons v. Paramount Film Service* (1934) 1 *Ch D* 593, 609 (CA); *King Features v. Kleeman* [1941] *AC* 417.

[66] *Johnstone Safety v. Peter Cook* [1990] *FSR* 161, 178. See also *Rose Plastics GmbH v. William Beckett & Co* [1989] *FSR* 113, 123; cf. *Billhöfer Maschinenfabrik v. Dixon* [1990] *FSR* 105, 120.

[67] *Cantor Fitzgerald International v. Tradition (UK)* [2000] *RPC* 95, 130, *Ibcos Computers v. Barclays Mercantile Highland Finance* [1994] *FSR* 275.

[68] Ibid.; *Electronic Techniques Anglia v. Critchley Components* [1997] *FSR* 401; cf. *Data Access Corp. v. Powerflex Services* (1999) 45 *IPR* 353 (HCA), citing with approval *Cantor Fitzgerald International v. Tradition (UK)* [2000] *RPC* 95.

[69] *Ladbroke (Football) v. William Hill (Football)* [1964] 1 *WLR* 273, 293 (Lord Pearce); *Designers Guild v. Williams* [2000] 1 *WLR* 2416, 2423 (Lord Hoffmann); *Merchandising Corp. v. Harpbond* [1983] *FSR* 32, 47; *IPC Media v. Highbury Leisure* [2005] *FSR* (20) 431, 443–4, [12]–[13].   [70] [1940] *AC* 112.

an infringement action against a person who made a film of the same name. In response, Lord Wright said that the 'copying which is complained of is the use of the title, and that is too unsubstantial on the facts of this case to constitute infringement'.[71] In other words, Lord Wright thought that there was no copyright in the title by itself. A similar approach was adopted in the parody case of *Williamson Music v. Pearson*,[72] in which the only parts left in the defendant's parody of the claimant's song 'There is Nothin' Like a Dame' were the words 'we got', which were repeated several times. Judge Baker QC held that the words were not a substantial part of the copyright work, noting that 'in themselves the words would not be copyright as a literary work'.[73]

(g) Repeated takings In certain situations, the question has arisen as to whether the taking of an insubstantial part of the copyright work over a period of time amounts to the taking of a substantial part of the work. This question arises in two situations. The first is where a defendant regularly takes insubstantial amounts from a *single copyright work*. For example, while students might not infringe the copyright in a 300-page textbook if they were to copy five pages, what if, over the course of an afternoon, the same student were to go to a photocopy machine 20 times and photocopy a different five-page section each time? While the copying of five pages may not amount to an infringement, what of the copying of 100 pages? The second scenario is where copyright works are created regularly and the defendant consistently takes insubstantial amounts from different works. For example, would it be an infringement for an evening newspaper to reproduce regularly an insubstantial amount taken from daily financial reports of foreign markets that appeared in a morning paper?

As regards the first situation—that is, where a defendant regularly takes insubstantial amounts from a *single copyright work*—the court in principle must decide whether there are a number of takings or only one: a person will infringe if the acts can reasonably be seen as a single act and the cumulative taking is 'substantial'.[74] Relevant factors would presumably include whether the taking were used for the same purpose and the time frame within which the activities took place. Beyond those limited situations in which a series of acts could be interpreted as a single act, it seems that the courts recognize a broader doctrine of 'repeated systematic copying from the same work'. Although Laddie J had indicated that the concept of infringement by taking small and regular amounts was problematical,[75] the Court of Appeal in *Newspaper Licensing Agency (NLA) v. Marks & Spencer* stated that such systematic copying could be infringement.[76] (The issue was not discussed in the House of Lords.) The Court of Appeal found support for its view from a case in which a defendant was held to infringe copyright in the fixture lists for the football season, because it had copied a part of the list every two weeks.[77] Nevertheless, the comments in *NLA* were obiter and the Court gave no indication as to when (or why) copying would be treated as 'systematic'.[78]

---

[71]   Ibid., 123–4.   [72]   [1987] *FSR* 97.   [73]   Ibid., 107.

[74]   *Electronic Techniques Anglia v. Critchley Components* [1997] *FSR* 401, 410. See further *Infopaq International A/S v. Danske Dagblades Forenung*, Case C-5/08, [2009] *ECR* I–6569 (ECJ), [49] (assuming that multiple searches of digitized version of daily paper, each followed by reproduction of an 11-word extract, might cumulatively infringe).

[75]   *Electronic Techniques Anglia v. Critchley Components* [1997] *FSR* 401, 407–11.

[76]   *Newspaper Licensing Agency v. Marks & Spencer* [2001] *Ch* 257, 269, [33] (Peter Gibson LJ). See also ibid., 288–9, [108] (Mance LJ).

[77]   *Football League v. Littlewoods Pools* [1959] *Ch* 637 (whether such fixture lists would now be protected by copyright depends upon whether, as a result of the selection or arrangement, they could be said to be their author's own intellectual creation).

[78]   Indeed, the fixture list case could have been an example of a single act, given that there was a preconceived course of action.

In contrast, where there is repeated copying of insubstantial parts from a series of the claimant's works, there can be no finding of infringement (despite certain nineteenth-century cases to the contrary).[79] Dismissing those authorities on the basis of the different statutory terms, Peter Gibson LJ said: 'I do not understand how in logic what is an insubstantial part of a work can when aggregated to another insubstantial part of another work become a substantial part of the combined work.'[80] Here, the only issue is whether, in each case, the claimant can show some use of a substantial part of the individual works.[81]

(iii) Judicial and practical responses to the complicated inquiry

Having set out a structured approach suited to a rigorous analysis of copyright infringement, we should conclude our discussion of the British approach to identifying whether a 'substantial part' has been taken by observing that courts have not always been as rigorous or structured in their analyses as we suggest is necessary in the preceding account. In most cases, in fact, the court has not examined carefully the nature of the claimant's work, instead taking for granted the boundaries of the work and that the work as a whole is protected. In these cases, the courts have often gone straight to the issue of substantiality of the taking.[82] In yet other cases, the court has avoided examining the substantiality issue with any rigour. In some such cases, the courts deployed the 'rough practical test' that 'what is worth copying is worth protecting'.[83] This might be thought to be justified where there is an indication that the defendant has deliberately copied, from which the court can at least draw an inference that the defendant regarded the material that they had appropriated as 'worth taking' and therefore as embodying original skill and labour.[84] In other circumstances, in particular where the issue of derivation has been determined through a process of inference from multiple similarities between the defendant's material and the claimant's work, the courts have sometimes indicated that further inquiry is superfluous.[85]

2.3.2 The European approach to authorial works

Article 4(1)(a) of the Software Directive,[86] Article 5(a) of the Database Directive,[87] and Article 2 of the Information Society Directive[88] all confer on the owners of copyright in computer programs, databases, and authorial works generally a right to control the

---

[79] Cate v. Devon Constitutional Newspaper (1889) 40 Ch D 500; Trade Auxiliary v. Middlesborough (1889) 40 Ch D 425. There is a possibility of infringing sui generis database right: see Chapter 13.

[80] Newspaper Licensing Agency Components [1997] FSR 401, 269, 288.

[81] PCR v. Dow Jones Telerate [1998] FSR 170, 183. But cf. International A/S v. Danske Dagblades Forenung, Case C-5/08 [2009] ECR I–6569 (ECJ), [49] (not being so scrupulous).

[82] Ibcos Computers v. Barclays Mercantile Highland Finance [1994] FSR 275.

[83] Ladbroke (Football) v. William Hill (Football) [1964] 1 WLR 273 (HL).

[84] For criticism, see Autospin (Oil Seals) v. Beehive Spinning [1995] RPC 683; Ibcos Computers v. Barclays Mercantile Highland Finance [1994] FSR 275, 289; Cantor Fitzgerald International v. Tradition (UK) [2000] RPC 95, 131 (Pumfrey J) (test 'proves too much').

[85] This was the view of the majority of the House of Lords in Designers Guild v. Williams [2000] 1 WLR 2416, 2418 (Lord Bingham), 2426 (Lord Millett), 2435 (Lord Scott). But cf. Baigent v. Random House [2007] EWCA Civ 247, [2007] FSR 579 (an inference of copying was drawn, but this was held not to be substantial) and Nova Productions v. Mazooma [2007] EWCA Civ 219, [2007] RPC 589, 599, [26].

[86] Software Dir., Art. 4(1)(a) ('in part or in whole').

[87] Database Dir., Art. 5(a) ('in whole or in part').

[88] Info. Soc. Dir., Art. 2 ('in whole or in part'), Recital 21. Strictly speaking, this relates to the reproduction right only, but Arnold J has said in his view it applies to other harmonized rights (communication, making available, as well as distribution): England & Wales Cricket Board v Tixdaq [2016] EWHC 575 (Ch), [67].

reproduction of the work in whole or 'in part'. Although the reference to 'part' appears only in the context of reproduction, it is inconceivable that a parallel criterion would not be applicable to other rights that are harmonized under European law (on which, see Chapter 6). The Court of Justice regards the question of what counts as a 'part' as a matter of European law.

In *Infopaq International A/S v. Danske Dagblades Forenung*,[89] the Court was responding to a reference from Denmark in relation to a 'press clippings service', which informed subscribers when certain specified search terms appeared in the daily newspapers. Infopaq, which provided the service, would scan the papers into TIFF form, subject the digital version to optical character reading, and then execute searches. The searches would reproduce the search term and the five words either side of it. One of the questions referred to the Court was whether such segments amounted to reproduction 'in part' for the purposes of Article 2 of the Information Society Directive. The Court reasoned that, to understand the scope of protection, it was necessary to understand the subject matter. Noting that Article 2(a) protected 'works', the Court asserted (on the basis of various provisions in directives and the Berne Convention) that this referred to 'intellectual creations'. The Court noted that there was nothing in the *acquis* that suggested that 'parts are to be treated any differently from the work as a whole', and concluded from this that parts 'are protected by copyright since, as such, they share the originality of the whole work'.[90] The Court added that 'the various parts of a work … enjoy protection … provided that they contain elements which are the expression of the intellectual creation of the author of the work'.[91]

The test established by the Court is not a model of clarity. In particular, the Court first talks about parts 'sharing' the originality of the whole—a standard that might be taken to imply that anything but a *de minimis* component of a work is protected. However, the Court goes on to indicate that a fragment of a work will be a protected 'part' only if that fragment itself contains elements that are themselves original. The latter understanding of the judgment seems preferable: if the fragment reproduced itself would be protected as original (in the European sense), then it is to be treated as a 'part' of the work that was reproduced.[92]

The approach in *Infopaq* has been followed by the High Court and the Court of Appeal in the United Kingdom, and by the Court of Justice (Grand Chamber). In *SAS Institute v. World Programming*,[93] Arnold J treated the question of whether parts of SAS's computer manuals (literary works) reproduced by WPL were 'substantial' as requiring analysis of whether the sections that were reproduced were original.[94] On appeal, Lewison LJ observed:

> In *Infopaq* the court said that parts of a work are entitled to the same protection as the work as a whole. But the parts in question must 'contain elements which are the expression of the intellectual creation of the author of the work': [39]. This is now the test for determining whether a restricted act has been done in relation to a substantial part of a work.[95]

---

[89] Case C-5/08 [2009] *ECR* I–6569 (ECJ).

[90] Ibid., [38]; *Nintendo Co v. PC Box Srl*, Case C-355/12, EU:C:2014:25 (ECJ), [22].

[91] *Infopaq International A/S v. Danske Dagblades Forenung*, Case C-5/08 [2009] *ECR* I–6569, [39].

[92] See ibid., [49] (perhaps suggesting that it is only in the case of 'lengthy fragments' that a finding of infringement would be routine).   [93] [2010] *EWHC* 1829 (Ch), [244], [263] (Arnold J).

[94] *SAS Institute v. World Programming* [2010] *EWHC* 1829 (Ch), [243], [244], [263] (Arnold J).

[95] [2013] *EWCA Civ* 1482, [38]. The broad terms of Lewison LJ's pronouncement may suggest that the English courts will apply the new European test even to parts of British law that have not been harmonized. One way in which to do so would be to highlight the similarities between the *Infopaq* test and that recognized by Lord Hoffmann in *The Newspaper Licensing Agency v. Marks and Spencer* [2003] *AC* 551.

In *Newspaper Licensing Association v. Meltwater & PRCA*,[96] the Court of Appeal applied the *Infopaq* test and held that the defendant's news-alert system, which forwarded links to web pages containing news stories relating to particular, preselected search terms, and a 256-character excerpt (which included the title) from the story, would from time to time amount to reproduction of a substantial part of the news article (a literary work). It would do so where what was reproduced was the author's own intellectual creation. In *Football Association Premier League v. QC Leisure*,[97] the Court of Justice (Grand Chamber) held that there would be infringement of copyright works contained in films where the amount held simultaneously in the 'buffer' system of the decoder or on the screen amounted to 'the author's own intellectual creation'.

(i) Differences from the British approach

The *Infopaq* approach involves a quite different logic or approach to the question of what counts as infringement from that which formerly occurred in the United Kingdom. Two important dimensions are worth noting. First, in contrast to an approach that looks at whether the part taken comprises a substantial part of the protected work and thus requires some consideration of the parameters of the protected work, the *Infopaq* approach merely asks whether what is taken is itself original. *Infopaq* thus avoids a lot of difficult questions about the parameters of the work. Jonathan Griffiths refers to this as the 'dematerialization' of copyright.[98]

Second, while the originality of the part taken is a necessary requirement for a finding of infringement under UK law, it has not been regarded as the only consideration. Rather, under the British approach, a component was regarded as 'substantial' only if it was sufficiently important (from a qualitative viewpoint). The reproduction from a newspaper article of the phrase 'a forthcoming sale of the telecommunications group TDC which is expected to be bought' would be treated as substantial under current UK jurisprudence only if it were thought to be an 'important' part of the literary labour, skill, and judgment involved in creating the article. The shift to the test in *Infopaq* thus represents an expansion in the scope of protection.[99]

Having said this, the British approach was evolving quite rapidly in the last decades of the twentieth century. As we noted earlier,[100] there had been a discernible shift towards allowing a copyright owner to control ever-smaller uses and reuses of their works. In the 1980s, it was still arguable that 'substantiality' was a criterion that would enable third parties to make 'fair use' of a work. However, authorities such as *Designer's Guild* supported a view that the threshold would only exempt a use of an 'insignificant' part or *de minimis* part.[101] Moreover, Lord Hoffmann's speech in *Newspaper Licensing Agency v. Marks and Spencer* offered up a similarly restrictive logic: copyright would be infringed by any use of a part that was qualitatively 'substantial', in the sense that it reproduced protected 'labour, skill, and judgment' of the author.[102] In so doing, he steered British law towards an understanding of 'substantiality' based on a logic that is close to that deployed by the Court of Justice in *Infopaq*.[103]

---

[96] [2011] *EWCA Civ* 890, [24]–[28] (Chancellor Andrew Morritt).

[97] Case C-403/08 [2011] *ECR* I–9083 (ECJ, Grand Chamber), [156]–[159].

[98] J. Griffiths, 'Dematerialization, Pragmatism and the European Copyright Revolution' (2013) 33(4) *OJLS* 767, esp. 784 *ff*. Cf. Yin Harn Lee, 'The Persistence of the Text' [2018] *IPQ* 22 and 107.

[99] Ibid., 788–90 (predicting judicial, or possibly legislative, responses).   [100] See section 2.3.1, p. 203.

[101] *Designers Guild v. Williams* [2000] 1 *WLR* 2416, 2418 (Lord Bingham). See also *Newspaper Licensing Agency v. Marks & Spencer* [2001] *Ch* 257, 268, 287.

[102] *Newspaper Licensing Agency v. Marks and Spencer* [2003] *AC* 551, [19].

[103] *SAS Institute v. World Programming* [2010] *EWHC* 1829 (Ch), [243] (Arnold J) (opining that *Infopaq* took 'the same approach' as Lord Hoffmann). See further J. Griffiths, 'Dematerialization, Pragmatism and the European Copyright Revolution' (2013) 33(4) *OJLS* 767, 771 *ff*.

Although the *Infopaq* test is not without its attractions, it should be recognized too that it is a substantial expansion in the protective scope of copyright. Consequently, it is more important than ever for policymakers in this field to ensure that appropriate flexibility for users is provided by way of exceptions (discussed in Chapter 9).

2.3.3 Entrepreneurial works and related rights

Although UK law refers to infringement of copyright in sound recordings, films, broadcasts, and typographical arrangements as dependent on whether the defendant has carried out a restricted act in relation to the whole or 'a substantial part' of the subject matter, as we have already observed, Article 2 of the Information Society Directive harmonizes the reproduction right not only for authorial works, but also for 'phonograms' (that is, sound recordings), films, and broadcasts.[104] That legislation envisages infringement by reproduction of 'a part' of the subject matter. In due course, the Court of Justice is likely to develop jurisprudence on how to identify what constitutes a 'part' of these productions. The existing *Infopaq* case law is not directly relevant, because it concerns authorial works that are subject, at international and regional levels, to an 'originality' standard, whereas no equivalent standard is stated for related rights.[105] Pending guidance from the Court of Justice, analysis must be based on the existing case law on 'substantial part'.[106] Even when such jurisprudence emerges, it will be worth noting that European law has for the moment left untouched the national rules that govern infringement of the copyright in typographical arrangements.

In determining the parameters of the protected subject matter, similar issues arise as with the 'British' approach to determining infringement of authorial works. Indeed, the *Hyperion Records* case[107] concerned questions of infringement of copyright in a sound recording. It is necessary first to identify what the work is and then to assess whether the defendant's act (being a restricted act) employs a 'substantial part thereof'.

(i) Identifying the work

(a) What is a sound recording? As we noted already, sound recording is defined in the Copyright, Designs and Patents Act 1988 (CDPA 1988) as involving either:

(a) a recording of sounds, from which the sounds may be reproduced, or
(b) a recording of the whole or any part of a literary, dramatic or musical work, from which sounds reproducing the work or part may be produced.[108]

---

[104] Info. Soc. Dir., Art. 2(c) (phonograms), (d) (films), (e) (broadcasts). The right also applies to performances: see *Heythrop Zoological Gardens v. Captive Animals Protection Society* [2016] *EWHC* 1370 (Ch), [41] (Birss J).

[105] In this respect, it is notable that there is no requirement of 'substantial investment' comparable to that referred to for '*sui generis* rights' in databases. The Court of Justice has used that requirement as a mechanism by which to side-step the issue of what comprises a 'database': A. Ohly, 'Economic Rights', in E. Derclaye (ed.), *Research Handbook on the Future of EU Copyright* (2009), 212, at 215–16; *Apis Hristovich EOOD v. Lakorda ad*, Case C-545/07 [2009] *ECR* I-1627 (ECJ, Fourth Chamber). See further Chapter 13, section 3.3, pp. 370–1.

[106] Speculating as to the appropriate approach, von Lewinski and Walter favour the view (discussed later) that there is infringement by use of any identifiable part: Walter and von Lewinski, 970, [11.2.21]. Ansgar Ohly, in contrast, proposes a test analogous to that for the *sui generis* database right—namely, whether the use endangers the 'producer's investment': A. Ohly, 'Economic Rights', in E. Derclaye (ed.), *Research Handbook* (2009), 212, at 215–16.

[107] *Hyperion Records v. Warner Music* (17 May 1991, unreported). See section 2.3.1, pp. 201–2.

[108] CDPA 1988, s. 5A. However, the European term, contained in Info. Soc. Dir., Art. 2(c), is 'phonogram'. This would likely be understood in light of the international conventions: in the Rome Convention (1961) and Geneva Convention (1971), 'phonogram' is defined as an 'exclusively aural fixation of sounds of a performance or of other sounds'. Moreover, 'performance' is further defined as a performance of a 'literary or artistic work'.

Where there is a recording of a 'work'—or, more properly speaking, the performance of a work—it seems reasonable to define the 'recording' by reference to the 'work'. So a sound recording of Beethoven's *Fifth Symphony* might be said to be a single sound recording, particularly insofar as it records a single performance of a single work.[109] However, with recordings 'of sounds' that are not performances of works, it is less clear how a tribunal would identify the parameters of the recording. Significant considerations might be how the initial recording was produced: whether the recording took place at a particular time, or related to particular types of sound.[110] However, there seems in principle to be no reason why a very short recording, for example of a lion's roar, should not count as a distinct recording.

(b) What is a fixation of a film? As observed in Chapter 3, CDPA 1988, section 5B(1) defines a film as 'a recording on any medium from which a moving image may by any means be produced'. As with the requirements that are used to identify a sound recording, little guidance exists on how to identify a film. Of course, if issued to the public under a particular title, a movie will itself be a 'film', as will a short advertisement. In some cases, the subject matter being fixed will help to delineate the boundaries of a film; a film of a football match will thus likely be considered a single entity. However, the processes of production may give rise to possible distinct works, which then are combined into a composite: in *Hyperion Records v. Warner Bros*,[111] Laddie J took the view that a film could include a single day's rushes and thus might be regarded as works distinct from the final film as released. Indeed, a televised broadcast of a football match was found to transmit at least ten films, some of which were used in many of the broadcaster's transmissions, others, prepared in advance for the particular transmission, and yet others, prepared contemporaneously.[112] Likewise, a televised broadcast of a cricket match might include separate films comprising action replays each 'the product of the editing process'. [113]

(c) What is a broadcast? In *Network Ten v. TCN Channel Nine*,[114] the Australian High Court was asked to determine the parameters of a television broadcast for the purpose of deciding whether there was infringement when excerpts of between 8 and 42 seconds were used as objects of satirical comedy in another television programme (*The Panel*). The full Federal Court had held that each and every image fell to be protected, in effect denuding the notion of 'substantial part' of any content. The High Court, by a majority of three to two, reversed that decision, taking the view that the parameters of a 'broadcast' were to be defined by reference to the 'programmes' transmitted and thus that separate programmes, each with their own titles, were to be regarded as distinct broadcasts. Although much of the reasoning of the majority drew on the complex labyrinth of Australian legislation surrounding broadcasting,[115] two key points suggest that the

---

[109] *The Newspaper Licensing Agency v. Marks and Spencer* [2003] *AC* 551, 557–8, [11] (Lord Hoffmann) (a sound recording of one musical work is by definition different from the recording of another, even if they are issued on the same CD).

[110] *Hyperion Records v. Warner Bros* (17 May 1991, unreported) (Deputy Judge Laddie QC).

[111] (17 May 1991, unreported).

[112] *Football Association Premier League v. QC Leisure* [2008] *EWHC* 1411, [2008] *FSR* (32) 789, [180] (opening sequence film; opening sequence graphics film; previous highlights film; match highlights film; special features film; next match preview film; on-screen graphics film; match film—via action replays; clean live feed film; world feed film). In the same case, however, it was accepted, at [208], that an 'action replay' would not constitute a film of its own (presumably, in part, because it would comprise a copy of an existing film).

[113] *England & Wales Cricket Board & Sky UK v. Tixdaq & Fanatix* [2016] *EWHC* 575 (Ch), [97] (arguable).

[114] [2004] *HCA* 14, reversing (2002) 118 *FCR* 417. For the first-instance decision of Conti J, see (2001) *FCR* 235.

[115] The majority drew heavily on M. Handler, 'The Panel Case and Television Broadcast Copyright' (2003) 25 *Sydney L Rev* 391, while the minority, especially Kirby J, sought to refute Handler's arguments.

finding could be a useful guide to the British position. First, the Australian Copyright Act 1968 was found to have been based on the British Copyright Act 1956, which, in introducing copyright protection for broadcasts, linked the subject matter of the right to the content—that is, 'programmes'. Second, the High Court was clearly conscious of the fact that the structure of the legislation implied that protection of entrepreneurial works would be weaker than that afforded authorial works, yet the effect of the decision of the full Federal Court would have been to make protection of broadcasts the strongest form of protection.

It therefore seems that the decision may be a useful precedent.[116] The parameters of a broadcast will often be readily determined by reference to the programme, publicized under a particular name and referred to in television listings. A live broadcast of a football match will be defined by reference to the match itself, as well as typically some introductory and concluding commentary. A broadcast of test cricket, lasting five days, will usually comprise a series of broadcasts of each two-hour session of play.[117] In addition, broadcasts of advertisements might constitute distinct broadcasts.

(d) What is a published edition? In *Newspaper Licensing Agency v. Marks and Spencer,*[118] the issue was whether the copyright in the typographical arrangements in a number of the newspapers had been infringed by copying and distributing individual articles. As a result, the House of Lords was called upon to consider whether the NLA had typographical copyright in each of the individual articles in the newspapers or only in each newspaper as a whole. The House of Lords held that 'the frame of reference for the term "published edition" is the language of the publishing trade' and therefore that 'the edition is the product, generally between covers, which the publisher offers to the public'.[119] Thus, each edition of the newspaper rather than each article benefited from the typographical copyright.

(ii) A 'substantial part' (or 'a part')

Once the parameters of the entrepreneurial works have been identified, it is necessary to assess whether what has been reproduced is a 'substantial part' or, under European law for phonograms, fixations of films, and broadcasts, 'a part'.

A number of commentators (and some foreign courts) have suggested that it was not possible to speak in a meaningful way about the 'important' part of an entrepreneurial work, contending that the quality of the entrepreneurial work will not change throughout the work.[120] For example, it has been argued that, while a three-second sample that contains the 'hook' of a song may be an important part of a musical work, it does not necessarily follow from this that the way in which the three seconds were recorded will be any different from the way in which the rest of the song was recorded. Indeed, it is more likely that the quality of the sound recording will be the same throughout the recording than that it will change from part to part.[121] Moreover, if a brief recording of a bird chirping is itself protected, why should the equivalent part of any other recording (however long or sophisticated the remainder may be) also be regarded as protected? This analysis implies

---

[116] Note also the Satellite Convention 1974, as well as the Satellite Dir. (referring to protection of 'programme-carrying signals', indicating that the relevant unit is the 'programme').

[117] *England & Wales Cricket Board & Sky UK v. Tixdaq & Fanatix* [2016] *EWHC* 575 (Ch), [96]–[98].

[118] [2003] *AC* 551 (HL).   [119] Ibid., [14].   [120] Laddie et al., 400, [6.29].

[121] In the case of a sound recording, it seems that, on this basis, it would be wrong to treat the part that embodies the most distinctive, unusual, or catchy sounds as automatically representing the important part of the sound recording. This is because those parts may reflect, for example, the musical work, performance, and so on, rather than labour, skill, and judgement in creating the recording itself.

that the slightest shred of all of these productions should receive protection. Such an approach has been adopted in relation to films and phonograms in Germany.[122]

Whatever the logical attraction of treating any identifiable reproduction as 'a part', such an approach is unattractive for three reasons. First, at least from a UK perspective, it would render the adjective 'substantial' in section 16(3) of the CDPA 1988 meaningless.[123] Second, it would confer stronger protection on 'entrepreneurial work' (related rights), which are mere products of investment, than on authorial works, which are the result of creative choices, and thus invert the conventional privileging of the latter.[124] Third, it would confer unnecessary and unjustified levels of control on such producers, given that only very limited freedoms are offered for downstream creators and users (on which, see Chapter 9).

In the United Kingdom, for the moment, the decision of the House of Lords in *Newspaper Licensing Agency* governs the issue. In that case, it was held in relation to typographical arrangements that it is necessary to assess whether there has been reproduction of a 'substantial part' from the perspective of the quality of the labour and skill invested in choosing the presentation and layout (as opposed to the particular words and images published in the edition).[125] One commentary says this suggests that the threshold may be set 'fairly high'.[126] Unless and until the Court of Justice indicates otherwise, the better view is that the approach in *NLA* should also apply to fixations of films, sound recordings, and broadcasts.[127] The question would be whether a substantial part of the investment (whether technical or organizational) in producing the recording is appropriated.

This was, in fact, the approach adopted by Arnold J in *England and Wales Cricket Board and Sky UK v Tixdaq and Fanatix*.[128] In that case the Court was called upon to assess the legitimacy of a mobile platform that was used by users to upload short segments from broadcast footage of cricket matches (e.g. wickets, dropped catches, or spectacular shots). Arnold J noted that broadcasts and fixations of films were entrepreneurial copyright, designed to protect investment. Referring to the Information Society Directive, the judge observed:

> parts of broadcasts and first fixations of films enjoy protection ... provided that they contain elements which reflect the rationale for protecting broadcasts and first fixations, that is to say, the investment made by the broadcaster or producer. I do not consider that ... reproduction of any part of a broadcast or first fixation amounts to an infringement.... [T]he correct test of substantiality is to consider the degree of reproduction both quantitatively and qualitatively, having regard to the extent to which the reproduction exploits the investment made by the broadcaster or producer.

Arnold J elaborated in relation to fixation and broadcasts of sports events. In such cases, broadcasters and producers invest knowing that some parts of the footage—goals in football, wickets or sixes in cricket—will be more interesting to viewers than other parts.

[122] *Metall auf Metall*, Case I ZR 182/11 (13 December 2012), I ZR 112/06 (20 November 2008) (BGH); *TV-Toyal*, Case I ZR 52/05 (20 December 2007). These cases are discussed in F. Niemann and L. Mackert, 'Limits on Sampling Sound Recordings' [2013] *EIPR* 356 and the first *Kraftwerk* decision is translated in N. Conley and T. Braegelmann, '*Metall auf Metall*: The Importance of the *Kraftwerk* Decision for the Sampling of Music in Germany' (2009) 56 *J Copyright Soc'y USA* 1017. Subsequently, the case was considered by the BVerfG (Federal Constitutional Court), 31 May 2016—*Metall auf Metall* (Metal on Metal), 2016 ZUM 626, and it has now been referred to the CJEU as Case C-476/16 *Hutter v Pelham*.

[123] *Hyperion Records v. Warner Bros* (17 May 1991) (unreported).

[124] A. Ohly, 'Economic Rights', in E. Derclaye (ed.), *Research Handbook* (2009), 212, 216.

[125] *Newspaper Licensing Agency v. Marks and Spencer* [2003] 1 *AC* 55.

[126] Laddie et al., 497, [9.20].   [127] Ibid., 400, [6.29].   [128] [2016] *EWHC* 575 (Ch).

Indeed, these incidents are often reworked by way of 'action replay' and related analytical technologies (to highlight whether players were off-side, whether the ball pitched in line, or a foot or ball crossed a relevant line). Moreover, the investment is made knowing that there is not a single market just for footage of the whole game, but also secondary markets for programmes with just the highlights. Consequently Arnold J rejected the proposition that different parts of a broadcast or film could not be identified as qualitatively more important: '[T]he footage is not undifferentiated either in terms of its interest to viewers or in terms of its commercial value or in terms of the equipment and skills that is required to produce it … '.

Having said this, it is widely assumed that quite small parts of sound recordings, films, and broadcasts might be protected. The matter has been frequently canvassed in relation to sampling of sound recordings (although without generating useful judicial guidance).[129] The courts have indicated that expert evidence, for example from musicologists, might help to determine the issue of whether a part is a 'substantial' part of a sound recording.[130] In a case decided in the early 1990s, in which one television company had broadcast football matches from the 1990 World Cup and another broadcaster showed clips of between 14 and 37 seconds (comprising the goals or near misses), it was conceded by the defendant that these were 'substantial' reproductions (the Court, however, holding that it was fair dealing).[131] Such parts would have been of real interest to viewers. More recently, Arnold J treated eight-second clips from cricket broadcasts as 'substantial' as they comprised 'highlights', 'something of interest, and hence value' and thereby 'substantially exploited the … investment in producing the relevant broadcast and/or film.'[132] In contrast, where four frames of a video stream were held in a decoder at a given moment, Kitchin J concluded that this was not a 'substantial part' of the film fixation, because it lasted 'a fraction of a second' and had 'no inherent value'.[133] In another case concerning buffering, Floyd J held that while the buffer copies might be a 'substantial part' of a film, they would not have been in relation to the broadcast.[134] It appeared that the issue would, however, be the subject of a reference to the Court, but this was not pursued.[135]

The question then of the meaning of 'a part' in relation to related rights is sorely in need of an authoritative decision. Fortuitously, the matter has now been referred to the ECJ by the German Federal Court of Justice, in a case which concerns 'very short audio

---

[129] *Produce Records v. BMG Entertainment* (unreported, 19 January 1999) (Jonathan Parker J) ('plainly arguable' that the sample amounted to a substantial part). For discussion, see R. Salmon, 'Sampling and Sound Recording Reproduction: Fair Use or Infringement?' [2010] *Ent L Rev* 174.

[130] *Produce Records v. BMG Entertainment* (unreported, 19 January 1999) (Jonathan Parker J); *Hyperion Records v. Warner Bros* (unreported, 17 May 1991) (Judge Laddie QC). See Laddie et al., 401, [6.30] (suggesting that many cases of use of samples will escape liability).

[131] *BBC v. British Satellite Broadcasting* [1992] *Ch* 141, 148.

[132] *England & Wales Cricket Board & Sky UK v. Tixdaq & Fanatix* [2016] *EWHC* 575 (Ch), [99]. See also *Football Association Premier League v. QC Leisure* [2008] *EWHC* 1411, [2008] *FSR* (32) 789, [208]–[209] (Kitchin J) (holding that 'action replays' lasting a few seconds were a 'substantial part' of a 90-minute film of a football match).

[133] *Football Association Premier League v. QC Leisure* [2008] *EWHC* 1411, [2008] *FSR* (32) 789, [234]. But cf. *Higgs* [2008] *EWCA Crim* 1324, [9] (suggesting that a single frame of a film might be protected, relying on CDPA 1988, s. 17(4)).

[134] *ITV Studios v. TV Catch Up* [2011] *EWHC* 1874 (Pat), [110], [112] (Floyd J). It seems that Floyd J accepted counsel's submission that '[t]he copyright which arises in a broadcast arises because of the collocation of subject matter which makes up the broadcast'.

[135] *ITV Broadcasting v. TV CatchUp* [2011] *EWHC* 2977, [27] (Floyd J) ('I cannot see any basis on which it can sensibly be argued that there is a reproduction of a substantial part of a broadcast').

snatches' from a recording entitled 'Metall auf Metall' by 1970s German electronic musicians, *Kraftwerk*. The samples were used by Pelham on a recording of performer Sabrina Setlur called 'Nur Mir'.[136] The Court asks whether such short snatches infringe the right conferred by Article 2 of the Information Society Directive, and how the Charter rights affect this conclusion. The ECJ is also asked to advise on the application of the exceptions (on which see Chapter 9, section 7).

For the reasons already explained, we suggest the Court approve the approach adopted by the House of Lords in *NLA*, and applied by Arnold J in the *Fanatix* case. In the context of Metall auf Metall, which is a 2' 11" recording in a 'minimalist' style, comprising the (sampled) repeating background, it may be more difficult for the Court to identify distinct components as qualitatively more significant (though the recording does build to a crescendo towards the end). It is to be hoped that the characteristics of the particular recording in issue does not lead the Court into ill-considered generalizations.

2.4 NON-LITERAL COPYING OF AUTHORIAL WORKS

As we explained in Chapter 6, the protection given to entrepreneurial works is limited to the form in which the work is fixed (in the case of a film, the specific images; in the case of a sound recording, the specific sounds recorded; for a broadcast, literally 'the signal'). As Mr Justice Richard Arnold has noted, these are 'signal copyrights'.[137] One of the consequences of this is that the only question that arises in relation to entrepreneurial works is whether a substantial part of the 'signal' has been taken. In relation to authorial works, however, the protection extends beyond the specific form in which the work is recorded or communicated to include other aspects—what Arnold calls 'the content'—of the work. For example, the protection afforded to a literary work, such as a novel, may extend beyond reproduction of the printed words on the page to include copying of the storyline, plot, and characters that form part of the novel.

In this section, we try to explain first what counts as the 'content'—that is, how far down beyond the 'signal' the protection of authorial copyright reaches. We go on to explain the principle that such protection does not extend to 'ideas', understood broadly as encompassing also facts and 'functions'. Finally, we consider the impact of European harmonization on these rules.

2.4.1 Non-literal components of an authorial work

Perhaps the best way in which to understand the scope of protection potentially available beyond the surface of the work is to provide some examples.

In relation to *literary and dramatic works*, as well as the words on the page (the literal aspect of the work), the non-literal elements of a novel or play (which may be protected by the copyright therein) may include the plot,[138] the storyline,[139] as well as the incidents

---

[136] Case C-476/17, *Hutter v Pelham* (pending).

[137] R. Arnold, 'Content Copyrights and Signal Copyrights: The Case for a Rational Scheme of Protection' (2011) 1 *QMJIP* 272 (explained in Chapter 6, section 2.2, pp. 147–8); *England & Wales Cricket Board v Tixdaq* [2016] *EWHC* 575 (Ch), [60].

[138] *Harman Pictures v. Osborne* [1967] 1 *WLR* 723, 728; *Rees v. Melville* [1914] *MacG CC* 168; *Brighton v. Jones* [2005] *FSR* (16) 288, [63]–[66]. In relation to literary works, the taking of a plot of a novel or play can certainly infringe—if the plot is a substantial part of the copyright work: *Designers Guild v. Williams* [2001] 1 *WLR* 2416; *Ibcos Computers v. Barclays Mercantile Highland Finance* [1994] *FSR* 275, 291.

[139] *Corelli v. Gray* (1913) 29 *TLR* 570; *Autospin (Oil Seals) v. Beehive Spinning* [1995] *RPC* 683, 697; *Kelly v. Cinema Houses* [1928–35] *MacG CC* 362.

and themes.[140] While the issue has not really been addressed in the United Kingdom, it is less likely that the characters of a novel or play will be protected.[141] As we explain later, the non-literal elements of a literary work do not include the general ideas that may have informed or underpinned a work.

In relation to *computer programs*, copyright protection potentially extends beyond the object and source code of the program to include non-literal elements such as the structure or architecture of the program.[142]

In relation to *musical works*, it seems that protection might include the melody, phrasing, or rhythm, the time, or the suggested orchestration, but not aspects such as timbre or pitch contour, which can be said to be purely aspects of performance style.

The question of the scope of protection available for *artistic works* was considered in *Krisarts SA v. Briarfine*.[143] The defendants commissioned an artist, G, to paint a number of scenes, including one of the Houses of Parliament with Westminster Bridge in the foreground. They showed G postcards of the scenes that they wanted her to paint, as well as prints taken from the painting of another artist, L. Many of G's paintings were made from the same view and the same angle as L's paintings. While Whitford J stressed that other painters should not be prevented from painting the same scenes, he did accept that there could be certain elements of the scenes that were 'distinctive' enough to warrant being protected.[144] As he said:

> When one is considering a view of a very well-known subject like the Houses of Parliament with Westminster Bridge and part of the Embankment in the foreground, the features in which copyright is going to subsist are very often the choice of viewpoint, the exact balance of foreground features or features in the middle ground and features in the far ground, the figures which are introduced, possibly in the case of a river scene the craft on the river and so forth. It is in choices of this character that the person producing the artistic work makes his original contribution.[145]

In light of this, Whitford J held that it was arguable that G's use of L's work was sufficiently substantial to amount to infringement of copyright. While it is highly unlikely that the style used by an artist could be protected (style being the equivalent of an idea), it has been suggested that if the 'feeling and artistic character' of the claimant's work has been taken, infringement might have occurred.[146]

2.4.2 Non-protection of ideas

Although copyright protection thus extends to copying of non-literal elements that fall below the 'surface' of a work, nevertheless it is a long-established principle that copyright protection is not granted to the ideas that are embodied in or which may have inspired the work.[147] In more positive terms, this means that third parties are able to make whatever use they wish of the ideas that are contained in a copyright work. Thus it is not an

---

[140] *Corelli* (1913) 29 *TLR* 570; *Rees v. Melville* [1914] *MacG CC* 168; cf. *Norowzian v. Arks (No. 2)* [2000] *FSR* 67, 74, 76 (rhythm and pace, theme, and editing style were not subjects of copyright).

[141] *Kelly v. Cinema House* [1928–35] *MacG CC* 362, 368. For a review, see J. McCutcheon, 'Property in Literary Characters: Protection under Australian Copyright Law' [2007] *EIPR* 140.

[142] *Ibcos Computers v. Barclays Mercantile Highland Finance* [1994] *FSR* 275, 292, 302; *Cantor Fitzgerald International v. Tradition (UK)* [2000] *RPC* 95, 133–4.   [143] [1977] *FSR* 557.

[144] While Whitford J was not willing to reach a final decision on copyright infringement, he was sympathetic to such a finding.   [145] [1977] *FSR* 557, 562.

[146] *Bauman v. Fussell* [1978] *RPC* 485; *Brooks v. Religious Tract Society* (1897) 45 *WR* 476.

[147] The principle that there can be no copyright in an idea has been described at the highest level as 'trite law': *L. B. (Plastics) v. Swish Products* [1979] *FSR* 145, 160 (Lord Hailsham), 165 (Lord Salmon).

infringement for someone to take the ideas or concepts 'behind' a painting, a book, or a computer program and incorporate them into their own work. In this context, it is important to note that 'idea' is a shorthand expression that covers an array of different things such as the ideas that prompted the work (for example to explore the impact of copyright law on artists), the subject matter of the work (for example a book on intellectual property law),[148] or the general style in which the work is created (such as a Cubist painting).[149]

Sometimes, the principle that copyright law does not protect ideas is referred to as the 'idea–expression dichotomy'. This is usually taken to mean that what is protected is not an idea, but its expression. Insofar as the dichotomy implies that copyright predominantly protects the mode of expression used by the author, rather than the ideas, the dichotomy is not inaccurate. It is unhelpful, however, in that it wrongly suggests that copyright protection is limited to the form or expression used by the author and that copyright does not protect against change of form or against non-literal copying:[150] as we noted earlier, copyright law will protect many of the ideas expressed in a work. As Lord Hoffmann explained in the *Newspaper Licensing Agency* case, copyright infringement:

> . . . is sufficiently flexible to include the copying of ideas abstracted from a literary, dramatic, musical or artistic work, provided that their expression in the original work has involved sufficient of the relevant original skill and labour [or presumably, now 'intellectual creation'] to attract copyright protection.[151]

In *Designers Guild v. Williams*,[152] Lord Hoffmann reviewed the case law on idea and expression, and concluded that it supported two quite distinct propositions. The first is that a copyright work may express certain ideas that are not protected 'because they have no connection with the literary, dramatic, musical or artistic nature of the work'.[153] Lord Hoffmann said that this would be the case with a literary work that described a system or invention: although the work would be protected, copyright would not entitle the author to claim protection for their system or invention as such. He gave, as a specific example, the case of *Kleeneze v. DRG (UK)*,[154] in which Whitford J found that there had been no infringement of copyright in the claimant's drawing of a letterbox draught excluder, where the defendant had merely taken the concept of the draught excluder.

The other proposition is that certain ideas expressed by a copyright work may not be protected because, although they are ideas of a literary, dramatic, or artistic nature, they are not original, or are so commonplace as not to form a substantial part of the work. Lord Hoffmann gave the example of *Kenrick v. Lawrence*.[155] This case concerned the copyright protection available for a rudimentary drawing of a hand pointing to a square on a ballot paper to be used by illiterate voters. While the court held that the drawing was protected by copyright, it also said that, because the level of skill, labour, and effort that was used in creating the work was minimal (it was a simple, functional work), nothing short of an exact literal reproduction of the drawing would constitute an infringement.[156] In that case, copyright subsisted in the drawing of a hand, but such copyright would not enable

---

[148] *Kenrick v. Lawrence* (1890) 25 *QBD* 99, 102.

[149] *Norowzian v. Arks* [2000] *EMLR* 67, 74, 76 (no copyright in film-editing style).

[150] For a warning about the use of this aphorism, see *Designers Guild v. Williams* [2000] 1 *WLR* 2416, 2422 (Lord Hoffmann); *Ibcos Computers v. Barclays Mercantile Highland Finance* [1994] *FSR* 275 (Jacob J).

[151] *The Newspaper Licensing Agency v. Marks and Spencer* [2003] 1 *AC* 55, 560, [20].

[152] [2000] 1 *WLR* 2416.

[153] Ibid., 2423. Discussed by Jacob LJ in *Nova Productions v. Mazooma* [2007] *EWCA Civ* 219, [2007] *RPC* 589, 601, esp. [35].

[154] [1984] *FSR* 399.   [155] (1890) 25 *QBD* 99.   [156] Ibid., 104.

the copyright owner to object to other people drawing hands, if in so doing all that was reproduced was the idea. As Lord Hoffmann explained: 'At that level of abstraction, the idea, though expressed in the design, would not have represented sufficient of the author's skill and labour as to attract copyright protection.'[157]

Lord Hoffmann's articulation of the rule that ideas are unprotected is helpful in that it recognizes that the vagueness of the concept of 'idea' is likely to lead to misinterpretation of the nature and scope of the exclusion. In fact, the exclusion is a relatively narrow one and does not encompass everything that might be referred to, in common speech, as an idea. However, his attempt to pin down the rule that copyright is not infringed by the use of some ideas is open to the criticisms that it lacks clarity,[158] is incomplete,[159] and (by collapsing the rule on the non-protection of ideas into a rule on originality, rather than acknowledging its basis in public policy) might produce an unduly limited account of the exception. Failing to acknowledge that the rule is based in public policy suggests that if general ideas embody substantial labour and skill, they will benefit from protection (unless they are 'unconnected' with the work). This would be a novel, and undesirable, outcome. The exclusion of 'ideas' from the scope of protection is an important judicial technique that is used to reconcile the divergent interests of copyright owners with those of users, creators, and the public more generally.[160] These interests include, but are by no means confined to: the public interest in ensuring that new works can be made dealing with the same topic, or subject matter;[161] the public interest in ensuring that copyright protection does not undermine the free use of functional ideas (other than those protected by designs);[162] the desirability of allowing multiple works using the same techniques of production (again, subject to the limitation of patent law); the public interest in free expression; and particularly the free dissemination of political and economic ideas and historical facts.[163] The rule on non-protection of ideas is thus primarily directed at leaving free from monopolization the building blocks of culture, communication, innovation, creativity, and expression.[164] It can be no surprise, then, that, given the potential variety of influences, the application of the rule has been somewhat unpredictable. Moreover, in an era in which there is increased international norm-setting in the definition of the rights of the copyright owner, the non-protection of ideas represents one of the few avenues by which the courts can take account of the individual circumstances and merits of particular decisions.

---

[157] [2000] 1 *WLR* 2416, 2423.

[158] In particular, his speech leaves unclear what kind of connections make ideas part of the protected elements.

[159] Lord Hoffmann's account seems to be incomplete, in that it omits techniques, methods, or style— matters that are usually considered unprotected: *Harman v. Osborne* [1967] 1 *WLR* 723, 728; *Norowzian v. Arks* [2000] *EMLR* 67, 74, 76; *Sawkins v. Hyperion* [2005] 1 *WLR* 3280, 3288, [29]; *IPC Media v. Highbury Leisure* [2005] *FSR* (20) 434, 444; *Baigent v. Random House* [2007] *EWCA Civ* 247, [146].

[160] There is an abundance of US literature: A. Yen, 'A First Amendment Perspective on the Idea/Expression Dichotomy and Copyright in a Work's "Total Concept And Feel"' (1989) 38 *Emory LJ* 393 (emphasizing the role and limitations of dichotomy in protecting freedom of speech); J. Litman, 'The Public Domain' (1990) 39 *Emory LJ* 965 (explaining the law's reluctance to protect ideas, information, short phrases, simple plots, themes, stock scenes, and utilitarian solutions to concrete problems on the ground that they are difficult to trace); S. Vaidhyanathan, *Copyright and Copywrongs: The Rise of Intellectual Property and How It Threatens Creativity* (2001) (arguing that the distinction has been steadily collapsing and that it is crucial that we rediscover, reinvent, and strengthen the idea–expression dichotomy).

[161] *Jones v. London Borough of Tower Hamlets* [2001] *RPC* (23) 407, 418–19.

[162] *Kleeneze v. DRG (UK) Ltd* [1984] *FSR* 399.

[163] *Ashdown v. Telegraph Group Ltd* [2001] 3 *WLR* 1368, 1379, [2002] *RPC* 235.

[164] *Jones v. London Borough of Tower Hamlets* [2001] *RPC* (14) 379, 418–19, [27].

While *Designers Guild* might have heralded a narrow interpretation of copyright law's refusal to protect 'ideas', subsequent cases indicate that the lower courts prefer to take advantage of the flexibility that the 'idea–expression dichotomy' provides to dismiss speculative claims. In *Navitaire v. EasyJet*,[165] the owner of copyright in a source code brought an action against a former licensee who, having never seen the source code, tried to emulate the functional behaviour of the program. Pumfrey J found no infringement, stressing that the functional behaviour of a program was different from the plot of a novel (which might gain protection) and that policy weighed against protecting the 'business logic' of a program through copyright.[166] In *Nova Productions v. Mazooma Games*,[167] Kitchin J held that similarities between video games were attributable to general ideas that had 'little to do with skill and effort' expended by the programmer. This was affirmed on appeal, Jacob LJ concluding that 'what was found to have inspired some aspects of the defendants' game is just too general to amount to a substantial part of the claimant's game'.[168] In *Baigent v. Random House* (the *Da Vinci Code* case),[169] Peter Smith J held that Dan Brown's book did not infringe copyright in Baigent and Leigh's *The Holy Blood and the Holy Grail*. In essence, Peter Smith J held that Brown had used Baigent and Leigh's book (along with other books), but that what was taken were facts and ideas at such a level of abstraction that there was no infringement.[170] In so holding, the judge observed that the line between idea and expression 'is to enable a fair balance to be struck between protecting the rights of the author and allowing literary development'.[171] The decision was affirmed on appeal, the Court unanimously agreeing that there was no reproduction of a substantial part of Baigent and Leigh's book because that which was in *The Da Vinci Code* was ideas rather than 'the form or manner in which ideas were expressed'.[172] Mummery LJ, in particular, emphasized that literary copyright does not give rights that enable persons 'to monopolise historical research or knowledge'.[173] A final example of a situation in which the defendant was 'inspired' by the claimant's copyright work, but was held not to have taken a substantial part, is provided by the 'World Cup Willie' case.[174] The claimant's work was the World Cup logo from 1966 comprising a lion in an England strip kicking a football. The defendant created a modernized version of a lion playing football for England. Although the defendant had copied the idea of a lion kicking a ball with its right foot, the postures were different (one leant back; the other, forward), the angle of the faces differed (the plaintiff's drawing depicted the lion's face from the side, whereas the defendant's showed the whole face). While the stylization was similar, the High Court concluded that all that had been reproduced was ideas rather than 'a substantial part of the original'.

On the other hand, in *Temple Island Collections v. New English Teas*,[175] the (then) Patents County Court took a rather narrow view of 'ideas' when it found infringement

---

[165] [2006] *RPC* (3) 111.   [166] Ibid., 162, [130].   [167] [2006] *RPC* (14) 379.

[168] [2007] *EWCA Civ* 219, [2007] *RPC* 589, 603, [44].

[169] [2006] *EWHC* 719, [2006] *FSR* (44) 893; (2007) *EWCA Civ* 247, [2007] *FSR* 579.

[170] [2006] *FSR* (44) 893, 952, [266].   [171] Ibid., 926, [153], 951, [255]. See also at 963, [348].

[172] [2007] *EWCA Civ* 247, [2007] *FSR* 579, 618, [92], 621, [99] (Lloyd LJ), 622–3, [105] (Rix LJ), and [137], [153]–[154] (Mummery LJ).

[173] Ibid., [156].   [174] *Jules Rimet Cup v. Football Association* [2008] *FSR* (10) 254.

[175] [2012] *EWPCC* 1. See also *Hodgson v. Isaac* [2010] *EWPCC* 37, in which the Patents County Court held that Isaac's film script 'Down among the Dead Men', the story of a wheelchair-bound football fan, was an infringing adaptation of the claimant's autobiography, *Flipper's Side*. The parties had initially been working towards an adaptation of Hodgson's story, but when the script began to deviate from his own account, Hodgson withdrew his consent. The judge rejected the defendant's argument that it had relied on conversations with Hodgson as opposed to reading *Flipper's Side*, and concluded that the amounts reproduced were substantial. More was taken than abstract biographical matters, including detailed incidents and, importantly, Hodgson's interpretation of those events: see [80]–[81].

of copyright in a photograph of a red double-decker crossing Westminster Bridge (the background all in black and white) (see Chapter 4, Fig 4.2, p. 109), when the defendants created a similar image (albeit from quite a different angle) of a red bus crossing Westminster Bridge with the background in black and white (Chapter 4, Fig. 4.3, p. 110). The case received widespread criticism on the basis that what had been reproduced by the defendant was the commonplace idea of a red foreground and monochrome background, and the idea of creating an image of an iconic London bus coupled with the setting of Westminster Bridge. Certainly, each was a commonplace idea. Perhaps the better view is that, in a case of relatively limited originality, there should be infringement only where there is near-perfect copying.[176]

2.4.3 European copyright law and non-literal copying

The *Infopaq* test has been developed primarily with copying of discrete parts or fragments of a work. However, as already noted, under traditional UK law, reproduction might also occur through copying 'non-literal' parts of a work (other than 'ideas'). Consequently, reproducing the general structure of a work—the plot of a novel or the layout of an artistic work—might count as reproduction of a substantial part. As yet, we have little indication of how to approach such cases in the post-*Infopaq* era.

The starting point is that the European legislature has taken different approaches to harmonization of, on the one hand, computer programs and databases, and on the other, 'authorial works'. As we saw in Chapter 6, in relation to computer programs and databases, the legislature harmonized both the reproduction right and the adaptation right. It also made express provision in the Software Directive to the effect that copyright did not protect ideas. In contrast, the Information Society Directive harmonized only the reproduction right and makes no explicit reference to non-protection of ideas. This structure might suggest that EU harmonization applies to non-literal copying of computer programs and databases, but not in relation to other authorial works.

However, in many countries (including the United Kingdom), the 'adaptation' right and the 'reproduction' right frequently overlap, the reproduction right also covering many non-literal uses.[177] It is quite conceivable that the Court of Justice will interpret Article 2 of the Information Society Directive broadly to cover non-literal copying (with the advantage that, by so doing, it will minimize the impact of the different approaches in the legislation).[178] Indeed, as we saw earlier, at least one Advocate-General has suggested that non-literal copying might be infringement of the reproduction right in authorial works. In *Painer v. SVGH*,[179] Advocate-General Trstenjak suggested that the making of a photofit image of a woman from a copyright-protected photograph such as to reflect the development of the woman's appearance might be a 'reproduction' if 'the personal intellectual creation which justifies the copyright protection of the photographic template is still embodied in the photo-fit'. If the photofit only appropriated raw data from the image (the size of the nose, the distance between the eyes) and none of the lighting, angle, etc., then the photofit would not count as a reproduction.

A second, related, matter is how the 'idea–expression dichotomy' applies to works falling within the Information Society Directive. The dichotomy is explicitly recognized in the Software Directive,[180] but does not feature in the Information Society Directive

---

[176] *Kenrick v. Lawrence* (1890) 25 QBD 99.   [177] IViR, *Recasting Copyright*, 53.

[178] Walter and von Lewinski, 970, [11.2.22]; J. Griffiths, 'Dematerialization, Pragmatism and the European Copyright Revolution' (2013) 33(4) *OJLS* 767, 784.

[179] *Eva-Maria Painer v. Standard VerlagsGmbH*, Case C-145/10 [2012] *ECDR* (6) 89, [AG129].

[180] Software Dir., Art. 1(2).

(perhaps for the reason that it covers only copying and not adaptation, and so was thought unlikely to be in issue).

However, the Court of Justice and English Court of Appeal decisions in *SAS Institute v. World Programming*[181] indicate that the exclusion from protection of 'ideas' applied in cases of non-literal copying of authorial works as much as in relation to infringement of copyright in computer programs. In that case, the defendants had developed a computer program that emulated the functioning of the claimant's integrated set of programs that was used in statistical analysis (and generated revenue for the claimant of more than £2 billion a year). There was no suggestion that the defendant had had access to the source code for the claimant's programs and the question arose whether, in creating the competing software, it had infringed copyright either in the computer program (protected under the Software Directive) or in the manuals for the SAS system, the latter being authorial works protected under the Information Society Directive.[182] SAS sought to distinguish between the law applicable to infringement under the Software Directive and that under the ordinary copyright rules (arguing that there was no exclusion of ideas from the latter or that it was a narrower exclusion).[183]

At first instance, Arnold J held that, whatever the position when enacted, the 1988 Directive must now be interpreted to give effect to Article 9(2) of TRIPS and Article 2 of the WIPO Copyright Treaty. Therefore copyright, whether in relation to software or generally, protects only expression, and does not protect 'ideas, procedures, methods of operation and mathematical concepts as such'.[184] Nevertheless, he referred various questions to the Court of Justice on the application of the idea–expression dichotomy within the Software Directive and its parallel application to the manual.

In relation to software, the Court of Justice explicitly held that neither the functionality of a computer program nor the programming language and the format of data files used in a computer program in order to exploit certain of its functions constitute a form of expression of that program. The Court's answer on the Information Society Directive was less clear-cut, merely reiterating the test of infringement that had emerged from *Infopaq*.[185]

The English Court of Appeal focused on the fact that Recitals 20 and 50 of the Information Society Directive specifically refer to the Software Directive.[186] Bearing in mind the international standards applicable and the jurisprudence of the Court of Justice (in particular as to originality), the Opinion of Advocate-General Bot in the *SAS* case, and 'well-established principles of copyright law', Lewison LJ concluded that:

> [T]he same concept of what is capable of protection (as a form of expression rather than as an idea) applies to both the Software Directive and the Information Society Directive. Since the court's avowed intention was to establish a harmonized legal framework for copyright, this is not surprising.[187]

However, the Court of Appeal emphasized the Court of Justice's reference to reproduction of the 'expression of the intellectual creation', not merely reproduction of the intellectual creation.[188] In the view of Lewison LJ, the simple answer to the question of whether copying the compilation of functional elements was infringing was that the copying was not a copying of 'the form of expression' of the intellectual creation. Thus it was unnecessary

---

[181] [2013] *EWCA Civ* 1482; Case C-406/10, EU:C:2012:259 (ECJ, Grand Chamber).

[182] [2010] *EWHC* 1829 (Ch), [64] (Arnold J) (explaining that there was no dispute that copyright subsisted in the manuals as original literary works).

[183] Ibid., [251]; [2013] *EWCA Civ* 1482, [67].   [184] [2010] *EWHC* 1829 (Ch), [205], [254] (Arnold J).

[185] *SAS Institute v. World Programming*, Case C-406/10, EU:C:2012:259. In the Court of Appeal, Lewison LJ called it 'disappointingly compressed, if not obscure': [2013] *EWCA Civ* 1482, [5].

[186] [2013] *EWCA Civ* 1482, [27], [68].   [187] Ibid., [69].   [188] Ibid., [61], [63].

for Arnold J to have rejected the claim on the ground that the intellectual creation that was copied lay in the programs rather than the manual.[189]

3 SECONDARY INFRINGEMENT

In an attempt to inhibit the negative impact that illegal acts have upon copyright owners, copyright law recognizes that it is not enough merely to provide remedies against those who copy or perform the copyright work. Instead, copyright law recognizes that it is also necessary to provide owners with protection against those who aid and abet the primary infringer. Such accessorial infringement is known as 'secondary infringement'.

There are two important differences between primary and secondary infringement. The first relates to the scope of protection: primary infringement is concerned with people who are directly involved in the reproduction, performance, etc. of the copyright work; in contrast, secondary infringement is concerned with people in a commercial context who either deal with infringing copies, facilitate such copying, or facilitate public performance. The second difference between the two forms of infringement relates to the mental element that the defendant must exhibit in order to infringe. As we explain later in this chapter, the state of mind of the defendant is not formally taken into account when deciding whether an act of primary infringement has occurred. In the case of secondary infringement, however, liability is dependent on the defendant knowing, or having reason to believe, that the activities in question are wrongful.[190]

3.1 TYPES OF SECONDARY INFRINGEMENT

Secondary infringement can be divided into two general categories: those who distribute or deal with infringing copies once they have been made; and those who facilitate copying by providing the equipment or means that enable the copying to take place.

3.1.1 The distribution of infringing copies

The first general category of secondary infringement is concerned with people who deal with infringing copies of the work in a commercial context. To this end, sections 22 and 23 of the CDPA 1988 provide that the copyright in a work is infringed by a person who, without the licence of the copyright owner:

(i) *imports* an infringing copy into the United Kingdom otherwise than for their private and domestic use;[191]

(ii) *possesses* an infringing copy in the course of business;[192]

(iii) *sells* or *lets for hire*, or offers or exposes for sale or hire, an infringing copy;

(iv) in the course of business, *exhibits* in public or distributes an infringing copy;[193] or

(v) *distributes* an infringing copy, otherwise than in the course of a business, to such an extent as to affect the copyright owner prejudicially.

---

[189] [2010] *EWHC* 1829 (Ch), [260] (Arnold J), rejected at [2013] *EWCA Civ* 1482, [74].

[190] CDPA 1988, ss 22–4, 27. See Laddie et al., ch. 20.   [191] CDPA 1988, s. 22.

[192] Business is defined in CDPA 1988, s. 178, as including a 'trade or profession'. See *Pensher Security Doors v. Sunderland City Council* [2000] *RPC* 249, 280–2.

[193] An art gallery carries on business even though certain paintings are not for sale: ibid., 282.

Section 27(2) provides that an article is an 'infringing copy' if its making constituted an infringement of the copyright in the work in question.[194] In the case of imported copies, infringing copy also includes 'notional infringements'—that is, copies that, if they had been made in the United Kingdom, would have infringed copyright at the time of making or would have constituted a breach of an exclusive licence agreement relating to the work.[195] This provision has proved to be problematic.[196] Its significance has been reduced, however, by the extension of liability for primary infringement to include the issuing of copies, including the importing of copies from outside the European Economic Area (EEA). Liability for secondary infringement by import remains important in cases of import from one EEA state to another; however, this right is subject to the TFEU and the principle of exhaustion.[197]

3.1.2 Providing the means for making infringing copies or performances

The second general category of secondary infringement is concerned with people who facilitate copying. This occurs, for example, where someone provides the equipment or the means that enables the copying to take place. There are a number of different situations in which the provision of the means for making infringing copies or performances will amount to a secondary infringement.

Section 24(1) of the CDPA 1988 provides that a person is liable for infringement where they supply an article that is specifically designed or adapted for making copies of the copyright work. More specifically, section 24(1) provides that:

Copyright in a work is infringed by a person who, without the licence of the copyright owner—

(a) makes,
(b) imports into the United Kingdom,
(c) possesses in the course of business, or
(d) sells, or lets for hire, or offers or exposes for sale or hire,

an article specifically designed or adapted for making copies of that work . . .[198]

It should be noted that section 24(1) states that the article must be *specifically* designed or adapted for the purpose of copying. This means that it is not enough that an article, such as a photocopier or a tape-to-tape recorder, has the potential to copy; rather, for the section to operate, the article must be specifically designed for the copying of a particular work. This would be the case, for example, if someone were to make a template or a mould of a copyright work that is used to create infringing copies.[199]

---

[194] However, note the many situations in which the making of a copy is not infringing because of the existence of a defence, but the statute requires the copy be treated as an infringing copy when subsequently dealt with in specified ways: CDPA 1988, s. 27(6) referring to ss 32(5), 35(3), 36(5), 37(3), 56(2), 63(2), 68(4), and 141.　　　　　　　　　　　　　　　　[195] CDPA 1988, s. 27(3), Sch. 1, para. 14(3).

[196] Described by Laddie et al., 818, [20.18], as 'far from straightforward'. One question that has been debated is who does the hypothetical making: the maker abroad, the importer, or someone else? Laddie et al. argue that the identity of the maker is not in issue; what is in issue is the purpose that the import is intended to fill.

[197] CDPA 1988, s. 27(5). See Chapter 1, section 4.1, pp. 13–15 and Chapter 6, section 3.3, pp. 151–5.

[198] Emphasis added.

[199] In between these two examples lies a device such as a media player (for example a so-called KODI box), which when adapted (by adding so-called 'add ons') and operated with a television may offer unauthorized access to pay-TV channels. Here, the device is specifically adapted to make transient copies of all the works streamed or broadcast. Nevertheless, it is suggested that this falls outside the scope of CDPA, s. 24, as the device is not specifically designed to make copies of particular works.

Special provisions are also made for people who *transmit the work* without the appropriate permission. Section 24(2) states that copyright in a work is infringed by a person who, without licence, transmits the work by means of a telecommunications system (such as a fax). It does not apply, however, to communications to the public. As with all forms of secondary infringement, infringement is dependent upon the defendant 'knowing or having reason to believe that infringing copies of the work will be made by means of the reception of the transmission in the United Kingdom or elsewhere'.

Where the copyright in a literary, dramatic, or musical work is infringed by a performance at a 'public place of entertainment',[200] any person who gave permission for that place to be used for the infringing performance is also liable for infringement. This does not apply, however, where the defendant gave permission on reasonable grounds that the performance would not be infringed.[201]

Special provisions also apply to those who facilitate an infringing performance. Section 26 deals with the situation in which copyright is infringed by a public performance or by the playing or showing of the work in public by means of apparatus for '(a) playing sound recordings, (b) showing films, or (c) receiving visual images or sounds conveyed by electronic means'. In these situations, the following people will infringe.

(i) The person who *supplies the apparatus* that enables the act of primary infringement to take place is liable for infringement. This covers someone who supplies equipment to play records or show films. Infringement here is conditional on the fact that, where an apparatus is normally used in public, the defendant did not believe on reasonable grounds that it would be used to infringe copyright.[202]

(ii) An occupier of premises who gave permission for an apparatus to be brought on to the premises will be liable if they knew or had reason to believe that the apparatus was likely to be used to infringe copyright.[203]

(iii) A person who *supplies a copy* of a sound recording or a film will be liable if they knew or had reason to believe that the copy was likely to be used to infringe copyright.[204]

Finally, it should be noted that special rules, analogous to provisions on secondary infringement, apply where persons do various acts that facilitate access to or duplication of works that have been protected by technological measures. We deal with these in detail in Chapter 13, section 4. For the moment, we merely need to note that these rights cover:

(i) acts that circumvent technological measures;[205]

(ii) the manufacture and distribution of devices either 'primarily designed, produced, adapted ... for the purpose of enabling and facilitating' circumvention, or 'promoted, advertised or marketed' for that purpose, and having 'only a limited commercially significant purpose or use other than to circumvent';[206] and

(iii) the provision of services for the purpose of enabling or facilitating circumvention.

Distinct, and narrower, provisions apply where the measures protect computer programs.[207]

---

[200] Defined in CDPA 1988, s. 25(2), to include premises occasionally used for public entertainment.
[201] CDPA 1988, s. 25(1).   [202] CDPA 1988, s. 26(2).
[203] CDPA 1988, s. 26(3). For a possible example, see *PRS v. Kwik-Fit Group* [2008] *ECDR* (2) 13 (OH CS).
[204] CDPA 1988, s. 26(4).   [205] CDPA 1988, s. 296ZA. See pp. 375–6.
[206] CDPA 1988, s. 296ZD. See pp. 376–8.   [207] CDPA 1988, s. 296(1). See pp. 380–1.

3.2 ACTUAL OR CONSTRUCTIVE KNOWLEDGE

One of the notable features of secondary infringement is that liability is dependent on the defendant 'knowing or having reason to believe' that the activities in question are wrongful—that is, liability is dependent on the defendant having either actual or constructive knowledge. The question of whether a defendant has the requisite knowledge is decided objectively.[208] As such, it does not matter that the defendant may not have believed that the act in question was wrongful; all that matters are the conclusions that a reasonable person would have reached in the circumstances.

The question that needs to be asked is whether the defendant knew or had reason to believe that they were dealing with or helping to facilitate the creation of an 'infringing copy' of the copyright work. In answering this question, the courts have stressed that the defendant must be in a position from which they are able to evaluate the information that is given to them.[209] This means that they must be given a reasonable period of time within which to consider the information.[210] It also means that the information that they are given must be sufficiently detailed as to the nature of the work in question: general allegations about infringement will not suffice.[211] The courts have also said that it is *not* enough for the facts to lead a reasonable person to *suspect* the relevant conclusion.[212] Although it will enhance the claimant's case if the defendant is supplied with a copy of, or given reasonable access to, the copyright work, the circumstances of the case may be such that the reasonable defendant could have 'known' about the wrongful nature of their activities without ever having seen the copyright work.[213]

---

[208] *Vermaat v. Boncrest (No. 2)* [2002] *FSR* (21) 331, [30]; Laddie et al., 810–11, [20.7]–[20.8].

[209] *LA Gear v. Hi-Tec Sports* [1992] *FSR* 121, 129.

[210] The normal period is often 14 days. Cf. *Monsoon v. Indian Imports* [1993] *FSR* 486.

[211] *Hutchinson Personal Communications v. Hook Advertising* [1995] *FSR* 365; *Metix UK v. Maughan* [1997] *FSR* 718.

[212] *ZYX Music GmbH v. King* [1997] 2 *All ER* 129.

[213] *Pensher Security Doors v. Sunderland City Council* [2000] *RPC* 249.

9

DEFENCES

1 INTRODUCTION

This chapter considers the exceptions on which a defendant may rely when sued for infringement of copyright. Most of these exceptions are found in Chapter III of Part 1 of the Copyright, Designs and Patents Act 1988 (CDPA 1988), as amended, where they are referred to as 'permitted acts'. The exceptions come into play only once a claimant has established that copyright has been infringed. Where this occurs, the onus of proof falls on the defendant to prove that one of the exceptions applies.[1]

At the most abstract level, the exceptions in the CDPA 1988 attempt to 'balance' the rights of copyright owners with a multiplicity of other rights, freedoms, and interests. The resulting body of legislation appears as anything but a rational scheme; rather, it is a strange collection of exceptions, many defined with 'extraordinary precision and rigidity'.[2] This remains the case, despite two reviews and their implementation by the addition of a number of additional exceptions in 2014.[3]

---

[1] Contrast various 'immunities', such as those for Internet intermediaries, discussed in Chapter 48, section 3.5, pp. 1275–8. These are not 'exceptions' because all they do is shield ISPs from liability for damages.

[2] *Pro Sieben Media v. Carlton UK Television* [1998] *FSR* 43, 48 (Laddie J).

[3] *Gowers Review*, ch. 4, 39, [3.26]; *Hargreaves Review*, 3, 8. New exceptions were added for 'data mining', quotation, and parody, while others, relating to education, libraries, persons with disability, and the administration, were substantially reformulated: The Copyright and Rights in Performances (Research, Education, Libraries and Archives) Regulations 2014 (SI 2014/1372), The Copyright and Rights in Performances (Disability) Regulations 2014 (SI 2014/1384), and The Copyright and Rights in Performances (Public Administration) Regulations 2014 (SI 2014/1385); Copyright and Rights in Performances (Quotation and Parody) Regulations 2014 (SI 2014/2356).

One reason that the form of the Act remains as it is can be found in the restricted legislative freedom at a national level. As we have observed, the Information Society Directive harmonizes the rights of reproduction, communication, and distribution, but it also regulates the circumstances in which exceptions to such rights may be recognized.[4] The Directive provides 'for numerous exceptions',[5] the aim being to provide 'a fair balance' between right holders and 'users'.[6] More precisely, the Directive contains one mandatory exception as regards transient or incidental acts of reproduction,[7] and a list of optional 'exceptions or limitations', many covering the analogue environment.[8] On the whole, member states have the choice not only whether to implement the optional exceptions, but also in relation to how the exception is implemented.[9] The list is exhaustive: member states may not maintain any other exceptions or limitations,[10] nor may they develop new ones in response to changes in the technological environment and cultural practices.

The interpretation of exceptions permitted under the Directive is a matter for the Court of Justice. In a number of cases, the Court has indicated a preference for a 'narrow' interpretation,[11] primarily on the basis that these are derogations from general rules.[12] However, in many of the same cases, the Court has also embraced a 'purposive'

---

[4] Info. Soc. Dir., Art. 5. Note also the requirements of the Rel. Rights Dir., Art. 10; Software Dir., Arts 5 and 6, Database Dir., Art. 6.

[5] *Padawan SL v. SGAE*, Case C-467/08 [2010] *ECR* I–10555, [AG43].

[6] *Microsoft Mobile Sales International Oy v. Ministero per i beni e le attività culturali*, Case C-110/15, EU:C:2016:326, [AG20] (AG Wahl).

[7] See section 3, pp. 235–9. Although not in mandatory form, the better view is that Info. Soc. Dir., Art 5(3)(d), recognizing a quotation exception, is also mandatory, because of it has that status under Berne, Art. 10. Note that the Proposal for a Directive on Copyright in the Digital Single Market, COM(2016) 593 final, Arts 3–5, includes three more mandatory exceptions: for text and data mining, teaching, and for preservation for cultural heritage institutions.   [8] Info. Soc. Dir., Art. 5.

[9] *Eva-Maria Painer v. Standard VerlagsGmbH*, Case C-145/10 [2012] *ECDR* (6) 89 (ECJ) ('*Painer*'), [AG148]–[AG150], [AG181] (AG Trstenjak); *Padawan SL v. SGA F.*, Case C-467/08 [2010] *ECR* I–10555, [AG43]; *Verwertungsgesellschaft Wort (VG Wort) v. KYOCERA Document Solutions Deutschland GmbH*, Joined Cases C-457/11, C-458/11, C-459/11 and C-460/11 EU:C:2013:426 (ECJ) ('*VG Wort*'), EU:C:2013:34, [AG35], [AG37] (AG Sharpston); *Vereniging Openbare Bibliotheken (VOB) v. Stichting Leenrecht*, Case C-174/15, EU:C:2016:856, [61] (allowing MS to set additional conditions in implementation of Rel. Rights Dir., Art. 6(1)). But cf. *DR, TV2 Danmark A/S v. NCB-Nordisk Copyright Bureau*, Case C-510/10, EU:C:2012:244 (ECJ), [36] (pointing out problems that arise if member states can set conditions, but in a case in which Danish law did not make reference to a condition in Art. 5(2)(d)); Opinion 3/15, EU:C:2017:114, [122]–[127] (ECJ, Grand Chamber) (referring to highly constrained freedom); J. Griffiths, 'Recent Developments Relating to Exceptions and Limitations in EU Copyright Law' (2013) 18 *Media & Arts L Rev* 268, 276; E. Rosati, 'Copyright In the EU: In Search of (In)flexibilities' (2014) 9 *JIPLP* 585 (arguing that member states that decide to implement Art. 5(2) (a), (b), (d), (e), and (3)(d), (f), (h), (i), and (m), must 'reproduce the very language of the Directive').

[10] See Info. Soc. Dir., Recital 32. Some flexibility is offered by Art 5(3)(o) which allows for exceptions in cases of 'minor importance' provided they only concern 'analogue uses'. In *AKM v Zürs.net Betriebs GmbH*, Case C-138/16, EU:C:2017:218, [37]–[38] (ECJ), this was interpreted strictly, and thus would not offer Member States freedom to permit the retransmission of broadcasts to groups of under 500 recipients. Although the Info. Soc. Dir. creates an exhaustive list of exceptions to the rights specified therein, note that this is without prejudice to prior directives (Art. 1(2)), so derogations to the lending right, or to copyright in software and databases, specified in earlier instruments can be maintained, and without prejudice to 'their legal provisions' (Art. 9). Note also the pending references in Case C-516/17, *Spiegel Online* (pending) (where the German BGH, Case I ZR 228/15, (27 July 2017) asks whether the listed exceptions are exhaustive in a case concerning linking).

[11] See, e.g., *Infopaq Int. v. Danske Dagblades Forening*, Case C-5/08 [2009] *ECR* I–6569 (ECJ) ('*Infopaq I*'), [57]; *Painer*, Case C-145/10 [2012] *ECDR* (6) 89 (ECJ), [109]; *AKM v Zürs.net Betriebs GmbH*, Case C-138/16, EU:C:2017:218, [37]–[38] (ECJ); *VCAST v RTI SpA*, Case C-265/16, EU:C:2017:913, [32].

[12] Cf. the traditional approach of the UK courts: *Newspaper Licensing Agency v. Marks & Spencer* [2000] 4 *All ER* 239 (CA), 257 (Chadwick LJ).

interpretation,[13] and emphasized the need to ensure a 'fair balance' between the rights and interests of authors and those of users.[14] In one Opinion, Advocate-General Szpunar even refers to 'user's rights',[15] and the Court itself has itself used similar language when discussing the rights of database users that cannot be overridden by contract.[16]

The defences listed in the Directive are also additionally declared subject to the so-called 'three-step test'. This requires that exceptions must be 'applied' only to 'certain special cases', must not interfere with the 'normal exploitation' of the work/subject matter, and must not prejudice the 'legitimate interests' of authors/right holders.[17] It remains unclear whether (or when) this constitutes an additional limitation,[18] and whether it is directed at 'application' by the legislature of member states when drafting exceptions,[19] or at the courts of member states when applying them,[20] or at both the legislatures *and* the courts of member states.[21] As yet, the Court of Justice has yet to confront the obvious tension between the 'three-step test' (with its focus directly purely on the effect of exceptions on rights holders) and the idea that exceptions are to fairly balance the fundamental rights and interests of owners and users.[22]

Before examining the exceptions contained in the CDPA 1988 individually, we begin by outlining some concepts that feature in many of the exceptions—fair dealing, non-commercial use, lawful use, and sufficient acknowledgment—as well as the rule, applicable to certain exceptions, that seeks to ensure that users' freedoms are not limited by contractual agreement.

---

[13] *Football Association Premier League v. QC Leisure* and *Karen Murphy v. Media Protection Services*, Joined Cases C-403/08 and C-429/08 [2011] *ECR* I–9083 (ECJ, Grand Chamber) ('*FAPL*'), [162]; *Painer*, Case C-145/10 [2012] *ECDR* (6) 89 (ECJ), [133]; *Deckmyn and Vrijheidsfonds v. Vandersteen*, Case C-201/13, EU:C:2014:458 (Opinion of AG Cruz Villalón), [AG 44].

[14] *FAPL*, Joined Cases C-403/08 and C-429/08 [2011] *ECR* I–9083 (ECJ, Grand Chamber), [163]; *Painer*, Case C-145/10 [2012] *ECDR* (6) 89 (ECJ), [132], [134]; *Deckmyn*, Case C-201/13, EU:C:2014:458), [27]; *England & Wales Cricket Board v. Tixdaq* [2016] *EWHC* 575 (Ch), [73].

[15] *EGEDA v Adminición del Estado*, Case C-470/14, EU:C:2016:24, [15] (AG Szpunar) (explaining rationale of private copying exception).

[16] *Ryanair v PR Aviation BV*, Case C-30/14, EU:C:2015:10, [39]–[40] (ECJ). Noted by T. Synodinou, 'Databases and Screen-Scraping', [2016] *EIPR* 313, 316 as 'the major contribution' of this ruling.

[17] Info. Soc. Dir., Art. 5(5); Marrakesh Dir, Art. 3(1) ('applied'); Rel. Rights Dir., Art. 10 ('applied'); Database Dir., Art. 6(3) ('interpreted in such a way as to allow its application to be used'); Proposal for a Directive on Copyright in the Digital Single Market, COM(2016) 593 final, Art. 6 (applying Art 5(5) to proposed new mandatory exceptions).

[18] *Infopaq I* [2009] *ECR* I–6569, [58] (viewing Art. 5(5) as a guide to the ECJ's own interpretation of Art. 5(1)); *VG Wort*, EU:C:2013:34, [AG68] (AG Sharpston) (Art. 5(5) explicitly requires a restrictive, rather than an extensive, interpretation); *FAPL*, Joined Cases C-403/08 and C-429/08 [2011] *ECR* I–9083 (ECJ, Grand Chamber), [181] (act that complies with the conditions of the exception in Art. 5(1) necessarily complies with Art. 5(5)); *Public Relations Consultants Association (PRCA) v. The Newspaper Licensing Agency (NLA)* [2013] *UKSC* 18, [25]; ibid., Case C–360/13, EU:C:2014:1195 (ECJ), [53] (treating three-step test as additional requirement).

[19] Opinion 3/15, EU:C:2017:114, [125] (ECJ, Grand Chamber) (referring to relevance when 'introducing' exception); *Stichting de Thuiskopie v. Mijndert van der Lee*, Case C-462/09 [2011] *ECR* I–5331, [AG42] (AG Jääskinen) (Art. 5(5) is 'in general aimed at national legislatures', but judges may also 'need to take account').

[20] *ACI Adam BV v. Stichting de Thuiskopie*, C-435/12, EU:C:2014:254 (ECJ), [24]–[25] (member states must consider when applying exceptions); *Painer*, Case C-145/10 [2012] *ECDR* (6) 89 (AG Trstenjak), [AG148] (member states must take into account when interpreting exceptions); *Deckmyn and and Vrijheidsfonds v. Vandersteen*, Case C-201/13, EU:C:2014:458, [AG29] (AG Cruz Villalón), (national courts must consider when applying an exception).

[21] *VCAST v. RTI SpA*, Case C-265/16, EU:C:2017:649, [AG58] (AG Szpunar); R. Arnold and E. Rosati, 'Are National courts the Addressees of the InfoSoc Three-Step Test?' (2015) 10 (10) *JIPLP* 741–9 (arguing national court as well as legislature should apply test).

[22] J. Griffiths, 'Fair dealing after *Deckmyn*', in M. Richardson and S. Ricketson (eds), *Research Handbook on IP in Media and Entertainment* (2017), ch. 3, 96–100.

2 BASIC CONCEPTS

In this section, we want to introduce six basic concepts that are frequently deployed in the specific exceptions.

2.1 'FAIR DEALING'

Perhaps the most significant concept in Chapter III is the concept of 'fair dealing'.[23] This requirement limits the operation of six defences:

(i)   fair dealing for the purposes of research or private study (section 29(1) and (1C));

(ii)   fair dealing for the purposes of criticism or review (section 30(1));

(iii) fair dealing exceptions will be available for 'quotation' (section 30(1ZA), introduced in 2014)

(iv)   fair dealing for the purpose of reporting current events (section 30(2));

(v)   fair dealing for purposes of 'parody, caricature or pastiche' (section 30A(1), also added in 2014) and

(vi)   fair dealing for the purposes of illustration for instruction (section 32).

In this context, all that is meant by 'dealing' is that the defendant has made use of the work. Dealing does not imply that there has to be some sort of transaction between the parties. Under these provisions (with the exception of fair dealing *by* quotation), 'fair dealing' is permitted only for the purposes specifically listed in the 1988 Act. This means that the dealing must be fair for the purpose of research or private study, criticism or review, quotation, the reporting of current events, parody,[24] or 'illustration for instruction'. As such, it is irrelevant that the use might be fair for a purpose not specified in the Act, or that it is fair in general. The restricted approach adopted in the United Kingdom should be contrasted with US copyright law, which has a general defence of *fair use* such that if the court is satisfied that the use is fair, then there will be no infringement.[25]

In deciding the purpose for which the work was used, the test does not depend on the subjective intentions of the alleged infringer;[26] rather, a more objective approach is adopted, so that the question is whether the dealing is 'in the context of' research, criticism, instruction, parody, or reporting.[27]

If a dealing falls within one of the specified purposes, it needs to be considered whether the dealing is fair.[28] 'Fairness' is said to be a question of degree and

---

[23] R. Burrell and A. Coleman, *Copyright Exceptions: The Digital Impact* (2005), ch. 9; M. de Zwart, 'An Historical Analysis of the Birth of Fair Dealing' [2007] *IPQ* 60; A. Sims, 'Strangling Their Creation: The Courts' Treatment of Fair Dealing in Copyright Law Since 1911' [2010] *IPQ* 192; A. Sims, 'Appellations of Piracy: Fair Dealing's Prehistory' [2011] *IPQ* 3.

[24] But see section 8, pp. 251–2, discussing whether the CJEU's requirement of 'fair balance' is the same as 'fair dealing'.   [25] US Copyright Act of 1976, §107.

[26] *Hyde Park Residence v. Yelland* [2000] *EMLR* 363, [21].

[27] *Pro Sieben Media v. Carlton TV* [1999] *FSR* 610 (CA), 620; *England & Wales Cricket Board v Tixdaq* [2016] *EWHC* 575 (Ch), [75]. But note some have suggested that whether something constitutes a 'parody' is a matter of intention: see section 8, pp. 250–1.

[28] 'Fairness' here is primarily a British concept, although it also appears in Berne, Art. 10 and Info. Soc. Dir., Art. 5(3)(d). The concept of fairness, in contrast with the three-step test (in Art. 9(2) Berne, and Info. Soc. Dir., Art. 5(5)), is a 'multifactor' test rather than a set of cumulative steps or conditions.

impression.[29] The courts have sometimes adopted the perspective of whether a 'fair-minded and honest person' would regard the dealing as 'fair', but whether this takes the analysis very far might be doubted.[30] As Lord Phillips MR stated: 'It is . . . essential not to apply inflexibly tests based on precedent, but to bear in mind that considerations of public interest are paramount.'[31] A number of factors might influence the way in which this question is answered,[32] although the relative importance of each of these factors will vary according to the case in hand and the type of dealing in question.[33]

2.1.1 Amount taken

The quantity and quality of what is taken will be a crucial factor in deciding whether a dealing is fair.[34] As Lord Denning MR said in *Hubbard v. Vosper*,[35] you 'must consider the number and extent of the extracts' and ask: are 'they altogether too many and too long to be fair'? This is because lengthy and numerous extracts, or extracts of the most important parts of a work, will reduce the expected returns to the copyright owner. By focusing on the quantity and quality of what is taken, the courts have recognized that fair dealing should not undermine the role that copyright plays in encouraging creativity. In general, therefore, the defence will apply only where part of a work is taken. Nevertheless, the courts have acknowledged that, in some cases, such as where the work itself is short, it may be fair to reproduce the whole work.[36]

2.1.2 Use made of the work

Another factor that may influence the decisions as to whether a dealing is fair is the use that is made of the work in question. In some instances, it may be 'fair' merely to reproduce someone else's work without comment or analysis (for example for research or instruction). However, in many cases, a use is more likely to be fair if the defendant can show that they have added to or recontextualized the part taken—that is, a defendant will have a stronger case if they can show that the dealing was transformative.[37] This is particularly the case with fair dealing for criticism or review, quotation, or parody.

It seems that the fact that a defendant derives a commercial benefit from the dealing will weigh against them when attempting to show that the dealing was fair.[38] As

---

[29] *Hubbard v. Vosper* [1972] 2 *QB* 84.

[30] *Hyde Park Residence v. Yelland* [2000] *EMLR* 363, [38], (Aldous LJ); *Newspaper Licensing Agency v. Marks & Spencer* [2000] 4 *All ER* 239 (CA), [44], (Peter Gibson LJ).

[31] *Ashdown v. Telegraph Group* [2002] *Ch* 149, 173, [71].

[32] Many countries offer a statutory list of factors and it seems surprising that such an approach was not adopted in the 2014 reforms.

[33] What follows is based on the established case law, so it is appropriate to note Arnold J's warning, *England & Wales Cricket Board v Tixdaq* [2016] *EWHC* 575 (Ch), [75] that this case law 'must be treated with a degree of caution, since they were mostly decided prior to the implementation of the Information Society Directive and all of them were decided well before the recent jurisprudence of the CJEU concerning the interpretation of that Directive. Moreover . . . there is no consideration in any of them of the three-step test.'

[34] In terms of Info. Soc. Dir, Art. 5(5), the factors listed at sections 2.1.1–2.1.3 relate to whether the defendant's use interferes with the normal exploitation of the work.   [35] [1972] 2 *QB* 84, 94.

[36] Ibid., 94–5, 98 (Megaw LJ) (example of a parishioner quoting an epitaph on a tombstone in the church-yard); *Sillitoe v. McGraw Hill* [1983] *FSR* 545; *Associated Newspapers Group v. News Group Newspapers* [1986] *RPC* 515, 520.   [37] *Newspaper Licensing Agency v. Marks & Spencer* [1999] *EMLR* 369, 380 (Lightman J).

[38] But note CDPA 1988, s. 29(1) (fair dealing for research defence applies only to research for a non-commercial purpose); Database Dir., Art. 6(2)(b)).

Chadwick LJ said in the Court of Appeal decision of *Newspaper Licensing Agency v. Marks & Spencer*:

> [A] dealing by a person with a copyright work for his own commercial advantage—and to the actual or potential commercial disadvantage of the copyright owner—is not to be regarded as a 'fair dealing' unless there is some overriding element of public advantage which justifies the subordination of the rights of the copyright owner.[39]

2.1.3 Consequences of the dealing

Another factor that will influence the decision as to whether a dealing is fair relates to the impact that the dealing will have upon the market for the work. This is particularly important where the parties are in competition and the defendant's use of the work acts as a substitute for the purchase of the original work.[40] This would be the case, for example, if, in criticizing it, a defendant were to show all of a film.

2.1.4 Is the work unpublished?

Where the dealing takes place in relation to a work that has not been published or made widely available to the public, this will weigh against the dealing being fair. [41] In fact, in the case of fair dealing for criticism or review, and fair dealing by quotation, the defence is specified to be unavailable if the work has not been previously 'made available' to the public.[42] In other cases, particularly that of reporting current event, the fact that a work has not been published will certainly stand against a defendant.[43] In this respect, it is likely that the weight that a court gives to the fact that a work is unpublished will vary according to the nature of the work in question, giving more weight in relation to private letters than it would for official reports that revealed matters of public importance.

2.1.5 How the work was obtained

The method by which the copyright material has been obtained has also been a factor in determining whether the dealing is fair.[44] It is less likely for a dealing to be fair if the dealing relates to a work that is leaked or stolen, or obtained by unauthorized access to a database, than to a work that is obtained legitimately.[45]

2.1.6 Motives for the dealing

Another factor that may influence the decision as to whether a use is fair relates to the motive of the alleged infringer.[46] For example, where a person acts dishonestly or for a

---

[39] *Newspaper Licensing Agency v. Marks & Spencer* [2000] 4 *All ER* 239 (CA), 257.

[40] *Hubbard v. Vosper* [1972] 2 *QB* 84.

[41] The factors considered at sections 2.1.4–2.1.7 may be thought of as relating the prejudice to the legitimate interests of the author or right holder.

[42] CDPA 1988, s. 30(1), (1A) (as amended to give effect to Info. Soc Dir., Art. 5(3)(d)); cf. Lord Denning in *Hubbard v. Vosper* [1972] 2 *QB* 84.

[43] *Hyde Park Residence v. Yelland* [2000] *EMLR* 363, 378, [34] (Aldous LJ); *HRH the Prince of Wales v. Associated Newspapers* [2007] 3 *WLR* 222, 264, [174] (Blackburne J), 280, [78]–[79] (Lord Phillips MR). But cf. *CCH Canadian v. Law Society of Upper Canada* [2004] *SCC* 13, [58].

[44] *Beloff v. Pressdram* [1973] 1 *All ER* 241.

[45] Ibid.; *The Controller of Her Majesty's Stationery Office, Ordnance Survey v. Green Amps* [2007] *EWHC* 2755 (Ch), [54]; *Queensland v. TCN Channel Nine* [1993] *IPR* 58 (Supreme Court of Queensland); *British Oxygen v. Liquid Air* [1925] 1 *Ch* 383; cf. *Time Warner v. Channel 4* [1994] *EMLR* 1.

[46] *Hyde Park Residence v. Yelland* [2000] *EMLR* 363 (CA), [36]; *Pro Sieben Media v. Carlton Television* [1999] *FSR* 610, 614 (Walker LJ); *Beloff v. Pressdram* [1973] 1 *All ER* 241, 263.

motive that the court finds questionable (such as being primarily motivated by financial gain), it is likely to weigh against them. In contrast, if an alleged infringer can show that they were acting benevolently or were motivated by some altruistic or noble cause, this will increase the chances of their establishing that the dealing was fair.

2.1.7 Could the purpose have been achieved by different means?

In some cases, the courts have asked whether the purpose could have been achieved in a manner that is less intrusive on the copyright holder's rights.[47] While there can be few objections to this test being used to determine whether a dealing is fair, problems may arise in the way in which it is applied by the courts. This can be seen in *Hyde Park Residence v. Yelland*.[48] This case concerned an application for summary judgment against *The Sun* newspaper for publishing stills of Dodi Fayed and Diana, Princess of Wales, taken from security film, the copyright in which was owned by the claimant. The defendant argued that the stills revealed the times when Fayed and Diana were present at Villa Windsor and therefore exposed the falsehood of statements made by Mohammed Al Fayed. The Court of Appeal held that it was not necessary for *The Sun* to have published the images taken from the video; the same result could have been achieved via written word. As Aldous LJ said:

> The information as to the timing of arrival and departure of Dodi and Princess Diana could have been given in the articles by the reporter in *The Sun* stating that he had seen the photographs which proved the Princess and Mr Dodi only stayed at the Villa for 28 minutes.[49]

2.2 NON-COMMERCIAL USE AND NOT-FOR-PROFIT USERS

Many of the exceptions depend on the use being 'non-commercial'.[50] This is said to cover not only uses that are directly commercial, but also uses that are indirectly commercial. The notion of 'commerce' here is almost certainly similar to the concept of 'trade' in trade mark law, which has been said to refer to 'economic activity'.[51] In these contexts, commerce is understood as more than a few one-off sales.[52]

Recital 42 of the Information Society Directive indicates that the test of non-commerciality relates to 'the activity as such'. The organizational structure and means of

---

[47] *Newspaper Licensing Agency v. Marks & Spencer* [1999] *EMLR* 369, 382–3 (Lightman J). Note also Info. Soc. Dir., Art. 5(3)(a), (c), (d). There is a tension between such an approach and ECHR-informed jurisprudence, which gives journalists leeway to determine what is necessary for a particular purpose: *Fressoz & Roire v. France* [2001] 31 *EHRR* 28, 60, [54]; *A v. B & C* [2002] 3 *WLR* 542, [11].   [48] [2000] *EMLR* 363.

[49] Ibid., 379.

[50] CDPA 1988, s 29(1) (research for a 'non-commercial purpose'), 29(1C), 178 (private study, defined as non-commercial), 29A(1)(a) (data analysis), 32(1)(a) (fair dealing for instruction), 35(1)(a) (recording of broadcasts for education), 36(1)(a) (copying for education), 42A(3)(c) (library making and supplying copies to users), 43(2)(c), and 61(4)(c) (library supply of unpublished works). Cf. CDPA 1988, s. 40B(3)(b) (not limiting research uses to 'non-commercial'). The limitation to non-commercial research is required under a number of the EU law provisions: Info. Soc. Dir., Art. 5(2)(b), (c), (e), 5(3)(a), (b); Database Dir., Art. 6(2)(b). See S. Karapapa, *Private Copying* (2012), ch. 4.   [51] See Chapter 40, section 7, p. 1106.

[52] Some further idea of what is meant might be gleaned from Recital 14 of the Enforcement Dir., Recital 14, which equates infringement on 'a commercial scale' with 'acts carried out for direct or indirect economic or commercial advantage', which 'would normally exclude acts carried out by end consumers acting in good faith'. See also *Schrems v. Facebook Ireland*, Case C-498/16, EU:C:2018:37 (broad interpretation of notion of 'consumer' in Art. 15 of Regulation No. 44/2001).

funding 'are not the decisive factors in this respect'.[53] It is worth observing that Recital 42 does not say that organizational structure and means of funding are not relevant: many activities by public sector and/or charitable and not-for-profit organizations will be 'non-commercial', and most activities of private sector, profit-making businesses will be per se commercial. Rather, the implication of Recital 42 is that an activity (such as in-house education) can be non-commercial even if it takes place in a for-profit, private sector organization, or in an environment in which students pay fees. Conversely, a not-for-profit organization might be involved in commercial use, for example where a university publisher makes and sells copies of a work.

Further problems exist in determining whether a use is to be regarded as 'indirectly commercial': how remote can the commercial benefit be and still be relevant? In our view, the answer is that the use must be closely integrated with a commercial activity before a use can be categorized as 'indirectly' commercial. For example, if a public house attracts customers by showing copyright films, this could be said to be indirectly commercial even if the pub does not charge directly, because it hopes to make money from the sale of food and drinks.[54] But if a person is studying law with a view to becoming a commercial lawyer, or researching a topic in the hope of publishing a book for which they might receive substantial royalties, we think that the commercial benefit is too remote for it to be said that the use is for a 'commercial purpose', even indirectly.

Other exceptions, such as that relating to making and supplying accessible copies to persons with a disability, are limited to not-for-profit organizations.[55] In many cases, this limitation replaced former requirements on the Secretary of State to designate or certify the scheme, and the reform is aimed at reducing bureaucracy.

2.3 LAWFUL USER

A number of exceptions under European law depend on the user being regarded as a 'lawful user' or 'lawful acquirer'.[56] Whether there was meant to be any distinction between these concepts may be regarded as doubtful.[57] The term 'lawful acquirer' covers a purchaser of a work, a subsequent recipient (such as a second-hand purchaser or borrower), and a licensee.[58] In *UsedSoft GmbH v. Oracle International Corp.*,[59] the Court of Justice held that a transferee of software from an original purchaser is a 'lawful acquirer' (even though a licence term affecting the original purchaser purported to prevent such transfer).[60] This is so even in the case of sale of software in intangible form and even after it has been subsequently patched or updated.[61]

---

[53] Note also Proposal for a Directive on Copyright in the Digital Single Market, COM(2016) 593 final, recital 15.

[54] *The Controller of Her Majesty's Stationery Office, Ordnance Survey v. Green Amps* [2007] *EWHC* 2755 (Ch), [23].

[55] CDPA 1988, s. 61 (recording of folk songs). See Info. Soc. Dir., Recital 40.

[56] CDPA 1988, s. 31A, as amended (accessible copies must be made from copy in lawful possession or lawful use of disabled person); Software Dir., Art. 5(1) (lawful acquirer), 5(2) (person having 'right to use'); Database Dir., Arts 6(1), 8(1), (2).

[57] W. Blocher, 'Computer Program Directive', in Walter and von Lewinski, [5.5.39]; T.-E. Synodinou, 'The Lawful User and a Balancing of Interests in European Copyright Law' (2010) 41 *IIC* 819, 824.

[58] The Commission has said that 'lawful acquirer' meant a 'purchaser, licensee, renter or a person authorized to use the program on behalf of the above': *Report on the Implementation and Effects of Directive 91/250/EEC* (April 2000) COM(2000) 199 final, 12. See also Blocher, op. cit., [5.5.11], [5.5.16].

[59] Case C-128/11 [2012] 3 *CMLR* (44) 1039.   [60] Ibid., [75], [80], [81], [82].   [61] Ibid., [85].

Some of the UK provisions use other terms in the same 'family': the text and data analytics defence is available only to a person who has 'lawful access';[62] the exceptions for persons with disabilities require 'lawful possession or lawful use'.[63] The differences, if they exist, between lawful acquisition, possession, access, and use, seem very subtle and such differentiation makes for an unnecessarily complex set of rules.

2.4 SUFFICIENT ACKNOWLEDGEMENT

In certain situations, for a defence to apply, the use must be accompanied by a 'sufficient acknowledgement'.[64] In essence, this means that the author and the work must be identified. It should be noted that even where sufficient acknowledgement is required as a general matter, the defence will still usually be available if 'this turns out to be impossible for reasons of practicality or otherwise'. [65] Moreover, section 178 of the CDPA 1988 indicates that there is no need for the author to be identified where a work is published anonymously or, in the case of an unpublished work, where it is not possible for a person to ascertain the identity of the author by reasonable inquiry.[66]

Where required, the defendant must show that they have identified both the work *and* the author of the work.[67] A work can be identified by its title or by some other description.[68] The author can be identified by name, pseudonym, or by other means, such as a photograph or a logo.[69] Whatever method is chosen, it must convey 'to a reasonably alert member of the relevant audience that the identified person is the author'.[70] It is important to note that it is the author and not the owner of the copyright work who must be identified.[71]

2.5 RELATIONSHIP WITH CONTRACT

As the CDPA 1988 reminds us, the mere fact that an activity falls within one of the permitted acts does not mean that it does not contravene some other legal right,[72] an obvious example being breach of contract. With the increasing use of digital means to make works available, users are often confronted by attempts to limit their freedoms under the

---

[62] CDPA 1988, s. 29A(1). See HM Government, *Technical Review of the Draft Legislation on Copyright Exceptions: Government Response* (2014) (the 'Technical Review'), 12.   [63] CDPA 1988, s. 31A(1).

[64] CDPA 1988, s. 29(1), (1B) (as amended to give effect to Info. Soc. Dir., Arts 5(3)(c)), 29A(1)(b) (data analytics), 30(1) (criticism, review, quotation), 30(3), 32(1) (fair dealing by illustration for instruction), 35(1)(b) (educational recording of broadcasts), 36(1)(b) (educational copying), and 59 (public reading or recitation).

[65] CDPA 1988, s. 29(1), (1B) (as amended to give effect to Info. Soc. Dir., Arts 5(3)(c)), 29A(1)(b) (data analytics), 30(1) (criticism, review), 30(3) (reporting current events by sound recording, film, or broadcast), 32(1) (fair dealing by illustration for instruction), 35(1)(b) (educational recording of broadcasts), and 36(1)(b) (educational copying). But not CDPA 1988, ss 30(2) (reporting current events by means other than sound recording, film, or broadcast), or 59 (public reading or recitation). See also Info. Soc. Dir., Art. 5(3)(a), (c), (d), and (f), and *Painer*, Case C-145/10 [2012] *ECDR* (6) 89 (ECJ), [147]–[148] (where work had been made available lawfully, but without author's name, it would be sufficient, to indicate 'the source', but not to attribute the author); *Renckhoff*, Case C-161/17, EU:C:2018:279, [AG119] (no need to identify author if acting with prudence).

[66] These might be understood as statutory examples of cases in which it is 'impossible' to name the author.

[67] CDPA 1988, s. 178.   [68] *Pro Sieben Media v. Carlton Television* [1999] *FSR* 610, 616 (Walker LJ).

[69] Ibid., 625; *Newspaper Licensing Agency* [1999] *EMLR* 369, 384 (Ch).

[70] *Pro Sieben Media* [1997] *EMLR* 509, 597 (Laddie J).

[71] *Express Newspapers v. Liverpool Daily Post* [1985] 3 *All ER* 680; cf. *Forensic Telecommunication Services v. Chief Constable of West Yorkshire* [2011] *EWHC*, [2012] *FSR* (15) 428, [114] (although presumably Arnold J meant that the author, Seyton Bradford, should have been credited, rather than his employer, FTS).

[72] CDPA 1988, s. 28(1).

Act. In some situations, European law has specified that particular exceptions may not be prevented by contract;[73] in other cases, it has left the matter to member states.[74] The 1988 Act goes beyond the EU requirements and, in a number of other situations, applies restrictions to contractual provisions that seek to override exceptions.[75]

The Act uses two different techniques. Sometimes, contractual provisions are declared to be 'void'.[76] In other cases, the same goal is achieved by stating that the relevant terms are 'unenforceable' (rather than void) insofar as they purport to restrict the availability of the particular exception.[77]

A related problem is that raised by the interface between the exceptions to copyright and technological measures of protection. If a person cannot take advantage of a defence because of the application of access or copy control mechanisms, can that person legally circumvent the measure in order to do so? So far, the UK legislature has answered this question with a clear 'no', leaving users deprived of the ability to utilize some of the exceptions, with the possibility of applying to the Secretary of State.[78] These provisions are reviewed in Chapter 13.

2.6 DEALINGS WITH COPIES MADE UNDER EXCEPTIONS

Because many of the permitted acts allow for the making of copies by particular people in specific circumstances and for particular purposes, the legislature has frequently sought to indicate that subsequent use beyond the purpose,[79] or dealing that places the copy in the hands of another person,[80] renders the copy an 'infringing copy'.[81] In other words, just because a copy has been made under an exception does not mean that the copy is able to circulate freely in the market. The precise language by which the legislature has sought to achieve this result is not always consistent.[82]

3 TEMPORARY TECHNOLOGY-DICTATED COPIES

In extending the notion of 'reproduction' to encompass transient copying,[83] the European legislature inevitably extended the remit of copyright into just about every corner of the

---

[73] Software Dir., Arts 5(2), 9; Database Dir., Art. 15 ('null and void'). See also Proposal for a Directive on Copyright in the Digital Single Market, COM(2016) 593 final, Art. 3(2) (text and data mining) ('unenforceable').

[74] Info. Soc. Dir., Art. 9 (provisions in Directive without prejudice to 'law of contract').

[75] Hargreaves Review, 8. Bizarrely, and presumably until the government embarks on the much-needed codification, the effect is that contractual limitations remain possible in relation to the core public interest exceptions—fair dealing for criticism and review and reporting current events.

[76] CDPA 1988, ss 36(4), 50A, 50B, 296A(1)(a), 296A(1)(b), 296A(1)(c), and 296B. See also Broadcasting Act 1996, s. 137.

[77] CDPA 1988, 29(4B) (research and private study), 29A(5) (data analytics), 30(4) (quotation), 30a(2) (parody etc), 32(3) (teaching), 31F(8) (disability), 32(3) (instruction), 41(5) (library copying for other libraries), 42(7) (library copying to replace missing parts), and 42A(6) (library copying of published works for user research). Cf. CDPA 1988, ss 40B (use on-site in cultural institutions), 43(3)(b) (prohibited copying of unpublished works), which are capable of being overridden by contract.

[78] CDPA 1988, ss 296ZA and 296ZE, Sch. 5A (as amended by SI 2014/1372, Sch., para. 10, and SI 2014/1384, Sch., para. 7, on disability); Info. Soc. Dir., Art. 6. See Chapter 13, section 4.1.3, pp. 378–80.

[79] CDPA 1988, s. 29A(2)(b) (copy for data analysis, use beyond purpose is infringement).

[80] CDPA 1988, ss. 29A(2)(a) (where copy made for data analysis, infringement occurs if copy is transferred to 'any other person') and 31A(4) (transfer of accessible copies to non-entitled persons).

[81] In many cases, the 'dealing' is an infringing act, being either a distribution or communication to the public.

[82] CDPA 1988, ss 29A(4) (data analytics), 31A(6) (disability), 31B(12) (defining 'dealt with' as sale), 35(6), and 36(9) (defining 'dealt with' to cover sale or communication).   [83] Info. Soc. Dir., Art. 2.

digital world. This is because digital communication—and digital tools generally—function through the generation of temporary copies. For example, digital networks operate processes of 'caching'—that is, the temporary storage of information in the user's computer or server, which allows for speedier access to websites.[84] Such activities are positively desirable, since they enable the Internet to function speedily and efficiently, and seem to have no obvious impact on the economic interests of content holders.

Recognizing this, the European legislature sought to exclude from copyright liability certain temporary copies that are transient or incidental to other activities.[85] Importantly, this was the only exception that was regarded as so significant that all member states were obliged to implement it. Nevertheless, the exception is subject to a number of conditions, so that its precise remit is uncertain. According to Article 5(1) of the Information Society Directive (implemented in the United Kingdom by section 28A of the 1988 Act[86]), a person making a temporary copy will escape liability only if:

(i)   the copy is transient or incidental;

(ii)   the making of the copy is an 'an integral and essential part of a technological process';

(iii) the copying either occurs to enable either transmission of the work in a network between third parties and an intermediary, or to enable a lawful use of the work; and

(iv)   the temporary copy has 'no independent economic significance'.

The conditions have made it difficult to predict when temporary acts of reproduction will be legitimate. Perhaps not surprisingly, the meaning of Article 5(1) has been considered a number of times already by the Court of Justice. The first three cases were *Infopaq I* and *Infopaq II*, and *Football Association Premier League (FAPL) v. QC Leisure*.[87] The first two concerned temporary copies made at various stages in an electronic news-clippings service (scanning, undertaking optical character recognition, or OCR, searching, and printing out), whereas *FAPL* related to copies created in the buffer of a satellite broadcast receiver. Importantly, the Court of Justice indicated that the goal of Article 5(1) was to 'ensure the development and operation of new technologies'.[88] The conditions thus need to be interpreted to ensure that the goal is achieved.

The first requirement—that the copy be transient or incidental[89]—was considered in *Infopaq I*. In that case, the Court indicated that, to be transient, the duration of an act must be limited to that necessary for completion of the process, and the copy must subsequently be deleted automatically and without human intervention.[90] A printout would

---

[84] See P. B. Hugenholtz, 'Caching and Copyright: The Right of Temporary Copying' [2000] *EIPR* 482, 483; *Newspaper Licensing Agency v. Public Relations Consultants Association* [2013] *UKSC* 18, [2] (Lord Sumption).   [85] Info. Soc. Dir., Recital 33.

[86] CDPA 1988, s. 28A, does not, on its face, extend the exception to broadcasts. However, Floyd J has held that it must be interpreted to apply to broadcasts: *ITV Studios v. TV CatchUp* [2011] *EWHC* 1874 (Pat), [47], [121].

[87] *Infopaq I*, [2009] *ECR* I–6569; *Infopaq International A/S v. Danske Dagblades Forening*, Case C-302/10, EU:C:2012:16 ('*Infopaq II*'); *FAPL*, Joined Cases C-403/08 and C-429/08 [2011] *ECR* I–9083 (ECJ, Grand Chamber).

[88] *FAPL*, Joined Cases C-403/08 and C-429/08 [2011] *ECR* I–9083 (ECJ, Grand Chamber), [179]; *PRCA*, Case C-360/13, EU:C:2014:1195, [24] (ECJ).

[89] *VG Wort*, EU:C:2013:34, [AG73] (AG Sharpston).

[90] *Infopaq I* [2009] *ECR* I–6569, [61], [64]. The Court assumed that caching and other acts that enable browsing would have this character: [63].

clearly not be a transient copy, nor would making a digital copy for access on the terminals of a library,[91] but a scan might (depending on the details of the process).[92]

The second requirement—that the reproduction be an 'integral and essential' part of a technological process—was considered in *Infopaq II*, in which the Court of Justice said that this 'requires the temporary acts of reproduction to be carried out entirely in the context of the implementation of the technological process and, therefore, not to be carried out, fully or partially, outside of such a process'.[93] Despite this language, the Court indicated that the condition could be satisfied even though the process is initiated by a human being, such as the scanning of the newspapers.[94] The copies so created could fall within the defence if the other requirements were met.[95]

The third requirement—that the purpose must be to enable a transmission in a network between third parties and an intermediary or to enable a 'lawful use'—was considered in *FAPL* and *Infopaq II*.[96] Both indicated a broad construction of lawful use. In *FAPL*, it was held that receipt of a satellite broadcast was lawful and thus the creation of the buffer copies did not give rise to liability.[97] In *Infopaq II*, it was suggested that the making of a summary of a newspaper article, being a use that the copyright owner could not prevent, might justify the making of temporary copies by a technological process that facilitated that use.[98]

The fourth requirement—that the acts be of no 'independent economic significance'—was also considered in both *FAPL* and *Infopaq II*. In *FAPL*, the Court of Justice indicated that, for a copy to have such significance, it must be attributable to the copy itself rather than the lawful use (in the case, the reception of the broadcast). Because the buffer copies had no such value, the Court indicated that they fell within the exception.[99] In *Infopaq II*, the Court elaborated on the reasoning in *FAPL*, stating that the defence would not apply if there were any economic benefit that was either distinct or separable from the economic advantage derived from the lawful use of the work concerned, or went beyond that derived from that use of the protected work.[100] Efficiency gains, for example that it was quicker or easier to search newspapers by digitizing them, were not relevant.[101]

The question of whether the exception allows for electronic copies that facilitate acts of browsing was considered by the UK Supreme Court and the CJEU in *Newspaper Licensing Agency (NLA) v. Public Relations Consultants Association (PRCA)*.[102] In that case, an electronic news-monitoring service used sophisticated search engines to identify stories contained in online versions of newspapers relating to particular search topics. The news-monitoring service sent its clients links to the relevant stories, accompanied by the titles and brief extracts surrounding the search term. In addition to raising controversial questions as to whether newspaper titles were original works,[103] the courts were

---

[91] *Technische Universität Darmstadt v Eugen Ulmer KG*, Case C-117/13, EU:C:2014:1795 [AG34] (AG Jääskinen).　　　　　　　　　　　　　　　[92] *Infopaq I*, [2009] ECR I–6569, [67].

[93] *Infopaq II*, Case C-302/10, EU:C:2012:16, [30].

[94] *Infopaq II*, Case C-302/10, EU:C:2012:16, [36]; *PRCA*, Case C-360/13, EU:C:2014:1195, [31] (ECJ) (the condition is met even if it takes human action to terminate the process).

[95] *Infopaq II*, Case C-302/10, EU:C:2012:16, [37]–[38].

[96] Lawful use is defined to include uses 'authorised by the rightholder or not restricted by law': Info. Soc. Dir., Recital 33.

[97] *FAPL*, Joined Cases C-403/08 and C-429/08 [2011] ECR I–9083 (ECJ, Grand Chamber), [171]–[173].

[98] *Infopaq II*, Case C-302/10 EU:C:2012:16, [44].

[99] *FAPL*, Joined Cases C-403/08 and C-429/08 [2011] ECR I–9083 (ECJ, Grand Chamber), [175]–[177].

[100] *Infopaq II*, Case C-302/10, EU:C:2012:16, [50].　　　[101] Ibid., [51].

[102] [2013] *UKSC* 18; Case C-360/13, EU:C:2014:1195 (ECJ).

[103] See, Chapter 3, section 2.2, pp. 64–5, and Chapter 4, sections 3.5.6, p. 107, and 3.7.2, pp. 111–12.

asked to rule on whether the recipient of links infringed when they clicked on the links and visited the sites. In turn, this raised the issue, in effect, of whether browsing websites might infringe copyright. Given the way in which digital technologies operate, browsing inevitably involves making temporary copies, in an Internet cache and on a browser's hard drive. The NLA argued that the browsing did not comply with the conditions of Article 5(1) and the Court of Appeal agreed. Relying heavily on *Infopaq I*, the Court stated that the copies in question met none of the conditions.[104]

The Supreme Court recognized that the case raised an issue of general public importance, Lord Sumption explaining that:

> [T]he . . . question potentially affects millions of non-commercial users of the internet who may, no doubt unwittingly, be incurring civil liability by viewing copyright material on the internet without the authority of the rights owner, for example because it has been unlawfully uploaded by a third party.[105]

Not insignificantly, by the time the case was heard by the Supreme Court, the Court of Justice had issued its decisions in *Infopaq II* and *FAPL*, both of which seemed to indicate a trend towards flexible purposive interpretation of Article 5(1). In light of these, the Supreme Court held that the acts of members of the PRCA in clicking on the links were not infringing. Giving judgment, Lord Sumption reasoned that the various components of Article 5(1) were overlapping and needed to be read together, rather than merely ticked off like separate items on a shopping list.[106] Having regard in particular to Recital 33 and also to *FAPL*, it was clear to the Supreme Court that Article 5(1) was intended to cover the making of copies to enable end-user acts of viewing content on the Internet (and was not confined, as NLA suggested, to copies created in transmission networks). Accordingly 'the various conditions laid down by that Article must be construed so far as possible in a manner consistent with that purpose'.[107] Lord Sumption said that it was beyond argument that the temporary copies were created as an integral part of a technological process and that they had no economic significance beyond that from the lawful act of viewing; the key question was whether they were temporary and 'transient or incidental'.[108] He explained that he thought there was no difference between a temporary and a transient copy.[109] Given that the copy could remain in the cache for a considerable length of time, the Court recognized that it was difficult to fit the circumstances within the literal term 'transient'. Nevertheless, because the cache copies are eventually, in the normal course of affairs, destroyed automatically, the Court found them to be transient in the sense (stated in *Infopaq I*) that the copies would be deleted without human intervention. Lord Sumption argued that, looked at in the round, the jurisprudence of the Court of Justice sought to elaborate a distinction between 'the use of a computer or other equipment simply to view the relevant material, and its use to record it'.[110] In his view, the case concerned the former not the latter. He also indicated that even if the copy was

---

[104] [2011] *EWCA Civ* 890, [35] (Morrit C).

[105] *Public Relations Consultants Association (PRCA) v. The Newspaper Licensing Agency (NLA)* [2013] *UKSC* 18, [4].

[106] Ibid., [11]. But cf. *Stichting Brein v. Jack Frederik Wullems*, Case C-527/15, EU:C:2017:300 (ECJ), [61] (emphasizing cumulative nature of conditions).

[107] *Public Relations Consultants Association (PRCA) v. The Newspaper Licensing Agency (NLA)* [2013] *UKSC* 18, [28].   [108] Ibid., [29].

[109] Ibid., [30].   [110] Ibid., [31].

not transient, it was incidental to the technological process;[111] therefore the copies all fell within the exception.

The Court of Justice affirmed the conclusion of the Supreme Court as to the first two conditions—no questions were referred on the issue of lawful use or independent economic significance,[112] finding temporary screen copies to be both transient and incidental to the process of viewing the material which had been placed on the Internet with the right holder's assent,[113] and the cache copies, though not transient, were incidental to that process.[114] Both acts, too, were an essential part of a technological process, because they were 'created and deleted by the technological process used for viewing websites, with the result that they are made entirely in the context of that process.'[115] It did not matter that the user, a human being, activated and terminated that process. Moreover, the process could not work 'correctly and efficiently' without the creation of these copies.

The Court conducted an additional analysis in which it found the conclusion consistent with the 'three-step test': the use in browsing websites was regarded as self-evidently a 'special case',[116] and was part of—rather than in conflict with—the normal exploitation of a work that had been placed on the Internet with the right holder's consent.[117]

However sensible the outcome in the *Meltwater* case,[118] it left a critical issue unanswered: would Article 5(1) also offer a defence to an end user who viewed, for example, an unauthorized stream? The CJEU has now answered that question, perhaps not surprisingly, with a categorical 'no'. In *Stichting Brein v. Jack Frederik Wullems*,[119] the question arose in the context of sale of a multimedia device (akin to a so-called 'Kodi Box') that was pre-programmed with add-ons that gave users access to unlawful streaming of broadcasts. If the user operated the device, inevitably, they would produce a transient copy of the stream. The Court indicated that this reproduction would fall outside Article 5(1), when read with Article 5(5). This was because the end user would access, for free and deliberately,[120] the protected work and the effect would be to reduce the number of lawful, paid, transactions.[121] Consequently, such access would conflict with normal exploitation of the work and/or prejudice the legitimate interests of the author.[122] The distinction between the circumstances and those in *FAPL* and *Meltwater*, where unauthorized reception/browsing of an authorized communication was treated as 'lawful' use, is not completely clear; though the holding is consistent with the CJEU's categorical position that exceptions and limitations do not justify acts with pirated or illegal material.[123]

---

[111] Ibid., [33].

[112] *Newspaper Licensing Agency (NLA) v. Public Relations Consultants Association*, Case C-360/13, EU:C:2014:1195, [25] (ECJ). The Court, at [22], [25], refers to three conditions, the other being that the copy is temporary: this is dealt with cursorily at [26]–[27].

[113] Ibid., [44]–[46]. This was so even though the user might, for example, leave the page on-screen while they went off to a meeting or to lunch, because the technological process was continuing.

[114] Ibid., [47]–[50].   [115] Ibid., [29].   [116] Ibid., [55].   [117] Ibid., [60]–[61].

[118] See also *Vereniging Openbare Bibliotheken (VOB) v. Stichting Leenrecht*, Case C-174/15, EU:C:2016:459, [AG58] (suggesting that temporary copies made by an electronic borrower from a public library would be exempt on this basis).

[119] *Stichting Brein v. Jack Frederik Wullems*, Case C-527/15, EU:C:2017:300 (ECJ).

[120] Ibid., [69].   [121] Ibid., [70].   [122] Ibid., [71]–[72].

[123] *ACI Adam BV v. Stichting de Thuiskopie*, C-435/12, EU:C:2014:254 (ECJ); (private copying); *Vereniging Openbare Bibliotheken (VOB) v. Stichting Leenrecht*, Case C-174/15, EU:C:2016:856, [68], [71]–[72] (public lending). See also *GS Media BV v. Sanoma Media Netherlands BV* et al., Case C-160/15, EU:C:2016:644 (ECJ), [53].

4 PERSONAL COPYING FOR PRIVATE USE

Apart from the exceptions relating to private study,[124] back-up copies of computer pro-grams,[125] and time shifting of broadcasts,[126] UK law contains no exception permitting private or personal use. Consequently, acts such as making a copy of legally purchased, copyright-protected CDs for use on a portable device, such as an MP3 player, iPhone, or iPod, constitute illegal acts of 'copying' the recording (and possibly the musical and literary works performed and recorded therein). This is so even though it is clear that the record industry neither offers licences to make such copies, nor would enforce the rights that exist in the recordings against such uses.

Article 5(2)(b) of the Information Society Directive allows member states to offer excep-tions that permit the making of 'reproductions on any medium by a natural person for private use and for ends that are neither directly nor indirectly commercial'. In many EU member states, a broad private copying exception exists, coupled with a levy system.[127] Some impose levies on blank media (such as blank CDs); some, on mp3 players; some, on printers; and some, on personal computers. This type of scheme is clearly what the EU leg-islature envisaged for Article 5(2)(b), and the details of many such schemes have already been ruled on by the Court of Justice.[128] That case law establishes that 'fair compensation' is intended to compensate right holders identified in Article 2,[129] and must be calculated on the basis of the criterion of the harm caused those persons,[130] although there is some inconsistency as to whether the harm for which compensation must be paid is merely the harm caused by the introduction of the private copy exception, or any harm caused

---

[124] See section 5.2, p. 243.   [125] See section 16.1, pp. 273–4.   [126] See section 20.3, p. 279.

[127] M. Kretschmer, *Private Copying and Fair Compensation: An Empirical Study of Copyright Levies in Europe* (2011) (22 out of the then 27 member states had such schemes); S. Karapapa, *Private Copying* (2012). For background, see B. Hugenholtz, 'The Story of the Tape Recorder and the History of Copyright Levies', in B. Sherman and L. Wiseman (eds), *Copyright and the Challenge of the New* (2012), ch. 7. See also *Microsoft Mobile Sales International Oy*, Case C-110/15, EU:C:2016:326, [AG23] (AG Wahl) (noting the increase in direct licensing of consumers and the diminishing importance of the private copy excep-tion and levy).

[128] *Padawan*, Case C-467/08 [2010] ECR I–10555 (ECJ), [32]–[33]; *Amazon.com International Sales Inc v. Austro-Mechana Gesellschaft zur Wahrnehmung mechanisch-musikalischer Urheberrecte Gesellschaft mbH*, Case C-521/11 EU:C:2013:515 (ECJ) ('*Amazon.com*'); *ACI Adam BV v. Stichting de Thuiskopie*, C-435/12, EU:C:2014:254 (ECJ) (such schemes cannot be applied to copying from illegal material) ('*ACI Adam*'); *Copydan Båndkopi v. Nokia Danmark A/S*, Case C-463/12 EU:C:2015:144; *EGEDA v Adminición del Estado*, Case C-470/14, EU:C:2016: 418 (ECJ), [26] (scheme raised through taxation must not charge those, e.g. corporations, who are not engaged in private copying) ('*Copydan*'); *Hewlett-Packard Belgium SPRL v. Reprobel SCRL*, Case C-572/13, EU:C:2015:750 (ECJ), [48] (on reprographic levy under Art 5(2) (a), noting that principles applicable should parallel those for private copying compensation schemes under Art 5(2)(b)) ('*Reprobel*').

[129] *Hewlett-Packard Belgium SPRL v. Reprobel SCRL*, Case C-572/13, EU:C:2015:750 (ECJ), [48] (a case on Art. 5(2)(a), the reprographic copying exception). Presumably, publishers and other licensees or assign-ees can claim such compensation in accordance with any contractual agreement made with the author (or right holder). The *Reprobel* decision has prompted a legislative response in the Commission's proposal for a Directive on Copyright in the Digital Single Market, COM(2016) 593 final, Art. 12 (specifying that a member state may specify that a transfer or licence to a publisher confers on the latter a 'sufficient legal basis' to be entitled to a share of compensation).

[130] Ibid. It seems strange that compensation should be calculated only in relation to harm to initial right holders and not assignees, such as publishers, whose interests are also (if not more) harmed by the acts of reprography and personal copying in relation to which compensation is payable.

by unauthorized reproduction.[131] Although, in principle, the compensation should be paid by end users who take advantage of the exception (and thus cause the harm),[132] it might alternatively be paid by those who are in possession of equipment and who make it available, or those who provide services to private users (the assumption being that they pass the charge on to purchasers),[133] or those who sell recording media (even if they do so from outside the country with the private copy exception).[134] Sales of such equipment other than to those involved in making private uses, for example to businesses, would not warrant such a levy.[135] Member states have a 'wide discretion' when deciding who must discharge the obligation to pay compensation,[136] but have an obligation to ensure that the mechanism is effective to secure the compensation to the authors.[137] The compensation collected need not be paid directly to right holders, so can be paid to social and cultural establishments to be used for the benefit of 'those entitled'.[138]

Relying on the freedom provided by Article 5(2)(b) of the Information Society Directive, the CDPA was amended so as to permit the making of personal copies of a work (other than a computer program) by an individual in certain restricted circumstances. Section 28B allowed an individual to copy content that they own and which they acquired lawfully to another medium or device for their own private use.[139] However, while Article 5(2)(b) requires that 'right holders receive fair compensation', section 28B made no provision for 'compensation'. The UK government claimed that no compensation was required, given the narrowness of the exception. Recital 35 of the Information Society Directive

---

[131] *Padawan, SL v. SGAE*, Case C-467/08 [2010] *ECR* I-10555, [38], [42] (harm caused by introducing exception); cf. *Stichting de Thuiskopie v. Mijndert van der Lee*, Case C-462/09 [2011] *ECR* I-5331 (ECJ) ('*Thuiskopie*'), [24] ('harm resulting for the author from the reproduction for private use of his protected work without authorization'); *VG Wort*, EU:C:2013:426 [37], [49] (harm caused by introducing the measure), [31], [75] (harm caused by unauthorized reproduction); *Amazon.com*, Case C-521/11 EU:C:2013:515 (ECJ), [47] (harm caused by unauthorized private use); *EGEDA v. Adminición del Estado*, Case C-470/14, EU:C:2016: 418, [26] (ECJ) (for non-authorized use); *Austro-Mechana Gesellschaft zur Wahrnehmung mechunisch-musikalischer Urheberrechte Gesellschaft mbH v Amazon EU Sàrl*, Case C-572/14, EU:C:2016:90, [AG33] (AG Saugmandsgaard Øe) (compensation for extinction of right). The significance of the distinction is that there will be harm caused by unauthorized copying *whether there is an exception or not*; on introducing an exception, the question arises as to whether compensation must cover only the new harm that results from legitimate private copying (but which would not have occurred had copying been prohibited), or also the harm that would have occurred whatever the legal position, but which is now legitimized. In *R (on the application of British Academy of Songwriters, Composers and Authors) v. Secretary of State for Business, Innovation & Skills* [2015] *EWHC* 2041 (Admin), [2015] *RPC* (26) 703, [176]–[207] Green J accepted that the relevant harm related to 'lost sales' as a result of introducing the exception.

[132] *Padawan, SL v. SGAE*, Case C-467/08 [2010] *ECR* I-10555, [45]; *Thuiskopie*, Case C-462/09 [2011] *ECR* I-5331, [26].

[133] *Padawan, SL v. SGAE*, Case C-467/08 [2010] *ECR* I-10555, [46]–[48]; *VG Wort*, EU:C:2013:426, [76]–[78].

[134] *Thuiskopie*, Case C-462/09 [2011] *ECR* I-5331, [39] (sellers into the Netherlands).

[135] *Padawan*, Case C-467/08 [2010] *ECR* I-10555, [52]–[53]. However, an indiscriminate approach might be permissible, so long as those who were not implicated in facilitating private copying can gain reimbursement of compensation that has been paid: *Amazon.com*, Case C-521/11 EU:C:2013:515 (ECJ, Second Chamber), [31]–[37]; *Copydan*, Case C-463/12 EU:C:2015:144, [47]–[52]; *Microsoft Mobile Sales International Oy*, Case C-110/15, EU:C:2016:717 (ECJ, Second Chamber).

[136] *Thuiskopie*, Case C-462/09 [2011] *ECR* I-5331, [23]; *Amazon.com*, Case C-521/11 EU:C:2013:515, [20].

[137] *Thuiskopie*, Case C-462/09 [2011] *ECR* I-5331, [23], [39].

[138] *Amazon.com*, Case C-521/11 EU:C:2013:515, [49].

[139] The Copyright and Rights in Performances (Personal Copies for Private Use) Regulations 2014, SI 2014/2361 (later invalidated). The conditions for so doing were that: (i) the person was an individual; (ii) they had lawfully acquired an initial copy ('the individual's own copy'); (iii) they held the initial copy on a permanent basis (rather than on loan); (iv) the further copy was for the individual's private use; and (v) the further copy was made for non-commercial ends.

states that 'where the prejudice to the rightholder would be minimal, no obligation for payment may arise'. The United Kingdom claimed that these acts are already 'priced into the purchase' and so entail no loss requiring compensation. When right holder groups brought proceedings for judicial review,[140] Green J examined the evidence upon which the government had determined that the economic impact of the exception would be minimal. The Court found the 'pricing in' evidence established that harm was diminished to some extent, but did not answer the 'specific legal question' whether it was so extensive as to render the harm minimal or non-existent.[141] While accepting that objective proof might not be possible, and emphasizing that the government was entitled to rely on a 'proper combination of quantitative and qualitative analyses (for instance surveys) in order then to draw inferences' of minimal harm, the government's conclusion was not 'not remotely supported' by the evidence offered, especially given potentially contradictory evidence submitted to the government by the film industry. As a result, the exception was held to be unlawful,[142] and subsequently (prospectively) quashed.[143] The UK private copying exception had survived from October 2014 until July 2015.

5 RESEARCH OR PRIVATE STUDY

Section 29(1) of the CDPA 1988 provides that fair dealing with a work for the purpose of non-commercial research or private study does not infringe copyright in the work.[144] The defence is of limited application to computer programs.[145] Contracts that attempt to exclude the operation of the defence are unenforceable.[146]

The rationale for this defence lies in the belief that research and study is necessary to generate new works. It also recognizes that non-commercial research and study does not normally interfere with the incentives and rewards that copyright provides to creators and owners. In effect, the defence helps to achieve copyright's goal of maximizing the production of works. The defence also takes account of the fact that dealings of this kind would often be difficult to detect.

In order for a defendant to rely upon the research or private study defence, they must show that the use made of the copyright work was either (i) for the purpose of non-commercial research or (ii) for private study, that (iii) the purpose was 'non-commercial', and that (iv) the dealing was 'fair'. In the case of research, the work and the author must be sufficiently acknowledged (with certain exceptions).

5.1 IS THE DEALING FOR THE 'PURPOSE OF RESEARCH'?

To fall within section 29(1), the defendant must show that the dealing was for the purpose of research.

---

[140] *R (on the application of British Academy of Songwriters, Composers and Authors) v. Secretary of State for Business, Innovation & Skills* [2015] *EWHC* 2041 (Admin), [2015] *RPC* (26) 703.   [141] Ibid., [272].
[142] Ibid., [274].
[143] *R (on the application of British Academy of Songwriters, Composers and Authors) v. Secretary of State for Business, Innovation & Skills* [2015] *EWHC* 1723 (Admin).
[144] Limitations as to the types of work to which the defence applied were removed by SI 2014/1372, reg. 3(1). For the previous position, see Bently and Sherman (2008), 207.
[145] CDPA 1988, s. 29(4)–(4A), excluding from the fair-dealing exceptions acts which are permitted in relation to computer programs under CDPA 1988, ss 50B (decompilaton) and 50BA (observing, testing, etc.), neither of which are limited to non-commercial acts. See section 16.2–16.3, pp. 274–6.
[146] CDPA 1988, s. 29(4B) (added by SI 2014/1372, reg. 3(e)).

An Australian case suggested that 'research' meant a systematic inquiry into a question.[147] This would certainly cover photocopying documents for the purposes of an academic research project, whether by a professor, doctoral student, or undergraduate researching an essay. It would also cover the acts of independent researchers investigating topics, as well as people researching their family history. There seems no reason why a research assistant, or designated agent, might not benefit from the exception when acting on behalf of the researcher (and a person who requests such copying will not be liable for authorization).

5.2 IS THE DEALING FOR 'PRIVATE STUDY'?

Although the 'private study' exception has existed since 1911,[148] its meaning has yet to be elaborated upon judicially. Giving the words 'private study' their normal meaning, the exception could cover any copying by a student when preparing for a seminar, or to assist in the writing of an essay, or even to help them to decide what type of stove to buy. However, as a general rule, in order to come within the defence, the dealing must be for a person's *own* study. Consequently, a publisher cannot rely on the exception to justify reproducing parts of copyright-protected works in 'study guides' for students.[149] Although it is possible for an agent to do the copying on behalf of the student, an important limitation to this possibility is imposed by section 29(3)(b).[150] This provides that copying by a person other than a researcher or student is not a fair dealing if the person doing the copying knows that it will result in 'copies of substantially the same material being provided to more than one person at substantially the same time and for substantially the same purpose'.[151] This means that lecturers are unable to use the research or private study defence where they make multiple copies of a work for their students.

5.3 IS THE PURPOSE OF THE ACTIVITY 'NON-COMMERCIAL'?

Both provisions are limited to 'non-commercial' activities. Private study is defined, in section 178, as not including any study that is directly or indirectly for a commercial purpose. The exceptions cover most research or private study for academic purposes or personal edification. In contrast, where a work (such as a database) is used in the market-testing of new drugs or for a commercial training course, the defence would not apply. Much research, however, will occupy a difficult middle ground.[152] In a recent case, the High Court appears to have approved the test of whether it is contemplated that the research will ultimately be used for a purpose that has some commercial value.[153]

---

[147] *De Garis v. Neville Jeffress Pidler* (1990) 18 *IPR* 292 (FCA). The 'research' exception is said to be justified by reference to Art. 5(3)(a) of the Directive, which refers to 'scientific research'. The term 'illustration' in Info. Soc. Dir., Art. 5(3)(a), qualifies the exception to 'teaching' not research: *Forensic Telecommunication Services v. Chief Constable of West Yorkshire* [2011] *EWHC* 2892 (Ch), [2012] *FSR* (15) 428, [109]; S. von Lewinski, 'Information Society Directive', in Walter and von Lewinski, 733–5, [9.6.27]–[9.6.29].

[148] Like the private copying exception under CDPA 1988, s. 28B, this is permissible under the Info. Soc. Dir., Art. 5(2)(a) and (b).

[149] *Sillitoe v. McGraw Hill* [1983] *FSR* 545; *Longman Group v. Carrington Technical Institute* [1991] 2 *NZLR* 574 (CANZ).   [150] See also CDPA 1988, s. 36, discussed in section 13.5, p. 266.

[151] CDPA 1988, s. 29(3); cf. *Longman v. Carrington*, [1991] 2 *NZLR* 574.   [152] See section 2.2, pp. 232–3.

[153] *The Controller of Her Majesty's Stationery Office, Ordnance Survey v. Green Amps* [2007] *EWHC* 2755 (Ch), [23].

5.4 DEALING MUST BE 'FAIR'

The mere fact that a defendant can show that the work was used for private study or non-commercial research does not necessarily mean that the dealing will be exempt from liability; it is also necessary to show that the dealing was fair. As explained earlier, a number of different factors will influence the decision as to whether a particular dealing is fair. In this context, the most important are likely to be the amount taken,[154] whether the work is readily available, and the effect that the dealing has on the market for the original work.

5.5 SUFFICIENT ACKNOWLEDGEMENT

Where a dealing is for purposes of non-commercial research, it can benefit from the exception only if there is 'sufficient acknowledgement'.[155] However, this can be dispensed with where the acknowledgement is impossible for reasons of practicality or otherwise. This requirement for sufficient acknowledgement seems to take account of the fact that research output, whether papers or articles, is often circulated. No such requirement must be satisfied as regards 'private study'.

6 TEXT AND DATA ANALYSIS

Following the Hargreaves Review, UK law was amended to introduce an exception for 'text and data mining'. Broadly speaking, text and data mining practices have been made possible by digital tools that can scan massive amounts of data (more than a human being could read in a lifetime) and identify hitherto unrecognized relationships between different pieces of data. A classic example would be a search tool that identifies a relationship between a particular trait or symptom and a disease.[156] However, the use of such research tools implicates copyright, in so far as they may require digitization of text, involve the generation of temporary copies, and breach the terms of licences with publishers.

From June 2014, a new section 29A has been introduced into the CDPA 1988 allowing a person to copy a work for the purposes of carrying out a 'computational analysis of anything recorded in the work', as long as it is done 'for the sole purpose of non-commercial research'.[157] The exception is subject to two further qualifications: first, the person must have 'lawful access' to a copy of the work; and second, any copy must be accompanied by sufficient acknowledgement. The exception is limited, in part because of the constraints of the Information Society Directive, to non-commercial research. This will restrict the value of the defence considerably. Nevertheless, the contractual override, contained in section 29A(5), will be of particular significance to those in research institutes who have acquired the right to use databases of material, but subject to restrictions that do not allow data mining.[158] However, licences may still impose conditions of access to the licensor's computer system, for example to maintain security or stability.

---

[154] *Universities UK v. Copyright Licensing Agency* [2002] *RPC* 693, 702, [34].

[155] Database Dir., Art. 6(2)(b); Info. Soc. Dir., Art. 5(3)(a). See section 2.4, p. 234.

[156] See further JISC, *The Value and Benefits of Text Mining* (2012), available online at https://www.jisc.ac.uk/reports/value-and-benefits-of-text-mining.

[157] CDPA 1988, s.29A, added by the Copyright and Rights in Performances (Research, Education, Libraries and Archives) Regulations 2014 (SI 2014/1372), reg. 3(2).

[158] Further, third parties who are developing data mining tools will at least be able to supply them to non-commercial users, confident that, by so doing, they will not incur accessory liability (because use of the tools is not infringing).

In 2016, inspired by the United Kingdom (and defeated in their attempts to produce voluntary solutions),[159] the European Commission's Proposal for a Directive on Copyright in the Digital Single Market included a mandatory exception (that is, one that all member states must enact) permitting the making of 'reproductions and extractions' by research organizations in order to carry out text and data mining of works or other subject matter to which they have lawful access for the purposes of scientific research.[160] The proposal defines 'text and data mining' as any automated analytical technique aiming to analyse text and data in digital form in order to generate information such as patterns, trends, and correlation.[161] The proposal restricts the availability of the exception to 'research organizations'. These are defined as 'a university, a research institute or any other organisation the primary goal of which is to conduct scientific research or to conduct scientific research and provide educational services.'[162] The organization must operate on a not-for-profit basis.[163] Right holders are specifically permitted to take measures to preserve the security and integrity of their networks.[164]

While the idea of an EU exception for text and data mining has received widespread approval, the particular form of this proposal has garnered significant criticism: the limitations by reference to beneficiary (research organization) and purpose (scientific research) seem difficult to justify, and are liable to create some unfortunate distortions. The European Copyright Society (a group of university professors) has argued that 'text and data mining' is an example of 'non-expressive use which should not fall within the scope of copyright at all' (because it does not use the copyright work as a work, but as a dataset).[165] Various amendments to the proposal are currently before the Parliament, so it is not possible to be certain what the final form of the exception is likely to be.[166]

7 CRITICISM, REVIEW; QUOTATION

Section 30(1) of the CDPA 1988 provides that fair dealing with any work for the purpose of criticism or review does not infringe the copyright in the work; section 30(1ZA) adds that copyright is not infringed by the use of a quotation from the work, whether for criticism, review, or otherwise.[167] The defences no doubt overlap significantly. Both defences only apply where (i) the work has previously been made available to the public, (ii) the dealing is 'fair', and (iii) the dealing is accompanied by sufficient acknowledgement. However, the (old) criticism of review defence is only available if the dealing is for the purpose of criticism or review, whereas the quotation defence is, in principle, available whatever the purpose. However, quotation is only permissible where it goes no further than is necessary to achieve the specific purpose for which the user requires the quotation.

---

[159] *Licences for Europe: Structured Stakeholder Dialogue* (2013), available online at http://ec.europa.eu/licences-for-europe-dialogue/en. WP4 was one the least successful of the 'dialogues'.

[160] COM(2016) 593 final, Art. 3(3).   [161] Ibid., Art. 2(2).   [162] Ibid., Art. 2(1).

[163] Ibid., Art. 2(1).   [164] Ibid., Art. 3(3).

[165] ECS, *General Opinion on the EU Copyright Reform Package* (2017) 5. For the concept of 'non-expressive uses', see Chapter 6, section 2, p. 145.

[166] Council Doc. 12533/17 (26 September 2017) suggests the Council has relatively few amendments, while the draft JURI Report of 10 March 2017, would universalize the beneficiaries and permitted uses.

[167] CDPA 1988, s. 30(1ZA), added by the Copyright and Rights in Performances (Quotation and Parody) Regulations 2014 (SI 2014/2356).

7.1 IS THE DEALING OF AN APPROPRIATE TYPE?

To fall within the exception provided by section 30(1), the dealing must be for the purpose of 'criticism or review' of the work, or of another work,[168] or the performance of a work. Although the courts have also said that criticism and review should be construed liberally,[169] it has been understood as requiring identification of a work or performance as the focus of the criticism or review. Thus it has been held to exclude criticism at large, for example of behaviour or political activity,[170] unless that can be connected plausibly to a work or performance.[171] This seemed unduly narrow given the international *acquis*.[172]

In contrast, section 30(1ZA), added in 2014, permits 'quotation' and is not limited by purpose.[173] What, then, counts as 'quotation'? Importantly, we suggest, that the meaning of quotation is not curtailed by the typical characteristics of textual quotation associated with the academic publishing sector. Rather, the term quotation must be understood broadly. This is for two reasons. First, because the quotation exception applies to all works,[174] so that any definition of necessary or sufficient conditions for a use to count as 'quotation' must fit with the ordinary use of the term across all cultural fields (including the visual arts, architecture, film, and music). In those contexts, we find the term quotation used to describe a very wide range of expressive reuses (including transformative reuses, but also stand-alone uses of fragments of text—as with a dictionary of quotations). Second, because quotation defence seeks to balance copyright with freedom of expression,[175] it is important not to interpret the concept too narrowly, lest freedom of expression be unduly restricted. Some legal systems have sought to add conditions: for example, that a quotation be unmodified, is incorporated in a 'quoting' text in a manner that comments on the quotation.[176] While Advocate-General Trstenjak seemed drawn irresistibly toward such conditions in the *Painer* case,[177] the Court did not embrace them (and implicitly, it seems, rejected them).[178] Quotation, then, can encompass a very wide range of reuses of copyright material for expressive or communicative purposes.[179]

---

[168] *Beloff v. Pressdram* [1973] 1 *All ER* 241; *Associated Newspapers Group v. News Group Newspapers* [1986] *RPC* 515.

[169] *Newspaper Licensing Agency v. Marks & Spencer* [2000] 4 *All ER* 239 (CA), 257 (Chadwick LJ); *Pro Sieben Media v. Carlton Television* [1999] *FSR* 610 (CA), 620. Criticism or review may be of the work as a whole or a single aspect of a work, the thought or philosophy underpinning a work, or its social and moral implications: *Hubbard v. Vosper* [1972] 2 *QB* 84, 94 *ff*; *Time Warner v. Channel 4* [1994] *EMLR* 1, 15; *Pro Sieben Media v. Carlton Television* [1999] *FSR* 610 (CA), 621.

[170] *Ashdown v. Telegraph Group* [2002] *Ch* 149, 171, [2002] *RPC* 235, 251. See also *Heythrop Zoological Gardens v. Captive Animals Protection Society* [2016] *EWHC* 1370 (Ch), [43] (noting distinction).

[171] Cf. *Time Warner v. Channel 4* [1994] *EMLR* 1, 15 (defence applied 'equally where the criticism is of the decision to withdraw from circulation a film in the public domain, and not just the film itself'); *Pro Sieben* [1999] *FSR* 610 (CA); *Fraser-Woodward v. BBC* [2005] *FSR* 762.

[172] Berne, Art. 10(1) ('It shall be permissible to make quotations from a work . . . '); Info. Soc. Dir., Art. 5(3)(d) ('quotations for purposes such as criticism or review . . . ').

[173] The government wanted to retain the existing defence to cover acts other than quotation, e.g. the summary of works: *Technical Review*, 9.   [174] S. Jacques, 'Mash Ups and Mixes' [2016] *Ent L Rev* 3.

[175] *Painer*, Case C-145/10 [2012] *ECDR* (6) 89 (ECJ), [134].

[176] T. Aplin and L. Bently, 'Whatever Became of Global, Mandatory, Fair Use?', in S. Frankel (ed.), *Is Intellectual Property Pluralism Functional?* (2018).

[177] *Painer*, Case C-145/10 [2012] *ECDR* (6) 89 (ECJ), [AG210]–[AG211] (AG Trstenjak) (requiring 'a material reference back to the quoted work').

[178] Ibid., [129]–[137] (ECJ) (declining to add conditions that are not in Art. 5(3)(d)).

[179] Note the pending reference in *Pelham v. Hutter*, Case 476/16 (concerning whether reuse of part of a sound recording—a sample—in a different recording constituted 'quotation' even where it would not be recognized as distinct in the derivative recording). We see no basis for adding such a condition as long as the reuse accords with fair practice and the attribution requirement.

7.2 WORK MUST HAVE BEEN MADE AVAILABLE

Both the criticism or review and quotation exceptions are available only where the work has been made available to the public.[180] 'Making available' is broadly defined to include the issuing of copies, making the work available by an electronic retrieval system, rental, or lending of copies to the public, the performance, exhibition, playing, or showing of the work, and the communication to the public.[181] Nevertheless, the condition limits the potential operation of the defence in relation to 'leaked' material. For example, in *HRH the Prince of Wales v. Associated Newspapers*,[182] it was held that Prince Charles's 'Hong Kong journals' had not been made available to the public, even though they had been distributed to as many as 75 people, because the recipients understood that the work was being disclosed in confidence.[183]

7.3 WAS THE DEALING FAIR?

Once a defendant has shown that the dealing was for the purpose of criticism or review, or was by way of quotation, they must then show that the dealing was fair.[184] As we explained earlier, a number of different factors will influence the decision as to whether a particular dealing is fair. In this context, the most important of these are likely to be the amount taken, the effect on the market,[185] and the nature of the dealing.[186]

When deciding whether dealing for the purpose of criticism or review is fair, the courts have not tended to consider whether the criticism itself is fair;[187] rather, they take account of whether the extent of the copying is fair to illustrate or support the criticism. As such, the criticism may be malicious, unbalanced, or motivated by insecurity without forfeiting the defence.[188] Although a 'quotation' is usually understood as the use of a part of a work, as with the 'criticism or review' defence, in some cases it might be fair to reproduce or make available the whole work (most obviously, perhaps, with visual works).[189]

Over and above the fairness requirement, a key limitation on the fair dealing for quotation exception is that the defence will operate only if the quotation is no more than required for the specific purpose for which it is used. Thus in the context of fair dealing for the purpose of quotation the issue of proportionality is explicitly addressed independently from the requirement that the dealing be 'fair'.

In considering the 'fairness' of a quotation, it is likely that the 'specific purposes' will be relevant. This is because different expressive purposes carry different weight (political

---

[180] CDPA 1988, s. 30(1), (1ZA)(a).

[181] CDPA 1988, s. 30(1A) (added by SI 2003/2498 to give effect to Info. Soc. Dir., Art. 5(3)(d)).

[182] [2007] 3 *WLR* 222, 265, [176] (Blackburne J).

[183] Note Case C-516/17, *Volker Beck v Spiegel Online* (pending) and Case C-469/17, *Funke Medien NRW* (pending), two references from the German BGH, the first in a case concerning a link from a newspaper report to a pdf of a manuscript, the author of which (the claimant) had not agreed to publication and the second concerning the publication of reports on German troops in Afghanistan.

[184] CDPA 1988, s. 30(1), (1ZA)(b). Cf. Info. Soc. Dir., Art. 5(3)(d) ('in accordance with fair practice').

[185] *IPC Media v. News Group Newspapers* [2005] *FSR* 752 (copying for own competing commercial purpose unfair); cf. *Pro Sieben v. Carlton UK Television* [1999] *FSR* 610 (CA).

[186] *Fraser-Woodward v. BBC* [2005] *FSR* 762.

[187] There is no need for the critical work to be representative of the original: *Time Warner v. Channel 4* [1994] *EMLR* 1, 12.

[188] *Pro Sieben Media v. Carlton Television* [1999] *FSR* 610 (CA), 619. An author's remedy for unjustified criticism lies in the law of defamation.

[189] *Painer*, Case C-145/10 [2012] *ECDR* (6) 89 (ECJ), [AG212].

and artistic purposes weighing heavier than mere commercial ones). If a given use provides some social, cultural, or informational benefit, that is likely to make a proportionate quotation automatically fair. Aggregating quotations, as with a 'book of quotations', might also be regarded as a fair purpose, particularly if the effect is to highlight the different opinions of a collection of people on similar topics.[190]

Although 'fairness' may well come to play an important part in ensuring that the quotation defence applies primarily to quotation for purposes that provide some social, cultural, or informational benefit, the fairness condition might also have a role in regulating the manner in which the quotations are presented. In the context of literary works, 'fair' dealing for the purpose of 'quotation' will be easier to establish through the use of grammatical conventions such as the use of quotation marks, or, if quotation is by paraphrase, a marker such as a footnote.

7.4 SUFFICIENT ACKNOWLEDGEMENT

To fall within the exception, criticism or review must be accompanied by 'sufficient acknowledgement' unless this would be impossible for reasons of practicality or otherwise.[191] The same condition applies to the quotation defence.[192] The issue of sufficient acknowledgement was discussed earlier.

Contracts are unenforceable to the extent to which they purport to restrict the freedom to quote provided under the section.[193] For reasons of history, rather than logic, no such rule applies to contracts excluding the criticism or review defence. No provision is made in relation to technological measures.

8 PARODY, CARICATURE, AND PASTICHE

Where parodies breach the rule against substantial taking,[194] it is necessary to consider whether such uses avoid liability through the 'fair dealing' exception. Prior to 1 October 2014, this involved assessing whether parody could count as criticism or review of a work, whether it is fair for that purpose, and whether implicit acknowledgement that is a prerequisite of effective parody is sufficient to comply with the sufficient acknowledgement requirement.[195] Meeting these conditions was anything but straightforward,[196] and commentators had long complained that the resulting legal position was unsatisfactory (and in tension with freedom of expression).[197]

Following the recommendations of both the Gowers and Hargreaves Reviews,[198] a new fair dealing exception for 'caricature, parody, or pastiche' has been introduced.[199] This

---

[190] CDPA 1988, s. 30(1ZA)(b), (c).   [191] CDPA 1988, s. 30(1).   [192] CDPA 1988, s. 30(1ZA).
[193] CDPA 1988, s. 30(4).   [194] See Chapter 8, section 2.3, p. 204.
[195] R. Burrell and A. Coleman, *Copyright Exceptions: The Digital Impact* (2005), 61; M. Spence, 'Intellectual Property and the Problem of Parody' (1998) 114 *LQR* 594; M. Spence, '*Rogers v Koons*: Copyright and the Problem of Artistic Appropriation', in D. McClean (ed.), *The Trials of Art* (2007), 213–34, 228.
[196] *Williamson Music v. Pearson* [1987] *FSR* 97, 103. The case law is reviewed in L. Bently, 'Parody and Copyright in the Common Law World', in *Copyright and Freedom of Expression: ALAI 2006 Barcelona* (2008), 360.
[197] R. Deazley, 'Taking Backwards the Gowers Review' (2010) 73 *MLR* 785; R. Jacob, 'Parody and IP Claims: A Defence? A Right to Parody?', in R. Dreyfuss and J. Ginsburg (eds), *IP at the Edge* (2014), ch. 20.
[198] Gowers Review, Recommendation 12; UK IPO, *Taking forward the Gowers Review of Intellectual Property* (2008), 31–6; Hargreaves Review, 50–1, [5.35] *ff*; UK IPO, *Modernising Copyright* (2012), 29–31.
[199] The Copyright and Rights in Performances (Quotation and Parody) Regulations 2014 (SI 2014/2356), adding CDPA 1988, s. 30A(1).

takes advantage of the freedom provided by Article 5(3)(k) of the Information Society Directive, but (presciently, as we explain) qualifies the breadth of that freedom by adding a requirement of fairness.[200] To benefit from this defence, there is no express requirement that a parodist acknowledge the work that is parodied or its authorship.

The meaning of 'parody' has been considered by the Court of Justice in *Deckmyn*.[201] The reference concerned a modified version of a comic book that caricatures the behaviour of a politician. The publisher of a Belgian comic book, *Spike and Suzy* (Fig. 9.1), brought an action against a member of a Flemish nationalist party, Johan Deckmyn, for copyright infringement, in relation to a calendar and brochure that were based on the cover of an issue of the comic entitled 'De Wilde Weldoener' (meaning 'The Wild Benefactor'). The defendant's image (Fig. 9.2) replaced the central figure from the comic, a man in a bowler hat scattering money, with the face of the mayor of Ghent, highlighting his wastefulness with public funds (which he distributes to a multi-ethnic public). Deckmyn claimed that this fell within the Belgian parody defence. The Court, sitting in Grand Chamber, found

Fig. 9.1 The Wild Benefactor cover of the Spike and Suzy comic
Source: © 2013 Standaard Uitgeverij/WPG Uitgevers Belgiënv

---

[200] A number of member states had such an exception: see, e.g., art. L 122–5.4 of the French Intellectual Property Code. For comparative study, see D. Mendis and M. Kretschmer, *The Treatment of Parodies Under Copyright Law in Seven Jurisdictions: A Comparative Review of the Underlying Principles* (2013).
[201] *Deckmyn and Vrijheidsfonds v. Vandersteen*, Case C-201/13, EU:C:2014:2132 (ECJ, Grand Chamber).

Fig. 9.2 Deckmyn's alleged parody

Source: Deckmyn and Vrijheidsfonds v. Vandersteen, Case C-201/13

that parody is an autonomous concept of European law,[202] and that its meaning was that which the term had in 'everyday language'. The Court defined the 'essential characteristics' of parody are, first, to evoke an existing work while being noticeably different from it, and, secondly, to constitute an expression of humour or mockery.[203] As a result it was neither necessary that the parody should display an original character of its own; nor that it should refer to the original source; nor that it could reasonably be attributed to a person other than the author of the original work itself.[204] In adopting this definition, the Court has clarified that parody is not limited to uses that parody the work itself (so-called 'target parody') but potentially extends to situations in which the work is used to target something else (sometimes called 'weapon parody').[205] On the other hand, the Court has left

---

[202] Ibid., [17].

[203] Ibid., [20]. Advocate-General Cruz Villalón referred to these two parts as 'structural' and 'functional': EU:C:2014:458, [AG48].   [204] Ibid., [21].

[205] However, the distinction may have a bearing on the 'fairness' analysis: Federal Supreme Court, 28 July 2016, Case No. I ZR 9/15- *Auf fett getrimmt*, [38], [2016] *GRUR* 1157, (2017) 48 *IIC* 474. For a valuable survey of US case law that sought to distinguish between 'parody' and 'satire', see B. Keller and R. Tushnet, 'Even More Parodic than the Real Thing' (2004) 94 *TMR* 979.

unclear whether the requirement of 'humour' is met if there is evidence of an intention to be 'humourous', or whether such 'humour' must be appreciated by the audience (and, if so, how that audience is identified). Probably the preferable conclusion is that 'humour' should be determined by reference to the reasonable audience, but that the particular character of the audience must depend on the type of work in issue.[206]

While offering a broad definition of parody, the Court introduced an additional condition that is not present in the wording of the Directive: fairness.[207] Identifying the policy aim of striking a balance between the rights of the copyright owner and the freedom of expression of the user, the Court observed that 'the application, in a particular case, of the exception for parody, . . . must strike a fair balance between, on the one hand, the interests and rights of persons referred to in Articles 2 and 3 of that Directive, and, on the other, the freedom of expression of the user of a protected work who is relying on the exception for parody.'[208] This 'fair balance' required an assessment of all the relevant circumstances, which in the Court's view included the 'discriminatory message' communicated by the defendant's reworking of the cartoon. In the light of Article 21 of the Charter, the Court suggested that 'holders of rights . . ., have, in principle, a legitimate interest in ensuring that the work protected by copyright is not associated with such a message'.[209]

The question as to when 'caricature, parody, and pastiche' must be regarded as 'fair' is unelaborated in the UK legislation.[210] It might have been expected that the courts will rely on jurisprudence from other areas of 'fair dealing',[211] but the CJEU's adoption of a parallel requirement suggests that a different methodology will be appropriate—that of 'balancing interests'. Probably the considerations that are relevant are no different (and indeed the outcomes are likely similar).[212] On either basis, it seems unlikely that use in

---

[206] BGH, 28 July 2016, Case No. I ZR 9/15—*Auf fett getrimmt*, [33] reported in German in [2016] *GRUR* 1157 and English at (2017) 48 *IIC* 474 ('Whether in the individual case a parody is present, rather, is essentially to be evaluated objectively according to whether this type of antithetical treatment is recognisable for the person who is familiar with the parodied work and who possesses the necessary intellectual understanding to recognise the new work as a parody. . . . Which goal the author of the new work was pursuing specifically with his adaptation is in this respect irrelevant. . . .'). Cf. J. Griffiths, 'Fair Dealing After *Deckmyn*', in M. Richardson and S. Ricketson (eds), *Research Handbook on IP in Media and Entertainment* (2017) 64, 80 (preferring intention); E. Rosati, 'Just a Laughing Matter' [2016] *CMLR* 511, 518–20; D. Jongsma, 'Parody After *Deckmyn*' (2017) 48 *IIC* 652, 655–6 (citing pre-*Deckmyn* case law from national courts that focus on intention), 672–3 (arguing for intention test). For a broader discussion of 'intentionalism', see B. Picozzi, 'What's Wrong With Intentionalism?' (2017) 126 *Yale LJ* 1408.

[207] Cf. Info. Soc. Dir., Art. 5(3)(c) (the quotation exception, which is explicitly subject to a 'fair practice' condition).

[208] *Deckmyn*, Case C-201/13, EU:C:2014:2132, [27]. In so doing, the Court converted a 'skeleton provision' into a 'usable defence': J. Griffiths, 'Fair Dealing After *Deckmyn*', in M. Richardson and S. Ricketson (eds), *Research Handbook on IP in Media and Entertainment* (2017), 64, 74.

[209] *Deckmyn*, Case C-201/13, EU:C:2014:2132, [31].

[210] Other member states have hitherto operated qualifications of this sort. In Belgium, parodic use must accord with 'fair practice'; in France, it must have 'due consideration for the laws of this genre'; in the Netherlands, it must be 'in accordance with what the rules of social intercourse reasonably permit'.

[211] The UK government had indicated that the 'fair dealing' condition would ensure that the exception would not be 'misused, and will preclude the copying of entire works where such taking would not be considered fair (for example if such works were already licensable for a fee)': UK IPO, *Modernising Copyright* (2012), 31.

[212] Cf. J. Griffiths, 'Fair dealing after *Deckmyn*', in M. Richardson and S. Ricketson (eds), *Research Handbook on IP in Media and Entertainment* (2017), 91–4, arguing that the results of the shift 'may be significant'.

commercial advertising would be regarded as fair, but likely that a liberal approach will be taken with much user-generated content. It should be noted, however, that the Court's reference to the 'discriminatory message' adds an unexpected factor into play. How far these considerations of third party interests are relevant is, as yet, unclear: if a person uses a copyright-protected photograph as a basis to parody the person portrayed, would fairness require consideration of those persons?[213] Would that depend on whether the use breached their fundamental rights under the Charter (or perhaps national constitutional law)?[214] Or does it depend on whether the use in some way tarnishes the reputation of the copyright owner (or author) of the used work?

There has as yet been no clarification of the concepts of 'caricature' or 'pastiche'. Some of the submissions from member states suggested that the Court should not differentiate between the three terms,[215] and the definition of 'parody' certainly seems broad enough to capture that of 'caricature'. However, 'pastiche' is a term that does not normally require humour, probably best being seen as a recognizable stylistic practice.[216]

9 REPORTING OF CURRENT EVENTS

Section 30(2) of the CDPA 1988 provides that fair dealing with any work (other than a photograph)[217] for the purpose of reporting current events does not infringe the copyright in the work, provided that it is accompanied by a sufficient acknowledgement. No acknowledgement is required, however, in connection with the reporting of current events by means of a sound recording, film, or broadcast where this would be impossible by reason of practicality or otherwise.[218]

As Gibson LJ has explained, the reporting of current events defence aims to strike a 'balance between protection of rights of creative authors and the wider public interest (of which free speech is a very important ingredient)'.[219] The courts have also said that the reporting of current events should be construed liberally.[220]

In order to rely upon the defence, a defendant must show that (i) the dealing was for the purpose of reporting current events, (ii) the dealing was 'fair', and (iii) there was sufficient

---

[213] As with the German 'fat-cropped celebrities' case: BGH, 28 July 2016, Case No. I ZR 9/15,—*Auf fett getrimmt*, [39]–[40] reported in German in *GRUR* (2016) 1157 and English at (2017) 48 *IIC* 474.

[214] For a narrow view, see *Deckmyn*, Case C-201/13, EU:C:2014:458, [AG85] (AG Cruz Villalón).

[215] Ibid., [AG46].

[216] R. Dyer, *Pastiche* (2007), 3 defines pastiche as 'a kind of aesthetic imitation', that is imitation of 'art' (broadly understood) by 'art' and that 'pastiche intends that it is understood as pastiche by those who read, see or hear it'; E. Hudson, 'The Pastiche Exception in Copyright Law: A Case of Mashed-Up Drafting?' [2017] *IPQ* 346 (arguing exception could cover mash-ups, fan fiction, music sampling, collage, appropriation art, and other forms of homage and compilation).

[217] This means that a newspaper is not able to take photographs from another paper and claim this defence; hence the need to rely on the criticism or review defence in *Banier v. News Group Newspapers* [1997] *FSR* 812. See C. Kelly, 'Current Events and Fair Dealing with Photographs: Time for a Revised Approach' [2012] 4 *IPQ* 242 (reviewing exclusion).

[218] CDPA 1988, s. 30(3).

[219] *Newspaper Licensing Agency v. Marks & Spencer* [2000] 4 *All ER* 239 (CA), 249. In *England & Wales Cricket Board v. Tixdaq & Fantatix* [2016] *EWHC* 575 (Ch), [112], Arnold J stated that 'The purpose of section 30(2) . . . is to provide an exception to, or limit upon, copyright protection in the public interest, namely freedom of expression.'

[220] The value placed on freedom of information and freedom of speech requires that gateway to be wide: *Newspaper Licensing Agency v. Marks & Spencer* [2000] 4 *All ER* 239, 382; *Ashdown v. Telegraph Group* [2002] *Ch* 149, 172.

acknowledgement.[221] Contractual restrictions on what would otherwise fall within the defence of fair dealing for the purpose of reporting current events are void insofar as the restriction relates to the inclusion of visual images taken from a broadcast in another communication to the public.[222]

9.1 WAS THE DEALING FOR THE PURPOSE OF REPORTING A CURRENT EVENT?

To fall within the defence, the dealing must take place (i) in relation to an event, (ii) which is *current*, and the dealing must be (iii) for the purpose of reporting such an event.

It seems that certain matters, by their very nature, will be treated as events. Thus matters of national or political importance,[223] as well as major sporting contests, such as the World Cup, are likely to be events.[224] In contrast, matters that are trivial, ephemeral, or immaterial will not be treated as events. For example, it has been said that comparisons of food products,[225] articles on clothing, and the times of television programmes are not 'events'.[226] The fact that a matter is currently of interest or in the press does not mean that it is a current event.[227] The mere fact that a fashion editor of a journal featured a Marks & Spencer garment did not make it a current event.[228] Occasionally, a trivial matter may be transformed into an 'event' through media coverage. This can be seen in *Pro Sieben Media v. Carlton UK Television*,[229] in which the sale to German television by a member of the public of an interview about a woman pregnant with octuplets was nonetheless treated as an 'event'. On this occasion, the volume and intensity of the media coverage was such as to justify its treatment as an 'event'.

An event will be *current* if it deals with a contemporary issue. The older the issue, the less likely it is that it will be treated as having any currency. An event that took place some time ago may, however, be current if it is still under discussion. For example, in *Hyde Park*, it was accepted, both at first instance and by the Court of Appeal (albeit grudgingly), that although the stills in *The Sun* were published more than a year after the visit by Fayed and Princess Diana to Villa Windsor, the events still had some currency.[230] As Jacob J said: '[A]t the time of publication the events were still very much under discussion that it would be pedantic to regard them as anything other than current.'[231]

The dealing must be concerned with 'reporting' the event. In *Newspaper Licensing Agency v. Marks & Spencer*,[232] the Court of Appeal held that private circulation of articles selected from newspapers was not *reporting* of current event. Similarly, in the more recent Court of Appeal decision in *Newspaper Licensing Agency v. Meltwater Holding*,[233] it was held that the distribution to commercial organizations of electronic links and text extracts

[221] CDPA 1988, s. 30(2).   [222] Broadcasting Act 1996, s. 137 (as amended).
[223] *Newspaper Licensing Agency* [2000] *4 All ER* 239 (CA), 267 (Mance LJ).
[224] *British Broadcasting Corporation v. British Satellite Broadcasting* [1992] *Ch* 141; cf. *Newspaper Licensing Agency v. Marks & Spencer* [2000] *4 All ER* 239, 257 (Chadwick LJ); *England & Wales Cricket Board & Sky UK v. Tixdaq & Fanatix* [2016] *EWHC* 575 (Ch), [106] ('a contemporary sporting event, such as a cricket match, is a current event').   [225] *Newspaper Licensing Agency* [1999] *EMLR* 369, 383.
[226] *Independent Television Publications v. Time Out* [1984] *FSR* 64.
[227] *Newspaper Licensing Agency* [1999] *EMLR* 369, 382.
[228] *Newspaper Licensing Agency* [2000] *4 All ER* 239 (CA), 250 (Gibson LJ), 267 (Mance LJ).
[229] [1999] *FSR* 610.   [230] *Hyde Park Residence v. Yelland* [1999] *RPC* 655.
[231] Ibid., 661. See also *Ashdown v. Telegraph Group* [2002] *Ch* 149, 172.
[232] [2001] *RPC* 76, 87–88 (Gibson LJ), cf. 105–6 (Mance LJ).
[233] [2011] *EWCA Civ* 890, [2012] *RPC* 1, [39] (not considered on appeal).

from news websites was outside the defence, either because there was no reporting or because the passage might not relate to current events. However, neither decision gives much useful guidance as to what counts as 'reporting'.[234] In contrast, in *England & Wales Cricket Board & Sky UK v. Tixdaq & Fanatix*,[235] faced with the question of whether a platform that hosted and made public clips of cricket matches was 'reporting current events', Arnold J emphasized that what was distinctive about reporting was its 'informatory purpose'.[236] This led him to the view that 'reporting' in not confined to traditional news media, but encompasses so-called 'citizen journalism'.[237] For example, if a member of the public captures images of a 'newsworthy event' using their mobile phone and uploads them to a social media site, they may be reporting current events. However, on the facts of the case, Arnold J thought the 'Fanatix platform' was not doing so.[238] This was because the clips were not used in order to inform the audience about a current event, but 'presented for consumption because of their intrinsic interest and value'.[239]

The material dealt with by the defendant must relate to or be relevant to the current event in question. Thus it was held that the *Daily Mail* newspaper was unable to rely on the death of the Duchess of Windsor to justify the republication of correspondence between the Duchess and her husband.[240] Similarly, in *Hyde Park*, the Court of Appeal held that the publication of the driveway stills that showed the arrival and departure times of Fayed and Princess Diana did not fall within the current events defence. This was because the material in question (the driveway stills) did not correlate with the event in question (the purpose being to expose the lies of Mohammed Al Fayed).[241] However, in other circumstances in which historical material is pertinent to current events,[242] its use would clearly fall within the defence.[243]

9.2 WAS THE DEALING FAIR?

Once a defendant has shown that their dealing was for the purpose of reporting current events, they must then show that the dealing was fair. According to the Court of Appeal, the defence should be available 'where the public interest in learning of the very words written by the owner of the copyright is such that publication should not be inhibited by the chilling factor of having to pay damages or account of profits'.[244] Although a number of different factors will influence the decision as to whether a particular dealing is fair, including whether the work is published or unpublished,[245] and the motive for the dealing,[246] the most important are likely to be whether the amount taken (in particular whether the effect is to damage the normal exploitation of the copyright owner's work),[247]

---

[234] *England & Wales Cricket Board v Tixdaq* [2016] *EWHC* 575 (Ch), [81].

[235] [2016] *EWHC* 575 (Ch).

[236] Ibid., [70]. Referring to Info. Soc. Dir., Art. 5(3)(c) which permits use 'to the extent justified by the informatory purpose', Arnold J concluded that 'an important consideration in the assessment of fair dealing is whether the extent of the use is justified by the informatory purpose.'   [237] Ibid., [114].

[238] Ibid., [129].   [239] Ibid., [129].

[240] *Associated Newspapers v. News Group Newspapers* [1986] *RPC* 515.

[241] *Hyde Park v. Yelland* [2000] *EMLR* 363, 374, 379–80.

[242] *Ashdown v. Telegraph Group* [2002] *Ch* 149, 166–7, [44].

[243] *Associated Newspapers* [1986] *RPC* 515.   [244] *Ashdown* [2002] *Ch* 149, 173, [69].

[245] *HRH the Prince of Wales v. Associated Newspapers* [2007] 3 *WLR* 222, 264, 287.

[246] *Newspaper Licensing Agency* [2000] 4 *All ER* 239 (CA), 258 (Chadwick LJ); *England & Wales Cricket Board v Tixdaq* [2016] *EWHC* 575 (Ch), [85].

[247] *England & Wales Cricket Board v Tixdaq* [2016] *EWHC* 575 (Ch), [137], [145]–[147].

and whether the use of the work was necessary to efficiently inform the public about the events in question.[248] It also seems that the courts will be influenced by what is taken to be normal behaviour in the circumstances. Thus, in the *World Cup* case, it was fair for the defendant to reshow the goals and match highlights, typically 30 seconds of a 90-minute match, even though these were clearly the most important extracts. This was because the sequences were the normal and obvious means of illustrating the news report.[249]

Reporting current events is frequently carried out by commercial operators, most obviously newspaper publishers and news broadcasters. Despite occasional suggestions to the contrary,[250] the commercial nature of a reporting organization rarely is a relevant factor against a finding of 'fair dealing'.[251] As Jacob J has noted, when newspapers publish stories, 'they will always expect to make money. They are not philanthropists'.[252]

9.3 SUFFICIENT ACKNOWLEDGEMENT

In order to benefit from the exception, the dealing must be accompanied by 'sufficient acknowledgement' (which was discussed earlier).[253] However, no acknowledgement is required in connection with the reporting of current events *by means* of a sound recording, film, or broadcast, where this would be 'impossible for reasons of practicality or otherwise'.[254]

10 INCIDENTAL USES

The urban landscape is full of works that are protected by copyright (such as murals, buildings, sculptures, and advertisements).[255] This creates a potential problem for those who wish to represent that landscape. For example, if a movie is filmed in a public place, it is highly likely that the final product will include a number of different copyright works. This gives rise to a potential problem in that the recording of these works is on its face an infringement of copyright.

To minimize such problems, section 31(1) of the CDPA 1988 provides that copyright in a work is not infringed by its 'incidental inclusion' in an artistic work, sound recording, film, or broadcast.[256] This means that a defence is available where a copyright work, such as a painting, is incidentally included in the background of another work, such as a film. Section 31(2) extends the defence to include the exploitation of works that incidentally

---

[248] *Associated Newspapers Group* [1986] *RPC* 515, 519; *Hyde Park* [2000] *EMLR* 363, 393, [78]; *England & Wales Cricket Board v. Tixdaq* [2016] *EWHC* 575 (Ch), [84], [149]–[151].

[249] *BBC v. British Satellite Broadcasting* [1992] *Ch* 141.

[250] *Newspaper Licensing Agency* [2000] 4 *All ER* 239 (CA), 267 (Mance LJ).

[251] Cf. *Initial Services v. Putterill* [1968] 1 *QB* 396.

[252] *Hyde Park Residence v. Yelland* [1999] *RPC* 655, 663; reversed on different grounds: *Hyde Park v. Yelland* [2000] *EMLR* 363 (CA), 379, [40]; *England & Wales Cricket Board v. Tixdaq* [2016] *EWHC* 575 (Ch), [138] (if use is for the purpose of reporting current events, the fact that user a commercial venture does not prevent the use from being fair dealing).   [253] CDPA 1988, s. 30(2). See section 2.4, p. 234.

[254] CDPA 1988, s. 30(3) (as amended to give effect to Info. Soc. Dir., Art. 5(3)(c)).

[255] See also CDPA 1988, s. 62 (public display of artistic works).

[256] CDPA 1988, s. 31(1). There is no defence of incidental inclusion in a website, because Internet transmissions fall outside the scope of the meaning of 'broadcast' in CDPA 1988, s. 8. However, the inclusion in a website of a work that incidentally includes another work and thus benefits from the exception in CDPA 1988, s. 31(1), will not infringe: CDPA 1988, s. 31(2).

include other works. This ensures that the showing, as distinct to the making, of a film does not infringe.

The question of when a work is 'incidentally included' in another work was considered in *Football Association Premier League v. Panini UK*.[257] In that case, the FAPL, its members, and Topps brought an action alleging that Panini had infringed copyright in their club emblems and the Premiership heraldic lion emblem by distributing stickers depicting well-known footballers, for purchase and collection in a book. Topps had obtained an exclusive licence from the claimant to use the emblems in this way and Panini had lost out in the tendering process for the licence, but had nevertheless gone ahead and produced an 'unofficial' product. In Panini's product, most players were in club strip, with their club emblems and the Premiership heraldic lion emblem often visible. The defendant argued that the emblems were artistic works that were incidentally included in other artistic works (photographs). Smith J rejected the defence and this was affirmed by the Court of Appeal. Mummery LJ declined to define the term 'incidental', stating that the term is 'sufficiently clear to enable the courts to apply it to the ascertainable objective context of the particular infringing act in question'.[258] The question of whether the uses were incidental did not have to be determined at the time that the photograph was taken, but rather when the sticker was created. The question was why one work was included in another, and the court could take account of commercial as well as artistic or aesthetic reasons. Given that a player in authentic club strip was 'something which would be attractive to a collector', the Court concluded that the inclusion of the emblem was 'essential to the object for which the image . . . was created' rather than incidental.[259] In an earlier case, the High Court held that, by featuring the claimant's magazine, *Woman*, in a television advertising campaign run for the defendant's own magazine, the defendant had infringed the claimant's artistic copyright in the masthead, the layout, and the photographs on the magazine cover. The defendant's argument that the use was incidental was rejected:

> . . . since the impact of the advertisement would be lost entirely if the front cover of *Woman* was not used. The inclusion of the copy of *Woman* was an essential and important feature of the advertisement. The impact could not be more obvious.[260]

The defence will apply irrespective of whether a work is accidentally or deliberately included.[261] This is not the case, however, with musical works or lyrics (as well as a sound recording, or broadcast of a musical work or lyrics). The reason for this is that section 31(3) says that musical works or lyrics shall not be regarded as being incidentally included if they are deliberately included. This means that the defence is not available where a song is chosen for the background of a film, or a song from a radio is deliberately played in the background to a broadcast. Thus if the makers of television soap opera *Eastenders* decide to have a scene in which a character is listening to a radio playing a Rolling Stones song, this is not an incidental inclusion. However, if a musical work is accidentally included in a live broadcast, this is within the defence. Thus a broadcast of a football match that accidentally includes a sound recording played over the public address system falls squarely within the defence.

---

[257] [2004] *FSR* 1. [258] Ibid., [39] (Mummery LJ). [259] Ibid., [27] (Chadwick LJ).

[260] *IPC Magazines v. MGN* [1998] *FSR* 431, 441. This was, evidently, a case of comparative advertising: the argument that it should therefore be permitted under the MCAD was rejected at 447. But cf. *O2 Holdings v. Hutchison 3G* [2007] *RPC* (16) 407 [45]–[47], [55] (indicating that this question will have to be answered one day by the Court of Justice). See Chapter 41, section 6, pp. 1142–5.

[261] *Football Association Premier League v. Panini UK* [2004] *FSR* (1) 1, [24].

11 DISCLOSURE IN THE PUBLIC INTEREST

Despite the lack of any statutory provision on point,[262] a defendant may resist an action for copyright infringement—probably, though, only in very rare instances—on the grounds that the use is justified 'in the public interest'. Although such a defence was recognized by the High Court in the 1970s and the Court of Appeal in the 1980s, the existence and scope of this defence has been heavily debated.[263] There are three key Court of Appeal decisions: *Lion Laboratories v. Evans*;[264] *Hyde Park Residence v. Yelland*;[265] and *Ashdown v. Telegraph Group*.[266]

In *Lion Laboratories v. Evans*, the manufacturers of a breathalyser sought to prevent the defendant newspaper from publishing extracts of a confidential internal memorandum that cast doubt on the accuracy of the device. The defendant claimed that the public had an interest in knowing that the breathalyser might be faulty. All three members of the Court of Appeal accepted that the public interest defence was available in an action for infringement of copyright. According to the Court of Appeal, if the alleged fault with the breathalyser were not investigated, a significant number of motorists could have been wrongly convicted of driving with excess alcohol. On the basis that there was a seriously arguable case that the disclosure was justified in the public interest, the Court refused to grant interim relief.

It will be recalled that *Hyde Park Residence v. Yelland* concerned an application for summary judgment against *The Sun* newspaper for publishing stills of Dodi Fayed and Diana, Princess of Wales, taken from security film, the copyright in which was owned by the claimant. The defendant argued that the stills revealed the times when Fayed and the Princess were present at Villa Windsor, and therefore exposed the falsehood of statements made by Mohammed Al Fayed; as such, the publication was in the public interest. The Court of Appeal found that there was no arguable defence. The Court did not consider that it was in the public interest to publish the stills to prove that Fayed's statements were false: the information could easily have been made available by *The Sun* without infringing the claimant's copyright. While the Court could have argued that the public interest defence did not succeed on the facts, the majority (Aldous LJ, with whom Stuart-Smith LJ agreed) said that there is no general public interest defence to an action for infringement of copyright in the United Kingdom (although this was not how *Ashdown*, a later case at which we look next, interpreted him). Aldous LJ gave three reasons: (i) on the basis that the statutory regime was exhaustive, he observed that no such defence is recognized in the code; (ii) he said that the defence of disclosure of information in the public interest was inappropriate, because copyright restricts reproduction of the form of a work, not the information that it contains; and (iii) he argued that the defence was incompatible with the Berne Convention.[267] In addition, Aldous LJ held that the reasoning in *Lion Laboratories* lacked any substantial basis in precedent.[268] In contrast, Mance

---

[262] The validity of the common law defence recognized in case law under the 1956 Act seemed to have been accepted by CDPA 1988, s. 171(3).

[263] *Lion Laboratories v. Evans* [1985] QB 526, 536 (Stephenson LJ), 550 (Griffiths LJ).

[264] [1985] QB 526.   [265] [2000] EMLR 363.   [266] [2002] Ch 149.

[267] Cf. Berne, Art. 17. See Ricketson and Ginsburg, 842 *ff*, [13.88].

[268] Although Aldous LJ denied the existence of a public interest defence, he recognized that the courts do retain a power under their 'inherent jurisdiction' to refuse to enforce copyright where it offends against the 'policy of the law'. For Aldous LJ, the courts would refuse to enforce copyright on the basis that it would be against the 'policy of the law' where the work is scandalous, immoral, or contrary to family life, where the work itself is injurious to public life, public health, and safety, or the administration of justice, or where a work incites or encourages others to act in a way that is injurious to public life, public health, and safety, or the administration of justice: *Hyde Park Residence v. Yelland* [2000] EMLR 363, 389.

LJ accepted that Parliament had intended, via section 171(3), that the courts should retain some discretion to refuse to enforce copyright on public interest grounds.

In *Ashdown v Telegraph*, a differently constituted Court of Appeal[269] rejected the approach of the majority in *Hyde Park*, preferring that of Mance LJ and referring with approval to *Lion Laboratories*. The *Ashdown* case concerned the publication in the *Sunday Telegraph* of sections of a secret memorandum written by Paddy Ashdown, leader of the Liberal Party, about a meeting that had taken place with Tony Blair concerning a possible pact between the Liberal Party and the Labour Party. Ashdown sought summary judgment and the newspaper sought to justify its infringement on the basis of the public interest defence (the criticism defence having failed because there was no criticism of a work and the current events reporting defence had failed because the use was not fair). Although the Court of Appeal rejected the *Sunday Telegraph*'s arguments on the facts, it reviewed the law relating to the 'public interest defence' in the light of the Human Rights Act 1998. While the Court explained that copyright was not normally in conflict with freedom of expression, because copyright does not prevent the publication of information,[270] there could be such a conflict where expression required reproduction of specific text or images.[271] In such cases, if fair dealing and refusal of discretionary relief would not protect the public interest, a defendant could invoke the public interest defence, as developed by the common law and acknowledged by section 171(3) of the CDPA 1988.[272]

In the absence of a decision of the House of Lords on this issue, the view favoured by the majority of the Court of Appeal over the three cases thus seems to be that a 'public interest' defence might justify an act otherwise infringing copyright—but in what circumstances? The Court of Appeal in *Lion Laboratories* failed to draw any distinction between the application of the public interest defence to a case of breach of confidence and one based upon copyright. The Court was clear that the defence was not confined to cases of iniquity, but covered situations in which there was 'just cause or excuse' for breaking confidence.[273] In *Hyde Park*, Mance LJ had declined to define the exact circumstances in which the defence would be available, but said that this discretion is much more limited than the defence recognized in breach of confidence cases. According to Mance LJ, the countervailing public interest was of more limited scope in the case of copyright, given that it is a property right and regulated by statute.[274] The Court of Appeal in *Ashdown* said that it agreed with Mance LJ that the circumstances in which the public interest may override copyright are not capable of precise categorization or definition, but indicated that the defence would succeed only in 'very rare' circumstances.[275] The more recent decisions therefore offer little assistance as to when the 'public interest defence' would apply, except to indicate that the circumstances are more limited than in cases of breach of confidence.[276]

---

[269] Lord Phillips MR, Keene LJ, and Robert Walker LJ.   [270] Ibid., 163, [31].

[271] Ibid., 166, [39].   [272] Ibid., 164, [34], 170–1, [58]–[59].

[273] *Lion Laboratories v. Evans* [1985] *QB* 526, 538 (Stephenson LJ), 548 (O'Connor LJ), 550 (Griffiths LJ).

[274] *Hyde Park v. Yelland* [2000] *EMLR* 363, 392. See R. Burrell, 'Defending the Public Interest' [2000] *EIPR* 394.

[275] *Ashdown v. Telegraph Group* [2002] *Ch* 149, 170, [59]. See P. Johnson, 'The Public Interest: Is It Still a Defence to Copyright Infringement?' [2005] *Ent LR* 1.

[276] The closest that a court has come to accepting the defence was in *In the Petition by the BBC in the Case of HM Advocate v. Hainey* [2012] *HCJDV* 10, [2012] *SLT* 476 (Lord Woolman) (allowing publication of photographs of child taken by mother who had been convicted of his murder), although even there the judge had accepted a defence of reporting judicial proceedings.

The Treaty on the Functioning of the European Union (TFEU) renders the European Charter of Rights and Fundamental Freedoms, and thus freedom of expression, part of the European legal order (and thus capable of direct application). According to Jonathan Griffiths, this means that the public interest defence is no longer needed to ensure that copyright does not interfere unduly with freedom of expression.[277] However, he has suggested a different role for section 171 of the CDPA 1988: to regulate the relationship between copyright and other national or EU norms. Thus where copyright and other intellectual property rights overlap, exceptions to those other rights may take precedence over, or 'pre-empt', copyright: for example, the repair exception to design rights, or the comparative advertising defence to use of trade marks, might be treated as equally applicable to copyright (even though no such exceptions are provided for in relevant national or EU regimes). Some basis for this approach might be found in Article 13 of the Database Directive and Article 9 of the Information Society Directive. Griffiths identifies a body of cases in which he claims copyright is 'disapplied' because the action is, in essence, one for breach of confidence, and in which the disclosure is not to be regarded as an actionable breach of confidence because the public interest in disclosure outweighs that of protecting confidentiality. From this basis, he suggests further situations in which the public interest defence might, in future, play a role in permitting the pre-emption of copyright law, for example where disclosure is required under the Freedom of Information Act 2000, but might involve the making and distribution of copies.

12 ACCESS TO WORKS BY/FOR PEOPLE WITH DISABILITIES

People with disabilities have been poorly served by copyright law. While the markets provided by such groups are rarely sufficient to attract private, market-based, suppliers, copyright law significantly impedes the capacity of others to provide access to such works that are commercially available. The CDPA 1988, as enacted, contained only one exception designed to help people with disabilities to gain access to copyright protected material—a provision relating to subtitling or modifying broadcasts.[278] Further exceptions were added in 2002 for the benefit of the visually impaired.[279] The Information Society Directive allows for the adoption of exceptions to the three harmonized rights for 'uses, for the benefit of people with a disability, which are directly related to the disability and of a non-commercial nature, to the extent required by the specific disability'.[280] The Hargreaves reforms seek to 'broaden and simplify the disability exceptions', with a view to giving 'more people equal access to cultural materials'.[281] However, as in the case of educational exceptions, it has been thought desirable to leave space for profit-making efforts to supply these markets, so the exceptions are subject to qualifications.

---

[277] J. Griffiths, 'Pre-empting Conflict' [2014] 34 *Legal Studies* 76, 95–6.

[278] CDPA 1988, s. 74 (as enacted). This has been repealed by SI 2014/0000. The general failure of copyright regimes to provide mechanisms that facilitate access to work by people with disabilities has now started to receive international attention, most importantly with the signing in 2013 of the Marrakesh Treaty.

[279] Copyright (Visually Impaired Persons) Act 2002.

[280] Info. Soc. Dir., Art. 5(3)(b). This was amended by Directive (EU) 2017/1564, by adding 'without prejudice' to that Directive.   [281] UK IPO, *Modernising Copyright* (2012), 43.

Section 31A, as amended, seeks to allow the making of modified versions of publicly available works that enable persons with a physical or mental impairment ('disabled persons') to have improved level of access to the work.[282] The provision applies to all disabilities that prevent a person from enjoying a copyright work to the same degree as a person who does not have the impairment,[283] and so would justify the making of Braille or sound versions of works for those with some impairment that makes reading print problematic ('the print-disabled'), or the making of subtitled versions of audiovisual works for those with impaired hearing. It contains one provision that allows for 'personal use' by a disabled person, and another that allows third parties to make and supply copies to such disabled persons.

12.1 PERSONAL USE BY PERSONS WITH DISABILITIES

Section 31A(1) deals with the creation of versions of works (of all types) for personal use. This is permitted where a person is disabled and that disability impairs access to a work that is lawfully in the possession of the disabled person (or of which they have lawful use).[284] Any creation of a copy of such a work that improves access is permitted, as long as four conditions are met: (i) the copy is for personal use;[285] (ii) it is derived from a copy of which the disabled person has lawful possession or use;[286] (iii) that a copy that would give the same level of access is not commercially available on reasonable terms with the authority of the copyright holder;[287] and (iv) where a person charges for making the copy, that charge does not exceed the cost of so doing.[288]

12.2 MAKING ACCESSIBLE COPIES FOR PEOPLE WITH DISABILITIES

In addition, an educational establishment, or a body not conducted for profit,[289] is permitted to make and supply, other than for profit, accessible copies of commercially published works for the use of disabled persons.[290] The exemption does not apply if copies making the works accessible are already commercially available.[291] Where the copy is made by an educational establishment, its use must be for educational purposes.[292] The making and supply of accessible copies is subject to a number of conditions: the body must have 'lawful possession' of a copy of the work;[293] the 'accessible copies' must state that they were made under section 31B, and must acknowledge the authorship and title of the work from which they were made;[294] the cost charged must not exceed the cost of making an supplying the accessible copy;[295] the records of to whom such copies have been

---

[282] CDPA 1988, s.31.

[283] CDPA 1988, s. 31F(2). This avoids complex definitions, e.g. of visual impairment. Cf. CDPA 1988, s. 31F(9) (as introduced in 2002, but now repealed).   [284] CDPA 1988, s. 31A(1)(a).

[285] CDPA 1988, s. 31A(2)(b).   [286] CDPA 1988, s. 31A(2).   [287] CDPA 1988, s. 31A(2)(c).

[288] CDPA 1988, s. 31A(3). The original CDPA 1988, s. 31A(4) (as added by the Copyright (Visually Impaired Persons) Act 2002), which applied to visual disability, contained two further requirements: (i) that the copy states that it was made under s. 31A; and (ii) that there is acknowledgement of author and title.

[289] CDPA 1988, s. 31F(6) (defining 'authorized body'). 'Educational establishment' is defined in CDPA 1988, s. 174 and The Copyright (Educational Establishments) Order 2005, SI 2005/223.

[290] CDPA 1988, s. 31B (added by SI 2014/1384).   [291] CDPA 1988, s. 31B(2), (4) (broadcasts).

[292] CDPA 1988, s. 31B(6).   [293] CDPA 1988, s. 31B(1), (3) (broadcasts).

[294] CDPA 1988, s. 31B(7).   [295] CDPA 1988, s. 31B(10).

supplied must be kept and made available to rights holders;[296] and the body making and supplying copies is under an obligation to contact a representative of the copyright owner or the copyright holder, notifying them.[297]

12.3 REFORM

Implementing the Marrakesh Treaty,[298] Directive (EU) 2017/1564 of 13 September 2017, adds a further EU dimension to the law.[299] From 11 October 2018, member states must allow certain acts in relation to copyright protected works for the benefit of persons who are blind, or in various other respects 'print disabled'.[300] As with the existing UK law, a distinction is made between acts by or on behalf of a 'beneficiary person' and activities of 'authorized entities' that make, communicate, or distribute versions that give access to works to such persons.[301] In short, member states are required to permit the making of 'accessible format copies' by or on behalf of a 'beneficiary person' or the making of such a copy by an 'authorized entity' and its communication, distribution, making available, or lending to a beneficiary person.[302] An authorized entity in one member state may carry out a relevant act for a beneficiary or an authorized entity in another member State. A parallel instrument, in the form of a regulation,[303] permits the export of accessible format copies from the European Union to authorized entities or beneficiaries in another Marrakesh signatory;[304] and importation into the European Union of such copies from authorized entities in another Marrakesh signatory.[305]

Apart from the difference in coverage (the UK regime at present covering all disabilities, the EU one just visual and print disability),[306] there tend to be more conditions and qualifications to the UK regime compared with the EU one. For example, in the United Kingdom, at present, the purpose of the use of the 'accessible copy' is limited to personal or educational use,[307] whereas under the EU regime the use must merely be for the 'exclusive use' of the beneficiary.[308] Commercial end uses, for example, might be within the exemption. Similarly, in the United Kingdom, the availability of the defence is predicated on the idea that there is no commercially available equivalent source.[309] No such condition applies under EU law.[310] On the other hand, the EU exception is explicitly to be

---

[296] CDPA 1988, s. 31BB.   [297] CDPA 1988, s. 31BB(3).

[298] See Chapter 2, section 6.6, pp. 49–50.

[299] Directive (EU) 2017/1564, *OJ L* 242/6 (20 September 2017).

[300] Art. 2(2) (identifying four categories: people who are blind; people with visual impairment that render them unable to read; people with perceptual or reading disability; and people who due to other physical disability are unable to hold or manipulate books) (largely replicating Marrakesh Treaty, Art. 3).

[301] 'Authorized entities' are defined in Marrakesh Treaty, Art. 2(4); 'accessible format copies' are defined in Marrakesh Treaty, Art. 2(3)

[302] Marrakesh Treaty, Art. 3(1). The Article requires member states to create exceptions to various copyright and related rights recognized under EU law (see also Recital 6) and does not affect freedom to provide exceptions to rights that are not harmonized (Recital 20). One might have thought the issue mostly related to the unharmonized adaptation right. Note, however, that the publication right, required under Directive 2006/116/EC, Art. 4, is not mentioned explicitly in Marrakesh Treaty, Art. 3(1), though presumably it is implicitly covered because the protection to be granted is to be 'equivalent to the economic rights of the author'.

[303] Regulation (EU) 2017/1563, *OJ L* 242/1 (20 September 2017) (in force from 12 October 2018).

[304] Regulation (EU) 2017/1563, Art. 3.   [305] Regulation (EU) 2017/1563, Art. 4.

[306] Regulation (EU) 2017/1563, Art. 2(2).   [307] CDPA 1988, s. 31A(2)(b), s. 31B(1) (personal use).

[308] Directive (EU) 2017/1564, Art. 3(1).   [309] CDPA 1988, s. 31A(2)(c), s. 31B(2), s. 31B(6).

[310] Directive (EU) 2017/1564, Art. 3(1), Recital 14 (prohibiting additional conditions 'such as the prior verification of the commercial availability of works in accessible format').

applied only in accordance with the three-step test,[311] and an accessible format copy must respect 'the integrity of the work or other subject matter'.[312] Note also that the definition of authorized entities may be slightly narrower under EU law.[313]

Because of the differences, in implementing the Directive, the United Kingdom will be forced to decide whether to operate a regime that differentiates between visual impairment and other disabilities; or to reform the disability regime in totality.[314] Whether that is feasible depends in part on the existing conditions in Article 5(3)(b) of the Information Society Directive.[315]

13 EDUCATIONAL USES

Education constitutes a particularly complex environment for copyright regulation.[316] On the one hand, it is an environment in which the transmission and use of information is at the very heart of what goes on. Access to relevant materials—in fact to as much material as possible for all concerned—is critical to the success of the process. For example, law students need to be able to read, examine, and appraise all relevant cases, legislation, statutory instruments, and commentaries. On the other hand, educational activities are served by a host of tailored services, such as those provided by educational publishers (offering textbooks, journals, and so forth) and those who broadcast educational programmes. These providers need to be able to stay in business and, without them, the information environment would likely be poorer.[317] One challenge is to establish a set of arrangements that allows for as much access as possible without jeopardizing the involvement of private interests in providing information services; another is to do so in a way that allows flexibility for individual instructors and is responsive to new technological opportunities. Rights holders tend to favour 'licensing' solutions, while those representing

---

[311] Directive (EU) 2017/1564, Art 3(3). The language is the same as Info. Soc. Dir., Art. 5(5).

[312] Directive (EU) 2017/1564, Art 3(2). But CDPA 1988, s. 31F(5) defines accessible copy in a manner that precludes 'must not include any changes to the work which are not necessary to overcome the problems suffered by the disabled persons for whom the accessible copy is intended.' Any difference is therefore to be found in the possibility that the 'integrity' of a work might be affected by something that might not be categorized as a 'change to the work': cf. Chapter 10, section 4.2, pp. 296–8 (discussion of 'treatment' in the context of UK moral rights).

[313] However, the definition of 'authorized entities' seems narrower under EU law than the existing definition of 'authorized body' under UK law: in particular, the UK law might cover educational establishments that are 'for profit'; and not-for-profit bodies that have characteristics other than those identified in Art. 2(4). See CDPA 1988, s. 31F(6) (an educational establishment or body that is not conducted for profit).

[314] Directive (EU) 2017/1564, Art. 3(1), Recital 20. It might be asked how far the EU Charter, Art. 20 ('Everyone is equal before the law') demands parallel treatment.

[315] Opinion 3/15, EU:C:2017:114, [111], [123]–[127] (ECJ, Grand Chamber) (noting that Info. Soc. Dir., Art. 5(3)(b) offers a highly constrained freedom to member states to derogate from the harmonized rights of reproduction, communication, and distribution, and Marrakesh implementation would affect this).

[316] The international norms governing educational defences are obscure in meaning. In particular, Berne, Art. 10(2), which explicitly permits use 'of illustration for . . . teaching' can be understood in different ways. For a valuable study, see R. Xalabarder, *Study on Copyright Limitations and Exceptions for Educational Activities in North America, Europe, Caucasus, Central Asia and Israel* (2009) SCCR/19/8.

[317] In some areas of education, particularly tertiary education, the role of private providers is being challenged. In part in response to increased pressure on library budgets, there has been a move to incentivize, or even compel, academics to publish materials by way of 'open access'. One way in which to do this is to pay publishers to publish work, but to require that they give access to all (immediately or after an embargo period).

educational interests argue for broad, flexible, exceptions. The UK government has stated that 'educational exceptions are intended both to complement and underpin educational licensing schemes'.[318] It rejects proposals for wide exceptions permitting mass copying as likely to cause unreasonable damage to rights holders and to undermine incentives, while at the same time attempting to offer flexibility to educators to use material in ways that 'modern technology allows'.[319]

Individual student activities are facilitated by the fair dealing for research and private study defences and the defences for library copying. Our concern here is with the activities of individual teachers and the institutions. These are governed by a complex web of provisions (although they are somewhat simpler after the Hargreaves reforms of 2014 than they were before):

(i) a general provision permitting fair dealing for purposes of illustration for instruction (section 32);

(ii) a narrow, virtually pointless, provision relating to educational anthologies (section 33);

(iii) a provision allowing performances at educational establishments (section 34);

(iv) an exception allowing for the recording and showing of educational broadcasts, but which gives way to various licensing schemes (section 35);

(v) an exception allowing for reprographic copying, but which underpins various licensing arrangements (section 36); and

(vi) an exception allowing for lending of copies by an educational establishment (section 36A).

Sections 34–36A apply only in relation to 'educational establishments' (which includes universities and colleges of further education).[320]

13.1 FAIR DEALING FOR INSTRUCTION AND EXAMINATION

Section 32 gives a 'fair dealing' exemption to those involved in 'instruction' and 'examination'.[321] The defence is applicable to all types of work and to all possible restricted acts.[322] The defence applies to dealings by the person giving instruction (the teacher or lecturer) and the person receiving instruction (the pupil or lecturer). Contracts that purport to exclude acts within the scope of the exception are unenforceable.

A key limitation is that the dealing must be 'for the sole purpose of illustration for instruction'.[323] Both the term 'instruction' and 'illustration' are awkward. 'Instruction'

---

[318] UK IPO, *Modernising Copyright* (2012), 40. See further R. Hooper, *Rights and Wrongs* (2012), 25–8, [65]–[71] (identifying 12 different organizations requiring licences in the schools sector and ten in further education colleges).   [319] UK IPO, *Modernising Copyright* (2012), 41.

[320] As specified by the Secretary of State under powers under CDPA 1988, s. 174(1)(b), (3). 'School' is defined by reference to the Education Act 1996, the Education (Scotland Act) 1962, and the Education and Libraries (Northern Ireland) Order 1986 (SI 1986/59: NI 3). Universities, theological colleges, and various institutions providing further education are 'educational establishment(s)': Copyright (Educational Establishments) Order 2005 (SI 2005/223). These provisions have been extended to apply to teachers employed by a local authority to give instruction to pupils unable to attend an educational establishment: Copyright (Application of Provisions relating to Educational Establishments to Teachers) (No. 2) Order 1989 (SI 1989/1067).   [321] CDPA 1988, s. 32 (as amended by SI 2014/1372).

[322] In this respect, it is much more significant that the provision in force prior to June 2014 that applied only to copying by non-reprographic processes.

[323] Info. Soc. Dir., Art. 5(3)(a) (illustration for teaching).

suggests a rather outdated understanding of learning, in which the student is a passive recipient of information or guidance. In turn, this might indicate that defence is limited to use by the teacher of copyright-protected material to 'illustrate a point', such as use of the materials in handouts and slides.[324] We suggest that this would be too narrow a view. First, the statutory provisions themselves acknowledge that the exemption includes the acts of the person 'receiving instruction' and preparing to receive instruction, as well as pupils' answers to exam questions. Thus some broader idea of 'illustration for instruction' seems intended. Second, the language in fact reflects the terms of the Information Society Directive and, in turn, Article 10(2) of the Berne Convention. In the latter, the permitted exception is 'by way of illustration *in publications, broadcasts or sound or visual recordings* for teaching'.[325] Immediately, it can be seen that the scope is much broader than offering examples 'in class'. Moreover, the legislative history of Article 10(2) of Berne supports a broad interpretation, so that the terms should be read to mean 'any reasonable use for the purpose of education or teaching'.[326]

The defence permits any 'fair dealing' by the instructor in preparing to teach or carrying out the act.[327] Thus making copies of materials with a view to deciding what to teach, and how to teach it, are covered. The defence also encompasses any fair dealing by the person receiving instruction,[328] for example, taking down notes, recording a lecture, singing a song, or playing a piece of music. The exception also permits fair dealing in preparation to receive instruction, for example making a copy of a document to take to class.[329] The 'fair dealing' exemption also covers examinations and indicates that there is no infringement in either setting or answering exam questions.[330]

The key qualification for the defence is 'fairness', a concept that is not elaborated.[331] The criteria explained already will likely be relevant.[332] The most important issue in assessing fairness will be whether the relevant act was proportionate to the use for instruction.[333] In addition, the exception will not apply unless the dealing is for a non-commercial purpose[334] and accompanied by a sufficient acknowledgement (where this is possible).[335] No acknowledgement is required where this would be impossible for reasons of practicality or otherwise.[336]

---

[324] See HM Government, *Technical Review of the Draft Legislation on Copyright Exceptions: Government Response* (2014) 7, which refers to the 'narrow focus' of the exception, and suggests that if private music tutors were to reproduce sheet music and give it to their students to play, this would fall outside the exception 'as it is . . . unlikely to be considered either illustrative or fair dealing'.

[325] Emphasis added.

[326] See R. Xalabarder, *Study on Copyright Limitations and Exceptions for Educational Activities in North America, Europe, Caucasus, Central Asia and Israel* (2009) SCCR/19/8, 15 (evidence from the Stockholm Conference suggests that this was not intended to limit the scope of the exception); cf. Ricketson and Ginsburg, 794, [13.45].   [327] CDPA 1988, s. 32(1)(b).

[328] CDPA 1988, s. 32(1)(b).

[329] It is not obvious that this would be fair dealing for the purpose of 'private' study within CDPA 1988, s. 29, although it might be so construed.   [330] CDPA 1988, s. 32(2).

[331] In this respect, the defence could conceivably be narrower than the old defence in s. 32(1) (as enacted). Although that applied only to non-reprographic copying, there appeared to be no limit on the quantity of copying.   [332] See section 2.1, pp. 229–32.

[333] 'Fairness' might justify use of reasonable portions of works and sometimes (e.g. with artistic works and photographs) whole works; cf. UK IPO, *Modernising Copyright* (2012), 40 ('*de minimis*'); *Technical Review*, 7 ('minor reasonable uses').

[334] Cf. *Technical Review*, 7 (a private music tutor would be using material for a commercial purpose). However, the status of the organization is not supposed to be determinative. See section 2.2, pp. 232–3.

[335] CDPA 1988, s. 32(1)(a), (c). See section 2.4, p. 234.

[336] CDPA 1988, s. 32(1)(c) (as amended by SI 2014/1372).

13.2 COPYING SHORT PASSAGES IN ANTHOLOGIES AND COLLECTIONS

Section 33 provides that copyright is not infringed where a 'short passage' from a published literary or dramatic work is included in a collection that is intended for use in an educational establishment.[337] This is subject to the proviso that (i) the collection consists mainly of material in which no copyright subsists, (ii) the inclusion is acknowledged, and (iii) the inclusion does not involve more than two excerpts from copyright works of the same author in collections published by the same publisher over any period of five years. These restrictions greatly restrict the utility of the defence.[338] The defence could be used, for example, to compile a collection of cases, many of which were out of copyright.

13.3 PERFORMING, PLAYING, OR SHOWING WORKS

A special defence exists to protect the performing, playing, or showing of literary, dramatic, or musical works before an audience consisting of teachers and pupils at an educational establishment.[339] Section 34(1) operates by deeming certain performances not to be public performances and hence not to be infringements of the performing right. To fall within the defence, the performance must be before an audience consisting of teachers and pupils at an educational establishment. The performance must be carried out either by a teacher or a pupil, or by any other person for the purposes of instruction. This will exempt performances, whether by students or outsiders, before students in a drama class. It does not cover pupil performances to audiences of parents.[340]

A similar defence exists with regard to the showing of films and broadcasts and the playing of sound recordings before an audience of teachers and pupils for the purposes of instruction.[341] While this would cover the showing of a documentary about the first moon landing to a primary school class, it presumably would not cover school film societies, since they are for pleasure and not instruction. Both provisions appear to permit the use of material in (computer or projector) slide shows (although the making of the slides—involving reproduction—as well as the distribution of copies or the making available online would not fall within the exception).

13.4 RECORDING OF BROADCASTS

Section 35 provides that, in the absence of a licensing scheme,[342] educational establishments may make a recording of a broadcast, or a copy of such a recording, for the educational purposes of that establishment, provided that there is sufficient acknowledgement of the broadcast and that the educational purposes are non-commercial.[343] Section

---

[337] CDPA 1988, s. 33.

[338] The work from which the passage is taken must itself not be intended for use in an educational establishment and no more than two excerpts from copyright works by the same author may be published in collections by the same publisher over any period of five years. Moreover, the collection in question must be described as being for use in educational establishments, must consist mainly of material in which no copyright subsists, and there must be a sufficient acknowledgement. [339] CDPA 1988, s. 34(1).

[340] CDPA 1988, s. 34(3).

[341] CDPA 1988, s. 34(2). However, it may now be arguable that these activities also fall within CDPA 1988, s. 20, and that because the s. 34 exception is an exception only to the s. 19 right (it says that the act is 'not a playing or showing of the work in public'), the immunity no longer survives. If so, the fate of the Advocate-General's opinion in *Renckhoff*, Case C-161/17, EU:C:2018:279, [AG117] (to the effect that posting an image on a school website where access is restricted to teachers and pupils is not communication 'to the public') may become important.

[342] CDPA 1988, s. 35(4) (as amended). [343] CDPA 1988, s. 35(1).

35(1A) permits the playing or showing of the recording not merely on the premises, but also off-site by means of a secure electronic network that is only accessible to staff or pupils of the establishment.[344] Because a number of broadcasters offer licences through the Educational Recording Agency (ERA), the practical importance of the section often concerns incidental material, such as advertisements, which do not fall within the licensing arrangements.[345] The extension of the exception in 2014 to secure networks offers some assurances as regards those incidental materials: the ERA had offered licences of this type from as early as 2007.[346]

13.5 MAKING AND SUPPLY OF COPIES

Section 36, much expanded by the 2014 amendments,[347] provides that, to the extent that licences are unavailable, educational establishments may copy 5 per cent of a work (other than an artistic work or broadcast) in any given year for the purposes of instruction without infringing copyright.[348] The copies may be distributed either as physical copies or electronically, as long as access is provided through a secure digital network that is accessible only to members of staff or pupils.[349] The exception operates only where the copies are accompanied by sufficient acknowledgement (unless this would be impossible), and the instruction is for a non-commercial purpose.[350] Again, the operation of the section 36 defence is limited as a result of the fact that educational establishments have entered into a number of relevant licensing schemes,[351] although it is significant that the terms of any such licence are ineffective insofar as they purport to restrict copying to less than that permitted under the section.[352]

13.6 LENDING OF COPIES

Copyright in a work is not infringed by the lending of copies of the work by an educational establishment.[353]

---

[344] CDPA 1988, s. 35(3), introduced by SI 2014/1372. This freedom to give access to broadcasts via secure networks probably has to be justified within Art. 5(3) of the Info. Soc. Dir., most obviously Art. 5(3)(a) ('illustration for teaching'). Art. 5(3)(n) is limited to 'dedicated terminals on the premises' of the establishment, and seems unlikely to cover 'virtual' access: *Technische Universität Darmstadt v. Eugen Ulmer KG*, Case C-117/13, EU:C:2014:1795, [AG48] (AG Jääskinen).

[345] The Educational Recording Agency licences cover broadcasts on the BBC, ITV, Channel 4, Five Television, s4C, and the Open University. For details on the ERA, see its website.

[346] The so-called 'ERA Plus agreement'.

[347] Section 36, as enacted, related only to 'reprographic copying' and only to extracts from 'published literary, dramatic and musical works'.   [348] CDPA 1988, s. 36.

[349] CDPA 1988, s. 36(3). It is not entirely clear whether this exception falls within those permitted by the Info. Soc. Dir.: Art. 5(2)(c) permits only 'reproduction' by educational establishments, and Art. 5(4) 'distribution', but electronic distribution probably implicates the right of communication to the public. Art. 5(3)(a) allows exception to the latter right for the purpose of 'illustration for teaching', the meaning of which phrase seems very obscure.   [350] CDPA 1988, s. 36(1).

[351] CDPA 1988, s. 36(6). The key administrator here is the Copyright Licensing Agency, which operates as agent for the Authors Licensing and Collecting Society, the Publishers Licensing Society, and the Design and Artistic Copyright Society. Examples of its licences for education can be seen on its website.

[352] Compare the CLA–HE Licence (2013–16), [3.4] (referring to a maximum of 5 per cent or, in the case of published law reports, a single case).

[353] CDPA 1988, s. 36A; Rel. Rights Dir., Art. 5(3).

13.7 PROPOSED EU REFORM

Article 4 of the Proposed Directive on Copyright in the Digital Single Market, if adopted, would introduce a mandatory exception allowing the digital use of works or other subject matter for the sole purpose of illustration for teaching and to the extent justified by the non-commercial purpose.[354] The use must occur on the premises of the educational establishment,[355] or through a secure electronic network.[356] Permitted uses extend beyond classroom (real or virtual) uses by a teacher,[357] and include 'digital uses of works and other subject-matter such as the use of parts or extracts of works to support, enrich or complement the teaching, including the related learning activities.'[358] In contrast with the existing optional exception in Article 5(3)(a) of the Information Society Directive, member states are obliged to provide compensation.[359] Perhaps because of this (though, oddly, given the provision's mandatory nature),[360] member states may choose to disapply the exception if and to the extent that 'adequate licences authorising the acts . . . are easily available in the market'.[361] Interestingly, the proposed Article 'deems' any use to occur where the educational establishment is established.[362]

14 LIBRARIES, ARCHIVES, AND MUSEUMS

Public libraries have long had a vital role, both as repositories of cultural output and as providers of public access to works. The former role has been achieved historically through legal deposit requirements, in particular requirements to deposit books with specified libraries.[363] For much of modern history, the ability of libraries to provide access has been secured by the principle of exhaustion, which meant that reading a book or magazine, or lending a work, did not implicate copyright. Objections that authors lost out as a result of such lending were met, in 1979, with the provision of a 'public lending right' (PLR) scheme paid for by taxpayers. Moreover, as photocopying technology became available, it became evident that certain freedoms should also be granted to libraries, for example to facilitate users creating copies for research purposes.

---

[354] COM(2016) 593 final, Art. 4.

[355] Ibid., Recital 15 indicates that this covers 'all educational establishments in primary, secondary, vocational, and higher education to the extent they pursue their educational activity for a non-commercial purpose.'   [356] Ibid., Recital 16 ('notably by authentication procedures').

[357] Ibid., Explanatory Memorandum ('teachers and students will be able to take full advantage of digital technologies at all levels of education'). The proposal does not explain why a teacher is not permitted to collect material for use in teaching from places other than educational establishments.

[358] Ibid., Recital 16.   [359] Ibid., Art. 4(4).

[360] ECS, *General Opinion on the EU Copyright Reform Package* (2017) 4.

[361] COM(2016) 593 final, Art. 4, Recital 17.

[362] For other situations where specific deeming provisions are used to overcome problems deriving from the territorial nature of rights, see Chapter 6, section 6.5.2, pp. 174–5 (satellite broadcasting), Chapter 12, section 6, pp. 349–50 (portability).

[363] Deposit requirements were initially in the 1710 Statute of Anne and the beneficiary libraries are commonly known as 'deposit libraries'. But it became clear that while the deposit was not a condition for protection, failure to deposit would lead to statutory penalties. See I. Alexander, *Copyright and the Public Interest in the Nineteenth Century* (2010), ch. 3, 47–63. The modern regime is contained in the Legal Deposit Libraries Act 2003 (requiring deposit of print works with the British Library and, on request, five other libraries: University of Oxford; University of Cambridge; the National Library of Scotland; the National Library of Wales; and Trinity College, Dublin).

The CDPA 1988 provided librarians and archivists with a number of defences, to facilitate use by readers, to maintain stocks, and to allow for cooperation between libraries.[364] These immunities, however, became outdated as digital technologies began to present new ways for libraries to fulfil their mission, for example by supplying digital copies. These technologies also mean that many acts that previously did not seem to implicate copyright (such as on-site browsing in electronic form) now do so. Following the Hargreaves Review and reflecting the flexibility available under the Information Society and other directives,[365] the exceptions in the 1988 Act have been modified and extended (in particular to encompass a wider range of copyright works), while new freedoms are offered to other cultural institutions.[366]

14.1 LENDING OF WORKS

Historically, a key function of libraries has been to lend books to members of the public. As we saw in Chapter 6, as a consequence of EU harmonization, copyright owners were given the right to control public lending of their works.[367] In order to ensure continued public access to literature, Article 6 of the Related Rights Directive permits member states to create a derogation to the public lending right as long as compensation is paid to affected authors. Taking advantage of this, section 40A of the 1988 Act provides that copyright in a work of any description is not infringed by the lending of a *book* by a *public library* if the book is eligible to be within the PLR scheme.[368] In addition, section 40A(2) provides that copyright is not infringed by the lending of copies of the work by a library or archive (other than a public library) that is not conducted for profit.[369] In *VOB*, the Court of Justice has interpreted Article 6 of the Related Rights Directive in a manner that would allow it to be applied to at least some remote 'e-lending' of works, though limited in that case to the situation where the library lends the number of copies in its holding (the so-called 'one copy, one user' rather than 'one copy, multiple user' model).[370] As explained in Chapter 13, there are plans to extend the Public Lending Right Scheme in this way, and thus in turn to extend the operation of section 40A.[371]

14.2 ON-SITE REFERENCE

Although not explicitly foreshadowed in the Hargreaves Review, during the subsequent consultation process, it was decided to introduce a new exception permitting cultural institutions to make works available from dedicated terminals,[372] thus taking advantage

---

[364] CDPA 1988, ss 37–44 (as enacted).

[365] The Court has tended to interpret these exceptions purposively and flexibly: *Technische Universität Darmstadt v. Eugen Ulmer KG*, Case C-117/13, EU:C:2014:2196, [27] (recognizing that the core mission of publicly accessible libraries is the 'dissemination of knowledge'); *Vereniging Openbare Bibliotheken v. Stichting Leenrecht*, Case C-174/15, EU:C:2016:856, [55] and [60] (noting the public interest in 'cultural promotion'); EU:C:2016:459, [AG58].

[366] UK IPO, *Modernising Copyright* (2012), 32–5. Such exemptions are permitted by Info. Soc. Dir., Art. 5(2)(c).　　[367] CDPA 1988, s. 18A; see Chapter 6, section 4, pp. 155–6.

[368] Rel. Rights Dir., Art. 5; see Chapter 13, section 6, pp. 385–6.

[369] CDPA 1988, s. 40A(2), as amended by SI 2014/1372, Sch., para. 3.

[370] The copy must not have come from an unlawful source: *Vereniging Openbare Bibliotheken (VOB) v. Stichting Leenrecht*, Case C-174/15, EU:C:2016:856, [68], [71]–[72].

[371] *Vereniging Openbare Bibliotheken (VOB) v. Stichting Leenrecht*, Case C-174/15, EU:C:2016:856. For an intelligent commentary, see V. Breemen, 'E-Lending According to the ECJ: Focus on Functions and Similar Characteristics in *VOB v. Stichting Leenrecht*' [2017] *EIPR* 249. For the UK reforms, see Digital Economy Act 2017, s. 31 (amending CDPA 1988, s. 40A(1ZA)).　　[372] CDPA 1988, s. 40B (as added by SI 2014/1372).

of the freedom provided in Article 5(3)(n) of the Information Society Directive. This could allow libraries to give on-site access to ebooks or to offer users facilities to listen to sound recordings in a sound archive, or to browse digital images of artworks in an art museum or gallery.[373]

The new exception is narrow. First, it applies only with respect to the act of communicating or 'making available'.[374] However, the Court of Justice has held that there is an 'ancillary right' to digitize the work under Article 5(2)(c),[375] at least as long as the library does not digitize its entire collection. The Court noted that the German legislation at issue ensured this freedom would not conflict with the three-step test, noting that the number of copies available on dedicated terminals was limited to the number of copies the library held in analogue form, and such making available was subject to a duty to pay 'compensation'.[376]

Second, the work or a copy of it must have been 'lawfully acquired' by the institution.[377] Although this might at first sight suggest that the cultural institution must possess its own physical copy, there is no reason to regard the word 'copy' as so limited. Thus if one museum sends another museum a digital copy of a work, so that the latter copy is lawfully acquired, there seems nothing to preclude the recipient from making the work available. Third, the making available must be only to 'individual members of the public'.[378] Fourth, the work must be made available for 'research or private study'.[379] This condition would appear to allow for works to be made available in a research library, but preclude the use of the work on terminals at a public exhibition (where members of the public might be present for purposes of recreation or entertainment). Fifth, access to the work must be provided through 'dedicated terminals on [the institution's] premises'.[380] Finally, section 40B provides that the act must comply with any purchase or licensing terms to which it is subject.[381] This reflects the limitation in Article 5(3)(n) of the Information Society Directive that the works or subject matter in issue are 'not subject to purchase or licensing terms'. In *Technische Universität Darmstadt*, the Court construed this condition narrowly, taking the view that it operated only where an actual contract had been entered into between a library and the relevant right holder establishing the circumstances in which the library might use the specific work.[382]

---

[373] CDPA 1988, s. 43A(3) (definitions).

[374] CDPA 1988, s. 40B(1). It is difficult to see how the 'making available' right is implicated if a person can access the work only from a dedicated terminal in a *specific library* during *opening hours*, rather than 'from a place and at a time chosen' by that person.

[375] *Technische Universität Darmstadt v. Eugen Ulmer KG*, Case C-117/13, EU:C:2014:2196, [43], [54] (ECJ). While a welcome interpretation, the framing of this as an 'ancillary right' raises the question whether it can be relied upon in national proceedings in the absence of implementation of the (optional) exception in Art. 5(2)(c) in national law. Our view is that the Court is suggesting that the 'right' might be implied into the terms of CDPA 1988, s. 40B. [376] Ibid., [48].

[377] CDPA 1988, s. 40B(3)(a).

[378] CDPA 1988, s. 40B(3)(b).

[379] CDPA 1988, s. 40B(3)(bb). It is curious that this is not limited to non-commercial research; cf CDPA 1988, s. 29(1), s. 42A.

[380] In *Technische Universität Darmstadt v. Eugen Ulmer KG*, Case C-117/13, EU:C:2014:2196, [54]–[55] (ECJ), the Court held that it might be permissible for users, who access the work on a dedicated terminal, to print it out or to copy it onto a USB drive if such acts are permitted under national legislation on private copying (giving effect to Arts 5(2)(a) or (b) of the Info. Soc. Dir.)—in the United Kingdom, the fair dealing exception in CDPA 1988, s. 29 (research and private study).

[381] CDPA 1988, s. 40B(3)(c).

[382] *Technische Universität Darmstadt v. Eugen Ulmer KG*, Case C-117/13, EU:C:2014:2196, [35] (ECJ).

14.3 INSTITUTIONAL AND PRESERVATION COPYING

Because library holdings vary, it may be that some works are contained in some libraries, but not others. In order to ensure that users of one library can benefit from the collections of others, provision is made for materials to be copied by one library and supplied to another. Under section 41, libraries are allowed to make copies of the whole or part of a published work in order to supply a not-for-profit library.[383] To ensure that this freedom does not become an opportunity to avoid paying for material provided by existing publishers (but is limited to old and obscure holdings), the exception does not apply if, at the time that the copy is made, the librarian knows or could reasonably ascertain the name and address of a person entitled to authorize the making of the copy.[384]

Libraries, archives, and museums also encounter situations in which material in their collections becomes fragile, is damaged, or is lost.[385] Examples include old newspapers starting to fade, old books becoming difficult to handle without disintegrating, or pages having been deliberately torn from a book. Section 42 provides that these institutions are free to copy from any 'item' in their permanent collection in order to preserve or replace that item or to replace an item from another institution's permanent collection that has been lost, destroyed, or damaged.[386] This does not apply to institutions that lend items to the public,[387] nor where it is reasonably practicable to purchase a replacement.

In its 2016 Proposal for a Directive on Copyright in the Digital Single Market, the Commission proposes to create a mandatory exception for 'cultural heritage institutions', that is a 'publicly accessible library or museum, an archive or a film or audio heritage institution',[388] that would permit preservation copying.[389] More specifically, proposed Article 5 would require member states to permit cultural heritage institutions 'to make copies of any works or other subject-matter that are permanently in their collections, in any format or medium, for the sole purpose of the preservation of such works or other subject-matter and to the extent necessary for such preservation.'[390] The existing British exception appears broader than the mandatory provision in the Proposal, though importantly the latter also extends to *sui generis* database right. As the terms of the Information Society Directive would be left unaffected, if the United Kingdom comes to be bound by the Directive (and its terms have not been altered),[391] little work would be necessary to implement it.

14.4 COPIES FOR RESEARCH OR PRIVATE STUDY

In many libraries, users are free to use photocopying machines, scanners, and cameras to copy works insofar as they are permitted to do so under the section 29 exception.

---

[383] CDPA 1988, s. 41, (2)(a) (defining recipient as 'not-for-profit').

[384] CDPA 1988, s. 41(2)(b). This condition does not apply in relation to parts of periodicals: s. 41(3).

[385] Info. Soc. Dir., Art. 5(2)(c), refers explicitly to libraries, archives, museums, and educational establishments, while Recital 40 talks of 'publicly accessible libraries or equivalent institutions, as well as archives'. CDPA 1988, s. 42, applies to libraries, archives, and museums, as defined in s. 43A(2), (3).

[386] CDPA 1988, s. 42.

[387] CDPA 1988, s. 42(2). This requires that the item be either for reference, inaccessible to the public, or available for loan only to other cultural institutions.   [388] COM(2016) 593 final, Art. 2(3).

[389] Ibid., Art. 6.   [390] Ibid., Recitals 18–20 of the Proposal.

[391] As of May 2018, the Proposal is currently still being considered in the Council and Parliament.

However, many libraries also offer copying services, in part to ensure that materials are appropriately handled when being copied. The Act makes provision for the making and supply of such copies if a series of prescribed conditions are complied with.[392] The copies can be supplied in any medium.

First, librarians are permitted, in specified circumstances, to copy published works and to supply them to individuals at cost *and* for purposes of non-commercial research or private study.[393] In the case of articles, they may copy up to one article in an issue of a periodical.[394] In the case of other published works, they may copy no more than a reasonable proportion of the work.[395] This latter criterion will prove problematic where the work is, for example, an illustration and thus an independent work in its own right.[396] Copying such a work by an individual researcher might well amount to fair dealing within section 29, and a librarian should be able to make and supply any copy that the recipient could themselves make within the latter provision. The person making a request must make a declaration stating, among other things, that the copy is required for 'the purposes of research for a non-commercial purpose or private study'.[397]

In the case of unpublished works,[398] librarians or archivists may make and supply single copies of a work as long as the copyright owner had not prohibited copying thereof.[399] A similar declaration is required of the recipient.[400]

The librarian (or archivist) is not required to investigate the truth of the recipient's statement and benefits from the defence as long as they are 'not aware that the declaration is false in a material particular'.[401] This will not merely save librarians from having to make judgements that even specialists on copyright law find difficult (such as what is a 'non-commercial' purpose), it will also keep talking in libraries to a minimum.

14.5 ARCHIVE CREATION

In addition to section 42, which allows for the making of preservation copies, a number of defences aid in the preservation of cultural objects.[402] A non-profit organization may record a song and make copies available for non-commercial research or private

---

[392] CDPA 1988, s. 42A.

[393] CDPA 1988, s. 42A. This much simplified provision, introduced by SI 2014/1372, reg. 5(2), replaces ss 37–40 (as enacted).

[394] CDPA 1988, s. 42A(1)(a) (formerly dealt with in s. 38 (as enacted)).

[395] CDPA 1988, s.42A(1)(b).

[396] Cf. CDPA 1988, s. 36(5).

[397] CDPA 1988, s. 42A(2) (declaration), (3) (identifying recipient and stating purpose of use, that it has not received the copy previously, and that others will not request the same material at the same time). CDPA 1988, s. 42A(4), limits the charges that a library may make when supplying copies under the section, but this is not expressed as a condition for operation of the defence.

[398] CDPA 1988, s. 43, is not in terms limited to unpublished works, but it offers no defence where a work 'has been published or communicated to the public before the date it was deposited in the library or archive': s. 43(3)(a).

[399] CDPA 1988, s. 43 (as amended by SI 2014/0000).

[400] CDPA 1988, s. 43(2). A parallel rule applies in relation to charging by the library for the copy: CDPA 1988, s. 43(4).

[401] CDPA 1988, ss 42A(2)(b), 43(1)(b).

[402] These have been amended in 2014 to render them simpler: SI 2014/1372.

study even though there is copyright in the words or music. This is subject to the proviso that the words are unpublished and are of unknown authorship.[403] In addition, where an article of cultural or historical importance cannot lawfully be exported from the United Kingdom unless a copy of it is made and deposited in an appropriate library or archive, it is not an infringement to make that copy.[404] Finally, a recording of a broadcast, or a copy of such a recording, may be made for the purpose of being placed in an archive maintained by a non-for-profit body without thereby infringing any copyright in the broadcast or in any work included in it.[405]

Although the legal deposit provisions ensure that the main libraries have a complete record of print works published in the United Kingdom,[406] the advent of digitization has led to huge amounts of non-print material. The Legal Deposit Libraries Act 2003 established a framework for collecting non-print publications and this has been put into operation from 6 April 2013.[407] This allows for the deposit of off-line non-print works (such as works published on CD-ROM) under similar conditions to print works. The Regulations also cover online publications and facilitate automated 'web-harvesting' (including works that are subject to conditional access). The obligations to permit web-harvesting apply in regard to online works that are published in the United Kingdom, and a provision elaborates on the localization of the activity.[408] The permissible uses of non-print works are defined restrictively,[409] and publishers may apply to have use by the public embargoed altogether for periods of three years at a time.[410] Section 44A of the 1988 Act, introduced by the 2003 Act, confers immunities on creators or users of non-print material archives that fall within the Regulations.

15 PUBLIC ADMINISTRATION

The CDPA 1988 contains a number of defences that facilitate involvement in, and the dissemination of information about, public administration.[411] To this end, the Act provides that copyright is not infringed by anything done for the purposes of parliamentary or judicial proceedings,[412] or for proceedings of a Royal Commission or statutory inquiry.[413] This means that copyright is not infringed if a barrister digitally scans a case report, or if a police officer photocopies a statement for use in a trial.[414] The 1988 Act also provides that copyright is not infringed by anything done for the purposes of

---

[403] CDPA 1988, s. 61 (as amended by SI 2014/1372, reg. 7). The making of the recording must not infringe any other copyright and must not have been prohibited by any of the performers. A special provision, s. 61(3), permits the supply of copies of such recordings under virtually identical terms to CDPA 1988, s. 43.

[404] CDPA 1988, s. 44.   [405] CDPA 1988, s. 75 (as amended by SI 2014/1372, reg. 8).

[406] Legal Deposit Libraries Act 2003, s. 1(1). Films and sound recordings are not subject to the obligation.

[407] Legal Deposit Libraries Act 2003, s. 6 (but subjecting such material to restrictions on its use under s. 7); The Legal Deposit Libraries (Non-Print Works) Regulations 2013 (SI 2013/777).

[408] SI 2013/777, reg. 18 (referring to the domain name and the activities of the publisher).

[409] Most notably, a deposit library may allow a particular work to be accessed at only one computer terminal at any one time.   [410] SI 2013/777, regs 23–5.

[411] Info. Soc. Dir., Art. 5(3)(e).

[412] CDPA 1988, s. 45(1). This includes arbitration proceedings: *London & Leeds Estates v. Paribas (No. 2)* [1995] 1 *EGLR* 102, 106.   [413] CDPA 1988, s. 46(2).

[414] *A v. B* [2000] *EMLR* 1007 (copying diary for use in divorce proceedings); *Vitof v. Altoft* [2006] *EWHC* 1678 (Ch), [175]; *Television New Zealand v. Newsmonitor Services* [1994] 2 *NZLR* 91, 100 (High Court of Auckland) (copying by legal advisers before proceedings start).

reporting such proceedings.[415] This means that law reports do not infringe copyright in the barristers' statements, a defendant's evidence, or a speech of a judge. It should be noted that these defences do not extend to the copying of the published reports of such proceedings. As such, the defence does not apply, for example, to the photocopying of law reports.

Special defences also enable the copying of material that is open to public inspection pursuant to a statutory requirement,[416] to material that is communicated to the Crown in the course of public proceedings,[417] and (in certain circumstances) to material on public records.[418]

16 EXCEPTIONS FOR COMPUTER PROGRAMS

Special provisions in the CDPA 1988, which follow from the Software Directive, govern how far it is permissible to copy and otherwise use computer programs without infringing. These defences ensure that a lawful user is able to make a back-up copy, to decompile a program for certain purposes, to study the program, and to adapt or copy the program where necessary for the lawful use of the program. The first three of these exceptions cannot be excluded or restricted by contract, and provisions attempting so to do are to be treated as null and void.[419]

16.1 MAKING BACK-UP COPIES

Section 50A(1) provides that it is not an infringement of copyright for a 'lawful user'[420] of a copy of a computer program to make any back-up copy of it, which is necessary for them to have for the purpose of their lawful use.[421] By enabling users to make back-up copies, it provides a form of insurance in case a computer program fails or is corrupted. Importantly, section 50A(3) provides that any term or condition in an agreement that purports to prohibit or restrict an act that is permitted under section 50A is void.[422]

The scope of the defence will depend on when it is 'necessary' for a lawful user to make a back-up copy. It is likely that this will depend on factors such as the relative stability of the program (the more vulnerable the program, the more the need for back-up), the environment in which the program operates, and the consequences of a program failing

---

[415] CDPA 1988, ss 45(2), 46(2). The latter, which relates to Royal Commissions and statutory inquiries, is limited to the reporting of any such proceedings held in *public*.

[416] CDPA 1988, s. 47 (as amended by SI 2014/1385, to facilitate the relevant registry or public authority making the material available online). For background, see UK IPO, *Modernising Copyright* (2012), 46–7. This would seem to justify the making available of patent, trade mark, and design documentation: RDA 1949, s. 17(4); PA 1977, s. 118 (once published, patent documents can be requested); TMA 1994, ss 40(4), 63(3)(a). If a third party makes the material commercially available to the public with the authority of the copyright holder, the exception does not apply: s. 47(2)(c).   [417] CDPA 1988, s. 48.

[418] CDPA 1988, ss 47 and 49. CDPA 1988, s. 50, provides a defence for acts specifically authorized by an Act of Parliament.

[419] CDPA 1988, ss 50A(3), 50BA(2), s50B(4), 296A(1), reflecting Software Dir., Art. 9(1), Recital 26.

[420] Defined as a person who has a right to use the program: CDPA 1988, s. 50A(2). See section 2.3, pp. 233–4.

[421] The Commission said that the notion of 'back-up' meant 'for security reasons' and that only one copy is permitted under Art. 5(2): *Report on the Implementation and Effects of Directive 91/250/EEC* (April 2000) COM(2000) 199 final, 18.   [422] CDPA 1988, ss 50A(3), 296A.

(it is more likely that a court will consider it necessary to make a back-up copy where the program is used for air traffic control or to assist in heart surgery than where it is a computer game). Indeed, in *Sony Computer Entertainment Inc. v. Owen*,[423] it was held that when a person buys a computer game on a CD, it is not 'necessary' for that person to make a back-up copy of the disk. Moreover, because a back-up copy is intended to meet 'the sole needs of the person having the right to use that program', a person cannot use that copy in order to sell the program to a third party.[424]

16.2 DECOMPILATION

One of the problems facing creators of computer programs is that they have to ensure that their creations can be used in conjunction with existing products and processes. In the same way as a manufacturer of spare parts for cars needs to ensure that its products are the appropriate size and shape, so too producers of computer programs and devices used in conjunction with existing programs need to ensure that their products comply with the existing standards. While some of this information will be generic and widely available, some of it may be hidden in the program. For a producer to ensure that its creations are compatible (or interoperable) with existing systems, it needs to have access to the information that is hidden in the program. Some developers (most famously IBM) publish such information to encourage others to construct further application programs or add-on devices, whereas others license the information. In some circumstances, the only way in which the relevant information can be obtained is by decompiling or reverse engineering the program. The process of decompilation reduces the object code in the program to a form that approximates with the source code. The potential problem with this is that, because decompilation involves intermediate copying of a program, it is on its face an infringement of copyright.[425]

After considerable debate, it was decided to include a defence for decompilation in the Software Directive.[426] This found its way into British law via section 50B of the CDPA 1988. Before looking at the defence, it should be noted that the parties cannot contract out of the decompilation defence.[427] It should also be noted that the importance of section 50B is reinforced by the fact that fair dealing for the purpose of research and study does not apply to the decompilation of computer programs.[428]

Section 50B provides that it is not an infringement of copyright for a lawful user of a copy of a computer program expressed in a low-level language to convert it into a higher-level language (that is, to 'decompile' it) or, incidentally in the course of converting the program, to copy it. This is subject to the proviso that:

(a) it is necessary to decompile the program to obtain the information necessary to create an independent program which can be operated with the program decompiled or with another program ('the permitted objective'); and

(b) the information so obtained is not used for any purpose other than the permitted objective.[429]

---

[423] [2002] *EMLR* (34) 742.

[424] *Aleksandrs Ranks, Jurijs Vasiļevičs v. Finanšu un ekonomisko noziegumu izmeklēšanas prokoratūra, Microsoft Corp.*, Case C-166/15, EU:C:2016:762, [43] (ECJ).

[425] See P. Samuelson, 'The Past, Present and Future of Software Copyright: Interoperability Rules in the European Union and United States' [2012] *EIPR* 229.   [426] Software Dir., Art. 6.

[427] CDPA 1988, ss 50A(3), 50B(4), 50D(2).   [428] CDPA 1988, s. 29(4).

[429] CDPA 1988, s. 50B(2).

These conditions will be not be met, for example, where (i) the relevant information is readily available to the lawful user, (ii) the decompilation is not confined to acts necessary to achieve the permitted objective, (iii) the lawful user supplies the information to any person to whom it is not necessary to do so in order to achieve the permitted objective, or (iv) the lawful user uses the information to create a program that is substantially similar in its expression to the program decompiled, or to do any act restricted by copyright.[430]

The European Commission has criticized the way in which the decompilation exception has been implemented in the United Kingdom. In particular, the Commission has said there are four reasons why section 50B may be non-conforming.[431] First, section 50B's use of 'lawful user' appears not to include a 'person authorized on behalf of the licensee or person having a right to use a copy of the program'. Second, while Article 6 of the Software Directive mentions 'reproduction of the code and translation of its form', this has been implemented in section 50B of the 1988 Act as 'expressed in a low-level language to convert it into a higher-level language'. Third, there is no restriction in the United Kingdom to 'parts' of the decompiled program; instead, section 50B is restricted to 'such acts as are necessary to achieve the permitted objective'. The final criticism is that the section 50B defence is not expressly subject to the three-step test (as is required under Article 6(3)). It is therefore likely that British courts will construe section 50B in such a way as to comply with many of the criticisms (if this were considered desirable).[432]

16.3 OBSERVING, STUDYING, AND TESTING PROGRAMS

Section 50BA, introduced in October 2003,[433] implements Article 5(3) of the Software Directive by providing that a lawful user of a copy of a program is not liable for infringement if, when carrying out an act that they are entitled to do (such as loading, displaying, running, transmitting, or storing the program), that person observes, studies, or tests the functioning of the program in order to determine the ideas or principles that underlie any element of the program. In *SAS Institute v. World Programming (WPL)*,[434] the defendant had developed its competing (but non-infringing) statistics program by studying the 'learning edition' issued by the claimant. The terms of the licence for the learning edition limited its use to purposes of learning how to use the SAS system.[435] Because WPL's purpose went well beyond learning how to use the system, there was an apparent breach of the licence terms.[436] The question thus arose as to whether the terms were valid in the light of the Directive and whether the defence of studying was nevertheless available. Arnold J found himself unable to reach a conclusion confidently and referred the question to the Court of Justice. Unfortunately, he found that neither the Court of Justice's reasoning, nor its answer was 'very clear'.[437] Nevertheless, Arnold J and the Court of Appeal interpreted the decision as drawing a distinction between 'acts' that were within the scope

---

[430] CDPA 1988, s. 50B(3).

[431] *Report on the Implementation and Effects of Directive 91/250/EEC* (April 2000) COM(2000) 199 final, 14.

[432] U.-M. Mylly, 'An Evolutionary Economics Perspective on Computer Program Interoperability and Copyright' (2010) 41 *IIC* 284.

[433] The specific implementation of Software Dir., Art. 5(3), seems to have been required now that the notion of fair dealing for research and private study in CDPA 1988, s. 29, has been limited to non-commercial ends. See *Navitaire Inc. v. Easy Jet Airline Co. & BulletProof Technologies Inc.* [2006] *RPC* (3) 111, [77].

[434] [2010] *EWHC* 1829 (Ch).   [435] Ibid., [271], [282], [286].   [436] Ibid., [290].

[437] [2013] *EWHC* 69 (Ch), [64] (Arnold J); cf. [2013] *EWCA Civ* 1482, [98] (saying that the Court of Justice gave a clear answer at [61]).

of a licence and a 'purpose' that formally took the acts outside the scope thereof. As long as the person with the licence was entitled to do the relevant acts, then the Article 5(3) defence operated.[438]

16.4 COPYING AND ADAPTING FOR LAWFUL USE

In the absence of contractual terms to the contrary, section 50C(1) allows a lawful user of a computer program to copy or adapt it if 'it is necessary for his lawful use'.[439] An example of a situation in which it will be necessary to copy for a lawful use given by section 50C(2) is where a person needs to correct errors in the program. In contrast, it has been held that a licence to use a computer game in Japan did not justify adaptation to circumvent copy protection so as to enable its use in the United Kingdom.[440] Given the limits of the licence to Japan, there was no lawful use in the United Kingdom. Another obvious example where copying is necessary relates to copying that occurs in the random-access memory (RAM) of a computer that enables the program to run (here, section 50 C(2) achieves a similar effect to section 28A/Article 5(1) of the Information Society Directive). However, the CJEU has indicated section 50C(2) has a more significant role still, that is, in facilitating an equivalent of 'exhaustion':[441] it is on this basis that the acquirer of an unlimited licence to use a program—whether an initial purchaser or 'transferee'—may make a copy by downloading it from the copyright owner's website.[442]

17 EXCEPTIONS FOR DATABASES

Section 50D of the CDPA 1988 provides that it is not an infringement of copyright in a database for a person who has a right to use the database or any part of the database (whether under a licence to do any of the acts restricted by the copyright in the database or otherwise) to do, in the exercise of that right, anything that is necessary for the purposes of *access to* and *use of* the contents of the database or of that part of the database. This means that if, in the course of searching a database, the database is downloaded into the memory of a computer, this will not be an infringement. Although in situations in which the copyright owner and the user are in a contractual relation (as a subscriber to *Lexis Library* would be), the user would have, at the very least, an implied licence covering these acts, this exception seems to operate in favour of others with a right to use the database, such as transferees of material copies of databases (for example the purchaser of a second-hand CD-ROM of the *Oxford English Dictionary*). It is important to bear in mind that

---

[438] [2013] *EWHC* 69 (Ch), [71] (Arnold J); cf. [2013] *EWCA Civ* 1482 [101]. The Court of Appeal found that there was nothing in the licence to prevent the licensee from being a legal person, such as WPL, so that it was unnecessary to grapple with the issue that Arnold J had considered, as to what happens if the user is not the formally recognized licensee.

[439] Note the contradictory provisions of Software Dir., Art. 5(1) and Recital 18. This defence does not apply to the making of back-up copies (s. 50A), to the decompilation of programs (s. 50B), or to acts carried out to study or test the program (s. 50BA).

[440] *Sony Computer Entertainment Inc v. Owen* [2002] *EMLR* (34) 742, 747.

[441] See Chapter 6, section 3.3, pp. 151–2.

[442] *UsedSoft*, Case C-128/11, EU:C:2012:407 (Grand Chamber), [75], [81]; *Aleksandrs Ranks, Jurijs Vasiļevičs v. Finanšu un ekonomisko noziegumu izmeklēšanas prokuratūra, Microsoft Corp.*, Case C-166/15, EU:C:2016:762, [49]–[50] (ECJ).

fair dealing for the purposes of research and study is not available for databases. This increases the relative importance of the section 50D defence. As with the defences for the making of back-up copies and decompilation, it is not possible to contract out of the section 50D defence.[443]

18 EXCEPTIONS FOR WORKS IN ELECTRONIC FORM

Under section 56 of the CDPA 1988, if the purchaser of a work in electronic form is entitled to make further copies or adaptations of the work, then, unless there is an express stipulation to the contrary, so too is anyone to whom the copy has been transferred. Any copies remaining with the original purchaser after transfer are infringing.[444] Given the parameters of the Software Directive, it is suggested that this section can have no role beyond that already provided by CDPA 1988, s 50C. Outside the field of computer programs, the section may apply only to sale in tangible form of electronic copies (eg on CD), as opposed to making available purely electronic copies (where the EU legislation hints that there is no exhaustion).[445]

19 EXCEPTIONS FOR ARTISTIC WORKS

A number of defences exist in relation to artworks. Given that artistic works protect a broad array of subject matter, from paintings and sculpture through to typefaces and industrial designs, it not surprising that these defences are similarly eclectic. In addition to the defences listed in the following sections, it should be noted that a number of defences exist in relation to industrial designs. These are discussed in Chapter 29.[446]

19.1 REPRESENTATION OF WORKS ON PUBLIC DISPLAY

A special defence exists in relation to the representation of artistic works on public display.[447] Section 62 of the CDPA 1988 provides that copyright in (a) buildings and (b) sculptures, models for buildings, and works of artistic craftsmanship if permanently situated in a public place or in premises open to the public, may be represented in a graphic work, photographed, filmed, or broadcast without a licence. The defence also applies to subsequent dealings with the representation. Thus a postcard of a sculpture in Trafalgar Square can be reproduced and distributed without infringing copyright in the sculpture. Similarly, a film of a new building could be made or broadcast without the consent of the owner of copyright in the building.[448] It seems that the defence applies to both private and public buildings. If so, this means that a company taking photographs of private homes to be stored on a database for use by real estate agents could rely upon the defence to avoid a claim for infringement of any copyright in the building.

---

[443] CDPA 1988, s. 50D(2). See Davison, 77–8.   [444] CDPA 1988, s. 56(2)–(3).

[445] See Chapter 6, section 3.3, p. 152.

[446] CDPA 1988, ss 51 and 53. See Chapter 29, section 3, pp. 811–15.

[447] See also incidental use defence in CDPA 1988, s. 31, discussed in section 10, pp. 255–6 (but with CDPA 1988, s. 62, there is no need for the use to be incidental: Info. Soc. Dir., Art. 5(3)(h)).

[448] While a film of a building could be placed on a website without infringing, a direct live feed of images of the building would appear to fall outside the scope of the exception.

One potential problem with the defence is that section 62 says that copyright in such a work is not infringed. As such, the defence seemingly would not apply to any preliminary drawings or plans that were used to create the public work. If so, it greatly reduces the scope of the defence.[449]

19.2 ADVERTISEMENTS FOR SALE OF AN ARTISTIC WORK

Section 63 declares that it is not an infringement of copyright in an artistic work to copy it or to issue copies to the public in order to advertise the sale of the work. This means that it is permissible, when selling a painting, to take a photograph of the painting and to publish it in a catalogue. Section 63 serves to reconcile the conflict that may arise where the artistic work and the copyright in that work are owned by different parties. It does this by preventing the copyright owner from exercising their copyright so as to hinder the owner of the artistic work from selling it. It should be noted that subsequent uses of the copy, such as selling it, are not covered by the defence.[450] This means that the sale of a catalogue formerly used to advertise the sale of the work is an infringement of copyright.[451]

19.3 SUBSEQUENT WORKS BY THE SAME ARTIST

It is common practice for artists to build upon and develop earlier works that they have created. A potential problem that arises for artists who sell the copyright in their works is that copyright owners may object to the artist continuing to work in the same style. Under general copyright principles, artists are able to develop the same ideas as long as they do not copy a substantial part of the expressive form of the earlier work. To ensure that owners of copyright in an earlier work are unable to stifle an artist's ability to work in the same style, section 64 adds that an artist is able to copy their earlier works, provided that they do not repeat or imitate a work's main design.[452]

19.4 RECONSTRUCTION OF BUILDINGS

Section 65 allows for the reconstruction of a building without infringement of any copyright in the building or in the original drawings or plans for it.[453] This ensures that an owner of a building is able to carry out repairs without having to seek the approval of the copyright owner.

19.5 USE OF TYPEFACES IN THE ORDINARY COURSE OF PRINTING

A special defence exists where typefaces (which are protected as artistic works) are used in the ordinary course of printing. Section 54 provides that it is not an infringement of copyright in an artistic work consisting of the design of a typeface to use the typeface in the ordinary course of printing activities. The section also provides

---

[449] R. Burrell and A. Coleman, *Copyright Exceptions: The Digital Impact* (2005), 233.
[450] CDPA 1988, s. 63.   [451] Info. Soc. Dir., Art. 5(3)(j).
[452] L. Bently, 'Copyright and Self Copying', in D. Hudson Hick (ed.), *The Aesthetics and Ethics of Copying* (2016).   [453] CDPA 1988, s. 65; Info. Soc. Dir., Art. 5(3)(m).

that it is not an infringement to possess or do anything in relation to the material produced by such a use.[454]

20 BROADCASTS

Various acts are permitted in relation to the making, retransmission, and reception of broadcasts. In addition to the provisions at which we have already looked in relation to archives,[455] education, and people with disabilities,[456] the following defences may apply.

20.1 INCIDENTAL RECORDING FOR THE PURPOSE OF BROADCASTING

A person authorized to broadcast a work may make a recording of it for purposes of the broadcast.[457] This is subject to the requirement that the recording should not be used for any other purpose and should be destroyed within 28 days of first being used.[458] This ensures that any temporary copies that are made in the course of broadcasting will not infringe.

20.2 RECORDING FOR PURPOSES OF SUPERVISION

As part of the regulatory framework that governs the broadcasting industry, a number of organizations are given the task of supervising broadcast programmes. To ensure that these bodies are able to perform these tasks, the 1988 Act provides that supervisory bodies (in particular, after the Communications Act 2003, the unitary body, Ofcom) may make recordings of broadcasts for the purpose of controlling broadcasting.[459]

20.3 TIME SHIFTING

Section 70 provides for a time-shifting defence, which allows for the private recording of broadcasts so that they may be watched at a later time. The making of a recording of a broadcast in domestic premises for private and domestic use, solely in order to view it or listen to it at a more convenient time, does not infringe any copyright in the transmission or of works included in the transmission.[460] This enables a person to record a television programme to watch at a more convenient time or to record a radio programme to which they want to listen later. Since broadcasts do not include most 'Internet transmissions', this defence cannot be employed to justify private copying from websites.

---

[454] CDPA 1988, s. 54. The typeface itself may be reproduced 25 years after the year of authorized marketing: CDPA 1988, s. 55. See J. Watts and F. Blakemore, 'Protection of Software Fonts in UK Law' [1995] *EIPR* 133.   [455] CDPA 1988, s. 75, discussed in section 14.5, p. 272.

[456] CDPA 1988, ss 31A, 32, 34(2), 35.

[457] CDPA 1988, s. 68; Info. Soc. Dir., Art. 5(2)(d); Rel. Rights Dir., Art. 10(1)(c); Berne, Art. 11*bis*(3). See *DR, TV2 Danmark A/S v. NCB-Nordisk Copyright Bureau*, Case C-510/10, EU:C:2012:244 (ECJ).

[458] *Phonographic Performance v. AEI Rediffusion Music* [1998] *Ch* 187, [1997] *RPC* 729.

[459] CDPA 1988, s. 69; Info. Soc. Dir., Art. 5(3)(e); Communications Act 2003, Sch. 17, para. 91(3).

[460] CDPA 1988, s. 71 (justified possibly by Info. Soc. Dir., Art. 5(2)(b), and Recital 35).

20.4 FREE PUBLIC SHOWING OR PLAYING

Although running a radio or television in public would normally count as a public performance (or communication to the public) of the broadcast and any works therein, a special defence limits the scope of such liability where a broadcast is shown or played to a non-paying audience.[461] In so providing, UK law takes advantage of the fact that international and regional norms only require that broadcasters are given the right to control communication to the public of their broadcasts if such communication is made in places accessible to the public against the payment of an entrance fee.[462] In utilizing this flexibility by way on an exception, section 72 further specifies that an audience will be treated as paying if they have paid admission, *or* if goods or services are supplied at that place at prices that are substantially attributable to the facilities afforded for seeing or hearing the broadcast or programme, or at prices exceeding those usually charged there and which are partly attributable to those facilities.[463] So a wine bar wishing to offer a television for the benefit of customers, but which does not alter its prices, would fall within the exception,[464] whereas a bar that charges an entry fee when broadcasts are being shown would not. The 'free showing' defence also covers the showing or playing of broadcasts to residents of hotels,[465] inmates in prisons, patients in hospitals, and members of clubs, and it covers free demonstrations of broadcast-receiving equipment, for example in shop windows. However, the defence would not be available to justify showing of a live broadcast of a sports event to fans who paid to enter the venue to view the broadcast.[466]

The 'free playing' defence applies only to claims relating to infringement of copyright in the broadcast,[467] and in certain specified situations, to the copyright in sound recordings. Permissions as regards other works included in the broadcast, for example music and lyrics of songs, will be required (from PRS for Music).[468] In the case of sound recordings, the section distinguishes between two categories of recording. If they either are not recordings of music or songs (for example recorded interviews with politicians), or are musical recordings of which the author is also the author of the broadcast (such as sound recordings created as theme music for the channel or to accompany a programme), it is not an infringement of the copyright in the recording to show in public a broadcast that includes the recording.[469] The exception does not, however, excuse any infringement of the copyright in other sound recordings—that is, those that are recordings of music and songs where the author of the recording is not the author of the music (termed 'excepted sound recordings'). These excepted sound recordings encompass most commercially distributed popular and classical music, so that the general 'free playing' defence would not apply to sound recordings featured on the radio or *Top of the Pops*. For these 'excepted sound recordings', a much more limited exception exists as regards the free playing or

---

[461] CDPA 1988, s. 72.   [462] Rome Convention, Art. 13(d); Rel. Rights Dir., Art 8(3).

[463] CDPA 1988, s. 72(2)(b).

[464] *Verwertungsgesellschaft Rundfunk GmbH v. Hettegger Hotel Edelweiss GmbH*, Case C-641/15, EU:C:2017: 131 (ECJ) ('*Rundfunk*').

[465] Ibid., [23] (referring to WIPO Guide to Rome Convention view that paying for meal in a restaurant or drinks in a bar where broadcast is shown is not 'against payment of an entrance fee').

[466] Ibid., EU:C:2016:795, [AG36] (AG Szpunar).

[467] Prior to amendment by the Copyright (Free Public Showing or Playing) (Amendment) Regulations 2016 (SI 2016/565), the exception also applied with respect to copyright in any film included in the broadcast. This was regarded as inconsistent with Info. Soc. Dir., Art. 3: *Football Association Premier League v. QC Leisure* [2012] *EWHC* 108 (Ch), [78], affirmed [2012] *EWCA Civ* 1708.

[468] Hence many electrical retailers allow the demonstration of television equipment with the sound off.

[469] CDPA 1988, s. 72(1A), introduced by SI 2003/2498 to implement Rel. Rights Dir., Art. 10(3).

showing of a broadcast for the purposes of repairing equipment for the reception of broadcasts, demonstrating that such repair has been carried out, or demonstrating such equipment.[470] So, while a wine bar, hotel, or even a National Health Service hospital or government-run prison will benefit from the broad 'free playing' defence as regards broadcasts, a Phonographic Performance Ltd licence will need to be obtained to cover the 'excepted sound recordings' included in the broadcast.

20.5 PHOTOGRAPHS OF TELEVISION BROADCASTS

The taking of a photograph of an image from a broadcast, in domestic premises for private and domestic use, is not an infringement of copyright in the broadcast or any film included in it.[471] The exception does not extend to photographs of artistic works included in television broadcasts.[472]

20.6 RECEPTION AND RETRANSMISSION OF WIRELESS BROADCAST BY CABLE

When the CDPA was passed, a special defence was included in section 73 dealing with the retransmission of wireless broadcasts by cable operators. The defence was designed to ensure that people in areas in which reception of the broadcast is very poor or restricted were able to get access to programmes. The defence also took account of the fact that certain cable operators are under a 'must carry' obligation.[473] The Court of Justice has indicated that retransmissions of this sort in fact require the copyright owner's permission,[474] and the government has decided, for other reasons, to repeal the exception.[475] This was done by section 34 of the Digital Economy Act 2017, with effect from 31 July 2017.[476]

21 MISCELLANEOUS DEFENCES

21.1 NOTES OR RECORDINGS OF SPOKEN WORDS

Given that a person who makes a speech may have copyright in the speech (once recorded),[477] a defence is provided to those who record speeches (such as journalists) to enable them to make use of their recordings. Section 58 provides that the copyright

---

[470] CDPA 1988, s. 72(1B)(b). A broader provision was removed in 2010: Copyright, Designs and Patents Act 1988 (Amendment) Regulations (SI 2010/2694), reg. 4.

[471] CDPA 1988, s. 71 (justifiable, possibly, under Info. Soc. Dir., Art. 5(2)(b) or (3)(i)).

[472] Other defences might assist, e.g. CDPA 1988, s. 31.

[473] Such obligations were imposed under the Communications Act 2003, s. 64.

[474] *ITV Broadcasting v. TV Catchup*, Case C-607/11, EU:C:2013:147, [2013] 3 CMLR (1) 1 (ECJ); *ITV Broadcasting v. TV Catchup* (in administration), Case C-275/15, EU:C:2017:144 (ECJ) (holding that exception not justified by Info. Soc. Dir., Art. 9).

[475] DCMS, *The balance of payments between television platforms and public service broadcasters: Consultation Paper* (March 2015); DCMS, *The Balance of Payments (etc): Government Response* (July 2016) 5; IPO UK, *Government Response to a technical consultation on transitional arrangements following the repeal of Section 73 of the Copyright, Designs and Patents Act 1988 (reception and re-transmission of wireless broadcast by cable)* (2017).

[476] Digital Economy Act 2017, s. 34; SI 2017/765, reg. 2(n).

[477] See Chapter 3, section 2, p. 62; Chapter 4, section 2, pp. 91–2, 110–11.

cannot be used to restrict the use of recordings made of their speech for the purpose of reporting current events, or recordings made for communicating to the public the whole or part of the work.[478] For the defence to operate, the recording must be a direct record of the spoken words and the speaker must not have prohibited the recording of their speech.[479]

21.2 PUBLIC RECITATION

Section 59(1) of the 1988 Act provides that the reading or recitation in public by one person of a 'reasonable extract' from a publicized literary or dramatic work does not infringe any copyright in the work so long as it is accompanied by a 'sufficient acknowledgement'.[480] Section 59(2) provides that copyright in a work is not infringed where a recording or recitation covered by section 59(1) is included in a sound recording or communicated to the public.

21.3 ABSTRACTS

Where an article on a scientific or technical subject is published in a periodical accompanied by an abstract indicating the contents of the article, it is not an infringement of copyright in the abstract or in the article to copy the abstract or to issue copies of it to the public.[481] The defence plays an important role in ensuring the circulation of scientific information.

21.4 DIFFICULTIES WITH IDENTIFYING AUTHORS

Where works are of unknown authorship, a fixed term of copyright replaces the normal *post mortem* term.[482] Similarly, in the case of films, where it is not possible to identify any of the persons by whom the calculation of the term of protection is normally made, a fixed term operates. In both situations, the possibility arises that while a user may rely on the fixed term, the author might later become known. If so, the longer, conventional term would apply.[483] In order to ensure that this does not create problems, there is a defence to infringement where reasonable inquiry cannot ascertain the identity of any author of a work and it is reasonable to suppose that copyright has expired in the work.[484] This provision should now be viewed alongside the provisions relating to orphan works that are discussed in Chapter 12.

21.5 EXPIRY OF FILM COPYRIGHT

As we saw earlier, one of the changes brought about as a result of the Term Directive is that copyright in films expires 70 years from the end of the calendar year in which the death of the last of the following occurs: the principal director; the author of the screenplay;

---

[478] CDPA 1988, s. 58; cf. Info. Soc. Dir., Art. 5(3)(f) (which requires that the source, including the author's name, is indicated).   [479] CDPA 1988, s. 58 (justifiable under Info. Soc. Dir., Art. 5(3)(o)).

[480] Defined in CDPA 1988, s. 178.

[481] CDPA 1988, s. 60(1) (justified under Info. Soc. Dir., Art. 5(3)(a) or (o)).

[482] CDPA 1988, s. 12(3).   [483] CDPA 1988, ss 12(4), 13(4); cf. s. 13(9) where there is no person.

[484] CDPA 1988, ss 57, 66A (justifiable under Info. Soc. Dir., Art. 5(3)(o)).

the author of the dialogue; or the composer of any music specifically created.[485] One of the consequences of this is that it may be difficult to determine when copyright in a film actually expires. To ensure that this uncertainty does not unduly hinder subsequent uses of the film, section 66A provides that copyright in a film is not infringed if (i) it is not possible by reasonable inquiry to ascertain the identity of any of the relevant persons, and (ii) it is reasonable to assume that the copyright has expired *or* that the last relevant person has been dead for longer than 70 years.

21.6 RIGHT OF REPAIR

As part of the general jurisdiction to refuse to enforce copyright where it would contravene public policy, the courts have sometimes treated a person as having a right to repair their property even though to do so would be a direct or indirect reproduction of a copyright work.[486] This was taken furthest by the House of Lords in *British Leyland v. Armstrong*,[487] holding that manufacturers were entitled to make spare parts for motor vehicles (even though to do so would be to reproduce the claimant's design drawings indirectly), so as to facilitate the repair of such vehicles. However, the defence enunciated in *British Leyland* has subsequently been qualified to such an extent that it is hard to imagine any situation in which it might apply. In *Canon Kabushiki Kaisha v. Metro-Goldwyn-Mayer Inc.*,[488] Lord Hoffmann said that, for the defence to apply, it must be plain and obvious that the circumstances are unfair to customers and that the monopoly is anti-competitive. Soon after that decision, in *Mars v. Teknowledge*,[489] Jacob J held that the *British Leyland* defence could not be applied to claims for infringement of copyright in computer software or to rights in databases because those rights stemmed from exhaustive European statutory regimes.[490] The upshot of this is that the right of repair has effectively been abolished.[491]

22 REFORM

Having had two British reviews of copyright exceptions already this century, it might have been assumed unnecessary to raise the issue of the desirability of further reform.[492] Nevertheless, two points are worth making (albeit briefly).

The first point is that there is growing worldwide discussion of a possible exemption for 'user generated content'. The idea is to legitimize the abundance of individual creative reuses of copyright-protected material currently visible on the Internet (typically on video-hosting platforms such as You Tube), but the legal status of which is often difficult to know (is it fair parody, pastiche, or quotation?). Such an exception has been adopted

---

[485] CDPA 1988, s. 13B(2). See Chapter 7, section 3, pp. 186–7.
[486] See Info. Soc. Dir., Art. 5(3)(l) (allowing exceptions relating to use in relation to repair of equipment).
[487] [1986] *RPC* 279.   [488] [1997] *FSR* 817.   [489] [2000] *FSR* 138.
[490] Ibid. (the defence was unlikely to succeed unless the court can be reasonably certain that no right-thinking member of society would quarrel with the result).
[491] See G. Llewellyn, 'Does Copyright Recognize a Right to Repair?' [1999] *EIPR* 596, 599.
[492] Indeed, at an EU level, legislative proposals have been adopted on the rights of the visually impaired (pp. 261–2), and are likely to be adopted on text and data mining (p. 245), education (p. 267), and preservation by libraries (p. 270). Assuming Brexit goes ahead, the former will require implementation, but the latter will probably not. Also, as noted also in Chapter 2, p. 55, further consideration of exceptions and limitations is progressing slowly at WIPO.

in Canada.[493] There, an individual may use a copyright-protected work or other subject matter in the creation of a new work or other subject matter and then authorize an intermediary to disseminate any resulting subject matter 'for non-commercial purposes'.[494] In Europe, similar proposals are circulating, often making the permitted use subject to a requirement of compensation that might be payable by any intermediary hosting the material.[495]

The second point is that, on the assumption that Brexit goes ahead, one part of the sovereignty that the United Kingdom will 'reclaim' is the ability to reformulate copyright law (at least within the limits set by international standards and the terms of any free trade agreements). One can imagine, then, that pressure will resurface to introduce flexibilities that previous reviews favoured, but were not possible because of EU constraints. The Gowers and Hargreaves Reviews were both attracted by the idea of 'fair use' and the flexibility associated with it.[496] The content industries in the United Kingdom are, of course, very effective lobbyists, but one can at the very least foresee a vibrant debate as to whether it would be desirable for the United Kingdom to introduce a fair use regime.[497]

---

[493] Copyright Act (Canada), s. 29.21.

[494] The exception is subject to a host of conditions: the material must have been made available to the public, and the individual must have had reasonable grounds to believe that those materials were not themselves infringing; the source (including the name of the author, performer, maker, or broadcaster) of prior materials used must be mentioned; and there must be no 'substantial adverse effect' on the exploitation of the prior materials, in particular, the user-generated content must not operate as a market-substitute for the material used.

[495] European Parliament Committee on the Internal Market and Consumer Protection (IMCO) Opinion on the Proposed Directive on Copyright in the Digital Single Market (Report 14 June 2017) 36 (new Art. 5b); European Parliament Committee on Culture and Education (CULT), Opinion on the Proposed Directive on Copyright in the Digital Single Market (14 July 2017) 5, 41 (proposed Art. 5a); M. Senftleben, *Recommendation on Measures to Safeguard Fundamental Rights and the Open Internet* (2017).

[496] *Gowers Review* (2006) ch. 4; *Digital Opportunity: A Review of Intellectual Property and Growth* (2011) (The Hargreaves Review), especially, 3, 8, 44–6.

[497] Copyright Act 1976 (US), s. 107. For a careful argument that the restrictive approach of British law would not necessarily change were a fair use defence adopted, see R. Burrell, 'Reining in Copyright Law: Is Fair Use the Answer?' [2001] *IPQ* 368; S. Halpern and P. Johnson, *Harmonising Copyright Law* (2014) 148–59.

10

MORAL RIGHTS

1 INTRODUCTION

Once a work qualifies for copyright protection, two distinct categories of right may arise. In addition to the economic rights that are granted to the first owner of copyright, the 1988 Act also confers moral rights on the authors of certain works.[1]

Moral rights[2] protect an author's non-pecuniary or non-economic interests.[3] The Copyright, Designs and Patents Act 1988 (CDPA 1988) provides authors and directors with the right to be named when a work is copied or communicated (the right of attribution), the right *not* to be named as the author of a work that they did not create (the right to object against false attribution), and the right to control the form of the work (the right of integrity). The moral rights recognized in the United Kingdom are more limited than the rights granted in some other jurisdictions, where, for example, authors are provided with the rights to publish or divulge a work, to correct the work, to object to the alteration or destruction of the original of a work, to object to excessive criticism of the work, and to withdraw a work from circulation on the ground that the author is no longer happy with it (because, for example, it no longer reflects the author's world view or because the person to whom the economic rights in the work have been assigned has failed to exploit it).

Infringement of a moral right in the United Kingdom is actionable as a breach of a statutory duty[4] and will result in an award of damages. The moral rights of integrity and attribution recognized under the 1988 Act last for the same time as the copyright in the relevant work. The right to object to false attribution is less extensive, lasting for only 20 years after the author's death.[5] After the author's death, moral rights usually are exercised

---

[1] See E. Adeney, *The Moral Rights of Authors and Performers: An International and Comparative Analysis* (2006); G. Davies and K. Garnett, *Moral Rights* (2010); W. Cornish, 'Moral Rights under the 1988 Act' [1989] *EIPR* 449; R. Durie, 'Moral Rights and the English Business Community' [1991] *Ent L Rev* 40; J. Ginsburg, 'Moral Rights in a Common Law System' [1990] *Ent L Rev* 121; Copinger, ch. 11; Laddie et al., ch. 13.

[2] The term 'moral rights' is derived from the French *droit moral*.

[3] J. Ginsburg, 'Moral Rights in a Common Law System' [1990] *Ent L Rev* 121, 121. This does not mean that they cannot be used to secure economic benefits. The estate of French painter Maurice Utrillo has benefited considerably from the grant of the right to use Utrillo's name in relation to certain paintings: see J. Merryman, 'The Moral Right of Maurice Utrillo' (1993) 43 *Am J Comp L* 445; A. Dietz, 'The Artist's Right of Integrity under Copyright Law: A Comparative Approach' (1994) 25 *IIC* 177.

[4] CDPA 1988, s. 103.

[5] UK law also describes a further right, that of privacy in photographs, as a 'moral right': CDPA 1988, s. 85. Breach of confidence may provide something akin to a divulgation right: see, e.g., *Prince Albert v. Strange* (1848) 2 *De G & Sm* 652, (1849) 1 *MacG CC* 25 (preventing unauthorized disclosure of previously unpublished artwork on grounds of common law copyright and breach of confidence).

by their heirs,[6] but in some countries may be enforced by executive bodies such as the Ministry for Culture.

The moral rights in the 1988 Act were introduced to give effect to Article 6*bis* of the Berne Convention,[7] which requires that members of the Berne Union confer on authors the right of attribution and integrity.[8] More specifically, it states that:

> Independently of the author's economic rights, and even after the transfer of the said rights, the author shall have the right to claim authorship of the work, and to object to any distortion, mutilation or other modification of, or other derogatory action in relation to, the said work, which would be prejudicial to his honour or reputation.

Instead of replicating Article 6*bis* verbatim, the British legislature chose to introduce a series of detailed statutory provisions, each of which contains a number of conditions, limitations, and exceptions.[9] This has led commentators to suggest that the manner in which Article 6 has been implemented in the United Kingdom is 'cynical, or at least half-hearted'.[10] Given that failure to give effect to Article 6*bis* does not represent a ground of complaint to the World Trade Organization (WTO),[11] it is unlikely that much will come of these criticisms.

While moral rights have received a considerable amount of support,[12] particularly from creators, they have also been subject to a degree of criticism.[13] At a general level, moral rights have been criticized for the fact that they are founded upon a romantic image of the author as an isolated creative genius who in creating a work imparts their personality upon the resulting work. Under this model, moral rights enable the author to maintain the 'indestructible creational bond' that exists between their personality and the work.[14] The notion of the romantic author, which became unfashionable in the second half of the

---

[6] The rights pass on death to the person nominated by testamentary disposition, or else to the person to whom copyright is being passed; otherwise, they are to be exercised by personal representatives: CDPA 1988, s. 95(1). As an exception, the right against false attribution passes to the author's personal representatives: CDPA 1988, s. 95(5).

[7] While various moral rights existed in the United Kingdom prior to 1989, it was widely believed that the protection was not sufficient to meet the criteria in the Berne Convention. The Gregory Committee, [219]–[226], had been reluctant to introduce such rights in 1956, anticipating difficulties in their drafting. The Whitford Committee, [51]–[57], impressed by the form of their implementation in Dutch law, recommended their adoption in 1977. See G. Dworkin, 'Moral Rights and the Common Law Countries' (1994) 5 *AIPJ* 5, 11; E. Adeney, *The Moral Rights of Authors and Performers: An International and Comparative Analysis* (2006), ch. 13.

[8] These were introduced at the Rome Conference in 1928. See Ricketson and Ginsburg, [3.28], 108, [10.07], 590–4; Adeney, op. cit., ch. 6. Article 6*bis* was, in many ways, a compromise. Durie tells us that the terms 'honour and reputation' were introduced in place of 'moral interests of the author' to satisfy objections of the common law jurisdictions: R. Durie, 'Moral Rights and the English Business Community' [1990] *Ent L Rev* 40; Ricketson and Ginsburg, [10.36], 614. Most importantly, Art. 6(3) leaves Union countries free to determine the conditions under which the rights are exercised.

[9] CDPA 1988, Ch. IV. The criticisms are that the provisions do not implement Berne, do not improve the position of authors, are, in practical terms, ineffective, and neglect the essential characteristics of moral rights.   [10] J. Ginsburg, 'Moral Rights in a Common Law System' [1990] *Ent L Rev* 121, 129.

[11] Cornish has suggested that the express recognition of moral rights might lay the foundation for less meagre treatment in future—particularly by penetrating judicial attitudes: W. R. Cornish, 'Moral Rights under the 1988 Act' [1989] *EIPR* 449.

[12] Although TRIPS requires member states to comply with Arts 1–21 Berne, it is notable that the agreement says that 'members shall not have rights or obligations under this Agreement in respect of the rights conferred under Art. 6*bis* of that Convention'.

[13] G. Dworkin, 'Moral Rights and the Common Law Countries' [1994] *AIPJ* 5, 34 (opposition to moral rights has at times bordered on the hysterical).

[14] A. Dietz, 'The Artist's Right of Integrity under Copyright Law' (1994) 25 *IIC* 177, 182.

twentieth century, has been criticized because it presents an unrealistic image of the process of authorship. In particular, it has been criticized for the fact that it fails to acknowledge the collaborative and intertextual nature of the creative process.[15]

Another criticism made about moral rights focuses on what is perceived as their foreign or alien nature.[16] More specially, it has been suggested that moral rights, which have their origin in continental copyright systems,[17] cannot readily be absorbed or transplanted into a common law system.[18] Any attempt to do so will not only fail, but will also upset the existing copyright regimes.

Moral rights have also been criticized on the basis that they represent an unjustified legal intervention in the working of the free market. Such arguments highlight the fact that moral rights typically secure authors' interests at the expense of entrepreneurs, disseminators, and exploiters of copyright.[19] Given this, it is not surprising that while authors' groups argue for further entrenchment of the rights (so that they are inalienable), the entrepreneurial interests lobby for further restrictions on the rights and their subjugation to voluntary market transactions.[20] Another criticism made of moral rights is that they prioritize private interests over the public interest. More specifically, it has been suggested that moral rights may inhibit the creation and dissemination of derivative creations, such as multimedia works and parodies.[21] For example, if an author were to use their moral right of integrity to prevent the publication of a parody of their work, this would conflict with the right to free expression, and thus with broader public interests.[22]

With these initial points in mind, we now turn to look at the moral rights that are recognized in the United Kingdom.

2 RIGHT OF ATTRIBUTION (OR PATERNITY)

The right of attribution or (as the statute prefers) the right of paternity is perhaps the best-known of all of the moral rights recognized in the United Kingdom. In essence, the right of attribution provides the creators of certain types of work with the right to be identified

---

[15] P. Jaszi, 'On the Author Effect: Contemporary Copyright and Collective Creativity' (1992) 10 *Cardozo AELJ* 293.

[16] For a discussion of tension along such 'comparative' lines, see I. Stamatoudi, 'Moral Rights of Authors in England: The Missing Emphasis on the Role of Creators' [1997] *IPQ* 478. For a less caricatured approach, see G. Dworkin, 'Moral Rights and the Common Law Countries' (1994) 5 *AIPJ* 5, 6.

[17] For the French and German histories, see D. Saunders, *Authorship and Copyright* (1992), chs 3 and 4. For a statement of the position in France, see P. Dulian, 'Moral Rights in France through Recent Case Law' (1990) 145 *RIDA* 126. For an exhaustive (if dated) account, see S. Stromholm, *Le Droit Moral de L'Auteur en droit Allemand, Française et Scandinave* (1966).

[18] While historically, there have been those who have wished to confine copyright to the protection of an author's pecuniary interests, they have not in general succeeded. The Engravings Act of 1735, for example, was directed, in part, to protecting an engraver against 'base and mean' imitations. See *Gambart v. Ball* (1863) 14 *CB (NS)* 306, 143 *ER* 463 (submission that Engravings Act could not be relied on to prevent photography on grounds that the Act's sole purpose was protection of reputation and quality, which was not diminished in a photograph, was rejected).

[19] Moral rights have been characterized as limits on the 'right of the owner of the copyright to do what he likes with his own': *Preston v. Raphael Tuck* [1926] *Ch* 667, 674.

[20] G. Dworkin, 'Moral Rights and the Common Law Countries' (1994) 5 *AIPJ* 5 36.

[21] G. Pessach, 'The Author's Moral Right of Integrity in Cyberspace: A Preliminary Normative Framework' (2003) 34 *IIC* 250.

[22] See *Confetti Records v. Warner Music UK Ltd* [2003] *EMLR* (35) 790, [161] (declining to 'read down' the integrity right to give effect to Art. 10 ECHR).

as the author of those works.[23] While the right of attribution cannot be assigned, as we will see, it can be waived. The moral right of attribution lasts for the same period of time as the copyright in the relevant work.

The right to be named as author of a work carries with it a number of symbolic, economic, and cultural consequences.[24] The reason for this is that the name of the author performs a number of different roles. It facilitates: the management of intellectual works (through indexes, catalogues, and bibliographies);[25] the channelling of royalties (for example from the public lending right scheme); the interpretation of the work (insofar as it provides a psychological or biographical history of the author); the celebration, reward, and sustenance of authorial talent or genius;[26] and the construction of the individual as the creator of an intellectual *oeuvre*. In many cases, the right to be named as author of a work will be unnecessary because it is in the interests of all of the parties concerned in the exploitation of the work to attribute it. Where this is not the case, however, the right of attribution is potentially a very important right.

Before looking at the right of attribution in more detail, it should be noted that an author may be able to rely on a number of mechanisms other than the right of attribution to ensure that they are named as author. Publishing contracts, for example, will often contain terms dealing with attribution that may be enforced against a publisher[27] and possibly also against third parties who knowingly induce such breaches. In some circumstances, such a term might be implied into a contract.[28] The right to be named as author of a work may also be ensured by other means such as union power and industry standards.[29] The law of reverse passing off might also be used to prevent another person from falsely claiming that they are the author of a work.

2.1 SUBSISTENCE OF THE RIGHT OF ATTRIBUTION

In order for the right of attribution to arise, it is necessary to show two things: that the work in question is the type of work to which the right applies; and that the right of attribution has been asserted.[30] We will deal with each of these requirements in turn.

2.1.1 Relevant works

The right of attribution is granted to the creators of only a limited number of works. More specifically, the right is recognized only in relation to original literary, dramatic, musical, and artistic works, and in films. In the case of literary, dramatic, musical, and artistic

---

[23] Cf. the information protected by rules on 'rights-management information' discussed in Chapter 13. See J. Ginsburg, 'Have Moral Rights Come of (Digital) Age in the United States?' (2001) 19 *Cardozo AELJ* 9; S. Dusollier, 'Some Reflections on Copyright Management Information and Moral Rights' (2003) 25 *Colum JL & Arts* 377.

[24] For experimental analysis of how such attribution is 'valued', see C. Buccafusco, C. Sprigman, and Z. Burns, 'What's a Name Worth?' (2013) 93 *Boston U L Rev* 1.

[25] See R. Chartier, 'Figures of the Author', in Sherman and Strowel, ch. 1.

[26] A link is frequently drawn between the right to be named and the ability to gain a reputation and make an income as an author or artist: see *Tolnay v. Criterion Film Productions* [1936] 2 All ER 1625.

[27] Ibid.   [28] *Miller v. Cecil Film Ltd* [1937] 2 All ER 464.

[29] See D. Read and D. Sandelson, 'Credit Where Credit's Due' [1990] *Ent L Rev* 42.

[30] The requirement of assertion and the rules governing who is bound by an assertion have the effect that the attribution right occupies a grey area between property rights and rights *in personam*. In many cases, third parties will be bound by the attribution right, whereas an author who was forced to rely on contract law might not succeed.

works, the right is granted to the author of the work. In the case of films, the right of attribution is granted to the director.[31]

Within these general categories, a number of specific types of work do not give rise to a right of attribution. The right of attribution does not arise in relation to works made for the purpose of reporting current events; nor does it apply to contributions to a newspaper, magazine, or periodical, or an encyclopaedia or similar work.[32] These exceptions, which are difficult to reconcile with the Berne Convention, reflect government concessions to the lobbying power of the newspaper and other publishing industries. The objections were informed by fears that the need to name the author of a work would interfere with the prompt delivery of news. It was also feared that enabling an author of a news story to be named would undermine the image of the news as being objective and neutral.

The CDPA 1988 also states that the right of attribution does not apply to computer programs,[33] computer-generated works,[34] typefaces,[35] or works protected by Crown or similar copyright.[36] No satisfactory policy-based justification has been given for denying authors of computer programs or typefaces a right of attribution.

2.1.2 The requirement of assertion

The right of attribution does not arise until it has been asserted.[37] Even if it has been asserted, in an action for infringement of the attribution right, the courts take into account any delay in asserting the right when considering remedies.[38] The imposition of the requirement of assertion is said to be justified because Article 6*bis* merely requires members of the Union to confer on authors the right 'to claim' authorship.[39] However, it has been suggested that such an interpretation is unsustainable given that Article 5(2) of the Berne Convention requires that an author's 'enjoyment and exercise of these rights shall not be subject to any formality'.[40] Because the Agreement on Trade Related Aspects of Intellectual Property Rights (TRIPS) does not require that Article 6*bis* of Berne be implemented, the merits of these arguments are unlikely to be tested before the WTO.

In general, the right can be asserted in one of two ways. First, when copyright in a work is assigned, the author or director includes a statement that asserts their right to be identified.[41] Second, the right may be asserted by an instrument in writing signed by the author or director. The form of assertion has an important impact on the extent to which third parties are bound to comply with the right.[42] If the first mode of assertion is chosen, it binds the assignee and anyone claiming through them, whether or not they have notice

---

[31] For such works created prior to 1 August 1989, see CDPA 1988, Sch. 1, para. 23(2)–(3) (the right applies: except in the case of a film made before that date, and other works the author of which died before that date or the author of which had assigned the copyright before that date).   [32] CDPA 1988, s. 79(6).

[33] TRIPS Art. 10 states that computer programs shall be protected as literary works under the Berne Convention. Thus while TRIPS Art. 9 does not require that members apply Art. 6*bis*, it seems (somewhat counter-intuitively) that Art. 10 requires that Art. 6*bis* be applied as regards computer programs.

[34] Perhaps on the ground that such works do not fall within Berne, i.e. a Union for the protection of the rights of authors: Berne Art. 1.

[35] CDPA 1988, s. 79(2). Typefaces are probably within the scope of Art. 2(7), which requires members to protect such works by copyright only if they do not offer protection as designs and models.

[36] CDPA 1988, s. 79(7). Perhaps justified because of Berne Art. 2(4).   [37] CDPA 1988, s. 78(1).

[38] CDPA 1988, s. 78(5).

[39] The requirement of assertion also helps to overcome some of the problems that may arise in tracing authors.   [40] See J. Ginsburg, 'Moral Rights in a Common Law System' [1996] *Ent L Rev* 121, 128.

[41] This may be difficult because the author need not be a party to such an assignment, e.g. where they are not first owner. But, in such circumstances, if there is an assertion, it does not seem to matter that the author was not party to the assignment.   [42] CDPA 1988, s. 78.

of the assertion. If the second mechanism is employed, however, the assertion binds only those who have notice of the assertion. The former is consequently the more effective mode of assertion. There seems to be no reason why an author or director should not use both methods or make a number of assertions.

Two additional modes of assertion exist in relation to artistic works.[43] First, the right will have been asserted if the artist is identified on the original, copy, frame, mount, or other attachment when the artist or the first owner of copyright parts with possession of the original.[44] Such an assertion binds anyone into whose hands the original or copy comes (including borrowers and purchasers), whether or not the identification is still present or visible.[45] If the work is exhibited in public thereafter, the artist should be named. Second, the right may be asserted by the inclusion of a specific statement to that effect in a licence that permits copies of the work to be made.[46] This kind of assertion binds the licensee and anyone into whose hands a copy made in pursuance of the licence comes, whether or not they have notice of the assertion.[47]

2.2 INFRINGEMENT

The attribution right provides that, when the work is dealt with in certain ways, authors and directors have the right to be identified as author of the work. In order for the right of attribution to be infringed, it is necessary to show that:

(i)   the author has not been properly identified;

(ii)   the work has been dealt with in circumstances under which attribution is required; and

(iii) none of the defences or exceptions applies.

2.2.1 Nature of the identification

For the attribution right to be infringed, it is necessary to show that the author has not been properly identified as an author. Merely thanking a person for 'preparing materials' was held not to have identified that person's authorship.[48] In order to be properly identified, the name of the author must appear in or on each copy of the work in a clear and reasonably prominent manner.[49] Where it is not appropriate for the name of the author to appear on each copy of the work, the name must appear in a manner that is likely to bring their identity to the notice of a person acquiring a copy of the work.[50] So long as the name becomes apparent during its use, there does not seem to be any need for the author to be named in a way that can be ascertained prior to acquisition of the copy.[51] Thus an author of a book might be named on the inside of the work. Where a performance, exhibition, showing, broadcast, or cable transmission is involved, the author has the right to be identified in a manner likely to bring their identity to the attention of a person seeing or hearing the communication. Where the relevant work is a building, the identification should be visible to persons entering or approaching the building.[52]

If, in asserting the right of attribution, the author specifies that a pseudonym, initials, or some other form of identification such as a symbol be used (as the musician

---

[43] See 491 Hansard (HL), 10 Dec. 1987, cols 346–56.   [44] CDPA 1988, s. 78(3)(a).

[45] CDPA 1988, s. 78(4)(c).   [46] CDPA 1988, s. 78(2)–(3).   [47] CDPA 1988, s. 78(4)(d).

[48] *Sawkins v. Hyperion Records* [2005] 1 *WLR* 3281.   [49] CDPA 1988, s. 77(7).

[50] CDPA 1988, s. 77(7)(a).

[51] Cf. Copinger, [11–20] (arguing that identification needs to be outwardly apparent).

[52] CDPA 1988, s. 77(7)(b).

Prince required between 1993 and 2000), then that form of identification should be adopted.[53] Otherwise, any reasonable form of identification may be used. It is not clear whether the attribution right gives rise to a right of anonymity, which may be valuable in raising public curiosity about the work and in protecting the author from vilification or criticism. However, it seems unlikely from the wording of the provisions that if an author were to make it clear that they wanted the work to be published anonymously, this would be treated as the particular form of identification that had to be used.

2.2.2 Circumstances under which attribution is required

The right to be identified as author or director of a work arises only when the work is dealt with in certain ways. While the particular circumstances in which the right arises vary depending upon the type of work in question, in all cases the right applies whether the act is carried out in relation to the whole work or a substantial part thereof.

An author of *literary or dramatic work* has the right to be identified whenever copies of the work are published commercially, or the work is performed in public or broadcast.[54] This means, for example, that the author of a play has the right to be named when copies of the play are sold in bookshops or the play is performed in public. Similarly, the writer of a film script has the right to be named when videos are sold to the public or the film is broadcast on television (but not, it seems, on rental copies).[55] The right applies equally to adaptations of the work—so the author of a French novel has the right to be named on copies of an English translation.

Songwriters are treated slightly differently. The author of the music or lyrics of a song has the right to be named on commercial publication of copies of the song—such as the issue of songbooks, sound recordings, or films containing a recording of the song. However, the right of attribution given to the author of a song does not extend to circumstances under which the song is performed in public or broadcast.[56] This limitation, often dubbed the 'disc jockey exception', was introduced so that DJs and broadcasters would not have to name the songwriters when songs are broadcast or played at clubs. It thus allows them to continue the current practice whereby only the name of the recording artist is mentioned.[57]

Where a right of attribution relates to an *artistic work*, the artist has the right to be identified where the work is published commercially, is exhibited in public, or where a visual image of it is broadcast or included in a cable transmission. If an artwork is filmed, the artist should be identified when copies of the film are issued to the public or if the film is shown in public. The 1988 Act also specifies that the creator of a building, sculpture, or work of artistic craftsmanship should be named where 'copies of a graphic work representing it, or of a photograph of it' are issued to the public.[58] The author of a work of architecture has the right to be identified on the building as constructed. If a series of buildings are made, however, the architect needs to be identified on only the first building to be constructed.

---

[53] CDPA 1988, s. 77(8).   [54] CDPA 1988, s. 77(7)(a).

[55] Although the practice of renting copies of films in plain packaging is common, this does not depend upon the absence of a right of attribution in relation to rental; in such cases, the director of a film, or the author of other works included therein, will usually be identified in the film credits.

[56] CDPA 1988, s. 77(2), (3).

[57] WPPT, Art. 5, confers moral rights on the performers of 'performances fixed in phonograms'. See Chapter 13, section 2.4, pp. 361–2.   [58] CDPA 1988, s. 77(4).

The director of a *film* has the right to be identified whenever the film is publicly shown, broadcast, or included in a cable service. The director also has the right to be named on copies of the film, but not (it seems) where the films are rented.

2.2.3 Exceptions

A number of exceptions and qualifications are placed upon the scope of the right of attribution by the 1988 Act. The right of attribution is constrained by section 79(3), which provides that if the employer or copyright owner authorized reproduction, etc. of the work, then the right does not apply.[59] It has been suggested that this exception can be explained on the basis that, because an employer has paid for the creation of the work, it should have complete freedom to exploit it. It is also said that the employer should not be required to keep detailed records of who contributes to a collaborative work.[60] Insofar as the right of attribution plays a role in the establishment of an author's or artist's reputation, the link between authorship and livelihood is less important when the creator is employed.

The 1988 Act also provides that the right of attribution will not be infringed where the act in question amounts to fair dealing for the purpose of reporting current events by means of a sound recording, film, or broadcast.[61] The Act provides too that the attribution right is not infringed where the work is incidentally included in an artistic work, sound recording, film, or broadcast, .[62] Exceptions also exist where the work is used for the purposes of examinations, parliamentary or judicial proceedings, and government inquiries.[63] It should be noted that while section 30A permits use of a work for 'caricature, parody or pastiche' without requiring 'sufficient acknowledgement' (on the basis that this would undermine a parody), no exception is provided to the moral right of attribution, with the effect that, in practice, parodists will take a risk of acting unlawfully if they do not make the authorship of the parodied work clear.

Further exceptions to the right of attribution exist in relation to works that lie at the interface between design law and copyright law. The defences to infringement of copyright granted by section 51 (and formerly also section 52) of the 1988 Act also apply to infringement of the attribution right. Consequently, if a person makes an article to a design document, there is no need to name the author of the design.

2.2.4 Waiver

Finally, it should be noted that an author can waive their right of attribution.[64] Waiver of the right of attribution, which is relevant for activities such as 'ghostwriting', is discussed in more detail later in this chapter in the context of the integrity right.

---

[59] CDPA 1988, s. 79(3).   [60] Laddie et al., 661, [13.22].

[61] CDPA 1988, s. 79(4)(a). This corresponds with CDPA 1988, s. 30(2)–(3), which requires 'sufficient acknowledgement' in cases of fair dealing for reporting current events by other means, such as in newspapers. The effect is that the fair-dealing defences parallel the moral rights provisions: fair dealings for which acknowledgement is required, but not provided, are likely to be infringements of both the copyright and the author's moral right.

[62] CDPA 1988, s. 79(4)(b).

[63] CDPA 1988, s 79(4A) (as inserted by SI 2014/1372, Sch., para. 4). The right of attribution applies to cases that would not infringe copyright because they amount to cases of fair dealing for purposes of criticism or review. However, because a finding of fair dealing requires 'sufficient acknowledgement' of the author, most cases of fair dealing will not infringe the moral right of attribution. See also E. Adeney, *The Moral Rights of Authors and Performers: An International and Comparative Analysis* (2006), 401, [14.44].

[64] CDPA 1988, s. 87(2).

3 RIGHT TO OBJECT TO FALSE ATTRIBUTION

The right to object to false attribution is the oldest of the United Kingdom's statutory moral rights.[65] Re-enacted in section 84 of the CDPA 1988, this right is effectively the flip side of the attribution right: the right of attribution provides authors with the right to be named on works that they have created, whereas the right to object to false attribution provides individuals with the right *not* to be named on works that they have *not* created.[66] Unlike the right of attribution, the right to object to false attribution applies whether or not the claimant is an author. The right to object to false attribution applies to persons[67] wrongly named as the authors of literary, dramatic, musical, or artistic works, or as the directors of films.[68] The right of false attribution lasts for only 20 years after the death of the person who is falsely said to be the author.

The right is infringed by a person who issues copies of a work to the public, or exhibits in public an artistic work, on which there is a false attribution (rather than by the person who makes the false attribution). The right can also be infringed by a person who performs, broadcasts, or shows the work and who knows that the attribution is false. Section 84(5) also provides for infringement where certain commercial acts are done with the knowledge that the attribution is false.[69]

Whether a work has been attributed to the wrong person depends on 'the single meaning which the . . . work conveys to the notional reasonable reader'.[70] There is no need for the complainant to prove that the attribution actually caused them any damage.[71] Examples of situations in which the right has been violated include the attribution to a member of the public of a newspaper article written by a journalist, but based on conversations between the two,[72] and a newspaper parody of a politician's diaries (see Fig. 10.1).[73]

In another decision, an author's work was held to be falsely attributed when it was attributed to the author after having been substantially added to by another person

---

[65] CDPA 1988, s. 84(6), re-enacts CA 1956, s. 43, which, in turn, was an expansion to literary, dramatic, and musical works of the Fine Art Copyright Act 1862, s. 7(4): Gregory Committee, [225]; CDPA 1988, Sch. 1, para. 22.

[66] For discussion of whether the Berne Convention implicitly requires recognition of such a right, see Ricketson and Ginsburg, 601, [10.19] (suggesting that Berne does not cover the case in which an author is seeking to deny rather than establish their authorship).

[67] *Clark v. Associated Newspapers* [1998] 1 *All ER* 959, 964. According to Lightman J, at 965, the section confers a personal or civic right.

[68] The provision does not contain the usual exceptions for computer programs or computer-generated works, so that while the author of a program has no right to be named, a person who is not the author of a program has the right not to be named as its author.

[69] CDPA 1988, s. 84(5), (6) (possessing or dealing with a falsely attributed copy of the work in the course of business or, in the case of an artistic work, dealing with it in business as the unaltered work of the artist when in fact it was altered after leaving their possession, knowing or having reason to believe that there is false attribution).   [70] *Clark v. Associated Newspapers* [1998] 1 *All ER* 959, 968.

[71] Ibid., 965.

[72] *Moore v. News of the World* [1972] 1 *QB* 441 (finding false attribution in a newspaper article entitled 'How my love for the Saint turned sour by Dorothy Squires', written in the first person by journalist on basis of conversations with Squires). It is not altogether clear whether the work was falsely attributed because Squires had not written the words or because she had not spoken them. In light of the changes in the 1988 Act, which confer copyright on spoken words, it seems that a verbatim account of a speech by a journalist should not be treated as having been falsely attributed to the speaker.

[73] *Clark v. Associated Newspapers* [1998] 1 *All ER* 959, [1998] *RPC* 261.

On the historic day Tony Blair made his Commons debut as Prime Minister, Alan Clark found himself in the ignominious position of sitting on the Opposition benches. PETER BRADSHAW imagines how the great diarist would record the event

It's wonderful to be back in the old place

Tuesday 6th May
Albany
Well, the Tory political landscape is a smoking ruin.

But as the dawn comes up, and Blair's Messerschmitts drone away over the horizon, I am delighted to report that the smart shops and elegant terraces of Kensington and Chelsea are unscathed. The only vote I seem to have lost is that of Michael Winner, the film director, who cut up rather rough over my comments about his house in this Diary.

We are in a mess, though, and every revolting little BBC functionary and Guardian scribbler with a colleague or homosexual "partner" on the New Labour benches is gloating.

Little Major has mumbled something about the show being over and it being time to leave the stage. This apparently was a phrase he learned at his father's knee as the old boy, wearing smeared make-up and floppy-toed clown shoes, hid in his dressing room with the lights off while the angry audience demanded their money back.

We have now started a spastic "leadership contest", which has about as much political significance as the election of a refreshments secretary in a suburban golf club. Heseltine is *hors de combat*, and while he was delirious with pain-killers on his hospital bed, his lady wife Anne typed out his withdrawal statement, then gripped his writing hand and wrote out his signature underneath. I'm not sure how he took the news of his standing down.

Clarke is standing for the collaboration with Kohl faction, Michael Howard is running on his iron-fist-in-the-iron-glove ticket, apparently with fresh-faced, apple-cheeked young Hague as his supporter, an arrangement toasted over champagne earlier this evening.

No one seems to be begging *me* to stand.

◇   ◇   ◇

Wednesday 7th May
Albany
Morning
Hague has dumped.

His claque of admirers encouraged him to think of himself as the Young Pretender, and he is believing this publicity whole-heartedly. So the engagement is broken off.

Now Dorrell is courting the bore vote and Redwood's candidacy is gravely damaged by the support of The Times.

A complete shower. I am going to the Commons.

◇   ◇   ◇

House of Commons
Evening
Extraordinary.

In the Commons I saw what appeared to be a crocodile of schoolchildren in the Central Lobby, moving unimpeded into the Chamber. When I complained, someone explained that this was the New Labour intake, all polytechnic lecturers, media folk and trades union press officers, with their electronic pagers dutifully turned off, and the person at their head barking instructions was little Mandelson — although what *he* knows about Parliament could be written on the back of a stamp.

It is *marvellous* to be back in the House; I simply can't believe it has been five years, although it was *very* strange to see the sides reversed. I couldn't get used to the through-the-looking-glass effect — I felt dizzy and disorientated and had a slight nose bleed.

We were in opposition when I first arrived in '74, when Ted Heath was Leader and it was a disagreeable shock to see that he is *still here*, Sir Edward Heath, Father of the House, still pompous and slow-witted — visibly bridling when Gwyneth Dunwoody, in her speech proposing dear Betty Boothroyd as Speaker, called him "Mr" Heath.

Later I was strolling towards the Strangers Bar, whistling a lively air, when I came across a *very* pretty girl in tears. "What's the matter?" I asked. The dear little thing gulped and pouted and said: "It's my first day. I'm lost ... " I twinkled, like Alec d'Urberville. "Never mind," I said, proffering a hanky. "It's easy for a secretary to get lost on her first day." She turned on me, her beautiful eyes flashing angrily. "I am the New Labour Member for Watford!" she shouted, and ran off down the corridor.

But she still has my handkerchief — an excuse to get back in touch!

How have I existed out of this place?

Fig. 10.1 'Alan Clark's Secret Political Diary', *Evening Standard* (May 1997)

Source: Evening Standard

without the author's consent.[74] On this basis, it seems that a replica of a painting that included the signature of the original artist could be said to be falsely attributed, since the replica painting would not be solely made by the original artist.[75] In the case of artistic works, the right to object to false attribution is extended by a special provision to circumstances in which the work has been altered, even if that alteration amounts only to deletion of part of the work. This would be the case, for example, if a detail were to be cut from a broader canvas and sold as an unaltered original.[76] The right would also be infringed where a black-and-white drawing was colourized.[77]

The right to object to false attribution of authorship is supplemented by various non-statutory causes of action, such as the action for passing off or defamation. Under the former, a person can complain where a work is misrepresented as being by the claimant, when it is in fact the work of the defendant.[78] In *Ridge v. English Illustrated Magazine*,[79] the defendant published a story that they attributed to the plaintiff, a well-known author, which in fact had been written by a grocer's assistant from Bournemouth. The court instructed the jury to find the publication to be defamatory if 'anyone reading the story would think that plaintiff was a mere commonplace scribbler'.[80] The jury awarded £150 in damages.

4 RIGHT OF INTEGRITY

The right of integrity is one of the most important of the innovations in the CDPA 1988. The moral right of integrity lasts for the same time as the copyright in the relevant work. The right of integrity is the right to object to derogatory treatment of a work, or any part of it. The basis for this authorial prerogative is that the artist, through the act of creation, has embodied some element of their personality in the work, which ought to be protected from distortion or mutilation.[81] In some cases, this carries with it the corollary that the artist feels some degree of responsibility for the work.[82] The desire to protect the reputation of authors was also a factor used to support the right.

---

[74] *Noah v. Shuba* [1991] *FSR* 14 (finding no false attribution of 17 words added to passage extracted from the plaintiff's work, since these words did not constitute a work, but that there was false attribution of the extract as a whole as attributed solely to the plaintiff). In effect, the plaintiff succeeded in protecting his right to endorse the defendant's services, and thus this indicates a potential usefulness in the context of 'personality merchandising'.

[75] *Preston v. Raphael Tuck* [1926] *Ch* 667 (replica with no signature would not be falsely attributed).

[76] CDPA 1988, s. 84(6) (introduced in response to a complaint of this sort by the English painter Landseer). For discussion of the extent of such alterations, see *Carlton Illustrators v. Coleman* [1911] 1 *KB* 771 (alteration must be material in the sense that it might affect the credit and reputation of the artist).

[77] *Carlton Illustrators v. Coleman* [1911] 1 *KB* 771 (a case in which colour was taken to be a very important element).

[78] See Chapters 32–34. Passing off requires a claimant to demonstrate not merely a misrepresentation, but also the existence of goodwill and likelihood of damage. It is broader than s. 84 in that s. 84 relies on a single meaning, whereas a misrepresentation can be established in passing off in circumstances under which a substantial or large number of consumers are likely to be misled. See *Clark v. Associated Newspaper* [1998] 1 *All ER* 959. [79] [1911–16] *MacG CC* 91 (KB, with special jury).

[80] Ibid., 92. See also *Marengo v. Daily Sketch* (1948) 65 *RPC* 242 (a cartoonist known as 'KIM' succeeded in a passing off action against another cartoonist using the name 'KEM'); *Samuelson v. Producers Distributing* [1932] 1 *Ch* 201 (passing off by giving film similar title to play).

[81] A. Dietz, 'The Artist's Right of Integrity under Copyright Law' (1994) 25 *IIC* 177, 181. See also B. Ong, 'Why Moral Rights Matter: Recognising the Intrinsic Value of Integrity Rights' (2003) 26 *Colum JL & Arts* 297.

[82] This was the case, e.g., with Stanley Kubrick's reaction to copycat violence (and the resulting media coverage) that followed the release of the film that he directed, *A Clockwork Orange* (1971).

4.1 SUBSISTENCE OF THE RIGHT

As with the other moral rights recognized under the 1988 Act, the right of integrity is given to the author of a literary, dramatic, musical, or artistic work, and the director of a film.[83] It is not given to computer programs or to computer-generated works.[84] With respect to computer programs, the exclusion is justified on the basis that it might be necessary to alter, debug, improve, or modify a program to render it suitable to achieve its purpose. The integrity right does not apply to a work made for the purpose of reporting current events,[85] to publications in newspapers, or to collective works of reference such as encyclopaedias.[86] In the latter case, the relevant publishers were keen to retain their power to edit or otherwise alter any submissions without having to consult contributing authors.[87]

4.2 INFRINGEMENT OF THE RIGHT

In order for the right of integrity to be infringed, an author or director must be able to show that:

(i)   there has been a 'derogatory treatment' of the work;

(ii)   the work has been dealt with in circumstances under which the author is protected from derogatory treatment;

(iii) none of the exceptions apply; and

(iv)   the right has not been waived or the action consented to by the author.

4.2.1 Derogatory treatment

In order for an author or director to show that the right of integrity has been breached, it is necessary to show that there has been a 'derogatory treatment' of their work. Before looking at the meaning of 'derogatory', it is necessary to explore what the Act means when it refers to a 'treatment' of the work.

(i) *Treatment* 'Treatment' of a work means any 'addition to, deletion from, alteration to or adaptation of the work'.[88] The concept of the work that is employed here is that of an autonomous artefact, which is born out of, tied to, or related to neither other works, nor its environment. Moreover, the work has its own internal integrity or logic (a beginning, middle, and end; a foreground, middleground, and background; line, shade, and colour).[89] For a treatment of the work to take place, it seems that the defendant must interfere with the internal structure of the work.[90] This idea of treatment, it seems, would cover a situation such as that in *Noah v. Shuba*,[91] in which 17 words were added to the claimant

---

[83] CDPA 1988, s. 80(1). For such works created prior to 1 August 1989, see Sch. 1, para. 23(2)–(3) (the right applies except in the case of a film made before that date, and other works the author of which died before that date or the author of which had assigned the copyright before that date). Colourization of pre-1989 black-and-white films would not infringe the moral right of integrity. However, insofar as the film consists of photographs of which the director is the author, colourization might incur liability on the basis of 'false attribution' under CDPA 1988, s. 84(6): cf. *Carlton Illustrators v. Coleman* [1911] 1 *KB* 77 (on Fine Art Copyright Act 1862, s. 7). This last caveat would not apply to films made after 1956.

[84] CDPA 1988, s. 81(2).   [85] CDPA 1988, s. 81(3).   [86] CDPA 1988, s. 81(4).

[87] See Copinger, [26–70].   [88] CDPA 1988, s. 80(2)(a).

[89] *Pasterfield v. Denham* [1999] *FSR* 168, 180.

[90] No indication is given as to the degree of significance to be attached to changing the 'meaning' rather than the structure, sequence, and organization of the work: Laddie et al., 664, [13.28] (actual physical treatment not as important as message).   [91] [1991] *FSR* 14.

author's medical guide. It would also cover situations in which a portion of a painting was cut from its original canvas and exhibited, a song was chopped up and inserted into a megamix,[92] a drawing was reproduced in reduced size or recoloured,[93] or a black-and-white film was 'colourized'.[94] In these cases, the internal composition or structure of the work is changed.

The definition of treatment that is used in the United Kingdom is narrower than that which is employed in Article 6*bis* of the Berne Convention, which requires that the author be able to object to 'any . . . derogatory action' in relation to a work. The broader definition used in Berne seems to acknowledge that a treatment of a work can take place even though the composition or structure of the work is not altered. Importantly, it suggests that a treatment of a work can take place where the meaning and significance of the work is affected. It has been suggested, for example, that the mere act of placing a work in a new context, such as the hanging of a religiously inspired artistic work alongside a piece of erotic art, probably would not amount to a treatment of a work under UK law. It would, however, amount to a treatment of the work under the Berne Convention.[95]

In the absence of much case law, we can only speculate as to which of the following scenarios would be considered to be a 'treatment' under UK law: placing two written works side by side in a bound volume? Changing the title of a work? Placing a book in an offensive or vulgar dust jacket?[96] Placing a caption on the frame of a painting? Placing a caption beside a painting?[97] Placing a ribbon around the neck of a sculpture of a goose? Placing a sculpture designed for a particular location in a different location? Performing a song's lyrics to a different tune or adding different words to a song's music?[98] Performing a tragedy in such a manner that it seems like a farce?[99] Adding recordings of the claimant's music to a film of which they did not approve?[100] Interrupting a film for advertising breaks?[101]

---

[92] *Morrison v. Lightbond* [1993] *EMLR* 144.

[93] In *Tidy v. Trustees of the Natural History Museum* (1998) 39 *IPR* 501, 503, neither party disputed that a reduction was an alteration.

[94] *Huston v. Turner Entertainment* (1991) 23 *IIC* 702 (French *Cour de Cassation*) (injunction granted to prevent television broadcast of colourized version of film *The Asphalt Jungle*). See B. Edelman, 'Applicable Legislation Regarding the Exploitation of Colourized Films' (1992) 23 *IIC* 629; J. Ginsburg, 'Colors in Conflicts' (1988) 36 *J Copyright Soc'y USA* 810.

[95] See G. Davies and K. Garnett, *Moral Rights* (2nd edn, 2016), [8.023]; E. Adeney, *The Moral Rights of Authors and Performers: An International and Comparative Analysis* (2006), 406, [14.63] (referring to the 'treatment' concept as 'unexpectedly narrow' in that it does not cover 'non-transformational uses of the work, such as its use in a particular context'). Thus playing electro-industrial music to inmates of a prison in order to 'torture them' would not breach the integrity right: a scenario suggested by S. Michaels, 'For Torture Services: Band Bill US for Use of Music at Guantanamo', *The Guardian* (8 February 2014).

[96] *Mosely v. Staley Paul & Co.* [1917–23] *MacG CC* 341 (such action was held to be defamatory).

[97] *Pasterfield v. Denham* [1999] *FSR* 168, 180.

[98] In *Confetti Records v. Warner Music UK Ltd* [2003] *EMLR* (35) 790, the defendants had 'rapped' over the claimant's 'track' (which comprised an insistent instrumental beat accompanied by the vocal repetition of the word 'burning'). The defendant accepted that this was a treatment, but the judgment of Lewison J leaves unstated what was 'treated': the musical work by the addition of the rap, or the literary work comprising the repetition of a single word? A more thorough analysis would have been helpful.

[99] Ricketson and Ginsburg, 603, [10.22].

[100] *Shostakovich v. Twentieth-Century Fox Film Corp.* 80 *NYS (2d)* 575 (Supreme Court, 1948) (failed). Apparently, the claim was successful in France: *Société le Chant de Monde v. 20th Century Fox* (Cour d'appel, Paris, 13 January 1953) *DA* 1954 16 80, cited in R. Durie, 'Moral Rights and the English Business Community' [1991] *Ent L Rev* 40, 42.

[101] T. Collova, 'Les interruptions publicitaires lors de la diffusion de films à la télévision' (1990) 146 *RIDA* 124.

In these cases, the internal composition or structure of the work is changed. In *Harrison v. Harrison*,[102] Judge Fysh QC observed:

> 'Treatment' of a work is . . . a broad, general concept; *de minimis* acts apart, it implies a spectrum of possible acts carried out on a work, from the addition of say, a single word to a poem to the destruction of the entire work. Where does one draw the line otherwise?[103]

The types of activity that will be considered to be a 'treatment' are further restricted by the fact that treatment is defined to exclude translations of literary and dramatic works, and arrangements or transcriptions of musical works involving no more than a change of key or register.[104] It is unclear why moral rights are deemed to be inappropriate here. One rather implausible explanation is that such acts never affect the internal structural or composition of a work.[105] Another possible explanation is that these activities would amount to adaptations of the work and, as such, require the consent of the copyright owner.[106] However, it is clear that an inaccurate translation may have a negative impact upon an author of a literary work.[107] It may be that, in order to minimize the incompatibility between UK law and Article 6*bis*, the courts might treat an inaccurate or poor-quality translation as if it were not a 'translation' at all, thus falling outside the scope of the exclusion.[108]

(ii) *'Derogatory'* Once it has been shown that there has been a treatment of the work, it is then necessary to show that the treatment was 'derogatory'. Section 80(2)(b) of the 1988 Act states that a treatment is derogatory if it amounts to a 'distortion' or 'mutilation' of the work, or if it is otherwise prejudicial to the honour or reputation of the author.[109]

As yet there is little indication of what the 1988 Act means when it talks about the 'distortion' or 'mutilation' of a work.[110] In *Tidy v. Natural History Museum*, the submission that the treatment was a 'distortion' was treated as an alternative to the submission that it was 'otherwise prejudicial'.[111] The same approach was taken in *Delves-Broughton v. House of Harlot*,[112] in which the (then) Patents County Court found cropping of a photo to be a distortion and thus an infringement of the photographer's moral right, even though it was not prejudicial to the honour or reputation of the author (although it is worth noting that neither party had legal representation in the latter case, so it must be regarded as of limited authority). The more prevalent view however, is that, in order for a work to be distorted or mutilated, the action must be prejudicial to the honour or reputation of the author.[113]

---

[102] [2010] *EWPCC* 3, [2010] *FSR* (25) 604.   [103] Ibid., 620, [60].   [104] CDPA 1988, s. 80(2)(a).

[105] See G. Dworkin, 'Moral Rights and the Common Law Countries' (1994) 5 *AIPJ* 22, 22.

[106] See P. Goldstein, 'Adaptation Rights and Moral Rights in the UK, the US and the Federal Republic of Germany' (1983) 14 *IIC* 43.   [107] See, e.g., the French case of *Leonide Zorine v. Le Lucernaire* [1987] *ECC* 54.

[108] There is authority that suggests that a 'translation' must be accurate: *Wood v. Chart* (1870) *LR* 10 *Eq* 193, 205; *Lauri v. Renad* [1892] 3 *Ch* 402.   [109] CDPA 1988, s. 80(1), (2).

[110] In *Tidy v. Natural History Museum* (1998) 39 *IPR* 501, 503, it was accepted that a reproduction in reduced size is not a mutilation.   [111] Ibid., 504.

[112] [2012] *EWPCC* 29, [24] (Douglas Campbell QC).

[113] *Confetti Records v. Warner Music UK Ltd* [2003] *EMLR* (35) 790, [149]–[150]; *Pasterfield v. Denham* [1999] *FSR* 168, 182; E. Adeney, *The Moral Rights of Authors and Performers: An International and Comparative Analysis* (2006), 408–9; Laddie et al., 664, [13.27]; Copinger, [11–48]; Ricketson, [8.107] (otherwise concepts of distortion and mutilation could lead to problems because they appear to be 'highly subjective'). See also *Snow v. The Eaton Centre* (1982) 70 *CPR* (2d) 105 (Canada) ('I am satisfied that the ribbons do distort or modify the plaintiff's work and the plaintiff's concern that this will be prejudicial to his honour or reputation is reasonable under the circumstances'). If this is right, then it is possible that highly distorting treatments, such as parodies, which might not be prejudicial to the author's reputation, do not infringe the integrity right. An alternative view is that distortions and mutilations are to be treated as prejudicial per se and that prejudice need be proved only for lesser cases of 'treatment'. The two views largely depend on differing interpretations of the words 'or otherwise', but also reflect disagreement as to interpretation of the Berne Convention itself: see Ricketson and Ginsburg, 609–10, [10.32], but note Adeney's categorical view that the qualification that the act must have a prejudicial effect on the honour or reputation of the author applies to distortions and mutilations: E. Adeney, *The Moral Rights of Authors and Performers: An International and Comparative Analysis* (2006), [6.52], [14.72].

The question of what the phrase 'prejudicial to honour and reputation' means was considered in the Canadian case *Snow v. The Eaton Centre*.[114] Michael Snow, a sculptor of international repute, created a work entitled *Flight-Stop*, which he sold to a shopping complex in Toronto called the Eaton Centre. The work comprised 60 geese flying in formation. The Eaton Centre tied ribbons around the necks of the geese as a Christmas decoration. Snow argued that this was prejudicial to his honour and reputation (the Canadian Copyright Act being in similar terms to the British 1988 Act). Snow was adamant that his naturalistic composition was made to look ridiculous by the addition of the red ribbons, which he likened to the addition of earrings to the Venus de Milo. Snow's views were shared by a number of well-respected artists and experts. Although the Eaton Centre produced another artist to deny the claim, the Ontario High Court ruled for Snow and ordered that the ribbons be removed. In so doing, the Court indicated that, so long as it was not irrational, the author's word on the matter would be sufficient. More specifically, O'Brien J said that the words 'prejudicial to honour and reputation' involved a certain subjective element or judgement on the part of the author, so long as it was reasonably arrived at.

In ascertaining what is meant by the phrase 'prejudicial to the honour or reputation of the author', as used in the 1988 Act, British courts have shown little inclination to follow the emphasis in the *Snow* case. In *Tidy v. Trustees of the Natural History Museum*,[115] the cartoonist Bill Tidy gave the gallery of the Natural History Museum the right to exhibit a series of black-and-white cartoons of dinosaurs that he had drawn. Tidy claimed that his right to integrity in the drawings had been violated when, in putting the cartoons in a book, the gallery reduced the size of the cartoons from 420 mm × 297 mm to 67 mm × 42 mm and added coloured backgrounds to the black-and-white originals. Tidy complained that the reduced cartoons had less visual impact, that the captions were unreadable, and that the process led to the inference that he had not bothered to redraw the cartoons so as to ensure that they were suitable for publication in a book. In the High Court, Rattee J refused Tidy's application for summary judgment for breach of his right of integrity, explaining that he was far from satisfied that the reductions amounted to a distortion of the drawings. The judge also suggested that, in order to find that the gallery's treatment of the cartoons was prejudicial to Tidy's honour, it was necessary to have evidence as to how the public perceived the defendant's acts. Referring to *Snow*, Rattee J said that he would have to be satisfied that the view of the artist was one that is reasonably held, which 'inevitably involves the application of an objective test of reasonableness'.[116] Without further evidence, Rattee J said that he could not see how he could draw such a conclusion.

A county court judge has recently gone further and argued that, for a treatment to be derogatory:

> ... what the plaintiff must establish is that the treatment accorded to his work is either a distortion or a mutilation that prejudices his honour or reputation as an artist. It is not sufficient that the author is himself aggrieved by what has occurred.[117]

Applying that test, the judge took the view that certain colour variations between the original and the artwork in question (the design of a brochure), the omission of trivial matter, and the reduction in size were not derogatory. The judge added that while the changes to peripheral matters were of the kind that 'could well be the subject of a Spot the Difference competition in a child's comic', it would be wrong to elevate such differences to a 'derogatory treatment'.[118]

---

[114] (1982) 70 *CPR* (2d) 105 (Canada).
[115] [1996] *EIPR* D–86; (1998) 39 *IPR* 501 (reductions of cartoons). See also Laddie et al., 666, [13.30] (court unlikely to treat author's own reaction as determinative).
[116] *Tidy v. Trustees of the Natural History Museum* [1996] *EIPR* D–86, (1998) 39 *IPR* 501.
[117] *Pasterfield v. Denham* [1999] *FSR* 168, 182.   [118] Ibid., 182.

In a third UK case, *Confetti Records v. Warner Music UK Ltd*,[119] Lewison J held that the claimant, Andrew Alcee (a member of the 'Ant'ill Mob'), had not made out a sufficient case for a finding of derogatory treatment where his garage track 'Burnin', which comprised an insistent instrumental beat accompanied by the vocal repetition of the word 'burning', had been superimposed with a rap by another garage act, 'The Heartless Crew' (the words of which were difficult to make out). The defendant accepted that this was a treatment, so the crucial issue was whether it was derogatory. The claimant had argued that it was, first, because the rap contained references to violence and drugs, by using phrases such as 'mish mish man', 'shizzle [or sizzle] my nizzle', and 'string dem up one by one', which was, according to the claimant, an 'invitation to lynching'. Alternatively, it was argued that the rap affected the 'coherence of the original work'. Lewison J rejected the claimant's argument. First, he stated that the fact that the words were difficult to decipher militated against them being derogatory. Second, he noted that the meaning of the words, which he described as being 'in a foreign language', could be determined only by way of expert evidence and no such evidence had been offered. Third, Lewison J took the view that 'string dem up' was not necessarily an 'invitation to lynching' and could be heard as merely advocating the return of capital punishment. Most importantly, however, he rejected the claimant's argument because the claimant had failed to provide evidence of his honour or reputation. In the absence of such evidence, even by the complainant himself, the judge was not prepared to infer prejudice. Lewison J was confirmed in this view by the fact that the Ant'ill Mob itself utilized the imagery of gangsters. As regards the claim based upon the effect of the rap on the coherence of the song, Lewison J seems to have been strongly influenced by indications that the song was written as a background for rapping and that the Ant'ill Mob's own mixes added rapping over the whole track.

Despite these decisions, it is still unclear how derogatory treatment will be construed in the United Kingdom. In particular, there is still some uncertainty as to whether the question of whether a treatment is prejudicial to the honour or reputation of an author is to be judged from an objective or subjective standpoint. Under UK law, one would expect that the notion of reputation used in this context would be similar to that which is employed in defamation law.[120] If this were the case, one would expect that the question of whether or not conduct was prejudicial to an author's reputation should be judged from the viewpoint of right-thinking members of society (that is, objectively).

While 'reputation' is a familiar concept in British law, the same cannot be said for 'honour'. If 'honour' is taken to refer to what a person thinks of themselves (and is thus similar to the Roman law concept of *dignitas*), it would seem that prejudice to honour might well involve a strong subjective element.[121] This distinction might be important where a defendant parodies the claimant's work in such a way that a member of the public would not believe the parody to be the claimant's work, so would be unlikely to find that the claimant's reputation was harmed.[122] Nonetheless, the claimant might feel offended.

4.2.2 Circumstances under which the author is protected from derogatory treatment

The right of an author or a director to object to, or prevent, the derogatory treatment of their work arises only when the work or copies thereof are dealt with in certain ways (section 80). While these acts vary according to the category of work involved, basically they arise where someone communicates, disseminates, or otherwise renders the derogatory

---

[119] [2003] *EMLR* (35) 790.

[120] Ricketson, [8.110]; Ricketson and Ginsburg, 592–3, [10.09], 594–6, [10.11], 606, [10.27] (explaining that these terms were preferred to the wider concept of 'moral or spiritual interest of the author').

[121] Laddie et al., 666, [13.30] (honour refers to integrity as a human being); Ricketson and Ginsburg, 606, [10.27].   [122] Copinger, [11–51].

treatment available *to the public*. As a result of this requirement, the right to integrity is not a right to prevent destruction of the work itself.[123]

In relation to *literary, dramatic, and musical works*, the right to object to derogatory treatment may be invoked when a derogatory treatment of the work is published commercially, performed in public, or communicated to the public. It is also triggered when copies of a film or sound recording embodying the derogatory treatment are issued to the public.[124] In turn, with an *artistic work*, the right may be invoked against a person who publishes commercially or exhibits in public a derogatory treatment of the work. The right is also triggered where someone communicates to or shows in public a film including a visual image of a derogatory treatment of the work.[125] Further acts are specified in relation to works of architecture, sculpture, and works of artistic craftsmanship.[126] In relation to *films*, the right of integrity is infringed whenever a derogatory treatment of the film is shown in or communicated to the public, or when copies of a derogatory treatment of the film are issued to the public.[127]

In addition, it should be observed that certain acts may amount to a secondary infringement of the right of integrity.[128] This will occur where, in the course of business, a person possesses, sells or lets for hire, offers or exposes for sale or hire, exhibits in public, or distributes an article that they know or have reason to know is an infringing article. In this context, an 'infringing article' means a work or a copy of a work that has been subjected to a derogatory treatment and has been, or is likely to be, the subject of any of the infringing acts in section 80. Secondary infringement takes place only if the dealing prejudicially affects the honour or reputation of the author. If the treatment itself is derogatory, it seems likely that the dissemination of the treatment will prejudice the honour or reputation of the author.

4.2.3 Exceptions and defences

A number of exceptions are placed upon the right of integrity by the 1988 Act. It is notable that there are no defences for fair dealing or for the design–copyright interface. Some commentators have therefore suggested that the defences are 'unduly narrow'.[129] In particular, objection is made that there is no transformative use exception, for example, relating to parody.[130] Many other legal systems subject the moral right of integrity to a 'reasonableness' defence.[131]

In the case of works created by employees,[132] the right of integrity does not apply to anything done by or with the authority of the copyright owner except in two particular

---

[123] Such a right has been accepted in the US Visual Artists Rights Act of 1990. At the Brussels Revision of Berne, one of the *voeux* adopted said that countries should introduce such a prohibition: see Ricketson and Ginsburg, 605, [10.26].

[124] CDPA 1988, s. 80(3)(a), (b). These are identical to the occasions on which an author has a right to be identified under CDPA 1988, s. 77(2); no differentiation is made for songs as in CDPA 1988, s. 77(3).

[125] CDPA 1988, s. 80(4)(a).   [126] CDPA 1988, s. 80(4)(c).   [127] CDPA 1988, s. 80(6).

[128] CDPA 1988, s. 83.   [129] Laddie et al., 674, [13.42].

[130] Many parodies might be said not to prejudice the honour or reputation of the author, because the audience would understand that the parodic variation had been created by a third party. Prejudice caused to an author from the critical quality of the parody is, strictly speaking, not relevant to infringement of the right, which protects only against prejudice that results from the treatment being thought to be the work of the author. The proposed new parody exception in CDPA 1988, s. 30A, applies only to economic rights. Even if an author is able to identify relevant prejudice, resort could be made by the defendant parodist to freedom of expression norms (under Art. 10 ECHR).

[131] Australia, Copyright Act 1968, s. 195AS; Israel Copyright Act 2007, s. 50. Under US law, 'fair use' operates as a defence to an action for infringement of the artists' moral rights recognized under the US Visual Artists Rights Act.

[132] CDPA 1988, s. 82. The same rules apply to works in which Crown or parliamentary copyright subsist and works in which copyright originally vested in an international organization under CDPA 1988, s. 168.

situations.[133] The general rule, then, is that an employer can deal publicly with derogatory treatments of an employee's work. In these circumstances, the authorial prerogative gives way to the demands of the employer for control.[134] This means, for example, that artists who work for a design firm will not be able to use their right of integrity where their artworks are modified either by their employer or by other employees. Similarly, an employee who drafts a report will not be able to restrain publication of a version that is rewritten on behalf of the employer.

The exceptions to this general position relate to circumstances in which the author/employee has been, or is to be, identified. Although the law privileges the needs of the employer and the copyright holder, those needs do not extend as far as continuing to name the employee where the work has been modified. Consequently:

> The right . . . does not apply to anything done in relation to such a work by or with the authority of the copyright owner unless the author or director—
>
> (a) is identified at the time of the relevant act, or
>
> (b) has previously been identified in or on published copies of the work . . . [135]

However, even in these cases, the right of integrity is not infringed if there is 'sufficient disclaimer'—that is, if there is a clear and reasonably prominent indication that the work has been subjected to treatment to which the author or director has not consented.[136]

There are also special defences to infringement of the moral right of integrity. In particular, the right is not infringed by anything done for the purpose of avoiding the commission of an offence (such as under the Obscene Publications Act 1959 or the Public Order Act 1986), complying with a duty imposed by or under an enactment, or (in the case of the BBC), 'avoiding the inclusion in a programme broadcast by them of anything which offends against good taste or decency or which is likely to encourage or incite crime or to lead to disorder or to be offensive to public feeling'.[137] In the case of a work of architecture, the right is limited. Where an architect is identified on a building that is subject to derogatory treatment, the architect is given the right to have their identification as architect removed from the building.[138]

4.2.4 Waiver

Although the moral right of integrity, like the other moral rights, cannot be assigned, section 87 of the 1988 Act ensures that they can be waived by way of agreement in writing. Such a waiver can be specific or general, and relate to existing or future works. It has been said that most 'objective observers would acknowledge that such wide waiver provisions, both in theory and in practice, erode significantly, indeed drive a coach and horses through the moral rights provisions'.[139] This is because the industries that exploit copyright works tend to oblige authors and artists to enter standard-form contracts that require them to waive the integrity rights. Even the requirement that waiver be in writing, which provides authors with some residual protection, is compromised by section 87(3), which states that the general law of contract and estoppel applies to informal waiver.

---

[133] The provision refers to the circumstance under which works vested in the director's employer by virtue of CDPA 1988, s. 9(2)(a). The Rel. Rights Regs amended the provisions on film authorship and ownership without altering the reference in CDPA 1988, s. 82(1)(a).

[134] See G. Dworkin, 'Moral Rights and the Common Law Countries' (1994) 5 *AIPJ* 5, 27.

[135] CDPA 1988, s. 82(2).   [136] CDPA 1988, s. 178.   [137] CDPA 1988, s. 81(6).

[138] CDPA 1988, s. 80(5).

[139] G. Dworkin, 'Moral Rights and the Common Law Countries' (1994) 5 *AIPJ* 5, 28; R. Durie, 'Moral Rights and the English Business Community' [1990] *Ent L Rev* 40, 48, calls this 'the greatest compromise in the Act'.

4.3 ALTERNATIVE AND RELATED FORMS OF RELIEF

If an argument based upon the moral right of integrity fails (or is dubious), an author may fall back on protection under common law or contract.[140] If a work is presented as being that of the author, but has been substantially altered, that representation could be defamatory. Thus, in *Humphries v. Thompson*,[141] a newspaper that serialized a story, but changed the names of the characters and omitted and added other text, was found by the jury to have defamed the author by damaging her literary reputation. Similarly, in *Archbold v. Sweet*,[142] an author successfully claimed that his reputation had been injured by the publication of a further edition of his work that contained a number of errors. The new edition would have been understood by the public to have been prepared by the author.[143]

Similarly, there are many situations in which an author may be able to rely on contract rather than moral rights to object to derogatory treatment of their work. In *Frisby v. BBC*,[144] the claimant had written a play for the BBC and the BBC had deleted the line 'my friend Sylv told me it was safe standing up . . .' on the ground that it was indecent.[145] The complex contractual arrangement prohibited the BBC from making 'structural', as opposed to 'minor', alterations to the script. The court decided that the contract was a licence and considered whether the alteration was structural or minor. The claimant alleged that it was essential to, and even the climax of, the play; in contrast, the BBC claimed that it was a minor deletion. Goff J granted the injunction, saying that the author 'prima facie would appear to be the best judge' of the significance of the line.[146]

4.4 THE FUTURE: HARMONIZATION

The existing directives have steered clear of moral rights.[147] Nonetheless, one would have thought that, however politically difficult it may seem, there would be clear justification (in terms of the internal market) for activity in this sphere.[148]

---

[140] For a general review of the common law analogues to moral rights, see G. Dworkin, 'Moral Rights: The Shape of Things to Come' [1986] *EIPR* 329. [141] [1905–10] *MacG CC* 148.

[142] (1832) 5 *Car & P* 219, 172 *ER* 947. See also *Springfield v. Thame* (1903) 89 *LT* 242.

[143] See also *Ridge v. English Illustrated Magazine* [1911–16] *MacG CC* 91. [144] [1967] *Ch* 932.

[145] The defence under CDPA 1988, s. 81(6)(c), means that claimant in *Frisby* would still have to rely on contract. [146] *Frisby v. BBC* [1967] *Ch* 932, 951.

[147] Term Dir., Art. 9, Recital 20; Database Dir., Recital 28; Info. Soc. Dir., Recital 19 ('moral rights remain outside the scope of this Directive'). The *travaux* indicate attempts to introduce moral rights provisions, but a failure to reach any consensus: see, e.g., the European Parliament amendment in the Related Rights Directive, which became Art. 4B of the Amended Proposal. However, the right of attribution is recognized in EU law insofar as the operation of a number of exceptions are conditioned on attribution: Database Dir., Art. 6(2) ('as long as the source is indicated'); Info. Soc. Dir., Art. 5(3)(a), (c), (d), (f) ('as long as the source, including the author's name, is indicated').

[148] Strowel et al., *Moral Rights in the Context of the Exploitation of Works through Digital Technology* (1990) (reviewing national laws and finding substantial differences in the detail of the laws of member states). Note M. Walter, 'Updating and Consolidation of the *Acquis*: The Future of European Copyright', Report of the Commission Meeting at Santiago de Compostela, June 2002 (proposing harmonization of moral rights). Cf. IViR, *Recasting Copyright*, 220, [7.3] (suggesting that, even with a European copyright code, moral rights might be left to member states).

11

EXPLOITATION AND USE OF COPYRIGHT

1 INTRODUCTION

As we saw in Chapter 6, copyright law confers on the first owner of copyright certain exclusive rights over the exploitation of the work. These rights are capable of being exploited in a number of ways. Most obviously, the rights enable copyright owners to control the sale of both the original work and copies of the work. By selling copies of the work at an appropriate price, copyright owners can ensure that they reap a reward sufficient to cover the costs of producing the work. This form of exploitation is most important where the market for the work is limited and the owner can easily be linked to a purchaser, such as with sales of limited editions of engravings or prints by artists.

If copyright law were to give the author only the right to exploit the work, its economic usefulness would be limited. While there has been a rise in self-publishing, and a reduction in the cost of selling works (particularly online), it remains the case that relatively few authors have the financial ability, economic acumen, or the willingness to print and sell their own works. Consequently, the law treats copyright as a form of personal property that can be exploited in a number of ways, most importantly by assignment or licence.[1] This enables copyright to be transferred to those who can exploit it more profitably. Where this occurs, the terms of the transfer agreement will determine how the profits are to be distributed. As we will see, such transfers are often arranged in advance of the creation of a work, for example where an author enters into a publishing contract prior to writing a book. Moreover, since some works can be exploited in a variety of ways, there may be many assignments, licences, and sub-licences. With new forms of exploitation, the web of transactions is becoming ever more complex.

One of the characteristics of the intangible property protected by copyright is that it has the potential to be used by a range of different people at the same time. For example, a sound recording can be played in numerous public places (such as pubs, shops, and clubs) simultaneously. As works are increasingly exploited in this manner, the role of licensing in exploitation becomes ever more important. In some situations, the copyright owner

---

[1] CDPA 1988, ss 1 and 90(1).

will be able to license the use of the work by the customer directly (for example where sale of software on a DVD includes a licence to make the immaterial copies necessary to run the program). In other cases, owner–user relations are mediated by an agency or collective management systems.

In this chapter, we look at the ways in which copyright can be exploited or transferred. After exploring the most important forms of exploitation—namely, assignment and licensing[2]—we consider the transfer of copyright in the case of mortgages, bankruptcy, or death. In turn, we examine situations in which the rights may be exploited by way of compulsory licence. We also consider briefly techniques for exploiting works that rely on the use of technological protection measures, techniques that are becoming increasingly important in the digital environment. (These are examined in detail in Chapter 13.) Finally, we look to the important role that collecting societies play in copyright exploitation.

Before doing so, it is important to note that assignment, licence, or other transaction in relation to copyright is effective only if the purported assignor was able to enter the transaction. Consequently, it is important to ensure that the person entering the transaction is the owner, or is appropriately authorized by the owner.[3] In this respect, it should be noted that where there are joint proprietors, all of them must consent to any transaction.[4] Particular difficulties may arise in relation to transactions made by minors who are creators. These are inviolable only if made for the benefit of the minor. If not so made, on reaching majority the minor can have such a transaction set aside.[5]

2 ASSIGNMENT

An assignment is a transfer of ownership of the copyright. As a result of an assignment, assignees stand in the shoes of the assignor and are entitled to deal with the copyright as they please. Although an assignment may be for payment of a royalty (as well as for a fixed sum), the nature of the assignment means that if the assignee transfers the copyright to a third party, the transferee takes free of the personal agreement to pay royalties.[6]

It is not necessary that all of the copyright be assigned.[7] In contrast with other types of property, where the tendency is to simplify transfers by limiting the ways in which the rights can be divided up, copyright law takes a liberal view of what may be assigned. In particular, copyright allows partial assignments by reference to 'times, territories and classes of conduct'.[8] For example, an agreement to write a book might include an exclusive grant of all rights. In turn, the publisher might parcel out the exploitation of the work by way of hardback, paperback, newspaper serialization, audiotape, reprography, electronic distribution, dramatization, and translation, as well as by being filmed.[9] Restrictions that

---

[2] UK IPO, *Copyright Works: Seeking the Lost* (2014), 1 ('The UK's copyright system is founded on the principle of licensing').   [3] *Beloff v. Pressdram* [1973] *RPC* 765.

[4] CDPA, s 173; also see *Powell v. Head* (1879) 12 *Ch D* 686.

[5] *Chaplin v. Frewin (Publishers)* [1966] *Ch* 71.

[6] *Barker v. Stickney* [1919] 1 *KB* 121 (royalty clause not enforceable against subsequent assignees, but only on the basis of contract against the initial assignee). See J. Adams, '*Barker v. Stickney* Revisited' [1998] *IPQ* 113; Copinger, [5–80].   [7] CDPA 1988, s. 90(2).

[8] *Kervan Trading v. Aktas* (1987) 8 *IPR* 583, 587.

[9] See further Copinger, [26.13]–[26.18]. For consideration of the limits of such parcelling, see Copinger, [5.97] *ff*.

are geographical in nature are subject to EU rules, so that agreements that are intended to divide up the internal market will be prohibited.[10]

In order for an assignment to be valid, it must be in writing and signed by or on behalf of the assignor. It has been held that sufficient writing might be provided by an invoice or receipt.[11] The assignment should identify the work concerned with sufficient clarity that it can be ascertained, although the courts have admitted oral ('parol') evidence to assist in the process of identification.[12] No special form of words is required, so a transfer of 'all of the partnership assets' will include a transfer of any copyright owned by the partnership.[13] Assignment of copyright is a distinct legal transaction and is not effected by mere sale or transfer of the thing itself.[14] Thus if a person sells an original painting or manuscript, this (of itself) transfers only the personal property right in the chattel; the copyright remains with its owner.[15] If a vendor wishes to transfer the copyright as well as the personal property in the chattel, this should be done explicitly.

Where an assignment is made orally, this will be ineffective *at law*. However, the general equitable rule that treats a failed attempt at a legal assignment as an oral contract to assign the interest will usually apply to attempted assignments of copyright. So long as there is valuable consideration, an oral contract of this nature will be specifically enforceable.[16] Where this occurs, a prospective assignee will be treated as the immediate equitable owner.[17] While such an equitable owner may commence an action against an infringer and secure interlocutory relief, the legal owner needs to be joined as a party before final relief can be secured.[18]

A prospective copyright owner (usually an author) can also make assignments of future copyright—that is, they can assign the copyright in works not in existence at the time of the agreement.[19] This will be useful, for example, where a painting is commissioned, or where a music publishing agreement is entered into before a songwriter creates the songs. However, it seems that the assignment of future copyright operates only where the agreement is for valuable consideration, since it is only in these circumstances that the assignee would be 'entitled as against the whole world'.[20]

There is no form of registration for assignments.[21] Priority is determined by reference to rules as to 'first in time' and bona fide purchase. In the case of legal assignments, the first transfer in time has priority over claims deriving from subsequent purported transfers of the same rights. Assignments effective in equity will be defeated only at the hands of a later bona fide purchaser for value without notice of the earlier assignment ('equity's darling').

---

[10] *IHT International Heiztechnik v. Ideal-Standard*, Case C-9/93 [1994] 1 *ECR* I–2789. Note also Proposal for a Regulation of the European Parliament and the Council addressing geo-blocking and other forms of discrimination based on customers' nationality, place of residence or place of establishment within the internal market and amending Regulation (EC) No 2006/2004 and Directive 2009/22/EC, COM(2016) 289 final, Art. 6. It seems that geographical restrictions may not be imposed so as to subdivide the United Kingdom: Copinger, [5.104]. Cf. *British Actors Film Co. v. Glover* [1918] 1 *KB* 299.

[11] *Savoury v. World of Golf* [1914] 2 *Ch* 566.

[12] Ibid.; *Batjac Productions v. Simitar Entertainment* [1996] *FSR* 139, 146–7.

[13] *Murray v. King* [1986] *FSR* 116, 124, 128, 130, 134–5 (FCA).   [14] Cf. CDPA 1988, ss 93 and 56.

[15] *Pope v Curl* (1741) 2 Atk 341, 26 ER 608; *Cooper v. Stephens* [1895] 1 *Ch* 567.

[16] *Western Front v. Vestron* [1987] *FSR* 66, 78.

[17] *Wilson v. Weiss* (1995) 31 *IPR* 423; *Ironside v. HMAG* [1988] *RPC* 197.

[18] *Batjac Productions v. Simitar Entertainment* [1996] *FSR* 139, 146–7.

[19] CDPA 1988, s. 91(1) (reversing *PRS v. London Theatre of Varieties* [1924] *AC* 1).

[20] Laddie et al., 1008, [24.6].

[21] In some countries, there are official mechanisms to record assignments for evidential purposes: see Canadian Copyright Act, s. 57.

2.1 PRESUMED TRANSFERS

Although transfer of ownership of copyright (or its component rights) is usually governed by contract, an important exception exists in relation to film production agreements. Where a contract concerning film production is concluded between an author and a film producer, the author is presumed to have transferred their *rental* right to the film producer.[22] The presumption operates only in relation to authors of literary, dramatic, musical, and artistic works, and therefore does not apply to the director of a film. Moreover, the presumption does not apply to the author of a screenplay, dialogue, or music specifically created for and used in a film.[23] The presumption is important in relation to the incorporation of existing works in films, for example where the author of a novel agrees to their work being made into a film, or a musical composer agrees to their work being used in a soundtrack. The presumption can be rebutted by an agreement to the contrary, which it seems can be express or implied.

3 VOLUNTARY LICENCES

The powers conferred on the copyright owner are most commonly employed by the copyright owner giving licences to particular individuals permitting them to carry out specified activities. At a basic level, a licence is merely a permission to do an act that would otherwise be prohibited without the consent of the proprietor of the copyright.[24] A licence enables the licensee to use the work without infringing. So long as the use falls within the terms of the licence,[25] it gives the licensee an immunity from action by the copyright owner.

In contrast with an assignment (where the assignor relinquishes all interest in the copyright), the licensor retains an interest in the copyright. Indeed, no proprietary interest is passed under a licence,[26] although in most circumstances a licence is binding on successors in title of the original grantor of the licence.[27] While the essential nature of a licence is that it is a mere permission, copyright law has developed a sophisticated repertoire of ways in which a work might be licensed.

Licences may take many forms, from a once-off permission through to an exclusive licence. Licences may be limited geographically, temporally, and in relation to specific modes of exploitation of the copyright work. A licence, even if non-exclusive, may (if the parties so choose) grant the licensee a right of action against infringers where the infringing act was directly connected to the prior licensed act of the licensee.[28] For the most part,

---

[22] CDPA 1988, s. 93A, implementing Rel. Rights Dir., Art. 2(6); member states are also allowed to have presumptions for transfers of other rights, provided they are not irrebuttable: see *Luksan v. van der Let,* Case C-277/10 [2013] ECDR (5) 125. The Beijing Treaty on Audiovisual Performances, Art. 12 also makes permissive provision in relation to transfers. At the time of writing neither the European Union nor the United Kingdom are parties. [23] CDPA 1988, s. 93A(3).

[24] *British Actors Film Co. v. Glover* [1918] 1 *KB* 299; *Canon Kabushiki Kaisha v. Green Cartridge Co.* [1997] *AC* 728, 735.

[25] Where a licensee breaches the agreement, the question arises whether there is an action merely for breach of contract or for infringement of copyright: if the act is outside the scope of the licence, it is an infringement; if the breach relates to a condition precedent for the licence, the action will also infringe (*Miller v. Cecil* [1937] 2 *All ER* 464); moreover, if the breach is sufficiently serious to amount to a repudiation of the contract, this may be accepted by the copyright owner and an action will lie for infringement of copyright as regards subsequent acts. [26] *CBS v. Charmdale* [1980] *FSR* 289, 295.

[27] CDPA 1988, s. 90(4).

[28] CDPA 1988, s. 101A; the purpose of this provision was to enable subscription broadcasters to bring proceedings where their programmes were copied.

the terms of a voluntary licence are up to the parties to choose. As such, terms will vary with the needs, capacities, and wishes of the parties.

3.1 EXCLUSIVE LICENCES

Of the different forms of licence, perhaps the most significant is the 'exclusive licence'. An exclusive licence is an agreement according to which a copyright owner permits the licensee to use the copyright work. At the same time, the copyright owner also promises that they will not grant any other licences and will not exploit the work themselves. The legal consequence of this is that the licence confers a right in respect of the copyright work *to the exclusion of all others including the licensor*.[29] In some ways, it is the intangible property's equivalent of a 'lease'.[30]

While a bare licensee acquires the right not to be sued in relation to the acts set out in the licence, an exclusive licence confers on the licensee a procedural status that is equivalent to that of the proprietor.[31] One significant aspect of this status is that exclusive licensees can sue infringers without having to persuade the proprietor to take action on their behalf.[32] Section 101(1) of the Copyright, Designs and Patents Act 1988 (CDPA 1988) declares that an exclusive licensee has the same rights and remedies in respect of matters occurring after the grant of the licence as they would have if the licence had been an assignment.[33] An exclusive licensee is given the same rights as a copyright owner and therefore has the right to bring proceedings in respect of any infringement of the copyright after the date of the licence agreement. Indeed, an action can be brought by both the copyright owner and an exclusive licensee: special provisions dealing with this situation are set out in section 102. Exclusive licences of legal interests in copyright have to be in writing and signed by or on behalf of the assignor[34] if the licensee wishes to take advantage of their statutory entitlement to sue for infringement.[35] This is in contrast to a non-exclusive licence, which may be made orally or in writing, and might be contractual or gratuitous, express or implied.[36]

In practice, the grant of an exclusive licence can often be seen as equivalent to an assignment.[37] Consequently, publishers are often happy to be granted exclusive licences, rather than full assignments, by authors.[38] However, there are legal differences between an assignment and an exclusive licence. The first difference arises from the fact that an assignee becomes the copyright owner, whereas an exclusive licensee does not. One of the consequences of this is that the remedies available to the exclusive licensee are limited to those that arise in an action for breach of contract against the copyright owner.[39] The second difference is that the rights given to licensees are less certain and can be defeated

---

[29] Cf. *Sega Enterprises v. Galaxy Electronics* (1998) 39 *IPR* 577.

[30] D. Vaver, 'The Exclusive Licence in Copyright' (1995) 9 *IPJ* 163, 165.   [31] Copinger, [5.215].

[32] The copyright owner is made party to the proceedings, if necessary by joining as a defendant. But note that a mere licensee may be able to bring an action under CDPA 1988, s. 101A, if the infringing act was directly connected to a previous licensed act of the licensee, the licence is in writing signed by the copyright owners, and it expressly grants the right of action.

[33] However, the exclusive licensee cannot sue the copyright owner for infringement of copyright (although if the terms of the contract are breached, the copyright owner will be liable for breach of contract): *CBS v. Charmdale* [1980] *FSR* 289, 297; and *Rapid Steel v. Blankstone* (1907) 24 *RPC* 529, 541.

[34] CDPA 1988, s. 90(3).   [35] CDPA 1988, s. 101.   [36] *Godfrey v. Lees* [1995] *EMLR* 307.

[37] *R. Grigg v. Evans* [2003] *EWHC* 2914, [58]; *Chaplin v. Frewin* [1966] *Ch* 71, 93.

[38] The Publishers' Association Code of Practice on Author Contracts (1982, updated 1997 and 2010), [2] states that, in some fields of publishing such as trade publishing, an exclusive licence should be sufficient, but in other areas, it may be appropriate for the copyright to be vested in the publisher, to make it easier for the publisher to protect the work as a whole.   [39] *CBS v. Charmdale* [1980] *FSR* 289, 297.

at the hands of a bona fide purchaser for valuable consideration and without notice (actual or constructive) of the licence.[40] Third, an exclusive licensee may not always be able to grant a sub-licence or transfer the benefit of their licence to a third party.[41] Fourth, the rights of an exclusive licensee may be limited by implied terms.[42] Finally, a copyright owner who wishes to permit another to exploit a work can retain better protection by giving an exclusive licence.[43]

In some situations, it may be difficult to determine whether a copyright owner has assigned their copyright or merely granted an exclusive licence.[44] Whether a person is an exclusive licensee or an assignee is a matter of construction of the agreement according to the ordinary rules of contractual construction. The question to be answered is whether there is evidence from which an intention to assign can be inferred. The way in which the parties describe the arrangement will be influential, but not conclusive. Use of terms such as 'grant', 'sole', and 'exclusive rights', and provisions on 'retransfer' if the copyright is not exploited, might indicate an assignment.[45] However, these descriptions may be ignored if the tenor of the agreement suggests that, in substance, there is an exclusive licence.[46] Occasionally, the courts have treated provisions concerning 'royalties' as suggesting that the arrangement is an exclusive licence rather than an assignment.[47] But in all cases the court should beware of linguistic formalism and infer the intention from all of the circumstances of the case.[48]

3.2 CREATIVE COMMONS, FREE SOFTWARE, AND VIRAL LICENCES

While it has been extremely common hitherto for an author to grant an exclusive licence to an exploiter, such as a publishing company, since the end of the twentieth century there has been a rise in popularity of 'open access' modes of distributing works—that is, the use of standardized licences allowing for particular reuses of works by any member of the public.[49]

The first popular version of such a licence was the so-called 'General Public License' (GPL) developed for use in relation to computer programs.[50] Given the manner in which computer programs build on existing programs, it was immediately evident to a few of those involved that the need to obtain copyright permissions could become a significant impediment to software development. Richard Stallman of the Free Software Foundation conceived that one way in which to avoid this would to be to grant permission in advance allowing anyone to use and modify material, but to make it a condition

---

[40] CDPA 1988, s. 90(4).   [41] Publishing contracts are generally non-assignable.

[42] For example, in *Frisby v. BBC* [1967] *Ch* 932 (in the case of a licence, the courts will more readily imply a term limiting the right of the licensee to alter the work).

[43] *Barker v. Stickney* [1919] 1 *KB* 121.

[44] *Western Front v. Vestron* [1987] *FSR* 66, 75. Nevertheless, the Supreme Court of Canada has called the distinction between an assignment and an exclusive licence 'important and meaningful': *Euro-Excellence Inc v. Kraft Canada Inc* (2007) SCC 37, [85].

[45] *Jonathan Cape v. Consolidated Press* [1954] 3 *All ER* 253; *Messager v. BBC* [1929] *AC* 151; *British Actors Film Co. v. Glover* [1918] 1 *KB* 299, 308.   [46] *Messager v. BBC* [1929] *AC* 151.

[47] *Western Front v. Vestron* [1987] *FSR* 66, 75–6.   [48] Ibid., 76.

[49] S. Dusollier, 'Sharing Access to Intellectual Property through Private Ordering' (2007) 82 *Chi-Kent L Rev* 1391.

[50] See http://www.gnu.org. There are three versions of the GPL, the last from 2007. See M. O'Sullivan, 'The Pluralistic, Evolutionary, Quasi-Legal Role of the GNU General Public License in Free/Libre/Open Source Software' [2004] *EIPR* 340; T. Rychlicki, 'GPLv3: New Software Licence and New Axiology of Intellectual Property Law' [2008] *EIPR* 232.

Fig. 11.1 Logo of the Creative Commons movement

Source: Creative Commons, http://creativecommons.org

of use that subsequent developers make their software available on the same terms.[51] The GPL therefore has been said to be 'viral' in nature, in that those who take advantage of the licences must subject their own work to the same conditions.[52] Developers are able to obtain remuneration by selling individual pieces of software, rather than by extracting licence fees based on copyright. The GPL has proved to be an amazing success,[53] although doubts exist over the enforceability of 'viral' clauses.[54]

Following in the wake of the GPL, the 'Creative Commons' movement (see Fig. 11.1) has attempted to develop similar standard open licences for other types of work.[55] In so doing, the Creative Commons movement has been forced to take account of different national legal systems.

In contrast with the GPL, Creative Commons offers copyright owners a menu of licences: some allow reuse of a work only in unmodified form ('CC BY-ND'); some allow reuse only with attribution ('CC BY'); some allow reuse only for non-commercial purposes ('CC BY-NC'); and some attempt to impose a 'share-alike' condition on users ('CC BY-SA'). As a result, a copyright owner has considerable flexibility and the take-up of such licences has been very widespread.[56] Nevertheless, it should be observed that the most commonly adopted licence is the 'attribution, non-commercial, no derivative works' licence ('CC BY-NC-ND'), which confers only the freedom to duplicate, distribute, play,

---

[51] GPL (v.1) states that:

[Y]ou may modify your copy or copies of the Program or any portion of it, and copy and distribute such modifications . . . provided that you . . . cause the whole of any work that you distribute or publish, that in whole or in part contains the Program or any part thereof, either with or without modifications, to be licensed at no charge to all third parties under the terms of this General Public License.

[52] The characterization of such contracts as viral is attributed to M. J. Radin, 'Humans, Computers, and Binding Commitment' (2000) 75 *Indiana LJ* 1125. The term 'copyleft' is also frequently used to describe this feature of the GPL and other licences. Non-viral licences, such as Apache or MIT licences, are in contrast called 'permissive licences'.

[53] Although the GPL is a very popular licence, the most commonly used open source licence is now the (non-viral) MIT licence http://redmonk.com/sogrady/2017/01/13/the-state-of-open-source-licensing/.

[54] A. Guadamuz Gonzalez, 'Viral Contracts or Unenforceable Document: Contractual Validity of Copyleft Licences' [2004] *EIPR* 331; cf. G. Westkamp, 'The Limits of Open Source' [2008] *IPQ* 14.

[55] See http://creativecommons.org. See S. Dusollier, 'The Master's Tools v. the Master's House: Creative Commons v. Copyright' (2005) 29 *Colum Jl. & Arts* 271; M. Fox, T. Ciro, and N. Duncan, 'Creative Commons: An Alternative, Web-Based, Copyright System' (2005) *Ent L Rev* 111.

[56] A purely practical difficulty with the system is that many things (such as blogs or social media) are purportedly licensed under Creative Commons licences where the content provider is not the original creator or copyright owners. This can present problems as a person cannot subject another person to particular licence terms. So for example, re-posts or extracts from other materials on a blog may not be the blogger's to license.

or perform the work in an unmodified state, for non-commercial purposes and with attribution of authorship.[57]

While both the GPL and the Creative Commons licences have become very widely used, these initiatives have not escaped criticism, even from those who share similar ideological goals or who desire similar practical results. Professor Elkin-Koren, for example, has emphasized the dangerous effect of 'open licensing' as constituting informational goods as property and creators as owners.[58] In fact, because Creative Commons licences depend on the prior existence of property right, there are those who advocate the expansion of such rights, for example the extension of legal protection to non-original databases, so that such products can effectively come within the terms of creative commons share-alike licensing schemes. More practically, Professor Dusollier has called attention to a number of potential limitations to the effectiveness of viral contracts,[59] in order to remind those in the open-access movement and beyond of the remaining importance of public law. It has also been suggested that in many cases the licences are bare licences (rather than contractual licences) and so certain types of term would be unenforceable (such as indemnities) and the licences could be revoked at will leaving users to rely on estoppel.[60]

Others, more sympathetic to traditional avenues of copyright exploitation, have emphasized the dangers of ill-considered adoption of these licences by aspiring authors. While it may seem attractive for a young or naive author to adopt an easy-to-use Creative Commons licence at a time when many others seem to be so doing, it is by no means obvious that such a move is always in their best interests. Rather, only those with a clear idea as to how they will be able to turn a profit if their works become popular should throw away the mechanism that has traditionally secured rewards to successful writers or composers. From this perspective, Creative Commons licences are primarily useful tools for those who do not need remuneration *from copyright* (or at all).

The popularity of Creative Commons licences amongst British academics seems likely to be endangered, too, by their use as what are, in effect, compulsory publication standards, by Research Councils UK (RCUK). The 2013 RCUK policy requires that outputs of Council-funded research be published under CC BY licences, which expressly permit the making of derivatives and commercial use.[61] The RCUK Open Access policy was reviewed in 2014 by Professor Sir Robert Burgess,[62] including the use of CC-BY licences.[63] It was found that while those in science, technology, engineering and mathematics (STEM) subjects were largely content with using Creative Commons licences, many in

---

[57] A. Chander and M. Sunder, 'The Romance of the Public Domain' (2004) 92 *Cal L Rev* 1331, 1361–2.

[58] N. Elkin-Koren, 'What Contracts Cannot Do: The Limits of Private Ordering in Facilitating a Creative Commons' (2005) 74 *Fordham L Rev* 375, 398. The dependence of open access licensing on copyright was earlier emphasized by Dusollier—S. Dusollier, 'Open Source and Copyleft: Authorship Reconsidered' (2003) 26 *Colum JL & Arts* 281, 286–7—but she also argues that creative commons may bring about a shift in the notion of the author from the romantic author-as-owner who controls the meaning of a text, to the post-modern author as the 'founder of a discursivity': S. Dusollier, 'The Master's Tools v. the Master's House: Creative Commons v. Copyright' (2005) 29 *Colum JL & Arts* 271, 285–6.

[59] Dusollier emphasizes three limits: the definition as to when the viral effect occurs; the validity of the licence itself; and the compatibility of different licences. On the potential problems posed by revocation, see L. P. Loren, 'Building a Reliable Semicommons of Creative Works: Enforcement of Creative Commons Licenses and Limited Abandonment of Copyright' (2007) 14 *Geo Mason L Rev* 271.

[60] See P. Johnson, '"Dedicating" Copyright to the Public Domain' (2008) 71 *MLR* 587.

[61] See RCUK, *Policy on Open Access and Supporting Guidance* (2013), 7–8, available online at http://www.rcuk.ac.uk/documents/documents/rcukopenaccesspolicy-pdf/.

[62] RCUK, *Review of the Implementation of the RCUK Policy on Open Access* (March 2015), available at http://www.rcuk.ac.uk/documents/documents/openaccessreport-pdf/. [63] Ibid., 18–20.

other disciplines, in particular those in the Arts, Humanities, and Social Sciences (which includes law) remained unhappy for practical reasons. One objection, common among art historians, whose articles often contain illustrative images, is that the policy requires open licensing of their articles in a mutilated form whenever the images are subject to rights of third-parties. Another objection was that work could be used commercially or in ways, or for things, in respect of which the academic did not approve. The Burgess Review concluded that there should be further work on the policy to ensure there is no detrimental impact.

3.3 IMPLIED LICENCES

In certain circumstances, the court may see fit to imply a licence to use a copyright work.[64] However, for the most part, the courts have been reluctant to imply licences from the circumstances.[65] They have indicated that they will normally imply terms into a contract only in two situations: terms may be implied 'by law' where they are 'inherent in the nature of the contract'; and terms may be implied to fill gaps left in an agreement where it is necessary to provide 'business efficacy'.[66]

In relation to terms implied by law, the court is primarily concerned with whether the contract falls into a particular class. However, that is not to say that the express terms are not important. This is because they may indicate that the parties did not intend the normal incidents of a particular class of contract to apply. The classes subject to such implied terms are not closed and change with the necessities of the times. An Australian case has indicated that one such class of contracts concerns 'persons who prepared written material with the intention it should be used in a particular manner'.[67] The specific terms to be implied in this class then depend upon the 'particular purpose'. For example, where an architect provides a client with plans, the court might determine the purpose (and the extent of any licence) from the fee, when viewed in light of the standard professional fee scales operating.[68]

Where courts are implying terms for particular cases, they look at the existing express terms and the surrounding context. It has been said that, for a term to be implied, it must be reasonable and equitable, necessary to give business efficacy to the contract, obvious that it 'goes without saying', capable of clear expression, and must not contradict any express term of the contract.[69] In *Ray v. Classic FM*,[70] Lightman J found that an expert in

---

[64] It is unclear how far the legal rules applicable to licensing, hitherto assumed to be ones of national law, are in fact implicitly harmonized: Info. Soc Dir., Art. 4, for example, specifically refers to 'consent' in defining exhaustion, but in other respects the other harmonized rights are simply couched as rights to 'authorize' acts. Nevertheless, the CJEU may be tempted to define when an author or right holder 'gives consent'. In *Marc Soulier, Sara Doke v. Premier Ministre, Ministre de la Culture et de la Communication*, Case C-301/15, EU:C:2016:878, [37], the CJEU held that consent included implied consent, but that 'the circumstances in which implicit consent can be admitted must be strictly defined' and concluded that even implied consent must be 'informed', in the sense that the author knows of the intended use of the work or subject matter. Section 3.3 should be read with this in mind.

[65] *Philips Electronique v. BSB* [1995] *EMLR* 472, 481; *Cescinsky v. Routledge* [1916] 2 *KB* 325, 319.

[66] As to implying terms in contracts more generally, see *BP Refinery (Westernport) Pty Ltd v. President, Councillors and Ratepayers of the Shire of Hastings* (1977) 52 *ALJR* 20 confirmed and approved in *Marks and Spencer plc v. BNP Paribas Securities Services Trust Company (Jersey)* [2015] *UKSC* 72, [2016] *AC* 742, [18], [21].

[67] *Acohs v. RA Bashford Consulting* (1997) 37 *IPR* 542 (FCA), [5.2].

[68] *Blair v. Osborne & Tompkins* [1971] 2 *QB* 78; *Stovin-Bradford v. Volpoint Properties* [1971] 1 *Ch* 1007. Note that *Ray v. Classic FM* [1998] *FSR* 622 treats these cases as ones in which the terms are implied to give business efficacy to the agreement.

[69] *BP Refinery (Westernport) v. Hastings Shire Council* (1977) 16 *ALR* 363, 376 (Lord Simon of Glaisdale); approved in *Ray v. Classic FM* [1998] *FSR* 622.   [70] [1998] *FSR* 622.

music who had been engaged by a radio station to catalogue its musical recordings had copyright in the catalogues produced. While the terms of his consultancy were silent as to copyright, the court held that the expert had granted an implied licence to the radio station to do certain things with the catalogues. The scope of the licence was limited to use of the material for the purpose of broadcasting in the United Kingdom. This meant that the claimant's copyright was infringed where copies were made for the purpose of exploiting the database abroad.[71]

In less formal circumstances (particularly those involving consumers), the courts have tended to react flexibly in deciding the nature and extent of any licence. For example, it seems that sale of an article to a consumer usually carries with it a licence to repair that article,[72] and that sale of a knitting pattern might carry with it an implied licence to the effect that a person can make the pattern for domestic, but not commercial, purposes.[73] Where the licence is claimed by a competitor who could have entered formal contractual arrangements, but neglected to do so, the courts have been reluctant to imply a licence.[74]

4 MORTGAGES

Like other forms of property, copyrights may be mortgaged—that is, assigned as security for a debt. This can be a useful technique that enables copyright owners to raise funds. It has proved to be particularly common where a work is extremely expensive to create, as in the film industry.[75] In this context, a mortgage is achieved by way of an assignment of the copyright by the copyright owner to the mortgagee (lender). This is subject to a condition that the copyright will be reassigned to the mortgagor when the debt is repaid (or, as the law describes this, on 'redemption'). In addition, it is important that the assignment reserves for the mortgagor a right to continue selling copies of the work. This is probably best achieved by reservation of an exclusive licence.[76] Alternatively, copyright can be used as security by way of a charge. While, in these circumstances, there is no assignment, the chargee does gain certain rights over the copyright as security.[77] In the case of both forms of security, the transaction must be in writing and signed by the parties in order to be valid. A mortgage or charge by a company of its copyright must also be registered within 21 days of its creation with the Registrar of Companies,[78] if it is not to be void against the

---

[71] *Grisbrook v. MGN Ltd* [2010] *EWCA Civ* 1399 (interpreting a freelance photographer's oral licence as limited to publication in a newspaper, rather than to global delivery of them via back issues hosted on website); *Celebrity Pictures Ltd v. B. Hannah Ltd* [2012] *EWPCC* 32 (implied licence to use photographs in magazine).

[72] *Solar Thomson v. Barton* [1977] *RPC* 537, 560–1; *Canon Kabushiki Kaisha v. Green Cartridge Co.* [1997] *AC* 728, 735; cf. *Sony Entertainment Inc v. Owen* [2002] *EMLR* (34) 742, 747 (Jacob J holding that, because a licence is territorial, a licensee must prove that a Japanese licence to use a computer game extended to the United Kingdom).

[73] *Patricia Roberts v. Candiwear* [1980] *FSR* 352. It may be that the making of a garment from written instructions is not an infringement in the first place: *Lambretta Clothing v. Teddy Smith* [2003] *RPC* (41) 728, [78]–[79]; also see *Abraham Moon & Sons v. Thornber* [2013] *FSR* (17) 312, [99]. See Chapter 6, section 2.1, pp. 146–7.

[74] *Banier v. News Group* [1997] *FSR* 812; cf. *Express Newspapers v. News (UK)* [1990] *FSR* 359 (tit-for-tat defence).   [75] M. Henry, 'Mortgages and Charges over Films in the UK' [1992] *Ent L Rev* 115.

[76] On the importance and delicacy of the terms of the licence, see M. Antingham, 'Safe as Houses? Using Copyright Works as Security for Debt Finance' (1998) 78 *Copyright World* 31, 32.

[77] Copinger, [5–202], seems to suggest that such a charge is equitable. While there is no definitional provision equivalent to PA 1977, s. 130, there seems no reason why it should not be legal.

[78] Companies Act 2006, s. 859A.

liquidator or a creditor of the company.[79] A legal mortgagee has the powers of proprietor and is therefore able to sue infringers,[80] even though, as a matter of practice, the borrower is in a better position to police infringements.

'Securitization' is the name given to a further way of raising money from copyright. Typically, securitization involves selling tranches of (that is, defined periods of entitlement over) the rights to royalties accruing from bundles of copyrights, a well-known example being in relation to David Bowie's recordings. The reasons for creating these financial arrangements stem from the desire to exchange future possible income for immediate capital, which will facilitate reinvestment of that capital in new projects.[81]

5 TESTAMENTARY DISPOSITIONS

Because copyright is personal property, it is capable of passing on the death of the proprietor either by will or according to the rules applicable in cases of intestacy. In the case of the death of one co-proprietor, because they hold copyright as tenants in common (rather than as joint tenants), the share of the deceased co-owner passes along with the rest of their estate.[82] A presumption exists that where a work is unpublished and a bequest is made of a document or other material thing containing the work, the bequest is to be construed as including the copyright in the work, insofar as the testator was the owner of the copyright immediately before their death.[83]

6 BANKRUPTCY

On bankruptcy, copyright passes via the Official Receiver to the trustee in bankruptcy by operation of law.[84] Where a court appoints a receiver to sell assets, both the appointment and subsequent sales by the receiver will involve transfers 'by operation of law' and therefore need not comply with the formal requirements.[85] Where copyright has been assigned in return for a royalty and the assignor subsequently becomes insolvent, that right also vests in the bankrupt's trustee in bankruptcy.[86]

7 COMPULSORY LICENCES

In general, if copyright owners choose not to allow others to exploit their rights, then that is their prerogative.[87] However, in certain exceptional circumstances, the law will intervene to force the copyright owner to license the work and require the 'licensee' to pay a fee. The basis for such action varies, as do the conditions on which the law permits the copyright owner's wishes to be overridden. Provisions of this nature are called 'compulsory licences'. In jurisprudential terms, the grant of a compulsory licence converts

---

[79] Companies Act 2006, s. 859H.   [80] See Copinger, [5–201].
[81] See A. Wilkinson, 'Securitization in the Music Industry' (1998), 86 *Copyright World* 26.
[82] *Lauri v. Renad* [1892] 3 *Ch* 402, 412–13.
[83] CDPA 1988, s. 93 and Sch. 1, para. 30; cf. *Re Dickens* [1935] 1 *Ch* 267.   [84] Copinger, [5.138].
[85] *Murray v. King* [1986] *FSR* 116 (FCA), 124, 130, 137.   [86] *PRS v. Rowland* [1997] 3 *All ER* 336.
[87] *Oscar Bronner v. Mediaprint*, Case C-7/97 [1998] *ECR* I–7791, 7811 [AG-56].

a property rule into a liability rule.[88] Compulsory licences can arise either as a result of various provisions in the CDPA 1988 or through the general powers of the European Commission. We discuss these in turn.

7.1 COMPULSORY LICENCES IN THE UNITED KINGDOM

Compulsory licences are made available under British law in only a small number of specifically defined circumstances. One reason why so few non-voluntary licences exist in the United Kingdom is because the international standards to which the United Kingdom has committed itself are generally incompatible with compulsory licensing. Although two provisions of the Berne Convention explicitly permit the national legislature to grant such licences,[89] the United Kingdom no longer takes advantage of these provisions. As regards rights in phonograms, the Rome Convention intimates that compulsory licences may be imposed only as regards the broadcasting or communication to the public of phonograms.[90]

Another reason for the limited circumstances in which compulsory licences are available is that they are generally seen as unsatisfactory when compared with full property rights. This is because, in contrast to exclusive property rights, the existence and terms of compulsory licences require some administrative procedure, which is costly and time-consuming when compared to negotiations in the free market. Critics of the compulsory licence also complain that the value of a licence can only ever be determined accurately by negotiations in the marketplace. It is also argued that compulsory licences unfairly deprive the copyright holder of the most significant element of their rights—namely, the right to bargain.

There are no common characteristics that explain the circumstances in which compulsory licences are granted.[91] In some cases, they are granted in response to past practices of 'abuse', usually where that abuse either prevented the production of a product for which there was a clear demand, or where the evidence showed that the copyright holder had imposed unjustifiable restrictive conditions. This is true of the compulsory licence relating to the publication of television schedules,[92] which was introduced to end the practice by television companies of licensing only the publication of daily listings, so that they could reserve for their own subsidiaries the market for weekly guides.[93] After a Monopolies and Mergers Commission (MMC) report,[94] the Broadcasting Act 1990 introduced provisions entitling publishers, once certain conditions are satisfied, to reproduce that information.[95] On other occasions, compulsory licences are granted where changes in market conditions unduly strengthen the copyright owner's interest. This sort of consideration

---

[88] See further R. Merges, 'Contracting into Liability Rules: Intellectual Property Rights and Collective Rights Organizations' (1996) 84 *Cal L Rev* 1293.

[89] Berne, Arts 11*bis*(2) (aka the 'jukebox licence'), Art. 13 (aka the 'mechanical licence'). Berne, Art. 17, is not intended to permit any general system of compulsory licences, but to cover such things as the maintenance of public order and morality.　　　　　　　　　[90] Rome, Art. 12. Note also Rome, Art. 15(2).

[91] For a full review, see Copinger, ch. 28.　　　[92] Broadcasting Act 1990, ss 175, 176, and Sch. 17.

[93] *ITP v. Time Out* [1984] *FSR* 64.

[94] MMC, *The British Broadcasting Commission and Independent Television Publications: A Report on the Policies and Practices of the BBC and ITP of Limiting the Publication of Advance Programme Information* (Cmnd. 9614, 1995).

[95] *News Group Newspapers v. ITP* [1993] *RPC* 173. Note also, CDPA 1988, ss 135A–G, introduced by the Broadcasting Act 1990 following MMC, *Collective Licensing: A Report on Certain Practices in the Collective Licensing of Public Performances and Broadcasting Rights in Sound Recordings* (Cm. 530, 1988) and applied in *The Association of Independent Radio Companies v. Phonographic Performance* [1994] *RPC* 143.

explains the introduction of compulsory licences where copyright had lapsed, but has been revived by the Duration Regulations.[96] There are also rights to use a work, similar to a compulsory licence, where a work qualifies for protection after a third party had started using the work.[97]

7.2 COMPULSORY LICENCES ORDERED BY THE EUROPEAN COMMISSION

Compulsory licences may also be made available by the European Commission if a copyright owner is found to have violated Article 102 TFEU which prohibits the 'abuse' of a 'dominant position'.[98] *RTÉ and Independent Television Publications v. Commission* (known as the 'Magill' case)[99] involved a battle between an Irish broadcaster (RTÉ), which produced copyright-protected television listings, but only licensed them on a daily basis (in order to reserve to itself the market for weekly guides to its own programmes), and a person wishing to publish a comprehensive weekly guide. The Commission held this refusal to license the copyright to be an abuse of the dominant position of the broadcaster and ordered it to license the listings.[100] The Court of Justice affirmed the legality of the action by the Commission. The substantive basis of this power to intervene—which it should be noted is limited to exceptional circumstances—is discussed in Chapter 12.[101] As Microsoft discovered, failure to comply with a Commission decision that it should grant a licence can result in a very substantial fine.[102]

8   TECHNOLOGICAL PROTECTION MEASURES

As already mentioned, copyright works have traditionally been exploited by the manufacture and sale of duplicated copies (where the processes of manufacturing and distribution have been controlled by the copyright owner). In light of the emergence of digital communication technologies and digital reproduction, many copyright owners are concerned that continued use of such a traditional model of exploitation will expose them to undue levels of infringement. More specifically, there is a concern that if digital versions of works are made available, it will result in widespread unauthorized copying, particularly by individual users in private. Since these digital copies will be perfect, this is seen as a much greater threat than that previously posed by photocopiers, for example. Relying on copyright against widespread copying by individuals is problematic. Copyright holders have consequently sought techniques outside copyright to protect their interests, in particular through the use of so-called 'technological measures of protection'—that is, they have sought to make available works only when they have additional protection systems through technologies that prohibit access, encrypt, or control copying. A familiar example of such a technology is the encryption of satellite broadcast

---

[96] Duration of Copyright and Rights in Performances Regulations 1995 (SI 1995/3297), reg. 24(1).

[97] Copyright and Performances (Application to Other Countries) Order 2016 (SI 2016/1219), Art. 13.

[98] I. Govaere, *The Use and Abuse of Intellectual Property Rights* (1996), 135–50.

[99] [1995] 4 CMLR 18.   [100] *Magill TV Guide/ITP, BBC and RTÉ*, Case IV/ 31.851 [1989] *OJ L* 78/43.

[101] Note also *IMS Health v. Commission*, T–184/01 R [2002] 4 CMLR 58, in which the Commission had also ordered a compulsory licence, but the (then) CFI overturned the interim measure.

[102] A fine of €899 million: European Commission, 'Antitrust: Commission Imposes €899 Million Penalty on Microsoft for Non-compliance with March 2004 Decision' (27 February 2008) Press Release IP/08/318.

signals and the provision to authorized service subscribers of cards that enable the use of decoding technology. Another example is the 'content scrambling system' used to protect DVDs and to ensure they can be used only on authorized players with CSS-descrambling software.

Technological measures are regarded as critically important for the so-called 'information society', because the feared duplication of works is thought to be likely to take place in private and thus be impossible to police. Technological measures provide an opportunity to police private uses, by forcing users to enter contractual arrangements before they can use or copy works. If users do not contact the copyright owner, they do not get a set of keys to open the technological locks. However, the potential for technological measures is much more than operating only to solve the problem of the digital shift in replication from public to private arenas; it also poses the possibility of radical transformation among the ways in which works are delivered. For example, technological measures might mean that a person could buy a digital newspaper for a single read with the advantage that the proprietor would not need to set the price on the basis that other readers will look at the newspaper (and so will not buy their own copy). The potential of technological measures is to enable consumers to get works delivered in the form that they want, with costs to the user tailored more closely to the use of the work.

The use of technological measures to support copyright, however, is not a complete answer to the problems of digital distribution and replication. This is because for every lock, there is some enthusiast willing to pick it. Those wishing to rely on technological measures have therefore sought government support for the use of such measures through the passage of laws prohibiting circumvention of the measures.[103] They argue that, by providing protection now, copyright owners will be given appropriate incentives to develop such systems. If such legal protection is not provided, that investment is vulnerable to being undermined by the rapid spread of circumventing technology. So there has been felt to be a need to act immediately. The problem with formulating legal principles to prevent circumvention, however, is that it is the locking systems currently being used that are crude. Strong protection of crude systems carries two problems: it may give users of technological protection too much control (or control of public domain dimensions of content); and it provides developers with little reason to make the systems more sophisticated.

The CDPA 1988, as amended, contains a formidable array of civil and criminal provisions dealing with situations in which a person facilitates access to works that the person concerned is not entitled to use or receive. Some of these relate to the circumvention of effective technological measures applied to copyright works other than computer programs and are designed to implement Article 6 of the Information Society Directive.[104] Others, somewhat less prescriptive in scope, apply only to computer programs (and implement Article 7(1)(c) of the Software Directive). The third category, in sections 297–9, relates to reception of transmissions (and implements the Conditional Access Directive).[105] We consider these provisions in Chapter 13. Whether these provisions will give copyright owners the confidence to exploit works, particularly in electronic form, by utilizing technological protection remains to be seen.

---

[103] S. Dusollier, 'Technological Measures and Exceptions in the European Directive of 2001: An Empty Promise' (2003) 34 *IIC* 62.   [104] See Chapter 13, section 4.1, pp. 375–80.

[105] Directive 98/84/EC of the European Parliament and of the Council of 20 November 1998 on the legal protection of services based on, or consisting of, conditional access [1998] *OJ L* 320/54 (29 November 1998).

9 COLLECTING SOCIETIES

One of the central problems facing copyright owners who wish to exploit their works is how to monitor or police infringements. Where the main form of copyright was the book and the main mode of exploitation the sale of printed copies, this policing (typically undertaken by a publisher) was ad hoc and depended on monitoring activities in the marketplace. However, as copyright expanded to encompass a wider array of subject matter and (particularly ephemeral) uses, the problems of policing copyright have changed. One of the main mechanisms developed by copyright owners to monitor infringement has been collective systems of management and enforcement of rights, in particular, the 'collecting society'.[106]

Collective administration is a system whereby certain rights are administered for the benefit of authors and/or copyright owners. The organizations that administer the rights are empowered to authorize various specified uses of their members' works, normally by way of a licence. The essential characteristic of these arrangements is that they are able to negotiate and act without individual consultation. In most cases, the copyright owner assigns their rights to the society. Where this occurs, the rights are pooled so as to create a repertoire of works at the disposal of potential users.

The main collecting societies in the United Kingdom are as follows.

(i)   The Performing Right Society (PRS) (now known as PRS for Music), formed in 1914, administers, as assignee, the performing and broadcasting rights in music and song lyrics. PRS annual income from all sources is in the region of £621 million.[107]

(ii)   The Mechanical-Copyright Protection Society (MCPS), formed in 1924, administers, as agent, the 'mechanical rights' in music and song lyrics—that is, the right to make a sound recording (part of the reproduction right).[108]

(iii)   Phonographic Performance Limited (PPL), formed in 1934, administers, as assignee, the performing and broadcasting rights in sound recordings, and from 2007 (when it merged with Performing Artists Media Rights Association, or PAMRA, and the Association of United Recording Artists, or AURA) has also represented performers.[109] In 2016, PPL collected £212 million.[110]

(iv)   Video Performance Limited (VPL), a sister company of PPL, administers, as agent, the performing and broadcasting rights in videos. While technically separate from PPL, it has the same management.

(v)   The Publishers Licensing Society (PLS), established in 1981, operates on behalf of the Publishers Association, the Association of Learned and Professional Society Publishers, and the Professional Publishers Association, in relation to the collective licensing of photocopying and digitization.[111]

(vi)   The Authors' Licensing and Collecting Society (ALCS), formed in 1977, represents writers and distributes the fees collected by the CLA for writers from

---

[106] For commentary, see Copinger, ch. 27; also see generally, D. Gervais (ed.), *Collective Management of Copyright and Related Rights* (2nd edn, 2010).

[107] On the history of the PRS, see T. Ehrlich, *Harmonious Alliance: A History of the Performing Right Society* (1989). For details of the PRS see http://www.prsformusic.com. In 2016, PRS collected £527.6 million: see Press Release, 'Over half a billion pounds in royalties paid out to music creators as PRS celebrates record financial performance in 2016' (21 April 2017).   [108] Also at http://www.prsformusic.com.

[109] See http://www.ppluk.com.   [110] PPL, *Annual Review* 2016.   [111] See http://www.pls.org.uk.

photocopying, scanning, and so forth.[112] In 2016, its licensing income was a little over £32 million.[113]

(vii) The Copyright Licensing Agency (CLA), formed in 1982, is owned by the PLS and ALCS, and collects on their behalf from various user constituencies involved on photocopying and scanning. It also operates as an agent for DACS. It enters blanket licences with educational authorities and universities.[114]

(viii) NLA Media access (formerly known as the Newspaper Licensing Agency) was established in 1996 by eight national newspapers to offer collective licences for news-clipping services. It now operates on behalf of 1,400 newspapers, offering a range of licences, [115] and in 2016 it collected £42 million.[116]

(ix) The Design and Artists' Copyright Society (DACS), formed in 1983, administers, as agent, the reproduction rights for painters, printmakers, sculptors, and photographers, as well as the resale royalty right.[117] In 2014, it collected £19.5 million.[118]

(x) The Artists Collecting Society (ACS), formed in 2006, administers the resale royalty right (in competition with DACS).[119]

(xi) The British Equity Collecting Society (BECS) was established in 1998 by the actors union, Equity, primarily to collect and distribute monies payable to audiovisual performers, in particular remuneration payable in other EU countries when audiovisual works are copied in private or retransmitted. In 2016, it collected £10.3 million.[120]

(xii) Directors UK, launched in 2008, represents film and television directors for purposes similar to those of BECS.[121]

(xiii) Eos (the Broadcasting Rights Agency), launched in 2012, represents musicians and publishers in Wales (its members withdrew from PRS to join Eos).[122]

(xiv) Picsel, launched in 2016, has been set up to collect monies from reprographic and secondary digital copying. Its income largely comes from the CLA.[123]

(xv) The Educational Recording Agency (ERA) licenses educational establishments to record broadcasts, distributing revenue to broadcasters and collecting societies (such as ALCS, DACS, MCPS, PPL, and PRS).[124]

9.1 ORGANIZATION

Because collecting societies are private organizations that have emerged in response to particular commercial environments, there is no great uniformity to their organizational structures. Nevertheless, it is worth considering the different dimensions of some of the existing societies.

---

[112] See http://www.alcs.co.uk.   [113] See ALCS, *Report and Accounts 2016–17*, 9.
[114] See http://www.cla.co.uk.   [115] See http://www.nlamediaaccess.com.
[116] NLA Media Access, *Annual Report 2017*.   [117] See http://www.dacs.org.uk.
[118] DACS, *Annual Report 2017*.   [119] See http://artistscollectingsociety.org.
[120] See http://www.equitycollecting.org.uk; see British Equity Collecting Society, *Annual Report 2015*, 1.
[121] See http://www.directors.uk.com.
[122] See http://www.eos.cymru (note most of the website is in Welsh).
[123] See http://www.picsel.org.uk.
[124] See http://www.era.org. See further Chapter 9, section 13.4, pp. 265–6.

9.1.1 Membership terms

In terms of copyright owner–collecting society relations, the relevant relationship will be determined in the membership agreement and the rules of the society. To ensure that each collecting society is capable of licensing the relevant right on behalf of the copyright owner, the owner has to assign the right to the society or appoint the society as its agent. The scope of any such assignment or agency will depend on the proposed function of the society. For example, a copyright owner joining the PRS is required to assign the 'small rights' relating to non-dramatic performances; the 'grand rights' relating to dramatic performances, which are not included, are administered by individual agreements. The rules of a society might also make provision for a member to assign rights in relation to works not in existence at the time of joining. A society may have different categories of membership (for example author members and publisher members). As a member, a copyright owner will have power to vote at meetings and thus to influence the way in which the society operates. A collecting society will distribute any licensing revenues that it collects in accordance with the rules of the society. Often, this will involve some kind of sampling mechanism that enables the society to estimate the amount to which each member is proportionally entitled. Usually, a society will first deduct its administration expenses. In some jurisdictions, a portion of the revenue is used for 'cultural purposes' (for example to fund indigenous music culture in the country making the deduction), and for pension and welfare payments. Provisions exist within the rules of a society specifying the circumstances in which a person may leave the society, which will usually require a substantial period of notice.

9.1.2 Licensing arrangements

The collecting societies enter into negotiations with copyright users, either as associations of users or on an individual basis. Negotiations with associations of users will often result in the establishment of tariffs. Sometimes, a society–user agreement will cover more than just a licence fee. Some associations of users will involve themselves in ensuring that licence fees are paid by their members, or help in other ways with the administration, in return for a reduced tariff. Although the terms of licences will vary, it is common for collecting societies to grant a 'blanket' licence entitling users to use any work in the repertoire of the licensing body without restriction.

9.2 ASSESSMENT

At a practical level, collecting societies are a convenient way of resolving some of the difficulties faced by copyright owners and users in reaching appropriate arrangements.[125] Collecting societies are useful insofar as they provide users with a focal point to locate and transact with copyright owners. Collecting societies reduce the 'transaction costs' that would otherwise exist in ascertaining and negotiating individual licences with individual copyright owners. This is particularly important where a user wishes to utilize a large number of copyright works, so that transacting on an individual basis would be time-consuming and costly.[126] Moreover, where the society grants a user a blanket

---

[125] G. Davies, 'The Public Interest in Collective Administration of Rights' (March 1989) *Copyright* 81.

[126] J. Fujitani, 'Controlling the Market Power of Performing Rights Societies: An Administrative Substitute for Antitrust Regulation' (1984) 72 *Cal L Rev* 103, 106 (breaking down the transaction costs in identifying and locating the copyright owner, obtaining the information necessary to negotiate a price, and transaction time costs).

licence, this offers users a degree of flexibility. For example, where a blanket licence is granted to a nightclub or a radio station, it means that it does not need to determine in advance the works that it is going to play.

For the copyright owner, collective administration relieves an otherwise impossible burden of policing and enforcing rights. It also provides copyright owners with a bargaining power that they would not possess as individuals. Moreover, the possibility of collective administration has enabled owners to argue for the extension of rights in relation to subject matter that might not otherwise have been protected on the basis that it was unenforceable.

Probably the most interesting thing about collecting societies is the way in which their emergence represents a significant shift in the character of copyright. As Thomas Streeter has observed, with collective administration, copyright loses much of its character as a property right exploited through distribution of copies bought and sold in the market-place.[127] Instead, copyright becomes more like the legal underpinning of an institutional bureaucracy that attempts to simulate a market through statistical mechanisms. Each copyright loses its individuality and the 'property form' is replaced by a liability form. In effect, collecting societies turn an author's property right into a right to receive welfare payments and a user's licence fee into a tax upon their activities.

9.3 INTERNATIONAL DIMENSIONS

Although collecting societies tend to operate at the national level, they form part of a global network of collecting agencies. For example, while performing rights are administered in the United Kingdom by the PRS, there are equivalent societies in the United States (Broadcast Music, Inc., or BMI; the American Society of Composers, Authors and Publishers, or ASCAP), Australia (the Australasian Performing Right Association, APRA), Germany (*Gesellschaft für musikalische Aufführungs- und mechanische Vervielfältigungsrechte*, or GEMA), France (*Société des Auteurs, Compositeurs et Editeurs de musique*, or SACEM), Belgium (*Société d'Auteurs Belge—Belgische Auteurs Maatschappij*, or SABAM), and so on. Typically, there will be 'reciprocal representation contracts' between national copyright management societies.[128] Under these arrangements, which date back as far as 1936, one national society (A) undertakes, on a reciprocal basis, to manage the rights attached to the repertoire of a foreign society (B) within its sphere of operation, normally its national territory. Society A collects royalties on behalf of foreign society B, pursues infringers, takes any necessary proceedings in respect of infringement, and transfers sums collected to B. Effectively, these agreements can mean that a particular national society controls within the territory the entire world repertoire of works.[129]

9.4 EUROPEAN DEVELOPMENTS

These national arrangements—under pressure from the EU authorities, as well as from business—are giving way to more flexible options. As markets for particular uses have

---

[127] T. Streeter, 'Broadcast Copyright and the Bureaucratization of Property' (1992) 10 *Cardozo AELJ* 567, 570, 576.

[128] The operation of CISAC and the role of such contracts, in described in *CISAC v. European Commission*, Case T-442/08 EU:T:2013:188 (General Court).

[129] In the present state of affairs, the Court of Justice has held that legislation that provides that a collecting society is the only source of licences does not breach Art. 56 TFEU: *Ochranný svaz autorský pro práva k dílům hudebním, o.s. (OSA) v. Léčebné lázně Mariánské Lázně a. s.*, Case C-351/12 EU:C:2014:110 (ECJ), [67]–[79].

become increasingly transnational, attempts have been made to develop EU-wide licences (so that users do not have to get permission on a territory-by-territory basis). For such EU-wide licensing to be possible, the collecting societies must agree that they can grant licences permitting uses outside their territories—so, for example, that GEMA can authorize webcasting in the United Kingdom or the PRS–For Music can do the same for Germany.[130] This sets the collecting societies up in competition with one another, which from one perspective could make them operate more efficiently. However, if collecting societies compete amongst themselves for users by reducing authors' (and copyright owners') remuneration, one might wonder whether the overall effect is in the public interest. One attempt to avoid this kind of competition was proposed by the music performing rights societies in an agreement that would have permitted all collecting societies to authorize Europe-wide licensing of public performance right, but would have required users to seek permission from their local society.[131] The Commission doubted whether this was compatible with competition law and has encouraged collecting societies to compete with one another.[132] The slow progress has led to the adoption of the Collective Rights Management Directive,[133] which was implemented in the United Kingdom by the Collective Management of Copyright (EU Directive) Regulations 2016.[134] This Directive provides that collecting societies which provide multi-territorial licensing of music may also be required to administer the repertoire of another collecting society that requests that it do so (and which is not offering such licences itself).[135] It also provides various rules on the proper conduct of collecting societies, such as acting in the best interest of right holder members,[136] regulating management fees and other deductions,[137] and ensuring there is a complaints procedure.[138]

9.5 EXTENDED COLLECTIVE LICENCES

Perhaps most analogous to compulsory licences,[139] section 116B of the CDPA 1988 allows for licensing bodies to be authorized to grant copyright licences in respect of works in which copyright is neither owned by the body nor by any of the persons on behalf of whom it acts.[140] The idea is that bodies that operate collective licensing schemes will be permitted or enabled to grant blanket licences relating to the complete array of works and

---

[130] This is referred to as the 'CELAS joint venture'—see http://www.celas.eu—but relates only to EMI-owned repertoire.

[131] The so-called 'Santiago agreement' is described in *CISAC v. European Commission*, Case T-442/08 EU:T:2013:188 (General Court), [28], [109] *ff*, [170] *ff*.

[132] European Commission, *Commission Staff Working Document: Impact Assessment Reforming Cross-Border Collective Management of Copyright and Related Rights for Legitimate Online Music Services* (11 October 2005), SEC (2005) 1254, 9; European Commission, *Communication from the Commission to the Council, the European Parliament and the European Economic and Social Committee: The Management of Copyright and Related Rights in the Internal Market* (16 April 2004) COM(2004) 261 final, 6–9.

[133] Directive 2014/26/EU of the European Parliament and of the Council of 26 February 2014 on collective management of copyright and related rights and multi-territorial licensing of rights in musical works for online use in the internal market [2014] *OJ L* 84/72 (the 'Collective Rights Management Directive', or CRM Directive); cf. European Commission, *Monitoring of the 2005 Music Online Recommendation* (7 February 2008).   [134] SI 2016/221 ('CMC Regs').

[135] CMC Regs, Pt 3.   [136] CMC Regs, reg. 3.

[137] CMC Regs, regs 11 and 14.   [138] CMC Regs, Pt 4.

[139] A critical difference is that copyright holders can opt out of such a regime: Hargreaves Review, 38, [4.51]; UK IPO, *Extending the Benefits of Collective Licensing* (2013), 15, [3.61].

[140] UK IPO, *Extending the Benefits of Collective Licensing* (2013).

rights that they purport to represent, and that users can feel secure that, having obtained a licence from such a society, they will not be liable to individuals who are not members. Precedents for such 'extended collective licensing' exist from the Scandinavian countries[141] and were approved of by the Hargreaves Review.[142]

The proposal is given effect by the Copyright and Rights in Performances (Extended Collective Licensing) Regulations 2014.[143] Essentially, this enables the Secretary of State to authorize an existing licensing body to operate extended collective licensing for the same type of works and rights as it is already administering.[144] The body must license works of the type which are proposed to be subject to the Extended Collective Licensing Scheme, its representation in relation to those types of works must be significant, and there must be adequate opt-out arrangements.[145] The application to set up the scheme needs to specify, amongst other things, the opt-out arrangements, the distribution policy, the licences being offered, and publicity arrangements.[146] The authorization lasts for five years,[147] but can be modified, renewed, or revoked.[148] Licences granted under the scheme are stated to have effect as if granted by the owner of the work or right.[149] Fees collected on behalf of non-members are, after nine months, to be put into separate accounts,[150] and if unclaimed after a specified period, transferred to the Secretary of State who may transfer them to fund social, cultural, and educational activities for the benefit of non-member rightholders.[151]

The CLA made the first application under the scheme. The IPO issued a consultation in December 2017, but the application was withdrawn in April 2018.

10 MANDATORY COLLECTIVE ADMINISTRATION: RETRANSMISSION

The Satellite and Cable Directive, adopted in 1993, sought to regulate, and simplify, the application of copyright law in the European Union to the retransmission of broadcasts.[152] In addition to requiring member states 'to ensure that when programmes from other member states are retransmitted by cable in their territory the applicable copyright and related rights are observed', the Directive requires that the right to grant or refuse authorization to a cable operator who wishes to retransmit a broadcast shall be exercised only through a collecting society.[153] This mandatory collective administration means that the retransmitter need only seek permission through collecting societies, rather than having to negotiate with all rights holders on an individual basis. The provision, it

---

[141] A. Strowel, 'The European Extended Collective Licensing Model' (2011) 34 *Colum JL & Arts* 665; also see T. Riis and J. Schovsbo, 'Extended Collective Licenses and the Nordic Experience—It's a Hybrid but is it a Volvo or a Lemon?' (2010) 33 *Colum JL & Arts* 471.   [142] Hargreaves Review, 37–8, [4.48]–[4.51].

[143] SI 2014/2588 (hereafter, 'ECL Regs').

[144] ECL Regs, reg. 4.   [145] ECL Regs, reg. 4(4).

[146] ECL Regs, reg. 5.   [147] ECL Regs, reg. 4(6).

[148] ECL Regs, reg. 9 (renewal), reg. 12 (modification), reg. 14 (revocation).

[149] One might wonder whether this is compatible with the CJEU's view that the author must be able to give informed consent: *Soulier*, Case C-301/15, EU:C:2016:878, [34]–[40], discussed in Chapter 12, section 5.3, p. 349.   [150] ECL Regs, reg. 18(3).

[151] ECL Regs, reg. 19.   [152] Satellite Dir., Arts 2 and 4.

[153] Satellite Dir., Art. 9.   [154] Satellite Dir., Art. 10.

should be noted, does not apply to the rights of the broadcasting organization: the right of the broadcaster to prohibit retransmission of its own transmissions can be exercised independently[154] (and this applies also to rights in the contents where they are owned by broadcasting organizations).

Legislation to extend this rule of mandatory collective administration is currently in front of the EU legislative bodies.[155] The Commission proposal would extend parallel rules to facilitate retransmissions of broadcasts (whether by wire or over the air, including by satellite) over closed electronic communication networks such as IPTV.[156] Like Article 9 of the Sat-Cab Directive, the Regulation seeks to simplify the rights-clearances necessary for these operators to retransmit broadcasts (and, for that reason, would not apply where retransmission is by the original broadcaster, who can identify right holders and clear the rights much more readily). Where there has been no relevant authorization by the right holder, the collecting society which manages rights of that category in the relevant member state 'shall be deemed to be mandated to manage the right on behalf of that rightholder'.[157]

11 DIGITAL COPYRIGHT EXCHANGES

For virtually a century, collecting societies proved to be an effective way of linking copyright holders with potential copyright uses. However, in the digital environment, even these organizational forms seem to have proved inadequate. Digitization has provided opportunities for individuals to become significant exploiters of copyright material held by others, whether by creating web pages or otherwise. Collecting societies have been seen to be ill-equipped to offer solutions to users who want to use a range of different types of work, of varying levels of obscurity, in low-value activities. One need only look at the 'IPKat' website, the leading UK blog on intellectual property, to see that a key feature of a blog is the inclusion of illustrative material designed to entertain alongside serious work of substantive commentary.

The question of establishing some sort of copyright clearing house was mooted in the Carter Report entitled *Digital Britain*.[158] Following the Hargreaves Review, the matter was taken forward in the Hooper Report. The first interim report, published in spring 2012, diagnosed the problems that needed attention to improve the 'efficiency and effectiveness' of copyright licensing;[159] the final report, dated July 2012, proposed a 'copyright hub'.[160] A non-for profit company was set up and, in 2013, a website www.copyrighthub. org was established. The idea of the hub is that it provides a portal (the website) which provides information how to get permission to use a particular content[161] via connected

---

[154] Proposal for a Regulation laying down rules on the exercise of copyright and related rights applicable to certain online transmissions of broadcasting organisations and retransmissions (14 September 2016) COM(2016) 594.   [156] Ibid., Proposed Art. 1(b) (defining retransmission).

[157] Ibid., Proposed Art. 3(2).

[158] BERR/DCMS, *Digital Britain: The Interim Report* (Cm. 7548, 2009); BIS/DCMS, *Digital Britain: Final Report* (2009), available online at https://www.gov.uk/government/uploads/system/uploads/attachment_data/file/228844/7650.pdf.   [159] UK IPO, *Rights and Wrongs* (March 2012).

[160] R. Hooper and R. Lynch, *Copyright Works: Streamlining Copyright Licensing for the Digital Age—An Independent Report* (July 2012).

[161] See Copyright Hub Manifesto (July 2014) available online at http://copyrightorg.wpengine.com/wp-content/uploads/2015/11/Manifesto-July2014.pdf.

websites. The original idea was that there would be a one-stop shop and the licensing would be through the portal itself to provide 'easy to use, transparent, low transaction cost copyright licensing'.[162] This has, to date, not proved possible due to the incompatibility of collecting society databases—in part because of different cataloguing and naming practices—and so the website currently provides information only about how to get a licence and then directs users to the relevant website of the collecting society.

The Hooper Report also recommended action favouring the further development of international standard identifiers (already under way in forums such as the Linked Content Coalition), backed up with severe sanctions for stripping metadata.[163]

---

[162] R. Hooper and R. Lynch, *Copyright Works: Streamlining Copyright Licensing for the Digital Age—An Independent Report* (July 2012), 2, [9] and [97].

[163] Ibid., [12] (organizations should sign up to a code of practice refusing to use images to which there is no metadata attached).

12

LIMITS ON EXPLOITATION

1 INTRODUCTION

The terms and conditions under which a copyright work is transferred or exploited are usually determined contractually by the parties. In this chapter, we look at the exceptional situations in which the law controls the way in which those rights are exploited.[1] We begin by looking at the various mechanisms that are used to regulate contracts between authors and entrepreneurs. We then go on to examine the impact that British and European competition law has on copyright owners' ability to exploit their copyright. In turn, we consider the ways in which copyright contracts are regulated in respect to users of copyright and situations in which their activities may be deemed to be licensed. Finally, we explore the various controls that are imposed on collecting societies.

Before reviewing these matters, it is important to note that there are many other restrictions placed on the owners' ability to exploit and use the copyright work that we will not examine here. Although copyright is described as a 'property right' and therefore might be expected to give absolute dominion, copyright law operates as an exclusionary right: it prevents all parties (other than the copyright holder) from exploiting the work. Copyright, however, does not confer on the proprietor of the copyright any positive rights to make and sell copies of the work. Consequently, the copyright owner will be subject to the regulatory regimes in the field in question (relating, for example, to the showing of films or broadcasts), and criminal laws (such as obscenity or public order legislation). Another factor that may affect the ability of a copyright owner to exploit a work is the rights that exist in any underlying works. For example, where the owner of the copyright in an English translation of a French novel wishes to exploit the copyright in the translation, it will be necessary for them to obtain the permission of the owner of copyright, if any, in the French novel that has been translated. With some copyright works, such as films or multimedia works, a whole host of prior right owners will have to be identified, approached, and persuaded to consent to the exploitation. It should be noted that one joint owner may not exploit the work without the licence of the other owners.[2]

---

[1] Note, too, the four non-voluntary mechanisms or other qualifications discussed in Chapter 11: implied licences, compulsory licensing, extended collective licensing, mandatory collective administration.

[2] CDPA 1988, s. 173(2); *Lauri v. Renad* [1892] 3 *Ch* 402; *Powell v. Head* (1879) 12 *Ch D* 686; *Cescinsky v. Routledge* [1916] 2 *KB* 325, 330.

2 LIMITS ON AGREEMENTS BETWEEN AUTHORS AND ENTREPRENEURS

This section considers the extent to which UK law will interfere to regulate the terms of transactions between authors and entrepreneurs, either to protect the psychological link between the author and their work, or to protect an author's financial interests. A number of other jurisdictions, notably France, Germany, the Netherlands, and Spain include within their copyright legislation provisions relating to the interpretation of copyright contracts. They also impose overriding terms that protect the financial interests of authors.[3] In the United Kingdom, there are very few provisions specifically directed at authors. The legal validity of such arrangements is generally dependent upon the law of contract, not the law of copyright. In the United Kingdom, the basic principle is that a contract freely entered into by an adult is binding. A court will not reopen the contract merely because the court thinks that the terms are unreasonable or unfair. The main way in which authors' interests are protected derives less from legal regulation than from collective processes, such as union activity or the promotion of standard contracts like those formulated by the Society of Authors and the Writers' Guild.[4] Individual authors and artists are also better able to secure reasonable terms by means of engaging literary agents.

Having said this, a contract entered into between an author and entrepreneurs may be regulated in a number of ways. On occasions, the general contractual doctrines of undue influence and restraint of trade have been used to protect particularly vulnerable authors from the more egregious of practices. In other cases, the courts may interfere with the sanctity of author–entrepreneur contracts where they are anti-competitive (under either domestic or European law). After looking at these, we will examine the specific terms that are implied by statute into certain contracts.

2.1 UNDUE INFLUENCE

If a disadvantageous bargain is the result of the exercise of undue influence, the court may set the bargain aside. An extreme example would be where an author assigned copyright to a publisher because of threats made by that publisher. However, the court's power to interfere extends beyond those extreme scenarios to all situations in which a 'person in a position of domination has used that position to obtain unfair advantage for himself, and so caused injury to the person relying on his authority or aid',[5] or as it is sometimes put, 'an exercise of improper of 'undue' influence, and hence unacceptable, whenever, the consent thus procured ought not fairly to be treated as the expression of the person's free will.'[6] For the courts to interfere in the sanctity of the contract, two elements need to be satisfied: first, it must be shown that the parties are in a relationship in which one

---

[3] See L. Bently, *Between a Rock and a Hard Place* (2002); W. Cornish, 'The Author as Risk-Sharer' (2002) 26 *Colum JL & Arts* 1; G. D'Agostino, *Copyright, Contracts and Creators: New Media, New Rules* (2010); W. Nordemann, 'A Revolution of Copyright in Germany' (2002) 49 *J Copyright Soc'y USA* 1041; M. Senftleben, 'Copyright, Creators and Society's Need for autonomous Art,' in R. Giblin and K. Weatherall, (eds), *What if We Could Reimagine Copyright* (2017), ch. 2; P. B. Hugenholtz, 'Towards Author's Paradise: The New Dutch Act on Authors' Contracts', in G. Karnell, A. Kur, P-J. Nordell, J. Axhamn, and S. Carlsson (eds), *Liber Amicorum Jan Rosén* (2016), 397–407.

[4] Even here, however, competition law may limit collective self-help: *In Re: Royal Institute of British Architects*, Case ref GP/908 (March 2003) ('fee guidance' infringed the Ch. 1 prohibition); CMA, *Conduct in the Modelling Sector*, Case CE/9859-14 (16 December 2016); CMA, *Letter to the Creative Industries on Competition Law* (12 September 2017).

[5] *National Westminster v. Morgan* [1985] 2 WLR 588, 599 (quoting Lord Shaw).

[6] *Royal Bank of Scotland v. Etridge* [2002] 2 AC 773, [7].

person has influence over another; and second, it must be shown that the influence was used to bring about a 'manifestly disadvantageous transaction'.[7] If undue influence exists, the contract is then voidable, and copyright assigned thereunder may be re-vested in the author. It seems that, since the contract is voidable (as opposed to void), contractual dealings with bona fide purchasers that take place before the contract is avoided will remain binding.

In order to have a contract set aside on the basis of undue influence,[8] it must first be shown that the parties are in a relationship in which one person has influence over another—that is, it is necessary to demonstrate a 'dominating influence'. The most common situation in which this occurs is where the parties are in a 'fiduciary' relationship—that is, one of trust. Where the relationship between the parties is deemed by the court to be fiduciary, the existence of a dominating influence is presumed. In most cases of copyright assignments, such as a publishing agreement, such a fiduciary relationship is unlikely to exist because there will rarely be any pre-existing relationship. An example of an exception to this is provided by *Elton John v. James*.[9] In that case, Elton John sought to avoid an agreement tying him to a publishing arrangement with James for six years. Nicholls J held that there was a 'dominating influence' even though the acquaintance of John and James was short before the publishing agreement was signed, because James 'really took charge', while the writer was young and eager, and received no independent advice, reposing trust 'in a man of stature in the industry that he would treat them fairly'.[10]

A similar position was reached in *O'Sullivan v. Management Agency*.[11] This decision arose as a result of the fact that a young and then unknown composer named Gilbert O'Sullivan entered into an exclusive management agreement with the defendant. The defendant operated through a number of companies with which O'Sullivan entered into publishing and other agreements. O'Sullivan later sought a declaration that these contracts were void and unenforceable on the ground that they had been obtained by undue influence. Mars-Jones J held that the defendant was in a fiduciary position and thus that the agreements were presumed to have been obtained by undue influence. The associated companies were equally subject to fiduciary obligations.[12] Although there had been no pressure placed on O'Sullivan to execute the agreements, because a fiduciary relationship existed, the onus was on the defendants to show that O'Sullivan had been fully informed and freely entered the agreements. Because O'Sullivan had no independent advice, the defendants were unable to establish that the agreements should stand.[13]

In order to have a contract set aside on the basis of undue influence, it must also be shown that the dominating influence was used to bring about a transaction that was 'manifestly disadvantageous'. The problem that confronts authors and artists here is that, in many cases, their grievances are collective, rather than individual, in nature. Consequently, the possibility exists for an assignee or exclusive licensee to deny that there is disadvantage by referring to agreements with other authors and the practices of other

---

[7] The relationship need not be one of domination: *Goldworthy v. Brickell* [1987] *Ch* 378, 404–6.

[8] *Chitty on Contracts* (32nd edn, 2015), ch. 8.   [9] *Elton John v. James* (1985) [1991] *FSR* 397.

[10] Ibid., 451.

[11] [1985] *QB* 428; see also *Samuel (Professionally Known As Seal) v. Wadlow* [2007] *EWCA Civ* 155, [47]–[63]; *Tolhurst v. Smith* [1994] *EMLR* 508 (relating to 'The Cure' and Robert Smith).

[12] *Tolhurst v. Smith* [1994] *EMLR* 448 (Dunn LJ).

[13] In an attempt to achieve 'practical justice', the Court of Appeal set aside the assignments of copyright and required the defendants to account for profits made from them, but subject to deduction of a service fee: [1985] *QB* 428, 458–9, 466–9, 471–3.

entrepreneurs. It should be noted that this tactic does not always work. For example, in *Elton John v. James*, some of the publishing agreements were found to be unfair even though James acted in a bona fide manner, imposing terms standard in the trade.[14] In that case (as with the *O'Sullivan* decision), the court was influenced by the fact that the royalty under the contract was less than that paid to other 'unknown' artists.

2.2 RESTRAINT OF TRADE

The second way in which vulnerable authors are protected is via the doctrine of 'restraint of trade'. As it suggests, this doctrine reflects a general policy of contract law that a person should be able to practise their trade.[15] Contracts that restrict this right will be scrutinized by the courts to ensure that they are justified.[16] In these circumstances, the courts have said that the terms must be no more than is reasonably required to protect the legitimate interests of the promisee and the public interest.[17] This doctrine has been important in relation to the long-term contracts that have been common in the music industry.

In *Schroeder Music Publishing Co. v. Macaulay*,[18] the House of Lords held that an agreement between a songwriter and a publisher was invalid because it was in restraint of trade. The agreement was in a standard form and required the songwriter to assign copyright in his works to the publisher. The duration of the agreement was to be five years, and if the royalties for those years exceeded £5,000, a further five-year period. In effect, the songwriter was bound to the publisher for ten years. However, the publisher was under no obligation to exploit the songs. Lord Reid said that it was an unreasonable restraint 'to tie the composer for this period of years so that his work will be sterilized and he can earn nothing from his abilities as a composer if the publisher chooses not to publish'.[19] Only a clause permitting the composer to terminate the agreement could save it.

In *Zang Tumb Tuum v. Holly Johnson*,[20] the Court of Appeal considered a publishing agreement and a recording agreement that the 1980s group Frankie Goes to Hollywood signed with Perfect and ZTT, respectively. The publishing agreement was for five years and the recording agreement possibly for nine years. Soon after the group became successful, Holly Johnson left the group. ZTT tried to enforce a 'leaving member' clause in the recording contract and sought an injunction to restrain Johnson from working for another record company. ZTT's action failed. Applying the doctrine of restraint of trade, the Court of Appeal set aside both agreements. The Court was particularly influenced by the duration of the agreement, Dillon LJ saying that:

> [S]tringent provisions such as many of those in the recording agreement may be justifiable in an agreement of short duration. But the onus must, in my judgment, be on the recording company to justify the length and the one-sidedness of the provisions as to its duration in this recording agreement.[21]

The Court held that ZTT had failed to justify the terms.

---

[14] *Elton John v. James* (1985) [1991] *FSR* 397, 453.

[15] *Schroeder Music Publishing Co. v. Macaulay* [1974] 3 *All ER* 616, 621 (Lord Reid). See Chapter 45, section 5.2, pp. 1244–7.

[16] Certain categories may be excluded from the doctrine: *Panayiotou v. Sony Music Entertainment* [1994] *EMLR* 229, 320. The doctrine has been held to apply to an exclusive agreement over image rights, even though it left unaffected the promisee's ability to trade in their primary field (football): *Proactive Sports Management Ltd v. Rooney* [2012] *FSR* (16) 475 [93] (Arden LJ).

[17] *Nordenfelt v. Maxim Nordenfelt* [1894] *AC* 535.   [18] [1974] 3 *All ER* 616.   [19] Ibid., 622.

[20] [1993] *EMLR* 61.   [21] Ibid., 73.

The doctrine's limitations were highlighted in *Panayiotou v. Sony Music Entertainment*.[22] Panayiotou, a songwriter and singer who worked under the name 'George Michael', sought to have the recording agreement into which he had entered with Sony in 1988 set aside. The background to the agreement was relatively complicated. In 1982, as a member of the group Wham!, Michael signed an agreement with a record company called Innervision. After some initial success, the validity of the agreement was called into question. Subsequent legal proceedings were settled and, in 1984, a new agreement was entered into between Wham! and Sony (which had been licensees of Innervision). This agreement placed Wham! under a potential obligation to record eight albums. When the group disbanded in 1986, Sony exercised its 'leaving member clause', which was to the effect that the 1984 agreement was to continue to bind Michael as an individual recording artist. After the success of Michael's first solo album (*Faith*), the 1984 agreement was renegotiated and replaced by a new agreement with Sony (the 1988 agreement). This also bound Michael, if the defendant so wished, to deliver a further eight albums and was to endure for 15 years. As part of the renegotiation, Michael was given much improved financial terms. As a result of changes in the corporate structure of the defendant company, Michael became disenchanted and, in 1992, sought to release himself from his obligations to Sony.

Parker J rejected Michael's claim that the 1988 agreement should be set aside. The main ground for rejecting George Michael's claim was that it was contrary to public policy to seek to reopen a previously compromised action and that the 1984 agreement was such a compromise: the 1988 agreement, being based on the 1984 predecessor, was covered by the same policy. However, Parker J went on to consider whether, had there been no compromise, the 1988 agreement would have been an unreasonable restraint of trade. He found that the agreement was restrictive of trade,[23] but that the restraint was reasonable. Although not explicit, Parker J appears to have accepted that the restraint was necessary to protect the defendant's interests not merely in recouping the investment that it had placed in Michael, but also the investment that it generally made in young artists who turned out to be unsuccessful.[24] Moreover, the restraint was reasonable as regards Michael's interests given the generous remuneration that was to be promised to the artist; the length of the agreement was simply a product of Michael's success. Parker J added that, when Michael's obligations under the 1984 agreement were taken into consideration, the 1988 agreement hardly restrained Michael at all.[25]

The *Panayiotou* case makes it clear that there are limits to the operation of the doctrine of restraint of trade. However, it has not provided any clear markers as to how to determine where those limits lie. More specifically, it is unclear what the legitimate interests of a recording or publishing company are and how the decision is to be made that the obligation (for example to produce eight albums, rather than three albums, or a five-year deal) is reasonable. Moreover, the case introduced a new limitation on the doctrine as a result of Parker J's final reason for dismissing Michael's claim: Parker J found that Michael, by requesting an 'advance' from Sony in 1992, had affirmed the existence of the contract

---

[22] [1994] *EMLR* 229. For criticism, see A. Coulthard, '*George Michael v. Sony Music*: A Challenge to Artistic Freedom?' (1995) 58 *MLR* 731.

[23] *Panayiotou v. Sony Music Entertainment* [1994] *EMLR* 229, 342.

[24] Ibid., 361.

[25] Cf. *Watson v. Prager* [1993] *EMLR* 275. In fact, the 1988 agreement effectively required Michael to produce eight albums, not the six that would have been needed to meet his remaining obligations under the 1984 agreement.

and could not thereafter argue that it should be set aside.[26] If this approach is followed,[27] authors, artists, and performers who seek to have lengthy or one-sided agreements set aside will have to take great care to ensure that they do not accept the benefit of the agreement after being informed of its potential unenforceability.

2.3 ANTI-COMPETITIVE CONTRACTS

A further ground on which a court might reopen an agreement between an artist and an entrepreneur is on the basis that it is anti-competitive. More specifically, a contract may be declared to be void by virtue of Article 101 of the Treaty on the Functioning of the European Union (TFEU).[28] As noted in Chapter 1, this renders void agreements (or clauses of agreements) that affect trade between member states and which have the object or effect of restricting competition within the internal market. Articles 101 and 102 TFEU are applicable only to the conduct of undertakings. The case of *RAI/Unitel*[29] indicates that, when contracting to perform an operatic work, singers operate as 'undertakings', so that the agreement may be subject to Article 101 TFEU. The Commission took the view that an exclusive agreement concerning the broadcast of the performance of *Don Carlos* at La Scala in Milan was subject to Article 101 TFEU.[30]

It seems possible that a contract between an author and an entrepreneur would fall outside the scope of Article 101 because the effect on competition might not be 'appreciable'.[31] Alternatively, as with exclusive distribution agreements, the contract might be justifiable under Article 101(3). An argument based on Article 101 TFEU was also raised, but rejected, in *Panayiotou v. Sony Music Entertainment*.[32] Parker J held[33] that the 1988 agreement between Michael and Sony had no effect on trade between EU member states because the agreement operated 'worldwide',[34] that, because the 1988 agreement replaced the 1984 agreement, it in fact had no effect on trade at all,[35] and that it did not have the object or effect of restricting competition.[36] Whether any or all of these conclusions are satisfactory has been doubted. However, had the contrary conclusion been reached—that the agreement infringed Article 101(1)—it is likely that the Commission would have been required to consider a deluge of individual applications for exemptions under Article 101(3).

---

[26] *Panayiotou v. Sony Music Entertainment* [1994] *EMLR* 229, 385–6.

[27] It has been in *Nicholl v. Ryder* [2000] *EMLR* 632, but not in *Proactive Sports Management Ltd v. Rooney* [2010] *EWHC* 1807, [708]–[713] (Judge Hegarty QC), in which *Nicholl* was treated as a case of equitable estoppel.

[28] Article 102 TFEU applies to unilateral conduct of dominant undertakings. A contract with a dominant undertaking will not be enforced when to do so will allow an abuse to become manifest.

[29] [1978] *OJ L* 157/39, [1978] 3 *CMLR* 306; European Commission, *Twelfth Report on Competition Policy* (1982), [90].

[30] Today such an agreement would likely be permissible under competition law unless one of the parties were to have a market share of more than 15 per cent.

[31] See Commission Notice on agreements of minor importance which do not appreciably restrict competition under Article 81(1) of the Treaty establishing the European Community (*de minimis*) [2001] *OJ C* 368/13 (22 December 2001). Below the threshold, the Commission considers that the competition authorities of member states should provide primary supervision.

[32] [1994] *EMLR* 229. See A. Coulthard, '*Panayiotou v. Sony Music Entertainment*' [1995] *J Bus L* 414.

[33] Because the agreement involved an assignment of copyright in the sound recordings to Sony, Parker J also held that it fell within Article 345 TFEU, which protects property. It has since been recognized that Art. 345, which was primarily directed towards matters such as state ownership, does not affect the Treaty rules on the free movement of goods, non-discrimination, or powers to legislate: see *UK v. Commission*, Case C-30/90 [1992] *ECR* I–829, [18]; *Phil Collins v. Imirat*, Cases C-92 and 326/92 [1993] *ECR* I–5144, [17]–[28]; *Spain v. Council*, Case C-350/92 [1995] *ECR* I–1985, [16]–[23].

[34] [1994] *EMLR* 229, 416.   [35] Ibid., 420.   [36] Ibid., 425.

Three developments that have taken place since the *Panayiotou* case are worth noting. The first is the Vertical Restraints Regulation (discussed in Chapter 42), which makes available a block exemption from Article 101 for 'vertical agreements' including exclusive supply agreements.[37] This means that even if an agreement falls within Article 101(1) TFEU, it may automatically benefit from exemption under Article 101(3) as long as the market share of the purchaser is less than 30 per cent.[38] However, while a publishing, recording, or songwriting contract would fall within the general definition of a 'vertical restraint' in the Regulation,[39] the exemption applies to assignment to the buyer or use by the buyer of intellectual property rights, provided that those provisions do not constitute the *primary object* of such agreements and are directly related to the use, sale, or resale of goods or services by the buyer or its customers.[40] We await a decision on whether the primary object of such an arrangement concerns intellectual property. This seems more likely with publishing than recording agreements. However, even if the block exemption does not apply, a restrictive agreement may be found exempt individually under Article 101(3).

The second significant development since *Panayiotou* is that section 2 of the Competition Act 1998 introduced into the United Kingdom a national provision (the so-called 'Chapter I prohibition') equivalent to Article 101.[41] It seems that an author or artist will be better served by the domestic provision, since it does not require the applicant to show that the contract had an adverse effect on trade between member states. This is because the Competition Act requires only that the agreement 'may affect trade within the United Kingdom'.[42] There is no express requirement that this effect must be 'appreciable' or 'substantial' (although there is an immunity from fines for 'small agreements' and 'conduct of minor significance'[43]). However, as with the EU provision, most vertical agreements are exempt from section 2 unless the agreement has as its primary object terms relating to the assignment or use of intellectual property.[44]

Third, and finally, it should be noted that, since 1 May 2004[45] is to render Article 101(3) directly applicable by competition authorities and courts of member states. (Previously, such decisions could be made only by the European Commission.) This means that a finding that an exclusive recording agreement breaches Article 101(1) will not now produce the bureaucratic consequences (in terms of notifications) that it formerly would have entailed. This may make a court willing to abandon the reasoning employed in the *Panayiotou* case and to treat exclusive recording arrangements as anti-competitive, but to rely on its own assessment of Article 101(3) in deciding whether such arrangements improve the production of goods, while allowing consumers a fair share of the resulting benefit.

---

[37] Commission Regulation (EU) No. 330/2010 of 20 April 2010 on the application of Article 101(3) of the Treaty on the Functioning of the European Union to categories of vertical agreements and concerted practices [201] *OJ L* 102/1 (23 April 2010) (the 'Vertical Restraints Regulation', or VRR).

[38] VRR, Art. 3, assuming that it has no 'hard core' terms.   [39] VRR, Art. 2(1).

[40] VRR, Art. 2(3). On the operation of the TTBE 2014, see Chapter 23.

[41] Competition Act 1998, s. 2. See J. Turner, 'The UK Competition Act 1998 and Private Rights' [1999] *EIPR* 181.   [42] Competition Act 1998, s. 2(1)(a).

[43] Competition Act 1998, ss 39 and 40; Competition Act 1998 (Small Agreements and Conduct of Minor Significance) Regulations 2000 (SI 2000/262). But the CMA (and previously the OFT) takes the view that an agreement will have no appreciable effect on competition if the parties' combined share of the market does not exceed 25 per cent.

[44] But the TTBE 2014 might operate: see Chapter 23. Agreements under UK law are treated in a similar manner to that which would be achieved under EU law: Competition Act 1998 (Land Agreements Exclusion and Revocation) Order 2004 (SI 2004/1260).

[45] By reason of the Council Regulation (EC) No. 1/2003 of 16 December 2002 on the implementation of the rules on competition laid down in Articles 81 and 82 of the Treaty [2003] *OJ L* 1/1 (4 January 2003).

2.4 STATUTORY RIGHT TO EQUITABLE REMUNERATION

Although UK copyright law treats the terms of a contract as essentially a matter for voluntary negotiation, an exception exists in relation to transfers of (once valuable) rental rights. This so-called 'unwaivable right to equitable remuneration' seemed to be a first step in the transplantation of provisions protecting authors from countries such as France and Germany to the UK, via the process of European harmonization.[46] Section 93B of the Copyright, Designs and Patents Act 1988 (CDPA 1988) specifies that where a person transfers the rental right 'concerning' a film or sound recording to the producer of the sound recording or film, 'he retains the right to equitable remuneration for rental'. The potential beneficiaries of the retained right are the authors of literary, dramatic, musical, or artistic works, and the principal director of a film.[47]

The right applies whether the transfer is presumed under section 93A (or with performers, section 191F) or is voluntarily transferred. The right to remuneration cannot be excluded by agreement.[48] The remuneration is to be claimed from the person 'for the time being entitled to the rental right', and the relevant time is presumably the time of rental rather than of claim. The right can be assigned only to a collecting society, by testamentary transmission, or by operation of law (for example on bankruptcy). The amount deemed equitable is to be determined by agreement or, failing this, by the Copyright Tribunal. In determining what is equitable, the Tribunal is directed to take into account the importance of the contribution of the author or performer to the film or sound recording. Remuneration is not to be considered inequitable merely because it was paid by way of a single payment or at the time that the rental right was transferred.[49]

2.5 HARMONIZATION?

As can be seen, with one or two exceptions, English law leaves authors free to make arrangements for the exploitation of their rights and rarely interferes to protect authors against decisions that are not in their long-term interests. In contrast, most EU member states have provisions regulating the terms and conditions of contracts between creators and exploiters. In the past, the Commission has stated that differences between contractual rules are not significant enough to require harmonization.[50] However, the 2016 proposal for a Directive on Copyright in the Digital Market addresses the matter.[51] It proposes that authors and performers are given 'sufficient' information on the exploitation of their works and performances from those who were licensed or to whom the

---

[46] More specifically, the Rel. Rights Dir., Art. 4.

[47] CDPA 1988, s. 191G, has the same effect as regards performers. It seems that CDPA 1988, s. 93B, applies not only to circumstances in which the work is incorporated in a film or sound recording (e.g. the music used on a film), but also where the work is to be rented with the sound recording or film, such as might occur with artwork on a record sleeve. This conclusion is consistent with the expansive definition of author in CDPA 1988, s. 93B(1)(a), as covering authors of artistic works, and the use in s. 93B(1) of 'concerning'. However, s. 93C(3) refers to the importance of the 'contribution ... to' the sound recording or film.   [48] CDPA 1988, s. 93B(5).

[49] The right applies even where transfers were made pursuant to agreements made prior to 1 January 1994, but only if the author asserted a claim to that effect between 1 December 1996 and 1 January 1997: Rel. Rights Regs, reg. 33(b).

[50] European Commission, *Communication from the Commission to the Council, the European Parliament and the European Economic and Social Committee: The Management of Copyright and Related Rights in the Internal Market* (16 April 2004) COM(2004) 261 final.

[51] European Commission, *Proposal for a Directive of the European Parliament and of the Council on copyright in the Digital Single Market* (14 September 2016) COM(2016) 593 final.

rights were transferred.[52] More significantly authors and performers will be entitled to *request* 'additional, appropriate, remuneration' from the other party when the remuneration originally agreed is 'disproportionately low' compared to the benefits the other party received. It must be intended that the right to request additional remuneration includes an entitlement to be paid such remuneration. Although this proposal has been described as a 'best-seller clause' (of the type that some member states have to deal with disproportionality of remuneration created when a work turns out to be unexpectedly successful), it is not clear that the proposed rule is so limited.[53] What is meant by 'disproportionately low' is unclear, but the assessment must take account of the specificities and practices of the relevant sector.[54] This suggests a view of a 'normal' share for authors and performers which is market sector dependent. The Proposal also requires member states to introduce voluntary alternative dispute resolution systems, and the Commission documents refer, as an example, to the Publishers' Association system of ADR. If adopted, this will breathe new life into that system, which appears defunct.

It is almost certain that the Directive will not require implementation before the United Kingdom leaves the European Union. Therefore, it is not clear what effect, if any, this provision would have on domestic law. If such a right were introduced in the United Kingdom it would be a significant departure from the traditional position of authors and performers.

3 COMPETITION LAW AND LIMITS ON THE EXPLOITATION OF COPYRIGHT

In this section, we look at the impact that UK and European competition law have on the copyright owner's ability to exploit copyright.

3.1 REFUSALS TO LICENSE

In general, copyright is regarded as a property right that its owner may use or not use as they so wish: an author cannot normally be compelled to publish their private letters or manuscripts, nor are publishers required to keep their books 'in print'. Nevertheless, just as, in exceptional circumstances, competition law will require a property owner to make available an 'essential facility' to an economic operator,[55] so—exceptionally—competition law might require a copyright owner to license their rights to other traders. The legal basis for this requirement is Article 102 TFEU, which prohibits the 'abuse' of a 'dominant position'. An operator holds a 'dominant position' when it holds a position of economic

---

[52] Proposed, Art. 14(1); it will not apply where there is not a 'significant' contribution from the claiming author/performer (proposed art. 14(3)). For a close analysis, see Bently, Kretschmer et al., *Strengthening the Position of Press Publishers and Authors and Performers* (Brussels: European Parliament, 2017) at http://www.europarl.europa.eu/RegData/etudes/STUD/2017/596810/IPOL_STU(2017)596810_EN.pdf.

[53] According to proposed recital 42 this right would be 'without prejudice' to contractual rights which exist under national law—though it is hard to see that it does not prejudice so-called 'freedom of contract.' Presumably, the aim is that the proposed right is without prejudice to various provisions that regulate the form and content of copyright contracts.   [54] Proposed recital 42.

[55] *Commercial Solvents v. Commission,* Cases C-6 and 7/73 [1974] *ECR* 223.

[56] *Compagnie Maritime Belge Transports and ors v. Commission,* Cases C-395 and 396/96P [2000] *ECR* I–365, [34].

[57] European Commission, *Article 102 Enforcement Priorities Guidance* [2009] *OJ C* 45/7, [75].

strength that enables it to behave to an appreciable extent independently of its competitors, customers, and consumers.[56] It is generally accepted that a dominant firm has the right to choose its trading partners.[57] However, operators in a dominant position are regarded as having a 'special responsibility' not to allow their conduct to impair competition and, in 'exceptional circumstances', the holder of an intellectual property right may be required to license others. If an operator in such a position fails to license its copyright, such refusal may be regarded as an abuse and can result not merely in the order of a compulsory licence, but also in very substantial fines.[58] It is also the case that an obligation to license may be imposed to remedy other competition law infringements.[59]

The first case in which the Court of Justice affirmed the application of Article 102 to copyright was *RTÉ and Independent Television Publications v. Commission* (known as the 'Magill' case).[60] The decision in *Magill* arose from the practice whereby the Irish broadcasting organization (RTÉ), which owned copyright in its television schedules,[61] refused to license newspapers to publish television listings in a weekly format. The effect of this was that the only weekly guides available were those issued separately by RTÉ and the other broadcasting organizations (BBC and ITV). As such, if a viewer were to want to plan their television viewing for the week ahead, they would have to purchase all three magazines. Magill, who proposed to publish a comprehensive guide, claimed that the refusal to license contravened Article 102. The Commission agreed and ordered the defendant to license the listings.[62]

The Court of Justice held that the broadcasting organization held a dominant position in the market for weekly television magazines.[63] The Court also agreed that the refusal to license was an abuse. It observed that the refusal to license an intellectual property right 'cannot of itself constitute abuse of a dominant position', but that 'the exercise of an exclusive right by the proprietor may, in exceptional circumstances, involve abusive conduct'.[64] The Court of Justice agreed with the General Court that this was a case of abuse, because (i) there was a specific, constant, and regular potential demand on the part of consumers for comprehensive weekly listings, (ii) demand was going unmet because the appellants refused to supply listing information to others, and (iii) there was no 'justification' for this behaviour related either to broadcasting or to the publishing of television magazines. The consequence of the refusal to license was that the broadcasters reserved to themselves the secondary market in weekly television guides by excluding all competition from that market.

Parties in subsequent cases have sought to explore the scope of the *Magill* holding,[65] but so far the courts have managed to make determinations within its parameters. In *IMS*

---

[58] In the case of Microsoft, the Commission's 2004 Order imposed a fine of €497 million: *Decision 2007/53 relating to a proceeding pursuant to Art. 82 EC and Art. 54 of the EEA Agreement against Microsoft Corp.*, COMP/C-3.37.792–*Microsoft* [2007] *OJ L* 32/23. The level of the fine was challenged by Microsoft before the CFI, but the Court affirmed: *Microsoft Corp. v. Commission*, Case T-201/04 [2007] 5 *CMLR* (11) 846, [1326]–[1367].   [59] *Volvo v. Veng*, Case 238/87 [1988] *ECR* 6211.

[60] [1995] 4 *CMLR* 18.   [61] *Radio Telefís Éireann v. Magill TV Guide Ltd* [1990] FSR 561.

[62] *Magill TV Guide/ITP, BBC and RTE* [1989] *OJ L* 78/43.

[63] [1995] 4 *CMLR* 18, 718, [50]. The Court's reasoning on this point has also been treated as less than fully satisfactory: T. Vinje, 'The Final Word on *Magill*' [1995] *EIPR* 297, 299. Subsequent commentaries have suggested that one distinguishing feature of *Magill* was that the dominance of RTÉ, ITV, and the BBC was in the provision of broadcasting services.   [64] [1995] 4 *CMLR* 718, [50].

[65] The differences between the Commission and the General Court (Court of First Instance) in the *IMS* case related to the very broad interpretation that the Commission was taking on when an abuse would be found under Art. 102: *IMS Health* [2002] *OJ L* 59/18; *IMS Health Inc v. Commission*, T-184/01 R [2002] 4 *CMLR* 58. Moreover, in the *Microsoft* case, the Commission argued that the application of *Magill* did not require the presence of all of the elements identified in *Magill*. Nevertheless, it argued, and the General Court found, that all those elements were present: *Microsoft Corp. v. Commission*, Case T-201/04 [2007] 5 *CMLR* (11) 846, [712].

Health GmbH & Co. OHG v. NDC Health GmbH & Co. KG,[66] for example, the Court of Justice indicated that it is 'sufficient' to constitute an abuse if these elements are present (leaving open the question of whether all elements of *Magill* must be present).

3.1.1 Indispensability

The first requirement is that the asset must be 'indispensable' for operation of another's business.[67] This means that it must be impossible, or at least unreasonably difficult, for an undertaking to operate in the relevant market without a licence.[68] In *IMS Health*, IMS provided information to pharmaceutical firms about sales by wholesalers to pharmacies (which gave the firms an indication of doctors' prescribing habits, and thus enabled the pharmaceutical companies to assess and respond to the effectiveness of their marketing to doctors). For privacy purposes, the information had to be collated from data relating to at least three pharmacies. With the assistance of pharmaceutical firms, over a number of years IMS had developed a geographical model for analysing the German pharmaceutical market—a so-called 'brick structure', comprising 1,860 segments—which it used from January 2000. IMS believed that NDC was using the same brick structure and brought an action for copyright infringement. The Frankfurt *Landgericht* (that is, regional court) granted an interim injunction, but referred various questions concerning the application of Article 102 TFEU to the Court of Justice.[69] One issue was whether use of the brick structure was 'indispensable' to NDC's operations.[70] It was clear that the brick structure had been developed with the assistance of the pharmaceutical companies and that there would likely be resistance (and costs) were NDC to adapt to a different basis for assessing data. In these circumstances, even were NDC to develop an alternative structure, it might 'be obliged to offer terms which are such as to rule out any economic viability of business on a scale comparable to that' of IDC.[71] The Court of Justice advised that these factors were relevant to the national court's assessment of the 'indispensability' of using the brick structure for the provision of data services.

In contrast, in *Tierce Ladbroke v. Commission*,[72] the proprietor of a chain of betting shops in Belgium complained that a refusal by the owner of rights in certain televised pictures of French horse races to allow retransmission in the applicant's betting shop amounted to a breach of Article 102. The General Court held that while the refusal to license the complainant was an exercise of power from a primary market (transmission of horse races) into a secondary market (betting shops), the refusal to license in no sense

---

[66] Case C-418/01 [2004] 4 *CMLR* (28) 1543, [38].

[67] In *Microsoft v. Commission*, Case T-201/04 [2007] 5 *CMLR* (11) 846, much time was spent contesting exactly what interoperability information was required, Microsoft claiming that the Commission's orders in effect required disclosure that would enable its competitors to clone its products and arguing that all that it should need to disclose was sufficient information to allow its competitors' products to connect with its system ('one-way' functionality). The CFI declined to overturn the Commission's ruling, agreeing that, for the competitors to remain viable, the information must be sufficient to enable 'two-way' functionality and observing that the requirements imposed fell well short of requiring the revelation of source code or enabling cloning.   [68] Ibid., [28].

[69] In light of the injunction, NDC sought a licence to use the 1,860-brick structure, offering an annual licence fee of about €5,000. When that was refused, NDC lodged a complaint with the Commission alleging an infringement of Art. 102. The Commission adopted a decision ordering interim measures, on the basis that IMS was abusing its dominant position: [2002] *OJ* L 59/18. The President of the General Court suspended the Commission's decision, because it had taken a very broad interpretation of *Magill*: *IMS Health Inc v. Commission*, T-184/01 R [2002] 4 *CMLR* 58.

[70] *IMS Health GmbH & Co. OHG v. NDC Health GmbH & Co. KG*, Case C-418/01 [2004] *ECR* I–5039 (ECJ, Fifth Chamber).   [71] Ibid., [29].   [72] Case T-504/93 [1997] *ECR* II–923.

prevented the defendant from operating in the secondary market. The provision of pictures was not essential for the applicant's activity.

3.1.2 New product

The second requirement—that of a new product—was also at issue in *IMS Health*.[73] A key question before the Court of Justice was whether it was necessary for NDC to establish that it was offering a 'new product', since, on the face of things, it appeared that NDC wanted to use the brick structure to compete with IMS in providing an identical service (pharmaceutical data services). The Court of Justice held that the refusal would be an abuse only where a licensee:

> . . . does not intend to limit itself essentially to duplicating the goods or services already offered on the secondary market by the owner of the copyright, but intends to produce new goods or services not offered by the owner of the right and for which there is potential consumer demand.[74]

The Court elaborated a little upon the requirement that there be an upstream and downstream market. While acknowledging that this leveraging from one market into another was an essential component in the *Magill* analysis, the Court of Justice admitted that a certain artificiality was possible in constructing the upstream market; it did not have to be a market that was actually offered. Thus, in the *IMS* case, the Court contemplated that the market for the 1,860-brick structure itself might be the primary market.

The 'new product' requirement was also discussed by the General Court in *Microsoft v. Commission*.[75] Here, the General Court was asked to review a Commission decision from 2004 fining Microsoft and ordering it to make available so-called 'interoperability information' about its work-group server systems to interested parties. 'Work-group server systems' are systems that connect PCs to each other, to common servers, and to printers, so that they can share files, share printers, and operate as efficient and secure networks.[76] Microsoft had a 60 per cent share of the work-group server market, so was in a dominant position.[77] While the Commission found that some information was available, it took the view that this was not sufficient to enable competitors to remain viably on the market. The 13-member Grand Chamber of the General Court therefore found that the refusal would prevent the appearance of a 'new product' because the refusal to permit full interoperability would limit technical development.[78] Evidence indicated that consumers preferred various facets (reliability, security) of the work-group server operating systems of Microsoft's competitors and that the chief quality associated with Microsoft's systems was their ability to interoperate.[79] In effect, people were buying Microsoft's items primarily because they were locked in, when they would have preferred the technical features offered by Microsoft's competitors. The refusal of Microsoft to make available relevant information was thus impeding 'innovation'.

3.1.3 Elimination of competition

The third *Magill* requirement is that the refusal must be *likely to exclude all competition in the secondary market*. In the *Microsoft* case, Microsoft argued that the continued existence of competitors in the work-group server system market—namely, Unix, Linux, and

---

[73] Case C-418/01 [2004] 4 *CMLR* (28) 1543.   [74] Ibid., [49].

[75] Case T-201/04 [2007] 5 *CMLR* (11) 846.

[76] The GC did not consider that the Commission had formulated the relevant market too narrowly: ibid., [531].   [77] Ibid., [555]–[558].   [78] Ibid.,[647].   [79] Ibid., [652], [407]–[412].

Novell—indicated that the refusal to license the information had not eliminated competition in the market. The Commission rejected that view and the General Court affirmed. The General Court stated that it was not 'necessary to demonstrate that all competition on the market would be eliminated. What matters . . . is that the refusal at issue is liable to or is likely to, eliminate all effective competition on the market.'[80] The existence of competitors with a marginal presence in niche markets was not evidence of effective competition.[81]

3.1.4 Objective justification

The final *Magill* requirement is that the refusal must *not be justified* by objective considerations. In the *Microsoft* case, the General Court said that the burden of proving objective justification lies on the operator holding the dominant position.[82] It is evident that the existence of intellectual property rights is not itself a sufficient basis (otherwise Article 102 could never apply to such rights).[83] In *Microsoft*, the General Court affirmed the Commission's view that the existence of secrets was not of itself a good reason to refuse to license,[84] but would, it seems, have accepted as an objective justification a substantiated argument that the requirement to license would seriously have affected Microsoft's incentives to innovate.[85]

3.2 EXCESSIVE PRICING

The competition provisions may also be applicable where a copyright (or database right) owner is willing to license, but only at a price that is unacceptable to the user. Some such issues arose in *Attheraces Limited, Attheraces (UK) Limited v. The British Horseracing Board Limited, BHB Enterprises plc,*[86] in which the Court of Appeal considered whether the British Horseracing Board was guilty of 'excessive pricing', and thereby abusing its admittedly dominant position, in relation to its charges for supplying pre-race data to horse-racing broadcaster, Attheraces. The Court of Appeal allowed an appeal from the judgment of Etherton J, who had held that there was abuse.[87] The Court recognized the difficulties with deciding the 'economic value of data', which was a preliminary to deciding whether BHB's pricing was excessive. The Court rejected Etherton J's approach of asking what the cost of creating the information was and allowing a reasonable profit on that cost; instead, the Court accepted that the value to the user might also be a relevant component of the 'economic value' of the data.[88]

3.3 TYING

If traders in a dominant position need to think carefully before refusing to license their copyright, they should also think carefully before giving away their copyright-protected software with their other products. In *Microsoft*,[89] the Commission held that Microsoft had breached Article 102 TFEU by its bundling of Windows Media Player with its operating system package. The Commission had found that Microsoft was dominant in the

---

[80] Ibid., [563].   [81] Ibid., [563].   [82] Ibid., [688], [697].   [83] Ibid., [690].
[84] Ibid., [693].   [85] Ibid., [701].
[86] [2007] *EWCA Civ* 38 (concerning supply of data, but not based on database right).
[87] [2006] *FSR* (20) 336.
[88] *Attheraces Limited, Attheraces (UK) Limited v. The British Horseracing Board Limited, BHB Enterprises plc* [2007] *EWCA Civ* 38, [218].   [89] Case T-201/04 [2007] 5 *CMLR* (11) 846.

operating system market, with a 90 per cent market share. During the early 1990s, it had offered (but not imposed) its competitor's media players (in particular that of RealNetworks), but from the end of the 1990s it had included its own audio-streaming software and stopped supporting the software of its competitors.[90] The General Court agreed with the Commission's analysis that there was abuse where (i) the tying (Windows OS) and tied (Media Player) products are two separate products, (ii) the undertaking concerned is dominant in the market for the tying product, (iii) customers are not offered the choice of buying the tying product alone, and (iv) the practice forecloses competition (in the market for the tied product).[91]

The General Court held that the operating system and the media player were, at the relevant time, two products. The Court was persuaded that these were two products as a result of evidence that Microsoft sometimes offered Windows without Media Player and sometimes marketed Media Player separately, and that there was demand (from employers) for Windows without Media Player.[92] The second factor, Microsoft's dominance in the operating system market was not contested. As to the third factor, consumer choice, Microsoft argued that consumers got the Media Player for free, and were able to install and use alternative media players.[93] Referring to Article 102(d), Microsoft argued that the circumstances were different from the classic case of abuse by tying, which involved imposing an additional obligation or expense (for example an obligation to buy expensive nails to go with a nail gun). The Court rejected the arguments: just because there was no separate charge for Windows Media Player, this did not imply that it was included gratis. Moreover, it found that it was not technically possible to remove Windows Media Player and that the bundling provided consumers with an incentive to use the Windows Media Player 'at the expense of competing media players, notwithstanding that the latter are of better quality'.[94] Turning to the fourth element, the General Court affirmed the Commission's view that the sheer ubiquity of Windows Media Player, which could not be removed from the operating systems with which it was installed, was likely to foreclose competition.[95] Given that most operating systems were pre-installed on PCs and laptops by 'original equipment manufacturers' (which were given no choice but to install Windows Media Player), such manufacturers and consumers were unlikely to choose to install a second, non-Microsoft, media player. In fact, had Microsoft not adopted the bundling tactic, the Court suggested that there would have been real competition with the market leader from the 1990s, Real Player. Finally, the Court considered whether there was an objective justification for the behaviour, through efficiency gains that outweighed the harm from the anti-competitive action. The Court found the claimed technical efficiencies unsubstantiated. Microsoft therefore had rightly been fined by the Commission and ordered to offer its Windows operating system without the Media Player (although it was also permitted to continue to sell the package).

3.4 ANTI-COMPETITIVE CONTRACTUAL TERMS

The key provision of European competition law affecting copyright agreements is Article 101 TFEU. This renders void all agreements that affect trade between member states and which have the object or effect of distorting competition within the internal market.[96]

---

[90] Ibid., [837].   [91] Ibid., [859].   [92] Ibid., [912]–[944].   [93] Ibid., [951]–[952].

[94] Ibid., [971]. Whether this would be so today is doubtful, because changes in bandwidth mean that consumers can readily download competing systems.   [95] Ibid., [1036]–[1037].

[96] *Football Association Premier League Ltd v. QC Leisure and ors* and *Karen Murphy v. Media Protection Services Ltd*, Joined Cases C-403/08 and C-429/08 [2011] *ECR* I–9083 (ECJ, Grand Chamber) ('*FAPL*'), [135].

The 'object' of an agreement is determined from its content, objectives, and economic and legal context.[97] If a tribunal is considering whether Article 101 has been breached by reference to the 'effect' of the agreement, it is necessary to show that competition has in fact been prevented, restricted, or distorted to 'an appreciable extent'.[98] Nevertheless, certain agreements that provide benefits may be exempt. In contrast with the fields of technology licensing and vertical restraints, the Commission has been slow to develop block exemptions in the copyright field. The Technology Transfer Block Exemption Regulation (TTBE 2014) exempts certain agreements that deal with copyright,[99] but only where such agreement is 'ancillary' to a pure patent licensing or know-how licensing agreement, or to mixed patent and know-how licensing agreements. The Vertical Restraints Regulation (VRR) is of more general applicability, exempting many agreements relating to the distribution of copyright works (for example the distribution of books or sound recordings). However, as we noted earlier, the exemption only applies to vertical agreements containing provisions which relate to the assignment to the buyer or use by the buyer of intellectual property rights, provided that those provisions do not constitute the primary object of such agreements and are directly related to the use, sale, or resale of goods or services by the buyer or its customers. Therefore it will rarely be applicable to copyright licences, such as software licences. However, the exemptions made may provide an important guide to the thinking of the Commission on terms in such agreements.

As a result of the Competition Act 1998, UK regulation of copyright agreements parallels European competition law. Section 2 introduces the 'Chapter 1 prohibition', which is equivalent to Article 101 TFEU.[100] An agreement will be deemed to be exempt from the national prohibition if it is exempt from Article 101 TFEU under the European Union's TTBE 2014 or VRR.[101]

With these general points in mind, we now look at the cumulative effect of the 'Chapter 1 prohibition' and Article 101 TFEU on various terms that are used in copyright contracts.

3.4.1 Agreements conferring exclusive territorial rights

A copyright licence commonly includes terms guaranteeing the licensee the exclusive right to sell the work in a particular territory. For example, the licence may grant someone the exclusive right to sell paperback versions of a book in the United Kingdom, or to show a film in public in Belgium. It may also include an undertaking by the licensor not to put the work on the market in that territory and an undertaking by the licensee not to sell the work in the territories of other licensees. The inclusion of such a guarantee of exclusivity may be important to a licensee, who has to invest in the advertising or marketing of the work, and who needs to ensure that they have a reasonable degree of control in the relevant market.

In related situations, the Commission has recognized *both* the value of such terms *and* the threat posed by exclusive licensing to the achievement of the internal market. Consequently, the Commission treats exclusive agreements as legitimate, but simultaneously prohibits certain terms that it considers will have an unduly restrictive effect on the practices of parallel importers. While the Commission allows terms that prohibit the

---

[97] Ibid., [136].   [98] Ibid., [135].

[99] Regulation No. 316/2014 of 21 March 2014 on the application of Article 101(3) of the Treaty on the Functioning of the European Union to categories of technology transfer agreements [2014] *OJ L* 93/17 (the '2014 Technology Transfer Block Exemption Regulation'). For more on the TTBE 2014, see Chapter 23.

[100] Competition Act 1998, s. 2. See OFT, *Intellectual Property Rights: A Draft Competition Act 1998 Guideline* (November 2001), OFT 418.   [101] Competition Act 1998, s. 10 (parallel exemptions).

active marketing of the work in the territory of another licensee, the agreement may not prohibit 'passive' sales.[102]

Where an exclusive territorial agreement covers the representation (or exhibition), as opposed to the distribution of copies of the work, it may also fall within Article 101 TFEU. In *Coditel II*,[103] a French company granted a Belgian company the exclusive right to exhibit the film, *Le Boucher*, in Belgium for seven years. The French company later licensed a German broadcasting company to broadcast the film on German television. When it did so, Coditel, a Belgian cable operator, included the film in its Belgian service. The question referred to the Court of Justice was whether the exclusive exhibition agreement was prohibited by Article 101 TFEU. The Court held that, in general, exclusive territorial licences do not infringe Article 101(1). However, the Court added that an exclusive licence might do so if the agreement were excessively long, or if the exercise of the right were to be likely to distort competition within the internal market.[104]

Coditel now needs to be viewed in the light of *Football Association Premier League Ltd (FAPL) v. QC Leisure and ors*.[105] In that case, FAPL licensed broadcasting rights for live transmission of football matches on a territorial basis for a term of three years. It awarded the rights on an exclusive basis, which it explained was to maximize its returns. To maintain the territorial exclusivity, each licensee broadcaster undertook to prevent the public from receiving its broadcasts outside the territory. This was done by means of encryption of the broadcast and making access to those broadcasts conditional on being in the territory.[106] FAPL brought an action against the importers of equipment and cards that enabled people in the United Kingdom to watch Greek broadcasts. The defendant argued that FAPL had breached Article 101 by requiring its Greek licensees to prevent the use of the cards outside Greece.[107] The Court of Justice held that the licence terms that obliged the Greek broadcaster not to supply decoding devices that could be used outside of the territory covered by the licence agreement were in breach of Article 101.[108] The Court referred to *Coditel II*, but (without casting doubt on the conclusions) noted that if the agreement were to tend 'to restore the divisions between national markets', that would frustrate the objective of integrating markets by making interpenetration of market 'more difficult'.[109] As a matter of principle, these agreements were to be regarded as having the object of restricting competition within Article 101(1) TFEU.[110] The Court recognized that it might be that the legal and economic context might justify such a provision,[111] or that there might be circumstances

[102] TTR, Art. 1(2), Recital 15; VRR, Art. 4(b); see *Re BBC* [1976] *CMLR* D–89. An OFT investigation into the CD market found evidence of past anti-competitive agreements requiring retailers of CDs not to import cheaper CDs from mainland Europe, or offering favourable terms to those who did not do so: see OFT, *Annual Report* (2002–03), 61.   [103] *Coditel SA v. Cine Vog Films SA (No. 2)*, Case 262/81 [1982] *ECR* 3381.

[104] Ibid., 3401–2, [15], [17], [19]. See also *FAPL*, Joined Cases C-403/08 and C-429/08 [2011] *ECR* I–9083 (ECJ, Grand Chamber), [137].

[105] *FAPL*, Joined Cases C-403/08 and C-429/08 [2011] *ECR* I–9083 (ECJ, Grand Chamber), See, e.g., W. Batchelor and T. Jenkins, '*FA Premier League*: The Broader Implications for Copyright Licensing' [2012] *ECLR* 157 (stating that *FAPL* 'effectively reverses or at least heavily distinguishes the *Coditel I* and *II* line of cases which held that territorial limits of content licensing were entirely legal').

[106] *FAPL*, Joined Cases C-403/08 and C-429/08 [2011] *ECR* I–9083 (ECJ, Grand Chamber) [32]–[35].

[107] So the case did not concern territorial limitations themselves, just attendant obligations to enforce them: ibid., [141].   [108] Ibid., [144], [146].

[109] Ibid., [139].   [110] Ibid., [139].

[111] Here, the Court referred back to [118]–[121], where it had considered whether there was any justification for the limitation on free movement of services that was a consequence of the rules prohibiting the use of decoder cards from one territory in another. There, it distinguished *Coditel I* as a case involving unauthorized retransmission by cable, whereas in *FAPL* the Greek broadcaster was authorized and provided remuneration.

in which a person could benefit from Article 101(3), but that no such justification had been persuasively offered.[112] The specific subject matter of any intellectual property rights in receiving 'appropriate remuneration' (not the 'highest possible remuneration') was sufficiently protected by the remuneration received from the Greek broadcaster, and there was no reason why that could not be calculated by reference to audiences not merely within Greece, but also outside that territory (on the basis of the numbers of decoders).[113]

Where does the *FAPL* case leave territorial licensing (and the related phenomenon of 'geo-blocking')? Some commentators have seen it as having radical implications, undermining the comfort that the *Coditel* case had been taken to provide.[114] However, others have observed the rather limited scope of the holding: the Court emphasized that territorial licensing was not in issue, but only clauses reinforcing such licensing.[115] Moreover, on its face, the Court decision explicitly limits itself to satellite broadcasting,[116] whereas contemporary distribution often includes distribution through cable and Internet.

In *Cross-Border Access to Pay-TV,*[117] the Commission read the FAPL decision as justifying it issuing a 'statement of objections' to seven film studios (Disney, NBC, Paramount Pictures, Sony, Twentieth Century Fox, Universal, and Warner Bros) and Sky TV in relation to their licensing agreements, which purport to offer Sky TV permission to broadcast (or otherwise transmit) the films, but only for access within the specified territory. Such agreements usually also commit the broadcaster to utilize technological measures that prevent access from outside the territory. One of the Commission's primary objections is that the effect of these licensing terms is to prevent broadcasters from offering their services in response to unsolicited requests from consumers located outside the licensed territory. Significantly, the Commission ceased proceedings against one of the film studios, Paramount Pictures, following its undertaking to vary the arrangements to allow for such 'passive sales'.[118]

As part of the Digital Single Market strategy, the Geo-Blocking Regulation has been adopted.[119] In operation from 3 December 2018, this seeks to prevent the use of blocking measures and discriminatory conditions in contracts between traders and customers that provide for different treatment based on the customer's nationality, place of residence, or place of establishment. However, its impact in our field is likely to be limited. This is

---

[112] *FAPL*, Joined Cases C-403/08 and C-429/08 [2011] *ECR* I–9083 (ECJ, Grand Chamber), [145], where the Court referred back to [105]–[124].   [113] Ibid., [105]–[117].

[114] See, e.g., B. Hugenholtz, 'Europe 1 Premier League 0', (9 October 2011) kluwercopyrightblog.com ('the judgment is likely to have far-reaching ramifications for current business practices in the broadcasting sector, as licenses conferring absolute territorial exclusivity are common, not only as regards televised football matches and other sporting events, but also in respect of motion pictures and other premium content offered by satellite pay TV services').

[115] D. Doukas, 'The Sky is not the (Only) Limit: Sports Broadcasting without Frontiers and the Court of Justice: Comment on Murphy' [2012] *ELR* 605, 625 (the ruling is not the 'gravedigger' of territorial exclusivity).

[116] *FAPL*, Joined Cases C-403/08 and C-429/08 [2011] *ECR* I–9083 (ECJ, Grand Chamber), [57].

[117] COMP/40023 *Cross-Border Access to Pay-TV Content*, IP/15/5432 (23 July 2015); G. Mazziotti, 'Is Geo-Blocking a Real Cause for Concern in Europe?' [2016] *EIPR* 365, 371 *ff*.

[118] Commission Press Release IP/16/2645 (26 July 2016).

[119] Regulation (EU) 2018/302 of the European Parliament and of the Council of 28 February 2018 on addressing unjustified geo-blocking and other forms of discrimination based on customers' nationality, place of residence or place of establishment within the internal market [2018] *OJ L* 60/1 2.3.2018. This was based on the proposal COM(2016) 289 final.

because it does not apply to audio-visual services at all,[120] and it has limited application to other services. More significantly, Article 4 of the Regulation, which prohibits discrimination in the conditions of access to goods and services, including electronically supplied services, is framed so as to be inapplicable to 'services the main feature of which is the provision of access to and use of copyright protected works or other subject matter.'[121] The effect is that legality of geo-blocking is unaffected in cases of, for example, customers in one EU Member State seeking access to sports broadcasts targeted at another Member State, or where customers from continental Europe seek access to Netflix (operating in the UK or Ireland).[122] In turn, providers can use technological measures to block the access, or impose conditions as to the place of residence of the consumer. However, in relation to ebooks or music, technical measures blocking access are not generally permitted,[123] but contractual conditions based on nationality or residence may be. In so far as the supplier of the services only has rights for particular territories, it would evidently be problematic to prohibit it from taking action to limit supply to the extent of the rights that have been granted. However, it is less clear that a service provider who has rights in multiple member states should be permitted through service conditions to divide up markets and subject them to different conditions based on nationality or residence.[124]

3.4.2 Restrictive field of distribution agreements

Where a work has a number of potential markets, a copyright owner may wish to limit the field in which the licensee exploits the work. For example, a copyright owner may wish to license a work for sale by a book club separately from its sale by retail outlets. Such agreements are akin to 'fields of use' limitations. Under the Vertical Restraints Regulation, these would be restrictions of the customers to whom the buyer may sell the contract goods or services. These would not be exempt unless the restriction were to be confined to active sales to an exclusive customer group allocated by the supplier to another buyer. If a copyright owner has given general retail rights exclusively to one person and book club rights to another, a restriction preventing the book club owner from actively selling outside the club would be exempt from Article 101. The Office of Fair Trading (now superseded by the Competition and Markets Authority) seems to have taken a similar stance as regards the application of the 'Chapter I prohibition'.[125]

3.4.3 Price limitations

A copyright owner may wish to restrict the price at which the licensee sells a particular product. They might also require the licensee to specify to subsequent purchasers that

---

[120] Art. 1(3) (excluding from scope of the Regulation 'the activities referred to in Article 2(2) of Directive 2006/123/EC'. Para (g) refers to 'audiovisual services, including cinematographic services . . . and radio broadcasting'). For the view that the division of markets for audio-visual works in the European Union is largely associated with maximizing profits, see G. Mazziotti, 'Is Geo-Blocking a Real Cause for Concern in Europe?' [2016] *EIPR* 365, 370 (exploring reasons for geo-blocking and noting that audiovisual producers typically possess all relevant rights for all member states).

[121] Geo Blocking Regulation, Art. 4(1)(b). This exclusion is to be subject to review by 23 March 2020: Geo Blocking Regulation, Art. 9(2).

[122] Geo Blocking Regulation, Recital 8.

[123] Geo Blocking Regulation, Art. 3. This would be subject to exceptions, in particular where blocking is necessary to ensure compliance with Union or national law: Art. 3(3).

[124] Consider, for example, Apple's iTunes service: see G. Mazziotti, 'Is Geo-Blocking a Real Cause for Concern in Europe?' [2016] *EIPR* 365, 369.

[125] See OFT, *Intellectual Property Rights: A Draft Competition Act 1998 Guideline* (November 2001) OFT 418, [2.21]; Competition Act 1998, s. 10.

they may not resell the product at anything other than a specified price. Although such agreements have traditionally been treated as being unlawful, the UK rather surprisingly went out of its way to tolerate one such price-fixing arrangement in the form of the 'Net Book Agreement' until as late as 1997. This was an agreement between members of the Publishers' Association to impose certain conditions on booksellers as regards the price at which certain books ('net books') could be sold (essentially restricting the discounting of books).[126] However, in 1995, the majority of publishers decided to abandon the net book system. As a result, the exemption previously afforded to the Agreement was removed.[127]

Under the Vertical Restraints Regulation, attempts at resale price maintenance constitute 'hardcore' restrictions that prevent the block exemption from operating.[128] An individual assessment would therefore be necessary.[129] The domestic position is similar: a provision relating to minimum price maintenance that is, on its face, anti-competitive would need to be justified on the ground that it (i) improves the production or distribution of goods or promotes technical or economic progress, and also (ii) allows consumers 'a fair share of the resulting benefit'.[130]

3.4.4 Site licences

The access and use of digitized works is commonly based on copyright licences and contractual restrictions. In the cases of software, databases, and journals in electronic form, it has become common to limit permitted use to a particular location. The question arises whether such a restriction is anti-competitive. It has been argued that, to the extent that site licences operate as restriction on output, they are anti-competitive and fall within Article 101 TFEU. For example, if the effect of licensing software to one particular terminal were to restrict the productive use of that software, such a licence may fall within Article 101. However, if a site licence is 'open', in the sense that it allows for expansion of output or has a clause allowing for further licences on commercial terms, then this objection does not operate.[131] Under the Technology Transfer Regulation,[132] restrictions on quantities of output will place agreement outside the block exemption.

4 REGULATION OF CONTRACTS FOR THE PROTECTION OF USERS

In this section, we consider the ways in which the law interferes with copyright contracts for the benefit of 'users', by which we primarily mean individual consumers who wish to utilize copyright-protected material. The idea of protecting users from unfair contracts imposed by copyright owners is a relatively new one. In part, this has arisen because

---

[126] *Re Net Book Agreement 1957* [1962] 1 *WLR* 1347.

[127] *Re Net Book Agreement 1957 (No. 4)* [1998] *ICR* 753.   [128] VRR, Art. 4(a).

[129] The ECJ held the UK Net Book Agreement to fall within the then Art. 101 prohibition, but said that it might be justifiable under Art. 101(3), overturning the views of the Commission and General Court: *Re Net Book Agreements: Publishers' Association v. EC Commission*, Case C-360/92P [1996] *FSR* 33, [1996] *ICR* 121, [1995] *EMLR* 185 (ECJ); *Publishers' Association v. EC Commission* [1992] 4 *All ER* 70, [1992] *ICR* 842 (CFI).

[130] Competition Act 1998, ss 9 (criteria for exemption), 10 (parallel exemption).

[131] M. Dolmans and M. Odriozola, 'Site Licence, Right Licence? Site Licences under EC Competition Law' [1998] *ECLR* 493; cf. J. Townsend, 'The Case for Site Licences' [1999] *ECLR* 169.

[132] TTR, Art. 3(5).

certain acts carried out by users have come to require the consent of copyright owners. In the past, a person who bought a book could do almost whatever they wished with the book without the need for further consent: the book could be read, lent to a friend, or sold to a charity shop without raising any potential liability. Today, as a result of technological developments, many similar acts (such as photocopying the book or reading an electronic version on screen) might now require permission. The second reason why contracts between copyright holders and users are becoming increasingly common is that techniques of distribution, particularly digital dissemination, are removing intermediaries from the distribution process. A consumer who formerly would have bought a hard copy of a CD from a retailer can now be supplied with an equivalent digital version over the Internet directly from the copyright holder. This direct contact allows the copyright owner to reinforce any rights that they may have under copyright with obligations imposed as part of the contract that they have with the owner.[133]

The main concern in these circumstances is that 'click-through contracts' will extend copyright owners' rights beyond their existing scope.[134] Consequently, such licences might impose conditions for use of works in which copyright has lapsed, or in the case of software might prohibit the making of back-up copies or decompilation, or in other cases might prohibit criticism or review.[135] As the use of electronic resources increases and such contracts become the norm, the 'delicate balance' between owners and users encapsulated in statutory copyright may be sacrificed.

Although the E-Commerce Directive specifies that 'electronic contracts' should be recognized as valid,[136] specific directives nevertheless indicate that certain exemptions may not be overridden by contract law.[137] For example, the Software Directive allows certain acts, including the decompilation of computer programs; it also renders void contracts that attempt to restrict those rights.[138] A similar clause has been introduced to prevent contractual circumvention of defences to infringement of copyright in databases.[139] In its implementation of the Hargreaves Review,[140] the UK government adopted a similar approach to the new and amended exceptions relating to private study and non-commercial research,[141] quotation,[142] parody,[143] data mining,[144] disability, education,[145]

---

[133] Issues of fitness for use and quality of digital content supplied by traders to consumers is regulated in part by the Consumer Rights Act 2015, Ch. 3. The European Commission, as part of the Digital Single Market strategy, has proposed harmonization: Proposal for a Directive on Certain Aspects Concerning Contracts for the Supply of Digital Content, COM(2015) 634 final. The proposal requires the supplier of digital content to have undertaken relevant rights clearances in relation to third party intellectual property rights, but in other respects the proposed legislation leaves intellectual property rights intact: ibid., Art. 8, Recital 21, Recital 31.

[134] As to the enforceability of these agreements see: P. Johnson 'All Wrapped Up? A Review of the Enforceability of "Shrink-Wrap" and "Click-Wrap" Licences in the United Kingdom and the United States' [2003] EIPR 98.

[135] SAS Institute v. World Programming Ltd [2013] EWCA Civ 1482, [108] (applying contra proferentem principle to interpretation of click-based, 'take it or leave it' licence).

[136] E-Commerce Dir., Art. 9(1).

[137] Broadcasting Act 1996, s. 137; giving effect to what is now art. 15 of the Audiovisual Media Services Directive (2010/13/EU). [138] CDPA 1988, ss 50A, 50B, 296A(1)(a), 296A(1)(b), 296A(1)(c).

[139] CDPA 1988, s. 296B. See also Database Regs, reg. 19(2).

[140] Hargreaves Review, Recommendation 5 and 51, [5.40]. See Chapter 9, section 2.5, pp. 234–5.

[141] CDPA 1988m, s. 29(4B). [142] CDPA 1988, s. 30(4). [143] CDPA 1988, s. 30A(2).

[144] CDPA 1988, s. 29A(5); the proposed Directive on Copyright in the Digital Single Market includes a requirement to provide an exception for data mining and also to restrict contractual obligations limiting the obligation. [145] CDPA 1988, s. 32(3),

and libraries.[146] Subsequent reforms of EU law, including the Marrakesh reforms, similarly preclude contractual overriding of the freedoms recognized.[147] Moreover, the Information Society Directive explicitly takes on board concerns about oppressive use of technological measures to prevent access to material falling within copyright's carefully defined exceptions. Article 6(4) of the Directive provided for a convoluted compromise. This, and its UK implementation in sections 296ZE and 296ZEA of the 1988 Act, is reviewed in Chapter 13.

5 ORPHAN AND OUT-OF-COMMERCE WORKS

One problem with exploiting copyright-protected material that has attracted increasing attention is that of so-called 'orphan works'. An orphan work is one the copyright owners ('parents') of which either do not exist or cannot be located. Orphan works exist in part because there is no formal structure for registering copyrights and keeping track of ownership. In some cases, the authors of works may not even appreciate that they have created something protected by copyright. In other cases, the ownership of copyright is impossible to trace, perhaps because a firm went bankrupt or the relatives of a deceased author cannot be identified. The fact that many works are protected by copyright, but that owners are not easy to identify, means that the market in copyright transactions is inefficient. It is inefficient because some transactions that would voluntarily occur—agreements to use copyright-protected material—are not occurring simply because the costs of locating the owner are greater than the value of the transaction to the potential licensee. In other cases, users simply take a risk or utilize litigation insurance in case the copyright holder does appear.

The issue of orphan works has become pressing for two reasons. The first is that the potential problem has grown as copyright term is extended. The British Library has estimated that 40 per cent of all print works are orphan works.[148] The second is that digital technologies have given rise to new potential uses of such largely forgotten or valueless works, for example in digital archives, but also because they can now be made available profitably to niche markets. If such projects are not to be impeded by heavy costs investigating copyright ownership, it is necessary to offer users some way of immunizing themselves from later liability.

In 2012, the European Union adopted the Orphan Works Directive which the United Kingdom implemented in 2014.[149] At the same time, the United Kingdom also adopted its own regime to enable further licensing of orphan works.[150] In addition, there is a proposal by the European Union to enable the use of out-of-commerce works for digitization, distribution, and communication to the public by cultural heritage institutions. An out-of-commerce work is one which is not public through customary channels of commerce and cannot be reasonably expected to become so.

5.1 EU ORPHAN WORKS REGIME

The EU regime is relatively limited in scope, being designed to enable digitization of the contents of public libraries, museums, and archives.[151] The regime extends beyond

---

[146] CDPA 1988, ss 41(5), 42(7), 42A(6), 75(2).
[147] Directive (EU) 2017/1564 of 13 September 2017, Art. 3(5).   [148] Gowers Review, [4.91].
[149] Copyright and Rights in Performances (Certain Permitted Uses of Orphan Works) Regs 2014 (SI 2014/2861).   [150] ERR 2013, s. 77 (introducing CDPA 1988, s. 116A).
[151] OWD, Art. 1(1); CDPA 1988, Sch. ZA1, para. 2 (defining 'relevant body').

authorial works to include related rights (phonograms) and also includes unpublished works that are publicly accessible as long as 'it is reasonable to assume that the rightholders would not oppose the uses'.[152] It does not, however, apply to stand-alone photographs.[153] The specified organizations are to be permitted to reproduce and make available 'orphan works'[154]—that is, works in relation to which all or some of the 'right holders' cannot be identified or located despite a 'diligent search' having been carried out.[155] Such a search must be carried out for each and every work by consulting appropriate sources for the category of work in question.[156] The search is targeted at the country of first publication,[157] but if there is 'evidence to suggest that relevant information on rightholders' is to be found in other countries, sources in such countries 'shall also be consulted'.[158] The details of such searches are to be recorded in a single publicly accessible online database managed by the European Union Intellectual Property Office. If a work is regarded as orphan in one member state, then that status should be recognized in other member states.[159] Should the right holder reappear, they may bring the orphan status of a work to an end[160] and the 'revenant' right holder is entitled to 'fair compensation' for past uses.[161]

After one year of operation, the Intellectual Property Office undertook a review of both the EU and domestic system. In relation to the EU regime, the review considered the number of entries on the database. Each entry is a work which has been given orphan status and so may be used by an eligible cultural heritage institution. This shows that in the United Kingdom there are ten beneficiary organizations and there are 61 across the European Union during the relevant period. During that period, between October 2014 and October 2015, there were 53 works declared to be orphan by British cultural heritage organizations and 1,374 so declared by organizations across the European Union. In relation to all those claims 25 authors subsequently came forward to make claims of ownership, two of whom were from the United Kingdom.[162]

5.2 THE UK ORPHAN WORKS REGIME

A specific UK regime was established by the Copyright and Rights in Performances (Licensing of Orphan Works) Regulations 2014 (Orphan Works Regulations).[163] The definition of 'orphan work' (that is, a work the owner of which has not been found after a 'diligent search') is more ambitious than in the EU regime.[164] The regulations entitle the authorizing body (that is, the Comptroller meaning, essentially, the Intellectual

---

[152] OWD, Art. 1(3); CDPA 1988, Sch. ZA1, para. 2(2) (defining 'relevant work').

[153] Groups representing photographers have lobbied effectively in opposition to orphan work legislation and believe that the difficulties with identifying authorship are particularly prevalent in their field. For a taste, see online at http://www.stop43.org.uk.   [154] OWD, Art. 6(1); CDPA 1988, Sch. ZA1, para. 3.

[155] OWD, Art. 2; CDPA 1988, Sch. ZA1, para. 4.   [156] OWD, Art. 3(1).

[157] OWD, Art. 3(3) ('a diligent search shall be carried out in the Member State of first publication'); CDPA 1988, Sch. ZA1, para. 4(4).   [158] OWD, Art. 3(4).

[159] CDPA 1988, Sch. ZA1, para. 6.   [160] OWD, Art. 5; CDPA 1988, Sch. ZA1, para. 7.

[161] OWD, Art. 6(5). Determined by the laws of the country in which the organization using the work is established: CDPA 1988, Sch. ZA1, para. 7(2).

[162] UK IPO, *Orphan works: Review of the first twelve months* (2015), 16.

[163] SI 2014/2863; these are made under CDPA, s 116A which was inserted by the Enterprise and Regulatory Reform Act 2013, s 77.

[164] 'Diligent search' is defined in Orphan Works Regs, reg. 4 ('shall comprise a reasonable search of the relevant sources to identify and locate the right holders of the relevant work'). Although the definition is the same as with the EU regime, the precise type of search that is appropriate may differ, because the proposed 'licence' might cover different acts.

Property Office) to license the use of 'orphan works',[165] and maintain a register of diligent searches, licences granted, and licences refused.[166] If satisfied, the Comptroller is able to grant non-exclusive licences for up to seven years.[167] Licence fees are payable 'up front' and correspond to comparable fees for non-orphan works.[168] Key differences between the UK regime and the EU one include: (i) the subject matter covered (the UK regime covers all works, including stand-alone photographs); (ii) the mechanism employed (a notional licence rather than an exception);[169] (iii) the types of potential licensee, which are not limited to 'publicly accessible cultural and heritage organisations' and thus might include commercial entities; and (iv) the types of act covered (going well beyond the mere digitization and 'making available', and covering commercial as well as non-commercial uses). The UK regime thus has potentially much greater reach than it European counterpart. In part, for this reason, at least one commentator has questioned the compatibility of the provision with European law.[170] However, the UK 'licences' can authorize acts only within the United Kingdom,[171] so while the legislation is more extensive, it is necessarily rather local in effect.

The Intellectual Property Office's review of the scheme after one year showed that in relation to the domestic regime there were 48 applications made covering 294 works. These works include 229 still images, 47 written works, 14 sound recordings, 2 musical notations, 1 script, and 1 moving image. There were seven commercial use licences granted in relation to 35 works with a value of a little under £8,000 and 20 non-commercial use licences for 212 works with a value of £21.20. No licences had been refused or appeals lodged during the 12-month period and no right holders had made themselves known.[172] It can be seen that both regimes have provided some benefit although the use of orphan works is still relatively limited in relation to the number of such works that exist and it does not appear that use of the system has slowed down since that time. [173]

5.3 OUT-OF-COMMERCE WORKS

In France, a law was introduced to allow collecting societies to collect licence fees for the use of out-of-commerce works, that is, works where the author is known but it is not

---

[165] Orphan Works Regs, reg. 6.   [166] Orphan Works Regs, reg. 5.

[167] Orphan Works Regs, reg. 6(2)(b). The 'licence' operates on the basis that moral rights have been asserted and thus require attribution (Orphan Works Regs, reg. 6(2)(e)). The UK IPO may refuse to grant a licence on the basis that the proposed use constitutes a derogatory treatment: reg. 6(5).

[168] Orphan Works Regs, reg. 10. Non-commercial licences may be at a nominal charge: UK IPO, *Copyright Works* (2014), 21. So-called 'relevant' rights owners is able to claim the fees from the IPO. After eight years, unclaimed fees may be applied by the IPO in respect of the costs of the scheme, or to 'fund social, cultural and educational activities': reg. 13.

[169] CDPA 1988, s. 116A(1) (empowering the Secretary of State to grant licences), 116A(5) (stating that the Regulations must provide for any licence 'to have effect as if granted by the missing owner'); reg. 6. Cf. CDPA 1988, s. 44B (introducing an exception for relevant bodies). One might wonder whether a notional licence is compatible with the CJEU's view that the author must be able to give informed consent: see section 5.3, p. 349 for the discussion of *Soulier*, Case C-301/15, EU:C:2016:878, [34]–[40].

[170] Rosati predicted that the UK scheme would outflank the EU one to such an extent that the latter would be rendered otiose: E. Rosati, 'The Orphan Works Provisions of the ERR Act: Are They Compatible with UK and EU Laws?' [2013] *EIPR* 724. For that reason, and others, she suggests that the EU Directive 'pre-empts' the UK action in the field, which is therefore disallowed.

[171] UK IPO, *Copyright Works* (2014), 13, 17; reg. 6(2)(a). This suggests that there may, in due course, be reciprocal agreements with other countries operating similar schemes.

[172] UK IPO, *Orphan works: Review of the first twelve months* (2015), 6–7.

[173] By May 2018, the number of works on the register had increased to 801 (584 still images, 186 written works, 18 sound recordings, 6 musical notations, 6 moving images, and 1 script).

possible to obtain the work commercially.[174] Under the regime, once the work had been in a database of out of print works for 6 months, and its status had not been opposed, a collecting society could collect remuneration from a third party for digitization and exploitation of the book. The Court of Justice held, in *Soulier & Doke*,[175] that the French law is incompatible with the Information Society Directive. This is because Articles 2 and 3 of the Directive conferred the exclusive right to authorize reproduction and communication, and for there to be consent (even of an implicit variety), the author must at the very least be aware of the proposed use. Under the system, the author would not necessarily be aware of the use.

It should be noted, however, as part of the proposed Digital Single Market Directive[176] the Commission has proposed that collective management organizations may grant licences to a cultural heritage organization to use 'out of commerce works' for non-commercial purposes.[177]

6 ONLINE PORTABILITY

As part of the EU's 'Digital Single Market' package,[178] the European Council and Parliament has adopted a Regulation[179] to provide for online portability. Put simply, from 1 April 2018, this allows users who are able to watch broadcast content on mobile devices in their own country to do so when they travel. To achieve this end, users who are temporarily abroad are deemed to be in their country of residence;[180] and providers are required to enable such subscribers to access the online content service 'in the same manner' as in the member state of residence, and may not charge an additional fee.[181] The rules apply only to 'online content services' that are 'portable'. An 'online content service' is either an audiovisual media service,[182] or a service 'the main feature' of which is the provision of access to, and use of works, subject matter, or transmissions of broadcasting organizations (whether linear or on-demand).[183] As a result, the rules would apply to those with subscriptions to Netflix or Spotify but be inapplicable to subscriptions to databases (such as Westlaw). A service is portable where subscribers can access and use the service in their member state without being limited to a specific location. The rules only apply to 'subscribers', a term limited to consumers who are entitled to access on the basis of a contract (another reason why the rules are inapplicable to Westlaw—most subscribers are not consumers but do so as part of their business or profession).[184] The provider of an online content service provided without the payment of money may decide to enable its subscribers who are temporarily elsewhere in the European Union to access

---

[174] For a discussion see, A. Bensamoun, 'The French Out-of-Commerce Books Law in the Light of the European Orphan Works Directive' (2014) 3 *QMJIP* 213.

[175] *Marc Soulier, Sara Doke v. Premier Ministre, Ministre de la Culture et de la Communication*, Case C-301/15, EU:C:2016:878, [34]–[40] (ECJ, Third Chamber).

[176] European Commission, *Proposal for a Directive of the European Parliament and of the Council on copyright in the Digital Single Market* (14 September 2016) COM(2016) 593 final.

[177] Ibid., Proposed Art. 7.   [178] COM(2015) 192 final.

[179] Regulation (EU) 2017/1128 of the European Parliament and of the Council of 14 June 2017 on cross-border portability of online content in the internal market, *OJ L* 168/1 (30 June 2017). Note the corrections at *OJ L* 198/42 (28 July 2017). The Regulation was based on Commission Proposal, dated 9 December 2015: COM(2015) 627 final.

[180] Regulation (EU) 2017/1128, Art. 4.   [181] Regulation (EU) 2017/1128, Art. 3.

[182] As defined in Directive 2010/13/EU, Art. 1.   [183] Ibid., Art. 2(5).

[184] Ibid., Art. 2(2) (thereby excluding, e.g., BBC services).

and use the service, and if it meets certain conditions, the Regulation will apply to such cases.[185] Contracts limiting cross-border portability are unenforceable.[186] According to the Commission's own impact assessment, the numbers of short-term migrants who might benefit from the portability rules is rather limited.[187]

7 CONTROLLING COLLECTING SOCIETIES

In Chapter 11, we looked at the ways in which copyright owners exploit their rights by way of collective administration. While collective licensing can clearly be beneficial to both copyright owners and users, the existence of single bodies solely responsible for administering rights may also cause a number of problems. The problems posed are of two sorts: problems with members and problems with users. Problems with members typically occur because a copyright owner has little alternative to joining the society, which can thus impose restrictive terms. The second set of problems arises from the relations with users, who similarly have little alternative but to take a licence from the collecting society on whatever terms it chooses.

This section looks at how these problems have been recognized and regulated at both national and European levels, including (i) EU and UK competition law, (ii) the UK's copyright tribunal, (iii) under EU law as implemented in the United Kingdom.[188] Until recently the picture was much more complicated as there were stronger elements of self-regulation[189] and some domestic regulation.[190] While the self-regulation continues to some degree, it has been largely overtaken by the EU collective management regime.

7.1 REGULATION OF MEMBER–SOCIETY RELATIONS

The terms of membership and control over the collecting society are a matter, first and foremost, for the rules of the society. If a sufficiently large number of member's object to these rules, they can be changed at the general assembly of members although it is possible for the society to delegate this role to an assembly of delegates.[191]

7.1.1 UK competition control

A powerful form of external control of society–member relations is provided by the UK competition authorities. As mentioned previously, the Competition Act 1998 contains prohibitions on agreements and concerted practices that restrict competition (the 'Chapter I prohibition') and 'abuse of a dominant position' (the so-called 'Chapter II prohibition'). Since collecting societies occupy a dominant position in the market (the supply of services of administering particular rights), relations are apt to be scrutinized to ensure there is no abuse. In addition, under Part IV of the Enterprise Act 2002, the

---

[185] Ibid., Art. 6.   [186] Ibid., Art. 7.

[187] Commission Staff Working Document, *Impact assessment*, SWD(2015) 270 final, 17 (72 million).

[188] For background, see European Commission, *Communication from the Commission to the Council, the European Parliament and the European Economic and Social Committee: The Management of Copyright and Related Rights in the Internal Market* (16 April 2004) COM(2004) 261 final.

[189] See, e.g., British Copyright Council, *Principles for Collective Management Organisations' Codes of Conduct* (2012).

[190] The now revoked Copyright (Regulation of Relevant Licensing Bodies) Regulations 2014 (SI 2014/898).

[191] See Collective Management of Copyright (EU Directive) Regulations 2016, reg. 7.

Competition and Markets Authority (CMA) is able (after conducting a preliminary infor-mal investigation) to constitute a group to investigate a market, the features of which it has grounds for suspecting prevent, restrict, or distort competition.[192] The group must investigate whether there is an adverse affect on competition, and report. As a result of such a finding, the CMA may require that action be taken to remedy the adverse affect and make orders or require undertakings to bring about appropriate changes.[193] In a pre-vious investigation, under powers similar to those now granted by the Enterprise Act, the Monopolies and Mergers Commission (a predecessor to the CMA) held that certain practices of the Performing Rights Society were unsatisfactory and the Society agreed to amend its rules.[194] An even earlier example was where that Monopolies and Mergers Commission found that the collective licensing of sound recordings by PPL improperly limited access to recorded music.[195] This was remedied by a compulsory licence being introduced by the Broadcasting Act 1990.[196]

7.1.2 EU competition law

Another form of control over the rules of the society is to be found in Article 102 TFEU. This prohibits the abuse by one or more undertakings of a dominant position. Rights organizations constitute 'undertakings' when they supply certain services to composers, authors, and publishers; they also often hold a dominant position in relation to the provi-sion of these services. The critical issue is the extent to which the conduct of the rights organization constitutes an abuse.

The balancing exercise required by Article 102 TFEU has been felt[197] in four important aspects of society–member relations:

(i)   It is clear that, under EU law, societies may not discriminate on grounds of nation-ality, for example by conferring associate status on foreign authors. All collect-ing societies must permit other nationals from the European Union to join the society.[198]

(ii) The Commission has stated that the rules of collecting societies should ensure that no group of members obtains preferential treatment from revenue collected from the membership as a whole.[199]

(iii) In *Belgische Radio v. SABAM*,[200] the Court of Justice held that an abuse would occur if a society were to impose obligations on members that were not absolutely neces-sary for the attainment of the society's objectives and which could encroach unfairly on members' freedoms.[201] A restriction imposed upon a member must be 'indis-pensable' to the operation of the society and must restrict the member's freedom to dispose of their works no more than is absolutely necessary (the 'equity' test).[202]

---

[192] Enterprise Act 2002, s. 131.   [193] Enterprise Act 2002, s. 134(4).

[194] *Report on the Supply in the UK of the Services of Administering Performing Rights and Film Synchronization Rights* (Cmnd. 3147, 1996).

[195] *Collective licensing. A report on certain practices in the collective licensing of public performance and broadcasting rights in sound recordings* (Cm. 530, 1988).

[196] Broadcasting Act 1990, s. 175, which inserted CDPA 1988, s. 135A to 135G.

[197] There was also an unsuccessful claim by the European Commission against 24 collecting societies across Europe alleging the societies had engaged in concerted practices to illegally agree the territorial scope of their licences and so precluded multi-territorial, multi-repertoire licensing (the so called 'CISAC Case'. Eventually, the General Court held that the Commission had insufficient evidence to make out their claim: *CISAC v. European Commission*, Case T-442/08, EU:T:2013:188.   [198] *Re GEMA (No. 1)* [1971] *CMLR* D–35.

[199] *Re GEMA's Statutes (No. 2)* [1972] *CMLR* D–115.   [200] [1974] *ECR* 313.   [201] Ibid., 317 [15].

[202] *Re GEMA (No. 1)* [1971] *CMLR* D–35; *Report on the Supply in the UK of the Services of Administering Performing Rights and Film Synchronization Rights* (Cm. 3147, 1996), [2.119]–[2.121].

(iv) Societies are not permitted to impose unduly lengthy notice periods. In *Belgische Radio*, the Court observed that rules operated by SABAM, the Belgian collecting society, allowing the society to retain rights for five years after a member withdrew 'may appear an unfair condition', but left the specific determination of whether this was so to the national authority.[203]

7.1.3 The Collective Rights Management Directive

In 2014, the European Commission adopted the Collective Rights Management Directive[204] which was implemented in UK law in 2016.[205] This sets out a general obligation that member states ensure that collecting societies act in the best interest of their members,[206] and that member states ensure that various rights are conferred on right holders and members,[207] and various obligations on societies relating to annual meetings,[208] collection and use of revenue,[209] deductions,[210] and so on.

7.2 REGULATION OF SOCIETY-SOCIETY RELATIONS

The Collective Rights Management Directive and implementing regulations contains a number of provisions that seek to ensure that societies that enter into reciprocal relations with other societies are able to ensure that their members' interests are secured. Importantly, for example, no deductions (such as for social and cultural purposes) are to be made by any society for fees that it collects on behalf of another society under a representation agreement.[211] There can also be no discrimination against right holders whose rights are managed under a representation agreement,[212] and that monies are distributed 'regularly, diligently and accurately'.[213]

7.3 REGULATION OF SOCIETY-USER RELATIONS

Another way in which collecting societies are regulated is in terms of their relationship with users of copyright. Here, the problem is that most people wishing to use copyright works have no alternative but to seek a licence from a collecting society. This places the society in a strong bargaining position, which may enable it to dictate terms of use to the licensee. In the absence of regulatory control, the society might charge exorbitant fees, discriminate unfairly between different kinds of user, or require parties to acquire

---

[203] *Belgische Radio* [1974] *ECR* 313, 317, [12], 325–6 (AG). See also *Re GEMA's Statutes (No. 2)* [1972] *CMLR* D–115.   [204] Directive 2014/26/EU of 26 February 2014 (the 'CRM Directive').

[205] Collective Management of Copyright (EU Directive) Regulations 2016 (SI 2016/221) ('CMC Regs').

[206] CRM Dir., Art. 4; CMC Regs, reg. 3.

[207] CRM Dir., Art. 5(2) (freedom to appoint collecting society from any member state), (3) (retention of right to license non-commercial uses), (4)–(6) (termination); CMC Regs, reg. 4.

[208] CRM Dir., Art. 8; CMC Regs, reg. 7.   [209] CRM Dir., Art. 11; CMC Regs, 10.

[210] CRM Dir., Art. 12; CMC Regs, regs 11 and 14; In some countries, there are very strong traditions regarding these funds, often leading to deductions of 10 per cent for social and cultural purposes such as pensions, grants, festival support. For example, it is said that the French collecting societies in 2004 set aside €95 million for cultural and social purposes: see KEA European Affairs, *The Collective Management of Rights in Europe: The Quest for Efficiency* (2006), 39. The CRM Directive permits collecting societies to make deductions from which to operate 'social, cultural or educational' funds. Such deductions may be approved in the annual general meeting under Art. 8(5)(d), but under Art. 12(4) 'such services shall be provided on fair criteria, in particular, as regards access to and the extent of those services'.

[211] CRM Dir., Art. 15; CMC Regs, reg. 19.   [212] CRM Dir., Art. 14; CMC Regs, reg. 13.

[213] CRM Dir., Art. 15(2); CMC Regs, reg. 14(2).

licences over many more works than they want. In order to ensure that this monopoly power is not abused, there are both domestic and European regulatory controls.[214]

7.3.1 The Collective Rights Management Directive

The Directive (which is a minimum harmonization instrument) includes provisions that relate to users. These include obligations to conduct negotiations for the licensing of rights 'in good faith',[215] to base licensing on 'objective and non-discriminatory criteria', and for tariffs to reflect the 'economic value of the use of the rights in trade' and 'the service provided by the collective management organisation'.[216] The Directive requires member states to provide for disputes to be 'submitted to a court, and if appropriate, to an independent and impartial dispute resolution body'.[217] The Directive has a swathe of more detailed provisions relating to multi-territory licensing.

7.3.2 The UK's Copyright Tribunal

The Copyright Tribunal[218] has wide-ranging powers to review licences and licensing schemes operated by collecting societies.[219] The Tribunal normally sits in panels of three, selected from a group of up to eight.

The Copyright Tribunal is primarily concerned with the operation of licensing bodies. A 'licensing body' is defined as a society or other organization that has as one of its main objects the negotiation or granting of copyright licences.[220] A body is still a licensing body if it is an agent, as well as when it becomes the owner of copyright. This means, for example, that the MCPS (which operates as an agent) is within the jurisdiction of the Copyright Tribunal. However, a body is a licensing body only if its object is the granting of licences covering works of more than one author.[221]

The CDPA 1988 distinguishes between two kinds of activity involving a licensing body—namely, 'licensing schemes' and 'one-off licences'. A 'licensing scheme' is defined as any regime that specifies the circumstances and terms on which a licensing body is willing to grant licences.[222] The Tribunal can consider complaints by representative organizations concerning the terms of a proposed scheme,[223] or complaints by organizations or individuals with respect to a scheme in operation.[224] The Tribunal has wide powers: it may approve or vary schemes, hold that particular applicants should be granted licences under such schemes, or approve or vary the terms of particular licences.[225] The Tribunal will also hear disputes over which applicants for licences fall within the scheme,[226] as well as refusals to grant licences. The Tribunal may make an order declaring that the complainant is entitled to a licence. After the Tribunal makes an order, a scheme may be referred again by its operator, a claimant for a licence, or a representative organization.[227]

The criterion against which the Tribunal judges matters is one of 'reasonableness'. As such, its role is more than one of 'arbitration'.[228] Indeed, where there are several reasonable

---

[214] A 'market investigation' reference could also be made under the Enterprise Act 2002.

[215] CRM Dir., Art. 16(1); CMC Regs, reg. 15(1)(a).   [216] CRM Dir., Art. 16(2); CMC Regs, reg. 15(2).

[217] CRM Dir., Art. 35; CMC Regs, reg. 15(4). The body must have 'expertise in intellectual property law'.

[218] It replaced the Performing Right Tribunal in 1989.

[219] Although, as is explained later, not every aspect of copyright is regulated by the Tribunal: see Rel. Rights Regs, reg. 17(4); CDPA 1988, s. 205B; Database Regs, Sch. 2.   [220] CDPA 1988, s. 116(2).

[221] See D. Zeffman and J. Enser, 'The Impact of UK Competition Law on the Music Industry' [1993] *Ent L Rev* 67, 71.   [222] CDPA 1988, s. 117.

[223] CDPA 1988, s. 118.   [224] CDPA 1988, s. 119.   [225] CDPA 1988, ss 118–20.

[226] CDPA 1988, s. 119. The Tribunal can make orders concerning matter excluded from a licensing scheme: *Universities UK v. Copyright Licensing Agency* [2002] *RPC* (36) 693, 707, [59].   [227] CDPA 1988, s. 120.

[228] *British Airways v. The PRS* [1998] *RPC* 581.

solutions, the Tribunal's job is to select whatever is the 'most reasonable'.[229] In considering whether to make an order, the Tribunal is instructed to have regard to a number of factors, of which the most important is to ensure that there is no 'unreasonable discrimination' between the scheme or licence in issue and comparable schemes or licences.[230] Apart from that, specific factors are to be considered in relation to different schemes.[231] For example, if the scheme concerns reprographic copying, the Tribunal is to have regard to the availability of published editions, the proportion of the work copied, and the nature of the use to which the copies will be put. In addition to the factors specifically listed in the 1988 Act, the Tribunal will take account of factors indicated as relevant in EU directives.[232]

In determining the reasonableness of licence fees, the Copyright Tribunal has often described its task as determining what a 'willing licensor and willing licensee' would have agreed.[233] The usual starting point for ascertaining what this might be is with previous agreements, which are evaluated by the Tribunal in light of changed circumstances.[234] Because the Tribunal is directed to ensure that there is no unreasonable discrimination, it will often be presented with evidence of allegedly equivalent arrangements.[235] These may include arrangements by the same licensing body with other categories of user,[236] or arrangements by similarly positioned licensing bodies with the same licensees.[237] While evidence of schemes in other jurisdictions is frequently put forward, it has rarely been influential.[238] Other factors that are often treated as relevant include the extent of use, the size of the audience, and the user's revenue. Ultimately, calculating fees is not a process of mathematics, but one of 'judicial estimation'.[239]

There is an appeal from any Tribunal decision to the High Court only on points of law[240] and the normal due deference is given to a specialist tribunal such as the Copyright Tribunal.[241]

7.3.3 Other avenues

A user who is dissatisfied with the terms of a licensing scheme or an individual licence from a collecting society might also be able to bring an action based upon either Articles 101 or 102 TFEU,[242] or the two prohibitions contained in the domestic Competition Act 1998.[243]

Applying Articles 101 and 102 TFEU, the Court of Justice has provided national courts with general guidance on legitimate collecting society behaviour. In particular, in *Ministère Public v. Tournier and Verney*,[244] it was argued that the arrangements between the French copyright management society SACEM and discotheques were prohibited under Articles 101 and 102 TFEU. In that case, SACEM granted a blanket licence for its whole repertoire and charged discotheques according to a percentage of gross receipts.

---

[229] *BPI v. MCPS* [1993] *EMLR* 86, 139.
[230] CDPA 1988, s. 129. Any discrimination should be 'logical': *BSB v. PRS* [1998] *RPC* 467, [5.4]. Cf. M. Freegard, 'Forty Years on: An Appraisal of the United Kingdom Copyright Tribunal, 1957–1997' (1998) 177 *RIDA* 3, 57 (comparisons rarely used as guides).   [231] CDPA 1988, ss 130–5.
[232] *BSB v. PRS* [1998] *RPC* 467 (Satellite Dir., Recital 17).
[233] For example, *Working Men's Club v. PRS* [1992] *RPC* 227, 232.
[234] *BACTA v. PPL* [1992] *RPC* 149; *BPI v. MCPS* [1993] *EMLR* 86, 139.
[235] See *BPI Ltd and ors v. MCPS and ors* [2008] *EMLR* (5) 147.   [236] *BACTA v. PPL* [1992] *RPC* 149.
[237] Ibid.; *AIRC v. PPL* [1994] *RPC* 143.   [238] *BA v. The PRS* [1998] *RPC* 581.
[239] *Universities UK v. Copyright Licensing Agency* [2002] *RPC* (36) 693, 726, [177].   [240] CDPA 1988, s. 152.
[241] See *ITV Network Limited v. Performing Right Society Ltd* [2017] *EWHC* 234 (Ch), [18].
[242] These prohibitions would also apply to society–society arrangements, such as reciprocal agreements.
[243] Competition Act 1998, ss 2 ('Ch. 1 prohibition'), 18 ('Ch. 2 prohibition').
[244] Case 395/87 [1989] *ECR* 2521, [1991] 4 *CMLR* 248.

Some discotheque owners complained that the charges were excessive and that SACEM refused to grant licences for part of its repertoire—namely, in relation to popular dance of Anglo-American origin. The public prosecutor brought criminal proceedings against Tournier, who was director of SACEM, for 'unfair trading'. As part of the action, certain questions were referred to the Court of Justice.

In relation to SACEM's refusal to license use of music from abroad separately, the Court noted that, coupled with similar stipulations by rights societies based in other member states, the behaviour might amount to strong evidence of a concerted practice (contrary to Article 101). The Court acknowledged that it might be possible to account for the parallel behaviour on the grounds that direct licensing would require each society to establish its own management and monitoring system in other countries.[245] With regard to SACEM's decision to grant only blanket licences, the Court suggested that the test was one of 'necessity'—that is, whether the terms or practices were 'necessary' to safeguard the interests of authors, etc. This was a matter for national courts to determine.

With respect to the charges, the Court of Justice found that if there exists an appreciable difference between the fees charged in one member state and those charged in other member states for the same services, such a discrepancy 'must be regarded as indicative of an abuse of dominant position'.[246] The burden of proof is effectively being reversed, so that it is for the relevant collecting society 'to justify the difference by reference to objective dissimilarities between the situation in the member state concerned and the situation prevailing in all the other member states'.[247]

Complaints about society–user relations are normally directed to national authorities. In the United Kingdom, this would be to the courts or the CMA if Articles 101 and 102 TFEU are implicated; otherwise, to the Copyright Tribunal.

---

[245] Ibid.   [246] Ibid., 2577, [38]; *Bassett v. SACEM*, Case 402/85 [1987] *ECR* 1747, 1769, [19].

[247] Case 395/87 [1989] *ECR* 2521, 2577, [38]. See further *Ochranný svaz autorský pro práva k dílům hudebním, o.s. (OSA) v. Léčebné lázně Mariánské Lázně a. s.*, Case C-351/12 EU:C:2014:110, [87] (ECJ, Fourth Chamber).

13

RIGHTS ASSOCIATED WITH COPYRIGHT

1 INTRODUCTION

If there is one characteristic that typifies the development of intellectual property law since the Second World War, it is the proliferation of new forms of intellectual property. In this chapter, we outline a number of regimes that are associated with, but which fall outside of, the remit of copyright law: performers' rights; the database right; rights relating to technological protection measures and rights management information; the public lending right; and the so-called *droit de suite*, or artist's resale royalty right.[1] In addition, we review an ongoing proposal for a news publishers' right.[2]

2 PERFORMERS' RIGHTS

While the creative or cultural contributions made by people who play instruments, read poetry, and act in plays have long been valued, nonetheless performers have been poorly served by intellectual property law. Indeed, it was not until technological changes at the beginning of the twentieth century (notably, the emergence of sound-recording technologies and radio broadcasting) threatened the livelihood of performers that the law intervened to protect performers. This occurred in 1925 when criminal sanctions were introduced to discourage people from abusing a performer's right to control the fixation and subsequent use of their performances.[3]

While it might have been expected that copyright law would have been expanded to accommodate performers, performers were considered to be subservient to the interests of the 'proper' rights holders—namely, authors, composers, and dramatists. While authors and composers create primary works, performers were seen merely to translate or

---

[1] Of these, in EU terminology, only performers' rights are 'related rights'.

[2] On 'publication right', see Chapter 7.

[3] Dramatic and Musical Performers' Protection Act 1925, consolidated and amended in the Performers' Protection Acts 1958 and 1972. See R. Arnold, *Performers' Rights* (5th edn, 2015).

interpret these works.[4] The second-rate status of performers was reflected in the decision that performers did not belong within the Berne Convention (along with the producers of phonograms and broadcasting organizations). Indeed, it was not until the Rome Convention of 1961 that performers were recognized at the international level.[5]

Eventually, the lobbying efforts of performers paid off when the Copyright, Designs and Patents Act 1988 (CDPA 1988) provided performers with the right to control the recording of live performances (and other related rights).[6] Because the rights were not assignable, they are described as 'non-property' rights. The 1988 Act also provided producers with certain rights when they entered into exclusive contracts to record performers.[7] The scope of the protection given to performers was further expanded as a result of European harmonization. To bring UK law into line with the Related Rights Directive, the 1988 Act was amended from 1 December 1996 to provide performers with fully assignable 'property rights' and certain 'rights to remuneration'. In a third significant development, the rights given to performers were expanded further in the WIPO Performances and Phonograms Treaty 1996 (WPPT), with Article 5 WPPT requiring contracting parties to grant moral rights of attribution and integrity to performers.[8] These have now been implemented in the United Kingdom. In all but two respects—namely, duration and depth of protection[9]—these bring performers' protection to a level virtually equivalent to that of authors.[10]

2.1 SUBSISTENCE

Protection is confined to dramatic performances (which include dance or mime), musical performances, readings and recitations of literary works, and also to 'a variety act or any similar presentation'.[11] This definition clearly encompasses the acting of a play in front of a live audience, or of a film script before a camera, or the performing of a ballet ('dramatic performances'); the playing of a classical piece, such as Beethoven's Fifth Symphony by an orchestra, or the rendition of a pop song by a band ('musical performances').[12] The term 'variety act' would include a performance given by magicians, clowns, jugglers, acrobats,

---

[4] For critical evaluation of the rationales for conferring a secondary status on 'performers', see M. Pavis, 'The Author-Performer Divide in Intellectual Property Law: A Comparative Analysis of the American, Australian, British and French Legal Frameworks', (Unpublished PhD thesis, University of Exeter, 2016).

[5] See Chapter 2, section 6.2, pp. 46–7.

[6] The Act has been held to confer rights on performers, such as Jimi Hendrix, who were long dead: *Experience Hendrix LLC v. Purple Haze Records Ltd* [2007] *EWCA Civ* 501.

[7] CDPA 1988, ss 180–4.

[8] See Chapter 2, section 6.5, pp. 48–9. The Beijing Treaty on Audiovisual Performances 2012 has not yet entered into force, nor has it been ratified by the United Kingdom.

[9] Performers are not protected against imitation.

[10] See A. Aguilar, 'Distributed Ownership in Music: Between Authorship and Performance' (2018) 27 *Social & Legal Studies* (published online October 2017).

[11] CDPA 1988, s. 180(2). The WPPT, Art. 2(a), defines performers as 'actors, singers, musicians, dancers and other persons who act, sing, deliver, declaim, play in, interpret, or otherwise perform literary or artistic works or expressions of folklore'. The form of definition—by way of a list—suggests uncertainty as to the underlying rationale of the regime. See O. Morgan, *International Protection of Performers' Rights* (2002), 27 (proposing a 'principled definition' of a performance as 'the transitory activity of a human individual that can be perceived without the aid of technology and that is intended as a form of communication to others for the purpose of entertainment, education or ritual').

[12] One may wonder whether performance of Cage's '4' 33' constitutes a musical performance. See the earlier discussion in Chapter 3, section 4, pp. 71–2 as to whether the piece is a 'musical work' for copyright purposes.

and the like.[13] In *Heythrop Zoological Gardens v. Captive Animals Protection Society*, Birss J. found that there was a 'variety act' and hence a performance where an animal trainer entertained an audience by causing the animals to do tricks: there was 'a performance by both animals and a human being in which each plays a necessary part', though for legal purposes the performer was the 'trainer'.[14]

However, the definition of 'performance' is not without its ambiguities and apparent restrictions.[15] First, there are ambiguities raised by the definition as to whether the work performed must exist before the performance takes place. The wording of section 180 of the CDPA 1988 suggests that this need not be so for musical or dramatic works, since sub-section (2) refers to musical or dramatic performances. Thus unscripted and improvised musical and dramatic performances are almost certainly covered.[16] However, in the case of readings or recitations, the definition suggests that the literary work must be in existence prior to the performance.[17] Consequently, a person who gives a spontaneous speech or an interview will not obtain protection as a performer. Another ambiguity relates to what constitutes a 'musical performance'. Presumably, a singer who sings a song gives a 'musical' performance, even though, in copyright terminology, there might be only a performance of a literary work. It is unclear whether the term covers the playing of the work from a recording, so that a disc jockey could be a performer.

Before moving on, it should be noted that international and regional treaties frequently distinguish between audiovisual performances and performances embodied on phonograms. While the reasons for the distinction are easy to understand (some parts of the film industry fearing that giving performers rights will potentially jeopardize a film company's ability to exploit a film), the distinction is not entirely satisfactory. This is because there is now a significant overlap and interchangeability between media, so that, for example, some performances start life as audiovisual before being recorded onto purely aural media and some aural performances are later fixed on audiovisual media. The boundary lines are, not surprisingly, highly contested.

2.2 PERFORMERS AND RELATED BENEFICIARIES

The beneficiary of the rights given in a performance is, on its face, the performer (or performers).[18] Although performers are typically freelance workers rather than employees, a performer is entitled to performance rights *even if* they are employed.[19] Two issues are worth further consideration: the first concerns exactly who counts as a performer;

---

[13] *Heythrop Zoological Gardens v. Captive Animals Protection Society* [2016] *EWHC* 1370 (Ch), [33] (referring, with approval, to R. Arnold, *Performers' Rights* (2015), [2.167].

[14] [2016] *EWHC* 1370 (Ch), [40].

[15] R. Arnold, *Performers' Rights* (2015) [2.18]–[2.19], suggests it even includes 'sporting performances'. Cf. Kamina (2016), 402, [248]. Nevertheless, the definition of 'performers' must reflect EU harmonization, and it seems eminently likely that the CJEU would draw on the definitions of performers and performances in international law, e.g. Rome, Art 3(a) and WPPT, Art 2(a). These are limited to the performance of 'literary or artistic works or expressions of folklore' and thus would be unlikely to extend beyond the performance of material that falls within the field of 'authors rights'. As sporting events do not do so, sporting performances would not, in our view, be regarded as being protected.   [16] Kamina (2016) 403, [248].

[17] *Heythrop* [2016] *EWHC* 1370 (Ch), [38] (Birss J) (placing emphasis on evidence on fact that the speech had been rehearsed). Cf. R. Arnold, *Performers' Rights* (2015), [2.13] (favouring protection of ex tempore performances).

[18] Each performer gains rights in their own performance: *Bamgboye v. Reed* [2004] *EMLR* (5) 61; *Experience Hendrix v. Purple Haze Records Ltd* [2005] *EMLR* (18) 417, [21]; *Bourne v. Davis* [2006] *EWHC* 1567, [7].   [19] R. Arnold, *Performers' Rights* (2015), [3.02].

the second, special provisions relating to the rights of those who are a party to exclusive recording agreements.

2.2.1 Main performers, ancillary performers, and other contributors

In contrast with some other jurisdictions, no attempt is made under UK law to exclude ancillary performers from the scope of protection.[20] This means that, in practice, care must be taken to deal contractually with all participants, including session musicians as well as named artists, extras as well as star performers. A person present in the audience at a performance would not normally be regarded as 'giving' a performance, although in situations in which a show depends upon active participation of members of the audience it is possible that a member of the audience might become a performer.[21] Although a director, or choreographer, or make-up artist may contribute significantly to the preparation of a performance, it cannot be said that they 'give' the performance.

2.2.2 Exclusive recording contracts

Special provisions exist in the 1988 Act that relate to exclusive recording contracts. Section 185 defines an exclusive recording contract as:

> . . . a contract between a performer and another person under which that person is entitled to the exclusion of all other persons (including the performer) to make recordings of one or more of his performances with a view to their commercial exploitation.

If the person having such rights is a qualifying person, then they are granted rights similar to a performer's non-property rights. More specifically, their consent is required by anyone else wishing to make a recording. A party who is the beneficiary of an exclusive recording contract may commence an action for breach of statutory duty against a person who makes such a recording,[22] or who shows a wrongful recording in public or broadcasts it,[23] as well as against those dealing commercially in such illicit recordings.[24] While performers' non-property rights are not transferable, the person with an exclusive recording contract may assign rights under that contract.[25]

2.3 RIGHTS

There are four types of right available to protect performers: non-property rights; property rights; remuneration rights; and moral rights.

2.3.1 Non-property rights

A performer has the right to authorize the recording of a live performance.[26] They also have the right to prevent the making of a recording of a live performance from a broadcast in which it has been included[27]—that is, the acts of 'bootlegging'. Performers also have the right to prevent their live performances from being broadcast. Prior to the mass distribution of fixed recordings, this right would have been very important. Where a recording

---

[20] Cf. Art. L. 212 of the French Intellectual Property Code.

[21] Cf. Copyright Act 1968, s. 248A(2)(d) (Australia) (excluding 'a participation in a performance as a member of an audience'). [22] CDPA 1988, s. 186.

[23] CDPA 1988, s. 187. [24] CDPA 1988, s. 188. [25] CDPA 1988, s. 185(2), (3).

[26] Including a 'substantial part' thereof. In *Heythrop Zoological Gardens v. Captive Animals Protection Society* [2016] *EWHC* 1370 (Ch), [41], Birss J took the view that this is a qualitative assessment, and that if the part 'represents' the whole performance, it is to be regarded as substantial. On the equivalent question for other related rights, see Chapter 8, section 2.3.3, pp. 210–15. [27] CDPA 1988, s. 182.

has been made without the consent of a performer, their rights are infringed when the wrongfully recorded performance is shown or played in public, or communicated to the public. This right is infringed only where the defendant knew or had reason to believe that the recording was made without the performer's consent.[28] This would cover the playing of obviously bootlegged recordings at nightclubs or on the radio. Performers are also given the right to control the distribution of illicit recordings. These are recordings made, otherwise than for private purposes, without the consent of the performer or the person, if any, having recording rights.[29] Import and sale of illicit recordings is prohibited where the person knows or has reason to believe that the recording is illicit.[30]

All of these non-property rights are non-transmissible, except on death.[31] Infringement is actionable as a breach of statutory duty. A person may also be subject to criminal liability if they knowingly commit certain commercial acts in relation to illicit recordings.[32]

2.3.2 Property rights

Performers are also given property rights in their performances. The performer's property rights include the right to make copies of a recording of a qualifying performance, the right to issue copies of a recording to the public, the right to rent or lend copies, and the right to include the performance in an on-demand service.[33] The definitions of these rights correspond to those of a copyright owner.[34] In contrast with the other rights given to performers, these property rights are transmissible. Any assignments made must be in writing and signed by the assignor.[35] In relation to film production agreements, a performer is presumed, in the absence of an agreement to the contrary, to have transferred the rental right to the producer.[36]

2.3.3 Right of remuneration

Performers are also given two 'remuneration rights', one in relation to rental,[37] the other for communication to the public. [38] The most important of these, at least financially, is the right to claim equitable remuneration from the owner of copyright in a *sound recording* (note, not an audiovisual work) of a qualifying performance where the sound recording is played in public, or communicated to the public (other than by way of 'making available').[39] This right formalized the existing practice whereby recording companies made *ex gratia* payments to bodies representing musicians. Under the new regime, performers must claim their revenue that accrues in the United Kingdom from the collecting society that administers the performing and broadcasting rights on behalf of the owners of copyright sound recordings—namely, Phonographic Performance Limited (PPL).[40]

---

[28] CDPA 1988, s. 183.   [29] CDPA 1988, s. 197.   [30] CDPA 1988, s. 184.
[31] CDPA 1988, s. 192A.   [32] CDPA 1988, s. 198. Illicit recording is defined in CDPA 1988, s. 197.
[33] CDPA 1988, ss 191A and 182A–C, 182CA (as added by Rel. Rights Regs, reg. 7).
[34] See Chapter 6.   [35] CDPA 1988, s. 191B.   [36] CDPA 1988, s. 191F.
[37] CDPA 1988, s. 191G. More specifically, where a performer has transferred their rental right concerning a sound recording or film to the producer, the performer retains the right to equitable remuneration for the rental of sound recordings or films.
[38] CDPA 1988, s. 182D (as amended by Rel. Rights Regs, reg. 7); Related Rights Dir., Art. 5(1), 8(2). Art. 8(2), in turn, reflects Rome Convention, Art. 12.
[39] CDPA 1988, s. 182D (as amended by Rel. Rights Regs, reg. 7). A sound recording is not played in public when a film in which the recording is incorporated is shown in public: CDPA 1988, s. 5B(3)(a).
[40] Occasionally, equitable remuneration may be collectable from the person playing a sound record in public or communicating it to the public: CDPA 1988, s. 182D(1) (where rights subsist in the performance embodied in the sound recording, but copyright therein has expired, as a consequence of termination for non-exploitation under s. 191HA(4)).

Both of the remuneration rights may be assigned only to a collecting society.[41] In the absence of a relevant agreement, the Copyright Tribunal may determine royalty rates.[42] As yet, there have been no cases in which the Tribunal has been asked to assess what an equitable remuneration should be. Although the concept of 'equitable remuneration' is an EU law concept, each national authority is left with a wide margin of appreciation, particularly as to determining relevant criteria: the Court of Justice has said that it was within this margin to calculate the money to be paid by a broadcaster by reference to: the number of hours of phonograms broadcast; the viewing and listening densities; the tariffs used in respect of such uses of musical works; the tariffs used in other member states; and the amounts paid by other (commercial) stations.[43]

In the case of the 'making available' right, the question of 'transmissibility' has been a source of some complaint by performers. This is because when performers enter recording contracts, they assign away the making available right. In contrast, performers receive 'equitable remuneration' when fixations of their performances on phonograms are 'communicated'. In practice, it seems, revenue streams from equitable remuneration rights are larger than those secured through the recording contract. As exploitation moves from traditional broadcasting and communication to Internet on-demand services, revenues payable under the remuneration right are falling, and the transmissible character of the 'making available right' proving more problematic. In response, performers representatives,[44] have launched a campaign for a 'fair Internet for performers'.[45]

2.4 MORAL RIGHTS

Performers are granted the moral rights of attribution and integrity.[46] Like authors' moral rights, these rights are not assignable, but may be waived, and are transmissible on death.[47]

The right of attribution applies in relation to live performances, live broadcasts of performances of all kinds, and the distribution and communication to the public of performances fixed on sound recordings.[48] Performers have the rights to have their identities brought to the notice of the relevant public; however, where a performance is by a group, attribution to the group may be sufficient.[49] As with the moral right of attribution granted to authors, the right is not infringed unless it has first been asserted.[50] The right is subject to various exceptions, the most important being that the right does not apply where it is not 'reasonably practicable' to identify the performer or, as appropriate, the group; also, among other things, it does not apply where the performance is for the purpose of reporting current events or where the performance is for the purpose of advertising any goods or services.[51]

---

[41] CDPA 1988, s. 191G(2).   [42] CDPA 1988, ss 182D(4), 191H.

[43] *Stichting ter Exploitatie van Naburige Rechten (SENA) v. Nederlandse Omroep Stichting (NOS)*, Case C-245/00 [2003] *ECR* I–1251 (ECJ, Sixth Chamber).

[44] In particular the Musicians Union (and its international affiliate FIM—the International Federation of Musicians), the Featured Artists Coalition (and its international affiliate IAO—the International Artist Organisation of Music), as well as the umbrella group of collecting societies which represent performers, AEPO-ARTIS.   [45] https://www.fair-internet.eu/.

[46] Performances (Moral Rights, etc.) Regulations 2006 (SI 2006/18). For background, see The Patent Office, *Moral Rights for Performers: Consultation Paper on Regulations Implementing Performers' Moral Rights in the UK Resulting from the WIPO Performances and Phonograms Treaty Obligations* (October 2004)

[47] CDPA 1988, ss 205J(2) (waiver), 205L (non-assignability), 205M (transmission on death).

[48] CDPA 1988, s. 205C.   [49] CDPA 1988, s. 205C(3), (4).

[50] CDPA 1988, s 205D. On such assertion, see Chapter 10, section 2.1.1, pp. 289–90.

[51] CDPA 1988, s. 205E.

The right of integrity applies in relation to live broadcasts of all qualifying performances, as well as to the playing or communication to the public of sound recordings embodying qualifying performances.[52] The performers have the right to object to any such performance insofar as it is subject to a distortion, mutilation, or other modification that is prejudicial to the reputation of the performer. Modifications 'consistent with normal editorial or production practice' are permitted, and other exceptions parallel those to author's moral rights.[53] The integrity right is also infringed by possession or distribution in the course of business of copies of a sound recording embodying a performance that has been so modified as to prejudice the reputation of the performer, but liability is dependent on a showing of *scienter*.[54]

2.5 DURATION, DEFENCES, AND REMEDIES

The term of protection offered to performers varies with the type of performance and its mode of embodiment. As a general matter, performers' rights last for at least 50 years from the end of the year in which the performance took place. However, if a recording incorporating the performance is released within this period,[55] the rights last for 50 years from the year of release.[56] Rights vested in a performer at the time of their death may be exercised only by a person specifically nominated in the performer's will or by their personal representative.[57]

However, if a performance has been embodied in a sound recording, the term of protection, initially 50 years from the fixation of the performance, is 70 years from the release of the recording.[58] This is a consequence of a legislative amendment that involved a complex compromise.[59] That compromise embodies three other key features all designed to ensure that performers—rather than those entitled under existing contracts—gain some benefit from the extension: the 'use it or lose it' mechanism; the waiver of deductions based on existing contracts when calculating royalties owing to featured artists; and the provision for remuneration for non-featured artists who assigned their rights for a lump sum.

First, there is a 'use it or lose it' obligation on the owner of copyright in the sound recording itself.[60] More specifically, once 50 years has run, the copyright in the sound recording might be determined if a performer decides to terminate an assignment of their

---

[52] CDPA 1988, s. 205F. The right exists in the actual performance and not the intended performance. So, for example, running on stage during a performance would not necessarily infringe the right to integrity.

[53] CDPA 1988, s. 205G(3). On parallel exceptions to authors' moral rights, see Chapter 10. It is suggested that these rights would not assist a person in the position of the singer Vera Lynn, as reported in *The Guardian*, 9 February 2009, who merely objected to the sale by the right-wing political party, the BNP, of a CD entitled 'The White Cliffs of Dover' that included a recording of a performance by Vera Lynn. The recording it appears had been included with the consent of the owner of the sound recording, and had not been distorted, mutilated, or modified. For examples of similar conflicts in the United States, see S. Knopper, 'Why Politicians Keep Using Songs without Artists' Permission' (9 July 2015), *Rolling Stone*.

[54] CDPA 1988, s. 205(H).

[55] CDPA 1988, s. 191(2). The requisite 'release' includes, if authorized, publication, playing or showing in public, or communication to the public: CDPA 1988, s. 191(3). For further details on these rights, see Chapter 6.

[56] CDPA 1988, s. 191.   [57] CDPA 1988, s. 192.

[58] CDPA 1988, s. 191(2)(c) (introduced with effect from 1 November 2013 by Copyright and Duration Regs, reg. 8, to implement Directive 2011/77/EU).

[59] Directive 2011/77/EU. A. Ramalho and A. Lopez-Tarruello, *Implementation of Directive 2011/77/EU*, PE 604.957 (European Parliament, 2018).

[60] Note the minor clarifying amendment to the terms of the Copyright and Duration Regs by SI 2014/434. Rather confusingly the copyright owner is referred to in the Copyright and Duration Regs as 'the producer' even though they may, in fact, not be a 'producer' as understood in CDPA 1988, s. 178, but may merely be an assignee of the copyright.

property rights therein on the basis that the sound recording is not being exploited. This 'use it or lose it' provision introduces an interesting concept into copyright law, although its practical effects are likely to be minimal. This is because the conditions under which a performer can terminate the assignment are strictly defined,[61] in particular the right to terminate does not exist if the recording is accessible over the Internet.[62]

Second, where the term of protection of a sound recording has been extended from 50 to 70 years, performers acquire some additional benefits for the additional period. First, performers who are entitled to royalty payments from record producers are, during the added period, to be paid those monies 'regardless of any provision in the agreement which entitles the producer to withhold or deduct sums from the amounts payable'.[63] The idea behind this was that a producer should no longer be entitled to deduct any 'advance against royalties'—that is, an initial lump sum paid to the performers—from these royalties if it has not been recouped in the first 50 years. Such advances are usually paid to provide performers who are starting out with some provision, but also often in respect of the costs of purchasing time in a recording studio. However, if a recording is generating significant revenues 50 years after its release, it seems unlikely that many advances would not already have been recouped. Nevertheless, the provision could conceivably apply to other terms in the recording agreement (the assignment), such as the notorious clauses relating to breakages,[64] thus giving performers what would be in effect a royalty uplift.

Third, with respect to performers who were entitled to be paid only a 'lump sum' (as might be the case with a so-called 'session musician' who was contracted to contribute to a particular performance), a complex provision requires the producer to pay an annual lump sum, comprising 20 per cent of the 'gross revenue' on sales (including Internet downloads) to a collecting society for distribution to the performer.[65] Because session musicians are rarely identified on the recordings,[66] considerable contractual archaeology is going to need to be undertaken to ascertain whether such payments are due—that is, whether any such musician performed on a recording (such that a payment is required)— and who, precisely, is entitled to the payment.[67] A good example of a situation where such work has been done was in relation to the various musicians who contributed tabla and tamboura to the Beatles recording 'Within You, Without You' on its 1967 release *Sergeant Pepper*.[68]

Performers' rights are subject to a host of defences that, rather inconveniently, are contained in Schedule 2 to the 1988 Act. The defences parallel those for copyright and include fair dealing for non-commercial research,[69] text and data analysis,[70] fair dealing

---

[61] CDPA 1988, s. 191HA(4) (introduced with effect from 1 November 2013 by Copyright and Duration Regs, reg. 9).   [62] CDPA 1988, s. 191HA(2)(b).

[63] CDPA 1988, s. 191HB(9) (introduced with effect from 1 November 2013 by Copyright and Duration Regs, reg. 9).

[64] These clauses supposedly date back to a time when records were made of shellac, which was brittle, and thus breakages were common. However, they continued to be utilized in recording agreements and sometimes entail deductions as high as 25 per cent.   [65] CDPA 1988, s. 191HB(3).

[66] A well-known exception is Billy Preston, who is attributed on The Beatles song 'Get Back' (but who also performed on other recordings).

[67] The operation of these provisions, which implement Directive 2011/77/EU, will be subject to review by the Secretary of State, which is to be completed by 1 November 2018.

[68] Press Association, 'Mystery Indian Musician on Sgt Pepper Album Track identified', *Evening Times* (Glasgow), 1 June 2017.

[69] CDPA 1988, Sch. 2, para. 1C. This was added, from June 2014, by the Copyright and Rights in Performances (Research, Education, Libraries and Archives) Regulations 2014 (SI 2014/1372), reg. 3(3).

[70] CDPA 1988, Sch. 2, para. 1D.

for criticism or review,[71] fair dealing for quotation,[72] as well as for caricature, parody, and pastiche,[73] fair dealing for reporting current events, and incidental inclusion, as well as a range of defences for persons with disabilities,[74] and for educational and library uses.[75] These are all discussed in Chapter 9 and the comments made there apply equally to performers (*mutatis mutandis*). However, the defence applicable to recording broadcasts for the purpose of watching or listening to the broadcast at a later time also applies to any performance included in the broadcast.

Like copyright, the property and non-property rights are enforceable in civil and criminal actions. The usual remedies for breaches of statutory duty are available—namely injunctions, damages, or account of profits. The right owner may also prosecute for a range of statutory offences, may seek orders that include delivery up and disposal, and may seize infringing articles from traders without premises. These remedies are discussed in Chapter 49.[76]

2.6 FOREIGN PERFORMANCES

Performances by foreign performers or performances that take place in foreign countries will be protected in the United Kingdom if the performance is 'qualifying'. A performance is a 'qualifying performance' if it is given by a 'qualifying individual' or takes place in a 'qualifying country'.[77] A 'qualifying individual' is a citizen of, or an individual resident in, a 'qualifying country'.[78] A 'qualifying country' is defined as the United Kingdom, another member state of the European Economic Area (EEA), a country which is party to the Rome Convention,[79] or a country designated under section 208 of the 1988 Act.[80] Section 208 empowers the Crown to designate other countries as qualifying countries by Order in Council.[81] The qualifying countries are divided up elaborately into four categories, as follows.

(i) Article 9 concerns countries that are parties to the Rome Convention, but have reservations under Article 16(1)(a), resulting in more limited protection that does not include the right to claim a single equitable remuneration for the communication of sound recordings to the public.

(ii) Article 10 concerns *countries that* are parties to the WPPT, but have made a declaration thereunder (such as Australia), resulting in more limited protection that does not include the right to claim a single equitable remuneration for the communication of sound recordings to the public.

---

[71] CDPA 1988, Sch. 2, para. 2. In *Heythrop Zoological Gardens v. Captive Animals Protection Society* [2016] *EWHC* 1370 (Ch), [42]–[44], Birss J held that showing a video of an animal performance was arguably fair dealing for criticism or review, the criticism being that the treatment was exploitative or inhumane.

[72] The Copyright and Rights in Performances (Quotation and Parody) Regulations 2014 SI 2014/2356 added CDPA 1988, Sch. 2, para. 2(1A). [73] Ibid., Sch. 2, para. 2A.

[74] CDPA 1988, Sch. 2 paras 3A–E. [75] CDPA 1988, Sch. 2, paras 4, 5, 6, 6ZA, 6C, 6D, 6E, 6F, 6G, 6H.

[76] CDPA 1988, ss 194–202.

[77] CDPA 1988, s. 181. Despite the use of the present tense in the legislation, once a country becomes a qualifying country or a person becomes a qualifying individual, the rights arise retrospectively in relation to past performances: see *Experience Hendrix LLC v. Purple Haze Records Ltd* [2007] *EWCA Civ* 501.

[78] CDPA 1988, s. 206. For a general analysis of concepts relevant to protecting foreign claims, see Chapter 1, section 3, pp. 6–7; Chapter 2, section 6.2, pp. 46–7; and Chapter 4, section 5, pp. 119–22.

[79] CDPA 1988 s 206(1)(bb), amended by the Intellectual Property Act 2014, s. 22(5).

[80] There is no distinction drawn between 'extension' and 'application', though CDPA 1988, s. 208(5), allows Pt II of the Act to be 'applied' to countries that, in Pt I, are subject to 'extension'.

[81] Copyright and Performances (Application to Other Countries) Order 2016 (SI 2016/1219).

(iii) Article 11 covers countries belonging to the WPPT, but not to the Rome Convention (such as Canada, China, Hong Kong, Indonesia, Malaysia, and Singapore). Performances with a required connecting factor to such a country receive more limited protection, which does not include public lending of copies.

(iv) Article 12 covers parties only to the World Trade Organization (such as India, New Zealand, Pakistan, and South Africa), resulting in more limited protection Article 11 countries, which does not include the 'making available' right.

Section 185 of the 1988 Act, which confers equivalent rights on a person who is party to an exclusive recording contract, does so only if they or one of their licensees is a 'qualifying person'. A 'qualifying person' is defined as a 'qualifying individual' or a body corporate sufficiently connected with a 'qualifying country'.[82]

3 DATABASE RIGHT

Many different technologies organize and order information: encyclopaedias, filing cabinets, and textbooks all play their role in placing information in a usable format. Databases are another obvious example. While databases have existed in one form or another for a very long time, digital technology has transformed and revitalized databases. In particular, the digital database has enabled the production of facilities that enable easy access to vast collections of information. Examples familiar to lawyers include *Lexis* and *WestLaw*, as well as CD-ROMs such as the *Index to Legal Periodicals and Books*. The value of these facilities is the comprehensive nature of the information that they contain and the ease of access, rather than the way in which that information is ordered. While databases can cost a considerable amount of money to construct, they are readily copied. This makes them an ideal candidate for intellectual property protection.[83]

Faced with the fact that the level of protection varied, sometimes considerably, between member states,[84] the European Commission decided to harmonize the law that protected the effort that went into creating databases.[85] Eventually, these efforts led to the Database Directive,[86] which was implemented into the United Kingdom on 1 January 1998, in the Database Regulations.[87] The Database Directive required member states to introduce a two-tier system of protection for databases. The first tier involves retaining copyright protection for databases that are 'original'.[88] This was discussed in Chapters 3 and 4.[89] The Directive also requires member states to provide a second tier of protection by way

---

[82] CDPA 1988, ss 181, 185(3), 206(1).

[83] At least in economic theory: see Davison, 239 *ff*, with criticisms; Derclaye, ch. 1.

[84] Some, such as the United Kingdom and Ireland, would probably have protected most databases by copyright; others would have done so by means of 'unfair competition'; the Nordic countries had adopted a special form of protection for catalogues and a burning issue remains as to what extent the Directive should be read as generalizing the latter position. On this, see Davison, 141.

[85] Complete uniformity has not been achieved because member states are able to retain unfair competition protection and to diverge in implementing exceptions: Database Dir., Arts 9, 13.

[86] See Davison, 50–68.

[87] Copyright and Rights in Databases Regulations 1997 (SI 1997/3032).

[88] Transitional provisions make it clear that databases that were already protected by copyright on 27 March 1996, but which would not reach the standards required under the Directive, continue to enjoy protection until the end of the copyright term.

[89] Chapter 3, section 2.6, pp. 66–8; Chapter 4, section 3.4, pp. 98–9 and sections 3.5.2–3.5.3, pp. 103–5.

of a new *sui generis* right known as the 'database right'.[90] Database rights arise in relation to databases, including those that fail to reach the copyright's originality threshold.[91] The database right is separate from and in addition to any copyright protection that may exist in relation to a database. According to Jacob LJ: 'the policy of the Directive is that databases which cost a lot of investment and can readily be copied should be protected. The right is created to protect the investment which goes into the creation of a database.'[92]

Although at its inception this database right was described as 'one of the least balanced and most potentially anti-competitive intellectual property rights ever created',[93] much of its apparent strength was curtailed by the Court of Justice in four decisions: *Fixtures Marketing v. Oy Veikkaus*;[94] *Fixtures Marketing v. Organismoa Prognostikon Agnon Podosfairou*;[95] *Fixtures Marketing v. Svenska*;[96] and *British Horseracing Board v. William Hill*.[97] The first three concerned whether there was a database right in Premier League fixture lists, and the Court clearly indicated that there is not; *British Horseracing Board* concerned cumulative lists of runners and riders in British horse races and, following the Court's advice, this was held by the Court of Appeal not to be protected.[98]

3.1 SUBSISTENCE

The database right is a property right that subsists in a database whether made before or after 1 January 1998.[99] A 'database' is defined as 'a collection of independent works, data or other materials that are arranged in a systematic or methodical way, and are individually accessible by electronic or other means'.[100] We reviewed the meaning of 'database' in Chapter 3,[101] noting its potentially awesome breadth. The concept of 'database' includes subject matter as varied as: library catalogues such as the English Short Title Catalogue; lists of sports data; websites cataloguing species of animals and plants or nucleotides;[102] collections of email addresses; lists of second-hand cars (for sale); and topographical maps.

The database right arises only if there has been a substantial investment in obtaining, verifying, or presenting the contents of the database. 'Investment' includes any

---

[90] For an assessment, see P. B. Hugenholtz, 'Something Completely Different: Europe's Sui Generis Database Right', in S. Frankel and D. Gervais (eds), *The Internet and the Emerging Importance of New Forms of Intellectual Property* (2016), 205–22.

[91] Database Regs, reg. 13(2) (reflecting Database Dir., Art. 7(4)), says that it is immaterial whether or not the database or any of its contents are copyright works.

[92] *Football Dataco v. Sportradar* [2013] *EWCA Civ* 27, [44].

[93] J. Reichman and P. Samuelson, 'Intellectual Property Rights in Data?' (1997) 50 *Vand L Rev* 51, 81; Davison, 285.

[94] Case C-46/02 [2004] *ECR* I–10365 (ECJ, Grand Chamber) ('*Veikkaus*').

[95] Case C-444/02 [2004] *ECR* I–10549 (ECJ, Grand Chamber) ('*OPAP*').

[96] Case C-338/02 [2004] *ECR* I–10497 (ECJ, Grand Chamber) ('*Svenska*').

[97] Case C-203/02 [2004] *ECR* I–10415 (ECJ, Grand Chamber) ('*BHB* (ECJ)').

[98] *British Horseracing Board v. William Hill* [2005] *RPC* 883. For commentaries on the cases, see T. Aplin, 'The ECJ Elucidates the Database Right' [2005] *IPQ* 204; E. Derclaye, 'The Court of Justice Interprets the Database *Sui Generis* Right for the First Time' [2005] *ELR* 420; M. Davison and B. Hugenholtz, 'Football Fixtures, Horseraces and Spin Offs: The ECJ Domesticates the Database Right' [2005] *EIPR* 113.

[99] Database Regs, regs 13(1), 27–8 (implementing Database Dir., Arts 14(3), 16). It is immaterial whether or not the database or any of its contents is a copyright work, so that there may be a database right where there is no copyright, or there may be both copyright and a database right. It may also be possible for a database to attract copyright, but not the database right, if the selection and arrangement renders the collection the author's own intellectual creation, but there is not substantial 'human' investment in presenting the contents of the database.   [100] Database Regs, reg. 12.

[101] Chapter 3, section 2.6, pp. 66–8.

[102] http://www.catalogueoflife.org/; http://www.ebi.ac.uk/ena.

investment, whether of financial, human, or technical resources.[103] Investment may be 'substantial' in terms of quality, quantity, or a combination of both. The former refers to 'quantifiable resources'; the latter, 'to efforts which cannot be quantified, such as intellectual effort or energy'.[104] Quite what level of investment the threshold 'substantiality' entails is yet to be clarified.[105] In the four fixtures cases, the Court of Justice did not comment on the Advocate-General's view that the Directive requires an absolute lower threshold for investments worthy of protection as a sort of *de minimis* rule, albeit at a low level; a high threshold level 'would undermine the intended purpose of the Directive, which was to create incentives for investment'.[106]

The act of 'obtaining' information is, it seems, to be distinguished from creating information: investment in creation is not relevant.[107] It is to be 'understood to refer to the resources used to seek out existing independent materials and collect them in the database, and not to the resources used for the creation as such of independent materials'.[108] So the investment in deciding which horses may run in a race was regarded as investment in the creation of data and thus to be disregarded when assessing whether a collection of such material was a database that resulted from substantial investment.[109] Equally, the resources deployed to determine the football league fixtures was an investment in creating data rather than the database. Finding and collecting, verifying, and presenting that existing data did not require 'any particular effort'.[110] The distinction between 'creating' and 'obtaining', however, will often not be straightforward: a number of commentators have suggested that scientific observation of natural phenomena 'creates' the resulting data.[111] In *Football Dataco v. Sportradar and Stan James*,[112] it was put to the English Court of Appeal that observations of events on a football field (who took throws, passed the ball, etc.) were not created as data until they were recorded. The Court rejected the argument as absurd.[113] It found the idea that data did not exist until it was recorded to be 'metaphysical' and one that would undermine the purpose of the Directive.[114] The distinction

---

[103] Database Regs, reg. 13; Database Dir., Recitals 7, 12, 39, 40 (right protects *any* investment and referring to various types). Note Derclaye, 74 (arguing that databases created by the state are unprotected because the state does not 'invest'); but cf. *Compass-Datenbank GmbH*, Case C-138/11, EU:C:2012:449 (ECJ), [47] (implicitly accepting that such public authority, such as a register of companies, could have *sui generis* database right even though in collecting the data and maintaining the database, it was not operating as an economic entity).

[104] *Svenska*, Case C-338/02 [2004] *ECR* I-10497 (ECJ, Grand Chamber), [28]; *OPAP*, Case C-444/02 [2004] *ECR* I-10549 (ECJ, Grand Chamber) [44]; *Veikkaus*, Case C-46/02 [2004] *ECR* I-10365 (ECJ, Grand Chamber), [38].

[105] £600,000 per annum was clearly enough: *Football Dataco v. Sportradar and Stan James* [2013] *EWCA Civ* 27, [69]. But under 100 hours seems to have been regarded as ample in *Technomed v. Bluecrest Health Screening* [2017] *EWHC* 2142 (Ch) (Judge D Stone)

[106] *Svenska*, Case C-338/02 [2004] *ECR* I-10497 (ECJ, Grand Chamber), [39] (AG Stix-Hackl).

[107] *BHB* (ECJ), Case C-203/02 [2004] *ECR* I-10415 (ECJ, Grand Chamber).

[108] *BHB* (ECJ), Case C-203/02 [2004] *ECR* I-10415 (ECJ, Grand Chamber), [31]; *Svenska*, Case C-338/02 [2004] *ECR* I-10497 (ECJ, Grand Chamber), [24]; *OPAP*, Case C-444/02 [2004] *ECR* I-10549 (ECJ, Grand Chamber), [40]; *Veikkaus*, Case C-46/02 [2004] *ECR* I-10365 (ECJ, Grand Chamber), [34].

[109] *BHB* (ECJ), Case C-203/02 [2004] *ECR* I-10415 (ECJ, Grand Chamber), [38]; *BHB v. William Hill* [2005] *RPC* 883 (CA).

[110] *Svenska*, Case C-338/02 [2004] *ECR* I-10497 (ECJ, Grand Chamber), [36]; *OPAP*, Case C-444/02 [2004] *ECR* I-10549 (ECJ, Grand Chamber), [49]; *Veikkaus*, Case C-46/02 [2004] *ECR* I-10365 (ECJ, Grand Chamber), [44].

[111] B. Hugenholtz and M. Davison, 'Football Fixtures, Horseraces and Spin-offs: The ECJ Domesticates the Database Right' [2005] *EIPR* 113; L. Bygrave, 'The Data Difficulty in Database Protection' (2013) 35 *EIPR* 25–33. [112] [2013] *EWCA Civ* 27.

[113] Ibid., [41]–[42]. [114] Ibid., [39].

between creating data and collecting it must be drawn pragmatically. The English courts, at least, are willing to interpret the criteria so as to confer protection on customer lists (even though the artificial incentive provided by the database right hardly seems relevant in such cases).[115]

In *British Horseracing Board*, 'verification' was described as monitoring the accuracy of the materials when the database is created and during its operation; it does not include verification during the stage of creation of data.[116] In the three *Fixtures Marketing* references, Advocate-General Stix-Hackl had observed that 'presentation' 'entails not only the presentation for users of the database, that is to say, the external format, but also the conceptual format, such as the structuring of the contents'.[117] The Court of Justice did not comment on this.

The basic term of protection is 15 years.[118] More specifically, the database right expires 15 years from the end of the calendar year in which the database was completed.[119] However, where a database is made available to the public before the end of the period of 15 years from the year in which it was made, rights in the database expire 15 years from the end of the calendar year in which the database was first made available to the public. It is possible that a database right might subsist for 30 years (and thereafter be extended, as discussed later). Where copies of the database as published bear a label or a mark stating that the database was first published in a specified year, the label or mark shall be presumed to be correct until the contrary is proved.[120]

It is important to note that a new period of protection may be acquired for a database. For this to occur, there must be a substantial change *to the contents* of the database.[121] This will include a substantial change resulting from the accumulation of successive additions, deletions, or alterations (so long as the changes constitute a substantial new investment in the database). In these circumstances, the 'new' database qualifies for its own term of protection, but probably only as regards those contents that reflect the new substantial investment. In many cases, therefore, it will be legitimate to extract contents that are more than 15 years old from the database, even if the accuracy of those contents has been verified.[122] While the idea of giving a new period of protection to an updated database may seem no less justified than the idea of giving the authors of the fourth edition of a textbook copyright in the new edition, problems exist in relation to databases because many are subject to a process of continual updating. For example, in *British Horseracing Board*, the BHB database was constantly being updated, so that 800,000 new records or changes to existing records were being made each year—that is, more than 2,000 a day. In these cases, which Laddie J has described as relating to 'dynamic databases',[123] there are clear difficulties in deciding when a sufficient alteration of the contents will have occurred as to render the database a new, separate database.

---

[115] *British Sky Broadcasting Group plc v. Digital Satellite Warranty Cover Ltd* [2011] *EWHC* 2662, [19]–[21]; *Flogas Britain Ltd v. Calor Gas Ltd* [2013] *EWHC* 3060 (Ch), [108] (Proudman J); cf. *Pintorex Ltd v. Keyvanfar* [2013] *EWPCC* 36, [11]–[13] (Alastair Wilson QC).

[116] *BHB* (ECJ), Case C-203/02 [2004] *ECR* I–10415 (ECJ, Grand Chamber), [34]; *Svenska*, Case C-338/02 [2004] *ECR* I–10497 (ECJ, Grand Chamber), [27]; *OPAP*, Case C-444/02 [2004] *ECR* I–10549 (ECJ, Grand Chamber), [43].

[117] For example, *OPAP*, Case C-444/02 [2004] *ECR* I–10549 (ECJ, Grand Chamber), [AG78].

[118] Where the making of a database was completed on or after 1 January 1983, the right began to subsist in the database for the period of 15 years beginning on 1 January 1998: Database Regs, reg. 30. These rights therefore should have lapsed.

[119] Database Regs, reg. 17 (implementing Database Dir., Art. 10).

[120] Database Regs, reg. 22(3); cf. Database Dir., Recital 53.

[121] Database Regs, reg. 17(3); Database Dir., Art. 10(3), Recitals 54, 55.   [122] Derclaye, 141–2.

[123] *British Horseracing Board v. William Hill* [2001] *ECDR* (20) 257, 283–5 (Laddie J), [2002] *ECDR* (4) 41 (CA).

3.2 MAKERS AND OWNERS

The 'maker' of a database is the first owner of the database right.[124] Subject to an exception as regards employees,[125] the maker of the database is the person who takes the initiative in obtaining, verifying, or presenting the contents of a database, and who assumes the risk of investing in that obtaining, verification, or presentation.[126] The implication of this is that the maker must take the initiative *and* the risk of the investment. If one person takes the risk and another person takes the initiative, joint making may occur. Where a database is made by an employee in the course of employment, unless otherwise stipulated the employer is regarded as the maker of the database.[127]

A number of presumptions simplify the task of proving ownership.[128] Where a name purporting to be that of the maker appears on copies of the database as published or on the database when it was made, the person whose name appeared is presumed to be the maker of the database and to have made it in an employment relationship. Where copies of the database as published bear a label or a mark naming a person as the maker of the database, the label or mark is presumed to be correct. Both presumptions are rebuttable.

The database right is an assignable property right, and sections 90–93 of the 1988 Act apply to the database right as they would to copyright works. It is also possible to license database rights, and licensing schemes and licensing bodies are subject to supervision in accordance with Schedule 2. The jurisdiction of the Copyright Tribunal has been extended accordingly.

3.3 INFRINGEMENT, RIGHTS, AND REMEDIES

The database right is infringed where a person, without the consent of the owner of the right, 'extracts' or 'reutilizes' all or a substantial part of the contents of the database. The owner of database right must prove that the alleged infringer has derived the material from the claimant's database, whether directly or indirectly.

'Extraction' means the permanent or temporary transfer of those contents to another medium by any means or in any form.[129] 'Reutilization' means making those contents available to the public by any means.[130] In *BHB*, the Court of Justice indicated that the concepts must be interpreted in the light of the objective pursued by the Directive—namely, promoting investment in the creation and maintenance of databases.[131] Consequently, the terms are defined widely, to refer to:

---

[124] Database Regs, reg. 15. For a discussion of some uncertainties, see M. Koščík and M. Myška, 'Database Authorship and Ownership of Sui Generis Database Rights' (2017) 31 *International Review of Law, Computers & Technology* 43.

[125] In fact, in the United Kingdom, much of the litigation over database right has involved actions by employers against former employees over customer or supplier lists: *Pennwell Publishing (UK) v. Ornstein and ors* [2007] *EWHC* 1570 (QB) (Judge Fenwick QC); *MPT Group v. Peel et ors* [2017] *EWHC* 1222 (Ch). For a decision in which the Court was rather disapproving of the addition of a database right claim to the sizeable arsenal of legal actions invoked against a former employee, see *Pintorex Ltd v. Keyvanfar* [2013] *EWPCC* 36, [11]–[13] (Judge Alastair Wilson QC). For attempts to claim rights in customer and supplier lists through the law of confidence, see Chapter 45, section 5, pp. 1232–5.

[126] Database Regs, reg. 14; Database Dir., Recital 41.   [127] Database Regs, reg. 14(2).

[128] Database Regs, reg. 22(1).

[129] Database Dir., Art. 7(2)(a); *Apis Hristovich EOOD v. Lakorda ad*, Case C-545/07 [2009] *ECR* I-1627 (ECJ) ('*Apis*'), [44].   [130] Database Dir, Art. 7(2)(b).

[131] *BHB* (ECJ), Case C-203/02 [2004] *ECR* I-10415 (ECJ, Grand Chamber), [46].

... any act of appropriating and making available to the public ... the results of his investment, thus depriving him of revenue which should have enabled him to redeem the cost
of the investment.[132]

This might include indirect, as well as direct, extraction or reutilization.[133] In the case at
hand, the Court held that William Hill had extracted data (albeit indirectly) and reuti-
lized those data by making them available to the public on its Internet betting site.[134] In
a later case, the Court clarified that there can be an extraction where a person consults a
database and uses the results, rather than physically transfers them from one database to
another.[135] The case concerned a database of poems, which the defendant had consulted
before making its own database, named *A Thousand Poems Everyone Should Have*. The
Court stated that the concept of extraction was to be given a broad construction and was
not limited by technology (the extraction need not be electronic) or by purpose,[136] or by
whether the contents were modified.[137] The Court left it to the referring court to determine whether the extraction had been substantial.

Extraction necessarily presupposes derivation. Inevitably, questions of proof will
arise similar to those discussed in Chapter 8, Section 2.2. In *Apis Hristovich EOOD v.
Lakorda ad*,[138] the Court of Justice indicated that the question was one of fact for the
national tribunal, but inferences might be drawn from the presence of the same material in the alleged infringing database, especially in the absence of any explanation of
such coincidence.

In *Innoweb*,[139] the operator of a website which advertised second-hand cars brought
an action against a 'meta-search engine' dedicated to car sales, which offered the user
improved search ability. The Court found that this amounted to making available of the
whole of the claimant's database, and thus a 'reutilization', irrespective of the number of
results actually found and displayed for every query keyed. In so holding, the Court recognized that the effect of the system was that users would not need to go to the claimant's
site, thereby reducing its attractiveness to advertisers. In the Court's view, the commercial
effect was similar to creating a 'parasitical competing product ...., albeit without copying
the information stored in the database concerned'.[140]

The act of extraction or reutilization must occur in relation to a 'substantial' part of
the contents of the database. This means substantial in terms of quantity or quality or
a combination of both. The Court in *BHB* held that this is assessed by reference to the
investment in the creation of the database and the prejudice caused to that investment by
the act of extracting or reutilizing that part.[141] The quantitative assessment compares the

---

[132] Ibid., [51].   [133] Ibid., [52].

[134] Ibid., [65]. On the location of the act, see *Football Dataco v. Sportradar*, Case C-173/11, [2013] 1 *CMLR*
(29) 903 (ECJ), [39].

[135] *Directmedia Publishing GmbH v. Albert-Ludwigs-Universität Freiburg and Professor Ulrich Knoop*,
Case C-304/07 [2008] *ECR* I-7565 (ECJ).

[136] Ibid., [46]–[47]; see also *Apis*, Case C-545/07 [2009] *ECR* I-1627 (ECJ), [46].

[137] *Directmedia Publishing GmbH v. Albert-Ludwigs-Universität Freiburg and Professor Ulrich Knoop*,
Case C-304/07 [2008] *ECR* I-7565[39]; *Apis*, Case C-545/07 [2009] *ECR* I-1627 (ECJ), [47]–[48].

[138] *Apis*, Case C-545/07 [2009] *ECR* I-1627 (ECJ), [50]–[55]. See further S. Vousden, '*Apis*, Databases and
EU Law' [2011] *IPQ* 215.

[139] Case C-202/12, EU:C:2013:850 (ECJ).

[140] Ibid., [48].   [141] Case C-203/02 [2004] *ECR* I-10415, [69].

volume of data extracted to the volume of the whole contents of the database. However, an extraction/reutilization of a part will also be substantial if it represents a significant part of the investment viewed qualitatively—that is, in terms of human, technical, or financial investment in obtaining, verification, or presentation of the database. The intrinsic value of the material taken is irrelevant;[142] so too is the investment in the creation of those data.[143] If a database comprises a bundle of modules (such as a legal database divided into legislation, case law, commentary, and journals), the question of whether there has been an extraction of a substantial part can be assessed against each module insofar as the module concerned reaches the threshold for protection (that is, is a result of substantial investment). If the module itself does not qualify, then an extraction must be assessed against the collection of modules as a totality.[144]

Regulation 16(2) provides that the repeated and systematic extraction or reutilization of insubstantial parts of the contents of a database may come to amount to the extraction or reutilization of a substantial part of those contents. This will be infringement only where it comprises acts 'which conflict with a normal exploitation of that database or which unreasonably prejudice the legitimate interests of the maker of the database'.[145] The Court of Justice has taken a purposive view: the Regulation on insubstantial parts is 'to prevent circumvention of the prohibition in Article 7(1)'; the systematic and repeated uses must be such that they would lead to the reconstitution of a substantial part of the database, and thus cumulatively would seriously prejudice the investment made by the maker of the database.[146] In the Court's view, William Hill's uses were systematic and repeated, but not infringing, because there was 'no possibility that, through the cumulative effects of its acts, William Hill might reconstitute and make available the whole or a substantial part of the contents of the BHB database'.[147]

The database right allows the maker to control the first sale, but not the subsequent distribution, of hard copies on which data is stored. Where a copy of a database has been sold within the EEA by, or with the consent of, the owner of the database right in the database, further sales within the EEA of that copy shall not constitute the extraction or reutilization of the contents of the database. It is interesting that the right is exhausted only by 'sale' and not by other forms of transfer.[148] Consequently, the sale by a customer of gratuitously distributed copies of databases, such as British Telecom telephone directories, may infringe. Oddly, where there has been first sale of hard copies on which data are stored, the Regulations permit only resale and not other forms of transfer. The Regulations appear to suggest that the lawful buyer of a copy of a database can neither give it away, nor rent it.[149]

In relation to the remedies available for breach of the database right, the Database Regulations provide that equivalent provisions of the 1988 Act apply in relation to the database right and databases in which that right subsists as apply in relation to copyright and copyright works.[150]

---

[142] Ibid., [72], [78].   [143] Ibid., [79].

[144] *Apis*, Case C-545/07 [2009] *ECR* I-1627 (ECJ).

[145] Database Dir., Art. 7(5).

[146] *BHB*, Case C-203/02 [2004] *ECR* I-10415 (ECJ, Grand Chamber), [86]-[87].

[147] Ibid., [91].   [148] Database Regs, reg. 12(3).   [149] Database Regs, reg. 12(2).

[150] See Chapter 49.

3.4 EXCEPTIONS AND DEFENCES

3.4.1 Lawful use

A lawful user of a database that has been made available to the public in any manner is entitled to extract or reutilize insubstantial parts of the contents of the database for any purpose.[151] This limitation may not be excluded by agreement.[152]

3.4.2 Fair dealing

Where a database has been made available to the public in any manner, the database right is not infringed by a fair dealing with a substantial part of its contents if three conditions are satisfied: (i) if that part is extracted from the database by a person who is a lawful user of the database; (ii) if it is extracted for the purpose of illustration for teaching or research and not for any commercial purpose; and (iii) if the source is indicated.[153] With respect to 'text and data mining', the government expressed the view that it was unnecessary to modify the exception to add something equivalent to the new section 29A (introduced in June 2014).[154] In its view, the existing exception was sufficiently broad to encompass acts falling within the new copyright exception.

3.4.3 Public lending

An exception is also made for public lending.[155] For lending to be 'public', it must take place through an establishment that is accessible to the public. Such an establishment is permitted to charge borrowers an amount that does not go beyond what is necessary to cover the costs of the establishment.[156] However, permitting remote access is not deemed to constitute a lending. Bizarrely, the exception for public lending does not apply to the making of a copy of a database available for on-the-spot reference use. Even if the lending is gratuitous and in a public establishment, the Regulations suggest that it may be an infringement.[157]

3.4.4 Other defences

Defences also exist in relation to parliamentary and judicial proceedings, royal commissions and statutory inquiries, material open to public inspection or on an official register, material communicated to the Crown in the course of public business, public records,

---

[151] Database Regs, reg. 19; Database Dir., Art. 8. The definition of 'lawful user' is problematic: see Chapter 9, section 2.3, pp. 233–4, section 17, pp. 276–7. See also Derclaye, 120–6.

[152] *Ryanair v. PR Aviation BV*, Case C-30/14, EU:C:2015:10, [39]–[40] (describing the right as 'mandatory rights for lawful users of databases', though holding that the only limits on contract in relation to databases that are not protected by copyright or database right are those inherent in national law). See further T. Synodinou, 'Databases and Screen-Scraping' [2016] *EIPR* 313, 315 (noting the possible role of competition law); P. Mysoor, (2017) 131 *LQR* 556; M. Borghi and S. Karapapa, [2015] *EIPR* 505; S. Vousden, 'Autonomy, Comparison Websites, and *Ryanair*' [2015] *IPQ* 386 (all, from different perspectives, critical of the CJEU decision).

[153] Database Regs, reg. 20(1); Database Dir., Art. 9(b). Criticized by the Royal Society as 'vague and unhelpful': Royal Society, *Keeping Science Open: The Effects of Intellectual Property on the Conduct of Science* (2003), [5.5].

[154] HM Government, *Technical Review of the Draft Legislation on Copyright Exceptions: Government Response* (2014), 13 (stating that the exception 'will permit the extraction of whole works if required for text and data mining through the provision for "fair dealing with a substantial part"').

[155] Database Regs, reg. 12(2); Database Dir., Art. 7(2).   [156] Database Regs, reg. 12(3).

[157] Database Regs, reg. 12(4).

and acts done under statutory authority.[158] The Regulations also provide a defence where the extraction or reutilization occurs at a time when the identity of the maker could not be ascertained by reasonable inquiry, or in pursuance of arrangements made at a time when such identification was not possible. It must also be reasonable to assume that the database right has expired.[159] Competition law will also apply to the database right in the same way as to other intellectual property rights.[160] This is considered in Chapter 12.

3.5 FOREIGN DATABASES

The database right will subsist only where, at the material time,[161] its maker was either: a national of an EEA state; habitually resident within the EEA; a body incorporated under the law of an EEA state; a body with its principal place of business or its registered office within the EEA; or a partnership or other unincorporated body that was formed under the law of an EEA state, which, at that time, satisfied certain conditions.[162]

3.6 ASSESSMENT

Although the Database Directive had been described by many as unduly protective, the Court of Justice cases have seriously curtailed the perceived excesses (by limiting the availability of protection of sole-source databases).[163] In December 2005, the Commission issued an evaluation of the effect of the Directive and was disappointed to find that the number of databases created in 2004 had declined to pre-Directive levels.[164] The Commission then embarked on a stakeholder consultation, asking whether stakeholders favoured maintenance of the status quo, repeal of the whole Directive (including its copyright components), repeal of the *sui generis* database right, or modification of the latter right.[165] Most respondents favoured reform of the right, but they were divided over whether the right should be strengthened or the exceptions broadened.[166] The Commission has now launched a new public consultation,[167] and commissioned a study. It is particularly concerned as to how the database right may operate in the changing digital economy associated with the 'Internet of Things'.

One possible set of reforms might be to subject the database right to the formality of prior registration, possibly with the EUIPO, thereby creating a unitary title.[168] We see this idea as attractive because the broad notion of 'database' renders many persons right

---

[158] Database Regs, Sch. 1. These correspond to the provisions of CDPA 1988, ss 45–50, and Database Dir., Art. 9(c). [159] Database Regs, reg. 21(1).

[160] Database Dir., Recital 47.

[161] Database Regs, reg. 18. The 'material time' means the time when the database was made or, if the making extended over a period, a substantial part of that period. [162] Database Regs, reg. 18(2).

[163] Derclaye, 96; M. Leistner, 'Case Comment' (2005) 36 *IIC* 581, 593–4; M. Leistner, 'The Protection of Databases', in E. Derclaye (ed.), *Research Handbook on the Future of EU Copyright* (2009), 427, 437–8; S. von Lewinski, in Walter and von Lewinski, [9.7.8], n. 251.

[164] European Commission, *DG Internal Market and Services Working Paper: First Evaluation of Directive 96/9/EC on the Legal Protection of Databases* (12 December 2005), [1.4], [4.23].

[165] Ibid., 25–7, [6.1]–[6.4].

[166] European Commission, *Protection of Databases* (2014), available online at http://ec.europa.eu/internal_market/copyright/prot-databases/index_en.htm.

[167] https://ec.europa.eu/digital-single-market/en/news/summary-report-public-consultation-legal-protection-databases.

[168] M. Leistner, 'Big Data and the Database Directive 96/9/EC: Current Law and Potential For Reform', in S. Lohsse (et al.) (eds), *Trading Data in the Digital Economy: Legal Concepts and Tools* (2017), 27, 57.

holders even where they might not know or care about obtaining exclusive rights. In relation to many websites, amateur and scientific databases, both for makers and users, the automatic quality of database right adds a wholly unnecessary set of regulatory burdens. A registration system would allow businesses that genuinely require exclusivity to 'opt in' to protection. Registration also seems particularly useful for a right that has a fixed term, because the register would provide notice to the public as to when a database is protected, and when it falls into the public domain. If a database maker reinvests substantially in the database, the registration system would facilitate renewal or re-registration (accompanied by an indication as to the investment made).

4 TECHNOLOGICAL PROTECTION MEASURES

As mentioned in Chapter 11, copyright owners have begun to exploit copyright-protected works using self-help mechanisms in the form of 'technological measures of protection'. This new mode of exploitation reflects real fears amongst the right holders that digital reproduction and communication technologies present the threat of such widespread private copying that copyright law, by itself, could not be relied upon to protect the investment involved in creating and publishing the work. Such technological protection measures include: encryption and similar access controls, which encode works so that only those with legitimate keys can obtain access; and copy controls, which allow users access to works, but operate to prevent the subsequent making of copies.

The use of technological measures to support copyright is reinforced by complex and extensive laws prohibiting circumvention of such measures. The reinforcement is by way of a mesh of overlapping civil and criminal actions. This complex topic deserves treatment separate from secondary infringement of copyright, but as 'related rights', for two reasons: first, because the measures are, in many cases, not limited to those applied to protect copyright works, but also protect performances and the *sui generis* database right; and second, because the civil rights of action are frequently conferred not only on the copyright holder who applies the measure to the work, but also on the person issuing copies to the public in protected form and any other person with intellectual property rights in the technological measure employed.

The CDPA 1988, as amended, contains three categories of provision dealing with situations in which a person facilitates access to works that the person concerned is not entitled to use or receive.[169] The first category, in sections 296ZA–ZF, relates to the circumvention of effective technological measures applied to copyright works other than computer programs and is designed to implement Article 6 of the Information Society Directive.[170] The second category, which is found in section 296, applies only to computer programs (and is intended to implement Article 7(1)(c) of the Software Directive). The third category, in

---

[169] P. Vantsiouri, 'A Legislation in Bits and Pieces: The Overlapping Anti-Circumvention Provisions of the Information Society Directive, the Software Directive and the Conditional Access Directive and Their Implementation in the UK' [2012] *EIPR* 587. Note that other causes of action might be available based on 'communication to the public' (see Chapter 6, section 6, pp. 160–71), or accessory liability (where the end user, for example, makes a copy) (see Chapter 48, section 3.4, pp. 1287–9), and other sources of criminal liability may exist under the Fraud Act 2006, ss 6, 7, and 11 and the Serious Crimes Act 2007, ss 44–46.

[170] CDPA 1988, ss 297ZA(1), (6), and 296 ZD(1), (8) (copyright works—other than computer programs— performances, database right, publication right); Info. Soc. Dir., Recital 50 (without prejudice to Software Dir.). In turn, Art. 6 implements WCT, Art. 11, and WPPT, Art. 18.

sections 297–9, relates to reception of transmissions (and is intended to implement the Conditional Access Directive).[171] Each needs to be considered in turn.

4.1 MEASURES APPLIED TO COPYRIGHT WORKS (OTHER THAN COMPUTER PROGRAMS)

Sections 296ZA–ZF are intended to implement Article 6 of the Information Society Directive, which requires member states to provide 'adequate legal protection' against a number of activities in relation to the circumvention of 'effective technological measures'. Because those provisions are not supposed to affect the provisions in the Software Directive, we are here concerned with cases in which effective technological measures have been applied to a copyright work other than a computer program.[172] Section 296ZF defines 'technological measures' as 'any technology, device or component that is designed, in the normal course of its operation, to protect a copyright work other than a computer program'.[173] A technological measure is 'effective' where the use of a protected work, etc., 'is controlled by the copyright owner through either (a) an access control or protection process such as encryption, scrambling or other transformation of the work, or (b) a copy control mechanism, which achieves the protection objective'.[174] This makes clear that the provisions apply both to access controls, such as encryption, and copy controls. In *Nintendo v. PC Box*,[175] the Court of Justice was asked whether protection was afforded to a games console (as opposed to the games themselves), such that use of a device that would enable other games to be played on the console counted as circumvention. The Court said that it could not see any reason why not, the copyright in the game being protected by the interaction between the console and the game, although it left to the national court the assessment of the purpose of the supposed circumvention device.[176] It remains unclear, however, whether it covers devices that monitor usage.[177]

Following largely the schema of the Directive, the Act distinguishes between two sorts of objectionable behaviour: on the one hand, protection is given against the act of circumvention itself; on the other, protection is given against those who make or sell devices that enable circumvention, or who supply services that achieve that end.

4.1.1 The act of circumvention

Section 296ZA of the 1988 Act gives specified persons civil rights of action where a person does anything that circumvents technological measures knowing, or with reasonable grounds to know, that they are pursuing that objective. The persons given the right to bring the action, who are described as having the same rights as those that a copyright owner has in respect of an infringement of copyright, are the copyright owners of the work protected (or their exclusive licensee) and the person issuing copies of the work or

---

[171] Directive 98/84/EC of the European Parliament and of the Council of 20 November 1998 on the legal protection of services based on, or consisting of, conditional access [1998] *OJ L* 320/54 (28 November 1998) (the 'Conditional Access Directive'). [172] CDPA 1988, s. 296ZA(1).

[173] CDPA 1988, s. 296ZF. This largely echoes Info. Soc. Dir., Art. 6(3). However, there the definition is worded so as to relate to devices designed 'to prevent or restrict acts, in respect of works or other subject matter, which are not authorised' by the right holder. A device that merely discourages infringement, rather than physically preventing it, is not covered: *R v. Higgs* [2008] *EWCA Crim* 1324.

[174] CDPA 1988, s. 298ZF(2), replicating Info. Soc. Dir., Art. 6(3).

[175] Case C-355/12, EU:C:2014:25 (ECJ). [176] Ibid., [28].

[177] L. Bygrave, 'The Technologisation of Copyright: Implications for Privacy and Related Interests' [2002] *EIPR* 51, 54–5.

communicating the work to the public in a form to which technological measures have been applied.[178] The *scienter* requirement means that users do not commit a wrong if they circumvent accidentally; it is only where a person knows or has reasonable grounds to know that they are trying to circumvent technological measures that they infringe. The wrong is committed only where a successful act of circumvention has taken place; mere attempts are not covered. The provision is inapplicable where a person circumvents a measure 'for the purposes of research into cryptography', unless, by so doing 'or issuing information derived from that research, he affects prejudicially the rights of the copyright owner'.[179]

4.1.2 Facilitating circumvention

The Directive requires member states to provide adequate legal protection of effective technological measures by preventing manufacture of and trade in circumvention devices. These include devices that are promoted, advertised, or marketed for the purpose of circumvention, or have only a limited commercially significant purpose or use other than to circumvent, or are primarily designed, produced, adapted, or performed for the purpose of enabling or facilitating the circumvention of any effective technological measures. In *Nintendo*,[180] the Court of Justice was asked to advise on whether a device that altered a games console and would allow it to play both pirated games and lawful, but unauthorized, games fell within the provision. The Court indicated that the Directive embraced a principle of proportionality: that the technological measures should not restrict activities beyond those necessary to protect the copyright in the works. Thus it was relevant to consider whether adequate protection could be achieved for copyright from measures directed at the games themselves, rather than the console. The Court of Justice suggested that, when assessing the purpose or effect of the defendant's device, the national court would need to assess how it was used in practice, in particular whether it was used to facilitate unauthorized copying of Nintendo games or instead to facilitate the use of alternatives to the authorized games.[181] If the court finds that the technological protection measures that have been deployed by the right holder in practice disproportionately exclude a high volume of legal acts, the court will withdraw the legal protection from such measures and allow circumvention that is required to achieve legal ends.

In the United Kingdom, the provision is implemented by civil and criminal measures.[182] The addition of criminal liability reflects the fact that these acts are regarded as the ones that seriously threaten the copyright holder's interests—after all, the general public does not have the time or means to break technological locks or controls. It is only with the assistance of commercially available circumvention devices or services that anti-circumvention is likely to become widespread.

There are two criminal provisions. The first applies to devices, products, or components 'primarily designed, produced or adapted for the purpose of enabling or facilitating the circumvention of effective technological measures'.[183] The limitation to devices 'primarily designed' for circumvention is important, and while it would cover forged smart cards for

---

[178] CDPA 1988, s. 296ZA(3); cf. the wider range of persons mentioned in ss 296ZD(2) and 296(2). In the case of so-called stream-ripping of music from a video-sharing platform such as You Tube, this gives a right to object to the circumvention both to You Tube and the copyright owner.

[179] CDPA 1988, s. 296ZA(2); Info. Soc. Dir., Recital 48. One may wonder whether circumvention ought not to be lawful where it is done in the public interest.

[180] Case C-355/12, EU:C:2014:25 (ECJ).   [181] Ibid., [31]–[38].

[182] Member states may also prohibit private possession of such devices: Info. Soc. Dir., Recital 49.

[183] CDPA 1988, s. 296ZB(1). See *R v. Higgs* [2008] *EWCA Crim* 1324.

decrypting copyright-protected broadcasts, devices that serve legitimate purposes (such as general-purpose PCs) fall outside its scope even if they can be used to avoid technological protection. A person commits an offence if they manufacture such a device for sale or hire, or distribute one in the course of business, or do so to such an extent as to affect prejudicially the copyright owner, unless they prove that they did not know and had no reasonable grounds for believing that the device enabled or facilitated the circumvention of effective technological measures.[184] One peculiar feature of this offence is that, in a situation in which a device is primarily designed for circumvention, but can be used for other legitimate purposes, a person commits an offence by making and selling such devices even where they were genuinely making and selling them for legitimate purposes. In such a situation, the defence is of no assistance, because while the person has good reason to believe that the device will not be used to circumvent, they know that it *could* be so used.

The second criminal provision relates to a service, the purpose of which is to enable or facilitate the circumvention of effective technological measures. A person commits an offence if, in the course of business or to such an extent as to affect prejudicially the copyright owner, they provide, promote, advertise, or market such a service.[185] As with devices, it is a defence for the accused to show that they did not know, nor had reasonable grounds for believing, that the service enabled or facilitated circumvention. In both cases, a further defence applies to acts of the intelligence services and law enforcement agencies.[186]

The civil actions cover broader ground than the criminal ones (and, in contrast to the criminal provisions, apply *mutatis mutandis* to effective technological measures used in relation to performances, the database right, and the publication right).[187] As regards manufacture and distribution of devices (etc.), liability exists not only in relation to devices 'primarily designed, produced, adapted . . . for the purpose of enabling and facilitating' circumvention, but also to devices 'promoted, advertised, or marketed' for that purpose and ones having 'only a limited commercially significant purpose or use other than to circumvent'.[188] This latter criterion was at issue in *Nintendo v. PC Box*,[189] in which the Court highlighted that the limitation was intended to embody the principle of proportionality. This meant that the right holder must not deploy technological measures that disproportionately inhibit lawful activities of third parties[190] and that a device that might enable circumvention should be permissible only where, in reality, it is used primarily for purposes other than to enable the use of copyright-infringing material.[191]

As regards services, civil liability is in some respects more narrowly defined than criminal liability, being confined to the *provision* of services (as opposed to the advertising, promoting, and marketing of a service). Civil liability exists, most obviously, where the service is performed for the purpose of enabling or facilitating circumvention. However, civil liability also exists in two other circumstances: where the service provided is merely

---

[184] CDPA 1988, s. 296ZB(5).

[185] CDPA 1988, s. 296ZB(2). The reference to non-business activities that affect the copyright owner prejudicially goes beyond the requirements of the Directive and seems designed to cover making available on the Internet of decryption codes. [186] CDPA 1988, s. 296ZB(3).

[187] CDPA 1988, ss 296ZD(8). 296ZE(11).

[188] CDPA 1988, s. 296ZD. The wrongful acts are more broadly defined too: any manufacture, as opposed to manufacture for sale or hire; import, compared to import 'otherwise than for his private and domestic use'; any distribution, rather than distribution in the course of business; selling or hiring, or offering or advertising for sale or hire, rather than doing so in the course of business. Moreover, civil liability extends to the situation in which a person has a device in their possession for commercial purposes.

[189] Case C-355/12, EU:C:2014:25 (ECJ), [29]. [190] Ibid., [32]–[33].

[191] Ibid., [36].

advertised or promoted for that purpose (even if the service does not achieve the advertised purpose!); and where a service is provided that has only a limited commercially significant purpose other than to circumvent (even, it seems, if it is provided for just such a non-circumventing use).

Civil actions to enforce these provisions can be brought by a number of parties: the copyright owner, or their exclusive licensee; the person issuing copies of the work to the public or communicating to the public the work to which technological measures have been applied; and the owner, or exclusive licensee, of 'any intellectual property right in the effective technological measures'.[192] There is no defence of ignorance, although damages may not be awarded against a defendant who demonstrates that they did not know, nor had reason to believe, that their acts enabled or facilitated an infringement of copyright.[193]

In a recent case under US law, record companies brought an action against the providers of the 'stream-ripping' service,[194] 'You-Tube-mp3.org', claiming that the service enabled users to circumvent You Tube's TPMs so that they could download music files from the video streams. The US case settled, and the service is now shut down, but it is notable that the complaint included arguments based on circumvention. Such an action would equally have been available in the United Kingdom.

4.1.3 Attempts to avoid digital lock-up

When the proposals to expand the scope of protection of technological measures were being debated representatives of consumers vigorously articulated their fear that such provisions would facilitate digital lock-up of material that the public is currently entitled to access and use (without payment). Those fears related in part to the supply of works in the public domain (for example the works of Shakespeare) in digital form, but subject to technical measures: why, it was asked, should the public not be able to circumvent such measures to access what are, after all, works in the public domain? The fears also related to the use of technical measures to prevent uses that fall within existing copyright exceptions: in a world in which works are protected by technical measures, and those measures are protected by law against circumvention, how are users to be able to access and copy works for research and private study, criticism and review, and so forth?

The first concern may seem to have been met through the definition of 'technological measure'. As already observed, 'technological measure' is defined as a technology designed in the normal course of its operation to protect a copyright work other than a computer program. Moreover, the provisions on civil liability for circumvention, or supplying devices or services that facilitate circumvention, apply only where 'effective technological measures have been applied to a copyright work other than a computer program'.[195] While this may seem, at first glance, to protect the public against 'digital lock-up', in practice the result is likely to be quite different: this is because if the measure protects at least one work, civil liability applies. Consequently, devices cannot be circulated, services provided, or acts of circumvention carried out where versions of public domain (that is, unprotected) works protected by technological measures include *any* copyright material: liability will exist, for example, where a person circumvents a measure to access the complete works of Shakespeare, because the collection also contains a recently written introductory essay.

---

[192] CDPA 1988, s. 296ZD(2).
[193] CDPA 1988, s. 296ZD(7).
[194] PRSforMusic and IPO, *Stream-Ripping: How it works and its Role in the UK Music Piracy Landscape* (2017).   [195] CDPA 1988, s. 296ZD(1).

In addition, one should note that the criminal provisions apply irrespective of the *particular* application of a technological measure. As long as the measure is 'designed' to protect a copyright work other than a computer program, criminal infringements occur in the circumstances that have been set out earlier. Imagine that an entrepreneur designs a technological measure to protect copyright works, but then decides to apply the measure to works in the public domain. The measure, even though now applied to such works, retains its quality of being designed to protect a copyright work. A person commits a criminal act by selling devices or advertising services to enable or facilitate the circumvention of such measures. The defence in section 296ZB(5) will not assist.

As regards the relationship between technological measures and exceptions to copyright, Article 6(4) of the Information Society Directive provides a strange, barely comprehensible, compromise.[196] The European Union was caught in the tricky position of wanting to legislate to protect technological measures from circumvention, but without being in a position to understand fully the implications of such strong protection.[197] As things currently stand, it is impossible to predict how dependent consumers are going to be on digital delivery or the extent to which consumers who previously relied on the limited scope of the rights conferred on copyright owners are going to be inconvenienced by such measures. Article 6(4) is intended to reassure the user community that the legislature will not stand by and let everything go horribly wrong. If technological measures start to impair user actions seriously, ways will be found in which to sort out the problems. Pending review at the EU level (under Article 12(1), every three years), national authorities may (or indeed, in some cases, must) take action to release content from its technological chains. Article 6(4) also operates to indicate to content holders that they should develop technological measures with as much sophistication as is possible, so that they can enable users to take advantage of limitations and exceptions traditionally recognized by copyright law. Article 6(4) of the Directive states that:

> Notwithstanding the legal protection provided for by paragraph 1, in the absence of voluntary measures taken by rightholders, including agreements between rightholders and other parties concerned, Member States shall take appropriate measures to ensure that rightholders make available to the beneficiary of an exception or limitation provided for in national law in accordance with Article 5(2)(a), (2)(c), (2)(d), (2)(e), (3)(a), (3)(b), or 3(e) the means of benefiting from that exception or limitation, to the extent necessary to benefit from that exception or limitation and where that beneficiary has legal access to the protected work or subject-matter concerned.[198]

The United Kingdom implemented Article 6(4) in section 296ZE of the CDPA 1988.[199] This allows for complaints to be made to the Secretary of State where an effective technological measure prevents a person from carrying out a permitted act. The relevant

---

[196] P. Akester, 'The Impact of Digital Rights Management on Freedom of Expression: The First Empirical Assessment' (2010) 41 *IIC* 32; V. Samartzi, 'Optimal vs Sub-optimal Use of DRM-Protected Works' [2011] *EIPR* 517; S. Dusollier, 'The Protection of Technological Measures: Much Ado about Nothing or Silent Remodelling of Copyright?', in R. Dreyfuss and J. Ginsburg (eds), *Intellectual Property at the Edge* (2014), ch. 12.

[197] For thoughtful consideration of ways of protecting users, see D. Burk and J. Cohen, 'Fair Use Infrastructure for Rights Management Systems' (2001) 15 *Harv JL & Tech* 41.

[198] Art. 6(4) is also to apply to the new EU mandatory exceptions in the Marrakesh Directive, Directive (EU) 2017/1564 of 13 September 2017, Art. 3(4), and the proposed exceptions in COM(2016) 593 final, Art. 3(3).

[199] IPO, *Guidance on TPMs Complaints Process* (2014).

permitted acts are listed in Schedule 5A.[200] It does not apply to copyright works that are made available on agreed contractual terms in such a way that members of the public may access them from a place and at a time individually chosen by them.[201] Given that this would cover most Internet supply of works (where a person accesses a work from their own terminal at a time chosen by them), this exclusion may confine the scope of the complaint procedure to circumstances involving encrypted broadcasts or technologically protected hard copies.[202] The Secretary of State is given wide powers to issue directions to ascertain whether voluntary measures are in place enabling such acts to be permitted, and if not, to ensure that the owner or exclusive licensee of the copyright work makes available to the complainant the means to carry out the permitted acts.[203] The order might be complied with by placing a copy lacking the technological measures at the disposal of the complainant, or possibly by giving the complainant access to a circumvention device. If the copyright owner fails to comply, the complainant is granted normal remedies for breach of statutory duty.[204] It is understood that the system has never been used, despite the widespread claims from users that access to the benefit of exceptions is hampered by technological measures.[205]

4.2 COMPUTER SOFTWARE

Section 296 confers a civil right of action where a person does either of two specified acts that facilitate the circumvention of any 'technical device' that has been applied to a computer program.[206] 'Technical device' is defined as 'any device intended to prevent or restrict acts that are not authorised by the copyright owner of that computer program and are restricted by copyright'.[207] The right is conferred on three sets of persons: the owner of copyright in the computer program, or their exclusive licensee; the person issuing or communicating the program to the public; and the owner (or their exclusive licensee) of 'any intellectual property right' in the technical device.[208] The right is infringed by two specified acts: the manufacture, distribution, or possession for commercial purposes of 'any means the sole intended purpose of which is to facilitate the unauthorised removal or circumvention of the technical device'; or the publication of information intended to enable or assist persons to remove or circumvent the technical device.[209] In either case, liability is predicated on *scienter*—that is, there is infringement only where a person does the act 'knowing or having reason to believe it will be used to make infringing copies'.[210]

---

[200] As amended, in particular by the Copyright and Rights in Performances (Research, Education, Libraries and Archives) Regulations 2014 (SI 2014/1372) Sch., para. 10. The contents of the list are determined by Art. 6(4), although the logic is hard to fathom.

[201] CDPA 1988, s. 296ZF(9), implementing Info. Soc. Dir., Recital 53.

[202] M. Hart, 'The Copyright in the Information Society Directive: An Overview' [2002] *EIPR* 58, 63. But note that this condition is not applied to the exception for the visually impaired in Directive (EU) 2017/1564, Art. 3(4) (applying 1st, 3rd and, 5th paras, but not para. 4, of Art. 6(4) of Info. Soc. Dir.). See Chapter 9, pp. 261–2. The same approach is proposed for the proposed directive on Copyright in the Digital Single Market, COM(2016) 593 final, Arts 3–5.

[203] CDPA 1988, s. 296ZE(3).   [204] CDPA 1988, s. 296ZE(6).

[205] See P. Akester, 'The Impact of Digital Rights Management on Freedom of Expression: The First Empirical Assessment' (2010) 41 *IIC* 31. For some suggestions as to why this might be the case throughout Europe, see S. Dusollier, 'The Protection of Technological Measures: Much Ado about Nothing or Silent Remodelling of Copyright?', in R. Dreyfuss and J. Ginsburg (eds), *Intellectual Property at the Edge* (2014), 264–5.

[206] CDPA 1988, s. 296(1).   [207] CDPA 1988, s. 296(6).   [208] CDPA 1988, s. 296(2).

[209] The wording of the first act follows closely that in Software Dir., Art. 7(1)(c).

[210] Infringing copies are made for these purposes when a computer is loaded into a console: *R v. Higgs* [2008] *EWCA Crim* 1324. See also *Sony Entertainment v. Ball* [2004] *ECDR* (33) 323, [15] (holding that infringing copies are limited to 'articles', but an article containing a transient reproduction is an infringing copy, and that where a person makes mod chips for export, these do not produce copies that infringe UK copyright law, but that a copyright owner might nevertheless sue in the United Kingdom in relation to foreign infringements).

It is useful here to observe how much more limited are the provisions related to software than those applicable to other copyright works. First, there is civil liability only in relation to circumvention of software (subject to what was said earlier about the possible application of measures 'designed' for copyright works—other than computer programs—to other material including computer programs). Second, there is no liability for the act of circumventing devices protecting software. Third, as regards software, liability applies only in relation to any means 'the sole intended purpose of which' is to facilitate circumvention, whereas the information society provisions cover the much broader array of devices advertised for, or primarily designed for, circumvention, or with only a limited commercially significant purpose other than circumvention. Fourth, liability in relation to the supply of devices to circumvent measures protecting software is predicated on a knowledge requirement that the person knows or has reason to believe the computer program will be used to make infringing copies; *scienter* is not relevant to section 296ZD except as part of a defence of innocence to an action for damages. Fifth, in relation to technological measures protecting software, no liability pertains to offering or carrying out circumvention services.[211] Although these differences might be taken to reflect a legislative awareness that too-strong control of technical measures applied to software might seriously limit access to and development of software, almost certainly they reflect a desire not to reopen the legislative compromise effected in the Software Directive of 1991. Nevertheless, the existence of such stark differences in the scope of protection is likely to prompt those who own copyright in software to argue that the technological measures that they employ simultaneously protect copyright software and other protected works, so that they too obtain the benefit of the generous protection granted by Article 6 of the Information Society Directive and sections 296ZA–ZF of the 1988 Act.

4.3 TRANSMISSIONS

A third set of provisions deals with protection measures used in relation to transmissions. Although the 1988 Act, as enacted, contained some such provisions, they have been amended to implement the Conditional Access Directive by the Conditional Access Regulations 2000.[212] These apply to broadcasts and 'information society services' that are encrypted and, among other things, prevent unauthorized dealings in decoders. The definition of 'information society service' is found in a directive that lays down a procedure for the provision of information in the field of technical standards, and covers any service that is normally provided for remuneration and which operates at a distance by electronic means and at the individual request of a recipient of the services.[213] However, applying Article 56 of the Treaty on the Functioning of the European Union (TFEU) (free movement of services), the Court of Justice has ruled that a broadcaster may not territorially limit reception of its broadcasts to consumers in particular member states,

---

[211] While the general effect of this comparison is that technological measures receive much stronger protection outside the field of computer programs, it should be noted too that the safeguard provisions of s. 296ZE (implementing Info. Soc. Dir., Art. 6(4)) do not apply to computer programs and that, in that minor respect, the provisions of s. 296 are stronger.   [212] SI 2000/1175.

[213] Council Directive 98/34/EC of 22 June 1998 laying down a procedure for the provision of information in the field of technical standards [1998] *OJ L* 204/37 (21 July 1998). The Directive excludes television and radio broadcasts from the definition, as well as providing an 'indicative list' of services that are not 'at a distance', 'by electronic means', nor 'at the individual request of a recipient', in Annex V.

so that decoders supplied to users in one EU country may be lawfully used elsewhere in the European Union.[214]

4.3.1 Fraudulent reception

Section 297 of the 1988 Act imposes criminal liability for dishonestly receiving a programme included in a broadcasting service provided from a place in the United Kingdom. It must be proved that the recipient intended to avoid payment of any charge applicable to the reception of the programme. Not unimportantly, in the light of the Court of Justice case law, section 297 is violated where a person utilizes a domestic decoder card to receive and display broadcasts to a commercial audience.[215] According to Laws LJ, the phrase 'any charge applicable to the reception of the programme' refers to 'whatever charge is properly applicable to the reception of the programme in the circumstances in question'.[216]

4.3.2 Unauthorized decoders

Section 297A imposes criminal liability on those who supply 'unauthorized decoders', which decode encrypted transmissions so as to enable access to the transmission without payment of the fee that the person making the transmission charges for access.[217] A 'transmission' is defined as any programme included in a broadcasting service from a place within the United Kingdom or any other member state, or 'an information society service'. It therefore covers transmissions of encrypted television services (which, as we saw in Chapters 3 and 6, do not include most 'on-demand' transmissions) and encrypted services providing video, music, or access to databases 'on demand', the latter falling squarely within the complex definition of 'information society service'. The wrongful acts include making, importing, distributing, selling, possessing (for commercial purposes), and advertising the sale or hire of unauthorized decoders, as well as installing, maintaining, and replacing for commercial purposes an unauthorized decoder. Obvious examples of such wrongs would include the unauthorized manufacture of 'digi-boxes', as well as re-enabling or extending the range of reception on old smart cards.[218] It may well also include KODI-boxes where the box offers unauthorized access to a stream (though it is less clear that facilitating access to unauthorized streams falls within the scope of the provision).[219] However, following the guidance of the Court of Justice in *Football Association Premier League Ltd v. QC Leisure*, it does not cover the importation of decoder cards from another

---

[214] See *Football Association Premier League Ltd v. QC Leisure* and *Karen Murphy v. Media Protection Services Ltd*, Joined Cases C-403/08 and C-429/08 [2011] *ECR* I–9083 (ECJ, Grand Chamber) ('*FAPL*'), [125].

[215] *FACT v. Ashton* [2013] *EWHC* 1923 (Admin).

[216] Ibid., [8]. This conclusion does not violate Conditional Access Dir., Art. 3(2): *FAPL*, [72]–[74].

[217] CDPA 1988, s. 297A(4). A transmission is 'encrypted' when it is 'subjected to scrambling or the operation of cryptographic envelopes, electronic locks, passwords or any other analogous application'. A 'decoder' is defined as an apparatus designed or adapted to enable an encrypted transmission to be decoded. A decoder is unauthorized where it is designed or adapted to enable an encrypted transmission to be accessed in an intelligible form without payment of the fee that the person making the transmission charges for access.

[218] See, e.g., *R v. Bridgeman & Butt* [1996] *FSR* 538 (re-enabling or extending the range of reception on old smart cards for Spain, where the transmitter did not supply the cards, violated CDPA 1988, s. 297A, and thus involved a conspiracy to defraud).

[219] IPO, *Illicit IPTV Streaming Devices: Call for Views* (February 2017) (setting out various grounds for potential criminal conviction) IPO, *Guidance, Illicit Streaming Devices* (20 November 2017). For convictions, see https://www.fact-uk.org.uk/cracking-down-on-digital-piracy/.

member state, even if that involves breach of contractual terms or the card was obtained only by making a misrepresentation (for example as to the recipient's residence).[220]

4.3.3 Civil liabilities

Section 298 gives civil rights of action, akin to those of a copyright owner, to persons who charge for the reception of programmes included in a broadcasting service, send encrypted transmissions, or provide 'conditional access services'.[221] This would cover many of the existing satellite broadcasters, such as Sky, Film Four, etc. A 'conditional access service' is defined as a service providing conditional access technology—that is, any technical measure or arrangement whereby access to encrypted transmissions in an intelligible form is made conditional on previous individual authorization.[222]

A person covered by section 298 has the same rights as a copyright owner against a person who makes or trades in various ways in apparatus that is 'designed or adapted to enable or assist persons to access the programmes or other transmissions or circumvent conditional access technology related to the programmes or transmissions when they are not entitled to do so'.[223] This would seem to cover the situation in which somebody made or sold fraudulent smart cards or decoders to enable reception of Sky channels by persons who were not subscribers. The rights also encompass a person who publishes any information calculated to enable or assist access.[224]

4.3.4 Relationship with sections 296ZA–ZF

As we saw earlier, a copyright owner and person communicating a work to the public have various rights under sections 296ZA and ZD where technological measures are applied to the work. These can operate cumulatively with the special transmission and conditional access provisions. For example, if a person installs a device enabling receipt of an encrypted transmission, they will violate section 296ZA if they knowingly circumvent a technological measure. They will also violate section 298(2)(a)(iii) if they install, maintain, or replace for commercial purposes 'an apparatus designed or adapted to enable or assist persons to access the programmes or transmissions or circumvent conditional access technology . . . when they are not entitled to do so'. If someone distributes an unauthorized decoder, they will both be distributing 'a device . . . primarily designed . . . for the purpose of enabling the circumvention of those measures'—that is, measures applied to the copyright-protected broadcast—and so violate section 297ZD(1)(b)(iii), and also be distributing an apparatus 'designed or adapted to enable or assist persons to access the programmes or transmissions or circumvent conditional access technology . . . when they are not entitled to do so'. In each situation, a careful analysis needs to be undertaken to decide which section is most suitable.

---

[220] See *FAPL*, [63]–[67]. But note that the FAPL decision does not offer a defence to a person using a decoder licensed only for domestic use in business: *R v. Luxton* [2016] *EWCA Civ* 1097 (domestic card acquired from Danish firm did not justify use to show football broadcasts in Swansea pub). See also *R v. Brent Magistrates' Court, ex p Helidon Vuciterni* [2012] *EWHC* 2140 (Admin) (holding that the magistrates had improperly issued warrants to search the premises of a supplier of decoder cards imported from Albania, a country outside the European Union, because sale of such cards was not an offence under s. 297A).

[221] CDPA 1988, s. 298 (as amended by the Conditional Access Regulations). The rights apply only to transmissions 'from a place in the UK or any other member state'.

[222] CDPA 1988, ss 298(7), 297A(4).

[223] CDPA 1988, ss 298, 299.

[224] CDPA 1988, s. 298, as amended by the Conditional Access Regulations, to implement the Conditional Access Dir.

5 RIGHTS MANAGEMENT INFORMATION

Article 7 of the Information Society Directive has required the introduction of provisions protecting 'electronic rights management information'. By 'rights management information' is meant any information provided by the copyright owner that identifies the work, the author, the copyright owner, the holder of any intellectual property rights, information about the terms and conditions of use of the work, or any numbers or codes that represent such information.[225] In effect, what we are concerned with is information equivalent to the copyright page of a book (author, publisher, ISBN, etc.) that is electronically attached to (typically being woven into the fabric of) a work that is distributed digitally. This is sometimes referred to as 'metadata'.[226] The information falls within the scope of protection when it (or any of it) is associated with a copy of a work or appears in connection with the communication to the public of a work.[227] The provision also applies to the *sui generis* database right.

Although the phrase 'rights management information' may not sound very glamorous, the European Commission sees its protection as the key prerequisite to an effective 'information society'.[228] This is essentially for two reasons. The first is that rights management information is seen as having the potential to enable direct contracting between content holders and consumers, to enable the 'metering' of uses of works, and to enable rights clearances more generally (for example in relation to the production of multimedia works). It is thus seen as the lubricant that will keep the legal cogs of the Internet turning. As Thomas Dreier has written:

> [Digital rights management] clearly goes beyond mere protection against piracy and illegal copying. Rather . . . [digital rights management] aims at implementing a technical structure which enables product and service differentiation together with, and on the basis of, price discrimination.[229]

Second, the Commission recognizes that works in digital form are 'plastic'—that is, that works in digital form are readily capable of modification and alteration. The protection of rights management information is needed to prevent the removal of various identifying insignia from works, and to enable users to keep track of what the information is and where it comes from.

Section 296ZG provides the copyright owner, its exclusive licensee, and any person communicating or issuing work to the public[230] with the ability to prevent the removal of rights management information and the further circulation of copies from which such information has been removed.[231] Liability is dependent in both cases on *scienter*. As regards removal or alteration, a person is liable where they 'knowingly and without

---

[225] CDPA 1988, s. 296ZG(7). It is clear from this that protection extends to all sorts of information that is electronic rather than being limited to information about 'electronic rights'.

[226] Dusollier has questioned whether the definition of 'rights management information' would cover digital watermarks, because some do not contain 'identifying information': S. Dusollier, 'Some Reflections on Copyright Management Information and Moral Rights' (2003) 25 *Colum JL & Arts* 377. For speculation as to whether it covers personal data about users, see L. Bygrave, 'The Technologisation of Copyright: Implications for Privacy and Related Interests' [2002] *EIPR* 51, 55–6.

[227] Info. Soc. Dir., Art. 7(2).

[228] See Commission Staff Working Paper, *Digital Rights: Background, Systems, Assessment* (14 February 2002) SEC(2002) 197.

[229] Thomas Dreier in the Rights Management Report of the Commission meeting Santiago de Compostela, June 2002.   [230] CDPA 1988, s. 296ZG(3)–(5).

[231] Info. Soc. Dir., Art. 7; cf. 17 *USC* §1202.

authority' remove or alter metadata in circumstances under which that person 'knows or has reason to believe that by so doing [they are] inducing, enabling, facilitating or concealing an infringement of copyright'.[232] Accidental removal of data is therefore permitted, as is deliberate removal of metadata where a person has no reason to think that there has been, is, or is likely to be an infringement. A researcher who deliberately deletes metadata when making an electronic copy of material from an electronic source for purposes of their own non-commercial research or private study will therefore not violate the section. As regards dealings in material that has been tampered with by the removal or alteration of metadata, a person infringes where they 'knowingly and without authority' distribute, import for distribution, or communicate to the public, copies of such material where that person 'knows or has reason to believe that by so doing [they are] inducing, enabling, facilitating or concealing an infringement of copyright'.[233] The provisions do not expressly prevent the publication of information on how to remove such information or the sale of devices that enable the removal of information, although the English legal system might regard this as joint tortfeasance.[234]

6 PUBLIC LENDING RIGHT

Although copyright in books enables authors to control (and seek compensation) where their works are copied, they have no right to prevent a range of people from reading the same book. Typically, this occurs when books are repeatedly borrowed from a library. Because borrowing reduces sales of a work, when it is carried out on a large scale (public libraries in England lend something like 250 million times a year),[235] it can substantially reduce an author's expected income. To remedy these problems, a public lending right (PLR) was established in the United Kingdom in 1979. The Public Lending Rights Act 1979 provides a framework for the scheme that is implemented in the Public Lending Right Scheme Order 1982.[236] The PLR scheme has been amended a number of times but the last consolidation was in a 1990 instrument.[237]

The PLR scheme entitles authors to remuneration where their works are loaned by public libraries. This is based on the principle that authors should be compensated for lost revenues, since such loans are substitutes for sales.[238] The right does not provide authors with large sums of money. Basically, an author[239] may register their right to receive a share of up to £6,600 per annum from a government fund of £8 million.[240] The right persists for the same period as copyright.[241] To qualify for the scheme, authors must have their principal homes in a listed country (at present, EEA countries).[242] The right which

---

[232] CDPA 1988, s. 296ZG(1). [233] CDPA 1988, s. 296ZG(2).

[234] See Chapter 48, section 3.4, pp. 1287–9.

[235] http://www.lboro.ac.uk/microsites/infosci/lisu/lisu-statistics/lisu-uk-library-statistics.pdf.

[236] Public Lending Right Scheme 1982 (Commencement) Order 1982 (SI 1982/719).

[237] SI 1990/2360 (as amended, including by SI 1991/2618 ('PLRS Order'). For fuller commentary, see Copinger, ch. 19.

[238] Rel. Rights. Dir., Art. 6(1) permits a derogation from the exclusive right of public lending 'provided that at least authors obtain a remuneration for such lending'.

[239] Defined in PLRS Order, Art. 4 to include illustrators, photographers and translators (and in relation to audio-books, narrators and producers). Note that the author's name should appear on the title page or be entitled to a royalty from the publisher: PLRS Order, Art. 4(2) . While the right is assignable and devolves on death, only the author may apply to register a book.

[240] Public Lending Right (Increase in Limit) Order SI 2003/839 and SI 2005/1519. [241] PLRS Order.

[242] In 2013, 3 per cent of the PLR fund was paid out to authors from elsewhere in Europe.

initially applied only with respect to books which had been 'printed and bound', has been extended (from July 2014) to cover audio and ebooks;[243] musical scores are excluded.[244] The scheme is administered by the British Library.[245] However, section 3(3) of the 1979 Act declares that the entitlement is to be 'dependent on, and its extent ascertainable by reference to, the number of occasions on which books are lent out from particular libraries'. Libraries thus have to provide information about the books that they have loaned.

7 DROIT DE SUITE

The final right 'related' to copyright is the *droit de suite*, or, as it is also known, the 'artist's resale royalty right'.[246] The *droit de suite* (literally translated as the 'right to follow' the work) enables artists to claim a portion of the price for which a work is resold. The idea is that an artist may sell a painting for a low price at a time when they are unknown and have little bargaining power. In due course, if the artist's reputation develops, that painting can be resold for continually increasing sums. The *droit de suite* enables the artist to claim a proportion of the increased value. The right is seen as justifiable not only because it encourages creation, but also because the artist is conceived (through the authorial link) as responsible for the increase in value (economic success) of their works.[247] Consequently, although the right is essentially economic in nature, it is sometimes categorized as a 'moral right'. Because of its specific *sui generis* nature, we have included it in this chapter on related rights.

Until recently, no such artists' resale right was recognized in British copyright law.[248] However, as many European countries introduced such a right and because there was thought to be a potential impact on the internal market from the differences in national

[243] The Public Lending Right Scheme 1982 (Commencement of Variations) Order, SI 2014/1457 (exercising a power conferred by the Digital Economy Act 2010, s. 43, in the light of an independent inquiry conducted by William Sieghert, *An Independent Review of E-Lending in Public Libraries in England* (March 2013) and DCMS, *Consultation on the Extension of the Public Lending Right to Rights of Holders of Books in Non-Print Formats* (February 2014)). Note that the extension to ebooks was of little initial significance, because the scheme did not cover 'remote lending' of ebooks, though following the CJEU decision *Vereniging Openbare Bibliotheken (VOB) v. Stichting Leenrecht*, Case C-174/15, EU:C:2016:856 (holding that 'e-lending' falls within the scope of the permitted derogation from the Rel. Rights Dir., Art. 6), DCMS announced on 24 February 2017 that it will extend the scheme to encompass such remote lending. The first step to so doing is effected by the UK reforms, see Digital Economy Act 2017, s. 31 (amending Public Lending Rights Act 1979, s. 5(2) (definition of lending)).

[244] Eligible books are defined in PLRS Order, Art. 6. 'Book' means printed and bound publication, but does not include books bearing corporate names, musical scores, and serial publications. The restriction to books of 32 pages has been removed.

[245] Replacing the Public Lending Right Registrar from October 2013: Public Bodies (Abolition of the Registrar of Public Lending Right) Order 2013 (SI 2013/2352) (made under the Public Bodies Act 2011, Sch. 1). A consultation on the future of the Registrar had occurred in 2012, but most respondents opposed the abolition of the Registrar; the government nevertheless had its own ideas.

[246] S. Stokes, *Artist's Resale Right (Droit de Suite): Law and Practice* (2nd edn, 2012). For an exploration of comparative historical perspectives, see A. O' Dwyer, 'The Nature of the Artists' Resale Right' [2017] *IPQ* 95.

[247] Cf. J. Merryman, 'The Proposed Generalisation of the *Droit de Suite* in the European Communities' [1997] *IPQ* 16, 22–3.

[248] See, for previous British views, Whitford Committee, ch. 17. The right is recognized, but effectively optional, under Berne, Art. 14ter. There is growing momentum at WIPO on this topic, with a 2015 study by Sam Ricketson entitled *Proposed International Treaty on Droit de Suite*, SG 15–0565. See also C. Jewell, 'The Artists' Resale Royalty Right: A Fair Deal for Visual Artists' (2017) (June) *WIPO Magazine*.

laws for modern artworks, the Resale Rights Directive was adopted requiring all member states to introduce such a right.[249] Prior to its adoption, the proposal was widely criticized, particularly from the perspective of the British art market. One particular fear that was expressed was that the effect of harmonizing 'upwards' would be to drive sales of modern artworks out of Europe, to the auction houses of New York, Switzerland, or Hong Kong, where no such 'tax' will be imposed on the seller. (Apparently, when California created a *droit de suite*, Sotheby's closed its auction house there.) These criticisms and questions, however, did not prove persuasive, although the *droit de suite*, as adopted, is much more limited than that originally proposed and gives considerable leeway to member states as regards implementation. The Directive was implemented in the United Kingdom by a statutory instrument, operative from February 2006.[250] The British government, rather surprisingly, did not take advantage of all of the flexibilities provided to implement the Directive in a minimal fashion. While in the period from 2006 to 2012 the right only applied to living artists, after 2012, it has applied also to deceased artists (and the sums raised have more than trebled).[251]

The Directive applies to original works of art—that is 'works of graphic or plastic art'; it does not apply to manuscripts of writers and composers.[252] The Directive includes within that definition works such as paintings, engravings, tapestries, ceramics, and photographs, and this implicitly suggests that the right is not available to designers of 'works of applied art'. The right applies not merely to unique works, but also to works produced in multiples, provided that they are made by the artist or are copies considered to be original works of art that have been made in limited number by the artist or under their authority.[253]

The Directive requires member states to confer the resale royalty right on the author of such a work.[254] The right is to last for the full term of copyright protection.[255] After death, the right passes with the author's estate.[256] The right is not assignable.[257] Royalties can be collected only through a collecting society, and provision is made for the administration of rights by a collecting society even without the holder's action.[258] Two societies, the Design and Artistic Copyright Society (DACS) and the Artists Collecting Society (ACS), collect the resale royalty.[259] Although the right applies to sales of existing works in which copyright subsists,[260] it may be exercised only by an artist who is, at the contract date,

---

[249] Resale Rights Dir. For an argument that the Directive was invalidly adopted, see J. Wuenschel, 'Article 95 EC Revisited: Is the Artist's Resale Right Directive a Community Act beyond EC Competence?' (2009) 4 *JIPLP* 130.

[250] The Artist's Resale Right Regulations 2006 (SI 2006/346). See IPI, *A Study Into the Effect on the UK Art Market of the Introduction of the Artists Resale Royalty* (2008) (reporting no evidence of diversion of trade); J. Collins, '*Droit de Suite*: An Artistic Stroke of Genius? A Critical Exploration of the European Directive and Its Resultant Effects' [2012] *EIPR* 305; S. Stokes, '10 Years of Artist's Resale Right' [2016] *Ent LR* 125.

[251] SI 2011/2873 (in effect from 1 January 2012). The impact was significant: in 2010, DACS collected and distributed £2.3 million to 868 artists; by 2016 this figure was £9.2 million to 1700 artists *and estates*. The increased burden after 2012 may reinforce the objection that the right in fact primarily benefits the heirs of deceased artists.   [252] Resale Rights Dir., Recital 19.

[253] Resale Rights Dir., Art. 2; ARR Regs, reg. 4.

[254] See Resale Rights Dir., Art. 6(1). The ARR Regulations define the term 'joint authors' in a different manner from that used for copyright: ARR Regs, reg. 5 (different from CDPA 1988, s. 10). The name appearing on the work is presumed to be the author: reg. 6.   [255] Resale Rights Dir., Art. 8.

[256] See Resale Rights Dir., Art. 6(1); ARR Regs, regs 9, 7(4).

[257] ARR Regs, reg. 7; nor is it waivable: regs 7(2), 8.   [258] ARR Regs, reg. 14.

[259] See http://www.dacs.org.uk; http://www.artistscollectingsociety.org.uk. DACS distributed £9.2 million and ACS £1.75 million in 2016. Each organization has administrative costs of around 15 per cent.

[260] ARR Regs, reg. 16(1)(b).

a national of an EEA state or a country that offers EEA artists reciprocal protection.[261] Where the artist is deceased, the right only exists if, at the time of their death, they would have been a qualifying person (an EEA national or a national of a state offering reciprocal protection).[262]

The right operates only in relation to 'resales' of such works—that is, sales by persons to whom the tangible property in the embodiment of a work has already been transferred[263]—and only when such resale is effected by an art market professional, such as salesrooms, galleries, and dealers.[264] It therefore seems to exclude transactions between individuals acting in their private capacity. A recital in the Directive also makes clear that the right is not to apply to resales by persons acting in their private capacity to museums that are not-for-profit and are open to the public.[265] The royalty is payable by the seller, and the seller's agent or, if there is no such agent, either by the agent of the buyer, if there is one, or by the buyer.[266]

As regards calculation of the sum due, it should be noted that member states may operate a threshold where the seller acquired the work directly from the author within three years of the resale and the resale price is less than €10,000.[267] Recital 18 implies that this is confined 'to the particular situation of art galleries which acquire works directly from the author'—but the Article is not so restricted. Since the maximum that such a seller would have to pay would be €500, the utilization of this exemption would seem particularly mean-minded.

Under the Directive, royalties are calculated on sales prices, net of tax.[268] The member states are given free rein in establishing a threshold (as long as it does not exceed €3,000) and setting royalty rates where the minimum threshold is lower than €3,000, as long as the rate is 4 per cent or above.[269] The United Kingdom, rather surprisingly (given its outright opposition to the Directive), elected to set a threshold of €1,000 at 4 per cent. After that, the royalty rates are set by the Directive and the percentage decreases as the resale price increases: up to €50,000, the artist is to be entitled to 4 per cent;[270] between €50,000 and €200,000, 3 per cent; for sales between €200,000 and €350,000, 1 per cent; for those fetching €350,000–500,000, a mere 0.5 per cent; and for those exceeding €500,000, 0.25 per cent. As if these sums were not measly enough—a sale for €1 million giving the artist €10,000 (exactly 1 per cent)—there is also a cap, so that the royalty may not

[261] Authors from non-EU countries may enjoy the right as long as authors from member states enjoy reciprocal treatment in those countries: Resale Rights Dir., Art. 7; ARR Regs, reg. 10. Over 81 Berne countries operate a resale royalty right, including Brazil and the Russian Federation, but not the United States: S. Ricketson, *Proposed International Treaty* (2015).

[262] ARR Regs, reg. 10 (as amended by SI 2011/2873).   [263] ARR Regs, reg. 3.

[264] Resale Rights Dir., Art. 1; ARR Regs, reg. 12(3)(a).   [265] Resale Rights Dir., Recital 18.

[266] ARR Regs, reg. 13; Resale Rights Dir., Art. 1(3), Recital 25. Note Resale Rights Dir., Art. 1(4) (member states may provide that a buyer or intermediary shall 'alone be liable or shall share liability with the seller for payment of the royalty'). Even if the national law chooses to make the seller's agent (an auction house) liable, it may choose to require the buyer to pay the resale royalty: *Christie's France v. Syndicat National des Antiquaires*, Case C-41/14, EU:C:2015:119 (ECJ).

[267] Resale Rights Dir., Art. 3(1); ARR Regs, reg. 12(3)(b). A sale price of €1,000 produces a royalty of a mere €40. No royalty is payable on a sale for less than €10,000 where the seller acquired the work directly from the author less than three years before the sale: reg. 12(4).   [268] Resale Rights Dir., Recital 20.

[269] Resale Rights Dir., Arts 3, 4(3). The threshold may help to avoid disproportionately high collection and administration costs: Recital 22. However, member states may desire to provide royalties below €3,000 'to promote the interests of new artists'. The Recital notes that variations are unlikely to have a significant effect on the proper functioning of the internal market.

[270] Resale Rights Dir., Art. 1(a), 1(2). If a member state elects, this figure can be set at 5 per cent. The United Kingdom chose 4 per cent.

exceed €12,500.[271] This cap was reached by the 2014 auction of Tracey Emin's 'Bed', which she originally sold to Charles Saatchi for £150,000, but which achieved a selling price of £2.5 million (from gallery operator, Jay Jopling). The rates are set so low in order to avoid the right having the effect of causing sales to relocate in order to circumvent the rules.[272] Provision is made for periodic review by the Commission,[273] and the Intellectual Property Office.[274]

Given the longstanding opposition to the Artists Resale Royalty right from the major London auction houses (Sotheby's, Christie's, and Bonhams), it will come as no surprise that Brexit has been recognized as an opportunity to campaign for abolition. With some might think indecent haste, a representative body, The British Art Market Federation, commissioned a report seeking to demonstrate the potential contribution made by the right to the decline of the British art market in comparison to say the New York market.[275] Abolition of the right might raise interesting questions under Article 1 of the first Protocol to the European Convention on Human Rights. Moreover, as with many issues, the future of the right might fall to be determined as part of the future trading arrangements between the European Union and the United Kingdom.[276]

8 PROPOSED ANCILLARY RIGHT FOR PRESS PUBLISHERS

In the 2016 proposal on Copyright in the Digital Single Market, the Commission has proposed a 'related right' for press publishers in Article 11 of the proposed Directive.[277] The idea is to confer on publishers their own 'related right', similar to the 'neighbouring rights' given to other investors in broadcasts, sound recordings, and film fixations. The goal is said to be to support 'a free and pluralist press'.[278] If press publishers have their own right, they would no longer have to prove ownership of copyright in each journalistic output.

The proposed press publishers right has the following features: it is an exclusive right comprising two elements corresponding to the reproduction and making available rights in Article 2 and 3 of the Information Society Directive; however, the rights are limited to 'digital uses'[279] and could be subject to the same limitation as are applicable to copyright

---

[271] Resale Rights Dir., Art. 4(2); ARR Regs, Sch. 1. The rates are cumulative: 4 per cent on the first €50,000, *plus* 3 per cent on the next €150,000, *plus* 1 per cent on the next €150,000, *plus* 0.5 per cent on the next €150,000. The right holder is entitled to 0.25 per cent on any part of the sale price above €500,000. The maximum royalty would be achieved only on a net sale of €2.3 million.

[272] Resale Rights Dir., Recitals 24 and 26.

[273] Resale Rights Dir., Recital 26. Commission Report, COM(2011) 878 final (14 November 2011).

[274] ARR Regs, reg. 17 (as substituted by SI 2011/2873). A report was due by 1 January 2017 but by May 2018 had yet to be published.

[275] Arts Economics, *The EU Directive on ARR and the British Art Market* (2016) available online at tbamf. org.uk. Note also PAIAM, *What Impact Might Brexit Have on Artist's Resale Right?* available online at www. paiam.org.   [276] See, e.g., EU-Moldova Association Agreement, Art. 290.

[277] Proposal for a Directive on Copyright in the Digital Single Market, COM(2016) 593 final. The idea was first mooted in European Commission, *Public Consultation on the Role of Publishers in the Copyright Value Chain and on the 'Panorama Exception'* (23 March to 15 June 2016), introductory section, 'The role of publishers in the copyright value chain', available online at https://ec.europa.eu/digital-single-market/ en/news/public-consultation-role-publishers-copyright-value-chain-and-panorama-exception. For background, see the working papers by R. Danbury available online at https://www.cipil.law.cam.ac.uk/projects/ copyright-and-news-project-2014-16.   [278] Ibid., Recital 31.

[279] Ibid., Recital 34.

under the Information Society Directive. The right would last for 20 years from first publication.[280]

The proposal has attracted considerable criticism and already generated a significant literature. Although some of this literature comes from interested parties,[281] much comes from independent sources, in particular academics from all over Europe. One comment, signed by 20 European copyright professors of the European Copyright Society (though before the text of the proposal had been released), advised caution, arguing that rights should only be granted when the case for them had been made out:

> IP rights, once created, have proved almost impossible to abolish. In a period of rapid technological and industrial change, the standards of evidence required must be particularly high. A fundamental point relates to the onus of proof. Any new intellectual property right is likely to bring costs. That is the point of rights; otherwise they could not perform an economic function. Someone needs to pay. It is therefore up to the proponents of new rights to show what these costs are, who will carry them, and that the costs are necessary and proportionate; and to provide verifiable evidence.[282]

Once the draft of Article 11 had been published (in September 2016), a further comment signed by 37 academics (based in the United Kingdom) went much further, highlighting problems with the proposal and concluding:

> we believe the proposed right *is unnecessary, undesirable, introduces unnecessary uncertainty and is unlikely to achieve anything apart from adding to the complexity and cost of operating in the copyright environment.*[283]

Despite the criticisms, as of May 2018, the proposal is still being considered in both the European Parliament and the Council and seems likely to be adopted, though the precise form remains difficult to predict.

---

[280] Ibid., Art. 11.

[281] See, e.g., on the one hand, CCIA (Computer and Communications Industry Association), 'The Ancillary Copyright for News Publishers: Why Its Unjustified and Harmful'; EDiMA, 'Directive Copyright in the Digital Single Market: The Impact of Article 11—Publishers' Right' (both opposed); and on the other, all the material endorsed by EMMA, ENPA, EPubC, and NME available online at http://www.publishersright.eu (supporting, and arguing for expansion to cover non-digital uses).

[282] https://europeancopyrightsocietydotorg.files.wordpress.com/2016/06/ecs-answer-to-ec-consultation-publishers-role-june16.pdf.

[283] https://www.cipil.law.cam.ac.uk/sites/www.law.cam.ac.uk/files/images/www.cipil.law.cam.ac.uk/documents/ipomodernisingipprofresponsepresspublishers.pdf.

PART II

PATENTS

14

INTRODUCTION TO PATENTS

1 INTRODUCTION

A patent is a limited monopoly that is granted in return for the disclosure of technical information. Under this Faustian pact, an applicant is required to disclose their invention so that it can be used (or worked) by a 'person skilled in the art'.[1] In return, the state (in the guise of the patent office) issues the applicant with a patent that gives them the exclusive right to control the way in which their patented invention is exploited for a 20-year period.

While the protection provided by a patent, which is limited to 20 years, is not as long as the protection provided by copyright law or (possibly) trade mark registration, the rights granted are more extensive. The rights granted to the patent owner cover most commercial uses of the patented invention. In addition, the rights will be infringed irrespective of whether or not the defendant copied from the patented invention. In part, the breadth of the patent monopoly is offset by the fact that patents are only granted if an applicant complies with a relatively onerous registration process. Unlike copyright, which arises automatically on creation of the work, patents are only granted after the applicant satisfies the requirements of registration. Although the granting process may not be as onerous as some would like, it does impose a number of limits and safeguards on the types of inventions that are patented, the scope of the monopoly granted, and the nature of the information that is disclosed in the patent. As such, rather than merely being seen as a prerequisite to grant, patent registration should be seen as a process in which policy goals are implemented and enforced.

Two bodies grant the patents that operate in the United Kingdom. The first and oldest granting authority is the UK Intellectual Property Office (UK IPO). (Until 2 April 2007, the IPO was known as the 'UK Patent Office'.[2]) Patents granted by the IPO only apply in the United Kingdom. A British patent cannot be infringed, for example, in Ireland or Germany. As of 1 June 1978, it is also possible to get a patent to protect inventions in the United Kingdom by applying to the European Patent Office (EPO). It should be noted that the EPO grants a bundle of national patents—that is, rather than granting a single pan-European patent, the EPO grants a series of national patents. While there are some subtle differences, once a patent has been granted by the EPO it is treated as if it had been issued by the UK IPO. As we will see later, there are plans to introduce yet another type of patent: the so-called 'unitary European patent', which, if it enters into force, will provide a single patent that spans most, but not all, of Europe.

---

[1] This is a notional person who has the requisite skill and knowledge appropriate to the type of invention in question.

[2] It legally retains the name Patent Office: Patents and Designs Act 1907, s. 62.

Applications for grant of a patent can be made directly to the UK IPO or the EPO. It is also possible to apply to these offices indirectly by way of an international filing under the Patent Cooperation Treaty (PCT). The European Patent Convention (EPC) has superseded the UK IPO as a source for applications for UK patents. As a result, the question has arisen as to whether there is much to be gained from retaining a national patent office.[3] In line with the fact that there are two routes by which a patent for the United Kingdom can be granted, there are also two (interrelated) legal regimes that need to be taken into account. These are set out in the European Patent Convention 2000 (EPC 2000) and the Patents Act 1977 (PA 1977), which is modelled on the EPC. In addition, there are also two different sets of tribunals that adjudicate on patent disputes: the tribunals at the EPO and the traditional British judicial structure (with some amendments for specialist tribunals for patents).

2 HISTORY OF THE BRITISH PATENT SYSTEM TO 1977

The passage of the Patents Act 1977 marked an important change in British patent law. As well as introducing procedural and substantive changes, it also saw Britain's entry into the European Patent Convention. While there are many important differences in the post-1977 law, in the following chapters we will encounter many concepts that pre-date the 1977 Act. For example, the image of the invention as the human intervention in nature that brings about a resulting physical change, which underpins much contemporary jurisprudence, was well entrenched in British law by the mid-nineteenth century.

Insofar as patents can be seen as monopolies offered by the state as rewards, there are many historical antecedents.[4] A notable example is the practice that came to prominence in sixteenth- and seventeenth-century Britain, where the Crown granted privileges to subjects in return for the subject carrying out some corresponding duty. Initially, these privileges were granted in letters patent—that is, as 'an open letter' from the Crown to a subject (from which the term 'patent' is derived). Unlike the present system, there were no formal checks or balances on the privileges granted by the Crown. As such, patents were frequently granted for activities that were already being performed by individuals. A famous example is the grant of a monopoly over the selling of playing cards.[5] Clearly, the grant of such a monopoly would have been detrimental to anyone who was already selling playing cards. As Crown grants of patents increased over the course of the sixteenth and seventeenth centuries, so too did the criticism. Eventually, the Crown's right to grant such privileges was challenged in the courts.[6] It was also subject to parliamentary intervention with various trials (impeachments) of patentees before Parliament[7]

---

[3] See W. Kingston, 'What Role Now for European National Patent Offices?' [2003] *EIPR* 289; J. Phillips, 'Time to Close the Patent Office Doors?' [1990] *EIPR* 151.

[4] See M. Biagioli, 'Patent Republic: Specifying Inventions, Constructing Authors and Rights' (2006) 73 *Soc Res* 1129.

[5] *Darcy v. Allin* (1602) 11 *Co Rep* 84b, 74 *ER* 1131; see M. Fisher, 'The Case That Launched a Thousand Writs, or All That Is Dross? Re-conceiving Darcy v Allen: the Case of Monopolies' [2010] *IPQ* 356.

[6] *Darcy v. Allin* (1602) 11 *Co Rep* 84b, 77 *ER* 1131, 1260; *The Clothworkers of Ipswich Case* (1614) *Godb R* 252, 78 *ER* 14.

[7] See E. R. Foster, 'The Procedure of the House of Commons against Patents and Monopolies, 1621–1624', in W. Appleton Aiken and B. Duke Henning (eds), *Conflict in Stuart England: Essays in Honour of Wallace Notestein* (1960); C. Tite, *Impeachment and Parliamentary Judicature in Early Stuart England* (1974); P. Johnson, *Privatised Law Reform: A History of Patent Law through Private Legislation, 1620-1907* (2017), ch. 3.

and then the passage of the 1623 Statute of Monopolies,[8] which imposed a general prohibition on the grant of patents by the Crown. While the Statute of Monopolies imposed a general prohibition on the grant of monopolies, an exception was made in section 6 where the grant related to 'a manner of new manufacture'. As well as limiting the circumstances in which a patent could be granted, the Statute also limited the duration of the patents for new manufacture to a period of 14 years: the period corresponding to two terms of apprenticeship. While it was not commonplace, some patents went further and included an 'apprenticeship clause' requiring the patentee to teach the new 'art' to two sets of apprentices.[9]

While patents have existed in one form or another for many centuries, the patent system that exists today is largely a creation of the nineteenth century. Indeed, many aspects of the registration process, as well as many of the legal concepts at which we look in subsequent chapters, crystallized over this period.[10] One of the most important changes that took place over the course of the nineteenth century was that patents changed from being primarily a creature of Crown prerogative to become a creature of bureaucracy. Although some of the trappings of the patent system's early connection with the Crown remained, patents are better seen as the product of an administrative process than as a form of Crown prerogative. The shift from Crown to administration was reinforced with the passage of the Patents Act 1977, which saw the United Kingdom enter the EPC and a patent become a purely statutory creature (and no longer an exercise of the prerogative). Another important, yet often overlooked, change that took place in the nineteenth century was the crystallization of patent law. Indeed, it was only after the publication of the first textbooks on patent law and the first series of judicial decisions to consider the validity and infringement of patents that a distinct and relatively coherent body of law came into existence.

Another important event that took place over the nineteenth century was that the emerging patent system was subject to a considerable amount of vocal and highly critical public scrutiny.[11] This scrutiny led not only to calls for the reform of patent law, but also, in some cases, to calls for the abolition of the whole patent system itself. Critics of the patent system said that it was unnecessarily complicated, technical, and obscure (as well as overly expensive). They also said that while applicants were able to benefit from the protection provided by the patent monopoly, the corresponding public interest in the disclosure of technical information was not being met.[12] In part, this was because in many cases, the information disclosed in the patent was of limited practical value. Given the lack of control exercised over the nature and content of the information disclosed in the patent, key aspects of inventions were often not disclosed. As a result, third parties were often not able to work or practise the invention from the information that

---

[8] The short title is the *Statute of Monopolies* but many commentators attribute a year to it. This varies between 1623 and 1624 due to dating conventions changing in the eighteenth century (or other mistakes), but if it carried a date it would be 1623: see P. Johnson, *Privatised Law Reform: A History of Patent Law through Private Legislation, 1620-1907* (2017), 31.

[9] See D. S. Davies, 'The Early History of the Patent Specification' (1934) 50 *LQR* 86, 104; P. Johnson, *Privatised Law Reform: A History of Patent Law through Private Legislation, 1620-1907* (2017), 104–6.

[10] See Sherman and Bently, 95–110.

[11] The patent controversy was also important insofar as it led to public discussions about the goals and functions of patent law (and intellectual property law more generally). See F. Machlup and E. Penrose, 'The Patent Controversy' (1950) 10 *J Ec Hist* 1; M. Coulter, *Property in Ideas: The Patent Question in Mid-Victorian Britain* (1991).

[12] Intriguingly, in an earlier period it looked possible that Parliament would be more likely to restrict disclosure of inventions than improve it: P. Johnson, *Privatised Law Reform: A History of Patent Law through Private Legislation, 1620-1907* (2017), 113–18.

was disclosed in the patent. Even where the information disclosed in the patent was potentially valuable, it was often very difficult for third parties to locate the relevant information. This was attributed to a range of factors, from the fact that the titles of many patents did not match the subject matter of the invention, to the fact that patent specifications were often not filed in a consistent or logical fashion. The criticisms of the patent system were also motivated by ideological concerns that focused on the monopolistic nature of the patents. Motivated by political economists who championed laissez-faire ideas that the government should interfere in the operation of the market only where it was absolutely necessary, patent monopolies were presented as unjustifiable inhibitions on the market that inhibited free trade. (This is in contrast with critics of the Crown grant of patents in the seventeenth century when monopolies were seen to be undesirable because of their association with the Stuart attempts to govern without Parliament.)

The criticisms made of the patent system had a long-standing impact on its shape and direction. Importantly, the shift away from patents being seen as a form of Crown prerogative opened the system up to the possibility of reform. Many of the objections to the existing patent laws were rectified in the Patents Designs and Trade Marks Act 1883 and by changes to Patent Office rules and guidelines. In turn, many of the criticisms made of the registration process were met by a raft of administrative reforms. For example, the patent system was rationalized with the establishment of the Office for the Commissioners of Patents in 1852 (which became the Patent Office in 1883). In addition, patents were organized alphabetically and rules were introduced that helped to ensure that the titles of the patent corresponded to the patented invention. The growing practice of including a description of the invention in the patent application (now called the 'specification') was made a statutory requirement. There was also more attention given to the form and nature of the information disclosed in the patent.

While many of the criticisms made of the patent system were met by legal and administrative reforms, nonetheless the criticisms made of the patent system continued to have an impact upon the way patents were viewed long after the debates had ended. In part, this may explain why from '1883 until after the end of the [Second World War], the courts tended to regard patent monopolies with some disfavour as being generally contrary to the public interest'.[13] It is interesting to contrast these attitudes with the approach after 1949, when it was said that:

> [T]he climate of opinion has changed. It is now generally recognized that it is in the public interest to encourage inventive genius. Accordingly the modern tendency of the courts has been to regard patent claims with considerably more favour than before.[14]

This trend has become even more marked in recent years as both UK courts and the EPO have grown increasingly inventive in their efforts to circumvent legislative obstacles to patent protection.

Another notable trend that developed over the nineteenth century was the growing influence that foreign patents systems had on the development of the British patent regime. As well as borrowing concepts from French and American patent law, aspects of the British registration process were modelled on foreign regimes. The second half of the nineteenth century also saw the growing internationalization of the patent system.[15]

---

[13] *Ethyl Corporation's Patent* [1972] *RPC* 169, 193.　　　　　　　　　　　　　　　[14] Ibid.
[15] Bilateral arrangements that dealt with patent-related issues were entered into in the early nineteenth century. These were usually in the form of treaties of freedom, commerce, and navigation.

These moves reached their peak with the signing of the 1883 Paris Convention (which, as of 1 May 2018, had 177 member countries).[16] One of the notable achievements of the Paris Convention was that it introduced the principle of 'national treatment'. This is the principle that a convention country must treat the nationals of other signatory countries in the same way as it treats its own.[17] Another notable aspect of the Convention was that it provided that an application for a patent in one member state should not prejudice subsequent applications in other member states.[18] This is achieved by requiring the later application to be treated as having the priority date of the earlier application. It should be noted that the Paris Convention does not impose minimum standards of protection for patents, as the Berne Convention does for copyright.[19]

3 JUSTIFICATIONS FOR PATENTS

Over time, a number of different justifications have been given in support of the patent system.[20] At times, the proponents of patent protection have emphasized the natural rights of inventors to the products of their mental labour.[21] Others have argued that justice demands that an inventor's contribution should be recognized by the grant of a reward.[22] While arguments of this ilk have occasionally been relied upon in discussing aspects of the patent system, they have not been as popular as the public interest rationales. Having said that, the current debates about how indigenous interests should best be accounted for in the patent system have seen a resurgence of interest in arguments about inherent rights and justice.

While commentators have occasionally drawn on natural rights in support of the grant of patents, the most common form of argument has concentrated on the public benefits that flow from the grant of patent monopolies. Although these arguments have changed over time, what they share in common is the basic idea that the public should only ever have to endure the harm caused by the grant of a patent if the public receives some corresponding benefit. These arguments have tended to dominate discussion of the function of the patent system since the nineteenth century.

Initially, the public interest in the patent system was said to flow from the fact that the patentee introduced a form of technology that had not previously been available in the United Kingdom. Often, this simply involved the patentee importing information about a trade or a craft from another country. Over time, this rationale was replaced by the argument that the public benefit lay in the disclosure of the invention that occurred on publication of the patent application—that is, the justifications focused on the role that the patent system played in the generation and circulation of technical information. (This is often referred to as the 'information function' of the patent system.) In particular, it is said that patents act as incentives to individuals or organizations to disclose information that might otherwise have remained secret.[23] Patents also encourage information to be

---

[16] See S. Ladas, *The International Protection of Industrial Property* (1930); S. Ricketson, *Paris Convention for the Protection of Industrial Property* (2015); E. Penrose, *The Economics of the International Patent System* (1951); *Asahi Kasei Kogyo* [1991] *RPC* 485, 532 (HL).

[17] Paris, Art. 2.   [18] Paris, Art. 4. The priority period is 12 months.

[19] Although Paris, Art. 4*ter*, requires mention of the inventor, Art. 4*quater* requires that patents are not refused on the ground that sale of the product is restricted in domestic law, and Art. 5 restricts the ability to forfeit the patent and the availability of compulsory licences.

[20] See R. Merges, *Justifying Intellectual Property* (2011).

[21] F. Machlup and E. Penrose, 'The Patent Controversy' (1950) 10 *J Ec Hist* 1, 11–17.   [22] Ibid., 17–21.

[23] See D. Davies, 'The Early History of the Patent Specification' (1934) 50 *LQR* 86.

disclosed in a way that is practically useful. At a more general level, the public interest in allowing patents is said to flow from the fact that the numerous patents that have been granted over time constitute a substantive and valuable database of technical and scientific information. The information function of the patent system was reinforced by the Patents Act 1977 and the European Patent Convention, which emphasized the need for the invention to be disclosed in such a way that it could readily be put into practice.[24] The value and effectiveness of the information was also bolstered by the publication of patent specifications on the Internet.

While the primary focus of the patent system is on the disclosure of technical information for scientific and industrial reasons, the information that is collected at patent offices throughout the world is occasionally used for other purposes. For example, historians have used the patent system as an indicator of public attitudes towards different technologies.[25] More bizarrely, the fact that patent applications had been lodged for ovens for the burning of human corpses was used in a defamation action as evidence of the existence of gas chambers at Auschwitz.[26]

Patents have also been justified by the fact that they provide an incentive for the production of new inventions.[27] As Lord Oliver said in *Asahi*:

> [The] underlying purpose of the patent system is the encouragement of improvements and innovation. In return for making known his improvement to the public the inventor receives the benefit of a period of monopoly during which he becomes entitled to prevent others from performing his invention except by his licence.[28]

More specifically, it is said that because patents provide the possibility for inventions to be exploited for a 20-year period, this means that investors will be more willing to fund research and development. In this sense, patents act as a vector that links scientific and technical research with commercial spheres.[29] Arguments of this nature have proved to be particularly important in situations in which an invention can be readily ascertained (or reverse-engineered) from the product that is put on the market (and no other form of protection exists).

The fact that a product is patented is often used by retailers trying to gain a competitive advantage to show the innovative nature of their products. There is also a sense in which the fact that a product has been patented suggests that the product (or process) has been publicly sanctioned in some way or other. This has proved to be an important consideration in the ethical debates about whether patents should be granted for genetically modified humans, animals, and plants.

If we reflect upon the way in which patent law has been viewed over the last century or so, a number of things stand out. The first notable feature is that the patent system has

---

[24] See Chapter 20, sections 1 and 2, pp. 599–609.   [25] T. O'Dell, *Inventions and Official Secrecy* (1994).

[26] *Irving v. Penguin Books* [2001] *EWCA Civ* 1197, [7.65]; G. Reimann, *Patents for Hitler* (1945).

[27] Kitch emphasized the way in which the grant of patents could be analogized to the grant of mineral rights, giving the grantee an incentive to invest in the exploitation of the 'prospect': E. Kitch, 'An Economic Review of the Patent System' (1977) 20 *J L & Econ* 265.

[28] *Asahi Kasei Kogyo* [1991] *RPC* 485, 523 (HL); E. Mansfield, 'Patents and Innovation: An Empirical Study' (1986) 32 *Manag Sci* 173; *Esswein/Automatic programmer,* T 579/88 [1991] *EPOR* 120, 125. See J. Aubrey, 'A Justification of the Patent System', in J. Phillips (ed.), *Patents in Perspective* (1985); A. Plant, 'The Economic Theory Concerning Patents for Inventions' (1934) *Economica* 30; C. Taylor and A. Silbertson, *The Economic Impact of Patents* (1973), chs 2 and 14.

[29] The role that the patent system played in inducing the invention and implementation of new industrial practices has been widely, but inconclusively, debated. See C. MacLeod, *Inventing the Industrial Revolution* (1988); H. Dutton, *The Patent System and Inventive Activity during the Industrial Revolution: 1750–1852* (1986); S. Bottomley, *The British Patent System During the Industrial Revolution 1700-1852* (2014).

widely been seen, both by supporters and critics alike, as a system of regulation—that is, as a regime that modifies behaviour. In some cases, this is explicit; in most cases, it is implicit in the way in which commentators think about patents.[30] Another notable and consistent trend has been that whenever commentators talk about the patent system in a *positive* sense—that is, as a system that regulates and controls behaviour in a desirable way—they have almost always seen it as a tool to promote economic ends, such as to encourage new industries, research and development, or innovation.[31] In contrast, whenever non-economic factors such as health, human rights, the environment, or ethics are discussed, they have either been treated as external (*negative*) constraints upon the core activities of the patent system or as undesirable side effects that need to be mitigated.

While there is no denying the important role that patents play in macro-economic policy, there is no reason why the patent system, as a regulatory tool, should only be used in the pursuit of economic ends, nor any reason why 'external' factors such as the impact of technology on the environment or health should not fall within the core remit of the patent system. That is, there is no compelling reason why the various practices, rules, and concepts that have been developed and fine-tuned over the last couple of centuries or so should be used only for economic ends. Given that modern patent law already performs a number of sometimes surprising non-economic roles, this is not as alien a proposition as it might first appear. For those who require an older lineage, there are also many examples from pre-modern patent law of instances in which the grant of a patent was used by the Crown to achieve political and personal, rather than economic, ends. As we will see later, arguments of this nature are beginning to have an influence on patent law, particularly in relation to its role in promoting food security, improving access to medicine, reducing climate change,[32] and protecting indigenous knowledge.[33]

4 CURRENT LEGISLATIVE FRAMEWORK

The law that regulates the creation and use of patents that operate in the United Kingdom is a hybrid mixture of national, European, and international elements. In this section, we provide an introduction to the legislation, conventions, and treaties that we will encounter in subsequent chapters. We begin by looking at the most important regimes—namely, the European Patent Convention and the Patents Act 1977. We then go on to look at the impact that the European Commission has had on patent law. After looking at the Community Patent Convention, we turn to look at some of the international treaties that have shaped British patent law. In particular, we look at the Patent Cooperation Treaty, the Agreement on Trade Related Aspects of Intellectual Property Rights (TRIPS), and the Convention on Biological Diversity.[34]

---

[30] Driven by a form of legal positivism that has long disappeared from most other areas of law, it is occasionally suggested that patent law does not regulate behaviour; rather, it merely grants property (or monopoly) rights in inventions. Invariably, however, the pretence of neutrality that underpins arguments of this nature disappears when commentators talk about the importance of patent protection in promoting technical innovation or investment in innovation.

[31] Occasionally, policy debates have also focused on the positive impact that patents have on the collection and distribution of technical information.

[32] For example, see E. Derclaye, 'Should Patent Law Help to Cool the Planet?' [2009] *EIPR* 168, 227; M. Rimmer, *Intellectual Property and Climate Change: Inventing Clean Technologies* (2012).

[33] See section 4.6.3, pp. 419–21. For general discussion, see G. Dutfield, 'A Critical Analysis of the Debate in Traditional Knowledge, Drug Discovery and Patent-Based Biopiracy' [2011] *EIPR* 238.

[34] There are a number of other regional patent agreements, most notably the Bangui Agreement (1997), the Harare Protocol on Patents (1982), and the Eurasian Patent Convention (1994).

4.1 EUROPEAN PATENT CONVENTION

The European Patent Convention (EPC) was signed in Munich in 1973 and came into operation on 1 June 1978.[35] The original Convention which we will refer to as the 'EPC 1973', was replaced by the European Patent Convention 2000 (EPC 2000) on 17 December 2007.[36] The provisions of the EPC 2000 apply unless the transitional provisions provide otherwise for the applicability of the EPC 1973.

The EPC 1973 was based upon the patent law of the various member states in force at the time. The EPC is an intergovernmental treaty that is distinct from the European Union. As such, membership extends beyond members of the European Union. In 2017 the EPC had 38 member states.[37] The EPC is primarily concerned with the granting of European patents.[38] This was facilitated by the establishment of the European Patent Office (EPO) in Munich, which acts as a centralized system for the grant of European patents. As the Enlarged Board of Appeal (EBA) said:

> [The] European Patent Organisation is an international, intergovernmental organisation, modelled on a modern state order and based on the separation of powers principle, which the sovereign contracting states have entrusted with some of their national powers in the field of patents.[39]

When an applicant wishes to protect their invention in a number of European countries, the EPO provides them with the benefit of a single application and search procedure, and a single grant of a bundle of national patents in each of the member states.[40]

Applications are made to the EPO in Munich or one of the other EPO Offices. It is also possible to file at a national office and have the application forwarded to the EPO. The application is submitted to the Examining Division and appeals are made from there to the Technical or Legal Board of Appeal. In rare cases, the Boards of Appeal (or the President of the EPO) may refer legal matters to the EBA.[41] While applications may be filed in any language,[42] if the application is not in an official language of the EPO (English, German, or French), the applicant is

---

[35] Work began on a European patent system in 1949 in the Council of Europe with the Longchambon Plan. For background, see K. Haertel, 'The Munich Diplomatic Conference on European Patent Law' (1973) 4 *IIC* 271; E. Ventose, 'In the Footsteps of the Framers of the European Patent Convention: Examining the *Travaux Préparatoires*' (2009) 31 *EIPR* 353.   [36] See section 4.1.1, pp. 401–3.

[37] As of 1 May 2018, the 38 members were Albania, Austria, Belgium, Bulgaria, Croatia, Cyprus, Czech Republic, Denmark, Estonia, Finland, France, Germany, Greece, Hungary, Iceland, Ireland, Italy, Latvia, Liechtenstein, Lithuania, Luxembourg, former Yugoslav Republic of Macedonia, Malta, Monaco, the Netherlands, Norway, Poland, Portugal, Romania, San Marino, Serbia, Slovakia, Slovenia, Spain, Sweden, Switzerland, Turkey, and the United Kingdom. In addition, there are two extension states: Bosnia and Herzegovina, and Montenegro, and four validation states: Cambodia, Republic of Moldova, Morocco, and Tunisia (these are countries where a European patent can be validated).

[38] This has cast doubts over the independence of the Office. Interestingly, the European Parliament suggested that the EPO reconsider the practice whereby it 'obtains payments for the patents that it grants as this practice harms the public nature of the institution': *Proposal for a Directive of the European Parliament and of the Council on the Patentability of Computer-implemented Inventions* (February 2002), COM(2002) 92 final, Recital 7b (introduced by European Parliament, Amendment 95). For a general overview of these problems, see P. Drahos, *The Global Governance of Knowledge* (2010).

[39] *President's Reference/Programs for Computers*, G 3/08 , [2011] *OJ EPO* 10, [7.2.1].

[40] The second planned element of the European patent system, the Community Patent Convention (CPC), provided for the establishment of a Community-wide patent. It has not yet come into force and has been supplanted by the EU's plan for a European patent with unitary effect. See section 4.1.1, pp. 401–3.

[41] EPC 2000, Art. 112a, provides that decisions of the boards of appeal can be contested on limited grounds including fundamental procedural defects.

[42] EPC 2000, Art. 14(2); EPC 2000 Regs, r. 40.

given two months in which to translate the application into an official language.[43] Upon grant, a European patent becomes a bundle of national patents that have effect in each of the member states for 20 years from the date of filing. The procedure for application to the EPO is similar to that at the UK IPO.[44]

When the EPC was being formulated, it was decided that for there to be an effective single granting process, it was necessary for the member states to harmonize the basic rules of patent law. This was particularly the case in relation to the rules on patentability and validity. As we will see, the tribunals at the EPO have had a substantial impact on this area of law. After some resistance, there has been a much greater recognition, as Lord Walker has said, of the 'importance of UK patent law aligning itself, so far as possible, with the jurisprudence of the EPO (especially decisions of the Enlarged Board of Appeal)'.[45] Jacob LJ took this one step further when he said that the Court of Appeal could, but was not bound to, depart from its own precedent if there were a 'settled view' of European patent law at the EPO that was inconsistent with earlier Court of Appeal decision.[46] While in some areas (such as patentable subject matter and inventive step), the approach in the United Kingdom is very different from that at the EPO, in other areas (such as sufficiency and novelty), both the approach and the outcomes are very similar.

The EPC only provides a mechanism for the grant of national patents. As such, while the EPC is concerned with the validity of European patents, matters of infringement, enforcement, revocation, renewal, and litigation are dealt with exclusively by national law. One of the consequences of this is that a patent granted at the EPO for two countries might be interpreted differently in each country. In order to reduce the chances of problems of this nature from arising, the EPO examiners, national judges, and examiners meet annually.[47] Further, a Protocol on the Interpretation of Article 69 of the EPC 2000 (reproducing Article 69 of the EPC 1973) provides guidance as to how patents should be interpreted.[48] Problems also arise because courts in the United Kingdom and the EPO have concurrent jurisdiction over questions of validity (infringement is only heard at the national level). As we explain later, this is potentially problematic insofar as it gives rise to the duplication of validity proceedings and conflicting decisions in the United Kingdom and at the EPO.[49] After some confusion, it is now clear that:

> [W]here judgement is given in an English court that a patent (whether English or European) is valid and infringed, and the patent is subsequently revoked or amended (whether in England or at the EPO), the defendant is entitled to rely on the revocation or amendment on the enquiry as to damages.[50]

4.1.1 EPC 2000

Over the course of the 1990s, there were growing calls for the EPC to be changed to take account of the technological, political, and legal changes that had occurred since it was

---

[43] EPC 2000 Regs, rr 6(1), 58.

[44] One important difference is that the EPC allows for third-party opposition to the grant during the nine months after publication of the details of the grant. Opposition is not possible under the UK system, but it is open to a person who objects to the patent to seek revocation on similar grounds.

[45] *Generics (UK) v. H. Lundbeck* [2009] *RPC* (13) 407 (HL), [35]. See also *Conor Medsystems v. Angiotech Pharmaceuticals* [2008] *RPC* (28) 716 (HL), [3]; *Human Genome Sciences v. Eli Lilly & Co.* [2011] *UKSC* 51, [83]–[95].   [46] *Actavis UK v. Merck* [2008] *EWCA Civ* 444, [107].

[47] On cooperation, see *Eli Lilly v. Human Genome Sciences* [2010] *EWCA Civ* 33, [6]–[10].

[48] PA 1977, s. 125(3). See B. Sherman, 'Patent Claim Interpretation: The Impact of the Protocol on Interpretation' (1991) 54 *MLR* 499.   [49] See Chapter 16, section 4.8, p. 450.

[50] *Virgin Atlantic Airways v. Zodiac Seats UK* [2013] *UKSC* 46, [35].

signed in 1973. To this end, a conference took place in Munich in November 2000 to discuss its revision.[51] The conference aimed to modernize the European patent system, while maintaining the proven principles of substantive patent law and procedure. The conference also aimed to undertake a comprehensive review of the EPC in light of technical and legal developments, and more than 20 years of practical experience. The conference also wanted to bring the EPC into line with TRIPS, the future Community patent, and provisions of the World Intellectual Property Organization (WIPO) Patent Law Treaty. In light of the leading political and legislative role that the European Union played in relation to the protection of biotechnological inventions, it was decided that it was inadvisable to open up parallel discussions in this area. It was also decided that further diplomatic conferences should be organized to consider the protection for computer programs and biotechnology inventions, as well as the changes required to implement the Community patent.

At the end of the conference, the member states of the EPC agreed to make a number of changes to the Convention.[52] The EPO Administrative Council adopted the revised Convention, known as the 'EPC 2000', and new Implementing Regulations on 28 June 2001. The EPC 2000 and its Implementing Regulations came into force on 13 December 2007. In so doing, the EPC 2000 replaced the EPC 1973. The new law applies to all European patent applications that were filed after the EPC came into force. In certain situations, the EPC 2000 also applies to applications that were pending on 13 December 2007 and to patents that had already been granted by that date. In this section, we provide an overview of some of the key features of the EPC 2000; we leave more detailed discussions (including the transitional arrangements) for the appropriate place in the text.

For the most part, the EPC 2000 did not bring about (or at least was not intended to bring about) many changes in the existing law. For example, Article 52(1) of the EPC 2000 did not make any substantial changes to the types of invention that were patentable under EPC 1973. Following Article 27(1) of TRIPS, EPC 2000 does, however, add the 'European patents shall be granted for any invention, in all fields of technology'. Contrary to the Basic Proposal for the Revision of the European Patent Convention, which proposed to delete 'computer programs as such' from Article 52(2)(c),[53] the conference decided not to remove computer programs from the list of non-patentable inventions in Article 52(2) of the EPC 2000.[54] As such, the statutory position under the EPC 1973 remains unchanged. The provisions in the EPC 2000 in relation to novelty, inventive step, and the internal requirements for patentability are basically the same as in the EPC 1973. The main change is that Article 54(4) of the EPC 1973 has been deleted. This means that the state of the art will include all previous European applications irrespective of their designation.

In other cases, existing provisions have been reworded to make them more transparent. For example, Article 52(4) of the EPC 1973 said that methods of treatment and diagnosis were lacking in industrial applicability and, as such, excluded from patentability. In contrast, Article 53(c) of the EPC 2000 takes a more direct approach insofar as it simply says that such methods are excluded from patentability. In other cases, the text has been changed to ensure that the EPC 2000 reflects current practice. As such, while there may have been a change in the language of the Convention, this was not intended to bring

---

[51] The Administrative Council of the EPO launched the revision project in 1998.

[52] Act Revising the Convention on the Grant of European Patents (EPC) (Munich) (29 November 2000), MR/3/00 Rev. 1e (the 'EPC Revision Act').

[53] CA/1000/00e, distributed by the German Federal Ministry of Justice on 27 June 2000; Diplomatic Conference on the Revision of the EPC, 20–29 November 2000.

[54] EPC 2000, Art. 52(2)(c) (which is identical to EPC 1973, Art. 52(2)(c)).

about changes to the existing law. For example, Article 54(5) of the EPC 2000 expressly allows for claims to second and further medical uses of known substances or compositions without the need for such claims to be expressed as 'Swiss-type claims', as was previously the case. The EPC 2000 also clarifies and strengthens the extent of protection conferred by European patents by expressly including the doctrine of equivalents in the revised Protocol on Article 69 of the EPC 2000.[55]

One of the most notable changes brought about by the EPC 2000 is that it provides patent owners with the option of limiting the protection afforded by their patents in a central procedure before the EPO.[56] The existence of a centralized procedure for amendment means that proprietors no longer have to go through the national patent offices. It also means that should a patent as granted turn out to be invalid, it can be amended quickly. It was hoped that this would act as an incentive to amend incorrectly granted patents promptly and at a lower cost. Article 138 of the EPC 2000 also enables proprietors to amend patents granted by the EPO in national proceedings relating to a patent's validity. As we will see, this has ramifications for the judicial discretion that exists in UK patent law as to whether an amendment should be allowed.

The EPC 2000 also made a number of amendments that simplified the patent grant procedure before the EPO.[57] These changes were intended to provide greater legal certainty for applicants and patent owners. It is now possible, for example, to file patent applications in any language, since a translation into one of the official languages of the EPO will not be required until a later date. The EPC 2000 also aims to streamline the European grant procedure. Notably, it was decided that the search and examination parts of the patent application should be brought together. Previously, search and examination were carried out in a number of different locations. On the basis that the EPO's vast collection of search documentation was available through databases at all of its duty stations, it was decided that there was no longer any need for the two tasks to be separated. It was hoped that this would improve the productivity and efficiency of the EPO. The EPC 2000 also made a number of other notable procedural changes. For example, in contrast to the EPC 1973, which required applicants to designate the states in which they wish to be protected,[58] Article 79(1) of the EPC 2000 provides that all EPC states will be deemed to be designated at the date of filing. The EPC 2000 has also created a legal basis for special agreements to be made between the contracting states concerning the translation of European patents. It provides for the introduction of a central court system for the enforcement of European patents, issues that are of importance for the proposed EU patent with unitary effect (and unified patent court).[59] In addition, the EPC 2000 authorizes the Administrative Council to adapt the EPC to international treaties and EU legislation.[60] Given the activity of the European Union in patent law, this may prove to be an important change.

4.1.2 London Agreement

One of the long-standing problems confronting the European patent system is the cost of translation. Given the informational role played by patents and the problems that arise where European patents are granted for 38 member states (with more than 23 different languages), it is not surprising that translation has been a key issue within the EPO. Many of these problems have been alleviated as a result of the optional London Agreement,

---

[55] EPC 2000, Protocol on the Interpretation of Art. 69, Art. 2: EPC Revision Act, Art. 2, item 2.
[56] EPC 2000, Art. 105 (a)–(c). See Chapter 16, section 5, p. 451.
[57] See, e.g., EPC 2000, Art. 15 ff; EPC 2000 Regs, rr 1–2. See also EPC Revision Act, Art. 1, items 27–43.
[58] See EPC 1973, Art. 79.   [59] EPC 2000, Art. 149a(1).   [60] EPC 2000, Art. 149a (2).

which came into operation in the European Union and the United Kingdom on 1 May 2008. As we will see later, as part of the unitary patent package, the Commission has recently passed a new regulation that will, if implemented, reduce the cost of translations even more.

One of the reasons why translation proved to be so problematic under the EPC and why the London Agreement was initiated in the first place was that Article 65 of the EPC 2000 (as was the case under EPC 1973) allows member states to require the patent to be translated into the national language as a prerequisite for validity.[61] Prior to 1 May 2008, for example, for a European patent (UK) not in English to be valid in the United Kingdom, the patent had to be translated into English within three months of grant. As the number of member states proliferated, so too did the cost of translation. Given the expense of translation (estimated to be 40 per cent of overall patent costs, with an average cost of €3,800),[62] it is not surprising that it attracted a lot of criticism. The concerns about translation cost were heighted by the fact that because most patent litigation was to be based on the 'authentic' text (published in English, German, or French) rather than the translated text, it was suggested that the national translations were redundant.[63] Given this, the contracting parties to the EPC decided to modify Article 65.[64] To this end, the London Agreement was adopted on 17 October 2000.[65] The Agreement came into force on 1 May 2008. By 1 May 2018, it had come into force in 21 of the 38 EPO Contracting States.

In order to reduce translation costs and thus the cost of patenting in Europe, Article 1(1) of the London Agreement provides that signatory parties that share an official language with the EPO (namely, Austria, Belgium, France, Germany, Ireland, Liechtenstein, Luxembourg, Monaco, Switzerland, and the United Kingdom) must waive, wholly or partially, the requirement under Article 65 of the EPC 2000 that a patent be translated into their national language. Article 1(2) provides that member states that do not have English, French, or German as their official language must also dispense with the translation requirement (allowed under Article 65 of the EPC 2000). Article 1(3) does, however, allow these countries to require that for a patent to be valid, the claims must be translated into the local language.[66] Under Article 2 of the Agreement, in the case of a patent dispute, the owner of the patent is required to supply a full translation of the patent to both the alleged infringer and the competent court.

The United Kingdom implemented Article 1(1) of the London Agreement as of 1 May 2008.[67] As a result, section 77(6) of the Patents Act 1977 no longer has effect in the United Kingdom. This means that European patents in French or German no longer have to be translated into English within three months of grant at the EPO for them to be valid in the United Kingdom. In line with Article 2 of the London Agreement, the rules of procedure

---

[61] EPC 2000, Art. 65. For an example of the impact of the London Agreement, see *IPCOM v. HTC* [2017] *EWCA Civ* 90, [5]–[7].

[62] See EPO, *The London Agreement* (14 November 2007), 1. In 1995, the cost of translation was estimated to be DM400 million per year.

[63] Interestingly, this does not take account of the informational value of the patents and what impact this might have, for example, in Portugal or Turkey. The EPO's response is to deny the value of the translation in providing information about new technologies, because they occur four or five years after filing: EPO, *The London Agreement*, 2.

[64] For previous EPO translation proposals, see Bently and Sherman (2014), 386, note 59.

[65] The full title is 'The Agreement on the application of Article 65 of the Convention on the Grant of European Patents made in London on 17th October 2000'.

[66] The Netherlands, Sweden, and Denmark require that the claims be translated into their official languages. They will also require the description to be published in English.

[67] Patents (Translations) Rules 2005 (SI 2005/682).

before British courts and the Comptroller may require the full text of the patent to be translated into English.

4.1.3 The United Kingdom and the EPC post-Brexit

While Britain's decision to leave the European Union will impact on the proposed pan-European patent system (discussed later), Brexit will not impact on the UK's membership of the EPC: patent protection will continue to be available in the United Kingdom via a European patent application in the same way as it is now. This is because as the EPC is a free-standing international agreement, membership of the EPC is *not* linked to the European Union. As a result, post-Brexit, the United Kingdom will be in a similar position to countries such as Switzerland, Turkey, and Norway, which are outside of the European Union but members of the EPC. While the President of the EPO was confident that Brexit will have 'no consequence on the membership of the United Kingdom to the European Patent Organisation, nor on the effect of the European Patents in the UK', there is a chance that issues may arise in the future, particularly in relation to initiatives by the European Commission (such as the Biotechnology Directive[68]) or where decisions of the CJEU conflict with British jurisprudence. For the most part, however, the UK's involvement in the EPC will not be affected by Brexit.

4.2 PATENTS ACT 1977

The law that regulates the creation and use of patents in the United Kingdom is found in the Patents Act 1977, as amended.[69] Because the bulk of the 1977 Act was based upon the EPC, the passage of the Act brought with it a number of substantive and procedural changes to British patent law. It also saw the United Kingdom's entry into the EPC.

Insofar as the provisions of the Patents Act 1977 are based on the EPC, the Act says that those provisions should be interpreted so as to give effect to the EPC and decisions made thereunder.[70] The important task of ensuring that the UK law remains consistent with the law at the EPO has been recognized by the English courts in numerous cases.[71] Interestingly, the EPO has occasionally reciprocated by taking notice of the decisions of national offices and courts so as to avoid lack of uniformity in the law of the EPC countries.[72] Although there is no consistent pattern, pre-1977 decisions have not been treated as being wholly irrelevant when deciding questions under the 1977 Act. In some cases the courts have said that the 1977 Act swept away the old law.[73] In other cases, however, they have acknowledged that because the intent of the EPC was to harmonize existing national rules, pre-1977 decisions are still important.[74] Despite this, as the jurisprudence at the EPO develops, it is clear that pre-1977 cases are becoming less important in the United Kingdom.

---

[68] See R. J. Aerts, 'The unitary patent and the Biotechnology Directive' [2014] *EIPR* 584.

[69] This replaced the PA 1949.

[70] PA 1977, s. 130(7); PA 1977, s. 91(1).

[71] *Wyeth's Application* [1985] *RPC* 545; *Gale's Application* [1991] *RPC* 305, 322–3 (Nicholls LJ) and 332 (Browne-Wilkinson V-C).

[72] *Wellcome Pigs*, T 116/85 [1989] *OJ EPO* 13, citing *Stafford Miller's Application* [1984] *FSR* 258; *ICI/Cleaning plaque*, T 290/86 [1991] *EPOR* 157, following *Oral Health Products (Halsteads) Application* [1977] *RPC* 612.

[73] *Unilever's Application* [1983] *RPC* 219; *Merrell Dow v. Norton Healthcare* [1996] *RPC* 76, 82; *Hallen v. Brabantia* [1990] *FSR* 134, 139.

[74] *Gale's Application* [1991] *RPC* 305.

4.2.1 Reform of the Patents Act 1977

In November 2002, the UK Intellectual Property Office and the Department of Trade and Industry released a Consultation Paper that outlined a number of possible amendments to the PA 1977.[75] While the aim of these changes was primarily to give effect to the EPC 2000, the Consultation Paper also suggested a number of other changes designed to improve the 1977 Act. The government's conclusions drawn from the consultation process were published in late 2003.[76] After a brief period of debate, the Patents Act received royal assent on 22 July 2004.

Many of the changes made by the Patents Act 2004 mirror those in the EPC 2000 (discussed earlier). The 1977 Act was amended to reflect the changes in the EPC 2000 by dealing with methods for treatment and diagnosis as exceptions to patentability under section 4A(1), rather than on the basis that they lacked industrial applicability, as had been the case previously.[77] Following Article 54(5) of the EPC 2000, the government also simplified and clarified the manner in which patent protection can be obtained for second and further medical uses. In particular, under the Patents Act 2004, claims to second or further medical uses of a known substance or composition are allowed.[78] The 1977 Act was also amended to reflect the fact that all applications for European patents form part of the state of the art under section 2(3).[79] The government's earlier proposal to amend section 1 of the 1977 Act to reflect Article 52(1) of the EPC 2000 (particularly that inventions 'should be granted in all fields of technology') was not adopted in the 2004 Act.[80]

A number of changes also related to the amendment of patents. As well as recognizing the new centralized limitation process available under the EPC 2000, the government changed the 1977 Act to remove a number of anomalies that previously existed in terms of when a patent may be amended.[81] The Patents Act 2004 also made a number of minor changes to the scheme developed to compensate employee-inventors.[82] It also clarified that co-owners have the ability to amend and revoke a patent if they act jointly.[83]

Infringement proceedings can only be brought before the Comptroller if both parties agree that this should happen. In order to provide patentees (particularly small and medium-sized enterprises) with an alternative dispute resolution process, the Consultation Paper suggested that the 1977 Act should be changed to allow infringement proceedings to be brought before the Comptroller at the request of one party. This

---

[75] *Consultation Paper on the Proposed Patents Act (Amendments) Bill* (29 November 2002).

[76] *Consultation on the Proposed Patents Act (Amendment) Bill: Summary of Responses and the Government's Conclusions* (13 November 2003). See also *Explanatory Notes to the Patents Bill* (2004).

[77] PA 2004, s. 1 (inserting new s. 4A into the 1977 Act). See *Consultation on the Proposed Patents Act (Amendment) Bill: Summary of Responses*, [19]–[20]; *Explanatory Notes to the Patents Bill* (2004), [15]–[21].

[78] PA 2004, s. 1 (inserting new s. 4A(4) into the PA 1977). See also *Consultation on the Proposed Patents Act (Amendment) Bill: Summary of Responses*, [25]–[27]. Until recently, this was in the form of what are known as 'Swiss-type claims'. These are no longer accepted in the United Kingdom or at the EPO. See Chapter 18, section 5.1.1, pp. 568–70.

[79] *Consultation on the Proposed Patents Act (Amendment) Bill: Summary of Responses*, [23]–[24].

[80] Ibid., [17]. On the basis that the revised Protocol to Art. 69 would operate in the United Kingdom under the current arrangements, it was decided that it was not necessary to make any changes in this regard: ibid., [40]–[41].

[81] PA 1977, s. 75, was changed to allow amendment during any proceedings in which validity may be in issue. This was a response to a problem highlighted by Jacob J in *Norling v. Fez-Away* [1997] RPC 160.

[82] PA 2004, s. 10 (amending PA 1977, ss 40–1); *Consultation on the Proposed Patents Act (Amendment) Bill: Summary of Responses*, [94]–[99]; see also *Consultation Paper on the Proposed Patents Act (Amendments) Bill*, [73]–[82].

[83] PA 2004, s. 9 (amending PA 1977, s. 36). See also *Consultation on the Proposed Patents Act (Amendment) Bill: Summary of Responses*, [115]–[124] (co-owners would be able to contract out of this requirement).

proposal was not supported.[84] Instead, the 2004 Act amended the 1977 Act to give the Comptroller a general power to undertake post-grant re-examination of a patent and also to make declarations as to whether a particular patent has been infringed. This is to be a non-binding opinion of the Intellectual Property Office, rather than a legally binding decision. It was hoped that this will provide a fast, fair, and effective way of resolving disputes, as an alternative to formal litigation.[85] The Patent Office Rules, which play a central role in many aspects of patent law in the United Kingdom, were overhauled and revised to modernize and simplify the patent process, as well as to improve patent litigation at the Office. The new rules, which are known as the 'Patent Rules 2007', came into force on 17 December 2007. The Rules have been amended a number of times, the most recent being in 2016 and 2017. All references to UK patent rules will be to the 2007 Rules (as amended) unless otherwise stated.[86]

4.3 COMMUNITY PATENT CONVENTION

As part of the plans for the establishment of a European patent system in the 1960s and the 1970s, it was decided that a dual system of protection should be introduced. The first element, which eventually emerged as the EPC, aimed to establish a centralized granting authority. The second part aimed to establish a single Community patent that was to be obtained by one central procedure and be binding in all member states. This came to be known as the 'Community Patent Convention' (CPC) and was signed in Luxembourg in 1975.[87] One of the key advantages said to flow from the Community patent was that it would lead to a rationalization of patent administration and thus to a reduction in costs. Unlike the EPC, however, the CPC has never come into force. These initial plans have been superseded by recent EU moves to establish a single EU-wide patent discussed later.[88]

4.4 IMPACT OF THE EUROPEAN UNION

While the European Union has not been involved in the reform of patent law anywhere near as much as it has been in relation to trade marks and copyright, to date the EU's legislature has had an impact on European patent law in two areas: in relation to the duration of patents, via the supplementary protection certificate (SPC) scheme; and biotechnological inventions.[89] As we will see later, another area in which the European Union may have a very important impact is in relation to the proposal to establish a unitary European patent. In this context it is important to recall that the EPC, the membership of which extends beyond the boundaries of the European Union, is a separate and distinct treaty that operates outside the remit of the European Union. The potential for overlap and conflict between the two regimes has been minimized by the fact that the two bodies

---

[84] See *Consultation on the Proposed Patents Act (Amendment) Bill: Summary of Responses*, [115]–[124].

[85] Ibid., [156]–[185]. On the current position, see Chapter 48, section 7.1.4, p. 1308.

[86] Patent Rules 2007 (SI 2007/3291). For an outline of changes in the way in which hearings are conducted at the UK IPO, see *Tribunal Practice Notice* (TPN 6/2007).

[87] A. Krieger, 'The Luxembourg Convention on the Community Patent: A Challenge and a Duty' (1988) 19 *IIC* 143; V. Scordamaglia, 'The Common Appeal Court and the Future of the Community Patent' (1991) 22 *IIC* 334; V. Scordamaglia, 'The Common Appeal Court and the Future of the Community Patent following the Luxembourg Conference' (1991) 22 *IIC* 458.

[88] For an overview of the CPC, see Bently and Sherman (2008), 348–9.

[89] EU competition law also plays a key role in shaping British patent practice: see Chapter 23, section 3, p. 682.

have worked in tandem on many issues (which, given the membership overlap, is not that surprising).

4.4.1 Supplementary protection certificates

The first area of patent law in which the European Union has intervened relates to the duration of patent protection. Faced with growing delays caused by the need for regulatory approval prior to marketing, patent owners argued that the time available during which they could exploit their inventions was much shorter than the planned 20-year period.[90] To remedy this problem, the European Union introduced the so-called 'supplementary protection certificate' (SPC), which extends patent protection where it has not been possible for the patent proprietor to take full advantage of their patent rights over the period of the grant.[91] In particular, SPCs compensate the owner where they have not been able to market the patented product because of delays in seeking regulatory approval. The effect of the basic patent can be extended for up to five years and in some cases five and a half years by means of this supplementary right. The right is characterized as a right distinct from patents in order to avoid the apparent conflict that would otherwise occur with the maximum term under Article 63 of the EPC 2000. A challenge made by the Spanish government to this regime in 1995 was dismissed by the Court of Justice.[92] A corresponding scheme for supplementary protection certificates has been introduced in the United Kingdom. The key features of the British scheme (including the impact that Brexit might have on this EU-based SPC scheme) are discussed later.[93]

4.4.2 Biotechnology Directive

A second area in which the EU has intervened in the patent field is in respect of biotechnological inventions. After a decade of heated debate, the Biotechnology Directive was formally adopted by the Council and the European Parliament on 6 July 1998.[94] The Directive deals with the patentability[95] and scope of protection conferred on biotechnological inventions.[96] As well as introducing special defences,[97] the Directive also establishes a scheme for compulsory licences and cross-licences to deal with the overlap between patent and plant variety protection.[98] In addition, it provides for the deposit of biological material.[99] The Directive was implemented in the United Kingdom.[100]

During the passage of the Directive, a question arose as to the nature of the relationship between the Biotechnology Directive and the EPC: what would a British court do, for example, if the EPC and the Directive were in conflict? Problems of this nature were resolved

---

[90] On the extent to which competitors may experiment prior to expiry of the patent, see Chapter 22, section 4.2, pp. 667–70.

[91] Council Regulation (EEC) No. 1768/2 of 18 June 1992 concerning the creation of a supplementary protection certificate for medicinal products [1992] *OJ L* 182/1 (now codified as Regulation (EC) No. 469/2009 concerning the supplementary protection certificate for medicinal products [2009] *OJ L* 152); Regulation (EC) No. 1610/96 of the European Parliament and of the Council of 23 July 1996 concerning the creation of a supplementary protection certificate for plant protection products [1996] *OJ L* 198/30–35.

[92] This was on the grounds that the Community (as it then was) did not have competence to legislate a new patent right and that intervention could not be justified by reference to the need to harmonize laws for the internal market: *Spain v. Council of the European Union*, Case C-350/92 [1995] *ECR* I–1985.

[93] See Chapter 24, section 3, pp. 708–15.

[94] EC Directive 98/44/EC of 6 July 1998 on the Legal Protection of Biotechnological Inventions [1998] *OJ L* 213/13 (the 'Biotech. Dir.'). [95] Biotech. Dir., Arts 1–7.

[96] Biotech. Dir., Arts 8–10. [97] Biotech. Dir., Art. 11. [98] Biotech. Dir., Art. 12.

[99] Biotech. Dir., Arts 13–14. It also deals with implementation and review procedures: Arts 15–18.

[100] Biotech. Dir., Arts 1–11, were introduced into British law by the Patents Regulations 2000 (SI 2000/2037) (in force 28 July 2000). Note also SI 2001/1412 and SI 2002/247.

when the Administrative Council of the EPO incorporated the Biotechnology Directive into the Implementing Regulations of the EPC.[101] In so doing, the Administrative Council aligned the EPC with the provisions of the Biotechnology Directive. The Council also provided that the Directive should be used as a supplementary means of interpreting the EPC. As a result, the Recitals to the Directive can be taken into account where relevant.[102]

The controversial nature of the patenting of biotechnological inventions, which delayed the passage of the Directive for so long, has continued since it was passed. In addition to ongoing public criticism of biotechnological patents, in November 1998 the Dutch government filed a challenge to the Biotechnology Directive in the Court of Justice. While the Court rejected the Dutch challenge to the Directive,[103] there are still many critics of the ongoing expansion of patent law in the life sciences.[104]

4.5 PROPOSED EUROPEAN CHANGES

There are currently a number of proposals for reform that have been put forward within Europe that will have an important impact upon patent law if and when they are finalized.[105] The most important are the plans for the establishment of a unitary European patent and a corresponding centralized patent court.[106]

4.5.1 Unitary patent package

The establishment of a unified and centralized European patent system has been a goal of many for nearly 50 years. While in early 2016, it seemed that the goal may finally have become a reality, the plans were derailed first by Brexit and then by a constitutional challenge in Germany. As a result, there are many legal and political uncertainties that make it difficult to predict whether a centralized European patent system will ever become a reality and, if so, what shape it might ultimately take.

Over the last few years, 25 member states and the European Parliament have (nearly) agreed on a scheme, known as the 'unitary patent package', designed to establish and enforce a common unitary patent.[107] The unitary patent package consists of three elements.

[101] Administrative Council of the EPO 16 June 1999 amending the Implementing Regulations of the EPC [1999] *OJ EPO* 437, 573 (in force from 1 September 1999).

[102] British Group of AIPPI, 'Report Q 150: Patentability Requirements and Scope of Protection of Expressed Sequence Tags (ESTs): Single Nucleotide Polymorphisms (SNPs) and Entire Genomes' [2000] *EIPR* 39, 40.

[103] *Netherlands v. European Parliament*, Case C-377/98 [2001] *ECR* I–7079, [2002] *OJ EPO* 231, [2002] *FSR* 575 (ECJ) (Italy intervened in support of the Dutch; France intervened in support of the Council of the EC). For the challenge, see [1998] *OJ C* 378/13. See A. Scott, 'The Dutch Challenge to the Bio-Patenting Directive' [1999] *EIPR* 212.

[104] See Commission on Intellectual Property Rights, *Integrating Intellectual Property Rights and Development Policy* (September 2001); Nuffield Council on Bioethics, *The Ethics of Research Related to Healthcare in Developing Countries* (2001). See also G. Dutfield, *Intellectual Property Rights and the Life Sciences Industries* (2nd edn, 2009).

[105] For an examination of the fate of the proposal for utility model protection under the European Union, see Bently and Sherman (2004), 338–40.

[106] Other recent examples, which are now largely dormant, relate to computer-related inventions (see Bently and Sherman (2014), 397) and innovation (see Bently and Sherman (2014), 390, note 101).

[107] The participating members are Austria, Belgium, Bulgaria, Czech Republic, Cyprus, Germany, Denmark, Estonia, Greece, Finland, France, Hungary, Ireland, Latvia, Lithuania, Luxembourg, Malta, the Netherlands, Portugal, Romania, Slovakia, Slovenia, Sweden, and the United Kingdom. Italy was not part of the Regulations, but was a signatory to the UPC Agreement. Poland was part of the Regulations, but not a signatory to the UPC Agreement. Spain was neither part of the Regulations nor a signatory to the UPC Agreement. Croatia subsequently acceded to the European Union in July 2013, but has not signed the UPC Agreement.

The first is the EU Regulation creating a unitary European patent.[108] The second is the EU Regulation that deals with the vexed issue of the language to be used in the unitary patent and the corresponding translation requirements.[109] Both of these Regulations, which were adopted in December 2012 using the little used 'enhanced co-operation mechanism',[110] entered into force in January 2013. The third and final part of the unitary patent package is the Agreement on a Unified Patent Court ('UPC Agreement').[111] Following the decision of the Court of Justice that a proposal to establish a unified patent was incompatible with EU law, it was decided that the unified patent court would need to be established via an intergovernmental treaty formed outside of the European Union. To this end, the 25 participating member states signed an international agreement on 19 February 2013 setting up a centralized patent court.[112] Once the Agreement and the Regulations enter into force, it will be possible to obtain a European patent with unitary effect across the 25 participating member states.

(i) A European patent with unitary effect: the 'unitary patent'

One of the key elements of the unitary patent package is the proposed pan-European unitary patent or, as the European Union prefers, a 'European patent with unitary effect'. Currently, applicants for a patent in Europe have a choice of one of two routes to grant: they can apply for national patents in the national patent offices in the countries in which they want protection; alternatively, they can apply to the EPO for a 'classical' or 'bundled' European patent. The EPO currently grants a bundle of national patents that are enforced separately through the courts of each country. The patent proprietor must choose the countries where they want protection and validate the European patent in those countries. The patent owner may also be required to pay a fee to the respective national patent office, comply with various formal requirements, and provide a translation of the patent in the official language of the country. Once validated, a bundled EPO patent has the same effect as a national patent granted in the respective territory.

There are a number of problems with the existing European patent system, not least that it is time-consuming, costly, and somewhat confusing. One of the goals of the unitary patent is to overcome these problems. To this end, the planned unitary patent, which will be a single patent that provides uniform protection in 25 member states, will be established. Under the new regime, an owner of a unitary patent will only be required to pay a single set of renewal fees to the EPO, which will manage the scheme

---

[108] Council Regulation (EU) No. 1257/2012 of 17 December 2012 implementing enhanced cooperation in the area of the creation of unitary patent protection (the 'Unitary Patent Reg.'). The Regulation will apply once the UPC Agreement enters into force. Decision of the Select Committee of the Administrative Council of 15 December 2015 adopting the Rules relating to Unitary Patent Protection (SC/D 1/15), (2016) OJEPO A39 ('Unitary Patent Rules').

[109] Council Regulation (EU) No. 1260/2012 of 17 December 2012 implementing enhanced cooperation in the area of the creation of unitary patent protection with regard to the applicable translation arrangements (the 'Translation Reg.'). The Regulation will apply once the UPC Agreement enters into force.

[110] The general arrangements for enhanced cooperation are laid down by the TEU, Title IV. This allows member states to move forward at different speeds and/or towards different goals. It does not allow extension of the powers as laid down by the Treaties, nor may it be applied to areas that fall within the exclusive competence of the Union. Enhanced cooperation may be undertaken only as a last resort, when it has been established within the Council that the objectives of such cooperation cannot be attained within a reasonable period by the Union as a whole.

[111] Agreement on a Unified Patent Court [2013] OJ C 175/1 (20 June 2013).

[112] This is the same 25 states that participated in the Regulations except for Italy (not part of the Regulations, but a signatory to the UPC Agreement) and Poland (part of the Regulations, but not a signatory to the UPC Agreement). Spain is still absent. See also Art. 142(1) of the EPC 2000.

centrally. In addition, only one validation (the request of the unitary effect with the EPO) will be needed to obtain patent protection in the 25 member states.

The unitary patent will be administered and granted by the EPO.[113] In order for a patent to have unitary effect across all of the participating member states, patent holders will need to request the unitary effect at the EPO no later than one month after the grant of their European patent has become effective. This will transform a European patent into a single patent for the 25 member states. Anybody, regardless of the country of origin, is able to opt for a unitary patent. When established, the unitary patent will coexist with existing national patents and with classical bundled European patents. This means that applicants for patent protection in Europe will be able to choose between national patents, classic bundled European patents, and unitary patents.

Translations costs have long been one of the factors hindering the effectiveness of European patents. One of the goals of the unitary patent package is to reduce the costs of patenting. The unitary patent aims to achieve this by ensuring that no further translations will be required after the grant of the European patent, except in the case of a dispute. The translation requirements of the unitary patent will be based on the current procedures within the EPO.[114] This means that an application for a European patent will need to be filed in either English, French, or German (which are the official languages of the EPO) or, if filed in any other language, translated into one of the official languages.[115] A compensation scheme has been designed to alleviate the translation costs that will inevitably arise where an application is not filed in one of the official languages. Under the scheme, European-based small and medium-sized enterprises (SMEs), natural persons, non-profit organizations, universities, and public research organizations that file an application in an official language of the European Union other than English, French, or German will be entitled to reimbursement (up to a ceiling) for the cost of translating the application into one of the official languages. This compensation scheme will be administered by the EPO.[116]

Following Article 14(6) of the EPC 2000, the unitary patent specification will be published in one of the three EPO languages and will include a translation of the claims in the other two official languages. Once a unitary European patent has been granted, no further translations will be required.[117] Patent owners will only have to provide (human) translations of their patents when, in a dispute, one is requested by an alleged infringer or by a court.[118]

A central aim of the proposed unitary patent system is to minimize costs by reducing the translation requirements post-grant. The problem with this, however, is that it potentially undermines a key feature of the patent system—namely, the information function of patents, which plays an important role in helping third parties to avoid infringement and to build technical and scientific information. One of the key features of the new scheme is that it relies on the free online translation service known as 'Patent Translate'—which the EPO has developed in conjunction with Google to produce machine translations of European patent applications and patents automatically—to ensure that the lack of human translations does not jeopardize the patent system's information function. At the time of writing, machine translation of patents are available for 28 languages of the 38 EPO member states, plus Chinese, Japanese, Korean, and Russian. The service has proved to be very popular: with around 15,000 translations requested per day. As the Translation Regulation notes, machine translations will not have any legal effect; they will only be used for information

---

[113] Unitary Patent Reg., Art. 9.   [114] Translation Reg., Recital 6.   [115] EPC 2000, Art. 14(2).
[116] Translation Reg., Art. 5, Recital 10. Unitary Patent Rules, Rules 8–23.
[117] Translation Reg., Art. 3(1).   [118] Translation Reg., Art. 4, Recital 8.

purposes.[119] One of the problems with the fact that granted patents will only be available in the official languages of the EPO is that third parties who do not understand the official languages of the EPO may not, even with the possibility of machine translation, be in a position in which they know that they are potentially infringing. To some extent, this problem will be alleviated because in deciding a claim for damages, the courts will take into account whether the party 'acted without knowing or without reasonable grounds for knowing that he was infringing the European patent with unitary effect'.[120]

The translation requirements of the unitary patent package are underpinned by the ability to make usable machine translations of patent documentation in all of the relevant languages. While the EPO has made progress, there are still issues with the quality of the translations. The service also needs to add a number of new languages. Given that Patent Translate is not yet fully operational, it was decided that there should be a transitional period until 2028 during which additional translations would be required. The transitional period will continue until a 'system of high quality machine translations into all official languages of the Union becomes available'.[121] During the transitional period, where the language of the proceedings at the EPO is French or German, a request for unitary effect will need to be accompanied by a full translation of the specification in English. Alternatively, where the language of proceedings at the EPO is English, the applicant will need to supply a translation in an official language of an EU member state.[122] As the Regulation says, this will ensure that during the transitional period all unitary patents are available in English, 'which is the language customarily used in the field of international technological research and publications'.[123]

There are several notable legal characteristics of the unitary patent. One of these is that a European patent with unitary effect will provide uniform protection and have equal effect in all of the participating member states.[124] While a unitary patent can only be limited, transferred, revoked, or lapse in respect of all participating member states,[125] it may be licensed in respect of the whole or part of the territories of the participating member states. For the purposes of exploitation, however, unitary patents will be treated as if they were national patents in member states.[126] As such, exploitation will be governed by local laws. The unitary patent package makes no changes in relation to patentability. It does, however, specify that a patent owner will have the right to prevent direct and indirect uses of the invention in certain situations.[127] It also provides for a series of defences including acts done for private and non-commercial purposes, acts done for experimental purposes, situations in which biological material is used for the purpose of breeding or discovering and developing new plant varieties, the pharmaceutical preparation of medicines, certain on-farm uses of patented plants and animals, and certain uses in relation to patented computer programs (such as decompilation and interoperability).[128]

(ii) Unified patent court

Another key part of the unitary patent package is the centralized patent court which, it is hoped, will simultaneously reduce litigation costs, unify patent law, and increase

---

[119] Translation Reg., Recital 11.

[120] Translation Reg., Art. 4(4), Recital 9. This is particularly the case with SMEs, natural persons, non-profit organizations, universities, and public research organizations.   [121] Translation Reg., Recital 12.

[122] Translation Reg., Art. 6(1)(a)(b).

[123] Translation Reg., Recital 12. These translations should not be carried out automatically.

[124] Unitary Patent Reg., Art. 3(2).   [125] Unitary Patent Reg., Art. 3(2).

[126] Unitary Patent Reg., Art. 7(1).   [127] UPC Agreement, Arts 25, 26.

[128] UPC Agreement, Art. 27(a)-(l).

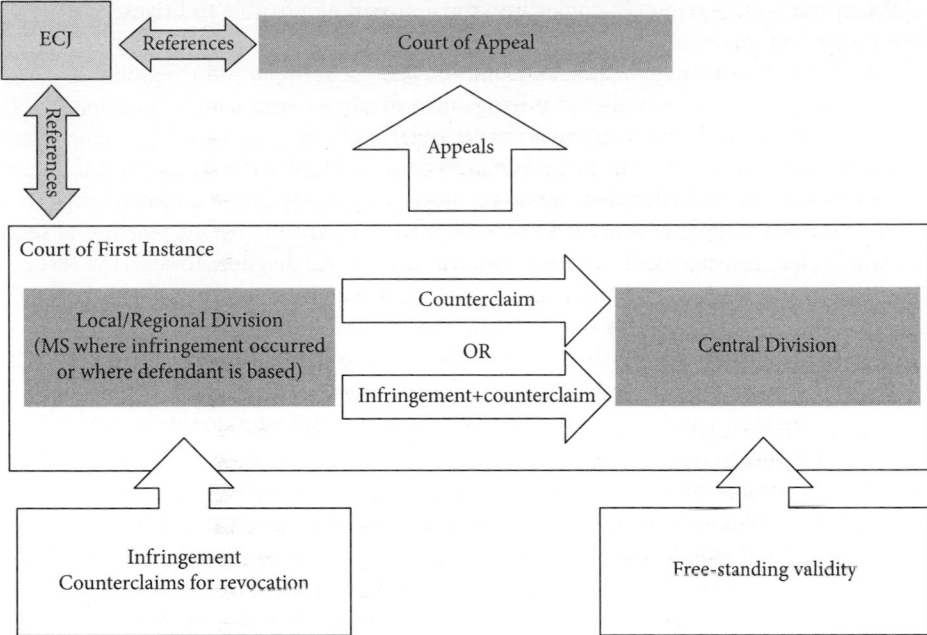

Fig. 14.1 Structure of the unified patent court

certainty. As we noted earlier, the Agreement that establishes the unified patent court was signed by 25 EU member states in February 2013. The UPC Agreement will enter into force on the first day of the fourth month after the 13th signatory state has deposited its instrument of ratification (so long as the United Kingdom, France, and Germany are all included).

The unified patent court will consist of a decentralized court of first instance which, in turn, will consist of local, regional, and central divisions located in the member states (see Fig. 14.1).[129] The central division of the court of first instance will be divided between London (responsible for chemical, pharmaceutical, and the life science patents), Munich (responsible for mechanical engineering patents), and Paris (responsible for all other patents).[130] There will also be a Court of Appeal, which will be based in Luxembourg. Decisions of the unified patent court will be enforced by the law of the country in which the enforcement takes place. Decisions of the Court of Justice will be binding on the unified patent court. References for preliminary rulings will be made whenever a question of Union law requires interpretation (like national courts).

The unified patent court will have exclusive jurisdiction over unitary European patents and, after a transitional period of seven years (extendable to 14), all classical bundled European patents. During the transitional period, individuals and companies with bundled European patents will be able to opt out of the jurisdiction of the unified patent court and continue to use national courts for litigation. The unified patent court will also have jurisdiction over infringement and validity actions in relation to supplementary protection certificates. The court will not, however, have jurisdiction over national patents (granted by the UK Intellectual Property Office or other national patent offices).

---

[129] UPC Agreement, Art. 7.
[130] The division is based on the International Patent Classification (IPC) system.

When the UPC Agreement comes into force, it will be possible to litigate European bundled patents and unitary patents at the unified patent court in single actions covering all relevant states. Infringement actions may be started at the local or regional division in the country in which the alleged infringement occurred or in which the defendant is based. Where the validity of a patent is challenged, the choice of court will be determined on the basis of the way in which the patent is classified under the International Patent Classification system. Where a defendant to an infringement action counterclaims that a patent is invalid, the judges at the local or regional division will decide whether to send the whole case (infringement and revocation) to the central division, to send the revocation case to the central division and hear the infringement case separately at the local/regional division, or to hear the entire case at the local/regional division.

The architects of the centralized patent scheme hope that a unified patent court will overcome some of the problems with the existing European patent system, particularly where a party wishes to bring an action in a number of different countries. Given that decisions relating to the infringement or validity of a unitary patent will have uniform effect across all participating member states, parties will no longer need to defend or challenge patents in different national courts. It is hoped that, in this way, the unified patent court will reduce litigation costs. It is also hoped that because decisions will be heard by a single centralized court rather than (potentially) by a number of different national courts, legal certainty will be improved. It is also hoped that the new centralized regime will reduce the differences that encourage the 'forum shopping' of European bundle patents (such as differences in the level of damages awarded, the speed of the decision making, and different jurisprudence).

(iii) Impact of the unitary patent package

In order for the unitary patent to come into operation in the United Kingdom, a number of changes will need to be made to domestic law. In particular, changes will be needed to be made to confer jurisdiction on the new unified patent court with 'respect to those actions for which the [unified patent court] will have competence, i.e. infringement and validity of European bundle and Unitary Patents.'[131] While the patentability requirements for European patents with unitary effect are identical to those of classical bundled European patents (and, as such, no changes will be needed to this area of law), changes will be needed to bring UK law into line with the infringement provisions and defences of the unitary patent. As noted earlier, the UPC Agreement sets out the infringement provisions for European bundle patents and for unitary patents. Currently, infringement of European bundle patents is a matter for national law. As a result, the Patents Act 1977 will need to be modified to ensure that UK law complies with the infringement provisions for European bundle patents and unitary patents in the UPC Agreement. According to the Intellectual Property Office, minor changes may also be necessary to ensure that British patent law is aligned with the UPC Agreement. For example, the law on infringement of patent rights may need to be amended to ensure that it is consistent with the provisions for European bundle and unitary patents.

---

[131] In order to facilitate Britain's entry into the UPC Agreement, the Intellectual Property Act 2014 amended the Patents Act to allow the Secretary of State to bring the unified patent court into effect (subject to approval by each House of Parliament, following public consultation). IP Act 2014, s. 17, which introduces new PA 1977, ss 88A, 88B. Building on this authority, the Patents (European Patent with Unitary Effect and Unified Patent Court) Order 2016 was passed on 2 March 2016. When in force, the 2016 Patents Order will amend the Patents Act to facilitate the adoption of the unitary patent and the Unified Patent Court. The Patent Orders will come into force when the Agreement on a Unified Patent comes into force: Patents Order 2016, Art. 1(2).

Following confirmation in November 2016 of its commitment to the Unified Patent Court, the UK signed the Protocol on Privileges and Immunities on 14 December 2016.[132] Secondary legislation designed to implement the Unified Patent Court in the UK was introduced into Parliament on 26 June 2017.[133] The United Kingdom ratified the Unified Patent Court Agreement on 27 April 2018. However, the Agreement will need modification after Brexit if the United Kingdom is to remain a member.

A number of different claims have been made about the benefits of a unitary patent administered by a centralized court. As the Regulation creating unitary patent protection states, unitary patent protection will make access to the patent system easier, less costly, and more legally secure.[134] One of the anticipated benefits of the new system is that it will reduce the costs of patenting. For example, the UK government has said that unitary patent protection for new inventions across 25 member states would offer businesses savings in translation and validation costs (against the current system for protection in the same states) of up to £20,000 per patent.[135] While there has been a lot of criticism made of the accuracy of claims such as these, there is little doubt that the proposed regime will lead to a reduction in the transaction costs associated with the grant of a European patent. It has also been said that, because patentees will only need to enforce their patents in one court, rather than in a number of national courts, the new regime will avoid duplicated litigation and, in so doing, will reduce the costs of enforcement.

There are a number of ongoing concerns with the proposed unitary patent. Concerns have been raised, for example, about the effect of bifurcation on forum shopping, the training and quality of the judges, and the prohibitive expense of using the unitary patent, particularly for SMEs.[136] It has also been said that instead of consolidating patent law in Europe, the unitary patent package will add to its fragmentation on both the territorial and substantive levels.[137] In part, this is because rather than simplifying things, the unitary patent package will add an additional type of patent to the existing national and bundled patents. It has also been said that the regime does not go far enough. This is particularly the case in relation to the fact that it leaves key matters—such as exploitation[138] and compulsory licensing[139]—to be regulated by national law and because it does not address issues such as a general research exception or compulsory licenses for biotechnological research tools. There is also a concern that the proliferation

---

[132] Cm 9405. The Protocol gives privileges and immunities to the Court, its judges, representatives, and staff.

[133] The Unified Patent Court (Immunities and Privileges) Order 2017. Equivalent legislation needs to be passed by the Scottish Parliament. [134] Unitary Patent Reg., Recital 4.

[135] House of Commons European Scrutiny Committee, *Draft Agreement on a Unified Patent Court and Draft Statute 30th Report of Session 2012–13* (3 February 2013), [8.28]. According to the EPO, obtaining patent protection in the territory of the 27 member states by means of a European patent costs about €36,000 (the majority of which goes on translation and other costs linked to validation, such as fees of local patent offices and costs for local patent agents). After full implementation of the unitary patent project, the costs will go down to about €5,000 (i.e. the fees up until the grant of the patent including the translation of the claims into the two other official languages of the EPO).

[136] Ibid. See also J. Pagenburg, 'Unitary Patent and Unified Court: What Lies Ahead?' (2013) 8 *JIPLP* 480.

[137] See R. Hilty et al., *The Unitary Patent Package: Twelve Reasons for Concern* (17 October 2013), online at http://www.ip.mpg.de/files/pdf2/MPI-IP_Twelve-Reasons_2012–10–17_final3.pdf; A. Strowel et al., *The Union cannot be stripped of its powers by the Member States: the dangerous precedent of the patent package* (13 March 2015). For a discussion of the vexed question of how patent claims might be interpreted by a Unified Patent Court, see P. England, 'The Scope of Protection of Patent Claims in Europe and the UPC' (2016) 11 *JIPLP* 689.

[138] Unitary Patent Reg., Recital 15. Basic rules, as contained in all previous proposals (transfer of right; rights *in rem*; treatment in execution and insolvency; *erga omnes* effect of restrictive contractual licensing; date of third-party effects of patent transactions), are missing: see Hilty et al., op. cit.

[139] Unitary Patent Reg., Recital 10.

in courts with competence to hear patent matters will fragment, rather than consolidate, patent jurisprudence. Within the United Kingdom, there are concerns about the impact that the unitary system will have upon domestic jurisprudence and, more seriously, about whether it will effectively mark the end of domestic law.

While a number of obstacles have been overcome,[140] aspects of the scheme are still under scrutiny. Brexit has given rise to a number of questions including whether a post-Brexit United Kingdom, as a non-EU country, would be eligible to become (or remain) a member of the UPC;[141] whether it is possible, as planned, for the divisional court to be based in London; and, perhaps most importantly, whether there is the political will in the United Kingdom to accept EU law and the autonomy and supremacy of the Court of Justice of the European Union (as is required under the existing scheme). These problems have been compounded by a constitutional challenge brought against the plans to ratify the Unified Patent Court Agreement made in Germany in July 2017. While this may not derail the push for a pan-European patent scheme, it will certainly delay things. Given that the Unified Patent system requires France, Germany, the United Kingdom and at least ten other EU countries to ratify the patent court before the scheme can begin, the problems in the United Kingdom and Germany are particularly important.[142] Until these matters are resolved, there will be a cloud over the unitary patent. At this stage, it is difficult to predict whether or not, and if so, when the unitary patent package will come into effect.

While a unitary patent will undoubtedly bring about a number of benefits, the fact that it is clearly the product of a political compromise will mean, almost inevitably, that the end product will not achieve all that is expected of it. In this sense, it seems that the dream of a harmonized, efficient, and centralized European patent system is still some way off. How close the final product comes to that dream is yet to be seen.

4.6 INTERNATIONAL TREATIES

As we mentioned earlier, international treaties have long played an important role in shaping aspects of British patent law. In addition to the Paris Convention (discussed earlier), the other treaties of note are the Patent Cooperation Treaty, TRIPS, and the Convention on Biological Diversity.

4.6.1 Patent Cooperation Treaty (PCT)

The Patent Cooperation Treaty (PCT) was signed in 1970 and came into operation from 1978. The key feature of the Treaty is that it provides for a system of international application and preliminary examination procedure. The PCT has 152 contracting states.[143] The Treaty only provides for an international application and search; the authority to grant

---

[140] *Spain and Italy v. Council,* Joined Cases C-274/11 and C-295/11, EU:C:2013:240 (ECJ, Grand Chamber) (dismissing the claim by Spain and Italy that the Council's decision to authorize enhanced cooperation in the area of the single European patent circumvented the requirement of unanimity). *Kingdom of Spain v. Council of the European Union*, Cases C-146/13 and C-147/13, EU:C:2015:298 (ECJ, Grand Chamber) (dismissing the action brought by Spain challenging the Unitary Patent Regulation and the Translation Regulation).

[141] This is primarily a result of Opinion 1/09 from the CJEU, which is often cited to mean that non-EU Member States are precluded from the unitary patent. For a different reading, see A. Ohly and R. Streinz, 'Can the UK Stay in the UPC System After Brexit?' (2017) 12 *JIPLP* 245.

[142] As of May 2018, 16 EU countries had ratified the Agreement: Austria, Belgium, Bulgaria, Denmark, Estonia, Finland, France, Italy, Latvia, Lithuania, Luxembourg, Malta, the Netherlands, Portugal, Sweden, and the United Kingdom.

[143] As of 1 May 2018.

the patent remains with the national patent office.[144] The PCT provides a second route through which applications for patents that operate in the United Kingdom and the EPO can be made.

Under the PCT, an applicant can apply to an international office and get an international search and an international preliminary examination. Once this is carried out, the application is sent to the designated national office(s) to decide whether to grant national patents. The centralized procedure is particularly useful for countries in which the patent office is not capable of carrying out its own examination. The patent cooperation system is attractive because it reduces the fees payable, and because of the lengthy period between the initial application to the international office and the time when that application is forwarded to the relevant national offices. The extra time, which is usually at least 18 months, gives applicants time in which to decide whether the invention is likely to be successful enough to warrant the translation costs that arise when the application is transferred to the national offices.

4.6.2 Agreement on Trade Related Aspects of Intellectual Property Rights (TRIPS)

While TRIPS had a dramatic impact upon many developing countries, it had little direct impact upon European or British patent law.[145] Perhaps the most significant change brought about by TRIPS relates to the limits imposed on compulsory licences. The impact of TRIPS may increase, however, as the jurisprudence at the World Trade Organization (WTO) takes shape. In an important decision in relation to the patenting of computer programs, the EPO Technical Board of Appeal noted that, because the EPO was not a signatory to TRIPS, it was not bound by it. However, on the basis that TRIPS aimed at setting common standards, the Board said that it acted as an indicator of modern trends.[146]

There were many critics of TRIPS, particularly in relation to the standards of protection that it imposed on developing countries. Given this, it is not surprising that reform of the 1994 Agreement has been a priority for many member states. Two areas of reform concern us here—namely, patents and public health, and the patentability of plants and animal inventions.

One issue that has attracted a lot of attention is the extent to which patents restrict access to life-saving drugs. This problem came to a head when patentees threatened to challenge legislation in South Africa that would have allowed their patented medicines (for the treatment of HIV/AIDS) to be sold at a price lower than they would have liked. Triggered by the dispute in South Africa, the Fourth WTO Ministerial Conference, held at Doha in November 2001, focused on access to patented medicines in developed and less-developed countries.[147] The delegates noted that compulsory licences, which are

---

[144] The PCT was signed in Washington 1970, amended in 1979, and modified in 1984 and 2001. See K. Pfanner, 'The Patent Cooperation Treaty: An Introduction' [1979] *EIPR* 98; D. Perrott, 'The PCT in Use' [1982] *EIPR* 67; C. Everitt, 'Patent Cooperation Treaty (PCT)' (1984) 13 *CIPAJ* 383; Anon., 'Patent Cooperation Treaty (PCT) in 1992' (1993) 75 *JPTOS* 354; J. Cartiglia, 'The Patent Cooperation Treaty: A Rational Approach to International Patent Filing' (1994) 76 *JPTOS* 261; J. Anglehart, 'Extending the International Phase of PCT Applications' (1995) 77 *JPTOS* 101. See Chapter 16, section 2.3, pp. 438–40.

[145] TRIPS, Art. 2, requires members to comply with Arts 1–12 of the Paris Convention (1967). In addition, TRIPS, Arts 27–34, increase the level of standards: Art. 27, as regards patentability; Art. 28, rights; Art. 29, disclosure requirements; Art. 30, exceptions; Art. 31, authorized uses; and Art. 33 requires a term of 20 years from filing date. [146] *IBM/Computer programs*, T 1173/97 [2000] *EPOR* 219, 224–5.

[147] See R. Roumet, 'Access to Patented Anti-HIV AIDS Medicine: The South African Experience' [2010] *EIPR* 137.

allowed under TRIPS, offer a possible solution for countries such as South Africa that have the domestic capacity to manufacture medicines. However, Article 31(f) of TRIPS, which provides that medicines produced under compulsory licence must predominantly be for the domestic market, creates problems for countries that are unable to manufacture the patented medicines themselves. In particular, it means that it is not possible to manufacture a patented drug under compulsory licence in Country A, with the intention of exporting the drug to Country B. While the delegates at Doha agreed that this problem needed to be resolved, they were unable to decide on how this should be done.[148] After heated public debate, on 30 August 2003, the WTO member states agreed that developed and less-developed countries that do not have the domestic capacity to manufacture drugs should be able to import cheaper generic drugs made under compulsory licences in other countries.[149] That is, the member states agreed to allow countries to manufacture patented pharmaceutical products under compulsory licence for export to developing countries. The decision covers patented products and products made using patented processes in the pharmaceutical sector, including active ingredients and diagnostic kits. The WTO member governments agreed that the obligations under Article 31(f) were to be waived, at least until the Article is amended.

A second area of the Agreement currently under review in the TRIPS Council is Article 27.3(b). This provides a limited exception to the general rule that patents should be granted in all areas of technology in relation to plant and animal inventions. In particular, it provides that members may exclude from patentability plants and animals other than micro-organisms and, essentially, biological processes for the production of plants or animals.[150] As part of the review process, a number of submissions have been made outlining the existing national patent protection for plants and animals, and also the plant variety protection. A number of countries have also made suggestions as to how Article 27.3(b) should be amended. These include discussions about whether patent applicants should be forced to disclose the origin of genetic materials and/or traditional knowledge used in the creation of their invention; the main debate here relates to the consequences of non-compliance.[151] At the same time, a group of African countries argued that there should be a general ban on the patenting of any life forms (including animals, plants, and micro-organisms) and that farmers should have a general right to save seed. Given the divergence of views on the question of patenting life forms, it is not surprising that reform of Article 27.3(b) has progressed slowly. The slow progress can also be attributed to the fact that the review touches on a number of contentious issues, such as patent protection for indigenous knowledge, the relationship between intellectual property and the protection of biodiversity, and the way in which TRIPS and the Convention on Biological Diversity

---

[148] WTO, *Declaration on the TRIPS Agreement and Public Health* (20 November 2001) WT/MIN(01)/DEC/2. See C. Correa, *Implications of the Doha Declaration on the TRIPS Agreement and Public Health*, WHO Health, Economics and Drugs EDM Series No. 12 (June 2002).

[149] WTO, *Implementation of Para. 6 of the Doha Declaration on the TRIPS Agreement and Public Health* (1 September 2003) WT/L/540 (decision of the General Council of 30 August 2003).

[150] TRIPS, Art. 27.3(b), also requires members to provide for the protection of plant varieties either by patent, an effective *sui generis* system, or both.

[151] The European Union has proposed that patent applicants disclose the origin of genetic material, with legal consequences outside the scope of patent law. Switzerland has proposed an amendment to WIPO's Patent Cooperation Treaty (and, by reference, WIPO's PLT), so that domestic laws ask patent applicants to disclose the origins of genetic resources and traditional knowledge. Failure to disclose could hold up a patent being granted or affect its validity. In turn, Brazil, Cuba, Ecuador, India, Peru, Thailand, and Venezuela want the TRIPS Agreement to be amended to make disclosure an obligation.

(discussed later) are to interact.[152] Given this, it is likely that the review of Article 27.3(b) may take some time.

The slow progress of the TRIPS review continued at the Fifth WTO Ministerial Conference which was held in Cancun from 10 to 14 September 2003. While intellectual property issues were not at the forefront of the discussions, the meeting ended in a deadlock with the parties unable to reach agreement as to the next phase of the Doha negotiations. It is currently unclear how future negotiations will proceed. Given that developing countries have little to gain from the TRIPS review (with the possible exception of extending protection for geographical indications of origin), it seems that there is little impetus for them to break this stalemate. As a result, we might expect to see a move away from multilateral treaties towards bilateral agreements (as is currently being favoured by the United States) in an attempt to extend the scope of patent protection beyond that permitted by TRIPS.

The only area where there has been any real change is in relation to the compulsory licensing of patented medicines for export to developing countries. In late 2005, the WTO General Council decided that the 2003 Doha Declaration should be permanently incorporated into the TRIPS Agreement.[153] In order for the amendment to enter into force, two-thirds of the WTO membership were required to adopt the changes. After some delays,[154] the threshold was met and the amendment came into force on 23 January 2017. As a result, TRIPS was amended to include a new Article 31bis and a new Annex. The amendments are very similar to the text of the 2003 Doha Declaration. Under the changes, member countries are able to grant compulsory licences to allow the manufacture and export of pharmaceuticals for public health reasons. This is permitted where the importing country is a developing country that lacks the capacity to produce the relevant pharmaceuticals (the proposed new Annex sets out the criteria to be used to determine whether a country lacks capacity). Importing countries have an obligation to take reasonable measures to prevent re-exportation. The first, and so far only, notification of a compulsory licence being granted to allow a company to make a generic version of a patented medicine for export was made by Canada on 4 October 2007. The licence allows the Canadian company to manufacture the AIDS therapy drug TriAvir and export it to Rwanda.[155] It may be that the regime is not used again as it does not fit the usual methods of drug procurement.[156]

4.6.3 Convention on Biological Diversity (CBD)

The Convention on Biological Diversity (CBD) was signed in June 1992.[157] While the Convention was not directly concerned with patent standards, it heralds a new approach to the way biological resources are treated. The Convention provided developing countries with an opportunity to voice their unhappiness at the exploitation of indigenous resources by firms from the developed world. Of late, there have been numerous examples of situations where this has occurred: the neem tree, traditionally used in India to make medicines and insecticides, has been the subject of 37 patents in Europe and the

---

[152] The Doha Declaration says that, in reviewing Art. 27.3(b), the TRIPS Council should look at the relationship between the TRIPS Agreement and the CBD, and that between the protection of traditional knowledge and folklore.

[153] General Council, *Amendment of the TRIPS Agreement: Decision of 6 December 2005* (8 December 2005) WT/L/641.

[154] WTO, *Amendment of the TRIPS Agreement: Third Extension of the Period for Acceptance by Members of the Protocol Amending the TRIPS Agreement* (5 December 2011), WT/L/829.

[155] (19 July 2007) IP/N/9/RWA/1.

[156] J. Gibson, *Intellectual Property, Medicine and Health* (2nd edn, 2017), pp. 158-9.

[157] On 13 July 2017, there were 196 parties (168 signatories) to the Convention. The United Kingdom signed on 12 June 1992; the EC on 13 June 1992.

United States;[158] there have been applications relating to the use of turmeric for treating wounds;[159] and inventions based on genetic material obtained from the Hagahai people, a small group in Papua New Guinea, have been patented.[160] The CBD offers a potential basis to control the uses made of traditional knowledge. The Preamble recognizes the close and traditional dependence of many indigenous and local communities embodying traditional lifestyles on biological resources. It also recognizes the desirability of equitably sharing the benefits arising from the use of traditional knowledge, innovations, and practices relevant to the conservation of biological diversity and the sustainable use of its components.

Faced with concerns about how the access and benefit-sharing aspect of the CBD were to be implemented, in 2002 the parties to the Convention adopted the Bonn Guidelines on access to genetic resources.[161] The Guidelines, which are voluntary in nature, were designed to assist parties, governments, and other stakeholders when establishing legislative, administrative, or policy measures on access and benefit-sharing and/or when negotiating contractual arrangements for access and benefit-sharing. The voluntary nature of the Guidelines did not endear them to developing nations, who, soon after their adoption, began to lobby for the development of a binding legal regime.

The push towards a more equitable sharing of benefits under the CBD took an important turn when the Nagoya Protocol was adopted in October 2012. The Protocol, which came into force on 12 October 2014, establishes a binding legal regime to govern access to genetic resources and the fair and equitable distribution of benefits derived from their use. The Protocol also regulates access to and use of the traditional knowledge and genetic resources of indigenous and local communities. The Protocol, which reaffirms the sovereign rights of states over their natural resources,[162] has as its primary objective the fair and equitable sharing of benefits arising from the utilization of genetic resources, including by appropriate access to genetic resources and by appropriate transfer of relevant technologies.[163] Article 1 of the Protocol makes it clear that such access must take into account 'all rights over those resources and technologies', which is clearly intended to include relevant intellectual property rights.

The Nagoya Protocol applies to genetic resources falling within the remit of Article 15 CBD—that is, genetic resources that are provided by contracting parties that are countries of origin of such resources or by the parties that have acquired the genetic resources in accordance with the Convention—and to traditional knowledge associated with genetic resources within the scope of the Convention, as well as to benefit-sharing for use of such resources and knowledge.[164] The Protocol obliges parties to adopt legislative, administrative, or policy measures to ensure fair and equitable sharing of benefits with the party providing resources and with indigenous and local communities where there is use of traditional knowledge or genetic resources over which they have established rights.[165]

[158] S. Kadidal, 'Subject Matter Imperialism? Biodiversity, Foreign Prior Art and the Neem Patent Controversy' (1996) 37 *IDEA* 371; E. Da Casta de Silva, 'The Protection of Intellectual Property for Local and Indigenous Communities' [1995] *EIPR* 546; M. Huft, 'Indigenous and Drug Discovery Research: A Question of Intellectual Property Rights' (1995) 89 *Nw UL Rev* 1678.

[159] (26 October 1996) *New Scientist,* 14.

[160] A. Pottage, 'The Inscription of Life in Law: Genes, Patents, and Bio-Politics' (1998) 61 *MLR* 740.

[161] Adopted by the Sixth Meeting of the Conference of the Parties to the Convention on Biological Diversity, The Hague, 2002.   [162] Nagoya Protocol, Preamble.

[163] Nagoya Protocol, Art. 1.

[164] Nagoya Protocol, Art. 3. For a discussion on the subject matter of the CBD, see M. Rourke, 'Viruses for Sale: All Viruses are Subject to Access and Benefit-Sharing Obligations Under the Convention on Biological Diversity' [2017] *EIPR* 78.   [165] Nagoya Protocol, Art. 5.

Access to genetic resources is subject to prior informed consent of the party providing such resources and must be on mutually agreed terms.[166] Parties are required to ensure that use of genetic resources within their jurisdiction is carried out in conformance with the domestic access and benefit-sharing laws of the providing party.[167] Where no domestic laws exist, the access and benefit-sharing provisions of the Protocol do not apply. The situation is somewhat different with regard to the genetic resources and traditional knowledge of indigenous and local communities, in which case prior informed consent and mutually agreed terms appear to be compulsory for access to their genetic resources[168] and traditional knowledge,[169] even where there is no national access and benefit-sharing legislation.[170] States are also required to take the customary laws of indigenous peoples and local communities into consideration in implementing the Protocol.[171] Users of indigenous peoples' and local communities' genetic resources and traditional knowledge will, in the future, need to ensure that requisite prior informed consent for its use has been obtained with due respect and recognition of customary law.[172]

While the CBD may not yet have had an immediate impact on patent law,[173] it does represent a change of attitude towards the way biological resources are exploited, which may impact upon the way patents are viewed. In particular, it may help to undermine the pro-patent attitudes that have dominated for the last 40 or so years. The impetus provided by the CBD to reconsider the aims and functions of the patent system has been reinforced by the growing body of literature that questions the often taken-for-granted assumption that technological development is both desirable and neutral. In so doing, commentators have emphasized the adverse physical and psychological effects of technology on individuals, their relations with society (alienation), and the planet in general (environmental problems). Technology is also seen as having vastly altered the nature of political government and reduced individual autonomy (computer databases, surveillance devices). Following this, some authors have called for the democratic control of technology, in particular arguing that some research and development should be prohibited (note, for example, the debate over the patenting of higher life-forms). In recent years, the CBD has begun to impact upon patent law in a variety of ways, the most notable being the possibility of making 'prior informed consent' a condition of patentability. This has been given a new impetus by the adoption of the Nagoya Protocol. Debates about this and related issues have become intertwined with the ongoing review of the TRIPS Agreement being conducted by the TRIPS Council and with WIPO's discussions about the protection of indigenous knowledge.[174] We look at these issues in more detail later.

---

[166] Nagoya Protocol, Art. 6.1.   [167] Nagoya Protocol, Art. 15.   [168] Nagoya Protocol, Art 6.2.

[169] Nagoya Protocol, Art 7.

[170] The Nagoya Protocol entered into force on 12 October 2017 as a result of EU Regulation 511/2014 of 16 April 2014 on compliance measures for users from the Nagoya Protocol on Access to Genetic Resources and the Fair and Equitable Sharing of Benefits Arising from their Utilization in the Union [2017] *OJ L* 150/59. In May 2015, the EU General Court rejected challenges by Dutch and German plant breeders to the validity of the EU Regulation. See *Ackermann Saatzucht v. European Parliament*, Case T-559/14, EU:T:2015:315 and *ABZ Aardbeien Uit Zaad Holding BV v. European Parliament*, Case T-560/14, EU:T:2015:314. For criticisms of the EU approach, see B. Tobin, 'Biopiracy by Law: European Union Draft Law Threatens Indigenous Peoples' Rights over their Traditional Knowledge and Genetic Resources' [2014] *EIPR* 124.

[171] Nagoya Protocol, Art. 12.

[172] B. Tobin, 'Bridging the Nagoya Compliance Gap: The Fundamental Role of Customary Law in Protection of Indigenous Peoples' Resource and Knowledge Rights' (2013) 9 *LEAD* 144.

[173] See T 1213/05 *Breast and ovarian cancer/UTAH UNIVERSITY* (27 September 2007), [4].

[174] See Chapter 16, section 6.2, pp. 455–7.

4.6.4 WIPO Patent Law Treaty (PLT)

Over the last two decades or so, the World Intellectual Property Organization (WIPO) has been engaged in an ongoing programme of reform of international patent law. The first concrete outcome from this process was the Patent Law Treaty (PLT) which was completed in June 2000.[175] The PLT, which opened for signature on 2 June 2000, entered into force on 28 April 2005.[176] In essence, the PLT is an international treaty that aims to simplify and streamline procedures for obtaining and maintaining a patent. It also aims to harmonize patent procedures relating to national and regional patent applications and the maintenance of patents.[177]

The PLT promises to reduce the cost of patent protection (as a result of changes such as national patent offices sharing the results of search and examination procedures), and to make the process more user-friendly and more widely accessible. The specific changes include: the use of standardized forms and simplified procedures that reduce the risk of error; cost reductions for inventors, applicants, and patent attorneys; the elimination of cumbersome and complicated procedures; improved efficiency of patent offices and lower operating costs; the possibility of introducing electronic filing of patent applications and related communications; the standardization of patent formalities in all countries party to the PLT (including the incorporation of provisions under the Patent Cooperation Treaty); exceptions from mandatory representation; and the possibility of obtaining a filing date even if the main part of the application (description) is filed in a foreign language.[178] Under the PLT, the requirements and procedures for national and regional patent applications and those for Patent Cooperation Treaty international applications have been harmonized.

4.6.5 Global harmonization of substantive patent law

The next stage in the WIPO reform of global patent law began in November 2000 when WIPO launched discussions on the harmonization of the substantive requirements of patent law.[179] These discussions go beyond the Patent Law Treaty of June 2000, which focused on the task of harmonizing the processes by which patents are granted, to consider substantive issues. It is hoped that standardizing the rules on patentability will mean that, because applicants will not have to prepare totally different patent documents

---

[175] WIPO, *Patent Law Treaty* (2 June 2000) PT/DC/47.

[176] There were 107 signatories to the Final Act of the Diplomatic Conference (including the United Kingdom and the EPO) on 2 June 2000. The Treaty had been ratified by 39 countries as of 13 July 2017. The United Kingdom ratified the Treaty on 22 March 2006.

[177] For criticisms, see R. Dreyfus and J. Reichman, 'Harmonizing without Consensus: Critical Reflections on Drafting a Substantive Patent Law Treaty' (2007) 57 *Duke LJ* 85.

[178] WIPO, 'Patent Law Treaty is Finalized' (1 June 2000) PR/2000/222; WIPO, *Patent Law Treaty* (2 June 2000) PT/DC/47.

[179] WIPO Standing Committee on the Law of Patents (SCP), *Suggestions for the Further Development of International Patent Law* (25 September 2000) SCP/4/2. Negotiators attended a meeting of the SCP on 6–10 November 2000. For the background, see R. Petersen, 'Harmonization. A Way Forward' (1987) 16 *CIPAJ* 234; R. Petersen, 'Harmonization—or Backward?' (1987) 17 *CIPAJ* 66; R. Petersen, 'Harmonization: Postponement' (1989) 18 *CIPAJ* 118, 293; R. Petersen, 'On to Harmonization' (1990) 19 *CIPAJ* 147; R. Petersen, 'Harmonization Again' (1990) 19 *CIPAJ* 356; J. Pagenberg, 'WIPO: Diplomatic Conference in the Hague on Harmonization of Patent Law' (1991) 22 *IIC* 682.

for different patent offices, the costs of patenting will decrease. It is also hoped that it will increase predictability about patentability of inventions.

Although the Patent Cooperation Treaty (PCT) contains some principles of substantive patent law, these are only taken into account at the international phase when an application is submitted under the PCT; PCT contracting states are free to apply any substantive conditions of patentability during the national phase of an international application. Importantly, it is at this stage that the national authorities make the important decision as to whether a patent should be granted.

15

NATURE OF A PATENT

1 INTRODUCTION

Patents have changed dramatically since they were first granted in England and Wales more than four centuries ago. Initially, patents were crude documents, often only one or two sentences long. Since then, patents have become much more sophisticated, complex, and lengthy. As we will see in the next chapter, the process by which a patent is granted has also changed dramatically. A lot of care and attention has been given to the form and content of the patent. If there is a kind of symmetry or logic to the patent system, the content of the patent is the key to that process. As such, to understand many facets of patent law, it is important to have a good grasp of the nature and content of the patent. This chapter is intended to provide an introduction to the nature of the patent. In so doing, we look at the different ways patents are described, the way patents are drafted, and the contents of a patent. To offer a sense of the nature of a patent, a patent for a relatively simple piece of technology is reproduced on the Online Resources: http://www.oxfordtextbooks. co.uk/orc/bently_sherman5e/.

2 TYPES OF PATENT

Patents are described in a number of different ways in the United Kingdom. Most commonly, a patent is seen as a legal document that confers a 20-year monopoly on the patentee. Patents are also characterized in terms of the organization that grants them. As we saw earlier, the patents that operate in the United Kingdom are granted by two authorities: the UK Intellectual Property Office (UK IPO) and the European Patent Office (EPO). The patents that operate in the United Kingdom are known either as 'British patents' or 'European patents (UK)'. British patents are issued by the IPO and are subject to British law. European patents are issued by the EPO in Munich; a European patent (UK) is a patent issued by the EPO and applies in the United Kingdom. Prior to the introduction of the 2000 European Patent Convention (EPC 2000), applicants had to designate the member states in which they wanted the patent to operate. In contrast, the EPC 2000 provides that all EPC states will be deemed to be designated as the country in which the patent will operate at the date of filing.[1] While there are a number of differences between the

---

[1] EPC 2000, Art. 79(1), provides that all EPC states will be deemed to be designated as the country in which the patent will operate at the date of filing (in contrast to Art. 79 of the EPC 1973, which required applicants to designate the states in which they wished the patent to operate).

two systems, once a European patent (UK) has been granted, it is treated as if it had been granted by the UK IPO.[2] As we noted in the previous chapter, there are plans to introduce a further type of patent: the unitary European patent which, if it ever enters into force, will be a single patent that spans most, but not all, of Europe.

Another way of classifying patents is in terms of the subject matter that they protect. In some instances, patents are described by reference to the industry or branch of science to which the patented invention relates. So, for example, it is common to speak of 'chemical patents' or 'biotechnology patents'. In other cases, patents are classified according to the nature of the interest that is protected—that is, whether it is a 'product patent', a 'process patent', or a 'product-by-process patent'. These are looked at in the following sections.

3 DRAFTING OF A PATENT

The drafting of patents, which is normally undertaken by patent agents, is a crucial part of the patent process. It is also a complex and difficult task. These difficulties can partly be attributed to the nature of the subject matter that is protected by patent law and partly to the fact that it is sometimes very difficult to explain particular forms of technology in the form demanded by patent law. In certain instances, notably in relation to biological inventions, patent law has been forced to develop specific rules and procedures to enable them to meet the requirements for patentability.[3]

Another reason why patent drafting is often such a difficult process is that patents are at once technical, commercial, and legal documents. As such, they are written with a number of different purposes in mind. As we saw earlier, one of the rationales for the grant of patents is that they encourage the dissemination of technical and scientific information. In the hypothetical patent bargain that views patents as though they were a contract between inventors and the state, the information contained in the application is treated as the 'consideration' for the grant of the monopoly.[4] It has been suggested that one of the reasons why inventors are given 'more or less complete freedom in the drafting of their patent applications' is because it is very 'difficult to legislate for future inventions'.[5] As well as encouraging inventors to disclose information that might otherwise remain secret, the patent system also attempts to ensure that the information that is made public is recorded in a format that is usable. To this end, a series of detailed rules and procedures regulate the way in which the patents are drafted.[6] To take one example, patent law stipulates that the patent specification ought to disclose the invention in a manner that is clear enough and complete enough for the invention to be performed by a person skilled in the art.[7]

While the patent system encourages inventors to disclose their technical creations, it would be incorrect to conclude from this that patentees necessarily draft their patents according to the rules and procedures set down by the law. In some cases, inventors may take out a patent, but attempt to manipulate the information in the patent application

---

[2] PA 1977, ss 77–78; EPC 2000, Art. 64.

[3] See A. Pottage and B. Sherman, *Figures of Invention* (2012).

[4] 'This is the price which the inventor pays in return for his twenty-year monopoly': *Mentor v. Hollister* [1993] *RPC* 7, 9. See also *Grant v. Raymond*, 31 *US* (6 *Pet*) 218, 247 (1832).

[5] *Hospira v. Genetech* [2014] *EWHC* 3857 (Pat), [126].

[6] For example, PA Rules, rr 14–15, Pts 1–4 of Sch. 2; EPC 2000 Regs, r. 47.

[7] PA 1977, s. 14(3); PA Rules, r. 12(4); EPC 2000, Art. 83; EPC 2000 Regs, r. 42. See Chapter 20, sections 1 and 2, pp. 599–609.

in a way that suits their own purposes. For example, as well as disclosing the invention, applicants may draft their patent in such a way as to attract sponsorship or to advertise the existence of the patent.[8]

Given that the information contained in a patent application may be used by an applicant's competitors, it is understandable that applicants may be tempted to provide only the minimum amount of information that is necessary for them to obtain a patent. While patentees may not now be able to obscure their inventions as they once were, applicants are only required to disclose such details of the invention as to enable a person skilled in the art to make the invention. As a result, a patent might not reveal important features about the invention, such as the cheapest or strongest starting materials.[9] This 'know-how' may provide the patentee with a strategic advantage over competitors that may be important when an invention is made available to the public. Ultimately, the degree to which applicants are able to draft patents for their own purposes depends upon how stringently the patent offices and the courts enforce the disclosure requirements.

Another factor that adds to the complexity of the drafting process relates to what has been called the 'infringement–validity dichotomy' (or, as it is also known, the 'Gillette defence'[10]). Because the scope of the monopoly is determined by what is claimed in the patent,[11] the applicants may be tempted to claim more than they perhaps ought. At the same time, however, applicants need to be mindful of the fact that if they draft claims too broadly, this increases the chance of the patent being declared invalid (primarily for lack of novelty). Because matters of infringement and validity are heard in the same tribunal, the infringement–validity dichotomy helps to ensure that the scope of the patent monopoly corresponds to what was actually invented.

4 CONTENTS OF A PATENT

Patents in Britain and the EPO are made up of four key parts:

(i)   an abstract;[12]

(ii)   a description of the invention;[13]

(iii) one or more claims;[14] and

(iv)   any drawings referred to in the description or claims.[15]

Before looking at these in more detail, it is important to bear in mind a number of preliminary issues.

---

[8] In *Cartonneries de Thulin v. CTP White Knight* [2001] *RPC* 107, 116, Robert Walker LJ said that patent attorneys in different industrial countries adopt perceptibly different approaches to drafting patent specifications: German (and other continental) draftsmen tend to a 'central' style, which concentrates on the 'centre of gravity' of an invention; British (and, still more, American) draftsman tend to a 'peripheral' style, which seeks to delimit the boundaries of an invention.

[9] Although there is no requirement of good faith, note PA 1977, ss 62(3), 63(2).

[10] This is based on the arguments before the House of Lords in *Gillette Safety Razor Company v. Anglo-American Trading Company Ltd* (1913) 30 *RPC* 465.

[11] But see Chapter 22, section 3.1, pp. 656 *ff* (suggesting that the monopoly may extend to 'equivalents' of parts specified in the claim).

[12] PA 1977, s. 14(2)(c); PA Rules, r. 15; EPC 2000, Art. 78(1)(e); EPC 2000 Regs, r. 47.

[13] PA 1977, s. 14(2)(b); PA Rules, r. 12(4)(a), Pts 1–4 of Sch. 2; EPC 2000, Art. 78(1)(b); EPC 2000 Regs, r. 42.

[14] PA 1977, s. 14(2)(b); PA Rules, r. 12; EPC 2000, Art. 78(1)(c); EPC 2000 Regs, r. 43.

[15] PA 1977, s. 14(2)(b); PA Rules, r. 12; EPC 2000, Art. 78(1)(d); EPC 2000 Regs, r. 46. Patent applications must also contain a request for the grant of a patent and designate the inventor.

The various components of a patent perform a number of different roles. Some of these, such as the abstract, are used both for administrative purposes and as a way of advertising the existence of the patented invention. The description and claims, which form the core of the patent, respectively disclose the invention in a usable form and demarcate the scope of the monopoly. It is also important to note that the contents of a patent application differ somewhat from the patent itself. While the patent and the application for a patent both contain a description and claims, the main difference is that the patent application contains additional information—the request for grant. The request for grant, which is used for administrative purposes, normally includes the title of the invention (which clearly and concisely states the technical designation of the invention), as well as relevant biographical details of the applicants and patent agents (if used). Because it is permissible to amend the patent application during and after the grant process, the final form that a patent takes may differ from the initial application. This process of amendment is examined in more detail later.[16]

While UK and European patents are very similar,[17] there are some differences that ought to be borne in mind. One of these relates to the language that is used to describe the components of the patent. More specifically, it relates to the fact that while the core of a British patent is known as the 'specification' (which comprises a description of the invention, the claims, and any drawings referred to in the description or claims), the EPC and the Patent Cooperation Treaty 1970 (PCT) speak instead of the contents of a 'patent application'.[18] Another difference between UK and European patents relates to the controls that are exercised over the form and content of the patent. While similar, in that both have to meet the statutory requirements for patentability, the rules of the EPC (but not the United Kingdom) provide detailed guidance as to the precise form that a patent should take. This is particularly the case in relation to the description and claims.

With these initial points in mind, we can now turn to look at the contents of a patent in more detail.

4.1 ABSTRACT

The first element of a UK and EPO patent is the abstract.[19] This is a brief summary (usually around 150 words) of the more important technical features of the invention. Normally, an abstract contains the title of the invention, a concise summary of the matter contained in the specification, and an indication of the technical field to which the invention belongs. The relevant rules also provide that the abstract should outline a technical explanation of the invention, and the principal use of the invention.[20]

Patent abstracts perform two main tasks. First, they are used by the patent offices as a search tool when examining other patent applications. To this end, the patent rules stipulate that abstracts ought to be drafted in such a way that they constitute an efficient instrument for searching in the particular technical field.[21] Abstracts, which are

---

[16] See Chapter 16, section 5, p. 451 and Chapter 20, section 4, p. 614.

[17] European patents that designate the United Kingdom are treated as UK patents: PA 1977, s. 77.

[18] PA 1977, s. 14. See *Genentech's Patent* [1989] *RPC* 147, 197–9, 236–7, 261; A. White, 'The Function and Structure of Patent Claims' [1993] *EIPR* 243; P. Cole, *The Fundamentals of Patent Drafting* (2006) ; G. Robert, *A Practical Guide to Drafting Patents* (2006).

[19] PA 1977, s. 14(2)(c); PA Rules, r. 15; EPC 2000, Art. 78(1)(e); EPC 2000 Regs, r. 47.

[20] PA Rules, r. 15(3); EPC 2000 Regs, r. 47(2) (abstract may be amended by the Comptroller).

[21] EPC 2000 Regs, r. 47(5), requires that the abstract be drafted in such a way that it constitutes an efficient instrument for purposes of searching in the particular technical field, in particular by making it possible to assess whether there is a need to consult the specification (or patent application) itself.

normally published around 18 months after the application was filed, also alert third parties to the existence of the application. To ensure that abstracts are only used for these purposes, the Patents Act 1977 (PA 1977) and the EPC 2000 stipulate that the abstract can only be relied upon to provide 'technical information'.[22] One of the consequences of this is that, for patent law purposes, the abstract does not form part of the state of the art until after publication.[23] This avoids the potential problem of the abstract anticipating the patent and, in so doing, rendering it invalid for lack of novelty. The fact that the abstract is only used for 'technical' purposes also means that it cannot be used to influence the scope of the monopoly.[24]

4.2 DESCRIPTION

The next element of a patent is the description.[25] As with the abstract, the description plays an important role in ensuring that the information function of the patent system is performed. In many ways, descriptions are similar to scientific or technical papers: they explain what has been created, the problems that the invention solves, why it is important, and how the invention differs from what has been created before.[26]

In most cases, a description will begin with an account of the background to the invention.[27] In so doing, the description will summarize the prior art, usually referring to existing patents and other published documents. This information is used to understand the nature of the invention, for carrying out the search report, and for the purposes of examination.[28] Typically, a description will then disclose the invention as claimed.[29] This is usually done by outlining the technical problem that the invention attempts to solve and the solutions that it offers (which are often couched in terms of the advantages that the invention offers over the 'background art').[30] Following a brief introduction to any drawings that are used,[31] the description will normally provide a detailed account of how the invention is carried out.[32]

---

[22] PA 1977, s. 14(7); EPC 2000, Art. 85.

[23] This is explicit in EPC 2000, Art. 85, and implicit in PA 1977, s. 14(7).

[24] *Bull/Identification system*, T 246/86 [1989] *OJ EPO* 199. (The TBA refused to allow an applicant to use an abstract that suggested that the apparatus was a credit card as a way of expanding the preliminary description and claims, which had not suggested that the apparatus could include a portable object.)

[25] PA 1977, s. 14(2)(b); PA Rules, r. 12(4)(a), Pts 1–4 of Sch. 2; EPC 2000, Art. 78(1)(b); EPC 2000 Regs, rr 42, 49. Unlike the EPC, which provides detailed guidance as to the contents of the description, the PA 1977 and the rules are silent as to the form that the description in a UK application ought to take.

[26] On the specification, see R. Merges and R. Nelson, 'On the Complex Economics of Patent Scope' (1990) 90 *Colum L Rev* 839, 844; G. Myers, 'From Discovery to Invention: The Writing and Re-writing of Two Patents' (1995) 25 *SSS* 57.

[27] EPC 2000 Regs, r. 42(1)(b); *EPO Guidelines*, F–II, 4.3–4.4. See *Sony/Television receivers*, T 654/92 [2000] *EPOR* 148 (on the meaning of 'background art').   [28] EPC 2000 Regs, r. 42(1)(b).

[29] EPC 2000 Regs, r. 42(1)(c); *EPO Guidelines*, F–II, 4.5.

[30] EPC 2000 Regs, r. 42(1)(c). For criticisms of EPC 1973 Regs, r. 27 (which is similar to EPC 2000 Regs, r. 42(1)(c)), on the basis that it is ambiguous and uncertain, see H. Ullrich, *Standards of Patentability for European Inventions: Should an Inventive Step Advance the Art?* (1977), 113.

[31] EPC 2000 Regs, r. 42(1)(d); *EPO Guidelines*, F–II, [4.7].

[32] The patent should include a specific description of at least one detailed embodiment, often referred to as the 'preferred embodiments'. Occasionally, this will be unnecessary: see *Toshiba/Semiconductor device*, T 407/87 [1989] *EPOR* 470. EPC 2000, r. 42(1)(f), adds that, where necessary, the applicant should state the way in which the invention is capable of industrial exploitation: *EPO Guidelines*, F–II, [4.9].

To ensure that the invention is disclosed in such a way that it is of practical use to people in the art, patent law imposes a number of constraints upon the way inventions are disclosed. At a general level, the application ought to describe the invention in a manner that is clear and complete enough for it to be performed by a person skilled in the art.[33] The description must also support the claims.[34] If the patent fails to meet these criteria, it may be declared invalid. These issues are dealt with in more detail later.[35]

4.2.1 Description of biological materials

One of the rationales for the inclusion of the description in a patent application is that it ensures that the public is able to access and make use of the invention that is disclosed in the application. This is based on the presupposition that it is possible to describe the invention, whether using words, figures, or diagrams, in such a way that third parties will be able to understand and make use of it. While this assumption holds true in relation to most technologies, it is not necessarily the case in relation to biological inventions. The reason for this is that where an invention depends on the use of living materials such as micro-organisms or cultured cells, it may be impossible to describe the invention so that the public is able to make the invention.[36]

The EPC 2000[37] and the PA 1977[38] attempt to address this problem by providing that if an invention involves biological material that cannot be described in a way that enables the invention to be carried out by a person skilled in the art, the applicant must deposit a sample of this biological material at a 'recognized institution' (or depositary).[39] These issues were also addressed in the Biotechnology Directive.[40] The application must contain such relevant information as is available on the characteristics of the biological material.[41] In depositing a sample, the applicant is treated as consenting to the depositary making the sample available after publication of the application.[42] An applicant may require that until the application has either been abandoned or patented, the deposit should only be released to experts who are allowed to use the culture only for experimental purposes.[43] Special rules also exist in relation to patent applications relating to nucleotide and amino acid sequences.[44]

---

[33] PA 1977, s. 14(3); EPC 2000, Art. 83.   [34] PA 1977, s. 14(5)(c); EPC 2000, Art. 84.

[35] See Chapter 20, sections 1 and 2, pp. 599–609.

[36] In *American Cyanamid (Dann)'s Patent* [1971] *RPC* 425, the House of Lords held that there was no obligation on a patentee under the PA 1949 to supply the microorganism to the public. See A. Pottage and B. Sherman, *Figures of Invention* (2012), 183*ff*; B. Hampar, 'Patenting of Recombinant DNA Technology: The Deposit Requirement' (1985) 67 *JPTOS* 569; V. Meyer, 'Problems and Issues in Depositing Micro-organisms for Patent Purposes' (1983) 65 *JPTOS* 455.

[37] EPC 2000 Regs, r. 31.

[38] PA 1977, s. 125A (introduced by CDPA 1988, Sch. 5, para. 30).

[39] Recognized depositary institutions include all international depositaries under the 1977 Treaty on the International recognition of the Deposit of Microorganisms (the Budapest Treaty) (modified 1980). This established minimum requirements for maintaining an international depositary for microorganisms (the United Kingdom joined on 29 December 1988). In May 2018, there were 80 member states, with 47 international depositary authorities (IDAs).

[40] Biotech. Dir., Arts 13–14; implemented in the United Kingdom by Patents (Amendment) Rules 2001, SI 2001/1412 (as of 6 July 2001).

[41] EPC 2000 Regs, r. 31(1)(b); PA 1977, s. 125A; PA Rules, r. 13(1), Sch. 1.

[42] EPC 2000 Regs, r. 31; PA Rules, r. 13(1), Sch. 1.

[43] EPC 2000 Regs, r. 32; PA Rules, r. 13(1), Sch. 1, paras 6–7.

[44] EPC 2000 Regs, r. 30; PA Rules, r. 13. See also *Decision of the President of the EPO 2 October 1998 concerning the presentation of nucleotide and amino acid sequences in patent applications and the filing of sequence listings* (1998) 11 *OJ EPO* Supp. No. 21.

4.3 CLAIMS

The next element of a patent is the claims.[45] While the purpose of the description is to ensure that the invention disclosed in the patent is of some practical use, the primary function of the claims is to set out the scope of the legal protection conferred by the patent.[46] As such, the claims play a key role in patent law.

Typically, a patent will consist of a number of claims that are arranged hierarchically.[47] Such patents will commence with a widely drawn 'principal', 'generic', or 'independent' claim that defines the invention by setting out its distinctive technical features. General claims of this sort are often followed by a series of narrower dependent or subsidiary claims (which may refer back to earlier claims).[48] For example, the primary claim may be for a product (such as a contact lens) having a particular character (such as being made up of recycled plastic), whereas the dependent claims may limit the principal claim to certain quantitative parameters (such as minimum or maximum length).

One of the reasons why claims are arranged hierarchically is that this provides patentees with the flexibility to respond to any legal challenges that are made to the patent.[49] More specifically, if claims are arranged hierarchically, a challenge to the patent might only lead to the principal or broadest claim being severed, leaving behind the more narrowly drafted claims.[50] Confident in the knowledge that the validity of narrower claims are not dependent on the validity of the more general claims, patentees are able to draft claims more generously than they would otherwise be able to do. The rules under the EPC 2000 require that, where appropriate, claims ought to be in two parts.[51] The first, which is called the 'preamble', sets out the technical features of the invention that are necessary for the definition of the claimed subject matter, but which are already part of the prior art. This is followed by a so-called 'characterizing portion', which sets out the novel technical features that the applicant wishes to protect.[52] The characterizing portion of the claim is neither required nor forbidden in the United Kingdom.[53] Following changes in 2016,

[45] PA 1977, s. 14(2)(b); PA Rules, r. 12; EPC 2000, Art. 78(1)(c); EPC 2000 Regs, r. 43. The requirement for a claim was first introduced in the United Kingdom by the Patents, Designs and Trade Marks Act 1883, s. 5(5). However, the practice of including claims had been common from at least the 1830s. Claims are central to the operation of the European patent system: *Mobil/Friction-reducing additive*, G 2/88 [1990] *OJ EPO* 93, 99; J. Kemp (ed.), *Patent Claim Drafting and Interpretation* (1983). On the history, see *British United Shoe Machinery v. Fussell* (1908) 23 *RPC* 631, 650.

[46] PA 1977, s. 14(5); EPC 2000, Art. 84. Given that the claims define the scope of protection, the way in which the claims are interpreted is very important: see Chapter 22, section 3, pp. 655–66. Note also that, in the light of the Supreme Court decision in *Actavis v. Eli Lilly* [2017] *UKSC* 48, [33] that a difference exists between 'a difference between interpreting a claim and the extent of the protection afforded by a claim'. For an interesting examination of the typical nature of the claims (and how they might differ from the abstract), see *R (on the application of Knight) v. Comptroller-General of Patents, Trade Marks and Designs* [2007] *All ER (D)* 125.

[47] The number has to be reasonable having regard to the nature of the invention claimed: EPC 2000, r. 43(5). In *Oxy/Gel forming composition*, T 246/91 [1995] *EPOR* 526, a patent with 157 claims violated EPC 1973, Art. 84 and r. 29(5): '[P]atents should not be allowed to erect a legal maze or smokescreen in front of potential users of the inventions to which they lay claim.'

[48] *Hallen v. Brabantia* [1990] *FSR* 134, 140–1.

[49] Following EPO practice, it is now clear that numbering claims will not impact on the construction of the claims in the United Kingdom: *Virgin Atlantic Airways v. Premium Aircraft Interiors UK* [2009] *EWCA Civ* 1062.

[50] See *Van der Lely v. Bamfords* [1964] *RPC* 54, 73, 76 (CA); *Chiron v. Organon (No. 7)* [1994] *FSR* 458, 460–6.

[51] This provision, apparently put in to appease British interests, enables UK patents to be drafted according to the traditional British approach.

[52] EPC 2000 Regs, r. 43(1)(b); *EPO Guidelines*, F–IV, [2.2].   [53] *CIPA*, [14.31].

so-called omnibus claims—that is, claims that largely mimics the way in which the invention is set out in the descriptions or the drawings[54]—will no longer be permitted in the UK (bringing British law into line with practice at the EPO).[55]

A notable feature of most patent claims is that they are difficult to understand, at least to the non-expert reader. This is not surprising, given that patents are written not for the general reader, but for the relevant person skilled in the art. As well as being written for specialists, the drafting and reading of claims builds upon well-established and sophisticated techniques and procedures that make them difficult for the uninitiated to understand.[56] Another reason why the claims may be difficult to understand is that they often use expressions not ordinarily employed in everyday speech. For example, while most people commonly talk about 'mice', a claim may refer to 'non-human mammals'. Similarly, a door handle may be called a 'rotatable actuating means'[57] and a train's sleeping car, 'a communal vehicle for the dormitory accommodation of nocturnal viators'.[58] Moreover, while in other contexts the rules of grammar are used to make the language that we use easier to understand, this is not so with patents, where claims are often made up of single lengthy, repetitive sentences.[59] Indeed, in one case an attempt to divide claims up into separate (shorter) phrases was considered to be ambiguous in scope.[60] One problem that has arisen is the number of claims incorporated in a patent. As part of their drafting strategy, some applications include a very large number of claims. To prevent this, higher fees are charged where the number of claims increases.[61]

4.3.1 Types of claim

Given that claims operate to demarcate and define the patented invention, they will always vary from case to case. Having said that, claims are usually grouped together on the basis either of the subject matter that is protected or the way in which the claims are formulated. While there are many different types of claim, such as 'Swiss claims', 'Markush claims', 'reach-through claims',[62] and 'novelty-of-use claims', in this section we wish to focus on some of the more common types.

(i) *Product claims* Product claims, which were the first type of patent to be recognized by British law, provide protection over physical entities or things (such as products, apparatuses, devices, and substances). Such a patent could be, for example, for a new type of contact lens or, as a patent agent might say, 'a new type

---

[54] *Raleigh Cycle v. Miller* (1948) 65 *RPC* 141; *Surface Silo v. Beal* [1960] *RPC* 154; *Deere v. Harrison McGregor & Guest* [1965] *RPC* 461.

[55] UK IPO, *Changes to Patent Rules* (1 September 2016). See, *CIPA Guide to the Patents Act: First Supplement to the Eight Edition* (2016), [14.35].

[56] For example, see *Virgin Atlantic v. Delta Air Lines* [2011] *EWCA Civ* 162, [19]; R. Macleod, 'What Does "for" Mean in "Means for"? The Role of Functional Limitations in Apparatus Claims' (2011) 33 *EIPR* 499.

[57] *Southco v. Dzus Fastener Europe* [1992] *RPC* 299.

[58] *Hookless Fastener v. GE Prentice* (CCA 2d, 1934) 68 F (2d) 940, 941. See also W. Woodward, 'Definiteness and Particularity in Patent Claims' (1948) 46 *Mich L Rev* 755.

[59] 'The repetitiveness of the claims and the lack of any indication of the strategic links between them is part of what makes them so hard for a non-lawyer to read': G. Myers, 'From Discovery to Invention' (1995) 25 *SSS* 57, 75. The technique of drafting claims in this way can have important implications for their interpretation: see *Glaverbel SA v. British Coal* [1995] *RPC* 255, 281.

[60] *Leonard's Application* [1966] *RPC* 269.

[61] *Decision of the President of the European Patent Office dated 22 November 2011 revising the Office's fees and expenses* [2011] *OJ EPO* 658; Patents (Fees) Rules 2007 (SI 2007/3291 as amended), r. 3B to 3D.

[62] These are 'claims directed to a chemical compound (or the use of that compound) defined only in functional terms with regard to the technical effect it exerts on one of the molecules': *EPO Guidelines*, F-III, [9].

of optical membrane being made up of at least one polymer and at least one solvent'.[63] Product claims (or, as they are also known, 'claims for a product per se') confer protection over all uses of that product, no matter how the product was derived.[64] As we will see, this has been the subject of some controversy, particularly in relation to claims for gene patents.

(ii) *Process claims* In contrast, process claims, which were recognized by patent law in the early part of the nineteenth century, protect activities or actions (such as methods, processes, or uses).[65] Such a patent would claim, for example, the particular method by which a contact lens is made (or 'the method of making an optical membrane from a solution comprising at least one polymer and at least one solvent').[66] Sometimes, a claim for a product per se will not be available because the product is already known in the field and a claim for the process or use is therefore all that is possible.

(iii) *Product-by-process claims* Beyond these two broad categories of claim there is a range of hybrids.[67] A well-known example is the 'product-by-process' claim.[68] To continue with the example used earlier, a product-by-process patent might claim 'a contact lens made by a particular method'. Where a product already exists, but a new process is devised for producing that product, it might be desirable to claim both the process and the product produced by the process. It is important to bear in mind the Court of Appeal's reminder that:

[I]t is not right to lump all claims which contain a process feature into a category called product-by-process claims . . . a patentee can define the monopoly claimed so as to disclaim products made by a particular process or only disclaim products which do not have the features of products made by a particular process. The two types of claims can be loosely called product-by-process claims, but to do so is likely to hide the differences between the two.[69]

For many years, product-by-process claims were viewed differently in the United Kingdom and at the EPO. As a result of the House of Lords' 2005 decision in *Kirin-Amgen*,[70]

---

[63] *Advanced Semiconductor Products/Limiting feature*, T 384/91 [1995] *EPOR* 97, [1994] *OJ EPO* 169.

[64] See *Mobil/Friction reducing additive*, G 2/88 [1990] *OJ EPO* 93; *Telectronics/Pacer*, T 82/93 [1996] *EPOR* 409, [1996] *OJ EPO* 274, 285. In *Moog/Change of category*, T 378/86 [1988] *OJ EPO* 386, the EPO explained:

> [The] division of patents into various categories (process or product) is legally important because the extent of protection depends to a crucial extent on the category selected, specific types of use being allocated to each category which in some cases differ substantially from each other. The difference in effect on the right conferred by a patent is the reason why it is at all justifiable to classify patents in categories.

[65] *Crane v. Price* (1842) 134 *ER* 239. See Sherman and Bently, 108.

[66] *Advanced Semiconductor Products/Limiting feature*, T 384/91 [1995] *EPOR* 97, [1994] *OJ EPO* 169.

[67] 'There are no rigid lines of demarcation between the various possible forms of claim': *Mobil/Friction reducing additive*, G 2/88 [1990] *OJ EPO* 93, 98–9. See also *IBM/Computer-related claims*, T 410/96 [1999] *EPOR* 318.

[68] *Ethylene Polymers/Montedison*, T 93/83 [1987] *EPOR* 144; *Eli Lilly/Antibiotic*, T 161/86 [1987] *EPOR* 366. For a useful general discussion of product-by-process claims see *Hospira v. Genetech* [2014] *EWHC* 3857 (Pat), [125]–[160] (the issue was not discussed on appeal [2016] *EWCA Civ* 780 (CA)).

[69] *Kirin-Amgen v. Transkaryotic Therapies* [2003] *RPC* 3 (CA), [27].

[70] *Kirin-Amgen Inc v. Hoechst Marion Roussel* [2005] *RPC* 9 (HL), [101].

however, the approach in the United Kingdom is now the same as that at the EPO. The EPO's Technical Board of Appeal (TBA) has consistently said that product-by-process claims are not recognized at the EPO, except where the 'product cannot be satisfactorily defined by reference to its composition, structure or other testable parameter'.[71] That is, product-by-process claims are only acceptable as 'a manner of claiming structurally indefinable product claims' or where a product cannot be satisfactorily defined by its features. In contrast, prior to *Kirin-Amgen*, British courts had expressly rejected the position at the EPO and said that, other than the general criteria for patentability, there were no limits either in the PA 1977 or in the EPC as to how the monopoly is defined.[72] As such, there were no additional limits on when product-by-process claims were allowed in the United Kingdom.[73] Recognizing the need for consistency between the approach adopted in the United Kingdom and that at the EPO, the House of Lords rejected previous British law and followed the approach at the EPO. The upshot of this is that where a product is known, product-by-process claims are no longer accepted in the United Kingdom on the basis that they lack novelty.

Product-by-process claims remain useful at the EPO and in the United Kingdom where there is no other information available to define the product by reference to its composition, structure, or other testable parameter.[74] This is particularly the case in relation to certain biotechnological and chemical inventions, where the product-by-process claim offers the only way to define certain or macromolecular materials of unidentified or complex composition which have yet to be defined structurally.[75]

(iv) *Representative claims* It has long been accepted practice for patents to be granted for extremely large classes of object. This is particularly the case in relation to chemical and biotechnological inventions, where patents may claim hundreds of thousands—sometimes even millions—of compounds, DNA sequences, and the like.[76] If patentees were required to outline every particular manifestation of their invention, it would make those patents unwieldy, cumbersome, and, in some cases, unworkable. Because of this, where a patent is for a class of compounds, it

---

[71] *IFF/Claim categories*, T 150/82 [1984] *OJ EPO* 309, [10]–[11]. This decision was made in the knowledge of the different approach in the United Kingdom.

[72] *Kirin-Amgen v. Transkaryotic Therapies* [2003] *RPC* 3 (CA), [29]–[31], upholding the finding of the Patents Court on this point in *Kirin-Amgen v. Roche Diagnostics* [2002] *RPC* 1, [296] ('as a matter of ordinary language, I find it impossible to construe a product-by-process claim in an absolute sense as the Board apparently felt able to do in T 219/83' *BASF/Zeolites* [1986] *EPOR* 247).

[73] In essence, the difference between the approach adopted at the EPO and the pre-*Kirin Amgen* approach turned on the way in which the invention was defined, the Board placing more emphasis on the interaction of the process and the product as a separate entity. On one level, the different approaches can be traced to different legal cultures (British compared to a more German approach). More specifically, the difference can be traced to differences in the way in which the invention is characterized. The crux of the difference is that the EPO sees the invention in terms of the relationship between the product and the process, whereas the UK tribunals seem to draw a clear divide between product and process. For example, at the EPO, it has been said that 'the effect of a process manifests itself in the result, i.e. in the product in chemical cases together with all its internal characteristics': *Gelation/Exxon*, T 119/82 [1984] *OJ EPO* 217. In a similar vein, 'the product is in consequence of the invention, without being the invention itself, which is rather the novel interaction represented by the process in such cases. Any attempt to claim the in itself non-inventive product by means of product-by-process claims is claiming the mere effects instead': *IFF/Claim categories*, T 150/82 [1984] *OJ EPO* 309. As we will see later this has important consequences when a patent is being examined for novelty.

[74] *IFF/Claim categories*, T 150/82 [1984] *OJ EPO* 309.

[75] *EPO Guidelines*, F–IV, [4.12]. The benefits of product-by-process claims are less important under the European Patent Convention, since infringement of a process occurs where a person disposes of, uses, or imports any product obtained directly by means of that process: PA 1977, s. 60(1)(c); EPC 2000, Art. 64(2).

is not necessary for applicants to spell out each and every product or process covered by the patent,[77] nor to show that they have 'proved their application in every individual instance'.[78] Instead, patentees are able to claim a broad range of products on the basis of a limited number of (representative) examples. This can be done, for example, through the use of functional language (particularly where the relevant features cannot be defined more precisely), the use of 'Markush claims'[79] (where a claim refers to a chemical structure by means of symbols indicating substituent groups), or the inclusion of a practical application of a theoretical principle or a formula. In other cases, a patent may include variations, analogues, or deemed equivalents that greatly expand the scope of the claims.[80]

Functional claims define the invention by reference to the function that the invention performs or its purpose, rather than the structure or elements of the invention—that is, instead of specifying what the invention is, a functional claim outlines what the invention does. For example, instead of claiming a modified form of bacteria in terms of its elements or structure, the invention might be described functionally as a bacterium that eats pollution.[81] Functional claims are permissible so long as they provide instructions that are sufficiently clear for the expert to reduce them to practice without undue burden[82] and 'if, from an objective point of view, such features cannot otherwise be defined more precisely without restricting the scope of the claim'.[83]

In some cases, patentees use functional claims because language and concepts are not available to describe the invention in any other way.[84] This is often the case with biological inventions.[85] In other cases, patentees might use functional language because it offers them a strategic advantage over competitors. For example, in describing how two metal plates are attached, a patentee might use functional language and claim a 'means for attaching' instead of claiming a 'nut and bolt'. This has the advantage of preventing a competitor from getting round the claim by using a screw.

4.3.2 Regulating the form and content of claims

A number of different rules and procedures regulate the form that claims ought to take.[86] At a general level, the contents of the claims must comply with the substantive

---

[76] See K. Luzzatto, 'The Support and Breadth of Claims to New Classes of Chemical Compounds' (1989) *Patent World* 21.

[77] *Biogen v. Medeva* [1997] *RPC* 1, 48 (HL) (Lord Hoffmann).

[78] *Kirin-Amgin v. Transkaryotic Therapies* [2003] *RPC* 31 (CA), 67.

[79] Named after US patent application 1,506,316 by Eugene Markush. See M. Franzosi, 'Markush Claims in Europe' [2003] *EIPR* 200.

[80] For problems that may arise, see *American Home Products v. Novartis Pharmaceuticals* [2001] *RPC* 159 (CA).

[81] See *Biogen v. Medeva* [1997] *RPC* 1 (HL), in which the claim was to a DNA molecule characterized by the way in which it was made (recombinant DNA) and what it did (display HBV antigen specificity).

[82] For US analogues, see *In re Donaldson* 16 *F.3d* 1189 (Fcd. Cir. 1994); K. Adamo, 'The Waiting at the Patent Bar is over: The Supreme Court decides Hilton Davis' (1996) 78 *JPTOS* 367.

[83] *Mycogen/Modifying plant cells*, T 694/92 [1998] *EPOR* 114, 119; *EPO Guidelines*, F–II, [4.3]; *CIPA*, [14.34].

[84] The TBA said that the use of structural description of chemical compounds by means of Markush-style formulae, which was part of the standard toolkit of the skilled-person chemist, is the most concise means of defining a class of chemical compounds in a claim: *Bayer CropScience/Safeners*, T 1020/98 [2003] *OJ EPO* 533, 540–1.

[85] *Genentech/Polypeptide expression*, T 292/85 [1989] *EPOR* 1, [1989] *OJ EPO* 275.

[86] Beyond the requirements that are set out in the PA 1977, British law provides no guidance as to the particular format that the claims ought to take. This is in marked contrast to the EPC, which provides detailed guidance as to the form and content that claims ought to follow.

requirements for patentability—namely, subject matter, novelty, and non-obviousness. The claims must also define the matter for which protection is sought in terms of the technical features of the invention,[87] be clear and concise,[88] be supported by the description,[89] and relate to one invention, or a group of inventions that are so linked as to form a single inventive concept.[90] We look at these criteria in more detail later.[91]

4.4 DRAWINGS

The final component of a patent is the drawings. These provide a representation of the invention.[92] Along with the description, the drawings may be used to interpret the claims.[93] The Patent Office Rules provide very detailed rules as to the nature and form of the drawings. These range from the quality of the paper,[94] the size of the margin,[95] and the use of shading,[96] through to the height of the letters or numerals used. The standardization of the way inventions are represented plays an important role in ensuring the usefulness of the information provided by the patentee.

---

[87] PA 1977, s. 14(5)(a); EPC 2000, Art. 84; EPC 2000 Regs, r. 43(1).
[88] PA 1977, s. 14(5)(b); EPC 2000, Art. 84.   [89] PA 1977, s. 14(5)(c); EPC 2000, Art. 84.
[90] PA 1977, s. 14(5)(d); PA Rules, r. 16; EPC 2000, Art. 82; EPC 2000 Regs, r. 44.
[91] See Chapter 20.
[92] PA 1977, s. 14(2)(b); PA Rules, rr 12(2), 18; EPC 2000, Art. 78(1)(d); EPC 2000 Regs, r. 46.
[93] PA 1977, s. 125(1).   [94] UK Manual of Patent Practice, [14.27].   [95] Ibid., [14.28].
[96] Ibid., [14.30].

16

PROCEDURE FOR GRANT
OF A PATENT

1 INTRODUCTION

Unlike the position under copyright law where rights arise without formality, patents are only granted after a series of formal procedures have been complied with. The process of registration plays a key role in defining many aspects of patent law and practice. In this chapter, we explore some of the key features of those processes. We begin by exploring some of the issues that would-be applicants ought to consider when deciding whether to take out a patent to protect their inventions in the United Kingdom. We then follow the trajectory of a patent through the administrative process, from its inception as a patent application through to grant. In so doing, we discuss the British and European patent systems, the Patent Cooperation Treaty (PCT), and how they intersect.

2 PRELIMINARY CONSIDERATIONS

2.1 DECIDING TO PATENT

A range of factors are taken into account when considering whether to patent an invention. A potential applicant will need to consider the benefits that may flow from patenting. Perhaps the most obvious benefit is that because a patent confers an exclusive right to make, use, and sell the patented invention for a period of up to 20 years, it provides the owner with associated monopoly profits. It should be noted that the economic value derived from a patent will vary according to the type of invention in question. For example, where competitors are able to develop new ways of achieving the same result that fall outside the scope of the monopoly (known as 'inventing around the patent'), the economic benefits are reduced. Another benefit associated with patenting flows from the fact that patenting translates inventions from the world of science and technology to the world of commerce. In so doing, patenting enables inventions to be included on the balance sheets of organizations and on the research returns of publicly funded institutions. This may be particularly important in attracting funds to pay for research.

Other less obvious benefits flow from patenting. These include the esteem or symbolic capital that flow from being recognized as an inventor. Indeed, in some cases it is the romantic appeal of becoming an inventor that encourages a person to enter into the patent system in the first place.[1] Another benefit of patenting is that it enables manufacturers to enhance the image of their goods. By advertising that their goods are patented, sellers are able to represent to consumers that they are buying cutting-edge technologies. There is also a sense in which the mere fact that something has been patented carries with it the belief that the product has public approval; this has been particularly important in relation to the patenting of life forms.

The benefits that flow from patenting need to be weighed against the associated costs. The financial costs of patenting include patent agent fees, the administrative charges imposed by national and international institutions as a condition of grant,[2] and (where a patent is sought in a non-English-speaking country) the costs of translation. A 2012 study commissioned by the European Patent Office (EPO) showed that the average cost of obtaining a patent directly at the EPO was €32,000.[3] Non-financial costs, such as the time and effort involved in transforming a practical technical idea into the form required by the patent system, also need to be taken into account. Another cost associated with patenting relates to the fact that the applicant must make their invention available to the public. While competitors may not be able to copy the patented invention, the disclosure of the invention makes it easier for them to invent around the patent. Another factor to be taken into account is whether the benefits that flow from patenting can be achieved through other means with fewer of the associated costs.[4] An important factor here is that an inventor (or owner) may be able to rely upon other techniques to protect their creations that do not require the invention to be disclosed to the public. These include contractual restrictions on the use or disclosure of the process, the law relating to breach of confidence, or non-legal techniques such as secrecy. The problem with these techniques is that they carry with them the risk that if the information is disclosed to the public (even if through a breach of contract or confidentiality), in most cases the invention becomes part of the public domain, free for all to use.[5] Another factor that may influence the decision to seek a patent is the ease with which the details of the invention can be ascertained or reverse-engineered when the invention or the products thereof are made available to the public.

Given that the decision to patent is influenced by a range of factors, it is not surprising that patenting practices vary from industry to industry. For example, in the pharmaceutical industry, where research and development costs are high and the products are readily and cheaply copied, the patent process is commonly relied on to protect inventions. In other industries, such as in the aviation field, where the expense of copying is very high, greater emphasis is placed on secrecy as a mode of protection.

2.2 ROLE OF PATENT AGENTS

It is common for decisions concerning patent applications to be made in consultation with a patent agent. Since emerging as a discrete profession during the nineteenth

---

[1] G. Myers, 'From Discovery to Invention: The Writing and Re-writing of Two Patents' (1995) 25 *SSS* 57, 59.

[2] Roland Berger Market Research on behalf of the EPO, *Study on the Cost of Patenting in Europe* (2004); EPO, 'Cost of Patenting in Europe' (1995) 26 *IIC* 650; M. Bednarek, 'Planning a Global Patent Strategy: Where to Get the Most "Bang for Your Buck"' (1995) 77 *JPTOS* 381; S. Helfgott, 'Why Must Filing in Europe Be So Costly?' (1994) 76 *JPTOS* 787.

[3] Commission Staff Working Paper, *Impact Assessment* (13 April 2012), SEC(2011) 482 final, 36.

[4] There may be a danger of another person patenting the invention. This has occasionally prompted defensive patenting, which, at one time, prompted a third of all applications in the United States: W. Davis (1947) 12 *L & CP* 796, 799–800.

[5] On the trade secret/patenting decision, see D. Munson, 'The Patent Trade Secret Decision: An Industrial Perspective' (1996) 78 *JPTOS* 689.

century,[6] patent agents have come to play a central role in the operation of the patent system. Under the European Patent Convention (EPC), a new breed of expert, the 'European patent agent', has developed to deal with the intricacies of the European patent system.[7] Patent agents normally have knowledge of the law, the patent administration process, and a particular branch of science. As well as assisting in the drafting and processing of patents, patent agents also offer advice as to whether a patent should be taken out and where and how patents are best exploited. In some cases, they are also able to litigate on behalf of patentees. In a sense, patent agents act as go-betweens who unite the technical–scientific domains with the legal and commercial.

2.3 CHOICE OF ROUTES TO GRANT

Once the decision is made to protect an invention in the United Kingdom by patent, it is then necessary to decide the particular route to take to secure grant of the patent. In particular, it is necessary to decide whether to take out a British patent or a European patent (UK).[8] In turn, it is necessary to decide whether to apply directly to the UK Intellectual Property Office (UK IPO) or the EPO, or whether it would be better to make use of the application system provided by the Patent Cooperation Treaty (PCT).[9] It should be noted that if the proposed unitary patent package is implemented, it will introduce yet another option: the unitary patent, which will provide uniform protection across 25 participating member states. The particular route that is chosen depends on a variety of factors; perhaps the most important are the countries where protection is desired.

When deciding whether to bring an application to the United Kingdom or the EPO, commercial and strategic considerations may come into play. From a commercial point of view, the primary variable is the fees charged by the respective patent offices. Because the cost of an application to the EPO is greater than to the UK IPO, if an applicant only wishes to file in the United Kingdom or in a few countries, it will be cheaper for them to apply to the respective national offices. There comes a point, however, where the cumulative cost of applying to several national offices will exceed the cost of a European application.[10]

---

[6] See D. Van Zyl Smit, 'Professional Patent Agents and the Development of the English Patent System' (1985) 13 *Int J Sociol L* 79; H. Dutton, *The Patent System and Inventive Activity during the Industrial Revolution 1750–1852* (1984), ch. 5; F. Kittel, 'Register of Patent Agents: A Historical Review' (1986–87) 16 *CIPAJ* 195.

[7] See EPC 2000, Arts 133–134a; L. Osterborg, 'The European Patent Attorney: A New Profession' (1994) 25 *IIC* 313.

[8] Applications to the EPO and UK IPO are alternatives, so a patentee cannot have patents via both mechanisms. To prevent this, PA 1977, s. 73(2), requires the Comptroller to revoke a UK patent where there is a European patent (UK) for the same invention, having the same priority date, which was applied for by the same applicant. Before revocation, the patentee is given an opportunity to justify holding two patents: PA 1977, s. 73(3), amended by CDPA 1988, Sch. 5, para. 19.

[9] There are four routes available to get a patent for the United Kingdom: directly to the UK IPO; indirectly to the UK IPO via the PCT; directly to the EPO; or indirectly to the EPO via the PCT. See *AstraZeneca/Priorities from India*, G 2/02 and G 3/02 [2004] *OJ EPO* 483 (not possible to claim priority for a European patent from first publication in India by way of TRIPS, because India was not a party to PCT).

[10] While translation costs have been a significant consideration in the decision whether to file for a European patent or a national patent, this became less important after 1 May 2008, when the London Agreement became operational.

Applicants may also be influenced by strategic considerations when they are considering whether to apply to the EPO or to national offices. An important factor relates to the fact that although the substantive law of the national systems and the EPC are largely the same, there are a number of other important differences.[11] In particular, while the EPC has a full examination system, some national offices do not require examination at all,[12] some allow for deferred examination, and some require patent agents to provide the examination service, while others will only reject applications on limited grounds (such as novelty).[13] Another factor that may influence the route taken is the relative vulnerability of the patent. In particular, while a national patent can only be challenged in national tribunals, the EPC allows for a central challenge to be made against a European patent (which takes the form of an 'opposition' to the grant and can be brought within the nine-month period after grant).[14] If a would-be-patentee believes that the application is likely to be challenged, the applicant might prefer to maximize the survival chances of the patent by registering in a range of national offices rather than to risk the possibility of a successful central attack, which would deprive the applicant of protection in all of the designated states.

Similar factors will influence inventors when they are considering whether to apply directly to the UK IPO or the EPC, or whether they want to make use of the international filing system provided by the PCT.[15] While the PCT does not issue patents, it does provide an alternative starting point by which both UK and European patents (UK) can be obtained.[16] Under the PCT,[17] an international application can be made to the patent office of one of the contracting states, which is called the 'receiving office'.[18] The application must contain a request, a description, at least one claim, drawings (where appropriate), and an abstract.[19] Prior to 1 January 2004, applicants also had to designate the states in which protection was sought.[20] This is no longer necessary,

[11] Early versions of the EPC proposed a two-stage approach: a provisional grant, which was subject only to formal examination and novelty report, followed by the possibility of confirmation as a final European patent within five years at the behest of applicant or a third party. See G. Oudemans, *The Draft European Patent Convention* (1963), 53–60, 164–76.

[12] There is no examination in Belgium, the Netherlands, Switzerland, or Ireland. On the latter, see *Rajan v. Minister for Industry and Commerce* [1988] 14 *FSR* 9; A. Parkes, 'The Irish Patent Act 1992' (1991–92) 21 *CIPAJ* 426.

[13] For example, the French Patent Office will not refuse on grounds of lack of inventive step: Law of 2 January 1968, Art. 16; J. Schmidt-Szalewski, 'Non-obviousness as a Requirement of Patentability in French Law' (1992) 23 *IIC* 725. For Germany, see E. Fischer, 'The New German Patent Procedure: From the View of a Corporate Patent Department' (1971) 2 *IIC* 277.   [14] EPC 2000, Arts 99–101.

[15] See Chapter 14, section 4.6.1, pp. 416–17; D. Perrott, 'The PCT in Use' [1982] *EIPR* 67; B. Bartels, 'Patent Cooperation Treaty: The Advantages for the Applicant in the UK' (1983) 13 *CIPAJ* 3; J. Cartiglia, 'The Patent Cooperation Treaty: A Rational Approach to International Patent Filing' (1994) 76 *JPTOS* 261; J. Anglehart, 'Extending the International Phase of PCT Applications' (1995) 77 *JPTOS* 101.

[16] This was signed in 1970 and came into operation from 1978. As of 1 May 2018, there were 152 contracting parties. PA 1977, s. 89, gives statutory effect to some of the Treaty's provisions.

[17] PCT, Art. 3.

[18] The receiving office retains one copy of the application, transmits another to the WIPO, and sends a third to an international search authority (ISA). The receiving office checks to ensure that a filing date should be granted (Art. 14) and that appropriate fees have been paid. The ISA conducts a search and reports its findings to the WIPO: PCT, Art. 15. The application can then be amended within two months—PCT, Art. 19; PCT Regs, r. 46—and it and the search report are then communicated to the patent offices of the designated states: PCT, Art. 20. The application must be published after the expiry of 18 months from the priority date: PCT, Art. 21(2).

[19] PCT Regs, rr 4–8.

[20] On the need to correct failure to designate during the international phase, see *Vapocure Technologies Application* [1990] *RPC* 1.

however, because the filing of a request automatically applies in all contracting states to the PCT (unless the applicant specifies otherwise).[21] Applicants can apply to their designated international offices for an international search and an international preliminary examination to be carried out, (this is the EPO for UK and EPO applicants).[22] At this point, the applicant can shift to the designated national offices, which will decide whether to grant national patents.[23] At this stage, the national office treats the application as if it has been filed in that office. Instead of going directly to the national stage, an applicant may ask for an international preliminary examination by an international preliminary examining authority.[24] The examining authority issues an international preliminary examination report indicating whether the invention appears to meet international standards of novelty, inventive step, or industrial applicability.[25] It should be noted that the examination is merely advisory and not binding on designated countries.[26]

The procedures are useful for countries in which the patent office is not capable of carrying out its own examination. Another factor in favour of the PCT is convenience. Rather than having to apply in each individual country, a single application can be submitted to a relevant PCT body. The PCT is also attractive because of the lengthy period between the initial application to the international office and the time when the application is forwarded to the relevant national offices, at which time the expensive process of translation must be completed.

3 FEATURES OF THE PATENT APPLICATION PROCESS

Before looking in detail at the procedures for grant of a patent, it may be helpful to highlight some of the key features of the UK and EPO patent application processes.[27]

3.1 REQUIREMENT OF REGISTRATION

Registration has long been a prerequisite for grant of a patent in the United Kingdom. In modern times, this is largely explained by reference to the type of monopoly that a patent confers. The decision to make patent protection dependent upon registration is said to result from the fact that patents confer an absolute monopoly that enables the patentee to prevent all others from practising the invention. This is the case even if the infringer developed the same invention independently from the patented invention. Consequently, as a matter of fairness, it is necessary to have a register that is open to the public. This

---

[21] PCT Regs, r. 53.7.

[22] There are 22 ISAs and international preliminary examining authorities (IPEAs).

[23] At 30 months after the priority date, the national stage begins, by formally initiating prosecution in the designated states, filing translations, and paying fees as necessary.

[24] PCT, Ch. II; PCT, Art. 22 (provides for a minimum period of 30 months, save in respects of a handful of countries who derogated from this requirement).   [25] PCT, Art. 35(2).

[26] PCT, Art. 33.

[27] The Strasbourg Agreement concerning International Patent Classification 1971 (which the United Kingdom joined on 7 October 1975) has led to a degree of uniformity in the presentation of patent documents. See A. Wittmann, R. Schiffels, and M. Hill, *Patent Documentation* (1979), 124–34.

ensures that third parties are able to ascertain whether they are infringing someone else's rights. The process of filing also helps to establish the priority of the invention and is a prerequisite to systems of pre-grant examination such as those that operate in the United Kingdom and EPO.

3.2 FIRST-TO-FILE

Most patent systems, including that of the United Kingdom and the EPC, operate on the basis that the first person to file an (acceptable) application for an invention should be granted a patent over the invention. The fact that patents are granted via a system of registration does not necessarily mean that the patent ought to be granted to the first person to file an application.[28]

While the first-to-file system may be incompatible with a regime of intellectual property predicated on natural rights, it avoids the need to consider difficult questions about who was the first person to have a particular idea or to reduce the idea to a working model (as occurs in first-to-invent systems).[29] Instead, the first-to-file system replaces such investigations with an administrative practice that delivers rough, but simple, justice.[30] The first-to-file system is also justified on the basis that it provides inventors with an incentive to disclose (or a reward for having disclosed) the invention: the first applicant to disclose the invention obtains the patent.[31] As we will see, the adoption of a first-to-file system has certain consequences that need to be taken into account later in the grant process.[32]

3.3 EXAMINATION

Another notable feature of the patent application processes in the United Kingdom and the EPO is that applications are subject to a full examination.[33] That is, all applications are examined to ensure that they comply with the formalities of filing, as well as the requirements of subject matter, novelty, non-obviousness, and sufficiency.

For most of their long history, British patents were granted without examination. The question whether examination as a prerequisite for grant should be introduced into the United Kingdom was considered and rejected on a number of occasions during the nineteenth century.[34] One of the main arguments against examination was that it would have made the recognition of property rights subject to the discretion of government officials.

---

[28] On 16 March 2013, the United States changed from first-to-invent to first-to-file: The America Invents Act of 2011 (Leahy-Smith Act, or AIA), Public Law 112-29.

[29] The preference for a first-to-file system, however, does not avoid all legal investigations into who was the 'inventor'. This is because inventors are entitled to be named on the patent, even if they are not the applicant: Paris Convention 4*ter* PA 1977, s. 13; EPC 2000, Arts 62, 81. If the inventor is not designated, the application is treated as having been withdrawn: PA 1977, s. 13(2); EPC 2000, Art. 90(3); EPC 2000 Regs, r. 57. However, there is no investigation into the correctness of the designation. Where the designated inventor and the applicant are different people, the practice is to inform the inventor of the application, thereby enabling the inventor to raise any objection that they may have. Procedures are also available for inventors to be omitted from published versions of the application if they wish: EPC 2000 Regs, r. 20(1).

[30] T. Nicolai, 'First-to-File vs First-to-Invent: A Comparative Study Based on German and United States Patent Law' (1972) 3 *IIC* 103; T. Roberts, 'Paper, Scissors, Stone' [1998] *EIPR* 89.

[31] For arguments for first-to-file, see Anon., 'Prior Art in Patent Law' (1959) 73 *Harv L Rev* 369, 380.

[32] See section 5, p. 451, and Chapter 20, section 4, p. 614.

[33] G. Smith, 'Why Examine?' (1982) 12 *CIPAJ* 9.   [34] (1864) 29 *PP* 321; (1871) 10 *PP* 603; (1872) 11 *PP* 395.

Examination would also have added to the cost and time of obtaining a patent[35]—changes that would have run counter to the spirit of much nineteenth-century reform, which aimed to simplify the system and to reduce the 'taxes' imposed on inventors.

After much deliberation, a limited system of examination was introduced into the United Kingdom in 1905.[36] An important factor that helped to support the case for examination was the finding of the 1901 Fry Committee that 40 per cent of the patents registered at the time were for inventions that had already been described in previous patents.[37] Because these patents would not have withstood litigation, they were theoretically harmless. Nevertheless, it was believed that they deterred others from working in the same field. Moreover, the lack of examination brought the system into disrepute and undermined the trust placed in valid patents. For some, the prospect of an examination system sanctioned and controlled by the state was attractive because it would have created a legal (and thus a commercial) presumption that any patents that had been granted were valid. Another factor that supported the case for examination was that fears of arbitrary or self-seeking exercise of discretion on behalf of those in charge of the register had been allayed by a growing trust in bureaucracy[38]—a trend that was cemented by the increased use of experts.[39]

The limited examination system established in 1905 was maintained until the passing of the Patents Act 1977, when the current full examination system was introduced.[40] While the examination system currently forms an integral part of the British patent system, there may come a time when the United Kingdom may wish to follow other countries in the EPC who, in the face of falling national applications, have abandoned full examination as part of national procedure. If this were to happen, it would provide applicants with greater choice, the alternatives being an unexamined national patent or an examined European patent.

3.4 AMENDMENT

Another notable feature of the grant system is that applicants are able to alter or amend their initial applications both during and after grant of the patent. The decision to give patentees the opportunity to amend their patents recognizes that the first-to-file system may encourage applicants to register without a full understanding of the invention or complete familiarity with the relevant prior art. It is also based on the fact that subsequent examination, either by the applicant or the patent office, may reveal the existence of a

---

[35] The most common criticism of examination today is delay. Many patent systems operate with time limits in an attempt to reduce such problems. In the United Kingdom, examination should occur not later than four years and six months from priority; PA 1977, s. 20; PR 2007, r. 30.

[36] Patents Act 1902. The Office began to search British patents in 1905.

[37] *Report of the Committee Appointed by the Board of Trade to Inquire into the Working of the Patents Act on Certain Specified Questions* (Cd. 506) (1901) 23 *PP* 59, 602, [6] (p. 4 of the report) (indicating that 42 per cent of the sample from the previous three years was wholly or partially invalid).

[38] EPC 2000, Art. 113, gives an applicant whose patent has been refused an opportunity to comment. This is of fundamental importance for ensuring a fair procedure and reflects the generally accepted notion of a right to be heard. The examiner must give the grounds for refusal—that is, the essential reasoning—sufficient for the case to be properly understood. See *NEC/Opportunity to comment*, T 951/92 [1996] *EPOR* 371, [1996] *OJ EPO* 53.

[39] *Electromagnetic Geoservices v. Petroleum Geo-Services* [2016] *EWHC* 881 (Pat), [6]–[10] (discussing the advantages of having a neutral scientific adviser to assist the court in understanding the technology in issue).

[40] Prior to the 1977 Act, examination was for patentability and novelty only. Examination for inventive step was introduced by the 1977 Act.

piece of prior art that requires the application to be reformulated to ensure its validity.[41] Similarly, an applicant may wish to amend the application (as filed) in light of subsequent experiments carried out on the invention. Where a patent is found to be partially valid,[42] it is desirable that the patent be amended by the deletion of the invalid claims, which otherwise might remain as a potential nuisance to industry.[43] At the end of this chapter, we look at the situations in which applicants and patentees are able to amend their applications and the restrictions under which they operate.

4 PROCEDURE FOR GRANT

The basic procedure for application for a patent to the UK Intellectual Property Office is roughly the same as at the European Patent Office. In this section, we provide an overview of some of the more important features of those processes (see Fig. 16.1).

4.1 WHO IS ENTITLED TO APPLY FOR A PATENT?

There are virtually no restrictions on who may apply for a patent. In contrast with the rules relating to copyright and trade marks, there are no limitations as regards the nationality or residency of the applicant.[44] Where appropriate, an application for a patent may be made by two or more applicants. While anyone may apply for a patent, there are a number of restrictions placed on those who are entitled to be granted a patent. The issue of entitlement to grant is dealt with later.[45]

During the application process, disputes over who is entitled to a patent that may subsequently be granted are dealt with differently, depending on whether it is a British or a European application.[46] For the purposes of proceedings before the EPO, it is assumed that the applicant is entitled to exercise the right to the European patent; issues about entitlement are determined elsewhere.[47] The EPO will only take account of the question of entitlement if a decision is made by an appropriate national court that a person other than the applicant is entitled to the patent.[48]

---

[41] G. Aggus, 'The Equities of Amendment' (1980–81) 10 CIPAJ 389. For the history of reissues in the United States, see K. Dood, 'Pursuing the Essence of Inventions: Reissuing Patents in the 19th Century' (1991) 32 Technol & Cult 999. For the history of 'intervening rights', see P. Federico, 'Intervening Rights in Patent Re-issues' (1962) 30 Geo Wash L Rev 603. [42] PA 1977, s. 63(1).

[43] Van der Lely v. Bamfords [1964] RPC 54, 73–4 (Pearson LJ).

[44] PA 1977, s. 7(1); EPC 2000, Art. 58; cf. Paris, Art. 2(1), which requires members to provide the same protection as nationals receive to nationals of any other country in the Union.

[45] See Chapter 21.

[46] Under EPC 2000, Art. 60, the right to a European patent belongs to the inventor or his or her successor in title. The rights of employees depend on the law of the state in which they are mainly employed or, if that cannot be determined, that in which the employer has its place of business. See Chapter 21, section 3.2, pp. 629–35.

[47] EPC 2000, Art. 60(3). See G. Le Tallec, 'The Protocol on Jurisdiction and the Recognition of Decisions in Respect of the Right to the Grant of a European Patent' (1985) 16 IIC 318; Kirin-Amgen/Erythropoietin, T 412/93 [1995] EPOR 629 (questions of entitlement could not be considered in opposition proceedings). For discussion of problems that arise when validity proceedings run concurrently at the EPO and UK courts, see P. England, 'Parallel Patent Proceedings between the European Patent Office and UK Courts' (2015) 10 JIPLP 509. On the criteria used to decide when national proceedings should be stayed, see IP Com v. HTC Europe [2013] EWCA Civ 1496, [68]; Acatvis Group v. Pharmacia [2014] EWHC 2265 (Pat).

[48] Three courses of action are available: prosecution of the application in place of the applicant; filing of a new application; or a request that the application be refused: EPC 2000, Art. 61(1). See Latchways/Unlawful applicant, G 3/92 [1995] EPOR 141.

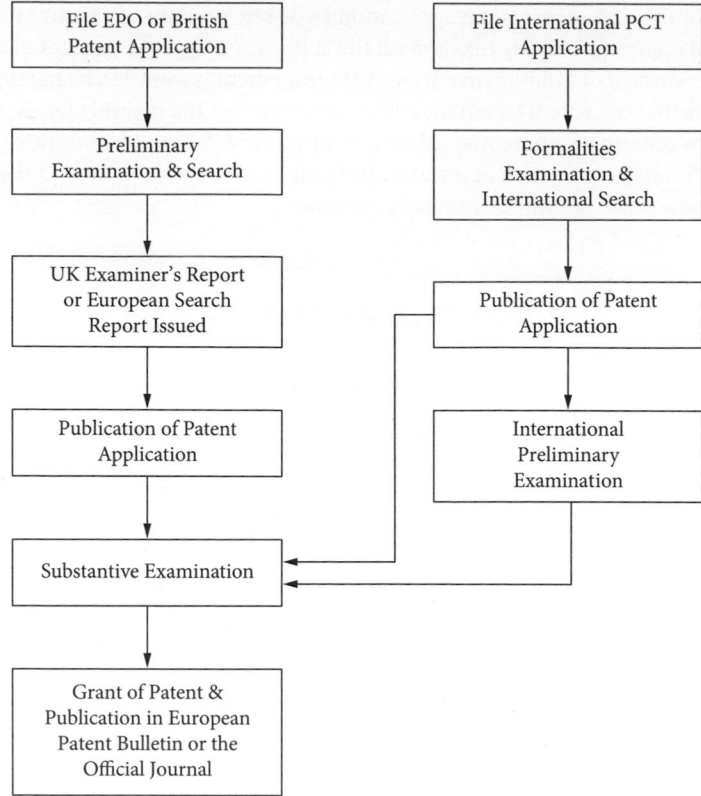

Fig. 16.1 Flowchart of a patent application

As with the EPC, an applicant for a British patent is presumed to be entitled to grant of the patent.[49] However, in contrast with the EPC, the Comptroller is able to consider issues of entitlement that are raised before grant.[50] If a person 'properly entitled' to a patent decides to submit a new application, they may be able to use the wrongful applicant's priority date.[51] The Comptroller of the UK IPO is given similar powers to determine entitlement where a patent has already been granted.[52]

4.2 FILING A PATENT APPLICATION

Applications for British patents are filed online, in person, or by post. The contents of all documents included in an application for a British patent must be in English or Welsh.[53] Applications for a European patent may be filed either with the EPO in Munich

---

[49] PA 1977, s. 7(4).

[50] PA 1977, ss 8 and 12. See T. Gold, 'Entitlement Disputes: A Case Review' [1990] *EIPR* 382.

[51] PA 1977, s. 8(3).

[52] PA 1977, s. 37. See *James Industries Patent* [1987] RPC 235 (applicant's claim for share of patent for net beds rejected in absence of contract evincing clear understanding that patent rights were to be shared); *Nippon* [1987] *RPC* 120; *Norris' Patent* [1988] *RPC* 159.

[53] PA Rules, r. 14(1).

or in The Hague, or with national patent offices in the contracting states.[54] Unlike the EPC 1973, under which applications had to be in one of three official languages and the text of the patent had to be in that language, the EPC 2000 allows European patent applications to be filed in any language.[55] If the application is not made in an official language of the EPO (English, German, or French), the applicant is given two months in which to translate the application into an official language.[56]

Applicants at the UK IPO and the EPO are faced with the choice of either making a 'full application' or alternatively of taking advantage of the facility that allows for 'early filing'.[57] A full application for a patent must contain a request for grant of a patent, a description of the invention, one or more claims, any drawings referred to in the description or the claims, and an abstract.[58]

In order to provide applicants with greater flexibility, the patent systems provide that instead of filing a full application, applicants are able to make an 'early filing'.[59] Early filing occurs where an applicant supplies an indication that a patent is sought, information identifying the applicant, and a description of the invention.[60] Essentially, early filing provides applicants with a 12-month breathing space in which they can decide whether they wish to pursue a patent, decide whether they are able to carry out further experiments on the invention, look for investors, and consider the countries in which they wish to seek patents.[61]

The applicant must file the claims and abstract within 12 months of the early filing (the so-called 'filing date') if an early application is not to lapse.[62] While early filing offers a breathing space 'for completion of the formalities and the interim preservation of priority', early filing was not intended 'to provide a cover for making improvements in the disclosed invention by bringing in new material not covered by the disclosure whilst preserving for it the priority conferred by the original filing date'.[63]

4.3 PRIORITY DATE OF THE APPLICATION

The initial application is important in that it sets in play the sequence of steps that may ultimately result in the grant of the patent. Irrespective of whether the filing is an early filing or a full application, filing is also important since it establishes the 'priority date' of the patent. In the absence of a claim to an earlier date, the priority date is the filing date of the application.[64] As we will see, the priority date is the date when the novelty,

---

[54] EPC 2000, Art. 75(1)(2). On designation costs, see O. Bossung, 'The Return of European Patent Law to the European Union' (1996) 27 *IIC* 287, 296. On the international status, see *Lenzing* [1997] *RPC* 245.

[55] EPC 2000, Art. 14(2); EPC 2000 Regs, r. 40.   [56] EPC 2000 Regs, rr 6(1), 58.

[57] Patent filing fees at the UK IPO were abolished from 1 October 2000.

[58] PA 1977, s. 14(2); EPC 2000, Art. 78(1); PCT, Arts 3–7; PCT Regs, rr 3–8, 10, 11, 13, and 32; *A. C. Edwards v. Acme Signs* [1990] *RPC* 621, 642. See also *Xerox/Amendments*, T 133/85 [1988] *OJ EPO* 441, 448. Patent applications must also designate the inventor: PA 1977, s. 13; PA Rules, r. 10; EPC 2000, Art. 81; EPC 2000 Regs, rr 19–21; *EPO Guidelines*, A–III, 1.

[59] PA 1977, s. 15(1); EPC 2000, Art. 80; EPC 2000 Regs, r. 49; PCT, Arts 11 and 14(2); PCT Regs, rr 7, 14.1(b), 15.4(a), 16, 20.2(a)(iii).

[60] It is no longer necessary for applications to the EPO to include one or more claims: EPC 2000 Regs, r. 40(1); see also EPC 2000 Regs, r. 57(c); PCT, Art. 4(ii).

[61] To clear up application backlogs and to speed up clearance times, the Intellectual Property Act 2014 allows the UK IPO to share information on unpublished patent applications: IP Act 2014, s. 18, which introduces the new PA 1977, s. 118(3)(aa), (3A)–(3C).

[62] See *Antiphon's Application* [1984] *RPC* 1, 9. On late submission of drawings, see *VEB Kombinat Walzlager* [1987] *RPC* 405.   [63] *Asahi Kaei Kogyo* [1991] *RPC* 485, 526 (HL) (Lord Oliver).

[64] PA 1977, s. 5; PA Rules, r. 6; EPC 2000, Arts 87–9. An application for which a date of filing has been accorded under the PCT is treated as an application for a patent under the 1977 Act.

inventiveness, and other aspects of the invention are assessed. As such, it is often of critical importance for the validity of the patent. The priority date is of practical significance
in several other ways. First, because novelty is assessed as of the priority date, once the
date is established, an applicant is able to exploit their invention without fear of invalidating the patent. Second, applicants are able to use the priority date established by filing in
the United Kingdom or EPO as the priority date for applications in other countries.

4.4 PRELIMINARY EXAMINATION AND SEARCH

The next formal step in the process of grant is the preliminary examination and search.[65]
Once the full application has been filed (description, claims, and abstract) and the application fee paid (if any), the Comptroller will refer the application to preliminary examination. Once preliminary examination is over, the applicant must request a search.[66]

On preliminary examination, the application is examined to see whether it complies
with certain formal requirements.[67] These are that the application contains a request for
grant, a description of the invention, one or more claims, any drawings referred to in
the description or claim, and an abstract. In addition, the preliminary examination also
ensures that the inventor(s) have been identified and that the application accords with
other formalities (such as meeting the language requirements).[68]

Applicants are alerted to any problems that may have been identified in the preliminary
examination in a report that is issued to them.[69] Applicants are then given the opportunity to respond to the report or, if necessary, to amend their application to overcome the
problems. If an applicant fails to change their application in a manner that satisfies the
respective patent offices, the application may be refused.

The examiner or (at the EPO) the Search Division also carries out a limited search of
the existing literature for relevant prior art—that is, information similar to the invention
in question.[70] The aim of the search is to identify the documents that may be used at the
substantive examination stage when the application is examined for novelty and inventive step.[71] The applicant is informed of the findings of the search by way of an examiner's
report or, as it is known at the EPO, the 'European search report'.[72]

As well as identifying the documents that may be relied upon when the application
is examined for novelty and inventive step, the application is also examined during the
search stage to ensure that it relates to one invention or to a group of inventions that form
a single inventive concept.[73] That is, it is examined to ensure that it meets the requirement
of 'unity of invention'.[74]

---

[65] PA 1977, ss 15A and 17; PA Rules, rr 23, 27; EPC 2000, Art. 90;PCT, Arts 14, 15, 17, and 18; PCT Regs,
rr 26–30, 33, 37, 38, 40, and 43.

[66] PA 1977, ss 15A(1) and 17(1). Under the EPC 2000, the search and examination stages of the application
process were combined.

[67] The receiving office retains one copy of the application, transmits another to the WIPO, and sends a
third to an ISA. The receiving office checks to ensure that a filing date should be granted and that appropriate
fees have been paid: EPC 2000, Art. 90.

[68] PA Rules, r. 25; EPC 2000 Regs, r. 40, 55; *EPO Guidelines*, A–II, [4].

[69] PA Rules, r. 29; EPC 2000 Regs, rr 57.   [70] PA 1977, s. 17(1); EPC 2000, Art. 92; EPC 2000 Regs, rr 61–4.

[71] PA 1977, s. 17(4)(5); EPC 2000, Art. 92; EPC 2000 Regs, r. 61(1).

[72] PA 1977, s. 17(5); EPC 2000 Regs, r. 65.

[73] PA 1977, ss 14(5)(d) and (6), 17(6); PA Rules, r. 16; EPC 2000, Art. 82; EPC 2000 Regs, r. 64.

[74] Lack of unity is not a ground for revocation: PA 1977, s. 26; PA Rules, r. 16. There is no EPC equivalent,
but see EPC 2000, Art. 82.

Where two or more inventions are claimed in the one application, the application will fail to comply with the requirement of unity of invention unless it can be shown that the inventions form a single inventive concept.[75] To do this, it is necessary to show that the inventions share the same 'special technical features'. Special technical features are the features that define the contribution that each of the claimed inventions considered as a whole makes to the claimed advance over the prior art.[76] There are at least two reasons for limiting patent applications to a single inventive concept. The first is that patent protection should not be available for two inventions for the price of one. The second, and more important, is that to allow more than one inventive concept to be included in a single patent is likely to undermine the administrative systems for locating, identifying, and searching for patents.

If it is found that the application contains more than one invention, the search is limited to the first invention that is set out in the claims.[77] In the face of a finding that an application contains more than one patent, applicants may simply pursue a patent for one of the inventions. Alternatively, they may divide the initial application into two (or more) fresh applications. So long as additional fees are paid and no new material is added, they may use the priority date for the original application for the new applications.[78]

Along with the search report, the EPO also provides applicants with a report into the patentability of the invention. This is called the 'Extended European Search Report'.[79] The report is to help applicants decide whether to proceed to the substantive examination of the application. If the application decides to progress, the report becomes the first examination report.

4.5 PUBLICATION

The next stage in the grant process is the publication of the patent application. The application will be published and made available for public inspection 18 months from the date of filing.[80] This process informs third parties that the application has been made. While third parties are not able to oppose the grant of a patent at this stage, they are able to make observations as to whether the patent should be granted.[81]

The documents published in the United Kingdom and the EPO include the description, claims, and drawings (if any) that have been filed. In the United Kingdom, the publication must include the original claims and any amendments that have been made to the claims, as well as any new claims. The UK IPO is also given power not to publish parts of the application that are offensive or disparaging,[82] or which might be prejudicial to

---

[75] PA 1977, s. 14(5)(d) and (6); PA Rules, r. 16; EPC 2000, Art. 82; EPC 2000 Regs, r. 64.

[76] PA Rules, r. 16(2); EPC 2000 Regs, r. 44. Technical features 'are the physical features which are essential to the invention'; with respect to a product, these are 'the physical parameters of the entity'; in relation to a process, the technical features are 'the physical steps which define such activity': *Mobil Oil/Friction Reducing additive*, G 2/88 [1990] *EPOR* 73, [1990] *OJ EPO* 93, 100. See also *May & Baker v. Boots* [1950] 67 RPC 23, 50; *Biogen v. Medeva* [1995] RPC 25, 92–3; *Bayer/Benzyl esters*, T 110/82 [1983] *OJ EPO* 274; *Siemens/Unity*, G 1/91 [1992] *OJ EPO* 253.

[77] *Hollister's Application* [1983] RPC 10, *Non-payment of further search fees*, G 2/92 [1993] *OJ EPO* 591.

[78] Failure to meet an objection of lack of unity is frequently remedied by the making of divisional applications: EPC 2000 Regs, r. 36; PA 1977, s. 18(3); PA Rules, r. 31(4)(b)(i).   [79] EPC 2002, r. 62.

[80] PA 1977, s. 16; PA Rules, r. 26; EPC 2000, Art. 93; EPC 2000 Regs, rr 67–70; PCT, Arts 21, 29; PCT Regs, rr 9.1, 48.   [81] PA 1977, s. 21; PA Rules, r. 33; EPC 2000, Art. 115; EPC 2000 Regs, r. 114.

[82] PA 1977, s. 16(2); PA Rules, r. 33.

national security.[83] At the EPO, the abstract and (where available) the search report are also published.[84]

Publication is important for two reasons. First, since the act of publication discloses the invention to the public, an unwanted publication may prevent applicants from relying on other ways of protecting their invention (such as confidentiality). Similarly, once a patent application has been published, the application can no longer be resubmitted (whereas if the application is withdrawn prior to publication, it is possible to make a later application).[85] Second, if the patent proceeds to grant, the date of publication is the date from which the patentee is able to sue for infringement of the patent. This is on the condition that the act would have infringed both the patent as granted and the claims in the form in which they were published.[86] In these circumstances, the patentee is only entitled to damages for infringement in the period between publication and grant.

As mentioned, a third party may respond to the publication of the application by submitting 'observations' to the patent office (at any time before grant).[87] Such observations should focus on whether the invention is a patentable invention.[88] Observations may be made by 'any person' and must be submitted in writing accompanied by appropriate reasons. The Comptroller of the UK IPO is instructed to consider the observations, whereas the EPO is merely required to communicate the observations to the proprietor, who, in turn, is permitted to comment on them. If the EPO wishes, it can take account of such observations when examining the application.[89] In both fora, the party submitting the observations does not become party to the proceedings and so will not be asked to any hearing, nor be made to pay the costs of any proceedings.

4.6 SUBSTANTIVE EXAMINATION

Once the requirements of preliminary examination and search have been satisfied, the next stage in the application process is the 'substantive examination'.[90] The applicant must request this within six months from the date of publication of the application or, at the EPO, the publication of the search report.[91] In some situations, it is possible for an applicant to request that the examination process is accelerated or fast-tracked.[92]

---

[83] PA 1977, s. 22 (no EPC 2000 equivalent). PA 1977, s. 23, provides that British residents who file an application (whether as an agent or applicant) for military technology or inventions which might prejudice national security or public safety, must file in the UK Intellectual Property Office first (and wait six weeks) or seek the Comptroller's permission to file abroad (including the EPO). If it does cause such prejudice then directions may be imposed to restrict publication or overseas filings.

[84] EPC 2000 Regs, r. 68(1).

[85] EPC 2000, Art. 128, specifies that the application prior to this point is confidential and may be viewed by third parties only with the consent of the applicant.

[86] PA 1977, s. 69(2); EPC 2000, Art. 67; PCT, Art. 29.   [87] PA 1977, s. 21; EPC 2000, Art. 115.

[88] That is, matters covered in PA 1977, ss 21(1), 1; EPC 2000, Arts 115, 52.   [89] EPC 2000, Art. 114.

[90] PA 1977, s. 18(1); PA Rules, rr 28, 29; EPC 2000, Art. 94; EPC 2000 Regs, rr 70, 71. Under the PCT, the national stage begins 30 months after the priority date by formally initiating prosecution in the designated states, filing translations, and paying fees as necessary. Instead of going straight into the national stage, an applicant may ask for an international preliminary examination by an examining authority: PCT, Art. 31. This is dealt with in Ch. II of the Convention. The IPEA establishes an international preliminary examination report indicating whether the invention appears to meet international standards of novelty, inventive step, or industrial applicability: PCT, Art. 35(2). Such examination is merely advisory and not binding on designated countries: PCT, Art. 33.

[91] PA Rules, r. 28(2); EPC 2000 Regs, r. 70(1). This distinction is not of great significance given that, in the United Kingdom, an applicant should receive the search report before the date of 'early' publication.

[92] In the United Kingdom, see *Relaxation of requirements for PCT (UK) Fast Track Practice Notice* (8 June 2012). For the EPO, see, e.g., 'Patent Prosecution Highway pilot programme between the Trilateral Offices based on PCT work products' (2012) *OJ EPO* 89.

The purpose of the substantive examination is to ascertain whether the application complies with the requirements of the Patents Act 1977 or, in the case of the EPO, the EPC 2000.[93] Unlike the preliminary examination, which is mainly concerned with ensuring the presence of certain documents, during the substantive examination the application is scrutinized to ensure that it is valid in all aspects. In particular, the invention is examined to ensure that it does not consist of subject matter excluded from patentability—that is, that it is novel, involves an inventive step, and is industrially applicable. The substantive examination also ensures that the application has been sufficiently disclosed, that the claims are concise, and that they are supported by the description.

The substantive examination takes the form of a dialogue between the examiner and the applicant. When examining the application, the examiner should consider whether if the matter in issue were to be fully investigated at trial with the aid of expert evidence, it would be resolved in the applicant's favour.[94] After the examination has taken place, the examiner draws up a report, which outlines any objections to the application that have been identified. The report is supplied to the applicant, who is given an opportunity to comment on the objections, often in the hope of persuading the examiner that any doubts they have about the application are ill-founded. Alternatively, the applicant may respond to the objections by amending the patent application.[95] If they think it necessary, the examiners may make or require further searches. Ultimately, the dialogue may lead in the United Kingdom to a hearing before the Senior Examiner or, at the EPO, before the full Examining Division of the EPO, and from there by way of appeal to the UK Patents Court or the Boards of Appeal of the EPO.[96]

4.7 GRANT OF THE PATENT

If the respective patent office is not satisfied that the application satisfies the various requirements for grant, the application will be refused.[97] If the respective patent office is satisfied that all of the necessary requirements have been satisfied, the patent will be granted.[98] The decision to grant a patent does not take effect until the date on which it is mentioned in the *Official Journal* (for a UK patent) or the *European Patent Bulletin* (for a European patent).[99] The protection afforded by a patent can last up to 20 years from the filing date.[100] Renewal fees must be paid after four years.[101] As we will see, the protection may extend beyond the 20-year period if a supplementary protection certificate is issued. The extent of protection conferred by a patent will be considered later.[102]

The date of the grant of a European patent is also the date of its transition from a European application to a bundle of separate national rights.[103] With the exception of opposition proceedings, questions of validity and infringement are thereafter considered at a national level.[104] Once granted, a European patent (UK) is given the same level of protection as those granted by the national patent office.[105] As discussed earlier, it is no

---

[93] Substantive examinations of EPO applications are carried out in Munich, The Hague, and Berlin.

[94] *Blacklight Power v. The Comptroller-General of Patents* [2009] *RPC* 173.

[95] PA 1977, s. 18(3); EPC 2000, Art. 94(3)(4); EPC 2000 Regs, r. 71; PCT, Ch. II (preliminary examination).

[96] PA 1977, s. 97(1); EPC 2000, Arts 106–112a; EPC 2000 Regs, rr 90–96. EPC 2000, Art 112a, provides parties with the ability to petition for review by the EBA in limited circumstances.

[97] PA 1977, s. 18(3); EPC 2000, Art. 97(2); *EPO Guidelines*, C–VI, [14].

[98] PA 1977, s. 18(4); EPC 2000, Art. 97(1).   [99] PA 1977, s. 24(1); EPC 2000, Art. 97(3).

[100] PA 1977, s. 25; EPC 2000, Art. 63(1).

[101] The fees increase over time to ensure that the Registry does not become cluttered with useless patents.

[102] See Chapter 22.   [103] EPC 2000, Art. 64(1); PA 1977, s. 77.   [104] EPC 2000, Art. 64(3).

[105] PA 1977, s. 77(1)(a).

longer necessary to translate European patents in French or German into English within three months of grant at the EPO for them to be valid in the United Kingdom.[106]

4.8 REVOCATION

While the patent examination processes at the UK IPO and EPO are relatively rigorous, they are not conclusive. As such, it is possible for patents to be revoked after grant on a limited number of grounds. The grounds on which a patent may be revoked are set out in section 72 of the 1977 Act and Article 138 of the EPC 2000. These are that:

(i)   the invention is not a patentable invention;[107]

(ii) the patent was granted to a person who was not entitled to that patent;[108]

(iii) the specification of the patent does not disclose the invention clearly enough and completely enough for it to be performed by a person skilled in the art;[109] or

(iv) the material in the patent extends beyond the material in the application as filed (impermissible amendment).[110]

In addition, the UK IPO has limited power to revoke patents on its own initiative.[111]

One of the notable features of section 72 is that it says that 'any person' can apply to have a patent revoked. This has been taken to mean that there is no need for a person to have any interest, whether commercial or otherwise, in the outcome of proceedings to bring an action to revoke a patent.[112] Unlike the position under the Patents Act 1949, a person who has no interest in the revocation is nevertheless entitled to apply to have the patent revoked. As Jacob J said: 'Parliament purposively made patents vulnerable to attack from anyone.'[113]

4.9 OPPOSITION PROCEEDINGS AT THE EPO

While the grant of a European patent generally brings the European stage to an end, a central challenge can be made to the validity of the European patent in the nine-month period following grant of the patent.[114] This process, known as 'opposition', has a number of advantages over leaving decisions about the validity of patents exclusively to national offices or courts. The most obvious advantage is cost: it is cheaper to launch or defend a single attack in one place than it is to engage in revocation proceedings in each of the countries in which the patent was issued.

---

[106] See Chapter 14, section 4.1.2, pp. 403–5; EPC 2000, Art. 97(1), EPC 2000 Regs, r. 71(3), (7). Under PCT, Art. 3, an international application can be made to a patent office of one of the contracting states, which is termed the 'receiving office'. Rules 4–8 of the PCT Regs set out the contents of a filing, i.e. a request, a description, at least one claim, drawings where appropriate, and an abstract. The application must designate the states in which protection is sought.

[107] PA 1977, s. 72(1)(a); EPC 2000, Arts 138(1)(a), 52–7.

[108] PA 1977, s. 72(1)(b); EPC 2000, Art. 138(1)(e).   [109] PA 1977, s. 72(1)(c); EPC 2000, Art. 138(1)(b).

[110] PA 1977, s. 72(1)(d)–(e); EPC 2000, Art. 138(1)(c)–(d).   [111] PA 1977, s. 73.

[112] *Cairnstores v. Aktiebolaget Hassle* [2002] *FSR* 564 (there were circumstances in which the commencement of revocation proceedings might amount to an abuse of process). See also *Indupack Genentech/Third party opposition*, G 3/97 [2000] *EPOR* 8.

[113] *Oystertec's Patent* [2003] *RPC* 559, [15]; cf. PA 1949, ss 14 and 32 (an applicant for revocation had to be a 'person interested').

[114] EPC 2000, Art. 99. See generally Bossung, 'The Return of European Patent Law to the European Union' (1996) 27 *IIC* 287, 296.

Any person may file a notice of opposition. For a period, it was common for the proprietor to file oppositions in order to make post-grant amendments (which otherwise would have to be made at national level).[115] This practice has now been curtailed.[116] Opposition has to be filed within nine months from grant and must be based on one of three grounds.[117] These are that:

(i) the subject matter of the European patent is not patentable under Articles 52–57 of the EPC 2000;[118]

(ii) the European patent does not disclose the invention in a manner sufficiently clear and complete for it to be carried out by a person skilled in the art;[119] or

(iii) the subject matter of the European patent extends beyond the content of the application as filed.[120]

Any opposition to a European patent is communicated to the patent proprietor, who may contest the opposition, make observations, and/or make amendments. The opposition proceedings will determine whether the patent should be revoked, maintained, or maintained in an amended form.[121] If the proceedings result in revocation, the patent is deemed from its outset not to have had any of the effects specified in the EPC.[122]

5 AMENDMENT

As we mentioned earlier, applicants are able to alter or amend their initial application both during and after grant of the patent. *Prior to grant*, applicants are able to amend their application where the examination reveals that the formal and substantive requirements are not complied with.[123] In addition, applicants have a general power to amend their application at any time before a patent is granted.[124] The ability to amend while the application is being processed is based on a belief that it would be unreasonable to expect applicants to be fully aware of all prior art at the point when they filed their application. This is especially the case given that the patent system provides for a search and examination at a later stage.

After a patent has been granted, the owner of a patent is also able to amend their patent.[125] In addition, the Comptroller is able to instigate proceedings that may prompt such amendment.[126] Under the EPC 1973, post-grant amendment only occurred in opposition

---

[115] *Mobil Oil/Opposition by proprietor*, G 1/84 [1985] *OJ EPO* 299, [1986] *EPOR* 39; *Mobil/Admissibility*, T 550/88 [1992] *OJ EPO* 117, [1990] *EPOR* 391.

[116] *Peugeot & Citroen/Opposition by patent proprietor*, G 9/93 [1995] *EPOR* 260.

[117] EPC 2000, Art. 100. The procedure for opposition is set out in EPC 2000 Regs, rr 75–89.

[118] EPC 2000, Art. 100(a).   [119] EPC 2000, Arts 100(b), 83.

[120] EPC 2000, Arts 100(c), 123(2). On the question of whether it is possible to amend a claim by way of a disclaimer under EPC 2000, Art. 123(2), see (identical decisions) *PPG/Disclaimer*, G 1/03 [2004] *OJ EPO* 413 and *Genetic Systems/Disclaimer*, G 2/03 [2004] *OJ EPO* 448.   [121] EPC 2000, Art. 101.

[122] EPC 2000, Art. 68.

[123] PA 1977, s. 18(3); PA Rules, r. 31; EPC 2000, Art. 123(1); EPC 2000 Regs, r. 137; PCT, Ch. II (preliminary examination).

[124] PA 1977, s. 19(1); PA Rules, r. 3; EPC 2000, Art. 123(1); PCT, Arts 19 and 34(2)(b); PCT Regs, rr 46 and 66.   [125] PA 1977, ss 27(1), 72, 75; EPC 2000, Art. 105a–c.

[126] PA 1977, s. 73.

proceedings;[127] otherwise, such matters were for national law.[128] Under the EPC 2000, however, patent owners are given a general power to revoke or limit European patents after grant at the EPO.[129] Article 138(3) of the EPC 2000 also provides proprietors of European patents with the right to amend a patent in national proceedings relating to the patent's validity. As we will see, this has ramifications for the way the judicial discretion to allow amendment is exercised. Under the procedures in the United Kingdom and EPO, the application to amend is advertised so that any person may oppose it within two months. If granted, the amendment is deemed to have taken effect from the grant of the patent. Following changes in 2004, a proprietor is able to amend their patent in any proceedings in which the validity of a patent *may* (rather than *is*) be put in issue.[130] This has overcome the lacuna in the (old) legislative scheme, which made no provision in circumstances where there were infringement proceedings and amendment was desired, but validity was not in issue.[131]

5.1 RESTRICTIONS ON AMENDMENT

In order to ensure that any amendments that are made comply with the overriding aims of the patent system,[132] a number of restrictions are placed on an owner's ability to amend their application/patent. The amended patent must comply with the requirements that have to be met by all patents. These include the requirements of subject matter, novelty, and inventive step. The amended claims must also be clear and concise, be supported by the description, and relate to one invention or group of inventions that are linked to form a single inventive concept.

There are a number of other provisions that restrict an owner's ability to amend either the application or the patent. Perhaps the most important of these, with which we deal in Chapter 20, strike at the validity of the patent. Under these provisions, if the amendment introduces subject matter that was not in the original application or the amendment

---

[127] *Advanced Semiconductor Products/Limited Feature*, G 1/93 [1994] *OJ EPO* 169. Amendments in opposition proceedings are considered only where they are appropriate and necessary—i.e. that they can fairly be said to arise out of the grounds of opposition: *Mobil/Admissibility*, T 550/88 [1992] *OJ EPO* 117, [1990] *EPOR* 391, 397. For a discussion of the situations in which amended claims will be allowed at the EPO, see *Minnesota Mining and Manufacturing Company*, G 1/99 [2001] *OJ EPO* 381 (EBA); *Lubrizol Corporation*, T 525/99 [2003] *OJ EPO* 452, 457–8.

[128] *Mobil/Admissibility*, T 550/88 [1992] *OJ EPO* 117.

[129] EPC 2000, Art. 105a–c. See also Art. 1, items 51, 62, of the Act Revising the Convention on the Grant of European Patents (Munich) (29 November 2000) MR/3/00 Rev 1e (the 'EPC Revision Act').

[130] PA 1977, s. 75(1) (amended by Patents Act 2004, Sch. 2, para. 19).

[131] *Norling v. Eez Away* [1997] *RPC* 160, 165: 'All this suggests that the sooner the whole procedure of amendment of a patent is rethought and provided for by an amended statute and rules the better. Preferably, so far as European patents are concerned, there should be one, effective and cheap, procedure.' In *Boston Scientific v. Palmaz* [2000] *RPC* 631, cited at [2000] *EIPR* N–115, the Court of Appeal held that if the EPO had amended a patent 'after judgment in UK patent litigation, but before an appeal of that judgment is heard, the Court of Appeal must consider the patent as amended'.

[132] R. Krasser, 'Possibilities of Amendment of Patent Claims during the Examination Procedure' (1992) 23 *IIC* 467, 471; Gunzel, *Staking Your Claim: Claiming Options and Disclosure Requirements in European Patent Practice* (1990), 29; A. Bubb, 'Implied Added Subject Matter: A Practitioner's View of History' (1991) *CIPAJ* 444.

extends the scope of protection beyond the initial application, the amended patent is liable to be revoked.[133] In this section, we focus on the situations in which validity is not at stake.

A post-trial application to amend a patent following revocation proceedings (in which the validity of the patent was at stake) will also be refused if it would lead to a second trial on validity (primarily because procedural fairness requires the parties to put forward their cases prior to trial).[134] Another important factor that limits the owner's ability to amend their application as filed arises from the fact that post-grant amendment is at the discretion of the Comptroller and the courts.[135] The onus is on the patentee to establish that the amendment should be allowed.[136] As a result of changes made in 2004, when deciding whether to allow an amendment, the courts and the Comptroller are directed to take account of 'any relevant principles applicable' under the EPC 2000.[137]

The courts have tended to use their discretion to deny amendments where the owner has not acted innocently. As Jacob J noted: 'No patent office is there for the purpose of enabling people deliberately to impose bogus monopolies on the public.'[138] There are two situations in which the discretion has been exercised against the patentee. The first is where a patentee knowingly and deliberately obtained claims that were wider than justified by what was invented.[139] The second situation in which discretion has not been exercised is where knowing of the doubtful validity of the patent, a patentee has been slow to take action to amend.[140] In *Raleigh Cycle v. Miller*,[141] the House of Lords emphasized that a patentee who suspects that a patent is too widely drawn should amend it promptly. If they do not, the discretion to amend will be refused. Lord Normand explained that 'the public interest is injured when invalid claims are persisted in so that inventors are illegitimately warned off an area ostensibly monopolised by the claims'.[142] In this situation, patentees should either litigate or amend. However, if they choose to litigate, they should not be permitted to amend later. It is reasonable for a patentee to delay where they believed on reasonable grounds that the patent was valid.[143]

---

[133] PA 1977, ss 72(1)(d) and (e), 76; EPC 2000, Art. 138(1)(c).

[134] *Nokia v. IPCom* [2011] *EWCA Civ* 6. See D. Wilson and A. Moir, 'Court of Appeal Warns Patent Holders Defending Revocation Proceedings to "Put up in Time or Shut up" if They Wish to Propose Amendments in Their Patent Claims' [2011] *EIPR* 326.

[135] PA 1977, ss 27(1), 75(1); EPC 2000, Art 105a. The Court of Appeal confirmed the general discretion of the courts to refuse post-grant amendments in the public interest under PA 1977, s. 75, in *Kimberly-Clark Worldwide v. Procter & Gamble* [2000] *RPC* 422, 435. In so doing, it overturned Laddie J's decision in the Patents Court in *Kimberly-Clark Worldwide v. Procter & Gamble* [2000] *RPC* 424; cf. *Palmaz's European Patent (UK)* [1999] *RPC* 47, 63–5, which distinguished Laddie J on this point. For the application of the CA decision, see *Oxford Gene Technology v. Affymetrix (No. 2)* [2001] *RPC* 310 (CA). See generally P. Cliffe, 'A Sorry Case of Making Amends' [2002] *EIPR* 277.

[136] *SKF v. Evans Medical* [1989] *FSR* 561, 569; *Chevron Research Company's Patent* [1970] *RPC* 580.

[137] PA 1977, s. 75(5).

[138] *Richardson-Vicks Patent* [1995] *RPC* 561. See also *Hallen v. Brabantia* [1990] *FSR* 134, 149; *Kimberly-Clark Worldwide v. Procter & Gamble* [2000] *RPC* 422 (CA), 435.

[139] *ICI (Whyte's) Patent* [1978] *RPC* 11. In *Richardson-Vicks Patent* [1995] *RPC* 561, 568, Jacob J observed that there was little EPO jurisprudence as regards post-grant amendment in opposition proceedings. Nonetheless, he assumed that if it were to be shown that an applicant had deliberately sought to patent an unjustifiably wide claim, the EPO would refuse leave to amend. Beyond this, however, Jacob J predicted that the EPO might allow a patent to be amended. Consequently, Jacob J held that, for purposes of consistency, nothing short of really blameworthy conduct by a patentee should act as bar to amendment in the United Kingdom. See also *Kimberly-Clark Worldwide v. Procter & Gamble (No. 2)* [2001] *FSR* 339, 342–3.

[140] *SKF v. Evans* [1989] *FSR* 561, 577.   [141] (1950) 67 *RPC* 226.   [142] Ibid., 230.

[143] On occasion, the courts have suggested that delay is more justified where the patentee operates outside the United Kingdom: *Bristol Myers Company v. Manon Freres* [1973] *RPC* 836, 857; *Mabuchi Motor KK's Patent* [1996] *RPC* 387 (not blameworthy for delay when involved in worldwide litigation in which the United Kingdom was not an important country).

Another factor that regulates the way in which patents are amended arises from the fact that the courts may limit the damages that are awarded where an amended patent is infringed. There are two situations in which this may occur. If an amended application expands the claims beyond those that were reasonably to be expected from the application as it was initially published, the courts may limit the damages that are available to the patentee. The question of whether the inference is reasonable is decided objectively. As such, it does not matter what the defendant (subjectively) thought.[144] Another factor that regulates the way patents are amended arises from the fact that when the court assesses damages prior to the date of the amendment it may take into account whether the specification was framed in good faith and with reasonable skill and knowledge.[145] In practice, it is rare for the courts to find that patents were not framed in these terms.

5.2 ERRORS AND CLERICAL MISTAKES

Instead of amending a patent, a patentee may seek to have the patent altered to correct errors and clerical mistakes.[146] Such corrections take effect retroactively. The ability to correct mistakes does not conflict with the general policy of protecting third parties, which forbids amendments that extend the patent beyond the scope of the application as filed. The reason for this is that 'if the mistake was obvious, it cannot have misled'.[147]

If the request to correct a mistake concerns the description, claims, or drawings, the correction must be obvious. A correction will be obvious where it is immediately evident that nothing else would have been intended other than what is offered as the correction.[148] If there are any doubts, a correction will not be allowed. A useful example of the limits imposed on a patentee's ability to correct mistakes can be seen in *PPG Industries Patent*.[149] In this case, it was said that faced with the proposition '2 + 2 = 5', a person might readily presume that this was obviously incorrect and that, to correct the mistake, the '5' should be changed to a '4'. However, as Dillon and Slade LJJ pointed out, since an alternative solution was to change one of the '2s to a 3', in the absence of an indication as to where the mistake lay, the correction was not obvious within the meaning of the 1977 Act.

6 REFORM

There are currently a number of different plans to reform patent procedure. These relate to the proposed unitary patent, the idea that patent applicants should be required to disclose any traditional knowledge that they are using in their patents, and suggestions that aim to improve patent examination.

---

[144] *Unilever v. Chefaro* [1994] *RPC* 567, 592.

[145] PA 1977, s. 62(3). PA 1977, s. 62(3), does not apply to an account of profits: *Codex Corporation v. Racal Milgo* [1983] *RPC* 369 (CA).   [146] PA 1977, s. 117(1); PA Rules, r. 105; EPC 2000 Regs, r. 139.

[147] *Holtite v. Jost* [1979] *RPC* 81, 91 (Lord Diplock). In *Correction under Rule 88*, G3/89 [1993] *EPOR* 376, it was held by the EBA that, as a matter of construction of the EPC, the correction must not extend protection contrary to EPC 1973, Art. 123(2) (which is the same as EPC 2000, Art. 123(2)).

[148] This was the position under PA 1949, s. 31(1): *Holtite v. Jost* [1979] *RPC* 81.

[149] [1987] *RPC* 469, 478, 483.

6.1 UNITARY PATENT SYSTEM

As we saw in Chapter 14, there are plans under way to introduce a new unitary European patent, which will provide uniform protection across the 25 participating member states. While the new unitary patent which will be issued by the EPO will build upon existing procedures at the EPO, a number of changes will need to be made to the procedures by which patents are granted to allow this to happen.

6.2 TRADITIONAL KNOWLEDGE AND PRIOR INFORMED CONSENT

In recent years, there has been increased attention given to the information that applicants have to disclose in their patent applications, particularly as a way of attempting to regulate the way in which indigenous knowledge is used by patentees. Discussions are taking place at the national, community, and international levels about the possibility of requiring inventors who draw upon or utilize genetic resources in the development of their inventions to disclose information in their patent application, such as the fact that they have prior informed consent to use the genetic resources. These discussions have been prompted by Article 15 of the Convention on Biological Diversity (CBD) (which recognizes equitable benefit sharing for access providers) and by Article 8(j) of the CBD which encourages the equitable sharing of benefits arising from the use of indigenous knowledge.[150] The discussions have also been prompted by the growing concern about biopiracy and the general misuse of genetic resources in the biodiscovery process. The idea that applicants should be required to disclose information about their invention builds upon the idea that patent law has the potential to modify behaviour to promote good corporate and scientific conduct.[151] The fact that an organization might not be able to patent products derived from genetic resources if it does not have the informed consent of the access provider in advance will act as a powerful incentive for such organizations to ensure that they have the necessary prior consent. As we mentioned earlier, debates are presently taking place over whether or not prior informed consent should be incorporated into patent law, and if so, how.[152]

This question has taken on a new significance following the adoption in 2012 of the Nagoya Protocol to the CBD (discussed earlier). This is because the Protocol requires parties to adopt legislative, administrative, or policy measures to monitor and enhance transparency about the utilization of genetic resources. This system includes the designation of checkpoints at which specified information regarding prior informed consent and mutually agreed terms may be required. It envisages the establishment of a standardized international system of certificates of compliance to act as evidence of prior informed consent and mutually agreed terms. Proposals for the inclusion in the Protocol of a disclosure-of-origin system requiring disclosure of information on prior informed consent and mutually agreed terms as a condition for the grant of patent rights were not included in the final text.

---

[150] See also the *Bonn Guidelines on Access and Benefit Sharing,* adopted at the Sixth Conference of the Parties to the CBD (The Hague, 2002). These are voluntary provisions that act as a guide to the implementation of CBD, Arts 1, 8(j), 10(c), 15, 16, and 19.

[151] See B. Sherman, 'Regulating Access and Use of Genetic Resources: Intellectual Property Law and Biodiscovery' [2003] *EIPR* 301.

[152] Particularly at the CBD, the TRIPS Council, and at WIPO. See Chapter 14, section 4.6.3, pp. 419–21.

Discussions have been taking place within Europe for some time about the best way in which the goals of the CBD might be achieved.[153] The issue of prior informed consent has already been recognized in Europe in the Biotechnology Directive, albeit only in the non-binding Recitals. In particular, Recital 27 encourages patent applications to include information on the geographical origin of biological material. In turn, Recital 55 requires member states to recognize Article 8(j) of the CBD when developing laws and regulations. To date, these have had minimal impact on member states.[154]

Early responses to the Convention were not positive. At one stage, the Commission suggested that there should be a debate over the unilateral development under EC law of 'a self-standing obligation for patent applicants to disclose the origin of genetic resources'.[155] This built upon existing requirements that encourage disclosure of information—namely, enabling disclosure, disclosure of relevant prior art for novelty examination, and the disclosure of the inventors.[156] Initial proposals by the Commission were fairly modest. These provided that prior informed consent would not be treated as an additional or formal requirement for patentability; rather, the Commission suggested that failure to comply with the requirement for prior informed consent would carry consequences outside patent law. For example, it might prompt civil law claims for compensation or administrative sanctions (such as a fee for refusal to submit relevant information). The Commission was also looking at introducing a similar requirement for plant variety rights.[157] Despite the modest nature of these proposals, they were not implemented.

Discussions about the way in which European law should deal with the question of access to genetic resources and related questions were reopened following the adoption of the Nagoya Protocol. In December 2012, the European Union published a draft legislative proposal for implementation of the Protocol. A modified version was adopted by the European Union on 16 April 2014.[158] While the Union, has taken the lead in the development of legislation to implement the Protocol, it seems that this is not being done in the spirit in which the Protocol was drafted. Indeed, the original draft law was criticized for, among other things, primarily focusing on enabling economic utilization of genetic resources and traditional knowledge, and restricting its temporal scope to genetic resources and traditional knowledge accessed after the Protocol comes into force.[159] Criticism has also been made of the law's adoption of a very narrow definition of protectable traditional knowledge,[160] which renders it almost meaningless as a tool for the protection of traditional knowledge rights. It has also been criticized for its failure to take into consideration customary law in both its preparation and redaction.[161] As such,

---

[153] See EC Thematic Report on Access and Benefit-Sharing, submitted to CBD Secretariat in October 2002, available online at https://www.cbd.int/doc/world/eur/eur-nr-abs-en.pdf.

[154] For discussion, see G. van Overwalle, 'Belgium Goes its Own Way on Biodiversity and Patents' [2002] EIPR 233.

[155] Communication from the Commission to the European Parliament and the Council, The Implementation by the EC of the 'Bonn Guidelines' on Access to Genetic Resources and Benefit-Sharing under the Convention on Biological Diversity (19 December 2003) COM/2003/0821 final.

[156] Ibid., 17. The proposal also builds on a Concept Paper submitted by the EC to the TRIPS Council in October 2003 on the relationship between TRIPS and the CBD.   [157] Ibid., 18.

[158] Regulation (EU) 511/2014 of 16 April 2014 on compliance measures for uses from the Nagoya Protocol on Access to Genetic Resources.

[159] L. Mulenkei and J. von Braun, 'Open Letter to the Committee on Environment, Public Health and Food Safety from Individuals and Organizations that Work with or Represent Indigenous Peoples and Local Communities' (2 July 2013).   [160] Ibid.

[161] B. Tobin, 'Bridging the Nagoya Compliance Gap: The Fundamental Role of Customary Law in Protection of Indigenous Peoples' Resource and Knowledge Rights' (2013) 9 LEAD 144.

it seems that little will change in the way in which European law deals with traditional knowledge and access to genetic resources.

6.3 PATENT EXAMINATION

Another area where reform might be considered is in relation to examination. Here, there are two issues that are currently attracting interest. The first relates to the rigour with which examinations are conducted. Some argue that, given the fact that the number of patent applications vastly exceeds the number of commercially significant inventions, it is a waste of resources to examine every application in detail. The most efficient approach, it is said, is to perform a cursory examination of all applications and to review seriously the validity of any grant that has commercial significance.[162] Because the validity of any commercially valuable patent will be subjected to a thorough review in any litigation, we should not bother to waste resources on pre-grant examination of patents. On the other hand, some argue that examination is important to protect the public—in particular, small traders—from threats of patent litigation on the basis of granted patents of dubious validity by well-resourced claimants. Essentially, the argument is that even invalid patents can be used to chill activity of legitimate traders or to extort settlements from risk-averse or poorly financed potential defendants. A related problem is said to be the activity of 'patent trolls'—that is, commercial organizations that acquire patents specifically with a view to bringing actions in the hope of making money by forcing settlements.[163] Although the causes and effects of patent trolling are controversial, some argue that the impact has been made much worse by the practices of some patent offices in granting patents that rigorous examination would have shown related to subjects that lacked novelty or were obvious.

The second issue that has arisen in relation to examination arises from increasing backlogs in the processing of applications. Filings at the EPO, for example, have more than quadrupled over the last 30 years to more than 296,000 in 2016, leaving substantial backlogs. As a result of a series of controversial 'efficiency' reforms, the EPO granted nearly 96,000 patents in 2016; a staggering increase of 40 per cent over 2015. While this has eased the pressure on the examination backlog, it has triggered other issues, one of which is a concern about the quality of the patents that have been granted.[164]

---

[162] M. Lemley, 'Rational Ignorance at the Patent Office' (2001) 95 *Nw UL Rev* 1495; A. Jaffe and J. Lerner, *Innovation and its Discontents* (2007), ch. 7.

[163] For a discussion of the use of remedies to deal with the behaviour of trolls, see M. Lemley and C. Shapiro, 'Patent Holdup and Royalty Stacking' (2007) 85 *Texas L Rev* 1991; J. Golden, '"Patent Trolls" and Patent Remedies' (2007) 85 *Texas L Rev* 2111.

[164] D. Smyth, 'Something is Rotten in the State of the EPO' (2016) 11 *JIPLP* 393.

17

PATENTABLE SUBJECT MATTER

1 INTRODUCTION

In the previous two chapters, we looked at the nature of patents and the processes by which patents are granted. In this and the following three chapters, we look at the criteria that an invention must satisfy to be patentable. These are that the invention must:

(i)   consist of subject matter that is patentable (this chapter);

(ii)   be new (Chapter 18);

(iii)   involve an inventive step (Chapter 19); and

(iv)   comply with the internal requirements of patentability (Chapter 20).

If an application fails to meet any one of these criteria, a patent will not be granted. If a patent has already been granted, failure may mean that the patent is revoked. With these general points in mind, we now look at the subject matter that is capable of being patented.

2 PATENTABLE SUBJECT MATTER

The exercise of deciding the types of subject matter that ought to be patentable often generates conflict and uncertainty. This is because patent law often finds itself dealing with technologies that it may not yet understand. It is also because the task of having to decide whether to grant property rights in a particular type of invention raises a complex mix of legal, cultural, political, and social questions. Over time, a range of different factors has restricted the subject matter protected by patents. Perhaps the most important is the image of the invention as something concrete and physical, which results from human intervention in nature.[1] A range of other more explicit policy factors has also limited the type of subject matter that is protected by patents.

---

[1] Sherman and Bently, 46, 150–7.

The subject matter that is potentially patentable under the Patents Act 1977 and the 2000 European Patents Convention (EPC 2000) is regulated in five ways.

(i) To be patentable, an invention must be capable of 'industrial application'.[2] While this is probably the least important of the five requirements, it has been important in relation to inventions involving naturally occurring substances.

(ii) The second restriction on patentable subject matter arises from the fact that patents are not granted for methods of medical and veterinary treatment.[3]

(iii) The third restriction on the subject matter protected by patents is set out in section 1(2) and Article 52(2)(3). In essence these provide a non-exhaustive list of things that are not regarded as inventions.[4] If the subject matter of an application falls within the scope of these provisions, it will not be patentable.

(iv) The fourth restriction on the subject matter excluded from patent protection provides that a patent shall not be granted for 'any variety of animal or plant or any essentially biological process for the production of animals or plants, not being a microbiological process or the product of such a process'.[5]

(v) The fifth factor that restricts the subject matter protected by patent law is that patents are not granted for immoral inventions or inventions that are contrary to public policy.[6] While rarely used in the past, this exclusion has taken on a new significance in light of developments in biotechnology. A number of specific exclusions relating to immoral biological inventions are also contained in Schedule A2, paragraph 3(a)–(d), to the Patents Act 1977 and Rule 28 of the EPC 2000 Implementing Regulations (EPC 2000 Regs).[7]

We will look at each of these in turn.

3 INDUSTRIAL APPLICATION

In order for an invention to be patentable, it must be capable of 'industrial application'.[8] This reflects the long-held view that patent protection should not be available for purely abstract or intellectual creations. The need to show industrial applicability also reflects the image of the patentable invention as having a concrete and technical character.[9]

---

[2] PA 1977, ss 1(1)(c), 4; EPC 2000, Art. 52(1).

[3] PA 1977, s. 4A(1); EPC 2000, Art. 53(c). Previously, methods of medical and veterinary treatment were excluded on the basis that they were not industrially applicable.

[4] PA 1977, s. 1(2); EPC 2000, Art. 52(2), (3).

[5] PA 1977, Sch. A2, para. 3(f), introduced by the Patents Regulations 2000 (SI 2000/2037) and replacing PA 1977, s. 1(3)(b) (as enacted); EPC 2000, Art. 53(b).

[6] PA 1977, s. 1(3), introduced by the Patents Regulations 2000 and replacing PA 1977, s. 1(3)(a) (as enacted); EPC 2000, Art. 53(a).

[7] Implementing Regulations to the Convention on the Grant of European Patents (2006). This provision was formerly EPC 1973 Regs, r. 23d   [8] PA 1977, s. 1(1)(c); EPC 2000, Art. 52(1).

[9] EPC 2000, Art. 52(1), provides that European patents 'shall be granted for any inventions *in all fields of technology*, provided that they are new, involve an inventive step and are susceptible of industrial application' (emphasis added). See Art. 1, item 17, of the Act Revising the Convention on the Grant of European Patents (EPC) (29 November 2000) MR/3/00 Rev., 1e (the 'EPC Revision Act'); Basic Proposal for the Revision of the European Patent Convention (2000) CA/100/00 e, 38. PA 1977, s. 1, was to be amended to reflect EPC 2000, Art. 52(1): HM Government, *Consultation on the Proposed Patents Act (Amendment) Bill: Summary of Responses and the Government's Conclusions* (13 November 2003), [17]. Despite earlier plans, this was not adopted in the Patents Act 2004.

An invention is capable of industrial application if it can be used or made in 'any kind of industry'.[10] 'Industry' is construed in its widest sense, including activities whether or not for profit.[11] It also expressly extends to include agriculture.[12] As such, the requirement that an invention be made or used in industry presents few problems. In a controversial decision, however, it was held that a private and personal activity (the application of a contraceptive composition to the cervix) was not industrial in character and thus not patentable.[13]

As well as being used or made in any kind of industry, for an invention to be industrially applicable, it is also necessary to show that it has a 'useful purpose'.[14] This is satisfied if a patent discloses 'a practical application' or has a 'concrete benefit'.[15] Because the Patents Act 1977 and the EPC 2000 provide that inventions only need to be *susceptible* or *capable* of industrial application, this implies that there is no need to show actual use; it is enough to show that the invention has the *potential* to be used or made in industry. The potential use must be 'reasonably credible' or 'plausible', rather than 'merely speculative'.[16] Where a product has been used (or put on the market), the commercial success of the product is not relevant when deciding its industrial applicability.[17] Inventions that contravene well-established scientific laws will be excluded on the basis that they are not industrially applicable. This is the case, for example, with inventions for perpetual motion machines and self-generating machines (which contravene the first law of thermodynamics that says that, in a closed system energy can neither be created or destroyed; it can only be transferred from one state to another).[18] In this context, the Technical Board of Appeal has stressed that it is not an appropriate forum in which to discuss new physical theories; these matters were to be decided in appropriate scientific arenas.[19]

The requirement that inventions need to exhibit a useful purpose is particularly important in relation to biological material. This is because while researchers have been successful in locating and identifying new gene structures, they have been less successful in ascertaining what many of these genes do.[20] While researchers have been able to identify the genes

---

[10] PA 1977, s. 4(1); EPC 2000, Art. 57. But not when the invention contravenes well-established natural laws: *Duckett v. Patent Office* [2005] *EWHC* 3140 (Pat) (application for machine that contravened the principle of conservation of energy was rejected); *Thompson v. Comptroller General of Patents, Designs and Trade Marks* [2005] *EWHC* 3064 (Ch) (invention that purported to contravene Newton's third law of motion was rejected); *Ward v. Comptroller-General* (unreported) (19 May 2000) (application for perpetual motion machine was rejected). [11] *Chiron v. Murex (No. 12)* [1996] *RPC* 535, 607.

[12] PA 1977, s. 4(1); EPC 2000, Art. 57.

[13] *British Technology Group/Contraceptive method*, T 74/93 [1995] *EPOR* 279, 284. For criticisms of the decision, see J. Pagenberg, 'Comment' (1996) 27 *IIC* 104. [14] *Chiron v. Murex (No. 12)* [1996] *RPC* 535, 607.

[15] *Max-Planck/BDP1 phosphatase*, T 870/04 [2006] *EPOR* 14, [6], [7], [21]; *Zymogenetics/Hematopoietic cytokine receptor*, T 898/05 [2007] *EPOR* 2, [2], [4], cited with approval by the Supreme Court in *Human Genome Sciences v. Eli Lilly* [2011] *UKSC* 51, [107].

[16] *Human Genome Sciences v. Eli Lilly* [2011] *UKSC* 51, [107] (Lord Neuberger), [149] (Lord Hope). See also *Warner-Lambert v. Generics* [2016] *EWCA Civ* 1006, [39]–[40] (CA).

[17] *Harvard/Onco-mouse* [2003] *OJ EPO* 473 (Opposition Division), 494. The fact that the transgenic mice were commercially unsuccessful was not relevant; all that mattered in this context was that they were on the market.

[18] *Blacklight Power v. Comptroller-General of Patents* [2008] *EWHC* 2763 (sets out criteria to be used when considering whether a scientific theory was true); *Nigel Buck's Applications*, BL O/106/13 (8 March 2013); *Peter Crowley's Application*, BL O/389/13 (27 September 2013); *Tecniq's Application*, BL O/42/14 (24 January 2014); C. Wadlow, 'Patents for perpetual motion machines' (2007) 2 *JIPLP* 136.

[19] *Zagyansky/New Atomic scale physics*, T 1358/05 (26 May 2006).

[20] This problem has been exacerbated by the success of the human (and other) genome projects that attempt to identify the thousands of genes that comprise the genetic blueprint of biological entities: see T. Wilkie, *Perilous Knowledge* (1993); BMA, *Our Genetic Future: The Science and Ethics of Genetic Technology* (1992); P. Gannon, T. Guthrie, and G. Laurie, 'Patents, Morality and DNA: Should There be Intellectual Property Protection of the Human Genome Project?' (1995) 1 *Med L Int* 321; J. Straus, 'Patenting Human Genes in Europe: Past Developments and Prospects for the Future' (1995) 26 *IIC* 920.

that make up the human genome, the role that many of these genes play remains unknown. Unless a useful purpose can be found for these genes, they will not be industrially applicable and, as such, not patentable.[21] This is reinforced by the Biotechnology Directive, insofar as it attempts to clarify the industrial applicability requirement in relation to biological inventions.[22] As the Recitals to the Directive explain, a mere DNA sequence without any indication of function does not contain any technical information and is therefore not a patentable invention.[23] In relation to gene sequencing, the Biotechnology Directive and the Patents Act 1977 (as amended) specify that the industrial application of a sequenced or a partial sequence of a gene must be disclosed in the application.[24]

The Opposition Division at the European Patent Office (EPO) applied this style of reasoning in *Icos Corporation*[25] to deny patent protection for a purified and isolated polynucleotide encoding for the amino acid sequence of the V28 protein.[26] The specification in question listed a number of predicted uses for the claimed protein (in relation to 'immunological and inflammatory events'). The problem for the applicant, however, was that these uses were based on the *predicted* function of the protein as a receptor.[27] Importantly, the applicants were unable to show that the receptor was actually involved in any specific immunological and/or inflammatory events. The Opposition Division said that it was not enough for the application to disclose uses that were merely speculative.[28] Echoing (but not citing) the Guidelines of the US Patent and Trademarks Office (USPTO),[29] the Opposition Division added that 'DNA sequences with indications of function which are not substantial, specific, and credible shall not be patentable inventions according to Article 52(1) EPC [2000]'.[30] On this basis, the Opposition Division said that the application lacked industrial applicability and, as such, was not patentable.

A somewhat more pro-industry approach was adopted by the UK Supreme Court in *Human Genome Sciences v. Eli Lilly*,[31] which concerned the validity of a patent that claimed the nucleotide sequence of the human Neutrokine-α gene, which encodes for a novel protein.[32] The patent also included predictions about the therapeutic activities

---

[21] On the proposal for a probationary or interim patent pending discovery of the function of a gene sequence, see M. Llewellyn, 'Industrial Applicability/Utility and Genetic Engineering: Current Practices in Europe and the United States' [1994] *EIPR* 473, 480.

[22] In *Icos Corporation/Seven transmembrane receptor* [2002] *OJ EPO* 293, [9]. The Opposition Division said that the Recitals to the Biotech. Dir. were relevant as supplementary rules of interpretation when examining European patent applications.　　　　　　　　　　　　　　　　　　[23] Biotech. Dir., Recital 23.

[24] Biotech. Dir., Art. 5(3), Recital 22; PA 1977, s. 76A and Sch. A2, para. 6. See also *Decision of the Administrative Council of the EPO of 16 June 1999 amending the Implementing Regulations of the EPC, EPC Rule 23e(3)* [1999] *OJ EPO* 437 (which introduced Biotech. Dir., Art. 5(3), into the EPC 1973).

[25] [2002] *OJ EPO* 293.

[26] The UK Patent Office said that it will follow *Icos Corporation* [2002] *OJ EPO* 293: UK Patent Office, *Biotechnology Examination Guidelines* (September 2002), [33]–[35].

[27] This was because the specification did not disclose any antibody substances that specially recognize V28 protein.

[28] This was based on Biotech. Dir., Recital 23 (which provides that 'a mere DNA sequence without indication of a function does not contain any technical information and is therefore not a patentable invention').

[29] The USPTO issued guidelines on the interpretation of the utility requirement under US patent law on 5 January 2001. These state that, for an invention to have requisite utility (which is similar to industrial application), there must be a 'specific, substantial and credible' use. See, *Manual of Patent Examining Practice*, §2107/II(A)(3)(ii).

[30] *Icos Corporation/Seven transmembrane receptor* [2002] *OJ EPO* 293 (Opposition Division), [11(ii)].

[31] [2011] *UKSC* 51, following *Human Genome Sciences/Neutrokine*, T 18/09 (21 October 2009).

[32] More accurately, the patent described the encoding nucleotide, the amino acid sequence, and certain antibodies of a novel human protein, which it calls 'Neutrokine-α', and includes contentions as to its biological properties and therapeutic activities, as well as those of its antibodies.

of the gene. There were three notable features of the invention. The first was that the Neutrokine-α gene had been found by (bioinformatic) data-mining techniques—that is, computer-assisted sequence homology studies, rather than wet lab techniques. The second was that the novel Neutrokine-α gene was a member of the TNF ligand superfamily of cytokines (which were proteins that acted as intercellular mediators in inflammation and other immune responses). The third was that the function of Neutrokine-α described in the patent was based on its homology (or similarity) to other members of the TNF ligand superfamily. The description of the function of the gene in the patent was not supported in any way by data obtained from *in vivo* or *in vitro* studies; rather, the application of the patented gene was essentially a prediction based on what was known about other members of the TNF superfamily—that is, the gene's function was determined on the assumption that, as a member of a general class of genes, it shared the same functions as other members of that group.

At first instance, Kitchen J held the patent to be invalid on the basis that 'there was nothing in the way of experimental evidence to support the claims about the effectiveness' of the patent.[33] Because the benefits were merely speculative, Kitchen J held that the patent lacked industrial application. The decision was upheld on appeal.[34] Following a similar approach to that of Kitchen J, the Court of Appeal said that to be industrially applicable, the patent needed to show a particular 'use' for the product that had actually been demonstrated—that is, the Court was looking for something more than a reasonable expectation that the molecule would be able to be used for the purposes of research work. A key factor in the Court of Appeal's finding that the patent lacked industrial applicability was that neither the patent nor the common general knowledge identified any disease or condition that Neutrokine-α could be used to diagnose or treat.[35] On the basis that the first step at the onset of research work did not provide an immediate and concrete benefit,[36] the Court held that the patent was too speculative to provide anything of practical value other than information on which a research programme could be based.[37]

In contrast, on appeal to the Supreme Court, the Court was satisfied with a more relaxed test of whether the product has plausibly been shown to be 'usable'.[38] In relation to a new protein and its encoding gene, the Court noted that it was not enough merely to identify the structure of a protein, without attributing a 'clear role' or a 'practical use' for the protein. The key question here was: what did an applicant need to do to show this practical use? The Supreme Court answered by saying that it was not enough to suggest 'a vague and speculative indication of possible objectives that might or might be achieved'.[39] While a merely speculative use would not suffice, the Court was willing to accept that a 'plausible' or 'reasonably credible' claimed use would. The Supreme Court was also willing to accept that an 'educated guess' about the use of an invention could suffice for a patent to be industrially applicable.[40]

[33] *Eli Lilly v. Human Genome Sciences* [2008] *EWHC* 1903 (Pat), [134].

[34] *Eli Lilly v. Human Genome Sciences* [2008] *RPC* 29 (CA).   [35] Ibid., [234].

[36] Ibid., [149].   [37] Ibid., [145].

[38] *Human Genome Sciences v. Eli Lilly* [2011] *UKSC* 51, [107] (which contains a useful summary by Lord Neuberger of the Board's approach to Art. 57).

[39] *Max-Planck/BDP1 phosphatase*, T 870/04 [2006] *EPOR* 14, [6], [7], [21]; *Zymogenetics/Hematopoietic cytokine receptor*, T 898/05 [2007] *EPOR* 2, [7], [10].

[40] The plausibility could be confirmed by later evidence; although this on its own will not do· *John Hopkins/Factor-9*, T 1324/04 [2006] *EPOR* 8, [6], [11]; *Genentech/Human PF4A receptors*, T 640/04 [2006] *EPOR* 8, [6]; *Zymogenetics/Hematopoietic cytokine receptor*, T 898/05 [2007] *EPOR* 2, [8], [21], [27], [31]; *Bayer/Serine protease*, T 1452/06 (10 May 2007), [6]; *Schering/IL-17 related polypeptide*, T 1165/06 (19 July 2007), [25].

As Lord Neuberger noted, the important question here was how are we to draw the line between permissible 'plausibility' or 'educated guesses' on the one hand, and impermissible speculation, on the other. That is: how are we to distinguish between a real possibility of exploitation and a purely theoretical possibility of exploitation?[41] In essence, the way this question is answered depends on the type of evidence that the Court is willing to accept: how specific and precise must the information be for a patent to be industrially applicable? While the lower courts had demanded concrete empirical evidence of use, the Supreme Court was willing to accept the predictions based upon Neutrokine-α's membership of the TNF ligand superfamily as evidence of its industrial applicability. As the Supreme Court said, the question to ask was whether, taking common general knowledge into account, it had *plausibly* been shown that the patented molecule was usable. On the facts, the Court held that the disclosure of the existence of Neutrokine-α, its gene sequence, and membership of the TNF ligand superfamily was sufficient to satisfy Article 57 of the EPC. Following the Technical Board of Appeal in *Human Genome Sciences/Neutrokine*,[42] the Supreme Court held that the patent had 'delivered sufficient technical information . . . to satisfy the requirement of disclosing the nature of the invention and how it can be used in industrial practice'.[43] The fact that further work was required to see whether the disclosure actually had therapeutic benefits did not affect its validity.[44] The upshot of this is that identification of a proposed function of a gene or protein based on homology will be enough to give rise to industrial applicability.[45]

While the threshold for showing industrial applicability for gene- and protein-related inventions may have been raised at the EPO over the last decade, the Supreme Court decision will no doubt please certain parts of the biotechnology industry.[46] Critics who argue that gene patents have a chilling impact on research will, however, be less pleased. In particular, it is now being suggested that the problem with patents over genes is that while a patentee only has to disclose one specific use to show industrial applicability, once this threshold is satisfied they are given control over *all* uses of the patented gene— even those uses that they had not discovered or even imagined. The problem here is that there is a lack of symmetry between what is disclosed and what is protected. This has led some to argue that protection should be limited to what is actually disclosed in the application.[47] Despite its importance, this issue has not yet been given the attention that it clearly requires.

---

[41] We can get a sense of the Supreme Court's approach to this issue in Lord Neuberger's statement that 'it would wrong to set the hurdle for patentability too high': *Human Genome Sciences v. Eli Lilly* [2011] *UKSC* 51, [120]; Lord Walker said that the policy goal was to 'reduce the risk of a chilling effect in investment in bioscience': ibid., [171]. Interestingly, Lord Neuberger based his argument on the views of the BioIndustry Association (which intervened in the decision) that the purpose of the patent system was to provide a temporary monopoly that acted as an incentive to innovation and also to facilitate the early dissemination of any such innovations: ibid., [99].   [42] T 18/09 (21 October 2009).

[43] *Human Genome Sciences v. Eli Lilly* [2011] *UKSC* 51, [155], following the TBA in *Human Genome Sciences/Neutrokine*, T 18/09 (21 October 2009), [27].

[44] *Human Genome Sciences v. Eli Lilly* [2011] *UKSC* 51, [120].

[45] It remains a requirement for polynucleotides that the industrial application must be fully established in the application as filed. UK IPO, *Examining Patent Applications for Biotechnological Inventions* (21 Oct 2016), [63].

[46] T. Minssen and D. Nilsson, 'The Industrial Applicability Requirement for Biotech Inventions in Light of Recent EPO & UK Law: A Plausible Approach or a Mere "Hunting License"?' [2012] *EIPR* 689, 701. See also A. Sharples, 'Industrial Applicability, Patents and the Supreme Court: *Human Genome Sciences Inc. v. Eli Lilly and Co* (2012) 34 *EIPR* 284.   [47] See Chapter 15, section 4.3.1, pp. 431–2.

4 METHODS OF MEDICAL AND VETERINARY TREATMENT

The second category of subject matter excluded from patentability are inventions for methods of medical and veterinary treatment.[48] Such inventions are excluded to ensure that people who carry out medical or veterinary treatments are not inhibited by patents.[49] As the Enlarged Board of Appeal (EBA) noted, this helps to achieve the socio-ethical and public health goal that '[m]edical and veterinary practitioners should be free to take the actions they consider suited to diagnose illness by means of investigative methods'.[50] Prior to the EPC 2000, methods of medical and veterinary treatment were excluded on the basis that they were not capable of industrial application.[51] Under the EPC 2000, however, methods of treatment and diagnosis are now directly excluded from patentability under Article 53(c), rather than on the basis that they are not capable of industrial application, as was the case previously. Article 53(c) of the EPC 2000 provides that 'a patent shall not be granted for methods of treatment of the human or animal body by surgery or therapy, and diagnostic methods practiced on the human or animal body'.[52] Similar changes were made in the United Kingdom to bring the Patents Act 1977 into line with EPC 2000; the exclusion is now in section 4A of the Act.[53] On the basis that the changes brought about by EPC 2000 in this area were primarily editorial in nature, the EBA has said that the 'actual legal position remains unchanged'.[54] Given this statement, the case law previously decided under the earlier European Patent Convention of 1973 (EPC 1973) is still applicable.

In thinking about the application of this, it is important to keep a number of things in mind. In the following section, we look at some of the more important of these.

4.1 METHODS

It is important to note that the exclusion is confined to *methods* of medical and veterinary treatment.[55] As such, it does not prevent the patenting of surgical, therapeutic, or diagnostic substances, compositions (such as drugs), apparatuses, or products (such as electrocardiogram, or ECG, machines, prosthetic ball and socket joints, or pacemakers).[56]

---

[48] See generally, D. Thums, 'Patent Protection for Medical Treatment: A Distinction between Patent and Medical Law' (1996) 27 *IIC* 423; G. Burch, 'Ethical Considerations in the Patenting of Medical Processes' (1987) 65 *Texas L Rev* 1139 (under US law, methods of medical treatment are patentable); Ana Nordberg, 'Patentability of methods of human enhancement' (2015) 10 *JIPLP* 19.

[49] *Medi-Physics/Treatment by surgery*, G 1/07 [2011] *OJ EPO* 134; *Wellcome/Pigs I*, T 116/85 [1989] *EPOR* 1, [1989] *OJ EPO* 13; *Telectronics/Pacer*, T 82/93 [1996] *EPOR* 409; *See-Shell/Blood flow*, T 182/90 [1994] *EPOR* 320. A technique that results in death of the animal does not fall within the exception.

[50] *Diagnostic methods*, G 1/04 [2006] *OJ EPO* 334 (EBA), 348.

[51] PA 1977, s. 4(2); EPC 1973, Art. 52(4) (both provisions have been repealed). TRIPS, Art. 27(3), allows members to exclude from patentability diagnostic, therapeutic, and surgical methods for the treatment of humans or animals.

[52] While EPC 2000, Art. 53, and PA 1977, s. 4A, are drafted (slightly) differently, it is unlikely that this will have any significant consequences.

[53] Patents Act 2004, s. 1 (inserting a new s. 4A into the Patents Act 1977). See also HM Government, *Consultation on the Proposed Patents Act (Amendment) Bill: Summary of Responses and the Government's Conclusions* (13 November 2003), [19]–[20]. Minor changes were also made to bring the language in the 1977 Act closer to that used in EPC 2000.   [54] *Diagnostic methods*, G 1/04 (2006) *OJ EPO* 334 (EBA), 360.

[55] PA 1977, s. 4A; EPC 2000, Art. 53(c).

[56] *Joint Medical Products/Ball and socket bearing for artificial joint*, T 712/93 [1998] *OJ EPO* (Special edn) 12; *Visx v. Nidek* [1999] *FSR* 405, 465.

4.2 SURGERY, THERAPY, OR DIAGNOSIS

For an invention to be caught by section 4A/Article 53(c), it must consist of a method of *surgery, therapy,* or *diagnosis*. We will look at each of these in turn.

4.2.1 Surgical methods

'Surgery' has been defined as the branch 'of medicine concerned with the healing of disease, accidental injury or bodily defects by operating on the living body'.[57] It is said to include both 'conservative (non-invasive) procedures such as repositioning and the far more numerous operative (invasive) procedures using instruments'.[58] In recent years, it has become clear that there are two inconsistent approaches to the way in which surgery is defined:[59] while one line of decisions focused on the *nature* of the physical intervention itself, a second line of decisions concentrated on the *purpose* of the intervention. Under the first and older approach, tribunals looked at the nature of the intervention and asked whether this could be classified as 'surgery'. This is the approach adopted in the UK. In a second series of decisions, the EPO moved beyond the nature of the intervention itself to focus on the *purpose* of the invention in question. In particular, this second line of decisions focused on whether the physical intervention 'is suitable for maintaining or restoring health, the physical integrity of the physical well being of a person or animal'.[60] The Enlarged Board of Appeal (EBA) seemed to support this approach when it said (*obiter*) that surgery 'includes any physical intervention on the human or animal body in which maintaining the life and health of the subject is of paramount importance'.[61]

By emphasizing the purpose of the intervention rather than its nature, a distinction was drawn between two different types of physical intervention in the body. The first, which falls within the definition of surgery, comprises curative practices that aim to maintain or promote health. As the Technical Board of Appeal said in the *General Hospital* decision, surgical treatment aims at protecting curative activities. This means that the exception applies to activities aimed at maintaining and restoring the health, physical integrity, and physical well-being of a person (and also preventing diseases).[62] The second type of physical intervention, which does not qualify as surgery for the purposes of Article 53(c), consists of interventions carried out for non-curative purposes. Under this approach, surgical treatments which were 'neither clearly suitable nor potentially suitable for maintaining or restoring the health, the physical integrity, or the physical well being of human beings or animals' did not fall with the exclusion in Article 52(4) of the EPC 1973 (now Article 53(c) of the EPC 2000).[63] On this basis, things such as hair removal, tattooing and piercing, the only possible object of which was to beautify the human or animal body, would not fall foul of Article 53(c). This was not the case, however, in relation to breast enlargement or nose reconstructions, which could be used to restore the physical integrity of the body following breast cancer or a car accident, for example.[64] The key difference is that the latter methods *are* potentially suitable for maintaining or restoring the health, physical integrity, or physical well-being of a person.

---

[57] *See Sholl/Blood flow,* T 182/90 [1994] *EPOR* 320, 323.   [58] Ibid.

[59] The TBA recognized that other approaches, including the risk of the activity, may be applied: *Medi-Physics/Treatment by surgery,* T 992/03 [2007] *OJ EPO* 557, 570.

[60] *General Hospital Corp/Hair removal method,* T 383/03 [2005] *OJ EPO* 159, 165.

[61] *Diagnostic methods,* G 1/04 [2006] *OJ EPO* 334 (EBA), 352.

[62] *General Hospital Corp/Hair removal method,* T 383/03 [2005] *OJ EPO* 159, 165 (the same applies to activities performed on animals).   [63] Ibid., 166.

[64] Ibid., 167.

In *Medi-Physics/Treatment by surgery*,[65] which is a comprehensive and wide-ranging review of European law on the exclusion of surgical methods, the EBA rejected the broad interpretation of 'surgery'. Instead, it adopted the narrow approach that has been followed in the United Kingdom which says that the definition of surgery relates to the nature of the treatment and not to it its purpose.[66] As the EBA said, 'the meaning of the term "treatment by surgery" is not to be interpreted as being confined to surgical methods pursuing a therapeutic purpose'.[67] As a result, the exclusion is not limited to surgical methods pursuing a therapeutic purpose; *any* method of surgical treatment, whether curative, prophylactic, cosmetic, or for non-therapeutic purposes (such as sterilization), will be caught by the exclusion. In so doing, the Board overturned previous practice in the EPO (such as the *General Hospital* decision), which had held that the only surgical methods to be excluded from patentability were to be those potentially suitable for 'maintaining and restoring the health, the physical well-being of a human being or animal, and to prevent disease'.[68] It also brought law at the EPO into line with British law.[69]

In reaching its decision in *Medi-Physics*, the EBA was at pains to point out that the speed of technical and medical change meant that it was not possible to provide a definitive definition of 'surgery'. It also stressed that the question was to be decided on a case-by-case basis. Nonetheless, the Board did say that the exclusion should be limited to the kinds of interventions that represented the core of the medical profession's activities—that is, the kind of activities for which professionals are specifically trained and for which they assume particular responsibility. More specifically, the Board held that 'a method should be excluded if it constitutes a non-significant physical intervention, which entails a substantial health risk even when carried out by a medical professional'.[70] In effect, what were excluded were physical interventions on the body that require professional medical skills to be carried out with the required medical professional care and expertise. This ruled out uncritical methods involving only minor intervention and no substantial health risks.[71] On this basis, it was held that invasive techniques of a routine character that are performed on uncritical parts of the body and generally carried out in non-medical commercial environments are not excluded, for example tattooing, piercing, hair removal by optical radiation, and micro-abrasion of the skin.[72] The position was the same in relation to non-critical medical interventions with no substantial health risks.

---

[65] G 1/07 [2011] *OJ EPO* 34.

[66] In so doing, the EBA endorsed the approach of the *EPO Guidelines*, which state that surgery is defined by 'the nature of the treatment rather than the purpose': *EPO Guidelines*, G-II, [4.2.11].

[67] *Medi-Physics/Treatment by surgery*, G 1/07 [2011] *OJ EPO* 34.

[68] This would not have been patentable under UK practice: UK IPO, *Examination Guidelines for Patent Applications Relating to Medical Inventions in the UK Intellectual Property Office* (14 October 2016), [51].

[69] In 2007, the UK IPO said that the second approach (as outlined in the *General Hospital* decision) was out of step with British practice: UK IPO, *Examination Guidelines for Patent Applications relating to Medical Inventions in the UK Intellectual Property Office* (June 2007), [46]. This was reconfirmed in UK IPO, *Examination Guidelines for Patent Applications Relating to Medical Inventions in the UK Intellectual Property Office* (May 2013), [46]. See now UK IPO, *Examination Guidelines for Patent Applications Relating to Medical Inventions in the UK Intellectual Property Office* (14 October 2016), [44]. *Medi-Physics* also aligned with a series of decisions by the TBA at the EPO: *See-Shell/Blood flow*, T 182/90 [1994] *EPOR* 320; *Georgetown University/Pericardial access*, T 35/99 [2000] *OJ EPO* 447; *Baxter/Blood extraction method*, T 329/94 [1998] *EPOR* 363 (focusing on the use of surgical instruments).

[70] *Medi-Physics/Treatment by surgery*, G 1/07 [2011] *OJ EPO* 34, [3.4.2.3].   [71] Ibid.

[72] This test has been followed in subsequent TBA decisions and at the UK IPO, where examiners ask 'Is the method invasive?', 'Does it require professional skill?', and 'Does it carry a potential risk?': ibid., [3.4.2.2]. See also *EPO Guidelines*, G-II, [4.2.1.1]. The Guidelines say that simple injection methods, either for taking blood samples or introducing compositions would not be regarded as methods of surgery because they involve relatively low levels of technical expertise. This is in contrast to more complicated procedures such as lumbar puncture to deliver epidural injections, which are likely to be excluded: ibid.

This is in contrast with methods that involve the implanting or insertion of devices by surgical means, or the injection of a contrast agent into the heart, catheterization, and endoscopy, which are excluded. These methods would be excluded on the basis that they encompass a substantial physical intervention on the body that requires professional medical expertise to be carried out and which entails a health risk. In this context, the Board noted that when deciding whether a method for introducing an agent (such as a pharmaceutical) is a surgical method, it is the risk of the invasive procedure and not the risk of side effects that are to be considered.[73]

It is important to remember that for a procedure to be excluded, there must be an *intervention* on the body. 'Intervention' has been defined broadly: it does not necessarily need to be invasive or the tissues penetrated; repositioning body limbs or manipulating a body part is 'surgery'. The need to show intervention on the *body* means that the exclusion does not apply to a process the end result of which is the death of a living being under treatment, either deliberately or incidentally.[74] It also means that a method such as an imaging method, which generates information about the body that is useful for or during surgery, or which allows a surgeon to make real-time decisions during a surgical intervention, is not a method of surgery as such.[75]

While the EBA in *Medi-Physics* held that the question of whether a method is excluded as a method of surgery cannot depend on who carries it out, not least because of changing medical roles in the healthcare systems, nonetheless it did find that the level of medical skill needed to perform a method could be a useful guide in determining whether a method was excluded.[76] This is reflected in the comment by the Board that any operation on the body that needs the skill or knowledge of a surgeon or medical practitioner would be a surgery (such as a method of embryo implantation that required the intervention of a surgeon or a veterinary surgeon).[77]

4.2.2 Therapeutic methods

'Therapy' has been interpreted broadly as the curing of a disease or malfunction of the human or animal body[78] and includes *prophylactic* treatments with a view to maintaining health by preventing ill effects that would otherwise arise.[79] It has also been held to include *curative* treatments that aim to cure diseases or bodily malfunctions that have already arisen.[80] On the basis that pregnancy and lice infestation are not diseases, inventions for methods of treatment that prevented pregnancies[81] or removed lice were not caught by the exclusion.[82] However, a method of immunizing against coccidiosis,[83] and another for controlling mange in pigs were held to relate to diseases and, as such, were excluded as methods of treatment by therapy.[84] The exclusion of therapeutic methods applies irrespective

---

[73] *Medi-Physics/Treatment by surgery*, G 1/07 [2011] *OJ EPO* 34, 134.

[74] *Georgetown University/Pericardial access*, T 35/99 [2000] *OJ EPO* 447, 451.

[75] *Medi-Physics/Treatment by surgery*, G 1/07 [2011] *OJ EPO* 34.

[76] Ibid., [3.4].   [77] Ibid., [50].

[78] *Cygnus/Diagnostic methods*, G 1/04 [2006] *OJ EPO* 334 (EBA), 352. See E. Ventose, 'Patent Protection for Therapeutic Methods under the European Patent Convention' [2010] *EIPR* 120.

[79] *Duphar/Pigs II*, T 19/86 [1988] *EPOR* 241, [1989] *OJ EPO* 24.

[80] Ibid.; *Unilever's (Davis) Application* [1983] *RPC* 219; *Salimen/Pigs III*, T 58/87 [1989] *EPOR* 125; *Thompson/Cornea*, T 24/91 (1996) 27 *IIC* 530; *Eisai/Second medical indication*, G 5/83 [1979–85] *B EPOR* 241.

[81] *Schering's Application* [1971] *RPC* 337; *British Technology Group/Contraceptive method*, T 74/93 [1995] *EPOR* 279, 284. But a method of contraception that includes a therapeutic method will be unpatentable even where that therapy is present only to counteract the side-effects of the contraceptive method: *General Hospital/Contraceptive methods*, T 820/92 [1995] *EPOR* 446.

[82] *Salimen/Pigs III*, T 58/87 [1989] *EPOR* 125.   [83] *Unilever's (Davis) Application* [1983] *RPC* 219.

[84] *Wellcome/Pigs I*, T 116/85 [1988] *EPOR* 1, [1989] *OJ EPO* 13. Fatigue is not a disease: T 469/94 (1998) *OJ EPO* 12.

of whether the disease or bodily malfunction that the invention seeks to prevent or cure is internal or external and whether it is a temporary or a permanent infliction.[85] It also applies irrespective of the origin of the pain, discomfort, or incapacity that the therapy seeks to remedy.[86] Therapeutic methods (which are seen as being carried out for noble purposes) are often contrasted with cosmetic methods (which are carried out for less important reasons). As such, a method that leads to weight loss for the purpose of curing or preventing obesity would fall within the exclusion;[87] in contrast, a method for weight loss that is undertaken for cosmetic purposes would not and, as such, might be patentable.[88]

4.2.3 Diagnostic methods

After some uncertainty, the nature and scope of the exclusion of diagnostic methods was clarified by the decision of the EBA in *Diagnostic methods*.[89] In this decision, the Board said that methods of diagnosis typically consist of four subsidiary steps.[90]

(i)   *Examination*   This involves the collection of data (recording the case history).

(ii) *Comparison*   This data is then to be compared with normal values.

(iii) *Identification*   Any significant deviation from the norm is to be identified (that is, any symptom).

(iv) *Diagnosis*   The 'deductive medical or veterinary decision phase' is the final stage at which the diagnosis for curative purposes is made (which represents a purely intellectual or non-technical exercise).

One of the questions that the Board was asked to consider was whether to fall within the exclusion, an application only needed to include the fourth 'deductive stage' (a narrow interpretation), or whether it had to include all four stages (a broad interpretation). Drawing on a range of factors, the Board adopted the narrow interpretation and said that to fall within the exclusion, *all* four steps needed to be present in an invention.[91] (In so doing, the EBA overturned the decision of the Technical Board of Appeal in *Cygnus*[92]

---

[85]   *Wellcome/Pigs I*, T 116/85 [1988] *EPOR* 1.

[86]   *Rorer/Dysmenorrhea*, T 81/84 [1988] *OJ EPO* 207.

[87]   A method of treating plaque, since it inevitably had a beneficial effect, was held not patentable: *ICI/ Cleaning plaque*, T 290/86 [1991] *EPOR* 157. A claim for the manufacture of the medicament for use in the treatment of certain respiratory disorders where the patient is suffering from a pre-existing heart condition fell foul of s. 4A(1)(a). This was because the inventiveness of the claim lay in the identification by the doctor of the patient as suffering from a heart problem: *Laboratorios Almirall v. Boehringer Ingelhem* [2009] *EWHC* 102, [289].

[88]   A cosmetic method is patentable unless it inevitably has a therapeutic effect. It was therefore possible to patent a method of dieting involving suppression of appetite, since the effect would not necessarily have been positive: *Du Pont/Appetite suppressant*, T 144/83 [1986] *OJ EPO* 301.

[89]   *Cygnus/Diagnostic methods*, G 1/04 [2006] *OJ EPO* 334 (EBA), 352.

[90]   As the EBA noted, these four steps overlap. The key point is that a diagnostic method is a multi-step process.

[91]   Where a method includes the first and final steps, the intermediate steps may be implied: UK IPO, *Examination Guidelines for Patent Applications Relating to Medical Inventions in the UK Intellectual Property Office* (14 October 2016), [55].

[92]   *Cygnus/Sampling substances*, T 964/99 [2002] *OJ EPO* 4, 13. The invention, which monitored sugar levels from the skin, thus avoiding the need for the pricking of fingers to collect blood and did not involve all of the steps in medical diagnosis (it only provided information used to make a diagnosis). The Board rejected *Bruker* (see next), and held that the patent was a method of medical diagnosis and, as such, was excluded from patentability. Drawing upon the French text of the EPC 2000, the Board in *Cygnus* said that the EPC 'does not favour an interpretation limiting the exception to patentability encompassing all steps required for reaching a medical diagnosis': ibid., 15. Instead, the Board said that 'any medical activity concerning the gathering of information in the course of establishing a diagnosis qualifies as a diagnostic method'.

and reinstated the earlier decision of *Bruker/Non-invasive measurement*.[93]) The EBA also said that no distinction should be drawn between essential method steps that have a diagnostic character and non-essential steps that do not.[94] The Board also said that the question of whether a method is excluded as a diagnosis is not dependent on who carries out the method or whether a medical or veterinary practitioner needs to be present;[95] rather:

> [W]hether or not a method is a diagnostic method within the meaning of [Article 52(4) of the EPC 1973; Article 53(c)of the EPC 2000] should neither depend on the participation of a medical or veterinary practitioner, by being present or by bearing the responsibility, nor on the fact that all method steps can also, or only, be practiced by medicinal or non-medicinal support staff, the patient himself or herself or an automated system.[96]

A general distinction is now drawn between the act of making a diagnosis (which involves using examination and data to reach a decision) and methods of data acquisition or data processing (the results of which may subsequently be used in diagnosis). If an invention only provides interim or preliminary results (data or information), the invention will not be excluded from patent protection under Article 53(c).[97] Put differently, the exclusion will only apply where an invention makes it immediately possible to decide on a particular course of medical treatment. As a result, a method of taking a sample or determining internal temperature or pH would not, in itself, identify a condition and, as such, would not be classified as a diagnostic method. This means that many diagnostic methods will no longer be caught by the exclusion despite the express language of the EPC 2000 and the Patents Act 1977. It also means that common diagnostic procedures practised on the human body, such as percussion or palpitation could, in principle, be patented because they do not constitute a complete diagnosis. The reasoning of the EBA has been applied in a subsequent decision, which concerned methods for magnetic resonance imaging.[98] On the basis that the invention only led to the acquisition of data, it was held that the invention was not a diagnostic method as defined in Article 52(4) of the EPC 1973 [now Article 53(c) of the EPC 2000].

The approach adopted by the EBA in *Diagnostic methods* has been followed by the UK Intellectual Property Office (IPO).[99] Given the willingness of judges in the United Kingdom to change British law to ensure that it mirrors the jurisprudence at the EPO, it is unlikely that British courts will deviate from the approach outlined in *Diagnostic methods*. By reading down the scope of the exclusion, it seems that the EBA may reopen concerns about the negative impact that patent law has upon healthcare and delivery (exemplified most famously by the patents granted to Myriad over both the genes that highlight the propensity to breast cancer and the diagnostic tests that use such genes). The Board has also raised interesting questions about the changing role of technology in the delivery of medical and veterinary care, and whether this should change the way in which we think about the role that patents play in these fields.

---

[93] *Bruker/Non-invasive measurement*, T 385/86 [1988] *EPOR* 357, [3.2]–[3.4] (for an invention to be classified as a non-patentable diagnostic method, *all* of the different steps had to present).

[94] *Cygnus/Diagnostic methods*, G 1/04 [2006] *OJ EPO* 334 (EBA), 356.

[95] Ibid.   [96] Ibid., 355.

[97] *Bruker/Non-invasive measurement*, T 385/86 [1988] *EPOR* 357. For criticisms, see R. Moufang, 'Methods of Medical Treatment under Patent Law' (1993) 24 *IIC* 18, 46–47.

[98] *Medi-physics/Treatment by surgery*, T 992/03 [2007] *OJ EPO* 557, 563.

[99] UK IPO, *Examination Guidelines for Patent Applications relating to Medical Inventions in the Intellectual Property Office* (April 2016), [54]–[61].

4.3 TREATMENT PRACTISED *ON* OR *IN* THE BODY

The third point to note is that the exclusion of methods of medical or veterinary treatment only applies to methods of treatment that are practised *on*[100] or *in*[101] the human or animal body. The ambit of this provision has been interpreted broadly to include 'any interaction with the human or animal body, necessitating the presence of the later'.[102] It has also been suggested that there is no need to show a specific type of interaction with the body. This means that the steps can be either invasive processes (which require physical contact with the body), or non-invasive ones that are practised at 'a certain distance to it'.[103] The key factor is that the step requires interaction with the body. This means that the exclusion does not apply to methods practised on substances that are removed from the body.[104] Thus neither the treatment of blood for storage in a blood bank nor the diagnostic testing of blood samples is excluded. Similarly, operations that occur at a cellular level (such as the incorporation of an oncogene into the fertilized egg of an animal) are not performed 'on' or 'in' the body.[105] While the use of a spectacle lens to correct a glass wearer's defective vision did lessen the effect of the poor vision, it was held not to be a therapeutic treatment because it did not change the user's eyes in any way, so much as change the light rays that travelled towards the glasses.[106] In contrast, a treatment of blood by dialysis, where the blood is returned to the same body, would be excluded.[107] To be excluded, diagnostic methods must be carried out on the living human or animal body; a method carried out on a dead body, for example to determine cause of death, would not be excluded.[108] While an invention may interact with or relate to a human or animal body, it will only be excluded if it is classed as a form of treatment on the body. In line with this, the Technical Board of Appeal held that 'a method and apparatus for preventing piglets from suffocat-ing' by blowing hot air under a mother pig to discourage piglets from going under her was patentable.[109] While the invention protected the body, it was still patentable because the method was not practised *on* the body of the piglet.

As we saw earlier, diagnostic methods typically consist of a number of steps, all of which much be present if an application is to fall within the ambit of the exclusion. While this is all well and good for the purposes of deciding whether an invention is a diagnostic method, it seems that a different approach is adopted when considering whether that diagnostic method is practised on or in the human or animal body. The reason for this is that some of the stages in a diagnostic method (particularly the final 'deductive phase') are intellectual exercises: they are carried out in the mind of the medical or veterinary prac-titioner. To get around the problems that this might pose, the Enlarged Board of Appeal said that the requirement that the invention be 'practised on or in the human or animal body' is only to be considered in relation to method steps of a *technical* nature; 'Thus, it does not apply to the diagnosis for curative purposes *stricto sensu*, i.e. the deductive

---

[100] *Salimen/Pigs III*, T 58/87 [1989] *EPOR* 125.

[101] *Siemens/Flow measurement*, T 254/87 [1989] *OJ EPO* 171.

[102] *Cygnus/Diagnostic methods*, G 1/04 [2006] *OJ EPO* 334 (EBA), 357.   [103] Ibid.

[104] The treatment of body tissues or fluids after removal from the body is not excluded: *EPO Guidelines*, G-II, [4.2.1].

[105] *Harvard/Onco-mouse* [2003] *OJ EPO* 473, 491 (Opposition Division). It added that 'the incorporation of the oncogene into the genome is a method which is neither surgical nor therapeutic nor diagnostic in nature'.

[106] *Rodenstock/Progressive spectacle lens with small magnification differences*, T 2420/13 (8 December 2016).

[107] *EPO Guidelines*, G-II, [4.2.1]. See *Baxter/Blood extraction method*, T 329/94 [1998] *EPOR* 363, 367.

[108] *EPO Guidelines*, G-II, [4.2.1].

[109] *Salimen/Pigs III*, T 58/87 [1989] *EPOR* 125; *Thompson/Cornea*, T 24/91 [1996] *EPOR* 19.

decision phase, which as a purely intellectual exercise cannot be practiced on the human or animal body.'[110] It also seems that the requirement would not be applied where the data gathered is compared to normal values. The requirement that the invention needs to be practised on or in the human or animal body would be important, however, where a step in an invention is deemed to be technical. This might be the case, for example, where part of the diagnosis makes use of a computer program, is carried out *in vitro*, or is carried out in a laboratory.[111] In these cases, because the (technical) step is not practised on the body, it would not fall within the exclusion in Article 53(c) of the EPC 2000.

4.4 DIRECT TREATMENT

In order for a patent to fall within the therapeutic method exclusion, it is necessary to show that the invention constitutes a *direct* treatment by therapy. This means, for example, that while the programming of a pacemaker to control the way in which it uses energy undoubtedly has an indirect effect on the human body, this was held to be more concerned with improving an apparatus than with health.[112] While it is difficult to draw the line between direct and indirect effects, a patent is more likely to fall within the exclusion if it can be shown that there is a 'corresponding functional link' between the invention and human or animal health.[113] That is, a method does not fall within Article 53(c) 'if there is no functional link and hence no physical causality between its constituent steps carried out in relation to a therapy device and the therapeutic effect produced on that body by that device'.[114] In a similar vein, it has been held that to fall within the exclusion, the invention must target a particular illness or disease,[115] and must also provide a 'defined, real treatment' of a pathological condition.[116]

4.5 TWO OR MORE USES

One issue that has arisen in this context relates to the familiar complaint about purpose-bound tests—namely, that the same physical activity may be used for different purposes. What would be the case, for example, in relation to the injection of a medicament (such as Botox), which might be administered both to treat a disease and for the purpose of reducing wrinkles? It is clear that so long as an application has a use that falls within the scope of section 4A/Article 53(c), it will be excluded. This is the case even if the invention has other uses that do not fall within the exclusion.[117] Thus an application for a method of cleaning plaque from human teeth that had both an (excluded) therapeutic effect and a (non-excluded) cosmetic effect was excluded from patentability by Article 53(c) of the EPC 2000 on the basis that the application claimed a therapeutic treatment.[118] While the

---

[110] *Cygnus/Diagnostic methods*, G 1/04 [2006] *OJ EPO* 334, 356 (EBA).   [111] Ibid., 357.

[112] *Ela Medical*, T 789/96 [2002] *OJ EPO* 364, 369, [2.2.2.1].   [113] Ibid., 369–70.

[114] *Siemens*, T 245/87 [1989] *OJ EPO* 171, [3.2.3].

[115] *Sequus Pharmaceuticals*, T 4/98 [2002] *OJ EPO* 139, 149–50.

[116] *Eli Lilly/Serotonin receptor*, T 241/95 [2001] *OJ EPO* 103, 109, [3.1.2]. See also *Norsk Hydro*, T 135/98 (20 November 2002) (a feed mixture for optimally satisfying the nutritional requirements of farmed fish was not a medical treatment practiced on an animal body).

[117] Unlike PA 1977, s. 1(2)/EPC 2000, Art. 52, the exclusion is not confined to methods of treatment 'as such'.

[118] *ICI/Cleaning plaque*, T 209/86 [1992] *OJ EPO* 414; *Du Pont/Appetite suppressant*, T 144/83 [1986] *OJ EPO* 30; *General Hospital/Contraceptive methods*, T 820/92 [1995] *EPOR* 446; *Meiji/Feeds*, T 438/91 [1999] *EPOR* 452; *Telectronics/Pacer*, T 82/93 [1996] *EPOR* 409 (if hybrid claims include a feature within the exception, the whole is unpatentable).

presence of a surgical step in a multi-step method for treatment of the human or animal body normally confers a surgical character on the method, there may be some instances where this is not the case.[119] On the basis that methods that have a destructive purpose do not fall within the aim of section 4A/Article 53(c), surgery is limited to processes that give 'priority to maintaining life or health of the human or animal body on which they are performed'.[120] As such, a process that has as its end result the death of a living thing (either deliberately or incidentally) will not be caught by the exclusion—even if the process involves a surgical step. Similarly, the fact that a chemical product has both a cosmetic and a therapeutic effect when used to treat the human or animal body does not render the cosmetic treatment unpatentable.[121]

4.6 METHODS WITH A NUMBER OF STEPS

Where a claimed method involves a number of steps, one or more of which constitutes a method of therapy or surgery (but not diagnosis), the method as a whole will be excluded.[122] Thus a method of producing a transgenic animal that includes a surgical method of embryo transplantation is objectionable under section 4A(1)/Article 53(c).[123] This is not the case, however, with diagnostic methods. This is because, since diagnostic methods are inherently multi-step methods, claims will only be excluded if they include *all of the* steps necessary for making a diagnosis.[124]

4.7 LIMITS

While section 4(A)/Article 53(c) impose important limits on the types of medical and veterinary inventions that may be patented, it would be wrong to assume that all medical and veterinary inventions are excluded from the scope of patent protection. The reason for this is that the potential scope of the exclusion is restricted by the fact that it must be read in light of section 4A(4)/Article 54(5). While we deal with this in more detail later,[125] it is enough to note that these provisions have been construed in such a way that they permit the patenting of uses of known substances for the *manufacture* of a medicament to treat a particular disease.[126] As we will see, while the so-called 'second medical use' patents continue to undermine the scope of the exception for methods of medical and veterinary treatment, the question of whether an application relating merely to a new dosage regime is patentable remains controversial.

Because section 4A(4)/Article 54(5) only apply to medical *methods* that use substances or compositions, the exclusion of methods of medical and veterinary treatment still

[119] *See-Shell/Blood flow*, T 182/90 [1994] *EPOR* 320; *EPO Guidelines*, G-II, [4.2.1].

[120] *Georgetown University/Pericardial access*, T 35/99 [2000] *OJ EPO* 447, 451. This is in contrast to processes the end result of which is the death of living things 'under treatment' either deliberately or incidentally.

[121] *General Hospital Corp./Hair removal method*, T 383/03 [2005] *OJ EPO* 159, 162.

[122] The mere presence of one therapeutic or surgical step in a multi-step method was enough to exclude that method from patentability: *Medi-Physics/Treatment by surgery*, G 1/07 [2011] *OJ EPO* 34, [3.2.3.2].

[123] UK IPO, *Examination Guidelines for Patent Applications Relating to Medical Inventions in the UK Intellectual Property Office* (14 October 2016), [72].

[124] *Cygnus/Diagnostic methods*, G 1/04 [2006] *OJ EPO* 334 (EBA).

[125] See Chapter 18, section 5.1, pp. 567–8.

[126] *ICI/Cleaning plaque*, T 209/86 [1991] *EPOR* 157 [1992] *OJ EPO* 414. For PA 1977, s. 2(6)/EPC 2000, Art. 54(3), to operate, the use must fall within PA 1977, s. 4(2)/EPC 2000, Art. 52(4): *Nycomed/Contrast agent for NMR imaging*, T 655/92 [1988] *EPOR* 206.

applies where apparatuses and objects are used. The residual scope of the exclusion was reaffirmed by the EPO's Technical Board of Appeal when it resisted attempts to extend the scope of Article 54(5) beyond the use of substances and compositions to include the surgical use of an instrument.[127]

5 EXCLUDED SUBJECT MATTER

Up until 1977, for a patent to be valid, it was necessary to show a 'manner of new manufacture'. This phrase, which was first used in the 1623 Statute of Monopolies, proved to be a remarkably versatile and flexible tool which enabled patent law to adapt to and accommodate many of the technological and scientific changes that have taken place over the last two-and-a-half centuries. The passage of the Patents Act 1977 saw a dramatic change in the way in which British patent law determined what was patentable subject matter. The reason for this was that, unlike previous legislation, neither the 1977 Act nor the EPC 1973 upon which it is based contains a definition of 'invention';[128] nor do they expressly require that applicants disclose an invention in order to be patentable. Instead, the 1977 Act and the EPC 2000 contain a non-exhaustive list[129] of creations that are deemed *not* to be inventions.[130] To this end, section 1(2) of the Patents Act 1977, which is the equivalent of Article 52(2) EPC 2000, states:

It is hereby declared that the following (among other things) are not inventions for the purposes of this Act, that is to say, anything that consists of:

(a)   a discovery, scientific theory or mathematical method;[131]
(b)   a literary, dramatic, musical or artistic work or any other aesthetic creation whatsoever;
(c)   a scheme, rule or method for performing a mental act, playing a game[132] or doing business, or a program for a computer;
(d)   the presentation of information;

but the foregoing provisions shall not prevent anything from being treated as an invention for the purposes of this Act only to the extent that a patent or application for a patent relates to that thing as such.

While the decision not to require the existence of an invention as an express requirement for patentability marked an important change in British patent practice, section 1(2) (and

[127]   In response to an attempt to patent a second use of a surgical instrument, the Board said that 'a surgical use of an instrument is not analogous to a therapeutic use (of a medicament) . . . since the former is not consumed in the application and could be repeatedly used for the same or even other purposes as well . . . medicaments on the other hand are expended in the process of use and thus have a once for all utility': *Codman/Second surgical use*, T 227/91 [1994] *OJ EPO* 491, [5.2].
[128]   Under PA 1949, s. 101, inventions were defined by the phrase 'manner of manufacture'.
[129]   See *Lux Traffic v. Pike Signals* [1993] *RPC* 107, 137 *ff*; *Christian Franceries/Traffic regulations*, T 16/83 [1988] *EPOR* 65.
[130]   G. Kolle, 'The Patentable Invention in the EPC' (1974) 5 *IIC* 140, 144. P. Johnson, 'Mr Skemp's preposterous provision: the drafting of the Patents Act 1977 and harmonization in the 1970s' (2015) 5 *QMJIP* 367.
[131]   For a discussion of 'mathematical methods', see *Citibank v. Comptroller General of Patents* [2006] *EWHC* 1676 (Ch), [19], [21] (concept did not merely operate at the rarefied atmosphere of calculus, but also extended to 'lower levels').
[132]   On games, see IPO Practice Notice, *Patents Act 1977: Patentability of Games* (25 November 2005, amended 2 November 2006); *Thomas Anderson's Application*, O/112/12 (9 March 2012) (application for a word game excluded).

Article 52) effectively codified the picture of the invention that had built up in Britain (and most other EPC countries) prior to 1977.[133]

On the face of it, the categories of excluded subject matter share little in common, other than that they are unable to be patented.[134] A number of different explanations are used to justify the exclusions. These vary from the fact that the subject matter is protected by other forms of intellectual property (used to explain the exclusion of computer programs, literary, dramatic, musical, and artistic works, and other aesthetic creations), through to the stifling effect that protection would have on research and development (used to explain the exclusion of discoveries, scientific theories, and mathematical methods). Lurking behind many of the categories of subject matter excluded from protection is an image of the invention as something concrete and technical in character. Whereas an invention leads to a practical concrete result, this is not the case with discoveries, mathematical methods, or scientific theories. Neither is it the case with schemes, rules, or methods for performing a mental act, playing a game, doing business, or the presentation of information—activities that are seen to be abstract and intellectual in nature, and thus not patentable.

While most, but by no means all, of the material listed in section 1(2)/Article 52(2) is excluded because it is abstract and non-technical,[135] this is not the case with computer programs which were excluded because it was thought at the time that the EPC 1973 was drafted, that they were better protected by copyright law,[136] or too difficult to search.[137] As we will see, a lot of time and effort has been expended in attempting to undo this decision.[138]

5.1 AN INVENTION AS A POSITIVE REQUIREMENT FOR PATENTABILITY?

Despite the absence of a need to show the existence of an invention as a precondition for patentability, it has been suggested that for an invention to be patentable, it is necessary to show that the application discloses an invention.[139] In the United Kingdom, support for this view came from the decision in *Genentech's Patent*,[140] where the Court of Appeal said that it was an essential requirement that 'must be satisfied before a patent can properly be granted . . . that the applicant has made an "invention"'. While Lord Mustill said, in *Biogen v. Medeva*,[141] that the requirement that there be an invention may be of relevance in the future, the question of whether the existence of an invention was a separate prerequisite for patentability was left unanswered. As such, the only issue which applicants need to concern themselves with is whether their invention falls within the scope of the subject matter excluded by section 1(2)/Article 52(2).[142]

---

[133] Because the exceptions were intended to harmonize existing laws, pre-1977 case law has been treated as of persuasive value when interpreting the exclusions: *Gale's Application* [1991] *RPC* 305. Over time, pre-1977 decisions have been replaced by decisions of the EPO and other member states.

[134] For a history of Art. 52, see *President's Reference/Patentability of programs for computers*, G 3/08 (12 May 2010).   [135] Cf. Jacob LJ in *Aerotel v. Telco Holdings* [2007] 1 *All ER* 225, [9].

[136] G. Kolle, 'The Patentable Invention in the EPC' (1974) 5 *IIC* 140, 147–8.

[137] See *Xanavi Infomatics/map database device* (14 April 2016), [3.2].

[138] 'Given the ubiquity of computers in modern life it is not surprising that the precise limitations of [PA 1977, s. (1)2(c)] have given rise to difficulty': *Autonomy Corporation v. Comptroller General* [2008] *EWHC* 146, [14].   [139] *EPO Guidelines*, G-I, [1.1], [2(ii)]; EPC 2000 Regs, rr 27 and 29.

[140] [1989] *RPC* 147, 262. Mustill LJ based his arguments on the wording of PA 1977, s. 1(2), EPC 1973, Art. 52, and the (then) *EPO Guidelines*, C-IV, 1.1, and 2.2 (now G-I, [1.1], [2(ii)]).

[141] [1997] *RPC* 1, 31; cf. 42 (Lord Hoffmann).

[142] EPC 1973, Art. 52, is repeated in EPC 2000, Art. 53(2). There are no substantive changes to the patentable subject matter: EPC 2000, Art. 1, item 17.

6 IS THE INVENTION EXCLUDED BY SECTION 1(2)/ARTICLE 52(2)?

The question of whether an invention is denied patent protection on the basis that it falls within one of the excluded categories in section 1(2)/Article 52(2) plays an important role in determining the types of invention protected by patents.[143] Reflecting a pro-patent position, the Enlarged Board of Appeal has recently stressed that the excluded subject matter should not be construed too broadly.[144] Determining whether something ought to qualify as patentable subject matter is an important and often problematic process. In part, this is an inevitable consequence of the fact that the law has to pass judgment over complex and rapidly changing technologies. It is also a consequence of the fact that this area of law has become caught up in a power struggle between the institutions of the European Union and the EPO as to who controls the future of patents in Europe. There was also an ongoing pressure for the threshold for patent protection to be lowered in Europe to ensure that it is on a par with that in the United States (where non-technical business methods are patentable).[145] At the same time, there is a growing concern about the number of trivial patents that have been granted (particularly for computer-related inventions) and the breadth of many gene-based patents. While all of these factors have played their part in muddying the waters, perhaps the single most important reason for the complexity that we now face is because two different approaches are used when deciding whether an invention falls foul of section 1(2)/Article 52(2).

The first approach, which is called the 'technical effect' approach, was developed in a series of decisions in the United Kingdom and at the EPO. This approach is currently applied in the United Kingdom. It is similar to the approach that was used at the EPO until (around) 2000. The second approach, often called the 'any hardware' approach, was suggested by the Technical Board of Appeal in the *Pension Benefit Systems Partnership* decision.[146] While focusing on the patentability of a business method invention, the decision has broader consequences for the way in which section 1(2)/Article 52(2) is applied. Although the 'any hardware' approach was followed in one (then) Patent Office decision in the United Kingdom[147] and incorporated into the EPO's *Guidelines for Examination*,[148] it was resoundingly rejected by the Court of Appeal in *Aerotel v. Telco Holdings*,[149] and later in *Symbian*,[150] in which the Court reaffirmed the technical effect approach in the United Kingdom. In contrast, the approach adopted in *Pension Benefits* has been applied and expanded in subsequent decisions at the EPO. It has also been confirmed by the EPO Enlarged Board of Appeal as the correct way to approach patentable subject matter.[151]

---

[143] In some cases, British courts have taken to using the text of EPC 2000, Art. 52, rather than that set out in PA 1977, s. 1(2): see *Aerotel v. Telco Holdings* [2007] 1 *All ER* 225, [6]. For a general discussion of the position at the EPO, see S. Sterckx and J. Cockbain, *Exclusions from Patentability: How Far Has the European Patent Office Eroded Boundaries?* (2012).

[144] *State of Israel/Tomatoes II*, G 2/12 [2015] *OJ EPO* A27, and *Plant Bioscience/Broccoli II*, G 2/13 [2015] *OJ EPO* A28.

[145] The situation in the United States has changed following the Supreme Court decision of *Alice Corp. v. CLS Bank* 134 *S. Ct.* 2347 (19 June 2014).

[146] *Pension Benefit Systems Partnership*, T 931/95 [2001] *OJ EPO* 441.

[147] *John Edward Rose*, O/075/01 (14 February 2001).

[148] See *EPO Guidelines*, G-II, [2] (amended as of 31 August 2001). See *Notice from EPO* [2001] *OJ EPO* 464.

[149] [2007] 1 *All ER* 225.

[150] *Symbian v. Comptroller-General of Patents* [2008] *EWCA Civ* 1066, [16].

[151] *President's Reference/Patentability of programs for computers*, G 3/08 [2011] *OJ EPO* 10.

6.1 'TECHNICAL EFFECT' APPROACH IN THE UNITED KINGDOM

While there may occasionally be problems in determining how the rules will be applied in particular situations, the approach taken in the United Kingdom to the question of whether an application falls foul of section 1(2) is relatively straightforward. Put simply, the question asked is: does the invention, when viewed as a whole, make a technical contribution to the art that does not fall within one of the areas excluded by section 1(2)?

One thing that has complicated the law in this area (like many areas of patent law) is the growing tendency for judges, as would-be treatise writers, to reduce the law to a set of rules or guidelines (which are invariably applied as if they were algorithms). This is what occurred in *Aerotel v. Telco Holdings*,[152] where the Court of Appeal said that, to determine whether an invention falls within one of the excluded categories of subject matter, it was necessary to undertake four separate tasks:

(i) to construe the claim;

(ii) to identify the contribution;

(iii) to ask whether the contribution falls within one of the excluded categories; and

(iv) to check to see whether the invention is technical.

While, as subsequent decisions have noted, the staged approach in *Aerotel* is a useful summary of the law, as the Court of Appeal subsequently said in *Symbian*, it should not be followed blindly.[153] The Court of Appeal in *Symbian* also said that the third and fourth questions in *Aerotel* could be conflated and that the order in which the stages are dealt with could be changed without affecting either the applicable principles or the outcomes. By downplaying the third stage set out in *Aerotel*, the Court of Appeal in *Symbian* restored technical contribution as the touchstone for determining patentable subject matter.[154] In so doing, the Court subtly changed the way in which UK courts approach the question of whether an invention falls foul of section 1(2). This is because while the Court of Appeal in *Symbian* said that it was dangerous to suggest that there was a clear rule to determine whether a program was excluded by Article 52(2), it did say that the key question to be asked when determining patentable subject matter is whether the invention, when considered as whole, makes a technical contribution to the known art that that does not fall within one of the areas excluded by section 1(2).[155] As we will see later, the decision in *Symbian* to refocus attention on the technical contribution of an application led the Court of Appeal to reject the argument that computer programs were only patentable when they brought about a novel effect outside of a computer. Instead, the question to be asked was whether the program brought about a technical effect or solved a technical problem, which could occur either within or outside the computer.

---

[152] [2007] 1 *All ER* 225, [40] (the patent was subsequently held to be invalid on other grounds).

[153] *Symbian v. Comptroller-General of Patents* [2008] *EWCA Civ* 1066, [16].

[154] Following *Gameaccount/Gamemachine*, T 1543/06 (29 June 2007), [2.5].

[155] This was on the basis of the Board's analysis in *Vicom/Computer-related invention*, T 208/84 [1987] *OJ EPO* 14, the two *IBM* decisions (*IBM/Data processor network*, T 6/83 [1990] *OJ EPO* 5 *IBM/Computer-related invention*, T 115/85 [1990] *EPOR* 107), and the UK decisions of *Merrill Lynch's Application* [1989] *RPC* 561 (CA) and *Gale's Application* [1991] *RPC* 305 (CA): *Symbian v. Comptroller-General of Patents* [2008] *EWCA Civ* 1066, [49], [51], [59].

In explaining the approach that is adopted in the United Kingdom to determine whether an invention falls foul of section 1(2), we will follow the approach outlined in *Symbian* (and subsequent decisions). This requires us to:

(i)   construe the invention;

(ii)   identify the contribution made by the invention; and

(iii) determine whether the contribution is technical and does not fall within one of the areas excluded by section 1(2).

We will look at each of these in turn.

6.1.1 Construe the claim: the 'whole contents' approach to interpretation

The first task that needs to be undertaken is that the claims need to be construed to determine the scope of the patented invention. While this may appear to be relatively inconsequential, it has proved to be crucially important in determining the validity of many patents.

In interpreting the scope of the claim, the courts adopt what is known as a 'purposive' approach to interpretation—that is, they look at the way the person skilled in the art would construe the claims (equivalents are not relevant for these purposes). This is discussed in Chapter 22. One question that arose in relation to section 1(2)/Article 52(2) was: what happens if an application contains a mixture of both excluded and permitted features? What should be done, for example, if an invention includes a discovery or a computer program that is expressly excluded under section 1(2)/Article 52(2) *as well as* other non-excluded elements? Initially, discussions in this area focused on the meaning that should be given to the proviso to section 1(2)/Article 52(2), which states that the listed exclusions apply only to the extent that the alleged invention relates to that thing *as such*.[156] Given the ambiguous nature of the proviso, it is not surprising that it lent itself to a number of different and sometimes conflicting styles of interpretation.[157]

In determining how applications should be interpreted, courts in the United Kingdom (and the EPO, even after *Pension Benefits*) have come down in favour of what is known as the 'whole contents' approach to interpretation.[158] In so doing, they rejected the so-called 'contribution' approach (under which the courts would only consider those aspects of the invention that were not excluded).[159] This means that, when considering whether an invention falls foul of section 1(2)/Article 52(2), the courts disregard the fact that the invention has as one of its elements say a computer program or a discovery, and focus instead on the invention *as a whole*. In so doing, the courts have stressed that, when determining whether an invention is patentable, it is not necessary to compare the non-technical and the technical elements of the

---

[156] PA 1977, s. 1(2); EPC 2000, Art. 52.

[157] It was initially suggested that, when determining whether an invention falls within PA 1977, s. 1(2)/EPC 1973, Art. 52, the courts should separate the excluded and non-excluded elements of the application and focus only upon the non-excluded components: *Merrill Lynch's Application* [1988] *RPC* 1.

[158] In the United Kingdom, see *Merrill Lynch's Application* [1989] *RPC* 561 (CA); *Genentech v. Wellcome* [1989] *RPC* 147, 204–14, 224 *ff.* At the EPO, see *Vicom/Computer-related invention*, T 208/84 [1987] *OJ EPO* 14, [1987] *EPOR* 74; *Kock & Sterzel/X-ray apparatus*, T 26/86 [1988] *EPOR* 72, [1988] *OJ EPO* 19.

[159] See *Aerotel v. Telco Holdings* [2007] 1 *All ER* 225, [26], [32]–[37], in which Jacob LJ said that there was a lot to be said for the contribution approach, but that he was bound by precedent to follow *Merrill Lynch* et al. See also *Cranway v. Playtech* [2009] *EWHC* 1588, [132]–[134] (which seems not to have followed the 'whole contents' approach).

invention. That is, it is irrelevant that an invention is made up of a mixture of technical and non-technical elements.[160]

6.1.2 Identify the contribution made by the invention

While the 'whole contents' approach offers guidance where a patent is made up of a mixture of excluded and non-excluded elements, it offers little assistance in helping us to answer the more general question of how the invention ought to be identified. In thinking about the nature of the invention, a number of different approaches could have been adopted. The courts, for example, could have attempted to distil the essence or kernel of the invention from the claims themselves. One of the interesting features of the way in which the invention has been interpreted by UK courts and by the EPO (pre-*Pension Benefits*) is that rather than attempting to identify the essential nature of the invention, they have focused on what the invention does or what it adds.[161] That is, when determining whether an invention falls within section 1(2)/Article 52(2), the courts concentrate upon the *contribution* or *effect* that the invention has upon the known art (or knowledge in the area in question). This is now captured in the second step in the *Aerotel* test, under which the court is required to identify the contribution made by the invention. As a result, when deciding whether an invention falls within one of the excluded categories, it is necessary to construe the claims to identify the contribution made by the invention. Once the invention has been characterized, it is then possible to determine whether it falls within the scope of section 1(2)/Article 52(2).

One of the problems that needs to be confronted when identifying the contribution made by an invention is that applicants may attempt to describe an invention that prima facie falls foul of section 1(2)/Article 52(2) in such a way that it appears to fall outside the scope of the excluded categories. Faced with the possibility of applicants dressing non-patentable inventions up in a way that makes them appear as if they are patentable, the courts have responded by ignoring the *form* of the claims and focusing instead on the *substance* of the invention.[162] In *Aerotel*, the Court of Appeal accepted that the test is an exercise in judgement, involving the problem to be solved, how the invention works, and what its advantages are. The Court also said that the second step was best summed up by the question: what has the inventor really added to human knowledge?[163]

6.1.3 Determine whether the contribution is 'technical'

Once the contribution made by an invention has been identified, it is then necessary to consider whether that contribution falls within any of the categories of excluded subject matter set out in section 1(2)/Article 52(2). Although, in many situations it is relatively easy to determine whether an invention falls within section 1(2)/Article 52(2), in some circumstances this is not the case. In the thirty or so years during which UK tribunals and the EPO (pre-*Pension Benefits*) have been thinking about how applications that are solely made up of excluded subject matter can be distinguished from inventions that happen to include something such as a computer program and are therefore prima facie patentable,

---

[160] *Kock & Sterzel/X-ray apparatus*, T 26/86 [1988] *OJ EPO* 1; *Pension Benefit Systems Partnership*, T 931/95 [2001] *OJ EPO* 441, 450; cf. *IBM/Text clarity processing*, T 38/86 [1990] *EPOR* 606.

[161] Cf *Epoch v Character Options* [2017] *EWHC* 556 (IPEC), where Hacon J focused on the objects in question—a child's decorative beads made of resin—and whether they were an aesthetic creation, rather than the contribution to the art (or effect) of the decorative beads. (Holding that the beads were not aesthetic creations as such and thus did not fall foul of PA s 1(2)(b), at [51].)

[162] *Merrill Lynch's Application* [1989] *RPC* 561; *IBM/Document abstracting and retrieving*, T 22/85 [1990] *OJ EPO* 12, [1990] *EPOR* 98, 105.   [163] *Aerotel v. Telco Holdings* [2007] 1 *All ER* 225, [43]–[44].

a somewhat surprising situation developed: in determining whether an invention falls within the scope of section 1(2)/Article 52(2), the courts have ignored the difficult question of whether the invention was, for example, a computer program or a mathematical method; instead, they asked whether the invention-as-claimed was 'technical'.[164] If the invention exhibits technical character or the problem that it solves is technical,[165] this is taken to mean that it falls outside the scope of section 1(2)/Article 52(2).[166] Conversely, the absence of technical character is treated as virtual proof that the invention falls within the scope of section 1(2)/Article 52(2) and that it is therefore unpatentable. In a sense, what happened—at least in difficult borderline cases—is that the negative criteria set out in section 1(2)/Article 52(2) were recast in more positive terms. This meant that for an invention to be patentable, it was necessary to show that the invention exhibited technical character or, in other words, that it made a technical contribution to the art.

The introduction of technical character (effect or contribution) as a de facto non-statutory requirement for patentability owes its origin to an imaginative interpretation of Article 52 of the EPC 1973 (now Article 52 of the EPC 2000). This stated that what the categories in Article 52(2) have in common is that they are non-technical, either because they are abstract (discoveries, scientific theories) or because they are clearly non-technical (aesthetic creations or presentations of information).[167] Because Article 52(1) and (2) only exclude from protection those inventions that are non-technical, it is a short inductive leap to conclude from this that the term 'invention' relates to inventions of a technical nature. This conclusion was reinforced by the rules and guidelines under the EPC, which clearly state that in order for an invention to be patentable, it must be technical.[168]

The use of technical character as a way of determining whether an invention falls within the scope of the excluded subject matter is set out in the leading EPO decision of *Vicom*.[169] In deciding that an application that related to a method of digitally filtering images using a device called an 'operator matrix', which aimed at producing enhanced images was patentable, the Technical Board of Appeal (TBA) stressed that even if the idea underlying an invention was a mathematical method, it could still be patentable if the invention as a whole made a technical contribution to the known art.[170]

---

[164] As Lewison LJ lamented, it was regrettable that, because the apparently simple words in Art. 52(2) have no clear meaning, British courts and the Boards of Appeal at the EPO have stopped even trying to understand them ('Instead of arguing what the legislation means, we argue about what the [technical] gloss means'): *HTC v. Apple* [2013] *EWCA Civ* 451, [143].

[165] *IBM/Data processor network*, T 6/83 [1990] *OJ EPO* 5; *IBM/Computer-related invention*, T 115/85 [1990] *EPOR* 107. The feature of using technical means for a purely non-technical purpose and/or for processing purely non-technical information does not necessarily confer technical character on any such individual steps of use or on the method as a whole; in fact, any activity in the non-technical branch of human culture involves physical entities and uses, to a greater or lesser extent, technical means.

[166] The mere occurrence of technical features in a claim is not enough: *Pension Benefit Systems Partnership*, T 931/95 [2001] *OJ EPO* 441, 450.

[167] *Sternmheimer/Harmonic vibrations*, T 366/87 [1989] *EPOR* 131. On aesthetic creations see *Epoch v. Character Options* [2017] *EWHC* 556 (IPEC); *Gram Engineering's Application* O/275/08 (9 October 2008); *Hettling-Denker/Translucent building materials*, T 686/90 [2004] *EPOR* 5.

[168] A patentable invention must relate to a technical field (EPC 1973 Regs, r. 27(1)(b)), it must be concerned with a technical problem (EPC 2000 Regs, r. 43(1)), and it must be characterized in the claims by means of technical features (EPC 2000 Regs, r. 43(1)(9b)): *EPO Guidelines*, G-I, [2(ii)].

[169] *Vicom/Computer-related invention*, T 208/84 [1987] *OJ EPO* 14. See also H. Beyer, 'Der Begriff der Information als Grundlage für die Beeurteilung des technischen Charakters von programmbezogenen Erfindungen' [1990] *GRUR* 399.

[170] *Hitachi/Auction method*, T 258/03 [2004] *OJ EPO* 575, 580 (the term 'invention' is to be construed as 'subject matter having a technical character').

While some doubts were initially raised in the United Kingdom about the use of technical character as a way of distinguishing inventions that are 'in reality' or 'in truth' patentable from those that are solely made up of excluded subject matter,[171] British courts followed the lead of the EPO and adopted technical character as a way of determining whether an invention falls within section 1(2).[172] This was highlighted in the Court of Appeal in *Merrill Lynch*, when Fox LJ said:

> [I]t cannot be permissible to patent an item excluded by section 1(2) under the guise of an article which contains that item—that is to say, in the case of a computer program, the patenting of a conventional computer containing that program. Something further is necessary. The nature of that addition is, I think, to be found in the *Vicom* case where it was stated 'Decisive is what technical contribution the invention makes to the known art'. There must, I think, be some technical advance on the prior art in the form of a new result.[173]

While Fox LJ's language differs in certain respects from that of the TBA, the Court of Appeal accepted that the presence of technical character was sufficient to show that an invention did not relate to a disqualified matter and that, as such, that it was patentable on its face.[174] While there was some uncertainty following *Aerotel* about the role that technical character should play in determining whether an invention is excluded under section 1(2),[175] it is now clear that technical effect is the touchstone to be used to determine whether an application falls foul of one of the excluded categories of subject matter in section 1(2). As Judge Birss said in *Halliburton Energy Service's Patent Application*,[176] at the heart of the law is the consistent principle that an inventor must make a technical contribution to the art that does not fall within one of the areas excluded by Article 52(2).

One of the advantages of shifting attention towards the idea of technical character is that the courts are able to avoid the difficult task of having to define the subject matter listed in section 1(2)/Article 52(2)—a task that is not only technically problematic, but also one that changes in technology are likely to render obsolete. Indeed, one of the major problems with specific formulations such as section 1(2) and Article 52(2) is that because they are drafted in light of contemporary technologies, they are prone to obsolescence or at least convoluted interpretations.

Whatever advantages there may be in using technical character as a de facto requirement for determining whether an invention falls within the ambit of section 1(2)/Article 52(2), it still leaves us with the difficult task of having to formulate and understand what is meant by the term 'technical'. As we will see, it is the difficulty in answering this question that led to adoption of the *Pension Benefits* approach at the EPO.

---

[171] *Wang Laboratories* [1991] *RPC* 463, 470; *Fujitsu's Application* [1996] *RPC* 511, 521. The Munich Diplomatic Conference on the establishment of the EPC abstained from limiting the concept of the invention by use of 'technical' as was earlier proposed: G. Kolle, 'Patentable Inventions in the EPC' (1974) 5 *IIC* 140, 145.

[172] Technical character has become decisive in determining whether or not a patent falls within the scope of s. 1(2): *CIPA*, [1.06].   [173] *Merrill Lynch's Application* [1989] *RPC* 561, 569.

[174] *IBM/Document abstracting and retrieving*, T 22/85 [1990] *OJ EPO* 12, [1]–[4].

[175] In part, this was prompted by the realization that the word 'technical' was inherently vague (which is not surprising, given that it is meant to act as a proxy for the equally vague 'invention'): *CFPH LLC v. Comptroller-General of Patents, Designs, and Trade Marks* [2006] *RPC* 259 ('technical' is 'a useful servant but a dangerous master'); *Aerotel v. Telco Holdings* [2007] 1 *All ER* 225, [121]–[124]; *IGT v. Comptroller of Patents* [2007] *EWHC* 134, [39]; *Re Oneida Indian Nation's Application* [2007] *EWHC* 954 (Pat), [9]; *Astron Clinica v. Comptroller General of Patents* [2008] *EWHC* 85, [45].   [176] [2011] *EWHC* 2508, [27].

(i) What is a 'technical' contribution?

Given that the law in this area is underpinned by the consistent principle that an inventor must make a technical contribution to the art that does not fall within one of the areas excluded by section 1(2)/Article 52(2), a key question for determining patentable subject matter is how a technical contribution is to be construed. While the way in which this question is answered changes depending on the technology in question (something at which we look at in more detail later), in this context we will limit ourselves to some general comments about the approach that is taken by the courts when determining whether a contribution is technical.

In the vast bulk of cases, it is relatively easy to determine whether an invention is technical. This is because it is generally accepted that certain types of creations, such as those in the fields of mechanical engineering or organic chemistry, are technical in nature and, as such, that they belong within the remit of patent law. This is made all the easier by the fact that applicants are required to specify the technical field to which their application relates.

While, in most circumstances, it may be easy to determine whether an invention is technical, in some situations this is not the case.[177] This has been the case with inventions in relation to financial systems, software-generating software, language processing, text-editing, and computer programs. In these borderline cases, determining whether an invention is technical is often very difficult. One of the reasons for this is that because computer programs and computer-related inventions are inherently technical, to give some meaning to section 1(2)/Article 52(2) it was not enough merely to say that any technical effect was sufficient for an invention to be patentable. As a result (as we see later), the tribunals have had to determine the type of technical effect that is sufficient to confer patentability.[178] The problems in this area were highlighted by the Comptroller of Patents who complained that 'in practice it is often very difficult to determine whether a particular invention does as a matter of fact involve the sort of technical contribution or result alluded to in the cases'.[179] The difficulty of this task was borne out by the fact that while the legal studies that prompted the revision of the EPO Guidelines were able to propose 'technical character' as one of the ways of determining whether subject matter was excluded from patentability, they were unable to provide a precise definition of what was meant by the term 'technical'.[180] Instead, they left the task of defining technology to the jurisprudence of the courts.

While the task of having to decide what is meant by a technical creation may have been left to the respective courts, so far they have provided little direct guidance in this matter. In many cases where this issue has arisen, no indication is given as to how a decision was reached as to whether something was technical. In other cases, the tribunals have offered the equally unhelpful 'it depends on the facts of the case'.[181] Given that the fate of many inventions depends on the way 'technology' is defined, it may be helpful to provide some guidance in this matter.

---

[177] See J. Thomas, 'An Epistemology of Appropriation: Patentable Subject Matter after *State Street Bank*' [2000] *IPQ* 27, 49 *ff*.

[178] As the EBA explained, the drafters of the EPC saw a computer algorithm as a non-technical, purely abstract, mathematical-logical exercise. The Board noted that computer programs could also validly be seen as defining a procedure to make a machine carry out a task: *President's Reference/Patentability of programs for computers*, G 3/08 [2011] *OJ EPO* 10, [13.5].

[179] *Fujitsu's Application* [1996] *RPC* 511, 521.   [180] WG/CP/I/1.

[181] *Wang Laboratories* [1991] *RPC* 463, 473. See also *Fujitsu's Application* [1997] *RPC* 608.

In determining whether an invention is 'technical', the courts have tended to fall back on the model of the invention that has long been employed in patent law.[182] This is one that sees the process of invention as the reduction of the abstract to the specific, or as a transformation from the general to the concrete—processes that are mediated by the agency of the human inventor. In turn, this model distinguishes between creations that are abstract, intellectual, mental, undefined, and non-patentable, and those that are concrete, physical, tangible, and patentable.[183] Drawing upon this model of the invention, it has been held that an invention is technical and patentable if it provides or leads to a concrete, causal, or non-abstract result or change in things. When translated into the context of section 1(2)/Article 52(2), this means that if it can be shown that the invention brings about a tangible physical change, this is taken as virtual proof that the invention is technical and that it therefore falls outside the scope of the excluded categories.[184] One question that is yet to be considered in this context is whether recent case law has extended the concept of invention beyond its physical roots to embrace a new type of (immaterial) information-based invention.[185]

The use of physical change to determine whether an invention is technical can be seen in *Vicom* where the Technical Board of Appeal explained how non-patentable mathematical methods could be distinguished from patentable inventions:

> [T]he fact that a mathematical method or a mathematical algorithm is carried out on numbers . . . and provides a result also in numerical form, the mathematical method or algorithm being only an *abstract* concept prescribing how to operate on numbers. No direct technical result is produced by the mathematical method as such. [While abstract creations are not patentable,] if a mathematical method is used in a technical process, that process is carried out on a physical entity (which may be a material object but equally an image stored as an electrical signal) by some technical means implementing the method and provides as its result a certain *change* in that entity.[186]

In a move that has important ramifications for many inventions, particularly in the field of information technology, the physical conception of technology has been interpreted very broadly. This is reflected in the comment that 'physical entities' includes 'a real thing, i.e. an image, even if that thing was represented by an electrical signal'.[187] The wide definition given to physical entity can also be seen in the EPO decision of *Kock & Sterzel*.[188] In this case, it was held that the fact that the invention controlled X-ray tubes in such a way as to ensure optimum exposure while minimizing the danger of overloading the tube was sufficient change for the application to be deemed technical.[189] Perhaps the best

---

[182] See *NRDC's Application* [1961] *RPC* 134, 142; *Rote Taube* (1970) 1 *IIC* 136, 137–8.

[183] The 'invention must belong not to the field of abstractions or speculations, but to that of practical achievement. It must concern not an abstract principle but a conception which is implemented in industry': *Christian Franceries/Traffic regulations*, T 16/83 [1988] *EPOR* 65, 70.

[184] The following inventions were held not to be patentable because they did not bring about a physical change: inventions for document abstracting (*IBM/Document abstracting and retrieving*, T 22/85 [1990] *EPOR* 98); linguistic expression processing (*IBM/Text clarity processing*, T 38/86 [1990] *EPOR* 606); a system for listing semantically related linguistic expressions (*IBM/Semantically related expressions*, T 52/85 [1989] *EPOR* 454); a method for automatically detecting and correcting contextual homophone errors in a text document (*IBM/Text processing*, T 65/86 [1990] *EPOR* 181).

[185] See M. Biagioli, 'Between Knowledge and Technology: Patenting Methods, Rethinking Materiality' (2012) 22 *Anthro Forum* 285.   [186] *Vicom/Computer-related inventions*, T 208/84 [1987] *EPOR* 74, 79.

[187] *IBM/Document abstracting and retrieving*, T 22/85 [1990] *EPOR* 98, 105.

[188] *Kock & Sterzel/X-ray apparatus*, T 26/86 [1988] *OJ EPO* 14.

[189] See also *IBM/Computer-related invention*, T 115/85 [1990] *OJ EPO* 30 (an invention that automatically gave visual indications of conditions prevailing in an apparatus or system was said to resolve a technical problem).

example of the way in which the meaning of 'physical entity' has been extended can be seen in *BBC/Colour television signal*,[190] where it was said that despite its transient character, because a television signal could be detected by technical means, it had a physical reality and therefore could not be considered to be an abstract entity. As such, it was prima facie patentable.

Another example of the way physical change has been used to help to decide whether an invention falls within section 1(2)/Article 52(2) is *Cappellini and Bloomberg's Application*.[191] While Pumfrey J stressed that he did not think that 'every result must be a physical article before the claim is allowed', he did reject a claim in the application in question on the basis that it was the 'pure manipulation of data without the production of any physical or real-world effect'.[192] Pumfrey J highlighted the important role that physical change plays in determining whether an invention is excluded under section 1(2) when he said that while a claim to an algorithm standing alone may be objectionable, this would not be the case if the claim were tethered to a physical article.[193] Using the language of *Aerotel*, Pumfrey J said that 'there is no contribution lying outside excluded matter until the claim also covers the result of performing the claimed algorithm'.[194]

While the British courts have embraced physical change as a guide to determine whether an invention falls within section 1(2)/Article 52(2), they have (at times) been careful to distance themselves from some of the more liberal readings at the EPO. For example, in *Shopolotto.com's Application*,[195] Pumfrey J cast doubt over the decision of the Technical Board of Appeal in *IBM/Computer program II*,[196] which held that material technical effect was found 'only in computer once programmed with the claimed software'. In so doing, Pumfrey J reinforced a more traditional (empirical) understanding of the invention that has long dominated in British patent law. As we will see later, however, British courts have recently been willing to construe 'technical' more broadly and, in so doing, have brought British law closer to the approach at the EPO.[197]

(ii) Limitations on the use of technical effect to determine patentability

It is important to note that not all technical contributions or effects will give rise to a patentable invention—that is, 'some apparently technical effects do not always count'.[198]

(a) *Where the technical contribution falls within one of the areas excluded by section 1(2)* One situation where a technical effect will not be sufficient to save an invention is where the contribution falls within one of the excluded categories set out in section 1(2)/Article 52. The fact that the exclusions are generic means that an application will be excluded if it falls within one of the excluded categories. This is the case even though it is otherwise 'technical' because, for example, it is carried out on a computer. As the Court of Appeal said in *Symbian*,[199] the computer program exclusion prevents other excluded material

---

[190] T 163/85 [1990] *OJ EPO* (Suppl.) 19. On this basis, the invention was held not to fall within EPC 1973, Art. 52(2)(d).

[191] [2007] *EWHC* 476. See also *Oneida Nation's Application* [2007] *EWHC* 954 (Pat), [9].

[192] *Cappellini and Bloomberg's Application* [2007] *EWHC* 476, [18]. See also *Oneida Nation's Application* [2007] *EWHC* 954 (Pat), [9].   [193] *Cappellini and Bloomberg's Application* [2007] *EWHC* 476, [8].

[194] Ibid.   [195] [2006] *RPC* 293, [11].   [196] T 935/97 [1999] *EPOR* 301.

[197] For an account of the standing of *Shopalotto* post-*Aerotel* see *Christopher Curtis' Application*, O/260/17 (1 June 2017), [8]–[9].

[198] *Halliburton Energy Service's Patent Application* [2011] *EWHC* 2508, [35] (the business method exclusion is generic).   [199] *Symbian v. Comptroller-General of Patents* [2008] *EWCA Civ* 1066.

becoming patentable merely by use of a computer in its implementation. Thus a business method, mathematical method, or presentation of information implemented on a conventional computer system or network would still be excluded. As we will see later, this logic does not apply to situations where a mental act is carried out on a computer, which would 'never be caught by the mental act exclusion because the claim does not encompass carrying out the calculation mentally'.[200] As a result, it does not matter that an invention leads to a faster, more efficient computer if the effect of the invention is limited to one of the excluded categories. Thus an improved way of presenting information using a computer would not be patentable; so too with a more efficient computerized book-keeping system. The generic nature of the exclusions can be seen in *Merrill Lynch's Application*,[201] where the Court of Appeal was called upon to consider whether an automatic share-trading system which operated using a computer program fell within the scope of section 1(2)(c). While the invention was clearly technical, the Court found that the contribution made by the invention was limited to the field of business (explicitly excluded by section 1(2)(c)) and, as such, was not patentable.[202]

(b) *Where the technical effect is not relevant*   Another situation where a technical effect will not be sufficient to save an application from being excluded is where it is deemed to be the wrong *type* of technical effect or, as the courts prefer, the effect is not '*relevant*'. The need to distinguish relevant and irrelevant technical contributions was promoted by the realization that because all computer-related inventions are technical in nature, if the presence of technical character of any sort were used as a shorthand for determining whether an invention fell within one of the excluded categories, this would have meant that all computer-related inventions would have satisfied the requirement.[203]

To ensure that section 1(2) is not rendered meaningless (which in the Court of Appeal's eyes is what has happened at the EPO[204]), the UK courts have been forced to deal directly with the issue that has driven a lot of the law in this area—namely, how to reconcile the fact that computer-related inventions are clearly technological with the fact that computer programs *as such* are explicitly excluded from the scope of protection.[205] Faced with this problem, Pumfrey J suggested that not all technical effects are relevant and that, in particular where computer programs are under consideration, 'the technical effect to be identified had to be technical effect over and above that to expected from the mere loading of a program into a computer'.[206] As Floyd J said:

---

[200] *Halliburton Energy Service's Patent Application* [2011] *EWHC* 2508, [43]. See also *Symbian v. Comptroller-General of Patents* [2008] *EWCA Civ* 1066, [27].

[201] [1989] *RPC* 561 (CA).   [202] Ibid., 569.

[203] A computer program's 'interdependence with the technical device makes the technical content hard to deny': Mellulis J, as cited in *Symbian v. Comptroller-General of Patents* [2008] *EWCA Civ* 1066, [31]. The technical effect test was 'singularly unhelpful' because the interaction of hardware and software in a computer was inherently technical: *HTC v. Apple* [2013] *EWCA Civ* 451, [147].

[204] In *Fujitsu/File search method*, T 1351/04 (18 April 2007), it was said that, because the claimed method required the use of a computer, it was technical in character and therefore an invention for the purposes of Art. 52. In *Symbian*, the Court of Appeal said that if this view 'represents the Board's view', the exclusion may have lost all meaning: *Symbian v. Comptroller-General of Patents* [2008] *EWCA Civ* 1066, [46].

[205] One of the reasons why it has been so difficult to determine whether an invention involving computer program has a technical effect or makes a technical contribution is because 'computers are self evidently technical in nature': *Halliburton Energy Service's Patent Application* [2011] *EWHC* 2508, [35].

[206] *Shopolotto.com's Application* [2006] *RPC* 293, [9]. See also *Cappellini and Bloomberg's Application* [2007] *EWHC* 476, [5]; *Oneida Indian Nation's Application* [2007] *EWHC* 954, [12] ('it does not follow, just because [a] system of gaming machines is technical, that everything they do (e.g. tracking and controlling the operation of the system) is technical *in the sense required*').

All the difficulties arise because, as matter of ordinary language, the programming of a computer is a technical exercise, and the consequences of so programming it can, in ordinary language, be regarded as achieving a technical effect. It is therefore the case that in applying the exclusion one is seeking to distinguish a relevant technical effect from one which is irrelevant.[207]

We look at what is meant by a *relevant* technical effect when we look at the specific applications later.[208]

6.2 'ANY HARDWARE' APPROACH AT THE EPO

The second approach used to determine whether an invention falls within Article 52(2)/section 1(2), which is currently applied at the EPO, is called (somewhat pejoratively) the 'any hardware' approach. This approach was developed by the Technical Board of Appeal (TBA) in the decision of *Pension Benefits Systems Partnership*[209] and subsequently expanded in *Hitachi*.[210] Under the 'any hardware' approach (in its expanded form), an invention will not fall within any of the excluded categories in Article 52(2) if it embodies or is implemented by some technical means (such as a computer). This is the case even if the technical means are used in relation to a non-technical activity. In effect, under the 'any hardware' approach, the tribunal will stand back from the invention—whether a method or an apparatus—and ask whether it can be classified as a form of technology (irrespective of whether it is novel or inventive); all that matters is that the invention makes use of, or embodies, some form of technology (or hardware).

The first key decision that outlined the 'any hardware' approach was the *Pension Benefits* decision, which was published in 2001. The patent at issue in *Pension Benefits* involved a computer-related invention that performed a number of different tasks which were integral to the operation of pension benefit schemes (such as calculating amounts payable and determining future assets). The patent included both method and apparatus claims for controlling a pension benefits system. The method claim (a method of controlling a pension benefits program by administering at least one subscriber employer account, which is to receive periodic payments) was made up of a series of steps, including the provision of data, determining the average age of all employees, and so on. The apparatus claim was for a data processing means that was arranged to receive and process information to be used to control a pension benefits system.

The approach that the TBA adopted in relation to the *method claim* in *Pension Benefits* was very similar to the approach previously adopted at the EPO and to the approach currently used in the United Kingdom. The Board began by noting that the question to be asked was whether the method claim represented a method of doing business as such. It then went on to characterize the invention, saying that all of the features of the method

---

[207] *Protecting Kids the World Over's Patent Application* [2011] *EWHC* 2720, [14]. In *Halliburton*, Judge Birss QC said that there 'are no doubt cases in which the task carried out [by the computer] is not within the excluded areas but nevertheless there is no technical contribution at all': *Halliburton Energy Service's Patent Application* [2011] *EWHC* 2508, [38].   [208] See section 7.2.1, pp. 496–505.

[209] *Pension Benefit Systems Partnership*, T 931/95 [2001] *OJ EPO* 441.

[210] *Hitachi/Auction method*, T 258/03 [2004] *OJ EPO* 575.

claim were 'steps of processing and producing information having purely administrative, actuarial and/or financial character. Processing and producing such information are typical steps of business and economic methods.'[211] On this basis, the Board concluded that the method claim was merely a method of doing business as such and was therefore excluded from patentability under Article 52(2)(c).[212] The mere fact that the invention operated on a computer did not turn the subject matter of the claim into an invention within the meaning of Article 52(1).[213] (As we will see, this aspect of *Pension Benefits* has been modified in *Hitachi*.)

While the Board found that the method claims fell foul of Article 52(2), this was not the case with the *apparatus claims*. The apparatus claims in question were for an apparatus consisting of a suitably programmed computer or system of computers. In considering whether the apparatus claims were patentable, the Board made a number of general comments. The Board began by noting that there are four basic requirements for patentability under the EPC—namely, that there must be an invention, and that the invention must satisfy the requirements for industrial applicability, novelty, and inventive step.[214] The Board also said that the basic test of whether there is an invention within the meaning of Article 52(2) is *separable and distinct* from the questions of whether the subject matter is susceptible of industrial application, is new, and involves an inventive step.[215] The Board added that, 'in addition to these basic requirements', the EPC and the Implementing Regulations implicitly contain the further requirement that the invention must be of technical character.[216]

The Board also considered the way in which an invention should be characterized when deciding whether it complies with Article 52(2). In particular, it looked at the 'contribution' approach (then) recommended in the EPO *Guidelines for Examination* (which is basically the same as the approach used in the United Kingdom). These said that when deciding whether an invention complied with Article 52, it was necessary to:

> . . . disregard the form or kind of claim and concentrate on its content in order to *identify the real contribution* which the subject matter claimed, considered as a whole, adds to the known art. If this contribution is not of a technical character, there is no invention within the meaning of Art 52(1).[217]

The Board said that there were a number of problems with the contribution approach.[218] The first and most general was that:

> [There] is no basis in the EPC for distinguishing between 'new features' of an invention and features of that invention which are known from the prior art when examining whether the invention concerned to be an invention within the meaning of Article 52(1) EPC.[219]

The contribution approach was also criticized because it failed to keep the Article 52(1) inquiry separate and distinct from industrial applicability, novelty, and inventive step.

---

[211] *Pension Benefit Systems Partnership*, T 931/95 [2001] *OJ EPO* 441, 449.   [212] Ibid.   [213] Ibid.

[214] *EPO Guidelines*, C-IV, [1.1]. (The Guidelines were changed as of 31 August 2001 to bring them into line with EPO case law on computer-related inventions.) See now *EPO Guidelines*, G-II, [3.6].

[215] EPO Guidelines, C-IV, 1.2.

[216] *Pension Benefit Systems Partnership*, T 931/95 [2001] *OJ EPO* 441, 454, following *EPO Guidelines*, C-IV, 1.2 (now G-I, [1(i), [2(ii)]).

[217] *EPO Guidelines*, C-IV, 2.2 (emphasis added). The revised Guidelines have taken out the reference to the contribution made by the invention.

[218] The Board said that the distinction drawn between a method of doing business and an apparatus situated to perform such a method was justified by the fact that while 'schemes, rules and methods' are non-patentable categories in the field of economy and business, the category of 'apparatus' in the sense of 'physical entity' or 'product' is not mentioned in EPC 1973. Art. 52(2) (now EPC 2000, Art. 52(2)): *Pension Benefit Systems Partnership*, T 931/95 [2001] *OJ EPO* 441, 452.   [219] Ibid., 454.

The Board also said that the contribution approach confused the requirement of 'invention' with the requirements of 'novelty' and 'inventive step'.[220] Moreover, the Board believed that the contribution approach incorrectly imported issues relating to inventive step into the inquiry into whether a patent complied with Article 52(1).[221] As a result, the TBA rejected the contribution approach saying that there 'is no basis in the EPC for applying this so-called contribution approach'.[222]

Rather than looking at the contribution made by the invention and determining whether this was technical, the Board focused on the *character* of the invention. That is, the Board attempted to distil the essence or kernel of the invention, rather than looking at what the invention did. On the facts, the Board said that what was claimed was a computer system suitably programmed for use in a particular field. Once the invention had been characterized, the next question to be decided was whether the invention exhibited the requisite technical character. In answering this question, the Board said that:

> [A] computer system suitably programmed for use in a particular field, even if that is the field of business and economy, has the character of a concrete apparatus in the sense of a physical entity, man-made for a utilitarian purpose.[223]

Given that an invention is likely to have a technical character if it leads to or produces a physical change in things, it is not surprising that the Board said that an 'apparatus constituting a physical entity or concrete product suitable for performing or supporting an economic activity, is an invention within the meaning of Article 52(1) EPC'.[224] Unlike the situation with the method claim, the apparatus claim could not be classified as a method of doing business and, as such, did not fall foul of Article 52(1). (It is important to note that the patent was refused on the basis that it lacked inventive step.) The upshot of the reasoning in *Pension Benefits* is that a claim to a *method* that consists of an excluded category will be excluded, even if hardware is used to carry out the method. In contrast, a claim to *an apparatus* itself, being concrete, is not caught by Article 52(2).

The reasoning that was developed by the TBA in *Pension Benefits* was applied and expanded in *Hitachi*.[225] The invention in *Hitachi* was an automatic auction method executed in a server computer. In essence, the invention was for a method of carrying out a Dutch auction—that is, an auction in which the seller starts at a high price, which is lowered until a bid is received. As in *Pension Benefits*, the application included both a product and a method claim. The Board began by reaffirming that there was no basis in the EPC for applying the contribution approach when deciding whether an invention falls foul of Article 52 of the EPC.[226] The Board also said that because the reasoning used in *Pension Benefits* was independent of the category of the claim, it would be inconsistent to reject the contribution approach for apparatus claims but not for method claims. On this basis, the Board held that:

> In order to be consistent with the finding that the so-called contribution approach . . . is inappropriate for judging whether claimed subject-matter is an invention within the

---

[220] The TBA cited the German Federal Court of Justice (BGH) decision of *Sprachanalyseeinrichtung (Speech Analysis Apparatus)*, X ZB 15/98 (11 May 2000) [2002] *OJ EPO* 415. For further discussion, see *Dell USA*, O/177/02 (24 April 2002), [24].

[221] The Board said that the contribution approach used to determine whether a patent complied with Art. 52(1) was 'so very closely related to examination with regard to the requirement of inventive step that the examining division decided in fact implicitly that there was lack of inventive step under Article 56 EPC': *Pension Benefit Systems Partnership*, T 931/95 [2001] *OJ EPO* 441, 455.

[222] Ibid., 442.   [223] Ibid., 452.   [224] Ibid., 453.

[225] *Hitachi/Auction method*, T 258/03 [2004] *OJ EPO* 575.   [226] Ibid., 581–2.

meaning of the Article 52(1) EPC there should be no need to further qualify the relevance of technical aspects of a method claim in order to determine the technical character of the method.[227]

While in *Pension Benefits*, the Board of Appeal had only been willing to apply the 'any hardware' approach to apparatus claims (preferring to retain the contribution approach for the method claim), this was not the case in *Hitachi*, where the Board applied the 'any hardware' approach to both apparatus *and* method claims.[228] That is, the Board concluded that a method involving a technical means is an invention within the meaning of Article 52(1). The upshot of *Hitachi*, which has been applied in subsequent decisions at the EPO,[229] is that (i) a claim to *hardware* is not caught by Article 52(2), and (ii) a claim to a *method* of using that hardware is also not excluded. This means that so long as a technical means such as a computer is used, the resulting invention will not fall foul of Article 52(1). This is the case even if the invention is for a purely non-technical purpose.

There are a number of notable features of the 'any hardware' approach. The first relates to the way in which the invention is characterized when determining whether it complies with Article 52(1). A key feature of the approach is the belief that it is not appropriate to look to the contribution made by the invention; instead, it requires the tribunal to look to the character or essence of the invention. The contribution made by the invention is only looked at when novelty and inventive step are examined. One of the consequences of this is that under the 'any hardware' approach, the tribunal is more concerned with categorizing the subject matter in question than with asking whether the application has disclosed an invention.

As the Board noted in *Hitachi*, the broad interpretation given to the term 'invention' under the 'any hardware' approach means that it will include activities that are so familiar that their technical character tends to be overlooked, such as the act of writing using pen and paper.[230] In the words of the EBA, a computer-readable data storage medium and a cup both have technical character.[231] The breadth of the 'any hardware' approach can be seen in the *Microsoft/Clipboard formats I* decision.[232] The application in question, which was for a way of 'facilitating data exchange across different formats', consisted of both method claims and a claim to a program on a computer-readable medium. The Board said that the 'method was implemented in a computer and this amounted to a technical means sufficient to escape the prohibition in Article 52'.[233] As Kitchin J said in *Astron Clinica*, 'the Board in *Microsoft/Clipboard formats* appears to have found that any program on a carrier has a technical character and so escapes the prohibition in Article 52'.[234] While the 'any hardware' approach has meant that more applications are now able to satisfy Article 52, it does not mean that the applications will necessarily be patentable. That is, while the approach has made it easier to satisfy the subject matter threshold at the EPO, this does not mean that all inventions will

---

[227] Ibid.

[228] In this sense, we see *Hitachi* as a continuation of the approach that was begun in *Pension Benefits*, T 931/95 [2001] *OJ EPO* 441. Cf. the comments by the UK Court of Appeal that these decisions were 'mutually contradictory': *Aerotel v. Telco Holdings* [2007] 1 *All ER* 225, [25].

[229] See, e.g., *Man/Provision of product-specified data* [2007] *OJ EPO* 421, 427 (the claims in question did not bear scrutiny in light of *Pension Benefits* and *Hitachi*); *Pitney Bowes/Undeliverable mail*, T 388/04 [2007] *OJ EPO* 16.   [230] *Hitachi/Auction method*, T 258/03 [2004] *OJ EPO* 575, 585.

[231] *President's Reference/Patentability of programs for computers*, G 3/08 [2011] *OJ EPO* 10, [9.2].

[232] *Microsoft/Clipboard formats I*, T 424/03 [2006] *EPOR* 414.   [233] Ibid., [5.1].

[234] *Astron Clinica v. Comptroller General of Patents* [2008] *EWHC* 85, [39].

necessarily cross the threshold. For example, in *Pitney Bowes/Undeliverable Mail*,[235] an application for a method of responding by a mailer to notice from a postal service that a piece of mail was undeliverable was held to fall within Article 52(1). The telling factor in this case was that no technical means whatsoever were described in the application. The fact that the invention *might* have been implemented by an unspecified technical process was not enough to prevent the application from being excluded on the basis that it was for a method of doing business for the purposes of Article 52(2)(c).[236] Another reason why the 'any hardware' approach does not necessarily mean that more inventions will now be patentable is because the invention still needs to be new, non-obvious, and susceptible to industrial application. One of the consequences of the 'any hardware' approach is that it has shifted the focus of attention at the EPO away from an inquiry into whether a patent complies with Article 52(1) towards an inquiry into whether there is an inventive step (and, arguably, also novelty and industrial applicability).[237] This is spelt out clearly in the revised EPO Guidelines which say that when examining computer-related inventions, it may 'be more appropriate for the examiner to proceed directly to the questions of novelty and inventive step, without considering beforehand the question of technical character'.[238] The shift towards inventive step is reinforced in the Guidelines by the fact that:

> [When] assessing whether there is an inventive step, the examiner must establish an objective technical problem. The solution of that problem constitutes the invention's technical contribution to the art. The presence of such technical information establishes that the claimed subject matter has a technical character and therefore is indeed an invention within the meaning of Art. 52(1).[239]

The shift has also been confirmed in subsequent decisions at the EPO, which have focused on inventive step rather than exclusion from patentability.[240]

6.3 COMPARING THE DIFFERENT APPROACHES

The 'any hardware' approach and the 'technical effect' approach represent very different ways of approaching the question of how patentable subject matter should be determined.[241] The key difference between the approach that has been adopted in the United Kingdom and that adopted at the EPO relates to the way the 'invention' is construed. In essence, the 'any hardware' approach differs from the UK approach in two ways. The first is in terms of the way the invention is characterized: while British courts look to the contribution made by the invention, this approach has been rejected at the EPO, where the focus is on the nature of the invention. As the

---

[235] T 388/04 [2007] *OJ EPO* 16.   [236] Ibid., 23.

[237] The 'inference from *Pension Benefit* . . . is that lack of technical contribution might be a matter for inventive step rather than exclusion from patentability': *Dell USA*, O/177/02 (24 April 2002), [27].

[238] *EPO Guidelines*, C-IV, 2.3 (modified in the revised Guidelines).   [239] Ibid.

[240] *Comvik/Two identities*, T 641/00 [2003] *OJ EPO* 352; *International Computers/Information modelling*, T 49/99 (5 March 2002). As the EBA said, the adoption of the any hardware approach does not mean that the 'list of subject-matters in Article 52(2) . . . has no effect on' patentability; rather, what has happened is that these factors are now taken into account when considering inventive step, where an 'elaborate system for taking that effect into account in the assessment of whether there is an inventive step has been developed': *President's Reference/Patentability of programs for computers*, G 3/08 [2011] *OJ EPO* 10, [10.13.1].

[241] For an examination of the difference, from the perspective of a member of the TBA, see W. Chandler, 'Patentability of computer-implemented inventions' [2015] *OJ EPO* 73 (Supplementary Publication).

Technical Board of Appeal said, 'the technical character of an invention is an inherent attribute independent of the actual contribution of the invention to the state of the art'.[242] The second way in which the two approaches differ is in terms of the way technical character is determined. Technical character may be implied at the EPO in at least three ways: (i) implied by the physical features of an entity; (ii) implied by the nature of the activity; or (iii) conferred on a non-technical activity by the use of a technical means.[243] While the UK courts have adopted the first two approaches, they have rejected the third.

One of the consequences of adopting the 'any hardware' approach at the EPO is that far fewer applications will be rejected on the basis that they do not have the appropriate subject matter. The impact that the different approaches have on the way in which an application is examined was highlighted by the Enlarged Board of Appeal (EBA), using the example of the fate of a patent application that claimed a cup carrying a picture (a company logo).[244] The effect of the application was information, brand awareness, and aesthetic pleasure. Under the 'technical effect' (or contribution) approach, 'cups are known, so that the "contribution to the art" is only in a field excluded from patentability'.[245] As such, it would be excluded. In contrast, according to the 'any hardware' approach, the claimed subject matter is considered without regard to the prior art. Applying this approach, a claim to a cup would not be excluded from patentability by Article 52(2) at the EPO. This is because 'whether or not the claim also includes the feature that the cup has a certain picture on it is irrelevant'.[246] It would, however, be rejected in the United Kingdom.

While initial reactions in the United Kingdom were mixed,[247] in *Aerotel* the Court of Appeal clearly rejected the 'any hardware' approach, suggesting that it 'must be wrong' and that it was 'not intellectually honest'.[248] The rejection of the approach was confirmed by the Court of Appeal in *Symbian*, which made it clear that the 'any hardware'

---

[242] *Quest International/Odour selection*, T 619/02 [2007] *OJ EPO* 63, 84.

[243] *Hitachi/Auction method*, T 258/03 [2004] *OJ EPO* 575, 585.

[244] *President's Reference/Patentability of programs for computers*, G 3/08 [2011] *OJ EPO* 10, [10.6]. The nature of the change brought about by *Pension Benefits* and the impact that it has on the way in which a patent is examined can be seen in the Patent Office decision in *James Shanley*, in which the contribution approach and the *Pension Benefits* approach were applied to the same facts: *James Shanley*, O/422/02 (16 October 2002). The invention in question was for dismountable partitions for buildings (which included both flat and curved panels). Using the contribution approach, the Hearing Officer said that the contribution made by the invention was wholly aesthetic insofar as it was solely directed 'to altering appearances'. Because the invention neither solved a technical problem nor made a contribution in a non-excluded field, the application was excluded by s. 1(2)(b). The Hearing Officer then went on to consider how the invention would have fared under the *Pension Benefits* approach. After reviewing the TBA's decision, the Hearing Officer said that 'what is claimed is a partition for buildings, and since this, taken as a whole and without regard to whether or not any technical contribution is involved, manifestly has a technical character . . . I would have to find that what is claimed . . . is an invention under section 1(2)': ibid., [22]. Because the Officer was bound by UK decisions, he did not follow the *Pension Benefits* approach. The interesting question here is whether the application would have satisfied the requirements of inventive step.

[245] *President's Reference/Patentability of programs for computers*, G 3/08 [2011] *OJ EPO* 10, [10.6].

[246] Ibid.

[247] In one Patent Office decision, the *Pension Benefits* approach was used to decide whether an application for 'behaviour modification' fell within s. 1(2): *John Edward Rose*, O/075/01 (14 February 2001) (as in *Pension Benefits*, the application was eventually excluded on the basis that it lacked inventive step).

[248] *Aerotel v. Telco Holdings* [2007] 1 *All ER* 225, [27]–[29]. Jacob LJ's arguments in this regard are far from convincing. In particular, it is difficult to imagine an application for an iPod loaded with a new piece of music being non-obvious. Interestingly, most of the criticisms of the EPO decisions are in relation to the way in which they applied inventive step, rather than how their approach excluded subject matter.

approach should not be followed in the United Kingdom.[249] A number of reasons have been given for not following the approach in the United Kingdom, perhaps the most pertinent being that the EPO's approach to patentability goes hand-in-hand with its approach to inventive step which is not followed in the United Kingdom.[250] Jacob LJ also said that *Pension Benefits* and like-minded decisions at the EPO were based on the mistaken assumption that the various categories of excluded subject matter were all limited to something abstract or intangible.[251] This reflects earlier criticisms of *Pension Benefits* that it runs contrary to a number of British Court of Appeal decisions that had held that claims directed to a system (hardware or apparatus) did not avoid the terms of section 1(2) of the Patents Act 1977.[252] The Board's decision was also criticized because it contradicts the established British view that questions of patentability should be decided as a matter of substance and not according to the actual form of the words.[253]

To date, there has been little to suggest that the different approaches adopted in the two jurisdictions have led to different results. Given that many of the applications excluded in the United Kingdom via the contribution approach under section 1(2) would be excluded under the 'any hardware' approach at the EPO because they lack inventive step, it is unlikely that the different approaches will lead to different results.[254] This was reflected in Kitchen's LJ's comment that 'whichever route is followed, one ought to end up at the same destination'.[255] Despite this, the growing divergence between the two jurisdictions is not desirable—particularly because there are suggestions that the 'any hardware' approach is having an impact in other areas of patent law at the EPO. Given that the EBA has confirmed existing practice at the EPO in this area, however, it seems unlikely that the EPO will change its approach in the future. One option is for legislative reform: as the EBA said, when 'judiciary-driven legal development meets its limits, it is time for the legislators to take over'.[256] However, given the problems that have prevented legislative changes in relation to computer-related inventions in the past, it is highly unlikely that reform will occur. As such, it seems that the only option for change is for the UK courts to adopt the 'any hardware' approach. Given that British courts are free, but not bound, to depart from previous jurisprudence on a specific issue in patent law where the EPO Boards of Appeal

---

[249] *Symbian v. Comptroller-General of Patents* [2008] EWCA Civ 1066, [48]–[51].

[250] *Halliburton Energy Service's Patent Application* [2011] EWHC 2508, [79(iii)].

[251] *Aerotel v. Telco Holdings* [2007] RPC 117, [30]. Jacob LJ added (ibid.) that we 'have already observed that the categories are disparate with differing policies behind each. There is no reason to suppose there is some common factor (particularly abstractness) linking them. The *travaux prépatoires* at least confirm this.'

[252] *Merrill Lynch's Application* [1989] RPC 561 (CA) (not possible to patent under the guise of an article that contains that item); *Fujitsu's Application* [1997] RPC 608 (CA) ('the fact that the invention was claimed as a method, a way of manufacture or an apparatus was irrelevant when the only invention claimed revolved around the use of a computer program'). Cf. '[A] computer system suitably programmed for use in a particular field, even if that use, for example, the field of business and economy, has the character of a concrete apparatus, in the sense of a physical entity or product and is thus an invention within the meaning of Article 52(1)': *EPO Guidelines*, C-IV, 2.3 (now modified).

[253] This has led the (then) Patent Office to conclude on a number of occasions that it is bound to follow the contribution approach set out in UK courts and not the approach advocated in *Pension Benefits*. See, e.g., *Hutchins' Application* [2002] RPC 264, 270; *Pintos Global Application*, O/171/01 (6 April 2001), [20]–[29].

[254] *Halliburton Energy Service's Patent Application* [2011] EWHC 2508, [79(ii)]; *Cappellini and Bloomberg's Application* [2007] EWHC 476, [9].

[255] *HTC v. Apple* [2013] EWCA Civ 451, [41]; *Cappellini and Bloomberg's Application* [2007] EWHC 47 (*Pension Benefits* was the correct result, but by the wrong approach).

[256] *President's Reference/Patentability of programs for computers*, G 3/08 [2011] OJ EPO 10, [7.2.7].

have developed a settled view (which was not 'plainly unsatisfactory'[257])—which, in the eyes of the EBA, has occurred—it will be interesting to see whether UK courts jettison the contribution approach in favour of the 'any hardware' approach. Given that there has been a consistent string of decisions in the United Kingdom in support of the contribution approach, this is unlikely. If this were to occur, it would mark a radical change in British patent law.

7 SPECIFIC APPLICATIONS

Having looked at the general approaches taken to the question of whether an invention falls within the scope of section 1(2)/Article 52(2), we now look at the way in which the law deals with a number of specific types of inventions. These are: (i) naturally occurring substances and discoveries; (ii) computer programs and computer-related inventions; (iii) methods of doing business; (iv) the presentation of information; and (v) methods for performing a mental act. After looking at these specific applications, we will look at possible reforms, particularly in relation to computer programs and computer-related inventions.

When thinking about these specific forms of subject matter, it is important to keep in mind the different approaches that are taken in the United Kingdom and at the EPO. While the EPO case law prior to *Pension Benefits* is still important in the United Kingdom, the liberalization brought about by the 'any hardware' approach means that it may no longer be as important at the EPO. Moreover, while the different approaches have not had much of an impact at least to date in relation to discoveries and natural substances, they have played an important role in the way in which the other forms of subject matter have been treated.

7.1 DISCOVERIES AND NATURAL SUBSTANCES

Advances in genetic engineering over the last few decades have enabled scientists to isolate and replicate a host of naturally occurring substances. Given the considerable investment that has been made in this research, it is not surprising that attempts have been made to patent the results of that research. In part, the extent to which this biological research is patentable depends on whether the resulting products and processes are treated as discoveries or inventions. The reason for this is that discoveries as such are excluded from the remit of patentable subject matter.[258] However, if it can be shown that when viewed as a whole, an application that incorporates a discovery brings about a technical change, it may be patentable. This means that if a person finds a new property of a known material or article, this will be treated as an unpatentable discovery—but if that person puts the property to a practical use, the invention may be patentable. For example, the discovery

---

[257] *Actavis UK v. Merck & Co.* [2008] *EWCA Civ* 444, [48]; *Human Genome Sciences v. Eli Lilly* [2011] *UKSC* 51, [3].

[258] PA 1977, s. 1(2)(a); EPC 2000, Art. 52(2)(a). On attempts to protect discoveries, see F. Neumeyer, 'Legal Protection of Scientific Discoveries' [1975] *Industrial Property* 348; K. Beier, 'Scientific Research, Patent Protection and Innovation' (1975) 6 *IIC* 367; E. Kitch, 'The Nature and Function of the Patent System' (1977) 20 *J L & Econ* 265, 288. For the current position in the United States, see *Mayo v. Prometheus*, 132 S. Ct. 3218 (2012).

that a known material is able to withstand mechanical shock would not be patentable—but a railway sleeper made from that material could well be patentable.[259]

In thinking about the extent to which biological products and processes are patentable, it is important to bear in mind that patent law distinguishes between naturally occurring substances (unpatentable discoveries) and the products and processes that result from the human effort in isolating those substances from their natural environment (patentable inventions).[260] To put it another way, a distinction is drawn between those things that freely exist in nature (and which can be only unearthed or discovered) and those things that are artificial (and which contain the necessary degree of human intervention for the resulting product to be called an invention).[261]

Given this, the important question that we need to consider is: what is the difference between something that is 'natural' and thus unpatentable, and something that is 'artificial' and thus potentially patentable? More specifically, given that the act of discovery and the act of invention often both involve a considerable amount of time, effort, skill, and labour, we need to ask: what type of effort is needed for an activity to be described as an artificial invention as distinct from a natural unpatentable discovery? In answering these questions, it becomes apparent that the borders between discovery and invention are far more vague and problematic than they might seem at first glance. Perhaps the best way in which to think about the extent to which biological inventions are patentable is to look at the different types of patent that may be granted.[262]

(i) If a process is developed that enables a substance found in nature to be isolated and obtained from its surroundings, the *process* may be patentable.[263]

(ii) The finding of a *substance* freely occurring in nature is a mere discovery and, as such, is unpatentable.[264] As the Opposition Division at the EPO explained, this means that the 'discovery' of the Moon (when the Americans landed on it in 1969), the finding of a 5,000-year-old mummy in the Italian/Austrian Alps, or the identification of a new animal would not be patentable.[265] This is reflected in Article 5(1) of the Biotechnology Directive, which says that the 'human body, at the various stages of its formation and development, and the simple discovery of one of its elements, including the sequence or partial sequence of a gene, cannot constitute a patentable discovery'. Similar provisions exist in the Patents Act 1977 and the EPC 2000.[266]

---

[259] *EPO Guidelines*, G-II, [3.1]. It is unclear whether the 'any hardware' approach will impact on the patentability of naturally occurring substances.

[260] See R. Whaite and N. Jones, 'Biotechnological Patents in Europe: The Draft Directive' [1989] *EIPR* 145, 149; A. White, 'The Patentability of Naturally Occurring Products' [1980] *EIPR* 37.

[261] For a different perspective on the issue of patenting of higher life forms, see *Harvard College v. Canada (Commissioner of Patents)* [2002] 4 *SCR* 45 (rejecting an application to patent the genetically altered OncoMouse).

[262] As yet, there has been no case directly on this point in the United Kingdom. There is little reason to doubt that the position in the United Kingdom will be the same as that at the EPO. Cf. *Chiron v. Murex Diagnostics* [1996] *FSR* 153, 177.   [263] *EPO Guidelines*, G-II, [3.1].

[264] *Tate & Lyle Technology v. Roquette Frères* [2009] *EWHC* 1312, [74]–[76].

[265] *Howard Florey/Relaxin* [1995] *EPOR* 541, 549. It is interesting to note that plant breeders' rights are available to those who 'discover' varieties, whether growing in the wild or occurring as a genetic variant, whether artificially induced or not: PVA 1997, s. 4(3) and (6). Apparently, the Braeburn apple was found in this way in 1952: see T. Boswell, Hansard (HC) (24 June 1997), col. 717.

[266] See PA 1977, Sch. A2, para. 3(a) (introduced by Patents Regulations 2000); EPC 1973 Regs, r. 23(e)(1).

(iii) If a natural substance that has been *isolated* from its surroundings can be properly characterized either by its structure, by the processes by which it is obtained, or by other parameters, the substance per se may be patentable. This means that as long as 'something' is inside a human or animal body or a plant, it is a natural element and cannot be considered to be patentable; once this 'something' is isolated from the human or animal body or plant by means of a technical process, it becomes eligible for patent protection.[267] This is the case even if its structure is identical to that of a natural element, since the processes used to isolate the element are technical processes.[268] This can be seen in the *Relaxin* decision, which concerned claims relating to DNA sequences of a naturally occurring substance that relaxes the uterus during childbirth, which was obtained from the human ovary.[269] The Opposition Division of the EPO held that the invention was not a discovery and, as such, was not excluded from patentability. Following the EPO Guidelines, the Opposition Division said that because a process had been developed to obtain Relaxin and the DNA that encoded it they were patentable under Article 52(2). This was because the substance Relaxin had not previously been recognized, because the products were characterized by their chemical structure, and because the products had a use.

This position was affirmed in the Biotechnology Directive,[270] and in equivalent provisions in the Patents Act 1977 and EPC 2000.[271] These provide that 'biological material that is isolated from its natural environment or produced by means of a technical process may be the subject of an invention even if it previously occurred in nature'.[272] More specifically, Article 5(2) of the Biotechnology Directive states that an element isolated from the human body or otherwise produced by means of a technical process, including the sequence or partial sequence of a gene, may constitute a patentable invention even if the structure of that element is identical to that of a natural element. Equivalent provisions have been introduced in the United Kingdom[273] and in the EPC 2000.[274]

This means that 'raw data' on the human genome (including the human DNA sequence and its variations:[275] human genes; partial gene sequences; the human body at various stages of its development), which are not isolated, purified, or somehow produced by a technical process, are not patentable.[276] However, if the genetic information (including

---

[267] See Biotech. Dir., Recitals 21–2. Similar arguments apply for the *purification* of a naturally occurring substance.

[268] S. Sterrckx, 'Some Ethically Problematic Aspects of the Proposal for a Directive on the Legal Protection of Biotechnological Inventions' [1998] *EIPR* 123, 124–5; cf. S. Crespi, 'Biotechnology Patents: The Wicked Animal Must Defend Itself' [1995] *EIPR* 431, 432–3.

[269] (1996) 27 *IIC* 704, 705–6. See *Icos Corporation/Seven transmembrane receptor* [2002] *OJ EPO* 293 (Opposition Division), [11(i)] (while 'the V28 protein exists as a segment of the human genome and thus is a part of nature, the purified and isolated nucleic acid having that sequence does not exist in nature and thus cannot be discovered').

[270] Biotech. Dir., Art. 3(2).   [271] PA 1977, Sch. A2, para. 2.

[272] Biotech. Dir., Art. 3(2); PA 1977, Sch. A2, para. 2, EPC 2000, reg. 27(a).

[273] See PA 1977, Sch. A2, para. 5.   [274] EPC 2000 Regs, r. 29(2).

[275] This was confirmed by the joint statement by Tony Blair and Bill Clinton, *Joint Statement to Ensure that Discoveries for the Human Genome Are Used to Advance Human Health* (14 March 2000).

[276] See S. Bostyn, 'Patentability of Genetic Information Carriers' [1991] *IPQ* 1; Hoffmann LJ adopted a similar approach in *Kirin-Amgen v. Transkaryotic Therapies* [2005] *RPC* 169, [76], [109], when he treated the information as to the makeup of DNA as an unpatentable discovery. But cf. Jacob LJ, speaking for the Court of Appeal, in *Aerotel Ltd v. Telco Holdings Ltd* [2007] *RPC* 117, [37] (doubting whether the revelation of the precise sequence of a piece of DNA, as opposed to its general existence, could be described as a discovery).

the sequence or partial sequence of a gene) has been isolated from the human body or somehow produced by a technical process, it will potentially be patentable. For example, consider the situation if a research team successfully isolated the gene responsible for migraines: while the underlying genetic information would be in the public domain, the technique used to isolate the gene (which may include complicated processes of identification, purification, and classification) would be patentable. On the basis that the isolated gene would not have been identified without the human intervention (*techne*), the isolated gene may also be patented.[277] This would also be the case in relation to transgenic plants or animals, which by definition do not exist in nature.[278]

The *Kirin-Amgen* decision, which involved Amgen's highly valuable patent for a method of producing erythropoietin (EPO), offers another useful example of the impact that the invention–discovery dichotomy has upon patentable subject matter. Erythropoietin is the hormone that promotes the production of red blood cells and is particularly useful in the treatment of anaemia. Underlying the patent was Amgen's discovery and subsequent sequencing of the gene that produces EPO. Building on this discovery, Amgen isolated and cloned the DNA sequence that produces EPO. The DNA sequence was then introduced into a host cell (a Chinese hamster ovary cell), which was used to manufacture the EPO. At first instance, Neuberger J said that the claim was:

> ... ultimately to the use of information first revealed in the patent, namely, the genetic code for EPO, for the purpose of expressing EPO cells by artificial manipulation of DNA. The essence of the invention was not the artificial manipulation but the use of the information.[279]

As a result, the technique used to manufacture the EPO was irrelevant. The Court of Appeal disagreed, saying that Neuberger J's definition was too broad.[280] While the Court of Appeal had no doubt that the discovery and sequencing of the gene that produced EPO was at the heart of the invention, the Court said that the gene sequence per se could not be claimed as the invention because it existed in nature. Instead, the Court held that what was claimed was an exogenous DNA sequence suitable for expressing EPO when introduced into a host cell. The House of Lords agreed.[281] While the decision did not directly focus on discovery as patentable subject matter, it is important insofar as it exemplifies the way in which the non-patentability of naturally occurring substances can influence not only the subject matter that is patentable, but also the decision as to whether a patent has been infringed.

While the patenting of processes used to isolate natural substances is relatively uncontroversial, the same cannot be said about the patenting of the substances that are isolated using those processes. In particular, doubts have been raised as to whether the act of isolation and characterization of a naturally occurring substance is really that different from the mere finding of the substance. As one commentator has noted, 'even if a natural element is isolated from the body by technical means, this does not change the "naturalness" of the element (neither does a purification of the element)'.[282] However valid

---

[277] The requirement that there be technical intervention is closely related to the requirement that the invention be non-obvious—*DSM NV's Patent* [2001] *RPC* 675, 709 (talking about obviousness over nature)— and also be industrially applicable: *Salk Institute for Biological Studies*, T 338/00 (6 November 2002).

[278] *Harvard/OncoMouse* [2003] *OJ EPO* 473 (Opposition Division), 491 ('transgenic animals of the present invention having an artificially inserted oncogene do not exist in nature as such but are the result of a technical intervention by man').   [279] *Kirin-Amgen v. Transkaryotic Therapies* [2002] *RPC* 187, 201.

[280] [2003] *RPC* 31 (CA).   [281] [2005] *RPC* 169 (HL), [76]. See Chapter 22, section 3, p. 655.

[282] S. Sterrckx, 'Some Ethically Problematic Aspects of the Proposal for a Biotech Directive' [1998] *EIPR* 123, 124–5. See also M. Davis, 'The Patenting of the Products of Nature' [1995] *Rutgers Comput Technol LJ* 331; cf. S. Bostyn, 'Patentability of Genetic Information Carriers' [1999] *IPQ* 1, 3–4.

these arguments may be, they have been outweighed by the policy goal outlined in the Biotechnology Directive that research aimed at obtaining and isolating elements valuable to medicinal production should be encouraged by the patent system.[283]

7.2 COMPUTER PROGRAMS AND COMPUTER-RELATED INVENTIONS

When the Patents Act 1977 and the EPC 1973 were enacted, it was commonly thought that copyright law rather than patents would be the area of intellectual property law that would regulate the creation and use of computer programs. While copyright has been important in this process, one of the most notable changes that have taken place since 1977 is the growing role played by patent law in relation to computer programs and computer-related inventions.[284] Given that computer programs are expressly excluded from patentability by section 1(2)(c)/Article 52(2)(c), it may come as a surprise to learn not only that many patents have already been granted for computer programs and for computer-related inventions, but also that it is also one of the fastest areas of growth in both the United Kingdom and at the EPO and that over the last 30 years, the EPO has reportedly dealt with over 100,000 cases involving computer-related inventions.[285]

In this section, we will look at the way the law has developed in this area. In so doing, we will look at the current position in the United Kingdom, which was similar to the position at the EPO prior to the adoption of the 'any hardware' approach. It is important to keep in mind that the case law at the EPO prior to *Pension Benefits* is still relevant in the United Kingdom. As such, in our analysis of the current UK position, we will make reference to the pre-*Pension Benefits* decisions from the EPO. We will then look at the standing of computer programs and computer-related inventions at the EPO.[286]

7.2.1 Approach in the United Kingdom

One of the most important changes that led to the liberalization of the protection offered to computer-related inventions in the United Kingdom (and at the EPO, pre-*Pension Benefits*) was the decision that an invention that includes a computer program could be patentable so long as the invention as a whole was technical. The upshot of the acceptance of the 'whole contents' approach was, as the Technical Board of Appeal said in *Vicom,* that 'an invention which would be patentable in accordance with conventional patentability criteria should not be excluded from protection by the mere fact that for its implementation modern technical means in the form of a computer program are used'.[287] This approach was adopted and endorsed by a number of decisions in the United Kingdom, notably the Court of Appeal in *Gale's Application*[288] and *Merrill Lynch.*[289]

---

[283] Biotech. Dir., Recital 17.

[284] A computer program claim 'referred to a sequence of instructions specifying a method rather than to the method itself', whereas a claim to a computer-implemented invention 'could not be divorced from the computer on which it was carried out': *President's Reference/Patentability of programs for computers*, G 3/08 [2011] *OJ EPO* 10, [11.2].

[285] W. Chandler, 'Patentability of computer-implemented inventions' [2015] *OJEPO* 73 (Supplementary Publication).

[286] One question that needs to be addressed is whether discussions at the EPO about the meaning of technical character in relation to inventive step are relevant in the United Kingdom in relation to subject matter (via 'technical character').

[287] *Vicom/Computer-related invention*, T 208/84 [1987] *OJ EPO* 14, [16].

[288] [1991] *RPC* 305.   [289] *Merrill Lynch's Application* [1989] *RPC* 561.

While a computer program per se remains unpatentable in the United Kingdom, following the acceptance of the 'whole contents' approach, it is clear that applications which contain a computer program are patentable on their face, so long as the invention as a whole makes a technical contribution to the art.[290] This can be seen, for example, in *Kearney*,[291] where the TBA held that a computer program that alerted machine operators when their machines needed to be repaired or a worn tool needed to be replaced solved a technical problem and, as such, was patentable subject matter. Similarly, in *Bosch*,[292] the TBA said that a device for monitoring computer components was technical because it considerably reduced 'the operating time of the computer component and thus undoubtedly improved the effectiveness of the device'. Both of these decisions were followed in the United Kingdom.

In contrast, if it *cannot* be shown that an application that contains a computer program is technical, then it will not be patentable. This was the case, for example, in *Gale's Application*, where the Court of Appeal decided that a ROM carrying a particular program was not distinguishable from the program itself and, as such, was unpatentable.[293] Following these decisions, it was clear that an invention that includes a computer program is potentially patentable so long as the invention as a whole is technical. With this question settled, the next question that arose for consideration was in relation to the exclusion of computer programs as such. The question of the scope of the exclusion of computer programs was considered in two decisions by the TBA, both involving applications by IBM. The invention in the first decision, *IBM/Computer programs* (T 935/97),[294] was a method for allowing information in a data-processing system that was displayed in one window to be altered if that window were obscured by another window. The application included claims for software and for software recorded in a computer-readable medium. While some of the claims were accepted, the Examining Division refused the application insofar as it was directed to a computer-program product. The second decision, *IBM/Computer programs* (T 1173/97),[295] related to 'resource recovery in a computer system'. Again, the Examining Division rejected the application insofar as it claimed a computer-program product. In both cases, the question for consideration related to the scope of the exclusion of computer programs *as such*. The reasoning in both cases was identical.

The Board began by noting that the language of Article 52(2) and (3) showed that the legislators did not want to exclude all computer programs from patentability;[296] instead, all that was excluded were computer programs *as such*. Drawing upon the logic that has been applied to Article 52(2) and (3) generally, the Board said that when the EPC referred to computer programs 'as such', it meant mere abstract creations, lacking in technical character. In more positive terms, this meant that computer programs that had a technical character were potentially patentable.[297] In so doing, the Board distinguished between

---

[290] This means that if it can be shown that the subject matter makes a technical contribution to the known art, patentability will not be denied merely on the ground that a computer program is involved in its implementation.   [291] *Kearney/Computer-related invention*, T 42/87 [1997] *EPOR* 236, 241.

[292] *Bosch/Electronic computer components*, T 164/92 [1995] *EPOR* 585, 592.

[293] *Gale's Application* [1991] *RPC* 305 (CA); cf. *Fujitsu's Application* [1997] *RPC* 608 (CA). The invention only achieved something that had previously been possible, albeit at a much faster speed and more conveniently than had previously been the case. As such, it was merely a conventional computer operating in a conventional way and so was not patentable. In light of subsequent decisions, notably *Symbian v. Comptroller-General of Patents* [2008] *EWCA Civ* 1066, [42], which questioned the way in which Aldous J interpreted 'technical', it is likely that *Fujitsu* would be decided differently today.

[294] [1999] *EPOR* 301.   [295] [2000] *EPOR* 219.

[296] *IBM/Computer programs*, T 935/97 [1999] *EPOR* 301, 309; T 1173/97 [2000] *EPOR* 219, 226.

[297] They did so on the basis of EPC 1973 Regs, rr 27, 29: *IBM/Computer programs*, T 1173/97 [2000] *EPOR* 219, 226.

computer programs as such (which are not patentable) and computer programs that had a technical character (which are patentable).[298]

This gives rise to the question: when does a computer program have a technical character? As with all inventions, the requisite technical character may exist either in technical effects or in the solution to a technical problem. In addressing this question, the TBA began by noting that a computer program cannot be assumed to have a technical character merely for the reason that it is a program for a computer. This means that *normal* 'physical modifications of the hardware (causing, for instance, the generation of electrical currents) deriving from the execution of the instructions given by programs for computers cannot per se constitute the technical character required for avoiding the exclusion of those programs'.[299] The Board added that such modifications were a common feature of all computer programs and therefore could not be used to distinguish programs with a technical character from programs 'as such'. Instead, the Board said that the technical character must be found elsewhere in the effects caused by the execution of the computer program by the hardware. That is, a computer program product could be patentable if it resulted in additional technical effects that went beyond the 'normal' physical interaction between the program (software) and the computer (hardware) on which it was run.

The TBA also noted that computer program products only produced and showed an effect when the program concerned was made to run on a computer. The effect only shows in 'physical reality' when the program is being run. On the basis that there was no good reason to distinguish between a direct technical effect and the potential to produce a technical effect, the Board accepted that a computer program that had the potential to cause a predetermined further technical effect was, in principle, not excluded from patentability under Article 52(2) and (3).[300]

After reviewing the scope of protection for computer programs, the Board remitted both cases to the Examining Division to determine whether the applications complied with this reading of Article 52(2)(c). While it is clear that the *IBM* decisions mark a victory for the proponents of greater protection for inventions relating to information technology, ultimately the extent to which computer programs are patentable depends on how 'technical character' is construed. One factor that suggests that the exclusion will be read narrowly flows from the Board's comment that it does not make any difference for the purpose of the exclusion whether a computer program is claimed by itself or as a record on a carrier.[301] This means that so long as a computer program is technical, the medium in which it is recorded (the carrier) is irrelevant.[302] This would allow, for example, patents to be granted for software-implemented inventions distributed over the Internet[303] and

---

[298] In so doing, the Board overturned *EPO Guidelines*, C-IV 2.3, which then stated that a 'computer program by itself or as a record on a carrier is not patentable, irrespective of its content'. The Board also distinguished *ATT/System for generating code*, T 204/93 (29 October 1993): *IBM/Computer programs*, T 935/97 [1999] *EPOR* 301, 308.

[299] *IBM/Computer programs*, T 935/97 [1999] *EPOR* 301, 310; *IBM/Computer program product*, T 1173/97 [2000] *EPOR* 219, 227.

[300] *IBM/Computer programs*, T 935/97 [1999] *EPOR* 301, 313; *IBM/Computer program product*, T 1173/97 [2000] *EPOR* 219, 230.

[301] *IBM/Computer programs*, T 935/97 [1999] *EPOR* 301, 317; *IBM/Computer program product*, T 1173/97 [2000] *EPOR* 219, 234.

[302] The Board said that if the 'computer program product comprises a computer-readable medium on which the program is stored, this medium only constitutes the physical support on which the program is saved and thus constitutes hardware': *IBM/Computer programs*, T 935/97 [1999] *EPOR* 301, 312; *IBM/ Computer program product*, T 1173/97 [2000] *EPOR* 219, 229.

[303] R. Hart, P. Holmes, and J. Reid, *The Economic Impact of Patentability of Computer Programs* (2000), 13.

to computer-program products directly loadable into the internal memory of a digital computer.[304]

To ensure that practice at the (then) Patent Office was consistent with the approach of the EPO, the UK Patent Office amended its practice guidelines in 1999 to follow the *IBM* decisions.[305] The resulting 1999 Practice Notice provided that the UK Patent Office would:

> . . . accept claims to computer programs, either in themselves or on a computer, provided that the program is such that when it is run on a computer it produces a technical effect which is more than would necessarily follow merely from the running of any program on a computer.[306]

While the law at the EPO may have changed after the *IBM* decisions, the law in the United Kingdom (which was reflected in the 1999 Practice Notice) remained stable for a number of years, at least until the 2007 decision in *Aerotel*.[307] As part of his wide-ranging judgment, Jacob LJ attempted to provide guidance as to how 'computer program' was to be construed. Jacob LJ began by noting that there are two views about what was meant by a computer program. Under the first narrow view, which has been followed in post-*Pension Benefits* case law at the EPO, a computer program is the set of instructions as an abstract thing, albeit that they could be written down on a piece of paper. The second wider view, which was adopted in pre-*Pension Benefits* case law at the EPO and in UK decisions such as *Gale's Application*, sees a computer program as including the 'instructions on some medium (floppy disk, CD, or hard drive) which cause a computer to execute the program—a program that works'.[308] Jacob LJ came down in favour of the later wider view, arguing that to do otherwise would render the exclusion meaningless.[309] He also suggested that the framers of the EPC 'really meant to exclude computer programs in a practical and operable form. They meant to exclude real computer programs, not just an abstract series of instructions'.[310] In so doing, Jacob LJ appeared to reaffirm British practice in this area. He also reinforced the divide that has opened up between the approach that is taken to section 1(2)/Article 52 in the United Kingdom and that taken at the EPO.

While the Court of Appeal expressly said that it was reformulating rather than changing the law in this area, nonetheless following *Aerotel*, the UK Intellectual Property Office (IPO) changed its practice in relation to the patenting of computer programs in November 2007 and reverted to its old practice of rejecting all computer program claims.[311] Following *Aerotel*, the UK IPO refused applications for computer-related invention 'unless it related to a technical process outside the computer or a solution to a technical problem within the computer', and, in so doing, it created a gap between the United Kingdom and EPO.[312]

---

[304] J. Lang, 'Patent Protection for e-Commerce Methods in Europe' [2000] *CTLR* 117, 119, contrasting the *IBM* decisions with the US decision in *Re Beauregard*, 53 *F.3d* 1583 (Fed. Cir. 1995), which held that computer programs embodied in a tangible medium, such as floppy discs, are patentable; R. Hart, 'Computer Program-Related Patents' [1999] *CLSR* 188, 189.

[305] PA 1977, s. 130(7); *Merrell Dow Pharmaceuticals v. Norton* [1996] *RPC* 76 (HL) (on the importance of unity of practice between UK Patent Office and EPO).

[306] IPO Practice Notice, *Patents Act 1977: Claims to Programs for Computers* (5 May 1999), 1.

[307] *Aerotel v. Telco Holdings* [2007] 1 *All ER* 225.   [308] Ibid., [31].

[309] On this, see *IGT v. Comptroller of Patents* [2007] *EWHC* 1341, [10] (Pat) (the definition also included a program that was actually open on a computer and operational, and not simply a program sitting, stored, unopened on a hard drive).   [310] *Aerotel v. Telco Holdings* [2007] 1 *All ER* 225, [31].

[311] IPO Practice Notice, *Patents Act 1977: Patentable Subject Matter* (2 November 2006). On this, see *Astron Clinica v. Comptroller General of Patents* [2008] *EWHC* 85, [46].

[312] *CIPA*, [1.10].

The question of whether the UK IPO's reading of *Aerotel* (and indirectly that of whether the decision itself) was correct was raised in the first-instance decision in *Astron Clinica v. Comptroller General of Patents*.[313] In this case, Kitchin J considered whether *Aerotel* prohibited the patenting of all computer programs, in particular those that would have been considered under the old approach to make a conventional computer operate in a new way, so as to deliver a relevant technical contribution.[314] For various reasons, Kitchin J said that he thought that the approach that had been adopted at the IPO after *Aerotel* was incorrect; instead, he inclined more to the approach that had been set out in the 1999 Practice Notice. Kitchin J concluded that 'where claims to a method performed by running a suitably programmed computer or to a computer programmed to carry out the method are allowable, then, in principle, a claim to the program itself should also be allowable'.[315]

Following the clear statements by Kitchin J in *Astron Clinica*, in February 2008 the UK IPO revised aspects of the Practice Notice issued in November 2007.[316] While the original 2007 Practice Notice said that claims for computer programs or for programs on a carrier were not patentable, the 2008 revision, which came into operation on 7 February 2008, followed the approach in *Astron Clinica*. As a result of the 2008 revisions, the (revised) 2007 Practice Notice said that so long as a claim to a computer program is drawn to reflect the features of the invention that would ensure the patentability of the method that the program is intended to carry out when it is run, examiners will no longer reject claims for a computer program or a program on a carrier.

Kitchin J's reading of section 1(2)/Article 52(2) was reconfirmed in *Symbian*,[317] where the Court of Appeal was called upon to determine whether Symbian's invention—which changed the way in which computers stored and used functions common to a number of different applications, meaning not only that computers were faster, but also that they needed less power and memory—was patentable. The UK IPO argued that computer programs were only patentable when they brought about a novel effect outside a computer. This would have meant that while a program that contained a method of carrying out a new procedure would be patentable, this would not have been the case if the effect of the procedure was solely within the computer itself. In contrast, Symbian argued that Article 52(2)(c) only excludes programs that do not provide a technical solution to a technical problem. Specifically, Symbian argued that a program that improves the performance of a computer would not be excluded any more than would a program that improved the performance of any machine. This was in contrast to a program that simply embodied a theory, which would have been excluded because it did not make a technical contribution.

The Court of Appeal agreed with Symbian and held that the question to be asked was whether the program brought about a technical effect or solved a technical problem, which could occur either within or outside the computer. A technical innovation 'whether within . . . or outside the computer will normally suffice to ensure patentability subject . . . to the claimed invention not falling foul of the other exclusions in Art. 52(2)'.[318] While the decision is important insofar as it clarified that inventions are potentially patentable even where their technical contribution is limited to the computer, in the end the result was straightforward given that the Court found that the effect of Symbian's invention was not limited

[313] [2008] *EWIIC* 85.   [314] Ibid., [46].

[315] Ibid., [50]. Kitchin J said that the approach outlined in *Aerotel* was consistent with the reasoning of the Board in the *IBM* decisions. He also thought that the decision was consistent with *Oneida Indian Nation's Application* [2007] *EWCA Civ* 954.

[316] IPO Practice Notice, *Patents Act 1977: Patentable Subject Matter* (7 February 2008).

[317] *Symbian v. Comptroller-General of Patents* [2008] *EWCA Civ* 1066.   [318] Ibid., [58].

to the computer programmed with relevant instructions, but also extended to cameras, mobile phones and other devices, and products connected to computer systems. Following *Symbian*, the UK IPO issued yet another Practice Notice in December 2008.[319] It began by noting that in the past, the Office had recognized two classes of computer-related invention as being potentially patentable: first, inventions that solved technical problems external to the computer; and second, inventions that solved technical problem within the computer. Following *Symbian*, another class of invention was now treated as potentially patentable:

> [I]nventions which improve the operation of a computer by solving a problem arising from the way the computer was programmed—for example, a tendency to crash due to conflicting library program calls—can also be regarded as solving 'a technical problem within the computer' if it leads to a more reliable computer.[320]

This meant that 'a program that results in a computer running faster or more reliably may be considered to provide a technical contribution even if the invention solely addresses a problem in the programming'.[321]

Following *Symbian*, it is clear that the question to be asked when determining whether an application falls foul of section 1(2)(c)/Article 52(2)(c) in the UK is whether the invention as a whole brings about a technical effect (which does not fall within one of the excluded categories). In some cases, this will occur outside of the computer. Thus, where the computer program represents something specific and external to the computer (a technical contribution), and it does not fall within one of the excluded categories, it is potentially patentable. In these cases, there was something more than 'just a computer program'; it 'evidently perform[s] a task which has real world consequences'.[322] Somewhat more controversially, the relevant technical effect may also occur only within the computer itself. It is clear that an invention that makes a technical contribution to the art is patentable even if it is entirely implemented on a computer and 'even if the way that it works is entirely as a result of a computer program operating on that computer'.[323] A contribution that is implemented entirely as a result of a computer program operating within a computer is not excluded if the contribution is technical in nature.[324] In these situations, as Birss J said, a 'patentee is entitled to claim the computer program itself'.[325] Thus a range of inventions involving computer programs have been held to be patentable, including 'a new method of communicating between programs and data files within the computer',[326] a new data structure system embodied in an algorithm that was faster and required less data storage than the state of the art (which displayed messages to users on the screen),[327] and programs that increase processing speed,[328] reliability, or simply lead to a 'better computer'.[329] Importantly, this is the case 'even if the invention solely addresses a problem in the programming'.[330]

---

[319] IPO Practice Notice, *Patents Act 1977: Patentable Subject Matter* (8 December 2008), [5]. In light of *Halliburton Energy Service's Patent Application* [2011] *EWHC* 2508, the December 2008 notice was replaced by IPO Practice Notice, *Patents Act 1977: Patentability of Mental Acts* (17 October 2011).

[320] IPO Practice Notice, *Patents Act 1977: Patentability of Computer Programs* (8 December 2008), [5].

[321] Ibid.   [322] *Halliburton Energy Service's Patent Application* [2011] EWHC 2508, [33].

[323] Ibid., [30].   [324] Ibid., [35].   [325] Ibid., [32].

[326] *Datenprozessornetz/IBM*, T 6/03 (6 October 1988), [6].

[327] *Computer-related invention/IBM*, T 115/85 [1990] *OJ EPO* 30.

[328] *Merrill Lynch's Application* [1989] *RPC* 561 (CA).

[329] An invention that solved the problem of how to deal with multiple simultaneous touches on a multi-touch device, which caused a 'device to operate in a new and improved way and the application software which it is running for that purpose', was held to be technical: *HTC Europe v. Apple* [2013] *EWCA Civ* 451, [56]–[59].

[330] IPO Practice Notice, *Patents Act 1977: Patentability of Computer Programs* (8 December 2008).

In *AT&T Knowledge Ventures*,[331] Lewison J set out a number of signposts that can help to determine whether an invention involving a computer program is excluded by section 1(2)(c) of the Patents Act 1977. In effect, this is a useful summary of the types of computer-related invention that have been patented to date. These are where:

(i)   the claimed technical effect had a technical effect on a process that is carried on outside the computer;

(ii)   the claimed technical effect operated at the level of the architecture of the computer—that is, where the effect was produced irrespective of the data being processed or the applications being run;

(iii) the claimed technical effect resulted in the computer being made to operate in a new way;

(iv)   the program made the computer a better computer, in the sense of running more efficiently and effectively as a computer;[332] or

(v)   the perceived problem was overcome by the claimed invention as opposed to merely being circumvented.[333]

Along with the staged approach in *Aerotel* (as modified in *Symbian*), these 'signposts' have been used by the examiners at the UK IPO[334] and by the Court of Appeal[335] when determining whether an application relating to a computer program is patentable.[336] While these are useful, it is always important to remember that the key issue here is whether, when viewed as a whole, the invention makes a technical contribution that does not fall within one of the excluded categories.

Although British courts have adopted a more liberal approach to the patenting of computer programs than might have been envisaged when the 1977 Act was passed, nonetheless there are still some important limitations on the types of thing that qualify as patentable subject matter. While some computer-based applications have been excluded on the basis that they are not technical,[337] as the Court of Appeal said in *Symbian*, if section 1(2) is not to be rendered meaningless, there must be some limits to the types of computer program that can be patented. As we explained earlier, this is because all inventions that use a computer are technical; as a result, it is not enough to show simply that a computer-related invention is technical. This means that the mere presence of conventional

[331] *AT&T Knowledge Ventures and CVON Innovations v. Comptroller General of Patents, Designs and Trade Marks* [2009] *EWHC* 343.

[332] Initially, the fourth signpost developed by Lewison J (as he then was) asked whether 'there was an increase in the speed or reliability of the computer'. In *HTC Europe v. Apple* [2013] *EWCA Civ* 451, Lewison LJ revised the fourth signpost. We have reproduced the revised signpost here.

[333] *AT&T Knowledge Ventures and CVON Innovations v. Comptroller General of Patents, Designs and Trade Marks* [2009] *EWHC* 343, [45].

[334] See, e.g., *Kube Partners'Application*, O/193/17 (20 April 2017) (scheme for storage of private information on a cloud computing platform in a way that did not contravene territorial privacy was an excluded computer program as such); *BQR Reliability Engineering Ltd's Application*, O/145/17 (27 March 2017) (computerized method for estimating the reliability of system at normal operating conditions excluded on the basis that it related solely to computer program per se and mathematical method).

[335] *HTC Europe v. Apple* [2013] *EWCA Civ* 451, [50]–[51].

[336] See, e.g., *Really Virtual v. UK Intellectual Property Office* [2012] *EWHC* 1086 (Ch); *Protecting Kids the World Over's Patent Application* [2012] *RPC* (13) 323; *HTC Europe v. Apple* [2013] *EWCA Civ* 451.

[337] A computer program that determined whether data that may be uploaded to a server 'relates to how information is administered and managed in a database on a server' was held to be a computer program per se and, as such, was not patentable: *Sony Corporation's Application*, O/240/12 (21 June 2012), [34].

computing hardware does not necessarily mean that an invention is patentable;[338] rather, something more is needed.

While the extent to which computer-related inventions will exhibit the relevant technical effect and thus be patentable will depend on the particular application in question, it can safely be said that an ordinary computer program used in a general-purpose computer would normally not be patentable in the United Kingdom. The reason for this is that while the implementation of the program in a computer transforms mathematical values into electrical signals, the electrical signals amount to no more than a reproduction of information, which would not be regarded as bringing about a relevant technical effect.[339] It is also clear that the mere inclusion of a program on a carrier is not enough to circumvent the exclusion; more is needed, such as a change in the speed with which the processor works.[340]

We can get a sense of what is meant by a relevant technical effect from *Gemstar v. Virgin*,[341] which concerned patents for electronic programming guides used to display information about television programs. One of the patents at issue, the so called 'Single Channel' patent, involved the delivery of information about television programming. The essential inventive step involved the formats in which that information was displayed on the television.[342] The invention worked by displaying programme listings in grid form, showing a number of programmes for a number of channels for various periods of time. The viewer was able to move a cursor to highlight a particular cell (and therefore a particular programme). If a cell were selected, the display would switch to 'single channel' mode. In this mode, the screen would show a list of the programmes appearing on the selected programme's channel (and no others) at and around the selected time. When this occurred, the focus of the display would shift from a survey of various channels to only the one. The user could scroll up and down that list, and if a particular programme was 'selected', then the screen would toggle back to the multi-channel mixed mode. Thus this patent was for a switch from a larger-scale grid to a single channel; hence the name given to it for the purposes of this action. Another feature of the invention was that whenever a programme was selected, the programme's information (cast list, etc.) was retrieved in a separate box or window superimposed onto part (but not the whole) of the listing display. The programme's listing could still be seen above or below the box.[343]

Mann J began by looking at the technical effects within the computer. While the computer program within the invention produced a technical effect in the sense that any functioning program did—the computer would not work in the same way without such effects—this was not enough. As Mann J said, '[m]ore is required to avoid the exclusion, and (in this context) that "more" is something which makes the computer work better'[344]—that is, the relevant technical effect needed for the program to be patentable in this case was one that 'made the computer a better computer in the sense of running more efficiently and effectively as a computer', or which solved a technical problem lying within

---

[338] See *Motorola Mobility's Application*, O/174/13 (29 April 2013), [14] (what is important was the contribution, not only the difference over the prior art; quicker user interaction was not technical); *Lantana v. Comptroller General of Patents, Designs and Trade Marks* [2014] *EWHC* Civ 1463 (CA) (effects within computer held to be non-technical).

[339] *Kock & Sterzel/X-ray apparatus*, T 26/86 [1988] *EPOR* 72.

[340] Ibid., [54]. See also *Aerotel v. Telco Holdings* [2007] 1 *All ER* 225, [92].

[341] [2009] *EWHC* 3068 (Ch). The question of the patentability of the subject matter was not discussed in the appeal (which focused on novelty): *Gemstar v. Virgin* [2011] *EWCA* Civ 302 (upholding decision of Mann J).

[342] While the decision dealt with three patents, we have limited our analysis to the first patent.

[343] *Gemstar v. Virgin* [2009] *EWHC* 3068, [4]–[5].   [344] Ibid., [42].

the computer itself. Unfortunately for Gemstar, Mann J said that in the case at hand, these traits were not present. This was because while the invention made the computer, as a computer, work differently in the sense of processing data in a different way, it did not make it work better, faster, or differently (in that sort of performance sense). While the invention was clearly technical, Mann J held that producing a different or better user interface was not a (relevant) technical effect.

Mann J then looked at whether there were any relevant technical effects outside of the computer.[345] Specifically, he looked at the question of whether the computer-generated appearance of the information on the screen of the computer (treating the screen as being separate from the computer for these purposes) was a relevant technical effect. Because of the technical consequences of firing electrons at phosphor, or applying charges across pixel cells, it was clear that the invention had a technical effect outside the computer. However, Mann J said that this was 'not the right sort of technical effect'; it 'is merely painting information on a screen so that it can be read, the user having had the opportunity to select the manner in which that happens by operating the controlling mechanism accordingly'.[346] There was no technical contribution in the sense that the cases require. While there was a different display on the screen, Mann J said that this was not enough: 'A different display to that shown before does not seem to me to go far enough to amount to a technical effect which makes a difference.'[347] This was because the technical effect relied on by Gemstar—namely, a better or a different interface—was not a relevant technical effect. The reason for this was that a better (or different) interface was an abstract concept; it did not describe some physical activity or effect.[348] Highlighting the problem that has long bedevilled patent law in this area, Mann J said:

> Many computers running a program are likely to have a display output, and if that were enough to be a technical effect then every program in such a computer would be likely to fall outside the exclusion, which is unlikely to have been the intention of the draftsman of the Act.[349]

Gemstar can usefully be contrasted with the decision of *Protecting Kids the World Over*,[350] which concerned an application for a system that monitored the content of electronic communications to ensure that children were not exposed to inappropriate content or language. Where certain content was identified on the monitored computer, an alarm was triggered alerting the user (parents) at a remote terminal (such as a mobile device) that inappropriate content was being processed on the monitored computer. This was seen to be qualitatively different from the invention in *Gemstar*, where information was 'simply displayed on a screen'. As Floyd J said, if, as in *Gemstar*,

> . . . the task that the program or computer performs is simply producing a different display, there is no relevant technical effect. Such an effect is too 'abstract' . . . [However,] if the effect outside the computer can in principle fairly be described as a physical concept, process or effect then the same considerations do not . . . apply.[351]

On the facts, Floyd J held that the invention in question was sufficiently technical for it not to fall foul of section 1(2)(c). This was because, unlike the abstract and ephemeral invention in *Gemstar*, the invention in *Protecting Kids* not only brought about a physical

---

[345] Ibid., [43].
[346] Ibid.   [347] Ibid., [50].   [348] An 'interface' was an abstract, not a physical, concept.
[349] *Gemstar v. Virgin* [2009] *EWHC* 3068, [42].   [350] [2011] *EWHC* 2720 (Pat).
[351] Ibid., [18].

change, but was also technically superior to what had gone before and solved a technical problem lying outside the computer.[352]

While the issue is far from clear, it seems that when determining whether something is a *relevant* technical effect, the courts simply apply the same test that they use to determine whether something is technical. While the courts will no doubt continue to pay lip service to the idea that certain types of 'technical' effect are not—at least for the purposes of patent law—technical, the reference to a relevant technical effect is perhaps best seen as a judicial fiction that allows the courts to resolve the conundrum of using technical effect to exclude things that are inherently technical (such as a computer program per se).

7.2.2 Approach at the EPO

As we mentioned earlier, one of the consequences of the adoption of the 'any hardware' approach at the EPO is that it is much easier for an invention to satisfy the subject matter requirement, whether for an apparatus or claim, than had previously been the case. Indeed, one commentator has suggested that Article 52 is now an insignificant bar to patentability, given that all that is required to 'impart the requisite technical character to a claimed method is the specification of some technical means, however banal or well-known'.[353] It should be noted that as in the United Kingdom, there are limits on the types of technical effect that will be taken into account when deciding whether an invention involving a computer program is patentable. In order to reconcile the exclusion of computer programs with the fact that all computer programs have technical effects, since they cause different electrical currents to circulate in the computer they run on, the Enlarged Board of Appeal (EBA) said that 'such technical effects are not sufficient to confer "technical character" on the programs, they must cause further technical effects', or that the 'programmer must have had technical considerations beyond "merely" finding a computer algorithm to carry out some procedure'.[354] While this does suggest some type of qualitative limitation on the types of technical effect that will suffice to confer patentability on computer programs, in practice it has had little impact. As in the United Kingdom, when determining whether a relevant technical effect exists, the tribunals have simply followed the usual approach to determining patentable subject matter.

If an invention is implemented by a computer, it will be considered to use technical means and, by that very token, will be taken to have technical character.[355] This means that so long as an invention makes use of, or is implemented by, a computer, it will fall outside the subject matter exclusion.[356] As the EBA said:

> [A] claim to a computer implemented method or a computer program on a computer-readable storage medium will never fall within the exclusion of claimed subject-matter under Articles 52(2) and (3), just as a claim to a picture on a cup will never fail under this exclusion.[357]

---

[352] Ibid., [35].

[353] D. Booton, 'The Patentability of Computer-Implemented Inventions' [2007] *IPQ* 92, 102; J. Pila, 'Dispute over the Meaning of Invention in Art 52(2) EPC: The Patentability of Computer-Implemented Inventions in Europe' (2005) 36 *IIC* 173.

[354] *President's Reference/Patentability of programs for computers*, G 3/08 [2011] *OJ EPO* 10, [13.5].

[355] *Infineon Technologies/Circuit simulation I*, T 1227/05 [2007] *OJ EPO* 574, 581.

[356] For a review of EPO case law, see *President's Reference/Patentability of programs for computers*, G 3/08 [2011] *OJ EPO* 10, [10.7]–[10.8] (a computer-readable storage medium is not excluded from patentability under Art. 52(2)(3)).   [357] Ibid., [10.13.1].

This can be seen in *Hitachi/Auction method*,[358] where a method of using a memory (clipboard) on a computer was held to be an invention for the purposes of Article 52(1). The liberal interpretation can also be seen in the decision in *Microsoft/Clipboard formats I*.[359] The application in question, which was for a way of 'facilitating data exchange across different formats', consisted of both method claims and a claim for a program on a computer-readable medium. The Technical Board of Appeal said that the 'method was implemented in a computer and this amounted to a technical means sufficient to escape the prohibition in Article 52'.[360] More specifically, the Board said that 'a method implemented in a computer system represents a sequence of steps actually performed and achieving an effect'.[361] Even though a method, in particular a method of operating a computer, may be put into practice with the help of a computer program, a claim relating to such a method does not claim a computer program as such.

The 'any hardware' approach has been extended beyond computer-implemented inventions in relation to the medium on which a computer program is supported. (Jacob LJ, in *Aerotel*, said that this presupposes that computer program is defined narrowly as an abstract set of instructions.[362]) As the Technical Board of Appeal said in *Microsoft/Clipboard formats I*, an invention will have technical character where it relates to a computer-readable medium (a technical product involving a carrier)—that is, a computer-readable medium is a technical product and thus has technical character. This means that where a computer program enhances the internal operations of a computer, it will have technical character—so long as it goes beyond the elementary interaction of hardware and software of data processing.[363] While the EBA noted that there was some inconsistency in EPO case law in this area,[364] it said that *Microsoft/Clipboard formats I* had been applied consistently and was good law. Applying the logic of the 'any hardware' approach, the Board said that a computer-readable data-storage medium ('storing computer program X') could not be excluded from patentability anymore than a cup, 'which was a technical article, could be excluded from patentability merely because it was decorated with picture X'.[365]

7.3 METHODS OF DOING BUSINESS

Despite its lineage, the exclusion of business methods from patentable subject matter has been somewhat controversial. In part, this is a consequence of developments in the United States, which have now backtracked somewhat, which provided more liberal protection to methods of doing business than had hitherto been the case.[366] The approach that has

---

[358] T 258/03 [2004] *OJ EPO* 575.   [359] T 424/03 (23 February 2006).   [360] Ibid., [5.1].

[361] Ibid.   [362] *Aerotel v. Telco Holdings* [2007] 1 *All ER* 225, [31].

[363] *Microsoft/Clipboard formats I*, T 424/03 [2006] *EPOR* 414; *IBM/Computer programs*, T 1173/97 [1999] *OJ EPO* 609. In *Astron Clinica*, Kitchen J said that the Board in *Microsoft/Clipboard formats* 'appears to have found that any program on a carrier has a technical character and so escapes the prohibition in Article 52': *Astron Clinica v. Comptroller General of Patents* [2008] *EWHC* 85, [39].

[364] *IBM/Computer programs*, T 1173/97 [1999] *OJ EPO* 609, was said to be inconsistent with *Microsoft/ Clipboard formats I*, T 424/03 (23 February 2006).

[365] *President's Reference/Patentability of programs for computers*, G 3/08 [2011] *OJ EPO* 10, [11]. See also *BDGB Enterprise/Classification method and apparatus*, T 1358/09 (21 November 2014).

[366] *State Street Bank & Trust v. Signature Financial Group* 149 F. 3d 1368 (Fed. Cir. 1998). The Federal Circuit Court of Appeals said, at 1374, that: [S]ince the 1952 Patent Act, business methods have been, and should have been, subject to the same legal requirements (utility, novelty, non-obviousness, disclosure) for patentability as applied to any other process or method 'so that a patent application relating to the transformation of data, representing discrete dollar amounts, by a machine, through a series of mathematical calculations into a final share price, constitutes a practical application of a mathematical algorithm, formula or calculation, and is thus patentable subject matter. There is no exception for methods of doing business'.

been used in the United Kingdom and at the EPO to determine whether an application is excluded on the basis that it consists of 'a method of doing business' under section 1(2)(c)/ Article 52(2)(c) is much the same as that which has been used with the other areas of section 1(2)/Article 52.[367]

7.3.1 Approach in the United Kingdom

The approach adopted in the United Kingdom (and at the EPO prior to *Pension Benefits*) is the same as the general approach discussed earlier. This can be seen in *Merrill Lynch's Application*,[368] where the Court of Appeal held that an automatic share-trading system operated by a computer program was unpatentable because it merely amounted to a method of doing business. This has been confirmed by a UK IPO Practice Notice[369] and in a number of subsequent decisions.[370] This has led to a range of applications being rejected, including a computer programmed to operate as a securities trading system,[371] a method of setting up a company,[372] an invention that 'calculates and moves currency electronically and turns that currency into other value systems (prizes, credits etc)',[373] an invention that provided decisions as to how to use employees to generate additional revenue streams,[374] and a payments advice system that allowed a payer to send a payment to a payee and associate it with a document stored in the advice system.[375] All of these alleged inventions were excluded on the basis that they were non-technical business methods.

A similar approach had been followed at the EPO. This can be seen in *Petterson/ Queueing system*,[376] which concerned a patent for a system for handling customers queuing at a number of service points. The patent consisted of a turn-number allocating unit, an information unit, a selection unit, and a computer program that decided which particular turn number was to be served at a particular service point. While the patent was rejected in Sweden, the Technical Board of Appeal at the EPO held that the claimed apparatus was clearly technical in nature and thus patentable.[377] Although the invention was

---

[367] See *Trilateral Report on Comparative Study on Business Method Related Inventions* (14 June 2000) for a summary of approaches at the European, US, and Japanese patent offices. See also H. Hanneman, 'The Patentability of "Methods of Doing Business"' [2000] *epi Information* 16; D. Booton and P. Mole, 'The Action Freezes? The Draft Directive on the Patentability of Computer-implemented Inventions' [2002] *IPQ* 289.

[368] [1989] *RPC* 561; *Stockburger/Coded distinctive mark*, T 51/84 [1986] *EPOR* 229.

[369] IPO Practice Notice, *Patents Act 1977: Interpreting Section 1(2)* (24 April 2002), 1, stressing that technical contribution is the basis for deciding patentability and, in so doing, rejecting the view that 'some excluded things cannot be patentable even if a technical contribution is present'. This means that 'inventions which involve a technical contribution will not be refused a patent merely because they relate to business methods or mental acts'.

[370] *Crawford v. Jones* [2005] *EWHC* 2417. The following applications were refused at the (then) UK Patent Office on the basis that they were business methods: a web-based online user system for ordering computer equipment (*Dell USA*, O/432/01 (4 October 2001)); a system for the exchange of information between providers and enquirers (*Pintos Global Services*, O/171/01 (6 April 2001)); a system for automating the ordering of food in a cafeteria (*Fujitsu Ltd*, O/324/03 (23 October 2003)); a method for allowing users to buy personalized financial products over the Internet (*Accucard Ltd*, O/145/03 (29 May 2003)); and a computer system for handling conflicting demands for resources, such as booking of meeting rooms (*Fujitsu*, O/317/00 (23 August 2000)). [371] *Merrill Lynch's Application* [1988] *RPC* 1.

[372] *Macrosson's Application* [2006] *EWHC* 705 (Ch).

[373] *IGT's Application*, O/140/13 (27 March 2013), [49].

[374] *Henri Duong's Application*, O/085/12 (24 February 2012).

[375] *Jagwood's Application*, O/114/12 (9 March 2012).

[376] T 1002/92 [1995] *OJ EPO* 605; See also *Texas Instruments/Language-understanding system*, T 236/91 [2000] *EPOR* 156; *Fujitsu's Application*, O/317/00 (23 August 2000).

[377] The possibility of patenting business method inventions received a boost as a result of the *Sohei* decision in which the TBA suggested that 'business' ought to be construed narrowly: *Sohei/General-purpose management system*, T 769/92 [1996] *EPOR* 253, 258 (generally acknowledged to have adopted an even more software-friendly approach in assessing patentability).

used in a business context, a telling factor in the Board's decision to uphold the validity of the patent was its finding that the essence of the invention lay in the way the elements of the system were combined.[378] More specifically, the validity of the patent was upheld because the problem that the invention solved related to the way in which the components of the system interacted, which was seen as a technical rather than a business problem.[379]

The Court of Appeal in *Aerotel* said that business method exclusion was not limited to abstract matters; it also said that there was no need for an activity to be completed—for the cash register to ring—for it to fall within the exclusion.[380] On the basis that the information was to be used in the conduct of the business, it was held that the idea of presenting information to be used in undertaking inventories in a pictorial form was a method of doing business.[381] It has also been said that the mere fact that an invention provides financial gains is not enough for it to be classified as a method of doing business; otherwise, nearly all patents would fall within the exclusion.[382]

7.3.2 Approach at the EPO

As we noted earlier, the fate of methods of doing business under the 'any hardware' approach at the EPO was clearly spelt out in the *Pension Benefits* decision.[383] (It is important to note that the reasoning developed in *Pension Benefits* was subsequently extended to both apparatus and method claims.) Given that the corresponding patent application was granted in the United States, the decision also highlighted that difference in approach between Europe and the United States in relation to patent protection for business method inventions.[384]

7.4 PRESENTATION OF INFORMATION

The approach that has been used in the United Kingdom and at the EPO to determine whether an invention consists of the presentation of information and thus falls foul of section 1(2)(d)/Article 52(2)(d) is similar to the approach that has been used in relation to the other categories of subject matter excluded from protection.[385]

---

[378] *NAT/Bagging plant* [1993] *EPOR* 517 (claims were allowed for a computer method that involved weighing and bagging on the quayside material transported in bulk by ship, because it used technical equipment to achieve a technical end—i.e. the production of sealed weighed bags of materials). See also *Pension Benefit Systems*, T 931/95 [2001] *OJ EPO* 441 (TBA) (a claim for a method of controlling a pension administration system).

[379] *Sohei/General purpose management system*, T 769/92 [1996] *EPOR* 253; *Pitney Bowes/System for processing mail*, T 767/99 (13 March 2002), [2.6].

[380] *Aerotel v. Telco Holdings* [2007] 1 *All ER* 225, [67]–[71].

[381] *Raytheon v. Comptroller General of Patents, Designs and Trade Marks* [2007] *EWHC* 1230, [40]. See also *Autonomy Corporation v. The Comptroller General of Patents* [2008] *EWHC* 146.

[382] *Quest International/Odour selection*, T 619/02 [2007] *OJ EPO* 63.

[383] This is reflected in the EPO Guidelines, which state that, 'in relation to an apparatus claim which contains computers, computer networks or other conventional programmable apparatus or a program thereof, for carrying out at least some steps of a scheme, it is to be examined as a computer-related invention': *EPO Guidelines*, G-II, [3.4].

[384] A patent had been granted on the appellant's pension system in the United States in *Pension Benefit Systems*, T 931/95 [2001] *OJ EPO* 441, 447, [iv], despite the fact that the reasoning of the Board was said to be reminiscent of USPTO, *Guidelines for the Examination of Computer-Related Inventions* (1996). See M. Likhovski, 'Fighting the Patent Wars' [2001] *EIPR* 267, 270.

[385] See, e.g., *Texas Instruments/Language-understanding system*, T 236/91 [2000] *EPOR* 156. See also *Hiroki Ashizawa*, O/235/03 (18 August 2003); *Crawford v. Jones* [2005] *EWHC* 2417 (application excluded on the basis that it was limited to display of information).

7.4.1 Approach in the United Kingdom

When considering whether a patent is excluded under Article 52(2) and (3), the EPO (pre-*Pension Benefits*) drew a distinction between ordinary (cognitive) information, which is excluded by section 1(2)(d)/Article 52(2)(d), and special (functional) information, which is not excluded.[386]

Ordinary cognitive information, which is the type of information excluded under section 1(2)(d)/Article 52(2)(d) as a presentation of information, includes subject matter that merely conveys cognitive or aesthetic content directly to a human.[387] In essence, ordinary cognitive information includes any representation of information that is characterized solely by the content of the information. This would include, for example, a television signal solely characterized by the information per se (for example moving pictures, modulated upon a standard television signal). Similarly, digital data that encodes cognitive content (such as a picture) in a standard manner would also be excluded.[388] As the EPO Guidelines explain, a claim will be excluded where it is directed to the presentation of information per se (for example acoustic signals, spoken words), to information recorded on a carrier where the carrier (that is, the book, the gramophone record, or magnetic computer tape) is characterized solely by the content being carried (the subject of the book, musical content, or data or programs), or to processes and apparatus for the presentation of information.[389] In all of these cases, the key aspect of the invention is the content of the message.

In contrast, a patent for *functional information* (or data) does not fall within the scope of Article 52(2)(d). As with all enquiries into excluded subject matter, if it can be shown that the information carrier or the process or apparatus for presenting the information, has a technical feature, the invention may be patentable. It is also possible that the arrangement or manner of representation, as compared with the content of the information itself, may be patentable. This would include instruments designed to measure information or the use of a code to represent characters. In explaining what is meant by functional information, the EPO supported the view that information (in its special sense) must not be confused with meaning. In fact, two messages, one of which is heavily loaded with meaning and the other of which is pure nonsense, can be exactly equivalent from the information technology point of view. Information in communication theory relates not so much to what you *do* say as to what you *could* say—that is, information is a measure of one's freedom of choice when one selects a message.[390]

Using this definition, the Technical Board of Appeal (TBA) said that information in the special (non-excluded) sense includes physical interactions within and between

---

[386] The Board said that, with the growth of information technology in the last half-century, information in its 'special sense had become much more important'. Nonetheless, the Board noted that the information mentioned in Art. 52(2)(d) was limited to information in the ordinary (cognitive sense): *Koninklijke Philips Electronics/Picture retrieval system*, T 1194/97 [2000] *OJ EPO* 525, [3.7.2].

[387] Ibid. The Board said that the only decision that appeared to have construed 'presentation of information' to include an aspect of the special sense of information was *Kock & Sterzal/X-ray apparatus*, T 26/86 [1988] *EPOR* 72. The Board noted that *Kock & Sterzal* dealt with the exclusion of computer programs and, as such, was 'strictly *obiter* as far as Article 52(2)(d) is concerned': *Koninklijke Philips Electronics/Picture retrieval system*, T 1194/97 [2000] *OJ EPO* 525, [3.7.4].

[388] In rejecting an application for a configuration for simultaneously displaying several images on a computer screen, the TBA said that imparting information on events in a screen window merely drew attention to the content of the images and, as such, was not technical: *Siemans*, T 599/93 [1997] *OJ EPO* (Special edn), 14.   [389] *EPO Guidelines*, G-II, [3.7].

[390] *Koninklijke Philip's Electronics*, T 1194/97 [2001] *EPOR* 193, [3.7.1], citing C. Shannon and W. Weaver, *The Mathematical Theory of Communication* (1949) [no page number provided].

machines that do not convey any humanly understandable meaning. It has also said that a television signal solely characterized by the information per se (for example moving pictures, modulated upon a standard television signal) would be an excluded presentation of information while, in contrast, a television signal defined in terms that included the technical features of the television system in which it occurs has been held not to be a presentation of information.[391] In a similar fashion, the TBA held that an invention that was defined in terms that inherently included the technical features of the system in which the record carrier operated was not excluded as a presentation of information.[392] In *Koninklijke*, the Board said that the difference between (excluded) cognitive information and (non-excluded) functional data was illustrated by the fact that if the cognitive data or content was lost, the result would be a humanly meaningless picture, like snow on a television screen. This would not have any effect whatsoever on the technical working of the system. In contrast, the loss of functional data would impair the technical operation of the system and might indeed bring the system to a halt.[393] The approach that was adopted at the EPO prior to *Pension Benefits* in relation to the presentation of information can be seen in *Broselow/Measuring tape*,[394] where the invention was for a method of ascertaining information about accident victims (such as drug dosage or defibrillation techniques). More specifically, the method involved an ambulance officer measuring the body length of the emergency victim using a particular tape, which provided information about how the patient was to be treated. Importantly, this was done without the need for clinical expertise or reference to other sources. Highlighting the importance of the way the invention is construed, the TBA held that the 'co-relation between the measured length and the information on the tape measure results in the tape ... becoming a new gauge for directly measuring the patient treatment values' and that such a new gauge, 'for directly measuring the patient values, is clearly technical in character'.[395]

After some uncertainty, it is now clear that UK courts will follow the approach adopted at the EPO (pre-*Pension Benefits*). This is a result of *Gemstar v. Virgin*,[396] where Mann J endorsed the approach that had been adopted at the EPO pre-*Pension Benefits*. Drawing on the EPO Examination Guidelines, Mann J said that to be patentable, there had to be some effect beyond the information being processed. While a representation of information defined solely by the content of the information would not be patentable, this is in contrast to situations where the presentation of information has some real-world technical achievement outside the information itself, which is potentially patentable. Mann J used this test to reject the application in *Gemstar*, arguing that because the invention in question only provided a better or new user interface that allowed the starting

[391] *BBC/Colour television signal*, T 163/85 [1990] *EPOR* 599, 603.

[392] On the facts, the Board held that the claim in question was not a presentation of information, since it had functional data recorded thereon (in particular a data structure of picture line syntonization, line numbers, and addressees): *Koninklijke Philip's Electronics/Picture retrieval system*, T 1194/97 [2001] *EPOR* 193. The Board followed *IBM/Computer programs*, T 1173/97 [1999] *OJ EPO* 609.

[393] *Koninklijke Philip's Electronics*, T 1194/97 [2001] *EPOR* 193.   [394] T 77/92 [1998] *EPOR* 266.

[395] Ibid., 270. The Board added that 'the subject matter as a whole of a claim consisting of a mix of known technical elements and non-technical elements is not excluded from patentability under Art. 52(2) and (3) when the non-technical elements interact with the known technical elements in order to produce a technical effect': ibid.

[396] [2009] *EWHC* 3068, [52]–[60]; upheld on appeal [2011] *EWCA Civ* 302. See also *Re Townsend's Patent Application* [2004] *EWHC* 482 ('presentation of information' was not limited to the way in which information is presented or expressed, in terms of the format, font, etc., but also includes the provision of information; as such, an application for an advent calendar designed so that it could be used simultaneously by more than one person was excluded under s. 1(2)(d)).

information to be presented in a different way, there was no new technical effect. As such, it was a mere presentation of information.

The upshot is that if it can be shown that an application has some real-world technical achievement outside the information itself, it will not be caught by the exclusion. This is the case, for example, with the slide lock features on the iPhone: while the slide lock provided visual information to users, it also brought about a real-world effect and, as such, it was a not a presentation of information.[397] A similar approach can be seen in *Samsung Electronic's Application*,[398] where it was held that an application for a method and apparatus for showing images embedded in an electronic map was *not* a mere presentation of information. The invention in question consisted of four stages. First, the user was presented with an electronic map. After the user selected a location on the map, the program analysed and then filtered the information contained in the map to identify images located within a certain radius of the selected location. In the final stage, the user was presented with images of nearby locations. A key feature of the application was that it identified and presented images of places of interest nearby the chosen location. This was in contrast to pre-existing electronic maps (such as Google Earth), which merely revealed images of the chosen location. While the invention was, at least from the perspective of the end-user, primarily concerned with the presentation of information, nonetheless it was held *not* to be a mere presentation of information. This was because while the invention began and ended by presenting information to the user (in the form of the initial map and the final map with the selected images), in between these two steps, the user selected the target point on the map, and the program analysed and filtered the information contained in the map. As the Hearing Officer held, the presence of the two middle steps meant that there was something more than the mere presentation of information; as such, the application was not excluded under section 1(2).[399] What was not clear, however, was why the selection of information by the end-user in *Gemstar* did not save the application, whereas in this case it did.

7.4.2 Approach at the EPO

The approach adopted at the EPO under the 'any hardware' approach in relation to presentations of information has been consistent with the general approach outlined earlier. Thus, if an invention employs some technical means, it will not fall foul of Article 52(2) (d)—even if the contribution made by the invention is limited to the presentation of information. One of the consequences of the adoption of the 'any hardware' approach is that some of the earlier decisions at the EPO, which were based on the contribution test, will no longer be followed.[400] In *Hitachi/Auction method*,[401] the Technical Board of Appeal said that the EPO Guidelines were inconsistent with the approach outlined in *Pension Benefits* insofar as they say that 'devices such as visual displays, books, gramophone records, traffic signs and apparatus are said not to be patentable . . . if defined solely by the content of the information'. It seems clear that applications of this nature will now pass the subject matter test in Article 52(2)(d) if they include *some* technical means—no matter how old, banal, or trivial.

---

[397] *HTC Europe v. Apple* [2012] *EWHC* 1789 (Pat).   [398] O/347/12 (8 October 2012).   [399] Ibid., [37].
[400] This can be seem, e.g., in the decision of the Board in *Infineon Technologies/Circuit simulation I*, T 1227/05 [2007] *OJ EPO* 574, 584–7, where the decisions of *IBM/Method for physical VLSI–chip design*, T 453/91 (31 May 1994) and *International Computers/Information modelling*, T 49/99 (5 March 2002) were not followed.   [401] T 258/03 [2004] *OJ EPO* 575, 583.

In *Gambro/Presentation of operating instructions*,[402] the Technical Board of Appeal provided guidance on the approach to adopt when considering the fate of inventions involving presentations of information. The Board distinguished between non-patentable *cognitive* data (only meaningful to a human mind) and potentially patentable *functional* data. The Board also distinguished between claims concerned with *how* the information was presented and claims directed to the content of the information (ie *what* is presented). While claims directed at how the information was presented were usually technical, the fate of what was presented depended on the further question of *why* the content was presented (ie for what purpose). In considering this later question, the Board distinguished between technical information that 'credibly enables the user to properly operate the underlying the technical system' (which has a patentable technical effect) and non-technical information which was 'exclusively aimed at the mental activities of the system user as the final addressee' and non-patentable.[403]

7.5 METHODS FOR PERFORMING A MENTAL ACT

At first glance, the exclusion of methods for performing a mental act seems to be relatively straightforward. While this is the case if an application is limited to a purely mental process (unaided by technology), this has not been the case where the mental process is carried out by a computer. One reason why this has been so problematic is that the courts have had to grapple with the fact that while computer-related inventions may perform tasks analogous to those carried out by humans, there comes a time when the analogy breaks down—that is, there is a point at which a process that is carried out by a computer is so qualitatively different from a functionally equivalent process carried out by the human mind that the two events cannot be equated with each other. The question that we look at next is where and how this line is drawn.

7.5.1 Approach in the United Kingdom

Of all of the categories of excluded subject matter, the one where there has been the greatest divergence, both within the United Kingdom and between the approaches adopted in the United Kingdom and at the EPO (pre-*Pension Benefits*), is in relation to the exclusion of methods, schemes, or rules for performing a mental act. As we will see later, there is now much more consistency both in the United Kingdom and between the approaches adopted in the United Kingdom and at the EPO (pre-*Pension Benefits*).

Although UK courts were largely in agreement that a patent would not be granted if the only contribution that the invention offers was mental (or intellectual), for some time there was disagreement as to what is meant by a 'mental act'.[404] More specifically, there was disagreement as to whether or not, and if so, in what circumstances a process that automatically performs a mental act fell within the scope of section 1(2)(c)/Article 52(2)(c).

Over time, two different readings of the provisions developed: a wide and a narrow construction of the exclusion. While there has been support for the wider construction, following *Halliburton Energy Service's Patent Application*,[405] the narrow approach is now applied in the United Kingdom. Given that this outcome is still somewhat fragile (and could benefit from the approval of a superior court), it is important to understand the difference between the two approaches.

---

[402] T 336/14 [2016] *EPOR* 112.   [403] Ibid., [1.2.3]–[1.2.4].

[404] See D. Wells, 'Expert Systems, Mental Acts and Technical Effects' (1995) *CIPAJ* 129; C. Muse, 'Patented Personality' (1988) 4 *Santa Clara Computer & High Tech LJ* 285.   [405] [2011] *EWHC* 2508.

Under the wide construction, an application that is *capable* of being performed mentally is excluded irrespective of whether it is in fact performed mentally. It does not matter if, in fact, the application only claims use of a computer. Thus a claim to a computer programmed to carry out a method of performing a calculation (say, a square root) would be excluded on the basis that it is a mental act. This is because calculations are the types of thing that are 'capable of being performed mentally'.[406] This is the case even if the invention does not actually cover performing the calculation mentally at all because the claim is limited to using a computer.

While the EPO (pre-*Pension Benefits*) had accepted that where a mental act is automatically performed by a computer, the activity may change in such a way that it can no longer be seen as the performance of a mental act, under the wide construction such activities remained a method for performing a mental act. This was the case even when the computer carried out the process in a way that could not be mimicked by the human mind.[407] This point was reinforced by the Court of Appeal in *Fujitsu's Application*,[408] where it was held that the concept for performing a mental act should be construed widely to include all methods of the type performed mentally, even if the particular method in question would not be carried out by the human mind. This was because a method 'remains a method for performing a mental act, whether a computer is used or not'.[409] As Aldous LJ said:

> [A] method of solving a problem, such as advising a person whether he has acted tortiously, can be set out on paper or incorporated into a computer program. The purpose is the same, to enable advice to be given, which appears to me to be a mental act.[410]

Aldous LJ added that:

> [The] method may well be different when a computer is used, but to my mind it still remains a method for performing a mental act, whether or not the computer program adopts steps that would not ordinarily be used by the human mind.[411]

Applying the wide construction, UK courts refused applications that amounted to the automation of operations that could otherwise be performed by humans.[412] This included inventions in the fields of expert systems,[413] pattern recognition systems,[414] and systems for rearranging conflicting demands for resources (such as room bookings).[415] Somewhat

---

[406] Ibid., [42].   [407] *Fujitsu's Application* [1996] *RPC* 511, 518–19.   [408] [1997] *RPC* 608.

[409] Ibid., 620, citing *Wang Laboratories' Application* [1991] *RPC* 463, 472. The suggestion was made that the provision be limited to those acts that can be carried out by the human mind. This was rejected on the basis that it would require the courts to engage in the extremely difficult task of deciding how the human mind actually works: ibid., 619–20.   [410] Ibid.

[411] Ibid. See also *Fujitsu's Application* [1997] *RPC* 620, 621 (CA). The Comptroller adopted a similar approach to reject an application for a computerized system for resolving disputes for resources (such as room or flight bookings) according to certain priorities more easily accessible to users: *Fujitsu's Application*, O/317/00 (23 August 2000), 11.

[412] Claims for an inference processor forming the core of an expert system have been allowed in a hearing at the Patent Office: see D. Wells, 'Expert Systems, Mental Acts and Technical Effects' [1995] *CIPAJ* 129.

[413] *Wang Laboratories* [1991] *RPC* 463 (expert system—comprising a conventional computer operating in the normal way, with an expert system program, the knowledge base of which was in the form of hierarchically defined terms and their definitions—was a mental act and was therefore excluded from protection).

[414] *Raytheon's Application* [1993] *RPC* 427 (patent for a method of 'pattern recognition and the matching of silhouettes, particularly those of ships', was rejected); *Fujitsu's Application* [1996] *RPC* 511 (application directed to methods for modelling a synthetic crystal structure by combining images of two structures to display a third image representing a further crystal structure rejected).

[415] *Fujitsu's Application*, O/317/00 (23 August 2000).

bizarrely, this was the case even if the invention could not be carried out by the unaided human mind.[416]

While there was support in the United Kingdom for the wide construction, over time there was growing support for a narrower, more limited, reading of the exclusion. Under the narrow approach, a claim is only excluded where it 'covers a method of arriving at a particular result by the exercise of rational processes alone'.[417] There are two notable features of the narrow reading. The first, which is based on the idea that the purpose of the mental act exclusion is to 'make sure that patent claims cannot be performed by purely mental means and that is all',[418] is that the exclusion only applies where the application *actually* claims a mental process. The fact that calculations are the type of things that are *capable* of being performed as mental acts is irrelevant. The second is that the exclusion will only apply where the application is limited to mental processes—that is, to processes that occur (exclusively) within the human mind.[419] This means that a process carried out on a computer would 'never be caught by the mental act exclusion because the claim does not encompass carrying out the calculation mentally'.[420]

The question of the correct way to approach the exclusion of mental acts in the United Kingdom was discussed in detail by Birss J in *Halliburton Energy Service's Patent Application*.[421] After reviewing UK case law, Birss J concluded that the balance of authority was in favour of the narrow approach to the exclusion.[422] He also said that he would have favoured the narrow reading in any case, not least because it prevented 'patents being granted which could be infringed by a purely mental process. Allowing for the possibility of patent infringement by thought alone seems to me to be undesirable'.[423] Following the clear statements in *Halliburton*, the UK IPO amended the relevant Practice Notice to make it clear that the mental acts exclusion will now be construed narrowly in the United Kingdom.[424]

The adoption of the narrow interpretation means that a claim will only ever be excluded where it is limited to a purely mental or rational process. One of the consequences of the adoption of the narrow approach is that whenever a mental process is implemented by a computer, it will not be caught by the exclusion. Another consequence is that the exclusion only applies where the application is limited to a purely mental process; the exclusion will not apply if there are appropriate non-mental limitations in the claim.[425] This means that where an invention consists of a mixture of mental and non-mental elements, the exclusion will not apply.

---

[416] *KK Toshiba* [1993] *IPD* 160 (19 February 1993).

[417] *Cappellini and Bloomberg's Application* [2007] *EWHC* 476, [8].

[418] *Halliburton Energy Service's Patent Application* [2011] *EWHC* 2508, [63].

[419] As Jacob LJ said, 'there is no particular reason to suppose that "mental act" was intended to exclude things wider than, for instance, methods of doing mental arithmetic . . . or remembering things': *Aerotel v. Telco Holdings* [2007] 1 *All ER* 225, [98]. One question is how much external (technical) assistance, if any, is permissible: what of paper, pen, chalk, abacus, calculators?

[420] *Halliburton Energy Service's Patent Application* [2011] *EWHC* 2508, [42].

[421] Ibid.   [422] Ibid., [57].   [423] Ibid.

[424] IPO Practice Notice, *Patents Act 1977: Patentability of Mental Acts* (17 October 2011) ('examiners will now take a narrow view of the mental act exclusion . . . claims which specify that the invention is implemented by a computer will not be considered to be excluded from patentability as a mental act'), adopted by the Comptroller in *Protecting Kids the World Over's Patent Application* [2011] *EWHC* 2720, [2]–[3]. The October 2011 Practice Notice replaced the Notice (of the same name) (8 December 2008), issued following *Symbian*, which adopted the wide construction of the mental act exclusion: *Symbian v. Comptroller-General of Patents* [2008] *EWCA Civ* 1066. For criticisms of the 2008 Practice Notice, see *Halliburton Energy Service's Patent Application* [2011] *EWHC* 2508, [78].

[425] *Kapur v. The Comptroller of Patents, Designs, and Trade Marks* [2008] *EWHC* 649, [19]–[20].

Another consequence of adopting the narrow approach is that UK law is now closer to the approach adopted at the EPO (pre-*Pension Benefits*). One difference, however, is that UK courts have tended to focus on the meaning of 'mental act', whereas the EPO followed the standard approach of using the existence of technical character to determine the scope of the exclusion. It also seems that the approach in the United Kingdom is not only more cut and dry (if a computer is used, a claim will not fall within the exclusion), but also a much restrictive reading of the exclusion.

Prior to the adoption of the 'any hardware' approach, the EPO accepted that patents would not fall foul of Article 52(2)(c) if the invention viewed as a whole was technical.[426] Many of the activities that are carried out by a computer, such as object recognition or the checking of text for spelling mistakes, are tasks that can also be performed by humans. Nonetheless, the EPO pre-*Pension Benefits* had been willing to accept that activities carried out automatically by machine may be *qualitatively* different from similar activities carried out by humans. That is, while a computer and a human may perform the same task, when this task is carried out automatically by computer, it might be done with such speed or accuracy that it is not the same as a functionally equivalent task performed by a human.[427]

Thus, when considering whether inventions based on text editing were patentable, the EPO pre-*Pension Benefits* largely followed the line of thought used in relation to other areas of Article 52(2). This meant that if an application only related to the internal, linguistic elements of the text (which are seen to be non technical), it fell foul of Article 52(2) and was thus unpatentable. This can be seen in *IBM/Text-clarity processing*,[428] where the Technical Board of Appeal (TBA) was called upon to decide whether an application for improving the clarity of texts was patentable. The invention in question was made up of a program that first identified linguistic expressions that were difficult to understand, then offered alternative expressions that were easier to understand. An important factor in the decision that the invention was directed to text editing and, as such, that it was not patentable was that the inventive element of the application lay in the mental elements of the process—namely, in the process of identifying parts of texts that were difficult to understand and offering alternatives.

In contrast, if it can be shown that the contribution made by the application is technical and not merely linguistic (mental) in nature, then it was prima facie patentable. That is, if it can be shown that the application extends beyond text processing to provide a technical contribution or to resolve some technical problem, then it will be patentable. A helpful example of this is provided by *IBM/Editable document form*,[429] which concerned an application for a method for transforming printer control items in word-processing documents from one format to another (which in turn allowed documents to be transferred from one text-processing format to another). Using the same logic that is used in relation to the other parts of Article 52(2), the TBA said that in considering whether the

---

[426] *Stockburger/Coded distinctive mark*, T 51/84 [1986] *EPOR* 229.

[427] *IBM/Text clarity processing*, T 38/86 [1990] *EPOR* 606. See also D. Wells, 'Patents for Software: The "Mental Act" Exclusion' [1993] *CIPAJ* 272, 273 (arguing that the UK Patent Office's decision in *Raytheon's Application* [1993] *RPC* 427 is 'completely at variance with the practice of the EPO'). For the position in Germany (following the approach at the EPO), see *Sprachanalyseeinrichtung (Language analysis device)*, X Z.B 15/98 [2002] *OJ EPO* 415 (BGH).

[428] T 38/86 [1990] *EPOR* 606 (application for a method for detecting and replacing incomprehensible expressions using conventional hardware and a dictionary); *IBM/External interface simulation*, T 833/91 [1998] *EPOR* 431 (method of designing external interfaces for a computer application program excluded).

[429] T 110/90 [1995] *EPOR* 185.

application was valid, it needed to 'investigate whether the claim seen as a whole constitutes nothing more than a method for performing mental acts as such, albeit carried out on a computer'.[430] After reviewing the nature of the invention in question, the Board found that the application could not be described as a method for performing a mental act (nor could it be described as a computer program). The reason for this was that the invention was concerned above all with (printer) control items in the source document. Given that the ultimate purpose of these control items was the control of hardware, the Board said that the application had nothing to do with the linguistic meaning of the texts being processed; rather, it represented features of the technical, internal working of that system.[431] As such, the application did not fall foul of Article 52(2)(c).

The adoption of the narrow reading of the mental act exclusion is out of step with other areas of section 1(2), in relation to which the courts have been careful to say that the mere use of a computer will not prevent an application claiming a business method, a mathematical method, or a presentation of information from falling foul of section 1(2).

One of the consequences of the narrow reading is that it renders the mental act exclusion all but meaningless. This is because while the exclusion will still apply where an application claims a purely mental process, it will not apply where a computer is involved. While the adoption of the narrow approach may mean that the mental act exclusion has effectively been rendered redundant, this does not necessarily mean that there will be a corresponding increase in the number of patents granted. This is because what has happened is that the focus of attention has shifted from the exclusion of mental acts to the exclusion of computer programs per se. This can be seen in *IBM/Text-clarity processing*[432] (which we discussed earlier). While the invention may not have fallen foul of the mental act exclusion, the Board found that the process by which these mental acts were placed in a format in which they could be performed automatically by a computer only involved the routine, straightforward application of conventional techniques. Given that the only contribution made by the application was in relation to the mental steps of the process and not (for example) in the way in which these steps were automatically carried out by a computer, the Board declared that the application was invalid. A number of other text-editing applications have been rejected on the basis that they used the same steps as mental processes and, when automated, merely employ conventional equipment ordinarily programmed.[433] A similar approach has been adopted at the UK IPO. For example, while the process of interpretation occurs solely within the interpreter's brain, nonetheless following the finding in *Halliburton* that mental acts performed by a computer cannot be considered a 'mental act', the Hearing Officer held that a claim to a method and apparatus for determining the competency of human language interpreters using a computer

---

[430] Ibid., [4].

[431] They were said to be akin to the technical functions carried out in mechanical typewriters, such as carriage return, new page, and new paragraph.

[432] T 38/86 [1990] *EPOR* 606 (application for a method for detecting and replacing incomprehensible expressions using conventional hardware and a dictionary); *IBM/External interface simulation*, T 833/91 [1998] *EPOR* 431 (method of designing external interfaces for a computer application program excluded).

[433] *Siemens/Character form*, T 158/88 [1992] *EPOR* 69 (methods for representing letters on a VDU was non-technical); *Beattie/Marker*, T 603/89 [1992] *EPOR* 221 (apparatus for a method for learning how to play a keyboard instrument was non-technical); *IBM/Document abstracting & retrieving*, T 22/85 [1990] *EPOR* 98 (abstracting a document), *IBM/Exclusion from patentability*, T 95/86 (23 October 1990) (processing data set out in table form); *IBM/Text clarity processing*, T 38/86 [1990] *EPOR* 606 (detecting linguistic expressions); *IBM/Text processing*, T 65/86 [1990] *EPOR* 181 (detecting contextual homophone errors, e.g. 'there' for 'their'). All were held not patentable because they were 'mental acts'.

program was not a mental act.[434] While this may have meant that the application was not excluded on the basis that it was a mental act, this did not mean that it was patentable. This was because in the absence of any technical effect either within or outside the computer, the invention was excluded on the basis that it was a computer program as such.

7.5.2 Approach at the EPO

For the most part, the approach adopted at the EPO under the 'any hardware' approach in relation to methods for performing mental acts has been consistent with the general approach outlined earlier. This can be seen, for example, in *Quest International/Odour selection*,[435] where the invention was directed to matching the tastes of the public to the design of perfumes. More specifically, it involved a 'perceptual evocation test' in which a person was presented with certain odours and with a target or priming stimulus of a visual or auditory nature. This was used to select an odour according to the response of the test subject. Insofar as the method in question involved physical activities ('activities in the physical world such as presenting test persons with odours and stimuli'), the Technical Board of Appeal held that the method did not constitute a mental act.[436] In this respect, the decision follows the 'any hardware' approach. In other respects, however, the Board seemed to adopt some of the techniques that had been applied under the contribution approach. The Board also provided a detailed analysis of what is meant by 'methods for performing mental acts'. In particular, the Board said that the selection method used in the application relies on the test subject's 'implicit odour memory'—that is, non-conscious associative recollections as opposed to explicit memory. It added that:

> [Such] perceptual processes (emotions, impressions, feelings etc) are psychological in nature and relate to—at least to a predetermined degree—subconscious processes that take place in the human mind, in contrast to the abstract nature of mental acts within the meaning of Article 52(2)(c)—are primarily based on cognitive, conceptual or intellectual processes conducted by the human mind.[437]

On this basis, the Board said that not even the perceptual processes in the mind of the test subject constituted mental acts within the meaning of Article 52(2)(c).

7.6 REFORM

The last four decades have seen a remarkable transformation in the way in which computer programs and computer-related inventions are dealt with under European law. From a situation in which computer programs 'as such' were expressly excluded from patentability, approximately 7 per cent of all applications for patents received by the EPO in 2017 were for computer technology.[438] The scope of protection available for computer-related inventions was enhanced by the fact that while computer programs per se have long been considered to be non-technical and thus outside the scope of patent law, this way of thinking about computer programs was called into question. In particular, a number of decisions at the EPO have recast computer programs as technical creations.[439] This reconfiguration of computer programs has been particularly important in light of Article 27 of the 1994 Agreement on Trade Related Aspects of Intellectual

---

[434] *Language Line Services' Application*, O/193/13 (14 May 2013), [22].
[435] T 619/02 [2007] *OJ EPO* 63.   [436] Ibid., 73.   [437] Ibid.
[438] EPO, *Annual Report 2017: European Patent Applications* (January 2018), 1; UK IPO, *Progress on Directive for Software Patents* (September 2003) (15 per cent of 30,000 applications received).
[439] *Bosch/Electronic computer components*, T 164/92 [1995] *EPOR* 585, 592.

Property Rights (TRIPS), which states that 'patents shall be available for any inventions, whether products or processes, in all fields of technology' and that 'patents shall be . . . enjoyable without discrimination as to . . . field of technology'.[440]

Notwithstanding (or possibly because of) these changes, there have been growing calls for reform of the scope of protection available for computer programs and computer-related inventions in Europe. In part, these debates were stimulated by changes in US patent law that facilitated the patenting of computer programs and business methods.[441] As well as setting a benchmark against which European law is judged, the liberalization of the level of protection in the United States also led to a flood of applications for computer-related inventions in Europe. In turn, these changes have led to the suggestion that the threshold for protection in Europe should be lowered to ensure that there is a level playing field between Europe and the United States. In response to such suggestions, a consortium of interests led by members of the open-source community has campaigned against greater protection.[442]

Despite the widespread calls for reform, to date there has been little change in the scope of protection for computer-implemented inventions in Europe. At best, there have been proposals for the law to be changed to make it clearer and more consistent. Notably, the former-US approach that protected business method inventions has not found favour at the EPO, the UK IPO, or in any of the EU agencies responsible for legislative change in Europe. The preference for the status quo can be seen in the revision of the EPC that took place in 2000. While it was suggested that 'computer programs as such' be deleted from the subject matter excluded from patentable status in Article 52(2)(c), delegates to the Diplomatic Conference voted against the proposal.[443] As a result, Article 52(2)(c) of the EPC 2000 replicates the exclusion of 'programs for computers' that was found in Article 52(2)(c) of the EPC 1973.

The UK government came out in support of the status quo. During a consultation process in 2000, respondents were asked to what extent computer programs and Internet business methods should be patentable. The resulting study found that while there was no consensus about the extent to which software should be patentable,[444] there was support for the ongoing patentability of computer-related inventions with technical effect. It was also clear from the responses that the law in this area was unclear. This led the UK government to conclude that clarification was needed, particularly as to 'how to define the boundary defining when software is, and is not, part of a technological innovation, so that what is patentable will be clear in specific cases in the future'.[445] The consultation process

---

[440] The Board noted that, because the EPO was not a signatory to TRIPS, it was not bound by it. However, on the basis that TRIPS aimed at 'setting common standards and it acted as an indicator of modern trends, the Board noted that it was the clear intention of TRIPS not to exclude from patentability any inventions, in particular, not to exclude programs for computers': *IBM/Computer programs*, T 1173/97 [2000] *EPOR* 219, 224–5. In *Symbian's Application* [2008] *EWHC* 518 (Pat), [47], Patten J said that the changes made to the language of EPC 2000, Art. 52(2)(c), to bring it into line with TRIPS, Art. 27(1), did not change the law.

[441] The situation in the US has changed as a result of the Supreme Court decision of *Alice Corp. v. CLS Bank*, 134 S Ct 2437 (2014).

[442] These include EuroLinux and the Association for the Promotion of Free Information Infrastructure (FFII).

[443] M. Delio, 'Europe Nixes Software Patents' (23 November 2000) *Wired News*, available online at http://www.wired.com; EPC 2000, Art. 1, item 17. As the explanatory remarks explained, the EPO Board of Appeal decisions that computer programs producing a technical effect are patentable subject matter meant that the 'current exception has become de facto obsolete': *Base Proposal for the Revision of the European Patent Convention* (2000) CA/100/00 e, 37. It was also suggested that Art. 52(2) ought to be abolished altogether. This was not put forward to the Diplomatic Conference for November 2000.

[444] See UK Patent Office, *Should Patents Be Granted for Computer Software or Ways of Doing Business? The Government Conclusions* (March 2001), [11].   [445] Ibid., [20].

also revealed that there was widespread opposition to patents for computer-implemented business methods that did not bring about some form of technological innovation.[446] This led the UK government to conclude that 'those who favour some form of patentability for business methods have not provided the necessary evidence that it would be likely to increase innovation. Unless and until that evidence is available, ways of doing business should remain unpatentable.'[447]

One of the consequences of the decision to retain the status quo in the EPC 2000 was that the debate on the patenting of computer-related inventions shifted to the European Commission and the European Parliament. After a period of consultation, which raised a number of questions about the scope, nature, and impact of patents for computer-related inventions,[448] the Commission's response took shape, with the publication of the draft Directive on the Patentability of Computer-Implemented Inventions in February 2002.[449] With the possible exception of the exclusion of a 'patent claim to a computer program, either on its own or on a carrier',[450] the draft Directive did not expressly alter existing law. For example, business methods, algorithms, and non-technical computer-implemented inventions were excluded from protection. However, given that the proposed Directive used concepts that are alien to British law, there was a chance that the Directive might have brought about a number of unexpected consequences. This is reinforced by the fact that although the Directive was very short (it consisted of six Articles), it lacked a coherent structure.

Faced with widespread criticisms of the draft Directive, particularly from the open-source community, not unsurprisingly the proposal was resoundingly rejected by the European Parliament in July 2005.[451] Given the legislative impasse, attention soon shifted to the possibility of a judicial solution to the perceived problems of the patenting of computer programs and computer-related inventions. In line with this, in 2007 the question of the patentability of computer-related inventions was reopened by the EPO President, who called for public discussion to fill the vacuum left by the rejection of the Directive. However, following the lukewarm response by the Enlarged Board of Appeal in the 2010 decision *President's Reference/Patentability of programs for computers*,[452] it seems that judicial reform is also unlikely, at least in the short term.

8 BIOLOGICAL SUBJECT MATTER

The fourth category of subject matter excluded from patent protection is set out in paragraph 3(f) of Schedule A2 to the Patents Act 1977[453] and Article 53(b) of the EPC 2000 (reproducing Article 53(b) of the EPC 1973). These provide that a patent shall not be granted for 'any variety of animal or plant or any essentially biological process for the

---

[446] Ibid., [21].   [447] Ibid., [24].

[448] The European Commission launched a process of consultation on 19 October 2000.

[449] *Proposal for a Directive on the Patentability of Computer-implemented Inventions* (2002) COM(2002) 92 final (the 'Proposed Computer-Implemented Inventions Directive'). The Council considered the proposal and reached a common position in November 2002: see Committee on Legal Affairs and the Internal Market, *Report on the Proposal for a Directive* (18 June 2003) final A5–0238/2003 (the 'McCarthy Report'). For a discussion of the proposed Directive, see Bently and Sherman (2004), 423: A. Guadamuz, 'The software patent debate' (2006) 1 *JIPLP* 196.

[450] Proposed Computer-Implemented Inventions Dir., Art. 5(1a).

[451] The proposed Directive was rejected 648 to 14.   [452] G 3/08 [2011] *OJ EPO* 10.

[453] Formerly PA 1977, s. 1(3)(b).

production of animals or plants, not being a microbiological process or other technical process or the product of such a process'.[454]

These provisions fall into two parts. First, they declare that patents should not be granted for 'animal varieties', 'plant varieties', and 'essentially biological processes'. The second part of paragraph 3(f)/Article 53(b) goes on to qualify and limit the subject matter that is excluded from patentability. As an exception to the exception, it provides that if an invention is 'a microbiological process or other technical process or the product of such a process', the invention may be patented.

Before looking at the exceptions, it might be useful to point out that there is no general bar on the patenting of biological material or biotechnological inventions.[455] Indeed, as the EPC 2000 and the 1977 Act (as revised) make clear, an invention shall not be considered unpatentable solely on the ground that it concerns a product consisting of or containing biological material or a process by which biological material is produced.[456] More specifically, the EPC 2000 and the 1977 Act explicitly state that it is possible to patent inventions for plants and animals, so long as they comply with the general requirements of patentability.[457] The exclusion under Article 53(b) is the denial of patents to the specified subject matter per se, rather than as under the morality exclusion in Article 53(a) (discussed later), 'which is to inventions covering such subject matter whose publication or exploitation must be measured by a moral or other standard'.[458]

8.1 ANIMAL VARIETIES

The first category of subject matter excluded from protection by paragraph 3(f)/Article 53(b) comprises those things that qualify as 'animal varieties'.[459] While the exclusion of plant varieties is usually explained on the basis that when the EPC 1973 was drafted, there was a ban on dual protection under the 1961 International Convention for the Protection of New Varieties of Plants (UPOV), the fact that there is no equivalent treaty for animal varieties has led some to question why animal varieties were also excluded. In discussing the rationale for the animal variety exclusion, the Opposition Division at the EPO said that 'the most obvious reason for this must have been the intention or at least the keeping open of the possibility to create such a law for the protection of animal varieties later

---

[454] The Biotech. Dir. prompted the introduction of the phrase 'or other technical process'; Biotech. Dir., Art. 4(1); EPC 1973 Regs, r. 23b(c).

[455] TRIPS, Art. 27(3), allows members to exclude 'plants and animals other than micro-organisms, and essentially biological processes for the production of plants or animals other than non-biological and micro-biological processes'. EPC 2000, Art. 53, provides that European patents shall not be granted in respect of 'plant or animal varieties or essentially biological processes for the production of plants or animals: this provision shall not apply to microbiological processes or the products thereof'. See EPC 2000, Art. 1, item 18. The TBA said that, when Art. 53(b) was drafted, 'the knowledge of the potential development in the field of biotechnology was rather limited': *Lubrizol/Hybrid plants*, T 320/87 [1990] *OJ EPO* 71. For a comparative study on the patentability of DNA fragments, see EPO, *Trilateral Project B3b: Comparative Study on Biotechnology Patents* (1998). See also J. Funder, 'Rethinking Patents for Plant Innovation' [1999] *EIPR* 551.

[456] PA 1977, Sch. A2, para. 1(a)–(b); Biotech. Dir., Art. 3; *Harvard/Transgenic animals*, T 315/03 (2006) *OJ EPO* 15, 78 (Art. 53(b) excludes only a limited category of animals and not all animals).

[457] PA 1977, Sch. A2, para. 4; EPC 2000 Regs, r. 27; Biotech. Dir., Art. 4(2).

[458] *Harvard/Transgenic animals*, T 315/03 [2006] *OJ EPO* 15, 56. The reference to publication was removed in EPC 2000, Art. 53(a).

[459] Biotech. Dir., Art. 4(1)(a); V. Di Cerbo, 'Patentability of Animals' (1993) 24 *IIC* 788; U. Kinkeldey, 'The Patenting of Animals' (1993) 24 *IIC* 777.

on'.[460] A more honest explanation for the exclusion of animal varieties is that they are simply 'not an appropriate subject matter'.[461] When Article 53(b) of the EPC 1973 was first drafted, the potential scope of the animal variety exclusion was straightforward and uncontroversial. This has changed, however, as patent law has been forced to confront the developments in biotechnology that have taken place since then.

The meaning of 'animal variety' was considered at the EPO in the early 1990s in the *OncoMouse* decisions. The claims in question related to a genetically modified non-human mammal (in particular a mouse), which had been modified so that it would be susceptible to cancer. The resulting products (the mice with cancer) were used in cancer research. At first instance, the Examining Division held that the exclusion not only covered groups of animals, but also animals in general; as such, the invention covered an unpatentable animal variety.[462] On appeal, the Technical Board of Appeal (TBA) held that the Examining Division had misconstrued the exclusion which, being an exception to patentability, ought to be construed narrowly.[463] Importantly, the Board said that Article 53(b) did not exclude animals in general. On this basis, the TBA remitted the matter to the Examining Division for reconsideration.

The Examining Division said that animal variety either meant a species or a subunit of a species. The Examining Division acknowledged that while the terms of EPC were not consistent—the English and French terms ('animal varieties' and *races animales*) meaning 'subunit of a species' and the German term (*Tierarten*) meaning 'species'—it was not necessary to decide which was the authoritative meaning for the purpose of the Convention.[464] This was because the claims in question related to non-human mammals, a category that was neither a species nor a subunit of a species. (In zoological terms, 'mammals' are of a higher taxonomic classification than species.) Consequently, the subject matter did not relate to an animal variety and, as such, was not excluded by Article 53(b).

The meaning of 'animal variety' was considered by the TBA in its 2006 decision in *Harvard/Transgenic animals*[465] (which is effectively a rerun of the earlier *OncoMouse* decisions). The Board began by noting that the reasoning of the Enlarged Board of Appeal (EBA) in relation to plant varieties in *Novartis* was applicable to the decision as to whether an invention fell within the animal variety exclusion.[466] In *Novartis* (which is discussed in the next section), the EBA held that where a specific plant variety is not individually claimed, the claim will not be excluded from patentability under Article 53(b). This is the case even though it may embrace plant varieties.[467] While the TBA accepted the reasoning of the EBA in *Novartis*, it was faced with the problem that the three official texts of the EPC use different taxonomic terms to refer to the excluded subject matter: the English version refers to 'animal varieties'; the German uses 'animal species'; and the

---

[460] *Harvard/OncoMouse* [2003] *OJ EPO* 473 (Opposition Division), 499.

[461] *Harvard/OncoMouse* [1989] *OJ EPO* 451 (Exam).

[462] *Harvard/OncoMouse*, T 19/90 [1990] *EPOR* 501 (TBA).

[463] *Harvard/OncoMouse* [1991] *EPOR* 525 (Exam).

[464] EPC 1973, Art. 177(1), says that the English, French, and German versions of the EPC are equally authentic. [465] T 315/03 [2006] *OJ EPO* 15.

[466] *Novartis/Transgenic plant*, G 1/98 [2000] *EPOR* 303 (EBA), 319. Whereas 'G1/98 makes reference to plants and not to animals, its holding can also be transferred to the interpretation of the exclusion of animal varieties in Article 53(b)': *Harvard/OncoMouse* [2003] *OJ EPO* 473, 499 (Opposition Division); *Harvard/Transgenic animals*, T 315/03 [2006] *OJ EPO* 15 (TBA), 58.

[467] The Opposition Division, which also adopted the reasoning in *Novartis*, said that this meant that, for a claim to be excluded because it was for an animal variety, the claim had to be for a variety per se. On this basis, the Division said that, because the invention was applicable to more than just varieties of mice, the patent was not excluded by Art. 53(b).

French version refers to 'animal races'.[468] (This was in contrast to the way in which plants are dealt with under Article 53(b), all three official languages referring to 'plant varieties'.) As the Board said, the fact that the three official texts of the EPC used different taxonomic categories potentially led 'to the absurd result that the outcome of an Article 53(b) objection depended on the language of the case'.[469] (Because species was a higher taxonomic order, it excluded more than a variety and race.) Faced with this problem, the TBA said that a 'definition by reference to taxonomical rank would be consistent with the position in relation to plant varieties and in the interests of legal certainty'.[470] While the Board noted that the uncertainty created by these linguistic differences was undesirable, nonetheless it said that it was unnecessary to pursue the matter further. The reason for this was that the claim for 'transgenic rodents' was for a taxonomic category that was higher than 'species', 'variety', and 'race'. This meant that the patent would not have been caught by either the English, French, or German versions of Article 53(b). The upshot of the decision in *Transgenic animals* is that Article 53(b) of the EPC 1973 (Article 53(b) of the EPC 2000) will only apply where a patent is for a specific animal variety (or species, or race, depending on the language that is used)—that is, it modified the reasoning of *Novartis* to take account of the different taxonomic terms used in the English, French, and German versions of the EPC. Until the problem is rectified, it will pose interesting challenges for those drafting animal patents.

As well as looking at the fate of the applicant's main request (which was for transgenic rodents), in the *Transgenic Animals* decision the TBA also looked at whether Article 53(b) acted as a bar to the patentability of the auxiliary request, which was restricted to 'transgenic mice'. Following *Novartis*, the Board said that an objection under Article 53(b) would only arise if 'one or more claims of the request are to a taxonomic category at least as narrow as an animal species—the broadest of the three taxonomic categories excluded in the three language texts of Article 53(b) EPC'.[471] Because the auxiliary claims did not fall within these criteria, the Board held that the auxiliary request did not fail under Article 53(b).[472]

8.2 PLANT VARIETIES

The second form of biological subject matter excluded from protection are 'plant varieties'.[473] The reason for the exclusion can be traced to the fact that the EPC 1973 was drafted in light of UPOV—a regime established in 1961 to grant property rights in new plant varieties. In order to ensure that plant breeders were not able to obtain patent protection *and* plant variety protection, it was decided that the two conventions should be

---

[468] While the English text of the EPC 1973 and the EPC 2000 both refer to 'plant or animal varieties', the German version refers to 'plant varieties or animal species' (*Pflanzensorten oder Tierarten*), while the French refers to 'plant varieties and animal races' (*les variétés végétales et les races animals*). The problems created by the fact that the three official texts use three different taxonomic terms—variety, species, and races—was compounded by the way in which EPC 1973 Regs, r. 23c, has been translated.

[469] *Harvard/Transgenic animals*, T 315/03 [2006] *OJ EPO* 15 (TBA), 60.   [470] Ibid., 58.

[471] Ibid., [13.3.1].

[472] The Board rejected the argument that the transgenic mice constituted a new species (primarily on the basis that it had not seen any evidence to this effect).

[473] PA 1977, Sch. A2, para. 3(f); EPC 2000, Art. 53(b); Biotech. Dir., Art. 4(1)(a). For the position before the PA 1977, see *Rau Gesellschaft* (1935) 52 *RPC* 362; *Lenard's Application* (1954) 71 *RPC* 190; *Commercial Solvents Case* (1926) 43 *RPC* 185; *Szuec's Case* [1956] *RPC* 25; *NRDC's Application* [1961] *RPC* 134; *Swift's Application* [1962] *RPC* 37. For an international overview, see T. Roberts, 'Patenting Plants around the World' [1996] *EIPR* 531.

mutually exclusive: a person could either be given *sui generis* plant breeder's right or patent protection, but not both.[474] Article 53(b) of the EPC 1973 and section 1(3)(b) of the Patents Act 1977 were drafted to give effect to this policy decision.[475] While the principle that the scope of the two regimes should be mutually exclusive was removed when UPOV was revised in 1991, nonetheless the exclusion of plant varieties still exists in both the EPC 2000 and the 1977 Act. Article 4(1) of the Biotechnology Directive confirms that plant varieties are not patentable. It also provides, as do the resulting changes to the 1977 Act and the changes to the EPC Implementing Regulations, that the concept of plant variety is to correspond to the definition used in Article 5 of the Community Plant Variety Regulation.[476]

The scope and operation of this exclusion depends on a number of factors. One is that it is not necessary to claim a 'plant' per se to qualify as a plant variety. This is because a plant variety may be represented not only by whole plants, but also by propagating material, such as seeds and other parts of plants that can be propagated.[477] It is also important to note that the question of whether a plant grouping constitutes a 'plant variety' does not depend on how it was obtained: the methods or steps for producing a new plant are not relevant for determining whether it is a variety. As such, it does not matter whether a plant was produced by genetic engineering technology or is the product of classical breeding techniques of crossing and selection;[478] all that matters is whether the application claims a variety. As the Technical Board of Appeal (TBA) said, it is clear that:

> [W]hether or not a plant is to be considered to be a plant variety depends only on whether or not it meets the criteria set out in the definition in Rule 26(4) EPC [2000 Regs] (former Rule 23b(4) EPC [1973 Regs]). The method for its production, be it by recombinant gene technology or by a classical plant breeding process, is not relevant for answering this question.[479]

Another important factor that impacts on the scope of the exclusion is the way in which 'plant variety' is defined for the purposes of Article 53(b)/section 1(3)(b). Rule 26(4) of the EPC 2000 Implementing Regulations says that a 'plant variety' means:

> any plant grouping within a single botanical taxon of the lowest known rank, which grouping, irrespective of whether the conditions for the grant of a plant variety are fully met, can be:
> (a) defined by the expression of the characteristics that result from a given genotype of combination of genotypes,
> (b) distinguished from other plant grouping by the expression of at least one of the said characteristics, and
> (c) considered as a unit with regard to its suitability for being propagated unchanged.

---

[474] UPOV, Art. 2(1).

[475] EPC 1973, Art. 53(b), was intended to express a general intention to exclude patent protection for subject matter capable of protection within UPOV: *Ciba-Geigy/Propagating material application*, T 49/83 [1984] *OJ EPO* 112; *Plant Genetic Systems/Glutamine synthetase inhibitors* (1993) 24 *IIC* 618.

[476] Council Regulation (EC) No. 2100/94 of 27 July 1994 on Community plant variety rights [1994] *OJ L* 227/1 (1 September 1994).

[477] *State of Israel/Tomatoes II*, T 1242/06 [2013] *OJ EPO* 42, [27] (claims 'directed to plant fruits which contain seeds and which are therefore to be regarded as plant parts capable of producing entire plans may well in general fall under the patent exclusion of plant varieties contained in Article 53(b) EPC').

[478] Ibid., [32]. See also *Novartis/Transgenic plant*, G 1/98 [2000] *EPOR* 303 (EBA), [5.3]; *Consejo Superior/Oil from seeds*, T 1854/07 (12 May 2010), [10.4]; *State of Israel/Tomatoes II*, T 1242/06 [2013] *OJ EPO* 42.

[479] *Consejo Superior/Oil from seeds*, T 1854/07 (12 May 2010), [10.4].

One of the earliest decisions to consider what is meant by the term 'plant variety' was *Ciba-Geigy's Application*.[480] The application in question claimed any plant-propagating material that had been chemically treated so as to make the material resistant to other agricultural chemicals. In deciding that the invention was not a 'plant variety', the TBA said that plant varieties were 'limited to claims to individually characterized plants which would have the detailed taxonomy and the reproductive capacity which is required in general for a plant variety right'.[481] The Board also stressed that a defining feature of a plant variety was that it contained certain features that distinguished the variety in question from other varieties. These distinguishing features needed to be stable enough so that the essential characteristics were passed on through subsequent generations. In so doing, the TBA highlighted the need for homogeneity between different generations. It also added that 'it is perfectly sufficient for the exclusion to be . . . restricted . . . to cases in which plants are characterized *precisely* by the genetically determined peculiarities of their natural phenotype'.[482]

On the facts, the TBA held that claims for plant-propagating materials that had been chemically treated so as to make the material resistant to other agricultural chemicals were not claims to a 'plant variety'. The reason for this was that while plant breeding (which is a form of human-induced genetic modification) introduced traits to plants that reappeared in subsequent generations, this did not occur with chemical treatment. As such, the Board held that the claims were not for plant varieties and thus not excluded from the scope of protection.

The definition of 'plant variety' for the purposes of Article 53(b) was clarified by the Enlarged Board of Appeal (EBA) in *Novartis*, where it was said that the reference in Rule 26(4)(a) of the EPC 2000 Implementing Regulations to the 'expression of the characteristics that result from a given genotype or combination of genotypes' means a reference to the entire constitution of a plant or a set of genetic information.[483] More specifically, the Board said that the concept of a 'plant variety' requires plant groupings to be defined by their whole genome, not merely by individual characteristics—that is, to qualify as a plant variety, a plant had to be defined by a multitude of characteristics resulting from a given genotype of combination of genotype.[484] Thus the EBA held that a claim to transgenic plants that were merely characterized by specific recombinant DNA sequences was not a plant variety.

The definition of plant variety developed in *Novartis* was applied in *Plant Bioscience/ Broccoli*,[485] where the TBA held that the application in question, which was for an edible *Brassica* (broccoli) plant with certain defined traits (an increased level of specific glucosinolates), was not a plant variety for the purposes of Article 53(b). As the Board said, a single trait is 'in general not sufficient to define a plant variety, without providing, apart from an indication of the species, further adequate information about the actual genotype of the plant grouping'.[486] This reasoning was also applied in *State of Israel/Tomatoes II*,[487] where it was held that the claim for a tomato fruit of the species *Lycopersicon esculentum*,

[480] *Ciba-Geigy/Propagating material application*, T 49/83 [1984] *OJ EPO* 112; followed in *Lubrizol/Hybrid plants*, T 320/87 [1990] *OJ EPO* 71 ('the present hybrid seed and plants from such seed, lacking stability in some trait of the whole generation population, cannot be classified as plant varieties'), and *PGS/Glutamine synthetase inhibitors*, T 356/93 [1995] *EPOR* 357 (practice is to allow claims directed to groups of plants larger than plant varieties if the invention is applicable to such larger plant groups).

[481] *Ciba-Geigy/Propagating material application*, T 49/83 [1984] *OJ EPO* 112, 113.

[482] Ibid., [4] (emphasis added).

[483] *Novartis/Transgenic plant*, G 1/98 [2000] *EPOR* 303 (EBA), [3.1], [3.8].   [484] Ibid., [3.1].

[485] T 83/05 [2014] *OJ EPO* A39.   [486] Ibid., [16].   [487] T 1242/06 [2013] *OJ EPO* 42.

which is naturally dehydrated, was not a 'plant variety' and thus not excluded by Article 53(b). What was important here was that the claimed tomatoes were not defined by a multitude of characteristics resulting in a given genotype, but only by one particular trait—that is, (natural) dehydration.[488] The Board noted that within the species *Lycopersicon esculentum*, there were thousands of tomato varieties, each with specific and distinct features with different genetic information.

In botany, a plant variety is typically defined by two things. One is that it is a member of a particular species and that, as such, it shares the defined traits of that species. (In turn, the species is defined by reference to the 'type specimen' deposited at a specific repository and a published description.) At the same time, the variety is defined in relation to the species as a whole and distinguished from other varieties of that species. Normally, these differences, which may and often are a single trait, are defined by external phenotypical characteristics such as colour of flower, stem length, or leaf shape;[489] rarely in this process is there any reference to the 'genotype of the plant grouping'. The approach that has been adopted at the EPO, which mixes (external) phenotypical traits with (internal) genomic traits, is an odd blend of approaches. It is also so restricted that it limits the scope of the exclusion to botanical innovations that are protectable under plant variety rights.

This reading of Article 53(b) has been reconfirmed in the way in which the EPO has approached the question of what happens when an application does not claim (or even mention) a specific plant variety per se, but nonetheless is broad enough to encompass a variety: what happens, for example, if someone claims a broader taxonomic category (such as a species) that necessarily encompasses all varieties of that species? This question was first considered in *Plant Genetic Systems*.[490] The claims in dispute related to plants, plant cells, and seeds that possessed a foreign gene, which made them resistant to a type of herbicide. Given that modified plants were immune to the application of the weedkiller, farmers were able to spray (modified) crops safe in the knowledge that the weedkiller would only affect the unmodified weeds. Greenpeace objected to the application, arguing, among other things, that the material claimed was a plant variety and thus excluded by Article 53(b).

At first instance, the Opposition Division held that the claims were not restricted to a specifically defined narrow group of plants (such as a variety), but related to a much broader group of plants.[491] As such, the claims were unobjectionable. In overturning this decision, the TBA acknowledged that 'the concept of plant variety under Article 53(b) refers to any plant grouping within a single botanical taxon [or classification] of the lowest known rank'.[492] On this basis, the Board said that plant cells as such, which modern technology allows to culture much like bacteria and yeasts, 'cannot be considered to fall under the definition of plant or of plant variety'.[493] Following *Ciba-Geigy*, the Board stressed that stability and homogeneity were important factors in determining whether something was a plant variety. More specifically, the Board noted that a plant variety 'is characterized by at least one single transmissible characteristic distinguishing it from other plant groupings and which is sufficiently homogeneous and stable in its relevant characteristics'.[494]

While the TBA in *Plant Genetic Systems* agreed with much of the reasoning in *Ciba-Geigy*, it disagreed with the way in which the ambit of the exclusion had been interpreted.

---

[488] Ibid., [29].

[489] This was acknowledged in *Tomatoes II*, when the Board said that, in some cases, a single trait may be sufficient to distinguish plant groupings: ibid., [30]. Nonetheless, the Board still followed the EBA in focusing on the whole genome.

[490] *Plant Genetic Systems/Glutamine synthetase inhibitors*, T 356/93 [1993] 24 *IIC* 618 (Opposition Division); [1995] *OJ EPO* 545 (TBA).

[491] (1993) 24 *IIC* 618.   [492] [1995] *EPOR* 357 (TBA), [23].   [493] Ibid., 375.   [494] Ibid.

More specifically, while in *Ciba-Geigy* plant varieties were restricted 'to cases in which plants are characterized precisely by the genetically determined peculiarities of their natural phenotype',[495] the Board in *Plant Genetic Systems* adopted a more expansive reading of the exclusion. In particular, it was willing to extend the exclusion beyond claims that were specifically directed to or characterized as plant varieties, to include claims that encompassed or included a plant variety within their scope. On the facts, the TBA held that what was being claimed was based upon or derived from genetically engineered cells (and that the application required the production of plant varieties to exemplify them). This meant that they were claiming rights over the plant varieties formed by those plants and seeds. As such, they were not patentable.

In summary, the TBA held that while claims relating to plant cells are potentially patentable, claims that 'encompass' or are 'based on' a plant variety are not.[496] (This is subject to the rider that the resulting plants have a distinguishable characteristic that is stable and homogeneous.) Given that plant varieties are frequently used as the starting point for the production of genetically engineered plants,[497] this meant that, in most cases, plants produced as a result of genetic engineering would not have been patentable[498]—a decision that, if followed, would have had important ramifications for the plant-breeding industry.[499] Given this, it is not surprising that the *Plant Genetic Systems* decision was subject to a considerable amount of criticism.[500]

Much of the cause for concern about the impact of the *Plant Genetic Systems* decision on plant genetics has now been alleviated. This is because two subsequent events have effectively overturned the decision: the enactment of the Biotechnology Directive and the decision of the EBA in *Novartis*.

Article 4(2) of the Biotechnology Directive provides that 'inventions which concern plants . . . shall be patentable if the technical feasibility of the invention is not confined to a particular plant . . . variety'.[501] Similar provisions have been introduced in the 1977 Act and the EPC 2000.[502] So long as a claim encompasses more than one variety, it is potentially patentable. The upshot of the Directive is that claims to plants will be allowed even if they encompass a plant variety. However, claims specifically directed to particular plant varieties (which are protected by a separate regime) will not be protected. This would appear to require member states to accept claims to genetically modified plants (such as those in *Plant Genetic Systems*) as being patentable.

---

[495] *Ciba-Geigy/Propagating material application*, T 49/83 [1984] *OJ EPO* 112, [4].

[496] On 'essentially derived variety', see UPOV, Art. 14(5).

[497] Most of the reaction was negative: U. Schatz, 'Patentability of Genetic Engineering Inventions in EPO Practice' (1998) 29 *IIC* 2; T. Roberts, 'Patenting Plants around the World' [1996] *EIPR*, 534; M. Llewellyn, 'The Legal Protection of Biotechnological Inventions: An Alternative Approach' [1997] *EIPR* 115.

[498] A. Schrell, 'Are Plants Still Patentable?' [1996] *EIPR* 242, 243.

[499] The President of the EPO, believing there to be a contradiction between *PGS* and *Ciba Geigy* (and also with the *OncoMouse* decision), referred the matter to the EBA. The Board refused to answer the question, which it ruled was improper because there was no conflict between the decisions: *Inadmissible referral*, G 3/95 [1996] *OJ EPO* 169.

[500] As Bostyn explained: '[There] is a difference between a claim embracing a plant variety and a claim to a variety. Every claim to plants will embrace plant varieties, since a plant variety is a plant grouping of the lowest possible rank. When claiming a species, or even a higher rank, it will always embrace plant varieties: all Golden Delicious Apples (variety) are apples (species), but not all apples are Golden Delicious.' See S. Bostyn, 'Patentability of Genetic Information Carriers' [1999] *IPQ* 1, 18. See also R. Crespi, 'Patents and Plant Variety Rights: Is There an Interface Problem?' (1992) 23 *IIC* 173.

[501] Biotech. Dir., Recitals 29–32. Recital 31 states that 'a plant grouping which is characterized by a particular gene (and not its whole genome) is not covered by the protection of new varieties and is therefore not excluded from patentability even if it comprises new varieties of plants'.

[502] PA 1977, Sch. A2, para. 4; EPC 2000 Regs, r. 27(b).

A similar position was reached by the EBA of the EPO in *Novartis*,[503] which related to plants that were genetically modified to render them resistant to fungi. In relation to the plant variety exclusion, the Board found that 'a claim wherein specific plant varieties are not individually claimed is not excluded from patentability under Article 53(b), even though it may embrace plant varieties'.[504]

The EBA noted that Article 53(b) serves to define the borderline between patent and plant variety protection. It also noted that the extent of the exclusion for patents is the obverse of the availability of plant variety rights[505] and that plant varieties are only granted for specific plant varieties (and not for technical teachings). On this basis, the Board held that in 'the absence of the identification of a specific plant variety in a product claim, the subject matter of the claimed invention is not directed to a plant variety or varieties within the meaning of Article 53(b) EPC'.[506] In short, the Board overturned the *Plant Genetics Systems* decision and held that a claim that encompasses more than one variety is not excluded under Article 53(b). That is, the mere fact that a patent encompasses a plant variety will not mean that the invention falls within the exclusion. Instead, the exclusion will only operate where the patent claims a plant variety per se (which should be protected by plant variety protection). As the TBA subsequently said, the core of the reasoning of the EBA was the 'consideration that the exclusion of plant varieties serves only to exclude from patentability those plant inventions which can be protected by plant breeders' rights'.[507]

While the proponents of patent protection for plants will welcome the *Novartis* decision, it gives rise to a potential problem, similar to those that arose when the 'whole contents' approach was first adopted in relation to the patenting of computer programs. This is the problem that patent claims will be dressed up to appear as though they do not fall within the exception.[508] While the jurisprudence on the patentability of computer programs may provide guidance in this area, the different rationales behind the exclusions means that the 'whole contents' and 'technical effect' approaches cannot be directly imported into paragraph 3(f) of Schedule A2 to the Patents Act 1977/Article 53(b) of the EPC 2000. It may, however, provide some useful insights into the potential problems that might arise.

8.3 ESSENTIALLY BIOLOGICAL PROCESSES

The third type of subject matter excluded from protection are inventions that are regarded as 'essentially biological processes for the production of animals and plants'.[509] As with the exclusion of animal and plant varieties, the exclusion of

---

[503] *Novartis/Transgenic plant*, T 1054/96 [1998] *OJ EPO* (Special edn) 149; R. Nott, 'You Did It: The European Biotechnology Directive at Last' [1998] *EIPR* 347, 351.

[504] *Novartis/Transgenic plant*, G 1/98 [2000] *EPOR* 303 (EBA), 319. The EBA gave the analogy of a patent for a copying machine: the fact that the machine could be used for copying counterfeit notes would not mean that the machine was excluded, since the improved properties could be used for other purposes. As we will see, this suggests a particular approach to morality that is not universally accepted.

[505] This was because 'inventions ineligible for protection under the plant-breeder's rights systems were intended to be patentable under the EPC provided they fulfilled the other requirements for patentability': *Lubrizol/Hybrid plant*, T 320/87 [1990] *OJ EPO* 71, [3].

[506] *Novartis/Transgenic plant*, G 1/98 [2000] *EPOR* 303 (EBA), 319.

[507] *State of Israel/Tomatoes*, T 1242/06 [2008] *OJ EPO* 523, [38].

[508] *Novartis/Transgenic plant*, T 1054/96 [1999] *EPOR* 123, 137.

[509] PA 1977, Sch. A2, para. 3(f); EPC 2000, Art. 53(b). The Biotech. Dir., Art. 53(b), affirms that essentially biological processes for the production of plants or animals are not patentable. EPC 2000, Art. 53(b), provides that European patents shall not be granted in respect of 'plant or animal varieties or essentially biological processes for the production of plants or animal: this provision shall not apply to microbiological processes or the products thereof': EPC 2000, Art. 1, item 18.

essentially biological processes was reconfirmed in the Biotechnology Directive,[510] and by corresponding changes made to the 1977 Act[511] and the EPC 2000. Four aspects of this exclusion are worth emphasizing.

8.3.1 Exclusion of the *production* of animals or plants

The first point to note is that the exclusion only applies where the process is for the *production* of animals or plants. As such, the exclusion will not apply if the process results in the death or destruction of animals or plants.[512] It will also not apply where the invention merely produces information that is used to manage plants or animals.[513]

8.3.2 Exclusion of the production of *plants* and *animals*

The second point to note is that Article 53(b) excludes essentially biological processes for the production of *plants* and *animals*, not plant and animal *varieties*. As such, Article 53(b) is not limited to processes for the production of plant and animal varieties, but extends to include the more abstract and open categories 'plants' and 'animals'.[514]

8.3.3 Essentially biological processes

Thirdly, the exclusion only applies where the process is 'essentially biological'. According to the Biotechnology Directive, a process for the production of plants and animals is essentially biological if 'it consists entirely of natural phenomena such as crossing or selection'.[515] This has been taken to mean that for the exclusion to apply, it must explicitly or implicitly involve plant breeding (i.e. the mixing of whole plant genomes).[516]

The key question that has arisen here is: how much human intervention is needed for a process that involves biological steps not to be classified as an essentially biological process?[517] This question was considered in *Lubrizol*,[518] where the Technical Board of Appeal (TBA) had to decide whether a process of producing high-quality hybrids was excluded from patentability on the ground that it was essentially biological. Drawing upon the image of the invention widely used in patent law, the Board said that the question of

---

[510] Biotech. Dir., Art. 4(1)(b).   [511] PA 1977, Sch. A2, para. 3(f).

[512] Cf. *NRDC's Application* [1961] *RPC* 134; *Swift's Application* [1962] *RPC* 37.

[513] *Lohmann/Fishy taint*, T 15/10 (14 October 2013), [9].

[514] A plant 'was an abstract and open definition which embraced an indefinite number of individual entities defined by a part of its genome or by a property bestowed on it by that part': *Plant Bioscience/Broccoli*, G 2/07 [2012] *OJ EPO* 130 (EBA), [6.1.1], citing *Novartis/Transgenic plant*, G 1/98 [2000] *EPOR* 303 (EBA), [3.1]. It has also been suggested that production of a fruit, rather than a plant per se, would not be excluded: *Syngenta/Seedless watermelons*, T 1729/06 [2015] *EPOR* 10.   [515] Biotech. Dir., Art. 2(2).

[516] *Syngenta/Seedless watermelons*, T 1729/06 [2015] *EPOR* 10 (claims were for a 'technical process' rather than the traditional processes covered by the UPOV Convention and, as such, outside the scope of the exclusion).

[517] Earlier drafts of the Directive defined 'essentially biological' as: 'a process in which human intervention consists in [no] more than selecting an available biological material and letting it perform an inherent biological function under natural conditions'; 'a process which, taken as a whole, does not exist in nature and is more than a mere production process shall be patentable'; and also 'a process which, taken as a whole, does not exist in nature and is more than mere breeding process'.

[518] *Lubrizol/Hybrid plant*, T 320/87 [1990] *OJ EPO* 71. (These were prior to the introduction of the definition.) See also *Ciba Geigy/Propagating material application*, T 49/83 [1984] *OJ EPO* 112 (propagating material not the result of an essentially biological process that involved treatment with chemical agents); *Harvard/OncoMouse* [1989] *OJ EPO* 451 (Exam) (process for producing transgenic mouse not essentially biological because it involved micro-injection); *Harvard/OncoMouse*, T 19/90 [1990] *OJ EPO* 476, 488 (agreeing that micro-injection is not essentially biological and noting also that sexual reproduction is not necessarily essentially biological).

whether a claim was for an essentially biological process had to be 'judged on the basis of the essence of the invention taking into account the totality of human intervention and its impact on the result achieved'.[519] Turning to the facts of the case, the Board noted that the process in question was divided into a number of steps. First, parent plants were selected and crossed. The resulting hybrids were then evaluated and suitable hybrids selected. The parent plants of the chosen hybrids were then cloned and, finally, the crossing was repeated. The Board held that while each step might be characterized as biological, the arrangement of steps *as a whole* represented an essential modification of known biological processes. On this basis, the TBA held that the process was not an essentially biological process and, as such, not excluded by Article 53(b).

The question of the degree of technical intervention needed for a process to fall outside the scope of the exclusion was also considered in the *Novartis* decisions. The TBA said that to decide whether a process was 'essentially biological', the tribunal must make a value judgement about the extent to which a process should be non-biological before it loses the status of 'essentially biological'.[520] The Board added that there were three possible approaches that could be taken when answering this question.

(i)   Under the first approach, an invention would be excluded if it included an aspect or step that was biological. To fall outside the exclusion, the claimed processes would have to be exclusively made up of non-biological process steps.[521]

(ii)   The second approach, which was taken from *Lubrizol*, requires the tribunal to weigh up the overall degree of human intervention in the process.[522] Under this approach, the decision regarding whether an invention is essentially biological is made on the basis of the essence of the invention, taking into account the totality of human invention and its impact on the result received.

(iii) The third option, which was the most liberal, provides that the mere presence of a single artificial (or technical) element in the process would be enough to prevent its being classified as an essentially biological process.[523] The TBA said that the third approach was reflected in Article 2(2) of the Biotechnology Directive.

Neither the TBA nor the Enlarged Board of Appeal (EBA) in *Novartis* provided any direct guidance as to which of these approaches was to be adopted.[524] The issue has now been clarified, however, as a result of a string of decisions in relation to patent applications for broccoli[525] and tomatoes,[526] which clearly rejected options (i) and (iii) and came down in favour of a version of option (ii).

---

[519] *Lubrizol/Hybrid plant*, T 320/87 [1990] *OJ EPO* 71, [6]. See also *PGS/Glutamine synthetase inhibitors*, T 356/93 [1995] *EPOR* 357 ('[i]n the present case the impact of human intervention is decisive since the claimed plants and plant material only exist as a result of the process of the invention').

[520] *Novartis/Transgenic plant*, T 1054/96 [1999] *EPOR* 123, 134.

[521] Ibid. This was drawn from the jurisprudence in association with the exclusion of methods of treatment by surgery and therapy: EPC 1973, Art. 52(4). See *General Hospital/Contraceptive method*, T 820/94 [1995] *EPOR* 446.   [522] *Lubrizol/Hybrid plants*, T 320/87 [1990] *EPOR* 173.

[523] *Novartis/Transgenic plant*, T 1054/96 [1999] *EPOR* 123 (TBA), 135.

[524] *Novartis/Transgenic plant*, G 1/98 [2000] *EPOR* 303 (EBA), 321.

[525] *Plant Bioscience/Broccoli*, T 83/05 [2007] *OJ EPO* 644; G 2/07 [2012] *OJ EPO* 130 (EBA); *Plant Bioscience/Broccoli II*, T 83/05 [2014] *OJ EPO* A39; G 2/13 [2016] *OJ EPO* A28 (EBA).

[526] *State of Israel/Tomatoes*, T 1242/06 [2008] *OJ EPO* 523; G 1/08 [2012] *OJ EPO* 206 (EBA); *State of Israel/Tomatoes II*, T 1242/06 [2013] *OJ EPO* 42; G 2/12 [2016] *OJ EPO* A27 (EBA). See A. Hubel, 'Essentials on Essentially Biological Processes for the Production of Plants' [2011] *EIPR* 328; J. Cockbain and S. Sterckx, 'Are Products of Essentially Biological Processes Patentable in Europe? The Purple Radish Sprouts Case in the Netherlands' (2012) 34 *EIPR* 422; S. Bostyn, 'Resolving the Conundrum of the Patentability of Plants Produced by an Essentially Biological Process: Squaring the Circle' [2013] *EIPR* 583.

The first of these decisions was the 2007 TBA decision in *Plant Bioscience/Broccoli*.[527] The central claim of the application in question was for a method for the production of broccoli (*Brassica*). This consisted of a number of steps traditionally used in breeding, including the crossing of specific species of broccoli and the subsequent selection of hybrids with certain defined features from those crosses. This was followed by backcrossing and further selection. Importantly, the application also involved the use of molecular markers to help to identify plants with the desired characteristics. It was argued in opposition that the application claimed an essentially biological process and that, as such, it should be excluded under Article 53(b).

As part of its deliberations, the TBA provided a general history of Article 53(b), noting that the drafters regarded 'biological' as being in opposition to 'technical' and that they had deliberately chosen the adverb 'essentially' to replace the narrower term 'purely'. The Board also noted that the drafters of the legislation intended that the exclusion apply to processes such as the selection or hybridization of existing varieties. This was the case even if, as 'a secondary feature, "technical" devices were involved (use of a particular type of instrument in a grafting process, or a special greenhouse in growing a plant)'.[528]

The Board also highlighted a number of problems with Rule 23(b)(5) of the EPC 1973 Implementing Regulations (now Rule 26(5) of the EPC 2000 Implementing Regulations), which (as we saw earlier) provides that a 'process for the production of plants or animals is essentially biological if it consists entirely of natural phenomena such as crossing or selection'. The Board noted that Rule 23(b)(5) says that processes will only be considered to be essentially biological where they consist *entirely* of biological processes for the production of plants. At the same time, the Rule also says that crossing and selection, which clearly involve human (technical) intervention, are examples of natural phenomena. As the Board said, this seems to be contradictory to the extent that 'the systematic crossing and selection as carried out in traditional plant breeding would not occur in nature without the intervention of man'.[529] The Board then went on to say that Rule 23(b)(5) (EPC 2000 Rule 26(5)) suggests that Article 53(b) should be read narrowly. In particular, the Board said that Rule 23(b)(5) meant that a process that 'contains an additional feature of a technical nature would be outside the ambit of the process exclusion'.[530] This would not be the case, however, in relation to 'natural phenomena' (which covered crossing and selection by way of a legal fiction).[531] The Board noted that on this reading of the exclusion, the use of molecular markers as part of a breeding process (which required the removal and *in vitro* analysis of plant tissues) would lead to the conclusion that the invention would fall outside the ambit of the exclusion. The Board also noted that this narrow reading of Article 53(b) would be contrary to the earlier decisions of *Lubrizol* and *Plant Genetic Systems*.[532] Faced with the uncertainty about the scope of Article 53(b), the TBA in *Plant*

---

[527] T 83/05 [2007] *OJ EPO* 644.

[528] *Preliminary Draft Convention of the Council of Europe* (Doc. EXP/Brev (61) 2 rev), 26; cited in *Plant Bioscience/Broccoli*, T 83/05 [2007] *OJ EPO* 644.   [529] Ibid., 660.

[530] Ibid., 661.

[531] The Board said that this did not reflect the approach that had been adopted by the boards of appeal prior to the introduction of the rule: see *Novartis/Transgenic plant*, T1054/96 [1999] *EPOR* 123, point 96.

[532] For example, in *Harvard/Transgenic animals*, T 315/03 [2006] *OJ EPO* 15, the TBA cited EPC 1973 Regs, r. 23b(5), and concluded that it was self-evident that a process that included genetic manipulation did not consist entirely of natural phenomena and was therefore not excluded by EPC 2000, Art. 53(b). Cf. *Novartis/Transgenic plant*, T 1054/96 [1999] *EPOR* 123, [3]. On the apparent clash of these decisions, see *Plant Bioscience/Broccoli*, T 83/05 [2007] *OJ EPO* 664, 665.

Bioscience/Broccoli decided to refer the matter to the EBA for deliberation. In particular, the TBA asked the EBA to consider the question:

> Does a non-microbiological process for the production of plants which contains the steps of crossing and selecting plants escape the exclusion of Article 53(b) merely because it contains, as a further step or as part of any of the steps of crossing and selection, an additional feature of a technical nature?[533]

The TBA also asked the EBA to identify the criteria that should be used to determine whether an invention fell within Article 53(b).[534]

Around the same time, the case of *State of Israel/Tomatoes* began to weave its way through the EPO. The application in question was for a method of breeding tomato plants that produced tomatoes with reduced water content. This involved a number of steps, including crossing, collecting, growing, and selection.[535] The fruit was allowed to stay on the vine past the normal point of ripening. The resulting fruit was then screened for reduced water content. The TBA was asked to consider whether this process was excluded under Article 53(b). The Board effectively said that in order to answer this question, it was first necessary to answer another question—namely: what kind of human intervention was required for an application not to be essentially biological?[536] Given that the referral to the EBA in *Broccoli* was still pending, the TBA decided to defer the case until the EBA handed down its decision. The TBA also decided to refer a number of additional questions to the EBA for consideration.

The EBA decided to consider the points of law raised by the TBA in the *Tomatoes* and *Broccoli* decisions in a single consolidated decision.[537] The EBA noted that there was considerable amount of confusion about the meaning of 'essentially biological'. In particular, there was uncertainty about how the existing jurisprudence was to be read in light of Rule 26(5) of the EPC 2000 Implementing Regulations and Article 2(2) of the Biotechnology Directive. The EBA felt that in light of this uncertainty, it was necessary to review what was meant by 'essentially biological'.

The Board began by noting the types of approach that should *not* be used to determine whether an application was essentially biological. It said that it was not appropriate to apply the approach used to determine whether an application was excluded as a method of surgery and therapy by Article 52(4), which would have seen the mere presence of one biological feature in a process as a basis on which to conclude that the process as a whole was essentially biological (option (i), discussed earlier). As the Board said, Article 52(4) clearly requires the claimed process as whole to have a biological essence; 'the mere presence of one biological feature in a process cannot automatically confer an essentially biological character on the process as a whole'.[538] The Board also rejected an approach based upon that used in relation to Article 52(2)/section 1(2), under which an application would not be caught by Article 53(b) where it included one non-biological (technical) step[539] (option (iii), discussed earlier).

---

[533] *Plant Bioscience/Broccoli*, T 83/05 [2007] *OJ EPO* 644.   [534] Ibid., 669.

[535] *State of Israel/Tomatoes*, T 1242/06 [2008] *OJ EPO* 523 (*Lycopersicon esculentum*—tomato—plant with a *Lycopersicon species* to produce a hybrid plant).

[536] The Board did not believe that the process of allowing tomatoes to remain on the vine past the point of ripening was 'technical', since it was characterized by an abstention, albeit deliberate, from human intervention: ibid., [14].

[537] But with two identical judgments: *State of Israel/Tomatoes*, G 1/08 [2012] *OJ EPO* 206; *Plant Bioscience/Broccoli*, G 2/07 [2012] *OJ EPO* 130.

[538] *State of Israel/Tomatoes*, G 1/08 [2012] *OJ EPO* 206, [6.2].   [539] Ibid., [6.3].

The EBA then turned to consider the key unanswered question—namely, what test was to be used to determine whether something was essentially biological? The Board said that the legislative history showed that the legislator's intention when drafting Article 53(b) was to exclude from patentability the kind of plant breeding processes that were conventionally used at that time (namely, crossing and selection). This was despite the fact that these classical breeding methods often used technical devices such as pruning shears, special tools to help with grafting, and special greenhouses for growing plants. As the Board said, 'while such technical devices may perfectly well be patented themselves, the biological process in which they are used may not'.[540] Given this, the Board concluded that 'the mere provision of a technical step in a process which is based on the sexual crossing of plants and on subsequent selection did not *necessarily* mean that the claimed invention escaped the exclusion'.[541] The willingness to accept that a process could still be essentially biological when it included technical steps gave rise to the question: how do we distinguish between a process that includes a technical step that is still an essentially biological process and a process that includes a technical step that takes the process outside the scope of the exclusion?

In essence, the way in which this question was answered was to focus on the role played by the technical step in the breeding of the plant or animal. Specifically, it was said that if a technical step modifies or introduces a trait into the genome of a plant or animal, the process will not be essentially biological. This would be the case, for example, where genetic engineering techniques are used to insert or modify one or more genes into a plant or animal. In contrast, where the modification to the genome of the plant or animal is a product of natural processes, and where the technical steps merely serve to enable or assist the performance of that process, the process as a whole will be essentially biological. This is the case, for example, where the technical step includes the use of special greenhouses to grow the plants, the use of specific tools to help with grafting or pollination, or the use of molecular markers to facilitate the selection for the desired properties. While technical means are used in these situations to assist with the breeding process, nonetheless they are 'characterised by the fact that the traits of the plants resulting from the crossing were *determined by* the underlying natural phenomenon of meiosis'[542]—that is, the traits of the plants (or animals) were primarily the result of natural forces.

As the EPO Guidelines explain, a method of crossing, interbreeding, or selectively breeding 'say horses involving merely bringing together those animals or their gametes having certain characteristics would be essentially biological and therefore unpatentable'.[543] The situation would remain unchanged even if it were to contain an additional feature of a technical nature, such as the use of genetic molecular markers to select either parent or progeny. In all of these instances, the resulting plant or animal is essentially the result of natural forces. The situation would change, however, in the case of a process in which a gene or trait was inserted into a plant by genetic engineering, which would be potentially patentable. In positive terms, this means that to fall outside the process exclusion in Article 53(b), there has 'to be a technical step which *by itself* introduced or modified a trait in the genome'.[544]

Interestingly, the EPO Guidelines also suggest that a process of treating a plant or animal to improve its properties or yield, or to promote or suppress its growth (such as a method of pruning a tree), would not be an essentially biological process, 'since it is not

---

[540] Ibid., [6.4.2.2].   [541] Ibid., [6.4.2.3].   [542] Ibid.

[543] *EPO Guidelines*, G-II, [5.4.2].

[544] *State of Israel/Tomatoes II*, T 1242/06 [2013] *OJ EPO* 42, [43] (emphasis added).

based on the sexual crossing of whole genomes and subsequent selection of plants and animals; the same applies to a method of treating a plant characterised by the application of a growth-stimulating substance or radiation'.[545] The same would be true of the treatment of soil by technical means to suppress or promote growth.

8.3.4 Product claims derived from essentially biological processes

The fourth point to about the exclusion relates to its application to product claims. Specifically, it relates to the question of whether the Article 53(b) exclusion only applied to processes, or whether it also extends to include product claims or product-by-process claims that were derived from essentially biological processes? This question came to a head when the dispute involving the tomato application was brought back to the TBA for reconsideration following the finding of the EBA in *Tomatoes*. Following the decision in the EBA, the process claims were deleted from the application; as a result, the claims were limited to product claims directed to tomato fruits or fruit products. As the TBA said in *Tomatoes II*, the removal of the process claims was not surprising given that they would have clearly fallen foul of the process exclusion in Article 53(b). (This was because they did not contain a technical step that, by itself, introduced or modified a trait in the genome.) Nonetheless, the appellants argued that the resulting product claims were still excluded from patentability under Article 53(b). This was on the basis that if the product claims were allowed to stand, it would render the exclusion of essentially biological processes for the production of plants completely ineffective, 'thereby frustrating the legislators aim not to provide patent protection for the excluded plant breeding processes'.[546]

This argument was based on the well-established principle that the protection conferred by a product claim is absolute.[547] This means that the patent owner has the right to exclude others from making or using the patented product. This is in contrast to a process claim for making a product, which is limited to the use of that process to make that product. The upshot of this, which was at the heart of the appellant's argument, is that 'a claim to a product provides the patent proprietor with protection that generally encompasses the protection provided by a patent claim for the process of making the product'.[548] In the case at hand, if the product claims were allowed, this would have meant that the patent owner would have been able to prevent others from using the essentially biological plant breeding methods that were the subject matter of the deleted method claims. As the TBA said:

> Disregarding the process exclusion in the examination of product claims would have the general consequence that, for many plant breeding inventions, patent applicants and owners could easily overcome the process exclusion of Article 53(b) EPC by relying on product claims providing a broad protection which encompasses that which would have been provided by an excluded process claim.[549]

The Board concluded that this would appear to be at odds with a purposive interpretation of Article 53(b). Given that these issues were of fundamental importance, the TBA decided to refer a number of questions concerning the standing of product claims directed to plants or plant material to the EBA for consideration.

Not to be outdone, the parties in the *Broccoli* case also brought their dispute back to the TBA for reconsideration following the EBA decision. In light of the earlier EBA finding, the patent application was amended to delete all method claims in the application. As a

---

[545] *EPO Guidelines*, G-II, [5.4.2].   [546] *State of Israel/Tomatoes II*, T 1242/06 [2013] *OJ EPO* 42, [20].
[547] *Friction Reducing Additive*, G 2/88, [1990] *OJ EPO* 93, [5].
[548] *State of Israel/Tomatoes II*, T 1242/06 [2013] *OJ EPO* 42, [45].   [549] Ibid., [47].

result, the subject matter was limited to an edible *Brassica* plant, produced according to a particular method. In considering whether the process exclusion contained in Article 53(b) has a negative impact on the respondent's product claims, the TBA endorsed the comments in *Tomatoes II*. The TBA in *Broccoli II* also decided to ask the EBA to consider the standing of product claims under Article 53(b).

As it had done earlier, the EBA decided to consider the points of law raised by the TBA in *Tomatoes II* and *Broccoli II* in a single consolidated decision.[550] In essence the question the EBA was asked to consider was whether the exclusion of essentially biological processes for the production of plants in Article 53(b) has a negative effect on the allowability of a product claim directed to plants or plant material such as plant parts?

Echoing the approach adopted in other areas[551] and the approach advocated by the President of the EPO,[552] the EBA decided that Article 53(b) does not apply to product claims or product-by-process claims directed to plants or plant material such as fruit. As such, they were potentially patentable. While the EBA acknowledged that the decisions had ethical, social, and ethical consequences, they were at pains to point out that the standing of plant-based product patents was to be decided by 'legal' criteria (which equated to a technical exercise in legislative interpretation).[553] Following a review of the wording, context, legislative purpose, and history (as evidenced in the *travaux preparatoires*), the EBA concluded that the process exclusion in Article 53(b) does not extend to product or product-by process claims directed to plants and plant materials.

While this decision was not unexpected, what was surprising was the response that it elicited from the European Commission and the EPO. Following the EBA decisions in *Tomatoes II* and *Broccoli II* (and reportedly motivated by Dutch and German plan breeders), the European People's Party announced that it was going to call on the European Commission to deal with the 'plant patent problem'. In part, this was motivated by a concern that allowing patent protection over plants in general and their traits in particular, would have a negative impact on traditional plant breeding practices. Heeding this call, the Commission issued a Notice in November 2016 outlining its views on the patentability of products emanating from essentially biological processes (under Article 4 of the Biotech Directive which is identical to Article 53(b) EPC 2000). Building on the drafting history of the Biotech Directive, the Commission said that the EU legislators' intention when adopting the Biotech Directive was 'to exclude from patentability products (plants/animals and plant/animal parts) that are obtained by means of essentially biological processes'.[554] The Commission concluded that this was the correct way to interpret the exclusion of essentially biological processes. That is, the Commission disagreed with the EBA in *Tomatoes II* and *Broccoli II*. Following the Commission's Notice, on 12 December 2016 the EPO announced that it had instigated a stay on all examination and opposition

---

[550] But with two identical judgments: *State of Israel/Tomatoes II*, G 2/12 [2016] *OJ EPO* A27; *Plant Bioscience/Broccoli II*, G 2/13 [2016] *OJ EPO* A28.

[551] In *OncoMouse*, it was irrelevant to the patentability of the invention that the claims included circumstances under which genetically modified rodents reproduced; the offspring of such an 'essentially biological process' (if sexual reproduction is such a process) were products and hence fell outside the exclusion: T19/90 [1990] *OJ EPO* 476, 488. See also, *Wisconsin Alumni Research Foundation/Use of embryos* G 2/06 [2009] *OJ EPO* 306 (EBA), [22]; *Oliver Brüstle v. Greenpeace*, Case C-34/10 [2011] *ECR* I-9821 (ECJ).

[552] *State of Israel/Tomatoes II*, G 2/12 [2016] *OJ EPO* A27; *Plant Bioscience/Broccoli II*, G 2/13 [2016] *OJ EPO* A28, VI (2), 27.

[553] *State of Israel/Tomatoes II*, G 2/12 [2016] *OJ EPO* A27; *Plant Bioscience/Broccoli II*, G 2/13 [2016] *OJ EPO* A28, VIII (2), 50.

[554] *Commission Notice on certain articles of Directive 98/44/EC of the European Parliament and of the Council on the legal protection of biotechnological inventions* (2016) *OJ* C411/3 (8 November 2016), 7.

proceedings in which the invention was for a plant or animal obtained by an essentially biological process. The capitulation at the EPO was confirmed when the EPO amended its Regulations, effective from 1 July 2017, to exclude from patentability plants and animals exclusively obtained by an essentially biological breeding process.[555] In so doing, the EPO followed the lead of the European Commission and overturned the EBA in *Tomatoes II* and *Broccoli II*.

The abrupt turn around by the EPO, which attempts to demarcate patent protection for plants and plant breeder's rights protection, gives rise to a number of questions. These include questions about the independence of the EBA, the relationship of the EPO and the European Commission (which, in turn, has ramifications for the UK post-Brexit), and what the decision to exclude plant and animal products from patentability means for other aspects of Article 53(b). And while this ruling may reflect existing practice in Germany and the Netherlands (which already exclude plant-related product claims produced by an essentially biological process),[556] it is contrary to existing law in the United Kingdom.[557] It will be interesting to see how the UK IPO and the courts respond, particularly as the United Kingdom moves to navigate patents post-Brexit.

8.4 MICROBIOLOGICAL OR TECHNICAL PROCESSES

As we saw earlier, the exclusion of animal varieties, plant varieties, and essentially biological processes from the scope of patentable subject matter is subject to the general qualification that the invention is not 'a microbiological process or other technical process or the product of such a process'.[558] If an invention is for a microbiological or technical process,[559] it will not be caught by the exclusion. In essence, the qualification restricts the subject matter excluded by paragraph 3(f) of Schedule A2/Article 53(b) to non-microbiological and non-technical processes. Given that the qualification restricts the scope of the subject matter excluded by paragraph 3(f)/Article 53(b), this means that if it were to be interpreted broadly, it would greatly undermine the impact of the provision as a whole. If this were the case, it would increase the scope of biological subject matter that is patentable.

It should be noted that when the 1977 Act and the EPC 1973 were first enacted, the qualification was limited to 'a microbiological process or the product of such a process'. This was changed as a result of the Biotechnology Directive to apply to 'a microbiological process *or other technical process* or the product of such a process'.

The question of what is meant by a 'microbiological process' was considered in *Plant Genetic Systems*,[560] where the Technical Board of Appeal (TBA) said that 'microbiological

---

[555] See Decision of the Administrative Council 27 June 2017 amending Rule 27 and 28 [2017] *OJ EPO* A56 (inserting a new EPC 2000 Regs, r. 28(2)).

[556] *German Patents Act of 1936* (last amended 2013), s. 2a(1); *Dutch Patent Act of 1995*, Art. 3(1)(d).

[557] For example, the UK IPO has said that it will use the 'guidance provided' by *Tomatoes II* and *Broccoli II* when interpreting claims which relate to essentially biological processes (and presumably also products related thereto). UK IPO, *Examining Patent Applications for Biotechnological Inventions* (21 Oct 2016), [106].

[558] PA 1977, Sch. A2, para. 3(f); EPC 1973 Regs, r. 23c(c); EPC 2000, Art. 53(b), refers only 'to microbiological processes or the products thereof'. See EPC 2000, Art. 1, item 18. TRIPS, Art. 27(b), requires only that microorganisms, non-biological, and microbiological processes be patentable; it does not require that products of microbiological processes be patentable. See also R. Teschemacher, 'Patentability of Microorganisms per se' (1982) 13 *IIC* 27; D. Cadman, 'The Protection of Micro-organisms under European Patent Law' (1985) 16 *IIC* 311; N. Marterer, 'The Patentability of Micro Organisms per se' (1987) 18 *IIC* 666.

[559] A microbiological process is defined as 'any process involving or performed upon or resulting in microbiological material': Biotech. Dir., Art. 2(2); EPC 2000 Regs, r. 26(6); PA 1977, Sch. A2, para. 11.

[560] *PGS/Glutamine synthetase inhibitors* (1993) 24 *IIC* 618, [1995] *OJ EPO* 545 (Opposition Division).

processes' refers to processes in which micro-organisms or their parts are used to make or to modify products. The Board also said that it refers to processes in which new micro-organisms are developed for specific uses. Products of microbiological processes encompass 'products which are made or modified by micro-organisms as well as new micro-organisms as such'; while cells and parts thereof were said to be microbiological, processes of genetic engineering were not.[561] The extension of the provision to include technical processes largely renders these issues obsolete.

When construing the qualification as enacted (that is, when it was limited to microbiological processes), most of the discussions focused on whether a process that was made up of a mixture of microbiological and technical steps fell within the qualification.[562] For example, when contemplating whether a process that involves a number of different steps is a microbiological process, the TBA in *Plant Genetic Systems* said that a process was not a microbiological process simply because a microbiological step was involved; instead, the process had to be judged as a whole. On the facts of the case, the Board said that while the introductory step of transforming plant cells or tissues with recombinant DNA *was* microbiological, subsequent steps of regeneration and transformation that played an important role in bringing about the final product *were not* microbiological processes. When viewed as a whole, the process was best described as a technical process that included a microbiological step, rather than a microbiological process (which would have justified the patenting of the process or a product of the process). As a consequence, the resulting plants were held not to be the product of a microbiological process within the meaning of Article 53(b) (as enacted).[563]

While *Plant Genetics Systems* provides us with some guidance as to the limits of the qualification, its precise scope remains unclear. It seems, however, that this may not matter too much. This is because the changes introduced to the exclusions so that they also include 'technical processes' means that the problems of the type discussed in *Plant Genetic Systems* have largely been overcome. Given that genetic manipulation is undoubtedly a technical process, this appears to demand the patentability of genetically modified plants and animals.[564] Because much of the research carried out in relation to biological subject matter involves a degree of human intervention, most of the processes will be captured by the qualification and thus fall outside the scope of the exclusions.[565] By increasing the scope of the qualification to section 1(3)(b)/Article 53(b), the changes initiated by the Biotechnology Directive will minimize the impact that the exclusion has upon the scope of patentable subject matter.

The scope of the subject matter excluded by paragraph 3(f)/Article 53(b) would have been further undermined if the approach suggested by the TBA in *Plant Genetic Systems* had been followed. In that case, the Board suggested that a plant variety that was a product

---

[561] Ibid.

[562] The issue of how you ascertain whether a process with a number of steps is a microbiological process is similar to the question whether a process is 'essentially biological'.

[563] While the point was not discussed at length, it was suggested in *PGS/Glutamine synthetase inhibitors*, T 356/93 [1995] *EPOR* 357, that a microbiological process was a purer process (with less human intervention) than a process that was essentially biological.

[564] Earlier drafts of the Directive defined microbiological to mean 'a process carried out with the use of or performed upon or resulting in a micro-organism', as 'a process consisting of a succession of steps', including 'at least one essential step of the process' that is microbiological, and as meaning 'a process involving or performed upon or resulting in microbiological material'. All were abandoned. See M. Llewelyn, 'The Patentability of Biological Material: Continuing Contradiction and Confusion' [2000] *EIPR* 191.

[565] A. Schrell, 'Are Plants Still Patentable?' [1996] *EIPR* 242, 243; O. Mills, *Biotechnological Inventions: Moral Restraints and Patent Law* (rev'd edn, 2016).

of a microbiological process would not have been caught by the exclusion and thus would have been patentable. This approach was rejected in *Novartis*, when the Enlarged Board of Appeal said that the plant variety exclusion applied irrespective of how the plant varieties were produced. The mere fact that a plant variety was obtained by means of genetic engineering does not give the producers of such plant varieties a privileged position.[566] This reflects the position set out in Recital 32 of the Biotechnology Directive, which says that:

> [I]f an invention consists only in genetically modifying a particular plant variety, and if a new plant variety is bred, it will still be excluded from patentability even if the genetic modification is the result not of an essentially biological process but of a biotechnological process.

9 IMMORAL INVENTIONS

It is a long-standing principle of patent law that patents should not be granted for immoral inventions. Until recently, the principle was rarely invoked. However, as a result of developments in biotechnology and related attempts to patent the products of that research, in recent years ethical considerations have played a more prominent role in patent law. While these provisions are potentially applicable to all patentable subject matter, more detailed provisions have also been introduced in relation to biotechnological inventions. What is most striking about the interaction of patent law and ethics is how uncomfortable the relationship has been and the difficulties that it has produced.[567]

When the EPC 1973 and the Patents Act 1977 were first drafted, the relevant statutory provisions in relation to immoral inventions were set out in section 1(3)(a) of the Act and Article 53(a) of the Convention.[568] Since then, the law in this area has undergone a number of important changes, notably to take account of the Biotechnology Directive.[569] When the Directive was first proposed, it made no reference to the morality of patenting. Over time, however, the Directive became a focal point for public concerns about the ethical and social dimensions of biotechnology generally, as well as specific concerns about the patenting of the products of such activities. In response, the proponents of patenting argued that the patent system was an inappropriate vehicle for dealing with concerns over morality. The reasons for this were said to be that the uses to be made of an invention are not clear at the application stage, that patent examiners are not qualified to deal with ethical questions, and most importantly because patents do not control whether or how an

---

[566] *Novartis/Transgenic plant*, G 1/98 [2000] *EPOR* 303 (EBA), 321. This is supported by Biotech. Dir., Recital 32.

[567] L. Bently and B. Sherman, 'The Ethics of Patenting: Towards a Transgenic Patent System' (1995) 3 *Med L Rev* 275.

[568] These are permitted by TRIPS, Art. 27(2), which says that members may exclude:

> ... inventions, the prevention within their territory of the commercial exploitation of which is necessary to protect *ordre public* or morality, including to protect human, animal or plant life or health or to avoid serious prejudice to the environment, provided that such exclusion is not made merely because the exploitation is prohibited by domestic law.

[569] It is likely that the Directive will bring about other changes. For example, Biotech. Dir., Art. 7, states that the Commission's European Group on Ethics in Science and New Technologies is to evaluate all ethical aspects of biotechnology. While this is unlikely to have a direct impact on patenting, there is a possibility that it may influence attitudes towards ethical issues. This is reinforced by the fact that the Commission is obliged under the Directive to report annually to the European Parliament and Council on the implications of patent law in the field of biotechnology and genetic engineering: Biotech. Dir., Art. 16(3).

invention is exploited. Instead, it was said that exploitation of biotechnological inventions was best controlled through other regulatory systems.[570] In the end, the Biotechnology Directive took a middle ground, insofar as it provides that inventions shall be unpatentable where their commercial exploitation would be contrary to *ordre public* or morality.[571] The Biotechnology Directive also provided specific examples of types of invention that were unpatentable.[572] These are now mirrored in the 1977 Act[573] and the EPC 2000.[574]

The upshot of these changes is that there are effectively two different types of morality provision that may be applied. The first, and more general, is found in Article 53(a)[575] and section 1(3).[576] These require an assessment 'as to whether or not exploitation of the invention in question would be contrary to morality or "*ordre public*".'[577] The Technical Board of Appeal refers to these as the 'real' Article 53(a) objections. The second, more specific, morality provisions are found in Rule 28(a)–(d) of the EPC 2000 Implementing Regulations[578] and paragraph 3(b)–(c) of Schedule A2 to the Patent Act 1977.[579] These provide specific guidance as to when an invention will be excluded under Article 53(a)/ section 1(3). Rule 28 provides that:

Under Article 53(a), European patents shall not be granted in respect of biotechnological inventions which, in particular, concern the following:

(a) processes for cloning human beings;[580]
(b) processes for modifying the germ line genetic identity of human beings;[581]
(c) uses of human embryos for industrial or commercial purposes;[582]
(d) processes for modifying the genetic identity of animals which are likely to cause them suffering without any substantial medical benefit to man or animal, and also animals resulting from such processes.[583]

---

[570] For an overview of some of the regulatory regimes, see J. Black, 'Regulation as Facilitation: Negotiating the Genetic Revolution' (1998) 61 *MLR* 621.

[571] This is mirrored in the new s. 1(3) and, in turn, reflects EPC 1973, Art. 53 (as enacted). Biotech. Dir., Art. 6(1), goes on to say that exploitation shall not be considered to be contrary to morality simply because it is prohibited by law or regulation. Similar provisions exist in the PA 1977 and the EPC 2000.

[572] Biotech Dir., Art. 6(2).   [573] PA 1977, Sch. A2, para. 3(b)–(e).

[574] EPC 2000 Regs, r. 28 (which is the same as EPC 1973 Regs, r. 23d). On the basis that EPC 1973 Regs, rr 23b–e, did not constitute a departure from previous law, it was held that they could be applied to matters that started prior to their enactment on 1 September 1999: *Harvard/OncoMouse* [2003] OJ EPO 473, 496 (Opposition Division).

[575] For the background, see EPC 2000, Art. 1, item 18; *Base Proposal for the Revision of the European Patent Convention* (2000) CA/100/00 e, 42.

[576] PA 1977, s. 1(3)(a) (as enacted), was replaced by a new s. 1(3) under the Patents Regulations 2000. The old s. 1(3)(a) provided that a patent should not be granted for 'an invention the publication or exploitation of which would be generally expected to encourage offensive, immoral or anti-social behaviour'. In contrast, the new s. 1(3) provides that a 'patent shall not be granted for an invention the commercial exploitation of which would be contrary to public policy or morality'. PA 1977, s. 1(4), states that, for the purpose of s. 1(3), exploitation shall not be regarded as contrary to public policy or morality only because it is prohibited by law in force in the United Kingdom. This replicates the language in Biotech. Dir., Art. 6(1).

[577] *Base Proposal for the Revision of the European Patent Convention* (2000) CA/100/00 e, 51.

[578] Formerly EPC 1973 Regs, r. 23a–d.

[579] PA 1977, Sch. A2, para. 3(b)–(c); Biotech. Dir., Art. 6(1).

[580] EPC 2000 Regs, r. 28(a) (ex EPC 1973 Regs, r. 23d(a)); PA 1977, Sch. A2, para. 3(b); Biotech. Dir., Art. 6(2)(a).

[581] EPC 2000 Regs, r. 28(b) (ex EPC 1973 Regs, r. 23d(b)); PA 1977, Sch. A2, para. 3(c); Biotech. Dir., Art. 6(2)(b).

[582] EPC 2000 Regs, r. 28(a) (ex EPC 1973 Regs, r. 23d(c)); PA 1977, Sch. A2, para. 3(d); Biotech. Dir., Art. 6(2)(c).

[583] EPC 2000 Regs, r. 28(a) (ex EPC 1973 Regs, r. 23d(d)); PA 1977, Sch. A2, para. 3(e); Biotech. Dir., Art. 6(2)(d).

After looking at the general prohibition in Article 53(a)/section 1(3), we will look at each of these specific cases in turn. Before doing so, it is important to note that if an application falls within any of the four types of invention, the application must ipso facto be denied a patent under Article 53(a)/section 1(3). In this situation, there is no need to consider Article 53(a)/section 1(3) any further. However, if an application falls outside the four categories of invention, the application needs to be assessed to determine whether it falls within Article 53(a).[584] That is, a case not falling within Rule 28 does not escape the operation of Article 53(a). The position is presumably the same in the United Kingdom.

9.1 INVENTIONS CONTRARY TO *ORDRE PUBLIC* OR MORALITY

Article 53(a) of the EPC 2000 provides that European patents 'shall not be granted in respect of inventions the commercial exploitation of which would be contrary to "*ordre public*" or morality'. While the UK provisions have changed so that they are more closely aligned to the EPC than was previously the case, the language in section 1(3) is slightly different, in that it provides that 'a patent shall not be granted for an invention the commercial exploitation of which would be contrary to public policy or morality'.[585]

The role and meaning of the morality exclusion under the EPC (as enacted) was first considered in the 1989 *OncoMouse* decision.[586] The case concerned the patentability of mice that had been genetically modified so that they would develop cancer—a result that the applicants hoped would be useful in cancer research.[587] Initially, the Examining Division declined to consider Article 53(a), taking the view that it was inappropriate for people who were essentially qualified as technicians to consider such an issue.[588] On appeal, the Technical Board of Appeal (TBA) took a very different view.[589] It observed that the genetic manipulation of mammalian animals is 'undeniably problematical in various respects', particularly in circumstances under which the modifications 'necessarily cause suffering'.[590] Moreover, the release of the mice into the environment might 'entail unforeseeable and irreversible adverse effects'.[591] Consequently, it was necessary to consider the application of Article 53(a).

The TBA, remitting the case to the Examining Division for reconsideration,[592] explained that the application of Article 53(a) 'would seem to depend mainly on a careful weighing-up of the suffering of animals and possible risks to the environment on the one hand, and the invention's usefulness to mankind on the other'.[593] Applying this utilitarian balancing test, the Examining Division held that the subject matter was patentable.[594] It reasoned that finding a cure for cancer was a highly desirable end and that the mouse would assist in achieving that end. In contrast, the Examining Division played down the harm caused by the invention. The Examining Division suggested that given that

---

[584] *Harvard/Transgenic animals*, T 315/03 [2006] *OJ EPO* 15, 40.

[585] For a general discussion, see Y. Min, 'Morality: An Equivocal Area in the Patent System' [2012] *EIPR* 261.

[586] See V. Vossius, 'Patent Protection for Animals' [1990] *EIPR* 250; R. Dresser, 'Ethical and Legal Issues in Patenting New Animal Life' [1988] *Jurimetrics Journal* 399; U. Schatz, 'Patentability of Genetic Engineering Invention' (1998) 29 *IIC* 2.

[587] More accurately, of a mammal into which malignancy-creating genes had been introduced, so that the mammal had an increased probability of developing tumours.

[588] [1989] *OJ EPO* 451 (Exam).   [589] *Harvard/OncoMouse*, T 19/90 [1990] *OJ EPO* 490 (TBA).

[590] Ibid., [5]. It has been suggested that the EPO was awaiting the outcome of the Directive before issuing a decision: see CIPA, *Briefing Paper Patentability of Animals* (May 1998), available online at http://www.cipa. org.uk/pages/info-papers-animals.   [591] *Harvard/OncoMouse*, T 19/90 [1990] *OJ EPO* 490, [5].

[592] Ibid.   [593] Ibid.   [594] *Harvard/OncoMouse*, T 19/90 [1991] *EPOR* 525 (Exam).

the research would take place anyway and that it would require vast numbers of mice to locate some that had 'naturally' developed cancer, the invention produced a benefit to mouse-kind in that large numbers of healthy mice would no longer need to be bred and then destroyed.

The utilitarian balancing test adopted in the *OncoMouse* decision was applied in 1991 when the EPO warned the pharmaceutical company Upjohn that it would not accept an application to patent a mouse into which a gene had been introduced that led the mouse to lose its hair. In weighing up the benefit that flowed from the invention (the usefulness of the mice in experiments to cure hair loss) as against the harm suffered by the mice, the EPO asserted that the invention was immoral and thus would not be patentable.[595]

The next occasion when the application of Article 53(a) was considered was by the Opposition Division in *Plant Genetic Systems*.[596] In this case, the opponents (Greenpeace) objected to the patent that had been granted for a genetically engineered plant (which rendered the plants resistant to herbicide) on the grounds that it was inherently immoral and that it created risks to the environment. Following the cost–benefit test suggested in *OncoMouse,* the opponents argued that these risks should be balanced against the benefits likely to accrue from the invention. The Opposition Division refused to apply the utilitarian cost–benefit analysis. On the basis that the patent system was primarily concerned with technical considerations and that it was not competent or qualified to decide ethical issues, the Opposition Division believed that it should not be routinely involved in considering ethical questions. Instead, the Opposition Division said that it was only necessary to consider the exclusion where the invention would be universally regarded as outrageous and where there was an overwhelming consensus that no patent should be granted—that is, it was only necessary to consider ethical questions once a certain ethical threshold had been crossed. The upshot of this is that, in most cases, it would not be necessary to consider the morality of patents.

The *Plant Genetic Systems* decision highlights a further difficulty in relation to the immorality examination. In an attempt to apply the balancing test outlined in *OncoMouse,* the Opposition Division was faced with the problem that it was unable to quantify the objections raised against the patent. This was compounded by the fact that no evidence was submitted to support these claims; instead, the examiners were asked to determine the opposition on the basis of personal philosophy or conviction. The Opposition Division rejected such an approach on the basis that it would produce 'individualistic' or 'arbitrary' decisions. Moreover, even if it were possible to convert abstractly formulated objections into a more concrete format (for example through the use of opinion poll evidence), the Opposition Division clung to the view that patent law should not be the forum in which such opinions should play a role.

The approach advocated in the *Plant Genetic Systems* decision was adopted by the Opposition Division in the *Relaxin* case.[597] This decision concerned an opposition by the Green Party to the Howard Florey Institute's patent for the DNA sequences of a naturally occurring substance that relaxes the uterus during childbirth, which is obtained from the human ovary. The Green Party objected to the patent on three grounds: (i) that the use of pregnancy for profit was offensive to human dignity; (ii) that the applicant was involved in patenting life, an activity that was intrinsically immoral; and (iii) that such patenting was equivalent to slavery. In rejecting the Green Party's objections, the EPO noted that the tissue used in the research was donated during the course of necessary gynaecological

---

[595] EP No. 0439553 rejected 25 July 1993.   [596] (1993) 24 *IIC* 618.
[597] *Howard Florey/Relaxin* [1995] *OJ EPO* 388 (Opposition Division).

operations and thus had not offended 'human dignity'. Moreover, the Opposition Division said that DNA was not 'life'; rather, it was a 'chemical substance which carries genetic code'.[598] The argument that the applicant was 'patenting life' was thus misconceived. Finally, the Opposition Division rejected the Green Party's assertion that such patenting was equivalent to slavery, on the ground that such an assertion misunderstood the nature of a patent. This was because, according to the Opposition Division, a patent does not give the proprietor any rights over a human being; all that a patent monopoly provides is the right to prevent someone from practising the same invention.

As with the *Plant Genetics* decision, the Opposition Division's decision in *Relaxin* further highlights the problems that confront patent law in accommodating ethical considerations. This was explicitly acknowledged in *Relaxin* when the Opposition Division said that the question of whether 'human genes should be patented is a controversial issue on which many persons have strong opinions . . . [T]he EPO is not the right institution to decide on fundamental ethical questions.'[599] The case also reveals the difficulties involved in translating the ethical concerns of critics into the language of patent law. Faced with a choice between a scientific understanding of DNA as a chemical substance and the social understanding of DNA as life, the Opposition Division preferred the former interpretation. This prioritization of the scientific view over the Green Party's approach illustrates the depth of the conflict between the logic of ethical objections and those of patenting, at least as it is currently understood.

The next development in this area came with the decision of the TBA in *Plant Genetic Systems*,[600] where the Board concluded that claims for genetically modified seeds did not contravene Article 53(a). Although this decision, which has attracted many critics,[601] represents a more flexible approach to the incorporation of ethics into patent law, it still highlights the uncertainty and ambiguity that exist in this relationship. The Board said that the concept of morality under the EPC was built upon the belief that some behaviour is right and acceptable, whereas other behaviour is wrong—a belief that was founded on norms deeply rooted in European society and civilization. Noting that patent offices exist 'at the crossroads between science and public policy', the Board said that *ordre public* in Article 53(a) covers the protection of public security, the physical integrity of individuals as part of society, and protection of the environment. On this basis, the TBA said that where the exploitation of an invention was likely to breach public peace or social order (for example through acts of terrorism) or seriously prejudice the environment, the invention would be excluded from patentability under Article 53(a).[602]

The TBA then attempted to clarify the way Article 53(a) was to be interpreted. As well as casting doubts on the value of opinion poll evidence, the Board said that the mere fact that the exploitation of a particular type of subject matter was permitted in some or all of the contracting states would not automatically influence the ethical status of the invention, at least in relation to its patentability. The Board observed that a balancing exercise was not the only way of assessing patentability, although it was useful in situations where actual damage and/or disadvantage existed. The Board added that although the morality provision is to be construed narrowly, it should not be disregarded. This is the case even if it is difficult to judge whether the claimed subject matter is contrary to *ordre public* or morality. Given the explicit wording of Article 53(a), it is difficult to see how the Board could have concluded otherwise.

---

[598] Ibid., [6.3.4].   [599] Ibid.   [600] [1995] *OJ EPO* 545.

[601] J. Straus, 'Patenting Human Genes in Europe' (1995) 26 *IIC* 920.

[602] *EPO Guidelines*, G-II, [4.1], gives the example of an anti-personnel mine. The UK takes a similar line by reason of the Landmines Act 1998, s. 2; see Patent Office Notice Anti-Personnel Mines (1998).

The scope of Article 53(a) was also considered by the TBA in its 2006 *Transgenic Animals* decision. In this case, the Board was called on to consider whether a patent for transgenic rodents containing an additional cancer gene was excluded from patentability under Article 53. This was an appeal from the 2003 decision of the Opposition Division to maintain the patent in an amended form.[603]

The TBA began by stressing that the words 'contrary to *ordre public* or morality' were not concerned with the morality of genetically manipulating a mouse, with the morality of the OncoMouse thereby produced, nor with the patenting of either the OncoMouse or the genetic manipulation method. Instead, the Board stressed that the morality provisions were only concerned with the morality of the publication or exploitation of the OncoMouse or that method.[604] (It should be noted that the EPC 2000 no longer refers to the publication of the invention; instead, it is now limited to the commercial exploitation of the invention.[605])

The Board reconfirmed that the balancing approach set out in the 1991 *OncoMouse* decision (T 19/90) was the correct approach to be adopted when deciding whether an invention fell within a 'real' Article 53(a) assessment. The Board reiterated that, unlike the balancing test mandated under Rule 23d(d) of the EPC 1973 Implementing Regulations (now Rule 28 of the EPC 2000 Implementing Regulations), the 'T 19/90 test' allowed a range of factors to be taken into account, including harm to the environment, possible use of non-animal alternatives, possible threats to human evolution, and so on.[606] As we will see later, the applicant's main request—which claimed 'transgenic rodents' and thus embraced all animals within the taxonomic order *Rodentia* including rats, mice, squirrels, beavers, and porcupines—was rejected on the basis that it failed the balancing test required under Rule 23d(d) (now Rule 28). Given this, the Board did not need to consider the fate of the main request under Article 53(a). Nonetheless, the Board said that the claims would have failed under the balancing test set out in the *OncoMouse* decision (T 19/90). This was on the basis that the balancing test in conjunction with Article 53(a) was able to take account of more factors than were permissible under Rule 23d(d) (now Rule 28). This meant that additional factors such as the degree of animal suffering and the availability of non-animal methods could also be taken into account. The Board said that when these factors were added to the inevitable harm created by the invention and the fact that there was no evidence that the medical benefits from the invention applied to all rodents, it further tilted the balance against the acceptance of the request.[607]

The fate of the main request under Article 53(a) needs to be contrasted with that of the auxiliary request, which was limited to 'mice' rather than 'rodents'. While it was accepted that the auxiliary invention caused actual suffering to mice, the auxiliary request differed from the main application in that the applicant was able to show that the invention also produced actual medical benefits. As the Board said, this meant that 'no suffering was envisaged

---

[603] *Harvard/OncoMouse* [2003] *OJ EPO* 473 (Opposition Division). In upholding the patent in an amended form, the Opposition Division set out what it saw to be the general principles underlying EPC 2000, Art. 53(a). In particular, it said that Art. 53(a) would only ever apply in exceptional cases. The Division also said that, in assessing whether a patent fell foul of Art. 53(a), it had no intention to apply 'extreme positions'. By this, it meant that it would not take account of possible abuses of the invention. The Opposition Division said that *ordre public* and morality had to be assessed 'primarily by looking at laws or regulations which are common to most European countries because these laws and regulations are the best indicators about what is considered right or wrong in a society': ibid., [9.3].

[604] *Harvard/Transgenic animals*, T 315/03 [2006] *OJ EPO* 15 (TBA), 29. The Board also said that *ordre public* and morality may form the basis of separate objections.

[605] This brings the EPC into line with TRIPS, Art. 27(2), and Biotech. Dir., Art. 6(1).

[606] *Harvard/Transgenic animals*, T 315/03 [2006] *OJ EPO* 15, 54.   [607] Ibid., 63.

to any animals without a corresponding prospect of benefit'.[608] As such, the Board concluded that the auxiliary request passed the *OncoMouse* (T 19/90) test under Article 53(a). Interestingly, while the Board accepted that additional factors (such as harm to the environment) could be taken into account if they were able to be substantiated,[609] it was highly critical of the arguments made by some of the opponents about the degree of suffering. This was rejected (presumably on the unsubstantiated moral basis) that it was distasteful even to attempt to draw a distinction between acceptable and unacceptable suffering.[610]

9.2 INVENTIONS DEEMED TO BE IMMORAL

In addition to the general morality provisions in Article 53(a)/section 1(3), there are a number of specific types of biological invention that are deemed to be immoral or contrary to *ordre public*. These are to be found in Rule 28 of the EPC 2000 Implementing Regulations (ex Rule 23d of the EPC 1973 Implementing Regulations) and paragraph 3 of Schedule A2 to the Patents Act 1977.[611]

9.2.1 Processes for cloning human beings

The first type of biological invention that is deemed to fall foul of Article 53(a)/section 1(3) are 'processes for cloning human beings'.[612] The exclusion of processes for human cloning reflects concerns about eugenics. Human cloning is defined as 'any process, including techniques of embryo splitting, designed to create a human being with the same nuclear genetic information as another living or deceased human being'.[613] It has been suggested that the scope of the exclusion will depend on how 'human being' is defined.[614] In particular, 'human being' may be defined in such a way as not to include human embryos and embryonic tissue. The UK Intellectual Property Office (IPO) has said that human totipotent cells (which have the potential to develop into an entire human body) would not be patentable 'because the human body at the various stages of its formation and development is excluded from patentability'.[615] In contrast, the UK IPO is willing to grant patents for human embryonic pluripotent stem cells (which arise from the division of totipotent cells, but do not have the potential to develop into an entire human body). The fact that a number of reports from key scientific bodies, including The Royal Society and the Nuffield Council on Bioethics, supported embryonic stem-cell research was taken as evidence that such research was not contrary to public policy or morality in the United Kingdom.[616] It should be noted that the EPO declared (on the basis of the 'old' law) that methods in a cloning process that fused human and pig cells were contrary to morality. As a consequence, the applicants did

---

[608] Ibid.

[609] Other factors, including the threat to evolution posed by the transgenic mice, the fact that the patent would have encouraged the use of transgenic mice in research, and the more general argument that genetically engineered mice were morally unacceptable to the public, were rejected: ibid., 69–72.

[610] Ibid., 67. The time at which a real Art. 53(a) assessment was to be made was the effective date of the patent (namely, either the filing or priority date), although later evidence may be taken into account so long as it is directed to the position at the relevant date.

[611] The TBA also said that the date at which the application should be assessed is the filing date or the priority date of the patent in question: ibid., 66.

[612] EPC 2000 Regs, r. 28(a) (ex EPC 1973 Regs, r. 23d(a)); PA 1977, Sch. A2, para. 3(b).

[613] Biotech. Dir., Recital 41. See also Biotech. Dir., Recital 40.

[614] S. Bostyn, 'Patentability of Genetic Information Carriers' [1999] *IPQ* 1, 11.

[615] UK Patent Office, *Practice Note: Inventions Involving Human Embryonic Stem Cells* (25 March 2015), 3(ii) (citing PA 1977, Sch. A2, para. 3(a)).   [616] Ibid.

not pursue the application any further.[617] As such, it seems that even if the cloning of human embryos were not caught by Rule 28(a) (ex Rule 23d(a)), it would fall under the general prohibition in Article 53(a).[618]

9.2.2 Processes for modifying the germ line genetic identity of human beings

The second type of biological invention that is deemed to fall foul of Article 53(a)/section 1(3) are 'processes for modifying the germ line genetic identity of human beings'.[619] The exclusion of such processes (which could alter the reproductive cells that are capable of transmitting genetic material to our descendants) also reflects concerns about eugenics. While somatic cell gene therapy is not caught by the provisions, germ cell line therapy inventions are.[620] It has been suggested that the exclusion of all forms of germ-line therapy is an overreaction. More specifically, it has been said that because it is conceivable that morally unobjectionable applications of germ-line therapy (for example for inheritable diseases such as cystic fibrosis) may arise in the future, the exclusion is 'retrograde and short-sighted'.[621] As Recital 42 of the Biotechnology Directive points out, the exclusion does not affect inventions for therapeutic or diagnostic purposes that are applied to the human embryo and are useful to it.

9.2.3 Uses of human embryos for industrial or commercial purpose

The third type of biological application that is deemed to fall foul of Article 53(a)/section 1(3) are those that claim 'uses of human embryos for industrial or commercial purpose'.[622] The scope of this exclusion, which has proven to be somewhat controversial,[623] depends on three factors: what is a *human embryo*; what is a *use* of a human embryo; and what is meant by an *industrial* or *commercial* purpose? We will look at each in turn. Before doing so, it is important to note that technical developments that take place after the filing date (such as the discovery of innocuous ways to make the invention) cannot be taken into account when assessing whether a claim contravenes Rule 28(c) of the EPC 2000 Implementing Regulations.[624]

(i) What is a human embryo?

Because the term 'human embryo' is not defined in the Biotechnology Directive or in the EPC, it is up to the courts to determine its meaning. One of the first to do so was the

---

[617] Patent applications for the cloning of embryos (including human embryos), as well as mixed-species embryos from pigs and humans: reported on Yahoo.news (27 October 2000).

[618] Such activities may also be caught by Biotech. Dir., Art. 5; EPC 1973 Regs, r. 23e(1); PA 1977, Sch. A2, para. 3(a).

[619] EPC 2000 Regs, r. 28(b) (ex EPC 1973 Regs, r. 23d(b)); PA 1977, Sch. A2, para. 3(c).

[620] S. Bostyn, 'Patentability of Genetic Information Carriers' [1999] *IPQ* 1, 8, n. 36 ('somatic cell gene therapy applies to differentiated cells of the foetus, the child or the adult, such as cells of the liver, blood or other organs'), n. 37 ('germ line therapy applies to non-differentiated cells, such as gametes or the fertile egg, and implies that the genetic modification will be transmitted to the individual's offspring').

[621] R. Nott, 'You Did It' [1998] *EPIR* 347, 349; M. Llewellyn, 'Legal Protection of Biotechnological Inventions' [1997] *EPIR* 115, 122.

[622] EPC 2000 Regs, r. 28(c) (ex EPC 1973 Regs, r. 23d(c)); PA 1977, Sch. A2, para. 3(d); Biotech. Dir., Art. 6(2)(c).

[623] See A. Plomer and P. Torremans (eds), *Embryonic Stem Cell Patents* (2009).

[624] *Wisconsin Alumni Research Foundation/Use of embryos*, G 2/06 [2009] *OJ EPO* 306, [33]. See S. Sterckx and J. Cockbain, 'Assessing the Morality of the Commercial Exploitation of Inventions Concerning Uses of Human Embryos and the Relevance of Moral Complicity: Comments on the EPO's *WARF* Decision' (2010) 7(1) *SCRIPTed* 83.

Enlarged Board of Appeal in *Wisconsin Alumni Research Foundation/Use of embryos*[625] which held that because the purpose of the exclusion is to protect human dignity and to prevent the commercial exploitation of 'embryos', it should not be given a narrow interpretation. This view was echoed in *Oliver Brüstle v. Greenpeace*,[626] where the Court of Justice was called on to consider the fate of a German patent for isolated and purified neural precursor cells produced from human embryonic stem cells (aimed at treating damaged organs). The Court said that, in drafting the Biotechnology Directive, the EU legislature intended to 'exclude any possibility of patentability where respect for human dignity could thereby be affected'.[627] As a result, the Court said that the concept of 'human embryo' within the meaning of Article 6(2)(c) of the Directive must be understood in a wide sense. More specifically, the Court interpreted 'human embryo' broadly to include any organism that 'is capable of commencing the process of development of a human being'.[628] On this basis, it said that any human ovum, as soon as it is fertilized is a 'human embryo' (since that fertilization commences the process of development of a human being).[629] The Court also added that a non-fertilized human ovum into which the cell nucleus from a mature human cell has been transplanted was a 'human embryo' and thus excluded insofar as it is capable of commencing the process of development of a human being.[630] A non-fertilized human ovum, the division and further development of which have been stimulated by parthenogenesis (a type of asexual reproduction in which the growth and development of embryos occurs without fertilization), insofar as it is capable of commencing the process of development of a human being, was also said to be a 'human embryo'.[631] This includes cells that are artificially stimulated or manipulated but not fertilized, which are able to trigger the development of a human being (parthenogenesis). In relation to stem cells obtained from a human embryo at the blastocyst stage (that is, five days after fertilization), the Court of Justice sent the matter back to the referring court to determine scientifically whether they are capable of commencing the process of development of a human being (and therefore fall within the concept of 'human embryo').[632]

The definition of human embryo adopted in *Brüstle* has been adopted in the United Kingdom. One area where there was some initial uncertainty was in relation to the Court of Justice's suggestion that a non-fertilized human ovum, the division and further development of which have been stimulated by parthenogenesis, was a 'human embryo'.[633] Doubts about the accuracy of the finding of the Court were raised in *International Stem Cell Corporation v. Comptroller General of Patents*,[634] which concerned applications for parthenotes developed from human embryonic stem cells. Notably, these parthenotes, which were developed without fertilization, are unable to develop into a human.

---

[625] G 2/06 [2009] *OJ EPO* 306, [20] (interpreting Biotech. Dir., Art. 6(2), which corresponds to EPC 2000 Regs, r. 28(c)).   [626] Case C-34/10, EU:C:2011:669 (ECJ, Grand Chamber).

[627] Ibid., [34].   [628] Ibid., [36].   [629] Ibid., [35].   [630] Ibid., [36].

[631] Ibid., [36]. While the UK Human Fertilisation and Embryology Act 1990, s. 1(1) defines 'embryo' to include the two-cell zygote and an egg in the process of fertilization, UK courts dealing with patents are bound to follow the Court of Justice, which described the human embryo as an autonomous concept of EU law: ibid., [26].   [632] Ibid., [37].

[633] While human totipotent cells are not patentable, the Office has no objections to the patenting of human pluripotent stem cells. This reflects the widespread (but not complete) consensus that while totipotent cells should be excluded from patentability, pluripotent cells should not. UK IPO, *Practice Notice: Inventions Involving Human Embryonic Stem Cells* (25 March 2015), [3(iv)]. See also *International Stem Cell Corporation v. Comptroller General of Patents* [2013] *EWHC* 807, [56].

[634] [2013] *EWHC* 807. More accurately, the case concerned 'parthenogentic activation of oocytes for the production of human embryonic stem cells' and 'for non-fertilised human-ova whose division and further development have been stimulated by parthenogenesis': ibid., [21].

As Judge Henry Carr QC said the findings of *Brüstle* would prima facie seem to mean that the applications in question were excluded on the basis that they involved the use of a human embryo. However, the International Stem Cell Corporation argued—and the Court agreed—that there was an inherent contradiction in *Brüstle*. While the Court of Justice had defined the concept of human embryo as something that was 'capable of commencing the process of development of a human being', this was not the case with a parthenote which, by definition, cannot develop into a viable human being. This is because while a parthenote is capable of developing into a blastocyst-like structure, it cannot develop to term because of the absence of any paternal DNA. The key question here is whether it is enough merely to start the process of development (that is, whether the focus was merely on whether the process had been started), or whether there was also a requirement that the process was able to be completed (that is, whether it also required the completion of the process of development leading to the birth of a viable human being). Judge Henry Carr QC agreed with the International Stem Cell Corporation that if the process of development is not capable of leading to a human being (as the Hearing Officer found to be the case in relation to parthenotes), then it should *not* be excluded from patentability as a human embryo.[635] Judge Henry Carr QC felt that the balance between the need to ensure that patent law supports biotechnological research and the need to respect fundamental principles safeguarding the dignity and integrity of the person was properly struck by excluding from patentability processes of development that are capable of leading to a human being. This was not the case, however, where a process of development that is incapable of leading to a human being is excluded. This was particularly the case in the case of parthenotes, which are not fertilized ova at any stage—the exclusion of which Judge Henry Carr QC equated to an unwarranted exclusion of the fruits of stem cell research from the remit of patent protection.[636] Despite this, Judge Henry Carr QC agreed with the Comptroller that there was insufficient clarity in *Brüstle* about what was meant by 'capable of commencing the process of development of a human being' to warrant a reference to the Court of Justice.[637]

The Court of Justice began by noting that a 'human embryo', which was 'an autonomous concept of EU law' that was to be understood 'in light of current scientific knowledge', was to be understood in a 'wide sense'.[638] Building on *Brustle* (and adopting the opinion of Advocate-General Cruz Villalon[639]), the CJEU said that as soon as a human ovum was fertilized it was a human embryo. The Court also said that a non-fertilized human ovum also fell within the definition in so far as it was capable of commencing the process of development of a human being. However, where a non-fertilized ovum does not have the 'inherent capacity of developing into a human being', the mere fact that the organism commences a process of development is not sufficient for it to qualify as a human embryo. Building on this analysis, the Court said that the question of whether a human parthenote was to be treated as a non-patentable human embryo was to be decided by the referring court in light of 'knowledge which is sufficiently tried and tested by international

---

[635] Ibid., [55].   [636] Ibid., [58].

[637] The question referred to the Court of Justice was 'Are unfertilised human ova whose division and further development have been stimulated by parthenogenesis, and which, in contract to fertilised ova, contain only pluripotent cells and are incapable of developing into human beings, included in the term "human embryos" in Article 6(2)(c) of [the Biotech. Dir.]?'

[638] *International Stem Cell Corporation*, Case C-364/13, EU:C:2014:2451 (Grand Chamber), [21], [24], [36].

[639] *International Stem Cell Corporation*, Case C-364/13, EU:C:2014:2104 (Opinion of Advocate-General Cruz Villalon).

medical science'.[640] Given that Judge Henry Carr QC had already held (and the parties agreed) that 'according to current scientific knowledge . . . a human parthenote is not capable of commencing the process of development which leads to a human being', the CJEU effectively ruled that for the purposes of patent law the human parthenote was not a human embryo and, as such, was potentially patentable.[641]

(ii) What is a use of a human embryo?

For the most part, the question of what constitutes a 'use' of a human embryo is straight-forward. For example, in one of the first decisions to consider the exclusion, the Opposition Division at the EPO held that the University of Edinburgh's controversial human embryo patent—which involved removing stem cells from human embryos, genetically manipulating these cells, and cultivating genetically manipulated embryos from them[642]—did not comply with Rule 23d(c) of the EPC 1973 Implementing Regulations (now Rule 28(c) of the EPC 2000 Implementing Regulations).[643] Here, there was no doubt that the invention involved a prohibited use.

One area where there was some uncertainty was in relation to the question of whether the exclusion is limited to situations where the invention directly involves use of an embryo or whether it also extends to activities that precede the invention. This question was addressed by the Enlarged Board of Appeal (EBA) in *Wisconsin Alumni Research Foundation/Use of embryos*.[644] The application in this case was for a cell culture made from primate embryonic stem cells. It was clear that the application covered human embryonic stem cells. It was also clear that to repeat the invention, the skilled person had to start from spare pre-implantation embryos and that they had to destroy them in the process. Given the importance of the area, the Technical Board of Appeal (TBA) referred a number of questions to the EBA for consideration. The EBA began by noting that the human embryo exclusion specifically refers to inventions (rather than claims). This meant that when deciding whether a patent falls foul of the exclusion, it was possible to look beyond the wording of the claims to the technical teaching of the application as a whole. It was also possible to look at how the invention was to be performed. The Board also noted that it was not the fact of patenting itself that was against order public or morality (although, for some, this is an issue); rather, it was the 'performing of the invention, which includes a step (the use involving its destruction of a human embryo) that has to be considered to contravene these steps'.[645] In the words of the Board, 'before human embryonic stem cell cultures can be used, they have to be made'.[646] As the Board noted, to restrict the application of Rule 28(c) to what an applicant had put in their claim would

---

[640] *International Stem Cell Corporation*, Case C-364/13, EU:C:2014:2451 (Grand Chamber), [36].

[641] UK IPO, *Practice Notice: Inventions Involving Human Embryonic Stem Cells* (25 March 2015), [2].

[642] After amendment, the patent no longer includes human or animal embryonic stem cells, but still covers modified human and animal stem cells other than embryonic stem cells.

[643] Patent EP 695,351, granted by EPO December 1999. The patent was allowed to continue in an amended form by the Opposition Division (hearing date 22–24 March 2002). See EPO Press Release, 'Edinburgh Patent Limited after European Patent Office Opposition Hearing' (24 July 2002).

[644] G 2/06 [2009] *OJ EPO* 306. Applied in *Stem Cells/California*, T 552/04 (28 May 2009) (claim 1 was directed to a method of proliferating *in vitro* a clonal population of neural crest stem cells of mammalian origin, which could only be prepared by a method that involved the destruction of human embryos); and *Technion/Culturing stem cells*, T 2221/19 (4 Feb 2014) (all steps preceding the use of a human embryonic stem cell were to be taken into account).

[645] G 2/06 [2009] *OJ EPO* 306, [29]. See also *Asterias/Embryonic stem cells*, T 1441/13 [2015] *EPOR* 78 (method of obtaining embryonic stem cells without the necessary destruction of human embryos fell outside the exception). [646] G 2/06 [2009] *OJ EPO* 306, [22].

have had the undesired consequence of making avoidance of the patenting prohibition merely a matter of clever drafting of the claims. On the facts, the Board held that because the only way to make the human embryonic stem cell culture claimed in the patent was to use human embryos in a way that led to their destruction, the patent fell foul of Rule 28(c).

A similar approach was adopted in *Oliver Brüstle v. Greenpeace*, where the Court of Justice said that an invention was not patentable where the implementation of the invention requires the destruction of human embryos.[647] This was the case even if the claims did not refer to the use of human embryos. The Court also added that it did not matter if the destruction occurred at a stage long before the implementation of the invention; rather, all that mattered was that the implementation of the invention required the destruction of human embryos. If this were not the case, it would have made the provision redundant by allowing a claim to avoid its application by skilful drafting of the claim.[648] On this basis, the Court held that the patent in issue, which related to neural precursor cells and the processes for their production from embryonic stem cells and their use for therapeutic purposes, was excluded.

Interestingly, the Court said that the Directive not only excludes an invention from patentability where the technical teaching that is the subject matter of the patent requires the prior destruction of human embryos, but also excludes inventions that require the use of human embryos as 'base material'.[649] This was the case whatever the stage at which these uses took place and even if the description of the technical teaching claimed did not refer to the use of human embryos. The prohibition on the use of human embryos as a 'base material' is broader than in *Wisconsin Alumni Research Foundation* (which was limited to situations in which the use resulted in the destruction of human embryos).[650]

The decision of the Court of Justice has been adopted by the UK IPO, which has said that it is now UK practice that where the implementation of an invention requires the use of cells that originate from a process that requires the destruction of a human embryo, the invention will be unpatentable.[651] Thus, where the implementation of an invention requires the use of a human embryonic stem cell line, the establishment of which originally required the destruction of a human embryo, the invention will not be patentable. This is not the case, however, in relation to human stem cells that are not derived from human embryos, such as induced pluripotent cells and adult stem cells, which are not caught by the exclusion.

(iii) Industrial or commercial purposes

One of the limitations on the operation of the exclusion is that it only applies when a human embryo is used for *industrial or commercial purposes*. The meaning of this phrase was considered by the Court of Justice in *Brüstle* when considering whether the concept of 'uses of human embryos for industrial or commercial purposes also covers the use of human embryos for the purpose of scientific research'.[652] While the Court of Justice recognized that scientific research needed to be distinguished from industrial or commercial purposes, it added that the use of human embryos for the purpose of (scientific) research that constitutes the subject matter of a patent application cannot be separated from the patent itself. This was because the 'grant of a patent implies, in principle, its

---

[647] *Oliver Brüstle v. Greenpeace*, Case C-34/10, EU:C:2011:669.   [648] Ibid., [50].

[649] Ibid., [52].

[650] See E. Bonadio, 'Biotech Patents and Morality after *Brüstle*' [2012] *EIPR* 433, 442 ('How far must patent officers and judges dig to find an immoral act upon which an invention is based?').

[651] IPO Practice Notice, *Inventions Involving Human Embryonic Stem Cells* (25 March 2015), 3(iii).

[652] *Oliver Brüstle v. Greenpeace*, Case C-34/10, EU:C:2011:669, [41].

industrial or commercial application'.[653] Thus use for industrial and commercial purposes also includes use for scientific research.

The exclusion of uses of human embryos for industrial or commercial purposes does not apply to inventions for therapeutic or diagnostic purposes that are applied to a human embryo.[654] This is because, in this situation, the invention is intended to benefit the embryo, rather than to lead to its destruction.[655] Presumably, this would not be the case, however, if the invention to be applied to the human embryo involved the destruction of a human embryo.

9.2.4 Processes for modifying the genetic identity of animals

The final category of inventions expressly excluded from protection are 'processes for modifying the genetic identity of animals which are likely to cause them suffering without any substantial medical benefit to man or animal, and also animals resulting from such processes', under Rule 28(d) of the EPC 2000 Implementing Regulations (ex Rule 23d(d)) of the EPC 1973 Implementing Regulations and paragraph 3(e) of Schedule A2 to the 1977 Act.[656] The fact that the provision is limited to the modification of animals means that it will not impact upon animal cloning (such as Dolly the sheep).

In the 2006 decision in *Harvard/Transgenic animals*,[657] the Technical Board of Appeal (TBA) was called on to consider whether a patent for transgenic rodents containing an additional cancer gene was excluded from patentability under Rule 23d(d) (now Rule 28(d)). In looking at this provision, the Board stressed that the balancing test in Rule 23d(d) only applies where suffering to animals is likely. This meant that a 'likelihood—but no more than a likelihood of such suffering is necessary to trigger the operation of Rule 23d(d)'.[658] While the balancing test in Rule 23d(d) (now Rule 28(d)) was based on the approach adopted in the *OncoMouse* (T 19/90) decision,[659] the tests differed. In particular, although the test in *OncoMouse* balances the suffering of animals against 'usefulness to mankind', the test in Rule 23d(d) (now Rule 28(d)) balances the suffering of animals against 'substantial medical benefit to man or animal'. It is clear from this that the test in *Harvard/Transgenic animals* was broader than the test that was developed in *OncoMouse*. It was also clear that if 'substantial medical benefit' is established for the purposes of Rule 23d(d), usefulness to mankind under *OncoMouse* T 19/90 would also be established.[660]

The Board also said that Rule 23d(d) (now Rule 28(d)) requires two matters to be evaluated: (i) whether animal suffering is likely; and (ii) whether likely substantial benefit has been established. While the criteria that need to be met may be different, the Board noted that the standard or level of proof to be applied in relation to the two integers of Rule 23d(d) was the same.[661] Since only a likelihood of suffering needs be shown, other matters such as the degree of suffering or the availability of non-animal alternatives do need to be considered. Evidence need not be limited to that available at the filing or priority date, but evidence available thereafter must be directed to the position at that date.[662]

In applying the test set out in Rule 23d(d) (now Rule 28(d)), the Board stressed that there needed to be a 'necessary correspondence between suffering and benefit'.[663] This

---

[653] Ibid.

[654] Ibid., [42]–[43]. Biotech. Dir., Recital 42. UK IPO, *Practice Notice: Inventions Involving Human Embryonic Stem Cells* (25 March 2015), [3(v)].See also *Wisconsin Alumni Research Foundation/Use of embryos*, G 2/06 [2009] *OJ EPO* 306, [25].

[655] *Wisconsin Alumni Research Foundation/Use of embryos*, G 2/06 [2009] *OJ EPO* 306, [27].

[656] This corresponds to Biotech. Dir., Art. 6(2)(d).   [657] T 315/03 [2006] *OJ EPO* 15.

[658] Ibid., 40–1.   [659] Ibid.   [660] Ibid., 42, 53–4.

[661] Ibid., 62.   [662] Ibid., 50–1.   [663] Ibid., 47.

was based on the understanding that Rule 23d(d) provided that a patent should only extend to those animals the suffering of which was balanced by a medical benefit. Taking a hypothetical example, the Board said:

> [I]f likely suffering to both cats and lions was established, it would none the less be contrary to Rule 23d(d) EPC [1973 Regs] to allow claims which encompassed both cats and lions when the only established likely medical benefit arose in relation to the use of cats.[664]

The impact that the principal of correspondence is able to play in limiting the scope of what may be patented, which is reminiscent of the requirement for sufficiency of disclosure, is evident from the way in which the TBA dealt with the main and auxiliary requests in *Harvard/Transgenic animals*. The main request considered by the Board was for 'transgenic rodents'. On the basis that the request embraced all animals within the taxonomic order *Rodentia*, the Board said that 'suffering will—and must—be present in the case of every such animal—not just mice but also squirrels, beavers, porcupines, and every other rodent'.[665] Applying this logic to the case in hand, the Board noted that no evidence had been produced that showed that there was a likelihood that a substantial medical benefit to man or animal would arise from applying the claimed process to all rodents, or indeed to any animals of the order *Rodentia* apart from mice. That is, there was no evidence that the medical benefits for cancer research that were meant to arise from the invention applied to all rodents. On this basis, the Board held that the likelihood of substantial medical benefit required by Rule 23d(d) had not been substantiated.[666] Given that animal suffering was 'not just a likelihood but an inevitable consequence of the very purpose of the patent', the Board concluded that the main request failed the balancing test of Rule 23d(d) and was therefore refused under Article 53(a).

The fate of the main request in *Harvard/Transgenic animals* needs to be contrasted with that of the auxiliary request, which was limited to 'mice' rather than 'rodents'. As with the main request, the Board noted that one of the inevitable consequences of the invention was that it would cause harm and suffering to mice. In contrast to the main claim, however, the applicant was able to produce evidence that showed that the invention (as defined in the auxiliary request) did have medical benefits. On this basis, the Board said that the subject matter of the auxiliary claims (which were limited to transgenic mice) satisfied the test in Rule 23d(d) (now Rule 28(d)). The Board then went on to consider the fate of the auxiliary application under Article 53(a) proper, which, as we saw earlier, was found not to apply to the claim for transgenic mice.

---

[664] Ibid.   [665] Ibid.   [666] Ibid., 63.

18

NOVELTY

1 INTRODUCTION

Both the Patents Act 1977 and the 2000 European Patents Convention (EPC 2000) stipulate that for an invention to be patentable it must be 'new'.[1] An invention is said to be new if it does not form part of the 'state of the art'.[2] The 'state of the art' is defined very broadly to include all matter that is available anywhere in the world before the priority date of the invention. Where an invention is disclosed or 'anticipated' by the state of the art, a patent will not be granted or, if it has been granted (because the prior art escaped the attention of the examiner), the patent is liable to be revoked.[3]

Novelty requires that the invention be *quantitatively* different from what has been disclosed previously—that is, the technical information disclosed by the patent must not already be available to the public. In this sense, novelty is different from the requirement that to be patentable an invention must have involved an inventive step (or be non-obvious), which is basically a *qualitative* examination to ascertain whether the contribution is creative enough to warrant a monopoly.

By ensuring that patents are not granted for products or processes that are already known, novelty helps to ensure that patents are not used to stop people from doing what they had already done before the patent was granted.[4] As we will see, this so-called 'right to work' argument has been modified as a result of changes in the way in which novelty is determined.[5] Another factor that is used to justify the novelty requirement relates to

---

[1] PA 1977, s. 1(1)(a); EPC 2000, Art. 52(1) (ex EPC 1973, Art. 52(1)).

[2] PA 1977, s. 2(1); EPC 2000, Art. 54(1) (ex EPC 1973, Art. 54(1)). PA 1977, s. 130(7), provides that s. 2 is framed so as to have, as nearly as practicable, the same effect in the United Kingdom as the corresponding provisions of the EPC.

[3] PA 1977, s. 72(1)(a); EPC 2000, Art. 138(1)(a). Lack of novelty is a ground of opposition at the EPO under EPC 2000, Art. 100(a).

[4] Prior to the 1623 Statute of Monopolies, the Crown granted patents for activities that had already been carried out, one of the most infamous examples being for the buying and selling of playing cards. This meant that those who were already practising the activities could no longer continue to do so. Not surprisingly, such persons were aggrieved. See *Clothworkers of Ipswich Case* (1614) *Godb R* 252, 78 *ER* 147; *Darcy v. Allin* (1602) 74 *ER* 1131. In part, the 1624 Statute of Monopolies was introduced to overcome these problems.

[5] On the right to work, see *Windsurfing International* [1995] *RPC* 59, 77; B. Reid, 'The Right to Work' [1982] *EIPR* 6. With respect to registered designs, see *Falk v. Jacobwitz* (1944) 61 *RPC* 116, 123.

the overall rationale for the grant of patents.[6] More specifically, it is argued that the public is only willing to pay the costs (or monopoly profits) of patenting if they are able to get access to information that would not otherwise have been available to them. To adopt the contract analogy that is often used to justify and explain patents, novelty ensures that the inventor provides the consideration necessary to warrant the patent being granted in the first place.

While the Patents Act 1977 retains many of the basic principles and rationales that have long been a feature of British law on novelty, Britain's entry into the EPC introduced some important changes in the way in which the novelty requirement is applied in the United Kingdom. One of these relates to the fact that the 1977 Act and the EPC operate on the principle of 'objective novelty'—that is an attempt, where possible, to avoid subjective judgements (which are seen to lead to uncertainty).[7] Perhaps the clearest example of this is that both British and European patent law have adopted the principle of 'absolute novelty'.[8] This means that the novelty of an invention is judged against all of the information that is available at the priority date of the invention, irrespective of where the information was released or the form in which it was released.[9]

Given the broad nature of the knowledge base against which the novelty of inventions is assessed, it is not surprising that it has been criticized on the basis that by allowing obscure materials to anticipate, absolute novelty produces harsh results. In its favour, however, absolute novelty is said to provide a 'bright line' test, thus 'avoiding subjectivity and most questions of degree'.[10] Given the sophisticated information tools that are currently available to researchers, there may be good reasons for providing disincentives to prevent the duplication of research that has already been carried out.[11] Another notable change in the post-1977 law is that in determining whether an invention is novel, the courts have placed increased attention on the information function of the patent system. As we will see, this has had important consequences for so-called 'secret' or 'inherent' uses, and their ability to anticipate.

The task of determining whether an invention is novel can conveniently be broken down into three separate questions, as follows.

(i)   What is the invention?

(ii) What information is disclosed by the prior art?

(iii) In light of (i) and (ii), is the invention novel—that is, is the invention part of the state of the art?

We will deal with each of these in turn. After doing so, we will look at three specific types of invention and the problems that have arisen when assessing their novelty.

---

[6] At the EPO, the purpose of the novelty requirement is to prevent the prior art from being re-patented: *Bayer/Diastereomers*, T 12/81 [1982] *OJ EPO*, [5] *Bayer/Amino acid derivatives*, T 12/90 [1991] *EPOR* 312, [2.6].

[7] See *Genentech's Patent* [1989] *RPC* 147, 198 (CA), 203 (Purchas LJ).

[8] Strasbourg, Art. 4. France and Italy already had such a standard.

[9] This is wider than under pre-1977 law, especially as regards the requirement of worldwide novelty. In other ways, it may be narrower, since the pre-1977 condition 'having regard to what was known and used' had no specific requirement that the use make 'the invention' available to the public. Some countries require novelty within the territory, exclude old documents, or confine the state of the art to printed documents. For an argument in favour of a more 'realistic standard', see Note, 'Prior Art in the Patent Law' (1959) 73 *Harv L Rev* 369.

[10] *Milliken Denmark AS v. Walk Off Mat* [1996] *FSR* 292.

[11] R. Merges, *Patent Law and Policy* (1992), 192–4 (examining the rationale behind the novelty doctrine from the point of view of its impact on search activities).

2 WHAT IS THE INVENTION?

Before being in a position to determine whether an invention is new, it is first necessary to identify what the alleged invention is.[12] While the way in which an invention is characterized often plays a key role in shaping many aspects of the novelty examination and consequently the fate of many inventions,[13] it has received very little attention.

3 WHAT INFORMATION IS DISCLOSED BY THE PRIOR ART?

Once the technical features of an invention have been identified, it is then necessary to ascertain the nature of the information that has been disclosed by the prior art. In order to do this, it is first necessary to ask: what material forms part of the state of the art? Once this has been ascertained (and the prior art that is relevant to the invention in question has been identified), it is then possible to determine the nature of the information (or teaching) that is disclosed by the prior art.

3.1 WHAT IS THE STATE OF THE ART?

The state of the art is defined in extremely broad and inclusive terms to include all matter (whether a product or process, information about either, or anything else) that, at the priority date of the application in question, has been made available to the public (whether in the United Kingdom or elsewhere) by written or oral description, by use, or in any other way.[14] There are a number of features of the way in which the state of the art is defined that should be borne in mind.

3.1.1 No geographical limits

There are no geographical limits on where the state of the art must be disclosed. As such, it includes information that is available *anywhere* in the world.

3.1.2 No restrictions on the mode of disclosure

Information will become part of the state of the art irrespective of the way in which it was made available to the public. Consequently, information may become part of the state of the art as a result of written descriptions (such as previously published patents[15] or journal articles[16]), through past uses,[17] exhibitions, sales,[18] or by oral communications

---

[12] *Merrell Dow Pharmaceuticals v. Norton* [1996] *RPC* 76, 82 (HL); *Evans Medical Patent* [1998] *RPC* 517.

[13] *Glaverbel v. British Coal* [1994] *RPC* 443; [1995] *RPC* 255 (CA); *CIPA*, [2.03].

[14] PA 1977, s. 2(2); EPC 2000, Art. 54(2).

[15] T 877/98 [2001] *OJ EPO* (Special edition) 3, 20 (a patent becomes part of the public domain on publication in the relevant Official Journal, not upon notification of the decision to grant).

[16] This includes a magazine available to the public one day before the priority date, but not a doctoral thesis that has been placed in a library archive and not yet been indexed: *Research Corporation/Publication*, T 381/87 [1990] *OJ EPO* 213. See also *Exxon Mobil*, T 314/99 (21 June 2001).

[17] *Luchtenberg/Rear-view mirror*, T 84/83 [1979–85] *EPOR* 793, 796. On previous use as prior art under the EPC, see A. Castro, 'Prior Use as Prior Art and Evidence Thereof' (1996) 27 *IIC* 190; under French law, see S. Mandelo, 'Prior Use under French Law' (1996) 27 *IIC* 203.

[18] *Telemecanique/Power supply unit*, T 482/89 [1992] *OJ EPO* 646.

(although, in the last case, difficult evidential questions may arise[19]). If the information is accessible, then its age, obscurity, duration, language, or location is irrelevant.[20] (As we will see later, limits are imposed in the case of confidential information and inventions disclosed at international exhibitions.) Similarly, there are no minimum requirements on how widely the information must be published for it to be disclosed. Thus a single copy of a document, or the sale of a single item, will be sufficient for the information to become part of the state of the art.[21]

3.1.3 Potential, rather than actual, disclosure

Material is factually available (and part of the state of the art) if it is open to or capable of being accessed by the public. As such, there is no need to demonstrate that anyone *actually* had access to the information in question; all that matters is that had they wanted to do so, they could have accessed the information.[22]

3.1.4 Priority date

Both the Patents Act 1977 and the EPC provide that the date at which the novelty is to be assessed is the 'priority date' of the invention in question.[23] The upshot of this is that the state of the art only includes information that is made available to the public *before* the priority date of the invention in question. While the priority date is normally the date on which an application was filed,[24] in some cases the priority date is earlier[25] (notably where an application is made in a Paris Convention country during the previous 12 months).

In contrast with some other patent regimes,[26] applicants for UK and European patents are not provided with a 'grace period'—that is, a period prior to filing during which they are able to practise their inventions.[27] Consequently, patents are frequently anticipated and thus rendered invalid for want of novelty as a result of the applicant's own acts and disclosures.[28] The priority date is thus important not only because it is the date when

---

[19] *Hooper Trading/T-cell growth factor*, T 877/90 [1993] *EPOR* 6; *CIPA*, [2.06]. See also *Genetech/Immunoglobulin preparations*, T 1212/97 [2002] *EPOR* 283 (discussing the problems in interpreting the information provided by a lecture given to an audience of more than 100 people).

[20] *Windsurfing International* [1995] *RPC* 59 (CA).

[21] *Fomento v. Mentmore* [1956] *RPC* 87; *Monsanto (Brignac's) Application* [1971] *RPC* 153 (a publication placed in the hands of salesmen was held to have been made available to the public, since there was no fetter on their use of that information). See also *Van Wonterghem*, T 1022/99 (10 April 2001) (sale of object to a single customer). However, supply to a manufacturer is likely to be treated as in confidence: *Strix v. Otter* [1995] *RPC* 607, 633–4. It should be noted that supply will make the invention available only if it reveals it: *Pall Corp v. Commercial Hydraulics* [1990] *FSR* 329.

[22] *Japan Styrene Paper/Foam particles*, T 444/88 [1993] *EPOR* 241. There is no requirement that a person be likely to examine the document: *Hoechst/Polyvinylester dispersion*, T 93/89 [1992] *OJ EPO* 718, [1992] *EPOR* 155; *Woven Plastics v. British Ropes* [1970] *FSR* 47; *Harris v. Rothwell* (1887) 4 *RPC* 225.

[23] PA 1977, s. 2(1); EPC 2000, Art. 54(2).   [24] PA 1977, s. 5(1); EPC 2000 Regs, r. 40.

[25] The law facilitates this by allowing for priority not only from full filing, but also from early filing: PA 1977, ss 14–15; EPC 2000 Regs, r. 40. On a situation in which early PCT filing is claimed under EPC 1973, Arts 87–88 (now EPC 2000, Arts 87–88), see *Requirement for claiming priority of same invention*, G/98 [2001] *OJ EPO* 413 (earlier priority could be claimed from an earlier application only if the skilled person could derive the subject matter of the later claim directly and unambiguously from the previous application as a whole).

[26] A grace period is provided by US law—35 *USC* §102(b)—in which the applicant's own acts are deemed to fall outside the state of the art.

[27] The Intergovernmental Conference of Member States of the EPO called for the EPO to examine the conditions under which a grace period should be introduced into the EPC. See F. Blakemore, 'Grace Periods in European Patent Law' (1998) 106 *Patent World* 18.

[28] See *Fomento* [1956] *RPC* 87; *Lux Traffic Controls v. Pike Signals* [1993] *RPC* 107, 134–5; *Research Corporation/Publication*, T 381/87 [1990] *OJ EPO* 213.

novelty is assessed, but also because it is the date from when inventors are able to exploit their inventions without jeopardizing any potential patents.[29]

3.1.5 Material specifically included within the state of the art

While, as a general rule, patent law provides that the state of the art only includes material in the public domain before the priority date of the invention, an exception is made in relation to patent applications that are published after the priority date of the application in suit. More specifically, the relevant laws provide that in addition to the matter published before the priority date of the invention, the state of the art also includes applications for other patents that are published after the priority date of the invention in question, but nonetheless have a priority date earlier than the application in question.[30] The reason why the state of the art is (effectively) backdated in this way is to avoid the possibility of 'double patenting'—that is, of patents being granted to different applicants for the same invention.[31] This potential problem is created by the fact that there is a time lag between the date of filing, which is normally the priority date, and the early publication of the application, when the application becomes part of the state of the art.

3.1.6 Material specifically excluded from the state of the art

There are two situations where material in the public domain is not taken into account when assessing novelty of inventions. The first is where the information was obtained unlawfully or was disclosed as a result of a breach of confidence.[32] In a sense, this reaffirms the old principle that material is only available to the public if the recipient is free in law and equity to divulge its contents.[33] The second situation where

---

[29] *Asahi Kasei Kogyo* [1991] *RPC* 485 (HL), 529 (Lord Oliver). In the United States, experimental use will not invalidate a patent even though the invention was in public use or on sale more than a year before the priority date.

[30] PA 1977, ss 2(3), 130(3); EPC 2000, Arts 54(3), 87(4). The test for novelty under PA 1977, s. 2(3), is the same as under s. 2(2): *SmithKline Beecham plc's Patent* [2003] *RPC* 114, [19]–[37] (CA); *Synthon BV v. SmithKline Beecham* [2002] *EWHC* 1172 (Pat). Article 54(3) does not treat existing national rights as part of the state of the art, so that a European patent (UK) would be granted at the EPO but not in the United Kingdom where the existing national right would anticipate: *Mobil/Admissibility*, T 550/88 [1992] *OJ EPO* 117, [1990] *EPOR* 391 (construing the term 'European patent application' in Art. 54(3) as excluding previous national applications, by reference to Arts 93 and 139); *Woolard's Application* [2002] *RPC* 767; *Zbinden's Application* [2002] *RPC* (13) 310 (discussing when a withdrawn application forms part of the state of the art). The effect of this is that the state of the art for a European application or patent now includes all previous European applications irrespective of their designation. The PA 1977 was amended accordingly. For discussion of so-called poisonous priorities (where an applicant's priority application is used against one of their subsequent applications), see *Infineum/Use of cold flow improvers*, G 1/15 [2017] *OJ EPO* A82 (EBA) (affirming partial priority).

[31] The section, however, may not always avoid double patenting, because the disclosure will anticipate only if it is enabling: *Asahi Kasei Kogyo* [1991] *RPC* 485 (HL).

[32] PA 1977, s. 2(4)(a)(b); EPC 2000, Art. 55(1)(a) (ex EPC 1973, Art. 55(1)(a)). Relevant examples include disclosure by employees (*Robert Bosch/Electrical machine*, T 1085/92 [1996] *EPOR* 381), submission of an article to a refereed journal (*Research Corporation/Publication*, T 381/87 [1989] *EPOR* 138), and disclosures at a meeting with a manufacturer (*Macor Marine Systems/Confidentiality agreement*, T 830/90 [1994] *OJ EPO* 713; *Telecommunications/Antioxidant*, T 173/83 [1987] *OJ EPO* 465. Cf. *Unilever/Deodorant detergent*, T 585/92 [1996] *OJ EPO* 129. On the timing of the disclosure, see *University Patents/Materials and methods for herpes simplex virus vaccination*, G 3/98 [2001] *OJ EPO* 62. See also *Aga Medical Corporation v. Occlutech* [2014] *EWHC* 2506 (Pat) (no presumption of confidentiality simply because of clinical trial).

[33] *Humpherson v. Syer* (1887) 4 *RPC* 407; *Bristol Myers Application* [1969] *RPC* 146; *James Industries' Application* [1987] *RPC* 235; T 818/93 and T 480/95 [1997] *OJ EPO* 20–1; *Robert Bosch/Electrical machine*, T 1085/92 [1996] *EPOR* 381; *Research Foundation/Translation inhibitor*, T 838/97 (14 November 2001) (oral presentation of an invention to a conference of 100 experts, who were told that the information could not be used without specific authorization, was a private communication that did not form part of the public domain).

information is excluded from the state of the art is where the disclosure was due to or made in consequence of the inventor displaying the invention at an 'international exhibition'.[34]

It is important to note that the exclusions only apply to disclosures that are made within the six-month period immediately preceding the date when the claim for the invention in question was filed.[35] Any disclosures that are made outside of this period will not be caught by the exceptions and will thus form part of the state of the art for the purposes of assessing novelty.

3.1.7 Information on the Internet

One of the criticisms made of the British patent system in the eighteenth and nineteenth centuries was that it was often very difficult to find the relevant patent information, which was often effectively hidden within the chaos of the (then) Patent Office. Similar problems potentially arise today as a result of the rapid increase in the amount of scientific and technical information that is available online—a situation that will only increase with the rapid push towards open-access scientific publishing. While earlier suggestions[36] that online publication required a higher standard of proof have not been followed in subsequent decisions, it has been recognized that in so far as internet publications could be changed in a way that were not easily traceable, online anticipation did present special problems.[37] As the Technical Board of Appeal (TBA) noted in *Philips*,[38] the size and nature of the Internet poses a number of potential problems, not least of which is the threat of hidden publications—that is, a document made available in theory, but hidden in practice because of its obscure location. This potentially gave authors the power to decide whether or not, and if so, when a document might be used to anticipate a patent. It also potentially undermines legal certainty. The Board said the public policy in preventing hidden publications means that in 'order to conclude that the document is available to the public', it is not enough for a document merely to be placed online; rather, it must also be shown that 'direct and unambiguous access to it by known means and methods is possible'.[39] While the TBA stressed that this question had to be considered on a case-by-case basis, it did say that for a document on the Internet that was accessible only via a specific URL to be disclosed to the public, the document had to: (i) be able to be found with the help of a public web search engine by using one or more keywords all related to the essence of the content of the document, and (ii) remain accessible at that URL for long enough a period of time that a member of the public might 'have direct and unambiguous access to the document'.[40] Exceptionally, the Board said that the URL may be so 'straightforward or

---

[34] PA 1977, s. 2(4)(c); EPC 2000, Art. 55(1)(b) (ex EPC 1973, Art. 55(1)(b)). 'International exhibitions' are defined in PA 1977, s. 130, and EPC 2000, Art. 55(1)(b), as relating to the Convention on International Exhibitions signed at Paris in 1928. See A. Serjeant, 'International Exhibitions' (1985–86) 15 *CIPAJ* 319.

[35] PA 1977, s. 2(4), refers to the period preceding the application date. According to the EBA, under EPC 2000, Art. 55(1), the 'relevant date is the date of the actual filing of the European patent application; the date of priority is not to be taken into account in calculating this period': *University Patents*, G 3/98 [2001] *OJ EPO* 62 (EBA).   [36] *Konami/Internet citations*, T 1134/06 (16 January 2007).

[37] *Bouygues/Sécurisation d'un accès à une ressource numérique* (21 May 2014), T 286/10 (21 May 2004). See also *Notice from the European Patent Office concerning internet citations*, [2009] *OJ EPO*, 456, *EPO Guidelines*, G-IV, [7.5.2].

[38] *Philips/Public availability of documents on the World Wide Web*, T 1553/06 [2012] *EPOR* 383; *Philips/Public availability of an email transmitted via the Internet*, T 2/09 [2012] *EPOR* 431 (information sent via email does not form part of the state of the art).

[39] *Philips/Public availability of documents on the World Wide Web*, T 1553/06 [2012] *EPOR* 383, [6.5.4].

[40] Ibid., [6.7.3].

predictable that it could be readily guessed'.[41] In this situation, a document available at the URL would form part of the state of the art.

3.2 WHAT INFORMATION IS DISCLOSED BY THE PRIOR ART?

The information disclosed by the prior art is restricted to the information that a person skilled in the art is able to derive from the prior art in question. In considering the way in which the prior art is interpreted by a person skilled in the art, it is useful to distinguish between situations where the relevant prior art consists of a document and those where it comprises a product.[42]

3.2.1 Interpreting documents

Documents are interpreted as if they were being read at the date of their publication[43] and not the priority date of the invention or the date of trial. Given that the act of interpretation usually takes place after the date when the document was published, it is important that documents are neither read retrospectively,[44] nor construed in light of events that have taken place since publication (notably the creation of the invention in question). The information available is that which a person skilled in the art would derive from reading the document in light of common general knowledge. In this respect, the skilled person has a limited ability to extend the meaning of the document beyond that which would be provided by a literal reading.[45] In line with this, the person skilled in the art is able to correct obvious mistakes, inconsistencies, or errors that may exist in the documents.[46]

Another important rule of interpretation is that the information must be drawn from a single document. This means that it is not possible to combine together (or 'mosaic') separate items in the prior art. In a similar vein, it is not normally possible to combine elements from within a single document.[47] The only occasion on which it is permissible to combine documents together is where a primary document inevitably leads to a second document. That is, where the person skilled in the art would read different documents as if they were one.[48]

3.2.2 Interpreting products

A number of special rules have been formulated to deal with situations where the prior art consists of a product, such as a drug or a machine, that has been released on the market.[49] In circumstances where the product is the same as the invention, few problems arise. The

[41] Ibid., [6.6.6].

[42] T 270/89 in G. Keller, 'Summary of Some Recent Decisions at the EPO' [1993] *JPTOS* 237.

[43] *General Tire & Rubber v. Firestone Tyre & Rubber* [1972] *RPC* 457; *Minnesota Mining v. Bondina* [1973] *RPC* 491; *Tektronix/Scottky barrier diode* [1995] *EPOR* 384. Cf. questions of sufficiency of disclosure where documents are read at the priority date of the invention.

[44] *Rhone-Poulenc/Taxoids*, T 77/97 [1998] *EPOR* 256.

[45] See *Bayer/Chimeric gene*, T 890/02 [2005] *OJ EPO* 497.

[46] *Toshiba*, T 26/85 [1990] *OJ EPO* 22; *Scanditronix/Radiation beam collimation*, T 56/87 [1990] *OJ EPO* 188; *ICI/Latex composition*, T 77/87 [1990] *OJ EPO* 280.

[47] *Draco/Xanthines*, T 7/86 [1988] *OJ EPO* 381; *Scanditronix/Radiation beam collimation*, T 56/87 [1990] *OJ EPO* 188.

[48] If the disclosure reveals one part of the product and another disclosure, another element, there is no anticipation: *Bayer/Diastereomers*, T 12/81 [1982] *OJ EPO* 296; *Texaco/Reaction injection moulded elatomer*, T 279/89 [1992] *EPOR* 294, 298; *Amoco Corporation/Alternative claims*, T 153/85 [1988] *OJ EPO* 1, [1988] *EPOR* 116, 123; *ICI/Latex composition*, T 77/87 [1990] *OJ EPO* 280, [1989] *EPOR* 246, 251.

[49] *Quantel v. Spaceward Microsystems* [1990] *RPC* 83.

task of interpretation becomes more problematic, however, where the technical information necessary to anticipate an invention is not immediately apparent from looking at the product, but can only be obtained if the product is analysed.[50]

It has long been recognized that the information disclosed by a product is not limited to the information that is immediately apparent from looking at the product. Importantly, the information available to the public also includes the information that a skilled person would be able to derive from the product if they were to analyse or examine it.[51] The person skilled in the art is able to make use of the analytical skills and techniques commonly available in the field before the priority date of the invention. This means that if the skilled person works in a field in which reverse engineering is commonly practised, then a machine placed on sale would reveal all of the information that a person skilled in the art would be able to obtain if they were to reverse-engineer the machine.

Any information that is obtained as a result of an analysis undertaken by a person skilled in the art must be obtained without undue burden or without the need to exercise any additional inventive effort.[52] If it were necessary for the person skilled in the art to embark on inventive or exploratory research to reveal the information in question, the information would not form part of the state of the art. The situation is the same where information is so submerged in a prior art document that it cannot be understood by a skilled person using their common general knowledge; in this case, the information would not form part of the state of the art.[53]

The amount of information that is revealed by an examination depends on the type of analysis undertaken.[54] This would vary with things such as the skills of the researchers in question, and the time and money spent on the examination.[55] Given this, the question has arisen as to whether limits should be placed on the type of (hypothetical) analysis that is undertaken. Following the principle of objective novelty, subjective factors such as the cost of carrying out the analysis or the time taken to find the relevant information are *not* taken into account when determining the nature of the information revealed by a product;[56] neither is it necessary that there be particular reasons that prompted the skilled person to examine the composition of the product in the first place.[57] The question is *could*, and not *would*, the product be analysed by the person skilled in the art?

---

[50] See L. Tournroth, 'Prior Use' (1997) 28 *IIC* 800, 800–1; Paterson, [10–07]. In *Lux Traffic Controls v. Pike Signals* [1993] *RPC* 107, Aldous J distinguished between cases of prior use in which the public had access to the invention and were able to handle it, and prior uses that allowed the public only to observe the object. The circumstances in which each would anticipate would differ, disclosure being much more likely in cases of handling. This, however, was not conclusive. In *Luchtenberg/Rear-view mirror*, T 84/83 [1979–85] *EPOR* 793, 796, the TBA accepted that the use of a mirror attached to a car in public for six months might be revealed if all aspects were disclosed. Cf. *Pfennigabsatz* [1966] *GRUR* 484, 486.

[51] *Thomson/Electron tube*, T 953/90 [1998] *EPOR* 415.

[52] *Availability to the Public Decision*, G 1/92 [1993] *OJ EPO* 277. Undue burden, however, seems to carry with it a subjective element. In *Packard/Liquid scintillatia*, T 952/92 [1997] *EPOR* 457, the TBA argued that the reference to 'undue burden' in G 1/92 was *obiter* and that the issue of burden in terms of time or work was irrelevant. See also *Siemens/Large scale vehicle*, T 1410/14 (14 October 2015) (features on a car test-driven in public that 'had been visible only briefly' were only publically available if it could be shown beyond doubt that the features had been clearly and directly apparent to the skilled person for that short time).

[53] *H. Lundbeck A/S v. Norpharma SpA* [2001] *EWHC* 907.

[54] It also depends on the general nature of the article: *Wesley Jessen Corp. v. Coopervision* [2003] *RPC* 355, 384 (the skilled addressee would have 'all the information he might require' from a contact lens in the public domain, which was 'not a product of high technical sophistication').

[55] *Novartis/Erythro-compounds*, T 990/96 [1998] *OJ EPO* 489 (disclosure for chemical compounds).

[56] *Packard/Liquid scintillatia*, T 952/92 [1997] *EPOR* 457.

[57] *Availability to the Public Decision*, G 1/92 [1993] *EPOR* 241.

4 IS THE INVENTION NOVEL?

Once the invention under examination and the information disclosed by the prior art have been identified, it is then possible to determine whether the invention is new. In many cases, particularly where the prior art and the invention are identical or the prior art leads directly to the patented invention, it will be relatively easy to determine whether an invention has been made available to the public. This task becomes more problematic, however, where there is a gap between the prior art and the invention. The reason for this is that the same thing may be known by the public in a number of different ways: things may be described in terms of what they look like, how they are made, what they do, the problems they solve, what they are made of, how much they cost, and so on.[58] This gives rise to the question: how does a patent need to be described for it to be known by the public? Put differently, how specific must a disclosure be for an invention to be 'known' or 'made available' to the public?[59] For example, will a chemical invention be anticipated if the formula of the chemical structure of the invention is made available to the public?[60] Or is it necessary for the formula and the means by which the formula is implemented both to be available to the public?

After some uncertainty,[61] it is now clear that an invention will lack novelty if at its priority date it has been 'made available' to the public.[62] Drawing upon the principle that patents should only be granted if the public has been provided with useful information, an invention is said to have been made available to the public if there has been an 'enabling disclosure'.[63] Following the House of Lords' decision in *Synthon BV v. SmithKline Beecham*,[64] it is clear that 'enabling disclosure' consists of two separate requirements that need to be satisfied if an objection of lack of novelty is to succeed. These are the requirements of *prior disclosure* and *enablement*. As Lord Hoffmann said in *Synthon*, it is important to keep in mind that disclosure and enablement are distinct concepts, each of which has to be satisfied and each of which has its own rules. He also stressed that there would be a serious risk of confusion if the two concepts were not kept separate. Before looking at

---

[58] *Merrell Dow Pharmaceuticals v. Norton* [1996] RPC 76, 88 (HL). As Lord Hoffmann reminds us, this is essentially an epistemological question: what does it mean for the public to know something so that it can anticipate? The problem is that there is often a marked difference between something being 'known' by the general public and something being known for the purposes of patent law; hence Lord Hoffmann's comments about the specific epistemological basis of patent law. In a similar vein, the TBA said that 'the concept of novelty must not be given such a narrow interpretation that only what has already been described in the same terms is prejudicial to it ... There are many ways of describing a substance': *Bayer/Diastereomers*, T 12/81 [1979–85] EPOR B–308, 312; *Hoechst/Thiochloroformates*, T 198/84 [1985] OJ EPO 209.

[59] While this question would have been relatively easy to answer if anticipation had been limited to circumstances in which the disclosure and the invention were identical, it is not necessary that an invention be replicated exactly in the prior art or that it be described in identical terms, for a disclosure to destroy novelty. A mere difference in wording or phraseology will not substantiate a claim to novelty. 'The term "made available" clearly goes beyond literal or diagrammatical description, and implies a communication, express or implicit, of technical information by other means as well. The inevitability of the outcome requires proof beyond reasonable doubt': *Allied Signal/Polyolefin fiber*, T 793/93 [1996] EPOR 104, 109.

[60] Similarly, would a patent for quinine be anticipated by the fact that Amazonian Indians have known for some time that the spirit of the cinchona bark possessed certain qualities that made it good for treating fevers?

[61] See, e.g., *PLG Research v. Ardon International* [1993] FSR 197, 218.

[62] Available 'carries with it the idea that, for lack of novelty to be found, all the technical features of the claimed invention in combination must have been communicated to the public, or laid open for inspection': *Mobil Oil/Friction reducing additive*, G 2/88 [1990] EPOR 73; *Chemie Linz/Reinforced channels*, T 242/85 [1988] EPOR 77.

[63] The same requirement operates in Germany: *Fluoron* (1989) 21 IIC 736.   [64] [2006] RPC (10) 323.

what is meant by 'disclosure' and 'enablement', it is important to note that in some situations, the same disclosure may satisfy both requirements. As Lord Hoffmann said:

> [T]he prior art description may be sufficient in itself to enable the ordinary skilled man, armed with general knowledge of the art, to perform the subject matter of the invention. Indeed, when the prior art is a product, the product itself, though dumb, may be enabling if it is 'available to the public' and a person skilled in the art can discover its composition or internal structure without undue burden.[65]

In other cases, however, different factors will be used to show disclosure and enablement. The difference between 'disclosure' and 'enablement' is clear from the facts in *Synthon*. The patent in question identified and claimed a crystalline chemical. The prior art contained both a description of such a product and a recipe for making it. If the skilled person tried to follow the recipe using their ordinary skill and knowledge, they would have failed. The recipe as such was not enabling. But even without it, the skilled man would have been able, with a little trial and experiment, to make the described product. So the prior art satisfied both the 'necessary result' and the 'enablement' requirements.[66]

4.1 DISCLOSURE

The first point that must be established to show that a patent has been anticipated is that there has been a 'disclosure'. Under what is sometimes called the 'reverse-infringement test', prior art will disclose a patent if it reveals subject matter that, if performed, would necessarily (or inevitably) result in an infringement of the patent.[67] With disclosure, there is no room for experiment. While the person skilled in the art is permitted to draw upon the general knowledge common to the field, the prior art must place that person in a position where they are able to work the invention without the need for further information, or to engage in new experiments, or for some other additional inventive activity.[68] As the Court of Appeal said in *General Tire*,[69] the prior disclosure must have planted the flag on the invention. In order for a combination from a single piece of prior art to anticipate, there must be clear and unambiguous teaching that the relevant combination can be made.[70] If it is an inevitable consequence of following the information disclosed in the prior art that the invention is made, the invention will have been disclosed.[71] If the instructions probably, normally, or only sometimes produce the product, however, there will be no anticipation.[72]

---

[65] Ibid., [29], citing *Availability to the Public*, G 1/92 [1993] *EPOR* 241 (EBA), [1.4].

[66] See *Ferag AG v. Muller Martini* [2007] *EWCA Civ* 15, [10].

[67] *Synthon* [2006] *RPC* (10) 323, [22], [24] (HL). It seems that this is judged on the basis of normal or purposive interpretation, rather than under the doctrine of equivalents: *Generics (UK) Ltd (t/a Mylan) v. Yeda Research and Development Company* [2017] *EWHC* 2629, [161]–[167]. On the doctrine of equivalents, see Chapter 22, section 3.1, p. 656.

[68] *Hills v. Evans* (1862) 31 *LJ Ch* 457, 45 *ER* 1195 (HL).   [69] *General Tire v. Firestone* [1972] *RPC* 457.

[70] *Glass v. Freyssinet* [2015] *EWHC* 2972, [49] (IPEC).

[71] See *Inhale Therapeutic Systems v. Quadrant Healthcare* [2002] *RPC* 419, in which Laddie J reviewed his earlier judgment in *Evans Medical Patent* [1998] *RPC* 517; *SmithKline Beecham PLC's Patent (No. 2)* [2003] *RPC* 607, 631.

[72] On inevitable disclosure, see *General Tire v. Firestone* [1972] *RPC* 457, 458–6. Inevitably, this has been defined to mean in 99 cases out of 100 (*Fomento* [1956] *RPC* 87) and 'tantamount to 100 per cent probability' (*Allied Signal/Polyolefin fiber*, T 793/93 [1996] *EPOR* 104). It seems that, at the EPO, the inevitability of the disclosure needs to be satisfied 'beyond all reasonable doubt': *Allied Signal*, ibid.

The question of whether a disclosure enables the public to work an invention is decided objectively.[73] Drawing upon the principle that patent infringement does not require that a person needs to know that they are infringing, Lord Hoffmann said that knowledge does not play a role when determining whether there had been a disclosure. Instead, all that matters is that the subject matter described in the prior disclosure is capable of being performed and is such that, if performed, it would result in the patent being infringed. This means that there is no need to show that a member of the public actually worked the invention, nor that they were aware of its existence. In these circumstances, there is no need for the person skilled in the art to know that they are producing the product in question; all that matters is that the prior art discloses information that, if followed, inevitably leads to the invention. To use the analogy often used in this context, 'if the recipe which inevitably produces the substance is part of the state of the art, so is the substance made by that recipe'.[74] It does not matter that the cook was ignorant of the fact that they were producing the product.

4.2 ENABLEMENT

The second point that needs to be demonstrated to show anticipation is that the prior disclosure was 'enabling'—or perhaps more accurately, enabled. A disclosure will be enabling and thus novelty destroying if the public is given sufficient information to enable the disclosed invention to be put into effect. That is, a disclosure will anticipate an invention if the disclosed matter could be 'worked' or 'practised'.[75] Enablement means that the ordinary skilled person would have been able to perform the invention, which satisfies the requirement for disclosure.[76] Lord Hoffmann said that the test for enablement of a prior disclosure for the purpose of anticipation was the same as the test for enablement for the purpose of sufficiency. This means that the authorities on sufficiency under section 72(1)(c) of the 1977 Act are applicable to enablement for the purposes of section 2(2) and (3).

As we saw earlier, for the purpose of disclosure, the prior art must reveal an invention that, if performed, would necessarily infringe the patent.[77] The disclosure must occur without further experiment or undue effort.[78] This is in contrast to the requirement for enablement under which the person skilled in the art is assumed to be willing to make trial-and-error experiments to get the invention to work.[79] Another way in which

---

[73] *Merrell Dow Pharmaceuticals v. Norton* [1996] *RPC* 76, 88, 89, 90 (HL). 'This does not affect the principle that the prior art directions or information that will inevitably result in the use of a patented process or creation of the patented product invalidates by anticipation': ibid., 90, 93. See also *Kaye v. Chubb* (1887) 4 *RPC* 289, 298.

[74] *Merrell Dow Pharmaceuticals v. Norton* [1996] *RPC* 76, [44]. See also *CPC/Flavour concentrates decision*, T 303/86 [1989] *EPOR* 95; *Bayer/Diastereomers*, T 12/81 [1979–83] *EPOR* B–308, 312; *Availability to the Public*, G 1/92 [1993] *EPOR* 241.

[75] *Merrell Dow Pharmaceuticals v. Norton* [1996] *RPC* 76, 89. This reiterates the old idea that, in order for a method or use claim to be anticipated, the prior art must provide 'clear and unmistakable directions to do what the patentee claims to have invented': *Flour Oxidizing v. Carr* (1908) 25 *RPC* 428, 457. On this, see *Regeneron v. Genetech* [2012] *EWHC* 657 (Pat) (disclosure that a compound *might* have a therapeutic effect is not a disclosure that it *has* that therapeutic effect, because there were not clear and unmistakable directions to do what the patentee had invented); *Hospira v. Genentech* [2015] EWHC 1796, [81]–[89] (Pat) (to anticipate, a therapeutic effect must be able to be directly and unambiguously derived from the prior disclosure).

[76] *Synthon* [2006] *RPC* (10) 323 (HL), [26]. [77] Ibid., [30].

[78] On this, see *SKB v. Apotex* [2005] *FSR* 524, in which Jacob LJ criticized the practice of 'litigation chemistry', i.e. the use of contrived experimental repetitions of the prior art. See also *Mayne Pharma v. Debiopharm* [2006] *EWHC* 164 (Pat), [10]–[11].

[79] *Synthon* [2006] *RPC* (10) 323 (HL), [30]. See also *Generics (UK) v. Lundbeck* [2009] *UKHL* 12 (where a product was available only as a 'racemate' and not as a single enantiomer, the single enantiomer was deemed not to be non-enabling and thus not available to the public).

'disclosure' and 'enablement' differ is in terms of the role that the person skilled in the art plays. As Lord Hoffmann said:

> [O]nce the meanings of the prior disclosure and the patent have been determined, the disclosure is either of an invention which, if performed, would infringe the patent, or it is not. The person skilled in the art has no further role to play.[80]

This is in contrast to the inquiry into whether the disclosure was enabling, where the 'question is no longer what the skilled person would think the disclosure meant but whether he would be able to work the invention which the court has held it to disclose'.[81]

It is very difficult to state with any precision the circumstances in which the prior art will enable an invention to be worked and thus be anticipated.[82] This is because the decision as to whether there has been an enabling disclosure always depends upon the facts of the case in question—that is, the information that is needed for an invention to be 'worked' always depends upon the particular invention under examination. As a result, it is impossible to specify in advance that to be novelty-destroying, the prior art must adopt a particular format. It is impossible to predict, for example, the nature of the information that needs to be disclosed for a chemical compound to be worked or practised. This can be seen if we look at the various ways in which chemical compounds can be anticipated. For example, in *Asahi Kasei Kogyo*,[83] the House of Lords held that the disclosure of the formula to a particular chemical compound did not anticipate a patent for that compound.[84] The reason for this was that for a skilled person to be in a position where they could work the invention in question, they not only needed to be given the chemical formulae, but also the means by which the compound could be produced. While on the facts of *Asahi* the formulae may have been non-enabling, as Lord Oliver said, there might 'be [other] cases where the means of producing the thing will be self evident to the man skilled in the art from the mere Recital of the formula of its composition'[85]—that is, there might be circumstances in which the disclosure of the formula to a chemical compound is sufficient to anticipate the compound. In other instances, in order to anticipate it might be necessary for the prior art to disclose not only the formulae and the means, but also the details of the starting materials.[86]

---

[80] Ibid., [32].   [81] Ibid.

[82] As such, it is not very helpful to attempt to quantify the situations in which a patent can be anticipated. Cf. *Inhale v. Quadrant* [2002] *RPC* 419, 436; *SmithKline Beecham plc's Patent (No. 2)* [2003] *RPC* 607, 630–1 (suggesting that a claim can be anticipated in two ways: if the prior art describes something falling within its scope; and where the inevitable result of carrying out what is described in the prior art falls within the claims).   [83] [1991] *RPC* 485 (HL).

[84] Drawing upon a series of cases decided under the Patents Act 1949, which utilized the reverse-infringement test (such as *Gyogyszeripari's Application* [1958] *RPC* 51), it was argued that, because the prior art disclosed the formulae of the chemical compound and there was an indication that the compound had actually been made, the chemical compound lacked novelty. This was the case irrespective of whether the chemical could have been made. In rejecting this line of argument (and, in so doing, finding that Asahi's patent had *not* been anticipated), the House of Lords stressed that, in order for a disclosure to destroy novelty, it needed to be 'enabling'. As such, the crucial question was whether the prior art provided sufficient information to enable the skilled person to make the chemical compound.   [85] [1991] *RPC* 485, 536.

[86] *ICI's Application/Herbicidal pyradine*, T 206/83 [1987] *OJ EPO* 5. In other instances, a chemical compound will not be 'known' unless the information disclosed in the prior art enables the compound to be prepared or, in the case of a naturally occurring compound, to be separated: *EPO Guidelines*, G-IV, [2].

4.3 SECRET OR INHERENT USE

One of the most important changes that has taken place with the shift to enabling disclosure is in relation to the issue of whether the existence of a previous secret or inherent use is enough to anticipate a subsequent patent. Basically, a secret or inherent use occurs where something is created, usually either accidentally or as an unknown by-product of some process, without the public knowing of its existence. While it was possible for a secret or inherent use to anticipate under the Patents Act 1949, this is no longer the case under the 1977 Act.[87] The position under the 1949 Act was set out in *Bristol-Myers' Application*,[88] where the question arose as to whether Bristol-Myers' patent for an ampicillin compound (an artificial antibiotic derived from penicillin) had been anticipated by the fact that before the priority date of the invention, Beecham had made small quantities of the ampicillin. At the time that the ampicillin was made, Beecham did not know about the invention, nor was it aware of its particular advantages. While the prior art conveyed no relevant information about the product to the general public, nonetheless the House of Lords held that the patent had been anticipated by the secret or uninformative use. The explanation for this was twofold: (i) had the patent been granted, the patentee would have been able to stop another trader from doing what it had done before (the 'right to work' doctrine); and (ii) the test for anticipation was coextensive with the test for infringement. Given that for a defendant to infringe, it was not necessary for them to have realized that what they were doing was an infringing act, such knowledge was therefore equally unnecessary when determining whether the invention was novel (the 'reverse-infringement test').

The question of the status of secret or inherent use under the Patents Act 1977 was considered by the House of Lords in *Merrell Dow v. Norton*.[89] This decision arose from the fact that in 1972 the claimant was granted a patent for the antihistamine terfenadine, a drug used in treating hay fever and other allergies. When terfenadine was taken by patients, it was transformed (or metabolized) in the body to produce a number of different products (metabolites). While terfenadine proved to be very effective in the treatment of hay fever, it had a number of unwanted side effects—notably, it led to heart-related problems in some patients. Because the initial patent was nearing the end of its duration, the claimant isolated and identified the particular metabolite that acted as an antihistamine. It was accepted that prior to this, the specific metabolite that acted as an antihistamine had not been identified. In 1983, the claimant obtained a patent for the newly identified metabolite. More accurately, it obtained a patent for the making of the metabolite with the antihistamine effects within the human body. This carried with it the obvious advantage that while it was useful in the treatment of hay fever, it did not have any of the side effects associated with terfenadine.

---

[87] The PA 1977 'introduced a substantial qualification into the old principle that a patent cannot be used to stop someone from doing what he has done before. If the previous use was uninformative, then subject to section 64 [which provides a defence for secret use before the priority date] it can': *Merrell Dow v. Norton* [1996] *RPC* 76, 86 (HL).

[88] [1975] *RPC* 127. Such an approach would mean that a previous secret use would anticipate a patent even if it were not clear how the invention worked. This is because such a use would give the public the benefit of the old invention even without their knowledge. Under the 1977 Act, it seems that there is nothing to prevent a person from concealing the use of their invention in this manner, although it has been suggested that, in a clear case of fraud, the Patent Office might decline to grant a patent. See H. Frost, 'Why Europe Needs a Sale Bar' [1996] *EIPR* 18; R. Jacob, 'Novelty of Use Claims' (1996) 27 *IIC* 170.

[89] [1996] *RPC* 76 (HL); I. Karet, 'A Question of Epistemology' [1996] *EIPR* 97; V. Vossius, 'Prior Written Disclosure and Public Prior Use under German Law and the EPC' [1994] *EIPR* 130.

After grant of the patent for the metabolic acid, Merrell Dow (the claimant) brought an action against Norton claiming that by supplying terfenadine, the defendant was facilitating the making of the patented metabolite, thus infringing the second patent.[90] The defendants counterclaimed, arguing that the second patent had been anticipated by prior use. The argument for anticipation by use relied on the fact that terfenadine had been made available to and used by volunteers in clinical trials before the priority date of the patent. Because the patented metabolite was produced in the livers of the volunteers when they took terfenadine, it was argued that the second patent had been anticipated and was thus invalid.

Lord Hoffmann said that while under the Patents Act 1949 mere uninformative use of this kind would have invalidated the patent, this was no longer the case under the 1977 Act.[91] Lord Hoffmann said that when deciding novelty, the starting point was whether there had been an enabling disclosure of the claimed invention.[92] Importantly, Lord Hoffmann said that while an invention might have been in existence before the priority date through a secret or inherent use, this was not sufficient in itself to destroy novelty. The reason for this was that 'the use of a product makes the invention part of the state of the art only insofar as that use makes available the necessary information'.[93] While the patented metabolite was inevitably produced in the body of the volunteers when they took terfenadine, this working of the invention was not as a result of information that had been made available to the public. The uninformative consumption of terfenadine, which secretly or inherently produced the metabolite, did not reveal or disclose information that would have allowed either the volunteers or the public more generally to make the metabolite in their bodies. On the basis that the use of terfenadine in the clinical trials conveyed no information that would have enabled anyone to work the invention (it was not enough that it had in fact been made), the House of Lords held that the prior use was not anticipatory.[94]

As Lord Hoffmann said in *Synthon*, problems of confusion between disclosure and enablement were acute in cases such as *Merrell Dow*, where the subject matter disclosed in the prior art is not the same as the claimed invention, but, if performed, will necessarily infringe:

> To satisfy the requirement of disclosure it must be shown that there will necessarily be infringement of the patented invention. But the invention which must be enabled is the one disclosed by the prior art. It makes no sense to inquire as to whether the prior disclosure enables the skilled person to perform the patented invention, since *ex hypothesi* in such a case the skilled person will not even realise that he is doing so. Thus in *Merrell Dow* the question of enablement turned on whether the disclosure enabled the skilled man to make terfenadine and feed it to hay-fever sufferers, not on whether it enabled him to make the acid metabolite.[95]

---

[90] This was on the basis that it amounted to a contributory infringement under PA 1977, s. 60(2).

[91] As such, *Bristol-Myer's Application* [1975] *RPC* 127 is no longer good law.

[92] 'The question to be decided is not what may have been "inherent" in what was made available (for example, by a prior written description or in what has previously been used (prior use). Rather it was what has been made available to the public': *Mobil/Friction reducing additive*, G 2/88 [1990] *EPOR* 73, 88.

[93] Lord Hoffmann emphasized that the invention, which was a piece of information, must have been made available to the public: *Merrell Dow v. Norton* [1996] *RPC* 76, 86.

[94] This rule applies whether the prior art is a previous application, a previous use, a description, or a set of instructions. The 'information deriving from a use is governed in principle by the same conditions as is information disclosed by oral or written description': *Availability to the Public*, G 1/92 [1993] *EPOR* 241, 243.

[95] *Synthon* [2006] *RPC* (10) 323 (HL), [33].

It should be pointed out that the invention in *Merrell Dow* was anticipated by the earlier patent. In the case of anticipation by use, the acts relied upon conveyed no information that would have enabled anyone to work the invention—that is, to make the acid metabolite in the body. In contrast, the earlier patent made information available to the public that enabled it to perform an act, the inevitable consequence of which was that the patented metabolite was produced. The terfenadine specification taught that the ingestion of terfenadine produced a chemical reaction in the body. For the purposes of working the invention in this form, this was a sufficient description of the making of the patented metabolite.

4.4 PRODUCT-BY-PROCESS CLAIMS

As we saw earlier, product-by-process claims are only allowed at the European Patent Office (EPO) only where it is impossible, or at least very difficult, to define the product in any other way.[96] The approach taken towards product-by-process claims manifests itself in the way in which the novelty of such claims are assessed. At the EPO, a product-by-process claim will only be novel if the product itself is novel; novelty cannot be conferred by the process alone (except in situations where there is no physical, chemical, or biological means for distinguishing the product from the prior art). In other words, the EPO does not recognize that novelty can be conferred on a known substance by a novel process for producing that substance.[97] This means that even if the process claimed is novel, a product-by-process claim will be anticipated (and thus held to be invalid) unless the product itself is also novel.

The approach that has been adopted at the EPO is in contrast to the approach traditionally taken to product-by-process claims in the United Kingdom. While product-by-process claims are only permitted at the EPO in exceptional circumstances, they were traditionally allowed in the United Kingdom. The different approach taken towards product-by-process claims manifested itself in the way in which the novelty of such claims were assessed in the United Kingdom and at the EPO. While the EPO has consistently refused to accept that the novelty of a product-by-process claim can arise from the novelty of the process used (that is, it must flow from the novelty of the product), the approach traditionally followed in the United Kingdom was different. For example, the practice under the Patents Act 1949 and earlier was 'to treat the fact that a product was made by a new process as sufficient to distinguish it from an identical product which was already part of the state of the art'.[98] The difference between the traditional British approach and the approach adopted at the EPO was made clear when the UK Court of Appeal in *Kirin-Amgen* explicitly rejected the EPO approach, saying that there was:

> . . . no reason why the limitation of claims to products produced by a process could not impart novelty . . . If a person invents a new method of extracting gold from rock, he can

---

[96] This is where there is no chemical or biological means for distinguishing a product from the prior art.

[97] UK IPO, *Examining Patent Applications for Biotechnological Inventions* (21 October 2016), [14]–[24]; *Kirin-Amgen v. Transkaryotic Therapies* [2003] *RPC* 31 (CA), [296]. For a useful summary of the novelty of product-by-process claims, see *Hospira v. Genentech* [2014] *EWHC* 3857 (Pat), [125]–[140]. See further P. Gilbert and S. Carter, 'Product-by-process claims' [2015] *EIPR* 314.

[98] *Kirin-Amgen v. Hoechst Marion Roussel* [2005] *RPC* 169 (HL), [88].

obtain a claim to the process and as Art 64(2) [of the EPC 1973 and EPC 2000] makes clear, he can also monopolise the gold when produced directly by the process.[99]

That is, a product-by-process claim was valid in the United Kingdom provided that the process itself was patentable. While this may have suggested that new monopolies could be established over old products (such as gold) every time a new process was invented, the protection only applied to products made by that process.

When *Kirin-Amgen* was appealed before the House of Lords in 2005, the Lords over-turned the Court of Appeal decision and, in so doing, brought British law into line with practice at the EPO. While Lord Hoffmann accepted that this meant a change in a practice that had existed in the United Kingdom for many years, he thought it was important that the United Kingdom should apply the same law as the EPO and other member states. In any case, Lord Hoffmann did not think that the adoption of the EPO approach would have much practical importance, since patentees could rely on the process claim and Article 64(2) to receive equivalent protection.[100] The upshot of the House of Lords' decision is that where the product is known a product-by-process claim will be rejected on the basis that it is not novel. The UK Intellectual Property Office (IPO) accordingly changed its practice to follow the approach at the EPO towards product-by-process claims.[101] As such, while a product defined by its method of production will be allowed if there is no other means for distinguishing that product from the prior art, they will not be allowed where there is an alternative chemical, physical, or biological way of defining that product.[102]

4.5 BIOTECHNOLOGIAL INVENTIONS

While a number of changes have been made to patent law to accommodate biotech-nological inventions, for the most part these are treated in a similar manner to other types of invention. The test for novelty is no exception to this general rule: a biotechno-logical invention will only be anticipated and thus be invalid where there has been an enabling disclosure.[103] Despite this, questions sometimes arise where biotechnological inventions are based on natural materials. In this context, it is important to note that a natural substance that has been isolated for the first time (such as a polynucleotide sequence) will not lack novelty because it was already present in nature (for example in the human genome). Here, patent law draws a distinction between the invention (the isolated 'artificial' polynucleotide) and the natural substance (the polynucleotide that exists in nature).[104] The artificial nature of the isolated substance provides the requisite difference between the prior art and the invention that is necessary to ensure novelty.

[99] *Kirin-Amgen* [2003] *RPC* 31 (CA), [33] ('I can discern no reason in principle or in practice why a claim to a product made by a certain process could be invalid simply because the product is not novel, if the process is novel, so that a claim to a process would be valid').

[100] *Kirin-Amgen* [2005] *RPC* 169, [101]. PA 1977, s. 60(1)(c), which accords to EPC 1973, Art. 64(2) (now EPC 2000, Art. 64(2)), states that protection provided by a claim for a process extends to the product of that process.

[101] UK IPO, *Examining Patent Applications for Biotechnological Inventions* (21 October 2016), [15].

[102] Ibid.

[103] See, e.g., *Asahi Kasei Kogyo* [1991] *RPC* 485; *Genentech's (Human Growth Hormone) Patent* [1989] *RPC* 613; UK IPO, *Examining Patent Applications for Biotechnological Inventions* (21 October 2016), [8]–[11].

[104] *Howard Florey Institute's Application*, T 74/91 [1995] *OJ EPO* 388. See also D. Schertenleib, 'The Patentability and Protection of DNA-based Inventions in the EPO and the European Union' [2003] *EIPR* 125; EPO/USPTO/JPO, *Trilateral Project 24.1: Biotechnology Comparative Study on Biotechnology Patent Practice—Comparative Study Report* (2001).

5 DISCOVERY OF A NEW ADVANTAGE OF AN OLD THING USED IN AN OLD WAY

In this final section, we move away from the general principles of novelty that have concerned us so far to concentrate on three specific types of invention and the problems that have arisen when assessing their novelty. In particular, we look at the novelty of inventions that relate to medical uses, non-medical uses, and so-called 'selection inventions'.

For many years, the primary goal of the research carried out in many areas of science and technology was the creation of either new products or new uses of old things. On the whole, the fruits of this research have been well served by patent law. This can be seen in the fact that patent law has long recognized both the discovery of new things[105] (such as the discovery of aspirin) and the discovery of new ways of using old things[106] (such as the discovery that aspirin rubbed on the skin acts as an effective insect repellent) as being novel.

In the last 40 years or so, a number of changes have taken place in the type of research undertaken in various industries. These changes were motivated by a realization that in certain fields (notably in relation to pharmaceutical and biological inventions), the possibility of discovering new things or finding new uses for old things was decreasing. As a result, the focus of research shifted to concentrate on the discovery of new uses (or purposes) of old substances used in old ways. The problem that confronted researchers working in this way was that British patent law traditionally refused to recognize the discovery of a new purpose or advantage of an old thing used in an old way as being novel. This meant, for example, that if someone discovered that as well as being useful in the curing of headaches that the consumption of aspirin also thinned the blood (and was thus useful in preventing blood clots), they would be unable to patent the invention. The reason for this was that the traditional British approach treated a claim to a 'product for a particular use' as a claim to the product per se, so that the product would lack novelty even if it had previously been employed for a different purpose.[107] The problem that confronted this 'new' style of research was that patent law was not willing to recognize 'novelty of purpose' as a basis on which an invention could be patented.

One of the notable trends in recent years is the way in which this principle has slowly been undermined. One of the first areas in which the general rule was relaxed was in relation to medical uses.[108] With the EPO leading the way and UK courts following, this was interpreted to include second and subsequent medical uses. While initially seen as an exception that left the general rule intact, the EPO and (arguably) now UK courts have recognized novelty of purpose irrespective of the field of technology.

5.1 NEW MEDICAL USES

As we saw earlier, when the EPC 1973 was being drafted, it was decided that methods for treatment of the human or animal body should not be patentable.[109] While the

---

[105] Claims for a substance provide protection not only over the thing itself, but also over all subsequent uses.

[106] Typically, new uses are claimed as a 'new method of using the old article'.

[107] See *Adhesive Dry Mounting v. Trapp* (1910) 27 RPC 341.

[108] It is arguable that selection patents, discussed in section 5.3, p. 573, were an early exception to the general rule about the non-patenting of novelty of purpose.

[109] PA 1977, s. 4(2); EPC 1973, Art. 52(4). See Chapter 17, section 4, p. 464.

pharmaceutical industry was able to patent new substances,[110] the proposed blanket exclusion of methods of medical treatment presented it with a problem.[111] The reason for this was that a lot of the research then being carried out was not into the creation of new substances or drugs; rather, much of the research focused on the discovery of new uses for old substances, or of new benefits from old substances. As such, the exclusion of methods of medical treatment from the scope of patent protection would have had a dramatic impact upon medical research. To appease the interests of the pharmaceutical industry, special provisions to 'compensate' for the exclusion of methods of medical treatment were introduced. Initially these provisions were found in section 2(6) of the 1977 Act (as enacted) and Article 54(5) of the EPC 1973. As part of the reforms instigated by the EPC 2000, the compensation provisions are now found in section 4A(3) of the 1977 Act and Article 54(4) of the EPC 2000. Section 4A(3) states that:

> In the case of an invention consisting of a substance or composition for use in any such method, the fact that the substance or composition forms part of the state of the art shall not prevent the invention from being taken to be new if the use of the substance or composition in any such method does not form part of the state of the art.[112]

Essentially, section 4A(3)/Article 54(4), which permit the patenting of new applications for old substances used in old ways (in a medical context), create a statutory exception to the traditional British view that the mere discovery of purpose could not confer novelty on an invention.[113] In essence, the provisions confer novelty via the new purpose ('the new pharmaceutical use of a known substance'), even though 'the substance itself is known and comprises part of the state of the art'.[114]

5.1.1 Second and subsequent medical uses of a known product

When enacted, it was widely believed that section 2(6)/Article 54(5) of the EPC 1973 (replaced by section 4A(3)/Article 54(4) of the EPC 2000) only applied to the discovery of the first medical use of known products—a position supported by a normal reading of the provisions. This reading would have meant that claims for second or further medical uses of products would have lacked novelty.

---

[110] PA 1977, s. 4(3), and EPC 1973, Art. 52(4), leave open the possibility of claims for new substances or compositions. Consequently, while it is not possible to obtain a patent for a method of preventing headaches involving the taking of aspirin, aspirin is patentable per se.

[111] When the EPC 1973 and the PA 1977 were enacted, the exclusion of methods of medical treatment was based on the fiction that they were not susceptible to industrial application: PA 1977, s. 4(2); EPC 1973, Art. 52(4). Under EPC 2000 and the revised UK Act, methods of medical treatment are directly excluded: PA 1977, s. 4A(1); EPC 2000, Art. 53(c).

[112] The old PA 1977, s. 2(6), was similar:

> [T]he fact that an invention consisting of a substance or composition for use in a method of medical treatment forms part of the state of the art, shall not prevent the invention from being taken to be new, if the use of the substance or composition in any such method does not form part of the state of the art.

This was apparently based on French law: Paterson, [9.61]; R. Singer, *The European Patent Convention* (1995), 167; *Hoffmann–La Roche/Pyrrolidine derivatives*, T 128/82 [1984] *OJ EPO* 164.

[113] See A. Benyamini, *Patent Infringement in the European Community* (1993), 80 *ff*; G. Paterson, 'The Patentability of Further Uses of a Known Product under the EPC' [1991] *EIPR* 16; G. Paterson, 'Product Protection in Chemistry: How Important for the Protection of an Apparatus, Device or Substance are Statements Made in a Patent as to their Purpose?' (1991) 22 *IIC* 852; G. Paterson, 'Novelty of Use Claims' (1996) 27 *IIC* 179.

[114] A. Horton, 'Methods of Treatment and Second Medical Use' (August 2000) *Patent World* 9.

The question of the scope of Article 54(5) of the EPC 1973 (now Article 54(4) of the EPC 2000) was considered by the Enlarged Board of Appeal (EBA) of the EPO in *Eisai/Second medical indication*.[115] Basing its arguments on the legislative history of the EPC and the principle that exceptions to patentability should be construed narrowly, the Board decided that as well as protecting first uses, Article 54(5) also applied to second and subsequent medical uses. The EBA went on to say, however, that this was conditional on the fact that claims were drafted in a style known as the 'Swiss form of claims'. Basically, this meant that the patent had to claim the 'use of a substance for the manufacture of a medicine for a specified new therapeutic use'.[116] This would mean that if the discovery that the consumption of aspirin was useful in thinning the blood were to be valid, the applicant would have to claim the 'use of aspirin in making a medicament for use in the prevention of blood clots'.[117]

One of the notable features of a Swiss claim is that it is directed at the *manufacture* of the known substance. This ensures that the invention is not excluded on the basis that it is a method of medical treatment under section 4(2)/Article 52(4).[118] At the same time, the novelty of a Swiss claim arises from the new therapeutic application (the drug and first medical use already being known).[119] As a result, the focus of the patent shifts, so that the novelty of the invention is not in the known way in which the substance is used, nor in relation to the substance itself; rather, the novelty of the invention is in the new therapeutic use (or purpose) that has been discovered. This is the case even 'where the process of manufacture does not differ from known processes using the same active ingredients'.[120]

In recognition of the need for the harmonization of patent law, the Patents Court, sitting *en banc* in *Wyeth's Application*,[121] followed the lead of the EPO and permitted the claims in the Swiss form in the United Kingdom. The finding in *Wyeth's Application* was confirmed, albeit somewhat reluctantly, by the Court of Appeal in *Bristol-Myers Squibb*.[122] Following this decision, it was clear that section 2(6) of the Patents Act 1977 included second and subsequent medical uses that were drafted in the Swiss form.

Any doubts that there might have been about the standing of second and subsequent medical use claims[123] were put beyond doubt as a result of changes made by EPC 2000. In order to promote certainty across member states, Article 54(5) of the EPC 2000 allows applicants to claim second and further medical uses of known substances or compositions, without having to make a Swiss-type claim.[124] Article 54(5) has been replicated in the United Kingdom in section 4A(4) of the 1977 Act (as amended).

[115] G 5/83 [1985] *OJ EPO* 64. See *EPO Guidelines*, G-IV, [7.1].

[116] *Second Medical Indication: Switzerland* [1984] *OJ EPO* 581. See also *Germany* [1984] *OJ EPO* 26; *Netherlands* [1988] *OJ EPO* 405.

[117] Patents have been allowed where the novelty lay in the frequency of drug administration.

[118] As the EBA said in *Eisai*, G 5/83 [1985] *OJ EPO* 64, the Swiss-type of use claim is not prohibited by Art. 52(4) and is capable of industrial application'.

[119] A. Horton, 'Methods of Treatment and Second Medical Use' (August 2000) *Patent World* 9.

[120] Ibid. For a general discussion, see *IGF-I–Genentech/Method of administration*, T 1020/03 [2007] *OJ EPO* 204.

[121] [1985] *RPC* 545. The patent in question in *Wyeth's Application* arose out of research carried out by Wyeth in relation to pharmaceuticals known as guanidines. While, prior to this, it was known that guanidines lowered blood pressure, Wyeth discovered that guanidines were also useful in treating and preventing diarrhoea: *Schering's Application* [1971] *RPC* 337.

[122] *Bristol-Myers Squibb v. Baker Norton Pharmaceuticals* [2001] *RPC* 1, 18, 24–6, [48] (Aldous LJ), [76]–[81] (Buxton LJ). See also *Actavis UK v. Merck & Co.* [2008] *EWCA Civ* 444.

[123] See, e.g., Jacob J's comments about the 'artificial construct of a Swiss form claim': *Merck & Co.'s Patent* [2003] *FSR* 498, [80].

[124] EPC 2000, Art. 54(5), applies to applications pending or filed after 17 December 2007.

The aim of Article 54(5) of the EPC 2000 and section 4A(4) of the 1977 Act was to eliminate any legal uncertainty over the patentability of further medical uses. In particular, the provisions aimed to put it beyond doubt that applicants were able to claim 'purpose-related product protection for each further new medical use of a substance or composition already known as a medicine'.[125] One of the consequences of these changes was that applicants were able to claim second medical use inventions more directly. In contrast with the convoluted Swiss claim ('Use of [known substance X] for the manufacture of a medicament to treat [medical condition Y]'), applicants were able to use a simpler and clearer form of second medical use claim in the form ('[Substance X] for treatment of [disease Y]').[126]

The standing of Swiss claims following the changes made by EPC 2000 was considered by the EBA in the 2010 decision *Abbott Respiratory/Dosage regime*.[127] The Board said that Swiss claims had been begrudgingly allowed in order to overcome the loophole that existed in the EPC 1973. However, Article 54(5) of the EPC 2000 (as with section 4A(4) of the Patent Act 1977) filled this loophole by allowing claims to the further specific use of a known drug. As a result, the EBA said that there was no longer any reason why the judge-made (praetorian) law should continue to exist. Given this, the Board decided that Swiss-type claims for the second or further medical use of a known substance should no longer be allowed.[128] The UK Intellectual Property Office (IPO) issued a Practice Notice on 26 May 2010, which said that in light of *Abbott* the IPO no longer allows claims in the Swiss format.[129] As a result, any claims in the Swiss format have to be deleted or replaced by claims of the form '[Substance X] for use in the treatment of [disease Y]'.[130]

While the aim of Article 54(5) of the EPC 2000 was to match as closely as possible the scope of protection provided by a 'Swiss type claim',[131] the TBA has held the scope of protection conferred by the new Article 54(5) of the EPC 2000 was in fact larger than the protection conferred by a Swiss-type claim. This was because while the Swiss-type claim ('use of X for the manufacture of a medicament for the treatment of Y') was a purpose-limited *process* claim, the Article 54(5) claims (typically in the form 'X for use in the treatment of Y') were purpose-limited *product* claims. The fact that it was generally accepted that a 'claim to the physical activity (eg. method, process, use) confers less protection than a claim to the physical entity' meant that a purpose-limited *process* claim confers less protection than a purpose-limited *product* claim.[132]

5.2 NON-MEDICAL USES OF KNOWN PRODUCTS: NOVELTY-OF-PURPOSE PATENTS

Shortly after the scope of the medical use exception was clarified, the question arose as to whether patent law should also recognize novelty of purpose in non-medical

---

[125] *Explanatory Notes to the Swiss Oroposal for Art. 54(5) EPC 2000* [2007] OJ EPO (Special edn), 4.

[126] UK IPO, *Patents Act 2004 Guidance Note No. 7: Methods of Treatment or Diagnosis* (2007), [7].

[127] G 2/08 [2010] OJ EPO 456, [5.9]–[5.10], [7.1.1]–[7.1.4]; S. Sterckx, 'Dosage Regime Claims in the EPO: The Dosage Regime/Abbott Hearing' [2010] *EIPR* 294.

[128] This came into effect at the EPO as of 29 January 2011.

[129] UK IPO, *Practice Notice: Patents Act 1977—Second Medical Use Claims* (26 May 2010).

[130] UK IPO, *Examination Guidelines for Patent Applications Relating to Medical Inventions in the Intellectual Property Office* (14 October 2016), [105]–[113].

[131] Preparatory Document MR/18/00, point 4, (as cited in *Abbott Respiratory/Dosage Regime* G 2/08 (2010) *OJEPO* 456, [5.10.4]).

[132] *Board of Regents, the University of Texas System/Cancer Treatment*, T 1780/12 [2014] EPOR 277, [16]–[24] (citing *Mobil Oil/Friction reducing additive*, G/2 [1990] OJ EPO 73, point 5.

fields.[133] That is, should patent law recognize the discovery of new applications for old substances used in old ways, irrespective of the field in which the invention was made? This question was particularly important given that a great deal of non-medical research is devoted to the discovery of new applications of known compounds.

The status of novelty-of-purpose patents under the EPC was considered by the EBA in *Mobil/Friction reducing additive*.[134] This decision arose from Mobil's attempt to patent a substance for use as a friction-reducing additive in lubricating oils. The application was opposed by Chevron on the basis that the substance was already known and was already being used to inhibit rust-formation in ferrous metals. In response, Mobil applied to amend its application by limiting it to the use of the substance for reducing friction, saying that its usefulness for this purpose had not previously been known. The question considered by the Board was whether the discovery of a new use of a known substance used in an old way could be patented.

The EBA held that while using an old substance in a new way to achieve a new purpose might be novel, the use of an old substance in an old way to achieve a new purpose would not. In the latter case, the only difference between the discovery and the old use was that it was carried out with a different purpose in mind; the applicant would be doing the same thing with the same substance. Given that on the facts of the case the same substance (the additive) was used in the same way (for example by pouring it into the engine), it might have been reasonable to presume that the attempt to patent its use as a friction reducer (when it was previously thought only to inhibit rust) would have failed. This was not the case.

The reason for this, as the Board went on to say, was that a claim for the use of an old compound in an old way for a new purpose could be interpreted to include 'the function of achieving the new purpose (because this is the technical result)'.[135] In such a case, the fact that the substance achieved the new purpose would be an objective 'functional technical feature' of the invention, rather than something that only resided in the mind of the user. In relation to the case in hand, the EBA said that the invention exhibited a functional technical feature in that the substance operated to reduce friction. As such, the Board held that claims for the use of a specified lubricant for the reduction of friction in engines were patentable, even though the lubricant had previously been used as a rust inhibitor. As a result of this decision, it is now clear that the discovery of a new purpose for an old thing used in an old way is potentially patentable at the EPO, irrespective of the technical field in which the invention takes place.[136]

As we will see, a number of criticisms have been made of the *Mobil* decision in the United Kingdom.[137] Nonetheless, it is clear that in Britain it is now possible to patent the

---

[133] See G. Paterson, 'The Patentability of Further Uses of a Known Product under the EPC' [1991] *EIPR* 16; R. Jacob, 'Novelty of Use Claims' (1996) 27 *IIC* 170; C. Floyd, 'Novelty under the Patents Act 1977: The State of the Art after *Merrell Dow*' [1996] *EIPR* 480.

[134] G 2/88 [1990] *EPOR* 73. See also *Bayer's Application*, G 6/88 [1990] *OJ EPO* 114.

[135] *Mobil/Friction reducing additive*, G 2/88 [1990] *EPOR* 73.

[136] The Court of Appeal in *Bristol-Myers v. Baker Norton* [2001] *RPC* 1 said that a Swiss claim was based on a different logic from that of *Mobil: Ortho/Pharmaceutical prevention of skin atrophy*, T 254/93 [1999] *EPOR* 1.

[137] See C. Floyd, 'Novelty under the Patents Act 1977: The State of the Art after *Merrell Dow*' [1996] *EIPR* 480; CIPA, [2.23]; A. White, 'The Novelty Destroying Disclosure' [1990] *EIPR* 315; J. Lane, 'What Level of Protection is Required to Anticipate a Patented Invention by Prior Publication or Use?' [1990] *EIPR* 462. These problems are particularly acute in the United Kingdom (and not at the EPO) because the EPO is concerned only with issues of validity, whereas British courts have to deal with validity and infringement.

discovery of a new purpose for an old thing used in an old way.[138] Unlike pre-1977 law, the mere fact that an invention's sole point of novelty lies in the discovery of a new purpose no longer means that the application will automatically be disallowed.

The key feature of a novelty-of-purpose claim is the discovery that a known use of a known substance achieves a new purpose. The only aspect of the invention that is novel is the third element—namely, the discovery of the new purpose. The step that facilitated the acceptance of novelty-of-purpose patents was the decision that a previous secret use did not destroy the novelty of a patent. As we explained earlier, under British law before 1977, it was possible for a past secret use to anticipate a later patent. Under the old law, the discovery that a known substance used in a known way could be put to a hitherto unknown purpose would not have been patentable. This was because the new purpose would have been seen as inherent in the existing use of the known substance. The fact that the use was secret would not have affected the fate of the invention.

As we pointed out earlier, under existing law a previously secret use will no longer destroy the novelty of a later patent.[139] As the EBA said in *Mobil*, the 'question to be decided is what has been "made available to the public": the question is not what may have been "inherent" in what was made available'.[140] 'Under the EPC, a hidden or secret use, because it has not been made available to the public, is not a ground of objection' to validity of a patent; as such, 'the question of "inherency" does not arise' under the EPC (nor under the Patents Act 1977).[141] In so ruling, this opened up the possibility for patent protection to be given to the discovery that a known substance used in a known way could be put to a new purpose. Once this step was taken, deciding the status of a discovery that a known substance used in a known way could be put to a new purpose is relatively straightforward. As the EBA said in *Bayer*, the question to be decided in these circumstances, as with all inventions, is whether the invention has already been made available to the public.[142] This has been reflected in subsequent case law, which has focused on whether the purpose that has been discovered is actually new.[143]

In those cases in which novelty-of-purpose patents have been accepted, the applicant has been able to show that they have 'two distinctly different effects, two distinctly different applications or uses of the same substances, which can clearly be distinguished from each other'.[144] For example, in *Mobil* the patent was for the use of an additive as a lubricant, whereas the state of the art revealed use of the same additive as a rust inhibitor. Similarly, in *Bayer* the patent application was directed to the use of a compound as a fungicide, whereas the state of the art described use of the same compound as an agent for influencing plant growth.[145] In both cases, the patent revealed that the known substance used in a known way could be put to a new purpose.

In contrast, in *Robertet/Deodorant compositions*[146] the patent was rejected on the basis that it lacked novelty. The applicants discovered that when used as an active ingredient in a deodorant composition, 'aromatic esters' can inhibit esterase-producing micro-organisms on the human skin. The prior art disclosed the use of aromatic esters as an active ingredient in deodorizing products. The Technical Board of Appeal (TBA) rejected the

---

[138] *Bristol-Myers v. Baker Norton* [2001] *RPC* 1, 18, [49] (Aldous LJ), noting that *Mobil* had been considered in some detail and applied by the House of Lords in *Merrell Dow* (admittedly on a different point). Aldous LJ said that 'it is unlikely that [the Court of Appeal] would conclude that [*Mobil*] was wrongly decided when the House of Lords did not so conclude': ibid. See also ibid., [81] (Buxton LJ).

[139] See section 4.3, pp. 563–5.   [140] *Mobil/Friction reducing additive*, G 2/88 [1990] *EPOR* 73 (EBA), 88.

[141] Ibid.   [142] *Bayer/Plant growth regulating agent*, G 6/88 [1990] *EPOR* 257 (EBA), 265.

[143] In many ways, the reasoning used in relation to new purpose is similar to that used in relation to second and subsequent medical uses. The main difference is that, in this context, there is no need to show manufacture.   [144] *Robertet/Deodorant compositions*, T 892/94 [1999] *EPOR* 516, 526.

[145] *Bayer/Plant growth regulating agent*, G 6/88 [1990] *EPOR* 257.   [146] T 892/94 [1999] *EPOR* 516.

application, saying that all that the patent did was disclose information about an existing purpose—that is, it was an *ex post facto* explanation of what had already taken place. While, in *Mobil* and *Bayer* a new purpose had been discovered, all that had been disclosed in this case was more information about a known purpose. The application was merely more information or an explanation of a past event, rather than the discovery of a new purpose per se. As such, it was held not to be novel. A similar conclusion was reached in *Ortho Pharmaceuticals*, in which the TBA said that:

> [T]he mere explanation of an effect obtained when using a compound in a known composition, even if the effect was not known to be due to this compound in the known composition, cannot confer novelty on a known process if the skilled person was aware of the occurrence of the desired effect.[147]

The principles used to determine novelty in new-purpose patents are similar to those used for other types of inventions. In other respects, however—notably, in terms of the problems that arise when deciding whether a novelty-of-purpose patent has been infringed—they mark a more radical change of direction. We look at this issue in more detail in our discussions of patent infringement.[148]

5.3 PATENTS: GENERIC DISCLOSURE

The third area which we wish to focus on is the novelty of so-called 'selection patents'. As with methods of medical treatment and novelty-of-purpose patents, selection patents developed in response to a particular problem. This arose from the fact that in some fields, such as organic chemistry, a researcher may discover that a particular combination of molecules produces certain results. In some instances, the researcher then extrapolates from this initial discovery to assert that the same qualities will be produced by a range of variants or homologues. This is referred to as a 'generic' or 'general' disclosure. In so doing, the researcher (potentially) discloses an extremely broad range of compounds.

Problems arise when it is subsequently discovered that some of the compounds that were outlined in the generic disclosure are particularly advantageous or have uses other than those that were initially envisaged. Because the compounds have already been made available to the public, the previous generic disclosure appears to prevent subsequent claims being made for individual members of the group.[149] This led to the potential problem that if the generic disclosure were able to anticipate, it would act as a disincentive for further research to be carried out in relation to the materials already disclosed. The question that underpins the doctrine of selection patents is whether, and if so, the extent to which a previous generic disclosure anticipates subsequent inventions in the same field.

In the United Kingdom, the classic answer to this problem was provided by the 1930 decision in *IG Farbenindustrie*.[150] This decision concerned an application to revoke IG

---

[147] *Ortho/Prevention of skin atrophy*, T 254/93 [1999] *EPOR* 1, 8. This was reinforced by the fact that the specific purpose in question was also known: ibid., 7.

[148] See Chapter 22, section 2.4, pp. 650–2.

[149] This is exacerbated by the fact that (at least until recently) patent law did not normally allow patents for discoveries of new advantages.

[150] (1930) 47 *RPC* 289, 322–3. See *Shell Refining and Marketing Patent (Revocation)* [1960] *RPC* 35, 52; P. Grubb, *Patents in Chemistry and Biotechnology* (1986), 132. While mechanical subject matter does not readily lend itself to the idea of selection, there have been a number of selection patents for mechanical inventions. See *Clyde Nail Russell* (1916) 33 *RPC* 291, 306 (Lord Parker); *Shell Refining and Marketing Patent (Revocation)* [1960] *RPC* 35, 54; *EI Du Pont de Nemours (Witsiepe's) Application* [1982] *FSR* 303, 314; *Hallen v. Brabantia* [1991] *RPC* 195.

Farbenindustrie's patent for a process of manufacturing certain azo and aromatic amine dyestuffs. This was on the ground that in light of a prior disclosure in an expired patent the invention lacked novelty. In response, IG Farbenindustrie claimed that there were potentially millions of combinations of azo and aromatic amine dyestuffs outlined in the expired patent. It also argued that the particular group of dyes that it had selected had peculiar and beneficial properties in that they withstood certain processing techniques required of cotton.[151] Maugham J said that if the compounds in question had previously been made, they would have lacked novelty. If the compounds had not been previously made, however, the patent might be valid if it could be shown that:

(i) the selection was based on substantial advantage resulting from the use of selected members;

(ii) all members of the selected class possessed the advantage in question; and

(iii) if the selection was in respect of a quality of a special character, it could fairly be said to be peculiar to the selected group.

While, on the facts, IG Farbenindustrie's patent was held to be invalid,[152] the decision helped to establish the principle that selection inventions are potentially patentable where it can be shown that the 'inventiveness' of the application lies in a particular selection from a known field. Selection patents:

> . . . enable a valid patent to be obtained for the selection of a product or process from a range of known or obvious products or processes because of surprising and non-obvious advantages over the others . . . The selection must be based on a substantial advantage of special character. The selected member or class must have the advantage, and the specification must direct the mind of the skilled reader to the advantage of the selection from the class.[153]

Although Maugham J's judgment was approved in subsequent decisions,[154] a number of issues remained unclear.[155] Many of the uncertainties result from a failure to distinguish clearly between novelty and inventive step. Another reason for the confusion can be traced to the fact that while Maugham J expressly said that the three propositions outlined in his judgment were not meant to be exhaustive, nonetheless they have often been treated as if they were definitive guidelines as to when a selection invention will have been anticipated. Another problem is that it is often forgotten that selection patents are not limited to new uses; they also apply, at least potentially, to the discovery of new substances, new uses for old substances, and new purposes for old substances used in old ways.[156]

Perhaps the greatest uncertainty that exists in relation to selection patents is whether the doctrine has any continued relevance under the Patents Act 1977. In light of recent changes—notably, the shift to enabling disclosure, the consequential move away from secret or inherent use, and the (apparent) acceptance of the discovery of new purposes as conferring novelty—there are good reasons for suggesting that it does not.

---

[151] More specifically, the advantage claimed was 'fastness to kier boiling under pressure in caustic liquor'.

[152] This was because the dyestuffs claimed did not have the property that the applicant alleged.

[153] *Boehringer Mannheim v. Genzyme* [1993] *FSR* 716.

[154] *Du Pont (Witsiepe's) Application* [1982] *FSR* 303, 309.

[155] It should be noted that there is some inconsistency in the EPO decisions in this area, e.g. *Pfizer/Penem*, T 1042/92 [1995] *EPOR* 207 is inconsistent with *Sanofi/Enantiomer*, T 658/91 [1996] *EPOR* 24.

[156] It is only if this is correct that selection patents provide obvious tactical advantages over patents for 'uses' that the EPO has recently recognized. Moreover, if this were not the case, the requirement demanded (particularly by the EPO) of novelty per se rather than mere novelty of use would be unnecessarily stringent.

To argue that under British law, the doctrine of selection patents should be jettisoned in favour of the more general rules about novelty is not as radical as it may first seem. This is because the issues that arise with selection patents are really no different from the question that Lord Hoffmann said underpinned the novelty examination more generally—namely, how specific must a disclosure be for an invention to be 'known' or 'made available' to the public? (The key difference is that with selection patents the question is rephrased to be: how specific must a generic or general disclosure be for it to destroy the novelty of a subsequent invention that incorporates the prior knowledge?) While Lord Hoffmann wisely answered that it always depends on the invention in question, the doctrine of selection patents has attempted the impossible and tried to stipulate in advance the type of disclosure that is needed to anticipate. Given the futility of this, it may be better if the novelty of selection patents were answered through the general rules about novelty.[157] If this approach were to be adopted, it would mean that a previous generic disclosure would only anticipate a selection invention if it is enabling—that is, if the disclosure placed a skilled person in a position from which they can 'work' the invention in question.

Arguments of this nature were accepted by the Court of Appeal in *Dr Reddy's Laboratories v. Eli Lilly*.[158] There are a number of notable things about this decision. The first is that Jacob LJ expressly rejected the approach in *IG Farbenindustrie*. As he said, the *IG Farbenindustrie* decision had not been used by the EPO, referred to in the EPO Guidelines for Examination, nor cited in a Board of Appeal decision. As a result, Jacob LJ said the best thing to do is to regard it 'as part of legal history, not as part of the living law'.[159] While these comments were made in relation to obviousness, they apply equally here. This means that generic disclosures will be examined for novelty in the same way as other disclosures.

The second notable thing about *Dr Reddy's Laboratories* is that it clearly states that the mere disclosure of a generic formula or class of compounds does not disclose every possible compound within that class; there also needs to be a clear indication that the substance had actually been prepared. Here, Jacob LJ agreed with the EPO approach which requires an 'individualised description' to anticipate a later compound or class of compounds. In this context, it was important to distinguish between:

> . . . the purely intellectual content of an item of information and the material disclosed in the sense of a specific teaching with regard to technical action. Only a technical teaching of this kind can be prejudicial to novelty. If any such teaching is to apply in the case of a chemical substance, an individualised description is needed.[160]

As a result, when considering anticipation in this situation it is necessary to look for an 'individualised description' of the later claimed compound or class of compounds.

As a result of *Dr Reddy's Laboratories*, British law is now in line with the approach that has been adopted at the EPO, where the rules on selection patents have been treated as being consistent with, rather than an exception to, the general rules about novelty. In these circumstances, a previous generic disclosure will only anticipate a substance if it can be characterized as an enabling disclosure.[161] This can be seen, for example, in *Bayer/*

---

[157] In *IG Farbenindustrie* (1930) 47 *RPC* 289, Maugham J argued that the rules applicable to 'selection patent' did not differ from the general rules of patent law—a view that was reaffirmed in *Shell Refining (Revocation)* [1960] *RPC* 35.

[158] [2009] *EWCA* 1362, [2010] *RPC* 222, [37].   [159] Ibid.

[160] *Hoescht/Enantiomers*, T 296/87 [1990] *EPOR* 337; approved in *Dr Reddy's Laboratories v. Eli Lilly* [2009] *EWCA* 1362, [30].

[161] *Sanofi/Enantiomer*, T 658/91 [1996] *EPOR* 24. On the EPO, see M. Vivian, 'Novelty and Selection Patents' (1989) 20 *IIC* 303.

Diastereomers[162]—a decision that concerned an application for the diastereomeric form of a compound, which was useful in treating mycoses (fungal diseases such as ringworm). The problem that confronted the applicants was that a prior patent had disclosed a group of compounds including the compound in question, as well as the method by which the compound could be produced. The TBA rejected the application on the basis that it was lacking in novelty. In so doing, the Board held that the teaching of a prior document was not confined to the detailed information given in the examples of how the invention is carried out; rather, it embraces any information in the claims and description enabling a person skilled in the art to carry out the invention. The TBA stressed that the essential point is what a person skilled in the art could be expected to deduce from the earlier disclosure in carrying out the invention.

---

[162] T 12/81 [1982] *OJ EPO* 296.

19

INVENTIVE STEP

1 INTRODUCTION

In this chapter, we focus on the requirement that to be patentable, an invention must involve an 'inventive step'.[1] An invention is said to involve an inventive step if it is not obvious to a person skilled in the art[2] (the terms 'inventive step' and 'non-obviousness' are used interchangeably).[3] The question of whether an invention is obvious can arise during examination in the national patent offices, where it is *ex parte*. It can also arise *inter partes* in opposition proceedings at the European Patent Office (EPO), or in revocation proceedings before the Comptroller or the courts. In each case, the onus is on the patent office, the opponent, or the party seeking revocation (as opposed to the applicant or patentee) to establish that the invention is obvious. While the inventive step requirement has long been a key element of patent law, it may become more important in the future. This is a result of changes that have taken place at the EPO, but not in the United Kingdom, in the way in which patentable subject matter is determined. As we explained in Chapter 17, as a result of the *Pension Benefits System* decision,[4] the Technical Board of Appeal has shifted the focus of attention away from subject matter to inventive step. (The Board held that while the claim for an apparatus for controlling a pension benefits system was an invention for the purposes of Article 52(1) of the European Patents Convention of 1973, or EPC 1973—now Article 52(1) of the EPC 2000—it lacked inventive step and thus was not patentable.) While there is a close relationship between the two requirements (particularly as a result of the focus on 'technical character' when determining subject matter), it is not clear what the consequences of this shift will be. It is, however, an important change that needs to be followed in the future.

As we will see, deciding where the line should be drawn between inventions that are obvious (or non-inventive) and those that are inventive (or non-obvious) is a difficult task. As well as being one of the most important requirements for patentability, inventive step is also one of the most problematic. Indeed, it has been said that inventive step is 'as fugitive, impalpable, wayward, and vague a phantom as exists in the whole paraphernalia

---

[1] PA 1977, s. 1(1)(b); EPC 2000, Art. 52(1) (ex EPC 1973, Art. 52(1)); PCT, Art. 33(3); TRIPS, Art. 27(1). See generally, J. Bochnovic, *The Inventive Step* (1982); H. Ullrich, *Standards of Patentability for European Inventions* (1977). [2] PA 1977, s. 3; EPC 2000, Art. 56 (ex EPC 1973, Art. 52(1)).

[3] However, a useful proposal (such as the idea to cover an umbrella with water-soluble textile) might be non-obvious, but lack inventive step: R. Singer, *The European Patent Convention* (1995), 181, n. 1; *Exxon/Gelation*, T 119/82 [1984] *OJ EPO* 217.

[4] *Pension Benefits Systems Partnership/Controlling pension benefits systems*, T 931/95 [2001] *OJ EPO* 413.

of legal concepts'.[5] In part, this is because the examination for inventive step is a factual inquiry; to this end, it has frequently been dubbed a 'question of fact' or a 'jury question' (although juries have not sat in patent cases in the United Kingdom since 1883). The corollary of the factual nature of the inquiry is that precedents should be treated with caution, even those that involve decisions on the same invention. The evaluative nature of the inquiry also means that reasonable people can easily reach different conclusions—thus making it extremely difficult to predict the outcome of an obviousness attack or objection.[6] This has led to accusations of uncertainty and to the arbitrary use of discretion.[7] It also means that on appeal, courts are often reluctant to overturn decisions of the lower courts.

While the novelty examination ensures that there is a quantitative difference between the invention and the state of the existing knowledge, non-obviousness ensures that this difference is of a quality deserving of patent protection.[8] By ensuring that patents are only granted for non-obvious inventions, the requirement that there be inventive step acts as a qualitative threshold that ensures that only meritorious inventions are granted protection. The need to show inventive step as a condition for patentability has been explained on the basis that 'if every slight difference in the application of a well-known thing [were to be] held to constitute a ground for a patent', it would lead to an unjustifiable interference with trade.[9] As the Court of Appeal said in *PLG Research v. Ardon International*,[10] the 'philosophy behind the doctrine of obviousness is that the public should not be prevented from doing anything which was merely an obvious extension or workshop variation of what was already known at the priority date'. In more positive terms, it has been suggested that the obviousness inquiry encourages people to carry out research that might not otherwise be undertaken. More specifically, the fact that patents are *not* granted for obvious inventions is said to encourage speculative or risky research. Or as Birss J put it, patents 'exist to provide incentives for costly and uncertain research but not all costly and uncertain research will lead to patentable inventions'.[11]

2 DETERMINING WHETHER AN INVENTION IS OBVIOUS

In order to harmonize the divergent approaches to obviousness that had been adopted in the member states prior to the passage of the EPC, the EPO set out to develop an

---

[5] *Harries v. Air King* 183 F.2d. 158, 162 (1950) (Judge Learned Hand). For the position in the United States, see *KSR International v. Teleflex*, 558 US 398 (2007).

[6] This 'contributes significantly both to the insecure commercial value of many patents and to the cost of litigating their validity': W. Cornish, 'The Essential Criteria for Patentability' (1983) 14 *IIC* 765, 771.

[7] H. Ullrich, *Standards of Patentability* (1977), 37; J. Schmidt-Szalewski, 'Non-obviousness as a Requirement of Patentability in French Law' (1992) 23 *IIC* 725, 737.

[8] While there has been a shift in the theoretical basis of the novelty requirement from a 'right to work' to an information-related understanding, such a shift has yet to be recognized in relation to inventive step.

[9] *Harwood v. Great Northern Railway Co.* (1865) 11 *HLC* 654, 682 (Lord Westbury). See also *Elias v. Grovesend* (1890) 7 *RPC* 455, 467; *Brugger v. Medic Aid* [1996] *RPC* 635, 653; *VDO Adolf Schindling/ Illuminating device*, T 324/94 [1997] *EPOR* 146, 153.

[10] [1999] *FSR* 116, 136. See also *Philips (Bosgra's) Application* [1974] *RPC* 241 (emphasizing right to work).

[11] *Actavis Group v. Actavis UK* [2016] *EWHC* 1955 (Pat), [279]; *Société Technique de Pulvérisation (STEP) v. Emson* [1993] *RPC* 513. Cf. *Mölnlycke v. Procter & Gamble (No. 5)* [1994] *RPC* 49; H. Ullrich, *Standards of Patentability* (1997), 103.

approach to the assessment of inventive step that was objective, economical, and transparent. In so doing, it also hoped to bring a degree of certainty to the area.[12] As the Chartered Institute of Patent Attorneys (CIPA) *Guide to the Patents Act 1977* says, the approach to inventive step at the EPO has two key characteristics. The first, which we encountered in our discussions about patentable subject matter in Chapter 17, is that it is 'an "effects-based" approach, so that whether or not a patent is granted ultimately depends on whether there is a new effect, a new function or result flowing from the claimed features'.[13] The second is that the examination for whether there is the requisite inventive step is conducted via 'the problem-and-solution approach'.[14] This is based on an image of the invention as a solution to a problem. Accordingly, an inventive step is seen as 'a step from the technical problem to its solution'.[15] As such, rather than asking whether an invention is obvious, the EPO asks whether the solution that an invention provides to the problem being addressed would have been obvious to the person skilled in the art. In more positive terms, this means that for an invention to be patentable, the solution must have been *not* obvious to the person skilled in the art at the priority date of the invention in question. There are a number of subsidiary steps that need to be undertaken when applying the problem-and-solution approach. In particular, it requires the tribunal to: ascertain the technical field of the invention (which is used, amongst other things, to determine the field of expertise of the person skilled in the art); identify the closest prior art in the field; identify the technical problem that can be regarded as solved in relation to the closest prior art; and finally, ascertain whether the technical feature(s) that form the solution claimed could be derived by the skilled person in a manner obvious from the state of the art.[16]

Over the period during which the problem-and-solution approach has been utilized at the EPO, it has proved to be a useful technique for determining inventive step. It is also one that was applied in nearly all situations. Despite this, aspects of the approach were called into question by the Technical Board of Appeal (TBA) in *Alcan/Aluminium alloys*.[17] In this decision, the Board said that while it was often assumed that the problem-and-solution approach was applicable in all situations, it was better seen as one of many possible approaches that could be adopted when assessing inventive step. The TBA said that there was no legal reason why all cases involving inventive step should be shoehorned into a single approach. In situations where the invention broke new ground, the test was inappropriate because there was no close prior art from which to formulate the problem. In these circumstances, the problem-and-solution approach was unnecessarily artificial. Because this approach proceeds on the basis of a search that is made with actual knowledge of the invention, it also suffered from the fact that it was inherently based on hindsight.[18]

Jacob LJ raised similar objections when he said that the key problem lay with the reformulation or retrospective construction of a problem was the weakest part of the problem-and-solution approach. This was particularly the case in those situations where the

[12] G. Knesch, 'Assessing Inventive Step in Examination and Opposition Proceedings at the EPO' (1994) *epi-Information* 95, 98.   [13] *CIPA*, [3.04].

[14] This was espoused in the first published decision of the TBA, *Bayer/Carbonless copying*, T 1/80 [1979–85] B *EPOR* 250.

[15] The problem-and-solution approach builds upon an image of research as an activity that sets out to solve particular problems: *ICI/Containers*, T 26/81 [1982] *OJ EPO* 211.

[16] *Comvik/Two identities*, T 641/00 [2003] *OJ EPO* 319, [5].   [17] T 465/92 [1995] *EPOR* 501.

[18] For a general discussion of need to avoid hindsight, see *Ferag v. Muller Martini* [2007] *EWCA Civ* 15, [13].

'invention involves perceiving that there is a problem or in appreciating that a known problem, perhaps "put up with" for years, can be solved'.[19]

In a sense, what the TBA did in *Alcan* was to align the problem-and-solution approach more closely with the types of research under consideration. By modifying (and narrowing) the circumstances where the test may be applied, the Board has served to strengthen the test. Despite these criticisms, the problem-and-solution approach is consistently applied by the EPO Boards of Appeal to determine whether or not there is the requisite inventive step.

2.1 APPROACH IN THE UNITED KINGDOM

Whatever the current state of the law at the EPO, English courts have largely remained isolated from and resistant to the adoption of the problem-and-solution approach.[20] Instead, when considering the way in which an invention is to be interpreted, they have relied on the approach set out in the *Windsurfing* decision.[21] In this decision, the Court of Appeal said that the court must begin by identifying the inventive concept embodied in the patent. The court should then identify the differences that exist between the cited prior art and the alleged invention. Finally, the court should ask whether, viewed without any knowledge of the alleged invention, those differences constitute steps that would have been obvious to the skilled man, or whether they required a degree of invention.[22] In the Court of Appeal decision of *Pozzoli*,[23] Jacob LJ reordered and elaborated on the *Windsurfing* test. While judicial attempts to restructure well-established rules, such as those in *Windsurfing*, are often counter-productive, Jacob LJ's reformulation is useful—particularly insofar as it takes the question of what is the invention more seriously. Under the new approach, which is known as the *Pozzoli* approach', the court asks four questions, as follows.

(i) Who is the notional 'person skilled in the art'? (This involves identifying the relevant common general knowledge of that person.)

(ii) What is the inventive concept of the claim? (If that cannot readily be identified, the court must construe it.)

(iii) What, if any, difference exists between the matter cited as forming 'part of the state' of the art and the inventive concept of the claim, or the claim as construed?

(iv) Viewed without any knowledge of the alleged invention as claimed, do those differences constitute steps that would have been obvious to the person skilled in the art, or do they require any degree of invention?[24]

---

[19] *Actavis v. Novartis* [2010] *EWHC Civ* 82, [35]. The Court noted, however, that the problem-and-solution approach worked very well when there was no need to reformulate the problem: ibid., [39]. This was the case in *Apimed Medical Honey v. Brightwake* [2011] *EWPCC* 2, in which the problem was that honey was runny at room temperature and the purpose of the invention (solution) was to immobilize liquid honey in such a way that it could be maintained at a wound site to act as a therapeutic dressing.

[20] Although these provisions are intended to be applied uniformly throughout the EPC states, inventive step appears to be an area in which British courts have taken little notice of EPC precedents and therefore an area in which harmonization seems at its most embryonic: *Hallen v. Brabantia* [1991] *RPC* 195, 212; *Hoechst Celanese v. BP Chemicals* [1997] *FSR* 547, 567, 572.

[21] *Windsurfing International v. Tabor Marine* [1985] *RPC* 59 (CA), followed in *Lux Traffic v. Pike Signals* [1993] *RPC* 107; *Hallen v. Brabantia* [1991] *RPC* 195; *Mannheim v. Genzyme* [1993] *FSR* 716, 724; *Mölnlycke v. Procter & Gamble (No. 5)* [1994] *RPC* 49, 115; *PLG Research* [1995] *FSR* 116; A. Griffiths, '*Windsurfing* and the Inventive Step' [1999] *IPQ* 160.

[22] For criticism, see J. Claydon, 'The Question of Obviousness in the *Windsurfer* decision' [1985] *EIPR* 218. See *Unilever v. Chefaro* [1994] *RPC* 567, 580.   [23] *Pozzoli SpA v. BDMO SA* [2007] *EWCA Civ* 588.

[24] Ibid., [15]–[19]. For further elaboration, see Jacob LJ in *Nichia Corporation v. Argos* [2007] *EWCA Civ* 741, [12].

While courts have occasionally reminded us that these questions are only a tool for answering the ultimate statutory question—'Was the invention obvious?'—and that adherence to any rigid formula can be a mistake,[25] nonetheless the *Pozzoli* approach is widely and consistently used to determine when an invention is obvious in the United Kingdom.

The decision to use the approach set out in *Pozzoli* rather than the approach used at the EPO was reinforced by the fact that the problem-and-solution approach has been subject to a considerable degree of criticism in the United Kingdom.[26] As well as being criticized for its use of hindsight,[27] the test is also said to be unnecessarily artificial because many inventions are developed without having a problem in mind. Perhaps the most important objection is that while the problem-and-solution approach is presented as being applicable to all types of research, there are situations in which its use is inappropriate. While this approach is sensibly applied to the improvement of existing techniques, it is not easy to formulate a problem for many inventions, particularly in the chemical/pharmaceutical field.[28] As well as being difficult to apply in situations involving the discovery of a new application for an existing technique or product, it is said to be wholly inappropriate where an innovation satisfies a latent need that has never previously been expressed.[29] In the case of so-called 'problem inventions', where the solution becomes obvious once the problem has been formulated, the reformulation of the research undertaken in terms of problem and solution 'is equivalent to emptying the definition of the problem of any substance, and thereby depriving the problem-and-solution approach of any effectiveness'.[30]

In determining obviousness under the Patents Act 1977, British tribunals have tended to utilize the *Pozzoli* approach rather than the problem-and-solution approach. Nevertheless, there has been a growing belief that the problem-and-solution approach ought to be used in the United Kingdom.[31] In part, this has been motivated by a realization that the two tests may not be as conceptually different as they first appeared,[32] by the fact that the EPO approach has precursors in UK patent law,[33] and by the fact that the *Alcan* decision goes some way towards resolving some of the criticisms that have been made of the EPO approach.[34] Perhaps the strongest support for the use of the

[25] See, e.g., *Regeneron Pharmaceuticals v. Genentech* [2013] *EWCA Civ* 93, [68]–[71]; *Conor v. Angiotech* [2008] *RPC* 28 (HL), [42]; *Generics (UK) v. Daiichi Pharmaceutical Co.* [2009] *EWCA Civ* 646, [17]; *Medimmune v. Novartis* [2012] *EWCA Civ* 1234, [34], [177]–[186].

[26] '[A]ttempts to force all questions of obviousness into a "problem-solution" approach can lead to trouble, though often the test can be a helpful guide': *Nichia Corporation v. Argos* [2007] *EWCA Civ* 741, [22]. Jacob LJ also noted that a similar view has been taken by the US Supreme Court in *KSR International v. Teleflex*, 550 US 398 (2007). See also A. White, 'The Problem-and-solution Approach to Obviousness' [1986] *EIPR* 387; J. Beton, 'Vote of thanks to G. Szabo' (1987) 16 *CIPAJ* 361.

[27] R. Singer, *The European Patent Convention* (1995), 186; *Grehal/Shear*, T 305/87 [1991] *EPOR* 389.

[28] F. Hagel and C. Menes, 'Making Proper Use of the Problem–solution Approach' [1995] *epi-Information* 14.   [29] *Rider/Simethicone tablet*, T 2/83 [1979–85] *C EPOR* 715.

[30] F. Hagel and C. Menes, 'Making Proper Use of the Problem–solution Approach' [1995] *epi-Information* 14, 16.

[31] P. Cole, 'Inventive Step: Meaning of the EPO Problem and Solutions Approach and Implications of the United Kingdom' [1998] *EIPR* 214, 271.

[32] *CIPA*, [3.04]. Descriptions in UK patents often begin by setting out the background of the invention and then explain the particular problem that the invention solves.

[33] See P. Cole, 'Inventive Step: Meaning of the EPO Problem and Solutions Approach and Implications of the United Kingdom' [1998] *EIPR* 214; *Sharp and Dohme v. Boots Pure Drug Company* (1928) 45 *RPC* 153, 173 (Sir Stafford Cripps); J. Beton, 'Vote of thanks to G. Szabo' (1987) 16 *CIPAJ* 361; S. Avery, 'Problem and Solution at the EPO: The Primary Consideration' (1984–85) 14 *CIPAJ* 166; G. Szabo, 'Questions on the Problem-and-solution Approach to the Inventive Step' (1986–87) 16 *CIPAJ* 351.

[34] See *Haberman v. Jackel International* [1999] *FSR* 683, 683, 699–700; *Dyson Appliances v. Hoover* [2001] *RPC* 26, [153].

problem-and-solution approach comes from the House of Lords' decision in *Biogen v. Medeva*,[35] where Lord Hoffmann said that a 'proper statement of the inventive concept needs to include some express or implied reference to the problem which it required invention to overcome'.

While it is important to keep in mind the different approaches that have been adopted in the United Kingdom and at the EPO, there are enough similarities for them to be dealt with together. Perhaps the best starting point for thinking about whether an invention is obvious is with section 3 of the 1977 Act/Article 56 of the EPC 2000 (ex Article 56 of the EPC 1973), which states that an invention is taken to involve an inventive step 'if it is not obvious to a person skilled in the art, having regard to any matter that forms part of the state of the art'. Stated in this way, the inquiry gives rise to three further questions.

(i)   Who is the 'person skilled in the art', and what skills and knowledge do they have?

(ii) What is the 'invention' that is being examined?

(iii) What does it mean to say that something is 'non-obvious'?

We will deal with each in turn.

3 PERSON SKILLED IN THE ART

As section 3 of the 1977 Act and Article 56 of the EPC 2000 make clear, obviousness is determined from the standpoint of the average person skilled in the art.[36] This means that when considering whether an invention is obvious, the tribunal views the invention through the eyes of a notional interpreter equipped with the attributes, skills, background knowledge, and qualifications relevant to the field in which they work.[37] While the person skilled in the art 'must have characteristics grounded in reality . . . no real person is the same as the notional person skilled in the art'.[38]

The objective nature of the inquiry means that the *actual* process by which the invention came about is irrelevant.[39] As such, it does not matter if an invention arose as a result of years of research by a team of leading experts, or as a chance result by an unskilled person. All that matters is whether the person skilled in the art would consider the invention to be non-obvious.[40]

---

[35] [1997] *RPC* 1, 45.

[36] Described as 'an assembly of nerds with different basic skills, all unimaginative': *Rockwater v. Technip* [2004] *RPC* (46) 919, [7], [10], and as 'a normative legal construct': *Positec Power Tools v. Husqvarna* [2016] *EWHC* 1061 (Pat), [8]. For early accounts, see J. Bochnovic, *The Inventive Step* (1982), 59; J. Pagenberg, 'The Evaluation of the "Inventive Step" in the European Patent System' (1978) 9 *IIC* 1, 16–17; J. Tresansky, 'PHOSITA: The Ubiquitous and Enigmatic Person in Patent Law' (1991) 73 *JPTOS* 37.

[37] *Technograph Printed Circuits v. Mills & Rockley (Electronics)* [1972] *RPC* 346, 355 (Lord Reid); *Polymer Powders/Allied colloids*, T 39/93 [1997] *OJ EPO* 134, 149. The person skilled in the art is not necessarily the same person skilled in the art for performing an invention when it is made: *Schlumberger Holdings Ltd v. Electromagnetic Geoservices AS* [2010] *EWCA Civ* 819, [61].

[38] *Positec Power Tools v. Husqvarna* [2016] *EWHC* 1061 (Pat), [8]. Citing *Teva v. Leo* [2015] *EWCA Civ* 779, [29] (CA) (which, giving the example of the 'bag-ridden' mindset of real vacuum cleaner designers in *Dyson v. Hoover* [2002] *RPC* 465, suggested that the skilled person 'includes the real prejudices and practices of persons skilled in the art').

[39] *Hoechst Celanese v. BP Chemicals* [1997] *FSR* 547, 565; *BASF/Metal refining*, T 24/81 [1979–85] *B EPOR* 354.

[40] For a summary of some of the attributes of the person skilled in the art, see Jacob LJ in *Rockwater v. Technip* [2004] *RPC* 919, [6]–[12].

The skills and qualifications of the person skilled in the art, as well as the resources and equipment that are available to that person, vary according to the particular invention in question.[41] More specifically, the qualities of the skilled person depend on the technical field into which the invention falls. Determining the technical field of the invention is made easier by the fact that at the EPO, the patent description should specify the technical field into which the invention falls.[42] Similarly, in the United Kingdom the description begins with a short title that indicates the general subject matter of the invention. The choice of technical field is particularly important in situations where the invention is made up of a mixture of technical and non-technical features. This is particularly the case in relation to computer-related inventions and business-method patents. To date, the tribunals have been careful to ensure that the person skilled in the art has expertise only in technical fields. For example, in *Comvik*,[43] which concerned the invention of a new single-user identity card (SIM card) which dealt with the way in which charges for different types of mobile phone call were organized for digital mobile telephones,[44] the Technical Board of Appeal said that:

> [The] skilled person will be an expert in a technical field. If the technical problem is concerned with a computer implementation of a business, actuarial or accountancy system, the skilled person will be someone in data processing, and not merely a businessman, actuary, or accountant.[45]

If the skills base of the expert were extended to include non-technical areas such as business or management skills, it would increase the patentability of business patents and other types of invention that are currently excluded from protection.[46]

The skills attributed to the person skilled in the art will vary depending on what is regarded as normal in the field in which they are deemed to operate. In some cases, the person skilled in the art may have a PhD and a well-established research record;[47] in other cases, they may have no formal academic qualifications and only have 'ordinary' skills.[48] While the person skilled in the art is normally an individual, in situations where research is carried out by groups of researchers, the court will adopt the standpoint of a notional research team.[49]

While the skill and qualities of the notional interpreter vary according to the art in question, one trait that is shared by skilled persons irrespective of the field in which they work is that they are uninventive.[50] It has also been said that the person skilled in the art

---

[41] *Genentech's Patents* [1989] *RPC* 147, 278 (Mustill LJ).

[42] EPC 2000 Regs, rr 42(1)(a), 47(2) (ex EPC 1973 Regs, rr 27(1)(a), 33(2)); *Luminescent Security Fibres/Jalon*, T 422/93 [1997] *OJ EPO* 24.

[43] *Comvik/Two identities*, T 641/00 [2003] *OJ EPO* 319, [vi].

[44] 'The inventor's merits resided in realizing the economical and administrative problem for certain subscribers that distribution costs for various categories of calls within one and the same subscription causes extra work': ibid., [vi].

[45] Ibid., [7] (ingenuity of the invention occurred in non-technical fields, which could not contribute to inventive step).

[46] *Pension Benefits Systems*, T 931/95 [2001] *OJ EPO* 413 (assessment for inventive step was to be carried out from the point of view of a software developer or application programmer).

[47] *Genentech's Patent* [1989] *RPC* 147, 241.

[48] *Dredge v. Parnell* (1899) 16 *RPC* 625, 628; cf. *Genentech's Patent* [1989] *RPC* 147, 214.

[49] *Genentech's Patent* [1989] *RPC* 147, 278; *Adolf Schindling/Illuminating device*, T 324/94 [1997] *EPOR* 146.

[50] This has been questioned in relation to the field of biotechnology: *Genentech's Patent* [1989] *RPC* 147, 214, 279–280. See also *Technograph Printed Circuit* [1972] *RPC* 346; *Polymer Powders/Allied colloids*, T 39/93 [1997] *OJ EPO* 134, 149.

is 'conservative', in the sense that they would not go against established prejudices, try to enter into sacrosanct or unpredictable areas, or take incalculable risks.[51]

3.1 STATE OF THE ART

In considering whether an invention is obvious, the person skilled in the art has regard to any matter that forms part of the state of the art at the priority date of the invention.[52] With two notable exceptions, the state of the art in an obviousness examination is the same broad concept as is used in a novelty examination (which was discussed in Chapter 18).[53]

The first difference is that patent applications that have priority over the application in suit but have not yet been published, are not included in the state of the art for the purposes of assessing inventive step.[54] The second difference is that when considering whether an invention is non-obvious (but not whether it is novel), it is possible to combine together (or 'mosaic') information from different sources. The act of combining documents must be 'natural and logical'.[55] It must also be a process that an unimaginative skilled person would (as opposed to could) follow.[56] Documents that conflict or are unrelated cannot be combined to demonstrate obviousness.[57]

The state of the art is made up of everything that is made available to the public before the date of filing—irrespective of the language of publication or how widely it has been circulated.[58] The potentially broad nature of the state of the art is restricted by the fact that the prior art is judged through the eyes of a person skilled in the art at the priority date. On this basis, the courts have accepted that a person skilled in a particular art may place greater emphasis on certain types of information than on others.[59] In more extreme cases, the fact that the person skilled in the art is able to evaluate the prior art may mean that certain types of information are discarded.[60]

The potentially broad nature of the state of the art is further restricted by the fact that the skilled person is only expected to have scrutinized the information available in their own or closely related fields. The impact that this has on the material available to the person skilled in the art can be seen in *Mobius/Pencil sharpener*,[61] which concerned an application for a patent over a hand-operated pencil sharpener with a device that prevented

---

[51] *Genentech/Expression in yeast*, T 445/91 [1995] *OJ EPO* 684.

[52] This date might be critical. For example, in *Biogen v. Medeva* [1995] *RPC* 25 (CA), it was acknowledged that, because recombinant DNA technology had developed so quickly, the invention would have been obvious by December 1979. As such, it was critical whether Biogen could take advantage of an earlier priority date from December 1978.

[53] See Chapter 18, sections 2 and 3, p. 553. On the approach the courts take when considering an order for disclosure of documents in an obviousness case, see *Positec Power Tools v. Husqvarna* [2016] *EWHC* 1061 (Pat), [7]–[43] (refusing to order disclosure).

[54] *BASF/Metal refining*, T 24/81 [1979–85] *EPOR* B–354.

[55] *Phillip Morris/Tobacco lamina filler*, T 323/90 [1996] *EPOR* 422, 430.

[56] *Technograph v. Mills & Rockley* [1972] *RPC* 346, 355.

[57] *Mobay/Nethylenebis*, T 2/81 [1982] *OJ EPO* 394. See also *Discovision/Optical recording*, T 239/85 [1997] *EPOR* 171.

[58] *Blaschim/rearrangement reaction*, T 597/92 [1996] *EPOR* 456; *Mitsoboshi/Endless power transmission*, T 169/84 [1979–85] *B EPOR* 354; *Hoechst Celanese v. BP* [1997] *FSR* 547, 563.

[59] *PLG Research* [1994] *FSR* 116, 137 ('Knowing of a piece of prior art is one thing; appreciating its significance to the solution to the problem in hand is another').

[60] Cf. *Brugger v. Medic Aid* [1996] *RPC* 635, 653 (the 'court should be wary of uncritical ageism in relation to prior art . . . The fact that a document is old does not, per se, mean that it cannot be a basis for an obviousness attack').   [61] T 176/84 [1986] *OJ EPO* 50.

pencil shavings from escaping. The application survived an obviousness attack on the basis of two pieces of prior art: one concerned with pencil sharpeners; the other, with savings boxes. The Technical Board of Appeal held that while the prior art concerning the pencil sharpener represented the closest prior art, it failed to suggest the answer employed in the invention and was thus of no relevance. Given the technological differences between the two fields, the prior art in relation to savings boxes was also of no relevance because it was not in a closely related or neighbouring field. Consequently, the person skilled in the art would not have utilized the solution set out in the prior art relating to the savings box.[62]

In addition to being confronted with specific material from the state of the art, the person skilled in the art is also presumed to have the benefit of the 'common general knowledge' of the particular art or technical field in question.[63] As well as being a valuable source of information in its own right,[64] the common general knowledge is also important because it enables the notional interpreter to combine different pieces of prior art, and to develop and build upon existing pieces of prior art (so long as they do not do anything inventive). The common general knowledge is also important because it acts as the basis from which documents are interpreted.[65]

To qualify as common general knowledge, 'a matter must be generally known and generally regarded as a good basis for further action by the bulk of those engaged in the art in question'.[66] While prior art may be published anywhere in the world, it seems that common general knowledge is more closely tied to the United Kingdom. As Arnold J said in relation to an obviousness challenge brought in the United Kingdom, for information to qualify as common general knowledge, it needs to be shown, at a minimum, that it was common general knowledge in the United Kingdom. As he said 'I do not think it matters that a fact was common general knowledge in (say) China, if it was not common general knowledge [in the United Kingdom]'.[67] The sources from which the notional skilled addressee acquires their general knowledge vary depending on the nature of the technical field in question.[68] Frequently, the tribunal assumes that the common general knowledge is that which can be found in encyclopaedias and standard dictionaries. Where this is the case, care must be taken to avoid a logical fallacy: common general knowledge will be in encyclopaedias, but that does not mean that everything in such works is common general knowledge.[69] Individual patent specifications are not normally regarded as forming part of the common general knowledge.[70] Scientific papers become part of the general knowledge only 'when it is generally known and accepted without question by the bulk of those

---

[62] *Kereber/Wire link bands*, T 28/87 [1989] *OJ EPO* 383. *Mobius* was distinguished in *Boeing/General technical knowledge*, T 195/84 [1986] *OJ EPO* 121.

[63] *Hoechst Celanese v. BP Chemicals* [1997] *FSR* 547, 563; *British Ore Concentration Syndicate v. Mineral Separation* (1909) 26 *RPC* 124, 138. For a general discussion, see *KCI Licensing v. Smith & Nephew* [2010] *FSR* 740, [105]–[121].

[64] Sometimes, information may fail to ground an invalidity attack when viewed as part of the prior art, but succeed in so doing once categorized as common general knowledge: *Boeing/General technical knowledge*, T 195/84 [1986] *OJ EPO* 121.

[65] To qualify as art of the common general knowledge, a fact must be 'generally known within the relevant art and not merely known to some people but not others'; in addition, 'requirements of quality and reliability must be satisfied': *Omnipharm v. Merial* [2011] *EWHC* 3393 (Pat). On this, see CIPA, [3.11].

[66] *Generics (UK) v. Warner-Lambert* [2015] *EWHC* 2548 (Pat), [125]. See also *Accord Healthcare v. Medac Gesellschaft* [2016] *EWHC* 24 (Pat), [119].

[67] *Generics (UK) v. Warner-Lambert* [2015] *EWHC* 2548 (Pat), [124] ('the position may be different if all the persons skilled in a particular art in the UK are acquainted with the position in China'. Ibid).

[68] *Beloit v. Valmet* [1997] *RPC* 489, 494.   [69] *Mars II/Glucomannan*, T 112/92 [1994] *EPOR* 249.

[70] See *General Tire and Rubber v. Firestone Tyre & Rubber* [1972] *RPC* 457, 482.

who are engaged in the particular art'.[71] Usually, information that is common general knowledge will have been used in some capacity or other. The fact that a concept has not been used does not mean that it is necessarily excluded, but only that it is unlikely to form part of the common general knowledge.[72]

While in many cases, common general knowledge will be used in conjunction with specific disclosures (such as 'particular concrete documents or well defined prior use'[73]), in some situations an obviousness challenge may be brought purely on the basis of common general knowledge or, as the judges prefer, 'obviousness over common general knowledge alone'. While it is theoretically possible to rely on common general knowledge on its own to challenge the obviousness of an invention, the courts have been at pains to point out the dangers of only using common general knowledge. The reason for this is that only using common general knowledge (particularly where a combination of individual pieces of common general knowledge is used) poses a 'particularly acute hindsight problem'. This is because while an obviousness challenge based on concrete items of prior art, even one based on combinations of features of the prior art, is 'not one which was created with hindsight knowledge of the invention', this is not the case where the challenge is based on common general knowledge alone (which requires an *ex post facto* review of what was known which is inevitably shaped by knowledge of the invention). As Birrs J said, if 'an invention is not obvious over the concrete prior art which is relied on, the court is entitled to be sceptical that an argument that it is nevertheless obvious over common general knowledge alone is correct'.[74]

4 WHAT IS THE 'INVENTION'?

As the Court of Appeal pointed out in the *Windsurfing* decision, when considering whether an invention is non-obvious, the court must identify the inventive concept embodied in the patent.[75] As we saw in relation to patentable subject matter and novelty, the way in which an invention is interpreted may play an important role in determining whether it is patentable. This is also the case with inventive step. As Lord Hoffmann said, before you can apply the test for obviousness stated in section 3 of the 1977 Act and ask whether the invention involves an inventive step, 'you first have to decide what the invention is'.[76] As we explained earlier, one of the consequences of *Pension Benefits Systems* is that it places greater emphasis on the requirement that there must be an inventive step. In particular, it places more emphasis on the way in which the invention is characterized—that is, on the way in which the 'inventive concept' is determined.

---

[71] *British Acoustic Films v. Nettlefordfold Productions* (1936) 53 *RPC* 221, 250.

[72] *Beloit v. Valmet* [1997] *RPC* 489, 494.

[73] *Accord Healthcare v. Medac Gesellschaft* [2016] *EWHC* 24 (Pat), [121].

[74] Ibid., [123]. For the ramifications this has for the way obviousness actions are pleaded, see *Meter-Tech v. British Gas* [2016] *EWHC* 2278 (Pat), [27]–[29]; *Unwired Planet International v. Huawei Technologies* [2016] *EWHC* 576 (Pat), [233].

[75] *Windsurfing International* [1985] *RPC* 59. The importance of the way in which an invention is interpreted is illustrated in *Genentech's Patents* [1989] *RPC* 147. See also B. Reid, 'Biogen in the EPO: The Advantage of Scientific Understanding' [2005] *EIPR* 98.

[76] *SABAF SpA v. MFI Furniture Centres* [2005] *RPC* 209 (HL), [24]. In particular, it was necessary to decide whether you were dealing with one or two or more inventions. The House of Lords said that it was not appropriate to combine separate inventions and then ask whether the combination would have been obvious: ibid., [28].

At the EPO, the task of identifying the invention is achieved via the problem-and-solution approach. More specifically, based on an image of the invention as a solution to a problem, to identify the 'thing' that must be non-obvious, it is necessary to identify the particular problem that the invention addresses. As with most aspects of the obviousness inquiry, this is understood from an objective point of view at the priority date of the invention.[77] The task of having to identify the problem that the invention solves is made easier by the fact that the EPC 2000 Implementing Regulations provide that 'the description should disclose the invention as claimed in such terms that the technical problem (even if not expressly stated as such) and its solution can be understood'.[78]

While, in many cases, it is possible to rely upon the problem that is disclosed in the patent application, in some cases the patent application cannot be used to provide an objective statement of the problem.[79] In situations where the problem is not properly set out in the application, the EPO may reformulate the problem.[80] In these circumstances, the nature of the problem is determined from the differences between the closest prior art[81] and the invention (which is seen in terms of its effects rather than its structure).[82] This may refer to the need to achieve the same kind of result, an improved result (for example a quicker, stronger, or cheaper result), or a different result from that which is achieved by the existing art.[83]

As we explained earlier, English courts have largely remained resistant to the problem-and-solution approach. While there have been criticisms of the problem-and-solution approach in the United Kingdom, there has been relatively little discussion of what alternative approach ought to be adopted.[84] It seems that British tribunals distil the 'invention' from the specification (presumably assessed in relation to the invention as understood from the 'normal' interpretation of the claims (that is, purposively from the perspective of the relevant person skilled in the art, as opposed to the scope of protection under the doctrine of equivalents).[85] It is important to recall that in *Biogen v. Medeva*,[86] Lord Hoffmann said that a 'proper statement of the inventive concept needs to include some express or implied reference to the problem which it required invention to overcome'.

---

[77] The problem that the applicant is required to specify should be a technical as opposed to a commercial one: *Esswein/Automatic programmer*, T 579/88 [1991] *EPOR* 120.

[78] EPC 2000 Regs, rr 42(1)(c), 47 (ex EPC 1973 Regs, rr 27(1)(c)], 33(2)).

[79] The problem might need to be reformulated in the light of information revealed by the search report, or the documents relied upon in opposition or appeal proceedings, if these represent a closer state of the art than that originally mentioned. Similarly, the technical problem might need to be reformulated in light of experiments that reveal that the claim is too broad: *Polymer Powders/Allied colloids*, T 39/93 [1997] *OJ EPO* 134, 144 *ff*.

[80] *Phillips Petroleum/Passivation of catalyst*, T 155/85 [1988] *EPOR* 164, 169; *Sperry/Reformulation of the problem*, T 13/84 [1986] *EPOR* 289.

[81] *IBM/Enclosure for data-processing apparatus*, T 9/82 [1997] *EPOR* 303; *Bayer/Thermoplastic moulding composition*, T 68/83 [1979–85] *C EPOR* 71; G. Knesch, 'Assessing Inventive Step in Examination and Opposition Proceedings at the EPO' (1994) *epi-Information* 95 ('the crucial question is whether the man skilled in the art would really have chosen that document as the starting point').

[82] *Pegulan/Surface finish*, T 495/91 [1995] *EPOR* 517.　　　　　　　[83] *CIPA*, [3.21].

[84] Cf. *Generics (UK) v. Daiichi Pharmaceutical Co.* [2009] *EWCA Civ* 646, [17]–[21]. Interestingly, *CIPA*, [3.04], suggests that much of the controversy in the United Kingdom in relation to the problem-and-solution approach is because of a misunderstanding: in the United Kingdom, it is generally understood to refer to a real-world problem; at the EPO, it usually relates to an artificially constructed problem.

[85] *Brugger v. Medic Aid* [1996] *RPC* 635, 656 (the inventive concept must be characterized in light of the claims and must apply to all embodiments in the claim). For a discussion as to how the invention is determined see Chapter 22, section 3.1, p. 656.

[86] [1997] *RPC* 1, 45. Lord Hoffmann identified the 'inventive concept' differently at different stages of his analysis.

More pertinently, in *Cipla v. Glaxo*,[87] Pumfrey J said that he was 'not persuaded that' the structured approach to obviousness at the EPO was 'substantially different from the *Windsurfing* approach subject to one qualification'—namely, that, unlike the case in the United Kingdom, the EPO will only consider obviousness on the basis of the closest prior art. Given the importance of this issue, it warrants more attention. This view was reiterated by the Court of Appeal in *Generics (UK) v. Daiichi Pharmaceutical*,[88] when Jacob LJ disagreed with the suggestion that the *Pozzoli/Windsurfing* approach was different from the EPO's problem-and-solution approach saying that the 'problem/solution approach only applies at stage 4 [of the *Pozzoli/Windsurfing* approach]. The first three stages must be carried out at least implicitly as much as for the problem/solution approach as for any other.'[89]

One question that arises in this context concerns the way inventions that are made up of a mixture of technical and non-technical features are to be characterized. While it is legitimate for there to be a mix of technical and non-technical features when deciding patentable subject matter under section 1(2)/Article 52(1),[90] this is *not* the case when deciding whether there is an inventive step. As the Technical Board of Appeal said in *Comvik*, non-technical factors are not relevant when deciding whether there was inventive step. This means that where an invention consists of a mixture of technical and non-technical characters, the non-technical features should be ignored:[91]

> This approach, which is actually a method of construing the claim to determine the technical features of the claimed invention, allows separating the technical from the non-technical features of the claimed invention even if they are intermingled in a mixed-type claim.[92]

The exclusion of non-technical features (which echoes the approach currently taken to subject matter in the United Kingdom) has important consequences for the fate of computer-related inventions (particularly those in relation to business and economics). Given that in many cases, the real innovations will be in solving managerial or business problems rather than in relation to information technology per se, the exclusion of non-technical features means that the inventive step is judged against standard computer technology. As *Pension Benefits Systems* and *Comvik* showed, one of the consequences of this is that such inventions are now excluded at the EPO on the basis that they lack inventive step. While UK courts have been highly critical of the way inventions are characterized for the purposes of an obviousness inquiry at the EPO, the approach outlined in *Comvik* and *Pension Benefits* has been adopted in subsequent decisions at the EPO.[93] This divergence in the way the invention is construed for the purpose of deciding inventive step must be seen in conjunction with the different approaches to patentable subject matter discussed earlier.[94] When seen in this broader perspective, it seems that while the tribunals in the United Kingdom and at the EPO may have adopted different approaches, in most cases they seem to lead to the same result.

---

[87] [2004] *EWHC* 477, [43]–[45].   [88] [2009] *EWCA Civ* 646.   [89] Ibid., [20].

[90] *Kock & Sterzel/X-ray apparatus*, T 26/86 [1988] *OJ EPO* 19.

[91] Non-technical meaning 'features relating to non-inventions within the meaning of Article 52(2)': *Comvik/Two identities*, T 641/00 [2003] *OJ EPO* 319, [4].

[92] Ibid., [7], following *Pension Benefits Systems*, T 931/95 [2001] *OJ EPO* 413.

[93] *Hitachi/Auction method*, T 258/03 [2004] *OJ EPO* 575, 583, 588; *Man/Provision of product-specific data*, T 1242/04 [2007] *OJ EPO* 421, 430.

[94] *Aerotel v. Telco Holdings* [2007] 1 *All ER* 225, [27], [105]–[106], *Pozzoli* [2007] *EWCA Civ* 588, [21].

5 IS THE INVENTION 'OBVIOUS'?

Once the person skilled in the art and the invention have been identified, it is then possible to consider whether the invention is non-obvious.[95] While the question of whether an invention is non-obvious is widely regarded as one of the most difficult questions in a difficult area of law, in some ways it is not that different from other questions that the courts are required to consider, such as whether a contractual term is fair or whether evidence is relevant to an issue. In other ways, however, the task of determining whether a particular invention is non-obvious is not only different, but also more problematic. One reason for this is that in patent law, the tribunals are frequently required to pass judgment on complex and novel technologies. While in deciding whether a person acted negligently, judges may be able to rely on their background experience and knowledge, there may be little to guide them when they are forced to consider, for example, the inventiveness of a genetic modification. These problems are exacerbated by the fact that questions about the obviousness of an invention may arise some time after the invention was made. It also means that the way in which inventive step is determined will change as a technical field develops. For example, while in the 1980s the futuristic nature of molecular biology meant that the threshold for inventiveness was easily crossed, advances over the last few decades or so mean that the criteria will be harder to satisfy. In particular, as more 'is known about the various genomes and the function of the constituent genes, the more difficult it will be to establish an inventive step for any isolated gene'.[96]

While ascertaining whether an invention is obvious is a difficult task, it is made easier by the fact that the question is asked from the perspective of the person skilled in the art. Although a non-specialist may find it difficult to assess whether an invention is obvious, a person who has knowledge of the area—particularly of what is regarded as normal progress in the field—will find it much easier to judge whether something is inventive. The task of determining whether an inventive step is present is also made easier by the fact that the courts invariably draw upon the evidence of experts. While experts are not able to take the place of the court in making the final decision as to whether an invention is obvious, they play an important role in providing the court with a sense of what would be normal in the field (and thus what would be unexpected and inventive).[97] However helpful these factors may be, it still leaves us with the question: what does it mean to say that an invention is 'obvious'?[98]

In recent years there has been increased attention given to concept of 'plausibility' and the role it plays in obviousness inquiries. In essence this requires an applicant to show that what has been claimed meets a specific standard; namely that it is plausible. While it has been suggested that plausibility as a concept arises from the EPO problem-and-solution approach,[99] it has a much older history which can be traced back to the emergence of formula-based chemical inventions in the later part of the nineteenth century. Then, as now, the particular nature of chemical inventions meant that a single patent

---

[95] Where the problem-and-solution approach is followed, this question becomes whether the solution that an invention provides to the problem being addressed would have been obvious to the person skilled in the art.

[96] UK IPO, *Examining Patent Applications for Biotechnological Inventions* (21 October 2016), [35].

[97] *Hoechst Celanese v. BP* [1997] *FSR* 547, 563; *British Westinghouse v. Braulik* (1910) 27 *RPC* 209 (Fletcher Moulton LJ); *Brugger v. Medic Aid* [1996] *RPC* 635, 661.

[98] While the *Windsurfing* decision and the 'problem-and-solution approach' provide guidance as to how the invention is to be interpreted, they provide no assistance in determining whether an invention is obvious.

[99] UK IPO, *Examining Patent Applications relating to Chemical Inventions* (5 June 2017), [41].

could potentially cover thousands of chemical compounds.[100] (Similar problems also now arise with genetic inventions.) Patent law's willingness to accept these speculative inventions without the need for an applicant to test whether they really worked created further issues. Given that it was not necessary (nor indeed often possible) to show that every possible manifestation of the invention was feasible, a secondary question arose: what was the threshold of proof that needed to be met for an application to be valid? While this question, which has been raised in relation to inventive step, industrial application, and sufficiency, has been described as a threshold test,[101] it is better seen as a qualitative evidential criterion (not unlike obviousness itself) that is designed to deal with a specific problem that arose with the acceptance of class or group-based inventions. While plausibility may appear to provide an answer to these problems, it really only defers the question to a new context. This is reflected in the different criteria that have been used to determine whether a claim is plausible ranging from the need for the claim to be 'credible as opposed to speculative',[102] to be 'more than incredible'[103] through to the idea that 'the standard for assessment of plausibility is not the same as assessment of obviousness'[104] or, as Kitchin LJ said, 'the patent must disclose a practical application for the claimed product and that a plausible or reasonably credible claimed use or even an educated guess as to such a use could be sufficient for that purpose. On the other hand, a merely speculative use does not suffice'.[105]

Perhaps the best approach to this issue is the approach adopted at the UK IPO which has expressly said that it will *not* follow the suggestion that plausibility is a threshold test.[106] Rather, the IPO will continue to apply the *Pozzoli/Windsurfing* test and will only make recourse to the question of whether it is plausible to work an invention across the scope of the claims as a sufficiency objection, rather than as an inventive step objection. Having said this, the IPO does recognize that the plausibility of a prima facie selection invention may need to considered as part of the *Pozzoli/Windsurfing* test. This is discussed later in the chapter.

5.1 MEANING OF 'INVENTIVE STEP'

One of the things on which courts and commentators regularly agree is that the qualitative and factual nature of the inquiry means that it is not possible to reduce obviousness to a precise verbal formula[107]—that is, it is not possible to define either 'inventive step' or 'non-obvious' in a meaningful or helpful way. While it may not be possible to formulate a test that enables us to predict with accuracy whether an invention will be regarded as obvious, it is possible to offer general guidance as to some of the factors that have shaped obviousness inquiries in the past.[108]

An important factor that has influenced decisions as to whether an invention is obvious is the extent to which the notional researcher would have had to exercise choice in the inventive process. In situations where there is no opportunity or need for an inventor to enter into and shape the research process—that is, where there is 'no real choice' or 'the

---

[100] Or, in some cases, they may cover a trillion compounds. See *Idenix Pharmaceuticals v. Gilead Sciences* [2014] *EWHC* 3916 (Pat), [444].   [101] *Actavis Group v. Eli Lilly* [2015] *EWHC* 3294 (Pat), [177]–[178].
[102] Ibid.   [103] *Human Genome Services v. Eli Lilly* [2011] UKSC 5.
[104] *Actavis Group v. Eli Lilly* [2015] *EWHC* 3294 (Pat), [177].
[105] *Idenix Pharmaceuticals v. Gilead Sciences* [2016] *EWCA Civ* 1089, [111] (CA).
[106] *Glaxosmithkline v. Wyeth Holdings* [2016] EWHC 1045, [94]; *Actavis Group v. Eli Lilly* [2015] *EWHC* 3294 (Pat), [177]–[178]. For discussion, see Paul England, 'Patents and Plausibility' (2014) 9 *JIPLP* 22.
[107] *John Manville's Patent* [1967] *RPC* 479, 493 (Diplock LJ). Singer suggests 13 subtests: R. Singer, *The European Patent Convention* (1995), 182–3.

skilled man is in an inevitable "one-way street"'[109]—the invention is likely to be obvious. In these situations, there is little or no scope for a researcher to act in a technically creative way. The converse of the need for choice is that there is a possibility that the research will fail. Where the research involves no risk or uncertainty—that is, where the results are predictable or likely—the invention is more likely to be obvious and thus unpatentable.

In a sense, the focus on the degree of choice or control exercised by the notional inventor builds upon the idea of invention as a process whereby the inventor (as creator) engages with 'nature' to produce something new. More specifically, it builds upon a model of the invention as a process in which the inventor is actively involved with, and ultimately shapes, the final product. It presumes that there is a degree of human intervention in the production of the invention. In situations where there is no real need nor opportunity for a researcher to make decisions about the shape and nature of the research, there is no real potential for 'human intervention' and, as such, no inventiveness. This is the case, for example, where an invention results from the application of a known technique to a known problem, or where it was obvious to try the technique in question.[110] It is also the case where the person skilled in the art is 'directly led as a matter of course' to the invention.[111]

The mere fact that the notional researcher must have exercised a degree of choice and control over the research process is not in itself enough for the final product to be non-obvious. Put differently, while the exercise of (mental) labour and effort is a *necessary* condition for an invention to be non-obvious, it is not a *sufficient* condition. In order for an invention to be non-obvious, it needs to be shown that the way in which the choice is exercised is technically creative[112]—a notion that changes not only across technologies (both in terms of how it is expressed and also the amount of ingenuity involved), but also over time.[113]

A number of different factors have been taken into account when determining whether an invention is technically creative. At a general level, a distinction is drawn (similar to the distinction drawn in copyright law between 'sweat of the brow' and creativity) between the exercise of routine skills (the results of which are non-patentable) and inventive skills (the results of which are). This is based upon the idea that inventions that are based on laboratory techniques, are routine, or which follow 'plainly or logically from the prior art'[114] do not contribute anything to 'the real advancement of the arts'[115] and, as such, are not worthy of protection.

The courts have also taken care to ensure that only *technical* factors are taken into account when determining inventive step. To this end, it was held that the fact that a particular route was not tried for some time because it was believed that the outcome would

[108] The inquiry was said to be based on myriad factors, which 'divide broadly into matters technical and matters historical': *Saint-Gobain Pam SA v. Fusion Provida* [2004] *All ER* (D) 44, [19].

[109] *Rider/Simethicone tablet*, T 2/83 [1984] *OJ EPO* 265, [6]. See also *Hallen v. Brabantia* [1991] *RPC* 195 (CA).

[110] For a discussion of 'obvious to try', see *Medimmune v. Novartis* [2013] RPC 659, [90]-[95].

[111] *Olin Mathieson v. Biorex* [1970] *RPC* 157.

[112] It has been suggested that proving obviousness by showing a technical contribution to the art is inherent in the problem-and-solution approach adopted at the EPO. *Idenix Pharmaceuticals v. Gilead Sciences* [2014] *EWHC* 3916 (Pat), [104]-[105]; *Generics (UK) v. Yeda Research and Development* [2013] *EWCA Civ* 925 (CA).

[113] *Tevea v. Leo* [2015] *EWCA* 779 (CA) (when considering whether something was obvious to try, it was important to take account of the expectations of the skilled person). For a useful discussion of the dangers of applying judicial tests (such as 'obvious to try') to determine obviousness, see: *Hospira v. Genentech* [2016] *EWCA Civ* 780, [9]-[17] (CA). [114] *EPO Guidelines*, G-VII, [4].

[115] *Atlantic Works v. Brady*, 107 *US* 192 (1883) (Justice Bradley).

not get regulatory approval did not make it a route that was not 'obvious to try'.[116] Equally, while the activities of a manager or accountant might play an important role in shaping the research process, their input is not regarded as 'technical' and, as such, is not taken into account when deciding whether an invention is non-obvious.[117] This was exemplified in the *Pension Benefits Systems* decision when the Technical Board of Appeal said that 'the improvement envisaged by the invention [which was for a computer apparatus for controlling a pension-benefits system] is an essentially economic one, i.e. lies in the field of economy, which, therefore cannot contribute to inventive step'.[118] As such, the claimed subject matter lacked inventive step. While the level of inventiveness required must be more than the mere application of time, money, and effort,[119] the courts have acknowledged that 'in practice what is technically feasible is unlikely to be wholly isolated from what is commercially feasible'.[120] This means that in some cases, commercial and technical considerations may be so inextricably linked that commercial factors may be relevant when considering whether a contribution is technical.[121]

5.2 SPECIFIC APPLICATIONS

Given that decisions about the obviousness of an invention are closely linked to the facts of each case, it may be helpful to look at the way in which inventive step has been approached in a number of different circumstances.[122]

5.2.1 Technique or avenue for research

In some situations, the inventive step may lie in the technique or the avenue of research that is followed. In these circumstances, an invention will be obvious if a person skilled in the art *would* (rather than *could*) have taken the route in question.[123]

The person skilled in the art is assumed to have tried all avenues that have a good prospect of producing valuable results.[124] Factors that might in reality mean that one route is tried before another—such as low cost, easy availability of starting materials, or the likely time before the outcome of an experiment is known—are ignored, since they are not pertinent to whether or not the route is technically obvious. As Laddie J explained in *Brugger v. Medic Aid*:

> [I]f a particular route is an obvious one to take or to try, it is not rendered any less obvious
> from a technical point of view merely because there are a number, and perhaps a large
> number, of other obvious routes as well.[125]

---

[116] *Richardson Vicks Patent* [1995] *RPC* 568, 579–80.

[117] *Genentech's Patent* [1989] *RPC* 147 (CA), 237 (Mustill LJ).

[118] *Pension Benefits Systems*, T 931/95 [2001] *OJ EPO* 413, [7].

[119] *Wiederhold/Two component polyurethane lacquer*, T 259/85 [1988] *EPOR* 209; *Medtronic/Defibrillator*, T 348/86 [1988] *EPOR* 159; *American Cyanamid (Dann's) Patent* [1971] *RPC* 425, 451.

[120] *Ward Building v. Hodgson*, C/47/97 (23 May 1997), unreported (Robert Walker J).

[121] If 'the intellectual horizon of practical research and innovation is in part set by the economic milieu, commercial realities cannot necessarily be divorced from the kinds of practical outcome which might occur to the law's skilled addressee as potentially worthwhile': *Dyson Appliances v. Hoover* [2002] *RPC* 465 (CA), 493 (Sedley LJ); see also Arden LJ at 494–5. Applied by Aldous LJ in *Panduit v. Band-It* [2002] *EWCA Civ* 465, [49].

[122] For discussions focusing on biotechnological inventions, see EPO/USPTO/JPO, *Trilateral Project 24.1: Biotechnology Comparative Study on Biotechnology Patent Practice—Comparative Study Report* (2001); D. Schertenleib, 'The Patentability and Protection of DNA-based Inventions in the EPO and the European Union' [2003] *EIPR* 125; UK IPO, *Examining Patent Applications for Biotechnological Inventions* (21 October 2016), [25]–[57].

[123] *Rider/Simethicone tablet*, T 2/83 [1984] *OJ EPO* 265; *Genentech/Expression in yeast*, T 455/91 [1996] *EPOR* 85.

[124] *American Cyanamid v. Ethicon* [1979] *RPC* 215, 266–7.   [125] [1996] *RPC* 635, 661.

The position is the same if the route to an invention requires the person to take a succession of obvious steps.[126]

In order for a particular avenue of research to be obvious, there is no need for a researcher to be 100 per cent certain that the chosen route will lead to a particular result; thus 'a route may still be an obvious one to try even if it is not possible to be sure that taking it will produce success, or sufficient success to make it commercially worthwhile'.[127] All that needs to be shown for an invention to be obvious is that there was a reasonable expectation of success, or that there was an expectation that the avenue of research 'might well produce a useful desired result'.[128] In *John Manville's Patent*,[129] Diplock LJ said that an invention would be obvious if the 'person versed in the art would assess the likelihood of success as sufficient to warrant actual trial'. The test of 'expectation of success' cannot be applied in all situations. While the test is useful where predictable methods are relied on to solve technical problems (for example methods of genetic engineering, such as cloning and expressing DNA sequences), as the Technical Board of Appeal noted, the test is not useful where an invention depends on random techniques (such as mutagenesis). Where the outcome of a process depends on random events, luck, or chance, the Board said that it was not appropriate to attempt to evaluate the expectation of success: 'Under these circumstances, as for example in a lottery game, the expectation of success always ranges irrationally from nil to high, so that it cannot be evaluated in a rational manner based on technical facts.'[130]

The inventiveness of a particular avenue of research can arise in a number of different ways.[131] In some fields, an avenue of research will not be obvious to try because the person skilled in the art considers the whole field to be unpredictable.[132] In other circumstances, the inventive step might arise from the fact that the research overcomes 'prejudices in the art'[133]—that is, it breaks with current views about an area of research. The decision to follow a particular line of research may be inventive where it had previously been thought that the area was either exhausted or fruitless. Similarly, the decision to follow a line of research may be inventive where all recent developments have exploited a different avenue.[134] As the EPO Guidelines explain:

[As] a general rule, there is inventive step if the prior art leads the person skilled in the art away from the procedure proposed by the invention. This applies in particular where a skilled person would not even consider carrying out experiments to determine whether these were alternatives to the known way of overcoming a real or imagined technical obstacle.[135]

---

[126] *VDO Adolf Schindling/Illuminating device*, T 324/94 [1997] *EPOR* 146. The number of alternative routes may be relevant, for if there is only one route, then even an unexpected result might be treated as being obvious: *Rider/Simethicone*, T 2/83 [1984] *OJ EPO* 265.

[127] *Brugger v. Medic Aid* [1996] *RPC* 635, 660.   [128] *Olin v. Mathieson Biorex* [1970] *RPC* 157, 187.

[129] [1967] *RPC* 479, followed under the 1977 Act in *Brugger v. Medic Aid* [1996] *RPC* 635, 661. See also *Chiron Corporation v. Murex Diagnostics* [1996] *RPC* 535, 557.

[130] *DMS/Astaxanthin*, T 737/96 [2000] *EPOR* 557, [11]. Patentees argued that there was no reasonable expectation of achieving the solution offered by the patent. The Board rejected this test because it was not possible to make reasonable predictions about the possibility of success since the success of the invention depended on chance events (mutagenesis).

[131] A distinction is drawn between an exercise of ingenuity and a voyage of discovery: see *Beechams Group (Amoxycillin) Application* [1980] *RPC* 261 (CA) (Buckley LJ).

[132] *Genentech/Expression in yeast*, T 455/91 [1995] *OJ EPO* 684.

[133] J. Schmidt-Szalewski, 'Non-obviousness as a Requirement of Patentability in French Law' (1992) 23 *IIC* 725, 735–6.

[134] If a particular route has not been considered for commercial reason, such a prejudice is irrelevant: see *Brugger v. Medic Aid* [1996] *RPC* 635.

[135] *EPO Guidelines*, G-VII, [4]. See also *Mobay/Nethylenebis*, T 2/81 [1982] *OJ EPO* 394 (documents revealed a prejudice or general trend pointing away from the invention).

Similarly, if a document in the prior art suggests that the route in question is unlikely to work but the patentee successfully took the route, it is likely that the invention will be patentable. In this context, it is important to keep in mind the comment by Lord Hoffmann that the mere fact that scientific opinion might have thought that something was 'perfectly useless' does not mean that practising it, or having the idea of making a preparation to do so, necessarily amounts to an inventive step. If this were allowed, it would lead to the paradoxical situation in which 'anyone who adopted an obvious method for doing something which was widely practised, but the best scientific opinion thought was pointless, could obtain a patent'.[136]

A particular line of research will also be inventive where it would not have been pursued by the person skilled in the art. It is important to show as well that the research was selected for technical reasons; factors such as the cost of the research are not taken into account. In this context, it is interesting to note that, in *Biogen v. Medeva*,[137] the evidence suggested that, whereas a person less skilled in the art might have regarded the route as being obvious, a person skilled in the art would consider it so beset by obstacles as not to be worth trying.[138]

5.2.2 Overcoming obstacles

In some cases, the ingenuity and skill needed for an invention to be non-obvious lies not so much in the identification of a research problem or in reaching the final goal as it does in the way in which the obstacles and problems that arise en route to reaching the final goal are overcome.[139] Where unforeseeable difficulties exist, the outcome will be non-obvious if the route chosen to overcome those difficulties is inventive.[140] However, where the obstacles are overcome through tenacity, sound technique, or trial and error, the outcome remains obvious.[141]

5.2.3 Selection of the problem

In some cases, the non-obvious nature of an invention may lie in the problem that has been selected, or in the selection of the goals to be pursued.[142] In situations where the inventiveness lies in the way in which the problem to be solved is chosen, for the resulting invention to be non-obvious, the perception of the problem must be beyond the capability of the person skilled in the art.[143] In *Boeing/General technical knowledge*,[144] the patent application related to a mechanism for extending a high-lift device (similar to a crane); the problem to be solved was how this could be done without using long cables. The solution developed by the applicant involved using short cables and pulleys. The Examining Division rejected the application on the basis of two pieces of prior art: one from the

---

[136]   *Ancare New Zealand Ltd's Patent* [2003] *RPC* 139, 143 (Lord Hoffmann); [2002] *UKPC* 8 (PC).

[137]   [1997] *RPC* 1. See also *Hoechst Celanese v. BP* [1997] *FSR* 547.

[138]   *Raleigh Cycle v. Miller* (1946) 63 *RPC* 113; *Phillips Petroleum/Passivation of catalyst*, T 155/85 [1989] *EPOR* 164.   [139]   *John Manville's Patent* [1967] *RPC* 479.

[140]   *Unilever/Chymosin*, T 386/94 [1997] *EPOR* 184, 194.

[141]   *Genentech's Patent* [1989] *RPC* 147 (CA), 276.

[142]   Buckley LJ said 'it will suffice if it is shown that it would appear to anyone skilled in the art but lacking in inventive capacity that to try the step or process would be worthwhile . . . Worthwhile to what end? It must, in my opinion, be shown to be worth trying in order to solve some recognized problem or meet some recognized need': *Beecham/Amoxycillin* [1980] *RPC* 261, 290–1. For a discussion of the approach to take to 'obvious to try', see *Medimmune v. Norvartis Pharmaceuticals* [2012] *EWCA Civ* 1234, [90]–[93].

[143]   *Rider/Simethicone*, T 2/83 [1984] *OJ EPO* 265. With problem inventions, dangers of hindsight are particularly pronounced: *Bonzel v. Intervention (No. 3)* [1991] *RPC* 553.

[144]   T 195/84 [1986] *OJ EPO* 121.

aircraft-engineering field; the other, a patent application directed at no specific field. The Technical Board of Appeal stated that inventiveness could not be found in the perception of the problem, since the overcoming of recognized drawbacks and the achievement of consequent improvements must be considered as the normal task of a skilled person.

5.2.4 Unexpected result

Another situation where the pursuit of an obvious route may result in a non-obvious invention is where the outcome is, in some important way, unexpected. If a route is obvious to try in response to a known problem, but the particular route chosen produces unexpected advantages, the result might be inventive. This is because the person skilled in the art would not associate the avenue of research with the final result.[145] Where the route taken merely produces a result of the sort that was expected, but more cheaply or efficiently, it is unlikely to be inventive. While an invention would be obvious where the skilled worker would think that there was a reasonable expectation if success, this would not be the case where the skilled worker required skills beyond the common general knowledge.[146]

5.2.5 Selection inventions

Particular problems arise where a patent is sought for a compound or class of compounds that are a selection from a broader class previously disclosed by a prior document. As we noted earlier, the patentability of the so-called 'selection inventions' in the United Kingdom was traditionally determined using the criteria set out in *IG Farbenindustrie AG's Application*.[147] However, following the Court of Appeal's 2010 decision in *Dr Reddy's Laboratories (UK) v. Eli Lilly*,[148] *IG Farbenindustrie* is no longer followed in the United Kingdom. Instead, the question to be asked now is: does the invention make a technical contribution or is it merely an arbitrary selection? If the latter, the invention is obvious. This approach is based on the approach that has been developed by the Enlarged Board of Appeal at the EPO:[149] a 'selection from the prior art which is purely arbitrary and cannot be justified by some useful technical property is likely to be held to be obvious because it does not make a real technical advance'.[150]

As the UK Intellectual Property Office (IPO) *Manual of Patent Practice* states, the 'unknown technical effect (ie advantage gained or disadvantage avoided) relied upon to justify a selection should be clearly identified or otherwise made plausible (eg discernable from tests provided in the application) in the specification at the time of filling'.[151] In order for a selection to be considered inventive, the UK IPO provides:

(i) If the alleged contribution is a technical effect which is not common to substantially everything covered by a claim, it cannot be used for the purposes of judging obviousness;

(ii) A selection from the prior art which is purely arbitrary and cannot be justified by some useful technical property is likely to be held to be obvious because it does not make a real technical advance;

---

[145] *Rider/Simethicone*, T 2/83 [1984] *OJ EPO* 265. The discovery of an as-yet-unrecognized problem may give rise to patentable subject matter and, as an unexpected bonus, might be interpreted as a solution of an as-yet-unknown problem.

[146] *Omnipharm v. Merial* [2011] *EWHC* 3393 (Pat).   [147] (1930) 47 *RPC* 289.

[148] *Dr Reddy's Laboratories (UK) v. Eli Lilly* [2009] *EWCA* 1362, [40]–[60].

[149] *Agrevo/Triazoles*, T 939/92 [1996] *OJ EPO* 309; *Wyeth/Dopamine agonists*, T 133/01 (30 September 2003) (a selection would be obvious if it did not make a real technical advance).

[150] *Generics (UK) v. Yeda Research and Teva Pharmaceutical Industries* [2013] *EWCA Civ* 925, [49].

[151] UK IPO, *Manual of Patent Practice*, [3.91].

(iii) A technical effect which is not rendered plausible by the patent specification may not be taken into account in assessing inventive step; and

(iv) Later evidence may be cited to support a technical effect made plausible by the specification.[152]

5.3 SECONDARY EVIDENCE

While the question of whether an invention is obvious is ultimately decided by the tribunals, at times they have been willing to accept so-called 'secondary evidence' that supports a claim that an invention is non-obvious.[153] In effect, secondary evidence is evidence that acts as virtual proof that the invention involved an inventive step. That is, it provides a basis from which it can be inferred that the invention is non-obvious.

While supporters of secondary evidence argue that it makes decision making simpler and adds a degree of realism to the inquiry,[154] there is a growing consensus of opinion against placing too much reliance on it.[155] As Laddie J warned, secondary evidence 'must not be permitted, by reason of its volume and complexity, to obscure the fact that it is no more than an aid in assessing the primary evidence'.[156] The growing suspicion about secondary evidence may reflect the fact that, with the increased specialization of the patent courts, the judges are happier to make technical judgments.[157] It also reflects a desire to keep the cost of patent litigation down, with secondary evidence seen as adding unnecessarily to the time and cost of litigation. With these general reservations in mind, we will now outline some of the forms of secondary evidence that have been used as proof of the non-obviousness of inventions.

5.3.1 Closeness to prior art

One factor that has been used to indicate that an invention is obvious is its proximity to the prior art. If, for example, an invention combines two documents from neighbouring fields, it is likely to be obvious. In a famous case, the Court of Appeal held that a design for a sausage machine that merely combined a better way of cutting sausages with an existing filler was obvious.[158] It would be possible, however, for elements from different areas to be combined in a non-obvious way. Similarly, where a patent application is for a 'new use' that is analogous to the existing known uses of the thing, it is unlikely to be inventive. The use of a substance to reduce friction when it was already known that the substance operated as a rust inhibitor was held not to be analogous.[159]

---

[152] UK IPO, *Examining Patent Applications relating to Chemical Inventions* (5 June 2017), [80].

[153] See J. Bochnovic, *The Inventive Step* (1982), 70; Singer, *The European Patent Convention* (1995), 196–205.

[154] See J. Pagenberg, 'The Evaluation of the "Inventive Step" in the European Patent System: More Objective Standards Needed' (1978) 9 *IIC* 1, 13; J. Pagenberg, 'Different Level of Inventive Step for German and European Patents? The Present Practice of Nullity Proceedings in Germany' (1991) 22 *IIC* 763, 764; E. Kitch, 'The Nature and Function of the Patent System' (1977) 20 *J L & Econ* 265, 283.

[155] *Glaverbel SA v. British Coal* [1995] *RPC* 255; *Hoechst Celanese v. BP* [1997] *FSR* 547, 566; R. Merges, 'Commercial Innovation and Patent Standards' (1988) 76 *Cal L Rev* 805.

[156] *Hoechst Celanese v. BP* [1997] *FSR* 547, 563, echoing *Mölnlycke v. Procter & Gamble (No. 5)* [1994] *RPC* 49.

[157] Cf. A. Cambrosio, P. Keating, and M. MacKenzie, 'Scientific Practice in the Courtroom' (1990) 37 *Soc Probs* 275.

[158] *Williams v. Nye* (1890) 7 *RPC* 62; J. Bochnovic, *The Inventive Step* (1982), 76–8; *Man/Intermediate layer for reflector*, T 6/80 [1979–85] *B EPOR* 266.

[159] *Mobil/Friction reducing additive*, T 59/87 [1990] *EPOR* 514; *Mars II/Glucomannan*, T 112/92 [1994] *EPOR* 249.

5.3.2 Comparative efforts

The efforts of researchers working in the same field as the inventor have also been used as evidence to support non-obviousness.[160] If a number of people working in the same field were pursuing the same goal, the fact that the inventor was the only person to solve the problem successfully might imply inventiveness. This is on the basis that the corresponding failure of others indicates that the solution was not obvious. On the other hand, if other researchers were to make the same invention shortly after the applicant, this might imply that the invention was obvious.[161]

The courts have emphasized that evidence of comparative effort should be treated with caution. In order to be of any value, the comparative inventors must have been working from the same prior art as that cited in the non-obviousness inquiry. They must have also been pursuing the same goal and working for some time. If different starting points were used, no inference can be drawn as to the obviousness of the invention from their relative activities. As Laddie J said, the fact that 'a particular researcher working from an unpleaded piece of prior art, arrived at the invention in suit is of no assistance to the court'.[162]

5.3.3 Long-felt want

A related form of evidence that is used to support claims for inventive step is evidence that the invention satisfies a 'long-felt want'. The logic of this is straightforward: if people had been trying to solve a particular problem for many years and the solution had been obvious, someone would already have invented it.[163] Given the existence of a long-felt want, the fact that no one had previously developed the invention means that the invention must have been non-obvious. While long-felt want may indicate inventiveness, there might be other reasons why a development was not made earlier.[164] As such, it is necessary to be careful when inferring non-obviousness from a long-felt want: the need must have been known about for some time; there must have been an interest in developing the field; and the materials and information that form the basis of the solution must have been known and available.[165]

5.3.4 Commercial success

In some situations, the fate of an invention after grant may provide evidence that suggests that the invention is non-obvious. For example, if an invention proves to be commercially successful or is widely copied by or licensed to competitors, it might be inferred that the invention involved a leap beyond what previously existed. As Tomlin J said in *Parkes v. Cocker*:

> When it has been found that the problem had awaited solution for many years and that the device is in fact novel and superior to what had gone before and has been widely used and indeed in preference to alternative devices, it is practically impossible to say that there is not present that scintilla of invention necessary to support the patent.[166]

---

[160] *Lucas v. Gaedor* [1978] *RPC* 297; *Fichera v. Flogates* [1984] *RPC* 227; *Chiron v. Organon (No. 3)* [1994] *FSR* 202; *Mölnlycke v. Procter & Gamble (No. 5)* [1994] *RPC* 49; *General Tire v. Firestone Tyre* [1976] *RPC* 197 (HL), 203.

[161] *Windsurfing International* [1985] *RPC* 59, 73–4; *Beloit Technologies* [1995] *RPC* 705, 753; *Genentech's Patent* [1989] *RPC* 147, 221.

[162] *Hoechst Celanese v. BP* [1997] *FSR* 547, 565.

[163] See *Teva UK v. Leo Pharma* [2015] *EWCA Civ* 779; *Brugger v. Medic Aid* [1996] *RPC* 635, 654; *Frisco-Findus/Frozen fish*, T 90/89 [1991] *EPOR* 42; *Air Products/Removal of hydrogen sulphide*, T 271/84 [1987] *OJ EPO* 405, [1987] *EPOR* 23.   [164] *Brugger v. Medic Aid* [1996] *RPC* 635, 654–5.

[165] *BASF/Metal Refining* [1979–85] *B EPOR* 354; *VDO Adolf Schindling/Illuminating device*, T 324/94 [1997] *EPOR* 146.   [166] (1929) 46 *RPC* 241, 248.

Evidence about the fate of an invention after grant that is introduced to prove inventive step needs to be treated with caution.[167] This is because there may be a number of reasons other than the non-obvious nature of an invention that explain the reaction of the market or competitors to the invention. For example, a competitor might have taken out a licence from a patentee to avoid threats of litigation, rather than because they regarded the patentee's invention as based on a significant technical advance. Similarly, commercial success might be attributable to factors such as advertising, distribution, marketing, or business acumen rather than to technical advance. For evidence of the fate of an invention after grant to be of value, it must suggest a link between the success of the product and the product's patented features.[168] As a result, commercial success will rarely be of significance unless it can be shown that there is evidence of a previous need for a solution to the particular problem, that the relevant prior art had been published for some time, and, most importantly, that the commercial success was attributable to the technical features of the invention.[169] It has also been suggested that the ability to rely on commercial success depends on being able to isolate what it is that has contributed to the success. As such, it has been suggested that commercial success would only ever be applicable for simple inventions.[170]

5.3.5 The belief and conduct of the inventor

While the factual nature of the obviousness inquiry, which requires the court to pass judgment on the relative 'inventiveness' of the patent, may seem to suggest that the views of the inventor would be critical, as Jacob LJ said, such evidence is at best secondary evidence, which must be kept firmly in place. This helps to protect against the inventor who 'may have thought that what he did was little short of, or actually [was], a work of genius—that he was a latter-day Edison'.[171]

---

[167] *Longbottom v. Shaw* (1891) 8 *RPC* 333, 336; *ICI/Fusecord*, T 270/84 [1987] *EPOR* 357; *EPO Guidelines*, G-VI, [10.2].

[168] R. Merges, 'Commercial Innovation and Patent Standards' (1988) 76 *Cal L Rev* 805; E. Walker, 'Objective Evidence of Non-obviousness: The Elusive Nexus Requirement' (1987) 69 *JPTOS* 175, 236; Comment, 'Non-obviousness in Patent Law: A Question of Law or Fact' (1977) 18 *WMLR* 612.

[169] *EPO Guidelines*, G-VI, [10.3]; *Raychem's Patent* [1998] *RPC* 31.

[170] See *Haberman v. Jackel* [1999] *FSR* 683 (the 'AnyWayUpCup'); *Conor Medsystems v. Angiotech Pharmaceuticals* [2007] *RPC* 487, [51]–[52]. The patent at issue in this decision can be examined on the Online Resources, http://www.oxfordtextbooks.co.uk/bently_sherman5e/.

[171] *Nichia Corporation v. Argos* [2007] *EWCA Civ* 741, [13]–[43].

20

INTERNAL REQUIREMENTS FOR PATENTABILITY

1 INTRODUCTION

In this chapter, we turn our attention away from the external criteria for patentability (subject matter, novelty, and inventive step) to focus on the internal criteria for patentability (so named because they focus on the way in which the patent is drafted). First, we consider the requirement of sufficiency of disclosure, which is the requirement that the invention be disclosed in a manner that is clear and complete enough for it to be performed by a person skilled in the art.[1] Second, we look at the form and content of the claims. In particular, we look at the requirements that the claims be clear and concise, be supported by the description, and relate to one invention.[2] Finally, we look at the requirement that the patent must not be amended in such a way that it acquires additional subject matter or extends the protection conferred by the patent.[3]

2 SUFFICIENCY OF DISCLOSURE

In determining how the scope of protection is to be determined, patent law has had to juggle a number of conflicting demands. On the one hand, it is necessary to ensure that patents offer sufficient rewards to encourage organizations to become involved in the patent process in the first place. To do this, the protection must be robust enough to ensure that competitors are unable to circumvent the patent, for example, by making minor changes to the invention. It is also important that the scope of protection coincides with the invention as disclosed in the patent. As Aldous LJ said:

> I do not believe that the patent system should be used to enable a person to monopolise more than that which he has described in sufficient detail to amount to an enabling disclosure. If it was, it would stifle research.[4]

It is also important that the information disclosed in the patent is useful. It makes little sense to reward someone for disclosing their invention with a patent if a key element of the invention is missing, or if members of the public have to undertake additional or

---

[1] PA 1977, ss 14(3), 72(1)(c); EPC 2000, Art. 83 (ex EPC 1973, Art. 83).
[2] PA 1977, s. 14(5)(c); EPC 2000, Art. 84 (ex EPC 1973, Art. 84).
[3] PA 1977, s. 76(2)–(3); EPC 2000 Regs, r. 136(1)–(2) (ex EPC 1973, Art. 123(2)–(3)).
[4] *American Home Products v. Novartis Pharmaceuticals* [2001] *RPC* 159 (CA), [46].

onerous research before they are in a position to reproduce the invention. At the same time, the law also has to deal with the fact that it is often difficult to describe an invention in words. In this section, we look at one of the most important rules used to regulate the scope of patent protection and, in so doing, help to resolve such issues.[5] This is the requirement that the patent application disclose the invention in a manner that is clear enough and complete enough for it to be performed by a person skilled in the art[6]—usually referred to as the 'requirement for sufficiency of disclosure'. Failure to comply with the requirement for sufficiency gives rise to an objection before grant and is also a ground for revocation once a patent has been granted.[7]

The question of whether the invention has been adequately disclosed is assessed as of the date of filing.[8] While the onus of establishing that an invention has been sufficiently disclosed initially falls upon the applicant/patentee, at trial the obligation is on the defendant to establish that the claims were insufficient. It is not enough for a defendant merely to allege that a patent has not been disclosed in a way that enables the invention to be performed by a person skilled in the art.[9] Instead, a patent can only be challenged on the basis that the invention is not sufficiently disclosed if there are 'serious doubts which are substantiated by verifiable facts'.[10] In the absence of evidence to this effect, the patent will be upheld.[11]

Underpinning the sufficiency requirement is the idea that a patentee should only receive protection for what they have disclosed to the public. In essence, this requires the court to compare what was claimed with what was disclosed. More specifically, as the Technical Board of Appeal at the European Patent Office (EPO) said, it requires the court to compare the extent of the patent monopoly as defined by the claims with the technical contribution to the art made by the patent.[12] In thinking about how this question is addressed, it is helpful to break it down into a number of subsidiary steps. First, it is necessary to determine the extent of the patent monopoly as defined by the claims. Second, it is then necessary to identify what is disclosed by the patent, which, as we will see, requires the court to identify the 'technical contribution' made by the invention. Once these two parameters have been identified, it is then possible to ask whether the technical contribution has been clearly and completely disclosed in the patent. We will look at each in turn.

2.1 WHAT IS THE EXTENT OF THE PATENT MONOPOLY?

In order to determine whether an invention has been sufficiently disclosed, it is first necessary to ascertain what has been claimed.[13] This process is essentially the same process as is used to determine the scope of protection as discussed in Chapter 22.[14]

---

[5] See B. Domeij, 'Patent Claim Scope: Initial and Follow-on Pharmaceutical Inventions' [2001] *EIPR* 326.

[6] PA 1977, ss 14(3), 72(1)(c); EPC 2000, Art. 83 (ex EPC 1973, Art. 83).

[7] PA 1977, s. 72(1); EPC 2000, Art. 100 (ex EPC 1973, Art. 100).

[8] *Biogen v. Medeva* [1997] *RPC* 1, 53–4 (Lord Hoffmann); *Kirin-Amgen v. Transkaryotic Therapies* [2003] *RPC* 31 (CA).

[9] PA 1977, ss 14(3), 72(1)(c); EPC 2000, Art. 83 (ex EPC 1973, Art. 83).

[10] The mere fact that a claim is broad is not in itself a ground for considering the application as not complying with the requirement for sufficient disclosure in EPC 1973, Art. 83 (now EPC 2000, Art. 83): *Harvard/OncoMouse*, T 19/90 [1990] *OJ EPO* 476.   [11] T 9182/89 [1991] *OJ EPO* 391.

[12] *Exxon/Fuel Oils*, T 409/91 [1994] *EPOR* 149, [3.3] (emphasis added).

[13] The test is conducted on the basis of the specification as a whole, including the description and the claims: *Eli Lilly v. Human Genome Sciences* [2012] EWCA Civ 1185, [11], citing Kitchin J in the same case at first instance ([2008] *EWHC* 1903 (Pat), [239]).

[14] It seems that this will be judged on the basis of normal or purposive interpretation, rather than under the doctrine of equivalents: *Generics (UK) Ltd (t/a Mylan) v. Yeda Research and Development Company* [2017] *EWHC* 2629, [161]–[167] (in relation to novelty).

2.2 WHAT IS THE 'TECHNICAL CONTRIBUTION'?

Once the scope of the monopoly has been ascertained, it is then necessary to determine the 'technical contribution' made by the invention. The potential importance of this preliminary inquiry can be seen from the decision of *Generics (UK) v. H. Lundbeck*, which concerned a patent for a chemical product—namely, an enantiomer (escitalopram) of a racemate (citalopram). At first instance, Kitchin J held that the claims in question were invalid for insufficiency.[15] This was in contrast with the Court of Appeal[16] and the House of Lords, which found the claims to be valid.[17] The different findings in this case were directly attributable to the way in which the relevant technical contribution was identified. For Kitchin J, the technical contribution was determined by identifying the elements of the invention that contributed to its inventive step: the two methods of isolating the enantiomer that the patentee had discovered.[18] The Court of Appeal and the House of Lords, however, held that the relevant contribution was the invention (or product) *itself* and not, as Kitchin J had held, the inventive step that underpinned the invention (which was the method of making the product). In reviewing the first-instance judgment, the Law Lords said that the problem with Kitchin J's judgment was that he had confused inventive step with invention. As Lords Walker and Neuberger explained, 'technical contribution' is different from 'inventive concept': inventive concept is concerned with the identification of the core (or kernel, or essence) of the invention, whereas the inventor's technical contribution to the art is concerned with the *evaluation* of its inventive concept—that is, how far forward it has carried the state of the art.[19] The mistake that Kitchin J had made was to focus on the elements of the invention that contributed to its inventive step—the method of isolating the enantiomer—rather than on what had been claimed—namely, the enantiomer as a product. As we will see later, the finding that the technical contribution was a product per se has important consequences for the type of information needed for a patent to satisfy the requirements of sufficiency.

The upshot of this is that when determining what the relevant technical contribution is, it is important to focus on the invention as claimed, and not the features or qualities that make that invention 'inventive' or, presumably, novel.

2.3 HAS THERE BEEN A CLEAR AND COMPLETE DISCLOSURE?

Once the scope of the monopoly and the relevant technical contribution have been identified, it is then necessary to ask whether the invention-as-claimed is disclosed in a manner that is clear enough and complete enough for it to be performed or carried out by a person skilled in the art. This is done to ensure that the claim does not 'exceed the technical contribution to the art embodied in the invention'.[20] This means, for example, that if an invention is a compound that reduces pain, the specification must contain sufficient information to enable compounds with that attribute to be manufactured.[21] It also means

---

[15] *Generics (UK) v. H. Lundbeck* [2007] *RPC* 729 (Pat).

[16] *Generics (UK) v. H. Lundbeck* [2008] *RPC* (19) 439 (CA).

[17] *Generics (UK) v. H. Lundbeck* [2009] *UKHL* 12.

[18] The problem for the patentee was that what had been claimed (the enantiomer made by *any* method) was greater than what had been disclosed (only two ways of making the enantiomer). Drawing on *Biogen* that a class of products could be enabled only if the person skilled in the art could perform or work the invention in respect of all members of the class, Kitchin J held that the claims were insufficient.

[19] *Generics (UK) v. H. Lundbeck* [2009] *UKHL* 12, [30] (Lord Walker).

[20] *Biogen v. Medeva* [1995] *RPC* 1, 25, 51 (HL).   [21] *Pharmacia v. Merck* [1997] *RPC* 1, 798 (CA).

that the scope of the monopoly must coincide with (or be less than) the technical contribution made by the invention.

Sufficiency is decided by the court judged through the eyes of a person skilled in the art. As the Patents Act 1977 and the EPC 2000 make clear, the specification must be disclosed in such a way that it can be performed by *the person skilled in the art*. The notional skilled person employed in this context is similar to the notional interpreter used to assess inventive step. One difference is that whereas for the purposes of evaluating inventive step the skilled person has only knowledge of the prior art, for the purpose of evaluating sufficiency of disclosure the skilled person has knowledge of the prior art *and* of the invention as disclosed.[22]

The sufficiency inquiry is often divided up according to the nature of the problem at issue into (i) classic insufficiency, (ii) insufficiency due to excessive claim breadth (or '*Biogen* insufficiency'[23]), or (iii) insufficiency due to ambiguity.[24] While this is a useful categorization, it is important to keep in mind that these are instances of a more general requirement that the disclosure in the specification must enable a person skilled in the art to manufacture the invention or, in Lord Hoffmann's words, that there must be an 'enabling disclosure'.[25]

2.3.1 Classical insufficiency

Classical insufficiency arises when the disclosure of the invention is not complete enough for the claim to be worked *at all* by a person skilled in the art from common general knowledge.[26] In recognition of the fact that many (if not most) patents require some degree of fine-tuning before they can be put into practice, the patent specification does not need to spell out every specific detail necessary for an invention to be performed.[27] In line with this, it has been accepted that in putting an invention into practice the skilled person is able to make use of common general knowledge,[28] to engage in routine laboratory tests, to correct obvious errors in the specification,[29] and does not have to be told

[22] *Mycogen/Modifying plant cells*, T 694/92 [1998] *EPOR* 114, 120; *Schlumberger Holdings v. Electromagnetic Geoservices* [2010] *EWCA Civ* 819, [61]. For the purposes of determining sufficiency of disclosure, the person skilled in the art is non-inventive, is able to make use of common general knowledge, and is able to perform non-inventive experiments. The notional interpreter 'is not to be expected to exercise any invention nor any prolonged research or inquiry or experiment. He must, however, be prepared to display a reasonable degree of skill and common knowledge of the art in making trials and to correct obvious errors in the specification if a means of correcting them can readily be found': *Mentor v. Hollister* [1993] *RPC* 7, 13. See also *Valensi v. British Radio Corporation* [1973] *RPC* 337; *Edison & Swan Electric Light v. Holland* (1889) 6 *RPC* 243. While the skilled reader is presumed to have *access* to everything in the state of the art, this does not mean that they also have *knowledge* of everything in the state of the art: *EPO Guidelines*, F-III, [1].

[23] *Biogen v. Medeva* [1997] *RPC* 1, 47 (Lord Hoffmann); *Asahi Kasei Kogyo* [1991] *RPC* 485, 536 (Lord Oliver), 547 (Lord Jauncey); *Pharmacia Corporation v. Merck* [2002] *RPC* 773, [54] (CA). *Eli Lilly v. Janssen Alzheimer Immunotherapy* [2013] *EWHC* 1737 (Pat), [248]–[254].

[24] See, e.g., *Sandvik v Kennametal* [2012] *RPC* 501, [106]–[124] (Arnold J).

[25] *Biogen v. Medeva* [1997] *RPC* 1, 47 (Lord Hoffmann); *Asahi Kasei Kogyo* [1991] *RPC* 485 (HL), 536 (Lord Oliver), 547 (Lord Jauncey); *Pharmacia Corporation v. Merck* [2002] *RPC* 775, [54] (CA). The question of how far different tests are appropriate to different sorts of insufficiency objection is at the heart of the pending appeal to the Supreme Court in *Warner-Lambert v. Mylan*, on appeal from [2016] *EWCA Civ* 1006 (CA), where the appellant argues that it is unnecessary to apply the test of 'plausibility' in relation to an insufficiency objection to a broad claim in a situation where the person skilled in the art could, without undue burden, confirm that the invention worked across the breadth of the claim.

[26] UK IPO, *Examining Patent Applications Relating to Chemical Inventions* (5 June 2017), [102].

[27] *Valensi v. British Radio Corp.* [1973] *RPC* 337, 375; *Mentor v. Hollister* [1993] *RPC* 7, 12.

[28] *Genentech/t-PA*, T 923/92 [1996] *EPOR* 275, 302.

[29] *Air Products/Redox catalyst*, T 171/84 [1986] *OJ EPO* 95.

what is self-evident.[30] While with manufactured objects and the like, the claims need to enable the person skilled in the art to produce something akin to a workable prototype, they do 'not have to be of sufficiently high quality to be ready to be sold'.[31]

There are two important limitations on the types of activity that the person skilled in the art can legitimately be called upon to engage in when implementing the invention. The first is that if the person skilled in the art needs to use any inventive skill when putting the invention into practice, the invention will not have been disclosed sufficiently and, as such, will be invalid.[32] The second limitation is that the invention must be able to be reproduced without 'undue burden'.[33] 'Undue burden' is a catch-all phrase that covers activities that the courts deem to be onerous.[34] This has been the case, for example, where the patent required the skilled person to undertake lengthy experiments before they are able to perform the invention,[35] or where the reproduction of the invention depended on a 'stroke of luck'.[36] Rejecting the argument that timescale should not be taken into account when assessing sufficiency, Jacob LJ said that:

> [P]atents are meant to teach people how to do things. If what is 'taught' involves just too much to be reasonable for all the circumstances including the nature of the art, then the patent cannot be regarded as an 'enabling disclosure'. That is the basic concept behind the requirement of sufficiency and one that lies at the heart of patent law . . . The setting of a gigantic project, even if merely routine, will not do.[37]

2.3.2 Insufficiency due to excessive breadth

A second form of insufficiency (often called *Biogen* sufficiency after Lord Hoffmann's judgment in *Biogen v. Medeva*) arises where the application only contains sufficient disclosure to enable part of the claims to be worked.[38] Although in reaching his decision in *Biogen v. Medeva,* Lord Hoffmann expressly referred to the jurisprudence of the Boards

---

[30] *Biogen v. Medeva* [1995] *RPC* 1, 25, 98 (HL); *Chiron v. Organon (No. 12)* [1994] *FSR* 153, 185.

[31] *Varian Medical Systems International v. Elekta* [2017] *EWHC* 712 (Pat), [166], citing *Mentor v. Hollister* [1993] *RPC* 7.

[32] *Mentor v. Hollister* [1993] *RPC* 7, 12; *Valensi v. British Radio Corp.* [1973] *RPC* 337, 377; *Wacker-Chemie*, T 931/91 (20 April 1993).

[33] *Unilever/Cleanser composition*, T 226/85 [1988] *OJ EPO* 336; *MedImmune v. Novartis Pharmaceuticals* [2011] *EWHC* 1669 (Pat), [458]–[484]; *Sandvik Intellectual Property v. Kennametal* [2011] *EWHC* 3311 (Pat), [106]–[124]; *Hospira v. Novartis* [2013] *EWHC* 516 (Pat), [182].

[34] The 'whole subject-matter which is defined in the claim should be enabled without undue burden by the teaching of the patent specification': *Weyershauser/Cellulose*, T 727/95 [2001] *OJ EPO* 1, [7]; *Mycogen/Modifying plant cells*, T 694/92 [1998] *EPOR* 114, 119 (in which the TBA said the 'claims need to provide instructions which are sufficiently clear for the skilled person to reduce them to practice without undue burden, i.e. with no more than a reasonable amount of experimentation and without applying inventive skill'). The person skilled in the art should not be called upon to make a prolonged study of matters that present some initial difficulty: *Valensi v. British Radio Corp.* [1973] *RPC* 337; *Badische Anilin v. Société Chimique* (1898) 15 *RPC* 359.

[35] *DSM NV's Patent* [2001] *RPC* 675, 712–16 (cloning, sequencing, and recombinant expression of the gene for phytsase from fungus held to be extremely broad and unworkable, because the skilled person would have had to depart from the patent and to experiment over what may have been a long period of time to achieve the desired goal); *Icos Corporation/Seven transmembrane receptor* [2002] *OJ EPO* 293 (OD), 300 (disclosure of a predicted function of a protein in combination with a method of verification of this function was insufficient because the skilled person was required to test millions of available compounds). Cf. *Bayer Crop Science/Safeners*, T 1020/98 [2003] *OJ EPO* 533, 542 (the actual time taken was not relevant when deciding whether a claim could be performed if clear and concise).

[36] *Weyershause/Cellulose*, T 727/95 [2001] *OJ EPO* 1, [10].

[37] *Halliburton Energy Services v. Smith International (North Sea)* [2006] *EWCA Civ* 1715, [17]–[18].

[38] *Biogen v. Medeva* [1997] *RPC* 1, 48–9.

of Appeal, in *Videojet Technologies* the Technical Board of Appeal said that there was no need to invoke the concept of 'Biogen sufficiency' at the EPO (as the opposition had done in that case). As the Board of Appeal said, 'the concept of "Biogen sufficiency" is not part of the established jurisprudence of the boards of appeal of the EPO and is not commonly used in EPO proceedings'.[39]

As we explained earlier, it is accepted practice for patents to be granted for extremely large classes of compounds, DNA sequences, and the like.[40] This is particularly the case in relation to chemical and biotechnological inventions, for which patents may claim hundreds of thousands (sometimes millions or trillions) of compounds. Strictly speaking the test for whether a patent for a large class of compounds has been suffi-ciently disclosed is the same test as is used to examine a patent for a simple mechani-cal device: so long as the patent equips a person skilled in the art with the means to perform the invention without undue burden[41] or the need to use inventive skills,[42] the invention will be sufficiently disclosed. Having said this, patents for large classes of inventions have given rise to very specific issues. This is largely due to the fact that British patent law has long accepted that in the case of patents for classes of inven-tions, it is not necessary for the patentee to prove that every last compound is enabled by the claims. While this facilitated the extension of patents to chemical inventions, it also gave rise to a series of new questions: the key one being what was needed to prove (or disprove) that a large class of inventions was sufficiently disclosed? The problems that arise here are magnified when the onus shifts to the defendant to show that such a patent is insufficient. In particular, questions have arisen in relation to the evidence that a defendant needs to produce to show that a class of compounds has not been disclosed in a manner that is clear enough and complete enough for it to be made by a person skilled in the art. Is it enough, for example, for an opponent to show that of a class of 1,000 compounds, one compound cannot be manufactured? If not one, how many?[43]

While there is no easy answer to these questions, it is possible to make some general comments as to how the insufficiency of large groups of inventions is calculated. The first and most straightforward point, which flows from the fact that the onus is on the defend-ant to show that claims are insufficient,[44] is that a patent will be upheld if the defendant fails to provide evidence showing that at least one of the claims cannot be performed.[45] The courts have also stressed that when carrying out experiments to test whether the invention is insufficient and thus invalid, the defendant should select representative

---

[39] *Videojet Technologies/Tape drive*, T 1727/12 (1 February 2016), [1.2].

[40] '[M]ost claims are generalizations from one or more particular examples. The extent of generalization permissible is a matter which the examiner must judge in each particular case in the light of the relevant prior art': *EPO Guidelines*, F-IV, [6.2]. See K. Luzzatto, 'The Support and Breadth of Claims to New Classes of Chemical Compounds' [1989] *Patent World* 21.

[41] *Unilever/Stable bleach*, T 226/85 [1989] *EPOR* 18.

[42] *Wacker-Chemie*, T 931/91 (20 April 1993).

[43] *Mycogen/Modifying plant cells*, T 694/92 [1998] *EPOR* 114, 119 (the *essential* features of the claimed invention must be capable of being performed); *Exxon/Fuel oils*, T 409/91 [1994] *EPOR* 149; *Sumitomo/Vinyl chloride resins*, T 14/83 [1984] *OJ EPO* 105; *Unilever/Stable bleaches*, T 226/85 [1989] *EPOR* 18.

[44] *Kirin-Amgen v. Transkaryotic Therapies* [2003] *RPC* 31 (CA), 71.

[45] The importance of this can be seen in *Kirin Amgen*, ibid., in which the absence of any evidence from the defendant that a single DNA sequence could not be worked meant that the ground of insufficiency was not established. Allowance is made for situations in which a few minor or marginal embodiments cannot be made to work: *Filtration/Fluid filter cleaning system*, T 126/89 [1990] *EPOR* 292; *Sumitomo/Vinyl chloride resins*, T 14/83 [1984] *OJ EPO* 105.

samples, rather than samples that are likely to fail. This follows from the fact that the person skilled in the art will be motivated by a desire to succeed, not to fail.[46] The courts have also suggested that where a defendant introduces experimental evidence that casts doubts over the sufficiency of a patent, it may hinder the patentee's case if they do not provide experimental evidence to the contrary.[47]

The specific information needed for a patent over a class of compounds to be disclosed sufficiently differs depending on the type of invention in question, the prior art in the field, and how developed the relevant discipline is.[48] In some situations, this might include details about the relationship between the chemical structure and the activities that the chemicals perform.[49] In the case of Swiss style or EPC 2000 claims, an applicant will need to show 'by appropriate experiments that the product has an effect on a disease process so as to make the claimed therapeutic effect plausible'.[50] In other cases, knowledge of an appropriate DNA sequence might provide the skilled person with enough information to rework the invention.[51] In some situations, the mere disclosure of a formula may be sufficient for the invention to be performed or worked.[52] In other cases, it may be necessary for both the formula and the starting materials (or means) to be disclosed for a person skilled in the art to put the invention into practice.

A useful example of the way sufficiency is applied to classes of compounds is offered by the *Genentech* decision[53] in which the applicants invented a general principle that enabled plasmids to control the expression of polypeptides in bacteria. Because there was no reason to believe that the invention would not work equally well with any plasmid, bacterium, or polypeptide, the patent for more general claims was granted. This is subject to the rider that the applicant must be able to show that the specification discloses a principle of general application that is shared by all members in the class. As Lord Hoffmann explained in *Biogen*, if 'the invention discloses a principle capable of general application, the claims may be in correspondingly general terms'.[54] This means that if the patentee has disclosed something 'which is common to the class, he will be entitled to a patent for all products of that class . . . even though he has not made more than one

[46] *British Thomson-Houston v. Corona Lamp Works* (1922) 39 *RPC* 49, 89; followed in *Kirin-Amgin v. Transkaryotic Therapies* [2003] *RPC* 31 (CA), 70–1.

[47] In *Pharmacia v. Merck* [2002] *RPC* 775 (CA), [75], Aldous LJ said that the 'patentees had ample opportunity to do experiments in reply to demonstrations that the compounds were not representative. They had equipment and the knowledge to do the experiments, but failed to do them.' See also *AgrEvo/Triazoles*, T 939/92 [1996] *OJ EPO* 309, [2.5.4].

[48] The tribunals seem to have taken a more relaxed approach in relation to biotechnological inventions than chemical inventions.   [49] See *Monsanto v. Merck* [2000] *RPC* 709, [7].

[50] *Regeneron v. Genentech* [2013] *EWCA Civ* 93, [103], citing *Salk Institute/AP-1 Complex*, T 609/02 (27 October 2004). The same approach was adopted by the Court of Appeal in *Warner-Lambert v. Mylan* [2016] *EWCA Civ* 1006 (CA) (finding that the use of a chemical was plausible to treat 'peripheral neuropathic pain' but not 'central neuropathic pain') but is the subject of a pending appeal to the Supreme Court.

[51] *Weyershauser/Cellulose*, T 727/95 [2001] *OJ EPO* 1.

[52] *Merck/Starting compounds*, T 51/87 [1991] *OJ EPO* 177.

[53] *Genentech/Polypeptide expression*, T 292/85 [1989] *EPOR* 1.

[54] *Biogen v. Medeva* [1997] *RPC* 1, 49 (HL). In so doing, Lord Hoffmann rejected a line of cases that had suggested that a single disclosure of one way of making the product was sufficient to disclose the invention, i.e. the so-called 'one way' rule derived from *Molnlycke v. Proctor and Gamble (No. 5)* [1992] *FSR* 549 and *Chiron Corporation v. Organon Teknika (No. 3)* [1994] *FSR* 202 (which is based on a misreading of *Genentech I/Polypeptide expression*, T 292/85 [1989] *EPOR* 1). On this, see R. Freeland and G. Blachman, 'The Law of Insufficiency: Is *Biogen* Still Good Law?' [2009] *EIPR* 478, 479.

or two of them'.[55] Problems arise, however, if the patentee is unable to show that there is something that unifies the general class. This would be the case, for example, where a patentee discovers:

> . . . a new product which has the beneficial effect but cannot demonstrate that there is a common principle by which that effect will be shared by other products of the same class[;] he will be entitled to a patent for that product but not for that class: even though some may turn out to have the same beneficial effect.[56]

In the absence of a unifying principle, the claim will be for a generalized description of a large number of compounds, rather than a true class.[57]

In recent years there has been a growing focus on the concept of 'plausibility' and the role it plays in relation to sufficiency. In part, this is based on the idea that it must be possible to make a reasonable prediction that the invention will work with substantially everything falling within the scope of the claim. This has been taken to mean that 'the assertion that the invention will work across the scope of the claim must be plausible or credible'. [58] Used in this way plausibility operates as a standard of proof (or a level of faith that the claims will work) that needs to be established. As Floyd LJ said, the EPO and UK cases indicate that 'the requirement of plausibility is a low threshold test . . . designed to prohibit speculative claiming . . . it is not designed to prohibit patents for good faith predictions which have some, albeit manifestly incomplete, basis'.[59] Arnold J took this one step further when he suggested that when considering whether an invention is capable of being performed over the whole scope of the claim, the court must undertake a two-stage inquiry. The first is to determine whether the disclosure of the patent read in the light of common general knowledge of the skilled team makes it plausible that the invention will work across the scope of the claim. (Here no evidence can be used which post-dates the patent).[60] Once this is done, it is then necessary to consider evidence as to whether the invention in fact can be performed across the scope of the claim without undue burden. At this stage, evidence which post-dates the patent is admissible.[61]

2.3.3 Insufficiency due to ambiguity

Insufficiency due to ambiguity arises when the disclosure is so ambiguous as to make it impossible for a skilled person to know whether they have worked the

---

[55] *Biogen v. Medeva* [1997] *RPC* 1, 49 (Lord Hoffmann). A principle of general application 'means an element of the claim which is stated in general terms. Such a claim is sufficiently enabled if one can reasonably expect the invention to work with anything that falls within the general term': *Kirin-Amgen v. Hoechst Marion Roussel* [2005] *RPC* 169, [112] (HL).

[56] *Biogen v. Medeva* [1997] *RPC* 1, 49 (Lord Hoffmann); *AHP v. Novartis* [2001] *RPC* 159, 176 (CA); *Pharmacia v. Merck* [2002] *RPC* 775 (inability to point to any characteristic that unified an otherwise unpredictable class of chemical compounds meant that the claims were insufficient and thus invalid).

[57] *Monsanto v. Merck* [2000] *RPC* 709, [67]; approved on appeal in *Pharmacia v. Merck* [2002] *RPC* 799 (CA). See also *Biogen v. Medeva* [1997] *RPC* 1 , 47 ('may claim every way of achieving a result, when it enables only one way and it is possible to envisage other ways of achieving that result which makes no use of the invention'), drawing on *Genentech I/Polypeptide expression*, T 292/85 [1989] *OJ EPO* 275.

[58] *Regeneron Pharmaceuticals v. Genentech* [2013] *EWHC Civ* 93, [100]; *GlaxoSmithKline v. Wyeth* [2016] *EWHC* 1045, [94]; *Merck Sharp and Dohme v. Shionogi* [2016] *EWHC* 2989 (Pat), [234] ('There must be a real reason for supposing that the claimed invention will indeed have the promised technical effect').

[59] *Warner-Lambert v. Mylans* [2016] *EWCA Civ* 1006, [46] (need to show the claims are not speculative). See also *Idenix Pharmaceuticals v. Gilead Sciences* [2016] *EWCA Civ* 1089, [111]–[112], [138].

[60] See also *Actavis Group v. Elli Lilly* [2015] *EWHC* 3294 (Pat) (plausibility was a threshold test).

[61] *Merck Sharp and Dohme v. Shionogi* [2016] *EWHC* 2989 (Pat), [233].

invention,[62] to put the invention into practice,[63] or to practice what is taught.[64] In this context a distinction is drawn between a fuzzy (or unclear) claim which is a by-product of the difficult task of trying to describe an invention in words (which is not objectionable) and, on the other, a truly ambiguous claim, (which is objectionable). If a skilled person needs to undertake a technical test to find out if a product or process is within the claim and the claims are such that they 'cannot know whether they are carrying out the right test', then the claim is truly ambiguous and therefore insufficient'.[65]

2.4 SUFFICIENCY FOR DIFFERENT TYPES OF CLAIMS AND INVENTIONS

The information that has to be disclosed for a person skilled in the art to perform an invention often varies depending on the nature of the invention.[66] We have already looked at some of the issues that arise in relation to chemical and genetic inventions where large classes of inventions are claimed. Here we look at two additional types of inventions that give rise to particular problems; product claims and biological inventions.

2.4.1 Product claims

Following the House of Lords' decision of *Biogen v. Medeva*, there was some uncertainty about the level of information needed for a product claim to satisfy the requirement of sufficiency of disclosure. As we explained earlier, one of the notable things about a product claim is that it not only covers the article or substance in question per se, but also extends to include the right to control how the product is made or used.[67] In this context, the question arose: was it necessary, following the approach in *Biogen*, for a patentee to disclose all of the different ways in which the product was made (and, in so doing, ensure that the scope of the monopoly coincided with what was disclosed)? Or was it sufficient for them merely to disclose the product (and one way of making the product)? After some confusion, following *Generics (UK) v. H. Lundbeck*,[68] it is now clear that there is no need for a patentee to disclose all of the ways in which a product might be made that fall within their control. So long as the patentee discloses one way of creating the product, they will disclose the product. As Lord Hoffmann said, 'when a product claim satisfies section 1 of the 1977 Act, the technical contribution to the art is the product and not the process by which it is made, even if the process was the only inventive step',[69] and importantly, with

---

[62] UK IPO, *Examining Patent Applications Relating to Chemical Inventions* (5 June 2017), [104] (noting that in *Kirin Amgen* this was distinguished from lack of clarity). For a discussion of insufficiency via ambiguity, see *Unwired Planet International v. Huawei Technologies* [2016] *EWHC* 576, [148]–[163]; *Actavis Group v. ICOS* [2016] *EWHC* 1955 (Pat), [469]–[471].

[63] See *Unwired Planet International v. Huawei Technologies* [2016] *EWHC* 576 (Pat), [156].

[64] The problem in *Kirin-Amgen* was 'not a "puzzle at the edge of the claim", it was a failure to disclose the invention clearly enough for it to be performed at all because the skilled person could never know if they were within it or not'. *Unwired Planet International v. Huawei Technologies* [2016] *EWHC* 576 (Pat), [159].

[65] Ibid., [163].

[66] Sufficiency is 'highly sensitive to the nature of the invention'. *Kirin-Amgen v. Hoechst Marion Roussel* [2004] *UKHL* 46, [200]; *H. Lundbeck A/S v. Generics (UK) Ltd and ors* [2008] *EWCA Civ* 311, [35]; *Mentor Corporation v. Hollister* [1993] *RPC* 7, 12; *Mycogen/Modifying plant cells*, T 694/92 [1998] *EPOR* 114, 120.

[67] On the difference between product claims and product-by-process claims, see *Generics (UK) v. H. Lundbeck* [2009] *UKHL* 12, [22]–[25].   [68] Ibid.

[69] *Biogen v. Medeva* [1997] *RPC* 1, 49 (Lord Hoffmann); *Generics (UK) v. H. Lundbeck* [2008] *RPC* (19) 439, [35] (Lord Hoffmann) (CA). For discussion, see *Generics (UK) v. H. Lundbeck* [2009] *UKHL* 12, [14] (HL).

an 'ordinary product claim, the product is the invention. It is sufficiently enabled if the specification and common general knowledge enable the skilled person to make it. One method is enough.'[70] As such, a patent for a product would be sufficiently enabled if the patent discloses at least one way of making it. While with product-by-process claims, it is necessary to disclose every way of making the product, with product claims, so long as the patent discloses (at least) one way in which to make the product in question, it would be sufficiently disclosed.[71]

It is important to ask, as Kitchin J did at first instance in *Generics (UK) v. H. Lundbeck*, whether the sufficiency requirement is doing its job properly in relation to product claims. The concern here is that with product claims, there is a potential discrepancy between what is invented and what is protected—a concern, as Jacob LJ said in the Court of Appeal, that the patentee gets 'more that he deserves'.[72] While Lord Hoffmann in *Lundbeck* was sympathetic to Kitchin J's 'instinctive reaction to the inherent breadth of a product claim',[73] he was not willing to accept that the requirement of sufficiency of disclosure could be used as a means to overcome the potential problem with per se claims—namely, that while they may disclose only one way of making a product, they are given control over the product and, as such, over all ways of making that product. Given that this undermines a core principle of patent law (namely, that the patentee receives protection only for what they have invented and disclosed) and that it is highly unlikely that this issue will be resolved at the legislative level, this is an area in which judicial creativity may be warranted.

2.4.2 Biological inventions

As we saw earlier, one of the problems that confronted applicants in their attempt to patent biological invention, whether it be new plants, microorganisms, or the products of modern biotechnological research, was the concern that they would not be able to describe their new creations in such a way that the inventions would satisfy the requirement for sufficiency of disclosure. The reason for this is that where an invention depends on the use of living materials such as microorganisms or cultured cells, or where the invention is for a new type of plant or animal, it may be impossible to describe the invention so that the public is able to make the invention.[74] Following a practice started in the United States in the 1930s (which borrowed directly from taxonomic practices),[75] the EPC 2000[76] and the Patents Act 1977[77] addresses this problem by providing that if an invention involves biological material that cannot be described in a way that enables the invention to be carried out by a person skilled in the art, the applicant must deposit a sample of this biological material at a 'recognized institution' (or depositary).[78] These issues were also addressed

---

[70] *Generics (UK) v. H. Lundbeck* [2008] *RPC* (19) 439, [27] (Lord Hoffmann) (CA).

[71] Arguably this would also apply to the situation in which the claim is to a product of a known goal, the properties of which are known, but which no one knows how to make. If the patentee finds, at minimum, one way of making the product, the claim would be sufficiently disclosed: *Kawasaki Steel Corporation*, T 595/90 [1994] *OJ EPO* 695. On this, see A. Batteson, '*Lundbeck v. Generics*: "*Biogen* Insufficiency" Explained' [2009] *EIPR* 51, 52.   [72] *Generics (UK) v. H. Lundbeck* [2008] *RPC* (19) 439, [57] (CA).

[73] See *Generics (UK) v. H. Lundbeck* [2007] *EWHC* 1040, [2007] *RPC* (32) 720 (Pat), [27].

[74] In *American Cyanamid (Dann)'s Patent* [1971] *RPC* 425, the House of Lords held that there was no obligation on a patentee under the PA 1949 to supply the microorganism to the public.

[75] See A. Pottage and B. Sherman, *Figures of Invention* (2010).

[76] EPC 2000 Regs, r. 31.   [77] PA 1977, s. 125A, introduced by CDPA 1988, Sch. 5, para. 30.

[78] Recognized depositary institutions include all international depositaries under the 1977 Treaty on the International recognition of the Deposit of Micro-organisms (the 'Budapest Treaty') (modified in 1980). This established minimum requirements for maintaining an international depositary for microorganisms (the United Kingdom joined on 29 December 1988). In December 2013, there were 79 contracting parties to the Treaty, with 42 international depositary authorities (IDAs).

in the Biotechnology Directive.[79] The application must contain such relevant information as is available on the characteristics of the biological material.[80] If an applicant intends to rely upon deposit as a way of satisfying the requirement for sufficiency of disclosure, it is important that the patent makes specific reference to the deposit; failure to do so may mean that the deposit cannot be relied upon.[81]

The extent to which an applicant needs to rely upon a deposit to satisfy the requirement for sufficiency depends on the nature of the invention in question. The material deposit is not mandated for biological inventions; it is an option that may be relied upon if needed. While it is more likely that traditionally bred plants will need to be deposited, this is not necessarily the case for many of the outcomes of molecular biology, which are able to be described in a way that enables the invention to be replicated by a person skilled in the art. This can be seen, for example, in the *Wisconsin Alumni Research Foundation/Stem cell* decision,[82] where the Technical Board of Appeal was called upon to consider whether in the absence of a reference to a deposit and of specific examples, the description contained sufficient information to enable the skilled person to prepare the claimed human embryonic stem-cell cultures without excessive burden or undue experimentation.[83] The Board accepted that the skilled person would have been in a position to prepare and grow human embryonic cell lines and, as such, that the invention complied with Article 83 of the EPC 1973 (now Article 83 of the EPC 2000).

3 CLAIMS

The claims play a crucial role in the patent system, not least because they define the scope of protection.[84] Given this, it is not surprising that there are a number of restrictions on how the claims are drafted. Here we focus on the requirements in section 14(5)(c)/ Articles 82 and 84 that the claims must be clear and concise (clarity), be supported by the description, and relate to one invention or group of inventions. Before looking at these in more detail, it is necessary to make some comments about the consequences of non-compliance with these provisions.

As we mentioned earlier, non-compliance with the requirement for sufficiency of disclosure gives rise to an objection before grant.[85] It is also a ground for revocation after grant. This is because insufficiency is specifically listed as a ground for revocation in section 72(1).[86] One of the notable features of the revocation provisions is that they do not mention any of the criteria listed in section 14(5)(c) or its EPC equivalents as the basis on which a patent may be revoked. (Because unity of invention has traditionally only ever arisen before grant, these discussions are limited to the requirements that the claims be 'clear and concise' and that they be 'supported by the description'.)[87] On a strict reading, this suggests that while non-compliance with section 14(5)(c)/Articles 82 and 84 will be a basis on which a patent will not be granted, non-compliance is *not* a ground for revocation once a patent has been granted. This strict reading was followed when the matter

---

[79] Biotech. Dir., Arts 13–14; implemented in the United Kingdom by the Patents (Amendment) Rules 2001 (SI 2001/1412).   [80] EPC 2000 Regs, r. 31(1)(b); PA 1977, s. 125A; PA Rules, r. 13 (1), Sch. 1.
[81] *Wisconsin Alumni Research Foundation/Stem cell*, T 1374/04 [2007] *OJ EPO* 313, [10].
[82] Ibid.   [83] Ibid.   [84] PA 1977, s. 14(5)(a).
[85] PA 1977, s. 14(3); EPC 2000, Art. 100 (ex EPC 1973, Art. 100).
[86] EPC 2000, Arts 100 (grounds for opposition), 138 (grounds for revocation) (ex EPC 1973, Arts 83, 100).
[87] *Siemens/Unity*, G 1/91 [1992] *OJ EPO* 253 (lack of unity is not an issue in opposition or oppositional appeal proceedings).

first came before the courts in the United Kingdom, where it was held that while failure to comply with section 14(5)(c) could be objected to prior to grant, it was not a ground on which a patent could be challenged after grant.[88]

This question was revisited by the House of Lords in *Biogen v. Medeva*, in which Lord Hoffmann said that:

> [The] substantive effect of section 14(5)(c), namely that the description should, together with the rest of the specification, constitute an enabling disclosure, is given effect by section 72(1)(c). There is accordingly no gap or illogicality in the scheme of the Act.[89]

A similar position was adopted at the EPO, where it was said that:

> Although Art. 84 is not open to objection under the terms of Art. 100 EPC [1973], it may nevertheless constitute a proper ground for revoking a patent if objections to either clarity or support arise out of amendments to the patent as granted.[90]

These rulings suggest that while failure to comply with Article 14(5)(c) is not a ground that could be *directly* argued against after grant, the requirements that the claims be 'clear and concise' and that they be 'supported by the description' could *indirectly* be taken into account when deciding insufficiency. In effect, it was suggested that the section 14(5)(c) requirements could be subsumed, after grant, within section 14(3)/section 72(1).

This reading of *Biogen* was thrown into doubt by the Court of Appeal decision in *Kirin-Amgen*,[91] where the Court considered whether the section 14(5)(c) requirements could indirectly be taken into account via section 14(3) to revoke a patent. This was triggered by the argument that there were problems in the way in which claims had been drafted (namely, that there was no standard against which the named recombinant polypeptide could be tested). The Court of Appeal began by reiterating the line taken pre-*Biogen* that while clarity and support were relevant when assessing whether to grant a patent, they were not express grounds for revocation under section 72(1).[92] (The Court noted that this was also the position under the EPC.) Because of this, the only way in which the claims could have been revoked in the circumstances was on the basis that they were insufficient. Following *Biogen*, the Court of Appeal said that the test for whether claims were insufficient under section 72(1)(c) was whether the disclosure was enabling. On the facts, the Court said that while the claims may have lacked clarity, nonetheless the person skilled in the art could still implement the invention—that is, because the invention could be performed without undue effort, there had been an enabling disclosure. As such, the claims were not insufficient. The Court also said that that it believed that the defendant's challenge was not an attack on the basis of insufficiency; rather, it was 'an attack of lack of clarity dressed up to look like insufficiency'.[93] In relation to the suggestion that the section 14(5)(c) criteria of clarity and support might indirectly be raised to undermine a patent after grant, the Court of Appeal said that 'the fact that a claim is not clear or is not supported by the specification is likely to be irrelevant'.[94] The Court also added that it could 'see no reason to stretch s72(1)(c) to seek to cover issues of lack of clarity of claiming as patentees will not be able to establish infringement of unclear claims'.[95]

---

[88] See *Genentech's Patent* [1989] *RPC* 147 (CA), 248; *Chiron v. Organon (No. 3)* [1994] *FSR* 202, 242; *Chiron v. Organon (No. 12)* [1994] *FSR* 202, 178–9 (CA).

[89] *Biogen v. Medeva* [1997] *RPC* 1, 47 (Lord Hoffmann).

[90] *Mycogen/Modifying plant cells*, T 694/92 [1998] *EPOR* 114, 119. EPC 1973, Arts 84 and 100, are the same under EPC 2000, Arts 84 and 100.   [91] *Kirin-Amgen v. Transkaryotic Therapies* [2003] *RPC* 31.

[92] Ibid., 69.   [93] Ibid.   [94] Ibid.   [95] Ibid.

The nature of the relationship between clarity and sufficiency, and the role that these concepts are able to play after grant, were also raised when *Kirin-Amgen* was heard by the House of Lords.[96] Lord Hoffmann began by noting that at first instance, the judge had held that lack of clarity had made the specification insufficient. He also noted that the Court of Appeal disagreed, saying that failure to specify which product the skilled person needed to use to make the invention was 'lack of clarity dressed up to look like insufficiency'. In reinstating the judge's finding at first instance that the claim in question was invalid for lack of sufficiency, Lord Hoffmann said:

> [I]f the claim says that you must use an acid, and there is nothing in the specification or context to tell you which acid, and the invention will work with some acids but not with others but finding out which ones work will need extensive experiments, then that in my opinion is not merely lack of clarity; it is insufficiency. The lack of clarity does not merely create a fuzzy boundary between that which will work and that which will not. It makes it impossible to work the invention at all until one has found out what ingredient is needed.[97]

In so ruling, the House of Lords in *Kirin-Amgen* not only reinstated the decision at first instance, but also clarified that clarity and lack of support continue to have a role to play in deciding questions of validity after grant.

3.1 CLARITY

During the nineteenth century, when anti-patent feelings were at their peak, many patents were struck down because they contained trivial errors in grammar or spelling. While patent law is no longer as harsh as it once was, it still demands that the public should not be left in any doubt as to the subject matter covered by a particular patent. Because the claims demarcate the scope of the monopoly, if the claims are unclear or not concise, the extent of protection cannot easily be discerned. This would lead to the undesirable situation that third parties would not be able to determine whether they were infringing the patent.[98] To ensure that this does not occur, patent law requires that the claims be clear and concise.[99] While clarity may not be an issue that can be used to challenge a patent after grant, it has been suggested that where a claim contains a vague and ambiguous term, it is less likely that the courts will find that there has been an infringement.[100] The requirement that the claims be clear and concise has been important in relation to structural and functional claims.[101]

Claims will be clear and concise if the skilled person is able to understand the language used.[102] The requirement that the claims be clear and concise applies to 'the choice of category of claims, to the terminology and also to the number and order of the claims'.[103] While claims should be internally consistent and free from contradiction, most of the problems tend to arise as a result of the use of relative or imprecise terms. Where this occurs, the test is whether the skilled person would have had difficulty in understanding

---

[96] *Kirin-Amgen v. Hoechst Marion Roussel* [2005] RPC 169.   [97] Ibid., [125]–[126].

[98] Another reason why the claims need to be clear and concise is because they will invariably be translated into another language. If a claim were not formulated in clear and precise terms, it would undermine the translation process and also cast doubts on 'foreign' patents.

[99] PA 1977, s. 14(5)(b); EPC 2000, Art. 84 (ex EPC 1973, Art. 84); EPC 2000 Regs, r. 43 (ex EPC 1973 Regs, r. 29).   [100] *Albany/Pure terfenadine*, T 728/98 [2001] *OJ EPO* 319, [3.1].

[101] P. Ford, 'Functional Claims' (1985) 17 *IIC* 325; *Efamol/Pharmaceuticals compositions*, T 139/85 [1987] *EPOR* 229; *Ciba-Geigy/Synergistic herbicides*, T 68/85 [1987] *EPOR* 302; *General Hospital/Contraceptive*, T 820/94 [1995] *EPOR* 446.   [102] *Strix Limited v. Otter Controls* [1995] RPC 607.

[103] Singer and Stauder, 378.

the language used when read in light of common general knowledge.[104] Because the skilled addressee reads the claims, this means that words and phrases that might not be understood outside the field of the invention may still be clear and concise.

The mere fact that a claim is very broad or takes a long time to understand does not necessarily diminish its clarity. As the Technical Board of Appeal said, there is no basis in the Article 84 clarity requirement 'for objecting that a claim is not simple but complex and hence takes too long to understand, as complexity is not tantamount to lack of clarity of a claim'.[105] All that Article 84 requires is that the claims 'define the subject matter for which protection is sought clearly and unambiguously for the skilled person'.[106] In contrast with the requirement for sufficiency of disclosure (where length of time may impose an undue burden on the public), the actual time required to determine whether a given compound falls within the scope of a claim 'does not really matter as long as the claim itself is clear'.[107] In reaching this position, the Board stressed that there was no justification for imposing quantitative criteria (such as the amount of time taken to understand a claim) on what is essentially a qualitative requirement that the claims be clear and concise.

The parameters of the invention may be defined by quantitative criteria (such as size, weight, volume, temperature) or qualitative criteria. While, in most cases, applicants will use precise measurements to define their inventions, applicants may confine their descriptions to general relationships between component parts in which nothing turns on finite limits.[108] Relative terms such as 'thin', 'fat', and 'slow' are admissible, but only if they have a generally recognized meaning in the field. Where no unequivocal generally accepted meaning exists in the relevant art, this casts uncertainty over the subject matter covered by the claim. On this basis, it was held that use of the term 'substantially pure' (the sole feature designated to distinguish the subject matter of a chemical invention), which had no clear and unequivocal meaning, meant that the patent was unclear and thus not in conformity with Article 84.[109]

3.2 SUPPORTED BY THE DESCRIPTION

The second requirement imposed on the claims is that they 'must be supported by the description'.[110] This helps to ensure that there is a correlation between what is invented and what has been claimed. The requirement that the claims must be supported by the description reflects the 'general legal principle that the extent of the patent monopoly as defined in the claims, must correspond to the technical contribution to the art'.[111] The requirement that the claim be supported by the description plays an important role in ensuring that the scope of the protection provided to the patentee does not exceed or differ from the invention disclosed in the patent.[112] By ensuring that the claims (which shape the scope of the legal monopoly) are supported by the description (which provides the necessary technical information), patent law enables potential users to ascertain without

---

[104] *Strix v. Otter* [1995] *RPC* 607; *ICI/Optical sensing apparatus*, T 454/89 [1995] *EPOR* 600.

[105] *Bayer CropScience/Safeners*, T 1020/98 [2003] *OJ EPO* 533, 542. In relation to a Markush formula for a class of chemical compounds, the TBA held that simplicity of a claim is not a criterion for the granting of a patent under the EPC.   [106] Ibid., 542–3.

[107] Ibid., 542.   [108] *No-Fume v. Pitchford* (1935) 52 *RPC* 231.

[109] *Albany/Pure terfenadine*, T 728/98 [2001] *OJ EPO* 319, [3.3].

[110] PA 1977, s. 14(5)(c); EPC 2000, Art. 84 (ex EPC 1973, Art. 84).

[111] *CIRD Galderma*, T 1129/97 [2001] *OJ EPO* 273, 287.

[112] *Exxon/Fuel oils*, T 409/91 [1994] *EPOR* 149, 154; *Mycogen/Modifying plant cells*, T 649/92 [1998] *EPOR* 114, 118.

undue burden or the need for inventive activity whether their planned commercial use is likely to infringe the patentee's monopoly.[113]

The approach that is used to decide whether the claims are supported by the description is similar to the approach that is used to decide whether the specification has been disclosed sufficiently.[114] As is the case with the requirement for sufficiency of disclosure, a description that outlines one way of performing the claimed invention may support broader claims. This would be the case, for example:

> . . . where the disclosure of a new technique constitutes the essence of the invention and the description of one way of carrying it out enables the skilled person to obtain the same effect of the invention in a broad area by use of suitable variants of the component features.[115]

As with sufficiency of disclosure, a single embodiment can only ever justify a broader claim if the class as a whole shares a common principle.[116] In other cases, more technical details and more than one example may be necessary to support claims of a broad scope.[117]

One situation in which claims may not be supported by the description is where the breadth of the claims extends beyond the technical contribution provided by the invention.[118] This might occur, for example, where the patent claims results that cannot be performed from the information in the claims. This would be the case where the patent claims the making of a wide class of products, but only enables one of those products to be made and fails to disclose a principle that enables the making of other products. Similarly, a patent may lack support where it claims every way of achieving a particular result, but only enables one way of making the product, and it is possible to envisage other ways of achieving that result that do not make use of the invention.[119]

3.3 UNITY OF INVENTION

As well as being clear, concise, and supported by the description, the claims must also relate 'to one invention or to a group of inventions which are linked as to form a single inventive concept'.[120] The requirement that there be unity of invention, which ensures that applications only contain a single invention or a single group of inventions, plays an important administrative role. It also helps to minimize some of the problems that might

---

[113] *Oxy/Gel-forming composition*, T 246/91 [1995] *EPOR* 526, 531.

[114] The phrase 'supported by matter disclosed' is also used in PA 1977, s. 5(2) (to establish whether priority from an earlier application is acceptable). A description would not support claims for the purpose of s. 14(5)(c) unless the specification were to contain sufficient material to constitute an enabling disclosure under s. 14(3): *Biogen v. Medeva* [1997] *RPC* 1, 47 (Lord Hoffmann); *Asahi Kasei Kogyo* [1981] *RPC* 485, 535–6 (Lord Oliver). A similar approach was adopted by the TBA in *Mycogen/Modifying plant cells*, T 649/92 [1998] *EPOR* 114, 119.   [115] *Mycogen*, T 694/92 [1998] *EPOR* 114, 120.

[116] *Mölnlycke AB v. Procter & Gamble* [1992] *FSR* 549, 600, based on *Genentech I/Polypeptide expression*, T 292/85 [1989] *OJ EPO* 275 and applied in *Chiron v. Organon (No. 3)* [1994] *FSR* 202, 241–2.

[117] This is the case where the achievement of a given technical effect by known techniques in different areas constitutes the essence of the invention and there are serious doubts as to whether the said effects can readily be obtained for the whole range of applications claimed: *Mycogen/Modifying plant cells*, T 649/92 [1998] *EPOR* 114, 120; *Xerox/Amendments*, T 133/85 [1988] *OJ EPO* 441, 448.

[118] *Biogen v. Medeva* [1997] *RPC* 1, 50–1 (Lord Hoffmann) ('whether the claims cover other ways in which they might be delivered: ways that owe nothing to the teaching of the patent or any principle which it discloses').   [119] *Mycogen/Modifying plant cells*, T 694/92 [1998] *EPOR* 114, 120.

[120] PA 1977, s. 14(5)(d); PA Rules, r. 16; EPC 2000, Art. 82 (ex EPC 1973, Art. 82); EPC 2000 Regs, r. 44 (ex EPC 1973 Regs, r. 30).

otherwise arise in the application of the substantive tests for patentability if a patent were to contain a number of distinct inventions.[121] For two or more inventions to appear in the same patent, there must be a single inventive concept that links them together. This might occur, for example, if there were an expectation in the art that the various inventions will behave the same way. Importantly, the unifying factor that links the different inventions must be an inventive concept and not some other feature of the invention.[122]

4 IMPROPER AMENDMENTS

The final internal requirement for patentability which we look at here concerns the extent to which patents can be amended. As we saw earlier, a number of restrictions are placed on the way in which patents can be amended.[123] In this section, we wish to concentrate on those amendments that throw the validity of the patent into doubt. There are two important limits on the way in which patents may be amended. The first is that an application must not be amended in such a way as to bring in subject matter that extends beyond the content of the application as filed. The second restriction is that amendments after grant must not extend the protection conferred by the patent.

The restrictions placed on the ability for patents to be amended have been criticized on the basis that the rules have been applied too rigorously.[124] It has been said that this denies legitimate inventors the protection they deserve and encourages loose filing.[125] Another problem with the law in this area is that there has been very little discussion about the principles on which the restriction of amendment is based. As Staughton LJ observed:

> [The] problem is not that the technology in this case is obscure or recondite, but that the law as to added matter is . . . A clear and precise test is not to be found in the Patents Act. Those who are engaged in the important business of inventing and manufacturers too, are to my mind entitled to more precise guidance as to how they should conduct their affairs. But they must seek it from Parliament, or from an international convention.[126]

4.1 RESTRICTIONS ON AMENDMENTS THAT ADD MATTER

The first limit is that an application must not be amended in such a way as to bring in subject matter that extends beyond the content of the application as filed.[127] Failure to comply with these requirements opens the patent up to the possibility of

---

[121] *Exxon*, T 314/99 (21 June 2001) (three different embodiments covered by the claim did not belong to the same single general inventive concept; while lack of unity could not be raised in opposition, it was held that the inventiveness of the claim as a whole was denied in the event that only one of the embodiments was obvious).

[122] *Draenert/Single general inventive concept*, W 6/90 [1991] *OJ EPO* 438. For the problems that this presents for gene patents, see D. Schertenleib, 'The Patentability and Protection of DNA-based Inventions in the EPO and the European Union' [2003] *EIPR* 125, 128–9.

[123] For a discussion on the role of disclaimers in amending patents at the EPO, see *PPG/Disclaimer*, G 1/03 [2004] *OJ EPO* 413.   [124] *Protoned BV's Application* [1983] *FSR* 110.

[125] R. Krasser, 'Possibilities of Amendment of Patent Claims during the Examination Procedure' (1992) 23 *IIC* 467, 471.   [126] *AC Edwards v. Acme Signs* [1992] *RPC* 131, 147.

[127] PA 1977, s. 76(2); EPC 2000, Art. 123(2) (ex EPC 1973, 123(2)); *EPO Guidelines*, H-IV; CPC, Art. 57(1). Despite obvious similarities, PA 1977, s. 76, is not listed in PA 1977, s. 130(7), as being framed so as to have as nearly as practicable the same effect as the corresponding provision of the Convention. Nevertheless, the UK courts have referred to EPO decisions. For a summary of UK law on added matter, see *AP Racing v. Alcon Components* [2014] *EWCA Civ* 40, [7]–[10].

revocation.[128] Consequently, applicants are confined by the scope of the description of the invention that is set out in the application. This ensures that patentees are not permitted to extend the patent so as to claim an invention developed after the priority date.[129] It also ensures, as the Technical Board of Appeal said, that applicants are not able to improve their position by adding subject matter not disclosed in the application as filed, giving them 'an unwarranted advantage and possibly being detrimental to the legal security of third parties relying on the contents of the application as filed'.[130]

As the Enlarged Board of Appeal said, a patent may only be amended 'within the limits of what a skilled person would derive directly and unambigiously using common general knowledge and seen objectively and relative to the date of filing, from the whole of these documents as filed'.[131]

While it is permissible for a patentee to claim the same invention in a different way, patentees are not able to amend their application so as to protect an inventive concept that was not disclosed in the original application.[132] The purpose of the restrictions on amendment is to stop patentees from inserting information after filing that enables them to support their claims.[133] As Aldous LJ said, this means that if a feature was omitted from a claim that the specification had made clear was essential, or if a feature were added that had not been disclosed in the application as filed, the amendment would add matter.[134] It is permissible to add information that explains, rather than expands, the scope of the claims. In this situation, the amendments 'harm no one and assist the public'.[135]

The basic issue is whether the amended patent contains any additional (technical) material that was not disclosed in the original application.[136] Basically, this requires the tribunal to compare the application as filed (the description, any claims, or drawings,[137] but not the abstract[138] or priority documents) with the amended application to determine whether the amended application contains any additional matter.[139] The crucial question here is

---

[128] *B & R Relay's Application* [1985] *RPC* 1. PA 1977, s. 72(1)(d) renders it a ground for revocation that the matter disclosed in the specification of the patent extends beyond that disclosed in the application as filed.

[129] *AC Edwards v. Acme Signs* [1992] *RPC* 131, 147 (CA).

[130] *British Biotech/Heterocyclic compounds*, T 684/96 [2000] *EPOR* 190, 197.

[131] G 2/10 *Disclaimer* [2012] *OJ EPO* 476 citing G 3/89 *Disclaimer* [1993] *OJ EPO* 117 and G 11/91 *Glu-Glu* [1993] *OJ EPO* 125. See also *Abbott Laboratories v. Medinol Limited* [2010] *EWHC* 2865 (Pat), [251]–[253]; *Brigade (BBS-TEK) v. Amber Valley* [2013] *EWPCC* 16, [74]–[89].

[132] *Southco v. Dzus Fastener Europe* [1990] *RPC* 587, 618. Consequently, amendment of a claim from 'handle' to a 'rotatable actuating means' would be read as not extending the disclosure.

[133] *Vector Corporation v. Glatt Air Techniques* [2007] *EWCA Civ* 805, [2007] *All ER* (D) 297, [3].

[134] *Texas Iron Works Patent* [2000] *RPC* 207, 246–7 (CA).

[135] *Vector Corporation v. Glatt* [2007] *EWCA Civ* 805, [3].

[136] 'Clearly the function of this provision is to prevent the addition of subject matter to a patent application after the date of filing. In contrast the reformulation of the same subject matter . . . would be permissible': *Xerox/Amendments*, T 133/85 [1988] *OJ EPO* 441, 449. See also *Milliken Denmark AS v. Walk Off Mats* [1996] *FSR* 292.

[137] *Amp/Connector*, T 66/85 [1989] *OJ EPO* 167; cf. *Sulzer/Hot gas cooler*, T 170/87 [1989] *OJ EPO* 441.

[138] *Bull/Identification system*, T 246/86 [1989] *OJ EPO* 199; *Abbott Laboratories v. Medinol* [2010] *EWHC* 2865 (Pat). The documents are looked at through the eyes of the notional skilled addressee: *Siegfried Demel v. Jefferson* [1999] *FSR* 204, 214.

[139] *Bonzel v. Intervention (No. 3)* [1991] *RPC* 553, 574; *Mölnlycke AB v. Procter & Gamble (No. 5)* [1994] *RPC* 49 (CA). Aldous J held that 'matter' included both structural features and inventive concepts: *Southco v. Dzus Fastener Europe* [1990] *RPC* 587, 616. However, this has proved to be controversial: see *AC Edwards v. Acme Signs* [1992] *RPC* 131, 144. For a more sympathetic reading, see *Sara Lee Household & Body Care v. Johnson Wax* [2001] *FSR* 261, following *Metal-Fren/Friction pad assembly*, T 582/91 [1995] *EPOR* 574.

'whether a skilled person would on looking at the amended specification, learn anything about the invention which he could not learn from the application as filed'.[140] As has been noted at the EPO, the issues that arise here are conceptually similar to those that arise in relation to the requirement for novelty. In both cases, the issue is whether something 'new' has been added: in the case of novelty, the invention must be new; in the case of amendment, the amended application must not contain anything new.[141] Under this approach, the test is whether a skilled person could derive any information in the amended patent that was not already in the application as filed.[142]

Unlike the position after grant, there is no reason per se to object to the broadening of the claims prior to grant.[143] This is because it is immaterial whether the amendment widens or narrows the monopoly claimed. The only restriction is the general one that prevents patentees from altering their claims in such a way that they claim a different invention from that which is disclosed in the application.[144] If the application as filed described the insertion of cancer genes in mice and flagged the potential application of the invention to other mammals, there is no reason why the claim should not be expanded to cover cats, dogs, or mammals in general.[145] The broadening of claims is legitimate as long as there is no new matter introduced. However, if the description as filed only mentioned mice, then such broadening of the claims would add subject matter and thus be invalid.[146]

A simple illustration of the way in which the courts determine whether the amendment has introduced additional matter is provided by *Ward's Application*,[147] which concerned an application for a patent for the packaging of flowerpots. The specification as filed referred to the packaging of a number of articles nested one within another. It also referred to nested flowerpots or similar containers. The Examiner objected to subsequent amendments that added references to plant pot bases on the basis that they extended the content of the application. Mr Bridges, in the Patent Office, concurred, saying that the question was whether:

> ... the amendment ... resulted in the specification disclosing matter which extends beyond that disclosed in the specification as filed ... matter must not be disclosed which extends, in the sense of enlarging upon the original disclosure, i.e. which increases the specificity or particularization of that disclosure.[148]

On the basis that plant pot bases are recognizably different from plant pots, the specification breached section 76(3)(a).[149]

While the question of whether an amended application contains additional subject matter always depends on the facts of the case, it may be helpful to outline some of the more common scenarios that may arise. It is not normally possible to amend a patent application

---

[140] *Sudarshan v. Clariant Produkte* [2013] *EWCA Civ* 919, [62].

[141] *EPO Guidelines*, H-IV, [2.1], [4.2], [4.4.3]; *Shell/Lead alloys*, T 201/83 [1984] *OJ EPO* 401; *General Motors/Electrodes*, T 194/84 [1990] *OJ EPO* 59, 65. It is different from the requirement that the claim be supported by the description, since support may justify broadening where novelty would not: *Xerox/ Amendments*, T 133/85 [1988] *OJ EPO* 441, 450. In the United Kingdom, the courts have referred to the novelty test employed at the EPO as a useful test, but one that should be applied with caution: *AC Edwards v. Acme Signs* [1992] *RPC* 131, 644.

[142] *British Biotech/Heterocyclic compounds*, T 684/96 [2000] *EPOR* 190, 197; *Advanced Semi-Conductor Products*, G 1/93 [1994] *OJ EPO* 541.

[143] *Spring Foam v. Playhut* [2000] *RPC* 327, 337–8.

[144] *Southco v. Dzus Fastener Europe* [1990] *RPC* 587, 615.

[145] Broadening is permissible where there is a basis for a claim lacking the feature in the application as filed: *Amp/Connector*, T 66/85 [1989] *EPOR* 283.   [146] *AC Edwards v. Acme Signs* [1992] *RPC* 131.

[147] [1986] *RPC* 50.   [148] Ibid., 54.

[149] For a more structured approach, see *European Central Bank v. Document Security Systems* [2007] *EWHC* 600 (Pat).

where the description was insufficient.[150] As Lord Hoffmann said in *Biogen v. Medeva*, the application may not add new matter to make an insufficient application sufficient.[151] At the EPO, applicants are prohibited from removing matter from a claim that appeared to be essential in the original application.[152] This is because if the feature that is being removed was essential in the original application, then the amended feature introduces novel subject matter.[153] The prohibition on removing essential features does not prevent an amendment that introduces an essential feature that was previously described as non-essential.[154]

Often, a patentee may wish to narrow the ambit of the patent. This usually occurs where a search reveals that some of the examples of prior art fall within the claims as originally filed or where subsequent experimentation reveals that some of the examples listed in the claims as filed do not work. Here, an applicant may amend the claim by disclaiming the examples.[155] While increasing the specificity of a claim, for example by narrowing it from mammals to mice, does not generally introduce new matter, it should not automatically be assumed that this is the case. The reason for this is that if the narrowing of the claims adds a technical feature (or something inventive), it will not be permissible.[156] However, if the limitation merely excludes protection for part of the subject matter of the application as filed, this would not give any unwarranted advantages to the applicant and, as such, is prima facie allowed.

4.2 AMENDMENTS THAT EXTEND THE SCOPE OF PROTECTION

In recognition of the fact that third parties may modify their behaviour in light of the patent as published, restrictions are placed on the degree to which the scope of protection conferred by the patent can be altered after grant.[157] To this end, section 76(3)/Article 123(3) provide that amendments after grant must not extend the protection conferred by the patent. That is, after the patent has been granted, a patentee may not amend the scope of the claims so as to extend the monopoly beyond that covered by the claims as granted.[158] Failure to comply with these provisions opens the amended patent up to the possibility of revocation.[159]

---

[150] *AC Edwards v. Acme Signs* [1992] *RPC* 131, 147.   [151] *Biogen v. Medeva* [1997] *RPC* 1, [81] (HL).

[152] This will be so if the feature was essential in the original disclosure, is indispensable in the light of the technical problem, or the removal requires other features to be modified: *Alza/Infuser*, T 514/88 [1990] *EPOR* 157, 161–2; adopted in *Southco v. Dzus Fastner Europe* [1992] *RPC* 299, 324 (Nicholls LJ), 327 (Staughton LJ).

[153] See *Alza/Infuser*, T 514/88 [1990] *EPOR* 157, 161–2.

[154] *Hymo/Water-soluble polymer dispersion*, T 583/93 [1997] *EPOR* 129. The rule against the removal of essential features may explain the criticized decision in *Protoned BV's Application* [1983] *FSR* 110. See D. Stanley, 'Euphemism v. Pragmatism of the Implication of Added Subject Matter' (1988) 17 *CIPAJ* 108; G. Dworkin, 'Implied Added Subject Matter: An Academic Overview' (1990–91) 20 *CIPAJ* 340.

[155] *Sulzer/Hot gas cooler*, T 170/87 [1989] *OJ EPO* 441; *Mölnlycke AB v. Procter & Gamble (No. 5)* [1994] *RPC* 49, 135.

[156] If a limiting feature is not disclosed in the application as filed or otherwise derivable therefrom, it will violate EPC 1973, Art. 123(2) (now EPC 2000, Art. 123(2)): *Advanced Semiconductor/Limited features*, G 1/93 [1994] *OJ EPO* 541. See also *Nokia v. IPCom* [2013] *RPC* 73 (CA).

[157] *Leland/Light source*, T 187/91 [1995] *EPOR* 199, 202–3.

[158] PA 1977, s. 76(3), says that no amendment of the specification of a patent shall be allowed under PA 1977, ss 27(1), 73, or 74, if it results in the specification disclosing additional matter or extends the protection conferred by the patent. PA 1977, s. 72(1)(e), provides for the revocation of patents on the ground that the protection conferred by the patent has been extended by an amendment that should not have been allowed. EPC 2000, Art. 123(3) (ex EPC 1973, Art. 123(3)), makes it clear that amendments of claims after grant (unlike those before) must not extend the scope of protection. The acceptance of post-grant amendments is subject to the discretion of the Comptroller or court, which have tended to employ that discretion to deny amendments to those whose behaviour is not perceived to have been innocent.

[159] While it would be possible to allow widening amendments that are prospective only, it might be thought that a person should be able to rely on the patent in its state as granted rather than to have to check constantly to see whether it has been altered.

The limits imposed on amendments that extend the scope of the patent operate in a similar way to the prohibition on amendments that introduce additional subject matter (discussed earlier). The provisions will not operate where claims are narrowed.[160] Perhaps the most notable situation in which amendments have been allowed under this head is where they contain changes to the types of claim employed.[161] Thus it is normally permissible to amend a claim from a compound to a use, since the claim to a use is narrower than the claim to the compound. Amendments of this type commonly arise where the patent application has been drafted on the basis that the compound was new per se, whereas it turns out that the compound was already within the state of the art, but the use was not.[162]

---

[160] *Strix v. Otter* [1995] *RPC* 607; *Mobil/Friction reducing additive*, G 2/88 [1990] *OJ EPO* 93, 100–1.

[161] In *Philips Electronic's Patent* [1987] *RPC* 244, the patentee was permitted to add an omnibus claim to a European patent (UK) on the ground that it did not extend the scope of protection.

[162] *Moog/Change of category*, T 378/86 [1988] *OJ EPO* 386 (an amendment of a process claim to include a claim to the apparatus for carrying out the process was allowed); cf. *Telectronics/Cardiac pacer*, T 82/93 [1996] *OJ EPO* 274 (change from a method of operating a device—a pacer—to the device itself was not allowed, because the latter claim extended the subject matter to cover the situation in which the pacer was ready for use, not only when it was being used).

21

OWNERSHIP

1 INTRODUCTION

Ownership plays a key role in shaping the way the rights and responsibilities that flow from the grant of a patent are organized. The owner or, as the Patents Act 1977 prefers, the proprietor of a patent is able to exploit and control the use that is made of a patent.[1] They are also able to make decisions about when and the conditions under which a patent can be assigned, licensed, or mortgaged.[2] The owner of the patent is also the person who is able to sue for infringement.[3]

The question of who is the owner of a patent is closely connected to the question of who is entitled to be granted the patent. This is because the chain of ownership begins with the person entitled to grant of the patent: they are treated as first owner (or proprietor) of the patent. It is important to note at the outset that the right to be granted a patent, which is the central focus of this chapter, is primarily given to the inventor or joint inventors. This presumption may be overridden in a number of situations—notably, in relation to employee inventions and where the right to the patent has been transferred to a third party.

While a particular individual or group of individuals might *initially* have been given the right to be granted the patent, it does not necessarily follow from this that they will also be the owner of the patent. One reason for this is that the person entitled to grant of the patent may have assigned their rights in the patent to someone else. Alternatively, the patent may have been transferred to a third party as a result of death or insolvency. Consequently, in ascertaining ownership, it is necessary to discover who was initially entitled to the grant of the patent, and thereafter whether there has been an effective transfer of the patent to another person.

2 ENTITLEMENT TO GRANT

Given the consequences that flow from the ownership of a patent, it is not surprising that disputes often arise over who is properly entitled to be granted a particular patent. Questions about who is properly entitled to be granted a patent can arise both during and

---

[1] 'Proprietor' is not defined in the 1977 Act.

[2] Under the 1977 Act, applications for a patent are also capable of being owned.

[3] The PA 2004 amended PA 1977, s. 36(3), to clarify that co-owners are able to seek, amend, and revoke a patent if they act jointly, and have not contracted out of this requirement. See further *Consultation on the Proposed Patents Act (Amendment) Bill: Summary of Responses and the Government's Conclusions* (November 2003), [115]–[124].

after the grant of a patent, and may even be heard prospectively—that is, before any application has been made for a patent. In practice, however, most disputes tend to be heard after the patent has been granted.[4]

When the European Patents Convention 1973 (EPC 1973) was being drafted, it was decided that matters relating to the ownership of patents were better dealt with by the national courts or tribunals, than under the EPC.[5] As a result, the European Patent Office (EPO) only has a limited procedural role in determining disputes over entitlement.[6] The upshot of this is that while the processes by which patents are granted in the United Kingdom and the EPO are very similar, the procedures by which a UK patent and a European patent (UK) may be challenged are somewhat different. As such, we will deal with them separately.

2.1 UK PATENTS

The starting point for determining who is properly entitled to the grant of a British patent is set out in section 7(4) of the 1977 Patents Act.[7] This creates a rebuttable presumption that the patent applicant is the person who is entitled to be granted the patent. The grounds on which this presumption may be rebutted, with which we deal later,[8] are set out in section 7(2). If none of these grounds can be established, the applicant will be treated as the proprietor of the patent. The significance of the presumption should not be underestimated: because the evidence about entitlement is often inconclusive,[9] the presumption frequently operates to maintain the status quo.[10] This is particularly the case where the court has to rely upon witness testimony.[11]

Prior to the grant of a patent for an invention, anyone may ask the Comptroller whether they are entitled to be granted (alone or with other persons) a patent for that invention.[12] They may also ask the Comptroller to determine whether they have or would have any

---

[4] This is because if an issue is raised during the application under PA 1977, s. 8(1), but has not been determined by the time of grant, the dispute is usually continued as if it were a dispute as to the entitlement of a granted patent (i.e. as if it were a PA 1977, s. 37, application). See PA 1977, s. 9; *Goddin & Rennie's Application* [1996] *RPC* 141.

[5] This was because disputes about entitlement potentially raise questions about legal personality, contract, equity, and labour law, rather than patent law.

[6] This issue was reopened in European Commission, *Green Paper on the Community Patent* (1997) COM(97) 314 final, in which, after noting that the application of these different rules has an impact on research work and management, the Commission asked respondents to indicate whether they thought that 'existing differences between member states laws on employees' inventions impacted on innovation and employment conditions and/or the freedom to provide services and/or the conditions of competition? Are they such as to justify harmonization at Community level?' See also European Commission, *Comparative Study of Employees' Inventions Law in Member States of the European Communities* (1977).

[7] In answering the question, 'who is the proprietor of the patent?', a useful starting point is the patent itself. This is because PA 1977, s. 13(2), provides that anyone who makes an application must state who the inventor is, or if the inventor is not applying, on what basis they are applying. See T. Gold, 'Entitlement Disputes: A Case Review' [1990] *EIPR* 382.

[8] See Chapter 16, section 4, pp. 443–51 and section 3, p. 635 later in this chapter.

[9] In part, this is because it is often difficult to determine the precise point in time and the circumstances under which an invention was created. The reason for this is, as Lord Wilberforce said, that 'it is often difficult to fix the point or points in a continuous line of discovery at which an invention has been made': *Beecham Group v. Bristol Laboratories International* [1978] *RPC* 521, 567.

[10] On the importance of the presumption, see *Staeng's Patent* [1996] *RPC* 183; *Viziball's Application* [1988] *RPC* 213.

[11] *Fireworks Fire Protection and Watermist v. Andrew James Cooke*, O/275/13 (23 July 2013).

[12] PA 1977, s. 8(1).

rights in or under any patent so granted. While these issues will normally be referred to the Comptroller, if the Comptroller considers that the question involves matters that would be better dealt with by the court, the Comptroller may refer the matter to the courts for consideration.[13]

The question of who is properly entitled to a UK patent may also be raised after grant. Any person claiming a proprietary interest in a patent may ask the Comptroller to clarify who is the true proprietor of the patent, whether the patent should have been granted to the person to whom it was granted, or whether any right in or under the patent should be transferred or granted to another person.[14]

2.1.1 Possible remedies

Where it has been decided that the wrong person has applied for a patent or a patent has been granted to the wrong person, the Comptroller has a number of options available. In deciding what action to take, it has been said that the main aim should be 'to reach a solution which would provide a reasonable opportunity for the patent to be exploited should there be a demand for it'[15]—a goal that reflects a desire to see that the invention enters the commercial domain, rather than a concern with recognizing entitlements.

Where a successful entitlement challenge has been made in relation to a patent application, the Comptroller can refuse, amend, or transfer the application.[16] If the application is refused and the person properly entitled to apply decides to submit a new application, they may be able to avail themselves of the wrongful applicant's priority date.[17] The Comptroller also has jurisdiction to reach more creative solutions. For example, they may grant the patent to one co-inventor, but order that the other co-inventor be given a non-exclusive, non-assignable licence, perhaps with payment of a royalty.

Where a patent has been granted, an order may be made directing that the person referring the issue to the tribunal shall be listed as the proprietor of the patent. Alternatively, the Comptroller may grant a licence to the claimant or revoke the patent on the ground that it was granted to the wrong person.[18] If it is decided that the patent should be revoked, the Comptroller may order that the person who made the application (or their successor in title) may make a new application for a patent. It is important to note that no order may be made to transfer the patent or to permit the

---

[13] PA 1977, s. 37(8).

[14] PA 1977, s. 37(1). See *Hughes v. Paxman* [2005] *All ER* (D) 255 (the Comptroller has wide discretion to grant licences to third parties); *Hughes v. Paxman* [2007] *RPC* 34 (the Comptroller has the jurisdiction to grant licence under s. 37(1) on the application of one co-proprietor).

[15] *Goddin & Rennie's Application* [1996] *RPC* 141, [23]. The factors that were considered relevant in this case included whether either of the joint inventors wished to exploit the patent themselves and the feasibility of their agreeing to license third parties.

[16] PA 1977, s. 8(2)(c). PA 1977, s. 8(2)(a), suggests that, where it is decided that the referent was the sole inventor, it will probably be ordered that the application shall proceed in the name of that person. Alternatively, if it is found that the invention was made jointly, the likely order is that the application will proceed jointly.   [17] PA 1977, s. 8(3).

[18] That is, to a person not entitled under PA 1977, ss 7(2), 36, or 72(1)(b); EPC 2000, Art. 138 (1)(e). While lack of entitlement is a ground of revocation, it appears that the right to demand revocation is available only to a person 'initially entitled' to the patent and not to someone to whom that right has been transferred: *Dolphin Showers and Brueton v. Farmiloe* [1989] *FSR* 1; *Henry Brothers v. Ministry of Defence* [1997] *RPC* 693. It remains unclear whether a declaration under PA 1977, s. 37, is required prior to an action for revocation under PA 1977, s. 72.

reapplication if the reference was made two years from the date of the grant. This exclusion does not apply, however, if the proprietor of the patent knew that they were not entitled to the patent.[19]

2.2 EUROPEAN PATENTS (UK)

As we mentioned earlier, the EPO only has a limited procedural role in determining disputes over entitlement. For the purposes of proceedings before the EPO, the applicant is deemed to be entitled to exercise the European patent, leaving issues of entitlement to be determined in national fora. As a result, the EPO only takes account of questions of entitlement if a decision has been made by an appropriate national court to the effect that a person other than the applicant is entitled to the patent. This means that questions relating to the ownership of European patents (UK)[20] both before and after grant[21] *may* be heard by the British Comptroller[22] or courts.[23]

In order to prevent a proliferation of ownership proceedings in different member states (and to prevent forum shopping), a Protocol to the EPC was formulated ('The Protocol on Jurisdiction and Recognition in Respect of the Right to a Grant of a European Patent').[24] The Protocol provides that questions about entitlement are only to be heard by one member state. The Protocol also establishes rules to determine which nation has jurisdiction to hear ownership disputes.[25] In the absence of an agreement between the claimant and the applicant stating the jurisdiction that is to operate, the Protocol provides that questions about entitlement are to be determined by the tribunals (and the law) of the country of which the applicant is resident (or in which the applicant has their place of business). If the applicant is not an EPC member state, ownership is decided by the tribunal of the country of the claimant.[26] Consequently, a UK court would decline to hear a case concerning a dispute between a French claimant and a German applicant, or between a British claimant and a French applicant. It would, however, consider disputes between a German claimant and a British applicant, and between a British claimant and an American applicant. Where both the applicant and claimant are not residents in EPC member states it is heard by the German courts in Munich.

2.2.1 Possible remedies

Once a national tribunal has made a determination as to entitlement, the EPO will take appropriate action. In these circumstances, Article 61 of the EPC 2000 provides that three

---

[19] Protection for third parties in these situations is offered by PA 1977, ss 37(6)–(7), 38(1), (3)–(4).

[20] PA 1977, ss 12(1), 77(1)(b). See *Norris's Patent* [1988] *RPC* 159; *Canning's US Application* [1992] *RPC* 459 (concerning international patent applications); *Kirin-Amgen/Erythropoietin*, T 412/93 [1995] *EPOR* 629 (questions of entitlement could not be considered in opposition proceedings).

[21] It seems that the issue of jurisdiction will be determined in accordance with the general rules of the Brussels Convention and that Art. 16(4), which requires issues relating to the validity and registration of patents to be dealt with by the tribunals of the country from which the patent issued, has no applicability. See *Duijnstee v. Goderbauer* [1985] *FSR* 221.

[22] PA 1977, s. 37(8). For a discussion of the principles by which the Comptroller should exercise the discretion conferred by PA 1977, s. 12(2), see *Luxim Corporation* [2007] *EWHC* 1624.

[23] PA 1977, s, 82, provides for rules as to UK jurisdiction over disputes as to ownership of European patents. See [1989] *FSR* 225.   [24] 5 October 1973.

[25] It also provided for the recognition of their decisions by other member states. See G. le Tallac, 'The Protocol on Jurisdiction and the Recognition of Decisions in Respect of the Right to the Grant of a European Patent (Protocol on Recognition)' (1985) 16 *IIC* 318, 356.

[26] These are reflected in PA 1977, ss 82 and 83.

courses of action are available: prosecution of the application in the applicant's home state; the filing of a new application; or a request that the application be refused.[27]

3 DETERMINING WHO IS ENTITLED TO GRANT

While the Patents Act 1977 provides that anyone is entitled to apply for a patent,[28] section 7(2) goes on to say that patents should only be granted to a limited category of people.[29] These provisions are the basis on which issues of entitlement are determined. As Lord Hoffmann said in *Yeda*,[30] section 7(2) and (3) provide an exhaustive code for determining who is entitled to the grant of a patent. This means that the question of whether a person is entitled to grant is solely dependent on them being able to show that they had been the actual inventor. In so ruling, the House of Lords rejected the argument that to prove entitlement, it was not enough for a person (A) to show that A and not the person (B) named on the patent was the actual inventor. In particular, the House of Lords rejected Jacob LJ's comment in *Markem*[31] that '[A] must be able to show that in some way B was not entitled to apply for the patent, either at all or alone. It follows that A must invoke some other rule of law'—typically by virtue of contract or breach of confidence—'to establish his entitlement—that which gives him title, wholly or in part, to B's application.' The upshot of *Yeda* is that the decision as to whether a person is properly entitled to grant of a patent turns solely on who came up with the inventive concept—a question at which we look shortly.

The starting point for determining issues of entitlement and ownership is section 7(2)(a). This provides that the right to be granted a patent is *primarily* given to the inventor or joint inventors. This focus upon the inventor follows the common practice whereby the creator is accorded the privileged status of first owner of intellectual property rights. Although the process of invention is frequently presented as being less creative than the production of literary or artistic works, patent law bears many of the marks of the romantic author. It is, at the very least, based on a model of an individual inventor—a matter emphasized in the 1977 Act by the requirement that the inventor be the 'actual deviser' of the invention.[32]

The assumption that the inventor is the person who is properly entitled to grant of the patent can be overridden in two situations. The first of these is set out in section 7(2)(b). This states that the presumption in favour of the inventor as owner does not apply where it can be established that at the time the invention was made, another person was entitled to the invention by virtue of (i) any enactment or rule of law, (ii) any foreign law, treaty, or international convention, or (iii) an enforceable term of any agreement entered into with the inventor before the making of the invention. Although the precise meaning of

---

[27] *Latchways/Unlawful applicant*, G 3/92 [1995] *EPOR* 141.

[28] PA 1977, s. 7(1).

[29] As we saw earlier, PA 1977, s. 7(4), creates a rebuttable presumption that the person who applies for a patent is the person who is entitled to grant of a patent. The grounds on which this presumption may be rebutted are set out in PA 1977, s. 7(2), which exhaustively sets out the parties to whom a patent may be granted.

[30] *Rhone-Poulenc Rorer International Holdings v. Yeda Research and Development Co. Ltd* [2007] *UKHL* 42, [2007] *All ER* (D) 373, [18].

[31] *Markem Corp. v. Zipher* [2005] *RPC* (31) 761 (CA), [79]. For similar statements by Jacobs LJ (which were also expressly rejected by the House of Lords in *Yeda*), see *University of Southampton's Applications* [2006] *RPC* 567 (CA), [8]. [32] PA 1977, s. 7(3).

the section is unclear,[33] it is widely accepted that it deals with employee inventions caught by section 39.

The second situation where the presumption that the inventor is the owner is overridden is set out in section 7(2)(c). This states that a patent may be granted to 'the successor or successors in title of any persons or persons mentioned in section 7(2)(a) or (b)'. This provision allows for the rights in the invention to be transferred to third parties. In all cases, it is important to note that in certain situations, the registered proprietor may be able to rely upon the equitable rules of proprietary estoppel to prevent or limit the transfer of a patent under section 7(2).[34]

While section 7(2) potentially covers a broad array of situations, in practice, questions relating to entitlement to grant tend to fall into two general areas: (i) inventors and joint inventors; and (ii) employee inventions. We will deal with each of these in turn.

3.1 INVENTORS AND JOINT INVENTORS

Being named as the inventor or joint inventor of a new product or process often carries with it a number of rewards. In addition to the prestige that is associated with being named as the creator of a new invention,[35] a lot flows from the presumption that patents are granted *primarily* to the inventor or joint inventors.[36] Given this, it is not surprising that the tribunals are often called upon to decide who is properly entitled to be named as inventor or joint inventor of a given invention.[37] Problems in this field tend to group together in two areas.

The first arises where someone claims that they, and not the named inventor, are the 'actual deviser' of the patented invention.[38] Problems also arise where an individual claims that their contribution to the invention has not been properly recognized.[39]

---

[33] Rather oddly, it would not appear to cover the position of an employee who was a joint inventor with someone who was not an employee, since the employer would not then be a person who, at the time of the making of the invention, was entitled to the *whole* of the property. It might have been assumed that such an anomaly would have been capable of being rectified by the use of express agreements between those concerned. However, the clause entitling a person to a patent as a result of being the beneficiary of 'an enforceable agreement entered into with the inventor before the making of the invention' is uncertain in scope too: see *Goddin & Rennie's Application* [1996] *RPC* 141. Because the provision excludes from its remit 'equitable interests', it is arguable that it would not cover a contractual agreement made prior to invention that a person was to assign their rights, because such an agreement creates a mere equitable right to the patent. However, such a pedantic interpretation seems to render redundant the provision relating to agreements, as well as to contradict the obviously desirable policy of encouraging the formation of such agreements allocating ownership.

[34] See *Rhone-Poulenc Rorer International Holdings v. Yeda Research and Development Co. Ltd* [2007] *UKHL* 42, [2007] *All ER* (D) 373, [22].

[35] Inventors are entitled to be named on the patent, even if they are not entitled to the patent: PA 1977, s. 13; EPC 2000, Arts 62 and 81 (ex EPC 1973, Arts 62 and 81). If the inventor is not designated, the application is treated as having been withdrawn: EPC 2000, Art. 90(5) (ex EPC 1973, Art. 91); EPC 2000 Regs, r. 60.

[36] PA 1977, s. 7(2)(a); EPC 2000, Art. 60(1). For a useful overview of the steps involved in determining whether parties were jointly entitled to an application, see *Minnesota Mining and Manufacturing Companies' International Patent Application* [2003] *RPC* 541.

[37] See *IDA v. University of Southampton* [2006] *EWCA Civ* 145, [44] (noting that there has been a recent rash of entitlement cases before the Comptroller and that these cases were particularly apt for mediation).

[38] 'Inventor' is defined in PA 1977, s. 7(3), to mean the 'actual deviser' of the invention. Joint inventors are construed accordingly.

[39] PA 1977, s. 10. For the application of PA 1977, s. 7, see *Cinpres Gas Injection v. Melea* [2008] *EWCA Civ* 9. On US law, see W. Fritz Fasse, 'The Muddy Metaphysics of Joint Inventorship: Cleaning up after the 1984 Amendments to 35 USC' (1992) 5 *Harv JL & Tech* 153.

In both situations, the courts are required to identify the 'inventive' elements of the invention. In turn, the courts are required to consider whether the claimant was responsible for the development of some or all of those elements.[40] In some cases, the courts have been willing to divide an invention up into parts, allocating responsibility for different claims to different inventors. In one case, the court emphasized that the appropriate way of determining who was the inventor was not to divide up the elements of a claim and ask who devised each; rather, it was necessary to interpret the claim so as to ascertain the essential inventive concept and then determine who contributed that concept.[41]

3.1.1 What is an inventive contribution?

In order to determine whether someone is entitled to be called an 'inventor' or 'joint inventor' under the 1977 Act, it is necessary to know what has been invented.[42] The courts have stressed that a person will not be regarded as an inventor merely because they have contributed to the claims: instead, to qualify as an inventor, a person needs to show that they have contributed to the 'inventive concept'.[43] As Lord Hoffmann explained in *Yeda*,[44] the reason why it was not enough for someone to show that they had contributed to the claims was because the claims might include non-patentable integers derived from the prior art. The task of determining whether someone has contributed an inventive concept is a difficult one, not least because the process of invention is often a complex process. As Lord Hoffmann went on to say, the complexity can be attributed in some cases to the fact that 'the inventive concept is a relationship of discontinuity between the claimed invention and the prior art. Inventors themselves will often not know exactly where it lies.'[45] While certain contributions (such as the posing of the problem to be solved or the answering of those problems) are usually treated as being inventive, other contributions (such as the supply of the test tubes used in the experiments) would usually be regarded as being non-inventive. In between these two extremes there are a range of other types of contribution that are more difficult to categorize. The question that arises here is which of the various contributions that are made to the production of an invention ought to be recognized as being inventive (or technically creative) and which ought not.[46] This is a particularly complex issue, not least because what is considered to be inventive not only changes over time,[47] but also changes between different areas of

---

[40] For an analysis of this in the United States, see *Mueller Brass v. Reading Industries*, 352 F. Supp. 1357, 1372–3 (ED Pa. 1972), aff'd without opinion, 487 *F.2d.* 1395 (3d Cir. 1973).

[41] *Henry Brothers v. Ministry of Defence* [1997] *RPC* 693.

[42] *Henry Brothers v. Ministry of Defence* [1999] *RPC* 442 (CA), 449 (Robert Walker LJ) (observing, at 452, that the 'whole question of co ownership called for clarification').

[43] *GE Healthcare v. Perkin Elmer* [2006] *EWHC* 214 (Pat), [146]. 'The task of the court is to identify the inventive concept of the patent or application and identify who devised it': *Stanelco Fibre Optics v. Biopress Technology* [2005] *RPC* 319, [12]. See also *Rhone-Poulenc Rorer International Holdings v. Yeda Research and Development Co.* [2007] *UKHL* 42.

[44] *Rhone-Poulenc Rorer International Holdings v. Yeda Research and Development Co.* [2007] *UKHL* 42, [20] (Lord Hoffmann).   [45] Ibid.

[46] 'The task of determining who is the inventor or joint inventor is similar to the non-obviousness inquiry. However, in contrast with the non-obviousness inquiry, which is determined 'objectively', the idea of inventorship carries a 'subjective' component. This arises because the inquiry can be undertaken even when no application has been made for a patent: PA 1977, s. 8(1)(a). See *Viziball's Application* [1988] *RPC* 213; *Goddin & Rennie's Application* [1996] *RPC* 141.

[47] For example, it is no longer possible to obtain a patent (as it was for a long time) merely for being the 'importer' of an invention: *Edgeberry v. Stephens* (1691) 1 *WPC* 35, 1 *HPC* 117.

science and technology.[48] Given this, and the fact that the definition of inventor offered in the 1977 Act offers little guidance in this regard,[49] perhaps the best way to approach this issue is by example.

It is commonly accepted that where a person has done something that helps to solve a particular problem or to answer a particular question, this will be regarded as an inventive contribution. As such, if it can be shown that an individual has done something that helps to solve a problem, it is likely that they will be treated as an inventor or joint inventor. While the answering of a problem is, in some ways, the archetypal inventive contribution, it is by no means the only type of contribution that is recognized as being inventive. For example, the perfection or improvement of a solution may also be regarded as an inventive contribution. Improvement of an existing device or process might itself provide for a patentable invention, in which case one would expect the patent to belong to the person who made the improvements (irrespective of the ownership of the starting invention). However, in practice, the process of devising a patent may incorporate a series of elements, some of which are mere improvements of an initial breakthrough. In those circumstances, the question arises as to whether these later contributions are sufficient for their author to become a joint inventor.[50]

The generation of the idea or avenue for research—that is, the formulation of the problem to be addressed—has also been treated as being inventive.[51] For example, in *Staeng's Patent*,[52] it was held that a person (A) was a joint inventor of a new method of securing electric cables where it was unlikely that the main inventor (B) would have turned his mind to the question without having been prompted by A. In this case, the (then) Patent Office was influenced by the fact that the principal inventor, who did not work in the field, was only alerted to the possibility of the improvement by A.

In other cases, however, the mere posing of a question to be answered (or the recognition of the problem to be solved) will *not* be treated as an inventive contribution. The reason for this is that in some circumstances, especially in the biotechnology industry, particular goals are commonly known (this is illustrated by the fact that a number of different companies often pursue the same goal).[53] In these circumstances, the decision to pursue a particular goal is unlikely to be treated as being sufficiently creative for it to be recognized as an inventive contribution.

3.1.2 What is a non-inventive contribution?

Just as certain types of contribution are normally considered to be inventive, so other types of contribution are not. Thus where a party has only contributed 'unnecessary

---

[48] The question who should be recognized as creators in intellectual property law is an important and often contentious issue. Over time, the law has witnessed many occasions on which interest groups have attempted to argue that they are creative enough to warrant the protection offered by intellectual property law. While these struggles may not be as visible in patent law as in other areas of intellectual property law, patent law is no exception to this general statement.

[49] Inventor is defined in PA 1977, s. 7(3), as the 'actual deviser'.

[50] In *Allen v. Rawson* (1845) 1 *CB* 551, 135 *ER* 656, Earle J said that, where a person collaborated in the elaboration of a 'main principle' and in so doing made valuable accessory discoveries, these were the property of the inventor of the original principle. The applicability and scope of this principle is, however, unclear: *Goddin & Rennie's Application* [1996] *RPC* 141.

[51] It was said in *Staeng's Patent* [1996] *RPC* 183, 189, that 'blowing the fire, rather than igniting it' can be sufficient for the contributor to be considered as the 'deviser' of the resulting invention.

[52] [1996] *RPC* 183. Under German law, the formula for calculating compensation for use of employee inventions gives equal weighting to those who 'elucidate' the problem and those who 'devise' the solution. See V. Schmied-Kowarzik, 'Employee Inventions under German Law' (1972) 54 *JPTOS* 807.

[53] See *Genentech v. Wellcome* [1989] *RPC* 147 (CA).

detail' to an invention, they will not be treated as an inventor;[54] so too merely recognizing a potential application of a general idea was said not to be an inventive contribution.[55] It also seems that managerial and entrepreneurial contributions, such as the provision of money, facilities, materials, support staff, and the like, will not be regarded as inventive contributions (although the provider of such contributions may obtain the right to apply for a patent).[56]

Another type of contribution that seems to be excluded from what may be labelled as an inventive contribution is the supply of crucial starting materials.[57] In a celebrated American case, doctors at the UCLA Medical Center extracted a cell line from the spleen of the patient (and plaintiff) John Moore, who was being treated for hairy-cell leukaemia. The cell line formed the basis of an invention that the university subsequently patented. The Supreme Court of California held that Moore had no proprietary interests in the invention (or patent).[58] More specifically, the Court held that he had no property rights in either the genetic information encoded in his cells or the cells themselves. In so ruling, the Court noted that everyone's genetic material contains information for the manufacture of lymphokines and, as a result, that Moore's cell line was 'no more unique to Moore than the number of vertebrae in the spine'.[59] The Court contrasted the mundane nature of the source materials with the skills of the researchers, noting that the 'adaptation and growth of human tissues and cells in culture is difficult—often considered an art'.[60] From the view of one commentator, the case illustrates the pervasive influence of the 'author construct', which leads intellectual property law to privilege certain kinds of contribution: the material basis of intellectual property is disregarded, while the researchers who manipulate that material are prioritized.[61]

A related issue arises in relation to bioprospecting. This is the practice whereby pharmaceutical firms, typically from the developed world, employ the knowledge of indigenous groups to identify the medicinal properties of local plants, which are then synthetically reproduced. Perhaps one of the best-known examples of this is the US patent, which has subsequently been revoked, directed to the medicinal application of turmeric in wound healing (a practice that has been known about in India for centuries).[62] In an attempt to

---

[54] *IDA v. University of Southampton* [2006] *EWCA Civ* 145, [39].

[55] *Fireworks Fire Protection and Watermist v. Andrew James Cooke*, O/275/13 (23 July 2013), [51]. A delay in raising inventorship as an issue was a possible factor to suggest that a person was not an inventor: ibid., [67]–[70].

[56] *Morgan v. Hirsch*, 728 *F.2d*. 1449, 1452 (Fed. Cir. 1984) (claimant confused entrepreneurship with inventorship); *Minnesota Mining & Mfg Co's Appn* [2008] *RPC* (28) 541, 556 (a party whose contribution was to identify or to draw attention to some prior art could qualify as an inventor in the appropriate circumstances).

[57] Cf. the novelty examination, during which the fact that prior art fails to disclose the starting materials may mean that the prior art does not destroy novelty. See Chapter 18, section 4.3, pp. 563–5.

[58] *Moore v. Regents of the University of California*, 793 *P.2d*. 479 (Cal. 1990), cert denied, 111 S. Ct. 1388 (1991). It was accepted that Moore had a cause of action for breach of fiduciary duty or lack of informed consent. For some of the many commentaries, see T. Dillon, 'Source Compensation for Tissues and Cells used in Biotechnical Research: Why a Source Shouldn't Share in the Profits' (1989) 64 *Notre Dame L Rev* 628; B. Edelman, 'L'Homme aux cellules d'or' (1989) 34 *Recueil Dalloz Sirey* 225; B. Edelman, 'Le Recherche biomedicale dans l'économie de Marché' (1991) 30 *Recueil Dalloz Sirey* 203; B. Hoffmaster, 'From the Sacred to the Profane' (1992) 7 *IPJ* 115.

[59] *Moore v. Regents of the University of California*, 1 Cal 3d 120, 139 (1990), cert denied 499 US 936 (1991).

[60] Ibid.

[61] J. Boyle, 'A Theory of Law and Information: Copyright, Spleens, Blackmail, and Insider Trading' (1992) 80 *Cal L Rev* 1413, 1516.

[62] See M. Uniyal, 'Trade: Biopirates Stake Claim to Southern Knowledge', Inter Press Service (29 August 1996).

argue that indigenous peoples should be compensated for the use that is made of their knowledge, the question has been raised as to whether the contribution of indigenous knowledge (such as the identification of starting materials) ought to be recognized as an 'inventive' contribution to the resulting synthetic drugs. As the law is currently formulated, it seems that the provision of information is unlikely to amount to co-inventorship.[63] The main reason for this is that the contribution of knowledge about a plant's whereabouts or uses, especially when the information is already in the public domain,[64] is unlikely to be seen as an essential part of the structure and composition of a synthetically produced drug. As a result, many now accept that the goal of providing proper rewards to indigenous communities is better served by other means (such as by the international recognition of a *sui generis* right or by mandated contractual benefit-sharing arrangements).

In order for a contribution to an invention to rise to the level of joint inventorship, the contribution must be concrete and specific rather than vague or general.[65] Having said this, the courts have said that to qualify as an inventor, there was no need for a person to show that they have (to use the American concept) brought about 'a reduction to practice'. Thus it was said that a person who comes up with and communicates an idea consisting of all of the elements in the claim, 'even though it is just an idea at that stage', will normally be treated as an inventor.[66] In contrast, if an inventor instructs an assistant or employee to carry out specific tests, it is unlikely that the assistant will be treated as a joint inventor. This is because the carrying out of instructions is likely to be seen as a process of execution rather than creation. For the purposes of determining ownership between employers and employees, a person who merely contributes advice or other assistance in the making of an invention is not an inventor.[67] Outside the employer–employee context, such contributions are also likely to be treated as non-inventive unless it can be shown that the advice or assistance was in some way inventive.[68] It is also clear that if a person's contribution is limited to applying common general knowledge, their contribution will not be regarded as inventive.[69]

While there has been little guidance as to the amount of mental labour that a person must contribute to an invention for them to qualify as a joint inventor, there may be grounds for arguing that where a person only makes a minor contribution to an invention, they should not be treated as a joint inventor. The reason for this is that joint inventors are sometimes able to control the ability of the other joint inventors to obtain or maintain a patent[70]—a power that might not be justified if the contribution is particularly small.[71] It should also be noted that in contrast with copyright law,[72] there is no explicit

---

[63] M. Huft, 'Indigenous Peoples and Drug Discovery Research: A Question of Intellectual Property Rights' (1995) 89 *Nw UL Rev* 1678, 1728; M. Blakeney, 'Access to Genetic Resources: The View from the South' (1997) 3 *Bioscience L Rev* 94, 99.

[64] Whether because the information is known within the community or because it has been documented by ethnobiologists. The classic anti-malarial drug, quinine, is derived from the bark of South American cinchona trees, the extract from which was first used to treat fever by the indigenous peoples of Peru in the eighteenth century: see Huft, op. cit., 1700. See the observations of Lord Hoffmann in *Merrell Dow v. Norton* [1996] *RPC* 76, 88.

[65] It has been suggested that the 'conceptual specificity of a person's contribution' is a critical factor in deciding whether or not they are joint inventor: R. Harris, 'Conceptual Specificity as a Factor in Determination of Inventorship' (1985) 67 *JPTOS* 315; *Garrett v. United States*, 422 *F.2d.* 874, 881 (Ct. Cl. 1970).   [66] *Stanelco v. Biopress* [2005] *RPC* 319, [14].

[67] PA 1977, s. 43(4); *Allen v. Rawson* (1845) 1 *CB* 551, 135 *ER* 656; *Smith's Patent* (1905) 22 *RPC* 57.

[68] *Staeng's Patent* [1996] *RPC* 183.   [69] *IDA v. University of Southampton* [2006] *EWCA Civ* 145, [35].

[70] PA 1977, s. 36.

[71] A co-inventor who refuses to apply for a patent can have any such patent that has been granted to a co-inventor revoked.   [72] CDPA 1988, s. 11.

requirement in patent law that for a person to be recognized as a co-inventor, the parties must have collaborated. Having said this, it is clear that where two persons independently create the same invention, they will not be treated as co-inventors: the first to file is the person entitled to the patent.[73]

3.2 EMPLOYEE INVENTIONS

Although the romantic image of the amateur inventor plays an important role in shaping the way we think about patent law, it has long been recognized that many inventions are made by professional researchers who are employed to invent, often by large corporations[74]—a situation that has expanded rapidly with the growth of so-called 'big science' since the Second World War.[75] Patent law recognizes the financial interests of such employers by providing that in certain circumstances, it will be the employer rather than the employee who will be the owner of inventions made by employees. In this way, patent law retains the romantic model of the inventor in name, but allocates the important monopoly rights to the commercial interests that support and maintain the research.[76]

When the EPC 1973 was being drafted, it was decided that questions relating to ownership of employee inventions were a matter that were better dealt with by national laws rather than the Convention.[77] While the EPC—as with the Community Patent Convention and the Patent Cooperation Treaty—makes no provision in relation to employee inventions, when the Patents Act 1977 was drafted, the (then) Labour government took the opportunity to regulate the position of employee inventors. In so doing, it effectively codified an area that prior to the enactment of the Act was primarily dealt with by case law.[78]

There are two notable features of the Patents Act 1977 relating to employee inventions. The first, which is the focus of the remainder of this chapter, is that sections 39–43 of the Patents Act provide detailed guidance as to the way in which ownership disputes between employers and employees should be determined. The second notable feature of the Act, which is dealt with in Chapter 23, is that employees are provided with a right of fair reimbursement (or compensation) where their inventions belong to their employers.

---

[73] The other inventor being left with such *in personam* defences as they can establish.

[74] Cf. S. Cherensky, 'A Penny for their Thoughts: Employee-Inventors, Preinvention Assignment Agreements, Property, and Personhood' (1993) 81 *Cal L Rev* 595; J. Hughes, 'The Personality Interest of Artists and Inventors in Intellectual Property' (1998) 16 *Cardozo AELJ* 81.

[75] See P. Galison and B. Hevly (eds), *Big Science: The Growth of Large Scale Research* (1992).

[76] For a comparative position, see H. Parker, 'Reform for Rights of Employed Inventors' (1984) 57 *S Cal L Rev* 603, 615 *ff*; V. Schmied-Kowarzik, 'Employee Inventions under German Law' (1972) 54 *JPTOS* 807; J. Joviczyk, 'Employee Inventions' (1989) 20 *IIC* 847.

[77] As such, national laws are free to determine ownership issues between employer and employee. All that the EPC 2000 does is specify which national law should operate. See European Commission, *Green Paper on the Community Patent* (1997) COM (97) 314 final, [4.3], explaining that there are great differences between member states' rules governing inventions by employees: that, in some member states, the question is dealt with in general terms by patent law (e.g. in France and the United Kingdom); in others, a specific law has been enacted (as in Germany and Sweden). Other laws distinguish between 'permanent', 'temporary', and 'occasional' inventive roles, with different rules for determining ownership of the patent in each case. Other laws, such as the German Act, contain a long series of provisions relating to the remuneration of employees with an inventive role and lay down the precise method for calculating additional remuneration.

[78] PA 1977, ss 39–43, apply only to inventions made after 1 June 1978. See J. Phillips and M. Hoolahan, *Employee Inventions in the UK* (1982); W. Cornish, 'Rights in Employee Inventions: The UK Position' (1990) 21 *IIC* 290; W. Cornish, 'Rights in University Inventions' [1992] *EIPR* 13.

In deciding whether an invention made in the course of employment should belong to the employee or the employer, patent law had to balance a range of competing interests. On the one hand, a desire to protect and promote freedom of labour, particularly for activities carried on outside the scope of employment, lent support to those who favoured employee ownership. These arguments were supported by the long-standing principle that the inventor is the first owner of a patent. Militating against this, however, was the powerful, and ultimately more influential, argument that where someone is employed to do something (such as to invent), the employer and not the employee should be the owner of the resulting products (or inventions).

Disputes between employers and employees over who is entitled to apply for a patent or, if a patent has already been granted, who is the rightful initial owner of the patent are governed by section 39 of the 1977 Act. Section 39 provides a 'complete code' for determining entitlement.[79] Following the common law position, the 1977 Act provides that an invention belongs to an employer in two situations.[80] Employee inventions that fall outside these two categories belong to the employee.[81]

(i)   The first situation where an employee invention belongs to the employer is set out in section 39(1)(a). This provides that an invention will belong to the employer where the invention was made in the course of the employee's normal or specifically assigned duties *and* the invention was made in circumstances under which an invention might reasonably have been expected to have resulted from the carrying out of those duties.

(ii) The second situation where an employee invention belongs to an employer is set out in section 39(1)(b). This provides that in certain circumstances, an employee's position and status within an organization will be such that they will be taken to be under a 'special obligation to further the interests of the employer's undertaking'. Thus, where an employee occupies a senior managerial or administrative position, any inventions that they produce belong to their employer.

3.2.1 Employer ownership of employee inventions

Before looking at the way that the ownership of employee inventions is allocated under the Patents Act 1977, it is necessary to take account of a number of preliminary points.

(i) Made in the course of employment   In order for section 39 to come into play, it is necessary to show that the invention was made by an 'employee' who was 'mainly employed' in the United Kingdom.[82] For the most part, showing that an invention was made in the course of employment is unlikely to present any major difficulties. Problems may arise, however, in situations where inventions are made by consultants, academics, visitors to universities, students, researchers on secondment, home-workers, and company

[79] *Fireworks Fire Protection and Watermist v. Andrew James Cooke*, O/275/13 (23 July 2013), [71]–[74], citing *French v. Mason* [1999] *FSR* 597, [13]. As such, PA 1977, s. 39, excludes the operation of other rules of law (such as law of constructive trust).

[80] PA 1977, s. 39(1)(a)–(b). Because the sections are not necessarily mutually exclusive, an employee may be caught by either subsection (a) or (b): *Memco-Med's Patent* [1992] *RPC* 403, 406.

[81] PA 1977, s. 39(2). PA 1977, s. 39(3), which was introduced by the CDPA 1988, provides that, where an employee is entitled to the patent, they may 'use material in support of the application in which the employer owns copyright or 'design'. For the common law position in the United States, see *United States v. Dubilier Condenser Corp.*, 289 US 178 (1933), amended by 289 US 706 (1933).   [82] PA 1977, s. 43(2).

directors.[83] While 'employee' and 'employer' are both defined in section 130 of the Act, this provides little guidance in these grey areas. In order to determine whether a particular inventor is in an employment relationship, a range of different factors are taken into account.[84] These include the relevant National Insurance and tax arrangements, the way in which the relationship is described by the parties, and the provision of materials, as well as the control and responsibility that is exercised by the parties in question.

(ii) 'Inventions' Another notable feature of section 39 is that it refers to 'inventions' rather than to 'patented inventions' (or some similar phrase). One of the consequences of this is that the section will operate to resolve issues of ownership irrespective of whether a patent application has been filed or a patent granted. It has also been suggested that the fact that the section refers to inventions may mean that the section extends beyond patentable subject matter to include things such as suggestion schemes.[85]

(iii) Onus of proof While evidential and procedural matters are often overlooked in discussions about patent law, decisions relating to the onus and standard of proof play an important role in shaping the way in which patent law operates in practice. Although the standard of proof in this context is clear enough—it is the civil standard of balance of probabilities—there is some uncertainty as to whether the onus of proof falls upon the employer or the employee. Given that the inventor is presumed to be the owner of the patent and that section 39 provides exceptions to this, it would seem reasonable to expect that the onus of proof falls upon the employer to establish that a particular employee invention belongs to them as a result of section 39(1)(a) or (b). Militating against this, however, is the fact that in a number of cases, the Comptroller has presumed that the onus of proof falls upon the person who is putting the question of entitlement in issue.[86] Because this approach concentrates on the person who makes the application, rather than on the relative bargaining powers of the parties, if it is not an untenable position, then it certainly is an undesirable one.[87]

(iv) It is not possible to diminish the rights of employees by contract In order to protect an employee whose inferior bargaining position may lead them to sign their statutory rights over to their employer, section 42 of the 1977 Act provides that any term in a contract of employment[88] that diminishes the rights of an employee in any invention shall be unenforceable against the employee.[89] The scope of the section is limited by the fact that it does not apply in relation to an employee's duty of confidentiality.[90] It is also limited in that section 42 does not seem to prohibit contracts dealing with inventions created

---

[83] See *CIPA*, [39.06]; B. Sherman, 'Governing Science: Patents and Public Sector Research in the United Kingdom' (1995) 26 *IIC* 15.

[84] *Ready Mix Concrete v. Minister of Pensions* [1968] 2 *QB* 497, 515; *Autoclenz v. Belcher* [2011] *UKSC* 41, [18]-[19]. For a discussion on equivalent provisions in copyright, see Chapter 5, section 3, p. 133.

[85] In other contexts, it has been held that 'invention' encompasses unpatentable subject matter: *Viziball's Application* [1988] *RPC* 213.   [86] Ibid. See also *Staeng's Patent* [1996] *RPC* 183.

[87] *CIPA*, [39.07]. In *Greater Glasgow Health Board's Application* [1996] *RPC* 207, in which an employee agreed to allow the employer to proceed with a patent application pending a decision, Jacob J said that it would be unfortunate if anything were to turn on the question of onus of proof.

[88] The provisions apply to contracts of employment, as well as to contracts made between employees and third parties either at the request of the employer or in pursuance of the employee's contract of employment. The section applies both to contracts made before and after the 1977 Act came into force.

[89] PA 1977, s. 42(2).

[90] On the question of employee's duty to disclose inventions and its relationship with PA 1977, s. 44, see *CIPA*, [42.02]. More generally, see J. Turner, 'Pre-invention Assignment Agreement Breach: A Practical Alternative to Specific Performance or Unqualified Injunction' (1997) 5 *JIPL* 631.

after an employee leaves employment.[91] The reason for this is that while such contracts may appear to fall within the terms of section 42, the section probably has no application because the inventions will have been made when the inventor was no longer in employment.[92] The exact scope of the provision, and the degree to which it modifies the common law rules in this area, remain unclear.

With these initial points in mind, we now turn to look in more detail at the two situations in which employee inventions will belong to an employer.

3.2.2 Persons employed to invent

The first situation in which an employee invention belongs to an employer is set out in section 39(1)(a). This provides that an invention made by an employee will belong to their employer if the invention was made in the course of the employee's normal or specifically assigned duties *and* the circumstances in which the invention was made were such that 'an invention might reasonably have been expected to result from the carrying out of those duties'.

(i) Scope of an employee's duties   In order to determine whether an employee invention belongs to the employer by virtue of section 39(1)(a), it is necessary to determine the scope and nature of an employee's duties. It is then necessary to ascertain whether the invention was made by the employee carrying out those duties.

The job description and the contract of employment are often used as a way of determining the precise nature of an employee's normal duties.[93] There has also been a willingness to look beyond the formal legal arrangement of the contract of employment to the activities that are *actually* undertaken by the employee.[94] Once the scope of an employee's normal duties has been ascertained, it is relatively easy to determine whether an employee has been assigned any additional duties.

Once the duties of the employee have been ascertained, it is then necessary to determine whether the invention was made 'in the course of those duties'. The factors to be considered here include when and where the invention was made, the facilities used by the employee, and the relationship between the invention and the field in which the employer operates.[95] So long as it can be shown that the activity in question falls within the general scope of employment, this is unlikely to present any major problems.

(ii) Duties that can be expected to result in an invention   As well as establishing that the invention was made in the course of an employee's normal or special duties, the second limb of section 39(1)(a) provides that it is also necessary to show that the invention was

---

[91] In the United States, these are called 'holdover' or 'trailer clauses'. See M. B. Hershovitz, 'Unhitching the Trailer Clause: The Rights of Inventive Employees and Their Employers' (1995) 3 *JIPL* 187.

[92] Even if these were not invalidated by s. 42, they would be subject to the doctrine of restraint of trade: see *Electrolux v. Hudson* [1977] *FSR* 312.

[93] *Staeng's Patent* [1996] *RPC* 183, 198 (the job description will normally be decisive).

[94] *LIFFE Administration and Management v. Pinkava* [2007] *RPC* 667 (CA), stressing that while the employment contract was an important starting point, the duties of an employee often evolved over time. In *Harris's Application* [1985] *RPC* 19, there was no evidence as to the contract of employment and Falconer J looked at what was actually done. See also *Greater Glasgow* [1996] *RPC* 207, 222. It should be noted that most of the cases begin, at least as a starting point, with the job description. See also *Fireworks Fire Protection and Watermist v. Andrew James Cooke*, O/275/13 (23 July 2013).

[95] In *Staeng's Patent* [1996] *RPC* 183, it was suggested that any invention that was useful to the employer would automatically fall within the employee's duties; cf. *Greater Glasgow* [1996] *RPC* 207, 222. See P. Chandler, 'Employee's Inventions: Inventorship and Ownership' [1997] *EIPR* 262.

made in circumstances under which an invention might reasonably have been expected to result from the carrying out of such duties.

One of the notable aspects of the second limb of section 39(1)(a) is that it requires that *the* invention be made in circumstances under which *an* invention might reasonably be expected to result from the carrying out of the employee's duties. The question of what is meant by 'an invention' in this context was considered by Falconer J in *Harris's Patent*,[96] where he said that 'an invention' did not mean *any* invention, nor did it mean 'the precise invention that was made'. While Falconer J's comments are useful in telling us what the phrase does not mean, it offers little positive guidance as to what it does mean.[97] One possibility is that it could be construed to mean an invention of the same description or type as the invention in suit.[98]

An important factor that is often relied upon when deciding whether there was an expectation that the carrying out of the employee's duties would lead to an invention is the extent to which the employee was engaged to invent or design.[99] Inventions that are made by an employee whose duties are limited to mechanical, routine, or non-creative tasks will ordinarily remain with the employee.[100] This can be seen in *Harris's Patent*,[101] an ownership dispute between Reiss, which manufactured valves under licence from Sistag, and Harris, who worked as a manager for Reiss. The particular issue in dispute was whether Reiss or Harris owned rights in a valve, invented by Harris, which controlled the flow of dust through ducts. A number of factors led the court to its finding that the invention belonged to Harris. These included the fact that Harris's normal duties were limited to the non-inventive tasks of sales and after-sales service. Importantly, in dealing with customer problems, Harris's role was limited to non-creative or routine application of known engineering practices. The fact that Reiss had no research laboratory, was not involved in research and development, and always referred major technical problems to Sistag for solution reinforced the conclusion that Harris had not been employed to design or invent. Indeed, when Harris made suggestions to Reiss as to how the valves could be improved, Reiss turned them down. Given that it was not part of the employer's business to solve design problems in valves, it could hardly have been a part of Harris's duties.[102]

Where a person is employed to invent or design, there will ordinarily be an expectation that the carrying out of the employee's duties would lead to an invention and, as such,

---

[96] *Harris's Application* [1985] *RPC* 19, [25].

[97] In this context, it is interesting to note that PA 1977, s. 40(7), speaks of 'inventions of the same description'. In *Harris's Application* [1985] *RPC* 19, 29, Falconer J said that the phrase an 'invention might reasonably have been expected to result from the carrying out of the duties' refers to 'an invention which achieves, or contributes to achieving, whatever was the aim or object to which the employee's efforts in carrying out his duties'.

[98] Another aspect of PA 1977, s. 39, that is unclear is that the section provides that the invention must be made in circumstances in which it might reasonably be 'expected'. It is unclear who it is that ought to expect the invention: the employee, the employer, or, most probably, an objective third party?

[99] Presumably, the status of the employee, a factor normally limited to PA 1977, s. 39(1)(b), would influence whether an invention would be 'expected'. It was said in *Greater Glasgow* [1996] *RPC* 207 that this was to be judged in terms of the circumstances in which the invention in suit was made and not the general circumstances of employment.

[100] Ibid., 222. It was said that a duty to treat patients did not impose a general duty to invent new ways of diagnosing and treating patients.   [101] [1985] *RPC* 19.

[102] Ibid., 32. See also *Fireworks Fire Protection and Watermist v. Andrew James Cooke*, O/275/13 (23 July 2013), [75]–[97].

that any inventions that are made will belong to their employer. This is the case even if the creative aspect of an employee's duties forms only a small part of an employee's overall duties. For example, in *Staeng's Patent*,[103] it was held that while an employee was primarily engaged in marketing, the fact that his job description also assigned to him the creative role of using discussions with customers to generate ideas for new products, as well as thinking of novel uses for existing products, meant that any inventions that he made belonged to his employer. As yet, it is unclear how small the creative contribution of an employee's duties needs to be for section 39(1)(a) not to apply.

3.2.3 Special obligations

The second situation where an invention made by an employee will belong to their employer is set out in section 39(1)(b). While section 39(1)(a) primarily deals with people who are employed to invent or design, section 39(1)(b) is concerned with inventions that are made by managerial or administrative employees. More specifically, section 39(1)(b) provides that in certain circumstances, an employee's position within an organization is such that they are deemed to be under a special obligation to further the interests of their employer. While the normal or special duties of an employee may not require them to invent or design, this is overridden by the fact that their seniority effectively places them under a legal obligation not to compete with the firm.[104] This fiduciary principle, which is embodied in section 39(1)(b), means that if an employee who occupies a senior position within an organization produces an invention and it can be shown that the invention was made in the course of the duties of the employee, the invention will belong to the employer.

Whether an employee is under a 'special obligation' largely depends upon the position that the employee occupies within an organization and the responsibilities that flow from that position. Employees who occupy senior positions, such as senior executives, directors, and managers, are treated as alter egos of their employers and are, as such, under a 'special obligation to further the interests of the employer's undertaking'.[105] In contrast, fewer obligations are imposed on less senior employees, such as sales managers or marketing managers.[106] The difficult issue here is deciding at what point within the hierarchy of an organization section 39(1)(b) ceases to apply: how junior must an employee be for them to retain the inventions that they produce?

We are able to gain some guidance as to where this line is to be drawn if we compare *Harris's Patent*, in which the employee was held not to be under a special obligation, with *Staeng*, in which section 39(1)(b) applied. As we saw earlier, *Harris's Patent* turned on the question of whether an invention made by Harris belonged to Harris, as an employee, or Reiss, as employer. As well as failing under section 39(1)(a), section 39(1)(b) was also held not to apply. This was because while Harris was called a 'manager', when the court looked at what Harris actually did, it found that he had no power to hire, fire, or agree holiday

---

[103] [1996] *RPC* 183.

[104] In many circumstances, this implied duty of good faith meant that an employee was under a duty to assign the patent to the employer: *Patchett v. Sterling* [1955] *RPC* 50; *British Syphon v. Homeword* [1956] *RPC* 330. The statutory rule may be stricter than the common-law position—on which, see *Worthington Pumping Engine Company v. Moore* (1903) 20 *RPC* 41.

[105] *Worthington Pumping Engine Company v. Moore* (1903) 20 *RPC* 46. It was said in *Harris's Application* [1985] *RPC* 19 that pre-1977 cases offered guidance as to the extent and nature of an employee's obligations to further the interest of the employer's undertakings.

[106] *Worthington Pumping Engine Company v. Moore* (1903) 20 *RPC* 37–8.

dates, never attended board meetings (even when his department was being discussed), and had limited financial control. As such, the court found that Harris did not owe a 'special obligation' to his employer; rather, it found that he was only under an obligation to do the best that he could to effect sales of the valves and related customer aftercare service. Consequently, the court concluded that because Harris was not under a special obligation, the invention in question belonged to Harris. In contrast, in *Staeng's* case, the employee operated at a very senior level: he attended board meetings; he often acted in a similar capacity to the directors; he had some control over budgetary matters (such as the product range); he was party to the company's profit-bonus scheme; and he had discretion whether to solve problems himself or to pass them on to others. From this basis, the court concluded that Staeng was under a special obligation under section 39(1)(b). As such, the invention that he made belonged to his employer.[107]

---

[107] For a comparison of these decisions, see *Fireworks Fire Protection and Watermist v. Andrew James Cooke*, O/275/13 (23 July 2013), [100]–[114].

22

INFRINGEMENT

1 INTRODUCTION

Patent infringement is a notoriously complex area of law.[1] In part, this is a consequence of the evidential nature of the inquiry, which often makes it difficult to generalize beyond the particular case in hand. Another factor that has added to this complexity (while simultaneously enhancing the effectiveness of the patent system) is that it has long been accepted that the scope of the patent monopoly should not be limited to situations where the infringing act takes place in relation to a product or process that is exactly the same as the patented invention. While extending the scope of the monopoly beyond a strict reading of the claims may have satisfied the law's desire to protect the equity of the patent, it generated a new question: how broadly can the patent be read? Similarly, when it was agreed that not all of an invention needed to be taken for a patent to be infringed, the question arose: how much of the invention needs to be taken? The difficulties that these questions generate further accentuate the problems that arise in understanding patent infringement.[2]

The complexity of the topic is also a consequence of Britain's entry into the European Patent Convention. When the EPC 1973 was drafted, it was decided that questions about the infringement of patents issued by the European Patent Office (EPO) were better dealt with by national courts.[3] Nonetheless, the close relationship between validity and infringement has meant that decisions at the EPO (particularly in relation to novelty) have impacted on the British law of infringement. These transitions have proved to be all the more problematic because of the absence of a common tribunal dealing with infringement.

As we mentioned earlier, this situation will change if the unitary patent package is implemented. One of the notable features of the unified patent package is that questions of infringement will no longer be the exclusive domain of national courts, nor of national law. Currently, infringement of European patents is a matter for national courts to be decided on the basis of the Patents Act 1977. Under the Agreement on a Unified Patent

---

[1] It is also potentially a very costly process. In one case, it was suggested that it cost £250,000 for a two-day trial in the county court and about £112,000 for the Court of Appeal: *Warheit v. Olympia Tools* [2003] *FSR* 6. The cost of cases has increased significantly since then.

[2] See A. Benyamini, *Patent Infringement in the European Community* (1993).

[3] Infringement proceedings can be also brought before the Comptroller so long as both parties consent: PA 1977, s. 61(3) (but it has not happened since long before the PA 1977 came into force). The suggestion that the 1977 Act be amended to remove the need for the consent of both parties was not adopted in the proposals for reform of the 1977 Act: see *Consultation on the Proposed Patents Act (Amendment) Bill: Summary of Responses and the Government's Conclusions* (Nov 2003), [115]–[124].

Court[4] (the 'UPC Agreement'), however, this will shift to the unitary patent courts (which will also have exclusive authority in relation to the infringement of the proposed new 'unitary patent'). In line with this, the UPC Agreement also sets out the relevant law rules to be used when deciding whether a bundled or a unitary patent is infringed.[5] The UPC Agreement also provides a series of defences that will apply (including acts done for private and non-commercial purpose, acts done for experimental purposes, situations in which biological material is used for the purpose of breeding or discovering and developing new plant varieties, the pharmaceutical preparation of medicines, certain on-farm uses of patented plants and animals, and certain uses in relation to patented computer programs, such as decompilation and interoperability).[6] While UK courts will still have jurisdiction over national patents issued by the UK Intellectual Property Office (IPO), the Patents Act 1977 will need to be modified to ensure that UK law complies with the infringement provisions for European bundle patents and unitary patents under the UPC Agreement.

Despite its complex and often uncertain nature, determining patent infringement can be separated into three tasks.

(i) First, it is necessary to determine the types of activity that constitute an infringement.

(ii) Next, it is necessary to ascertain whether the activity complained of falls within the scope of the patent monopoly.

(iii) Finally, it needs to be determined whether the defendant is able to make use of any of the defences that are available to them.

Each of these tasks will be dealt with in turn.

2 TYPES OF INFRINGING ACTIVITY

It is important to note at the outset that patent law draws a general distinction between direct and indirect infringement. The main difference between them is that *direct* infringement involves some immediate engagement with the patented product or process,[7] whereas *indirect* infringement applies where a person facilitates the act of infringement[8]—in effect, patent law's version of aiding and abetting. Before looking at direct and indirect infringement in more detail, it is important to note that to infringe, the activity must be carried out without the consent of the patentee (that is, the activity must not be covered by licence),[9] must occur within the United Kingdom,[10] and must take place during the duration of the patent.[11]

---

[4] *Agreement on a Unified Patent Court* [2013] *OJ C* 175/1 (20 June 2013).

[5] UPC Agreement, Arts 25, 26 (the right to prevent direct and indirect uses of the invention in certain situations).

[6] Ibid., Art. 27(a)–(l).   [7] PA 1977, s. 60(1).

[8] PA 1977, s. 60(2); CPC, Art. 26. The PA 1977 also contains provisions in relation to contributory infringement.   [9] See Chapter 23, section 2.3, pp. 676–9.

[10] The United Kingdom includes the Isle of Man and the territorial waters of the United Kingdom: PA 1977, s. 132(2), (3).

[11] A patentee may sue only with respect to acts that occur after publication of the application and then only if the patent has been granted. PA 1977, s. 62(3), introduces certain qualifications where the patent application is amended after publication. PA 1977, s. 62(2), deals with the position where the patentee fails to renew the patent promptly. For considerations of duration and SPCs, see Chapter 24, section 3.4 *ff*, pp. 714–15.

2.1 DIRECT INFRINGEMENT

For a patentee to succeed in an infringement action, they must show on the balance of probabilities that the defendant performed one of the activities that falls within the patent owner's control.[12] The primary rights given to a patent owner are set out in section 60(1) of the 1977 Act. As we will see, section 60(1) covers a wide array of activities, from the making or using of a product or a process, through to the sale or import of the product. As a result most, if not all, commercially valuable activities fall within the owner's control.

The rights given to an owner differ depending on whether the patent is for a product, a process, or a product obtained directly from a process. With the exception of the situation in which an infringer uses a process or 'offers a process for use' under section 60(1)(b), direct infringement takes place irrespective of the knowledge of the defendant. This means that liability is absolute in relation to a patent for a product, or where a product has been obtained directly from a patented process. As such, there is no need for a patentee to show that the defendants knew that they were infringing. In these cases, independent, accidental, or unintentional creation of the same invention will infringe.

2.2 PATENT FOR A PRODUCT

The owner of a patent for a *product* is given the right to make, dispose of, offer to dispose of, use, import, or keep the product, whether for disposal or otherwise.[13] It is important to note that in this context, liability is absolute: the knowledge of the defendant is not relevant when deciding whether they have carried out one of the activities within the owner's control.[14] While intention to infringe is not relevant to the determination of liability, *mens rea* might play a significant role in relation to the remedies granted by the court.[15]

Three different rationales are usually given to explain why patent liability is absolute.[16] The first is that the principle is necessary to allow patentees full enjoyment of their monopoly rights.[17] This is often said to be more pressing because of the onerous nature of the validity requirements imposed on patent applicants. When thinking about assertions of this nature, it is important to remember that property rights are never absolute and that the rights recognized in patents are no exception to this.[18] For example, patents are limited in terms of duration, scope of operation, subject matter, and types of activity

---

[12] PA 1977, s. 60(1)–(2); CPC, Arts 25–8.

[13] PA 1977, s. 60(1)(a).

[14] *Schenck v. Universal Balancing* [2012] *EWHC* 1920 (Pat), [86].

[15] PA 1977, s. 62(1). See further Chapter 49, section 5, pp. 1326–33.

[16] The following cases are usually cited in support: *Proctor v. Bennis* (1887) *RPC* 333, 356–7 (no real justification given); *Curtis v. Platt* (1863) 3 *Ch D* 135, 140n; *Valensi v. BRC* [1972] *FSR* 273, 306 (adds nothing); *Stead v. Anderson* (1847) 2 *WPC* 151, 156; *Wight v. Hitchcock* (1870) *LR* 37, 47 (argument based on a version of parallel importing: 'if the law were otherwise . . . another might by merely crossing the Channel, and manufacturing abroad, and selling for far less than the original price . . . wholly deprive the patentee of the benefit of the invention'); *Walton v. Lavater* (1860) 8 *CB (NS)* 162, 186, 29 *LJ (CP)* 275, 279; *Betts v. Neilson* (1865) 34 *LJ (Ch)* 537; *Elmslie v. Boursier* (1869–70) *LR* 9 *Eq* 217.

[17] *Lishman v. Erom Roche* (1996) 68 *CPR (3d)* 72, 77 (FCTD).

[18] See R. Gordon, 'Paradoxical Property', in J. Brewer and S. Staves (eds), *Early Modern Conceptions of Property* (1995), 95. See also Lord Irvine of Lairg, 'The Law: An Engine for Trade' (2001) 64 *MLR* 333, 346:

> [P]atents do not create wholly controlled monopolies. They confer on their owners the narrower benefit of exclusive commercial exploitation for a duration limited to twenty years. Even during the currency of the patent, members of the public are free to conduct experiments on the patented invention.

that are protected. As such, there is little, if anything, in this argument that demands that infringement ought to be absolute.

A second explanation offered as to why the intention of the defendant is not relevant when determining whether someone has infringed can be traced to the so-called 'reverse-infringement test', which is used to determine whether an invention is novel.[19] Under this test, which conceives of the novelty examination as a mirror of the test for infringement, the court asks the following hypothetical question: if the disclosure were to be made or take place after grant, would it infringe the patent (if granted)? If so, then the disclosure is anticipatory.[20] The next step in the argument is to remind us that when considering whether information in the public domain anticipates an invention, the intention of the person who made that information public is irrelevant (that is, novelty is decided objectively). On the basis that novelty and infringement are mirrors of each other and that novelty is determined objectively, it is therefore suggested that infringement should also be decided objectively. However, while the 'reverse-infringement' test may have brought conceptual clarity to the novelty examination, it offers little real guidance when considering whether intention *should* be a factor taken into account when deciding infringement.

A third argument in support of the principle that the intention of the defendant is irrelevant in deciding infringement focuses on the existence of the patent register and the information function performed by the patent system more generally. Here, the potential harm that third parties might endure as a result of infringement being absolute is mitigated by the fact that as part of the patent process, the invention is made available to the public. More specifically, it is argued that because information about the patented invention is in the public domain, third parties are able to access the information and subsequently alter their behaviour (or license the patent), and thus avoid infringing the patent. While this rationale *might* carry some weight in relation to mechanical inventions, it is not as easily applied to biological inventions. This is because the rationale for strict liability is based on an image of the invention as something inert, static, and (largely) immutable. In the case of mechanical inventions (in which it is the behaviour of the defendant that determines whether they infringe), would-be defendants are able to modify their conduct to ensure that they do not do so. However, in the case of (some) biological inventions, which are dynamic and active, there may be very little (if anything) that a defendant can do to avoid infringing. Given that the infringement might be traced to the action of the invention (rather than the defendant), this may be the case even if the defendant had known about the patented invention.

The potential problems that arise in relation to biological inventions were highlighted by the Canadian decision *Monsanto v. Schmeiser*,[21] in which a farmer was successfully sued for infringing Monsanto's patent for glyphosate-resistant plants, when patented plants were found growing on his property. Importantly, it was held that the principle of strict liability meant that it did not matter whether the defendant farmer had planted the infringing plants or whether, as he claimed, the plants were there as a result of conduct outside his control (including cross-field breeding by wind or insects, seed blown from passing trucks with loose tarpaulins, seed dropped from farm equipment, and seed that had escaped when a neighbour dropped a bag of Monsanto's seed from his truck); all that mattered was that there had been an unauthorized use of the patented invention. The decision is important since it highlights the possibility of, and some of the problems

---

[19] See, e.g., *Synthon v. SmithKline Beecham* [2006] *RPC* (10) 323, [22], [24] (HL), discussed in Chapter 18, section 4.1, p. 560; *PLG Research v. Ardon International* [1993] *FSR* 197, 218; *Robert Alfred Young and Robert Neilson v. Rosenthal* (1884) *RPC* 29, 31–3.

[20] The classic statement is provided by Sachs LJ in *General Tire & Rubber v. Firestone Tyre & Rubber* [1972] *RPC* 457, 485–6.   [21] [2004] 1 *SCR* 902.

associated with, what could be called 'passive infringement' of biological inventions. This is the fact that farmers, through no fault of their own, may be liable for patent infringement when a patented plant 'invades' their property and cross-pollinates with one of their plants. (Similar problems could arise with genetically modified animals.) The possibility of passive infringement has important ramifications for the traditional farming practice whereby seeds saved from one year's harvest are used to sow crops in the following year. Even if this does not occur, the mere possibility of passive infringement of biological inventions will increase the pressure on farmers to obtain licences to use patented inventions of this nature. It is, however, a problem that could easily be remedied through the introduction of a defence for passive infringement.

2.2.1 The right to make the product

Perhaps the most important right given to the owner of a patent for a product is the exclusive right to 'make' the product. Few problems have arisen in determining what is meant by the right to make a product. One exception to this is where the defendant repairs or modifies the patented product. Patent law has long recognized that purchasers of patented products should be able to repair and modify those products. As Lord Hoffmann said in *United Wire*,[22] 'repair is one of the concepts (like modifying or adapting) which shares a boundary with "making" but does not trespass on its territory'. He added that:

> [A]s a matter of ordinary language, the notions of making and repair may well overlap. But for the purposes of the statute, they are mutually exclusive. The owner's right to repair is not an independent right conferred upon him by licence, express or implied. It is a residual right, forming part of the right to do whatever does not amount to making the product.[23]

At the same time, however, patent law has been keen to ensure that while a person who obtains a patented product is able to repair or modify the product, they may not go so far as to make the product anew.[24] In these circumstances, the question arises: how much of a product is a person able to repair or modify before they infringe the owner's right to make the product? To put it another way: when does the legitimate act of repair or modification switch to become the illegitimate making of the patented product?

These questions were considered at length by the Supreme Court in *Schütz v. Werit*.[25] This was an infringement action brought by Schütz in relation to a patent for an intermediate bulk container—that is, a device used to transfer large quantities (around 1,000 litres) of liquids (such as chemicals, soft drinks, or cosmetics). The patent consisted of two parts: the large plastic bottle, which held the liquid; and the metal cage, which protected the bottle in transit and storage (see Fig. 22.1).[26] The novel and inventive part of Schütz's patented intermediate bulk container was the particular way in which the cage was made. One of the notable things about intermediate bulk containers is that it was often necessary to replace the plastic containers, either because the bottle had become damaged

---

[22] *United Wire v. Screen Repair Services* [2000] 4 *All ER* 353 (HL), 358.

[23] Ibid. Prior to this decision, the right to repair had sometimes been based on the idea of implied licence: *Solar Thomson Engineering v. Barton* [1977] *RPC* 537, 555; *British Leyland v. Armstrong* [1986] *RPC* 279, 358, 361–2; cf. *Canon v. Green Cartridge Co.* [1997] *FSR* 817, 822; *Hazell Grove v. Euro League Leisure* [1995] *RPC* 529, 537–41.

[24] *Solar Thomson Engineering v. Barton* [1977] *RPC* 537; *Sirdar Rubber v. Wallington Weston* (1907) 24 *RPC* 537; *British Leyland v. Armstrong* [1986] *RPC* 279, 376.

[25] [2013] *UKSC* 16. See B. Whitehead, 'Manufacture or Repair: The Final Word—*Schütz v. Werit* [2013] *EIPR* 42.

[26] There was a third part of the invention—the pallet on which the container sat—but this was not considered in the decision.

Fig. 22.1 Intermediate bulk container
Source: Schütz Ltd

or because they contained residue of a toxic material. Many secondary organizations, known as 'reconditioners', undertake this work. This usually consists of them removing the old bottles, repairing the cage if needed, and putting in a new bottle (either of the same type as that which had been removed or a different one). Delta and Werit worked in the reconditioning industry. Delta purchased second-hand intermediate bulk containers that had been made by Schütz. Delta replaced the plastic bottles made by Schütz with new bottles that it had bought from Werit. The resulting reconditioned intermediate bulk containers were a mixture of the old Schütz cage and a new Werit bottle. Schütz objected to this, arguing that, in producing the reconditioned intermediate bulk container, Werit and Delta had infringed its exclusive right to 'make' the patented invention.

In considering this issue, the Supreme Court was called upon to determine how much of a product a person could modify before they infringed the owner's right to make the product. Lord Neuberger stressed that the answer to this question depended on how 'make' was interpreted. He also emphasized the 'somewhat slippery nature of the meaning of the word, and the very important role which context plays in determining whether a particular activity involves "making" an article'.[27] Thus while placing a Schütz bottle in a Schütz cage would clearly have been a 'making', replacing the detachable lid would not.[28] What, then, of the situation in which someone placed a Werit bottle in a Schütz cage?

---

[27] *Schütz v. Werit* [2013] *UKSC* 16, [53].   [28] Ibid., [58].

In answering this question, Lord Neuberger began by critically examining some of the approaches that had previously been used to determine whether, in replacing part of an article, a person had repaired or made the article. One approach that has been used to answer this question focuses on the inventive concept of the patented article. Under this approach, if the defendant's activities were to relate to the inventive part of the patented article, they would infringe. Conversely, if their conduct were limited to replacing the non-inventive parts of the article, they would be engaged in non-infringing repair. Thus if a patented product were to relate to the invention of a pool table with a novel and inventive coin-operating system, it would almost certainly be legitimate for a person to replace the cloth on the pool table. Under this approach, it would probably not be legitimate, however, for them to replace an old coin-operating system with a new one, since it is likely that this would be an essential component of the invention.[29] This is the approach that was adopted by Floyd J at first instance in *Schütz v. Werit*,[30] who held that the reconstituted bulk containers were non-infringing because the defendant had only replaced the non-inventive plastic bottle and not the inventive part, which was the cage. Using the inventive part of the invention as a touchstone for determining whether someone has 'made' the patented invention has the advantage of providing certainty (although it may be difficult to determine the inventive element of the invention in some cases).

While Lord Neuberger was willing to accept that the question of whether a defendant had replaced the inventive part of an article was a factor to be taken into account when deciding whether a particular activity constituted a making of the article, he stressed that it was wrong to use the inventive concept as a single touchstone for deciding whether, in replacing or modifying part of an article, a person had repaired or made the article. Specifically, Lord Neuberger was critical of the 'oversimplified approach' adopted by Floyd J at first instance, who had said the 'correct approach is to ask whether, when the part in question is removed, what is left embodies the whole of the inventive concept of the claim'.[31]

Lord Neuberger was also critical of approaches that used the relative importance of the part that had been replaced to the article as a whole to determine whether the article had been made or repaired. Under this approach, if the part replaced was a material part of the article as a whole, it would be a making. In contrast, where the part in question was an immaterial part of a product, it was less likely for a court to hold that a person has made a patented product.[32] Lord Neuberger rejected this approach, saying that the 'mere fact that an activity involves replacing a constituent part of an article does not mean that the activity involves "making" of a new article rather than constituting a repair of the original article'.[33] Thus if an original Schütz intermediate bulk container was reusable except for the detachable lid, which had been damaged, Lord Neuberger said that it 'could not be plausibly contended that the replacement of the lid constituted "making" the claimed article, even though the [intermediate bulk container] would be unusable without the new 'lid'.[34]

It is important to note that Lord Neuberger did not reject out of hand the use of the inventive concept or the relative importance of the part taken as tools for determining whether replacing part of an article constituted a making of the article. Instead, what he objected to were situations in which these factors were treated as the *only* factor to be taken into account. Drawing upon the idea that 'making' was to be decided contextually, Lord Neuberger said that it was important to focus on a range of factors, which would

[29] *Hazell Grove v. Euro League Leisure* [1995] *RPC* 529. In *United Wire v. Screen Repair Services* [2001] *RPC* 439 (HL), the inventive concept lay in the frame (which was retained) and not in the wire (which was replaced). [30] *Schütz v. Werit* [2010] *EWHC* 660 (Pat).
[31] *Schütz v. Werit* [2013] *UKSC* 16, [196] (Lord Neuberger).
[32] *United Wire v. Screen Repair Services* [2001] *RPC* 439.
[33] *Schütz v. Werit* [2013] *UKSC* 16, [50]. [34] Ibid., [58].

vary from case to case. On the facts before him, Lord Neuberger found that placing a Werit bottle in a Schütz cage did not constitute a 'making' of the patented article and, as such, was non-infringing. In reaching this conclusion, Lord Neuberger drew on a number of factors, including the fact that the bottle was a free-standing replaceable part of the patented article and that it had no connection to the claimed 'inventive' part of the intermediate bulk containers—namely, the metal cage. Another important factor was that the bottle had a much shorter life expectancy than the metal cage. It was also important that the bottle could not be described as the main component of the article. Lord Neuberger also said that it was important that apart from replacing the bottle and undertaking very minor repairs, Delta did not undertake any additional work on the bulk container.

In light of *Schütz v. Werit*, the question of whether something is 'made' or whether it is merely repaired or modified is decided by looking at the facts of the case as a whole. This will include quantitative factors, such as the amount of the product that is repaired and the relative life expectancy of the part that is being replaced. It will also include qualitative considerations, such as whether the inventive part of the patented invention has been replaced and the relative importance of the part of the patented product that has been repaired. While the test for determining whether someone has made a patented article takes account of a wide range of factors, there are limits. For example, it is does not matter who carries out the work,[35] nor how a party views or markets its products (such as claiming that it is 're-manufactured').[36] While the courts now need to take a more holistic approach when deciding whether something has been repaired or made, it seems that this is unlikely to lead to different results.[37]

Where purchasers of a patented article are entitled to repair the product:

[They] must be entitled to carry out what is a genuine repair whether it is economical to do so or not, and whether the part repaired or replaced in the course of what is truly a repair is crucial to the function of the patented article or not.[38]

It also seems that if the repaired article does not work as well or as safely as the original product, this will not affect the decision as to whether the repair is legitimate.[39]

2.2.2 The right to dispose of the product

Another important right given to the owner of a product patent is the right to sell (or vend) the product. The right to sell, which is part of the general right to dispose of the invention,[40] includes the sale of individual articles.[41] It also applies where the patented product is sold to people who intend to use the article in non-infringing activities (such as sale to a

---

[35] Ibid., [46].   [36] Ibid., [47].

[37] See, e.g., *Nescafé v. Dualit* [2013] *EWHC* 923 (Pat), [200]–[205], in which it was held that owners of Nespresso coffee machines did not 'make' the patented system when they purchased non-Nespresso capsules for their Nespresso machines. Here, what was important was the fact that the machines and the capsules had an independent commercial experience; purchasers of the machine had an expectation that they could purchase capsules from wherever they wanted; the capsules did not embody the inventive element of the patent; and the owner of the machine did nothing that could be described as repairing, let alone making.

[38] *Solar Thomson Engineering v. Barton* [1977] *RPC* 537, 555.

[39] Ibid., 556–7; *Dellareed v. Delkin Developments* [1988] *FSR* 329; approved in *Hazell Grove v. Euro League Leisure* [1995] *RPC* 529, 541.

[40] *Gerber Garment v. Lectra* [1995] *RPC* 383. An 'offer' to dispose of a product in this context is not the same as 'offer' in contract law: ibid., 411. See also *Musion Systems v. Activ8-3d* [2011] *EWPCC* 12, [46]–[48]. To be an infringing act, an 'offer to dispose' must be made in the United Kingdom and propose disposal within the United Kingdom: *Kalman v. PCL Packaging* [1982] *FSR* 406. For issues relating to joint tortfeasance where the joint tortfeasor is located outside the jurisdiction, service out of the jurisdiction, and actions for infringement of foreign patents, see Chapter 48, section 3, pp. 1286–97.

[41] *Hadley Industries v. Metal Sections and Metsec (UK)* (unreported, 13 November 1998) (Pat).

person who intends to use the article for experimental purposes).[42] A patent owner's right to dispose of a product will be infringed where a person supplies the product in kit form. As with all infringement actions, the kit must fall within the scope of the claims.[43] If the kit partially falls outside the claims, a patentee will have to rely on indirect or contributory infringement to prevent sale of the kits.[44] These matters are discussed later.[45]

Implied licences and exhaustion[46] A patent owner's ability to control the way patented products are disposed of is limited by the common law doctrine of implied licence and the doctrine of exhaustion as developed under EU law.[47] According to the doctrine of implied licence, in the absence of any limitation to the contrary, where the patentee sells a patented product, the patentee is unable to rely on the patent to prevent the resale of the article. This is because the sale of a product carries with it an implied licence to keep, use, and resell the product.[48] However, where there is an express limitation, it will bind those who receive the goods with notice of the limitation—unless the limitation contravenes Article 34 or 101 of the Treaty on the Functioning of the European Union.

Under the doctrine of exhaustion,[49] a patentee is unable to use a patent to prevent the further disposal of an article that has been placed on the market in the European Economic Area (EEA) with the patentee's consent.[50] Consequently, an express limitation on further disposal of a patented article will contravene Article 34 and thus be void if it prevents import into or resale in another member state. However, such a limitation might enable a UK patentee to prevent export to Australia, or perhaps further disposal within the United Kingdom.[51]

2.2.3 The right to import the product

The patentee has the right to control the import of products that fall within the scope of the product. It seems that where the patented product is passively imported (that is, where the patented product is of no importance as far as any question of carriage is concerned),

---

[42] *Hoffman La Roche v. Harris Pharmaceuticals* [1977] *FSR* 200 (under the PA 1949).

[43] *Rotocrop v. Genbourne* [1982] *FSR* 241; *Furr v. CD Truline (Building Products)* [1985] *FSR* 553, 565; A. Benyamini, *Patent Infringement in the European Community* (1993), 68–74 (suggesting that kits are dealt with as direct infringements unless they lack one or more essential elements).

[44] *Rotocrop v. Genbourne* [1982] *FSR* 241, 258–9.

[45] See section 2.5, pp. 651–4.

[46] As Lord Hoffmann said, the difference between an implied licence and exhaustion is that 'an implied licence may be excluded by express contrary agreement or made subject to conditions, while the exhaustion doctrine leaves no patent rights to be enforced': *United Wire v. Screen Repair Services* [2001] *RPC* 439, [68]–[69].

[47] For an overview, see *HTC Corporation v. Nokia Corporation* [2013] *EWHC* 3247, [151]–[169].

[48] *Betts v. Willmott* (1871) 2 *Ch LR* 6; *Incandescent Gas Light Co. v. Cantelo* (1895) 12 *RPC* 262; *National Photograph Co. of Australia v. Menck* [1911] *AC* 336. While the common law has tended to adopt an implied licence approach, there is some evidence that this case law may be being reinterpreted as part of an 'exhaustion of rights' principle like that found within European law. In *Canon v. Green Cartridge* [1997] *FSR* 817, 822, Lord Hoffmann said that the notion of 'a general implied licence to use the patented product at all, which is sometimes used to explain why mere user does not infringe the patentee's monopoly . . . is perhaps better regarded as a consequence of the exhaustion of the patentee's rights in respect of the particular article when it is sold'.   [49] See Chapter 1, section 4.1, pp. 13–16.

[50] The doctrine of exhaustion has been held inapplicable to products made under a compulsory licence: *Merck v. Stephar*, Case C-187/80 [1981] *ECR* 2063.

[51] *Roussel Uclaf SA v. Hockley International* [1996] *RPC* 441 (for a limited licence applied to sales of a patented product outside the EEA to be effective, notice of it must be brought to the attention of every person down the chain of supply).

the patent will not be infringed.[52] As Tomlin J said: 'I cannot think . . . that the employment of a patented cutting blow-pipe or a patented hammer in the manufacture of some part of a locomotive would necessarily render the importation of the locomotive an infringement.'[53] A person will infringe where they deal with the patented product in the course of trade or for the purposes of profit.[54] Because an importer must have a legal and beneficial interest in the infringing goods, foreign parties will not infringe where they transfer their interests in the infringing object outside the United Kingdom (although they might be liable as a joint tortfeasor).[55] As with the right to dispose of the product, the patentee's right to prevent import is limited by the common law principle of implied consent and by the doctrine of EU/EEA exhaustion.

2.2.4 The right to keep the product

The patentee's monopoly also includes situations where an infringer keeps the product, whether for disposal or otherwise. The scope of this right was considered in *SKF v. Harbottle*,[56] where the court was called upon to decide whether the storage of a product in a London warehouse fell within the meaning of 'keep' in section 60(1) of the Patents Act 1977. This decision arose from the fact that British Airways, which was in the process of transporting an antihistamine drug called Cimetidine from Italy to Nigeria, stored 20 kg of the drug in a warehouse in London. While the drug was being stored, a patent infringement action was brought by the UK patentees (SKF) against the owner and importer of the drug, Harbottle. British Airways was joined as co-defendant in the infringement action on the basis that it had infringed the owner's right to keep the product. Finding in favour of British Airways, the court held that the act of passively storing a patented drug in a warehouse in London could not be construed as the 'keeping of a product' within the meaning of section 60(1). While declining to arrive at a definitive meaning of the term 'keep', the court was strongly influenced by the 'very much more limited' terms employed in Article 29(a) of the Community Patent Convention (CPC), where the equivalent wording refers to 'stocking' a patented product. On this basis, it was said that 'keep' implied 'keeping in stock' rather than acting as a custodian.

Despite the approach adopted in *Harbottle,* a broader interpretation of the right to keep a product was adopted in *McDonald v. Graham*.[57] In this case, the patentee asserted that the defendant (a marketing consultant who had been introduced to the patentee), who retained certain articles (and later made them available to a third party), had infringed their right to 'keep' the patented product. In response, the defendant argued that the materials had not been kept 'for disposal or otherwise'. The Court of Appeal held that the defendant had kept the product 'in the sense of keeping them in stock for the purposes of his business in order to make use of them as and when it would be beneficial to him to do so'.[58] As such, the patent had been infringed.

---

[52] See *SABAF SpA v. MFI Furniture Centres* [2005] *RPC* 209 (HL), [40]–[46] (on the definition of 'importer').

[53] *Wilderman v. Berk* (1925) 42 *RPC* 79, 88.

[54] This is the case irrespective of whether the ultimate destination is the United Kingdom or elsewhere: *Hoffmann-La Roche v. Harris Pharmaceuticals* [1977] *FSR* 200 (under the PA 1949).

[55] *SABAF v. Meneghetti* [2003] *RPC* 264 (CA), [57]–[63]. As the Italian defendants passed legal title in the 'infringing' article (which was subsequently imported into the United Kingdom) to another party in Italy, it could not be said that they imported the goods into the United Kingdom, although they did organize and pay for the haulage of the articles. In so finding, the Court of Appeal expressly disregarded *Waterford Wedgwood v. David Nagli* [1988] *FSR* 92 (re-import under TMA 1994).

[56] [1980] *RPC* 363; M. Howe, 'Infringing Goods and the Warehouseman' [1979] *EIPR* 287.

[57] [1994] *RPC* 407.   [58] Ibid., 431.

In circumstances where the patentee has placed the product on the market, a person will be free from liability under the implied licence theory. However, if no such licence is implied, liability for mere possession or use is absolute (irrespective of knowledge or intent).

2.2.5 The scope of protection for biotechnological inventions

In the lead-up to the Biotechnology Directive,[59] questions arose about the scope of protection for biotechnological inventions. The issues were dealt with by Articles 8–10 of the Directive. The Patents Act 1977 has been amended to take account of these provisions.[60] The scope of protection of product patents for biological material is dealt with in Articles 8(1) and 9 of the Directive.

Article 8(1) provides that the protection conferred by a patent on biological material (possessing specific characteristics) extends to any biological material derived from that biological material by propagation or multiplication in an identical or divergent form. This would apply, for example, to inventions for herbicide-resistant plants and genetically manipulated animals.[61] For the derivative biological material to be covered by the patent, it must possess the same characteristics as the patented biological material. This means that a patent for a genetically modified animal would extend to include future generations (so long as they retain the 'specific characteristics' of the 'original' animal).[62]

Article 9 (which is mirrored in the United Kingdom in paragraph 9 of Schedule A2 to the Patents Act 1977)[63] deals with the scope of protection for a product that contains genetic information. More specifically, it provides that the protection conferred on a patent containing or consisting of genetic information shall extend to all material, save as provided in Article 5(1),[64] in which the product is incorporated and in which the genetic information is contained or performs its function.

In recent years, there has been a growing concern about the nature of the protection granted to biotechnological inventions, particularly in relation to product patents granted for genes, DNA sequences, and the like. The main problem with product patents is that they give the patentee control over subsequent uses of the product, even for uses that they did not envisage or know about. For example, if a research team were to discover that the ABC gene caused acne, it might be possible for them to obtain a product patent over the isolated ABC gene. If another research team were subsequently to discover that the ABC gene also played a role in the development of skin cancer, this would be covered by the earlier product patent. One objection to a situation such as this is that the reward granted to the patentee outweighs the benefits that flow from their disclosure. Another related problem is that product patents may stifle research into new uses of a patented product In *Monsanto v. Cefetra*[65] the Court of Justice considered the scope of Article 9. It concluded that where an isolated DNA sequence is protected as a patented product and it is contained in the material, but it no longer performs its function (the enzyme made the plant roundup ready and so resistant to that herbicide during its lifetime) then it falls outside the scope of protection conferred even if the product could be taken from the biological material and used again.[66] There is therefore no absolute protection granted and if modified crops are grown outside Europe and once grown, provided the function

---

[59] See Chapter 14, section 4.4.2, pp. 408–9.

[60] Patents Regulations 2000 (SI 2000/2037). regs 8–10, were said to be declaratory of the (then) existing law.

[61] S. Bostyn, 'The Patentabilty of Genetic Information Carriers' [1999] *IPQ* 1, 28.   [62] Ibid.

[63] Introduced by Patents Regs 2000.

[64] Biotech. Dir. Art. 5(1)/PA 1977, Sch. A2, para. 3(a), states that the human body at the various stages of its formation and development, and the elements thereof (including gene sequences), cannot be patented.

[65] C-428/08, [2010] *ECR* I-6765.   [66] Ibid., [50].

is no longer performed, they can be sold within the EU without infringing the patent.[67] In 2016, an Expert Group appointed by the European Commission published a report which considered two interpretations of *Monsanto*.[68] The minority view of the Group was that the decision took DNA sequences out of the scope of protection of patents.[69] The majority of the Expert Group said the relevant question was whether the patented product was *capable* of performing the function protected by the patent. The example they used was the sale of DNA in a dry state, where it could not perform its function; however, if the dry substance was put in an aqueous environment, it was able to perform its function once more. The sequence was 'capable' of performing its function, but it was not performing the function during the manufacture, sale, or importation of the product and so would not infringe.[70] However, if it is used after being rehydrated then that use would infringe. While special defences have been introduced to minimize the impact of product patents for biological inventions,[71] many commentators believe that further action is necessary. One solution that has been suggested is that the scope of protection for gene patents should be limited to the use that is actually disclosed in the patent.[72] To continue with the example mentioned earlier, this would mean that the initial patent would only be granted for the ABC gene insofar as it triggers acne. In this situation, the protection reflects the disclosure. The more limited protection also means that the patent would not act as a disincentive for others to look for other uses of the ABC gene. It has been suggested that this proposal is supported by Recital 25 of the Biotechnology Directive insofar as it limits product claims to the parts of the product that are essential to the invention—that is, it restricts the scope of DNA-product patents based on their disclosed function.[73] Another more radical suggestion, which harks back to the way in which chemical inventions were treated in the early part of the twentieth century, is to limit gene patents to process claims—that is, product production would simply not be available for gene-based inventions.

2.3 PATENTS FOR A PROCESS

The owner of a patent for a process is given the right to use the process or to offer it for use in the United Kingdom.[74] This is subject to the proviso that the right is only infringed where it can be shown that the defendant knew, or it would have been obvious to a reasonable person in the circumstances that the unauthorized use of the process would be an infringement of the patent. It is important to note that in contrast with the rights given to owners of patents for products (discussed earlier) and the rights given to patents for products derived from processes (discussed later), liability for infringement of a patent for a process[75] is *not* absolute—that is, liability depends upon the owner proving that the defendant knew, or that it would have been obvious to a reasonable person in the circumstances, that the unauthorized use of a process would be an infringement of the patent. In

---

[67] Ibid., [69]; also see M. Lock, 'Patent protection for DNA sequences – to be or not to be?' (2010) 5 *JIPLP* 754.

[68] EU Commission, Final Report of the Expert Group on the Development and Implications of Patent Law in the Field of Biotechnology and Genetic Engineering (17 May 2016).   [69] Ibid., [89].

[70] Ibid., [203].   [71] See section 4.4, pp. 671–2.

[72] See D. Schertenleib, 'The Patentability and Protection of DNA-based Inventions' [2003] *EIPR* 125, 136–8; A. White, 'Gene and Compound per se Claims: An Appropriate Reward?' [2001] 6 *Bioscience L Rev* 239; P. Jacobs and G. Van Overwalle, 'Gene Patents: A Different Approach' [2001] *EIPR* 505.

[73] Where the claimed DNA sequences 'overlap only in parts which are not essential to the invention, each sequence will be considered as an independent sequence in patent law terms: Schertenleib, op. cit., 136.

[74] PA 1977, s. 60(1)(b).   [75] *Warner-Lambert v. Actavis Group* [2015] *RPC* 665, [129].

essence, the owner of a patent for a process is given the right to practise the invention or to put the invention into effect. For the most part, there have been few problems in interpreting this provision (although discovering how a defendant makes a particular product may be one).[76] Problems may arise, however, in relation to patents for 'novelty-of-use' claims, which are discussed later in this chapter.

2.3.1 DIRECT PRODUCTS OF PATENTED PROCESSES

It has long been accepted that where a patent is granted over a process, the protection includes both the process in question and the products that flow from that process. This principle is now to be found in section 60(1)(c) of the Patents Act 1977, which provides that a person infringes a process patent if they dispose of, offer to dispose of, use, import, or keep any product derived from that process.[77] This protection is particularly important where no claim has been made to a product as such. It is also important where the process is carried on outside the United Kingdom and a product derived from that process is imported into the United Kingdom.[78] As we have already looked at the way these terms are construed, there is no need to examine them again.

The protection given to process patents is potentially very wide. In part, this is because where a range of different products flow from a single process, all of the products fall within the remit of the patent. It is also because the scope of protection not only includes the products that flow from the process, but also the products that are based upon the products that flow from the process—that is, the derivatives of the derivative. To ensure that the scope of the monopoly is kept within justifiable limits, an important restriction is placed on the products that are protectable by process patents. This has been done by stipulating that for protection to arise, there must be a direct *relationship* between the process and the product in question.[79]

The question of what is meant by a 'direct' relationship was considered by the Court of Appeal in *Pioneer Electronics v. Warner Music*.[80] This action arose when the claimant argued that its process patent for a method of manufacturing compact discs had been infringed after the defendant imported optical discs into the United Kingdom that were a by-product of the patented process. While there was no doubt that the imported discs had been derived from the patented invention, it was unclear whether there was a 'direct' relationship between the process patent and the imported discs.

After considering the way equivalent provisions were interpreted in other European jurisdictions, the Court of Appeal concluded that 'directly' meant 'without intermediary'. More specifically, Nourse LJ said that when the Patents Act 1977 stipulated that for protection to arise, there had to be a direct relationship between the process and product, this meant that there were no material or important steps that intervened between the process and the product in question. In situations where material and important steps did intervene, the process patent could not be used to control the use that was made of the product. This situation would only change if it could be shown that the intervening steps were immaterial or trivial.

---

[76] For some of the problems that arise in proving infringement of a process patent where the process is carried out overseas, see *Nutrinova Nutrition Specialties & Food Ingredients v. Sanchem UK* [2001] *FSR* 797.

[77] CPC, Art. 25(c); EPC 2000, Art. 64(2) (ex EPC 1973, Art. 64(2)).   [78] CIPA, [60.06].

[79] PA 1977, s. 60(1)(c). For the common-law position, see *Saccharin Corp v. Anglo Continental Chemical* (1900) 17 *RPC* 307.

[80] [1997] *RPC* 757 (CA). See H. Hurdle, 'What is the Direct Product of a Patented Process?' [1997] *EIPR* 322; F. Russell and H. Hurdle, 'What is the Direct Product of a Patented Process?' [1995] *EIPR* 249.

The process patent for the production of the master discs was not infringed when the final discs were imported into the United Kingdom. The reason for this was that a number of important and material steps separated the product from the process. A key factor in the finding of non-infringement was that the production of the master discs was only an initial stage in the production of the final optical discs. The master discs were used to produce 'mothers', which in turn were converted into 'sons', which subsequently acted as the basis from which the moulding of the final discs took place. While the patented invention may have acted as a platform that aided in the production of the final discs, because there were a number of important and material steps that separated them, there was not a direct relationship and thus no infringement. The requirement that there be a direct relationship is in accord with the general logic of patent law. While a product may draw upon a process patent, if the product only comes into existence as a result of material steps that occur outside the process, the products are no longer derivative; rather, they are new products that warrant separate patent protection. If patentees were able to regulate the use that was made of such products, this would extend the ambit of the monopoly beyond the scope of the invention disclosed in the patent.[81]

The question of what is meant by a direct relationship was also considered in *Monsanto v. Cargill*.[82] In this case, Monsanto argued that by importing into the United Kingdom a cargo of soybean meal produced in Argentina, Cargill had infringed Monsanto's patent for Round Up Ready soybeans—the main claim being for 'a method of producing genetically transformed plants'. There was no doubt that the soybean meal imported into the United Kingdom (or at least a substantial part of it) was produced from Round Up Ready soybeans in Argentina. In deciding whether the method claims in the patent had been infringed, the court had to consider whether the soybean meal had been 'directly obtained' from the process in question under section 60(1)(c). Pumfrey J said that the phrase 'directly obtained by means of the process' means the 'immediate product of the process, or where the patented process is an intermediate stage in the manufacture of some ultimate product, that product, but only if the product of the intermediate process retains its identity'.[83] Following *Pioneer Electronics v. Warner Music*, Pumfrey J said that a product that is derived from a patented process will be directly obtained so long as the product retains its essential characteristics. However, where a product has 'lost its identity and become something else', it will not be directly obtained. As Pumfrey J noted, intermediate processes in chemical cases often suffer this fate.

In considering whether the method claim in Monsanto's patent had been infringed by the importing of the soybean meal, Pumfrey J said that the method claim consisted of the isolation and insertion of a recombinant DNA molecule with prescribed characteristics into the genome of a plant cell. The DNA molecule was inserted into one original plant, which was named and identified in the patent as the parent of all Round Up Ready plants in Argentina. Pumfrey J noted that the transformation of the original plant had occurred many generations ago and that since then, soybeans had been grown by seedsmen or retained by farmers for planting. After some generations, the harvested beans were processed into the meal that had been imported in the United Kingdom. Pumfrey J was willing to accept that all of the Round Up Ready soybean plants in Argentina were lineal descendents of the original plant and also that the 'huge mountain of soybean meal' could be described as the ultimate product of the original transformation of the parent plant. Pumfrey J was unable to accept, however, that the soy meal was the ultimate product of the original transformation of the parent plant—a phrase that he reserved for the original transformed plant. On this basis, Pumfrey J held that the imported soybean meal was not

---

[81] If a 'patentee wants appropriate cover . . . they should secure a product-by-process claim': *Report of the Committee to Examine the Patent System and Patent Law* (Cmnd. 4407, July 1970) (the Banks Committee), [297].

[82] *Monsanto Technology LLC v. Cargill International SA* [2008] FSR 153, [34]–[35].   [83] Ibid.

'directly obtained' for the purposes of section 60(1)(c) and, as such, did not infringe. In so doing, Pumfrey J rejected Monsanto's argument that the product retained its essential characteristics when it was made into meal. In rejecting the hereditary nature of the relationship between the Round Up Ready sequence (as inserted in the parent plant) and the soybean meal, Pumfrey J said that Monsanto's argument confused the 'informational content of what passed between the generations (the Round Up Ready genomic sequence) with the product, which is just soybean meal with no special intrinsic characteristics from one of the generations of plants'.[84] As well as clarifying what it means for a product to be directly obtained, the decision is also important in that it provides some insight into the approach that UK courts may take towards the infringement of biological inventions.

2.3.2 DIRECT PRODUCTS OF BIOTECHNOLOGICAL PROCESSES

The question of the scope of protection for patents for biotechnological processes is dealt with in Article 8(2) of the Biotechnology Directive. A similar provision now exists in the Patents Act 1977 as a result of amendments made in July 2000.[85] Article 8(2) provides that:

> The protection conferred by a patent on a process that enables a biological material to be produced possessing specific characteristics as a result of the invention shall extend to biological material directly obtained through that process and to any other biological material derived from the directly obtained biological material through propagation or multiplication in an identical or divergent form and possessing those same characteristics.

As with the protection given to product patents for biological materials, the derived material must possess the same characteristics as the 'original' material. It should be noted that the protection under Article 8(2)/paragraph 8 of Schedule A2 to the Patents Act 1977 is limited to material 'directly obtained' from the patented process. It seems that 'directly obtained' would be construed in a way similar to how a 'direct' relationship was construed in *Monsanto v. Cargill*[86] and *Pioneer Electronics v. Warner Music*[87] (discussed earlier).

2.4 NOVELTY-OF-USE CLAIMS

For the most part, when determining whether a defendant has carried out one of the activities within the patentee's control, the key question is the way in which the language of the patent is construed. One situation in which problems may arise, however, is in relation to patents for a new use of a known substance used in an old way, which have been recognized at the EPO and in the United Kingdom.

The decision to accept novelty-of-use patents has met with considerable resistance in the United Kingdom.[88] As Lord Hoffmann said in *Merrell Dow*,[89] the Board's decision

---

[84] Ibid., [38].   [85] PA 1977, Sch. A2, para. 8 (introduced by Patents Regs 2000).

[86] [2007] *EWHC* 2257, [34]–[35].   [87] [1997] *RPC* 757 (CA).

[88] To 'hold that every new use of an old composition may be the subject of a patent upon the composition would lead to endless confusion and go far to destroy the benefits of our patent laws': *In re Thuau*, 135 F.2d. 344 (CCPA 1943).

[89] *Merrell Dow Pharmaceuticals v. Norton* [1996] *RPC* 76 (HL), 92. In *Mobil*, it was said that the analogous problems concerning infringement would arise in relation to second and subsequent medical uses: *Mobil/Friction reducing additive*, G 2/88 [1990] *EPOR* 73, 89. However, in such cases, the regulation of packaging is often a sound indication of the intended use: *Actavis v. Merck* [2008] *EWCA Civ* 444, [8]. For an unusual case where such marketing rules did not clarify the purpose for which the medicine was to be used, see *Warner-Lambert v. Mylan* [2015] *EWCA Civ* 556, [127], [129], [184] ff, [206]–[208], currently on appeal to the Supreme Court.

in *Mobil* has been criticized on the 'ground that a patent for an old product used in an old way for a new purpose makes it difficult to apply the traditional UK doctrine of infringement'. The problem with novelty-of-use claims is that it may be difficult to ascertain when a product is being used in the relevant way. Unless use claims are confined to uses of products that are distinct, it seems that a patentee of an invention that consists of a new use must demonstrate that the infringer intended to produce the particular effect.

The reason why the recognition of use claims is incompatible with the traditional UK doctrine of infringement can be traced to the fact that the infringement of a patent turns exclusively on the physical conduct of the defendant. A person will infringe if, for example, they manufacture or sell the patented invention without permission. In so doing, the alleged infringer's state of mind is irrelevant; it does not matter whether the alleged infringer knew that they were dealing with the patented product. In most cases, this presents few problems. For example, because claims to a new use of an old thing will be physically different from previous uses of the same thing, the earlier use can continue to be performed without infringing the subsequent patent. Problems may arise, however, in relation to novelty-of-use patents. This is because, for infringement purposes, the discovery that a known product used in a known way can be put to a new purpose is physically identical to the previous use, the only difference between the two uses being in the mind of the user. Given that the physical acts protected by a novelty-of-use patent would be the same as the steps taken during the previous use, when someone uses an old substance in an old way, there is no obvious way of telling whether they are using the substance to achieve the old purpose or whether they are using the substance to achieve the new purpose. As Lord Hoffmann said:

> [L]iability for infringement is, as I have said, absolute. It depends upon whether the act in question falls within the claims and pays no attention to the alleged infringer's state of mind. But this doctrine may be difficult to apply to a patent for the use of a known substance in a known way for a new purpose. How does one tell whether the person putting the additive into his engine is legitimately using it to inhibit rust or infringing by using it to reduce friction?[90]

The problem raised by novelty-of-use patents is that while the only feature that enables a novelty-of-use patent to be distinguished from the previous use is the purpose for which it is used (which exists in the mind of the user), the purpose of the alleged infringer is not taken into account when determining whether a patent has been infringed; all that matters is whether the physical act of infringement has taken place. The consequence of this is that a patent granted for the discovery of a new purpose of an old thing used in an old way could prevent someone from doing what they had done before—thus denying the user their previous right to work.[91]

While it has been suggested that these problems are based on an artificial distinction,[92] the inherent conflict between the physical nature of infringement and the mental nature of novelty-of-use patents gives rise to real problems in the United Kingdom that will need to be resolved if such patents are allowed. If novelty-of-use patents are not to impinge upon the

---

[90] *Merrell Dow v. Norton* [1996] *RPC* 76 (HL), 92. See also *Bristol-Myers Squibb v. Baker Norton Pharmaceuticals* [2001] *RPC* 1 (CA), [49] (Aldous LJ said that it was unlikely that the Court of Appeal would suggest that *Mobil* was wrongly decided when the House of Lords 'did not so conclude').

[91] 'New use patents raise vexing questions about the patentee's right to prevent others from selling the old compound': *Dawson Chemical Co. v. Rohm & Haas Co.*, 448 *US* 176 (1980).   [92] Paterson, [10–31].

legitimate (existing) activities of others,[93] it may be necessary to limit the scope of the monopoly (possibly to the making, using, and commercial supply of the thing for the specified use) or to modify the defence of prior use.[94] In *Warner-Lambert v. Actavis Group*[95], Floyd LJ reviewed the approach to purpose bound claims in countries around the world, before concluding the law was 'far from settled'. This led Floyd LJ to consider the two candidates for a test: (a) foreseeability that the drug will intentionally be used for the patented indication and (b) a subjective intention to that effect.[96] He concluded that the better way to consider the matter as to whether there is an infringement is to ascertain whether a person knows or could reasonably foresee the end use of the product being an infringing purpose.[97] For these purposes the person will not be taken to have foreseen an outcome when he or she has taken all reasonable steps within their power to prevent the consequences occurring. In such circumstances his true objective is a lawful one, and one would be entitled to say that the foreseen consequences were not intended, but were an unintended incident of his otherwise lawful activity.[98] The problem with use or purpose claims outside prescribed pharmaceuticals is more difficult. But we suggest that the principles outlined above should equally apply to other products.

2.5 INDIRECT INFRINGEMENT

In addition to the prohibited activities set out in section 60(1), the Patents Act 1977 also provides that a patent is infringed where a person contributes to, but does not directly take part in, the infringement.[99] This is particularly important where the maker or user is difficult to detect (for example where the manufacture or use occurs in private) or they are not worth suing. Section 60(2) states that a person infringes a patent where they supply or offer to supply any means relating to an essential element of the invention for putting the invention into effect.[100] Thus a patent for a glue that is produced by combining two chemicals A and B may be infringed by a person who supplies either A or B to a person who then manufactures the glue.[101] The question of what it means for an online invention to be put into effect in the United Kingdom was considered by the Court of Appeal.[102] The patent in question was for a gaming system consisting of a host computer, terminal

---

[93] In response to arguments of this type, the EBA in *Mobil* offered the following unhelpful advice: '[T]here is a clear distinction between the protection which is conferred and the rights which are conferred by a European patent.' While the 'protection conferred by a patent is determined by the terms of the claims (Art. 69(1) EPC [1973]) and in particular by the categories of such claims and their technical features . . . [i]n contrast, the rights conferred on the proprietor of a European patent (Art. 64(1) EPC [1973; now EPC 2000, Art. 64(1)]) are the legal rights . . . [conferred] upon the proprietor': *Mobil/Friction reducing additive*, G 2/88 [1990] *EPOR* 73, 80–1.   [94] See section 4.3, pp. 669–70.

[95] [2015] *RPC* 665.   [96] Ibid., [122].   [97] Ibid., [126] and [132].

[98] *Warner-Lambert v. Generics (UK) (t/a Mylan)* [2015] *RPC* 1, [208].

[99] PA 1977, s. 60(2); CPC, 26(1); *Dow Chemical v. Spence Bryson* [1982] *FSR* 598, 628–30 (inducing or procuring infringement by persuading infringer to adopt process, teaching how to operate it). See Chapter 48, section 3, pp. 1286–97.

[100] The 'means in question' must contribute to implementing the technical teaching of the invention; there is no need to show that the feature in question 'served to distinguish the subject matter of the claim from the prior art ie was novel in its own right': *Nescafé v. Dualit* [2013] *EWHC* 923 (Pat), [170] (following the German BGH decision of *Impeller Flow Measure* Case X ZR 48/03) (2005) 36 *IIC* 963.

[101] The policy of expanding the patentee's monopoly to cover contributory infringement seems to conflict with the policy underpinning the rules preventing a patentee from requiring licensees to utilize particular suppliers. On these, see Chapter 23, section 3, pp. 682–4. The connection is recognized in US jurisprudence, where the Supreme Court has observed that the 'doctrines of contributory infringement and patent misuse have long and interrelated histories': *Dawson Chemical Co. v. Rohm & Haas Co.*, 448 US 176 (1980).

[102] *Menashe Business Mercantile v. William Hill Organization* [2003] *RPC* 575 (CA).

computers, and software that operates the system. The invention enabled end-users on terminal computers to engage in interactive gaming with the host computer. The defendant, William Hill, operated an online gaming system for punters in the United Kingdom. British punters were supplied with a computer program (either via CD or downloaded from the net) that transformed their computer into a terminal computer of the defendant's system. The claimant argued that when the defendant's system was in use, it infringed its patent. The defendant argued that it did not infringe the patent because its host computer was located abroad and not in the United Kingdom (in Antigua, and then in Curaçao in the Netherlands Antilles). Aldous LJ said that it was 'not straining the word "use" to conclude that the UK punter will use the claimed gaming system in the United Kingdom, even if the host computer is located in, say, Antigua'.[103] Focusing on the way in which the end-user related to the invention, Aldous LJ said that a punter who used the William Hill system would be using the whole system as if it were in the United Kingdom. The punter would, in substance, use the host computer in the United Kingdom, it being irrelevant to the punter where it was situated. Aldous LJ concluded that in supplying the computer program in the United Kingdom, the defendant intended to put the invention into effect in the United Kingdom and, as such, infringed the claimant's patent.[104]

For indirect infringement to take place, three criteria must be satisfied. First, the proprietor of the patent must establish that the means supplied by the defendant relate to an essential element of the invention.[105] A person will also indirectly infringe where they supply a number of the essential components of a patented invention. This would occur, for example, where a patent is for an oil lamp (which is made up of a vessel holding the oil, a burner and wick, an outer glass container, and a chimney) and the defendant supplied all of the parts other than the chimney.[106]

Second, the supplier must know, or it must be obvious to a reasonable person in the circumstances, that the means are both 'suitable' for and are 'intended' to be used in putting the invention into effect.[107] It is important to note that the Court of Appeal has said that the reference to 'intention' in section 60(2) is not linked to any specific person (such as the supplier, the direct customer, or the ultimate users). Instead, the inquiry is whether the means and the circumstances surrounding it being offered or supplied 'are such that some ultimate users will intend to use or adapt the "means" so as to infringe'.[108] The knowledge requirement will be satisfied if 'at the time of supply or offer of supply, the supplier knows, or it is obvious in the circumstances, that ultimate users will intend to put the invention into effect'.[109] The imposition of a knowledge requirement, which is construed objectively, ensures that parties who do not knowingly benefit from the misuse of a patent are not caught as indirect infringers. As Jacob LJ said, the section is 'clearly intended to apply to, among other things, products which are perfectly capable of being used in a manner which will not constitute a direct infringement within s. 60(1)'.[110]

---

[103] Ibid., 584–5, upholding Jacob J's first-instance decision—[2002] *RPC* 951—but for different reasons.

[104] *Menashe Business Mercantile v. William Hill Organization* [2003] *RPC* 57.

[105] *Hazell Grove v. Euro League Leisure* [1995] *RPC* 529, 541.

[106] See *Wallace v. Holmes*, 29 F.Cas. 74 (No. 17, 100) (CC Conn. 1871).

[107] Thus, it did not matter for the purposes of indirect infringement that drugs supplied to doctors or pharmacists were not identical to the patented invention in the form they were sold, given that when the drugs were dissolved in a saline solution (which was needed for them to be administered to patients), the defendants either knew or it was obvious in the circumstances that they produced solutions that were chemically identical to the patented invention. *Actavis v. Eli Lilly* [2017] *UKSC* 48, [103]–[112] (direct infringement is discussed in section 2.1, p. 638–51).

[108] *Grimme Maschinenfabrik v. Derek Scott* [2010] *EWCA Civ* 1110, [107].   [109] Ibid., [131].

[110] Ibid., [102]. See P. Johnson, 'Contributing to the Wrong: Indirect Infringement of Patents' (2010) 5 *JIPLP* 514.

Third, in recognition of the fact that there might be legitimate reasons why a person supplies or offers to supply something that enables the means for putting the invention into effect, section 60(3) provides that the supply of a staple commercial product will not constitute an indirect infringement under section 60(2).[111] The meaning of 'staple commercial product' is not clear, although it might be assumed that it covers basic products that are readily available.[112] The staple commercial product exemption does not apply where the product is specifically supplied for the purpose of *inducing* an infringement.[113]

2.5.1 Novelty-of-use claims

Given the difficulty in establishing direct liability in relation to novelty-of-use patents (discussed earlier), indirect liability may take on a greater significance. Taking the example of a patent for the use of a substance in oil as a lubricant, where it was previously known that the substance inhibited rust, it would seem that a defendant would infringe if they supplied the oil to people and advertised it as a lubricant. However, a person would not infringe if they were to continue to supply the oil as a rust inhibitor. While it might be known that the oil could be used as a lubricant, it would be difficult to prove that the defendant 'intended' that the oil be used in this way (as is required under section 60(2)). In these circumstances, secondary factors may be helpful, such as the documentation that accompanies the product, which might indicate the way in which the product was expected to be used.[114] It would be more difficult to determine whether a defendant indirectly infringes where they supplied the oil saying that it acted both as a rust inhibitor and a friction reducer. The liability of the defendant would also be uncertain if they were to supply the oil saying that it acted as a rust inhibitor, where it was widely known that the oil could also be used to reduce friction. In these circumstances, the likelihood of the user using the oil as a lubricant is high, but not certain. Jacob J, who has expressed doubts about the role of novelty-of-use claims, has called for these issues to be considered in detail by the European Patent Office whenever it gives further consideration to claims for uses.[115] So far, these pleas have fallen on deaf ears.

2.6 ADDITIONAL LIABILITY

In addition to the rights set out in sections 60(1) and 60(2), patentees are also able to make use of a limited number of provisions that exist outside the Patents Act 1977. These provisions will be particularly important where a party acts in such a way as to undermine the value of a patent, yet the activities fall outside of the scope of section 60(1) or (2).

Perhaps the most important non-statutory mechanism available to a patent owner is the concept of joint tortfeasance.[116] This provides that even if a party does not fall within the scope of section 60, the patentee can enjoin the third party as a joint tortfeasor if it can be shown that they have acted in a 'common design' with a party who is liable for a

---

[111] In *Pavel v. Sony*, C/14/93 (22 March 1996, unreported), the (then) Patents County Court defined staple commercial product as meaning 'products of regular kind needed daily and generally available'.

[112] A. Benyamini, *Patent Infringement in the European Community* (1993), 234–5.

[113] *Furr v. Truline (Building Products)* [1985] FSR 553, 565.

[114] It has been said that German case law supports the view that, in this form, there is direct infringement, either because a use claim is seen as primarily a product claim and this amounts to sale of the product, or because such an act is an offering of a process for use: see A. Benyamini, *Patent Infringement in the European Community* (1993), 84–90 (advocating direct infringement approach). See further A. Horton, 'Methods of Treatment and Second Medical Use' (August 2000) *Patent World* 9, 12.

[115] *Bristol-Myers Squibb v. Baker Norton Pharmaceuticals* [1999] RPC 253, 280.

[116] See *CIPA*, [60.28].

statutory tort of infringement under section 60 (and that they jointly inflicted damage on a patentee).[117] For a party to be liable as a joint tortfeasor, they must be 'so involved in the commission of the tort as to make himself liable for the tort'.[118]

It has also been suggested that the law of restitution provides patentees with an additional ground on which to found liability. More specifically, it has been argued that independently of the rights set out in the 1977 Act, the law also recognizes unjust enrichment as a separate cause of action. Proposals of this type were considered and rejected in *Union Carbide Corporation v. BP Chemicals*,[119] where Jacob J said that the law of restitution could *not* be used to supplement the law of patents to the extent of providing a cause of action for unjust enrichment. Jacob J did say, however, that there might be cases in which the strict rights set out in section 61 of the 1977 Act might not limit what a court could do in furtherance of the policy of patent law—but what this policy is and what it might mean in this context was left unclear.

3 SCOPE OF PROTECTION

Once it is clear that a defendant has carried out one of the activities listed in section 60 of the 1977 Act, it is then necessary to consider whether in so doing they fall within the scope of the patent. The starting point for determining the scope of protection is section 125 of the Patents Act 1977, which corresponds to Article 69 of the EPC 2000 (ex Article 69 of the EPC 1973).[120] This provides that the extent of the protection conferred by a patent shall be 'taken to be that specified in a claim of the specification of the application or patent, as the case may be, as interpreted by the description and any drawings contained in that specification'. Once the scope of the patented invention has been determined, it is then necessary to compare it with the defendant's alleged infringing process or product. Where the claimant's invention and the alleged infringing product or process are very different, there will be no infringement. Likewise where the two are identical, the defendant will clearly infringe. A defendant will also infringe where they incorporate the patented invention into a larger process or product. This is the case even if the addition improves upon the patented invention. It is also clear that the defendant will infringe where they supply a patented product in parts or in kit form.[121] A defendant will not infringe, however, if the consumer needs to exercise inventive skill in putting the kit together.[122]

While these situations are relatively unproblematic, problems arise where there is only a slight difference between the patented invention and the defendant's alleged infringing product. This would be the case, for example, if, rather than adding to the patented invention, a defendant altered or omitted part of the patented invention in their product or process, and on this basis argued that their invention fell outside the scope of the monopoly.[123] Problems also arise where a defendant changes one aspect of an invention,

---

[117] See further Chapter 48, section 3.4.2, pp. 1274–5.

[118] *Celem SA v. Alcon Electronics* [2006] *EWHC* 3042 (Pat), [33].   [119] [1998] *FSR* 1.

[120] While the EPC 1973 version said that the scope of protection 'shall be determined by the terms of the claims', Art. 69(a) of the EPC 2000 simply says that the scope 'shall be determined by the claims'.

[121] *Rotocrop v. Genbourne* [1982] *FSR* 241.

[122] *Virgin Atlantic v. Delta* [2010] *EWHC* 3094 (Pat), [135] (a claim to a product consisting of a number of parts was not infringed by the manufacture, disposal, etc. of an incomplete kit of parts in circumstances in which (i) the missing part/s were obtained by the defendant's customers themselves, and (ii) the assembly was carried on outside the relevant territory).

[123] A related situation arises where a defendant supplies most, but not all, of the patented invention in kit form.

or uses a different means to reach the same end result as the patented invention. In these situations, the decision as to whether a defendant infringes largely turns on the way in which the scope of protection is determined.[124]

3.1 DETERMINING THE SCOPE OF PROTECTION

In determining how the scope of protection is to be determined, patent law is faced with a choice. The easiest and most straightforward option would be to construe the patent strictly (or literally). In this situation, the patentee's protection would be limited to what was clearly stated in the claims. A spade would be a spade. This accords with the basic idea that a patentee should only get protection for what they have disclosed. Where this approach is applied, it would mean that a patent that said that an angle in an invention had to be at 90 degrees would not be infringed by a competing product where the angle was at 89 or 91 degrees. While this has the advantage of providing third parties with guidance about the limits of the patent, it undermines the scope of protection for the patentee. This is because as it is often very difficult to describe the invention, patentees may be forced to use language that third parties can easily avoid. While the pendulum between the competing interests of third party certainty and fairness for the patentee has constantly moved, British patent law has consistently recognized that patentees should not be limited to a strict literal reading of the claims. That is, the courts have allowed patentees to extend their monopoly beyond a strict reading of the text of the claims so as to prevent 'the unscrupulous copyist [from making] unimportant and insubstantial changes and substitutions in the patent which, though adding nothing, would be enough to take the copied matter outside the claim, and hence outside the reach of the law'.[125] While the decision to extend protection beyond a strict reading of the claims has ensured that patentees are not exposed to unscrupulous competitors who take the inventive aspect of an invention but frame it in a way that falls outside the literal reading of the claims, it also creates the possibility that patentees may get more protection than they deserve (in terms of what they have invented).

One of the consequences of the shift away from a literal reading of the claims is that it gives rise to a further question: *how far outside the literal wording of the claims is it permissible to go?*[126] Over time, there have been numerous attempts to answer this question. The latest iteration being the 2017 Supreme Court decision of *Actavis v. Eli Lilly*.[127] Before looking at *Actavis*, it may be helpful to outline recent judicial and legislative attempts to provide guidance on where and how the limits on claim drafting are to be set.[128]

3.1.1 Purposive interpretation

While there is an important but largely neglected pre-history,[129] the history of patent claim interpretation in the United Kingdom usually begins with Lord Diplock's celebrated 1982

---

[124] For a summary of the approach to be taken in construing patent claims, see *Mayne v. Pharmacia* [2005] *EWCA Civ* 137, [5], which is a restatement of the summary made by Jacob LJ in *Rockwater v. Technip France SA* [2004] *RPC* 919, [41], following the qualified approval of *Rockwater* by Lord Hoffmann in *Kirin-Amgen v. Hoechst Marion Roussel* [2005] *RPC* 169.

[125] *Kirin-Amgen v. Hoechst Marion Roussel* [2005] *RPC* 169, [37] (Lord Hoffmann) quoting Jackson J in *Graver Tank & Manufacturing v. Linde Air Products* 339 US 605, 697 (1950). See also *Actavis v. Eli Lilly* [2017] *UKSC* 48, [42] (SC).

[126] '[I]f one departs from ordinary language, it is necessary to have some guidance or to draw some lines'. *Actavis v. Eli Lilly* [2017] *UKSC* 48, [53] (SC) (Neuberger LJ).   [127] Ibid., [54].

[128] For commentary, see *CIPA*, [125.04]–[125.30].

House of Lords' judgment in *Catnic v. Hill and Smith*[130] (decided under the 1949 Patents Act), which held that the fundamental principal that underpins claim interpretation is the idea that the claims should be construed 'purposively'. This means that rather than limiting the meaning of a claim to a literal or strict meaning, it was necessary to interpret claims from the perspective of the person skilled in the art.[131] As Lord Hoffmann said in *Kirin-Amgen*, the key question to ask was:

> [W]hat would a person skilled in the art have understood the patentee to have used the language of the claim to mean? . . . Everything else . . . was only guidance to a judge trying to answer that question.[132]

We can get a sense of the impact that a purposive interpretation can have on the way in which claims are interpreted from the facts in *Catnic v. Hill and Smith*.[133] In *Catnic*, the House of Lords was called upon to decide whether in manufacturing the steel lintels, the defendants had infringed the claimant's patent for galvanized steel lintels. (A lintel is a load-bearing beam that spans open spaces, such as doors and windows, in cavity walls.) While it was evident that the defendant's lintel and the patented invention (see Fig. 22.2) were very similar, one issue remained unclear. This arose from the fact that while the patent specified that the rear side of the lintel should be 'vertical', the defendant's lintel (see Fig. 22.3) was at an angle of 84 degrees. In order to determine whether the claimant's patent had been infringed, the House of Lords had to decide whether a claim that specified that the rear support be vertical encompassed a lintel whose rear support was not 'precisely' vertical.

While a literal reading of the claims would have limited the claimant's patent to lintels at 90 degrees (and thus to a finding of non-infringement), Lord Diplock said that the patent ought to be construed *purposively*. A purposive interpretation demands that the claims are to be read through the eyes of the person skilled in the art and that the purpose or function of the invention be borne in mind when the patent is interpreted.[134] This meant that when deciding whether 'vertical' included lintels at an 84 degree angle, the person skilled in the art would take into account the function or purpose of the invention. On reading the patent, it was decided that the person skilled in the art would have understood that the reason why the patent specified that the rear support member was to be 'vertical' related to the load-bearing capacity of the lintel. An important factor in the finding that the patent had been infringed was that a 6 degree movement away from 90 degrees only led to a 0.6 per cent reduction in the load-bearing capacity of the lintel. This meant that the defendant's lintel effectively performed the same purpose or function as the claimant's lintel.

---

[129] H. Laddie, 'Kirin-Amgen: The end of equivalents in England?' (2009) 40 *IIC* 3; *Clark v. Adie* (1877) 2 *App Cas* 315.

[130] [1982] *RPC* 183.

[131] *Catnic v. Hill and Smith* [1982] *RPC* 183 (HL), 241. For the application of the purposive interpretation to '1 per cent' and '25 per cent' in the phrase 'the agent being present in a concentration between 1 per cent and 25 per cent of the total volume of treatment', see *Smith & Nephew v. Convatec Technologies* [2013] *EWHC* 3955 (Pat) (finding that 1 per cent extended to 0.95 per cent, while 25 per cent extended to 25.5 per cent).

[132] *Catnic v. Hill and Smith* [1982] *RPC* 183 (HL), 241. As Lord Hoffmann said in *Kirin-Amgen v. Hoechst Marion Roussel Ltd* [2005] *RPC* 169, the only compulsory factor to be taken into account when determining the extent of protection conferred by a European patent—namely, the rules as set out in EPC 2000, Art. 69, and its Protocol.

[133] [1982] *RPC* 183. Although *Catnic* was decided under the PA 1949, it is still relevant under the 1977 Act. In *PLG Research v. Ardon* [1993] *FSR* 197, 309, the Court of Appeal argued that *Catnic* was no longer good law under the 1977 Act. However, the promotion of Aldous LJ to the appellate court led to an immediate reversal of this view. This has been confirmed in a range of subsequent decisions, including *Kirin-Amgen v. Hoechst Marion Roussel* [2005] *RPC* 169, [48]. See, e.g., J. Turner, 'Purposive Construction: Seven Reasons Why *Catnic* is Wrong' [1999] *EIPR* 531; cf. the critical response by M. Franzosi, 'In Defence of *Catnic*' [2000] *EIPR* 242.

[134] *Kastner v. Rizla* [1995] *RPC* 585.

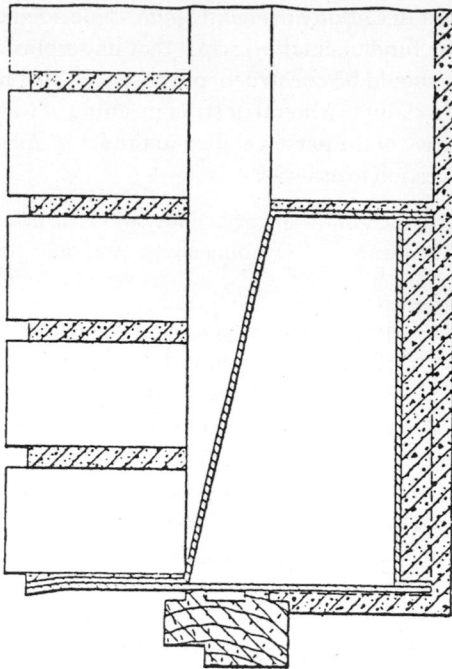

Fig. 22.2 Claimant's lintel
Source: *Catnic v. Hill and Smith* [1982] *RPC* 183

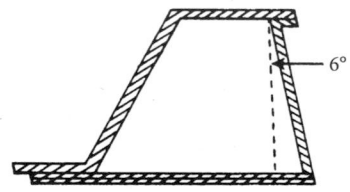

Fig. 22.3 Defendant's lintel
Source: *Catnic v. Hill and Smith* [1982] *RPC* 183

While the patent specification is read from the perspective of the person skilled in the art, the question of the construction of the claims is ultimately a matter for the court. In some cases, the courts will draw on external assistance to help it to determine the meaning of a claim. In some cases, a court can hear expert evidence on the meaning of technical terms.[135] Although a purposive interpretation may allow the courts to extend the scope of the claims beyond that which would be allowed by a literal reading, this does not mean that a purposive approach is an open-ended and unconstrained process. Indeed, there are a number of factors that shape the way in which purposive interpretation is applied, one of which is the fact that the person skilled in the art is presumed to proceed on the basis that the purpose of the specification:

> . . . is both to describe and demarcate the invention—a practical idea which the patentee has had for a new product or process—and not to be a textbook in mathematics or chemistry or a shopping list of chemicals or hardware.[136]

[135] *Glaverbel SA v. British Coal Corporation* [1995] *RPC* 269.   [136] Ibid., [33]–[34].

It will also be presumed that the patentee is attempting to describe something that is new, with all of its attendant problems. It is also presumed that the skilled person will read the patent specification as a whole,[137] and will draw upon the description and drawings to interpret the claims.[138]

A lot will turn on the skill and expertise that is attributed to the person skilled in the art, which will always vary depending on the invention in question. The person skilled in the art is presumed to read the specification 'with common general knowledge of the art available at the time of its publication'.[139] It is also presumed that the notional skilled reader would be aware, and take account, of the drafting conventions by which the patent and its claims were framed.[140] They are also presumed to be aware of the language conventions that have developed over time, which ascribe particular meanings to words such as 'comprising' and 'suitable for'.

While the use of a purposive style of interpretation often means that the scope of the monopoly is broader than that which would arise if the claims were to be interpreted literally, purposive interpretation does not necessarily require that the claims be read broadly or indeed in the patentee's favour. All that the purposive approach requires is that the court interprets patents through the eyes of the person skilled in the art, while taking into account the purpose of the invention—nothing more, nothing less. How broadly claims will be read in any particular case *always* depends on the approach undertaken by the person skilled in the art in the case in hand, which in turn is influenced by the purpose of the invention and the way in which the claims are drafted.[141]

3.1.2 The Protocol on the Interpretation of Article 69 EPC

One of the problems that confronted the drafters of the EPC 1973 was that some member states—notably, the United Kingdom and Germany—approached the task of interpreting patent claims differently. While the British were said to favour a strict, literal reading of the claims, it was suggested that in Germany, the claims simply acted as a guide for determining the scope of protection. Given the potentially important role that claim interpretation plays in determining the scope of protection, if these different styles of interpretation were allowed to continue under the EPC, it would have undermined the aim of a standardized pan-European patent system. In an attempt to overcome these (perceived) differences and to harmonize the way in which patents are interpreted across member states, the Protocol on Interpretation of Article 69 of the EPC 1973 was introduced to provide guidance as to how patent claims should be interpreted.[142] The Protocol,

---

[137] *EMI v. Lissen* (1939) 56 *RPC* 23; *Glaverbel SA v. British Coal Corporation* [1995] *RPC* 255, 269. The statement of the problem that the invention is intended to solve may be particularly influential: *Minnesota Mining & Manufacturing Co. v. Plastus Kreativ AB* [1997] *RPC* 737 (CA); *SEB v. De'Longhi* [2002] *EWHC* 1556 (Pat), [2] (when one encounters a word of degree, the problem is to ascertain its function in the claim so as to obtain a handle on its meaning).

[138] PA 1977, s. 125; EPC 2000, Art. 69 (ex EPC 1973, Art. 69). In *Rosedale v. Carlton Tyre* [1960] *RPC* 59, the Court of Appeal used the drawings and descriptions in determining that 'holes' did not have to be round.

[139] *Hoechst Celanese Corporation v. BP Chemicals* [1999] *FSR* 319 (Aldous LJ). On common general knowledge, see *Beloit Technolgies v. Valmet Paper Machinery* [1997] *RPC* 489, 494.

[140] *Virgin Atlantic Airways v. Premium Aircraft Interior* [2009] *EWCA Civ* 1062, [15], citing *Kirin-Amgen v. Hoechst Marion Roussel* [2005] *RPC* 169, [34]. [141] See section 3.1, p. 651.

[142] On the Protocol generally, see B. Sherman, 'Patent Claim Interpretation: The Impact of the Protocol on Interpretation' (1991) 54 *MLR* 499. See the Protocol on the Interpretation of Article 69 EPC ('Protocol on Art. 69'), as revised by the Act Revising the Convention on the Grant of European Patents (EPC) (Munich) (29 November 2000) MR/3/00 Rev, 1e (the 'EPC Revision Act'), Art. 2, item 2.

which is said to bear 'all the hallmarks of a compromise agreement',[143] was replicated in EPC 2000 in a slightly modified form.[144]

There are three notable features of the Protocol under EPC 2000. The first is that it stipulates the standpoint of interpretation that should *not* be adopted when interpreting a patent. In particular, it says that the courts should not read the claims literally. The Protocol also says that the claims should not be used as a mere guide to interpretation; instead, it says somewhat cryptically, that the courts should adopt a position in between these extremes.[145] The second, more positive, feature of the Protocol is that it says that the courts should interpret the claims in a way that combines a fair protection for the patentee with a reasonable degree of certainty for third parties.[146] The third feature of the Protocol is that it provides that when determining the scope of protection due account should be taken of any element which is equivalent to an element specified in the claims.[147]

3.1.3 The *Improver* questions

The next important intervention on claim interpretation was Hoffmann J's 1990 judgment in *Improver v. Remington*.[148] This decision was concerned with the potential infringement of a patented hair removal device, known as 'Epilday' (which operated by trapping hairs in a rotating coiled helical spring which then pulled them out of the skin) by the defendant's device (which operated in the same way but used a slotted rubber rod to capture and remove the hairs). While the alleged infringing device clearly fell outside the scope of a strict literal reading of the claim, Hoffman J was willing to consider whether it nonetheless still infringed. Holding that the purposive interpretation outlined by Lord Diplock in *Catnic* was consistent with the 1977 Patents Act, the EPC 1973, and the Protocol, Hoffmann J went on to suggest a three-step approach to determine whether a patent was infringed. As he said, when the issue was whether a feature embodied in an alleged infringement fell outside the 'primary, literal or a contextual meaning of a descriptive word or phrase in the claim' (what he called 'a variant') was 'nonetheless still within its language as properly interpreted', three questions, which have come to be known as the *Improver* questions,[149] should be asked:

(i) Does the variant have a material effect on the way in which the invention works? If yes, the variant is outside the claim. If no—

(ii) Would this (i.e. that the variant has no material effect) have been obvious to a reader skilled in the art at the date of the publication of the patent? If no, the variant is outside the claim. If yes—

(iii) Would a reader skilled in the art nevertheless have understood from the language of the claim that strict compliance with the primary meaning was an essential requirement of the invention? If yes, the variant is outside the claim.[150]

Applying these questions to the facts of the case, Hoffmann J found that the difference between the patented invention and the allegedly infringing device (namely, the difference between the coiled helical spring and the slotted rubber bar) did not have a material effect on the way the invention worked: both functioned to capture and remove body hair. He also found that this would have been obvious to the skilled reader. However, on the

---

[143] *Actavis v. Eli Lilly* [2017] *UKSC* 48, [32] (SC) (Neuberger LJ).

[144] The new Protocol includes, in Art. 2, provision in relation to equivalents.

[145] Protocol on Art. 69, Art. 1.

[146] On the background, see *American Home Products v. Novartis Pharmaceuticals* [2000] *RPC* 547, 557

[147] Protocol on Art. 69, Art. 2 (often called the 'doctrine of equivalents').   [148] [1990] *FSR* 181, 189.

[149] While these were renamed the three Protocol questions in *Wheatley v. Drillsafe* [2001] *RPC* 7, [23], the original name is still used.   [150] *Improver v. Remington* [1990] *FSR* 181, 189.

basis that it would have been obvious to the skilled reader that the rubber had problems . . . which might have been difficult to overcome', Hoffmann J found that the patentee failed to satisfy the third test and as such that there was no infringement.[151]

3.1.4 *Kirin-Amgen*

The next important development in this area was the 2005 House of Lords decision of *Kirin-Amgen*.[152] In considering 'whether a protein manufactured by gene-activation infringed a patent relating to production of the same protein by recombinant DNA technology', Lord Hoffmann reviewed the existing law on patent claim interpretation. There are three notable things about the decision. The first relates to the way it promoted purposive interpretation at the expense of the Improver questions. While Lord Hoffmann thought that the purposive interpretation as outlined in *Catnic* was the 'bedrock of patent construction, universally applicable',[153] he said that the Protocol and the Improver questions were 'simply guidelines for applying [purposive interpretation] to equivalents . . . more useful in some cases than in others'.[154] In so doing, he called into question the practice that had developed in the UK post-*Improver* whereby the Improver questions were routinely applied in UK patent infringement cases.[155] Following *Kirin-Amgen* the *Improver* questions fell out of favour in infringement actions in the United Kingdom, to be replaced by the purposive interpretation that asked: what would the person skilled in the art have understood the patentee to mean?[156]

The second notable point about *Kirin-Amgen* was in relation to the so-called doctrine of equivalents and its place within British law.[157] Prior to the passage of the Patents Act 1977, under the doctrine of equivalents, elements of an invention were not only considered to be the same when they were identical, but also when they were functionally equivalent.[158] This meant that 'there may be infringement even if the accused product falls outside the meaning of the words of the claim when understood in context'.[159] Given that neither Article 69 of the EPC 1973[160] nor the Protocol (under EPC 1973) made specific reference to the doctrine of equivalents,[161] when the 1977 Act was passed doubts were raised as to whether the doctrine of equivalents was still applicable under the new law. In many ways, it seemed that the uncertainty about the status of the doctrine of equivalents was answered by the EPC 2000. In affirming the continued role of the doctrine of equivalents, Article 2 of the Protocol on Interpretation of Article 69 in the EPC 2000 reads that for 'the purposes of determining the extent of protection conferred by a European patent, due account shall be taken of any element which is equivalent to an element specified in the

---

[151] Ibid., 197.

[152] *Kirin-Amgen v. Hoechst Marion Roussel* [2004] *UKHL* 46, [2005] *RPC* 169, [82]. On this, see *Virgin Atlantic Airways v. Premium Aircraft Interior* [2009] *EWCA Civ* 1062, [5].

[153] *Kirin-Amgen v. Hoechst Marion Roussel* [2004] *UKHL* 46, [52].   [154] Ibid.

[155] *Actavis v. Eli Lilly* [2017] *UKSC* 48, [40] (SC) (Neuberger LJ).

[156] R. Cox and S. Spink, 'UK Claim Construction: Return of the Protocol Questions and File Wrapper Estoppel' (2015) *JIPL* 167, 168.

[157] For an overview of the history of the doctrine of equivalents in the UK, see Bently and Sherman, (2014), 632–4.

[158] See *Kirin-Amgen v. Hoechst Marion Roussel* [2005] *RPC* 169, [36] *ff*; *Van der Lely v. Bamfords* [1963] *RPC* 61 (HL); *Rodi & Weinenberger v. Showell* [1969] *RPC* 367 (HL); *Beecham Group v. Bristol Laboratories* [1978] *RPC* 153.

[159] *Celltech* [2003] *FSR* 433, 436. See generally M. Franzosi, 'Equivalence in Europe' [2003] *EIPR* 237.

[160] PA 1977, s. 125.

[161] *Beloit Technologies v. Valmet Paper Machinery* [1995] *RPC* 705, 720; *Celltech* [2003] *FSR* 433 436 (no express provision in Europe for doctrine of equivalents).

claims'.[162] As a result, it seemed clear that the doctrine of equivalents needed to be taken into account when deciding whether a patent has been infringed.

The belief that the EPC 2000 might have reinstated the doctrine of equivalents under British law was temporarily undermined by the House of Lords in *Kirin-Amgen*,[163] when Lord Hoffmann said that the amendment changed nothing; the provision only made it clear that equivalents need to be considered, not that there was a 'doctrine of equivalents' allowing a court to extend protection beyond that covered in the claims (as interpreted by the person skilled in the art). As Lord Hoffmann said: '[It] seems to me that both the doctrine of equivalents in the United States and the pith and marrow doctrine in the United Kingdom were born of despair. Since the *Catnic* case we have article 69 which, firmly shuts the door on any doctrine which extends protection outside the claims'.[164] One of the consequences of *Kirin-Amgen* was that the doctrine of equivalents was subsumed within the purposive approach to interpretation. Thus while the Court of Appeal may have been able to say in 2009 that 'there is no general "doctrine of equivalents"',[165] nonetheless it also accepted that a purposive interpretation could 'lead to a conclusion that a technically trivial or minor difference between an element of a claim and the corresponding element of the alleged infringement nonetheless falls within the meaning of the element when read purposively'.[166] In a strange (literal) reading, this was said not to be because there was a doctrine of equivalents; rather, it was because it was the fair way to read the claims in context[167]—a doctrine of equivalents in all but name?

3.1.5 *Actavis v. Lilly*

The 2017 Supreme Court decision of *Actavis v. Lilly* was an infringement action that concerned a chemotherapy drug patented by Eli Lilly.[168] It has long been known that while a class of chemicals known as antifolates had valuable therapeutic effects on cancerous tumours, the antifolates had a number of serious, sometimes fatal, side-effects that undermined their value as an anti-cancer drug. Eli Lilly discovered that the side-effects could be avoided if a compound called pemetrexed disodium (which was a type of antifolate) was taken with vitamin B12. Accordingly, the patent claimed the use of antifolate pemetrexed disodium in the manufacture of a medicament for use in combination with vitamin B12 (and, optionally, folic acid) for the treatment of cancer. From 2004, Eli Lilly sold a medicament that combined the antifolate, pemetrexed disodium, and vitamin B12.

The allegedly infringing products that Actavis were considering selling in the United Kingdom (France, Italy, or Spain) were similar to Eli Lilly's in that they combined antifolates and vitamin B12 together in a single medicament. They differed however in that rather than using pemetrexed disodium with vitamin B12, Actavis used pemetrexed diacid, pemetrexed ditromethamine, or pemetrexed dipotassium.[169] Actavis argued that because they did not use pemetrexed disodium, Eli Lilly's patent would not be infringed. In contrast, Eli Lilly argued that the Actavis products infringed because they were medicaments consisting of pemetrexed diacid with vitamin B12 to be used as a treatment for cancer. At first instance, Arnold J agreed and held that none of the Actavis products either directly or indirectly infringed. While the Court of Appeal agreed that there was

---

[162] Protocol on Art. 69, Art. 2, item 2.
[163] *Kirin-Amgen v. Hoechst Marion Roussel* [2004] *UKHL* 46, [2005] *RPC* 169.   [164] Ibid., [44].
[165] *Virgin Atlantic Airways v. Premium Aircraft Interior* [2009] *EWCA Civ* 1062, [5].
[166] *Kirin-Amgen v. Hoechst Marion Roussel* [2004] *UKHL* 46, [2005] *RPC* 169, [82]. On this, see *Virgin Atlantic Airways v. Premium Aircraft Interior* [2009] *EWCA Civ* 1062, [5].
[167] *Kirin-Amgen v. Hoechst Marion Roussel* [2004] *UKHL* 46, [82].
[168] *Actavis v. Eli Lilly* [2017] *UKSC* 48 (SC).   [169] Also known as pemetrexed 'salts'.

no direct infringement, they did find that there would be an indirect infringement. On appeal the Supreme Court found in favour of Eli Lilly, holding that the Actavis products would directly and indirectly infringe.

Given that the Actavis products and the Eli Lilly patent utilized different chemical compounds, it was clear that on a strict literal reading of the claims, there was no infringement.[170] For Eli Lilly to sustain its infringement action, it needed to show that, despite this literal reading, the claims should be construed in a way that encompassed Activis's medicaments. To do so, they relied on the Protocol on the Interpretation of Article 69 which, as Lord Neuberger noted, provided that the scope of protection afforded to a patentee was not limited to the literal meaning of the claims. The problem with the Protocol, however, was that 'it was not at all clear how far a court is permitted to move away from a literal meaning'.[171] In addition, while Article 2 made it clear that equivalents needed to be taken into account, it provided no guidance as to how this was to be done. As a result, in determining whether Eli Lilly's patent had been infringed, the Supreme Court was led to consider the question at the heart of patent claim interpretation, namely: 'how far one can go outside the wording of a claim to enable the patentee to enjoy protection against products or processes which are not within the ambit of the actual language'?

After reviewing *Catnic*, the *Improver* questions, *Kirin-Amgen* (all discussed earlier), and the approach to claim interpretation adopted in a number of other EPC states,[172] the Supreme Court outlined what it considered to be the proper approach to claim interpretation. As Lord Neuberger said, infringement is best approached by addressing two issues,[173] each of which is to be considered through the eyes of the person skilled in the art. These are:

(i) Does the variant[174] infringe any of the claims as a matter of normal interpretation;[175] and, if not,

(ii) Does the variant nonetheless infringe because it varies from the invention in a way or ways which is or are immaterial?

If the answer to either question was yes, there is an infringement.

In relation to the first question, Lord Neuberger said that, according to the 'normal principles of interpreting documents' in the case at hand, there was no infringement. This was because when read normally there was 'no sensible way' in which pemetrexed diacid, pemetrexed ditromethamine, or pemetrexed dipotassium could 'be said to fall within the expression, "pemetrexed disodium" in claim 1 of the Patent'.[176] As a result, Lord Neuberger turned to the second question which raised a difficult matter of principle; namely, what is it that makes a variation immaterial?[177] To answer this question, Lord Neuberger relied on the *Improver* questions; which he said were helpful guidelines, but in need of reform.

---

[170] Eli Lilly's patent was limited to the specific chemical compound, pemetrexed disodium in combination with vitamin B12, whereas Actavis's products combined vitamin B12 with pemetrexed diacid (or pemetrexed salt), pemetrexed ditromethamine, or pemetrexed dipotassium.

[171] *Actavis v. Eli Lilly* [2017] *UKSC* 48, [33] (SC) (Neuberger LJ).

[172] Germany, France, Italy, and Spain. Ibid., [44]–[52].

[173] Ibid., [55]. This was in contrast to Lord Hoffmann in *Kirin-Amgen* who suggested that there was a single question to be asked (namely, what would a purposive interpretation lead to?).

[174] A 'variant' is the thing that is different between the patented invention and the alleged infringing product or process.

[175] Although Lord Neuberger does not explain what he meant by 'normal' interpretation, later case law has understood it as involving no departure from 'purposive interpretation'. See, e.g., *Illumina v. Premaitha* [2017] *EWHC* 2930 (Pat), [200]–[202] (Carr J) ('normal interpretation means purposive interpretation').

[176] *Actavis v. Eli Lilly* [2017] *UKSC* 48, [58] (SC) (Lord Neuberger).   [177] Ibid., [59].

Lord Neuberger began by noting that the first *Improver* question, which asks whether the variant has a material effect on the way the invention works, requires the court to focus on whether 'the variant achieves the same result in substantially the same way'.[178] Lord Neuberger said that when answering this question, the emphasis should not be on how 'the invention' works, so much as on the 'problem underlying the invention', 'the inventive core', or the 'inventive concept'.

While the first *Improver* question escaped any real criticism, the same cannot be said for the second *Improver* question which asks: would the fact that the variant has no material effect have been obvious to a reader skilled in the art at the date of the publication of the patent? For Lord Neuberger, the problem with the second question related to the information that the notional addressee was presumed to have when they asked whether it was obvious that the variant would not have a material effect on the way the invention works. The problem here was that as the notional addressee was presumed not to know whether the variant worked, it required the 'addressee to figure out for himself whether the variant would work'. While this may have been possible with mechanical inventions, it was more problematic with certain types of chemical research where it was not possible to predict in advance whether a variant would have a material effect on the invention. As a result, this inevitably meant that in these cases the 'second *Improver* test could not be answered yes'. For Lord Neuberger, this ran counter to Article 1 of the Protocol which requires fair protection for the patentee. Given this, Lord Neuberger said that the second test should be reformulated to ask: whether, on being told what the variant does, would the notional addressee consider it obvious that it achieved substantially the same result in substantially the same way as the invention?[179]

While Lord Neuberger thought that the third *Improver* question, which asks whether the notional addressee would have understood from the language of the claim that the patentee wanted to limit the claims to a strict literal reading was a valid question, he felt that it was open to misunderstanding. To prevent this, he attempted to clarify a number of issues. The first was that the notional addressee's understanding was not limited to the language of the claim, but also extended to include the specification and 'all the knowledge and expertise' normally attributed to them. Second, the fact that the language of the claim did not, 'on any sensible reading', cover the variant was not in itself a reason why a patentee should fail the third test. Rather, it was more of a reason to ask the *Improver* questions in the first place. Third, while it was appropriate to ask whether the 'component at issue' was an essential part of the invention, this was not to be mistaken with the overall product or process which the invention was part of. And finally, when considering whether a variant was obvious at the date of infringement (rather than priority date), the notional address would be imbued with more information.[180]

In light of these changes, Lord Neuberger reformulated the *Improver* questions to read:

(i)   Notwithstanding that it is not within the literal meaning of the relevant claim(s), does the variant achieve substantially the same result in substantially the same way as the invention, ie the inventive concept revealed by the patent?

(ii) Would it be obvious to the person skilled in the art, reading the patent at the priority date, but knowing that the variant achieves substantially the same result as the invention, that it does so in substantially the same way as the invention?

(iii) Would such a reader of the patent have concluded that the patentee nonetheless intended that strict compliance with the literal meaning of the relevant claim(s) of the patent was an essential requirement of the invention?[181]

---

[178] Ibid., [60].
[179] Ibid., [62]. The reformulated test also applies to variants which rely on developments after the priority date.
[180] Ibid., [65].   [181] Ibid., [62].

To establish non-literal infringement, it would be necessary to answer 'yes' to the first two questions and 'no' to the third.

Lord Neuberger then applied the revised *Improver* questions to the facts-at-hand. Given that the Actavis products worked in the same way as the patented invention (they all involved a medicament that combined the active pemetrexed ingredient (namely pemetrexed anion[182]) and vitamin B12), the answer to the first question was 'yes'. In contrast to the lower courts, Lord Neuberger felt that the answer to the second question was also 'yes'. The reason why Lord Neuberger differed from the lower courts was because of the knowledge imputed to the person skilled in the art. While the lower courts had followed the unmodified *Improver* questions (which led them to presume that the notional addressee did not know that the Actavis products worked), Lord Neuberger assumed that the notional addressee would know that the Actavis products worked. Armed with this knowledge and the fact that the notional addressee would have regarded the testing of the different pemetrexed compounds as a 'purely routine exercise', Lord Neuberger said that it would have been obvious to the notional addressee at the priority date that the Actavis products worked in the same way as the patented invention.

Lord Neuberger also disagreed with the Court of Appeal's decision that the answer to third question was 'no'. Unlike with the second question, the difference here had more to do with how the patent was interpreted than with Lord Neuberger's modifications. For Lord Neuberger, the Court of Appeal decision had relied too much on a straightforward reading of the claims and not enough on Article 2 of the Protocol (which calls for a non-literal reading). For Lord Neuberger it was wrong to treat the third question as one of 'normal interpretation', not least because it made a nonsense of asking the three questions. This was because 'if one cannot depart from the language of the claim when considering those questions, what is the point of those questions in the first place?'[183] While the Court of Appeal had found reason in the specification to limit the patent to pemetrexed disodium,[184] Lord Neuberger disagreed and held that there was no good reason why the patentee would have wanted to limit the patent to a literal reading of the claims. On this basis, the Supreme Court held that the Actavis products provisionally infringed Eli Lilly's patent.

The reason for treating this conclusion as 'provisional' was because the court wanted to consider what effect, if any, the prosecution history (that is, the information exchanged between the applicant and the patent office during the grant of the patent) had on the way the claims were interpreted. Here, Actavis argued that the prosecution history at the EPO suggested that the claims should be limited to pemetrexed disodium. Signaling a move away from *Kirin-Amgen*,[185] Lord Neuberger said that the UK courts should adopt a 'sceptical, but not absolutist' approach to the suggestion

---

[182] This important point, about what the active ingredient was, was not discussed in any detail in the judgment.   [183] Ibid., [71].

[184] The Court of Appeal held that the fact that the specification referred to 'anti-folates' but only claimed 'pemetrexed disodium' suggested that it was limited to this specific chemical compound.

[185] In *Kirin-Amgen v. Hoechst Marion Roussel* [2005] *RPC* 169, [35] Lord Hoffmann indicated that the British courts generally do not look at 'prosecution history': The courts of the United Kingdom, the Netherlands and Germany certainly discourage, if they do not actually prohibit, use of the patent office file in aid of construction. There are good reasons: the meaning of the patent should not change according to whether or not the person skilled in the art has access to the file and in any case life is too short for the limited assistance which it can provide. Despite such an authority, counter-examples exist: *Furr v. CD Truline (Building Products)* [1985] FSR 553, 560–4; *Rohm and Haas v. Collag* [2002] FSR 445, 457–8 (letter to EPO held to contain objective information that was of assistance in resolving aspects of the specification that were unclear); *Wesley Jessen v. Coopervison* [2003] RPC 355, 382 (prosecution history at the EPO, which showed that application was changed from pattern to dots to avoid prior art, was used to limit 'dots' to mean 'small roundish marks' and nothing else). For the position of prosecution history estoppel in the United States, see *Festo Corporation v. Shoketsu Kinzouku Kogyo KK*, 535 US 722 (2002), [2003] FSR 10 (patentee bound by representations made at US patent office).

that the history of the patent at the patent office could be used to interpret the claims post-grant.[186] Specifically, he said that reference to the file would only be appropriate where the file history unambiguously resolves a point of uncertainty, or where it would be contrary to public interest not to do so.[187] In any case, as the contents of the file did not justify departing from the preliminary conclusion, the court held that the Actavis products directly infringed the Eli Lilly patent.

While it will take some time to see how *Actavis* is received,[188] it is possible to draw some preliminary conclusions. One thing that is clear is that *Actavis* has reinstated the importance of the now-modified *Improver* questions in determining how far a patent can be construed beyond a 'normal' reading of the claim. While this is clear, what is less clear is the continued importance of purposive interpretation. Given some of Lord Neuberger's sweeping claims, it would seem that the purposive interpretation has been subsumed within the second stage of his two-step infringement test.[189] It will be interesting to see whether the courts follow this lead and replace the purposive test with the modified-*Improver* questions or whether they continue to selectively use the purposive test when dealing with more straightforward cases (as in *Catnic*).[190] Another subtle but important consequence of *Actavis* is that it has increased the scope of protection for patentees, particularly in relation to chemical inventions. This is because presuming that the notional addressee knows that the variant works increases the likelihood that the second *Improver* question will be answered positively and thus that there is a finding of infringement. A third, as yet unexplained issue is whether the variants which might be covered under the test of equivalents outlined by Lord Neuberger can include material which formed part of the state of the art at the priority date. Such an outcome seems undesirable, and might be avoided by applying the third guideline so as to assume that in such a case the patentee would want strict compliance with the literal meaning of the claim.[191] Alternatively, it might be necessary to develop a doctrine (such as the so-called 'Formstein defence') that equivalents cannot include matter which would not have been patentable in the light of the state of the art.[192]

---

[186] *Actavis v. Eli Lilly* [2017] *UKSC* 48, [87] (SC) (Neuberger LJ).   [187] Ibid., [88].

[188] An important issue is whether the new approach is adopted in relation to the 'reverse infringement' test embraced in the context of novelty. If so, it may become harder to establish novelty, and the line between novelty and inventive step will become blurred. So far, the courts have suggested that the 'reverse infringement' test is to be conducted on a normal interpretation of the claim in issue, and thus without reference to equivalents: *Generics (UK) v. Yeda Research* [2017] *EWHC* 2629 (Pat), [157]–[167] (Arnold J) (considering the impact of *Actavis* on the *Synthon* novelty assessment and observing, at [161], that it will require another decision of the Supreme Court to supply a definitive answer to the question . . .'; *Fisher & Paykel Healthcare v. ResMed* [2017] *EWHC* 2748 (Ch), [74]–[86] (Deputy Judge Meade QC).

[189] But cf. *Illumina v. Premaitha* [2017] *EWHC* 2930 (Pat), [200]–[202] (Carr J).

[190] In *Actavis v. Eli Lilly* [2017] *UKSC* 48, [55], Lord Neuberger acknowledged that 'normal principles of interpretation could . . . accommodate the notion that "vertically" extended to an item which was not at precisely 90° to another item'). It is unclear how the *Actavis* approach will affect the interpretative practices that have developed in relation to claim interpretation, for example, the conventions on scientific numbers and numerical ranges: see *Smith & Nephew v. ConvaTec* [2015] *EWCA Civ* 607, [19]–[22]; *Napp Pharmaceutical v. Dr Reddy's Laboratories* [2016] *EWHC* 1517 (Pat).

[191] However, if (as *Actavis*, [33], implies) the extent of protection is severed from the process of interpretation of the claim, and the question of equivalents is only relevant to infringement (and not novelty) (as started in *Generics (UK) v. Yeda Research* [2017] *EWHC* 2629 (Pat), [157]–[167]), it is not obvious that a reader of the patent would necessarily conclude merely from the fact that an equivalent of a claim existed in the prior art that the patentee intended that strict compliance with the literal meaning of the relevant claim.

[192] *Formstein* (29 April 1986) [1991] *RPC* 597, 606 (BGH) (recognizing a 'defence that the alleged infringement which is claimed to be an equivalent is not a patentable invention in the light of the prior art').

4 DEFENCES TO PROCEEDINGS FOR INFRINGEMENT

Once the claimant has proved that the defendant has performed an activity that falls within the scope of the patent monopoly, the obligation then shifts to the defendant to show that the activity is exempted from liability by one of the defences to patent infringement that are available. There has been surprisingly little discussion about the defences to patent infringement actions and the policies that inform them.[193] At a general level, the exceptions balance the interests of patentees against the interests of other groups, such as competitors, previous users, traders, users, and non-profit-making bodies, as well as teaching and research establishments. In some cases, the defences operate to overcome the market failure that occurs where a patentee declines to license a socially beneficial use because of the transaction costs involved. It should be noted that if the unitary patent package is implemented, the defences will need to be revisited. With these general points in mind, we now turn to look at some of the more important defences that may exempt a defendant from liability.

4.1 PRIVATE NON-COMMERCIAL USES

Section 60(5)(a) of the 1977 Act provides that acts that are done privately *and* for non-commercial purposes do not infringe.[194] The private use exception is usually explained on the basis that while private uses may increase scientific knowledge and thus be socially beneficial, high transaction costs may mean that they are unlikely to be licensed.[195] Another factor in favour of the defence is that private non-commercial uses do not pose much of a threat to the patent monopoly. While private uses need not be secret or confidential, they must be 'for the person's own use'.[196] Where an activity has both commercial and non-commercial benefits, it is necessary to ascertain the subjective intention of the user. If the infringer were motivated by commercial interests, the defence would not apply. However, if the subjective purposes were non-commercial, the defendant could rely on the immunity. This is the case even if the resulting information has a commercial benefit.[197]

4.2 EXPERIMENTAL USES

Section 60(5)(b) provides immunity for acts done for experimental purposes relating to the subject matter of the invention.[198] This defence gives effect to a number of related policies, the most obvious being that the patent monopoly should not be allowed to inhibit scientific developments. It is likely that the experimental use defence will become increasingly important as patenting (especially in relation to biotechnology) enters the

---

[193] D. Gilat, *Experimental Use and Patents* (1995); R. Eisenberg, 'Patents and the Progress of Science: Exclusive Rights and Experimental Use' (1989) 56 *U Chi L Rev* 1017; J. Karp, 'Experimental Use as Patent Infringement' (1991) 100 *Yale LJ* 2169.

[194] CPC, Art. 31.

[195] See D. Gilat, *Experimental Use and Patents* (1995), 25. The US courts have occasionally employed the principle of *de minimis non curat lex* ('the law does not concern itself with trifles'): e.g. *Finney v. United States* 188 *USPQ* 33 (CCTD 1975).

[196] *SKF Laboratories v. Evans Medical* [1989] FSR 513, 518; *McDonald v. Graham* [1994] RPC 407.

[197] *SKF Laboratories v. Evans Medical* [1989] FSR 513.

[198] CPC, Art. 27(b). See W. Cornish, 'Experimental Use of Patented Inventions in European Community States' (1998) 29 *IIC* 735. T. Cook, *A European Perspective as to the Extent to which Experimental Use and Certain Other Defences to Patent Infringement Apply to Differing Types of Research* (2006).

traditional domains of 'pure' scientific research carried out within the universities.[199] For the defence to apply, a defendant must show that the act (i) was done for experimental purposes and (ii) that it relates to the subject of the invention.

(i) Experimental purpose To a large extent, the scope of the defence depends on the way in which 'experimental purpose' is defined.[200] If it can be shown that the purpose of the activity was to discover something unknown or to test a hypothesis, it would be regarded as an experiment.[201] An act will also be experimental where a person is attempting to discover whether the patented invention works.[202] This may occur, for example, where a party is thinking whether to license a patent or they believe that the patent is invalid on grounds of insufficiency. Given the public interest in determining whether a monopoly has been validly granted, it is desirable that competitors undertake this kind of policing task. In the absence of an experimental use defence, such acts might require the licence of the patentee, which in the circumstances may not be forthcoming.[203]

If the purpose of the activity is to prove something that is already known, to demonstrate to a third party that the product works in the way in which the maker claims, or to obtain official approval for a product,[204] these would *not* be regarded as acts done for experimental purposes.[205] In one case, it was held that trials that were carried out to obtain safety clearances and to gather information to support an attempt to gain approval for a new use of a patented product (to be used once the patent had expired) were for commercial, rather than scientific, purposes.[206] While the issue has yet to be considered in any detail, it seems that if there is a commercial motive behind the experimental use, or where the purpose of the trial was 'mainly directly or indirectly to generate revenue',[207] it is more likely to fall outside the scope of the exception.[208]

Where an act is done for a number of purposes—such as establishing confidence in the market, generating income, and gathering information—the courts look to the

---

[199] E. Barash, 'Experimental Uses, Patents and Scientific Progress' (1997) 91 *Nw UL Rev* 667 (recommending expansion of experimental-use defence for non-profit research).

[200] The 'purposes for which tests or trials are carried out may in some cases be mixed and in some cases may be difficult to discern': *Monsanto v. Stauffer Chemical* [1985] *RPC* 515 (CA), 542.   [201] Ibid., 515.

[202] The decision of the SCC in *Micro-Chemicals v. Smith Kline and French InterAmerican* (1971) 25 *DLR* 79, 89 (that use by a defendant to establish that it could manufacture a quality product in accordance with the specification was not an infringement) was explicitly approved by Dillon LJ in *Monsanto v. Stauffer* [1985] *RPC* 515, 538. Trials directed to discovering whether something that is known to work in certain conditions will work in different conditions could fairly be regarded as experiments: see section 4.2, p. 667; D. Gilat, *Experimental Use and Patents* (1995), 20.

[203] The situation is analogous to the criticism-or-review defence in copyright law, which is based on the idea that criticism would be stifled if the law were to require a prospective critic to obtain a licence from the copyright owner before criticizing the work.

[204] *Auchinloss v. Agricultural and Veterinary Supplies* [1999] *RPC* 397, 405. *Meter-Tech v. British Gas* [2016] *EWHC* 2278 (Pat), [235].   [205] *Monsanto v. Stauffer* [1985] *RPC* 515 (CA), 542.

[206] Ibid., 515; *Auchinloss v. Agricultural and Veterinary Supplies* [1997] *RPC* 649, [1999] *RPC* 397 (CA). Another situation in which a person may wish to rely on the defence is where they test someone else's patented invention for the purposes of obtaining regulatory approval, either by providing data or samples to the relevant authority. In *Upjohn v. Kerfoot* [1988] *FSR* 1, Whitford J held that the mere application for a marketing authorization in respect of a medicinal product, even when accompanied by test results, did not constitute an infringement of the patent, since it did not amount to use of the patent. In the United States, such samples are permitted under the Drug Price Competition and Patent Term Restoration Act 1984, 35 *USC* §271. The European Commission argued that a similar Canadian provision, which permits making and stockpiling of the drug up to six months prior to the expiry of the patent, contravened TRIPS. The matter was referred to the WTO on 12 November 1998. See WTO, *Canada: Patent Protection of Pharmaceutical Products—Report of the Panel* (17 March 2000) WT/DS114/R.

[207] *Meter-Tech v. British Gas* [2016] *EWHC* 2278 (Pat), [235].

[208] *Inhale Therapeutic Systems v. Quadrant Healthcare* [2002] *RPC* 419, 463.

'preponderant purpose' for the activity to decide whether the activity falls within the exemption.[209] In *CoreValve v. Edwards Lifesciences*,[210] the court held that clinical trials were not exempted by section 60(5)(b) because the main purpose was to 'generate immediate revenue of a substantial character'. The standing of commercial research will undoubtedly become more pressing given the growing trend for public sector agencies that have traditionally relied upon the defence, such as universities, to commercialize their research results.[211] So far, there has been no consideration given to the question of whether a person who tests an invention to improve it, to invent around the patent, or to invent something else falls within the defence.[212] However, the German Supreme Court has held that experiments to discover the most appropriate form that a patented product should take to alleviate a specific disease fell within the experimental use defence under German law.[213]

(ii) 'Relates to the subject matter of the invention' Once it has been shown that a use has been carried out for an experimental purpose, it is then necessary to show that the experiment relates to the subject matter of the patent.[214] This means, for example, that a person who wished to test a cure for cancer that they had developed by applying it to a genetically modified mouse could not rely on the defence against a claim by the patentee of the mouse. If the law were otherwise, the patentees of diagnostic test kits would never receive any remuneration because all uses of the kit would be experimental.[215] Where a researcher wishes to use patented processes or products to test other subject matter, they would need to obtain a licence.[216]

In addition to the experimental use defence, researchers may also be able to rely on the more specific, but related, medical regulatory use defence in section 60(5)(i) .[217] This provides a defence for an act done in conducting a study, test, or trial that aims to produce medicinal products for either human[218] or veterinary use.[219]

In 2014, the 1977 Patents Act was amended to allow clinical trials, field trials, and health technology assessments to be carried out without infringing a patent.[220] The new section 60(6D) clarifies that activities that are carried out for the purposes of obtaining regulatory approval or health technology assessment for drugs fall within the scope of section 60(5)(b) of the Patents Act 1977. The new provisions do not cover commercial uses of patented medical products.[221] Section 60(6D) is designed to deal with the

---

[209] *Corevalve v. Edwards Lifesciences* [2009] *EWHC* 6 (Pat), [79].   [210] Ibid.

[211] For the approach taken in the United States in this situation, see *Madey v. Duke University* 64 *USPQ 2d* 1737 (Fed. Cir. 2002) (Duke University could not rely on experimental-use defence because of the commercial nature of the university, among other things).

[212] *McDonald v. Graham* [1994] *RPC* 407 ('no doubt the defendant would be right to submit that supplying a patented article to a designer with a request that he design a non-infringing equivalent would be, in principle, an unobjectionable use of the article if the article were a "franked" article, but the defendant used infringing articles which he was well aware were not supposed to be in his possession at the material time').

[213] *Klinische Versuche (Clinical trials) II* [1998] *RPC* 423 (s. 11(2) of the German Patent Act). See P. Tauchner, 'Experimental Use Exemption in Germany' (December 1997) *Patent World* 23.

[214] In *Auchinloss v. Agricultural and Veterinary Supplies* [1999] *RPC* 397 (CA), 406, Aldous LJ said that the 'subject matter' of the invention must be ascertained from the patent as a whole.

[215] *SKF v. Evans* [1989] *FSR* 513, 523.   [216] *Monsanto v. Stauffer* [1985] *RPC* 515, 522.

[217] This was added by the Medicines (Marketing Authorisations etc.) Amendment Regulations 2005 (SI 2005/2759).   [218] Directive 2001/83/EC, Art. 10(1)–(4).

[219] Directive 2001/82/EC, Art. 13(1)–(5).

[220] Legislative Reform (Patents) Order 2014, cl. 2 introducing new PA 1977, s. 60(6D)–(6G) (with effect, 1 October 2014).

[221] UK IPO, *Changes to patents legislation made by the Legislative Reform (Patents) Order 2014 from 1 October 2014*.

patent-related problems that arise because of the fact that in order to obtain regulatory approval to market a new drug product, companies must undertake trials to demonstrate to the regulatory authorities that the product is safe and effective. It is hoped this will encourage companies to conduct clinical trials in the United Kingdom.

4.3 PRIOR USE

As we saw earlier, one of the changes brought about by the 1977 Act was that novelty was redefined to exclude inventions that had been 'made available to the public'. As a result, secret third-party use does not destroy novelty.[222] One of the consequences of this is that the rights conferred by a patent might cover secret activities carried out by a third party prior to grant.[223] In recognition that it would be wrong if patents were allowed to be used to prevent a person from carrying on an activity that they were doing prior to grant (the so-called 'right to work' doctrine), section 64(1) provides previous users with a personal defence.[224]

There are a number of points to note about the defence. The first is that it only applies where the previous acts were committed in the United Kingdom (or possibly the EEA).[225] Given that the novelty standard is worldwide, this raises the possibility that a person carrying out an activity in Japan, which is then patented by another person in the United Kingdom, will not be able to practise the invention in the United Kingdom.

It is also important to note that the defence is only available where the acts were carried out in good faith. Although the notion of good faith has yet to be interpreted by the courts, this might prevent a member of a research team from relying on the prior use defence where they left the research team contrary to an understanding between them. Similarly, if a former employee was preparing to use trade secrets obtained while in employment to compete with their ex-employer, the ex-employee would not be able to rely on the preparatory acts as a defence to patent infringement actions.[226]

The prior use defence is only available where the defendant has done the acts or, before the priority date of the patent, made 'serious and effective preparations' to do an act that would be infringing if it were carried out after the grant of the patent. It has been said that the preparations 'must be so advanced as to be about to result in the infringing act being done'.[227] The defence allows a past user to continue to do the same act after the patent has been granted. While it is not necessary for a defendant to show unbroken use, they must show a clear link or a 'chain of causation' between the previous use and the

---

[222] This reinforces the policy that the patent should be granted to the first to file and disclose the invention rather than the first to invent. See P. Hubert, 'The Prior User Right of H.R. 400: A Careful Balancing of Competing Interests' (1998) 14 *Santa Clara Computer & High Tech LJ* 189; Symposium (1996) 36 *IDEA* 345.

[223] Paris, Art. 4(B), leaves such matters to the domestic legislation of contracting states. See R. Rohrback, 'Prior User Rights: Roses or Thorns?' (1993) 2 *U Balt IPJ* 1; N. Marterer, 'The Prior User's Right' (1990) 21 *IIC* 521.

[224] *Helitune v. Stewart Hughes* [1991] *FSR* 171, 206.

[225] The latter modification may be required to prevent the provision being contrary to Art. 28 EC (ex Art. 30 of the Treaty), as interpreted in *EC Commission v. United Kingdom*, Case C-30/90 [1993] *RPC* 283, [1992] 2 *CMLR* 709, [1992] *ECR* I–829. There is no EU harmonization of this issue. See L. Osterborg, 'Towards a Harmonized Prior User Right within the Common Market Patent System' (1981) 12 *IIC* 447; J. Neukom, 'A Prior Use Right for the Community Patent Convention' [1990] *EIPR* 165; J. Neukom, 'A Prior Use Right for the Community Patent Convention: An Update' [1991] *EIPR* 139.

[226] Subject to the 'springboard principle', the action for breach of confidence might not be available once the employee's patent is published, so it is important that the ex-employee cannot rely on the s. 64 defence. See Chapter 44, section 5.2, pp. 1215–17.

[227] *Lubrizol Corporation v. Esso Petroleum* [1998] *RPC* 727 (CA), 770; *Helitune* [1991] *FSR* 171 (serious and effective preparations required more than general research into the same field).

infringing use.[228] Because the 'past secret use' defence is a personal defence, the continued use must be by the same person (or partner). The exact scope of the act is therefore
crucial. The defence is not available to a defendant who does a thing that is wholly different in nature. This would mean, for example, where the previous use was in relation to a
process, that the previous user would not be able to use the defence for acts carried out
(after grant) in relation to products of the process.[229] It is important to note that some
variation is allowed between the previous use and the alleged infringing act;[230] the difficult question is: how much of a variation is possible?

If the act or preparations were done in the course of business, the previous user has the
right to authorize the doing of the act by their business partners at that time. They also
have the right to assign that right or to transmit it on death to any person who acquires
the part of the business in the course of which the act was done or the preparations were
made.[231] Importantly, the defence does not extend to include licensees.[232]

4.4 DEFENCES FOR BIOTECHNOLOGICAL INVENTIONS

As a part of the regime dealing with biotechnological inventions, three new defences to
the infringement of patents for biotechnological inventions have been formulated. These
are set out in Articles 10 and 11 of the Biotechnology Directive and in changes made to
the Patents Act 1977 by the Patents Regulations 2000.

4.4.1 Exhaustion of biological patents

Article 10/paragraph 10 of Schedule A2 provide that the protection conferred by a patent
shall not extend to biological material obtained from the propagation or multiplication
of biological material placed on the market by the owner of the patent (or with their consent) where the multiplication or propagation necessarily results from the application for
which the biological material was marketed.[233] This is subject to the proviso that the material obtained is not subsequently used for other types of propagation or multiplication.

In effect, Article 10 introduces a specific form of exhaustion for biological patents. For the
patent rights to be exhausted under Article 10, it is necessary to establish that the multiplication or propagation (which potentially infringes the patent) is 'an incident of what might be
called the true purpose of the sale'.[234] The upshot of this is that a person who used a patented
yeast to make beer would, on its face, infringe the patent in the yeast. This is because the
process of making the beer necessarily involves the multiplication of the yeast. However, if
the patented yeast was sold in a home-brew shop for the purpose of beer making, Article 10
(and its British equivalent) would provide the defendant with a 'defence'. Nonetheless, if the
defendant was to propagate the yeast and offer it for sale, the defence would not apply.[235] The
defence will allow farmers to sow a patented seed, and to harvest and sell the resulting crop
(for example to sell the wheat for flour); they will not be permitted, however, to sell the seed
to other farmers for the purpose of propagating new crops.[236]

---

[228] *Hadley Industries v. Metal Sections* (unreported, 13 November 1998) (Pat).   [229] Ibid.

[230] *Helitune v. Stewart Hughes* [1991] *FSR* 171, 206; *Lubrizol v. Esso Petroleum* [1992] *RPC* 281, 295, [1998]
RPC 727 (CA).

[231] PA 1977, s. 64(2), provides an equivalent to exhaustion when a previous user disposes of the product.
The person who acquires the product is entitled to deal with the product in the same way as if it had been
disposed of by a sole registered proprietor.   [232] PA 1977, s. 64(3).

[233] As set out in Biotech. Dir. Arts 8 and 9; PA 1977, Sch. A2, paras 7–9. These were discussed in
section 2.2.5, pp. 646–7.

[234] See S. Bostyn, 'Patentability of Genetic Information Carriers' [1999] *IPQ* 1, 30.   [235] Ibid.

[236] R. Nott, 'You Did It: The European Biotechnology Directive at Last' [1998] *EIPR* 347, 349.

4.4.2 Farmers' privilege

In the debates surrounding the Biotechnology Directive, one of the fears raised was that patent protection of biological inventions would have a negative impact on traditional farming practices. In particular, it was feared that patent protection would mean that farmers would not be able to use the seeds that they harvested from their crops to resow in future, nor would they be able to breed patented animals. The potential problem was that sowing and breeding carried out in relation to a patented product would infringe. To remedy problems of this sort, Article 11(1) and (2) of the Biotechnology Directive provide farmers with specific defences. These provisions have been mirrored in section 60(5)(g) and (h) of the Patent Act 1977, introduced under the Patents Regulations 2000.

Section 60(5)(g) provides a defence where a farmer uses the product of their harvest for propagation or multiplication by them on their farm after there has been a sale or other form of commercialization of plant-propagating material to the farmer by the patent owner for agricultural use. In effect, the defence enables farmers to save seeds from one year's crop to sow crops in the following year. The defence in section 60(5)(g) only applies to the plant species and groups set out in paragraph 2 of Schedule A1 to the Patents Act 1977. This covers various types of fodder plant, cereal, potato, and oil and fibre plant. In situations where a farmer successfully relies on the defence in section 60(5)(g), the farmer must pay the relevant rights holder equitable remuneration.[237] The remuneration must be 'sensibly lower than the amount charged for the production of the protected material of the same variety on the same area with the holder's authority'.[238] The need to pay equitable remuneration does not arise if a farmer can prove that they are a 'small farmer'.[239] Where requested, the rights holder and the farmer must supply each other with certain information.[240] The use of the defence is subject to a number of other restrictions (such as ability of the farmer to move protected material from their farm).

Section 60(5)(h) provides farmers with a defence in relation to the breeding of animals. More specifically, it provides that 'the use of an animal or animal reproductive material by a farmer for an agricultural purpose . . . of breeding stock or other animal reproductive material which constitutes or contains the patented invention' is non-infringing. The farmer's defence for the breeding of animals is potentially very broad. In part, the scope of the defence will depend on how the phrase 'use for an agricultural purpose' is construed. The Act tells us that 'use for an agricultural purpose' includes situations in which the animal or animal reproductive material is made available for the purposes of pursuing the farmer's agricultural activity; it does not include 'sale within the framework, or for the purposes of a commercial reproduction activity'.[241]

It will be interesting to see what impact these defences have upon farming practices. It will also be interesting to see how the biotechnology industry responds to these defences. It has been suggested that defences such as those provided in section 60(5)(g)–(h) may act as a stimulus for the development of techniques such as terminator genes or special hybrids that operate to ensure that seeds will not regerminate.[242]

---

[237] PA 1977, Sch. A1, para. 3(1) (introduced by Patents Regs 2000).
[238] PA 1977, Sch. A1, para. 3(3) (introduced by Patents Regs 2000), says that a remuneration will be sensibly lower if it would be 'sensibly lower within the meaning of Art. 14(3) third indent of the Council Regulation on Community plant variety rights'.
[239] PA 1977, Sch. A1, para. 4(1)–(2) (introduced by Patents Regs 2000). A 'small farmer' is defined via Art. 14(3), third indent of the Council Regulation on Community plant variety rights.
[240] PA 1977, Sch. A1, paras 5–11 (introduced by Patents Regs 2000).
[241] PA 1977, s. 60(6B)(a)(b). Sale is defined to include any other form of commercialization: PA 1977, s. 60(6C).
[242] R. Nott, 'You Did It: The European Biotechnology Directive at Last' [1998] *EIPR* 347, 349 n. 27.

4.5 MISCELLANEOUS DEFENCES

A number of other exceptions to infringement exist. Section 74(1)(a) expressly provides that the validity of a patent may be put in issue by way of a defence to proceedings for infringement. This is the most commonly used defence: an alleged infringer will normally argue that the patent is invalid because the invention lacks novelty or is obvious. A particular example of this is the so-called 'Gillette defence',[243] where a defendant attempts to demonstrate that the infringing activity was being carried out in public before the priority date of the patent, thus forcing the patentee either to require the patent to be interpreted so as to exclude the activity or to accept that the patent covers the activity and is therefore invalid (for want of novelty).

A defence is available where a person in a pharmacy makes an extempore preparation of a medicine in accordance with a prescription.[244] A defence also exists where products or processes are used on ships, aircraft, hovercraft, or vehicles that have temporarily or accidentally entered UK airspace or waters.[245] The Crown has a broad immunity from infringing the exclusive rights of patentees.[246] The Crown may use an invention without obtaining a licence in advance, so long as it pays compensation. More specifically, the defence permits 'any government department and any person authorized in writing by a government department' to do certain acts,[247] in return for which the department must provide payment,[248] including 'compensation' for loss of profits.[249] In some cases, the doctrines of exhaustion of rights and implied licence, reviewed earlier, also (effectively) provide defences to accusations of infringement.

Prior to the passage of the Competition Act 1998, section 44 of the 1977 Act provided a defence where a patentee imposed a requirement on a licensee:

> . . . to acquire from the licensor or his nominee, or prohibit him from acquiring from any specified person, or from acquiring except from the licensor or his nominee, anything other than the product which is the patented invention or (if it is a process) other than any product obtained directly by means of the process or to which the process has been applied.

The defence was available to any person against whom the licensor brought an infringement action.[250] Section 44, which was widely criticized, was repealed by the Competition Act 1998.[251]

---

[243] A defence that is based on the arguments before the House of Lords in *Gillette Safety Razor Company v. Anglo-American Trading Company Ltd* [1913] 30 *RPC* 465 (HL).

[244] PA 1977, s. 60(5)(c).

[245] PA 1977, s. 60(5)(d)(e). See *Stena Rederi v. Irish Ferries* [2003] *RPC* 668 (CA). A ship that sailed between Dublin and Holyhead in the United Kingdom three or four times a day (each visit, the ship was in UK waters for about three hours), was held to have temporarily entered the United Kingdom. Here, 'temporarily' meant 'transient' or 'for a limited period of time', rather than the frequency of the visits. See further R. Sharma and H. Forrest, 'A Lifeline for Infringing Ships' [2003] *EIPR* 430.   [246] PA 1977, s. 55.

[247] Listed in PA 1977, s. 55(1)(a)–(e).

[248] PA 1977, s. 55(4). An exception, in which case no royalty need be paid, operates under PA 1977, s. 55(3).

[249] PA 1977, s. 57A.   [250] PA 1977, s. 44(3).

[251] See The Competition Act 1998 (Transitional, Consequential and Supplemental Provisions) Order 2000 (SI 2000/311) for transitional provisions.

23

EXPLOITATION

1 INTRODUCTION

As forms of personal property,[1] patents and patent applications may be assigned, licensed, or mortgaged, and they may devolve by operation of law (notably through death or bankruptcy).[2] One of the consequences of this is that patents have become part of the commercial currency; they can be traded, exploited, and included on the balance sheet of companies. As such, patent exploitation is a central aspect of the patent system. The importance of the way in which patents are exploited has taken on a new significance in recent years, as increased attention is given to the question of how innovative modes of exploitation might be used to achieve non-commercial goals, such as improving food security and the accessibility of science, particularly for biotechnological research.[3]

The terms and conditions that control the way in which patents are exploited are usually determined contractually by the parties: patent law merely provides a framework within which parties are able to manoeuvre. Where parties have agreed upon the way a patent is to be exploited, the law has been reluctant to interfere with the sanctity of the contract. There are some situations, however, in which this is not the case. Apart from the general vitiating factors of contract law (such as unreasonable restraint of trade), special provisions exist in the Patents Act 1977 in relation to co-owners,[4] employee inventions, and (at least until recently) certain types of contractual terms. Competition law, both domestic and European, also places important limits upon the nature and content of transactions entered into by a patentee. In recognition of the fact that non-use of a patent may produce undesirable consequences, in certain situations the law may order a patent owner to grant a licence to work the invention.

This chapter is divided into four parts. First, we consider the various ways in which patents may be exploited. We then look at some of the limits that are imposed on the way in which patents are exploited to minimize any possible anti-competitive effects. We then examine situations in which compulsory licences are available (for example where a patent is not used or is underused). Finally, we look at the compensation payable where the patent is used via a compulsory licence, as well as when an employer or the Crown uses the invention.

---

[1] PA 1977, s. 30(1); although it is not a thing in action (it is therefore a *sui generis* type of property).

[2] PA 1977, s. 30(3).

[3] J. Hope, *Bio Bazaar: Biotechnology and the Open Space Revolution* (2008); S. Dusollier, 'Sharing Access to Intellectual Property through Private Ordering' (2007) 82 *Chi-Kent L Rev* 1391; J. D'Silva, 'Pools, Thickets and Open Source Nanotechnology' [2009] *EIPR* 300.   [4] PA 1977, s. 36(3), (7).

2 MODES OF EXPLOITATION

In this section, we examine some of the ways patents are exploited. After considering the situation in which patentees exploit the patent themselves, we look at some of the more common forms of voluntary uses—namely, assignment and licence. We then turn to consider situations where the patent is exploited by way of a compulsory licence or a licence as of right.

2.1 EXPLOITATION BY THE OWNER

In many cases, the owner of a patent may decide to manufacture or use the patented invention themselves. While in most cases self-exploitation presents few legal problems, difficulties may arise when the patent is owned by a number of different parties. The most significant issue that arises here is whether one co-owner is able to practise the invention without the consent of the other co-owners. In some cases, the conditions of use will be dealt with contractually between the parties. As well as setting out the way each of the co-owners is able to exploit the patent, ideally such a contract should also specify the obligations that the parties have to each other. In situations in which there is no contract between co-owners of a patent,[5] the Patents Act 1977 declares that each of the co-owners is entitled to work the invention[6]—that is, each owner is permitted to use and benefit from their undivided share of the patent.[7] The possibility for opportunistic behaviour that this presents is limited by the fact that a joint owner cannot license others to use the patent without the permission of the other co-owners.[8]

2.2 ASSIGNMENT

A common way in which patented products and processes are exploited is for the owner to assign their interests to another party.[9] An assignment is a transfer of ownership of the patent (or application). As a result of an assignment, an assignee stands in the shoes of the assignor and is entitled to deal with the patent as they see fit. In contrast to a licence (where the licensor retains an interest in the patent), once a patentee has assigned the patent, they no longer have any interest in, or responsibility to maintain, the patent.[10]

For an assignment to be valid,[11] it must be in writing and signed by or on behalf of the assignor.[12] Where the patent or application is owned by more than one party, for the

---

[5] A patent may be co-owned where the invention is a product of joint inventorship, or as a result of dealings with a patent that was initially solely owned, such as an assignment to two persons.

[6] PA 1977, s. 36. The PA 2004 amended PA 1977, s. 36(3), to clarify that co-owners are able to seek, amend, and revoke a patent if they act jointly and have not contracted out of this requirement. Disputes between co-owners may be resolved via PA 1977, s. 37. See R. Merges and L. Locke, 'Co-ownership of Patents: A Comparative and Economic View' (1990) 72 *JPTOS* 586.

[7] The general rule is that co-owners are entitled to equal undivided shares, unless there is an agreement to the contrary: PA 1977, s 36(1).

[8] *Henry Brothers v. Ministry of Defence* [1997] *RPC* 693; cf. M. Anderson, 'Applying Traditional Property Laws to Intellectual Property Transactions' [1995] *EIPR* 236, 240.   [9] PA 1977, s 30(2); s 31(2) (Scotland).

[10] The assignor once comes under a personal disability in that they may not challenge the validity of the assigned patent: *Chambers v. Crichley* (1864) 33 *Beav* 374, 55 *ER* 412 (assignor prohibited from challenging validity of patent on basis of non-derogation from grant). But see A. Robertson, 'Is the Licensee Estoppel Rule Still Good Law? Was It Ever?' [1991] *EIPR* 373.

[11] In respect of a European patent application, it is necessary for the transaction to be signed by all parties: EPC, Art. 72.

[12] PA 1977, s. 30(6). Differently worded, but largely equivalent, provisions for Scotland are set out in PA 1977, s. 31. An oral assignment might take effect as an agreement to assign and be enforceable in equity: *Stewart v. Case* (1891) 8 *RPC* 259, (1892) 9 *RPC* 9.

assignment to be valid, all of the co-owners must consent to the assignment.[13] While assignments need not be registered to be valid, certain advantages flow from registration, and we review these.[14]

2.3 VOLUNTARY LICENCES

Another common way in which patents are exploited is by licence. A licence provides a party with permission to do an act that would otherwise be prohibited. Licences may be made orally or in writing,[15] and may be express or implied.[16] Where a patent is owned jointly, all of the co-owners must provide their consent for the licence to be valid.[17] In contrast with an assignment, no proprietary interest is passed under a licence.[18]

Licences may take many forms—from a one-off permission, through to an exclusive licence. An exclusive licence is an agreement under which the owner of a patent not only grants the licensee permission to use the patented technology, but also promises that they will not grant any other licences, nor exploit the technology themselves. The legal consequence of this is that an exclusive licence confers rights upon the licensee to the exclusion of all others, including the licensor.[19]

While the grant of an exclusive licence is very similar to an assignment,[20] an exclusive licence does not need be made in writing.[21] Indeed, as with other licences, an exclusive licence may be made orally or in writing,[22] and may be express or implied.[23] While a 'bare licensee' acquires the right not to be sued in relation to the acts set out in the licence,[24] an exclusive licence confers powers on the licensee that are equivalent to those of the proprietor. Undoubtedly the most significant of these is that exclusive licensees can sue infringers in their own right; they do not need to persuade the proprietor to take action on their behalf.[25] Non-exclusive licences, which are a very common way of exploiting patents, take many forms and one particular form for patents for essential standards is discussed later.

2.3.1 Common licence conditions

(i) Field of use restriction

A licence may only grant a person a right to use the patented invention in relation to a particular type of product. Thus, an invention might work with both fan heaters and

---

[13] PA 1977, s. 36(3), (7). For a situation in which the (then) Patent Office ordered an assignment of a patent where one of seven co-owners was opposed to the agreement, see *Florey's Patent* [1962] *RPC* 186.

[14] See section 2.6, p. 680.   [15] *Crossley v. Dixon* (1863) 10 *HLC* 293.

[16] See *Morton-Norwich v. Intercen and United Chemicals (No. 2)* [1981] *FSR* 337. A voluntary and exclusive licence is granted 'under' and not 'in' a patent, therefore PA 1977, s. 30(6), does not apply: *Instituform v. Inliner* [1992] *RPC* 83; *CIPA*, [30.05].   [17] PA 1977, s. 36(3), (7).

[18] *Allen & Hanbury v. Generics* [1986] *RPC* 203, 246. A licence itself can be dealt with: PA 1977, s. 30(4)(a).

[19] PA 1977, s 130(1); cf. *Peaudouce SA v. Kimberly Clark* [1996] *FSR* 680, 690–1.

[20] There are a number of differences between an assignment and an exclusive licence. For example, while an assignment of a patent must be in writing, an assignment of an exclusive licence need not: *Instituform v. Inliner* [1992] *RPC* 83. In addition, note the weak position of the exclusive licensee in relation to the compulsory licence-of-right provisions operating in relation to the extension of patent terms: *Kaken Pharmaceutical Patent* [1990] *RPC* 72.

[21] Cf. the position in relation to copyright: CDPA 1988, s. 92 (exclusive licences must be in writing); *Morton-Norwich v. Intercen and United Chemicals* [1981] *FSR* 337.

[22] *Crossley v. Dixon* (1863) 10 *HLC* 293.   [23] *Morton-Norwich* [1981] *FSR* 337.

[24] A bare licence is simply permission to do what is otherwise unlawful: *Thomas v. Sorrell* (1673) *Vaugh* 330, 124 *ER* 1098.

[25] PA 1977, s. 67. The proprietor is made party to the proceedings, if necessary by joining them as a defendant.

cooling fans, but the licence may restrict the licensee to using the invention with cooling fans only.[26]

(ii) Territorial restrictions

A patent can be licensed for the whole or part of the United Kingdom. It is therefore possible to license a person to only use a patented process in Scotland or to only make the patent product at a particular factory in Birmingham. However, territorial restrictions on the disposal (sale) of products made under such a licence are at risk of being anti-competitive and so contrary to Article 101 of TFEU.

(iii) 'Best endeavours'/'reasonable endeavours' clauses

Licences may include an obligation on the licensee to use the licensee's best endeavours (or reasonable endeavours) to do certain things, such as maximize sales of licensed products.[27] Where a royalty is dependent on profits being made, turnover of product or units being sold, a requirement to work an invention is important protection for patentees, particularly where an exclusive licence is granted. It is the only way the licensor can ensure that it makes money.

Terrell v. Mabie Todd & Co Ltd[28] gives the traditional meaning of 'best endeavours' within the context of intellectual property. The agreement contained clauses requiring the licensees to use 'all diligence' to promote sales of the inventions and designs, and to use their 'best endeavours' to exploit the invention and design. The meaning of best endeavours was relaxed by the Court of Appeal in *IBM United Kingdom Ltd v. Rockware Glass Ltd*[29] as it was described as:

> [best endeavours mean a person is] bound to take all those steps in their power which are capable of producing the desired results … being steps which a prudent, determined and reasonable owner, acting in his own interests and desiring to achieve that result, would take.

(iv) Most favoured licensee clauses

A term which requires a licensor to offer an existing licensee the same (favourable) terms as a new licensee can be important, but a mechanism for the existing licensee to be notified and a procedure for those terms to be incorporated may be needed to make such a term effective.

For example, A contracts with B at a 3 per cent royalty. A then negotiates with C. C can require disclosure of the existing licence fees being paid before contracting. If C, knowing of A's royalty, accepts a royalty of 4 per cent then this is a commercial decision. However, if A offers C a 2 per cent royalty and B is bound to a 3 per cent royalty then C can undersell B and there is nothing B can do about it. Accordingly, a most favoured licensee clause enables B to be entitled to get no worse terms than C (or any subsequent licensee).

(v) Duty to account and allowing auditing of records

It is a common term in a licence to require the licensee to produce accounts and to allow the licensee to inspect them. Such a requirement may also allow a licensor to query whether the books offered for inspection are the only relevant ones and he or she may

---

[26] A field of use restriction may be seen as anti-competitive for dividing the market: see *Windsurfing International* [1983] L 229/1; upheld: *Wind-surfing International v. Commission*, Case 193/83 [1986] *ECR* 611.

[27] What the endeavours must be directed towards must be sufficiently certain to be enforceable: *R & D Construction Group Limited v. Hallam Land Management*, 2011 *SC* 287, [37].

[28] (1952) 69 *RPC* 234 (Terrell was a well-known patent lawyer who wrote the then leading patent text of the day). [29] [1980] *FSR* 335.

demand that other books be produced where there is reason to believe they contain relevant information. In general, however, a contractual term that a licensee will render accounts is generally auxiliary to the covenant to pay a royalty and so the failure to provide the accounts will usually lead to the termination of the licence.[30]

(vi) Requirement to bring or defend proceedings for infringement

Where a clause requires a licensor to take reasonable steps to prevent infringement, the licensor must take the steps a reasonably energetic patentee would take to protect what he or she thought was a valuable patent.[31]

(vii) No challenge clauses

A licensor sometimes tries to include a condition in the licence that the licensee will not challenge the validity of the patent (a no challenge clause). The validity of these is usually a matter of competition law,[32] but where they do not offend competition law they are enforceable.[33]

2.3.2 Standard Essential Patents

An important example of a non-exclusive licence are those granted by patent holders who participate in standard-setting arrangements. One example would be the mobile telephone standards established by the European Telecommunication Standardization Institute (ETSI). ETSI will only consider the adoption of a patented technology as part of a standard if the patentee can show that they license the technology on FRAND terms. Another emerging licensing practice is the grant of 'open licences' allowing subsequent researchers to use patented material on the condition that they apply similar terms to any improvements. One example of such a licence is that offered in the field of agricultural biotechnology, known as the 'Biological Innovation for Open Society agreement'. A similar approach has been adopted in relation to so-called 'humanitarian' licences, which allow a patentee to exploit their innovations in developed countries, but not in developing countries. Such clauses are increasingly being used by philanthropic funding agencies, particularly where the research is conducted by public–private consortiums.

These sorts of agreements create particular, and unusual, issues. There are sometimes issues whether a particular patent is used in a particular standard, and declarations of non-infringement have been used for determining this question.[34] Once it is clear that a patent needs to be licensed for a particular standard to be used, the patentee may be asked to provide an undertaking to only license the technology on so called 'fair, reasonable and non-discriminatory terms' (FRAND); absent such an undertaking being forthcoming the standard would not be adopted using that technology. The benefits of these licences were summarized by Birss J in *Unwired Planet v. Huawei*:[35]

> The point of FRAND in standard setting is fairly easy to understand. Standards exist so that different manufacturers can produce equipment which is interoperable with the result that the manufacturers compete with one another. So the phone makers compete in the market for phones and the public can select a phone from any supplier and be sure (for example) that if it is a 4G phone, it will work with any 4G network. As a society we want the best, most up to date technology to be incorporated into the latest standards and

---

[30] *Bower v. Hodges* (1853) 13 *CB* 765, 75–6, 138 *ER* 1402, 1407.
[31] *Splendor Gloeilampen Fabrieken NV v. Omega Lampworks Ltd* (1933) 50 *RPC* 393, 404.
[32] See section 3, pp. 682–4.   [33] *Apple Corp. Ltd v. Apple Computer Inc.* [1992] *FSR* 431.
[34] See Chapter 48, section 2.2, pp. 1284–6.
[35] [2017] *EWHC* 2988 (Pat), [83] (this judgment was handed down in a redacted form as [2017] *EWHC* 711(Pat)).

that will involve incorporating patented inventions. While the inventor must be entitled to a fair return for the use of their invention, in order for the standard to permit interoperability the inventor must not be able to prevent others from using the patented invention incorporated in the standard as long as implementers take an appropriate licence and pay a fair royalty. In this way a balance is struck, in the public interest, between the inventor and the implementers. The appropriate licence is one which is fair, reasonable and non-discriminatory. That way a standard can safely incorporate the invention claimed in a patent without giving the inventor or his successors in title unwarranted power over those who implement the standard. Thus the public interest is served because telecommunication standards can be set using the best and most up-to-date technical expedients available and the inventor's private interest is served because the FRAND undertaking ensures they or their successors will obtain a fair reward for their invention.

Yet the assessment of how to calculate what constitutes FRAND terms remains somewhat unclear, at least in Europe.[36] When FRAND terms are set there should be a single set of FRAND terms based on what a truly willing licensor and truly willing licensee would have agreed on in the particular circumstances.[37] The terms are not conjured out of thin air, but rather comparable rates and agreements are used to set the rate (in the same way that patent damages are set).[38]

Additionally, issues have arisen in relation to competition law. For instance, many standards agreements involve the formation of so called patent pools—that is an agreement where patentees agree to cross-license their patents for mutual benefit and, sometimes, to agree that third parties can license the entire portfolio in a single transaction. These arrangements potentially raise issues under both Article 101 and 102 of TFEU[39] and the Commission has set out strict guidance on how to decide which patents are included in the pool and which are not.[40] Difficulties can also arise where, despite a FRAND undertaking, a potential licensee disagrees that the fee is not FRAND compliant. This raises the issue of whether it is permissible for a proprietor of a standards essential patent to then bring infringement proceedings. In *Huawei v. ZTE*[41] the Court of Justice held that such a patentee can bring infringement proceedings provided that the patentee has notified the alleged infringer of the activity first and the alleged infringer has not, reasonably diligently, agreed to accept a licence which is FRAND compliant.

2.4 MORTGAGES

Like other forms of property, patents may be mortgaged (or assigned as security for a debt).[42] This can be a useful technique to enable patentees to raise the funds necessary to exploit the patented invention. In this context, a mortgage is achieved by way of an

---

[36] K. Henningsson, 'Injunctions for Standard Essential Patents under FRAND Commitment: A Balanced, Royalty-Oriented Approach' (2016) 47 *IIC* 438, 448–49; in the United States, see *TCL Communications v. Telefonaktiebologet LM Ericsson* (21 December 2017, CD Cal) for a US approach to setting FRAND damages.

[37] *Unwired Planet International Ltd v. Huawei Technologies Co. Ltd and anor* [2017] *EWHC* 2988 (Pat), [156].

[38] *Unwired Planet International Ltd v. Huawei Technologies Co. Ltd and anor* [2017] EWHC 2988 (Pat), [169]; as to damages, see Chapter 49, section 5, p. 1340.

[39] See Roughton, Johnson, and Cook, [21.114–21.127].

[40] See Guidelines on the application of Article 101 of the Treaty on the Functioning of the European Union to technology transfer agreements [2014] *OJ* C89/3, [244–273].

[41] Case 170/13, EU:C:2015:477.

[42] A mortgage includes a charge for securing money or money's worth: PA 1977, s. 130(1). See M. Bezant and R. Punt, *The Use of Intellectual Property as Security for Debt Finance* (1997); D. Townend, *Using Intellectual Property as Security* (1996); M. Henry, 'Mortgages of Intellectual Property in the United Kingdom' [1992] *EIPR* 158.

assignment of the patent by the patentee-mortgagor to the mortgagee-lender. This is subject to a condition that the patent will be reassigned to the mortgagor when the debt is repaid (or, as the law says, 'on redemption'). It is important that the assignment reserves for the mortgagor a right to continue practising the invention. This is probably best achieved by the reservation of an exclusive licence. Alternatively, a patent can be used as security by way of a legal charge, in which case there is no assignment.[43] In this case, the chargee gains certain rights over the patent as security.

In order to be valid, a mortgage must be in writing and signed by the parties.[44] Where there are joint proprietors, all of them must consent to the mortgage.[45] A mortgage need not be registered at the Intellectual Property Office to be valid, but there are advantages to registration, which are reviewed later. Furthermore, where the mortgage or security relates to a patent owned by a company it is necessary to register it at Companies House.[46]

2.5 TESTAMENTARY DISPOSITIONS

Because a patent is personal property, it is capable of passing on the death of the proprietor either by will or via the rules of intestacy. Co-owners hold patents as tenants in common (rather than as joint tenants).[47] This means that if a co-proprietor dies, their share passes along with the rest of the estate, rather than accruing to the other co-owners. In the absence of any successors it passes to the Crown as bona vacantia (and the Crown has a policy of not paying renewal fees so the patent lapses). In devolving the patent, the personal representative must sign a written consent.[48]

2.6 REGISTRATION OF INTERESTS AND TRANSACTIONS

There is no need for transactions to be registered in order for them to be valid. Nonetheless, the Patents Act 1977 provides that assignments, mortgages, licences, sub-licences, and certain equitable interests may be registered.[49] While non-registration will not affect the validity of transactions made in relation to a patent, there are two reasons why a transaction should be registered.

The first is that registration gives the registrant priority against anyone who has an earlier unregistered right, subject to the proviso that the registrant had no notice of the earlier right.[50] In so doing, registration helps to allocate priorities between the parties who have interests in a patent. The act of registration enables a person with an interest to secure priority over those who engage in subsequent transactions. The effect of this can be illustrated as follows.

(i)   On 1 July 2017, X assigns their patent to Y. On 1 August 2017, X licenses the patent to Z. At the time of the licence, Y had not registered the assignment, nor did Z have any knowledge of the assignment to Y. On being informed by Y of their interest, Z registered their licence on 1 September 2017. In this case, Y is bound by Z's licence.[51]

---

[43] Charges are included within the definition of mortgage in PA 1977, s. 130.   [44] PA 1977, s. 30(6).

[45] PA 1977, s. 36(3).   [46] Companies Act 2006, s. 859A to 859H.

[47] On an attempt to alter this (which failed), see *Florey's Patent* [1962] *RPC* 72.   [48] PA 1977, s. 30(6)(b).

[49] PA 1977, ss 32–3.

[50] The relevant date on which to assess whether the registrant knew of the right is the date on which the later registrant acquired their interest. Both the fact of registration and the knowledge of the party are assessed at the time of the transaction (which is registered), not the date of registration.

[51] It is possible, but yet to be decided, whether the rule *nemo dat quod non habet* trumps the priority rules on the register.

(ii) On 1 July 2017, X grants an exclusive licence to Y, which Y duly registers on 15 July 2017. On 1 August, X grants another licence to Z. Y can sue Z if Z attempts to exercise the 'rights' that they were purportedly granted.

(iii) X grants a mortgage of their patent to Y. Z, aware that Y has not registered the mortgage, obtains an exclusive licence from X, which Z immediately registers. Y's mortgage binds Z.

The second reason why registration is advisable is because in the case of assignments and exclusive licences, non-registration may affect a party's right to costs.[52] This is because a proprietor or exclusive licensee who does not register within six months—unless it was not practicable to register within that period—of the transaction cannot claim costs in relation to actions for infringements that occurred within the period prior to registration.[53] Given that an infringement action might relate to acts of a defendant that occur during a period extending both before and after registration, courts can be faced with some difficult questions of apportionment.

2.7 LICENCES OF RIGHT

A patentee who is willing to license the technology to all comers may take advantage of the facility that allows them to put a note on the register that licences are to be available as of right.[54] Once a 'licences of right' note is entered on the register, anyone is able to apply for a licence and establish the scope of the licence that they desire (whether it be to manufacture, sell, or import the invention). There are three reasons why a patentee might want to render a patent subject to licences as of right: (i) the endorsement of a licence of right acts as an advertisement that the owner of the patent is willing to grant licences to parties who wish to exploit the invention; (ii) such an endorsement halves the renewal fees payable; and (iii) it precludes any finding of anti-competitive behaviour.

One of the consequences of making licences available as of right is that the patentee is no longer able to dictate who can exercise the patent, nor control the terms of such licences. The terms of any licence are set by the parties or, if they cannot agree, by the Comptroller. The courts have accepted that they have a wide discretion in the determination of terms.[55] When deciding the terms under which the licences should be exercised, the courts have taken into account the guidelines provided for the grant of compulsory licences.[56] A patentee who has previously rendered a patent subject to 'licences of right' can apply to the Comptroller for cancellation of the entry. If accepted, the patentee must pay the balance of all the renewal fees (i.e. the other half of the renewal fees excused during the time the entry was made). Applications to remove the entry may be opposed.[57]

2.8 COMPULSORY LICENCES

The final mode of exploitation worth noting is the compulsory licence. A compulsory licence is a licence compulsorily imposed on the patentee. In contrast to a licence of right,

---

[52] A previous incarnation of the section, which prevented the patentee from claiming damages or an account of profits for the relevant period, was described as intended to protect infringers: *Mölnlycke AB v. Procter & Gamble* [1992] *FSR* 549, 606–10.

[53] PA 1977, s. 68; as to how it works see *Schütz (UK) v. Werit (UK)* [2013] *RPC* 395, [97] to [107].

[54] On the history, see *Allen & Hanbury v. Generics* [1986] *RPC* 203, 246.

[55] *Cabot Safety Corp.'s Patent* [1992] *RPC* 39. In that case, the tribunal made decisions about to whom the licence should be granted.

[56] PA 1977, s. 50. See, e.g., *Smith Kline & French Laboratories (Cimetidine) Patents* [1990] *RPC* 203, 250.

[57] PA 1977, s. 47.

which is usually initiated voluntarily, the decision as to whether a compulsory licence should be granted, and if so, the terms on which it is to be granted, is made by the relevant tribunals. We deal with the situations in which compulsory licences may be granted in more detail later.[58]

3 LIMITS ON EXPLOITATION: ANTI-COMPETITIVE BEHAVIOUR

A number of limits are imposed on the ability of the patent owner to exploit the invention. When a patent owner exploits an invention, they must comply with the general laws and regulations. These require patent owners to respect the rights of other patentees, and to comply with health and safety, environmental regulation, product liability, and criminal laws.[59] While these non-economic restrictions on patent exploitation should not be neglected, our particular concern here is with the potentially anti-competitive effects of patent exploitation. There are three areas of law that minimize the potential for patent misuse—namely, British patent law, British competition law, and EU competition law.

3.1 BRITISH PATENT LAW

For most of its long history, patent law has used various techniques to minimize the potential for abuse that a patent monopoly confers. These have included rules prohibiting the use of certain terms in patent licences,[60] as well as provisions permitting the use of patented inventions by third parties where the patent was being underused or misused by the patentee. Despite this long tradition, it was decided that it was more appropriate for the potential abuse of patents to be regulated by competition law than by patent law. This farming out of patent regulation took place when the draconian provisions of sections 44 and 45 of the Patents Act 1977 were repealed by section 70 of the Competition Act 1998.

3.2 BRITISH COMPETITION LAW

The introduction of the Competition Act 1998 marked an important change in the way British law regulated anti-competitive behaviour.[61] The Act establishes a system that parallels European competition law. It does this by enacting a prohibition (the 'Chapter I prohibition') that is equivalent to Article 101 of the Treaty on the Functioning of the European Union (TFEU).[62] Section 2 of the 1998 Act prohibits agreements that may affect trade within the United Kingdom and have as their object or effect the prevention, restriction, or distortion of competition within the United Kingdom.[63] It is most significant where the activity is not subject to Article 101 TFEU because they do not affect trade between member states.[64]

---

[58] See section 4, pp. 684–8.   [59] Biotech. Dir. (98/44/EC), recital 14.

[60] PA 1977, ss 44 and 45 (now repealed).

[61] S. Rose, A. Clark, and M. Burdon, 'A New UK Competition Law: More Restrictions on Restrictions' (January 1997) *Patent World* 27.

[62] This was previously Article 81, and before that Article 85 of the EC and EEC Treaty respectively.

[63] Conduct that amounts to the abuse of a dominant position in a market within the United Kingdom or a part thereof is also prohibited—known as the 'Chapter II prohibition'.

[64] Competition Act 1998, s. 10.

3.3 EU COMPETITION LAW

The key provision of EU competition law affecting patent licences and exploitation agreements is Article 101 TFEU.[65] This provides that all agreements that affect trade between member states and which have the object or effect of distorting competition within the internal market shall be void.[66] However, under certain conditions, agreements falling within Article 101(1) may be exempt from Article 101 as a result of Article 101(3). Whether a transaction is exempt depends either on an individual assessment (now made by the tribunal *ex post*) or on whether the transaction falls within the scope of a block exemption.[67] The most important block exemption for patent licences is Technology Transfer Block Exemption 2014 (TTBER) and the related Guidelines.[68] The effect of TTBER is considered in detail in specialist texts, but we will briefly outline here its scope and application to a few typical patent licence terms.

TTBER applies to technology rights, that is, know-how, patents, utility models, and supplementary protection certificates and the combination thereof (as well as designs and software copyright).[69] The TTBER only applies if the Research and Development (R&D) Block Exemption Regulation[70] or the Specialization Agreements Block Exemption Regulation[71] are not applicable. A notable feature of TTBER is that it treats agreements differently depending on whether the parties are 'competing undertakings' or 'non-competing undertakings'. 'Competing undertakings' are defined as undertakings that compete on the relevant technology market and/or the relevant product market.[72] Other undertakings are dealt with on the basis that they are non-competing. In any event, there is a threshold that parties must not cross if they are to benefit from the block exemption: the combined market share of the parties cannot exceed 20 per cent for competing undertakings or 30 per cent for non-competing undertakings.[73] Failure to remain below these market ceilings does not mean that agreements are illegal per se; rather, it simply means that they are outside the block exemption and so their compliance with Article 101(3) TFEU is judged on a case-by-case basis.

TTBER contains a series of so called 'hardcore restrictions'.[74] Where an agreement contains a hardcore restriction, it will fall outside the scope of the block exemption and thus carry the risk that the agreement (or at least part of the agreement) is void. The

---

[65] This includes agreements to settle litigation. There have been a series of cases where a defendant has paid a claimant money to withdraw litigation. Such agreements have, sometimes, been found to be anti-competitive: see *Lundbeck v. European Commission* T-472/13, EU:T:2016:449.

[66] A licence term was held to be 'incompatible with EC Art. 81 [Art. 101 TFEU] if it sought to regulate the commercial market by controlling not only what was made with the licensed technology but also the use which was made of it thereafter': *Intel Technologies v. Via Technologies* [2003] *FSR* 574, [72].

[67] Organizations have to determine for themselves whether their agreements come within the block exemptions.

[68] Commission Regulation (EU) No. 316/2014 of 21 March 2014 on the application of Article 101(3) of the Treaty on the Functioning of the European Union to categories of technology transfer agreements [2014] *OJ L* 93/17 (28 March 2014); Guidelines on the application of Article 101 of the Treaty on the Functioning of the European Union to technology transfer agreements [2014] OJ C89/3.   [69] TTBER, Art. 1(1)(b).

[70] Commission Regulation (EU) No. 1217/2010 of 14 December 2010 on the application of Article 101(3) of the Treaty to categories of research and development agreements [2000] *OJ L* 335/36 (18 December 2010).

[71] Commission Regulation (EU) No. 1218/2010 of 14 December 2010 on the application of Article 101(3) of the Treaty on the Functioning of the European Union to certain categories of specialisation agreements [2010] OJ L 335/43 (18 December 2010).

[72] TTBER, Art. 1(1)(e), (j), and (k) (which also defines 'relevant technology market' and 'relevant product market').   [73] TTBER, Art. 3(1)–(3).

[74] TTBER, Art. 4.

hardcore restraints include things like price fixing, restricting a company from using its own technology, or carrying out research and development.

In addition to hardcore restrictions, there are a list of forbidden clauses.[75] Where an agreement includes such a clause, the clause alone falls outside the block exemption. An example of a forbidden clause is a grant-backs clause—that is, provisions that require the licensee to assign to, or exclusively license, the licensor the licensee's own improvements to the licensed technology.[76]

No challenge clauses are another example of a forbidden clause.[77] This precludes any agreement which directly or indirectly obliges a party not to challenge the validity of an intellectual property right. However, a clause is allowed which permits an exclusive licence to be terminated where the licensee challenges the validity of the intellectual property right.

4 LIMITS ON NON-EXPLOITATION: COMPULSORY LICENCES

Another way in which patents can be misused is if the owner uses the patent to prevent the product from being manufactured or if demand for the product is being met from some other source. In contrast with trade mark law, there is no obligation on a patentee to work, or to intend to exploit, the invention. However, provisions exist in the form of compulsory licences that allow people other than the patent owner to exploit the invention in situations where the patentee is either unable or unwilling to do so.[78]

Compulsory licensing provisions were first introduced into British patent law at the end of the nineteenth century.[79] The law evolved during the early twentieth century to broaden the powers of compulsory licensing. These were motivated by a fear that large (often foreign) organizations that were in a dominant market position might buy up patents and decline to exploit them. There was also a concern that technical progress might be impeded by the holder of a basic patent who refused to license people to make improvements to patented inventions. In addition, there was a perceived risk that patents might be used to prevent the adequate supply of essentials, such as food or medicine.[80] While applications are now rarely made for compulsory licences,[81] it would be wrong to conclude from this that the provisions are of little effect. This is because the threat of such licences being granted may stimulate the patentee into working or voluntarily licensing the patent. Compulsory licences have become a topic of debate recently, primarily as a result of discussions at the World Trade Organization (WTO) about access to medicines in developing countries.[82]

Under the Paris Convention, members of the Paris Union are able to provide for compulsory licences 'to prevent the abuses which might result from the exercise of the exclusive rights conferred by the patent, for example, failure to work'.[83] The ability to

---

[75] TBBER, recitals (14) and (15)l   [76] TTBER, art 5(1)(a).   [77] TTBER, art 5(1)(b).

[78] See, e.g., C. Fauver, Comment, 'Compulsory Patent Licensing in the US: An Idea Whose Time Has Come' (1988) 8 *Nw J Intl L & Bus* 666.   [79] Patents, Designs and Trade Marks Act 1883, s 22.

[80] See P. Johnson, 'Access to Medicines and the Growth of the Pharmaceutical Industry in Britain', in Dinwoodie, *Methods and Perspectives in Intellectual Property* (2013), 329.

[81] Since 2000, there have been applications made in relation to four patents. Two applications were withdrawn and two were dismissed by a joint decision of the comptroller: *Swansea Imports v. Carver Technology*, O/170/04.

[82] See Chapter 14, section 4.6.2, pp. 417–19.

[83] Paris, Arts 5A(2) and 5(4).

grant compulsory licences was curtailed by Article 31 of the Agreement on Trade Related Aspects of Intellectual Property Rights 1994 (TRIPS)[84] As we will see, these changes have restricted the circumstances in which compulsory licences are available. One of the changes brought about by the TRIPS amendments is that the grounds on which a compulsory licence will be granted depend on whether the patent is owned by a WTO proprietor.

The Patents Act 1977 distinguishes between five general situations in which compulsory licences can be granted:[85]

(i)   the various grounds set out in section 48 (which in turn distinguishes between patents with WTO owners and patents with non-WTO owners);

(ii)   following a report of the Competition Commission (now, the Competition and Markets Authority);

(iii) for Crown use;

(iv)   in relation to biotechnological inventions; and

(v)   for licences granted on public health grounds.

Before looking at these in more detail, it is necessary to make some preliminary comments.

4.1 COMPULSORY LICENCES UNDER SECTION 48

The general conditions under which a compulsory licence may be issued are set out in section 48 of the Patents Act 1977. There are different approach depending on whether a WTO proprietor or a non-WTO proprietor[86] owns the patent. As we will see, the grounds on which compulsory licences will be granted are more onerous in the case of WTO owners than that of non-WTO owners.[87] Given the number of members of the WTO, it is unlikely that the more generous provisions will be used very often.

In both cases, a compulsory licence granted under section 48 is not available until three years after the grant of the patent.[88] This gives patentees a reasonable amount of time within which to exploit the invention or to arrange for others to do so.[89]

4.1.1 Compulsory licences in relation to WTO proprietors

The relevant grounds on which a compulsory licence will be granted in relation to a patent owned by a WTO proprietor are set in section 48A. Before looking at the grounds on which such a licence will be granted, it is important to note that, as with all compulsory licences, the onus is on the applicant for a licence to establish a case that the grounds relied upon apply on its face.[90] It is also important to note that a compulsory licence (for a WTO patent) will not be granted unless the applicant has made efforts to obtain a licence from the proprietor on reasonable commercial terms and conditions, and can

---

[84] This was given effect in British law by the Patents and Trade Marks (WTO) Regulations 1999 (SI 1999/1899).

[85] There have also been compulsory licences under non-patent legislation: see for instance, White Phosphorus Matches Prohibition Act 1908, s. 4.

[86] There are no significant industrialized countries which are not members of the WTO. Thus, the non-WTO proprietor rules may be seen as moribund.

[87] A proprietor is a WTO proprietor if they are a national of, or domiciled in, a country that is a WTO member, or they have a real and effective industrial or commercial establishment in such a country: PA 1977, s. 48(5)(a)–(b).   [88] PA 1977, s. 48(1); see PA 1977, s. 48B(2).

[89] Paris, Art. 5. In some cases, three years may be too little, so the Comptroller may reject an application for compulsory licences if it is considered that the patentee ought to be given more time in which to attempt to exploit the patent themselves.   [90] *Monsanto's CCP Patent* [1990] *FSR* 93, 98.

establish that their efforts have not been successful within a reasonable period.[91] In addition, compulsory licences are not available if the patented invention is within the field of semiconductor technology.[92]

A compulsory licence may be granted where:

(i)   demand in the United Kingdom for a patented product is not being met on reasonable terms;[93]

(ii)   the owner's failure to license a patent on reasonable terms has a blocking effect on later improvements[94] (in which case, the Comptroller must be satisfied that the proprietor of the patent for the later invention is 'able and willing to grant to the proprietor of the patent concerned and his licensees a licence under the patent for the other invention on reasonable terms'[95]);

(iii) the owner's failure to license a patent on reasonable terms unfairly prejudices the 'establishment or development of commercial or industrial activities in the United Kingdom';[96] or

(iv)   as a consequence of limitations imposed on the grant of licences under the patent, on the disposal or use of the patented product, or on the use of the patented process, the manufacture, use, or disposal of materials not protected by the patent, or the establishment or development of industrial activities in the United Kingdom is unfairly prejudiced.[97]

The power vested in the Comptroller to grant a compulsory licence under section 48 is discretionary. Section 50 provides a list of 'purposes' and 'factors' that the Comptroller ought to take into account when exercising this discretion.[98] The recognized purposes are that:

(i)   it is in the public interest to work an invention in the United Kingdom;[99]

(ii)   an invention should be worked 'without undue delay' and 'to the fullest extent that is reasonably practicable';[100]

(iii) the patentee should receive 'reasonable remuneration having regard to the nature of the invention';[101] and

(iv)   the interests of the person who has worked the invention ought not to be unfairly prejudiced.[102]

The factors that the Comptroller is directed to take into account include the nature of the invention, the time that has elapsed since the grant of the patent, and the measures taken by the proprietor or exclusive licensee to make full use of the patent.[103]

The grant of a compulsory licence in relation to a patent with a WTO owner is subject to the further restrictions that the licence should:

(i)   not be exclusive;

(ii)   not be assigned except to a person to whom there is also assigned the part of the enterprise that enjoys the use of the patented invention, or the part of the goodwill that belongs to that part;

[91] PA 1977, s. 48A(2).   [92] PA 1977, s. 48A(3).   [93] PA 1977, s. 48A(1)(a).

[94] PA 1977, s. 48A(1)(b)(i). It may be possible in such cases to claim that licences should be made available by the European Commission to prevent abuse of a dominant position contrary to Art. 102 EC. Laddie J's suggestion in *Philips Electronics v. Ingman* [1998] 2 *CMLR* 1185 that *Magill* might have no application to patents was rejected in *Intel v. Via* [2003] *FSR* 574. See Chapter 1, section 4.2, pp. 16–18, and Chapter 11, section 7.2, p. 316.

[95] PA 1977, s. 48A(4).   [96] PA 1977, s. 48A(1)(b)(ii).   [97] PA 1977, s. 48A(1)(c).

[98] *Monsanto's CCP Patent* [1990] *FSR* 93, 97.   [99] PA 1977, s. 50(1)(a).   [100] PA 1977, s. 50(1)(a).

[101] PA 1977, s. 50(1)(b).   [102] PA 1977, s. 50(1)(c).   [103] PA 1977, s. 50(2).

(iii) predominantly be for the supply of the market in the United Kingdom;

(iv) include conditions entitling the proprietor of the patent concerned to remuneration that is adequate in the circumstances of the case, taking into account the
economic value of the licence; and

(v) be limited in scope and in duration to the purpose for which the licence was
granted.[104]

In addition, the Act provides that compulsory licences should not be assigned except to a
person to whom the patent for the other invention is also assigned.[105]

4.1.2 Compulsory licences in relation to non-WTO proprietors

In the case of an application for a compulsory licence made in respect of a patent whose
proprietor is not a WTO proprietor,[106] the relevant grounds are set out in section 48B of
the 1977 Act.[107] These are where:

(i) the patented invention is not being commercially worked in the United Kingdom,
or is not being worked to the fullest extent that is reasonably practicable[108] (under
which head a compulsory licence will not be granted if the patented invention is
being commercially worked in a country that is a member state of the WTO and
demand in the United Kingdom is being met by import from that country);[109]

(ii) the demand for a patented product in the United Kingdom is not being met on
reasonable terms, or is being met to a substantial extent by import from a country
that is *not* a member state of the WTO;[110]

(iii) the patented invention is prevented or hindered from being commercially worked
in the United Kingdom by the import (from a country that is not a member state)
of a patented product, a product obtained directly by means of a patented process,
or to which the process has been applied;[111]

(iv) the owner's failure to license a patent on reasonable terms means that:

(v) a market for the export of any patented product made in the United Kingdom is
not being supplied;[112] or

(vi) the working or efficient working in the United Kingdom of any other patented
invention that makes a substantial contribution to the art is prevented or hindered;[113] or

---

[104] PA 1977, s. 48A(6)(a)–(e); TRIPS, Art. 31.   [105] PA 1977, s. 48A(5).

[106] A proprietor is a WTO proprietor if they are a national of, or domiciled in, a country that is a WTO
member, or they have a real and effective industrial or commercial establishment in such a country: PA 1977,
s. 48(5)(a)–(b).

[107] For discussions under the law prior to the 1999 amendments, see *Penn Engineering & Manufacturing
Corp. Patent* [1973] *RPC* 233; *Monsanto's CCP Patent* [1990] *FSR* 93, 100.   [108] PA 1977, s. 48B(1)(a).

[109] PA 1977, s. 48B(3).

[110] PA 1977, s. 48B(1)(b). These changes overcome the problem identified in *EC v. UK and Italy,* Case C-30/90
[1993] *RPC* 283. See M. Hodgson, 'Changes to UK Compulsory Patent Licensing Laws' [1992] *EIPR* 214.

[111] PA 1977, s. 48B(c).

[112] PA 1977, s. 48B(d)(i). This is subject to the proviso that a compulsory licence granted under this head
should not contain such provisions as appear to the Comptroller to be expedient for restricting the countries
in which any product concerned may be disposed of or used by the licensee: PA 1977, s. 48B(4).

[113] PA 1977, s. 48B(1)(d)(ii). The Comptroller must be satisfied that the proprietor of the patent for the
other invention is able and willing to grant to the proprietor of the patent concerned and their licensees a
licence under the patent for the other invention on reasonable terms: PA 1977, s. 48B(5).

(vii) it unfairly prejudices the establishment or development of commercial or industrial activities in the United Kingdom;[114] or

(viii) as a consequence of limitations imposed on the grant of licences under the patent, on the disposal or use of the patented product, or on the use of the patented process, the manufacture, use, or disposal of materials not protected by the patent, or the establishment or development of industrial activities in the United Kingdom is unfairly prejudiced.[115]

In deciding whether to grant a patent, the Comptroller must take into account the factors set out in section 50. The only additional limit in relation to non-WTO-owned patents arises where an application is made on the ground that the patented invention is not being commercially worked in the United Kingdom, or is not being so worked to the fullest extent that is reasonably practicable. In these cases, if, for any reason, there has been insufficient time since the publication of the patent to enable the invention to be so worked, the Comptroller may adjourn the application for a period to allow the invention to be worked.

4.2 COMPETITION AND MARKETS AUTHORITY

The third situation in which compulsory licences may be made available is where a report of the Competition and Markets Authority (CMA) concludes that an undesirable monopolistic situation exists or an anti-competitive practice is operating against the public interest.[116] The provision gives the appropriate minister the power to respond to the report by applying to the Comptroller to have the patent endorsed as a licence as of right. The application may be opposed.

4.3 CROWN USE

A special form of compulsory licence exists for the benefit of the Crown.[117] The elaborate provisions contained in sections 55–59 entitle any government department[118] and any person authorized in writing by a government department to do certain acts,[119] in return for which the department must provide payment[120] (including 'compensation for loss of profits').[121] In contrast with the compulsory licences described earlier, there is no requirement that the department needs to apply to the Comptroller (or any other authority) before acting.[122] The Crown use of a patent is only legitimate where it is done by or with authorization of 'a government department', and 'for the services of the Crown'. This is defined to include the supply of anything for foreign defence purposes, the production of specified drugs and medicines, and certain purposes relating to the production or use of

---

[114] PA 1977, s. 48B(1)(d)(iii).   [115] PA 1977, s. 48B(1)(e).

[116] PA 1977, s. 51; see TRIPS, Arts 8, 31(k), 40.

[117] For background, see *Pfizer Corporation v. Ministry of Health* [1965] *AC* 512.

[118] A 'government department' does not have legal personality (that is reserved to the Minister) and, furthermore, the term has no clearly defined meaning (in some statutes it has an inclusive, rather than exclusive definition). It originally meant one of the organization units of central government headed by a Minister of the Crown. Its definition is now wider and might include executive agencies: see *Jowitt's Dictionary of English Law* (3rd edn, 2010), p 1031.   [119] Listed in PA 1977, s. 55(1)(a)–(e).

[120] PA 1977, s. 55(4). An exception where no royalty needs to be paid operates under s. 55(3). Payment may have to be made to others: *Patchett's Patent* [1963] *RPC* 90.   [121] PA 1977, s. 57A.

[122] There is a duty to inform the proprietor that the department is using the invention.

atomic energy.[123] Furthermore, it is possible to authorize Crown use retrospectively and so turn an infringing act into a permitted Crown use.[124] Disputes relating to the exercise, terms, or payment for Crown uses are referable to the court provided the patent has been granted.[125]

The modern government practice is to license patents on a commercial basis. Today most Crown use matters are considered by the Ministry of Defence,[126] usually in response to claims of infringement by patentees. Nevertheless, there are very few cases involving claims of Crown use raised in recent years.[127]

4.4 BIOTECHNOLOGICAL INVENTIONS

One of the features of the packages of reforms initiated by the Biotechnology Directive is that it introduced a new regime for compulsory licensing and cross-licensing of biotechnological inventions. In essence, the new scheme attempts to manage the interrelationship between patent protection for biological inventions and plant variety protection. A similar scheme was introduced into the United Kingdom on 1 March 2002 by the Patents and Plant Variety Rights (Compulsory Licensing) Regulations 2002.[128]

The 2002 Regulations introduced two new forms of compulsory licence in the United Kingdom. The first of these is set out in regulation 3.[129] This provides that where a person is unable to acquire or exploit a plant breeder's rights or a Community plant variety right without infringing a prior patent, they are able to apply to the Comptroller of Patents for a non-exclusive compulsory licence to use the invention. This is subject to the requirement that the applicant pay an appropriate royalty and that the holder of the patent be entitled to a cross-licence to use the protected variety on reasonable terms.[130] In order for a compulsory licence to be granted under regulation 3, the applicant must show that they have unsuccessfully applied to the holder of the patent to obtain a licence. They must also show that the new plant variety in relation to which they wish to acquire or exploit the plant breeder's rights or Community plant variety right 'constitutes significant technical progress of considerable economic interest in relation to the invention protected by the patent'.[131] It seems that the latter requirement may impose limitations on the grant of compulsory licences for biotechnological inventions. In part, this will depend on how the 'significant technical progress' and 'considerable economic interest' are interpreted.

The second compulsory licence is set out in regulation 11.[132] This provides that where the holder of a patent for a biotechnological invention is unable to exploit the invention without infringing prior plant breeders' rights, the patent owner is able to apply to the

---

[123] PA 1977, s. 56(2).   [124] PA 1977, s 55(6); also see *Dory v. Sheffield Health Authority* [1991] *FSR* 221.

[125] PA 1977, s. 58; significantly, the most secret inventions (those subject to directions under PA 1977, s 22) are not granted but merely found to be ready for grant. This means that they cannot ever be litigated before the court (but they can be licensed and payments made for Crown use albeit there is no mechanism to deal with disputes between the Crown and the applicant patentee).

[126] During the 1960s there was a period where the Ministry of Health used the provision to obtain cheaper pharmaceuticals: see P. Johnson, 'Access to Medicine: The Rise of the British Pharmaceutical Industry', in G. Dinwoodie (ed.), *Methods and Perspectives in Intellectual Property* (2013), 329–59.

[127] Based on a Freedom of Information request, in the period between 2013 and 2017, the Ministry of Defence intended to use the provisions once (in 2014) but ultimately did not use it at all during that period.

[128] SI 2002/247.   [129] Based on Biotech. Dir., Art. 12(1).

[130] Patents and Plant Variety Rights (Compulsory Licensing) Regulations 2002 (SI 2002/247), reg. 7(1)–(5).

[131] Patents and Plant Variety Rights (Compulsory Licensing) Regulations 2002 (SI 2002/247), reg. 3(2)(c); Biotech. Dir., Art. 12(3)(a).   [132] Biotech. Dir., Art. 12(2).

Controller of Plant Variety Rights for a non-exclusive compulsory licence to use the protected plant variety.[133] This is subject to the requirement that the patent owner pay an appropriate royalty and that the holder of the plant breeder's rights be entitled to a cross-licence to use the patented invention on reasonable terms.[134] For a compulsory licence to be granted under regulation 11, the applicant must show that they made an unsuccessful application to the holder of the patent or plant variety right to obtain a licence. As with the compulsory patent licence, an applicant for a compulsory plant variety licence is subject to the onerous requirement that the biotechnological invention protected by the patent 'constitutes significant technical progress of considerable economic interest in relation to the plant variety protected by the prior plant breeders' rights'.[135] It seems that this second requirement may impose considerable limitations on the grant of compulsory licences for biotechnological inventions.

In relation to prior Community plant variety rights that restrict the ability of patentees to exploit their invention in the United Kingdom, the patentee must first apply to the Community Plant Variety Office for a 'compulsory exploitation right'.[136] Where such a right is granted to a patentee for a biotechnological invention who could not otherwise exploit their invention in the United Kingdom without infringing the prior Community plant variety right, the patentee is entitled to apply to the Comptroller of Patents for a cross-licence to use their biotechnological invention in the United Kingdom.[137]

4.5 COMPULSORY LICENCES FOR PUBLIC HEALTH

In order to follow through on commitments made at the Doha round of TRIPS to minimize the negative impact of patent law on access to medicines in developing countries, the European Commission introduced a new regulation in 2006 that allows for the compulsory licensing of patents relating to the manufacture of pharmaceutical products for export to countries with public health problems.[138] In effect, this allows for the grant of compulsory licences in relation to patents, and supplementary protection certificates (SPCs) for the sale and manufacture of pharmaceutical products intended for export to 'eligible importing countries in need of such products to address public health problems'.[139] To be 'eligible', a country must either be regarded by the United Nations as a 'least-developed country', have notified the TRIPS Council of its intention to use the system as an importer, or be listed by the Organisation for Economic Co-operation and Development (OECD) as a low-income country.[140] To accommodate these changes in the United Kingdom, section 128A was introduced into the Patents Act 1977 as of 17 December 2007.[141] The regime is unlikely to ever be used. The TRIPs mechanism which

---

[133] The applicant must also comply with the Plant Breeders' Rights Regulations 1998 (SI 1998/1027), established under reg. 23.

[134] Patents and Plant Variety Rights (Compulsory Licensing) Regulations 2002, reg. 11(1), (2)(b).

[135] Patents and Plant Variety Rights (Compulsory Licensing) Regulations 2002, reg. 11(c); Biotech. Dir., Art. 12(3)(a)–(b).   [136] Biotech. Dir., Art. 12(3).

[137] Patents and Plant Variety Rights (Compulsory Licensing) Regulations 2002, reg. 15.

[138] Regulation (EC) No. 816/2006 of the European Parliament and of the Council of 17 May 2006 on compulsory licensing of patents relating to the manufacture of pharmaceutical products for export to countries with public health problems [2006] *OJ L* 157/1 (9 June 2006). This implements TRIPS, Art. 31*bis*. The required number of ratifications of TRIPS, Art. 31*bis* for it to come into force was only reached in January 2017.

[139] Regulation (EC) No. 816/2006, Art. 1.   [140] Regulation (EC) No. 816/2006, Art. 4(a)–(c).

[141] The Patents (Compulsory Licensing and Supplementary Protection Certificates) Regulations 2007 (SI 2007/3293).

it implements has only ever been used once.[142] A 2012 international report[143] highlighted why the provision has not been used, in particular it pointed out that it does not cover the most common procurement scenarios. Those scenarios being that there is no patent in force or the patentee of the drugs will reduce the price following negotiations. The importance of the regime is its soft power which lead pharmaceutical companies to change their behaviour so as to be more willing to make their essential drugs available.[144]

5 COMPENSATION FOR USE

In the vast bulk of cases, the amount that is paid for the use of a patent is largely left to the market and the negotiating skills of the parties. In a number of exceptional circumstances, however, the Comptroller or court may be called upon to determine the amount payable for use of the patent. The question of the compensation payable arises in relation to employer use of employee inventions, compulsory licences, licences of right, and Crown use. In each case, the tribunal has to make difficult qualitative judgements about the value of the patent and how the profits that have been or might be made are to be allocated. In due course, international agreements may require that the contributions of indigenous groups are compensated where their knowledge and resources are used to develop pharmaceuticals.[145]

5.1 COMPENSATION FOR EMPLOYER USE

While the fate of a creator's relationship with their creations is normally left to the vagaries of contract law and the negotiating skills of the creator, intellectual property law occasionally recognizes that creators have residual interests in their creations.[146] One of the most notable examples of this is found in section 40(1) and (2) of the Patents Act 1977, which provides employee-inventors with a statutory right to compensation where their inventions are exploited by their employer.[147]

The compensation provisions apply when an invention made by an employee is owned by the employer by virtue of section 39(1)(a) or (b) and it can be shown that the patented invention is of outstanding benefit to the employer.[148] The compensation provisions also apply where an employee invention has been assigned to or exclusively licensed by the employer and it can be shown that the remuneration that the employee received from the transaction was inadequate. In both of these situations, inventors have a statutory right of compensation.[149] Awards for compensation will only be made if it is 'just' to do so.[150]

While these provisions may appear to provide employee-inventors with a potentially valuable source of income, they have mostly been construed in such a way as to provide little direct benefit to employees. Whether the compensation scheme provides indirect

---

[142] The importing country being Rwanda and the exporting country being Canada.

[143] WTO-WIPO-WHO, *Promoting Access to Medical Technologies and Innovation* (2012), 179.

[144] See J. Gibson, *Intellectual Property Aspects of Medicine: Current Debates* (2nd edn, 2017), 155–9.

[145] CBD, Art. 15(7).

[146] The most obvious examples are to be found in copyright law, where the creator's personality interests are protected by moral rights, and their financial interests by the *droit de suite* and unwaivable rights to remuneration.

[147] See A. Chandler, 'Employee Inventions: Outstanding Compensation?' [1992] *J Bus L* 300; K. Witherspoon, 'Employee Inventions Revisited' (1993) 22 *ILJ* 119, 131; J. Hughes, 'The Personality Interest of Artists and Inventors in Intellectual Property' (1998) 16 *Cardozo AELJ* 81, 138.   [148] PA 1977, s. 40(1).

[149] PA 1977, s. 40.   [150] PA 1977, s. 40(1) and (2)(d).

benefits to employees, for example acting as an impetus for the introduction of in-house compensation schemes, is another matter.

Applications for compensation can be made to the Comptroller or the court during the life of the patent and up to one year after the patent has expired. In recognition of the fact that the fate of a patented invention may change over time, if an initial application for compensation is rejected, employees can reapply for compensation at a later stage.[151] After some initial uncertainty,[152] it is now clear that the onus of proving that the patent is of outstanding benefit to the employer falls upon the employee.[153]

In order to protect employees, the 1977 Act provides that contractual terms that attempt to undermine the employee's right to compensation are unenforceable.[154] In recognition of the fact that unequal bargaining power might be mitigated by collective action, provision is made for collectively bargained schemes to override the individual claim machinery. Thus section 40(3) states that any employee who is a member of a trade union that has a 'relevant collective agreement' with the employer is unable to bring a claim for compensation.[155] For the provision to apply, the collective agreement must provide for the payment of compensation in respect of inventions of the same description as made by the employee.[156]

5.1.1 Compensation where an invention automatically belongs to employer

The first situation where employees are entitled to apply for compensation is set out in section 40(1). This states that where an employee has made an invention belonging to the employer via section 39(1), the employee may be entitled to compensation. For an award for compensation to be made, the applicant must show that:

(i)   they have made an invention belonging to the employer that has been patented;

(ii)   the invention *or* the patent for it is of benefit to the employer;

(iii) the benefit is outstanding; and

(iv)   it is *just* that the employee be awarded compensation.

We will deal with each of these in turn.

(i) The applicant has made a patented invention owned by the employer In order to qualify for compensation, an employee must show that they were the inventor, or actual deviser, of the invention in question. The test here is the same as determining whether someone is initially entitled to grant of a patent or is a joint inventor (discussed earlier). It is not enough for a person to show that they merely contributed to the invention (in a non-inventive way); rather, to be eligible for compensation, they must show that they came up with the inventive concept.[157]

(ii) 'The invention or the patent is of benefit to the employer' The benefits that flow to the employer can come either from the invention or from the patent that is taken out for the invention in question.[158]

The employer for this purpose includes not only the legal entity which employs the person, but the whole group of companies of which it forms part. This is to avoid the legal structure of an employer depriving a person from compensation.[159]

---

[151] PA 1977, s. 41(7).   [152] Cf. *GEC Avionics' Patent* [1992] RPC 107, 112.
[153] *Memco-Med's Patent* [1992] RPC 403.   [154] PA 1977, s. 42(2).   [155] PA 1977, s. 40(3) and (6).
[156] PA 1977, s. 40(3).   [157] *Kelly and Chiu v. GE Healthcare* [2009] RPC (12) 363, [9]–[11].
[158] It previously had to come from the patent. This changed following PA 2004, s. 10.
[159] *Shanks v. Unilever* [2011] RPC (12) 352, [17].

Determining whether the benefit that an employer has derived from an invention or a patent is outstanding is a complex task.[160] The valuation of the benefit must be in light of all of the available evidence as to what the patent has actually achieved and *not* what revenues the patent would have raised had it been exploited optimally or even ordinarily.[161]

The process of calculation is made somewhat easier as a result of 'benefit' means 'money or money's worth'.[162] This means that non-financial benefits, such as the prestige that flows from a patent, are excluded from the equation. Section 40 does not require the court to value the benefit precisely only what it might be.[163] In *Memco-Med's Patent*,[164] the court said that it was useful 'to examine what the employer's position would have been if the patent had never been granted, in comparison with the actual position'. The courts have also stressed that the patent must be the cause of the benefit, although it does not have to be the only cause.[165]

However helpful these principles may be, the courts have tended to rely upon more concrete information when calculating benefit, such as licence fees.

While sales figures of patented products, licence fees, and the like provide a useful basis from which to calculate the benefit that an employer has derived from a patent, they cannot be relied upon to provide an exact figure. The reason for this is that while the existence of a patent over a manufactured product will frequently influence sales, the number of products sold (as with the licence or assignment fees that are paid for use of the patent) may be a consequence of a range of factors—such as the advertising and marketing campaigns used to sell the product.[166]

Given that sales figures and licence fees may be influenced by an array of factors other than the patented invention, when they are being used to calculate benefit, it is necessary to isolate the *net* benefits that flow from the patent (or invention) to the employer from any other contributing factors.[167] *British Steel's Patent*[168] offers another useful example of the care that needs to be taken when calculating the net benefit that flows to an employer from a patent. The particular accounting problem that arose in this case stemmed from the fact that a number of technical obstacles had to be overcome before the patented invention could be put into practice. In this situation, the Hearing Officer accepted that in calculating the net benefit that flowed to the employer, it was necessary to subtract the costs that the employer had incurred in moving the invention from its initial conception to a practical profitable reality.

The care that needs to be taken in using sales figures as an indicator of benefit was also highlighted in *Memco-Med's Patent*,[169] in which Aldous J was called upon to resolve a remuneration dispute over a patented invention that detected when someone was near lift doors and prevented the doors from closing on them. In response to the argument that high sales of the patented detection device was evidence that the employer had derived

[160] *British Steel's Patent* [1992] *RPC* 117, 121. The calculation may take into account the benefits received under foreign patents and equivalent rights (such as utility models): PA 1977, s. 43(4); *GEC Avionics' Patent* [1992] *RPC* 107, 111.   [161] *Shanks v. Unilever* [2011] *RPC* 12, [8].

[162] PA 1977, s. 43(7).

[163] *Memco-Med's Patent* [1992] *RPC* 403, 413; *Kelly v. GE Healthcare* [2009] *RPC* (12) 363, [23].

[164] [1992] *RPC* 403, 413.

[165] *Kelly and Chiu v. GE Healthcare* [2009] *RPC* (12) 363, [60]. See A. Odell-West, '*Kelly v. GE Healthcare*: Employee Innovations in Health Care' [2010] *EIPR* 449.

[166] Whether an employer can circumvent the provision by deciding not to patent, but to utilize another form of protection such as confidentiality agreements, remains unclear. PA 1977, s. 43(4), defines 'references to a patent' as covering 'a patent or other protection'—arguably including confidentiality.

[167] The figure should not be net of corporation tax however: *Shanks v. Unilever* [2017] *RPC* (15) 522, [43].

[168] [1992] *RPC* 117.   [169] [1992] *RPC* 403.

high levels of benefit from the patent, the court found that the high sales were attributable more to the price and quality of the product and to the fact that the manufacturer had a long and established relationship with the purchaser, than to the patent itself.[170] From this basis, the court concluded that the benefit that flowed to the employer from the patent was minimal.

(iii) Is the benefit 'outstanding'? Once the level of benefit that an employer has derived from a patent has been calculated, it is then necessary to determine whether it is 'outstanding'. It has been suggested that the reason why compensation is only awarded where the benefit is outstanding is that the employees making a claim under section 40(1) would already have received some remuneration for the invention as part of their salary package.[171] While 'outstanding' is not defined in the Act, it is clear that it is restricted to exceptional cases[172] and it is a threshold question. In *GEC Avionics' Patent*,[173] an application for compensation was rejected on the ground that although the patent conferred some benefit, the employer achieved similar benefits in relation to products not involving the invention.

Whether a patent is of outstanding benefit to an employer depends on the circumstances of the case in question. The only guidance that the Act provides is that the 'size and nature of the employer's undertakings' ought to be taken into account when determining whether a patent is of outstanding benefit.[174] In *Shanks v. Unilever*[175] it was argued by Unilever that £24.5 million benefit was not an outstanding benefit due to its size and turnover. In the Court of Appeal, Patten LJ accepted that the size of the company was a relevant factor, but should not be the only factor, in assessing the benefit.[176] Briggs LJ went further and indicated that the benefit of Shank's invention might have been outstanding in a smaller company.[177] He continued and indicated that sometimes the size of the company compared to the benefit might, in some circumstances, be decisive.[178]

(iv) Is it just that compensation should be awarded? For compensation to be awarded, as well as establishing that the patent is of outstanding benefit to the employer, employees must also show that it is 'just' that they be awarded compensation.[179] The decision as to whether an award for compensation is just is based is not confined to the same factors that are taken into account when deciding whether the patent provides the employer with an outstanding benefit. Floyd J in *Kelly v. GE Healthcare*[180] took the view that the types of situation where an award is unjust cannot be categorized, but the court will recognize them when they arise. It appears, therefore, that the requirement is a safety value where for some reason compensation is not warranted.

5.1.2 Compensation where an employee-invention has been assigned to an employer

The second situation where an award for compensation may be made to an employee is set out in section 40(2) of the 1977 Act. This provides that additional compensation may be paid where the initial entitlement to an invention lay with an employee, but the employee assigned or licensed the invention to the employer. Here, the employee must demonstrate that the remuneration for the transaction is inadequate in comparison with the remuneration derived by the employer from the patent. They must also show that it is just that additional compensation be paid.

---

[170] Ibid., 417. There is a presumption that sales from non-patented goods are not attributable in any way to the patent: *GEC Avionics' Patent* [1992] *RPC* 107, 114.   [171] Ibid., 115.
[172] *Shanks v. Unilever* [2017] *RPC* (15) 522, [12].   [173] [1992] *RPC* 107.   [174] PA 1977, s. 40(1).
[175] [2017] *RPC* (15) 522.   [176] Ibid., [59]–[64].   [177] Ibid., [68].   [178] Ibid., [69].
[179] PA 1977, s. 40(1).   [180] [2009] *RPC* (12) 363, [41].

To determine whether compensation is payable under section 40(2), it is necessary to ascertain the benefit that the employee derived from the contract with their employer and the benefit that the employer derived from the patent. Once these two figures have been calculated, it is then necessary to determine whether the remuneration was adequate. This appears to require the court to estimate what remuneration might have been achieved in a market transaction between a willing seller and purchaser. However, given that an employee who makes an application under section 40(2) will have had an opportunity to bargain with their employer, it is unlikely that the tribunal will hold that remuneration is inadequate in circumstances where it would not treat the benefit as outstanding.

5.1.3 Calculating the amount of compensation

Once it has been decided that compensation should be awarded to the employee, the question arises: how much? Section 41(1) directs that the award should secure for the employee a 'fair share' of the benefit that the employer has derived. Compensation may be awarded as a lump sum or in periodic payments.[181] There is a power to vary the amount at a later stage.[182] In *British Steel*,[183] the Hearing Officer said that the question was similar to the question that arose when determining the royalty payable in licence-of-right proceedings. The relevant considerations included the size of the benefit that had been and was likely to be derived from the patent, and the salary and awards that the employee had already received. In that case, these would have included a £10,000 *ex gratia* payment from British Steel and an MBE.[184] In other cases, the tribunal might take account of the contribution made by other people, such as co-inventors, other employees, and the employer.

We can get a sense of how the courts construe the provisions in section 41 from *Kelly and Chiu v. GE Healthcare*,[185] where the court found that the patent delivered, at minimum, £50 million benefit to the employer. Based on all of the factors, the court felt that 3 per cent of the value of the benefit to the employer represented a just and fair award to the claimants. Based on different contributions made by the claimants to the development on the invention, one employee was awarded £1 million, while the other was awarded £500,000.

5.2 COMPENSATION FOR COMPULSORY LICENCES AND LICENCES AS OF RIGHT

Another situation where the tribunals may be called upon to determine the compensation that ought to be paid for the exploitation of a patent is where the patent is subject to a compulsory licence or a licence as of right. In these circumstances, the principal goal is to ensure that the owner of the patent receives reasonable remuneration for the use that is made of the invention.[186]

Three techniques have been used to reach an appropriate sum. These are commonly referred to as the 'comparable royalties', 'costs', and 'profits available' approaches.

(i) Comparable royalties The 'comparable royalties', or willing licensee/willing licensor, test is regarded as 'by far the best and surest approach'.[187] It involves utilizing evidence from comparable licences to estimate what would have been agreed by the parties. The kinds of evidence used will vary from evidence relating to standard royalty rates for patented products in a particular field,[188] through to the actual examples of licence

---

[181] PA 1977, s. 41(6).   [182] PA 1977, s. 41(7), (9)–(11).   [183] *British Steel's Patent* [1992] RPC 117.
[184] It is not clear why the MBE is relevant as it is not awarded by the employer.
[185] [2009] RPC (12) 363, [173]–[207].   [186] *SKF Cimetidine* [1990] RPC 203, 236 (CA).   [187] Ibid.
[188] *Cabot Safety* [1992] RPC 39, 61; *Chiron Corp. v. Murex Diagnostics (No. 13)* [1996] FSR 578.

agreements voluntarily entered into by the patentee. In deciding whether a situation is comparable, the most important factor is the nature of the patentee's invention: if the patentee's invention is unusual and the comparator licence covered the same invention, it is likely to offer a useful comparison (although it may be necessary to make adjustments in relation to market size and other terms in the licence).[189] If the invention is unusual and the licence that is used as a basis for comparison relates to a different product, it is likely to be of little value (even if the size of the market is similar).[190]

(ii) Costs Where no comparable licence exists, the terms are calculated by the so-called 'costs' approach.[191] Under this approach, the tribunal tries to assess the value of the patent in terms of a return on costs. This involves an examination of the patentee's expenditure on research and development, promotional expenditure, and an appropriate annual increase. The idea behind this approach is that the patentee should receive a fair and reasonable return for their financial outlay. Once the costs have been calculated, it is necessary to determine what an appropriate increase would be. This may be done by looking at the average annual return that the patentee makes on other inventions.[192]

(iii) Profits available The third approach, which is called the 'profits available' approach, is used as a last resort.[193] The approach requires the tribunal to determine the profit that the applicant will make (if licensed), and then to divide the available profits between the patentee and the licensee. One problem with this approach is that it will often be difficult to decide how to split the profits.[194] It has been said that the 'profits available' approach is particularly dubious because it gets matters the wrong way round: it 'makes the licensee's reasonable remuneration the measure of what is an appropriate royalty instead of the patentee's reasonable remuneration'.[195] There is also a danger that it might leave the patentee with no royalty at all.[196] Despite these problems, it has been acknowledged that 'some assistance may often be derived from looking at what are the expected profits, if only as a cross-check on the end result'.[197]

5.3 COMPENSATION FOR CROWN USE OF PATENTS

Where an invention is used for the services of the Crown, the government department concerned is required to inform the proprietor of the patent and negotiate to pay such terms as may be agreed. In the absence of an agreed rate, the matter is determined by the courts, who, following the approach taken in compulsory licence proceedings, attempt to second-guess what a willing licensor and licensee would have agreed.[198] In addition, the patentee can be awarded compensation to cover lost contracts.[199] This arises from the way that tenders work. A person who tenders to manufacture an unpatented product for the government would include in their price a reasonable profit. If a patentee had won the contract, therefore, it would have included in its price both a notional licence fee for using the patent *and* a reasonable profit from the simple manufacture. The compensation for lost contracts is intended to give remuneration to cover this additional 'profit' element.

---

[189]   *Cabot Safety* [1992] *RPC* 39.   [190]   *Research Corp.'s (Carboplatin) Patent* [1990] *RPC* 663, 701.

[191]   See *Geigy SA's Patent* [1964] *RPC* 391; *SKF Cimetidine* [1990] *RPC* 203, 253.

[192]   Where the outcome of comparison and PA 1977, s. 41, are in conflict, the comparability figure is generally preferred: *American Cyanamid Co.'s (Fenbufen) Patent* [1990] *RPC* 309.

[193]   *SKF Cimetidine* [1990] *RPC* 203, 244.

[194]   Ibid., 230. See also *American Cyanamid Fenbufen* [1990] *RPC* 309, 338; *Cabot Safety* [1992] *RPC* 39, 63.

[195]   *SKF Cimetidine* [1992] *RPC* 39.   [196]   *Research Corp.'s (Carboplatin) Patent* [1990] *RPC* 663, 700.

[197]   *SKF Cimetidine* [1992] *RPC* 39, 257.   [198]   *Patchett's Patent* [1967] *RPC* 237, 247, 253.

[199]   PA 1977, s. 57A(3).

24

RIGHTS RELATED TO PATENTS

1 INTRODUCTION

In this chapter, we examine two areas of law that are related to but do not traditionally form part of patent law. The first and oldest of the two regimes is the system of plant variety protection. This gives protection to the breeders of new varieties of plants. We then go on to look at supplementary protection certificates (SPCs), which currently operate in the United Kingdom to extend the length of patent protection. In essence, the SPC scheme was introduced to compensate owners for time lost while they were waiting to get regulatory approval to market their patented products.

2 PLANT VARIETIES

While the value of new plant varieties has long been recognized in the United Kingdom, a system of protection was only introduced in 1964. (In contrast, a system of protection existed in the United States from 1930.[1]) In part, this was because of the belief that the development of new varieties was part and parcel of traditional farming practices rather than a distinct activity of breeders (which required separate protection). Moreover, for much of the twentieth century, the leading breeders' organizations were publicly funded institutions that did not prioritize intellectual property protection.[2] However, during the Second World War, the desire to improve agricultural yields became a matter of national significance. In addition, by the 1950s it had become clear that the few private seed firms that operated in the United Kingdom were losing ground to foreign competitors—and the lack of property protection was seen as one possible cause.[3]

---

[1] See B. Greengrass, 'The 1991 Act of the UPOV Convention' [1991] *EIPR* 466; M. Llewelyn, 'The Legal Protection of Plant Varieties in the European Union: A Policy of Consensus or Confusion?' [1997] 2 *Bioscience L Rev* 50; M. Llewelyn, 'European Plant Variety Protection: A Reactionary Time' [1999] *Bioscience L Rev* 211. On the US Plant Patent Act of 1930, see A. Pottage and B. Sherman, 'Organisms and Manufactures: On the History of Plant Inventions' (2007) 31 *Melb U L Rev* 539.

[2] See P. Palladino, 'Science, Technology, and the Economy: Plant Breeding in Great Britain, 1920–1970' (1996) 49 *Econ Hist Rev* 116 (reporting that 83 per cent of wheat grown by British farmers in the 1990s was derived from seeds grown in publicly financed plant-breeding centres).

[3] See ibid., 131 (another alleged cause was lack of capital).

The production of successful varieties is thought to be highly desirable insofar as it increases yields resistance to pests and disease, and the sheer number and diversity of varieties.[4] While the breeding of new varieties takes a considerable amount of time and is often very costly,[5] once a variety is made available to the public, it can readily be duplicated.[6] Indeed, one of the features of plant varieties is that they produce their own reproductive material. Consequently, it was thought that it would be 'equitable to give plant breeders the opportunity of a fair reward for their work, effort, and investment in breeding, and to grant them protection against unauthorized exploitation'.[7] It was also intended 'to provide plant breeders with an incentive to produce improved varieties of a wide selection of plant species to the benefit of farmers, growers, and private gardeners'.[8]

However, in the same way as agriculture was long seen as being non-industrial (and thus outside the remit of patent law), so too the results of plant breeding were not thought to be appropriate subject matter for patent protection. In part, this was because prior to the acceptance of Mendelian theories of genetics, the production of varieties was seen more as an art than as a scientifically informed activity.[9] This was reinforced by the fact that there were technical problems in describing plant varieties in a way that met the requirements of patent law. However, the most significant reason why plant varieties were thought to be inappropriate subject matter for patent protection was that new plant varieties were unlikely to satisfy the inventiveness threshold of patents: most breeds were obvious. Consequently, it was decided that the protection needed could best be provided by a *sui generis* system tailored to the characteristics of plant varieties and the needs of breeders, growers, and traders.[10]

The United Kingdom first adopted a system of plant variety protection in 1964. This was in response to the report of the Committee on Transactions in Seeds[11] and to the International Convention for the Protection of New Varieties of Plants (UPOV), originally formulated in 1961.[12] The Plant Varieties and Seeds Act 1964 was substantially amended in 1978 and 1991 to take into account revisions of UPOV.[13] In 1997, it was

---

[4] Ibid. (describing a doubling in yields of cereals and potatoes and attributing half of this gain to genetic improvements). See the benefits listed by the British Association of Plant Breeders, cited in G. Dworkin, 'The Plant Varieties Act 1983' [1983] *EIPR* 270, n. 3.

[5] For a discussion of the costs of production of a variety of barley, see *Golden Promise Spring Barley* [1981] *FSR* 562. A successful variety might take between 8 and 20 years to develop: Hansard (HC), 24 June 1997, Vol. 296, col. 711.

[6] CPVR, Recital 5. For criticism of plant variety rights (PVRs), particularly from a developing country perspective, see P. Mooney, *Seeds of the Earth: A Private or Public Resource?* (1979); S. Verma, 'TRIPS and Plant Variety Protection in Developing Countries' [1995] *EIPR* 281; V. Shiva, 'The Seed of Our Future' [1996] *Development Journal* 4. For a defence against some of these attacks, see G. Dworkin, 'The Plant Varieties Act 1983' [1983] *EIPR* 270.　　　　　　　　　　　[7] Dworkin, op. cit., 271.

[8] Ibid.

[9] Many of these themes are explored in P. Palladino, 'Between Craft and Science: Plant Breeding, Mendelian Genetics, and British Universities 1900–1920' (1993) 34 *Technol & Cult* 300.

[10] For a general account, see Mark Janis et al, *Intellectual Property Law of Plants* (2014).

[11] *Report of the Committee on Transactions in Seeds* (Cmnd. 1092, 1960). See P. Murphy, 'Plant Breeders' Rights in the United Kingdom' [1979] *EIPR* 236; M. Llewelyn, 'The Legal Protection of Biotechnological Inventions: An Alternative Approach' [1997] *EIPR* 115, 117.

[12] UPOV had 75 members as of 1 May 2018. For a detailed account of UPOV, see J. Sanderson, *Plants, People and Practices* (2017).

[13] UPOV was also modified on 10 November 1972 and revised in 1978. The 1991 version came into force in April 1998. For commentary, see B. Greengrass, 'UPOV and the Protection of Plant Breeders: Past Developments, Future Perspectives' (1989) 20 *IIC* 622; N. Byrne, *Commentary on the Substantive Law of the UPOV* (1991).

repealed and replaced by the Plant Varieties Act 1997.[14] In 1994, the European Union adopted a Community Plant Variety Regulation (CPVR), which made it possible, from 27 April 1995, for breeders to apply for a single EU-wide right for varieties.[15] Community plant variety rights have uniform effect within the territory of the European Union[16] The grant of a Community right leads to the suspension of any equivalent national rights that may exist.[17] Because the international, regional, and national systems are similar, we will look at them together.

2.1 PROCEDURE FOR GRANT

As with patents, plant variety rights arise as a result of a process of registration. The initial application is made to a relevant granting authority: either the UK Plant Variety Rights Office in Cambridge; or the Community Plant Variety Office (CPVO) in Angers in France.[18] Anyone may apply for national rights irrespective of their nationality. However, a person may only apply for a Community right if they are a national of, or domiciled in, a country that is a member of UPOV.[19] As well as identifying the botanical taxon, the applicant must also provide the name of the breeder, a provisional designation for the variety, a technical description of the variety, the geographical origin of the variety, details of any previous commercialization of the variety, and information about applications made in respect of the variety.[20] In some cases, a colour photograph of the variety must also be supplied. An applicant must select a name for the variety.[21] Provision is made for objections by third parties.[22] Fees are payable.[23]

The CPVO examines the application in three stages.

(i)   First, there is a formal examination.[24]

(ii) This is followed by a substantive examination, whereby the Office examines the application to ensure that it relates to appropriate subject matter (that is, a

---

[14] In force 8 May 1998: Plant Varieties Act 1997 (Commencement) Order 1998 (SI 1998/1028); Plant Breeders' Rights Regulations 1998 (SI 1998/1027). The four major changes are that: the regime extends to all genera and species; the rules on previous exploitation are liberalized to allow market testing; there is a simplified system of rights pending grant; and breeder's rights are strengthened. The plant breeders' regime falls under the control of Defra rather than BIS. For an introductory guide, see MAFF, *UK Plant Breeders' Rights Handbook 1998* (1998). The 1964 Act had previously been amended by the Plant Varieties Act 1983, which was intended to enable UK ratification of the 1978 revision of UPOV.

[15] See M. Llewelyn and M. Adcock, *European Plant Intellectual Property* (2006); P. van der Kooij, *Introduction to the EC Regulation on Plant Variety Protection* (1997); J. Sanderson, 'Reconsidering Plant Variety Rights in the European Union after *Monsanto v. Cefetra*' [2012] *EIPR* 387. UK IPO, *The UK Plant Breeding Sector and Innovation* (February 2016).   [16] CPVR, Art. 2.

[17] CPVR, Art. 92; PVA 1997, s. 11(3). The Regulation is otherwise 'without prejudice' to the rights of member states to grant national rights. While there is no 'approximation directive', the common need to satisfy the requirements of UPOV and good sense have produced a high level of harmonization. Most EU member states have a parallel national system, with the exception of Greece and Luxembourg.

[18] See http://www.cpvo.fr. In 2017 there were 3,421 PVR applications and 2,865 PVR granted. CPVO, *CPVO Statistics* (2017).

[19] CPVR, Art. 12. The Commission may extend qualification to nationals and domiciliaries of other countries that provide corresponding protection.   [20] PVA 1997, s. 3(2); CPVR, Art. 50.

[21] PVA 1997, s. 18(2)(a); CPVR, Art. 50(3).   [22] CPVR, Art. 59.

[23] The Plant Breeder's Rights (Fees) Regulations 1998 (SI 1998/1027 as amended by SI 2002/1677). The application fee is £300, but the tests fees and renewal fees vary according to the species involved, e.g. tests are £815 for cereals and £130 for roses, while renewals are £475 for cereals and £80 for roses.

[24] CPVR, Art. 53.

variety), that the variety is new, and that the applicant is the person entitled to plant breeders' rights.[25] The Office also considers the suitability of the name proposed for the variety and takes account of a host of considerations, including previous registrations.[26]

(iii) The third stage is the technical examination of the characteristics of the variety. At this stage, the CPVO examines the application to ensure that the variety is distinct, uniform, and stable,[27] requirements sometimes referred to as 'DUS'.[28] An applicant must supply propagating material that the Office can use to test DUS by planting and growing the variety.[29] The tests may be carried out at more than one site. In most cases, DUS tests will take between one and three years.[30] As a result, it may be some years between application and grant.[31] Indeed, the crop is grown throughout the period of the monopoly, and if it becomes apparent that the variety does not satisfy the requirements of the Act, grant is liable to be revoked.[32]

2.2 SUBJECT MATTER

All three systems of plant variety protection cover varieties of 'all plant genera and species', from ornamental roses, to vines, potatoes, and wheat.[33] Section 1(3) of the Plant Variety Act 1997 defines a variety as:

> . . . a plant grouping within a single botanical taxon of the lowest known rank, which grouping . . . can be—
>
> (a) defined by the expression of the characteristics resulting from a given genotype or combination of genotypes,
> (b) distinguished from any other plant grouping by the expression of at least one of those characteristics, and
> (c) considered as a unit with regard to its suitability for being propagated unchanged.[34]

A botanical 'taxon' means a 'group' of plants; the requirements that it be of the lowest known rank is to make it clear that protection could not be granted for a 'family', 'genus', or 'species', which are groups higher in the taxonomical classification system.[35]

---

[25] CPVR, Art. 54.   [26] CPVR, Art. 63.

[27] UPOV, Art. 5; CPVR, Art. 6; PVA 1997, s. 4(2). On the power of the President of the CVPO to insert new characteristics, see *Schniga v. CVPO,* Case C-625/15P, EU:C:2017:435, [45]–[67].   [28] CPVR, Art. 55.

[29] For the United Kingdom, this work is mainly carried out by the National Institute of Agricultural Botany (NIAB), the Scottish Agricultural Science Agency (SASA), and the Department of Agriculture and Rural Development for Northern Ireland (DARDNI). See also UPOV, Art. 12; CPVR, Arts 53–5.

[30] Usually one year for ornamentals, three for herbage varieties and trees, and two years for other species.

[31] Provisional protection is provided: UPOV, Art. 13; CPVR, Art. 95; PVA 1997, s. 5(1). The fact that a PVR has been tested in other UPOV member states (Australia, New Zealand, the United States, and South Africa) did not oblige the Community Office to accept the test reports. This was on the basis that the 'Community system is independent—and different from their systems': *Prophyl v. CPVO,* Case A 3/2003 (4 June 2004) (CPVO BA), [1].   [32] CPVR, Arts 20–1; PVA 1997, ss 21–2.

[33] CPVR, Art. 5 (all botanical genera and species, including, among others, hybrids between genera and species); PVA 1997, s. 1(2).

[34] CPVR, Art. 5(2); PVA 1997, s. 1(3). See further *Van Den Bout and Ten Hoopen,* A 1/2002 (1 April 2003) (CPVO BA), 5.

[35] A wild rose is in the species '*carolina*', which is in the genus '*rosa*', which is in the family '*rosaceae*', which is in the order '*rosales*', which is in the class 'dicotyledons', which is in the subphylum '*angiospermae*', which is in the phylum '*spermatophyte*', which finally is in the kingdom 'plants'.

2.3 VALIDITY

In order to be protected, the variety must be 'new'. It is also necessary for the variety to be 'distinct', 'uniform', and 'stable'.[36]

2.3.1 Novelty

The requirement that the variety be new is nowhere near as onerous as the worldwide novelty requirement in patent law. A variety is new if there has been no sale or disposal of propagating or harvested material within the territory (under the Plant Variety Act 1997, the United Kingdom; under the case of the CPVR, the European Union) more than one year prior to the application. The novelty of a variety may also be lost if there has been a sale or disposal outside the relevant territory either, in the case of trees and vines, more than six years before the application date, or for other plants, more than four years prior to the application date.[37]

Three features of the novelty requirement should be noted. The first is that novelty is not lost by previous use (for example growth) of the variety, but only by previous sale or disposal. As such, a plant can be grown in someone's garden for years prior to application and an application will still succeed. In part, this reflects the desire to reward the discovery as much as the breeding of new varieties. Indeed, it seems that the applicant can still obtain a plant variety right even if they have given away propagating or harvested material, as long as this was not 'for the purposes of exploiting the variety'.

The second notable feature is that the novelty provisions allow for substantial 'grace periods'—that is, they allow for periods during which the applicant can commercialize the plant prior to grant without prejudicing the application. As a result, a person can sell vines outside the United Kingdom for up to six years before they need apply for a plant variety right.

Third, and perhaps most significantly, the only disposals or sales taken into account when considering the novelty of a particular variety are those made *by the applicant themselves or with their consent*.[38] Sales of material by third parties who have independently developed the same variety will not destroy the novelty of the variety. In such circumstances, priorities are accorded to the first to apply.[39] However, no protection is given to the independent developer via prior user's rights. In such circumstances, a monopoly may be granted to a person over an activity or trade that someone else was doing already.

2.3.2 Distinct, uniform, and stable

As well as being novel, to be the subject of plant breeders' rights, the variety must also be 'distinct', 'uniform', and 'stable'.[40] These are referred to as the 'DUS', or 'agro-technical', requirements.

---

[36] UPOV, Art. 5; CPVR, Art. 6; PVA 1997, s. 4(2).

[37] UPOV, Art. 6; CPVR, Art. 10; PVA 1997, Sch. 2, para. 4. See also *Agriculture and Agri-Food Canada v. CVPO*, Case A 1/2007 (15 December 2007) (CPVO BA) (farm catalogues offering to make a plant available to the public for fruiting trials were held to be commercial disposal).

[38] See A. Christie, 'The Novelty Requirement in Plant Breeders' Rights' (1988) 19 *IIC* 646; cf. P. van der Kooij, *Introduction to the EC Regulation on Plant Variety Protection* (1997), 15.

[39] PVA 1997, Sch. 2, Pt II, para. 5.

[40] UPOV, Art. 5; CPVR, Art. 6; PVA 1997, s. 4(2). If a variety is not uniform, it is 'impossible to judge the distinctness criterion because the variety is not precisely defined and the official plant material does not have the status of a variety within the meaning defined by CVPO': *Rogalski v. CVPO*, A 9/2011 (17 January 2012), [2.3.1].

(i) Distinct A variety is 'distinct' if it is 'clearly distinguishable by one or more characteristics which are capable of a precise description from any other variety whose existence is a matter of common knowledge at the time of application'.[41] Distinctiveness may
arise through visible differences in outward appearance, such as height, size of leaves, leaf
colour, or in the ears of cereals. It may also arise through physiological differences associated with the variety's particular chemical or biological structure, such as resistance to
disease,[42] or ability to withstand certain conditions.[43] Any difference will suffice;[44] there
is no need for the distinguishing feature to confer any particular aesthetic or economic
advantage. Distinctness is a comparative test and may require the claimed variety to be
compared with similar varieties. The variety must only be compared with 'other' varieties
and not with examples of 'itself'.[45] In practice, the comparison is made with the varieties of the same species in the Office's 'reference collection'. The reference collection is
made up of those varieties for which rights already exist or are being sought. The types
of characteristic and the extent of the deviation necessary for a variety to be distinct will
vary with the grouping concerned. Moreover, the characteristics needed for a variety to
be distinct may be different for each comparison (for example variety A might differ from
variety B by being higher, but differ from variety C by being hardier).[46]

(ii) Uniform A variety is 'uniform' if 'it is sufficiently uniform in those characteristics' that make it distinct.[47] This means that nearly all examples of the variety must bear
the characteristics that make the plant distinct. During the early stages of the breeding process, a proportion of the plants grown may not bear the relevant characteristics.
Where this is the case, it may be necessary to undertake further breeding to eradicate
deviant strains. However, there comes a point at which uniformity requires effort that is
out of proportion to the improvement in uniformity gained by the removal of deviants.
Consequently, it is not necessary for a variety to be completely uniform. This means that
a variety will still be uniform even if a few of the plants that are grown do not exhibit
the critical characteristics. To this end, the CPVO has stated that a variety is sufficiently
uniform if there is:

> . . . the degree of uniformity a capable breeder skilled in the art can reasonably be expected
> to achieve having regard generally to the nature of plant material and more particularly
> to the biological possibilities of the species in which he is working including its mode of
> reproduction, and to any special features of the variety under consideration.[48]

(iii) Stable A variety is 'stable' if the characteristics that make it distinct 'remain unchanged
after repeated propagation'.[49] The idea is that while a first generation might be distinct and
uniform, when a second generation is grown, a large number of deviants appear (resulting

[41] UPOV, Art. 7; CPVR, Art. 7 (clearly distinguishable by reference to the expression of characteristics
that results from a particular genotype or combination of genotypes); PVA 1997, Sch. 2, para. 1.

[42] *Maris Druid: Spring Barley* [1968] *FSR* 559 (resistance to mildew accepted as a characteristic).

[43] Under the 1964 Act, these two types of distinctiveness were referred to as 'morphological' and
'physiological'.

[44] It seems that a mere modification of genetic structure that is not revealed or expressed in the variety
will not make it distinct: P. van der Kooij, *Introduction to the EC Regulation on Plant Variety Protection*
(1997), 16.   [45] Ibid.

[46] For an illustration (although under the differently worded provision in the 1964 Act), see *Daehnfeldt
v. Controller of Plant Varieties* [1976] *FSR* 95.

[47] UPOV, Art. 8; CPVR, Art. 8; PVA 1997, Sch. 2, para. 2. For an example illustrating the difficulties of
determining uniformity in tests in which variants can arise through 'out-pollination' from nearby crops and
spontaneous mutants, see *Moulin Winter Wheat* [1985] *FSR* 283.

[48] *Zephyr: Spring Barley* [1976] *FSR* 576, 579.

[49] UPOV, Art. 9; CPVR, Art. 9; PVA 1997, Sch. 2, para. 3.

from residual 'heterozygosity'). This requires an assessment to be made of the inherent capability of the variety to remain true to its original characteristics. As with the testing of uniformity, deviants that appear as a result of pollination by nearby crops are ignored.

2.4 OWNERSHIP

The person entitled to the grant of plant breeders' rights is the person who breeds the plant variety, or who discovers and develops it.[50] As the Board of Appeal at the CPVO has said, '"breeding" . . . does not necessarily imply inventing something totally new but includes the planting, selection and growing on of pre-existing material and its development into a finished 'variety'.[51] In a different decision, the Board said that 'discover' means that 'somebody comes across a variety either by search or chance, being conscious of the fact that it is a new variety, which was unknown to him before and which in his opinion is unknown to other persons as well'.[52] Where the breeding, discovery, and development occur in the course of a person's employment, the employer is presumed to be the person entitled to grant of the plant breeder's rights.[53] Plant breeder's rights are property rights and, as such, are assignable, although the 1997 Act forbids a separate assignment of rights in the protected variety and rights in 'dependent' varieties. The Community right cannot be assigned other than for the European Union as a whole. Where this occurs, the assignment must be in writing and should be entered in the register kept by the CPVO.[54]

2.5 DURATION

The duration of rights varies with the type of plant concerned: UPOV requires members to provide a minimum duration of 20 years for most plants, and a minimum of 25 years for trees and vines.[55] However, the European and UK systems go further than these minima, protecting potatoes, trees, and vines for 30 years, and other genera and species for 25 years.[56] Throughout the period for which the grant operates, rights holders should ensure that they are in a position to produce propagating material to the Office.[57] A national right will become ineffective on grant of a Community right for the same variety.[58]

2.6 RIGHTS AND INFRINGEMENT

A valid plant breeder's right gives the proprietor (initially, the breeder or discoverer) a number of rights.[59] While these rights are primarily in relation to the

---

[50] PVA 1997, s. 4(3); UPOV, Art. 1(iv); CPVR, Art. 11(1). The fact that rights are available to 'discoverers' has sometimes proved controversial: see G. Dworkin, 'The Plant Varieties Act 1983' [1983] *EIPR* 270, 272.

[51] *Sakata Seed Corporation*, A 17/2002 (3 April 2003) (CPVO BA), 8–9.

[52] *Keith Kirsten Horticulture International v. CPVO*, A 1/2004 (16 December 2004) (CPVO BA), 6. Thus 'it was possible that one and the same variety is discovered by two or more persons independently, on different moments on the same spot, or on different spots': ibid.

[53] PVA 1997, s. 4(4); UPOV, Art. 1(iv). As far as the CPVR is concerned, entitlement shall be determined in accordance with the national law applicable to the employment relationship in the context of which the variety was bred, or discovered and developed.   [54] CPVR, Arts 2 and 23(2).

[55] UPOV, Art. 19.

[56] CPVR, Art. 19; Council Regulation (EC) No. 2470/96 of 17 December 1996 (extending protection for a further five years for potatoes); PVA 1997, s. 11.   [57] PVA 1997, s. 16.

[58] CPVR, Art. 92(1).

[59] CPVR, Art. 11; PVA 1997, s. 4(3)–(5). The rights are assignable: CPVR, Art. 23; PVA 1997, s. 12. For a discussion of how damages and account of profits for infringement are calculated, see *Jorn Hansson v. Jungpflanzen*, Case C-481/14, EU:C:2016:419.

commercialization of propagating material, they may also apply to harvested material and to derivative varieties.[60] The rights given to breeders are more limited than in the cases of patentees.[61] Moreover, it should be noted that as with other intellectual property rights, these are negative. It is also important to note that, with the exception of ornamentals and fruit, the breeder must gain relevant regulatory approval before a variety is marketed.[62]

2.6.1 Propagating material

The fundamental right conferred on a proprietor of a plant breeder's right is the exclusive right to authorize certain acts in relation to 'propagating material' (referred to in the 1997 Act as 'reproductive material';[63] and in the Community Regulation as 'variety constituents'). In particular, a plant breeder is given the rights to produce or reproduce the material, to 'condition' the material for the purposes of propagation, and to sell, offer for sale, stock, export, or import the material.[64] While 'propagating material' is not defined, it includes seeds for sowing, seed potatoes, seedlings, bulbs, rhizomes, grafts, and the like. The nature of plant material and breeding technology is such that a variety can be propagated from a much wider array of plant material than has traditionally been the case, including material such as cut blooms. Consequently, material will be treated as propagating material if it is intended to be used as a propagating material. Obviously, a person will infringe the fundamental right if, for example, they sell seeds, produce cuttings, or import bulbs. However, if such a person (who has legitimately grown the plant) sells beans for canning, grain for milling, or blooms or rose bushes for personal use, and these are subsequently used for propagation, it is unlikely that the vendor will be liable. In these cases, the user will be liable because they will have reproduced or 'conditioned' the material for the purposes of propagation.

2.6.2 Harvested material

In most cases, the rights conferred in relation to the exploitation of propagating material also apply to harvested material obtained through the *unauthorized* use of propagating material (for example crops of wheat grown from unauthorized seed). 'Harvested material' is defined to include entire plants and parts of plants.[65] As such, it will encompass things such as cut blooms from flowers.[66] An exception to this right arises where, prior to harvest, the rights holder has had a reasonable opportunity to exercise their rights in relation to the unauthorized use of the propagating material.[67]

The plant breeder's rights also extend to any product that is made directly from such harvested material (such as flour made from wheat), which falls within the categories

---

[60] UPOV, Art. 14; CPVR, Art. 13; PVA 1997, ss 6–7.

[61] *Report of the Committee on Transactions in Seeds* (Cmnd. 1092, 1960), [141].

[62] They must pass tests of value for cultivation and use, i.e. of yield, quality, and disease resistance. Once this is done, the variety is entered on the National List: Seeds (National Lists of Varieties) Regulations 1982 (SI 1982/844), as amended (no seed of the major agricultural and vegetable species may be marketed in the United Kingdom unless the variety is on a UK National List or in the EC Common Catalogue). See J. Harvey, 'UK Plant Breeders' Rights and the European Seed Regime' [1990] *Patent World* 22.

[63] For a discussion of definitional problems, see G. Dworkin, 'Plant Breeders' Rights: The Scope of United Kingdom Protection' [1982] *EIPR* 11, 12.

[64] PVA 1997, s. 6; UPOV, Art. 14(1)(a); CPVR, Art. 13(2). Although these rights are limited within EU law: *Re the Plant Royalty Bureau* [1979] *FSR* 644 (Commission investigation on restriction of exports).

[65] PVA 1997, s. 6(6)(b).   [66] The scheme under Sch. 3 to the 1964 Act has been abolished.

[67] PVA 1997, s. 6(3).

prescribed by the ministers.[68] Certain procedures and presumptions operate to assist the holder of plant breeder's rights in proving that harvested material and products made directly from such material were obtained through unauthorized use of propagating material. The rights holder may issue an information notice to a defendant requesting certain information as to the source of specified material. If the recipient fails to provide the relevant information within a particular time, the material is presumed to have been obtained by way of an unauthorized use.[69]

2.6.3 Derivative varieties

The plant breeder's rights extend beyond the registered variety to cover varieties that are 'dependent' on the protected variety. 'Dependent varieties' include varieties the production of which requires the repeated use of the protected variety, as well as 'essentially derived' varieties.[70] A variety is deemed to be 'essentially derived' where it is predominantly derived from the initial variety. In addition, the variety must retain the expression of the essential characteristics that result from the genotype of the initial variety and, at the same time, be clearly distinguishable from the initial variety.

2.6.4 Naming rights

Registration is conditional on the applicant providing a suitable name for the variety. This prevents the confusion that would otherwise arise if a number of different names were to be used to describe the same variety.[71] Once approved, anyone who sells or markets propagating material is obliged to use that name. This duty, breach of which is punishable under criminal law,[72] applies to the proprietor as much as to the public at large.[73] The duty subsists indefinitely—that is, even after expiry of plant breeders' rights.[74] The proprietor of a British plant variety right is also able to control the wrongful use of that name. As a result, the right holder may bring an action against anyone who uses the name of a protected variety in marketing material of a *different* variety within the same class, or uses a name so nearly resembling the registered name that it is likely to deceive or cause confusion.[75]

2.7 EXCEPTIONS

One important feature of the plant variety system is the careful way in which the competing interests of developers, users, and other interested parties have been accommodated

---

[68] PVA 1997, s. 6(4). The provision applies only if no relevant consent has been gained in relation to dealing with the propagating material and the right holder has not had a reasonable opportunity to enforce those rights, e.g. where the wheat was produced in a country that did not recognize plant breeders' rights. It will also operate only as regards varieties prescribed in regulations by the ministers. For background, see J. Rooker (Minister for Agriculture, Fisheries and Food), Hansard (HC), 24 June 1997, Vol. 296, cols 692–4.

[69] PVA 1997, ss 14–15; Plant Breeders' Rights (Information Notices) (Extension to European Community Plant Variety Rights) Regulations 1998 (SI 1998/1023).

[70] PVA 1997, s. 7; UPOV, Art. 14(5); CPVR, Art. 13(5). On essential derivation, see J. Rooker, Hansard (HC), 24 June 1997, Vol. 296, cols 693–4; J. Sanderson, 'Essential Derivation, Law and the Limits of Science' (2006) 24 *Law in Context* 34; Charles Lawson, 'Plant Breeder's Right and Essential Derivation' [2014] *EIPR* 499.

[71] M.-C. Piatti and M. Jouffray, 'Plant Variety Names in National and International Law' [1984] *EIPR* 283; B. Sherman, 'Taxonomic Property' (2008) 67(3) *CLJ* 560.

[72] PVA 1997, s. 19. Failure to use the name is a crime punishable by a fine. See also UPOV, Art. 20(7).

[73] UPOV, Art. 20; CPVR, Art. 63. For a discussion of CPVR, Art. 63(3), see *Vegetal-Progress v. Giovanni Ambrogio*, A 4/2004, (18 July 2005) (CPVO BA), 5–8.   [74] UPOV, Art. 20(7).

[75] PVA 1997, s. 20(2).

through the use of exceptions and compulsory licences.[76] UPOV permits members of the European Union to impose various restrictions on the operation of the monopoly.[77]

There are certain limitations that parallel those that apply to patents. Acts done privately and for non-commercial purposes, and acts done for experimental purposes, are non-infringing.[78] Moreover, acts done for the purpose of breeding or discovering and developing other varieties do not infringe plant breeders' rights. There are also the customary rules relating to EU exhaustion of rights where material is 'disposed of to others by the holder or with his consent'.[79]

As regards certain varieties, farmers are authorized to use 'in the field, on their own holding' the product of a harvest that they have obtained by planting a variety.[80] Small farmers are permitted to use such saved seed without payment, whereas others must provide equitable remuneration.[81] Remuneration is required in relation to lists of fodder plants (such as vetch and clover), cereals, and potatoes, as well as oil and fibre plants such as rape.[82] The equitable remuneration must be paid no later than the (next) 30 June following the date of reseeding.[83]

2.8 COMPULSORY LICENCES

Compulsory licences may be granted by the Controller of Plant Variety Rights (who is different from the Comptroller of Patents, Designs and Trade Marks) in certain circumstances two years after grant of plant breeder's rights.[84] The first condition is that the holder of a plant breeder's right has either unreasonably refused to grant a licence or has proposed an unreasonable term for such a licence.[85] It has been said that this is a heavy burden to discharge.[86] The Controller must also be satisfied that such licences are needed to ensure that the variety is available to the public at reasonable prices, is widely distributed (although not necessarily that demand is fully met),[87] or is maintained in quality. The applicant must be intending to exploit the rights and be in a position to do so.[88] The Controller sets the terms of the licence as they think fit, having regard to the desirability of securing reasonable remuneration to the plant breeder, but the licence must not be an exclusive

---

[76] Users are represented largely through the National Farmers Union; breeders are represented by the British Society of Plant Breeders.   [77] UPOV, Art. 17.

[78] CPVR, Art. 15; PVA 1997, s. 8.   [79] CPVR, Art. 16; PVA 1997, s. 10.

[80] CPVR, Art. 14(2); PVA 1997, s. 9. On the importance of these sorts of provisions for developing countries, see S. Verma, 'TRIPS and Plant Variety Protection in Developing Countries' [1995] *EIPR* 281, 286.

[81] CPVR, Art. 14(3); PVA 1997, s. 9(3)–(4). Small farmers are further defined: Plant Breeders' Rights (Farm Saved Seed) (Specified Information) Regulations 1998 (SI 1998/1026).

[82] CPVR, Arts 14, 29; Commission Regulation No. 1768/95 of 24 July 1995 implementing rules on the agricultural exemption provided for in Article 14 (3) of Council Regulation (EC) No. 2100/94 on Community plant variety rights [1995] *OJ L* 173/14 (25 July 1995). Collections of remuneration for farm saved seed began in autumn 1996. For a discussion on the information that a farmer needs to supply in this context, see *Raiffeisen-Waren-Zentrale Rhein-Main v. Saatgut-Treuhandverwaltungs*, Case C-56/11, EU:C:2012:713 (ECJ, First Chamber). For the way in which compensation is calculated, see *Geistbeck v. Saatgut-Treuhandverwaltungs*, Case C-509/10, EU:C:2012:416 (ECJ, First Chamber). More generally see E. Paunio, 'Plant Variety Rights revisited' [2014] *EIPR* 482.

[83] *Saatgut v. Gerhard* Case, C-242/14 , EU:C:2015:422, [19]–[32].

[84] CPVR, Art. 29 (compulsory exploitation rights); PVA 1997, s. 17; Plant Breeders' Rights Regulations 1998 (SI 1998/1027), reg. 10 (compulsory licences operate only two years after grant); *Cama Wheat* [1968] *FSR* 639, 643 (explaining that plant breeders should have complete control at the first introduction of a variety when seed supplies may be limited and demand uncertain).   [85] PVA 1997, s. 17(1).

[86] *Cama Wheat* [1968] *FSR* 639, 644.

[87] Ibid., 645 (where the breeder's licensees supplied 2,000 tons of seed, a refusal to license the applicant to sell 30 tons did not result in the seed not being 'widely distributed').

[88] PVA 1997, s. 17(2)(b)–(c).

licence. The Controller can require the plant breeder to supply propagating material to the holder of the licence.

As we saw earlier, a new regime for compulsory licensing and cross-licensing of biological innovations was introduced into the United Kingdom in 2002. In essence, the new scheme attempts to manage the interrelationship between patent protection for biological inventions and plant variety protection.[89]

2.9 RELATIONSHIP TO THE PATENT SYSTEM

The plant breeders' rights system was initiated because of the belief that plant varieties fell outside the types of creation that were traditionally considered to be patentable.[90] Nonetheless, when the EPC 1973 was formulated, a specific exclusion was placed in the definition of patentable subject matter to avoid the possibility of dual protection.[91] For most of the history of the operation of the EPC, it was thought that the patent and plant variety systems were mutually exclusive. Indeed, the 1961 version of the UPOV seemed to require that members allow either patenting or *sui generis* protection, but not both.[92]

However, developments in techniques for modifying plants, such as somatic cell hybridization and genetic engineering more generally, have thrown the relationship of mutual exclusivity into doubt. This has been reinforced by the fact that biotechnology companies have attempted to use the patent system to obtain protection for their innovations (for example claims directed to plant cell strains or to groups of plants at a taxonomical level higher than a 'variety').[93] Such attempts increase the possibility of overlap with the plant breeders' system. As a result of the 1991 revision of the UPOV, the patent and plant variety systems are no longer mutually exclusive.[94] This increased the possibility for overlap between the regimes. As we noted earlier, following growing concerns about the negative impact arising from the increased use of patent protection for plants, changes have been made at the EPO, effective from 1 July 2017, to exclude from patentability plants and animals exclusively obtained by an essentially biological breeding process.[95] While this may not go as far as some may wish, and is yet to be implemented in the United Kingdom, it seems that it will strengthen the plant variety system.

At the same time, frustration with what are seen as overly broad exceptions in the plant breeders' rights systems has led some breeders to resort to technological measures, such as the controversial terminator technology (which renders plants sterile), to protect their research. The use of genetic use restriction technologies (GURTs) poses a direct threat to the plant variety systems. While plant variety rights are granted only to botanical innovations that satisfy certain criteria, are limited in time, and provide a number

---

[89] Patents and Plant Variety Rights (Compulsory Licensing) Regulations 2002 (SI 2002/247). See Chapter 23, section 4.4, pp. 689–90.

[90] Most importantly, it was seen not as being capable of meeting the requirements of sufficient disclosure. For an international overview, see T. Roberts, 'Patenting Plants around the World' [1996] *EIPR* 531.

[91] EPC 1973, Art. 53(b); *Ciba-Geigy/Propagating material application*, T 49/83 [1984] *OJ EPO* 112 (legislator did not wish to afford patent protection under the EPC to plant varieties within 1961 Convention); *Plant Genetic Systems/Glutamine synthetase inhibitors*, T 356/93 [1995] *EPOR* 357 ('the purpose of Art. 53(b) EPC . . . is to draw an appropriate dividing line between plant variety and patent law'; it is 'important that no grey area in which protection is not given exists between the above two systems').

[92] UPOV 1961, Art. 2(1).   [93] See Chapter 17, section 8, p. 519.

[94] Recital 8 states that the definition of plant variety is not intended to alter definitions applicable in relation to other intellectual property rights, especially in the patent field.

[95] EPC, r. 28(2); see 'EPO clarifies practice in the area of plant and animal patents' (29 June 2017), available online at www.epo.org/news-issues/news/2017/20170629.html. See Chapter 17, section 8.3.4, p. 533.

of exceptions to protect breeders and farmers, this is not the case with genetically based protection regimes. Although it may be some time before GURTs are put to work, if they are implemented they are likely to shape the way in which intellectual property deals with biological inventions in the future.

3 SUPPLEMENTARY PROTECTION CERTIFICATES

Supplementary protection certificates (SPCs) are intellectual property rights that are based on and similar in nature to patents. SPC's extend patent protection where a patent proprietor has been unable to take full advantage of their patent rights over the period of the grant because of delays in obtaining the regulatory approval needed to market a patented invention.[96] The need for additional protection arose because obtaining the requisite marketing approval is often an expensive and lengthy process. For example, in 1990 the average period for approval of medicines was 12 years. Such delays erode the time available to the patent owner to market their inventions under the protection of the patent monopoly.

Following a proposal by the Commission in 1990,[97] two Council regulations were passed creating new rights related to patents for 'medicinal products' (in 1992)[98] and 'plant protection products' (in 1996).[99] Following a series of amendments to the 1992 Regulation on Medicinal Products, a new Regulation for the Protection of Medicinal Products was introduced in 2009.[100] Because this merely codified previous changes, the case law under the 1992 regulations is still relevant. As such, in this section we focus on the 1996 SPC Plant Protection Products Regulation[101] and the 2009 SPC Protection for Medicinal Products Regulation.

---

[96] The relevant regulatory authorities are the European Medicines Agency, the Veterinary Medicines Directorate, the Medicines and Healthcare Products Regulatory Agency, and the Chemicals Regulation Directorate.

[97] European Commission, *Proposal for a Council Regulation (EEC) Concerning the Creation of a Supplementary Protection Certificate for Medicinal Products* (April 1990) COM(90) 101 final. The United States introduced 'patent term restoration' in 1984 and Japan, in 1987. In 1991, France and Italy introduced so-called 'certificates of complementary protection'. See P. Kolker, 'The Supplementary Protection Certificate: The European Solution to Patent Term Restoration' [1997] *IPQ* 249. D. Culey, *Extending Rewords for Innovative Drug Development: A Report on Supplementary Certificates for Pharmaceutical Products* (2007).

[98] Council Regulation (EEC) No. 1768/92 of 18 June 1992 concerning the creation of a supplementary protection certificate for medicinal products [1992] *OJ L* 182/1 (the 'SPC (MP) Reg.'). The Spanish unsuccessfully challenged the SPC (MP) Reg. on the grounds that the European Union did not have competence to legislate a new patent right and that intervention could not be justified by reference to the need to harmonize laws for the internal market: *Spain v. Council of the European Union*, Case 350/92 [1995] *ECR* I–1985, [1996] *FSR* 73. Note also the Canadian complaint, WTO/DS 153.

[99] Council Regulation (F.C) No. 1610/96 of the European Parliament and of the Council of 23 July 1996 concerning the creation of a supplementary protection certificate for plant protection products [1986] *OJ L* 198/30 (the 'SPC (PPP) Reg.').

[100] Council Regulation (EC) No. 469/2009 of the European Parliament and of the Council of 6 May 2009 concerning the creation of a supplementary protection certificate for medicinal products [2009] *OJ L* 152/1 (the 'SPC (PM) Reg.'). The Commission announced in June 2008 that it was considering codification of the regulations relating to SPCs: European Commission, *Proposal for a Regulation Concerning the Supplementary Protection Certificate for Medicinal Products (Codified Version)* (June 2008) COM(2008) 369 final.

[101] See generally, V-C. Arunasalam and F. De Corte, 'Supplementary Protection Certificates for Plant Protection Products' (2016) 11 *JIPLP* 833.

To avoid conflict with the maximum patent term allowed under Article 63 of the EPC 2000, an SPC is characterized as a supplementary right, distinct from a patent. Because SPCs operate at the interface between the patent system and the systems for marketing approval, the availability, scope, and duration of protection is defined by concepts drawn from both systems, coupled with the hybrid concept of the 'product'.

There are a number of points of uncertainty in relation to SPCs. As will become apparent, the jurisprudence in this area is far from clear. To remedy these problems, and to 'strengthen EU-based manufacturing and competitiveness in industry sectors whose products are subject to regulated market authorisations', the Commission announced plans to review certain aspects of patent and SPC protection.[102] These problems are compounded by the fact that the standing of SPCs if (or when) the unified patent regime is introduced is unclear. While the Commission has recognized that the uncertainties over how the Unitary Patent will work with national patents and national SPCs need to be clarified, we are still awaiting details.[103] We are also still waiting details on what a unitary European-SPC might look like and how this would be implemented. In the United Kingdom these problems are compounded by Brexit. Given that SPCs are granted under EU law, the United Kingdom will presumably no longer be part of the SPC regime (nor the EU-based regulatory schemes). While UK companies will still be able to make use of SPC protection in EU countries where they have a patent, it is not clear what the law and practice in the United Kingdom will be. While it may be relatively easy for this to be clarified, it is unlikely that SPCs will be a high political priority in the United Kingdom so this may take some time.

3.1 AVAILABILITY

In order to receive an SPC, a person must apply to the national patent office (and not the European Patent Office).[104] The application must be made within six months of receipt of authorization to market the medicinal or plant protection product.[105] At the time of application, the applicant must be the proprietor of a basic patent that is in force.[106] Applications lodged outside the six-month period[107] will not be accepted.[108] Taking into

---

[102] European Commission, *Upgrading the Single Market: more opportunities for people and business* (28 October 2015) COM(2015) 550 final, [3.3]. The Commission has subsequently announced plans to review the legal and economic basis of the SPC system. [103] Ibid.

[104] From 17 December 2007, this is done by virtue of PA 1977, s. 128B and Sch. 4A, introduced by The Patents (Compulsory Licensing and Supplementary Protection Certificates) Regulations 2007 (SI 2007/3293), and the Patent Rules 2007 (SI 2007/3291), r. 116(1)–(5). See generally, UK IPO, *Supplementary Protection Certificates* (16 May 2014).

[105] SPC (PM) Reg., Art. 7, replacing SPC (MP) Reg., Art. 7; SPC (PPP) Reg., Art. 7; *Yamannouchi Pharmaceuticals v. Comptroller-General*, Case C-110/95, [1997] *ECR* I-3251. A valid authorization does not include a mere authorization of clinical trials: *British Technology Group SPC Application* [1997] *RPC* 118. Nor, where the UK marketing authorization had not yet been granted, does it include an email from the relevant German national competent authority described as the 'End of Procedure communication of approval'. *Merck, Sharp & Dohme v. Comptroller* [2016] *EWHC* 1896 (Pat).

[106] To overcome the problem where the underlying basic patent is revoked after the application date for an SPC, the UK IPO now checks whether the basic patent is in force before the related SPC comes into force. UK IPO, *Invalidity and surrender of Supplementary Protection Certificates* (12 September 2016).

[107] Calculated from the date of grant of authorization and not the date of publication of grant in the relevant Official Gazette: *Abbott Laboratories' SPC Application*, [2004] *RPC* 391, [10].

[108] *Hässle AB v. Ratiopharm*, Case C-127/00, [2003] *ECR* I-4781, [80]–[89] '('Where a mistake has been committed regarding the date of first marketing authorisation in the Community . . . the certificate must be declared invalid').

account third-party observations,[109] the national patent office assesses whether an SPC should be granted (that is, whether the patent covers the product[110] and whether appropriate authorizations exist);[111] there is no reinvestigation into the validity of the patent.

The relevant authorization must be the *first* authorization.[112] The first authorization must be in relation to the product that is in issue. Thus, in one decision it was held that the existence of a prior authorization for the same active ingredient as in the basic patent (that was used in a medical product) was not relevant because the prior authorization was for a veterinary product.[113] A product that is placed on the market in the European Union as a medicinal product for human use *before* undergoing a relevant marketing authorization is not able to be protected under an SPC.[114] The first authorization must be a marketing authorization in accordance with the relevant European directives and not some other authorization required by national law.[115] For pharmaceutical products, the relevant directive is the Directive on Medicinal Products for Human Use.[116] For veterinary products, it is the Veterinary Medical Products Directive.[117] It is only possible for the person who applies for the first marketing authorization to apply for an SPC; it is not possible for a person to apply for an SPC based on a marketing authorization obtained by a third party when the two people have no connection with each other.[118]

First authorization must be in relation to products that are covered by the basic patent. As the Court of Justice said, the mere existence of an earlier marketing authorization for a product does not 'preclude the grant of an SPC for a different application of the same product for which an [marketing authorization] has been granted'. This is on the condition that 'the application is within the limits of the protection conferred by the basic patent relied upon for the purposes of the application of the SPC'.[119]

If a patentee applies for an SPC, but is unable to submit the appropriate marketing authorization (for example because it was granted to the patentee's licensee and that person refuses to cooperate), the national patent office may contact the relevant authority.[120] However, the office will first require the applicant to provide evidence of the patentee's inability to supply the authorization, as well as Official Gazette information that will enable them to verify the identity of the product and the date

---

[109] On this, see *BASF AG's SPC Application* [2000] *RPC* 1. Documents are usually open to public inspection within 14 days of being filed. Observations should be made in writing.

[110] If a patent is granted for a combination of ingredients, but a certificate relates to one of the ingredients only, no certificate should be granted: *Centacor SPC Application* [1996] *RPC* 118. Whether a patent for a product would cover its salts or esters will be a matter of interpretation of the patent claims, applying principles explained in Chapter 22, section 3, pp. 654–66: see *Takeda Chemical Industry's Application* [2003] *EWHC* 649 (Pat).

[111] *BTG SPC Application* [1997] *RPC* 118 (refusing an SPC because no relevant authorization).

[112] SPC (PM) Reg., Art. 7, replacing SPC (MP) Reg., Art. 7; SPC (PPP) Reg., Art. 3(1)(d).

[113] *Neurim Pharmacueticals (1991) v. The Comptroller-General of Patents*, Case C-130/1, EU:C:2012:489.

[114] *Generics (UK) v. Synaptech*, Case C-427/09 [2012] *RPC* 70 (ECJ), [33]; *Synthon BV v. Merz Pharma*, Case C-195/09 [2012] *RPC* 37 (ECJ).

[115] *Hässle v. Ratiopharm*, Case C-127/00, [2003] *ECR* I-4781, [58]–[59]. It is not possible to rely on an emergency marketing authority issued under Art. 8(4) of Dir. 91/414/EEC of 15 July 1991 concerning the placing of plant protection products on the market [1991] *OJ L* 230/1 (19 August 1991) as the basis for a SPC: *Sumitomo Chemical v. Deutsches Patent-und Markeamt*, Case C-210/12, EU:C:2013:413, [38].

[116] 2001/83/EC [2001] *OJ L* 311/119 (which repealed and replaced Dir. 65/65/EEC).

[117] 2001/82/EC [2001] *OJ L* 311/1 (which repealed and replaced Dir. 81/851/EEC).

[118] *Eli Lilly v. Human Genome Sciences* [2012] *EWHC* 2290, [3]–[5].

[119] *Neurim Pharmacueticals (1991) v. The Comptroller-General of Patents*, Case C-130/1, EU:C:2012:489 (ECJ).   [120] *Biogen v. SmithKline Beecham Biologicals SA*, C-181/95, [1997] *ECR* I-357.

of authorization.[121] Once an SPC is granted, the relevant authority may demand an annual fee to maintain it in force. In addition to £250 application fee and £600 paid at the start date, in the United Kingdom an owner must pay £1,300 for the second year, £2,100 for the third, £3,000 for the fourth, and £4,000 for the fifth and final year (which must all be paid in advance of the SPC coming into force).[122]

3.2 SUBJECT MATTER

The aim of the SPC system is to ensure that patentees are not short-changed in terms of the time they have to exploit a patented invention because of unavoidable delays caused by the regulatory schemes that need to be complied with before a patented invention can be placed on the market. At the same time, it is also important that patentees do not use SPCs either to extend the duration of their patent that is not warranted or to obtain 'protection for different monopolies'.[123] These conflicting demands are mediated by way of the 'product', which is defined as the 'active substance' (in the case of plant protection) or the 'ingredient' (in the case of medicinal products) for which approval was gained.[124] The product ties together the SPC, the marketing authorization, and the basic patent in a way that ensures, at least in theory, that the protection provided by the SPC is justified and appropriate. Specifically, this is done by stipulating that: (i) an SPC will only be granted if the 'product is protected by a basic patent'; (ii) the protection conferred by the SPC only extends to the product covered by the marketing authorization; and (iii) the SPC will confer the same rights as conferred by the basic patent.[125] This requires a comparison to be made and a correspondence established between the basic patent, the product that has been subject to marketing approval, and the SPC (which should in theory cover the same thing). This gives rise to all of the problems that arise with claim interpretation discussed earlier, compounded by the fact that it requires a comparison to be made between three (rather than two) entities.

Given that a basic patent may cover a number of different products, it is possible to obtain different SPCs for each of the different products. This is on the condition that each of the products is covered by the basic patent and the products meet the necessary requirements for SPCs.[126] Where a basic patent covers a family of compounds, it is not possible for a patentee to obtain a new SPC whenever they place a new medical product on the market containing the principle active ingredient in the basic patent coupled with another active ingredient not protected by the patent.[127] The situation would change, however, if a combination consisting of an innovative active ingredient in respect of which an SPC had already been granted and another active ingredient was subject to a new basic patent.

---

[121] See Patent Office, *Supplementary Protection Certificates for Medicinal Products and Plant Protection Products: A Guide for Applicants* (2014), SPM 8.04.1.

[122] SPC (PM) Reg., Art. 12, replacing SPC (MP) Reg., Art. 12; SPC (PPP) Reg., Art. 12; Patents Rules 2007, r. 116(4)(b); Patents (Fees) Rules 2007 (SI 2007/3292), r. 6(2).

[123] *Takeda Chemical* [2003] *EWHC* 649, [12]. On the balancing of interests, see the Opinion of AG Trsenjak in *Neurim Pharmaceuticals (1991) v. Comptroller*, Case C-130/11, EU:C:2012:489.

[124] SPC (PM) Reg., Art. 1(b), replacing SPC (MP) Reg., Art. 1(b) (defining 'product'); SPC (PPP) Reg., Art. 1(8) (defining 'product'), 1(3) (defining 'active substance'), and 1(2) (defining 'substances').

[125] SPC (PM) Reg., Art. 4, replacing SPC (MP) Reg., Art. 4; SPC (PPP) Reg., Art. 4.

[126] *Georgetown University v. Octrooicentrum Nederland*, Case C-484/12, EU:C:2013:828, [30].

[127] The concept of a 'product' cannot include the therapeutic use of an active ingredient protected by a basic patent: *Yissum Research and Development Company*, Case C-202/05 [2007] *ECR* I–2839, [16]–[20].

The scope of the SPC is limited to the active ingredients that are identified in the claims of the basic patent.[128] As the Court of Justice said, 'Art 3(a) of the Regulation precludes the grant of a SPC relating to active ingredients which are not specified in the wording of the claims of the basic patent'.[129] In so doing, the Court rejected the so-called 'infringement test', which is based on the idea that the concept of a product corresponded to substances of a medicinal product that directly infringed the patent. As a result, the issue for national courts is to determine the active ingredients specified in the wording of the claims. The problem here, however, is that it is not clear what the Court of Justice meant when it said that the active ingredient must be 'specified or identified in the claims'. As Arnold J said in *Novartis*, it was unclear whether it was 'sufficient for the product to fall within the scope of the claim on its true construction' or whether 'something more [was] required and if so what?'[130] While the Court of Justice did not answer this question, it did say that 'there must be some wording indicating that [the active ingredients] are included in the claims'.[131] It has also been said that because the Court of Justice said that the product must be specified in the *wording of the claims*, this pointed to a test that was 'more demanding than merely requiring that the product be within the scope of the claim, although it is not clear how much more demanding'.[132]

The important question of how to determine the active ingredient in a basic patent was considered by the Court of Justice in *Eli Lilly v. Human Sciences*.[133] Stressing that an SPC can only be granted in relation to active ingredients that are specified in the basic patent (and the key role played by the claims for that purpose), the Court said that this does not mean that the ingredient necessarily had to be described in a specific way (particularly, that it had to be described structurally rather than functionally). Following basic principles, the Court said that the task of determining the active ingredient in the basic patent was to be done by interpreting the claims as required by Article 69 EPC 2000 and the Protocol on Interpretation. Given that the Court of Justice does not have jurisdiction to interpret the EPC (the European Union not being a Convention member), the question of whether the 'claims relate, implicitly but necessarily and specifically, to the active ingredient in question' (using broad functional language) was to be determined by the national court.

While it may have been thought that, given how active the Court of Justice has been in this area, the law would be settled, there is still some uncertainty, particularly in relation to 'the test to be applied in order to determine whether a product is "protected" by a basic patent' within the meaning of Article 3(a).[134] As Arnold J said, the broadest tenable

---

[128] *Medeva v. Comptroller-General*, C-322/10 [2011] *ECR* I-12051. *Daiichi Sankyo v. Comptroller General of Patents, Designs and Trade Marks*, Case C-6/11 [2011] *ECR* I-12255 (ECJ).

[129] *Medeva BV v. Comptroller-General of Patents, Designs and Trade Marks*, Case C-322/10 [2011] *ECR* I-12051, [25] (ECJ).   [130] *Novartis Pharmaceuticals v. Medimmune* [2012] *EWHC* 181, [53].

[131] *Medeva BV v. Comptroller-General of Patents, Designs and Trade Marks* [2012] *EWCA Civ* 523, [33]– [34]; cf *Yeda Research and Development v. Comptroller-General of Patents, Designs and Trade Marks*, Case C-518/10 [2011] *ECR* I–12209 (adopting a broader non-literal reading of the claims).

[132] *Novartis Pharmaceuticals v. Medimmune* [2012] *EWHC* 181, [56]. It seems that there is a narrower test for process claims than for product claims: *University of Queensland v. Comptroller-General of Patents, Designs, and Trade Marks*, Case C-630/10 [2011] *ECR* I–12231, [41] (requiring that the 'product to be identified in the wording of the claim as the product deriving from the process in question').

[133] Case C-493/12, EU:C:2013:835.

[134] *Teva UK v. Gilead Sciences* [2017] *EWHC* 13 (Pat), [91]. See also *Teva UK v. Merck Sharp & Dohme* [2017] *EWHC* 539 (Pat); *Sandoz v. Searle* [2018] *EWCA Civ* 49; *Novartis Pharmaceuticals v. Medimmune* [2012] *EWHC* 181, [53] (the tests laid down by the CJEU were 'unclear save in [their] rejection of the infringement test in combination cases').

interpretation is that for Article 3(a) to apply, the product must fall within at least one claim of the patent.[135] The problem however is that this interpretation has been rejected by the CJEU, which has said instead that the product must be 'specified'[136] or 'identified'[137] in the wording of the claims. For Arnold J, the problem here is that while the CJEU has said that it is not enough merely to show that the product falls within a claim, they have not specified what more is required for the product to be protected by a basic patent.[138] Given the uncertainty, in *Teva v Gilead* Arnold J asked the CJEU to clarify what the criteria were for deciding whether the product is protected by a basic patent.[139] To assist the CJEU, Arnold J answered his question by stating that a product is protected by the basic patent if: (i) the product falls within the scope of the claim when interpreted in accordance with Article 69 EPC 2000 and the Protocol on Interpretation (the 'Extent of Protection Rules'); and (ii) the product does so because it contains an active ingredient, or a combination of active ingredients, which embodies the inventive advance (or technical contribution) of the patent'. Put differently, the product must infringe 'because it contains an active ingredient, or a combination of active ingredients, which embodies the inventive advance (or technical contribution) of the basic patent'.[140] This seems a straightforward and sensible approach to a matter that has become unnecessarily complicated. Given that Arnold J's approach mirrors the basic two-step approach to interpretation proposed by the Supreme Court in *Actavis*,[141] it seems likely that it (or something similar) will be followed in the United Kingdom. What is less clear is whether the CJEU will also agree (and whether this matters post-Brexit). While we wait the outcome of this referral, it is possible to outline some of things that we do know about the way that the legitimate scope of an SPC is determined. These include:

(i)   The claims must be construed in light of Article 69 EPC and the Protocol on the Interpretation of Article 69 (the 'Extent of Protection Rules') rather than national laws which define the acts that amount to an infringement ('Infringing Act Rules').[142]

(ii) The fact that the product in the SPC would infringe the patent should not be used as a guide for determining the scope of the SPC because it may lead to protection being given for new and different monopolies.[143]

(iii) There is no particular form that the active ingredient must take in the claim: the identification of the active ingredients in the claims by way of a structural formula (or Markush formula) is permissible (but not essential).[144]

---

[135] Interpreted by way of the EPC Art. 69 and the Protocol on interpretation ('Extent of Protection Rules'). *Sandoz v. Searle* [2017] *EWHC* 987 (Pat), [61].

[136] *Medeva BV v. Comptroller-General of Patents, Designs and Trade Marks*, Case C-322/10 [2011] *ECR* I-12051, [28].

[137] *University of Queensland v. Comptroller-General of Patents, Designs, and Trade Marks*, Case C-630/10 [2011] *ECR* I–12231, [23]–[24].

[138] In relation to functional descriptions, the CJEU said that the claims must 'relate, implicitly but necessarily and specifically, to the active ingredient'. *Eli Lilly v. Human Genome Sciences*, Case C-493/12, EU:C:2013:835, [39], [44] (which Arnold J said was 'an unclear test which is difficult to apply': *Teva UK v. Gilead Sciences* [2017] *EWHC* 13, [81]. See also *Sandoz v. Searle* [2017] *EWHC* 987, [63]).

[139] *Teva UK v. Gilead Sciences* [2017] *EWHC* 13 (Pat), [95].   [140] Ibid., [96].

[141] *Actavis v. Eli Lilly* [2017] *UKSC* 48, (SC).

[142] Section 60(1)(2) 1977 PA; *Teva UK v. Gilead Sciences* [2017] *EWHC* 13 (Pat), [35]–[38].

[143] This is because if the patent was for X and an SPC was for X & Y, the SPC would infringe (because it takes X), but also extends protection beyond the patent to Y. See *Takeda Chemical Industries SPC Application* [2003] *EWHC* 649, [7]–[12]; *Teva UK v. Gilead Sciences* [2017] *EWHC* 13 (Pat), [39]–[43].

[144] *Sandoz v. Searle* [2017] *EWHC* 987, [65]; *Eli Lilly v. Human Genome Sciences*, Case C-493/12, EU:C:2013:835.

(iv) It is not necessary for a claim to 'individually name or depict the active ingredient', nor does it matter that a claim covers a number of compounds in addition to
the active ingredient.

3.3 LIMITS

The rights granted under an SPC are subject to the same limitations and obligations as
applied to the basic patent.[145] An SPC will therefore be subject to licences of right if the
patent would have been subject to such a licence prior to its expiry.[146]

3.4 DURATION

The SPC comes into operation at the expiry of the patent. This is subject to the requirement that the patent is maintained until the end of its potential term.[147] If the patent
is permitted to lapse, is declared to be invalid, or is revoked, the SPC will not come
into effect. The duration of an SPC will vary depending on the length of time it took
to receive regulatory approval. The maximum period for an SPC is five years. The
period is ascertained by calculating the difference between the date of application for
the basic patent and the date of the grant of the first authorization, less five years. This
means that if a patent application was made in 2005 and authorization was granted
in 2014, the relevant certificate should last for four years. However, because there is a
maximum duration of five years, if the authorization was granted in 2017, the duration of the SPC would be five years. The average term of the SPCs granted in the United
Kingdom in 2000 was just over three years.[148] Amendments effected to encourage
investigation into diseases affecting children can lead to a six-month addition to the
certificate taking it to a maximum of five and a half years (even where no paediatric
indication is achieved).[149]

The duration of the SPC is formulated in such a way as to ensure harmonization within
Europe regarding the date of the *expiry* of all national SPCs. Consequently, although for
the purposes of an application the relevant authorization is the first national authorization, for the purposes of calculating the duration of the SPC, the relevant authorization is
the first *EU* authorization.[150] For example, if A applies for a patent for aspirin on 1 January
2010 and gets marketing authorization for the sale of aspirin in the United Kingdom

---

[145] SPC (PM) Reg., Art. 5, replacing SPC (MP) Reg., Art. 5; SPC (PPP) Reg., Art. 5.

[146] PA 1977, s. 128B and Sch. 4A, para. 1(2); *Research Corps SPC* [1994] *RPC* 667. On terms, see *Research Corps SPC (No. 2)* [1996] *RPC* 320.

[147] SPC (PM) Reg., Art. 13, replacing SPC (MP) Reg., Art. 13; SPC (PPP) Reg., Art. 13.

[148] B. Domeij, *Pharmaceutical Patents in Europe* (2000), 268.

[149] Regulation (EC) No. 1901/2006 of the European Parliament and of the Council of 12 December 2006 on medicinal products for paediatric use [2006] *OJ L* 378/1, Arts 7, 8, 36, 52. For a discussion, see *W I Du Pont De Nemours v. UK Intellectual Property Office* [2009] *EWCA Civ* 966; *Merck's SPC Extension Application* [2010] *RPC* 99; *Dr Reddy's Laboraties v. Warner-Lambert* [2011] *EWHC* 3715 (Pat); U. Resse et al., 'The Legal Scope and Content of the Right to SPC Extension under the Paediatric Regulation 1901/2006' [2010] *EIPR* 146.

[150] This would include relevant EEA authorizations, e.g. in Iceland, Norway, and Liechtenstein. The question of the status of the first authorization as the basis for calculating duration was considered by the Court
of Justice in *Novartis*, Case C-207/03 [2005] *ECR* I-3209, on referral from *Novartis AG and University College London's SPC Application*, O/044/03 (12 February 2003).

on 1 January 2017, but had already received marketing authorization in Portugal on 1 January 2016, the UK SPC will only last for one year. If national regulatory procedures are particularly quick in other member states, UK SPCs may not be available to compensate owners for the loss of the opportunity to exploit the patent in the United Kingdom. To a number of commentators this is unfair, since the patent owner suffers delays, but gets no compensation.[151]

---

[151] B. Domeij, *Pharmaceutical Patents in Europe* (2000), 273.

PART III

LEGAL REGULATION
OF DESIGNS

1 INTRODUCTION

Designs play an important, but often neglected, part in our lives. As well as influencing the appearance of the clothes that we wear, the shape of the chairs in which we sit, and the surfboards that we ride, design also influences the decisions that we make as consumers—why it is that we choose one toothbrush over another.[1] The practice of design covers a variety of domains ranging from industrial design,[2] urban planning, graphic design, and stage design, through to costume design, fashion design, product design, and packaging design.[3] In reflection of this diversity, the role played by design varies greatly. In some cases, an object may be designed for frivolous or trivial reasons; in other cases, the way in which an object is designed may play an important role in how effectively the designed article works. Whatever role design performs, it is widely recognized to be a time-consuming, costly, and valuable activity. Given that the art of designing is concerned with the nature and appearance of objects, one of the notable aspects of designing is that the results are readily copied. Not surprisingly, therefore, intellectual property protection plays an important role in regulating the creation and use of designs. While technological developments such as the photocopier, tape recorder, video recorder, and digital technologies—which changed both where copying occurred and who did the copying—played

---

[1] For emphasis in legal commentaries on designs as marketing instruments, see A. Kur, 'The Green Paper's Design Approach: What's Wrong with It' [1993] *EIPR* 374, 376; F.-K. Beier, 'Protection for Spare Parts in the Proposals for a European Design Law' (1994) 25 *IIC* 840, 841. A UK IPO report suggests that £33.5 billion was spent in the United Kingdom on design in 2008: see J. Haskel and A. Persole, *Design Services, Design Rights, and Design Life Lengths in the UK* (2011), i.

[2] C. Woodring, 'A Designer's View on the Scope of Intellectual Property Protection' (1996) 24 *AIPLA QJ* 309 (defining industrial design as 'the professional service of creating and developing concepts and specification that optimize the function, value, and appearance of products and systems for the mutual benefit of user and manufacturer').

[3] V. Papanek, *Design for the Real World: Human Ecology and Social Change* (1984), 3–4 (defining design as 'the planning and patterning of any act towards a desired, foreseeable end').

a key role in shaping copyright law over the last century, design law has for the most part escaped unscathed from such changes. While new technologies have delivered new ways of creating designs, these have been readily accommodated within the existing legal frameworks. The spectre of readily accessible 3D-printing technologies, which effectively allows three-dimensional objects to be recreated in the home, seems set to change this situation. While the long-term impact will depend on a range of factors, such as the cost of copiers and the strength of the three-dimensional copies, it seems that 3D-printers are set to change the landscape in which design law operates.[4] As the Hargreaves Report noted: 'Digital technology is altering the nature of design. It has radically altered the way in which many designs are produced, and the development of fabrication through "3D printing" can be expected to have a substantial impact.'[5]

Over time, a number of different areas of intellectual property, such as trade marks,[6] passing off,[7] and the law of breach of confidence,[8] have been used to protect designs. In the next six chapters, we concentrate on those areas of intellectual property law more commonly used to protect designs:

(i) the UK registered design system established by the Registered Designs Act 1949 (modified in 2001 to comply with the Designs Directive);

(ii) the Community registered design system;

(iii) the unregistered Community design system;

(iv) copyright protection provided by the Copyright, Designs and Patents Act 1988 (CDPA 1988); and

(v) UK unregistered design right protection, which was established by Part III of the CDPA 1988.

1.1 DESIGNS AND BREXIT

Brexit will impact on design law in a number of ways. As with other areas of intellectual property, the precise nature of the impact will depend on the changes that are made, the transitional provisions agreed to, and the nature of any new provisions introduced. Post-Brexit, designs in the United Kingdom will be protected by the UK registered design

---

[4] See B. Depoorter, 'Intellectual Property infringements and 3D printing' (2014) *Hastings Law Journal* 1483; S. Bechtold, '3D Printing, Intellectual Property and Innovation Policy' (2016) *IIC* 517; S. Bradshaw, A. Bowyer, and P. Haufe, 'The Intellectual Property Implications of Low-Cost 3D Printing' (2010) 7(1) *SCRIPTed* 5.

[5] I. Hargreaves, *Digital Opportunity: A Review of Intellectual Property and Growth* (2011), [7.10].

[6] *Philips Electronics BV v. Remington Consumer Products* [1998] *RPC* 283. It seems that, in light of harmonization, words can be protected as designs, and this raises the issue of the relation of design law to trade mark law and practical questions as to whether a person is better off registering a logo as a design (or relying on unregistered design right in a logo) rather than a trade mark: Musker, 14; C.-H. Massa and A. Strowel, 'Community Design: Cinderella Revamped' [2003] *EIPR* 68, 77. Indeed, it might be noted that the effect of the *Arsenal* litigation (see Chapter 40, section 7, p. 1114) led to an increase in the number of UK design registrations. On the extent to which overlap between the new designs law and trade marks should be seen as a concern, see A. Kur, 'Protection of Graphical User Interfaces under European Design Legislation' (2003) 34 *IIC* 50, 60–2 (arguing that these concerns are exaggerated and observing that the possibility of such overlap has long existed in Germany without raising problems).

[7] *Benchairs v. Chair Centre* [1974] *RPC* 429. But cf. *Hodgkinson & Corby and Roho v. Wards Mobility Services* [1995] *FSR* 169.

[8] For recent examples, see *Carflow Products v. Linwood Securities* [1996] *FSR* 424; *Valeo Vision SA v. Flexible Lamps* [1995] *RPC* 205.

system, UK unregistered designs, and copyright. Given that the Community registered design and the unregistered Community design are both EU initiatives, these rights would cease to apply in the United Kingdom. While UK nationals will be able to make use of Community registered designs to protect their designs in the remaining member states (but not the United Kingdom), there may be some changes to the existing practice. For example, while UK nationals and businesses are currently not required to be represented in design proceedings before EUIPO, the situation may change post-Brexit.[9]

2 NORMATIVE BASIS OF DESIGN PROTECTION

It is a notable feature of the commentary on the legal protection of designs that very little consideration has been given to the question of why we protect designs.[10] Rather, it is assumed that the general arguments that justify the protection of works by copyright or inventions by patents, whether based on instrumental philosophies or ethical beliefs, are equally applicable to designs.

These assumptions are, no doubt, often warranted: the design process involves investment of time and money,[11] and successful designs can and are readily copied. Those who favour ethical arguments of a reap-and-sow nature argue that design protection is required to prevent second-comers reaping where they have not sown. Those who cling to a utilitarian approach argue that protection is necessary to provide sufficient incentives to encourage investment in the design process.[12] It is notable that the legal protection of designs has rarely been justified by reference to the natural rights of individual designers in their creations. This reflects a commonly held assumption that designs are less creative than artistic works because designing is subject to a number of inevitable constraints.[13] For example, the potential scope for the design of a table is constrained by our existing idea of a table, the functions that it must perform, the need for it to be comfortable, its cost, and the possibilities presented by available materials.[14]

The erroneous but widely held view that designers are somehow less creative than artists and authors has not only shaped the discussions justifying the legal protection of

---

[9] EUIPO, *Guidelines for Examination of Registered Community Designs* (1 February 2017), [3.6.1].

[10] J. Lahore, 'The Protection of Functional Designs: The Amended Proposal for a European Designs Directive' (1997) 1 *IPQ* 128, 132 (registering surprise at lack of analysis of benefits of design protection).

[11] Apparently, the development costs for the outer appearance of the Ford Sierra in the 1980s amounted to US$140 million, or 20 per cent of the total cost: M. Levin, 'Recent Developments in Nordic Design Protection' (1988) 19 *IIC* 606.

[12] *Electronic Techniques (Anglia) v. Critchley Components* [1997] *FSR* 401, 418. The CDR, Recital 7, states that 'enhanced protection for industrial design not only promotes the contribution of individual designers to the sum of Community excellence in the field, but also encourages innovation and development of new products and investment in their production'. See also *In the Matter of Morton's Design* (1900) 17 *RPC* 117, 121 (Farwell J) (the purpose of the design portion of the Act is the same as the patent portion of it); *Allen West & Co. v. British Westinghouse Electric 8 Manufacturing Co.* (1916) 33 *RPC* 157, 162 (design protection was said to be 'primarily to advance our industries and keep them at a high level of competitive progress'); *Dart Industries v. Décor Corporation* (1989) 15 *IPR* 403.

[13] R. Denicola, 'Applied Art and Industrial Design' (1983) 67 *Minn L Rev* 707, 741–3, and n. 165; J. Reichman, 'Design Protection in Domestic and Foreign Copyright Law' [1983] *Duke LJ* 1143, 1160, 1220–1, 1235.

[14] Moreover, there is a tendency to place greater emphasis on the potential social costs that the legal protection of designs cause to competitors of the proprietors of such right. As designs are applied to 'articles', it is feared that any impediments placed on the reproduction of the design will also interfere with free competition for the article itself. One commentator describes this as the 'two-market conundrum', which arises because designs operate to render articles desirable both as (useful) articles and as attractive objects: Reichman, op. cit.

designs, it has also served to marginalize the role that the designer plays within design law.[15] There are two main reasons for this. The first is that designing is seen as being less creative than authorship: designers are seen to be more constrained by the market, by the laws of physics, by the needs of users, and by fashion.[16] As a result, the designer is seen to have less of an intimate relationship with their design than an artist has with their creations.[17] The second reason is that designing is rarely undertaken by an individual; usually, a designer will be part of a team, will be given a design brief, and will be asked to develop a number of possible solutions. A design that reaches the marketplace will often be the product of many individuals, not only one, and the role of the draughtsman in the design process may by no means be the most significant.[18] As a consequence, design law is more concerned with designs as assets[19] and their effects on the market than with the individuals who create the designs.[20] It has also focused on designs rather than designers. This can be seen in the fact that protection commences either from the date on which the design was first made available (for unregistered Community designs) or registered (for national registered designs and registered Community designs), rather than that on which the design was created, in the absence of moral rights for designers (or, in the case of the right to be named on the register, the practical impossibility of using such a right),[21] in the fact that duration is not linked to the life of the author, and in the relatively insignificant position of the designer in determining entitlement.

3 BRITISH HISTORY

While the story of how designs came to be protected in intellectual property law is a long and important one, we must deal with it here in outline. The story starts in 1839,[22] when, out of a desire to improve the aesthetic quality of industrially manufactured goods, Parliament introduced a registered design system.[23] Under this system, if an applicant submitted representations of a new and original design for an article of manufacture,

---

[15] Some 87 per cent of companies have their own design departments: OHIM, *Prospective Study about the Design Registration Demand at the European Union Level: Executive Summary* (May 2002), 7.

[16] The Designs Directive and CDR specifically acknowledge that the designer's freedom may be limited: see Designs Dir., Arts 5(2), 9(2), and Recital 13; CDR, Arts 6(2), 10(2), and Recital 14.

[17] Indeed, the designer is referred to as 'developing' rather than 'creating' a design: Designs Dir., Recital 13; CDR, Art. 14(2), Recital 14. The requirement of 'creation', however, is employed in framing an exception to the unregistered Community design: see CDR, Art. 19(2). And cf. the French version, which uses the terms '*le créateur*' and '*l'élaboration du dessin ou modèle*'.

[18] The CDR, Recital 7, does recognize the role of individual designers, but sees the more significant benefit from 'enhanced protection for industrial designs' as the encouragement of 'innovation and the development of new products and investment in their production'. The CDR explicitly refers to teamwork: CDR, Art. 18.

[19] Designs Dir., Recital 15, and CDR, Recital 11, both attribute the need to protect design features of modular products by reference to the fact that such features 'present a major marketing asset'.

[20] CDR, Recitals 8, 15 (although CDR, Recital 24, contemplates that the Community system might be used by individual designers).

[21] European Commission, *Green Paper on the Legal Protection of Industrial Design* (June 1991), III/ F/5131/91–EN (henceforth 'EC Green Paper'), [7.1.4], stating that a moral right 'hardly appears to be desirable and probably also not practical'.

[22] Prior to this, the Calico Printers Acts 1787 and 1794 conferred protection upon new and original patterns for linens, cotton, calico, and muslins *automatically*.

[23] Copyright of Designs (Registration) Act 1839. While design law was one of the first areas of modern intellectual property law to take shape, over time it has been eclipsed by copyright and patent law. This has led to the (inaccurate) claim that designs law is the stepchild of patents and copyright. See Sherman and Bently, chs 3, 4, pp. 163–6, 210–12.

the law would grant a monopoly over the design for up to three years. This registration system seemed to operate successfully for the rest of the century, with many thousands of designs being registered.[24] Insofar as there were problems with the design system, they largely concerned the relationship between the design system and the patent system in the protection of useful mechanical devices, and these problems seemed to disappear with improvements in the administration of the patent system.

However, just as the popularity of the registered design system reached a peak at the turn of the twentieth century, issues were raised about the relationship between design law and the copyright system. In large part, these questions arose as copyright law was expanded and rationalized to give effect to the Berlin revision of the Berne Convention of 1908. These reforms not only created the possibility of many designs being protected by copyright law for the first time (especially on the basis of the design drawings that were artistic works), they also threatened the viability of the registration system. This was because copyright offered a system of protection that was automatic (no longer requiring registration), potentially longer, and (in some respects) stronger.

The initial response of the legislature was to draw a boundary between designs, which required registration, and artistic works (such as works of artistic craftsmanship), which were protected under the copyright system. As a result, the Copyright Act 1911 included a provision excluding from copyright protection works that were 'capable' of being registered as designs and which were intended to be used as the basis for multiplication by an industrial process. Later statutes employed different techniques to regulate the boundary between copyright and design. In one way or another, all of these proved to be unsatisfactory. Perhaps the most bizarre consequence of the last such attempt to establish a boundary was that designs that were unregistrable because they were 'dictated by function' received longer protection than those that were registered. Such protection was widely referred to as 'industrial copyright'.

In response to these failings, the CDPA 1988 fashioned a new 'design–copyright interface'. It did so by modifying the Registered Designs Act 1949 so that registration was confined to aesthetic designs, adding important defences to copyright infringement (sections 51 and 52), and establishing a new unregistered design right regime. As we will see, from July 2016 important changes were made to this scheme to bring industrially manufactured items into line with other artistic works.

4 INTERNATIONAL FLEXIBILITY

While the United Kingdom pursued its own ideas as how best to protect designs, other countries took different approaches. Some placed emphasis on copyright; others, on unfair competition law; others, on registration.[25] There was little consensus and consequently few international norms could be agreed.[26] The Paris Convention contains provisions on national treatment and the priority dates of design applications, but nothing of substance

---

[24] L. Bently, 'Requiem for Registration? Reflections on the History of the UK Registered Design System', in A. Firth (ed.), *Perspectives in Intellectual Property, Vol. I: The Prehistory and Development of Intellectual Property* (1997), 1.

[25] J. Reichman, 'Design Protection in Domestic and Foreign Copyright Law' (1983) 32 *Duke LJ* 1143; H. Cohen Jehoram, 'Designs Law in Continental Europe and Their Relation to Copyright Law' [1981] *EIPR* 235; C. Fellner, *The Future of Legal Protection for Industrial Design* (1985), ch. 6.

[26] A. Kingsbury, 'International Harmonisation of Designs Law: The Case for Diversity' (2010) 32(8) *EIPR* 382.

on registered design protection.[27] The Berne Convention is only a little more prescriptive. While 'applied art' is included in the subject matter covered by the Convention,[28] countries of the Berne Union are given free rein with regard to the scope of protection and to whether any formalities may be required.[29] The only specific requirement in relation to designs in the Berne Convention is that if special protection is not granted, then such works shall be protected as artistic works. Even the Agreement on Trade-Related Aspects of Intellectual Property Rights (TRIPS) only has two articles on designs.[30] Design laws are allowed to vary on a national basis.

Not surprisingly, the variation in national design protection across Europe was seen to present a problem for the European Union and in particular the internal market.[31] In 1991, the Commission issued a Green Paper laying out a scheme to tackle the problems raised by the enormous variation in national designs laws.[32] The Green Paper was notable for its advocacy of a 'designs' approach—treating designs as a distinct field of law rather than as a branch or extension of copyright or patents. The Green Paper advocated a three-pronged approach, involving harmonization of national registered designs law, the establishment of a Community registered design system, and the introduction of an unregistered Community design right. It seemed that this would require the passage of two pieces of Community legislation—namely, a directive to harmonize national law and a regulation to establish the two Community-wide rights. Following consultation, two Proposals were published.[33] The Commission decided to start with the directive, it being understood that the regulation—where relevant—would be substantively the same. Following criticisms of the initial proposal, in particular in the European Parliament, an amended Proposal for a Directive was published in 1996.[34] Although there were a number of significant amendments for designs generally, the legislative process was dogged by the issue of the appropriate form of protection for car spare parts. Ultimately, as is explained in Chapter 26, differences could not be resolved. Consequently, in the so-called 'standstill plus' compromise, the Directive left the question to member states. Once the Directive was adopted in July 1998, the Commission's focus returned to the regulation. Amended proposals were published in 1999 and 2000, and the Regulation was adopted in December 2001.

---

[27] Paris, Arts 2 and 4C(1). Indeed, until the Lisbon revision of 1958, the Convention did not even require countries of the Paris Union to protect industrial designs: Paris, Art. 5*quinquies*. This does not specify how protection is to be conferred, so that compliance may be achieved through copyright or unfair competition rather than *sui generis* designs law.   [28] Berne, Art. 2.

[29] Berne, Art. 2(7). Under Berne, Art. (7)(4), applied art should be protected for a minimum period of 25 years.

[30] TRIPS, Arts 25 and 26. This requires members to provide protection for independently created industrial designs that are new or original. More specifically, it provides that the owner of a protected industrial design shall have the right to prevent third parties from making, selling, or importing articles bearing or embodying the design for at least ten years. Certain limited exceptions are permitted. See Gervais, [2.240]–[2.250]; A. Kur, 'TRIPS and Design Protection', in Beier and Shricker.

[31] *Keurkoop BV v. Nancy Kean Gifts BV*, Case 144/81 [1982] *ECR* 2853; *Consorzio Italiano della Componentistica de Ricambio per Autoveicoli 8 Maxivar v. Regie Nationale des Usines Renault*, Case 53/87 [1988] *ECR* 6039; *AB Volvo v. Erik Veng (UK)*, Case 238/87 [1988] *ECR* 6211.

[32] European Commission, *Green Paper on the Legal Protection of Industrial Design* (June 1991), III/F/5131/91–EN. For useful accounts of national laws prior to harmonization, see B. Gray and E. Bouzalas, *Industrial Design Rights: An International Perspective* (2001).

[33] For commentaries, see A. Horton, 'European Designs Law and the Spare Parts Dilemma: The Proposed Regulation and Directive' [1994] *EIPR* 52; F.-K. Beier, 'Protection for Spare Parts in the Proposals for a European Design Law' (1994) 25 *IIC* 840.

[34] See G. Dinwoodie, 'Federalized Functionalism: The Future of Design Protection in the European Union' (1996) 24 *AIPLA QJ* 611; T. Margoni, 'Not for Designers: On the Inadequacies of EU Design Law and How to Fix It' (2013) 4(3) *JIPITEC* 225.

The Directive attempts to harmonize the features of national registered design systems that most obviously affect the functioning of the internal market.[35] It refers to this as 'limited approximation' rather than as full-scale harmonization.[36] Harmonization was required in relation to the 'conditions for obtaining registration', the rights of the design owner, the term of protection, and grounds on which the registration can be invalidated.[37] In contrast, issues of procedure and remedies were left to member states.[38] The Designs Directive also allows member states to protect designs by other regimes such as (national) unregistered design rights or competition law.[39] The Directive requires that member states do not treat the existence of registered design protection as pre-empting protection by copyright, a regime referred to as 'cumulation of copyright'.[40] The Directive was to be implemented by 28 October 2001, and the British government did so by amending the Registered Designs Act 1949 from 9 December 2001.[41]

The Community Design Regulation established a Community-wide system of registered design protection with a Community Design Office based at the Office for Harmonization in the Internal Market (OHIM) in Alicante, Spain. This became operational on 1 April 2003.[42] On 23 March 2016, OHIM was renamed the European Union Intellectual Property Office (EUIPO). Like the Community trade mark, the vision that drives the registered Community design is the replacement of national design systems (which, even if harmonized, present the possibility of national rights owned by different people) with a unified system for obtaining a Community design with uniform effect throughout the entire Community.[43] The registered Community design is acquired by an application to EUIPO, but there is no substantive examination. A registered Community design can last for up to 25 years and confers an 'absolute monopoly' on the proprietor. The validity of the designs can be challenged in proceedings at the Community Design Office,[44] or by way of a defence to an infringement action in a Community design court.[45]

The registered Community design is supplemented by the unregistered Community design right, available under the Community Design Regulation since 7 March 2002.[46] The unregistered Community design right is intended to provide short-term protection for those industries (such as clothing manufacture) for which registration is not appropriate—primarily because designs are of value for only a limited period of time.[47] Unregistered Community designs are also intended to provide temporary protection while proprietors consider whether a design is worth registering.

---

[35] Designs Dir., Recitals 1, 2, 3. [36] Designs Dir., Recitals 1, 3, 5.

[37] Designs Dir., Recitals 9, 10; CDR, Recitals 17, 21. [38] Designs Dir., Recitals 5, 6.

[39] Designs Dir., Art. 16, Recital 7; CDR, Recital 31. [40] Designs Dir., Art. 17, Recital 8; CDR, Recital 32.

[41] Perhaps not surprisingly (although no doubt rather annoyingly), the UK legislature has implemented the Directive into UK law by way of statutory instrument and, on occasion, has decided to alter the wording. We can be relatively certain that the UK courts will ignore these modifications and rely, where appropriate, on the Directive itself. Even the UK IPO has been irritated by the redrafting: *Design Practice Notice: Component Part of Complex Product Visible in Normal Use* (7 January 2003) DPN 1/03.

[42] The substantive provisions are aligned with those in the Directive: CDR, Recital 9. The constitutional validity of the Registered Designs Regulations 2001 (which implemented the Directive in the United Kingdom) was upheld by the Court of Appeal in *Oakley Inc v. Animal Ltd and ors* [2006] *Ch* 337. See M. Howe, '*Oakley Inc. v. Animal Ltd*: Designs Create a Constitutional Mess' (2006) 28(3) *EIPR* 192.

[43] CDR, Recital 1. [44] CDR, Art. 25. [45] CDR, Arts 24, 25.

[46] The aim of the unregistered Community design right is to strengthen the competitive position of European industries (not to complete the internal market): EC Green Paper, [4.3.9].

[47] J. Reichman, 'Design Protection and the New Technologies: The US Experience in a Transnational Perspective' (1989) 19 *U Balt L Rev* 6, 23.

An unregistered Community design right arises automatically when a design that is novel and has an 'individual character' is first made available in the Community.[48] The protection lasts for three years from the date on which the design was first made available.[49] Unlike the registered Community design (which protects against independent creation), the unregistered Community design right only protects against copying. The right is enforced by an action in a national Community design court. It is at this stage that the validity of the right may be challenged.

5 UK REFORM: THE INTELLECTUAL PROPERTY ACT 2014

After years of complaint by designers, lawyers, and academics, the UK government has recently turned its attention to the topic of design law. While the reforms, which have been described as piecemeal, do not provide the wide-ranging review that is clearly needed, they do provide some needed changes. The trigger for the reform was the 2011 Hargreaves Review of intellectual property and growth, which was a review of the impact of digital technologies on intellectual property law and policy, with a particular emphasis on growth and innovation. While, tellingly, the terms of reference for the Hargreaves Review did not explicitly mention design law, nonetheless the report did look at the impact of digital technologies on the law. The key recommendation of the Review was that the UK Intellectual Property Office (IPO) should conduct a further review of design law and policy.[50] Following the government's acceptance of this recommendation, the UK IPO launched a 'call for evidence' in 2011 to identify areas where reform was needed.[51] This was followed by a consultation process that sought feedback on a number of proposed reforms.[52] While most of the initial proposals were adopted, a number of initial suggestions were not. One of the most important was the suggestion that the UK unregistered design right should be abolished.[53] Despite a number of problems with the UK unregistered design right, it was decided to retain a modified unregistered design right, not least because there was evidence that because it was used as a safety net by British companies, it was 'a very useful protection for industry'. Another initial suggestion that was not taken up was the idea that the design legislation should be amended to state explicitly that design protection does not apply for general concepts and ideas.[54]

---

[48] It is the first Community-wide right to be available automatically.

[49] V. Saez, 'The Unregistered Community Design' [2002] *EIPR* 585, 588 (thereby avoiding problems with using creation as the key date).

[50] I. Hargreaves, *Digital Opportunity: A Review of Intellectual Property and Growth* (2011), ch. 7. See HM Government, *The Government Response to the Hargreaves Review of Intellectual Property and Growth* (August 2011).

[51] This was followed by UK IPO, *IPO Assessment of the Need for Reform of the Design Intellectual Property Framework* (December 2011) and, subsequently, another consultation process: UK IPO, *Consultation on the Reform of the UK Designs Legal Framework* (July 2012). For a summary of responses, see UK IPO, *Consultation on the Reform of the UK Designs Legal Framework: Summary of Responses* (December 2012).

[52] UK IPO, *Consultation on the Reform of the UK Designs Legal Framework Government Response* (April 2013).

[53] UK IPO, *Consultation on the Reform of the UK Designs Legal Framework* (2012), [4.2] (noting that the United Kingdom is alone in retaining unregistered design right alongside the Community unregistered design right).

[54] Ibid., [4.18]–[4.22]. For response, see UK IPO, *Consultation on the Reform of the UK Designs Legal Framework: Summary of Responses* (December 2012), [22]–[24]; UK IPO, *Consultation on the Reform of the UK Designs Legal Framework Government Response* (April 2013), [35]–[37].

Eventually, the remaining recommendations were included in the Intellectual Property Bill 2013–14, which was introduced into the House of Lords on 9 May 2013. After a number of revisions, the Intellectual Property Act 2014 was given royal assent on 14 May 2014.

In relation to *UK registered designs*, the new Act removes the requirement that an applicant for a design needs to be the owner, changes the rules in relation to ownership of commissioned designs, removes the rule prohibiting the UK IPO from registering an interest in a registered design unless it is satisfied that the same interest applies to any associated unregistered designs, and introduces a right of prior use into UK law. Changes have also been made to allow the United Kingdom to become a signatory state to the Hague System for the International Registration of Design.[55] The new Act also introduces changes that ensure that businesses that have permission to use a Community registered design are able to defend themselves against accusations of infringement of UK artistic copyright. Changes also took place to allow appeals to be made from decisions at the IPO to newly established 'Appointed Persons',[56] and to reduce fees for electronic filing.

A number of changes have also been made in relation to the *UK unregistered design right*, including amending the definition of design to prevent rights holders from using a very small part (or 'aspect') of their design as the basis for a claim that a third party is infringing their design. Changes have also been made that clear up some of the uncertainty in relation to the requirement that unregistered design right must not be commonplace in the relevant design field, that simplify the rules in relation to who can qualify as owner of unregistered design right, and which remove the rule that said that UK rights were automatically owned by commissioners, to make the designer the initial owner of commissioned designs. A number of new exceptions have also been introduced. We will look at each of these changes in the relevant sections later in this Part.

6 PLAN OF DISCUSSION

The effect of the combination of British and European law is to create a system of design protection that is multi-layered, complex, and lacking in logic. The United Kingdom affords registered protection to virtually all new designs and unregistered protection to most three-dimensional designs that are not commonplace. There is also the possibility of copyright protection for designs for three-dimensional artistic works, patterns, and surface decoration. In addition to these national schemes, there are two further layers of Community protection that arise either by registration (and last for up to 25 years) or automatically on publication of the design (and last for three years thereafter). To summarize, there are currently five different ways to protect a design. These are via:

(i) a UK registered design;

(ii) a registered Community design right;

(iii) an unregistered Community design right;

(iv) copyright protection of design drawings for artistic works (such as sculptures), two-dimensional designs, and surface decoration; and

(v) a UK unregistered design right.

---

[55] Discussed in Chapter 25, section 3, p. 729.

[56] RDA, 1949, s. 27A-27B. For the first designs decision by an Appointed Person see *Erol's Design Application*, Appeal O/253/17 (18 May 2017).

Since the substantive law dealing with UK registered designs, registered Community designs, and unregistered Community designs are virtually identical, we will look at them together over the next four chapters. In the next chapter (Chapter 25), we look at the way in which design rights arise—whether, in the case of UK registered designs and registered Community designs, by registration, or, in the case of unregistered Community designs, automatically. In the following two chapters, we look at the criteria which UK registered designs, registered Community designs, and unregistered Community designs need to comply with to be valid. In Chapter 26, we examine the subject matter requirement that there be a 'design'. In Chapter 27, we explore the concepts of 'novelty', 'individual character', and other aspects of validity. In Chapter 28, we consider who is entitled to apply for a design registration, and the rules relating to ownership and exploitation. We also look at infringement and exceptions in the three harmonized systems. In Chapters 29 and 30, we consider the two other main forms of protection for designs in the United Kingdom: in Chapter 29, we examine UK copyright law as it applies to designs; in Chapter 30, we look at the UK unregistered design right.

7. A NOTE ON LANGUAGE

As was noted earlier, the United Kingdom implemented the Designs Directive in 2001 by amending the Registered Designs Act 1949. One development that is helping to simplify this complex area of law is that a custom has developed in the United Kingdom whereby counsel and the courts refer directly to the Regulation and the Designs Directive rather than to the 1949 Act.[57] Where possible, we will follow this practice.

---

[57] See, e.g., *Dyson v. Vax* [2010] *EWHC* 1923, [9] (Arnold J) (also noting, at [10], that the provisions in the Designs Directive were to be construed in the same way as the provisions in the Community Designs Regulation).

25

HOW DESIGN PROTECTION ARISES IN THE UNITED KINGDOM AND THE EUROPEAN UNION

1 INTRODUCTION

This chapter is concerned with the way UK registered designs, registered Community designs, and unregistered Community designs come into being. The chapter is not concerned with copyright protection of designs nor with the UK unregistered design right, which are examined in Chapters 29 and 30. While the bulk of the chapter focuses on design registration, it also looks at the conditions that need to be satisfied for an unregistered Community design right to come into being. An understanding of the process by which a design comes into being is critical to understanding design law generally, not least because it has a direct bearing on the substance of design protection.

2 DECISION TO REGISTER

The decision whether to register a design is primarily a question of business strategy.[1] The critical issue is whether the advantages of registration outweigh the disadvantages, particularly when compared to alternative modes of protection. This will depend upon a range of factors, including the type of design in question, the cost of the design, the importance of monopoly protection, the likelihood of a competitor independently creating a similar

---

[1] For some empirical work, see OHIM, *Prospective Study about the Design Registration Demand at a European Union Level: Executive Summary* (May 2002), available online at http://oami.europa.eu/en/design/pdf/3830000.pdf. Although we set out some factors that would be taken into account by someone deciding whether to register or not, often there will be an established practice in a particular sector.

design,[2] and the scope of the potential market. While registration has been popular in the electronics and furniture industries, the textile and fashion industries have tended to rely more on unregistered design right.[3]

One of the features of the UK and EU registration systems is that the designs registration process is virtually automatic. There is no examination to see whether the application complies with the requirements for protection and no possibility for third-party opposition or intervention during the registration process; instead, there is only a formal review of the application. The simplified procedures are 'intended to keep to a minimum the formalities and other procedural and administrative burdens, as well as the cost to applicants, thereby making registration more readily available to small-and-medium sized enterprises and to individual designers'.[4]

The registration systems confer a number of benefits on the design proprietor. First, registration provides some certainty, which justifies further investment in exploitation of a design. The certainty largely derives from filing and the manner in which this establishes priority over later designs.[5] The second advantage of registration is that the rights conferred on the proprietor tend to be stronger than unregistered rights. This is true of the European harmonized national systems and Community designs. Unregistered rights (copyright, the unregistered Community design, and the UK unregistered design right) are only infringed where the user of the design has copied the design. The registered rights enable proprietors to object to use of a design even where the design is independently created by a third party.[6] A third advantage is that the registered system potentially provides protection for 25 years, whereas the unregistered design rights tend to be shorter: unregistered Community design rights last for only three years, while the UK unregistered design right only last for ten years from marketing. (The exception is copyright for artistic works which, as of 28 July 2016, lasts for life plus 70 years—replacing the previous 25-year protection where more than 50 copies of an artistic work were made.) As a result, a prudent designer or design owner will need to take a range of factors into account when deciding whether to register a design. These include the likelihood that someone will copy or independently create a similar design, the difficulty of proving copying, the intended (and likely) markets for the design, and the likely longevity of the design. If automatic protection is deemed to be wanting, the design proprietor will need to consider whether the advantages of registration are sufficient to justify the cost of registration. As we will see, much has been done, particularly at the European Union Intellectual Property Office (EUIPO)—which until 23 March 2016 had been called the Office of Harmonization in the Internal Market (OHIM)—to make the system cheaper and administratively more attractive. The expense of registering a design is nothing like the expense associated with patenting.

Designers also have a choice as to where they register a design. Although the Designs Directive harmonized the salient substantive features of the design registration systems in member states, it left procedure to national law. As we have already intimated, this has resulted in divergences in the protection available in different member states. These differences will affect decisions as to whether to apply to register in the UK, to apply for a bundle of national registrations, to apply for a single Community registration, or to apply for a combination of national and Community registrations. Important differences include: how 'design' is defined (whether by reference to a deposit or graphic representations, and the

---

[2] This question is much disputed. In European Commission, *Green Paper on the Legal Protection of Industrial Design* (June 1991), III/F/5131/91–EN (henceforth 'EC Green Paper'), [4.3.9], the European Commission saw the risk of independent creation as slight.

[3] Especially in the light of the House of Lords' decision in *Designers Guild v. Williams* [2000] 1 *WLR* 2416.

[4] *Federation Cynologique Internationale v. Federacion Canina Internacional de Perros de Pura Raza*, Case C-561/11 (15 November 2012), Opinion of Advocate-General Mengozzi, [26].

[5] EC Green Paper, [6.2.4.2].　　　[6] Ibid., [6.4.2]–[6.4.4].

extent to which written delimitations on what is protected are allowed); whether the systems allow for single applications for multiple designs;[7] whether the systems allow registrations in secret or deferral of publication and with what consequences;[8] whether the systems permit applications relating to designs that do not identify a product; how the systems define priority; whether the systems provide for substantive examination, and if so, as to which potential grounds of objection;[9] whether the systems carry out a search of existing designs, and if so, how rigorous the search is; whether the systems demand declarations by the applicant to the effect that they believe the design to be new and have individual character, or that they intend to apply the designs to products; and whether the system allows for opposition.[10]

3 APPLYING TO REGISTER IN THE UNITED KINGDOM

National registered design protection in the United Kingdom is acquired by applying to the Designs Registry at the UK Intellectual Property Office (IPO). The registration process is governed by the Registered Designs Act 1949, (modified in 2001 to comply with the Designs Directive). In this section, we look at some the key features of the registration process in the United Kingdom. Before doing so, it should be noted that the Intellectual Property Act 2014 makes changes that allow the United Kingdom to give effect to the Hague Agreement concerning the International Registration of Industrial Designs.[11] The Hague Agreement enables the owner of an industrial design to obtain protection in a number of countries by filing a single application with the World Intellectual Property Organization (WIPO), in one language and with one fee. The European Union and, since 13 March 2018, the United Kingdom are members of the Hague Agreement. This means, even post Brexit, UK business will be able to use the scheme to enable more targeted country-specific protection.

3.1 APPLICATION

Section 1(1) of the Registered Designs Act 1949 states that '[a] design may . . . be registered under this Act on the making of an application for registration'.[12] To bring UK

---

[7] Prior to harmonization, the Benelux countries and Germany allowed applications containing up to 50 designs, while France and Italy permitted up to 100. In contrast, the United Kingdom required each application to relate to a single article or set of articles.

[8] Prior to European harmonization, many countries allowed for deferral, although the periods differed: in Scandinavia, deferral was for six months only; in the Benelux countries, for 12 months; in Austria, for 18 months; and in France, for three years.

[9] Art. 14 of the Swedish Act No. 2002: 570, amending the Design Protection Act No. 1970: 485 (requiring examination as to whether the application relates to a design, and whether the design is immoral or a misuse of a protected emblem, proprietorship, classification, representations). Prior to harmonization, some form of substantive examination took place in Austria, Portugal, and Scandinavia: see Suthersanen, 327, 337, 357.

[10] Art. 18 of Swedish Act No. 2002: 570 (allowing opposition for two months).

[11] IP Act 2014, s. 8, the enactment of which will introduce new RDA 1949, s. 15ZA (enabling the Secretary of State to make necessary changes).

[12] The UK registration process was modified on implementation of the Directive to reduce differences between the national process and that at EUIPO. In particular, 'statements of novelty' were abolished, as was the requirement that the applicant specify an 'article' to which the design was to be applied. Substantive examination based on a previous search was removed in 1999 even before harmonization made it desirable.

registration into line with EUIPO practice, since 1 October 2006 applicants have been able to incorporate any number of new designs into a single application (in contrast with previous practice, which limited applicants to one design per application).[13] Previously, the application to the Design Registry in the UK IPO had to be made by the person claiming to be the owner of the design.[14] On the basis that this created unnecessary delays in the registration process, the Intellectual Property Act 2014 removed the requirement that an applicant needed to be the owner of the design.[15]

The application should include two identical representations of the design (including, if desired, an explanatory description), a statement as to the product to which the design is to be applied, and (if desired) a 'partial disclaimer' identifying the features of the appearance for which protection is sought.[16] The applicant, or their representative, also needs to sign a declaration to the effect that 'the owner believes that the design is new and has individual character'. The fee is £60 per application (which includes a fee for publication). The cost of applying to register additional designs in the same application is £40 per additional design.[17]

3.2 REPRESENTATIONS

Undoubtedly, the most significant part of the application are the 'representations' of the design or 'specimens',[18] and any partial disclaimer indicating that the design is only for the appearance of part of a product.[19] The representations can be conceived as the positive claims, from which the disclaimer excludes matter, so that in combination they define the property. Other than being 'suitable for publication', the applicant is able to present a design in whatever format suits them. The most common types of representation are pencil drawings, black line drawings, photographs, or computer-generated graphic images.[20] Where design detail is very refined, it is also possible to include magnified views of the design.[21] As the Supreme Court decision of *PMS International Group v. Magmatic* shows, the style of representation chosen may play a pivotal role in determining the fate of a design.[22]

---

[13] The Regulatory Reform (Registered Design) Order 2006 (SI 2006/1974) changed the RDA 1949 to allow for multiple applications.

[14] RDA 1949, s. 3(2). If unregistered design right subsists, the applicant should be that person.

[15] RDA 1949, s. 3(2), repealed by IP Act 2014, s. 6(2).

[16] The IP Act 2014 allows applicants to include more information about the design, including who is the designer, whether the design was made public before the design was applied for, and whether the applicant is willing to license the design.

[17] Registered Designs (Fees) Rules 2016 (SI 2016/889).

[18] It is for the Registrar to decide whether specimens are acceptable, by reference, amongst other things, to ease of mounting: RDR, r. 21.

[19] RDR, rr 15 (partial disclaimer), 17 (representations). It should be noted that the register may be rectified under RDR, r. 20, and if a design has been declared partially invalid, such a declaration should appear on the register.

[20] UK IPO, *Guidance on use of representations when filing Registered Design applications* (1 June 2016), [2]. For guidance on accepted representation practices at EUIPO and UK IPO see *Convergence on graphic representations of designs: Common Communication* (15 April 2016) (aiming to harmonize EU design practice).

[21] UK IPO, *Guidance on use of representations when filing Registered Design applications* (1 June 2016), [2]. For guidance on accepted representation practices at EUIPO and UK IPO see *Convergence on graphic representations of designs: Common Communication* (15 April 2016) (aiming to harmonize EU design practice).

[22] [2016] *UKSC* 12. On this see UK IPO, *Registered Designs Examination Practice Guide* (16 March 2017), [11.06]–[11.07]; UK IPO, *Guidance on use of representations when filing Registered Design applications* (1 June 2016). For discussion of the SC decision see Chapter 27, section 2.1, p. 751.

The UK rules permit the inclusion of a 'brief description explaining the representation' on the front of the first sheet of each representation or specimen.[23] This can be used to specify the material from which the design is made, to identify a colour (for example using the Pantone system),[24] or to specify dimensions if they are important. Applicants are able to use 'disclaimers' to limit the scope of protection to specific aspects of a design. These should appear on the representations and thus be available to the public.[25] The disclaimer can take many forms including visual techniques (such as blurring or the use of broken lines) or a written disclaimer (for example, that 'protection is sought for the head of the toothbrush, the handle being disclaimed').[26] Alternatively, especially in cases in which the representation includes a photograph of the designed product, it may be appropriate to disclaim aspects of appearance of the whole product (such as 'protection is sought for the shape of the toothbrush, the materials, colours, words and patterns being disclaimed'), or a particular aspect of part of the product (such as 'protection is sought for the shape and texture, but not colour, of the handle of the toothbrush').

If there is no disclaimer, a tribunal will treat the full contents of the representation as the design.[27] While this may mean that the design might be valid, it might also make it easier for competitors to avoid infringement by altering or adding features so as to give a different overall impression (while perhaps still taking the features that embodied the registered proprietor's primary design investment). Imagine, for example, that an application relates to a toothbrush and the design investment went into developing a bend in the brush. The applicant submitted a photographic representation of the brush, including multicoloured bristles, coloured plastic stem, and Colgate logo, but failed to disclaim the colours, the bristles, logo, or the colour of the stem. A competitor could foreseeably reproduce the bend in the brush, apply a different logo, make the brush out of blue plastic with white bristles, and thus make a product that creates a different 'overall impression' on an informed user. (In an extreme case, the bend may be so striking that even the competitor's version would be regarded as creating the same overall impression.)

3.3 IDENTIFICATION OF THE PRODUCT

Although applicants for registration in the United Kingdom have to identify the product which they intend to apply the design to,[28] the significance of this should be made clear: design protection is *not* limited to the particular product mentioned in the registration[29] and, as a corollary, a design may lack novelty in the face of the design of a different product.[30] The identification of a product in the application is primarily procedural:[31] it enables the design to be classified, searches to be made, and so on. Thus, if a person designs a motif for use on wallpaper and identifies the product as wallpaper, the protection granted by registration is not limited to wallpaper: the use of the motif

---

[23] Note to Form 2A, which adds that 'any such description shall not be taken to limit the scope of protection conferred by registration of a design'.

[24] Verbal techniques could also usefully clarify colour, because 'subtle shades of colour do not photograph or reproduce well': Musker, 15.   [25] RDA 1949, s. 22(1); RDR, rr 15(2), 67.

[26] UK IPO, *Designs Practice Note 2/03: Apply to register part of a product* (January 2003).

[27] As was the practice formerly: *Kestos v. Kempat and Vivien Fitch Kemp* (1935) 53 *RPC* 139, 150.

[28] RDR, r. 14.

[29] See *Easy Sanitary Solutions v. EUIPO*, Cases C-361/15 and C-405/15, EU:C:2017:720.

[30] RDR, r. 14(3).

[31] It is also financial, since designs for lace and textile products are cheaper, and will affect whether the designs can be inspected.

by a third party on curtain fabric or duvet covers would infringe. Equally, a design for a 'whistling kettle' might be rejected in the face of an identical design for a 'kettle', while a toy car might infringe the registered design of a full-scale automobile. While the primary role of the designed product is procedural (and, as such, does not directly affect the scope of protection), it may have some indirect consequences. For example, it is unlikely that a registered design for the shape of a chair would be infringed by its use on the shape of a table, because an informed user would be unlikely to find that the two designs give rise to the same impression. Where the appearance of the product and the nature of the product are inseparably connected, the product will matter. As we will see, the product which a design is ultimately linked to (which may be different from the product indicated in the application)[32] also plays an important role in identifying who the notional 'informed user' is and the degree of design freedom available—factors that shape questions of validity (notably novelty and individual character), as well as the scope of protection.

3.4 GROUNDS FOR REFUSAL AND EXAMINATION

A design application can only be refused on certain specified grounds.[33] In order to bring the UK system into line with EUIPO practice, from 1 October 2006 the grounds for refusal in the United Kingdom were greatly restricted.[34] The Registrar *may* refuse to register a design if the application fails to comply with rules made under the Act,[35] and *must* do so if the application has not been made by the person claiming to be the proprietor of the design and, where relevant, the owner of a UK unregistered design right.[36] In addition, the Registrar *must* refuse an application if it does not comply with the definition of design,[37] if the design is dictated by function,[38] if it is contrary to public policy or morality,[39] or if the application is for an emblem mentioned in Schedule A1 to the Registered Designs Act 1949.[40] The Registrar *no longer* has the power to refuse registration on the grounds that the design lacks novelty or individual character. As a result of these changes, from 1 October 2006 the Registrar no longer examines applications for novelty and individual character (as had been past practice), effectively ending substantive examination in the United Kingdom. These issues can only now be addressed in invalidity proceedings or as a counterclaim in proceedings for infringement.[41] One of the consequences of the United Kingdom ending substantive examination of designs is that it increased the importance of post-grant challenges to the validity of designs.

---

[32] On this, see *Grupo Promer Mon Graphic SA v. OHIM*, Case T-9/07, [2010] *ECR* II-981, [54]–[60], in which the General Court found that the relevant class of products was for 'pogs', 'rappers', and 'tazos', rather than the more general category 'promotional items for games'.

[33] RDA 1949, s. 3A (as amended).

[34] RDA 1949, s. 1A (repealed by the Regulation Reform (Registered Designs) Order 2006).

[35] RDA 1949, s. 3A(2). In many cases, refusal can be avoided and the Registrar can ask the applicant to amend the application. RDA 1949, s. 1(1), refers to applications to register 'a design' and, in stark contrast with the approach of EUIPO, the UK Registry operates a rule of one design per application. If an applicant mistakenly submits an application relating to more than one design, the examiner may raise a 'divide out' request', under s. 3B(3), leaving the original application as a 'parent' and treating additional designs as 'child' applications: UK IPO, *Designs Practice Note 3/03: Dividing-out design applications* (March 2003).

[36] RDA 1949, ss 3A(3), (2)(3), 14.   [37] RDA 1949, ss 3A(4)(a), 1(2).

[38] RDA 1949, ss 3A(4), 1C.   [39] RDA 1949, ss 3A(4), 1D.

[40] RDA 1949, s. 3A(4)(c) and Sch. 1A.   [41] RDA 1949, ss 11ZA(1), 11ZB.

3.5 REGISTRATION AND PUBLICATION

On registration, the applicant is issued with a certificate and the design is open to inspection.[42] Registration gives the proprietor the exclusive rights set out in section 7 of the 1949 Act and described in Chapter 28. Registration is treated as being made as of the date of application (despite a typical three-month processing period).[43] As part of the reform of design law that took place in 2006, the Registrar is now required to open all new designs to public inspection[44] (thus ending the previous practice, which limited public access in relation to registered designs for textiles, wallpaper, or lace for two or three years[45]). As part of the reform of design law brought about by the Intellectual Property Act 2014, changes have been made to allow documents to be viewed online.[46] Under the 2006 regime, applicants were able to defer publication for 12 months; to bring UK law into line with European law, this has been changed by the 2014 Act to allow delay in publication for up to 30 months.

4 APPLYING TO REGISTER AT THE EUROPEAN UNION INTELLECTUAL PROPERTY OFFICE

Registered Community design protection is acquired directly by application to the European Union Intellectual Property Office (EUIPO) at Alicante or indirectly through the offices of member states.[47] The procedure is governed by the Community Design Regulation[48] and the Community Design Implementing Regulation,[49] as supplemented by EUIPO's *Guidelines for Examination of Registered Community Designs*.[50] From 1 January 2008, applicants have also been able to make use of the international registration system for industrial designs (established under the Hague Agreement and administered by WIPO) to obtain registration of a Community design.[51]

4.1 APPLICATION

The application, which must be signed, should include a request for registration, the name and address of the applicant (and their representative, if one is used), a representation of the design, an indication of the products in relation to which the design is intended to

---

[42] RDA 1949, ss 18, 22 (as amended); RDR, r. 67.   [43] RDA 1949, s. 3C.

[44] RDA 1949, s. 22(1).

[45] RDA 1949, s. 22(2) (repealed by Regulatory Reform (Registered Designs) Order 2006); RDR, r. 69.

[46] IP Act 2014, s. 9(2), introduces a new RDA 1949, s. 22(1)(aa). Section 9(3)–(6) makes consequential changes to RDA 1949, s. 22(5)–(6).

[47] CDR, Art. 35(1); Community Design (Fees) Regulations 2002 (SI 2002/2942) (UK charge: £15); M. Schlotelburg, 'The Community Design: First Experience with Registrations' [2003] *EIPR* 383.

[48] Council Regulation (EC) No. 6/2002 on Community designs [2002] *OJ L* 3/1 (5 January 2002).

[49] Commission Regulation (EC) No. 2245/2002 of 21 October 2002 implementing Council Regulation (EC) No. 6/2002 on Community designs [2002] *OJ L* 341/28 (17 December 2002).

[50] *Examination of Applications for Registered Community Designs* (1 August 2016). See also, EUIPO *Guidelines for Examination of Registered Community Designs: Examination of Registered Community Designs* (1 February 2017). See also EUIPO, *Convergence on graphic representation of designs* (15 April 2016) ('Common Practice Guidelines').

[51] The Hague Agreement Concerning the International Deposit of Industrial Designs 1999 allows applicants to make a single application to WIPO for a number of countries.

be used,[52] any relevant declaration of priority, a specification regarding languages,[53] and payment of the registration fee of €230. The application *may* also include a description, a request for deferment of publication, an indication as to classification, and citation of the designer.[54] Of these elements, the most important are the representation of the design[55] and the description. If an application fails to include the necessary data, the Office will not accord a filing date.[56]

4.2 REPRESENTATIONS

The representation should consist of a 'graphic or photographic reproduction of the design in black and white or colour'.[57] (In contrast with the United Kingdom, where the Registrar may accept specimens, which can be mounted in the register, specimens can only be accepted at EUIPO for registrations for which deferred publication is requested, since the process of publication in the Community Designs Bulletin by definition demands that the design be represented.[58]) Each representation must consist of at least one 'view' and may involve a maximum of seven views.[59] As the representation is the means to specify the features of design for which protection is sought, 'it is of the utmost importance that it is clear and complete and that nothing regarding the design is left to conjecture'.[60] As an official at EUIPO said, 'the selection of the means for representing a design is equivalent to the drafting of the claims in a patent: including features means claiming them'.[61] The choice of the mode of representation is up to the applicant; the only requirements are that the features for which protection is sought are distinguished clearly and the representation is 'suitable for publication'.[62]

The representation should only cover one design.[63] Where registration is for a repeating pattern, 'the representation of the design shall show the complete pattern and a sufficient portion of the repeating surface'.[64] Where registration consists of a 'typographic typeface', the representation should include the complete alphabet and all of the Arabic numerals, as well as five lines of text.[65]

The representation may also contain a single description per design not exceeding 100 words explaining the representation of the design or specimen.[66] However, this should not refer to novelty, individual character, or the technical value of the design.

---

[52] CDR, Art. 36(2); CDIR, Art. 1(d). The indication of a product should state clearly the nature of the product and EUIPO requests applicants to utilize the 'Euro-Locarno List', which takes Locarno's 32 classes and elaborates in the region of 4,000–5,000 products: CDIR, Art. 1(d).

[53] The application can be made in any of the official languages of the European Union, but must specify a second language from one of the five languages of the Office (Spanish, German, French, English, and Italian).

[54] CDIR, Art. 1(2).   [55] CDR, Art. 36(1)(c); CDIR, Art. 1(c).   [56] CDIR, Art. 10.

[57] CDIR, Art. 4.

[58] Alternatively, a specimen can be supplied (but only in relation to two-dimensional designs and where publication is deferred): CDIR, Art. 5(1). This facility seems to be made available to those who need time deciding whether to proceed to full registration, and presumably the submission of a specimen is regarded as minimizing the costs of securing protection to such undecided designers.

[59] CDIR, Art. 4(2).

[60] OHIM, *Examination Guidelines: Community Designs*, [4.4] (not repeated in the revised Guidelines).

[61] M. Schlotelburg, 'The Community Design: First Experience with Registrations' [2003] *EIPR* 383, 385.

[62] See generally *Mast-Jägermeister v. EUIPO*, Case T-16/16, EU:T:2017:68 (General Court, Eighth Chamber).

[63] For a discussion, see *Ball Beverage Packaging Europe v. EUIPO*, Case T-9/15, EU:T:2017:386 (General Court, First Chamber).   [64] CDIR, Art. 4(3).

[65] CDIR, Art. 4(4).   [66] CDIR, Art. 1(2)(a); CDR, Art. 36(3a); EC Green Paper, [8.6.7].

The description is used both positively to explain aspects of the representation and nega-tively to disclaim features for which protection is not desired. Although Article 1(2)(a) of the Community Design Implementing Regulations states that the description 'shall not contain statements as to the purported novelty or individual character of the design or its technical value', the description may be useful in ascertaining what the design is. (Rather than say that 'the novel part of the design is the pattern', the applicant should say that 'the design for which protection is sought is the pattern, the shape of the teapot being disclaimed'.[67])

It is also permissible for applicants to include a disclaimer in their application where they disclaim part of the design.[68] The EUIPO Design Guidelines suggest a number of techniques for delimiting the representation including dotted lines to indicate elements for which no protection is sought; 'or boundaries' or 'colouring' (of black-and-white rep-resentations) to identify features for which protection is sought.[69] (A distinct facility is provided for 'partial disclaimers' to be added after registration.[70])

4.3 MULTIPLE DESIGNS

In order to make the system as cheap and attractive as possible, particularly to those industries producing large numbers of short-lived designs,[71] several designs may be com-bined in one application.[72] Multiple applications are permitted so long as the designs are intended to be applied to products within the same class of the Locarno Convention, and even that restriction does not apply in the case of ornamentation.[73] Where an application includes a number of designs, the application may be divided.[74] The process of using a single application for multiple designs has proved to be very popular.

4.4 SECRET DESIGNS AND DEFERRED PUBLICATION

Provision exists for the registration of secret designs, which can remain unpublished for 30 months.[75] This is seen to be desirable because publication can 'destroy or jeopardise the success of a commercial operation involving the design'.[76] The EUIPO deferred pub-lication procedure, which is available in relation to all designs, can occur earlier if the applicant so requests.[77] In cases in which deferred publication is sought, an applicant does not have to prepare representations and may prefer to submit five copies of a specimen of each design (although these must be two-dimensional if they are to comply with practi-cal requirements).[78] A request for deferment is required and a small fee has to be paid

---

[67] Musker, 156–8, with useful examples.

[68] See *Green Lane Products v. PMS International* [2008] *EWCA Civ* 358, [31], citing Lewison J in *Green Lane Products v. PMS International* [2007] *EWHC* 1712 (Pat), [31] (a disclaimer limits the scope of the design rather than the design's application to certain product classes); RDR, rr 15 (partial disclaimer), 17 (repre-sentations). It should be noted that the register may be rectified under RDR, r. 20, and if a design has been declared partially invalid, such a declaration should appear on the register. See Musker, 157.

[69] EUIPO, *Examination of Applications for Registered Community Designs* (1 August 2016), [5.3].

[70] CDIR, Art. 18.   [71] CDR, Recital 25.

[72] CDR, Art. 37, Recital 25; CDIR, Art. 2; EC Green Paper, [4.3], [8.7.1]. Fees are reduced for the second to the tenth designs; further reductions are available per design for the 11th design onwards.

[73] CDIR, Art. 2(2).   [74] CDIR, Art. 10(3).   [75] CDR, Art. 50; CDIR, Art. 1(2)(b).

[76] CDR, Recital 26; EC Green Paper, [8.11.3].

[77] CDIR, Arts 15–16; EC Green Paper, [8.11.1] (explaining that deferred publication is desirable in the automobile and textile industries).   [78] CDIR, Art. 5.

(€40), followed by the normal publication fee (€120) when the design is finally published. Protection during the period of deferred publication is, however, limited to situations in which the design proprietor can prove that there was copying of the design.

4.5 DESIGNER'S ATTRIBUTION

Another feature of the EU system worth noting is the designer's 'moral' right of attribution—that is, the designer (or the design team) has the right to be 'cited as such before the Office and in the register'.[79] It is rather strange that the procedural rules then state that the application may—but need not—mention the designer.[80] Perhaps this might be to enable the designer to remain anonymous, if they so wish, but the effect is to leave unstated exactly how issues of citation are to be resolved.[81] Pending the formulation of specific rules by the Commission, existing legal procedures will need to be employed. In the case of a designer who has not been named by the legitimate proprietor, the most obvious way in which to enforce their right would be to bring an action against EUIPO. Conflicts between teams and individuals would probably need to be resolved before national Community design courts, seeking a declaration as to who has the right to be cited as the designer before the Office and in the register. Such a declaration could then be the basis of a further action against EUIPO. These procedural difficulties remove much of the significance of the designer's right to be cited.

4.6 GROUNDS FOR REFUSAL AND EXAMINATION

EUIPO does not conduct a substantive examination (for example as to subject matter, novelty, or individual character).[82] This is to minimize the procedural burdens on applicants, and to make protection cheaper and more readily available.[83] The idea is that examination is difficult, expensive, and inconclusive, and it is better that the validity of a given design be decided on the basis of an *inter partes* dispute (and thus disputes only over those designs with a significant market value).[84] Nevertheless if, on a formal examination, the Office 'notices' that the design does not satisfy the definition of design in Article 3a of the Community Design Regulation, or is contrary to public policy or accepted principles of morality, it shall notify the applicant, and, if the applicant fails to remedy the objection, EUIPO shall refuse the application.[85] EUIPO cannot, however, refuse obviously old designs.[86]

---

[79] CDR, Art. 18. However, if the design is a result of teamwork, the citation of the team may replace that of the individual designers.   [80] CDIR, Art. 1(2)(d).

[81] Musker, 119–20.

[82] CDIR, Art. 11. A formal examination is conducted: CDR, Art. 45; CDIR, Art. 10. See also *Celaya Emparanza y Galdos Internacional SA v. Proyectos Integrales de Balizamientos SL*, Case C-448/10 [2012] ECDR 17 (ECJ, First Chamber), [43] (describing the examination as an 'essentially formal, expeditious check'); cf. the *ex officio* examination of trade marks by OHIM.

[83] CDR, Recitals 18, 24. See also European Commission, *Explanatory Memorandum: Amended Proposal for a Council Regulation (EC) on Community Design* [2000] OJ C 248E, 3; Musker, 173.

[84] EC Green Paper, [2.3.4], [4.3.10]–[4.3.11]. A suggestion that OHIM (now EUIPO) provides an optional examination facility was not taken up: EC Green Paper, [8.9.1].

[85] CDR, Art. 47; CDIR, Art. 11. EUIPO, *Examination of Applications for Registered Community Designs* (1 August 2016), [4.1], states: 'Whether the product is actually made or used, or can be made or used, in an industrial or handicraft manner, shall not be examined'.

[86] Musker, 177 (noting no basis on which to refuse obviously old designs or ones owned by others).

4.7 REGISTRATION AND PUBLICATION

As long as the application meets the formal requirements, the Office is obliged to register the design and (except in cases of deferred publication) publish it in the Community Design Bulletin.[87] The published design registration includes the representations, indication of the product, and the name of the designer, but not any description lodged with the application.[88]

5 COMMUNITY UNREGISTERED DESIGN RIGHT

One of the distinguishing features of the unregistered Community design right is that it is not dependent on registration; instead, it arises automatically when certain conditions are satisfied. For a claimant to establish that they are the holder of an unregistered Community design right, they must do two things: (i) they must show that the design was initially made available to the public within the Community; and (ii) they must indicate what constitutes the individual character of their Community design. Once established, the onus falls on the defendant to contest the validity of the design either as a plea or a counterclaim in an infringement action. In the case of unregistered Community designs, jurisdiction to determine invalidity is confined to Community design courts, whether on an application for a declaration of invalidity or as a counterclaim to an infringement action.[89] As a preliminary matter, however, claimants first need to outline their design. This means that the claimant's pleadings are particularly important. As courts dealing with the UK unregistered design right have noted, this allows claimants to limit their claim to those parts of an article that have been copied—thus increasing their chances of a successful infringement action.[90]

To establish the existence of an unregistered Community design, the claimant must show that the design was first made available to the public within the Community.[91] If, as often will be the case, the question of the existence of the unregistered Community design arises in an infringement action, the claimant will also have to prove that the prior disclosure occurred within three years of the alleged infringement. It is clear that an unregistered Community design right cannot arise from a disclosure that occurs outside of the European Union; the initial disclosure *must* occur within the European Union.[92] If a design is initially disclosed outside of the European Union, this not only means that the design will not be protected as an unregistered Community design, but also undermines the possibility of registering the design (because of a lack of novelty). In this situation, the only real option is for

---

[87] CDR, Arts 48, 49, and 73; CDIR, Art. 13. The publication fee is €120.   [88] CDIR, Art. 14.

[89] CDR, Arts 24, 25. The High Court, which would include the IPEC, is designated for England: Community Designs (Designation of Community Designs Courts) Regulations 2005 (SI 2005/696).

[90] See *Ocular Sciences v. Aspect Vision Care* [1997] *RPC* 289, 422; *Fulton v. Totes Isotoner* [2004] *RPC* (16) 301, [34]; *Virgin Atlantic Airways v. Premium Aircraft Interiors Group* [2009] *EWHC* 26, [27]–[28].

[91] CDR, Art. 11.

[92] To provide certainty, in May 2004, the Commission introduced CDR, Art. 110a(5). This provides that, '[p]ursuant to Article 11, a design which has not been made public within the . . . Community shall not enjoy protection as an unregistered Community design'. See also the decision of the German BGH, *Gebäckpresse* ['Pastry Press'] I ZR 126/06 [2009] *GRUR* 79. On this, see A. Gartner, '*Bundesgerichtshof* (*Pastry Press*): The disclosure of designs outside the European Community' [2010] *EIPR* 181.

an applicant to rely upon the one-year grace period that is provided for in limited situations (discussed in Chapter 27).[93]

The second thing that a claimant must do to establish the existence of an unregistered Community design is 'to indicate what constitutes the individual character of their Community design'.[94] This means that, as well as setting out their design, a claimant also has to indicate those elements of the design that 'create a different overall impression on an informed user from any design that has been previously made available to the public'.[95] In *Karen Millen v. Dunnes Stores*,[96] the Irish High Court rejected the defendant's argument that to establish the existence of an unregistered Community design right, a claimant needed to *prove* that the design has individual character (rather than the much easier requirement of merely *indicating* what the individual character was). The Court rejected this argument on the basis that because the unregistered Community design was meant to provide designs with a short market life with protection without the burden of registration, this would have imposed a greater burden on claimants to unregistered designs than was imposed on parties who made use of registered designs. While this seems to be the correct approach, the Irish Supreme Court made a request for a preliminary ruling from the Court of Justice on this issue. In particular, the Irish Supreme Court asked:

> Is a Community design court obliged to treat an unregistered Community design as valid for the purposes of Article 85(2) of the Regulation where the rights holder merely indicates what constitutes the individual character of the design, or is the right holder obliged to prove that the design has individual character?[97]

As expected, the Court of Justice responded by stating that while the lack of registration formalities for unregistered designs meant the holder of the design was obliged to 'specify what he wants to have protected', the right holder was 'not required to prove that [the unregistered design] has individual character'. Instead, all that was needed was for them to 'identify the features of his design which gives it individual character'.[98]

6 WHICH AVENUE TO CHOOSE?

The registered Community design right and the UK registered design right can exist cumulatively[99] or as alternatives. If only one form of registration is wanted, the registered Community design may be preferable to a UK registered design (and other national rights) for a number of reasons, including that it is a EU-wide right, it is cheaper,[100] it is administratively more convenient (for example because of the possibility of making a single application with multiple designs), or because it offers the benefits of deferred

---

[93] One question that needs clarification is whether, to establish the existence of an unregistered Community design, a claimant must also prove that the design has been disclosed in a way that could reasonably have become known in circles specialized in the sector concerned (as per CDR, Art. 11(2)).

[94] CDR, Art. 85(2).   [95] CDR, Art. 6.

[96] [2007] *IEHC* 449. See also *Bailey v. Haynes* [2006] *EWPCC* 5, [53]–[54].

[97] *Karen Millen v. Dunnes Stores*, Case C-345/13, C:2014:2013, [22].   [98] Ibid., [46]–[47].

[99] CDR, Art. 95.

[100] EUIPO charges a fee of €230 for registration and €120 for publication. In the case of multiple applications, the basic fee must be paid only for the first design; thereafter, for the second to tenth designs, the fee is halved (to €115), and if the application contains 11 or more designs, the registration fee is reduced to €50. In the United Kingdom, the fee is £60 per application (except if the design is for lace or consists substantially of stripes or checks to be applied to textiles, in which case it is £35).

publication. However, in some circumstances national registration may be preferable to a registered Community design. Local protection may be preferred because in some countries—but not the United Kingdom—local protection may enable the proprietor to obtain a registration for, and protection over, spare parts. Many of the reasons for choosing the UK system over the Community scheme that existed in the past—notably the benefits of substantive examination and, for the textile industries, the United Kingdom's (temporarily) closed register (with full monopoly rights)—no longer exist. Given that registration in the United Kingdom no longer offers many substantial advantages over a Community registration, it is not surprising that the opening of OHIM in April 2003 (now renamed EUIPO) prompted a notable decline in the number of UK applications. Since it was opened, the number of registrations at EUIPO have steadily increased, with more than 105,000 designs registered in 2016. This is compared to 8,481 designs registered in the United Kingdom in 2016 (which was up from the 5,690 registered in 2016).[101]

---

[101] EUIPO, *Facts and Figures Report 2016* (Version 2) (28 February 2017). In comparison, in the United Kingdom in 2002 there were 9,505 design applications and 9,192 registrations. EUIPO received 6,204 design applications from the United Kingdom in 2016. For analysis of UK registered design applications from 1989 to 2005, see Gowers Review, 43. Between 2009 and 2012, the numbers stood at just over 4,000 per year.

26

SUBJECT MATTER: THE REQUIREMENT THAT THERE BE A DESIGN

1 REQUIREMENTS FOR PROTECTION

Prior to harmonization (and with one or two exceptions, notably in Scandinavia), most European countries set a low threshold that needed to be satisfied for a design to be protected—asking only that the design meet some standard of local novelty.[1] An advantage of a low threshold is that it allows protection for different designs. However, a disadvantage of making protection readily available is that the protection conferred is necessarily very limited. If design protection is permitted at a low threshold and protection is strong, this could lead to unwarranted interference with the development of subsequent designs. To prevent this, it has been common to match a low threshold with weaker rights. Such an approach is frustrating for the developers of highly innovative designs because it means that they will often find it difficult to establish infringement.[2]

Initially, the European Commission proposed to reinvigorate design protection by setting the threshold of protection at a higher level.[3] The Commission planned to protect fewer designs, but proposed that the protection that was granted was to be worth having.[4] To this end, a Green Paper proposed that designs should be only protected if they possessed 'distinguishing character'.[5] After consultation, it was accepted that the idea was impractical and likely to cause confusion with trade marks—'distinguishing character' being similar (in English, at least) to the concept of distinctive character in Article 3(1)(b) of the Trade Marks Directive.[6] Moreover, in the course of consultation and during

---

[1] European Commission, *Green Paper on the Legal Protection of Industrial Design* (June 1991), III/F/5131/91–EN (henceforth the 'EC Green Paper'), [2.3.7], 18. See M. Franzosi commentary, in Franzosi, 46; M. Levin commentary, in Franzosi, 64–5.

[2] M. Levin commentary, in Franzosi, 67. It was a common complaint that, prior to harmonization, the UK registered design system rarely produced a monopoly worth having.

[3] Fellner, [6.017]; cf. M. Franzosi commentary, in Franzosi, 58–9 (a halfway standard).

[4] EC Green Paper, [5.5.6.3]; 'Official Commentary on Regulation', in Franzosi, 56.

[5] Even in the EC Green Paper, the Commission proposed that this was to be assessed using a limited prior art. More specifically, it proposed that design should be protected only 'if the design is distinct to designs known to the circles specialised in the sector concerned' and that the design 'distinguishes itself from any other design known to such circles . . . through the overall impression it displays in the eyes of the relevant public': EC Green Paper, 5.

[6] M. Franzosi commentary, in Franzosi, 59, n. 50; M. Levin commentary, in Franzosi, 68 (the change 'has its real grounds in a translation problem', noting that the German word *Eigenart* remains).

the legislative process,[7] it came to be accepted that a higher threshold would not work well for some industries, such as textiles.[8] In order to accommodate the differing needs of different industries and the cyclical nature of fashion, a new formula was employed. This is now captured in the requirements for validity that are set out in Article 25(1) of the Community Design Regulation.

1.1 REQUIREMENTS FOR VALIDITY

In order to be valid,[9] UK registered designs, Community registered designs, and unregistered Community designs need to satisfy a number of different criteria.[10] These are that:

(i)   there must be a 'design';

(ii) the design must be 'new';

(iii) the design must have 'individual character';

(iv) the applicant or right holder must be entitled to the design; and

(v)   the design must not conflict with earlier relevant rights (which include earlier design applications, trade mark rights, copyright, and rights relating to certain types of emblem).

In this chapter, we focus on the first of these criteria—namely, the requirement that there must be a design. We then turn in Chapter 27 to look at the remaining requirements for validity—namely, novelty, individual character, and the question of whether an applicant or rights holder was entitled to grant, as well as conflict with earlier rights.

2 WHAT IS A DESIGN?

The scope of the design system is delimited at the most basic level in the way the subject matter is defined.[11] In design law, this is reflected in the basic requirement of validity that there must be a 'design'. For the purposes of UK registered designs, registered Community designs, and unregistered Community designs, the definition of 'design' is identical. Article 3(a) of the Community Design Regulation defines a design as 'the appearance of the whole or part of a product resulting from the features of, in particular, the lines, contour, colours, shape, texture and/or materials of the product itself and/or

---

[7] The threshold included in the original proposal to the effect that the design must 'differ significantly' from previous designs was further reduced by removal of the adverb 'significantly' in the European Parliament: see Musker, 30. Note, however, that Designs Dir., Recital 13, left in 'differs clearly'—'a small difference [that] may be "clear" but not "significant"': Musker, 31.

[8] R. Posner commentary, in Franzosi, 6; M. Franzosi commentary, in Franzosi, 62. The Scandinavians favoured a high threshold; the automobile industry was opposed to such a standard: F. K. Beier, 'Protection for Spare Parts in the Proposals for a European Design Law' (1994) 25 *IIC* 840, 852–5.

[9] Similar to the situation in relation to registered designs, once an unregistered Community design has been found to exist, the obligation falls upon the defendant to challenge its validity.

[10] In *Grupo Promer v. OHIM and PepsiCo*, Case T-9/07 [2010] *ECR* II-981, [30], the General Court held that the grounds for invalidity in CDR, Art. 25(1), were exhaustive and, in line with this, that the bad faith of the rights holder was not a ground for invalidity.

[11] If an application for a UK registration does not relate to a design, it should be refused: RDA 1949, s. 1A(1)(a). If it comes to be registered, such a design can be declared invalid: RDA 1949, s. 11ZA(1). In the case of an application to register a Community Design, the fact that the design does not 'correspond to the definition under Article 3(a)' constitutes a ground for non-registrability: CDR, Art. 47(1)(a). It is also a ground for invalidity, under CDR, Art. 25(1)(a), and this can be raised against registered and unregistered Community designs.

its ornamentation'.[12] This definition is exceedingly broad—broader than the definitions previously used in many member states.[13]

There are three key elements to this definition of design which we will look at in turn—namely, appearance, features, and product.

2.1 APPEARANCE

The first thing to note about the way 'design' is defined is that it focuses on the *appearance* of products. While this directs attention to the look of products, there is no requirement that a design needs to be attractive, decorative, ornamental, or aesthetically pleasing; nor is there anything that limits protection to aesthetic designs: it is possible to protect functional designs, so long as some consideration is given to the look of the design.[14] 'Appearance' is defined very broadly. It includes moving designs (such as symbols or lines moving across computer screens); it may extend to include microscopic designs not visible to the naked eye (which would have important ramifications for nanotechnology);[15] and while single colours are unlikely to be registrable, complex patterns and combinations may.[16] While it is possible to register an ornamentation independently of the product to which it is applied, it has been held that words written in black standard script cannot be registered 'because they do not contain any features of appearance and therefore cannot be considered as ornamentation'.[17]

For the most part, the focus on the appearance of products is straightforward. One question that remains unclear, however, is whether the focus on the appearance of products means that protection is confined to visual features or whether the definition is broad enough to encompass materials, textures, smells, and sounds that are perceived by senses other than the eye. The reference to 'texture' and 'materials' in Article 3(a) of the Regulation implies that touch may be an important attribute of a design. This suggests that a conventional style of clothing might be protected when it is made of a new material with a distinct texture (as lycra once was).[18] Equally, the weight and flexibility of materials might be an important part of the design. Whatever merit there might be in recognizing (and rewarding) the non-visual aspects of design,[19] it seems that design law

---

[12] Designs Dir., Art. 1(a); CDR, Art. 3(a); RDA 1949, s. 1(2).

[13] Previous British law (RDA 1949, as amended by the CDPA 1988) had defined designs as 'features of shape, configuration, pattern or ornament applied to an article by an industrial process, being features which in the finished article appeal to and are judged by the eye'. It also required that the article be one for which appearance was material—that is, that persons acquiring the article took appearance into account when deciding which article to acquire.

[14] No aesthetic criteria are applicable: Designs Dir., Recital 14; CDR, Recital 10. See also European Commission, *Explanatory Memorandum to the Proposal for a Regulation for a Council Regulation (EC) on Community Design* [2000] *OJ* C 248E/3, [8.2]; M. Levin commentary, in Franzosi, 83.

[15] A 'design is something that is discernable or recognizable (not necessarily to the naked eye)': *A Fulton v. Totes Isotoner (UK)* [2004] *RPC* (16) 301, [31].

[16] 'It goes without saying that a colour in itself or a material as such are not eligible for protection': 'Official Commentary of Proposal for Regulation', in Franzosi, 36. See further Stone, [4.16].

[17] *Baw London v. EUIPO*, Case R 1266/2016–3 (17 February 2017), [10].

[18] M. Franzosi commentary, in Franzosi, 41 ('all those . . . elements of the product which may be perceived by the human eye or by touch'). It was not the Commission's initial intention that the definition be limited to aspects perceptible by the eye: EC Green Paper, [5.4.7.2] (referring to the texture of textiles).

[19] Designs Dir., Recital 11, speaks of protection 'for those design features of a product, in whole or in part, which are shown visibly in an application'. Nonetheless, it does not require that protected features be solely or fully comprehended and appreciated from the visible representation: *Lindner Recyclingtech GmbH v. Franssens Verkstäder AB*, Case R 690/2007–3 (22 October 2009) (OHIM, Third Board of Appeal), [34] ('Community design law is concerned with the visual appearance of products'); *Gimex International Groupe Import v. The Chill Bag Co. Ltd* [2012] *EWPCC* 31, [25].

Fig. 26.1 Design of biscuit

Source: Biscuits Poult v. Banketbakkerij Merva, Case T-494/12, EU:T:2014:757, [2]–[3]

is fixated on the visual appearance of objects.[20] As such, it seems that texture and feel will only be protected insofar as they form part of the visual appearance of a product—that is, they will only be protected when they can be seen. In line with this sounds, smells, and taste have been held to fall outside the definition of design because they do not relate to the appearance of products.[21]

While the internal features of products—but not 'complex products', which are subject to special rules discussed later—such as the inside of suitcase may be protected so long as the features can be represented,[22] questions have arisen about *when* a design needs to be visible. This is particularly important for designs that are only visible after a product has been purchased. Here, the question arises: does a design have to be visible at the time of purchase or is it acceptable that hidden features are revealed during normal use of the product? What would be the case, for example, if a design for the inside of a chocolate were visible only when it is eaten? While it has been argued that there is nothing in the Regulation that restricts designs to those aspects of appearance that are visible at the time of purchase,[23] the Polish Supreme Administrative Court has held that an application to register a design of an ice cream, which consisted of a ball-shaped, uncut solid, which contained filling that was not visible until the ice cream was eaten, was not registrable as a design. This was because 'all features of the product appearance or its parts that give it a certain image of the design had to be present at the time' that the product was purchased.[24] In a similar vein, the General Court held that the layer of filling inside a biscuit

---

[20] For arguments that 'appearance' is limited to the visual, see Musker, 12 (it is questionable whether the word is appropriate to any sense other than sight). The equivalent terms in the Directive are *l'apparence d'un produit* (French), *la apariencia* (Spanish), *l'aspetto* (Italian), and *Erscheinungsform* (German). This is consistent with the requirement in Recital 13 that the design be protected only if it has individual character, a determination to be made by reference to an 'informed user *viewing* the design', and with the requirement in Recital 11 that protection corresponds to the features 'shown *visibly* in an application'. This provision was included as part of a compromise justifying rejection of parliamentary amendments that designs were to protect only 'outwardly visible' features: see H. Speyart, 'The Grand Design' [1997] *EIPR* 603, 605–6. See Chapter 25, section 3.2, pp. 722–3.

[21] See *Eli Lilly*, Case R-120/2001–2 (4 August 2003) (OHIM Board of Appeal). On this, see Stone, [4.09].

[22] Patent Office, *Legal Protection of Designs: A Consultation Paper on the Implementation in the United Kingdom of EC Directive 98/71/EC* (February 2001), 4, [3].   [23] Stone, [4.39]–[4.46].

[24] K. Maciaszek, 'Poland: Are the Designs within an Ice-Cream to be Registered as an Industrial Design?' [2012] *EIPR* 656, 658, citing *Przedsiebiorstwo Produkcji Lodow v. Patent Office* (20 March 2007). Stone criticized this decision on the basis that protection extends to stocking, importing, making, and various other uses of the design: Stone, [4.43]. It could be said that, in these situations, the 'hidden' design would still not be visible.

that was only visible after the biscuit was broken open could not be taken into consideration for the purpose of determining individual character.[25] (See Fig. 26.1.)

2.2 FEATURES

According to the definition of design used in the Community Design Regulation and the Designs Directive, the appearance that is protected must result from the *features* of a product.[26] The definition of design provides a non-exhaustive list of characteristics that can produce the requisite appearance, including lines, contours, shape, texture, or materials. This is a broad list that covers most types of design including aspects of conventional graphic design, industrial design, product and packaging design, and fashion design.[27] In the case of a mobile phone, for example, it would include the overall shape, the arrangement of buttons, the positioning of the earpiece and screen, the colour of the screen, the lettering, and the numbering. In the case of an item of clothing, such as a shirt, it would include the shape of the collar, the proportions, pattern, embroidered features (such as buttonholes), and potentially also the colours.

2.3 PRODUCT

The third notable feature of the way 'design' is defined is that it focuses on the appearance of *products* or *parts of products*. 'Product' is defined exhaustively and very broadly in Article 3(b) of the Regulation as 'any industrial or handicraft item, including inter alia parts intended to be assembled into a complex product, packaging, get ups, graphic symbols and typographical typefaces, but excluding computer programs'.[28] This definition is very broad, covering items such as clothes, fabric, furniture, electrical goods, and motor vehicles. It also includes packaging, get-up, graphic symbols, and typefaces. It does not, however, extend to computer programs, which are expressly excluded. The reference to *part of a product* allows someone to claim the design of aspects of a product, such as a handle of a cup or the spout of a teapot. 'Part of a product' needs to be distinguished from a 'component part of a complex product' which, as we will see, needs to satisfy different criteria to be valid.

2.3.1 Products associated with copyright

One question that has arisen is whether paintings, drawings, or buildings are 'products' within the meaning of the Directive and Regulation. If so, it seems that a number of types of work typically protected by copyright might also be protectable as designs—either through national or Community registration, or automatically (as unregistered Community designs) after being made available to the public.[29] In turn, this creates the possibility of monopoly protection over designs for up to 25 years.

---

[25] *Biscuits Poult v. Banketbakkerij Merva*, Case T-494/12, EU:T:2014:757, [24]–[26]. For argument that the decision was incorrect, see Stone, [4.41]–[4.42].

[26] Although some commentators have suggested that design law can protect the 'cachet' or 'coolness' of a product, insofar as such cachet arises from images associated with a product, it cannot be treated as an aspect of appearance that 'results from' the identified features.

[27] M. Franzosi commentary, in Franzosi, 40 ('as neutral and broad as possible in order to cover any marketing value attached to the form or shape of a product').

[28] Designs Dir., Art. 1(b); RDA 1949, s. 1(3); CDR, Art. 3(b).

[29] One could also protect such works when copyright has lapsed if they have previously not been widely published.

(i) Paintings For a painting to be protected as a design, it would have to be able to be classified as a 'handicraft item'. A preliminary question here is whether a painting is an 'item' for the purposes of Article 3(b). Under old British case law on registered designs, where the definition of registrable design included 'pattern and ornament . . . applied to an article', it was held that the article had to have a distinct existence from the design— so that a design of a football pools coupon was not registrable because the design *was* the article.[30] The fact that graphic symbols are listed as 'items' in Article 3(b) seems to suggest, however, that the EU's definition of design does not require a distinction to be drawn between product and design. Thus, it seems that a painting could be an item for the purposes of Article 3(b). Next, it is necessary to ask: is a painting an *industrial or handi-craft* item? Presumably, it could be argued that a painting is neither, because painting is non-industrial and is artistic rather than handicraft. While this would mean the design of a painting would fall outside the definition of a design and thus would prevent design law from duplicating the protection conferred by copyright, tribunals are likely to find it difficult to draw a boundary between art and handicraft.[31]

(ii) Buildings One of the stumbling blocks to using design law to protect the efforts of architects is the uncertainty about whether the objects to which the design is applied— namely, buildings and structures—fall within the definition of a product. Again, the issue here is whether a building could be classified as an 'industrial or handicraft item'. Under old case law, it had been held that building was not an 'industrial process' and, as such, that a design for a petrol filling station was unregistrable.[32] If followed, this would suggest that buildings and structures are not 'industrial items', and thus not products for the purposes of Article 3(b). This would be consistent with the fact that infringement is defined in such a way to suggest that the Directive and Regulation had portability in mind.[33] However, it should be observed that some commentators have taken a different view, arguing that environmental designs, whether internal or external, are protectable.[34] One factor that may be relevant here is that the Euro-Locarno Classification System, which was specially designed for classification of designs by the European Union Intellectual Property Office (EUIPO), includes houses, buildings, and buildings (transportable) in Class 25, 'Building Units and Construction Elements'.[35]

(iii) Computer programs Article 3(b) of the Regulation specifically excludes computer programs from the definition of a product.[36] Consequently, the appearance of computer programs are unable to be protected by a UK registered design, a registered Community design, or an unregistered Community design right. Determining what this exclusion

---

[30] *Re Littlewood's Pools* (1949) 66 *RPC* 309. British law also excluded many items from the definition of 'article' and thus from the design regime, through RDR, r. 26 (relating to articles of primarily a literary or artistic character).

[31] See Stone, [4.83] (noting that the EUIPO has accepted more than 400 registered Community designs for 'sculptures', and more than 50 'paintings').   [32] *Collier & Co.'s Application* (1939) 54 *RPC* 253.

[33] Musker, 18.

[34] C.-H. Massa and A. Strowel, 'Community Design: Cinderella Revamped' [2003] *EIPR* 68, 71 (giving examples of amusement parks and gardens).

[35] Under the Locarno Agreement Establishing an International Classification for Industrial Designs 1968, which is administered by WIPO and open to members of the Paris Union.

[36] At one stage, the Commission said that this was because computer programs 'cannot be designed': European Commission, *Explanatory Memorandum to the 1993 Proposal for a Council Regulation on the Legal Protection of Designs* [1994] *OJ C* 29/20, COM(1993) 342 final. Franzosi disagreed, stating that '[i]n reality this is not completely correct': M. Franzosi commentary, in Franzosi, 43. However, it should be noted that the Commission continues by saying that: '[It] may be useful, however, to state explicitly that the copy-right protection provided under the umbrella of the aforementioned Directive cannot be supplemented or reinforced by a protection of the 'look and feel' of a computer program by way of design protection'.

covers may prove to be tricky. One possible construction is that the appearance of a computer program is the appearance of the source or object code and thus that this is not capable of protection. Such a construction, which has been favoured by a number of commentators, would exclude from design protection the sort of material that is covered by copyright under the Software Directive. However, such a construction would not exclude the effects of running the program in a computer: the user interface or images that appear on the computer screen might be protected individually or in the overall appearance.[37] Indeed, Article 3(b) of the Regulation refers to 'graphic symbols' as products and it is widely accepted that this includes computer icons.[38] Insofar as they can be reduced to the form needed to meet the procedural requirements of national or criminal EU law, it is possible to protect certain aspects of web design.[39] However, it may be difficult to represent dynamic effects and sound effects visibly in the application.[40]

2.3.2 Corporeal and biological products

In an era during which there is widespread interest in the medical and cosmetic design of the human body, it might be asked whether designs for things such as body parts, tattoos, artificial limbs, and genetically modified animals (such as a scarlet-coloured cat) can be protected. The Euro-Locarno Classification System includes artificial eyes, limbs, and teeth in Class 24, and hairpieces in Class 28, suggesting that the appearance of prosthetics and wigs are designs. As such, there seems little reason not to treat these as 'industrial items'. Tattoos are probably not designs, since it is unlikely that the courts would think it acceptable to call the human body an 'industrial or handicraft item'.[41] (However, were a tattoo design to be registered as a painting, if this were possible, it might be an infringement of a registered design right to apply the image to a body, because this might amount to using the design.[42])

Given that plant breeding, particularly of ornamental plants, is often concerned with the appearance of plants, whether as a whole or elements thereof such as flowers, fruit or leaves, the question might also be asked: to what extent can a new type of plant or a new shaped fruit be protected as designs? A key stumbling block here is that design protection is only available where an item has gone through an industrial process or has been crafted in some way.[43] While the shape of artificial fruit, vegetables, or animals (such as a plastic apple) may be registered, it seems that in their 'natural' state fruit, vegetables, plants, and animals will not be regarded as 'industrial items' and thus will not be classified as

---

[37] See Patent Office, *Legal Protection of Designs* (February 2001), [4] (stating that the exclusion covers the programs themselves, i.e. the lines of code and the functionality); Musker, 16 ('the exclusion of screen displays seems either unnecessary or harmful', so that the scope of the exclusion should be confined to what is protected by copyright); A. Kur, 'Protection of Graphical User Interfaces under European Design Legislation' (2003) 34 *IIC* 50 (arguing that the exclusion may apply to the visual appearance generated by a computer program in its entirety, but not to individual graphic elements). Note also *Bezpecnostni Softwarova Asociace—Svaz Softwarove Ochrany v. Ministerstvo Kultury*, C-393/09 [2011] *FSR* (18) 465 (ECJ, Third Chamber) (graphic user interface is not software protected under the Software Directive, but may be a graphic work protected by copyright).

[38] M. Schlotelburg, 'The Community Design: First Experience with Registrations' [2003] *EIPR* 383, 386.

[39] See Stone, [4.94]–[4.95].

[40] Musker, 17. See Chapter 25, section 3.2, pp. 722–3, and section 4.2, pp. 726–7.

[41] But cf. RCD [Registered Community Design] 744347–0001 for a tattoo registered to Gillette (interestingly, the product is listed as a tattoo). See Stone, [4.57].

[42] But note the private and non-commercial use defence: Designs Dir., Art. 13(1); RDA 1949, s. 7A(2); CDR, Art. 20(1).

[43] UK IPO, *Registered Designs Examination Practice Guide* (16 March 2017), [2.09]. See also Stone, [4.53]–[4.56].

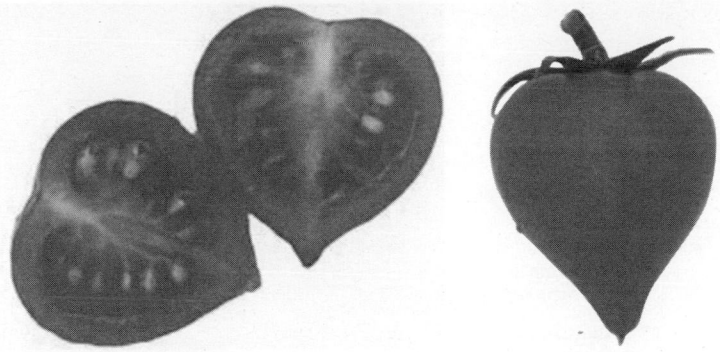

Fig. 26.2 Heart-shaped tomatoes

Source: EUIPO, *Guidelines for Examination: Invalidity Applications* (1 October 2017), [5.1.1]

products. This was the approach adopted at EUIPO, which rejected a Polish application on the basis that 'the representation showed a real animal'.[44] In another decision, the Board of Appeal rejected an application for heart-shaped tomatoes (which took on this shape naturally as they grew) (see Fig. 26.2). This was primarily because as living organisms the tomatoes were not products.[45] While not as clear cut, the situation would probably be the same where young fruit is placed into plastic moulds to shape the fruit into a particular form as it matures. While it may be possible to register the plastic moulds used to grow heart-shaped strawberries (or rectangular watermelons), it seems that it would not be possible to register the design of the resulting heart-shaped strawberry itself (see Fig. 26.3). One of the lessons to draw from the gradual inclusion of biological innovations into other areas of intellectual property (notably patents) is that it has been accompanied by a reconfiguration of basic concepts.[46] At this stage, it seems unlikely that this will occur in design law, although given the industrial nature of modern agriculture, it is an issue that may arise in the future.

2.3.3 Semiconductor chip products

It is worth noting that the design of the surface features (or topographies) of semiconductor chips falls within the ambit of the definition of design. Member states must therefore protect topographies as registered designs. Topographies are also protectable by registered Community designs and automatically by unregistered Community designs. This raises difficulties because member states are already obliged by the 1986 Chip Directive[47] to protect chip topographies that are the result of the creator's own intellectual effort and are not commonplace. As if this accumulation of different modes of protection were not inconvenient enough, the registered design system has important variations from those operating under the Chip Directive. For example, where the Chip Directive works on the basis of reciprocity, national treatment principles apply to registered designs under

---

[44] RCD 1982380 (23 February 2012).

[45] *Groente en fruit*, Case R 595/2012–3, (18 February 2013).

[46] The EPC 2000, Art. 57, in defining when an invention is 'capable of industrial application', talks of the use 'in any kind of industry, including agriculture', which might support an argument in favour of the protection of such artefacts by designs law.

[47] Council Directive 87/54/EEC of 16 December 1986 on the legal protection of semiconductor products [1986] *OJ* L 24/36 (27 January 1987) (Chip Dir.).

Fig. 26.3 Heart-shaped strawberries ('Seduberries')

Source: Seduberry Trading Co

the Paris Convention.[48] Similarly, the rules on ownership are different.[49] Thankfully, it is unlikely that the semiconductor industry will take advantage of design protection.

2.3.4 Complex products

As indicated, the Community Design Regulation allows for the protection of designs of 'parts intended to be assembled into a complex product'.[50] Many products will be classified as complex products: nearly anything bought from stores such as Ikea, where the final product (such as a bookshelf, bed, or chair) is sold in parts to be put together by consumers using Allan keys and screwdrivers would qualify. A 'complex product' is defined as 'a product which is composed of multiple components which can be replaced permitting disassembly and reassembly of the product'.[51] The meaning of this phrase is important because component parts of complex products need to meet a special standard of novelty

[48] Cf. Chip Dir., Recital 6 (on the extension of protection to persons outside the European Union). See Chapter 30, section 8, pp. 834–5.

[49] Chip Dir., Art. 3(2) (allowing, but not requiring, member states to allocate ownership to employer 'where a topography is created in the course of the creator's employment', or to a commissioner); CDR, Art. 14(3) (allocating ownership to employer, but only where 'developed by an employee in the execution of his duties or following the instructions given by his employer'). Given that topographies might also be protected by patents, utility models, or copyright, the domain seems to be absurdly overregulated.

[50] Designs Dir., Art. 1(b); RDA 1949, s. 1(3); CDR, Art. 3(b). As a result, it seems that the rule in *R v. RDAT, ex p Ford* [1995] *RPC* 167 has been reversed.

[51] Designs Dir., Art. 1(c); RDA 1949, s. 1(3); CDR, Art. 3(c). The British implementation of Art. 1(c), contained in s. 1(3), as amended, redefined 'complex product' to mean 'a product which is composed of at least two replaceable component parts permitting disassembly and reassembly of the product'.

and individual character before they can be protected—namely, the only features of a 'complex product' that are taken into account when determining novelty and individual character are those features that are visible during 'normal use'.[52] It is also important because they are subject to special (as yet unharmonized) limitations.[53]

In 2003, the UK Designs Registry suggested that a complex product was something that consisted of a number of parts, one of which will need maintenance, service, or repair during the life of the complex product (usually a product with mechanical, electrical, and/or electronic features, such as a motor car).[54] This approach, which would have limited the scope of complex products, has not been followed. Instead, the courts and tribunals have adopted a more straightforward approach. As well as including complex technical objects such as cars,[55] machines for shredding materials for recycling,[56] and lawnmowers,[57] a number of less technical objects have also been found to be 'complex products'. These include a skirting board made up of several components, which could be taken apart and put back together if, for example, the cables behind the skirting board needed to be changed or the floor refurbished,[58] a window blind system with a number of component parts (including the head rail, plastic ends, pulley, and track),[59] and a fireplace.[60]

A key hurdle for something to be classified as a complex product is the requirement that the final product must be able to be disassembled and reassembled. This means that where a final product (which is made up of a number of component parts) is put together in such a way that it cannot subsequently be taken apart and reassembled (presumably without unreasonable effort), it will not be a complex product. Thus, wire mesh that was designed to act as reinforcement in concrete was held not to be a component part of a complex product, the reason being that once the wire was put to its normal use and encased in concrete, it could not be disassembled and reassembled.[61] The situation is similar for products such as ice creams and chocolates which, although they may be made up of a number of subsidiary parts that are combined together, are often difficult to disassemble into the component parts and cannot (usually) be reassembled after they have been broken open.[62]

It is also important that the final product is able to be conceptualized as a single product. Thus in one case, it was held that a cot bumper that was able to be attached to baby cots was an attachment rather than a component part of a complex product. In part, this was because a 'product "protected cot" of which a cot bumper could form a component part does not exist'.[63]

---

[52] CDR, Art. 4(2).   [53] Designs Dir., Arts 3(3), 14; RDA 1949, ss 1B(10), 7A(5); CDR, Arts 4(2), 110.

[54] UK IPO, *Designs Practice Notice 1/03: Component Part of Complex Product Visible in Normal Use* (7 January 2003).

[55] *Estrella Dominguez Martinez v. BMW*, Case ICD 8701 (22 May 2013) (Invalidity Division) (component part was the wheels).

[56] *Lindner Recycling v. Franssons Verkstader*, Case R 690/2007–3 (22 October 2009) (Board of Appeal) (component part was the chaff cutters).

[57] *Kwang Yang Motor v. OHIM*, Case T 10/08 [2011] *ECR* II-265 (GC), [20]–[21] (component part was the internal combustion engine).

[58] *Profile Vox v. Cezar Przedsiebiorstwo*, Case R 442/2011–3 (15 April 2013) (Third Board of Appeal), [30].

[59] *Louver-Lite v. Harris Parts* [2012] *EWPCC* 53, [23] (component part was the headrail of the window blind).

[60] *Euro Fire v. Tarnavva*, Case R 316/2008–3 (14 October 2009) (Board of Appeal) (component part was the fireplace inserts).

[61] *Drahtwerk Plochingen v. AVI Alpenländische Verundululungs-Industries*, Case ICD 3218 (16 February 2007) (Invalidity Division). See further Stone, [4.114].

[62] K. Maciaszek, 'Poland: Are the Designs within an Ice-Cream to be Registered as an Industrial Design?' [2012] *EIPR* 656, 658, citing *Przedsiebiorstwo Produkcji Lodow v. Patent Office* (20 March 2007).

[63] *Mamas and Papas v. Jane Wall-Budden*, Case R 208/2016 (25 July 2017), [27]–[28].

In a similar vein, it was held that a ceiling into which a sensor was to be placed could not be seen as a component part of a complex product that consisted of the ceiling with the sensor inserted. This was on the basis that the place or location where an object is installed or fixed can never become a part of that object.[64]

One question that has arisen is whether a component part includes a part that is exhausted and disposed of such as a printer cartridge. The UK Designs Registry has indicated that consumable items that are intended to be 'used up' are not 'component parts'; it prefers the test that, absent the part, the item would not be seen as a complete product.[65] A laser printer would be seen as a complete product without its cartridge (although it would not function), so the cartridge is not a component part (although the printer may be a complex product). However, the Design Registry said that:

> Parts which are not 'used up' in the same sense as consumables but which might require replacement from time to time in order to enhance the performance of the complex product (e.g. parts of engines such as spark plugs) are considered to be component parts and so may face objections to registration.[66]

The Design Registry's definition has limited authority and its formulation and/or application is difficult to support. To say that a part is a component only if, absent the part, the item would not be seen as a complete product raises the question of when an item would be seen as a complete product: is a car a complete product without its hubcaps, tyres, wing mirrors, fenders, seats, fan belt, or spark plug? The question also arises whether, when Article 3(b) of the Regulation defines a product as 'any industrial or handicraft item', it excludes combinations of more than one item from being protected. For example, is design protection available for a suite of furniture or a kitchen design made up of a number of units? It is clear that it is possible to register each unit individually—'including . . . parts intended to be assembled into a complex product'—and it is implicit that if the individual units form a 'complex product', the unit as a whole can be registered. But what if the whole is not a 'complex product'? While the European Commission contemplated the registration of kitchen designs in its Green Paper, it is unclear whether they would be considered to be complex products under Article 1(c) of the Regulation.[67] Probably, the critical question is whether the combination of items results in something that can, in itself, be called 'an item'. This, in turn, will depend on whether the component elements are attached or linked to one another, whether the design value of the whole is greater than the sum of its parts, and whether there is a distinct market for the combination.[68] If the totality can be called 'an item', it should be registrable. The General Court provided support for this view in noting that it was possible for a group of articles to constitute a product so long as they 'are linked by aesthetic and functional complementarity and are usually marketed as a unitary product'.[69]

---

[64] *Everspring Industry v. Theben,* Case R 255/2014–3 (23 September 2015), [23]–[25] (overturning the Invalidity Division decision that the ceiling and the sensor formed a complex product).

[65] UK IPO, *Designs Practice Notice 1/03: Component Part of Complex Product Visible in Normal Use* (7 January 2003). [66] Ibid., 1.

[67] EC Green Paper, [5.4.1]–[5.4.2].

[68] Former German law required that there be 'unity of design' before such combinations could be protected: see *Bernhard Pflug GmbH v. Interlübke KG,* Case 1 ZR 35/73 (1976) 8 *IIC* 270, in which the BGH held that furniture belonging to a 'furniture program' could be protected in its entirety. The ensemble comprised a bed, chest of drawers, shelf units, and corner elements, which were intended to be used together and regarded by the public as a unity.

[69] *Ball Beverage Packaging Europe v. EUIPO,* Case T-9/15 EU:T:2017:386, [60].

3 EXCLUSIONS: WHAT IS *NOT* A DESIGN

Three types of design are excluded from the very broad definition of design:[70]

(i)   designs dictated solely by technical function;

(ii)   designs for products that must be produced in a specific way to enable them to connect to another product; and

(iii) designs that are contrary to morality.

We will examine each in turn.

3.1 FUNCTIONAL FEATURES

Article 8(1) of the Regulation (which corresponds to Article 7(1) of the Designs Directive) states that a design 'shall not subsist in features of appearance of a product which are solely dictated by its technical function'.[71] As the EUIPO Board of Appeal has said, the exclusion operates 'to deny protection to those features of a product's appearance that were chosen exclusively for the purpose of designing a product that performs its function'. This is in contrast to 'features that were chosen, at least to some degree, for the purpose of enhancing the product's visual appearance'.[72] The task of judging whether design features are dictated by function is 'assessed from the standpoint of a reasonable observer who looks at the design and asks . . . whether anything other than purely functional considerations could have been relevant when a specific feature was chosen'.[73] The exclusion of designs solely dictated by technical function aims to prevent design rights from being used to obtain 'monopolies over technical solutions without meeting the more stringent conditions laid down in patent law'.[74] In so doing, the exclusion aims to prevent technological innovation from being hampered.[75]

It is notable that Article 8(1) does not say that these features are not designs; rather, it says that a design right shall not subsist in features that are solely dictated by technical function. This means that it is possible to register (or to obtain protection for) a design that includes functional features. A design will only be excluded in totality where the design as a whole was dictated by function.[76] If a design includes functional features falling within Article 8(1), these are not taken into account for the purposes of assessing novelty or individual character.[77] In addition, there is no infringement of a design where a person reproduces the functional features (because no design right subsists in them).

---

[70] If an application for a UK registration is confined to excluded matter, it should be refused: RDA 1949, ss 1A(1)(b), 1C, 1D. If it comes to be registered, such a design can be declared invalid: RDA 1949, s. 11ZA(1). In the case of an application to register a Community design, the fact that the design is contrary to public policy or accepted principles of morality constitutes one of only two grounds for non-registrability: CDR, Art. 47(1)(b). The other exclusions can be raised only as grounds for invalidity, under CDR, Art. 25(1)(b), against both registered and unregistered Community designs.   [71] RDA 1949, s. 1C(1); CDR, Art. 8(1).

[72] *TrekStor v. Zagg*, Case R 1997/2012–3 (12 May 2014), [22].   [73] Ibid., [28].

[74] *Lindner Recyclingtech v. Franssons Verkstäder*, Case R 690/2007–3 [2010] *ECDR* 1, [28].

[75] Designs Dir, Recital 13; CDR, Recital 10.

[76] *Austrotherm v. Termo Organika*, Case R 998/2013–3 (12 February 2015), [45] (design will be only invalid as a whole if '*all of the essential features* of the appearance of the product were solely dictated by its technical function').   [77] Designs Dir., Recital 14; CDR, Recital 10.

3.1.1 Technical function

Although Article 8(1) excludes features dictated by technical function,[78] we are not given any guidance about what 'technical' means in this context.[79] The exclusion of technical features achieves three related goals. First, by preventing features necessary to achieve a technical function from being protected, the Regulation leaves the protection of those features to patent law (and, where it exists, utility model protection).[80] It thereby prevents applicants from gaining protection for technical features at a lower cost and without having to comply with the standards of inventiveness demanded by patent law.[81]

Second, by leaving features necessary to achieve a technical function unprotected, the law enables different people to reproduce and utilize features of shape that are necessary to achieve a particular function. In so doing, it ensures that there is potential for competition in functional products.

Third, the exclusion recognizes that in situations where a shape is dictated by function, a designer has no design freedom and, as such, is unable to contribute any relevant design effort. In this situation, a designer should not be able to benefit from design protection.[82] If such a person makes a contribution, it is as an inventor and not as a designer.[83]

3.1.2 When is a feature solely dictated by technical function?

One issue that has bedevilled Article 8(1) jurisprudence is the question: what does it mean to say that features are 'solely dictated' by technical function?[84] While a number of different approaches have been adopted over the last decade or so, two stand out. The first, which is known as the 'multiplicity-of-forms' approach (and which has been widely employed in member states), provides that a design will only be dictated by technical function where the designer was unable to exercise any control whatsoever over the final shape of the article. Under this approach, the exclusion only applies if the technical function cannot be achieved by any other configuration; if the designer has a choice between two or more alternative configurations, the form is *not* dictated by the function.[85] If a designer has a choice between two (or more) different forms (even if both are functional), the resulting design will not fall foul of Article 8(1).[86] In positive terms, the 'multiplicity-of-forms'

---

[78] This limitation was probably required because TRIPS, Art. 25(1), permits members only to provide that protection shall not extend to 'designs dictated essentially by technical or functional considerations'.

[79] Where products are subject to patent and design protection, the patent has been used to identify the technical function of the product for the purposes of design law (but with no real discussion of the meaning of 'technical' in patent law). See *Benmore Ventures v. 2WF Société par actions simplifiée,* Case R 1341/2–15–3 (6 June 2016), [20]–[31]; *Nintendo v. Compatinet,* Case R 1772/2012–3 (14 April 2014), [24]–[34]. See also C.-H. Massa and A. Strowel, 'Community Design: Cinderella Revamped' [2003] *EIPR* 68, 72 ('technical function' may extend further to cover 'economic or marketing constraints').   [80] EC Green Paper, [5.4.6.1].

[81] This is often referred to as the 'channelling function'. How effective Art. 7(1) is in achieving the function will depend on how robustly it is interpreted, but certainly there are dangers that, with a narrow interpretation, the EU designs regime may be viewed as an attractive means by which to protect technical products, insofar as examination is limited and protection can last up to 25 years—five years longer than patent law: Beier, op. cit., 851 ('design protection . . . finds its natural limits when it comes to technical–functional features for which no design alternative exists').   [82] EC Green Paper, [5.4.6.2].

[83] Musker was opposed to the exclusion altogether, seeing little harm in protecting technical contributions by a broad design law: Musker, 41–3.

[84] The French language version refers to *les caractéristiques de l'apparence d'un produit qui sont exclusivement imposé par sa fonction technique;* the German to *die ausschließlich durch dessen technische Funktion bedingt sind.* Compare the parallel discussion in the context of exclusion from trade marks under TMD, Art. 3(1)(e), in Chapter 36, section 3, pp. 950–63.

[85] For a critical discussion see, *Benmore Ventures v. 2WF Société par actions simplifiée,* Case R 1341/2–15–3 (6 June 2016), [15]–[16].

[86] *Landor & Hawa International Ltd v. Azure Designs Ltd* [2007] *FSR* 181, [2006].

approach says that a functional design may be eligible for protection if it can be shown that the same technical function could be achieved by a different form.

The operation of the approach can be seen in the UK Court of Appeal decision of *Landor & Hawa International Ltd v. Azure Designs Ltd*,[87] where the Court had to consider whether the design of rigid or shell suitcases, which were fitted with an expandable section (that enabled the size of the suitcase to be increased), fell within the ambit of Article 8(1) of the Regulation. In deciding whether the claimant's design for an expandable suitcase was solely dictated by the technical function and thus excluded, the Court of Appeal asked whether the design was 'driven without options'—that is, the Court looked at whether, in creating the design in question, the designer exercised a degree of choice. On the facts of the case, the Court found that because the designer had exercised choice in many aspects of the design—including 'the spatial position of the constituent elements (big piping/zip/normal piping, zip/big piping) and the presence of the piping elements themselves'—this introduced 'an essentially non-functional and even capricious element to the final appearance of the ensemble'.[88] As such, the design was not excluded on the basis that it was solely dictated by function.

The alternative approach—which has now been adopted in the United Kingdom and at EUIPO—has its origins in the 1971 English decision of *Amp v. Utilux*,[89] where the House of Lords was called on to interpret section 1(3) of the (pre-harmonized) Registered Designs Act 1949, which is very similar to Article 8(1) of the Regulation. In this case, the House of Lords held that a product's configuration is solely dictated by its technical function if every feature of the design was determined by technical considerations.[90] Under this approach, a design will be solely dictated by function and thus excluded if a product was created without any consideration for how it looks—that is, if the product was developed purely with functional considerations in mind. This is the case even if the function could be performed by other shapes (which is not the case with the 'multiplicity-of-forms' approach). It is only where aesthetic considerations are completely irrelevant that the features of design will fall foul of Article 8(1). As the EUIPO Board of Appeal said in *Linder Recyclingtech*, this is not 'tantamount to introducing a requirement of aesthetic merit into the legislation'; instead, it simply recognizes that:

> [W]hen aesthetics are totally irrelevant, in the sense that no one cares whether the product looks good, bad, ugly or pretty, and all that matters is that the product functions well, there is nothing to protect under the law of designs.[91]

The 'multiplicity-of-forms' approach has been widely criticized, primarily because it undermines the policy aim of Article 8(1)—namely, to prevent design law (rather than patents) from being used to monopolize functional designs.[92] As the EUIPO Board of Appeal said, if adopted, the multiplicity-of-forms theory would deprive Article 8(1) of any purpose and content, rendering it virtually redundant.[93] In *Doceram* the Court of Justice rejected the multiplicity-of-forms approach and essentially adopted the approach in *Amp v. Utilux*.[94] After some uncertainty,[95] there is now a consensus in the UK, at

---

[87] Ibid.   [88] Ibid., [32] (citing Judge Fysh QC).   [89] [1971] *FSR* 572 (HL).

[90] See *Dyson v. Vax* [2010] *EWHC* 1923 (Pat), [23]–[31] (Arnold J).

[91] *Linder Recyclingtech GmbH*, Case ICD 3150 (3 April 2007) (OHIM, Invalidity Division), [35].

[92] See *Dyson v. Vax* [2010] *EWHC* 1923 (Pat), [23]–[31]; *Linder Recyclingtech GmbH*, Case ICD 3150 (3 April 2007) (OHIM, Invalidity Division), [35]. The extent to which the mandatory approach excludes features will often depend on the level of abstraction from which the product is considered.

[93] *Benmore Ventures v. 2WF Société par actions simplifiée*, Case R 1341/2–15–3 (6 June 2016), [15].

[94] *Doceram v. CeramTec*, Case C-395/16, EU:C:2018:172, [22]–[23].

[95] In the United Kingdom, support for the 'multiplicity-of-forms' approach came from *Landor & Hawa International Ltd v. Azure Designs* [2007] *FSR* 181. L. Brancusi, 'Designs determined by the product's technical function' [2016] *EIPR* 23.

EUIPO, and the Court of Justice.[96] This means that Article 8(1) will only deny protection to features of a product's appearance that were chosen *exclusively* for the purpose of designing a product that performs its function.[97] This is opposed to features that were objectively chosen, at least to some degree, for the purpose of enhancing the product's visual appearance. The question of why certain features were chosen is decided objectively: it is not necessary to 'determine what actually went on in the designer's mind when the design was being developed'; rather, the 'matter must be assessed from the standpoint of a reasonable observer who looks at the design and asks himself whether anything other than purely functional consideration could have been relevant when the specific features were chosen'.[98] That is, the test must be 'assessed objectively, not in the perception of the informed user who may have limited knowledge of technical matters'.[99]

3.2 INTERCONNECTIONS

The second type of design that is expressly excluded are designs for products that must be produced in a specific way to enable them to connect to another product. As Article 8(2) of the Regulation (which corresponds to Article 7(2) of the Designs Directive) states:

> [A design] shall not subsist in features of appearance of a product which must necessarily be reproduced in their exact form and dimensions in order to permit the product in which the design is incorporated or to which it is applied to be mechanically connected to or placed in, around or against another product so that either product may perform its function.

The reasoning behind the exclusion seems to be that while the harmonized definition of design includes the appearance of parts of products, features that enable mechanical parts to be connected together should not be protected because this might enable the proprietor of a design for a particular article to prevent competition in a secondary market.[100] For example, protection of the design of the external ports of a laptop could operate to allow the designer to control the sale of keyboards; protection of the design of the parts of a laser printer could allow the designer to control the sale of printer cartridges; and a design right over a pod-based coffee machine could enable the designer to control sale of the coffee pods used.

The provision is similar to the 'must fit' exclusion recognized in the British law of unregistered designs (discussed in Chapter 30).[101] However, given differences in wording, it is unlikely that the case law on the 'must fit' exclusion will be of much assistance in the application of Article 8(2) of the Regulation. One reason for this is that while the British

---

[96] *Linder Recyclingtech GmbH*, Case ICD 3150 (3 April 2007) (OHIM, Invalidity Division), [28]–[36]; *ACV Manufacturing NV v. AIC SA* [2012] *ECDR* 13, [24]; *Nordson Corporation v. UES AG*, Case R 211/2008–3 (29 April 2010) (OHIM, Third Board of Appeal), [26]–[35]. Cf. Stone, 70 (suggesting yet another approach at EUIPO).

[97] But this does not require an objective observer: *Doceram v. CeramTec*, Case C-395/16, EU:C:2018:172, [38].

[98] *Linder Recyclingtech GmbH*, Case ICD 3150 (3 April 2007) (OHIM, Invalidity Division), [36]. In July 2016, the Oberlandesgericht Düsseldorf asked the CJEU to consider whether the standpoint of an objective observer should be adopted when deciding whether features have been chosen for functional purposes: *Doceram*, Case C-395/16 (pending). The CJEU in *Doceram* was also asked what the position was where the 'design effect is of no significance for the product design, but the (technical) functionality is the sole factor that dictates the design'. Ibid.

[99] *Austrotherm v. Termo Organika*, Case R 998/2013–3 (12 February 2015), [47].

[100] Designs Dir., Recital 14, and CDR, Recital 10, state that 'the interoperability of products of different makes should not be hindered by extending protection to the design of mechanical fittings'. See also EC Green Paper, [5.4.10.1].

[101] CDPA 1988, s. 213(3)(b) ('Design right does not subsist in . . . features of shape and configuration of an article which . . . enable the article to be connected to, or placed in, around or against another article so that either article may perform its function'). See Chapter 30, section 2.2.3, pp. 816–19.

Act excludes features that 'enable' connections, Article 7 sets a more taxing requirement before the exclusion comes into play: the features 'must *necessarily* be reproduced in their *exact* form and dimensions'.[102] Where the shape of a designed artefact merely influences the shape of another product—for example where one must fit inside another, but need not correspond exactly to the internal dimensions—the European exclusion would not come into play. Another reason is that the European provision is confined to features that must be reproduced so that the design-protected product can be '*mechanically* connected to, or placed in, around or against another product'. The Recitals to the Directive and Regulation reiterate that the exclusion is targeted at 'mechanical fittings', but do not clarify whether the adverb 'mechanically' applies where the product is 'placed in, around or against' another product (or whether 'placement' might be regarded, necessarily, as 'mechanical').[103] While the connection of an exhaust pipe to the chassis of a car might be regarded as a classic example of a 'mechanical' fitting, it is less clear whether the fitting of a lampshade to a table lamp, a filter to a coffee maker, or a candle to a candelabrum would be regarded as mechanical.[104] Given that the term 'mechanical' is often used in contrast to 'electrical', the possibility also arises that electrical fittings can be the subject of design protection, although the distinction has nothing to recommend it on policy grounds. Yet another difference between the interconnection and 'must fit' exclusions is that the only interconnections covered by the exclusion in Article 8(2) are those that relate to other products—that is, 'industrial or handicraft items'. This would certainly not cover interconnections to parts of the human body, such as to the eye by a contact lens, as the British 'must fit' exclusion has done.

3.2.1 Modular products

The interconnections exclusion is subject to an express derogation. Article 8(3) states that, notwithstanding the interconnections exclusion in Article 8(2), 'design right shall . . . subsist in a design serving the purpose of allowing multiple assembly or connection of mutually interchangeable products within a modular system'.[105] Recital 15 justifies the exclusion on the basis that 'the mechanical fittings of modular products may nevertheless constitute an important element of the innovative characteristics of modular products and present a major marketing asset and therefore should be eligible for protection'. The real explanation for the exclusion is that it was a product of lobbying by the Danish government, keen that the key features of lego bricks should remain protectable (although, since lego, with its stud and tube coupling system, has been available to the public since 1958, there can be very few regimes in which the basic design protection has not lapsed). Other examples of modular design systems include meccano construction sets, modular seating systems, and shelving arrangements.[106]

3.3 DESIGNS CONTRARY TO MORALITY OR PUBLIC POLICY

According to Article 9 of the Regulation, 'design right shall not subsist in a design which is contrary to public policy or to accepted principles of morality'. This exclusion

---

[102] Although in one case the British courts held that 'enablement' required such a level of exactitude: see *Amoena v. Trulife* [1995] *EIPR-D* 346.

[103] The limitation of the exclusion to mechanical connection was not in the initial proposal in the EC Green Paper.

[104] Cf. R. Durie, 'European Community Design Law', in B. Gray and E. Bouzalas (eds), *Industrial Design Rights: An International Perspective* (2001), 75, 91 (giving example of television set and stand as a mechanical interface).

[105] RDA 1949, s. 1C(3); CDR, Art. 8(2), Recital 11.

[106] Patent Office, *Legal Protection of Designs* (February 2001), [24].

corresponds to equivalent provisions in European patent and trade mark law, and previous provisions under many national design systems.[107] Importantly, this exclusion operates as a ground for refusal of registration (both at national and EU levels) and as a ground for invalidity.[108] Aldous J stated that the test was not whether a section of the public would be offended; rather, the test is whether the moral principles of right-thinking members of the public would think it very wrong for the law to grant protection.[109] While the appearance of objects does not usually give rise to moral objections[110] it has been suggested that designs which contain racist or homophobic messages,[111] textile designs that utilized a swastika,[112] or functional design for landmines or man-traps, might fall within the exclusion.[113] Given that the Directive 'does not constitute a harmonization of national concepts of public policy or accepted principles of morality',[114] one can expect that some designs would be considered immoral in some countries, but not others. It is unlikely that many designs will be excluded from protection in the United Kingdom on the basis that they are immoral or against public policy. In the pre-harmonization case of *Masterman's Design Application*,[115] the Court (on appeal) allowed the application to register a design for a male Highlander doll, which when its sporran was lifted revealed its genitals (see Fig. 26.4).

Fig. 26.4 Front view of the doll in *Masterman's Design*

Source: Keith Beresford

[107] Prior to amendment to implement the Directive, RDA 1949, s. 43(1), had stated that nothing in the Act should be construed as 'authorising or requiring the Registrar to register a design the use of which would, in his opinion, be contrary to law or morality'.
[108] RDA 1949, ss 1A(1)(b), 1D, 11ZA(1); CDR, Arts 47(1)(b), 25(1)(b).　　[109] [1991] *RPC* 89, 103–4.
[110] UK IPO, *Registered Designs Examination Practice guide* (16 March 2017), [5.03] (rare for the Register to raise an objection on public policy grounds).　　[111] Ibid.
[112] EC Green Paper, [8.9.2]. A swastika on the packaging of a board game about the Second World War would presumably not cause offence.　　[113] Musker, 52 (design of landmines).
[114] CDR, Recital 16.　　[115] [1991] *RPC* 89.

27

GROUNDS FOR INVALIDITY: NOVELTY, INDIVIDUAL CHARACTER, AND RELATIVE GROUNDS

1 INTRODUCTION

In Chapter 26, we looked at the first of the criteria which a design needs to comply to be valid—namely, the requirement that there be a 'design'. In this chapter, we look at the other criteria which a design—whether a national registered design, a registered Community design, or an unregistered Community design—must comply with in order to be valid.[1] These are that:

(i) the design must be 'new';

(ii) the design must have 'individual character';

(iv) the applicant or the right holder must be entitled to the protected design; and

(v) the design must not conflict with earlier relevant rights (which include earlier design applications, trade mark rights, copyright, and rights relating to certain types of emblem).

We will look at each of these in turn.

2 NOVELTY

In order to be valid, national registered designs, registered Community designs, and unregistered Community designs must be novel or new. A design is new if no identical design, or designs the features of which only differ in immaterial details, has been made available to the public before the date of application (or, in the case of unregistered Community designs, the date on which the design was first made available to the public).[2]

---

[1] Designs Dir., Art. 11 (listing four mandatory grounds, and three optional ones); RDA 1949, ss 3A (grounds for refusal), 11ZA (grounds for invalidity), Sch. A1 (emblems); CDR, Art. 25 (listing seven grounds of invalidity).

[2] RDA 1949, s. 1B(2); Designs Dir., Art. 4; CDR, Art. 5(2). If priority is claimed, the relevant date is the priority date.

This is a historical or objective test that requires the design to be compared with the body of existing materials. As such, it can be contrasted with copyright's originality test, which is a psychological or subjective test that focuses on the relationship between the creator and the creation. To assess whether a design is new, we need to ask three questions:

(i)   What is the design that is being examined?

(ii)   What material is the design to be compared with? In patent jargon: what is the state of the art?

(iii)   What difference needs to exist between a design and the state of the art for the design to be new?

We will look at each question in turn.

2.1 WHAT IS THE DESIGN?

In many cases, the preliminary task of determining the ambit of the protected design will play an important role in determining whether a design is novel.[3] It also potentially plays an important role in relation to the other grounds for invalidity, and in relation to ownership, exploitation, and infringement. While there are differences, for the most part the task of determining the scope of a design is similar in all areas. As such, in this section we look generally at the question of how the scope of the design is determined.

While the definition of design is very broad, there are a number of types of design that are excluded. Three are of interest here. The first, which was discussed in Chapter 26, are those features of a design that are solely dictated by function. The second, which was also discussed in Chapter 26, are those features that must be produced in a specific way to enable them to connect to another product. The third type of design that is excluded relates to component parts of complex products—which are subject to the requirement that the only aspects of the design that will be recognized are those features that are visible in normal use. This requirement is discussed later in this chapter. It is important to note that in all three situations, a design may be valid although certain features are excluded. The design as a whole will only be invalid if all of the features are either dictated by function, if all of the features of a product must be produced in a specific way to enable that product to connect to another product, or if none of the features of a component part of a complex product are visible when in normal use. Once the excluded features of a design have been clarified, the next step is to determine what the design at issue is. The approach adopted will differ depending on whether the design is registered or unregistered.

(i) British and Community registrations The key factor that will determine the ambit of a registered design are the representations which specify the features of design for which protection is sought. As Lord Neuberger said, the extent of protection afforded by a registered design 'must ultimately depend on the proper interpretation of the registration in issue, and in particular of the images included in that registration'.[4] Importantly, these images will 'almost exclusively identify the nature and extent of the monopoly' claimed.[5]

As we saw earlier, a large body of rules and procedures have been developed to guide the crafting of representations. These range from rules about the techniques applicants can use to identify what is disclaimed in an application through to rules about the role descriptions play in how the representations are read. These rules play an important role in shaping

---

[3] For a discussion of why it is not appropriate to talk here about the 'scope' of a design (as in patents), see *Erol's Design Application*, Appeal O/253/17 (18 May 2017), [59]–[62].

[4] *PMS International Group v. Magmatic* [2016] *UKSC* 12, [30].   [5] Ibid., [31].

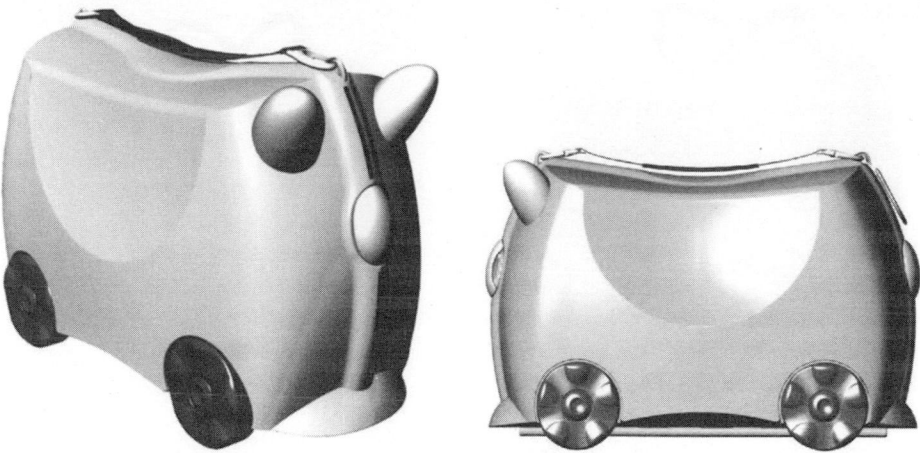

Figure 27.1 Magmatic's Community Registered Design

Source: PMS International Group Plc v. Magmatic [2016] *UKSC* 12, [1]

how the representations are interpreted. Within the frame of these rules, applicants have a degree of flexibility in how they represent their designs. They also have a great degree of flexibility in terms of what is represented and thus what is protected. An applicant may, for example, limit protection to the shape of a product, to features of surface appearance, or a combination thereof. As the Supreme Court decision of *PMS International Group v. Magmatic* ('*Trunki*') shows, the style of representation chosen and the way that this is construed by the courts may play a pivotal in determining the fate of a design.[6]

The *Trunki* decision involved an infringement action in relation to a registered Community design for ride-on suitcases for young children. The registered design consisted of six images prepared by 3D Computer Assisted Design (CAD) in 'monochrome with grey-scale shading and distinct tonal contrasts' (see Fig. 27.1). Magmatic had manufactured and sold ride-on suitcases for children under the trade mark 'Trunki' since 2004. Trunki was initially sold with the body and strap in one colour, the horns and wheels another, and the strips, clasps, and wheel-spokes a third colour. Over time, the design of the suitcases evolved to include different colours and ornamentation (see, for example, Fig. 27.2). In 2013, Magmatic brought infringement proceedings claiming that in importing and selling the 'Kiddee Case' in the United Kingdom (see Fig. 27.3) PMS infringed Magmatic's registered Community design (Fig. 27.1).

In determining the features of design which were protected, the Supreme Court was called on to interpret the images that had been registered (see Fig. 27.1). While the Supreme Court discussed a number of issues, one is of particular importance here: namely, whether the registered image was limited to the specific shape of the suitcase or whether it also included the contrasting colours (or shades).

Agreeing with Kitchin LJ in the Court of Appeal, Lord Neuberger said that the tonal differentiation used in the representations meant that the design as claimed was *not* for the shape alone. Rather, the design was for the shape with a strap, strips, wheels, and spokes in a colour (or possibly colours) which contrasted with the remainder of the product. The

---

[6] [2016] *UKSC* 12. On this see UK IPO, *Registered Designs Examination Practice Guide* (16 March 2017), [11.06]–[11.07]; UK IPO, *Guidance on use of representations when filing Registered Design applications* (1 June 2016).

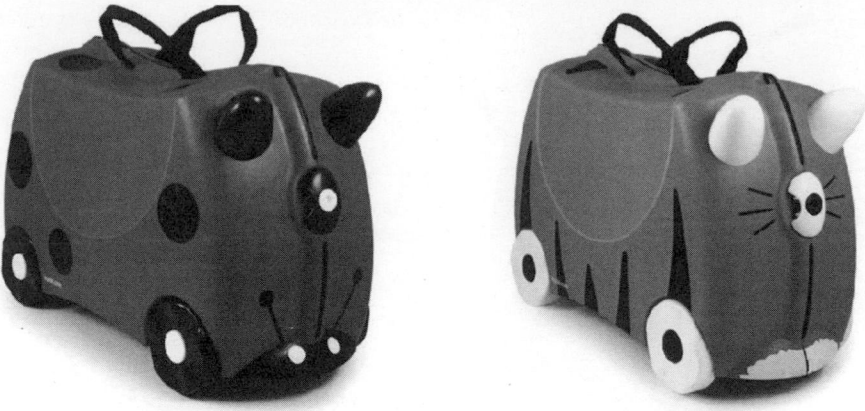

Figure 27.2 Examples of Magmatic's Trunki as sold
Source: PMS International Group Plc v. Magmatic [2016] UKSC 12, [3]

Figure 27.3 PMS's Kiddee Cases
Source: PMS International Group Plc v. Magmatic [2016] UKSC 12, [4]

decision that the registered design included both the shape of the suitcase and the strap, strip, and wheels narrowed the scope of the design and almost inevitably led the court to conclude that the design had not been infringed.

While many commentators (including Lord Neuberger) have celebrated the innovation and skill of Robert Law in creating the original ride-on suitcase (and correspondingly lamented his loss in the Supreme Court),[7] it seems that the lack of protection is attributable to the lack of clarity in the representations and the way they were interpreted by the courts. To some extent, problems of this nature may be less common now given

---

[7] See D. Stone, 'Trunki: How Did Things Go So Wrong?' (2016) 11 *JIPLP* 662; S. Ashby, 'The UK Supreme Court and the Trunki case' [2016] *EIPR* 527 ('getting the representations right is crucial'); B. Trimmer and G. Parsons, 'Trunki's Crazy (Registered Design) Ride' [2016] *EIPR* 451.

the 2016 agreement by EUIPO, the UK IPO, and many other EU design offices to adopt common practice guidelines in relation to the drafting of representations.[8] In the United Kingdom, the specific problems raised in *Trunki* may be less common following the 2016 UK IPO's *Guidance Notes* which clarify what applicants need to do when they want to claim shape alone.[9]

While the representations provide the foundation for determining the ambit of the protected design, other factors may help to identify the features for which protection is sought. For example, it has long been the practice for the courts to look at a physical embodiment of a registered design, where one exists, to help them to determine what a design is.[10] While the physical manifestations of the design are often used as helpful concrete examples of a registered design, it is important that the physical object actually corresponds to the design that has been registered. Thus, in one of the many decisions between Samsung and Apple, the court stressed that Apple's iPad should not be confused with the design that Apple had registered, which differed slightly from the product that was marketed.[11] The gap between the design as registered and the design as marketed was also a key reason why the claimant lost in *Trunki*.

(ii) Unregistered Community designs While the rules about the types of design that are excluded (such as features dictated solely by function) apply equally to UK registered designs, Community registered designs, and unregistered Community designs, there is an obvious difference between registered and unregistered designs. This is that in the case of unregistered Community designs, none of the bureaucratic aids that are used to determine the scope of a registered design are available to assist the court in identifying the unregistered design in question. As we already noted, the question of the novelty of an unregistered Community design only arises before a Community design court, either in infringement or invalidity proceedings. In such cases, the court will have to examine the appearance of the article in issue to determine whether the design is novel and has individual character. In an infringement action, the procedural rules of the member state where the action is commenced will require the claimant to identify the design that they allege has been infringed. In principle, however, there seems no reason why a person should not claim a collection of features as a design, as well as each of the features individually.

2.1.1 Component parts of complex products: visibility in use

We have already noted that the European reforms were forged amidst strenuous lobbying by the automobile manufacturing industry on the one side and spare parts manufacturers on the other. One of the outcomes of this messy compromise was that features dictated solely by function, along with features that function as 'interconnections', are excluded from design protection. A further limitation, which we look at here, is found in Article 4(2) of the Community Design Regulation. This provides that:

A design applied to or incorporated in a product which constitutes a component part of a complex product shall only be considered to be new and to have individual character:

(a) if the component part, once it has been incorporated into the complex product, remains visible during normal use of the latter, and

(b) to the extent that those visible features of the component part fulfil in themselves the requirements as to novelty and individual character.[12]

---

[8] EUIPO, *Convergence on graphic representation of designs* (15 April 2016).

[9] UK IPO, *Guidance on use of representations when filing Registered Design applications* (1 June 2016).

[10] *The Procter & Gamble Company v. Reckitt Benckiser* [2007] *EWCA* 936, [12].

[11] *Samsung v. Apple* [2012] *EWHC* 1882, [8].

[12] Designs Dir., Art. 3(3); CDR, Art. 4(2); RDA 1949, s. 1B(8).

There are a number of things to note about the so-called 'visibility in use' exclusion, which excludes 'under the bonnet' or non-visible spare parts from the remit of design protection.[13] One of these is that the exclusion only applies to 'component parts' of 'complex products', which were discussed in Chapter 26.[14] Where a design is applied to a component part of a complex product, the novelty of the design (along with its individual character) is decided on the basis of those features of the design that are visible in 'normal use'; all other features are ignored. It seems that the mere possibility that something might be used in a way that allows them to be seen may suffice. Thus, in one case involving the design of insulation blocks, the Board of Appeal (BoA) held that while insulation blocks are 'normally affixed to walls and covered with plaster' (and thus hidden from view), 'they may also be left exposed to view either as a decorative feature of a wall, or in the course of construction'.[15] Article 4(3) of the Regulation defines 'normal use' as 'use by the end-user, excluding maintenance, servicing, or repair work'.[16] The decision about the nominal end-user is important because it determines the perspective from which a complex product is viewed and what is to be considered 'normal use'. As is evident from the many cases in which Article 4(2) has arisen, the fact that the design is limited to those features that are visible in normal use makes it harder to establish that a design is new (or has individual character). It also correspondingly limits the scope of what is protected.[17]

The impact of the exclusions can be seen, for example, in *Kwang Yang Motors*[18]—a decision of the General Court, which concerned the design for an internal combustion engine that was held to be a component part of a complex product (namely, a lawnmower) (see Fig. 27.4). In determining the aspect of the engine that formed part of the design, the General Court had to answer two subsidiary questions: who was the end-user and what was the normal use of a lawnmower? The General Court found that the end-user was the person who used the mower to cut lawns and that normal use was the cutting of lawns. More specifically, the General Court said that during normal use, a lawnmower was placed on the ground with the user standing behind it. Importantly, this was the perspective (literally) from which the visible features of the product were to be determined. As a result, the design was limited to those aspects of the engine that a person standing behind the lawnmower would see—namely, the top upper side of the engine. Importantly, it was this feature of the engine that had to be novel (and also show individual character).[19]

While the decision of the tribunals have been fairly consistent in the way in which they have approached the visibility-in-use exclusion, in *Lindner Recyclingtech*,[20] the Board of Appeal construed the phrase 'remains visible during normal use' in such a way as to narrow the operation of the exclusion. The design in question was for a 'chaff cutter' (a metal cylinder with knives attached), which was a component part of a complex

---

[13] See G. Dinwoodie, 'Federalized Functionalism: The Future of Design Protection in the European Union' (1996) 24 *AIPLA QJ* 611, 680.

[14] *Argo Development and Manufacturing v. OHIM*, Case T-41/14 EU:T:2015:53.

[15] *Austrotherm v. Termo Organika*, Case R 998/2013–3, (12 February 2015).

[16] RDA 1949, s. 1B(9); CDR, Art. 4(3), Recital 12 ('those component parts which are not visible during normal use of a product, or to those features of such part which are not visible when the part is mounted, or which would not, in themselves, fulfil the requirements as to novelty and individual character; whereas features of design which are excluded from protection for these reasons should not be taken into consideration for the purpose of assessing whether other features of the design fulfil the requirements for protection'). On the legislative history, see B. Posner commentary, in Franzosi, 7.

[17] *Euro Fire v. Tarnavva*, Case R 316/2008–3 (14 October 2009) (Third BoA), [26] (the fireplace insert was limited to the front sides of the insert, since this was the only part visible).

[18] *Kwang Yang Motors v. OHIM*, Case T-11/08 [2011] *ECR* II-265 (GC).   [19] Ibid., [21]–[22].

[20] *Lindner Recyclingtech v. Franssons Verkstäder*, Case R 690/2007–3 (22 October 2009) (Third BoA).

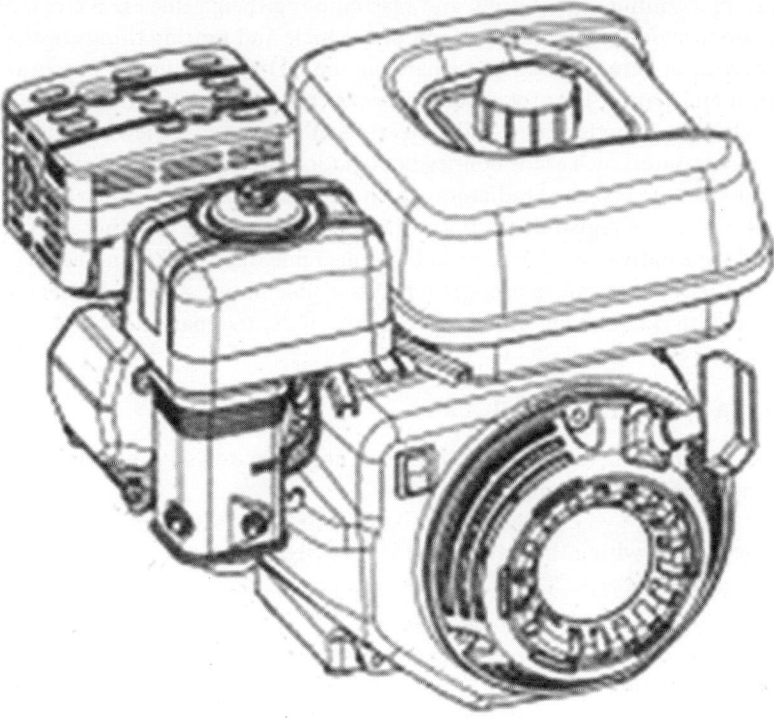

Figure 27.4 Image of internal combustion engine in *Kwang Yang Motors*
Source: Kwang Yang Motors

product—namely, a machine for shredding used paper, cardboard, plastic, and glass for recycling purposes. Given that the chaff cutters were a component part of a complex product, the question arose: what aspects of the chaff cutter were visible in normal use? The problem here was that when the recycling machines were being used, it was difficult to see the chaff cutters. This was a consequence of safety regulations which required the cutters to be covered to prevent users from getting direct access to the rotating parts of the shredder, of the fact that when the cutters were in use they rotated at high speed making them difficult to see, and of the fact that when the machines were in operation the cutters were largely covered by the material being shredded. In a decision that has important ramifications for designs for moving parts, the Board of Appeal held that despite these considerations, Article 4(2)(a) of the Community Design Regulation:

> . . . does not require a component part to be clearly visible at every moment of use. It is sufficient if the whole of the complement part can be seen some of the time in such a way that all its essential features can be comprehended.[21]

One of the notable features of the way 'normal use' is defined in Article 4(3) of the Regulation is that it specifically excludes 'maintenance, servicing, or repair work'. This gives substance to the exclusion, which might otherwise have been undermined by the claim that normal users include car and bike enthusiasts who spend their weekends

---

[21] Ibid., [21].

dismantling, cleaning, fine-tuning, and reassembling their vehicles. We can infer that normal use includes getting into and out of a vehicle and putting things in the boot, as well as driving or being a passenger. Changing the oil or adjusting the points are almost certainly maintenance. The protectable parts of a car would include the internal features, such as the seats, gearstick, handbrake, steering wheel, and rear-view mirrors, as well as the external features, such as the bonnet, boot, doors, hubcaps, wipers, and wing mirrors. The designs for things such as radiators (which are usually only seen when the car is being repaired) will not be registrable.[22] If a part is visible in normal use, those parts must be novel and have individual character to be protectable. It should be noted that where a component part of a complex product remains visible in use, a special defence exists in Article 110 of the Regulation, which allows a third party to repair the complex product.[23]

2.2 WHAT IS THE PRIOR ART?

Once the design has been identified, it is then necessary to ascertain what the relevant prior art is for the design in question.

2.2.1 The date on which the state of the art is assessed

Since the prior art changes as new designs are published, it is crucial to work out the relevant date when the prior art is to be assessed.

(i) British and Community registrations Similar rules apply to Community and UK registrations. A design application or registration is assessed for novelty against designs made available to the public before the filing date for the application for registration, or if priority is claimed, the date of priority.[24] The most important mechanism for claiming priority relates to a claim based on an earlier application to a 'Convention country' made not more than six months before the UK filing.[25] In the case of a Community application, priority may also be claimed from an earlier exhibition. However, in contrast to the British position, the Community Design Regulation allows applicants to claim priority from the date of disclosure at an officially recognized international exhibition.[26] Since there are very few such exhibitions, the difference in the approach taken by the UK Designs Registry and EUIPO is unlikely to be important.[27]

(ii) Unregistered Community designs In the case of unregistered Community designs, novelty is assessed at the date on which the design was first made available to the public.[28] This is also the date from which the three-year term of protection commences.

---

[22] H. Speyart, 'The Grand Design: An Update on the E.C. Design Proposals, Following the Adoption of a Common Position on the Directive' [1997] *EIPR* 605, 609, argues that the exclusion is unnecessary, for such designs will be functional or made up of interconnections.   [23] See Chapter 28, section 5.7, pp. 793–5.

[24] Designs Dir., Art. 4; RDA 1949, s. 14; CDR, Arts 38 (date of filing), 41 (right of priority). For speculation as to whether priority might be claimed from a patent application, see Musker, 169. For the European Union position, see CDR, Arts 41–44; CDIR, Art. 8. On exhibition priority, see CDIR, Art. 9.

[25] RDA 1949, s. 14(1). The Convention countries are identified by way of an Order in Council under RDA 1949, s. 13. See Designs (Convention Countries) Order 2007 (SI 2007/277 as amended). As regards the Community design right, a six-month priority is accorded to applications for design right or for utility model protection made in a state that is party to the Paris Convention or the WTO Agreement, or which accords an equivalent right of priority.   [26] CDR, Art. 44.

[27] As we will see, in both the United Kingdom and at the EUIPO, the exposure of a design at an exhibition by the applicant or with their consent during the 12 months preceding an application will not invalidate an application, because of the grace period. The inability to claim priority from the exhibition is of significance only if a third party who independently develops the design tries to register in the period between exhibition and application. Such cases are likely to be quite rare.   [28] CDR, Art. 5(1)(a).

2.2.2 The contents of the state of the art

The state of the art consists of all designs made available to the public before the relevant date. Taken alone, this would create a state of the art that was comparable to that used in patent law—that is, without geographical or temporal limits. As we will see, however, this broad definition is subject to a number of exceptions. A design is deemed to have been made available to the public 'if it has been published following registration or otherwise, or exhibited, used in trade or otherwise disclosed'.[29] The definition is very broad;[30] disclosure of a design by any means, anywhere in the world will—subject to the limits discussed later—form part of the prior art against which a design's novelty will be assessed. As Arnold J said, 'any disclosure which makes the design public in any part of the world will suffice'.[31] Typically, a design will be made available in one of two ways. First, a representation of the design will include pictures, photographs, drawings, graphic representations, or sketches of the design. A design may also be made available to the public in a physical form, for example the sale of a chair would disclose the design. Reflecting design law's focus on the appearance of things, it is highly unlikely that a written description will ever count as a relevant disclosure for the purposes of determining novelty. While patents and designs cover different matter, it is possible for a patent to form part of the state of the art for design law purposes. This is on the condition that in addition to the technical description, the patent also discloses the appearance of the design in question.[32]

Although the legislation starts by defining the state of the art broadly, it then excludes certain matters—namely, disclosures that derive from obscure events (the 'safeguard clause'), disclosures that are confidential, disclosures that are a consequence of a breach of confidence, and disclosures by the applicant within the grace period.[33] We will look at each in turn.

(i) The safeguard clause The first exclusion is found in Article 7(1). This provides that the prior art does not include events that could not reasonably have become known in the normal course of business to the circles specialized in the sector concerned operating within the European Union, before the date of filing of the application for registration, or if priority is claimed, the date of priority.[34] This is a safeguard clause that aims to prevent designs from being rendered invalid on the basis of obscure disclosures. The clause was promoted by the fear that a broadly defined state of the art might lead to claims of invalidity based on the citation of obscure prior art, such as that in museums. In principle, the safeguard clause applies to a wide range of obscure disclosures; these could be very old disclosures, geographically remote disclosures, or disclosures made to a very narrowly defined group of people. In positive terms, the safeguard clause allows for the protection of designs that, while previously disclosed as a matter of objective fact, have been lost or have not been available to the design market within the European Union. In negative

---

[29] Designs Dir., Art. 6; RDA 1949, s. 1B(5)(a); CDR, Art. 7(1).

[30] This includes technical catalogues (even though it did not include prices). See *Watt Drive Antriebstechnik v. Nanotehnologija*, Case R 1053/2012–3 (25 February 2013) (Third BoA), [13]–[18].

[31] *Magmatic v. PMS* [2013] *EWHC* 1925 (Pat), [33], not discussed on appeal: [2014] *EWCA Civ* 181. An incorrectly registered design forms part of the state of the art: *Cheng-Kang Chu v. Fitness Brands*, Case R 346/2012–3 (21 February 2013) (Third BoA), [17].

[32] *Senz Technologies v. OHIM*, Joined Cases T-22/13 and T-23/13, EU:T:2015:310, [24].

[33] Designs Dir., Art. 6; RDA 1949, s. 1B(6); CDR, Art. 7. Private business correspondence in the form of email was a private communication and thus not part of the state of the art. *CTA Digital v. Bigben Interactive*, Case R 1103/2012–3 (6 August 2015).

[34] Designs Dir., Art. 6(1); RDA 1949, s. 1B(6)(a); CDR, Art. 7(1). This is a reversal of the Max Planck Institute's original proposal of a relative novelty requirement according to which designs were assessed against other products 'made accessible to interested business circles in the EC'.

terms, the provision enables monopolies to be granted over designs that are not really new and possibly are not even original in a copyright sense.[35]

The onus of proving that a disclosure could not reasonably have been known falls upon the party relying on the exception. Typically, this will be the design proprietor defending a design's alleged invalidity in the face of a disclosure presented by the applicant. Once it is shown that the disclosure relied upon is obscure, the onus shifts to the other party.[36] The safeguard clause does not ask whether 'the design' could reasonably have become known, but whether 'the event'—that is, the exhibition, use in trade, or publication that disclosed the design—could reasonably have become known.

In applying the safeguard clause, tribunals are asked to speculate on the normal behaviour of a specific group of people: the circles specialized in the sector concerned. As such, the first question that we need to ask is: what is the 'sector concerned'? In many cases, this will be unproblematic, because the earlier design and the design in issue will relate to the same sector (for example where a design for a chair had been disclosed at an exhibition in Japan and the issue was whether a similar design registered at EUIPO after the exhibition was novel). However, it is easy to foresee more complex situations: where the earlier design was a painting exhibited in a small art gallery and the later design is an application of a similar image to a teapot, is the relevant design sector painters or ceramic designers? Some commentators have argued that the 'sector concerned' must be the sector to which the earlier design belongs (here, painters),[37] while others have argued that the sector will be determined by the prior art in question. Yet another approach was raised by the European Commission, which suggested that the relevant sector was determined by the goods which the design was applied to.[38] The question of how the relevant sector is to be determined was discussed by the Court of Appeal in *Green Lane Products*,[39] who held that 'the relevant sector is the sector that consists of or includes the sector of the alleged prior art. It is not limited to the sector specified in the application for registration.' Following the decision of the Court of Justice in *Easy Sanitary Solutions*, the position in Europe is now the same as in *Green Lane Products*: the 'sector concerned' is not limited to the product in which the design was intended to be incorporated or applied.[40]

Once we have identified the relevant sector for the design in question, we then need to identify who 'the *circles specialized* in the sector' are. It has been said that 'the circle' extends beyond designers working in the field to include all individuals who conduct trade in relation to products in that sector including those who design, make, advertise, market, distribute, or sell such products in the course of trade in the European Union.[41]

---

[35] In TRIPS terms, this seems unproblematic, because TRIPS, Art. 25, merely requires members to protect designs that are new or original, but does not say that members should not protect designs that are neither new nor original: see Tritton ('just permissible as the agreement can be argued to be permissive in this respect'); Musker, 23–4 (if one takes TRIPS as mandating particular requirements, 'one would struggle to find any country in compliance with TRIPS').

[36] *Magmatic v. PMS* [2013] *EWHC* 1925 (Pat), [41], not discussed on appeal: [2014] *EWCA Civ* 181.

[37] See Musker, 36.

[38] European Commission, *Green Paper on the Legal Protection of Industrial Design* (June 1991), III/F/5131/91–EN (henceforth 'EC Green Paper'), [5.5.5.1].

[39] *Green Lane Products v. PMS International Group Ltd* [2008] *EWCA Civ* 358, [10]–[11]; followed in *Magmatic v. PMS* [2013] *EWHC* 1925 (Pat), [37], not discussed on appeal: [2014] *EWCA Civ* 181, [2016] *UKSC* 12.

[40] *Easy Sanitary Solutions v. EUIPO*, Case C-361/15 EU:C:2017:720. The Board of Appeal at EUIPO reached the opposite conclusion in *Ferrari SpA v. Dansk Supermarked*, Case R 84/2007–3 (25 January 2008) (Third BoA); *Crocs v. Holey Soles Holdings*, Case R 9/2008–3 (26 March 2010) (Third BoA), [62].

[41] *Green Lane Products v. PMS International Group Ltd* [2007] *EWHC* 1712 (Pat), [34]; EC Green Paper, [5.5.5.2] ('the specialists, designers, merchants, and manufacturers operating in the sector concerned'); upheld by the Court of Appeal in *Green Lane Products v. PMS International Group Ltd* [2008] *EWCA Civ* 358, [10]–[11].

In line with this, it has also been suggested that circles includes experts and all of the businesses involved in the trade (including importers).[42] This approach was confirmed by the Court of Justice in *Gautzsch*, who rejected the suggestion that the specialized circles should be limited to people who created designs or developed or manufactured products based on those designs, holding instead that there were no 'restrictions relating to the nature of the activity of natural or legal persons who may be considered to form part of the circles specialized in the sector concerned'.[43]

Once the circles specialized in the sector have been identified, it is then necessary to determine whether the events 'could reasonably have become known in the normal course of business'. In effect, this requires a tribunal to speculate on normal practices within the specific sector. It is always important to keep in mind that the question of what could become known in any particular case always depends on what is normal in the sector in question. Thus the mere fact that the disclosure took place in a remote location is not of itself enough; the relevant question is always whether the disclosure could reasonably have become known in the normal course of business.[44] This also means that it is not appropriate to speak generally—as the Board of Appeal did when considering whether a patent available on the US Patent and Trademark Office (USPTO) website was an obscure disclosure for the purposes of a design for an umbrella[45]—about the quality of innovation or design in the United States or about the strong trade links between the United States and the European Union; all that matters is the practice of the umbrella sector and whether, objectively,[46] the design could be known in the European Union. It has been suggested that in the context of a validity challenge to a design of a garden pavilion, prior exhibition in a company showroom in China may not of itself qualify as a disclosure that could reasonably have become known in the normal course of business.[47] The situation would have been different, however, if the presentation had been made at an international fair in China attended by European professionals of the sector in question. In the same decision, Advocate-General Wathelet said that communication to a single operator in the European Union (a sample of a garden pavilion was sent to a Belgian firm before the design had been registered) was not sufficient to conclude that the design had become known in the relevant circles. This was because of the language of the Community Design Regulation and the Designs Directive which speak in the plural, of 'circles specialized'.[48] While the quality of contemporary search engines means that online disclosures outside of the European Union will usually mean that the design will be treated as being known to relevant circles within the European Union,[49] it is possible to imagine situations in which this is not the case.

[42] *Harron SA v. THD Acoustics*, Case R 552/2008–3 (25 July 2009) (Third BoA).

[43] *H. Gautzsch Großhandel v. Münchener Boulevard Möbel Joseph Duna*, Case C-479/12, EU:C:2014:75. See also *H. Gautzsch Großhandel v. Münchener Boulevard Möbel Joseph Duna*, Case C-479/12, EU:C:2013:537 (Opinion of AG Wathelet), [38] (the 'circles specialized in the sector concerned' should be construed very broadly to include all operators that take part in the trade of the foods at issue, including designers, advertisers, producers, distributors, wholesalers, and retailers).

[44] *H. Gautzsch Großhandel v. Münchener Boulevard Möbel Joseph Duna*, Case C-479/12, EU:C:2014:75, [34].

[45] *Senz Technologies v. Impliva*, Case R 2453/201–3 (26 September 2012) (Third BoA), [17].

[46] *Magmatic v. PMS* [2013] *EWHC* 1925 (Pat), [39], not discussed on appeal: [2014] *EWCA Civ* 181; [2016] *UKSC* 12.

[47] *H. Gautzsch Großhandel v. Münchener Boulevard Möbel Joseph Duna*, Case C-479/12, EU:C:2014:75. See also Opinion of Advocate-General Wathelet, Case C-479/12, EU:C:2013:537, [55].

[48] See also *H. Gautzsch Großhandel v. Münchener Boulevard Möbel Joseph Duna*, Case C-479/12, EU:C:2013:537 (Opinion of AG Wathelet), [44]–[45].

[49] *Magmatic v. PMS* [2013] *EWHC* 1925 (Pat), [91], not discussed on appeal: [2014] *EWCA Civ* 181; [2016] *UKSC* 12.

In most instances, the obscurity of a design will be a product of where, how, or the parties to whom the design is disclosed. In some situations, the potential obscurity of a design may arise because of *when* it was disclosed. When the European Union law was being developed, there was a desire to ensure that very old designs were excluded from the relevant prior art.[50] Because this did not make it into the Directive or Regulation, very old designs will be treated the same as any other design: their relative obscurity will depend on whether the design could reasonably be known at the priority date.

The tribunals have adopted a liberal approach when considering whether a disclosure would be something that could be known to the interested circles in the European Union.[51] As a result, the concern that the safeguard clause might have transformed the broad, objective novelty notion into a peculiar and complex form of local novelty has not eventuated.[52] The approach taken to the safeguard clause can be seen, for example, in a decision in relation to a design for a children's ride-on suitcase (known as the 'Rodeo'). In a challenge to the novelty of the design, the question arose as to whether disclosure of a concept board at the 1998 BASF/Institute of Materials Designs Awards that showed the product in use was an obscure disclosure. It was agreed that the relevant sector was the suitcase sector. The question here was whether as a result of the awards ceremony, the design of the Rodeo could reasonably have become known in the normal course of business to circles specializing in suitcases within the European Union. The court found that the disclosure was not obscure and that it formed part of the relevant prior art for the design in question. This was because while the Designs Awards were for plastics, the Awards were well known in the field of product design in the United Kingdom. This was reinforced by the fact that the theme of the 1998 Awards was luggage.[53] In another decision, the Board of Appeal found that the sale in Florida and Colorado of 10,000 pairs of Crocs shoes (plastic clogs) made according to the challenged design could reasonably have reached the relevant circles in the European Union. This was because of the volume of sales, the fact that shoes were design items that would have been proudly worn in public, because the commercial success of the plastic clogs would have attracted the attention of competitors, and the fact that the sales occurred 10 months prior to registration—an 'eternity in the field of fashion'.[54]

(ii) Confidential disclosure The provisions dealing with confidential disclosures are more straightforward. A disclosure made under conditions of confidentiality will *not* make the design available to the public.[55] One potential difficulty is that the legislation is silent as to when conditions of confidentiality will exist. The law of confidence has hitherto been treated as a matter of national law.[56]

(iii) Disclosures in breach of confidence A related but distinct exclusion from the 'state of the art' applies 'if a design for which protection is claimed . . . has been made available to the public as a consequence of an abuse in relation to the designer or his successor in title'.[57] The

---

[50] EC Green Paper, [5.5.5.2] ('if the design is unknown to them, then it should be eligible for protection even if an identical design has existed in the past and has completely vanished from the collective memory'); Musker, 37.

[51] *Magmatic v. PMS* [2013] *EWHC* 1925 (Pat), [38] (the words are to be broadly interpreted), not discussed on appeal: [2014] *EWCA Civ* 181, [2016] *UKSC* 12.

[52] Musker, 61 ('parochial novelty').

[53] *Magmatic v. PMS* [2013] *EWHC* 1925 (Pat), [54], not discussed on appeal: [2014] *EWCA Civ* 181, [2016] *UKSC* 12.   [54] *Crocs Inc v. Holey Soles Holdings Ltd*, R 9/2008-3, [64]–[70].

[55] Designs Dir., Art. 6; RDA 1949, s. 1B(6)(b); CDR, Art. 7.

[56] British law has failed to decide, conclusively, whether implicit obligations of confidentiality are to be assessed by subjective or objective criteria: see Chapter 45, section 2.3, p. 1224.

[57] Designs Dir., Art. 6(3); RDA 1949, s. 1B(6)(e); CDR, Art. 7(3).

most obvious example of such an abuse is a breach of confidence, such as where an employee publishes the design. This exclusion is subject to the limitation that the disclosure must have taken place in the 12 months preceding the priority date.

(iii) Grace period The most important of the exclusions from the state of the art is the grace period. This excludes from consideration the designer's own disclosures in the 12-month period preceding the priority date.[58] The purpose of the grace period is to allow applicants to test their designs in the marketplace before deciding whether to register or to rely upon the protection given to unregistered designs.[59] It should be noted that the grace period not only applies to disclosures by the designer, but also to disclosures by their successor in title 'or a third person as a result of information provided or action taken by the designer or his successor in title'.[60] The obligation is on the person relying on the grace period to establish that they are either the creator of, or the successor in title to, the design.[61]

The reference to disclosures by 'a third person *as a result of* information provided or *action* taken by the designer' is ambiguous. It may be interpreted to encompass the activities of a third party who copies a design made available by the designer and places imitations (or variations) on the market. The third-party disclosure may be 'as a result of' the action of the designer, in that it could not have occurred without the designer's disclosure. A narrower and more natural construction of the phrase 'as a result of action' might confine the limitation to disclosures that have been initiated or authorized by the designer, for example publication by authorized advertisers or exhibition by distributors. While this latter interpretation might seem to raise doubts over the usefulness of the grace period, it should not be forgotten that the state of the art is defined elsewhere to exclude disclosures that have been made 'as a consequence of an abuse in relation to the designer'. If a third party has made illegitimate or unauthorized copies of the design available, these are made available as a consequence of 'an abuse', the abuse being an infringement of the designer's unregistered Community design.

While the grace period has been widely welcomed, two limitations are worth observing. The first is that the grace period only exempts a designers' own action from invalidating their own later application for registration; it does not backdate the application to the time of initial disclosure, nor establish priority over an independent design. Consequently, a design application by A will still be invalidated by disclosures of identical designs by third parties in the 12 months between A's first disclosure and application for registration. The second limitation is that the grace period only applies to disclosures of 'a design for which protection is claimed'. On a literal reading, this would be unfortunate for an applicant who had been market-testing a design that differed either in immaterial details, or in material details which were nonetheless insufficient to create a different overall impression on an informed user: in these cases, it must have been the legislative intention that the designer's own (or authorized) actions would not invalidate a later application (albeit for a non-identical design). Such a result could be achieved, albeit artificially, by saying the 'design for which protection

---

[58] Designs Dir., Art. 6(2), RDA 1949, s. 1B(6)(c)–(d), CDR, Art. 7(2)(b). Musker refers to this as creating 'a regrettably long period of uncertainty for competitors': Musker, 38. Existing national laws had sometimes been even more generous: see French Intellectual Property Code, art. L.511–6 (no time limit). However, Germany had given six months only. See E. Ferrill and J. Roorda, 'Amazing Grace Periods for Registered Designs and Design Patents' (2016) 11 *JIPLP* 762.

[59] CDR, Recital 20; EC Green Paper, [4.3.2]–[4.3.6].

[60] RDA 1949, s. 1(b), (6)(d); Designs Dir., Art. 6(2)(a); CDR, Art. 7(2)(a).

[61] *Min Lu v. OHIM*, Case T-813/14, EU:T:2015:868, [21]–[23].

is claimed' is that in the representations *and all others that would create the same over-all impression on an informed user*. A designer could then argue that insofar as their own previously disclosed variations would infringe the Community registered design if published by a third party after the date of registration, they are 'designs for which protection is claimed'.

2.3 ARE THE DESIGNS IDENTICAL?

Once we have ascertained the nature of the design in question and the relevant prior designs, we then need to decide whether the design in question is novel. Article 5 of the Regulation (which corresponds to Article 4 of the Directive) states that a design is new if no identical design has been made available to the public before the priority date. According to Article 5(2), designs will be identical if their features only differ in 'immaterial details'.[62]

In most situations, determining whether two designs are identical will be straightforward. In this context, it is important to note that the point of comparison is the physical form (or appearance) of the designs. It does not matter if the ideas or concepts that lie behind the designs are the same; all that matters is whether the tangible physical forms (or appearance) of the designs are identical.[63] It is also important to recall that when undertaking the novelty examination, we are comparing *appearance* not function, nor (at least in most cases) the products to which the appearance is applied. In making the assessment, we should recall that appearance not only includes lines, contours, and shapes, but also colours, texture, and materials. The appearance of a red plastic teapot may therefore not be identical to a red crockery teapot, even if the shape and size are identical, and an orange-coloured leather football of standard size may not be identical to a conventional white-lacquered leather football of the same size. The issue here is whether the appearance is precisely the same. In these cases, novelty will often depend on the way the design is represented. This can be seen, for example, in two related cases before the Invalidity Division, which concerned the novelty of a registered design for a sponge that consisted of a thick white layer and a thin yellow layer. In one decision, where the design was represented in colour, it was held that the design was novel.[64] In contrast, in another decision, it was held that the design for the same sponge, this time represented in black and white, lacked novelty.[65] In both cases, the prior art was the same: the fate of the designs turned on the way they were represented.

The main difficulty that arises in this context is determining whether, when two designs differ slightly, the difference is immaterial. In a process not unlike the children's game of 'spot the difference', tribunals begin by identifying the points of difference between the prior art and the registered design. Once this is done, they then need to decide whether the identified differences are material. In most cases, there is little guidance from the tribunal as to why they have decided that differences are immaterial or not. In the many challenges to the validity of Community registered designs that have been raised to date, a very strict approach has been adopted, requiring almost exact similarity between the

---

[62] Rather strangely, the Green Paper contrasts this with a 'creative independent development': EC Green Paper, [5.5.5.4].

[63] *Rolawn v. Turfmech Machinery* [2008] *RPC* (27) 663, [79]; EC Green Paper, [5.4.3.1]–[5.4.3.4] (design law does not protect the idea or overall concept).

[64] *Bümag v. Procter & Gamble*, ICD 1741 (15 May 2006) (Invalidity Division) (also held to have individual character).

[65] Ibid., 1758 (also lacked individual character).

registered design and the prior art for the design to be declared invalid. A key consideration is whether the point of difference contributes to the overall appearance of the product. It has been said that immaterial details are 'details that are not immediately perceptible and that they would not therefore produce differences, even slight, between . . . designs'.[66] This is reflected in the suggestion that the definition would exclude differences that are only noticeable when 'conducting a close forensic analysis'.[67] As the Board of Appeal said, a 'detail is "immaterial" if it does not invest in the project as such, but is "outside" or accessory to it'.[68]

Perhaps the best way in which to get a sense of how the question of whether a difference is immaterial might be decided is by looking at some examples. In a decision that concerned a design for the shape of wine glasses with sealed lids, the point of difference between the registered design and the prior design lay in the shape of the stem of the wine glasses: the shape of the stem was faceted (or angular) in the registered design, while it was round in the prior design.[69] The Invalidity Division held that because the faceted stem was 'easily recognisable' and 'contributed to the appearance of the product', the difference was not immaterial. In a decision concerning the design of a helicopter, it was held that the differences between the prior design and the contested design—the bottom of the windshields and the shape of the bottom of the doors were different—were material differences and, as such, that the design was novel (see Fig. 27.5).[70] In another case, it was held that differences between the registered design for a golf tee and the prior art (a 1925 patent)—namely, the angle or splaying of the bristles, and the spike and shoulder of the tee—were material differences and, as such, that the prior art did not anticipate the design (see Fig. 27.6).[71]

One question that arises is the perspective from which the point of difference should be addressed. The legislation does not explain to whom the differences must be immaterial, and the other provisions of the Regulation and Directive point to various candidates: the designer; the design expert; the consumer; the informed user; and relevant circles.[72] While the General Court said that this should be addressed from an objective point of view,[73] it still leaves this question open (although the Court did suggest that it would not include the informed user). No doubt, the issue will rarely arise, and variations from previously disclosed designs will probably either be material to all of the potential candidates or to none of them. But there might be variations of detail that a design expert might notice, which a consumer would not.[74] And there might be minor differences of appearance that might be regarded by the designer as crucially important, which are of no consequence to a consumer. Whatever uncertainties may exist in relation to the novelty examination, they are unlikely to be significant, primarily because the novelty requirement will almost always be overshadowed by the more exacting inquiry into individual character.

---

[66] *Erich Kastenholz v. OHIM*, Case T 68/11, EU:T:2013:298 (GC), [37].

[67] *Central Vista v. Pemi Trade* [2009] *ECDR* 363, [23].

[68] *Antrax v. The Heating Company*, Case R 1451/2009–3 (2 November 2010) ('Third BoA) (an immaterial detail may be 'the presence of a sign printed on a template, such as a product code or brand quality').

[69] *Guy Jackson-Eben v. Wine Innovations*, ICD 8610 (27 February 2013) (Invalidity Division). See also *Central Vista v. Pemi Trade* [2009] *ECDR* 363.

[70] *Trendak v. Celier*, ICD 8900 (18 June 2013) (Invalidity Division).

[71] *In the Matter of Registration No 2054,094 (Michael St John) 0–023–09* (26 January 2009).

[72] In *Erich Kastenholz v. OHIM*, Case T-68/11, EU:T:2013:298 (GC), [37], it would not be the 'overall impression produced on the informed user'.

[73] Ibid., [40].   [74] EC Green Paper, [5.5.5.3].

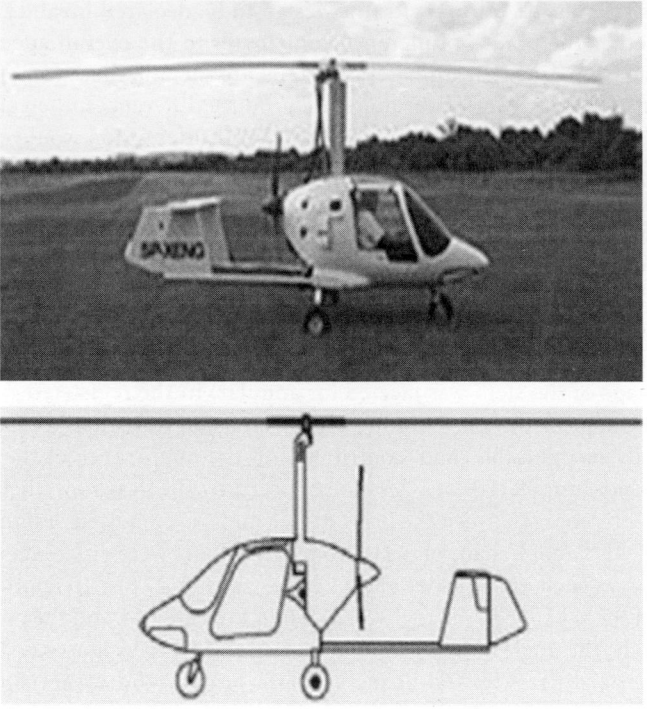

Figure 27.5 Applicant's representation of a design of a helicopter and prior art
Source: Trendak v. Celier, ICD 8900 (18 June 2013) (Invalidity Division)

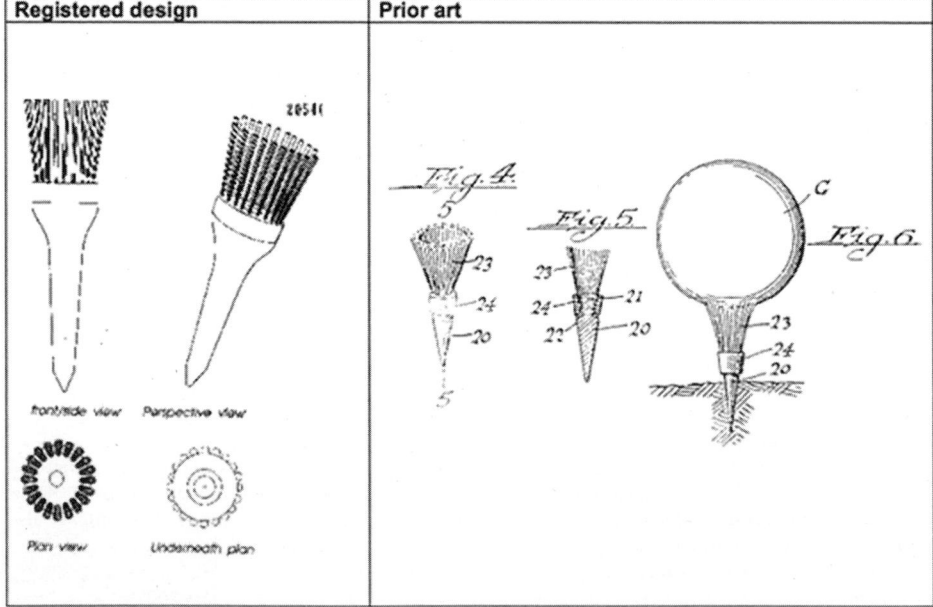

Figure 27.6 Design of a golf tee and prior art
Source: Michael J. St John

3 INDIVIDUAL CHARACTER

As well as complying with the definition of design and the requirement that the design be novel, to be valid a design must also possess 'individual character'.[75] The test of individual character is whether 'the overall impression [the design] produces on the informed user differs from the overall impression produced on such a user by any design which has been made available to the public'.[76] This has been described as 'the overall dominant and decisive criterion',[77] and is the most difficult aspect of any design to judge.[78] It is also one of the most common matters that arises before the tribunals.

One of the notable things about the test for individual character is that it mirrors the test used to determine the scope of design protection and thus infringement. This is reflected in Article 10(1) of the Regulation, which states that 'the scope of the protection conferred by a Community design shall include any design which does not produce on the informed user a different overall impression'. Although individual character looks back in time (from the design in question to relevant designs in the prior art), whereas infringement looks forward (from the design in question to subsequent designs), nonetheless the concepts used are the same. As a result, the comments in this section apply equally when determining the scope of protection and whether there has been an infringement. It also means that cases in one area are relevant in the other.

Questions have been raised about whether the requirement for individual character is consistent with EU obligations under the Agreement on Trade Related Aspects of Intellectual Property Rights 1994 (TRIPS), which obliges members to provide protection of 'independently created industrial designs that are new or original'.[79] This is because, at first blush, individual character looks like an additional, and therefore illegitimate, hurdle. One attempt to justify the individual character standard argues that individual character can be equated with the independent creation standard,[80] although this is unconvincing. A preferable approach is to see individual character as being equivalent to 'significant difference': Article 25 of TRIPS permits members to provide that 'designs are not new or original if they do not significantly differ from known designs or combinations of known design features'. Viewed in this manner, TRIPS can also help us to define the limits of the 'individual character' inquiry.

As with the novelty examination, to determine whether a design has individual character, it is necessary to compare the design in question with relevant designs in the prior art. A key difference, however, is that with individual character the perspective from which the evaluation is made is explicit—namely, that of the informed user. The task of determining whether a design has individual character can be broken down into a number of subsidiary questions,[81] as follows.

---

[75] Designs Dir., Art. 3(2); RDA 1949, s. 11ZA(1)(b); CDR, Art. 4(1). Recital 9 of the Directive explains that the needs of the internal market require the adoption of 'a unitary definition of the notion of design and of the requirements as to novelty and individual character with which registered design rights must comply'. In the other four official languages of the Office, individual character is: *présente un caractère individuel* (French), *carácter singular* (Spanish), *un carattere individuale* (Italian), and *Eigenart* (German).

[76] Designs Dir., Art. 5.   [77] M. Levin commentary, in Franzosi, 69.

[78] UK IPO, *Designs Practice Note 4/03: Requirement of Novelty and Individual Character* (24 June 2003) ('a much broader and more difficult test than the simple novelty test').   [79] TRIPS, Art. 25(1).

[80] Suthersanen, 437, n. 65 ('arguably, the concept of "individual character" under the EC designs law may be a re-formulation of the "independently created" criterion').

[81] For a different breakdown see *H&M v. EUIPO*, Case T-525/13, EU:C:2014:2254, [32].

(i)   What is the design in question?

(ii)   What is the relevant prior art?

(iii) Who is the informed user?

(iv)   Does the design have individual character?

We will look at each in turn.

3.1 WHAT IS THE DESIGN IN QUESTION?

The first task that must be undertaken when considering whether a design has individual character is to clarify what the design in question is. This was discussed earlier in the context of the novelty examination.

3.2 WHAT IS THE RELEVANT PRIOR ART?

Once the design in question has been clarified, it is then necessary to determine the design(s) with which the challenged design is to be compared. To determine whether a design has individual character, it is necessary to compare the challenged design with relevant prior designs and *not* with the design corpus (that is, with a 'hypothetical amalgam of a number of prior designs'[82]). In rejecting the so-called 'amalgam theory', the Court of Justice said that it was not appropriate to compare the design in question with 'a combination of features taken in isolation and drawn from a number of designs'. Instead, the comparison was to be made in 'relation to one or more specific, individualised, defined and identified designs from all the designs which have been made available to the public previously'.[83] While the informed user will be aware of the design corpus, as with the novelty examination the examination is always with specific designs. The question of whether a particular design forms part of the prior art for the purposes of individual character is the same as with the novelty inquiry that was discussed earlier.

3.3 WHO IS THE INFORMED USER?

One of the notable features of the inquiry into individual character is that it is undertaken from the perspective of the 'informed user'—a fictitious character used to set the standard by which the designs are judged.[84] As well as setting the benchmark for deciding individual character (and thus infringement), the notional informed user is also used when deciding whether an application is in conflict with earlier rights (discussed later).[85]

---

[82] Stone, [12.152], citing the Irish High Court in *Karen Millen v. Dunnes Stores* [2008] *ECDR* (11) 156, [83].

[83] *Karen Millen v. Dunnes Stores,* Case C-345/13, EU:C:2014:2013, [23]–[25]. On this see D. Stone, 'Justice delayed: in 2015, Karen Millen's 2007 design infringement case comes to an end' [2015] *EIPR* 617.

[84] In the other four official languages of the Office: *l'utilisateur averti* (French); *usuario informado* (Spanish); *utilizatore informato* (Italian); *informierten Benutzer* (German). The Green Paper had originally proposed a test of distinctive character to be determined by the relevant public or ordinary consumer: EC Green Paper, [5.5.6.2]. See V. Torelli, 'The Informed User's Perception and a Design's Individual Character' (2015) 10 *JIPLP* 737.

[85] In *Samsung v. Apple* [2012] *EWHC* 1882 (Pat), [189], Judge Birss highlighted the importance of the standard, saying that, when he first compared the Samsung and Apple tablets, he 'was struck how similar they looked'. However, once he educated himself and was able to look at the designs from the perspective of the informed user, the way in which he looked at the tablets changed considerably.

The decision about who the fictitious informed user is, and the attributes and knowledge that they have, is important.[86] This is because the more knowledge and experience an informed user has of a product, the more likely it is that small differences will lead to a conclusion that the design gives rise to a different overall impression. In contrast, where the informed user has less knowledge, they are more likely to conclude that the designs are the same.

The informed user is not an expert in the sector who would know too much and identify every difference;[87] thus they are neither a designer, technical expert,[88] or manufacturer, or a seller of the products in which the designs are incorporated.[89] While the informed user is not an expert, they are also not the 'real' or 'average consumer' (who might be too ready to see individual character).[90] Instead, the informed user is a regular user of articles of the same sort as the registered design.[91] As the Court of Justice said in *PepsiCo*,[92] the concept of the informed user refers 'not to a user of average attention, but to a particularly observant one, either because of his personal experience or his extensive knowledge of the sector in question'. We also know that the informed user uses the product in which the design is embodied in accordance with the purpose for which it was intended, and that they are reasonably discriminatory in that they show a relatively high degree of attention when they use the product.[93] The informed user also has some awareness of the existing designs in the sector,[94] 'without knowing which aspects of that product are dictated by technical function'.[95] The informed user is someone who 'habitually purchases and uses' the products in question, who has 'become informed on the subject by browsing through catalogues, or making telephone inquiries, visiting the relevant stores, downloading information from the Internet'.[96]

3.4 DOES THE DESIGN HAVE INDIVIDUAL CHARACTER?

Once we have identified the design in question, the prior designs which the challenged design is to be compared with, and the attributes of the informed user, the next step is to ask whether, in light of this, the design has individual character. In other words, we need to ask: does the overall impression that the design produces on the informed user differ from the overall impression produced on such a user by any design that

---

[86] Occasionally, the tribunals have worked on the basis that there is more than one informed user. Thus, in *Grupo Promer Mon Graphic v. OHIM-PepsiCo*, Case T-9/07 [2010] *ECR* II–981, the GC worked on the basis that the informed users of the rapper were a 5–10-year-old child and a marketing manager. It is unclear how these two differ.

[87] They were not the 'person skilled in the art' in patent law (whose 'nerd-like' attributes were said to be too technical): *Woodhouse v. Architectural Lighting Systems* [2006] *ECDR* 11, [50].

[88] *Shenzhen Taiden Industrial v. OHIM*, Case T 153/08 [2010] *ECR* II–02517, [47].

[89] *Grupo Promer Mon Graphic v. OHIM-PepsiCo*, Case T-9/07 [2010] *ECR* II–981 (GC), [62]. See also *El Hogar Perfecto del Siglo XXI v. OHIM*, Case T-337/12, EU:T:2013:601 (ECJ, Sixth Chamber).

[90] *Grupo Promer Mon Graphic v. OHIM-PepsiCo*, Case T-9/07 [2010] *ECR* II–981, [24]–[26]; aff'd in *PepsiCo v. Grupo Promer*, Case C-281/10P [2011] *ECR* I-10153 (ECJ, Fourth Chamber). *Gamet v. EUIPO*, Case T-306/16, EU:T:2017:466, [40].   [91] *Woodhouse v. Architectural Lighting Systems* [2006] *ECDR* 11, [50].

[92] *PepsiCo v. Grupo Promer*, Case C-281/10P [2011] *ECR* I-10153 (ECJ, Fourth Chamber), [53]; reiterated in *Neuman v. OHIM*, Joined Cases C-101/11P and C-102/11P [2012] *ECR* I–641 (ECJ, Sixth Chamber), [53]–[54].

[93] *Shenzhen Taiden Industrial v. OHIM*, Case T-153/08 [2010] *ECR* II–02517, [47]. See also *Dyson v. Vax* [2011] *EWCA Civ* 1206, [15].

[94] *PepsiCo v. Grupo Promer*, Case C-281/10P [2011] *ECR* I-10153 (ECJ, Fourth Chamber), [62].

[95] *Kwang Yang Motor Company v. OHIM*, Case T-10/08 [2011] *ECR* II-265 (General Court).

[96] *Hook of Sweden v. Jukka Heininen*, Case R 650/2012–3 (19 February 2013) (Third BoA), [23].

has been made available to the public? To do this, the informed user will be presumed to compare the registered design with existing designs. While 'individual character' might suggest that the test is whether the design has a 'personality' of its own, this is not what is required by the definition; instead, it merely focuses on the impression made by the registered design on the notional informed user and whether that differs from the impression made by the existing designs. Ultimately, the decision as to whether a design has individual character is a factual question that will depend on the circumstances of the case.

Given that the test for individual character is a comparative test, the question arises: how different does a design have to be for it to have individual character? After some confusion,[97] it is now clear that a design will have individual character if the overall impression that the design produces on the informed user *differs* from the overall impression produced by designs that have previously been made available to the public. As the General Court said:

> 'the individual character of a design results from an overall impression of difference, or lack of déjà vu, from the point of view of an informed user in relation to any previous presence in the design corpus, without taking account of any differences that are insufficiently significant to affect that overall impression'.[98]

When examining the designs for individual character, it is also important to keep in mind that the informed user will focus on the *appearance* of the designs.[99] As such, the informed user is not concerned with the motivations of the parties,[100] how the design features were formed,[101] how the designed article behaves,[102] or that a design is a poor quality imitation;[103] all that matters is the overall impression given by the appearance of the designs in question.

It is important to note that the informed user's impression of the designs needs to be determined in light of the way the product at issue is used, 'in particular on the basis of the handling to which it is normally subject on that occasion'.[104] This means that in many

---

[97] In *Procter & Gamble* [2007] *EWCA Civ* 936, [19], on the basis of Designs Dir., Recital 13, Jacob LJ said that a higher standard should be imposed—namely, that the impression given by the design must 'clearly differ' from the impression produced on them by the 'existing design corpus'. Jacob LJ subsequently admitted that he was wrong and that all that had to be shown was that there was a difference: *Dyson v. Vax* [2011] *EWCA* 1206, [34].

[98] *Thomas Murphy v. EUIPO*, Case T-90/16, EU:T:2017:464, [43]; *Gamet v. EUIPO*, Case T-306/16, EU:T:2017:466, [38].

[99] But cf. the Austrian court, cited with approval by Jacob LJ in *Procter & Gamble* [2011] *EWCA Civ* 1206, [34], in which the Court noted that the febreze sprayer fits the hand differently from the airwick sprayer: ibid., [61].

[100] *Pepsico v. Grupo Promer Mon-Graphic*, Case R 1003/2005–3 (27 October 2006) (Third BoA), [23] (the fact that the appellant was acting in bad faith and copied the design was irrelevant; the question is not whether the design was copied, but whether it produced the same overall impression).

[101] *HK Ruokatalo Group Oyj v. Heinonen*, ICD 1964 (12 September 2006) ('meat foodstuffs'). In this case, it did not matter that the stripes on the surface of the meat were formed by grooves and ridges pressed into the raw meat (as was the case with the CRD) or whether the stripes were burnt onto the surface of the meat by frying them in a pan with ridges. The informed user was not concerned with how the stripes were formed; what mattered was that the resulting surface pattern was the same.

[102] The behaviour of dolls in use was not part of the appearance of the product and thus not to be taken into account in the assessment of the overall product: *Aktiebolaget Design Rubens Sweden v. Advikatefirnab Vinge KB*, ICD 461 (20 December 2005), [11].

[103] *J. Choo (Jersey) v. Towerstone* [2008] *EWHC* 346 (Ch) (the quality of a copy was not relevant for infringement).

[104] *Shenzen Taiden Industrial v. OHIM*, Case T-153/08 [2010] *ECR* II–02517 (GC, Second Chamber).

cases, the informed user will make a direct side-by-side comparison between the goods. However, where this is impractical or uncommon in the sector concerned, it will be necessary to:

> . . . envisage a comparison which, although not based exclusively on vague recollection, as in the field of trade marks, may none the less be made over a period of time and at different locations, so far as it is required in the specific case.[105]

Thus, in an action concerning the design for streetlights, which were often 8–10 metres off the ground, the question arose: should the comparison be side-by-side or from a distance? Should the designs be viewed at night or during the day? Rejecting the way in which the designs were actually sold as the basis by which the designs should be evaluated, the court said that the informed user would have in mind the visual impact of the street light *in situ*—during the daytime and a little distance from the base of the pole upon which the light is suspended.[106]

What matters is what strikes the mind of the informed user *when* the design is carefully viewed, not what sticks in the user's mind *after* it has been carefully viewed. While the test of imperfect recollection makes sense in trade mark law, where the main rationale for the protection is to prevent consumer confusion or deception, this is not the case with design protection; instead, the goal of design law is to protect the design *as a design*. What matters is the overall impression created by the design: will the informed user 'buy it, consider it, or appreciate it for its *individual character*? That involves the user looking at the article, not half-remembering it.'[107]

When an informed user compares the challenged design with existing designs, they are interested in the 'overall impression', which is to be contrasted with the idea of detailed dissection.[108] While it is appropriate to consider similarities and differences between the respective designs, 'what matters is the overall impression produced on the informed user by each design having regard to the design corpus and the degree of freedom of the designer'[109]—or, as the Court of Appeal put it, 'the two designs must . . . be considered globally'.[110]

Because the notion of 'overall impression' can be apt to mislead, it is helpful to remind ourselves that the design can lie in the appearance of the whole or part of a product, and that design protection exists irrespective of the product to which the design is applied. Given this, it is not surprising that one issue that has arisen is the specificity at which the comparison between the designs should be made. As Jacob LJ said, the 'level of generality to which the court must descend is important',[111] given that the more general the level of comparison, the more likely it is that the design will lack individual character (although

---

[105] *PepsiCo*, Case C-281/10P [2011] *ECR* I-10153 (Opinion of AG), [52].

[106] *Woodhouse v. Architectural Lighting Systems* [2006] *ECDR* 11, [52]. See also *Louver-Lite v. Harris Parts* [2012] *EWPCC* 53, [29] (the 'informed user will be able to encounter [the headrail of a window blind] as free standing items and see them side by side but will always think about them in the overall context that what really matters is the appearance of the product in use when fixed to a ceiling').

[107] *Procter & Gamble* [2007] *EWCA Civ* 936, [27] (emphasis in original).

[108] The European Commission, from the start, proposed that the threshold be determined by 'a synthetic approach, letting the design act on him as a whole and comparing this impression with the one produced by a similar design': EC Green Paper, [5.5.8.2].

[109] *Magmatic v. PMS International* [2013] *EWHC* 1925 (Pat); *Procter & Gamble* [2011] *EWCA Civ* 1206, [3]; *Dyson v. Vax* [2011] *EWCA Civ* 1206, [8]; *Samsung v. Apple* [2012] *EWHC* 1882 (Pat), [28].

[110] *Magmatic v. PMS International* [2014] *EWCA Civ* 181, [46]–[54] (agreeing with the reasoning of Arnold J at first instance, but overturning the decision on the basis of the way in which he applied the relevant legal principles to the facts at hand).

[111] *Procter & Gamble* [2007] *EWCA Civ* 936, [35(vii)].

this may not be the case with very novel designs). While the informed user is attentive to detail, they will not undertake a detailed and specialist appraisal; rather, the informed user will show a relatively high degree of attention when using the designs.

The question of the way designs are interpreted will always depend on the nature of the design in question. In some cases (for example with Apple products), this may mean that an important feature of the design is the lack of ornamentation.[112] In other cases, however, ornamentation may play a key role in influencing the overall visual impression created by a design.[113]

One factor that plays an important role when evaluating overall impression is the degree of freedom that the designer had in developing the challenged design.[114] As the General Court said:

> [The] greater the designer's freedom in developing the challenged design, the less likely it is that minor differences between the designs at issue will be sufficient to produce a different overall impression on an informed user. Conversely, the more the designer's freedom is restricted in developing the challenged design, the more likely minor differences between the designs at issue will be sufficient to produce a different overall impression on an informed user.[115]

The upshot of this is that minor differences between designs will have little impact on the overall impression in situations where the designer had considerable freedom.[116] In contrast, 'the more the designer's freedom in developing the contested design is restricted, the more likely minor differences between the design at issue will be sufficient to produce a different overall impression on the informed user'.[117]

The notion of 'design freedom' refers to the various constraints a designer would be under when developing the appearance of a product,[118] including constraints created by the fact that the product needs to perform a particular function[119] and statutory requirements applicable to the product.[120] A designer's freedom may also be constrained by the

---

[112] *Samsung Electronics (UK) v. Apple* [2012] *EWCA Civ* 1339, [2013] *FSR* 9, [15]–[16]. For a discussion of how the absence of decoration can operate as a feature of a registered design see *PMS International Group v. Magmatic* [2016] *UKSC* 12, [44].

[113] *PMS International Group v. Magmatic* [2016] *UKSC* 12. See also *Magmatic v. PMS International* [2014] *EWCA Civ* 181, [47] (CA).

[114] See J. Cornwell, 'Dyson and Samsung Compared: Functionality and Aesthetics in the Design Infringement Analysis' [2013] *EIPR* 273.

[115] *Kwang Yang Motors v. OHIM*, Case T-10/08 [2011] *ECR* II-265, [33]; applied in *BS Studio v. Naturkram Giot*, Case R 991/2011–3 (27 September 2012) (Third BoA), [28].

[116] Thus 'if the designer enjoys a high degree of freedom in developing a design, that reinforces the conclusion that the designs which do not have significant differences produce the same overall impression in an informed user': *Kwang Yang Motors v. OHIM*, Case T-10/08 [2011] *ECR* II-265, [33]; applied in *BS Studio v. Naturkram Giot*, Case R 991/2011–3 (27 September 2012) (Third BoA), [28].

[117] *Grupo Promer Mon Graphic v. OHIM-PepsiCo*, Case T-9/07 [2010] *ECR* II–981 (GC), [72]–[76]; *Erich Kastenholz v. OHIM*, Case T 68/11, EU:T:2013:298, [62].

[118] RDA 1949, s. 1B(4); Designs Dir., Art. 5(2).

[119] In the case of the design of a rug, other than the need to be reasonably flat to fulfil their purpose, in all other respects—particularly shape, colour, and the materials used—the designer's freedom was almost unlimited: *BS Studio v. Naturkram Giot*, Case R 991/2011–3 (27 September 2012) (Third BoA), [29]. A designer of door handles had almost unlimited freedom since 'handles can take any combination of colours, patterns, shapes and materials'; the only limitation was that the handle had to have a grip and be able to be mounted onto a door: *Neves & Fihos v. Alcides de Sá Pinto Castro*, Case R 1083/2011–3 (31 October 2012) (Third BoA), [37].

[120] *Procter & Gamble* [2007] *EWCA Civ* 936, [29]; *Grupo Promer Mon Graphic v. OHIM-PepsiCo*, Case T-9/07 [2010] *ECR* II–981 (GC), [67].

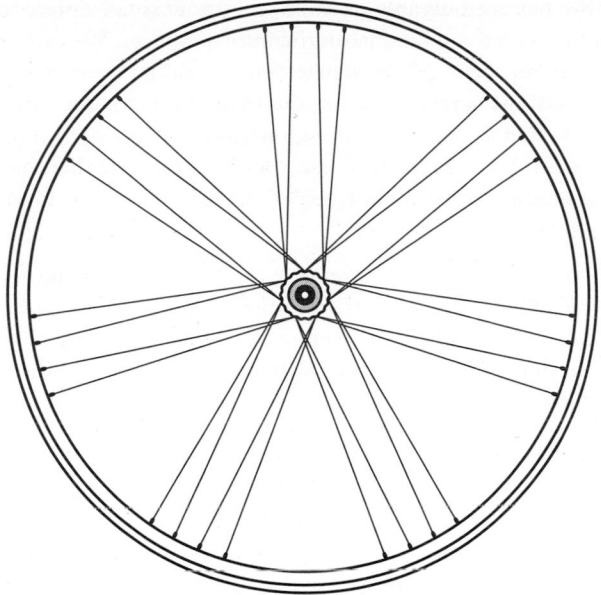

Figure 27.7 Bicycle wheel

Source: Rodi Comercial SA v. Soldatini Andrea, ICD 0271 (30 August 2005)

need to incorporate features common to the product[121] and by economic considerations (such as the need for the item to be inexpensive).[122] It seems, however, that constraints imposed by the expectation of the market and by fashion will not be taken into account (although it is an issue that could do with some clarity).[123] Because the test is an objective one, this means that the constraints actually imposed on the designer are not relevant.[124]

When evaluating a design, the informed user will focus on those aspects of the design (if any) where the designer was able to express themselves and, in so doing, imbue the design with 'individual character'. This means that where a designer has little opportunity to express themselves (that is, where they have little design freedom), even relatively small differences will suffice to create a different overall impression.[125] (It should be noted that the scope of protection available is correspondingly limited.) In contrast,

[121] Ibid., [70]. The designer's freedom in designing a children's toy known as a 'rapper' or 'tazo', which were small, flat, or slightly curved discs made of plastic or metal, was severely restricted, 'since he had to incorporate those common features in his design for the product in question'. Clearly, the decision about the nature of the product in issue is crucial.

[122] *Gimex International Groupe Import Export v. The Chill Bag Company* [2012] *EWPCC* 31, [66]; *Dyson v. Vax* [2010] *EWHC* 1923 (Pat), [34], upheld on appeal [2011] *EWCA Civ* 1206.

[123] Both mentioned in EC Green Paper, [5.5.8]. Trends in communication equipment favouring small, flat rectangular devices was not relevant to the examination of individual character: *Shenzhen Taiden Industrial v. OHIM*, Case T-153/08 [2010] *ECR* II-2517, [58]; cf. *Samsung v. Apple*, ICD 8720 (13 May 2013) (Invalidity Division), [63] (holding that, where the market is saturated with designs, the informed user will be more sensitive to differences between products).

[124] While certain elements (such as fuel tank, vent, etc.) must be present in an internal combustion engine, the designer had considerable freedom in where and how the elements were placed (appearance was not determined by technical considerations). As such, the designer had a high degree of freedom: *Kwang Yang Motors v. OHIM*, Case T-10/08 [2011] *ECR* II-265, [36]–[37].

[125] *Grupo Promer Mon Graphic v. OHIM-PepsiCo*, Case T 9/07 [2010] *ECR* II-981 (GC), [62]. A photograph of the rapper can be seen in the case report. See also CDR, Recital 14.

where the designer has considerable freedom, the same small differences are unlikely to create a different overall impression on the informed user. We can get a sense of the way design freedom impacts on the way in which individual character is assessed in the series of EUIPO decisions in relation to designs of bike wheels. On the basis of the functional limitations facing the designer of bike wheels and the high number of existing designs,[126] it was held that the informed user would appreciate that the designer would not be able to exercise much freedom when creating a new shape for a wheel. On this basis, it was said that:

> [T]he informed user will pay more attention to the features where the designer was not limited in his creativity, such as the pattern of distribution of the spokes around the hub and between the hub and the rim, including . . . the distances and angles among the spokes, the angles among the spokes and the hub flange and among the spokes and the rim, the limitations on the freedom [and so on].[127]

Focusing on these features of the designs (the distribution of the spokes), the Invalidity Division held that the design had individual character and was thus valid (see Fig. 27.7).[128]

4 RELATIVE GROUNDS FOR INVALIDITY

Design law contains a number of other grounds for refusal or invalidity that we have yet to discuss. Two of these are mandatory; three, optional. We can call these 'relative grounds' for invalidity because they concern conflicts between the rights of the putative design proprietor and other competing claims. The 'relative' nature of these grounds for objection is reflected in the fact that the Community Design Regulation regulates who is entitled to rely on them.[129]

4.1 APPLICANT OR RIGHT HOLDER IS NOT ENTITLED TO DESIGN RIGHT

The Directive requires that design registrations be treated as invalid 'if the applicant for or the holder of design right is not entitled to it under the law of the Member State concerned'.[130] This ground may only be invoked by the person who is appropriately entitled.[131] As we will see in the next chapter, the Directive says nothing about ownership of designs, leaving this matter to national law. In the United Kingdom, ownership in the first instance vests in the designer, or their employer or commissioner. The British implemented the relative ground for refusal or invalidity in two ways. First, if an application is made to the UK Designs Registry by a person who does not 'claim to be' the proprietor of the design and, where relevant, the owner of a UK unregistered design right, the Registrar is required to refuse the application.[132] Second, a registration may be declared invalid on the ground that the registered proprietor is not the proprietor of the design.[133] In normal

---

[126] Specifically, that the degree of freedom that the designer is able to exercise is limited by the 'requirement that such a wheel has to be laced with the spokes between the hub and the rim in order to support the rim and transfer the weight of the rider to the rim': *Rodi Comercial SA v. Soldatini Andrea*, ICD 0271 (30 August 2005), [27].

[127] Ibid., [27].   [128] Ibid.   [129] Designs Dir., Art. 11(5)–(6).

[130] Designs Dir., Art. 11(1)(c).   [131] Designs Dir., Art. 11(3).

[132] RDA 1949, ss 3A(3), 3(2), and 3(3). Rather oddly, given the wording of the Directive, this is not dependent upon the real design owner objecting.   [133] RDA 1949, s. 11ZA(2).

circumstances, however, the person properly entitled is much more likely to seek rectification of the register, so that they are entered thereon as the proprietor.[134]

The Community Design Regulation implements the same ground for objection purely as a ground for invalidity. Before applying, the person truly entitled must previously have obtained a court decision to that effect. This should be done in a national court, usually in the jurisdiction where the registered proprietor is domiciled.

4.2 CONFLICTS WITH EXISTING DESIGNS

The Directive requires member states to refuse registrations or to treat them as invalid in cases where:

> … the design is in conflict with a prior design which has been made available to the public after the date of filing of the application or if priority is claimed, the date of priority, and which is protected from a date prior to the said date by a registered Community design or an application for a registered Community design or by a design right of the Member State concerned, or by an application for such a right.[135]

This ground can be invoked by the applicant for, or the holder of, the conflicting right, or if the member state elects, the appropriate authority of the member state on its own initiative.[136] Essentially, the conflicts provision requires member states to operate a 'first to file' system to determine priority between registrants in cases where the earlier application was not published by the priority date of the later application. The earlier application might not have been published by the time of the later application for a number of reasons, including because the earlier application was outside the European Union but was the basis of a later application to a national registry of a member state (or EUIPO) claiming priority,[137] or because there was deferred publication of the earlier Community registration. The fact that the Directive is satisfied that this ground would only be capable of being invoked by the right holder implies that the policy behind this ground of invalidity is not to avoid 'double design registration' in cases where two individuals come up with similar designs in close succession. Indeed, the effect of the provision leaves it open to member states to decide whether to allow two (or more) such proprietors to have rights over identical designs.

The UK Registered Designs Act 1949 implements the conflicts as a ground for invalidity that can only be invoked by the registered proprietor or applicant.[138] The relevant earlier designs are ones 'protected by virtue of a registration under this Act or the Community Design Regulation or an application for such registration'. It does not include, as it might have done,[139] earlier UK unregistered designs published after the date of application. In contrast, the Community Design Regulation only recognizes conflict with a previous design as the basis of an invalidity action.[140] Like the United Kingdom, it limits the relevant

---

[134] RDA 1949, s. 20.   [135] Designs Dir., Art. 11(1)(d).   [136] Designs Dir., Art. 11(1)(d), (4), (6).

[137] For example, A applies in the United States on 1 January 2003; B applies for registration of an identical design in the United Kingdom on 1 May 2003; A applies in the United Kingdom on 31 May, claiming priority from its earlier US registration, and that application is published on 15 August 2003. In such circumstances, B's application is in conflict with A's, and A's is earlier. So A has a ground for invalidity. A's is a prior design and has been made available after B's filing, but is protected from before.

[138] RDA 1949, ss 11ZA(1), 11ZB(3)–(4).

[139] EC Green Paper, [6.5.2.2].

[140] See, e.g., *Servicios de Distribucion e Investigacion v. Sola*, Case ICD 396 (20 Sept 2005); *Burberry v. Duran-Corretjer & Partners*, Case ICD 1568 (8 February 2006).

earlier designs to earlier Community applications and registrations, and earlier applications and registrations for a 'registered design right of a Member State'.[141] If the invalidity action is before EUIPO, the only person who is permitted to invoke this ground is the applicant for or holder of the earlier right. If the invalidity action is before a Community design court on the basis of a counterclaim in infringement proceedings, it seems that the appropriate authority of the member state may invoke the ground on its own initiative.

There is a 'conflict' where the later registration lacks novelty or individual character when compared with a prior design. Building of the logic that sees individual character as a mirror of the scope of protection, the General Court held that a design will be 'in conflict with a prior design, taken into consideration the freedom of the designer in developing the . . . design, that design does not produce on the informed user a different overall impression from that produced by the prior design relied on'.[142] The concepts here have been discussed earlier.

4.3 CONFLICTS WITH DISTINCTIVE SIGNS

Article 25(1)(e) of the Regulation (which corresponds to Article 11(2)(a) of the Directive) provides that a design will be invalid 'if a distinctive sign is used in a subsequent design, and Community law or the law of the member state concerned governing that sign confers on the right holder of the sign the right to prohibit such use'.[143] This provision covers conflicts with trade mark rights with effect in the European Union or in one of its member states.[144] Thus, if a person tries to register the design of a football shirt with a purple body, yellow collar, orange arms, blue cuffs, and bearing the Arsenal club crest (being a registered trade mark for clothing), such a registration could be declared invalid (even though, in other respects, it might be novel and have individual character). To be declared invalid, the design must be the same as, or conceptually similar to, an earlier mark. As the contested design must be compared with the earlier marks as if it were perceived as a trade mark and not a design, conceptual similarity, which can be visual, phonetic, or conceptual, is based on the overall impression of the signs.[145] As the General Court said, Article 25(1)(e) does not 'necessarily presuppose a full and detailed reproduction of an earlier distinctive sign in a subsequent Community design'.[146] Given that the public 'only retains an imperfect memory of a registered mark', this means that even though the design may lack 'certain features of an earlier distinctive sign or may have different, additional features, this may constitute "use" of that sign, particularly where the omitted or added features are of secondary importance'.[147] The upshot of this it is sufficient if the design and trade mark are similar; there is no need for them to be identical for Article 25(1)(e) to apply. In *José Manuel Baena*,[148] the Court of Justice said

---

[141] CDR, Art. 25(1)(d).   [142] *Grupo Promer v. OHIM-PepsiCo*, Case T 9/07 [2010] *ECR* II-981, [52].

[143] RDA 1949, s. 11ZA(3).

[144] *Solen Cikolata v. Elka Zaharieva*, Case R 1144/2015–3 (12 September 2016), [17] (a Turkish trade mark could not be used to challenge the validity of a design under CDR Art. 25(1)(e)).

[145] *Juliuis Sämann v. Kubi*, Case R 1999/2013–3 (4 January 2016), [45]–[58].

[146] *Su-Shan Chen v. OHIM*, Case T-55/12, EU:T:2013:219, [23].

[147] *Beifa Group v. OHIM- Schwan-Stabilo Schwanhaüßer*, Case T-148/08 [2010] *ECR* II-1681, [50]–[51]. See also *Beifa Group v. OHIM Schwan-Stabilo Schwanhaüßer*, Case T-608/11, EU:T:2013:334 (affirming earlier decision).

[148] *Herbert Neuman (OHIM) v. José Manuel Baena Grupo*, Joined Cases C-101/11P and C-102/11P, EU:C:2012:641, [57], citing with approval the GC in *Baena Grupo v. OHIM: Herbert Neuman*, Case T-513/09 [2010] *ECR* II–00289, [20]–[22]. See also *Rackzek v. Śnieżka-Invest*, Case R 1148/2010–3 (7 November 2011) (Third BoA).

Figure 27.8 Registered design and prior trade mark in *José Manuel Baena*

Source: Beifa Group v. OHIM- Schwan-Stabilo Schwanhaüßer, Case T-148/08 (12 May 2010) (General Court)

that when considering whether an earlier right holder has the 'right to prohibit the use of the sign', it was necessary to compare the overall impression of the design and the overall impression on the informed user—that is, the approach to be adopted here is the same as the approach that is used when determining individual character, conflict with an earlier design, and infringement. As such, the discussion earlier about individual character is applicable here. The scope of Article 25(1)(e) can be seen from the decision of the General Court in *José Manuel Baena* (approved by the Court of Justice), which concerned a possible conflict between a design of a figure for caps, T-shirts, etc. and an earlier mark. The General Court said that the differences between the trade mark and the design, particularly when focusing on the 'fundamental characteristics' that will be remembered by the user (namely, the facial expressions), were enough to create a different overall impression on the informed user. As such, the design was declared invalid (see Fig. 27.8).[149]

As well as basing an attack on registered trade marks, an earlier right holder may be able to rely on analogous regimes protecting 'distinctive signs',[150] which could include passing off and, possibly, protected designations of origin (PDOs) and protected geographical indications (PGIs). In some circumstances, this ground may be capable of being used by famous personalities to prevent the registration of designs for merchandise bearing their name, signature, or image. This is important, since no other grounds of objection are available.[151] Presumably the same approach will adopted here as is used when considering conflict with earlier trade marks.

---

[149] *Baena Grupo v. OHIM: Herbert Neuman*, Case T-513/09 [2010] *ECR* II–00289 (GC), discussed, but not re-examined, by the Court of Justice in *Herbert Neuman (OHIM) v. José Manuel Baena Grupo*, Joined Cases C-101/11P and C-102/11P, EU:C:2012:641, [57].

[150] Whether all signs that are registered as trade marks, being not exclusively 'descriptive' or 'devoid of distinctive character', can be said to be 'distinctive signs' will, no doubt, have to be resolved in due course.

[151] Cf. art. 4(4)(b) of the Swedish Act No. 2002:570 amending the Design Protection Act 1970:485, which states that design right shall not subsist if the design 'contains, without authorization, another person's portrait or anything that can be perceived as another person's family name, artistic name or similar name, unless the portrait or the name obviously relates to a person who is long deceased'.

4.4 CONFLICTS WITH EARLIER COPYRIGHT PROTECTED WORKS

Article 21(1)(f) of the Regulation (which corresponds to Article 11(2)(a) of the Directive) provides that a design will be invalid 'if the design constitutes an unauthorised use of a work protected under the copyright law of a Member State'.[152] This ground may only be invoked by the 'holder' of the copyright.[153] An obvious example of a case where this would occur is if a design for a T-shirt was based upon an unpublished painting.[154]

4.5 CONFLICTS WITH PROTECTED BADGES

Finally, the Regulation (and Directive) provide that a design will be invalid if it constitutes improper uses of items listed in Article 6*ter* of the Paris Convention, as well as 'badges, emblems and escutcheons . . . which are of particular public interest in the Member State concerned'.[155] Article 6*ter* requires members of the Paris Union to refuse or invalidate the registration of trade marks that are, or which contain, prohibited emblems—such as armorial bearings, flags and other state emblems, official signs and hallmarks of countries of the Union, or those of intergovernmental organizations. With the exception of flags, these insignia have to be notified to the World Intellectual Property Organization (WIPO). The Directive allows for this ground to be raised by 'the person or entity concerned by the use' (such as an official representative of the state concerned), or if a member state so chooses, an 'appropriate authority' of the member state may invoke this ground *ex officio*.[156]

The United Kingdom has treated this as a ground for refusal,[157] as well as invalidity.[158] Schedule A1 to the 1949 Act elaborates the emblems concerned. The domestic ones include royal arms, the Crown, 'a representation of Her Majesty or any member of the Royal Family', the Union Flag, flags of the home nations, and coats of arms granted by the Crown. The Community Design Regulation treats conflicts with protected badges as a ground for invalidity.

---

[152] RDA 1949, s. 11ZA(4). This refers to the 'owner' of copyright, which almost certainly would be taken to include exclusive licensees—CDPA 1988, s. 101(2)—but not the owner of moral rights. It is expected that other countries will interpret the 'holder' of the right to include the author.

[153] CDR, Art. 25(1)(f), (3). For application, see *Erich Kastenholz v. OHIM- Qwatchme A/S*, Case T-68/11, EU:T:2013:298; *Viejo Valle v. Établissements Coquet*, Joined Cases T-566/11 and T-567/11, EU:T:2013:549 (GC, Second Chamber).

[154] If the painting were well known, the design would probably lack novelty, although this depends upon whether a painting is a design, i.e. 'the appearance of a product'.

[155] Designs Dir., Art. 11(2).   [156] Designs Dir., Art. 11(6).   [157] RDA 1949, s. 3A(4)(c), Sch. A1.

[158] RDA 1949, s. 11ZA(1). The application may be made by 'any person concerned by the use': RDA 1949, s. 11ZB(2).

28

OWNERSHIP, EXPLOITATION, AND INFRINGEMENT: UK REGISTERED DESIGNS, REGISTERED COMMUNITY DESIGNS, AND UNREGISTERED COMMUNITY DESIGNS

This chapter deals with issues key to the operation of UK registered designs, registered Community designs, and unregistered community designs; namely, ownership, exploitation, and infringement.

1 INITIAL ENTITLEMENT

The question of who is initially entitled to a design is a key issue in design law. In the pre-harmonized era, most European countries awarded the rights to the designer or their employer, but the rules differed in their details (for example whether all designs created by an employee in the course of employment belonged to the employer or only those that could be expected to result from the employee carrying out their duties). Consequently, a registered design right in country A might have vested in the designer, while in country B it belonged to the designer's employer. Harmonization would thus have reduced the potential for a national design right to vest in different people—a situation that, as we have seen, can produce barriers to the free movement of goods made to particular designs. However, it was probably thought unlikely that such barriers would arise in practice, because subtle differences in the national laws of member states could (and would) be rectified by express contractual dealings between the designer and their employer. For example, an employer wanting to obtain protection in a number of European countries through national registration could readily enter into an agreement with the designer assigning (or affirming the employer's ownership of) worldwide rights. While the Designs Directive deals with entitlement in relation to Community registered and unregistered designs, it does not deal with the question of who is entitled to a national registered design, so this remains a matter of national law. Given this, we will look at the national position and the position in relation to Community registered and unregistered designs separately.

1.1 ENTITLEMENT UNDER THE UK REGISTERED DESIGNS ACT 1949

The initial owner of a UK registered design (or as the Registered Designs Act 1949 prefers, the 'original proprietor') is the designer—that is, the author of the design.[1] The author of a design is defined as 'the person who creates it'.[2] The person who creates a design is the person who gives the design its specific form and appearance.[3] There is case law prior to harmonization that suggests that a person is not a creator if all that they have done is to bring a design into the United Kingdom from overseas (despite the fact that it may be 'new' in the European Union).[4] Nor is a person who is given the right to register,[5] or the exclusive right to distribute a design in the United Kingdom, a creator.[6]

There are two exceptions to the general principle that the initial owner of a UK registered design is the designer. First, where a design is created by an employee in the course of employment, the employer is treated as the original proprietor.[7] The second limited exception applies to commissioned designs. Prior to the enactment of the Intellectual Property Act 2014, all designs created in pursuance of a commission were owned by the commissioner.[8] In order to bring UK law into law with EU design law, the Act removed the exception in relation to commissioned works,[9] so that commissioned designs are now owned by the designer. It should be noted that the 2014 Act does not apply where (i) the design was created before the operation of the Act, or (ii) the commissioning contract was entered into before the commencement of the Act.[10] In these limited situations, the old law will still apply: the commissioner will be the owner of the design. In all other cases, designs created in pursuance of a commission will be initially owned by the designer. As

---

[1] RDA 1949, s. 2(1).

[2] RDA 1949, s. 2(3). RDA 1949, s. 2(4), defines the author of a computer-generated design as 'the person by whom the arrangements necessary for the creation of the design are made'.

[3] *A. Pressler & Co v. Gartside & Co.* (1933) 50 *RPC* 240 (Luxmoore J).

[4] *Lazarus v. Charles* (1873) *LR* 16 *Eq* 117 (importer not entitled to register under s. 5 of the 1842 Act); cf. *Barker v. Associated Manufacturers (Gowns and Mantles)* (1933) 50 *RPC* 332, 337 (possible to obtain registration of a design that was used by the Ancient Egyptians 6,000 years ago, if it had not been previously used in the United Kingdom).

[5] *Jewitt v. Eckardt* (1878) 8 *Ch D* 404; *Re Guiterman's Registered Design* (1886) 55 *LJ Ch* 309.

[6] In *Neville v. Bennett* (1898) 15 *RPC* 412, it was held that where one person selected an idea for a design from existing Persian designs, which was then rendered into a workable design by someone else, they were joint designers. This suggests that the process of selecting the basic design was considered a relevant act of creation, a proposition that seems difficult to reconcile with the 'import' cases.

[7] RDA 1949, ss 2(1B), 44; *Coffey's Registered Designs* [1982] *FSR* 227 (suggesting that the employer is the first proprietor only where employment carries with it a duty to make the design for the benefit of the employer).

[8] RDA 1949, s. 2(1A), repealed under IP Act 2014, s. 6(1). Where a person requests a design and agreement is that the designer will have exclusive distribution in some places, the commissioner is the proprietor: *Breville Europe v. Thorn EMI Domestic Appliances* [1995] *FSR* 77.

[9] IP Act 2014, s. 6(1), omits RDA 1949, s. 2(1A), and corresponding changes to s. 2(1B).

[10] While this is not directly dealt with by the 2014 Act, this would seem to be the case on the basis of the transitional arrangements for commissioned unregistered designs: see IP Act 2014, s. 2(3), and Chapter 30, section 3, p. 825. It is also in line with transitional arrangements previously used in registered design law in this area.

such, the designer will normally be the first owner of any design right in a design, unless it is created in the course of employment.

1.2 ENTITLEMENT: THE EU PROVISIONS

Registered and unregistered Community designs vest in the designer or their successor in title.[11] There is no further guidance as to who is the 'designer'. However, it is clear that the first person to disclose a design to the public is not, for that reason, the designer. Provision is made for the designer (or person entitled) to make a claim as to ownership of an unregistered Community design that has been 'disclosed or claimed by … a person who is not entitled to it'. The Community Design Regulation recognizes the possibility of joint design where 'two or more persons have jointly developed a design'.[12]

As with the United Kingdom, an exception is made to the general rule that Community designs vest with the designer where the design is made by an employer. (Notably, no equivalent provision exists for commissioned designs.) Article 14(3) of the Regulation provides that where a design is 'developed by an employee in the execution of his duties or following instructions given by his employer, the right to the Community design shall vest in the employer, unless otherwise agreed or specified under national law'.[13] The Court of Justice has clarified that Article 14(3) only applies to 'employers and employees', and that it does not extend to include other relationships, such as designs that have been produced as a result of a commission.[14]

Four points should be noted about Article 14(3). First, in contrast to the British provision, which ascribes rights to an employer where a design 'is created by an employee in the course of employment', Article 14(3) refers to both 'the execution of his duties' and 'following instructions'. The difference can be demonstrated by means of an example of a situation in which a person is employed as an administrator, but the employer specifically requests the employee to design the cover of a brochure. It seems that under UK law, the employee might be the owner, because the design was not created 'in the course of employment';[15] if Article 14(3) applies, the employer would be the owner, since the design was made 'following instructions given by his employer'. Although it is not easy to think of many situations that would fall within one provision but not the other, the divergence in terminology is unfortunate.[16]

Second, in its British form no provision is made for 'agreements to the contrary'.[17] In contrast, the Regulation allows for variation from the provision 'where it is agreed or specified under national law'. Such an agreement would not necessarily have to comply with the rules on formalities for transfer, only those for agreements.

---

[11] CDR, Art. 14(1).   [12] CDR, Art. 14(2).

[13] CDR, Art. 14(3). The designer has a right to be named on the register—CDR, Art. 18—unless waived, under CDR, Art. 36(3)(e).

[14] *Fundacion Española para la Innovación de la Artesania (FEIA) v. Cul de Sac Espacio Creativi SL*, Case C-32/08 [2009] *ECR* I–561, [49].

[15] Possibly, the design would be treated as having been commissioned.

[16] It is copied from the Software Directive: European Commission, *Green Paper on the Legal Protection of Industrial Design* (June 1991), III/F/5131/91–EN (henceforth 'EC Green Paper'), [7.2.3].

[17] This leaves unclear whether the normal rules on transfer must be complied with if an employee is to be made owner. If a court sees the rule on employers as a statutory variation of the orthodox rule that the designer is the owner, it may take the view that the retention of the rights in the design by the designer is not a 'transfer' and so need not comply with the normal formalities. However, if a court wishes to emphasize the evidential importance of the transfer formalities, it may insist that any variation from the statutory rule is a transfer. See *Ultraframe (UK) v. Eurocell Building Plastics* [2005] *RPC* 894, an unregistered design right case, discussed in Chapter 30, section 2.3, p. 818.

Third, the reference in the Regulation to specification under national law seems to enable member states to have their own rules about the allocation of rights to designs made by employees, and for these to override the EU rules.

Finally, the EU rules say nothing about commissioners and thus leave the initial rights with the designer: a commissioner who wishes to own design right must secure their prospective rights by assignment.

The person named on a Community registered design is 'deemed to be the person entitled'.[18] Although this is put in categorical terms, it is a presumption that can be rebutted. Provision is explicitly made for claims to be recognized as 'the legitimate holder of the Community design' and for the change in ownership to be entered on the Register.[19] In the absence of a provision giving the European Union Intellectual Property Office (EUIPO) the power to decide, the matter must be for the relevant national courts, with jurisdiction governed by the Brussels Regulation.[20] The effect is that the action should usually be brought in the state in which the defendant, the current proprietor, is domiciled.[21] The Regulation does, however, provide a limitation period for such actions. In general, an incorrect ascription of rights can be rectified for up to three years following the publication of the registered Community design. However, this limitation is not applicable where the registrant has acted in bad faith. Alternatively, a Community design may be declared invalid 'if, by virtue of a court decision, the right holder is not entitled to the Community design under Article 14'.[22]

Prior to the enactment of the Intellectual Property Act 2014, the effect of these differences was to create a possible distinction between the person entitled under national design law and the person entitled to the Community design right—and thus to produce two different right holders with equivalent rights. For example, in the United Kingdom a commissioner of a design was entitled to national design right,[23] whereas under the EU regime such rights belong to the designer.[24] As was mentioned earlier, this anomaly is now rectified by the new Act, which removes the provisions in relation commissioned designs in the United Kingdom. As a result, UK law is now the same as EU provisions: the first owner of a commissioned design is the designer, subject to any contractual assignments.

2   ASSIGNMENT AND LICENCES

2.1   ASSIGNMENT AND LICENCES IN THE UNITED KINGDOM

The proprietor of a design may assign or mortgage the design, or license others to make articles bearing it.[25] Assignments should be made in writing, as should licences.[26] As a chose in action, design right may be assigned either in law or equity. For design right to be assigned in equity, it is necessary to show 'sufficient expression of an intention to assign in the context of a transaction from which it can be inferred that the property was intended to pass'.[27] No provision exists for the assignment of future designs, and it is probably necessary for the original proprietor to register and then execute the relevant

---

[18] CDR, Art. 17.

[19] CDR, Art. 15. Third parties whose activities are affected by such changes in the register are protected by the availability of licences upon reasonable terms: CDR, Art. 16.

[20] CDR, Art. 79.   [21] This follows from *Duijnstee*, Case C-288/92 [1985] 1 *CMLR* 220.

[22] CDR, Art. 25(1)(c).   [23] RDA 1949, s. 2(1A), repealed under IP Act 2014, s. 6(1).

[24] CDR, Art. 14(1).   [25] RDA 1949, s. 19.   [26] *Jewitt v. Eckardt* (1878) 8 *Ch D* 404.

[27] *Victor Ifejika v. Charles Ifejika Lens Care* [2010] *EWCA Civ* 563, [26].

dealing.[28] An offer of exclusivity in distribution is not an assignment, because it is not a grant of the 'right to apply' the design to a product.[29] Neither an exclusive licensee nor the sole distributor of a design has a right of action against an infringer; this right belongs to the proprietor alone.[30]

2.1.1 Registration of transactions

Information concerning assignments and other transactions of registered designs is maintained at the UK Designs Registry at the Intellectual Property Office.[31] Any person who becomes entitled to an interest in a registered design should apply to the Registrar to have their interests entered on the register.[32] The interests that can be entered include assignments, mortgages, co-ownership, and licences, but not beneficial interests relating to trusts.[33] A strong incentive exists to register such a transaction: any document in respect of which no entry has been made in the register may not be admitted as evidence of such title 'unless the court otherwise directs'.[34] Moreover, a transferee of a registered design will take subject to any interests that have been registered[35]—the position in relation to unregistered interests, it seems, being governed by the general law. There are two notable effects here: first, licences, as interests that would not bind a purchaser under the general law (being non-proprietary), acquire a proprietary character as a consequence of registration; and second, equitable interests—such as an equitable charge on the design—will bind a purchaser with notice, but in the absence of registration, not one without notice. Until recently, the UK Intellectual Property Office (IPO) would not register an interest in a registered design unless it was satisfied that the same interest applied to any associated unregistered designs.[36] On the basis that this created uncertainty and was out of step with EU design law, the Intellectual Property Act 2014 removed this requirement.[37]

2.2 ASSIGNMENT AND LICENCES: EUROPEAN UNION PROVISIONS

As Community design rights are unitary in nature, they can only be transferred for the European Union as a whole.[38] While it is possible to license a Community design in different parts of the European Union, the rights cannot be assigned or surrendered in different member states. While the Regulation does not establish the rules relating to transfers, leaving those to member states, it does provide a scheme for deciding which member states' rules apply. The basic rule is that national laws of the member state in which the holder has their seat or domicile apply. So if a design proprietor is British and she assigns an unregistered Community design to a French citizen, British laws govern the transaction. If the French owner assigns the design to a Spaniard, the rules that operate are French.

2.2.1 Registration

In the case of registered Community designs, an additional requirement is that the transfer be entered in the register. Pending an entry, the successor in title may not invoke

---

[28] Ibid.   [29] *Leary Trading Co.'s Designs* [1991] *RPC* 609.

[30] *Oren & Tiny Love v. Red Box Toy Factory* [1999] *FSR* 785, 800 (speculating as to whether an exclusive licensee could be registered as a proprietor); *Woolley v. Broad* [1892] 9 *RPC* 208.

[31] RDA 1949, s. 17(1)(b).   [32] RDA 1949, s. 19(1).   [33] RDA 1949, s. 17(2).

[34] RDA 1949, s. 19(5).   [35] RDA 1949, s. 19(4).

[36] RDA 1949, s. 19(3A), repealed under IP Act 2014, s. 9(1).

[37] RDA 1949, s. 19(3A), repealed under IP Act 2014, s. 9(1).   [38] CDR, Arts 1(3), 27.

the rights 'arising from the registration of' the Community design.[39] The same is true of grants of registered Community designs as security.[40]

2.2.2 Licences

A licence may be granted for the whole or part of the European Union.[41] Any licence relating to part of the European Union will need to be scrutinized to ensure it does not breach Article 101 of the Treaty on the Functioning of the European Union (TFEU). Licences may be exclusive or non-exclusive: an exclusive licensee may bring proceedings for infringement, but a licensee needs the consent of the proprietor to do so. Licences can be entered in the register. The effect of this is likely to depend on the law of the member state of the proprietor,[42] but registration may well be a prerequisite for the licence to bind a third-party transferee of the Community registered design. This would be so in the case of a transfer governed by British law.[43] A licensee is able to bring infringement proceedings of a registered Community design whether or not the licence has been entered in the register.[44] Licensees are also able to claim damages for loss suffered by them.[45]

3 DURATION

Because the subject matter covered by design law is so wide, calculating an optimal period of protection was difficult. While some designs will be the product of considerable investment, others are the result of minimal effort. Some designs will have a very brief commercial life, whereas other design classics might last much longer.[46] While it was not possible to tailor the duration to suit all of the different types of design, a different approach was taken to registered designs to that provided for unregistered designs.

3.1 NATIONAL AND COMMUNITY REGISTERED DESIGNS

Upon registration, national and Community registered designs are protected for five years from the date of filing. Registered designs can be renewed (in five-year periods) for up to a maximum of 25 years.[47] In contrast to the position in relation to copyright, the harmonization of which was 'upwards', the 25-year period was not the longest provided under existing law: France had previously protected registered designs for 50 years.[48] The Commission could claim some international consensus for the 25-year period (an easier course than justifying the term by reference to economic or philosophical arguments):[49] the term corresponds to the minimum period of copyright protection for works of applied art under the Berne Convention.[50]

---

[39] CDR, Art. 28(b).   [40] CDR, Art. 29.

[41] CDR, Art. 32.   [42] See CDR, Art. 33.

[43] RDA 1949, s. 19(4). A court might direct otherwise to prevent the statute being used as an instrument of fraud.   [44] *Thomas Phillips v. Grüne Welle Vertriebs,* Case C-419/15, EU:C:2016:468, [16]–[25].

[45] Ibid., [26]–[32].   [46] EC Green Paper, [4.3.16]–[4.3.18], [6.3].

[47] CDR, Art. 12; Designs Dir., Art. 10.

[48] French Intellectual Property Code, L 513(1). The Benelux countries had 15 years; Germany, 20 years; the United Kingdom, 25 years; Italy, as single period of 15 years; Scandinavia, 15 years; Austria, 15 years; Spain, 20 years; Portugal, 25 years.

[49] CDR, Recital 16, refers to the term as 'corresponding to the foreseeable market life of their products'.

[50] TRIPS, Art. 26(3), requires only a ten-year term.

3.2 UNREGISTERED COMMUNITY DESIGNS

Unregistered Community designs are protected for three years from the date when the design was first made available to the public within the European Union.[51] The period was chosen by the Commission in preference to the two-year term suggested by the Max Planck Institute.[52] It is notable that the period starts irrespective of whether or not the making available was lawful; thus disclosures in breach of confidence or as a consequence of industrial espionage or theft can trigger an unregistered Community design coming into being. The onus is on the claimant to prove subsistence of unregistered Community design and thus to demonstrate when the design was first made available within the European Union.

4 INFRINGEMENT

In this section, we look at infringement of national registered designs, registered Community designs, and unregistered Community designs. With a limited number of exceptions, which are detailed later, the approach taken to infringement is the same for UK registered designs, registered Community designs, and unregistered Community designs.

4.1 RIGHT TO 'USE' THE DESIGN

One of the defining features of intellectual property law is that protection is never absolute. The rights are limited in terms of jurisdiction, duration, and scope. One of the most important limitations is that the rights holder is only ever granted the ability to control the intangible property in certain limited ways. Thus, while a copyright owner in a book can stop someone from reproducing the book, they cannot stop them from reading the book. Design law is no different. Design owners—whether of national registered designs, registered Community designs, or unregistered Community designs—are given the exclusive right *to use* the design and to prevent a third party not having the owner's consent from using it.[53] 'Use' is defined to cover, in particular, 'the making, offering, putting on the market, importing, exporting or using of a product in which the design is incorporated or to which it is applied, or stocking such a product for those purposes'.[54] This is a very broad (and open ended) definition that would seem to cover most situations that a design owner might want to control. Thus it may be that the list includes the marketing of a complete kit, which when made up, constitutes the design, on the basis that this is 'putting on the market ... *a product* ... to which [the design] is applied'.[55] If not, such an activity is likely to

---

[51] CDR, Art. 11.

[52] EC Green Paper, [6.3.1.2]. The Commission wanted the unregistered Community design to be valuable to industries that change their designs after a limited number of years.

[53] Designs Dir., Art. 9, and CDR, Art. 10, deal with 'scope of protection'. In turn, Designs Dir., Art. 12, and CDR, Art. 19, deal with the rights conferred by design right.

[54] Designs Dir., Art. 12; RDA 1949, s. 7(1); CDR, Art. 19. The UK provisions formerly covered 'exposing for sale or hire' rather than offering, because such exposure fell short of an offer: see Fellner, [5.151]. Although this has been deleted, the same act will almost certainly be covered, either as 'stocking' or 'use'.

[55] Designs Dir., Art. 12(1); RDA 1949. s. 7(2)(a); CDR, Art. 19(1).

infringe on the basis that it is a 'use' of the design, even though it is a form of use that has not been explicitly listed.[56]

An important question will be whether 'use' is limited to activities of the same sort as those listed (*ejusdem generis*), which relate to the manufacture and distribution of *products*. The better view is that it should be limited in this way, especially given that the definition of design is broad enough to encompass subject matter previously the preserve of copyright and trade mark law. For example, if a cartoon character has been registered as a design, the question might arise as to whether the design is 'used' when the cartoon is broadcast for reception on television or placed on a website. In Spain, prior to the harmonization directive, the broadcasting of a design was held to be non-infringing,[57] and such a conclusion under the harmonized and European Union regimes would be welcome. Recital 21 of the Regulation states that the right 'should also extend to trade in products embodying infringing designs', and supports a view that the meaning of 'use' is to be confined to 'trade in products'.[58] On this basis, 'use' would not cover broadcasting.

4.2 PROTECTION FOR THE USE OF ANY PRODUCT

The second point to note is that infringement is not confined to dealings with the same product which the design had been applied to or which is mentioned in the application; instead, the rights are infringed by the use of *any* product in which the design is incorporated or to which it is applied. Once a design is registered, it is not only protected in relation to the products specified in the application, but also in relation to *any* product in which the design is used.[59] So a wallpaper design might be infringed by making curtains bearing a similar pattern and a design for a car by making a toy version of it.[60] It also does not matter if the purpose or use of the product changes. Thus an application for the design for a spiky ball that specified use as 'flat iron and washing, cleaning and drying equipment' (when placed with wet clothes in a tumble dryer, the ball improved the drying process) was not limited to use as a laundry ball. Instead, the registration prevented third parties from using the designed product irrespective of whether it was used as a massage ball, dog toy, Christmas decoration, or 'anything else that an ingenious marketer can think of'.[61] This was a dramatic change for UK registered designs law, which formerly confined the scope of infringement to use of substantially the same design on the article for which the design had been registered.[62] As such, it made registration much more attractive and

---

[56] Formerly such acts were explicitly dealt with by RDA 1949, s. 7(4), with 'kit' being defined as 'a complete or substantially complete set of components intended to be assembled into an article'. Would the sale of a computer program that enabled a printer to employ a particular design-protected font be treated as use of a product into which the design is incorporated? The answer seems to be that such 'indirect use' is not covered by the harmonized and Community regimes, although it might well be by national rules on joint tortfeasance: for the position in the United Kingdom, see Chapter 48, section 3.4, pp. 1287–96. See D. Ohlgart commentary, in Franzosi, 137–8.

[57] Cf. *Heirs to Eduardo MS v. Television Espanola en Canarias SA,* discussed by L. Gimeno, 'Spain: Design Right' [1997] *EIPR* D 216.

[58] The definition of 'design', however, indicates clearly that the appearance of graphic symbols is to be protected. In this respect, confining use to use on material products, rather than immaterial media such as the web, seems unduly limiting. The effect of this narrow construction is also to exclude web design from the field of designs law.

[59] *Green Lane Products v. PMS International* [2007] *EWHC* 1712, [12].

[60] See J. Wessel, 'Germany: Registered Designs' [1996] *EIPR* D200, discussing *BMW v. Carrera* (unreported).   [61] *Green Lane Products v. PMS International* [2007] *EWHC* 1712, [12].

[62] *Best Products v. Woolworth & Co.* [1964] *RPC* 226; *Bourjis v. British Home Stores* (1951) 68 *RPC* 280.

saved design proprietors from having to register a design for articles which they did not intend to apply the design to, but to which they suspected competitors might apply their design.[63] After some uncertainty, the position is now the same for Community designs.[64]

One problem raised by the legal separation of designs from their use in relation to a particular product relates to the treatment of 'books' (and other communication media) as products. It seems safe to proceed on the assumption that books constitute 'industrial or handicraft items' and so are products—otherwise, the regime would fail to protect designs of book covers. If this is the case, design law may now be a potential tool of censorship. For example, if a design has been registered for a cartoon figure to be applied to wallpaper, the depiction of the design in a book may constitute a 'use' of the design by its application to a product. Indeed, in one German case the owner of a Community design right in the shape of a train succeeded in bringing an action against a trader who used an image of the train on its brochure.[65] Although, as we will see, a 'citation' defence exists, it is subject to certain limitations (in particular, it only applies to acts of reproduction not distribution) and so may not adequately protect free speech interests. It would be preferable for tribunals to interpret the statute so as to avoid having to look for such an exception in the first place.[66]

4.3 ABSOLUTE AND QUALIFIED PROTECTION

One of the key differences between an infringement action in relation to a registered design (whether at national or EU level) and an infringement action in relation to an unregistered Community design relates to the conduct of the defendant. More specifically, it relates to the question of whether infringement might occur, as in patent law, irrespective of whether a defendant has copied or even seen the protected subject matter, or whether a claimant needs to prove, as in copyright, copying as part of their action. In reflection of the different goals of the registered and unregistered design protection, different standards are applied.

4.3.1 Independent creation: registered national and Community designs

Reflecting the Commission's view that registered designs should be 'an efficient and strong right, sought after by industry',[67] the protection conferred on registered national designs and registered Community designs is 'absolute': the rights are exclusive (akin to patents), rather than qualified rights of the sort given by copyright that only control the use of reproductions of the registered designs. Because protection extends to independent creations, it does not matter whether a defendant copied a registered design; all that matters is that they used the design (and that the designs are the 'same'). As a result, the proprietor of a registered design does need to be concerned about whether the defendant copied the design or arrived at the design independently.

---

[63] See J. Phillips commentary, in Franzosi, 94.

[64] *Easy Sanitary Solutions v. EUIPO*, Case C-361/15 and C-405/15, EU:C:2017:720.

[65] BGH I ZR 56/09 (KG) *Intercity-Express (ICE)* (7 April 2011).

[66] This might be done by focusing on the informed user of the product in question, whose particular interests might well lead them to have quite a different interpretation of the design than that of the informed user of the product for which it was initially used: *Gimex International Export v. The Chill Bag Co.* [2012] *EWPCC* 31, [115] (informed user of chill bags would notice differences in prior-art bag, which was not used or usable as a chiller bag).

[67] EC Green Paper, [6.4.4]. The CDR, Recital 21, states that such a right 'is consistent with its greater legal certainty'. The position before harmonization had not been uniform. Whilst most countries conferred a full monopoly, some, such as Germany, required derivation to be proved. See Suthersanen, 201.

4.3.2 Copying: unregistered Community designs and unpublished Community registered designs

In contrast to registered national designs and registered Community designs, the rights conferred by unregistered Community designs are confined to situations where the defendant copied the protected design.[68] As such, proof of copying is an essential element in an infringement action involving an unregistered Community design. It should be noted that the situation is the same for registered Community designs that are yet to be published; proof of copying is also necessary in an infringement action involving an unpublished registered Community design.[69]

The decision to make copying an element of an infringement action of unregistered Community designs and registered designs yet to be published is based on the belief that it would be wrong to stop a third party from using a design that they had developed in circumstances under which they could not have ascertained that the design was already protected.[70] In the absence of a means by which users could be placed on notice of earlier rights, a person should only be prevented from using a design if they have copied that design from the claimant. The design proprietor must prove copying on the balance of probabilities and it is for a given Community design court to rely on its own rules of evidence.[71]

The question of whether a design has been copied is a question of fact. In some cases, this can be easily proved. In the majority of cases, however, it will be difficult to show actual copying. To overcome this problem, the courts have been willing to infer copying from the circumstances of the case: relevant factors have included similarities between the designs, evidence of the defendant's access to the claimant's work, and the plausibility of independent creation. Thus, in *J Choo v. Towerstone*,[72] the UK High Court said that when the claimant's and defendant's bags were viewed side-by-side, the 'inference of copying' was 'overwhelming'. This was because the 'likelihood that these two designs could have been arrived at independently, given the large number of identical features in a design field as free as the present one, seems to me to be truly fanciful'.[73] Article 19(2) of the Regulation elaborates that use:

> . . . shall not be deemed to result from copying the protected design if it results from an independent work of creation by a designer who may reasonably be thought not to be familiar with the design made available to the public by the holder.

Although the Regulation clearly imposes a requirement of copying for unregistered Community designs and for registered Community designs yet to be published, it is silent on two further matters. First, it does not state whether copying can be indirect as well as direct. Second, it does not state whether a person who sells a product to which the design has been applied is liable for infringement even though that person was ignorant of the

---

[68] CDR, Art. 19(2), (3). It had been proposed that liability should turn on bad faith, but this was rejected. See Musker, 122; V. Saez, 'The Unregistered Community Design' [2002] *EIPR* 585, 586–7.

[69] CDR, Art. 19(3). Article 50 allows for deferred publication for up to 30 months. On this, see Stone, [15.60], [15.166], [19.77].

[70] Although this would be the case in the United Kingdom for secret designs.

[71] *H. Gautzsch Großhandel v. Münchener Boulevard Möbel Joseph Duna*, Case C-479/12 , EU:C:2013:537 (Opinion of Advocate-General Wathelet), [69]–[71]. While the determination of burden of proof is, in principle, a matter for national law, the Advocate-General said that the issue affects the substance of the right and is therefore governed by European law. See D. Ohlgart commentary, in Franzosi, 121–2, arguing that the rules as to evidence in such cases are Community rules.　　[72] [2008] *EWHC* 346 (Ch).

[73] Ibid., [23].

fact that the product carried a design that had been copied from a protected design. On a literal reading, in both situations 'the contested use results from copying the protected design' and falls outside the clause clarifying when a use 'shall not be deemed to result from copying'. Nevertheless, it does seem harsh to hold a secondary infringer liable in the absence of any *mens rea,* and at least one commentator has asserted that the relevant Article can be interpreted in accordance with general principles to avoid such an outcome.[74]

4.4 SAME OVERALL IMPRESSION ON THE INFORMED USER

One of the key questions that arises in an infringement action is whether the allegedly infringing design is the 'same' as the design in question. In the peculiar language of EU design law, designs will be the same (and thus infringe) when they create the 'same overall impression' on the informed user. As Article 10(1) of the Regulation states, the scope of protection 'includes any design which does not produce on the informed user a different overall impression'.[75] As we mentioned earlier, the test for whether a design is infringing is a mirror of the test to determine individual character.[76] The concepts used and the questions asked are, subject to a temporal difference, identical (or very nearly so).[77] As such, there is no need to repeat what was said earlier. All of the comments made in relation to the inquiry into individual character apply equally here. Having said this, there are a number of additional points about design infringement that should be noted.

The first point to note is that the date on which the overall impression of the allegedly infringing design will be compared with the overall impression of the design in question is the date of registration, not the date of infringement.[78] This may be important when determining the design corpus and the freedom of the designer. Presumably, the logic would be the same for unregistered designs, in which case the relevant date would be the date when the design was first made available to the public within the European Union. It is also important to note that when comparing the defendant's allegedly infringing design with the claimant's design, matter added by the defendant will be ignored. This is because when comparing designs, the informed user will ignore aspects of the design that are considered to be optional accessories, such as a trailer attached to a (protected) toy cement truck[79] or the heel strap on a shoe.[80] While these additions might justify the defendant registering a new design (for the additions individually), they would not be taken into account when deciding

---

[74] D. Ohlgart commentary, in Franzosi, 124–6; Musker, 122.

[75] Designs Dir., Art. 9(1); RDA 1949, s. 7(1); CDR, Art. 10(1). But cf. TRIPS, Art. 26, requiring that protection extend to use of a design that 'is a copy, or substantially a copy, of the protected design'.

[76] *Celaya Emparanza y Galdos Internacopnal SA v. Proyectos Integrales de Balizamientos SL,* Case C-448/10 [2011] *ECR* I-147 (ECJ, First Chamber), [52].

[77] One difference is that the informed user is referred to certain factors in the context of the assessment of individual character that are not mentioned in relation to the scope of protection. Specifically, the informed user is to have regard to the existing design corpus, the product, and the industrial sector: Designs Dir., Recital 13. To date, these have not led to any notable differences.

[78] *Dyson v. Vax* [2010] *EWHC* 1923 (Pat), [42]–[45]. The scope of the rights are determined objectively: *Celaya Emparanza y Galdos Internacional SA v. Proyectos Integrales de Balizamientos SL,* Case C-448/10 [2011] *ECR* I-147 (ECJ, First Chamber), [55].

[79] *Geobra Brandstätter v. Shantou Wanshun Toys Industrial,* Case R 1701/2010-3 (12 July 2011) (BoA), [26]–[28].   [80] *Crocs v. Holey Shoes Holdings,* Case R 9/2008-3 (26 March 2010) (BoA), [102]–[103].

whether the design was identical or produced a different overall impression on an informed user. It should also be noted that in this context at least, size does not seem to matter. Thus it does not matter whether the alleged infringing design is the same size as the design in question: 'It could be half the size or a hundred times the size. Use of the design is prohibited.'[81]

Following a logic that is widely applied in intellectual property law, the ideas or concepts that lie behind a design are not protected; instead, protection is limited to the tangible physical form (or appearance) of the design that is embodied either in an article or a design document.[82] It is also important to note that a design that solely claims shape will only infringe by making a product (or dealing with a product made) to that shape. This means that a design for a three-dimensional product, such as the design of an automobile, would not be infringed by use on two-dimensional products, such as posters or tablemats. This is because in this context, the design—that is the shape—has not been 'applied' to the poster or tablemat. For the same reason, a book featuring images of the designs will not infringe, although, as we already observed, this may not be the case if the designer not only claimed shape, but also features of colour, line, or pattern.

Although protection is not limited to the product for which the design was registered, there are substantive limits to the principle of the 'irrelevance of the product'. This is particularly the case where the design comprises the shape of a three-dimensional item. In such cases, the design and product will be inseparable, so that use of a similar design for a different product will usually fail to produce the same overall impression on the informed user. This can be seen if we consider two designs which are intended to be complementary, such as a dining table and a sideboard. Each may be made out of similar materials (say, oak), use simple lines, and give off a chunky, although not inelegant, appearance—yet it would be difficult in such a situation for an informed user to say that the two designs produced the same 'overall impression', because one design has drawers, cupboards, and handles, whereas the other has a flat top and four legs. The designs may be in the same 'style', but the *appearance* of the two products will differ. Where the appearance of the product and the nature of the product have an inseparable connection, the product will matter.[83]

5 EXCEPTIONS AND DEFENCES

The Directive and Regulation provide for, and the UK Act implements, certain 'limitations of the rights conferred' by a UK registered design, a Community registered design, and unregistered Community designs.[84] Three of these relate specifically to ships and aircraft,

---

[81] *Green Lane Products v. PMS International* [2007] *EWHC* 1712, [12]. Presumably, there might come a point at which a product is either so very small or very large that it *might* produce a different overall impression on the notional informed user.

[82] *Rolawn v. Turfmech Machinery* [2008] *RPC* (27) 663, [9]; EC Green Paper, [5.4.3.1]–[5.4.3.4] (design law does not protect the idea or overall concept).

[83] However, the former Benelux position that a change in the function of the product will take it outside the scope of protection, even if appearance is the same, can no longer be good law.

[84] TRIPS, Art. 26(2), permits 'limited exceptions ... provided that such exceptions do not unreasonably conflict with the normal exploitation of protected industrial designs and do not unreasonably prejudice the legitimate interests of the owner of the protected design, taking account of the legitimate interests of third parties'.

and need not be discussed here;[85] four others merit at least a brief discussion.[86] Article 20(1) of the Regulation (which corresponds to Article 13(1) of the Directive) states that:

> The rights conferred by a design right upon registration shall not be exercised in respect of:
> (a) acts done privately and for non-commercial purposes;
> (b) acts done for experimental purposes;
> (c) acts of reproduction for the purposes of making citations or of teaching provided that such acts are compatible with fair trade practice and do not unduly prejudice the normal exploitation of the design, and that mention is made of the source.[87]

The Directive and Regulation also contain provisions on exhaustion of rights and the repair of complex products. In addition, the UK Act and the Regulation contain other specific limitations. We will look at all of these in turn.

5.1 ACTS DONE PRIVATELY AND FOR NON-COMMERCIAL PURPOSES

Designs law has traditionally been concerned with uses of designs in trade.[88] However, since the delineation of rights is not restricted to commercial uses, Article 20(1)(a) of the Community Design Regulation specifically excludes acts done privately and for non-commercial purposes.[89] The meaning of 'private' and 'non-commercial' was discussed in relation to section 60(5)(a) of the Patents Act 1977,[90] and there is no reason to suppose that a different construction will be placed on the exception to national registered design or Community designs (whether registered or unregistered Community designs).

5.2 ACTS DONE FOR EXPERIMENTAL PURPOSES

The next limitation on the scope of the rights relates to acts done for experimental purposes. This defence corresponds to the exception available under section 60(5)(b) of the Patents Act 1977, and the related case law will provide useful guidance on the scope of this limitation.[91] Given that it is possible to protect designs informed by functional considerations (but not those features 'dictated by function'), the inclusion of the defence seems warranted,[92] although its use may be rare. Imagine, for example, a company trying to

---

[85] Designs Dir., Art. 13(2); RDA 1949, s. 7A(2)(d)–(f); CDR, Art. 20(2).

[86] It is not a defence to an action to rely on a later registration. See *Celaya Emparanza y Galdos Internacional SA v. Proyectos Integrales de Balizamientos SL*, Case C-448/10 [2011] *ECR* I–147 (ECJ, First Chamber). For a similar conclusion in relation to trade marks, see Chapter 41, section 1, p. 1121.

[87] Designs Dir., Art. 13(1); RDA 1949, s. 7A(2)(a)–(c), (3); CDR, Art. 20(1). The curious phrasing in terms of a prohibition on exercise of the rights is difficult to account for and has not been adopted in the UK implementation.

[88] EC Green Paper, [6.4.7.2].

[89] TRIPS, Art. 26(1), requires rights to be granted only over acts that are undertaken for commercial purposes. [90] See Chapter 22, section 4.1, p. 667.

[91] See Chapter 22, section 4, pp. 667–9. One difference worth observing between the PA 1977 provision and that in relation to designs is that the exempted experimental purposes are not restricted to ones relating to the 'subject matter' of the design; in principle, a design may be employed for experiments that do not relate to the design itself.

[92] Cf. D. Ohlgart commentary, in Franzosi, 143 ('there is no reason for a design-developer to base his design work on somebody else's protected design').

discover the optimal shape of a car chassis in terms of air resistance: the company might create five designs for testing, one of which falls within the design proprietor's protection. Such tests would be non-infringing.

5.3 ACTS OF REPRODUCTION FOR CITATION AND TEACHING

The next exclusion relates to acts of reproduction undertaken for the 'purposes of making citations or of teaching'. This is on the condition that the 'acts of reproduction' are (i) compatible with 'fair trade practice', (ii) that they 'do not unduly prejudice the normal exploitation of the design', and (iii) that mention is made of the source.[93] The defence recognizes that the breadth of the harmonized design law means that design protection potentially inhibits a range of activities that had hitherto only been subject to copyright law.[94] As we have seen, the reproduction of the image of a three-dimensional design in a book or newspaper will probably not infringe because the later use would create a different overall impression on the informed user of the book. However, it is not possible to be completely confident even in such a situation[95]—and even less so about the reproduction of designs comprising other features. For example, a cartoon character or logo may be protected as a Community or national design, and this may give the design proprietor the right to prevent the sale of products, such as books and newspapers, which the design is applied to. The citation defence allows such uses in the specified circumstances (namely, that such acts are compatible with fair trade practice, that they do not unduly prejudice the normal exploitation of the design, and that mention is made of the source). A book about cartoons, logos, or a company that makes the products or the designer thereof (for example a book about Terence Conran or Phillip Starck), might be able to reproduce the designs in the book.

There are a number of elements to the defence. The first is that it only applies to reproductions for *the purposes of teaching and citation*. A school teacher of carpentry or metalwork may want to demonstrate how to produce certain design-protected features, and this exception makes such acts non-infringing. Equally, a teacher of intellectual property law might want to reproduce logos as part of the process of teaching when a design or figurative trade mark is infringed. The defence is also likely to be important in schools of art and design.[96] There seems to be no reason why 'teaching' should be limited to the activities of educational establishments. As such, 'teaching' might include demonstrations for apprentices in the private sector. It is important, however, that the overall purpose is educational. Thus the defence did not apply where an image of a design-protected train was reproduced in an advertising brochure, because 'advertising was not a form of citation— the use in the brochure was solely for marketing purposes, and did not serve any intellectual debate': therefore unlawful.[97] While this had been accepted by some commentators, a broader reading was given by the Court of Justice in *Nintendo v. BigBen*. This was an infringement action brought by Nintendo in relation to its design protected Wii video game console and accessories against BigBen, who sells video game accessories in the

---

[93] CDR, Art. 20(1)(c); Designs Dir., Art. 13(1)(c); RDA 1949, s. 7A(2)(a)–(c), (3).

[94] The French term *illustration* and German term *Zitierung* confirm a broad understanding of citation as quotation or illustration.

[95] Especially given the decision of the BGH in *Deutsche Bahn v. Fauhofer Gesellschaft*, Case I ZR 56/09 (7 April 2011) [2012] *GRUR* (BGH), 1117.   [96] EC Green Paper, [6.4.7.3].

[97] Stone, [20.71] citing *Deutsche Bahn v. Fauhofer Gesellschaft*, Case I ZR 56/09 [2012] *GRUR* (BGH) (7 April 2011), 1117.

European Union that are compatible with the Nintendo video game console. Nintendo's complaint was that BigBen had reproduced images of Nintendo's design protected products on the BigBen website and on the packaging BigBen used to sell accessories that were compatible with the Nintendo video game console. In response, BigBen argued that this use fell within Article 20(1)(c). After the Landesgericht Düsseldorf found in BigBen's favour, Nintendo appealed to the Oberlandesgericht Düsseldorf who, in turn, asked the Court of Justice to clarify the scope of Article 20(1)(c). Finding in favour of BigBen (and agreeing with Advocate-General Bot's opinion that draws heavily on trade mark jurisprudence), the Court held that the defence included reproductions 'in order to explain or demonstrate the joint use of the goods' being sold 'and a product corresponding to a protected design'.[98]

Another limitation on the defences is that it is confined to 'acts of reproduction'. On one construction, dealings in products involving reproductions are not covered. This would seem to be unobjectionable, because there is no reason to allow a teacher or student to sell the designed product. Despite this, the defence could be undermined by the fact that it is limited to reproductions. Perhaps, one way around this is to interpret the prohibition on the design proprietor exercising rights 'in respect of' reproductions broadly, so that selling a book featuring a reproduction of a design is seen as an activity 'in respect of' the act of reproduction.[99] Although limitations on rights are usually interpreted narrowly under European intellectual property law, a broader interpretation seems to be justified here, given that the defence is subject to further limitations, to which we should now turn.

The citation and teaching defence is subject to a rather strange version of the three-step test, which we have already encountered in the Berne Convention, and which has been extended through the Agreement on Trade Related Aspects of Intellectual Property Rights 1994 (TRIPS) to designs and patents. However, in contrast to the TRIPS provision, which states that limitations should not 'unreasonably conflict with the normal exploitation' or 'unreasonably prejudice the legitimate interests of the owner',[100] the citation defence specifies that the acts should be 'compatible with fair trade practice' and 'not unduly prejudice the normal exploitation of the design'.[101] A third condition—namely, that 'mention is made of the source'—is also added.[102] This has been described as the grant of 'a moral right of paternity on the Community design holder'.[103] Because it is not clear whether 'the source' is the manufacturer, designer, or design proprietor, a cautious user might be advised to mention all three.[104]

5.4 EXHAUSTION

Although importation is specifically included in the list of prohibited uses, EU exhaustion applies under the Directive and, for Community designs, under the Regulation.[105]

---

[98] *Nintendo v. Big Ben Interactive*, Joined Cases C-24/16 and C-25/16, EU:C:2017:724, [77]. For criticisms of the AG's opinion see D. Stone, 'Design Law misplayed in Nintendo AG Opinion' (2017) 12 *JIPLP* 558.

[99] D. Ohlgart commentary, in Franzosi, 144, favours a broad construction to cover any form of use of the protected design.　　　　　　　　　　　　　　　　　　　　　　　[100] TRIPS, Art. 26(2).

[101] On this see *Nintendo v. Big Ben Interactive*, Joined Cases C-24/16 and C-25/16, EU:C:2017:146, Opinion of Advocate-General Bot, [82] ('fair trade' linked to consumer confusion).　　　　[102] Ibid., [80]

[103] D. Ohlgart commentary, in Franzosi, 144.

[104] *Nintendo v. Big Ben Interactive*, Joined Cases C-24/16 and C-25/16, EU:C:2017:146, Opinion of Advocate-General Bot, [79]–[80] (linking mention of source to consumer knowledge). For criticisms of this, see D. Stone, 'Design Law misplayed in Nintendo AG Opinion' (2017) 12 *JIPLP* 558, 563 ('previously thought that a reference to a RCD number would suffice').

[105] Designs Dir., Art. 15; RDA 1949, s. 7A(4); CDR, Art. 21.

This is EU exhaustion only and occurs when the product has been 'put on the market in the [EU] by the holder of the Community design or with his consent'. The implication is that member states may not provide for international exhaustion, because such a provision would undermine the internal market objectives of the Directive. For discussion of the merits of such a position, see Chapter 41.

5.5 ACTS COMMITTED BEFORE REGISTRATION (UNITED KINGDOM ONLY)

In relation to UK registered designs (but not Community designs), a limitation applies to acts committed before the date when registration was granted. The date from when the first five-year monopoly commences is the application date.[106] However, since applications are not open for inspection until registration, it would have been unfair to allow a design proprietor to sue in relation to acts that occur between application and registration. (This is contrary to the position in trade mark and patent law.) Such a limitation is not clearly permissible under the Directive, although one commentator has suggested that member states are free to provide for defences (and, since the Community Design Regulation contains a prior use defence that is not provided for in the Directive, this may be correct).[107] Certainly, the impact of this defence is unlikely to be of important significance given that most registrations occur within three months of the application, and if the design has been made available to the public, the design proprietor will be able to rely on the protection offered by unregistered Community designs (if not, they may be able to rely on copyright or a UK unregistered design right).

5.6 CROWN USE (UNITED KINGDOM ONLY)

Although there is nothing in the Directive permitting it,[108] the United Kingdom has retained certain provisions relating to 'Crown use'.[109] The 'Crown use' defence allows any government department and any person authorized in writing by such a department to use a UK registered design 'for the services of the Crown'.[110] A classic example is the use of a design for a gun, nuclear missile, or mask suitable for use in the case of an attack with chemical or biological weapons. Compensation should be paid to the design proprietor or exclusive licensee, on the basis of lost profits.[111] If the sum cannot be agreed, it may be determined by a court.[112] From 1 October 2005, the UK Community Designs Regulations[113] also allow for Crown use of Community designs (with a similar scheme for compensation as that for for UK registered design).

---

[106] RDA 1949, s. 3C(1).

[107] Musker, 67. As we will see, the Commission is still working to harmonize the market in spare parts.

[108] Nevertheless, the CDR implies, by recognizing a similar derogation, that the provisions of the Directive are not exhaustive on such matters: see CDR, Art. 23 (which allows member states to permit use of Community design by or for the government, but only to the extent that the use is 'necessary for essential defence or security needs').   [109] RDA 1949, s. 12, Sch. 1.

[110] It has not been used by the Crown since at least before 2000.

[111] RDA 1949, Sch. 1, para. 2A.   [112] RDA 1949, Sch. 1, para. 3.

[113] (SI 2005/2339), Sch. 5, reg. 5. For an overview of the fate of spare parts in the United Kingdom, see *Dyson v. Qualtex* [2006] *RPC* 769 (CA), [3] *ff.*

5.7 REPAIR OF COMPLEX PRODUCTS: SPARE PARTS

As we have seen, the question of how harmonized design law was to treat car spare parts was a highly politicized and troubling issue. Given this, it is perhaps not surprising that the European legislature was unable to formulate an acceptable set of laws relating to spare parts that would allow their manufacture for the purposes of ensuring competition in the spare parts market. However, a compromise was reached to the effect that the existing laws in member states should be maintained or possibly 'liberalized', pending further work by the Commission.[114] After the adoption of the Directive, the Commission consulted with manufacturers of original parts and spare parts, with the aim of arriving at a voluntary agreement that provided fair and reasonable remuneration.[115] Given that (in the words of the Commission) the parties were completely opposed, it is not surprising that the voluntary agreement failed. In light of this breakdown, the Commission undertook a study on the possible options for harmonizing the aftermarkets in spare parts.[116] While the study focused on the automotive sector, the subsequent proposals applied to any sector in which replacement and repair of complex products occurs. Drawing upon this study, the Commission decided that 'the option to exclude design protection in the aftermarket for spare parts is the only effective one to achieve an internal market'.[117] To this end, in 2004 the Commission proposed that the Directive be amended so as to introduce what is, in effect, a right of repair. If adopted, the new provision would have provided that 'protection as a design shall not exist for a design which constitutes a component part of a complex product ... for the purposes of repair of that complex product so as to restore its original appearance'.[118] To alleviate concerns about quality control and safety, member states would also have been obliged to ensure that consumers were duly informed about the origin of spare parts. While the proposal to end design protection for spare parts has been subject to considerable criticism, in November 2007, the Commission's proposal received the approval of the Legal Affairs Committee. Despite this, the Commission's proposal has not been adopted. Given the fate of earlier proposals, it seems that there are still a number of important obstacles that need to be overcome before we see any change in this area.[119] The upshot is that we are left with the provisions in the Regulation and equivalent provisions in national law. It is to this topic that we now turn.

As we have seen, one of the concerns that arose during the consultations on the proposed Community design law was that design law should not be able to be used by original manufacturers to monopolize the aftermarkets in spare parts. This was particularly the case where the owner of a product had no realistic alternative but to replace the part with one of the same design if the original part were to become damaged.[120] While the

---

[114] Designs Dir., Recital 19. Article 18 of the Directive required the Commission to submit an analysis of the consequences of the provisions of the Directive for Community industry by 2004 and to propose any necessary changes by 2005. As we will see, the Commission is still working to harmonize the market in spare parts.

[115] Parliament finally accepted the Council's request that this provision should not be incorporated into the text after receiving assurances from Commissioner Mario Monti that the Commission would issue a declaration referring to such a consultation exercise and that this would appear in the Official Journal along with the text of the Directive.

[116] European Commission, *Proposal for Directive of the European Parliament and the Council amending Directive 98/71/ERC on the legal protection of designs* (September 2004) COM(2004) 582 final, 6–7.

[117] Ibid., 7. See J. Strauss, 'Design Protection for Spare Parts Gone in Europe?' [2005] *EIPR* 391.

[118] European Commission, *Proposal for Directive of the European Parliament and the Council amending Directive 98/71/ERC on the legal protection of designs* (September 2004) COM(2004) 582 final, [3].

[119] For a history, see *Bayerische Motoren Werke Aktiengesellschaft v. Round and Metal* [2012] *EWHC* 2099 (Pat), [18] *ff.*   [120] Ibid., [78].

provisions in relation to complex products, interconnections, and functionality (which were discussed earlier) went some way toward ensuring that many spare parts would not be protected (and thus that competition in the production of such spares was possible), there were still some spare parts that were able to be protected. In particular, where designs were visible in use, but not dictated by function, or designed so as to enable objects to be connected together, they would often fall outside those exclusions and, as such, would be protected in principle. This would be the case, for example, for components parts such as car doors, body panels, bumpers, and windows. In order to 'avoid the creation of captive markets in certain spare parts',[121] Article 110 of the Regulation (which has been taken to be the same as the differently worded Article 14 of the Directive)[122] was introduced. This states that 'protection as a Community design shall not exist for a design which constitutes a component part of a complex product used … for the purpose of the repair of that complex product so as to restore its original appearance'.[123] The British implementation assumed (probably correctly) that absolute exclusions were not permitted under the Directive, deleted the previous exclusion of so-called 'must match' features,[124] and replaced it with an exception in section 7A(5) of the Registered Design Act 1949, as amended. This states that the right in a registered design of a component part (which may be used for the purpose of the repair of a complex product so as to restore its original appearance) is not infringed by the use for that purpose of any design protected by the registration. Section 7(2) indicates that 'use' for these purposes includes making and putting a product on the market in which the design is incorporated.[125]

While there was initial concern about the wording of Article 110(1) of the Regulation, as Arnold J said in *BMW v. Round and Metal*,[126] the wording of the provision is reasonably clear. The defendant in this case, the aptly named Round and Metal, imported and sold replica alloy wheels for cars, including replica wheels for BMWs. BMW argued that, in importing and selling the replica wheels, the defendant had infringed the registered designs that BMW had in the wheels. In response, the defendants argued that Article

---

[121] *Explanatory Memorandum to the Proposal for a Regulation on the Council Regulation on the Community Design* (December 1993) COM(93) 342 final.

[122] Designs Dir., Art. 14, states that:

> Member States shall maintain in force their existing legal provisions relating to the use of the design of a component part used for the purpose of the repair of a complex product so as to restore its original appearance and shall introduce changes to those provisions only if the purpose is to liberalize the market for such parts.

The Council had previously sought to allow a 'free for all', i.e. giving the member states carte blanche to introduce or change national legal provisions in this area: see H. Speyart, 'The Grand Design' [1997] *EIPR* 603, 609. Parliament had wanted a harmonized system of fair and reasonable remuneration for right holders covering any use of the design of a component part in the repair of a complex product.

[123] See F.-K. Beier, 'Protection for Spare Parts in the Proposals for a European Design Law' (1994) 25 *IIC* 840, 868–9 (considering whether the limitation to three years in a previous proposal was compatible with TRIPS).

[124] RDA 1949, s. 1(1)(b)(ii), prior to amendment, excluded from protection 'features of shape and configuration of an article which are dependent upon the appearance of another article of which the article is intended by the author of the design to form an integral part'. Such an exclusion continues to exist for the UK unregistered design right under CDPA 1988, s. 213(3)(b)(ii), and is discussed in Chapter 30, section 2.2.2ff, p. 816.

[125] While this is a genuine attempt at compliance, it is difficult to see how it can be said to 'liberalize' the market. Following the practice common in the United Kingdom, we will refer here, as we have done elsewhere, to the language of the Regulation rather than the RDA 1949.

[126] *Bayerische Motoren Werke Aktiengesellschaft v. Round and Metal* [2012] *EWHC* 2099 (Pat), [76].

110(1) provided Round and Metal with a valid defence. Arnold J clarified that Article 110(1) operates as an exception to the right conferred on the design owner (and not as a limitation on what could be protected in the first place). As such, the onus of proof was on a defendant to show that the exception applies.[127] Arnold J also held that the exception only applies to component parts that are dependent on the appearance of the complex product.[128] This meant that the defence allows the replacement of parts that 'must match' the overall design of the product. The test here was whether a consumer has some 'realistic choice' in what they replace a part with. Thus, while body panels, bumpers, and windows would be covered, it was held that the replica wheels for cars were not covered, because the 'replacement of wheels of one design with wheels of a different design [was] a perfectly realistic option'.[129] The key question here is: what level of choice must a consumer be able to exercise for the defence to kick in? It seems that, where a consumer has some choice in what part they use, the defence will not apply. Thus although BMW only sold wheels that were 'sympathetic to the design of each model of car', nonetheless the consumers still had a range of different types of wheel to choose from. As such, the replica wheels were *not* dependent on the appearance of the complex product. In June 2016, following litigation over the applicability of the repair defence, the Corte d'appello di Milano asked the Court of Justice to clarify the scope of Article 110, particularly in terms of its applicability where the customer has a choice about the shape of the product.[130] Hopefully this will clarify the scope of the defence.

Article 110(1) only applies to component parts that are used 'for the *purpose of the repair* of that complex product'. This requires us to ask: how was the component part normally used in practice? Was it normally used to repair a complex product when the part was broken, damaged, or worn? Or was it used for another purpose, such as upgrading the complex product (improving its appearance)?[131] In *BMW v. Round and Metal*, it was held that the replica wheels were not normally used for the purpose of repairing cars, but for the purpose of upgrading them. As such, the replica wheels were not used for the purpose of repair. This was based on the facts that the replica wheels were normally sold in sets of four and that there was no evidence that customers regularly took advantage of the price differential when replacing damaged wheels to purchase a set of four replica wheels instead of a single BMW wheel (which was more expensive than the four replica wheels).

The defence only applies where the part is used to restore the complex product to its '*original appearance*'. 'Original appearance' has been taken to mean the appearance of the complex product when it was sold by the manufacturer. In *BMW*, this was not limited to the appearance when the car left the factory, but also included parts fitted by authorized dealers.[132] The repair clause does not extend to include trade marks attached to the original designed part. Thus, it was held that a manufacturer of replacement parts for motor vehicles (such as wheel covers) could not rely upon Article 110 to affix to their products a trade mark registered for such products without obtaining the trade mark owner's consent.[133]

---

[127] Ibid., [51].

[128] Ibid., [57]. The defendants argued that this was not the case because the rider 'upon whose appearance the design is dependent' (which is in CDR, Art. 110(1), and Designs Dir., Art. 14) does not appear in CDR, Recital 13, and Designs Dir., Recital 19.

[129] *Bayerische Motoren Werke Aktiengesellschaft v. Round and Metal* [2012] *EWHC* 2099 (Pat), [78].

[130] *Audi v. Acacia & Pneusgarda*, Case C-397/16 (pending).

[131] *Bayerische Motoren Werke Aktiengesellschaft v. Round and Metal* [2012] *EWHC* 2099 (Pat), [73].

[132] Ibid., [74].   [133] *Ford Motor Company v. Wheeltrims*, Case C-500/14, EU:C:2015:680.

5.8 PRIOR USE

Article 22 of the Regulation confers a right for a third party to continue activities that they were doing, or preparing to do, before the priority date.[134] This provision, which parallels section 64 of the Patents Act 1977, recognizes that a person who has secretly been using a design would be unfairly prejudiced by the grant of monopoly rights over that design to someone else. To benefit from the right, the user must establish that before the priority date 'he has in good faith commenced use within the [European Union], or has made serious and effective preparations to that end'.[135] The 'user right' is inapplicable if the design being used has been copied from the registered Community design.[136] The right allows the previous user to 'exploit the design for the purpose for which its use had been effected, or for which serious and effective preparations had been made',[137] before the priority date. The previous user will therefore not be able to expand their activities into other arenas, for example by applying the design to new articles. The right is a personal right, in the sense that it cannot be exploited by way of licensing and can only be transferred as part of the business.

One of the changes made by the Intellectual Property Act 2014 is to introduce a right of prior use into UK law. The new provision, which is similar to Article 22 of the Regulation, permits a person who, before the application date, used a registered design in good faith or made serious and effective preparations to continue to do so.[138]

5.9 FREEDOM OF EXPRESSION

One question which we have touched in passing is the increased potential for design law to censor behaviour and to limit free speech. The exceptions provided in the Directive and Regulation, which seem to have been modelled on patent law, fail to provide sufficient flexibility to accommodate free speech concerns. Consequently, it has already proved necessary for at least one national court to refer to the European Convention for Human Rights (ECHR) to resolve this oversight. The case, *Plesner v. Louis Vuitton*,[139] involved a painting by the artist Nadja Plesner called *Simple Living*, which consisted of an African child holding a pink Chihuahua and a Louis Vuitton handbag (see Fig. 28.1). The painting, which was a reference to Paris Hilton, was intended to highlight the situation in Sudan. Like much of Plesner's work, it also aimed to highlight the difference between luxury and affluence, and poverty and famine. *Simple Living* was a central part of Plesner's work: the image appeared in subsequent paintings, on T-shirts, posters, and invitations to art exhibitions, and as an 'eye-catcher' to advertise her work (see Fig. 28.2). Louis Vuitton objected to the fact that Plesner had incorporated its Community design-protected pattern on the handbag into the painting.[140]

In early 2011, the District Court of The Hague issued an *ex parte* injunction against Plesner and her gallery, prohibiting the defendants from 'further infringement of Vuitton's registered design'. Plesner appealed to the District Court of The Hague, which lifted the injunction. The Court held that Plesner's right to freedom of expression under

---

[134] CDR, Recital 23. At least the Benelux countries had such a rule prior to harmonization.

[135] CDR, Art. 22(1).   [136] Although if varied sufficiently, such a copied design might not infringe.

[137] CDR, Art. 22(2).   [138] IP Act 2014, s. 7, introduces a new RDA 1949, s. 7B.

[139] *Nadia Plesner Joensen v. Louis Vuitton Malletier*, Case 389526/KG ZA 11–294 (4 May 2011) (District Court of The Hague). An English translation of the case is appended to L. Guibault, 'The Netherlands: Darfurnica, Miffy and the Right to Parody!' (2011) *JIPITEC* 236.

[140] Louis Vuitton applied the registered design for graphic symbols, known as the 'Multicolor Canvas Design', to a handbag known as the 'Audra'.

Fig. 28.1 *Simple Living*
Source: Nadia Plesner

Fig. 28.2 Eye-catcher
Source: Nadia Plesner

Article 10 ECHR outweighed Louis Vuitton's right to the protection of property (including its designs rights) under Article 1 of the first Protocol of the ECHR.[141] The Court based its decision on the fact that Plesner's right to express her opinion through her art was 'high in a democratic society's priority list', that she had no intention to free-ride on Louis Vuitton's reputation for commercial purposes, and Louis Vuitton's considerable reputation implied that it 'must accept critical use … to a stronger degree than other rights holders'.[142] This is a potentially very important decision, not least because it highlights the important role that human rights might play in design law in the future. The decision is also important in that it raised the question of the proper role of design law. This is because, as the Court noted, Louis Vuitton based its action against Plesner on the potential damage to its reputation.[143] As the Court said, however, the main objective of design law is to protect the appearance of products. While the Court left open the question of whether design law might also extend to the protection of the reputation of a design or the right holder, it seems that this is something that should be beyond the reach of design law.

---

[141] *Nadia Plesner Joensen v. Louis Vuitton Malletier*, Case 389526/KG ZA 11–294 (4 May 2011) (District Court of The Hague), [4.8].   [142] Ibid., [4.8].
[143] Ibid., [4.7].

29

COPYRIGHT PROTECTION FOR DESIGNS

1 INTRODUCTION

The fourth regime that can be employed for the protection of designs is copyright law. The relationship between designs and copyright has been the focus of a great deal of attention over the last 100 years, and different countries have attempted to draw lines between the two forms of protection in a number of different of ways.[1] France, classically, allowed for the cumulation of registered design protection with that offered by copyright under the so-called theory of 'unity of art'. In contrast, Italy attempted to make the two regimes mutually exclusive. Although the British position varied through the twentieth century,[2] the Copyright, Designs, and Patents Act 1988 (CDPA 1988) sought to limit the operation of copyright in much of the design field—particularly three-dimensional designs, covered by the new 'unregistered design right'.

EU harmonization of designs only deals partially with the interface between designs and copyright. While Article 17 of the Designs Directive and Article 96(2) of the Community Designs Regulation require member states to adopt a policy of cumulation of copyright, they leave it to member states to determine 'the extent to which, and the conditions under which, such protection is conferred, including the level of originality required'. This was understood to mean that 'no design should be denied protection under copyright law for the 'sole' reason that it has been registered either at national or at [EU] level'.[3]

This failure to harmonize the degree of protection afforded to designs through the copyright law of member states inevitably detracted from the goal of harmonization and has rightly been criticized.[4] Perhaps recognizing this, in *Flos v. Semararo*,[5] the Court of Justice indicated that member states are obliged to protect all original designs (not only registered designs) by copyright. They also added that this implicitly

---

[1] E. Derclaye (ed.), *The Copyright/Design Interface: Past, Present and Future* (2018).

[2] L. Bently, 'The Design/Copyright Conflict in the United Kingdom: A History', in Derclaye, op. cit., ch. 6.

[3] European Commission, *Green Paper on the Legal Protection of Industrial Design* (June 1991) 111/F/5131/91-EN (henceforth 'EC Green Paper'), [11.3.4], point (a).

[4] L. Bently, 'The Shape of Things to Come: European Design Law', in P. Coughlan (ed.), *European Initiatives in Intellectual Property* (1993), 63, 86–7; D. Musker, *Community Design Law: Principles and Practice* (2002), 80 ('requiring copyright protection, yet not harmonizing it, is a curious strategy').

[5] *Flos SpA v. Semararo Case e Famiglia SpA*, Case C-168/09 [2011] *ECR* I-181 (ECJ). The decision related purely to a transitional issue peculiar to Italian law.
[6] Ibid., [36].

precludes the possibility of imposing conditions on acquisition. Importantly, the Court stated that:

> [T]he second sentence [of Article 17 of the Designs Directive] cannot be interpreted as meaning that Member States have a choice as to whether or not to confer copyright protection for a design protected by a design right registered in or in respect of a Member State if the design meets the conditions under which copyright protection is conferred.[6]

In essence, conditions on 'the extent' of protection could not prevent its 'existence'. Moreover the Court added that 'the extent' of protection could not cover 'term' because term had already been harmonized by the Term Directive.[7] Even if the designs had not been registered, as appeared to be the case with the 'Arco' lamp design at the centre of the litigation, the Court stated that:

> It is conceivable that copyright protection for works which may be unregistered designs could arise under other directives concerning copyright, in particular Directive 2001/29, if the conditions for that directive's application are met, a matter which falls to be determined by the national court.[8]

Moreover, the Court's reasoning not only explicitly prohibits limitations on the term of protection afforded by such copyright, but implicitly disallows limitations that cabin the scope of the rights conferred or regulate the relationship with other protection regimes. In so doing, the Court virtually deleted Article 17 of the Designs Directive.[9]

The United Kingdom responded to the *Flos* decision by repealing section 52 of the CDPA 1988, which limited the term of protection of copyright for mass-produced designs to 25 years.[10] However, the United Kingdom continues to retain limitation on copyright for designs in sections 51 and 53 of the 1988 Act.

In this chapter, we first consider the conditions under which copyright law might protect designs, before examining those limitations. We then reflect upon the demise of section 52.

2 SUBSISTENCE OF COPYRIGHT IN DESIGNS

Copyright can provide protection for designs by two routes: either directly, by protecting the form and decoration of articles as artistic works (in particular as sculptures, engravings, or works of artistic craftsmanship); or indirectly, through the protection that copyright confers on the author of a preliminary document on which a design is based. In the latter situation, the design document will normally be protected as a graphic work, but may be protected, exceptionally, as a literary work.

2.1 PROTECTION OF THE DESIGN ARTICLE AS AN ARTISTIC WORK

In order for an article embodying a design to qualify for copyright protection as an artistic work, it must fall within the terms of section 4 of the CDPA 1988.[11] The most obvious

---

[7] Ibid., [39].   [8] Ibid., [34].
[9] For critical comment, see L. Bently, 'The Return of Industrial Copyright?' [2012] *EIPR* 654.
[10] ERR 2013, s. 74.   [11] CDPA 1988, s. 4. See Chapter 3, especially section 5, pp. 72–9.

ways in which designs might be protected are as engravings, sculptures, or works of artistic craftsmanship. In each case, only some designs will qualify as artistic works and hence get copyright protection, and exactly which designs will do so is very difficult to predict with any precision.

2.1.1 As an engraving

In some cases, it will be possible to argue that features of surface decoration (even functional ones) amount to engravings. Indeed, as we saw in Chapter 3, in *Wham-O v. Lincoln Industries*,[12] the New Zealand Court of Appeal held that both the mould from which a frisbee was pressed and the frisbee itself were engravings. However, we cannot assume from this decision that all surface designs will be protected by copyright as engravings. For example, the Australian Federal Court declined to hold the drive mechanism of a lawnmower to be an engraving, on the basis that no consideration of policy or other approach 'could justify straining the English language so far as to call the moulds engravings'.[13]

2.1.2 As a sculpture

Many designs for the shape of three-dimensional artefacts will be susceptible to protection by copyright as 'sculptures'. In *Breville Europe v. Thorn EMI Domestic Appliances*,[14] Falconer J held that scallop-shaped moulds for toasted sandwich makers were sculptures; in *Wham-O*,[15] the New Zealand Court of Appeal held that a wooden model prototype for a plastic frisbee was a sculpture (see Chapter 3, Fig. 3.5, p. 75). However, not all designed artefacts will be sculptures. For example, the plastic Frisbees themselves, which were created by injecting plastic into a mould, were said not to be sculptures. Moreover, Laddie J signalled that the term 'sculpture' will not be construed broadly so as to encompass designs for products where the main considerations are achieving a functional effect: in *Metix UK v. G.H. Maughan*,[16] Laddie J said that to constitute a sculpture, the maker must be concerned with shape and appearance rather than only with achieving a precise functional effect. The Supreme Court approved Laddie J's approach in *Lucasfilm v. Ainsworth*[17] (which is discussed in Chapter 3).

2.1.3 As a work of 'artistic craftsmanship'

Designs may also be protected by copyright if they are taken to be 'works of artistic craftsmanship'.[18] Although, in *George Hensher v. Restawhile Upholstery*,[19] the House of Lords rejected a claim that the prototype of an upholstered chair was a work of artistic craftsmanship, a significant body of designed artefacts may nevertheless fall within the category. In this respect, it should be observed that the decision admits that a work can be a work of artistic craftsmanship even though it is a utilitarian article. More significantly, despite *Hensher*, there is room to argue that a work may qualify as a work of artistic craftsmanship even though it is intended to be mass-produced. Although Lord Reid and Viscount Dilhorne suggested that craftsmanship implied 'hand-made',[20] Lord Simon

---

[12] [1985] *RPC* 127. See Chapter 3, section 5.1.3, pp. 74–5.

[13] *Greenfield Products v. Rover–Scott Bonnar* (1990) 17 *IPR* 417 (FCA) (Pincus J) (the term 'engraving' has to do with marking, cutting, or working the surface, usually the flat surface, of an object).

[14] [1995] *FSR* 77, 94.   [15] *Wham-O v. Lincoln Industries* [1985] *RPC* 127.

[16] [1997] *FSR* 718, 722.

[17] *Lucasfilm v. Ainsworth* [2008] *EWHC* 1878 (Ch), [141]; aff'd on point [2009] *EWCA Civ* 1328, [87]; aff'd [2011] *UKSC* 39, [2012] 1 *AC* 208. See Chapter 3, section 5.1.6, pp. 76–9.   [18] CDPA 1988, s. 4(1)(c).

[19] [1976] *AC* 64.   [20] Ibid., 77 (Lord Reid), 84 (Viscount Dilhorne).

concluded that 'craftsmanship' in the statutory phrase cannot be limited to handicraft; nor is the word 'artistic' incompatible with machine production.[21]

2.1.4 *Infopaq, BSA*, and their implications

As we noted in Chapters 3 and 4, the case law of the Court of Justice may demand a rather different approach to copyright subject matter and the originality inquiry than the UK courts have hitherto adopted: *BSA*[22] suggests that it may not be appropriate to operate a closed list of subject matter, so that any original work—in that case, a graphic user interface—falling within the Berne Convention must be protected; *Infopaq*[23] suggests that the threshold of protection for all such (authorial) works is the European standard of the author's intellectual creation. The implications for UK law are that: (i) narrow interpretation of the list of subject matter in sections 1–4 of the CDPA 1988, such as 'sculpture', may be inappropriate if the effect is to exclude from protection 'works' within the Berne Convention; and (ii) it is no longer appropriate to adopt qualitative thresholds, such as 'artistry', when assessing whether a work is protected—the only question being whether the work is the author's own intellectual creation. In turn, *Flos v. Semararo* can be read as confirming that the freedom apparently reserved to member states in the Designs Directive and Community Design Regulation no longer exists, at least insofar as it relates to the 'the conditions under which, such protection is conferred, including the level of originality required'.[24]

2.2 INDIRECT PROTECTION

Although some designs will benefit from copyright protection as artistic works, many more will benefit from copyright protection indirectly—that is, through the copyright in the documents that were prepared in the process of devising the finished design. These may be protected as drawings or as literary works.

2.2.1 Design drawings

Copyright protection for designs may arise through the creation of preliminary drawings for the design—that is, through the creation of two-dimensional graphic works on which the final article is based. Because these works are protected irrespective of artistic quality, this is the most common way copyright is used to protect designs for articles. As copyright protection extends to three-dimensional reproductions of two-dimensional works and also includes indirect, as well as direct, reproductions, a person who replicates a three-dimensional design will infringe the rights in the two-dimensional drawing. For example, if copyright exists in a drawing for an exhaust pipe or a lego brick, reproduction of the manufactured exhaust pipe or lego brick would infringe (subject to what will be said later).[25]

As noted in Chapter 4, the relevant standard of originality is the *Infopaq* standard of the author's own intellectual creation. Compared with the British position hitherto, the effect is likely to preclude protection of some very simple design documents. Thus, for

---

[21] Ibid., 90; *Coogi Australia v. Hysport International* (1998) 41 *IPR* 593 (FCA).

[22] *Bezpečnostní softwarová asociace*, Case C-393/09 [2010] *ECR* I–13,971 (ECJ).

[23] *Infopaq International v. Danske Dagblades Forening*, Case C-5/08 [2009] *ECR* I–6569 (ECJ).

[24] *Flos SpA v. Semararo Case e Famiglia SpA*, Case C-168/09 [2011] *ECR* I-181 (ECJ), [35]. But note that other Member States, such as Italy and Portugal, do impose requirements of artistic character. Whether this is permissible may become clear when the Court of Justice answers the questions referred in *Cofemel v. G-Star Raw*, Case C-683/17 (pending).

[25] See, classically, *British Leyland v. Armstrong* [1986] *RPC* 279.

example, older cases that recognized that drawings of a rivet, bolt or screw,[26] washers,[27] pulley wheels,[28] spare parts for vacuum cleaners,[29] and exhaust pipes[30] were protectable must now be regarded as dubious. As Christine Fellner explained, the protection in such cases had largely been justified on the basis that a technical draftsperson had put in an hour or two of work.[31] It seems unlikely that the requirement of an 'own intellectual creation' would be met by such efforts: it is no longer sufficient that labour and skill has been expended; there must be real creative freedom. Moreover, where technical requirements limit that freedom, it will be difficult to establish originality. The worst excesses of what was called 'industrial copyright' seem paradoxically to have been removed by the Court of Justice.[32]

2.2.2 Protection of designs as literary works

Copyright law may also protect certain design documents as 'literary works'. This is the case, for example, in relation to a knitting pattern which describes a series of stitches to be employed to create a pullover of a particular style. The protection offered by copyright in this context is very limited. While the copyright owner is able to control reproduction of the pattern, the owner is probably not able to prevent the production of pullovers made to the pattern. The reason for this is that because the pattern and the pullover are not objectively (or visually) similar (as is required to establish infringement of copyright), these are not reproductions.[33] While the courts have sometimes suggested that infringement of copyright in literary works ought to be expanded,[34] as yet there have been no circumstances where a court has held that a written description of a design has been reproduced by the making of articles embodying the design.

3 LIMITATIONS ON THE USE OF COPYRIGHT

The CDPA 1988 sought to limit the role of copyright protection of designs, while offering tailor-made protection under the UK unregistered design right.[35] Section 51 plays a critical role here.

3.1 SECTION 51

Section 51 of the 1988 Act states that copyright is not infringed by making an article from a design document, or a model that records or embodies a design where the design is for 'anything other than an artistic work or a typeface'. The upshot of this is that copyright in a blueprint for a three-dimensional industrial design (such as an exhaust pipe) will not be

---

[26] *British Northrop Ltd v. Texteam Blackburn Ltd* [1973] *FSR* 241, 255 (Megarry J).

[27] *Ocular Sciences Ltd v. Aspect Vision Care Ltd and ors* [1997] *RPC* 289, 421 (Laddie J).

[28] *Solar Thomson Engineering Co. Ltd v. Barton* [1977] *RPC* 537 (CA), 558.

[29] *Hoover plc v. George Hulme (Stockport) Ltd* [1982] *FSR* 565, 571–2 (Whitford J).

[30] *British Leyland Motor Corporation v. Armstrong Patents Co. Ltd* [1986] *RPC* 279.

[31] C. Fellner, *Industrial Design Law* (1995), [1.023], 9.

[32] L. Bently, 'The Return of Industrial Copyright?' [2012] *EIPR* 654, 654–6.

[33] *Brigid Foley v. Ellott* [1982] *RPC* 433 (Sir Robert Megarry VC) (referring to the guide as comprising 'words and numerals'); cf. *Autospin (Oil Seals) v. Beehive Spinning* [1995] *RPC* 683.

[34] But cf. *Moon v. Thornber* [2012] *EWPCC* 37, [98]–[99] (Birss J).

[35] *Mackie Designs v. Behringer Specialised Studio Equipment (UK)* [1999] *RPC* 717, 723 (intention of the legislature that copyright protection be removed from 'ordinary functional commercial articles').

infringed where a person makes articles (here, exhaust pipes) that embody the drawing. The section provides immunity from copyright liability because the blueprint is a 'design document', and the exhaust pipes are 'articles made to the design' or copies thereof.

Section 51, however, is not intended to remove all protection from such design drawings; rather, by limiting the role of copyright in relation to three-dimensional designs (as we will see in Chapter 30), section 51 opens up a corresponding space for the operation of unregistered design right. This is because, according to section 236, if the making of an article to a design drawing is an infringement of copyright, then it is not an infringement of unregistered design right.[36] However, if there is a defence to infringement of copyright in the design document, there *may be* an infringement of unregistered design right. Judicial interpretation of section 51 will consequently be critical in defining the relative roles of copyright and unregistered design right in the protection of designs: if the defence is construed broadly, then unregistered design right has a greater role; if the defence is construed narrowly, then the role of copyright dominates.[37]

There are three critical elements to the operation of section 51:

(i)   there must be a 'design document';

(ii)   the design document must be 'for something other than an artistic work'; and

(iii) the defence only applies where the defendant has made an article to the design or copied an article made to the design.

We consider each in turn.

3.1.1 Design documents

Section 51 only applies where there is either a 'design document' or a 'model recording or embodying a design'. A 'design document' means 'a record of a design, whether in the form of a drawing, a written description, a photograph, data stored in a computer or otherwise'.[38] It covers design documents that are both literary and graphic works.

It should be noted that in this context, 'design' has a particular and restricted meaning—that is, 'any aspect of the shape or configuration (whether internal or external) of the whole or part of an article, other than surface decoration'.[39] Thus the exception does not affect copyright in any decorative feature that will be applied in two dimensions to industrial articles.[40] It does, however, affect three-dimensional applications embodying the shape or configuration of an article. The term 'configuration' has also been held to

---

[36] *Mark Wilkinson Furniture v. Woodcraft Designs (Radcliffe)* [1998] *FSR* 63, 65 (copyright and unregistered design right described as mutually exclusive); cf. *Lambretta Clothing Co. Ltd v. Teddy Smith (UK)* [2003] *RPC* 744, [60]–[68] (Etherton J) (discussing how CDPA 1988, s. 51, demarcates the relationship between copyright and unregistered design right, but observing that it seeks to achieve more than that and refusing to accept propositions in *Wilkinson v. Woodcraft*).

[37] *Mackie v. Behringer* [1999] *RPC* 717, 723 (approving broad construction of 'design', so as to ensure protection by design right not copyright).   [38] CDPA 1988, s. 51(3).

[39] Ibid.

[40] On the meaning of 'surface decoration', see *Mark Wilkinson Furniture v. Woodcraft Designs (Radcliffe)* [1998] *FSR* 63, discussed in the context of unregistered design right in Chapter 30, section 2.2.1, at pp. 813–15. But cf. *Lambretta Clothing Co. Ltd v. Teddy Smith (UK)* [2003] *RPC* 728 (copying of design for sweater, including colourways, protected by s. 51 defence); *Abraham Moon & Sons Ltd v. Thornber* [2012] *EWPCC* 37 (copyright in designs for fabric related to 'surface decoration', so s. 51 gave no defence); *Flashing Badge Co. v. Groves* [2007] *EWHC* 1372 (examining Court of Appeal's decision in *Lambretta Clothing* and concluding that s. 51 defence inapplicable to design for surface decoration of flashing badges).

encompass the arrangement of features (resistors, diodes, etc.) on a circuit diagram.[41] As we will see, this definition corresponds to the definition of 'design' used for the purposes of unregistered design right. It is unclear how important the intention of the designer is in determining whether the contents of a document constitute a 'design'. While still unsettled, it seems that something is only a 'design' if it is intended by its creator, at the outset, to be a 'design'.[42]

Section 51 also applies to 'models'—that is, to three-dimensional prototypes—so, for example, the wooden prototype for a frisbee could not be relied upon to claim copyright infringement in the reproduction of mass-produced frisbees.

3.1.2 'For something other than an artistic work'

Section 51 only applies where the design or model 'is for something other than an artistic work or a typeface'. Consequently, there is no defence where the design document or model embodies a design 'for an artistic work'. This means, for example, that a sketch of the sitter for a portrait sculpture or a plan for a building will not be caught by the defence, since they are designs for artistic works.[43]

The section once again raises the question of what is an artistic work. Section 4(1) states that artistic work means a graphic work, photograph, sculpture, work of architecture, or work of artistic craftsmanship. This means that a design drawing for a chair will be a design for an artistic work if the chair is treated as a work of artistic craftsmanship. Moreover, given that the 1988 Act protects 'sculptures' and 'engravings' as artistic works irrespective of any artistic quality, it is uncertain which industrial objects would fall within these concepts. However, in *Lucasfilm v. Ainsworth* the courts found that designs for helmets for the Stormtroopers in *Star Wars IV* (Chapter 3, Fig. 3.6, p. 76) were not designs for artistic works, because the helmets were not sculptures or works of artistic craftsmanship. As such, the defence was applicable.[44]

3.1.3 Making articles to the design (or copying articles)

The section 51 defence only applies where a person makes an article that corresponds to the 'design' or makes 'a copy' of 'an article made to the design'. The upshot of this is that the section appears to allow a person to make articles (such as exhaust pipes) to the design, or to copy an article (such as an exhaust pipe) that has been made to the design. The defence does not apply, however, where a person merely photocopies a design document, which remains an infringement of copyright.[45]

It has been suggested that the section 51 defence also provides a defence to a person who makes a two-dimensional copy of a (three-dimensional) article that has been made to a design document. In *BBC Worldwide v. Pally Screen Printing*,[46] the BBC brought an action for infringement of copyright in the children's television characters, the Teletubbies. These characters were played by actors wearing costumes, and the defendants sold T-shirts bearing pictures of children's television characters. The claimant sought

---

[41] *Mackie v. Behringer* [1999] *RPC* 717, 722–3.

[42] *BBC Worldwide v. Pally Screen Printing* [1998] *FSR* 665, 672 (design must have been for something other than an artistic work from the outset).

[43] Ibid., 672 (emphasizing that if the drawings of the Teletubbies had been prototypes for a cartoon series, the s. 51 defence could not have applied).

[44] *Lucasfilm v. Ainsworth* [2008] *EWHC* 1878 (Ch), [141]; aff'd on point [2009] *EWCA Civ* 1328, [87]; aff'd [2011] *UKSC* 39, [2012] 1 *AC* 208.

[45] *Lambretta Clothing Co. Ltd v. Teddy Smith (UK)* [2003] *RPC* 728, [65] (Etherton J).

[46] [1998] *FSR* 665, 672.

summary judgment, asserting infringement of copyright in the drawings upon which the characters' costumes were based. The defendants sought to resist summary judgment, on the basis that there was an arguable defence under section 51. While the defendants admitted that they had derived the characters from the television broadcast (and thus, indirectly, from the documents), they alleged that the T-shirts were copies (albeit in two dimensions) of the costumes which, in turn, were articles made to design drawings. Laddie J said that while he did not find the defendants' case 'terribly attractive', it was arguable. Summary judgment was consequently refused.[47]

3.1.4 The impact of *Flos*

As noted, the Court of Justice's decision in *Flos*[48] suggests that designs, whether registered or not, may be 'works' protected under the Information Society Directive. As will be recalled, Article 2 of that Directive harmonizes the reproduction right in such works, and Article 5 contains an exhaustive list of permissible limitations on that right. There is no exception that corresponds to section 51 of the CDPA 1988. Does this mean that section 51 must be repealed? Lobbyists for the designs industry have suggested that it does.[49]

The answer to this question depends on three matters: first, on whether section 51 is a limitation on the harmonized 'reproduction right' or the unharmonized 'adaptation right'; second, on whether, if section 51 implicates 'reproduction' rather than adaptation, it 'limits' that right rather than merely 'defines it'; and third, whether, if it limits the reproduction right, some other justification might be found outside Article 5 of the Information Society Directive. It will probably take a number of decisions of the Court of Justice before we have a clear answer.

3.2 SECTION 53 (ACTS DONE ON THE BASIS OF RIGHTS IN THE REGISTERED DESIGN)

Section 53 deals with the situation where the ownership of copyright and the proprietorship of a registered design (or registered Community design) are vested in different people.[50] This may occur by means of voluntary transactions or as a result of the fact that the principles by which ownership of copyright are determined differ from those relating to registered designs.[51] Section 53 effectively provides a defence to a person who relies on permission from the registered design proprietor but has failed to gain the authorization of the copyright owner. More specifically, section 53 states that copyright in an artistic work is not infringed by anything done 'pursuant to an assignment or licence' made by the proprietor of the registered design. The idea behind the section is to protect a person who transacts with the registered proprietor by giving that person immunity from copyright infringement.

The defence is qualified, however: it only applies where the person claiming the immunity has acted in good faith in reliance upon the registration and without notice of proceedings for cancellation or rectification of the design (if they exist). In normal

---

[47] Affirmed in *Mackie v. Behringer* [1999] *RPC* 717, 723–4.

[48] *Flos SpA v. Semararo Case e Famiglia SpA*, Case C-168/09 [2011] *ECR* I-181 (ECJ).

[49] See, e.g., *Memorandum submitted by The Alliance Against IP Theft* [2011] *ECR* I-181 *ERR* 22, to the Public Bill Committee on the Enterprise and Regulatory Reform Bill. On the legal issues, see L. Bently, 'The Return of Industrial Copyright?' [2012] *EIPR* 654, 668–9.

[50] CDPA 1988, s. 53, as modified by IP Act 2014, s. 5, to make the provision applicable to registered Community designs.

[51] But note that this is now changed as a result of IP Act 2014, ss 2 and 6, which remove the principle of commissioner ownership from the law of registered and unregistered designs.

circumstances, the registered design displaces the copyright as far as third parties need be concerned. As soon as the legitimacy of the registration becomes questionable, however, the copyright regains its force. The acts of the registered proprietor do not fall within the scope of the defence.

4 SECTION 52 AND ITS DEMISE

As noted, the United Kingdom formerly operated an exception (section 52), that limited the term of copyright to 25 years as regards artistic works that were used as the basis for designs that were put into mass production. In so doing, section 52 was intended to prevent copyright from providing a longer term of protection for industrially exploited designs than would be gained via registration. In this section, we consider the scope of the section and its repeal.

4.1 SCOPE OF OLD SECTION 52

Section 52 was never unproblematic. It operated where the artistic work had been exploited (by or with the licence of the copyright owner) by making 'by an industrial process' and marketing articles that were copies of the work. An article was said to have been 'made by an industrial process' if more than 50 articles were made (whether or not by hand), all of which were copies.[52] However, certain articles (specified in delegated legislation) did not fall within the scope of the section.[53] The excluded articles included some sculptures, medals, and 'printed matter primarily of a literary and artistic character' such as greeting cards. The division frequently seemed arbitrary: an artistic work used as a design for a book jacket remained protected for the full copyright term; a label for a paint tin was subject to the defence.[54] Moreover, section 52 operated to reduce the duration of copyright to 25 years from the first legitimate marketing of articles that were copies of the copyright work by providing a defence to an action for copyright infringement.[55] The defence allowed a person to make articles of any description that corresponded to the artistic work. This meant that if the artistic work had been applied to teapots, 25 years from the first marketing of the teapots, it would no longer be an infringement of copyright to apply the same work to pillowcases. However, the defence left the copyright intact where the design was applied to things other than articles—so that, after 25 years of marketing the teapot, it was still an infringement to photograph the artistic work (in its unapplied state). Anything might, however, have been done in relation to an article which the artistic work had been applied to without infringing copyright in the work.

4.2 REPEAL

The defence in section 52 was repealed by the Enterprise and Regulatory Reform Act 2013.[56] The justification for doing so was European harmonization—in particular the

---

[52] CDPA 1988, s. 52(4)(a); Copyright (Industrial Process and Excluded Articles) (No. 2) Order 1989 (SI 1989/1070).   [53] CDPA 1988, s. 52(4)(b); Copyright (Industrial Process, etc.) Order 1989.

[54] *Gary Fearns t/a Autopaint International v. Anglo-Dutch Paint and Chemical Co. Ltd* [2007] *EWHC* 955 (Ch) (labels for paint tins were not articles of primary literary and artistic character).

[55] CDPA 1988, s. 52(2). The author's moral right of integrity is left intact, while CDPA 1988, s. 79(4)(f), denies the author the right of paternity.   [56] ERR 2013, s. 74.

view that as a result of *Flos v. Semararo*, what was (in effect) a limitation on the term of copyright was no longer permissible in relation to designs. It seems that significant pressure had been brought to bear on the UK government from lobbyists in the design field, particularly rights holders in furniture. The effect of repeal is that the term of protection by copyright is now the regular term of life plus 70 years, except for works created before 1957.[57]

In October 2013, the UK IPO began consulting on transitional provisions associated with the repeal of section 52.[58] Issues included how long people with stocks of goods made at a time when it was legal to make such goods would be given to sell off those goods, and the fate of users of existing two-dimensional images of out-of-copyright designs. While the repeal was initially planned to have become operational in 2020 (with a five-year transitional period), the government responded to criticism that the transitional period was too long and withdrew the Commencement Order.[59] Following fresh public consultation, it was decided that the repeal would come into effect on 28 July 2016, with a transitional period running until 28 January 2017.[60] As a result, designs protected as artistic works now last for life-plus seventy years irrespective of the number of copies of the work that are made. The changes also apply to artistic works whose term had expired under the old section 52. As a result, many artistic works whose term had lapsed under the old regime have been revived. These now run for the life-plus 70-year period.[61]

[57] In the case of works created before 1957, which were registrable as designs, no copyright protection had existed, and the 1956 and 1988 Acts did not alter the position: CDPA 1988, Sch. 1, para. 6. However, subsequent representations led to copyright being conferred on any such works which were protected in any Member State on July 1, 1995: CDPA 1988, Sched. 1, para. 6A, introduced by Copyright (Amendment) Regulations 2016 (2016/1210), Reg. 2(3) (qualifying CDPA 1988, Sched. 1, para. 6, which had preserved the public domain status of artistic works excluded from copyright under Copyright Act 1911, s. 22, where such works were capable of registration and designs).

[58] UK IPO, *Call for Evidence: Transitional Provisions for Repeal of Section 52 of the Copyright, Designs and Patents Act 1988* (2013).

[59] Commencement Order (Enterprise and Regulatory Reform Act 2013) (Commencement No. 8 and Savings Provisions) Order 2015 (revoked on 23 July 2015 following a judicial review challenge to the Order).

[60] Enterprise and Regulatory Reform Act 2013 (Commencement No. 10 and Savings Provisions) Order 2016 (SI 2016/593). As of 28 July 2016, a limit was placed on the *manufacture or importation* of affected artistic works. This was extended from 28 January 2017 to *all protected dealings* with the affected artistic works.

[61] UK IPO, *Repeal of section 52 of the Copyright, Designs and Patents Act 1988* (March 2017).

30

UK UNREGISTERED DESIGN RIGHT

1 INTRODUCTION

The fifth way in which designs may be protected is by way of the UK unregistered design right. The UK unregistered design right, which is governed by Part III of the Copyright Designs and Patents Act 1988 (CDPA 1988),[1] was developed as part of the reconceptualization of the way designs were protected in Britain in the 1980s. Prior to 1988, the boundary between the UK registered design system and the copyright system was placed under pressure as a result of the decision that non-registrable designs—such as the design of car exhaust pipes—could be protected by copyright (so-called 'industrial copyright'). In an attempt to remedy the bizarre situation whereby unattractive designs were protected by copyright but attractive ones were not, the unregistered design right was introduced to provide short-term, automatic protection for functional designs.[2] In so doing, the new right was meant to provide 'limited protection against unfair misappropriation of time skill and effort expended by the author of the design in the creation of the work'.[3] Consequently, it was decided to limit the registered system to designs for articles for which appearance mattered, and copyright to the protection of two-dimensional designs or designs for artistic works. As we noted in the previous chapter, the protection given to the proprietor of an unregistered design is intended to dovetail with the protection conferred by the copyright system in respect of design drawings for three-dimensional designs.

The logic of that division has been undermined both by the harmonization of European registered design law, which covers functional as well as aesthetic designs, and by the

---

[1] *Guild v. Eskandar* [2003] *FSR* 23, [8] ('a new, wholly statutory right'). The right was modelled on principles enunciated in Directive 87/54/EEC of 16 December 1986 on the legal protection of semiconductor chips [1986] *OJ L* 24/36 (27 January 1987), upon which the Semiconductor Products (Protection of Topography) Regulations 1987 (SI 1987/1497) were based. See A. Christie, *Integrated Circuits and Their Contents: International Protection* (1995), ch. 4.

[2] *Fulton v. Totes Isotoner (UK)* [2003] *RPC* 499, [71] ('a medley of political and practical compromise').

[3] *Farmers Build v. Carier Bulk Materials Handling* [1999] *RPC* 461, 480 (Mummery LJ). In *Landor and Hawa International Ltd v. Azure Designs Ltd* [2006] *ECDR* 413, [11], Neuberger LJ described the function of the system as the rewarding of 'imagination and inventiveness'.

establishment of the unregistered Community design, which covers a broader field than the UK unregistered design right, albeit for a shorter period of time. While academics and policymakers might raise questions about whether there are any good reasons for maintaining the UK unregistered design right, a knowledge of this *sui generis* right remains essential for understanding the current law of designs.

2 SUBSISTENCE OF THE UK UNREGISTERED DESIGN RIGHT

As with copyright, unregistered design rights arise automatically on the creation of a design. An important preliminary step in any litigation in respect of an unregistered design right is that the 'claimant must identify with precision each and every "design" he relies upon'.[4] This has been, and remains, an important issue. Prior to 2014, the definition of design allowed claimants to assert design right in 'aspects' of a larger article. The decision to extend the definition of design to include aspects of a design allowed claimants to claim a design right in different aspects of an article (which meant that questions of subsistence and infringement often had to be considered separately for each aspect relied upon).[5] It also allowed claimants to craft complex and potentially oppressive legal claims, and to trim the right to match what they believe a defendant had copied.[6]

In 2014 the definition of design was amended to prevent rights holders from inappropriately using a very small part of their design as the basis for a claim that a third party is infringing.[7] This was achieved by removing the reference to '*any aspect of*' a design from the definition of a design.[8] As a result, a UK unregistered design is now defined, as in EU law, to mean 'the design of the shape or configuration (whether internal or external) of the whole or part of an article'. This limits protection to new designs and parts of designs. The revised definition only applies to designs created after 1 October 2014.[9] While it has been suggested that the removal of '*any aspect of*' from the definition of a design was merely declaratory of the existing law and had thus had no real effect,[10] a better view is that the change narrowed the scope of what can constitute a design.[11] This accords with the government's suggestion that the reform would reduce the tendency for design owners to overstate the breadth of their unregistered design right. This is what Henry Carr J

---

[4] *Dyson v. Qualtex* [2006] *RPC* 769, [62]; *Albert Packaging v. Nampak Cartons & Healthcare* [2011] *EWPCC* 15 (Pat), [14]–[15]. See generally S. Clark, 'Design Rights All Wrapped up' (2012) 34 *EIPR* 343.

[5] *Albert Packaging v. Nampak Cartons & Healthcare* [2011] *EWPCC* 15 (Pat).

[6] See *Bailey (t/a Elite Anglian Products) v. Haynes (t/a RAGS)* [2007] *FSR* (10) 199, [18]; *Ocular Sciences v. Aspect Vision Care (No. 2)* [1997] *RPC* 289; *Virgin Atlantic v. Premium* [2009] *EWHC* 26 (Pat), [27]–[29]; *A Fulton v. Totes Isotoner (UK)* [2003] *EWCA Civ* 1514 (enables design owners to manipulate their claims by cropping the scope of the design).

[7] This only applies to designs created after 1 October 2014.

[8] IP Act 2014, s. 1(1), (2), amending CDPA 1988, ss 51 and 213(2).

[9] *Neptune v. Devol Kitchens* [2017] *EWHC* 2172 (Pat), [42] (the removal of '*any aspect of*' a design 'does not extinguish accrued rights of action for infringements which occurred prior to 1 October 2014').

[10] See *DHK Retail v. H. Young* [2014] *EHWC* 4034 (common ground amongst the parties); *Copinger and Skone James on Copyright* (17th edn, 2016), [13-58]–[13-60].

[11] *DKH Retail v. H. Young* [2014] *EWHC* 4034, [10]–[14]. HH Judge Hacon suggested that one of the consequences of the reform was that it was no longer possible for a design right to be claimed in designs extending beyond those embodied in an article. That is, it was no longer possible to claim 'unregistered design rights in abstract designs': [15]–[16]. See also *Whitby Specialist Vehicles v. Yorkshire Specialist Vehicles* [2014] *EWHC* 4242, [41], [45]; *Action Storage Systems v. G-Force Europe* [2016] *EWHC* 3151, [14]–[16].

held when he said that the changes to section 213(2) were not merely declaratory of the existing law. Rather, the reforms made a substantive change to the law by 'preventing claims in respect of disembodied features, arbitrarily selected, which are not, in design terms, parts of the design'.[12]

While the removal of the reference to aspects of a design may make it more difficult for claimants to claim more than they deserve, the fact that the definition of design still extends to part of an article means that it will still be possible to crop an article to enhance a claim for infringement. Given this, it seems that if the design right is not to be abused, the courts will need to develop rules to ensure that the scope of litigation is limited (by requiring the claimant to identify what they regard as their best case), and that there is a level of correspondence between what is created and what is 'claimed'. To some extent, the courts have begun to do this. Building on the concept of a design and a number of the doctrinal rules (including the definitions of 'design' and 'designer', and the exclusion of methods of construction), it has been held that design protection is limited to specific aspects of shape and configuration, rather than 'improperly wide abstract ideas or principles'.[13] Based on this, it has been said that the UK unregistered design right 'does not protect ideas, but only the actual physical manifestation of them',[14] and that the right cannot exist until there is an embodiment of the design in an article or a design document. This has been taken to mean that it is not possible to claim design right in abstract ideas or design concepts. Thus, it was not possible to claim design right in the 'concept of a mower which has arms folding back on themselves at the mid-way point'.[15]

In order to establish the existence of a UK unregistered design right, it is necessary to show (i) that there is a design, (ii) which falls outside the exclusions from design right, (iii) which is 'original', and (iv) which qualifies for protection in the United Kingdom. We will deal with each requirement in turn.[16]

2.1 'A DESIGN'

In order for a design to be protected as a UK unregistered design right, it is necessary to show that there is a 'design'. In this context, 'design' was initially defined to mean 'the design of any aspect of the shape or configuration (whether internal or external) of the whole or part of any article'.[17] As noted earlier, the Intellectual Property Act 2014 amended this definition by removing the reference to 'any aspect of' a design.[18] As a result, a design is now defined as 'the design of the shape or configuration (whether internal or external) of the whole or part of an article'.

The subject matter of the UK unregistered design right is more limited than the harmonized registered design systems, insofar as the UK unregistered design right does not

---

[12] *Neptune v. Devol Kitchens* [2017] *EWHC* 2172 (Pat), [33].

[13] *Sealed Air v. Sharp Interpack* [2013] *EWPCC* 23 (Pat), [91].

[14] *Rolawn v. Turfmech Machinery* [2008] *EWHC* 989 (Pat), [79]–[84]; *G-Star Raw v. Rhodi* (2015) *EWHC* 216, [31] (the design right does not protect ideas).

[15] *Rolawn v. Turfmech Machinery* [2008] *EWHC* 989 (Pat), [84]. HHJ Hacon said that this approach was not achieved until the 2014 reforms which changed the definition of design: *Action Storage Systems v. G-Force Europe* [2016] *EWHC* 315, [54].

[16] See *Dyson v. Qualtex* [2006] *RPC* 769, [14], in which Jacob LJ is scathing in his criticism of s. 213, which he describes as having only one virtue: its brevity. In other respects, it is badly drafted and there is no clear indication of what is intended.   [17] RDA 1949, s. 1(2).

[18] IP Act 2014, s. 1(1), (2), amending CDPA 1988, ss 51 and 213(2).

protect most two-dimensional features.[19] In many other respects, however, the subject matter of UK unregistered design rights is as broad as UK registered designs, Community registered designs, and unregistered Community design rights. In particular, it should be noted that the UK unregistered design right protects designs that are not aesthetic; in fact, there is no requirement that the design features need to be visible to the naked eye.[20] Indeed, in one case, it was held that detailed dimensions of the shape of contact lenses could be a design despite the fact that the lenses would appear identical to any normal observer and could only be distinguished with the aid of sophisticated measuring equipment.[21] The definition of designs for a UK unregistered design right also extends to designs that are purely functional.[22] One of the leading cases, for example, concerned the internal features of a farming machine used to separate the solid and liquid parts of slurry.[23]

A key feature of the definition of design is that it only applies to the *shape or configuration* of articles (or parts thereof). 'Shape and configuration' has the same meaning for unregistered designs as it previously did (prior to EU harmonization) for registered designs.[24] Configuration includes 'the relative arrangement of parts or elements of an article', so that the way in which different components of a medical kit are layered within a polythene pack amounts to configuration.[25] It is clear that this does not limit designs to three-dimensional shapes. As Jacob LJ said, 'you can have 2D features of shape or configuration, e.g. one produced by cutting one out from a piece of paper'.[26] There is no reason why a design should 'not subsist in what people would ordinarily call a flat or 2-dimensional thing—for instance a new design for a doily would have shape and could in principle have [unregistered design right] in it'.[27] Having said this, the courts have also made it clear that patterns (such as a patchwork quilt) and articles coloured in a novel way would not fall within the definition of 'shape' or 'configuration' and, as such, would not be protected.[28]

---

[19] The courts have speculated as to whether 'configuration', in contrast to shape, is not confined to three-dimensional characteristics. See *Mackie Designs v. Behringer Specialised Studio Equipment (UK)* [1999] *RPC* 717, 722–3 (holding that 'configuration' should be broadly construed to cover circuit diagrams); *Baby Dan SA v. Brevi* [1999] *FSR* 377, 383 ('configuration' implies some form of arrangement of elements, e.g. the ribbing arrangement of a hot-water bottle); *Lambretta Clothing Co. Ltd v. Teddy Smith (UK)* [2003] *RPC* 728, [48] (there is nothing to suggest that configuration is not confined to three-dimensional aspects of an article); *Dyson v. Qualtex* [2006] *RPC* 769, [74] (cutting pattern out of piece of paper is 'configuration'). It was held that design right did not protect stitching on mobile phone cases: *Parker v. Tidball* [1997] *FSR* 680, 696. But cf. *Fulton v. Grant Barnett* [2001] *RPC* 257, [78] (stitching on case for umbrella treated as protected in case in which it produced accentuated rectangular character).

[20] To some extent, this may be true of registered designs, Community registered, and unregistered designs.

[21] *Ocular Sciences v. Aspect Vision Care* [1997] *RPC* 289; *Fulton v. Totes Isotoner (UK)* [2003] *RPC* 499, [30] ('unregistered design right extends beyond the visually appreciable to other aspects of the design of an article').

[22] *Fulton v. Grant Barnett* [2001] *RPC* 257, [34]. But quite how significant depends on what the EU tribunals make of the 'dictated by function' standard.

[23] *Farmers Build v. Carier Bulk Materials Handling* [1999] *RPC* 461. See also *Dyson v. Qualtex* [2006] *RPC* 769, [26] ('UDR can subsist in aspects of detail').

[24] *Lambretta Clothing Co. Ltd v. Teddy Smith (UK)* [2005] *RPC* 88, [15].

[25] *Magmatic v. PMS International* [2013] *EWHC* 1925(Pat), [81]; *CliniSupplies v. Park* [2012] *EWHC* 3452 (Ch), [36]–[53]. Having reviewed the case law, Arnold J concluded that while the matter was not entirely free from doubt, Pumfrey J's broad interpretation of 'configuration' in *Mackie Design v. Behringer Specialised Studio Equipment* [1999] *RPC* 717, 721–23, represented the law.

[26] *Dyson v. Qualtex* [2006] *RPC* 769, [74].

[27] *Lambretta Clothing Co. Ltd v. Teddy Smith (UK)* [2005] *RPC* 88, [24].

[28] Thus it was held that mere choice of different colours for a standard track top was not an aspect of 'shape or configuration': ibid., [29].

Unregistered design right protects designs for 'articles'. The term is not defined further, but needs to be contrasted with the concept of 'products' that is used in relation to UK registered designs, Community registered designs, and unregistered Community designs.[29] The UK unregistered design right applies to designs for whole articles, as well as parts of articles. This means that an article may embody a number of different designs. In the case of a teapot, for example, an unregistered design right could reside in the shape of the whole pot, or in a part, such as the spout, the handle, or the lid.[30] For designs made *prior* to the commencement of the 2014 Act,[31] the main limitation is that the design must be of *an aspect* of the whole or part of the article—which means a 'discernible or recognizable' part of the article.[32] While *aspects* of a design includes 'disembodied features which are merely recognisable or discernible', *parts* of a design are 'concrete parts which can be identified as such'.[33] Thus, in relation to a teapot, aspects of design might include the combination of the end portion of the spout and top portion of the lid of a teapot, which are disembodied from each other and from the spout and lid (and as such not parts of the design).[34] As we noted earlier, the Act removed the reference to 'any aspect of' a design from the definition of a UK unregistered design.[35] This means, at least for designs created after the commencement of the Act, that it is now more difficult for claimants to 'define the shape of a design at a higher level of abstraction than its physical manifestation in the relevant article'.[36]

2.2 EXCLUSIONS

In order for a design to be protected by the UK unregistered design right, it is necessary to ensure that it does not fall within the list of excluded features contained in section 213 of the CDPA 1988. This provides that unregistered design right does not subsist in 'surface decoration', 'methods or principles of construction', or features that 'must fit' or 'must match'.[37]

2.2.1 Surface decoration

Section 213(3)(c) provides that unregistered design right does not subsist in features of 'surface decoration'. As Jacob LJ explained in *Dyson v. Qualtex*,[38] the exclusion of 'surface decoration' is related to its inclusion within 'ordinary' copyright law. This led Jacob LJ to suggest that the exclusion is confined to 'that which can fairly be described as a decorated surface'.[39]

---

[29] It is possible that the shape and configuration of buildings may be protected by unregistered design right. For similar argument as to whether buildings are 'products' in relation to the harmonized definition of designs, see Chapter 26, section 2.3.1, p. 744–6.

[30] *Ocular Sciences v. Aspect Vision Care* [1997] *RPC* 289, 422; *Fulton v. Totes Isotoner (UK)* [2004] *RPC* (16) 301 (CA) (part of a cloth case for portable umbrella).　　　　　　　[31] See section 2, p. 810.

[32] *Dyson v. Qualtex* [2006] *RPC* 769, [23]. A photograph of the Dyson wand can be seen in the case report.

[33] *Neptune v. Devol Kitchens* [2017] *EWHC* 2172 (Pat), [44].　　　[34] Ibid.

[35] IP Act 2014, s. 1(1), (2), amending CDPA 1988, ss 51 and 213(2).

[36] *Neptune v. Devol Kitchens* [2017] *EWHC* 2172 (Pat), [60].

[37] An initial problem with the drafting of s. 213 should be observed. This arises from the fact that while the nature of unregistered design right and the way in which the right is infringed are defined in relation to 'designs', the exclusions relate to 'design rights'. A literal construction of s. 213 would produce the nonsensical result that it would be possible for an infringement to take place in relation to subject matter excluded from the scope of protection: *Mark Wilkinson Furniture v. Woodcraft Designs (Radcliffe)* [1998] *FSR* 63. This problem has been avoided in relation to the exclusion of 'surface decoration'. This was done by incorporating the exclusion of 'surface decoration' into the meaning of 'design': ibid., 72 (relying on the definition of design in CDPA 1988, s. 51(3)). It is hoped that similar strategies can be applied to the other exclusions. The reasoning employed in *Mark Wilkinson Furniture* would not resolve the problem for 'must fit' or 'must match' features.

[38] [2006] *RPC* 769, [76]. Although there may be rare situations in which a design may fall between the gaps of the two regimes.　　　　　　　[39] Ibid., [81].

It is clear that surface decoration covers the application of colour in two dimensions (such as stripes on a shirt),[40] but is not confined to two-dimensional features (strictly defined). This means, for example, that surface decoration would include both where 'a surface is covered with a thin layer and where the decoration, like in Brighton rock, runs throughout the article'.[41] In some situations, 'surface decoration' may be three-dimensional; there is no need for it to be 'essentially flat'. As such, it includes both 'decoration lying on the surface of the article (for example, a painted finish) and decorative features of the surface itself (for example, beading or engraving)'.[42] Consequently, in *Mark Wilkinson Furniture v. Woodcraft Designs (Radcliffe)*,[43] Jonathan Parker J held that the painted finish, V-grooves, and cock-beading on the kitchen furniture the claimant had created was surface decoration and thus not protectable. Other features, such as cornices, quadrants, and handles were not surface decoration and, as such, were protected by unregistered design right (see Fig. 30.1).

Fig. 30.1 The plaintiff's kitchen

Source: Mark Wilkinson Furniture

---

[40] *Lambretta Clothing Co. Ltd v. Teddy Smith (UK)* [2005] *RPC* 88 (CA), [30] (over-arm stripes on sleeves of track top were surface decoration; mere juxtaposition of colours, not 'configuration').   [41] Ibid.

[42] *Mark Wilkinson Furniture v. Woodcraft Designs (Radcliffe)* [1998] *FSR* 63, 73; *Neptune v. Devol Kitchens* [2017] *EWHC* 2172 (Pat), [26]–[28] (cock-beading and moulding that was a prominent part of the shape of cabinet doors, which was 'truly three dimensional', was an important design feature and therefore not surface decoration).

[43] [1998] *FSR* 63, 73. Cited with approval by Jacob LJ in *Lambretta Clothing Co. Ltd v. Teddy Smith (UK)* [2005] *RPC* 88, [31]. See also *Jo Y Jo v. Matalan Retail* [2000] *ECDR* 178 (embroidery on ladies' garments was surface decoration, but other aspects of knitted cardigans, such as the choice of knit or fabric and edging, were not).

In other cases, three-dimensional features may not be regarded as decoration but as part of the overall shape and configuration: ultimately, the court has to make a value judgment. So, in *A. Fulton v. Grant Barnett*,[44] Park J took the view that although stitching on the seams of a rectangular umbrella case existed 'in a small third dimension', it was not excluded as surface decoration because it gave the case its 'box-like character'. On the basis that unregistered design right was developed to protect functional designs, it has been suggested that surface features that have 'significant function' would not be excluded on the ground that they were surface decoration. Thus, the Court of Appeal in *Dyson* held that because the ribbing on the handle of a vacuum cleaner functioned to provide grip, it was not excluded as surface decoration (see Fig. 30.2).[45]

In situations where a design feature is both functional *and* decorative, the courts have said that a subsidiary functional purpose does not take the design aspect out of the exemption if the primary purpose is surface decoration. As Mann J said in *Dyson*, this will limit the scope of the exception, because if an item of decoration has a functional purpose:

> [I]t will be difficult to say that functional purpose is sufficiently subsidiary to make the feature surface decoration . . . I think that the subsidiary purpose of beading that is used to conceal a joint can also fairly be described as decorative.[46]

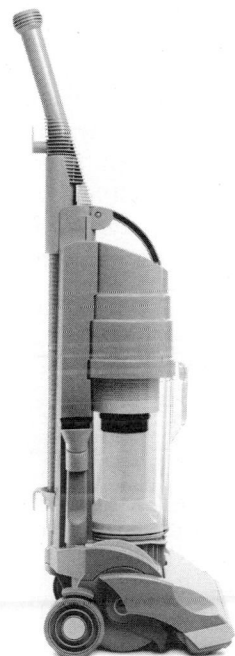

Fig. 30.2 Dyson
Source: Dyson, http://www.dyson.com

---

[44] [2004] *RPC* (16) 301, [78]–[79]. See also *Christopher Tasker's Design Right References* [2001] *RPC* 39 (features must be decorative).   [45] *Dyson v. Qualtex* [2004] *EWHC* 298 (Ch).

[46] Ibid., [38]. For a situation in which a design with both a decorative and functional feature was held to be surface decoration, see *Helmet Integrated Systems v. Mitchell Tunnard* [2006] *FSR* 813, [99]–[101] (concerning the scalloping on the visor of a firefighter's helmet).

2.2.2 Methods of construction

Section 213(3)(a) provides that unregistered design right does not subsist in 'a method or principle of construction'.[47] The provision, which is to be construed narrowly, does not preclude a design from being protected merely because it has a functional purpose.[48] The exclusion of methods of construction from the remit of protection, which has its origins in now-repealed (that is, pre-harmonization) British registered designs law,[49] confines design protection to shape, rather than to the ideas or principles underlying a shape. In so doing, it ensures that protection does not exist in the method by which a shape is produced, as opposed to the shape itself.[50] That is, it ensures that designers are unable to obtain patent-style protection over the way in which articles of a particular style are made.[51] In some cases, the courts have suggested that section 213(3)(a) not only excludes the methods or processes by which a shape is produced (as opposed to the shape itself), but also excludes underlying ideas from being protected. It has also been suggested that section 213(3)(a) ensures that design protection is limited to physical manifestations of an idea, rather than to abstract design proposals.[52] In this sense, the exclusion in section 213(a) has been construed to operate, in effect, like a design law version of the idea expression dichotomy.

The application of the exclusion can be seen in *A. Fulton Co. Ltd v. Grant Barnett*,[53] which concerned a claim to unregistered design right in rectangular umbrella cases, where the rectangular shape was created in part by the use of stitching. While Park J accepted that the stitching used in making the umbrella cases was a technique, he was happy to protect the shape produced by that method. Accordingly, it appears that the exclusion only bites where the protection of the shape would prevent others from using the method. That is, where the use of a method can only result in one shape or configuration.[54] In contrast, in *Bailey v. Haynes*[55] Fysh J held that a claim for infringement of unregistered design right in the shape of stitching of micromesh bags for fishing bait failed because the claim related to a method of construction. The judge seems to have been influenced by the fact that there were no dimensional limitations on the pattern of threads being claimed (see Fig. 30.3).

2.2.3 'Must fit'

Section 213(3)(b)(i) of the 1988 Act provides that 'design right does not subsist in . . . features of shape or configuration of an article which . . . enable the article to be connected

---

[47] CDPA 1988, s. 213(3)(a).

[48] *Landor & Hawa International v. Azure Designs* [2007] *FSR* (9) 181 (CA), [10].

[49] *Clinisupplies v. Park* [2012] *EWHC* 3453 (Ch), [55]–[56]; *JCM Seating Solutions v. James Leckey Designs* [2002] *EWHC* 3218 (Ch), [29].

[50] *Landor & Hawa International v. Azure Designs* [2006] *FSR* 427 (PCC), 433 (explaining that while the language was 'a little opaque', it would be wrong in principle to attempt to define it further as opposed to applying it, but leaving unclear whether a shape that was the best way of achieving a function would be excluded from protection); decision upheld on appeal: [2006] *EWCA* 1285.

[51] *Bailey v. Haynes* [2007] *FSR* (10) 199, [62].

[52] *Albert Packaging v. Nampak Cartons & Healthcare* [2011] *EWPCC* 15, [14]–[15] ('the more abstract the definition, the more likely it is that the design will be excluded'); *Landor & Hawa v. Azure* [2006] *EWCA* 1285, [13]; *Rolawn v. Turfmech Machinery* [2008] *EWHC* 989 (Pat), [91], [92], [96]; *Virgin Atlantic Airways v. Premium Aircraft Interiors* [2009] *EWHC* 26 (Pat), [24].   [53] [2001] *RPC* 257.

[54] Ibid., [70]; cf. *Parker v. Tidball* [1997] *FSR* 680, 696 (claimant claimed design right in mobile phone cases; the judge excluded stitching in seams as a method of construction). Copinger, [13]–[55], sees the different results as attributable to the fact that, in *Fulton*, the seam was intended to produce a design feature, whereas in *Parker* the seam was an unintended result of a method of construction. Perhaps it would be easier simply to regard the remarks in *Parker* as *obiter*, the stitching not being shape or configuration.

[55] [2007] *FSR* 199.

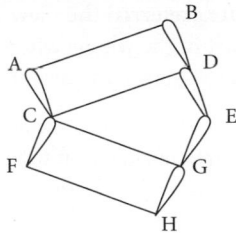

The 1cm Design, showing how it is made of the repeats;

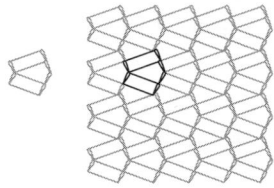

Fig. 30.3 Micromesh bags

Source: Bailey and anor v. Haines and ors [2006] *EWPCC* 5

to, or placed in, around or against, another article so that either article may perform its function'. This is known as the 'must fit' exclusion (although the courts have stressed that it is important to apply the statutory language, rather than the language of the epithet).[56] This exclusion (along with the 'must match' exclusion) is intended to minimize the significance of unregistered design right in the protection of spare parts (particularly for cars). It has been said that the exclusion should be interpreted 'purposively' and 'should not be given a breadth which would take it far beyond what it was intended to achieve'.[57] There are a number of notable aspects of the exclusion.

(i) *The article*   The first is that the exclusion specifies that designs are excluded to the extent that they enable an *article* to be connected (etc.) to another *article*. In this context, article has been interpreted very broadly as being synonymous with the word 'thing'.[58] Following from this, it has been held that 'article' not only includes machines and objects, but also includes the human body. Thus it has been held that the aspects of the shape of contact lenses that enable the lenses to fit the eyes of their users, or the aspects of the shape of a mobile telephone that enable it to fit the hand of a person holding the phone, fall outside the scope of unregistered design right.[59]

(ii) *Integrated parts*   Where two articles are joined together to make a single article, the 'must fit' exception not only applies to the parts as separate articles, but also to the interfaces that become elements of the integrated whole.[60] However, this view has the potential to produce odd results (apparently, for example, that there would be no unregistered design right in the wing of an aeroplane). Consequently, in *Baby Dan v. Brevi*,[61]

---

[56] See *Dyson v. Qualtex* [2006] *RPC* 769, [27].   [57] *Fulton v. Grant Barnett* [2001] *RPC* 257, [73].
[58] *Ocular Sciences v. Aspect Vision Care (No. 2)* [1997] *RPC* 289, 425.
[59] Ibid., 425–8; *Parker v. Tidball* [1997] *FSR* 680, 697; *Dyson v. Qualtex* [2006] *RPC* 769, [28]. For criticism, see L. Bently and A. Coulthard, 'From the Commonplace to the Interface: Five Cases on Unregistered Design Right' [1997] *EIPR* 401.
[60] *Electronic Techniques (Anglia) v. Critchley Components* [1997] *FSR* 401, 417–19.
[61] [1999] *FSR* 377, 382.

Judge David Young QC preferred the view that when units are assembled, unregistered design right may subsist in the whole; whereas when design right is asserted in the parts, protection is confined to parts of the design other than the 'must fit' features.

(iii) *No need for designer to have intention to fit* The 'must fit' exclusion operates where the shape of an article enables it to be attached or connected to another article. In assessing whether an article must fit another article, the designer's intention is irrelevant. This is because 'the subsection does not require that the designer should know that the features enable the interface, it is sufficient if they do so in fact'.[62]

(iv) *Closeness of fit* Features are only excluded as 'must fit' features if they 'enable' one article to fit with another article.[63] Perhaps the most important question is how closely shapes need to correspond to each other for the feature of one article to enable the articles to be connected.[64]

In *Amoena v. Trulife*,[65] Judge Sumption QC (now Lord Sumption) suggested that the provision should be read very narrowly. In particular, he said that the 'must fit' exclusion was 'concerned with a . . . precise correspondence between two articles, as with a rigid plug and socket, where the functional requirement that one article should fit in or against another displaces original design work'. Consequently, the design of breast prostheses was not excluded under the 'must fit' exception, because while the prostheses were shaped so that they fitted into bras, the shape of the bra would only *influence*, rather than *determine*, the details of the design; the prostheses were highly flexible and pliable, so that they would fit a number of different bras. However, other High Court decisions have taken a different approach, suggesting instead that features may fall within the 'must fit' exclusion even though other shapes might do equally well. For example, in *Ocular Sciences* Laddie J said:

> There is . . . nothing in the provision which requires the feature to be the only one which would achieve the proper interface. If a number of designs are possible each of which enables the two articles to be fitted together in a way which allowed one or other or both to perform its function, each falls within the statutory exclusion.[66]

Consequently, Laddie J held that the shape of the claimant's soft contact lenses was not protected because evidence showed that it enabled the lenses to fit onto the eyeball. This approach was approved by Judge Englehart QC in *Parker v. Tidball*,[67] where he held that features of mobile phone casings, which permitted use of the phone while inside the case, were excluded on the basis that they were 'must fit' features. This was despite the fact that

---

[62] *Ocular Sciences v. Aspect Vision Care (No. 2)* [1997] *RPC* 289, 424–8 (features of the claimants' lenses were excluded even though they were chosen without the fit requirement in mind).

[63] The term can be contrasted with three related notions: the notion in the 'must match' exclusion that the appearance of one article must be 'dependent' on that of another, and the two exclusions in the registered design arena of features 'dictated' by function, and features that 'must necessarily be reproduced in their exact form and dimensions' to enable functional connection to another product. See Chapter 26, section 3.1, pp. 751–4, and Chapter 30, section 2.2.4, pp. 819–21. Elements that enable parts to fit together to 'look nicer' are not within the exception: *Ultraframe v. Fielding* [2003] *RPC* 435, [80].

[64] For a discussion about whether parts need to touch and how this issue applies to the 'must fit' exemption, see *Dyson v. Qualtex* [2006] *RPC* 769, [37]–[38].

[65] C/72/95 (25 May 1995), Jonathan Sumption QC; *Fulton v. Grant Barnett* [2001] *RPC* 257, [75] (emphasizing importance of exactness, so that a rectangular umbrella case was not excluded because it had to accommodate a rectangular umbrella handle; 'any case of the same approximate dimensions would do that').

[66] *Ocular Sciences v. Aspect Vision Care (No. 2)* [1997] *RPC* 289, 424–8.   [67] [1997] *FSR* 680.

the function that the shape performed could have been achieved by a number of other designs.[68]

While the 'must fit' exclusion may apply where the 'article' that the design must fit is part of the human body, this does not mean that the 'exclusion must apply to every design which in some way fits the human body . . . such as a handle or seat'.[69] As with other designs, the key question is whether the design 'enables' one article to fit with another article. Thus, in a decision involving design right in a sling and a portable frame from which the sling could be hung for use during sexual activities involving bondage, the question arose whether the sling was excluded because of the 'must fit' exclusion. It was held that while the sling was designed to support a person's body, at most 'the user would lie on the sling or parts of it'.[70] This meant that none of the features of the sling were 'dictated by the need to fit the user', nor did they 'connect' with the user. As such, the design was not excluded by section 213(3)(b)(i).

(v) *Enabling an article to perform its function*   The 'must fit' exclusion only applies to features of shape or configuration that enable the article to be connected to, or placed in, around, or against, another article *so that either article may perform its function*. Applying this provision, the Court of Appeal in *Dyson* held that, insofar as holes in the handle of the wand of a vacuum cleaner (so-called 'bleed holes') enabled the handle to be placed against a flat surface (such as a stair carpet), the holes allowed the handle to perform its function as a vacuum-cleaner handle. As such, the bleed holes fell within the exception and thus were not protected.[71]

2.2.4 'Must match'

Section 213(3)(b)(ii) of the 1988 Act excludes from unregistered design right features of shape or configuration of an article that are dependent upon the appearance of another article of which the article is intended by the designer to form an integral part.[72] As with the 'must fit' exclusion, the idea behind this exclusion was to limit the protection afforded to spare parts, particularly for cars.

(i) *Appearance*   The 'must match' exclusion is only concerned with the *appearance* of objects. This is to be contrasted with the 'must fit' provision, which concerns the interconnection of parts so that either can perform their *function*. If we consider a classic example such as a car door, there will probably be both 'must fit' and 'must match' features: the 'must fit' features will enable the door to fit into the chassis and the handle to fit onto the door; the 'must match' features will relate to the general shape of the door, in particular any styling features that must match the rest of the car in order to be of an acceptable appearance.

(ii) *'Dependent' upon the appearance of another article*   The 'must match' exclusion only operates where designs are 'dependent' upon the appearance of another article. The fact that designs are aesthetically linked to (or dependent upon) the appearance of the article as a whole lies at the heart of the rationale for the 'must match' exclusion.

A part will be dependent and thus unprotected if it is *not* possible for it to be replaced with a different part without radically altering the appearance or identity of the vehicle

---

[68] Ibid., 694; cf. *Dyson v. Qualtex* [2006] *RPC* 769, [29], in which Jacob LJ said that 'the actual decision may be questionable'.   [69] *UWUG v. Derek Ball* [2013] *EWPCC* 35, [29].

[70] Ibid., [30].   [71] *Dyson v. Qualtex* [2006] *RPC* 769, [42]–[43].

[72] Prior to reform of the registered design system, the 'must match' exclusion also operated in this context: see Bently and Sherman (2001), 590–2.

as a whole. A Mercedes-Benz with a Volkswagen roof is no longer a Mercedes-Benz, but a cannibalized mismatch. Where the owner of a complete article is obliged to replace a worn, damaged, or missing component with an identical component to maintain the appearance of the article, the part will be dependent. Where a part is dependent, the maker of the spare part has to produce a part that looks exactly like the original or it is unable to be sold. The maker has no design freedom. Consequently, parts such as the main body panels, doors, bonnet lids, and so forth will probably be treated as being 'dependent' on the appearance of the car as a whole.[73]

In contrast, a part will be independent and therefore able to be protected, if it can be replaced by a part with a different shape and configuration in such a way that it does not alter the appearance of the article as a whole. If it is possible to substitute a part with another part with a different shape and configuration, while leaving the general shape and appearance of the vehicle unaffected, the part will not be dependent. One of the defining aspects of an independent part is that while it (necessarily) contributes to the appearance of the vehicle, it is *subsidiary* to the overall shape—that is, it can be replaced without 'radically altering' the appearance of the vehicle (or article) as a whole. As Jacob LJ said in *Dyson v. Qualtex*,[74] 'if there is, as a practical matter, design freedom for the part, then there is no dependency'.

For example, a steering wheel may be replaced with an alternative wheel of a sportier design while leaving the general appearance of the vehicle unchanged. Likewise, an owner might choose to substitute seats with more comfortable seats. Although the owner of a car might wish the component to blend in with the general style of the vehicle, such items would *not* be dependent on the appearance of another article. This reflects the goal of the 'must match' exclusion, which is to 'protect spare parts to the extent that they have features of shape and configuration which do not have to be copied in order to fit or to match aesthetically'.[75]

(iii) *'Dependence' does not require the other article to exist*   The 'must match' exclusion only prevents protection of those features of an article that must match those of another article. One shape can be dependent upon another article even though the latter may not yet exist. The provision requires the court to assume the existence of another article and decide whether the shape or configuration of the article depicted in the design is dependent on the appearance of the other article.[76]

(iv) *Defining the 'other' article*   Another notable aspect of the 'must match' exclusion is that design features are only excluded where they are dependent on the shape of 'another article'. This gives rise to the difficult question of what is meant by 'another article'—an issue that was discussed under the old law of registered designs in *In re Ford Motor Co. & Iveco Fiat SpA*.[77] In that case, it was agreed that there were basically two ways of construing the phrase in the context of a part for a car: 'another article' could mean the vehicle as a whole minus the part in question[78]—known as the 'n–1' approach; alternatively, 'another article' could mean the whole car including the part in question. While the

---

[73] See *In re Ford Motor Co. & Iveco Fiat SpA* [1993] RPC 399 (a pre-harmonization registered designs case). The question was not considered by the House of Lords: *R v. Registered Designs Appeal Tribunal, ex parte Ford* [1995] RPC 167. For unregistered design right cases, see *Fulton v. Grant Barnett* [2001] RPC 257, 279–80 (particular shape of umbrella case claimed held not dependent on shape of umbrella); *Ultraframe UK v. Fielding* [2003] RPC 435, [79] (parts of conservatory roof assembly system that gave 'consistent theme' were not 'dependent').   [74] [2006] RPC 769, [63].

[75] Lord Beaverbrook, Hansard (HL), 1 March 1988, Vol. 494, col. 110.

[76] *Valeo Vision SA v. Flexible Lamps* [1995] RPC 205 (a registered design case).   [77] [1993] RPC 399.

[78] Ibid., 411.

decision is not altogether clear (nor convincing in its reasoning), the Registered Design Appeal Tribunal ultimately favoured the latter approach.[79] On appeal, the High Court confirmed that in relation to spare parts, 'other article' meant the vehicle as a whole.[80]

(v) *Integral part*   The exclusion only operates where the features relate to an article that forms an 'integral part' of another article. A part is integral if it is essential to the overall design or look and feel of the article. As such, it excludes inessential parts (the extras), such as a toolkit or a car jack. Because most articles or parts of articles that are non-integral will also be independent, it seems that it adds little to the scope of the provision.

The provision is important, however, insofar as it helps to clarify that although a particular item may not stand alone, this does not necessarily mean therefore that the item forms part of another article. While articles such as cups and saucers, or knives and forks may fit together, this does not necessarily mean that they fall within the scope of the exclusion.[81] For example, while an article such as a cup might need to match a saucer, it is unlikely that the designer would have intended the cup to form an 'integral part' of the saucer.

In order for an article to be treated as an integral part of another article, the designed article in question must be subservient to the appearance of the other article. As such, where the articles play an equal part in the overall product, the design will not fall within the scope of the exclusion. This can be seen, for example, in relation to a unit in a range of kitchen cupboards, which was held not to be an article that formed an integral part of another article; instead, it was seen as one of a 'series of matching articles none of which forms an integral part of another'.[82]

2.3 ORIGINALITY

Unregistered design right only subsists in 'original' designs. A design is not 'original' if, at the time of its creation, it is 'commonplace in the design field in question'.[83] Deciding whether a design is original involves two stages. First, it is necessary to decide whether the design is original in the copyright sense—that is, in the sense that the design originated with the designer and was not slavishly copied from an existing design.[84] One question that has arisen is whether for the purpose of UK unregistered design law, the traditional British idea of copyright originality applies (which requires the author to have spent sufficient time, labour, and skill in the creation of the work), or whether the new test of originality as espoused by the Court of Justice applies (which talks of the work comprising the expression of the authors intellectual creation). To date, we have judicial opinion supporting both the traditional approach[85] and the newer approach of

---

[79] Ibid., 412, 420. The Registered Designs Tribunal no longer exists.

[80] In *Dyson v. Qualtex* [2005] *RPC* 395, [55], Mann J also rejected the 'n–1' approach stating that, as a matter of logic, if 'article 1 is intended by the designer to form an "integral part" of article 2, then article 2 must comprise article 1'.   [81] *In re Ford Motor Co. & Iveco Fiat SpA* [1993] *RPC* 399, 419.

[82] *Mark Wilkinson Furniture v. Woodcraft Designs (Radcliffe)* [1998] *FSR* 63, 73.

[83] CDPA 1988, s. 213(4). See generally, *Whitby Specialist Vehicles v. Yorkshire Specialist Vehicles* [2014] *EWHC* 4242, [44]–[45].

[84] *Farmers Build v. Carier Bulk Materials Handling* [1999] *RPC* 461, 481; *Fulton v. Grant Barnett* [2001] *RPC* 257, [42] (must have been consciously designed rather than arising accidentally); cf. *Guild v. Eskandar* [2003] *FSR* 413, [44]–[56] (recognizing that an accidental feature could contribute to originality of design because it was perpetuated on purpose, but holding in the circumstances that the design lacked originality).

[85] *Raft v. Freestyle of Newhaven* [2016] *EWHC* 1711 (IPEC), [43].

the Court of Justice.[86] While it has been suggested (probably correctly) that the difference between the two tests is largely semantic,[87] it is something that could benefit from clarification.

Second, if the tribunal is satisfied that the design is original, it is then necessary to determine if the design is 'commonplace in the field in question'. The concept of 'commonplace designs' is peculiar to this right. In *Farmers Build v. Carier Bulk Materials Handling*,[88] the Court of Appeal said that it would be wrong to attempt any further definition of what 'commonplace' meant; rather, the Court preferred to look at the term in light of its legislative history and purpose. Given that unregistered design right is intended to protect functional designs, only provide relatively weak protection, and include safeguards excluding the protection of spare parts, Mummery LJ concluded that it would be wrong to interpret 'commonplaceness' broadly. Instead, he said that its purpose was 'to guard against situations in which even short-term protection for functional designs would create practical difficulties'.[89] Consequently, once it is shown that the design was not copied, all that is required is that the design must be different in some respects from other designs, so that it can be fairly and reasonably described as 'not commonplace'. This second inquiry itself has three stages.

(i) *Design field*   The first stage is to decide what is the design field. This is an important stage of the inquiry because the broader the design field, the more likely it is that a particular design will be held to be commonplace. One of the questions that has arisen in this context relates to the geographical scope of the design field. In particular, there has been uncertainty as whether the design field is limited to the United Kingdom, the European Union, or a wider area. In order to resolve this uncertainty, the Intellectual Property Act 2014 amended section 231(4) of the 1988 Act to specify the relevant geographic area. Specifically, the revised definition provides that 'a design is not "original" . . . if it is commonplace in a qualifying country in the design field in question: and qualifying country has the meaning given in section 217(3)'.[90]

It has been suggested that the courts should adopt a reasonably broad approach when deciding what the appropriate design field is.[91] What matters is the type of design with which 'a notional designer of the article concerned would be familiar'.[92] A similar approach was adopted by the Court of Appeal in *Scholes Windows v. Magnet*.[93] In this case, the defendant argued that the claimant's design for decoratively shaped window

[86] In *Whitby*, Arnold J. assumed 'without deciding' that the approach at the CJEU (see, e.g., *Football Association Premier League v. QC Leisure*, Case C-145/10 [2011] *ECR* I–9083, which requires creativity on the part of the designer) was the correct approach: *Whitby Specialist Vehicles v. Yorkshire Specialist Vehicles* [2014] *EWHC* 4242, [43].

[87] *Newspaper Licensing Agency v. World Programming* [2013] *EWCA Civ* 1482, [36]–[37]; *Action Storage Systems v. G-Force Europe* [2016] *EWHC* 3151, [22]; cf. *SAS Institute v. World Programming* [2013] *EWCA Civ* 1482 (CJEU approach may impose a higher standard).

[88] [1999] *RPC* 461, 479; *Dyson v. Qualtex* [2006] *RPC* 769, [98] ('a far from easy concept').

[89] *Farmers Build v. Carier Bulk Materials Handling* [1999] *RPC* 461, 481; *Scholes Windows v. Magnet* [2000] *FSR* 432, 443; *Fulton v. Grant Barnett* [2001] *RPC* 257, [50] (commonplace to be interpreted narrowly rather than widely).

[90] IP Act 2014, s. 1(3) (only for unregistered designs created after the commencement of the section).

[91] *Lambretta Clothing Co. Ltd v. Teddy Smith (UK)* [2005] *RPC* 88, [45].

[92] Ibid., [30]. This is similar to the reading that is given to 'design field in question' in the Semiconductor Products Directive (which is where the phrase was taken from): ibid., [46].

[93] [2002] *ECDR* 196. See also *Ultraframe (UK) v. Eurocell Building Plastics* [2005] *RPC* 894, [54] *ff* (what matters is the kind of material that would be well known to designers of articles of the type in question).

frames made in unplasticated PVC was commonplace. The defendant said that the assessment of whether a design was commonplace should be made by considering traditional window designs for wooden frames. The claimant disputed this, arguing that the design field was for 'PVC window designs'. The Court of Appeal rejected that view. It said that while the words 'design field' bear their 'ordinary and natural meaning', the bounds of which are issues 'of fact and degree', the definition of 'design' in this context relates to shape and configuration, rather than materials or the nature and purpose of the article. Consequently the design field is not to be defined by reference to limitations of this sort. In the case in hand, therefore, the design field was that of window frames generally.[94]

(ii) *Design of other articles in the field*   The second stage of the inquiry requires the court to examine the design of other articles in the same field, including any allegedly infringing articles. When considering this issue, it is important to bear in mind that a design that is commonplace in a design field will 'be ready to hand', rather than something that 'has to be hunted for and found at the last minute'.[95] The Court of Appeal in *Scholes* emphasized that the courts should be concerned with those designs in the field at the time when the design issue was created.[96] This may include old designs, even if they are no longer available for purchase, if such designs were still available to be viewed by designers and interested members of the public. Consequently, the claimant's design in *Scholes* was considered in light of the continued presence of Victorian sash windows in the built environment in 1994 (the date when the claimant's design was created).[97] Other decisions have suggested that the issue of 'commonplaceness' is concerned primarily, and possibly exclusively, with designs that were available in the United Kingdom. As a result, designs only available in foreign countries or are in other ways 'obscure' are unlikely to be taken into account.[98]

(iii) *Similarity of the designs*   Finally, the court should examine the design in question to determine how similar it is to designs in the same field.[99] The closer the similarities, the more likely it is that the design will be commonplace.[100] This is because if different designers have independently come up with similar designs, but each is given protection,

---

[94] In a case concerning designs of kitchen cabinets, the court held that the design field was 'fitted kitchen furniture' rather than 'cabinetry generally', because kitchen furniture was 'a discrete design field, with its own particular problems and characteristics': *Mark Wilkinson Furniture v. Woodcraft Designs (Radcliffe)* [1998] FSR 63, 74. Presumably, *L. Woolley Jewellers v. A & A Jewellery* [2003] FSR 255 (treating design field as '*coin-mounted* jewellery design') and *Spraymiser & Snell v. Wrightway Marketing* [2000] ECDR 349, 363 (defining field as 'the design of *wooden configurable* figures of the human form') defined the field too narrowly.   [95] *Ultraframe (UK) v. Eurocell Building Plastics* [2005] RPC 894.

[96] *Scholes Windows v. Magnet* [2000] FSR 432, esp. [45].

[97] Old designs will not necessarily remain present in the field—whereas sash windows have a long life, umbrellas break and are quickly thrown away: *Fulton v. Totes Isotoner (UK)* [2003] RPC 499, [83].

[98] *Fulton v. Grant Barnett* [2001] RPC 257, [52] (an obscure piece of prior art does not render commonplace); *Fulton v. Totes Isotoner (UK)* [2003] RPC 499, [73], [78] (Judge Michael Fysh QC) (Australian and Japanese examples irrelevant; this is not a novelty inquiry); upheld on appeal: *A. Fulton v. Totes Isotoner* [2004] RPC (16) 301 (CA). But cf. *Guild v. Eskandar Ltd* [2001] FSR 645 (design field described as 'global one of ladies' luxury fashion' as opposed to the 'sensual/philosopher' market proposed by the defendant); *Spraymiser & Snell v. Wrightway Marketing* [2000] ECDR 349, 364 (comparison with US design).

[99] The court usually looks at the designs through the eyes of the customer: *Fulton v. Totes Isotoner* [2003] RPC 499, 509; *Scholes Windows v. Magnet* [2002] ECDR 196, [49]–[50] (expressly rejecting suggestion that comparison should be from the point of view of a designer who is an expert in the field).

[100] Although where similarities that existed between a design and one already in the field were a result of the fact that both designs were modelled on the human form, the court held the later design not to be commonplace, because of differences in the detail of the features: *Spraymiser & Snell v. Wrightway Marketing* [2000] ECDR 349.

practical difficulties of proof of copying and enforcement arise. These are precisely the difficulties that the requirement that the design not be commonplace was meant to avoid. If, however, there are aspects of the claimant's design that are not found in the field in question, the design is probably not commonplace.[101]

'Commonplaceness' is a question of fact on which little further guidance can be provided. However, three observations are worth making. The first relates to the question of whether a collection of commonplace designs can give rise to design that is protected. In what has been described as the legal form of *Gestalt*—in which the whole is more than the sum of its individual parts—it has been held that unregistered design right can exist in 'an assembly of individual commonplace parts'.[102] The second is that the test for whether a design is commonplace seems to operate more harshly against decorative designs than against functional ones. This is because in the case of decorative designs, there is likely to be a larger reservoir of existing designs in the field. This can be seen by comparing *Farmers Build* with the *Scholes Windows* case. In *Farmers Build*,[103] the Court of Appeal held various components of the slurry separator (such as the hopper design), as well as the combination of elements, to be original and protected. In part, this was because slurry separators were relatively new machines and there were not many comparators. Consequently, the (albeit visually unexceptional) functional differences between some of the claimant's parts and those of comparators meant that the claimant's design was not commonplace. In *Scholes Windows*,[104] however, the claimant's design was in the crowded field of window frame design where the requirement that the design should not be commonplace posed more of a hurdle. The design—a design of a PVC window frame that was intended to evoke a traditional Victorian sash window—was held to be similar to existing window designs and not to be sufficiently different to lift it out of the ordinary run of such designs.[105] The third is that following the 2014 removal of 'any aspect of' from the definition of design in section 213(2) (discussed earlier), it is now harder for a defendant to prove that a design is commonplace.[106]

2.4 QUALIFICATION

Unregistered design right is only available in a design that meets one of the following criteria:[107]

(i)   the designer is a 'qualifying person'—namely, a citizen or subject of, or an individual habitually resident in, a 'qualifying country' (the United Kingdom, the European Union, a country to which the relevant Part of the 1988 Act 'extends', or a 'designated country');

---

[101] For a discussion of the fate of well-known designs in this context, see *Dyson v. Qualtex* [2006] *RPC* 769, [100] *ff*.   [102] *Ultraframe v. Eurocell Building Plastics* [2005] *RPC* 864 (CA), [64]–[66].

[103] [1999] *RPC* 461, 484.   [104] [2000] *FSR* 432; aff'd on appeal [2002] *ECDR* 196, [45].

[105] *Scholes Windows v. Magnet* [2000] *FSR* 432, 442. See also *Sales v. Stromberg* [2006] *FSR* 89, [58] (design of decorative pendants, although simple geometric shapes common in rock art and 'native American culture', was original and not commonplace in field of complementary medical devices, including ones that were ornamental and decorative devices).

[106] *Neptune v. Devol Kitchens* [2017] *EWHC* 2172 (Pat), [60]; *Whitby Specialist Vehicles v. Yorkshire Specialist Vehicles* [2014] *EWHC* 4242, [45].

[107] CDPA 1988, s. 218. However, if the design was created in pursuance of a commission or in the course of employment, then it must qualify by that route or by first marketing.

(ii) the designer has been commissioned by or is employed by a 'qualifying person';[108] or

(iii) the design has been first marketed by a 'qualifying person' in the United Kingdom, the European Union, or a country to which the Part 'extends'.[109]

Because of the limited scope of these provisions, many foreign designs will not qualify for protection in the United Kingdom.[110]

One of the goals of the Intellectual Property Act 2014 was to overcome some of these shortfalls by simplifying the existing provisions. For designs created after the commencement of the relevant sections, the new Act relaxes the qualification requirement to anyone of *any* nationality, provided that either:

(i) the designer is habitually resident in a qualifying country (the European Union and other nominated countries); or

(ii) the organization or person who employed the designer to create the design was either 'formed under the law of the UK or another qualifying country', or has a place of business in a qualifying country at which 'substantial business activity is carried on'.[111]

3 OWNERSHIP

Unregistered design right initially vests in the designer (subject to two exceptions).[112] The designer is the person who creates the design.[113] The case law has yet to develop, although it seems that neither a person who provides an idea for a product,[114] nor a person who merely executes instructions, will be regarded as a creator.[115] As with copyright, it seems that the creator is the person who gives the expressive form—the shape and configuration—to the design.[116]

There are two exceptions to the general principle of first ownership. The first relates to designs created in the course of employment—which are owned by the employer.[117] Prior to the enactment of the Intellectual Property Act 2014, all designs created in pursuance of

---

[108] CDPA 1988, s. 219. A design that was commissioned or made in the course of employment cannot qualify via the s. 218 route (designer a 'qualifying individual').

[109] CDPA 1988, s. 255, allows for orders 'extending' the Part of the Act to the Channel Islands, the Isle of Man, or any colony, while s. 256 allows for orders to be made 'designating' countries as enjoying reciprocal protection. See Design Right (Reciprocal Protection) (No. 2) Order 1989 (SI 1989/1294) (designating countries such as Anguilla, Bermuda, Hong Kong, and New Zealand).

[110] *Mackie Designs v. Behringer Specialised Studio Equipment (UK)* [1999] *RPC* 717, 724.

[111] IP Act 2014, s. 3, amending CDPA 1988, ss 217(1)(4), 218(2),(4), 219, and 220 (only for designs created after the commencement of s. 3).   [112] CDPA 1988, s. 215(1).

[113] CDPA 1988, s. 214.

[114] *Spraymiser & Snell v. Wrightway Marketing* [2000] *ECDR* 349 (person who provided the idea of an articulated, reconfigurable, wooden figure that could be put to various uses, e.g. a magazine rack or plant stand, was not the designer).

[115] *Fulton v. Grant Barnett* [2001] *FSR* 257 (mould makers or stitchers working pursuant to instructions held not to be designers).

[116] *Spraymiser & Snell v. Wrightway Marketing* [2000] *ECDR* 349 (the designer was the person who developed the wooden figure—albeit with the assistance of a person who was commissioned to help him—and who knew precisely how he wanted the figure to look).

[117] CDPA 1988, s. 215(3). See *Ultraframe UK v. Fielding* [2004] *RPC* (24) 479 (CA) (managing director not employee, or commissioned, but held unregistered design right on trust for company under fiduciary principles); *Fulton v. Grant Barnett* [2001] *RPC* 257, 281 (director of the claimant company was held to be an employee).

a commission were owned by the commissioner.[118] In order to bring UK law into line with EU design law, the 2014 Act removes the exception in relation to commissioned works, so that commissioned designs are now owned by the designer. It should be noted that the 2014 Act does not apply where (i) the designs was created before its coming into force, or (ii) where the commissioning contract was entered into before the Act came into force.[119] In these limited situations, the old law will still apply: the commissioner will be the owner of the design. In all other cases, designs created in pursuance of a commission will be initially owned by the designer. As such, the designer will always be the first owner of any design right in a design, unless it is created in the course of employment.[120] Hopefully, these changes will overcome the problem that arose from the fact that the old rules on ownership of commissioned designs were different from those in copyright law. This created an unfortunate situation where the copyright in design drawings was able to vest in one person (the designer), whereas unregistered design right in the design embodied therein was able to vest in another (the commissioner).[121]

4 DURATION

Unregistered design right lasts for 15 years from creation,[122] or if the design was 'made available' within five years of creation, ten years from the date of such marketing.[123] The maximum period of protection is therefore 15 years. The dual system of protection means that designers have a reasonable period in which to interest manufacturers or purchasers before they market the design.[124] The right is subject to licences of right 'in the last five years of the design right term'.[125]

5 INFRINGEMENT

5.1 RIGHTS

The owner of unregistered design right has the exclusive right to reproduce the design for commercial purposes, among other things by making articles to that

---

[118] CDPA 1988, ss 215(2), 263 (amended by IP Act 2014, s. 2). See *Spraymiser & Snell v. Wrightway Marketing* [2000] *ECDR* 349, 365 (where a person did not charge to create a prototype in the hope of being remunerated from the process of mass production, the design was nevertheless made for money's worth).

[119] IP Act 2014, s. 2(3).

[120] IP Act 2014, s. 2(1), amending CDPA 1988, s. 215(1) and (3), and deleting s. 215(2). IP Act 2014, s. 2(2), makes consequential changes to CDPA 1988, ss 213(5)(a), 218, 219(1)–(3), 220, and 263–4.

[121] *APPS v. Weldtite Products* [2001] *FSR* 703, [97].

[122] More specifically, from the end of the year in which the design was 'first recorded in a design document, or an article was first made to the design, whichever first occurred'.

[123] CDPA 1988, s. 216(1). See *Dyson v. Qualtex* [2006] *RPC* 769 (CA), 802–3 (Jacob LJ complaining that 'the provision is not well-thought out', but affirming Mann J's view that something can be made available only if it exists, so that advanced orders would not necessarily suffice). Making available for sale, on any scale, was relevant for the section to apply; there was no need to show that a particular level of sales for term to begin: *Victor Ifejika v. Charles Ifejika and Lens Care* [2011] *EWPCC* 31, [128].

[124] Fellner, [3.046]–[3.053].

[125] CDPA 1988, s. 237. For an application of the licence of right and some of the complications that arise, see *NIC Instruments Licence of Right (Design Right) Application* [2005] *RPC* 1; *Penny Hydraulics v. Reid Lifting*, O/101/11 (11 March 2011). This has potential ramifications for assessing damages: see CDPA 1988, s. 239. On this, see Neuberger LJ in *Ultraframe v. Eurocell* [2005] *RPC* 894 (CA), [103] *ff.*

design.[126] Reproduction of a design by making articles to that design is defined to mean 'copying the design so as to produce articles exactly or substantially to that design',[127] or making a design document recording the design for the purpose of enabling such articles to be made. The owner of unregistered design right also has an 'authorization right'—that is, a right to authorize someone else to do any of the acts.[128] Since this is likely to be treated in the same way as the concept of 'authorization' in copyright law, the reader is referred back to Chapter 6. One of the consequences of the 2014 removal of 'any aspect of' from the definition of design in section 213(2) (discussed earlier), is that in specifying what their design is, claimants are now more closely tied to the physical manifestation in the article. As a result, it is now harder to prove infringement.[129]

The owner of unregistered design right can also object to various acts of secondary infringement. These concern commercial dealings with infringing articles: importing infringing articles into the United Kingdom; possessing such articles for commercial purposes; selling the articles; and exposing them for sale. These will often be of great importance because the primary act will frequently take place abroad (where labour and material costs are lower). As with secondary infringement of copyright, there is a *mens rea* requirement—namely, that the alleged infringer 'knows or has reason to believe' that the article is infringing.[130] The concept of 'reason to believe' has been interpreted in the same way as the equivalent copyright provisions,[131] and thus the reader is referred back to Chapter 8 for further analysis.

Once it is clear that the defendant's activities fall within the scope of the protected rights, it is necessary to show that there has been 'substantive' infringement. The three key elements of substantive infringement are (i) derivation, (ii) so as to produce articles, (iii) which are substantially similar in design.

5.2 DERIVATION

In order for a UK unregistered design right to be infringed, it must be copied. As a result, to show infringement it is necessary to demonstrate a causal connection between the two designs. It is not enough to show that the designs are similar. In some cases, this will be unproblematic: there will be direct proof of copying. Often, this will occur where the alleged infringer was supplied by the claimant of design right, but decided (for whatever reason) to start manufacturing similar designs.[132] Occasionally, there will be evidence that the defendant's designer used the claimant's design as 'inspiration'.[133] However, in

---

[126] CDPA 1988, s. 226(1).   [127] CDPA 1988, s. 226(2).   [128] CDPA 1988, s. 226(3).

[129] *Neptune v. Devol Kitchens* [2017] *EWHC* 2172 (Pat), [60]; *Whitby Specialist Vehicles v. Yorkshire Specialist Vehicles* [2014] *EWHC* 4242, [45].

[130] CDPA 1988, s. 233(2), limits the damages in a situation in which the defendant acquired the infringing goods innocently. The test of innocent acquisition, as defined in s. 233(3), was said to be 'an objective test': *Badge Sales v. PMS International Group Ltd* [2006] *FSR* 1, [8].

[131] *Baby Dan SA v. Brevi* [1999] *FSR* 377, 392; *Fulton v. Grant Barnett* [2001] *RPC* 257 (knowledge of the existence of a registered design); *Fulton v. Totes Isotoner* [2003] *RPC* 499, 530–1 (inference of knowledge based on knowledge of Fulton's action against Barnett in separate litigation).

[132] *Baby Dan SA v. Brevi* [1999] *FSR* 377, 387 (the defendant's design retained certain functional features of the claimant's design, even though in the defendant's design these features were not necessary to achieve the function); *Parker v. Tidball* [1997] *FSR* 680; *Farmers Build v. Carier Bulk Materials Handling* [1999] *RPC* 461, 466.

[133] It has been suggested that similar fact evidence, i.e. evidence of a defendant having mimicked a claimant's products a number of times in the past, may be of some use in deciding infringement (although the court stressed that such evidence would be of only minor probative value and would require wide-ranging investigations): *Mattel Inc v. Woodbro (Distributors)* [2004] *FSR* 12, [14], [21]–[22].

many cases, there will be no direct proof of derivation, and proof of copying will depend on proving 'access' and 'similarity'.[134] Often, the court will compare the designs and ask: do the similarities between the designs 'call for an explanation'?[135] The mere fact that designs are the same does not necessarily mean that the design has been copied: in the field of functional design, substantial similarity may be an inevitable consequence of the functional nature of the design and not a result of copying.[136]

The way in which the courts determine whether a design has been copied can be seen in *Amoena v. Trulife*,[137] where the defendant began to market PVC breast prostheses similar to ones that the claimant had been selling during the previous year. Judge Jonathan Sumption QC dismissed Amoena's allegation of infringement of unregistered design right on the ground that it had failed to prove that Trulife had copied the design. Although the defendant would have had access to the claimant's product and had produced a similar product comparatively swiftly, Judge Sumption said that he was unable to infer copying merely from the fact that the form of the designs was the same. The reason for this was that a number of design constraints limited the range of possible forms that the design could take. As such, it was reasonable to conclude that the similarity could be explained on grounds other than copying. In designing breast prostheses, a designer needed to emulate the appearance of a breast in a bra, take into account the shape and size of scarring left by a mastectomy, as well as consider surgical practices. The judge concluded that 'designers pursuing similar objectives determined by bra design, surgical practice and stocking requirements are quite likely to arrive at designs which have a great deal in common'. While such similarities might have been the result of copying coupled with the deliberate introduction of differences, the two designs were not so similar that this was the only explanation—or even the most inherently probable. The degree of similarity was capable of being explained on the basis that two designers had independently sought to achieve the result suggested to them by the design of the bra and the location of the scars produced by current surgical methods.

5.3 COPIED SO AS TO PRODUCE THE SAME 'ARTICLES'

In order to infringe unregistered design right, it is necessary to show that the defendant copied the design so as to produce *articles* exactly or substantially similar to the protected design. Two questions arise in relation to this requirement. First, is there infringement where a defendant uses the design on different articles? Second, in the case of designs for parts of articles, is the comparison to be made between the parts themselves or between the part claimed and the whole of the defendant's alleged infringement?

5.3.1 Application to different articles

As with UK registered designs, Community registered designs, and unregistered Community designs,[138] it seems that a UK unregistered design right will be infringed where a substantially similar design is used on other articles. In *Electronic Techniques v. Critchley Components*,[139] Laddie J said that since unregistered design right is 'presumably

---

[134] *Farmers Build v. Carier Bulk Materials Handling* [1999] *RPC* 461, 481. Compare *Fulton v. Grant Barnett* [2001] *RPC* 257 (inference of copying by manufacturer in Taiwan drawn from multiplicity of similarities), with *Guild v. Eskandar* [2003] *FSR* 23 (no copying proven).

[135] *Albert Packaging Ltd and ors v. Nampak Cartons & Healthcare Ltd* [2011] *EWPCC* 15 (PCC), [153].

[136] *Virgin Atlantic v. Premium* [2009] *EWHC* 26 (Pat), [35], citing *Farmers Build* [1999] *RPC* 461.

[137] C/72/95 (25 May 1995, unreported), Jonathan Sumption QC.

[138] See Chapter 28, section 4, pp. 783–5.   [139] [1997] *FSR* 401, 418.

intended to reward and encourage design effort, it seems unlikely that the effort should only be protected and rewarded if the infringer happens to use the design on precisely the same type of article'. However, Laddie J added an important qualification to the general proposition that unregistered design right is infringed by use of the design on other articles. He said that this did not mean that the nature of the defendant's article was irrelevant:

> It may be that a design applied to certain articles has a different impact to the same design applied to other articles. In such cases it may well be that the design, in the context of other features of shape and configuration of the article itself, may be viewed differently to the same or a similar design in a different context.[140]

5.3.2 The test with partial designs

The fact that the definition of infringement refers to the use of the claimant's design in relation to articles rather than to parts of articles has posed particular problems where the claimant's design is for part of an article. This is because although design right subsists in 'the design of any aspect of the shape or configuration . . . of the whole or part of any article', infringement occurs where the defendant is shown to have copied 'the design so as to produce *articles* exactly or substantially to that design'. The statutory provisions are thus inconsistent. The 'linguistic mismatch between the subsistence of design right and the right it confers' was considered in *Virgin Atlantic v. Premium*,[141] where it was said that:

> [It] must obviously have been Parliament's intention that if design right subsisted in part of an article (e.g. the teapot spout) the right would be infringed by incorporating a copy of that spout in another teapot, even if the infringing spout is not itself a whole article.[142]

This seems to be a sensible way of resolving the drafting problems in the 1988 Act.

5.4 SUBSTANTIAL SIMILARITY

In order to infringe a UK unregistered design right, it must be shown that the defendant copied the design so as to produce articles that are exactly the same as or *substantially similar* to the claimant's design.[143] This is a somewhat different test from that for copyright infringement, where (as we saw in Chapter 8) the focus is on whether the defendant has reproduced a 'substantial part' of the claimant's work.[144] In the case of designs, we are concerned with overall similarity, not only appropriation of part of an article.[145] It is important to recall that what is protected from copying in design right cases is the design, meaning the physical manifestation of the design; it is not some underlying physical abstraction or idea.[146]

In cases where the design is for the appearance of an article, the question of whether the designs are the same is determined through the eyes of the relevant customer.[147]

---

[140] Ibid. See Chapter 28, section 4, p. 783.   [141] [2009] *EWHC* 26 (Pat).

[142] Ibid., [31]. See also *Dyson v. Qualtex* [2006] *RPC* 769, [113]–[114] (seeming to suggest the comparison is of relevant parts); cf. *Parker v. Tidball* [1997] *FSR* 680, 691.   [143] CDPA 1988, s. 226(2).

[144] *Neptune v. Devol Kitchens* [2017] *EWHC* 2172 (Pat), [53] (it is not an infringement of a UK unregistered design to reproduce a substantial part of a design).

[145] *L. Woolley Jewellers v. A & A Jewellery* [2003] *FSR* 255, 261.

[146] *Rolawn v. Turfmech Machinery* [2008] *EWHC* 989, [81].

[147] *Mark Wilkinson Furniture v. Woodcraft Designs (Radcliffe)* [1998] *FSR* 63, 75; *Fulton v. Totes Isotoner* [2003] *RPC* 499, 528.

Substantial similarity is a matter of overall impression and, as such, the courts often find it difficult to explain why they reached a particular conclusion.[148] In one case, it was suggested that the question is whether a consumer looking at the two designs side-by-side would say that they are made to substantially the same design.[149] However, a visual test is inappropriate where the design features lie in details that cannot be seen by the eye. It will be recalled that in *Ocular Sciences*, Laddie J accepted the claimant's argument that each of its lenses, although only differing from its neighbour's in fine dimensional details, might constitute a separate design.[150] Indeed, Laddie J observed that the designs were protectable despite the fact that a member of the public would not be able to distinguish the design of one lens in a particular range from another in the same range by mere visual inspection. If protection is to be meaningful, the question of whether the articles copied were exactly or substantially the same as the protected design should not simply be a question of visual similarity.

A visual test is also inappropriate where the features of shape or configuration protected by unregistered design right are functional.[151] In these circumstances, the question should be whether the defendant's design embodies a form that is similar (taking into account the way in which the form operates to achieve the function). Although it was not necessary to decide the point, this was the approach taken by Pumfrey J in his discussion in *Mackie Designs* of what would amount to infringement of the unregistered design right in a circuit board.[152] The question of similarity would not be one of visual comparison of the shapes and colours from the point of view of someone unversed in electronics but a comparison through the eyes of someone versed in electronics, and interested in the functioning of the circuit, of the units, their order, and interconnections.

6 DEFENCES: THE RELATIONSHIP BETWEEN THE UNREGISTERED DESIGN RIGHT AND COPYRIGHT

When the unregistered design was introduced, the key defence available was the special defence in relation to overlap with copyright. This was found in section 236 of the CDPA 1988, which states that 'it is not an infringement of design right in the design to do anything which is an infringement of copyright in that work'.[153] Consequently, to the extent that there is dual protection, copyright pre-empts unregistered design right. However, as we have seen, section 51 severely limits the impact of copyright protection in this area. This is because where copyright and unregistered design right both exist, section 51 provides a defence so that making an article to the design does not infringe copyright, but might nevertheless still infringe unregistered design right. An exhaust pipe produced indirectly from design drawings would not infringe copyright in those drawings; it would, however, infringe unregistered design right as regards those features of the exhaust pipe that are not excluded as 'must fit' or 'must match' features.[154]

---

[148] *Ultraframe UK v. Fielding* [2003] *RPC* 435, [85].

[149] *Fulton v. Grant Barnett* [2001] *RPC* 257, 283.

[150] *Ocular Sciences v. Aspect Vision Care (No. 2)* [1997] *RPC* 289.

[151] Cf. *C. & H. Engineering v. Klucznik* [1992] *FSR* 421, 428 (applying visual test to functional design).

[152] *Mackie Designs v. Behringer Specialised Studio Equipment (UK)* [1999] *RPC* 717, 723; *Mark Wilkinson Furniture v. Woodcraft Designs (Radcliffe)* [1988] *FSR* 63.   [153] CDPA 1988, s. 236.

[154] However, where a design comprises surface decoration as well as configuration, the division of the creative elements amongst two forms of protection may have undesirable effects: *Jo Y Jo v. Matalan* [2000] *ECDR* 178, 200.

The Intellectual Property Act 2014 introduced a number of new exceptions for infringement of unregistered design right.[155] A new section 244A of the 1988 Act provides that:

Design right is not infringed by—
(a) an act which is done privately and for purposes which are not commercial;
(b) an act which is done for experimental purposes; or
(c) an act of reproduction for teaching purposes or for the purpose of making citations provided that—

  (i) the act of reproduction is compatible with fair trade practice and does not unduly prejudice the normal exploitation of the design, and
  (ii) mention is made of the source.

A new section 244B also creates exceptions for acts carried out in overseas ships and aircraft. Because these new exceptions are based on the exceptions for registered designs, readers should refer to Chapter 28.

7 SYNTHESIS

The legal protection of designs is a complicated matter. As a result, it may be helpful to conclude with some simple examples.

Example 1   *A has designed a double-barrelled syringe, which he marketed. It is registered as a design in the United Kingdom and at EUIPO. A similar syringe has subsequently appeared on the UK market, where it is being sold by X.*

First, we should consider the validity of A's national or registered Community designs. Both regimes afford protection to the 'appearance of . . . a product'.[156] One question will be whether the features are 'solely dictated by its technical function'.[157] Parts of the handle might be excluded as 'mechanical interconnections'[158]—where an exact fit is required with the plunger. A more difficult hurdle will be whether the design is new and has individual character.[159]

On the assumption that the registrations are valid, we would need to decide whether X infringes. X is using a design by selling articles bearing it.[160] There is no need to prove that the design was copied. The critical issue will be whether X's design produces a different overall impression on an informed user. If it does, there is no infringement.[161]

If A can prove copying, he will also be able to rely on unregistered Community design at least for the period of three years from the date on which the design was made available.[162]

A will not be able to rely on copyright. The syringe is not itself an artistic work.[163] The drawings, if any exist, are designs for something 'other than an artistic work'. It is not an infringement to make articles to the design or copy articles made to the design.[164]

A may be able, however, to rely on a UK unregistered design right. This protection would arise automatically as regards features of shape and configuration.[165] Surface decoration (such as the measure) would not be protected. Parts of the handle might be excluded on

---

[155] IP Act 2014, s. 4.   [156] Designs Dir., Art. 1(a); CDR, Art. 3(a); RDA 1949, s. 1(2).
[157] Designs Dir., Art. 7; RDA 1949, s. 1C(1); CDR, Art. 8.   [158] Designs Dir., Art. 7(2).
[159] Designs Dir., Art. 3(2); RDA 1949, s. 1B; CDR, Art. 4.
[160] Designs Dir., Art. 12; RDA 1949, s. 7(1); CDR, Art. 19.
[161] Designs Dir., Art. 9; RDA 1949, s. 7; CDR, Art. 10.   [162] CDR, Art. 11.
[163] CDPA 1988, s. 4. It is not a sculpture: *Metix v. Maughan* [1997] *FSR* 718.   [164] CDPA 1988, s. 51.
[165] CDPA 1988, s. 213.

the grounds that it must fit both the syringe barrel and, possibly, the hand of the user.[166] If the shape is 'not commonplace', it may be protected.[167] (It is conceivable that the syringe might lack 'individual character' and yet be not commonplace.) Assuming that the syringe is protected, A will need to prove X is dealing in 'infringing articles'—that is, articles made without A's permission, by copying A's design (directly or indirectly), and which are articles made substantially to the design.[168] Whether the articles are 'substantially to [the] design' is a matter of impression and only in a few cases would the result differ from that based on the registered design. A will also need to prove that X is either a primary infringer, or knows or has reason to believe the articles are infringing articles. The defence in section 236 will not apply, because making articles to the design is not an infringement of copyright.

Example 2   *B has designed a steering wheel for a new car and has retained her preliminary drawings. The steering wheel is of a conventional circular design and characterized by having four radiating spokes in the shape of a 'CND' sign. B is about to commence production.*

B may be able to obtain a UK registered design or a registered Community design for the shape of the steering wheel. The design relates to the appearance of a product, which includes 'parts intended to be assembled into complex products'.[169] The main question will be whether the design is new and has individual character. For parts to be used in complex products, the European Union-based regimes require the part to be visible in use—which should not be a problem for steering wheels.[170] The fact that the design is known as a 'CND' symbol might be thought to raise issues of novelty. However, the design of the symbol is two-dimensional, whereas the three-dimensional version is different—it will have spatial presence, texture, and weight. The design would almost certainly produce, on an informed user, a different impression to, say, a CND sticker. However, a registration might be declared invalid as an infringement of copyright.[171] Pending an application for registration, B benefits from the grace period for 12 months, and if she chooses not to register, from the unregistered Community design right for three years from making the design available.

B will be able to rely on copyright in any design drawings. However, such copyright will not enable her to prevent anybody from replicating the steering wheel.[172]

B will be able to rely on the UK unregistered design right insofar as the steering wheel is a shape, which is original and not commonplace. Unregistered design right will not protect 'must fit' nor 'must match' features.

Example 3   *C has developed a design for a door handle shaped like an eagle's head. C has original drawings and preliminary clay models.*

C could register the design at a national or EU level, and will also have protection automatically (for three years from making available the design) by virtue of the unregistered Community design right. There may be issues as to whether the door handle is new and has individual character.

C could rely on copyright protection in the drawings and the clay model, if the latter were treated as a 'model for the purposes of sculpture'.[173] The mass-produced version of the handle is unlikely to be treated as a sculpture.[174] It could nevertheless be a work of

---

[166] CDPA 1988, s. 213(3)(b)(i); *Ocular Sciences v. Aspect Vision Care (No. 2)* [1997] *RPC* 289.
[167] CDPA 1988, s. 213(4).   [168] CDPA 1988, ss 228 (defining infringing article), 226.
[169] Designs Dir., Art. 1(b); RDA 1949, s. 1(3); CDR, Art. 3(c).
[170] Designs Dir., Art. 3(3); CDR, Art. 4(2); RDA 1949, s. 1B(8).
[171] Designs Dir., Art. 11(2)(a); RDA 1949, s. 11ZA(4); CDR, Art. 25(I)(f).   [172] CDPA 1988, s. 51.
[173] Cf. *J & S. Davis (Holdings) v. Wright Health Group* [1988] *RPC* 403.
[174] *Lucasfilm v. Ainsworth* (2011) UKSC 39.

artistic craftsmanship.[175] The extent of copyright protection will depend on the application of section 51 of the 1988 Act. If the design is a work of artistic craftsmanship, full protection would apply—either based on direct infringement of the work, or indirect infringement via the sculpture or drawings. If the door handle is an artistic work, then the design drawing is a design document for an artistic work; thus the section 51 defence does not apply. If the door handle is not an artistic work, the question arises whether the drawings, on which the sculpture was based, are designs for an artistic work, or whether they will be treated as designs for the door handle (a non-artistic work).

C could also attempt to rely on unregistered design right as regards the shape of the handles. However, according to section 236 of the 1988 Act, there will be no infringement of unregistered design right insofar as there is an infringement of copyright. The operation of unregistered design right is therefore significant only if there is no infringement of copyright.

Example 4 *D, an artist, produces an abstract painting (in the style of Mondrian), which is widely exhibited. It is later applied by E to ties, with D's consent. Y has now made trays bearing the painting.*

E can apply to register the design for the tie at national or EU level. The application relates to the appearance of a product. The first issue that will need to be addressed is whether the design of the tie is new, given the existence of the painting. The EU-based regime provides no clear answer: whether an identical design has been made available depends, first, on whether the painting itself counts as a design. Is a painting the appearance of 'a product'—namely, the canvas?[176] Assuming that the painting is a design, has it been made available? Making available includes exhibition, so it seems that the painting has been made available.[177] Is the design of the tie identical to the design of the painting? Would the change in size, texture, and possibly colours (as well as the very nature of the product) be such that the design of the tie differs only in 'immaterial details'?[178] Does the design have individual character? If not, can the use of the artistic work within the previous 12 months be ignored on the basis of the grace period?[179] Here, the hurdle is that the painting was made available by D, rather than the design of the tie by E—a situation that does not fall easily into the exclusion.

If the painting is not a design, it would seem that the design for the tie is a new design. This would mean that E would obtain monopoly rights as regards use of the tie on any product. E consequently could bring an action against Y and the issue would be whether the design produced a different overall impression on an informed user. Would the design on a tray give a different impression from the design on a tie? If E had registered the design without D's permission, D could invalidate the registration on the ground that it infringed E's copyright.[180] This ground would not, however, be available to Y.

D can rely, as against E or Y, on copyright in the painting. This is infringed where anybody applies the work to an artefact, because that amounts to reproduction of the work.[181] Section 51 has no application (because the painting was not a design 'for' anything, being simply an artistic work).[182] It is difficult to see how E could claim any copyright in the tie.

Neither D nor E can rely on unregistered design right. The design is not a shape.[183]

---

[175] *Coogi Australia v. Hysport International* (1998) 41 *IPR* 593 (FCA).
[176] RDA 1949, s. 1(B)(2); Designs Dir., Art. 4; CDR, Art. 5(2).
[177] RDA 1949, s. 1B(5)(a); Designs Dir., Art. 6; CDR, Art. 7(1).
[178] RDA 1949, s. 1B(2); Designs Dir., Art. 4; CDR, Art. 5(2).
[179] RDA 1949, s. 1B(6); Designs Dir., Art. 6(2); CDR, Art.7(2)(b).
[180] RDA 1949, s. 11ZA(4); Designs Dir., Art. 11(2)(a); CDR, Art. 25(1)(f), (3).   [181] CDPA 1988, s. 17.
[182] In any case, the painting is not a 'design', a term that relates to shape and configuration.
[183] CDPA 1988, s. 213.

Example 5   *F, an artist, creates an abstract sculpture, which is exhibited in Holland Park. Z is thinking of selling paperweights in a similar shape.*

F may attempt to register the design of the sculpture at national or EU level. The critical question will be whether a sculpture is a product—that is, 'an industrial or handicraft item'.[184] It seems improbable that the UK Designs Registry, EUIPO, or the courts will refuse to register such things, but they will require that F specify a product (and identify its place in the Euro-Locarno Classification System).[185] If this has occurred, Z's use of a similar design will infringe if the resemblance is such that it does not produce a different overall impression.

F could rely on copyright, a sculpture being one of the 'artistic works' enumerated in section 4 of the CDPA 1988 and protected 'irrespective of artistic quality'. F will thus be able to bring an action against Z on the ground that Z has infringed by reproducing the sculpture or by issuing copies of it to the public.[186] However, F will need to prove that Z made the paperweights by copying the sculpture. If Z bought the paperweights from a third party, F will need to prove that the paperweights are copies of the sculpture, and that Z knew, or ought reasonably to have been aware, that these were infringing copies.[187]

F may have unregistered design right if the sculpture is treated as the design of the shape of an article. However, F will not be able to use unregistered design right against Z because of section 236: '[I]t is not an infringement of design right in the design to do anything which is an infringement of the copyright in that work.'

Example 6   *G has produced a photograph and proposes to make birthday cards bearing the image.*

G can register, either nationally or at EUIPO. The design relates to the appearance of a product and will obtain protection for up to 25 years. It will also benefit from an unregistered Community design right for three years from the first making-available of the design. G cannot rely on a UK unregistered design right: there is no shape or configuration. G can rely on copyright. The photograph is an original artistic work. Section 51 does not apply.

8 SEMICONDUCTOR TOPOGRAPHIES

A special form of legal protection based on unregistered design right, which has been described as being 'clearly rather esoteric',[188] has been created to afford protection for the layouts of semiconductor chips (which are colloquially known as 'computer chips', or 'silicon chips'). This section briefly explains this *sui generis* right.[189]

---

[184] RDA 1949, s. 1(B)(2); Designs Dir., Art. 4; CDR, Art. 5(2).   [185] RDA 1949, s. 3(2).

[186] CDPA 1988, ss 17, 18. If F permits the exploitation of the sculpture by the making of more than 50 articles (which are copies of the sculpture) and marketing them, F's ability to restrain further uses of the sculpture after 25 years from such marketing may be compromised: s. 52(2). Although Copyright (Industrial Process and Excluded Articles) (No. 2) Order 1989 (SI 1989/1070), Art. 3(1)(a), excludes 'sculptures' from the operation of CDPA 1988, s. 52, it does so only for sculptures 'other than casts or models used or intended to be used as models or patterns to be multiplied by any industrial process'. The better view is that F's copyright is unaffected if F sells multiple copies of the sculpture as a sculpture, but CDPA 1988, s. 52, comes into play if F permits the sale of articles modelled on the sculpture.   [187] CDPA 1988, s. 23.

[188] UK IPO, *The Consultation on the Reform of the UK Designs Legal Framework Government Response* (April 2013), [6].

[189] As noted in Chapter 26, chips are also now protectable by registered Community design, national registered design, and the unregistered Community design right.

When the question of the protection for the designs of semiconductor chips arose in the 1980s, it was widely assumed in the United States that copyright protection would not be available (or, if available, would not be adequate) given that the design of semiconductor chips is essentially functional. As a result, in 1984, the United States passed a Semiconductor Chip Protection Act introducing a *sui generis* protection regime. Because the United States was only prepared to recognize the claims of foreign designers of semiconductor chips where the country of origin recognized the rights of US chip designers, the European Commission decided to adopt an equivalent system of protection. Consequently, the Semiconductor Chip Directive was adopted, in December 1986, requiring member states to bring into effect protection for semiconductor topographies.[190] In the United Kingdom, this was initially implemented by means of the Semiconductor (Protection of Topography) Regulations 1987[191]—an instrument that was later repealed and replaced by the Design Right (Semiconductor Topographies) Regulations 1989.[192]

8.1 UK SCHEME

Semiconductor topographies are now protected in the United Kingdom as unregistered designs, with certain modifications. Protection is afforded to the pattern(s) fixed, or intended to be fixed, in or upon a layer or layers of a semiconductor product. A semiconductor product is defined as:

> . . . an article the purpose, or one of the purposes, of which is the performance of an electronic function and which consists of two or more layers, at least one of which is composed of semi-conducting material and in or upon one or more of which is fixed a pattern appertaining to that or another function.[193]

The prerequisite of design right protection—namely, that the design be 'original' and 'not commonplace'—applies equally to topographies. Protection is provided against copying, but there is a defence for private reproduction for non-commercial aims and generous provision is made for reverse engineering.[194]

While the concept of 'qualifying country' is confined to the United Kingdom or another member state of the European Economic Area (EEA), the notion of 'qualifying person' includes citizens, subjects, habitual residents, and bodies corporate listed in Schedule 1 to the 1989 Regulations.[195] Consequently, if a design for a topography is commissioned by a 'qualifying person' who is also the first owner of design right, is created by a designer who is a 'qualifying person',[196] or the first marketing of a topography is by a 'qualifying person' in Europe, the design qualifies for protection in the United Kingdom. The countries listed include Australia, the United States, Japan, and others.[197]

---

[190] Directive 87/54/EEC of 16 December 1986 on the legal protection of semiconductor chips [1986] *OJ L* 24/36 (27 January 1987).

[191] SI 1987/1497. [192] SI 1989/1100.

[193] Design Right (Semiconductor Topographies) Regulations 1989 (SI 1989/1100), reg. 2(1).

[194] Design Right (Semiconductor Topographies) Regulations 1989 (SI 1989/1100), reg. 8; cf. Software Dir., Arts 4 and 6.

[195] This is every WTO country (or at least those who were members in 2006 and 2008 respectively).

[196] The commissioner/employer and the designer routes are mutually exclusive, so that a commissioner or employer who is not a 'qualifying person' cannot claim the benefit of the designer being a 'qualifying individual'; rather, if the commissioner or employer was first owner, it must be qualified. However, if the designer was first owner pursuant to an agreement to that effect, then the designer must qualify.

[197] See A. Christie, Integrated Circuits and their contents: International Protection (1995), 67–71.

PART IV

TRADE MARKS AND PASSING OFF

This part of the book is concerned with three related forms of intellectual property—namely, the common law tort of passing off, the statutory regime that protects registered trade marks found in the Trade Marks Act 1994, and the registration based regime for the EU-wide protection of geographical indications. The first two regimes regulate certain signs or symbols, usually words or pictures,[1] when used in trade in connection with particular goods or services. Examples include APPLE for computers and phones, the 'golden arches' in the shape of an M for restaurant services, and the 'swoosh' or rounded tick symbol for (NIKE) sports clothing. These two legal regimes transform signs into forms of property. In so doing, they enable the proprietors to prevent other traders from using the signs on the same or similar goods or services. Both forms of legal protection are available simultaneously. Under the law of passing off, the sign must have been used in trade so as to have acquired a reputation. In the case of the statutory regime, the sign must have been registered, either at the UK Trade Mark Registry or at the EU trade mark office—that is, the European Union Intellectual Property Office (EUIPO). Signs which qualify are protected against unauthorized uses by third parties which produce harmful effects in the minds of consumers. Consumer confusion (or its likelihood) is the paradigmatic category of harm. These forms of legal protection underpin the enormous value of some of these brands. In 2017, the brand valuation agency Interbrand calculated that 100 brands are now worth over US$4 billion each. The most valuable, APPLE, GOOGLE, and MICROSOFT, are each worth in the region of $184, $141, and $80 billion each, respectively.[2]

Actual or potential brand value also explains the economic motivation for protecting geographical indications, the third category of signs considered in this section. They represent regional products, such as Champagne, Parmigiano Reggiano, and Darjeeling, which are collectively developed and used by multiple producers based within a defined geographical region and where the attributes of the product can be linked to the region of origin.

---

[1] Marks are often referred to according to the nature of the sign. A 'word' mark is a registration of a word alone (irrespective of its depiction). A 'figurative' mark is usually made up of a visual image, such as a picture. Marks that have both figurative and verbal elements are commonly referred to as 'composite' marks. As we will see, there are new possibilities to register 'three-dimensional marks', 'colour marks', and 'sensory marks' (such as sounds or smells).

[2] See http://www.interbrand.com. There are important differences between the legal rights conferred by trade mark law and the more nebulous commercial notion of a 'brand': see J. Davis, 'Between a Sign and a Brand', in Bently, Davis, and Ginsburg.

31

INTRODUCTION TO PASSING OFF AND TRADE MARKS

This chapter has three aims. First, it provides a brief history of the development of the law in this area. Second, it considers the ways in which legal protection of signs and symbols are justified. Third, the chapter provides an introduction to the international and regional framework that informs and constrains this area of the law in the United Kingdom.

1 HISTORY

Most accounts of the history of trade marks tend to focus on two intertwined themes: one is a history of the social practices and understandings attached to the activity of applying marks to goods; the other, a positivist history of trade mark law. These two histories are often conflated in a way that suggests that the law inevitably evolves with, or ought to reflect the changes in, the nature and function of marks.[1] While acknowledging that many developments in trade mark law have been made in response to changes in the functions that marks perform, we would prefer to keep the histories separate to avoid any implication that a change in the function of marks requires corresponding action by the legislature or judiciary to alter (typically, to expand the scope of legal protection afforded by) trade mark law.

1.1 HISTORY OF MARKS

In the earliest times, traders applied marks to their goods to indicate ownership. These are called 'proprietary' or 'possessory' marks. For example, farmers commonly branded cattle and earmarked sheep as a way of identifying their livestock. In a similar way, merchants also marked their goods before shipment, so that, in the event of a shipwreck, any surviving merchandise could be identified and retrieved. From medieval times, marks were used for a slightly different purpose within guild structures. Guilds were trade organizations that had control over who could make certain goods or provide certain services. They were also concerned to ensure that the goods were of a satisfactory quality.

---

[1] F. Schechter, *The Historical Foundations of the Law Relating to Trade Marks* (1925); T. Drescher, 'The Transformation and Evolution of Trademarks: From Signals to Symbols to Myth' (1992) 82 *TM Rep* 301, 309–21; *Scandecor Development AB v. Scandecor Marketing AB* [2002] *FSR* (7) 122, 128–38 (Lord Nicholls).

In order to be able to identify the source of unsatisfactory goods, the guilds required their members to apply identifying marks or signs to the goods.[2]

With the demise of the guilds during the eighteenth century, it was no longer obligatory for traders to apply particular marks or signs to goods. However, with the growth of regional (as opposed to local) trading and the rise of factory production that accompanied the Industrial Revolution, many traders applied marks to the goods that they manufactured.[3] Moreover, with the growth of mass media and the reading public, traders started to advertise their goods by reference to these marks.[4] In turn, purchasers of goods started to rely on the signs that the goods bore as truthful indications of the source of the goods. Importantly, they began to use them to assist their purchasing decisions. Over time, as consumers started to realize that some marks indicated a particular manufacturer—and, in turn, goods of a certain standard—the nature of the mark changed from being a source of liability to become an indicator of quality.

Another important change in the role played by marks took place around the beginning of the twentieth century. During this period, trade marks changed from being indicators of origin (and thus signs from which consumers could assume consistency of quality) to become valuable assets in their own right.[5] Thus it is said that some marks, by virtue of their distinctiveness or appeal, were able to convey some sort of emotional allure to potential consumers. Literally, the sign attracted custom, not as a result of some idea or assumption of origin or quality, but as a result of a so-called 'advertising' quality.[6] Indeed, the mark *itself* (reinforced by advertising) gave rise to a desire for the product that was distinct from a desire based on a belief that the product would be of a particular quality. The trade mark served more as a marketing tool and less as a means of identifying a product's source or sponsorship. This change in the function of trade marks has been described as a transformation from 'signals' to 'symbols'.[7] As signals, trade marks trigger an automatic response and serve to identify the maker of the product. In contrast, as 'symbols', trade marks evoke a broader set of associations and meanings. Here, they are used to identify the product or to give the product an identity. In so doing, 'the mark became . . . a poetic device, a name designed to conjure up product attributes whether real or imagined'.[8]

More recently, trade marks have taken on new roles.[9] In one commentator's words, marks have come to take on a 'mythical status'.[10] In their mythical form, trade marks help to provide consumers with an identity—for example as a FERRARI or VOLVO driver, or BUDWEISER or BUDVAR drinker. When the consumer purchases a product bearing a mark, they purchase an 'experience envelope' that helps to construct their identity. The conception of trade mark as 'myth' can be seen in the increased attention given to 'brands'.

---

[2] P. Mollerup, *Marks of Excellence: The History and Taxonomy of Trademarks* (1997), 15–42; S. Diamond, 'The Historical Development of Trademarks' (1975) 65 *TM Rep* 265, 272.

[3] B. Pattishall, 'Trade Marks and the Monopoly Phobia' (1952) 42 *TM Rep* 588, 590–1.

[4] S. Diamond, 'The Historical Development of Trademarks' (1975) 65 *TM Rep* 265, 281; R. Church, 'Advertising Consumer Goods in Nineteenth-Century Britain: Reinterpretations' (2000) 53 *Economic History Review* 621.   [5] *Eastman Photographic Material Co. v. John Griffith Cycle Corp.* (1898) 15 *RPC* 105.

[6] R. Brown, 'Advertising and the Public Interest: The Legal Protection of Trade Symbols' (1948) 57 *Yale LJ* 1165, 1189.

[7] T. Drescher, 'The Transformation and Evolution of Trademarks: From Signals to Symbols to Myth' (1992) 82 *TM Rep* 301.

[8] Ibid., 338. See also, K. Moore and S. Reid, 'The Birth of Brand: 4000 Years of Branding' (2008) 50(4) *Business History* 419.

[9] R. Dreyfuss, 'Expressive Genericity: Trademarks as Language in the Pepsi Generation' (1990) 65 *Notre Dame L Rev* 397, 397–8.   [10] Drescher, op. cit.

While the definition of brands varies in both marketing and legal analysis,[11] it normally extends beyond a word or device mark to encompass the personality, style, or aura associated with a particular product. For those who would have us believe in the ontological status of brands, COCA-COLA is more than a product, a reputation for quality, and a mark; instead, it is an image and a way of life, which is instituted through the presentation, marketing, advertising, and packaging (as well as the production) of the product.[12]

1.2 HISTORY OF THE LEGAL PROTECTION OF MARKS

The history of the legal protection of trade marks has been less well charted than most areas of intellectual property, and the early developments are particularly obscure. It seems that the courts first began to protect 'marks' at the behest of traders in the sixteenth century.[13] Acknowledging that such signs operated as an indication of source, the courts held that if another trader were allowed to use the same sign, this would allow a fraud to be committed on the public. Initially, protection was provided by the common law courts.[14] The idea was that if a trader had already used a mark, the deliberate use of the same mark by another trader would amount to a form of deceit. After some hesitation, from the early nineteenth century, the courts of Chancery used the action for 'passing off' to protect a trader who had developed a reputation or 'goodwill' through use of a particular sign or symbol.[15] This included protection against innocent misrepresentations. The passing off action is still available today and recognizes the proprietary interest in goodwill.[16] Passing off has always required a trader to establish that there had been a misrepresentation that deceived consumers. In effect, this meant that the action was always concerned with confusion as to source. Notwithstanding an expansion in scope, the action remains anchored in misrepresentation. It has not developed into a general action for misappropriation of intangible value or unfair competition of the type recognized by other European legal systems.

A system for registration of marks was first introduced in 1875.[17] The impetus for this came more from foreign sources, as well as from domestic pressure. With increasing interest in international recognition of industrial property rights, foreign traders were unconvinced that British law provided them with the same level of protection against the misuse of their signs that foreign laws afforded to British traders in similar

[11] J. Davis, 'The Value of Trade Marks: Economic Assets and Cultural Icons', in Y. Gendreau (ed.), *Propriété intellectuelle: Entre l'art et l'argent [Intellectual Property: Bridging Aesthetics and Economics]* (2006) 97–125.

[12] J. Litman, 'Breakfast with Batman: The Public Interest in the Advertising Age' (1999) 108 *Yale LJ* 1717; D. Gangjee, 'Property in Brands: The Commodification of Conversation', in H.R. Howe and J. Griffiths (eds), *Concepts of Property in Intellectual Property Law* (2013) 29.

[13] On the early role of the Star Chamber, see F. Schechter, *The Historical Foundations of the Law Relating to Trade Marks* (1925), 126–7.

[14] For eighteenth-century cases at common law, see L. Bently, 'The First Trade Mark Case at Common Law? The Story of *Singleton v. Bolton (1783)*' (2013) 47 *U Cal Davis L Rev* 969.

[15] L. Bently, '*Day v Day, Day and Martin* (1816)', in J. Bellido (ed.), *Landmark Cases in Intellectual Property Law* (2017), 87 (exploring the first instances of injunctive relief for misuse of trade marks).

[16] On the history of 'goodwill' as a requirement, see I. Tregoning, 'What's in a Name? Goodwill in Early Passing Off Cases' (2008) 34 *Monash U L Rev* 75. For an analysis of the US history, see R. Bone, 'Hunting Goodwill: A History of the Concept of Goodwill in Trademark Law' (2006) 86 *Boston U L Rev* 549; M. McKenna, 'The Normative Foundation of Trademark Law' (2007) 82 *Notre Dame L Rev* 1839.

[17] L. Bently, 'The Making of Modern Trade Marks Law: The Construction of the Legal Concept of Trade Mark (1860–1880)', in Bently, Davis, and Ginsburg.

circumstances.[18] When the registration system was initially adopted, registration had a rather limited role: the system allowed for the registration of a limited range of marks that the Registry subjected to examination prior to their entry on the register.[19]

Trade mark registration brought with it a number of benefits. The most obvious was that it reduced the difficulties of proving goodwill and distinctiveness that arose in a passing off action.[20] In addition, registration brought with it the possibility of a sign being protected prior to use. Other advantages of registered trade marks over passing off developed later—most notably, when the Trade Marks Act 1938 permitted the assignment of marks separately from the goodwill of the business.[21] Despite this, passing off remained valuable insofar as the criteria of registrability were restrictive, the process of registration was inappropriate or unnecessarily onerous, and the rights granted were broader.[22] The action continues to have relevance in contemporary litigation, since it may succeed where claims based upon registered trade marks are unsuccessful.[23]

Perhaps the most vexing question that has arisen has been that of determining the appropriate scope of protection. Reflecting its relationship with passing off, the Trade Marks Act 1875 worked on the assumption that trade marks operated to indicate origin.[24] However, as we just observed, around the beginning of the twentieth century, marks began to function in other ways—notably, as a 'silent salesman' that could sell products irrespective of consumer understandings about origin or associated quality. The recognition of the changed function of trade marks was soon coupled with a claim that trade mark proprietors *deserved* stronger protection to reflect the new ways in which marks were being understood. One of the most important advocates for greater protection was Frank Schechter, who is also the leading historian of trade marks.

Schechter radically asserted that modern trade mark law should have a single rational basis.[25] More specifically, Schechter proposed that 'the preservation of the uniqueness of a trade mark should constitute the only rational basis for its protection'.[26] For Schechter (and his cohort of followers), marks should be protected as a species of property. Importantly, this would mean that the owner would be protected when the marks were used on dissimilar goods as well as similar goods. Schechter argued that trade mark law was no longer adequate if it was wedded to a prerequisite of consumer confusion. The reason for this was that:

> [T]he real injury in all such cases . . . is the gradual whittling away or dispersion of the identity and hold upon the public mind of the mark or name by its use upon non-competing

---

[18] Ricketson (2015), 12–13; P. Duguid, 'French Connections: The International Propagation of Trade Marks in the Nineteenth Century' (2009) 10(1) *Enterprise and Society* 3.

[19] It was soon accepted that the registered trade marks system was a statutory supplement to the common law doctrine of passing off: *Great Tower v. Langford* (1888) 5 *RPC* 66; *Faulder v. Rushton* (1903) 20 *RPC* 477. Protection remains cumulative: TMA 1994, s. 2.

[20] *Spalding v. Gamage* (1915) 32 *RPC* 273, 284–5 (Lord Parker).   [21] TMA 1938, s. 22.

[22] M. Shúilleabháin, 'Common Law Protection of Trade Marks: The Continuing Relevance of Passing Off' (2003) 34(7) *IIC* 722.

[23] *The Sofa Workshop Ltd v. Sofaworks Ltd* [2015] *EWHC* 1773 (IPEC) (registered marks for SOFA WORKSHOP were descriptive and therefore invalid or *arguendo* liable to be revoked but the passing off claim succeeded); *The Ukulele Orchestra of Great Britain v. Clausen and anor (t/a the United Kingdom Ukulele Orchestra)* [2015] *EWHC* 1772 (IPEC) (registered mark THE UKULELE ORCHESTRA OF GREAT BRITAIN held to be descriptive and therefore invalid but passing off succeeded).   [24] TMA 1875, s. 10.

[25] F. Schechter, 'The Rational Basis of Trade Mark Protection' (1927) 40 *Harv L Rev* 813, 831. See S. Stadler, 'The Wages of Ubiquity in Trademark Law' (2003) 88 *Iowa L Rev* 731; B. Beebe, 'The Suppressed Misappropriation Origins of Trademark Anti-dilution Law', in Dreyfuss and Ginsburg (2014), ch. 3.

[26] F. Schechter, 'The Rational Basis of Trade Mark Protection' (1927) 40 *Harv L Rev* 813, 831.

goods. The more distinctive or unique the mark, the deeper its impress upon the public consciousness, and the greater its need for its protection against vitiation or dissociation from the particular product in connection with which it has been used.[27]

Schechter's article soon became 'a talisman to members of the trademark bar who [sought] to expand the protection available to their clients'.[28] In fact, its impact was not confined to the Bar. Today, many commentators treat the subsequent period as one during which Schechter's insights came to fruition. In particular, the arguments that he made for expansion have gradually been acknowledged and implemented in national law (even if in a much distorted fashion). Notable examples include the expansion of the rights given to a trade mark proprietor to include: certain uses of marks on *dissimilar* goods, even where consumers appreciate that there is no connection; the recognition by the Court of Justice that trade marks protect their holders not only from damage to the mark as an indicator of origin, but also in respect of the other 'functions' (which it recognizes as the quality, advertising, investment, and communication functions);[29] the recognition of signs as assets;[30] and the gradual abandonment of various restrictions on dealings with marks.[31]

2 COSTS OF TRADE MARKS

One of the major charges against the protection of trade marks is that trade marks are monopolies and that monopolies are inefficient.[32] In most situations, the characterization of trade marks as monopolies is unhelpful. As one commentator has noted, '[m]onopoly is merely an ugly word used by people to put a curse on any kind of property they do not like'.[33] In any case, trade marks are not properly treated as monopolies. This is because, in contrast with patents, design right, and copyright, a trade mark does not normally give exclusive control over the sale of particular goods or services; rather, it merely provides control over the use of the sign in connection with goods or services. Trade marks do not create monopolies[34] unless the sign is treated in combination with the goods or services as a product in its own right.[35] As one commentator pointed out, a trade mark 'quite

---

[27] Ibid., 825.

[28] J. Swann and T. Davis, 'Dilution: An Idea Whose Time Has Gone—Brand Equity as Protectable Property, the New/Old Paradigm' (1994) 84 *TM Rep* 267, 285.

[29] See in particular Chapter 40, section 10, pp. 1116–25. The influence of reasoning by reference to functions is not, however, confined to cases of use of identical marks on identical goods, but also appears in other contexts. See, e.g., Chapter 38, section 2.2.3, p. 1031 (discussing relative grounds), and section 2.5, pp. 1071–2 (the discussion of 'without due cause'), and Chapter 49, section 3.3, pp. 1338–9 (grant of EU-wide injunctive relief).

[30] *Mirage Studios v. Counter-Feat Clothing* [1991] *FSR* 145. C. Corrado and J. Hao, *Brands as Productive Assets: Concepts, Measurement and Global Trends* (WIPO Economic Research Paper No. 13, 2014).

[31] With increasingly less attention being paid to the role of the consumer: J. Davis, 'To Protect or Serve? European Trade Mark Law and the Decline of the Public Interest' [2003] *EIPR* 180.

[32] N. Economides, 'The Economics of Trademarks' (1988) 78 *TM Rep* 523, 532.

[33] E. Rogers, 'The Social Value of Trade Marks and Brands' (1947) 37 *TM Rep* 249, 249.

[34] While this proposition is true for arbitrary word and device marks, it is less obviously so for three-dimensional marks. Reflecting these concerns, the law excludes shapes from registrability where the shape has some non-trade mark value to consumers. See Chapter 36, section 3, pp. 958–71.

[35] See, e.g., P. Behrendt, 'Trademarks and Monopolies: Historical and Conceptual Foundations' (1961) 51 *TM Rep* 853.

simply, is not a monopoly in the underlying good, and no product market has ever been defined as narrowly as a single brand'.[36]

Even if the charge that a trade mark is a monopoly has little to be said for it, this does not mean that trade mark law does not impose certain costs that require justification. Indeed, the grant of exclusive rights over certain signs has a number of social costs.[37] Probably the most obvious is that it restricts other people (most importantly, other traders) from using the same or a similar sign. As the scope of the subject matter of trade mark rights has expanded to cover shapes, to avoid infringement a trader may need to design different packaging or shapes for goods. As the rights conferred by trade mark law expand, the costs increase for traders, even if they are not trading in the same or a similar field—that is, the costs of developing suitable marks, searching registers, and (where necessary) negotiating with owners of related marks. This is particularly so for new entrants.

To a large extent, the way in which the 'harm' caused by trade marks is evaluated depends on the way in which signs and language are viewed. If we take the view that the number of suitable signs is infinite and the inherent value of all signs is fairly consistent, then the cost of adopting a different sign from one already used or protected by another trader should not be that great. If, however, we take the view that some signs are better than others and that the pool of available marks is limited, then the costs to other traders of one trader being granted ownership of a particular mark may be significant.[38] As the better marks are used up, a trader will have to invest more and more money in establishing and building suitable associations with their signs. Business practices suggest that many traders consider that the choice of trade symbols is an important one and that some signs are better than others. This explains why firms such as Standard Oil spend so much time and money developing marks such as EXXON. It also explains why so many marks are selected for their 'suggestive' or 'allusive' qualities.[39] It has also been argued that the specific institution of trade mark registration—justified in similar 'information efficiency' terms to other forms of property registration—is unhelpfully opaque and imposes costs.[40] In addition, registers create their own problems (and costs), most obviously, the problem of clutter or deadwood—the existence of marks on the register that are partly or wholly unused by their owners.[41]

More expansive trade mark protection, which gives a trade mark holder the ability to control non-trade mark uses or uses of similar marks in relation to dissimilar goods, imposes further costs. Some such regulations may even restrict free speech.[42] To the extent that the law confers power over words and symbols, it places some of the ability to make and control meaning in private hands. Some obvious examples include the use of

---

[36] J. Swann and T. Davis, 'Dilution: An Idea Whose Time Has Gone—Brand Equity as Protectable Property, the New/Old Paradigm' (1994) 84 *TM Rep* 267, 272.

[37] W. Landes and R. Posner, 'The Economics of Trademark Law' (1988) 78 *TM Rep* 267, 268–9 (referring, among other things, to the costs of transferring marks, enforcing them, and from the restriction on others from using similar marks).

[38] Recent empirical research from the United States suggests this may indeed be the case: B. Beebe and J. C. Fromer, 'Are We Running Out of Trademarks? An Empirical Study of Trademark Depletion and Congestion' (2018) 131 *Harv L Rev* 945.

[39] J. Cross, 'Language and the Law: The Special Role of Trade Marks, Trade Names and other Trade Emblems' (1997) 76 *Neb L Rev* 95.

[40] R. Burrell, 'Trade Mark Bureaucracies', in Dinwoodie and Janis (2008), 95.

[41] G. von Graevenitz et al., *Cluttering and Non-Use of Trade Marks in Europe* (UK IPO Report 2015/48); US PTO, *Post Registration Proof of Use Pilot Final Report* (25 August 2015).

[42] W. Sakulin, *Trade Mark Protection and Freedom of Expression* (2010); see further Chapter 41, section 9, pp. 1164–5.

these laws to control the connotations of the word 'Olympics', the name 'Champagne', or the name 'Barbie'. As such, intellectual property laws:

> ... play a fundamental role in determining what discourses circulate in the public realm and achieve dominance, and how these 'languages' are spoken, while providing both enabling conditions and limiting obstacles for those who seek to construct identities and compel recognition.[43]

3 JUSTIFICATIONS FOR THE LEGAL PROTECTION OF TRADE MARKS

In this section, we ask the question: why should we protect trade marks? In contrast with commentaries on copyright and patents, this topic has received relatively little attention. One possible reason for this is that the negative impact of trade mark rights is less obvious. Another reason is that, for much of the last 50 years, the flourishing of brands has been equated with the success of capitalism (in terms of increasing consumer choice).[44] However, blind faith in the value of trade marks is difficult to sustain and the time is ripe for a more open and critical examination of the justifications for protecting trade marks.[45]

A number of different rationales have been used to justify trade mark protection. As we will see, there have been few problems in justifying the protection given to signs and symbols insofar as they operate as indicators of origin (to identify the origin or ownership of goods to which the mark is affixed), or as guarantees of quality (to signify that all goods bearing the mark are of a certain quality).[46] However, more problems have arisen in justifying the extensive protection that is currently granted to marks as 'brands'.

3.1 CREATIVITY AND INNOVATION

The arguments that are used to justify copyright, design rights, and patents, which focus on the protection of labour and personality (whether as recognition of a right, as a reward, or as an incentive) are difficult to apply to trade marks. This is because, while some trade marks may be invented, novelty is not a prerequisite to protection.[47] These differences have not prevented some commentators from trying to extend the idea of 'creation' to encompass trade marks. This has been done by claiming that a trader creates goodwill as much as an author creates a work; that a trade mark is to be regarded as having been created in that it is either invented, or if not, that a new association has been created between the mark and a product and thus 'a new meaning'.[48] Additionally, the evolving brand

---

[43] R. Coombe, 'Tactics of Appropriation and the Politics of Recognition in Late Modern Democracies' (1993) 21 *Political Theory* 411, 414–5.

[44] E. Rogers, 'The Social Value of Trade Marks and Brands' (1947) 37 *TM Rep* 249, 253.

[45] See, e.g., N. Klein, *No Logo: Taking Aim at the Brand Bullies* (2000); R. Coombe, *The Cultural Life of Intellectual Properties* (1998).

[46] E. Hamak, 'The Quality Assurance Function of Trademarks' (1975) 65 *TM Rep* 318, 319.

[47] D. Gangjee, 'Innovation and Creativity: New Justifications for Trade Mark Protection', in G. Dinwoodie and M. D. Janis (eds), *Trademark Law and Change* (2018) (forthcoming).

[48] S. Maniatis, 'Trade Mark Rights—A Justification Based on Property' [2002] *IPQ* 123; J. C. Fromer, 'The Role of Creativity in Trade Mark Law' (2011) 86 *Notre Dame L Rev* 1885.

dimension of trade marks invites parallels with the creativity usually associated with copyright law rationales.[49]

Nevertheless, attempts to justify trade marks or goodwill as creations are weak, in part because while the associations between the mark and a source of goodwill may be instigated and nurtured by the trader, they are as much created by the customers and the public.[50]

Perhaps the most plausible argument made along these lines sees trade marks as a reward for investment. This argument was summed up by Justice Breyer of the US Supreme Court when he said that trade mark law helps 'to assure a producer that it (and not an imitating competitor) will reap the financial, reputation-related rewards associated with a desirable product'.[51] In so doing, trade mark law thereby encourages:

> ... the production of quality products ... and simultaneously discourages those who hope to sell inferior products by capitalising on a consumer's inability quickly to evaluate the quality of an item offered for sale. It is the source-distinguishing quality ... that permits it to serve these basic purposes.[52]

In the same vein, the European Commission claimed that the 'mark works . . . as an engine of innovation'.[53] An emerging innovation rationale posits that trade mark registrations may either mirror innovation in underlying commercial sectors, or—in a more causally connected sense—reflect innovations and improvements in marketing or the underlying product itself.[54] However such claims are premised on a number of unverified assertions. For example, it is not clear that the grant of trade mark owners encourages 'quality' products, and it is not at all obvious that businesses will not vary the quality of the products that they sell from time to time in order to maximize profits.[55]

3.2 INFORMATION AND 'SEARCH COSTS'

Perhaps the most convincing, and certainly the most prevalent,[56] of the arguments for the protection of trade signs is that they operate in the public interest insofar as they increase the supply of information to consumers and thereby increase the efficiency of the market. These arguments highlight the fact that trade marks are a shorthand way of

---

[49] I. D. Manta, 'Branded' (2016) 69 *Southern Methodist University L Rev* 713; J. M. Kiser, 'Brands as Copyright' (2016) 61 *Villanova L Rev* 45.

[50] S. Wilf, 'Who Authors Trademarks?' (1999) 17 *Cardozo AELJ* 1; Gangjee, 'Property in Brands' op. cit.

[51] *Qualitex v. Jacobson Products*, 115 S. Ct. 1300, 1303 (1995).

[52] Ibid., 103–4; *SA-CNL SUCAL v. HAG*, Case C-10/89 [1990] *ECR* I–3752 ('*Hag II*'), [AG18] (AG Jacobs).

[53] European Commission, *Proposal for a Directive of the European Parliament and of the Council to Approximate the Laws of Member States relating to Trade Marks (Recast)* (2013) COM(2013) 162 final, Explanatory Memorandum, 1, [1.1].

[54] WIPO, *Brands—Reputation and Image in the Global Marketplace* (2013) 109–137 (brands help firms to recoup investments in innovation).

[55] J. Aldred, 'The Economic Rationale for Trade Marks: An Economist's Critique', in Bently, Davis, and Ginsburg, ch. 12.

[56] B. Beebe, 'Semiotic Analysis of Trademark Law' (2004) 51 *UCLA L Rev* 621, 623–4 (Chicago 'search costs' analysis is the theory of trade marks most widely adhered to in the United States). See also S. Dogan and M. Lemley, 'A Search-costs Theory of Limiting Doctrines in Trademark Law', in Dinwoodie and Janis (2008), ch. 3. Significantly, their arguments would suggest that many aspects of European trade mark law, which does not possess the same limitations as US law, are inconsistent with search costs theory. See further Chapter 41, section 6, pp. 1142–5 (comparative advertising); Chapter 42, section 3.2, pp.1168–9 (assignment in gross), and Chapter 40, section 10, pp. 1116–25 (trade mark functions).

communicating information that purchasers need in order to make informed purchasing choices. By 'preventing others from copying a source-identifying mark', trade mark law reduces:

> ... the customer's costs of shopping and making purchasing decisions ... for it quickly and easily assures a potential customer that this item—the item with this mark—is made by the same producer as other similarly marked items that he or she liked (or disliked) in the past.[57]

The information provided by trade marks is particularly important in relation to goods that a consumer cannot judge merely through inspection (known as 'experience goods'). Where the quality and/or variety of goods is not readily apparent, trade marks enable consumers to choose the product with the desired features. Trade marks also encourage firms to maintain consistent quality and variety standards, and to compete over a wide quality and variety. Consequently, it has been said that:

> [The] primary reason for the existence and protection of trade marks is that they facilitate and enhance consumer decisions and ... they create incentives for firms to produce products of desirable qualities even when these are not observable before purchase.[58]

The idea that trade mark protection is necessary and desirable to minimize consumer 'search costs' has not gone without criticism. First, while generally supportive of search costs theory, Professors Dogan and Lemley point out that reducing search costs is not an end in itself; rather, more competitive markets are the ultimate goal.[59] Thus trade mark rights should not, for example, be provided over product shapes if the effect of doing so is to prevent competition (even if search costs are increased for some). Second, the economist Jonathan Aldred has attacked many of the assumptions on which search cost theory is based.[60] For example, he has probed the assumption that trade marks provide consumers with information, suggesting that the only real information of which consumers can be confident when they see a trade mark is that the trade mark owner is being paid some share of the cost of the product![61] Aldred is also critical of the assumption that trade mark owners will not vary the quality of the products, noting that, even taking a profit-maximizing approach, there may be many occasions on which it is in the trade mark owner's interest to reduce the quality of the goods. The trade mark owner may, for example, know that there is no long-term future for the market in the particular goods and thus take the view that there is no need to preserve the 'repute' of the mark. In these situations, trade marks do worse than increase consumer search costs.

In some respects, it is impossible, when assessing the protection of trade marks, to divorce considerations about trade marks from considerations about advertising. This is because '[t]rade symbols are a species of advertising: their special characteristics are brevity and continuity in use, both of which are essential to their symbolic function'.[62]

---

[57] *Qualitex v. Jacobson Products*, 115 *S. Ct.* 1300, 1303 (1995) (Breyer J).

[58] N. Economides, 'The Economics of Trademarks' (1988) 78 *TM Rep* 523, 525–6. Landes and Posner call this the 'economizing function': W. Landes and R. Posner, 'The Economics of Trademark Law' (1988) 78 *TM Rep* 267, 270. See also A. Griffiths, 'The Law and Economics of Trade Marks', in Bently, Davis, and Ginsburg, ch. 11.

[59] S. Dogan and M. Lemley, 'A Search-costs Theory of Limiting Doctrines in Trademark Law', in Dinwoodie and Janis (2008), ch. 3, 69, 90–2.

[60] J. Aldred, 'The Economic Rationale for Trade Marks: An Economist's Critique', in Bently, David, and Ginsburg, ch. 12. See also A. Bartow, 'Likelihood of Confusion' (2004) 41 *SDLR* 721, 729–38.

[61] See also G. Lastowka, 'The Trademark Function of Authorship' (2005) 85 *BULR* 1171, 1191.

[62] R. Brown, 'Advertising and the Public Interest: The Legal Protection of Trade Symbols' (1948) 57 *Yale LJ* 1165, 1185.

If trade marks function as a vehicle for advertising, one obvious question is whether we value advertising.[63] In a very influential article, American academic Ralph Brown tied the legitimacy of trade mark protection to advertising.[64] He said that:

> [A]dvertising depends on the remote manipulation of symbols, most importantly of symbols directed at a mass audience through mass media or imprinted on mass-produced goods. The essence of these symbols is distilled in the devices variously called trade marks, trade names, brand names or brand symbols.[65]

Importantly, Brown drew a distinction between what he called 'informational' and 'persuasive' advertising: 'From the point of view of the economic purist, imparting information is the only useful function of advertising.'[66] However, most advertising was 'persuasive advertising' and was socially unjustifiable. This was because it added costs and effectively insulated traders from competition: 'By differentiating their products in order to carve out a separate market in which demand, price, and output can be manipulated . . . The main drive of advertising is to facilitate this latter form of control.'[67] Brown was sceptical about the idea that, in buying brands, consumers were buying the associations, intangible allure, etc. Given his negative view of persuasive advertising, Brown argued that the task of the courts in trade marks cases was to 'pick out, from the tangle of claims, facts and doctrines they are set to unravel, the threads of informative advertising, and to ignore the persuasive'.[68]

Brown argued that, in addition to being justified insofar as trade marks were used to indicate source and quality, trade mark protection was also justified where it supported the informational aspect of advertising. For Brown, the so-called 'advertising' or persuasive function of marks is 'of dubious social utility. There seems little reason why the courts should recognize or protect interests deriving from it.'[69] He considered likelihood of confusion to be the 'universal judicial touchstone'.[70] Persuasive, rather than informational, advertising can lead to distortion of incentives in a competitive economy.[71] Therefore in order to justify a corresponding extension of protection, these costs need to be shown to be worth sacrificing to some greater goal.

Attempts have, however, been made to justify protection of trade marks against uses on dissimilar goods that are non-confusing by reference to the 'search costs' theory. In one US case, Judge Posner developed the idea of 'imagination costs', arguing that the 'search costs' of consumers included the time taken to recall the associations and meaning of a mark.[72] For Posner, these costs might justify protecting the 'uniqueness' of a mark. Others, such as Rebecca Tushnet, have drawn on empirical work to demonstrate that such 'imagination costs' are, in fact, trivial.[73] The better view is that a 'search costs' theory would justify only a relatively narrow field of protection for trade mark holders.

3.3 ETHICAL JUSTIFICATIONS

Ethical arguments have also been used to justify the trade marks regime.[74] The main ethical argument for the protection of trade marks is based on the idea of fairness or justice. In particular, it is said that persons should not be permitted 'to reap where they have not

---

[63] A. Greenbaum, 'Trademarks Attacked' (1968) 58 *TM Rep* 443. [64] Brown, op. cit.
[65] Ibid., 1166. [66] Ibid., 1168. [67] Ibid., 1171. [68] Ibid., 1184. [69] Ibid., 1190.
[70] Ibid., 1195. [71] N. Economides, 'The Economics of Trademarks' (1988) 78 *TM Rep* 523, 533.
[72] *Ty Inc. v. Perryman*, 306 *F.3d.* 509, 511 (7th Cir. 2002) (Posner J).
[73] R. Tushnet, 'Gone in 60 Miliseconds' (2008) 86 *Texas L Rev* 507.
[74] J. N. Sheff, 'Marks, Morals and Markets' (2013) 65 *Stanford L Rev* 761.

sown'.[75] More specifically, it is said that, by adopting another trader's mark, a person is taking advantage of the goodwill generated by the earlier trader. Through this agricultural metaphor, the justification for protecting trade marks is linked to the broader arenas of the protection of traders against 'unfair competition' and 'unjust enrichment'.[76]

While a misleading use of a mark—or 'classic' trade mark infringement—is clearly objectionable under the principle that a person should not reap where they have not sown, the principle has also been used to justify more extensive protection. For example, it is said that one objection to 'comparative advertising' is that, even though it does not confuse consumers, it takes advantage of the reputation that the earlier trader has built up. Similarly, one of the objections that are made to marks being used on dissimilar goods (for example the ROLLS ROYCE café) is that it takes advantage of the repute of the earlier mark. 'Reap–sow' arguments thus have the potential to justify very broad protection of trade marks.[77]

Problems arise from such attempts to use the principle that a person should not reap where they have not sown to justify more extensive forms of protection. The first problem is that it is not always easy to determine what the trade mark owner has sown: the mere selection of signs and symbols from the public domain seems a meagre basis on which to found such a claim (especially against a trader who is not aware that a mark may be registered). Also, it is not obvious that we should necessarily treat the associations that develop in the minds of the public as something of value that the trade mark owner has nurtured.[78]

Second, it is often unclear whether another person is reaping from the cultivated soil of the trade mark owner or has obtained their fruits from the uncultivated commons. Although the causal link can be substantiated in cases of misrepresentation leading to confusion, it is difficult to justify protection where consumers are not 'confused'.[79]

Third, and more generally, the law does not penalize every case of reaping without sowing (for example copying an unpatented business idea).[80] Indeed, copying has been described as the lifeblood of competition. As such, the onus falls on the advocates of the reap–sow principle to provide guidance as to the other factors that trigger the legal operation of the principle.[81]

Other ethical arguments have also been used to justify trade mark protection.[82] For example, it is sometimes argued that the misuse of trade marks is justified by reference

---

[75] Also referred to as 'free-riding', the argument can be put, and refuted, in economic terms as well as ethical ones: see D. Gangjee and R. Burrell, 'Because You're Worth It: L'Oréal and the Prohibition on Free Riding' (2010) 73 *MLR* 282.

[76] A. Kamperman Sanders, *Unfair Competition Law: The Protection of Intellectual and Industrial Creativity* (1997).

[77] A. Chronopoulos, 'Goodwill Appropriation as a Distinct Theory of Trade Mark Liability: A Study on the Misappropriation Rationale in Trade Mark and Unfair Competition Law' (2014) 22 *Texas Intellectual Property Law Journal* 253; M. E. Kenneally, 'Misappropriation and the Morality of Free-Riding' (2014) 18 *Stanford Technology Law Review* 289.

[78] M. Spence, 'Passing Off and the Misappropriation of Valuable Intangibles' (1996) 112 *LQR* 472, 479–80; M. Chon, 'Trademark Goodwill as a Public Good: Brands and Innovations in Corporate Social Responsibility' (2017) 21 *LCLR* 277.

[79] Jacob LJ referred precisely this question to the Court of Justice in *L'Oreal SA v. Bellure NV* [2007] *EWCA Civ* 968.

[80] D. Gangjee and R. Burrell, 'Because You're Worth It: L'Oréal and the Prohibition on Free Riding' (2010) 73 *MLR* 282, 289–90.

[81] For discussion of the extent to which Lockean arguments can justify trade mark protection, see D. Scott, A. Oliver, and M. Ley Pineda, 'Trade Marks as Property: A Philosophical Perspective', in Bently, Davis, and Ginsburg, ch. 13.

[82] W. Howarth, 'Are Trademarks Necessary?' (1970) 60 *TM Rep* 228 (business morality).

to moral norms that treat 'truth-telling' as a core 'good' (rather than as necessary for the maintenance of efficient markets).[83] Under this approach, it is argued that the law ought to allow a person who suffers harm as a result of lying to bring an action against the liar. Misrepresentations of the source of goods are equivalent to lying or deception and are simply 'wrong'.[84] While arguments of this sort would justify a law of trade marks and passing off in some form, they would not appear to justify the protection of one trade mark owner against the innocent adopter of a mark, nor against uses that the public would not understand as indicating a business connection with the owner. As such, they would support only a very narrowly confined law of trade marks.[85]

Michael Spence has also proposed an ethically grounded argument that could justify broader protection.[86] Justifications for protecting freedom of expression, grounded in notions of autonomy, might be used to explain why third parties should not be permitted to use trade marks in certain ways. Spence draws an analogy between misuse of trade marks and 'compelled' speech: if a person uses someone else's trade mark on goods (or in any way), that use implicates the expressive autonomy of the trade mark owner insofar as the third party's speech is understood as communicating a message from the trade mark owner (for example 'I made these goods').[87] What is useful about Spence's argument is that both trade mark owner and user might be viewed as having claims grounded in speech rights, the conflicting interests thus being rendered 'commensurable'. However, while this kind of balancing is the sort of activity that the judiciary have already been compelled to undertake in the context of the protection of privacy, it is hard to imagine either judges or traders supporting such a radical rethinking of trade mark principles.

4 INTERNATIONAL AND REGIONAL DIMENSIONS

Trade marks have always been connected to particular geographical conditions. Indeed, one impetus for legal recognition of marks has been the decline of the local economy, which meant that consumers became dissociated from the source of the goods.[88] It is therefore not surprising that further changes in the geographical aspects of trade have prompted alterations in trade mark law.[89] These have largely taken two forms. First, growth in international trade led to the establishment of international systems of registration, thereby enabling traders to gain protection swiftly and cheaply in all relevant markets. Second, changes in international trade prompted the establishment of international minimum standards of protection.

---

[83] Cf. J. Cross, 'Language and the Law: The Special Role of Trade Marks, Trade Names and other Trade Emblems' (1997) 76 *Neb L Rev* 95, 111.

[84] B. Pattishall, 'Trade Marks and the Monopoly Phobia' (1952) 42 *TM Rep* 588, 600.

[85] M. Spence, 'Passing Off and the Misappropriation of Valuable Intangibles' (1996) 112 *LQR* 472, 480.

[86] M. Spence, 'The Mark as Expression/The Mark as Property' (2005) 58 *CLP* 491; M. Spence, 'An Alternative Approach to Dilution Protection: A Response to Scott, Oliver and Ley Pineda', in Bently, Davis, and Ginsburg, ch. 14.

[87] Spence characterizes this in terms of the 'freedom from compulsion to subsidise a message with which the person from whom the subsidy is sought chooses not to be associated': Spence, 'An Alternative Approach', op. cit., 308–312.   [88] B. Paster, 'Trademarks: Their Early History' (1969) 59 *TM Rep* 551, 551–2.

[89] I. Calboli and E. Lee (eds), *Trademark Protection and Territoriality Challenges in a Global Economy* (2014).

4.1 INTERNATIONAL REGISTRATION

Traders who operate on more than a local level will wish to protect their marks on a transnational basis. Various mechanisms have been developed to assist in this regard. The earliest of these was the Paris Convention of 1883, which requires members to apply the principle of national treatment—that is, it requires members to treat foreign nationals of contracting states as they would their own nationals.[90] This ensures the possibility for foreign protection of trade marks. This is further facilitated by provisions that give registrants in one country a short period of priority,[91] and provisions obliging national offices of Paris Convention members to register any trade mark that has been registered in its country of origin.[92]

While the Paris Convention was of some assistance to transnational traders,[93] it failed to create a mechanism for the international application for marks. However, the Madrid Agreement on the International Registration of Marks of 1891 and the Madrid Protocol of 1989 provide just such mechanisms. Under these arrangements, after making a 'home registration' or 'home application', an individual or company may apply to the Bureau of the World Intellectual Property Organization (WIPO) for an international registration. The Bureau passes the application on to relevant national trade mark offices. If the office of the contracting party does not refuse the application within a limited time, it is treated as registered. The simplification of the process of international registration has obvious advantages for trade mark owners. While the United Kingdom long resisted invitations to join the Madrid Agreement (mainly on the ground that the Agreement worked unfavourably against those who first registered in the United Kingdom, where examination of all applications is required), the United Kingdom is now a party to the Protocol.[94]

While the Madrid Agreement and Protocol provide useful simplified mechanisms for obtaining national registrations, they necessarily result in the proprietor holding a portfolio of national marks, each of which needs to be managed, licensed, and enforced separately. In contrast, the European Union Trade Mark (EUTM) regime (formerly the Community trade mark (CTM) regime), which became fully operational on 1 April 1996, confers on a trade mark owner a single legal right that operates throughout the European Union. Such unitary rights are acquired by the filing of a single application for a EUTM with the European Union Intellectual Property Office (EUIPO) (formerly the Office for Harmonization in the Internal Market (Trade Marks and Designs) (OHIM)), which is located at Alicante in Spain. The EU registration system has also been linked to the Madrid Protocol: international applications can be based on EUTMs, and the applicants under the Madrid Protocol can themselves designate the European Union.

4.2 INTERNATIONAL STANDARDS

There has been relatively little action, either at the international or regional level, on the protection of *unregistered* marks. The most important provision is Article 10*bis* of the Paris Convention, which obliges member countries to assure 'effective protection against unfair competition', which, in turn, is defined as any 'act of competition contrary to honest practices in industrial or commercial matters'.[95] UK law has not expressly implemented

---

[90] Paris, Art. 2. The Trademark Law Treaty, signed on 28 October 1994, is a limited agreement relating mostly to prosecution procedure.   [91] Paris, Art. 4.

[92] Paris, Art. 6*quinquies* (the *telle-quelle* obligation).   [93] Ricketson (2015), ch. 12.

[94] See Chapter 35, section 4, pp. 949–53.

[95] TRIPS, Art. 39, requires member states to protect undisclosed information under Paris, Art. 10(2).

this provision, presumably on the assumption that the existing rules relating to passing off and malicious falsehood (as well as registered marks) already deal with it adequately.

In part, this lack of international standardization of the laws protecting unregistered trade marks can be explained by the fact that if a business operates on a transnational level, it typically will have the resources to protect its interests via registration. As a result, the protection of unregistered marks tends to be a matter of concern only for small enterprises; hence it has not prompted activities at the diplomatic level. Moreover, the forms and conditions for protection of unregistered marks vary widely, very much reflecting local legal principles. (In the United Kingdom, the main form of protection is through the judge-made law of passing off.)

That said, the geographical expansion in the operations of many businesses has given rise to a form of opportunism, against which international action has been taken. More specifically, the Paris Convention has been revised to prevent the pre-emptive adoption of such marks by interlopers in countries in which the 'proprietor' has not yet commenced marketing. Article 6*bis* of the Paris Convention imposes an obligation to recognize and protect well-known marks even where they have not been registered.[96] The concept of 'well-known marks' (as distinct from distinctive marks, marks with a reputation, and famous marks) is left undefined and has been contested.[97] Article 16(2) of the Agreement on Trade Related Aspects of Intellectual Property Rights 1994 (TRIPS) indicates that, in assessing whether a mark is well known, members shall take account of the knowledge of the trade mark in the relevant sector of the public, including knowledge in the member concerned that has been obtained as a result of the promotion of the trade mark.[98] The UK law on well-known trade marks is examined further in Chapter 32.

In relation to registered marks, TRIPS provides by far the most detailed international prescription of the substantive rules relating to their protection. Article 15 defines the protectable subject matter expansively, to include, for example, service marks. It also prohibits discrimination as to registrability based on the nature of the goods and services to which a trade mark is to be applied. Article 16 requires recognition of certain rights, in particular over the use of an identical or similar mark on identical or similar goods or services where such use would result in a likelihood of confusion (although not extending to dilution). Articles 17 and 18 provide, respectively, for limited exceptions to the rights conferred by a trade mark,[99] and for the potentially indefinite registration of marks on the basis of renewable terms each of a minimum of seven years. Article 19 limits the circumstances in which registrations may be revoked for non-use, Article 20 prevents certain conditions being imposed on the use of marks,[100] and Article 21 prohibits the compulsory

---

[96] For an international and comparative study, see F. W. Mostert (ed.), *Famous and Well-Known Marks: An International Analysis* (2nd edn, 2004).

[97] WIPO, *Joint Recommendation Concerning Provisions on the Protection of Well-Known Marks* (1999); A. Kur, 'Joint Recommendation on Well-known Marks' [2000] *IIC* 824. On the adoption of global common standards for well-known marks, see E. Lee, 'The Global Trade Mark' (2014) 35 *U Penn J Int L* 917.

[98] TMA 1994, s. 56.

[99] The scope of Art. 17 was considered by the WTO Dispute Body when considering whether the EU Geographical Indications (GI) Regulation, discussed in Chapter 43, violated TRIPs insofar as it gave primacy to users of a protected GI over prior trade mark holders: *US v. EC*, WTO DS 174/R (15 March 2005), [7.638]–[7.688].

[100] TRIPS, Art. 20. This provision is at the centre of the ongoing debate over the legitimacy of laws that regulate the use of marks on tobacco products. Five countries have brought proceedings against Australia alleging infringement of TRIPS: WTO DS 434, *Ukraine v. Australia*; WTO DS 435, *Honduras v. Australia*; WTO DS 441, *Dominican Republic v. Australia*; WTO DS 454, *Cuba v. Australia*; and WTO DS 467, *Indonesia v. Australia*. See T. Voon and A. Mitchell, 'Face off: Assessing WTO Challenges to Australia's Scheme for Plain Tobacco Packaging' (2011) 22(3) *Pub L Rev* 218. The Panel Report is still pending: https://www.wto.org/english/tratop_e/dispu_e/cases_e/ds467_e.htm.

licensing of marks. The significance of these standards for UK law is mainly in the restrictions that they place on potential future developments, most obviously the adoption of plain packaging regulations for tobacco products.

4.3 REGIONAL HARMONIZATION

It is impossible to understand current UK law without reference to regional harmonization initiatives. The most significant of these is the European Trade Marks Directive adopted in 1988 and codified twice since then, first in a 2008 version,[101] and most recently amended and recast in 2015 (though this is not due for implementation until January 2019).[102] As we explained in Chapter 1, disparities among the trade mark laws of individual member states (which gave trade mark owners different rights in different circumstances) were thought to impede the free movement of goods and freedom to provide services, and to distort competition within the European Union.[103] In response, the Trade Marks Directive was designed to approximate 'those national provisions of law which most directly affect the functioning of the internal market'.[104] The original Directive therefore harmonized the general conditions for obtaining and continuing to hold a registered trade mark, and the rights conferred by a trade mark.[105] In certain areas, however, it was decided that harmonization was not necessary. Consequently, member states are given discretion to decide whether to adopt certain of the rules provided for in the Directive. For example, there are certain optional grounds for refusing to register or invalidating a trade mark.[106] The Directive also leaves to the member states matters such as the procedure concerning the registration, revocation, and invalidity of trade marks.[107]

In addition to the Trade Marks Directive, the European legislature also adopted a Regulation establishing a European Union Trade Mark (known until 2016 as the Community Trade Mark).[108] Adopted in 1994, this established the EUIPO (formerly known as the OHIM) as an agency that could grant trade marks with EU-wide effect. The conditions that an applicant must meet to be granted a trade mark, as well as the rights conferred by such marks, correspond in general to the rules in the Directive, but whereas some matters were left in the Directive to the discretion of member states, the EU regime was necessarily obliged to adopt particular positions on those issues. As of May 2018, the EUIPO had received more than 1.7 million applications and has registered nearly 1.5 million marks.[109] Following a comprehensive review of the

---

[101] Directive 2008/95/EC of the European Parliament and of the Council of 22 October 2008 to approximate the laws of the Member States relating to trade marks [2008] *OJ L* 299/25 (8 November 2008).

[102] Directive (EU) 2015/2436 of the European Parliament and of the Council of 16 December 2015 to Approximate the Laws of the Member States Relating to Trade Marks [2015] *OJ L* 336/1.

[103] TMD 1989, Recital 3.

[104] TMD 1989, Recital 4. See *David West, trading as Eastenders v. Fuller Smith* [2003] *FSR* (44) 816, [69] (Arden LJ) (acknowledging the divergence between the EU approach to assessing the distinctiveness—and therefore registrability—of a mark and the prior UK approach).

[105] A. Kur, 'Harmonisation of the Trademark Laws in Europe—An Overview' [1997] IIC 1. These optional provisions must be implemented in full or not at all: *Adidas-Salomon AG and Adidas Benelux BV v. Fitnessworld*, Case C-408/01 [2004] 1 *CMLR* (4) 448 (ECJ), [20].

[106] TMD 1989, Recital 8; see also TMD 2015, Recital 14.   [107] TMD 1989, Recitals 4–6.

[108] Council Regulation (EC) No 40/94 of 20 December 1993 on the Community trade mark [1994] *OJ L* 011/1 (14 January 1994), as amended. This was revised and codified in 2009 and most recently in 2017. See Chapter 35, section 3, pp. 945–9.

[109] *SSC009—Statistics of European Union Trade Marks* (November 2017); available online at https://euipo.europa.eu/ohimportal/en/the-office.

operation of the EU system,[110] both the Directive and the EUTM Regulation have been recently recast.[111] The most important of these changes will be referred to in the chapters that follow.

While there has thus been almost complete 'Europeanization' of *registered* trade mark law, it is notable that there has been comparatively little activity in relation to unfair competition law (at least insofar as it concerns rights of business, as opposed to consumers). The primary exception is a Directive on Misleading and Comparative Advertising, which harmonizes the circumstances under which comparative advertising is permissible.[112] While the European Union has adopted a more general Directive on Unfair Competitive Practices, this is restricted to business-to-consumer practices.[113] In due course, this might be made the basis of full harmonization of unfair competition law as it affects businesses.

Finally, we should note that the Union has a number of initiatives dealing with 'protected designations of origin' (PDOs) and 'protected geographical indications' (PGIs) for wines, spirits, agricultural products, and food. These are considered in Chapter 43.

5 CHALLENGES

The advent of electronic commerce and the possibility of direct sales of goods over the Internet has brought with it new questions for trade marks. Initially, questions arose about the relationship between trade marks and domain names. This issue attracted a lot of attention, both at the national and international levels, and UK law responded to these pressures through existing legal regimes, rather than attempted to promulgate new statutes. Where a domain name is used to trade in the same sphere as an existing trade mark owner, the courts have found little difficulty in employing the laws of passing off and registered trade marks.[114] Moreover, these laws have often been applied somewhat generously to enable existing businesses to prevent opportunistic 'cyber-squatting'.[115]

There has also been an international response of an interesting sort: the establishment by the Internet Corporation for Assigned Names and Numbers (ICANN) of a Uniform

---

[110] Max Planck Institute, *Study on the Overall Functioning of the European Trade Mark System* (2011).

[111] See Chapter 35, section 1.1, pp. 929–30.

[112] Directive 2006/114/EC of the European Parliament and of the Council of 12 December 2006 concerning misleading and comparative advertising [2006] *OJ L* 376/21 (27 December 2006).

[113] Directive 2005/29/EC of the European Parliament and of the Council of 11 May 2005 concerning unfair business-to-consumer commercial practices in the internal market and amending Council Directive 84/450/EEC, Directives 97/7/EC, 98/27/EC and 2002/65/EC of the European Parliament and of the Council and Regulation (EC) No. 2006/2004 of the European Parliament and of the Council [2005] *OJ L* 149/22 (11 June 2005). Implemented in the United Kingdom by the Consumer Protection from Unfair Trading Regulations 2008 (SI 2008/1277). See generally H. Collins (ed.), *The Forthcoming EC Directive on Unfair Commercial Practices* (2004); G. Howells, H. W. Micklitz, and T. Wilhelmsson (eds), *European Fair Trading Law: The Unfair Commercial Practices Directive* (2nd edn, 2016); J. Glöckner, 'The Scope of Application of the UCP Directive' (2010) 41 *IIC* 570. On the potential for this to develop into a business-to-business regime, see C. Wadlow, 'The Emergent European Law of Unfair Competition and its Consumer Law Origins' [2012] *IPQ* 1; P. Johnson and J. Gibson, 'The "New" Tort of Passing Off' (2015) 131 *LQR* 476.

[114] There are, of course, real problems about jurisdiction where a foreign trader uses a similar name on a website run from overseas and who targets a different market. [115] See Chapter 33, section 2.2, pp. 889–90.

Domain Name Dispute Resolution Policy (UDRP).[116] This involves arbitration to resolve disputes concerning the abusive registration of a domain name. The UDRP is a mandatory administrative procedure incorporated into the agreements between ICANN and the top-level domain registries that it regulates (such as .com).[117] The registries in turn contractually ensure that accredited registrars and ultimately domain name applicants submit to this procedure, making it the primary recourse for any abusive registration challenges. At present, five organizations, including WIPO and the National Arbitration Forum, provide such arbitration services.

As of May 2018, WIPO panellists had decided 40,505 cases.[118] The UDRP is considered attractive because of its remedial effectiveness. Panellists may cancel an abusive registration or transfer the domain name to the complainant. An abusive registration is one where (i) the domain name is identical or confusingly similar to the complainant's trade mark, whether registered or unregistered; (ii) the registrant has no rights or legitimate interests in the trade mark; and (iii) the registration has been made and is being used in bad faith.[119] An extensive body of panel reports elaborates on these three requirements.[120] A recently introduced, cheaper and faster variant of the UDRP is the Uniform Rapid Suspension System (URS), 'for rapid relief to trade mark holders for the most clear-cut cases of infringement'.[121] In such cases of abuse, involving a higher burden of proof, the domain name can be temporarily or permanently suspended. Instead of transferring control to the trade mark owner, this system is designed to block others from using the domain name, especially where misleading variants of the mark may be in play.

Since *ex post* solutions to domain name conflicts continue to be costly and time-consuming, attention has turned towards pre-emptive solutions.[122] These include the establishment of the Trademark Clearinghouse (to enable verified rights holders to apply for domains during an advance window) as well as the Domains Protected Marks List (DPML), which relies on prior Clearinghouse authentication and subsequently enables brand owners to block their trade marks from being registered as domains by third parties for five years.

Alongside technological challenges, the wider recognition of brands has provided further fuel for those with expansionist tendencies. One particular campaign that has rumbled on in the United Kingdom for at least two decades would offer 'brand owners' broader control over imitation (especially in relation to 'lookalikes' and 'me-toos').[123]

---

[116] Initially adopted in 1999, the current version is available online at https://www.icann.org/resources/pages/help/dndr/udrp-en. On its adoption, see L. Helfer and G. Dinwoodie, 'Designing Non-national Systems: The Case of the Uniform Dispute Resolution Policy' [2001] 43 *WMLR* 141; see also T. Bettinger and A. Waddell (eds), *Domain Name Law and Practice: An International Handbook* (2nd edn, 2015).

[117] Nominet operates a similar policy for '.uk' domains, including '.co.uk' and '.plc.uk': see http://www.nic.uk. Nominet does not control some other second-level domains, such as '.ac.uk' and '.gov.uk'.

[118] See http://www.wipo.int/amc/en/domains/statistics/cases.jsp.

[119] WIPO, *UDRP Policy*, para. 4a.

[120] See WIPO, *Overview of WIPO Panel Views on Selected UDRP Questions* (2nd edn, 2011) available online at http://www.wipo.int/amc/en/domains/search/overview2.0/.

[121] Available online at https://newgtlds.icann.org/en/applicants/urs.

[122] See WIPO, *Update on Trade mark-Related Aspects of the Domain Name System* (25 February 2016) (SCT/35/5).

[123] Gowers Review, [5.82]–[5.88]. See, e.g., *European Parliament Resolution on a More Efficient and Fairer Retail Market* (2010) 2010/2109 (INI), [31], describing 'parasitic copying' as an 'unacceptable practice which should be addressed without delay'; P. Johnson, J. Gibson, and J. Freeman, *The Impact of Lookalikes: Similar Packaging in Fast Moving Consumer Goods* (2013) (offering an overview and pointing to possible extension of a right of action to businesses to enforce the obligations under the Unfair Commercial Practices Directive).

Brand owners argue that lookalikes exploit their goodwill built up through considerable investment and mislead customers into making unwanted purchases. Lookalike producers, including supermarkets with their own brands, respond that the similarity in packaging effectively signals quality equivalence at a cheaper price, which benefits consumers. Successive governments have resisted the lobbyists, but during the committee stage of the Intellectual Property Act 2014, David Willets announced a review to examine whether there is a need to give businesses a private right of action to help to protect brand owners from lookalikes.[124] Eventually, it was decided that no action would be taken.

---

[124] BIS, *Consumer Protection: Review of the Enforcement Provisions of the Consumer Protection from Unfair Trading Regulations 2008 in Respect of Copycat Packaging—Call for Evidence* (April 2014).

32

PASSING OFF

1 INTRODUCTION

The oldest of the modern legal regimes for the protection of trade symbols is the action for passing off.[1] In essence, the action allows trader A to prevent competitor B from passing their goods off as if they were A's. Lord Langdale MR summed up the rationale for the passing off action in *Perry v. Truefitt*[2] when he said:

> A man is not to sell his own goods under the pretence that they are the goods of another man; he cannot be permitted to practise such a deception, nor to use the means which contribute to that end. He cannot therefore be allowed to use names, marks, letters or other indicia, by which he may induce purchasers to believe, that the goods which he is selling are the manufacture of another person.[3]

While the early history of passing off is unclear,[4] it is widely thought that an action of this sort was first recognized in the Elizabethan case of *JG v. Samford*.[5] It is also generally acknowledged that the common law roots of the action are found in the torts of deceit and misrepresentation,[6] with the strictures of the common law action being mollified in a number of Chancery cases in the early nineteenth century.[7] The modern

---

[1] The pre-modern regimes included guild regulation, heraldry, and cutlers' marks: see Sherman and Bently, 166–8.

[2] (1842) 6 *Beav* 66, 49 *ER* 749.   [3] Ibid., 752.

[4] W. Morison, 'Unfair Competition and Passing Off' (1956) 2 *Sydney L Rev* 50, 53; *Henderson v. Radio Corporation Pty* (1960) [1969] *RPC* 218, 236.

[5] (1584) reported in J. Baker, *Baker and Milsom: Sources of English Law* (2nd edn, 2010), 673; first cited as a precedent in *Southern v. How* (1617) *Cro Jac* 468, 79 *ER* 400. See the discussion in F. Schechter, *The Historical Foundations of the Law Relating to Trade Marks* (1925), 10.

[6] For a discussion of the common law in the late eighteenth century, see L. Bently, '*Singleton v. Bolton*: The First Common Law Trade Mark Case?' (2014) 47 *U Cal Davis L Rev* 969. The first report of a common law case in which the claimant succeeded seems to be *Sykes v. Sykes* (1824) 3 *B & C* 543, 107 *ER* 834.

[7] In particular, Equity judges abandoned the requirement of bad faith in *Millington v. Fox* (1838) 3 *My & Cr* 338, 40 *ER* 956. See L. Bently, 'Day v Day, Day and Martin (1816)', in J. Bellido (ed), *Landmark Cases in Intellectual Property Law* (2017) 87 (exploring the first instances of injunctive relief for misuse of trade marks). Quite what became of the common law action is unclear. There is some authority for the view that it was abolished by the legislature when registration was introduced, because that prohibited any action based on an unregistered mark. Passing off, in contrast, survived because the basis of the action was not the mark itself, but the trader's goodwill. For arguments that there remains a common law action based on fraud, without a requirement of goodwill, see Gummow J in *10th Cantanae Pty v. Shoshama Pty* (1989) 10 *IPR* 289; *ConAgra Inc. v. McCain Foods (Australia) Pty* (1992) 23 *IPR* 193.

or classic formulation of the action (usually classified as a tort) emerged in the second half of the nineteenth century. In its classic form, the basis of the action was the existence of a 'misrepresentation'. Typically, a misrepresentation occurs where a person says or does something that incorrectly suggests that the goods or services they are selling are the goods or services of the claimant. In order to justify injunctive relief, the courts believed that it was necessary for the action to be based on a property right. It was initially suggested that this property right was located in the name or symbol employed.[8] This approach was rejected in the early twentieth century, when it was said that the basis of equitable intervention was the property in 'goodwill'.[9] The concept of goodwill, which will be examined in detail later, remains a prerequisite for a successful passing off action today.

It is important to recognize that the modern action, if it can be called a single action,[10] has moved beyond the classic case.[11] Indeed, as a result of adapting to changes in the commercial environment, the tort now extends beyond the sale of goods to cover services, beyond pretences concerning the origin of goods to cover pretences concerning their quality, and beyond simple pretences that the goods are those of another trader to cover pretences that the goods have been licensed by another trader.[12] As a result, the tort continues to play a central role in the legal regulation of trade behaviour.[13] The common law nature of the action also gives it a flexibility that makes it attractive in situations that are not covered by the statutory regimes. This is particularly important where business practices change and the legislature is slow to respond.[14]

With these developments, it has become increasingly difficult to state the law of passing off with any clarity or precision. Indeed, it has been said that the law 'contains sufficient nooks and crannies to make it difficult to formulate any satisfactory definition in short form'.[15] The difficulty in formulating a precise and accurate statement of the law has not been made any easier by the fact that recent authoritative statements of the law, which are found in the House of Lords' decisions in *Warnink v. Townend* (the 'Advocaat'

---

[8] L. Bently, 'From Communication to Thing: Historical Aspects of the Conceptualisation of Trade Marks as Property', in Dinwoodie and Janis (2008).

[9] *Spalding v. Gamage* (1915) 32 *RPC* 273, 284.

[10] Phillips and Coleman have argued that passing off is better seen as a family of actions, each with particular characteristics: J. Phillips and A. Coleman, 'Passing Off and the Common Field of Activity' (1985) 101 *LQR* 242, 244–5. Despite the strength of this argument, the courts have continued to treat passing off as a unitary action, only occasionally distinguishing 'classic' passing off, from 'extended' passing off. See, e.g., *Chocosuisse Union des Fabricants Suisses de Chocolat v. Cadbury* [1998] *RPC* 117, 127 (distinguishing between 'extended' and 'classic' passing off and describing the question of whether it is the same tort as 'a matter of semantics'). Note also *British Diabetic Association v. Diabetic Society* [1996] *FSR* 1, 11 (Robert Walker J) (warning against the assumption that principles from one set of facts can be applied to very different facts).

[11] *Arsenal FC plc v. Reed (No. 2)* [2003] *RPC* 39, [70] (Aldous LJ).

[12] However, the law of passing off has not expanded into a tort of unfair competition. See Chapter 34, section 3, pp. 924–7.

[13] *Cadbury Schweppes Pty v. Pub Squash Co.* [1981] *RPC* 429, 490 (Lord Scarman) (the tort 'is no longer anchored in its early nineteenth-century formulation'); cf. *Hogan v. Koala Dundee* (1988) 12 *IPR* 508 (FCA), 517 (Pincus J) (little progress in English law beyond the traditional notion of passing off). See also M. Shúilleabháin, 'Common Law Protection of Trade Marks: The Continuing Relevance of Passing Off' (2003) 34(7) *IIC* 722.

[14] Passing off operates as a basis for relief where a trader has failed to register a mark, while also retaining a role within the registered trade mark system. As will be seen at Chapter 38, section 3.1, pp. 1073–4, it is not possible for a person to register a sign as a trade mark if its use would amount to passing off.

[15] *ConAgra v. McCain Foods (Australia) Pty* (1992) 23 *IPR* 193 (FCA), 247.

decision),[16] and *Reckitt & Colman v. Borden* (the 'Jif' lemon decision),[17] are in very different terms.[18] Having said that, it is possible to formulate a general statement regarding the elements of the action. In order to succeed in an action for passing off, a claimant must establish that:

(i)   the claimant has 'goodwill' (discussed in this chapter);

(ii) the defendant made a 'misrepresentation' that is likely to deceive the public (Chapter 33); and

(iii) the misrepresentation damages the goodwill of the claimant (Chapter 34).

Before turning to examine goodwill in more detail, two caveats are in order. The first is that each of the three elements must be shown to have existed or occurred at the time when the conduct which the claimant objects to took place (as opposed, for example, to the time of proceedings).[19] The second point to note is that the three elements are interrelated. As a result, the same facts may be important in proving goodwill, deception, and/or damage. Consequently, the courts may dismiss an action for lack of misrepresentation where it might as easily involve a lack of goodwill.[20] The interrelationship is also important because developments in one area, such as misrepresentation, may impact on another area, such as damages. This can be seen, for example, with the recognition of dilution as a form of damage, which has thrown into doubt the need for the defendant's misrepresentation to cause confusion or deception.[21]

2 REQUIREMENT OF GOODWILL

The first factor that needs to be proved to establish an action for passing off is goodwill.[22] The mere fact that consumers are confused about the source of a product or service is not enough for a trader to bring a successful passing off action against another trader with

---

[16] *Erven Warnink BV v. Townend (J.) & Sons* [1979] *AC* 731. The case contains two different formulations of the requirements for the action. Lord Diplock laid down five 'characteristics' that must be present to create a valid cause of action in passing off: (i) a misrepresentation, (ii) made by a trader in the course of trade, (iii) to prospective customers of that trader or ultimate consumers of goods or services supplied by that trader, (iv) which is calculated to injure the business or goodwill of another trader (in the sense that this is a reasonably foreseeable consequence), and (v) which causes actual damage to a business or goodwill of the trader by whom the action is brought or (in a *quia timet* action) will probably do so: ibid., 742. Lord Fraser also set out five requirements: (i) that the claimant's business consists of, or includes, selling in England a class of goods to which the particular trade name applies; (ii) that the class of goods is clearly defined and that, in the minds of the public, or a section of the public, in England, the trade name distinguishes that class from other similar goods; (iii) that, because of the reputation of the goods, there is a goodwill attached to the name; (iv) that the claimant, as a member of the class of those who sell the goods, is the owner of goodwill in England that is of substantial value; and (v) that the claimant has suffered, or is really likely to suffer, substantial damage to their property in the goodwill by reason of the defendant selling goods that are falsely described by the trade name to which the goodwill is attached: ibid., 755–6.   [17] [1990] 1 *WLR* 491.

[18] In the latter case, Lord Oliver reduced the elements of the action to three—reputation, deception, and damage: ibid., 499. This formulation was adopted by Lord Neuberger in *Starbucks (HK) Ltd v. British Sky Broadcasting Group PLC* [2015] *UKSC* 31, [15].

[19] *J. C. Penney v. Penneys* [1975] *FSR* 367; *Barnsley Brewery Co. v. RBNB* [1997] *FSR* 462, 470; *Chocosuisse Union des Fabricants Suisse de Chocolat v. Cadbury* [1999] *RPC* 826, 836, 846; *Interlotto (UK) Ltd v. Camelot Group plc* (2003) *EWHC* 1256 (Ch) (Laddie J); (2003) *EWCA Civ* 1132, [7].

[20] See, e.g., *Chivers & Sons v. Chivers & Co.* (1900) 17 *RPC* 420.

[21] *Harrods v. Harrodian School* [1996] *RPC* 697.

[22] *Star Industrial Co. v. Yap Kwee Kor* [1976] *FSR* 217, 223; *Warnink v. Townend* [1979] *AC* 731, 742, 755–6.

whom their products are being confused.[23] Before any such action, traders must show that they have goodwill in relation to the product or service in question.

Goodwill is a form of intangible property that is easy to describe, but difficult to define. It is that ineffable thing, that magnetism, which leads customers to return to the same business or to buy the same brand. In *IRC v. Muller & Co.'s Margarine*, Lord Macnaghten said that:

> [Goodwill] is the benefit and advantage of the good name, reputation, and connection of a business. It is the attractive force that brings in custom. It is the one thing which distinguishes an old-established business from a new business at its first start. The goodwill of a business must emanate from a particular centre or source. However widely or extended or diffused its influence may be, goodwill is worth nothing unless it has power of attraction sufficient to bring customers home to the source from which it emanates. Goodwill is composed of a variety of elements. It differs in its composition in different trades and in different businesses in the same trade. One element may preponderate here and another element there.[24]

As Lord Macnaghten stressed, for goodwill to exist, there must be some 'causative' impact upon customer behaviour. Goodwill is the attractive force that 'brings in' custom. The goodwill must have a 'power of attraction sufficient to bring customers home to the source from which it emanates'.[25] One consequence of this is that just because a trader has started business does not necessarily mean that there will be goodwill. This is because consumers might use the business—that is, purchase the goods or services—because it is conveniently located or simply because it is there. For goodwill to exist, customers must be buying the goods or using the services as a result of the reputation that the business has developed.[26]

2.1 MANIFESTATIONS OF GOODWILL

The law of passing off is concerned with goodwill when it manifests itself in certain ways. Passing off is usually concerned with the signs or badges that are understood as indicating that a product or service emanates from a particular trade source. These badges can take a variety of forms. Typically, goodwill arises in relation to the name, symbol, or logo that has been employed by a trader and thus has come to be associated with the business. For example, it is clear that there is goodwill associated with the name MARKS & SPENCER, and the NIKE 'swoosh' or tick. In these situations, the law is relatively straightforward. However, the courts have recognized that goodwill may arise in a number of other situations. These include goodwill associated with the packaging, get-up, or trade dress of products, and advertising style. In this section, we will limit our discussions to some of the less straightforward situations.

2.1.1 Goodwill in descriptive words

While goodwill is typically developed through the use of words such as NIKE, GUCCI, or ROLLS-ROYCE to distinguish one trader's goods or services from those of its competitors,

---

[23] *HFC Bank v. Midland Bank* [2000] *FSR* 176, 182–3; *Starbucks (HK) Ltd and ors v. British Sky Broadcasting Group Plc and ors* [2012] *EWHC* 3074 (Ch), [153]–[158].

[24] *IRC v. Muller & Co.'s Margarine* [1901] *AC* 217, 224 (Lord Macnaghten). Although a tax case, it has been frequently employed in passing off cases and the Court of Appeal has said that 'no one, judge or jurist, has yet improved' on it as a description: *Scandecor Development AB v. Scandecor Marketing AB* [1999] *FSR* 26, 41.

[25] *IRC v. Muller & Co.'s Margarine* [1901] *AC* 217, 224 (Lord Macnaghten).

[26] *HFC Bank v. Midland Bank* [2000] *FSR* 176, 183.

in some circumstances goodwill may come to be associated with words that initially were capable of being understood as descriptive of the goods themselves.[27] For example, FRUIT PASTILLES might be taken to be a description of a product delivered in pastille form, which tastes of or is made from fruit. However, most children (and adults) in the United Kingdom will understand the words as indicating a particular brand of sweet confectionary, in fact made by Rowntree's, now owned by Nestlé. Consequently, such words have become the manifestation of the goodwill that Rowntree's owns in the sweets.

While it is possible for a descriptive term to become associated with a claimant, the courts are extremely reluctant to allow a person to obtain a monopoly in descriptive words.[28] In part, this is because policy considerations favour allowing other traders to make use of words that are part of the common stock-in-trade. It is also because in relation to descriptive words, it will be more difficult for a trader to show that the words indicate source, rather than what they ordinarily describe. In short, the more descriptive the words of the goods or services that the trader sells, the more difficult it will be to establish the existence of goodwill attaching to those words.

For a trader to show that they have goodwill in a descriptive word, they need to show that the word has become 'distinctive in fact' or has taken on a 'secondary meaning'.[29] This can be seen, for example, in *Reddaway v. Banham*,[30] where the House of Lords acknowledged that the claimant's use of the term CAMEL HAIR to describe its belting (which was in fact substantially made out of hair from camels) had acquired a secondary meaning amongst those who purchased it for use in their machinery. Other examples of (largely) descriptive words that acquired secondary meaning include: OVEN CHIPS for potato chips to be cooked in the oven rather than fried;[31] FLAKED OATMEAL;[32] MALTED MILK;[33] and MOTHERCARE for clothing for expectant mothers and children.[34]

For a trader to show that they have goodwill in a descriptive word, the trader needs to demonstrate that the words have acquired a secondary meaning, not only of goods or services of that description, but also specifically of the goods or services of which they are the source.[35] The descriptive terms should be demonstrably distinctive of one source.[36] Thus where two publishers are competing to launch magazines with a title such as LEISURE NEWS, it is unlikely that either will be able to bring a passing off action until the magazine

---

[27] In between the category of invented or coined words and descriptive words, are many allusive or quasi-descriptive terms. The courts will be willing to protect these terms soon after they are used in trade: see, e.g., *Phones4U Ltd v. Phone4u.co.uk Internet Ltd* [2006] *EWCA Civ* 244, [24]–[25], [30]–[34] (first-instance judge had wrongly held that there was no goodwill in PHONES4U because it was descriptive, even though turnover was £42 million and it held 19 per cent of the market); *Knight v. Beyond Properties Pty Ltd* [2007] *FSR* 34 (goodwill in MYTHBUSTERS for children's books as a result of sales numbering in the thousands).

[28] *Spalding v. Gamage* (1915) 32 *RPC* 273, 284; *Cellular Clothing Co. v. Maxton & Murray* [1899] *AC* 326, 339.

[29] See Wadlow (2016), [8–076]. See also: *The Sofa Workshop Ltd v. Sofaworks Ltd* [2015] *EWHC* 1773 (IPEC) ('The Sofa Workshop' acquired sufficient secondary meaning to succeed in passing off against 'Sofaworks'); *The Ukulele Orchestra of Great Britain v. Clausen* [2015] *EWHC* 1772 (IPEC) ('The Ukulele Orchestra of Great Britain' acquired sufficient secondary meaning to succeed in passing off against 'The United Kingdom Ukulele Orchestra'). For acquisition of secondary meaning in the context of registered marks, see Chapter 37, section 3.5, pp. 1005–12.

[30] [1896] *AC* 199 (HL) (reversing the Court of Appeal decision that the defendant should not be liable for telling the simple truth).

[31] *McCain International v. County Fair Foods* [1981] *RPC* 69.   [32] *Parsons v. Gillespie* [1898] *AC* 239 (PC).

[33] *Horlick's Malted Milk Co. v. Summerskill* (1916) 33 *RPC* 108.

[34] *Mothercare v. Penguin Books* [1988] *RPC* 113, 115.

[35] Secondary meaning is essential not only where the name describes the product, but also where it embodies a reference to quality. For example, THE HIT FACTORY was descriptive of a quality of the claimant's recording studio and, in the absence of a demonstration of secondary meaning, could not form the basis of a passing off action: *Peter Waterman v. CBS* [1993] *EMLR* 27.   [36] Ibid.

has been in the marketplace for a sufficient period of time to build up a public association between the name and a particular source.[37] As Farwell J said, the name should:

> ... have to the whole of the trade and to all persons who have any knowledge of the article in question the sole meaning sought to be attached to it by the plaintiffs—that is to say, the original primary meaning must have been eliminated from the dictionary of persons who deal in this article in the trade and all other persons whom it may concern to know it.[38]

In proving secondary meaning, it will be common for a claimant to submit evidence such as the length of use and the amount of money spent on advertising.[39] It will certainly be easier to find that a name is distinctive and thus protected where a trader has used the name separately rather than in conjunction with another sign that designates source.[40] Moreover, distinctiveness will be acquired more readily if the sign is not exclusively descriptive, as was the case with FARM FLUID for farm disinfectant.[41] A trader may acquire secondary meaning in a descriptive phrase through public adoption rather than their own action.[42] In these cases, the most important evidence is evidence of the trade or public.

On the whole, the association must be in the mind of the general public, so that it is not normally legitimate 'to slice the public into parts'.[43] However, in *Starbucks (HK) Ltd v. British Sky Broadcasting Plc*[44] Arnold J held that there might be goodwill amongst a distinct segment of the population, such as the Chinese-speaking community. The Court of Appeal saw no problem with such an approach.[45]

Similar principles apply to geographic words and personal names. In general, the adoption of a geographic term or a personal name will not prevent another trader from using the same designation.[46] In certain circumstances, however, secondary meaning can attach to such signs. For example, in *Montgomery v. Thompson*[47] the claimant had operated a brewery in the small town of Stone in Staffordshire for more than 100 years. Over time, its beer had become widely known as STONE ALE. The defendant, who had recently established a brewery in Stone, was prevented from using the term stone to describe its beer.[48] Similarly, it was held by the Court of Appeal that the term SWISS CHOCOLATE had come to be understood by a significant section of the public to mean, and to mean only, chocolate made in Switzerland and that this was understood as being of a particular quality.[49]

---

[37] *Marcus Publishing v. Leisure News* [1990] *RPC* 576, 584.

[38] *Chivers v. Chivers* (1900) 17 *RPC* 420, 430 (Farwell J) (in the context of personal names); Wadlow (2016), [8–73]–[8–88] (reviewing comparative case law on generic and descriptive names).

[39] Such factors, of themselves, will not give rise to recognition. Advertisement distinguished from trade is nothing: *Chivers v. Chivers* (1900) 17 *RPC* 420, 431 (Farwell J) (describing the act of advertising as an atrocious disfigurement of the fairest landscape in the kingdom); *Burberrys v. Cording* (1909) 26 *RPC* 693 (slip-on).

[40] *McCain v. County Fair* [1981] *RPC* 69 (oven chips used with MCCAIN's). See more generally in Chapter 37, section 3.5.5 ff, at pp. 1010–12.

[41] *Antec International v. South Western Chicks (Warren)* [1997] *FSR* 278, [1998] *FSR* 738, 743–4.

[42] *Edge & Sons v. Gallon & Son* [1900] *RPC* 557; *Peter Waterman v. CBS* [1993] *EMLR* 27.

[43] *Peter Waterman v. CBS* [1993] *EMLR* 27 (rejecting arguments that it was sufficient that the claimant's recording studio was known as THE HIT FACTORY to popular music press and the 'non-pompous end of market', when other sectors treated the phrase as referring to others).

[44] *Starbucks (HK) Ltd v. British Sky Broadcasting Plc* [2012] *EWHC* 3074 (Ch), [130], [134].

[45] *Starbucks (HK) Ltd v. British Sky Broadcasting Group Plc* [2013] *EWCA Civ* 1465, [59], [63].

[46] *Chivers v. Chivers* (1900) 17 *RPC* 420.   [47] [1891] *AC* 217.

[48] See also *My Kinda Town v. Soll* [1983] *RPC* 407 (CHICAGO PIZZA); *CPC (United Kingdom) v. Keenan* [1986] *FSR* 527 (OXFORD marmalade, OXBRIDGE marmalade).

[49] *Chocosuisse v. Cadbury* [1999] *RPC* 826, 832.

Words, once distinctive, may later lose their ability to indicate source whereupon a passing off action will no longer be available. A classic example is LINOLEUM, which is the name used for a floor covering made of solidified oil. The floor covering had been the subject of a patent and, during that time, the claimant was its only manufacturer. After expiry of the patent, other manufacturers began to make and sell the floor covering under the name linoleum. Fry J refused to prevent competitors using this term on the basis that it had become generic. That is, the public had begun to use the term to refer to the product generally, without connoting the source of manufacture.[50]

2.1.2 Goodwill associated with packaging, get-up, and trade dress

A person may acquire goodwill through use of particular packaging or 'get-up' for their products.[51] For example, in *Reckitt & Colman*,[52] since the 1950s, the claimant had sold lemon juice in plastic containers that resembled a lemon in size, shape, and colour. The House of Lords held that if the defendant went ahead with its plans to use plastic lemons that were very similar to the claimant's, the defendant would be passing their juice off as the claimant's. This was because the evidence indicated that the claimant had succeeded in persuading the public that lemon juice sold in plastic lemon-sized containers had been manufactured by them. It made no difference that the claimant's juice was labelled JIF and the defendant's REALEMON, because purchasers did not look closely at the labels.

The protection that passing off provides over trade dress, get-up, and the packaging of goods is particularly important where consumers identify products by their external features rather than by words. This will be the case where goods are sold in foreign-language markets where little attention is likely to be paid to the words,[53] or where the goods are sold to people who are illiterate.[54] Get-up is also more likely to be an identifying feature in the case of common household goods,[55] rather than goods that are bought under professional supervision.[56]

In order to establish that the claimant has goodwill associated with the get-up, including both the shape and/or packaging of a product, a claimant must be able to prove that the public recognizes that the get-up is distinctive of the claimant's goods or services.[57] In practice, a claimant may experience a number of difficulties in establishing such an association, particularly where the claim relates to the shape rather than the packaging of a product. Consumers may not consider that the get-up indicates any commercial source, especially where it is used alongside an established brand name.[58] Alternatively

---

[50] *Linoleum Manufacturing Co. v. Nairn* (1878) 7 Ch D 834, 836.

[51] J. Evans, 'Passing Off and the Problem of Product Simulation' (1968) 31 *MLR* 642; Wadlow (2011), [8.132]–[8.165], 725–49; *Edge v. Nicholls* [1911] *AC* 693 (washing soap sold in a calico bag with a stick attached). It should be remembered that design protection exists for product shapes, although there are limits upon such protection (for instance, technical shapes are excluded). See Part III of this book.

[52] [1990] *RPC* 341, 406.

[53] *Modus Vivendi v. Keen (World Marketing)* [1996] *EIPR* D-82 (sale of butane gas by defendant in similar get-up in China); *Johnston v. Orr Ewing* (1882) 7 *App Cas* 219, 225.

[54] *Edge v. Nicholls* [1911] *AC* 693.   [55] *United Biscuits (UK) v. Asda Stores* [1997] *RPC* 513.

[56] *Hodgkinson & Corby v. Wards Mobility Services* [1995] *FSR* 169.

[57] However, while it is clear that imitation of get-up or packaging may constitute a misrepresentation, this does not mean that in all cases it will do so: *Reckitt & Colman* [1990] *RPC* 341, 406.

[58] *The London Taxi Corporation Ltd v. Frazer-Nash Research Ltd* [2016] *EWHC* 52 (Ch), [287], [295] (Arnold J) (identifying reliance on the sign as a source indicator as the 'acid test' for establishing goodwill in a product shape or feature); *George East Housewares Ltd v. Fackelmann GmbH* [2016] *EWHC* 2476 (IPEC), [34]–[40] (reviewing the authorities on this point, in the context of assessing goodwill in various aspects of the get-up of a measuring cup); *Gama Healthcare Ltd v. Pal International Ltd* [2016] *EWHC* 75 (IPEC) (get-up not clearly defined).

consumers may understand a product shape or feature to be merely functional or aesthetically pleasing. Since such features may be legitimately copied with an eye to competitive substitutability, it is therefore important to distinguish between situations where the shape of the product is copied and those where product packaging is copied.

While there is no public policy exception to the passing off action for 'functional features' and no requirement that features of get-up be 'capricious',[59] it will be very difficult for a trader to demonstrate that the public view functional or non-capricious features of an article as indicating source. As Jacob J said in *Hodgkinson & Corby v. Wards Mobility Services*,[60] the claimant must prove a misrepresentation, which will be hard where there is no manifest badge of trade origin. This is because people tend to buy things for what they are and what they do, rather than out of interest in their origin. Accordingly, Jacob J found that a defendant who produced cushions that were used to help alleviate bed sores had not passed them off as the claimant's. This was the case even though the claimant's cushions were memorable and striking, and the defendant's cushions were similar in appearance.

2.1.3 Advertising style

A trader may also attempt to establish that they have goodwill associated with particular advertising techniques or slogans, and thus that a defendant is liable for passing off where they use techniques or slogans that are similar to those used by the claimant. In *Cadbury Schweppes v. Pub Squash*,[61] the claimant produced a lemon-flavoured soft drink called SOLO. As a part of its Australian marketing campaign, television advertisements featured 'ruggedly masculine and adventurous men' drinking SOLO. The defendant promoted its lemon-flavoured soft drink with a similar campaign. While the Privy Council rejected the passing off claim, Lord Scarman said that there was no reason *in principle* why the claimant could not have acquired goodwill associated with a particular advertising style. The reason for this was that:[62]

> [T]he tort is no longer anchored as in the early nineteenth-century formulation to the name or trade mark of a product or business. It is wide enough to encompass other descriptive material, such as slogans or visual images, which radio, television or newspaper advertising campaigns can lead the market to associate with the plaintiff's product, provided always that such descriptive material has become part of the goodwill of the product.[63]

While the Privy Council recognized that passing off may protect a claimant's advertising campaign, it seems that claimants will have difficulties in demonstrating that the public associates a specific style of advertising with a particular source.[64]

2.1.4 Use of image, likeness, or voice

Finally, it is worth observing that in principle there is no reason why goodwill might not also arise through the use of a celebrity's image,[65] likeness, or voice.[66] Whether this is the

[59] *Hodgkinson & Corby v. Wards Mobility Services* [1995] *FSR* 169, 177. However, the House of Lords in *Reckitt & Colman* [1990] *RPC* 341 did indicate that such imitation of get-up might not amount to a misrepresentation when it was the only way in which to present the product. Lord Oliver noted that the association of the plastic shape with the claimant arose because 'there is nothing in the nature of the product sold which inherently requires it to be sold in the particular format': ibid., 416.

[60] [1995] *FSR* 169.   [61] [1981] *RPC* 429.   [62] Ibid., 490.   [63] Ibid.

[64] For further consideration of advertisements, see the cases discussed by Wadlow (2016), [8–235]–[8–238].

[65] *Henderson v. Radio Corporation* (1960) [1969] *RPC* 218; *Fenty v. Arcadia Group Brands Ltd (t/a Topshop)* [2013] *EWHC* 2310 (Ch).

[66] *Sim v. H. J. Heinz Co.* [1959] 1 *WLR* 313.

case will always be a question of fact. In particular, it will depend on whether the public believe that there is a relevant connection between the celebrity and the goods or services in issue. It should be noted that, unlike the position in many continental jurisdictions[67] and in several US states,[68] British law does not recognize a general right of publicity or personality.[69]

2.2 'TRADER OPERATING IN TRADE'

As we indicated earlier, in order to demonstrate goodwill, a claimant must be a trader and operate in trade. We will look at each of these in turn.

2.2.1 The claimant must be a 'trader'

For a claimant to be in a position to show that they have the goodwill necessary to sustain a passing off action, they must show that they are engaged in a very general sense in a business or commercial activity. The upshot of this is that the action is not available where one person changes their name to that of another, or calls their cat, boat, or house by the same name as that of their neighbour (however inconvenient or confusing that may be).

For the most part, the requirement that the claimant be in a trade has presented few problems. This is because the courts have been quite generous when deciding whether someone is engaged in business.[70] For example, the courts have recognized authors,[71] performers,[72] unincorporated associations,[73] and charities[74] as businesses that potentially give rise to goodwill.

The courts have only occasionally rejected a claimant's claim to passing off because of a lack of business status. One instance where a passing off action was denied was in *Kean v. McGivan*,[75] where the claimant claimed the exclusive right to the name social democratic party. The Court of Appeal refused relief on the basis that the claimant was involved in a non-commercial activity. This was because the claimant was a small northern-based political party, whose commercial activities were limited to the hiring of halls for meetings. If the claimant had been one of the major political parties, which received and spent large sums of money, the answer may have been different. It should be noted that the decision in *Kean v. McGivan* has been distinguished by the Court of Appeal in *Burge v. Haycock*,[76] where a lobbying organization known as the 'Countryside Alliance' (best known for campaigning in support of fox hunting) was granted injunctive relief to prevent the defendant, a former member of the right-wing British National Party, from

---

[67] H. Beverley-Smith, A. Ohly, and A. Lucas-Schloetter, *Privacy, Property and Personality: Civil Law Perspectives on Commercial Appropriation* (2005).

[68] M. Bartholomew, 'A Right is Born: Celebrity, Property, and Postmodern Lawmaking' (2011) 44 *Connecticut L Rev* 301; J. T. McCarthy, *The Rights of Publicity & Privacy* (2nd edn, 2017).

[69] As recently confirmed in *Fenty v. Arcadia Group Brands Ltd* [2015] *EWCA Civ* 3, [29] (Kitchin LJ) ('There is in English law no "image right" or "character right" which allows a celebrity to control the use of his or her name or image'). For arguments in favour of such control, see D. Tan, *The Commercial Appropriation of Fame* (2017).

[70] 'The word "trade" is widely interpreted': *Kean v. McGivan* [1982] *FSR* 119, 120 (Ackner LJ).

[71] *Alan Clark v. Associated Newspapers* [1998] *RPC* 261, 269.

[72] *Henderson v. Radio Corporation* (1960) [1969] *RPC* 218; cf. *Kaye v. Robertson* [1991] *FSR* 62 (Kaye, an actor, not a trader in relation to story about accident).

[73] *British Legion v. British Legion Club (Street)* (1931) 63 *RPC* 555, 562.

[74] *British Diabetic Association* [1996] *FSR* 1, 5.

[75] [1982] *FSR* 119. The defendants were a high-profile breakaway group from the Labour Party, known as the 'Gang of Four'. In due course, the defendants' Social Democrats merged with the Liberal Party to form the Liberal Democrats.   [76] [2001] *EWCA Civ* 900.

standing in a parish council election under the banner of the Countryside Alliance. Distinguishing *Kean* on the basis that it was 'a decision on its particular facts',[77] the Court of Appeal said that the right to protect goodwill did not depend on the precise legal status of an entity (such as whether it was a charity or a political party); instead, all that mattered was they had established goodwill.[78]

Another potentially problematic situation relates to professionals: do they merely have a professional reputation as opposed to protectable goodwill? The authorities were reviewed in *Bhayani*,[79] which addressed the issue of whether a law firm or an individual partner owns the goodwill generated in the course of her professional duties and whether the partnership could be prevented from using her name when she left. In the usual course, the goodwill generated by a partner's acts will vest in the partnership, as was the case here. However in certain circumstances an employee or partner may generate goodwill of their own, such as where they conduct activities outside the scope of employment or partnership duties or where the employee was a writer for a newspaper and the public assumed they bore sole responsibility for the quality of their work.

A further situation where the requirement that the claimant be a trader has been problematic is where an action for passing off is brought by a trade association. If the trade association does not manufacture or sell any particular product, it will be unable to bring a passing off action against a defendant who has merely passed off their products as those of the members of the trade association.[80] However, where a trade association organized exhibitions, it could own goodwill through its members, which would form the basis for an action in passing off. In such a case, the action would have to be commenced by a member of the association acting in a representative capacity.[81]

2.2.2 The claimant must be trading

Once it has been shown that a claimant is engaged in a trade activity, there will usually be few problems in establishing that they have the goodwill necessary to sustain a passing off action. Traders, however, have experienced problems in establishing goodwill in three situations: (i) before they have started trading; (ii) after trading has ended; and (iii) where the trader is situated overseas. We will deal with each in turn.

(i) Pre-trading goodwill

Given that goodwill 'has no independent existence apart from the business to which it is attached',[82] difficult questions arise when a person is setting up a business. In these circumstances, the question may arise: at what point can a person claim to have goodwill? Is there any way in which a trader who is about to launch their business, and who has spent time and money on advertising and marketing, can prevent a competitor from taking advantage of their pre-launch publicity?

---

[77] Ibid., [69] (Hale LJ).

[78] Ibid. The Court cited *Holy Apostolic & Catholic Church of the East (Assyrian) Australia New South Wales Parish Association v. Attorney General (New South Wales)* [1989] 18 *NSWLR* 291, 294 (Court of Appeal of New South Wales) (no reason why a religious organization should not have the same protection over the goodwill in its name as is afforded to commercial organizations).

[79] *Bhayani v. Taylor Bracewell* [2016] *EWHC* 3360 (IPEC).

[80] A trade consortium may sue in its own name, but cannot bring a representative action: *Consorzio del Prosciutto di Parma v. Marks & Spencer* [1991] *RPC* 351. See also *Chocosuisse v. Cadbury* [1999] *RPC* 826, 843–4. The Court of Appeal did acknowledge, however, that it might be convenient if a trade association were able to sue on behalf of its members in such circumstances.

[81] *Artistic Upholstery v. Art Forma (Furniture)* [1999] 4 *All ER* 277, 286–7.

[82] *Star Industrial v. Yap Kwee Kor* [1976] *FSR* 217, 223; *IRC v. Muller* [1901] *AC* 217, 223.

The traditional position is that before a passing off action can be brought, trading must actually have commenced.[83] This can be seen, for example, in *Maxwell v. Hogg*.[84] Maxwell proposed to launch a magazine called BELGRAVIA in October 1866. As a part of the pre-launch publicity, in August and September of 1866 Maxwell advertised the forthcoming launch of BELGRAVIA in a magazine run by Hogg. On 25 September 1866, Hogg issued a magazine also called BELGRAVIA. Despite noting that this was hardly fair and candid dealing, the court held that Maxwell could not restrain Hogg from using the same name. This was because a declaration of intention to use a name did not secure any protection.

In contrast, where there has been substantial pre-launch publicity, claimants have occasionally succeeded in gaining interim relief prior to the launch of their products. In *Allen v. Brown Watson*,[85] the publisher of a book entitled *My Life and Loves* by Frank Harris, which had been widely advertised prior to publication, was granted an interim injunction against the defendant, who proposed to publish an abridged version also called *My Life and Loves* by Frank Harris.[86] Similarly, in *BBC v. Talbot Motor Co. Ltd*,[87] the BBC had publicized its forthcoming traffic information service named CARFAX, which required motorists to have special car radios fitted or conventional ones adapted. The BBC was granted an interim injunction preventing the defendant from selling spare parts for vehicles under the name CARFAX. Sir Robert Megarry V-C noted that, '[a]lthough that scheme has not yet been launched, that does not prevent the BBC from having built up goodwill in it which is entitled to protection'.[88] While these authorities represent individual victories based on pre-launch publicity, they have not established conclusively that the courts will recognize goodwill prior to trading. In part, this is because the cases were interim,[89] aspects of the reasoning are unconvincing,[90] and neither really turned on a demonstration of goodwill.[91]

Other cases exhibit a more hard-line approach, holding that while pre-launch advertising and publicity assists in the acquisition of goodwill, it is necessary for a trader to have customers for them to demonstrate that they have goodwill. This can be seen, for example, in *My Kinda Bones v. Dr Pepper's Stove Co*.[92] where the claim to goodwill was based exclusively on pre-launch publicity. While the court refused to strike out the claimants' action on the ground that their case was not 'manifestly unarguable', nonetheless Slade J said that he thought that the claimants' prospects of success were very doubtful. The reason for this was that there was a requirement that 'a substantial number of customers or potential customers must at least have had the opportunity to assess the merits of those goods or services for themselves'.[93] Slade J added that customers 'will not have sufficient opportunity to do this until the goods or services are actually on the market'.[94]

---

[83] The period of time and the types of activity that are needed to generate goodwill will vary from case to case: *Stannard v. Reay* [1967] RPC 589 (three weeks' trade under the name 'Mr Chippy' was sufficient to establish goodwill on the Isle of Wight).   [84] (1867) *LR 2 Ch App* 307.

[85] [1965] *RPC* 191.   [86] However, the claimant's book had been published by the time of the hearing.

[87] [1981] *FSR* 228.   [88] Ibid., 233.

[89] But, in *BBC v. Talbot*, the court was considering the parties' prospects of success, not merely whether there was a serious question to be tried.

[90] For example, *BBC v. Talbot* may have misunderstood *Allen v. Brown Watson* [1965] *RPC* 191. See Wadlow (2016), [3–070]–[3–071].

[91] Wadlow explains that, in 'reality, neither *Allen v. Brown Watson* nor *BBC v. Talbot* actually turned on the existence of goodwill', because both Allen and the BBC had long-established businesses: Wadlow (2016), [3–071].

[92] [1984] *FSR* 289 (concerning restaurants selling spare ribs, both to be called 'rib shack').

[93] Ibid., 303. *BBC v. Talbot* meant that it was not impossible to argue the case.

[94] Ibid., 299. See also *Marcus Publishing v. Leisure News* [1990] *RPC* 576.

While it might be inappropriate to protect a trader who has only made preparations to launch a product, fewer objections can be made about a trader being able to rely on passing off where they have engaged in widespread pre-launch advertising. This is because in these circumstances, competitors are likely to be aware of the claimant's intention to use the name in a business context. Consumers are also more likely to expect a product with specific associations.

While the law in this area is unclear, it is important to note that even if there is no pre-launch goodwill, if goods or services are placed on the market after extensive preparatory publicity, goodwill may well be generated after a very short time.[95] It is also important to recognize that different businesses have different relationships with their customers. For example, the launch of a radio programme requires very little, if any, active involvement by the public. Indeed, the Court of Appeal has argued that even before a service is launched, a business may generate goodwill through publicity and advertising. In *Starbucks v. BSB*,[96] the claimant sought to prevent the defendant from using the sign NOW TV for its Internet broadcast service. Rejecting the claim, the Court of Appeal said:

> It was insufficient for a passing off action for Now TV simply to be planned. It was necessary either to have or promote and publicise or advertise a customer base here in order to establish a goodwill protectable by law. The preparations did not establish a goodwill in the sense of acquiring a protectable exclusive right created by the attraction of custom in this country.[97]

While the reasoning implies that goodwill could arise even before a service is accessible, it was not necessary to decide whether this was the case on the facts.

Although other jurisdictions have been more flexible in recognizing the rights of traders based upon pre-launch publicity than has been the case in the United Kingdom,[98] in *Starbucks*, the Supreme Court declined to develop the law in this way, Lord Neuberger stating that it was 'better to decide the point in a case where it arises.'[99]

(ii) Goodwill after trading ends

Given that goodwill is directly linked to the existence of a business, it follows that once a business ceases to trade that goodwill starts to wither away.[100] As Lord Macnaghten said in *Commissioners of Inland Revenue v. Muller & Co.'s Margarine*,[101] goodwill 'cannot subsist by itself. It must be attached to a business. Destroy the business and the goodwill perishes with it.' Nevertheless, in recognition of the commercial reality that businesses may recede, change hands, or close temporarily, the courts have held that goodwill is an asset that does not dissipate immediately after a business ceases to operate. As a result, when trading stops, 'elements remain which may perhaps be gathered up and revived again'.[102] Whether goodwill continues to exist depends on two matters: first, whether the public retains relevant associations between the sign and a particular trader; and second, whether there is evidence of an intent to resume the business.

In contrast with the law relating to registered marks, which adopts a rule that the mark is revocable after five years,[103] the continued survival of repute (without the support of a

---

[95] *My Kinda Bones v. Dr Pepper's Stove Co.* [1984] *FSR* 289.   [96] [2013] *EWCA Civ* 1465.

[97] Ibid., [105].

[98] *Pontiac Marina Private v. Cdl. Hotels International* [1998] *FSR* 839, 861 (Court of Appeal for Singapore); *Turner v. General Motors* (1929) 42 *CLR* 352 (Australia); *Windmere Corp. v. Charlescraft Corp.* (1989) 23 *CPR* (3d) 60 (Canada).

[99] *Starbucks (HK) Ltd v. British Sky Broadcasting Group PLC* [2015] *UKSC* 31, [66].

[100] Wadlow (2011), [3–220]–[3–230], 243–8.   [101] [1901] *AC* 217, 224.   [102] Ibid.

[103] In the context of registered marks, five years' non-use, without due cause, is treated as a ground for revocation: see Chapter 39, section 2, p. 1078–93.

business) will simply depend on the facts. Relevant factors include the extent of the original reputation, the existence of continuing promotion or other activities, the nature of the goods, and the nature of the mark.[104] If the extent of the goodwill is small, it will likely wither quickly;[105] if there is nationwide familiarity with a trade mark, the reputation may remain for many decades.[106] Moreover, it may be that some goods remain in the public eye, for example where films or television programmes are re-run, music tracks played,[107] or vintage cars are repaired and restored.

The trader must intend to resume business. If a trader assigns their goodwill to a third party, that is taken to be an indication that they did not intend to resume business.[108] Intention to resume business may be evident from the trader's acts or may be inferred from the fact that trading was brought to an end by outside forces.[109] In *Ad-Lib Club v. Granville*,[110] for example, the claimant was forced to shut its nightclub ('The Ad-Lib Club') because of noise problems. Pennycuick V-C granted an interlocutory injunction against the defendant who, four years later, announced that they were going to open a disco under the same name. This was because the public still associated the name with the club and, because the claimant had been seeking an alternative venue since the club had closed, there was no reason to think that they had abandoned the business. In the 'World Cup Willie' case,[111] Deputy Judge Roger Wyand QC held that even though the Football Association had not used the 'World Cup Willie' device for 40 years and had allowed its trade mark registrations to lapse, the circumstances did not indicate that the Association had no intention to resume use of the sign. This was because since the sign related to the World Cup, the Football Association was not able to contemplate reusing it until it became a realistic prospect that England would host the event again.

(iii) Foreign traders

The next situation where questions about the existence of goodwill arise is in relation to foreign traders. Where a business located in a foreign country acquires an international reputation, this may lead the foreign trader to set up business in the United Kingdom. In this case, the UK-based business will normally have goodwill. In many situations, however, something short of this may occur. For example, the foreign business may merely have an agent in the United Kingdom, or only respond to orders taken directly from customers in the United Kingdom. Alternatively, a trader may only have a reputation that connects them with England and Wales, but no place of business or customers to speak of in those countries. In these circumstances, the question arises: can a foreign trader rely on passing off to protect their interests in the United Kingdom? The case law, which is by

---

[104] *Knight v. Beyond Properties* [2007] *FSR* 34, [68]; *Jules Rimet Cup Ltd v. Football Association Ltd* [2007] *EWHC* 2376 (Ch), [2008] *FSR* 10.

[105] *Knight v. Beyond Properties* [2007] *FSR* 34 (author of MYTHBUSTER books had goodwill in 1996, but by 2003 this was not more than trivial).

[106] *Jules Rimet Cup Ltd v. Football Association Ltd* [2007] *EWHC* 2376 (Ch), [2008] *FSR* 10 (Football Association retained goodwill in the mascot device from 1966 World Cup despite 40 years of inactivity).

[107] Compare with *Knight v. Beyond Properties* [2007] *FSR* 34 (rejecting argument that children's books 'remain on the shelves'); *Sutherland v. V2 Music Ltd* [2002] *EMLR* 568 (funk band using name 'Liberty', which was reasonably well-known in mid-1990s, retained sufficient goodwill, so that pop group formed in 2001 under same name was passing itself off).

[108] *Star Industrial v. Yap Kwee Kor* [1976] *FSR* 256 (PC).

[109] *A. Levey v. Henderson Kenton (Holdings)* [1974] *RPC* 617 (closure for two years of claimant's department store, because of fire, coupled with notices saying that it was reopening, held to maintain goodwill).

[110] [1971] *FSR* 1, [1972] *RPC* 673.

[111] *Jules Rimet Cup Ltd v. Football Association Ltd* [2007] *EWHC* 2376 (Ch), [2008] *FSR* 10.

no means conclusive, appears to distinguish between three situations. We will deal with each in turn.

(a) Evidence of business activity If the claimant can demonstrate a trading link with the United Kingdom, they will normally succeed in establishing goodwill. The courts have been generous when considering whether a foreign trader has a sufficient trade presence and, consequentially, goodwill in the United Kingdom. It is clear that there is no need to have a registered business in the United Kingdom. The generous approach taken by the courts can be seen, for example, in *Sheraton*.[112] In this case, the claimant company, which ran a chain of high-class hotels, but at the time had none in England, was granted an interim injunction to prevent the defendant from using the name, 'Sheraton Motels'. The court held that although the claimant did not have any hotels in the United Kingdom at that time, the fact that bookings for its hotels abroad were frequently made both through an office that Sheraton maintained in London and through travel agencies was sufficient to entitle it to relief.

(b) No business activity, but customers The second situation where a foreign trader may attempt to claim goodwill is where they have customers in the United Kingdom.[113] The law on this point is unclear. In the first instance, there is a line of cases that suggest that, for a foreign trader to establish goodwill in the United Kingdom, they must show *both* that they have customers *and* that they carry on business in the United Kingdom. This can be seen in the *Crazy Horse* decision.[114] In this case, the claimant was proprietor of the CRAZY HORSE SALOON in Paris. The defendant opened a place of the same name in London. Pennycuick J refused to grant an interlocutory injunction to restrain the defendant from using the CRAZY HORSE SALOON name in London. While the claimant had distributed leaflets in England advertising the saloon, there was no evidence that there were English customers of the Paris saloon (at least in the sense of persons who made bookings in the United Kingdom). The judge explained that:

> [A] trader cannot acquire goodwill in this country without some sort of user in this country. His user may take many forms and in certain cases very slight activities have been held to suffice . . . I do not think that the mere sending into this country by a foreign trader of advertisements advertising his establishment abroad could fairly be treated as a user in this country.[115]

The *Crazy Horse* decision has been criticized by commentators and distinguished by the courts in the so-called 'soft line' of cases.[116] In this second line of cases, it was held that if a foreign business can demonstrate that it has customers in the United Kingdom (other than foreign customers who have merely moved here),[117] it is likely that the court will

---

[112]　*Sheraton Corporation v. Sheraton Motels* [1964] *RPC* 202.

[113]　There is some authority to the effect that this is insufficient to justify a passing off action, but the preponderance of authority now appears to be to the contrary.

[114]　*Bernadin v. Pavilion* [1967] *RPC* 581.　　　[115]　Ibid., 584.

[116]　The terms 'hard' and 'soft' were characterizations used in *Athlete's Foot* [1980] *RPC* 343, 349. See also *Baskin-Robbins Ice Cream v. Gutman* [1976] *FSR* 545, 548; *Maxim's v. Dye* [1978] 2 *All ER* 55, 59.

[117]　Customers on US forces bases who bought Budweiser beer from PX stores were excluded from consideration in *Anheuser-Busch v. Budejovicky Budvar Narodni Podnik* [1984] *FSR* 413, even though sales numbered 65 million bottles per annum. However, in *Jian Tools for Sales v. Roderick Manhattan Group* [1995] *FSR* 924, Knox J treated as relevant customers resident in the United Kingdom who had been influenced by foreign advertising and ordered goods from the US business: these were customers on the open market. But note the Trade Mark Registry's approach in cases under TMA 1994, s. 5(4): *In re Speciality Retail Group's Application (Suit Express)*, O/124/00 (5 April 2000), [42] ('it is doubtful whether an overseas retail outlet that UK residents have used casually whilst on business or holiday abroad can be said to be in business here merely because those customers returned here after doing business with the retailer whilst abroad').

treat this as sufficient to establish goodwill. That is, it is not necessary for the business to establish that it carries on business in the United Kingdom (in any formal sense). For example, in *Athlete's Foot Marketing Association Inc. v. Cobra Sports*,[118] an American retailer selling shoes under the name ATHLETE'S FOOT sought to prevent a UK business from using the same name in the UK. While the American firm had a reputation in the United Kingdom at the relevant time, it had not yet conducted business in the United Kingdom. Moreover, the claimant was unable to demonstrate that a single person in England and Wales had purchased its shoes. In considering whether the claimant had goodwill, Walton J said 'it does not matter that the plaintiffs are not at present actually carrying on business in this country, provided they have customers here', the reason being that:

> [N]o trader can complain of passing off as against him in any territory . . . in which he has no customers, nobody who is in a trade relation with him. This will normally . . . be expressed by saying that he does not carry on any trade in that particular country (obviously, for present purposes, England and Wales) but the inwardness of it will be that he has no customers in that country: no people who buy his goods or make use of his services (as the case may be) there.[119]

Given that the claimant had no customers in the United Kingdom, the court held that they did not have the goodwill necessary to sustain the passing off action.

Perhaps the most formidable critique of the approach adopted in the *Crazy Horse* decision was offered in *Peter Waterman v. CBS*.[120] In this case, CBS was proposing to refurbish studios in London and call them THE HIT FACTORY. The claimant, who ran a recording business nicknamed THE HIT FACTORY, brought an action to stop CBS from using the same name. Based on the running of a recording studio in New York, which was also called THE HIT FACTORY, CBS responded by arguing that it had goodwill in the United Kingdom that was at the very least concurrent with any goodwill of the claimant. Browne-Wilkinson V-C held that the claimant failed to establish the distinctiveness of THE HIT FACTORY and that, as such, consideration of the defendant's position was unnecessary. Nevertheless, Browne-Wilkinson V-C went on to review the authorities on the issue of whether the English courts will protect a foreign trader in the United Kingdom.

Browne-Wilkinson V-C began by noting that the essence of goodwill is the ability to attract customers and potential customers to do business with the owner of the goodwill. Consequently, any interference with the trader's customers is an interference with their goodwill. Browne-Wilkinson V-C added that prior to the *Crazy Horse* decision, there was nothing in the authorities inconsistent with that view. For the Vice-Chancellor, that case law merely required the use of the name and the presence of customers in this country. To the extent that the *Crazy Horse* decision required that the trader had conducted some business (however slight) in England and Wales, Browne-Wilkinson V-C said that the case was wrongly decided.[121] The judge took the view that the presence of customers in this country was sufficient to constitute the carrying on of business here. This is the case

---

[118] [1980] *RPC* 343.

[119] Ibid., 350. See also *SA des Anciens Etablissements Panhard et Levassor v. Panhard Levassor Motor Co.* (1901) 18 *RPC* 405.   [120] [1993] *EMLR* 27.

[121] For Browne-Wilkinson V-C, if the foreign trader uses their name for the purposes of trade in the United Kingdom, the piracy of that name is an actionable wrong wherever the goodwill is located. Browne-Wilkinson V-C acknowledged that there is binding authority to the effect that the basis of claim must be a goodwill situated in England.

whether or not there is a place of business in England and Wales, or services are provided there. On this basis, Browne-Wilkinson V-C held that since the defendant's New York recording studio had *a substantial number* of customers in England, it would have been entitled to protect its name in the United Kingdom against third parties.

While the Court of Appeal has affirmed that there is goodwill in England where a business has 'customers' in England, it has also recognized that determining when this is the case is not altogether straightforward. In the *Hotel Cipriani* decision,[122] the claimant operated a hotel in Venice under the name hotel CIPRIANI. 'Cipriani' was the name of the Italian family that ran the hotel. The defendant, another member of the Cipriani family, opened a bar in Grosvenor Square, London, called BAR CIPRIANI. On being sued, the defendant denied that the claimant had goodwill in England. At the same time, the defendant also argued that they had goodwill in England as a consequence of the bar that they operated in Venice. At first instance, Arnold J rejected these arguments, finding that the claimant had goodwill because bookings for the hotel were made from England. Arnold J also found that the operation of the bar in Venice did not confer concurrent goodwill on the defendants. While the Court of Appeal affirmed Arnold J's decision, Lloyd LJ indicated that in light of the development of e-commerce, which meant that hotels could be booked through websites from anywhere in the world, it might be appropriate to review the requirement for direct bookings in relation to the question of goodwill in services.[123]

In *Starbucks (HK) v. British Sky Broadcasting*,[124] affirming the decision of the Court of Appeal and Arnold J, the Supreme Court confirmed that 'a claimant in a passing off claim must establish that it has actual goodwill in this jurisdiction, and that such goodwill involves the presence of clients or customers in the jurisdiction for the products or services in question.'[125] The Supreme Court therefore agreed that the claimant had no goodwill in the designation NOW TV in relation to its Internet broadcast service, which originated in Hong Kong. This was so even though the service was accessed by Chinese speakers in the United Kingdom. The Court explained that '[i]n order to establish goodwill, the claimant must have customers within the jurisdiction, as opposed to people in the jurisdiction who happen to be customers elsewhere. Thus, where the claimant's business is carried on abroad, it is not enough for a claimant to show that there are people in this jurisdiction who happen to be its customers when they are abroad.'[126] Consequently, the claimant could not rely upon the fact that its service was accessed by residents in England to show the existence of goodwill in England.[127]

(c) Mere reputation The third situation where the question of whether a foreign trader has goodwill in the United Kingdom arises is where the claimant merely has a reputation, but no customers as such in the United Kingdom. This might be the case where there is 'spillover' advertising, or where the product becomes known through films, television, or via the Internet.[128] Given that it is necessary for a foreign trader to have customers in the United Kingdom for them to establish goodwill (or, on a more extreme view, customers and business), it would seem reasonable to assume that where a foreign trader merely has a reputation in the United Kingdom, they would not be able to prove that they had the goodwill necessary to sustain a passing off action.

---

[122] *Hotel Cipriani SRL v. Cipriani (Grosvenor Street)* [2008] *EWHC* 3032 (Ch), [2009] *FSR* (9) 209 (Arnold J); [2010] *ECWA Civ* 110, [2010] *RPC* (16) 485.   [123] Ibid., [124].

[124] *Starbucks (HK) Ltd v. British Sky Broadcasting Group PLC* [2015] *UKSC* 31.

[125] Ibid., [47].   [126] Ibid., [52].   [127] Ibid., [103].

[128] *In re Readmans Ltd's Application (Luxor)*, O/39/02 (30 January 2002) (mere existence of Internet site accessible from United Kingdom does not give rise to goodwill).

The case law on this point has, however, vacillated. Very occasionally courts—particularly first instance courts—have suggested that a foreign trader who only has a reputation in the United Kingdom may nonetheless still be able to show that they have goodwill. In *Maxim's v. Dye*,[129] for example, the claimant was the world-famous restaurant in Paris known as MAXIM'S. In 1970, the defendant opened a restaurant in Norwich also called MAXIM'S. In considering whether the claimants were entitled to protect their reputation, even though they were not running any business in England, Graham J held that the claimants *did* have sufficient goodwill to bring a passing off action. After noting that globalization was making the 'world grow smaller', Graham J said that the true legal position was that the 'existence and extent of the claimants' . . . goodwill [in their business] in every case is one of fact however it may be proved and whatever it is based on'.[130] Graham J added that the claimants' existing goodwill in the United Kingdom, 'which is derived from and is based on a foreign business . . . may be regarded as prospective but none the less real in relation to any future business which may be later set up by the plaintiff in this country'.[131]

However, the predominant view of the English courts is that where a trader only has reputation in the United Kingdom, they will *not* have the goodwill necessary to justify an action for passing off.[132] This can be seen, for example, in the *Budweiser* case.[133] In this decision, Anheuser-Busch, an American company that manufactured BUDWEISER beer, sued the Czech brewers, Budejovicky Budvar, for passing off. The Czech brewers began selling their boutique beer in England under the name BUDWEISER BUDVAR in 1973.[134] While, at this time, the claimant's sales of BUDWEISER were confined to stores on US Air Force bases, the beer was widely known throughout the United Kingdom. The Court of Appeal rejected the claimant's claim on the basis that there was no goodwill in the United Kingdom. Because the beer sold on the Air Force bases was not available for general purchase, the Court held that these sales were to be ignored.[135] In rejecting the action, the Court supported the view that mere reputation alone would not justify an action for passing off.

The requirement that for a foreign trader to have goodwill they must be able to show that they have customers in the United Kingdom has been criticized by those who consider the geographical division of goodwill to be out of step with the commercial reality of globalized trade.[136] Support for this criticism comes from the fact that a number of comparable jurisdictions have recognized the international character of goodwill. The Full Federal Court of Australia in *ConAgra v. McCain Foods (Australia)*,[137] has perhaps gone the furthest in this regard. In this case, Lockhart J said that:

> [The] real question is whether the owner of the goods has established a sufficient reputation with respect to his goods within the particular country in order to acquire a sufficient level of consumer knowledge of the product and attraction for it to provide custom which, if lost, would likely result in damage to him. This is essentially a question of fact.[138]

---

[129] [1978] 2 *All ER* 55.

[130] Ibid., 59, quoting from *Baskin-Robbins Ice Cream v. Gutman* [1976] *FSR* 545, 548.

[131] *Maxim's v. Dye* [1978] 2 *All ER* 55, 60.

[132] *Athlete's Foot* [1980] *RPC* 343; *Jian Tools v. Roderick Manhattan Group* [1995] *FSR* 924.

[133] *Anheuser-Busch v. Budvar* [1984] *FSR* 413.

[134] 'Budweis' is the old German name of the town in which the Czech beer is brewed.

[135] In *Anheuser-Busch v. Budvar* [1984] *FSR* 413, 462, Oliver LJ defined the question as follows: 'How far is it an essential ingredient of a successful claim in passing off that the plaintiff should have established in this country a business in which his goods or services are sold to the general public on the open market?'

[136] A. Coleman, 'Protection of Foreign Business Names and Marks under the Tort of Passing off' [1986] *LS* 70, 76; F. Mostert, 'Is Goodwill Territorial or International?' [1989] *EIPR* 440.

[137] (1992) 23 *IPR* 193, 234.   [138] Ibid.

In the *Peter Waterman v. CBS* case, Browne-Wilkinson V-C commented on the need for passing off to be adapted to modern business environments in this way:

> The changes in the second half of the twentieth century are far more fundamental than those in nineteenth-century England. They have produced worldwide marks, worldwide goodwill and brought separate markets into competition with the other. Radio and television with their attendant advertising cross national frontiers. Electronic communication via satellite produces virtually instant communication between all markets. In terms of travel time, New York by air is as close as Aberdeen by rail. This has led to the development of the international reputation in certain names, particularly in the service fields, for example Sheraton Hotels, Budget Rent A Car . . . In my view, the law will fail if it does not try to meet the challenge thrown up by trading patterns which cross national and jurisdictional boundaries due to a change in technical achievement.[139]

Despite these comments and his liberal interpretation of the case law, the Vice Chancellor was not prepared to abandon the requirement that to establish goodwill, a foreign trader must have customers in the United Kingdom. This reluctance to allow an action based merely on reputation may have been grounded in a fear that if such a prerequisite was abandoned, it would enable claimants with an international reputation to enforce a worldwide monopoly without any guarantee that they would ever expand into the domestic market.[140] In addition, it has been pointed out that too-ready recognition of rights of foreign traders may render it difficult for domestic traders to find marks that can be lawfully used in the United Kingdom.[141] Indeed, in *Starbucks*, Lord Neuberger stated that a 'claimant who has simply obtained a reputation for its mark in this jurisdiction in respect of his products or services outside this jurisdiction has not done enough to justify granting him an effective monopoly in respect of that mark within the jurisdiction.'[142] That decision, it seems, will put an end to attempts to base reputation on 'spill-over reputation' for the next few decades.

(d) Well-known marks Despite the fact that mere reputation is an insufficient basis for a passing off action, the Trade Marks Act 1994 provides foreign traders who lack local goodwill with a potential remedy.[143] Section 56, which gives effect to Article 6*bis* of the Paris Convention,[144] states that:

> The proprietor of a trade mark which is entitled to protection under the Paris Convention as a well-known trade mark is entitled to restrain by injunction the use in the United Kingdom of a trade mark which, or the essential part of which, is identical or similar to his mark, in relation to identical or similar goods or services, where the use is likely to cause confusion.

---

[139] *Waterman v. CBS* [1993] *EMLR* 27.

[140] In Australia, this objection has been met by emphasizing the need for a claimant to show damage, diversion of trade that it is about to commence, or the tarnishment of reputation: *ConAgra v. McCain* (1992) 23 *IPR* 193, 235.

[141] *In re Tara Jarmon's Application (Tara Jarmon)*, O/311/99 (7 September 1999), [36].

[142] *Starbucks (HK) Ltd v. British Sky Broadcasting Group PLC* [2015] *UKSC* 31, [62].

[143] This remedy is less attractive than passing off in three obvious respects: (i) TMA 1994, s. 56, is available only if the mark is 'well known'; (ii) s. 56 results only in injunctive relief rather than compensation or restitution; and (iii) s. 56 does not extend to dissimilar goods, whereas passing off might. Note, however, that many of the limitations on registrability of trade marks (e.g. s. 3(2)), and statutory defences to infringement of registered marks (ss 11–12), do not appear to apply to the s. 56 action.

[144] Trademark Law Treaty, Art. 16, and TRIPS, Art. 16(2), require application of Paris, Art. 6*bis*, to service marks.

Importantly, this provision applies to a proprietor of a 'well-known' trade mark 'whether or not that person carries on business, or has any goodwill, in the United Kingdom'.[145] (In fact, if the proprietor is a national of the United Kingdom, they will not benefit from the provision.[146]) The key limitation in section 56 is not goodwill; rather, it is whether the mark is 'well known'. It seems that a number of considerations will be taken into account when deciding whether a mark is well known. These include: trade recognition and public recognition in the United Kingdom;[147] the inherent distinctiveness of the mark; the duration and extent of any use (whether in the United Kingdom or neighbouring territories), or promotion or advertising (especially in territories covered by the same media); sales made abroad to British residents (such as those on holiday); and the value of the goodwill.[148] It seems that this evidence must point to a high level of recognition amongst the relevant consumers in the United Kingdom. In *General Motors v. Yplon SA*,[149] the Advocate-General described the protection afforded to well-known marks under the Paris Convention as 'exceptional' and therefore concluded that it 'would not be surprising . . . if the requirement of being well-known imposed a relatively high standard for a mark to benefit from such exceptional protection'.

Rather surprisingly, section 56 has rarely been relied upon by foreign traders. One case in which the claimant did succeed was the *Hotel Cipriani* case, where Arnold J found that the claimant's hotel was a well-known mark in the United Kingdom.[150]

3 SCOPE OF GOODWILL

Once it has been decided that the claimant has goodwill, the next question to consider is its scope. This is an important question, because it may influence whether the defendant's representation amounts to a passing off.[151] While similar inquiries take place with other

---

[145] *Starbucks (HK) Ltd v. British Sky Broadcasting Group PLC* [2015] *UKSC* 31, [64] (taking comfort in the existence of section 56 which 'substantially reduces the likelihood . . . [of] harsh results' from the rule on goodwill).

[146] See TMA 1994, s. 55(1)(b); *Jules Rimet Cup Ltd v. Football Association Ltd* [2007] *EWHC* 2376, [73] (Wyand QC). Nor need the proprietor of a well-known mark have registered the mark in a Convention country: *In re Sharif's Application (Advanced Health Products)*, O/112/00 (23 March 2000), [52].

[147] TRIPS, Art. 16(2), requires that account be taken of the knowledge of the trade mark in the relevant sector of the public, including knowledge that has been obtained as a result of the promotion of the trade mark. WIPO, *Joint Recommendation Concerning Provisions on the Protection of Well Known Marks* (2000) refers to: (i) the degree of knowledge or recognition of the mark in the relevant sector of the public; (ii) the duration, extent, and geographical area of any use of the mark; (iii) the duration, extent, and geographical area of any promotion, advertising, and publicity; (iv) the duration and geographical area of any registrations; (v) previous recognition by authorities of the well-known status of the mark; and (vi) the value associated with the mark. These factors were cited and applied by Arnold J in *Hotel Cipriani v. Cipriani* [2008] *EWHC* 3032, [2009] *FSR* (9) 209, [237]–[239].

[148] For an example of such an assessment at the EUIPO, see *Maurice Emram v. Guccio Gucci SpA*, Case R 620/2006–2 (3 September 2007) (OHIM, Second BoA).

[149] Case C-375/97 1999] *ECR* I–5421, [33] (AG Jacobs). A mark is only well known in a member state if it is well known in a substantial part of that state, as opposed to only in a city or its surrounding area: *Alfredo Nieto Nuño v. Leonci Monlleó Franquet*, Case C-328/06 (22 November 2007) (ECJ, Second Chamber).

[150] *Hotel Cipriani v. Cipriani* [2008] *EWHC* 3032, [239].

[151] *Associated Newspapers Ltd v. Express Newspapers* [2003] *FSR* 51, [23] (considering whether repute of the *Mail* was limited to papers that were sold or whether it extended to free papers); *Boxing Brands v. Sports Direct International* [2013] *EWHC* 2220 (Ch) (use of QUEENSBERRY as name of a boxing club in Bedford gave rise to goodwill, but that goodwill would not support a passing off claim against a person selling clothing under the mark QUEENSBERRY).

forms of intellectual property, there is one important difference which relates to the territorial scope of the property. For example, when considering whether a patent has been infringed, the question of the geographical scope of the protection is not an issue. This is because the patent operates throughout the whole of the United Kingdom. This is not the case, however, in relation to an action for passing off where the territorial or geographical scope of the goodwill must first be ascertained. Despite the apparent dominance of nationwide firms and franchises, there are many businesses that only trade in a small and relatively confined area. In these circumstances, the way in which the physical limits of the goodwill are determined may be crucial to the success or otherwise of a passing off action.[152]

4 OWNERSHIP OF GOODWILL

In principle, the owner of goodwill is the business that generates it. While goodwill will normally be owned by a single trader or business, the courts have recognized that a group of traders may share goodwill in a name or feature of a product that they have in common. Where the singularity of a product is shared by a group of traders (normally in a specific region), they may share goodwill in the identifying feature: the name, image, logo, etc. The courts have recognized shared goodwill in relation to CHAMPAGNE,[153] SHERRY,[154] SCOTCH WHISKY,[155] ADVOCAAT,[156] SWISS CHOCOLATE,[157] VODKA,[158] and GREEK YOGHURT.[159]

Problems arise, however, where a number of different people, companies, or businesses cooperate in the making and distribution of a product. In these circumstances, the courts are forced to decide whether the goodwill is individually or jointly owned, and if so, by whom.

The difficulties in deciding how the ownership of goodwill is to be ascribed have become all the more problematic with the expansion of international trade, the globalization of markets, and the growth of multinational corporations.[160] In such cases, it is common for a firm in one country to expand into another through a subsidiary, distributor, agent, or licensee. In the absence of a carefully formulated contract dealing with the relationships between the parties, difficult questions can arise as to ownership of the goodwill generated by the actions of the local distributor and foreign supplier. This is especially the case when the arrangements between the parties end. This can be seen, for example, in *Scandecor Development v. Scandecor Marketing*.[161] In this case, a Swedish art-poster business founded in the 1960s was rearranged so that a subsidiary, Scandecor Marketing (the defendant), had responsibility for marketing the claimant's products in the United Kingdom. The claimant supplied poster products for sale. The defendants also sold ancillary products, such as calendars and cards, not supplied by the claimant and

---

[152] *Evans v. Eradicure* [1972] *RPC* 808; *Levey v. Henderson-Kenton* [1974] *RPC* 617; *Associated Newspapers* [2003] *FSR* 51, [29] (a trader's reputation in Birmingham might be different from that in London).
[153] *Bollinger v. Costa Brava Wine Co.* [1960] *Ch* 262; *Taittinger v. Allbev* [1994] 4 *All ER* 75 (champagne companies able to prevent use of elderflower champagne).
[154] *Vine Products v. Mackenzie* [1969] *RPC* 1.
[155] *John Walker & Sons v. Henry Ost* [1970] 2 *All ER* 106.
[156] *Erven Warnink BV v. Townend (J.) & Sons* [1979] *AC* 731.
[157] *Chocosuisse v. Cadbury* [1998] *RPC* 117.
[158] *Diageo North America Inc. and anor v. Intercontinental Brands (ICB)* [2010] *EWCA Civ* 920.
[159] *Fage UK Ltd v. Chobani UK* [2013] *EWHC* 630 (Ch).
[160] *Scandecor Development v. Scandecor Marketing* [1999] *FSR* 26 (CA), 38–9.
[161] [1998] *FSR* 500, [1999] *FSR* 26 (CA); not considered by the House of Lords.

over which the claimant had no control. The defendant's marketing occasionally referred to the fact that it was connected with the world's largest poster company. In the 1980s, the claimant was taken over. The new owners terminated the agreement with the defendant. After further negotiations failed, the claimant demanded that the defendant stop using the SCANDECOR mark.

At first instance, Lloyd J held that the goodwill was shared between the claimant and defendant, effectively finding two different, yet connected, forms of goodwill: a distributor's goodwill and a publisher's goodwill. The Court of Appeal rejected that view, holding instead that the goodwill belonged to the defendant. The Court of Appeal observed that where the goodwill originates from a common source overseas, but then expands and is developed by different companies in different territories, it is necessary to analyse the effect of the changes occurring from time to time in the control and ownership of the businesses that generate the goodwill.[162] Reviewing that history, the Court of Appeal noted that the contact with customers had been largely through the defendant. The Court also denied that there was any 'rule of law or presumption of fact that the goodwill generated by the trading activities of a wholly owned subsidiary company belongs to the parent company'.[163] Instead, 'what matters is who retailers identified as the person carrying out the trading activities in the local territory'.[164] In this respect, the Court of Appeal placed less emphasis than Lloyd J had done on the fact that the defendant had occasionally referred to the international scope of its activities. The evidence showed that the customers treated the supplier—that is, the defendant—as being more significant than the publisher.

There have also been considerable problems in determining ownership of goodwill in association with bands. This is particularly problematic when band members leave, form new groups, and reuse or modify the original name, or where disbanded groups regroup (often with a differently configured membership). In these circumstances, the question of who owns the goodwill in the name of a band (or indeed any collective) will depend on the relationship that the members have with each other. As Laddie J said in *Byford v. Oliver*,[165] which was a dispute between former members of the heavy metal band SAXON about ownership of the goodwill in the band name, many of the problems that arise in this context could be avoided if the band members were to enter 'into a partnership agreement which expressly provide[s] for the partnership to continue on the departure of one or more of the members'.[166] Laddie J also said that it would be advisable to ensure that the agreement 'expressly confirmed the rights of the continuing and expressly limit[ed] the rights of departing partners to make use of the partnership name and goodwill'.[167] In the absence of such an agreement, ownership will depend on the nature of the relationship between the members. Thus if the band members were partners, but had no agreement about how the rights in the name were to be dealt with, the name (as an asset of the partnership) would be dealt with along with the other assets of the partnership. In this situation, members would not own the name or the goodwill built up under it; they would, however, have an interest in the realized value of the partnership assets (which would include the goodwill in the name). If, however, the band members performed together as

---

[162] The Court of Appeal in *Scandecor Development v. Scandecor Marketing* [1999] *FSR* 26, 42, accepted that, in an appropriate case, it is legally and factually possible for a business based overseas to acquire goodwill in this country by the supply of its products or services through a subsidiary, agent, or licensee. Whether or not that occurs must depend on the facts of the particular case. Cf. *Habib Bank v. Habib Bank AG Zurich* [1981] 2 *All ER* 650 (international parent may retain international goodwill); *Gromax Plasticulture v. Don & Low Nonwovens* [1999] *RPC* 367.

[163] *Scandecor Development v. Scandecor Marketing* [1999] *FSR* 26, 43.

[164] Ibid., 45.   [165] [2003] *EWHC* 295, [2003] *FSR* 39 (Ch).   [166] Ibid., [26].   [167] Ibid., [26].

independent traders, it is likely that each member would acquire a 'discreet interest in the name and the reputation which they could use against third parties but not against each other'.[168] Where there is no contractual or other arrangement governing the relationship between and among members—where the band is an unincorporated association of individuals—the 'goodwill and reputation built up and acquired by the group' belongs 'to the "last man standing"'.[169] In this situation, the key issue will be whether any of the band members have abandoned their rights.

4.1 GOODWILL AS PROPERTY

Goodwill is a form of property that is transmissible by assignment, on death, or by operation of law.[170] There are no formalities laid down for assignment of goodwill *inter vivos*. However, it is relatively settled that goodwill cannot be assigned in 'gross'—that is, separately from the business to which it is attached.[171]

---

[168] Ibid., [19]. See also *Gill v. Frankie Goes to Hollywood Ltd* [2008] *ETMR* 4.

[169] *Eric Burdon v. John Steel* (9 September 2013) SRIS O-369–13, [8]–[9] (in relation to the band name THE ANIMALS); *Powell v. Turner* [2013] *EWHC* 3242 (IPEC) (WISHBONE ASH).

[170] *Artistic Upholstery v. Art Forma (Furniture)* [1999] 4 *All ER* 277, 286 (goodwill is property in context of assignment, nationalization, bankruptcy, and can be owned by unincorporated association through its members). In circumstances in which the relationship is purely personal, as with a barrister or conductor, goodwill will be regarded as inalienable: see *Newman v. Adlem* [2006] *FSR* 16, [26] (Jacob LJ) (holding the rule inapplicable to the goodwill of a funeral director).

[171] *Barnsley Brewery Co. v. RBNB* [1997] *FSR* 462, 469.

33

MISREPRESENTATION

1 INTRODUCTION

The second element of the passing off action, which we consider in this chapter, is the requirement that there be a misrepresentation.[1] Historically, the need for a misrepresentation, which is one of the factors that distinguishes passing off from a law of unfair competition, is explained by the fact that the passing off action grew out of the common law action for deceit.[2] Typically, a misrepresentation occurs where the defendant says or does something that indicates (expressly or impliedly) that the defendant's goods or services derive from (or are otherwise economically connected with) the claimant. Initially, liability for passing off was limited to situations where the defendant's actions gave rise to the suggestion that their goods or services had come from the claimant. That is, that there was confusion as to the source of the goods. Over time, however, the action has expanded to include representations that relate to the quality of the goods or services, and to representations that suggest that there is a relevant connection between the claimant and the defendant.

This chapter is divided into four parts. First, we consider the type of conduct that forms the basis of the defendant's misrepresentation. Second, we look at the types of suggestion that are actionable. Third, we look at the requirement that, for a statement to be a misrepresentation, it must be likely to cause confusion. Fourth, we note that a passing off action can not only be brought against a person who carries out the misrepresentation, but also against someone who provides the means that enables the misrepresentation to occur.

---

[1] In *Spalding v. Gamage* (1915) 32 *RPC* 273, 284, Lord Parker referred to false representation by the defendant as 'the basis of a passing-off action'.

[2] See J. Phillips and A. Coleman, 'Passing off and the Common Field of Activity' (1985) 101 *LQR* 242, 243, for a comparison of passing off with deceit.

2 NATURE OF THE DEFENDANT'S REPRESENTATION

As passing off hinges on misrepresentation, it helps to begin by distinguishing this requirement from closely related concepts.[3] Courts have consistently held that mere confusion in the minds of consumers is not enough ('I wonder if there is a connection between traders A and B'). Something additional is required, which some suggest is more aptly reflected in the standard of deception. However deception, which can be traced back to the tort of deceit, inaccurately implies that a subjective fraudulent intention is required. As we will see later, passing off is objectively assessed. The additional element which separates misrepresentation from mere confusion is instead better described as a materiality requirement: the defendant's use must have causal potency and move consumers to mistakenly buy their product instead of the claimant's. In summary, the misrepresentation must be material or 'really likely' to be material.

Otherwise there are no formal restrictions on the types of representation that are actionable. Indeed, as Lord Parker said in *Spalding v. Gamage*,[4] it is 'impossible to enumerate or classify all the possible ways in which a [trader] may make the ... representation relied upon'. So long as the representation confuses the public in a relevant way, the means by which this comes about is irrelevant. Having said this, it may be helpful to consider some of the more important points about the types of conduct that might constitute a misrepresentation.

2.1 DEFENDANT'S STATE OF MIND

In deciding whether a misrepresentation has taken place, the key concern is with the *consequences* of the defendant's actions and the effect that these have upon the public, rather than the state of the defendant's mind. As such, to succeed in a passing off action, there is no need for the misrepresentation to be conscious, deliberate, intentional, or fraudulent.[5] It also does not matter whether the misrepresentation was made deliberately or innocently. Similarly, the fact that a statement is true does not matter, so long as the defendant's actions or representations generate the requisite confusion in the mind of the public.

A misrepresentation is actionable even if it is unintentional or can be explained on what seem to be legitimate grounds.[6] For example, if a person trades under their own name, they might still be passing off their goods as those of the claimant.[7] In *Parker Knoll v. Knoll International*,[8] the defendant, Hans Knoll, established a furniture manufacturing business that he called KNOLL INTERNATIONAL. Another firm of furniture makers, established by the defendant's uncle, already traded as PARKER KNOLL. Despite dicta to the effect that individuals have a 'natural and inherent right' to use their own name,[9] the

---

[3] For a useful review of authorities and principles, see *Moroccanoil Israel Ltd v. Aldi Stores Ltd* [2014] *EWHC* 1686 (IPEC), [8]–[12]; *The National Guild of Removers and Storers Ltd v. Bee Moved Ltd* [2016] *EWHC* 3192 (IPEC), [10]–[11]; *Comic Enterprises Ltd v. Twentieth Century Fox Film Corporation* [2016] *EWCA Civ* 41, [2016] *FSR* 30 at [157]–[159].

[4] (1915) 32 *RPC* 273, 284.

[5] *HFC Bank plc v. Midland Bank* plc [2000] *FSR* 176, 181. But there are advantages for a claimant who can show that use was deliberate: *Irvine v. Talksport* [2002] *FSR* 943; Wadlow (2016), [5–57] ('An intention to deceive the public is strong evidence that deception will occur').

[6] *Montgomery v. Thompson* [1891] *AC* 217, 220.

[7] G. Kodilinye, 'Passing off and the Use of Personal Names' (1975) 26 *NILQ* 177; Wadlow (2016), [9–55]–[9–75].

[8] [1962] *RPC* 265; *NAD Electronics Inc v. NAD Computer Systems* [1997] *FSR* 380, 392; *Reed Executive v. Reed Business Information* [2004] *RPC* 767, [109]–[112].   [9] *Marengo v. Daily Sketch* (1948) 65 *RPC* 242.

House of Lords denied that a person was entitled to use their own name to indicate that their goods are the goods of another. Consequently, their Lordships granted an injunction.[10] Given that there is no defence where a person uses their own name, it is not surprising that there is no defence where someone changes their name or uses a nickname.[11]

2.2 FORM OF THE MISREPRESENTATION

The courts have been very flexible in deciding whether a defendant has made the requisite misrepresentation. The flexible nature of the misrepresentation is reflected in the fact that the misrepresentation can arise through the use of words or actions. We will look at each of these in turn.

(i) Words The commonest form of misrepresentation involves the use of words, whether oral or written. In some cases, this will occur where the defendant makes a statement that links them either explicitly or implicitly to the claimant. Often, the defendant will use a name that is identical or very similar to the trade name used by the claimant. Thus, in *Taittinger v. All Bev*,[12] the Court of Appeal held that, by calling their drink ELDERFLOWER CHAMPAGNE, the defendants had made a misrepresentation that they were part of the group of CHAMPAGNE producers. One of the consequences of the fact that words are able to form the basis of a misrepresentation is that passing off may prevent a person from calling their book, film, record, or band by the same name or title as that used by someone else.[13]

(ii) Action In some cases, the relevant misrepresentation may be implied from the action of the defendant. Perhaps the clearest example of this is where the defendant manufactures their goods to look like the claimant's. It will also occur if a customer asks a trader to supply them with someone else's goods, but the trader instead supplies the customer with their own goods: this would be an actionable misrepresentation.[14] Indeed, in some circumstances where a trader knows that a consumer is susceptible to a particular understanding concerning the origin of goods or services,[15] that trader must 'take such care as will prevent his chosen marketing method from conveying any misrepresentation to the effect that there is such a connection'.[16] A misrepresentation can also occur where the defendant places their product in close proximity to that of the claimant. For example, in *Associated Press v. Insert Media*,[17] the court held that by inserting advertisements inside the claimant's newspaper after the paper had been delivered to newsagents, the defendant passed the inserts off as if they were the claimant's. The position might have been different, however, if the two products were delivered at the same time. It does not seem likely

---

[10] G. Kodilinye, 'Passing off and the Use of Personal Names' (1975) 26 *NILQ* 177, preferring Lord Denning's dissenting speech to those of the majority, argues that the case, 'far from laying down any coherent principles, seems to have thrown the law into even greater confusion than before'.

[11] *Biba Group v. Biba Boutique* [1980] *RPC* 413, 420.   [12] [1993] *FSR* 641.

[13] Wadlow (2016), [8–117]–[8–135]; R. Stone, 'Titles, Character Names and Catch Phrases in the Film and Television Industry: Protection under the Law of Passing off' (1996) 7 *Ent L Rev* 263.

[14] *Bovril v. Bodega Co. Ltd* (1916) 33 *RPC* 153 (supplying oxo when customer requested BOVRIL); *Bristol Conservatories v. Conservatories Custom Built* [1989] *RPC* 455; *LEEC v. Morquip* [1996] *EIPR* D–176 (speculating on the possible significance of body language in forming the misrepresentation); *BSB Group plc v. Sky Home Services Ltd* [2007] *FSR* 14.

[15] For example, where one trader has previously had a monopoly over the goods and the junior trader is one of the first competitors.

[16] *BSB v. Sky Home Services* [2007] *FSR* 14, [82] (the defendant was offering warranty contracts relating to Sky equipment in circumstances under which it was aware that many consumers considered it to have been authorized to do so by Sky).   [17] [1991] *FSR* 380.

that where products are placed side-by-side on a supermarket shelf this would amount to a misrepresentation.

Another situation where the action of a defendant may give rise to an actionable misrepresentation is in relation to the adoption of domain names used on the Internet. This can be seen in *British Telecommunications v. One in a Million*,[18] which was one of the earliest British cases to deal with the practice of 'cyber-squatting'. The defendant in this case was a dealer in Internet domain names who had secured domain name registration for prestigious names such as 'virgin.com' and 'tandy.com'. The domain names were registered without the consent of the organization that owned the goodwill in the names. The defendant's aim was either to sell the names that they had registered to the owners of the goodwill (using the blocking effect of the registration to negotiate for a better price),[19] or to sell them to other people (such as collectors). The Court of Appeal held that the act of registering names such as 'marksandspencer.co.uk' amounted to an actionable misrepresentation. This was particularly the case where the name denoted a particular trader and no one else. Aldous LJ explained that:

> [The] placing on a register of a distinctive name such as 'marksandspencer' makes a representation to persons who consult the register that the registrant is connected or associated with the name registered and thus the owner of the goodwill in the name.[20]

This decision, which is not without its critics, has important ramifications for the legal regulation of the Internet.[21] Courts have continued to develop the application of passing off principles to e-commerce contexts, such as the use of protected terms on search engines.[22]

3 WHAT TYPE OF SUGGESTIVE CONDUCT IS ACTIONABLE?

In the previous section, we looked at the various types of conduct that constitute misrepresentation. In this section, we turn to look at the *consequences* that flow from that conduct. In so doing, it is important to note that in order to promote the sale of their products or services, a trader might act or make statements that are suggestive of a number of things. For example, trader A might act in such a way that the public comes to believe that trader A's products are cheaper than those of trader B or that they are better for the environment. Trader A might also suggest that their goods are very suitable to be used in connection with those of trader B. Equally, trader A might suggest that their goods are similar to or better than those of trader B. While trader A's conduct in each of these cases

---

[18] [1998] 4 *All ER* 476. For criticism, see M. Elmslie, 'The *One in a Million* Case' [1998] *Ent L Rev* 283, 284 (questioning the conclusion reached that no evidence of how users view the register was given in the case). See also *French Connection v. Sutton* [2000] *ETMR* 341.

[19] For example, the defendants offered to sell the domain name 'burgerking.co.uk' to Burger King for £25,000.   [20] *One in a Million* [1998] 4 *All ER* 476, 497.

[21] *Phones4U Ltd v. Phone4u.co.uk Internet Ltd* [2006] *EWCA Civ* 244, [2007] *RPC* 5; *Tesco Stores Ltd v. Elogicom Ltd* [2006] *EWHC* 403 (Ch), [2007] *FSR* (4) 83. See the discussion of ICANN in Chapter 31, section 5, at pp. 862–3.

[22] *Victoria Plum Ltd v. Victorian Plumbing Ltd* [2016] *EWHC* 2911 (Ch) (applying passing off in the context of bidding for keywords for internet search engine advertising); *Jadebay v. Clarke-Coles Ltd* [2017] *EWHC* 1400 (IPEC) (use of a sign similar to the claimant's mark as part of Amazon product listings was an actionable misrepresentation).

may harm trader B, this does not mean that trader B will succeed in a passing off action. This is because passing off only protects against certain types of suggestion. In this section, we examine the types of suggestive conduct that are actionable.

3.1 MISREPRESENTATION AS TO SOURCE

The traditional form of misrepresentation occurs where the defendant's actions give rise to a suggestion that the defendant's goods or services are those of the claimant. That is, the defendant somehow suggests that the claimant is the 'source' of the goods.[23] Such a misrepresentation is objectionable because it confuses the public and attempts to ride on the back of the claimant's reputation.

A misrepresentation as to source occurs, for example, where the defendant suggests that they are the manufacturer, marketer, or retailer of the product. It also occurs where the defendant uses a word or name that the public associates with the claimant's business. In both of these situations, the defendant's conduct gives rise to the suggestion that their goods emanate from the claimant. The representation may also give rise to a suggestion that the goods or services of the claimant and the defendant are related. For example, in *Kimberley Clark v. Fort Sterling*,[24] as a part of the defendant's campaign to promote the NOUVELLE toilet roll, the defendant offered to placate customers who had brought NOUVELLE but were dissatisfied with it, by replacing NOUVELLE with ANDREX toilet paper. The claimant, who owned the goodwill in ANDREX, objected. The court held the offer to be a misrepresentation, because it was likely to lead purchasers into thinking that NOUVELLE was a product from the ANDREX stable, or that ANDREX was in some way behind the promotion.

3.2 MISREPRESENTATION AS TO QUALITY

The courts have also recognized that a misrepresentation may occur where a defendant makes a representation about the quality of the claimant's goods. The objection here is not so much to the fact that the defendant is riding on the back of the claimant's reputation (although this may occur) as it is to the negative impact that the defendant's actions have upon the claimant's goodwill. This can be seen in *Spalding v. Gamage*.[25] In this case, the claimant, who manufactured and sold footballs, brought a passing off action against the defendants, who had obtained some of the claimant's old disused stock and sold them as if they were new and improved footballs. Lord Parker held that this was a misrepresentation. The reason for this was that:

> [The] proposition that no one has the right to represent his goods as the goods of somebody else must, I think … involve as a corollary the further proposition, that no one, who has in his hands the goods of another of a particular class or quality, has a right to represent these goods to be the goods of that other of a different quality or belonging to a different class.[26]

The extension of the passing off action to include representations about the quality of the claimant's goods may enable a trader to control the parallel importing of their goods. This has been particularly important where a trader places goods of one quality on a foreign

---

[23] It is irrelevant that the customers are not actually familiar with the source: *Birmingham Vinegar Brewery v. Powell* [1897] *AC* 710, 715; *Edge v. Nicholls* [1911] *AC* 693; *United Biscuits (UK) v. Asda Stores* [1997] *RPC* 513. This is referred to as the 'anonymous source' doctrine.
[24] [1997] *FSR* 877.   [25] (1915) 32 *RPC* 273.   [26] Ibid., 284.

market under a particular sign and goods of a different quality on the UK market under the same sign. In these circumstances, the trader may be able to use passing off to prevent goods marketed abroad from being imported into the United Kingdom. In *Colgate-Palmolive v. Markwell Finance*,[27] the claimants were all members of an international group of companies, which marketed toothpaste in different countries. While the external appearance of the toothpaste tube that was sold in different countries was very similar (the mark and get-up were the same), the quality of the contents varied from country to country. For example, the COLGATE toothpaste sold in Brazil was of a lower quality than that which was available in the United Kingdom. This was because the Brazilian toothpaste used a number of cheaper raw materials, such as local chalk, instead of the better quality ingredients that were used in the United Kingdom. Colgate UK, a wholly owned subsidiary of Colgate US, instigated an action to prevent Markwell from importing lower-quality COLGATE toothpaste, which had been sold in Brazil, into the United Kingdom. Markwell argued that Colgate UK had no right to rely upon the reputation for superior quality toothpaste that it had in the United Kingdom, when the COLGATE trade marks and the get-up were used as worldwide presentation for different quality toothpaste. Markwell also argued that Colgate US must have foreseen that different quality toothpaste would circulate around the world. In effect, what Markwell argued was that it was Colgate, and not Markwell, that had made the relevant misrepresentation.

Applying *Spalding v. Gamage*, the Court of Appeal held that traders who placed the same mark on distinct classes of articles were entitled to bring a passing off action against a person who resold the inferior goods in circumstances that constituted a false representation that the goods were of the superior class and thereby damaged the trader's reputation.[28] Given that the defendant had made a misrepresentation to consumers in the United Kingdom as to the character and quality of the Brazilian toothpaste, it was irrelevant that the goods were originally produced and sold by a subsidiary of Colgate US.

Another situation where the courts have recognized misrepresentation of the quality of goods is in relation to the so-called 'extended form' of passing off, which was first recognized by Danckwerts J in *Bollinger v. Costa Brava Wine Co*.[29] As we explained earlier, this case recognized that a class or group of traders may share goodwill in a name (or some other indicator) that is distinctive of a particular class of goods. In particular, it was recognized that champagne producers who made sparkling wine with grapes from the Champagne region of France using the *champenois* process had goodwill in the name CHAMPAGNE. It was also recognized that individual members of the class of traders were able to bring an action against anyone who uses the distinctive name in relation to products of a different quality. On this basis, French champagne houses have been able to stop other traders who do not make drinks with those characteristics, for example producers of the drinks SPANISH CHAMPAGNE or ELDERFLOWER CHAMPAGNE, from using the term 'champagne'.[30] The House of Lords approved this line of authority in *Warnink v. Townend*.[31] In so doing, they granted relief to a producer of egg-based alcoholic drink ADVOCAAT. The action has subsequently been used by the producers of PARMA HAM

---

[27] [1989] *RPC* 497.

[28] Ibid., 514 (Slade LJ), 529 (Lloyd LJ); cf. *Champagne Heidsieck v. Buxton* [1930] 1 *Ch* 330, which was distinguished because, on the facts, resale in COLGATE carried with it a misrepresentation as to quality: ibid., 513

[29] [1960] *RPC* 16. See Chapter 32, section 4, pp. 884–6. For historical background, see D. Gangjee, '*Spanish Champagne*: An Unfair Competition Approach to GI Protection', in Dreyfuss and Ginsburg (2014), 105.

[30] *Taittinger v. Allbev* [1993] *FSR* 641 (elderflower champagne). But not BABYCHAM: *H.P. Bulmer and Showerings v. J. Bollinger SA* [1978] *RPC* 79.

[31] *Erven Warnink BV v. Townend (J) & Sons (Hull)* [1979] *AC* 731, 742.

(albeit unsuccessfully), SWISS CHOCOLATE, VODKA and GREEK YOGHURT.[32] The specifics of the action, which has a number of idiosyncratic characteristics, are considered later.[33]

3.3 MISREPRESENTATION THAT THE CLAIMANT HAS CONTROL OR RESPONSIBILITY OVER THE GOODS OR SERVICES

The courts have also recognized that a misrepresentation may occur where the defendant's conduct gives rise to the suggestion that the claimant has some type of control or responsibility over the defendant's goods or services. In *British Legion v. British Legion Club (Street)*,[34] Farwell J held that an organization formed to assist First World War veterans called the 'British Legion' could rely on passing off to prevent the words 'British Legion Club (Street)' from being used to describe a local social club. This was because members of the public would have thought that the social club was:

> ... either a Branch of the plaintiff association, or at any rate that it was a club in some way amalgamated with or under the supervision of the plaintiff association for which the plaintiff association had in some way made itself responsible.[35]

It should be noted that the mere fact that a defendant suggests that they are somehow connected to the claimant will not necessarily amount to passing off. This is because the connection will only be relevant if the defendant's misrepresentation suggests that the claimant has some type of control or responsibility over the goods or services in question. The nature of the connection that is necessary to sustain a misrepresentation was considered in *Harrods v. Harrodian School*.[36] In this case, the famous London department store was refused an injunction to prevent a preparatory school known as 'The Harrodian Club', which was built on the site of the former Harrods club, from calling itself the 'Harrodian School'.[37] (Harrods claimed that Harrodian was the adjectival form of Harrods.) In the Court of Appeal, Millett LJ explained that:

> [T]he relevant connection must be one by which the plaintiffs would be taken by the public to have made themselves responsible for the quality of the defendant's goods or services ... It is not in my opinion sufficient to demonstrate that there must be a connection of some kind between the defendant and the plaintiff, if it is not a connection which would lead the public to suppose that the plaintiff has made himself responsible for the quality of the defendant's goods or services. A belief that the plaintiff has sponsored or given financial support to the defendant will not ordinarily give the public that impression.[38]

The *Harrods* decision places an important limit on the scope of passing off, particularly in relation to sponsorship.[39] For example, it seems that if a trader was to adopt the logo of the Diana Memorial Fund, this would not amount to passing off. This is because the public would most probably take this to mean that the trader had made a donation to the Diana

---

[32] *Consorzio del Prosciutto di Parma v. Marks & Spencer* [1991] *RPC* 351 and *Consorzio del Prosciutto di Parma v. Asda Stores* [1988] *FSR* 697 (Parma ham); *Chocosuisse Union des Fabricants Suisses de Chocolat v. Cadbury* [1999] *RPC* 826; *Diageo North America Inc v. Intercontinental Brands (ICB) Ltd* [2010] *EWHC* 17 (Ch) (vodka); *Fage UK Ltd v. Chobani UK Ltd* [2013] *EWHC* 630 (Ch) (Greek yoghurt).

[33] See Chapter 34, section 2, pp. 918–23.   [34] (1931) 63 *RPC* 555.   [35] Ibid., 564.

[36] [1996] *RPC* 697; H. Carty, 'Passing off at the Crossroads' [1996] *EIPR* 629, taking the view that Millett LJ's restrictive approach is less in line with existing authorities than Sir Michael Kerr's dissenting judgment.

[37] In so doing, the Court of Appeal criticized *Bulmer v. Bollinger* [1978] *RPC* 79, 117, in which Goff LJ said that the connection must 'lead people to accept them on the faith of the plaintiff's reputation'.

[38] [1996] *RPC* 697, 712–13.   [39] *Irvine v. Talksport* [2002] *FSR* 943.

Fund, rather than that the Fund had any control over the trader's business.[40] However, where a trader inaccurately suggests that it is a member of a trade association and satisfies its membership criteria, this falls within the scope of actionable misrepresentation.[41]

3.3.1 Personality merchandising

The expansion of passing off to include situations in which the defendant makes a representation that the claimant has some type of control or responsibility over their goods or services helps to ensure that the action continues to be relevant in the modern commercial environment. It has also given rise to the possibility that celebrities may be able to utilize passing off to control the use that is made of their images or other personal indicia. This is potentially very important given that personality merchandising—that is, the practice whereby celebrities use their names and images to endorse and associate themselves with products and services—has become a common feature of modern marketing and that, at present, UK law refuses to recognize a right of personality.[42]

Despite the flexible nature of the passing off action, it has provided limited protection against traders who appropriate aspects of someone else's personality.[43] In *Lyngstrad v. Annabas Products*,[44] the pop group ABBA complained that the defendant was selling paraphernalia that bore the name and image of the group. Refusing to grant relief, Oliver J said that he did not think anyone could reasonably imagine that the pop stars had given their approval for the paraphernalia. He also added that the defendants were not doing 'anything more than catering for a popular demand among teenagers for effigies of their idols'.[45]

The courts in Australia have adopted a more generous approach to the application of passing off to personality and character merchandising. For example, in *Henderson v. Radio Corporation*,[46] the defendants reproduced a picture of the claimants, who were ballroom dancers, on one of their record covers. The Supreme Court of New South Wales held that in so doing the defendants had made a misrepresentation that there was a 'connection' between the claimants and the defendants. This was because 'the class of persons for whom the record was primarily intended would probably believe that the picture of the respondents on the cover indicated their recommendation or approval of the record'.[47]

An even more liberal approach was adopted by the Federal Court of Australia in *Hogan v. Koala Dundee*,[48] where Pincus J said that it was no longer necessary to show misrepresentation to prove passing off. In this case, the claimant, who was the writer and star of the film *Crocodile Dundee*, brought an action against two tourist shops that sold clothing, hats, and T-shirts that were 'of a particularly Australian nature'. The basis of the claimant's complaint was that the defendants had used the name Dundee and had also used an image of a koala bear, which, like the hero in the claimant's film *Crocodile Dundee*, was

---

[40]   B. Isaac, 'Merchandising or Fundraising? Trade Marks and the Diana, Princess of Wales Memorial Fund' (1998) *EIPR* 44 (use of Diana logo not an indication of source, but rather an indication that the user has given the fund financial support).

[41]   *The National Guild of Removers and Storers Ltd v. Bee Moved Ltd* [2016] *EWHC* 3192 (IPEC) (the first defendant, through its checklists and advertising, made an implied statement that it continued to be a member of the NGRS when it had in fact ceased to be one).

[42]   H. Beverley-Smith, *The Commercial Appropriation of Personality* (2002); G. B. Dinwoodie and M. Richardson, 'Publicity Right, Personality Right, or Just Confusion?', in M. Richardson and S. Ricketson (eds), *Research Handbook on Intellectual Property in Media and Entertainment* (2017), ch. 16. On protection of non-pecuniary or dignitary interests through the law of confidence, see PartV, section 1.3, pp. 1216–17.

[43]   For other impediments, in particular, the difficulty with demonstrating damage, see Chapter 34, section 1.3, pp. 914–15.   [44]   [1977] *FSR* 62.

[45]   Ibid.   [46]   [1969] *RPC* 218.   [47]   Ibid., 232.   [48]   (1988) 12 *IPR* 508.

dressed in a sleeveless shirt, wore a bush hat with teeth in the band, and carried a knife. The Court granted the claimant relief, denying that there was a need for a misrepresentation. It grounded the decision on the basis of 'wrongful appropriation of a reputation, or, more widely wrongful association of goods with an image properly belonging to an applicant'.[49]

However, in a second *Crocodile Dundee* case, *Hogan v. Pacific Dunlop*,[50] the full Federal Court reverted to the conventional position that to succeed in a passing off action, the claimant must show that there has been a misrepresentation. Here, the claimant advertised shoes by reference to a particular scene (the knife scene) in the film *Crocodile Dundee*. The Federal Court of Australia said that there was a misrepresentation 'involving use of the image or indicium in question to convey a representation of a commercial connection between the plaintiff and the goods and services of the defendant, which connection does not exist'.[51]

English cases have stuck to the view that passing off requires a misrepresentation. They have also held that while the public does not need to believe that the personality made the goods or services, the public must have thought that the personality endorsed them. As a result, while labelling a product with the words 'official' or 'approved by' a particular personality would probably be treated as a misrepresentation, the unauthorized use of a celebrity's image on an advertisement might or might not.[52] In a similar vein, in the *Elvis Presley* decision,[53] Laddie J said that the public would not assume that the use of the words ELVIS, ELVIS PRESLEY, or the signature ELVISLY YOURS on toiletries and perfumes indicated any connection with Elvis's estate. This was because when people buy such articles, they probably do not care one way or the other who made, sold, or licensed them. Similarly, it has been said that people buying stickers showing the Spice Girls are unlikely to believe that the stickers were published by the band or that the quality of the stickers was authorized by them. This was because the traders who supplied the merchandise were merely responding to a demand 'for effigies and quotes of today's idols'.[54]

A somewhat more sympathetic approach to the protection of a celebrity's image can be seen in the decision of Laddie J in *Irvine v. Talksport*.[55] In this case, a Formula 1 racing driver, Eddie Irvine, brought an action against Talksport for using his image on a promotional brochure (used to attract advertising to the radio station). The brochure comprised a picture of Irvine that had been modified so that he was listening to a radio bearing the Talksport logo. Irvine brought an action for passing off and Laddie J found in his favour. Laddie J reviewed the cases on personalities and passing off, and held that they indicated that a person might be able to utilize passing off to prevent a misrepresentation by a trader that its products or services had been endorsed by the personality. (In so doing, the judge made it clear that endorsement was a narrower notion than merchandising.) On the facts before him, Laddie J found that Talksport's brochure had given the impression that Irvine had endorsed the radio station. In particular, Laddie J was impressed by evidence from an associate of Irvine that he sought a free radio from the racing driver, an act that indicated that he believed Irvine had done a deal with

---

[49] Ibid., 520.   [50] (1989) 12 *IPR* 225.   [51] Gummow J, at first instance.

[52] *Elvis Presley Trade Marks* [1997] *RPC* 543, 558.   [53] Ibid.

[54] *Halliwell v. Panini SpA* (6 June 1997) (Lightman J), echoing *Lyngstrad v. Annabas Products* [1977] *FSR* 62 and refusing the claimant an *ex parte* injunction demanding no further sale of the albums without a disclaimer.

[55] [2002] *FSR* 943. The decision has been regarded by some as marking a shift in judicial attitudes to personality merchandising; see H. Carty, 'Advertising, Publicity Rights and English Law' (2004) *IPQ* 209, 240 (describing the case as 'a radical re-alignment of the tort, at least where image rights are concerned').

the radio station. The Court of Appeal affirmed Laddie J's decision, emphasizing in particular that the actual image of Irvine listening to the radio gave an impression of endorsement.[56] At best, the case indicates that British courts will be sympathetic to any unauthorized use of a personality's image or likeness that wrongfully implies endorsement of a trader's products.

This view was echoed by Birss J in *Robyn Rihanna Fenty v. Arcadia Group Brands*.[57] This was a passing off action brought by Rihanna, who was described by the court as a 'world famous pop star' with a 'cool, edgy image', against Topshop, the well-known fashion retailer, for selling a T-shirt with a large picture of her on it. Birss J began by reiterating that English law did not recognize a general right for a person, famous or otherwise, to control the reproduction of their image. As a result, Rihanna had to show passing off, which required her to show goodwill, misrepresentation, and damage. As is often the situation in cases involving personalities, the main issue was whether, in selling the T-shirt with the picture of Rihanna on it, Topshop had made a misrepresentation about trade origin. As Birss J stressed, 'selling a garment with a recognisable image of a famous person is not, in and of itself, passing off'; instead, to constitute passing off, 'a false belief engendered in the mind of the potential purchaser must play a part in their decision to buy the product'.[58] While there was nothing on the swing tag or the other labelling to suggest that Rihanna had authorized the garment, nonetheless Birrs J found that there had been a misrepresentation. In a judgment that reflects a changing and much more realistic attitude about the knowledge of customers about merchandising and endorsement (at least among the 13–30 age group that Rihanna appealed to), Birrs J found that a substantial number of the customers who brought the T-shirt would have thought that it 'was an authorised product ... approved by Rihanna herself'.[59]

3.3.2 Misrepresentations in character merchandising

Character merchandising involves the application of images of cartoon and other fictional characters to merchandise. While the Australian approach has not been followed in the United Kingdom in relation to personality merchandising, it has been more enthusiastically applied to character merchandising. For example, in *Mirage Studios v. Counter-Feat Clothing*,[60] the defendants were found liable for passing off when they applied the claimant's characters, the Teenage Ninja Mutant Turtles, to their clothing. Browne-Wilkinson V-C explained that:

> [T]he critical evidence in this case was that a substantial number of the buying public now expects and knows that where a famous cartoon or television character is reproduced on goods, that reproduction is the result of a licence granted by the owner of the copyright or owner of other rights in the character.[61]

As a result, he concluded that sale of the merchandise involved two misrepresentations: first, a (mis)representation to the public that the goods were 'genuine' (that is, that the drawings were the claimants' drawings); and second, a misrepresentation that the goods

---

[56] *Irvine v. Talksport* [2003] *FSR* 619 (CA).

[57] [2013] *EWHC* 2310 (Ch). The reasoning was confirmed on appeal: *Robyn Rihanna Fenty v. Arcadia Group Brands Ltd* [2015] *EWCA Civ* 3.   [58] [2013] *EWHC* 2310 (Ch), [36].

[59] Ibid., [72]. The nature of the recognizable photographic image (taken while shooting an official music video), the fact that Topshop had previous commercial interactions with Rihanna, and the retailer's track record of endorsement or design agreements with other famous personalities all contributed to the finding of liability.

[60] [1991] *FSR* 145.   [61] Ibid., 155.

were licensed.[62] Browne-Wilkinson V-C went on to say that he regarded the Australian authorities as 'sound'.[63]

While the *Ninja Turtle* case has received a mixed reaction,[64] the indications are that the English courts will treat the decision as being limited to its particular facts.[65] As we have seen, the decision has not been extended to personality merchandising cases;[66] nor does it appear to extend to the use of names, as opposed to the use of copyright images.[67] This is because, in the case, the judge distinguished a number of authorities on the ground that they were concerned with the licensing of names in which no copyright subsists, rather than the copyright material.[68] Moreover, even where the merchandising is protected by copyright, the courts have subsequently indicated that to succeed in a passing off action, the claimant must show that the public understood that the goods were licensed *and* that they bought the merchandise on that basis. This can be seen in *BBC Worldwide v. Pally Screen Printing*.[69] The BBC owned copyright and merchandising rights to the popular children's characters known as the Teletubbies. The defendants printed pictures of the Teletubbies on various items such as T-shirts. In response to the BBC's action for passing off, Laddie J explained that to succeed:

> [T]he plaintiffs will need to show that they have built up the necessary reputation so that members of the public would look at this type of artwork and consider it to represent the plaintiffs or products made with the plaintiffs' approval. It seems to me that it is quite possible that members of the public will look at T-shirts bearing this artwork and think no more than it is artwork bearing illustrations of well-known television characters without having any regard whatsoever to the source of supply and without having any regard as to whether or not these T-shirts were put out with the sanction of or under the aegis of the plaintiffs.[70]

Laddie J refused to grant the BBC summary judgment against the defendants because it was 'not unforeseeable' that the defendants might succeed.

3.4 REVERSE PASSING OFF

'Reverse', or 'inverse', passing off is the name given to the situation where a trader tries to claim the benefit of another trader's goods or service to enhance their own reputation.[71] In the classic passing off action, the defendant's misrepresentation gives rise to a suggestion that the defendant's goods or services are those of the claimant. However, with reverse

---

[62] The reference to 'genuineness' was interpreted by Laddie J as perhaps referring to the creator of the character or his successors: *Elvis Presley* [1997] *RPC* 543, 553.

[63] The authorities did not, however, include the two *Dundee* cases. For a comparison of English and Australian law, see S. Burley, 'Passing off and Character Merchandising' [1991] *EIPR* 227, 228.

[64] Wadlow (2016), [7–151], is critical of the decision. More approving sentiments can be found elsewhere: J. Holyoak, 'United Kingdom Character Rights and Merchandising Rights Today' [1993] *J Bus L* 444, 451 (in general arguing that character merchandising is now adequately protected).

[65] *Elvis Presley* [1997] *RPC* 543, 553.

[66] As the UK Court of Appeal recently confirmed, 'simply because the name or image of a celebrity appears upon a consumable commercial item, the public will [not necessarily] assume that it has in some way been endorsed by that celebrity'; in *Robyn Rihanna Fenty v. Arcadia Group Brands Ltd* [2015] *EWCA Civ* 3, [41]. [67] *Nice and Safe Attitude v. Piers Flook* [1997] *FSR* 14, 21.

[68] See, e.g., *Wombles v. Womble Skips* [1977] *RPC* 99; *Tavener Rutledge v. Trexapalm* [1975] *FSR* 179. He also asserted that *Lyngstrad v. Annabas Products* [1977] *FSR* 62 could be distinguished on that basis.

[69] [1998] *FSR* 665. [70] Ibid., 674.

[71] J. Cross, 'Giving Credit where Credit is Due: Revisiting the Doctrine of Reverse Passing off in Trademark Law' (1997) 72 *Wash L Rev* 709.

passing off, the defendant's misrepresentation gives rise to the suggestion that the defendant is the source of the claimant's goods or services (or is somehow responsible for the quality of the claimant's goods or services). That is, instead of the defendant pretending that their goods are the claimant's, the defendant claims the claimant's goods as their own.

It is not clear whether reverse passing off amounts to an actionable wrong.[72] In principle, it depends on whether the standard requirements of the 'classic trinity' are met. The problem here is in establishing misrepresentation and damage. If a person merely resells the goods of another trader, this will not usually amount to a misrepresentation. This is the case even if they have added a new sign to the goods. Moreover, given that the claimant-manufacturer will have already placed the goods on the market, it is difficult to see where the damage lies. Although a defendant may derive benefit where they resell the goods, this does not in itself harm the manufacturer. In some circumstances, however, the activities of the reseller may cross into the realm of passing off. A good example of this is where a person represents the claimant's goods as their own, but subsequently supplies their own goods. For example, in *Bristol Conservatories v. Conservatories Custom Built*,[73] both the claimant and the defendant were engaged in the business of designing and selling conservatories. The defendant's salesmen showed potential customers photographs of the claimant's conservatories. In so doing, they led customers to believe that the conservatories were examples of the defendant's own design and craftsmanship. The defendant's application to strike out the statement of claim as disclosing no reasonable cause of action was successful at first instance. This decision was, however, overturned by the Court of Appeal. The Court of Appeal held that the defendant had made a misrepresentation that its goods were of the same quality as the claimant's. The Court added that because the claimant's goodwill was 'asserted and demonstrated as the photographs were shown', it did not matter that the customer might not have known of the claimant. The damage caused was the diversion of sales from the claimant to the defendant. The Court of Appeal took the view that it did not matter that there was no confusion because the misrepresentation 'left no room for confusion'. Whether it is helpful to categorize the case as one of reverse passing off is a matter of debate.[74]

3.5 COMPARATIVE ADVERTISING

'Comparative advertising' is the term used to describe advertisements in which the goods or services of one trader are compared with the goods or services of another trader. To show the advertiser's wares in a favourable light, comparative advertisements usually emphasize differences in things such as price, value, durability, or quality.[75] The question of whether a person engaged in comparative advertising is liable for passing off depends on the nature of the comparison. In some situations, the comparison will not be treated as a misrepresentation. For example, in *Bulmer v. Bollinger*,[76] Goff LJ said that there is no actionable passing off 'if one says that one's goods are very suitable to be used in

---

[72] H. Carty, 'Inverse Passing off: A Suitable Addition to Passing off?' [1993] *EIPR* 370.

[73] [1989] *RPC* 455, 464–5. See also *Boehringer Ingelheim KG v. Swingward Ltd* [2004] *EWCA Civ* 129, [55]–[58].

[74] Wadlow (2016), [7–192] (not a nominate tort in its own right, but a further example of an actionable misrepresentation to which the normal principles apply); J. Drysdale and M. Silverleaf, *Passing off: Law and Practice* (1995), [4.14] (doubting that the concept of reverse passing off is of any value).

[75] For the position of comparative advertising under the registered trade marks regime and non-legal regulation, see Chapter 40, sections 2, 6, and Chapter 41, section 6, pp. 1142–5.

[76] [1978] *RPC* 79, 117.

connection with the plaintiffs'. Equally, for a defendant to say that their goods are similar to or better than the claimant's does not amount to passing off.

In other circumstances, however, comparative advertising may be treated as a misrepresentation. For example, in *McDonald's Hamburgers v. Burger King*,[77] Burger King advertised its hamburgers in the London Underground with the slogan 'It's Not Just Big Mac'. Opinion poll evidence indicated that members of the public treated these as advertisements for a Burger King hamburger called 'Big Mac', or as an improved version thereof. The evidence also indicated that people were likely to respond to the advertisement by going to Burger King restaurants and ordering a 'Big Mac'. Consequently, Whitford J held that the advertisement was a misrepresentation. In *Kimberley Clark v. Fort Sterling*,[78] the defendant promoted its NOUVELLE toilet roll with an offer to placate dissatisfied customers by replacing their NOUVELLE with ANDREX toilet roll. The NOUVELLE packaging said, prominently, 'Softness guaranteed (or we'll exchange it for ANDREX ®)'; the claimant, who owned the ANDREX brand, claimed that the defendant's promotion amounted to passing off. The court agreed, holding that this was a misrepresentation because it was likely to induce purchasers into thinking that NOUVELLE was another product 'from the ANDREX stable or that ANDREX is in some way behind the promotion'.[79]

4 IS THE MISREPRESENTATION DECEPTIVE?

As we explained earlier, in deciding whether a misrepresentation has taken place, the key concern is not with the state of the defendant's mind; instead, it is with the *consequences* of the defendant's actions and the effect that these have upon the public. In particular, the claimant must show that the defendant's actions either have confused or are likely to confuse the public or a substantial part thereof. That is, to succeed in a passing off action, the claimant must show that the defendant's misrepresentation is *deceptive*.[80] Lord Jauncey made this clear in *Reckitt & Colman Products v. Borden*[81] when he said that one of the prerequisites of a successful passing off action was that 'the misrepresentation has deceived or is likely to deceive and that the plaintiff is likely to suffer damage by such deception. Mere confusion which does not lead to a sale is not sufficient.'

The question of whether the misrepresentation is deceptive is a question of fact that requires the court to predict how the public will interpret the defendant's actions.[82] It does not matter that the defendant's representation is true, honest, or legitimate if it deceives the public. Equally, it does not matter if the defendant uses their own name, a relevant geographical name, or a descriptive term, if it is used in a way that was deceptive.[83]

In deciding whether the misrepresentation is deceptive, a number of different questions may arise. While the nature and relative importance of each will vary from case to case, these include the following.

(i)   Who must be deceived?

(ii) How many people must be deceived?

(iii) When must the deception occur?

---

[77] [1986] *FSR* 45.   [78] [1997] *FSR* 877.   [79] Ibid., 885.

[80] *Phones4U* [2006] *EWCA Civ* 244 (Jacob LJ) (contrasting 'confusion' and 'deception'); *Hodgkinson & Corby v. Wards Mobility Services* [1995] *FSR* 169, 175; *Nice and Safe v. Flook* [1997] *FSR* 14, 20; *Barnsley Brewery Company v. RBNB* [1997] *FSR* 462, 467 (confusion but no deception).   [81] [1990] *RPC* 341, 417.

[82] This is a 'jury question': *Harrods v. Harrodian School* [1996] *RPC* 697, 717; *Neutrogena Corporation v. Golden Ltd* [1996] *RPC* 473, 482.   [83] *Montgomery v. Thompson* [1891] *AC* 217, 220.

After looking at these questions, we will consider the types of evidence that may be used by the courts in this context. We will then look at some of the factors that may be taken into account in deciding whether the misrepresentation is deceptive.

4.1 WHO MUST BE DECEIVED?

The question of whether the misrepresentation operates to deceive the public is largely looked at by the courts through the eyes of the general public.[84] However, where the goods or services are not marketed to the general public, the courts consider the impact that the misrepresentation has upon that part of the public for whom the product or services were intended. Although there are dicta to the effect that the appropriate part of the public is the defendant's customers, the better view is that the 'relevant public' should vary according to the type of misrepresentation being alleged. Thus where the allegation is that the defendant has made a misrepresentation that suggests that the claimant is the source of the defendant's goods, and that the goods of the claimant and the defendant are similar, the court would consider the impact that the misrepresentation has upon the claimant's customers.[85] Where the parties' goods or services are different, so that some other type of connection is being alleged, the court will focus on customers who are familiar with the claimant's activities, but who are in the market for goods and services of the defendant. This kind of approach was adopted in *Harrods v. Harrodian School*,[86] where the relevant public was described by Millett LJ as 'affluent members of the middle class who live in London, shop at Harrods and wish to send their children to fee-paying schools'.

The attributes and skills of the notional customer will vary depending on the facts in question.[87] Indeed, as Lord Oliver said in *Reckitt & Colman*,[88] the 'customers have to be taken as they are found'. In some cases, the relevant public might be quite discerning. For example, in a decision involving a passing off action between two banks, it was said that 'potential customers wishing to borrow large sums of money from a bank could reasonably be expected to pay rather more attention to the details of the entity with whom they were doing or seeking to do business'.[89] In other situations, however, the notional customer might be careless and uninterested—for example supermarket shoppers, who apparently spend less than ten seconds examining each purchase. A defendant cannot escape liability by arguing that customers would not have been misled if they were 'more literate, careful, perspicacious, wary or prudent'.[90] While the attributes and skills of the notional customer may vary depending on the facts in question, the court will not take account of situations where the notional customer does not care one way or another about the goods that they are buying.[91] If customers are indifferent to the goods that they are

---

[84] *Marengo v. Daily Sketch* (1948) 65 *RPC* 242, 250.

[85] *Okotoks Ltd v. Fine & Country Ltd (formerly Spicerhaart Ltd)* [2012] *EWHC* 2230 (Ch), [75]. Hildyard J holding that:

> [T]he expressions 'the public' or 'people' connote customers or purchasers (actual or prospective) of the claimant or others with whom the claimant has business relations.

See further *Okotoks Ltd v. Fine & Country Ltd* [2013] *EWCA Civ* 672.

[86] [1996] *RPC* 697, 716.   [87] *Reckitt & Colman (Products) v. Borden* [1990] *RPC* 341, 423.

[88] Ibid., 415–16.   [89] *HFC Bank v. Midland Bank* [2000] *FSR* 176, 185.

[90] *Reckitt & Colman v. Borden* [1990] *RPC* 341, 415–16; *Clark v. Associated Newspapers* [1998] *RPC* 261, 271.

[91] As Lightman J said in *Clark v. Associated Newspapers* [1998] *RPC* 261, 271, 'no claim lies if they are indifferent or careless as to who is the author'. See also *Politechnika Ipari Szovetkezet v. Dallas Print Transfers* [1982] *FSR* 529.

purchasing, a claimant will be unable to show that the defendant's misrepresentation was deceptive. This is because in these circumstances, the misrepresentation has no impact upon the relevant consumers.[92]

4.2 HOW MANY PEOPLE MUST BE DECEIVED?

The next question to consider is how many people must be deceived? It is clear that for an action to succeed, it is not necessary for a claimant to show that *all* of the consumers in the relevant section of the public were deceived by the misrepresentation. As Jacob J said, 'there is passing off even if most of the people are not fooled most of the time but enough are for enough of the time'.[93] But what is 'enough'? The courts' response to this has been that a 'substantial' part of the public must be confused. As Falconer J said in *Lego*,[94] passing off only arises if there is a 'real risk that a substantial number of persons among the relevant sections of the public will in fact believe that there is a business connection between the plaintiff and the defendant'.

This, in turn, gives rise to the further question: what is meant by a 'substantial' part of the relevant group? There is no clear answer to this question. For the most part, the courts have defined the term negatively. Thus it is clear that 'substantial' does not mean either a large proportion or a majority of the public.[95] For example, in the *Chocosuisse* case, those people confused into thinking that a chocolate bar called SWISS CHALET was made from Swiss chocolate were fewer than those who had not been deceived. Nevertheless, this was substantial enough to amount to a passing off.[96] The Court of Appeal has said that references to 'more than *de minimis*' and 'above a trivial level', which had been used in some cases, were best avoided.[97] Beyond these comments, the courts have been unwilling to give much guidance as to what 'substantial' entails.

4.3 WHEN MUST THE DECEPTION OCCUR?

One issue that remains largely unexplored in English law relates to the question: at what point of time must the public be misled? The way in which this question is answered depends on the facts of the case. In most cases, the answer is straightforward: the confusion must occur at the time of purchase. This can be seen in *Bostik v. Sellotape GB*.[98] The

---

[92] This explains Foster J's exclusion from consideration of a 'moron in a hurry': *Morning Star Co-operative Society v. Express Newspapers* [1979] *FSR* 113. See also *Newsweek v. BBC* [1979] *RPC* 441, 447 (test is whether ordinary, sensible members of the public would be confused; not sufficient that the only confusion would be to a very small unobservant section of society). The Court of Appeal has employed the touchstone of the notional consumer developed in European trade marks law, i.e. confusion is to be assessed from the point of view of the consumer who is reasonably well informed, reasonably observant, and reasonably circumspect: *Asprey & Garrard v. WRA (Guns) Ltd* [2002] *FSR* 487, [35].

[93] *Neutrogena Corp. v. Golden Ltd* [1996] *RPC* 473, 481.

[94] *Lego v. Lemelstrich* [1983] *FSR* 155, 188. See also *Reed Executive v. Reed Business Information* [2004] *RPC* 767, 797, [111]; *Phones4U* [2006] *EWCA Civ* 244, [17]; *Knight v. Beyond Properties Pty Ltd* [2007] *FSR* 34, [80].

[95] *Neutrogena v. Golden Ltd* [1996] *RPC* 473 (claimant had only 0.25 per cent of the market, but it was held that a substantial number of members of the public would be misled into thinking the defendant's products were those of the claimant).

[96] *Chocosuisse v. Cadbury* [1999] *RPC* 177, 143, aff'd by the Court of Appeal on the basis that the conclusion was not one that could be regarded as 'perverse': [1999] *RPC* 826 (CA), 838.

[97] *Neutrogena v. Golden Ltd* [1996] *RPC* 473, 494.

[98] [1994] *RPC* 556. See also *Julius Sämaan Ltd v. Tetrosyl Ltd* [2006] *FSR* 42, [118] (Kitchin J) (no passing off where air freshener shaped like a Christmas tree was sold in different packaging and at a higher price than the claimant's pine tree).

claimant in this case manufactured and sold a blue reusable adhesive called BLU-TAK. To compete with the claimant, the defendants launched a blue-coloured adhesive called SELLOTAK, which was sold in a similarly sized wallet to that of BLU-TAK. Except for being approximately the same size, the competing products were 'wholly different in appearance'. As a result the claim for passing off rested entirely on the colour of the tack. The court held that the defendant had not passed its product off as BLU-TAK when it sold blue adhesive putty. The reason for this was that the defendant's blue adhesive putty was not visible at the point of sale.

In other cases, the relevant time to consider whether consumers were deceived is the point in time when the product is consumed or used, rather than when it is purchased. For example, in relation to an action for passing off brought in relation to the authorship of a newspaper story, it was said that the relevant time to consider whether the public is confused is when the person reads the story, rather than when the newspaper was purchased.[99] Post-sale confusion may also be significant in other environments. This may be the case, for example, with designer goods such as clothes or kitchen equipment, where the manufacturer's label is often visible long after purchase.[100]

One question that remains unresolved is whether there is passing off where a defendant's misrepresentation causes immediate confusion, but that confusion vanishes by the time the consumer makes the decision whether to purchase the defendant's goods or engage the defendant's services. This is also referred to as pre-transaction or 'initial interest confusion'.[101] This will be a realistic scenario as regards transactions that are preceded by lengthy formalities, etc., such as those involving financial services. In *HFC Bank v. Midland Bank*,[102] it seemed that a number of customers had mistakenly gone to Midland because it was using the name HSBC, which was similar to HFC. However, in no case did customers do business with Midland without first having been disabused of the error. Lloyd J accepted that to amount to passing off, the deception must be more than momentary or inconsequential,[103] but beyond that declined to venture a view. Subsequent cases seem to have taken a broader view of the sorts of confusion encompassed by passing off to include so-called 'initial interest confusion' (or 'switch selling'). In *Fine and Country v. Otokoks*, Hildyard J observed:

> Damage may occur even if deception is dispelled before the moment of purchase (or other commitment), if the claimant's goodwill is nonetheless harmed; and dispelled deception is actionable accordingly. Thus damage caused by passing off may successfully be claimed if a customer is deceived into going into one shop thinking it to be another if it can be established that, but for the deception, he or she might have gone in to the claimant's shop.[104]

---

[99] *Clark v. Associated Newspapers* [1998] *RPC* 261, 271; *Marengo v. Daily Sketch* (1948) 65 *RPC* 242, 250.

[100] *Chelsea Man Menswear v. Chelsea Girl* [1987] *RPC* 189, 204 (Slade LJ, when considering risk of damage, observed that labelled garments can readily move about the country with their wearers).

[101] *Moroccanoil Israel Ltd v. Aldi Stores Ltd* [2014] *EWHC* 1686 (IPEC), [17]–[28]. For consideration in the trade mark context, see Chapter 38, section 2.3.3, pp. 1043–4.

[102] [2000] *FSR* 176, 186, 202; cf. *Phones4U* [2006] *EWCA Civ* 244, [21] (*HFC* was a case 'on its facts').

[103] See also *Cadbury Schweppes Pty Ltd v. Pub Squash* [1980] *UKPC* 30, [1981] 1 *WLR* 193; *Woolley v. Ultimate Products* [2012] *EWCA Civ* 1038, [4] (Arden LJ) ('The misrepresentation must be more than transitory: it is not sufficient that a purchaser is misled initially but his misunderstanding is dispelled before any material step is taken. In this case, for example, trade purchasers who were confused as to HENLEYS watches checked the position with Mr Woolley so that any misrepresentation to them was not operative'); *Newsweek v. BBC* [1979] *RPC* 441, 449.

[104] *Fine and Country v. Otokoks* [2012] *EWHC* 2230 (Ch), [91].

Arnold J reached a similar conclusion in *Och-Zif Management Europe v. OCH Capital*,[105] noting that it did not necessarily matter that a defendant had ceased to be misled by the time a transaction was concluded: if a 'defendant successfully induces the public to do business with him by making a misrepresentation then it ought not to matter that the falsity of the representation would become apparent at some stage'.

It should be noted that confusion in an abstract sense is not sufficient and a material misrepresentation is required, in the sense of being really likely to cause damage.[106] Even if such misrepresentation is treated as sufficient to give rise to passing off, it remains necessary for a claimant to show a likelihood of damage. In *Knight v. Beyond Properties*,[107] Richards J considered that there was no deception where the defendant called its television programme *Mythbusters*. The claimant had written and sold children's books under the name MYTHBUSTERS, and the judge acknowledged that some people who had read the books might initially have wondered whether the programme was from the same source. However, he did not think that the initial confusion (which would have quickly been dispelled by the content of the programmes, which were directed at 'lads and dads') was such as to cause the claimant any damage.

4.4 EVIDENCE OF CONFUSION

While the question of whether there is a likelihood of confusion is ultimately decided by the court,[108] the courts frequently base such decisions on evidence introduced by the parties. Four types of evidence have been commonly used, often in combination: evidence of actual confusion of consumers; trade evidence; expert evidence; and survey evidence. Processes of proof in trade mark and passing off cases have received quite some judicial scrutiny of late.[109] The courts have been especially concerned to keep the costs of proceedings down by ensuring that only evidence that has some probative value is led. This means that in future, courts will probably focus less on survey evidence, in particular.[110] As Lewison LJ said, 'the classic way in which passing off cases are decided' is by reference to 'the evidence of the live witnesses and [the judge's] own independent assessment'.[111]

While there is no requirement that to succeed in a passing off action, the claimant must show evidence of actual deception, evidence that people have actually been misled will be highly significant.[112] The lack of such evidence may also be probative, but only where the products have been on the market for some time.[113] If, after a lengthy period of time, there

---

[105] [2010] *EWHC* 2599 (Ch), [2011] *FSR* 11, [156], citing Wadlow (2004), [7–39]; approved and applied in *Doosan Power Systems Ltd v. Babcock International Group* [2013] *EWHC* 1364 (Ch), [166], [178].

[106] Wadlow (2016), [5–180]–[5–182].   [107] [2007] *FSR* 34, [80]–[84].

[108] *North Cheshire & Manchester Brewery v. Manchester Brewery* [1899] *AC* 83, 86; *Mothercare v. Penguin Books* [1988] *RPC* 113, 116. The court must not surrender its own independent judgment to any witness or number of witnesses: see *Spalding v. Gamage* (1915) 32 *RPC* 273, 286–7 (Lord Parker). But note that it is the court's (rather than the judge's personal) judgment as to whether it would be deceived that is relevant: *Chocosuisse Union des Fabricants Suisses de Chocolat v. Cadbury* [1998] *RPC* 117, 136.

[109] *Marks & Spencer plc v. Interflora Inc.* [2012] *EWCA Civ* 1501, [2013] 2 *All ER* 663; *Interflora Inc v. Marks & Spencer plc* [2013] *EWCA Civ* 319.

[110] A court might be more amenable to survey evidence in a passing off case because the question to be answered is different from that in a trade mark infringement action: *Marks & Spencer plc v. Interflora Inc.* [2012] *EWCA Civ* 1501, [26]–[34].   [111] *Fine & Country v. Okotoks* [2013] *EWCA Civ* 672, [75].

[112] *Harrods v. Harrodian School* [1996] *RPC* 697, 716. See also *Marks & Spencer plc v. Interflora Inc.* [2012] *EWCA Civ* 1501, [136], [137(i)]; *Marks & Spencer plc v. Interflora Inc.* [2013] *EWCA Civ* 319, [10], [20] (evidence of real-world confusion, in the sense of spontaneous reaction to the allegedly infringing sign, could be of real value).   [113] *Phones4U* [2006] *EWCA Civ* 244, [41]–[47].

is no evidence of actual confusion, this will weigh against a claimant, primarily because it suggests that there is no confusion.[114] However, before inferring a lack of confusion from this, it is important to note that a lack of evidence of confusion might arise for other reasons. For example, it may simply be because the relevant consumers have not been found or are not willing to come forward.

The courts have also been willing to accept expert evidence in relation to matters about which the court is ignorant and needs to be informed. Often, this involves information about the particular trade involved and includes evidence of things such as the class of people, how the goods are displayed or purchased, the numbers sold,[115] and the amount of attention that average shoppers give to the appearance of products at the point of purchase.[116] Thus, in deciding whether the public was deceived into thinking that a chocolate bar called SWISS CHALET was made from Swiss chocolate, the Court of Appeal made extensive use of the expert evidence of the person responsible for selecting products (notably the chocolate) for Marks & Spencer.[117] In another decision, the court went so far as to admit expert evidence as to whether consumers were likely to be deceived.[118] Although this is the very question that the court itself must determine, and therefore one on which evidence is not normally admitted, Browne-Wilkinson V-C saw no good reason why the court should not be assisted by experts in making that judgment.

It has long been commonplace for the courts to admit and rely upon survey evidence when deciding whether the public is deceived by a misrepresentation.[119] The courts have been careful to scrutinize the nature of the survey.[120] To this end, the courts frequently hear evidence from experts criticizing the methodology of the survey undertaken. The courts also scrutinize the survey to take account of issues such as who was interviewed, the questions asked, and whether or not the interviewees were prompted.[121] Following the Court of Appeal decision in *Interflora v. Marks & Spencer*,[122] however, the use of such evidence must now be justified. As Lewison LJ explained, a judge should not admit survey evidence unless satisfied that the survey is likely to be of real value and that the likely value of the evidence justifies the cost.[123] While surveys therefore remain admissible in principle, it seems that their cost will rarely be proportionate to their evidentiary value.[124]

---

[114] *Kimberley Clark* [1997] *FSR* 877, 887–9. See also *Antec International v. South-Western Chicks (Warren)* [1998] *FSR* 738, 745.   [115] *Slazenger & Sons v. Feltham & Co.* (1889) 6 *RPC* 531, 534.

[116] *Kimberley Clark* [1997] *FSR* 877, 884.   [117] *Chocosuisse v. Cadbury* [1999] *RPC* 826, 836.

[118] *Guccio Gucci SpA v. Paolo Gucci* [1991] *FSR* 89, 91; *Sodastream v. Thorn Cascade Co.* [1982] *RPC* 459, 468.

[119] It seems that the problem of survey evidence being excluded because it is hearsay has been avoided. This has been achieved by treating surveys as situations that do not involve proof of the truth of the opinion stated, so much as its existence: *Lego v. Lemelstrich* [1983] *FSR* 155, 178–9. See, e.g., Wadlow (2016), [10–23]–[10–24]. In any case, hearsay evidence is admissible in civil cases: Civil Evidence Act 1995, s. 1.

[120] *Imperial Group PLC v. Phillip Morris* [1984] *RPC* 293 (the Whitford Guidelines); *Interflora Inc. v. Marks & Spencer plc* [2012] *EWCA Civ* 1501, [61] (Lewison LJ).

[121] *Mothercare v. Penguin* [1988] *RPC* 113, 117 (Dillon LJ). Even when flawed, some courts sometimes still find surveys to be 'qualitatively valuable', although others find surveys unhelpful: *Kimberley Clark* [1997] *FSR* 877, 886–7.

[122] [2013] *EWCA Civ* 319.   [123] Ibid., [26].

[124] *Zee Entertainment Enterprises Ltd v. Zeebox Ltd* [2013] *EWHC* 1644 (Ch) (rejecting an application to adduce survey evidence of the views of the UK's Asian community, bearing in mind the costs of the survey—£150,000 out of total expected costs of £1 million—its probative value, and that inferences the court would be able to draw from other 'primary' evidence). But note Birss J's view that a survey may be useful in 'an intrinsically weak passing off case': ibid., [54]. For similar reasoning rejecting surveys, see: *Zee Entertainment Enterprises Ltd v. Zeebox Ltd* [2014] *EWCA Civ* 82; *The London Taxi Corporation Ltd v. Frazer-Nash Research Ltd* [2015] *EWHC* 1840 (Ch).

4.5 FACTORS TO BE TAKEN INTO ACCOUNT IN DECIDING WHETHER THE MISREPRESENTATION IS DECEPTIVE

In deciding whether a defendant's misrepresentation is deceptive, the court will take a number of factors into consideration, including:

(i) the strength of the public's association with the claimant's sign;

(ii) the similarity of the defendant's sign;

(iii) the proximity of the claimant's and defendant's fields of business;

(iv) the location of the claimant's and defendant's businesses;

(v) the characteristics of the market;

(vi) the intention of the defendant;

(vii) whether the defendant has made a disclaimer; and

(viii) whether the defendant is attempting a parody or satire.

We will consider these in turn. It is important to note that the relative importance of each of these will vary according to the facts in question and that the various factors are often closely interrelated.

4.5.1 The strength of the claimant's sign

One factor that will influence a court when deciding whether a misrepresentation is deceptive is the relative strength of the claimant's sign. If the claimant's mark is highly distinctive, the courts are more likely to find that the use of similar marks in a different field of trading is likely to cause confusion. The classic example of this is provided by the *Lego* case,[125] where it was held that the claimant's mark LEGO for children's toys was so strong that confusion resulted from use of the name on coloured plastic garden equipment.

Where a mark or sign is less distinctive, slight differences between the claimant's and the defendant's marks, or between their fields of trading, may mean that there is no passing off. Where a claimant has adopted a descriptive word as a mark, a defendant may be able to avoid passing off by changing the word slightly.[126] Thus where a claimant used the term FURNITURELAND, the court refused to hold a furniture retailer liable for passing off for using the name FURNITURE CITY.[127] In contrast, BUSINESSPLAN BUILDER for software was held to be sufficiently similar to BIZPLAN BUILDER to constitute passing off. This was because BIZPLAN BUILDER was not wholly descriptive, the words 'Biz' and 'Business' were virtually interchangeable, and the capital 'P' and the style of script were common to both.[128]

---

[125] *Lego v. Lemelstrich* [1983] FSR 155, 187; *British Sky Broadcasting Group Plc v. Microsoft Corp* [2013] *EWHC* 1826 (Ch).

[126] *Office Cleaning Services v. Westminster Window and General Cleaners* (1946) 63 *RPC* 39. In *Phones 4u Ltd v. Phone4u.co.uk. Internet Ltd* [2007] *RPC* 5, [21], Jacob LJ explained that:

> [T]here are cases where what at first sight may look like deception and indeed will involve deception, is nonetheless justified in law. I have in mind cases of honest concurrent use and very descriptive marks. Sometimes such cases are described as 'mere confusion' but they are not really—they are cases of tolerated deception or a tolerated level of deception.

[127] *Furnitureland v. Harris* [1989] FSR 536, 539–40; *Associated Newspapers Ltd v. Express Newspapers* [2003] FSR 51 (the *Mail* and the *London Evening Mail*); *Evegate Publishing Ltd v. Newsquest Media (Southern) Ltd* [2013] *EWHC* 1975 (Ch), [170]–[177] (no deception of consumers of the magazine *South-East Farmer* as a result of the publication of *The Southern Farmer*).

[128] See also *Jian Tools for Sales v. Roderick Manhattan Group* [1995] FSR 924.

4.5.2 The similarity of the signs

Another factor that may influence the court when considering whether a misrepresentation deceives the public is the similarity of the signs. It is important to note that the approach adopted by the courts in deciding whether the signs are similar always depends on the facts in hand. As such, the points below should be treated as providing no more than general guidance.

In deciding whether two signs are similar enough to cause confusion, the marks are rarely looked at side-by-side. Instead, the courts tend to ask the hypothetical question: if a person was to see the signs separately, would they mistake the defendant's product for that of the claimant? When deciding whether signs are similar, the courts also tend to look at the signs as a whole and in the context in which they are used. The impact that this has upon the scope of passing off can be seen, for example, in *Wagamama v. City Centre Restaurants*.[129] The claimant in this case ran a chain of Japanese restaurants called WAGAMAMA. Laddie J held that the defendant was liable for passing off when the defendant used the name RAJAMAMA for its chain of Indian restaurants. The judge was influenced by the similar form (the shared second half) of the word, which might give an impression of similarity and connection. This was important in an area in which it was common for recommendations to be made orally and in which recollections were imperfect.

The fact that signs are looked at as a whole has important ramifications where only part of the claimant's sign or mark is appropriated. Where this occurs, the likelihood of there being a passing off depends on the relative distinctiveness of the element that is different. It also depends on the importance that consumers place on the part when purchasing the product in question. For example, where the distinctive feature of the claimant's get-up for water bottles was that the bottles were cobalt blue and were made in a particular shape, it was held that the defendant was not liable for passing off when it sold water in cobalt-blue bottles of a very different shape.[130] This can be usefully contrasted with *Reckitt & Colman*[131] which, as we saw earlier, was a passing off action in relation to the get-up of lemon-juice containers. While the shape, colour, and size of the two containers were the same, the labels on the two products were different. Nonetheless, the courts held that there had been passing off. This was because the labels were only a minor part of the get-up and not an element to which a customer would pay particular regard.

In judging the similarity of signs, the courts sometimes emphasize the 'idea of the mark'—that is, they do not focus on the detail of the mark so much as the general idea that it conveys. For example, in one case the shared idea of 'seabirds' was a significant factor in holding that the defendant had passed its PUFFIN biscuits off as those of the claimant, who sold its biscuits under the name PENGUIN.[132] Given the type of audience in question and the similarity of the get-up, the court held that a substantial number of customers would have been deceived into incorrectly thinking that the biscuits were produced by the same manufacturer.

4.5.3 The proximity of the claimant's and the defendant's fields of business

For some time, it was thought that to succeed in a passing off action, the claimant and defendant had to share 'a common field of activity'. Thus where a radio presenter's name was used for a breakfast cereal, it was held that there was no passing off. This

---

[129] [1995] *FSR* 713; *Neutrogena v. Golden Ltd* [1996] *RPC* 473.

[130] *Ty Nant Spring Water v. Simon Feeney Associates* (28 April 1998), Scott VC refusing interlocutory injunction where both used bottles of the same colour (cobalt blue).

[131] *Reckitt & Colman v. Borden* [1990] *RPC* 341, 423.   [132] *United Biscuits v. Asda* [1997] *RPC* 513.

was because the fields of radio presentation and the sale of breakfast cereals did not overlap.[133] However, even at its inception, the need to show a common field of activity was difficult to reconcile with a number of earlier decisions.[134] It has since been reinterpreted,[135] diluted,[136] and ultimately declared to be heretical.[137] If a claimant can demonstrate a misrepresentation and likelihood of damage to their goodwill, they will succeed; there is no additional requirement that they need to establish a common field of activity.

Having said this, it is clear that the ability to demonstrate a 'common field of activity' will greatly assist a claimant's action for passing off. This is because if two traders share a common field of activity, it will be easier for a court to hold that there is a misrepresentation that is likely to deceive the public and thus cause damage to the claimant.[138] Indeed, the abandonment of the requirement for a common field of activity has meant that a comparison of the trade activities of the parties is a factor that is taken into account in determining the likelihood of deception. The similarity of the fields also interacts with other factors, such as the distinctiveness of the claimant's sign.

The courts have adopted a liberal approach when deciding whether the claimant and defendant operate in the same field. For example, in one decision the use of CARFAX for spare parts for motor vehicles was held to be likely to amount to a passing off, given the claimant's plans to launch a traffic information service under the same name.[139] Similarly, a claimant who used the name MARIGOLD for household rubber gloves was granted an injunction to prevent the defendant from using the mark on toilet tissue.[140] The court was confident that a customer—or, more specifically a 'housewife'—who was familiar with the claimant's gloves would expect toilet roll sold under the same name to be a product of the same business. In a trade mark case, however, the Registry took the view that the owner of the EVER READY mark for batteries would not be able to succeed in a passing off action against a person who used the same words for condoms.[141] Consequently, the mark was registerable for condoms.

4.5.4 The location of the claimant's and defendant's businesses

Goodwill is recognized as being local and, in principle, there is no actionable misrepresentation where a person uses the sign in a different geographical area. This can be seen from the decision of *Bignell v. Just Employment Law Ltd*[142] In this case, the claimant

---

[133] *McCulloch v. May* (1948) 65 *RPC* 58.

[134] See, e.g., *Eastman Photographic Materials Co. v. John Griffiths Cycle Corp.* (1898) 15 *RPC* 105 (cameras and bicycles); *Walter v. Ashton* [1902] 2 *Ch* 282 (*The Times* newspaper and bicycles); as argued by J. Philips and A. Coleman, 'Passing Off and the Common Field of Activity' (1985) 101 *LQR* 242 and accepted by Millett LJ in *Harrods v. Harrodian School* [1996] *RPC* 697, 714.

[135] In the 'Abba' case, *Lyngstad* [1977] *FSR* 62, Oliver J interpreted *McCulloch* as merely requiring a 'real possibility of confusion'.   [136] *Lego v. Lemelstrich* [1983] *FSR* 155.

[137] *Mirage v. Counter-Feat* [1991] *FSR* 145, 157 (Browne-Wilkinson V-C) (referring to the common field of activity theory as discredited); *Harrods v. Harrodian School* [1996] *RPC* 697; *Irvine v. Talksport* [2002] *FSR* 943.

[138] *Nice and Safe v. Flook* [2002] *FSR* 943, 21 (Robert Walker J) ('the *Lego* case, though it illustrates a relaxation of the common field of activity concept does not mark its extinction. It must still be very relevant to the likelihood of deception'); *Oasis Stores' Trade Mark Application* [1998] *RPC* 631, 644 (where the fields of activity are far apart, the burden of establishing a likelihood of confusion or deception will be significantly greater).

[139] *BBC v. Talbot* [1981] *FSR* 228.   [140] *LRC v. Lila Edets* [1972] *FSR* 479.

[141] *Oasis Stores' Trade Mark Application* [1998] *RPC* 631 (in the context of TMA 1994, s. 5(4)).

[142] [2007] *EWHC* 2203 (Ch), [2008] *FSR* 125.

was a solicitor specializing in employment law, who had practised for about ten years in Guildford under the name JUST EMPLOYMENT. The defendant was a Scottish company, incorporated in 2004 as Just Employment Law Ltd (JEL). When the defendant ran a radio campaign on Capital Radio, a number of listeners contacted Bignell's office on the assumption that it was his firm's advertisement, whereupon he sued JEL, alleging passing off. There was no evidence of anyone contacting the defendant in the belief that it had anything to do with the claimant's firm. Deputy Judge Engelhart QC dismissed the claim, finding that Bignell's goodwill was inherently local.[143] The claim for passing off failed, because there was no actual damage, only some confusion, which was to be expected from two such similar names. However, the court left open the possibility that incidental passing off might occur if JEL were to open an office and solicit work near Guildford.

4.5.5 The characteristics of the market

In deciding whether a misrepresentation is deceptive, the courts take account of 'the background of the type of market in which the goods are sold, the manner in which they are sold, and the habits and characteristics of purchasers in that market'.[144]

The characteristics of the market have a particularly pronounced impact on decisions as to whether two signs are similar. Where consumers are well informed or particularly attentive to detail,[145] small differences between signs may be sufficient to avoid a finding of deception. For example, the defendant's use of *Mother care/Other care* as a title for its book was held not to be a misrepresentation that the book was connected with the shop MOTHERCARE.[146] As Bingham LJ explained, the claimant's lettering was not employed, the words were not spelled as one word, the PENGUIN mark was liberally used on the books, and no one who was familiar with the claimant's literary output could see any similarity of style, content, or format. Bingham LJ added that reasonably literate people would not see the title as an indication that the contents bore any reference to the claimant. The better the consumer's memory for detail, the closer the marks must be to cause deception.

Ultimately, the level of detail remembered by the consumer will depend on the goods or services in question. While there may be exceptions, the courts do not normally assume that consumers have a perfect memory of the goods in question. Instead, they tend to assume that the notional consumers have a vague and hazy memory of the goods or services—that is, it is often assumed that consumers have 'imperfect recollection'. Consequently, where a defendant adds laudatory or commonplace words such as 'International' or 'Super' to a name, this will not mean that they will be able to escape liability.[147] The reason for this is that while the addition of the prefix may mean that the signs are not identical, nonetheless they may be similar enough to deceive a consumer with a hazy and imperfect memory. It is usually assumed that consumers pay little attention to detail in purchasing cheap necessities in supermarkets.[148] It will also usually be assumed that non-English-speaking audiences will pay little attention to verbal or textual, as opposed to visual references.[149]

---

[143] Ibid., 145–7.   [144] *Reckitt & Colman v. Borden* [1990] *RPC* 341, 415–16.

[145] Although evidence as to consumer behaviour might reveal that, even with elite goods, consumers are oddly inattentive: *Guccio Gucci v. Gucci* [1991] *FSR* 89.

[146] *Mothercare v. Penguin* [1988] *RPC* 113, 121–2.

[147] *Pontiac Marina* [1998] *FSR* 839 (Court of Appeal of Singapore); *Antec International* [1998] *FSR* 738, 745.

[148] *Kimberley Clark* [1997] *FSR* 877, 884.

[149] *Modus Vivendi v. Keen (World Marketing)* [1996] *EIPR* D–82.

4.5.6 The intention of the defendant

It is well established that it is not a prerequisite to liability that the claimant be able to show that the defendant intended to pass their goods off as those of the claimant.[150] However, it will assist a claimant if they can show that a defendant has acted fraudulently.[151] In these circumstances, the likelihood of deception is more readily inferred. This is because the defendant is assumed to have achieved their goal.[152] Occasionally, a similar attitude has been taken to a defendant who makes a conscious decision to live dangerously and use a sign as close to that of the claimant as is legally possible.[153]

4.5.7 Disclaimers

Because the representation is to be viewed in context, it is sometimes possible for a defendant to correct any misunderstandings that their actions may potentially create.[154] For example, a defendant was able to avoid what would otherwise have been passing off by placing the word 'sliced' in front of the claimant's distinctive designation 'Parma ham'. This was held to be sufficient to counteract the potential misrepresentation.[155]

It is a question of fact whether a defendant succeeds in correcting any misunderstandings the public may have as a result of their misrepresentation.[156] The relative effectiveness of a disclaimer depends on a number of things. To be effective, a disclaimer must be as 'bold, precise and compelling as the trade description itself and must be as effectively brought to the notice of any person to whom the goods may be supplied'.[157] In effect, the disclaimer must negate the misrepresentation. The precise form that the disclaimer needs to take will depend upon the nature of the misrepresentation. In the old case of *Edge v. Nicholls*,[158] the claimant produced distinctive calico bags. The defendant produced a calico bag with a similar get-up to the claimant's, to which it added a label saying NICHOLLS. The disclaimer was ineffective because consumers of the goods (being the 'poorer classes') relied on the get-up, rather than the name of the product.

The point in time at which the disclaimer is communicated to the consumer will also influence whether or not it is effective. As a general rule, the disclaimer must reach the relevant consumer before the misrepresentation brings about the requisite damage. Thus a disclaimer will be ineffective where customers have already been lured into examining the defendant's product as a result of the defendant's use of the claimant's name. Another case exemplifying the importance of the timing of the disclaimer is *Associated Newspapers v. Insert Media*.[159] It will be recalled that by placing advertising inserts inside the claimant's newspaper without its permission or knowledge, the defendant was held to be liable for passing off. In response, the defendant indicated that it would be prepared

---

[150] *Chocosuisse v. Cadbury* [1998] *RPC* 117, 137.   [151] *Burberrys v. Cording* (1909) 26 *RPC* 693, 701.

[152] *Slazenger v. Feltham* (1889) 6 *RPC* 531, 538; *Irvine v. Talksport* [2003] *FSR* 619. In *Parker Knoll v. Knoll International* [1962] *RPC* 265, 290, Lord Devlin questioned the basis of the rule, stating: '[I]t is not easy to see why the defendant's own estimate of the effect of his representation should be worth more than anybody else's. It seems probable that the rule is steeped in history rather than in logic.' *Slazenger* was applied by the Court of Appeal in *L'Oréal v. Bellure* [2008] *RPC* 9.

[153] *United Biscuits v. Asda* [1997] *RPC* 513.   [154] *Chivers v. Chivers* (1900) 17 *RPC* 420.

[155] *Consorzio Parma v. Marks & Spencer* [1991] *RPC* 351, 371 (Nourse LJ), 374 (Balcombe LJ), and 379 (Leggatt LJ).

[156] The public can be surprisingly easily confused, e.g. confusing 'elderflower champagne' with champagne: *Taittinger v. Allbev* [1993] *FSR* 641.

[157] *Norman v. Bennett* [1974] 1 *WLR* 1229, 1232 (a case on the Trade Descriptions Act 1968); *Clark v. Associated Newspapers* [1998] *RPC* 261, 272; cf. *Allen v. Redshaw* [2013] *EWPCC* B1, [35]–[41] (disclaimer ineffective).

[158] [1911] *AC* 693.   [159] [1991] 3 *All ER* 535.

to include on its inserts a statement to the effect that the material did not appear with the approval or knowledge of the newspaper publishers. Browne-Wilkinson V-C said that this would not nullify the misrepresentation. The reason for this was that:

> [The] inclusion in the insert of a disclaimer of that kind would be most unlikely to come to the attention of a person reading the advertisement contained on the insert. It is just inappropriate in this field for the matter to be corrected by a disclaimer which is unlikely to come to the attention of the reader and may well confuse him further if it does come to his attention.[160]

A disclaimer may also fail for the simple reason that it is likely to become detached from the misrepresentation and, as a result, will be unable to nullify the misrepresentation.[161]

4.5.8 Parody

One area in which special considerations may apply is where the defendant sets out to parody or satirize the claimant's goods or services (or some more general target).[162] In these cases, the owner of the goods that have been parodied may bring a passing off action. The key problem here is that for a parody or satire to be effective, the audience needs to understand that the defendant's aim is to ridicule the original. If a parody is effective, there will normally be no misunderstanding and hence no possibility of confusion. This can be seen from *Miss World v. James St Productions*.[163] The claimants in this case, who were the proprietors of goodwill in the 'Miss World' beauty contest, sought to prevent the showing of a film entitled *Miss Alternative World*, which was described as a spoof of the Miss World pageant, with sado-masochistic overtones.[164] The Court of Appeal declined to intervene on the ground that there was no danger that ordinary members of the public would be confused.

However, any confidence that parody will not amount to passing off has been undermined by the *Alan Clark* case.[165] In this decision, the politician and author Alan Clark wished to prevent the *Evening Standard* from publishing a satirical column called 'Alan Clark's Secret Diaries' that bore Clark's name and photograph.[166] The main issue was whether Clark could establish that there had been a misrepresentation or a 'false attribution'.[167] In turn, this required Clark to establish that a substantial number of readers of the *Evening Standard* had been, or were likely to have been, misled in a manner that was more than momentary and inconsequential. Looking at the column and having regard to the evidence of the witnesses, Lightman J held that a substantial body of readers would be misled. The counter-messages (or disclaimers) that appeared on the column, such as the use of the word 'secret' and the statement that 'Peter Bradshaw imagines how the great diarist might record', were said not to be sufficiently forthright to counteract the suggestion that the claimant was the author of the column. As one commentator rightly observed, as a result of this decision '[t]he author of even the most obvious parody cannot assume that his work is [not] a misrepresentation under the law of passing off'.[168]

---

[160] Ibid., 542.

[161] In *Reckitt & Colman v. Borden* [1990] *RPC* 341, 423 (Lord Jauncey), the label was not effective to prevent misrepresentation because it would easily be detached from the product.

[162] For consideration of parody in the context of copyright and trade mark infringements, see Chapters 8 and 41. For reflections, see M. Spence, 'Intellectual Property and the Problem of Parody' (1998) 114 *LQR* 594.

[163] [1981] *FSR* 309.   [164] Ibid., 310.   [165] *Clark v. Associated Newspapers* [1998] *RPC* 261.

[166] See Chapter 10, Fig. 10.1, p. 294.

[167] Clark also based his claim on CDPA 1988, s. 84 (false attribution of authorship). On this, see Chapter 10, section 3, pp. 293–5. It is interesting to note that the constituents of false attribution in s. 84 were treated as different from those under the law of passing off, with s. 84 requiring consideration.

[168] See M. Spence, 'Intellectual Property and the Problem of Parody' (1998) 114 *LQR* 594, 599.

5 PROVIDING DECEPTIVE MEANS OR
INSTRUMENTS OF FRAUD

It is important to note that an action for passing off can not only be brought against a person who carries out the act of misrepresentation, but also against someone who provides the means or facilities that enable the passing off to take place in the first place. This can be seen, for example, in *Lever v. Goodwin*,[169] where the claimant sought relief against a defendant who had been selling soap in a similar get-up. In the circumstances, while consumers might have been deceived by the similarity of the get-up, the defendant did not sell the soap directly to the public; instead, they only sold the soap to retail buyers, who, in turn, sold the soap to members of the public. The problem for the claimant was that the retailers were not deceived about the origin of the goods: they knew exactly what they were purchasing. The defendant argued that because they did not sell the soap directly to the public and because the retailers were not confused, they were not liable for passing off. Chitty J, whose judgment was approved on appeal, denied that a defendant could escape liability in this way. What a manufacturer did in these circumstances, he explained, was to put 'an instrument of fraud' into the retailer's hands. In these circumstances, it was necessary to ask: has the defendant 'knowingly put into the hands of the shopman ... the means of deceiving the ultimate purchaser'?[170] On the facts, Chitty J found that it had. This doctrine was also applied in a character merchandising case, where the suggestion that an official licence to use the image of 'Betty Boop' being granted by the defendant to its own licensees would constitute an 'instrument of fraud'.[171]

This variant of the passing off action can also be applied in the Internet context, as confirmed by the *One in a Million* decision.[172] In this case, the Court of Appeal held that persons who registered and dealt in Internet domain names such as 'marksandspencer. co.uk' were likely to be restrained. This was on the basis that they were 'equipped with or intending to equip another with an instrument of fraud'.[173] Aldous LJ said that a 'name which will, by reason of its similarity to the name of another, inherently lead to passing off is an instrument of fraud'.[174] Even if a name does not inherently lead to passing off, Aldous LJ said that it may nevertheless be an instrument of fraud. In deciding whether this is the case, the court should consider 'the similarity of the names, the intention of the defendant, the type of trade and all the surrounding circumstances'.[175] Aldous LJ added that if the court concludes 'that the name was produced to enable passing off, is adapted to be used for passing off, and, if used, is likely to be fraudulently used, an injunction will be appropriate'.[176]

On the facts, it was held that the domain names in question were 'instruments of fraud'. This was because any 'realistic use of them as domain names would result in passing off'.[177]

---

[169] (1887) 4 *RPC* 492, 498.   [170] Ibid.

[171] *Hearst Holdings Inc and anor v. AVELA Inc and ors* [2014] *EWHC* 439 (Ch).

[172] [1998] 4 *All ER* 476. For criticism of the reasoning, see M. Elmslie, 'The *One in a Million* Case' [1998] *Ent L Rev* 283, 285; C. Thorne and S. Bennet, 'Domain Names: Internet Warehousing—Has Protection of Well-known Names on the Internet Gone too Far?' [1998] *EIPR* 468 (referring to *One in a Million* as 'a policy decision rather than a straight application of the law of passing off'). See also H. Carty, 'Passing off and Instruments of Deception' [2003] *EIPR* 188, arguing that the doctrine requires (i) circulation of (ii) an instrument (iii) calculated to deceive and that, in *One in a Million*, there simply was no instrument of deception. Carty prefers the view that the decision is to be justified as a case of threatened passing off, or threatening to authorize another's passing off. However, the case has been followed: *Phones4U* [2006] *EWCA Civ* 244, [27]; *Tesco v. Elogicom* [2006] *EWHC* 403, [41]–[50]; *Thomson Ecology Ltd v. Apem Ltd* [2013] *EWHC* 2875 (Ch).

[173] *One in a Million* [1998] 4 *All ER* 476, 493.   [174] Ibid.

[175] Ibid.   [176] Ibid.   [177] Ibid., 497.

Because the value of the names lay in the threat that they would be used in a fraudulent way, the Court held that the 'registrations were … made for the purpose of appropriating the respondent's property, their goodwill, and with an intention of threatening dishonest use by them or another'.[178]

In contrast, in *French Connection v. Sutton*,[179] Rattee J refused to grant summary judgment to French Connection (UK) against a defendant who had registered 'fcuk.com'. The judge reasoned that, in contrast to the examples in *One in a Million*, the defendant might succeed in establishing a defence at trial—namely, that the domain name was not registered with a view to passing off, but for 'use by himself of what he thought would be a useful internet and email name'. According to Rattee J, this was not an 'incredible' argument, because the letters FCUK were widely used by Internet users as an alternative to the word 'fuck', usually to access sites containing pornographic material. As is clear from this, much will turn on when a court is willing to infer potential legitimate use of the name. In particular, it is not easy to predict whether a so-called 'typo-squatter', who registers a name that is similar to that of a well-known business (for example 'tescp.com'), in the hope of attracting visitors who mistype the name of that business ('tesco.com'), will face liability under the 'instruments of fraud' doctrine. The registrant might intend to collect revenue by forwarding such traffic to Tesco's own site, or may have other goals.

---

[178] Ibid., 498. See also *Reallty Group v. Chance* [2002] *FSR* 13 (where the claimant sought to stop the defendant's alleged 'blocking registration' of a Community trade mark, Patten J referred to *One in a Million* when refusing to strike out).

[179] [2000] *ETMR* 341. For other cases in which passing off has been used to prevent use of websites in trade, see *Easyjet Airline Co. v. Dainty* [2002] *FSR* 6; *Bonnier Media v. Smith (GL)* [2002] *ETMR* 86.

34

DAMAGE

The third and final element that a claimant must prove to sustain a passing off action is that they have suffered, or are likely to suffer, damage as a result of the defendant's misrepresentation.[1] After looking at the third limb of the passing off action, we turn away from the classic passing off action to consider the notion of extended passing off and then unfair competition.

1 HEADS OF DAMAGE

There are four types of damage that have been recognized by the courts in connection with misrepresentation: loss of existing trade and profits; loss of potential trade and profits; damage to reputation; and dilution.[2] In each case, there must be more than trivial or minimal damage.[3] Where the damage to reputation relates to future losses, the damage must also be reasonably foreseeable.[4]

1.1 LOSS OF EXISTING TRADE AND PROFIT

One of the most common forms of damage is where the misrepresentation diverts trade and thus profit from the claimant to the defendant. This will occur where the misrepresentation generates confusion about the source or origin of the goods or services. In this situation, the damage is self-evident: it is the loss of profit on the sale of goods or services that the claimant suffers. This type of damage will only occur where the parties deal in similar goods or services or operate in similar fields.

1.2 LOSS OF POTENTIAL TRADE AND PROFIT

The courts have also recognized that a claimant may incur damage where the misrepresentation leads to a loss of future profit. This will occur, for example, where a defendant trades in a field or geographical area into which the claimant intends to expand in the

---

[1] A requirement of damage is specified in both Lord Diplock and Lord Fraser's fifth 'probanda'—*Erven Warnink v. Townend* [1979] *AC* 731, 742, 756—and the third branch of Lord Oliver's classic trinity.

[2] Wadlow (2016), ch. 4; H. Carty, 'Heads of Damage in Passing off' [1996] *EIPR* 487; but see P. Johnson and J. Gibson, 'The "New" tort of passing off' (2015) 131 *LQR* 476, 491.

[3] Lord Fraser's reference, in *Erven Warnink v. Townend* [1979] *AC* 731, 756, to 'substantial' damage was reinterpreted in this way by Peter Gibson LJ in *Taittinger SA v. Allbev* [1993] *FSR* 641, 664.

[4] Not 'hypothetical' or 'far-fetched': *Mothercare v. Penguin Books* [1988] *RPC* 113, 116.

future. In this situation, the damage suffered arises as a result of the potential trade that is lost rather than the existing trade that is diverted.[5]

Importantly, the loss of potential profits includes the loss of a chance to expand into a new field. This can be seen, for example, in *Lego v. Lemelstrich*,[6] which was an action brought by Lego, the well-known manufacturer of children's building blocks, against Lemelstrich, who sold brightly coloured plastic garden sprinklers marketed under the name, LEGO. On the basis that Lego's reputation extended beyond children's toys to include garden sprinklers, Falconer J found that the defendant's use of the LEGO name in relation to garden equipment was likely to damage Lego's goodwill. Given that the LEGO goodwill extended to garden equipment, the claimant would have had the potential to use its name to operate in the field of garden equipment, or to have licensed or franchised other traders in that field.

1.3 LOSS OF LICENSING REVENUES

Loss of future profit may also include situations where the defendant's conduct undermines the claimant's ability to license their own mark and thus brings about a loss of potential licensing revenues. The recognition of the loss of future licensing revenue as a relevant form of damage may enable celebrities to use passing off to prevent the misappropriation of their image or personality.[7] (Without this form of damage, celebrities face the problem that if they had not already licensed their image, they would have difficulties in proving the requisite damage.) In *Mirage Studios v. Counter-Feat Clothing*,[8] Browne-Wilkinson V-C held that the creators of the Teenage Mutant Ninja Turtles (fictitious cartoon characters), suffered damage when the defendant licensed others to reproduce the cartoon characters on clothing. This was because they would lose the royalties that would otherwise have been paid to them to use the images. This line of reasoning has been criticized on the basis of its circularity.[9] The reasoning is said to be circular because a person is only entitled to licensing revenue if they have the legal ability to control the use that is made of their image (etc.). In turn, this only arises where the unauthorized use amounts to passing off. While this criticism may be technically correct, it overlooks the fact that parties may enter into licensing schemes even though there is no legal requirement to do so.[10] Despite doubts about the impact of passing off on character and personality merchandising, it remains a profitable business. As long as the courts only recognize damage through loss of royalties where licensing is likely to take place, it is difficult to see that the circularity objection carries much force.

This must be contrasted with *Stringfellow v. McCain*.[11] The defendant in the case manufactured a new brand of long, thin oven-ready chips called stringfellows. The television advertisements for the defendant's chips featured a choreographed disco number set in a kitchen. The claimant was the owner of a well-known nightclub called STRINGFELLOW'S, which consisted of a restaurant and a discotheque. The claimant argued that the defendant's misrepresentation was likely to prejudice his future chances of exploiting the goodwill associated with the name STRINGFELLOW'S. The court refused to grant relief on the ground that it was unlikely that the misrepresentation would cause Peter Stringfellow, the

---

[5] *LRC v. Lila Edets* [1973] *RPC* 560 (use on toilet tissue of same name, in a similar style, as claimant used for household gloves and nappies caused damage because claimant was planning to move into the field).

[6] [1983] *FSR* 155, 194. See also *Dunhill v. Sunoptic* [1979] *FSR* 337.

[7] *Robyn Rihanna Fenty v. Arcadia Group Brands* [2013] *EWHC* 2310 (Ch).   [8] [1991] *FSR* 145.

[9] H. Carty, 'Heads of Damage in Passing off' [1996] *EIPR* 487, 490.

[10] Wadlow (2016), [4–42]–[4–45].   [11] [1984] *RPC* 501.

proprietor of the club, any damage. Slade LJ found that the television advert would not prejudice the proprietor Stringfellow's ability to exploit his name through the establishment of (say) franchises. In part, Slade LJ was influenced by the fact that there was no evidence that Stringfellow had any intention to exploit his name. Stephenson LJ said that in a case such as this, there must be clear and cogent proof of actual damage or real likelihood of damage. Along with Slade LJ, he said that where there is a tenuous overlap between the fields of activity of the protagonists, he doubted whether damage in the form of loss of future franchising or merchandising revenue was ever recoverable.[12]

1.4 DAMAGE TO REPUTATION

The courts have also recognized that damage may occur where the misrepresentation has a negative impact on the claimant's reputation.[13] This form of damage is particularly important where the misrepresentation is made in respect of non-competing goods or services. While the claimant may not lose any trade, the misrepresentation may nonetheless have a negative impact upon the claimant's reputation. This is particularly so where the claimant deals in high-quality goods or services. As we explained earlier, damage from loss of existing or potential trade arises where the public is confused about the origin of the goods or services; in contrast, damage to reputation arises where the defendant's misrepresentation leads the public to believe that the goods or services of the claimant and the defendant are somehow related. The resulting damage arises from the negative impact that this has upon the claimant's reputation. As Warrington LJ explained:

> [To] induce the belief that my business is a branch of another man's business may do that other man damage in various ways. The quality of goods I sell, the kind of business I do, the credit or otherwise which I enjoy are all things which may injure the other man who is assumed wrongly to be associated with me.[14]

Another example of the way reputation may be damaged is offered by *Associated Newspapers v. Insert Media*.[15] The claimant in this case was the publisher of two national newspapers. The defendant arranged with retail newsagents to have advertising materials inserted into the papers, without the publisher's knowledge or consent. The Court of Appeal held that since there was a real risk that the publisher would be thought to be responsible for the accuracy and honesty of the inserts, there was an obvious, appreciable risk of loss of goodwill and reputation by the publisher.

One situation where damage to reputation may be important is where the claimant deals in high-quality goods and the defendant acts in a way that undermines that reputation. This would be the case, for example, where the defendant trades under the same name as the claimant, but in a market in which the claimant would never operate. In these circumstances, the defendant's misrepresentation would not impact upon the claimant's sales. The reason for this is that the claimant would never have made the sales in the first place. Nonetheless, the courts have recognized that the defendant's conduct may damage the claimant's reputation. This can be seen, for example, in *Annabel's Berkeley Square v.*

---

[12] Ibid., 546–7.

[13] But cf. *Harrods v. Harrodian School* [1996] *RPC* 697, 718 ('damage to reputation without damage to goodwill is not sufficient to support an action for passing off', so that even if the school had a poor reputation, it would not rub off on the department store).

[14] *Ewing v. Buttercup Margarine Co.* [1917] 2 *Ch* 1, 14. Applied by Laddie J in *Associated Newspapers v. Express Newspapers* [2003] *FSR* 51, [46], and by Mann J in *Sir Robert McAlpine Ltd v. Alfred McAlpine* [2004] *EWHC* 630, [2004] *RPC* (36) 711, [4]–[45].   [15] [1991] *FSR* 380.

Schock,[16] where a well-known London club called 'Annabel's' was granted relief to prevent the defendant from trading as 'Annabel's Escort Agency'. The court accepted that the defendant's use of the name 'Annabel's' could have tarnished and thus undermined the claimant's reputation.

Another situation in which a misrepresentation may damage a claimant's reputation is in relation to the unauthorized use of the name, image, or likeness of a celebrity. Where the name or image of a celebrity is used without permission and the celebrity can show that the public (incorrectly) thought that they had endorsed the use of their image, this may damage the celebrity's reputation. This would be the case, for example, if the picture of a sports star who has a reputation for healthy living was used to advertise a brand of cigarettes.[17] Damage to reputation may also be important in relation to character merchandising. For example, in *Mirage Studios v. Counter-Feat Clothing*,[18] the claimants brought an action against the defendant for licensing the reproduction of images of Teenage Mutant Ninja Turtles on T-shirts and clothing. Browne-Wilkinson V-C said that since the public 'associates the goods with the creator of the characters, the depreciation of the image by fixing the Turtle picture to inferior goods and inferior materials may seriously reduce the value of the licensing right'.[19] A similar approach was adopted by the Supreme Court of New South Wales in *Henderson v. Radio Corporation*.[20] It will be recalled that in this case, the unauthorized use of a photograph of two ballroom dancers on a record cover was held to be a misrepresentation that the dancers had endorsed the product. On the basis that the 'wrongful appropriation of another's professional or business reputation is an injury in itself', the Court found that the misrepresentation had caused the requisite damage. This was because it had deprived the dancers of the right to bestow recommendations at will.[21] Whether this is really a case of damage to reputation or a loss of an opportunity to profit is, however, questionable.

1.5 DILUTION

The final form of damage recognized by the courts is where the misrepresentation dilutes the claimant's goodwill. This occurs where the defendant's misrepresentation causes the claimant's sign to become familiar or commonplace and, as a result, undermines the ability of the sign to summon up particular goods or values. That is, the defendant's misrepresentation dilutes the pulling power or goodwill of the claimant's sign. Importantly, this applies where the public is not confused about the source or origin of the goods, or where it is unlikely that the reputation will be damaged.

The notion of damage through dilution was acknowledged in English law in *Taittinger v. Allbev*.[22] The claimant was a member of a group of producers from the Champagne district, who made a naturally sparkling wine that had long been known in the United Kingdom as 'Champagne'. Notably, the claimant's Champagne was produced by a process of double fermentation from grapes grown in the Champagne district. The claimant

---

[16] [1972] *RPC* 838. See also *British Medical Association v. Marsh* (1931) 48 *RPC* 565.

[17] Courts have additionally recognized that reputation may be endangered by the 'loss of control' over one's image and the corresponding loss of autonomy in deciding whom to endorse or merchandise with, without the need to establish that the defendant's products are of lower quality or the context of use is incompatible with the image. See *Robyn Rihanna Fenty v. Arcadia Group Brands* [2013] EWHC 2310 (Ch), [74].

[18] [1991] *FSR* 145.   [19] Ibid., 156.   [20] [1969] *RPC* 218.   [21] Ibid., 236.

[22] [1993] *FSR* 641. A number of earlier cases had referred to a trader's interest in maintaining the exclusivity of their signs: *Lego v. Lemelstrich* [1983] *FSR* 155; *Dalgety Spillers Food v. Food Brokers* [1994] *FSR* 504; *Peter Waterman v. CBS* [1993] *EMLR* 27.

brought an action against the producer of a non-alcoholic sparkling beverage called ELDERFLOWER CHAMPAGNE that was produced in England. At first instance, it was held that the claimant had goodwill in 'Champagne' and that the labelling of the defendant's product amounted to a misrepresentation. However, the court found that while a small number of people might be confused by the defendant's misrepresentation, the claimant had not established that there was any real likelihood of serious damage if the defendant continued to sell its product as ELDERFLOWER CHAMPAGNE.

The Court of Appeal overturned the first-instance decision, finding that the defendant was liable for passing off. While the Court of Appeal agreed with the judge's findings at first instance in relation to goodwill and misrepresentation, it disagreed as to the question of damage. In particular, the Court held that the defendant's use of 'Champagne' had caused the requisite damage to sustain a passing off action. Importantly, the Court found that the relevant injury to the Champagne house's goodwill occurred under a head of damage not considered at first instance: the damage arose from the fact that there would have been a blurring or erosion of the uniqueness associated with the name 'Champagne', which would have debased the claimant's reputation. The use of the name 'Champagne' for the elderflower drink brought about 'a gradual debasement, dilution or erosion of what is distinctive'.[23] This was because, as Cross J explained in another context:

> [I]f people were allowed to call sparkling wine not produced in Champagne 'Champagne' even though preceded by an adjective denoting the country of origin, the distinction between genuine Champagne and 'champagne-type' wines produced elsewhere would become blurred; that the word 'Champagne' would come gradually to mean no more than 'sparkling wine' and that part of the plaintiff's goodwill which consisted in the name would be diluted and gradually destroyed.[24]

The explicit recognition of dilution as a form of damage was greeted enthusiastically by many commentators, especially in light of similar extensions in trade mark law.[25] However, the status of dilution as a head of damage in passing off has subsequently been thrown into doubt by *Harrods v. Harrodian School*.[26] In this decision, Millett LJ said that while:

> . . . erosion of the distinctiveness of a brand name has been recognized as a form of damage to the goodwill of the business with which the name is connected in a number of cases, particularly in Australia and New Zealand . . . unless care is taken this could mark an unacceptable extension of the tort of passing off.[27]

Millett LJ also said that he had problems with an action based on confusion that recognized a distinct head of damage that did not depend on confusion.[28] On the facts, Millett LJ held that it was highly unlikely that as a result of the defendant's activities, the Harrods name would lose its distinctiveness or become a generic term to refer to shops that sold luxury goods. As such, the passing off action failed.[29]

As a result of the *Harrods* decision, there is now some uncertainty over the extent to which dilution will be recognized as a distinct head of damage. One view treats dilution

---

[23] *Taittinger v. Allbev* [1993] *FSR* 641, 670, 674, 678 ('singularity and exclusiveness of the description Champagne').   [24] *Vine Products v. Mackenzie* [1969] *RPC* 1, 23.

[25] TMA 1994, s. 10(3), discussed in Chapter 38, section 2.4, pp. 1051–6.

[26] [1996] *RPC* 697.   [27] Ibid., 715–16.

[28] See Wadlow (2016), [4–58]. Similar concerns were echoed in *TWG Tea Co Pte Ltd v. Tsit Wing (Hong Kong) Co. Ltd* [2016] *HKCFA* 2, [23]–[24] (Gummow NPJ).

[29] Sir Michael Kerr, in a dissenting judgment, applied the dilution doctrine from *Taittinger v. Allbev* [1993] *FSR* 641.

as an appropriate form of damage only in extended passing off cases.[30] Other authorities, however, have been willing to accept dilution in the context of classic passing off. In *British Telecommunications v. One in a Million*,[31] the Court of Appeal held that people who registered and dealt in Internet domain names, such as 'marksandspencer.co.uk', were liable for passing off. This was because 'registration of the domain name including the words Marks & Spencer is an erosion of the exclusive goodwill in the name which damages or is likely to damage Marks & Spencer'.[32] Similarly, in *Sir Robert McAlpine Ltd v. Alfred McAlpine plc*,[33] Mann J held that the defendant was guilty of passing off when it decided to rebrand itself as MCALPINE. While the two McAlpine forms had been long established as 'Robert McAlpine' and 'Alfred McAlpine', and shared goodwill in the 'McAlpine' name, the decision to use the surname by itself would blur the distinctive character of Sir Robert McAlpine's mark. 'Once the prefix goes', the judge explained, 'there is scope for a greater amount of elbowing (or blurring, or diminishing, or erosion) ... to which Robert has not consented.'[34]

2 EXTENDED PASSING OFF

As should be clear by now, the classic passing off action contains a host of subcategories and sub-rules. The courts have developed one variant, known as 'extended passing off', which deserves special attention. The extended form of passing off was first recognized by Danckwerts J in the *Bollinger* decision,[35] in which the claimants, who were champagne producers, brought a successful action to prevent the defendant from calling its product SPANISH CHAMPAGNE. The action for extended passing off represents a radical departure from the classic form, which is based on misrepresentation as to source.[36] As Laddie J said in *Chocosuisse*,[37] although extended passing off grew from passing off roots, it displays marked differences from the classic form of the cause of action. These differences are best looked at in terms of the three elements of the action: goodwill; misrepresentation; and damage.

2.1 GOODWILL

The first point to note about extended passing off is that it recognizes that a class or group of traders may share goodwill in a name (or some other indicator) that is distinctive of a particular class of goods, such as ADVOCAAT, CHAMPAGNE, SCOTCH WHISKY,

---

[30] *Chocosuisse Union des Fabricants Suisses de Chocolat v. Cadbury* [1998] *RPC* 117, 127 (damage by dilution only in case of famous yet descriptive marks). Caution is also advocated in: H. Carty, 'Heads of Damage in Passing off' [1996] *EIPR* 487. See also H. Carty, 'Passing off at the Crossroads' [1996] *EIPR* 629, 631; H. Carty, 'Dilution and Passing off: Cause for Concern' (1996) 112 *LQR* 632; *TWG v. Tsit Wing* [2016] *HKCFA* 2, [14]–[37] (Gummow NPJ reasoning that the Hong Kong Court of Final Appeal should not endorse the concept).

[31] [1998] 4 *All ER* 476, 497. See also *Pontiac Marina Private v. CDL Hotels International* [1998] *FSR* 839 ('anything which dilutes the distinctiveness of Millennia causes damage').

[32] [1998] 4 *All ER* 476, 497.   [33] [2004] *RPC* (36) 711, [43], [49].   [34] Ibid., [49].

[35] *Bollinger v. Costa Brava Wine Co.* [1960] *RPC* 16. For historical background, see D. Gangjee, 'Spanish Champagne: An Unfair Competition Approach to GI Protection', in Dreyfuss and Ginsburg (2014) 105.

[36] See S. Naresh, 'Passing off, Goodwill and False Advertising: New Wine in Old Bottles' (1986) 45 *CLJ* 97, 98.

[37] *Chocosuisse Union des Fabricants Suisses de Chocolat v. Cadbury* [1998] *RPC* 117, 124; on appeal, Chadwick LJ focused on two differences—the shared nature of the goodwill and the fact that the class of traders was capable of continued expansion: [1999] *RPC* 826, 830.

VODKA, or GREEK YOGHURT. This can be seen, for example, in the *Bollinger* decision,[38] in which the claimants were members of a group of producers from the Champagne district in France, who made a naturally sparkling wine that had long been known in the United Kingdom as 'Champagne'. The claimant's Champagne was produced by a process of double fermentation from grapes grown in the Champagne district. The claimant brought a passing off action against the defendant for selling a product called SPANISH CHAMPAGNE. The claimant did so on the basis that because the defendant's drink was made in Spain and/or from grapes grown in Spain, it did not qualify to be called 'Champagne'. Danckwerts J reviewed the cases concerning geographical expressions as trade descriptions and the cases on shared goodwill. He said that passing off would restrain a trader who sought to attach to their product a name or description with which they have no natural association, 'so as to make use of the reputation and goodwill which has been gained by a product genuinely indicated by the name or description'.[39] Danckwerts J added that it did not matter 'that the persons truly entitled to describe their goods by the name and description are a class producing goods in a certain locality, and not merely one individual'.[40] In essence, the court recognized that the claimant, along with the other members of the class, had the requisite goodwill in the name 'Champagne' since the collective goodwill nevertheless added a little lustre to each individual claimant. The collectively generated goodwill had arisen on the basis that CHAMPAGNE indicated a sparkling wine that came from the Champagne district in France, was made by a particular method, and was made only from grapes sourced from the Champagne region. As such, champagne had a distinctive reputation that could only be used by producers from that region.

The extended form of passing off was approved and elaborated on in *Warnink v. Townend*.[41] In this decision, the House of Lords held that extended passing off was not confined to drinks or to indications of geographical origin; instead, the action applied equally where any product had a particular characteristic or quality. In this case, the claimant produced ADVOCAAT, a drink manufactured from eggs and a spirit called 'brandewijn'. The defendant sold its drink, made out of eggs and wine, under the name 'Advocaat'. The House of Lords held that this amounted to passing off. Previous case law had been confined to cases in which a particular product had been manufactured in a particular way using ingredients from a particular geographical source, such as Champagne or Scotch whisky.[42] In *Warnink*, no such geographical connection was claimed; instead, the claimant based its case on the association that existed between the name—ADVOCAAT—and a particular product with particular ingredients—namely, a drink manufactured from eggs and brandewijn.[43]

---

[38] *Bollinger v. Costa Brava Wine* [1960] *RPC* 16. See also *Vine Products v. Mackenzie* [1969] *RPC* 1 (Sherry—wine produced by the solera process in the province of Jerez de la Fontera in Spain); *John Walker & Sons v. Henry Ost* [1970] *RPC* 489 (Scotch whisky—blended whisky distilled, but not necessarily blended, in Scotland); *Taittinger v. Allbev* [1993] *FSR* 641 (Champagne); *Consorzio del Prosciutto di Parma v. Marks & Spencer* [1991] *RPC* 351 and *Consorzio del Prosciutto di Parma v. Asda Stores* [1988] *FSR* 697 (Parma ham).

[39] *Bollinger v. Costa Brava Wine* [1960] *RPC* 16, 31–2.   [40] Ibid.   [41] [1979] *AC* 731.

[42] For example, in *Bollinger v. Costa Brava Wine* [1960] *RPC* 16, 'champagne' was taken to refer to a drink made from grapes from the Champagne region, which was produced by the champenois process. In *Walker v. Ost* [1970] *RPC* 489, 'Scotch whisky' referred to a blended whisky, the ingredients of which were all whiskies distilled in Scotland.

[43] See also *Diageo North America Inc. and anor v. Intercontinental Brands (ICB)* [2010] *EWHC* 17 (Ch), [155] (evidence established that the 'alcohol-consuming public in the United Kingdom, and in particular the vodka consuming public, have come to regard the term "vodka" as denoting a particular class of alcoholic beverage').

Lord Fraser said that it was not necessary that the class of traders should be defined by reference to the locality in which the product was produced; instead, the crucial thing was that the name was distinctive of a particular class of goods. He added that the name must have a 'definite meaning', so that its use in relation to a different product was a misrepresentation.[44] In a similar vein, Lord Diplock said that the name must denote 'a product endowed with recognizable qualities which distinguish it from others of inferior reputation that compete with it in the same market'.[45]

Lord Fraser's sentiment that the crucial thing in relation to extended passing off was that the name was distinctive of a particular class of goods was echoed in *Chocosuisse v. Cadbury*,[46] in which Laddie J recognized that the Swiss Chocolate Industry Association had collective goodwill in the term 'Swiss chocolate'. The Swiss body argued that by introducing a chocolate product called SWISS CHALET, Cadbury had made a misrepresentation to the public that the product was made of Swiss chocolate. Laddie J (whose judgment was affirmed by the Court of Appeal) said that for a claimant to succeed, it was necessary for them to show that 'a significant part of the public took the words "Swiss chocolate" to indicate a particular group of products having a discrete reputation as a group'.[47] On the evidence, he held that it had: a significant part of the public understood the words 'Swiss chocolate' to denote a group of products of distinctive reputation for quality. The fact that the public could not define what those distinctive features were was of little relevance.[48]

In many ways, the concept of goodwill recognized in extended passing off is similar to that recognized in the so-called 'classic' action. Indeed, as Patten LJ said in *Diageo v. Intercontinental Brands*:

> [The] classic and extended forms of passing-off are not different torts but are simply convenient labels to describe the two most obvious situations in which the law will intervene to render actionable the misappropriation of established goodwill by a seller based in a misrepresentation by him as to the nature and province of his own goods.[49]

In line with this, the courts have made it clear that the shift away from the name and reputation of the seller (classic passing off) to the reputation associated with a product (which is a defining feature of extended passing off) does not change the fundamental principal that the claimant needs to show goodwill in the name.[50] That is, they need to show that the 'trade name has a pulling power that brings in custom, so that reputation and goodwill can properly be said to be enjoyed by all producers within the class which use that name for their product'.[51] To establish the requisite goodwill, it is necessary to show that 'a significant section of the public believe that the trading name denoted a sufficiently defined and distinctive class, with the requisite pulling power'.[52] The relevant time for testing whether the use of a particular name or get-up has the reputation and goodwill necessary to found an extended passing off claim is the moment when the alleged offending product first appears in the market.[53]

In establishing goodwill, it is not enough for a claimant merely to show that a trade name is descriptive of the geographical location where the product was manufactured.[54] At the other extreme, it is not necessary for a claimant to show that the goods or services

---

[44] *Erven Warnink v. Townend* [1979] *AC* 731, 754.   [45] Ibid., 744.   [46] [1998] *RPC* 117.

[47] Ibid., [28].   [48] Ibid., 133. See also *H. P. Bulmer and Showerings v. J. Bollinger SA* [1978] *RPC* 79, 119.

[49] *Diageo North America Inc. and anor v. Intercontinental Brands (ICB)* [2010] *EWCA Civ* 920, [23].

[50] See ibid.   [51] *Fage UK Ltd v. Chobani UK* [2013] *EWHC* 630 (Ch), [125].

[52] Ibid., [127]–[132].

[53] Ibid., [81]. The manner in which the alleged offending product is marketed and sold is relevant only to the question of misrepresentation: ibid.   [54] Ibid.

have a reputation for being luxury goods or goods of 'higher quality or cachet'. That is, there is no 'legal requirement that the distinctiveness of the claimant's mark should also be a badge of quality'.[55] Nor is it necessary for a claimant to show that the place or country of origin imposed strict regulations as to the mode of manufacture of the product in question.[56] There is also no need for a claimant to be able to show that consumers are knowledgeable about the manufacturing processes typical of the product in question.[57] Instead, all that matters with extended passing off is that there is goodwill in the name.

While the shared goodwill that underpins the extended passing off action is similar to goodwill that is jointly owned by a number of parties, there are a number of differences. One important difference relates to who can control the goodwill where it is jointly owned. Where classic goodwill is owned jointly, each owner cannot prevent other owners from using the particular sign; all joint owners, however, may prevent others from using the sign. By contrast, the goodwill recognized by extended passing off differs in that other traders may participate in the shared goodwill without the consent of existing owners.[58]

In determining whether a claimant has the requisite goodwill to bring an extended passing off action, a distinction is drawn between establishing the distinctiveness of the descriptive term in the minds of the public and establishing who is entitled to use the term. This distinction was brought out clearly in the *Chocosuisse* decision.[59] Acknowledging that different manufacturers who called their chocolate 'Swiss chocolate' employed very different recipes, the Court of Appeal said that this did not prevent them from collectively acquiring a reputation for quality. Equally, it did not matter that the public did not know or appreciate the identifying characteristics of the class.[60] All that was required was that the designation 'Swiss chocolate' was taken by a significant section of the public to indicate a particular group of products (chocolate made in Switzerland) having a discrete reputation distinct from other chocolate.[61]

Despite the assistance provided by the *Chocosuisse* case, a number of issues are unclear in relation to the operation of collective goodwill. One issue that is uncertain relates to the question: how extensive must the trade of an individual be for them to participate in the collective goodwill? In other words, what does an individual trader need to do to establish that they are a member of a class? According to *Warnink v. Townend*,[62] the mere fact that a person has begun to trade in relation to a particular product does not mean that they are therefore entitled to share in the extended goodwill. As Lord Diplock noted:

> As respects subsequent additions to the class, mere entry on to the market would not give any right of action for passing off; the new entrant must have himself used the descriptive term long enough on the market in connection with his own goods and have traded successfully enough to have built up a goodwill for his business.[63]

This requirement was doubted at first instance in *Chocosuisse*.[64] There, Laddie J said that the courts would allow a joint action by new users without inquiring into how extensive

---

[55] *Diageo North America Inc. and anor v. Intercontinental Brands (ICB)* [2010] *EWCA Civ* 920, [29]. This leaves open the question of how far the notion of goodwill may be extended: do everyday product categories such as butter also enjoy relevant goodwill?

[56] *Fage UK Ltd v. Chobani UK* [2013] *EWHC* 630 (Ch), [125].   [57] Ibid., [126].

[58] As Lord Diplock noted in *Erven Warnink v. Townend* [1979] *AC* 731, 744, the size of the class of traders will influence the scope of the goodwill.

[59] [1998] *RPC* 117 (Laddie J); [1999] *RPC* 826 (CA). See also *Bulmer v. Bollinger* [1978] *RPC* 79, 119.

[60] [1999] *RPC* 826, 849.   [61] Ibid., 832.   [62] [1979] *AC* 731.

[63] Ibid., 744. Lord Fraser said that '[a] new trader who begins to sell the genuine product would become a member of the class when he had become well enough established to have acquired a substantial right of property in the goodwill attached to the name': ibid., 754.

[64] *Chocosuisse v. Cadbury* [1998] *RPC* 117.

their trade had been. The Court of Appeal made no comment on this issue when affirming Laddie J's decision.

A second question that remains unclear is exactly how the courts are to define the class of persons who are to participate in the goodwill. In many cases, this will be uncontroversial, because the reputation will have arisen in relation to a discrete class of traders who are themselves subject to regulatory control. However, the potential for difficulty of definition can be seen from the *Chocosuisse* case. There, the claimants had proposed a definition of the class based on the recipes used to manufacture Swiss chocolate.[65] However, Laddie J rejected this on the ground that it excluded a number of those who were already using the designation and were represented by the Association. Instead, Laddie J took the defining feature of 'Swiss chocolate' to be that the chocolate was made in Switzerland, according to Swiss food regulations. However, on appeal, the Court of Appeal held that the group of traders entitled to use the goodwill was that identified by the claimant—that is, those who made chocolate in Switzerland, other than those who made chocolate with vegetable fat as an ingredient.[66] Since none of the claimants supplied a product with such added fat, nor wished to do so, Chadwick LJ said that he saw no reason to define the product in less precise terms. Since, on either view, Cadbury's chocolate was not entitled to share in the goodwill (as it was made in England), the finding did not matter. However, had the dispute been with a Swiss producer of chocolate who added vegetable matter, the Court would have been called on to locate its own basis for defining the product.

A third question relates to the extent to which the participants in the shared goodwill can modify the criteria by which the class is defined. If the majority of champagne makers were to decide to abandon the double fermentation process, perhaps because it was discovered to be unhealthy, would they then be able to exclude others who continued to do so from using the term 'Champagne'?

2.2 MISREPRESENTATION

In establishing misrepresentation in an extended passing off action, the critical factor is what the public understands about the way the name is used. As with classic passing off, this is a question of fact. Although extended passing off and classic passing off both require the claimant to show that there has been a misrepresentation, there are important differences between the way in which this is approached in the two actions. In relation to extended passing off, 'protection is given to a name or word that has come to mean a particular product rather than a product from a particular trader'.[67] It follows from this that the descriptiveness of the term will not be sufficient to defeat the action. Moreover, there will be no misrepresentation if the defendant uses the distinctive term accurately; rather, the misrepresentation 'lies in marketing the goods in a way which will lead a significant section of the public to think that those goods have some attribute or attributes which they do not truly possess'.[68] Thus, in the situation in which UK customers believed that the phrase 'Greek yoghurt' meant that the yoghurt was made in Greece, it was held that the defendant's use in the United Kingdom of the term 'Greek yogurt' to describe yoghurt made in the United States 'plainly involve[d] a misrepresentation'.[69]

Another difference between the classic and extended actions relates to the use that the owner of the goodwill can make of the distinctive name. In conventional passing off, a

---

[65] Ibid., 133–5.   [66] [1999] *RPC* 826, 840.
[67] *Chocosuisse v. Cadbury* [1998] *RPC* 117, 125. See also on appeal: [1999] *RPC* 826, 832.
[68] Ibid., 837.   [69] *Fage UK Ltd v. Chobani UK* [2013] *EWHC* 630, [136].

trader can change the quality of the goods or services that they offer under a particular sign. However, in extended passing off, an existing user is not able to use the sign on products for which it is not a correct designation.[70] Thus an individual champagne producer would not be able to use 'Champagne' to describe another product. Each trader within the class, however, is able to use their own trade name in association with the distinctive name shared by the class of traders. This will not prejudice their right to share in the goodwill associated with the product. Thus there is no problem with Bollinger using its name in association with Champagne, nor with Warninck using its name in relation to Advocaat.

2.3 DAMAGE

A final feature of the extended form of passing off worth observing is the treatment of damage. The most relevant form of damage is the reduction of the distinctiveness of the descriptive term—that is, *dilution*. For regional products with a valuable reputation, dilution potentially takes the form of an erosion of origin-indicating ability, also referred to as 'genericide'. An example would be where the unregulated use of Champagne on sparkling wines would lead to the term designating a class or type of wine, as opposed to wine specifically from designated regions in France.[71] While doubts have been raised about the ongoing relevance of dilution in the classic passing off action, it seems that it will continue to operate in relation to extended passing off.[72] Thus, in *Fage v. Chobani*[73] it was held that the 'loss of distinctiveness in the description Greek yoghurt as meaning (inter alia) yoghurt made in Greece occasioned by the introduction into the market of Greek yoghurt made in the USA' was obvious. While likelihood of damage remains a prerequisite of extended passing off, it is not essential for a claimant to demonstrate that they would have been damaged individually.[74]

2.4 ACTIONS RELATED TO EXTENDED PASSING OFF

It is worth observing that the use that is made of names that designate the geographical origin or quality of goods is regulated by a number of regimes other than passing off. For example, a person's ability to use an incorrect designation of origin or quality may lead to criminal liability under consumer protection laws such as the Consumer Protection from Unfair Trading Regulations 2008[75] (and formerly the Trade Descriptions Act 1968).[76] The European Council and Parliament has also adopted a number of regulations dealing with 'protected designations of origin' (PDOs) and 'protected geographical indications' (PGIs) for wines, spirits, agricultural products, and food. These are discussed in Chapter 43.

---

[70] The points are all drawn from Laddie J's analysis in *Chocosuisse v. Cadbury* [1998] *RPC* 117, 124–6.
[71] See Wadlow (2016), [4–58].   [72] *Chocosuisse v. Cadbury* [1998] *RPC* 117, 126–7, 143.
[73] [2013] *EWHC* 630, [140].   [74] *Erven Warnink v. Townend* [1979] *AC* 731, 756.
[75] SI 2008/1277.
[76] In general, these do not impose statutory duties that give rise to civil liability: *Bollinger v. Costa Brava Wine* [1960] *RPC* 16, 34 (claim under the Merchandise Marks Acts 1887–1953). But see Consumer Protection from Unfair Trading Regulations 2008, regs 3 (unfair practices include misleading action), 5(2)(a) (misleading action defined as action that contains false information likely to mislead average consumer as to matter in reg. 5(4)), 5(4) (relevant misleading information includes information as to 'main characteristics' of the product), and 5(5)(p) (main characteristics includes geographic origin). Note also reg. 5(3)(a) (misleading by using distinguishing marks of competitor).

Finally, it is worth noting that marks that designate the geographical origin or quality of goods can be registered in the United Kingdom as certification or collective trade marks, or as Community collective marks.[77] Certification marks indicate that the goods or services meet certain standards.[78] This mechanism has been used to protect products such as 'Stilton' cheese.[79] In turn, collective marks serve to distinguish the goods or services of the members of relevant associations.

3 UNFAIR COMPETITION

In the final part of the chapter, we consider the principles of unfair competition and their relevance to the United Kingdom. The law of unfair competition occupies the role of the referee in a competitive marketplace. It enforces the rules of the game by providing remedies for traders affected by unfair trading methods. Stated as a general proposition, it prohibits any 'act of competition contrary to honest practices in industrial or commercial matters'.[80] Marketplace competition inevitably creates winners and losers, so it is not the harm suffered by the complainant per se—losing sales or market share—that is unfair. Instead competitive conduct should not violate norms prohibiting (i) misrepresentation, (ii) denigration, or (iii) misappropriation.[81] The focus is therefore on regulating unfair conduct, as opposed to recognizing protected categories of intellectual property subject matter. However if the conduct involves wrongful imitation or misrepresentation in relation to intangibles, unfair competition effectively complements intellectual property protection.

Inevitably, such flexibility comes at a price. The intuitive appeal of fairness must be offset against the inescapable vagueness that accompanies it. A longstanding challenge has therefore been to develop a methodology for delineating unfairness in specific instances; to translate general norms into detailed, context-specific rules. 'The question [of] where the line should be drawn between fair competition and unacceptable competitive behaviour has created abundant debate and literature'.[82] In legal systems with well-established unfair competition regimes, a two-tiered response has emerged to address this. An open-ended general clause prohibiting unfair competition is often followed by enumerated instances (a 'blacklist') of unfair conduct. The best known example of this is the German *Gesetz gegen den unlauteren Wettbewerb* (UWG) statute. The general proscription in Article 3(1) of the UWG (2015) states that 'unfair commercial practices are prohibited' and Article 3(2) further refines this to acts 'contrary to the requirements of professional diligence and [which] are likely to materially distort the economic behaviour of consumers'. This general algorithm is supplemented by specific instances of unfair competition such as conduct denigrating a competitor, making false allegations, offering replica products to the public, or illegitimately interfering with the business of a competitor (Article 4); aggressive commercial practices (Article 4a); misleading commercial practices (Articles 5 and 5a); comparative advertising which does not comply with EU standards (Article 6); and so on. The general prohibition provides flexibility while the

---

[77] See Chapter 36, section 7, pp. 973–5.   [78] TMA 1994, s. 50.

[79] *Stilton Trade Mark* [1967] RPC 173.   [80] Paris, Art. 10*bis*(2).

[81] M. Spence, *Intellectual Property* (2007), 37.

[82] M. Hopperger and M. Senftleben, 'Protection against Unfair Competition at the International Level', in R. M. Hilty and F. Henning-Bodewig, (eds), *Law Against Unfair Competition: Towards a New Paradigm in Europe?* (2007), 61, 61.

specific instances channel claims and enhance predictability. The second technique to reconcile stability with adaptability is a common law (i.e. judge-made) process of refinement and elaboration. This is equally true in civil law jurisdictions, where the judiciary incrementally develops the law, adding new categories of conduct deemed to be unfair over time.

Besides legal uncertainty, a general prohibition also gives rise to a second concern. Within a market paradigm premised upon liberal economic values, an overly solicitous articulation of unfair competition could inhibit conduct otherwise beneficial to consumers. The 'freedom to compete implies a right to induce prospective customers to do business with the actor rather than with the actor's competitors'.[83] Courts in common law jurisdictions have expressed reservations when invited to recognize open-ended norms preventing copying per se or to move beyond established categories of harm.[84] The Supreme Court once again confirmed this stance when setting out the limits to passing off:

> [It] is not enough for a claimant to establish copying to succeed. All developments, whether in the commercial, artistic, professional or scientific fields, are made on the back of other people's ideas: copying may often be an essential step to progress. Hence, there has to be some balance achieved between the public interest in not unduly hindering competition and encouraging development, on the one hand, and on the other, the public interest in encouraging, by rewarding through a monopoly, originality, effort and expenditure . . . [85]

Common law courts have also sought to avoid any 'judicial indulgence of idiosyncratic notions of what is fair in the market place'.[86]

Having identified the basis for enduring national divergences,[87] the apparent lack of ambition in international obligations is easier to comprehend. The only general standard is contained in Article 10*bis*(2) of the Paris Convention, which prohibits any 'act of competition contrary to honest practices in industrial or commercial matters'. By contrast, Article 10*bis*(3) is more potent and specifies three mandatory categories: (i) acts which create confusion; (ii) false allegations which discredit a competitor; and (iii) indications likely to mislead the public as to the characteristics of the defendant's goods. Besides these three mandatory categories, the drafting history of this provision reveals that the intention was to defer to national legal approaches as regards the form and content of unfair competition law.[88] In several countries, the protection offered under unfair competition extends beyond the three specified situations to cover dilution as a form of harm, denigrating another trader, free-riding on another's efforts or reputation, certain forms of comparative advertising, and slavish imitation.[89]

Therefore Article 10*bis* provides methodological guidance at best: (i) the claimant need not be a direct competitor producing competing or substitutable products; (ii) dishonesty

---

[83] *Restatement (Third) on Unfair Competition* (American Law Institute, March 2016 update), § 1.

[84] Prominently: *Victoria Park Racing and Recreation Grounds v. Taylor* (1937) 58 *CLR* 479, 509; *Hodgkinson & Corby Ltd v. Wards Mobility Ltd* [1994] 1 *WLR* 1564, 1569; *L'Oréal SA v. Bellure* [2007] *EWCA Civ* 968, [139]–[142] (Jacob LJ).

[85] *Starbucks (HK) Ltd and anor v. British Sky Broadcasting Group PLC and ors* [2015] UKSC 31, [61] (Neuberger J).

[86] *Moorgate Tobacco Ltd v. Philip Morris Ltd (No. 2)* [1985] *RPC* 219, 239–40.

[87] For an overview of national systems, see Henning-Bodewig (2013).

[88] G. H. C. Bodenhausen, *Guide to the Application of the Paris Convention for the Protection of Industrial Property* (1968), 142–8; Wadlow (2016) [2–21]–[2–31]; Ricketson (2015), [13.33]–[13.59].

[89] WIPO, *Protection against Unfair Competition: Analysis of the Present World Situation* (1994), 48, 54–60.

is assessed objectively, in terms of effects produced, rather than subjective dishonest intention; (iii) 'honest practices' does not refer to abstract, universal ethical standards but should inductively reflect sector-specific marketplace practices; and (iv) the various interests implicated (traders, consumers, the competitive marketplace) need to balanced. Beyond the Paris Convention, TRIPS incorporates the Article 10*bis* standards in the specific instances of geographical indications protection (Article 22.2(b)) and undisclosed or confidential information (Article 39).[90]

3.1 UNFAIR COMPETITION FOR THE UNITED KINGDOM?

While all unfair competition regimes seek to prevent certain forms of objectionable conduct between traders, the institutional forms these laws take varies considerably across jurisdictions.[91] Thus France can trace its regime back to the general tort (delict) provisions contained in Arts 1382 and 1383 of the *Code Civil* while Germany has relied upon successive iterations of its UWG legislation for over a century. In the United Kingdom, the question has periodically arisen as to whether an unfair competition law exists in this jurisdiction. An awareness of the relatively undemanding obligations imposed by Article 10*bis* of Paris Convention suggests that the answer is an emphatic yes. The United Kingdom offers up an unfair competition menu consisting of individual torts or equitable wrongs (primarily passing off, injurious falsehood, defamation, and the breach of confidence), the prohibition of misleading practices under consumer protection law, trade mark law, and codes of advertising regulation.[92] In terms of coverage, this agglomeration of options overlaps considerably with the claims available under civilian unfair competition regimes. Yet a crucial difference is that the general clause is missing; there is no functional equivalent to Article 10*bis*(2) of the Paris Convention. One explanation for this may be that the common law approach to tort law has conventionally preferred particularized claims and specific causes of action, such as passing off.

This leads on to a related point of comparison between the United Kingdom (as well as other common law jurisdictions) and civilian jurisdictions. For some, unfair competition is considered synonymous with an open-ended tort claim directed against the misappropriation of valuable intangibles.[93] Regimes lacking such an action are therefore considered to stop short of possessing full-fledged unfair competition law. Without the general clause to rely on, attempts have been made to repurpose existing options by suggesting that passing off is evolving or should evolve into a general tort of wrongful trading. This evolution would accommodate claims sounding in misappropriation or free-riding, independently of any misrepresentation requirement. During the 1970s and 1980s, a series of decisions suggested that passing off was indeed evolving into this broader tort.[94]

However the decision of the Privy Council in *Cadbury Schweppes v. Pub Squash*[95] clearly signalled that this would be an over-extension. The approach taken by the Privy Council was echoed by a strong judgment of the Court of Appeal in the 2008 decisions of *L'Oréal SA v. Bellure*,[96] a case in which the defendant was selling smell-alike perfumes in packaging that, by adopting some of the features of the fine fragrance brand packaging,

---

[90] C. Riffell, *The Protection of Unfair Competition in the WTO TRIPS Agreement* (2016).

[91] Summarized in D. Gangjee, 'Trade Marks and Allied Rights', in Dreyfuss and Pila (2018), 550–1.

[92] R. Arnold, 'English Unfair Competition Law' [2013] *IIC* 63; J. Davis, 'Unfair Competition: The United Kingdom', in Henning-Bodewig (2013), 600.

[93] *Moorgate Tobacco Ltd v. Philip Morris Ltd (No. 2)* [1985] *RPC* 219, 235–6; M. Spence, 'Passing Off and the Misappropriation of Valuable Intangibles' [1996] *LQR* 472.

[94] See Bently and Sherman (2014) 885–6.   [95] [1981] *RPC* 429.   [96] [2008] *ETMR* 1.

indicated to consumers that the smells were equivalent. Having struggled with its trade mark infringement claims and failed in its passing off argument, the claimant tried to persuade the Court that this was a form of unfair competition that the law should prohibit. Jacob LJ was unimpressed, arguing that recognition of such a rule was unnecessary, undesirable, and inappropriate. It was *unnecessary* because the UK's international obligations under Article 10*bis* of the Paris Convention required no more than a prohibition on deceptive conduct.[97] It was *undesirable* because it was a basic rule that competition was 'not only lawful but the mainspring of the economy',[98] because there were real difficulties in formulating a clear and rational line between that which is fair and unfair,[99] and because the tort would create unnecessary uncertainty.[100] Moreover it was *inappropriate* for the courts, at least at the level of the Court of Appeal, to step in 'and legislate into existence new categories of intellectual property rights'.[101]

In the last few years, the question of whether the United Kingdom should recognize a tort of unfair competition has been reopened. In particular, it has been argued that rather than pretending to find goodwill, misrepresentation, and damage where there is not really any, the courts should be honest about what they are really doing—which is objecting to free-riding.[102] In contrast, others have come out in defence of the existing approach, saying that the courts should stick to the three core requirements—namely goodwill, misrepresentation, and damage. In line with this, these commentators are also critical of decisions that deviate from the traditional approach (such as *Irvine*, which assumed damage).[103] While much ink has been spilled debating the merits of unfair competition law, it is unlikely that British judges will develop the existing regimes into a generalized action for unfair competition. Moreover, the domestic legislature has been reluctant to legislate in this field, either generally or in response to specific issues (such as look-alike brands).[104] Because this is an area of law in which it will be difficult to reach commonly agreed principles, European harmonization also appears unlikely in the near future although, in the longer term, European harmonization of consumer protection law may pave the way for the introduction of a parallel regime of business regulation.[105] For the time being, then, those who complain about unfair competitive practices will have to continue to bring their grievances under existing causes of action.

---

[97] Ibid., [147] ('Moreover, even if the United Kingdom is in derogation, it has been so for over 80 years without complaint. It is not a matter for the judges').

[98] Ibid., [140].   [99] Ibid.   [100] Ibid., [160].   [101] Ibid., [141].

[102] J. Davis, 'Why the UK Should Have a Law against Misappropriation' [2010] *CLJ* 561.

[103] H. Carty, 'Passing off: Frameworks of Liability Debated' [2012] *IPQ* 106. For a more flexible approach, see C. Wadlow, 'Passing off at the Crossroads Again' [2011] *EIPR* 447.

[104] See, e.g., the Copyright and Designs Bill 2000: Hansard (HL) (17 March 2000), cols 1885 *ff*. While the Gowers Review, [5.82]-[5.88] was supportive of brand owners' objections to copycat packaging, recent research for the UKIPO presents a more complex picture; see P. Johnson, J. Gibson, and J. Freeman, *The Impact of Lookalikes: Similar Packaging in Fast Moving Consumer Goods* (2013), 19-58.

[105] The Unfair Commercial Practices Directive requires member states to prohibit certain forms of commercial practice, but is concerned explicitly with business-to-consumer, rather than business-to-business, practices. Nevertheless, Recital 8 states that 'the Commission should carefully examine the need for Community action in the field of unfair competition beyond the remit of this Directive and, if necessary, make a legislative proposal to cover these other aspects of unfair competition'.

35

TRADE MARK REGISTRATION

1 INTRODUCTION

In this chapter, we look at the process by which registered trade marks come into being. While registering a trade mark can be a costly and time-consuming process, it confers on the proprietor certain exclusive rights to use a particular sign in relation to specified commercial activities. In contrast with the law of passing off, registration enables traders to protect their marks before they are put on the market. Registration is also advantageous in that, once a mark is registered, there is a presumption, although not a guarantee, that the registration is valid. A third advantage to registering a trade mark is that it reduces the possibility of disputes and confers on the trade mark proprietor increased certainty, in so far as the registration determines the scope of the property protected as a trade mark. The process of registration attempts to delineate what sign is protected and in which commercial spheres it is to be protected. The register, which is open to the public, also acts as an important source of information.[1]

There are three possible routes that UK traders might take to register a trade mark: national; at the EU level; or international. A national registration system for trade marks has existed in the United Kingdom since 1875. The UK Trade Marks Registry, which is based in Newport in Wales, provides successful applicants with rights in the United Kingdom in relation to the sign as registered. Registration at the EU level involves a single application to the European Union Intellectual Property Office (EUIPO; formerly the Office for Harmonization in the Internal Market or OHIM), which is based in Alicante in Spain. A successful application to the EUIPO results in the grant of a single EU trade mark (EUTM; formerly Community trade mark or CTM) that operates throughout the European Union.[2]

---

[1] TMA 1994, s. 63(3)(a). For a sceptical view of the public benefits of registration, see R. Burrell, 'Trade Mark Bureaucracies', in Dinwoodie and Janis (2008), ch. 4. On the distinct logics of use-based and registration-based protection, see R. Tushnet, 'Registering Disagreement: Registration in Modern American Trade Mark Law' (2017) 130 *Harv L Rev* 867.

[2] With the expansion of the EU by ten new states on 1 May 2004, and the further expansion to encompass Bulgaria and Romania from 1 January 2008 and Croatia on 1 July 2013, the protection afforded by existing applications and registrations was automatically extended to cover the new territories. Transitional arrangements clarify that earlier rights in those states cannot be relied upon to found objections to the validity of an EUTM granted before accession. However, the proprietors of such existing rights in accession states are permitted to continue using such signs and are rendered immune from liability for infringing an EUTM. For a useful explanation, see a series of communications from the President of the OHIM: *No. 5/03* (2004); *No. 2/06* (2006); and *No. 4/12* (2013). See also *EUIPO Examination Guidelines*, Part A, Section 9, [3] ('Rules Concerning Oppositions and Cancellations').

A person can apply for both an EUTM and a national registration, and—in contrast with the position in relation to European patents (UK), the grant of which leads to the revocation of an equivalent domestic patent—both, if granted, may subsist. Recent reforms to the EUTM system are outlined in the following sub-section of this chapter.

In contrast with registration at a national or EU level, the international filing systems merely facilitate the acquisition of national marks. International registration, which is administered by the International Bureau of the World Intellectual Property Organization (WIPO) at Geneva, will be carried out either under the 1891 Madrid Agreement or the 1989 Madrid Protocol. The main advantage of the international system is administrative: instead of traders having to file separate applications in the countries in which they would like protection, the international system enables traders to obtain protection in a number of different jurisdictions via a single application.

While there has been a degree of standardization of trade mark procedure at both the regional and international levels, there are many important differences between the three regimes. In particular, although the procedures and documentation needed for national, regional, or international applications are similar, there are significant variations in the way in which applications are examined.[3]

1.1 TRADE MARK REFORM IN THE EU

At the time of writing, both unitary and national registration regimes across the European Union are concluding a series of significant reforms. Approximately two decades after the promulgation of the first Trade Marks Directive, the Max Planck Institute for Intellectual Property, Competition and Tax Law conducted a comprehensive review of the functioning of the European trade mark system for the European Commission. It produced a study in 2011,[4] which formed the basis for a legislative reform package with two major components. First, a series of amendments to the Community Trade Mark Regulation were introduced in Regulation (EU) 2015/2424,[5] which were subsequently amalgamated into the recast EU Trade Mark Regulation (EU) 2017/1001 (EUTMR).[6] As noted earlier, two name-changes are significant: OHIM is now the EUIPO and the EUTM has replaced the CTM. The majority of the amendments came into force on 23 March 2016, with the remainder entering into force on 1 October 2017. New implementing legislation has also been introduced.[7] Second, the TMD 2008 has been amended and recast as Directive (EU)

---

[3] For example, under TMD 2008, Recital 5, procedural matters are left to member states. Despite this, the Court of Justice has been happy to rule on what is 'graphic representation' and on the need for a full *a priori* examination on absolute grounds, as well as the inappropriateness of certain types of disclaimer: see *Ralf Sieckmann v. Deutsches Patent-und Markenamt*, Case C-273/00 [2002] *ECR* I-11737; *Koninklijke KPN Nederland NV v. Benelux-Merkenbureau*, Case C-363/99 [2004] *ECR* I-1619; *CIPA v. Registrar of Trade Marks (IP Translator)*, Case C-307/10 [2012] *ETMR* 42 (ECJ, Grand Chamber). See further *Génesis v. Boys Toys SA*, Case C-190/10, EU:C:2012:157; *Strigl v. Deutsches Patent- unt Markenamt*, Case C-90/11, EU:C:2012:42, [AG24]–[AG26] (AG Jääskinen) (disclaimers).

[4] Max Planck Institute, *Study on the Overall Functioning of the European Trade Mark System* (2011).

[5] Regulation (EU) 2015/2424 of the European Parliament and of the Council of 16 December 2015 amending Council Regulation (EC) No. 207/2009 on the Community trade mark [etc] [2015] *OJ L* 341/21.

[6] Regulation (EU) 2017/1001 of the European Parliament and of the Council of 14 June 2017 on the European Union trade mark [2017] *OJ L* 154/1.

[7] Commission Implementing Regulation (EU) 2018/626 of 5 March 2018 laying down detailed rules for implementing certain provisions of Regulation (EU) 2017/1001 of the European Parliament and of the Council on the European Union trade mark, and repealing Implementing Regulation (EU) 2017/1431 [2018] *OJ L* 104/37. See also Commission Delegated Regulation (EU) 2018/625 of 5 March 2018 supplementing Regulation (EU) 2017/1001 of the European Parliament and of the Council on the European Union trade mark, and repealing Delegated Regulation (EU) 2017/1430 [2018] *OJ L* 104/1 (Detailed rules inter alia on the procedure for opposition, amendment and appeals). This delegated legislation also addresses transitional arrangements.

2015/2436 (TMD 2015).[8] It entered into force in early 2016. However, the new Directive does not repeal the TMD 2008 until 15 January 2019, leaving members states with a three-year implementation window. With Brexit intervening, the United Kingdom Intellectual Property Office has commenced a consultation on implementing the TMD 2015 into UK law, making it likely that the new changes will be accommodated within national law.[9]

2 REGISTRATION IN THE UNITED KINGDOM

A registration system for trade marks was introduced in the United Kingdom in 1875. Earlier attempts to introduce a registration system had been resisted on the basis that it would have been complicated, expensive, and unnecessary.[10] Eventually, the benefits of registration were seen to outweigh the potential disadvantages. In particular, it was thought that a registration system would help to reduce the difficulties that traders faced in proving reputation (which was necessary to sustain an action for passing off). It was also thought that a trade mark registry would enable third parties to discover whether other traders had claimed the right to use a particular sign and, where necessary, to locate the proprietor of the sign. The introduction of a registration system also helped to relieve the pressure that foreign powers were exerting on the British government to introduce a registration system for trade marks.

It is common for applicants to use trade mark attorneys in the drafting and process-ing of applications. While 'trade mark agents' (as they used to be called) emerged in the United Kingdom late in the nineteenth century, the professional association that governs them, the Chartered Institute of Trade Mark Attorneys (CITMA), in its previous incarna-tion as the ITMA, was not formed until 1934.[11] While few restrictions were placed on who could act as a trade mark attorney until recently, the Trade Marks Act 1994 now places limits on the use of the title 'registered trade mark agent'.[12]

The registration process in the United Kingdom can be divided into four stages: (i) the filing of the application; (ii) examination; (iii) publication, observation, and opposition; and (iv) registration (see Fig. 35.1).

2.1 FILING OF THE APPLICATION

Any person (natural or legal) can apply for the registration of a trade mark. Section 32 of the 1994 Act provides that an application for a trade mark must contain:

(i) a request for registration, including the name and address of the applicant;[13]

(ii) a statement of the goods or services for which the mark is to be registered;[14]

---

[8] Directive (EU) 2015/2436 of the European Parliament and of the Council of 16 December 2015 to approximate the laws of the Member States relating to trade marks [2015] *OJ L* 336/1.

[9] See https://www.gov.uk/government/consultations/implementation-of-the-trade-mark-directive-2015.

[10] See, e.g., W. Hindmarch, giving evidence to the Select Committee on Trade Marks Bill and Merchandise Marks Bill, 'Report, Proceedings and Minutes of Evidence' (1862) 12 *PP*; A. Ryland, *Trade Marks Registration: Essential to Successful Litigation* (1862).

[11] See http://www.citma.org.uk. A Royal Charter was obtained in 2016.

[12] TMA 1994, ss 82–6; Institute of Trade Mark Attorneys Order 2005 (SI 2005/240). The profession is regulated by the Intellectual Property Regulation Board, known as 'IPReg': see http://www.ipreg.org.uk. IPReg publishes an annually updated register of individuals and other bodies who are qualified to practice as trade mark attorneys.

[13] TMA 1994, s. 32(2)(a)–(b).   [14] TMA 1994, s. 32(2)(c).

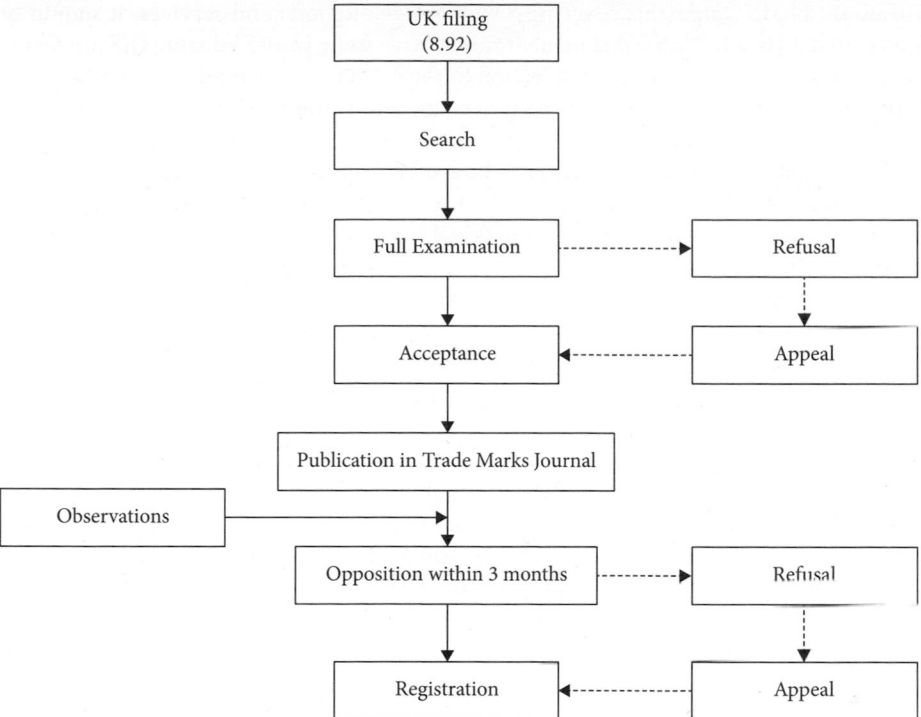

Fig. 35.1 Registering a trade mark in the United Kingdom

(iii) a representation of the mark;[15] and

(iv) a declaration that the mark is being used or that there is a bona fide intention to use the mark.[16]

The filing date of the application (which is the date from which things such as duration are calculated) is the date on which (i)–(iii), but not (iv), are provided to the Registrar.[17] It may be possible to claim a priority date from an earlier application elsewhere.[18] This may be important where there are independent conflicting applications for the same trade mark.

2.1.1 The statement (or specification) of the goods or services

A trade mark application must define the goods and services for which protection is sought.[19] The statement shapes the scope of the rights in the registered mark. In *CIPA v. Registrar of Trade Marks (IP Translator),*[20] the Court of Justice indicated that the specification 'must be formulated with sufficient clarity and precision to enable the relevant competent authorities and economic operators to be able to determine, on that basis alone, the extent of protection sought or conferred'.[21] While applicants may be tempted

---

[15] TMA 1994, s. 32(2)(d).   [16] TMA 1994, s. 32(3).

[17] TMA 1994, s. 33. See *Ty Nant Spring Water* [2000] *RPC* 55, 60–1.

[18] TMA 1994, s. 35, TMR, r. 6; Paris, Art., 4(A)(1), (C)(1) (six months).

[19] For the relevance of TMA 1994, s. 3(6), that applications should be made in good faith, see Chapter 37, section 4.4, pp. 1017–23. Some trade mark regimes permit extremely broad registrations and subsequently regulate undue scope through the provisions on revocation for non-use.

[20] Case C-307/10 [2012] *ETMR* 42 (ECJ, Grand Chamber), [49], [64].

[21] This requirement was extensively reviewed in *Sky v. Skykick* [2018] *EWHC* 155, [140]–[174] (Arnold J).

to submit broad statements covering a wide range of goods and services, it should be noted that a broadly defined statement might have to be limited during the process of registration in order to avoid an objection to the validity of the mark,[22] and might later have to be confined to the goods or services for which the registrant can demonstrate actual use.[23]

A question which inevitably arises is how much freedom does an applicant have to define classes tactically in order to avoid objections such as descriptiveness? The Court of Justice stated in *Postkantoor*[24] that national registries may not accept marks 'subject to the condition that they do not possess a particular characteristic', such as allowing PENGUIN for 'books (other than books about penguins)'. This was said to be because third parties would not be aware of the condition and might refrain from selling goods under the mark. The distinction appears not to be one between defining categories positively or negatively,[25] but between 'characteristics' and 'subcategories'. It seems that a subcategory is defined by reference to the nature, purpose, or function of the goods (or services), whereas a characteristic pertains to some specific quality or feature that can be present or not without altering the nature, function, or purpose of the goods/services.[26] A specification for 'luxury shoes' (or shoes 'other than luxury shoes') would thus be impermissible as referring to style or quality,[27] but 'children's shoes' would be allowed, because children's shoes identifies features of size (that is, nature, purpose, and function) and 'dress shoes' would also be permitted for similar reasons.

2.1.2 Classification

Section 34 of the 1994 Act provides that goods and services shall be classified for the purposes of registration according to a 'prescribed system of classification'.[28] The classification system, which is based in the international system adopted at Nice in 1957, has 34 classes of goods and 11 classes of service.[29] Each class is represented by a class heading, which gives general information about the type of goods or services covered. For example, Class 25 has 'clothing, footwear, headgear' as its general class heading and includes one further level of detail—aprons, bath robes, and caps all have express identification codes within Class 25. For applicants looking to map their products on to these administrative classes, the EUIPO provides a helpful electronic tool (*TMclass*) that enables users to select preapproved terms in order to build their list of goods and services more quickly and effectively.[30] It is possible for an application to relate to a number of classes.[31] The

---

[22] See, e.g., *Mister Long Trade Mark* [1998] *RPC* 401, 407.

[23] On revocation for non-use and the processes for recalibrating a broad specification, see Chapter 39.

[24] *KPN Nederland*, Case C-363/99 [2004] *ECR* I–1619, [115]. See also *Patak (Spices) Ltd's Application*, Case R 746/2005–4 [2007] *ETMR* (3) 66 (OHIM Board of Appeal), [24]–[25]; *Croom's Trade Mark Application* [2005] *RPC* (2) 23, [27]–[29].

[25] *Merlin Trade Mark*, O/043/05 (17 February 2005), [27]–[29] (AP, Arnold QC) (accepting negative disclaimer); *Omega Engineering Inc v. Omega SA* [2012] *EWHC* 3440 (Ch), [50] (Arnold J). Cf. *Croom's Trade Mark Application* [2005] *RPC* (2) 23, 35, [29] (AP, Hobbs QC) (applicant may not identify the goods 'negatively'); *Wisi Trade Mark* [2006] *RPC* (22) 580, 586, [16] (AP, Hobbs QC)).

[26] *Omega Engineering Inc v. Omega SA* [2012] *EWHC* 3440 (Ch) (Arnold J).

[27] *Croom's Trade Mark Application* [2005] *RPC* (2) 23 (clothing excluding 'haute couture' impermissible); *Merlin Trade Mark*, O/043/05 (17 February 2005), [27]–[29] (AP, Arnold QC) (reinterpreting *Croom*).

[28] TMA 1994, s. 34; TMR, r. 7 and Sch. 3. For an excellent account of the emergence of indexing and classification systems, see J. Bellido and H. Y. Kang, 'In Search of a Trade Mark: Search Practices and Bureaucratic Poetics' (2016) 25 *Griffiths Law Review* 147.

[29] The latest edition of the Nice classification system is the eleventh edition, in force from 1 January 2017.

[30] See http://euipo.europa.eu/ec2/.   [31] TMR, r. 8.

Registrar, whose decision is final, resolves any doubts over how the goods and services are to be classified.[32]

The purpose of the classification process is primarily administrative—namely, to facilitate searching for earlier competing marks.[33] In contrast with the specification, which helps to define the boundaries of trade mark protection, the way in which a mark is classified does not ordinarily impact upon substantive matters such as the scope of the rights given to the trade mark owner. Thus the fact that a mark is used by a competitor on goods or services in a different class from those of the registered proprietor does not necessarily mean that it is not being used on 'identical' or 'similar' goods or services (which is the test for infringement). Having said that, there are some situations in which the way in which a mark is classified *might* impact on the scope of the proprietor's rights. This will be the case where, in their statement of the goods and services, an applicant makes reference to the classes used at the Registry[34]—that is, where applicants tie the list of goods or services claimed to the bureaucratic categories used at the Trade Marks Registry.

Can the class headings or classes be used in formulating the specification? In *CIPA's Application (IP Translator)*,[35] the Chartered Institute of Patent Attorneys applied to register 'IP Translator' for various services, using the general terms of the heading of Class 41 of the Nice Classification—that is, 'Education; providing of training; entertainment; sporting and cultural activities'. On the basis that the reference to the class headings should be understood as an application for 'all services in Class 41', which would include translation services, the Registry rejected the application on the ground that the mark was descriptive of those services. CIPA appealed and the Appointed Person (AP) referred a number of questions to the Court of Justice.

The Court answered that use of class headings was permissible, provided that the effect was to define the goods or services clearly and precisely.[36] Where it is unclear whether the application is intended to cover all goods and services within a class, or only those in the normal meaning of the class headings, the applicant must indicate what precisely is intended.

In terms of the immediate reference, CIPA indicated that it had not intended to include translation services—the application 'meant what it said'. Its appeal was allowed and the application was remitted for further processing.[37] The *IP Translator* endorsement of the literal or 'means what it says' approach has been incorporated into both the EUTMR 2017 and the TMD 2015.[38] The European Trade Mark and Design Network (TMDN), which seeks to collaboratively streamline the practices and procedures of the EUIPO and national IP Offices including the UKIPO, has supplemented this with helpful guidance. The TMDN has (i) outlined the impact of the changes on registry practices; (ii) identified the criteria to be used when assessing whether a description of goods is clear and precise

---

[32] TMA 1994, s. 34(2). The exception to this rule is classifications contained in International Applications under the Madrid Protocol.

[33] *Cal-U-Test Trade Mark* [1967] *FSR* 39, 45; *Carless Capek & Leonard v. Pilmore-Bedford 8 Sons* (1928) 45 *RPC* 205.

[34] See also *GE Trade Mark* [1969] *RPC* 418, 458; *Avnet v. Isoact* [1998] *FSR* 16; *Altecnic's Trade Mark Application* [2002] *RPC* (34) 639.

[35] *CIPA v. Registrar of Trade Marks (IP Translator)*, Case C-307/10 [2012] *ETMR* 42 (ECJ, Grand Chamber).

[36] The EUIPO and national offices have identified a number of class headings that do not meet the criteria, including 'goods of common metal not included in other classes' (a heading from Class 6) and 'repair' (a heading in Class 37).

[37] *In re CIPA's Application*, O/197/13 [2013] *ETMR* 42 (AP, Geoffrey Hobbs QC). The Registrar would be required to record formally that the words of identification used in the statement were not intended to cover anything that did not fall within the natural and ordinary meaning of those words as written and recorded in the application. [38] EUTMR 2017, Art. 33(2)–(5); TMD 2015, Art. 39(2)–(5).

(by resorting to their characteristics, purpose, and market sector); and (iii) from amongst the 204 general class headings of the Nice classification, identified five which lacked sufficient clarity and would need further qualification (for example, 'machines' in class 7 and 'repair' in class 37).[39]

2.1.3 Representation of the sign

The trade mark applicant is also required to provide a graphical representation[40] of the sign and, before an application is accepted, that representation must be 'adequate'.[41] This reflects the fact that the trade mark registration system is built around a notion of 'representative registration'[42]—that is, rather than depositing an actual sample of the mark, applicants are required to deposit a representation of the mark.[43] This representative registration has a number of rationales (as well as having some significant effects).[44] One function of the representation (which might be called the 'property' function and is analogous to the role of patent claims) is to define the scope of the trade mark owner's rights and delineate with a degree of precision exactly what sign is protected. A second function of graphic representation (which might be called the 'information function') is to enable publicity to be given to the fact that an applicant is seeking registration, the publicity being provided by publication in the *Trade Marks Journal*. In particular, it helps to ensure that third parties are able to search the register, to ascertain things such as the scope of existing marks, and to determine whether a fresh application conflicts with earlier marks. A third and related function of the graphic representation requirement (which might be called the 'administrative function') is to make the bureaucratic dealing with the sign—its classification and comparison with other signs—more manageable.

While each of these functions demands different things, in effect, for a graphic representation to be adequate, it must achieve all three goals. As the Court of Justice held in *Ralf Sieckmann*,[45] a graphic representation is one that utilizes images, lines, or characters. In order to render a sign registrable as a trade mark, the graphic representation must be clear, precise, self-contained, easily accessible, intelligible, durable, and objective (known as the '*Sieckmann* criteria'). While the *Sieckmann* case is useful in that it articulates criteria that a graphic representation must meet, it remains difficult to say in particular situations whether a representation is *sufficiently* stable, durable, objective, or intelligible to satisfy the criteria. It seems that a representation is not sufficiently intelligible if it is intelligible only to a few, or to a limited section, of the population (such as with a chemical formula). In the *Libertel* case,[46] reviewed later, Advocate-General Léger indicated that

---

[39] See respectively: *Common Communication on the Implementation of 'IP Translator'*, v1.2 (20 February 2014); *Common Communication on the Common Practice on the Acceptability of Classification Terms*, v1.0 (20 February 2014); *Common Communication on the Common Practice on the General Indications of the Nice Class Headings*, v1.2 (28 October 2015).   [40] TMA 1994, s. 1(1).

[41] The furnishing of a representation of the mark is one of the few elements necessary to obtain a filing date. The applicant is given two months in which to remedy any inadequacies.

[42] Sherman and Bently, 180–93. See M. Handler and R. Burrell, 'Making Sense of Trade Mark Law' [2003] *IPQ* 388; Kerly, [2–049] *ff*:

> Any registration system is going to be an imperfect way of capturing all the attributes of trade marks which operate in the market. The best that can be achieved is to have a registration system which records the most concrete attributes of each trade mark.

[43] The EUIPO now recognizes a broader range of deposit methods. See the EUTMIR, Art. 3(1) ('The trade mark shall be represented in any appropriate form using generally available technology, as long as it can be reproduced on the register . . . ').

[44] *Ralf Sieckmann v. Deutsches Patent-und Markenamt*, Case C-273/00 [2002] *ECR* I–11737, [48]–[49].

[45] Ibid.   [46] *Libertel Groep BV v. Benelux-Merkenbureau*, Case C-104/01 [2003] *ECR* I–3793, [AG71].

a representation was sufficiently accessible and intelligible if it did not require excessive efforts to be taken for the public to understand it. Moreover, in *Shield*,[47] the Court noted that accessibility and intelligibility did not require 'immediate' intelligibility, but only that intelligibility should be 'easy', so that a music score would suffice as a representation of sound.

There are a number of different techniques that applicants may use to represent their marks graphically. These include words and images (such as line drawings and photographs). With the vast majority of marks, the process of graphic representation is straightforward: 'word marks' are written, and device or 'figurative' marks are represented by pictures.[48] However, difficulties arise because, as we will see, since the Trade Marks Act 1994 liberalized the definition of marks, it is now possible to register various 'exotic' marks, such as sounds, shapes, colours, holograms, gestures, etc. In these cases, graphic representation can be more problematic.[49] The particular mode of description that is used will vary according to the type of mark in question.[50] Identifying the mark type is therefore an important preliminary step. If the applicant does not do this voluntarily on the relevant form, the UKIPO will allocate a type to the mark to facilitate examination.[51]

(i) *Shape and appearance of products* It has been held that a verbal description of a shape or packaging—such as 'vacuum packing' or 'a chewy sweet on a stick'—will rarely ever be satisfactory because it will not convey the precise appearance of the sign; rather, design drawings or photographs will be necessary.[52] An attempt to protect the appearance of tiles for the board game scrabble by use of the description, a 'three-dimensional ivory-coloured tile on the top surface of which is shown a letter of the Roman alphabet and a numeral in the range 1 to 10' was said to lack clarity, precision, and objectivity.[53]

(ii) *Colours* One area in which trade mark law has long had problems is in relation to colour marks. Indeed, the reason why colour marks initially were not registrable was because the technology did not exist to enable colour marks to be reprinted in the *Trade Mark Journal*.[54] In *LibertelGroep BV v. Benelux-Merkenbureau*,[55] the

---

[47] *Shield Mark BV v. Joost Kist*, Case C-283/01 [2003] *ECR* I–14313, [2004] *ETMR* 33, [63].

[48] It should be noted that certain conventions surround the registration of marks. First, word marks are regarded as covering the word in any form, so that graphic or stylistic variations are regarded as falling within the scope of the rights. In contrast, figurative marks are taken to be limited to the specific representation. However, even in the case of a figurative mark, colour is presumed not to be an element of a trade mark unless the application contains a statement to that effect and specifies the colour: TMR, r. 5(3); EUTMIR, Art. 3(3)(a) and (b). Similar rules operate under Madrid, Art. 3, and Madrid Prot., Art. 3(3). In principle, a figurative mark registered in black and white is protected against the use of the same sign irrespective of the colour used. See further *Faber Chimica v. OHIM—Nabersa (Faber)*, Case T-211/03 [2005] *ECR* II–1297 (CFI, Second Chamber), [33]–[40]; TMDN, *Common Communication on the Common Practice of the Scope of Protection of Black and White ('B&W') Marks* (15 April 2014).

[49] Given the extensive jurisprudence, it is perhaps worth noting that, since it opened in 1996, over 99 per cent of EUTM applications relate to word or figurative marks, 0.56 per cent to shapes, and 0.06 per cent to colours. See *SSC009—Statistics of European Union Trade Marks* (December 2017).

[50] For an emerging consensus, see WIPO, 'Methods of Representation and Description of New Types of Marks', 29 March 2007 (SCT/17/2).

[51] UKIPO, *Trade Marks Manual*, [2.2]. On the extent to which the representation, description, and type-classification of the mark should define its scope, see D. Gangjee, 'Paying the Price for Admission: Non-Traditional Marks across Registration and Enforcement'. in I. Calboli and M. Senftleben (eds), *The Protection of Non-Traditional Marks: Critical Perspectives* (2018).

[52] *Swizzels Matlow Ltd's Trade Mark Application* [1998] *RPC* 244.

[53] *JW Spear & Son Ltd, Mattel Inc v. Zynga Inc.* [2012] *EWHC* 3345 (Ch), [48] (not intelligible), aff'd [2013] *EWCA Civ* 1175, [32]. [54] See Sherman and Bently, 190.

[55] Case C-104/01 [2003] *ECR* I–3793.

Court of Justice considered the extent to which trade marks comprising a single colour could be registered. In this case, the applicant had sought to register the colour orange for telephone books in Class 9 and telecommunication services in Classes 35–8. While the Court clearly accepted that colours per se could be represented graphically, it stated that an assessment was required—in light of the facts of the case and the mode of representation proposed by the applicant—as to whether the seven *Sieckmann* criteria would be met. So a mere sample of a colour would not satisfy those requirements, because the exact shade of colour on paper cannot be protected from the effects of the passage of time. Equally, the Court said that a verbal description would not normally satisfy the conditions. However, the Court reiterated that it was necessary to decide whether a given description was satisfactory on the particular facts. Finally, the Court noted that a designation using an internationally recognized identification code *might* be considered to constitute a graphic representation, adding that such codes are precise and stable. Moreover, the use of a sample, verbal description, and international code—in combination—*might* satisfy the seven *Sieckmann* criteria.[56]

Libertel clearly prohibits member states from operating a categorical exclusion prohibiting pure or abstract colours from being registered. In the period following this decision, a registry-level consensus has emerged whereby marks consisting of single colour (in the abstract, without contours) or combinations of such colours can be represented 'by submitting . . . a reproduction of the colour and an indication of that colour by reference to a generally recognised colour code'.[57] This is the format adopted for an EUTM consisting of a single colour.[58] Similarly, while the United Kingdom previously treated samples of colours as acceptable, following *Libertel* colour samples on paper are no longer treated as graphic representations, but a written description coupled with the relevant code from an internationally recognized colour identification system—Pantone®, RAL, and Focoltone® are mentioned—will be regarded as acceptable.[59] However an electronic submission can incorporate an image of the colour, along with the RGB profile for that image, which should not contradict the shade depicted by the colour code.

Marks consisting of combinations of abstract colours can also—in principle—be registered provided they are adequately represented. In *Heidelberger Bauchemie*,[60] the Court of Justice addressed the related issue of the graphic representation of two colours, blue and yellow, for various goods including adhesives, solvents, and paints. The application indicated that the colours would be used 'in every conceivable form'. The Court held that, in the case of a sign consisting of two or more colours, designated in the abstract and without contours, a graphic representation would be sufficiently clear and precise only if the application specified that the colours would be 'systematically arranged by associating the colours concerned in a predetermined and uniform way'.[61] In contrast, the Court said that the mere juxtaposition of two or more colours, without shape or contours, or a reference to two or more colours 'in every conceivable form', did not exhibit the qualities

---

[56] Ibid., [28]–[38]. The Court focused on the problem of identifying the precise shade of colour being registered. Unlike the Advocate-General, it seemed less perturbed by the fact that an abstract colour—red per se as opposed to a red square—is necessarily represented without contours and can manifest in a variety of ways on goods and services.

[57] TMDN, *Common Communication on the representation of new types of trade marks* (4 December 2017) 4.

[58] EUTMIR, Art. 3(3)(f)(i).

[59] UK IPO, *Libertel: Graphical Representation of Colour Marks Filing Requirements* (October 2003) PAN 3/03. This practice is reiterated in UK IPO, *Graphical Representation* (May 2007) PAN 2/07.

[60] Case C-49/02 [2004] *ECR* I-6129.   [61] Ibid., [33]; see also ibid., [49].

of precision and uniformity and would not satisfy the requirements of Article 2 of the TMD 1988.

Applying these principles, the Court of Appeal has held that the Trade Marks Registry should have rejected Cadbury's application for 'the colour purple (Pantone 2685C), . . . applied to the whole visible surface, or being the predominant colour applied to the whole visible surface, of the packaging of the goods'. The notion of purple being the 'predominant colour' introduced a multitude of possibilities, and these were not capable of graphical representation in a manner that satisfied the *Sieckmann* criteria.[62] In contrast, it seems that an application might succeed if it specifies the colours, and explains their distribution on the product and in relation to each other, for example by stating that the colour blue, comprising 50 per cent of the surface area, runs horizontally above the colour red, forming a striped whole.[63]

A final point to note is one that has arisen in the context of colour combinations but has more general significance. When the representation and written description do not align and one is drafted more broadly than the other, a court or registry can objectively assess the application to construe the mark that is *really* being applied for. Glaxo had applied for a colour combination mark described as 'the colour dark purple (Pantone code 2587C) applied to a significant proportion of an inhaler, and the colour light purple (Pantone code 2567C) applied to the remainder of the inhaler'.[64] Defining the scope of the mark became relevant because—following *Cadbury*—it otherwise risked failing the graphical representation requirement, to the extent that it permitted unlimited permutations and combinations of purple. On an objective assessment, the specific photographic image of one model of an inhaler, submitted as the representation, could not rein in or take precedence over the much broader written description, which more accurately reflected the scope of protection being claimed.

(iii) *Smells* After a period of uncertainty in which the OHIM rather surprisingly held that a verbal description of a smell was sufficient,[65] in *Ralf Sieckmann*, the Court of Justice indicated that a smell will not be adequately graphically represented by a verbal description because it will not be 'sufficiently clear, precise or objective'.[66] Sieckmann had sought to register the smell of cinnamon as a trade mark in Germany and, as well as providing a verbal description, had also attempted to represent the mark by way of a chemical formula and a sample. The Court also indicated that these other mechanisms would not meet the requirements of the Trade Marks Directive: a deposit of a sample is not a graphic representation, but in any case would not be sufficiently durable or stable; and a chemical formula (although probably a representation of a chemical rather than an odour) would not be sufficiently intelligible, clear, or precise. While the Court has not ruled out the possibility of there ever being an acceptable graphic representation

---

[62] *Société des Produits Nestlé SA v. Cadbury UK Ltd* [2013] *EWCA Civ* 1174 (reversing the judgment of HH Judge Birss QC [2012] *EWHC* 2637 (Ch)).

[63] UK IPO, *Graphical Representation* (May 2007) PAN 2/07, citing CTM No. 2177566. See also the examples provided in the EUIPO *Examination Guidelines,* Part B, Section 4, Chapter 2, [2.4] ('Colour marks').

[64] *Glaxo Wellcome v. Sandoz* [2016] *EWHC* 1537 (Ch), aff'd [2017] *EWCA Civ* 335. For a very similar outcome, see *Red Bull GmbH v. EUIPO, Opium Mark,* Joined Cases T-101/15 and T-102/15, EU:T:2017:852. On the extent to which applicants can tactically characterize the mark to avoid substantive examination requirements, see D. Gangjee, 'Paying the Price for Admission: Non-Traditional Marks across Registration and Enforcement', in I. Calboli and M. Senftleben (eds), *The Protection of Non-Traditional Marks: Critical Perspectives* (2018).

[65] *Vennootschhap Onder Firma Senta/The smell of freshly cut grass,* R156/1998–2 [1999] *ETMR* 429.

[66] Case C-273/00 [2002] *ECR* I–11737, [70].

of a smell,[67] other possible techniques—such as through chromatography or so-called 'digital noses'—would not seem to satisfy the requirement of intelligibility. Even accepting a degree of variation between different countries and forums in the application of concepts such as 'intelligibility', it is unlikely that there will be many (if any) marks granted for smells.[68]

(iv) *Sounds* In *Shield Mark BV v. Joost Kist*,[69] the Court considered the application of the graphic representation requirement to sounds. The case concerned two marks: the first nine notes of the melody for Beethoven's 'Für Elise' and the crowing of a cock, both for advice and services in the field of intellectual property and marketing. The applicant had used musical notation (including the instructions to be played on the piano) and onomatopoeic representation ('kukelekuuuuuu'), as well as a verbal description ('the crowing of a cock'). The Hoge Raad asked the Court whether such marks were registrable as trade marks, and if so, whether the requirement of graphic representation of a sound was met by a note bar, a description in words, a voice picture or sonogram, a sound carrier, a digital recording that can be listened to via the Internet, or a combination of these.[70] The Court stated that a score that comprised a stave with a clef, musical notes, and rests, the form of which indicates relative values, and, where necessary, accidentals (sharp, flat, etc.) would satisfy the seven *Sieckmann* requirements. This was so even though not everyone can read music: the requirement is 'intelligibility', not 'immediate intelligibility'.[71] In contrast, the mere verbal description of sounds (of the type involved in the case) lacked clarity and precision.[72] The Court held that onomatopoeic representation was problematic for two reasons: first, because 'there is a lack of consistency' between the onomatopoeia itself and the sound; and second, because perceptions of an onomatopoeia are individual (and hence subjective), or at least culturally determined (in English, for example, such a sound would be represented as 'cock-a-doodle-doo'). Consequently, 'a simple onomatopoeia cannot without more constitute a graphical representation of the sound or noise of which it purports to be a phonetic description'.[73]

Since the Court declined to comment on whether a digital recording or a sonogram would suffice,[74] the EUIPO first tentatively embraced and then retreated from sound spectrograms or sonograms, which were technically precise but relatively hard to interpret.[75] The settled—and eminently sensible—current position is to represent the mark 'by submitting an audio file reproducing the sound or by an accurate representation of the sound in musical notation'.[76]

(v) *Tastes* Following the earlier facilitative case law of the OHIM as regards registration of smells, Eli Lilly applied to register the taste of artificial strawberry in respect of pharmaceuticals. This application was initially rejected on the ground that the

---

[67] *Eden SARL v. OHIM*, Case T–305/04 [2005] *ECR* II–4705, [2006] *ETMR* (14) 181, [28]; cf. *Sieckmann*, Case C–273/00 [2002] *ECR* I–11737, [AG44].

[68] TMDN, *Common Communication on the representation of new types of trade marks* (4 December 2017) (No common practice for registering scent or taste marks). For a review of the arguments, see S. Karapapa, 'Registering Scents as Community Trade Marks' (2010) 100 *TMR* 1335.

[69] Case C-283/01 [2003] *ECR* I–14313.   [70] *Shield Mark*, Case C-283/01 [2003] *ECR* I–14313.

[71] Ibid., [63], [AG40].   [72] Ibid., [59].   [73] Ibid., [60].   [74] Ibid., [54].

[75] See respectively: *MGM Lion Corporation*, R781/1999–4 [2004] *ETMR* (34) 480 (a lion's roar); *Edgar Rice Burroughs, Inc.*, Case R 708/2006–4 (27 September 2007) (Tarzan's yell).

[76] EUTMIR, Art. 3(3)(g); TMDN, *Common Communication on the representation of new types of trade marks* (4 December 2017).

mere verbal description was not sufficiently precise, but ultimately the examiner based her objection on lack of distinctiveness. Rejecting an appeal, the OHIM Board of Appeal affirmed the examiner's finding that the taste was not distinctive, but added that, following *Sieckmann*, a verbal description would not be acceptable as a graphic representation of a gustatory sign.[77]

(vi) *Reform* As a result of the European trade mark reform package, the new legislation has discarded the 'graphical' requirement while embracing new technological possibilities for representing marks. The new standard is best summarized as adequate or enabling representation: '[A mark should be represented] in a manner which enables the competent authorities and the public to determine the clear and precise subject matter of the protection afforded to its proprietor'.[78] However, the *Sieckmann* criteria and existing approaches continue to be relevant, as suggested by Recital 13 of the TMD 2015:

> In order to fulfil the objectives of the registration system for trademarks, namely to ensure legal certainty and sound administration, it is also essential to require that the sign is capable of being represented in a manner which is clear, precise, self-contained, easily accessible, intelligible, durable and objective. A sign should therefore be permitted to be represented in any appropriate form using generally available technology, and thus not necessarily by graphic means, as long as the representation offers satisfactory guarantees to that effect.

The existing approaches to various categories of non-traditional marks, developed under the former graphical representation standard, have been clarified and given formal recognition, while leaving room to develop standards for new categories of non-traditional marks which use generally available representation technology and otherwise meet the seven *Sieckmann* criteria.[79]

(vii) *Classification of figurative marks* In 2013, the United Kingdom became a party to the Vienna Agreement Establishing an International Classification of the Figurative Elements of Marks. This agreement, like that on the classification of goods and services, is administrative. The UK Trade Marks Registry is required to code components of figurative marks according to a complex taxonomy. The idea is that this will assist in searching these marks when it is sought to discover conflicting marks.

2.1.4 Bona fide intention to use

A UK application must also contain a declaration that the mark is being used, or that there is a bona fide intention to use the mark.[80] According to section 3(6) of the 1994 Act, a trade mark shall not be registered if or to the extent that the application is made in bad faith.[81] While we examine this ground of invalidity in detail later,[82] the declaration operates to warn the applicant that the register is intended to confer rights only on persons

---

[77] *Eli Lilly/The taste of artificial strawberry flavour*, R120/2001–2 [2004] *ETMR* (4) 59 (OHIM Board of Appeal). See further J. C. Ginsburg, '"See Me, Feel Me, Touch Me, Hea[r] Me" (and maybe smell and taste me too): I Am a Trademark—A U.S. Perspective', in Bently, Davis, and Ginsburg, ch. 4.

[78] TMD 2015, Art. 3(2); see also EUTMR, Art. 4(b).

[79] EUTMIR, Art. 3(3); TMDN, *Common Communication on the representation of new types of trade marks* (4 December 2017); EUIPO *Examination Guidelines*, Part B, Section 2, [9] ('Mark type').

[80] TMA 1994, s. 32(3). This is not required by the EUIPO.

[81] Pursuant to an optional provision: TMD 1988, Art. 3(2)(d); there is no corresponding provision in the EUTMR.   [82] See Chapter 37, section 4.4, pp. 1017–23.

who genuinely intend to use the particular mark in trade; it is not to be used for bogus applications in order to get in the way of opponents, blocking registrations or ghost registrations.[83] In addition, the Registry has used the objection to induce applicants to restrict the specifications to a more limited range of goods and services. Although it makes less use of section 3(6) to limit specifications than it did when the 1994 Act first came into force, so as to bring the UK approach more closely into line with that at the EUIPO, the Registry will refuse to accept very broad applications such as those 'for all goods or services' in a particular class.

2.1.5 Series of marks

It is possible to register a series of marks in a single registration, thereby saving expense.[84] A 'series of marks' is defined as 'a number of trade marks that resemble each other as to their material particulars and differ only as to matters of a non-distinctive character not substantially affecting the identity of the trade mark'.[85] An attempt to retrospectively 'split' a vulnerable mark into a series of two marks, in order to preserve the priority date, was rejected. The very basis for its invalidation—that multiple differing interpretations of the mark were possible—also meant that it did not meet the definition in section 41, which required that the marks in a series resemble one another as regards their material particulars.[86] The application should include a separate representation of each mark in the series.[87] Individual marks may be deleted from the series at any time. In the context of whether such marks are compatible with EU law, the Court of Appeal has clarified that an application for a series does not create a single registered trade mark made up of a number of signs (thereby vulnerable to an attack on the basis of lacking precision and certainty), but instead creates a series of distinct, individually registered trade marks under a single registration number.[88] As a supplementary, purely administrative provision, section 41 cannot create new trade mark rights.

2.2 EXAMINATION

Once the filing process has been completed, the Registrar conducts a search[89] and an examination of the application[90] to ensure that the proposed mark satisfies various requirements set out in the Act. In particular, the Registrar will ensure that the application complies with section 1(1) and that none of the absolute grounds for refusal apply.[91] Since 1 October 2007, the Registrar will not object to registration on 'relative grounds'.[92] The Court of Justice has indicated that this examination of the absolute grounds is to be

---

[83] See *Origins v. Origin Clothing* [1995] *FSR* 280, 285 (Jacob J).

[84] The practice is explained in UK IPO, *Applications to Register a Series of Trade Marks* (2003) PAN 1/03 following the decision of the AP in *Logica's Trade Marks*, SRIS O/068/03 (5 March 2003) (holding that logica followed by various domain name suffixes did not resemble each other as to their material particulars). See also *In re Digeo Broadband Inc.'s Trade Marks* [2004] *RPC* (32) 639 (Digeo plus domain name suffixes not a series).

[85] TMA 1994, s. 41.

[86] *Cadbury UK Limited v. The Comptroller General of Patents, Designs and Trademarks* [2016] *EWHC* 796 (Ch).   [87] TMR, r. 28.

[88] *Comic Enterprises Ltd v. Twentieth Century Fox Films* [2016] *EWCA Civ* 41.

[89] TMA 1994, s. 37(2).   [90] TMA 1994, s. 37(1).

[91] In addition (and in contrast to the EUIPO), the Registrar may object to the application on the basis that the applicant does not have a bona fide intention to use the mark.

[92] Trade Mark (Relative Grounds) Order 2007 (SI 2007/1976), made under TMA 1994, s. 8, bringing UK procedure into line with that at the EUIPO; followed by the Trade Marks (Earlier Trade Marks) Regulations 2008 (SI 2008/1067). For background, see Patent Office, *Future of Official Examination on Relative Grounds* (2001).

taken seriously.[93] The applicant is required to respond and, if they fail to do so, the application will be refused.[94] In some situations, in which the objection pertains to only some of the goods or services to which the application relates, a process of reformulation of the specification is called for. So, for example, an application that relates to motor vehicles and bicycles might be objectionable in relation only to motor vehicles. Reformulation may be done by the applicant voluntarily, or by the Registrar, although the extent to which the Registrar can impose different wording is controversial.[95]

If the Registrar has no valid objections to the application, it will be *accepted*. The Registrar does not have a general discretion to reject applications: if an application satisfies the requirements set out in the Act, it must be accepted.[96] Acceptance of the application is not the same as registration. It merely marks the end of the *ex parte* procedure—registration occurs only after the period for opposition has elapsed.

2.3 PUBLICATION, OBSERVATIONS, AND OPPOSITION

Once an application has been accepted by the Registrar, it is published in the *Trade Marks Journal*.[97] In the two-month period following publication, there is an opportunity for third parties to comment on the application. This will either take the form of observations on, or oppositions to, the application. Any person may make observations to the UK Registry, which will be forwarded on to the applicant.[98] It seems that third-party observations may prompt the Registry to reconsider the registrability of an application. Alternatively, a proprietor of an earlier mark or right may formally oppose the registration.[99] This must be lodged within three months of the publication of the application and should specify the grounds for opposition. Where an opposition is made, it sets in play a procedural process that is structured to encourage the parties to reach an amicable settlement, but, failing such, may lead to a hearing and a determination by the Registrar.[100] A 'fast-track opposition' procedure was introduced in 2013, for cases not requiring evidence from parties.[101]

2.4 CHANGING THE APPLICATION AS FILED

While applicants should take great care in the way in which they draft their applications, for a variety of reasons, an applicant may wish to make alterations to the application as filed. This may be in response to the results of the examination, to third-party observations and oppositions, or to changes in circumstances. There are a number of ways in which an application may be changed, the most common being by way of amendment, division, merger, or disclaimer.[102] Before looking at these, it should be noted that many

---

[93] *Libertel*, Case C-104/01 [2003] *ECR* I–3793, [58]–[59]; *Henkel KgaA v. OHIM*, Joined Cases C-468/01P–472/01P [2004] *ECR* I–5089, [AG51]–[AG52] (AG Colomer) (stating, in the context of the CTM, that the examination 'must not be brief, but must be stringent and thorough in order to prevent marks from being improperly registered'); *Nichols v. Registrar of Trade Marks*, Case C-404/02 [2004] *ECR* I–8499, [AG51]–[AG52] (AG Colomer).

[94] TMA 1994, s. 37(4); *Postperfect Trade Mark* [1998] *RPC* 255.

[95] *Citybond Trade Mark* [2007] *RPC* (13) 301 (AP, Hobbs QC); *Sensornet Ltd's Trade Mark Application* [2007] *RPC* (10) 185.   [96] DTI, *Reform of Trade Marks Law* (Cm. 1203, 1990), [3.11].

[97] TMA 1994, s. 38; TMR, r. 16. TMA 1994, s. 67(2), prohibits the Registrar from issuing details prior to publication.   [98] TMR, r. 22.

[99] TMA 1994, s. 34(2). The original TMA 1994, s. 38(2), which states that any person may oppose, must be read in light of Trade Mark (Relative Grounds) Order 2007 (SI 2007/1976), art. 2.

[100] TMR, r. 13.   [101] Trade Mark (Fast Track Opposition) Amendment Rules 2013 (SI 2013/2235).

[102] TMA 1994, ss 13, 39, and 41.

of these changes, such as amendment, may occur either before or after grant. Other techniques, such as disclaimers, may be included in the initial application or added later.

2.4.1 Pre-grant amendment

Section 39 of the 1994 Act provides that an applicant may amend the application, at any time, in such a way as to restrict the goods or services covered by the application. Applications may also be amended to correct the name or address of the applicant, to alter errors of wording or copying, or to correct obvious mistakes.[103] Such amendments are permissible only where they do not substantially affect the identity of the mark or extend the goods or services covered by the application.[104] So, for example, it was stated in the *Polo* case that it is permissible to limit an application for 'sugar confectionery' to one for 'mint-flavoured compressed confectionery'.[105] However, the Court of Appeal held that, in the case of shape registrations, in which the identity of the goods and the mark may be linked, it is not permissible to attempt to amend the *mark* being registered by amending the *goods* for which registration is sought. So it was not permissible to amend a shape mark by adding a reference to the colour and size of the goods.[106] An amendment that affects the representation or specification must be published and an opportunity provided for objections.[107]

The failure to allow amendment of the representation, except as to the name or address of the owner, is a remarkably restrictive feature of the trade mark system, with potentially significant consequences. If a mark is registered in monochrome (and thus for all colours), it is conceivable that it might be opposed on the basis of an earlier colour mark or subject to revocation for non-use in relation to certain specified colours. The owner will not be able to amend the mark so that it relates only to colours some distance from the opponent's mark or to avoid the objection for non-use. It seems strange that limitations should not be permitted, as they are in patent law, where the effect is to narrow the scope of the claim. Nor do disclaimers appear to offer an alternative route.[108] The registrant must simply reapply for a new mark in the more limited form.[109]

2.4.2 Division

It is also possible for an applicant to transform a single application into several 'divisional applications'.[110] At any time before registration, an applicant may request that their application be divided into two or more separate applications, with each relating to different goods or services. The main reason for dividing an application up in this way is to isolate the problematic parts of an application. In so doing, it increases the chances of the uncontroversial parts being registered. Divided applications have the same filing date as the original application. Where division occurs after the application has been published, any objections to the original application apply to each of the divisional applications.

---

[103] TMA 1994, s. 39(2). According to a Practice Notice, the Registry takes the view that correcting the name of a proprietor is a serious matter. For parallels, see EUTMR, Art. 49.

[104] The Court of Appeal has held that an amendment to change the classification was impermissible: *Altecnic's Application* [2002] RPC (34) 639.

[105] *Nestlé Trade Mark* [2005] RPC (5) 77, [40].   [106] Ibid., [41].

[107] TMA 1994, s. 39(3); TMR, rr. 25, 57. A request to restrict a specification may not be made conditionally: *Sensornet* [2007] RPC (10) 185, [64]–[65], following CFI authorities on CTMR, Art. 44 (now EUTMR, Art. 49), such as *Ellos v. OHIM*, Case T-219/00 [2002] ECR II–753, [58]–[63].

[108] *Swizzel Matlow's Application* [1999] RPC 879; *Robert McBride Ltd's Trade Mark Application* [2004] RPC (19) 343; *Nestlé Trade Mark* [2005] RPC (5) 77.

[109] DTI, *Reform of Trade Marks Law* (Cm. 1203, 1990), [4.09].

[110] TMA 1994, s. 41; TMR, r. 26.

2.4.3 Merger

A corresponding facility exists for the *merger* of separate applications. Applicants will normally merge marks to simplify a trade mark portfolio and to save on fees. Merger occurs only if the applications are for the same mark, and have the same application date, and have the same proprietor.[111] If two or more marks have already been registered, those registrations can also be merged so long as they are in respect of the same trade mark. If one of the registrations is subject to a disclaimer or limitation, the merged registration is restricted accordingly. Similarly, if they bear different dates, the date applicable for the merged registration is the latest date.

2.5 DISCLAIMERS

Section 13 of the 1994 Act enables applicants (or the proprietor) to disclaim any right to the exclusive use of specified elements of the trade mark. Applicants are also able to agree that the rights conferred by the registration shall be subject to a specified territorial or other limitation.[112] Where the registration of a trade mark is subject to a disclaimer or limitation, the rights conferred on the proprietor are restricted accordingly.[113] Use of disclaimers may assist an applicant in overcoming a potential objection to registration,[114] but will not enable the applicant to alter the nature of the mark that is registered. Thus an attempt to limit the (three-dimensional) sign in an application relating to confectionery by restricting its size and colour was held by the Court of Appeal not to be a disclaimer of any *right*.[115]

The practices relating to disclaimers expose the limitations of the registration system as an effective mechanism for defining the boundaries of intangible property rights.[116] The courts have recognized that disclaimers are of limited value because they appear only on the register and do not follow goods into the market.[117] Consequently, because consumers and competitors would normally be unaware that aspects of a mark had been disclaimed, often a disclaimer will not save a mark from objection.[118]

2.6 REGISTRATION

In the absence of an effective opposition, the Registrar should register the trade mark.[119] The registration is then published in the *Trade Marks Journal*.[120] The date of registration

---

[111] TMR, r. 27.

[112] The Registrar cannot impose a disclaimer: *Patron Calvert Cordon Bleu* [1996] *RPC* 94, 103.

[113] *General Cigar Co. Inc. v. Partagas y Cia SA* [2005] *FSR* (45) 960 (considering effect in opposition proceedings); *Phones4U Ltd v. Phone4u.co.uk Internet Ltd* [2006] *EWCA Civ* 244, [2007] *RPC* (5). See also *Strigl v. Deutsches Patent- unt Markenamt*, Case C-90/2011 (26 January 2012), [AG24]–[AG26] (AG Jääskinen) (acknowledging that disclaimers are part of the procedural matters left to member states).

[114] See, e.g., *Diamond T* (1921) 38 *RPC* 373; *Laura Ashley's Trade Mark* [1990] *RPC* 539, 549.

[115] *Nestlé Trade Mark* [2005] *RPC* (5) 77 (the 'Polo' case).

[116] Kerly, [10–159] (describing use of disclaimers as 'very patchy'). See also Max Planck Institute, *Study on the Overall Functioning of the Community Trade Mark System* (2011), 74–7 (stating that the UK Registry does not use disclaimers). Following on from the Study, the reformed EUTM regime no longer permits the EUIPO to request a disclaimer; nor does it allow applicants to voluntarily submit them. See EUIPO *Examination Guidelines*, Part B, Section 4, Chapter 1, [8] ('Disclaimers').

[117] *Granada Trade Mark* [1979] *RPC* 303, 308.

[118] Moreover, in composite marks, the disclaimer may mean that it is no infringement to use only the disclaimed component, but the disclaimed component is still one element of the composite whole: ibid., 306. Consequently, matter that is disclaimed is not necessarily disregarded when questions of possible confusion are being decided. Cf. *Paco/Paco life in colour* [2000] *RPC* 451, 467.   [119] TMA 1994, s. 40.

[120] TMR, r. 16.

of the trade mark is deemed to be the date of filing the application.[121] This is the date from which matters such as duration are calculated[122] and the rights of the proprietor are enforceable against third parties.[123] While registration in the United Kingdom lasts for an initial ten years, trade marks may be renewed for further ten-year periods.[124] One characteristic that distinguishes trade marks from other forms of intellectual property is that there is no maximum period of protection. So long as they are renewed, trade marks can potentially last forever. As with patents and designs, the reason why renewal is required is to ensure that the only marks that are on the Register are those in which proprietors have some interest.[125] Proprietors are normally provided with some leeway for late renewal[126] and, in certain circumstances, are able to restore lapsed registrations.[127] Generally, alteration of registered marks is not permitted.[128] The Registrar may, however, allow the proprietor's name or address to be altered. This is permissible only where the alteration does not 'substantially affect the identity of the mark'.[129]

2.7 TRADE MARK SYMBOL

Although the trade mark symbols™ and ® are used widely, there is no legal requirement that proprietors use these symbols to indicate that a mark has been registered. Criminal liability does, however, exist for anyone who uses these symbols, the word 'registered', or any other word or symbol that suggests that a mark is registered when, in fact, it is not.[130]

2.8 VALIDITY AND REVOCATION

Once a mark is registered, there is a presumption, although not a guarantee, that the registration is valid.[131] As with all forms of registered intellectual property, it is possible for trade marks to be withdrawn after they have been registered. This may be because the mark should not have been registered in the first place, or because changes in circumstances mean that it should no longer be registered. The grounds on which a registered mark may be challenged by third parties are set out in sections 46 and 47 of the 1994 Act. Section 46(1) sets out the grounds on which a mark may be *revoked*—that is, (i) where it has not been used for five years, (ii) where, as a result of the way in which it has been used, it has lost its distinctiveness, or (iii) where, as a result of the way in which it has been used, the further use of the mark has become likely to 'mislead the public'. In addition, a mark that should never have been registered can be declared *invalid* under section 47. A registration will be liable to be declared invalid where it should not have been registered on absolute grounds because of a potential objection under section 3 (for example because it lacks distinctiveness) and where relative grounds for refusal existed under section 5. These issues are dealt with in later chapters.

---

[121] TMA 1994, s. 40(3).

[122] TMA 1994, s. 42. But note TMA 1994, s. 46(1)(a), calculating period of non-use from 'the date of completion of the registration procedure'.

[123] TMA 1994, s. 9(3), explains that the rights have effect from the date of registration, i.e. filing, but no infringement proceedings may be begun before the date on which the mark is in fact registered and no criminal liability is incurred for acts done before the date of publication of the registration. This has no parallel in the TMD 1989; see *Interlotto UK Ltd v. Camelot plc* [2004] *RPC* (9) 186, [19]–[20].

[124] TMA 1994, s. 42; EUTMR, Art. 52; Madrid Prot., Art. 7(1).

[125] TMA 1994, s. 43(5); TMR, rr. 34–37.　[126] TMA 1994, s. 43(3).

[127] TMA 1994, s. 43(5); TMR, rr. 36, 37.　[128] TMA 1994, s. 44.

[129] TMA 1994, s. 64; TMR, r. 44.　[130] TMA 1994, s. 95. See Chapter 49, section 10, pp. 1354–5.

[131] TMA 1994, s. 72.

3 REGISTRATION OF EUROPEAN UNION TRADE MARKS

Registration at the EU level involves the filing of a single application with the EUIPO, which is based in Alicante in Spain.[132] In its former incarnation as the OHIM, the EUIPO began receiving applications on 1 April 1996.[133] In contrast with the procedure for European patents, during which the European Patent Office (EPO) issues a series of national patents, a successful application to the EUIPO results in the grant of a single trade mark that operates for the whole of the European Union; such marks are said to have a 'unitary character'.[134] The main benefit of the EU system is that it enables traders to protect their marks throughout the European Union on the basis of a single application, rather than having to file separate applications in each of the member states.

While the procedure at the EUIPO differs in certain respects from the procedure at the UK Trade Marks Registry, there is close similarity between the two regimes. As is the case with the UK Registry, traders who wish to have their signs protected as EU trade marks (EUTMs) often rely upon the expert advice of trade mark agents/attorneys. Legal representation before the EUIPO is more strictly prescribed than in the United Kingdom. Although legal representation is not required in all cases,[135] businesses that are not domiciled and do not have their principal place of business in the EU must be represented before the EUIPO. Representation can be undertaken only by a legal practitioner qualified in a member state of the European Economic Area (EEA) or a professional representative recognized by the EUIPO.[136] To be duly recognized, a representative must be a national of a member state with a place of business in the EU. In addition, they must be entitled to act as an agent before the trade marks office of the member state in which that business is located.[137]

3.1 APPLICATION

The application for an EUTM, which can be made by anyone, should be made directly to the EUIPO in Alicante (see Fig. 35.2).[138]

An application for an EUTM may be filed in any of the official languages of the EU. The applicant should also specify a second language in which opposition, revocation, or invalidity proceedings may be conducted.[139] As in the United Kingdom, an application for an EUTM must include: a request for registration; the name and address of the applicant; a list of the goods or services for which the mark is to be registered; and a representation of the mark.[140] The date of filing is the date on which these documents are furnished to the EUIPO. As in the United Kingdom, it may be possible to claim a priority date from an earlier application elsewhere.[141]

Three other points of comparison are worth emphasizing. First, as regards the goods or services for which a mark is registrable, the EUIPO was previously more generous,

---

[132] EUTMR, Arts 1–2.

[133] Strictly speaking, that was the date of opening and applications could be submitted from 1 January 1996.

[134] EUTMR, Art. 1(2).   [135] EUTMR, Art. 119.   [136] EUTMR, Arts 119, 120.

[137] EUTMR, Art. 120(2).

[138] EUTMR, Art. 30. As the relevant annual office reports indicate, during 2016, the EUIPO received over 135,000 trade mark applications, compared with the UK IPO's 54,800 applications in 2015–16 and 64,818 applications in 2016–17. Total EUIPO registrations now exceed 1.4 million.

[139] EUTMR, Art 146; EUTMIR, Art. 2(1)(j). The second language must be English, French, German, Italian, or Spanish.   [140] EUTMR, Art. 31; EUTMIR, Art. 2.

[141] EUTMR, Arts 34–36.

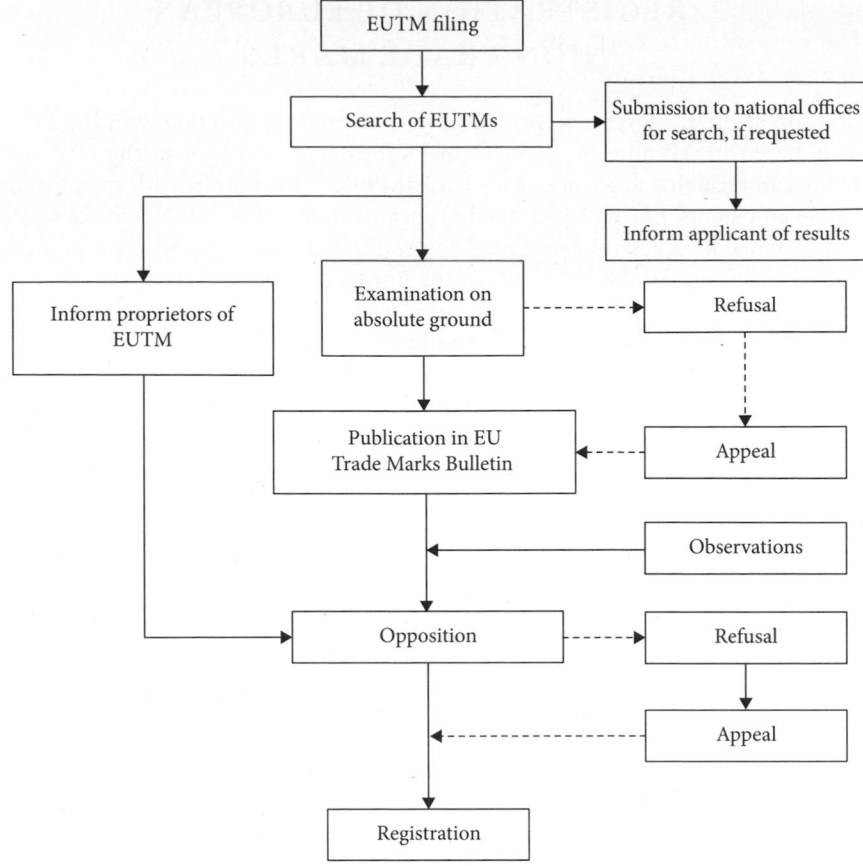

Fig. 35.2 Registering an EUTM

permitting applications, for example, relating to 'all goods in class x'. After *IP Translator*, which has been considered earlier in this chapter, general indications included in the class headings of the Nice Classification may still be used, provided that they comply with the requisite standards of clarity and precision, as set out in Article 33 of the EUTMR. In a move away from previous practice, the general class headings will also be literally interpreted ('means what it says'), within the context of the class in which they appear.[142] Second, and related, there is no requirement that an applicant state that they intend to use the mark(s).[143] Third, with the EUIPO opening up to new representation technologies, the UK will need to modify its 'graphical' representation standard, in order to avoid future divergences in representation practices for new types of marks.

3.2 SENIORITY AT THE EUIPO

Applicants who seek registration of an EUTM may claim the seniority of earlier national registrations of the same mark of which they are the proprietor.[144] Seniority can be

---

[142] EUIPO, *Examination Guidelines*, Part B, Section 3, [4] ('Building a List of Goods and Services').
[143] The applicant's good faith is presumed: *pelicantravel.com v. OHIM*, T-136/11, EU:T:2012:689, [57].
[144] EUTMR, Art. 39.

claimed either before or after registration of the EUTM.[145] To apply for seniority, an applicant must be able to show that the earlier national mark is for the same sign, the same goods and services, and has the same proprietor as the EUTM.[146]

The effect of a seniority claim is that, even though the national registration ceases to exist (because of lack of renewal or because it was surrendered),[147] the proprietor of the EUTM continues to have the same rights as if the national mark had continued to be registered.[148] Effectively, it allows the EUTM owner to let the national registration lapse without being prejudiced in any way.[149] As the Board of Appeal observed, seniority is a useful way of encouraging proprietors of national marks to use the EU system and thereby consolidate the management of their national marks.[150] As a result of its popularity, problems occurred in processing seniority claims and many were let through without formal examination.[151]

3.3 EXAMINATION

Once the filing process has been completed, the application is then examined. Initial examination at the EUIPO is restricted to an inquiry as to whether the application complies with the absolute grounds for refusal.[152] The absolute grounds for refusal will apply to the mark across the whole EU, even if they arise in only one member state.[153] Where the application fails to comply with the absolute grounds for refusal, the application may be amended or withdrawn.[154] While the Office could previously request that the applicant disclaim any exclusive right in a particular element, this is no longer possible.[155]

While the EUIPO does not examine applications to see if the relative grounds for refusal apply, it does provide third parties (and applicants) with some assistance. In particular, the EUIPO searches the EUTM register for similar marks and, if requested to do so by the applicant, asks member states that participate in the search system to do the same, which results in both EUTM and national search reports.[156] The results of the

---

[145] EUTMR, Arts 39, 40.

[146] EUTMR, Art. 39(1) (so-called 'triple-identity rule'). The EUIPO examines only the question of identity of signs: OHIM, *Communication No. 2/00 of the President of the Office of 25 February 2000 Concerning the Examination of Seniority Claims* (2000). For general guidance on the identity of signs, see *Shang v. OHIM (justing)*, Case T-103/11, EU:T:2012:19; *Langguth Erben v. OHIM (MEDINET)*, Case T-378/11, EU:T:2013:83, aff'd in Case C-412/13P, EU:C:2014:269 (later black-and-white mark not identical to earlier version in gold). On identity of the specification, see OHIM, *Communication No. 1/97 of the President of the Office of 17 June 1997 Concerning the Examination of Seniority Claims* (1997). On identity of proprietorship, see *BatMark, Inc./Viceroy*, R 5/97-1 [1998] *ETMR* 449.

[147] EUTMR, Art. 39(3); *Allied Telesyn Inc. v. Rapier 1 Ltd*, O-170-07 (13 June 2007) (AP Hobbs QC).

[148] There is no obligation on the EUIPO to treat the EUTM as valid just because seniority is claimed for an identical national mark: *Develey Holdings GmbH v. OHIM*, T-129/04 [2006] *ETMR* (85) 1190.

[149] EUTMR, Art. 39(3).   [150] *BatMark, Inc./Viceroy*, R 5/97-1 [1998] *ETMR* 449, 455-6.

[151] Examination of seniority claims, which was suspended, has now resumed, but is confined to comparison of marks: OHIM, *Communication No. 2/00 of the President of the Office of 25 February 2000 Concerning the Examination of Seniority Claims* (2000).

[152] EUTMR, Arts 41-42. Absolute grounds are set out in EUTMR, Art. 7(1). One difference between the EUTM and UK law is that the United Kingdom will examine whether the application is in bad faith, whereas, under the EUTMR, this is only a ground for invalidity (not refusal).

[153] EUTMR, Art. 7(2).   [154] EUTMR, Arts 42(2), 50.

[155] Formerly, CTMR, Art. 37(2); See also *Technopol v. OHIM*, Joined Cases T-425/07 and T-426/07 [2009] *ECR* II-04275, [19]. However the arguments against disclaimers eventually carried the day and they are no longer recognized under the EUTMR; see Max Planck Institute, *Study on the Overall Functioning of the Community Trade Mark System* (2011), 74-7.

[156] EUTMR, Art. 43. Those offices that participate are the Czech Republic, Denmark, Lithuania, Hungary, Romania, and Slovakia.

EUTM search are also sent to the owners (or applicants, if still pending) of any potentially conflicting EUTM registrations that are found.[157] The search, however, does not lead to an examination on relative grounds; instead, it is left up to the holders of prior rights to bring opposition proceedings[158] or, if the mark has been registered, cancellation proceedings.[159]

3.4 PUBLICATION, OBSERVATIONS, AND OPPOSITION

Once an application has successfully been examined, it will then be published in the EU Trade Marks Bulletin.[160] Publication takes place one month after the applicant is provided with the search report. At the same time, the application file, which is previously closed, is opened up for public inspection.[161]

Following publication, there is an opportunity for third parties to make 'observations' on and 'opposition' to the proposed registration of the application. While an EUTM covers the whole of the European Union, a single objection to the application can result in the entire application being refused. Third parties may make 'observations' explaining why the trade mark should not be registered under Article 7 of the EUTMR (which are the absolute grounds for refusal). Although the Regulation states that the observations are to be communicated to the applicant, 'who may comment on them', the EUIPO has indicated that, where observations raise serious doubts about registrability, the Office will re-examine the application.[162]

Within three months of publication, the application may be *opposed* on relative grounds.[163] As in the United Kingdom, only a limited set of persons is entitled to bring opposition proceedings—these include the proprietors of earlier registered trade marks and their licensees, the proprietors of well-known trade marks under Article 6*bis* of the Paris Convention, those entitled to claim on the basis of earlier signs used in trade, as well as oppositions based on prior geographical indications.[164] Once an opposition is accepted, the EUIPO notifies the applicant and a 'cooling-off period' of up to 24 months ensues.[165] If the parties have not resolved the conflict (for example through a delimitation agreement allowing the registration), the 'adversarial' process begins. The opponent will be asked to substantiate the existence of an earlier right and, where this consists of a mark granted more than five years previously, the applicant may request the opponent prove use of its mark.[166] In response, the applicant is entitled to make observations on the opponent's evidence and grounds of opposition. Ultimately, these matters are decided by the EUIPO.[167] In contrast to the process in the United Kingdom, oral hearings are practically unknown. While it was anticipated that oppositions at the EUIPO would be very common, it seems that they affect only about a sixth of all applications.[168] Most oppositions

---

[157] EUTMR, Art. 43(7).   [158] EUTMR, Arts 8, 47.   [159] EUTMR, Art. 60.

[160] EUTMR, Art. 44; EUTMIR, Art. 7. See also EUTMR, Arts 111 (register open to public inspection) and 116 (explaining EUTM Bulletin).

[161] Prior to publication, the file cannot be inspected without an applicant's consent: EUTMR, Art. 114.

[162] EUTMR, Art. 45; OHIM, *Communication No. 02/09 of the President of the Office of 09/11/2009 Concerning Third Party Observations* (2009); the Office now explicitly has the authority to reopen examination on absolute grounds: EUTMR, Art. 45(3).

[163] EUTMR, Art. 46; EUTMDR, Arts 2–10. For analysis of the grounds, see Chapter 38. The opposition must be in one of the languages of the Office: English, French, German, Italian, or Spanish. See F. Gevers and D. Tatham, 'Opposition Procedure in the Community Trade Mark System' [1998] *EIPR* 22.

[164] EUTMR, Art. 46(1).   [165] EUTMDR, Art. 6(1).   [166] EUTMR, Art. 47(2); EUTMDR, Art. 10.

[167] EUTMR, Art. 47(5).

[168] As of May 2018, the EUIPO had received nearly 1.8 million applications and there had been 305,224 oppositions: EUIPO, *SSC009—Statistics of European Union Trade Marks* (May 2018).

are resolved within the cooling-off period, with only about a third leading to an office decision.[169]

If an application to the EUIPO is rejected or withdrawn, it may be converted back into a series of national applications, which retain the filing date used at the EUIPO.[170] Conversion is not possible, however, in those member states to which the grounds for refusal of the EUTM relate.[171] As with UK applications, it is possible for an application for an EUTM to be changed or amended after it has been lodged. While the way in which this is done at the EUIPO is similar to the techniques used in the United Kingdom,[172] one important difference is that whereas disclaimers are used voluntarily by UK applicants, they have been phased out by the EUIPO.[173]

3.5 REGISTRATION

In the absence of an effective opposition, the mark will be registered.[174] The date of registration is the filing date, which is the date from which matters such as duration are calculated.[175] As regards the EUTM, a proprietor is entitled only to 'reasonable compensation' for acts occurring between publication of the application and publication of the registration.[176] Registration at the EUIPO lasts for ten years.[177] An EUTM may be renewed for further periods of ten years.[178] Alteration of registered marks is generally not permitted.[179] As in the United Kingdom, it is possible for an EUTM to be revoked or declared invalid after it has been registered—and this may occur either as a counterclaim in proceedings in an EUTM court, or by application to the Cancellation Division of the EUIPO.[180]

4 INTERNATIONAL FILING

The third way in which UK traders are able to protect their marks is via the international filing systems established under the 1891 Madrid Agreement and the 1989 Madrid Protocol. It should be noted at the outset that international registration does not lead to something such as an 'international mark', so much as it does facilitate the acquisition of national marks. The main advantage of international registration is that instead of trade mark holders having to file a series of applications in each of the jurisdictions in which they would like protection, they are able to obtain protection in a range of jurisdictions with a single application.

---

[169] As of May 2018, 272,360 oppositions had been finally settled: 66,249 by decision and 206,111 by 'not proceeding to judgment': ibid.

[170] EUTMR, Art. 139; EUTMIR, Art. 22.   [171] EUTMR, Art. 139(2)(b).

[172] EUTMR, Art. 49; EUIPO, *Examination Guidelines*, Part B, Section 1, [5] ('Amendments to an EUTM Application').   [173] See section 2.5 of this chapter p. 943.

[174] EUTMR, Art. 51.   [175] EUTMR, Art. 52.   [176] EUTMR, Art. 11(2).

[177] EUTMR, Art. 52.   [178] EUTMR, Arts 52, 53.

[179] EUTMR, Art. 54; EUTMIR, Art. 10.

[180] As of May 2018, there had been 16,049 cancellation requests. However only a minority of these result in a successful cancellation. As of 2009—the most recent year for which there are figures—there were 4,099 cancellation requests but only 1, 644 marks had been cancelled and surrendered. See *SSC009—Statistics of European Union Trade Marks* (May 2018). This seems a relatively small figure, given that registrations have exceeded the 1 million mark.

4.1 MADRID AGREEMENT

The oldest international filing system is the 1891 Madrid Agreement.[181] Under the Agreement—to which the United Kingdom is *not* a party—it is possible to register a trade mark at a national level and then to apply to have the mark recognized by the WIPO in Geneva as an 'international registration'. Despite it being over 100 years old, only a relatively small number of countries have signed up to the Agreement.[182]

To apply for international registration, the applicant must have a trade mark registered in its country of origin, which must be a contracting state of the Agreement. Applications must be in English, French, or Spanish and include: the name and address of the applicant; information about the registration in the country of origin; a reproduction of the mark; and a statement of the goods and services to which the mark is applied.[183] The application should also nominate the countries of the Agreement in which the applicant wishes the mark to be protected.[184] The Madrid Agreement can be used only by a person or business that has headquarters or a real and effective establishment in a country that is a party to the Agreement. Given that the United Kingdom is not a party to the Madrid Agreement, UK businesses will be able to take advantage of the system only if they have a base outside the United Kingdom.[185]

Once the national office of the country of origin is satisfied that the application is complete, it sends the international application to the WIPO International Bureau in Geneva. On receiving the international application, the Bureau examines the application to ensure that it complies with various formalities; there is no substantive examination of the application. An application that satisfies the procedural requirements is immediately registered.[186] The registration date is the date on which the International Bureau receives the completed application.

The Bureau then sends applications to the national offices nominated by the applicant. Article 4 of the Agreement provides that, from the date of the international registration, the application is to be treated in each of the designated countries as if it had been filed directly at that country's national office.[187] Upon receipt of the international registration, the national offices have the opportunity to reject the application. Registration under the Madrid Agreement lasts for 20 years and is renewable for further 20-year periods.[188]

One of the major problems with the Madrid Agreement is that it provides for the possibility of a 'central attack'.[189] This means that if, within five years from the date of international registration, the mark is declared invalid or otherwise lost in the country of origin, *all of the* national registrations that are based upon it are also lost. At the end of the five-year period, the opportunity for central attack ends. From this point, the non-country of origin registrations are not dependent upon the fate of the mark in the country of origin.

---

[181] Madrid Agreement Concerning the International Registration of Marks of 14 April 1891, as revised.

[182] The Madrid Agreement covers only 55 countries (as of May 2018). The United States and Japan are not members.

[183] Madrid, Art. 3; Common Regulations under the Madrid Agreement Concerning the International Registration of Marks and the Protocol Relating to that Agreement (as in force on 1 May 2018), rr 6, 9.

[184] Madrid, Art. 3*bis*.

[185] G. Souter, 'The Rights of Nationals of Non-Madrid Union Countries to Own International Registrations' [1995] *EIPR* 333.

[186] Madrid, Art. 3(4).   [187] Madrid, Art. 4.   [188] Madrid, Arts 6, 7(1).

[189] Madrid, Art. 6(3).

4.2 MADRID PROTOCOL

The Madrid Protocol[190] was established in 1989 to provide an alternative mechanism to the Madrid Agreement for the international filing of marks. In particular, it was hoped that it would overcome some of the perceived shortcomings of the Agreement that led to its membership being so small.[191] Given that there are, at time of writing, 91 parties to the Protocol (as distinct from 56 to the Agreement), the Protocol has been a success, at least in this regard. While the Protocol and the Agreement are similar there are, as we will see, some important differences. The United Kingdom became a party to the Madrid Protocol on 1 December 1995[192] and the Protocol became operational on 1 April 1996. The European Union joined with effect from 1 October 2004.[193] The system established under the Protocol is run by WIPO in Geneva.

4.2.1 Application

In order to apply for international registration for a mark under the Protocol, an application for registration must have been made in a country that is party to the Protocol.[194] The existing registration or application provides the 'national basis' that grounds the Protocol application. Applications for international registration are filed in the office in which the national basis was filed;[195] WIPO will not accept applications that are filed directly with it.[196] For British traders, this would normally be the UK Trade Marks Registry. International applications governed exclusively by the Protocol may be in English, French, or Spanish (although the office of origin may restrict the applicant's choice to one of these languages).

An international application can also be based upon an application or a registration at an 'intergovernmental organization',[197] and a Council Decision enabled the EUIPO to take advantage of this possibility.[198] Since the autumn of 2004, both applicants and holders of EUTMs have been able to apply for international protection of their marks through the filing of an international application under the Protocol. Conversely, holders of international registrations under the Madrid Protocol can apply for protection of their marks as an EUTM.[199]

The national office or EUIPO examines the international application to ensure that the international application corresponds to the basic application or registration—that

---

[190] Protocol Relating to the Madrid Agreement Concerning the International Registration of Marks (as signed at Madrid on 28 June 1989).

[191] I. Kaufman, 'Madrid Agreement: Will Reform Proposals Attract More Members?' [1990] *EIPR* 407; G. Kunze, 'The Madrid System for the International Registration of Marks as Applied under the Protocol' [1994] *EIPR* 223. For an assessment, see E. McDermott, 'Measuring the Merits of Madrid' [2008] 177 *Managing IP* 62.

[192] In order to give effect to its obligations under the Protocol, the United Kingdom passed delegated legislation in the form of the Trade Marks (International Registration) Order (SI 1996/714), as amended by SI 2000/138 and eventually replaced by SI 2008/2206, which is the current applicable legislation. The 2008 Order was amended by SI 2009/2464 and SI 2013/445.

[193] The Madrid Protocol allows for accession by intergovernmental organizations: Madrid Prot., Art. 14. The authority to join was conferred by Council Regulation (EC) No. 1992/2003 of 27 October 2003 amending Regulation (EC) No 40/94 on the Community trade mark to give effect to the accession of the European Community to the Protocol relating to the Madrid Agreement concerning the international registration of marks adopted at Madrid on 27 June 1989 [2003] *OJ L* 296/1 (14 November 2003).

[194] Madrid Prot., Art. 2(1).   [195] On fees, see Madrid Prot., Art. 8.   [196] Madrid Prot., Art. 2(2).

[197] Madrid Prot., Art. 14(1)(b).

[198] Council Regulation (EC) No. 1992/2003, op. cit. See J. Weberndorfer, 'The Integration of the OHIM into the Madrid System' [2008] *EIPR* 216.

[199] EUTMR, Arts 183, 189 *ff.*

is, that it is for the same mark, has the same owner as, and covers the same goods and services as the 'basic application'.[200] An application for international registration must also designate the countries in which the mark is to be protected. Although this should be done at the application stage, further countries may subsequently be added.[201]

Once it is satisfied that the formalities have been complied with, the national office will then forward the application to WIPO, which examines the application to ensure that it complies with the Protocol. Once it is satisfied that an application is in order, the International Bureau then places the mark on the International Register of Trade Marks, advertises the mark, and passes on details of an application to each of the designated countries listed in the application.[202] As with the Madrid Agreement, the application is treated in each of the designated countries as if it had been filed directly at that country's national office.[203] Each designated country then examines the application against its own criteria for registration.[204] Any refusal can be based only on the grounds that would apply under the Paris Convention.[205]

Countries normally have up to 12 months within which to notify WIPO of any objections.[206] However, in accordance with a special provision, the United Kingdom has declared that the time limit to notify a refusal of protection is 18 months.[207] Where a refusal to protect results from an opposition to the granting of protection, such refusal may be notified after the expiry of the 18-month time limit. Such a refusal is notified to WIPO, which then sends notification of the refusal to the international registrant, who is able to contest, amend, and appeal the decision.[208] Where a national registry fails to notify WIPO of a decision to refuse registration within the relevant time limit, the mark is deemed to be protected as if it had been registered by the authorities of that country.[209]

Registration under the Protocol lasts for ten years,[210] with the possibility of being renewed for further ten-year periods.[211] Where a mark that is the subject of a national or regional registration is the subject of a later international registration and both registrations stand in the name of the same person, the international registration is deemed to replace the national or regional registration, without prejudice to any rights acquired by virtue of the latter.[212] This occurs only if all of the goods and services listed in the national or regional registration are also listed in the international registration in respect of the said contracting party. Rights in all of the countries can then be renewed by a single transaction.

4.2.2 Central attack

Under the Madrid Agreement, the fate of the international registration (and all of the subsidiary registrations made under it) depends on the fate of the trade mark registered in the country of origin: if it is lost, all of the other registrations are also lost. While an international registration under the Protocol is vulnerable to a central attack (most obviously

---

[200] Madrid Prot., Art. 3(1); EUTMR, Art. 184. A country can insist that, insofar as it is designated, the applicant must indicate a bona fide intention to use the mark. The United Kingdom has such a requirement and, in *Red Bull v. Sun Mark* [2012] *EWHC* 1929 (Ch), [113] *ff*, [126] *ff*, [167]–[174], the Court treated the international requirement as having a similar significance to a statement made under TMA 1994, s. 32(3) when assessing whether the application had been made in bad faith.

[201] Madrid Prot., Arts 3*bis,* 3*ter.*

[202] Madrid, Art. 3(4). The WIPO advertises an applicant's mark in the WIPO Gazette of International Marks.   [203] Madrid Prot., Art. 4.

[204] In the case of the EUIPO, EUTMR, Art. 193 provides for examination on absolute grounds.

[205] Madrid Prot., Art. 5(1).   [206] Madrid Prot., Art. 5(2).   [207] Madrid Prot., Art. 5(2)(b)–(c).

[208] Madrid Prot., Art. 5(6).   [209] Madrid Prot., Art. 4(1)(a).   [210] Madrid Prot., Art. 6(1).

[211] Madrid Prot., Art. 7(1).   [212] Madrid Prot., Art. 4*bis.*   [213] Madrid Prot., Art. 6(3).

where the basic application is refused by the national authority),[213] the consequences of a successful attack are not as drastic as they are under the Agreement. As we saw earlier, a successful attack under the Agreement means that all of the national registrations made in pursuance of the international registration are also lost. Where a central attack is successful under the Protocol, however, it is possible to transform the international registration into a series of national or regional applications.[214] Under this provision, if, within three months of cancellation, the person who was the holder of the international registration files an application for the registration of the same mark with the office of any of the designated territories, that application shall be treated as if it had been filed on the date of the international registration. This takes place, however, only if the goods and services listed in the application correspond to the list of goods and services contained in the international registration. The fresh application must comply with the requirements of the applicable law.

5 DECIDING WHICH ROUTE TO TAKE

Because of the interaction between these systems, an applicant is faced with a complex array of possible avenues through which to acquire trade mark protection. The most obvious of the existing routes are by:

(i) application directly to the United Kingdom;

(ii) application to a Paris Convention country, then to the United Kingdom;[215]

(iii) application to the EUIPO leading to an EUTM;

(iv) application to a Paris Convention country, then to the EUIPO;

(v) application to a Paris Convention country, then international registration designating the United Kingdom;

(vi) application to a Paris Convention country, then international registration designating the EUIPO; or

(vii) application to the EUIPO, followed by an international application.[216]

Decisions to register, and the choice of routes, are likely to involve commercial judgements as to the likely markets in which protection is desired compared with the cost of obtaining registrations for such territories. Probably the most significant factor determining choice of application process is the cost. If trade mark protection is required in several countries, it may be cheaper to use the EUTM or the Madrid Protocol than to make national applications in each country.[217] As well as savings in office fees, associated savings can be achieved by using the Madrid Protocol in terms of lower costs of trade mark agents. There are also obvious advantages to the EUIPO or Madrid in terms of the simplicity of completing the EUTM or Madrid forms rather than numerous national forms in various national languages. One of the advantages with the regional and international systems lies in the fact that they avoid the obligation to submit applications in the language of each

---

[214] Madrid Prot., Art. 9*quinquies*.

[215] Under the 'telle quelle' provision contained in Paris, Art. 6*quinquies*, a member of the Paris Union is obliged to accept for registration any trade mark that has been duly registered in its country of origin.

[216] From 1 October 2004.

[217] See Max Planck Institute, *Study on the Overall Functioning of the Community Trade Mark System* (2011), 46.

country where protection is sought. Moreover, in the long term, maintenance of regional or international marks will be easier, requiring only one renewal at each office instead of several renewals. Finally, the application of the substantive or procedural law might be perceived as being more favourable at the EUIPO than in the local registry.[218]

That is not to suggest there may not be reasons (especially for small enterprises) to use national registration systems. It may be difficult to find appropriate marks to operate in all countries: trade mark lawyers love to tell anecdotes about word marks adopted in one country and transported to another without considering what the mark suggests in that territory. Moreover, it is foreseeable that valid marks will be harder to obtain at the EUIPO than in some national registries, given the broader field in which the mark has to operate. Words that are distinctive in the United Kingdom may lack distinctiveness at the EU level (for example because the word is a description in a foreign language or indicates a geographical origin). In addition, the number of similar marks in use or already registered, which form the potential basis for opposition, is likely to be substantially greater for EUTMs than for national marks. One consequence of this will be that those who are seeking protection quickly might prefer to seek national registrations, rather than to begin with a filing to the EUIPO, because of the substantial risk that the mark will be rejected or prove invalid at the EU level.

6 BREXIT AND TRADE MARKS

At present, UK trade mark law is highly integrated into EU trade mark law. Brexit will change this in two fundamental ways. First, it could lead to a divergence between the substantive standards of national UK trade mark law and the harmonized trade mark regimes across the other EU Member States. The European Union (Withdrawal) Bill 2017–2018,[219] also known as the 'Great Repeal Bill', aims to ensure that European law will no longer apply in the United Kingdom after Brexit. However all existing EU legislation will be copied into domestic law, thereby preserving the status quo as of 2019. By that stage most EU members should have implemented the TMD 2015 into national law and there has been a recent indication—in the form of a consultation regarding an amending statutory instrument—that the United Kingdom will update the TMA 1994 to incorporate the new features of the TMD 2015.[220] For example, under the definition of a trade mark, domestic law still refers to graphical representation while EU law has moved on to 'adequate' representation, which need not necessarily be graphical.[221] And the United Kingdom presently adopts an EU-wide exhaustion rule but its future is uncertain.[222] Even after the TMD 2015 changes are incorporated, the extent to which future UK trade mark law will continue to track harmonized EU trade mark law depends on the nature of the trading relationship that will develop between the United Kingdom and the European Union. One potentially positive aspect of any divergence is that areas of EU trade mark law which have proven controversial, such as the usefulness of 'functions' theory and the extent to which it supplants trade mark use,[223] or the scope of the protection against free-riding or 'unfair advantage',[224] could be revisited by UK courts in a post-Brexit future. A

---

[218] For example, the EUIPO permits broad specifications.

[219] Available online at https://services.parliament.uk/bills/2017-19/europeanunionwithdrawal.html.

[220] UKIPO, *Implementation of the EU Trade Mark Directive 2015* (February 2018), available online at https://www.gov.uk/government/consultations/implementation-of-the-trade-mark-directive-2015.

[221] See Chapter 35, section 2.1.3, pp. 934–9.   [222] See Chapter 41, section 8, pp. 1146–63.

[223] See Chapter 40, section 10, pp. 1116–25.   [224] See Chapter 38, section 2.4, pp. 1065–70.

more sobering counter-argument is that new bilateral or multilateral commitments could rapidly reintroduce these standards as binding legal obligations, thereby reducing any future room to manoeuvre.[225]

The second major constellation of changes relates to the EUTM regime. At present, 1.4 million registered EUTMs have effect within the United Kingdom, as a consequence of unitary rights having effects across the entire EU. On Brexit, these marks will cease to have effect in the United Kingdom, subject to any transitional arrangements. This has been identified as a concern by the EU.[226] It is also true for registered EU geographical indications for wines, spirits, agricultural products and foodstuffs under unitary, harmonized EU regimes. The EU suggests that the 'holder of any intellectual property right having unitary character within the Union and granted before the withdrawal date should, as of that date, be recognised as the holder of an enforceable intellectual property right in relation to the United Kingdom territory, comparable to the right provided by Union law—if need be on the basis of specific domestic legislation to be introduced'.[227] Various models for incorporating the corpus of registered EUTMs into United Kingdom trade mark law have been proposed, ranging from unilaterally deeming EUTMs to have domestic effects without the need for registration to facilitating *en masse* registration of all valid EUTMs into the United Kingdom's trade marks register, in a vast 'data dump'.[228] Accompanying issues include the extent to which such EUTMs would need to be actively used in the United Kingdom to be maintained and the related risk of 'cluttering' the national trade mark register with marks that are not in fact used in this jurisdiction.

Two additional issues are considered important. First, how can existing rights of legal representation be preserved to the greatest extent possible? United Kingdom trade mark practitioners desire rights of representation before the EUIPO as well as the Court of Justice, while EEA professionals would require reciprocal rights before the UKIPO. Second, licensing agreements, as well as delimitation and coexistence agreements, will need to be reconsidered where they presently refer to the territory of the EU. These are some of the more prominent unsettled issues, in terms of the implications of Brexit for trade mark law. It is hoped there will be greater clarity by the next edition of this book.

[225] L. Bently, 'Fantasy Island. What Policy-Freedom will the UK gain from leaving the European Union?' (Presentation at Bournemouth University, 3 November 2016).

[226] European Commission, *Position Paper on Intellectual Property Rights (including Geographical Indications)*, TF50 (2017) 11/2 (20 September 2017); see also EUIPO, *Impact of the United Kingdom's Withdrawal from the European Union on the European Union Trade Mark and the Community Design—Frequently asked Questions and Answers* (18 January 2018). In light of the European Commission's proposed draft withdrawal agreement, in March 2018 the UK government has indicated its intention to grant all EUTM holders an equivalent UK right after the transition period. For further updates, see online at https://www.citma.org.uk/membership/brexit/brexit.

[227] European Commission, *Position Paper*, op. cit. 2.

[228] The various options are set out in: CITMA, 'EU Registered Rights—Trade Marks' (19 August 2016), available online at https://www.citma.org.uk/membership/brexit/eu_registered_rights_-_trade_marks; CIPA, *The Impact of Brexit on Intellectual Property* (5th edn, October 2017); CITMA, *Post-Brexit Registered Trade Mark and Design Rights, and Rights of Representation* (July 2017). See also, C. Morcom, 'The Implications of "Brexit" for Trade Marks and for Practitioners in the UK: What Are the Likely Effects and What Needs to Happen Now?' (2016) 38 *EIPR* 657; G. B. Dinwoodie and R. C. Dreyfuss, 'Brexit and IP: The Great Unravelling?' (2018) 39 *Cardozo L Rev* 967; M. Mimler, *The Effect of Brexit on Trademarks, Designs and Other 'Europeanized' Areas of Intellectual Property Law in the United Kingdom* (British Institute of International and Comparative Law, Paper No. 7, December 2017).

36

SUBJECT MATTER

1 INTRODUCTION

The first requirement that a sign must satisfy to be validly registered or, if it is already registered, to ensure that it is not subsequently declared invalid is that it must conform to the definition of a trade mark in section 1(1) of the Trade Marks Act 1994/Article 4 of the European Union Trade Mark Regulation (EUTMR).[1] In particular, it is necessary to show that there is (i) a sign, (ii) which can be represented adequately on the register, and (iii) which is capable of distinguishing the goods or services of one undertaking from those of other undertakings. Failure to comply with any of these requirements means that the sign will not be registered; this is one of the absolute grounds for refusal set out in section 3(1)(a). Alternatively, if a mark is incorrectly registered, the registration of the mark may be declared invalid under section 47(1).

Before looking at these three elements in more detail, it is important to recall that the requirement that the sign must possess the qualities of a trade mark that are set out in section 1(1)/Article 4 is only the first of three general limitations that are placed on what can be registered as a trade mark. In addition, it is also necessary to ensure that the mark is not excluded by one of the absolute grounds for refusal found in section 3/Article 7.[2] It is also necessary to show that the mark is not excluded by any of the relative grounds for refusal found in section 5/Article 8.[3]

2 WHAT IS A SIGN?

For a trade mark to be validly registered, it is necessary to show that it consists of a 'sign'. No statutory definition is given as to what is meant by this term. Indeed, one of the notable features of the current law is that there are very few *a priori* restrictions placed on what may be registered as a trade mark.[4] The starting point for considering what may be

---

[1] In this chapter, any reference to an Article, without further qualification, will be to the EUTMR.

[2] See Chapter 37.   [3] See Chapter 38.

[4] The current definition of what constitutes a trade mark is to be contrasted with the restrictive definition formerly found in TMA 1938, s. 68.

protected as a sign is section 1 of the 1994 Act, which provides a non-exhaustive list of the types of sign that may be protected as trade marks. These include words (including personal names), designs, letters, numerals, or the shape of goods or of their packaging.[5] Although all of the matters referred to in section 1 of the Act are visually perceptible, the Court of Justice has held that the concept of a sign is not limited to visually perceptible matter; as a result, both sounds and smells have been held to fall within the notion of a sign.[6] Over time, the EUIPO has come to recognize the following categories of signs which have the potential to be marks: words, letters or numerals; figurative marks which include both pictorial elements as well as stylized words or numerals; three dimensional shapes including product packaging; the specific position of a sign upon a product; regularly repeated patterns; both single colours per se and colour combinations; sounds; elements or images in motion; multimedia, combining images and sound; holograms; and a residual 'other' category.[7] The recently amended Article 4 now expressly refers to sounds, as an illustration of a non-visual mark category.

The more open approach adopted under the EU trade mark regime has been welcomed by trade mark owners. It has also been welcomed because of the fact that, by increasing the features of products that may indicate source, it benefits consumers from different cultural backgrounds and with varying standards of literacy.[8] Some, however, have questioned whether the potential problems that are raised by some of the more exotic marks are justified by the benefits that they confer on their owners.[9]

Although it is clear that the concept of a 'sign' is broad, it is not without limits. In two cases, the Court of Justice has indicated that attempts to register must be refused if the subject matter was not a 'sign' for the purposes of trade mark law. The first occasion related to an attempt to register a combination of colours (blue and yellow) howsoever they were applied to articles or packaging.[10] The Court held that while a colour *could be* a sign, it was not necessarily so: in many situations, colour is simply a property or characteristic of a thing. According to the Court, in order to prevent trade mark law from being used by one trader to obtain an unfair advantage over other traders, an applicant for a colour mark must establish that the colour in question is seen as a 'sign'. Unfortunately, the Court of Justice provided little guidance on how an applicant was to establish (or an office to assess) the semiotic status of a colour or colour combination. If the requirement is that

---

[5] In response to a reference from Germany, the Court has held that the concept of 'a sign' can encompass the appearance of a shop that offers retail services on the basis that it is represented as a design or figurative drawing: *Apple v. German Patent Office*, Case C-421/13 [2014] *ETMR* 48. The issue of whether any given Apple store-in-reality varies from the store-as-represented seems to have been relocated from representation to distinctiveness (i.e. is the sign stable enough to be distinctive).

[6] *Ralf Sieckmann v. Deutsches Patent-und Markenamt*, Case C-273/00 [2002] *ECR* I–11737, [43]–[44]; *Shield Mark BV v. Joost Kist*, Case C-283/01, [2003] *ECR* I–14313.   [7] EUTMIR, Arts 3(3), 3(4).

[8] G. Dinwoodie, 'Reconceptualising the Inherent Distinctiveness of Product Design Trade Dress' (1997) 75(2) *NC L Rev* 471, 561.

[9] Those advocating caution include: B. Elias, 'Do Scents Signify Source? An Argument against Trade Mark Protection for Fragrances' (1992) 82 *TM Rep* 475; A. Bartow, 'True Colors of Trademark Law: Greenlighting a Red Tide of Anti Competition Blues' (2008–2009) 2 *Kentucky Law Journal* 263; A. Gilson LaLonde and J. Gilson, 'Getting Real with Nontraditional Trademarks: What's Next after Red Oven Knobs, the Sound of Burning Methamphetamine, and Goats on a Grass Roof' (2011) 101 *TM Rep* 186; K. Port, 'On Nontraditional Trademarks' (2011) 38 *N Kentucky Law Review* 1; G. Lea, 'Special Marks: After 20 years, not so Special After All?' (2015) *Communications Law* 40. See generally, I. Calboli and M. Senftleben (eds), *The Protection of Non-Traditional Marks: Critical Perspectives* (2018).

[10] *Heidelberger Bauchemie*, Case C-49/02 [2004] *ECR* I–6129. Similar remarks had been made in *Libertel Groep BV v. Benelux-Merkenbureau*, Case C-104/01 [2003] *ECR* I–3793, [27].

the applicant must show that consumers see the colour combination as indicating origin, the requirement seems to add nothing over the demand that the mark be not devoid of distinctive character.

The second case, *Dyson Ltd v. Registrar of Trade Marks*,[11] concerned an attempt to register a trade mark which consisted 'of a transparent bin or collection chamber forming part of the external surface of a vacuum cleaner as shown in the representation'. Along with this description, Dyson also submitted representations in the form of photographic images of two vacuum cleaner models with external bins, but the mark as claimed extended beyond these two exemplars. An externally mounted transparent collection bin has functional utility; customers can visually verify when the bin needs emptying while it is easy to detach. However since it was very emphatically not a shape, the (then applicable) EU functionality objections didn't apply. The Court of Justice reasoned that since a multitude of bin shapes and configurations could satisfy the representation and description of the sign, it related to non-specific subject matter.[12] Recognizing exclusive trade mark rights in such an abstract, technical concept would allow Dyson to obtain an unfair competitive advantage in a (useful) property of the underlying product. Since it related to an abstract property of the product which could be implemented in a variety of ways, it was not a specific sign.[13]

This reasoning has been subsequently applied by the Court of Appeal in two cases heard together, *Nestlé v. Cadbury*[14] and *Spear v. Zynga*.[15] In *Nestlé*, the Court of Appeal reversed the decision of the UK Trade Marks Registry and HH Judge Birss QC, and held that Cadbury's application for 'the colour purple (Pantone 2685C), . . . being the predominant colour applied to the whole visible surface, of the packaging of the goods' should not have been accepted as it referred to a 'multitude of permutations, presentations and combinations of the subject matter of the registrations'.[16] For the same reason, in *Spear*, the Court affirmed Arnold J's decision invalidating the registration of a 'three-dimensional ivory-coloured tile on the top surface of which is shown a letter of the Roman alphabet and a numeral in the range 1 to 10', on the grounds that it potentially covered many signs.

3 LIMITATIONS FOR SHAPES AND OTHER CHARACTERISTICS

While, in extending trade mark protection to the shape of goods, trade mark law took account of the realities of consumer buying habits, it also gave rise to a problem: that trade mark rights could operate to limit competition in ways that were contrary to the public interest. In order to avoid such undesirable effects, section 3(2) provides for a 'preliminary

---

[11] Case C-321/03 [2007] *ECR* I-687. A photograph of the bin can be seen in the case report and also in Chapter 30, Fig. 30.2, p. 823.

[12] Ibid. The Advocate-General seems to provide a test for determining whether the application relates to an abstract concept (at [AG53]–[AG54]): while a sign can be perceived by one of the five physical senses, a concept is only conceived by the mind.

[13] Ibid., [37]–[40]. The general proposition that an abstract concept cannot be claimed as a sign has been subsequently confirmed in *Schunk GmbH v. OHIM* Case T-7/09, EU:T:2010 153, [25].

[14] *Société des Produits Nestlé SA v. Cadbury UK Ltd* [2013] *EWCA Civ* 1174, reversing [2012] *EWHC* 2637 (Ch).

[15] *JW Spear & Son Ltd, Mattel Inc v. Zynga Inc.* [2012] *EWHC* 3345 (Ch), aff'd [2013] *EWCA Civ* 1175, [32].

[16] *Société des Produits Nestlé SA v. Cadbury UK Ltd* [2013] *EWCA Civ* 1174, [51].

obstacle' to registration[17]—namely, that a sign shall not be registered as a trade mark if it consists exclusively of a shape that:

(i)   results from the nature of the goods themselves;

(ii) is necessary to obtain a technical result; or

(iii) gives substantial value to the goods.

After the recent reform package, EU trade mark law extends this preliminary obstacle beyond shapes, to a broader range of signs. Consequently, for each indent Article 7(1)(e) presently refers to 'the shape, or another characteristic'.[18] The latter is understood to include other product characteristics which might be applied for as a trade mark, such as a colour which may be chosen for its technical function (radiating heat or increasing visibility).

3.1 PRELIMINARY ISSUES

Before looking at each of the exclusions in detail, it is worth noting five features that they have in common.

(i) The exclusions seem generally to be understood as aimed at promoting competition. In *Phillips v. Remington*,[19] the Court of Justice referred to Article 3(1)(e) in general as being:

> . . . intended to prevent the protection conferred by the trade mark right from being extended . . ., so as to form an obstacle preventing competitors from freely offering for sale products incorporating such technical solutions or functional characteristics in competition with the proprietor of the trade mark.[20]

The 'natural, functional or ornamental' shape of goods is a feature that consumers might value in their own right, and thus a feature in relation to which (absent any other intellectual property protection) there should be competition.[21] If such shapes (or other characteristics) could be protected indefinitely under trade mark law, this would subvert the logic of having finite terms of protection under other intellectual property regimes. Without such an exclusionary filter, a shape which was sufficiently technical to qualify for a 20-year term of patent protection could then rely upon that period of exclusivity to claim trade mark protection on the basis of acquired distinctiveness, thereby gaining indefinite protection, since trade marks can be renewed every ten years. Trade mark law, which is intended to facilitate competition by reducing consumer search costs in the marketplace, would instead inhibit competition.[22] In this respect, section 3(2) plays a similar role to that played in US trade mark law by the doctrines of 'mechanical functionality' and 'aesthetic functionality'.[23]

---

[17]   *Koninklijke Philips Electronics NV v. Remington Consumer Products*, Case 299/99 [2002] *ECR* I–5475. But this description did not preclude the OHIM from rejecting an application on this basis after it had already reviewed distinctiveness: *Bang & Olufsen v. OHIM*, Case T-508/08, [2011] *ECR* II–6975, [40].

[18]   As does TMD 2015, Art. 4(1)(e); cf. TRIPS, Art. 15(1).

[19]   *Koninklijke Philips Electronics NV v. Remington Consumer Products*, Case 299/99 [2002] *ECR* I–5475, [2002] 2 *CMLR* 5.   [20] Ibid., [78].

[21]   Ibid., [AG16] (AG Colomer).

[22]   *Lego Juris A/S v. OHIM*, Case C-48/09P [2010] *ECR* I–8403, [43]–[47] (ECJ, Grand Chamber); *Hauck GmbH & Co. KG v. Stokke A/S*, Case C-205/13, EU:C:2014:322, [AG25]–[AG40] (AG Szpunar).

[23]   It is perhaps reassuring that US scholars have recognized similar difficulties with its jurisprudence: see M. McKenna, '(Dys)Functionality' (2011) 48 *Hous L Rev* 823.

(ii) The section 3(2) exclusions apply only to 'shapes', as did the equivalent EUTMR and TMD provisions until recently. Although this might seem a significant limitation, the courts have interpreted it flexibly. The Court of Justice has held that it applies to packaging of products that have no intrinsic shape of their own (such as liquids or granules).[24] Moreover, the Court has confirmed that figurative marks which depict the underlying products may themselves be treated as 'shapes'.[25] In *Yoshida Metal v. OHIM*,[26] the General Court considered whether the exclusion might apply to a figurative mark representing the handle of a kitchen knife (Fig. 36.1). The Court found that Article 7(1)(e) made 'no distinction between three-dimensional shapes, two-dimensional shapes, or two-dimensional representations of three-dimensional shapes'.[27] This, perhaps, reflects the fact that there seems no good reason why the 'competition policy' should not, in fact, be equally applied to such marks.[28] On appeal, the Court of Justice endorsed this approach and additionally clarified that the mode of representation of a mark could not restrict the registry. While the graphical representation requirement had a scope definition objective—'in order to determine the precise subject of the protection afforded by the registered mark to its proprietor'—that could not be abused to 'restrict the competent authority's examination under' the functionality objections.[29] The registry was entitled to look beyond the (supposedly two dimensional) representation and consider the application in the round, as well as the 'the actual use made of the trade mark following its registration', provided that use shed light on the situation at the time of filing the application.[30]

(iii) To be excluded, the sign must consist 'exclusively' of an excluded 'natural, functional or ornamental' shape. Does this require the sign in its entirety—one hundred percent of it—to be natural, ornamental, or functional? If so, it would be all too easy to bypass the exclusion via the addition of a single capricious element that is not affected by the relevant indent. In *Lego*,[31] the Court of Justice reinterpreted this by asking instead

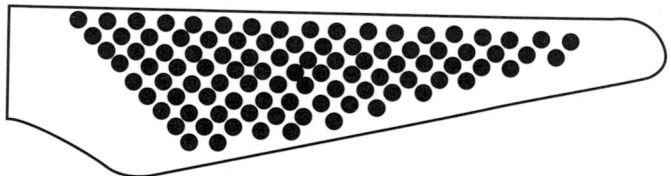

Fig. 36.1 Yoshida kitchen knife handle design

Source: Pi-Design AG v. Yoshida, Case C-340/12P (6 March 2014) (ECJ, Seventh Chamber)

---

[24] *Henkel's Application*, Case C-218/01 [2004] *ECR* I–1725, [35], [37].

[25] *Storck v. OHIM*, Case C-25/05P [2006] *ECR* I–5739, 5755, [29] (CTMR, Art. 7(1)(b), case law on shapes was deemed equally applicable to application to register a two-dimensional image of sweets). In contrast, the English Court of Appeal has held that the shape exclusions do not operate in relation to two-dimensional device marks representing excluded three-dimensional shapes: *Koninklijke Philips Electronics NV v. Remington Consumer Products* [2006] *FSR* (30) 537, [94]–[100]. This is now questionable authority.

[26] *Yoshida Metal v. OHIM*, Case T-416/10 (8 May 2012) (GC), aff'd *Pi-Design AG v. Yoshida*, Joined Cases C-337/12P–C-340/12P [2014] *ETMR* 32.   [27] *Yoshida v. OHIM*, Case T-416/10 (8 May 2012) (GC), [24].

[28] Especially where it is a tactical move to repackage a three-dimensional mark as a two-dimensional or figurative representation, in order to escape the more rigorous scrutiny reserved for the former: D. Gangjee, 'Paying the Price for Admission: Non-Traditional Marks across Registration and Enforcement', in Calboli and Senftleben (2018). In EU law, these exclusions have now been broadened to apply to other characteristics as well. Cf. *Koninklijke Philips Electronics NV v. Remington Consumer Products* [2006] *FSR* (30) 537, [94] (competition policy does not apply in the case of abstract representations of shapes).

[29] *Pi-Design AG v. Yoshida*, Joined Cases C-337/12P–C-340/12P [2014] *ETMR* 32, [57]–[58].

[30] Ibid., [60]–[61].

[31] *Lego Juris v. OHIM*, Case C-48/09P [2010] *ECR* I–8403 (ECJ, Grand Chamber).

whether the 'essential characteristics' of the shape fall within the exclusions. The effect of this is that the addition of trivial features to a shape that is otherwise excluded will not render the sign registrable.[32] In contrast, a shape is not excluded if there is a 'major' non-excluded element.[33] Consequently, one technique for avoiding this exclusion is to combine the sign being applied for with other non-excluded elements, such as a word mark, whereupon the sign in question no longer consists *exclusively* of an objectionable shape or other characteristic.[34]

In determining which characteristics are 'essential' and which are 'trivial', the Court of Justice has offered some guidance. In *Lego*, the Court indicated that the essential characteristics were to be identified by the authority deciding on the application (i.e. the registry) and not from the perspective of the relevant consumer for those products.[35] The essential characteristics are the 'most important elements of the sign'.[36] Precisely which elements qualify has to be assessed on a case-by-case basis, which gives examiners considerable discretion.[37] The examiner may either base the 'assessment directly on the overall impression produced by the sign, or first examine in turn each of the components of the sign concerned'.[38] Depending on the degree of difficulty, this could involve a simple visual analysis or a more detailed examination, taking into account 'surveys or expert opinions, or data relating to intellectual property rights conferred previously in respect of the goods concerned' such as prior patent or design registrations.[39] In identifying the essential characteristics, consumer perception is not in any way dispositive—these exclusions apply notwithstanding how distinctive a sign may in fact be—but it remains a relevant criterion of assessment,[40] which may have additional significance for the 'ornamental' exclusion (are consumers likely to see the identified elements as having aesthetic appeal?).[41] It has recently been suggested that the function of the goods concerned (as indicated in the registration application) will provide guidance in both identifying the essential characteristics and determining whether they perform a technical function.[42]

The fact that the exclusions apply only where the sign applied for consists 'exclusively' of the excluded features, even when interpreted liberally, leaves open at least two difficulties. First, what happens if some features of a shape are excluded under one exclusion and the remainder under another? Is the mark registrable because, when viewed

---

[32] Ibid., [52]. See *Koninklijke KPN Nederland NV v. Benelux-Merkenbureaus*, Case C-363/99 [2005] 2 *CMLR* (10) 184, 209, [AG70]–[AG74]; *DKV Deutsche Krankenversicherung v. OHIM*, Case C-104/00P [2002] *ECR* I–7561, [AG51]–[AG54].

[33] *Lego Juris v. OHIM*, Case C-48/09P [2010] *ECR* I–8403, [54] (referring to a 'major non-functional element, such as a decorative or imaginative element which plays an important role in the shape'; Lego unsuccessfully argued that since it had applied for the shape of a red toy brick as a mark, the colour red—from the perspective of the relevant consumer—would be a distinctive and dominant, yet non-technical element, allowing it to escape the 'technical result' exclusion).

[34] For a successful attempt at combining a logo with a shape, see *Lidl Stiftung & Co. KG v. Crocs Inc.*, R 3021/2014–5 (OHIM, Fifth BoA) (CROCS shoes with crocodile logo). For an unsuccessful attempt at adding a visually insignificant word mark to a shape, see *Flamagas, SA v. EUIPO, MatMind Srl*, Case T-580/15, EU:T:2017:433 (CLIPPER on a lighter). [35] *Lego Juris v. OHIM*, Case C-48/09P [2010] *ECR* I–8403, [68].

[36] Ibid., [69]. [37] See *Reddig v. OHIM*, Case T-164/11, EU:T:2012:443.

[38] *Lego Juris v. OHIM*, Case C-48/09P [2010] *ECR* I–84, [70]. [39] Ibid., [71].

[40] Ibid., [75]–[76].

[41] *Hauck GmbH & Co. KG v. Stokke A/S*, Case C-205/13, EU:C:2014:322, [AG90]–[AG95] (AG Szpunar); [2014] *ETMR* 60, [34] (CJEU).

[42] *Simba Toys GmbH v. EUIPO*, Case C-30/15P, EU:C:2016:350, [83] (AG Szpunar) (where the shape of the Rubik's Cube toy was applied for, 'the function of the goods concerned [related to a] three-dimensional puzzle, that is to say a brain-teaser consisting of a logical arrangement of movable elements'. These moveable elements formed part of the essential characteristics and enabled (functional) rotation capacity).

from the perspective of each exclusion, the sign cannot be said to be 'exclusively' natural, functional, or ornamental? Bearing in mind the policy goal of the exclusions, the answer should be 'no': for a sign to be registrable, it must not subsist exclusively of matter covered by any of the three exclusions. However the Court of Justice held otherwise, on a reference in relation to a child's high-chair (Fig. 36.2), some features of which appeared to be 'natural' while others were 'ornamental'.[43] It subsequently confirmed this stance when the English High Court referred the same issue in relation to the shape of a chocolate bar (Fig. 36.3), all features of which were said to be excluded, but some as 'natural' and others as 'functional'.[44] Therefore the so-called mosaicking of exclusions—combining ornamental characteristics with natural or functional ones in order to reject the sign—is not permitted.

A further and related problem concerns the *consequences* of a finding that a sign does not comprise 'exclusively' excluded matter. The present approach to section 3(2) considers signs as a whole, in terms of their essential characteristics. What if a very significant part of the sign is entirely functional or ornamental but this falls short of all the essential characteristics? There is a real danger that if excluded features form a substantial part of a registered sign, a competitor using these features might be treated as having used a 'similar sign' for the purposes of infringement. The infringement tests rely on the perspective of the average consumer who will not ignore substantial natural, technical, or ornamental

Fig. 36.2 Stokke TRIPP-TRAPP chair design
Source: Hauck GmbH & Co. KG v. Stokke A/S, Case C-205/13

---

[43] *Hauck GmbH & Co. KG v. Stokke A/S*, Case C-205/13 [2014] *ETMR* 60, [39]–[41] (design for the TRIPP-TRAPP chair).
[44] *Société des Produits Nestlé SA v. Cadbury UK Ltd*, Case C-215/14 [2015] *ETMR* 50, [45]–[51]; cf. [2014] *EWHC* 16 (Ch), [68]–[71], [75] (Arnold J).

Fig. 36.3 Nestlé's chocolate bar trade mark

Source: Société des Produits Nestlé SA v. Cadbury UK Ltd [2014] *EWHC* 16 (Ch) (reference to ECJ pending as Case C-215/14)

elements.[45] As we will see in Chapter 40, there is no explicit exception permitting a competitor to utilize freely the excluded aspects of a registered shape, even if they do so honestly (although the recent reforms may have implicitly created a defence in this regard).[46] In contrast, US law offers just such a defence.[47]

(iv) Perhaps most importantly, these objections cannot be overcome by showing that the sign is recognized as distinctive. The Court of Justice thus stated that if the shape of jeans (having an oval kneepad and two lines of sloping stitching from hip height to crotch height) gave substantial value to the goods and so was unregistrable, it was of no consequence—for trade mark law—that consumers would recognize the shape and understand it as indicating that G-Star had made the jeans.[48] This result might be open to criticism, on the basis that consumers who do consider a shape as indicating trade origin might be deceived when competitors sell the same shape.[49] However, it seems that the law of passing off might operate in such circumstances at the very least to ensure that the product is sold in such a way that no deception occurs.[50]

(v) Unlike section 3(2), Article 7(1)(e) has been amended to include not just shapes but other characteristics as well, across all three indents.[51] This expansion is premised on the same policy rationales outlined earlier. Certain product features or characteristics which consumers may seek in the goods of competitors should be left freely available. These characteristics are more likely to be found in non-traditional marks. Under the 'nature of the goods' exclusion, the EUIPO gives the examples of a sound mark representing the

---

[45] Cf. *Lego Juris v. OHIM*, Case C-48/09P [2010] *ECR* I–8403, [72] (the Court assumes that if an 'important' part of the sign were functional, another trader's use of merely the functional element would not be use of a similar mark. It implies that the scope of protection is reduced for the purposes of infringement analysis.)

[46] Although it might be said that such features are inherently non-distinctive, so that the new extension of the descriptiveness exception (reflected in TMD 2015, Art. 14(1)(b) but not yet incorporated into s. 11(2)(b)) to allow for use of non-distinctive elements of a registered mark would offer a defence. See Chapter 41, section 4.3 p. 1139.   [47] US Trademark Act of 1946, §33(b)(8), 15 *USC* §1115(b)(8).

[48] *Benetton v. G Star*, Case C-371/06 [2007] *ECR* I–7709. See also *Yoshida Metal v. EUIPO, Pi-Design*, Case C-421/15P, EU:C:2017:360, [34].

[49] G. Dinwoodie, 'The Death of Ontology: A Teleological Approach to Trademark Law' (1999) 84 *Iowa L Rev* 611 (arguing that courts 'should explore the possibility of conditioning a defendant's right to copy a functional design on compliance with labelling or other requirements that minimize consumer confusion').

[50] See Chapter 32, section 2.1.2, pp. 871–2; Chapter 33, section 4.5.2, p. 906. Indeed, the Court in *Lego Juris v. OHIM*, Case C-48/09P [2010] *ECR* I–8403, [61], seems to hint that unfair competition rules might operate to prevent 'slavish imitation'.   [51] See also the amended TMD 2015, Art. 4(1)(e).

sound of motorbikes for motorbikes as goods, or an olfactory mark of a scent for per-fumes.[52] Similarly, a colour could add substantial (aesthetic) value to a product.[53] One cat-egory of two-dimensional signs which may be affected by this expansion is pattern marks, since they apply to the surface of goods and potentially add ornamental value.[54] However 'characteristics' should not extend to cover conventional figurative marks (in the form of images or drawings), since Article 7(1)(e) seeks to regulate characteristics or features that are intrinsic to the goods, as opposed to appearing on labels applied to them. Since the Trade Marks Act 1994 has not yet been amended to include 'characteristics', the analysis that follows is restricted to shapes. Nevertheless the reasoning which follows should be more generally applicable to other characteristics as well.

3.2 WHERE THE SHAPE RESULTS FROM THE NATURE OF THE GOODS THEMSELVES

Section 3(2)(a) provides that a sign shall not be registered where it consists exclusively of a shape that results from the nature of the goods themselves.[55] The Court of Justice has now clarified that this exclusion applies in three situations: (i) for natural products which have no substitute, such as the shape of a banana for bananas; (ii) for regulated products, whose dimensions are prescribed by legal standards, such as a rugby ball; as well as (iii) for 'shapes with essential characteristics which are inherent to the generic function or func-tions of such goods'.[56] In doing so, the Court endorsed the Advocate-General's reasoning, which is instructive as regards this third category. Certain generic features of a product—such as the lid, handle, or spout of a kettle—usually result from its practical function. Users are likely to seek these features in the products of all manufacturers. Where the shape consists of little else besides these generic and practically functional features, for which—in economic terms—there is no equally good substitute, it falls within the exclu-sion and cannot be registered, notwithstanding evidence of acquired distinctiveness.[57] In extending the exclusion beyond the first two categories to cover 'generic' shapes as well, the Advocate-General rejected a restrictive interpretation of this provision which would have it only apply 'to goods which do not have alternative shapes' and for which there is no design freedom i.e. only natural or regulated shapes.[58]

---

[52] EUIPO *Examination Guidelines*, Part B, Section 4, Chapter 6, [2] ('Shape or Other Characteristics Resulting from the Nature of the Goods').

[53] See *Christian Louboutin v. Van Haren Schoenen BV*, Case C-163/16, EU:C:2017:495 (AG Szpunar) (as this related to the pre-amendment exclusion, which was restricted to shapes, the positioning of the colour red on the undersoles of high heeled shoes was held to be 'in relation' to the shape of the product and conse-quently, to add substantial aesthetic value. However the reference is being re-heard at present).

[54] Previously pattern marks have been excluded on the basis of lacking distinctiveness. See *Louis Vuitton Malletier v. OHIM, Nanu-Nana Handelsgesellschaft mbH*, Case T-359/12, EU:T:2015:215. However Art. 7(1)(e), if applicable, would now override even acquired distinctiveness arguments for such marks.

[55] EUTMR, Art. 7(1)(e)(i); TMD 2015, Art. 4(1)(e)(i) (extending beyond shapes to other characteristics).

[56] *Hauck GmbH & Co. KG v. Stokke A/S*, Case C-205/13 [2014] *ETMR* 60, [24]–[25].

[57] *Hauck GmbH & Co. KG v. Stokke A/S*, Case C-205/13 (14 May 2014) EU:C:2014:322, [AG49]–[AG63] (AG Szpunar) (however, the creative expression of an otherwise functional element—such as a stylized gui-tar shape which departs from the standard template of a guitar shape—would result in the exclusion not applying; [AG64])

[58] Ibid., [AG45]. For similar reasoning, where the existence of alternatives does not disable the exclusion, see *Société de Produits Nestlé SA v. Cadbury UK Ltd*, O/257/13 (20 June 2013) (A. James); [2014] *EWHC* 16 (Ch), [28], [30] (Arnold J). Cf. *Philips v. Remington* [1999] *RPC* 809 (CA), 820; *Société de Produits Nestlé SA v. Unilever plc* [2003] *ETMR* (53) 681, 688, [14]–[15].

The policy rationale or public interest underlying this indent is similar to the functional and ornamental exclusions. If trade mark protection is granted to the characteristics of a product which a user is likely to seek in the products of a competitor, trade mark law descends into becoming an obstacle to healthy competition. 'All three grounds serve to keep in the public domain the essential characteristics of particular goods which are reflected in their shape'.[59]

One question that is raised by the exclusion is: what is meant by the phrase, 'the goods themselves'? The way in which this question is answered is important, given that the more narrowly the 'goods themselves' is defined, the more likely it is that the shape will correspond to the goods in question and thus be excluded. This question was considered in *Philips v. Remington* both at first instance[60] and by the Court of Appeal,[61] where the issue was whether the shape of a three-headed rotary shaver fell within the scope of section 3(2)(a) (see Fig. 36.4).

At first instance, Jacob J said that it was possible for the 'goods themselves' to be defined either as 'three-headed rotary shavers', 'electrical shavers', 'mechanical shavers', or 'shavers' as such. As opposed to their formal classification on the application form, the judge preferred an approach which prioritized the manner in which the goods were regarded as a 'practical business matter'; in other words, how they were viewed as articles of commerce. On this basis, he concluded that the relevant goods were 'electrical shavers'.[62] By contrast, the Court of Appeal placed greater reliance on the way in which the mark was classified, with the caveat that registries and courts should be alert to the possibility of applicants tactically classifying goods and services broadly to escape the exclusion.[63]

While the Court of Justice has not yet addressed the issue, it has been considered in the context of a challenge to the registration of the shape of Lego mini-figures, which had been applied for in relation to 'games and playthings' in Class 28. The invalidation applicant argued in favour of a functional approach to construing the goods; narrowing it down from the broader 'games and playthings' in the registration to the specific toys depicted (here, figures) which had the ability to interlock with other toy bricks.[64] However

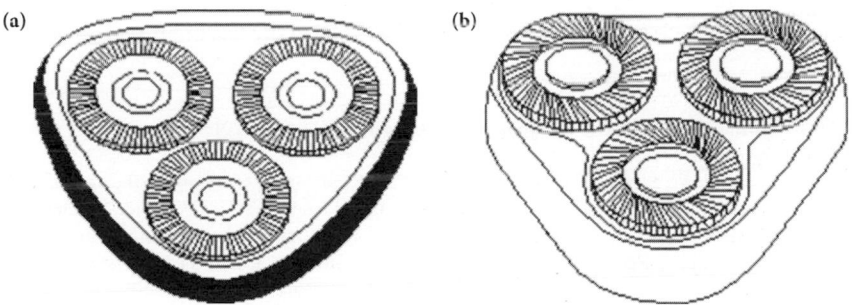

Fig. 36.4 Philips three-headed electric shaver mark
Source: Koninklijke Philips Electronics NV

[59] *Hauck GmbH & Co. KG v. Stokke A/S*, Case C-205/13, EU:C:2014:322, [AG27]–[AG28]; aff'd by the CJEU, [17]–[20].   [60] *Philips v. Remington* [1998] *RPC* 283 (Pat).
[61] *Philips Electronics NV v. Remington Consumer Products* [1999] *RPC* 809 (CA).
[62] *Philips v. Remington* [1998] *RPC* 283 (Pat), 305.
[63] *Philips Electronics NV v. Remington Consumer Products* [1999] *RPC* 809 (CA), 820.
[64] *Best-Lock (Europe) Ltd v. Lego Juris A/S*, R 1695/2013–4 (OHIM, Fourth BoA).

the argument was insufficiently developed to be pursued on appeal.[65] More revealingly, the issue was again considered in an invalidation challenge to the shape of the Rubik's Cube toy, applied for in relation to 'three-dimensional puzzles' in Class 28. The Advocate-General reasoned that since the assessment of the nature of the goods was a question of fact, it could not be reassessed on appeal save in exceptional circumstances.[66] However the reasoning suggests that in different circumstances, the broad registration classification of 'three-dimensional puzzles' (which come in many different shapes) could give way to the narrower commercial category of puzzle cubes or 'magic cubes', which was a known category in the market at the time of the trade mark application, based on evidence submitted by the cancellation applicant.[67]

3.3 WHERE THE SHAPE IS NECESSARY TO OBTAIN A TECHNICAL RESULT

The second limitation on the types of shape that can be registered as trade marks is set out in section 3(2)(b) of the 1994 Act.[68] These provide that a sign shall not be registered where it consists exclusively of a shape that is necessary to obtain a technical result. In many ways, section 3(2)(b) is very similar to section 3(2)(a). In *Philips v. Remington* and *Lego*, the Court of Justice has offered two explanations for the exclusion. On the one hand, it has said that the exclusion is designed to ensure that trade mark rights do not impede traders from offering products incorporating 'technical solutions or functional characteristics' that a user or consumer might want.[69] In addition, the Court has noted that the exclusion would also prevent individuals from using registration 'to acquire or perpetuate exclusive rights relating to technical solutions', thereby bypassing the finite duration of patent protection.[70] Nevertheless, it seems that the Court does not restrict the concept of 'technical result' to the meaning given to it in patent law.[71] While clearly a higher threshold than merely functional—since almost every shape has a function or purpose (a glass contains the liquid within it)[72]—this concept includes desirable and practically useful aspects of shapes. Consequently, the exclusion should encompass shapes that facilitate convenient storage or transportation of the goods, or which provide the purchaser with other 'convenience features' such as enhanced strength or the use of the least material.[73]

---

[65] *Best-Lock (Europe) Ltd v OHIM, Lego Juris A/S*, Case T-395/14, EU:T:2015:380, aff'd Case C-451/15P, EU:C:2016:269.

[66] *Simba Toys GmbH v. EUIPO*, Case C-30/15P, EU:C:2016:350, [46] (AG Szpunar) (the appellant would have to establish that the General Court distorted the facts or evidence).   [67] Ibid., [AG36]–[AG50].

[68] EUTMR, Art. 7(1)(e)(ii); TMD 2015, Art. 4(1)(e)(ii) (extending beyond shapes to other characteristics).

[69] *Koninklijke Philips v. Remington*, Case 299/99 [2002] *ECR* I–5475, [78]; *Lego Juris v. OHIM*, Case C-48/09P [2010] *ECR* I–8403, [43].

[70] *Koninklijke Philips v. Remington*, Case 299/99 [2002] *ECR* I–5475, [82]; *Lego Juris v. OHIM*, Case C-48/09P [2010] *ECR* I–8403, [45]–[46].

[71] *Yoshida Metal Industry Co. v. OHIM, Pi-Design*, Joined Cases T-331/10 RENV and T-416/10 RENV, EU:T:2015:302, [59] ('It must moreover be noted that Article 7(1)(e)(ii) . . . is aimed at protecting the shape of goods which is necessary to obtain a technical result, and not only the innovative technical results that may be patented.').

[72] *Yoshida Metal v. EUIPO, Pi-Design*, Case C-421/15P, EU:C:2017:360, [26] (as opposed to merely functional shapes, by 'the terms "exclusively" and "necessary", [Art. 7(1)(e)(ii)] ensures that solely shapes of goods which only incorporate a technical solution, and whose registration as a trade mark would therefore actually impede the use of that technical solution by other undertakings, are not to be registered'). However, merely functional shapes which approximate the generic template may now be excluded under section 3(2)(a).

[73] EUIPO *Examination Guidelines*, Part B, Section 4, Chapter 6, [3] ('Shape or Other Characteristics of Goods Necessary to Obtain a Technical Result').

In *Nestlé SA v. Cadbury*, the question arose as to whether 'technical result' is broad enough to cover how the goods are manufactured, rather than how they are to be used. The application concerned the shape of a four-fingered KIT-KAT chocolate wafer bar. The grooves between each chocolate finger allowed consumers to easily separate them, while the angles of the sides and grooves were determined by a specific chocolate moulding process. The Advocate-General agreed with the referring court that the underlying rationale of the provision sought to keep 'technical solutions', including manufacturing processes, freely available to competitors and thereby excluded from registration.[74] Remarkably, the Court of Justice disagreed, favouring a more literal interpretation that could be reconciled with previous doctrine and concluding that the technical result exclusion applied 'only to the manner in which the goods at issue function and [not] to the manner in which the goods are manufactured'.[75]

(i) When is a shape 'necessary' to achieve a technical result? The key issue in relation to section 3(2)(b) is: when is a shape *necessary* to achieve a technical result? In *Philips v. Remington*, the reference arose from an action brought by Philips against its competitor Remington to prevent the latter from selling three-headed rotary shavers. Having developed such rotary shavers in 1966 and having registered a figurative mark depicting the shaver in 1985, Philips commenced infringement proceedings against Remington in 1995. Remington counterclaimed for invalidity, on the basis that this was a shape *necessary* to achieve a technical result. Philips retaliated by arguing that 'necessary' implied that the shape must be 'the only one' capable of performing the technical function. Demonstrating the existence of other shapes which could achieve the same result (a close and effective shave) would establish that the shape was therefore not absolutely 'necessary' or indispensable to achieve the result. By contrast, Remington argued that 'necessary' required only causal necessity. If the shape was chosen to cause the desired result (a close shave) it was 'necessary' within the meaning of the provision. The trial court initially found for Remington[76] and the Court of Appeal subsequently sought clarification from the Court of Justice on this issue.[77] After outlining the pro-competitive policy basis for this provision, the Court favoured a causal understanding of necessity. It concluded that the exclusion applies where the essential characteristics of the shape 'perform a technical function and were chosen to fulfil that function'.[78] The mere existence of other shapes that could achieve the same technical result is not of itself sufficient to overcome this ground for refusal.[79]

Further guidance on whether a shape is 'attributable to a technical result' has been provided in *Lego Juris*, in which the famous makers of LEGO bricks had registered an image of a red brick as a CTM for, among other things, 'teaching apparatus' in Class 8 and 'games and playthings' in Class 28 (see Fig. 36.5). In the context of an invalidation challenge by a competitor, the Cancellation Division had identified each of the brick's important features (the bosses or studs on top; the secondary projections; the smooth sides; the hollow skirt; and overall shape) and attributed a particular technical function to each feature. This approach was confirmed in all subsequent appeals, up to and including the Court of Justice.[80] Following *Lego*, an EUIPO Board of Appeal has also provided more specific

---

[74] *Société des Produits Nestlé SA v. Cadbury UK Ltd*, Case C-215/14, EU:C:2015:395, [AG72]–[AG78]; agreeing with [2014] *EWHC* 16 (Ch), [68], [72] (Arnold J).

[75] *Société des Produits Nestlé SA v Cadbury UK Ltd*, Case C-215/14 [2015] *ETMR* 50, [52]–[57].

[76] *Philips v. Remington* [1998] RPC 283 (Pat).

[77] *Philips Electronics NV v. Remington Consumer Products* [1999] *RPC* 809 (CA).

[78] *Koninklijke Philips v. Remington*, Case 299/99 [2002] *ECR* I–5475, [80].   [79] Ibid., [81].

[80] *Lego Juris v. OHIM, Mega Brands*, R 856/2004-G [2007] *ETMR* 11(OHIM, GBoA), [54]; Case T-270/06 [2009] *ETMR* 15, [39], [70]–[75]; Case C-48/09P [2010] *ECR* I–8403, [72]–[74].

Fig. 36.5 LEGO Brick
Source: Lego Juris v. OHIM, Case C-48/09P [2010] *ECR* I–8403

guidance: 'the test is whether if the respective element was absent, the technical result would not be obtained, and if the respective element was altered substantially, the technical result would also alter substantially'.[81]

(ii) Reliance on prior patents?   To what extent is the existence of a prior patent relating to the same product considered to be a 'smoking gun', which confirms the technical nature of the shape being applied for? Prior patents are not dispositive but clearly relevant considerations when assessing whether the essential characteristics are necessary to produce a technical result.[82] Much will turn on the scope of the prior patent's claims. Where the prior patent includes the features of the shape applied for as a trade mark to be the preferred embodiment of the invention, this generates a very strong presumption, or 'practically irrefutable' evidence, that those features are technical.[83] However the existence of a prior patent has been considered irrelevant where the overall shape was found to be non-technical (although individual features of the shape had been reflected in the patent claims).[84]

3.4 WHERE THE SHAPE GIVES SUBSTANTIAL VALUE TO THE GOODS

The third restriction placed on the types of shape that may be registered as trade marks is found in section 3(2)(c) of the 1994 Act.[85] These provide that a sign shall not be registered where it consists exclusively of a shape that gives substantial value to the goods.[86] The Court of Justice has now addressed this exclusion in *Hauck*, which related to an application for the shape of a children's chair. The Advocate-General suggested that the teleological purpose of the provision is to establish a demarcation between the protection conferred by trade mark law and that conferred by industrial designs and copyright.[87]

---

[81] *L&D v. Julius Sämann Ltd*, R 1283/2013–4 (OHIM, Fourth BoA), [36].

[82] *Lego Juris v. OHIM, Mega Brands*, Case C-48/09P [2010] *ECR* I–8403, [85]; *Yoshida Metal Industry Co. v. OHIM, Pi-Design*, Joined Cases T-331/10 RENV and T-416/10 RENV, EU:T:2015:302, [54]–[59].

[83] *Lego Juris v. OHIM, Mega Brands*, R 856/2004-G [2007] *ETMR* 11, [8], [40], [47], (OHIM, GBoA).

[84] *Best-Lock (Europe) Ltd v. Lego Juris A/S*, R 1695/2013–4 (OHIM, Fourth BoA) (shape of a LEGO mini-figure).

[85] EUTMR, Art. 7(1)(e)(iii); TMD 2015, Art. 4(1)(e)(iii) (extending beyond shapes to other characteristics).

[86] For discussion, see A. Kur, 'Too Pretty to Protect? Trade Mark Law and the Enigma of Aesthetic Functionality', in J. Drexl et al. (eds), *Technology and Competition: Essays in Honour of Hans Ullrich* (2009), 139–60, updated in 2011 and available online at http://papers.ssrn.com/sol3/papers.cfm?abstract_id=1935289.

[87] *Hauck GmbH v. Stokke*, Case C-205/13, EU:C:2014:322, [AG70] (AG Szpunar).

Its rationale is to 'prevent the monopolization of the external features of goods which do not perform a technical or practical function and at the same time substantially enhance the attractiveness of goods and strongly influence consumer preferences'.[88] Its coverage therefore extends beyond works of fine or applied art to cover even 'practical objects', where 'design is one of the fundamental elements which determine their attractiveness, and thus the market success of the goods concerned'.[89] Aesthetic appeal is thereby translated into economic value. Adopting this line of reasoning, the Court of Justice rejected a narrow interpretation of this provision, which would have restricted its application to those products which are solely or primarily purchased on the basis of their aesthetic appeal, such as jewellery or sculptures.[90] The exclusion would also 'apply to a sign which consists exclusively of the shape of a product with several characteristics each of which may give that product substantial value'.[91] It would therefore apply to 'blended' shapes like the TRIP TRAPP chair, which appealed to consumers not only on the basis of its visual style but also on the basis of its safety, comfort, and reliability. Consequently, aesthetic appeal is a necessary requirement but need not be the only or even primary basis for the product's appeal to consumers, so long as it is a significant factor.[92]

Restated as a workable test, the objective is to assess whether the aesthetic value of the shape is sufficiently substantial, in its own right, to determine to a large extent the commercial value of the product and a consumer's decision to purchase it.[93] In terms of the factors to be considered when assessing this, the Court clarified that (i) alongside the relevant consuming public's perception of the shape of the product, additional criteria would include (ii) the nature of the category of goods (is visual appeal usually important for that category?), (iii) the artistic value of the shape in question, (iv) its dissimilarity from other shapes in common use on the market concerned, (v) a substantial price difference in relation to similar products, and (vi) the development of a promotion strategy which focuses on accentuating the aesthetic characteristics of the product in question.[94]

Bang & Olufsen conveniently illustrates the nature of evidence that can be provided under these headings.[95] While consumer perception was not dispositive, for the category of high-end speakers, the slender, stylistic design of the speaker was clearly a motivating factor for consumer purchases. The manufacturer also emphasized that design as part of its branding efforts. Evidence from the trade— in the form of distributors and resellers—also suggested that 'the shape [was] perceived as a kind of pure, slender, timeless sculpture for music reproduction'. The fact that consumers also appreciated its other characteristics, such as technical sound quality, did not detract from the conclusion that its aesthetic value significantly added to its overall commercial value and appeal.[96] More recently, Arnold J. applied the *Hauck* criteria in a dispute relating to the shape of a London taxi.[97] He made two important preliminary clarifications. First, the shape should add *substantial* aesthetic value (in a sense relevant for design law) and

---

[88] Ibid., [AG80].   [89] Ibid., [AG81]–[AG84].

[90] *Hauck GmbH & Co. KG v. Stokke A/S*, Case C-205/13 [2014] *ETMR* 60, [31]–[32].

[91] Ibid., [36].

[92] *Bang & Olufsen v. OHIM*, Case T-508/08 [2012] *ETMR* 10, [73]–[77] (pencil-shaped loudspeaker, which had considerable aesthetic appeal but was also purchased for its sound quality and brand appeal).

[93] EUIPO *Examination Guidelines*, Part B, Section 4, Chapter 6, [4] ('Shape or Other Characteristics Giving Substantial Value to the Goods').

[94] *Hauck GmbH & Co. KG v. Stokke A/S*, Case C-205/13 [2014] *ETMR* 60, [34]–[35].

[95] *Bang & Olufsen v. OHIM*, Case T-508/08 [2012] *ETMR* 10.   [96] Ibid., [73]–[77]

[97] *The London Taxi Corporation Ltd v. Frazer-Nash Research Ltd* [2016] *EWHC* 52 (Ch), [196]–[215].

therefore 'goodwill derived from sales and advertising is not relevant'. Brand value did not count. Second, a relevant (but not sufficient) indicator of *substantiality* would be to compare the shape in question with the shapes of equivalent articles.[98] A systematic analysis of the evidence in accordance with criteria (i)-(vi) listed earlier led to the conclusion that the shape added substantial value. Arnold J observed that in seeking both registered trade mark and design protection for the shape, the mark would also offend the underlying policy of preventing a finite, 25-year design monopoly from being indefinitely extended via trade mark law.[99]

(i) Does substantial value extend beyond aesthetic appeal? Or stated differently, would other characteristic product features—besides aesthetic appeal—that also add substantial value trigger the exclusion? There are two reasons for thinking this might be the case. First, the sweeping conclusion of the Court of Justice seems to leave this possibility open: 'the ground for refusal of registration set out in [TMD 1989, Article 3(1)(e)(iii)] may apply to a sign which consists exclusively of the shape of a product with several characteristics each of which may give that product substantial value'.[100] However this must be qualified in light of the question referred. The Court was asked if the provision would apply to 'blended' shapes which appealed to consumers for a range of reasons (aesthetics, ergonomic design, comfort, safety, etc.). Its reasoning suggests that it is sufficient if aesthetic appeal is *an* important product characteristic which motivates consumers to purchase the shape; there may be others as well and this does not prevent the exclusion from applying.[101] Second—and more convincingly—the policy rationale underlying this provision would also apply to situations where consumers valued a shape based on these other characteristics. In the absence of patent protection, a desirable safety or comfort feature ought to be excluded from trade mark protection, since it would add substantial (albeit non-aesthetic) value to a product. Some EUIPO Boards of Appeal apparently favour this broader interpretation,[102] although the Court may not have intended *Hauck* to be read this expansively.

(ii) What is excluded from 'substantial value'? The EUIPO has clarified that not any shape which is pleasing or attractive will be caught by the exclusion, 'given that in modern business there is no product of industrial utility that has not been the subject of study, research and industrial design before its eventual launch on the market'.[103] Therefore 'substantial' seems to have significance in this regard. Additionally, if a shape is attractive to consumers on the basis of reputation or brand appeal, the exclusion is inapplicable.[104] However where a shape has both aesthetic and brand appeal, the exclusion will still apply.[105]

---

[98] Ibid., [209].   [99] Ibid., [213]–[215].

[100] *Hauck GmbH & Co. KG v. Stokke A/S*, Case C-205/13 [2014] *ETMR* 60, [36].

[101] Additionally, the factors adopted by the Court (at [34]–[35]) revolve around assessing the aesthetic appeal of a product.

[102] *Consorzio Origini v. Vitra Collections AG*, R 664/2011-5, (OHIM, Fifth BoA), [15] ('The [exclusion] is not limited simply to aesthetic value in a shape, but may apply to other characteristics as well, which may be more functional (safety, comfort and reliability are mentioned in the judgment)—but also add value'); *Chocoladefabriken Lindt & Sprüngli AG*, R 2450/2011 G (EUIPO, GBoA), [31]. However both these decisions conclude that the exclusion applies on the basis of the substantial aesthetic value that is added to the shape.

[103] *Gancino Quadrato Singolo*, R 395/1999-3 (OHIM, BoA), [33].

[104] *Christian Louboutin v. Van Haren Schoenen BV* Case C-163/16, EU:C:2017:495, [70] (AG Szpunar) (the 'analysis relates exclusively to the intrinsic value of the shape, and must take no account of attractiveness of the goods flowing from the reputation of the mark or its proprietor.'); *The London Taxi Corporation Ltd v. Frazer-Nash Research Ltd* [2016] *EWHC* 52 (Ch), [209].

[105] *Benetton v. G-Star*, Case C-371/06 [2007] *ECR* I–7709.

4 CAPABLE OF BEING REPRESENTED GRAPHICALLY

The second general hurdle that must be met for a trade mark to be validly registered under section 1(1) of the 1994 Act is that the sign must be 'capable of being represented graphically'. This requirement was discussed in the previous chapter.[106]

5 CAPACITY TO DISTINGUISH

The third and final hurdle that must be met for a trade mark to be validly registered under section 1(1)/Article 4 is that the sign must be 'capable of distinguishing the goods or services of one undertaking from the goods or services of another'. Corresponding to this, section 3(1)(a) provides that failure to comply with any of the requirements of section 1(1) is one of the absolute grounds under which a sign will not be registered.

Following the passage of the Trade Marks Act 1994,[107] the British courts spent a great deal of effort trying to define 'capacity to distinguish' in a way that would both give it meaning and avoid it undermining the other substantive requirements relating to distinctiveness (which we examine in the next chapter). In particular, the courts sought to make sense of the interrelationship between the requirement that a sign be 'capable of distinguishing' and the exclusion in section 3(1)(b) relating to marks that are 'devoid of distinctive character'. The goal was to resolve the seeming conundrum raised by the statute, which seemed to presuppose the possibility of a sign that was simultaneously 'capable of distinguishing' and 'devoid of distinctive character'. The judicial efforts produced a series of inconsistent decisions and impossible tests.[108] Thankfully, in *Philips v. Remington*,[109] the Court of Justice made it clear that these efforts were unnecessary.

As already noted, Remington challenged Philip's registration of the shape of a three headed electrical razor. The Court of Appeal held that the requirement that a sign be 'capable of distinguishing' the goods of one trader from those of another was a preliminary requirement.[110] As such, the Court needed to consider this matter before examining whether the mark was 'devoid of distinctive character'. On the facts, the Court of Appeal held that the three-headed rotary shaver failed the test. This was because the Court considered that a sign needed to have some 'capricious addition'—and not be purely functional—in order to render it capable of distinguishing. A sign with such a capricious alteration could pass the first step (that is, be capable of distinguishing in principle), but fail the second (that is, be devoid of distinctive character on the actual evidence).

The Court of Justice held that there was no 'capricious alteration' test in European law.[111] It also made it clear that if a sign was, in fact, distinctive (either by nature or by use), then it would be treated by definition as 'capable of distinguishing' the goods of one undertaking from those of others.[112] More specifically:

[T]here is no category of marks which is not excluded from registration by Article 3(1)(b), (c), and (d) and Article 3(3) [of the TMD 1989] on the ground that such marks are incapable of distinguishing the goods of the proprietor of the mark from those of other undertakings.[113]

---

[106] See Chapter 35, section 2.1.3, pp. 934–9.   [107] Bently and Sherman (2001), 769–73.
[108] *Dyson v. Registrar of Trade Marks* [2003] *ETMR* (77) 937, 945, [16].
[109] *Koninklijke Philips v. Remington*, Case 299/99 [2002] *ECR* I–5475.
[110] *Philips v. Remington* [1999] *RPC* 809 (CA).
[111] *Koninklijke Philips v. Remington*, Case 299/99 [2002] *ECR* I–5475, [41]–[46].   [112] Ibid., [39].
[113] Ibid., [40].

The Court of Justice suggested that Articles 2 and 3(1)(a)–(d) of the TMD 1989 needed to be 'read together'. Each provides flavour to the other. Article 3(1)(a) 'is intended essentially to exclude from registration signs which are not generally capable of being a trade mark'.[114] In this respect, it is 'like the rule laid down by Article 3(1)(b), (c), (d)'.[115] The three specific exclusions are elaborations of the basic requirement of capacity to distinguish. If a mark is devoid of distinctive character, it lacks capacity to distinguish; if a sign is descriptive, it lacks capacity to distinguish, and so forth. But Article 3(1)(a) does not 'constitute a separate ground for refusing registration in connection with lack of distinctiveness'.[116] In effect, Article 3(1)(a) was reduced to testing whether the 'sign' and 'graphical representation' requirements were met.

6 PROTECTION OF SERVICE MARKS FOR RETAIL SERVICES

Service marks—that is, signs that are used in connection with the provision of services—first became registrable in the United Kingdom as a result of the Trade Marks (Amendment) Act 1984. Service marks are treated in the same way as trade marks by the 1994 Act. This enables the providers of professional, financial, commercial, or personal services to obtain the same statutory protection for their goodwill as is given to the manufacturers and sellers of goods.

Although not listed in the Nice System of Classification, it is now clear that the EUIPO and member states must allow for registration of marks for 'retail services'. In *Praktiker Bau-und Heimwerkermärkte AG*,[117] the applicant had sought to register 'Praktiker' in Germany for 'retail trade in building, home improvement and gardening goods for the do-it-yourself sector'. The German Federal Patent Court (*Bundespatentgericht*) referred various questions to the Court of Justice relating to registration for retail services. The Court held that there was nothing in the Trade Marks Directive that required the concept of 'services' to be restrictively defined and noted that retail trade included the selection of goods, as well as the provision of services 'aimed at inducing the consumer to conclude transactions with the trader rather than a competitor'.[118] The Court stated that objections

---

[114] Ibid., [37].

[115] Ibid., [38]. It has been argued that this decision still leaves room for an understanding of s. 1 as concerned with whether a sign has capacity to distinguish in the abstract, whereas s. 3(1)(b)–(d) concerns whether a sign is distinctive for the particular goods or services for which registration is sought: D. Keeling, 'About Kinetic Watches, Easy Banking and Nappies that Keep a Baby Dry' [2003] *IPQ* 131, 134–6; *Sat. 1 v. OHIM*, Case C-329/02P [2004] *ECR* I–8317, [AG16]–[AG17] (AG Jacobs). Indeed, the Court of Justice has stated that the fact that a sign is, 'in general, capable of constituting a trade mark' does not mean that the sign necessarily has distinctive character for the purposes of CTMR, Art. 7(1)(b), in relation to a specific product or service: *Henkel v. OHIM*, Joined Cases C-456/01P and C-457/01P [2004] *ECR* I–5089, [32]; *OHIM v. BORCO-Marken-Import Matthiesen GmbH & Co. KG*, C-265/09P [2010] *ECR* I–8265, [29]. This view has been dubbed by Kerly 'the German theory' and heavily critiqued: Kerly, [2–104], [2–108]–[2–111]. The authors of Kerly instead argue that the phrase introduces and encapsulates the 'essential function' of any trade mark.   [116] *Koninklijke Philips v. Remington*, Case 299/99 [2002] *ECR* I–5475, [46].

[117] Case C-418/02 [2005] *ECR* I–5873.

[118] Ibid., [34]. But see *Apple Inc. v. German Patent Office*, Case C-421/13 [2014] *ETMR* 48, [26], where the Court recognizes that a mark can be registered for services 'where those services do not form an integral part of the offer for sale of those goods' such as 'demonstrations by means of seminars of the products that are displayed there.' The Court notes that such services might be 'remunerated'. The tenor of the judgment is quite different from that in *Praktiker*, which specifically rejected the need to specify the services in any detail, and thus casts considerable doubt over the breadth of that holding. Probably the Court in *Apple* intended to clarify that a trader which was selling its own goods (rather than a variety of goods of diverse manufactures), might still offer relevant retail services.

to such registration being of undue breadth could largely be accommodated by judicious application of the 'global assessment' of likelihood on confusion in relation to relative grounds for refusal or infringement. Consequently, a specification would be acceptable in principle if it were to use general words such as 'bringing together a variety of goods, enabling customers to conveniently view and purchase those goods' as long as the goods or type of goods to which the service related was specified.

7 COLLECTIVE AND CERTIFICATION MARKS

UK trade mark law additionally recognizes two forms of collectively used or 'group' marks, which may be used by persons other than the proprietor of the mark, if they satisfy certain conditions.[119] A collective mark is one which distinguishes 'the goods or services of members of the association which is the proprietor of the mark from those of other undertakings'.[120] It indicates that the trader using such a mark is a member of a 'club' or association. This membership helps to distinguish the products of that trader from those of other non-members and an examples would be the mark BIID REGISTERED INTERIOR DESIGNER.[121] In contrast, a certification mark indicates that 'the goods or services in connection with which it is used are certified by the proprietor of the mark in respect of origin, material, mode of manufacture of goods or performance of services, quality, accuracy or other characteristics'.[122] The proprietor of the mark certifies that the products of those using it possess a specific characteristic. Examples that may be familiar include STILTON[123] and the KITEMARK logo.[124] As the first of these suggests, certification or even collective marks can also be used to protect geographical indications (GIs).[125]

Unlike individual trade marks, collective and certification marks pass through two stages of examination. There is the initial examination of the application itself, where the mark is assessed against (slightly modified) absolute and relative grounds. Next, the registry reviews the regulations that govern the use of both types of marks. The Trade Marks Act 1994 contains specific provisions in relation to collective marks in Schedule 1. An applicant is required to file regulations which specify inter alia 'the persons authorised to use the mark, the conditions of membership of the association and, where they exist, the conditions of use of the mark, including any sanctions against misuse'.[126] Schedule 2 sets out the equivalent requirements for certification marks. These include an 'arms' length' condition—the proprietor cannot carry on a business in relation to the products which are being certified[127]—and the need to file regulations setting out 'who is authorised to use the mark, the characteristics to be certified by the mark, how the certifying

---

[119] These types of marks are recognized in several other jurisdiction as well. For an overview, see WIPO, 'Technical and Procedural Aspects Relating to the Registration of Certification and Collective Marks', 15 February 2010 (SCT/23/3).

[120] TMA 1994, s. 49(1). Paris, Art. 7*bis* requires its membership to recognize collective marks.

[121] Reg. No. UK00003127914. BIID stands for the British Institute of Interior Design.

[122] TMA 1994, s. 50(1).

[123] Reg. No. UK0000831407. The mark certifies both the geographical origin as well as method of production for this blue cheese.

[124] Reg. No. UK00002265372 (certifying product safety to standards set by the British Standards Institution, the mark was surrendered in 2012, seemingly in favour of an EUTM registration).

[125] M. Gonzalez, 'Collective, Guarantee and Certification Marks and GIs: Connections and Dissimilarities' (2012) 7 *JIPLP* 251; For GIs, see Chapter 43.　　　[126] TMA 1994, Sch. 1, para. 5.

[127] TMA 1994, Sch. 2, para. 4.

body is to test those characteristics and to supervise the use of the mark, the fees (if any) to be paid in connection with the operation of the mark and the procedures for resolving disputes'.[128] Issues specific to such marks include the modified distinctiveness test that applies to collective and certification marks, the (legal) nature of associations which can own such marks, grounds for revocation and infringement, as well as the extent to which such marks offer legally binding guarantees to consumers.[129] While both marks accommodate groups of users and the governing regulations need to be publicly accessible, collective marks may be seen as relatively more discretionary; certification marks may be used by anyone who complies with the certification specifications.[130]

At the EU level both types of marks are recognized in the TMD 2015.[131]

The former CTM regime recognized collective marks and this has continued into the new EUTM system.[132] However the accommodation of certification marks within the EUTM system is a new development.[133] Curiously, certification marks which certify a product's geographical origin cannot be accepted as EUTMs,[134] although national certification marks, national collective marks, or collective EUTMs which verify geographical origin (for example, as a condition of association membership) can all be registered. Geographical indications are therefore selectively, albeit inexplicably, excluded from being registered as certification marks under the EUTMR.

While both collective marks and certification (or guarantee or standardization) marks have a respectable vintage,[135] the integration of such marks within a system designed primarily around individual marks has been partial. The Court of Justice recently emphasized the functional differences between individual and 'group' marks, on a reference where the proprietor of an individual trade mark was licensing it on the basis that it functioned as a mark of quality in the cotton textiles sector.[136] In other words, the proprietor was using conventional trade mark licensing to indirectly approximate product certification. In the context of a revocation challenge to an EUTM—as a counterclaim to infringement proceedings—the Court was asked whether the mark had been put to 'genuine use'. It concluded that for a mark to be able to fulfil 'its essential role [or function] in the system of undistorted competition [in the internal market] it must offer a guarantee that all the goods or services bearing it have been manufactured or supplied under the control of a single undertaking which is responsible for their quality'.[137] While 'group' marks might guarantee quality without guaranteeing a single commercial source for the

---

[128] TMA 1994, Sch. 2, para. 6(2).

[129] See J. Belson, *Certification and Collective Marks: Law and Practice* (2017); Kerly, Ch 14.

[130] This is encouraged by the UK Registry. See UKIPO, *Manual of Trade Marks Practice* (February 2018), [3.4.2] ('Most certification marks are available for use by any person whose goods or services demonstrate the relevant characteristic being certified').

[131] TMD 2015, Arts 1, 27 (definitions), 28 (guarantee or certification marks, as an optional measure), 29–36 (collective marks, as a mandatory requirement). Under the TMD 2008, Art. 15 it was optional for EU member states to recognize and register such marks.   [132] EUTMR, Arts 74–82.

[133] EUTMR, Arts 83–93.

[134] Confirmed by the EUIPO *Examination Guidelines*, Part B, Section 4, Chapter 16 ('European Union Certification Marks'), [2.1].

[135] Collective marks were first incorporated into Paris, Art. 7*bis* at the Washington revision conference in 1911. See Ricketson (2015) 586–592. Standardization marks were introduced into UK trade mark law via the Trade Marks Act, 1905, s. 62. See N. Dawson, *Certification Trade Marks: Law and Practice* (1988), 15.

[136] *W. F. Gözze Frottierweberei GmbH v. Verein Bremer Baumwollbörse*, Case C-689/15 [2017] *Bus LR* 1795.

[137] Ibid., [41]–[51]. But cf., *The Tea Board v. EUIPO*, Joined Cases C 673/15P–C 676/15P, EU:C:2017:702, [50], [63] (collective marks also have a distinguishing function similar to individual trade marks; they distinguish the goods or services of the members of the association which is the proprietor of the trade mark from those of other undertakings).

products being certified, individual trade marks could not discard the essential origin requirement. The mark was not being used to indicate a single commercial source for the products on which it appeared. Such use was therefore unlikely to sustain the EUTM registration.

As a result of this fundamental difference—'group' marks cannot be distinctive in the same way as individual trade marks, because they are used by multiple and otherwise unrelated traders—the scope of protection for such marks risks being diminished. Distinctiveness is one the regulatory devices for enhancing the scope of protection of a mark. If certification or collective marks with multiple users are considered 'weakly distinctive' in the classical trade mark sense, proprietors or legitimate users will find enforcement challenging.[138] Yet at the same time, such marks are growing in importance and visibility. With the increasing privatization of regulatory functions and the adoption of private governance models in market sectors, trade mark law has the potential to empower consumers by providing reliable, objective information facilitating their choices about where products come from, how they are made, and the values to which a manufacturer is willing to commit. Certification and collective marks are increasingly relevant in this context.[139]

---

[138] *Organismos Kypriakis Galaktokomikis Viomichanias v. OHIM*, Case T-535/10 [2012] *ETMR* 55, [50]–[55].

[139] M. Chon, 'Marks of Rectitude' (2009) 77 *Fordham L Rev* 2311; J. C. Fromer, 'The Unregulated Certification Mark(et)' (2017) 69 *Stanford L Rev* 121.

37

ABSOLUTE GROUNDS FOR REFUSAL

1 INTRODUCTION

In this chapter, we explore the 'absolute' grounds for refusing to register a trade mark. The absolute grounds for refusal are set out in section 3 of the Trade Marks Act 1994, Article 3 of the Trade Marks Directive 2008, and Article 7 of the European Union Trade Mark Regulation (EUTMR).[1] The 'absolute grounds' share two key characteristics. First, with one or two exceptions, the term 'absolute' indicates that the ground for objection relates intrinsically to the sign itself, rather than to the rights of individual third parties. For this reason, these grounds concern matters that can be scrutinized easily by the various offices without reference to third parties.[2] Second, the 'absolute' grounds for refusal are grounds that give effect to a 'public' or 'general' interest (although the public interest underpinning each ground may vary).[3] One consequence of this is that if a sign is registered, which should have been refused on absolute grounds, any person may bring proceedings to have the mark declared invalid.[4]

The absolute grounds for refusal can conveniently be grouped into three general categories. The first is concerned with whether the sign falls within the statutory definition of a trade mark found in sections 1(1) and 3(1)(a) and (2). The second category of grounds, each of which is contained in section 3(1)(b)–(d), excludes from registrability marks that are non-distinctive, descriptive, and generic. The third and more eclectic category, which covers the absolute grounds for refusal set out in section 3(3)–(6), provides that trade marks shall not be registered if they are contrary to public policy or morality, if they are likely to deceive the public, if they are prohibited by law, or if the application was made in bad faith. Specific provisions also exist for specially protected emblems.

---

[1] See also TMD 2015, Art. 4.

[2] This is the chief contrast with 'relative' grounds, discussed in Chapter 38. An absolute ground cannot, in general, be overcome by demonstrating the 'consent' of the right holder to registration. For exceptions, relating to state emblems and, possibly, geographical indications, see section 4.3, p. 1017, and section 4.5, pp. 1023–4.   [3] *Sat. 1 Satellitenfersehen GmbH v. OHIM*, Case C-329/02P [2004] *ECR* I–8317, [25].

[4] TMA 1994, s. 47. A registered mark may be challenged at any stage by any person, by application to the UK Registrar or before the Cancellation Division at the EUIPO (EUTMR, Art. 59), or as a counterclaim to an action based on a national or EUTM (EUTMR, Arts 59 and 128). Such applications cannot be rejected on the ground that the applicant is guilty of 'abuse of rights': *Ultra Air GmbH v. OHIM*, Case T-396/11, EU:T:2013:284, aff'd Case C-450/13P, EU:C:2014:2016.

Before considering each of these general categories in turn, it is perhaps useful to step back and consider the question: when should a legal system deny the possibility of registration to an applicant? We suggest that there are at least five reasons. The first reason for denying registration is that the sign has not been sufficiently precisely defined—perhaps it is incapable of the precise definition that is necessary to define a property right. This explains the rejections relating to the sign and representation requirements under sections 1 and 3(1)(a), which were discussed in Chapter 35. A second reason why a trade mark regime might want to reject an application is where it is impossible, or unlikely, that the sign will function as a trade mark. If consumers will not see the sign as a trade mark, there is simply no justification for its protection as such. This consideration is also reflected in Chapter 35, when discussing whether 'capable of distinguishing' in section 1 was a requirement that differed from 'devoid of distinctiveness' in section 3. A third reason for refusing registration is that granting rights in the particular sign might limit, rather than promote, competition. This reason goes some way towards explaining the exceptions with respect to shapes that were reviewed in Chapter 36, but, as we will see, similar reasoning arises in the context of other grounds of refusal, particularly descriptiveness. Fourth, a legal system might exclude some types of mark from registration simply because it does not want to encourage the use of those types of sign (as would be the case with immoral or deceptive marks), or because it wants to preserve the use to particular contexts (as is the case perhaps, with state emblems). Finally, applications might be thought to need rejection not because of the character of the signs themselves, but because of the behaviour of the applicant. If the applicant appears in some way to be abusing the system, or using it opportunistically, this may be considered a good reasons to reject the application.[5]

2 SUBJECT MATTER

Section 3(1)(a) of the 1994 Act provides that a sign that does not satisfy the requirements of a trade mark as set out in section 1(1)(a) will not be registrable. In practical terms, the requirements to be tested are whether the candidate is specific enough to (i) be a sign and (ii) satisfy the representation requirements. These two requirements, along with the identification of goods or services, are concerned with establishing boundaries to the property rights that registration confers. The types of sign that are potentially registrable are further restricted by section 3(2), which provides special rules in relation to the registration of shapes as trade marks. Because these topics were dealt with in Chapters 35 and 36, it is not necessary to look at them again here.

3 NON-DISTINCTIVE MARKS

The second category of absolute grounds for validity relates to what can be described as non-distinctive, descriptive, or generic marks. More specifically, section 3(1)(b)–(d) and Article 7(1)(b)–(d) of the Regulation provide that the following trade marks shall *not* be registered:

(b) trade marks which are devoid of any distinctive character;

---

[5] *Red Bull v. Sun Mark* [2012] *EWHC* 1929 (Ch), [135] (explaining TMA 1994, s. 3(6), on this basis and identifying two forms of abuse).

(c) trade marks which consist exclusively of signs or indications which may serve, in trade, to designate the kind, quality, quantity, intended purpose, value, geographical origin, or the time of production of the goods or of the rendering of the service, or other characteristics of the goods or service;

(d) trade marks which consist exclusively of signs or indications which have become customary in the current language or in the bona fide and established practices of the trade;[6] . . .

Because each ground represents a separate basis for refusal (or invalidity), if it is to be valid, a mark must not fall within any of the three grounds. While each provision has a distinct sphere of operation, they will often be applied cumulatively[7]—that is, a mark will often be rejected on the basis of more than one ground. In many cases, the tribunals have said that a mark that is descriptive falls within section 3(1)(c) and, as a result, also lacks distinctive character, thus is excluded under section 3(1)(b). In contrast, a sign that is not descriptive may well lack distinctive character and thus be excluded under section 3(1)(b), even though it is not excluded under section 3(1)(c).

Subsections (b)–(d) are all subject to a proviso—namely, that a sign that falls within any of the provisions (that is, a sign that is non-distinctive, descriptive, or generic) is not to be treated as invalid if, as a result of use, it has 'acquired distinctive character'. In other words, the objections in section 3(1)(b)–(d) apply to the 'inherent' characteristics of the sign and can be overcome if the sign comes to be understood by consumers as, in fact, communicating that the particular goods or services in relation to which the sign is used come from one particular trade origin. Sometimes, this distinction between inherent and acquired characteristics of a sign is likened to the characteristics that an individual has from 'nature' and those that they acquire as a result of 'nurture'. A word perceived by consumers as intrinsically empty or meaningless (such as ANDREX or NOXEMA) will be innately distinctive from its 'nature', whereas a descriptive word (DOUBLEMINT for mint chewing gum or OPTIONS for insurance services) will acquire 'distinctive character', if at all, only if there has been such use as to educate the public that the sign operates to distinguish the goods of one undertaking from those of another.

3.1 GENERAL APPROACH

3.1.1 What is the mark?

In order to decide whether a sign is excluded under section 3(1)(b)–(d), it is first necessary to decide what the sign is. In many ways, this is straightforward: we have seen that the sign is that for which registration is sought. This task is made somewhat easier by the fact that the applicant has to submit documentation identifying the mark and indicating whether protection is sought as a word mark, a figurative mark, a colour mark, or a three-dimensional mark.[8]

---

[6] Both the TMD and the EUTMR (formerly CTMR) absolute grounds provisions are derived from Paris, Art. 6*quinquies* (2). See also TRIPS, Art. 15(2).

[7] *Linde AG, Winward Industries, Rado Watch Co Ltd*, Joined Cases C-53/01, C-54/01, C-55/01 [2003] *ECR* I–3161, [45], [67]; *Société des Produits Nestlé SA v. Mars UK Ltd* [2003] *ETMR* (101) 1235, 1250, [42] (Mummery LJ) (although the grounds overlap, they are independent grounds and have to be separately examined).

[8] It has been argued that the system might be more exacting if the Registry were to view the mark in the context of its actual or proposed use: Kerly, [2–047]. The courts do look at such use in the context of assessing infringement (see Chapter 38, section 2.3.1, p. 1040, and Chapter 40, section 4, pp. 1106–8), so it is a fair question. The mark as used was historically the starting point for assessing the object of protection in use-based systems like that of the United States.

3.1.2 The average consumer

In making the necessary predictive assessment, the relevant class from whose perspective the sign must be assessed has been defined as comprising the average consumers of the category of goods.[9] In turn, the relevant consumer has been construed as 'reasonably well-informed and reasonably observant and circumspect'.[10] Although the consumer is assumed to be reasonably observant, the cases make clear that levels of attentiveness vary from sector to sector: the general consumer's level of attentiveness in relation to everyday goods is lower than that of the consumer for expensive goods.[11]

In the case of national marks in the United Kingdom, the average consumer has the characteristics of a British person; whether marks in a foreign language will be treated as registrable or as descriptive will depend on whether the average consumer is likely to understand the meaning of the sign. In turn, this will depend on the extent to which the mark is recognized in its original language, how widely the language is spoken in the United Kingdom, how familiar the word is, and how common it is for foreign words to be used in that trade.[12] Even though this approach could lead to division in the Internal Market, the Court of Justice has given its imprimatur in a case in which the German word for mattresses—MATRATZEN—had been registered in Spain for mattresses![13]

In contrast, Article 7(2) EUTMR provides that the exclusions 'shall apply notwithstanding that the grounds for non-registrability obtain in only part of the Union'. OLUT would thus be unregistrable as a EUTM for alcoholic beverages, given that *olut* means beer in Finnish.[14] As part of the reform package, the Commission had proposed the expansion of this basis for exclusion, on the basis that 'the grounds of non-registrability obtain . . . in other Member States' or 'where a trade mark in a foreign language is translated or transcribed in any script or official language of the Member States'.[15] This approach is known as the doctrine of 'foreign equivalents' in US trade mark law. However,

---

[9] The 'average consumer' is a pivotal figure in trade mark law, akin to the 'person skilled in the art' in patent law. For discussion of the historical origins of the 'average consumer', see J. Davis, 'Locating the Average Consumer: His Judicial Origins, Intellectual Influences and Current Role in European Trade Mark Law' [2005] *IPQ* 183. The extent to which trade mark law requires this consumer to be empirically fleshed out (for example, by survey evidence) or operate as a hypothetical vantage point instead has been considered in: J. Davis, ' Revisiting the Average Consumer: An Uncertain Presence in Trade Mark Law', [2015] *IPQ* 15; G. B. Dinwoodie and D. S. Gangjee, 'The Image of the Consumer in European Trade Mark Law', in D. Leczykiewicz and S. Weatherill (eds), *The Image(s) of the Consumer in EU Law* (2015) 339; K. Weatherall, 'The Consumer as the Empirical Measure of Trade Mark Law' (2017) 80 *MLR* 57; R. Burrell and K. Weatherall, 'Towards a New Relationship between Trade Mark Law and Psychology' (2018) *CLP* (forthcoming).

[10] *Linde AG, Winward Industries, Rado Watch Co Ltd*, Joined Cases C-53/01, C-54/01, C-55/01 [2003] *ECR* I–3161, [41]; *Société des Produits Nestlé v. Mars UK Ltd ('Have a Break')* [2004] *FSR* (2) 16, [23].

[11] Cf. *Henkel KgaA v. OHIM*, Joined Cases C-456/01P and C-457/01P [2004] *ECR* I–5089; *Procter & Gamble v. OHIM*, Joined Cases C-473/01P and C-474/01P [2004] *ECR* I–5173, [62]. In *Smart Technologies*, Case C-311/11P, EU:C:2012:460, [48], the Court of Justice observed that 'it does not necessarily follow that a weaker distinctive character of a sign is sufficient where the relevant public is specialist'.

[12] UK IPO, *Foreign Descriptive Use: Interpretation of the Internet and Registrability of Non-English Words* (May 2007) PAN 1/07.

[13] *Matratzen Concord AG v. Hukla Germany SA*, Case C-421/04 [2006] *ECR* I–2303; *House of Donuts International v. OHIM*, Joined Cases T-333/04 and T-334/04 [2007] *ETMR* (53) 877 (CFI) (donuts not lacking distinctiveness in Spain). Contrast the much stricter US position: *Otokoyama Co. Ltd v. Wine of Japan Import Inc.*, 175 F. 3d. 266 (2nd Cir. 1999).

[14] With the expansion of the EU in 2004, 2011, and 2013, the potential for such objections increased. Note, however, that while existing registrations are automatically extended to these countries, absolute grounds for refusal under Art. 7 (or invalidity based on Art. 59) do not operate where such grounds became applicable merely because of the accession of a new member state: EUTMR, Art. 209(2).

[15] See Bently and Sherman (2014), 931–2.

as a result of the opposition to it by the EU Parliament and national trade mark offices, it was dropped from the final EUTMR.

The tribunal must interpret the sign in the application as the notional consumer would. This process of interpretation will take into account so-called 'normal' and 'fair' use, including use on packaging and in advertising. Thus the assessment takes account of the possibility that the mark will normally be used not only in its represented form, but also orally. Consequently, the mark will be interpreted in terms of the overall impression that it makes on the average consumer—aurally, conceptually, and visually. In the past, British tribunals would operate a general rule that a word that was 'phonetically equivalent' to an unregistrable word was itself unregistrable. It seems today that there is no concrete rule; rather, the Registrar must consider the impression that is produced by the sign aurally and visually, taking account of the goods or services.[16] In situations in which purchasers are attentive and purchase is rarely made orally, a visual variation of a descriptive word (such as KA for cars) may render a sign registrable (even though the sign is phonetically equivalent to a description). However, where the goods are of the sort that are purchased orally, or advertised on the radio or television, mere visual alterations, such as misspellings, of otherwise non-distinctive marks are unlikely to render the sign registrable.

It is important to note in this respect that the sign will normally be viewed as a whole; a sign will not be rejected just because parts of the sign lack distinctiveness or are descriptive or customary in the trade.[17] Nevertheless, consumers may ignore certain elements that they regard as trivial or insignificant. Equally, consumers may readily expand abbreviated forms into their full unabbreviated form. Another situation in which the tribunal will have to assess how the 'reasonably circumspect' consumer interprets a sign is where an applicant combines, shortens, or telescopes two (or more) unregistrable terms. Although consumers tend to interpret signs as a whole, rather than to dismember them into their component parts, certain obvious combinations or abbreviations may immediately be translated back into their (non-registrable parts). Thus EUROLAMB would immediately be interpreted as European lamb and thus, being descriptive (for lamb), be unregistrable. CJEU guidance indicates that the mere fact that an abbreviation derives from two descriptive terms is not dispositive. Actual, or likely, consumer usage of those terms in a descriptive sense or consumer recognition of their descriptive content is more important.[18]

3.1.3 Assessment

Distinctiveness is assessed by the Registrar or the EU Intellectual Property Office (EUIPO) at the time of examination or in response to observations.[19] It is assessed as of the date of application.[20] Where an application is made and it is held that the sign lacks distinctiveness for certain goods, but not others, it should be refused only as regards those goods for

---

[16] *Koninklijke KPN Nederland NV v. Benelux-Merkenbureau*, Case C-363/99 [2004] *ECR* I–1619, [99]; *Campina*, Case C-265/00 [2004] *ECR* I–1699, [40].

[17] *Procter & Gamble Co. v. OHIM (Baby Dry)*, Case C-383/99P [2001] *ECR* I–6251; *Campina*, Case C-265/00 [2004] *ECR* I–1699, [37].

[18] *Strigl and Securvita*, Joined Cases C-90/11 and C-91/11, EU:C:2012:147 (MULTI MARKETS FUND MMF); *Flexi*, Case T-352/12, EU:T:2014:519.

[19] TMA 1994, ss 37 (examination), 38(3) (observations). In the United Kingdom, absolute objections can be raised in opposition proceedings by any person: TMA 1994, s. 38(2).

[20] *Imagination Technologies Ltd v. OHIM*, Case C-542/07P [2009] *ECR* I–4937; *OHIM v. Froch Touristick GmbH*, Case C-332/09P [2010] *ECR* I–49. The Max Planck Institute proposed (without success) that this be altered to the date of examination: Max Planck Institute, *Study on the Overall Functioning of the Community Trade Mark System* (2011), 79, [2.60].

which it lacks distinctiveness.[21] Conversely, where the same ground for refusal is given for a group of goods or services, the registrar may use general reasoning for all of the goods and services that are sufficiently directly and specifically connected, provided the group or category is sufficiently homogeneous.[22] In deciding whether a sign is excluded, the tribunal should take account of all relevant facts and circumstances, including (where pertinent) opinion poll evidence.[23]

Ultimately, the assessment is one of fact. This has at least three consequences. First, care must be taken about making broad generalizations on the basis of previous decisions. It also means that it is not possible to formulate with any precision general rules about whether types of mark will be distinctive. A second consequence of the factual nature of the distinctiveness inquiry is that it is a subject on which different minds may well take different views. In *Doublemint*,[24] Advocate-General Jacobs indicated that, in many situations, 'an element of subjective judgment' will be required in order to determine whether a sign is within the exclusions. Third, the factual assessment in each individual case means that evidence of similar registrations at the UK Trade Marks Registry itself, or that the sign has been regarded as registrable elsewhere, will be of limited value. Although the Court of Justice has yet to confirm the approach,[25] the General Court and English courts have emphasized that each application must be assessed on its merits by the relevant registry.[26] The general principles of equal treatment and sound administration require the EUIPO to treat like cases alike and therefore give due consideration to the reasoning of other EU trade mark registrars in relation to the same mark for similar goods. However, the Office is not bound by these decisions; it must interpret the applicable legal criteria in light of the specific facts of the case before it, to ensure the rigour of the examination process. The rationale for a (possibly illegitimate) national registration elsewhere cannot supplant the reasoning of the Office.[27]

Nevertheless this can generate inconsistency, as a dispute pending before the Court of Justice for NEUSCHWANSTEIN in relation to the well-known Bavarian castle quite starkly illustrates. In the context of a national trade mark registration, the German Federal Court of Justice (*Bundesgerichtshof*) previously held the term to lack distinctiveness in Germany—concluding that the term referred to the castle as a national monument but not the commercial source of souvenirs—and invalidated it,[28] while the EUIPO reasoned that it nevertheless could be distinctive across the European Union, including Germany.[29] British courts have gone one step further and said that evidence about 'other

---

[21] TMD 2008, Art. 13; TMD 2015, Art. 7; EUTMR, Art. 41(8); *Koninklijke KPN Nederland NV v. Benelux-Merkenbureau*, Case C-363/99 [2004] *ECR* I-1619, [112]–[117]. See UK IPO, Partial Refusal (2012) TPN 1/2012.

[22] See for example *salesforce.com, Inc. v. EUIPO*, Case T-134/15, EU:T:2016:366 (SOCIAL.COM rejected across a range of social media products).

[23] *Koninklijke KPN Nederland NV v. Benelux-Merkenbureau*, Case C-363/99 [2004] *ECR* I-1619, [33]–[37].

[24] *Wrigley (Doublemint)*, Case C-191/01P [2003] *ECR* I-12447, [AG56]–[AG57] (AG Jacobs); *Nichols plc v. Registrar of Trade Marks*, Case C-404/02 [2004] *ECR* I-8499, [AG34] (AG Colomer).

[25] So far, the Court of Justice has stated only that a decision in respect of the registrability of a particular mark in one member state is non-binding when another member state or the EUIPO is considering registration of the same mark for similar goods: *KPN Nederland NV*, Case C-363/99 [2004] *ECR* I-1619, [43]; *Develey v. OHIM*, Case C-238/06P [2007] *ECR* I-9375, [72]–[73] (ketchup bottle); *Lindt v. OHIM*, Case C-98/11P, EU:C:2012:307, [50].

[26] *Sykes Enterprises Inc. v. OHIM (Real People, Real Solutions)*, T-130/0 [2002] *ECR* II-5179, [31].

[27] *Agencja Wydawnicza Technopol v. OHIM*, Case C-51/10P [2011] *ECR* I-01541, [73]–[77].

[28] BGH (8 March 2012) I ZB 13/11.

[29] *Bundesverband Souvenir—Geschenke—Ehrenpreise e.V. v. EUIPO*, Case T-167/15, EU:T:2016:391; aff'd by AG Wathelet in C-488/16P, EU:C:2018:3.

marks on the Register is in principle irrelevant when considering a trade mark tendered for registration'.[30]

With these general principles in mind, we now turn to examine in detail the exclusions relating to signs that are intrinsically or innately lacking distinctiveness, are descriptive, or customary. After looking at these three heads, we then turn to consider how signs can be shown to have acquired distinctive character through use.

3.2 DEVOID OF DISTINCTIVE CHARACTER

Section 3(1)(b) of the 1994 Act/Article 7(1)(b) EUTMR provide that trade marks that are devoid of any distinctive character shall not be registered. The primary function of this exclusion is to exclude marks that do not even perform the 'distinguishing function'.[31] As the Court of Justice stated in *Linde, Winward & Rado*,[32] distinctive character means 'for all trade marks, that the mark must be capable of identifying the product as originating from a particular undertaking, and thus distinguishing it from other undertakings'. The focus is therefore on how the trade mark would be perceived by the relevant public, which consists of average consumers of the goods or services in question.[33] The focus of the tribunal is on the anticipated performance of the mark in relation to the goods or services for which it is proposed to be used: an informed guess at what the relevant class of consumers would understand from the sign. To avoid rejection under section 3(1)(b), the tribunal must conclude that the sign will be perceived as an indication that goods or services come from a single source—in other words, that it is a 'badge of trade origin'.

With the benchmark established—does the sign possess origin indicating ability—the analytical framework adopted to test for it consists of three basic elements: (i) assess the sign, as applied for, (ii) against the backdrop of the goods and services specified, (iii) from the perspective of well informed, reasonably observant, and circumspect consumers for those categories of products.[34]

Consumers will readily recognize as indicating origin words that have no relation to the goods, such as NOXZEMA (for shaving cream) or APPLE (for computers), and equally will see abstract logos as having the same function. It is more difficult to predict whether consumers would see colours, shapes, slogans, and the like as indicating origin.

Article 3(1)(b) excludes those signs that the average consumer 'does not identify as reliably indicating the commercial origin of the product'.[35] Consequently, the provision excludes from registration those signs that would not be perceived to communicate any message (because they would be treated simply as part of the goods or the appearance thereof),[36] and those that while perceived as conveying information, are not perceived as indicating information as to trade source (for example where the sign is seen as a product number or perhaps as a slogan urging a person to do something). According to the Court of Justice, 'it suffices that the trade mark should enable the relevant public to identify the

---

[30] *British Sugar v. James Robertson & Sons* [1996] *RPC* 281, 305.

[31] *Bio-ID*, Case C-37/03P [2005] *ECR* I–7975, [61]–[63]. If a mark that is descriptive under Art. 7(1)(c) is necessarily devoid of distinctive character under Art. 7(1)(b)—on which, see *Campina*, Case C-265/00 [2004] *ECR* I–1699, [19]—is it logical to say that the public interest underpinning Art. 7(1)(c) is not relevant under Art. 7(1)(b)? See further Max Planck Institute, *Study on the Overall Functioning of the Community Trade Mark System* (2011), 58, [1.48].

[32] *Linde AG, Winward Industries, Rado Watch Co. Ltd*, Joined Cases C-53/01, C-54/01, and C-55/01 [2003] *ECR* I–3161, [47].   [33] *KPN Nederland NV*, Case C-363/99 [2004] *ECR* I–1619, [34].

[34] *Linde AG, Winward Industries, Rado Watch Co. Ltd*, Joined Cases C-53/01, C-54/01, and C-55/01 [2003] *ECR* I–3161, [41].   [35] *Nichols v. Registrar*, Case C-404/02 [2004] *ECR* I–8499, [43].

[36] *Libertel Groep BV v. Benelux-Merkenbureau*, Case C-104/01 [2003] *ECR* I–3793.

origin of the goods or services protected thereby and to distinguish them from those of other undertakings'.[37] There is no requirement that the sign be inventive, imaginative, unusual, or linguistically or artistically creative, or that it differs from those 'which from the point of view of the relevant public are commonly used in trade in connection with the presentation of goods or services or in respect of which they could be used in that way'.[38] Signs are excluded only if they are 'devoid' of distinctive character; some tribunals have indicated that a 'smidgeon' or minimal degree of distinctive character suffices for the absolute ground not to apply but this approach has gradually receded.[39] The principles for assessing distinctive character have been conveniently summarized by Arnold J in a dispute concerning the distinctiveness of the shape of a KITKAT chocolate bar.[40]

Although the courts have repeatedly indicated that the same tests are applicable to all marks, whether words, pictures, shapes, or colours, it is useful to look at the way in which the tribunals deal with these different types of sign. This is because the perception of the relevant section of the public is not necessarily the same for exotic marks, such as colours or shapes, as for words or figurative devices which bear no relation to the appearance of the goods.[41] Moreover, in its application to marks such as colours, section 3(1)(b) has been interpreted as requiring the tribunal to consider not only how the sign would be perceived by the average consumer of the goods, but also whether giving a single trader a monopoly over the sign would confer an unjustified competitive advantage on the applicant. The courts, however, have indicated that such considerations of 'public' or 'general interest' are not relevant in the case of words, names, slogans or shapes.[42] How far these kinds of consideration should extend to other sorts of sign is controversial.[43]

While not specifically considered later in this chapter, it should be noted that the case law on figurative signs or logos has now developed to encompass a range of issues, including the extent to which a figurative dimension (a graphic element or stylized font) can compensate for an otherwise weakly distinctive word mark[44] and when the figurative element might be descriptive or commonly used in relation to the goods and services being applied for.[45]

3.2.1 Simple signs: letters, numbers, and grammatical signs

In most cases, single letters, numbers, grammatical signs, and simple geometric shapes will be treated as 'devoid of distinctive character'.[46] This is because consumers would not

---

[37] *Sat. 1 v. OHIM*, Case C-329/02P [2004] *ECR* I–8317, [41].   [38] Ibid., [35]–[36].

[39] *Sat. 1 Satellitenfersehen GmbH v. OHIM*, T 323/00 [2002] *ECR* II–2839, [35] (not discussed on appeal); *Henkel KgaA v. OHIM*, Case T-393/02 [2004] *ECR* II–4115, [42]; *Nestlé v. Mars* [2003] *ETMR* (101) 1235, [23]. For criticism, see Kerly, [10.046]–[10.061].

[40] *Société des Produits Nestlé v. Cadbury* [2014] *EWHC* 16, [40]–[45].

[41] For a representative statement in relation to product packaging, see *August Storck KG v. EUIPO*, Case C-417/16P, EU:C:2017:340, [33]–[36].

[42] *Henkel v. OHIM*, Joined Cases C-456/01P and C-457/01P [2004] *ECR* I–5089; *Sat. 1 v. OHIM*, Case C-329/02P [2004] *ECR* I–8317, [36].

[43] *In re Bongrain's Application* [2005] *RPC* (14) 306, [24] (Jacob LJ) (refusing to accept that the 'depletion' public interest is confined to colour marks). Advocate-General Szpunar also argued against such a limitation in *Christian Louboutin SAS v. Van Haren Schoenen BV*, Case C-163/16, EU:C:2017:495.

[44] See TMDN, *Common Communication on the Common Practice of Distinctiveness—Figurative Marks containing descriptive/non-distinctive words* (2 October 2015).

[45] See EUIPO, *Examination Guidelines,* Part B, Section 4, Chapter 3, [6]–[8].

[46] UK IPO, *Letter and Numeral Marks* (May 2006) PAN 10/06; *Cain Cellars v. OHIM*, Case T-304/05 [2007] *ECR* II–112*, [22] (pentagon shape for wine would not be perceived as a mark); *Evonik Industries v. OHIM*, Case T-499/09 [2011] *ECR* II–225*, [28] (in French or German only) (a rectangle with a convex side would be understood as ornamental or decorative rather than as conveying a trade mark message).

be able to assume that such signs indicated one particular source. Even in these cases, however, the question of whether the sign lacks distinctive character must be assessed on the facts. In the context of an application for the alpha symbol (α) the Court of Justice confirmed that the EUIPO could not presume that consumers were less likely to categorically perceive all single letters as non-distinctive, thereby increasing the applicant's burden, without taking into consideration the specific goods and services being applied for (alcoholic beverages), as the general test for distinctiveness requires.[47] The Registry and the courts should consider carefully how relevant consumers of the particular goods or services would react to the specific sign. Taking the example of numerals, the tribunal should consider whether the number would be taken to indicate catalogue numbers, sizes, model numbers, quantity, date of production, etc., as opposed to being understood to be a trade mark.[48] The same is true of combinations of these elements, although in general the longer the combination, the more likely it would be thought to be a trade mark.

3.2.2 Colour marks

Abstract or 'pure' colour marks—which include both single colours and colour combinations—are likely to be treated as devoid of distinctive character.[49] This is because, in the case of colours, the sign forms part of 'the look of the goods' and consumers are not in the habit of assuming the origin of goods merely based on the colour of packaging. Consequently, the Court of Justice in *Libertel* observed that '[a] colour per se is not normally inherently capable of distinguishing the goods of a particular undertaking'.[50] In addition, the Court has recognized that there is a strong public interest in favour of keeping colours free. This is because the number of colours actually available is limited and so a small number of trade mark registrations could exhaust the entire range of the colours available (an understanding sometimes referred to as 'colour depletion theory'). Exclusive trade mark rights over any such colour would potentially create 'an unjustified competitive advantage for a single trader'.[51] Consequently, in the case of a colour per se, 'distinctiveness without any prior use is inconceivable save in exceptional circumstances, and particularly where the number of goods or services for which the mark is claimed is very restricted and the relevant market very specific'.[52] Prior to the judgment in *Libertel*, the General Court had allowed registration of a shade of orange in relation to 'technical and business consultancy services in the area of plant cultivation, in particular the seed sector' in Class 42.[53] This exceptional decision may be justified, given the relatively narrow scope of the specification to which the mark related. Apart from these exceptional circumstances, colours have otherwise been rejected on the basis that they descriptively signal a particular characteristic of the goods[54] or that they are not uncommon in the sector concerned.[55]

---

[47] *OHIM v. BORCO-Marken-Import*, Case C-265/09P [2010] *ECR* I-08265.

[48] *Agencja Wydawnicza Technopol v. OHIM*, Case C-51/10P [2011] *ECR* I-01541 (the application for '1000' was rejected since it could indicate the number of pages or puzzles included, for periodicals including puzzle-related magazines).   [49] *Libertel*, Case C-104/01 [2003] *ECR* I-3793.

[50] Ibid., [65].   [51] Ibid., [54]–[55].   [52] Ibid., [66].

[53] *KWS Saat AG v. OHIM*, T-173/00 [2002] *ECR* II-3843 (CFI), aff'd Case 447/02P [2004] *ECR* I-10107.

[54] *Enercon GmbH v. EUIPO, Gamesa Eólica, SL*, Case T 36/16, EU:T:2017:295 (shades of green on wind energy convertors indicating the ecological advantages of this form of energy).

[55] *Deutsche Bahn AG v. OHIM*, Case C-45/11P, EU:C:2011:808 (upholding the EUIPO's rejection of a horizontal combination of red and light gray for rail transport services, given the use of red and white signaling on railway barriers and road signs).

3.2.3 Shapes

Another area in which the exclusion relating to marks that are 'devoid of distinctive character' may have an important impact is in relation to shape marks. Although the courts have repeatedly stated that the same test is applicable to shape marks as is applied to word or device marks, because consumer perception of such marks is different, the result of applying the tests will not necessarily be the same.[56] This is because the relevant consumers are unlikely to think of a shape as communicating at all, let alone as being indicative of a particular trader's goods.[57] Consequently, the vast majority of such applications are refused.

In the case of shapes, an assessment of whether the shape is registrable requires an appraisal of whether the shape 'significantly departs from the norm or customs of the sector and thereby fulfils its essential original function'.[58] In turn, this requires, first, an assessment of whether there is anything unusual or idiosyncratic about the shape such that the relevant consumer would notice it and remember it, and then, if there is such individuality, an assessment as to whether the consumer would think of the shape as indicative of source, rather than being merely functional or decorative. The results of this assessment may change as practices change, and with them, consumer perceptions and expectations. Moreover, they may vary from sector to sector or in accordance with the goods or services being applied for.[59] A particular shape could be perceived as a trade mark in one field, but not in another.

The test of 'significant departure' is designed to ensure that consumers of the goods can perceive the difference between the shape in question and other shapes.[60] Basic geometric shapes will not be noticed by consumers and so will not perform the distinguishing function; nor will shapes that are not readily differentiable from those ordinarily used in trade.[61] In one case, the Court of Justice affirmed the (then) Court of First Instance (CFI) decision that the brown colour and shape of WERTHER'S ORIGINALS (see Fig. 37.1) was not a significant departure from those commonly used.[62] The Court said that the mark comprised 'a combination of presentational features which come naturally to mind and which are typical of the goods in question, that it is a variation of certain basic shapes commonly used in the confectionery sector'.[63] Given that the alleged differences are not 'readily perceptible', the Court agreed that the shape in question could not be sufficiently distinguished from other shapes commonly used for sweets, and that it did not enable the relevant public to distinguish immediately and with certainty the appellant's sweets from those of another commercial origin.[64] Similar reasoning led the Court to affirm the ruling

---

[56] *Linde AG, Winward Industries, Rado Watch Co Ltd*, Joined Cases C-53/01, C-54/01, and C-55/01 [2003] *ECR* I-3161, [42], [46], [49]; *Freixenet SA v. OHIM*, Joined Cases C-344–345/10P [2011] *ECR* I-10205, [46].

[57] See, e.g., *Henkel*, C-218/01 [2004] *ECR* I-1725, [52]; *August Storck KG v. OHIM*, Case C-24/05P [2006] *ECR* I-5677, [25]. Whether the public distinguishes certain types of goods by reference to shapes is a question of fact. The public, apparently, are used to identifying vehicles by reference to the design of the grille: *Daimler Chrysler Corp. v. OHIM*, Case T-128/01 [2003] *ECR* II-701, [42]. It seems that the Office may 'infer' that consumers do not normally see certain sorts of sign as an indication of origin and, in such cases, 'it is for the applicant for a trade mark to show that consumers' habits on the relevant market are different': *Unilever NV v. OHIM*, T-194/01 [2003] *ECR* II-383, [18].

[58] *Henkel*, C-218/01 [2004] *ECR* I-1725, [49]; *Henkel v. OHIM*, Joined Cases C-456/01P and C-457/01P [2004] *ECR* I-5089, [39]; *Mag Instrument*, Case C-136/02P [2004] *ECR* I-9165, [32].

[59] *Jaguar Land Rover Ltd v. OHIM*, Case T-629/14 [2016] *ETMR* 12 (the shape of a Range Rover car was distinctive for vehicles for locomotion by 'air and water').

[60] A 'significant departure' is a lower threshold than 'a marked difference': *August Storck*, Case C-24/05P [2006] *ECR* I-5677, [28].   [61] *Procter & Gamble v. OHIM*, T-63/01 [2002] *ECR* II-5255 (CFI), [43].

[62] *August Storck*, Case C-24/05P [2006] *ECR* I-5677.   [63] Ibid., [29]–[30].   [64] Ibid., [25].

Fig. 37.1 The shape of WERTHER'S ORIGINALS

Source: August Storck KG

of the General Court that a chocolate rabbit covered in gold foil, with a red bow and a bell around its neck, was not a significant departure from what was common in the trade.[65]

Even if a shape is a significant departure from those ordinarily used in the sector, it does not follow that it is registrable. The shape must be one that the average consumer would view as indicating trade origin.[66] If average consumers would see a shape as simply there to 'do a job',[67] or as merely decorative, they are less likely to think of the shape as indicating source.[68] Hence the Court of Appeal has refused registration for a floral shape, comprising six lobes, for cheese (SAINT ALBRAY) (see Fig. 37.2),[69] and the Court of Justice has affirmed that the attractive, well-designed cylindrical shape of a MAG-LITE® torch would not function as an indicator of origin (see Fig. 37.3)[70] and neither would an abstract design comprising countless tiny strokes for application to the surface of glass products (showers, windows, etc.) (see Fig. 37.4).[71] In the cheese case, Jacob LJ explained that an average consumer would 'be astonished to be told that one of the shapes was a trade mark. Consumers do not expect to eat trade marks or part of them.'[72] In the *Mag* case, the Court of Justice explained that 'the fact that goods benefit from a high quality of design does not necessarily mean that a mark consisting of the three-dimensional shape of those goods enables *ab initio* those goods to be distinguished from those of other undertakings'.[73] In a rare counter-example, the CFI allowed registration of the distinctive shape of the grille of a jeep, explaining that consumers had come to understand car grilles as signs of origin, so that the applicant's grille could serve as a trade mark (see Fig. 37.5).[74] Similarly, the CFI reversed a decision of the Examiner that the shape of a speaker was devoid of distinctive character: in the Court's view, the shape was different from the customary shapes of

---

[65] *Lindt v. OHIM*, Case C-98/11P, EU:C:2012:307, [41]–[49]. See Fig. 37.10, p. 1018.

[66] *Bongrain's Application* [2005] *RPC* (14) 306 (CA).

[67] *Philips v. Remington* [1999] *RPC* 809 (CA), 819.

[68] *Procter & Gamble (Soap Bar Shape)*, T-63/01 [2002] *ECR* II-5255.

[69] *Bongrain's Application* [2005] *RPC* (14) 306 (CA).

[70] *Mag Instrument*, Case C-136/02P [2004] *ECR* I-9165. However, the three-dimensional shape of the Mag-Lite® flashlight was awarded a CTM registration on the ground of 'acquired distinctiveness'.

[71] *Glaverbel (Patterned Glass)*, Case C-445/02P [2004] *ECR* I-6267.

[72] *Bongrain's Application* [2005] *RPC* (14) 306, [29].

[73] *Mag Instrument*, Case C-136/02P [2004] *ECR* I-9165, [68].

[74] *DaimlerChrysler (Grille)*, Case T-128/01 [2003] *ECR* II-701.

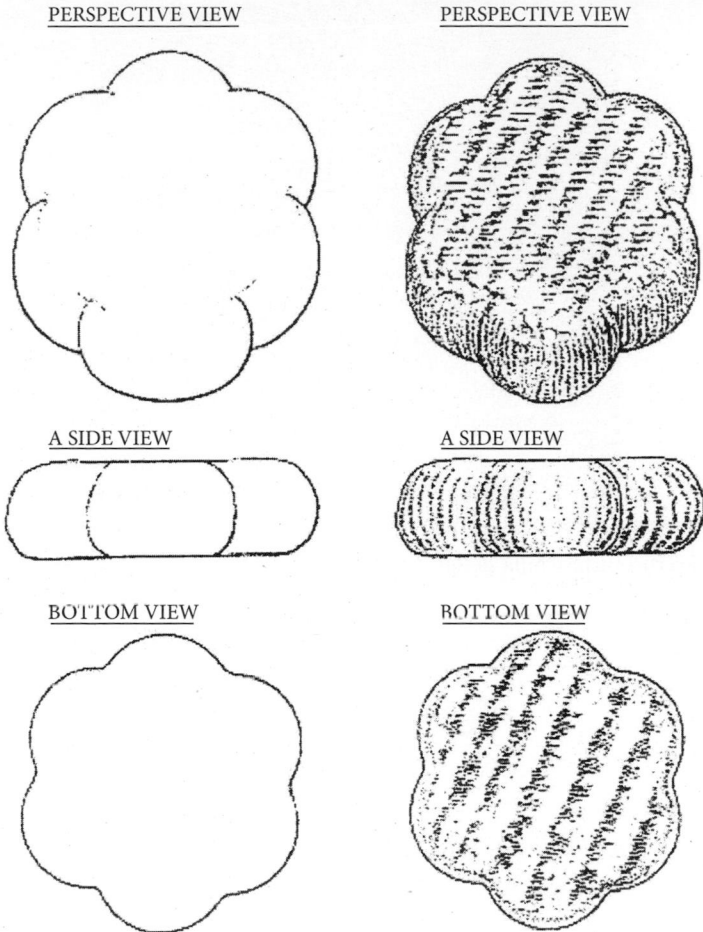

PERSPECTIVE VIEW   PERSPECTIVE VIEW

A SIDE VIEW   A SIDE VIEW

BOTTOM VIEW   BOTTOM VIEW

Fig. 37.2 SAINT ALBRAY cheese

Source: Bongrain's Application [2005] *RPC* (14) 306 (CA)

Fig. 37.3 The MAG-LITE® flashlight

Source: Mag Instruments Inc.

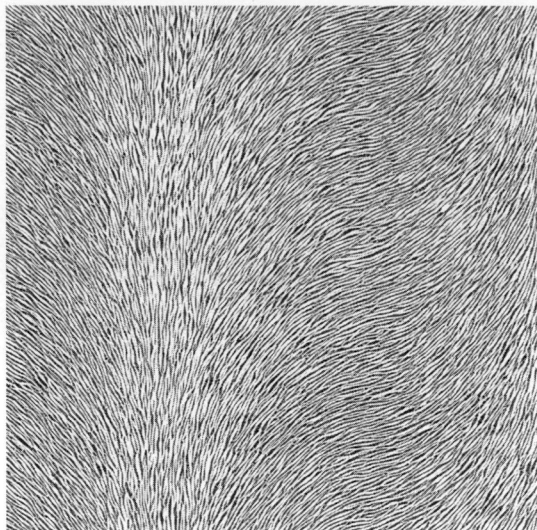

Fig. 37.4 Glaverbel's 'Chinchilla' design for glass

Source: AGC Flatglass

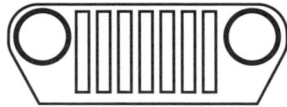

Fig. 37.5 The JEEP design

Source: DaimlerChrysler (Grille), Case T-0128/01 [2003] *ECR* II–701

loudspeakers, and was characterized by specific and arbitrary features that would retain the attention of the average consumer.[75] Notwithstanding the considerable merits of the 'different does not always mean distinctive' approach, an issue which remains unresolved is the extent to which the two requirements (significantly departs; *thereby* indicates origin) are (i) independent and cumulative requirements, or (ii) whether the latter can be presumed once the former is established.[76]

3.2.4 Get-up and trade dress

Although it is not possible to say that the overall packaging of a product ('get-up' or 'trade dress') can never be inherently distinctive, in most cases these matters will be devoid of distinctive character. This is for the simple reason that (as with shapes) average consumers do not treat the majority of packaging or get-up as indicating source; rather, they treat packaging as comprising protective material, which has decorative, attractive, or eye-catching features. In part, this is a matter of current social practice: consumers have long been invited to focus on the literature on packaging as indicating source and, as a result, the overall look of the get-up is ignored, at least in this regard.

---

[75] *Bang & Olufsen v. OHIM*, Case T-460/05 [2007] *ECR* II–4207. The registration was however subsequently invalidated on the basis that the distinctive stylistic features added 'substantial value' to the shape. See Chapter 36, section 3.4, pp. 960–2.

[76] *The London Taxi Corporation v. Frazer-Nash Research* [2017] *EWCA Civ* 1729, [40]–[42].

Fig. 37.6 Long-necked bottle with lemon in spout

Source: Eurocermex SA v. OHIM, Case C-286/04P [2005] ECR I-5797

In *Proctor & Gamble v. Registrar of Trade Marks*,[77] Robert Walker LJ confirmed the rejection by the Registrar of applications for registration in Class 3 of a three-dimensional bottle bearing a label for floor-cleaning products. The hearing officer had described the application as having three component parts—namely, the shape of the bottle, the pattern on the label, and the colours applied to both. Having concluded that none of the three components was individually distinctive, the hearing officer had found that the combination was lacking in distinctiveness. Affirming the Registry's conclusion, Robert Walker LJ emphasized that, in order to overcome an objection based on section 3(1)(b) of the 1994 Act, the applicant's trade mark must *readily* distinguish the applicant's product, and that where a close examination was required to identify differences, the get-up was not distinctive.

The Court of Justice has been faced with a steady trickle of appeals from refusals of the EUIPO to register get-up on the ground that it is lacking in distinctiveness. In one

---

[77] [1999] *RPC* 673, 680.

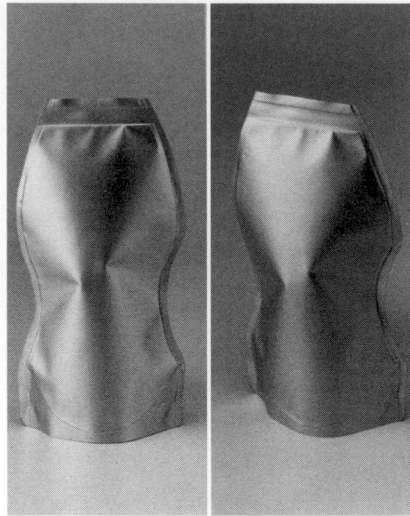

Fig. 37.7 Deutsche 'Si-Si' pouches

Source: Grünecker, Kinkeldey, Stockmair & Schwannhäusser

case, the Court of Justice affirmed that the (then) CFI had not erred in law when it found that the shape of a long-necked bottle with a piece of lemon placed in the spout was not distinctive of beer (see Fig. 37.6).[78] The CFI had found that this was a common way of presenting beer for consumption and that, given that consumers paid little attention, the combination would not be viewed as indicating source. In another case, the Court of Justice affirmed that no error existed in the (then) CFI's decision that stand-up pouches for packaging fruit juices and fruit drinks were not distinctive (see Fig. 37.7).[79]

In contrast, in *Nestlé Waters France v. OHIM (Bottle shape)*,[80] the (then) CFI allowed the registration of the shape of a bottle for non-alcoholic beverages (see Fig. 37.8). The CFI took the view that, because of repeated attempts over a number of years by various traders to educate consumers into treating bottle shapes as trade marks, the average consumer is now 'quite capable of perceiving the shape of the packaging of the goods as an indication of commercial origin' if the shape possessed characteristics that are sufficient to hold their attention.[81] The CFI reversed the OHIM's view that the bottle was commonplace, finding that the whole formed a design 'which is striking and easy to remember'. It was a combination capable of holding the public's attention and distinguishing the goods from those with a different commercial origin. As a result, the mark had a minimum degree of distinctiveness and fell outside Article 7(1)(b) of the Regulation.

Similarly, in *Henkel KgaA v. OHIM*,[82] the CFI overturned the finding of the OHIM Board of Appeal that a container resembling the shape of an upturned pear, with flattened

---

[78] *Eurocermex SA v. OHIM*, Case C-286/04P [2005] *ECR* I-5797 (Corona beer), affirming Case T-399/02 [2004] *ECR* II-1391. Although not the original image submitted by Eurocermex, this photograph gives an idea of what Eurocermex was trying to register.

[79] *Deutsche Sisi-Werke GmbH & Co. Betriebs KG v. OHIM*, Case C-173/04P [2006] *ECR* I-551.

[80] T-305/02 [2003] *ECR* II-5207. But cf. *Adelholxener Alpenquellen GmbH v. OHIM*, Case T-347/10, EU:T:2013:201, [22]–[38] (French and German only) (complex mark comprising bottle shape with surface decoration representing mountain held to be non-distinctive).

[81] *Nestlé Waters France v. OHIM (Bottle shape)*, T-305/02 [2003] *ECR* II-5207, [40].

[82] Case T-393/02 [2004] *ECR* II-4115. A picture of the container can be seen in the case report.

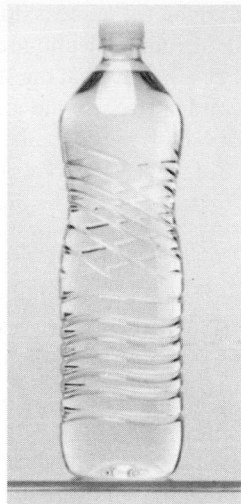

Fig 37.8 The bottle design in *Nestlé Waters France v. OHIM*

Source: Nestlé Waters

sides and coloured white and transparent, lacked distinctive character for washing liquids and detergents. The CFI found that the combination of elements had a 'truly individual character', commenting on its flat character and crystal shape.

The touchstone therefore appears to be whether traders in the sector have educated consumers to view packaging as indicative of commercial origin. If this has been achieved, then whether particular packaging is devoid of distinctive character is likely to turn on whether the get-up is sufficiently noticeable in the circumstances to catch the attention of consumers. If this is not the case, such as where a compact disc of a sound recording is suddenly sold in unusual packaging, the position is problematic. On the one hand, the packaging will be memorable; on the other, it is unlikely to be perceived as an indication of origin.

3.2.5 Names and signatures

Traditionally under UK law, surnames had been considered non-distinctive and thus unregistrable.[83] In part, the decision to exclude surnames was motivated by the inconvenience that the grant of a right would cause to other traders who shared the same name. The courts also stressed that third parties who made legitimate use of their names ought not to be forced to rely on a defence equivalent to that contained in section 11(2).[84] However, under the 1994 Act, there is no *a priori* exclusion of surnames, or personal names, and the question of registrability is determined by the same standards as for other marks. The question in any given case will be whether the average consumer of the goods would assume that the name operates to indicate one particular manufacturer or supplier. In making this assessment, the Court of Justice has indicated, in *Nichols's Trade Mark Application*,[85] that an examining authority tribunal may not use *general* criteria, such as

---

[83] *Elvis Presley Trade Marks* [1997] *RPC* 543, 558.

[84] *Cadbury Bros's Application* (1915) 32 *RPC* 9, 12.

[85] *Nichols v. Registrar*, Case C-404/02 [2004] *ECR* I–8499, [25]–[26]. The registration of the mark NICHOLS for vending machines was subsequently confirmed on 26 May 2006: TM 2241893.

predetermined rules about how common the name is (for example a rule that if the name appears more than 500 times in the London telephone directory, it should not be registered). Moreover, the Court of Justice was clear that the 'unfair advantage' obtained by the first person to register a name over other traders who might wish to use it is irrelevant.[86] However, commonness may be relevant to the consumer's likely appreciation of the *specific* name as an indication of origin of the *specific* goods. The scope of protection available for names registered as trade marks may therefore be limited.[87]

The removal of the traditional rules for determining registrability of surnames has left something of a void, which has not yet been filled with much guidance from subsequent decisions. However, the Appointed Person provided some useful insights in *Oska's Ltd's Trade Mark Application*.[88] In the course of opposition proceedings, it was necessary to assess the distinctiveness of the opponent's earlier mark, MORGAN, for clothing. Following the guidance of the Court of Justice, Richard Arnold QC took into consideration the commonness of the name 'Morgan', the frequency with which names were used in the clothing trade, and the number of traders in the clothing field, and concluded that the average consumer would regard the surname as devoid of distinctive character. Before the average consumer would consider a common surname in the clothing trade as an indication of source, they would expect the addition of a forename (as with PAUL SMITH or TED BAKER).

One peculiarity should be noted here: the full name of a famous personality may well be devoid of distinctive character (at least for goods that would be understood as merchandise). In *Elvis Presley Trade Marks*,[89] the Court of Appeal refused to allow registration of ELVIS and ELVIS PRESLEY for toiletries, perfumes, cosmetics, and soaps. It had been argued by the applicants that, as a result of changes in public awareness about character merchandising, consumers seeing the name ELVIS would assume that the product to which it was attached was 'genuine'—that is, they would assume that the goods originated from Elvis Presley's estate or from someone with rights granted by the estate. At first instance, Laddie J was not willing to accept that this was an accurate portrayal of how the general public thought about the way in which the names of celebrities were used and the Court of Appeal affirmed that view: people treat a name as part of the product that they are purchasing, not as a feature that distinguishes the goods of one trader from those of another. For consumers, the goods are memorabilia or mementos of which the name is an essential component, rather than a different class of consumable commercial goods that people purchased because they came from a specific trader.[90]

In those cases in which a name itself lacks distinctiveness, registration may nevertheless be obtained where an application is for the name in conjunction with a device or represented in a special or particular manner, so that the whole is distinctive. Perhaps the most obvious example of this is where the name takes the form of a person's signature. Signatures were specifically treated as registrable under the 1938 Act because they were seen as 'a substantially unique and frequently highly distorted way of writing the author's

---

[86] Ibid., [31]. The Court of Justice referred to the defence contained in Art. 6(1)(a).

[87] Ibid., [AG46] (AG Colomer); *Barbara Becker v. Harman International Industries*, Case C-51/09P [2010] *ECR* I–5805, [36] (in analysing relative grounds, the Court indicated that the commonness of a surname was relevant to its distinctive character); *Oska's Ltd's Trade Mark Application* [2005] *RPC* (20) 525 (AP, Arnold QC), [27]–[28].   [88] [2005] *RPC* (20) 525 (AP, Arnold QC), [27]–[28].

[89] [1999] *RPC* 567; [1997] *RPC* 543, 558. Cf. *Annette von Droste zu Hülshoff Stiftung*, 33 W (Pat) 550/11 (of 2 July 2013) (German Federal Patent Court held that the mere fact than a mark comprised the name of a famous person—here, the early nineteenth-century novelist Annette von Droste-Hülshoff—did not mean that it was devoid of distinctive character).

[90] *Elvis Presley Trade Marks* [1997] *RPC* 543 (Laddie J); [1999] *RPC* 567 (CA), 585. Although the case was decided under the 1938 Act, the reasoning, relating to an issue of fact, seems applicable under the 1994 Act.

name. They are in a sense a private graphic tied to one person'.[91] Under the 1994 Act, a 'signature' may be registrable even if it is not written in a distinctive graphic style—a simple cursive rendition of Elvis's signature 'Elvis A. Presley' would probably be distinctive.[92] This may be the case even if the signature is not authentic.[93]

3.2.6 Slogans

The question of whether slogans can be registered highlights some of the real difficulties with assessing whether a particular sign will, when used, be understood to indicate origin. On the one hand, slogans are mostly understood as promotional communications and thus would not be understood as indicating origin. On the other hand, in many fields, slogans are used as marks, for example I CAN'T BELIEVE IT'S NOT BUTTER for margarine. Which form of use is the relevant authority to assume when it considers an application? Although English courts have tended to suggest that slogans lack distinctive character[94] and the General Court has often taken a similar view,[95] the Court of Justice has reiterated on a number of occasions that there are no special requirements for slogans. The case law of the Court demonstrates a reluctance to offer any concrete indications of what will make a slogan inherently registrable. While the Court acknowledges that consumers do not normally consider slogans to be trade marks,[96] the Court will not tolerate any suggestion that a slogan be imaginative or creative to be registrable,[97] although the presence of those qualities is likely to endow that mark with distinctive character.[98] Moreover, the Court of Justice has denied that the mere capacity of a slogan to be understood as promotional does not mean that the slogan necessarily lacks distinctive character. In *Audi AG v. OHIM*,[99] an application to register VORSPRUNG DURCH TECHNIK (meaning 'advancement through technology') had been refused for various goods and services on the basis that it was a slogan carrying an objective laudatory message.[100] The Court of Justice annulled the decision, observing that 'the mere fact that a mark is perceived by the relevant public as a promotional formula . . . is not sufficient, in itself, to support the conclusion that that mark is devoid of distinctive character'.[101] A slogan could be promotional and distinctive. In effect, the Court is saying that there are no 'sub-rules': each application needs to be looked at in relation to its own individual characteristics—the nature and meaning of the slogan, as well as the goods or services for which registration is sought. Of course, slogans will be refused registration if they are descriptive.[102]

---

[91] *Elvis Presley Trade Marks* [1997] *RPC* 543, 558 (Laddie J).

[92] Ibid. *In re Applications by the Estate of the Late Diana, Princess of Wales* (25 January 2002) (TM Registry) (Diana signature registrable, signatures being 'a unique sign of authenticity').

[93] *Elvis Presley Trade Marks* [1999] *RPC* 567 (CA), 586, although the Court presumed, at 576, that the signature was authentic and ultimately the application was refused on relative grounds: see 587.

[94] *Nestlé v. Mars* [2003] *ETMR* (101) 1235 (CA) (rejecting HAVE A BREAK for confectionery).

[95] For examples, see Bently and Sherman (2014) 944, n. 81; EUIPO, *Examination Guidelines*, Part B, Section 4, Chapter 3, [5] ('Slogans: Assessing Distinctive Character'). See also J. Davis and A. Durant, 'To Protect or not to Protect? The Eligibility of Commercially used Short Verbal Texts for Copyright and Trade Mark Protection' [2011] *IPQ* 345.

[96] *OHIM v. Erpo Möbelwerk GmbH*, Case C-64/02P [2004] *ECR* I–10031, [35].   [97] Ibid.

[98] *Audi v. OHIM*, Case C-398/08P [2010] *ECR* I–535, [47]. *Pro-Aqua International v. OHIM*, Case T-133/13, EU:T:2015:46 (WET DUST CAN'T FLY was sufficiently fanciful—since dust is usually dry—to be distinctive).

[99] Case C-398/08P [2010] *ECR* I–535, [47].

[100] The slogan had been registered for cars on the basis of acquired distinctiveness. Ibid., [5].

[101] Ibid., [44]. At [59], the Court suggests that the mark is not devoid of distinctive character for these goods, because it is well known in relation to cars. This surely is inconsistent with the general principle that a mark is assessed independently for each category of goods or services.

[102] *RheinfelsQuellen H. Hovelmann GmbH & Co. KG v. OHIM*, Case T-28/06 [2007] *ECR* II–4413.

3.2.7 Sounds

While there is presently limited authority for sound marks, the General Court has upheld the EUIPO's refusal of an application for a 'ringtone' across a range of goods and services.[103] Since the mark consisted of a simple and banal ringing sound—and not, as the applicant had argued, a short yet sufficiently complex melody—it would go unnoticed and not be remembered by consumers, thereby inhibiting its ability to indicate origin. The Court confirmed that the perception of the relevant public is not necessarily the same for sounds, so it could prove more difficult to register them. The degree of difficulty will vary across product sectors; while consumers of television broadcasting services, computer software, or media services may rely on sounds for distinguishing source, in other situations sounds are perceived as functional or indicators without any inherent characteristics. The ringtone belonged to the latter group, since it would remain self-referential (conveying a ringing sound) regardless of the context of use.[104]

3.2.8 Position marks

A position mark 'consist[s] of the specific way in which the mark is placed or affixed on the product'.[105] Registration attempts have included the position of a metal button attached to the ears of soft toys such as teddy bears[106] and a particular shade of orange applied to the toes of socks.[107] While the overarching distinctiveness test applies to this category as well, factors which are relevant for three dimensional/shape marks are also relevant here: is the positioning of the mark a departure from the norms in that sector and is it likely to be 'read' as having origin indicating significance, as opposed to (say) a decorative purpose.

The recent interest in position marks is partially attributable to the varied fortunes of Christian Louboutin's attempts to register red soled high-heeled shoes as a trade mark.[108] The mark (see Fig. 37.9) consists 'of the colour red (Pantone 18.1663TP) applied to the sole of a shoe as shown (the outline of the shoe is therefore not part of the trade mark but serves to show the positioning of the trademark)' for high-heeled shoes (except orthopaedic footwear) in class 25.[109] Besides issues surrounding the characterization of the mark—is

Fig. 37.9 Louboutin's red soled shoe

Source: *Christian Louboutin v. Van Haren Schoenen*, Case C-163/16 (22 June 2017)

---

[103] *Globo Comunicação e Participações S/A v. EUIPO*, Case T-408/15, EU:T:2016:468.

[104] Ibid., [41]–[46], [52]–[53].   [105] EUTMIR, Art. 3(3)(d).

[106] *Margarete Steiff GmbH v. OHIM*, Joined Cases T-433 and 434/12, EU:T:2014:8 (buttons were commonly—and decoratively—used for these products and would not attract attention). See also *K-Swiss Inc v. OHIM*, Case T-3/15, EU:T:2015:937 (five parallel stripes on the side of a shoe not distinctive).

[107] *X Technology Swiss v. OHIM*, Case T-547/08, EU:T:2010:235, aff'd Case C-429/10 [2011] *ECR* I-00076 (such use was likely to be perceived as decorative).

[108] C. Gommers and E. De Pauw, '"Red Sole Diaries": A Tale on the Enforcement of Louboutin's Position Mark' (2016) 11 *JIPLP* 258; D. Gangjee, 'Paying the Price for Admission: Non-Traditional Marks across Registration and Enforcement', in Calboli and Senftleben (2018) (forthcoming).

[109] For example, in EUTM No. 008845539.

it a pure colour, akin to a shape or a position mark[110]—and the ensuing representation requirements, the distinctiveness of this mark has also been contested.[111]

3.3 DESCRIPTIVE MARKS

The second category of marks excluded from registration relates to what may be called 'descriptive marks'. More specifically, section 3(1)(c) of the 1994 Act/Article 7(1)(c) EUTMR excludes from registration trade marks that consist *exclusively* of signs or indications that may serve, in trade, to designate the (i) kind, quality, or quantity, (ii) the intended purpose, (iii) the value, (iv) the geographical origin, (v) the time of production of the goods or of the rendering of the service, or (vi) other characteristics of the goods or service.

3.3.1 The function of section 3(1)(c): the requirement for availability

Whereas section 3(1)(b) is largely aimed at ensuring that the only signs that are registered are those that could be perceived as trade marks, section 3(1)(c) has an additional purpose (which we can call the 'protective function')—namely, to minimize the negative impact that the grant of trade marks may have upon traders working in the same or related fields. If trade mark law were to permit one trader to obtain property protection over descriptive or generic marks, it could have a dramatic impact upon other traders. For example, if one greengrocer were given trade mark protection over the word 'orange' or 'fruit' (for oranges), it would interfere with the ability of other greengrocers to convey information about their goods or services. In other words, where there are a limited number of possible ways of describing or presenting one's goods, the provision of legal monopolies over such signs might enable one trader to keep other traders completely out of the market.[112] The Court of Justice calls this 'the requirement of availability'.[113]

The first occasion on which the Court of Justice considered Article 3(1)(c) of the TMD 1989 was in *Windsurfing Chiemsee v. Attenberger*.[114] In this case, the question before the Court was whether the word CHIEMSEE, the name of a lake in Bavaria, could be a trade mark for sports clothing or whether such a mark fell within Article 3(1)(c). More specifically, the Court was asked to consider whether the application of Article 3(1)(c) depends on whether there is a 'real, current, or serious need to leave the sign or indication free'. In answering this question, the Court acknowledged that one of the aims of the Article was to protect the public interest (referred to as the 'general interest' in subsequent cases)[115]

---

[110] *Christian Louboutin v. Van Haren Schoenen*, Case C-163/16, EU:C:2017:495 (Advocate-General Szpunar concluded the mark was sufficiently three dimensional for the specific shape mark policy exclusions to apply). Despite a second opinion confirming the AG's reasoning (EU:C:2018:64) the Grand Chamber ultimately held that the sign was not a shape whereupon the exclusions did not apply: EU:C:2018:423.

[111] Compare *Société Christian Louboutin et Monsieur Christian Louboutin v. Société Zara France*, Cour de cassation, Chambre Commerciale, No. 11–20724, 30 May 2012 (a variant of this mark was insufficiently distinctive, since it was a concept relating to contrasting colours and not a mark) with *Christian Louboutin* R 2272/2010–2 (OHIM, Second BoA) (the mark is inherently distinctive as an EUTM).

[112] Although the protective function is usually talked about in terms of the needs or desires of other traders, it can equally be expressed in terms of a trader's rights to free commercial expression: see P. N. Leval, 'Trademark: Champion of Free Speech' (2004) 27 *Colum JL & Arts* 187.

[113] *Adidas AG and ors v. Marca Mode CV and ors*, Case C-102/07 [2008] *ECR* I–2439, [23], [AG27]–[AG45].

[114] Joined Cases C-108/97 and C-109/97 [1999] *ECR* I–2779.

[115] For a review of the public interest across registration, validity, and infringement, see I. Fhima, 'The Public Interest in European Trade Mark Law' [2017] *IPQ* 311.

by keeping descriptive signs or indications free for use by all traders.[116] The Court observed that:

> Article 3(1)(c) of the Directive pursues an aim which is in the public interest, namely that descriptive signs or indications relating to the categories of goods or services in respect of which registration is applied for may be freely used by all, including as collective marks or as part of complex or graphic marks. Article 3(1)(c) therefore prevents such signs and indications from being reserved to one undertaking alone because they have been registered as trade marks.[117]

It continued:

> As regards, more particularly, signs or indications which may serve to designate the geographical origin of the categories of goods in relation to which registration of the mark is applied for, especially geographical names, it is in the public interest that they remain available, not least because they may be an indication of the quality and other characteristics of the categories of goods concerned, and may also, in various ways influence consumer tastes by, for instance, associating the goods with a place that may give rise to a favourable response.[118]

The view that section 3(1)(c) must be understood in light of this public interest has, with one notorious exception,[119] been reiterated on many occasions.[120]

3.3.2 General

To avoid objection under section 3(1)(c), the applicant will need to establish that the sign is not used (and is unlikely to be used in the future) as a description of the characteristics of the goods or services. Consequently, invented words such as MARANTZ (for hi-fi equipment), or PEPSI (for drinks), are likely to be registrable, because it is unlikely that traders could use them descriptively or that consumers would perceive them to be anything other than an indication of origin. In contrast, TREAT would be understood as describing the fact that the product was especially good, and EUROLAMB would be understood as usable in describing the fact that the product was a particular type of meat from a particular place. In between these extremes is a huge array of signs, not wholly descriptive, but partly suggestive of a product's quality; in such cases, the tribunal will have to make a judgment as to how consumers will interpret the sign.

3.3.3 Exclusively

Trade marks are excluded from registration by section 3(1)(c) only if they consist *exclusively* of signs that characterize the goods and services. This means that the mark *as a whole* must be descriptive for it to be excluded. The converse of this is that if it can be shown that part of a mark is non-descriptive, then it will fall outside the remit of the section, as long as that part is not *de minimis*. Thus marks that are made up of descriptive and non-descriptive matter may be protected. However the non-descriptive elements should be sufficiently prominent to divert attention away from the purely descriptive ones, which

---

[116] *Windsurfing*, Joined Cases C-108/97 and C-109/97 [1999] *ECR* I–2779, [30].   [117] Ibid., [25].
[118] Ibid., [26].
[119] *Procter & Gamble v. OHIM (Baby Dry)*, Case C-383/99P [2001] *ECR* I–6251, [2002] *ETMR* (3) 22.
[120] *Wrigley (Doublemint)*, Case C-191/01P [2003] *ECR* I–12447 (AG); *Linde AG, Winward Industries, Rado Watch Co. Ltd*, Joined Cases C-53/01, C-54/01, and C-55/01 [2003] *ECR* I–3161, [73]; *Campina*, Case C-265/00 [2004] *ECR* I–1699, [34]–[36]; *KPN Nederland NV*, Case C-363/99 [2004] *ECR* I–1619.

will otherwise convey the (descriptive) message.[121] In the famous *Baby Dry* case (in which the Court of Justice held the words BABY DRY not to be exclusively descriptive of diapers), the Court suggested that 'any perceptible difference' between the applicant's sign and a descriptive term or terms is 'apt to confer distinctive character on the combination enabling it to be registered as a trade mark'.[122] Subsequent rulings have raised this threshold, which is generally considered a positive development. In *Campina Melkunie BV v. Benelux-Merkenbureau*,[123] the Court of Justice stated that the mere combination of elements that are each descriptive will not normally create a neologism that is registrable; rather, there must be some 'unusual variation, in particular to syntax or meaning', which produces an impression on the relevant consumer of something that is 'sufficiently far removed from that produced by the mere combination of meanings lent by the elements of which it is composed, with the result that the word is more than the sum of its parts'.[124] The application of this test would leave the words BABY DRY as registrable for nappies, while rendering BIO-MILD and DOUBLEMINT unregistrable for natural yoghurt and chewing gum (respectively). In the first case, the words 'baby' and 'dry' each alluded to the function of diapers, but because of 'the syntactically unusual juxtaposition', it was not a familiar expression for designating nappies nor for describing their essential characteristics. The phrase was a 'lexical invention', bestowing distinctive power on the mark. In the last case, the subtraction of the space left the sign as no more than a designation of the characteristic of its being mint-flavoured.[125]

3.3.4 Multiple meanings

The requirement of 'exclusivity' does not mean that a sign is excluded only if all possible meanings of a sign fall within the exclusion. Consider, for example, a word with two or more meanings, such as 'pen' (referring to a writing implement, a female swan, and a small enclosure for animals). In assessing whether 'pen' would be registrable for writing implements, the tribunal should not be content simply to find that there is one signification—that of a female swan—which is not excluded. If that were the case, then the existence of a single obscure meaning would render the mark not exclusively descriptive (and hence registrable). In *Doublemint*, the Court of Justice rejected an approach suggesting that the conceptual ambiguity generated by having to choose between alternative descriptive meanings prevented a term from being immediately descriptive. The ambiguity in the types of mintiness (spearmint, peppermint) and the notion of doubling (the types or strength) could not render DOUBLEMINT registrable. The Court concluded that a sign is excluded from registration if 'at least one of its possible meanings designates a characteristic of the goods concerned'.[126] The test in Article 7(1)(c) is not whether the sign is 'exclusively descriptive', but rather whether the trade mark consists exclusively of signs or indications that may have a descriptive capacity. The mere existence of another, non-descriptive, meaning is irrelevant.[127]

---

[121] *Castel Frères v. OHIM*, Case C-622/13P, EU:C:2015:297, [71]–[80] (minor spelling change insufficient to prevent geographically descriptive connotations for CASTELL). See also *Zitro IP v. OHIM*, Case T-318/15, EU:T:2016:1 (despite the stylized font, TRIPLE BONUS would still convey to consumers the notion of games of chance where earnings could be tripled).

[122] *Procter & Gamble v. OHIM (Baby Dry)*, Case C-383/99P [2001] *ECR* I–6251, [2002] *ETMR* (3) 22, [40].

[123] Case C-265/00 [2004] *ECR* I–1699.

[124] Ibid., [41]. See also *KPN Nederland NV*, Case C-363/99 [2004] *ECR* I–1619.

[125] *Wrigley (Doublemint)*, Case C-191/01P [2003] *ECR* I–12447.

[126] *Streamserve*, T-106/00 [2002] *ECR* II–723, [42].

[127] See, e.g., *Revolution LLC v. EUIPO*, Case T-654/14, EC:T:2016:268 (notwithstanding its other political meanings, REVOLUTION would convey the sense of 'new and innovative' for financial services. It was laudatory, emphasizing the positive qualities of the services provided).

3.3.5 'May serve': the element of futurity

Article 3(1)(c) of the TMD 2008 excludes from registration trade marks that consist of signs or indications that *may serve*, in trade, to designate the characteristics of the goods or service.[128] The requirement that the tribunal should consider not only the current use of a term, but also its future associations, was recognized by the Court of Justice in *Windsurfing*,[129] in which the Court said that the relevant tribunal was to ask whether there was 'an association in the mind of the relevant class of persons between the geographic name and the category of goods in question' or, where there was none at the relevant date (that is, the date of application), 'whether it is reasonable to assume that such an association may be established in the future'. The *Windsurfing* approach has been confirmed by the *Doublemint* decision, in which the Court stated that, for the exclusion in Article 7(1)(c) EUTMR to operate, it is not necessary for the sign in question actually to be in use as a description of the goods or their characteristics; it is sufficient 'that such signs could be used for such purposes'.[130] The test therefore has an element of 'futurity' about it.

3.3.6 Broad specifications and disclaimers

A final general point worth noting is that, when considering whether a sign is excluded, the tribunal should consider it in relation to each and every category of goods included in the specification. In many cases, a sign will be excluded only in relation to some categories of goods or services and not others. However, an application will be refused registration if it is descriptive of the characteristics of any of the goods or services in a specific category of the specification. So if an application relates to orange for 'beverages', it will be refused registration on the grounds that it is descriptive (of orange-flavoured drinks) even though it would not be descriptive of apple-flavoured drinks.[131] In some cases, an applicant may be able to avoid such an objection by amending the application to 'apple drinks', but not, it seems, to 'beverages (other than those made from, coloured, or flavoured orange)'.[132] It should also be noted that in appropriate cases, the same descriptiveness rationale can be 'globally' applied across a wide range of goods and services. Consequently SOCIAL.COM was found sufficiently directly descriptive for goods and services across several classes in relation to social media, since they all related to 'social interaction on the internet'.[133]

3.3.7 Any characteristic of the goods or services

In the *Postkantoor* case,[134] the Court of Justice indicated that a sign falls within Article 3(1)(c) if it is capable of being used to designate the characteristics of goods or services, even if the characteristic in question is of peripheral significance to the goods in question. Thus STINKY might be unregistrable for a weedkiller, even though the most important characteristic of a weedkiller is whether it is effective in killing weeds. 'Capability' should not be understood as presenting a purely abstract test, but rather should be considered in the context of the existing market and foreseeable developments therein. In *Agencja Wydawnicza Technopol v. OHIM*,[135] the Court added further language: a descriptive

---

[128] See also TMD 2015, Art. 4(1)(c); EUTMR, Art. 7(1)(c).

[129] *Windsurfing*, Joined Cases C-108/97 and C-109/97 [1999] *ECR* I–2779, [31].

[130] *Wrigley (Doublemint)*, Case C-191/01P [2003] *ECR* I–12447, [32].

[131] *DaimlerChrysler AG v. OHIM*, T-355/00 [2002] *ECR* II–1939.

[132] *Giorgio Armani v. Sunrich Clothing* [2010] *EWHC* 2939 (Ch), [52]–[53] (Mann J); UK IPO, *Partial Refusals* (2011) PAN 2/11; UK IPO, *Partial Refusals* (2011) TPN 1/11. See Chapter 35, section 2.4 *ff*, pp. 941–2.

[133] salesforce.com, *Inc. v. EUIPO*, Case T-134/15, EU:T:2016:366.

[134] *KPN Nederland NV*, Case C-363/99 [2004] *ECR* I–1619, [102].

[135] Case C-51/10P [2011] *ECR* I–1541, [50].

mark is one that designates a property, 'easily recognisable by the relevant class of persons', of the goods or the services in respect of which registration is sought. It there agreed that '1,000' would be such a term in relation to puzzle magazines.

3.3.8 Must the association be 'specific and direct'?

The General Court requires that, for a sign to be descriptive, the association between a sign and goods or services must be 'sufficiently specific and direct to show that that sign enables the relevant public to identify those goods and services immediately'.[136] The effect of this is that vague references to the character of the goods, including via laudatory epithets, may not be excluded under this provision (although they might nevertheless be excluded under section 3(1)(b) or (d)). So, for example, the (then) CFI treated ULTRAPLUS as registrable for ovenware, and the English Court of Appeal held that E.S.B. (an abbreviation of 'extra strong bitter') was protectable for bitter beer.[137] AROMA was also registrable for cooking utensils and appliances, since it referred to the scent of the food cooked in the appliances and was not a characteristic of the appliances themselves.[138] The registrability of such 'indirectly' descriptive or laudatory terms seems to have been endorsed by the Court of Justice[139] and, in some ways, seems at odds with the general approach taken by the Court in *Doublemint* and *Postkantoor*. In *Doublemint*, in particular, Advocate-General Jacobs had offered three guidelines as to when marks might be descriptive, one of which related to the 'specificity' and the second, the 'immediacy' of the meaning conveyed by the sign in relation to the goods.[140] However, the Court of Justice gave no hint that it found them to be useful and (as we noted in the previous paragraph) in fact explicitly rejected the third (the significance of the characteristic in the purchases of the goods or services) in *Postkantoor*. Moreover, the Appointed Person, Geoffrey Hobbs QC, has said that he has 'misgivings' about such a narrow interpretation. In his view, signs such as BEST EVER or SERIOUSLY GOOD should be regarded as excluded descriptions.[141] Marks with laudatory connotations continue to generate seemingly conflicting decisions.[142] By contrast, it is well settled that the sign in question does not necessarily have to be reflected in a dictionary entry in order to be descriptive. Combinations of descriptive terms, which are not otherwise found in dictionaries but where the semantic sum is not greater than its parts, will still be excluded from the register.[143]

---

[136] See, e.g., *DKV Krankenversicherung AG v. OHIM (Eurohealth)*, Case T-359/99 [2001] *ECR* II-1645, [35]–[36]; *O2 (Germany) GmbH v. OHIM*, Case T-344/07 [2010] *ECR* II-153, [34], [54], [65]; *Psytech International Ltd v. OHIM*, Case T-507/08 [2011] *ECR* II-165*, [24].

[137] *Dart Industries Inc. v. OHIM*, Case T-360/00 [2002] *ECR* II-3867, [27] (ultraplus); *West (Eastenders) v. Fuller Smith & Turner* [2003] *FSR* (44) 816 (although the case was based on an application of *Baby Dry* and may need reviewing in the light of *Doublemint*).

[138] *Chung-Yuan Chang v. EUIPO, BSH Hausgeräte*, Case T-749/14, EU:T:2016:286, aff'd Case C-389/16P, EU:C:2016:876.

[139] See *PTV Planung Transport Verkehr AG v. OHIM*, Case C-512/06P [2007] *ECR* I-148 (in French and German only), affirming by Order the CFI decision Case T-302/03 [2006] *ECR* II-4039, [40], without criticizing the test applied; *Telefon & Buch VerlagsgmbH v. OHIM*, Case C-326/01P [2004] *ECR* I-1374, [33] (stating that the CFI had 'acted correctly and committed no error in law').

[140] *Wrigley (Doublemint)*, Case C-191/01P [2003] *ECR* I-12447, [AG 61] *ff*.

[141] *In re Interactive Intelligence Inc's Application*, O/325/07 [2007] *InfoTLR* 319; *Starbucks (HK) Ltd and anor v. British Sky Broadcasting Group Plc and ors* [2012] *EWHC* 3074 (Ch), [95] (Arnold J) (adopting CFI standard, but stating that he was uncertain whether it added anything).

[142] Compare *Mühlbauer Technology GmbH v. EUIPO*, Case T-218/16, EU:T:2017:334 (MAGICROWN for goods related to dental repair was descriptive) with *provima Warenhandels GmbH v. OHIM*, Case T-543/14, EU:T:2016:102 (HOT SOX induced so many meanings that the public would not immediately think of trendy socks).

[143] *Research Engineering & Manufacturing v. OHIM*, Case T-558/14, EU:T:2015:858, [50] (TRILOBULAR would evoke the nature and technical function of 'metal threaded fasteners' or screws).

3.3.9 Marks that are not words

Although section 3(1)(c) is most frequently applied to word marks, it can in principle be applied to all types of marks. In joined cases *Linde AG, Winward Industries, and Rado Watch Co. Ltd*,[144] the applicants sought to register three-dimensional marks comprising the shape of a forklift truck, a torch, and a watch, respectively. The Court of Justice held that Article 3(1)(c) of the Trade Marks Directive was equally applicable to shape marks. Although the Court did not provide any examples, two obvious ones are the bone shape of BONIO dog biscuits and the plastic lemon shape used by Reckitt's for its JIF lemon juice.[145] In one case in which the descriptiveness of a shape was contested, the Court held that the shape of a pine tree was not inherently descriptive of pine-scented air freshener.[146] Descriptiveness analysis is also frequently applied to figurative marks or figurative elements of composite marks.[147]

3.3.10 Excluded significations

With these general points in mind, we now turn to look at the categories of descriptive mark excluded by section 3(1)(c).

(i) Kind, quality, or quantity The first group of marks excluded from registrability are those that consist exclusively of signs that may serve to designate the 'kind, quality, or quantity' of goods and services. Undoubtedly, the greatest problem faced by a tribunal in this context is that of distinguishing between unregistrable terms or descriptions, and registrable allusions or suggestions. The General Court has affirmed EUIPO findings that BASICS is descriptive of paint,[148] GOLF USA of sports clothing,[149] MAP&GUIDE of computer software,[150] and TEK (the French and Italian word for 'teak') of metal shelves,[151] but that EUROPREMIUM is not descriptive of packaging.[152]

(ii) Intended purpose A mark that describes what the product does, suggests what the consumer is to do with the product, or outlines what happens when the product is consumed will not be registrable. Consequently, for example, health was held to be descriptive of the intended purpose of 'medical services', because the sign indicated that such services were to restore the recipient's good health.[153]

(iii) Value Trade marks that consist exclusively of signs that refer to the value of the goods or services will not be registrable. The reason for this is that consumers are unlikely to treat references to value as indications of origin. The provision also ensures that other traders are free to use common words and expressions to refer to things such as price and value. On this basis, signs such as CHEAP, ECONOMY, PREMIUM, or BEST BUY would

---

[144] Joined Cases C-53/01, C-54/01, and C-55/01 [2003] *ECR* I–3161.

[145] For an image, see [1990] RPC 341, 343.

[146] *Julius Sämaan Ltd v. Tetrosyl Ltd* [2006] *FSR* (42) 849, [39]–[40] (Kitchin J).

[147] *Universal Protein Supplements Corp. v. EUIPO*, Case T-335/15, EU:T:2016:579 (black silhouette of a body builder had a sufficiently direct link with nutritional supplements to be descriptive); Cf. *Novartis v. EUIPO,* Joined Cases T-678 and T-679/15, EU:T:2016:749 (stylized grey and green curves sufficiently abstract and would not be seen as representing a pill for pharmaceuticals).

[148] *Colart/Americas Inc v. OHIM*, Case T-164/06 [2007] *ECR* II–116.

[149] *Golf USA*, Case T-230/05 [2007] *ECR* II–23.

[150] *PTV Planung*, Case T-302/03 [2006] *ECR* II–4039, aff'd Case C-512/06P [2007] *ECR* I–148 (in French and German only).

[151] *Tegometall International AG v. OHIM*, Case T-458/05 [2007] *ECR* II–4721 (since they could be given the appearance of teak).

[152] *Deutsche Post Euro Express*, Case T-334/03 [2006] *ECR* II– 65, [25] (an appeal was lodged, but withdrawn). The case relies heavily on the discredited parts of *Baby-Dry*.

[153] *Diagnostiko v. OHIM*, Case T-7/10 [2011] *ECR* II-136*.

lack inherent distinctiveness, but could, of course, acquire distinctiveness through use (as with BUDGET for car-hire services).

(iv) Geographical origin While trade mark law has long been reluctant to grant protection to signs that consist of geographical names and places,[154] not every sign that happens also to be the name of a stream, village, lake, mountain, or other geographical reference will be unregistrable. The precise application of the exclusion depends on careful consideration of what the average consumers of the goods or services would be likely to understand from their naming. In *Windsurfing*,[155] the question was whether the word CHIEMSEE, the name of the largest lake in Bavaria, could be a trade mark for sports clothing or whether such a mark fell within Article 3(1)(c) of the Directive. The Court of Justice said that the tribunal must assess whether a geographical name designates a place that is currently associated in the mind of the relevant class of persons with the category of goods concerned, or whether it is reasonable to assume that such an association may be established in the future.[156] As the Court explained, the exclusion does not necessarily preclude the registration of geographical names that are unknown to the relevant class of persons—or at least unknown as the designation of a geographical location—or of names in respect of which, because of the type of place they designate (say, a mountain or lake), such persons are unlikely to believe that the category of goods concerned originates there.[157]

If there is an established connection between the place and the products in question—as with CUBA for CIGARS, SHEFFIELD for steel, FRANKFURT for financial services, or SILICON VALLEY for computers[158]—registration will normally be refused. In the *Windsurfing Chiemsee* case, the Court of Justice observed that the connection was not necessarily confined to a belief that the goods were *manufactured* in a particular place, but 'might depend on other ties, such as the fact that the goods were conceived and designed in the geographical location concerned'.[159] For example, an application to register SAVILE ROW for spectacle frames was refused because of the proximity that spectacles had to the goods for which Savile Row in London is famous (namely, tailors' services), both being fashion items.[160]

One key factor in deciding whether a sign of geographical origin should be excluded is the size of the place, since this affects how consumers are likely to understand the sign (and, in turn, whether other traders are likely to want to use it). The larger the place, the more likely it is that another trader may wish to use the name. Hence the reluctance to register EUROLAMB for meat,[161] or NORDIC for buildings and building materials,[162] and the willingness to register TOTTENHAM for various goods (all relating to Tottenham Hotspur Football Club).[163]

Where no connection exists between place and the products in issue, such as with SWEDISH FORMULA for cosmetics, the signs will be registrable.[164] Even the names of sizeable places may be registrable if there is no realistic connection with the goods concerned: an example that has often been given is that of NORTH POLE for bananas.[165] Where a mark

---

[154] *Yorkshire Copper Work's Trade Mark Application* (1954) 71 *RPC* 150, 154.

[155] Joined Cases C-108/97 and C-109/97 [1999] *ECR* I–2779.   [156] Ibid., 2824–5, [29]–[31].

[157] Ibid., 2825, [33].   [158] In the United States, this is referred to as the 'goods/place association'.

[159] Joined Cases C-108/97 and C-109/97 [1999] *ECR* I–2779, 2826, [36].

[160] *Savile Row Trade Mark* [1998] *RPC* 155.   [161] *Eurolamb Trade Mark* [1997] *RPC* 279.

[162] *Nordic Sauna Ltd's Trade Mark Application* [2002] *ETMR* (18) 210 (Thorley QC).

[163] *Tottenham Trade Mark* (6 January 2003) (AP, Prof. Annand).

[164] *Procter & Gamble/Swedish Formula*, R 85/98–2 [1999] *ETMR* 559.

[165] *British Sugar v. Robertson* [1996] *RPC* 281; *Yorkshire Copper* (1954) 71 *RPC* 150, 154, 156.

refers to a certain type of place, which contains a strong concentration of luxury or high quality products and this type of place can be found at different real-world locations, this is not sufficient to render the registration objectionably geographical.[166]

(v) The time of production of the goods or the time of rendering of the services Marks such as NOW for on-demand television services,[167] 24 HOURS (for restaurant services), SUNDAY (for newspapers), or SUMMERTIME for travel agency services would be inherently unregistrable as descriptive of the time of production or rendering of the goods or services.

(vi) Other characteristics The final part of section 3(1)(c) excludes signs that exclusively serve to designate 'other characteristics' of the goods or service.[168] Perhaps the most troublesome set of cases under this head concern the situation in which a trader gives their goods or services an arbitrary quality and seeks to register as a trade mark a description of that quality. In *OHIM v. Zapf Creation*,[169] Advocate-General Jacobs advised the Court of Justice to annul the CFI's finding that NEW-BORN BABY was not excluded from registration for toys and accessories for dolls under Article 7(1)(c) CTMR. While the Advocate-General agreed that NEW-BORN BABY was not a description of toys, he considered that the word combination was unregistrable, because it was a reference to the 'characteristics' of the goods—namely, that the toys represented or looked like newborn babies.[170] In contrast, in *Psytech International*,[171] the General Court agreed that the sign 16PF was not descriptive of various goods (software, printed matter) and services concerned with 'personality testing'. It was argued by Psytech that '16PF' referred to a test developed by Raymond Cattell in the 1940s, which focused on 16 different personality factors (such as warmth, dominance, sensitivity, and privateness). Viewing the relevant public as both the general public and specialists, the Court concluded that the general public would consider 16PF as 'devoid of meaning', while for specialists the term 16PF was primarily associated with the trade mark holder (which owned copyright in the questionnaire and was thus its main supplier). The Court of Justice observed that:

> [I]f a section of the relevant public could perceive, without further thought, the intervener's mark as referring to Dr Cattell's 16 factor personality test, that would suggest that that mark performs the essential function of a trade mark which is to allow identification of commercial origin.[172]

Importantly, perhaps, the Court did not think that there was any '16PF' theory (so allowing a monopoly over the sign would not, in practice, prevent anyone else from offering—and being able to describe—functionally equivalent tests).

The exclusion of marks that refer to 'other characteristics' has also been applied to certain insignia used in merchandising. In *Linkin Park LLC's Application*,[173] the Appointed Person held that LINKIN PARK, the name of a rock band, was unregistrable for posters,

---

[166] *Juan Moreno Marin et al. v. Abadia Retuerta SA*, Case C-139/16, EU:C:2017:518 (LA MILLA DE ORO, which is Spanish for the Golden Mile).

[167] *Starbucks (HK) Ltd v. British Sky Broadcasting Group Plc* [2013] *EWCA Civ* 1465 (referring to 'nowness' as a characteristic of the service).

[168] This is not included in Paris, Art. 6*quinquies*(B)(2), and thus may fall to be construed *ejusdem generis*.

[169] Case C-498/01P [2004] *ECR* I–11349 (AG). However there was no final judgment since the trade mark registration was subsequently withdrawn.

[170] It is notable that he considered that this was an essential characteristic of the goods—a contrast with the Court of Justice decision in *Koninklijke KPN Nederland NV v. Benelux-Merkenbureau*, Case C-363/99 [2004] *ECR* I–1619, which indicated that the commercial significance of a characteristic was irrelevant when deciding whether it was excluded.

[171] *Psytech International Ltd v. OHIM*, T-507/08, [2011] *ECR* II–165*, [24].   [172] Ibid., [41].

[173] [2006] *ETMR* (74) 1017 (AP, Arnold QC), [44].

because the term was descriptive of posters of the band (which consumers would doubtless refer to as 'Linkin Park posters'). He rejected an argument that 'other characteristics' is confined to the 'measurable properties' rather than the 'information content' of the goods.[174] Similarly, in *Score Draw Ltd v. Finch*,[175] Mann J held that the 'CBD' device was so associated with the Brazilian football team that it could be said to designate the characteristics of goods bearing the device—Brazilian football shirts, boots, etc.

3.4 CUSTOMARY AND GENERIC MARKS

Section 3(1)(d) of the 1994 Act/Article 7(1)(d) EUTMR provide that 'trade marks which consist *exclusively* of signs or indications which have become customary in the current language or in the bona fide and established practices of the trade' shall not be registrable.[176] Although it has been stated by the Court of Justice that the reason for this exclusion is that such signs are 'incapable of distinguishing' the goods or services of one undertaking from those of another,[177] it should be noted that the section is especially concerned with the languages and practices 'of the trade'. In the view of Advocates-General Colomer and Jacobs, the so-called 'requirement of availability' or 'protective function' also underpins this exclusion: signs that are customary in the trade are ones that other traders should be free to use.[178] However, in contrast to the operation of the protective function under section 3(1)(c), the terms of section 3(1)(d) refer to the meaning that has already developed by the time of the application. Consequently, the possibility of the sign becoming a designation in the future is not relevant.

While the scope of the section has yet to be fully explored, it seems that it will cover so-called 'generic' marks. A mark, particularly a name mark, is generic if, even though when it was first adopted it was distinctive, over time it has come to designate a genus or type of product rather than a particular product originating from a particular source. Well-known examples include LINOLEUM, YO-YO, ASPIRIN, and CELLOPHANE. One of the features of a generic mark is that it is no longer capable of distinguishing the goods or services of different traders. Where a word comes to describe a class of products, it can

---

[174] It should also be noted that distinctiveness seems to be more readily acquired for characters than the names of individuals. In a case concerning the 1930s cartoon character 'Betty Boop', Birss J found that the name and character were indicative of trade origin despite the fact that it might be equally possible for a consumer to ask in a shop for a 'Betty Boop T-shirt': *Hearst Holdings Inc v. A.V.E.L.A. Inc.* [2014] *EWHC* 439 (Ch), [97], [108], [109]. The judge emphasized that the issue is one of fact, and while there is no general rule, it may be easier to acquire distinctiveness in relation to a character: ibid., [107]. On the facts, he found that the reaction of the average consumer was 'multi-faceted'—i.e. the image would be seen as aesthetic or decorative, but also as indicating trade origin. He rejected the attacks on the validity of the marks: ibid., [140].

[175] [2007] *FSR* (20) 508. The Court had already found that the device was devoid of distinctive character.

[176] The terms of this category are not dissimilar to those of TMA 1994, s. 46, on revocation (on which, see Chapter 39, section 3, pp. 1094–7), although the differences are worthy of note. This ground covers not merely names, but all signs, and applies where the mark is customary in the 'current language' (which arguably may not be confined to trade). For the view that there are two exclusions in s. 3(1)(d), one relating to customary language and another to custom in the bona fide practices of the trade, see *Backaldrin Österreich The Kornspitz Company GmbH v. Pfahnl Backmittel GmbH*, Case C-409/12, EU:C:2013:563 (AG Cruz Villalón), [AG56], although the issue was not mentioned in the judgment of the Court: [2014] *ETMR* 30.

[177] See *Merz & Krell*, Case C-517/99 [2001] *ECR* I–6959. See also *Psytech International Ltd v. OHIM*, Case T-507/08, [2011] *ECR* II–165*, [56]; *Backaldrin Österreich The Kornspitz Company GmbH v. Pfahnl Backmittel GmbH*, Case C-409/12, EU:C:2013:563 (AG Cruz Villalón), [AG55]; EU:C:2014:130 (ECJ).

[178] *Nichols v. Registrar*, Case C-404/02 [2004] *ECR* I–8499, [AG43]; *Sat. 1 v. OHIM*, Case C-329/02P [2004] *ECR* I–8317, [AG21]–[AG23]. In the United States, these interests are regarded as overriding, so that a sign that is generic is unable to become a trade mark: *Abercrombie & Fitch Co. v. Hunting World Inc.*, 537 F.2d. 4 (2nd Cir. 1976).

no longer be relied upon to separate the products in the class from each other. In *Alcon Inc. v. OHIM*,[179] the Court of Justice held that the CFI had not erred in law when it found that BSS was unregistrable for sterile solutions for ophthalmic surgery. The CFI had found that ophthalmologists and ophthalmic surgeons practising in the European Union would have understood BSS as an abbreviation for 'buffered saline solution': scientific dictionaries and articles used the abbreviation, and many companies marketed products under designations containing 'BSS'. The Court held that there was no error in deciding that the relevant public (for assessing whether the sign was customary) was the specialist medical public, nor in its assessment of the facts. In *Backaldrin*, the Court of Justice clarified that the relevant public to be considered included not only consumers or end users but also, depending on the features of the product market, commercial intermediaries trading in the product.[180] Thus, where bakers were aware that KORNSPITZ was a trade mark for the baking mixture used to make a popular Austrian whole wheat bread roll but consumers used the term to refer to that type of roll, the perception of both groups was relevant. However, consumer perception and usage would ultimately be determinative; intermediary or trade usage was only relevant to the extent that it could influence consumer usage, whereas the bakers in this case did not emphasize the existence of the trade mark. In contrast, in *Psytech International*, the General Court agreed that the sign 16PF was not a generic designation of goods (software, printed matter) and services concerned with 'personality testing' because it was understood as referring to a questionnaire designed by a particular person and used by authorized users rather than as referring to a type of test.[181]

Quite what is covered by section 3(1)(d) beyond 'generic' marks is less than clear. In *Merz & Krell*,[182] the Court of Justice was asked whether, in the case of terms such as BRAVO, which were used purely as terms of praise, or as incitements to purchase, or in advertising, there was a requirement that, before they fell within Article 3(1)(d), they had to be understood by the trade *as descriptions of specific goods and services*. The Court answered that the application of the provision needed to be considered in relation to the mark and goods or services concerned (which, in the case in hand, were writing implements).[183] However, the exclusion was not confined to terms that *described* the properties or characteristics of the goods or services covered by them; the exclusion also covered signs that 'designate' the characteristics of the goods or services. The Court failed, however, to elaborate on the distinction between a description and a designation. It seems that designation involves a looser association with the goods or services than description.[184] The Court of Justice also said that while the term need not describe the goods (as under Article 3(1)(c)), the mere use of the term in advertising did not of itself indicate that the term 'designated' the goods concerned.

Section 3(1)(d) may occasionally exclude pictorial marks. In *RFU & Nike v. Cotton Traders*,[185] a registration by the Rugby Football Union (RFU) of an image of a rose for

---

[179] *Alcon Inc. v. OHIM*, Case T-237/01 [2003] *ECR* II-411, aff'd on appeal Case C-192/03 [2004] *ECR* I-8993.

[180] *Backaldrin Österreich The Kornspitz Company GmbH v. Pfahnl Backmittel GmbH*, Case C-409/12, EU:C:2014:130. The Court also confirmed that a brand owner's inactivity—in not preventing generic use—was a relevant factor when assessing generic status under revocation proceedings.

[181] *Psytech International Ltd v. OHIM*, T-507/08, [2011] *ECR* II-165*, [59].

[182] Case C-517/99 [2001] *ECR* I-6959, [36]-[40].   [183] Ibid., [29].

[184] Advocate-General Colomer drew a distinction between Art. 3(1)(c), which he saw as concerned with 'description' by *direct* reference to characteristics, and Art. 3(1)(d), which was not so confined and did not specify the degree of association that must exist between the sign and the goods/services: ibid., [AG48]–[AG50]. In his view, bravo—a mere expression of enthusiasm—would be registrable for typewriters, but not for sports clothing or services, because in the sporting field the term is 'habitually used' and, in bullfighting, it even refers to a characteristic of a fighting bull.

[185] [2002] *ETMR* (76) 861, 876 (Lloyd J); cf. *Score Draw v. Finch* [2007] *FSR* (20) 508, [45].

clothing was held to be invalid. Evidence of sales of shirts bearing a rose crest by undertakings not associated with the RFU indicated that it was customary to associate the rose with the England rugby team. Consequently, the sign was customary and not distinctive of the goods of the RFU.

3.5 USED MARKS: ACQUIRED DISTINCTIVENESS

So far in our discussions of section 3(1)(b)–(d), we have been concerned with whether marks are inherently registrable—that is, we have been looking at marks in their 'natural' or unused state. In this section, we turn to look at the ways in which an unregistrable mark—one which is non-distinctive, descriptive, or generic—becomes registrable through use. As the proviso to section 3 of the 1994 Act states, 'a trade mark shall not be refused registration . . . if, before the date of application for registration, it has in fact acquired a distinctive character as a result of the use made of it'.[186] Similarly, section 47(1) provides that a mark that is wrongly entered into the Register (because it lacks inherent distinctiveness) shall not be declared to be invalid where the mark has acquired distinctiveness after registration.[187] The result of these provisions is that even if a mark inherently lacks distinctiveness, it is now possible to register the mark if it does *in fact* become distinctive.

Consequently, the only question that needs to be asked where a mark has been used is: has the mark in fact acquired a distinctive character?[188] The inquiry in relation to used marks is exclusively concerned with customer perception (that is, the 'distinguishing function'); the 'protective function' (the needs of other traders) is irrelevant.[189] As a result, consumer recognition becomes the litmus test for whether a mark is registrable.[190] The primary goal is to minimize consumer confusion by preventing other traders from using a similar mark. To successfully establish acquired distinctiveness, an applicant must be able to show that the primary significance of the word or sign indicates a source rather than, for example, merely describes or praises the product as it might have done in its natural state. The sign must have acquired 'secondary meaning'. In *Windsurfing*,[191] the Court of Justice explained that an unregistrable name (in that case, a geographical one):

> . . . may be registered as a trade mark if, following the use which has been made of it, it has come to identify the product in respect of which registration is applied for as originating from a particular undertaking and thus to distinguish that product from goods of other undertakings.[192]

---

[186] The same requirement applies to EUTMs: the use to support this form of distinctiveness must have been prior to the date of the application: *Imagination Technologies v. OHIM*, Case C-542/07P [2009] *ECR* I-4937, [49], [51]. However evidence of use of the mark after registration *may* be relevant as regards its situation prior to registration. A noteworthy recent development relates to EUTMIR, Art. 2(2). An EUTM applicant can now include acquired distinctiveness as a subsidiary claim; only after the Office has taken a decision on the inherent distinctiveness of a mark will the analysis turn to acquired distinctiveness, if required.

[187] A parallel is found in EUTMR, Art. 59(2).

[188] Note that it is not necessary to know the identity of the source; only that the product or service comes from a single source. This is sometimes termed the 'anonymous source doctrine'.

[189] *Windsurfing*, Joined Cases C-108/97 and C-109/97 [1999] *ECR* I-2779, 2829, [48]; *Audi Ag v. OHIM*, T-16/02 [2003] *ECR* II-5167, [50]. The interests of others are accommodated via specific exclusions (such as for shapes) or the defences in TMA 1994, s. 11.

[190] The ability for marks to become registrable through use, which is provided for under the 1994 Act, is in marked contrast to the position in the 1938 Act, under which held that certain marks could never become registrable irrespective of how distinctive they were 'in fact': *York TM* [1984] *RPC* 231.

[191] Joined Cases C-108/97 and C-109/97 [1999] *ECR* I-2779.   [192] Ibid., [46].

By acknowledging this new meaning, the law is merely recognizing what has already happened in practice. Nevertheless, there are concerns that if the threshold for recognizing this is set too low, individual traders could appropriate descriptive and cultural signs, or non-traditional signs such as colours, primarily on the basis of an advertising investment over time.[193]

Before turning to consider the requirements for acquired distinctiveness, a threshold question—which has recently generated controversy—relates to the precise significance of the mark, as a consequence of its commercial use. Is *recognition* of the mark and its *association* with a particular trader sufficient in order to establish acquired distinctiveness, or is something more specific required? Recognition suggests that the sign is merely familiar (but perhaps as a decorative feature), while association with a specific trader is not necessarily the same as indicating commercial source. One associates the colour red with Coke, but also with Vodafone, Santander, Virgin, and Target. Associations per se may be too promiscuous for trade mark purposes. While this issue had previously arisen on several occasions, it was finally addressed by the Court of Justice in a reference from the English High Court.[194] The reference arose in the context of determining whether the 'naked' shape—without any trade marks embossed on the surface—of a four fingered KIT KAT chocolate wafer bar had established distinctiveness through long-standing use. Both the end point (eventual consumer perception) and the means by which it is achieved are important aspects of this enquiry.

In referring the matter, Arnold J contrasted two end point mental states—the potentially looser *recognition and association* requirement, as opposed to *reliance* on the shape instead of any other trade marks that may also be present upon the goods.[195] The means used suggested that consumers did not have the opportunity to rely on the 'naked' bar as a trade mark, since the chocolate had been sold accompanied by word marks both on the external packaging as well as embossed on the surface of the individual chocolate fingers. While the Advocate General rejected the recognition and association standard,[196] the Court of Justice reformulated the (end point) question: would consumers '*perceive* the goods or services designated exclusively by [the mark applied for], as opposed to any other mark which might also be present, *as originating* from a particular company'. [197] The Court also confirmed that a sign could reach this end point whilst in the company of other trade marks on the same product, but the sign was ultimately expected to be capable of signalling origin on its own.[198]

On remand to the national court, Arnold J incorporated the reliance standard within a perception-focused approach. In upholding the UKIPO's rejection of the shape mark, the judge concluded that it was legitimate for the 'competent authority, when assessing whether the applicant has proved that a significant proportion of the relevant class of person perceives the relevant goods or services as originating from a particular undertaking *because of the sign in question,* to consider whether persons would *rely upon the sign as denoting the origin* of the goods if it were used on its own (i.e., without other trade marks being present)'.[199] Seemingly significant consumer survey evidence was attributed to

---

[193] L. Anemaet, 'The Public Domain Is Under Pressure—Why We Should Not Rely on Empirical Data When Assessing Trademark Distinctiveness' (2016) 47(3) *IIC* 303.

[194] *Société des Produits Nestlé SA v. Cadbury UK Ltd*, Case C-215/14 [2015] *ETMR* 50; on referral from *Société des Produits Nestlé SA v. Cadbury UK Ltd* [2014] *EWHC* 16 (Ch) (Arnold J).

[195] *Société des Produits Nestlé SA v. Cadbury UK Ltd*, Case C-215/14 [2015] *ETMR* 50, [26].

[196] Ibid., [AG42], [AG55] (AG Wathelet).   [197] Ibid., [58], [67] (emphasis added).

[198] Ibid., [65].

[199] *Société des Produits Nestlé SA v. Cadbury UK Ltd* [2016] *EWHC* 50, [60] (emphasis added). Arnold J. interpreted the Court's guidance as requiring that 'a significant proportion of the relevant class of persons [should perceive] the relevant goods or services as originating from a particular undertaking *because of* the sign in question (as opposed to any other trade mark which may also be present)', [57].

establishing merely recognition and association, rather than reliance.[200] In turn, Arnold J's conclusion was upheld on appeal, with Kitchin LJ articulating a potential reconciliation between the different ways of framing the analysis: 'Perception by consumers that goods or services designated by the mark originate from a particular undertaking means they can rely upon the mark in making or confirming their transactional decisions. In this context, *reliance is a behavioural consequence of perception*'.[201] At the time of writing, the chocolate shape mark remains unregistrable. Perhaps the most useful lesson to be drawn is that the means matter; the applicant had not made 'standalone', origin-indicating use of the sign in question since the accompanying word marks did the source-signification work. Had it done so, the outcome might be different.[202] The significance of this reasoning therefore extends beyond shape marks to all manner of non-traditional marks, which will face the same challenges.[203]

3.5.1 Displacement of the primary meaning

While the various authorities make it clear that, to be registrable, a sign must have become distinctive, there is less guidance as to the nature of the relationship between the old and new meanings. At the most extreme, some authorities seem to suggest that the new trade mark meaning must have completely replaced the original meaning. This seems to be what Jacob J required in *Philips v. Remington*[204] when he said that 'unless the word, when used for the goods concerned, has in practice displaced its ordinary meaning, it will not properly denote the trader's goods and none other'.[205] However, to require that there be nothing left of the original meaning in any circumstances would be going too far (and indeed would be inconsistent with the idea that allusive marks will be registrable as long as the immediate impression given to consumers is not exclusively descriptive).[206] Other authorities acknowledge that it is possible for a sign to become distinctive even though the 'primary meaning' still exists. For example, in *Windsurfing Chiemsee*, the Court of Justice explained that, where a geographical name has come to identify the product as originating from a particular undertaking and thus to distinguish that product from goods of other undertakings, the geographical designation 'has gained a new significance and its connotation, no longer *purely descriptive*, justifies its registration as a trade mark'.[207] The critical displacement of meaning is that which operates when the sign is used in relation to the particular goods or services, and the question is whether, in such a situation, the average consumer of the product immediately understands the sign as referring to source.

---

[200] Ibid., [67]–[68]. By contrast, the General Court concluded that acquired distinctiveness had been acquired in the United Kingdom, when assessing the registrability of the equivalent EUTM: *Mondelez UK Holdings & Services Ltd v. EUIPO*, Case T-112/13, EU:T:2016:735, [78]–[94]; appeal pending as C-84/17P.

[201] *Société des Produits Nestlé SA v. Cadbury UK Ltd* [2017] *EWCA Civ* 358, [82] (emphasis added).

[202] As a possible example of (quite literally) flagging up trade mark significance, see *Bonbonverpackung mit Fähnchen* (30 June 2016) Case No. 25 W (Pat) 33/13, German Federal Patent Court (BPatG) (an extruding 'flag' on a cough lozenge wrapper had been used since the 1920s with the claim 'Only genuine with the flag'; it was clearly being used to indicate commercial source).

[203] G. Dinwoodie, 'Non-Traditional Marks in Europe: Conceptual Lessons from their Apparent Demise', www.ssrn.com.   [204] [1998] *RPC* 283, 303.

[205] Having said this, a distinctive mark may contain other messages, such as suggestions or allusions as to quality or origin. As long as these are not deceptive, and thus contrary to TMA 1994, s. 3(3)(b), registration may proceed; see section 4.2, pp. 1015–17.

[206] *West (Eastenders)* [2003] *FSR* (44) 816, 841, [68] (Arden LJ); Kerly, [7-103]–[7-112], [7-179]–[7-183].

[207] Joined Cases C-108/97 and C-109/97 [1999] *ECR* I-2779, 2829, [47].

3.5.2 Numerical extent of recognition

It is clear that, for an unregistrable mark to become registrable, it is necessary for consumers to think about the sign as an indication of origin. One question that arises is: how widespread must the consumer recognition be? In *Windsurfing*, the Court of Justice said that the question is whether 'the relevant class of persons, or at least a *significant proportion* thereof*', identify goods as originating from a particular undertaking because of the trade mark.[208]

The Court made it clear that it is not possible to say whether a mark is distinctive by reference to predetermined percentages.[209] This is because the evidence that is needed to support a claim that a mark has become registrable through use (or, where wrongly registered, that it deserves to stay on the register) depends on how descriptive (etc.) the mark is in its 'natural' state. Thus if the objections to the word are not strong, then it is likely that less evidence of acquired distinctiveness will be required. However, the more descriptive a mark is, the more convincing the evidence of acquired distinctiveness must be.[210] In *Windsurfing*, the Court said that, where a geographical name is very well known, it can acquire distinctive character only if there has been long-standing and intensive use of the mark by the undertaking applying for registration.[211]

3.5.3 Geographical extent of recognition

How widespread geographically must the acquired distinctiveness be? In *Bovemij Verzekeringen*,[212] the Court of Justice had to advise on the registrability of the mark EUROPOLIS for insurance services with the Benelux Trade Mark Office (which grants rights for Belgium, Luxembourg, and the Netherlands). The sign was descriptive to Dutch speakers, who understood the word *polis* as referring to insurance policies, but not to French speakers. The Court indicated that, to be registrable, the sign must be shown to have acquired distinctiveness by use throughout the territory where the ground of objection subsisted, in effect for a 'significant proportion' of Dutch speakers.

In the case of a UK trade mark, acquired distinctiveness would thus need to be demonstrated amongst a 'significant part' of consumers as a result of use throughout the United Kingdom. Consequently, in *Bignell v. Just Employment Law Ltd*,[213] a trade mark was held to be invalid on the basis that the fact that it had acquired distinctiveness within Surrey and the neighbouring counties was not sufficient evidence that a significant proportion of the relevant class of persons *in the United Kingdom as a whole* would have identified goods as originating from a particular undertaking because of the trade mark. However, in *Evegate Publishing Ltd v. Newsquest Media (Southern) Ltd*,[214] Asplin J declined to

---

[208] Ibid., 2830, [52]; *Koninklijke Philips v. Remington*, Case C-299/99 [2002] *ECR* I–5475, [65] (substantial portion of the relevant class); *Bovemij Verzekeringen NV v. Benelux-Merkenbureau*, Case C-108/05 [2006] *ECR* I–7605 (ECJ, First Chamber); *Oberbank AG v. Deutscher Sparkassen- und Giroverband eV*, Joined Cases C-217 and 218/13, [2014] *ETMR* 56, [42].

[209] This was subsequently confirmed in *Oberbank AG*, Joined Cases C-217 and 218/13, [2014] *ETMR* 56.

[210] See *Fine & Country v. Okotoks* [2013] *EWCA Civ* 672, [96], [97], [106], drawing attention to the statement of the Court of Justice in *Lloyd Schuhfabrik Meyer & Co. GmbH v. Klijsen Handel BV*, Case C-342/97 [1999] *ECR* I–3819, [23], that the assessment of distinctiveness required consideration of 'the fact that [the sign] does or does not contain an element descriptive of the goods or services for which' registration is sought. See also *Oberbank AG*, Case C-217/13, [2014] *ETMR* 56, [45]–[48] (while it may be practically more difficult to establish acquired distinctiveness for certain categories of marks, such as abstract colours, this does not justify imposing more demanding predetermined percentage requirements for such categories).

[211] Joined Cases C-108/97 and C-109/97 [1999] *ECR* I–2779, 2830, [50].

[212] Case C-108/05, [2006] *ECR* I–7605.   [213] [2008] *FSR* (6) 125 (Englehart QC).

[214] [2013] *EWHC* 1975 (Ch), [238].

invalidate a mark, SOUTH EAST FARMER, because even though use was demonstrated primarily in three counties in southeast England (Kent, Surrey, Sussex, and parts of Hampshire), it was not restricted to these areas. The Court concluded that the paper was advertised nationally, and so while its 'reputation' was geographically limited, its 'distinctiveness' existed outside the southeast.

In respect of EUTMs, parallel issues arise as to the geographical dimensions of acquired distinctiveness. Here, however, the issue is coloured by the linguistic diversity of the European Union and geopolitical assumptions about whether the Union is a single entity or really a bundle of nation states (as well as the logic of the relationship with national trade mark regimes). Acquired distinctiveness arises in two types of situations—where the mark is not distinctive in a part of the EU, because it is (say) descriptive according to one of the official languages; and where it is deemed to lack inherent distinctiveness across the whole of the EU, because it is (say) a colour or shape mark.

As an introduction to the first scenario, let us return to the example of OLUT, which is descriptive of beer in Finnish, but not in English. Acquired distinctiveness would have to be proved in all the territories where the mark lacks distinctiveness; in this case, Finland. In *Ford Motor's Application/Options*,[215] the applicant sought to register OPTIONS for, among other things, insurance services. In response to the examiner's objection that the sign was devoid of distinctive character in French and English, the applicant filed evidence of use in a number of countries including the United Kingdom, but not France. It was argued that this was sufficient since the United Kingdom was a substantial part of the territories for which acquired distinctiveness was required. The (then) CFI disagreed, reasoning that, in order to be accepted for registration, a sign must possess distinctive character throughout the European Union. Since the mark lacked distinctiveness in France, it was not registrable as a CTM. Subsequent EUIPO registration practice has consolidated the position on the geographical extent required for an EUTM—for example by indicating where a language is considered official. Consequently, where a term is descriptive in German, acquired distinctiveness will have to be established in Austria, Belgium, Germany, and Luxembourg, while for English terms the relevant territories are Ireland, Malta, and the United Kingdom.[216]

The second scenario involving acquired distinctiveness for EUTMs primarily relates to non-traditional marks, such as colours, surface patterns, or shapes. Since consumers are unlikely to perceive such signs as trade marks *ab initio*, they are considered devoid of any distinctive character across the European Union as a whole.[217] Consequently acquired distinctiveness for such marks must be established throughout the Union. However does 'throughout' the Union mean 'in each and every member state' or rather amongst a 'significant proportion' of European citizens, irrespective of their geographical distribution?

In *Lindt,* which concerned the registration of a shape mark consisting of a golden rabbit for chocolate confectionaries (see Fig. 37.10), the Court of Justice reiterated the requirement for acquired distinctiveness to be established throughout the European Union. Such evidence in relation to only 16 out of the (then) 25 member states was insufficient. However since EUTMs had a unitary character, an approach reliant upon usage in individual national markets was inappropriate; for marks lacking inherent

---

[215] Ibid. See also *Audi v. OHIM (TDI)*, T-16/02 [2003] *ECR* II-5167, [52], [60], [66].

[216] See EUIPO, *Examination Guidelines*, Part B, Section 4, Chapter 14, [6] ('Territorial Aspects').

[217] *August Storck KG v. OHIM*, Case C-25/05P [2006] ECR I-5719, [83]; *Louis Vuitton Malletier v. OHIM, Nanu-Nana*, Case T-359/12, EU:T:2015:215, [91]–[93] (representation of a brown and beige chequerboard pattern).

distinctiveness 'it would be unreasonable to require proof of such acquisition for each individual Member State'.[218]

At present, the threshold for those marks which are required to prove acquired distinctiveness 'throughout' the EU remain unclear. The EUIPO has developed an extrapolation model, such that failure to prove acquired distinctiveness in one or more specific national markets is not decisive, provided that the 'missing pieces' of the puzzle do not affect the conclusion that a significant proportion of the relevant European public now perceives the sign as a trade mark, as a result of the use made of it.[219] Extrapolating, by drawing from selective evidence to reach broader conclusions, is permitted where two cumulative conditions are met:

(i)   The market is homogeneous, in the sense that market conditions and consumer habits are comparable. Where these criteria are satisfied, the findings from surveys covering some member states could reflect consumer perception in other member states that have not been surveyed.

(ii) At least some evidence of use of the mark is submitted for all the areas where the extrapolation is required. This second limb continues to impose a significant evidentiary burden, since it apparently requires that a candidate (non-traditional) sign has to at least be used throughout the European Union.

It remains to be seen whether the Court of Justice will endorse or subsequently adapt this approach.

3.5.4 The relevant consumers

On general principles, distinctiveness needs to be acquired across the full range of goods or services for which registration is sought. This needs to be established for both actual and prospective purchasers of the goods or services. For prospective purchasers, this principle may cause problems where a mark is used in relation to goods or services targeted at a niche market, because the sign might come to be known by an elite, but not by the mass of consumers of goods of the relevant type. It has now been confirmed that if the claimed goods (say, watches) are broader than the sub-category of goods on which the mark is actually used (say, luxury watches), the broader category—the general watch purchasing public—will still set the benchmarks. Acquired distinctiveness will have to be established in relation to this broader category.[220]

3.5.5 Types of supporting evidence

A range of different types of evidence may be used to support a claim for registrability through use. In *Windsurfing Chiemsee*,[221] the Court of Justice listed the following considerations: (i) the market share held by the mark; (ii) how intensive, geographically

---

[218] *Chocoladefabriken Lindt & Sprüngli AG v. OHIM*, Case C-98/11P, EU:C:2012:307. As an alternative to each member state being included in the assessment, the Max Planck review had suggested the majority of the markets making up the respective territory. Max Planck Institute, *Study on the Overall Functioning of the Community Trade Mark System* (2011), 147, [3.74].

[219] EUIPO, *Examination Guidelines*, Part B, Section 4, Chapter 14, [6.3] ('Extrapolation'). Cf. *Mondelez UK Holdings & Services Ltd v. EUIPO*, Case T-112/13, EU:T:2016:735, [141]–[143] (merging all member states and regions into a single market is an incorrect approach); appeal pending as C-84/17P.

[220] *Raimund Schmitt Verpachtungsgesellschaft v. EUIPO*, Case T-56/15, EU:T:2016:618, [106]–[111], [138]–[139] (evidence relating to specialized brewing magazines insufficient to support claims to magazines as a broader category); EUIPO *Examination Guidelines*, Part B, Section 4, Chapter 14, [4]–[5].

[221] Joined Cases C-108/97 and C-109/97 [1999] *ECR* I–2779, 2830, [51].

widespread, and long-standing the use of the mark has been; (iii) the amount invested by the undertaking in promoting the mark; (iv) the proportion of the relevant class of persons who, because of the mark, identify goods as originating from a particular undertaking; and (v) statements from chambers of commerce and industry or other trade and professional associations.[222] The General Court has also confirmed that there is a hierarchy of significance for categories of evidence. Those circumstantial categories over which the applicant has greater control, such as the extent of use and advertising expenditure, are relevant only insofar as they produce objective results, by influencing the perception of the relevant public.[223] Thus sales figures and advertising material constitute a form of secondary evidence which support more direct evidence of acquired distinctiveness, such as consumer surveys.[224]

(i) Evidence of use Acquired distinctiveness must be proved 'on the basis of specific and reliable data'.[225] A tribunal may take into account evidence of the length of time for which the product has been on the market, the volume of the goods marketed, or the extent of services provided. Such evidence might be supplied by way of statutory declarations. Typically, examples of uses on packaging, marketing, and advertising, as well as details of expenditure, will also be submitted. These uses should occur prior to the trade mark application, while the geographical territory to which they relate is an important consideration. The credibility of evidence submitted by certain parties, such as the applicant's employees, is open to being challenged.[226] However, as observed earlier, the critical evidence concerns the impact of such activities; do they influence the perception of the sign amongst the relevant public?

Earlier in this chapter, when considering the *Kit Kat* shape mark, it was established that an important consideration for acquired distinctiveness is whether the sign in question has been used in a trade mark sense, to indicate the commercial origin of the goods. The Court of Justice identified this as a requirement in *Philips*, another case relating to shape marks.[227] The Court has additionally clarified that there is no need for the sign to be used alone; other trade marks may also be present. Thus a slogan on a product (for example HAVE A BREAK) might acquire distinctive character even though it had been used only when accompanied by a registered mark (KIT KAT) in the PHRASE HAVE A BREAK . . . HAVE A KIT KAT.[228] Equally, a shape might acquire distinctive character even though it is accompanied by a verbal mark.[229]

As we have previously identified, in the context of the *Kit Kat* shape mark, the means (manner of use) is what allows us to successfully reach the end (establishing acquired distinctiveness). Here we consider the means. Where a trader has a legal monopoly (for instance, exclusivity based on patent protection) or commercially dominates the market, the public

---

[222] One of the factors is stated to be the proportion of the relevant class of persons who, because of the mark, identify goods as originating from a particular undertaking': ibid., [51]. However, in our view, this is not really a 'factor' so much as the essence of the inquiry: see ibid., [52]. Consequently, we think it is more helpful to distinguish, as patent law does in its non-obviousness inquiry, between 'primary' and 'secondary' evidence. See *Glaverbel*, Case T–141/06 [2007] *ECR* II–114*, [41], aff'd Case C–513/07P [2008] *ECR* I–146*.

[223] *Compagnie des bateaux mouches SA v. OHIM, Castanet*, Case T–365/06 [2008] ECR II–310, [59].

[224] *The Coca-Cola Company v. OHIM*, Case T–411/14, EU:T:2016:94, [83] (shape of a contour bottle without fluting). [225] *Koninklijke Philips v. Remington*, Case C–299/99 [2002] *ECR* I–5475, [65].

[226] *Heinrich Deichmann-Schuhe GmbH v. OHIM*, Case T–86/07 [2008] ECR II–321*, [46]–[50].

[227] *Koninklijke Philips v. Remington*, Case C–299/99 [2002] *ECR* I–5475, [64] ('as a result of use of the mark *as a trade mark*, and thus as a result of the nature and effect of it', emphasis added); *Nestlé*, Case C–353/03 [2005] *ECR* I–6135, [26]. This means that the sign must be used 'for the purpose of the identification by the relevant class of persons of the product or service as originating from a given undertaking': ibid., [29].

[228] Ibid. The mark—which had been the subject of several contested applications over many years—was finally registered in July 2006: TM 2015684.

[229] *August Storck*, Case C–24/05P [2006] *ECR* I–5677, [59].

may come to associate the sign being claimed—such as a three-headed electrical rotary shaver—with this trader.[230] However mere longstanding use of a certain feature or sign, without signalling that it is intentionally being used as a trade mark, is not sufficient. Once other traders begin to use the sign—it may be an attractive or useful product feature—the initial association with the original trader dissipates in the face of competing uses. This logic applies to word marks as well, since words may be perceived as merely descriptive of the products or laudatory, as opposed to indicating commercial origin.[231] This 'use as a mark' requirement is especially relevant for non-traditional marks, such as colours or shapes, since consumers are likely to otherwise attribute functional or aesthetic significance to them instead.[232]

(ii) *Advertising expenditure* Although the Court of Justice specifically stated that tribunals may take account of the amount invested by the undertaking in promoting the mark, British courts have been more sceptical as to the value of matters such as advertising expenditure or evidence of sales success as indicators of acquired distinctiveness. This is because evidence of use will not inevitably lead to a finding of distinctiveness *through* use. It is not the extent of promotional efforts that is crucial so much as it is the effect on consumers.[233] Consequently, evidence that the word TREAT had been used for five years did not, on its own, demonstrate that the mark had become a badge of trade origin. A concluding point worth noting is that the expenditure should specifically relate to the mark that is being applied for.

(iii) *Evidence of the trade* Moreover, although the Court of Justice also refers to the relevance of 'statements from chambers of commerce and industry or other trade and professional associations', UK courts have treated these as of only marginal significance.[234] The reason for this is that the relevant class of persons is not trade buyers, but the average customer of the product.[235]

(iv) *Consumer surveys* Since the inquiry is focused upon consumer attitudes to the sign, direct evidence from consumers and consumer surveys will most likely prove to be of value. The Court of Justice has stated that, in this context, EU law 'does not preclude the competent authority, where it has particular difficulty in that connection, from having recourse, under the conditions laid down by its own national law, to an opinion poll as guidance for its judgment'.[236] Under UK law, opinion polls are not precluded, but must be scrutinized with considerable care and their real probative value appraised.[237]

---

[230] *Koninklijke Philips v. Remington,* Case C-299/99 [2002] *ECR* I–5475. The Court was asked for guidance on this question but did not directly address it, which eventually led to the referral in *Kit Kat.*

[231] *Reed Exhibitions Ltd v. OHIM,* Case T-633/13, EU:T:2015:674 (the use of INFOSECURITY for various information security products and services was not sufficiently emphasized to acquire distinctiveness).

[232] *Työhönvalmennus Valma Oy v. OHIM,* Case T-363/15, EU:T:2016:149 (shape of a games chest containing wooden blocks was not used such that it would indicate origin); *The Coca-Cola Company v. OHIM,* Case T-411/14, EU:T:2016:94, [83] (shape of a contour bottle without fluting was not itself used as a mark and also not implicitly visually contained within the well-known fluted bottle, which did function as a mark).

[233] *British Sugar v. Robertson* [1996] *RPC* 281. See also *L & D SA v. OHIM,* Case C-488/06P [2008] *ECR* I–5725, [AG86] (AG Sharpston) (some evidence must be presented that the mark in issue is actually perceived as linking the products that bear it with a particular undertaking, and such evidence cannot come solely from data such as market share and advertising investment or duration of use), and [75]–[76] (such evidence sufficed at least when coupled with 'prolonged use').

[234] *Wickes's Trade Mark Application* [1998] *RPC* 698.   [235] *Re Dualit* [1999] *RPC* 890, 898, [33].

[236] *Windsurfing,* Joined Cases C-108/97 and C-109/97 [1999] *ECR* I–2779, 2830, [53].

[237] *Nestlé v. Unilever* [2003] *ETMR* (53) 681, [22]. In general, the question of admissibility will depend on the court balancing the probative value against the cost of the survey: *Interflora Inc. v. Marks & Spencer plc* [2012] *EWCA Civ* 1501, [2012] *FSR* (21) 415, [150]. However, it is notable that Lewison LJ implied that such a survey (or related witness-gathering exercise) might have greater probative value where the issue is whether a registered mark has acquired distinctiveness than in determining whether there is likely confusion: ibid., [137]. See Chapter 38, section 2.3.4, pp. 1050–1.

4 OTHER ABSOLUTE GROUNDS FOR INVALIDITY

The third and more eclectic category of absolute grounds for refusal is set out in section 3(3)–(6) of the 1994 Act. This provides that trade marks shall not be registered if they are contrary to public policy or morality, if they are likely to deceive the public, if they are prohibited by law, or if the application was made in bad faith. Particular provisions also exist for specially protected emblems.

4.1 PUBLIC POLICY AND MORALITY

Section 3(3)(a) provides that a trade mark shall not be registered if it is contrary to public policy or to accepted principles of morality.[238] The two exceptions relate to the intrinsic qualities of the sign, rather than the manner in which it is used.[239]

4.1.1 Morality

Rather like the corresponding ground for invalidity in the European Patent Convention,[240] this provision has generated a rather inconsistent case law, particularly with respect to the application of the notion of 'morality'.[241] The UK Trade Marks Registry and the EUIPO seem to have made matters all the more confusing by trying to interpret the notion in the light of Article 10 of the European Convention on Human Rights (ECHR), and permissible exceptions thereto.[242] In our view, the implications for 'free speech' of refusal to register a trade mark are negligible and these considerations irrelevant.[243] However, the topic is one that would benefit from the authoritative views of a higher tribunal.

In the United Kingdom, the question of morality has come before the Appointed Person four times. The test, which has repeatedly been mentioned as helpful in distinguishing cases of mere bad taste (which can be registered) from those that contravene principles of morality, has been said to be whether use of the sign would 'justifiably cause outrage or would be the subject of justifiable censure as being likely significantly to undermine current religious, family or social values'.[244] Despite the apparently high threshold, the test has been applied to reach the surprising conclusions that TINY PENIS,[245] JESUS,[246]

---

[238] Note also that a trade mark that contains a representation of one of the flags of the countries of the United Kingdom, the use of which would be 'grossly offensive', shall not be registered: TMA 1994, s. 4(2).

[239] *Durferrit GmbH v. OHIM, Kolene Corp. Intervening*, Case T-224/01 [2003] *ECR* II–1589, [76].

[240] EPC 1973, Art. 53(a). See Chapter 17, section 9, pp. 537–50.

[241] The United States is presently undergoing a seismic shift in relation to this exclusion. In *Matal v. Tam* 137 *S. Ct.* 1744 (2017), the US Supreme Court evaluated the constitutionality of the 'disparagement' absolute ground under federal trademark law (15 *USC* §1052(a)). Eight justices unanimously agreed this provision violates the free speech clause of the First Amendment to the Constitution, since the government discriminates based on viewpoint and targets offensive expression with an intent to discourage its use.

[242] *In re Basic Trademark SA's Application* [2005] *RPC* (25) 611 (AP, Hobbs QC), [26]; *FCUK Trade Mark* [2007] *RPC* 1 (AP, Arnold QC), [60]. However, the General Court has been quick to cite fundamental rights as a reason for excluding certain signs from registration: *Paki Logistics GmbH v. OHIM*, T-526/09 [2011] *ECR* II–346, [15] (referring to discrimination under Arts 2 and 3(3) TEU, Arts 9 and 10 TFEU, and Art. 21 of the Charter of Fundamental Rights of the European Union). See also S. Snedden, 'Immoral Trade Marks in the UK and at OHIM: How Would the Redskins Dispute be Decided There?' (2016) 11(4) *JIPLP* 270.

[243] J. Griffiths, 'Is There a Right to an Immoral Trade Mark?', in P. Torremans (ed.), *Intellectual Property and Human Rights* (2008).   [244] *Ghazilian's Application* [2002] *RPC* (33) 628.

[245] Ibid.

[246] *Basic Trademark* [2005] *RPC* (25) 611 (Hobbs QC). Registration was sought for various goods in Classes 3, 9, 14, 16, 18, 24, 25, and 28.

and FOOK (all for, among other things, clothing) were 'contrary to accepted principles of morality',[247] while FCUK (for jewellery) was not.[248] TINY PENIS was held to be unregistrable for clothes because (according to Simon Thorley QC) use of the words would undermine an important social value—namely, that anatomical terms for parts of the genitalia should be retained for serious (educational) use and not tainted by 'use as a smutty trade mark for clothing'.[249] JESUS was rejected for clothing and other goods because:

> [B]randing which employs words or images of religious significance can quite easily have a seriously troubling effect on people whose religious beliefs it impinges upon and others who adhere to the view that religious beliefs should be treated with respect in a civilised society.[250]

FOOK was rejected because it was the phonetic equivalent of 'fuck', the use of which would apparently cause 'justifiable outrage' when used on clothing (despite its frequent use in football stadiums),[251] but FCUK was acceptable because, even though it could be used to evoke the swear word, it was not a phonetic or visual equivalent of 'fuck'.[252] In reaching the last conclusion, Richard Arnold QC (as he then was) seems to have been particularly influenced by the fact that other regulatory authorities (such as the Advertising Standards Agency and Ofcom) had allowed the use of FCUK and that 16 million articles of FCUK-branded clothing had been sold.

The EUIPO has also struggled to apply the corresponding provision of the EUTMR.[253] For example, the Board of Appeal accepted DICK and FANNY as registrable for clothing: this was merely in poor taste, having a 'rather smutty flavour'.[254] The Board was particularly taken by the fact that the words 'merely designate things', rather than proclaim an opinion, incite behaviour, or convey an insult. In contrast, the Grand Board of Appeal rejected SCREW YOU for sunglasses, clothing, and beverages (but not for sex toys and condoms).[255] Recognizing that 'screw' was a slightly less offensive profanity than 'fuck', the Board nevertheless held that 'a substantial number of citizens with a normal level of sensitivity and tolerance would be upset by regular commercial exposure to the term'.[256] The sign therefore should not be registered for the goods that, in normal use, would be exposed to the general population, including children. However, because sex toys are normally sold in specialist shops, 'a more relaxed attitude' was appropriate and the sign was registrable. More strangely, perhaps, the Board held that a person who is 'sufficiently interested in [condoms] to notice the trade marks under which they are sold is unlikely to be offended by a term with crude sexual connotations'.[257] The OHIM Board of Appeal

---

[247] *Scranage's Trade Mark Application*, O/182/05 (24 June 2005) (AP, Kitchin QC).

[248] *FCUK* [2007] *RPC* 1 (AP, Arnold QC).

[249] *Ghazilian's Application* [2002] *RPC* (33) 628. The reasoning is therefore consistent with the result at the OHIM in *Dick Lexic/Dick & Fanny*, R111/2002–4 (25 March 2003), since 'Dick' and 'Fanny' are not proper anatomical terms for genitalia. But Thorley QC's conclusions were doubted in *FCUK* [2007] *RPC* 1 (AP, Arnold QC), [61].

[250] *Basic Trademark* [2005] *RPC* (25) 611 (AP, Hobbs QC). Would the decision have been different if the Church of England or Jesus College, Cambridge, had been the applicant? If so, why should this make a difference? The Grand Board of Appeal of the OHIM has suggested that cases of religious offence might best be dealt with under the heading of 'public policy' rather than 'morality': *Application of Kenneth (trading as Screw You)*, Case R 495/2005–G [2007] *ETMR* (7) 111, [20].

[251] *Scranage's Trade Mark*, O/182/05 (24 June 2005), [11] (AP, Kitchin QC).

[252] In *FCUK* [2007] *RPC* 1, [74], Arnold QC notes the widespread use of 'fuck'.

[253] EUTMR, Art. 7(1)(f). For a candid compilation of examples drawn from decided cases, see EUIPO, *Examination Guidelines*, Part B, Section 4, Chapter 7.

[254] *Dick Lexic*, R 111/2002–4 (25 March 2003) (for various goods in Classes 9, 16, and 25).

[255] *Application of Kenneth (t/a Screw You)*, Case R 495/2000–G [2007] *ETMR* (7) 111 (OHIM, Grand Board).

[256] Ibid., [26].   [257] Ibid., [29].

also accepted REVA, a slang Finnish term for female genitalia, as registrable for electric cars because, in that context, it carried no rude or disrespectful message.[258] The General Court also seems to favour the prohibition of registrations which may lie closer to the distasteful side of the dividing line.[259]

4.1.2 Public policy

The exclusion relating to 'public policy' has been invoked less frequently. According to the OHIM, 'obviously malevolent racial and cultural slurs, whether by word or pictorial representation, should not be allowed on a trade mark register'.[260] The matter is judged not from the point of view of those who will be easily offended, but from the perspective of 'a reasonable person with average levels of sensitivity and tolerance'.[261] The ground has been held to justify refusal of registration of a sign that included the hammer and sickle and a red star, on the basis that these were 'symbols of despotism' that, given its political and cultural history, would be offensive in Hungary.[262] The ground also justifies the exclusion of marks that promote illegal activity, for example by glamorizing drug-taking or terrorism. The exclusion is not concerned with economic grounds for objection, such as the effect that registration would have on competition.[263]

4.2 DECEPTIVE MARKS

Section 3(3)(b) of the 1994 Act states that a trade mark shall not be registered if it is 'of such a nature as to deceive the public (for instance as to the nature, quality or geographical origin of the goods or service)'.[264] This prohibition tends to be applied to marks that, although distinctive, contain some kind of suggestion or allusion that is inaccurate. This is likely to be assessed from the viewpoint of the consumer who is reasonably well informed, observant, and circumspect.[265] The risk of deception must be a real one and relate to the mark itself (as opposed to the way it is used). In *Elizabeth Emanuel*,[266] the opponent was a well-known designer of wedding clothes, Elizabeth Emanuel. Although she had assigned her business to a third party (including a trade mark application), she later opposed registration of the mark ELIZABETH EMANUEL on the absolute ground that its nature was such as to deceive the public into believing that the clothes sold by the trade mark owner were of her design. The Examiner refused the opposition and, on appeal, the Appointed Person

---

[258] *Reva Electric Car Co. (PVT) Ltd*, Case R 558/2006–2 (OHIM, BoA).

[259] *Constantin Film Produktion GmbH v. EUIPO*, Case T-69/17, EU:T:2018:27 (in a combined analysis of morality and public policy, FACK JU GÖHTE for a popular German film was rejected since it translated into 'Fuck you Göhte'. The German speaking general public would find this to be not just in bad taste but shocking and vulgar).

[260] *Kenneth*, Case R 495/2005–G [2007] *ETMR* (7) 111, [19]–[20]; *Paki Logistics GmbH v. OHIM*, Case T-526/09 [2011] *ECR* II–346 (French and German only) (affirming OHIM's refusal to register 'Paki' for packaging, pallets, and transportation services, because in the United Kingdom the term would be understood as a racial slur).

[261] *Couture Tech Ltd v. OHIM*, Case T-232/10 [2011] *ECR* II-6469, [51]; *Paki Logistics GmbH v. OHIM*, Case T-526/09 [2011] *ECR* II–346, [12].

[262] *Couture Tech Ltd v. OHIM*, Case T-232/10 [2011] *ECR* II-6469. It was relevant evidence that such symbols are illegal in Hungary.   [263] *Philips v. Remington*, Case C-299/99 [2002] *ECR* I–5475.

[264] EUTMR, Art. 7(1)(g); TMD 1989, Art. 3(1)(g). See Chapter 39, section 4, pp. 1098–101.

[265] Consequently, mere advertising 'puff', as lawyers call it, as was present in the application KENCO THE REAL COFFEE EXPERTS, will not be misleading: *Kraft Jacobs Suchard Ltd's Application; Opposition by Nestlé UK* [2001] *ETMR* (54) 585.

[266] *Elizabeth Florence Emanuel v. Continental Shelf 128 Ltd*, Case C-259/04, [2006] *ECR* I–3089.

referred several questions to the Court of Justice. According to the Court, the ground for refusal (and the corresponding ground for opposition) requires 'the existence of actual deceit or of a sufficiently serious risk that the consumer will be deceived'.[267] The Court denied that the assignment of the mark of itself (as opposed to how the proprietor utilized it) gave rise to such a serious risk of deception. Even if the average consumer 'might be influenced in his act of purchasing a garment bearing the trade mark ELIZABETH EMANUEL by imagining that the appellant in the main proceedings was involved in the design of that garment', there was no deception because the 'characteristics and the qualities of that garment remain guaranteed by the undertaking which owns the trade mark'.[268] Although the questions referred to, and answers given by, the Court of Justice related to a rather specific set of circumstances (and accordingly left some questions to be decided on another occasion),[269] the case appears to set a high threshold for the ground for refusal to apply. The Court also considered the application of this exclusion in the context of invalidity proceedings for an EUTM. A (regular) figurative trade mark was being used as a certification mark, to certify the composition and quality of cotton textiles, via the use of licence agreements. Would such a mark be deceptive 'where the proprietor of the mark fails to ensure, by carrying out periodic quality controls at its licensees, that expectations relating to the quality which the public associates with the mark are being met'?[270] The Court left it to the referring national court to decide whether there was a sufficiently serious risk that the use of the mark per se—as opposed to the mismanagement of its licensing—would deceive consumers.

The exclusion has been applied to signs that misleadingly suggest official approval and to signs that wrongly suggest goods are made out of particular materials or come from particular locations. The General Court has held that the mark Caffè Nero which means black coffee in Italian would be deceptive if it was used on tea.[271] The UK Trade Marks Registry refused an application for a collective mark, CHARTERED FINANCIAL ANALYST (for financial services), reasoning that the sign would give the impression to the average consumer that the users of the mark were members of a professional organization of the sort that benefits from a royal charter.[272] The OHIM Board of Appeal rejected an appeal from a decision refusing registration of TITAN (which means 'TITANIUM' in German, Swedish, and Danish) for building units made of non-metallic materials,[273] and of WINE OH! for, among other things, beverages.[274] The term TITAN was misleading because consumers could be led into taking an interest in the products on the basis of an indication that they were made of titanium. The term WINE was misleading for water and the addition of OH! merely emphasized this. The Board was not able to assume that the misleading connotation would be corrected as a result of the nature of the packaging of the water. In contrast, if the mis-description is obvious and

---

[267] Ibid., [47], citing *Consorzio per la Tutela del Formaggio Gorgonzola v. Kaserei Champignon Hofmeister GmbH*, Case C-87/97 [1999] *ECR* I–1301, [41].

[268] *Elizabeth Florence Emanuel v. Continental Shelf 128 Ltd*, Case C-259/04, [2006] *ECR* I–3089, [48].

[269] In particular, the questions/answers were confined to the case in which the trade mark came to be assigned with goodwill of the business, leaving open the possibility of a different conclusion in cases of assignment or licensing 'in gross'. For comment, see R. Moscona, 'What really Matters? The Designer's Name or the Name on the Label?' (2007) 29(4) *EIPR* 152.

[270] *W. F. Gözze Frottierweberei GmbH v. Verein Bremer Baumwollbörse*, Case C-689/15, EU:C:2017:434, [52]–[56].

[271] T-29/16, EU:T:2016:635; see also *Tea Marks*, O/358/17 (24 July 2017) (AP, Johnson).

[272] *CFA Institute's Application; Opposition of the Chartered Insurance Institute*, O/315/06 [2007] *ETMR* (76) 1253; UK IPO, *Trade Marks which Contain the Word 'Chartered'* (2013) PAN 02/13 (deceptive because implies 'chartered status', which the UK IPO states thus 'deceives the public as to the quality of the services claimed').

[273] *Portakabin Ltd/Titan*, R 789/2001-3 (OHIM, BoA); cf. *Lord Corp./Metaljacket*, R314/2002-1 (23 October 2002) (ambiguous mark METALJACKET for non-metallic coatings for metals not misleading).

[274] *Wine Oh! LLC's Application*, R 1074/2005-4 [2006] *ETMR* (95) 1319.

is such that it would immediately be corrected on further observation by the consumer, such mis-descriptions will not render the sign invalid.

Another situation in which a trade mark may be refused is if it gives rise to a real, but inaccurate, expectation that the goods come from a particular locality. For example, an application to register MCL PARFUMS DE PARIS for toiletries including perfumes was refused by the UK Registry, on the grounds that the mark created an expectation that the perfume would be manufactured in Paris, so that (if it were not) the trade mark would deceive the public not only as to the geographic origin of the goods, but also as to their nature and quality.[275] The refusal of signs involving geographical mis-descriptions parallels the role of section 3(4) discussed later. However, the circumstances in which the owner of a protected designation of origin can object to use of that designation or a similar one may be broader than the situations in which a mark will be treated as misleading.

4.3 MARKS PROHIBITED BY LAW

Section 3(4) provides that 'a trade mark shall not be registered if or to the extent that its use is prohibited in the United Kingdom by any enactment or rule of law or by any provision of EU law'. Thus a mark will not be registered if it is unlawful under statutes such as the Geneva Conventions Act 1957 (protecting symbols of the Red Cross), the Plant Varieties Act 1997,[276] or the Hallmarking Act 1973.[277] The illegality must be intrinsic or inherent in the mark, rather than in the goods for which its use is proposed.[278] The reference to EU law prevents the registration of 'protected designations of origin' (PDOs) and 'protected geographical indications' (PGIs) for wines, spirits, agricultural products, and food, as well as Traditional Speciality Guarantees (TSGs).[279]

4.4 BAD FAITH

According to section 3(6), a trade mark shall not be registered if, or to the extent that, the application is made in bad faith.[280] The courts, tribunals, and offices have struggled to find a satisfactory definition of 'bad faith'—in particular whether it is a question of conscious dishonesty or whether it is to be decided by reference to objective standards.[281]

---

[275] *Madgecourt's Application; Opposition by Federation des Industries de la Parfumerie* [2000] *ETMR* 825.

[276] A parallel provision has now been added to the EUTMR, Art. 7(1)(m).

[277] See also Scotch Whisky Regulations 2009 (SI 2009/2890). See UK IPO, *Practice in Relation to Trade Marks Containing the Words 'Scotch' and 'Scotch Whisky'* (2011) PAN 1/11.   [278] Paris, Art. 7.

[279] EUTMR, Art. 7 (1)(j), (k), (l): see Chapter 43, which describes the manner in which the protection for PDOs and PGIs is broad, extending beyond confusion to the notion of 'evocation' or merely making a mental connection between the products on the basis of similar signs being used.

[280] Pursuant to optional provision in the TMD 2008, Art. 3(2)(d); TMD 2015, Art. 4(2) (absolute grounds), Art. 5(4)(c) (optional relative ground); EUTMR, Art. 59(1)(b) (registration liable to be declared invalid where application was made in bad faith). See N. Dawson, 'Bad Faith in European Trade Mark Law' [2011] *IPQ* 229; A. Tsoutsanis, *Trade Mark Registrations in Bad Faith* (2010).

[281] *Gromax Plasticulture v. Don & Low Nonwovens* [1999] *RPC* 367, 379 (concept of bad faith is to be understood as requiring 'dishonesty' or at most 'conduct falling short of acceptable commercial behaviour'); *Knoll AG's Trade Mark* [2003] *RPC* (10) 175, 182, [27] (Neuberger J). For broader views, see *Road Tech. Computer Systems v. Unison Software UK* [1996] *FSR* 805; *Postperfect Trade Mark* [1998] *RPC* 255; *Artistic Upholstery v. Art Forma (Furniture)* [1999] 4 *All ER* 277, 290.

Ultimately, the Court of Appeal has decided to align the definition in trade mark law with that operating in other areas of civil liability, particularly so-called 'knowing assistance' in breach of trust.[282] This definition requires, first, an inquiry into what the applicant actually knew, and then an assessment as to whether a reasonable person would regard the applicant's behaviour, given that knowledge, as 'conduct falling short of acceptable commercial behaviour'.[283] The views of the applicant as to whether its behaviour is dishonest are of no consequence; the issue is whether the act of applying for the registration was dishonest as judged by the 'ordinary standards of honest people'.[284]

The Court of Justice has yet to indicate whether this test is appropriate. In *Lindt v. Hauswirth*,[285] Lindt registered the appearance of a golden rabbit with a red bow around its neck for chocolate (see Fig. 37.10) and relied on the registration to bring an action against Hauswirth, which was also selling chocolate rabbits (see Fig. 37.10) and had done so in

Fig 37.10 Lindt chocolate rabbit

Source: Chocoladefabriken Lindt & Sprüngli AG v. Franz Hauswirth GmbH, Case C-529/07 [2009] *ECR* I–4893

---

[282] *Harrison v. Teton Valley Trading Co.* [2005] *FSR* (10) 177 (CA). The case was heavily criticized by Richard Arnold QC, sitting as AP in *Robert McBride Ltd's Application* [2005] *ETMR* (85) 990, [27]–[31]. However, he has subsequently observed, in *Target Fixings v. Brutt* [2007] *RPC* (19) 462, that much of the force of the criticisms has been removed by the clarification of Prof. Annand QC in *Ajit Weekly Trade Mark* [2006] *RPC* (25) 633. The point made by Arden LJ in *Harrison*, at [40], and reiterated by Arnold QC in *Robert McBride*, at [30], that 'good faith' is a European concept, the meaning of which must be found in the 'language, scheme and structure' of the Directive, remains significant: ultimately, it will be the Court of Justice that determines the meaning of bad faith in the TMD and the EUTMR.
[283] *Ajit Weekly Trade Mark* [2006] *RPC* (25) 633 (AP, Ruth Annand); *Target Fixings v. Brutt* [2007] *RPC* (19) 462.
[284] *Ajit Weekly Trade Mark* [2006] *RPC* (25) 633, [41]; *Jules Rimet Cup Ltd v. Football Association Ltd* [2008] *ECDR* (4) 43, 65, [94] (Deputy Judge Wyand QC).
[285] *Chocoladefabriken Lindt & Sprüngli AG v. Franz Hauswirth GmbH*, Case C-529/07 [2009] *ECR* I–4893.

Fig. 37.11 Hauswirth chocolate rabbit

Source: Chocoladefabriken Lindt & Sprüngli AG v. Franz Hauswirth GmbH, Case C-529/07 [2009] *ECR* I–4893

Austria since 1962. Hauswirth counterclaimed that the application had been made in 'bad faith'. The Austrian Oberster Gerichtshof referred various questions to the Court of Justice, in particular as to whether it was bad faith to apply for a mark in circumstances in which the applicant knew others were using the same or similar mark. In a curious decision, the Court declined to define good faith at all, but merely indicated that the national court should assess bad faith by taking into account 'all the relevant factors'. The Court said that particular attention should be paid to: (i) whether the applicant *knows or must know* that a third party is using an identical or similar sign for an identical or similar product capable of being confused with the sign for which registration is sought; (ii) the applicant's *intention* to prevent that third party from continuing to use such a sign; and (iii) the degree of legal protection enjoyed by the third party's sign and by the sign for which registration is sought.

In a subsequent case, the Court reiterated that mere knowledge that a third party is using or intends to use a particular mark is not of itself sufficient to establish bad faith.[286] If the applicant has their own legitimate reasons for seeking protection, the mere knowledge that someone else has an interest in the field does not amount to bad faith.

It may seem rather odd that the Court has avoided defining bad faith[287] and has merely endorsed a close analysis of all of the facts. In *Frost Products*,[288] in which a registrant

---

[286] *Malaysia Dairy Industries Pte Ltd v. Ankenaernet*, Case C-320/12 [2013] *ETMR* 36.

[287] See A. Kur, 'Not Prior in Time, but Superior in Right: How Trademark Registrations Can be Affected by Third-party Interests in a Sign' [2013] *IIC* 790, 810 (defining bad faith is 'no easy task, if at all feasible'). In contrast, other commentators have either found the potential created by the decision to be welcome or worrisome: N. Dawson, 'Bad Faith in European Trade Mark Law' [2011] *IPQ* 229, 258 (welcoming the interpretation as a 'powerful pro-competitive weapon'); R. Moscona, 'Bad Faith as Grounds for Invalidation under the Community Trade Mark' [2010] *EIPR* 48 (criticizing the decision as introducing considerable uncertainty).

[288] *Frost Products Ltd v. FC Frost Ltd* [2013] *EWPCC* 34, [128].

was found to have applied for the mark FROST in bad faith, Vos J suggested that the tests are consistent with one another, the English courts 'defining' bad faith, while the Court of Justice has merely suggested 'factors that may be taken into account in determining whether it exists'.

In many respects, this is a broad test that the courts have applied to a wide range of situations. The cases can be placed in three categories: where there is no intention to use the mark; where there is an abuse of a relationship; and where the applicant was aware that a third party had some sort of claim to the goodwill in the mark.

4.4.1 No intention to use the mark

The first situation in which a mark may be refused because it was applied for in bad faith is where the applicant had no intention of using the mark in trade. Such applications might be said to be in 'bad faith' under UK law because the applicant declares, under section 32(3), that the trade mark is being used or that the applicant has a bona fide intention to use the mark in relation to those goods or services. If there is no such intention, the declaration is dishonest and the dishonesty taints the application.[289] However, because there is no such declaration required by the EUIPO, it is not clear whether registering with no intention to use a mark would be regarded as bad faith. Nevertheless, the General Court has recognized that registering repeatedly merely to avoid the consequences of revocation for non-use could well be bad faith.[290] The Court has also held that where there is no intention to use the mark coupled with an intention to obtain tactical commercial advantages instead, this amounts to bad faith.[291] On the assumption that merely lacking an intention to use the mark would not be bad faith at the EUIPO,[292] the question arises whether UK law would itself be regarded as incompatible with the Trade Marks Directive.[293] In *Red Bull v. Sun Mark*,[294] Arnold J indicated that, in an appropriate situation, the question would need to be referred to the Court of Justice for resolution. At the time of writing, the opportunity has arisen and the following issue is being referred: 'Can it constitute bad faith to apply to register a trade mark without any intention to use it in relation to the specified goods or services?'[295]

---

[289] *Demon Ale Trade Mark* [2000] *RPC* 345; *In re Ferrero SpA's Trade Marks (Kinder)*, O/279/03 [2004] *RPC* (29) 253, [25] (AP, Kitchin QC). Merely drafting a specification broadly will not mean that the application is in bad faith: to say that one intends to use a mark, e.g. for pharmaceutical substances, where one intends to use the mark only in relation to a specific category of pharmaceutical products is not sufficient to warrant a finding of bad faith: *Knoll AG* [2003] *RPC* (10) 175, 182, [27] (Neuberger J). Cf. *Betty's Kitchen Coronation Street Trade Mark* [2000] *RPC* 825 (finding application to have been in bad faith because no intention to use all four words together as a single mark and used on only some goods).

[290] *pelicantravel.com v. OHIM*, Case T-136/11 EU:T:2012:689, [27]. There is some suggestion in this case that an applicant for cancellation might establish on the facts that there was no such intention to use the mark and that this might lead to a finding of bad faith: ibid., [58].

[291] *Copernicus-Trademarks Ltd v. EUIPO, Maquet*, Case T-82/14, EU:T:2016:396 (applying for a mark solely to be able to use the application to oppose an EUTM and thereby gain a commercial advantage was bad faith), aff'd C-101/17P, EU:C:2017:979.

[292] 53447/03 (OHIM Cancellation Division), discussed in *Robert McBride* [2005] *ETMR* (85) 990, [20]. For an overview of practices which are/are not considered bad faith, see EUIPO *Examination Guidelines*, Part D, Section 2, [3.3] ('Bad Faith—Article 59(1)(b) EUTMR').

[293] Cf. *Knoll AG* [2003] *RPC* (10) 175, 185, [33]–[34] (Neuberger J) (warning against relying on the s. 32(3) declaration, on the basis that the requirement 'may be inconsistent with the Directive').

[294] [2012] *EWHC* 1929 (Ch) (where Red Bull had registered BULLIT for drinks and alleged that the defendant's use of BULLET infringed, the defendant counterclaimed that the BULLIT registration had been made in bad faith; on the facts, the judge found that there was sufficient evidence of intent to use).

[295] *Sky v. Skykick* [2018] *EWHC* 155 (Ch), [258]. It was also argued that the specifications of goods and services lack clarity and precision, which raised issues in relation to *IP Translator* guidance.

There will be no problem with a UK tribunal finding bad faith where absence of intent to use on the part of the applicant themselves is coupled with some other goal. Thus there may be bad faith where a person applies to register a mark with the intent either of preventing a competitor from registering the mark or selling ('trafficking in') the registered right. So, for example, where an antique dealer realized that 'demon ale' was an anagram of 'lemonade' and applied to register DEMON ALE as a mark, with a view to selling the mark and with no intention of brewing, the Appointed Person held that the application was in bad faith.[296] As well as regulating the 'trafficking' in marks, the requirement of good faith can be used to prevent the registration of 'ghost marks'—that is, the registration of marks that are similar to an unregistrable mark that the trader is, in fact, using. A famous example, from pre-1994 case law, was the illegitimate registration of NERIT for cigarettes, when the applicant really intended to use the mark MERIT, but realized that it would not be accepted for registration (because it lacks distinctiveness).[297] However, where an applicant intended to use a three-dimensional mark and registered a two-dimensional device comprising an image of the mark, the Appointed Person held that the applicant had not lacked good faith because, in some circumstances, use of the shape could in fact count as use of the two-dimensional mark.[298]

4.4.2 Abuses of relationships

The second situation in which an applicant may be held to lack good faith is where, in applying for the mark, they are knowingly abusing a relationship with a third party. The most obvious example of such abuse of a relationship is where the registration would give rise to a breach of trust or contract between them. This might be the case where the applicant is an employee or an agent, a partner or former partner, or co-venturer.[299] If the applicant is aware that their behaviour is wrongful in law, then an honest person would likely regard that behaviour as 'conduct falling short of acceptable commercial behaviour'.[300] However, an application may be treated as in bad faith where the abuse falls short of a breach of a legal relationship, for example where the parties were in pre-contractual negotiations as to a licensing arrangement and, when this fell through, the disappointed potential licensee registered the mark.[301]

4.4.3 Knowledge of third-party claims

Another situation in which an application may be rejected on the basis that it was made in bad faith is where a party attempts to register a mark when it knows that a third party has some better claim to the reputation or goodwill attaching to the sign. However, bad faith should not be presumed too lightly, based merely on one party's awareness of another's

---

[296] Ibid.   [297] *Imperial Group v. Philip Morris & Co.* [1982] *FSR* 72.

[298] *Robert McBride* [2005] *ETMR* (85) 990.

[299] *Mickey Dees (Nightclub) Trade Mark* [1998] *RPC* 359.

[300] *Target Fixings (Brutt Trade Marks)* [2007] *RPC* (19) 462, 485, [100]; *Mary Wilson Enterprises Inc's Trade Mark Application* [2003] *EMLR* (14) 259 (bad faith application to register THE SUPREMES contrary to agreement with Motown Records); *Saxon Trade Mark* [2003] *FSR* (39) 704 (bad faith application by former member of heavy metal band to register SAXON, which Laddie J considered to be a partnership asset); *Gromax Plasticulture* [1999] *RPC* 367 (bad faith on part of distributor not established); *SA.PAR Srl v. OHIM*, Case T-321/10, EU:T:2013:372 (registration of GRUPPO SALINI by former member of group of Salini family-held companies cancelled as lacking good faith).

[301] *John Arthur Slater v. Prime Restaurant Holdings, Inc.*, Case R 582/2003–4 (OHIM, BoA) (concerning the sign EAST SIDE MARIOS registered in the United States and Canada).

mark, and may not even operate in situations where one party seeks to 'free-ride' off the goodwill of another's mark.[302]

One important example of bad faith occurs where an applicant identifies a foreign business that is expanding and races to the Trade Marks Registry to register a UK mark.[303] In *Ajit Weekly Trade Mark*,[304] a trade mark had been granted for a Punjabi word (meaning 'invincible') in relation to printed matter. The owner of a Punjabi newspaper of the same name, which had been sold in India since 1959 and which was a 'household name' in the Punjab, applied to have the mark cancelled on the grounds that the application had been made in bad faith. The Examiner concluded that the proprietor of the mark had known of the Punjabi paper and its reputation, and that use of the mark in the United Kingdom would confuse the substantial Punjabi community present in the country. The Appointed Person affirmed the decision, holding that (as a matter of law) it was unnecessary to show that the applicant thought what he was doing was dishonest and that the Examiner had been entitled to reach a conclusion that an honest person would regard such behaviour as 'conduct falling below acceptable standards'.

A second situation in which bad faith might exist is where an applicant seeks, through registration of a sign, to prevent a third party from continuing acts that they have already been doing and are entitled to do. The *Lindt* case[305] can be seen as a possible example: if the goal of registration of the shape of the *Lindt* rabbit was primarily to prevent an existing competitor with established rights from continuing to sell its chocolate bunnies, then the application might have been regarded in bad faith (unless Lindt could establish that it had legitimate reasons of its own to seek registration, for example to prevent other third parties from making and selling counterfeit chocolate rabbits).

A similar argument was run unsuccessfully in the *Hotel Cipriani* case. As we saw in Chapter 32, this case concerned an action by the Venice hotel, Hotel Cipriani, against a London restaurant, Cipriani London. The claimant relied on a CTM for cipriani, for which it had applied in 1996. The defendant counterclaimed that the registration was invalid. At first instance, Arnold J conducted an elaborate examination of 'bad faith', rejecting the counterclaim.[306] He particularly emphasized the claimant's legitimate reasons to register and the ways in which its rights would be limited vis-à-vis earlier users and third parties.[307] The Court of Appeal, equipped with the Court of Justice judgment in *Lindt*, affirmed.[308] The application had not been made in bad faith because, being for hotels, it would not prevent any of the Cipriani family from carrying on any of their existing activities. The registration would not have conferred rights on the claimant that would implicate the freedoms of Villa Cipriani or Locanda Cipriani.

---

[302] *Socks World International Ltd Trade mark Application* [2011] *RPC* 11 (where BEKO SPORT was seemingly inspired by BEKO, the mark for the well-known white goods manufacturer, the opposition under the unfair advantage/free-riding heading was successful but this did not amount to bad faith).

[303] TMD 2008, Art. 4(4)(g), allows member states to provide that a trade mark application may be opposed, or a registered trade mark declared invalid, where the trade mark is liable to be confused with a mark that was in use abroad on the filing date of the application and which is still in use there, provided that, at the date of application, the applicant was acting in bad faith. It is proposed to introduce an equivalent relative ground into the CTMR. See generally A. Kur, 'Not Prior in Time, but Superior in Right: How Trademark Registrations Can be Affected by Third-party Interests in a Sign' [2013] *IIC* 790, 811–12 *ff*.

[304] [2006] *RPC* (25) 633.

[305] *Chocoladefabriken Lindt & Sprüngli AG v. Franz Hauswirth GmbH*, Case C-529/07 [2009] *ECR* I–4893.

[306] *Hotel Cipriani srl v. Cipriani (Grosvenor St) Ltd* [2008] *EWHC* 3032 (Ch), [2009] *RPC* (9) 209, [165]–[202].

[307] Ibid., [189].   [308] *Hotel Cipriani srl v. Cipriani (Grosvenor St) Ltd* [2010] *EWCA Civ* 110, [54]–[57].

A finding of bad faith may also occur where a person seeks to appropriate for themselves the residual goodwill of a trader who has stopped trading. In *Jules Rimet Cup Ltd v. Football Association Ltd*,[309] the applicant sought to register an image of a lion in the English football strip, the World Cup logo from 1966, known as 'World Cup Willie'. Before doing so, it had approached the Football Association to find out whether it still held rights in the mark, and had done searches and employed a trade mark attorney. As a consequence, it believed itself entitled to use the image of 'World Cup Willie'. Nevertheless, because it was knowingly taking advantage of the Football Association's residual goodwill, Deputy Judge Wyand QC held that the application was not in good faith and that the Association's opposition should succeed.

4.5 SPECIAL EMBLEMS

Section 4 excludes from registration trade marks that consist of, or contain, 'specially protected emblems'.

(i) Section 4(1) precludes registration of signs that include symbolic elements connected to the Crown. These include emblems such as the royal arms, the royal crown, and flags. The exclusion also covers any representation of any member of the royal family, or any other sign suggesting that the applicant has royal patronage.

(ii) Section 4(2) excludes various national flags—that is, the Union Flag and the flags of the various British nations. Here, the criterion is that their use would be either misleading or grossly offensive.

(iii) Section 4(3) has a similar exclusion for international emblems and flags that are protected under sections 57 and 58 of the Act.[310] Sections 57 and 58 contain a similar list of excluded emblems, flags, etc., for other countries that are members of the Paris Union. Applying the equivalent provision of the CTMR, the General Court held that an application relating to a flag containing a circle of 12 stars was unregistrable for computer programs and arranging conferences, in light of the European Union's own flag, which it described, in heraldic terms, as 'on a field azure a circle of 12 mullets or, their points not touching'.[311] Whatever the 'geometric' differences, the Court ruled, the two signs were to be compared 'from a heraldic point of view' and because the applicant had not specified colour, from such a perspective, it was an unregistrable imitation.[312]

---

[309] [2008] *ECDR* (4) 43 (Deputy Judge Wyand QC). See also *Pavel Maslyyukov v. Diageo Distilling* [2010] *EWHC* 443 (Ch), [2010] *ETMR* (37) 641 (application to register DALLAS DHU for whisky was bad faith given that DALLAS DHU was name of defunct distillery).

[310] In accordance with Paris, Art. 6*ter*; TRIPS, Art. 15(2); EUTMR, Art. 7(1)(h).

[311] *Concept—Anlagen u. Geräte nach 'GMP' für Produktion u. Labor GmbH v. OHIM*, Case T-127/02 [2004] *ECR* II-1113. See also *American Clothing v. OHIM*, Joined Cases C-202/08P and 215/06P [2009] *ECR* I-6933 (affirming rejection of application of maple leaf with letters RW for clothing and holding that CTMR provision applied to applications for service marks, even if Paris, Art. 6*ter*, did not); *Kreyenberg v. OHIM*, Case T-3/12, EU:T:2013:364; cf. *European Union v. Ten EWIV*, R 5/2011–4 (Fourth BoA); *European Union v. EASI*, R 1991/2010–4 (Fourth BoA) (the appeal to the GC was withdrawn in both cases).

[312] In this case, the interpretation of the heraldic description, a verbal description, has more in common with patent interpretation than traditional trade mark infringement analysis.

(iv) Section 4(4) restricts registration of marks that include coats of arms, subjecting trade marks to the rules of the law of arms.

(v) Section 4(5) also prohibits the registration of marks that consist of or contain a 'controlled representation' under the Olympic Symbol (Protection) Act 1995 (as amended by the London Olympic Games and Paralympic Games Act 2006). These controlled representations include the Olympic and Paralympic symbols, mottos, and various protected words ('Olympics', 'Paralympics', 'Olympiad', 'Olympian', etc.).[313]

---

[313] Exclusion from registrability as a trade mark is only one aspect of a broader constellation of regimes protecting mega-sporting events against so-called 'ambush marketing'; see P. Johnson, *Ambush Marketing and Brand Protection: Law and Practice* (2nd edn, 2011); S. Ericsson, 'Ambush Marketing: Examining the Development of an Event Organizer Right of Association', in N. Lee, G. Westkamp, A. Kur, and A. Ohly (eds), *Intellectual Property, Unfair Competition and Publicity Convergences and Development* (2014).

38

RELATIVE GROUNDS FOR REFUSAL

1 INTRODUCTION

In this chapter, we explore the 'relative grounds' for refusing to register a trade mark. These are set out in section 5 of the Trade Marks Act 1994 and Article 8 of the European Union Trade Marks Regulation (EUTMR), and are a basis of opposition to an application for registration, or for cancellation of registration of a mark that has been registered.[1]

The relative grounds for refusal fall into two general categories: those concerned with 'earlier trade marks'; and those concerned with 'earlier rights'. We deal with each in turn.

2 RELATIVE GROUNDS IN RELATION TO EARLIER TRADE MARKS

The objections relating to earlier trade marks are found in section 5(1)–(3) of the 1994 Act and Article 8(1) and (5) EUTMR. These provide that a trade mark shall not be registered if, when compared with an earlier mark, it is found that:

(i) the marks are identical *and* the goods or services are identical;[2]

(ii) the marks are identical, *and* the goods or services are similar, *and* there is a likelihood of confusion, which includes the likelihood of association, with the earlier mark;[3]

(iii) the marks are similar, *and* the goods or services are either identical or similar, *and* there is a likelihood of confusion, which includes the likelihood of association, between the marks;[4] or

(iv) the marks are either identical or similar, the earlier trade mark has a reputation, and use of the applicant's mark would take unfair advantage of, or be detrimental to, the distinctive character or the repute of the earlier trade mark (irrespective of whether the goods or services are similar or not).[5]

---

[1] TMA 1994, s. 47(2)(a), (b); EUTMR, Art. 60. See also TMD 2008, Art. 4; TMD 2015, Art. 5.

[2] TMA 1994, s. 5(1); EUTMR, Art. 8(1)(a).   [3] TMA 1994, s. 5(2)(a); EUTMR, Art. 8(1)(b).

[4] TMA 1994, s. 5(2)(b); EUTMR, Art. 8(1)(b).   [5] TMA 1994, s. 5(3); EUTMR, Art. 8(5).

These grounds for refusal mirror the provisions dealing with trade mark infringement. In particular, section 5(1)–(3) corresponds to section 10(1)–(3), which deal with trade mark infringement. Effectively, these relative grounds for refusal enable the owner of an earlier mark (A) to prevent the registration of a sign by another (B) where the use of that sign would infringe A's rights. One of the consequences of this symmetry is that much of the case law on infringement is relevant to the relative grounds for refusal.[6] As such, in this chapter, we draw upon trade mark infringement cases where relevant. As we describe later, the principal difference is that relative grounds analysis is largely 'paper based' whereas infringement analysis can take into consideration the real world use of the claimant or defendant's marks.[7]

2.1 PRELIMINARY QUESTIONS

When considering section 5(1)–(3)/Article 8(1) and (5), it is necessary to ask three preliminary questions, as follows.

(i)   What is an 'earlier trade mark'?

(ii)   Does the opponent (or applicant for cancellation) have an appropriate interest on which to base a challenge?

(iii) Has the earlier mark been used?

2.1.1 What is an earlier trade mark?

In the United Kingdom, the definition of 'earlier trade mark' is quite complex. In essence, it covers earlier UK trade marks, earlier international trade marks (designated 'EU' or 'UK'), and earlier European Union Trade Marks (EUTMs). The provisions make it clear that the concept of 'earlier trade marks' includes 'earlier trade mark applications' with priority over the application under scrutiny. They also indicate that earlier trade marks include earlier 'well-known' marks, which are protected under the Paris Convention, even though these marks may not have been registered.[8] The concept of a 'well-known mark' was discussed in Chapter 34. The specific list of earlier marks is as follows:

(i)   under section 6(1)(a), a registered British mark, an EUTM, or an international trade mark (UK or EU)—that is, a mark registered under the Madrid Protocol designating the United Kingdom or European Union[9]—which has a priority date earlier than the trade mark in question;[10]

(ii)   under section 6(1)(b), an EUTM or international trade mark (EU) that has a valid claim to seniority from an earlier registered trade mark or international trade mark (UK);[11]

(iii) under section 6(1)(ba), a registered trade mark or international mark (UK) that had been converted from an EUTM or international trade mark (EU), which itself had a valid claim to seniority from an earlier registered trade mark or international mark (UK) and accordingly has the same claim to seniority;[12]

---

[6] *SA Société LTJ Diffusion v. SA Sadas*, Case C-291/00 [2003] *ECR* I-02799, [43], [AG19].

[7] G. B. Dinwoodie and D. S. Gangjee, 'The Image of the Consumer in EU Trade Mark Law', in D. Leczykiewicz and S. Weatherill (eds), *The Image(s) of the Consumer in EU Law* (2015) 339, 357–360.

[8] In such cases, an applicant cannot require the earlier trade mark owner to establish use in the previous five years: Trade Marks (Earlier Trade Marks) Regulations 2008 (SI 2008/1067).   [9] TMA 1994, s. 53.

[10] TMA 1994, s. 51.

[11] TMA 1994, s. 6(1)(b). For EUTM seniority rules, see Chapter 35, section 3.2, pp. 946–7.

[12] TMA 1994, s. 6(1)(ba).

(iv)   under section 6(2), an application for a mark, which, when registered, would be an earlier trade mark;[13] and

(v)   under section 6(1)(c), a trade mark that is entitled to protection as a well-known trade mark.[14]

If the registration of a mark falling within the first two categories (section 6(1)(a) or (b)) has lapsed, the mark can form the basis of an objection for a period of one year after expiry. However, this will not be the case if the Registrar is satisfied that there was no bona fide use of the mark during the two years immediately preceding expiry.[15]

In relation to oppositions brought against EUTMs, the definition of earlier marks differs in some respects from in the Trade Marks Act. Under the EUTMR, 'earlier trade marks' include not only EUTMs and international trade marks specifying the EU (under the Madrid Protocol), but also all trade marks registered in *any* member state or at the Benelux Trade Marks Office, and international registrations under the Madrid Agreement and the Madrid Protocol nominating a member state.[16] Thus they include registrations in other member states—which could not be the basis for an opposition to a UK mark. The important consequence of this is that, in many circumstances, marks will be capable of being registered in national registries, but not at the European Union Intellectual Property Office (EUIPO). As for earlier but unregistered well-known marks, the national and EU regimes adopt the same approach, in accordance with Article 6*bis* of the Paris Convention. For reputed but unregistered marks, the EUTMR prevents the same (or a similar) mark being registered (i) for similar goods or services and (ii) where it is liable to create confusion.[17] To prevent the use of well-known marks on dissimilar goods or services, registration is a prerequisite.[18]

2.1.2 Does the opponent (or applicant for cancellation) have an appropriate interest on which to base a challenge?

An opposition (or application for cancellation) on relative grounds can be commenced only by a person who has a relevant interest in an earlier mark.[19] Neither the office nor third parties may object if the same or a similar mark is registered for the same or similar goods—however much confusion this might produce. In the case of opposition to a UK registration, it is only the proprietor of the earlier trade mark who can bring proceedings. In contrast, a cancellation action can be brought by the proprietor or a licensee of an earlier mark (or, in the case of a certification mark, an authorized user). This latter position is perhaps most easily explained by the fact that a cancellation action may be by way of a counterclaim to infringement: it would be unfair were it not possible for a licensee of the earlier trade mark who is accused of infringing a later mark to be able to challenge that mark. At the EUIPO, opposition (or an application for cancellation based on an earlier trade mark) may be brought by the proprietor or a licensee authorized by the proprietor.[20]

---

[13]   TMA 1994, s. 6(2).

[14]   TMA 1994, s. 56(1), as amended by the Patents and Trade Marks (WTO) Regulations 1999 (SI 1999/1899). See Chapter 32, section 2.2.2, pp. 882–3.

[15]   TMA 1994, s. 6(3). The concept of genuine use is explored at some length at Chapter 39, section 2.3, pp. 1085–8 in the context of revocation.   [16]   EUTMR, Art. 8(2).

[17]   EUTMR, Art. 8(2)(c); TRIPS, Art. 16(3).

[18]   *Padilla v. OHIM*, Case T-255/08 [2010] *ETMR* 55, [47]–[48].

[19]   Trade Marks (Relative Grounds) Order 2007 (SI 2007/1976), Arts 2 (opposition), 5 (invalidity).

[20]   EUTMR, Arts 46(1), 60. If the earlier mark is revoked during proceedings, then the basis for objection falls away: *Just Music Fernsehbetriebs v. OHIM*, Case T-589/10, EU:T:2013:356.

2.1.3 Has the earlier trade mark been used?

Where an applicant for a mark is faced with an opposition on relative grounds on the basis of an earlier trade mark registered more than five years previously, the applicant can demand that the opponent produces evidence of use of the trade mark in the previous five years or proper reasons for non-use.[21] If the opponent fails to do so, the opposition will be rejected.[22] This requirement reflects the fact that a trade mark may be revoked if it has not been used for five years, and so an application should not be prevented by opposition based on a mark that itself could be revoked. The issue of revocation and the jurisprudence on when a mark is to be regarded as having been 'used' are discussed in Chapter 39. If the mark has not been used but this is within the five-year grace period, fair and notional use of the marks will be assumed when conducting relative grounds analysis.

2.2 DOUBLE IDENTITY: SECTION 5(1)/ARTICLE 8(1)(A)

The first relative ground for refusal, the so-called 'double identity' ground, is found in section 5(1) of the 1994 Act and Article 8(1)(a) EUTMR.[23] This provides that a trade mark shall not be registered if it is identical to an earlier trade mark *and* the goods or services to which the trade mark application relates are identical to the goods or services for which the earlier trade mark is protected. Because earlier trade marks are protected unconditionally as against a later application to register an identical mark for identical goods and services, there is no need to prove confusion.[24] However, if the applicant is able to demonstrate that registration will not adversely affect any of the functions of the trade mark, the later application may be registrable.

In considering whether a mark falls foul of section 5(1)(a)/Article 8(1)(a), three questions arise, as follows.

(i)   When are marks 'identical'?

(ii)   When are the goods and services 'identical'?

(iii) When will registration of the later mark be, nevertheless, regarded as legitimate?

2.2.1 Are the marks identical?

The first question to ask in relation to section 5(1)/Article 8(1)(a) is: are the marks identical? In answering this question, it is necessary to compare the representation of the earlier trade mark contained in the registration certificate with the trade mark that has been applied for (or, in the case of infringement, that being used by the defendant).

When considering the earlier mark, it is particularly important to bear in mind some of the conventions associated with representation of marks—in particular, the rules that a

---

[21] TMA 1994, ss. 6A, 47(2A)–(2E). For EUTMs and international marks designating the European Union, use need only be demonstrated in the European Union. For well-known marks, the opponent is not required to demonstrate use.

[22] TMA 1994, s. 6A(2)–(7); EUTMR, Art. 47(2) (formerly CTMR, Art. 42(2)).

[23] See also TMD 2008, Art. 4(1)(a); TMD 2015, Art 5(1)(a); A. Griffiths, 'The Trade Mark Monopoly: An Analysis of the Core Zone of Absolute Protection under Art. 5(1)(a)' [2007] *IPQ* 312.

[24] The rationale for this is that confusion will necessarily result: TRIPS, Art. 16(1); TMD 2008, Recital 11; TMD 2015, Recital 16; Griffiths, op. cit., 317 *ff*.

word mark represents that word in any form,[25] and that matter disclaimed in the registration will be ignored.[26] If the mark has been used by the opponent, no attention is usually paid to how the mark was in fact used; rather, the exercise is a 'paper one'.[27]

In contrast with the position on infringement,[28] under which the court has to decide on the parameters of the defendant's sign, in the context of assessing relative grounds of validity, the comparison is between the earlier trade mark (as registered) and the sign in the applicant's application. The two marks are considered as a whole; nothing in the applicant's mark is ignored.

While few problems are likely to arise in determining whether marks are identical, one particular issue warrants consideration—namely, whether marks that are slightly different may nonetheless still be treated as being identical. While specific provisions exist that prevent a mark that is similar to an earlier mark from being registered, the reason why owners of earlier marks might wish to argue their case under section 5(1)/Article 8(1)(a) is that, unlike the other relevant relative grounds, there is no need to prove confusion.[29] Given this, it would seem reasonable for the courts to construe section 5(1)/Article 8(1)(a) narrowly. Applying this logic, in *SA Société LTJ Diffusion v. SA Sadas*,[30] the Court of Justice concluded that the criterion 'must be interpreted strictly. The very definition of identity implies that the two elements should be the same in all respects.' The Court then elaborated that there is identity where a sign reproduces 'without any modification or addition, all the elements constituting the [trade mark]'.[31] However, it qualified this strict interpretation by observing that the test is to be applied from the viewpoint of the average consumer and that such a person will usually assess two signs globally, looking at the overall impression. Consequently 'insignificant differences between the sign and the trade mark may go unnoticed by the average consumer'.[32] The existence of such 'insignificant differences', then, would not cause the signs to be lacking in identity. The Court has provided little further guidance, taking the view that this is a matter of factual appraisal

---

[25] *Faber Chimica v. OHIM and Nabersa*, Case T-211/03 [2005] *ECR* II-1297, [33]-[40]; *Present-Service Ullrich GmbH v. OHIM*, Case T-66/11, EU:T:2013:48, [57]; *Ontex v. OHIM and Curon Medical*, Case T-353/04, EU:T:2007:47, [74]; *British Sky Broadcasting v. Microsoft Corp.* [2013] *EWHC* 1826 (Ch), [75] (Asplin J). It appeared to be British practice that a device mark registered in black and white was interpreted as giving the right to the device in any and every colour. The ECJ decision in *Specsavers Int'l Healthcare Ltd v. Asda Stores Ltd*, Case C-252/12 [2013] *ETMR* 46, was seen as requiring a deviation from such an approach in the case of used trade marks. However, the various offices of member states and the EUIPO have agreed to a different practice: see TMDN, *Common Communication on the Common Practice of the Scope of Protection of Black and White ('B&W') Marks* (April 2014). An earlier trade mark in black and white is *not identical* to the same mark in colour unless the differences in colour are insignificant.

[26] *Torremar Trade Mark* [2003] *RPC* (4) 89, 98, [29]; *The European v. The Economist Newspaper* [1998] *FSR* 283, 289; *General Cigar Co. Inc. v. Partagas y Cia SA* [2005] *FSR* (45) 960 (Collins J). At the EUIPO, although the Office can no longer impose a disclaimer, for existing marks disclaimed matter is treated as lacking distinctiveness: EUIPO *Examination Guidelines*, Part C, Section 2, Chapter 4, [3.2.3.4] ('Disclaimers').

[27] *Reed Executive plc v. Reed Business Information Ltd* [2004] *RPC* (40) 767, [50] (Jacob LJ); *British Sky Broadcasting v. Microsoft Corp.* [2013] *EWHC* 1826 (Ch), [75] (Asplin J); cf. *Specsavers Int'l Healthcare v. Asda Stores*, [2010] *EWHC* 2035 (Ch), [2011] *FSR* (1) 1, discussed in sections 2.3.1, pp. 1032-40, and Chapter 40, section 3, pp. 1105 6.   [28] See Chapter 40, section 4, pp. 1106-8.

[29] Moreover, as explained in Chapter 40, in assessing conflicts in cases of 'double identity', the Court of Justice's jurisprudence allows regard to be had to all of the recognized functions of trade marks (not only the origin function, but also the so-called 'quality', 'communication', 'advertising', and 'investment' functions). See Chapter 40, section 10, pp. 1116-25.

[30] Case C-291/00 [2003] *ECR* I-2799, [50]. The concept of 'identity' here is the same as that used in EUTMR, Art. 34, in relation to assessing 'seniority' of marks: see Chapter 35, section 3.2, pp. 945-9.

[31] Ibid., [51].   [32] Ibid., [53].

for national courts.[33] It is a question of fact whether consumers would see differences as significant.[34] Applying the test, Lewison J has held that consumers of computer software would not notice the difference between WEBSPHERE and WEB-SPHERE[35]—but Hart J held that KCS HERR VOSS was not identical to HERR-VOSS.[36]

2.2.2 When are goods or services identical?

The second element that must be proved for a mark to fall foul of section 5(1)/Article 8(1)(a) is that the goods or services to which the application relates must be identical with the goods or services for which the earlier mark is protected.[37] If the category of goods or services protected by an earlier trade mark is broader than, but includes, the category of goods or services to which the application relates, then the applicant's goods are identical to those of the earlier mark.[38] So if an earlier trade mark were to relate to 'broadcasting services', a later application relating to radio broadcasting services would be understood as being identical.[39] Equally, if the specifications of the trade mark applicant overlap with those of the earlier trade mark owner/opponent, those goods within the overlap will be regarded as identical.[40]

While the specification of goods or services for which the earlier mark is registered is the starting point for determining whether goods or services are identical, in some cases the language of the trade mark specification may need to be interpreted.[41] So, for example, courts may have to decide whether 'vermin' includes insects,[42] or whether 'cosmetics'

---

[33] In *Portakabin Ltd v. Primakabin BV*, Case C-558/08[2010] *ECR* I–6963, [47]–[49], the Court contemplated that the referring tribunal might regard 'portacabin', 'portokabin' and 'portocabin' as identical to PORTAKABIN. More surprisingly, in *Die BergSpechte GmbH v. trekking-at-reissen GmbH*, Case C-278/08 [2010] *ECR* I–2517, [25]–[27], the Court left it to the referring court to decide whether the word BERGSPECHTE was identical to a registered composite mark, which included as well a figurative element (a bird on skis) and other words *Outdoor-Reisen und Alpinschule Edi Koblmüller* (meaning 'outdoor travel and alpine school') and the name of an Austrian mountaineer.

[34] *Lewis v. Client Connection* [2011] *EWHC* 1627 (Ch), [18] (Norris J) (debate can become 'metaphysical').

[35] *Websphere Trade Mark* [2004] *FSR* (39) 796.

[36] *Blue IP Inc v. KCS Herr-Voss Ltd* [2004] *EWHC* 97 (Ch), [49]. Note also *Bayer Cropscience SA v. Agropharm* [2004] *EWHC* 1661 (Ch) (Patten J) (issue whether PATRIOT C and PATRIOT P were identical to PATRIOT not suitable for summary judgment); *Datacard v. Eagle Technologies* [2011] *EWHC* 244 (Pat), [314]–[315] (holding that DATACARD is identical to Datacard and Data Card); *Lewis v. Client Connection* [2011] *EWHC* 1627 (Ch), [18](b) (MONEY SAVING EXPERT and MONEY CLAIMING EXPERT not identical); *United Airlines Inc. v. United Airways Ltd* [2011] *EWHC* 2411 (Ch), [40]–[41] (UNITED/UNITED AIRLINES and UNITED AIRWAYS were identical); *Powell v. Turner* [2013] *EWHC* 3242 (IPEC), [105] ('www.wishboneash.co.uk' not identical to word mark WISHBONE ASH); *Hasbro Inc v. 123 Nahrmittel GmbH* [2011] *ETMR* 25, [193] (PLAY DOUGH not identical to PLAY-DOH).

[37] The reference to the goods or services *protected by* the earlier trade mark ensures that the section covered well-known marks (which may not have been registered): Kerly, [11–037]–[11–039].

[38] *Oberhauser v. OHIM and Petit Liberto (Fifties)*, Case T-104/01 [2002] *ECR* II–4359, [32]–[33] (applicant's goods 'Denim clothing' identical to opponent's goods 'clothing'); *Aventis Parma v. OHIM*, Case T-95/07 [2008] *ECR* II–229, [35] (applicant's mark related to 'medicines'—a category that fell within the opponent's specification for 'pharmaceuticals'—and therefore the goods were identical); *British Sky Broadcasting v. Microsoft Corp.* [2013] *EWHC* 1826 (Ch), [76] (Asplin J).

[39] *Discovery Communications v. Discovery* [2000] *ETMR* 516.

[40] *Galileo Trade Mark* [2005] *RPC* (22) 569 (AP, Prof. Annand).

[41] The interpretation of the specification is done as of the date of registration: *Reed Executive plc v. Reed Business Information Ltd* [2004] *RPC* (40) 767, [46] (Jacob LJ). Where the specification itself expressly referred to a class, e.g. 'widgets included in Class X', the question of whether any particular goods fall within the specification is to be answered by reference to the Registrar's practice at the date of registration: see *Omega Engineering Inc. v. Omega SA* [2010] *EWHC* 1211 (Ch), [2010] *FSR* (26) 625, [4]–[25]; *Datacard v. Eagle Technologies* [2011] *EWHC* 244 (Pat), [320]–[326].

[42] *Bayer Cropscience v. Agropharm* [2004] *EWHC* 1661 (Ch).

includes 'skin-lightening cream'.[43] The dominant approach today seems to be that the words used in a specification should be given their 'natural', 'ordinary', 'usual' or 'core' meaning.[44] After the *IP Translator* decision of the Court of Justice, the EUIPO has moved closer to this position in interpreting general class headings, which are given their natural and ordinary meanings.[45]

2.2.3 Registration of later mark will not adversely affect the functioning of the earlier mark

The Court of Justice has held, in the context of infringement, that there will be no liability in the case of use of an identical mark in relation to identical goods or services where the use does not adversely affect the functions of the mark.[46] It is difficult to envisage many circumstances under which normal and fair use of a later mark as a mark for identical goods would not adversely affect the capacity of a mark to indicate origin (let alone interfere with the owner's capacity to use the earlier mark as a vehicle for advertising, investment, or communication). Two related issues have arisen in an infringement context but are relevant for relative grounds as well. First, upon whom does the burden of proof lie to establish that there is harm to a mark's functions? Can harm be presumed in cases of double identity (once identical marks and products are established), or does the claimant have to additionally demonstrate that it is likely? Second, if a rebuttable presumption of harm exists and the onus shifts to the defendant, how should the defendant set about rebutting that presumption?[47] Neither issue has been directly addressed by the Court of Justice to date.

The Court of Justice has also indicated that the doctrine of functions might apply in a relative-grounds case in which the later applicant can demonstrate a lengthy period of honest concurrent use during which no such adverse effect has occurred. In *Budejovicky Budvar v. Anheuser-Busch Inc.*,[48] both Anheuser Busch and Budvar had been granted registration in the United Kingdom of the BUDWEISER word mark for beer and had been using it concurrently for 30 years. Anheuser-Busch sought to invalidate Budvar's registration on the ground that Budvar's application had a later priority date. The Court indicated that it would be open to the national authority to refuse such a request if Budvar could show that there was no likely adverse affect on Anheuser-Busch's ability to use the BUDWEISER mark as an indicator of the origin of its beer.[49] The Court did, however, describe the factual background in the case as 'exceptional'.[50]

2.3 CONFUSING SIMILARITIES: SECTION 5(2)/ARTICLE 8(1)(B)

According to section 5(2)/Article 8(1)(b) (which correspond to Article 4(1)(b) of the Trade Marks Directive), a trade mark shall not be registered where it is:

(i) identical or similar to an earlier trade mark;

---

[43] *Beautimatic International v. Mitchell International Pharmaceuticals* [1999] *ETMR* 912, 921 ('skin-lightening cream' and 'dry-skin lotion' were identical to earlier trade registration relating to 'toilet preparations and cosmetics').

[44] *You View TV Ltd v. Total Ltd* [2012] *EWHC* 3158 (Ch), [12] (Floyd J) (avoid either a broad interpretation such that the limits of the specification become fuzzy, or a narrow meaning); *Omega Engineering Inc. v. Omega SA* [2012] *EWHC* 3440 (Ch), [2013] *FSR* (25) 534 (Arnold J).

[45] *CIPA v. Registrar of Trade Marks (IP Translator)*, Case C-307/10 [2012] *ETMR* 42.

[46] See Chapter 40, section 10, pp. 1116–25.

[47] The issues are comprehensively reviewed by Arnold J in *Supreme Petfoods Ltd v. Henry Bell & Co (Grantham) Ltd* [2015] *EWHC* 256 (Ch), [83]–[181]. [48] Case C-482/09 [2011] *ECR* I-8701.

[49] Ibid., [74].   [50] Ibid., [76]. Note the qualification at [83].

(ii) to be registered for goods or services similar to those for which the earlier trade mark is protected; *and*

(iii) there exists a likelihood of confusion on the part of the public, which includes the likelihood of association with the earlier trade mark.

In considering whether a mark falls foul of section 5(2)/Article 8(1)(b), a number of questions arise.[51] A convenient summary of the likelihood of confusion factors has been provided by the Court of Appeal in *Maier v. ASOS Plc*.[52] We have already considered what is meant by an 'earlier trade mark' and the situations in which marks and services will be 'identical'. As such, it remains only to consider when goods or services are 'similar', when marks are 'similar', and what is meant by 'likelihood of confusion'.

Before looking at these in more detail, it is important to note that, in *Canon Kabushiki Kaisha v. Metro-Goldwyn-Mayer*,[53] the Court of Justice said that the various elements of Article 4(1)(b) of the TMD 1989 are interdependent. This means that difficulties in proving one of the requirements may be offset by the way in which one of the other requirements is met. For example, low levels of similarity between goods might be offset by a high degree of similarity between marks.[54] This has been called the 'interdependency principle'. In other cases, however, the Court of Justice has indicated that the requirements—similarity of marks, similarity of goods, and a likelihood of confusion—are cumulative.[55] There are therefore circumstances in which a tribunal is correct to reject an opposition (or to find infringement) on the ground purely that the signs (or goods) are dissimilar—so dissimilar, at least, that there could be no confusion even were the goods (or signs) to be identical and the mark highly distinctive.[56] The seemingly contradictory approaches ('interdependence' and 'cumulation') are reconciled by saying that the interdependence of the factors falls to be assessed only once a 'minimum level' of similarity of marks or a 'slight' similarity of goods/services has been reached. In practice, registries and tribunals use a sliding scale when assessing similarity, resorting to categories such as (i) strong or high, (ii) medium or average, and (iii) weak or low.[57] Finding the signs to be weakly similar satisfies the cumulation requirement and allows the analysis to proceed to the next stage of comparing goods or services. Finding the signs to be dissimilar brings the analysis to a halt, as the first limb of the test is not satisfied.

2.3.1 Similarity of marks

The case law provides voluminous guidance on when marks will be treated as similar. However, the starting point is *Sabel v. Puma*,[58] in which the Court of Justice laid down a basic framework that has been followed ever since: the so-called 'global appreciation'

---

[51] The likelihood of confusion test is comprehensively analysed in I. Fhima and D. Gangjee, *The Confusion Test in European Trade Mark Law* (2018).   [52] [2015] *EWCA Civ* 220, [2015] *ETMR* 26, [75].

[53] Case C-39/97 [1998] *ECR* I–5507. See also *Marca Mode CV v. Adidas AG*, Case C-425/98 [2000] *ECR* I–4861.

[54] *BSH Bosch und Siemens Hausgeräte GmbH v. EUIPO, LG Electronics*, Case C-43/15, EU:C:2016:837 (where the mark was weakly distinctive, this factor could be offset by other factors favouring a likelihood of confusion).

[55] *Vedial v. OHIM*, Case C-106/03 [2004] *ECR* I–9573, [51]; *Il Ponte Finanziaria v. OHIM*, Case C-234/06P [2007] *ECR* I–7333, [48]–[50]; *OHIM v. riha WeserGold Getränke GmbH*, Case C-558/12P, EU:C:2014:22, [41]–[45].

[56] *Ferrero SpA v. OHIM*, Case C-552/09P [2011] *ECR* I–2063, [65]–[66] (TIMI KINDERJOGHURT not similar to kinder, so that the issue of the reputation of KINDER was irrelevant); *Vedial*, Case C-106/03 [2004] *ECR* I–9573, [51]; *Il Ponte Finanziaria*, Case C-234/06P [2007] *ECR* I–7333, [48]–[50].

[57] I. Fhima and C. Denvir, 'An Empirical Analysis of the Likelihood of Confusion Factors in European Trade Mark Law' (2015) 46 *IIC* 310, 319.

[58] *Sabel BV v. Puma AG, Rudolf Dassler Sport*, Case C-251/95 [1997] *ECR* I–6191, I–6224.

approach. According to this approach, the tribunal should compare the marks as a whole, in the way in which an average consumer would see them. As the Court of Justice has observed, the average consumer *normally* perceives a mark as a whole and does not proceed to analyse its various details.[59] Consequently, attention should be paid particularly to the dominant and distinctive components of the mark. The tribunal should examine the degree of aural, visual, or conceptual similarity between the marks. In so doing, the tribunal will take into account the inherent or acquired distinctiveness of the mark.[60] Negligible elements may not be taken into consideration, but these have to be identified and the classification is interpreted strictly; for example, text in very small font may not be noticed by the relevant public.[61] One of the consequences of looking at the marks as a whole is that the courts will not necessarily examine the marks in too much detail.

(i) Visual, aural, and conceptual similarity The marks should be assessed from the point of view of their visual, aural, and conceptual similarities (or, as the Americans put it, by reference to 'sight, sound and meaning').[62] Typically, tribunals consider each in turn, before reaching an overall conclusion. In so doing, they have observed that a trade-off can occur: visual and conceptual differences, for example, can offset aural similarities.[63]

Although the marks are compared as a whole, emphasis is placed on the 'dominant' components.[64] The tribunals therefore struggle, particularly in the case of composite marks, to identify which are the dominant elements. In much of the case law, there is a tendency to emphasize the textual elements.[65] So, in *Claudia Oberhauser v. OHIM*,[66] an application for the word mark FIFTIES for denim clothing was successfully opposed because of similarities with the opponent's composite mark, registered for clothing, including words MISS FIFTIES in its lower part. Likewise, in *Matratzen Concord GmbH v. OHIM*,[67] the earlier word mark MATRATZEN was a successful basis for opposition to registration of a composite mark, comprising MATRATZEN MARKT CONCORD and including a figure carrying a mattress, because the word MATRATZEN was found to be the dominant feature of the applicant's composite mark. Difference in textual matter can also lead to a conclusion that marks are not similar. A dramatic example occurred in a UK infringement case in which Specsavers alleged that Asda had infringed its logo mark comprising two overlapping ovals (see Fig 38.1).[68] Finding no infringement, Mann J highlighted that the Asda mark (see Fig 38.2) comprised two abutting white ovals and contained the words 'Asda Opticians'. He reasoned that:

> [W]hile the ovals are an important part of the Specsavers sign they do not dominate so as to subordinate the wording as a matter of overall appearance. The wording is equally significant. That being the case, a different form of wording (in the form of the Asda wording)

---

[59] Ibid., [23].   [60] Ibid., [23]. On disclaimed matter, see Chapter 35, section 2.5, and section 2.2.1, n. 26.

[61] EUIPO, *Examination Guidelines*, Part C, Section 2, Chapter 4, [1.5].

[62] See, e.g., *King of the Mountain Sports Inc. v. Chrysler Corp*, 185 *F.3d* 1084, 1090 (10th Cir. 1999); *AMF Inc. v. Sleekcraft Boats*, 599 *F.2d* 341, 351 (9th Cir. 1979).

[63] *Il Ponte Finanzaria*, Case C-234/06P [2007] *ECR* I-7333, [34]; *T.I.M.E. Art v. OHIM*, Case C-171/06 [2007] *ECR* I-41, [49].

[64] In the context of visual, aural or phonetic, and conceptual similarity, the focus on distinctive and dominant *elements within marks* is different from distinctiveness of the earlier mark *as a whole*, considered later in the chapter. A further difference is that dominance may be due either to distinctiveness in the classic sense or the visual prominence of the element, even if it is (say) descriptive and has no inherent distinctiveness. See, e.g., *Intermark v. OHIM, Coca-Cola* Case T-384/13 [2015] ECR II-0000, [37] (COLA dominated in RIENERGY COLA, on grounds of its size and position, even though it clearly would not be inherently distinctive).

[65] Sometimes it is said that 'words "speak louder" than devices': *Oasis Stores' Trade Mark Application* [1998] *RPC* 631, 644.   [66] Case T-104/01 [2002] *ECR* II-4359, [47].

[67] Case T-6/01 [2002] *ECR* II-4335.

[68] *Specsavers Int'l Healthcare v. Asda Stores* [2010] *EWHC* 2035 (Ch), [2011] *FSR* (1) 1.

Fig. 38.1 Specsavers logo mark

Source: Specsavers Int'l Healthcare v. Asda Stores [2012] EWCA Civ 24, [2012] FSR (19) 555

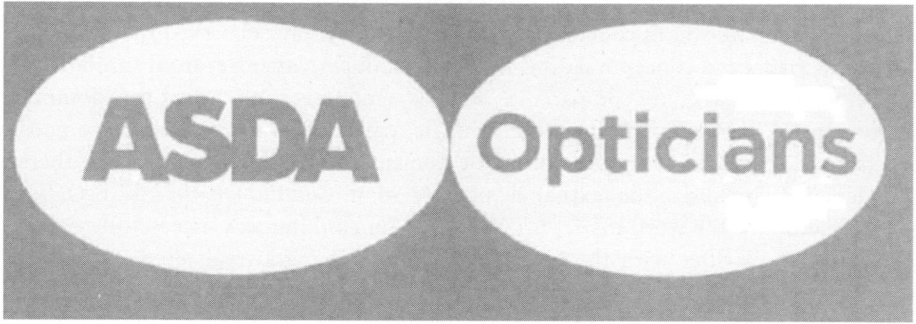

Fig. 38.2 Asda Opticians logo mark

Source: Specsavers Int'l Healthcare v. Asda Stores [2012] EWCA Civ 24, [2012] FSR (19) 555

introduces a very significant difference. In my view a very different overall impression is given. Taking that comparison by itself, I do not see how the reasonably circumspect consumer would be confused by the only real element in common, namely the presence of ovals, and thereby think that the two marks connote the same trade origin. Asda is itself a well-known name, and I do not readily understand how its name expressly spelled out, in prominent letters, could leave a reasonably circumspect consumer thinking that the mark is, or even might be, Specsavers.[69]

Although, in a composite mark, text frequently dominates, the Court of Justice has provided a reminder that the assessment is a global one. In *Shaker de Laudato v. Limiñana y Botella*,[70] an applicant for a composite mark for alcoholic beverages that included the word LIMONCELLO above an image of a plate decorated with six lemons (see Fig. 38.3) was opposed by the owner of the Spanish word mark LIMONCHELO, also relating to goods in Class 33. The (then) Court of First Instance (CFI) had held that the signs were dissimilar because of the dominance of the dish feature in the applicant's mark, a feature that was absent in the opponent's. (This finding was itself surprising, given the general tendency to emphasize verbal components.) The Court of Justice overturned this finding, reminding the Court that the assessment was a global one and could not be conducted by comparing

---

[69] Ibid., [136] (Mann J). The Court of Appeal affirmed this finding, but found that there was infringement under s. 10(3): [2012] *EWCA Civ* 24, [2012] *FSR* (19) 555.

[70] *Shaker de L. Laudato & C. Sas v. Limiñana y Botella, SL*, Case C-334/05P [2007] *ECR* I–4529.

Fig. 38.3 'Limoncello'

Source: Shaker de L. Laudato & C. Sas v. Limiñana y Botella, SL, Case C-334/05P [2007] ECR I–4529

only one element. It is only where all other aspects are negligible that the assessment can be carried out on the basis solely of the dominant element.

The relative importance of each sort of similarity will vary with the circumstances in hand—in particular, the goods and the types of mark. In the case of certain kinds of goods, such as clothes or furniture, visual similarity between the marks in issue will be the most important form of similarity.[71] In contrast, it has been said that wine marks will be perceived 'verbally';[72] with restaurant services (in which word-of-mouth recommendation is highly important), it is likely that phonetic similarity will be key.[73] Each case is therefore to be viewed in its own context. However, the Court of Justice has ruled that, in an appropriate case, mere aural similarity may make marks so similar as to be likely to cause confusion.[74] In the case of device marks (as well as three-dimensional marks), visual similarity will usually be the most important factor,[75] and in the case of sound marks, clearly, the inquiry will depend chiefly on aural similarity.

In the case of word marks, a determination of visual similarity typically involves looking at the length of the marks, their structure (whether there are the same number of words), and whether the same letters are used. The courts also bear in mind that consumers may not be able to remember a mark perfectly (a notion known as 'imperfect recollection'). The average consumer only rarely has the chance to make a direct comparison between marks and so must place their trust in the 'imperfect picture of them

---

[71] *Inter-Ikea Systems BV v. OHIM*, Case T-112/06 [2008] *ECR* II–6, [79]; *Calida Holding v. OHIM*, Case T-597/13, EU:T:2015:804, [70]–[71]; cf. *Claudia Oberhauser*, Case T-104/01 [2002] *ECR* II–4359, esp. [48].

[72] *Castellani SpA v. OHIM*, Case T-149/06 [2007] *ECR* II–4755, [53]; *Osotspa v. OHIM*, Case T-33/03 [2005] *ECR* II–763, [63]–[64] (energy drinks).

[73] *Mystery Drinks GmbH v. OHIM*, Case T-99/01 [2003] *ECR* II–43, [48]; *Warsteiner Brauerei v. OHIM*, Case T-243/12, EU:T:2013:344 , [42] (French and German only) (beers).

[74] *Lloyd Schuhfabrik Meyer v. Klijsen Handel BV*, Case C-342/97 [1999] *ECR* I–3819.

[75] *Julius Sämaan Ltd v. Tetrosyl Ltd* [2006] *FSR* (42) 849, [54] (Kitchin J).

that he has kept in his mind'.[76] In many cases, this means that while, at first glance, two marks may appear to be dissimilar, when the possibility of imperfect recollection is taken into account, the marks may in fact be similar. While the courts have used the notion of imperfect recollection to expand the ambit of protection given to earlier marks, they are always mindful of the need for the marks to be similar.[77]

When comparing marks aurally, some attention must be paid to the relevant linguistic context. Words that might not seem similar aurally to an English-speaker may seem so to a person with a different linguistic background. In the case of EUTMs to which oppositions arise from earlier national marks, it is the linguistic context of the country of registration of the opposing marks that is of relevance. Thus while the words CULTRA and SCULPTRA might seem aurally distinct in English, according to the General Court, for the relevant Hungarian and Czech public, the words were liable to give rise to similar sounds.[78]

The pertinent tribunals have tended to carry out a quantitative assessment: do the two signs have more syllables in common than not? For example, the (then) CFI held that GIORGIO AIRE was not aurally similar to MISS GIORGI because only one syllable out of four was the same,[79] whereas MYSTERY and MIXERY were treated as similar.[80] In a short word, a slight variation may be sufficient to render the marks dissimilar. For example, BASS and PASH were treated as dissimilar by the CFI,[81] although in a different case it held ILS to be similar to ELS.[82] In assessing similarity, the tribunal will typically be more influenced by the first than the last syllable. So the CFI treated BUD and BUDMEN, ZERO and ZERORH+, SEVEN and SEVEN FOR ALL MANKIND as similar, the English High Court held VIAGRA and VIAGRENE to be similar,[83] and the General Court has confirmed that SKYPE is similar to SKY.[84] Consistently with this logic, the CFI held words with common endings—NUTRIDE and TUFFTRIDE, ASTERIX and STARIX—not to be similar.[85] In other cases, similarity of the first syllable has proven insufficient to establish similarity, for example the CFI held that GIORGI LINE was not similar to GIORGIO AIRE.[86] Despite emphasis on the first part, the CFI also has held LA MER to be confusingly similar to LABORATOIRES DE LA MER (both in closely related goods in the cosmetics area).[87] These counter-examples are a

---

[76] *Lloyd Schuhfabrik*, Case C-342/97 [1999] *ECR* I-3819, [22]–[26].

[77] *Equinix, formerly Ancotel v. OHIM,* Case T-443/12, EU:T:2013:605, [54] (even consumers with high levels of attention rely on imperfect recollection).

[78] *Aventis Pharmaceuticals v. OHIM*, Case T-142/12, EU:T:2013:374, [44].

[79] *Laboratorios RTB, SL v. OHIM*, Case T-156/01 [2003] *ECR* II-2789, [77].

[80] *Mystery Drinks*, Case T-99/01 [2003] *ECR* II-43.

[81] *Phillips–Van Heusen*, Case T-292/01 [2003] *ECR* II-4335, [50]. For further examples, see *Inter-Ikea Systems*, Case T-112/06 [2008] *ECR* II-6 (CFI), [79] (IDEA and IKEA); *Grether AG v. OHIM*, Case T-167/05 [2007] *ECR* II-63 (FENNEL and FENJAL).

[82] *Institut für Lernsysteme GmbH v. OHIM*, Case T-388/00 [2002] *ECR* II-4301.

[83] *José Alejando SL v. OHIM*, Case T-129/01 [2003] *ECR* II-2251, [49]; *Zero Industry v. OHIM and zero Germany,* Case T-400/06 [2009] *ECR* II-150*, [49]; *Seven for All Mankind v. Seven SpA,* Case C-655/11P, EU:C:2013:94 , [75]–[77]; *Pfizer v. Eurofood Link (UK)* [2000] *ETMR* 187 (EWHC); *L'Oréal v. OHIM and Spa Monopole (SPA THERAPY),* Case T-109/07 [2009] *ECR* II-675, [30].

[84] *Skype v. OHIM, Sky,* Case T-183/13, EU:T:2015:259; appeal withdrawn Case C-382/15P, EU:C:2016:31.

[85] *Durferrit GmbH v. OHIM*, Case T-224/01 [2003] *ECR* II-1589; *Les Éditions Albert René v. OHIM*, Case T-311/01 [2003] *ECR* II-4625, [56].

[86] *Laboratorios RTB*, Case T-156/01 [2003] *ECR* II-2789 (GIORGI was not thought particularly distinctive for perfumes). See also *Aldi GmbH & Co. v. OHIM*, Case T-505/11 [2014] *ETMR* (8) 162 (annulling Opposition Division decision that DIALDI was dissimilar to ALDI, noting that the middle syllable can be as important as the opening one).

[87] *La Mer Technology Inc. v. OHIM*, Case T-418/03 [2008] *ETMR* (9) 169; *Julian James; Opposition of Smart* [2005] *ETMR* (93) 1096 (AP, Arnold QC) (CARSMART similar to SMART, both for cars, in part because while 'car' was at beginning, it was descriptive).

useful reminder that the rulings are fact-specific, so that previous decisions are helpful only to provide a sense of the standards being applied; they have virtually no value as precedents.

Because similarity is assessed conceptually, as well as visually and phonetically, in thinking about whether marks are similar, it is necessary to take account of the ideas that lie behind or inform the earlier mark.[88] The important role that conceptual or non-visual features may play in deciding whether marks are similar can be seen in the 'Betty Boop' case.[89] Here, the claimant had various registrations for the words BETTY BOOP, the name of a 1930s cartoon character, which had been held to have acquired distinctive character. The defendant had been licensing an image of the cartoon character, which it had acquired from out-of-copyright material. The court held that using the image infringed the word trade mark, because the average consumer seeing the image would immediately summon up the words 'Betty Boop'.[90] The Court distinguished a case in which there was found to be no similarity between the word ALLIGATOR and Lacoste's well-known registered device of a crocodile, because, on the facts, seeing the words would not cause the average consumer to perceive the earlier device mark.[91] Inevitably, conceptual similarity might be found at a certain degree of abstraction—thus the outline of a pheasant with a top hat is similar to a pigeon with a top hat since both are birds.[92] Yet the higher the level of abstract similarity, the greater becomes the concern that trade mark exclusivity is being granted to the concepts underlying signs.[93]

(ii) Distinctiveness The question of whether marks are similar will often be dependent on the inherent or acquired distinctiveness of the mark (for the goods or services for which it is registered).[94] Distinctiveness here should be understood as the strength of the mark;[95] it does not refer to whether the mark has sufficient origin indicating ability to qualify as a trade mark. This has a number of effects.[96]

First, the less distinctive the earlier trade mark, the less literal or visual alteration is necessary to ensure that the later mark is not similar. For example, comparing two words CASTELLANI and CASTELLUCA for wine from the point of view of a German consumer, the General Court found the two marks to be dissimilar, because the 'castel' element is a common descriptive component in wine names and the applicant's suffix 'luca' would be

---

[88] *Sir Terence Conran v. Mean Fiddler Holdings* [1997] *FSR* 856 (ZN similar to ZINC); *Osotspa v. OHIM*, Case T-33/03 [2005] *ECR* II–763, [51] (some conceptual similarity between SHARK and the word HAI, the latter being Finnish for 'shark'); *Golden Balls Ltd v. OHIM*, T-437/11 [2014] *ETMR* (1) 1, [41]–[51] (in the context of printed matter, GOLDEN BALLS was regarded as having weak conceptual similarity with BALLON D'OR).

[89] *Hearst Holdings Inc. v. A.V.E.L.A. Inc.* [2014] *EWHC* 439 (Ch).　　[90] Ibid., [156].

[91] *La Chemise Lacoste SA v. Baker Street Clothing Ltd* [2011] *RPC* 5 (AP, Hobbs QC). In Germany, conceptual similarity was at issue where Haribo argued that Lindt's three dimensional golden foil covered chocolate bears infringed the word mark GOLDBEAR. Since several different meanings could be attributed to the shape of Lindt's bear—such as chocolate teddy and not merely gold bear—there was no immediate similarity of meaning: *Goldbären* (23 September 2015) I ZR 105/14 (Bundesgerichtshof).

[92] *Jack Wills Ltd v. House of Fraser (Stores) Ltd* [2014] *EWHC* 110 (Ch), [94].

[93] See, e.g., *The Polo/Lauren Company, LP v. OHIM*, Case T-265/13, EU:T:2014:779 (polo players on bicycles found to be conceptually similar).

[94] *Picasso v. OHIM*, Case C-361/04 [2006] *ECR* I–643, [32] (PICASSO was highly distinctive for painting, but not for cars).

[95] Cf. B. Beebe and C. Scott Hemphill, 'The Scope of Strong Marks: Should Trademark Law Protect the Strong More than the Weak?' (2017) 92 *NYU L Rev* 1339 (strong marks tend to be better insulated against confusion).

[96] The status of some of these propositions—whether they are legal rules, presumptions of fact, or merely guidelines—has been a matter of dispute. Given the Court of Justice's role, particularly on references from member states, it has been assumed that some statements must be propositions of law: *Reed Executive plc v. Reed Business Information Ltd* [2003] *RPC* (12) 207, 241, [103], [2004] *RPC* (40) 767 (CA), [83].

seen as the Italian name and thus sufficient to differentiate the marks.[97] In *Reed Executive plc v. Reed Business Information Ltd*,[98] Jacob LJ stated that 'where a mark is descriptive small differences may suffice to avoid confusion', giving an illustration from the law of passing off concerning the terms OFFICE CLEANING ASSOCIATION and OFFICE CLEANING SERVICES. Where the distinctiveness of the earlier trade mark is very low, the later mark will have to be in close proximity for it to be similar.[99] The same principle applies to common names that intrinsically have a low level of distinctiveness.[100] When assessing similarity, what matters most is the similarity in the distinctive components of the marks being compared (so-called 'distinctive similarity'), rather than in their descriptive elements.[101] Despite the force of this argument—distinctiveness is not a one way ratchet leading inevitably to enhanced protection—the Court of Justice has repeatedly affirmed that where two trade marks correspond only in relation to non-distinctive elements, this is still sufficient to establish the likelihood of confusion.[102] The 'global appreciation' test focuses on the overall similarity of the marks from the perspective of the relevant consumer and distinctiveness is only one limb of this analysis; weak distinctiveness cannot entirely counteract findings of similarity in relation to other parts of the test. The contrasting position—weakly distinctive marks or non-distinctive elements within marks are only entitled to a correspondingly reduced scope of protection—remains appealing to many tribunals.[103]

Second, if the earlier mark is highly distinctive, then a mark that has been substantially modified might nonetheless still be similar.[104] This enhanced distinctiveness has to be proved and cannot be easily presumed.[105] When measuring its strength, the registrar will usually first consider the overall inherent distinctiveness of the earlier mark before considering whether it has acquired enhanced distinctiveness.[106] However—at least for the purposes of relative grounds analysis—any acquired distinctiveness being claimed in favour of the later mark being applied for cannot counteract the likelihood of confusion.[107]

---

[97] *Castellani*, Case T-149/06 [2007] *ECR* II–4755 (CFI). However, the Court of Justice has held that the so-called 'requirement of availability' is irrelevant to the determination of similarity between marks, goods, or likelihood of confusion: *Adidas AG and ors v. Marca Mode CV and ors*, Case C-102/07 [2008] *ECR* I–2439.

[98] [2004] *RPC* (40) 767, 792, [84].

[99] But cf. *Václav Hrbek v. OHIM*, Case C-42/12P, EU:C:2012:765 (two composite marks containing word alpine were similar even though the common feature was of weak distinctiveness).

[100] *Reed Executive* [2004] *RPC* (40) 767, [86] (common surnames); *Barbara Becker v. Human International Industries*, Case C-51/09P [2010] *ECR* I–5805.

[101] Kerly, [11–090].

[102] See, e.g., *BSH Bosch und Siemens Hausgeräte GmbH v. EUIPO, LG Electronics*, Case C-43/15, EU:C:2016:837 (KOMPRESSOR and KOMPRESSOR PLUS successfully used to oppose a figurative mark including 'compressor technology', for household appliances including refrigerators); *Mr Kebab v. EUIPO*, Case T-448/16, EU:T:2017:459 (Mr Kebap versus Mr Kebab; both figurative with only the descriptive word in common).

[103] *Starbucks (HK) Ltd v. British Sky Broadcasting Group plc* [2012] *EWHC* 3074 (Ch), [117] (Arnold J) (asking trade mark registries to reflect upon 'registering descriptive marks [such as NOW for telecommunication services] under the cover of a figurative figleaf of distinctiveness'); *Supreme Petfoods Ltd v. Henry Bell & Co. (Grantham) Ltd* [2015] *EWHC* 256 (Ch), [185] (Arnold J) (common element SUPREME was non-distinctive, so confusion was unlikely); TMDN, *Common Communication on the Common Practice of Relative Grounds of Refusal—Likelihood of Confusion (Impact of non-distinctive/weak components)* (2 October 2014).

[104] *Sabel v. Puma*, Case C-251/95 [1997] *ECR* I–6191, [24]; *Lloyd Schuhfabrik*, Case C-342/7 [1999] *ECR* I–3819, [21]–[22]; *Canon KK v. MGM*, Case C-39/97 [1998] *ECR* I–5507, [17]–[18].

[105] *Arav Holding v. EUIPO*, Case C-379/12P, EU:C:2013:317, [71] (cannot presume enhanced distinctiveness because the mark is (descriptively) unrelated to the underlying goods).

[106] Evidence of acquired distinctiveness can compensate for the weak inherent distinctiveness of a mark: *Shoe Branding Europe v. adidas*, Case C-396/15P, EU:C:2016:95.

[107] *Skype v. OHIM, Sky* Case T-183/13, EU:T:2015:259, [49]-[50]; aff'd Case C-382/15P, EU:C:2016:31.

Puma

Sabel

Fig. 38.4 The 'bounding felines' in *Sabel v. Puma*
Source: Sabel v. Puma, Case C-251/95 [1997] *ECR* I–6191

Third, the chance of there being a likelihood of confusion on the basis of the ideas (or concepts) that underlie a mark is particularly influenced by the distinctiveness of the earlier mark.[108] In *Sabel v. Puma*,[109] which concerned two images of bounding felines, the Court of Justice suggested that *if* the earlier mark were well known by the public and/or the image of the puma were imaginative, mere conceptual similarity might be sufficient to give rise to a finding of a likelihood of confusion (see Fig. 38.4).[110]

Fourth, although the comparison is to be made between the particular mark registered and the sign applied for,[111] the relevance of acquired distinctiveness may permit the tribunal to consider the earlier mark in the context of a 'family of marks'. Most readers will be familiar with the range of products marketed by Apple Inc., such as the iMac, iPad, iPhone, as well as services such as iTunes.[112] On the assumption that these are registered as trade marks, it might be that the existence of a 'family' allows each mark to reinforce each other and gain a broader scope of protection than they would otherwise have. This might mean that an application by a third party for 'iSoft' (for software), 'iBroadcasting' (for broadcasting services), or even 'iBank' (for financial services) would be refused.[113] The Court of Justice, in *Il Ponte Finanzaria SpA*,[114] has affirmed that the existence of a family of marks is a relevant factor when assessing similarity, although it emphasized at the same time that the status of being a 'family' can be conferred only on marks that have been used in such a way that they would be

---

[108] *Sabel v. Puma*, Case C-251/95 [1997] *ECR* I–6191, [24].   [109] Ibid.   [110] Ibid., [25].
[111] *Ener-Cap* [1999] *RPC* 362.
[112] However, Apple's application to register iWATCH was refused based on the earlier mark iSWATCH: see *iWATCH*, O/307/16 (27 June 2016).
[113] There would, of course, need to be finding of a minimal level of similarity of the services with the goods or services covered by the Apple registrations. This is easier to foresee for software and broadcasting than for financial services, but might be the case if the latter were to be seen as including an Internet banking service.   [114] Case C-234/06P [2007] *ECR* I–7333.

recognized in the market as a family. Merely registering a series of marks will not confer this added strength.[115] Moreover, there needs still to be at least minimal similarity between the opponent and applicant's mark. The Court subsequently indicated that the likelihood of confusion standard is satisfied if consumers are mistaken into thinking the mark being applied for is part of the earlier family. The later mark should inter alia include the key element that is common to the family of marks, such that consumers think it is a new member of that family.[116]

Fifth, because there is a global assessment, account may be taken of how the earlier mark has in fact been used. This may seem surprising, given the focus in the case law on the importance of 'graphic representation' defining the mark. Nevertheless, in *Specsavers Int'l Healthcare v. Asda Stores*,[117] the Court of Justice indicated that even though the claimant's registered mark (Fig. 38.1) comprising two overlapping ovals was represented in black-and-white (and might have been assumed to cover use of the device in any colour), it was relevant to the assessment of likelihood of confusion that the claimant had used the device in a particular shade of green and that the defendant used the device in the same colour. Admittedly *Specsavers* involved an infringement claim, as opposed to relative grounds analysis. However the latter mode does allow evidence of acquired distinctiveness—and the manner in which it has been acquired—as part of the analysis of the strength of the mark under the distinctiveness factor. The conclusion undermines the role of the register as a mechanism for defining the bounds of the property conferred by trade mark law, and may well be seen as reflecting the Court's frustration with the fact that as yet there has been no harmonization of the law of unfair competition.

(iii) Deviation from the global approach Having adopted the 'global approach', the Court of Justice was confronted by a difficult case: what to do with an application for a mark that added a well-known 'house mark' or company name to a third party's earlier registered mark. For example, where the distinctiveness of an earlier mark is weak, as with, say, SENSATIONS for crisps, does it inevitably follow from the global appreciation approach that there is no similarity with WALKERS SENSATIONS, where WALKERS is a highly distinctive component of the latter mark? If so, this leaves big firms with established names free to swamp the goodwill engendered by smaller proprietors. Rather than accept the injustice that would arise from strict application of the global appreciation approach, the Court of Justice has added a qualification for cases in which elements of a mark retain some 'independent distinctive role' in a later 'composite mark'. In *Medion AG v. Thomson Multimedia Sales*,[118] the Court of Justice stated that in such cases, at least where there is identity of goods or services, it suffices that 'because the earlier mark still has an independent distinctive role, the origin of the goods or services covered by the composite sign is attributed by the public also to the owner of that mark'.[119] While it is easy to understand the motivation behind this approach, one cannot help but wonder whether this does not drive the proverbial 'coach and horses' through the global appreciation test.[120]

---

[115] Ibid., [63]–[64].

[116] *Debonair Trading v. OHIM*, Case C-270/14P, EU:C:2015:688 (the key element 'so …?', which was common to the earlier family of marks, did not coincide with the element 'sô' in the application).

[117] *Specsavers Int'l Healthcare Ltd v. Asda Stores Ltd*, Case C-252/12 [2013] *ETMR* 46.

[118] Case C-120/04 [2005] *ECR* I–8551, [36].

[119] See also *L'Oréal v. OHIM and Spa Monopole (SPA THERAPY)*, Case T-109/07 [2009] *ECR* II–675; *Zero Industry v. OHIM and zero*, Case T-400/06 [2009] *ECR* II–150*, [51], [78], [79].

[120] In *Barbara Becker v. Harman International Industries*, Case C-51/09P [2010] *ECR* I–5805, [AG53], [AG56], AG Cruz Villalón has referred to the circumstances in which *Medion* is applicable as 'exceptional'.

The *Medion* test has been held to be applicable to the situation in which one component of an applicant's mark is not necessarily identical but highly similar to an earlier mark,[121] at least where that component has an 'independent distinctive role' within the later mark. In *Aveda Corp. v. Dabur India*,[122] an application to register DABUR UVEDA for specified goods in Classes 3 and 5 was opposed by Aveda on the basis of its earlier Community and UK marks for the word AVEDA also covering goods in Classes 3 and 6. Although the UK Trade Marks Registry rejected the opposition, applying the orthodox 'global appreciation', Arnold J upheld Aveda's appeal (at least in relation to some of the goods). He found that the Registry should have considered whether UVEDA had independent significance of its own, and if so, whether that would have been likely to lead the average consumer to be confused as to the existence of an economic connection between the earlier mark owner and the sellers of DABUR UVEDA. Given that DABUR had been used as a 'house mark' with other product names, that normal and fair use of DABUR UVEDA was admitted to include use of UVEDA in a distinct script, coupled with the high distinctive character of the opponent's AVEDA mark, the court found that there would have been confusion in relation to some identical and some similar goods. Ultimately, satisfying the *Medion* test often turns on the extent to which the common element is truly independent and distinctive within the composite mark.[123]

2.3.2 When are goods or services similar?

The next question is whether goods or services are similar. When deciding whether a trade mark application falls foul of one of the relative grounds for refusal, the comparison is normally between the goods or services for which the earlier mark has been registered and the goods or services to which the application relates. This is largely a paper exercise. However, in an infringement action, the court will usually compare the defendant's goods as they have actually been used with the goods in the claimant's specification. This requires the court to interpret the specification and then to characterize the defendant's goods or services to see if they fall within the specification.

In *Canon Kabushiki Kaisha v. Pathé Communications*,[124] the Japanese company Canon opposed MGM's registration of the sign CANNON for films in the German Trade Marks Registry. The opposition was based upon Canon's registration of CANON for 'still and motion picture cameras and projectors, television filming and recording devices, etc'. The question arose whether the goods were not similar. In response to a reference from the German Federal Court of Justice, the Court of Justice explained that, when assessing the similarity of the goods or services concerned, 'all the relevant factors' should be taken into account. Those factors include, among others, 'their nature, their end-users, and their method of use, and whether they are in competition with each other or are complementary'.[125] The methods by which the goods are distributed may also be a pertinent

---

[121] *Bimbo SA v. OHIM*, Case C-591/12P [2014] *ETMR* 41 (while the overall impression conveyed remained the test and BIMBO was the dominant element in BIMBO DOUGHNUTS, the analysis had to include DOUGHNUTS, which retained an independent distinctive role. On this basis the earlier mark DOGHNUTS could successfully oppose it).   [122] [2013] *EWHC* 589 (Ch).

[123] Components would not have independent significance where they are linked as with ERIC CANTONA CANTO, where the CANTO would be understood as an abbreviated nickname for the former French footballer-turned-actor: *Novartis Seeds BV's Application* [2006] *ETMR* (82) 1158 (AP, Hobbs QC). See also *Whyte & Mackay Ltd v. Origin Wine UK Ltd* [2015] *EWHC* 1271 (Ch) (overruling the registry hearing officer, ORIGIN as the common element, in relation to use on wine and whisky, had low independent distinctiveness); *Pia Hallstrom Ltd's Trade Mark Application* [2018] *FSR* 5 (AP, Alexander QC) (upholding the hearing officer, the common element PIA, as a name, had a very limited independent distinctive role); cf. *BGW v. Bodo Scholz*, Case C-20/14, EU:C:2015:714.   [124] Case C-39/97 [1998] *ECR* I–5507.

[125] Ibid., [17].

factor.[126] In an infringement scenario, the tribunal might also have relevant evidence of how the defendant has marketed its goods.[127]

British Sugar v. Robertson[128] illustrates how the courts have applied the factors in the case of a non-distinctive mark (namely, TREAT). In that case, the question was whether a sweet syrup to be poured over desserts was similar to a sweet-flavoured spread. Jacob J concluded that the goods were not similar, explaining that the goods were used differently (the spread could be used on desserts, but generally would not be), were not in direct competition, were located in different places in supermarkets (the spread with jams, the dessert sauce with desserts), were physically different (the spread was more viscous than the sauce), and were treated differently by market researchers.[129] In contrast, in *Balmoral Trade Mark*,[130] whisky and wine were held to be similar goods: although the two products have very different producers, it is common to find them being bought and sold by the same merchants, and sold through the same outlets.

It is clear that the fact that goods or services are registered in different classes does not inevitably mean that they are not similar. For example, the (then) CFI held that the development of correspondence courses was similar to educational textbooks and printed materials.[131] The fact that the signs relate to different classes is irrelevant because the way in which the goods or services are classified is an administrative matter, whereas the question of whether goods or services are similar is an issue for substantive law.[132] It is also clear that if an earlier trade mark relates to goods, whereas the applicant's mark relates to services, they may nonetheless still be similar (and vice versa).[133] In one case, an application for the sign BALMORAL for wines was rejected because of the existence of an earlier trade mark BALMORAL for bar services.[134]

Although application of the *Canon* test has generally proved unproblematic, one question that has raised concern is the application of the 'complementarity' factor. The basic idea seems straightforward: consumers of some goods under a particular mark (say, KENZO for clothes) might believe complementary goods (say, shoes, scent, or bath towels) sold under the same (or a similar) mark are made under the authority of the trade mark

---

[126] *Ampafrance SA v. OHIM*, Case T-164/03 [2005] *ECR* II–1401, [53]; *El Corte Ingles*, Case T-443/05 [2007] *ECR* II–2579, [43]; *Serrano Aranda v. OHIM and Burg Groep (LE LANCIER)*, Case T-265/09, EU:T:2012:472, [40] (French and Dutch only) (sale in supermarkets a weak indication of similarity of goods).

[127] *Canon*, Case C-39/97 [1999] 1 *CMLR* 77, 95, [18]; *Pfizer v. Eurofood* [2000] *ETMR* 187.

[128] [1996] *RPC* 281, 297; cf. esp. *Vedial SA v. OHIM*, Case T-110/01 [2002] *ECR* II–5275 (CFI) (edible fats were similar to vinegars and sauces, among other things, because they are offered for sale on the same shelves), not discussed on appeal in Case C-106/03 [2004] *ECR* I–9573, and *Pedro Díaz v. OHIM*, Case T-85/02 [2003] *ECR* II–4835 (condensed milk and cheese held to be similar because they are in the same family of 'milk products', so consumers might think that they both come from the same enterprise).

[129] *Serrano Aranda v. OHIM and Burg Groep (LE LANCIER)*, Case T-265/09, EU:T:2012:472, [40] (French and Dutch only) (finding 'little similarity' between 'edible oils, vinegar, mustard, salt and spices', on the one hand, and 'fresh fruit and vegetables', on the other).   [130] [1999] *RPC* 297, 302.

[131] *Institut für Lernsysteme*, Case T-388/00 [2002] *ECR* II–4301.

[132] *El Corte Ingles*, Case T-443/05 [2007] *ECR* II–2579, [38]; *Isdin SA v. OHIM*, Case C-597/12P, EU:C:2013:672, [27]–[28].

[133] The characterization of a defendant's activities may be such that it can be said that they are simultaneously using the sign in relation to both goods *and* services. For example, advertising BMW vehicle repairs can be use in relation to both cars and repair services: *Bayerische Motorenwerke AG v. Ronald Karel Deenik*, Case C-63/97 [1999] *ECR* I–905, [38]–[42]. However, such cases of simultaneous use are limited to situations in which there is a 'specific and indissociable link' between the products and services: *Adam Opel AG v. Autec*, Case C-48/05 [2007] *ECR* I–1017, [27]–[28]. Otherwise where the goods and services share the same overall purpose (here, beauty and healthcare) soap and cosmetics can be similar to spa and sauna services: *Costa Crociere Spa v. OHIM*, Case T-388/13, EU:T:2015:118.   [134] *Balmoral* [1999] *RPC* 297, 301.

holder, whereas such a connection might not be made in relation to non-complementing goods (say, hairdryers or fridges).[135]

Nevertheless, the General Court has tried to formulate a notion of 'aesthetic complementarity' that is unduly exacting. In one case, the Court said that goods would be regarded as complementary only where there is 'a true aesthetic necessity', such that consumers would think it 'unusual or shocking' if the two items did not match.[136] On this basis, footwear and bags were not complementary, nor were perfumes and clothes, but bags and clothes were.[137] The narrowness of this test may be appropriate, since establishing complementarity alone can potentially carry the day. The Court of Justice has confirmed that the autonomous criterion of complementarity can be the sole factor which establishes similarity between goods or services, notwithstanding countervailing evidence that their nature, methods of use or distribution channels diverge.[138]

Finally, as a practical resource, the EUIPO has developed a Similarity search tool, which can be used during opposition or cancellation proceedings to assess, for the goods or services in question, whether participating trade mark offices have previously considered them similar or dissimilar and to what degree.[139]

2.3.3 Likelihood of confusion

The final, and critical, element that has to be shown for a mark to fall foul of section 5(2)/ Article 8(1)(b) is that (as a result of the similarities) there is 'a likelihood of confusion on the part of the public, which includes the likelihood of association with the earlier trade mark'.

(i) The standpoint of interpretation: who must be confused? The likelihood of confusion is considered from the point of view of the average consumer of the products concerned, comparing the marks as a whole. As the Court of Justice observed in *Sabel v. Puma*,[140] 'the average consumer of the type of goods or services in question plays a decisive role in the global appreciation of the likelihood of confusion'. EU law thus applies its own understanding of the consumer, rather than focusing on actual consumers (who might be ignorant or uninterested). In subsequent decisions, the Court of Justice has said that the average consumer is 'reasonably well informed' and 'reasonably observant and circumspect'.[141] There is no confusion if only a minority of particularly inattentive consumers might possibly be confused.[142] However, these are the default characteristics of the 'average consumer' and the tribunals accept that the characteristics of the average consumer of the goods may vary with the sector concerned.[143] For example, consumers purchasing cars

---

[135] Complementarity exists where 'there is a close connection between [the goods or services], in the sense that one is indispensable or important for the use of the other in such a way that consumers may think that the responsibility for the production of those goods or provision of those services lies with the same undertaking'; *Nanu-Nana Joachim Hoepp v. EUIPO*, Case T-39/16, EU:T:2017:263, [73].

[136] *Sergio Rossi SpA v. OHIM*, T-169/03 [2005] *ECR* II-685 (CFI), [62].

[137] Ibid. (footwear and bags); *Mühlens v. OHIM*, T-150/04 [2007] *ECR* II-2357 (indispensable or important); *El Corte Ingles*, T-443/05 [2007] *ECR* II-2579 (CFI, Fourth Chamber, extended composition), [38] (bags and clothes). See also *Serrano Aranda v. OHIM and Burg Groep (LE LANCIER)*, T-265/09, EU:T:2012:472, [36] (French and Dutch only) (seasoning and vegetables are complementary).

[138] *Kurt Hesse v. OHIM,* Case C-50/15P, EU:C:2016:34, [23].   [139] See http://euipo.europa.eu/sim/.

[140] Case C-251/95 [1997] *ECR* I-6191, [23].

[141] *Lloyd Shuhfabrik*, Case C-342/7 [1999] *ECR* I-3819, [26]. The average consumer is also relevant when assessing distinctiveness. See Chapter 37, section 3, pp. 979-80.

[142] *Reed Executive v. Reed Business Information* [2004] *RPC* (40) 767, [82] (approach guards against 'too "nanny" a view of protection').

[143] The relevant goods or services determine the degree of attention of the consumer. Deciding whether consumers are particularly attentive or not, when purchasing a specific category of products (say, sports shoes) goes on to influence whether they will notice differences between marks: *Shoe Branding Europe v. adidas*, Case C-396/15P, EU:C:2016:95.

take more care than those buying sweets.[144] In some circumstances in which consumers are advised (for example by medical professionals), they may be particularly attentive and thus unlikely to confuse superficially similar marks.[145] Beyond this, however, there has been as yet little discussion of the characteristics that ought to be attributed to the average consumer.[146] Where the consumers of particular goods or services include some who are particularly attentive, but others who are less so, the General Court has indicated that the assessment is to be made from the perspective of the least attentive.[147]

(ii) Which public? Very frequently, the potential markets for an applicant and opponent's goods or services overlap and the objective is identify those overlapping segments of the relevant public. But sometimes one or the other might have quite some niche. The question then arises: is it the opponent's public that must be confused, or the applicant's public?[148] We have seen, for example, that the linguistic competencies of the average consumer are defined by reference to the territory of the earlier mark (so, for example, an opposition based on an Italian mark will be viewed from the perspective of Italian consumers). The General Court has observed that 'the relevant public for the assessment of the likelihood of confusion is composed of users likely to use *both* the goods or services covered by the earlier mark and those covered by the mark applied for'.[149] In identifying this 'overlap', the tribunal will consider the full breadth of the opponent's and applicant's specifications.[150] Where an applicant applies in relation to a particular category of goods, such as wines, the average consumer in determined by reference to the consumers of those goods in general, rather than the specific section to which the applicant in fact intends to market the goods (say, drinkers of kosher wine). This is because the applicant might change its strategy.[151]

(iii) About what must the public be confused? The next question to consider is what is meant by 'likelihood of confusion' in section 5(2)/Article 8(1)(b). In its 'classic' form, consumers must be confused about the source or origin of the goods or services—that is, they must be confused as to the designer, manufacturer, selector, or supplier of the goods or services. In other words, classic confusion is concerned with the situation in which consumers believe that the goods or services emanate from one organization, but they, in fact, come from a different, independent organization. This classic form of confusion has been extended to accommodate broader understandings of the source of goods or services.

---

[144] *Picasso v. OHIM*, Case C-361/04P [2006] *ECR* I–643, [39]; *Reed Executive* [2003] *RPC* (12) 207, 241, [103] (Pumfrey J); [2004] *RPC* (40) 767, [78]. Apparently, purchasers of tobacco products have an enhanced level of attention: *GRE Grand River Enterprises Deutschland GmbH v. OHIM*, Case T-206/12, EU:T:2013:342, [23] (in French).

[145] *Ratiopharm's Trade Mark* [2007] *RPC* (28) 630 (AP, Hobbs QC), [18] (in the case of prescription medicines, the only relevant consumers are medical professionals); *Aventis Pharmaceuticals v. OHIM*, Case T-142/12, EU:T:2013:374, [24]–[28] (with medical products, the degree of attention of end consumers is relatively high).

[146] G. B. Dinwoodie and D. S. Gangjee, 'The Image of the Consumer in EU Trade Mark Law', in D. Leczykiewicz and S. Weatherill (eds), *The Image(s) of the Consumer in EU Law* (2015), 339,

[147] *Yorma's v. OHIM and Norma Lebensmittelfilialbetrieb (YORMA'S)*, Case T-213/09 [2011] *ECR* II–19, [25], aff'd by Order, Case C-191/11P, EU:C:2012:62 (in French/German only).

[148] A variation of this is where the goods are the same but the claimant and defendant are targeting different market segments, such as high-end or budget conscious consumers; see *Jack Wills Ltd v. House of Fraser* [2014] *ETMR* 28, [85]–[86] (Arnold J).

[149] *Apple Computer v. OHIM and TKS-Teknosoft (QUARTZ)*, Case T-328/05 [2008] *ECR* II–104*, [23] (emphasis added); *ancotel v. OHIM and Acotel*, Case T-408/09 [2011] *ECR* II–151*, [38] (French and German only); *The Cartoon Network v. OHIM*, Case T-285/12, EU:T:2013:520, [19]; aff'd C-670/13P, EU:C:2014:2024.

[150] *Zero Industry v. OHIM and zero Germany*, Case T-400/06, EU:T:2009:331, [39].

[151] *Ella Valley Vineyards (Adulam) v. OHIM*, Case T-32/10, EU:T:2012:118, [29]; *Zero Industry v. OHIM and zero Germany*, Case T-400/06, EU:T:2009:331, [38].

Consequently, a person will be confused for the purposes of section 5(2) if they incorrectly assume that there is some broader kind of *economic connection* between the users of marks,[152] for example that the goods are being provided by a subsidiary or licensee of the trade mark owner.[153] Confusion might also arise if the use of a sign leads consumers to believe that a person's repair business is 'authorized' by the trade mark owner.[154]

(iv) Likelihood as risk The 'likelihood' requirement of this test is often underappreciated. While the term 'likelihood' indicates probability rather than possibility, courts have interpreted this as requiring the possibility of confusion: trade mark proprietors need not argue that it is more likely than not (on a balance of probabilities) that confusion *will inevitably occur* based on the subsequent application for registration (or use).[155] The owner need only argue that there is a *risk* of this mental state occurring.[156] As Arnold J put it, this 'is not a binary question: is the average consumer confused or is the average consumer not confused? Rather it requires an assessment of whether it is likely that there is, or will be, confusion, applying the standard of perspicacity of the average consumer. It is clear from the case law that this does not mean likely in the sense of more probable than not. Rather it means sufficiently likely to warrant the court's intervention'.[157] When combined with the 'substantial proportion of the public' requirement, considered later, the test lends itself to speculation. It is receptive to arguments that there is *a risk* that a significant-yet-undefined *minority* of the relevant public *might* be confused in the future.[158] It is therefore important to counteract this by recalling that the risk needs to be substantial. Tribunals must consider whether there is a genuine and properly substantiated likelihood of confusion;[159] it is not enough that confusion is hypothetical and remote.[160] In *Marca Mode*,[161] the Court of Justice indicated that the mere inability to rule out the possibility of confusion was not sufficient.

(v) How much confusion? In the law of passing off, it is necessary to show deception of 'a substantial proportion of the public'.[162] In contrast, by adopting the legal construct of the average consumer, European trade mark law seems to suggest that concern with how many real people are confused is not relevant; the question is simply whether the notional consumer would be confused. In some ways, this implies that the law would acknowledge only a single view of the impact of one sign on another. However, in *Interflora Inc. v. Marks & Spencer plc*,[163] the High Court rejected an argument that there was a 'single

---

[152] *Canon KK v. MGM*, Case C-39/97 [1998] *ECR* I–55077, [29]–[30].

[153] In the context of pre-harmonization, free-movement case law, the Court of Justice identified a 'number of situations [that] are covered: products put into circulation by the same undertaking, by a licensee, by a parent company, by a subsidiary of the same group, or by an exclusive distributor'; see *IHT v. Ideal Standard GmbH*, Case C-9/93 [1994] ECR I–2789, [34].

[154] Opinion of Advocate-General Jacobs in *BMW v. Deenik,* Case C-63/97 [1999] 1 *ECR* I–905, [AG45]; *BMW v. Technosport London Ltd* [2017] *EWCA Civ* 779.

[155] Cf. UKIPO *Trade Marks Manual* (2017) 184 ('Likelihood of confusion means that it is more likely than not that confusion will arise in the mind of the average consumer … ').

[156] Case C-39/97 [1998] *ECR* I–5507, [29] ('the *risk* that the public *might believe* that the goods or services in question come from the same undertaking or, as the case may be, from economically linked undertakings, constitutes a likelihood of confusion') (emphasis added).

[157] *Interflora Inc. v. Marks & Spencer plc* [2013] *EWHC* 1291 (Ch), [224], [185].

[158] For critiques in the equivalent US context, see B. Beebe, 'Search and Persuasion in Trade Mark Law' (2005) 103 *Mich L Rev* 2020; M. Grynberg, 'Trade Mark Litigation as Consumer Conflict' (2008) 83 *NYU L Rev* 60; M. A. Lemley and M. McKenna, 'Irrelevant Confusion' (2010) 62 *Stanford L Rev* 413; A.C. Yen, 'The Constructive Role of Confusion in Trade Mark' (2014–15) 93 *NC L Rev* 77.

[159] *Lloyd Schuhfabrik*, Case C-342/97 [1999] *ECR* I–3819, [AG24].

[160] Ibid., [AG20]. See also *Marca Mode CV v. Adidas AG*, Case C-425/98 [2000] *ECR* I–4861, [AG35] ('marks should be registrable in the absence of a genuine and properly substantiated risk of confusion').

[161] Case C-425/98 [2000] *ECR* I–4861, [40]–[42].   [162] See Chapter 33, section 4, p. 901.

[163] [2013] *EWHC* 1291 (Ch).

meaning rule' operative in trade mark law (analogous to that which formerly was recognized in the English law of malicious falsehood and defamation). Arnold J, after carefully reviewing the case law, found that the average consumer indicated a standard of assessment (involving ignoring the likely understandings of especially sophisticated and attentive, as well as those of particularly ignorant or careless, consumers), but not necessarily that all average consumers would reach the same conclusion. The question was whether a significant number would be confused.[164] In so holding, he seemed to prefer the views of Jacob LJ in *Reed Executive v. Reed Business Information*[165] to those of Lewison LJ in *Interflora v. Marks & Spencer (No. 1).*[166] At some point, it would be useful to obtain clarification of these matters from the Court of Justice.

(vi) Is 'mere association' confusion? A hotly contested issue, which emerged in the aftermath of the first Trade Marks Directive, was whether establishing merely the likelihood of association, where one mark brought the other to mind, satisfied the likelihood of confusion test.[167] The matter was resolved in *Sabel v. Puma,* where the Court of Justice established that mere association was not prohibited under this test.[168] Sabel had applied for a German composite trade mark consisting of an image of a 'bounding feline' with the word SABEL underneath it. Puma—not the familiar sportswear brand but another less well known commercial entity—objected on the basis of a prior purely graphic or pictorial mark consisting of the silhouette of a bounding feline (see Fig. 38.4). The referring court found that no consumer confusion as to commercial source had been established, so the question was whether an association between the marks, based on the shared concept of a 'bounding feline', nevertheless satisfied the test. In answering this negatively, the Court of Justice held that 'the concept of likelihood of association is *not* an alternative to that of likelihood of confusion, but serves to define its scope'.[169] This was subsequently reiterated by the Court in *Marca Mode.*[170]

(vii) Initial interest confusion While the potential for confusion is usually assessed at the point of sale, does the analysis include so-called 'initial interest confusion'—that is, confusion engendered prior to a particular commercial transaction, but which comes to be corrected by the time of the transaction?[171] An oft-deployed example is that of a roadside cafe (say, 'Sherman's Cafe'), which erects signs on a motorway suggesting that travellers can obtain the goods or services of a particular trade mark holder (say, MCDONALDS), but when the driver has turned off, it becomes apparent that sustenance can be provided only at Sherman's. A certain proportion of travellers will stay and try Sherman's burgers, and they will not at that point imagine that there is any connection with MCDONALDS—yet it was the 'initial interest' in MCDONALDS that got them there. Such practices may be objected to on the economic ground that the use of trade mark is not reducing the consumer's search costs and also, perhaps, by reference to intuitive ideas of what is unethical.[172]

---

[164] Ibid., [224].

[165] *Reed Executive Plc v. Reed Business Information Ltd* [2004] *EWCA Civ* 159, [2004] *RPC* (40) 767, [82]. Note also *Société de Produits Nestlé SA v. Unilever plc* [2003] *ETMR* 681, 692, [30] (Jacob J) ('it is enough if a significant proportion of the public, exercising reasonable care, is confused').

[166] [2012] *EWCA Civ* 1501, [2013] *ETMR* (11) 152, [33]–[36].

[167] See Bently and Sherman (2014), 990–1.

[168] Case C-251/95 [1997] *ECR* I-6191.   [169] Ibid., [18].

[170] *Marca Mode*, Case C-425/98 [2000] *ECR* I-4861, [40] [42].

[171] INTA Board Resolution, *Initial Interest Confusion* (18 September 2006); available online at http://www.inta.org/Advocacy/Pages/InitialInterestConfusion.aspx.

[172] I. Fhima, 'Initial Interest Confusion' (2013) 8(4) *JIPLP* 311; J. Rothman, 'Initial Interest Confusion: Standing at the Crossroads of Trademark Law' (2005–6) 27 *Cardozo L Rev* 105.

In *Och-Ziff Management Europe Ltd v. OCH Capital Ltd*,[173] the High Court held that 'likelihood of confusion' could include so-called 'initial interest confusion'.[174] Arnold J reasoned that because the acts that were deemed infringing uses included using a trade mark in advertising,[175] so it followed that 'likelihood of confusion' could not refer merely to confusion at the point of sale. Moreover, the 'keyword advertising' cases (discussed in Chapter 40) also seem to suggest that there can be a likelihood of confusion where an initial representation—the ad that appears immediately in response to an Internet search—is unclear, even though matters would become clear if the consumer were to 'click through' to the advertiser's web page.[176] However, the Court of Appeal has subsequently criticized this doctrine and severely curtailed its application.[177] Initial interest confusion would impose an onerous burden on the advertiser, in excess of that required by a balanced system of competition. As articulated in *Och-Ziff*, it would impose a duty upon advertisers to avoid confusion altogether, rather than a duty to enable consumers to make informed choices.

(viii) Post-sale confusion Attempts have also been made to extend trade mark holders' rights to encompass confusion of consumers who see the product away from the point of sale.[178] When discussing issues such as distinctiveness and trade mark 'use', the Court of Justice has indicated that familiarity with a mark in the post-sale environment can either confer acquired distinctiveness or jeopardize the sign's ability to function as a mark.[179] So, in *Arsenal*,[180] the Court held that use of the mark ARSENAL on football scarves was a use likely to jeopardize the essential function of the mark, even though, at the time of selling the goods, a sign informed consumers that the goods were not official goods manufactured under the control of the football club. This was said to be because those who saw the sign away from the point of sale might have believed that the scarves in fact came from the football club. However this finding was in relation to a double identity claim. By contrast, in the context of likelihood of confusion, a stricter approach seems to have been taken in the *Picasso* decision.[181] Here, the owners of the PICASSO mark for cars objected to registration at the OHIM of the mark PICARO for cars. With lower tribunals rejecting the opposition, the owners of the earlier PICASSO mark appealed to the Court of Justice, arguing that the average consumer was not particularly attentive, since many consumers would see the PICARO car after-sale (on the roads) and, at such times, would be much less attentive. In rejecting this argument, the Court distinguished *Arsenal* as a case that did not concern likelihood of confusion and in which it had not been intended to establish a general rule, particularly one that would conflict with the many authorities that define the 'average consumer'.

In *Datacard v. Eagle Technlogies*,[182] Arnold J reviewed the case law and found that 'post-sale' confusion might be relevant in certain circumstances. The judge said that he did not think that the *Picasso* decision was intended to undermine the holding in

---

[173] [2010] *EWHC* 2599 (Ch), [2011] *ETMR* 1, [79]–[101].

[174] See also *Interflora Inc. v. Marks & Spencer plc* [2013] *EWHC* 1291 (Ch), [306]; *BSB Group v. Microsoft* [2013] *EWHC* 1826 (Ch), [82] (Asplin J).   [175] See Chapter 40, section 6.4, p. 1112.

[176] See Chapter 40, section 6.5, pp. 1112–13.

[177] *Interflora v. Marks and Spencer plc* [2014] *EWCA Civ* 1403, [152]–[158] (Kitchin LJ).

[178] For discussion, see P. O'Byrne and B. Allgrove, 'Post-sale Confusion' [2007] *JIPLP* 315 (arguing that post-sale confusion is not irrelevant, but will not itself justify a finding of likelihood of confusion). See also M. McKenna, 'A Consumer Decision Making Theory of Trademark Law' (2012) 98 *VLR* 67, 130–3.

[179] See Chapter 40, section 10.1, pp. 1118–22.

[180] Case C-206/01 [2002] *ECR* I–10273. For a review of the functions, see Chapter 40, section 10.

[181] *Claude Ruiz Picasso v. OHIM*, Case 361/04P [2006] ECR I–643, [60].

[182] [2011] *EWHC* 244 (Pat).

Arsenal. One situation in which post-sale confusion might be relevant is where it leads to repeat purchases. The facts of *Datacard v. Eagle* were suggestive of such a possibility: consumers purchased printer ribbons from the defendant's website, knowing them to be created by third parties and merely compatible with Datacard's printers. However, on receiving packaging bearing Datacard branding, those customers might have had second thoughts, now wondering whether the products were made by Datacard or whether the website operator was licensed to produce the ribbons. If such a person were then to make a further purchase, the 'post-sale' confusion would have materialized into real, material, point-of-sale confusion. Whether that was what Arnold J had in mind, however, is unclear.

(ix) The relevance of distinctiveness and repute Although the signs and the goods or services of the parties must reach a minimal level of similarity before a tribunal need assess likelihood of confusion, the Court of Justice has made it clear that the inherent and acquired distinctiveness of the earlier sign may be a very significant factor when assessing whether there is a likelihood of confusion. In other words, the tribunal should also take into account 'the distinctive character of the earlier trade mark, and in particular its reputation' when determining whether the similarity 'between the goods or services covered by the two trade marks *is sufficient to give rise to the likelihood of confusion*'.[183]

(x) The public interest/requirement of availability In some circumstances, a person's use of a registered trade mark might reflect the existence of a rather limited choice of obvious terms or devices. In considering likelihood of confusion, must the tribunal bear in mind the need to protect the freedom of such traders? In *Adidas v. Marca Mode*,[184] this question was put to the Court in a case concerning the use of two stripes on sportswear, a feature that was said to infringe Adidas's three-stripe mark. The point was that if two and four stripes were regarded as similar to three stripes, the freedom of sportswear manufacturers would be severely limited.[185] The Court rejected the contention, saying that the requirement of availability had no role to play in the assessment of confusion, which was a matter of perception of the relevant public.[186] It argued that if such considerations were taken into account, the rights of trade mark holders would be undermined. On the particular facts, it noted that Adidas's mark related to vertical stripes in particular positions, so that use of stripes in other ways were unaffected by Adidas's trade mark registration,[187] and that the rules on acquisition (in particular distinctiveness) were sufficient to ensure the maintenance of freedoms of competitors.

2.3.4 Questions of proof

The question whether a mark is likely to be confused with another mark is 'a matter upon which the judge must make up his mind and which he, and he alone, must decide. He cannot, as it is said, abdicate the decision in that matter to witnesses before him.'[188] The EUTMR contains an indicative list of means for providing evidence, which includes categories of evidence relevant for the likelihood of confusion test.[189]

---

[183] *Canon KK v. MGM*, Case C-39/97 [1998] *ECR* I–55077, [24]. In *Intermark Srl v. OHIM, Coca Cola*, Case T-384/13, EU:T:2015:158, the enhanced distinctiveness or strength of Coca Cola's marks counteracted the fact that the only word in common with the applicant's RIENERGY COLA was the generic term Cola; the likelihood of confusion was established.   [184] Case C-102/07 [2008] *ECR* I–2439.

[185] Ibid., [17].   [186] Ibid., [30].

[187] Ibid., [32]. This relates to the scope of protection for marks having weakly distinctive, descriptive, or commonplace elements; see the analysis of distinctiveness in section 2.3.1, pp. 1037–40.

[188] *Electrolux Ltd v. Electrix Ltd* (1954) 71 *RPC* 23, 31; *The European v. The Economist* [1998] *FSR* 283, 291.

[189] EUTMR, Art. 97 (referring inter alia to sales brochures, catalogues, advertising figures, customer and/or market surveys and affidavits).

The nature of the inquiry into whether there is a likelihood of confusion will vary depending on whether the mark has been used. Normally (although not necessarily), where the relative grounds are heard by the Registrar, the mark will not have been used, thus there will be no evidence of actual confusion. Therefore many of the categories of evidence considered later have greater relevance for infringement claims. In contrast, where it is argued that a mark should be declared invalid after registration because it falls foul of a relative ground for refusal, it is highly likely (as with an infringement action) that the mark will have been used and thus there might be evidence of actual confusion.[190]

In the absence of evidence, the tribunal makes an intuitive and speculative judgement about whether there is a likelihood of confusion. In so doing, the tribunals assume that the marks are used in a normal and fair way.[191] The reason for assuming normal and fair use is that:

> [Unless] one assumes notional use of the earlier mark, the answer to the question of whether a later trade mark gives rise to a likelihood of confusion on the part of the public will always be no. If the public have never seen the earlier mark the later mark cannot cause confusion. Thus it is necessary to assume use of the earlier mark (and the later mark) when considering the likelihood of confusion.[192]

In situations in which the mark has been used, the courts will usually be able to draw on different forms of evidence to help them to decide whether there is confusion. For example, the tribunal might be informed by evidence of actual confusion where the applicant has used the mark prior to the application or in a post-grant application for a declaration of invalidity. A claimant will be in a strong position if they can produce testimony of a reasonably prudent purchaser who was in fact confused, or can provide examples of conduct probative of actual confusion (such as telephone calls to the registered proprietor about the defendant's goods or services, or misdirected letters).[193]

In some cases, the absence of evidence of actual confusion *may* also be probative (especially where the marks have been used in parallel for a considerable time).[194] However, an inability to produce evidence of confusion is not always fatal to an action.[195] This is because there may be extraneous reasons that explain the absence of confusion. These include the possibility that the confusion has been so complete that customers are not

---

[190] However even in the infringement context, evidence of actual consumer confusion is not mandatory: *BMW v. Technosport London Ltd* [2017] *EWCA Civ* 779, [24] (Floyd, LJ).

[191] This assumption is also relevant for infringement: *Roger Maier v. ASOS Plc* [2015] *EWCA Civ* 220 (infringement should be assessed based on the notional and fair use of the mark across the full specification for goods or services; not just actual use).

[192] *React and Device Trade Mark* [1999] *RPC* 529, 532; *Reed Executive* [2004] *RPC* (40) 767, [80]–[81] (Jacob LJ).

[193] In an infringement context: *Comic Enterprises Ltd v. Twentieth Century Fox Film Corporation* [2016] *EWCA Civ* 41, [102] (evidence of actual confusion, including 'wrong way round' confusion where the relevant public thought the claimant was affiliated to the more famous defendant, was persuasive); *Enterprise Holdings, Inc v. Europcar Group UK Ltd* [2015] *EWHC* 17 (Ch), [208]–[215].

[194] *Stichting BDO v. BDO Unibank* [2013] *EWHC* 418 (Ch), [167] (Arnold J); *Assos of Switzerland SA v. Asos plc* [2013] *EWHC* 2831 (Ch), [96] *ff* (Rose J). However the Court of Appeal subsequently reversed on this point; [2015] *EWCA Civ* 220, [80]–[90] (Kitchin LJ). While *actual sales* for the claimant's casual clothing had occurred through specialized channels on a small scale, if the trial judge had considered *the notional and fair use* of the claimant's CTM ASSOS across the goods (even for the pared-back specification), this approach would presume the sale of casual wear through ordinary retail outlets and on the Internet, on a reasonably substantial scale and bring the marks into conflict.

[195] *Phones 4U Ltd v. Phones4u.co.uk Internet Ltd* [2006] *EWCA Civ* 244, [2007] *RPC* (5) 83; *32Red plc v. WHG (International) Ltd* [2011] *EWHC* 62 (Ch), [102] (Henderson J); *The Cartoon Network v. OHIM*, T-285/12, EU:T:2013:520, [54] *ff*; aff'd C-670/13P, EU:C:2014:2024.

conscious of their mistakes.[196] In other cases, the appropriate evidence may simply be too difficult to obtain.

(i) Trade and expert evidence Sometimes, parties seek to rely on trade and expert evidence.[197] Whether such evidence will be admitted depends on precisely the issue to which it is said to relate.[198] It has long been held that expert evidence must not relate to the key question of whether the use is confusing;[199] instead, it should be confined to factual explanations of things such as how the trade is structured.[200]

(ii) Surveys Parties sometimes wish to offer survey evidence to demonstrate that marks are confusingly similar, or to introduce evidence from a selected group of witnesses gathered via such a survey. Before such evidence can be introduced, the permission of the Court is required,[201] and recent case law suggests that judges will permit this kind of evidence only in 'special or unusual' cases.[202] This is because the court must balance the cost of the evidence against its probative value.[203] The costs of surveys are typically high, not least because, in addition to the cost of conducting the survey, there will inevitably be further expense spent on determining its validity. In contrast with the inevitable costs, the courts rarely regard surveys as being of much probative value. One reason for this is that surveys are always subjected to criticism.[204] However, more importantly, the survey will rarely offer any insights that cannot be gained by the judge from the evidence of the parties. This is particularly so in a case concerning ordinary consumer goods and services, in which the court is able to put itself into the position of the average consumer without requiring expert evidence or a consumer survey.[205] If a survey is not of any value, then the evidence of consumers located while conducting such a survey will be even less useful (at least as far as the question on which evidence is sought is likelihood of confusion).[206] A similar approach is taken in application proceedings before the Registrar.[207]

---

[196] *Sämaan v. Tetrosyl* [2006] *FSR* (42) 849, [58] (Kitchin J).

[197] *Rihanna Fenty v. Arcadia* [2013] *EWHC* 1945 (Ch) (Birss J) (distinguishing between trade witnesses and experts).

[198] Permission must be sought under CPR, r. 35.4, and in the Registry: see UK IPO, *Survey Evidence and Expert Witness Evidence* (2012) TPN 2/2012.

[199] *esure Insurance Limited v. Direct Line Insurance Plc* [2008] *EWCA Civ* 842, [2008] *ETMR* (77) 1258, [62] (Arden LJ); *The European v. The Economist* [1998] *FSR* 283; cf. *Guccio Gucci SpA v. Paolo Gucci* [1991] *FSR* 89.

[200] *George Ballantine v. Ballantyne Stewart* [1959] *RPC* 273; *The European v. The Economist* [1998] *FSR* 283, 291 (Millett LJ).

[201] *Interflora Inc. v. Marks & Spencer plc* [2012] *EWCA Civ* 1501, [2012] *FSR* (21) 415, [149]. Permission is not needed to conduct a pilot study.

[202] Ibid., [150]. See further *Interflora Inc. v. Marks & Spencer plc (No. 2)* [2013] *EWCA Civ* 319, [2013] *FSR* (26) 559.

[203] *Interflora Inc. v. Marks & Spencer plc* [2012] *EWCA Civ* 1501, [2012] *FSR* (21) 415, [150] (a 'cost–benefit' analysis); *Interflora Inc. v. Marks & Spencer plc (No. 2)* [2013] *EWCA Civ* 319, [2013] *FSR* (26) 559, [26]–[27] (the evidence generated must be of *real* value).

[204] The criteria for a rigorous survey are the so-called 'Whitford Guidelines', from *Imperial Group plc v. Philip Morris* [1984] *RPC* 293, 310. Note Jacob LJ's comment in *Interflora Inc. v. Marks & Spencer plc (No. 2)* [2013] *EWCA Civ* 319, [2013] *FSR* (26) 559, [33], that '[i]t is possible to conduct fair surveys and they may indeed lead to witnesses of value'.

[205] *Interflora Inc. v. Marks & Spencer plc* [2012] *EWCA Civ* 1501, [2012] *FSR* (21) 415, [45]–[56]; cf. *Schuh Ltd v. Shhh … Ltd* [2011] *CSOH* 123, [16] (stating that court should distrust its own reactions).

[206] In *Interflora Inc. v. Marks & Spencer plc* [2012] *EWCA Civ* 1501, [2012] *FSR* (21) 415, [137], Lewison LJ acknowledged that the court might need to be informed about 'shopping habits', 'the characteristics of the market', and the means by which goods are marketed. Moreover, witnesses might provide useful evidence of their 'spontaneous reactions' in relation to goods that are not within the judge's experience or to amplify the results of a reliable survey. For the argument that a greater range of surveys should be admissible, see K. Weatherall, 'The Consumer as the Empirical Measure of Trade Mark Law' (2017) 80 *MLR* 57.

[207] UK IPO, *Survey Evidence and Expert Witness Evidence* (2012) TPN 2/2012; *esure Insurance Ltd v. Direct Line Insurance Plc* [2008] *EWCA Civ* 842, [2008] *ETMR* (77) 1258, [82] (Kay LJ).

(iii) Intention Intention is a factor more likely to be considered in infringement proceedings, rather than relative grounds analysis. As noted, whether an applicant's mark is in conflict with an earlier mark, as well as whether use of a later mark infringes the rights in an earlier mark, does not depend on whether there was any intention to cause confusion. But that is not to say that intention can never be relevant. In fact, the British courts have historically taken the view that intention is, at the very least, a relevant factor. The courts typically cite the Court of Appeal decision in *Slazenger v. Feltham*,[208] in which the claimant's mark, an image of the devil's head with the word demon for tennis racquets, was held infringed by the defendant's use of DEMOTIC. Although the evidence was finely balanced, the Court took account of the fact that the defendant deliberately sought out a word as close to the claimant's mark as it could find in the dictionary. Lindley LJ observed:

> One must exercise one's common sense, and, if you are driven to the conclusion that what is intended to be done is to deceive if possible, I do not think it is stretching the imagination very much to credit the man with occasional success or possible success. Why should we be astute to say that he cannot succeed in doing that which he is straining every nerve to do?[209]

In *Specsavers v. Asda Stores*,[210] the Court of Appeal considered the operation of this principle in the context of an advertising campaign by Asda that had deliberately set out to target Specsavers (an operation with something like 39 per cent of the UK market for spectacles). Initially, it was proposed to parody the Specsavers mark, but along the way a combination of legal advice and marketing strategy had led Asda to modify its campaign. In the end, it adopted a logo comprising two abutting white ovals containing the words 'Asda Opticians' in green (see Fig. 38.2), in contrast to Specsavers' overlapping green ovals with 'Specsavers' in white writing (see Fig. 38.1). It used the straplines 'Be a real spec saver at Asda' and 'Spec savings at Asda'. When determining whether there was a likelihood of confusion, the Court considered the role of intention. At first instance, Mann J had acknowledged that Asda had chosen to 'live dangerously', but also observed that its intention was to not confuse. As already noted, he found no likelihood of confusion as between the logos.[211] On appeal, Kitchin LJ agreed that the *Slazenger* principle was limited to the case in which someone intends to cause deception and deliberately seeks to take the benefit of another trader's goodwill, and even then, that 'intention' was only one factor in the global assessment.[212] There was therefore nothing wrong with the trial court's treatment of the matter.

2.4 PROTECTION OF NON-ORIGIN FUNCTIONS: SECTION 5(3)/ ARTICLE 8(5)

The third relative ground for refusal is found in section 5(3) of the 1994 Act and Article 8(5) EUTMR.[213] Section 5(3), which implements the optional Article 4(4)(a) of the original TMD 1988,[214] recognizes that the value of a trade mark may lie not simply in its ability to indicate source, but also in 'the image conveyed by the trade mark'—its so-called

---

[208] (1889) 6 *RPC* 531.   [209] Ibid., 538.

[210] *Specsavers Int'l Healthcare v. Asda Stores* [2012] *EWCA Civ* 24, [2012] *FSR* (19) 555.

[211] *Specsavers Int'l Healthcare v. Asda Stores* [2010] *EWHC* 2035 (Ch), [2011] *FSR* (1) 1, [95]–[96], [141].

[212] [2012] *EWCA Civ* 24, [2012] *FSR* (19) 555, [115].

[213] See also TMD 2008, Art. 4(3); TMD 2015, Art. 5(3)(a).

[214] *General Motors Corporation v. Yplon*, Case C-375/97 [1999] *ECR* I–5421, [29]. Previously this used to be an optional ground, albeit one that was almost universally adopted by member states. Under TMD 2015, Art 5(3)(a), it is now mandatory.

'advertising function'.[215] As the CFI stated in *Sigla SA v. OHIM*, as well as operating as an indication of trade origin:

> [A] mark also acts as a means of conveying other messages concerning . . . for example, luxury, lifestyle, exclusivity, adventure, youth. To that effect the mark has an inherent economic value which is independent of and separate from that of the goods and services for which it is registered. The messages in question which are conveyed inter alia by a mark with a reputation or which are associated with it confer on that mark a significant value which deserves protection, particularly because, in most cases, the reputation of a mark is the result of considerable effort and investment on the part of its proprietor.[216]

Section 5(3) introduces protection for this 'advertising function' by protecting the mark against various forms of non-confusing mental associations between an earlier mark with a reputation and a subsequent mark. An illustration helps to convey the fact patterns which trigger such claims: should Louis Vuitton, the luxury leather goods manufacturer, have a claim against a pet products manufacturer who makes inexpensive 'Chewy Vuitton' dog chew toys, even though no consumer is likely to be confused as to origin or commercial affiliation?[217] The provision seeks to prohibit a mental association which either harms the reputed mark's ability to communicate certain messages or because the association confers an undeserved advantage upon the defendant, enabling them to 'free-ride'. It should be noted that the provision seeks to prevent both detriment as well as free-riding, which may not cause detriment to the reputed mark at all. While the first stage—is a mental association likely between two signs—is relatively straightforward, the second stage—what are the consequences flowing from this association—has proved enduringly controversial, in theoretical, doctrinal, and empirical terms.

Section 5(3) incorporates a version of trade mark 'dilution', first articulated by Frank Schechter almost a century ago.[218] According to Advocate-General Jääskinen:

> Trade mark dilution relates to the idea that the proper purpose of trade mark law should be to protect the efforts and investments made by the trade mark proprietor and the independent value (good will) of the trade mark. This 'property-based' approach to trade marks differs from the 'deception-based' idea that trade mark law primarily protects the origin function with a view to preventing consumers and other end users from erring as to the commercial origin of goods and services. The property-based approach also protects the communication, advertising and investment functions of trade marks with a view of creating a brand with a positive image and independent economic value (brand equity or good will). Consequently, the trade mark [as brand] can be used for various goods and services having nothing in common apart from being under the control of the trade mark proprietor.[219]

---

[215] See further Chapter 40, section 10.2.2, pp. 1123–4. See also M. Senftleben, 'The Trademark Tower of Babel' [2009] *IIC* 45.

[216] T-215/03 [2007] *ECR* II–711, [35]. See also *Intel Corporation*, Case C-252/07 [2008] *ECR* I–8823, [AG8] (AG Sharpston). For a description of these as 'atmospherics', see J. Litman, 'Breakfast with Batman: The Public Interest in the Advertising Age' (1999) 108 *Yale LJ* 1717.

[217] The fact pattern is taken from *Louis Vuitton Malletier v. Haute Diggity Dog*, 507 F.3d 252 (4th Cir 2007). The clearly parodic reference to a strong mark was unlikely to dilute its distinctiveness.

[218] F. I. Schechter, 'The Rational Basis of Trademark Protection' (1927) 40 *Harv L Rev* 813. In turn, Schechter relied upon contemporary German case law, as well as English cases such as *Eastman Photographic Materials Co. v. John Griffiths Cycle Corporation* (1898) 15 *RPC* 105 (KODAK confusing on bicycles). See further B. Beebe, 'The Suppressed Misappropriation Origins of Trademark Antidilution Law', in Dreyfuss and Ginsburg (2014), ch. 3; I. Simon Fhima, 'Exploring the Roots of European Dilution' [2012] *IPQ* 25.

[219] *Interflora Inc. v. Marks & Spencer*, Case C-323/09 [2011] *ECR* I–8625, [AG50]. Whether there is a justification for offering legal protection to such investments might be regards as doubtful: see H. Sun, B. Beebe, and M. Sunder (eds), *The Luxury Economy and Intellectual Property: Critical Reflections* (2015); see more generally Chapter 31, section 3, pp. 853–6.

The protection offered by section 5(3) encompasses: (i) the erosion of a mark's distinctiveness by its use on the goods of another (what is referred to as 'blurring'); (ii) the related concept of 'tarnishment', whereby the repute or goodwill associated with a mark becomes tainted by its use in connection with products of an unsavoury quality, or as a consequence of being portrayed in an unwholesome context; and (iii) the prevention of free-riding by another trader on the repute of the mark.[220] We will return to these concepts in the course of this chapter.

Section 5(3)/Article 8(5) provide that a trade mark will not be registered where:

(a) the later mark is identical with or similar to an earlier (registered) mark;

(b) the earlier trade mark has a reputation in the United Kingdom or, in the case of an EUTM, in the European Union;

(c) the use of the later mark must either take unfair advantage of, or be detrimental to, the distinctive character or the repute of the earlier trade mark; and

(d) the use of the later mark is without due cause.

Before looking at these, it might be worth observing two critical features of section 5(3), which distinguish it from section 5(2): first, there is no requirement for the earlier trade mark holder to prove a likelihood of confusion;[221] and second, section 5(3) applies where the goods are identical, similar, or even dissimilar.[222]

2.4.1 Reputation

The first requirement that must be satisfied for a mark to fall foul of section 5(3)/Article 8(5) is that it has to be shown that the earlier trade mark has a 'reputation' in the United Kingdom or, in the case of an EUTM, in the European Union. The concept of reputation is thus a crucial threshold that must be crossed before the whole provision comes into play. In *General Motors Corporation v. Yplon*,[223] the Court of Justice provided guidance in relation to this threshold requirement. The reference was prompted by an application by General Motors, the proprietor of the sign CHEVY for motor vehicles, to restrain Yplon from using the identical sign for detergents. The Court stated that 'reputation' involved a knowledge threshold, so that 'a mark would have a reputation where it was known by a significant part of the public concerned by the products or services covered by the trade mark'.[224] It was only when there was:

> . . . [a] sufficient degree of knowledge of the mark that the public, when confronted with the later trade mark may possibly make an association between the two trade marks, even when used for non-similar products or services, and that the trade mark may consequently be damaged.[225]

A mark's reputation therefore laid the ground for recognition and mental association, which were preconditions for any injury or free-riding. To establish this reputation, indicative criteria included 'the market share held by the trade mark, the intensity,

---

[220] In the context of interpreting TMA 1994, s 10(3) (the equivalent infringement provisions), the Court of Appeal has provided general guidance in *Comic Enterprises v. Twentieth Century Fox Film Corp.* [2016] *EWCA Civ* 41, [107]–[123] (Kitchin LJ).

[221] *Adidas-Salomon AG and Adidas Benelux BV v. Fitnessworld*, Case C-408/01 [2003] *ECR* I–12537, [27].

[222] *Davidoff & Cie SA v. Gofkid*, Case C-292/00 [2003] *ECR* I–389; TMD, Art 5(3)(a). Cf. *32Red plc v. WHG (International) Ltd* [2011] *EWHC* 62 (Ch), [127] (criticizing the effect of *Davidoff* decision); M. Spence, 'Section 10 of the Trade Marks Act 1994: Is There Really a Logical Lapse?' [2001] *EIPR* 423.

[223] Case C-375/97 [1999] *ECR* I–5421. [224] Ibid., [22]. [225] Ibid., [23].

geographical extent, and duration of its use, and the size of the investment made by the undertaking in promoting it'.[226] Subsequent decisions have confirmed that this reputation should relate to the mark in relation to its use on specific products, as opposed to the general reputation of a corporate house name or an individual's name, such as a fashion designer.[227] A closely related issue is whether that reputation has to be in relation to be the goods and services contained in the registration.[228] The earlier mark being relied upon may also acquire a reputation in the course of being used as part of another mark, provided it plays a significant or predominant role within that other mark.[229]

Yplon also clarified two further elements of the reputation enquiry. First, although we have seen these indicative criteria before, in the context of acquired distinctiveness, the threshold serves a different purpose and is potentially higher in the context of this provision. The proprietor of the earlier registered mark has to do more than merely show the mark has acquired distinctiveness; reputation is therefore used synonymously with 'well-known' status.[230] Nevertheless, there is a suggestion by the High Court that for EUTMs, in accordance with *Yplon*, this is not a 'particularly onerous requirement'.[231] Second, the test for reputation is quantitative.[232] While the focus at this stage is on establishing how many consumers are aware of the mark, at a subsequent stage of analysis, the qualitative reputation of the mark—what do consumers think of it—becomes relevant, when considering whether there has been any harm or benefit.[233] After all, under a tarnishment claim only a mark with a good or positive reputation can claim it has something to lose by the later mark's allegedly degrading use.[234] The same is true for an unfair advantage claim, which responds to the misappropriation of an attractive brand image that needs to be qualitatively established.

---

[226] Ibid., [27]. The absence of evidence under any one factor, such as market share, is not fatal: *Antartica v. OHIM, Nasdaq Stock Market*, Case T-47/06 [2007] *ECR* II-42*, [51]–[52]; not considered on appeal in Case C-320/07P [2009] *ECR* I-28*.

[227] *Unicorn v. EUIPO*, Case T-123/15, EU:T:2016:642; *Pierre Balmain, Société Anonyme v. Carrington*, R 201/2010–2 (OHIM BoA).

[228] *Lifestyle Equities CV v. Santa Monica Polo Club Ltd* [2017] *EWHC* 3313 (Ch) (Recorder Douglas Campbell QC), [113]–[114] (accepting evidence of reputation in relation to products beyond the registration, since anti-'dilution' protection extends to dissimilar goods as well). This appears irreconcilable with the requirement that in 'order to satisfy the requirement of reputation, the earlier mark must be known by a significant part of the public concerned by the goods or services covered by that trade mark': *Helena Rubinstein v. OHIM, Allergan*, Joined Cases T-345 and 357/08 [2010] *ECR* II-279*, [42]; aff'd Case C-100/11P [2012] *ETMR* 40.

[229] *Formula One Licensing BV v. OHIM, Idea Marketing*, Case T-55/13, EU:T:2015:309, [46]–[47].

[230] *Nieto Nuño v. Franquet*, Case C-328/06 [2007] *ECR* I-10093, [17]; *Pago v. Tirolmilch*, Case C-301/07 [2009] *ECR* I-9429, [AG32] ('kindred concepts'); *L'Oréal SA and ors v. Bellure NV and ors*, Case C-487/07 [2009] *ECR* I-5185, [AG37], [AG57], [AG58], [AG73], [AG91] (AG Mengozzi, using terms interchangeably). Well-known status is elaborated upon in the WIPO, *Joint Recommendation Concerning Provisions on the Protection of Well-Known Marks* (2000): A. Kur, 'Well-known Marks, Highly Renowned Marks and Marks Having a (High) Reputation: What's it all about?' (1992) 23 *IIC* 218; F. W. Mostert (ed.), *Famous and Well-Known Marks: An International Analysis* (2nd edn, 2004).

[231] *Red Bull v. Sun Mark* [2012] *EWHC* 1929 (Ch), [90] (Arnold J).

[232] *General Motors v. Yplon*, Case C-375/97 [1999] *ECR* I-5421, [26] (the earlier mark must be 'known by a significant part of the public concerned'); *Azumi Ltd v. Zuma's Choice Pet Products Ltd* [2017] *EWHC* 609 (IPEC), [51]–[52] (reputation established amongst general public based on positive press coverage); *Jadebay Ltd v. Clarke-Coles Ltd* [2017] *EWHC* 1400 (IPEC), [90]–[95] (Insufficient evidence of reputation even within the niche market of flagpole purchasers in the United Kingdom).

[233] *Roger Maier v. ASOS* [2015] *ETMR* 26, [120]–[122] (Kitchin LJ).

[234] *Sigla v. OHIM*, Case T-215/03 [2007] *ECR* II-711, [35]. See also *Aktieselskabet af 21 November 2001 v. OHIM*, Case C-197/07P [2008] *ECR* I-193*, [21].

Less obviously, *Yplon* opened the door to arguments that a niche reputation in a certain product sector, also referred to as being a 'big fish in a small pond',[235] would be sufficient to satisfy the reputation requirement. This is because reputation must be judged 'by reference to the perception of the relevant public, which consists of average consumers *of the goods or services for which that mark is registered*'.[236] Thus while a reputation amongst specialist purchasers could be sufficient, the relevant public could also—depending on the product—encompass both professionals as well as the general public.[237] By contrast, the comparable fame threshold in the United States stipulates that 'a mark is famous if it is widely recognised by the general consuming public of the United States'.[238] Anti-dilution law in the United States is therefore directed at protecting nationally famous brands or household names.[239]

A related issue is whether a geographical niche reputation is also recognized.[240] In the case of national marks, in *Yplon*, the Court of Justice said that while the reputation must exist in the member state, it need not exist throughout the territory; it is sufficient if the reputation exists in a substantial part of it.[241] Similarly, in the case of EUTMs, in *Pago Intl v. Tirolmich*,[242] the Court has held that the relevant reputation must exist in a substantial part of the European Union, but that this might be achieved even if the reputation is confined to a single member state. In that case, the claimant had a strong reputation in Austria, and the Court intimated that this would be sufficient to bring an action under Article 9(1)(c) CTMR against a defendant whose use was also in Austria. However, even though an EUTM owner might be able to access Article 8(5) by demonstrating that it has a reputation in only part of the European Union, the claim may falter when it comes to proving a link and consequent detriment or advantage. This was at issue where Unilever, the EUTM proprietor of IMPULSE for deodorants, opposed the registration of a figurative mark including the words 'BE IMPULSIVE' in Hungary. Unilever could establish a reputation in the United Kingdom and Italy but not in Hungary. The Court of Justice concluded that the proprietor of an EUTM 'may benefit from [the equivalent provision in the TMD 2008] where it is shown that a *commercially significant part* of [the public in the Member State of the dispute] is familiar with that mark, makes a connection between it and the later national mark, and that there is, taking account of all the relevant factors in the case, either actual and present injury to its mark, for the purposes of that provision or, failing that, a serious risk that such injury may occur in the future'.[243] In suggesting that there must exist a segment of the relevant public familiar with the earlier mark within the jurisdiction of dispute, the Court has proposed a less demanding threshold, which falls short of proving the mark is reputed. Yet without this segment there can be no infringement since

[235] X-T. Nguyen, 'Fame Law: Requiring Proof of National Fame in Trademark Law' (2011) 33(1) *Cardozo L Rev* 89.

[236] As confirmed in *Intel Corporation*, Case C-252/07 [2008] *ECR* I–8823, [34] (emphasis added); I. Simon Fhima, *Trade Mark Dilution in Europe and the United States* (2011), 29–31.

[237] *Helena Rubinstein v. OHIM, Allergan* Case C-100/11P [2012] *ETMR* 40 (BOTOX would be familiar to both health care professionals and the general public).

[238] 15 USC §1125(c)(2)(A).

[239] B. Beebe, *Trade Mark Law: An Open-Source Casebook* (Version 4.0, July 2017) Part II: Trademark Infringement, 150–5 available online at http://tmcasebook.org/.

[240] For criticisms of product as well as geographical niche fame recognition, see R. Burrell and M. Handler, 'Reputation in European Trade Mark Law: A Re-examination' (2016) 17 *ERA Forum* 85.

[241] Case C-375/97 [1999] *ECR* I–5421, [28]. For the application of this principle, see: *K&K Group AG v. EUIPO, Pret A Manger Ltd*, Case T-2/16, EU:T:2016:690 (reputation in the United Kingdom for PRET A MANGER sufficient).   [242] Case C-301/07 [2009] *ECR* I–9429.

[243] *Iron & Smith v. Unilever*, Case C-125/14, EU:C:2015:539, [34] (emphasis added).

the public are unlikely to make a connection between the marks. Finally, even assuming the risk of infringement under Article 8(5) can be established on the basis of very modest levels of recognition of the earlier mark, injunctive relief may be limited to territories in which the function(s) of the mark are likely to be damaged.[244]

2.4.2 Similarity of marks

The second requirement is that the marks be identical or similar. Where there is no similarity between the marks, claims under section 5(3) fail.[245] We have already considered these comparisons in the context of section 5(1) and (2). While the general approach is much the same, it is worth observing that a finding of similarity or dissimilarity of marks in a case under section 5(2) does not necessarily mean that those marks are similar or dissimilar for the purpose of section 5(3).[246] This is because the concept of 'similarity' is interpreted in light of the purpose of each provision. So while a tribunal must look at the marks as a whole, taking into account their dominant and distinctive components, and is required to assess similarity from a visual, aural, and conceptual viewpoint,[247] what it is looking for under section 5(3) is not the same as what it is looking for under section 5(2). Whereas, under section 5(2), the tribunal is asking whether the marks are 'confusingly similar', under section 5(3), the tribunal must assess whether the marks are sufficiently similar that the average consumer will *make a link* between them.[248] As the Court of Justice observed in *Adidas v. Fitnessworld*, '[i]t is sufficient for the degree of similarity between the mark with a reputation and the sign to have the effect that the relevant section of the public *establishes a link* between the sign and the mark'.[249] Without the link, there can be none of the 'cross-pollination' needed to transfer value to the applicant (or defendant). The Court has also confirmed that a lesser degree of similarity between the signs may suffice, since the link for 'dilution' can be more attenuated than the link for confusion.[250]

All that is required is that the marks are sufficiently similar such that 'the later mark would call the earlier mark to mind … [This] is tantamount to the existence of such a link', even though there is no likelihood of confusion.[251] In *Intel*, the Court of Justice said that

---

[244] *DHL Express France SAS v. Chronopost SA*, Case C-235/09 [2011] *ECR* I–2801 (ECJ, Grand Chamber), [46]–[48]; *Combit Software v. Commit Business Solutions*, Case C-223/15, EU:C:2016:719, discussed in Chapter 49, section 3.3, pp. 1338–9.

[245] *Alma-The Soul of Italian Wine v. EUIPO, Miguel Torres*, Case T-637/15, EU:T:2017:371 (earlier mark VIÑA SOL not similar to figurative mark including the word elements 'sotto il sole italiano' and 'sotto il sole', notwithstanding the reputation of the former); aff'd C-499/17P, EU:C:2017:978.

[246] *Ferrero v. OHIM*, Case C-552/09P [2011] *ECR* I–2063, [53] (those provisions differ in terms of the degree of similarity required); cf. *Gateway, Inc. v. OHIM*, Case C-57/08P [2008] *ECR* I–188, [62]–[64]; *Ravensburger AG v. OHIM and educa Boras*, Case C-370/10P [2011] *ECR* I–27* (14 March 2011), [63].

[247] *Adidas-Salomon AG and Adidas Benelux BV v. Fitnessworld*, Case C-408/01 [2003] *ECR* I–12537, [27]–[31]; *Ferrero SpA v. OHIM*, Case C-552/09P [2011] *ECR* I–2063, [52]–[53].

[248] *Adidas-Salomon AG and Adidas Benelux BV v. Fitnessworld*, Case C-408/01 [2003] *ECR* I–12537, [27]–[31].   [249] Ibid., [31].

[250] *Intra-Presse v. OHIM, Golden Balls*, Joined cases C-581 and 582/13P, EU:C:2014:2387, [72]–[78] (the low degree of conceptual similarity between GOLDEN BALLS and BALLON D'OR might be sufficient to establish the link and the issue needed to be considered); *El Corte Inglés v. OHIM*, Case C-603/14P, EU:C:2015:807, [39]–[42] (EL CORTE INGLÉS was not sufficiently similar to 'The English Cut' for establishing confusion. However low conceptual similarity, based on the latter being a literal translation of the former, was sufficient to require dilution analysis).

[251] *Intel Corp. v. CPM UK Ltd*, Case C-252/07 [2008] *ECR* I–8823, [60] (whether INTELMARK, registered for marketing services, could be invalidated for creating a mental association with INTEL for microprocessors, that harmed the distinctiveness of the reputed mark); *Specsavers International Healthcare Ltd v. Asda Stores Ltd* [2012] *EWCA Civ* 24, [120]–[121].

assessing whether there is sufficient similarity to give rise to a link will depend on a global appreciation of the marks.[252] The Court suggested a multifactor approach to identifying whether such a link would be made. The factors include the degree of similarity of the marks, the similarity of the goods or services, the strength of the earlier mark's reputation, and its distinctive character (whether inherent or acquired), as well as the existence of a likelihood of confusion.[253] For example, a link can be established based on the structure of the reputed mark; PRET A DINER evoked the structure and format of PRET A MANGER.[254] It can also arise where there is 'wrong way round' confusion; a later mark that is more reputed may threaten to swamp an earlier mark with a modest reputation, such that the relevant consumers assume the earlier mark is affiliated with the later but more famous mark.[255] However, where a sign is perceived purely as decorative, no such link would exist.[256]

The first factor mentioned is the similarity of the marks. Clearly, a link is more likely to be established where marks are identical, such as where the stock exchange that had registered its mark NASDAQ objected to use of an identical mark for bicycle helmets.[257] Nevertheless, identity is not to be regarded as sufficient.[258] Where marks are not identical, similarity will depend on appreciation of the dominant components of the earlier and later marks. In cases concerning the SPA mark, which has a reputation in Benelux for mineral water, it has been held there would be a link with SPALINE, but not with SPAGO. In the former case,[259] the additional feature ('linc') was highly descriptive, so the link would be formed, whereas in the latter case,[260] the 'spa' element was absorbed within what would appear as an invented word. While in some cases, marks which share only descriptive or commonly used elements will not lead to consumers making a link,[261] in others—as we have seen in the context of likelihood of confusion analysis—marks which share descriptive or commonly used elements may nevertheless be found to be similar enough to do so.[262]

The second factor mentioned in *Intel* is the degree of similarity of goods or services.[263] Factors relevant for establishing such similarity in the context of the likelihood of confusion also apply here. Courts have found links readily where good or services are in adjacent markets, such as jewellery and women's clothing.[264] A degree of complementarity or relatedness between products is relevant here; thus the provision of theatrical services was held to be sufficiently related to restaurant services, on the basis that theatres had bars or provided catering during intervals.[265] However, where goods and services

[252] *Intel Corp. v. CPM UK Ltd*, Case C-252/07 [2008] *ECR* I–8823, [41]. It seems that the *Medion* principle applies: *Ella Valley Vineyards (Adulam) v. OHIM*, Case T-32/10 (9 March 2012).

[253] *Intel Corporation*, Case C-252/07 [2008] *ECR* I–8823, [42]; *Japan Tobacco, Inc. v. OHIM, Torrefacção Camelo*, Case C-136/08P [2009] *ECR* I–70*, [26] (French).

[254] *K&K Group AG v. EUIPO, Pret A Manger Ltd*, Case T-2/16, EU:T:2016:690.

[255] *Comic Enterprises Ltd v. Twentieth Century Fox Film Corp* [2016] *EWCA Civ* 41, [130]–[144].

[256] *Adidas-Salomon AG and Adidas Benelux BV v. Fitnessworld*, Case C-408/01 [2003] *ECR* I–12537, [27]–[31].　　　　　　　　　　　　　　　　　[257] *Antartica Srl v. OHIM*, C-320/07P [2009] *ECR* I–28*.

[258] *Intel Corporation*, Case C-252/07 [2008] *ECR* I–8823, [45].

[259] *L'Oréal v. S.A. Spa Monopole*, Case T-21/07 [2009] *ECR* II–31*.

[260] *Spa v. OHIM and De Francesco Import*, Case T-438/07 [2009] *ECR* II–04115.

[261] *FCC Aqualia v. OHIM*, Case T-402/14, EU:T:2016:100, [93] (common element 'aqua' insufficient for expert water management professionals to link ACQUALOGY and AQUALIA).

[262] *Jaguar Land Rover Ltd v. EUIPO*, Case T-71/15, EU:T:2017:82 (LAND ROVER successfully opposed LAND GLIDER, on the basis of the common element 'land'); *Starbucks Corp v. Hasmik Nersesyan*, Case T-398/16, EU:T:2018:4 (the only common elements were concentric black circles and the descriptive word 'coffee') cf. *Alma-The Soul of Italian Wine v. EUIPO, Miguel Torres*, Case T-637/15, EU:T:2017:371.

[263] *Intel Corporation*, Case C-252/07 [2008] *ECR* I–8823, [82]; *Audi-Med Trade Mark* [1998] *RPC* 863, 874 (reputation would not easily transfer from cars to deafness aids).

[264] *Nute Partecipazioni SpA v. OHIM*, T-59/08 (7 December 2010).

[265] *Jackson International v. OHIM, Royal Shakespeare*, Case T-60/10, EU:T:2012:348.

are dissimilar, the question of drawing a link can become more complex. The goods or services might, for example, be so dissimilar that their users do not overlap (so no link is ever made); even if they do overlap, they may be so distant that the relevant consumers would not connect them.[266] However, even if goods or services are dissimilar—as in the *Nasdaq* case—if the repute of the earlier mark is so great as to reach the general public, then a link may be drawn.[267]

The third factor, the strength of the earlier mark (its repute and inherent or acquired distinctiveness) will often be critical. Certainly, it is easier to establish a link where the earlier mark is unique or invented than when it has some dictionary meaning.[268] This probably explains why a link would be drawn between BEATLE and BEATLES in the rather distant fields of wheelchairs and sound recordings,[269] but not between ONLY and a figurative mark including the words 'only' and 'Givenchy'.[270]

In addition to the *Intel* factors, the General Court held that the existence of a family of marks—those beginning with Mc and owned by McDonald's in this case—was a relevant factor in determining whether MACCOFFEE would create a link and be declared invalid on the basis of leading to an unfair advantage under Article 8(5).[271] In infringement proceedings, the context of the usage and surrounding words could increase the likelihood of a mental association.[272] The intention of the junior user has also emerged as a relevant—but not sufficient or dispositive—factor.[273] In *L'Oréal v. Bellure*,[274] a case relating to the packaging of various smell-alike perfumes, the claimant had registrations relating to certain names (including TRÉSOR and MIRACLE), and for various forms of bottle and packaging (see Figs 38.5 and 38.6). The issue arose whether the defendant's packaging of its imitation scents was 'similar', and whether the names COFFRET D'OR and PINK WONDER were similar to the name marks (see Fig. 38.7).

Lewison J had found that some of the packaging was similar (for example the old packaging of LA VALEUR was similar to that of TRÉSOR and the bottle for the PINK WONDER perfume was similar to the MIRACLE bottle), but in other cases (for example the PINK WONDER and MIRACLE boxes) it was not. Both parties appealed. The Court of Appeal rejected the defendant's appeal, noting with seeming approval that the judge had considered the appearance of the products, the public reaction, and the intention of the designers. Where the packaging was intended to convey the message 'this is a bit like … ', the Court agreed that it is 'a small step' for a tribunal to conclude that the designer succeeded (and thus that the signs were similar enough to create a link).[275] Finally, the Court also affirmed the finding that the word marks were not sufficiently similar to create a 'link'; while in French there was 'some similarity at a high level of generality' between COFFRET

---

[266] *Intel Corporation*, Case C-252/07 [2008] *ECR* I–8823, [48]–[49]; *Arnoldo Mondadori Editore v. OHIM*, Case C-548/14P, EU:C:2015:624 (along with other factors, the dissimilarity of goods and services precluded a link, so there was no need to proceed to analyse unfair advantage).

[267] *Antartica Srl v. OHIM*, C-320/07P [2009] *ECR* I–28*.

[268] *Intel Corporation*, Case C-252/07 [2008] *ECR* I–8823, [56].

[269] *YOU-Q BV v. Apple Corp.*, Case C-294/12P, EU:C:2013:300 .

[270] *Aktieselskabet af 21 November 2001 v. OHIM and Parfums Givenchy*, Case T-586/10, EU:T:2011:722.

[271] *Future Enterprises v. EUIPO, McDonald's*, Case T-518/13, EU:T:2016:389.

[272] *Azumi Ltd v. Zuma's Choice Pet Products Ltd* [2017] *EWHC* 609 (IPEC), [69]–[76].

[273] I. Simon Fhima and R. Jacob, 'Unfair Advantage Law in the European Union', in D. Bereskin (eds), *International Trademark Dilution* (2017), [11.22].   [274] [2007] *EWCA Civ* 968, [2008] *ETMR* (1) 1.

[275] Ibid., 31, [97], referring to *Slazenger v. Feltham* (1889) 6 *RPC* 531, 538 (Lindley LJ).

Fig. 38.6 MIRACLE bottle designed by Charles Boussiquet and used by Lancôme (a member of the L'Oréal Group)

Source: Baker & McKenzie

Fig. 38.7 PINK WONDER packaging from the Creation Lamis range marketed by Bellure

Source: Baker & McKenzie

Fig. 38.5 MIRACLE packaging used by Lancôme (a member of the L'Oréal Group)

Source: Baker & McKenzie

D'OR and LA VALEUR, this would have been lost on the average British consumer. The claim that there was sufficient similarity between MIRACLE and PINK WONDER to establish a link was described as 'near fantastic'.[276]

The intention of the user of the later mark was again held to be relevant when assessing whether a link existed in the *Specsavers* case. Here, Asda's design process had started with Specsavers' logo, but ended up as two non-overlapping ovals in white with green writing, giving only a 'resonance' (see Figs 38.1 and 38.2). The Court of Appeal affirmed the view of the High Court that a link would be drawn between the Asda logo and the Specsavers mark. The Court of Appeal said that, although the test is objective, intention is relevant as evidence of someone familiar with the market.[277] More importantly, and in stark contrast with the decision in *L'Oréal*,[278] the Court of Appeal thought that the use of the logo needed to be viewed in the context of the campaign as a whole, including use of straplines such as 'Be a real spec saver at Asda'.[279] Seen in this way, there was no doubt that a link would have been established.

2.4.3 Unfair advantage or detriment

The third requirement that must be met for a mark to fall foul of section 5(3) is that it must be shown that the use of the later mark *either*:

(i)   is detrimental to the distinctive character of the earlier trade mark; *or*

(ii)   is detrimental to the reputation of the earlier trade mark; *or*

(iii) takes unfair advantage of the earlier trade mark.

The provision is not intended to prevent *any* use of a mark with a reputation; it is essential in any case that the opponent establishes that use of a similar mark would have one of these three effects.[280] The EU courts have held that, as with the determination of likelihood of confusion, so when assessing whether one of the injuries exist requires a global assessment. In addition to the factors used when assessing whether there is a link, other factors that are relevant to such an assessment are the strength of the reputation and inherent or acquired distinctiveness of the earlier mark, and whether the earlier mark owner has registrations and has used a family of marks.[281] On the other hand, the requirement of availability is irrelevant.[282] Because the analysis will often be prospective (the later mark not having been used), the opponent will need to establish evidence on its face of future risk that is not hypothetical. We will deal with each of these in turn.

(i) Detrimental to the distinctive character of the earlier mark The first type of 'injury' recognized is that the use of the later mark would be detrimental to the distinctive character of the earlier mark. This is usually equated with 'blurring'[283]—that is, 'the gradual whittling away or dispersion of the identity and hold upon the public mind of the mark or name by its use upon non-competing goods'.[284]

---

[276] When the case returned from the Court of Justice, packaging was no longer in issue, the defendants having accepted the historic acts amounted to infringement.

[277] *Specsavers Int'l Healthcare v. Asda Stores* [2012] *EWCA Civ* 24, [2012] *FSR* (19) 555, [158].

[278] [2008] *ETMR* (1) 1, [133].   [279] Ibid., [164].

[280] *Spa finders*, T-67/04 [2005] *ECR* II–1825, [40]; *Sigla SA v. OHIM*, T-215/03 [2007] *ECR* II–711, [46].

[281] *IG Communications Ltd v. OHIM and Citigroup*, T 301/09, EU:T:2012:473.

[282] *Adidas AG and ors v. Marca Mode CV and ors*, Case C-102/07 [2008] *ECR* I–2439, [43].

[283] *Premier Brands UK v. Typhoon Europe* [2000] *FSR* 767, 787; *DaimlerChrysler AG v. Alavi* [2001] *RPC* (42) 813, [88]; *Adidas v. Fitnessworld*, Case C-408/01 [2003] *ECR* I–12537, [AG37].

[284] F. Schechter, 'The Rational Basis of Trademark Protection' (1927) 40 *Harv L Rev* 813, 825.

The concern here is that the unauthorized use on similar or dissimilar products may undermine an established trade mark's uniqueness, and thus its selling power and 'commercial magnetism'. As Schechter said, 'if you allow Rolls-Royce Restaurants, and Rolls-Royce cafeterias, and Rolls-Royce pants and Rolls-Royce candy, in ten years you will not have the Rolls-Royce mark any more'.[285]

In *Intel Corp. v. CPM UK Ltd*,[286] the Court of Justice understood 'detriment to distinctive character' as blurring. In this case, the question was whether a (prior) registration of INTELMARK for marketing services would be detrimental to the distinctive character of the INTEL mark registered for microprocessor chips and therefore liable to be invalidated. Intel played to its strengths, arguing that harm would inevitably or presumptively arise once a mental connection was established and emphasizing the apparent uniqueness of its mark and its vast reputation. Meanwhile Intelmark emphasized the dissimilarity between Intel's goods and its services, as well as the absence of any economic harm or other meaningful detriment.

The Court of Justice began by defining 'detriment to distinctive character' as 'dilution', 'whittling away', or 'blurring', which occurs where there is a weakening of a mark's ability to identify the goods or services for which it is registered and used, because the use of the later mark leads to 'dispersion' of the earlier mark's 'identity and hold upon the public mind'.[287] The Court referred to the impact of such blurring on the length of time that the consumer would take to associate the mark with the goods—this potential 'mental slowdown' or disambiguation time is what some US scholars have referred to as 'imagination costs'.[288]

In addition to identifying the factors necessary to establish a link or mental association, *Intel* provides us with an indicative list of factors to determine whether detriment to distinctive character occurs as a consequence of this link.[289] (i) Merely establishing a mental link is not a sufficient basis to presume that this detriment will inevitably follow. (ii) A mark need not be unique for this sort of damage to be possible, and that any mark with a reputation, and thus acquired distinctive character, could have that character damaged. However, where the mark is truly unique—best understood as highly inherently distinctive—then detriment is more likely. Conversely, where it is more widely used due its descriptive meaning, detriment should be less likely.[290] (iii) The first use of an identical or similar mark can damage distinctiveness, rather than waiting for the fabled 'death by a thousand cuts'. (iv) As a related point, the likelihood of detriment—as opposed to actual detriment—is sufficient for this provision. The Court then made a valiant attempt to reconcile this prospective 'likelihood' standard, which could anticipate harm, with the need for some meaningful detriment. Otherwise any mark with a reputation which could satisfy the link requirement might routinely succeed without showing more. The Court indicated that detriment to the distinctive character of the earlier mark:

> . . . requires evidence of a change in the economic behaviour of the average consumer of the goods or services for which the earlier mark was registered consequent on the

---

[285] Hearings before the House Committee on Patents, 72nd Congress, 1st Session, 15 (1932). For a compelling critique, see R. Tushnet, 'Gone in 60 Miliseconds' (2008) 86 *Texas L Rev* 507.

[286] Case C-252/07 [2008] *ECR* I–8823; *Adidas v. Fitnessworld*, Case C-408/01 [2003] *ECR* I–12537, [AG37] (AG Jacobs); *Marca Mode*, Case C-425/98 [2000] *ECR* I–4861, [AG44].

[287] *Intel Corporation*, Case C-252/07 [2008] *ECR* I–8823, [29]. See also *Interflora Inc. v. Marks & Spencer*, Case C-323/09 [2011] *ECR* I–8625, [73] [AG52].

[288] *Intel Corporation*, Case C-252/07 [2008] *ECR* I–8823, [29] (blurring occurs 'when the earlier mark, which used to arouse immediate association with the goods and services for which it is registered, is no longer capable of doing so'). See *Ty Inc. v. Perryman*, 306 *F.3d*. 509, 511 (7th Cir. 2002) (Posner J).

[289] *Intel Corporation*, Case C-252/07 [2008] *ECR* I–8823, [65]–[81].

[290] *SIGLA SA v. OHIM*, Case T-215/03 [2007] *ECR* II–711, [38] (VIPS).

use of the later mark, or a serious likelihood that such a change will occur in the future.[291]

The requirement of 'a change in economic behaviour' initially seemed to present a significant evidentiary hurdle.[292] However, subsequent courts continued to infer such detriment,[293] often paying only lip service to the test adopted in *Intel*. In *Environmental Manufacturing v. OHIM*,[294] where the figurative image of a wolf's head was the common element, the Court of Justice overruled the General Court, categorically rejecting any 'watering down' of this behavioural change requirement. The Court of Justice clarified that this requirement applied regardless of whether the goods or services were similar or dissimilar (since *Intel* had concerned only the latter).[295] It confirmed that the 'concept of "change in the economic behaviour of the average consumer" lays down an objective condition ... [which] cannot be deduced solely from subjective elements such as consumers' perceptions'.[296] However, since anticipatory claims could be accommodated, evidence of actual detriment was not required; 'the serious risk of detriment' could be established via 'logical deductions' that were not 'the result of mere suppositions but ... [based on] an analysis of the probabilities and by taking account of the normal practice in the relevant commercial sector as well as all the other circumstances of the case'.[297] Despite the unambiguous reminder in *Environmental Manufacturing* that *Intel* raised the threshold, tribunals continue to rely on the 'logical deductions' proviso. When concluding that detriment to distinctiveness is likely, they sometimes build (plausibly) on a prior finding of the likelihood of confusion but at other times (less plausibly) on little else besides the reputation of the earlier mark and the link or mental association.[298] Therefore in the absence of a likelihood of confusion, how easily should we infer detriment? Arnold J openly acknowledges the difficulty: 'The dividing line between legitimate inference and impermissible speculation is not always easy to discern'.[299]

Besides mental slowdown, in the form of impeding a sign's ability to recall the associated goods or services (in the *Intel* sense), or diminishing its exclusivity (in the Schechter

---

[291] Ibid., [77].

[292] D. Slopek, 'Case Comment' [2009] *IIC* 348, 352; A. Breitschaft, '*Intel, Adidas* & Co' [2009] *EIPR* 497, 503; D. Meale and J. Smith, 'Enforcing a Trade Mark When Nobody's Confused' (2010) 5(2) *JIPLP* 96; C. Davies, 'To Buy or Not to Buy' [2013] *EIPR* 373 (suggesting that a change in consumer behaviour should be only one way in which to establish blurring); cf. S. Middlemiss and S. Warner, 'The Protection of Marks with a Reputation' [2009] *EIPR* 326, 328 (criticizing the test as lacking clarity, but arguing that it is 'likely to give the right result in at least the majority of cases'). See also Bently and Sherman (2014), 1003–1004.

[293] See, e.g., *Fine and Country Ltd v. Okotoks Ltd* [2012] *EWHC* 2230 (Ch), [270]; *32Red plc v. WHG International Ltd* [2011] *EWHC* 62 (Ch), [2011] *RPC* (26) 721, [133] (Henderson J); cf. the more demanding approach in *Och Ziff v. Och Capital* [2010] *EWHC* 2599 (Ch), [138].

[294] Case C-383/12P, EU:C:2013:741, overruling Case T-570/10 [2012] *ETMR* (54) 972, [53]–[54], [62].

[295] Case C-383/12P, EU:C:2013:741, [45].   [296] Ibid., [37].

[297] Ibid., [42]–[43]. On remand, the General Court held that—notwithstanding arguments relating to the 'uniqueness' of the opponents mark, the similarity of the goods and the lack of an explanation for the applicant's choice of a wolf's head—the 'change in economic behaviour' requirement had not been satisfied, so the dilution claims failed: T-570/10 RENV, EU:T:2015:76.

[298] *Comic Enterprises v. Twentieth Century Fox Film Corp* [2016] *EWCA Civ* 41, [113]–[118], [142]–[144] (Kitchin LJ) (behavioural change derived from evidence of 'wrong way round' confusion); *Skyscape Cloud Services Limited v. Sky plc, Sky UK Limited and Sky International AG* [2016] *EWHC* 1340 (IPEC) (no evidence of behavioural change but detriment likely, following from a finding of likelihood of confusion); *Lifestyle Equities CV v. Santa Monica Polo Club Ltd* [2017] *EWHC* 3313 (Ch), [133]–[134] (no evidence of behavioural change but detriment likely, following partially from a finding of likelihood of confusion and partially from the intention to copy the claimant's sign).

[299] *Enterprise Holdings, Inc. v. Europcar Group UK Ltd* [2015] *EWHC* 17 (Ch), [221]–[222] (once the confusion arguments were filtered out, an independent claim for detriment to distinctive character was unsuccessful).

sense), a third form of blurring, best characterized as 'genericide', has been recognized. Where the sign is used by a junior user—a subsequent applicant or competitor in the marketplace—on identical or very similar products, the reputed mark might become the general name for that class or category of products. Thus in *Interflora*,[300] the (ultimately unsubstantiated) concern was that the defendant Marks & Spencer's purchase of 'Interflora' as a keyword, to advertise its own flower delivery services, could lead to that mark becoming a generic term for flower deliver services. Unauthorized use which risks genericide is clearly detrimental to the origin indicating ability of a trade mark, i.e. its distinctiveness (for instance, if the keyword advertisement had read: 'If you want an Interflora-type service, try us instead').

It is worth concluding with a review of why blurring or detriment to distinctiveness has proved so enduringly controversial. First, what attribute of the mark is being harmed?[301] Is it uniqueness or exclusivity per se, or distinctiveness? The two conceptions lead down diverging paths, since detriment to exclusivity can be approached formalistically—first there was one mark and now there are two. Harm is a logical consequence. By contrast, detriment to distinctiveness (in the origin indicating sense) additionally requires that consumers experience increased internal search costs or greater recall time, after exposure to the junior user's identical or similar mark, to an extent which materially impedes decision making. Marks that are not unique can nevertheless be perfectly distinctive. This explains why three unrelated commercial entities can claim POLO as their trade mark—Ralph Lauren (for clothing and cosmetics), Nestlé (for the 'mint with the hole' confectionaries) and Volkswagen (for cars). The logic of the trade mark register is premised on similar marks being allowed to coexist when used on dissimilar products. Conflating detriment to exclusivity with detriment to distinctiveness is doctrinally unsound and normatively undesirable.

Second, if detriment to distinctiveness is our target, then how should we go about measuring it? In the European Union, 'logical deductions' seem to be on the ascendant, such that no one is ever required to prove any detriment. However, those who have engaged more seriously with this question doubt that blurring exists in any meaningful form. Empirical research from the United States indicates that independent third parties continue to register identical marks in dissimilar classes and even use famous marks as trade names at the local level, without any apparent harm to the famous national brands.[302] Marks can therefore coexist in different categories, since consumers are able to compartmentalize brand information and retain multiple sets of messages simultaneously. Mental associations between marks may also produce a so-called 'echo effect', whereby the junior use reinforces the associations between the famous mark and its underlying products. While consumer surveys or laboratory experiments can establish mental associations and measure slowdowns associated with disambiguation, these delays are measured in milliseconds and unlikely to affect real world purchasing decisions.[303]

[300] *Interflora Inc. v. Marks & Spencer*, Case C-323/09 [2011] *ECR* I–8625, [79], [AG82]–[AG84] (AG Jääskinen).

[301] The contrasting approaches are evident in: F. I. Schechter, 'The Rational Basis of Trade Mark Protection' (1927) 40 *Harvard L Rev* 813; M. Senftleben, 'The Trademark Tower of Babel—Dilution Concepts in International, US and EC Trade Mark Law' (2009) 40 *IIC* 45; I. Simon Fhima, 'Dilution by Blurring—A Conceptual Roadmap' [2010] *IPQ* 44; A. Dworkowitz, 'Ending Dilution Doublespeak: Reviving the Concept of Economic Harm in the Dilution Action' (2011–2012) 20 *Texas IP LJ* 25.

[302] J. N. Sheff, 'Dilution at the Patent and Trade Mark Office' (2015) 21 *Michigan Telecommunications and Technology Law Review* 79; R. Brauneis and P. J. Heald, 'The Myth of Buick Aspirin: An Empirical Study of Trade Mark Dilution by Product and Trade Names' (2011) 32 *Cardozo L Rev* 2533.

[303] Contrast J. Jacoby, 'Considering the Who, What, When, Where and How of Measuring Dilution' (2007) 24 *Santa Clara High Tech LJ* 601 with the powerful critique by R. Tushnet, 'Gone in 60 Milliseconds: Trade Mark Law and Cognitive Science' (2008) 86 *Texas L Rev* 507.

Experimental measurements of slowdown also exclude the course-correcting cues available in real-world shopping contexts. We wouldn't expect to find cars in the biscuit aisle of a supermarket.[304] Furthermore, the slowdown observed in experiments may be due to experimental subjects becoming wary and cautious in general, upon being exposed to any diluting stimuli.[305] Cumulatively, there is little compelling evidence that blurring exists as a meaningful form of harm to distinctiveness. The real complaint may instead be that the junior user is free-riding on the brand's exclusivity and image.[306]

(ii) Damage to reputation The second form of injury recognized by section 5(3) is 'detriment to the repute of the earlier mark'. This is often referred to as 'degradation', or 'tarnishment'.[307] To those with a legal background, this claim 'has seemingly clear parallels with other areas of the law that seek to prevent harm to reputation, such as the torts of defamation or injurious falsehood, or moral rights protections for authors of copyright works, as well as with laws regulating obscenity'.[308] The Court of Justice has held that it occurs:

> ... when the goods or services for which the identical or similar sign is used by the third party may be perceived by the public in such a way that the trade mark's power of attraction is reduced. The likelihood of such detriment may arise in particular from the fact that the goods or services offered by the third party possess a characteristic or a quality which is liable to have a negative impact on the image of the mark.[309]

The owner of the earlier trade mark must establish that the negative association will be real, not fanciful. This involves not only substantiating the existence of a particular image in the earlier mark, but also the way in which the later mark will bring about the damage.[310]

There are two obvious ways in which tarnishment might occur. The first, suggested by the Court of Justice, is where the proposed use on the applicant's goods would reflect badly on the opponent's reputation. This would be the case where the mark is to be used on ineffective goods,[311] but there might equally be damage to reputation where there is some other negative association with goods—or, as it is sometimes called, 'antagonism' between the goods. So, in a classic pre-harmonization example (referred to with approval in some post-harmonization case law), the Benelux Court held that KLAREIN for detergent would tarnish CLAERYN for gin because 'no one likes to be reminded of a

---

[304] Unless it's a Jammie Dodgem.

[305] B. Beebe, R. Germano, C. J. Sprigman, and J. H. Steckel, 'Is Dilution a Unicorn? An Experimental Investigation' (Forthcoming, 2018).

[306] B. Beebe 'The Suppressed Misappropriation Origins of Trade Mark Antidilution Law' and G. B. Dinwoodie, 'Dilution as Unfair Competition: European Echoes', in Dreyfuss and Ginsburg (2014) 59, 81; D. Franklyn, 'Debunking Dilution Doctrine: Toward a Coherent Theory of the Anti-Free-Rider Principle in American Trademark Law' (2004) 56 *Hastings Law Journal* 117.

[307] *L'Oréal SA and ors v. Bellure NV and ors*, Case C-487/07 [2009] *ECR* I–5185, [40]; *Interflora Inc. v. Marks & Spencer*, Case C-323/09 [2011] *ECR* I–8625, [73], [AG52].

[308] M. Handler, 'What Can Harm the Reputation of a Trademark? A Critical Re-Evaluation of Dilution by Tarnishment' (2016) 106 *TMR* 639, 640. Handler critically re-evaluates whether tarnishment is a form of 'harm' that the law should take cognizance of, since it rests upon an oversimplified notion of the brand reputation that is being protected. He questions whether 'unsavory' mental associations actually lead to lasting harmful perceptions in the minds of consumers. Consequently, is tarnishment really about harm to the reputed mark or regulating the (im)morality of trade behaviour?

[309] *L'Oréal SA and ors v. Bellure NV and ors*, Case C-487/07 [2009] *ECR* I–5185, [40]; *Interflora Inc. v. Marks & Spencer*, Case C-323/09 [2011] *ECR* I–8625, [AG82]–[AG92] (AG Jääskinen).

[310] *DaimlerChrysler v. Alavi* [2001] *RPC* (42) 813, 844, [94]. Mere assertions about the lack of product quality should not be recognized: *TDK Kabushiki Kaisha v. Dosteba AG*, R 2090/2013–2 (OHIM BoA), [92].

[311] *Sihra's Trade Mark Application* [2003] *RPC* (44) 789.

detergent when drinking their favourite tipple'.[312] Trade mark owners commonly object to association with sexual products or services, and the tribunals are generally sympathetic.[313] Other 'antagonisms' might exist between cigarettes or alcohol and goods associated with health.[314] However, the General Court has held that there was no antagonism between mineral water and travel agency services such that the use of SPA-FINDERS for a travel agency would harm SPA for mineral water,[315] or between self-service restaurants and hotel computer systems such that the use of VIPS for the latter would tarnish the mark VIPS for the former.[316] Tribunals are also hesitant to endorse claims that merely because a product is cheaper and relatively less prestigious, there will be tarnishment (such as where a mark for relatively cheaper Cava is associated with one for more exclusive Champagne).[317]

The second circumstance in which tarnishment might be thought to occur is where the later mark modifies the earlier sign in a denigratory way. Perhaps the most obvious example would be the modification of COCA-COLA in its familiar cursive script to 'Cocaine'—a modification that might tarnish the contemporary image of COCA-COLA by suggesting that it contains cocaine.[318] It is notable that the Court of Justice's definition of 'tarnishment' talks only in terms of damage to repute, which results from the character of the goods or services in relation to which a third party uses a mark. Such a narrow definition of tarnishment could be justified on the basis that it would prevent trade mark owners from unduly limiting the free speech of others (such as parodists).[319] However, such a narrow interpretation of the notion of detriment, is an abrupt contrast to the broad notion of 'repute' as relating to the image or atmospherics associated with a mark. It thus seems likely that, when faced with a case of denigratory modification of a mark, the Court will modify its definition.[320] It is hoped that it will nevertheless adopt a high threshold test for the demonstration of damage to repute, which excludes from any prohibition the sorts of humorous modifications of marks that circulate widely on the Internet and which do not appear to do any harm at all to trade mark proprietors.[321]

(iii) Unfair advantage The final form of 'injury' recognized in section 5(3)/Article 8(5) occurs where the use of the applicant's mark would take 'unfair advantage' of the earlier mark. According to the authorities, this is intended to enable a trade mark owner to prevent another trader from registering (or using) a similar mark when to do so would involve 'parasitism' or taking a 'free-ride' on the reputation of the earlier mark.[322] Although it is referred to as an 'injury', the Court of Justice stated in *L'Oréal v. Bellure,* the 'concept

---

[312] *Colgate Palmolive v. Lucas Bols (Claeryn/Klarein)* [1976] *IIC* 420. This case was referred to with seeming approval in *Adidas v. Fitnessworld,* Case C-408/01 [2003] *ECR* I-12537, [AG38] (AG Jacobs); *British Sugar v. Robertson* [1996] *RPC* 281, 295; *Premier Brands,* [2000] *FSR* 767, 787.

[313] *C.A. Sheimer (M.) Sdn Bhd's Trade Mark Application* [2000] *RPC* 484, 506–7; cf. *Oasis Stores* [1998] *RPC* 631.

[314] *Souza Cruz v. Hollywood,* R283/1999–3 [2002] *ETMR* (64) 705, [85]–[86]; *Inlima SL's Application; Opposition by Adidas AG* [2000] *ETMR* 325, 336. Cf. *Éditions Quo Vadis v. OHIM, Francisco Gómez Hernández,* Case T-517/13, EU:T:2015:816, [41]–[44].   [315] *Spa finders,* Case T-67/04 [2005] *ECR* II-1825.

[316] *Sigla SA v. OHIM,* T-215/03 [2007] *ECR* II-711, [66]–[67].

[317] *Champagne Louis Roderer v. J Garcia Carrion SA* [2015] *EWHC* 2760 (Ch), [89]–[90] (Rose J).

[318] For examples of such distortions, see R. Burrell and D. Gangjee, 'Trade Marks and Freedom of Expression: A Call for Caution' (2010) 41 *IIC* 544.

[319] Indeed, it might be observed that damage from altering the mark can occur without any 'use' to distinguish goods or services at all. The Court of Justice thus might be intending to restrict the notion of tarnishment that is caused by use of the mark as a trade mark. Even the 'Cocaine' example might well fall outside such use.   [320] O/504/13 (12 December 2013), [23] (TMR, Pike).

[321] See *Red Bull v. Sun Mark* [2012] *EWHC* 1929 (Ch).

[322] *Adidas v. Fitnessworld,* Case C-408/01 [2003] *ECR* I-12537, [AG39].

relates not to the detriment caused to the mark but to the advantage taken by the third party'.[323] The Court explained:

> It covers, in particular, cases where, by reason of a transfer of the image of the mark or of the characteristics which it projects to the goods identified by the identical or similar sign, there is clear exploitation on the coat-tails of the mark with a reputation.[324]

The principle underpinning this ground for objection seems to be the prevention of 'misappropriation' or free-riding. As we explained earlier, and as a number of commentators have elaborated at greater length,[325] there are good economic reasons to doubt the desirability of legal sanctions against free-riding, and it is not entirely obvious why free-riding on the reputation of another person's trade mark should be regarded as special circumstances under which the law provides a remedy. A blanket prohibition on gaining from the efforts of others would be overbroad, since cultural and economic life relies on interdependence. We share and reference to create or renew relationships, while copying is essential for learning, competing, as well as cultural transmission.[326] The front cover of this very book you are reading concisely conveys this point. Amongst others, comparative advertisers, novelists, scriptwriters, producers of compatible products, social media users, and parodists (including those with the creative appetite to produce a Game of Scones recipe book)[327] evoke reputed trade marks. Should the default setting be a prohibition on all such uses, with a narrow exception (due cause) available for a circumscribed range of uses? It is notable that there is no equivalent to a free-riding prohibition in the US federal dilution law.[328] This suggests that it would be desirable to give this ground a narrow construction.

However, difficulties of proof with blurring and tarnishment mean that tribunals prefer to rely on the 'unfair advantage' ground. In applying the provision, it is necessary for the tribunal to proceed in three stages. First, it should identify the 'power of attraction, reputation and prestige' of the earlier mark.[329] Second, the tribunal should establish whether any advantage has been shown to have transferred (or to be seriously likely to transfer) to the user of the later (identical or similar) mark. Unlike blurring and tarnishment, where the reactions of the consumers of the reputed mark are central, here the focus is on the impact assessed from the perspective of the average consumer of the goods or services that are alleged to free-ride.[330] Third, it must be established that the advantage thereby secured has been 'unfairly taken'.

---

[323] *L'Oréal SA and ors v. Bellure NV and ors*, Case C-487/07 [2009] *ECR* I–5185, [41].

[324] Ibid. See also *Interflora Inc. v. Marks & Spencer*, Case C-323/09 [2011] *ECR* I–8625, [AG53].

[325] See pp. 818–19; R. Burrell and D. Gangjee, 'Because You're Worth It' (2010) 73 *MLR* 282, 288–92; G. Austin, 'Tolerating Confusion about Confusion' (2008) 50 *Ariz L Rev* 157, 161–2; *Interflora Inc. v. Marks & Spencer*, Case C-323/09 [2011] *ECR* I–8625, [AG94] (AG Jääskinen); cf. *Helena Rubinstein SNC v. OHIM and Allergan*, Case C-100/11P, EU:C:2012:95 [AG31].

[326] Drawing on parallels with copyright, if creativity is understood as cumulative and collaborative, then copying becomes a necessary part of it and is objectionable in a narrower range of circumstances: A. Drassinower, *What's Wrong with Copying?* (2015); R. Deazley and B. Meletti, 'Copying, Creativity and Copyright', CREATe Working Paper 2016/02 (February 2016); J. P. Fishman, 'Honest Copying Practices' (2017) 93 *Notre Dame L Rev* 267 (should the issue of whether copying is easy or hard affect liability?).

[327] Published by Orion books and authored by Jammy Lannister, it includes the aptly named recipe for Jaime and Cersei's Family Mess.

[328] *Interflora Inc. v. Marks & Spencer*, Case C-323/09 [2011] *ECR* I–8625, [AG53], G. Dinwoodie, 'Dilution as Unfair Competition: European Echoes', in R. Dreyfuss and J. Ginsburg (eds), *Intellectual Property at the Edge* (2014), ch. 4, 88–9.

[329] *L'Oréal SA and ors v. Bellure NV and ors*, Case C-487/07 [2009] *ECR* I–5185, [40].

[330] *Intel Corporation*, Case C-252/07 [2008] *ECR* I–8823, [36].

The first stage then is to establish the qualitative repute (or atmospherics) of the earlier mark—that is, 'the image of the mark or of the characteristics which it projects'.[331] In relation to the latter, the General Court seems to have readily adopted the characterizations used in the field of marketing, identifying a brand of mineral water as conveying messages of 'health, beauty, purity and mineral richness',[332] a mark for fast food as being associated with qualities of 'speed', 'availability', and 'youth',[333] a mark for a stock exchange as having associations with 'modernity',[334] and a mark for cigarettes as having an image of 'relaxation'.[335] In order to establish the 'repute', it seems that tribunals can both take account of the characteristics of the goods or services that are sold under the mark, and examine the specific manner in which the mark is advertised and promoted, insofar as they draw attention to particular characteristics. Not every attribute or feature contained in a marketing campaign, however, can be assumed to constitute a relevant component of the 'image' that is created: some such features may simply be incidental, while others may have achieved no impact on consumers.

The second stage is to examine closely whether the reputation, or the repute (the image conveyed), will 'transfer' to the later mark (and the goods or service to which it relates), so as to confer an 'advantage' on the applicant (or user of the mark). This appears to require the court to revisit the various components involved in the 'global appreciation' and to examine closely the benefit, if any, which would accrue to the user of an identical or similar mark. Following *Intel*, *L'Oréal* identifies the same indicative factors: the strength of the marks reputation and the degree of its (inherent) distinctiveness; the similarity between the marks; and the nature as well as degree of proximity between goods or services.[336] In the case of identical or similar goods, that transfer may be almost self-evident, but in the case of dissimilar goods or services, the possibility of such 'cross-pollination' is often unthinkable. Consider, for example, the use of TWIX, a well-known mark for chocolate, as the name of a garden plant (a viola or pansy): it is difficult to imagine how any advantage could accrue in relation to the plant.[337] Where the goods or services are dissimilar, the most critical consideration is likely to be the distinctiveness of the earlier mark. As the Court of Justice said:

> [T]he more immediately and strongly the mark is brought to mind by the sign, the greater the likelihood that the current or future use of the sign is taking, or will take, unfair advantage of the distinctive character or the repute of the mark.[338]

So far, there has been no suggestion that the benefit needs to be articulated in terms of increased sales; rather, tribunals seem to be looking for plausible explanations of consumer thought processes by which particular characteristics will be transferred.[339] In

---

[331] *L'Oréal SA and ors v. Bellure NV and ors*, Case C-487/07 [2009] *ECR* I–5185, [41].

[332] *L'Oréal v. OHIM and Spa*, Case T-21/07 [2009] *ECR* II–31*, [40]; *Interflora Inc. v. Marks & Spencer*, Case C-323/09 [2011] *ECR* I–8625, [74].   [333] *Sigla v. OHIM*, Case T-215/03 [2007] *ECR* II–711.

[334] *NASDAQ*, Case T-47/06 [2007] *ECR* II–42*.

[335] *Japan Tobacco, Inc. v. OHIM and Torrefacção Camelo*, Case C-136/08P [2009] *ECR* I–70* (French).

[336] *L'Oréal*, Case C-487/07 [2009] *ECR* I–5185, [44]. For a recent summary of the test to be applied, see: *Shoe Branding Europe BVBA v. EUIPO, Adidas*, T-85/16, EU:T:2018:109, [48]–[55] (two stripes on shoes would bring to mind adidas' three stripes position mark in a manner which risks unfair advantage).

[337] *Flowil International Lighting v. EUIPO*, Case T-430/15, EU:T:2016:590 (a reputation for lamps and lighting goods was too dissimilar to foodstuffs to pose a risk) Cf. *PP Gappol Marzena Porczyńska v. EUIPO*, Case T-411/15, EU:T:2017:689 (despite the differences between clothing and furniture, the applicants mark GAPPOL might take advantage of GAP's reputation for clothing, since fashion designers were moving into furniture design and fashion brands were moving into interior decoration accessories).

[338] *L'Oréal*, Case C-487/07 [2009] *ECR* I–5185, [44].

[339] Sometimes, tribunals have set the threshold absurdly low: *NASDAQ*, Case T-47/06 [2007] *ECR* II–42*; aff'd Case C-320/07P [2009] *ECR* I–28*.

L'Oréal v. OHIM and Spa,[340] the (then) CFI thought it likely that the image that the mark SPA conveyed in relation to mineral water—namely, health, beauty, purity, and mineral richness—might be transferred to the applicant's goods, cosmetics, were it to use the mark SPA-LINE because both products were used to preserve and improve health or beauty. Similarly, the General Court thought that the reputation of the mark BOTOX for pharmaceuticals would readily transfer onto the applicant's marks BOTOLIST and BOTOCYL, both relating to cosmetics including wrinkle creams, and the Court of Justice saw no reason to interfere with those conclusions of fact.[341] In contrast, the CFI said that the use of the mark SPA-FINDERS would not take unfair advantage of the distinctive character or the repute of the mark SPA (registered for mineral water), because there was no evidence that the reputation of the mark SPA would in any way transfer to the travel agency.[342] Similarly, despite suggestions that 'cigarettes' and 'coffee' were both associated with relaxation, the Court of Justice found no error when the CFI had not found any transfer of advantage from camel cigarettes to the applicant's figurative trade mark for coffee, which included an image of a camel, a pyramid, and palm trees, and the word CAMELO (in precisely the same configuration as the opponent's earlier mark).[343]

In other cases, a 'transfer of image' can occur because of the way in which the earlier trade mark has been promoted. In *Aktieselskabet af 21 November 2001 v. OHIM and TDK*,[344] for example, the reputation associated with the earlier mark 'TDK' for cassettes was sufficient to oppose 'TDK' for clothing, due to the use of the former on clothing at sponsorship events. This could give rise to a likelihood of a commercial connection by suggesting licensed use. Conversely, the context of the usage of the later mark can ward off the potential for image transfer and ensuing unfair advantage.[345]

In the case of three-dimensional marks, the English courts have been reluctant to assume any transfer of 'image' merely because products have similar features. In *Whirlpool v. Kenwood*,[346] the claimant had been selling a premium price food mixer under the mark KITCHENAID ARTISAN. This was a stand mixer, of a general shape that had been used for 70 years. It had an EUTM registration for the shape of the mixer (see Fig 38.8), which mark was distinctive, 'but not strongly so'.[347] Whirlpool objected to similarities in the bodywork on Kenwood's KMIX MIXER (see Fig. 38.9). While the similarities were regarded as sufficient to warrant the view that, on seeing the KMIX, the consumer would call to mind (and thus draw a link with) the reputed mark, affirming the decision of the deputy judge, Geoffrey Hobbs QC, that there was no infringement, the Court noted that the similarities were a consequence of the fact that both products were stand mixers designed to a high standard of style, so as to be attractive products on the kitchen work surface. The two products bore the same 'basic shape' and the 'reminder' was not strong. Accordingly, there was no advantage to Kenwood (or if there was, it was not an 'unfair one').[348]

The third stage is to determine whether the advantage has been 'unfairly taken'. The Court of Justice initially seemed to have offered a rather narrow interpretation, which

---

[340] Case T-21/07 [2009] *ECR* II–31*, [40].

[341] *Helena Rubinstein SNC and L'Oréal SA v. OHIM*, Case C-100/11P [2012] *ETMR* 40, [96]–[98], affirming T-345/08 [2010] *ECR* II–279*.   [342] *Spa Monopole v. OHIM*, T-67/04 [2005] *ECR* II–1829, [52].

[343] *Japan Tobacco, Inc. v. OHIM and Torrefacção Camelo*, [2009] ECR I–70* (French). See, to similar effect, *Sigla v. OHIM*, T-215/03 [2007] *ECR* II–711, [73]–[74].

[344] Case T-477/04 [2007] *ECR* II–399, aff'd in Case C-197/07P [2008] *ECR* I–193*, [21]. See also *L'Oréal v. OHIM and Spa*, Case T-21/07 [2009] *ECR* II–31*, [35].

[345] In an infringement scenario, the defendants other trade marks used in close proximity, its status as a leading player in the car rental market, as well as its own independent advertising efforts were all relevant: *Enterprise Holdings, Inc. v. Europcar Group UK Ltd* [2015] *EWHC* 17 (Ch), [223]–[225] (Arnold J).

[346] [2009] *EWCA Civ* 753.   [347] Ibid., [137] (Lloyd LJ).   [348] Ibid., [138] (Lloyd LJ).

Fig. 38.8 KITCHENAID ARTISAN food mixer
Source: Whirlpool v. Kenwood [2009] *EWCA Civ* 753

Fig. 38.9 KMIX food mixer
Source: Whirlpool v. Kenwood [2009] *EWCA Civ* 753

highlights the underpinning concern as being the *deliberate* misappropriation of repute. In *L'Oréal*, it stated that:

> The advantage arising from the use by a third party of a sign similar to a mark with a reputation is an advantage taken unfairly . . . where that party *seeks by that use* to ride on the coat-tails of the mark with a reputation in order to benefit from the power of attraction, the reputation and the prestige of that mark and to exploit it, without paying any financial compensation, the marketing effort expended by the proprietor of the mark in order to create and maintain the mark's image.[349]

Some doubt exists as to the vitality of the criterion of 'unfairness'.[350] It appears that intentional referencing to another sign is potentially unfair, as is any other (even unintended) use which leads to a benefit without compensation—taking without giving back. However,

---

[349] *L'Oréal SA and ors v. Bellure NV and ors*, Case C-487/07 [2009] *ECR* I–5185, [50] (emphasis added).
[350] *Helena Rubinstein SNC and L'Oréal SA v. OHIM*, Case C-100/11P [2012] *ETMR* 40; *Interflora Inc. v. Marks & Spencer*, Case C-323/09 [2011] *ECR* I–8625, [AG32].

this second broader conceptualization assumes there is an obligation to give back in the first place. While one panel of the English Court of Appeal considered that there must be an added factor of some kind for that advantage to be categorized as 'unfair',[351] the Court of Justice, in *Interflora v. Marks & Spencer*, seems now to have confirmed that 'unfair' indeed has no meaning in a situation in which there has been an intentional riding on the coat-tails of the reputation of an earlier mark.[352]

In an opposition action, in which it will often be the case that the applicant has yet to use the mark, the tribunal will need to assess whether an advantage will be 'taken' if the mark comes to be used for the goods or services for which registration is sought. In *Helena Rubinstein*,[353] the Court of Justice indicated that the proprietor must adduce evidence on its face of a future risk, which is not hypothetical, of unfair advantage. As with detriment (through blurring or tarnishment), unfair advantage may be established on the basis of 'logical deductions made from an analysis of the probabilities and by taking account of the normal practice in the relevant commercial sector as well as all the other circumstances of the case'.[354]

Much depends on one's starting point when approaching a prohibition on 'free-riding'. Does socio-economic life inevitably involve the ongoing enjoyment of benefits from positive externalities (how many of us have appreciated a fireworks display without contributing to it)? Or, more individualistically, are we only permitted to succeed by relying upon our own unaided efforts? To avoid the dangers of circular reasoning and to give unfairness some meaningful content, an advantage may be considered objectionable if it is (i) detrimental or harmful (but this was absent in *L'Oréal*); (ii) removes the incentive for further creation and product differentiation (but brands thrive in the United States despite no such federal prohibition against free-riding); (iii) immoral or unethical because those who create are not compensated (but moral philosophy only justifies a narrow form the of the claim where there is a legitimate expectation worth protecting); (iv) or based on the protection of a proprietary interest.[355] As regards this fourth argument, if brands are to be justified as the objects of property rights, based on a narrative of creation by the trade mark owner ('I made it, I own it'), marketing research reveals that, increasingly, brand image content and value arise from consumer efforts and investment, while the content of brand image is itself dynamic. If a brand is more analogous to an evolving and many-sided conversation, proprietary claims to a stable brand image projected by the trade mark owner are less convincing.[356]

---

[351]   *Whirlpool Corp. v. Kenwood Ltd* [2009] *EWCA Civ* 753, [114], [136]; cf. *L'Oréal v. Bellure* [2010] *EWCA Civ* 535, [49] ('All free riding is unfair').

[352]   *Interflora Inc. v. Marks & Spencer*, Case C-323/09 [2011] *ECR* I–8625, [89]. See *Interflora Inc. v. Marks and Spencer Plc* [2013] *EWHC* 1291 (Ch), [279]; Kerly, [11–135], [16–116], [16–125] (in its insistence on a demonstration of 'unfairness', *Whirlpool* must be regarded as incorrect).

[353]   *Helena Rubinstein SNC and L'Oréal SA v. OHIM*, Case C-100/11P [2012] *ETMR* 40.

[354]   Ibid., [95].

[355]   See M. Lemley and M. P. McKenna, 'Owning Mark(et)s' (2010) 109 *Mich L Rev* 137; D. S. Gangjee and R. Burrell, 'Because You're Worth It: *L'Oréal* and the Prohibition on Free Riding' (2010) 71 *MLR* 282; A. Chronopoulos, 'Goodwill Appropriation as a Distinct Theory of Trade Mark Liability: A Study on the Misappropriation Rationale in Trade Mark and Unfair Competition Law' (2014) 22 *Texas Intellectual Property Law Journal* 253; M. E. Kenneally, 'Misappropriation and the Morality of Free-Riding' (2014) 18 *Stanford Technology Law Review* 289.

[356]   D. Gerhardt, 'Consumer Investment in Trade Marks' (2009–10) *NCL Rev* 427; D. S. Gangjee, 'Property in Brands: The Commodification of Conversation', in H. Howe and J. Griffiths (eds), *Concepts of Property in Intellectual Property Law* (2013), 29; L. McDonagh, 'From Brand Performance to Consumer Performativity: Assessing European Trade Mark Law after the Rise of Anthropological Marketing' (2015) 42 *Journal of Law & Society* 611.

2.5 WITHOUT 'DUE CAUSE'

Once an opponent has established that its earlier mark has a reputation and that use of the applicant's mark will take unfair advantage of, or be detrimental to, the earlier mark, the obligation then falls upon the applicant to show that the use would not be 'without due cause'. It had hitherto been imagined that the threshold that an applicant would have to meet to demonstrate 'due cause' would be particularly onerous—perhaps requiring something akin to real commercial necessity, where the junior user cannot be reasonably required to refrain from using the mark.[357] Recent decisions from the Court of Justice have confirmed that due cause may be found in a wider range of circumstances, although the nature of the enquiry and its outer limits are still being established.[358]

As we have seen earlier, the Court of Justice presently deems all deliberate references to a reputed mark to be unfair advantage. To counterbalance this, in *Interflora* the Court indicated that a use that was 'fair competition' would be regarded as a use with 'due cause'.[359] Thus, it said, the use of a trade mark with a reputation (such as INTERFLORA) as a keyword that would generate Internet advertising could be justified on the basis that the advertiser is offering a competing product (as Marks and Spencer was with its flower service). The four conditions to which the Court referred were: (i) that the advertiser offered an 'alternative' to the goods associated with the reputed mark; (ii) that the competing product that was offered was not a 'mere imitation of the goods or services of the proprietor of that trade mark'; (iii) that the use did not dilute or tarnish the mark; and (iv) that the use did not (otherwise) adversely affect the functions of the trade mark.[360]

This case clearly suggests that (in an infringement context) a later user need not show a 'compelling need' to use the earlier mark, but rather merely a legitimate interest in so doing.[361] What seems to be required is a 'balancing of interests' as between the owner of the reputed mark and the later applicant or user.[362] In *Leidseplein Beheer*,[363] the defendant had, since the 1970s, run a bar in Amsterdam known as 'The Bull Dog'; in essence, it had made prior use of the sign, but as a trade name. The claimant registered its RED BULL trade mark for non-alcoholic beverages in 1983 and later developed a reputation for the mark for energy drinks. The defendant registered its THE BULL DOG mark for hotel, restaurant, and cafe services soon after the claimant's registration. Later, the defendant marketed an energy drink under the same name. The Dutch courts found that there was sufficient similarity between the marks to give rise to a link and that the defendant was taking unfair advantage of the reputation that red bull had acquired. The question arose whether there was 'due cause' to justify the actions of the defendant. The Court of Justice indicated that due cause did not require 'objectively overriding reasons' (necessity of use), but could also

---

[357] *Premier Brands UK v. Typhoon Europe* [2000] *FSR* 767, 789–92; *L'Oréal v. OHIM and Spa*, T-21/07 [2009] *ECR* II–31*, [40], [43]; *BSB v. Microsoft* [2013] *EWHC* 1826 (Ch), [193], [234] (Asplin J). This standard was found in the former Benelux approach: *Colgate-Palmolive BV v. NV Koninklijke Distilleerderijen Erven Lucas Bols*, Case A 74/1 [1979] *ECC* 419.   [358] I. Fhima, 'Due Cause' (2017) 12 *JIPLP* 897.

[359] *Interflora Inc. v. Marks & Spencer*, Case C-323/09 [2011] *ECR* I–8625, [91]. This has been acknowledged to be a significant development: *Specsavers Int'l Healthcare v. Asda Stores* [2012] *EWCA Civ* 24, [2012] *FSR* (19) 555, [141]. Indeed, Graeme Dinwoodie has suggested that the *L'Oréal v. Bellure* decision 'may already be seen to represent the high water mark of European dilution law': G. Dinwoodie, 'Dilution as Unfair Competition: European Echoes', in R. Dreyfuss and J. Ginsburg (eds), *Intellectual Property at the Edge* (2014), 97.   [360] Functions are further discussed in Chapter 40, section 10, pp. 1116–25.

[361] The distinction is drawn out well by Advocate-General Kokott in *Leidseplein Beheer BV v. Red Bull GmbH*, Case C-65/12 [2014] *ETMR* 24.   [362] Ibid., [AG34]–[AG36].

[363] *Leidseplein Beheer BV v. Red Bull GmbH*, Case C-65/12 [2014] *ETMR* 24. Cf. *Shoe Branding Europe BVBA v. EUIPO, Adidas*, Case T-85/16, EU:T:2018:109, [56]–[67], [137]–[148] (prior long-standing use in Germany not sufficient to establish due cause, albeit only in the relative grounds context).

relate to 'the subjective interests' of the defendant.[364] The latter interests may be found in the historical investment in the later conflicting mark as well as the intention ('good faith') of the person when choosing to use the same mark for different goods or services (to which objection was being made). The Court of Justice left it to the national court to decide whether Leidseplein Beheer's decision to sell the bull dog energy drink involved a good faith, natural extension into an adjacent field of a mark registered and whether it had occurred before the RED BULL mark had acquired its own reputation. If so, Leidseplein's use of 'The Bull Dog' was something that Red Bull would have to tolerate.

The *Leidseplein* and *Interflora* cases thus identify two specific situations in which a use might be regarded as with 'due cause': to facilitate fair competition and to acknowledge subjective, good faith reasons for adopting the later mark (such as prior use as a trade name and a reasonable extension into a new product market). The extent to which this embryonic methodology has started to align with that required by the 'honest practices' proviso—a necessary condition for trade mark defences[365]—has been considered by some courts.[366] However, legitimate interests could also include an interest in exploiting the descriptive qualities of a mark,[367] or freedom of expression more generally.[368] By contrast, arguments involving the use of a personal name, or a pet's name for that matter, as the basis for a later trade mark have proved less successful.[369]

Moreover, neither case considered by the Court of Justice concerned an attempt to register a mark that was being opposed on relative grounds by the owner of a mark with a reputation. Could 'due cause' be used to affirmatively support registration, as opposed to excusing the defendant's use of the sign in an infringement context? On the one hand, the Court in *Leidseplein Beheer* suggested that due cause should not lead to the recognition 'for the benefit of that third party, of the rights connected with a registered mark, but rather obliges the proprietor of the mark with a reputation to tolerate the use of the similar sign'.[370] This might be taken to suggest that registration of the later mark—say, the BULL DOG for energy drinks—is not envisaged. But the language of 'due cause' is present in section 5(3) of the 1994 Act, Article 4(4)(a) of the TMD 2008 (now Art 5(3)(a) of the TMD 2015), and Article 8(5) EUTMR. If there is a legitimate interest in using the mark, it is difficult to see why the same mark should not be registrable.[371]

---

[364] *Leidseplein Beheer BV v. Red Bull GmbH*, Case C-65/12 [2014] *ETMR* 24, [45], [48].

[365] See Chapter 41.

[366] *The London Taxi Corporation v. Frazer Nash* [2016] *EWHC* 52 (Ch), [268], [273]–[282] (suggesting the relevant factors under both enquiries overlap); *Lifestyle Equities CV v. Santa Monica Polo Club Ltd* [2017] *EWHC* 3313 (Ch), [121], [139]–[150].

[367] *Evegate Publishing Ltd v. Newsquest Media (Southern) Ltd* [2013] *EWHC* 1975 (Ch), [208] (use of the SOUTHERN FARMER for periodical was fair competition and thus with due cause). Cf. *Ukulele Orchestra of Great Britain v. Clausen* [2015] *EWHC* 1772 (IPEC), [71].

[368] *Comic Enterprises Ltd v. Twentieth Century Fox Film Corp* [2016] *EWCA Civ* 41, [122]–[123] (endorsing the balancing of interests approach); [145]–[147] (while a television series was an expressive work, there were alternative choices for its title as a trade mark, which diminished the potency of the expression argument).

[369] *Kenzo Tsujimoto v. OHIM*, Case T-414/13, EU:T:2015:923, [58] (no unconditional right to register one's own name as a trade mark, which might constitute due cause); *Arrom Conseil v. EUIPO*, Case T-358/15, EU:T:2016:490, [79]–[85] (belonging to the same family as the opponent NINA RICCI did not constitute due cause to use the family name Ricci); *Azumi Ltd v. Zuma's Choice Pet Products Ltd* [2017] *EWHC* 609 (IPEC), [86]–[87] (selection of the trade mark DINE IN WITH ZUMA for pet foods based on defendant's pet's name Zuma not due cause).   [370] *Leidseplein Beheer BV v. Red Bull GmbH*, Case C-65/12 [2014] *ETMR* 24, [46].

[371] The EUIPO decisions cited earlier in the context of an 'own name' due cause indicate it is at least arguable. The General Court directly addressed this in *Shoe Branding Europe BVBA v. EUIPO, Adidas*, Case T-85/16, EU:T:2018:109, [137]–[148] (prior long-standing use in Germany not sufficient to establish due cause, albeit only in the relative grounds context; while the two stripe mark could not be registered, its use might still be preserved if due cause was reconsidered in an infringement context).

3 RELATIVE GROUNDS IN RELATION TO EARLIER RIGHTS

In addition to refusal on the basis of earlier trade marks, a mark may also be rejected on the basis that it conflicts with 'earlier rights'. The relative grounds for refusal in relation to *earlier rights* are found in section 5(4)(a) and (b), and Article 8(4) EUTMR, respectively.[372] These provide that a trade mark shall not be registered where the use of the applicant's mark would be restrained under the law of passing off—section 5(4)(a)/Article 8(4)—or by some other right, such as copyright—section 5(4)(b)/Article 60(2) (in the context of invalidation of an EUTMR). We consider each in turn.[373]

3.1 UNREGISTERED MARKS

Section 5(4)(a) provides that a trade mark shall not be registered if, or to the extent that, its use in the United Kingdom is liable to be prevented by virtue of any rule of law (in particular, the law of passing off) protecting an unregistered trade mark or other sign used in the course of trade. It seems this section is intended to implement Article 4(4)(b) of the TMD 2008 (Article 5(4)(a) of the TMD 2015), although that provision uses the narrower language of 'rights to a non-registered trade mark'.[374]

Section 5(4)(a) will cover passing off if the requisites of goodwill,[375] misrepresentation, and likely damage can be established.[376] The burden of proving the existence of the earlier right falls upon the opponent.[377] In this context, it is important to note that 'in an action for passing off the likelihood of misrepresentation and the prospect of damage to goodwill must be sufficiently real and substantial to warrant the intervention of the court'.[378] Although it may be more costly and time-consuming to base an opposition on section 5(4) rather than section 5(2), there may be advantages in so doing, in that the tribunal may focus more upon how the mark has been used by the opponent and understood by the public. The Appointed Person has clarified that a likelihood of confusion claim under trade mark law is sufficiently distinct from a passing off claim to require the latter to be independently considered.[379] Under the

---

[372] EUTMR, Art. 60(1)(c) (formerly CTMR, Art 53(2)), recognizes the equivalent relative ground for invalidity.

[373] These 'earlier rights' are unharmonized. In *OHIM v. National Lottery Commission*, Case C-530/12P, EU:C:2014:186, it was held that while it is normally for the opponent or applicant for cancellation to demonstrate that the law, as well as the facts, establish its earlier right, the OHIM and General Court were entitled to apprise themselves independently as to the relevant national law. See also *macros consult GmbH v. OHIM*, Case T-579/10, EU:T:2013:232. For an overview of the types of rights that have been asserted and recognized, see EUIPO *Examination Guidelines*, Part D, Section 2, 20–7 (these include a right to a name, a right of personal portrayal, a copyright, or an industrial property right); *Cellap Laboratoire S.A. v. G.M. Holdings,* R 0581/2016–5 (8 March 2017) EUIPO BoA (recognizing company names, trade names, and Internet domain names as prior rights).   [374] *Wild Child Trade Mark* [1998] *RPC* 455, 457. See also EUTMR, Art. 8(4).

[375] But the objection is not available if the goodwill is residual and there is no continuing use in the course of trade: *Dimian AG v. OHIM*, T-581/11, EU:T:2013:553.   [376] See Chapters 32, 33, and 34.

[377] One as-yet-unresolved problem relates to the date on which the opponent must establish that there would have been passing off: is it the date on which the applicant commenced using the mark, or the date of application for the registration, or the date of registration? Cf. *Interlotto (UK) v. Camelot Group plc* [2004] *RPC* 186 (CA) (date of registration); *Last Minute Network v. OHIM*, Joined Cases T-114 and T-115/07 [2009] *ECR* II–1919 (General Court), [96] (implying date was application date); *Boxing Brands Ltd v. Sports Direct International* [2013] *EWHC* 2200 (Ch), [77], [95]–[96]; *Roger Maier v. Asos plc* [2013] *EWHC* 2831 (Ch), [71]–[81] (Rose J).   [378] *Corgi Trade Mark* [1999] *RPC* 549, 557.

[379] *Eriks Industrial Services Ltd v. Volvo Trademark Holding Aktiebolag*, O-061–15 (30 January 2015) Trade Marks Registry, [80]–[83] (Professor Annand, AP).

EUTMR regime, the EUIPO and General Court are gradually becoming more familiar with the doctrinal contours of passing off, as the basis for an opposition or invalidation based on relative grounds.[380]

In the case of EUTMs,[381] the owners of rights in unregistered marks—which (depending on national laws) may include appellations of origin, company names, and trade names—may oppose registration only if the sign is 'of more than mere local significance'.[382] The aim of the provision is to prevent a person from opposing registration of an EUTM by relying on a right that has no real presence on the relevant market.[383] The threshold appears to be quite high. In *Anheuser-Busch*,[384] the Court of Justice offered some useful guidance as to how this fell to be assessed.

(i) The criterion is directed at the use of the sign, rather than the scope of its protection.[385] The fact that a sign is protected, for example, throughout England and Wales does not demonstrate that its use was of more than mere local significance.

(ii) The use must be in the course of trade—that is, it must be commercial use, but not necessarily, given the varied nature of the rights, use 'as a trade mark' or 'genuine use'. [386]

(iii) There are two dimensions to the appraisal: first, was the use of the sign in the course of trade 'sufficiently significant'; and second, was the geographical extent of the use more than merely local—that is, 'in a substantial part of the territory' for which protection is claimed?[387] Although there are no *a priori* standards, this would typically exclude uses in a town or province.[388] Under section 47 of the Trade Marks Act (invalidity challenges), the Court of Appeal has clarified that while reputation may sometimes exist on such a small scale that it does not generate the requisite goodwill, as a general rule prior goodwill in a particular locality will be sufficient to oppose registration as well as subsequently invalidate a registered mark.[389]

---

[380] *Tilda Riceland Pvt Ltd v. OHIM*, Case T-136/14, EU:T:2015:734 (recognizing that under extended passing, an individual trader may claim a share in the goodwill in BASMATI rice, which generates a sufficient proprietary interest for an opposition); *Nelson Alfonso Egüed v. EUIPO, Jackson Family Farms*, Case T-45/16, EU:T:2017:518, [86]–[90] (while goodwill must have been acquired by the opponent before the contested EUTM was applied for, evidence of its continued existence at the date opposition is also required; the latter need not be proved if the temporal gap between the application and opposition is modest, since passing off recognizes residual goodwill).　　　　[381] Cf. *Saxon Trade Mark* [2003] *FSR* (39) 704, [32] (Laddie J).

[382] EUTMR, Art. 8(4).

[383] *Moreira de Fonseca Lda v. OHIM*, Joined Cases T-318–T-321/06 [2009] *ECR* II–663, [36]; *Anheuser-Busch Inc v. Budejovicky Budvar*, Case C-96/09P [2011] *ECR* I–2131 (ECJ, Grand Chamber), [157].

[384] Case C-96/09P [2011] *ECR* I–2131 (ECJ, Grand Chamber).

[385] Ibid., [158]. See also *Peek & Cloppenburg v. OHIM*, aff'd in Cases C-326/13P and C-325/13P, EU:C:2014:2059 (affirming the General Court's reasoning that 'more than mere local significance' does not require that the geographical scope of the right to prohibit the contested trade mark extends to the entire territory of a Member State, as opposed to a part of it); *Ugly Inc v. OHIM*, Case T-778/14, EU:T:2016:122 (evidence relating to a film and its soundtrack—COYOTE UGLY—could not be used to demonstrate that the chain of bars, on which the film was based, had reached the knowledge threshold required by Art. 8(4))

[386] *Anheuser-Busch Inc v. Budejovicky Budvar*, Case C-96/09P [2011] *ECR* I–2131 (ECJ, Grand Chamber), [144], [152].

[387] Ibid., [159]–[163]. It is worth noting the Court's qualification, however, that the test of use in a substantial part of the territory is appropriate only where the territory itself is 'other than local'. Presumably, Malta and Luxembourg might be regarded as merely local territories, from the perspective of the European Union.

[388] *Moreira de Fonseca Lda v. OHIM*, Joined Cases T-318–321/06 [2009] *ECR* II–663, [36]–[42]; cf. *Frost Products Ltd v. FC Frost Ltd* [2013] *EWPCC* 34.

[389] *Caspian Pizza Ltd v. Shah* [2017] *EWCA Civ* 1874 (Patten LJ) (also confirming that partial invalidity was not an option in these circumstances; the mark as a whole was invalidated based on the prior right).

3.2 COPYRIGHT, DESIGN RIGHT, AND REGISTERED DESIGN RIGHT

Section 5(4)(b) of the 1994 Act states that a trade mark shall not be registered if, or to the extent that, its use in the United Kingdom is liable to be prevented 'by virtue of any earlier right … in particular by virtue of the law of copyright, design right or registered designs'. This provision is permitted by, but does appear at first sight not take complete advantage of, Article 4(4)(c) of the TMD 2008 (now Article 5(4)(b) of the TMD 2015).[390] In contrast, there is no provision for opposition on this ground at the EUIPO. Article 60(2) EUTMR, however, does recognize conflict with a non-exhaustive list of earlier rights as a ground of invalidity.[391]

If someone owns copyright in the design of a device, the effect of section 5(4)(b) is that the applicant cannot obtain protection for the device as a trade mark without the copyright owner's consent. For example, in *Karo Step Trade Mark*,[392] an applicant succeeded in having a registered proprietor's device mark cancelled on the basis that the applicant owned artistic copyright in the mark.[393] Similarly, in *Oscar Trade Mark*,[394] the Academy of Motion Pictures successfully opposed the registration of a device mark comprising a silhouette of the famous Oscar statue given out at the annual Academy Awards. Graham J held that the statue was protected by copyright as a sculpture and that the silhouette device had been copied from it.[395] It should be recalled that, because single invented words and short phrases do not ordinarily provide information, instruction, or literary pleasure, they are not usually protected by copyright as literary works.[396] Therefore section 5(2)(b) will not enable the creator of a word or short phrase to prevent someone else from using the word or short phrase as a trade mark.[397]

3.3 UNAUTHORIZED REGISTRATION BY AGENT

An application for registration of a trade mark by an agent or representative of a person who is the proprietor of the mark in a Convention country is to be refused if that proprietor opposes the application.[398] The CFI has explained that this provision is intended to

---

[390] Although Art. 4(4)(c) refers also to a person's right to 'names' or 'personal portrayal' and s. 5(4)(b) does not refer to these, such interests may be protected under the law of passing off where use of a person's image implies endorsement (see Chapter 33, section 3.3.1, pp. 894–6) and through the extended law of confidentiality in circumstances that would implicate the individual's privacy (see Chapter 47). The former circumstances are covered by TMA 1994, s. 5(4)(a), but it is an open question whether the latter could be protected as an 'earlier right' under s. 5(4)(b). Insofar as the ECtHR has formulated rights to one's own name or image, it seems arguable that, despite having been shoehorned into the law of confidence, they should count as relevant rights.

[391] This provision, formerly CTMR, Art. 53(2), allows invalidity proceedings to be brought on the basis of earlier national or EU-wide rights, including a right to a 'name' or a right of 'personal portrayal'. On the former, see *Edwin v. OHIM*, Case C-263/09P [2011] *ECR* I–5853 (ECJ, Grand Chamber). The protection is, in contrast to Art. 8(4), not subject to requirements of use in the course of trade and that the sign be a more than mere local significance. It suggests that an invalidity claim as a form of 'other right' is easier to establish than an opposition to registration based on prior rights under passing off.

[392] [1977] *RPC* 255. The device must, in fact, amount to an infringement: *Jules Rimet Cup Ltd v. Football Association Ltd* [2008] *ECDR* (4) 43 (Deputy Judge Wyand QC).

[393] *Karo Step Trade Mark* [1977] *RPC* 255, 273.   [394] *Oscar Trade Mark* [1980] *FSR* 429.

[395] Ibid., 439, 440.   [396] See Chapter 4, section 3.7.2, pp. 111–12.

[397] But this is subject to a possible 'bad faith' challenge; see TMA 1994, s. 3(6), discussed in Chapter 37, section 4.4, pp. 1017–23.

[398] TMA 1994, s. 60; Paris, Art. 6*septies*; EUTMR, Art. 8(3). See A. Kur, 'Not Prior in Time, but Superior in Right: How Trademark Registrations Can be Affected by Third-party Interests in a Sign' [2013] *IIC* 790, 804–8 (discussing the existing situation and potential reforms).

prevent the former agent from unjustly benefiting from the knowledge and experience of its principal.[399] The opponent must establish that it is the proprietor of a mark in a Convention country, that the applicant is (or was) its 'agent or representative',[400] and that the application was not 'authorized'.[401] Where an agent applies for a trade mark using a corporate front, it may be necessary for the examiner to 'pierce the corporate veil' in order to reveal the true agency relationship. It has been observed that it is frequently easier to establish bad faith than that the applicant was an agent of the 'real trade mark owner'.[402]

---

[399] *DEF-TEC Defense Technology GmbH v. OHIM and Defense Technology Corporation of America*, Case T-6/05 [2006] *ECR* II–2671, [38]. For an overview, see EUIPO, *Examination Guidelines,* Part C, Section 3 ('Unauthorised Filing by Agents').

[400] *Safariland LLC v. OHIM*, Case T-262/09 [2011] *ECR* II –1629, [64]–[74].

[401] As regards the final element, the CFI has said that the consent must be 'clear, specific and unconditional': *DEF-TEC Defense Technology GmbH v. OHIM and Defense Technology Corporation of America*, Case T-6/05 [2006] *ECR* II–2671, [38]. See also *Ursula Adamowski v. OHIM*, Case T-537/10, EU:T:2012:634.

[402] *Target Fixings v. Brutt* [2007] *RPC* (19) 462, [101].

39

REVOCATION

1 INTRODUCTION

In spite of the examination process, the trade mark register is not a guarantee of the validity of trade marks.[1] There are two reasons why a mark might be removed from the register. The first is if it is held to be invalid. The grounds for invalidity are set out in section 47 of the Trade Marks Act 1994 and Articles 59 and 60 of the European Union Trade Marks Regulation (EUTMR).[2] These provide that a mark may be declared to be invalid on the basis that it was registered in breach of one of the absolute or relative grounds for refusal—topics that were dealt with earlier.[3]

The second reason why a mark might be removed from the register, which is the focus of this chapter, is if it is 'revoked'. There are four grounds for revocation and these are found in section 46 of the 1994 Act and Articles 18(1) and 58 EUTMR.[4] These grounds largely correspond to the provisions in Articles 10 and 12 of the TMD 2008 (and Articles 19 to 21 of the TMD 2015). Section 46/Article 58 provides that a mark may be revoked (in relation to all or some of the goods and services in respect of which it is registered)[5] on the grounds that:

(i) the trade mark has not been used for five years following the date of completion of the registration (that is, *non-use*);

(ii) use of the trade mark has been suspended for an uninterrupted period of five years;

(iii) the trade mark has become the 'common name in the trade' (that is, *generic*); or

(iv) the trade mark has been used in such a way that it is liable to mislead the public (that is, it is *deceptive*).

Section 46(4) of the Act provides that an application for revocation may be made by any person and may be made either to the Registrar or to the court.[6] The onus of proving that a mark should be revoked falls upon the party seeking revocation of the mark.[7] In relation to revocation for non-use, however, section 100 modifies the general position by

---

[1] TMA 1994, s. 70.   [2] Formerly, CTMR, Arts 52 and 53.

[3] See Chapters 36, 37, and 38. TMA 1994, s. 47(6), provides that, where the registration of a trade mark is declared invalid to any extent, the registration shall to that extent be deemed never to have been made.

[4] Formerly, CTMR, Art. 51.   [5] TMA 1994, s. 46(5); EUTMR, Art. 58(2) (ex CTMR, Art. 51(2)).

[6] As regards EUTMs, an application for revocation may be made either directly to the Cancellation Division of the EUIPO or by way of counterclaim to an action for infringement: EUTMR, Arts 58(1) and 128(1) (ex CTMR, Arts 51(1) and 100(1)). Non-use can also be put in issue in opposition proceedings at the EUIPO: EUTMR, Art. 47 (2) (ex CTMR, Art. 42(2)).   [7] TMA 1994, s. 72.

stating that the proprietor must show the use that has been made of the registered mark.[8] It should be noted that while the language of section 46(1) appears to confer a discretion on the Registrar to leave an otherwise revocable mark on the register (but not to remove a mark that is not revocable), the better view is that no such discretion exists.[9]

With these general points in mind, we now consider the grounds on which a registered mark may be revoked. It is convenient to deal with the two non-use grounds together.

2 NON-USE

The first ground on which a mark may be revoked is on the basis of 'non-use'. Revocation for non-use reflects the notion—also found in the law of passing off—that protection for marks is justified as a result of their use.[10] As Recital 24 EUTMR explains, 'there is no justification for protecting EU trade marks or, as against them, any trade mark which has been registered before them, except where the trade marks are actually used'.[11] It is only by virtue of use that marks come to communicate information to consumers and thus operate in a way that merits legal protection. Consequently, if a mark is not put into use within a reasonable period of registration, or use comes to be suspended, there is no good reason for preventing another trader from adopting that mark. Revocation for non-use helps to ensure that such unused marks, as well as marks that have been registered and used, but use of which has ceased,[12] can be removed from the register so that other traders can safely use similar, as well as identical, marks.[13] In recent years the problem of clutter or deadwood—the existence of marks on the register that are partly or wholly unused by their owners—has attracted the attention of policymakers, since clutter increases clearance costs for subsequent applicants.[14] Revocation for non-use also deters opportunistic

---

[8] Where an EUTM faces a revocation challenge, the burden of proof is on the proprietor to demonstrate relevant use; see EUTMR Art. 51(1)(a) read with EUTMDR, Art. 19(1).

[9] *Premier Brands UK v. Typhoon Europe* [2000] FSR 767, 811.

[10] *Invermont Trade Mark* [1997] RPC 125; *Cabanas Havana (Device) Trade Mark* [2000] RPC 26, 34. TMD 2008, Recital 9 refers to a desire to reduce the number of registered marks in order to prevent needless conflicts. This is reiterated in TMD 2015, Recital 31.

[11] The equivalent was CTMR, Recital 9.

[12] Jacob J figuratively referred to these signs as 'abandoned vessels in the shipping lanes of trade': *Re Laboratories Goëmar SA* [2002] ETMR (34) 382, 389, [19]. Advocate-General Colomer has called them 'corpses': *Silberquelle*, Case C-495/07 [2009] ECR I–137, [AG45]. See also Mummery LJ in *La Mer Technology v. Laboratoires Goëmar SA* [2006] FSR (5) 49, [14].

[13] Since the EUIPO previously allowed applications for very broad specifications, revocation plays a very significant role in restricting the rights of trade mark proprietors within appropriate confines. Many have expressed concern with cluttering of the register, but empirical evidence remains inconclusive: G. von Greavenitz et al., *Trade Mark Cluttering: An Exploratory Report* (2012) (not finding evidence of a systemic problem); Max Planck Institute, *Study on the Overall Functioning of the Community Trade Mark System* (2010), [1.32] *ff* (reviewing evidence), [1.39] ('There is no sustainable documentation showing that access to trade marks is substantially impaired by congestion of registers'), [4.44] ('Opinions differ as to whether congestion actually is a real problem in Europe').

[14] G. von Graevenitz, R. Ashmead, and C. Greenhalgh, *Cluttering and Non-Use of Trade Marks in Europe* (UK IPO Report 2015/48); US PTO, *Post Registration Proof of Use Pilot Final Report* (25 August 2015). For the related issue of whether we are running out of viable trade marks, see B. Beebe and J. Fromer, 'Are We Running Out of Trademarks? An Empirical Study of Trademark Depletion and Congestion' (2018) 131 *Harv L Rev* 945 (challenging the assumption that there is an inexhaustible supply of trade marks that are competitively effective). Cf. Max Planck Institute, *Study on the Overall Functioning of the Community Trade Mark System* (2011), [1.32] *ff*, [1.39], [4.44] (expressing scepticism about the impact of clutter).

stockpiling of good marks.[15] The relevant principles applicable to revocation have been conveniently summarized by Arnold J in *London Taxi* and in *W3*.[16]

2.1 RELEVANT PERIOD OF NON-USE

As indicated, there are two distinct types of non-use. The first ground for non-use is set out in section 46(1)(a)/Article 58(1)(a),[17] which provides that a trade mark may be revoked on the basis that:

> ... within the period of five years following the date of completion of the registration procedure it has not been put to genuine use in the United Kingdom, by the proprietor or with his consent, in relation to the goods or services for which it is registered, and there are no proper reasons for non-use ...[18]

In order for a mark to be revoked under section 46(1)(a), it is necessary to show that, in the five-year period after registration, the mark has not been put to genuine use.[19] The fact that the non-use must be for a five-year period recognizes that the registrant should be given a reasonably lengthy period of time in which to arrange the use of the mark. The Court of Justice has confirmed that a revocation challenge for non-use within this five-year grace period, for any of the goods or services applied for, is inadmissible; invalidation, based on the application being in bad faith, is the only alternative.[20]

The second ground of revocation for non-use is found in section 46(1)(b) and refers to an extended interruption or suspension of use. This states that a mark may also be revoked where 'use has been suspended for an uninterrupted period of five years, and there are no proper reasons for non-use'. The fact that the non-use must be for a five-year period recognizes that the goodwill built up from the use of a mark does not immediately disappear when the owner stops using the mark.[21]

A mark will not be revoked on the basis of non-use if use is commenced or resumed after the expiry of the five-year period and before the application for revocation is made.[22] Section 46(3) goes on to say, however, that the commencement or resumption of use is to be disregarded if it takes place 'within the period of three months before the making of the application'. This provision will not apply, however, 'where preparations for the commencement or resumption began before the proprietor became aware that the application might be made'. The three-month cut-off period operates to prevent trade mark

---

[15] As we saw in Chapter 37, section 4.4, pp. 1017–23, the United Kingdom treats applications without intent to use the mark as made in bad faith, contrary to s. 3(6), and thus treats any resulting registration as liable to be held invalid. However, 'bad faith' can be difficult to establish in cases of 'greedy', rather than dishonest, applications and s. 46 is better suited to dealing with such cases. While revocation for non-use has sometimes also been said to reflect a public interest in maintaining the register as a reflection of enforceable marks—see, e.g., *Imperial Group v. Philip Morris* [1982] *FSR* 72, 84—the truth is that neither the national or EUTM registers come close to mirroring the enforceable marks.

[16] *London Taxi Corp v. Frazer-Nash Research Ltd* [2016] *EWHC* 52 (Ch), [219], [227]; *W3 Ltd v. Easygroup Ltd* [2018] *EWHC* 7 (Ch), [194]–[202].

[17] Ex CTMR, Art. 51(1)(a);. For the international standards limiting such powers, see Paris, Art. 5C; TRIPS, Art. 19.

[18] This has been interpreted as five years from the day after registration, so that the earliest date of revocation for a mark registered on 9 February 1999 was 10 February 2006: *Valent Biosciences Trade Mark* [2007] *RPC* (34) 829.

[19] TMD 2008, Art. 12; TMD 2015, Art. 19. On the issue as to whether the Directive defined the precise dates, see *Armin Häupl v. Lidl Stiftung & Co. KG*, Case C-246/05 [2007] *ECR* I–4673.

[20] *Länsförsäkringar AB v. Matek A/S*, Case C-654/15, EU:C:2016:998, [26].

[21] Note the corresponding rules in relation to passing off in Chapter 32, section 2.2.2, pp. 876–7.

[22] TMA 1994, s. 46(3). But the Court of Justice has recognized that use after this period may be of relevance when assessing the extent to which use during the relevant period was genuine: *La Mer Technology Inc. v. Laboratoires Goëmar SA*, Case C-259/02 [2004] *ECR* I–1159, [31].

proprietors who have not used the mark from defeating an application for revocation for non-use by (re)commencing use as soon as they get wind of the interest of the applicant. Thus applicants are theoretically able to write to the proprietor before they apply to have a mark revoked and ask whether there has been any use of the mark. In so doing, they will be safe in the knowledge that, although their inquiry may prompt the trade mark proprietor to use the mark, this will not defeat their application for non-use.

One question that has arisen is whether it was possible to register the same mark twice. If so, the further question arises: how does this impact on the five-year non-use rule? In *Origins Natural Resources v. Origin Clothing*,[23] the claimant, who had taken an assignment of a mark registered for various clothes in Class 25, applied to register the same mark for a wider range of clothes. The defendant argued that this should not be allowed because it would undermine the five-year non-use rule. Jacob J disagreed:

> [I]f a man were to keep registering the same mark with no genuine intention of using it then he would lose his mark . . . If, on the other hand, a man had registered a mark with a bona fide intention to use it and found himself unable to use it for a number of years so that the mark was removable . . . but he still had genuine plans to use the mark then I see no reason why he should not apply again.[24]

The Court of Justice has recognized that registering repeatedly merely to avoid the consequences of revocation for non-use could well be bad faith.[25]

2.2 WHAT IS USE OF THE MARK?

The next question to ask in relation to section 46(1)(a)–(b)/Article 58(1)(a) is what is meant by 'use' of the mark. One preliminary point to note is that not all uses of a trade mark that would infringe (if made by a third party) amount to use for the purposes of defending an application for revocation.

2.2.1 Use

The most obvious way in which a registered proprietor will be able to show use is by demonstrating sales of articles that are marked with the sign. Other uses, such as advertising, may also be sufficient (as long as they are in connection with the anticipated sale of products bearing or provision of services under the mark).[26] Preparatory acts, such as gearing up a business to launch a product, are probably insufficient, at least if they are internal to the trade mark owner's organization. Similarly, negotiations between businesses referring to possible licensing of a mark do not count as use of the mark for the purposes of section 46.[27] In *Ansul BV v. Ajax Brandbeveiliging BV*, the Court indicated that what is required is:

> . . . use of the mark on the market for the goods or services protected by that mark and not just internal use by the undertaking concerned . . . Use of the mark must therefore relate to goods or services already marketed or about to be marketed and for which preparations by the undertaking to secure customers are under way, particularly in the form of advertising campaigns.[28]

---

[23] [1995] *FSR* 280.

[24] Ibid., 284.   [25] *pelicantravel.com v. OHIM*, Case T-136/11, EU:T:2012:689, [27]–[28].

[26] *Verein Radetzky Orden v. Bundesvereinigung Kameradschaft Feldmarschall Radetzky*, Case C-442/07, [2009] *ETMR* 14, [24] (use on publicity materials sufficient for a charitable organization).

[27] *Philosophy Inc v. Ferretti Studios* [2003] *RPC* (15) 287, 295–6, [18], [21] (Peter Gibson LJ). If this does count as use, it is not 'genuine use'.

[28] *Ansul BV v. Ajax Brandbeveiliging BV*, Case C-40/01 [2003] *ECR* I–2439, [37].

According to EUIPO practice, evidence indicating use in relation to an intermediary or distribution company will not be discounted as internal use.[29] On several occasions the General Court has considered the categories of evidence relevant for establishing genuine use for an EUTM, as well as the probative value of each category.[30] One interesting question that may need to be decided in due course is whether 'oral use' is relevant. Under section 103(2) of the Act, use is said to include 'use . . . otherwise than by means of a graphic representation'. This would suggest that oral use might suffice,[31] but in *Anheuser-Busch v. Bedejovicky Budvar*,[32] Deputy Judge Simon Thorley QC said that whether oral use by customers counts as use for section 46(1) 'raised complex questions of trade mark law'.

2.2.2 Use as a trade mark

It seems that 'use' must be 'as a trade mark' in the sense of indicating trade origin of the goods or services in question. In *Animated Music Ltd's Trade Mark*,[33] the UK Trade Marks Registry revoked the registration of the mark NELLIE THE ELEPHANT even though the proprietor had been able to show some use of the sign on brochures and invoices relating to the licensing of cartoons. The Registry found that the evidence was at best evidence of use of the sign as the title of the cartoon or name of the character, not use 'as a trade mark'—that is, to indicate the trade origin of any of the services. Where a figurative 'cotton flower' mark was being used to certify the composition and quality of cotton textiles from a variety of different commercial sources via a licensing scheme—in other words, being tacitly used as a certification mark despite being registered as an individual mark—the Court of Justice confirmed that use which did not align with the essential origin-indicating function of a mark would not save it from revocation.[34] This was notwithstanding the fact that the use reinforced other recognized functions such as the quality or guarantee function of a trade mark. Use of the sign to indicate a distinct commercial origin for products was an essential prerequisite for withstanding a revocation challenge. It follows from the case law that use of marks to decorate products—or which would be understood (by the average consumer) in that way—will not amount to 'genuine use'; similarly, use in a descriptive sense will not amount to relevant use of the mark.[35] Use as a corporate name

---

[29] EUIPO, *Examination Guidelines*, Part C, Section 6, [2.3.2]. See also *Fruit of the Loom, Inc. v. EUIPO*, Case T-431/15, EU:T:2016:395 (external use of a mark does not necessarily mean use aimed at end consumers; use directed at professional intermediaries, including resellers, is relevant).

[30] See, e.g., *Futbol Club Barcelona v. EUIPO*, Case T-614/14, EU:T:2016:448 (evidence should establish extent, place, and time of use); *Marcas Costa Brava, SL v. EUIPO*, Case T-686/15, EU:T:2017:53, [56]–[63] (simply producing copies of promotional material is not sufficient; evidence of its distribution to the public is required); *M.I. Industries, Inc. v. EUIPO*, Case T-30/16, EU:T:2017:77, [35]–[48] (reviewing case law on probative value of trade mark owner's own affidavit in support of use).

[31] *Ensure Plus Trade Mark*, O/389/02 (26 September 2002), [39].

[32] [2002] *RPC* (38) 748, [51]. See also *Second Skin Trade Mark* [2002] *ETMR* (CN3) 326 (TM Registry) (even if oral use would suffice, mere use by customers would not).   [33] [2004] *ETMR* (79) 1076.

[34] *W.F. Gözze Frottierweberei GmbH v. Verein Bremer Baumwollbörse*, Case C-689/15, EU:C:2017:434.

[35] *Henkell & Co v. EUIPO*, Case T-20/15, EU:T:2016:218 (PICCOLO used on bottles of sparkling wine to describe a bottle of a certain size and not as a trade mark); *Futbol Club Barcelona v. EUIPO*, Case T-614/14, EU:T:2016:448 (CULE, the mark being challenged, was conventionally used to denote a supporter or player of FC Barcelona and not use to indicate commercial origin); *Polytetra v. OHIM, EI du Pont de Nemours*, Case T-660/11, EU:T:2015:387, [80] (the 'presence of the TEFLON mark on third parties' final products guides the consumer's choice towards the product by reference to the positive experience relating to the coating or certain functional characteristics of the product owing to the presence of the raw material designated by that mark', which means it does not satisfy the essential function). Other jurisdictions have also adopted this approach to genuine use. See, e.g., *FMTM Distribution Ltd v. Van Cleef & Arpels SA* [2017] SGIPOS 6 (IPO Singapore) (instead of being used to indicate commercial origin, MYSTERY SET described the setting of gemstones with no visible mounting).

may not of itself justify maintenance of the mark.[36] Equally, evidence of use of a mark on the top of invoices, with addresses, etc. does not of itself prove genuine use.[37]

2.2.3 Use via associated marks

There are two ways in which a trade mark, despite not being used as registered, may nevertheless satisfy the genuine use requirement. The first is where the mark is used in a modified form. The second is when the mark is used as part of a composite mark or constellation of other marks. Each is considered in turn later, but the underlying reason for not requiring strict conformity between the mark as registered and as used is so that it can 'be better adapted to the marketing and promotion requirements of the goods or services concerned'.[38]

As long as the changes do not alter the distinctive character of the mark, the use of the modified mark will be recognized as use of the registered mark (unless the modified version is registered in its own right).[39] Section 46(2) explains that 'use of a trade mark includes use in a form differing in elements which do not alter the distinctive character of the mark in the form in which it was registered'.[40] According to Lord Walker in *Anheuser-Busch v. Bedejovicky Budvar*,[41] it is for the tribunal first to ascertain the points of difference between the mark as used and the mark as registered. Having done this, the tribunal should then ask whether the differences alter the distinctive character of the mark as registered. The distinctive character in issue is what makes the mark 'in some degree striking and memorable', as judged from the point of view of the Registrar (rather than the average consumer), who is concerned with 'the mark's likely impact on the average consumer'.[42]

The question of whether a change to a mark alters the distinctive character of that mark is one of 'first impression' (and thus one that an appeal court should be reluctant to overturn).[43] Much will depend upon the type of mark (whether a word or device mark), the way in which the mark is typically used and understood (whether visually, aurally, or conceptually), and the way in which the mark is varied. To change the distinctive character of the mark, it is necessary to alter the identity or individuality of the mark.[44] The registered mark and variant being used are compared for equivalence on visual, aural, and conceptual grounds.[45] According to the General Court, for composite marks consisting of elements this 'calls for an assessment of the distinctive or dominant character of the

---

[36] While use as a trade name is not necessarily use as a trade mark, certain uses of a trade name might be: *Céline SARL v. Céline SA*, Case C-17/06 [2007] *ECR* I–7041. See Chapter 40, section 9, pp. 1115–16. More specifically, where the proprietor affixes the sign consisting of the company name to products it sells, or uses it in such a manner that an origin-indicating link is established in the minds of consumers, this may qualify as the type of use which prevents revocation. Cf. *M.I. Industries, Inc. v. EUIPO*, Case T-30/16, EU:T:2017:77 [64]–[66] (company name not being used as a trade mark).

[37] *Orient Express Trade Mark* [1996] *RPC* 25, 42. In *Euromarket Designs Inc. v. Peters* [2000] *ETMR* 1025, [56], Jacob J stated that use as a shop name was not use in relation to goods.

[38] *Specsavers International Healthcare Ltd v. Asda Stores Ltd,* Case C-252/12 [2013] *ETMR* 46, [29].

[39] *Il Ponte Finanziaria SpA v. OHIM*, Case C-234/06P [2007] *ECR* I–7333, [86]. See further *Bernhard Rintisch v. Klaus Eder*, Case C-553/11, EU:C:2012:671, [21], [22]. Cf. *Alcohol Countermeasure Systems v. EUIPO*; Case T-638/15, EU:T:2017:229, [21]–[25] (prior word mark registered by the same proprietor could be relied on to establish use for the later mark being challenged, which did not vary in terms of its distinctiveness); on appeal as C-340/17P.   [40] TMD 2008, Art. 10(1)(a); TMD 2015, Art 16(5)(a).

[41] [2003] *RPC* (25) 477 (CA), 490, [41].

[42] Ibid. Sir Martin Nourse said that the Registrar's failure to apply the right test would not have affected his view of the mark because the Registrar 'would necessarily have to view the matter through the eyes of the average consumer': ibid., 483, [10].   [43] Ibid.

[44] The Court of Justice talks about 'a slightly different form': *Il Ponte Finanziaria*, Case C-234/06P [2007] *ECR* I–7333, [86].   [45] *EUIPO v. Cactus SA*, Case C-501/15P [2018] *ETMR* 4, [68]–[71].

components added, on the basis of the intrinsic qualities of each of those components, as well as on the relative position of the different components within the arrangement of the trade mark'.[46] In the case of short or simple marks, or marks with very little distinctive character, a slight modification may mean that use will not sustain the registration.[47] So, for example, the (then) Court of First Instance (CFI) has held that the mark J. GIORGI was not used on invoices that bore the terms GIORGI, MISS GIORGI, or GIORGI LINE, because the distinctive character of the J. GIORGI mark was affected by such uses.[48] ('Giorgi' was viewed as a common name and so of low inherent distinctiveness.) In contrast, in the case of a word-and-device mark, substantial alteration to the device may have little impact if the average consumer sees the word as dominating the mark.[49] This was the case in *Budweiser*,[50] in which a registration of BUDWEISER BUDBRÄU in a stylized form was successfully maintained by relying on use of the words in block capitals as a circular surround to a device consisting of a castle and shield.[51] Similar reasoning almost certainly explains the CFI's decision that variations in the style of QUANTIÈME (capitalization, modifying, and underlining the 'Q') did not alter the distinctive character of the mark for watches.[52] If a mark includes a distinctive word or logo as its dominant element, additions or deletion of descriptive terms to a mark will not ordinarily affect the distinctive character.[53] Similarly, minor stylistic changes which are ornamental in nature will not be considered relevant for revocation purposes.[54]

In *Specsavers*, the Court of Appeal has held that when assessing genuine use, it is relevant that a mark registered in black and white has been used in a specific colour, provided

[46] See, e.g., *hyphen GmbH v. EUIPO, Skylotec Gmbh*, Case T-146/15, EC:T:2016:469, [37] (disagreeing with the EUIPO and somewhat controversially holding that the addition of a surrounding circle to an otherwise simple 'dog bone' or dumbbell figurative mark would *not* alter its distinctive character, since the circle itself was a basic geometric shape).

[47] The converse is also true: *Toni Klement v. EUIPO*, Case T-211/14, EU:T:2015: 688, [27]–[42]; aff'd C-642/15P, EU:C:2016:918 (French) (where a sufficiently distinctive shape mark for a stove was regularly used along with the word mark BULLERJAN, it could withstand the addition of the word, which would not alter its distinctiveness).

[48] *Laboratorios RTB, SL v. OHIM*, T-156/01 [2003] *ECR* II–2789, [44]. See, to similar effect, *El Corte Inglés, SA v. OHIM*, T-39/10, EU:T:2012:502 (E. TUCCI altered distinctive character of EMIDIO TUCCI).

[49] *J & F Participações SA v. OHIM/Plusfood Wrexham*, Case T-324/09 [2011] *ECR* II 24*, [36] (addition of ribbon to registered word FRIBO did not alter distinctive character), *Victor International GmbH v. EUIPO*, Case T-204/14, EU:T:2016:448, [23]–[42] (the word element VICTORIA remained sufficiently stable, despite being accompanied by a figurative element which varied slightly, or was written in colour, or set within a circle and accompanied by other figurative and word elements).

[50] *Anheuser-Busch v. Bedejovicky Budvar* [2003] *RPC* (25) 477 (CA).

[51] The Registrar accepted that the use of the words in this way was use of the mark in a form that did not alter its distinctive character, because the average consumer would view the graphic as use of the words (the underlining and different fonts not detracting from, or adding anything to, 'the central message'). In the Court of Appeal, Sir Martin Nourse observed that the Registrar had legitimately found that 'the words have a dominance which reduces to insignificance the other recognisable elements': ibid., 483, [12]. Lord Walker, sitting in the Court of Appeal, said that if it had been for him to decide, he would have taken a view more like that of the judge than the Registrar—but since the Registry had not erred in principle, it was not for the High Court or the Court of Appeal to replace the Registrar's assessment with its own: ibid., 491, [52] ff.

[52] *Devinlec Développement Innovations Leclerc SA v. OHIM*, T-147/03 [2006] *ECR* II–11, appealed on a different ground and aff'd as *T.I.M.E. ART v. OHIM*, Case C-171/06P [2007] I–41*.

[53] *GfK v. OHIM and BUS*, T-135/04 [2005] *ECR* II–4865, [35]–[41]; *New Yorker SHK Jeans GmbH & Co. KG v. OHIM*, T-415/09 [2011] *ECR* II–366, [63]–[64]; *Nirvana Trade Mark*, O/262/06 (18 September 2006) (AP, Arnold QC); *OAO Alfa-Bank v. alpha Bank AE* [2011] *EWHC* 2021 (Ch) (Briggs J).

[54] *Galletas Gullón v. EUIPO, O2 Holdings*, Case T-404/16, EU:T:2017:745 (where the mark consisted of the trade dress of a packet of biscuits, alterations to some of the colours or geometrical shapes used on the packaging did not significantly alter the overall impression of the mark).

the use in that colour affects the perception of the mark by the average consumer in a way that could affect its distinctiveness.[55] On a related note, the EUIPO has issued a common practice communication, which departs from the previous practice that marks registered in black and white were deemed to be registered for all colours.[56] For participating registries, the registration will now be restricted to the black and white depiction, thereby limiting the scope of the mark. However when assessing genuine use, a change in colour in the marketplace context will not be considered to alter distinctive character, provided the word and figurative elements are the same, the contrast of shades remains stable, and the combination of colours does not independently possess distinctiveness.

Turning to the second scenario where there is a gap between registration and actual usage, difficult questions have been raised about whether use of a mark in combination with other marks amounts to 'genuine use'. In *Rintisch*,[57] the Court of Justice ruled that the mark PROTI had been used, even though the only use was PROTI-PLUS and the combination PROTI-PLUS was itself a registered mark. It is notable that the combination derived its distinctiveness primarily from its incorporation of the word PROTI. However, the Court has found there to have been use of a mark even in situations in which its use is combined with a distinctive sign that has itself been registered. Thus, in *Colloseum Holding*,[58] the Court held that there might be use of a registered mark comprising a red tab (to be positioned on the back pocket of jeans) even though the only examples of use of the tab were in tandem with the word LEVI's, the word superimposed over the red flag. Likewise, the Court held that Specsavers' registered mark comprising two black intersecting ovals was used, even though the only use was of the mark with the words SPECSAVERS superimposed (see Fig. 38.1, section 2.3.1, p. 1034).[59]

These cases are, at first blush, difficult to square with the general rule that use of a mark that is different from the mark as registered counts as use of the latter mark only where the differences do not alter the distinctive character of the earlier mark. After all, the words LEVI's and SPECSAVERS are themselves distinctive (as demonstrated by their registration, but also as evident from their use), and their addition must therefore have altered the distinctive character of the red flag or overlapping oval marks. However, the explanation appears to be that, despite the combination of the two marks physically (by superimposition of the words on the devices), both marks are regarded as retaining their distinctness to consumers, who view the combination as the use of two (or possibly three) individual marks: the word, the device, and the combination itself. In some situations, the mark being challenged loses its significance amidst the other signs and the revocation action is successful.[60]

2.2.4 Use by a licensee

According to section 46(1)(a)–(b)/Article 18 read with Article 58(1)(a), the use must be by the proprietor or with *their consent*.[61] It will be for the proprietor of a mark to demonstrate

---

[55] *Specsavers International Healthcare Ltd v. Asda Stores Ltd (Registrar of Trade Marks Intervening)* [2014] *EWCA Civ* 1294, [22], [33] (Kitchin LJ).

[56] TMDN, *Common Communication on the Common Practice of the Scope of Protection of Black and White Marks* (15 April 2014).   [57] *Bernhard Rintisch v. Klaus Eder*, Case C-553/11, EU:C:2012:671.

[58] *Colloseum Holding AG v. Levi Strauss & Co.*, Case C-12/12 [2013] *ETMR* 34.

[59] *Specsavers International Healthcare Ltd v. Asda Stores*, Case C-252/12 [2013] *ETMR* 46.

[60] *Labeyrie v. EUIPO*, Case T-766/15, EU:T:2017:123 (French) (where a figurative mark consisting of a pattern of golden fish on a blue background, registered for foodstuffs including fish (which had low inherent distinctiveness to begin with) was used along with the word mark LABEYRIE, this altered the distinctive character of the pattern).

[61] TMD 2008, Arts 10, 12; TMD 2015, Arts 16, 19; TRIPS, Art. 19(2); *Martin Y Paz Diffusion SA v. Depuydt*, Case C-661/11 [2014] *ETMR* 6, [AG64].

consent, although a tribunal may infer this from the fact that the proprietor has evidence of use by a third party.[62] In *Hebrew University of Jerusalem v. Continental Shelf 128 Ltd (Einstein)*,[63] the applicant sought revocation of the mark EINSTEIN for clothing on the basis that it had not been used between 1999 and 2004. The proprietor provided a statement by a sales executive from a different company, Hornby Street Ltd, that it had used the mark on swing tags, sew-in labels, and invoices. Hornby Street Ltd was described as a sister company of the proprietor, but no further evidence of a connection was given. While the examiner accepted that the evidence established use, he held that the proprietor had not shown the use was *with its consent*. This was because, in his view, what was required was not mere consent, but some level of control. On appeal, the Appointed Person, Geoffrey Hobbs QC, conducted a thorough analysis of the history of the Trade Marks Directive to conclude that there was no requirement that the proprietor control the quality of the goods sold under the sign, so long as they have consented to the use—that is, that there existed an economic link between the proprietor and the user. Here, the common owner-ship of the two firms was sufficient. In the context of EUTMs, the General Court has also confirmed the relevance of use by a licensee in helping to sustain the registration.[64]

2.3 GENUINE USE

For a mark to remain on the register, it is necessary to show that it has been put to genu-ine use in the United Kingdom (or, in the case of an EUTM, in the European Union). Two understandings of 'genuine use' have been employed in the case law.[65] According to the first understanding, any use that is not artificial, non-sham, or merely to retain the mark will suffice. In contrast, the second view, of 'genuineness' of use, demands real substantial use in the marketplace, such as to bring the mark to the attention of consum-ers. Sometimes, these tests are articulated in terms of the subjective genuineness of the use (where the test is whether there was honest intent) and objective genuineness (where the test is ordinary commercial standards).[66] The key difference is that if the test is honest use, it can be *de minimis* (although it is also possible that substantial use in a trade mark protection programme might be disregarded); for objective genuineness, there must be substantial use (although what is 'substantial' will vary from sector to sector).

It is now clear that the Court of Justice has adopted a test that is much closer to the 'sub-jective approach', but where the use must still be real or meaningful. The present approach stresses that there is no *de minimis* threshold—subjectively honest but very modest use can preserve a mark—but tribunals cannot entirely escape from the question of whether 'enough' use has been made of the mark to preserve it. This approach was developed by the Court of Justice in two important decisions. In *Ansul BV v. Ajax Brandbeveiliging BV*,[67] Ansul had registered the mark MINIMAX in the Benelux countries in 1971 for fire extinguishers and associated products. However, it had not sold any extinguishers since

---

[62] *The Sunrider Corp. v. OHIM*, Case C-486/04P [2006] *ECR* I–4237.

[63] *Einstein Trade Mark* [2007] *RPC* (23) 539.

[64] See, e.g., *Matrazen Concord v. OHIM*, Case T-258/13, EU:T:2015:207, [38]–[44]; *Windrush Aka LLP v. EUIPO*, Case T-336/15, EU:T:2017:197 (where the EUTM proprietor claims third party use constitutes genuine use, this implies use with consent and the burden of proof shifts to the revocation applicant to show no consent), on appeal as Case C-325/17P; *IR v. EUIPO*, Case T-132/15, EU:T:2017:162, [81]–[86] (evidence relating to licence agreements being merely offered or negotiated was insufficient to establish actual use).

[65] L. Bently and R. Burrell, 'The Requirement of Trade Mark Use' (2002) 13 *AIPJ* 181.

[66] *Gerber Trade Marks* [2003] *RPC* (34) 637, 641 (Auld LJ) (a 1938 Act case).

[67] Case C-40/01 [2003] *ECR* I–2439.

1989. Nevertheless, Ansul had sold component parts for the extinguishers, repaired and maintained them, and used the mark MINIMAX on invoices in relation to such services. A German company called Minimax GmbH had made and sold fire extinguishers, and had owned a German registration for MINIMAX for 50 years. In 1994, Ajax, a subsidiary of the German company, began to use the MINIMAX trade mark in the Netherlands. Ajax sought revocation of Ansul's 1971 registration and Ansul sought an injunction against Ajax to prevent it from using the MINIMAX mark in the Benelux countries. The outcome of the case depended on whether Ansul's mark had been put to genuine use in the period after 1989, when it had been used in relation to components and repairs.

The Court of Justice stated that the notion of genuine use required a uniform interpretation throughout the European Union. It said that token use, serving solely to attempt to preserve rights, was not genuine use.[68] Genuine use must be consistent with the essential function of a trade mark, to guarantee the identity of the origin of goods or services to the consumer. It concluded that such use required:

> . . . use of the mark on the market for the goods or services protected by that mark and not just internal use by the undertaking concerned . . . Use of the mark must therefore relate to goods or services already marketed or about to be marketed and for which preparations by the undertaking to secure customers are under way, particularly in the form of advertising campaigns.[69]

Moreover, the Court observed that, when assessing whether use was genuine, it was necessary to take account of all of the facts and circumstances to decide whether 'the commercial exploitation of the mark is real, in particular whether such use is warranted in the economic sector concerned to maintain or create a share in the market for the goods or services protected by the mark'.[70] Use of a mark need not always be quantitatively significant for it to be genuine. Finally, the Court indicated that use in relation to components or after-sales services could be use that 'related to' goods, even though the goods for which the mark was registered were no longer being sold. The Court declined to say anything about the specific case between Ansul and Ajax, pointing out that this was a matter for the national courts.

Although some aspects of the Court's judgment are a little vague, further clarification was offered in response to a reference from the United Kingdom. In *Re Laboratories Goëmar SA*,[71] the question was whether there was 'genuine use' sufficient to resist a section 46 revocation of the sign LABORATOIRE DE LA MER for cosmetics containing marine products. The proprietor was a small French company specializing in seaweed products and the applicant for revocation, Huber Laboratories, intended to launch a huge range of skincare products under the LA MER name. The proprietor had made sales worth only £800 to a Scottish agent. There was no suggestion that the use by Goëmar was 'token'— that is, merely for the purpose of maintaining the mark on the register. Jacob J referred a number of issues to the Court of Justice.

The Court responded that even minimal use (not quantitatively significant) can qualify as genuine, 'on condition that it is deemed to be justified, in the economic sector concerned, for the purpose of preserving or creating market share for the goods or services protected by the mark'.[72] That requires an assessment by the national court, on the facts in front of it. In certain cases, the criterion might be met by use of a mark by a single client, but it would have to appear that the operation had 'a genuine commercial justification

---

[68] Ibid., [36].   [69] Ibid., [37].   [70] Ibid., [38].   [71] [2006] *FSR* (5) 49.
[72] *La Mer v. Goëmar*, Case C-259/02 [2004] *ECR* I–1159, [21]–[27].

for the proprietor of the mark'. However, the need for such an assessment on the facts precludes any *a priori*, abstract, quantitative threshold.

Armed with the advice of the Court of Justice, Blackburne J held that the sales were not sufficient to constitute genuine use.[73] However, on appeal, the Court of Appeal reversed.[74] The Court said that the use could not be considered 'internal': the Scottish agent was an independent entity and not, for example, a subsidiary of Goëmar. Goëmar was genuinely trying to sell its goods—that is, to gain a share in the market; the fact that it had not been particularly successful and that the goods had not reached the attention of consumers was irrelevant. It was enough that there was a genuine attempt to sell goods bearing the mark. The Court of Appeal warned that any other approach would have amounted to setting a quantitative threshold (contrary to the Court of Justice's view). Neuberger LJ (as he then was) indicated that an approach that required the courts and offices to assess whether use was substantial would be difficult, expensive, and time-consuming to apply.[75]

The Court of Justice had stated that genuine use requires use that is warranted in the marketplace to maintain or establish market share. This criterion, which requires the assessor to take account of the kind of goods concerned and not to decide mechanically by reference to predetermined percentages, could easily have been understood as requiring some substantial presence. In contrast, the Court of Appeal has interpreted *Ansul* and *Goëmar* as merely requiring use as a trade mark that is neither token nor purely internal. This position had already been advocated by the Appointed Person and the Irish Patents Office,[76] and it looks likely to remain the standard at least for the foreseeable future.[77] However, courts continue to return to the issue of whether very modest commercial use (that is neither token nor sham) will constitute genuine use.[78] It has been clarified that every commercial use will not automatically qualify as genuine use.[79] After all, a trade mark proprietor is given a five-year period of exclusivity in which to establish usage. If the proprietor cannot show that it has made an impression on the market by then, ought they really be allowed to retain their registration?[80]

The Court has held that promotional use will not be 'genuine use'.[81] Thus where the mark WELLNESS had been registered for clothing and non-alcoholic drinks, but the only occasion on which it had been used for drinks was as a promotional gift when WELLNESS

---

[73] *La Mer Technology Inc. v. Laboratoires Goemar SA* [2004] *EWHC* 2960, [2005] *FSR* (29) 668.

[74] *Laboratoires Goemar SA v. La Mer Technology Inc.* [2005] *EWCA Civ* 978.   [75] Ibid., [46].

[76] *Police Trade Mark* [2004] *RPC* (35) 693 (Arnold QC); *Stefcom SPA's Trade Mark; Application for Revocation by Travel Hurry Projects Ltd* [2005] *ETMR* (82) 960.

[77] See also *MFE Marienfelde GmbH v. OHIM*, Case T-334/01 [2004] *ECR* II-2787; *La Mer Technology, Inc. v. OHIM*, Case T-418/03 [2007] *ECR* II-125, in which the CFI viewed minimal use as sufficient in relation to the relevant goods.

[78] In some situations the use will be too modest—bearing in mind the economic sector concerned and with an eye to market share—to preserve the mark. See *J and J Crombie Ltd v. Nutter (Holdings) Ltd* [2013] *EWHC* 3459 (Ch) (Asplin J) (trade mark examiner's decision upheld that minimal use did not amount to genuine use); *Reber Holding GmbH & Co KG v. OHIM*, Case C-141/13, EU:C:2014:2089 (French and German) (in the context of the German confectionary market, a small volume of handmade chocolates sold in one town did not amount to genuine use).

[79] *Reber Holding GmbH & Co KG v. OHIM*, Case C-141/13, EU:C:2014:2089, [32] (French and German); *SdS InvestCorp AG v. Memory Opticians Ltd* [2016] *ETMR* 8 (AP, Prof. Annand); *Nike Innovate C.V.'s Trade Mark Application* [2017] *FSR* 8 (AP, Alexander QC) (for an EUTM, establishing non-sham and commercial use may still be insufficient to prevent revocation, where the use is otherwise small scale and geographically restricted).

[80] See Kerly, [12–064]; cf. the concept of signs of more than 'local significance', where the Court has required some evidence of impact on the market: Chapter 38, section 3.1, pp. 1073–4.

[81] *Silberquelle*, Case C-495/07 [2009] *ECR* I-137, [20]-[22].

clothing was sold, the Court indicated that there was no genuine use in relation to drinks. This was because the use was not 'to create or preserve an outlet for' drinks.[82] In so holding, the Court emphasized that, given the number of marks and potential conflicts, it was 'essential' to maintain rights only where the mark has been used on the market for the relevant goods or services.[83]

2.4 USE IN RELATION TO THE GOODS OR SERVICES FOR WHICH THE MARK IS REGISTERED

While the paradigmatic use of a trade mark is considered to be its application directly to products or their packaging, legislation broadens this out to cover use 'in relation to' or 'in connection with' products (including brochures, flyers, invoices, and advertisements at places of sale). To ensure that a mark is not revoked because of non-use, the mark must be used in relation to *the* goods or services for which the mark is registered.[84] In general, therefore, use in relation to similar goods is *not* use in relation to the goods for which the mark is registered. However, it seem there may be use *in relation to* the goods or services for which the mark is registered, when the proprietor applies the marks either on parts to be used in the repair of the goods for which the sign is registered, or in connection with services involving repair or maintenance of the goods.[85]

A related problem arises if a proprietor uses the registered mark on promotional goods such as T-shirts: does this amount to use *in relation to* T-shirts or only in relation to the goods that are being promoted? This is probably a question of fact, the answer being dependent on how the average consumer would perceive the use.[86] It should be observed, however, that such use could be seen as both use in relation to T-shirts *and* the goods promoted on the shirt. In *Premier Brands UK v. Typhoon Europe*,[87] the proprietor of the TYPHOO mark for domestic utensils and containers resisted revocation by claiming that it had used the mark on tea canisters, biscuit barrels, etc. Neuberger J said that although the public would understand the use as promoting TYPHOO tea, it did not follow that the public would not *also* assume that the goods had been marketed by or with the approval of the makers of TYPHOO tea.

Evidence relating merely to advertising or promotional activities, without corresponding evidence of the actual sales and distribution of products, is unlikely to sustain a registration.[88] Finally, the difficult question of partial revocation—where the mark has been used only in relation to a subset of the goods or services applied for—is considered in greater detail later in this chapter.

[82] Ibid., [18]. But cf. *Antartica Srl v. OHIM*, C-320/07P [2009] *ECR* I–28*, [28]–[30] (on non-profit-making uses).

[83] *Silberquelle*, Case C-495/07 [2009] *ECR* I–137, [19], referring with approval to Advocate-General's description of unused trade marks as 'corpses' and the goal of preventing trade mark offices becoming 'cemeteries': ibid., [AG45], [AG55].

[84] TMA 1994, s. 45(1)(a); TMD 2008, Art. 10; TMD 2015, Art. 17; EUTMR, Art. 18(1) (ex CTMR, Art. 15(1)).

[85] *Ansul v. Ajax*, Case C-40/01 [2003] *ECR* I–2439, [41]–[42]. This perhaps reflects an inclination to interpret the requirement of use more generously in relation to marks that have been used and retain residual goodwill than to marks for which a substantial goodwill has never been established.

[86] *Young v. Medici* [2004] *FSR* (19) 383, [3] (Jacob J) (no use for boxes and packaging by selling trade marked goods in packaging). [87] [2000] *FSR* 767. See also *Elle Trade Marks* [1997] *FSR* 529.

[88] *Arrieta D. Gross v. OHIM*, Case T-298/10, EU:T:2012:113, [60]–[70] (advertising in specialist circles did not establish whether the services were sold or offered for sale to the public).

2.5 PLACE OF USE

In relation to British marks, the relevant use must take place in the United Kingdom. An advertisement released in a foreign jurisdiction may also constitute use, so long as the advertisement is available in the United Kingdom. For example, in *Elle Trade Marks*,[89] the proprietor of the mark ELLE for soap and perfume sought to rely on the fact that soaps and other cosmetics branded with ELLE had been offered for sale in the French edition of a well-known woman's magazine, of which the appellant was also proprietor. It was accepted that the French edition was sold in the United Kingdom and that it contained an advertisement for ELLE soap, which could be obtained by readers in Britain either by going to Paris or by ordering it by phone. Although there was no evidence of actual sale, Lloyd J held that this was a genuine use within the relevant class of goods. In contrast, mere use on an Internet site is not use in the United Kingdom: as the Registrar, Mr Salthouse, has said, were the position to be otherwise, 'the simple creation of a website would provide use in every country in the world on the basis that it could be accessed globally'.[90] It seems that, in such cases, what is required is evidence of a site targeting customers in the United Kingdom.[91]

A special provision of a trade mark includes situations in which the mark is affixed to goods or to the packaging of goods in the United Kingdom solely for export.[92] This has been interpreted broadly as including the situation in which the proprietor attaches the mark to goods in the United Kingdom and transfers them to a foreign subsidiary, rather than only circumstances in which export is made to an independent business abroad.[93] If this is right, the provision must be understood as an exception to the general requirement that the use be other than internal to the proprietor's organization.

In relation to EUTMs, the relevant use must be in the European Union.[94] It was unclear for some time whether this required use in more than one EU Member State.[95] In *Leno Marken*,[96] the Court rejected the 'one state' solution—that is, the view that use in one state was necessarily sufficient. In this case, Hagelkruis applied to the Benelux trade mark office to register OMEL for advertising and marketing services. The application was opposed by Leno Merken on the basis of a Community trade mark registration for ONEL, also for services in Class 35. It was accepted that there was a likelihood of confusion, but the opponent had demonstrated that it had used ONEL only in the Netherlands. The question arose whether this was sufficient to maintain a Community mark (under Article 15 CTMR). The Court indicated that Council and Community Minutes on this issue were non-binding[97] and that the question of whether there was genuine use in the European Union was to be assessed without reference to the territorial borders of member states.[98] The question is whether there has been use to maintain or create a market share in the EU market for those goods or services (which might require more use than to create or maintain a

---

[89] Ibid. Cf. Chapter 40, section 8, pp. 1114–15.

[90] *Platinum Trade Mark*, O/133/01 (15 March 2001), [35]. *DeLorean Motor Co.*, O/317/16 (4 July 2016) (AP, Annand) (weak evidence relating to websites containing 'parked' domain names and shared websites did not constitute genuine use in the United Kingdom).

[91] *Euromarket Designs v. Peters* [2000] *ETMR* 1025. The case law on targeting has been comprehensively reviewed in *Argos Ltd v. Argos Systems Inc* [2017] *EWHC* 231 (Richard Spearman QC), [144]–[244]. See Chapter 40, section 8, pp. 1114–15.   [92] TMA 1994, s. 46(2). Cf. Chapter 40, section 6.3, at pp. 1111–12.

[93] *Imaginarium Trade Mark* [2004] *RPC* (30) 594 (TM Registry).

[94] CTMR, Art. 15(1), (1)(a) ('genuine use in the Community').

[95] For background, see Bently and Sherman (2014), 1025.

[96] *Leno Merken v. Hagelkruis Beheer B.V.*, Case C-149/11 [2013] *ETMR* 16.   [97] Ibid., [45]–[47].

[98] Ibid., [44], [AG48].

share in the national market).[99] Although the geographical extent of use was one factor in the assessment of whether there had been genuine use 'in the Community',[100] it could not be categorically stated that use in a single state was (or was not) sufficient.[101] Not insignificantly, however, the Court rejected submissions, based on the analogous question of the location of marks with a reputation for the extended protection afforded against dilution,[102] to the effect that the use must be in a 'substantial part' of the Community.[103] The Advocate-General gave what she called a 'slightly light-hearted example':

> [A] successful vendor of deep-fried chocolate bars in Scotland might formulate a marketing plan to expand his business into France, Italy, Estonia and Hungary. To that end, he registers an appropriate Community trade mark. Despite his best commercial endeavours, the plan proves ill-conceived: unaccountably, consumers in those Member States appear wedded to their own national culinary delicacies and unwilling to be tempted by the new offering. The lack of commercial success would not affect the analysis of whether there had been genuine use of the mark. By contrast, the fact that demand for a particular product in question was concentrated, at a particular point, in a specific geographical area would be relevant to the assessment.[104]

In the example, there would probably be genuine use 'in the Community', because the European market for deep-fried chocolate bars is limited to Scotland. In analysing the market share of the product when assessing genuine use, the Court emphasized that all the relevant circumstances must be considered, including 'the characteristics of the market concerned, the nature of the goods or services protected by the trade mark and the territorial extent and scale of the use as well as its frequency and regularity'.[105] The General Court has subsequently concluded that even use restricted to London and the Thames Valley can be sufficient to sustain an EUTM, taking into account not only the territorial extent, but also the high population density, London's status as a leading global financial and cultural centre, and a disproportionately high profile for the electronic network access services in question.[106]

2.6 PROPER REASONS FOR NON-USE

Section 46(1)(a)–(b) of the 1994 Act and Article 58(1)(a) EUTMR provide that failure to use a mark will not affect the fate of the mark if there are 'proper reasons for non-use'.[107] The Court of Justice has interpreted this in a manner that makes it difficult for a proprietor to rely on. *Armin Häupl v. Lidl Stiftung & Co. KG*[108] concerned an Austrian mark, LE CHEF DE CUISINE, owned by the German supermarket chain Lidl. Lidl had faced bureaucratic obstacles in opening its supermarkets in Austria and, after five years had

---

[99] Ibid., [AG50].   [100] Ibid., [56].

[101] Ibid., [50]. As Advocate-General Sharpston explained, 'if the national court finds, for example, that the internal market for the services covered by "ONEL" is particularly concentrated in the Netherlands and possibly in surrounding areas, use of the mark in only the Netherlands may be given particular weight': ibid., [AG57].   [102] On which, see Chapter 38, section 2.4, pp. 1051–70.

[103] *Leno Merken v. Hagelkruis Beheer B.V.*, Case C-149/11 [2013] *ETMR* 16, [53].

[104] Ibid., [AG50, n. 31].   [105] Ibid., [58].

[106] *Now Wireless v. OHIM, Starbucks (HK)* Case T-278/13, EU:T:2015:57, [42]–[58]. Cf. *The Sofa Workshop Ltd v. Sofaworks Ltd* [2015] *EWHC* 1773 (IPEC) (fairly extensive use in the United Kingdom insufficient to sustain an EUTM).

[107] Ex CTMR, Art. 50(1)(a). Under the 1938 Act, a similar exclusion was made where non-use was attributable to 'special circumstances in the trade'.   [108] Case C-246/05 [2007] *ECR* I-4673.

elapsed, Häupl sought revocation. In response to various questions from the Austrian Supreme Patent and Trade Mark Adjudication Tribunal, the Court of Justice indicated that, in order to rely on the proviso, a proprietor would need to demonstrate that (i) the obstacle arose independently of the will of the proprietor, (ii) there is a direct relationship between the obstacle and the failure to use the trade mark, and (iii) the obstacle is such as to make the use of the mark impossible or unreasonable. We will examine each element in turn, but it should be clarified at the outset that establishing justified reasons for non-use will not have an effect equivalent to establishing use. The period of justified non-use will merely not count towards the five-year grace period.

2.6.1 Circumstances arising independently of the will of the proprietor

The Court of Justice interpreted the notion of 'proper reasons' in the light of Article 19 of the Agreement on Trade Related Aspects of Intellectual Property Rights 1994 (TRIPS).[109] This states that '[c]ircumstances arising independently of the will of the owner of the trademark which constitute an obstacle to the use of the trademark . . . shall be recognised as valid reasons for non-use'. While Article 19 tells a tribunal about certain circumstances that shall be treated as 'proper reasons for non-use', the Court of Justice has gone further than this, indicating that these are the only reasons that will be regarded as proper.[110]

The idea of an obstacle arising 'independently of the will of the proprietor' is capable of being interpreted more or less broadly. It could be taken to refer only to matters wholly outside the proprietor's control, or more broadly to cover all matters that the proprietor has not 'willed'. While classic examples of such obstacles are 'import restrictions or other government requirements',[111] it is not obvious that one would say that other circumstances, such as a lack of resources, financial problems, lack of staff, marketing problems, or difficulties in perfecting technology, are ones that a proprietor 'wills'. Nevertheless, these latter kinds of difficulty are regarded as not being 'independent of the will of the proprietor' because they are matters that are 'within the businessman's own control', for which the businessperson should plan accordingly.[112] The General Court has stated that:

> [T]he concept of proper reasons . . . must be considered to refer essentially to circumstances unconnected with the trade mark owner which prohibit him from using the mark, rather than to circumstances associated with the commercial difficulties he is experiencing.[113]

---

[109] TRIPS, Art. 19, in full, reads:

Circumstances arising independently of the will of the owner of the trademark which constitute an obstacle to the use of the trademark, such as import restrictions or other government requirements for goods or services protected by the trademark, shall be recognised as valid reasons for non-use.

[110] *Häupl v. Lidl*, Case C-246/05 [2007] *ECR* I–4673 (ECJ, Third Chamber).

[111] TRIPS, Art. 19; *Invermont Trade Mark* [1997] *RPC* 125, 130 (non-use said to be justified under the 1994 Act to include 'delays occasioned by some unavoidable regulatory requirement, such as the approval of a medicine'); *British American Tobacco UK Ltd and ors, R (on the application of) v. The Secretary of State for Health* [2016] *EWCA Civ* 1182, [78]–[80] (legislative prohibitions on the use of tobacco trade marks qualifies as a proper reason for non-use). External obstacles to use need not be ones imposed by the state. The UK Registry held that there were proper reasons for non-use of Team Lotus where the proprietor had applied for, but been refused, entry to Formula 1 racing: *Team Lotus Trade Mark* (29 May 2003) (TM Registry).

[112] *Invermont Trade Mark* [1997] *RPC* 125; *Philosophy v. Ferretti* [2003] *RPC* (15) 287 (CA), 298, [25].

[113] *RTB v. OHIM*, T-156/01 [2003] *ECR* II–2789, [41]. See also *Kaane American International Tobacco Company FZE v. EUIPO*, Case T-294/16, EU:T:2017:382, [43].

The Court of Justice has also clarified that arguments which may be relevant as proper reasons for non-use cannot be repackaged as reasons justifying limited use, which is otherwise so modest that it fails to satisfy the genuine use threshold.[114]

2.6.2 A sufficiently direct relationship between the obstacle and the mark

For the 'proper reasons' proviso to operate, the Court of Justice requires there to be a direct relationship between the obstacle and the use of the mark. Bureaucratic obstacles in gaining building permits for supermarkets, it is implied by the Court in *Häupl*, did not have a sufficiently direct relationship with the use of the mark LE CHEF DE CUISINE on foodstuffs (the goods or services for which it is registered).[115] In contrast, a sufficiently direct relationship would exist, for example, if use of a particular name for the goods were dependent on obtaining authorization from a regulatory authority (such as the European Medicines Evaluation Agency). If the concept of obstacles arising 'independently of the will' is interpreted broadly to include matters such as lack of resources or financial problems, there is probably an insufficient connection between these circumstances and the use of a specific mark on specific goods for these to ever count as a proper reason for non-use.[116]

2.6.3 Rendering use impossible or unreasonable

The Court of Justice has noted that many circumstances arising independently of the will of the owner should only hinder preparation for use of the mark rather than prevent its use. As a consequence, these will not suffice to justify non-use and bring the proprietor within the proviso. To do this, the obstacle should make the use of the mark impossible or at least unreasonable. The Court has said that, where an obstacle seriously jeopardizes 'the appropriate use of the mark, its proprietor cannot reasonably be required to use it nonetheless'.[117]

Cases of 'impossibility' will be rare. In most cases, the question will be whether the obstacle is one to which the trade mark proprietor should respond flexibly to ensure that the mark is used (or lose it), or one that justifies retention of the mark until the impediment evaporates. This will be a fact-specific inquiry.[118] The tribunal can examine the proprietor's existing corporate strategy (and the amount invested in it), any goodwill already achieved by the proprietor, the likely duration of the obstacle,[119] alternative strategies available to the owner (such as using the mark in a different form),[120] or licensing others to use the mark. The Court of Justice has stated that 'the proprietor cannot reasonably be required to sell its goods in the sales outlets of its competitors'.[121] In one UK case, it was held that non-use of a mark for cigarettes was not justified where health regulations merely limited the tar content of cigarettes, because such regulations did not prevent use of the mark on cigarettes in general.[122] In another case, the court found that failure to

---

[114] *Naazneen Investments v. OHIM, Energy Brands*, Case T-250/13, EU:T:2015:160; aff'd Case C-252/15P, EU:C:2016:178.   [115] *Häupl v. Lidl*, Case C-246/05 [2007] *ECR* I–4673, [52].

[116] *Anglian Mode Trade Mark SRIS*, O/181/00 (19 May 2000) (economic downturns, etc., 'do not constitute a proper reason for non-use of a trade mark over an extended period of time'); *Naazneen Investments v. OHIM, Energy Brands*, Case C-252/15P, EU:C:2016:178, [96]–[99] (commencement of revocation proceedings against the mark did not have a sufficiently direct relationship with the non-use).

[117] *Häupl v. Lidl*, Case C-246/05 [2007] *ECR* I–4673, [53].   [118] Ibid., [54].

[119] If obstacles continue indefinitely (as with the US trade embargo on Cuba, which was first imposed in 1962), they come to be 'the normal conditions in the trade': *Cabanas Habana* [2000] *RPC* 26, 33.

[120] Ibid. (where use of the mark in a modified form, by removing the word HABANA, was treated as relevant).   [121] *Häupl v. Lidl*, Case C-246/05 [2007] *ECR* I–4673, [53].

[122] *K-2 Trade Mark* [2000] *RPC* 413, 421.

perfect the technology for manufacturing certain sweets was a proper reason for non-use of the mark MAGIC BALL.[123] Both cases were pre-*Häupl,* and now careful consideration is required as to whether it would be reasonable to require the proprietor in either case to have used the mark K-2 on low-tar cigarettes or MAGIC BALL on other confectionery.

Proper reasons for non-use may pertain, of course, to only a part of the specification. In such a case, a tribunal may permit the registration to be maintained for those goods or services in relation to which non-use was justified. For example, in the *Team Lotus* case,[124] the proprietor's registration was for 'advertising services in Class 35', but its efforts had (unsuccessfully) been directed towards gaining entry for its team to the Formula 1 motorsport championships: if successful, advertising activities would have followed as a matter of course. The UK Trade Marks Registry accepted that the peculiar barriers were a proper reason for non-use in relation to advertising in connection with Formula 1, although they would not have justified non-use for advertising in general or advertising related to motorsport. The Registry allowed maintenance of the mark, but only in relation to advertising services included in Class 35, 'all relating to Formula One motor racing'.

2.7 REWRITING THE SPECIFICATION

More difficult questions arise where the proprietor can demonstrate use (or proper reasons for non-use) for only part of the goods or services of the specification. If the Registry is to limit the scope of the registration, there arise issues of characterization of the goods for which the sign has actually been used. In many cases, this should be straightforward, for example there may be a registration for clothing and drinks, but only use in relation to drinks, so the mark will be struck off for clothing. But what if there is a registration for alcoholic drinks, but use only in relation to whisky? Should the specification be rewritten? Should it limit the party to whisky? Or to malt whisky? Or to Scottish single malt whisky? The question is significant, not least because the specification defines the core of the trade mark owner's rights with respect to which, if any, use of an identical mark is prohibited (without any need to establish likelihood of confusion).

Therefore partial revocation is an issue of considerable practical importance, as reflected in section 46(5): 'Where grounds for revocation exist in respect of only some of the goods or services for which the trade mark is registered, revocation shall relate to those goods or services only'.[125] Applicants often adopt broad language when drafting the product specification during registration. In an infringement context, the defendant will invariably counterclaim for revocation, as a method of narrowing the list of goods or services relied upon by the claimant.[126] Using an example from *Asos*, should use in relation to specialist cycling clothing sustain a registration for clothing in general?[127]

The question of how to characterize the scope of usage initially prompted a division of opinion among the intellectual property judges at the High Court, some being willing to rewrite the specification, while others were prepared only to eliminate items from the proprietor's existing list.[128] In *Thomson Holidays v. Norwegian Cruise Line,*[129] the Court of Appeal expressed its approval of the former approach, thereby

---

[123] *Magic Ball Trade Mark* [2000] *RPC* 439 (Park J).   [124] *Team Lotus Trade Mark* (29 May 2003).
[125] EUTMR, Art. 58(2) (ex CTMR, Art. 51(2)).
[126] *Stichting BDO v. BDO Unibank* [2013] *EWHC* 418 (Ch), [50]–[88] (Arnold J) (reviewing both European and English authorities on the approach to be adopted).
[127] *Roger Maier v. Asos Plc* [2015] *EWCA Civ* 220.   [128] See Bently and Sherman (2014), 1029.
[129] [2003] *RPC* (32) 586. See also *Young v. Medici* [2004] *FSR* (19) 383 (Jacob J).

resolving the debate. In attempting to rewrite a 'fair specification' while having regard to actual usage, the Court suggested that the manner in which the average consumer would perceive the use on products was relevant when (re)classifying them.

The CFI, in *Reckitt Benckiser*,[130] took a rather different approach. In this case, an opposition was based on a registration of the mark ALADDIN for 'polish for metals', but the opponent was able to prove use only in relation to 'magic cotton'—that is, cotton impregnated with a polishing agent. The Court considered what was the breadth of a specification that would correspond to such use, distinguishing between 'coherent categories' and 'subcategories', which 'cannot be divided other than in an arbitrary manner'.[131] If use is demonstrated in relation to one commercial variant in a subcategory that cannot be divided other than arbitrarily, that use justifies retention of the trade mark for the subcategory itself. In making this assessment, the CFI paid particular regard to the categories and subcategories of the Nice Agreement, concluding that 'polish for metals' was a 'particularly precise and narrowly defined subcategory' of the Nice System of Classification, which mentioned 'cleaning, polishing, scouring and abrasive preparations'. Consequently, there was no justification for defining it further, by reference to the use of impregnated cotton. One might question whether the CFI is correct in relying on Nice in this way, since it treats the bureaucratic Nice categories as representing some universal logic.[132]

The subsequent approach in the United Kingdom has been to amalgamate both sets of tests. The Court of Appeal has identified the conflicting imperatives that require reconciliation in such situations: a trade mark owner should not be able to monopolize a general category of products based on use in relation to only certain sub-categories, since the exclusive rights enjoyed by the trade mark owners are conditioned upon actual use of the mark. At the same time, commercial realities must be acknowledged; 'a proprietor cannot be reasonably expected to use his mark in relation to all possible variations of the particular goods or services covered by the registration'.[133] Consequently, the 'court must identify the goods or services in relation to which the mark has been [actually] used in the relevant period and consider how the average consumer would fairly describe them', thereby permitting some degree of abstraction.[134] If independent sub-categories can be identified within the broader category, then proof of use needs to relate to each sub-category. For instance, clothing can be further divided into casual wear, knitwear, baby clothes, and so on. If it is not possible to identify commercially relevant sub-categories, then proof of use in relation to some goods or services will be sufficient to demonstrate use across the entire category.

3 GENERIC MARKS

The second reason why a mark may be revoked is because it has become generic—that is, it may have come to designate a genus or type of product rather than a particular

---

[130] T-126/03 [2005] *ECR* II–2861 (ALADDIN). See also *Mundipharma AG v. OHIM*, T-256/04 [2007] *ECR* II–449.   [131] T-126/03 [2005] *ECR* II–2861 (CFI, Fourth Chamber), [45]–[46].

[132] The Agreement is designed for administrative classification, rather than defining property rights: see Chapter 35, section 2.1.2, pp. 932–4. See also Kerly, [12–126]. Ultimately, a reference to the Court of Justice is likely on this issue.   [133] *Roger Maier v. Asos Plc* [2015] *EWCA Civ* 220, [56]–[60] (Kitchin LJ).

[134] Ibid., [64]–[65]; see also *Comic Enterprise Ltd v. Twentieth Century Fox Film Corp* [2014] *EWHC* 185 (Ch), [74]–[94]. For a comparison of the EU and UK approaches, see Kerly, [12–113]–[12–132].

product from a particular source.[135] As section 46(1)(c)/Article 58(1)(b) says, a mark may be revoked on the ground 'that in consequence of the acts or inactivity of the proprietor, it has become the common name in the trade for a product or service for which it is registered'. Examples of marks that have become generic include GRAMOPHONE[136] and SHREDDED WHEAT.[137]

It has been argued that the revocation of generic marks is not justifiable. For example, Pendleton has suggested that the arguments for expunging generic marks seem 'weak but rarely examined'.[138] Moreover, he argues that the rule is 'an open invitation to commercial sharp practice through campaigns by a competitor to render a successful mark generic'.[139] In contrast, others have suggested that while the arguments for the revocation of generic trade marks may not have been articulated well, consumers and competitors would be harmed if generic marks were allowed to stay on the register.[140] This is because, where a mark has become generic, it loses its capacity to distinguish one trader's goods or services from those of another.

The harm to consumers lies in the possible responses that a seller would give if consumers were to ask for the trade marked product by its generic name. If consumers are offered only the trade mark owner's version of the product, consumers are not being offered the full range of prices, qualities, etc. that are available.

Another problem that arises where a mark becomes generic is that competitors are not legally able to use the term that most consumers use to refer to the product. While competitors may be able to develop alternative names for the product, explain the situation to the consumer, or take licences from the trade mark holder, these are potentially ineffective and costly.[141]

3.1 NAME

For a mark to be revoked on the basis that it has become generic, it is necessary to show that it has become the common *name* in the trade for a product or service for which it is registered.[142] Although marks that become generic are often name marks, the restriction of the scope of section 46(1)(c)/Article 58(1)(b) to 'names' seems unnecessary and unsatisfactory. This is because it is possible to imagine situations in which what is generic does not involve words, for example the initially arbitrary use of a certain colour on a pharmaceutical, which may come to be taken as indicating its nature,[143] or the shape of

---

[135] TMD 2008, Art. 12(2)(a); TMD 2015, Art. 20(a). See *Backaldrin Österreich The Kornspitz Company GmbH v. Pfahnl Backmittel GmbH*, Case C-409/12 [2014] *ETMR* 30, [AG40]–[AG46] (AG Cruz Villalón), (explaining that genericism relates to loss of the 'origin' function, and it is irrelevant whether consumers continue to understand a designation as referring to a particular quality in the product), [19]–[23] (ECJ).

[136] [1910] 2 *Ch* 423.   [137] (1940) 57 *RPC* 137.

[138] M. Pendleton, 'Excising Consumer Protection: The Key to Reforming Trade Mark Law' (1992) 3 *AIPJ* 110, 116.   [139] Ibid.

[140] R. Folsom and L. Teply, 'Trademarked Generic Words' (1980) 89 *Yale LJ* 1323, 1326; D. R. Desai and S. L. Rierson, 'Confronting the Genericism Conundrum' (2007) 28 *Cardozo L Rev* 1789.

[141] Folsom and Teply argue that the question of whether a mark is generic should be decided by reference to any harm that may be caused. On this basis, the question would be whether 'the challenged mark substantially increases ultimate consumer search costs or raises real entry barriers to new firms': R. Folsom and L. Teply, 'Trademarked Generic Words' (1980) 89 *Yale LJ* 1352.

[142] Although the statutory text refers to the sign becoming *the* common name in the trade, it has been held to suffice if it has become *a* common name for the goods: *Hormel Foods Corp. v. Antilles Landscape Investment NV* [2005] *RPC* (28) 657, 700, [167].

[143] On the significance of a competitor being able to imitate shape and colour for pharmaceuticals, see J. A. Greene, 'The Materiality of the Brand: Form, Function, and the Pharmaceutical Trademark' (2013) 29(2) *History and Technology* 210.

a bottle, which may come to be taken as indicating the type of contents, or (through the standardization of technology) aspects of computer-user interfaces, such as icons. In fact, a reference to the Court of Justice concerned the potential for the stitching on the pockets of denim jeans to be seen as generic—although no point seems to have been raised about whether such a sign could sensibly be described as a 'name'.[144] In these cases, the same policy concerns exist as with words and revocation should be available. Hopefully, therefore, the Court of Justice will offer a broad construction of the clause (as its case law has done with other aspects of this ground of revocation).

3.2 COMMON IN THE 'TRADE'

The wording of section 46(1)(c)/Article 58(1)(b) suggests that the name must have become common in the *trade*, rather than amongst the public. Numerous examples show that this is an important distinction, because trade mark owners, by aggressive policing, can ensure that traders continue to appreciate the trade mark significance of signs (such as GRAMOPHONE or ASPIRIN) even though consumers have come to see them as generic. However, in *Björnkulla v. Procordia*[145] and again in *Kornspitz*[146] the Court of Justice held that, in most cases, the assessment was to be undertaken from the point of view of the consumer. The former case concerned the mark BÖSTONGURKA registered in Sweden by Procordia for pickled gherkins. Evidence before the Swedish courts showed that consumers saw the sign as descriptive of the goods, but traders (grocers and stall holders) appreciated that it indicated the gherkins of a particular manufacturer, Procordia. The Court stated that both Articles 3 and 12 of the TMD 1988 reflected the need for a mark to perform the function of indicating origin in order to be placed on, or be permitted to remain on, the register.[147] The Court has subsequently confirmed that the matter should normally be interpreted from the viewpoint of consumers or end-users rather than those in the trade.[148] Nevertheless, as ever fearful of laying down categorical rules, the Court provided for the possibility of exceptional situations in which 'features of the product market' meant that traders' perceptions of the trade mark must also be considered.[149] Although it did not provide any examples, one circumstance in which this might be the case is in relation to prescription pharmaceuticals, where the influence of medical professionals on the choice of drug could make them the relevant class when assessing whether the trade mark for a drug has become generic.[150]

---

[144] *Levi Strauss & Co. v. Casucci SpA*, Case C-145/05 [2006] *ECR* I–3703; cf. *Julius Sämaan Ltd v. Tetrosyl Ltd* [2006] *FSR* (42) 849, [113] (Kitchin J).

[145] *Björnekulla Fruktindustrier Aktiebolag v. Procodia Food Aktiebolag*, Case C-371/02 [2004] *ECR* I–5791.

[146] *Backaldrin Österreich The Kornspitz Company GmbH v. Pfahnl Backmittel GmbH*, Case C-409/12 [2014] *ETMR* 30

[147] In so doing, the Court in *Björnekulla* implicitly suggests that it is appropriate to adopt a broad reading of this ground for revocation, so that it potentially encompasses any situation in which a sign has lost its capacity to distinguish.

[148] *Backaldrin Österreich The Kornspitz Company GmbH v. Pfahnl Backmittel GmbH*, Case C-409/12 [2014] *ETMR* 30, [28]–[30] (kornspitz, understood by the public as common name for a bread roll made from dark flour with two pointed ends, but understood by bakeries to be made with the trade mark holder's bread mix, was generic).

[149] *Björnekulla Fruktindustrier Aktiebolag v. Pocodia Food Aktiebolag*, Case C-371/02 [2004] *ECR* I–5791, [25].

[150] *Backaldrin Österreich The Kornspitz Company GmbH v. Pfahnl Backmittel GmbH*, Case C-409/12 [2014] *ETMR* 30, [AG59] (AG Cruz Villalón).

3.3 REQUIREMENT OF FAULT

Even if a mark has become the common name in the trade for a product or service for which it is registered, the mark will be revoked only if it has become generic as 'a consequence of the acts or inactivity' of the proprietor. The Court of Justice has referred to this as a 'requirement of vigilant conduct'.[151] This requirement means that the proprietor must not only abstain from using a mark in a way that causes it to become generic (for example using the mark as a description of the product in their own advertising or labelling), but must also take action to ensure that other operators do not jeopardize the distinctiveness of the mark, for example by bringing infringement proceedings.[152] Beyond bringing infringement actions against traders, the exact steps that owners need to take are less clear. The EUTMR provides the trade mark owner with an express power to have the trade mark status of certain words recognized in dictionaries and encyclopaedias, although there is no corresponding provision in UK law (and it seems doubtful whether such use would fall within current understandings of infringement).[153] There are, of course, non-legal steps that a trader can take to try to maintain the perception of their signs as trade marks: many have explicitly used advertising to inform consumers and ask them not to use the trade mark as a verb ('to XEROX' or 'to HOOVER') or as a noun (LEGO or LYCRA), but to use it as a proper adjective (LEGO bricks, XEROX copiers, or LYCRA fibre), accompanied by a ® or ™.

In light of the *Björnkulla* holding, the courts will need to decide to what extent 'the requirement of vigilant conduct' requires trade mark proprietors to take these kinds of step, so as to prevent consumers from seeing the sign as generic.[154] Subsequently, Advocate-General Villalón has indicated that 'due diligence requires that the [trade mark] holder monitors the market and do everything that is reasonably practicable to protect its brand against the transformation generic designation'.[155] He has said that the owner of the mark must take all steps reasonably possible to prevent generic use by third parties, and must draw attention of the public to the fact that it is a trade mark. This could include advertising and labelling indicating the product name, and asking publishers of dictionaries to indicate that the particular word is a mark. Moreover, a trade mark owner

---

[151] *Levi Strauss v. Casucci*, Case C-145/05 [2006] *ECR* I-3703, [30]–[31]. The act/inactivity of the proprietor must be 'a' cause of the mark becoming generic, but need not be the only cause: *Hormel Foods* [2005] *RPC* (28) 657, 700, [171]–[172].

[152] *Levi Strauss v. Casucci*, Case C-145/05 [2006] *ECR* I-3703, [34]; *Hormel Foods* [2005] *RPC* (28) 657 (spambusters generic because owner had not policed its use, whereas spam was not so, because it had been subject to policing).

[153] EUTMR, Art. 12. See the material on trade mark use in Chapter 40, section 7, p. 1114, and that on the exceptions in Chapter 41, section 4, pp. 1136–9. There is an important, and yet underexplored, interrelationship between these three legal spheres. If a competitor uses a sign descriptively with the deliberate intent of genericizing the mark, as in *Stix Products, Inc. v. United Merchants and Manufacturers, Inc.*, 295 F.Supp. 479 (SDNY 1968), will the trade mark owner be able to take any action? The answer appears to be 'yes', at least insofar as the marks used are identical or insofar as detriment to distinctiveness (blurring) can be argued. First, it seem that such use 'jeopardises one of the essential functions of the mark' (i.e. its distinctiveness) even though no consumers are likely to be deceived, and so is infringement. Moreover, such use appears to fall outside the descriptiveness defence in TMA 1994, s. 11(2)(b), on the ground that the use is contrary to honest practices. But, is there use 'in relation to' goods or services?

[154] See also Case No. 4 Ob 269/01 (29 January 2002) (Austrian Supreme Court) (walkman), [2003] *IIC* 966 (holding walkman to be generic because there was no other term available to describe the portable cassette player); *Jenken v. Creeks*, Paris Court of Appeal, Case No. 04/03753 (20 April 2005) (vintage) [2006] *IIC* 347 ('vintage' generic for clothing).

[155] *Backaldrin Österreich The Kornspitz Company GmbH v. Pfahnl Backmittel GmbH*, Case C-409/12 [2014] *ETMR* 30, [AG83]–[AG84] (AG Cruz Villalón), [34] (ECJ).

should protect a mark from genericism by requiring licensees, if any, to use a mark in an appropriate fashion, and should take steps to enforce such obligations.

The Court of Justice explains the requirement of 'vigilant conduct' as a component in the balancing of the interests of the proprietor with those of other economic operators. In certain respects, it is difficult to understand the policy underpinning the requirement. First, it is not clear why any mark that lacks or has lost distinctive character should be allowed to remain on the register. Why should the efforts made to stem semantic erosion deny the fact that semantic erosion has nevertheless occurred?[156] Second, some commentators argue that money spent on policing is wasted and should be a factor in support of, rather than against, revocation.[157] This is because 'from an economic perspective, such measures normally do not stimulate demand for a firm's product and are therefore economically inefficient'.[158] However, the requirement of policing might be justified on the basis of the general principle that property should not be lost without acquiescence on the part of the owner.[159]

4 MISLEADING USES

The third reason why a mark may be revoked is on the basis that it has been used in a way that misleads the public. To this end, section 46(1)(d) of the 1994 Act/Article 58(1)(c) EUTMR says that a mark may be revoked where:

> . . . in consequence of the use made of it by the proprietor or with his consent in relation to goods or services for which it is registered, it is liable to mislead the public, particularly as to the nature, quality, or geographical origin of the goods or services.[160]

Section 46(1)(d) corresponds to the absolute ground of refusal in section 3(3)(b), but recognizes that changes might occur after registration, leading the mark to become misleading over time. If the mark was deceptive at the time of registration, it should be invalidated under Section 3(3)(b).[161]

4.1 REQUIREMENT OF FAULT

In order for a mark to be revoked under section 46(1)(d), the mark must have become misleading *either* as a result of the acts of the proprietor *or* as a result of acts done with their consent.[162] Given that a mark can become misleading as a result of the conduct of third

---

[156] A. Pickett, 'The Death of Genericide? A Call For a Return to the Text of the Lanham Act' (2007) 9 *Tulane Journal of Technology and Intellectual Property* 329, 331.

[157] R. Folsom and L. Teply, 'Trademarked Generic Words' (1980) 89 *Yale LJ* 1323, 1354.

[158] Ibid.

[159] *Backaldrin Österreich The Kornspitz Company GmbH v. Pfahnl Backmittel GmbH*, Case C-409/12 [2014] *ETMR* 30, [AG31], (citing Art. 17(2) of the Charter) (AG Cruz Villalón); [32]–[34] (ECJ referring to the balancing of interests).

[160] TMD 2008, Art. 12(2)(b); TMD 2015, Art. 20(b). See Chapter 37, section 4.2, pp. 1015–17.

[161] It has been suggested that the underlying 'vice'—the sign being misleading or deceptive—is the same; the only difference is whether this vice was always inherent in the sign or arose as a consequence of its use: Kerly, [12–155].

[162] In *Bostitch Trade Mark* [1963] *RPC* 183, the licensee had begun selling certain articles of his own manufacture without the permission of the trade mark owner. Such actions would not be such as to render the proprietor's mark liable to be expunged.

parties, it is good counsel for trade mark owners to include provisions in their licence agreements that ensure that the licensee does not misuse the mark in a way that might jeopardize the mark's viability.

4.2 MISLEADING THE PUBLIC

In order for a mark to be revoked under section 46(1)(d), it must be shown that the use misleads the public, particularly as to the nature, quality, or geographical origin of the goods or services. The Court of Justice has held that, for the ground to apply, there must be evidence of 'the existence of actual deceit or of a sufficiently serious risk that the consumer will be deceived'.[163]

A mark may become misleading if, for example, a garment made entirely of wool, to which the mark ORLWOOLA is affixed, is subsequently manufactured with other materials (such as nylon), in which case the connotation of a homogeneous woollen garment arising from the verbal pronunciation of the mark ('all wool' with a meaningless suffix) is misleading as to the true nature of the goods.[164] A mark may also be misleading where a proprietor alters the geographical location of their business in such a way that a mark that was formerly suggestive of origin becomes deceptive.[165] However, in thinking about the situations in which a use may be misleading, it should be borne in mind that a trade mark proprietor is perfectly entitled to change the quality of its goods or services without informing the consumer, is perfectly entitled to move geographical locations or change the sources from which it gains its resources, and is perfectly entitled to assign the mark to a third party or license it to others.[166] Where an individual trade mark was being used to certify the quality and composition of cotton textiles, via a licensing programme, the Court of Justice has clarified that a mark may not be invalidated on the basis of being deceptive, 'because the proprietor of the mark fails to ensure, by carrying out periodic quality controls at its licensees, that expectations relating to the quality which the public associates with the mark are being met'.[167] To be revoked, the mark needs to be capable per se of deceiving the consumer; the subsequent management of the mark and licences for its use are irrelevant.

One question that arises in this context is whether a use that misleads the public as to the *trade origin of the goods* or services constitutes a misuse for the purposes of section 46(1)(d). If so, this gives rise to the further question of whether the very act of licensing a mark would justify removal under section 46(1)(d).[168] In *Elizabeth Emanuel*,[169] a famous designer who had assigned her business and mark ELIZABETH EMANUEL to a third party, sought revocation of that mark on the grounds that consumers believed that she had been involved in designing the garments sold under the mark. The Court of Justice was not persuaded that this fell within the purview of the section. This was because the mark

---

[163] *Elizabeth Florence Emanuel v. Continental Shelf 128 Ltd*, Case C-259/04 [2006] I–3089, [47] citing *Gorgonzola v. Kaserei Champignon Hofmeister GmbH*, Case C-87/97 [1999] *ECR* I–1301, [41].

[164] *Orlwoola Trade Mark* (1909) 26 *RPC* 683.

[165] *Biscosuisse and Chocosuisse v. Mövenpick Holding*, R 697/2008–1, (OHIM, First BoA) (revocation of registered mark Mövenpick of Switzerland for biscuits, because biscuits had been sold by a licensee in Germany indicating that the product was made in Germany).

[166] *Bostitch* [1963] *RPC* 183, 197 (Lloyd Jacob J).

[167] *W.F. Gözze Frottierweberei GmbH v. Verein Bremer Baumwollbörse*, Case C-689/15, EU:C:2017:434, [56]–[57]. It is not entirely clear whether this was primarily addressed to invalidity on the basis of absolute grounds or revocation under the CTMR, since both were argued in combination.

[168] H. Norman, 'Trade Mark Licences in the UK' [1994] *EIPR* 154, 158.

[169] *Elizabeth Florence Emanuel v. Continental Shelf 128 Ltd*, Case C-259/04, [2006] *ECR* I–3089.

had been assigned and the goods were, in fact, manufactured by or under the control of the owner of the mark. Consequently, the mark continued to carry out its function of indicating trade origin. Even if the average consumer imagined that Elizabeth Emanuel was personally involved in the design process, this was not misleading as to the nature or quality of the goods.

The exact reasoning is a little opaque and it may be worth teasing out some possibilities. The Court of Justice could be saying that the legal reality is that trade marks may comprise personal names, that these may be legally assigned or licensed, and if so, that the mark cannot be of itself misleading, even if consumers believe the individual is involved in production and their role has a significant impact on the quality or value of the goods. Alternatively, the case might simply be about what the average consumer would understand in the light of the legal reality—that is, the 'average consumer' is reasonably well informed about trade mark law and knows that a trade mark only signals that the goods have been made with the consent of the trade mark proprietor. Further, the case could instead be saying that misunderstandings as to trade origin are not relevant when assessing this ground for revocation, which is concerned with the nature, quality, or geographic origin of the goods. This leaves open the question of whether trade origin can affect the perceived qualities or nature of the goods. Finally, the Court might instead be saying that 'imagining a person is involved' is different from real deceit. While this could leave open the possibility of a trade mark comprising a personal name being deceitful, it is difficult to think of exactly when: one wonders whether the assignment by a visual artist of a mark comprising their signature for paintings and sculptures would be an example.

Although the *Elizabeth Emanuel* case indicates that revocation is not possible on this basis where there has been an assignment with goodwill, the logic probably extends further to encompass assignments in gross and licensing of a mark without any exercise of quality control. These questions were considered by the House of Lords in *Scandecor Developments AB v. Scandecor Marketing AB*.[170] In that case, an international group of companies operated in a way that afforded a degree of autonomy to its subsidiaries. While the international company held the marks, the local companies dealt with retailers. When one of the subsidiaries was sold off and the parent company refused to continue to license the mark to it, the (former) subsidiary argued (in a counterclaim to the claimant's action for infringement) that, by allowing the defendant to affix the trade mark to its goods, the claimant had allowed the trade marks to become deceptive. More specifically, it was argued that the mark had come to acquire distinctiveness in relation to the defendant's, rather than the claimant's, goods. Because trade marks operate as indications of origin, the defendant therefore asserted that the claimant's mark had become misleading and should be revoked. The House of Lords held that it was not possible to reach a conclusion in the case without first receiving guidance from the Court of Justice. In particular, the House asked whether use of a mark by a bare licensee (that is, without quality control being exercised by the trade mark owner) necessarily renders a trade mark liable to mislead. However, the case was settled before the Court of Justice was able to provide any guidance, so an understanding of the current law must be deduced, for the moment, from the decision of the House. Lord Nicholls was clear that, in his view, such use was not inherently liable to mislead, at least during the term of any such exclusive licence. However, at the end of the licence, whether the trade mark would become misleading would depend on how the respective parties operated—in particular, whether the former licensee carried on trading in the relevant goods or services. If customers of the former

---

[170] [2002] *FSR* (7) 122.

licensee associate goods bearing the mark, incorrectly, with the former licensee, the mark will have become deceptive. Whether it does so, according to Lord Nicholls, is a question of fact. The decision of the Court of Justice in *Elizabeth Emanuel* is consistent with this position.

5 EFFECT OF REVOCATION

Section 46(6) states that the rights of the proprietor cease to have effect from the date of application for revocation, or if the registrar or court is satisfied that the grounds for revocation existed at an earlier date, that date.[171] If a party wants revocation to take effect from a date earlier than the date of application for revocation, it should explicitly allege that the grounds for revocation existed at the earlier date.[172] The importance of this can be seen in *Riveria Trade Mark*.[173] In that case, the mark RIVERIA, registered as of 1973, was the successful basis of an invalidity objection to a registration of FRANCO'S RIVERIA CONE, which had been registered as of 2000. Just over a month later, RIVERIA was held to be revocable for non-use, with effect from May 2001 (the date of application for revocation). The later revocation, however, was unable to affect the earlier holding as to the validity of FRANCO'S RIVERIA CONE. Had revocation been sought with earlier effect, however, the position might have been different.

Where a person began using a trade mark at a time when it was not revocable, but it later became so, no injunctive relief may be awarded; instead, the trade mark proprietor will be limited to financial remedies of damages and an account of profits.[174]

Finally, it is worth recalling that even if a mark is revoked for insufficient use—and EUTMs may be especially vulnerable where they have a commercial presence restricted to only a part of the EU—the tort of passing off remains a viable option.[175]

---

[171] *K-2 Trade Mark* [2000] *RPC* 413 (revocation from end of five-year period following completion of registration procedure).

[172] *Omega SA v. Omega Engineering Inc.* [2003] *FSR* (49) 893, 896 (Jacob J); *Datasphere Trade Mark* [2006] *RPC* (23) 590 (AP, Hobbs QC). Note also *WISI Trade Mark* [2006] *RPC* (22) 580 (revocation granted from five-year period following completion of registration procedure in a case in which the question of use at any time since registration had been addressed). [173] [2003] *RPC* (50) 883.

[174] *Levi Strauss v. Casucci*, Case C-145/05 [2006] *ECR* I–3703, [36].

[175] *Sofa Workshop Ltd v. Sofaworks Ltd* [2015] *EWHC* 1773 (IPEC); *The Ukulele Orchestra of Great Britain v. Clausen and anor (t/a the United Kingdom Ukulele Orchestra)* [2015] *EWHC* 1772 (IPEC). Both are cases where the EUTM was revoked but passing off was successful.

40

INFRINGEMENT

1 INTRODUCTION

One of the most remarkable aspects in the recent development of trade mark law has been the expansion in the scope of the rights conferred on the proprietor. In the United States, a leading commentator has talked of equivalent developments as 'the death of common sense'.[1] Indeed, the rights granted to the owners of registered trade marks have expanded to such an extent that it could be said that they now confer a form of quasi-copyright protection that protects traders rather than consumers.

The rights of the owner of a British trade mark are set out in sections 9 and 10 of the Trade Marks Act 1994 and the rights conferred on the owner of a European Union trade mark (EUTM), which are largely the same as those given to UK trade mark owners, in Article 9 of the European Union Trade Marks Regulation (EUTMR).[2] EUTMs are enforced in national courts that have been designated as 'European Union trade mark courts'.[3] When dealing with the infringement of an EUTM, the national courts apply the EUTMR, supplemented, where appropriate, by national law.[4] When sitting as a EU trade mark court, national courts are invested with the jurisdiction to grant relief in the territory of any member state.[5] Where an alleged infringement takes place in different member states, the appropriate forum is determined by jurisdictional rules that are similar to those operating under the Brussels Regulation. Normally, it will be the state of the defendant's domicile or where they have an establishment.[6]

---

[1] M. Lemley, 'The Modern Lanham Act and the Death of Common Sense' (1999) 108 *Yale LJ* 1687.

[2] It is notable that EUTMR, Art. 12 (ex CTMR, Art. 10), gives trade mark proprietors a specific right to require the publishers of dictionaries, encyclopaedias, and other reference works to indicate that the mark is a registered mark. This was recently introduced in TMD 2015, Art. 12 as well. This prohibition is presumably on the basis that indiscriminate usage in reference works could erode the (specific commercial) origin indicating function of a mark and result in genericide. For antecedents, see J. Bellido and A. Pottage, 'Lexical Properties: Trademarks, Dictionaries and the Sense of the Generic' (2018) *History of Science* (forthcoming).

[3] EUTMR, Art. 123 (ex. CTMR, Art. 95, which refers to Community Trade Mark Courts). See Chapter 48, section 7.1.5, p. 1308. [4] EUTMR, Art. 129 (ex CTMR, Art. 101).

[5] EUTMR, Art. 126 (ex CTMR, Art. 98). See Chapter 49, section 3.3, pp. 1338–9.

[6] EUTMR, Arts 122, 125–128 (ex CTMR, Arts 94, 97–100). See Chapter 48, section 10, pp. 1312–21.

While trade mark infringement proceedings will normally be brought by the owner of the mark,[7] it is also possible for an action to be brought by an exclusive licensee.[8] Where licensees are not entitled to bring proceedings in their own right, they are usually able to call on the proprietor to take proceedings on their behalf.[9]

Proceedings to enforce a trade mark may be brought as soon as a mark is registered. It should be noted that the rights of the proprietor are enforceable against third parties with regard to acts done after the date of registration (which is the date of filing).[10] The rights continue for ten years from registration[11] and may be renewed for further ten-year periods, possibly indefinitely.[12] Similar principles apply in relation to EUTMs, with the exception that the proprietors of EUTMs are entitled only to 'reasonable compensation' for acts that occur between publication of the application and registration.[13]

2 INFRINGING ACTS

The circumstances in which a mark may be infringed are set out in sections 10(1)–(3) of the 1994 Act and Article 9 EUTMR. Before looking at the circumstances in which a trade mark may be infringed, it is important to note that, to infringe, there is no requirement for knowledge, intention, or derivation on the part of the defendant.[14] This is because, as with patents and registered designs, liability for trade mark infringement is strict: the monopoly is an 'absolute' one. Moreover, and in contrast with passing off, there is no need for a trade mark owner to demonstrate damage. Indeed, a trade mark owner is able to commence an action for infringement even though the mark has not been used. It is also important to note that section 10(1)–(3) clearly provides that, in order to infringe, it must be shown that the defendant used the mark 'in the course of trade'. We discuss the meaning of this phrase later.

In order to determine whether a trade mark has been infringed, it is necessary to compare the registered mark with the alleged infringing sign. The circumstances in which a mark may be infringed are set out in sections 10(1)–(3). These are where:

(i)   the marks are identical *and* the goods or services are identical;[15]

(ii) the marks are identical, *and* the goods or services are similar, *and* there is a likelihood of confusion, which includes the likelihood of association, with the registered mark;[16]

(iii) the marks are similar, *and* the goods or services are either identical or similar, *and* there is a likelihood of confusion, which includes the likelihood of association, between the marks;[17] or

(iv) the marks are either identical or similar, the registered trade mark has a reputation in the United Kingdom, and use of the defendant's mark would take unfair advantage of, or be detrimental to, the distinctive character or the reputation of the registered trade mark.[18]

---

[7] A co-proprietor may bring an action, TMA 1994, s. 23(5).   [8] TMA 1994, s. 31.

[9] TMA 1994, s. 30; EUTMR Art. 25 (ex. CTMR, Art. 22).

[10] TMA 1994, s. 9(3). No criminal liability can be incurred for acts done before the date of publication of the registration.

[11] TMA 1994, s. 42.   [12] TMA 1994, s. 43.   [13] EUTMR, Art. 11(2) (ex CTMR, Art. 9(3)).

[14] *Frisdranken Industrie Winters BV v. Red Bull GmbH*, Case C-119/10 [2011] *ECR* I–13179, [AG43] (AG Kokott); *Specsavers International Healthcare Ltd v. Asda Stores* [2010] *EWHC* 2035 (Ch), [95] (Mann J).

[15] TMA 1994, s. 10(1); EUTMR, Art. 9(2)(a) (ex CTMR, Art. 9(1)(a)).

[16] TMA 1994, s. 10(2)(a); EUTMR, Art. 9(2)(b). (ex CTMR, Art 9(1)(b))

[17] TMA 1994, s. 10(2)(b); EUTMR, Art. 9(2)(b).   [18] TMA 1994, s. 10(3); EUTMR, Art. 9(2)(c).

The grounds for infringement in section 10(1)–(3) mirror the relative grounds for refusal in section 5(1)–(3). One of the consequences of this is that a mark will fall foul of the relative grounds for refusal in situations in which use of the later mark would amount to an infringement under section 10(1)–(3). Another consequence of the fact that the relative grounds for refusal mirror the provisions dealing with infringement is that the concepts used when deciding whether a mark has been infringed—such as whether two signs are sufficiently similar—are the same as those used when deciding whether a mark falls within one of the relative grounds for refusal. Because we have already looked in Chapter 38 at the concepts that arise in deciding whether a mark will be refused on relative grounds, it is not necessary to look at them again here. However, a number of key differences exist between an action for infringement and the relative grounds for refusal. Some of these arise because the focus is on a specific real-life situation, rather than the speculative analysis called for in relation to many cases of relative grounds. As Advocate-General Mengozzi stated, compared with opposition proceedings that involve hypothetical situations, infringement proceedings involve an *ex post* analysis of use on the market.[19]

Revisions to EU trade mark law have now confirmed that comparative advertising, which is not otherwise permitted in accordance with the Directive on Misleading and Comparative Advertising (MCAD),[20] will fall within the scope of the three categories of infringement outlined earlier.[21] The revisions have also created two new categories of infringing acts. Article 9(4) of the EUTMR extends the application of exclusive rights to goods transiting through the European Union, even when they will not be placed on the market in the EU.[22] The prohibition was introduced to prevent counterfeits from passing through the EU, since its scope is restricted to the use of 'identical or essentially identical marks' on identical goods.[23] This is achieved by drawing on the assistance of customs authorities.[24] However the Recitals expressly refer to the need to balance this prohibition against the guarantee of freedom of transit in Article V of GATT as well as the danger that the international trade in legitimate generic medicines might be undesirably impeded by this.[25] The second new addition is contained in Article 10 of the EUTMR and recognizes a right to prohibit preparatory acts in relation to the use of packaging or any other means of affixing a mark to a product.[26] This applies where 'the risk exists that the packaging, labels, tags, security or authenticity features or devices or any other means to which the mark is affixed could be used' in the course of trade, in ways that constitute an infringement. The right holder can prevent the affixation of an identical or similar marks upon such tags or labels, or prevent the commercial distribution of such labelling or packaging

---

[19] *Fédération Cynologique Internationale v. Federación Canina Internacional de Perros de Pura Raza*, Case C-561/11 [2013] *ETMR* 23 (AG Mengozzi), [AG36].

[20] See Chapter 41, Section 6, pp. 1142–5.   [21] EUTMR, Art. 9(3)(f); TMD 2015, Art. 10(3)(f).

[22] It states in relevant part, that—subject to priority rules—the 'proprietor of [an] EU trade mark shall also be entitled to prevent all third parties from bringing goods, in the course of trade, into the Union *without being released for free circulation there*, where such goods, including packaging, come from third countries and bear without authorisation a trade mark which is identical with the EU trade mark registered in respect of such goods, or which cannot be distinguished in its essential aspects from that trade mark' (emphasis added). See also TMD 2015, Art. 10(4).

[23] EUTMR, Recitals 15–18; TMD 2015, Recitals 21–24.

[24] See Commission notice on the customs enforcement of Intellectual Property Rights concerning goods brought into the customs territory of the Union without being released for free circulation including goods in transit [2016] *OJ* C 244.

[25] EUTMR, Recitals 15 and 19; TMD 2015, Recitals 21 and 25. See M. Senftleben, 'Wolf in Sheep's Clothing? Trade Mark Rights against Goods in Transit and the End of Traditional Territorial Limits' (2016) 47 *IIC* 941.   [26] See also TMD 2015, Art. 11.

materials which bear the infringing mark. These two new additions have not yet been incorporated within the Trade Marks Act 1994.

Reverting to the three principal categories of infringement—double identity, the likelihood of confusion and 'dilution'—UK courts have developed a structured analytical approach for each category.[27] However certain stages of analysis are common across all three categories. It is first necessary to identify the scope of the trade mark owner's property (the mark and the goods or services). Second, we need to identify the defendant's mark (a task that, in the context of relative grounds for validity, the applicant for the later mark carries out). In assessing whether there is liability, the court will consider the specific use of the mark by the defendant, whereas in the case of relative grounds, the tribunal would have to consider other 'notional uses'. The third difference is that, to establish infringement, it is necessary to show that the mark was (i) 'used', (ii) 'in the course of trade', (iii) in the relevant territory (for a UK mark, the United Kingdom; for an EUTM, the European Union), and, most controversially, (iv) in a way that affects one of the relevant functions of the mark. We treat each in turn.

3 WHAT IS THE CLAIMANT'S TRADE MARK?

The starting point for assessing infringement of a registered trade mark, evidently, is the register. As we saw in Chapter 35, it is the register that defines the property, via the graphic representation, which delineates the mark,[28] and the specification, which identifies the core of the goods or services in relation to which protection is granted.[29] However, both are, in material respects, 'starting points'.

First, and most obviously, if the registration is more than five years old, the specification of goods and services may need to be reformulated. Indeed, it is relatively common for an alleged infringer to challenge the scope of the registration, especially if it is more than five years old, through a counterclaim for revocation for non-use. As described in Chapter 39, this will often lead to a reformulation of the scope of the trade mark specification, so that it represents a fair description of the goods or services for which the claimant can demonstrate genuine use.

Moreover, in evaluating infringement, the court may be concerned with how the mark has been used.[30] As explained in Chapter 38, the assessment of confusion is 'global'. According to the Court of Justice, attention can be paid in the global appraisal to how the mark has been used: the greater the intensity and geographical extent of the use, the greater the acquired distinctiveness of the mark, and the greater the likelihood of confusion.[31] Moreover, if the mark has been used in particular ways and the defendant uses

---

[27] For double identity, see: *Supreme Pet Foods Ltd v. Henry Bell & Co Ltd* [2015] *EWHC* 256, [83] (Arnold J). For likelihood of confusion assessment, see: *Interflora Inc v. Marks & Spencer* [2015] *ETMR* 5, [67]–[69] (Kitchin LJ); *Roger Maier v. ASOS plc* [2015] *EWCA Civ* 220, [75]–[80] (Kitchin LJ); *W3 Ltd v. Easygroup Ltd* [2018] *EWHC* 7 (Ch), [229]–[232] (Arnold J). For 'dilution', see: *Enterprise Holdings Inc v. Europcar Group UK Ltd* [2015] *EWHC* 17 (Ch), [119] (Arnold J).

[28] Disclaimed matter in the earlier trade mark will usually be ignored: *Saville Perfume v. June Perfect and F.W. Woolworth* (1941) 58 *RPC* 147; *The European v. The Economist Newspaper* [1998] *FSR* 283, 289. However disclaimers are no longer recognized in the case of EUTMs. See Chapter 35, Section 2.5, p. 943.

[29] *Praktiker Bau-und Heimwerkermärkte AG*, Case C-418/02 [2005] *ECR* I–5873, [AG61]–[AG62] (AG Léger).

[30] See *Specsavers International Healthcare Ltd v. Asda Stores Ltd* [2012] *EWCA Civ* 24, [161] (Kitchin LJ).

[31] *Canon v. MGM*, Case C-39/97 [1998] *ECR* I–5507, [18].

its mark in a similar way, this could form part of the 'global appreciation'. In *Specsavers International Healthcare Ltd v. Asda Stores Ltd*,[32] the claimant's mark comprised two intersecting oval shapes and had been registered in black, which, under the prevailing conventions was assumed to confer rights irrespective of the colour in which the shape is used by the defendant. Nevertheless, the mark had been used primarily in a particular shade of green. The Court was asked whether this was relevant and it unhesitatingly replied that it was, both to the global appreciation of likely confusion, and also in appraising whether unfair advantage had been taken of the mark.[33] However the contextual appraisal of the trade mark owner's sign has limits. An additional element otherwise not visible on the register—such as use in a specific colour—is relevant only because it affects consumer perception of the registered mark in question. The Court of Appeal has rejected an argument that the gameplay mechanics of the application software for a word game, sold under the protected mark, should—as part of its context—be included in the likelihood of confusion assessment.[34]

4 WHAT IS THE DEFENDANT'S SIGN?

In determining whether a person infringes a registered trade mark, it is necessary to compare the sign as registered (and, as just explained, in the light of any use) with the sign used by the defendant.[35] The question of exactly what constitutes the defendant's sign is of primary importance when considering section 10(1)—the 'double identity' provision: if the marks and goods or services are identical, then a defendant will infringe irrespective of any confusion. However, determining exactly what the defendant's sign comprises can prove problematic.

In *LTJ Diffusion*,[36] the owners of a figurative mark including the word ARTHUR in handwritten form for clothes brought infringement proceedings against a company selling children's clothing under the name ARTHUR ET FÉLICIE. The French court sought clarification as to whether Article 5(1)(a) covers only identical reproduction without addition or can extend to reproduction of the sign with added matter. The Court of Justice, in stating that there is identity where a sign reproduces 'without any modification *or addition*, all the elements constituting the [trade mark]',[37] seems to imply that there is no doctrine of 'added matter' or 'ineffective addition'. Although the Court's decision provides no specific guidance as to whether the defendant's sign was ARTHUR or ARTHUR ET FÉLICIE, the clear implication is that it is to be regarded as the latter.[38]

While the *LTJ Diffusion* case indicates that member states are not free to ignore added matter, it gives virtually no guidance on the critical question of how a tribunal is to identify the parameters of the defendant's mark. If we consider simple examples of signs featured in advertising or on packaging, it will be very rare for the sign to appear by itself,

---

[32] Case C-252/12 [2013] *ETMR* 46. See Chapter 38, Fig. 38.1, p. 1034.

[33] Ibid., [37]–[41]. This was the view of the Court of Appeal: [2012] *EWCA Civ* 24, [96] (although Kitchin LJ indicated that it would not affect the conclusion that there was no likelihood of confusion). See also *Evegate Publishing Ltd v. Newsquest Media (Southern) Ltd* [2013] *EWHC* 1975 (Ch), [180].

[34] *JW Spear & Sons Ltd and ors v. Zynga Inc.* [2015] *EWCA Civ* 290, [46]–[48], [178] (Floyd LJ) (SCRABBLE); cf. *Comic Enterprises Ltd v. Twentieth Century Fox Film Corporation* [2016] *EWCA Civ* 41, [102]–[106] (where evidence of the claimant's mark-as-used supported the conclusion that there was a risk of confusion).

[35] *SA Société LTJ Diffusion v. SA Sadas*, Case C-291/00 [2003] *ECR* I–02799.   [36] Ibid.

[37] Ibid., [51] (emphasis added).

[38] *Reed Executive plc v. Reed Business Information* [2004] *RPC* (40) 767, [33].

without any other material (slogans, images, colouring, decoration, ingredients, instructions, etc.). Nevertheless the mere proximity of other material surely does not mean that a defendant's use of a sign is not identical. Consequently, some rules or practices will need to be adopted to help tribunals to decide the limits of the defendant's sign. Put differently, how are we to 'zoom in' on it? Perhaps the most plausible guide is that a tribunal will be justified in ignoring extraneous matter only if, in the eyes of the average consumer, it would not be regarded as being part of the sign.[39] One factor would be whether the matter is visually or syntactically interlinked so as to be perceived as part of a single visual or semiotic entity (for example the use of the same font might suggest that words form part of a single sign, the use of different fonts suggesting the opposite).[40] So REED BUSINESS INFORMATION in capitals might be regarded as a single semiotic entity (for trade mark purposes) whereas 'REED business information' (with only reed in capitals) might be taken to be use of REED as the trade mark.[41] Likewise, the combination RITZPOKER.NET involves the sign RITZPOKER, which is not identical to RITZ.[42] Such semiotic interlinking might also be conveyed by adding an adjective in front of a trade mark. So, for example, THE EDIBLE PLAY DOUGH would not be identical to PLAY-DOH, nor would TRANSPORT YELLOW PAGES be identical to YELLOW PAGES, because the adjective, correctly positioned from a syntactical perspective, renders EDIBLE PLAY DOUGH and TRANSPORT YELLOW PAGES individual semiotic entities.[43] Moreover, use of a term grammatically correctly within a slogan (for example 'designed to keep your baby dry') might render the slogan as a whole the relevant sign, but if, within the slogan, there were some changes in font or stylization that made a component distinct, then that alone might constitute the sign.[44] Thus the defendant used the sign 'spec saver' even though the context was the slogan 'Be a real spec saver at Asda', because 'spec saver' is by no means a normal way in which to describe a careful purchaser of the cheapest spectacles (and was evidently meant to allude to the market leader, Specsavers).[45] Another factor is whether the element is perceived as functioning in a distinct way—as might be the case if the extraneous matter were regarded as having no trade mark significance, for example where it is regarded as a list of ingredients or instructions, or a description or designation of the product. Thus, in the case of a person using the words CADBURY'S CHOCOLATE in advertising, a tribunal may treat the word 'chocolate' as a description rather than as part of the mark.[46] The prefix and suffix components of an email might also be seen as distinct entities (with different roles), and this would explain why HERR-VOSS@KCS-INDUSTRY.COM was held to be use of a sign identical to the claimant's registered mark HERR VOSS.[47] The same might be the case

---

[39] *SA Société LTJ Diffusion v. SA Sadas*, Case C-291/00 [2003] *ECR* I–02799, [AG49]; cf. *Specsavers International Healthcare Ltd v. Asda Stores* [2010] *EWHC* 2035 (Ch), [127] (Mann J).

[40] If the claimant's mark itself is not a single semiotic entity, but a composite of disparate signs, the answer may be less obvious: see further R. Burrell and M. Handler, *Australian Trade Mark Law* (2016), 393–6.

[41] *Reed Executive plc v. Reed Business Information* [2004] *RPC* (40) 767, [33].

[42] *Ellerman Investments Ltd, The Ritz Hotel Casino Ltd v. Elizabeth C-Vanci and Eduardo C-Vanci* [2006] *EWHC* 1442 (Ch), [10]; *Och Ziff v. Och Capital* [2010] *EWHC* 2599 (Ch), [71] (finding OCH CAPITAL not identical to OCH).

[43] *Hasbro v. 123 Nahrmittel GmbH* [2011] *EWHC* 199 (Ch), [193]; *Yell Ltd v. Giboin* [2011] *EWPCC* 9, [123].

[44] *Specsavers International Healthcare Ltd v. Asda Stores* [2010] *EWHC* 2035 (Ch), [127].

[45] Ibid., [128].

[46] Ibid., [37]. See also *Compass Publishing v. Compass Logistics* [2004] *EWHC* 520 (Ch), [21] (COMPASS LOGISTICS not identical to COMPASS, but 'at Compass logistics are king' would have been).

[47] *Blue IP Inc. v. KCS Herr-Voss Ltd* [2004] *EWHC* 97 (Ch), [53]. In *Antoni Fields v. Klaus Kobec Ltd* [2006] *EWHC* 350 (Ch), [68]–[72], Deputy Judge Sheldon QC held that KLAUS KOBEC LIMITED and klauskobec.com were identical to KLAUS KOBEC, but that KLAUSKOBECRUGBY.COM was not; cf. *Powell v. Turner* [2013] *EWHC* 3242 (IPEC), [105] ('www.wishboneash.co.uk' not identical to word mark WISHBONE ASH).

if the composite were regarded not as a trade mark plus a description, but as two trade mark, such as where there is a house mark—say, CADBURY'S—and a product line—such as DAIRY MILK.[48]

Where it is unclear whether consumers would consider an element to be outside the mark, the 'strict' approach in *LTJ* suggests that the tribunal should treat the mark as a whole, and the comparison should be under section 10(2) not section 10(1). If the rationale for section 10(1) is to improve simplicity of decision making, its application should be confined to obvious cases; complex tests of 'identity', with commensurably protracted debate, are inappropriate.

5 SPECIFICS OF THE DEFENDANT'S USE

The third difference between assessing relative grounds and assessing infringement relates to the specificity of the defendant's acts. In the case of relative grounds, the tribunal has to imagine the likely forms of use of the mark by the defendant and assess whether any of them would give rise to an objection. In contrast, in the case of infringement, the defendant will have committed, or will be about to commit, specific acts.[49] Assessment of liability relates to the specific acts, viewed in their context.[50] In *Specsavers*,[51] Kitchin LJ reiterated that the assessment involved taking account of *all of the circumstances* that are likely to operate on the average consumer; thus, even though the trial court had held that Asda used the sign 'spec saver' in the slogan 'be a real spec saver at Asda', in assessing the likelihood of confusion, the court had been right to consider such use in the context of the slogan as a whole and, indeed, of the posters in which the slogan featured.

Moreover, in *Specsavers*, the Court of Justice indicated that the relevant context was broader that that: in the case of Asda's alleged infringement of Specsavers' logo trade marks,[52] a relevant circumstance was the fact that Asda was itself associated with the colour green. The Court indicated that this might reduce the likelihood of confusion or support a plea of 'due cause' for taking advantage of the distinctiveness of the registered mark.[53] While the context surrounding a defendant's actual use will be relevant for infringement analysis, the use of the defendant's own mark, adjacent text and signs as well as specific retail arrangements may not be sufficient to avert the risk of confusion.[54]

---

[48] *Datacard v. Eagle Technologies* [2011] *EWHC* 244 (Pat), [314]–[315] (holding that DATACARD PLUS-RIBBON™ is use of two signs, so identical to DATACARD); *Powell v. Turner* [2013] *EWHC* 3242 (IPEC), [105] ('Martin Turner's Wishbone Ash' not identical to word mark WISHBONE ASH).

[49] *O2 Holdings Ltd v. Hutchison 3G UK Ltd*, Case C-533/06 [2008] *ECR* I–4231, [66]–[67]; Kerly, [11–030].

[50] *O2 Holdings Ltd v. Hutchison 3G UK Ltd*, Case C-533/06 [2008] *ECR* I–4231, [64]–[67]; *Och Ziff v. Och Capital* [2010] *EWHC* 2599 (Ch), [78]. Some judges now include a 'contextual assessment' preface to infringement analysis: *W3 Ltd v. Easygroup Ltd* [2018] *EWHC* 7 (Ch), [211] (Arnold J).

[51] *Specsavers International Healthcare Ltd v. Asda Stores* [2012] *EWCA Civ* 24, [87]–[88], approving [2010] *EWHC* 2035 (Ch), [145]. See ibid., [101]. It is not clear whether Kitchin LJ regarded Arnold J's characterization of the context as too narrow.   [52] See Chapter 38, Fig. 38.1, p. 1034.

[53] *Specsavers International Healthcare Ltd v. Asda Stores*, Case C-252/12, EU:C:2013:497, [48]–[49].

[54] *Thomas Pink v. Victoria's Secret Ltd* [2014] *EWHC* 2631 (Ch), [128] (Birss J) (four contextually specific uses by defendant to be assessed separately); *Jack Wills Ltd v. House of Fraser (Stores) Ltd* [2014] *EWHC* 110 (Ch), [97]–[98] (Arnold J); *Enterprise Holdings, Inc. v. Europcar Group UK Ltd* [2015] *EWHC* 17 (Ch), [206] (Arnold J) (use with defendant's own marks, straplines, and additional advertising context); *BMW v. Technosport* [2017] *EWCA Civ* 779, [18], [26]–[35] (Floyd LJ) (the context helps to establish whether the message is likely to be misleading or confusing). The approach is *BMW* should be contrasted with the narrower focus—sans context—in *AB Volvo v. Heritage* [2000] *FSR* 253. We are grateful to Luis Porangaba for some of these references.

There is a geographical aspect here, too, which has significant ramifications in cases of infringement of EUTMs. This is because the particular infringement may be localized, whereas in assessing relative grounds of refusal (for an EUTM applicant), use must be assumed to be going to take place throughout the European Union. A good example is provided by a Dutch court decision, concerning the EUTM SPAM for meat, which had a reputation in the United Kingdom, but not elsewhere. The defendant used that mark SPAM for an energy drink in the Netherlands. Had the defendant been applying for an EUTM, use in the United Kingdom (the place of reputation) would have been assumed, thereby triggering the conflict at least on paper. But, in the specific circumstances of the alleged infringement, the use was outside the United Kingdom and in a place where the relevant public was unfamiliar with SPAM as a mark for meat. There was thus no infringement.[55]

6 TYPES OF USE

Section 10(4) of the 1994 Act/Article 9(3) EUTMR provides a non-exhaustive list of the situations in which a person uses a sign.[56] These are where someone:

(i) affixes the sign to the goods or to the packaging thereof;

(ii) offers or exposes goods for sale, puts them on the market or stocks them for these purposes under the sign, or offers or supplies services under the sign;

(iii) imports or exports goods under the sign; or

(iv) uses the sign on business papers or in advertising.

Two additional forms of use, which are now explicitly recognized within the remit of infringement analysis, are (v) 'using the sign as a trade or company name or part of a trade or company name'; and (vi) 'using the sign in comparative advertising in a manner that is contrary to the' Directive on Misleading and Comparative Advertising (MCAD).[57]

6.1 WHERE THE SIGN IS AFFIXED TO GOODS

Section 10(4)(a)/Article 9(3)(a) provides that a sign is used where it is affixed to the goods or the packaging thereof. This is probably the most common form of trade mark infringement. This would occur, for example, if a counterfeiter were to place scented liquid in bottles to which they have attached the CHANEL label.[58] In order to affix a sign to goods, it seems that the defendant must engage in some positive act, such as stamping, engraving, or gluing a label onto the goods. However, filling cans with drink for a third party has been held not to be 'use'. In *Frisdranken Industrie Winters BV v. Red Bull GmbH*,[59] the

---

[55] *Hormel Foods Corporation v. Dukka B.V. and Van Doorne Beverages B.V.* (9 October 2013) (District Court, The Hague) (Judge P. H. Blok). Conversely, where such a 'paper' conflict does arise in the case of an EUTM *claimant*, tribunals may nevertheless deny relief where there is no meaningful harm to the functions of a mark; for instance, no detrimental effect on the origin function since consumers in an EU member state with no use footprint are unaware of the EUTM and unlikely to be confused. See *Enterprise Holding Inc. v. Europcar Group UK Ltd* [2015] *EWHC* 300 (Ch); G. B. Dinwoodie, 'Territorial Overlaps in Trademark Law: The Evolving European Model' (2017) 92(4) *Notre Dame LR* 101, 154–155 (in the context of dilution).

[56] TMD 2008, Art. 5(3); TMD 2015, Art. 10(3).

[57] Respectively, EUTMR, Arts 9(3)(d) and (f); TMD 2015, Art. 10(3)(d) and (f).

[58] See *Glaxo Group v. Dowelhurst* [2004] *ETMR* (39) 528, 551, [97].

[59] Case C-119/10 [2011] *ECR* I–13179, [2012] *ETMR* (16) 340.

defendant, a Dutch company, filled cans on behalf of Smart Drinks, a firm based in the British Virgin Islands. Smart Drinks supplied the drink extract, as well as the empty cans and lids (which bore signs that were said to infringe the claimant's trade marks). After filling the cans with the made-up drink, the defendant placed the filled cans at the disposal of Smart Drinks, which then exported them to countries outside the Benelux region. The Dutch appellate court had held that filling the cans was akin to affixing a mark to the goods, reasoning that, in relation to a liquid, a sign cannot be affixed in any other way than by placing it in packaging that already bears the sign, but the Dutch Supreme Court referred the issue to the Court of Justice. The Court answered that, in these circumstances, a party such as the defendant was not using the mark because it 'merely executes a technical part of the production process of the final product without having any interest in the external presentation of those cans and in particular in the signs thereon'.[60]

To 'affix a sign', the mark must be used directly rather than indirectly on the goods; it is not enough if a mark incidentally appears on the defendant's goods. This can be seen in *Trebor v. Football Association*,[61] an infringement action involving the Football Association's 'three lions' logo. The action arose when a sweet manufacturer, Trebor, included photographs of footballers in packets of sweets that it sold. The Football Association argued that, because some of the footballers were wearing the English team strip, which had the 'three lions' logo attached to it, this amounted to an infringement of its mark. In dismissing the action, Rattee J explained that Trebor was 'not even arguably using the logo, as such, in any real sense of the word "uses", and [was] certainly not . . . using it as a sign in respect of its cards'.[62] Rattee J added that it was 'unreal' to suggest that Trebor was affixing the English football logo to its cards, and therefore to goods, within the meaning of section 10(4)(a). Whether this reasoning will be extended to situations in which a mark is deliberately used in the background, has yet to be determined. Because this would not be an incidental or accidental use, it would most probably fall within section 10(4)/Article 9(3)(a).

Affixing a trade mark owner's mark to packaging, but not to goods, is not an infringement under section 10(4)(a), but falls under section 10(5). This states that a person who applies the mark to 'material intended to be used for labelling or packaging goods, as business paper or for advertising goods or services' is liable for any infringing use of the material. Unlike an action for primary infringement, in which knowledge is not a relevant factor, secondary infringement under section 10(5) arises only where the person who applied the mark 'knew or had reason to believe that the application of the mark was not duly authorized by the proprietor or a licensee'.[63] It should also be noted that Article 10 of the EUTMR now recognizes a right to prohibit preparatory acts in relation to the use of packaging or any other means of affixing a mark to a product, without any knowledge requirement.[64]

6.2 USE 'UNDER THE SIGN'

Section 10(4)(b)/Article 9(3)(b) provides that a person uses a sign where they offer or expose goods for sale, put them on the market, or stock them for these purposes 'under the sign', or offer or supply services 'under the sign'. The key concept in section 10(4)(b) is that the goods are dealt with *under the sign*. This suggests that, although a sign may not be

---

[60] Ibid., [30]. See also ibid., [AG37]–[AG39], considering injunctive relief under Art. 11 of the Enforcement Directive and joint tortfeasance, discussed in Chapter 48, sections 3.4, pp. 1287–9, and 3.5, pp. 1289–96.

[61] [1997] *FSR* 211.   [62] Ibid., 216.

[63] See *Beautimatic International v. Mitchell International Pharmaceuticals and Alexir Packaging* [1999] *ETMR* 912.   [64] See also TMD 2015, Art. 11.

physically attached to the goods in question, a sign may nonetheless still be 'used' where it is placed in proximity to, or is connected with, the goods. This might be the case, for example, where it is sold from a place that is named as the sign.

One question that arises here is whether section 10(4)(b)/Article 9(3)(b) would apply in situations in which a consumer specifically asks for a product by a particular trade name, but is supplied with a competing product. This would be the case, for example, if, in response to a request for a particular brand of pharmaceutical, such as the painkiller NUROFEN, customers were provided with the generic product ibuprofen. While this would undermine the value of the mark, it is unlikely that this would be treated as a situation in which a mark was sold 'under a sign' for the purposes of section 10(4)(b)/Article 9(3)(b).

Although the situations in which goods are used under a sign are potentially very wide, the scope of section 10(4)(b)/Article 9(3)(b) is limited by the fact that the defendant must play a direct and positive role in ensuring that a connection is drawn between the sign and the goods in question. It is not enough that the connection is incidental or accidental. This can be seen, for example, in *Trebor v. Football Association*,[65] in which the decision that the sweet manufacturer had not put 'the cards on the market under the sign comprising the England logo within section 10(4)(b)' was influenced by the fact that the inclusion of the sign on the card was not a direct consequence of the manufacturer's actions—that is, the sign was there because the player was wearing the shirt when the photograph was taken, rather than being a direct result of the defendant's actions. In these circumstances, it is more accurate to say that the goods were sold *with*, rather than *under*, the sign. On this basis, it seems that if a photograph of a cricketer with the trade mark of the team sponsor on their shirt were to appear on the cover of a book, this would not amount to a 'use' of the mark under section 10(4)(b)/Article 9(3)(b).

6.3 IMPORT OR EXPORT

Section 10(4)(c) states that a sign is also 'used' when someone imports or exports goods under the sign.[66] This provision is important because it means that a trade mark owner can prevent the importing of goods that bear the mark into the United Kingdom. As we will see, this right can sometimes be used even where those goods have been marketed elsewhere with the trade mark owner's consent. The consequence of this is that a trade mark owner is empowered through this right to divide up markets on a territorial basis (and thus, possibly, to set prices differently for each territory). In terms of the scope of this provision, a person need not have title to the goods to be treated as an importer.[67] This was counterbalanced by the position under UK law that merely transporting a product bearing a trade mark through a territory (that is, where the destination is somewhere else) is not an infringing use.[68] However, as we noted earlier, goods in transit through

---

[65] [1997] *FSR* 211.

[66] EUTMR, Art. 9(3)(c). Under a proposed reform, this would cover the situation in which the consignor acts commercially, but the recipient is a private individual: European Commission, *Proposal for a Directive of the European Parliament and of the Council to Approximate the Laws of the Member States Relating to Trade Marks* (March 2013) COM(2013) 0162 final, proposed Art. 10(4).

[67] *Miller Brewing Co. v. The Mersey Docks and Harbour Co.* [2004] *FSR* (5) 81, 98 [68].

[68] *Philips Electronics v. Lucheng Meijing Industrial Co.; Nokia v. HMRC*, Joined Cases C-446/09 and C-495/09 [2012] *ETMR* 13 (goods in transit were not 'counterfeit goods' for the purposes of the Border Measures Regulation, because there is no trade mark infringement unless the goods are imported into the European Union). See Chapter 49, section 2, pp. 1331–4. But cf. *Frisdranken Industrie Winters BV v. Red Bull GmbH*, Case C-119/10 [2011] *ECR* I–13179, [AG56] (AG Kokott) (organizing the manufacture and labelling of a product for export is infringing use, because the goods when made up are not subject to a customs procedure).

the European Union now fall within the remit of infringement under Article 9(4) of the EUTMR,[69] although there is presently no corresponding provision in the Trade Marks Act 1994. Although right holders support this, doubts have been raised as to whether seizing goods in these circumstances is compatible with the Agreement on Trade Related Aspects of Intellectual Property Rights 1994 (TRIPS).[70]

6.4 USE ON BUSINESS PAPERS OR IN ADVERTISING

Section 10(4)(d)/Article 9(3)(e) provides that a person uses a sign where they 'use the sign on business papers or in advertising'. It seems that 'use on business papers' covers things such as use on letterheads, envelopes, and invoices.[71] Whether such uses are 'in relation to goods' will depend on whether they refer to the goods (as opposed, for example, merely to the packaging).[72]

Use 'in advertising' might encompass a wide range of promotional activity—from advertisements at the cinema, on television, on billboards, and in magazines, as well as 'below the line' promotion (on beer mats and T-shirts). Because section 103(2) provides that reference to use of a trade mark includes use otherwise than by means of a graphic representation, this means that oral advertisements also fall within the notion of use. 'Advertising' also includes 'comparative advertising'.[73] Use of a third party's trade marks to generate advertising has been held to amount to use by the advertiser, even where the trade mark is typed into a search engine by a third party and the advertisement appears in a set of the search results designated 'sponsored links'.[74] It seems that section 10(4)(d) would also apply to the use of another person's trade mark as 'meta-tags' to attract people to a particular website.[75]

One of the notable features of section 10(4)(d)/Article 9(3)(e) is that, unlike the other examples listed in section 10(4)/Article 9(3), the section makes no mention of the goods. This means, for example, that where someone uses a sign on an advertising billboard, they will infringe, even though the goods are not pictured. In these circumstances, it seems that it is necessary only for the advert to 'relate to' goods of a relevant kind.

6.5 USE ON THE INTERNET

Use on publicly accessible websites will almost certainly count as use within section 10(4). This may be because there is an offer of goods 'under the sign', or use 'in advertising', or simply because this is a use of the same sort as those contained in the illustrative list provided by section 10(4) of the 1994 Act, Article 6(3) of the Trade Marks Directive, and

---

[69] See also TMD 2015, Art. 10(4).

[70] H. Grosse Ruse-Khan, 'A Trade Agreement Creating Barriers to International Trade? ACTA Border Measures and Goods in Transit' (2011) 26 *Am U Int'l L Rev* 645.

[71] *Broad v. Graham (No. 2)* [1969] *RPC* 295, 298; *Cheetah Trade Mark* [1993] *FSR* 263; *Beautimatic International* [1999] *ETMR* 912, 925 (invoices).   [72] Ibid., 927.

[73] *O2 Holdings Ltd v. Hutchison 3G UK Ltd*, Case C-533/06 [2008] *ECR* I-4231, [32]-[36]; EUTMR, Art. 9(3)(f).

[74] *Louis Vuitton v. Google France*, Cases 236/08-238/08 [2010] *ECR* I-2417 (ECJ, Grand Chamber), [51]-[52], [64] *ff*; *Die BergSpechte GmbH v. trekking-at-reissen GmbH*, Case C-278/08 [2010] *ECR* I-2517, [19]; *Portakabin Ltd v. Primakabin BV*, Case C-558/08 [2010] *ECR* I-6963, [28]; *Eis.de GmbH v. BBY*, Case C-91/09 [2010] *ECR* I-43, [18]. There is use in relation to the advertiser's goods or services, even where the sign selected as a keyword does not appear in the advertisement itself.

[75] *Belgian Electronic Sorting Technology v. Bert Peelaers*, Case C-657/11, EU:C:2013:516 (use of sign in meta-tag was advertising for purposes of MCAD); cf. *Reed Executive plc v. Reed Business Information Ltd* [2004] *RPC* (40) 767, [149] (Jacob LJ) (uncertain).

Article 11(2) CTMR. Use as a domain name in such a context is regarded as relevant use within section 10(4).[76] But mere registration of a trade mark as a domain name, absent more, would probably not be advertising.[77]

So-called 'keyword' advertising, such as Google's AdWords, has generated considerable jurisprudence (as well as academic commentary).[78] We have already noted that advertisers who use third-party trade marks as keywords to generate their advertisements 'use' those marks and thus may incur liability.[79] However, in a pioneering case, it was held that the act of the search engine provider in suggesting the mark as a keyword and generating the adverts in response to the keyword does not 'use' the mark,[80] the Court of Justice explaining that use 'implies, at the very least, that that third party uses the sign in its own commercial communication'. For the same reason, an Internet market service provider, such as eBay, which provides a service that allows its customers to offer goods for sale under signs that may correspond to trade marks, does not itself 'use' those signs.[81] It should be observed that while these key decisions mean that search engines and auction sites are not primarily liable for wrongful use of trade marks, the possibility exists that they may be liable as joint tortfeasors (subject to the immunity offered to 'hosters' under Article 14 of the e-Commerce Directive),[82] and, whether liable or not, may be subject to remedies under Article 11 of the Enforcement Directive.[83] At the very least, such intermediaries will need to take action when they know about unlawful uses of marks by advertisers and sellers.

As regards internet advertisers—the purchasers of keywords which consist of or contain a trade mark—they are considered to make relevant use of a mark for the purposes of infringement. They consequently remain (potentially) liable for creating a likelihood of confusion where the use risks harming the origin indicating function of a trade mark,[84] as well as for one of the three categories of 'dilution' where the use risks harming other functions such as the investment or advertising functions.[85]

---

[76] *Argos Ltd v. Argos Systems Inc* [2017] *EWHC* 231 (Ch) (use of the registered mark ARGOS in the defendant's domain name and advertising on its website was within the ambit of infringement, albeit non-infringing on the facts of the case) For discussion of cyber-squatting in the context of passing off, see Chapter 33, sections 2, pp. 889–90 and 5, pp. 911–12. For discussion of dispute resolution outside the court system, see Chapter 31, section 5, pp. 862–3.

[77] *Belgian Electronic Sorting Technology v. Bert Peelaers*, Case C-657/11, EU:C:2013:516, [43].

[78] S. Dogan and M. Lemley, 'Trademark and Consumer Search Costs on the Internet' (2004) 41 *Hous L Rev* 777; G. Dinwoodie and M. Janis, 'Confusion over Use: Contextualism in Trademark Law' (2007) 92 *Iowa L Rev* 1597; R.C. Goodstein et al., 'Using Trademarks as Keywords: Empirical Evidence of Confusion' (2015) 105 *TMR* 732; A. Blythe, 'Trade marks as Adwords: An Aid to Competition or a Potential Infringement?' [2015] *EIPR* 225.

[79] The key question is whether the advert affects the functions of the registered mark: see sections 6.4, p. 1112 and 10, pp. 1116–25.

[80] *Louis Vuitton v. Google*, Case C-236/08 [2010] *ECR* I–2417, [56]. Bechtold and Tuckerhave studied the effect of the *Google* decision, finding as a general matter that the freedom granted to providers of search engines to offer 'sponsored links' by reference to third-party trade marks has not altered consumer search behaviour significantly, although it affects different groups of searchers (those looking specifically for the trade mark owner and those more generally trawling for information) in different ways: S. Bechtold and C. Tucker, 'Trade Marks, Triggers and Online Search' (2014) 11(4) *Journal of Empirical Legal Studies* 718.

[81] *L'Oréal SA v. eBay International AG*, Case C-324/09 [2011] *ECR* I–6011, [102]. On the possibility of accessorial liability, see ibid., [104]. See also, J. Riordan, *The Liability of Internet Intermediaries* (2016).

[82] On joint liability, see Chapter 48, section 3.4, pp. 1287–9. On the e-Commerce Directive, see this chapter, section 11.   [83] On which, see Chapter 49, section 3.2.3, pp 1337–8.

[84] See section 10, pp. 1116–25. See also *Cosmetic Warriors Ltd v. Amazon.co.uk Ltd* [2014] *EWHC* 181 (Ch) (Amazon was liable for creating confusion as an advertiser where the sponsored advertisement contained the LUSH mark, but not otherwise; Amazon was liable for its own internal search functionality on its website when LUSH was suggested as a search term, since it did not clarify that no LUSH products were available on its website).   [85] *Interflora v. Marks & Spencer* [2015] *ETMR* 5 (CA);

7 IN THE COURSE OF TRADE

In order to infringe the sign must be used 'in the course of trade'.[86] In *Arsenal v. Reed*,[87] the Court of Justice stated that a sign is used in the course of trade where it is used 'in the context of commercial activity with a view to economic advantage and not as a private matter'. It is not clear whether these criteria (economic advantage, non-private) are two cumulative requirements, or whether 'not as a private matter' merely clarified when usage is in the context of a commercial activity.[88] Given that the Court has indicated that use itself requires use in a person's own commercial communication, it has been argued that 'internal' uses are not uses at all and that, implicitly, the phrase 'course of trade' relates purely to the existence of economic activity.[89] In *L'Oréal v. eBay*,[90] the Court gave guidance on how this would apply to sales by individuals on Internet market services. In general, such sales do not take place in the context of commercial activity. However, if, as a result of their volume and frequency, the sales 'go beyond the realms of private activity', the seller will be regarded as acting in the course of trade. Quite where the line will be drawn is unclear, but the Court appeared to approve Arnold J's assumption that the fourth to tenth defendants in the case were selling in the course of trade.[91] Although these were not subject to those proceedings, Arnold J described the level of activity (many had sold many thousands of items) and found that, in eBay's own terms, these were 'business sellers'.[92]

8 IN THE TERRITORY

In order to sustain an action for infringement of a British trade mark, the infringing act must take place in the United Kingdom.[93] Although it is usually relatively easy to say whether an act has occurred in the United Kingdom or not, particular problems arise in relation to Internet uses, because foreign sites can easily be accessed by consumers from the United Kingdom. Although such uses might appear to constitute a use in the United Kingdom per se, the Court of Justice has indicated that mere accessibility is insufficient to constitute use of a mark in a particular territory and that the assessment of whether

[86] TMD 1989, Art. 5(1); CTMR, Art. 9(1). Trade is defined in the UK Act as including any business or profession: TMA 1994, s. 103(1).

[87] Case C-206/01 [2002] *ECR* I–10273, [40]. See also *Google France SARL v. Louis Vuitton Malletier SA*, Joined Cases C-236/08 to C-238/08 [2010] *ECR* I–2417 (ECJ, Grand Chamber), [50]; *Frisdranken Industrie Winters BV v. Red Bull GmbH*, Case C-119/10 [2011] *ECR* I–13179, [28].

[88] *Och Ziff v. Och Capital* [2010] *EWHC* 2599 (Ch), [55]–[66]. Use of trade marks in political campaigns is not use in the course of trade: *Unilever v. Griffin* [2010] *EWHC* 899 (Arnold J).

[89] *Frisdranken Industrie Winters BV v. Red Bull GmbH*, Case C-119/10 [2011] *ECR* I–13179, [28] (filling bottle was 'in the course of trade', but not 'use'); *Anheuser-Busch Inc. v. Budejovicky Budvar*, Case C-96/09P [2011] *ECR* I–2131 (ECJ, Grand Chamber), [144]; *Och Ziff v. Och Capital* [2010] *EWHC* 2599 (Ch), [66] (Arnold J); cf. *Divineo v. Sony Computer Entertainment France* (15 January 2014) (Paris Court of Appeal) (importing the latest games consoles in order to investigate their operation was regarded as 'in the course of trade').

[90] *L'Oréal SA v. eBay International AG*, Case C-324/09 [2011] *ECR* I–6011, [55].

[91] Ibid., [56].

[92] [2009] *EWHC* 1094 (Ch), [2009] *RPC* (21) 693, [4] (explaining that L'Oréal had settled with four of the six and obtained default judgments against the other two), [92]–[246] (reviewing their activities).

[93] TMA 1994, s. 9(1). And the Isle of Man: TMA 1994, s. 108(2).

such use exists depends on whether there is 'targeting' at consumers in that territory.[94] Indications of whether a mark is targeted would include the top level domain (a '.co.uk' domain being on its face targeted at a UK audience),[95] the places to which the site indicates it will deliver or dispatch goods,[96] and the currencies in which payment can be made.[97] Subsequently, the Court of Justice has indicated that the sale of an item from a website outside the European Economic Area (EEA) to an individual customer constitutes infringement in the territory, such that the goods can be confiscated at the borders under the Border Measures Regulation.[98]

9 IN RELATION TO GOODS OR SERVICES

To infringe, a defendant must have used a sign 'in relation to goods and services' covered by the claimant's rights (identical, similar to, or possibly even dissimilar to the claimant's goods). The requirement that there be use 'in relation to' itself constitutes an important limitation on the scope of trade mark (compared, for example, with copyright). Some communications that might be damaging to the reputation of a mark, for example a news report, simply could not be said to be use 'in relation to' goods or services: featuring a mark in a news article, for example, cannot sensibly be said to distinguish the newspaper from other newspapers (that task being achieved by the name and logo). However, there are at least two difficulties in interpreting and applying the notion of use 'in relation to'.

First, the breadth of 'in relation to' remains uncertain. The implication of Article 5 of the TMD 2008 is that 'in relation to' means 'to distinguish'.[99] It is likely that 'in relation to' goods or services has emerged as the functional equivalent of the former 'use as a trade mark' precondition for infringement.[100] This is because Article 5(5) confers on member states the option of offering additional protection to signs 'other than for the purposes of distinguishing goods or services'.[101] The Court of Justice has tended to adopt this approach, but has taken a flexible approach to when a person uses a mark to distinguish goods or services. In *Céline SARL*,[102] the Court held that while use as a trade name was

---

[94] *L'Oréal SA v. eBay International AG*, Case C-324/09 [2011] *ECR* I–6011 (ECJ, Grand Chamber), [61]–[64]; *Euromarket Designs Incorporated v. Peters and anor* [2001] *FSR* 288; *Stichting BDO v. BDO Unibank, Inc.* [2013] *EWHC* 418 (Ch), [100]–[109] (Arnold J reviewing the ECJ authorities); *Argos Ltd v. Argos Systems Inc* [2017] *EWHC* 231 (Ch), [144]–[224] (comprehensively reviewing the law on when a website can be said to target consumers in a territory).

[95] *L'Oréal SA v. eBay International AG*, Case C-324/09 [2011] *ECR* I–6011, [66].

[96] Ibid., [65] (a factor of 'particular importance').

[97] *Yell Ltd v. Giboin* [2011] *EWPCC* 9, [56], [162]–[170].

[98] *Blomqvist v. Rolex SA*, Case C-98/13 [2014] *ETMR* 25, [28]. Such use was 'in the course of trade' because the vendor was so acting. [99] TMD 2015, Art. 10.

[100] *Supreme Petfoods Ltd v. Henry Bell & Co (Grantham) Ltd* [2015] *EWHC* 256 (Ch), [85] (Arnold J) ('The CJEU has held that use of a sign "in relation to" goods or services means use "for the purpose of distinguishing" the goods or services in question, that is to say, as a trade mark as such').

[101] Although the United Kingdom has not taken advantage of TMD 2008, Art. 5(5), it has enacted provisions governing the registration of company names that may produce a similar effect. Companies Act 2006, s. 69, allows persons to object to the registration of a company name that is 'the same' as a name associated with the applicant in which the applicant has 'goodwill' (which is defined as including 'reputation of any description'), or which is 'sufficiently similar' to such a name that its use in the United Kingdom would be 'likely to mislead by suggesting a connection between the company and the applicant'. Objections fall to be heard by a company names tribunal. By preventing the registration of company names that are likely to be confused with (used) trade marks, the trade mark owner can go some way toward ensuring that use of its trade mark as a trade name does not take place. [102] *Céline Sarl v. Céline SA*, Case C-17/06 [2007] *ECR* I–7041.

not of itself use within Article 5, for that required use to distinguish the goods or services of the user from those of other traders, a shop might use a trade name in a way that was perceived as distinguishing the goods of the shop from those of other traders. In such a case, the use would be infringing. Moreover, the Court has held that use in comparative advertising is use in relation to the advertiser's goods (rather than the goods of the owner of the mark).[103]

Second, whatever the scope, difficult questions can arise when deciding in relation to what goods a mark is being used. This is important, because it logically precedes the inquiry as to whether those goods and services are identical or similar (or dissimilar) to those for which the claimant' mark has been registered. In *Frisdranken v. Red Bull*, as we have noted already, W filled bottles supplied by SD and returned the filled bottles to SD.[104] The Court held that if it could be said that W was 'using' a mark (which might infringe Red Bull's mark), it was being used 'in relation to' the services that W provided—filling bottles—rather than in relation to drinks.

A similar problem arises in relation to composite products: is the mark that features on a component being used 'in relation to' the component or the product as a whole? The answer appears to be that it depends on the understanding of the average consumer. As has been remarked, the average consumer of cars recognizes that the marks on the tyres relate to the tyres alone and not to the car as a whole.[105] Other cases may be less straightforward.

10 USE AS A MARK: THE CONTROVERSY OVER FUNCTIONS

An enquiry into whether the various functions of a trade mark have been harmed has relevance beyond the confines of infringement.[106] However this enquiry has emerged as a crucial—yet frequently opaque—stage in the analysis of infringement. Its emergence can be traced to case law interpreting the scope of the double identity provision.[107] On its face, the protection afforded under Article 5(1)(a) (double identity) appears absolute. All a claimant must do is establish that the signs are identical and the products are identical. Nevertheless, according to the Court of Justice, whether a use infringes depends upon whether the use affects or is liable to affect the functions of the trade mark, 'in particular its essential function of guaranteeing to consumers the origin of the goods'.[108] For some time, the only function to which the Court would refer

---

[103] *O2 (UK) Ltd v. Hutchison 3G UK Ltd*, Case C-533/06 [2008] *ECR* I–4231; *Louis Vuitton v. Google France*, Cases 236/08–238/08 [2010] *ECR* I–2417 (ECJ, Grand Chamber), [67]–[73].

[104] *Frisdranken Industrie Winters BV v. Red Bull GmbH*, Case C-119/10 [2011] *ECR* I–13179.

[105] *Schütz (UK) Ltd v. Delta Containers Ltd* [2011] *EWHC* 1712 (Ch), [80], [85] (Briggs J).

[106] Most trade mark defences are subject to an 'in accordance with honest practices' proviso, which in turn imposes a duty to act fairly with regard to the legitimate interests of a trade mark owner in protecting the functions of a mark. In the exhaustion context, rights to oppose the resale of a product within the European Union also turn on whether a mark's functions are threatened. Both these aspects are considered in Chapter 41. Successfully defending against a revocation challenge requires genuine use to have been made of the mark, which in turn means use in accordance with the essential function. See Chapter 39.

[107] *Supreme Petfoods Ltd v. Henry Bell & Co (Grantham) Ltd* [2015] *EWHC* 256 (Ch), [86] (Arnold J) (highlighting the interpretative difficulties as regards double identity).

[108] *Arsenal v. Reed*, Case C-206/01 [2002] *ECR* I–10273, [51]; *O2 (UK) Ltd v. Hutchison 3G UK Ltd*, Case C-533/06 [2008] *ECR* I–4231, [57].

in Article 5(1)(a) of the TMD 2008 was the origin function (although it had already referred to other functions when considering questions of exhaustion under Article 7 and the Treaty).[109] However, in *L'Oréal v. Bellure*,[110] the Court announced that it was also necessary to consider other functions, 'in particular that of guaranteeing the quality of the goods or services in question and those of communication, investment or advertising'.[111] Subsequent case law, including that of the Grand Chamber, has reiterated the statement.[112]

Before going on to examine the content of the functions further, a few points are worth making. First, by limiting infringement under section 10(1)/Article 5(1) of the TMD 2008 to situations in which functions were affected, the Court was initially narrowing the extent of protection afforded on a literal reading of the Directive (which referred to protection in such cases as 'absolute').[113] In addition to proving identical signs and identical products, the element of harm was introduced as a further requirement. Second, it seems structurally inevitable that an interpreter would have to recognize a broader set of circumstances as infringing under section 10(1)/Art 5(1)(a) than under section 10(2)/Article 5(1)(b) (which, by requiring a likelihood of confusion, is necessarily concerned with one function only—the origin function).[114] Thus it is perhaps not surprising that the Court is inclined to offer protection to trade mark owners that goes beyond the origin function. Third, the notion of 'effect' seems synonymous with 'adverse effect'[115] or 'detriment',[116] and the courts have been clear that the question is whether there is a 'risk' that the function will be affected in this way.[117] In contrast with Article 5(2) liability, which includes unfair advantage (free-riding), benefit to the user is irrelevant to Article 5(1) liability.[118] This consequently gives rise to a paradox—if harm to functions is a common preface for all the infringement claims under Article 5, what is a provision solely focusing on benefit or unfair advantage doing within this catalogue?

---

[109] *Parfums Christian Dior SA v. Evora BV*, Case C-337/95 [1997] *ECR* I-6013, [39]–[48]; *Copad SA v. Christian Dior Couture SA*, Case C-59/08 [2009] *ECR* I-3421, [52]–[59].

[110] Case C-487/07 [2009] *ECR* I-5185, [58].

[111] In so holding, the Court contradicted House of Lords' authority that the rights conferred were limited to the origin function: *R v. Johnstone* [2003] *FSR* (42) 748, 755, [13] (Lord Nicholls).

[112] *Louis Vuitton v. Google France*, Cases C-236/08–238/08 [2010] *ECR* I-2417 (ECJ, Grand Chamber), [77], [AG95].

[113] *Interflora Inc. v. Marks & Spencer*, Case C-323/09 [2011] *ECR* I-8625, [2012] *ETMR* 1, [36]–[37]; *Leidseplein Beheer BV v. Red Bull GmbH*, Case C-65/12 [2014] *ETMR* 24, [32]. See C. Morcom, 'Trade Marks and the Internet: Where Are We Now?' [2012] *EIPR* 40 (suggesting that the Court went wrong in requiring an adverse affect of functions because protection should be absolute); L. P. Ramsey and J. Schovsbo, 'Mechanisms for Limiting Trade Mark Rights to Further Competition and Free Speech' [2013] *IIC* 671, 679.

[114] *Louis Vuitton*, Cases C-236/08–238/08 [2010] *ECR* I-2417 (ECJ, Grand Chamber), [78].

[115] *Céline SarL v. Céline SA*, Case C-17/06 [2007] *ECR* I-7041, [16]; *L'Oréal NV v. Bellure NV*, Case C-487/07 [2009] *ECR* I-5185, [58]; *Louis Vuitton*, Cases C-236/08–238/08 [2010] *ECR* I-2417 (ECJ, Grand Chamber), [79].

[116] *Arsenal Football Club plc v. Matthew Reed*, Case C-206/01 [2002] *ECR* I-10273, [54]; *L'Oréal NV v. Bellure NV*, Case C-487/07 [2009] *ECR* I-5185, [60]; *Louis Vuitton*, Cases C-236/08–238/08 [2010] *ECR* I-2417 (ECJ, Grand Chamber), [76]; *Die BergSpechte GmbH v. trekking-at-reissen GmbH*, Case C-278/08 [2010] *ECR* I-2517, [30]; *Portakabin Ltd v. Primakabin BV*, Case C-558/08 [2010] *ECR* I-6963, [29].

[117] *Louis Vuitton*, Cases C-236/08–238/08 [2010] *ECR* I-2417 (ECJ, Grand Chamber), [88] (a risk thereof); *Die BergSpechte*, Case C-278/08 [2010] *ECR* I-2517, [37] ('or a likelihood thereof').

[118] *Leidseplein Beheer BV v. Red Bull GmbH*, Case C-65/12 [2014] *ETMR* 24, [39]–[40]; M. Senftleben, 'Trade Mark Protection: A Black Hole in the Intellectual Property Galaxy?' [2011] *IIC* 383, 386. However unfair advantage or free-riding could always be repackaged as harm to the seemingly capacious investment or advertising functions.

10.1 DAMAGE TO THE ORIGIN FUNCTION

The 'origin' function—also described as the essential function of a trade mark—has been described as the function of 'guaranteeing' that goods or services bearing a registered mark have been placed on the market with the authority of the proprietor.[119] It is most clearly likely to be adversely affected if another person markets goods or services under the mark or in a way that leads consumers to believe that they originate with the trade mark proprietor. In this respect, the circumstances in which a trade mark is infringed under Article 5(1)(a) parallel those in which it would be infringed under Article 5(1)(b)— that is, where the use produces a 'likelihood of confusion'. In the case of use of an identical mark on identical goods or services, such a likelihood can be presumed, so—although there is a divergence of opinion at present—the more plausible argument is that it is for the defendant in every case to demonstrate that the function would not, in fact, be implicated.[120]

One circumstance in which the origin function may be unaffected is where a mark is used for purely descriptive purposes.[121] For example, in *Hölterhoff v. Freiesleben*,[122] the trade mark owner of the words SPIRIT SUN and CONTEXT CUT for 'precious stones for further processing as jewellery' had brought an action alleging infringement by Hölterhoff as a result of certain commercial dealings in which he had been asked to cut diamonds in the shape of 'spirit sun'. The dealings were oral, and neither the customer nor the jeweller considered the term 'spirit sun' to indicate that the goods came from the claimant. The Court of Justice, in a decision focused on the specific facts that underpinned the reference, held that the rights conferred by Article 5 of the TMD 1989 did not cover these specific circumstances, in which there was no question of the trade mark used being perceived as a sign indicative of origin.[123]

A second example of a use that would not implicate the origin function is a purely decorative use. In *Adam Opel AG v. Autec AG*,[124] the well-known car manufacturer Opel had registrations of its logo (see Fig. 40.1) for cars and toys. The defendant sold remote-controlled scale models of the Opel Astra V8 Coupé bearing the OPEL logo on its radiator grille. Opel sued and the Landgericht Nürnberg-Fürth asked the Court of Justice for a ruling as to whether such use infringes Article 5(1)(a) of the TMD 1989 in circumstances under which consumers are used to scale models and accord importance to absolute fidelity, so that, viewing the toy, they would appreciate that it was a reduced-scale version of the Opel car. The Court of Justice responded that, as long as consumers did not think that the toys came from Opel or an economically linked undertaking, then the use did not affect the essential function of the mark.[125]

However, the circumstances in which an identical mark used for identical goods will not affect the function of indicating origin are relatively few. Certainly, the Court has indicated that third-party uses on merchandising do not escape the trade mark owner's monopoly. In *Arsenal Football Club plc v. Matthew Reed*,[126] Arsenal Football Club, which

---

[119] *Hoffman-La Roche v. Centrafarm*, Case C-102/77 [1978] *ECR* I–1139, [7]; *Martin y Paz Diffusion v. Depuydt*, Case C-661/11, EU:C:2013:252 (AG Cruz Villalón), [AG75].

[120] The burden of proof question has been considered at length by Arnold J in *Supreme Petfoods Ltd v. Henry Bell & Co (Grantham) Ltd* [2015] *EWHC* 256 (Ch), [87]–[134]. Cf. *Interflora Inc. v. Marks & Spencer* [2014] *EWCA Civ* 1403, [84], [131]–[151] (Kitchin LJ) (rejecting the argument that a reverse onus exists).

[121] *Arsenal v. Reed* [2003] *RPC* (9) 144.   [122] Case C-2/00 [2002] *ECR* I–4187.

[123] Ibid., [17] (the reference was to a certain style of cutting gems to maximize reflective facets); *Rxworks* [2007] *EWHC* 3061 (Ch) (Deputy Judge Daniel Alexander QC).

[124] *Adam Opel AG v. Autec AG*, Case C-48/05 [2007] *ECR* I–1017.   [125] Ibid., [24].

[126] Case C-206/01 [2002] *ECR* I–10273.

Fig. 40.1 Opel corporate logo
Source: Opel

owned the trade mark for ARSENAL in respect of clothing and footwear, brought an action for infringement against a stall holder, Reed, who sold scarves bearing the mark from a stall located outside Arsenal FC's ground. The evidence indicated that the marks were not perceived by purchasers as indicating that the goods were made or supplied by the club; rather, they were seen as badges of support, loyalty, or affiliation, used to indicate that those who possessed them supported Arsenal FC. On a reference to the Court of Justice, the Court indicated that the exercise of a trade mark owner's right was confined to cases in which a third party's use of the sign affects or is liable to affect the functions of the trade mark—in particular, its essential function of guaranteeing to consumers the origin of the goods.[127] The Court then went on to make some observations on the case itself. It noted that the use of the sign takes place in the context of sales to consumers 'and is obviously not intended for purely descriptive purposes'.[128] The use was 'such as to create the impression that there is a material link in the course of trade between the goods concerned and the trade mark proprietor'.[129] This was so even if the initial consumers were not confused because 'some consumers, in particular if they come across the goods after they have been sold . . . and taken away from the stall . . . may interpret the sign as designating Arsenal FC as the undertaking of origin of the goods'.[130] So the use was liable to jeopardize the guarantee of origin, which constitutes the essential function of the mark.[131] Interpreting the judgment of the Court of Justice, the Court of Appeal held that Reed had infringed Arsenal's trade mark.[132] According to the Court of Appeal, unchecked, non-descriptive use would damage the trade mark because it 'can no longer guarantee origin'; the 'wider and more extensive the use, the less likely the trade marks would be able to perform their function'.[133]

According to the House of Lords in *R v. Johnstone*, it will be a question of fact whether use of registered marks to identify the performers on CDs or similar items constitutes a use that is liable to jeopardize the origin function of the mark.[134] This case concerned a

---

[127] Ibid., [51].   [128] Ibid., [55].   [129] Ibid., [56].

[130] Ibid., [58]. See also *Viking Gas A/S v. Kosan Gas A/S*, Case C-46/10 [2011] *ECR* I–6161, [AG40] (AG Kokott) (implying that post-sale confusion as to origin may damage the origin function).

[131] *Arsenal Football Club plc v. Matthew Reed*, Case C-206/01 [2002] *ECR* I–10273, [62].

[132] *Arsenal FC plc v. Reed (No. 2)* [2003] 3 *All ER* 865, reversing Laddie J's judgment: [2003] 1 *CMLR* 13, [2003] 1 *All ER* 137. See also *Dyer v. Gallacher* [2007] *JC* 125.

[133] *Arsenal FC plc v. Reed (No. 2)* [2003] 3 *All ER* 865, [48].

[134] [2003] 1 *WLR* 1736, [2003] 3 *All ER* 884, [2003] *FSR* (42) 748.

criminal action against a bootlegger, who had made and sold recordings of (among others) a performance of Bon Jovi. It was alleged that, by using the words 'Bon Jovi' on the
CDs, the defendant had infringed the trade mark BON JOVI. Their Lordships indicated
that such use might be purely descriptive of the contents of the disc and nothing more, or
might indicate origin. Lord Walker suggested some factors that might be relevant, including the prominence of the mark, use of other marks, the terms and prominence of any disclaimer, and any other matters 'going to the alleged infringer's good faith and honesty'.[135]

Is the origin function damaged by use of trade marks in 'keyword advertising'? In
a series of cases, the Court has ruled that the origin function *might* be damaged by the
display of 'ads' (understood as the link, a heading, and a brief message) even though
those ads do not themselves include the trade mark, but are generated in response to a
consumer entering a particular trade mark into a search engine.[136] The cases involved
a range of situations, including the use of trade marks to generate advertisements that
link to sites selling variously counterfeit goods,[137] goods of competitors,[138] and second-
hand versions of the trade mark proprietor's goods.[139] Beginning with the *Louis Vuitton
v. Google France* case,[140] the Court indicated that the relevant test turned on the impact
of the advertisement (that is, the link and short message) on the 'normally informed and
reasonably attentive Internet user'[141]—terminology that is rather odd, given the ubiquity
of the 'average consumer' within European trade mark jurisprudence.[142] The key question
was whether the 'ad' enables such users:

> . . . or enables them only with difficulty, to ascertain whether the goods or services referred
> to by the ad originate from the proprietor of the trade mark or an undertaking economi-
> cally connected to it or, on the contrary, originate from a third party.[143]

The Court emphasized the importance of clarity in Internet communication[144] and
adopted, it seems, a version of the 'likelihood of confusion test'.[145] Indeed, in two cases,
the Court has outlined the same test for damage to the origin function as 'likelihood of
confusion'.[146]

---

[135] The reference to 'good faith and honesty' seems inappropriate in the context of determining whether
use indicates origin.

[136] Moreover, the 'ads' appear under the heading 'sponsored links'. The Court declined to consider the
position were the 'ads' to appear in the 'organic' search results: *Die BergSpechte GmbH v. trekking-at-reissen
GmbH*, Case C-278/08 [2010] *ECR* I–2517, [43]; *Portakabin Ltd v. Primakabin BV*, Case C-558/08 [2010] *ECR*
I–6963, [38]. It should be noted that in early 2016, Google completely removed the list of sponsored links on
the right hand side of the search results and transitioned to up to four ads (flagged as such) at the beginning
of the organic results list.

[137] *Louis Vuitton*, Cases C- 236/08–238/08 [2010] *ECR* I–2417 (ECJ, Grand Chamber), [84].

[138] Ibid.; *Die BergSpechte*, Case C-278/08 [2010] *ECR* I–2517, [35]; *Eis.de GmbH v. BBY*, Case C-91/09
[2010] *ECR* I–43.

[139] *Portakabin Ltd v. Primakabin BV*, Case C-558/08 [2010] *ECR* I–6963, [34].

[140] Cases C-236/08–238/08 [2010] *ECR* I–2417 (ECJ, Grand Chamber), [84].

[141] *Eis.de GmbH v. BBY Vertriebsgesellschaft mbH*, Case C-91/09 [2010] *ECR* I–43, [18] (reasoned order), [27].

[142] *Interflora Inc. v. Marks & Spencer* [2013] *EWHC* 1291 (Ch), [231].

[143] *Die BergSpechte*, Case C-278/08 [2010] *ECR* I–2517, [35]; *L'Oréal SA v. eBay International AG*, Case
C-324/09 [2011] ECR I–6011, [94]–[97].

[144] *Louis Vuitton*, Cases C-236/08–238/08 [2010] *ECR* I–2417, [86]; cf. *Viking Gas A/S v. Kosan Gas A/S*,
Case C-46/10 [2011] *ECR* I– 6161, [AG38] (AG Kokott) (treating the test as one of general application).

[145] *DataCard Corp. v. Eagle Technologies Ltd* [2011] *EWHC* 244 (Pat), [2011] *RPC* (17) 443, [263]; *Interflora
Inc. v. Marks & Spencer* [2013] *EWHC* 1291 (Ch), [233], [241], [256], [266] (Arnold J) (describing the tests as
'a test of likelihood of confusion, but with a reversed onus).

[146] *Die BergSpechte*, Case C-278/08 [2010] *ECR* I–2517, [35] and [39]; *Portakabin Ltd v. Primakabin BV*,
Case C-558/08 [2010] *ECR* I–6963, [34] and [52].

The Court's test does not suggest that use of trade marks as keywords is inherently objectionable,[147] but rather requires attention to be paid specifically to the facts of any given particular use.[148] Consequently, national courts have reached different conclusions.[149] An important national decision which applies the guidance is *Interflora Inc. v. Marks & Spencer.*[150] The claimant, Interflora, is a flower delivery network, comprising 1,618 independent florists with 1,879 shops (whose business comprises 10–15 per cent of the UK flower market).[151] It is owner of the registered mark INTERFLORA. The defendant, Marks and Spencer, used purchased advertising services that enabled it to display ads for its own flower-delivery service in response to user searches for INTERFLORA. The 'ads' generated simple phrases such as 'M&S Flowers' and did not mention INTERFLORA. At the end of litigation lasting five years, and involving hearings before the Court of Justice and two trips to the Court of Appeal (concerning evidential questions), the High Court had to decide whether this practice damaged the origin function of the claimant's mark. The Court considered that, as of 2008, the relevant date, average Internet users did not appreciate that Google operated a keyword system that produced results as part of a paid service.[152] The Court of Justice had indicated that, in assessing the effect on the average (reasonably well-informed and reasonably observant) Internet user, it was relevant to consider the general context—in particular, whether they knew that Marks and Spencer is not part of the Interflora network. If they did, there would probably be no liability.[153] However, Arnold J found that such general knowledge did not exist.[154] Moreover, the Court rejected the defendant's argument that the presentation of the page would mean that the Internet user would realize that this was a competitive offering. The judge emphasized that there was nothing in the 'ad', such as a disclaimer, to clarify that there was no connection between the two organizations.[155] Moreover, given the peculiar nature of the Interflora network, which operated through businesses both big (it has a link with Tesco) and small, which used their own names, the average Internet user would not be able to infer that Marks and Spencer was not part of the Interflora network.[156] The Court was also impressed by a statistical study, which showed that a high proportion of those who entered INTERFLORA as a search term, but clicked through to the defendant's site, then went on and looked at the Interflora site. The inference drawn was that these consumers were looking for Interflora, and that the intermediate visit to Marks and Spencer's site occurred because they believed that Marks and Spencer was part of the network

---

[147] If anything, according to Arnold J, it has recognized that 'as a general rule, keyword advertising promotes competition': *Interflora Inc. v. Marks & Spencer* [2013] *EWHC* 1291 (Ch), [288].

[148] For the view that use of keywords should not be regarded as affecting the origin function in any circumstances, see G. Psaroudakis, 'In Search of the Trade Mark Functions: Keyword Advertising in European Law' [2012] *EIPR* 33.

[149] The national case law is reviewed in *Interflora Inc. v. Marks & Spencer* [2013] *EWHC* 1291 (Ch), [282]–[287]. Of the cases referred to the Court of Justice, liability was found in relation to the ads in *BergSpechte* and *CNRRH*, but not *Eis.de: Die BergSpechte Outdoor Reisen und Alpinschule Edi Koblmüller GmbH v. Guni* [2011] *GRUR Int* 173 (Oberster Gerichtshof); *BANANABAY II* (13 January 2011) (BGH); *CNRRH v. Google France SARL* (13 July 2010) (French Cour de Cassation). See T. Bednarz, 'Keyword Advertising before the French Supreme Court and Beyond: Calm at Last after Turbulent Times for Google and its Advertising Clients?' [2011] *IIC* 641, 663 *ff.*

[150] [2013] *EWHC* 1291 (Ch). Subsequent decisions are: *Cosmetic Warriors Ltd v. Amazon.co.uk Ltd* [2014] *EWHC* 181 (Ch); *Victoria Plumb Ltd v. Victorian Plumbing Ltd* [2016] *EWHC* 2911 (Ch).

[151] Full details can be found at [2013] *EWHC* 1291 (Ch), [21]–[64].   [152] Ibid., [290].

[153] *Interflora Inc. v. Marks & Spencer*, Case C-323/09 [2011] *ECR* I-8625, [51].

[154] *Interflora Inc. v. Marks & Spencer* [2013] *EWHC* 1291 (Ch), [295].   [155] Ibid., [296].

[156] Ibid., [297].

(or at least were not certain that it was not).[157] Having regard to all of these matters, the Court concluded that the defendant's keyword use of the INTERFLORA mark damaged the origin function.[158]

On appeal, the decision was remanded on the basis that Arnold J was mistaken in adopting a reverse burden of proof approach when assessing harm to functions under Article 5(1)(a) of the TMD 2008. It was incorrect to conclude 'that the onus lies on the third party advertiser to show that the use of the sign in context is sufficiently clear that there is no real risk of confusion on the part of the average consumer as to the origin of the advertised goods or services'.[159] This reverse burden in turn influenced many of the evidential findings.[160] The Court of Appeal was also critical of the notion of initial interest confusion, which had been relied upon to establish the likelihood of confusion under Article 5(1)(b).[161] This underscores the significance of the legal standards adopted—including the perspicacity of the hypothetical average consumer construct—which will prove influential in determining whether there is harm to trade mark functions.

10.2 OTHER FUNCTIONS

In *L'Oréal NV v. Bellure NV*,[162] the Court had been asked about whether it was permissible for a maker of smell-a-like perfumes to use 'comparison lists', which referred to the trade marks by which the imitated perfumes were known. Almost certainly there was no damage to the 'origin function', because the consumer understood that the smell-a-like was not from the trade mark proprietor. So the restrictive effect of existing jurisprudence limiting liability to damage to the origin function was presented squarely to the Court: comparative advertising using trade marks would simply be exempt from liability. This unpalatable conclusion led the Court to sift through its own case law to identify other functions. It therefore recognized that a person would infringe under Article 5(1)(a) where they use an identical sign in a manner that, while it does not damage the origin function, does have an adverse affect on the other functions—'in particular those of guaranteeing the quality of the goods or services in question and those of communication, investment or advertising'.[163]

Importantly, trade mark proprietors can use trade marks to achieve these functions even though the mark has yet to develop a reputation.[164] The precise nature of these other functions remains extremely unclear. So far, the Court has offered guidance on only the 'quality', 'advertising', and 'investment' functions.

10.2.1 The quality function

The 'quality' function seems the most straightforward. In *SA-CNL SUCAL v. HAG*, the Court of Justice observed:

> [A]n undertaking must be in a position to keep its customers by virtue of the quality of its products or services, something which is possible only if there are distinctive marks which enable customers to identify products and services. For the trade mark to be able to fulfil

---

[157] Ibid., [301]–[306]. Arnold J treats this as 'initial interest confusion': on this concept, see Chapter 38, section 2.3.3, pp. 1046–8.

[158] *Interflora Inc. v. Marks & Spencer* [2013] *EWHC* 1291 (Ch), [318].

[159] *Interflora Inc. v. Marks & Spencer* [2014] *EWCA Civ* 1403, [151] (Kitchin LJ).

[160] Ibid., [174], [177]–[184].   [161] Ibid., [152]–[158].

[162] Case C-487/07 [2009] *ECR* I–5185.

[163] Ibid., [58]. These functions were first referred to by Advocate-General Jacobs in *Parfums Christian Dior SA v. Evora BV*, Case C-337/95 [1997] *ECR* I–6013.

[164] *Interflora Inc. v. Marks & Spencer*, Case C-323/09 [2011] *ECR* I–8625, [40].

[its] role, it must offer a guarantee that all goods bearing it have been produced under the control of a single undertaking which is accountable for their quality.[165]

Of course, there is no legal guarantee of quality. Trade mark proprietors are not obliged to maintain the standards of the products that they market under particular marks. However, they frequently do so, and they rely on the trade mark as a signal to consumers that the goods or services do in fact retain the characteristics of which the consumer has been apprised (either through advertising or experience).[166] In *Dior v. Evora*,[167] Advocate-General Jacobs observed that the quality function could properly be regarded as part of the origin function. The Court of Justice has subsequently clarified that the two functions are sufficiently distinct, such that using a mark only to certify quality (via licensing) will not be sufficient to establish the origin function and thereby insulate that mark from a revocation challenge.[168]

Furthermore, the Court has appeared to offer the quality function a surprisingly broad construction. In *Copad SA v. Christian Dior Couture SA*,[169] the Court indicated that, in the case of luxury goods, quality was not confined to their physical or material characteristics, but also included an 'aura of luxury'.[170] While this broad reading of the quality function served the Court's purpose in that case, it seems to blur the analysis unnecessarily. In assessing whether there is damage to the quality function, we suggest that tribunals confine consideration to issues relating to the physical or material qualities and characteristics of products or services. The quality function is thus damaged where the goods bearing the unauthorized mark do not have the same physical characteristics that consumers associate with the goods or services that bear the mark.

10.2.2 The advertising function

In *Google France*,[171] the Court considered whether using keyword advertising might damage any of the functions of the trade mark. The Court identified a function of a trade mark as that of advertising the goods,[172] and consequently suggested that the proprietor of a trade mark is thus entitled to prevent any use that 'adversely affects the proprietor's use of its mark as a factor in sales promotion or as an instrument of commercial strategy'.[173] However, the Court indicated that this function was not harmed by third parties' use of LOUIS VUITTON as a keyword merely because their bidding on the keyword meant that the trade mark owner would itself have to pay a higher price to obtain a better ranking for its own sponsored links.[174]

---

[165] *SA-CNL SUCAL v. HAG*, Case C-10/89 [1990] *ECR* I–3752, [13]; *L'Oréal SA and ors v. Bellure NV and ors*, Case C-487/07 [2009] *ECR* I–5185, [AG53] (AG Mengozzi) (referring to 'the guarantee of quality, or perhaps, to be more precise, consistency (or uniformity) in the quality of products'). See A. Griffiths, 'Quality in European Trade Mark Law' (2013) 11(7) *Northwestern Journal of Technology and Intellectual Property* 622.
[166] Ibid., [AG18].
[167] *Parfums Christian Dior SA v. Evora BV*, Case C-337/95 [1997] *ECR* I–6013, [41]. See also *Viking Gas A/S v. Kosam Gas A/S*, Case C-46/10 [2011] *ECR* I–6161, [AG45], [AG47] (collective or certification marks indicate quality rather than origin).
[168] *W.F. Gözze Frottierweberei GmbH v. Verein Bremer Baumwollbörse*, Case C-689/15, EU:C:2017:434, [41]–[46] (use merely certifying quality does not qualify as genuine use of a mark, which requires use in accordance with the origin function).
[169] Case C-59/08 [2009] *ECR* I–3421.   [170] Ibid., [24].
[171] *Louis Vuitton v. Google France*, Cases C-236/08–238/08 [2010] *ECR* I–2417 (ECJ, Grand Chamber), [91].
[172] Ibid., [91]. For the argument that the advertising function deserves to be recognized, since brand image is a distinct and complementary 'product' that consumers value, see A. Chronopoulos, 'Legal and Economic Arguments for the Protection of Advertising Value through Trade Mark Law' (2014) 4(4) *QMJIP* 256.
[173] Ibid., [92].   [174] Ibid., [94].

When would the 'advertising function' be damaged? Arnold J has held that the advertising function of a trade mark is its function of conveying a particular image to the average consumer of the goods or services in question.[175] Thus the advertising function is most likely to be in issue when the trade mark has been used by the trade mark proprietor in relation to prestigious goods that have a luxurious image. There will be an adverse affect if the defendant's use associates the prestigious mark with down-market goods, marketing methods, or advertising.

10.2.3 Investment function

What about the 'investment' function? In *Interflora Inc. v. Marks & Spencer*,[176] the Court of Justice also provided some guidance on the investment function. It noted that trade marks are often used as 'an instrument of commercial strategy', so as to enable the proprietor to 'acquire a reputation in order to develop consumer loyalty'.[177] It was this purpose that was the 'investment' function. Although the Court acknowledged that this might overlap with the 'advertising' function,[178] it is nonetheless distinct. Advertising was, according to the Court, only one commercial technique by which a trade mark could be used to acquire or preserve a reputation.[179] The Court then explained that this function would be damaged where a third party's use of a mark '*substantially* interferes with the proprietor's use of its trade mark to acquire or preserve a reputation capable of attracting consumers and retaining their loyalty'.[180]

Despite this, the investment function remains something of a mystery.[181] Arnold J made a valiant attempt to make sense of it in the context of alleged damage to the investment function through keyword advertising.[182] He argued that the 'investment function' is damaged if the use 'adversely affects the reputation of the trade mark, as for example where the image the trade mark conveys is damaged'.[183] In effect, damage to the investment function is what, in the context of Article 5(2), has been called 'tarnishment'.[184]

10.2.4 Communication function

So far, the Court of Justice has had nothing to say about the 'communication' function. However, in *L'Oréal v. Bellure*,[185] Advocate-General Mengozzi observed that a trade mark can convey to consumers various kinds of information about the goods identified by it. This could be within the sign itself (such as where a sign alludes to certain characteristics of the product) or, more commonly, by associating information with the sign through advertising and promotion. He treated the 'communication' function as encompassing informative advertising and communications that cultivate an image of the product (quality, trustworthiness, reliability, luxury, strength, etc.). In his view, this capacity of the trade mark to

---

[175] *Datacard v. Eagle Technologies* [2011] *EWHC* 244 (Pat), [2011] *RPC* (17) 443, [272] (Arnold J).

[176] Case C-323/09 [2011] *ECR* I–8625.

[177] Ibid., [39]; cf. *Viking Gas A/S v. Kosam Gas A/S*, Case C-46/10 [2011] *ECR* I– 6161, [AG58], in which Advocate-General Kokott appeared to understand the investment function in terms of the ability of the proprietor to license the mark and thereby gain income.

[178] But cf. *Louis Vuitton v. Google France*, Cases C-236/08–238/08 [2010] *ECR* I–2417, [AG96], in which Advocate-General Poiares Maduro indicated that the functions of guaranteeing quality, advertising, and communication were all specific examples of the function of promoting 'innovation and commercial investment'.

[179] *Interflora Inc. v. Marks & Spencer*, Case C-323/09 [2011] *ECR* I–8625, [60]–[61].   [180] Ibid., [66].

[181] For the view that investment is not a function of a mark, so much as an 'attribute of the mark' see Kerly, [2–005].

[182] *Interflora Inc. v. Marks & Spencer* [2013] *EWHC* 1291 (Ch).   [183] Ibid., [274].

[184] For damage to reputation, see Chapter 38, section 2.4.3, pp. 1064–5.

[185] Case C-487/07 [2009] *ECR* I–5185, [AG54].

communicate information merits protection.[186] Unfortunately, it is not clear when this function would be damaged, other than—yet again—by confusion, blurring, or tarnishment.

10.2.5 Criticism and reform

The Court of Justice case law on 'functions' has come under criticism from courts, commentators,[187] and policymakers. The most common criticism is that the concepts are incomprehensible. In *Interflora*, Arnold J complained that it was difficult to understand precisely what the functions referred to and what their interrelationship was.[188] In *L'Oréal v. Bellure*,[189] Jacob LJ was more acerbic, calling the functions 'vague and ill-defined'. A second objection is that the Court has developed these concepts without any legislative basis for so doing.[190] Further, it is argued that it is difficult to understand how this interpretation of Article 5(1)(a) of the Directive can be reconciled with Article 5(2).[191] There are important limitations built into the protection conferred by Article 5(2)—most obviously, the requirement that, to infringe, the use of the trade mark be 'without due cause'. No such requirement is contained explicitly in Article 5(1)(a), leading to the possibility the uses that would be excusable under Article 5(2) in relation to marks with a reputation might not be permissible under Article 5(1)(a), irrespective of whether the proprietor's mark has a reputation.[192] Finally, it has been suggested that there is no justifiable reason for protecting many of these types of use of trade marks.[193]

Accepting some of these criticisms, the Max Planck Institute's study recommended that the functions no longer play an autonomous role in Article 5(1)(a) determinations.[194] Subsequently, the European Commission also acknowledged that the 'recognition of additional trade mark functions under Article 5(1)(a) of the Directive has created legal uncertainty'.[195] However neither recommendation was incorporated into the recast EUTMR and TMD 2015. Functions analysis resolutely remains a part of the European trade mark landscape.

---

[186] Cf. *Viking Gas A/S v. Kosam Gas A/S*, Case C-46/10 [2011] *ECR* I– 6161, [AG56]–[AG58] ('communication function' refers to the understandings of those who see a mark at a distance). See also Max Planck Institute, *Study on the Overall Functioning of the Community Trade Mark System* (2011), [2.186].

[187] A. Ohly, 'Keyword Advertising or Why the ECJ's Functional Approach to Trade Mark Infringement does not Function' [2010] *IIC* 879; A. Horton, 'The Implications of *L'Oréal v. Bellure*: A Retrospective and Looking Forward' [2011] *EIPR* 550; A. Kur, 'Trade Marks Function, Don't They? CJEU Jurisprudence and Unfair Competition Practices' [2014] *IIC* 434; M. Senftleben, 'Function Theory and International Exhaustion—Why it is Wise to Confine the Double Identity Rule to Cases Affecting the Origin Function' [2014] EIPR 518. [188] *Interflora Inc. v. Marks & Spencer* [2013] *EWHC* 1291 (Ch), [271].

[189] [2010] *EWCA Civ* 535, [30]. [190] Ibid.

[191] *L'Oréal v. eBay* [2009] *EWHC* 1094 (Ch), [2009] *RPC* (21) 693, [300] (Arnold J); *Datacard v. Eagle Technologies* [2011] *EWHC* 244 (Pat), [2011] *RPC* (17) 443, [272] (Arnold J); *Interflora Inc. v. Marks & Spencer*, Case C-323/09 [2011] *ECR* I–8625, [AG58] (AG Jääskinen); European Commission, *Proposal for a Directive of the European Parliament and of the Council to Approximate the Laws of the Member States Relating to Trade Marks* (March 2013) COM(2013) 0162 final, 6.

[192] On 'due cause', see Chapter 38, section 2.5, pp. 1071–2. Various Advocates-General have sought to overcome this problem by requiring a balancing of interests when considering the functions other than the origin function: see *Louis Vuitton v. Google France*, Cases 236/08–238/08 [2010] *ECR* I–2417 (ECJ, Grand Chamber), [AG102] (AG Poiares Maduro); *Viking Gas A/S v. Kosan Gas A/S*, Case C-46/10 [2011] *ECR* I–6161, [AG59]–[AG64] (AG Kokott). This 'solution' seems merely to add extra uncertainty to the already problematic notion of functions. The Court seems to have accepted that Art. 5(1)(a) may give rise to liability even where there would be no such liability under Art. 5(2): *Leidseplein Beheer BV v. Red Bull GmbH*, Case C-65/12 [2014] *ETMR* 24, [36].

[193] *L'Oréal v. Bellure* [2010] *EWCA Civ* 535, [30]; N. Dawson, 'Non-Trade Mark Use' [2012] *IPQ* 204, 224–5.

[194] Max Planck Institute, *Study on the Overall Functioning of the Community Trade Mark System* (2010), [2.184].

[195] European Commission, *Proposal for a Directive of the European Parliament and of the Council to Approximate the Laws of the Member States Relating to Trade Marks* (March 2013) COM(2013) 0162 final, 6.

11 ACCESSORY LIABILITY

Doctrines of secondary liability for trade mark infringement fall outside the scope of the Directive and Regulation, and remain therefore unharmonized.[196] In France, they fall to be dealt with under the Civil Code, whereas in Germany, special remedies are frequently made available under a doctrine called *Storerhaftung* ('interferer liability') against third parties who wilfully make a causal contribution to the primary infringements of others without themselves carrying out infringing acts.[197] In the United Kingdom, there are two sources of potential liability for accessories: limited statutory protection for so-called 'secondary infringement', and the general rules of joint torts.

Statutory liability is provided for in section 10(5), which states that a person who applies the mark to 'material intended to be used for labelling or packaging goods, as business paper or for advertising goods or services' is liable for any infringing use of the material. Unlike an action for primary infringement, in which knowledge is not a relevant factor, secondary infringement under section 10(5) arises only where the person who applied the mark 'knew or had reason to believe that the application of the mark was not duly authorized by the proprietor or a licensee'.[198]

Defendants may also indirectly infringe the rights in a trade mark where they act as a joint tortfeasor. The principles are reviewed in Chapter 48: the alleged infringer must do more than facilitate infringement; they must be actively implicated in a 'common design' to infringe.[199]

These matters are of increasing commercial importance (and legal contest). These doctrines regulate, for example, the suggestion by a search engine provider that offers keyword advertising services of certain keywords that might be terms used by users looking for counterfeits,[200] or of sales on eBay facilitating the auction of infringing goods.[201]

Even if liability can be established under the principles of joint tortfeasance, Article 14 of the e-Commerce Directive offers important 'safe harbour' limitations on financial liability (but not on injunctive relief). This applies in relation to what is usually referred to as 'hosting'. More specifically, where an information society service is provided that consists of the 'storage of information' provided by a recipient of the service, the service provider is not liable for the information stored at the request of a recipient of the service if it complies with certain conditions. These conditions are that the provider does not have actual knowledge of illegal activity or information and is not aware of facts or circumstances from which the illegal activity or information is apparent, and that the provider, upon obtaining such knowledge or awareness, acts expeditiously to remove or to disable access to the information.

---

[196] However, in the Internet context, immunities are harmonized through the e-Commerce Directive, esp. Art. 14 (hosting). See generally M. Leistner, 'Structural Aspects of Secondary (Provider) Liability in Europe' (2014) 9 *JIPLP* 75. For a comparative assessment of secondary liability for trade mark infringement, see the symposium issue (2014) 37 *Colum JL & Arts*; G. B. Dinwoodie (ed.), *Secondary Liability of Internet Service Providers* (2017).

[197] Leistner, op. cit., 78–81.

[198] The knowledge requirement is in similar terms to that employed in the context of copyright. See Chapter 8.

[199] Direct tort liability, in the form of negligent omission, has also been considered. See A. Roy and A. Marsoof, 'Negligent Omissions as a Basis for Holding Internet Intermediaries Liable for Infringements of Trade Mark Rights: Approaches under the English Common Law' [2017] *IPQ* 52.

[200] *Louis Vuitton v. Google France*, Cases 236/08–238/08 [2010] *ECR* I–2417 (ECJ, Grand Chamber), [57], [AG114]–[AG125] (AG Poiares Maduro).

[201] *L'Oréal SA v. eBay International AG*, Case C-324/09 [2011] *ECR* I–6011 (ECJ, Grand Chamber), [104], [AG55]–[AG56]; *Frisdranken Industrie Winters BV v. Red Bull GmbH*, Case C-119/10 [2011] *ECR* I–13179, [35].

The core idea behind the immunity for hosting lies in the 'passive' role of the service provider. As the Court of Justice stated in the *Google* case, the role played by the service provider must be 'neutral, in the sense that its conduct is merely technical, automatic and passive, pointing to a lack of knowledge or control of the data which it stores'.[202] Such passivity is not inconsistent with being paid, but rather requires the services to be provided in a neutral, blind, and responsive manner. It seems likely that a provider of automated advertising in response to keywords chosen by the advertiser, or a site that offers a marketplace for the sale of goods that are selected and described by the seller, would be regarded as falling within the scope of the immunity.[203] It is, however, less clear whether a search tool that actively suggests trade marks as keywords would constitute a sufficiently passive role. Indeed, the Court in *Google* highlighted that the role 'played by Google in the . . . selection of keywords' was 'relevant' to whether the test of passivity was met.[204]

Even if the host is passive, the immunity will not apply where a service provider knows of the wrongdoing. This leaves open critical questions as to when there is such knowledge.[205] Is a host able to rely on the immunity where it specifically designs a system such that it cannot be said to have knowledge of acts, infringing or otherwise? Might it be sufficient that the host has generalized knowledge that the system is likely to be used to infringe and yet does nothing to prevent or deter such activity? In considering the concept of 'knowledge' in this context, it is important also to bear in mind that Article 15 of the e-Commerce Directive forbids member states to impose a 'general obligation' on providers 'to monitor the information which they transmit or store, nor a general obligation actively to seek facts or circumstances indicating illegal activity'.[206] Thus it seems that any concept of imputed or constructive knowledge cannot assume that the provider monitors its users.

The Court in *eBay* stated that the service would lose immunity:

> . . . if [it were] aware of facts or circumstances on the basis of which a diligent economic operator should have realised that the offers for sale in question were unlawful and, in the event of it being so aware, failed to act expeditiously.[207]

The relevant knowledge could be provided by third parties, or arise from the service provider's own actions. The application of these rather vague criteria was left to the courts of member states and the *eBay* case has now been settled.

---

[202] *Louis Vuitton v. Google France*, Cases C-236/08–238/08 [2010] *ECR* I–2417 (ECJ, Grand Chamber), [114].

[203] *L'Oréal SA v. eBay International AG*, Case C-324/09 [2011] *ECR* I–6011 (ECJ, Grand Chamber), [115] (indicating that merely storing offers for sale on its server, setting the terms of its service, and providing general information to its customers did not make the auction site 'active'). Nevertheless, the French Cour de Cassation has held that eBay is, in fact, active and thus does not benefit from the immunity: *eBay Inc. v. LVMH* (3 May 2012) (Cour de Cassation, Comm. Ch).

[204] *Louis Vuitton v. Google France*, Cases C-236/08–238/08 [2010] *ECR* I–2417, [118]. It also referred to the role in 'drafting of the commercial message which accompanies the advertising link', but it seems clear that the advertisers draft the text and insert the link: ibid., [AG126], [AG138]. Along with the extent to which an intermediary must be passive, the definition of an intermediary has been considered in *Tommy Hilfiger Licensing LLC v. Delta Center*, Case C-494/15, EU:C:2016:582; *McFadden v. Sony Music Entertainment Germany*, Case C-484/14, EU:C:2016:689.

[205] For reflections based on the US experience, see S. Dogan, 'Principled Standards vs. Boundless Discretion: A Tale of Two Approaches to Intermediary Trademark Liability Online' (2014) 36 *Colum JL & Arts* 1; M. Senftleben, 'An Uneasy Case for Notice and Takedown: Context Specific Trademark Rights' (March 2012), available online at http://www.ssrn.com/abstract/=2025075.

[206] See, however, e-Commerce Dir., Recital 48 (recognizing that some specific monitoring may be required without violating Art. 15).

[207] *L'Oréal SA v. eBay International AG*, Case C-324/09 [2011] *ECR* I–6011 (ECJ, Grand Chamber), [120].

Although one might have expected the question of accessory liability (particularly the creation of positive criteria in which liability would arise) to have been included in the ongoing EU reforms, so far all that has been incorporated is the prohibition contained in Article 10 of the EUTMR, which recognizes a right to prohibit preparatory acts in relation to the use of packaging or any other means of affixing a mark to a product.[208]

Beyond this, the most that has been achieved is a 'memorandum of understanding' between brand owners and intermediaries—particularly 'auction sites' (including eBay and Amazon)—by which the latter commit themselves to take down adverts when notified that the items are counterfeit and to take steps against users who are generally engaged in counterfeiting.[209] There appears to be no ongoing effort at the level of the World Intellectual Property Organization (WIPO).[210]

---

[208] See also TMD 2015, Art. 11.

[209] European Commission, *Memorandum of Understanding on the Sale of Counterfeit Goods via the Internet* (May 2011), available online at http://ec.europa.eu/internal_market/iprenforcement/docs/memo-randum_04052011_en.pdf. See also European Commission, *Report from the Commission to the European Parliament and the Council on the Functioning of the Memorandum of Understanding on the Sale of Counterfeit Goods via the Internet* (April 2013) COM(2013) 0209 final; G. Dinwoodie, 'Secondary Liability for Online Trademark Infringement: The International Landscape' (2014) 36 *Colum JL & Arts* 463; EUIPO, *Study on voluntary collaboration practices in addressing online infringements of trade mark rights, design rights, copyright and rights related to copyright* (September 2016). Voluntary measures have also been incorporated into proposed legislation under the EU Digital Single Market Strategy which could affect the scope of safe harbours: see G. F. Frosio, 'Reforming Intermediary Liability in the Platform Economy: A European Digital Single Market Strategy' (2017) 112 *Nw U L Rev* 19.

[210] For discussions at WIPO, albeit with little progress, see WIPO, Information Meeting on the Role and Responsibility of Intermediaries in the Field of Trademarks (August 2012) SCT/INFO/NET/GE/12/INF.1; WIPO, Report of the Standing Committee on the Law of Trademarks, Industrial Designs and Geographical Indications (27th Session, Geneva, 18–21 September 2012) SCT/27/11; cf. the study for the Advisory Committee on Enforcement by F. W. Mostert, *Study on Approaches to Online Trademark Infringement* (1 September 2017) (WIPO/ACE/12/9 REV.2).

41

TRADE MARK DEFENCES

1 INTRODUCTION

In this chapter, we explore the various defences that are available to a person who has been charged with trade mark infringement. While the defences to trade mark infringement have always been important, the expanded scope of protection provided under the Trade Marks Act 1994 means that defendants are now likely to try to rely much more frequently on the defences provided.[1] It should be noted that a common tactic for a defendant who is accused of infringement is to assert that the claimant's registered right was invalidly registered or that it ought to be revoked.[2] These issues have been considered in Chapters 36, 37, 38, and 39.

2 USE OF REGISTERED MARK

The first defence to a claim of infringement of a UK trade mark is set out in section 11(1) of the 1994 Act. This provides that a trade mark is not infringed by the use of another registered trade mark in relation to goods or services for which the latter mark is registered. In effect, section 11(1) provides that registration gives a defence to an action for infringement. This is in contrast to the situation in copyright law where a person can simultaneously exploit their own work and infringe someone else's. The immunity conferred by registration acts as an incentive for traders to apply for trade mark registration.

---

[1] G. Dinwoodie, 'Developing Defenses in Trademark Law' (2009) 13 *LCLR* 99, 152; see also W. McGeveran, 'Rethinking Trademark Fair Use' (2008) 94 *Iowa L Rev* 49; M. Grynberg, 'Things are Worse than We Think: Trademark Defenses in a "Formalist" Age' (2009) 24 *BTLJ* 897; W. McGeveran, 'The Trademark Fair Use Reform Act' (2010) 90 *Boston U L Rev* 2267; R. G. Bone, 'Notice Failure and Defenses in Trademark Law' (2016) 96 *Boston U LR* 1245 (proposing defences as a method of offsetting the chilling effects generated by having fuzzily defined exclusive rights).

[2] Note also CTMR, Art. 99(3) (formerly Art. 95(3) of Regulation 40/94), providing a limited defence short of a counterclaim for revocation or invalidity.

On its face, this exception appeared to be incompatible with EU law.[3] In *Fédération Cynologique International v. Federación Canina Internacional de Perros de Pura Raza*,[4] the Court of Justice ruled in relation to the Community Trade Marks Regulation (CTMR, now EUTMR) that the exclusive right of the proprietor of a Community trade mark (CTM, now EUTM) to prohibit 'all third parties' from using its trade mark applies even in respect of a third-party proprietor of a later registered CTM. The proprietor does not need to apply to invalidate the later mark *before* they can bring proceedings for infringement. While that case concerned CTMs, the same language of 'all third parties' appears in Article 5 of the TMD 2008.

However, on closer examination, the question of incompatibility looks less straightforward. On the one hand, section 11(1) of the 1994 Act appears to be an exception to the trade mark proprietor's rights that is not permitted under the Directive. But if one thinks through what happens in practice, it is perhaps easier to see that the defence does not preclude an action by the earlier trade mark owner unless there has been invalidation of the later mark 'beforehand'.[5] This is because where a defendant relies on the section 11(1) defence, the claimant will usually respond by challenging the validity of the registered mark under section 47(3). This can (indeed, must) be done in the same proceedings, so it does not operate as a procedural bar to continuing with the action.

In practice, the ability of the claimant to nullify the section 11(1) defence by challenging the validity of the defendant's registration may be restricted if the claimant has acquiesced in the use of the later trade mark. This is because, where the owner of an earlier trade mark has knowingly acquiesced in the use of the mark for a continuous period of five years, section 48 of the 1994 Act provides that they lose the ability to apply for a declaration that the registration is invalid or to oppose the use of the mark.[6] Unless the defendant's registration was in bad faith, where a claimant has acquiesced in the use of the later mark, they lose the ability to counteract the section 11(1) defence.

The focus may now shift to compatibility of section 11(1) with newly introduced provisions of European trade mark law, which now also contains an 'intervening rights' defence. A subsequent (or intervening) trade mark registration may withstand an infringement claim based upon a prior trade mark in qualified circumstances. In effect, this defence introduces a form of coexistence for both prior and subsequent registered marks, by additionally insulating the prior mark against an infringement claim based upon the later mark.[7] Each is protected against the other in certain circumstances. However the circumstances vary depending on whether a later EUTM is being considered,[8] or a national mark.[9] For both types of marks, the defence applies where the right holder of the prior mark has acquiesced to the use of the later mark, or where the earlier mark was vulnerable to revocation at the filing or priority date of the later mark. The EUTMR recognizes the consent of the owner of the earlier mark as a means of activating the defence, while the TMD 2015 stipulates that if an invalidation challenge against the later mark, at its filing or priority date, would fail on specified grounds such as non-use or not having acquired distinctiveness or a sufficient reputation, the defence will operate at the national level.

---

[3] Although it is notable that the Spanish Supreme Court has persisted with it: *Editorial Prensa Canarias, S.A. v. Radio Pública de Canarias SA* (24 July 2013). See also recent legislative developments towards the end of this section.   [4] Case C-561/11 [2013] *ETMR* 23.

[5] Note the operative part of the Court ruling: ibid.

[6] TMD 1989, Art. 9; *Budejovicky Budvar v. Anheuser Busch*, Case C-482/09 [2011] *ECR* I–8701.

[7] EUTMR, Recital 22.   [8] EUTMR, Art. 16 (ex CTMR, Art. 13a after the initial recasting in 2015).

3 USE OF NAME OR ADDRESS

Section 11(2)(a) of the 1994 Act//Article 14(1)(a) EUTMR provides that a registered trade mark is not infringed by 'the use by a person of his own name or address'.[10] Significantly, both the TMD and EUTMR now specify that only natural persons can avail of this defence. As with all of the defences in section 11(2), this is subject to the proviso that the use is 'in accordance with honest practices in industrial or commercial matters'.

3.1 USE OF NAME

In contrast with the law of passing off,[11] trade mark law provides a defence to a claim of infringement where a person uses their own name. This defence is all the more important because of the way in which section 3(1)(b) of the Act has been interpreted in relation to surnames, which leaves open the possibility that the first person to apply to protect a surname as a trade mark in a given field will be able to obtain protection,[12] and that there will on its face be a case of infringement where others utilize their own names.[13]

In *Anheuser-Busch*,[14] the owner of the BUDWEISER mark for beer sued its Czech trade rival, which was importing its BUDVAR beer into Finland. The defendant's beer bore the BUDVAR mark, but also stated below the trade mark—and in considerably smaller lettering—that the product had been 'brewed and bottled by the brewery Budweiser Budvar national enterprise'. The Court of Justice provided guidance on the interpretation of Article 6(1)(a) of the TMD 1989, which, in its view, was necessary for the Finnish court to dispose of the case. Most significantly, the Court held that the defence was not confined to personal names. This was in spite of a Council and Commission Minute stating that the exception was so limited.[15] The Court of Justice noted that these Minutes were non-binding and that there was nothing in the text of the Directive to suggest such a limitation. While this resolved the most important question about the scope of the exception, which had existed since its enactment, tribunals continued to refine the scope of the concept of one's 'own name'. The English courts had favoured a restrictive interpretation, permitting slight variation from the formal registered company name, for example by dropping 'Ltd',[16] but not more substantial abbreviations,[17] nor the adoption of a trading name.[18] However, the Court of Appeal decision in *Hotel Cipriani*[19] signals a more flexible approach. There is no per se rule that a trading name is not a person's own name, although

---

[9] TMD 2015, Art. 18.   [10] Ex CTMR, Art. 12(a); TMD 2008, Art. 6(a); TMD 2015, Art. 14(1)(a).

[11] See Chapter 33, section 2.1, pp. 888–9.

[12] The debate over the appropriate test for distinctiveness, explained in Chapter 37, has been informed by different views as to the scope and usefulness of the defences: see *Nichols plc's Trade Mark* [2003] *RPC* (16) 301, 305–6; cf. esp. *Procter & Gamble v. OHIM (Baby Dry)*, Case C-383/99P [2001] *ECR* I–6251; *Wrigley v. OHIM (Doublemint)*, Case C-191/01P [2003] *ETMR* (88) 1068 (AG Jacobs).

[13] *McCartney*, R 1802/2011–2 (OHIM BoA).

[14] *Anheuser-Busch v. Budvar*, Case C-245/02 [2004] *ECR* I–10989 (ECJ, Grand Chamber), [75]–[84].

[15] For a draft version, see European Council, *Note from General Secretariat to COREPER on Amended Proposal for a Council Regulation on the Community Trade Mark* (11 May 1988) Note 5865/88, available online at https://www.cipil.law.cam.ac.uk/projecteuropean-travaux/community-trade-mark-regulation.

[16] *Scandecor Developments AB v. Scandecor Marketing Ltd* [1998] *FSR* 500, 521–2 (Lloyd J); *Daimler Chrysler AG v. Alavi* [2001] *RPC* (42) 813, 846, [100].

[17] *Premier Luggage & Bags Ltd v. Premier Company (UK) Ltd* [2003] *FSR* (5) 69, 88–9, [44].

[18] *Asprey & Garrard Ltd v. WRA (Guns) Ltd* [2001] *EWCA Civ* 1499, [2002] *FSR* (31) 487, [15].

[19] *Hotel Cipriani Srl v. Cipriani (Grosvenor Street) Ltd* [2010] *EWCA Civ* 110, [2010] *RPC* (16) 485.

a substantial variation from it is not. Thus Cipriani Grosvenor Street was able, in principle, to rely on the defence to justify using the name 'Cipriani (London)', its trading name, even though such use would otherwise have infringed the claimant's CIPRIANI mark, but not 'Cipriani' (which was not its name at all).[20] The High Court had previously held that the section 11(2)(a) defence would not apply to the use of a nickname,[21] but the Court of Appeal indicated the opposite—that:

> [I]n principle an individual ought to be able to use the defence in relation to an adopted name by which he or she is known for business purposes or generally, for example an actor's stage name or a writer's nom de plume.[22]

Where the 'own name' defence has been unsuccessful, this is frequently due to the evaluation of the various factors relevant for the honest practices proviso.[23] Nevertheless the defence has been successfully relied upon by those using a corporate or trading name.[24] The recent legislative contraction to personal names is therefore significant.[25] While infringing acts carried out prior to the new EUTMR provisions coming in to force will be grandfathered and insulated,[26] the contraction to personal names has been unsuccessfully challenged on the grounds that it constitutes an unjustified or disproportionate interference with EU fundamental rights, including the freedom of expression and freedom to conduct a business.[27] While an interference with both rights could be established, the contraction of the scope of the defence was justified by its legitimate objectives and did not exceed the limits of what was necessary to achieve those objectives. Considered against the backdrop of legislative discretion to achieve these objectives (the protection of trade marks as property), this contraction was not manifestly inappropriate.

3.2 HONEST PRACTICES

The notion of 'honest practices in industrial and commercial matters' has its origins in the provisions of the Paris Convention that require member states to take steps to prohibit unfair competition.[28] The thinking behind its use in Article 6 of the TMD 2008 is that certain uses of a registered mark by third parties should be permissible, but only insofar as they do not legitimize unfair competitive practices by the third party. Simply fitting into one of the specified categories—using one's own name or using a sign descriptively—is

---

[20] Ibid., [73].   [21] *NAD v. NAD* [1997] *FSR* 380.

[22] [2010] *EWCA Civ* 110, [2010] *RPC* (16) 485, [66].

[23] The honest practices proviso proved to be the stumbling block in *Och-Ziff v. OCH Capital* [2010] *EWHC* 2599; *Redd Solicitors LLP v. Red Legal* [2012] *EWPCC* 54; *Property Renaissance Ltd (t/a Titanic Spa) v. Stanley Dock Hotel Ltd (t/a Titanic Hotel Liverpool) & ors* [2016] *EWHC* 3103 (Ch) [89]–[111] (Carr J) (the defence was narrowly unsuccessful in relation to past practices; however with some finessing the defence would be applicable in the future). It is also restricted to natural or legal persons and cannot be extended to the names of pets: *Azumi Ltd v. Zuma's Choice Pet Products Ltd* [2017] *EWHC* 609 (IPEC).

[24] *Stichting BDO v. BDO Unibank* [2013] *EWHC* 418 (Ch); *Roger Maier v. ASOS plc* [2015] *EWCA Civ* 220 (note the dissent by Sales LJ); *Argos Ltd v. Argos Systems Inc* [2017] *EWHC* 231 (Ch).

[25] Justification for this was offered in the Max Planck Institute, *Study on the Overall Functioning of the Community Trade Mark System* (2011), [2.254]–[2.254] (referring to the 'priority principle' which should consistently mediate conflicts between all distinguishing signs).

[26] *Argos Ltd v. Argos Systems Inc* [2017] *EWHC* 231 (Ch), [312].

[27] *Sky v. SkyKick* [2018] *EWHC* 155 (Ch), [336]–[355] (Arnold J).

[28] Paris, Art. 10*bis*(2). Note also *Anheuser-Busch v. Budvar*, Case C-245/02 [2004] *ECR* I–10989 (ECJ, Grand Chamber) (referring to TRIPS, Art. 17, requiring regard to be had to the legitimate interests of the proprietor).

not enough to avail of the defence. The basis for that use and its effects upon the trade mark proprietor must also be factored in. The Court of Justice has therefore interpreted the proviso as imposing 'a duty to act fairly' towards the trade mark owner.[29] The same approach is taken in relation to all three defences in section 11(2) (Article 6 of the TMD 2008; Article 14 of the EUTMR),[30] although the application may vary from one situation to another.

As opposed to purely subjective honesty assessed from the defendant's perspective, this is an objective test. It requires the circumstances to be viewed globally,[31] taking into account how the sign came to be adopted,[32] the impact of the use on the interests of the proprietor of the mark, the knowledge of the alleged infringer,[33] and the efforts that they make to ensure that there is no confusion or unfair advantage.[34] It is now clear that the proviso does not preclude use of a sign as a trade mark.[35] In deciding whether use of a trade mark is in accordance with honest practice, a tribunal needs to examine the overall presentation of the goods (or advertising of the services) by the defendant.[36]

Despite the framing of the test of honest practices in terms of broad notions of fairness, dependent on an overall understanding of the circumstances, in at least one case the Court of Justice appears also to have indicated that there are some minimum conditions that must be met before the defence can come into play.[37] More specifically, the Court has indicated that a use will not be in accordance with honest practices if it is done in such a manner that it may give the impression that there is a commercial connection between the reseller and the trade mark proprietor,[38] if the use affects the value of the trade mark

[29] *BMW v. Deenik*, Case C-63/97 [1999] *ECR* I–905, [61]; *Céline Sàrl v. Céline SA*, Case C-17/06 [2007] *ECR* I–7041, [32]; *Gerolsteiner Brunnen GmbH & Co. v. Putsch GmbH*, Case C-100/02 [2004] *ECR* I–691, [24]; *Anheuser-Busch v. Budvar*, Case C-245/02 [2004] *ECR* I–10989 (ECJ, Grand Chamber), [82]; *Gillette Co. v. L.A-Laboratories Ltd Oy*, Case C-228/03 [2005] *ECR* I–2337, [41]; *Portakabin Ltd v. Primakabin BV*, Case C-558/08 [2010] *ECR* I–6963 (ECJ, First Chamber), [67].

[30] For example, the Court of Justice in both 'own name' cases *Anheuser-Busch v. Budvar*, Case C-245/02 [2004] *ECR* I–10989 and *Gillette Co. v. L.A-Laboratories Ltd Oy*, Case C-228/03 [2005] *ECR* I–2337 cites the earlier 'descriptive fair use' case of *Gerolsteiner Brunnen GmbH & Co. v. Putsch GmbH*, Case C-100/02 [2004] *ECR* I–691. See also *Samuel Smith Old Brewery v. Lee* [2011] *EWHC* 1879 (Ch), [2012] *FSR* (7) 263, [113].

[31] *Gillette Co. v. L.A-Laboratories Ltd Oy*, Case C-228/03 [2005] *ECR* I–2337, [46] ('an overall assessment of all the relevant circumstances').

[32] *Céline Sàrl v. Céline SA*, Case C-17/06 [2007] *ECR* I–7041, [AG53]–[AG57]; *Hotel Cipriani SRL v. Cipriani (Grosvenor St) Ltd* [2009] *RPC* (9) 209, [151].

[33] *Céline Sàrl v. Céline SA*, Case C-17/06 [2007] *ECR* I–7041, [34]; *Anheuser-Busch v. Budvar*, Case C-245/02 [2004] *ECR* I–10989, [83]; *Portakabin Ltd v. Primakabin BV*, Case C-558/08 [2010] *ECR* I–6963, [67], [70].

[34] *Gillette Co. v. L.A-Laboratories Ltd Oy*, Case C-228/03 [2005] *ECR* I–2337, [46]. The question of how the user of the sign responded to changing appreciation of the effects of use of the mark was emphasized in *Samuel Smith Old Brewery v. Lee* [2011] *EWHC* 1879 (Ch), [2012] *FSR* (7) 263, and *Maier v. Asos plc* [2013] *EWHC* 2831 (Ch), [157].

[35] *Reed Executive plc v. Reed Business Information Ltd* [2004] *RPC* (40) 767, [121], [124], [125].

[36] There are now many examples applying the standard. In the context of the 'own name' defence, see *Hotel Cipriani SRL v. Cipriani (Grosvenor St) Ltd* [2009] *RPC* (9) 209, [153]–[164], on appeal at [2010] *EWCA Civ* 110, [2010] *RPC* (16) 485, esp. at [58]–[86]; *Och Ziff v. Och Capital* [2010] *EWHC* 2599 (Ch), [141]–[151]; *Stichtung BDO v. BDO Unibank Inc.* [2013] *EWHC* 418 (Ch); *Frost Products Ltd v. FC Frost Ltd* [2013] *EWPCC* 34, [138]–[139] (Vos J); *Maier v. Asos plc* [2015] *EWCA Civ* 220, [145]–[160] (Kitchin LJ) (with a dissent from Sales LJ, who was critical of the defendant's failure to conduct a comprehensive clearance search before adopting a name) *Sky v. SkyKick* [2018] *EWHC* 155 (Ch), [327]–[335] (Arnold J).

[37] *Gillette Co. v. L.A-Laboratories Ltd Oy*, Case C-228/03 [2005] *ECR* I–2337, [42]–[45], [49]; *BMW v. Round and Metal Ltd* [2012] *EWHC* 2099 (Pat), [113].

[38] *BMW v. Deenik*, Case C-63/97 [1999] *ECR* I–905, [51]; *Gillette Co. v. L.A-Laboratories Ltd Oy*, Case C-228/03 [2005] *ECR* I–2337, [42]; *Anheuser-Busch v. Budvar*, Case C-245/02 [2004] *ECR* I–10989, [83].

by taking unfair advantage of its distinctive character or repute,[39] if it discredits or denigrates that mark,[40] or if it presents its product as an imitation or replica of the product bearing the trade mark.[41] These latter factors seem to have been drawn from the Directive on Misleading and Comparative Advertising (under which they operate as conditions, rather than factors). English case law, like the earlier Court of Justice jurisprudence,[42] treats these as 'important factors' in the overall assessment, rather than as conditions.[43] As will become clear, this more flexible approach has much to be said for it—after all, we are assessing 'fairness'.

The first two of the conditions (or factors) warrant a little further elaboration. In the first instance, the defence will not be available if consumers would understand the use of the trade name to be implying a link with the trade mark owner,[44] for example by suggesting that the trader's business is part of or affiliated with the trade mark owner's business.[45] This will doubtless depend on exactly how the defendant used the sign (in displays, advertising, packaging, or on the product) and how observant the average consumer is likely to be. The Court of Justice said that this was a question of fact to be decided by national courts.[46] However, it has also indicated that some confusion may be permissible: the Court in *Gerolsteiner*[47] acknowledged that the defences might be available even though there was some limited evidence of aural confusion. Presumably, the greater the level of confusion, the more likely that the use will be regarded as falling outside the defence.[48] A distinction is also drawn between actual instances of confusion or harm to other functions of the mark, which makes a successful defence less likely and the risk or possibility of harm, where the defences remains in play.[49] Later cases have added that it is important also to consider the extent to which the defendant was aware, or ought to have been aware, that the consumer would consider there to be a link. If it is obvious to the defendant that such a conclusion would be drawn by consumers, then most likely the use will not be regarded as honest.

In *Portakabin Ltd v. Primakabin BV*,[50] the Court indicated that even if the defendant's use of the sign on its goods falls within the terms of section 11(2)/Article 6, it will rarely be in accordance with honest practices to utilize that trade mark as a keyword to generate adverts, at least if it is not clear from those adverts that the two enterprises are unconnected economically. The Court did not close the door completely, however.[51]

---

[39] *BMW v. Deenik*, Case C-63/97 [1999] *ECR* I–905, [52]; *Gillette Co. v. L.A–Laboratories Ltd Oy*, Case C-228/03 [2005] *ECR* I–2337, [43].   [40] Ibid., [44].

[41] Ibid., [45].

[42] *Céline Sàrl v. Céline SA*, Case C-17/06 [2007] *ECR* I–7041, [34]; *Anheuser-Busch v. Budvar*, Case C-245/02 [2004] *ECR* I–10989, [83].

[43] *Hotel Cipriani SRL v. Cipriani (Grosvenor St) Ltd* [2009] *RPC* (9) 209, [145] (Arnold J); *Samuel Smith Old Brewery v. Lee* [2011] *EWHC* 1879 (Ch), [2012] *FSR* (7) 263, esp. [116], [118]; *Maier v. Asos plc* [2013] *EWHC* 2831 (Ch), [148] (Rose J). The justification for so doing seems to be that it is only if these are 'factors' that the conclusion in *Gerolsteiner Brunnen*, Case C-100/02 [2004] *ECR* I–691, [25], that some confusion does not preclude a finding of honest practices, can be reconciled with the statement in *Gillette*.

[44] *Anheuser-Busch v. Budvar*, Case C-245/02 [2004] *ECR* I–10989, [83].

[45] *BMW v. Deenik*, Case C-63/97 [1999] *ECR* I–905, [52], [63], [64].   [46] Ibid., [55].

[47] Case C-100/02 [2004] *ECR* I–691. See also *Roger Maier v. ASOS plc* [2015] *EWCA Civ* 220 [149] (Kitchin LJ) ('The possibility of a limited degree of confusion does not preclude the application of the defence, however. It all depends upon the reason for that confusion and all the other circumstances of the case').

[48] *Fine & Country v. Okotoks* [2012] *EWHC* 2230, [2013] *EWCA Civ* 672, [123].

[49] *Sky Plc v. Skykick UK Ltd* [2018] *EWHC* 155 (Ch), [330]–[331].

[50] *BMW v. Deenik*, Case C-63/97 [1999] *ECR* I–905, [53]. See *Mercedes Star* (5 July 2001) (Düsseldorf Court of Appeal) (2003) 34 *IIC* 438.   [51] Case C-558/08 [2010] *ECR* I–6963, [68]–[72].

Second, the Court has emphasized that the defendant's use must not take 'unfair advantage' of the reputation associated with the mark. However, the mere accrual of some 'advantage' is not determinative: the Court of Justice has said that if there is no risk that the public will be led to believe that there is a commercial connection between the trader and the trade mark proprietor, the mere fact that the trader derived an advantage from using the mark (for example because the advertisements lend an aura of quality to their business) would not of itself mean that the use was dishonest.[52]

The emphasis in the case law on 'unfair advantage' is, in many respects, understandable, but any attempt to elevate it into a condition for the operation of the defence must be regarded as regrettable for two reasons. Both reasons stem from the fact that the same language appears as a condition for liability in the context of 'dilution', discussed in detail in Chapter 38, and the concepts have been assumed to be identical.

The first objection is that this understanding of section 11(2)/Article 6 denudes it of any role in actions for infringement based on section 10(3)/Article 5(2).[53] Because 'unfair advantage' is one of the conditions for liability, if 'unfair advantage' precludes a defence, then there can never be a defence to any such claim. The danger of circular reasoning is worth highlighting: (i) infringement is established, (ii) whereupon the defendant reaches for the defences, (iii) only to find themselves unable to establish 'honest practices', since the same factors giving rise to infringement resurface as obstacles under the proviso.[54] The same reasoning applies insofar as section 10(3) provides for liability based on blurring and tarnishment, and the existence of any blurring or tarnishment could also been said to preclude the defence. All of this is regrettable because it is precisely in situations in which liability extends beyond confusion that most commentators regard there to be a pressing need for exceptions. The inevitable effect of removing the availability of the section 11(2)/Article 6 exceptions from section 10(3)/Article 5(2) claims is to force tribunals to develop the vague language of 'due cause' (so that there is no liability to begin with). Thus while use of a sign comprising a third party's keyword may necessarily confer an unfair advantage, in *Interflora*[55] the Court seemed to recognize that a trade might have 'due cause' to utilize a keyword (there, in order to offer alternatives to the trade mark proprietor's goods to the consumer).

The second objection to a rule that the existence of unfair advantage precludes the operation of the section 11(2) defences is that the concept of 'unfair' advantage has itself been deprived of much content. Indeed, as we saw in Chapter 38, the notion of 'unfairness' has been equated with the deliberateness of the use. One possible way in which to avoid an undesirably restrictive application of the defences would be to give 'unfairness' a different meaning when deciding whether an act is in accordance with honest practices (as the

---

[52] Ibid., [71]. See also *Maier v. Asos plc* [2013] *EWHC* 2831 (Ch), [165] (Rose J); *Argos Ltd v. Argos Systems Inc* [2017] *EWHC* 231 (Ch), [283], [326]–[327] (Richard Spearman QC) (any unremunerated advantage is not unfair).

[53] *Céline Sàrl v. Céline SA*, Case C-17/06 [2007] *ECR* I–7041, [AG47]. Cf. Max Planck Institute, *Study on the Overall Functioning of the Community Trade Mark System* (2010), [2.250] (uses of reputation marks that would benefit from one of the exceptions are made 'with due cause').

[54] P-J. Yap, 'Honestly, Neither Celine nor Gillette is Defensible' [2008] *EIPR* 286. For the argument that interpretative approaches to defences have been undesirably restrictive, see I. Fhima, 'The Trade Mark Defences Meet Copyright: Fair use or Three Step Test?' (2014) 4 *QMJIP* 297; M. Senftleben et al., 'The Recommendation on Measures to Safeguard Freedom of Expression and Undistorted Competition: Guiding Principles for the Further Development of EU Trade Mark Law' [2015] *EIPR* 337.

[55] *Interflora v. Marks & Spencer*, Case C-323/09 [2011] *ECR* I–8625.

Court did in the *BMW* case[56]). It might be added that similar problems would be caused were it to be concluded that it is a condition for the operation of the defence that a use must not be detrimental to the distinctive character of a mark, given that jurisprudence suggests that if there is a likelihood of confusion, then there is detriment to distinctive character.[57] Because there is no 'due cause' limitation on section 10(1) (double identity) or section 10(2) (confusing similarity) liability, elevating these factors into conditions could potentially deprive the defences of all operation.[58]

Drawing back from the specifics of unfair advantage, the recent reforms to EU trade mark law have explicitly acknowledged the need to balance the interests of trade mark proprietors with competitors and other third parties. The content of honest practices has now been expanded to include considerations relating to artistic expression and the freedom of expression, as well as fundamental rights more generally.[59]

4 DESCRIPTIVE USE

Section 11(2)(b) of the 1994 Act/Article 14(1)(b) of the EUTMR[60] provides that a registered trade mark is not infringed where the mark is used to indicate the kind, quality, quantity, intended purpose, value, geographical origin, time of production (goods) or of rendering (services), or other characteristics of goods or services. This is subject to the proviso that the use is in accordance with honest practice in industrial or commercial matters. Although descriptive terms are inherently unregistrable,[61] as noted in Chapter 37, if a descriptive term becomes registrable because it has 'acquired distinctiveness' through use, the section 11(2)(b) defence ensures that the rights conferred on the proprietor do not restrict other traders from using the same word or sign to describe goods or services.

4.1 DESCRIPTIVENESS

The notion of descriptive use is not limited to 'purely descriptive' uses such as those that have no effect on the functions of a trade mark, and thus might include, for example, descriptive use in advertising.[62] The most obvious situation in which the section 11(2)(b) defence applies is where a trader uses a sign that is a registered trade mark to describe their own goods, for example where, in the face of the trade mark BABY DRY registered for diapers, a competitor advertises its own nappies with the slogan 'guaranteed to keep your baby dry'.

---

[56] *BMW v. Deenik*, Case C-63/97 [1999] *ECR* I-905. But cf. *L'Oréal NV and ors v. Bellure NV*, Case C-487/07 [2009] *ECR* I-5185, [77] (unfair advantage has the same meaning in TMD 1989, Art. 5(2), and MCAD, Art. 4(f)); *O2 Holdings Ltd v. Hutchison 3G UK Ltd*, Case C-533/06 [2008] *ECR* I-4231, [49] (confusion has the same meaning in both legal instruments).

[57] *Fine and Country Ltd v. Okotoks Ltd* [2012] *EWHC* 2230 (Ch), [270] (Hildyard J).

[58] A proposal to codify these two conditions in a non-exhaustive definition of 'honest practices' was ultimately not incorporated adopted as part of the European legislative reform inititaive: Max Planck Institute, *Study on the Overall Functioning of the Community Trade Mark System* (2011), [2.265]

[59] TMD 2015, Recital 27; EUTMR, Recital 21.

[60] Ex CTMR, Art. 12(b); TMD 2008, Art. 6(b); TMD 2015, Art. 14(1)(b).

[61] The debate over the appropriate test for descriptiveness has been informed by different views as to the scope and usefulness of the descriptiveness defence. cf. *Procter & Gamble v. OHIM (Baby Dry)*, Case C-383/99P [2001] *ECR* I-6251 and *Wrigley v. OHIM (Doublemint)*, Case C-191/01P [2003] *ETMR* (88) 1068 (AG Jacobs).

[62] *L'Oréal NV and ors v. Bellure NV*, Case C-487/07 [2009] *ECR* I-5185, [61]-[62]. On 'purely' descriptive uses that do not jeopardize the 'origin function', see Chapter 40, section 10.1, pp. 1118-22.

The defence can also apply where a person uses a descriptive indication as part of their own trade mark. For example, in *Gerolsteiner Brunnen GmbH & Co. v. Putsch GmbH*,[63] the question referred to the Court of Justice was whether bottled water bearing the mark KERRY SPRING could rely on the defence to an action brought by the owner of the registered GERRI for mineral water. Although the defendant used the sign 'as a trade mark', the Court accepted that the sign KERRY SPRING was also an indication of geographical origin within Article 6(1)(b). The fact that a sign is used additionally as a mark is a factor pertinent to the assessment whether the use is in accordance with honest practice, rather than whether the sign indicated geographical origin.

However, there are now a number of relatively clear situations in which the descriptiveness defence cannot be relied upon. It does not apply where a person uses the mark to describe the claimant's goods, also referred to as nominative or referential use (as with 'PAMPERS soak up twice as much liquid as BABY DRY'),[64] nor to the use of third-party marks as 'keywords' to generate advertising.[65] Moreover it does not justify 'decorative' use. In *Adidas AG v. Marca Mode CV*,[66] the Court of Justice explained that a decorative use (in the case of two stripes on athletic clothing) is not a descriptive indication.

A more difficult case is the use of a trade marked feature of a product to indicate that what is being sold is a representation or miniature model of the product (that the seller is entitled to make or sell). In *Adam Opel AG v. Autec AG*,[67] the well-known car manufacturer Opel had registrations of its logo for cars and toys (see Fig. 40.1, section 10.1, p. 1119), and brought an action against Autec, which featured the Opel logo on its replica toys. The defendant asserted that this could be regarded as use to describe the goods—that is, to indicate that the goods were replicas of cars made by Opel. The Court of Justice indicated that Article 6(1)(b) of the Directive could not be stretched to exempt such uses (if indeed they fell within Article 5 of the Directive). The Court stated bluntly that:

> The affixing of a sign which is identical to a trade mark registered, inter alia, in respect of motor vehicles to scale models of that make of vehicle in order to reproduce those vehicles faithfully is not intended to provide an indication as to a characteristic of those scale models, but is merely an element in the faithful reproduction of the original vehicles.[68]

It therefore contradicted Advocate-General Colomer's view that such use should be within the exception. Unfortunately, it is unclear why the use of the logo is not regarded by the Court of Justice as a use that indicates that the toy is a replica of the Opel car.

4.2 HONEST PRACTICES

A descriptive use will provide a defence only if it is in accordance with 'honest practices in industrial and commercial matters'.[69] Readers are referred back to the discussion of this

---

[63] Case C-100/02 [2004] *ECR* I–691 (ECJ, Fifth Chamber); cf. *Windsurfing Chiemsee*, Cases C-108 and 109/97 [1999] *ECR* I–2779, [28]; *Adidas AG and ors v. Marca Mode CV and ors*, Case C-102/07 [2008] *ECR* I–2439, [AG77].

[64] *L'Oréal SA v. Bellure*, Case C-487/07 [2009] *ECR* I–5185, [AG25] (AG Mengozzi); *Portakabin Ltd v. Primakabin BV*, Case C-558/08 [2010] *ECR* I–6963, [60]–[61].   [65] Ibid., [60].

[66] Case C-102/07 [2008] *ECR* I–2439, [48]; cf. *Samuel Smith Old Brewery v. Lee* [2011] *EWHC* 1879 (Ch), [2012] *FSR* (7) 263, esp. [127].

[67] *Adam Opel AG v. Autec AG*, Case C-48/05 [2007] *ECR* I–1017; cf. ibid., [AG51] (AG Colomer).

[68] Ibid., [44].

[69] For examples in this context, see *Samuel Smith Old Brewery v. Lee* [2011], *EWHC* 1879 (Ch), [2012] *FSR* (7) 263; *Fine and Country Ltd v. Okotoks Ltd* [2012] *EWHC* 2230 (Ch), [270] (Hildyard J).

Fig. 41.1 O$_2$'s bubble trade mark
Source: O$_2$

in the previous section. One factor that is worth drawing attention to here, however, is the impact of linguistic diversity in the European Union. Although the question of infringement, like distinctiveness,[70] is viewed from the perspective of the average consumer with the particular characteristics associated with the territory,[71] it may be that, when considering honest practices, it will be relevant that the sign was adopted as descriptive in the member state from which the goods originate. In *Gerolsteiner*,[72] the Court observed that a certain amount of confusion might need to be tolerated in an economic union of the size and diversity of the European Union. The Court stated that, given the great linguistic diversity, 'the chance that there exists some phonetic similarity between a trade mark registered in one Member State and an indication of geographical origin from another Member State is . . . substantial'.[73] Such confusion was not conclusive evidence that a defendant was not acting in accordance with honest practices. That case concerned a geographical indication, but the observations are all the more relevant to descriptive terms from different languages.

---

[70] Recall *Matratzen Concord AG v. HuGermany SA*, Case C-421/04 [2006] *ECR* I–2303, discussed in Chapter 37, section 3.1.2, pp. 979–80, in which the German word for mattresses, *Matratzen*, was registrable as a trade mark in Spain for mattresses.

[71] It may be worth considering whether a country-of-origin rule (similar to that adopted recently for orphan works and discussed in Chapter 12, section 5, pp. 346–9) should be applicable to the question of whether an indication is descriptive: if it is descriptive in its country of origin, then the defence should be applicable (subject to a finding of honest practices). This, presumably, is the situation under the EUTM, so the system would have greater coherence if it were also the rule for TMD 2008, Art. 6.

[72] *Gerolsteiner Brunnen*, Case C-100/02 [2004] *ECR* I–691.   [73] Ibid., [25].

4.3 EXTENSION TO NON-DISTINCTIVE ELEMENTS

The 'descriptiveness' defence in Article 14(1)(b) of the EUTMR/Article 14(1)(b) of the TMD 2015 has recently been extended to cover the use of 'non-distinctive' signs.[74] This amendment has not yet been incorporated into UK law. One reading is that it embodies the teachings of *Hölterhoff,* insulating purely descriptive uses of the whole sign by the defendant against infringement.[75] However the preferred reading is that this new addition seeks to filter out non-distinctive elements within otherwise-distinctive trade marks. It emerges as a counterweight to the proposal in the Max Planck study to do away with disclaimers in European trade mark law, which was eventually adopted.[76] At the time of registration if trade mark applicants can no longer volitionally disclaim non-distinctive elements of a complex mark, or be asked to do so by registries, alternative mechanisms are required to permit the use of these elements by third parties. Because trade mark applications are rejected only when they consist *exclusively* of elements that are non-distinctive, it is possible to register marks that include non-distinctive components. This new defence might enable traders to use non-distinctive components of earlier registered marks as decorations or in their own marks, or to selectively use functional or ornamental elements of shape marks that have been registered on the basis that they are not 'exclusively' functional or ornamental.[77] While this new addition seems desirable, certain aspects lack clarity. Presumably, the new defence would not allow the use of inherently non-distinctive signs (as a whole) that have acquired distinctiveness, but only the use of those components of registered marks that remain non-distinctive. In this respect, its application would be rather different from the broader descriptive use exception within which it appears; the imagery of 'holes in Swiss cheese' is more apt.

5 USE TO INDICATE THE INTENDED PURPOSE OF A PRODUCT OR SERVICE

Section 11(2)(c) of the 1994 Act/Article 14(1)(c) EUTMR provides that a registered trade mark is not infringed where the defendant finds it necessary to use the mark to indicate the intended purpose of a product or service (in particular, as accessories or spare parts) and—as is outlined later—EU law has recently been amended to include referential use in general.[78] This is subject to the proviso that the use must be in accordance with honest practice in industrial or commercial matters. It is peculiar that these acts warrant an explicit defence, because section 11(2)(b) itself encompasses the use of 'indications' of the 'intended purpose' of the

---

[74] See also EUTMR, Recital 21 ('The exclusive rights conferred by an EU trade mark should not entitle the proprietor to prohibit . . . the use of descriptive or non-distinctive signs or indications in general').

[75] See Chapter 40, section 10.1, pp. 1118–22.

[76] Max Planck Institute, *Study on the Overall Functioning of the Community Trade Mark System* (2011), [2.38]–[2.48]. On disclaimers, see Chapter 35, section 2.5, p. 943. For additional interpretations, see A. Kur, 'Yellow Dictionaries, Red Banking Services, Some Candies and a Sitting Bunny: Protection of Colour and Shape Marks from a German and European Perspective', in I. Calboli and M. Senftleben (eds), *The Protection of Non-Traditional Marks: Critical Perspectives* (2018).   [77] See Chapter 36, Section 3.1, pp. 959–64.

[78] See also TMD 2008, Art. 6(c); TMD 2015, Art. 14(1)(c). This would also count as comparative advertising within the MCAD, since it implicitly states that the two products have equivalent technical features: *Toshiba Europe GmbH v. Katun Germany GmbH,* Case C-112/99 [2002] 3 *CMLR* (7) 164, [32]–[40]. As we have noted in section 3.2, pp. 1132–6, the Court of Justice has increasingly used the conditions from MCAD, Art. 4, to define the notion of 'honest practices' under TMD 2008, Art. 6(1)(c).

goods or services. However, it has been assumed that section 11(2)(c) constitutes a special provision, explicitly referring to the use of a 'trade mark', and thus controls exclusively cases falling within its ambit.[79]

In effect, this defence recognizes that while a trader may not be formally linked to the trade mark owner, they might find it necessary to refer to the trade mark as a part of the normal course of their trade. This would occur, for example, where a trader sells spare parts for a particular type of product.[80] In these circumstances, the trader will wish to inform consumers that the parts fit particular products. The most efficient way in which this can be done is by referring to the trade mark for that product. Another situation in which it will be necessary to use a trade mark in the course of trade is where a trader repairs a particular brand of goods (such as SONY televisions). If trade mark owners were able to control such uses, they would unfairly restrict trade. As the Court of Justice said, the defence in Article 6(1)(c) of the Directive seeks to reconcile the 'fundamental interests of trade mark protection with those of the free movement of goods and freedom to provide services'.[81]

The nature of this defence was considered by the Court of Justice in *BMW v. Deenik*.[82] The defendant in this action ran a garage that specialized in repairing and maintaining BMW cars. Notably, he was not a part of the official BMW dealer network. BMW claimed that when the defendant described himself as specializing in the repair and maintenance of BMWs, he made unlawful use of the BMW mark. The Court of Justice disagreed, explaining that, in these circumstances, the defendant could rely on the defence in Article 6(1)(c) of the Directive. This was because the defendant could not communicate the fact that he repaired and maintained BMW cars without using the BMW mark.[83] In relation to the question of whether the use was *necessary* to indicate the intended purpose, the Court of Justice said that 'if an independent trader carries out the maintenance and repair of BMW cars or is in fact a specialist in the field, that fact cannot in practice be communicated to his customers without using the BMW mark'.[84]

The Court of Justice revisited the question of the scope of this exception in *Gillette*.[85] In this case, the claimant, Gillette, had registered trade marks for the words GILLETTE and SENSOR for razors. The defendant was selling blades under its mark PARASON FLEXOR, with a sticker on the packaging stating that 'all PARASON FLEXOR and GILLETTE SENSOR handles are compatible with this blade'. When Gillette sought to prevent this, the Finnish courts were uncertain as to whether the blades constituted 'spare parts' and therefore referred the matter to the Court. The Court of Justice responded by observing that the scope of the exception was not limited to spare parts and accessories, which were simply examples of possible intended uses of goods that would likely fall within the exception. The Court therefore stated that it was unnecessary to decide whether blades were accessories or spare parts; instead, the key issue was whether it was 'necessary' to refer to Gillette's marks to indicate the intended purpose of the blades. The Court helpfully explained that this would be so only if it were necessary to use the trade mark to provide the public with comprehensible and complete information about the intended purpose of the product (including its compatibility). Having given a generally broad definition

---

[79] *BMW v. Round and Metal Ltd* [2012] *EWHC* 2099 (Pat), [113].

[80] *PAG v. Hawk-Woods* [2002] *FSR* (46) 723, 729 (J).

[81] *Bayerische Motorenwerke AG and BMW Nederland Pumfrey BV v. Deenik*, Case C 63/97 [1999] *ECR* I–905, [64].   [82] Ibid.

[83] Ibid., [54].   [84] Ibid., [AG54], [60].

[85] *Gillette Co. v. L.A–Laboratories Ltd Oy*, Case C-288/03 [2005] *ECR* I–2337, [24]–[39]. See also *Portakabin Ltd v. Primakabin BV*, Case C-558/08 [2010] *ECR* I–6963, [62]–[66].

of the scope, the Court gave a rather narrow interpretation of 'necessary' when it stated that this meant that use of the claimant's trade mark must be the only way of conveying the relevant information. Consequently, where technical standards and other norms are available that are well understood by the public, it would not be necessary to use the claimant's trade mark to convey full information about compatibility. Armed with this advice, the Helsinki Supreme Court held that the reference to GILLETTE and SENSOR was indeed 'necessary' (and in accordance with honest practices).[86]

5.1 HONEST PRACTICES

For the defence to be available, the use must be 'in accordance with honest practices in industrial and commercial matters'. Readers are referred back to the discussion in section 3.2 of this chapter. In this context, the key danger that a trader must avoid is that consumers believe there to be an affiliation, for example that a repairer of automobiles is an 'authorized repairer' or that a provider of spare parts is, in fact, associated with the original manufacturer.[87] Where the defendant's use of the mark misleadingly suggests a connection—for example, being an authorized repairs garage—this should be initially analysed as part of the infringement analysis.[88] Evidence of misleading uses is relevant once again as it reduces the prospects for satisfying the 'honest practices' proviso.[89] Although we have argued that the question of honest factors should be assessed by reference to 'factors', it is particularly significant in this context that the Court of Justice has emphasized that absence of confusion, unfair advantage, blurring, and tarnishment operate as conditions.

5.2 REFERENTIAL USE IN GENERAL

As a consequence of the recasting and reform of EU trade mark law, the 'intended purpose' defence has been extended to be a more general referential use defence. In the United States, a body of case law has emerged in which traders are permitted to use trade marks to refer to the trade mark owner's goods or services. The amended EU law would offer equivalent freedom to European actors. Any use of a trade mark 'for the purpose of identifying or referring to goods or services as those of the proprietor of the trade mark' is permitted, as long as the use complies with the proviso.[90] The amended legislation now clarifies that referential use in order to honestly indicate the resale of genuine goods bearing the trade mark is permitted under this provision. So is fair referential use, 'for the purpose of artistic expression', provided it satisfies the honest practices proviso.[91] There is recognition that EU trade mark legislation—including defences—'should be applied in a way that ensures full respect for fundamental rights and freedoms, and in particular the freedom of expression'.[92]

---

[86] *Gillette Co. v. L.A.-Laboratories Ltd Oy* [2007] *ETMR* (17) 235 (Supreme Court, Helsinki).

[87] *Datacard v. Eagle Technologies* [2011] *EWHC* 244 (Pat), [347]; *BMW v. Round and Metal Ltd* [2012] *EWHC* 2099 (Pat), [113].

[88] *Bayerische Motoren Werke AG v. Technosport London Ltd* [2017] *EWCA Civ* 779, [14].

[89] *Bayerische Motorenwerke AG v. Ronayne (T/A BMW Care)* [2013] *IEHC* 612.

[90] EUTMR, Art. 14(1)(c); TMD 2015, Art. 14(1)(c). See also EUTMR, Recital 21 ('the proprietor should not be entitled to prevent the fair and honest use of the EU trade mark for the purpose of identifying or referring to the goods or services as those of the proprietor').

[91] EUTMR, Recital 21; TMD 2015, Recital 27.   [92] Ibid.

6 COMPARATIVE ADVERTISING

'Comparative advertising' is the term used to describe advertisements in which the goods or services of one trader are compared with the goods or services of another trader.[93] To show the advertiser's wares in a favourable light, comparative advertisements usually emphasize differences in aspects such as price, value, durability, or quality. In so doing, advertisers often refer to the competitor's products or services by their trade mark. The European Union has created specific legislation—the Directive on Misleading and Comparative Advertising (MCAD)[94]—dealing with the circumstances in which comparative advertising is permissible, and those in which it should be prevented.[95] However, the exact relationship between these rules and those relating to trade marks was unclear until relatively recently.[96]

In principle, the Directive requires member states to permit comparative advertising,[97] but does so only if the advertisement satisfies the eight conditions specified in Article 4:

(a) it is not misleading within the meaning of Articles 2(b), 3, and 8(1) of this Directive ... [these oblige member states to provide a minimum of protection against 'misleading' advertising, although leave that concept undefined];[98]

(b) it compares goods or services meeting the same needs or intended for the same purpose;[99]

(c) it objectively compares one or more material, relevant, verifiable, and representative features of those goods and services, which may include price;[100]

(d) it does not discredit or denigrate the trade marks, trade names, other distinguishing marks, goods, services, activities, or circumstances of a competitor;[101]

---

[93] See A. Ohly and M. Spence, *The Law of Comparative Advertising* (2000).

[94] Directive 2006/114/EC of the European Parliament and of the Council of 12 December 2006 concerning misleading and comparative advertising [2006] *OJ L* 376/21 (27 December 2006).

[95] For background, see A. Ohly and M. Spence, *The Law of Comparative Advertising* (2000); J. Glockner, 'The Regulation of Comparative Advertising in Europe' [2012] *IIC* 35.

[96] The curious provision in TMA 1994, s. 10(6), is now being treated by the UK courts as redundant: *O2 v. Hutchison* [2007] *RPC* (16) 407, [58]. For the case law on this, see Bently and Sherman (2004), 917–20.

[97] MCAD, Art. 2(c), defines 'comparative advertising' as 'any advertising which explicitly or by implication identifies a competitor or goods or services offered by a competitor'. This is 'particularly broad': *L'Oréal NV and ors v. Bellure NV*, Case C-487/07 [2009] *ECR* I–5185, [52]. On whether registration of a domain name counts as advertising and meta-tags, see *Belgian Electronic Sorting Technology v. Bert Peelaers*, Case C-657/11, EU:C:2013:516 (use of sign in meta-tag was advertising). On when advertising is 'comparative', see *De Landtsheer Emmanuel SA v. Comité Interprofessionnel du Vin de Champagne, Veuve Clicquot Ponsardin SA*, Case C-381/05 [2007] *ECR* I–3115. On whether 'keyword advertising' might be so regarded, see *Interflora Inc. v. Marks & Spencer plc* [2013] *EWHC* 1291 (Ch), [325] (Arnold J).

[98] See *Pippig Augenoptik GmbH & Co. KG v. Hartlauer Handelsgesellschaft mbH*, Case C-44/01 [2003] *ECR* I–3095, [53], [65]; *Lidl Belgium GmbH & Co. KG v. Etablissementen Franz Colruyt NV*, Case C-356/04 [2006] *ECR* I–8501 (ECJ, Grand Chamber); *Lidl v. Vierzon*, Case C-159/09 [2010] *ECR* I–11761; *Kingspan Group plc v. Rockwool* [2011] *EWHC* 250 (Ch); *Carrefour Hypermarchés SAS v. ITM Alimentaire International SASU*, Case C-562/15, EU:C:2017:95.

[99] *Emmanuel v. Veuve Clicquot*, Case C-381/05 [2007] *ECR* I–3115; *Lidl Belgium GmbH & Co. KG v. Etablissementen Franz Colruyt NV*, Case C-356/04 [2006] *ECR* I–8501, esp. [28], [34], [36]; *Lidl v. Vierzon*, Case C-159/09 [2010] *ECR* I–11761.

[100] *Lidl Belgium GmbH & Co. KG v. Etablissementen Franz Colruyt NV*, Case C-356/04 [2006] *ECR* I–8501, [47], [49], [61],[70]–[74]; *Carrefour Hypermarchés SAS v. ITM Alimentaire International*, Case C-562/15, EU:C:2017:95.   [101] See *Pippig*, Case C-44/01 [2003] *ECR* I–3095, [80].

(e)   for products with designation of origin, it relates in each case to products with the same designation;[102]

(f)   it does not take unfair advantage of the reputation of a trade mark, trade name, or other distinguishing marks of a competitor or of the designation of origin of competing products;[103]

(g)   it does not present goods or services as imitations or replicas of goods or services bearing a protected trade mark or trade name;[104]

(h)   it does not create confusion among traders, between the advertiser and a competitor or between the advertiser's trade marks, trade names, other distinguishing marks, goods or services and those of a competitor.

These conditions are to be interpreted in the sense most favourable to the comparative advertiser.[105] Member states are to ensure that 'adequate and effective' means exist to combat misleading advertising and to enforce compliance with the rules on comparative advertising 'in the interests of traders and competitors'. Such means are to include the taking of legal action.

The United Kingdom implements its obligations under the Directive through a patchwork of provisions.[106] One of the most important of these is the UK Code of Non-Broadcast Advertising, Sales Promotion and Direct Marketing (the 'CAP Code'), which was drafted by the Committee on Advertising Practice (CAP) and is administered by the Advertising Standards Authority (ASA).[107] The CAP Code establishes what is primarily a self-regulatory system, and was drawn up by representatives from relevant trade and professional bodies. The Code applies to advertisements in newspapers and other printed publications, cinema and video commercials, and promotions. A parallel code, applicable to broadcast media— the UK Code of Broadcast Advertising (the 'BCAP Code')—is also administered by the ASA.

The CAP Code permits comparative advertising so long as the comparisons comply with the terms of MCAD.[108] Conformity with these requirements is assessed according to the advertisement's probable impact, taken as a whole and in context. The impact that an advertisement has will depend on the audience, the medium, the nature of the product, and any additional material distributed to consumers at the time. Before releasing an advertisement, advertisers must have documentary evidence to prove all claims, whether

---

[102] Although products outside a designation can be compared with ones within: *De Landtsheer Emmanuel SA v. Comité Interprofessionnel du Vin de Champagne, Veuve Clicquot Ponsardin SA*, Case C-381/05 [2007] *ECR* I–3115.

[103] See *Toshiba v. Katun*, Case C-112/99 [2001] *ECR* I–7945; *Pippig*, Case C-44/01 [2003] *ECR* I–3095, [84]; *L'Oréal NV and ors v. Bellure NV*, Case C-487/07 [2009] *ECR* I–5185, [2010] *EWCA Civ* 535. For criticisms, see D. Gangjee and R. Burrell, 'Because You're Worth It' (2010) 73 *MLR* 282, 288–92.

[104] *L'Oréal NV and ors v. Bellure NV*, Case C-487/07 [2009] *ECR* I–5185, [75]–[76] (comparison list for smell-a-likes implicitly presented goods as imitations of fragrances, so breached condition), [2010] *EWCA Civ* 535, [38]. On the latter, see A. Kur, L. Bently, and A. Ohly, 'Sweet Smells and a Sour Taste: The ECJ's *L'Oréal* Decision' (2009), available online at http://papers.ssrn.com/sol3/papers.cfm?abstract_id=1492032. However in principle comparison lists are a form of comparative advertising: *Supreme Petfoods Ltd v. Henry Bell & Co. (Grantham) Ltd* [2015] *EWHC* 256 (Ch), [130] (Arnold J).

[105] *Toshiba v. Katun*, Case C-112/99 [2001] *ECR* I–7945, [37]. Despite this, the EU regime is considered more restrictive than the US equivalent: T. W. Dornos and T. Wein, 'Trademarks, Comparative Advertising, and Product Imitations: An Untold Story of Law and Economics' (2016) 121 *Penn State Law Review* 421.

[106] See D. Fitzgerald, 'Self-regulation of Comparative Advertising in the UK' [1997] *Ent L Rev* 250.

[107] This, along with the ASA, dates back to 1962, but has been amended many times. The ASA is funded by a levy on marketing and advertising. The CAP Code can be accessed online at https://www.asa.org.uk/codes-and-rulings/advertising-codes.html.

[108] CAP Code, [3.33]–[3.37], [3.41]–[3.44] (corresponding with the eight conditions of MCAD, Art. 4).

direct or implied, that are capable of being objectively substantiated.[109] The adequacy of this evidence will be judged against whether it supports both the detailed claims and the overall impression created by the advertisement.

The ASA investigates complaints.[110] The ASA may request that a company withdraw or amend its advertisements or promotions.[111] The judgment of the ASA Council on interpretation of the Code is final,[112] although there is some provision for appeal.[113] A number of sanctions exist to counteract advertisements and promotions that conflict with the Code. The media may deny access to space, the publication of a ruling on the ASA's website may generate adverse publicity, trading sanctions may be imposed or recognition revoked by the advertiser's, promoter's, or agency's professional association, and financial incentives provided by trade, professional, or media organizations may be withdrawn.[114]

The self-regulatory system is reinforced by the Business Protection for Misleading Marketing Regulations 2008.[115] Under these Regulations, an enforcement authority, such as the Competition and Markets Authority (CMA), can seek injunctive relief in relation to advertisements that do not comply with the requirements of the MCAD.[116]

The MCAD refers to trade mark law only in its Recitals and, for some time, there was uncertainty as to how trade mark rights and the MCAD related to one another.[117] The position has, however, been clarified: a comparative advertisement that uses another's trade mark, but complies with the eight conditions, is exempt from liability for trade mark infringement.[118] If such an advertisement does not comply with the conditions, it almost certainly infringes the proprietor's trade marks rights. This position has now been formally incorporated into EU trade mark law. Article 9(3)(f) of the EUTMR/Article 10(3)(f) of the TMD 2015 recognize that 'using the [protected] sign in comparative advertising in a manner that is contrary to' the MCAD will constitute trade mark infringement.[119]

To begin with, the use of the mark in comparative advertising is regarded as use in relation to the advertiser's goods.[120] If it uses an identical mark to that registered and the goods being advertised are identical, there is infringement under section 10(1).[121] If there is a similar mark and/or the use is for similar goods, there is liability under section 10(2)—and the use necessarily fails Article 4(h) of the MCAD (ex Article 3a(1)(d) CAD).[122] If the

---

[109] CAP Code, [3.7].

[110] Ibid., 104, [60.4], [60.6], [60.28] *ff.* Complaints are normally not pursued if the point at issue is the subject of simultaneous legal action: BCAP Code, [60.32].   [111] CAP Code, 104.

[112] Ibid., 9(IVa).   [113] Ibid., 101.   [114] Ibid., 104.–5.

[115] SI 2008/1276, regs 4 (setting out the conditions for permissible comparative advertising), 15 (enforcement authority may seek injunction to prevent breach of reg. 3), 18 (court powers).

[116] CAP Code, 105. See OFT, *Business to Business Promotions and Comparative Advertisements* (2009); CMA, *Consumer Protection: Guidance on the CMA's Approach to the Use of its Consumer Powers: Consultation Document* (September 2013).   [117] MCAD, Recitals 13–15.

[118] *O2 Holdings Ltd v. Hutchison 3G UK Ltd*, Case C-533/06 [2008] *ECR* I–4231, [45], [51]; *L'Oréal NV and ors v. Bellure NV*, Case C-487/07 [2009] *ECR* I–5185, [54], [71].

[119] See also EUTMR, Recital 14 and TMD 2015, Recital 20 ('In order to ensure legal certainty and full consistency with specific Union legislation, it is appropriate to provide that the proprietor of a trade mark should be entitled to prohibit a third party from using a sign in comparative advertising where such comparative advertising is contrary to [the MCAD]').

[120] *O2 Holdings Ltd v. Hutchison 3G UK Ltd*, Case C-533/06 [2008] *ECR* I–4231, [35]; *L'Oréal NV and ors v. Bellure NV*, Case C-487/07 [2009] *ECR* I–5185, [53].   [121] Ibid., [55]–[56].

[122] *O2 Holdings Ltd v. Hutchison 3G UK Ltd*, Case C-533/06 [2008] *ECR* I–4231, [46]. The possibility exists that the use of a similar mark may not produce a likelihood of confusion and yet might, for example, be disparaging and thus breach MCAD, Art. 4(d). If the earlier mark does not have a reputation, it is conceivable it could not comply with the MCAD, but not give rise to liability for trade mark infringement. In such a case, a trade mark owner might use the CAP Code, or bring an action for a declaration that the use breaches the MCAD and/or Business Marketing Regulations 2008.

earlier mark has a reputation, then comparative advertising will usually count as taking unfair advantage of the repute of the trade mark.[123] Because one of the MCAD conditions (Article 4(f)) is that no unfair advantage is taken, and this has the same meaning as with Article 5(2) of the Trade Marks Directive (section 10(3) of the 1994 Act),[124] the logical conclusion is that the owner of a mark with a reputation can always prevent a competitor from using that mark in comparative advertising.[125] This final conclusion seemed wholly unsatisfactory.[126] The solution that has emerged is to substitute the analytical frame of 'unfair advantage' in trade mark law in such situations,[127] since a legitimate comparison should not be 'unfair' or alternatively, the safety valve of 'due cause' recognizes the pro-competitive benefits of certain referential uses.[128]

Given that the MCAD provides a defence to trade mark infringement, the question has been raised whether, in addition to the eight conditions in Article 4 (then Article 3(a)), the Recitals imposed a further condition of 'indispensability'. In *O2 v. Hutchison*,[129] the defendant had advertised its mobile phone service using bubble imagery similar to that for which the claimant had a registered mark (in relation to tele-communication services) (see Fig. 41.1). It was argued by the claimant that, to be per-missible under the MCAD, the use of a trade mark in a comparative advertisement must be 'indispensable' and that while it might have been necessary for Hutchison to refer to O_2, it was not necessary for it to use the bubble marks. Advocate-General Mengozzi's opinion was that there is no such requirement for 'indispensability',[130] but the Court did not deal with this question.

7 LOCAL USE

Section 11(3) of the 1994 Act provides that a UK registered trade mark is not infringed by the use in a particular locality of an earlier right that applies only in that locality.[131] An earlier right applies in a locality 'if, or to the extent that, its use in that locality is protected

---

[123] *Specsavers International Healthcare Ltd v. Asda Stores* [2012] *EWCA Civ* 24, [150]–[151].

[124] *L'Oréal NV and ors v. Bellure NV*, Case C-487/07 [2009] *ECR* I–5185, [77] (unfair advantage has the same meaning in TMD 1989, Art. 5(2), and MCAD, Art. 4(f)). It may be that this proposition needs reconsideration. It would be better to say that a comparative advertisement breaches MCAD, Art. 4(f), only where greater advantage of the repute of a mark is taken than is inevitable in any effect comparative advertisement.

[125] Recall from Chapter 38, section 2.4.3, pp. 1065–70, that deliberately taking advantage of that rep-utation is invariably unfair—*L'Oréal NV and ors v. Bellure NV*, Case C-487/07 [2009] *ECR* I–5185, [50]; *Interflora v. Marks & Spencer*, Case C-323/09 [2011] *ECR* I–8625, [89]—and a comparative advertisement always deliberately takes advantage of the visibility (repute) of the earlier mark: *Specsavers Int'l Healthcare v. Asda Stores* [2012] *EWCA Civ* 24, [2012] *FSR* (19) 555, [164].

[126] Indeed, it might imply that comparative advertising using trade marks is never permissible, because no one would ever comparatively advertise using an unknown trade mark and a known trade mark almost certainly has a reputation: see Chapter 38, section 2.4.1, pp. 1053–6. Such a conclusion would, however, be inconsistent with the premise under which *Pippig Augenoptik GmbH & Co. KG v. Hartlauer Handelsgesellschaft mbH*, Case C-44/01 [2003] *ECR* I–3095 and *Toshiba v. Katun*, Case C-112/99 [2001] *ECR* I–7945 were decided.

[127] *L'Oréal NV and ors v. Bellure NV*, Case C-487/07 [2009] *ECR* I–5185, [77].

[128] *Interflora v. Marks & Spencer plc*, Case C-323/09 [2012] *ETMR* 1, [89]–[92].

[129] *O2 Holdings Ltd v. Hutchison 3G Ltd*, Case C-533/06 [2008] *ECR* I–4231.   [130] Ibid., [AG43].

[131] TMA 1994, s. 11(3). This reflects TMD 2008, Art. 6(2); TMD 2015, Art. 14(3). See further Kerly, [17–032]–[17–044].

by virtue of any rule of law (in particular, the law of passing off)'. The defence arises only if the use of the earlier right began before both the use and the registration of the claimant's mark.[132]

The relationship between local uses and European Union trade marks (EUTMs) is complex. Article 137 of the EUTMR (formerly Article 110 of the CTMR) allows the owner of any earlier right to rely on national law against the EUTM owner.[133] Thus the owner of a national mark who has not opposed the grant of an EUTM may utilize its national rights in national fora to prevent use of that EUTM (including, presumably an action for infringement against it).[134] Article 138 of the EUTMR additionally recognizes prior rights applicable to particular localities. To the extent permitted by the law of the Member State in question, the 'proprietor of an earlier right which only applies to a particular locality may oppose the use of the EU trade mark in the territory where his right is protected'. This is subject, however, to the principle of acquiescence—that is, five years of continuous use by the owner of the EUTM in the member state in which the earlier local right operates.[135] Even where the prior local right can no longer be invoked against the EUTM, the proprietor of that earlier right will have a defence to an action brought by the owner of the EUTM.[136]

These provisions are of increasing importance since the expansion of the Community from 15 to 25 states in 2004, to 27 in 2008, and 28 in 2013. While existing registrations of EUTMs will automatically apply to new territories, Articles 137 and 138 of the EUTMR protect those who previously were operating in those territories from the otherwise potentially devastating effect of such automatic extension.

8 EXHAUSTION

Traditionally, trade marks have been territorial in nature, so that a proprietor may own distinct rights in different territories. Typically, those rights have included the right to prevent the import of goods bearing the mark into the territory in which the rights apply.[137] This led to the situation in which the owner of a trade mark was able to use the rights in one territory (A) to prevent the import of goods from another territory (B). This was the case *even where* the goods had been put on the market in territory B with the consent of the owner. In practice, there are a number of reasons why the import of goods from one country to another may be desirable. The most obvious is where the price of the goods is cheaper in territory B than territory A, or where demand in territory A is not being met. At first glance, it seems that if import were permitted, it would be to the advantage of all concerned. The

---

[132] *Caspian Pizza Ltd v. Maskeen Shah* [2017] *EWCA Civ* 1874 (Hacon J) (where the claimant commenced trading under the name Caspian elsewhere in the United Kingdom but the defendants commenced trading under that name first in Worcester—the locality where prior goodwill was defensively asserted—the defendants had relevant priority in accordance with the TMD 2008, Art. 6(2)). Cf. *Redd Solicitors LLP v. Red Legal Ltd* [2012] *EWPCC* 54 (which is no longer good law on this issue).

[133] As defined in EUTMR, Arts 8 and 60(2). However, while these provisions exclude mere local rights, EUTMR, Art. 138, provides similar protection for precisely such local rights.

[134] As we saw in Chapter 38, section 3, pp. 1073–4, according to EUTMR, Art. 8(4), use of rights of no more than mere local significance cannot prevent registration on relative grounds.

[135] EUTMR, Art. 138(2). However acquiescence is irrelevant if the EUTM was applied for in bad faith.

[136] EUTMR, Art. 138(3).

[137] TMA 1994, s. 10(4)(c); EUTMR, Art. 9(3)(c) (ex CTMR, Art. 9(2)(c)); TMD 2008, Art. 5(3)(c); TMD 2015, Art. 10(3)(c).

public in territory A would benefit from cheaper products, while the trade mark owner's interests would be satisfied by sale in territory B. However, first impressions give way to more complex realities. This is because trade mark owners may have good reasons for wishing to divide markets up and to prevent parallel imports.[138] Given that it may be difficult to distinguish between legitimate and counterfeit goods at the border, parallel importing may also weaken the trade mark owner's capacity to prevent the import of counterfeit goods.

8.1 DEVELOPMENT OF THE BASIC RULES

Prior to the adoption of the Trade Marks Directive, the Court of Justice developed a series of sophisticated rules that detailed the situations in which the owner of a national trade mark for one member state could prevent goods put on the market elsewhere in the European Union from being distributed in that member state.[139] Since Article 7 of the TMD 2008 and section 12 of the 1994 Act embody the notion of exhaustion developed under the case law, it is worth noting the basic features of that case law.[140]

The jurisprudence that developed prior to the passage of the Trade Marks Directive recognized the conflicting demands of Articles 34 and 36 of the Treaty on the Functioning of the European Union (TFEU). Under Article 34 TFEU, 'quantitative restrictions on imports or measures having equivalent effect' are prohibited. However, under Article 36 TFEU, prohibitions or restrictions on imports between member states are permissible if they can be justified on grounds of the protection of industrial and commercial property. This is subject to the proviso that they do not constitute a means of arbitrary discrimination or a disguised restriction on trade between member states.

As we observed in Chapter 1, in striking a compromise between the demands of the internal market and national industrial property rights,[141] the Court of Justice recognized the principle of exhaustion of rights, where the goods were placed on the market under a trade mark with the consent of the trade mark proprietor.[142] This principle, also known as the 'first-sale' rule, exists to prevent a trade mark owner from controlling resale or subsequent distribution of products bearing the mark via infringement claims. Upon first sale of the products bearing the trade mark, the owner's rights are exhausted. On the other hand, in order to ensure that trade marks continue to function as indicators of origin and as guarantors of quality to the consumer,[143] the Court also said that the rights

---

[138] In the case of pharmaceuticals, the price differentials are largely the result of the fact that regulatory mechanisms for price setting differ on a national basis. If parallel importing were always possible, effectively the trade mark owner would have to live with the lowest price set by any of the national authorities. On the legality of controlling markets by restricting supply, see section 8.3.6, p. 1158.

[139] See generally C. Stothers, *Parallel Trade in Europe: Intellectual Property, Competition and Regulatory Law* (2007); L. G. Grigoriadis, *Trade Marks and Free Trade: A Global Analysis* (2014), ch. 7; I. Calboli and E. Lee (eds), *Research Handbook on Intellectual Property Exhaustion and Parallel Imports* (2016).

[140] See also TMD 2015, Art. 15; EUTMR, Art. 15 (ex CTMR, Art. 13).

[141] *Bristol-Myers Squibb v. Paranova A/S and C. H. Boehringer Sohn; Boehringer Ingelheim KG and Boehringer Ingelheim A/S v. Paranova A/S; and Bayer Aktiengesellschaft and Bayer Danmark A/S v. Paranova A/S*, Joined Cases C-427/93 and C-429/93 [1996] *ECR* I-3457, I-3528, [31].

[142] The principle of exhaustion applies where the same person owns the mark in the country of import and export. It also applies where the parties are economically linked—e.g. as subsidiaries of the same group: *Centrafarm BV and Adriaan De Peijper v. Sterling Drug*, Case C-15/74 [1974] *ECR* 1147—and where the distribution is effected by a licensee, as long as it does not breach core terms of the licence. However, economic linkage does not cover the situation in which an assignment of the trade mark rights has occurred: *IHT Internationale Heiztechnik v. Ideal Standard*, Case C-9/93 [1994] *ECR* I-2789, I-1850, [43]-[45].

[143] See, e.g., *Hoffmann-La Roche v. Centrafarm*, Case C-102/77 [1978] *ECR* 1139, [7]; *IHT Internationale Heiztechnik v. Ideal Standard*, Case C-9/93 [1994] *ECR* I-2789, [33].

were not exhausted where the trade mark owner had a legitimate reason for opposing further circulation of the goods.[144]

This jurisprudence on exhaustion of rights was carried over into Article 7(1) of the Directive[145] and section 12(1) of the 1994 Act.[146] This provides that a 'registered trade mark is not infringed by use of the trade mark in relation to goods which have been put on the market in the European Economic Area under that trade mark by the proprietor, or with his consent'.[147] As with the pre-Directive jurisprudence, the principle of exhaustion found in Article 7(1) and section 12(1) is subject to the general rider that, in certain circumstances, the rights of the owner will not be exhausted. As Article 7(2) says, '[p]aragraph 1 shall not apply where there exist legitimate reasons for the proprietor to oppose further commercialisation of the goods, especially where the condition of the goods is changed or impaired after they have been put on the market'.[148]

8.2 CONDITIONS FOR EXHAUSTION

In order for the trade mark owner's rights to be exhausted, two conditions must be satisfied: (i) the goods must have been put on the market in the European Economic Area (EEA); and (ii) this must have been done by the proprietor or with its consent. It has been said that these two components constitute the 'decisive factors' that extinguish the rights of the trade mark holder (with respect to further commercialization of those goods).[149]

8.2.1 Put on the market

In most cases, assessing whether this has occurred will be straightforward. The question is whether the power of disposal of the goods has passed from the mark owner (or its licensee) to a third party. If it has, those goods have been placed on the market.[150]

In *eBay*,[151] however, the Court of Justice, sitting in Grand Chamber, reasoned that the testers and samples of perfumes had not been put on the market at all because they had been distributed to the retailers for free. In so holding, it explicitly contradicted a German Supreme Court decision that had been cited by the referring court.[152] The Court of Justice instead cited its own jurisprudence in the *Silberquelle* case on when there was 'genuine use' of a mark.[153] The reasoning is unpersuasive. In particular, reliance on *Silberquelle* misconstrues that decision. As a leading commentary observes, that case 'does not mean that use on promotional items can never be considered genuine use. The test is whether the proprietor of the mark is using the mark in order to create an outlet for the goods in

---

[144] See *Hoffmann-La Roche v. Centrafarm*, Case C-102/77 [1978] *ECR* 1139; *Centrafarm v. American Home Products Corporation*, Case C-3/78 [1978] *ECR* 1823.

[145] *Bristol-Myers*, Joined Cases C-427/93 and C-429/93 [1996] *ECR* I–3457, I–3528, 3529.

[146] To the extent that TMD 2008, Art. 7, is narrowly drafted, Arts 34 and 36 TFEU operate as previously: see *Pharmacia & Upjohn SA v. Paranova*, Case C-379/97 [2000] 1 *CMLR* 51, 81, [28]; cf. *Oracle America Ltd v. M-Tech Data* [2012] *UKSC* 27, [13] (Lord Sumption).

[147] Although TMD 2008. Art. 7(1), refers to marketing in the Community and TMD 2015, Art. 15 refers to the Union, the principle of the exhaustion of rights was extended for certain purposes to the EEA. See Annex XVII and Art. 2(1) of the Protocol to the Agreement for the European Economic Area [1994] *OJ L* 1/3.

[148] In TMA 1994, s. 12(2), the expression 'further dealings' should be read as synonymous with further 'commercialization of goods'.

[149] *Viking Gas A/S v. Kosan Gas A/S*, Case C-46/10 [2011] *ECR* I– 6161, [27].

[150] *Peak Holding AB v. Axolin-Elinor ABR*, Case C-16/03 [2004] *ECR* I–11313.

[151] *L'Oréal SA v. eBay International AG*, Case C-324/09 [2011] *ECR* I–6011.

[152] *L'Oréal SA v. eBay International AG*, [2009] *EWHC* 1094 (Ch), [2009] *RPC* (21) 693, [320]–[326] (Arnold J).   [153] See Chapter 39, section 2.3, p. 1088.

question.'[154] In *eBay*, promotion was precisely the purpose of giving the samples away. The Court's conclusion that where 'items are supplied free of charge, they thus cannot, as a rule, be regarded as being put on the market by the trade mark proprietor' thus seems incorrect.[155]

Two days later, the Court of Justice decided *Viking Gas A/S v. Kosan Gas A/S*,[156] and again seemed to make exhaustion dependent on sale. The case concerned the sale of refilled gas bottles, and the initial question was whether the rights in the bottles were exhausted. In contrast with *eBay*, the Court said that they were, going out of its way to reason that the bottles had been purchased. The purchase was not merely of the gas, because the bottles of gas cost more than gas in canisters and 'are intended for reuse a number of times, do not constitute mere packaging of the original product, but have an independent economic value and must be regarded as goods in themselves'.[157]

Despite this case law, we think that it would be better for the Court to recognize that exhaustion is a consequence not of 'sale', but of any transfer of property rights in the goods. This is the position in relation to copyright, where transfers other than 'sales' can exhaust rights.[158] Moreover, as a general matter, focusing on the issue of consideration seems to leave downstream actors in some difficulty: goods do not normally indicate whether they were sold or given away, and such actors will not readily obtain access to the contractual details of any initial marketing. Indeed, even if it were clear that the parties designated a transfer of particular items as 'free', an economist would often be sceptical about whether that represented a truthful account of the transaction: think, for example, of 'buy one, get one free'.

For all of these reasons, we are unpersuaded by the rationale offered in *eBay* (and seemingly perpetuated in *Viking*) as to why the trade mark proprietor's rights in the tester bottles and samples were not exhausted. Perhaps the Court should have considered distinguishing between the demonstration units and the samples: it seems plausible to say that the demonstration units, supplied only to the retailers and distinguishable in form from the goods that were being marketed, were not put on the market at all; with respect to the samples, if they were given to customers by the retailers (as intended), they would have been placed on the market at that point, but if (as seems likely) there had been no such authorized transfer of the units that were being resold on eBay,[159] then the conclusion is best explained as a situation in which there was no consent to transfer of the units at all.[160]

8.2.2 Consent

Exhaustion occurs only where the goods have been placed on the market with the 'consent' of the trade mark holder. The concept of consent has been harmonized at the EU level.[161] Consent must amount to an unequivocal demonstration of an intention to renounce the right to control further distribution.[162] Such consent will usually be express,

---

[154] Kerly, [12–081].

[155] *L'Oréal SA v. eBay International AG*, Case C-324/09 [2011] *ECR* I–6011, [71].

[156] Case C-46/10 [2011] *ECR* I– 6161 (ECJ, First Chamber). Four of the five members of the Chamber, including Rapporteur Judge Ilešič, were in the Grand Chamber in *eBay*.　　　　　[157] Ibid., [30].

[158] Cf. Info. Soc. Dir., Art. 4 (which provides for the exhaustion of the distribution right in the event of first sale or *first other* transfer of ownership of an 'object'), discussed in Chapter 6, section 3.3, pp. 151–2.

[159] [2009] *EWHC* 1094 (Ch), [323].

[160] But cf. *Coty Prestige Lancaster Group GmbH v. Simex Trading AG*, Case C-127/09 [2010] *ECR* I–4965; note also *L'Oréal SA v. eBay International AG*, Case C-324/09 [2011] *ECR* I–6011, [AG67].

[161] *Zino Davidoff*, Joined Cases C-414/99 and C-416/99 [2001] *ECR* I–8691, [43]; *Makro v. Diesel spA*, Case C-324/08 [2009] *ECR* I–10019. See Stothers, 345–7.

[162] *Makro v. Diesel spA*, Case C-324/08 [2009] *ECR* I–10019, [22].

but could be implied.[163] The Court has stated that consent may be inferred from facts and circumstances prior to, simultaneous with, or subsequent to the placing of the goods on the market, if those facts and circumstances unequivocally demonstrate that the proprietor has renounced their exclusive rights.[164]

If a licensee markets goods under a licence, this is treated as marketing with the consent of the trade mark proprietor. However, what if goods are placed on the market by a licensee of the trade mark owner, but outside the scope of the licence? In *Copad SA v. Christian Dior Couture SA*,[165] Dior marketed its lingerie through a selective distribution agreement that forbade licensees from selling to, among others, discount stores. SIL, a licensee with a stock of Dior products, found itself in financial difficulty and sold goods, in breach of the agreement, to a discount store operator, Copad. The Court of Justice held that there would be no exhaustion if the marketing occurred in breach of a clause in the licence equivalent to one of those listed in Article 8(2) of the Directive. This indicates that a licensee infringes trade mark rights where they breach terms relating to duration, the form of the trade mark, the scope of the goods or services, the territory in which the mark may be affixed, and the quality of the goods manufactured or services provided by the licensee. If the breach was of one of these five types of term, the marketing was not to be said to be with the consent of the proprietor.[166] Although the list is exhaustive, the Court offered the concept of 'quality' a broad interpretation, saying that, in the case of luxury goods such as those at issue, it was not confined to their physical or material characteristics, but also included its 'aura of luxury'.[167] Whether the breach of the term not to sell to discount stores related to the quality of the goods depended on whether doing so would damage 'the allure and prestigious image which bestows on the goods an aura of luxury'.[168] That was a matter to be assessed by the national court, the Court of Justice offering a series of factors that might be taken into account (the nature of the luxury goods, the volume of sales, whether the sales outside the selective distribution arrangement are regular or occasional, the practices of the purchaser, and the methods of marketing that are normal in the sector).

In *Coty v. Simex*,[169] the question arose as to whether a trade mark proprietor's rights had been exhausted in relation to 'tester bottles' of perfume. The testers had been made available to retailers to use freely in demonstrations, but in formal terms the claimant retained property in the goods. The tester bottles were packaged bearing the words 'demonstration' and 'not for sale', but nevertheless had come into the defendant's hands. As with the decision in *eBay*, the Court found that the trade mark proprietors' rights were not exhausted, but the Court in *Coty* (sitting in Chamber, a couple of years before the *eBay* decision) offered a quite different explanation. The Court reasoned that there was no consent to marketing, rather than that the goods had not been placed on the market at all. Although it was clear that some of the items came from outside the EEA, the Court considered whether the trade mark proprietor could be said to have 'consented' to the marketing of the tester bottles even if they had supplied them to retailers in the EEA. The Court suggested that providing tester bottles in this way would not amount to 'consent' to placing the goods on the market, given the labelling.[170]

---

[163] Ibid., [45]. [164] Ibid., [22]. [165] Case C-59/08 [2009] *ECR* I–3421 (ECJ, First Chamber).
[166] Ibid., [51]. [167] Ibid., [24].
[168] Ibid., [37]. See also *Coty Germany GmbH v. Parfümerie Akzente GmbH*, Case C-230/16 [2018] 4 *CMLR* 9 (holding that certain selective distribution agreements for luxury goods, which imposed bans on sales via third party online platforms, could withstand a competition law challenge; the Court confirmed that when the distributor breached the terms of agreement, this amounted to trade mark infringement).
[169] *Coty Prestige Lancaster Group GmbH v. Simex Trading AG*, Case C-127/09 [2010] *ETMR* 41.
[170] Ibid., [48].

8.3 LEGITIMATE REASONS TO PREVENT FURTHER DEALINGS IN GOODS BEARING THE MARK

Trade mark owners are able to utilize their rights to prevent further dealings in goods bearing their mark that have been placed on the market in the EEA only when there are 'legitimate reasons' to do so.[171] The mere fact that the further dealing is to another trader's advantage is not a legitimate reason for the trade mark owner to prevent the use from taking place.[172] However, there are a number of situations in which a trade mark owner may have a legitimate reason to oppose further dealings in goods bearing the mark. These include situations in which the goods are altered or repacked, or in which the mark is altered, or in which the goods or services are advertised. We will consider each in turn.

8.3.1 Altering the goods

One situation in which a trade mark owner has a legitimate reason to oppose further dealings in a mark is where the condition of the goods has changed or been impaired after they have been put on the market. For example, a trader that manufactures and sells video-game consoles under a particular registered mark in France may wish to prevent another trader from exporting the console from France to the United Kingdom, opening the packaging, adding adaptors to enable the console to work in the United Kingdom, and selling the repackaged goods. The trade mark owner may have a legitimate reason to object to the resale of such goods, for example if the adaptor is of a different standard from that which the trader would supply in the authorized UK packages—at least where the repackaged goods do not clearly indicate the origin of the adaptors.[173] If the owner were unable to control such acts, the role that the mark plays in enabling the trade mark proprietor to control the quality of products placed on the market under the mark would be undermined.

Change in the characteristics of the goods is not only objectionable where it interferes with the capacity of the mark to guarantee origin (and thus quality), but also may be objectionable if it seriously affects the reputation associated with the mark. In *Viking Gas A/s v. Kosan*,[174] the Court of Justice held that while trade mark rights in the shape of bottles that had been sold as gas containers were exhausted, the trade mark holder might nevertheless have grounds on which to object to the later sale of such bottles refilled with gas from other sources. Whether this was so would depend on how they were labelled and the circumstances in which the bottles were resold or exchanged. For the sales to be unobjectionable, the labelling must make clear that there is no commercial connection between the trade mark holder and both the reseller and the provider of gas that it contains. Whether an erroneous impression exists depends on the practices in the sector, but clearly where an individual consumer gets their gas bottle refilled that absence of connection will be most apparent.[175]

---

[171] *Oracle America Ltd v. M-Tech Data* [2012] *UKSC* 27, [16].

[172] Moreover, there are some risks that are inherent in trade in second-hand goods; the trade mark proprietor must live with these. See *Viking Gas A/S v. Kosan Gas A/S*, Case C-46/10 [2011] *ECR* I– 6161, [AG25] (AG Kokott). But, even with resale, the reseller must not give the impression that there is a commercial connection between it and the trade mark proprietor.

[173] *Sony Computer Entertainments v. Tesco Stores* [2000] *ETMR* 104.

[174] Case C-46/10 [2011] *ECR* I–6161.

[175] See also *Schütz (UK) Ltd v. Delta Containers Ltd* [2011] *EWHC* 1712 (Ch), [80], [85] (Briggs J).

8.3.2 De-packaging

A trade mark owner may seek to oppose the resale of goods that have been removed from their packaging. The Court of Justice considered this question in the *eBay* case,[176] in which a number of sellers had been selling goods on the defendant's auction site without the original packaging. The Court indicated that the trade mark owner would have a legitimate reason to oppose further commercialization if the effect of removing the packaging were that essential information, such as information relating to the identity of the manufacturer or the person responsible for marketing the cosmetic product, was missing. Moreover, the trade mark owner would be also able to oppose resale if it could establish that the removal of the packaging had damaged the image of the product and thus the reputation of the trade mark.

8.3.3 Repackaging

Another situation in which a trade mark owner may have a legitimate reason to control further dealings is where the goods are repackaged.[177] In *Bristol-Myers v. Paranova*,[178] Bristol-Myers marketed pharmaceutical products in various member states. It was the owner of certain trade marks for those pharmaceuticals in Denmark. Paranova purchased products sold by Bristol-Myers in member states such as Greece and the United Kingdom, in which the prices were relatively low, and then imported them into Denmark. The pharmaceuticals had originally been marketed as tablets in blister packs, flasks, phials, and ampoules. For the purposes of sale in Denmark, Paranova repackaged all of the pharmaceuticals in new external packaging. In so doing, Paranova gave the pharmaceuticals a uniform appearance—namely, white with coloured stripes corresponding to the colours of the manufacturers' original packaging. The new packaging displayed the respective trade marks of the manufacturer (namely, BRISTOL-MYERS). It also included statements that the products had been manufactured by Bristol-Myers, and were imported and repackaged by Paranova. Bristol-Myers claimed that the import infringed various trade marks that it had registered in Denmark. The matter was referred to the Court of Justice for consideration.

The Court of Justice began by noting that Article 7(1) of the Trade Marks Directive provides that owners of a trade mark cannot rely on their rights in the mark to prevent the importing or marketing of a product that has been put on the market in another member state by them or with their consent. However, where those goods had been repackaged, the trade mark owner was entitled to prevent further commercialization, because the repackaging jeopardized the 'guarantee of origin'.[179]

Nevertheless, the Court in *Bristol Myers* acknowledged that this may create problems insofar as it enables owners to exercise their rights in a way that constitutes a disguised restriction upon the free movement of goods under Article 34 TFEU. To ensure that this did not occur, the Court said that the owner could *not* prevent the parallel import of repackaged goods where the use of the trade mark right by the owner contributes to the artificial partitioning of the markets between member states. In so doing, the Court of Justice limited the scope of the trade mark owner's rights.

---

[176] *L'Oréal SA v. eBay International AG*, Case C-324/09 [2011] *ECR* I–6011 (ECJ, Grand Chamber).
[177] See Stothers, 74–103.   [178] Joined Cases C-427/93 and C-429/93 [1996] *ECR* I–3457, I–3528.
[179] Ibid., 3532–3, [47]. See also *Boehringer Ingelheim KG, Boehringer Ingelheim Pharma KG v. Springward Ltd; Merck, Sharp & Dohme GmbH v. Paranova Pharmazeutica Handels GmbH*, Joined Cases C–143/00 and 443/99 [2002] *ECR* I–3759, [30].

To ensure that this derogation from the owner's rights did not adversely affect the subject matter of the trade mark, the Court said that parallel importing of repackaged goods is permissible only where the parallel importer satisfies certain conditions. These are that:

(i)   the repackaging does not adversely affect the original condition of the product;

(ii)   the parallel importer complies with certain obligations as to labelling and provision of samples; and

(iii)   the quality of the repackaging does not adversely impact on the reputation of the mark.[180]

After looking at the question of what is meant by 'artificial partitioning of the market', we will look at each of the three conditions imposed on the parallel importer.

(i) Artificial partitioning of the markets between member states Repackaging by a parallel importer is justified only where and insofar as it is necessary to avoid artificial partitioning of the market.[181] The test for whether there has been an 'artificial partitioning' of the market is decided by objective standards. This means that the importer does not need to show that the trade mark owner deliberately intended to partition the markets between member states. The Court of Justice said that partitioning is artificial if it prevents access to the market. In other words, the power of the trade mark cannot be used to prevent repackaging that is *necessary* for the importer to market the product in the member state of import.[182]

One situation in which repackaging would be justified is if the goods were marketed in different packaging in different member states and the goods could not be sold in the second member state unless they were repackaged.[183] For example, if a whisky were marketed as 'pure whisky' in one country, but regulations in another member state meant that the whisky could not be described as 'pure', it would be necessary to remove the word 'pure' from the packaging before the product could be imported into the latter state.[184]

Equally, a trade mark owner cannot oppose the repackaging of a product where the size of the original packet cannot be marketed in the importing member state.[185] This would occur, for example, where the size of the packaging was dictated by national regulations. In *Bristol-Myers*, the Court of Justice made it clear that a 'need' to repackage may exist even where a number of different types of packaging are used in the importing state.[186] This is so even if this includes the form of packaging in which the goods in question have been marketed. The reason for this is that 'partitioning of the markets would exist if the importer were able to sell the product in only part of his market'.[187] It is possible too that repackaging may be justified in response to consumer practices. In *Boehringer Ingelheim (No. 1)*,[188] the Court of Justice indicated that while consumer resistance would not always

---

[180]   Joined Cases C-427/93 and C-429/93 [1996] *ECR* I–3457, I–3528, 3533–4, [54].   [181]   Ibid., [56].

[182]   *Boehringer Ingelhem v. Swingward*, Case 143/00 [2002] *ECR* I–3759, [46]. See also *Ferring Lægemidler v. Orifarm*, Case C-297/15, EU:C:2016:857 (repackaging can be objected to where (i) the medicinal product at issue can be marketed in the importing EEA member state in the same packaging as that in which it is marketed in the exporting EEA member state; and (ii) the importer has not demonstrated that the imported product can only be marketed in a limited part of the importing member's market. The Court also provided examples of when repackaging would be necessary, at [20]–[23]).

[183]   *Bristol-Myers*, Joined Cases C-427/93 and C-429/93 [1996] *ECR* I–3457, I–3528, 3536, [57].

[184]   *Frits Loendersloot v. George Ballantine & Son*, Case C-349/95 [1997] *ECR* I–6227, 6260, [45].

[185]   *Bristol-Myers*, Joined Cases C-427/93 and C-429/93 [1996] *ECR* I–3457, I–3528, 3534–5, [53]. This is a matter of fact for the national tribunal to determine: *Aventis Pharma Deutschland GmbH v. Kohlpharma GmbH and MTK Vertbriebs-GmbH*, Case C-433/00 [2002] *ECR* I–7761, [AG66].

[186]   *Bristol-Myers*, Joined Cases C-427/93 and C-429/93 [1996] *ECR* I–3457, I–3528, 3534–5, [54].

[187]   Ibid., [54].   [188]   *Boehringer Ingelheim v. Springward*, Case 143/00 [2002] *ECR* I–3759.

constitute an impediment to effective market access such as to render repackaging necessary, it might do so. More specifically, it stated that 'there may exist on a market, or on a
substantial part of it, such strong resistance from a significant proportion of consumers to
relabelled pharmaceutical products that there must be held to be a hindrance to effective
market access'.[189]

The question of necessity is a threshold question.[190] Thus the 'necessity' requirement 'is
directed solely at the fact of repackaging not at the manner and style of repackaging'.[191]
Details of the repackaging need be scrutinized only when assessing whether there has
been compliance with the other conditions.

(ii) Whether the original condition of the product is adversely affected Even if it is necessary to repackage to gain access to a market, a trade mark owner may oppose this if
it involves either a risk that the product inside the package might be tampered with or
that the original condition of the goods will be adversely affected.[192] This is sometimes
referred to as the doctrine of 'adverse effects'. In order to constitute a legitimate reason for
a trade mark owner to oppose further commercialization of goods that have been repackaged, the risks of adverse effects must be *real*; the hypothetical risk of isolated error will
not do. An example of this is provided by *Bristol-Myers*, in which it was argued that the
repackaging of blister packs might affect the condition of the drugs.[193] It was suggested
that combining blister packs with different use-by dates into single sets might lead to the
sale of products that might have been stored for too long—but the Court of Justice did not
consider this to be a real risk.

To determine whether the repackaging adversely affects the original condition of the
product, both the nature of the product and the method of repackaging must be taken
into account. Parallel importation is permissible where the repackaging affects only the
external layer, leaving the inner packaging intact, or where the repackaging is carried
out under the supervision of a public authority to ensure that the product remains intact.
Similarly, the addition of accurate information by the repackager will not constitute a
legitimate reason to oppose the further circulation of the goods.[194]

The Court of Justice has recognized that the original condition of the product inside
the packaging might be indirectly affected where the repackaged product omits important information, or gives inaccurate information about the nature, composition, effect,
use, or storage of the product.[195]

(iii) The parallel importer must comply with certain obligations Moreover, to protect
the owner against misuse, an importer of repackaged pharmaceuticals must comply with
certain requirements.[196] First, the packaging should indicate both who manufactured

---

[189] Ibid., [51]–[52].
[190] *Boehringer Ingelheim v. Swingward Ltd,* Case C-348/04 [2007] *ECR* I–3391.   [191] Ibid., [38].
[192] *Bristol-Myers,* Joined Cases C-427/93 and C-429/93 [1996] *ECR* I–3457, I–3528, 3536, [59].
[193] Ibid., [62]–[63].
[194] Ibid., 3537, [66]; *Phytheron International SA v. Jean Bourdon SA,* Case C-352/95 [1997] *ECR* I–1729,
I–1748, [23].
[195] *Bristol-Myers,* Joined Cases C-427/93 and C-429/93 [1996] *ECR* I–3457, I–3528, 3538, [65].
[196] Ibid., [49]. In *Frits Loendersloot v. George Ballantine & Son,* Case C-349/95 [1997] *ECR* I–6227,
[48], which concerned the relabelling of alcoholic drinks, the Court of Justice suggested that while, in the
case of pharmaceuticals, it was necessary for a parallel importer to comply with the requirements set out
in *Bristol-Myers*, it might not be necessary to do so in the case of other goods. In the case of the parallel
import of alcohol, the interests of the trade mark owner, particularly to combat counterfeiting, required
only that the relabeller/importer provide them with advance notice that the relabelled products are to be
put on sale.

the product[197] and who repackaged it.[198] That indication must be clearly shown on the repackaged product[199] and must be printed in such a way as to be understood by a person with normal eyesight, exercising a normal degree of attentiveness.[200] It is not necessary that a statement be made that the repackaging was carried out without the authorization of the trade mark owner.[201]

Second, the trade mark owner must be given advance notice that the repackaged product is being put on sale.[202] The owner may also require that they be supplied with a specimen of the repackaged product before it goes on sale. This enables the owner to check that the repackaging does not affect the original condition of the product or damage the reputation of the trade mark. This also affords trade mark owners with a better opportunity to protect themselves against counterfeiting.[203] It is incumbent on the parallel importer itself to give notice, which must provide the proprietor with 'a reasonable time to react to the intended repackaging'.[204] In one case, the Court indicated that, were a sample to be provided along with the notice, a period of 15 working days would be a reasonable time.[205] Failure to comply with the notice requirements renders the commercialization of the goods an infringement.[206]

(iv) Quality of packaging The repackaging must not adversely affect the reputational interests of the trade mark proprietor. In *Bristol-Myers*,[207] the Court of Justice recognized 'the possibility that the reputation of the trade mark and thus of its owner may nevertheless suffer from an inappropriate presentation of the repackaged product'. This is particularly the case if the repackaging is defective, untidy, or poor quality. When assessing whether the presentation of the repackaged product is liable to damage the reputation of the trade mark, it is necessary to take account of the nature of the product and its market.[208] In the case of pharmaceutical products that are marketed directly to the public, packaging could be crucial in maintaining or inspiring public confidence in the quality and integrity of the product. In these cases, defective, poor-quality, or untidy packaging could damage the trade mark's reputation.[209] However, where a pharmaceutical is sold to hospitals, the presentation of the product will be of little importance.[210] In the intermediate situation, in which the product is sold on prescription through pharmacies, presentation may be important to consumers even though some degree of confidence in the quality of the product would flow from the fact that the products were sold only on prescription.[211] The reputation of the trade mark holder might be damaged through 'de-branding' (where, in

---

[197] *Pfizer v. Eurim-Pharm*, Case C-1/81 [1081] *ECR* 2913, [11]; *Bristol-Myers*, Joined Cases C-427/93 and C-429/93 [1996] *ECR* I-3457, I-3528, [74].

[198] *The Wellcome Foundation Ltd v. Paranova Pharmazeutika Handels GmbH* [2008] *ECR* I-10479 (this need not be the actual packager in cases in which that act has been delegated, but can be simply the person who arranged for the repackaging).

[199] *Hoffmann-La Roche*, Case C-102/77 [1978] *ECR* 1139, 1165, [12]; *Pfizer v. Eurim-Pharm*, Case C-1/81 [1081] *ECR* 2913, [11]; *Bristol-Myers*, Joined Cases C-427/93 and C-429/93 [1996] *ECR* I-3457, I-3528, [71].

[200] Ibid., [71].   [201] Ibid., [72].

[202] *Hoffmann-La Roche*, Case 102/77 [1978] *ECR* 1139, 1165, [12].

[203] *Bristol-Myers*, Joined Cases C-427/93 and C-429/93 [1996] *ECR* I-3457, I-3528, 3540-1, [77].

[204] Case C-143/00 [2002] *ECR* I-3579, [64].

[205] Ibid., [67]; *Glaxo v. Dowelhurst* [2004] *EWCA Civ* 129, [127].

[206] *Boehringer Ingelheim v. Swingward*, Case C-348/04 [2007] *ECR* I-3391, [59], [61]–[62]. If the notice requirement is breached, the matter is treated just like any other trade mark infringement: *Hollister Inc. v. Medik Ostomy Supplies* [2012] *EWCA Civ* 1419, [2013] *FSR* (24) 502.

[207] *Bristol-Myers*, Joined Cases C-427/93 and C-429/93 [1996] *ECR* I-3457, I-3528, 3540, [75]; *Frits Loendersloot v. George Ballantine & Son*, Case C-349/95 [1997] *ECR* I-6227, 6255, [29].

[208] Ibid.   [209] Ibid., [76].   [210] Ibid., [77].   [211] Ibid.

repackaging, the parallel importer removes many of the manufacturer's trade marks) and 'co-branding' (where the parallel importer adds its own brand).[212]

8.3.4 Rebranding

Another situation in which the trade mark owner may have a legitimate reason to restrict further dealings of goods bearing their trade mark arises where the parallel importer alters the mark. In *Pharmacia & Upjohn v. Paranova*,[213] Upjohn marketed an antibiotic called clindamycin under the trade mark DALACIN in Denmark, Germany, and Spain, and under the mark DALACINE in France. Paranova bought DALACINE capsules in France, with the intention of reselling the antibiotic in Denmark. When Upjohn sought to prevent this, the question arose as to whether it was legitimate for Paranova to replace the DALA-CINE mark with DALACIN. The Court of Justice said that there is no difference between this situation and that of repackaging.[214] Applying the *Bristol-Myers* conditions, to justify affixing the DALACIN mark, the parallel importer needed to show that it was objectively necessary for it to do so to access the market. In so stating, the Court made it clear that the suggestion that had been made in *American Home Products*[215] that, to justify reaffixing the mark, the parallel importer had to prove that the owner had a subjective intention to divide up the market, was not correct. The Court of Justice indicated that the 'condition of necessity' would be satisfied if, for example, consumer protection legislation were to prohibit use of the mark DALACINE, or if use of the mark were not allowed because it was misleading.[216] The Court added that the requisite 'conditions of necessity' did not exist, however, if the replacement of the trade mark was 'explicable solely by the parallel importer's attempt to secure a commercial advantage'.[217]

In *Speciality European Pharma Ltd v. Doncaster Pharmaceuticals Group*,[218] the Court of Appeals reversed the lower court's finding that such necessity was not proven in a case in which the claimant, who was licensed by Medeus to use the mark REGURIN in the United Kingdom, had only 8 per cent of the UK market for tropsium chloride (used in the treatment of incontinence), and 60 per cent of the market was supplied by generics (the drug having come off patent). Asplin J had held that permitting the parallel importer to rebrand products sold by licensees of Medeus in France as CÉRIS and in Germany as URIVESC with the REGURIN mark would merely give it a 'commercial advantage' (allowing it to be sold at a higher price than other generics). There was no need to rebrand to access the market in general and it was inappropriate to define the market to tropsium chloride sold as REGULIN.[219] By contrast, the Court of Appeal preferred the evidence establishing that, despite generic competition, there remained a proportion of the prescription market which was resistant to it and demanded REGURIN. Consequently, rebranding went no further than was necessary to overcome artificial barriers to effective market access.

In the rebranding context, the Court of Appeal has also clarified that for the *Bristol-Myers* analysis to apply in order to excuse the defendant, they must establish that the product they seek to import was placed on the market in the exporting EEA member state by or under the control of the same entity that is now trying to prevent its import. Stated another way, the goods in question must have been put on the market elsewhere in the EEA by the same entity that seeks to restrain the rebranding.[220]

---

[212] *Boehringer Ingelheim v. Swingward*, Case C-348/04 [2007] *ECR* I–3391, [38]; *Boehringer Ingelheim v. Swingward Ltd* [2008] *EWCA Civ* 83.   [213] Case C-379/97 [1999] *ECR* 6927.

[214] Ibid., 82, [37].   [215] *Centrafarm v. AHP*, Case C-3/78 [1978] *ECR* 1823, 1841–2, [21]–[23].

[216] Case C-379/97 [1999] *ECR* I–6927, [43].   [217] Ibid., [44].

[218] [2015] *EWCA Civ* 54, overruling [2013] *EWHC* 3624 (Ch).   [219] Ibid., [67].

[220] *Flynn Pharma Ltd v. Drugsrus Ltd* [2017] *EWCA Civ* 226, affirming [2015] *EWHC* 2759 (Ch).

8.3.5 Advertising the goods

In *Christian Dior v. Evora*,[221] the Court of Justice indicated that while commercial resellers had a legitimate interest in using a trade mark proprietor's mark to advertise those goods, there might be situations in which the proprietor could prevent such advertising. The reference to the Court arose out of a complaint by perfume maker, Dior, that Evora infringed its trade marks by advertising that it was selling Dior perfume in Evora's chemist shops in the Netherlands. The Court of Justice held that the damage done to the reputation of a trade mark might, in principle, be a legitimate reason for opposing the advertising of goods that have been put on the market in the European Union,[222] but that 'a balance must be struck' between the legitimate interest of the trade mark owner and that of the reseller.[223] In the case of prestigious luxury goods, resellers must endeavour to prevent their advertising from affecting the value of the trade mark by detracting from the allure and prestigious image of the goods in question, and from their aura of luxury.[224] However, if the reseller is merely employing techniques that are customarily used for goods of the kind, but not necessarily of the same quality in issue, then an objection to such advertising is legitimate only if it '*seriously damages* the reputation of the trade mark'.[225] The Court suggested that this would occur if, in advertising goods bearing the mark, the trade mark were placed in a context that seriously detracted from the image that the trade mark owner had succeeded in creating around their trade mark.[226]

Is use of 'keywords' of the trade mark holder justified in the case of resellers of the trade marked goods? The issue was broached by the Court of Justice in *Portakabin v. Primakabin*,[227] in which the defendant used the PORTAKABIN mark (and other variants thereof) to generate sponsored links that fed through to its website, which sold, among other things, second-hand structures made by the claimant. The Court noted that, for liability to exist in the first place, the ads (being the few lines generated under the 'sponsored links' heading when the consumer entered the claimant's trade mark in the search engine) must leave the relationship between the trade mark owner and the advertiser unclear, and this itself meant that there was a legitimate reason for the trade mark proprietor to object to the commercial practice.[228] Nevertheless, the Court sought to elaborate three further points. First, because of the widespread sale of second-hand goods, consumers would not assume there to be any commercial link between a trade mark owner and a seller of second-hand goods.[229] Second, there would be legitimate reasons to oppose the use of the keyword if the goods sold by the defendant, although originating with the trade mark proprietor, had subsequently been subjected to processes of 'de-branding' (removal of the PORTAKABIN mark) and rebranding (with the PRIMACABIN mark).[230] Third, the Court indicated that it was not determinative that the defendant sold second-hand goods

---

[221] *Parfums Christian Dior SA v. Evora BV*, C-337/95 [1997] *ECR* I–6013. See Stothers, 71–4. See also *Coty Germany GmbH v. Parfümerie Akzente GmbH*, Case C-230/16 [2018] 4 *CMLR* 9 (preservation of a luxury image can justify a restriction upon competition, in the form of conditions attached to exclusive distribution agreements).   [222] *Parfums Christian Dior SA v. Evora BV*, Case C-337/95 [1997] *ECR* I–6013, [43].

[223] Ibid., [44].   [224] Ibid., [45].   [225] Ibid. (emphasis added).

[226] Ibid., [47]. In *BMW v. Deenik*, Case C-63/97 [1999] *ECR* I–905, [64], the Court of Justice added that if there is no risk that the public will be led to believe that there is a commercial connection between the trader and the trade mark proprietor, the mere fact that the trader derived an advantage from using the mark (e.g. because the advertisements lend an aura of quality to their business) would not of itself mean that the use was dishonest. See section 3.2, pp. 1132–6.   [227] Case C-558/08 [2010] *ECR* I–6963.

[228] Ibid., [81].   [229] Ibid., [84].

[230] Ibid., [86]. See also *Viking Gas v. Kosan Gas A/S*, Case C-46/10 [2011] *ECR* I–6161, [AG31]. Despite these statements, there is no basis in trade mark law for an objection to the resale of goods from which all of the marks have been removed.

that originated with traders other than the claimant. The Court accepted that it might be tolerable to allow use of the claimant's trade mark as a keyword, as long as volume, presentation, and quality of the other goods did not create a risk of 'seriously damaging the image which the proprietor has succeeded in creating for its mark'.[231]

8.3.6 Competition law and parallel imports

Given the rule on exhaustion within Europe, some pharmaceutical firms have sought to limit parallel trade by restricting the supply of drugs in low-priced markets. In *Sot. Lelos kai Sia EE v. GlaxoSmithKline*,[232] it was argued that the refusal of GSK to supply Greek wholesalers with more LAMICTAL than it regarded to be necessary to meet demand in that market was an abuse of a dominant position. GSK argued that, given the regulatory context—in particular, the fixing of drug prices in Greece—all that it was doing was protecting its legitimate commercial interests: were it to be obliged to supply the Greek wholesalers, the ultimate effect would be that it would have to supply the whole European market at the price set by the Greek authorities. The Greek competition authority referred several questions to the Court of Justice. The Court ruled that while refusal to supply within the European Union that was motivated by a desire to limit parallel imports would ordinarily amount to an abuse of a dominant position, there were circumstances in which a trader in a dominant position might justify such a refusal to protect their legitimate commercial interests. Importantly, the Court drew a distinction between 'ordinary orders' and other 'out of the ordinary' orders (assessed in light of previous business relations and the requirements of the market in the member state). The Court held that the refusal to meet ordinary orders would be an abuse, but refusal to meet extraordinary orders might be permissible to counter 'in a reasonable and proportionate way the threat to its own commercial interests' posed by the recipient exporting the medicines to other (higher-priced) markets.[233]

Although only indirectly related to exhaustion, it is worth noting that the Court of Justice has also affirmed the validity of selective distribution systems established by luxury brands, which restrict an authorized distributer from using a third party website, such as Amazon, to sell their luxury goods (perfumes in this instance).[234] If the purpose of any such restrictive clause was to preserve the luxury image of a brand, the contractual restrictions were proportionate to achieving this goal and the resellers were selected on objective criteria such that potentially any reseller meeting them might qualify, the clause would not offend Article 101(1) of the TFEU.[235]

8.4 PARALLEL IMPORT OF TRADE MARKED GOODS AND COPYRIGHT IN LABELS

While a parallel importer may be entitled to relabel goods for resale, the question may arise as to whether the proprietor can prevent import by relying on any copyright that

---

[231] *Portakabin Ltd v. Primakabin BV*, Case C-558/08 [2010] *ECR* I–6963, [91].

[232] *Sot. Lelos kai Sia EE v. GlaxoSmithKline Anonimi Emporiki Viomikhaniki Etairia Farmakeftikon Proionton*, Case C-468/06 [2008] *ECR* I–7139 (ECJ, Grand Chamber). See Stothers, 254–62.

[233] *Sot. Lelos kai Sia EE v. GlaxoSmithKline Anonimi Emporiki Viomikhaniki Etairia Farmakeftikon Proionton*, Case C-468/06 [2008] *ECR* I–7139 (ECJ, Grand Chamber).

[234] *Coty Germany GmbH v. Parfümerie Akzente GmbH*, Case C-230/16, EU:C:2017.941 (at issue was whether the preservation of a luxury image might justify a restriction on competition).

[235] Ibid., [22] (under this provision 'all agreements between undertakings . . . and concerted practices which may affect trade between Member States and which have as their object or effect the prevention, restriction or distortion of competition within the internal market are incompatible with that market and are prohibited').

they have in the label. Since the parallel importer would presumably reproduce and issue copies of such labels, there is on its face infringement of copyright. Nevertheless, a different approach has been taken in relation to labels. This can be seen in *Christian Dior v. Evora*,[236] in which Christian Dior sought to rely on its copyright in the picture marks to prevent Evora from reproducing the marks on advertising leaflets. The Court of Justice held that, in these circumstances, 'the protection conferred by copyright as regards the reproduction of protected works in a reseller's advertising may not . . . be broader than that which is conferred on a trade mark owner in the same circumstances'.[237] The Court added that the holder of copyright may not oppose the use of a trade mark by a reseller who habitually markets articles of the same kind, but not necessarily of the same quality, as the protected goods unless it is established that the use of those goods seriously damages the reputation of those goods.[238]

8.5 INTERNATIONAL EXHAUSTION

The scope of Article 7 of the TMD 2008 and section 12 of the 1994 Act is confined to products placed on the market in the EEA.[239] It does not matter that the product bearing the mark has been manufactured in a non-member country if it has been lawfully put on the market in the member state from which it has been imported by the owner of the mark or with their consent.[240] Article 7 gives no explicit guidance as to what happens if the product is imported from outside the EEA and has not yet been placed on the market in the EEA with the consent of the trade mark owner. It is to this issue that we now turn.

8.5.1 Background

Prior to the passage of the Directive, the question of international exhaustion was a matter for individual member states.[241] The Commission's original proposal would have imposed international exhaustion—that is, trade mark owners would not have been permitted to oppose the resale of products that had been put on the market with their consent anywhere in the world.[242] The Commission subsequently changed its view and its amended proposal explicitly limited the exhaustion principle to goods that had been put on the market 'in the Community'.[243] This left unclear the position in relation to goods placed on the market outside the European Union.

8.5.2 *Silhouette*

This issue was addressed in *Silhouette International v. Hartlauer*,[244] in which the Court of Justice was called upon to decide whether the principle of international

---

[236] Case C-337/95 [1997] *ECR* I–6013.   [237] Ibid., [58].   [238] Ibid., [59].

[239] Since the rules differ so dramatically, it is important to know when goods are placed on the market in the EEA and when outside it: see *Glaxo Group v. Dowelhurst Ltd* [2004] *ETMR* (39) 528, [2004] *EWCA Civ* 290.   [240] *Phytheron v. Bourdon*, Case C-352/95 [1997] *ECR* I–1729, I–1748, 1748, [21].

[241] *EMI Records v. CBS United Kingdom*, Case 51/75 [1976] *ECR* 811, 845.

[242] [1980] *OJ C* 351/80, proposed Art. 6; for the Explanatory Memorandum, see European Commission, *Proposal for a First Council Directive to Approximate the Laws of the Member States Relating to Trade-marks; Proposal for a Council Regulation on the Community Trade-Mark* (November 1980) COM(80) 635 final. See also Stothers, 335–6.

[243] European Commission, *Amended Proposal for a Council Regulation on the Community Trade Mark* (July 1984) COM(84) 470 final; [1985] *OJ C* 351/80, 4; Stothers, 336–7.

[244] Case C-355/96 [1998] *ECR* I–4799. For commentary, see A. Carboni, 'Cases about Spectacles and Torches: Now, Can We See the Light?' [1998] *EIPR* 471; Stothers, 342–4.

exhaustion applied under the Directive.[245] Silhouette manufactured high-quality fashion spectacles, which it distributed worldwide under the trade mark SILHOUETTE. The claimant was the registered proprietor for the mark in Austria and many other countries. Silhouette sold an out-of-date range of frames to a firm in Bulgaria. The defendant, Hartlauer, acquired the out-of-date frames from the Bulgarian firm and then imported them into Austria for resale. Silhouette sought an order prohibiting Hartlauer from marketing the spectacles in Austria under its trade mark. It did this on the basis that the frames had not been put on the market in the EEA by it or with its consent. As such, Silhouette had not exhausted its trade mark rights. Silhouette argued that the Directive provides that such rights can be exhausted only by reason of marketing within the EEA.

The Supreme Court of Austria sought a ruling from the Court of Justice as to whether EU law requires member states to provide for exhaustion only when the goods have been marketed in the EEA, or whether member states may (or perhaps must) provide for exhaustion when the goods have been marketed in a third country. The Court rejected the argument that the Directive left the member states free to provide for exhaustion in their national law. In light of Recitals 1 and 9, the Court said that Articles 5–7 of the Directive must be construed as 'embodying a complete harmonization of the rules relating to the rights conferred by a trade mark'.[246] A single rule was also necessary to safeguard the functioning of the internal market. Given the terms of Article 7, the only plausible harmonized rule was that member states are obliged to confer on trade mark owners the ability to prevent imports of trade marked goods from outside the EEA (even where the same trade mark owner has consented to that marketing).

8.5.3 Consent

Although *Silhouette* made clear that member states were not to apply rules of international exhaustion, it took another Court of Justice decision to clarify the next logical question: what amounts to consent to import goods into the EEA? In *Zino Davidoff*,[247] Laddie J asserted that even though, in principle, the trade mark owner has the right to stop importation into the EEA of goods not previously marketed in the EEA by or with their consent, this right cannot be used where the trade mark owner had consented to such import—and, remarkably, he held that, at least under English law, consent existed where the proprietor 'has agreed, expressly or otherwise to such entry, or he has, directly or otherwise, placed the goods in the hands of a third party under conditions which give the third party a right to distribute and onward sell them without restriction'.[248] In effect, in the absence of full and explicit restrictions being imposed on the purchasers at the time of purchase, according to Laddie J a trade mark owner is treated as impliedly consenting to further distribution of those goods (including their import into the EEA). On the facts of the case, placing goods on the market in Singapore was sufficient consent to their import into the EEA.

---

[245] The question had already been decided differently by the EFTA court in *Mag Instrument v. California Trading Company Norway*, Case E–2/97 [1998] 1 *CMLR* 331, [28], in which the Court concluded that it was for each of the EFTA states to decide whether to introduce or maintain the principle of international exhaustion with regard to goods originating outside the EEA. That conclusion was reversed in the light of *Silhouette*: *L'Oréal Norge AD v. Per Aarskog*, Cases E–9/07 and E–10/07 [2008] *ETMR* (60) 943 (EFTA Ct).

[246] *Silhouette*, Case C-355/96 [1998] *ECR* I–4799, [25].

[247] *Zino Davidoff v. A. & G. Imports* [1999] 3 *All ER* 711.   [248] Ibid., [38].

The Court of Justice, following the logic of *Silhouette*, rejected Laddie J's approach.[249] First, it held that it was implicit from the Directive that there must be a harmonized concept of consent in this context.[250] Second, the Court held that consent need not be express, but could be implied. Nevertheless, that consent must indicate an intention to renounce one's right to object to the import of the item into the EEA unequivocally.[251] Consequently, while in some cases consent could be inferred from facts and circumstances prior to, simultaneous with, or subsequent to the placing of goods on the market outside the EEA, consent could not be implied from the failure to express positively that goods were not to be imported into the EEA, or from silence.

In effect, it will be very difficult for a parallel importer to persuade a court that consent exists in the absence of evidence of express agreement. One example might be a situation in which the trade mark owner has known about and facilitated, but not objected to, a practice of importing trade marked goods into the EEA.[252]

8.5.4 Proving consent

The *Davidoff* decision seemed to imply that a trader operating within the EEA who is faced with an allegation that the goods have been imported from outside the EEA must be able to show that a trade mark proprietor has consented to the circulation of goods in the EEA. In *van Doren + Q GmbH v. lifestyle + sportswear Handelsgesellschaft mbH*,[253] the Court of Justice indicated that the issue of the onus of proof was one for member states, but that the national rule should not itself inhibit the free movement of goods within the EEA. Here, Stüssy Inc., a company based in California, owned the mark STÜSSY for clothes and Van Doren was the exclusive distributor of the STÜSSY clothes for Germany. Lifestyle was selling STÜSSY clothes in Germany and Van Doren claimed that there was trade mark infringement. Van Doren alleged that the goods came from the United States, whereas Lifestyle alleged that it had sourced them in the EEA (so that the trade mark rights were exhausted), but refused to name its suppliers. Under German law, it was for the defendant to prove exhaustion, although the appeal court had sought to place some onus on the claimant. The Court of Justice was asked whether Article 34 TFEU required there to be an exception to the rule that the full burden of proof fall on the defendant.

First, the Court held that the German rule of evidence is consistent with Community law, including Articles 5 and 7 of the Directive. However, the Court qualified this by stating that such a rule of evidence might need to be qualified where its application might lead to a 'real risk of partitioning of national markets'.[254] In such circumstances, Article 34 TFEU requires the rule of evidence to be qualified and, instead, a national court should divide up the different matters to be proved. More specifically, the onus would fall on the proprietor of the mark to prove that the goods were first marketed outside the EEA; it would then be for the parallel importer to prove consent to subsequent import of the products.

The Court gave an example of a situation in which there could be such a risk of partitioning as to qualify the general approach—that is, where European marketing is by

---

[249] Joined Cases C-414/99 and C-416/99 [2002] *Ch* 109, [2001] *ECR* I-8691, [2002] 1 *CMLR* 1. The test is the same as that for assessing whether there was consent to goods being placed on the market directly (rather than imported): *Makro v. Diesel spA*, Case C-324/08 [2009] ECR I-10019. See section 8.2.2, pp. 1149–50.

[250] Joined Cases C-414/99 and C-416/99 [2001] *ECR* I-8691, [43].   [251] Ibid., [45].

[252] The courts have found implied consent in at least two cases: *Corporation Habanos SA v. Mastercigars* [2007] *EWCA Civ* 176; *Honda Motor Co. v. Naseem* [2008] *EWHC* 338 (Ch). But cf. *Roche Products Ltd v. Kent Pharmaceutical* [2006] *EWCA Civ* 1775. See also *Levi Strauss v. Tesco* [2002] 3 *CMLR* 11, [2002] *ETMR* (95) 1153 (Pumfrey J).   [253] Case C-244/00 [2003] *ECR* I-3051.

[254] Ibid., [38]–[39].

way of an exclusive distribution system. In such cases, the effect of requiring the parallel importer to prove consent is tantamount to requiring it to reveal its sources (and hence to expose the breaches in the trade mark owner's exclusive distribution system). Such exposure would enable the trade mark proprietor to remove its leaky distributor from the supply chain and thus prevent the parallel importer from continuing to obtain supplies in this way. In such cases, therefore, the Court requires the trade mark proprietor to prove that the goods were marketed outside the EEA. It might do so by referring to batch numbers, or other characteristics that demonstrate that first marketing was outside the EEA.

In *Oracle America Ltd v. M-Tech Data*,[255] the claimant was a manufacturer of computer hardware that it had placed on the market bearing its trade marks in China, Chile, and the United States. The defendant imported them into the United Kingdom and supplied a third party (who was, in fact, acting on behalf of the claimant). When the claimant sought summary judgment in an action for infringement of its trade mark, the defendant argued that the claimant's trade mark rights were not enforceable because the object and enforcement was to partition the EEA market in Oracle hardware contrary to Articles 34–36 TFEU. The argument was made that the defendant could not know whether these were goods that Oracle had permitted to be marketed in the EEA. This was said to be the case because the market in disks (and computer hardware) was a global market, and Oracle could easily provide the information by making available a list of the serial numbers of disks that had been marketed in the EEA. M-Tech argued that Oracle refused to do so precisely so that it could prevent unauthorized trade in its legitimate products in Europe.[256] Unfortunately, M-Tech was unable to show that the particular sales in issue in the case had been affected by Oracle's alleged wrongful behaviour,[257] and so sought to claim that its general practice rendered its trade marks unenforceable on the basis that Article 5 of the TMD 2008 'is subject to an implied limitation to be derived as a matter of construction from Articles 34 to 36 of the EU Treaty'.[258] At first instance, Kitchin J rejected the defence, but on appeal the Court of Appeal found that the defence was not unarguable, so that the case should have been permitted to go to trial. On appeal to the Supreme Court, the judgment at first instance was reinstated. Lord Sumption, with whom the Court unanimously agreed, found that, once the distinction was understood between the rules relating to goods placed on the market in the EEA and goods that had not been so placed, it was apparent that there was no arguable defence. The conduct to which the defendant objected was 'collateral to the particular right which [the claimant was] seeking to enforce'[259]—namely, the absolute right to oppose first marketing in the EEA. The defence could not succeed and no reference to the Court of Justice was required.

8.5.5 Competition rules

Even if the rule that there is no international exhaustion is now quite clear, there are unresolved issues concerning the interrelationship between European trade mark policy and European competition law, particularly Article 101 TFEU. The relevance of the latter was made clear by the Court of Justice in the *Javico v. Yves St Laurent* decision.[260] In that case, Yves St Laurent sought to terminate a distribution contract with Javico under which Javico undertook to sell products only in Russia and the Ukraine, because it had

---

[255] [2012] *UKSC* 27.

[256] Ibid., [9]. For the purposes of the hearing, the Court assumed this to be true.

[257] If so, it might have been able to rely on a Euro-defence: ibid., [11].   [258] Ibid., [11].

[259] Ibid., [24].

[260] *Javico International and Javico AG v. Yves St Laurent Parfums SA*, Case C-306/96 [1998] *ECR* I–1983.

been discovered that some of the products had found their way to the United Kingdom. The Cour d'Appel of Versailles sought the advice of the Court of Justice as to whether such a contract might be prohibited by Article 81 (now Article 101). The Court held that the agreement had as its object the restriction of competition, so that the key question was whether it was capable of affecting trade between member states. If the agreement specifically prohibited imports into the EEA, it would have as its object the restriction of competition in the EEA and would be likely to be void. However, here, the contract specified that there were to be no sales outside the territory (whether to the EEA or not). Consequently, the Court said that the question was: what was the 'effect' of the agreement? This involved assessing the economic context, particularly the relative position and importance of the parties on the market in question. However, if the effects were insignificant, the contract would be outside the prohibition and hence valid. If the EU market is oligopolistic, or the price differentials are significant, it is necessary to examine the likely impact of the disputed contract. If the market outside the EU is relatively small compared to that within the EU, the impact is likely to be insignificant. However, assessing such matters is the task of national courts.

While, in *Silhouette*, the Court of Justice clearly indicated that trade marks law should enable a proprietor to keep legitimate goods first marketed outside the EEA out of the market, when examining competition policy, the Court in *Javico* suggested that agreements that prohibit marketing in the EEA are contrary to Article 101 TFEU (ex Article 81 EC and Article 85 of the Treaty). The two policies are in conflict, and the likely reconciliation is through a limited application of *Javico*. In any case, *Davidoff* reduces the likely application of *Javico* for two reasons: first, because the definition of 'consent' (and onus-of-proof issues) means that the trade mark proprietor need not support their trade mark rights through contractual prohibitions on import into the EEA, and so can avoid Article 101 (which applies to agreements rather than unilateral acts); and second, because even if a contract selling goods outside the EEA obliges the purchaser not to resell within the EEA, it is arguable that such a clause has no effect on competition over and above that attributable to the proprietor's rights under trade marks law.[261]

8.5.6 Reform?

Following the *Silhouette* decision, the European Commission raised the question of reform of the rules relating to international exhaustion. It commissioned a study of the economic effects of changing to international exhaustion, which, in turn, indicated that the issues were complex (there might be effects not only on pricing, but also on matters such as product quality or after-sales services) and that the price benefits to consumers of changing the regime would probably be limited (in some sectors, up to 2 per cent).[262] The Commission then consulted widely with member states and interested parties, mooting various possible options, such as having international exhaustion only for certain products (for example excluding pharmaceuticals and sound recordings).[263] However, in May 2000, the Commission decided not to propose any action in this field.

[261] Commission Staff Working Paper, *Possible Abuses of Trade Mark Rights within the EU in the Context of Community Exhaustion* (May 2003) SEC(2003) 575 (finding the current legal position to be satisfactory).

[262] National Economic Research Associates/SJ Berwin, *The Economic Consequences of the Choice of Regime of Exhaustion in the Area of Trade Marks: Final Report for DG XV of the European Commission* (February 1999).

[263] Select Committee on Trade and Industry, *Eighth Report: Trade Marks, Fakes and Consumers* (8 July 1999).

Unsurprisingly, Brexit has reopened some of these debates. If the United Kingdom leaves the EU without staying in the European Economic Area, the EU-wide concept of regional exhaustion will no longer apply. The choice of models to be adopted in the future includes (i) continuing with regional exhaustion, as part of any future trade agreement with the EU; (ii) adopting a restrictive notion of national exhaustion, where only goods first placed upon the domestic market will have rights of control exhausted; or (iii) reverting to the pre-harmonization position of international exhaustion.[264]

9 FREEDOM OF EXPRESSION

The preceding analysis alludes to the interface between trade marks and competition law. A final relationship to consider is that between expressive values or recognized speech interests and trade mark law. Digital technology and social media have made this an increasingly relevant interface. A painting, parody, song, or satirical blog post may use a mark to critique an undertaking's environmental record or the treatment of its workers. Since trade marks function as convenient registers of social meaning, critics may also use leading brands to critique an entire sector, such as fossil fuels, the luxury goods industry, or big tobacco. There are two techniques for responding to such conflicts within trade mark law.[265] The first is to apply existing rules with a sensitivity to the freedom of expression values at stake in a given dispute. The critic's use may be non-commercial, while a defence such as referential use or due cause may also be available. The second is to craft a specific legislative defence which responds to speech interests.[266] While each has its advantages and drawbacks, EU law exhibits a preference for the former approach.

In general, trade mark rights rarely create significant limitations on free speech. For example, use of a trade mark to criticize a company or its products will not normally amount to an infringement of trade mark rights. This is because such speech will rarely be regarded as an act occurring in the 'course of trade',[267] nor in relation to the user's goods or services.[268] A *Which?*-style review of the merits of goods or services may utilize trade marks, but will not do so 'in relation to' the publisher's goods (only to refer to the trade mark owner's goods). It is less clear whether there could be infringement by use of a sign as the subject matter of a painting (as with Warhol's famous depictions of CAMPBELL's soup cans) or even as the title of a pop song (as with The Undertones' song 'Mars Bars' or Scandinavian dance act Aqua's use of the mark BARBIE in its song 'Barbie Girl').[269] On the

---

[264] M. Mimler, *The Effect of Brexit on Trademarks, Designs and Other 'Europeanized' Areas of Intellectual Property Law in the United Kingdom* (BIICL, Paper No. 7, December 2017) 10–11.

[265] W. Sakulin, *Trade Mark Protection and Freedom of Expression* (2010); R. Burrell and D. S. Gangjee, 'Trade Marks and Freedom of Expression: A Call for Caution' (2010) 41 *IIC* 544; L. P. Ramsey, 'Reconciling Trade Mark Rights and Free Expression Locally and Globally', in D. Gervais (ed.), *International Intellectual Property: A Handbook of Contemporary Research* (2015) 341; S. Jacques, 'A Parody Exception: Why Trade Mark Owners Should Get the Joke' [2016] *EIPR* 471 (arguing for a specific parody exception in trade mark law, similar to that found in EU copyright law).

[266] As some US courts prefer. See *Rogers v. Grimaldi*, 875 F 2d 994 (2nd Cir. 1989) (which adopts a two stage enquiry: expressive use of the mark will be restrained (i) only where the work has 'no artistic relevance'; or (ii) if it has such relevance, where it nevertheless explicitly misleads consumers as to commercial source or content).   [267] *Unilever v. Griffin* [2010] *EWHC* 899 (Ch), [11]–[14] (Arnold J).

[268] Ibid., [15].   [269] *Mattel, Inc. v. MCA Records.* 296 F.3d. 894, 902 (9th Cir. 2002).

assumption that these acts occur in the course of trade,[270] there would be a serious issue as to whether the use was in relation to (that is, as a distinguishing sign for) the painting or song (which is marginally more plausible in relation to the song titles). In that case, liability would probably depend on whether these uses took unfair advantage of, or were detrimental to, the repute of the CAMPBELL's mark, and if so, whether they were 'without due cause'.[271] We have argued (in Chapter 38) that 'due cause' might leave room to accommodate freedom of speech. As we have noted earlier, there is now an explicit steer that EU trade mark legislation—including infringement and defences provisions—'should be applied in a way that ensures full respect for fundamental rights and freedoms, and in particular the freedom of expression'.[272]

While, for the most part, trade mark law should not compromise freedom of speech, sometimes a person may trade in goods that have expressive qualities that could infringe trade marks: an obvious example is a T-shirt that parodies trade marked goods, for example mimicking the blue oval FORD logo, but replacing the word 'Ford' with the word 'Fraud'. Another example, drawn from US case law, would be the sale of dog toys as CHEWY VUITTON, which could be understood as a parody of LOUIS VUITTON.[273] In these cases, trade mark law may come into conflict with freedom of expression (especially if Louis Vuitton has acquired trade mark rights in relation to 'textile goods' in Class 24 or 'playthings' in Class 28).[274] Might there be liability under section 10(2) or (3) of the 1994 Act? If so, in these situations, there is a possibility that an appeal could be made to fundamental freedoms recognized in national, regional, or international law.[275]

---

[270] Case C-206/01 [2002] *ECR* I 10273, [40]. See also *Travelex Global and Financial Services Ltd & Interpayment Services Ltd v. Commission*, Case T-195/00 [2003] *ECR* II-1677, [93]–[104]; cf. *Arsenal v. Reed*, Case C-206/01 [2002] *ECR* I-10273, [AG63].   [271] See Chapter 38, section 2.5, pp. 1071–2.

[272] TMD 2015, Recital 27; EUTMR, Recital 21.

[273] *Louis Vuitton Malletier v. Haute Diggity Dog, LLC*, 507 *F.3d.* 252 (4th Cir. 2007).

[274] W. Sakulin, *Trademark Protection and Freedom of Expression* (2011); W. Sadurski, 'Allegro without Vivaldi: Trademark Protection, Freedom of Speech, and Constitutional Balancing' [2012] *EUConst* 456; L. Ramsey and J. Schovsbo, 'Mechanisms for Limiting Trade Mark Rights to Further Competition and Free Speech' (2013) 44 *IIC* 671; R. Burrell and D. Gangjee, 'Trade Marks and Freedom of Expression: A Call for Caution' (2010) 41 *IIC* 544. Burrell and Gangjee suggest that resort to freedom of expression 'concedes too much', and that the problem (and solution) is to be found in the problematic and unjustified extension of trade mark rights through 'dilution' and extended concepts of confusion. Moreover, they argue that appeals to freedom of expression may not be sufficient to counter the undesirable effects of trade mark law's expansion (among other things), noting how unreceptive some common law judges have been to draw on Art. 10 ECHR in English courts. Finally, they suggest that while some of these difficulties with utilizing freedom of expression might be reduced by deploying particular categories of exception (such as 'parody'), such a strategy brings its own problems (in part of arbitrariness).

[275] Human Rights Act 1998, s. 12; EU Charter, Art. 11; ECHR, Art. 10. See also, L. Zelechowski, 'Invoking Freedom of Expression and Freedom of Competition in Trade Mark Infringement Disputes: Legal Mechanisms for Striking a Balance' (2018) ERA Forum, available online at https://link.springer.com/article/10.1007/s12027-018-0498-3.

42

EXPLOITATION AND USE OF TRADE MARKS

1 INTRODUCTION

Given that the law of registered trade marks developed from the law of passing off, it is not surprising that it has long carried with it limitations derived from the law of passing off. One such limitation is that passing off does not protect property in the mark; instead, it protects traders against misrepresentations affecting a distinct proprietary interest—namely, 'goodwill'. While this limitation has gradually been removed from the law of registered trade marks (trade marks are now treated as forms of property in their own right),[1] the law relating to the exploitation of trade marks has yet to embrace wholeheartedly the idea that a trade mark is an asset over which its proprietor should have full control.[2] Although it is now common practice for trade marks to be included on the balance sheets of companies,[3] the law still imposes a number of restrictions on the use that can be made of marks. We begin this chapter by looking at the ownership of trade marks, focusing in particular on the problems that arise in relation to co-ownership. After going on to look at the ways in which trade marks can be exploited, we will focus on the limitations placed on the uses that can be made of a trade mark.

Before examining these matters in more detail, it is worth observing that while the exploitation of British trade marks is governed by the Trade Marks Act 1994, the European Union Trade Mark Regulation (2017/1001) (EUTMR) sets out only a partial code for dealing with European Union trade marks (EUTMs). In the absence of harmonized EU laws on transfers, assignments, security interests, testamentary dispositions, and insolvency, the drafters of the Regulation decided that the most appropriate approach would be for transactions in relation to EUTMs to be governed by the laws of the most closely connected member state. As a result, EUTM transactions will normally be dealt with by the laws of the country in which the proprietor has their seat or domicile on the relevant date.[4]

---

[1] TMA 1994, s. 22 (personal property); EUTMR, Art. 19 (an object of property). For a history of the same trend in the United States, see L. Johnston, 'Drifting towards Trademark Rights in Gross' (1985) 85 *TM Rep* 19.

[2] DTI, *Reform of Trade Marks Law* (1990 Cm. 1203), [4.34]–[4.39]; K. Lupton, 'Trade Marks as Property' (1991) 2 *AIPJ* 29.

[3] In particular, where they have been purchased: B. Sherman and M. Power, 'Law, Accounting and the Emergent Positivity of Intangible Property' (1994) 3 *S & LS* 477; P. Cussons, 'Trade Marks on the Balance Sheet', in D. Campbell, H. Harmeling, and E. Keyzer (eds), *Trademarks: Legal and Business Aspects* (1994), 235.

[4] EUTMR, Art. 19(1). See also EUTMR, Art. 23(2) (levy of execution); cf. Art. 24(1) (applicable rules on insolvency are to be those of the state in which the debtor has its 'centre of main interests').

2 OWNERSHIP

2.1 PROPRIETORSHIP

The owner of a trade mark is the person who registers it.[5] In contrast with patent law, which recognizes the concept of the 'inventor' and 'person entitled' as entities that have an existence prior to (and thus independently of) the application for a patent, the 1994 Act does not recognize that a trade mark may have a proprietor before an application is made. In short, the Act treats the first person to register as the proprietor, and the only proprietor is the registered proprietor. Where there is competition as to who should be entitled to a trade mark, those disputes are decided by reference to the relative grounds for invalidity and by the requirement that all applications be made in good faith.

2.2 CO-OWNERSHIP

One potential problem that arises in the exploitation of a trade mark is when the mark is owned by two or more parties. In these circumstances, the question arises as to whether one co-owner can utilize the trade mark without the consent of other co-owner(s). Where there is no contract between two or more co-owners of a trade mark, the Trade Marks Act 1994 declares that each of the co-owners is 'entitled to an equal undivided share in the registered trade mark'.[6] This means that each owner is permitted 'by himself or his agents, to do for his own benefit and without the consent of or the need to account to the other or others, any act which would otherwise amount to an infringement of the registered trade mark'.[7] The power and immunity given to each co-proprietor is limited because, without the consent of the other co-owner(s), the joint owner cannot license others to use the trade mark.[8]

3 MODES OF EXPLOITATION

Trade marks can be exploited in a number of different ways.[9] Perhaps the most common technique is for owners to exploit the mark themselves. Trade marks may also be assigned, licensed, mortgaged, or devolve by operation of law (notably through death or bankruptcy).[10] We will look at each in turn.

3.1 SELF-EXPLOITATION

One of the most common ways in which trade marks are used is for owners to exploit the marks themselves. Often, this will involve the owner making the goods, applying the mark, and selling the goods. While trade mark owners may do all of these acts themselves, they often use third parties. For example, a trade mark owner will use goods manufactured by someone else, a 'contract manufacturer', to which they apply their marks. In

---

[5] In fact, an application is itself regarded as an object of property that can be transferred and has value, and is even protected as property under the ECHR: *Anheuser-Busch v. Portugal*, App. No. 73,049/01 [2007] *EHRR* (36) 830, [2007] *ETMR* (24) 343.

[6] TMA 1994, s. 23.   [7] TMA 1994, s. 23(3).   [8] TMA 1994, s. 23(4).

[9] For a discussion of the many issues that may arise in the exploitation of trade marks, see N. Wilkof, *Trade Mark Licensing* (2005).   [10] TMA 1994, s. 24(1); EUTMR, Art. 24 (insolvency).

these circumstances, the mark is not used to indicate that the goods were manufactured by the trade mark owner; instead, the mark indicates that the goods were selected and approved by the trade mark owner.[11] By and large, such relationships are not problematic. However, if they break down, for example through bankruptcy or failure to meet contractual stipulations, difficulties may arise in determining whether parties other than the trade mark owner can sell the goods that have been marked with the trade mark proprietor's consent.[12]

Trade mark proprietors use a number of strategies when placing their goods on the market. In many instances, they will be happy for the goods to reach the market by any means. In other cases, however, to maintain the allure of the product, they may wish to restrict distribution to particular persons. This is the case with perfumes, which many manufacturers have deemed unsuitable for sale in certain kinds of outlet, such as supermarkets.[13]

Once the goods are on the market in the European Economic Area (EEA), the rights of the trade mark owner are exhausted. Usually, therefore, distributors of the trade marked goods do not need permission to sell goods bearing the mark. A trade mark owner may, however, wish to control certain uses of the mark by such a distributor. As we noted in Chapter 41, there will be limitations on the ways in which the distributor may use the mark in advertising and as regards any alteration of the goods.

3.2 ASSIGNMENT

3.2.1 Registered trade marks

An assignment is a transfer of ownership of the trade mark (or application). As a result of an assignment, the assignee stands in the shoes of the assignor and is entitled to deal with the trade mark as they please. In contrast with a licence, under which the licensor retains an interest in the trade mark, once a trade mark owner has assigned the trade mark, they no longer have any interest in, or responsibility to maintain, the trade mark.[14]

Assignments of trade marks can occur without any corresponding transfer of business or goodwill.[15] This is a critical difference between passing off and registered trade marks. An owner of an unregistered mark can assign the benefit of the mark only by assigning the goodwill of the business with which it has been used.[16] This common law distrust of the trading in marks reflects the understanding that marks are protected because they operate in the consumers' eyes as indications of source. Following this logic, if assignments were allowed, it would create confusion as to the source of the goods or services. With registered trade marks being treated increasingly as assets, this rationale for restricting assignments carries less weight.

An assignment can be made in part or in a limited manner. A national trade mark may be assigned in relation to part of the goods and services for which the mark is registered,

---

[11] Indeed, Millett J has noted that a trade mark owner 'may have the components made by one company, assembled by another, the trade mark affixed by a third and the goods marketed by a fourth': *Accurist Watches v. King* [1992] *FSR* 80, 88.

[12] As in *Accurist Watches,* ibid. (sale by manufacturer in exercise of retention of title clause); N. Wilkof, *Trade Mark Licensing* (2005), ch. 8.

[13] Ibid., ch. 7.   [14] TMA 1994, s. 24.

[15] Goodwill can of course be assigned: *Reuter v. Mulgens* (1953) 70 *RPC* 235.

[16] *Pinto v. Badman* (1891) 8 *RPC* 181; *Thorneloe v. Hill* [1894] 1 *Ch* 569.

limited in the manner of its use,[17] or geographically[18] (subject to compliance with the Treaty on the Functioning of the European Union).[19] In contrast, an EU trade mark must be dealt with 'in its entirety, and for the whole area of the Union'.[20]

In order for an assignment to be valid, it must be in writing and signed by the assignor. In the case of a European mark, the assignment must be signed by all of the parties to the transaction.[21] In situations in which the trade mark or application is owned by more than one party, each co-owner can assign only their share and then only if the others consent to such an assignment.[22] It follows that a full assignment of a mark would require the cooperation and signatures of all co-owners. While the assignment does not need to be registered to be effective, there are a number of advantages that follow from registration, which are reviewed later. With respect to the assignment of EU trade marks, the EU Intellectual Property Office (formerly, OHIM) is obliged not to register any transfer that is likely to mislead the public as to the nature, quality, or geographical origin of the goods or services in respect of which it is registered. In contrast, the UK Trade Marks Registry has relinquished even a minimal supervisory role.[23]

3.2.2 'Unregistered' trade marks

The law of passing off protects the goodwill associated with the mark. Furthermore, goodwill cannot be assigned without also assigning the business to which it attaches.[24] This means that an assignment of the mark without the goodwill—an assignment of the mark in gross[25] as is called—is not possible.[26] Where a business, and its goodwill, is assigned the new owner can carrying on the business under the mark and sue third parties for passing off.[27] It is also possible to divide the goodwill in the business (sometimes called a partial assignment). The classic instance of this occurring was *Dent v. Turpin*[28] where a father died and left a shop to both of his stepsons in different parts of London: one in the Strand and one in the Royal Exchange. The shops passed on again and the goodwill transferred. The court was content that each had their own goodwill and could sue third parties (but not each other) for passing of the mark. Similarly, in *Sir Robert McAlpine v. Alfred McAlpine*[29] the business had been divided on geographical lines (which had long since ceased to be applied) and continued to co-exist as Alfred McAlpine and Robert McAlpine. When the former wanted to rebrand as simply McAlpine, it was held that this would amount to passing off. This demonstrates that while severance of the business and its goodwill is possible it does not mean that the divided businesses do not have to pay attention to the actions of each other.

---

[17] TMA 1994, s. 24(2).

[18] Issues may arise where the use of the same trade mark by different trade mark owners within one jurisdiction becomes deceptive, but this cannot affect the freedom to assign: *Elizabeth Emanuel v. Continental Shelf*, C-259/04 [2006] *ETMR* 56.

[19] TMA 1994, s. 24(2)(b).   [20] EUTMR, Art. 19(1).

[21] TMA 1994, s. 24(3) (must be signed by assignor); EUTMR, Art. 20(3) (must be signed by parties to the contract).   [22] TMA 1994, s. 23(4).

[23] For refusal of transfer to be justified, such deception must be clear from the transfer documents. Moreover, the EUIPO should accept the transfer insofar as the transferee agrees to limit registration of the European mark to goods or services in respect of which it is registered: EUTMR, Art. 20(4). In addition, under EUTMR, Art. 20(2), a presumption exists that a transfer of the whole of an undertaking includes the transfer of the EU trade mark.   [24] *Adrema v. Custodian* [1957] *RPC* 49.

[25] This can also arise where the goodwill is purported sold without the business as well (see for example, *Barnsley Brewery v. RBNB* [1997] *FSR* 462) but this is not relevant for the current purposes.

[26] *Pinto Badman* (1891) 8 *RPC* 181; *Thorneloe v. Hill* [1894] 1 *Ch* 579.

[27] *Newman v. Adlem* [2006] *FSR* 16, [27]; citing with approval *Reuter v. Mulhens* (1953) 70 *RPC* 102.

[28] (1861) 2 *Johnson & Hemming's Chancery Reports* 139; 70 *ER* 1003.   [29] [2004] *RPC* 36.

3.3 VOLUNTARY LICENCES

3.3.1 Registered trade marks

Another common mode of exploitation is for a trade mark owner to grant a licence that enables others to carry out specified activities in relation to the mark. The licensing of trade marks, which facilitates merchandising, franchising, and distribution agreements more generally, is at the heart of a multibillion-pound industry,[30] which 'pervades the way . . . goods and services are distributed, marketed and sold, both domestically and internationally'.[31] At a basic level, a licence is merely a permission to do an act that would otherwise be prohibited without the consent of the trade mark owner.[32] A licence enables the licensee to use the trade mark for specified goods or services without infringing.[33] So long as the use falls within the terms of the licence, the licensee is immune from an action by the trade mark owner.[34] For the most part, the terms of a voluntary licence are up to the parties to determine, and thus will depend on the needs, capacities, and wishes of the parties.[35]

However, under trade mark law, a licence amounts to much more than a mere permission to use a mark. In the absence of an agreement to the contrary, a trade mark licence binds a successor in title to the grantor's interest.[36] In addition, it enables a licensee of a trade mark to enforce their rights against third parties.[37] Given the almost proprietary nature[38] of a trade mark licence,[39] it is not surprising that the law requires the licence to be in writing for it to be 'effective'[40] (a consent agreement need not be in writing however). A licence need not be registered to be valid as against the licensor, but there are several advantages from registration, which are discussed later.[41]

Licences may take many forms, from a one-off permission through to an exclusive licence. Licences (even of EU trade marks) may be limited geographically,[42] temporally, in relation to particular goods or services, or as to manner of use.[43]

Of the different forms of licence, perhaps the most significant (in terms of law, at least) is the 'exclusive licence'. An exclusive licence is an agreement according to which the registered proprietor of a trade mark not only confers permission on the licensee to use the trade mark, but also promises that they will not grant any other licences and that they will not exploit the mark themselves.[44] The legal consequence of this is that an exclusive

---

[30] G. Battersby and C. Grimes, 'Merchandising Revisited' (1986) 76 *TM Rep* 271, 275.

[31] N. Wilkof, *Trade Mark Licensing* (2005), 1.

[32] This basic view of a licence (more generally) is ancient: see *Thomas v. Sorrell* (1673), 124 *ER* 1098 (*Vaugh* 330).

[33] *Martin Y Paz Diffusion SA v. Depuydt*, Case C-661/11, EU:C:2013:252 (Opinion of Advocate-General Cruz Villalón), [AG62] ('A licence is the most common way in which consent to the use of the trade mark in the course of trade is given'). See also *Pie Opitiek v. Bureau Gevers*, Case C-376/11, EU:C:2012:502 (ECJ, Second Chamber).

[34] *Sport International v. Inter Footwear* [1984] 2 *All ER* 321.

[35] If provision is made for such action, the law recognizes that a licensee may grant sub-licences: TMA 1994, s. 28(4).

[36] TMA 1994, s. 28(3); EUTMR, Art. 27(1). But note EUTMR, Art. 27(2).

[37] TMA 1994, s. 30; EUTMR, Art. 25(3); unless the licence provides otherwise. It is not necessary to register the licence to have these rights under the EUTMR: see *Youssef Hassan*, C-163/15, EU:C:2016:71.

[38] Although the courts have held that it is not *actually* proprietary: *Northern & Shell v. Cond Nast* [1995] *RPC* 117.

[39] See N. Wilkof, *Trade Mark Licensing* (2005), ch. 12. For discussion of the distinction between licences and proprietary interests in the context of relief from forfeiture, see esp. ibid., [12.43]–[12.55], 278–84.

[40] TMA 1994, s. 28(2). Presumably, the law will continue to recognize implied licences and oral consents, as well as to apply the traditional principles relating to estoppel.

[41] Where there are joint proprietors, all of them must consent to any licence: TMA 1994, s. 23(4)(a).

[42] TMA 1994, s. 28(1)(b); EUTMR, Art. 25(1).   [43] TMA 1994, s. 28(1).

[44] TMA 1994, s. 29(1). See *Scandecor International v. Scandecor Marketing* [2002] *FSR* 122, [14].

licence confers a right in respect of the trade mark *to the exclusion of all others including the licensor (i.e. the trade mark owner).*

An exclusive licence confers powers on the licensee that are equivalent to those of an assignee.[45] Undoubtedly, the most significant aspect of this is that, unlike a mere licensee,[46] an exclusive licensee can sue infringers without having to persuade the proprietor to take action on their behalf.[47] An exclusive licensee is given the same rights as an assignee and therefore has the right to bring proceedings in respect of any infringement that occurs after the date of the licence agreement. Indeed, an action can be brought by both the trade mark proprietor and an exclusive licensee.[48] The statute provides guidance where concurrent rights exist.[49]

Although the law distinguishes between bare, contractual, and exclusive licences, commercial dealings are less precise in the way in which the term 'licence' is used. Indeed, it has been said that 'both business executives and lawyers use the word "licence" indiscriminately and conclude agreements they call "licences" when no licence is really necessary'.[50] From a commercial point of view, it is possible to characterize licences and similar arrangements in a more functional manner as product trade mark licences, franchise agreements, and distributorship agreements.[51]

Under a *product trade mark licence*, the licensee will manufacture the product and be permitted to apply the mark to it. This often occurs with character merchandising, and also with the manufacture of many products (such as soft drinks, where the trade mark owner supplies the syrup, but the licensee makes up, bottles, and sells the drink). Product trade mark licences are also often linked to licences of patents and technology.

It has been said that franchising accounts for a third of retail turnover with the United Kingdom.[52] Under a *franchise agreement*, the franchisor provides the framework within which the franchisee operates. While the nature of the agreement varies from case to case, the franchisor effectively provides the system by which the business operates. The franchisor may provide things such as the corporate image (including the mark), the advertising, training, premises, know-how, and support service.[53] Familiar examples of franchises include STARBUCK's coffee, pronuptia's wedding attire, and kall-kwik photocopying shops.[54]

A *distributorship agreement* is merely a means by which a producer regulates how their goods reach the market.[55] Although distribution agreements are not usually trade mark licences, such agreements may include clauses requiring the distributor to sell the goods under the producer's trade mark in a manner specified by the producer. Alternatively, they may require a licensee to use particular distributor's marks.[56] In order to protect the reputation of the brand, a supplier may restrict distribution to certain specialist shops, a recent example of which has been the refusal of perfume manufacturers to supply supermarkets.

---

[45] TMA 1994, s. 31(1).   [46] For the position of a mere licensee, see TMA 1994, s. 28(2)–(5).
[47] TMA 1994, s. 31(1).   [48] TMA 1994, s. 31(2).   [49] TMA 1994, s. 31(4)–(8).
[50] R. Joliet, 'Trademark Licensing Agreements under the EEC Law of Competition' (1983–84) 5 *Nw J Intl L & Bus* 755, 765.   [51] Ibid., 765–6.
[52] M. Abell, 'Clouds on the Horizon for Franchisors in the EU' (August 1998) *Trademark World* 34.
[53] *Kall-Kwik v. Rush* [1996] *FSR* 114.
[54] Franchises can be subdivided into three categories: 'service franchise agreements', which concern the supply of services (e.g. kall-kwik); 'production' or 'industrial franchise agreements', which concern the manufacturing of goods; and 'distribution franchise agreements', which involve the sale of goods (e.g. pronuptia).
[55] In some circumstances, distribution franchises can share many facets of distribution agreements: R. Joliet, 'Trademark Licensing Agreements under the EEC Law of Competition' (1983–84) 5 *Nw J Intl L & Bus* 755, 764–5.   [56] *Consten & Grundig v. EC Commission*, Case C-56/64 [1966] *CMLR* 418.

3.2.2 'Unregistered' trade marks

The licensing of 'unregistered' trade marks—that is a mark which is protected under the law of passing off—is complicated.[57] The difficulty arises essentially because an intellectual property licence is usually seen as an asset (that is, property). In relation to licences of 'common law' marks in gross the situation can be greatly simplified once it is understood that a licence can create an inalienable personal right but not a property right.

The absence of a proprietary right in a licence arises from the fact that the common law does not recognize the assignment of licences in gross.[58] Accordingly, the licensee of an 'unregistered' trade mark has no rights against third parties and (potentially) such a licence is not an asset to be distributed upon the insolvency of the 'licensee'.

This personal right means that one person (A) can contract with another (B) not to sue them for passing off where B uses A's mark. This licence can (but need not) include use conditions (that is, conditions under which the use of the A's mark will not lead to be B being sued).[59] A difficulty with this sort of arrangement was demonstrated in *Fine & Country v. Okotoks*.[60] Fine & Country created an estate agent 'brand' and it licensed independent estate agents to use its brand. Fine & Country did not itself trade as an estate agent, it merely provided a shop front for its licensees to do so. It was held that the goodwill in such a circumstance was shared in the Fine & Country brand between the licensees and the licensors.[61]

A further difficulty arises from the fact that to avoid issues of shared goodwill licence agreements (and more commonly, franchise agreements) usually provide that the goodwill in the brand is vested in the licensor (franchisor).[62] While the Court of Appeal in *Fine & Country* has implicitly accepted that this is correct,[63] it is difficult to see how it is not an impermissible assignment of goodwill without the underlying business.

3.4 MORTGAGES

3.4.1 Registered trade marks

Like other forms of property, trade marks may be used as security for a debt. This can be a useful technique to enable the proprietors of trade marks to raise funds. One form of such security is the legal mortgage, which involves an assignment of the trade mark by the trade mark owner (mortgagor-borrower) to the mortgagee-lender. This is subject to a condition that the trade mark will be reassigned to the mortgagor when the debt is repaid (or, as the law says, 'on redemption'). It is important that the assignment reserves for the mortgagor a right to continue using the trade mark. This is probably best achieved by reservation of an exclusive licence.[64] An alternative form of security is to subject the trade mark to a 'charge',[65] in which case there is no assignment; instead, the charge gains certain rights over the trade mark. In the case of both forms of security, to be valid, the transaction must be in writing and signed by the parties.[66] Where there are joint proprietors, all

---

[57] See generally, S. Lane, 'The Status of Licensing Common Law Marks' (1991).

[58] *Star Industries v. Yap Kwee Kor* [1976] *FSR* 256, 270–2.

[59] See, for instance, *British Legion v. British Legion Club (Street) Ltd* (1931) 48 *RPC* 55.

[60] [2012] *EWHC* 2230 (Ch).

[61] Ibid., [71]; the Court of Appeal [2013] *EWCA Civ* 672 at [56]–[57] drew comparisons with franchise businesses and relied on Wadlow (2011), [7-110–7-111]

[62] In *Fine & Country* the licence referred to the goodwill being held on trust by the licensee for the licensor.   [63] [2013] *EWCA Civ* 672 at [56]–[57].

[64] D. Campbell, H. Harmeling, and E. Keyzer (eds), *Trademarks: Legal and Business Aspects* (1994), 250–2 (advising that the legal mortgage technique be avoided).

[65] TMA 1994, s. 24(5).   [66] TMA 1994, s. 24(3)–(5).

of them must consent to the grant of a security interest.[67] While such an interest need not be registered to be valid, there are advantages from registration, which are reviewed later.

3.4.2 'Unregistered trade marks'

It is possible to charge or mortgage goodwill,[68] however the rights this give are somewhat circumscribed. It is not possible, for instance, for the mortgagee to bring a claim for passing off when the mortgagor is still carrying on the business.[69] The impossibility in assigning the goodwill without the business also makes the enforcement of such a mortgage difficult as there is no property that can be seized unless the whole business can be taken. Accordingly, these sorts of securities are often tied up into wider company finance structures such as debentures.

3.5 TESTAMENTARY DISPOSITIONS

Because a trade mark is personal property, it is capable of passing on the death of the proprietor either by will or according to the rules applicable in cases of intestacy.[70] In the case of the death of one co-owner, because co-owners hold the trade mark as tenants in common (rather than as joint tenants),[71] the share of the deceased co-owner passes along with the rest of its estate rather than accrues to the other co-owners. In devolving the trade mark, the personal representative must sign a written assent. The transfer of goodwill at the death of the proprietor of a business follows the same rules as it does for assignment. The goodwill can only pass with the business.

3.6 REGISTRATION OF INTERESTS AND TRANSACTIONS

We observed earlier that trade mark registration performs a number of different functions:[72] it helps to overcome difficulties in proving the existence of goodwill; it allocates priorities between competing traders wishing to secure rights over a particular trade mark; and it acts as a repository of information that alerts third parties who might independently wish to use the same or a similar mark about the proprietor's rights.

Although legal transparency might be an admirable goal, because there is no statutory obligation to register marks or transactions therewith, and indeed transactions are valid in the absence of registration, the register cannot be said to operate as a 'mirror' of legal rights over commercial signs in the way that the Land Registry system purports to be a reflection of proprietary rights over real property. Nevertheless, the usefulness of the register is ensured because of the existence of incentives for parties to transactions in marks to enter them on the register: because unregistered transactions are vulnerable to later dealings, it is highly advisable to register them immediately.[73] Registrable transactions are listed in section 25(2) of the 1994 Act as assignments, the making of assents, the granting of securities, and the grant of licences.[74] Notice of trusts may not be registered.[75]

---

[67] TMA 1994, s. 23(4).   [68] See *Reuter v. Mulhens* (1953) 70 *RPC* 235.

[69] *Beazley v. Soares* (1882) 22 *Ch D* 660.

[70] It can even pass as *bona vacantia*: see *Joe Cool (Manchester) TM* [2000] *RPC* 926.

[71] TMA 1994, s. 23(1).   [72] See Chapter 35, section 1, pp. 920–1.

[73] See N. Wilkof, *Trade Mark Licensing* (2005), chs 3 and 4.

[74] The EUTMR provides that, on request of one of the parties, the following shall be entered on the register and published—a transfer, security, levy of execution, licence (or transfer thereof): EUTMR, Arts 20(5), 22(2), 23(3), 24(3), and 25(5).   [75] TMA 1994, s. 26.

While similar transactions may be registered with the UK Trade Marks Registry and at the EUIPO, the consequences of failing to register a transaction differ between the two regimes. As such, they will be considered separately.

Registration of transactions with regards to UK marks at the UK office has three distinct effects. First, registration ensures that the interest of the registrant survives further inconsistent transactions in relation to the mark. More specifically, section 25(3) states that an unregistered transaction is 'ineffective' as against a person acquiring a conflicting interest in or under the mark in ignorance of it.[76] Second, as regards licences, registration enables the licensee to acquire the full scope of available rights and remedies.[77] Third, costs in an unsuccessful infringement action are withheld from assignees and licensees who do not register promptly—that is, within six months of the transaction—as regards any acts of infringement that occur prior to registration.[78]

According to the EUTMR, similar consequences flow from non-registration of transactions affecting European Union trade marks. Article 27 states that transfers, grants of security, and licences of EUTMs shall only have effect vis-à-vis third parties after entry in the register, unless that third party knew of the relevant transaction at the date on which they acquired their interest. The effect of levies of execution and bankruptcy on third parties are matters for the law of the relevant member states.

A special incentive to register is placed on transferees of EUTMs. According to Article 20(11) of the EUTMR, as long as the transfer has not been entered in the EUIPO, the successor may not invoke the rights arising from registration of the EUTM. For refusal of a transfer to be justified, the deception must be clear from the transfer documents. Moreover, the EUIPO should accept the transfer insofar as the transferee agrees to limit the registration of the EUTM to goods or services in respect of which it is registered.

3.7 COMPULSORY LICENCES

In contrast with other areas of intellectual property law such as designs, copyright, and patents, there are no compulsory licences in relation to trade marks. Such a remedy is formally prohibited under the Agreement on Trade Related Aspects of Intellectual Property Rights 1994 (TRIPS).[79] However, occasionally, competition authorities may seek to remedy abuses of monopolistic position by requiring the trade mark proprietor to license a number of manufacturers.[80] Presumably, this is justified under TRIPS by reference to its competition provision.

4 LIMITS ON EXPLOITATION

The terms and conditions under which a trade mark is exploited are usually determined contractually by the parties; the Trade Marks Act 1994 merely provides a shell

---

[76] The effect of this can be illustrated as follows: A assigns the trade mark to B on 1 July 2017, and A then licenses the trade mark to C on 1 August 2017; B had not registered the assignment and C had no knowledge of it on 1 August—but B is bound by C's licence. See N. Wilkof, *Trade Mark Licensing* (2005), 58.

[77] TMA 1994, s. 25(3)(b).

[78] TMA 1994, s. 25(4); this corresponds to PA 1977, s. 68, discussed in Chapter 23, section 2.6, pp. 680–1.

[79] But see T. Riis and J Schovsbo, 'Compulsory Licenses and Trade Marks' (2012) *EIPR* 651.

[80] Licensing obligations are also used to remedy competition problems in merger control. See European Commission, *Merger Regulation Remedies Notice* [2008] *OJ C* 267/1, [65].

within which parties are able to manoeuvre. Where parties have agreed upon the way in which a trade mark is to be exploited, the law has been loath to substitute its view of what should have been agreed. Having said this, as with all forms of intellectual property law, the power conferred by trade mark law on a proprietor is limited in a number of ways.

The major restriction on licensing arises through the operation of the revocation provisions contained in section 46[81] because, if the terms or extent of the licensing (or assignment) are such that the mark becomes deceptive, the registration may be revoked. As a result, in exploiting a trade mark, the proprietor should take care to ensure that the mark does not become deceptive or generic. In order to avoid the mark becoming deceptive, trade mark owners would be wise to include quality control provisions in any licences that they grant and to operate some sort of monitoring policy to ensure that those standards are complied with.

Another important limitation placed on the use that can be made of a trade mark is provided by UK and European competition law. In the next section, we outline the general nature of these regulations, before considering the ways in which these regimes treat a selection of commonly used trade mark licence terms.

4.1 EU COMPETITION LAW

The key provision of European competition law affecting trade mark licences and exploitation agreements is Article 101 of the Treaty on the Functioning of the European Union (TFEU). This renders void all agreements that affect trade between member states and which have the object or effect of preventing, restricting, or distorting competition within the internal Market.[82] The issue of whether an element in an agreement 'restricts trade' is usually looked at by the Commission in terms of whether it restricts the activities of the parties to the agreement (or third parties) to an 'appreciable extent'.[83]

For minor agreements, the Commission has issued a Notice on Agreements of Minor Importance,[84] which treats agreements between firms that are not competitors as falling outside of Article 101(1) if the market share held by each of the parties does not exceed 15 per cent of any of the relevant markets affected by the agreement. This does not apply, however, where those agreements contain provisions relating to resale price-fixing or territorial protection.

Even if an agreement falls within the Article 101 TFEU prohibition, it may nonetheless fall within one of the block exemptions issued by the Commission. The two block exemptions that are relevant relate to (i) technology transfer agreements (the Technology

---

[81] See Chapter 39, section 4, pp. 1090–3.   [82] TFEU, Art. 101(2).

[83] This is often called 'freedom of action theory' and has been widely criticized as casting the prohibition too broadly. The Court, e.g. in *Javico v. Yves Saint Laurent*, Case C-306/96 [1998] *ECR* I–1983, [23]–[26], has tended to look at the effect in the market and has treated a number of agreements as falling outside Art. 101(1) TFEU because they are objectively necessary for particular kinds of transactions. For discussion, see N. Green, 'Article 85 of the EC Treaty in Perspective: Stretching Jurisdiction, Narrowing the Concept of a Restriction and Plugging a Few Gaps' [1988] *ECLR* 190; H. P. Lugard, 'Vertical Restraints under EC Law: A Horizontal Approach' [1996] 17 *ECLR* 166. The Commission seems to be signalling a change towards a less formalistic approach: see R. Whish, 'Regulation 2790/99: The Commission's "New Style" Block Exemption for Vertical Agreements' (2000) 37 *CMLR* 887, 889–90.

[84] [2001] *OJ C* 368/13. Below the threshold, the Commission considers that the competition authorities of member states should provide primary supervision.

Transfer Block Exemption Regulation 2014, or TTBE 2014[85]) and (ii) vertical agreements (the Vertical Restraints Regulation, or VRR).[86]

We considered the TTBE 2014 in Chapter 22. Here, it should be noted that the Regulation applies only where trade marks are ancillary to the main purpose of the agreement—namely, the licensing of patents or know-how.[87] If trade marks are a central component, the agreement cannot fall within the TTBE 2014.[88] However, much more important for trade mark licences is VRR.[89] The idea behind this block exemption is that vertical agreements often have positive consequences by increasing inter-brand competition and are anti-competitive only in limited circumstances, such as where the supplier has a high level of market power.

The VRR applies to 'vertical agreements', which are defined as agreements or concerted practices entered into between two or more undertakings, each of which operates (for the purposes of the agreement) at a different level of the production or distribution chain, and relating to the conditions under which the parties may purchase, sell, or resell certain goods or services.[90] However, while it is explained that this covers agreements containing provisions that relate to the assignment to the buyer or use by the buyer of intellectual property rights, those provisions must be directly related to the use, sale, or resale of goods or services by the buyer or its customers.[91] However, the VRR does not apply if those provisions relating to intellectual property constitute the primary object of such agreement.[92] It should be noted from the outset, then, that the block exemption does not cover many trade mark transactions: it does not cover assignments, or such things as merchandising arrangements.[93] However, for the most part, it will be potentially applicable to franchising and distribution agreements, where trade mark issues often arise, but the provisions are directly related to the use, sale, or resale of goods or services.[94]

The VRR declares initially that vertical agreements are not prohibited by Article 101 TFEU[95] and provides for the exemption of many agreements that contain restraints. In particular, agreements containing 'vertical restraints' are permitted where the market share of the supplier is less than 30 per cent.[96] Nevertheless, even some agreements between

---

[85] Council Regulation (EU) No. 316/2014 of 21 March 2014 on the application of Article 101(3) of the Treaty on the Functioning of the European Union to categories of technology transfer agreements [2014] *OJ L* 93/17 (28 March 2014). See Chapter 23, section 3, pp. 683–4.

[86] Commission Regulation (EU) No. 330/2010 of 20 April 2010 on the application of Article 101(3) of the Treaty on the Functioning of the European Union of categories of vertical agreements and concerted practices [2010] *OJ L* 102/1 (23 April 2010) (the 'Vertical Restraints Regulation', or VRR).

[87] TTBER 2014, Art. 1 (defining technology transfer agreement by reference to technology rights).

[88] *Commission Decision of 23 March 1990: Moosehead/Whitbread* [1990] *OJ L* 100/36 (in which the agreement was held to fall outside the Know-How BER because the trade mark licence was central to the agreement). See R. Subiotto, '*Moosehead/Whitbread*: Industrial Franchises and No-challenge Clauses Relating to Licensed Trade Marks under EEC Competition Law' [1990] 11 *ECLR* 226.

[89] Note also European Commission, *Guidelines on Vertical Restraints* [2010] *OJ C* 130/1 (19 May 2010) ('VRR Guidelines').

[90] VRR, Art. 1(1)(a).   [91] VRR, Art 2(3).   [92] VRR, Art. 2(3).

[93] VRR Guidelines, [33]. But the Commission intimates such agreements would be treated in a similar way: ibid., [43].

[94] Ibid., [42]–[44] (on franchising).   [95] VRR, Art. 2(1).

[96] VRR, Art. 3. In the case of an 'exclusive supply obligation', the relevant share is that of the purchaser. The Commission may withdraw the benefit of a block exemption regulation, pursuant to Council Regulation (EC) No. 1/2003 of 16 December 2002 on the implementation of the rules on competition laid down in Articles 81 and 82 of the Treaty [2003] *OJ L* 1/1 (4 January 2003), Art. 29(1), where it finds in a particular case that an agreement to which the exemption provided for in this Regulation applies nevertheless has effects that are incompatible with Art. 101(3) TFEU. Under Recitals 15–16, the Commission may withdraw the benefit of the VRR where 50 per cent of the market is covered by similar agreements.

small undertakings will not be exempt where they include provisions on the 'hard core' list (for example, price-fixing and strict territorial restraints): these are prohibited in all agreements.[97] If the agreement constitutes a vertical restraint, does not contain a forbidden ('hard core') term, and does not fall outside the market share limitation, then the agreement is exempt. This is so irrespective of the other terms of the agreement: the exemption works on the basis that anything not forbidden is permitted. If, on the other hand, the VRR does not apply, a restrictive agreement may be contrary to Article 101 TFEU.[98]

4.2 UK COMPETITION LAW

UK competition law is made up of a complex mixture of common law principles restricting the terms that may legitimately be imposed in contracts, such as the doctrine of restraint of trade, and statutory interventions, of which the most important is the Competition Act 1998. This Act establishes a system that parallels European competition law, by enacting a provision equivalent to Article 101 TFEU.[99] An agreement may be regarded as falling outside the prohibition under section 9 of the 1998 Act (which parallels Article 101(3) TFEU) without any need for prior notification or exemption. Nevertheless, an agreement will be deemed to be exempt from the national prohibition if it is exempt from the EU prohibition.[100]

4.3 COMMONLY USED TRADE MARK LICENCE TERMS

In this section, we look at terms that are commonly used in trade mark licence agreements and the approach that competition law takes towards them.

4.3.1 Exclusivity

A trade mark licence commonly includes terms guaranteeing the licensee the exclusive right to sell the goods or to provide the services under the mark in a particular territory, such as the United Kingdom. It may also include associated undertakings by the licensor not to put the goods on the market under the same mark in that territory or to compete with the licensee by providing the same services. In turn, the licensee may undertake not to sell goods bearing the mark in territories of other licensees.[101] The guidelines on vertical restraints treat these arrangements as exclusive distribution.[102] The inclusion of a guarantee of exclusivity may be important to a licensee who has to make a considerable investment in the establishment of production facilities (in the case of trade mark product licences) or retail outlets (in the case of distribution or service franchisees). In these cases, the licensee may wish to ensure that they have a reasonable degree of control over the relevant market.[103] In the absence of exclusivity, the licensee would not only

---

[97] VRR, Art. 4. Where an agreement includes a term under Art. 5, these can be severed.

[98] There is no longer a system of notification.

[99] Competition Act 1998, s. 2; see OFT, *Vertical Agreements* (April 2004) OFT 419a.

[100] Competition Act 1998, s. 10 (parallel exemptions). But note *Days Medical Aids v. Pihsiang Machinery* [2004] *EWHC* 44 (Comm), [254]–[266] (raising doubts about application of the common law restraint of trade doctrine in a manner inconsistent with an outcome required by Art. 101 TFEU. See also *Jones v. Ricoh UK Ltd* [2010] *EWHC* 1743, [49].

[101] R. Joliet, 'Trademark Licensing Agreements under the EEC Law of Competition' (1983–84) 5 *Nw J Intl L & Bus* 755, 789–90 (distinguishing between territorial licences, exclusive territorial licences, and territorial sales restrictions). [102] VRR Guidelines, [39].

[103] As to the importance, or otherwise, of quality controls, see N. Wilkof, 'Trademark Licensing: The Once and Future Narrative' (2014) 104 *TM Rep* 895.

be exposed to competition that exists in the market in the goods or services, but also to competition from others dealing in goods or services bearing the brand name, and (not surprisingly) may prefer not to risk such investment. Consequently, exclusivity agreements may encourage the production and dissemination of goods and services with the mark into the market—and thus foster competition. Simultaneously, exclusive licences cause little detriment to third parties because the trade mark owner had such exclusivity as a result of the ownership of the trade mark. On the other hand, exclusive licensing—by dividing up territories—may have serious detrimental effects on the achievement of the internal market.

The VRR recognizes a compromise position: Article 4(b) states that the exemption will not be available where the object of the agreement is 'the restriction of the territory into which, or of the customers to whom, the buyer may sell the contract goods and services'. However, it is permissible to impose a restriction on active sales into 'the exclusive territory or to an exclusive consumer group reserved to the supplier or allocated by the supplier to another buyer where such a restriction does not limit sales by the customers of the buyer'. The key distinction is thus between 'passive' and 'active' sales—that is, between sales that are a response to customer action and sales that involve the trader actively approaching the customer.[104] The basic idea underpinning the various exemptions is that an agreement is exempt only if the prohibition is limited to active selling outside the territory.

4.3.2 Manufacturing standards

To ensure that certain standards are maintained, a trade mark proprietor who is either involved in franchising or licensing others to manufacture and sell goods to which a mark is applied will often wish to impose conditions on the manufacture or operation of the licensee's business.[105] Since one of the functions of a mark is to guarantee quality,[106] such clauses are readily justified and, in general, are not treated as restrictions on trade. However, because such clauses might require the licensee to purchase ingredients, components, or other material from certain limited sources, such obligations may look like anti-competitive tie-ins. Nevertheless, the competition authorities have treated such clauses with less severity than they have patent agreements that include tie-ins.[107]

If such clauses are caught by Article 101 TFEU, the VRR appears to permit them as long as they are not too long in duration or too extensive in scope. Article 5(a) excludes from the block exemption 'any direct or indirect non-compete obligation, the duration of which is indefinite or exceeds five years'. Article 1 defines 'non-compete' obligations as including 'any obligation on the buyer to purchase from the supplier or from an undertaking designated by the supplier more than 80 per cent of the buyer's total purchases of the contract goods or services and their substitutes on the relevant market'. Consequently, in many cases, such clauses will be permissible.

4.3.3 Non-competition

A trade mark owner may be keen to prevent licensees from selling other goods. In *Campari*,[108] the European Commission approved such a clause on the ground that it

---

[104] VRR Guidelines, [51]–[52] (advertising and Internet selling are treated as passive).

[105] R. Joliet, 'Trademark Licensing Agreements under the EEC Law of Competition' (1983–84) 5 *Nw J Intl L & Bus* 755, 779–85.

[106] On functions, see Chapter 40, section 10, pp. 1108–17.

[107] OFT, *Intellectual Property Rights: A Draft Competition Act 1998 Guideline* (November 2001) OFT 418, [2.25]–[2.27].   [108] *Re the Agreements of Davide Campari Milano SpA* [1978] *FSR* 528 (European Commission).

would ensure that licensees focused on selling the licensed product. The Commission said that although such clauses in patent licences might be objectionable on the basis that they constituted barriers to technical and economic progress, such a prohibition in trade mark licences 'makes for improved distribution of the relevant product in the same way as do exclusive distribution agreements'.[109]

Trade mark owners might also wish to protect their interests by prohibiting licensees from competing in the same goods after termination of the licence. This is particularly desirable where the licence of the trade mark has been part of a deal involving trade secrets. It may be equally desirable to protect the trade mark owner's goodwill. Under the VRR, it seems that such restrictions are permitted in limited circumstances: the restriction must not exceed one year; it must be confined to sales of competing goods or services from the point of sale at which the buyer operated during the contract period; and the restriction must be indispensable to protect 'know-how' transferred from the supplier to the buyer.[110]

In domestic law, such matters are also governed by the doctrine of restraint of trade, which requires restraints to be reasonable having regard to the legitimate interests of the parties and the public interest. In *Kall-Kwik Printing (UK) v. Rush*,[111] a franchise agreement for a photocopying shop contained a restraint not to engage directly or indirectly in any business competitive with the business of the franchisor. It also said that the restraint operated within a 10-mile radius of the premises of any franchisee of the franchisor for two years after termination. During the term of the franchise, the franchisee set up a competing shop a short distance from the franchised premises. The court held that the clause was too widely drawn geographically. This was because, since the franchisor had 191 franchisees, the effect of the clause would have been tantamount to a nationwide prohibition. However, the judge construed the clause as being confined to businesses competitive with that of the business and this allowed him to uphold it. Judge Cooke said that he considered the two-year period to be reasonable.[112]

4.3.4 No-challenge clauses

Trade mark licence agreements often include undertakings prohibiting the licensee from challenging the validity of the registration. These are known as 'no-challenge clauses'. These are not dealt with in the VRR and are probably permissible. In *Moosehead/Whitbread*,[113] a no-challenge clause was upheld in the context of a trade mark licence between the Canadian beer manufacturer and its UK licensee. A distinction was drawn in the case between obligations not to contest the validity of the registration and no-challenge clauses concerned with the ownership of the mark. Clauses preventing the licensee from challenging ownership did not contravene what is now Article 101 TFEU, because, according to the Commission, they did not restrict competition. However, a clause preventing the challenge to the validity of the mark might be a restriction within Article 101 TFEU. In the case itself, the Commission held that, because the obligation related to

---

[109] Ibid., 540, [72].

[110] VRR, Art. 5(b). This obligation is without prejudice to the possibility of imposing a restriction, which is unlimited in time on the use and disclosure of know-how that has not entered the public domain.

[111] [1996] *FSR* 114; also see *Dyno-Rod plc v. Reeve and anor* [1999] *FSR* 148; and *Carewatch Care Services v. Focus Caring Services* [2014] *EWHC* 2313 (Ch).

[112] See also *Kall-Kwik (UK) v. Bell* [1994] *FSR* 674 (18 months not unreasonable restraint); *Prontaprint v. London Litho* [1987] *FSR* 315 (three years).

[113] *Moosehead/Whitbread* [1990] *OJ L* 100/36, [1991] 4 *CMLR* 391. See R. Subiotto, 'Moosehead/Whitbread: Industrial Franchises and No-challenge Clauses Relating to Licensed Trade Marks under EEC Competition Law' [1990] 11 *ECLR* 226.

both, it did not constitute an appreciable restriction on competition. In the main, this was because the moosehead mark was new to the market.

We will return to the question of no-challenge clauses in the context of trade mark delimitation agreements, which are discussed later.

4.3.5 Price restrictions

A trade mark owner may wish to restrict the price at which the licensee sells the trade marked product. Such restrictions are treated as anti-competitive under Article 101(1) TFEU, and exemptions are not possible under Article 101(3) unless the agreement allows consumers a fair share of resulting benefit. Unsurprisingly, such terms fall within the 'hard core' prohibited terms, which, if present, prevent an agreement from benefiting from the VRR.[114] Nevertheless, it is possible for an agreement to contain price recommendations. Similarly, under the Competition Act 1998, agreements that 'directly or indirectly fix purchase or selling prices' are specifically referred to as examples of prohibited agreements under section 2(2)(a).

4.4 TRADE MARK DELIMITATION AGREEMENTS (CO-EXISTENCE AGREEMENTS)

In the previous section, we examined the application of competition regulations to various common clauses in vertical arrangements relating to trade marks—that is, to agreements that operate down the chain from manufacturer to consumer, such as those between trade mark owner and franchisee or distributor. We now need briefly to consider horizontal arrangements—that is, arrangements at the same level of distribution between competing manufacturers or trade mark owners. These are generally treated as much more likely to be anti-competitive. Our interest in them extends as far as 'consent agreements' or 'trade mark delimitation agreements'. Trade mark delimitation agreements are contracts between owners of similar marks that are intended to settle conflicts (or potential conflicts) between them.[115] Such agreements can be particularly complicated where interests have to be represented on the internet.[116] While these arrangements may not be licences at all, because they contain many terms similar to those found in licence agreements, which are regulated by competition law, we will consider them in this section.[117]

There seems to be a number of typical ways of resolving such conflicts:

(i)   by agreeing that only one party may use the mark, so that the other must adopt a new mark;

(ii) by agreeing that one party will use the mark only in one field and the other, in a distinct field, so as to avoid the possibility of overlap;

(iii) by agreeing that one party will use the mark in a particular geographical area and the other, in a different one; and

(iv) by agreeing that each will use the mark only with specified get-up, so that consumer confusion is minimized.

---

[114] VRR, Art. 4(a).

[115] See generally, N. Wilkof, 'Out of the Shadows: The Unique World of Trade Mark Consent Agreements', in I. Calboli and J. de Werra (eds), *The Law and Practice of Trademark Transactions* (2016), ch. 11; M. Fawlk, 'Trademark Delimitation Agreements under Article 85 of the Treaty of Rome' (1992) 82 *TM Rep* 223.

[116] A. Peukert, 'The Coexistence of Trade Mark Laws and Rights on the Internet, and the Impact of Geolocation Technologies' [2016] 47 *IIC* 60.

[117] R. Joliet, 'Trademark Licensing Agreements under the EEC Law of Competition' (1983–84) 5 *Nw J Intl L & Bus* 755, 765.

The contents of trade mark delimitation agreements will vary,[118] but in each case they will need to be scrutinized under both European and domestic law. As regards European competition law, the key provision is Article 101 TFEU. The Commission and the Court of Justice have indicated that such settlement agreements may be acceptable because, by resolving protracted litigation between the parties, they eliminate restraints on competition and the internal market that conflicting rights under national laws might cause.[119] The Commission has indicated, however, that, in forging the compromise, the enterprises should try to reach the least restrictive solution possible.[120]

If the agreement restricts competition or produces market sharing, it will contravene Article 101(1) TFEU. Whether the agreement restricts competition has been said largely to depend on the use to which the mark was previously being put. In *BAT Cigaretten-Fabrik GmbH v. EEC*,[121] for example, an agreement restraining a Dutch competitor of British American Tobacco from using its toltecs mark in Germany was an unlawful restraint, because BAT's dorcet mark was dormant (or unused). Where, however, the party who submits to the restraint has not used the mark (or was not utilizing it to a significant extent), the Commission has taken the view that assignment of that mark to the other party will not amount to a restriction on the assignor's ability to compete.[122] Indeed, the Commission seems to take the view that an unused mark has no value, and that a person can simply choose a different mark for their goods or services.

However, in most cases of conflict, both parties will have been using their marks to some extent. As indicated, the Commission then favours the least restrictive solution. If conflict can be avoided by the parties merely agreeing to utilize different 'get-up', that is likely to be treated as outside Article 101.[123] Alternatively, it may be that the conflict can be settled by assigning one mark to one party and a different mark to another. Although the effect will be to force the party to re-establish goodwill under other marks and this may have a restrictive effect, bringing it within Article 101, such an arrangement might be acceptable if there is a transitional phasing out and/or the party is allowed to continue using the name as a trade name. It seems that the Commission has looked least favourably on agreements that give different parties use of the mark in different parts of the Common Market.[124] It has also indicated that it disapproves of widely drawn or lengthy 'no-challenge' clauses.[125]

As regards UK law, trade mark delimitation agreements have until now been treated as enforceable commercial contracts. The only ground for objection that seems to have been raised in the case law is restraint of trade. While, in principle, this would require a person imposing a restraint to demonstrate that it is reasonable, according to the Court of Appeal in *WWF–World Wide Fund for Nature v. World Wrestling Federation Entertainment Inc.*,[126] there is a presumption that the restraint represents a reasonable division of their

---

[118] There are instances when very old agreements have to be applied to modern issues (such as when a 1970 agreement was applied to domain name allocation): see *KGaA v. Merck Sharp & Dohme Corp and ors* [2016] *EWHC* 49 (Pat).

[119] *BAT Cigaretten-Fabrik v. EEC* [1985] *FSR* 533, 541, [33]; however, an agreement which pays someone not to enter a territory as part of a co-existence agreement might be problematic (such agreements have found to be anti-competitive in patent law: see Chapter 23, section 2.3.1(i), p. 677).

[120] *Commission Decision 78/193/EEC of 23 December 1977 relating to a proceeding under Article 85 (Penney's)* [1978] *FSR* 385, 395.

[121] [1985] *FSR* 533.   [122] *Penney's* [1978] *FSR* 385, 396.   [123] Ibid.

[124] *Sirdar/Phildar* [1975] 1 *CMLR D* 93; *Community v. Syntex/Synthelabo* [1990] *FSR* 529.

[125] *BAT Cigaretten-Fabrik* [1985] *FSR* 533. In other cases, more flexibility has been shown: *Penney's* [1978] *FSR* 385, 396–7 (acceptable if under five years).

[126] [2004] *FSR* (10) 161. See also *Fenchurch Environmental Group Ltd v. Bactiguard AG* [2007] *RPC* (31) 701 (TM Registry).

interests. Consequently, the defendant must show that the restraint is unreasonable, for example by demonstrating that there was no goodwill to justify the restraint. In *Apple Corp. Ltd v. Apple Computer Inc.*,[127] when considering various difficult procedural questions concerning litigation over a consent agreement, the Court of Appeal held that restraints contained in such agreements were legitimate only where they were necessary to protect the legitimate interests of the parties. The ownership of registered marks would not of itself justify such an agreement; rather, the restraint would be justified only where it was necessary to protect the goodwill of the restrainer. As a consequence, such a restraint would be justified only where the mark had been used. The Court of Appeal observed that the approach under what is now Article 101 TFEU and under the common law were largely similar.[128]

---

[127] [1991] 3 *CMLR* 49.

[128] Such an agreement may include a no-challenge clause: *Apple Corp. v. Apple Computer Inc.* [1992] *FSR* 431. For subsequent litigation over the scope of the delimitation, see *Apple Corp. Ltd v. Apple Computer Inc.* [2006] *EWHC* 996 (Ch), [2006] *Info TLR* 9 (Ch D).

43

GEOGRAPHICAL INDICATIONS OF ORIGIN

1 INTRODUCTION

Over time, the European Union has introduced a raft of measures to control the way agricultural products are described and labelled. These vary from laws regulating the marketing standards for olive oil[1] and the labelling of beef products,[2] through to complicated laws that regulate the description, designation, presentation, and protection of wines.[3] In this chapter, we look at three regimes that form part of this overarching legal framework. First, we look at the scheme developed by the European Union to regulate geographical indications (GIs) for agricultural products and foodstuffs under the Quality Scheme Regulation.[4] These are the names that are used to describe foods and other agricultural products that originate from particular geographic areas. Some well-known regional products include Kalamata olives and Parma ham.[5] Since the agricultural products regime is increasingly viewed as the template for future internal EU reforms as well as external bilateral and multilateral negotiations, it forms the primary focus of this chapter. The reader interested in the EU regimes for wines and spirits is directed to more specialized literature.[6] Second, we look at the traditional specialities guaranteed scheme developed by the European Union to protect the names of traditional foods and recipes. Third, we look at the optional quality terms scheme that was introduced in 2013.

---

[1] Regulation (EC) No. 2815/98 of 22 December 1998 concerning marketing standards for olive oil [1998] *OJ L* 349/56 (regulates designations of origin on the labelling and packaging of virgin and extra virgin olive oils).

[2] Regulation (EC) No. 1760/2000 of 17 July 2000 establishing a system for the identification and registration of bovine animals and regarding the labelling of beef and beef products [2000] *OJ L* 204/1, Recital 31, Art. 16(6).

[3] Regulation (EU) No. 1308/2013 of the European Parliament and of the Council of 17 December 2013 establishing a common organisation of the markets in agricultural products and repealing Council Regulations (EEC) No. 922/72, (EEC) No. 234/79, (EC) No. 1037/2001, and (EC) No. 1234/2007 [2013] *OJ L* 347/671.

[4] Presently Regulation No. 1151/2012 of the European Parliament and of the Council of 21 November 2012 on Quality Schemes for Agricultural Products and Foodstuffs [2012] *OJ L* 323/1 ('Quality Schemes Reg.'). It replaces Regulations 2081/1992 and 510/2006.

[5] Protected EU names can be searched for on the Database of Origin and Registration (DOOR), available online at ec.europa.eu/agriculture/quality/door/list.html.

[6] V. Mantrov, *EU Law on Indications of Geographical Origin: Theory and Practice* (2014), chs 7–9; M. Blakeney, *The Protection of Geographical Indications: Law and Practice* (2014), chs 4–5.

While it may seem that an emphasis on the regional provenance of foodstuffs is a recent phenomenon, in fact they have a very old lineage.[7] This is especially the case in countries such as Spain, France, Italy, Portugal, and (to a lesser extent) Germany. Given the important role that food and agricultural products play in all cultures, it is not surprising that special legal regimes have long been used to regulate geographical designations. For example, special legislation existed in fourteenth-century France to protect Roquefort cheese. However, the legal bases and institutional forms adopted by these regulatory regimes has varied across time and place. In common law countries, the names of agricultural products and foodstuffs have been protected by passing off, trade marks, and certification marks.[8] While civil law countries have relied on collective marks and unfair competition, they have also developed more specialized regimes, such as appellations of origin, to regulate the use that is made of agricultural names. Civil law countries have also entered into a series of bilateral and (occasionally) multilateral treaties that recognize rights in the names given to wines, cheeses, olive oils, and other agricultural products. More recently, the European Union has introduced a series of regulations to standardize the protection available for regional and traditional food names within Europe.

One of the questions that sometimes arises in discussions about the legal regimes that regulate geographical designations is their status as a form of intellectual property. Archival research reveals that these signs were initially recognized within the Paris Convention framework for the same reasons that trade marks were—in order to protect the goodwill or brand value of reputed regional products. However their (descriptive) geographical connotations and collective use dimensions led to GIs being perceived as a poor fit within mainstream trade mark law. So the intangible object being protected—the sign—is one that is shared with trade mark law but the rationales and methodologies of protection go further. Over time a raft of additional policy agendas to support the product behind the sign, such as facilitating sustainable rural development by anchoring production to a region, or supporting cultural heritage, have been recognized as additional justifications for protection.[9] In Europe, there is little doubt that GIs are a form of intellectual property, given that both the Court of Justice and the House of Lords have explicitly acknowledged that the geographic designations protected under European law are categorized as such.[10] What sets them apart from other categories of protected

---

[7] For engaging historical accounts, see P. E. McGovern et al. (eds), *The Origins and Ancient History of Wine* (1996); K. M. Guy, *When Champagne Became French: Wine and the Making of a National Identity* (2003); P. Boisard, *Camembert: A National Myth* (2003). Despite this history, the legal regimes protecting them as a specific category of intellectual property emerged only in the late nineteenth century.

[8] See WIPO Secretariat, '*Document SCT/6/3 Rev. on Geographical Indications: Historical Background, Nature of Rights, Existing Systems for Protection and Obtaining Protection in Other Countries*' 2 April 2002 (SCT/8/4), D. Gangjee, 'Spanish Champagne: An Unfair Competition Approach to GI Protection' and D. Gervais, 'A Cognac after Spanish Champagne? Geographical Indications as Certification Marks', in Dreyfuss and Ginsburg (2014).

[9] D. Gangjee, *Relocating the Law of Geographical Indications* (2012); I. Calboli, 'Of Markets, Culture and *Terroir*: The Unique Economic and Culture-Related Benefits of Geographical Indications of Origin', in D. Gervais (ed.), *International Intellectual Property: A Handbook of Contemporary Research* (2015). Cf. T. Broude, 'From Chianti to Kimchi: Geographical Indications, Intangible Cultural Heritage, and Their Unsettled Relationship with Cultural Diversity', in I. Calboli and W.L. Ng-Loy (eds), *Geographical Indications at the Crossroads of Trade, Development, and Culture in the Asia-Pacific* (2017); S Frankel, 'The Mismatch of Geographical Indications and Innovative Traditional Knowledge' (2011) 29 *Prometheus* 253.

[10] See *Consorzio del Prosciutto di Parma v. Asda Stores Ltd* [2002] *FSR* 3 (HL), 38, [6] (Lord Hoffmann) ('a PDO is a form of intellectual property right'). It is also one of the explicit legislative bases for the EU agricultural GI regime, which refers to TFEU, Art. 118 (mandating the creation of intellectual property rights to further internal market objectives): see the Preamble to the Quality Schemes Reg.

signs such as trade marks or trade names is the notion of an exclusive or distinctive link between product and place, which generates the goodwill collectively shared by producers in that region. As with the idea of the unique expression of the author or the novelty of patented inventions, the 'uniqueness' of this link is intended to ensure that the granting of property rights does not jeopardize the rights of third parties.[11]

In this chapter, we focus on the names given to agricultural products and foodstuffs. However, it is important to note that geographic designations potentially apply to all products. This has led to the suggestion that indigenous creations could be protected via a style of law modelled on geographic designations. This is an interesting possibility, since it recognizes both collective rights and the connection between 'product' and 'place' that are so important for many indigenous groups.[12]

1.1 TYPES OF PROTECTION

There are subtle and often important differences between the various forms of legal protection that have been adopted to protect the names given to agricultural products and foodstuffs.[13] While the enactment of European legislation regulating the naming of wines, spirits, and agricultural products has gone some way towards alleviating this problem in Europe, widely different approaches are still adopted elsewhere. The failure of the World Trade Organization (WTO) negotiations in Cancún, combined with the hostile reception that greeted the EU proposal to extend the level of protection required under the Agreement on Trade Related Aspects of Intellectual Property Rights 1994 (TRIPS), suggests that this situation is likely to continue for some time in the future. Given this, it may be helpful to define some of the key terms used in this area.

(i) Indication of source   An 'indication of source'—which is also known as an 'indication of provenance' or as a simple or qualified 'geographical indication of origin'—is the most general of the terms used to describe geographical designations.[14] A defining feature of an indication of source is that it connects a product to a particular geographical location; there is no requirement that there be any correlation between the characteristics or quality of a product and the place from which the product originated. Instead, an indication of source simply informs consumers that the product bearing the sign comes from a particular place, region, or country.[15] As a result, indication of source is broader than both appellations of origin and geographical indications.

(ii) Geographical indication   Article 22(1) of TRIPS defines geographical indications as 'indications, which identify a good as originating in the territory of a member, or a region or locality in that territory, where a given quality, reputation or other characteristic of the good is essentially attributable to its geographical origin'. Somewhat perplexingly, the TRIPS definition recognizes two distinct and alternative forms of linkage—the

---

[11] For contextualization and criticisms of this 'unique link' claim, see the contributions in Gangjee (2016).

[12] For problems, see B. Sherman and L. Wiseman, 'From Terroir to Pangkarra: Geographical Indications of Origin and Traditional Knowledge', in Gangjee (2016). Cf. T. W. Dagne, 'The Identity of Geographical Indications and Their Relation to Traditional Knowledge in Intellectual Property Law' (2014) 5 *WIPOJ* 137.

[13] See generally Gangjee (2012).

[14] Used in the Paris Convention and the Madrid Agreement for the Repression of False or Deceptive Indications of Source of Goods of 1891.

[15] See *Exportur*, Case C-3/91 [1992] 1 *ECR* 5529, [11]; *Jacques Pistre*, Cases C-321–324/94 [1977] *CMLR* 565 (ECJ), 587.

seemingly more objective causal connection between a product's qualities or characteristics and its origin, or the potentially more subjective reputation that is 'essentially attributable' to geographical origin.[16]

(iii) Appellation of origin   An 'appellation of origin' is a specific type of geographical indication.[17] It is the 'geographic name of a country, region, or locality, which serves to designate a product originating therein, the quality or characteristics of which are due exclusively or essentially due to the geographical environment, including natural and human factors'.[18] The defining feature of an appellation of origin is that the 'product for which an appellation of origin is used must have a quality and characteristics which are due exclusively or essentially to its geographic environment'.[19]

The indication of source is the most general of these three modes of protection: it simply signals that a product originates from a particular geographic location (for example 'French perfume'). In contrast, geographical indications of origin and appellations of origin both require the geographic location to imbue the product with particular traits or characteristics. Where they differ is in terms of the nature of the relationship and the types of trait that they recognize. In particular, with an appellation of origin, the quality or characteristics of the product must be exclusively or essentially as a result of the geographical environment—that is, there must be a link between product and place. In contrast, geographical indications of origin extend beyond the quality of the product to include 'reputation or other characteristic of the good'. By shifting the focus beyond the strict connection of product to place, it subtly changes the nature of the protected interest away from something that mirrors the model of creation used in patents, copyright, and design law, toward something more akin to that used in trade mark law.[20]

As part of its ongoing reform of agricultural policy in Europe, the European Union has passed a series of laws that regulate geographic designations. In so doing, it has introduced a number of new terms into the legal lexicon.

(i) Protected designation of origin (PDO)[21]   This is the term used to describe a designation of origin that has been registered under the Quality Schemes Regulation. In this context, a 'designation of origin' is defined as the name of a region, a specific place, or, in exceptional cases, a country used to describe an agricultural product or foodstuff. To qualify as a PDO, the named product must originate in the specified place. It is also necessary to show that the quality or characteristics of the product are 'essentially or exclusively due to a particular geographical environment with its inherent natural and human factors',[22] and that the production, processing, and preparation take place in the defined geographical area. Registration as a PDO now requires producers to use the appropriate designation and logo on their labelling (see Fig. 43.1).[23]

---

[16] It may be possible to objectively attribute reputation to geographical origin by drawing on meaningful historical evidence. See D. Gangjee, 'From Geography to History: Geographical Indications and the Reputational Link', in I. Calboli and W.L. Ng-Loy (eds), *Geographical Indications at the Crossroads of Trade, Development, and Culture in the Asia-Pacific* (2017).

[17] Derived from the French *appellation d'origine*.

[18] Article 2 of the Lisbon Agreement for the Protection of Appellations of Origin and their International Registration of 1958. See section 1.2.3, pp. 1188–9.

[19] For comparisons, see F. Gevers, 'Geographical Names and Signs Used as Trade Marks' [1990] *EIPR* 285.

[20] On the different models of creation used in intellectual property (other than trade marks), see Sherman and Bently, 166–72.

[21] This is the translation of *appellation d'origine contrôlée* (AOC).

[22] Quality Schemes Reg., Art. 5(1).

Fig. 43.1 PDO, PGI, and TSG logos
Source: © European Union, 1995–2012

(ii) Protected geographical indication (PGI) This term is used to describe a geographical indication that has been registered under the Quality Schemes Regulation. 'Geographical indication' is defined as the name of a region, a specific place, or, in exceptional cases, a country used to describe an agricultural product or foodstuff. To qualify for protection, a geographical indication must originate in the specified place. The product or foodstuff must also possess a specific quality, reputation, or other characteristic attributable to that geographical origin. It is also necessary to show that the production, processing, or preparation takes place in the defined geographical area.[24] The link is considered to be less demanding than the PDO, since reputation can be the basis for satisfying it, while only one of the preparation stages needs to take place within the specified place.[25] Again, registration as a PGI requires producers in certain situations to use the appropriate designation and logo on their labelling (see Fig. 43.1).

(iii) Traditional speciality guaranteed (TSG) This is the term used in relation to traditional foods and recipes registered under the Quality Schemes Regulation.[26] For a name to be registered as TSG, it must be specific, express the specific character of the foodstuff or product, and be traditional or established by custom. 'Specific character' in this context means 'the features or set of features which distinguishes an agricultural product or a foodstuff clearly from other similar products or foodstuffs belonging to the same category'.[27] As well as granting rights over use of the registered name, registration as a certificate of special character also enables producers to use the designation 'Traditional Speciality Guaranteed (TSG)' and the accompanying logo (see Fig. 43.1).

(iv) Optional quality term A fourth term that was introduced by the Quality Schemes Regulation refers to the optional quality term scheme, which was established by the Quality Schemes Regulation and came into effect on 3 January 2013. The aim of the scheme is to 'facilitate the communication within the internal market of the value-adding characteristics or attributes of agricultural products by the producers thereof'.[28]

---

[23] Quality Schemes Reg., Art. 12(3), provides that for products marketed under a PDO or PGI, 'the Union symbols associated with them *shall* appear on the labeling' (emphasis added). This is in response to empirical research indicating that the vast majority EU consumers did not understand the significance of the PDO and PGI logos; European Court of Auditors, *Do the design and management of the geographical indications scheme allow it to be effective?* (Special Report No. 11, 2011) 25–33.

[24] Quality Schemes Reg., Art. 5(2).

[25] For criticisms of this loosening, see I. Calboli, '*In Territorio Veritas*: Bringing Geographical Coherence in the Definition of Geographical Indications of Origin under TRIPs' (2014) 6 *WIPOJ* 57.

[26] Quality Schemes Reg., Art. 18. Previously, this category was governed by Regulation (EC) No. 509/2006 Council Regulation (EEC) No. 2082/1992.

[27] Quality Schemes Reg., Art. 3(5).   [28] Quality Schemes Reg., Art. 27.

1.2 INTERNATIONAL TREATIES

In this section, we look at some of the more important of the international treaties that impact upon the legal regulation of geographic designations.[29]

1.2.1 Paris Convention for the Protection of Industrial Property

The 1883 Paris Convention for the Protection of Industrial Property provides for limited protection over geographical designations. Article 1(2) provides that the protection of industrial property has as its purpose, among other things, indications of source or appellations of origin. Article 10(1), read in conjunction with Article 9, provides for the seizure of goods on import where there is 'direct or indirect use of a false indication of the source of the goods'. These provisions are limited to false indications; they make no reference to the situation in which a term is translated, or where the name is accompanied by suffixes such as '-type', '-like' or '-style'. It has been argued that use of a false indication of source may constitute an act of unfair competition covered by Article 10*bis*(2)(3).

1.2.2 Madrid Agreement for the Repression of False or Misleading Indications of Source on Goods

The Madrid Agreement for the Repression of False or Misleading Indications of Source on Goods, finalized in Madrid in 1891, aims to protect consumers against false indications of source.[30] The Agreement requires seizure or import prohibition of all goods bearing a false or misleading indication. The question of whether an indication has become generic is decided by member states, with the exception of regional appellations for wine, which cannot be declared to be generic.

The primary aim of the Madrid Agreement was to protect consumers from being misled. To this end, the Madrid Agreement was designed to cover all false indications of source, irrespective of the intention of the user. When the Madrid Agreement was drafted, this was particularly important given that, prior to the Lisbon revision of the Paris Convention in 1958, Article 10 of the Paris Convention protected indications of source only if there was fraudulent intent. However, with the Lisbon revision in 1958, Article 10 of the Paris Convention now protects indications of source without the need to show fraud. As a result, the continuing need for the Madrid Agreement was thrown into doubt.[31]

1.2.3 Lisbon Agreement for the Protection of Appellations of Origin and their International Registration

The Lisbon Agreement for the Protection of Appellations of Origin and their International Registration, which was concluded on 31 October 1958,[32] establishes an international system for the protection of appellations of origin.[33] The Agreement defines an 'appellation

---

[29] Contemporary GI protection regimes draw heavily on their predecessors. For bilateral and multilateral antecedents, see Ricketson (2015), chs 2, 13; Gangjee (2012), 176–7.

[30] 14 April 1891, revised in Washington (2 June 1911), The Hague (6 November 1925), London (2 June 1934), and Lisbon (31 October 1958), and by the Additional Act of Stockholm (14 July 1967). In May 2018, there were 36 members of Madrid, including the United Kingdom, France, and Germany.

[31] See M. Leaffer, *International Treaties on Intellectual Property* (1990), 270.

[32] Revised in Stockholm on 14 July 1967 (amended 28 September 1979). In May 2018, there were 28 members.

[33] The bulk of these were for French wines: M. Hopperger, 'International Protection of Geographical Indications: The Present Situation and Prospects for Future Developments' [1999] *WIPO Symposium: South Africa* 5.

of origin' as the 'geographic name of a country, region, or locality, which serves to desig-nate a product originating therein, the quality or characteristics of which are due exclu-sively or essentially due to the geographical environment, including natural and human factors'.[34]

Article 1 of the Lisbon Agreement provides that member states must protect the appel-lations of origin of other member states that are registered with the World Intellectual Property Organization (WIPO). For a name to be placed on the international register administered by WIPO, an appellation of origin must first be protected in its country of origin. An application for registration at WIPO can be made only by the relevant admin-istrative agencies in the member states, who act on behalf of the group who 'owns' the appellation. The appellation is published and member states are notified of the registra-tion. Upon notification, member states have 12 months in which to make a declaration that they are unable to protect the appellation. If no declaration is made, the member state must protect the appellation of origin, so long as it is protected in its country of origin.

The Lisbon Agreement requires member states to provide protection against a broad range of misuses, which can be analytically divided into (i) prohibiting misleading uses, (ii) preventing generic use, and (iii) proscribing so-called free riding on the reputation of an appellation. While the Madrid Agreement was primarily concerned with the protec-tion of consumers, the Lisbon Agreement also protects producers against misuse, even where consumers may not be deceived about the nature or origin of the product.[35] More specifically, the Lisbon Agreement requires member states to protect against usurpation or imitation, even if the true origin of the product is indicated (for example 'Cornish clotted cream' made in Queensland), or if the appellation is translated or accompanied by terms such as 'kind', 'type', 'make', or 'imitation'.[36] Importantly, once an appellation is validly registered, it is legally insulated from being found to be generic for a type of product.[37]

The Lisbon Agreement has been significantly amended, leading to a separate Geneva Act of 2015.[38] In order to broaden the appeal of robust registration-based international GI protection, the Geneva Act contains a number of amendments, including (i) two parallel doorways into registration—a term may qualify for registration either as an appellation of origin or as a geographical indication in accordance with Article 22.1 of TRIPS;[39] (ii) the appellation definition has been modified to recognize indirect geographical terms (such as *Feta* for the Greek cheese in brine);[40] (iii) besides applying via a national com-petent authority, applicants can also directly apply to WIPO;[41] (iv) the legal and institu-tional form of protection as well as the scope of protection have been clarified;[42] and (v) the prohibition against subsequent generic use has been retained.[43] It remains to be seen whether the amended agreement will prove attractive enough to expand its appeal and membership.[44]

---

[34] Lisbon Agreement, Art. 2.   [35] Gangjee (2012), 157–76.   [36] Lisbon Agreement, Art. 3.

[37] Lisbon Agreement, Art. 6 (once registered, the appellation 'cannot, in [the] country [of the dispute], be deemed to have become generic' so long as it is protected in the country of origin).

[38] Geneva Act of the Lisbon Agreement on Appellations of Origin and Geographical Indications (as adopted on May 20, 2015) ('Geneva Act').   [39] Geneva Act, Art. 2(1).

[40] Ibid.   [41] Geneva Act, Art. 5.   [42] Geneva Act, Arts 9–11.   [43] Geneva Act, Art. 12.

[44] D. Gervais, 'Irreconcilable Differences? The Geneva Act of the Lisbon Agreement and the Common Law' (2015) 53 *Hous L Rev* 339; M. Geuze, 'Geographical Indications under WIPO-Administered Treaties', in Gangjee (2016); A. Micara, 'The Geneva Act of the Lisbon Agreement for the Protection of Appellations of Origin and Their International Registration: An Assessment of a Controversial Agreement' (2016) 47 *IIC* 673.

1.2.4 TRIPS

Perhaps the most important international treaty in this area, not the least because of its broad membership, is the 1994 Agreement on Trade Related Aspects of Intellectual Property Rights. TRIPS requires member states to provide legal means for interested parties to prevent:

(i) the use of any means in the designation or presentation of an item that indicates or suggests that it originates in a geographic area other than the true place of origin in a manner that misleads the public as to the geographical origin of the item; or

(ii) any use that constitutes an act of unfair competition within the meaning of Article 10*bis* of the Paris Convention.

As we saw earlier, geographic indications are defined in TRIPS as 'indications, which identify a good as originating in the territory of a Member, or a region or locality in that territory, where a given quality, reputation or other characteristic of the good is essentially attributable to its geographical origin'.[45] It is important to note that TRIPS applies to all products, and not only agricultural products or foodstuffs.

All GIs benefit from a certain degree of protection against misleading uses. TRIPS prohibits the use of indications which mislead the public (Article 22.2(a)), or are false despite being literally true—consider *haute couture* from the runways of Paris, Texas (Article 22.4); or uses amounting to unfair competition (Article 22.2(b)); and trade marks consisting of GIs may be refused or invalidated where they mislead the public (Art 22.3). A notable feature of TRIPS is that it provides for higher levels of protection for wines and spirits than for other agricultural products. In particular, Article 23 requires member states to provide protection even where the true origin of the goods is indicated, the geographical indication is used in translation, or is accompanied by expressions such as 'kind', 'type', 'style', 'imitation', or the like. It also requires member states to determine the status of homonymous names. Article 23(4) also provides that the TRIPS Council should undertake negotiations for the establishment of a multilateral system of notification and registration for wines. Article 24 sets out certain exceptions (for example in relation to overlap between geographical indications and trade marks).

Despite protests from the United States and other WTO members, a group of WTO members led by the European Union succeeded at the 2001 WTO Ministerial Conference in Doha to get reform of geographical indication protection placed on the agenda.[46] In particular, the Doha Declaration set a mandate for the negotiation of a multilateral system of notification and registrations of geographical indications for wines and spirits, and the possibility of extending the higher level of protection given to wines and spirits under Article 23 TRIPS to all agricultural products.[47] In a sense, what was proposed was that TRIPS should adopt the approach adopted in Europe as a global standard. However progress on both tracks has stalled in the intervening two decades. Despite having a mandate to discuss an international register for wines (and spirits), the most recent development dates back to 2011, when a composite text containing the various diverging proposals

---

[45] TRIPS, Art. 22(1). See generally T. Kongolo, 'Any New Developments with Regards to GI Issues Debated under WTO?' (2011) 33 *EIPR* 83.

[46] See WTO Ministerial Conference, *Ministerial Declaration* (20 November 2001) WT/MIN(01)/DEC/1, available online at http://www.wto.org/english/thewto_e/minist_e/min01_e/mindecl_e.htm.

[47] Ibid., [12], [18].

emerged.[48] The reforms contained in the Geneva Act of the Lisbon Agreement, considered earlier in this chapter, can therefore be read against this backdrop. Lisbon is being projected as an alternative international registration system for all products. As for the proposal to extend Article 23 levels of protection beyond wines and spirits to all products, opposition to it rests primarily on the basis that the original provision was a negotiating concession to European wine lobbies; whether there is a normative or principled rationale for its extension remains contested.[49]

1.2.5 Bilateral agreements

The European Union has entered into a number of bilateral agreements to protect agricultural products and foodstuffs. For example, it has negotiated treaties with Australia (wine),[50] Chile (wines, spirit drinks, and aromatized drinks),[51] and Mexico (spirits).[52] Given the limited membership of the international treaties regulating geographic designation and the impasse in the TRIPS negotiations at Cancún, the European Union has proactively developed a policy to use bilateral agreements as a way of protecting European products in other jurisdictions.[53]

1.3 EU REGULATIONS

Specific laws regulating the way in which agricultural products are named were introduced in the European Union in 1993 by two regulations. The first, which introduced PDOs and PGIs into the EU, was the 1992 GI Regulation.[54] The second, which established the TSG scheme, was the 1992 Traditional Specialties Regulation.[55]

As part of a dispute between the European Union and a number of ex-colonies over geographical indications, a complaint was made by Australia and the United States to the WTO Dispute Settlement Body that aspects of the 1992 GI Regulation were in breach

---

[48] The draft text is annexed to the TRIPs Council, 'Report by the Chairman to the Trade Negotiations Committee' 21 April 2011 (TN/IP/21). For background, see J. M. Cortes Martin, 'International Protection of Geographical Indications: The WTO Multilateral Register Negotiations', in Gangjee (2016).

[49] M. Handler, 'Rethinking GI Extension', in Gangjee (2016); J. Hughes, 'Champagne, Feta, and Bourbon—the Spirited Debate about Geographical Indications' (2006) 58 *Hastings Law Journal* 299.

[50] Council Decision 94/184/EC of 24 January 1994 concerning the conclusion of an Agreement between the European Community and Australia on trade in wine [1994] *OJ L* 086/1 (31 March 1994) (the Australia–EU Agreement).

[51] Agreement establishing an association between the European Community and its Member States, of the one part, and the Republic of Chile, of the other part: Final Act [2002] *OJ L* 352/3 (30 December 2002) (the EU–Chile Association Agreement).

[52] Council Decision 97/361/EC of 27 May 1997 on mutual recognition and protection of designations for spirits and drinks [1997] *OJ L* 152/15 (11 June 1997) (the EU–Mexico Agreement).

[53] A. Moroni, 'New Generation of Free Trade Agreements: Towards 'International' European Geographical Indications' (2017) 8(3) *George Mason Journal of International Commercial Law* 286. An assessment of the effectiveness of the GI provisions is included in periodic reviews. See European Commission, *Report from the Commission to the European Parliament, the Council, the EESC and the Committee of the Regions on Implementation of Free Trade Agreements* COM(2017) 654 final (9 November 2017).

[54] This Regulation was amended in an attempt to ensure the procedure for obtaining Community geographical indications was available to producers from third countries: Regulation (EC) No. 535/97 of 17 March 1997 amending Regulation (EEC) No 2081/92 on the protection of geographical indications and designations of origin for agricultural products and foodstuffs [1997] *OJ L* 83/3; Regulation (EC) No. 692/2003 of 8 April 2003 amending Regulation (EEC) No. 2081/92 on the protection of geographical indications and designations of origin for agricultural products and foodstuffs [2003] *OJ L* 99/1.

[55] Regulation (EC) No. 2082/92 of 14 July 1992 on certificates of specific character for agricultural products and foodstuffs [1992] *OJ L* 201/9 (the 'Traditional Specialties Reg. 1992').

of TRIPS.[56] Finding in favour of Australia and the United States, the Panel said that the 1992 GI Regulation did not provide national treatment to non-European WTO members because registration of a geographical designation from a country outside the European Union was contingent on the government of that country adopting a system of reciprocal protection. The Panel also said that the requirement for government-monitored inspection structures under the 1992 GI Regulation discriminated against foreign nationals.

However the lasting legacy of this dispute lies in the WTO Panel's approval of a particular approach for resolving priority conflicts between GIs and trade marks. At issue was whether Article 14(2) of the 1992 GI Regulation—which permitted the coexistence of a subsequent GI with a prior trade mark—inhibited the right to exclusivity guaranteed to that prior mark under Article 16(1) of TRIPS. The United States and Australia argued that the principle of 'first in time, first in right' should resolve such conflicts. After unsuccessfully exhausting the possibilities for coexistence within Articles 24(3) and 24(5) of TRIPS, the European Union achieved its desired outcome by turning to the limitations to trade mark rights contained in Article 17. These limitations included (geographically) descriptive fair use and since all GIs faithfully describe the geographical origin of the product, coexistence was justified under Article 17.[57]

If the WTO dispute generated external pressures for reform—requiring foreign GI regimes to mirror the EU system violated WTO national treatment obligations—internal pressures had been building as well. Considerable evidence in relation to the operation of the various EU GI regimes suggested that they could be simplified and further consolidated, while the application process could be more streamlined.[58] This extended period of introspection would ultimately result in the Quality Schemes Regulation of 2012. The European Union continues to monitor the operation of this Regulation and has recently turned its attention to assessing the market value generated by GI products, the internal monitoring of GIs (inspection structures and regulatory oversight), as well as the scale of infringement and enforcement issues.[59] A potentially major expansion is being contemplated, with the Commission proposing that the coverage of the EU regimes be extended to non-agricultural products, which would include crafts and textiles.[60] Beyond

---

[56] *US v. EC*, WT/DS174; *Australia v. EC*, WTO DS/290. See M. Handler, 'The WTO Geographical Indications Dispute' (2006) 69 *MLR* 70; M. Handler, 'The EU's Geographical Indications Agenda and its Potential Impact on Australia' (2004) 15 *AIPJ* 173.

[57] D. Gangjee, 'Quibbling Siblings: Conflicts Between Trademarks and Geographical Indications' (2007) 82(3) *Chi-Kent L Rev* 1253; cf. B. Goebel and M. Groeschl, 'Learning to Love My PET—The Long Road to Resolving Conflicts between Trade Marks and Geographical Indications', in Gangjee (2016).

[58] See Bently and Sherman (2014), 1118–19; G. Evans, 'The Simplification of European Legislation for the Protection of Geographical Indications: The Proposed Regulation on Agricultural Product Quality Schemes' (2012) 34 *EIPR* 770; V. Mantrov, 'Protection Norms of Indications of Geographical Origin in the Applicable Regulations: Recent Changes and the Necessity for Further Unification' (2012) 43 *IIC* 174.

[59] See respectively Tanguy Chever et al., *Value of Production of Agricultural Products and Foodstuffs, Wines, Aromatised Wines and Spirits Protected by a Geographical Indication (GI)* (Final Report, October 2012) AGRI–2011–EVAL–04 (the worldwide estimated sales value of EU GIs was €54.3 billion in 2010); EUIPO, *Protection and Control of Geographical Indications for Agricultural Products in the EU Member States* (December 2017) (on inspection structures in Member States); EUIPO, *Infringement of Protected Geographical Indications For Wine, Spirits, Agricultural Products and Foodstuffs in the European Union* (April 2016).

[60] European Commission Green Paper, *Making the most out of Europe's traditional know-how: a possible extension of geographical indication protection of the European Union to non-agricultural products* COM(2014) 469 final (15 July 2014); see D. Marie-Vivien, 'Do Geographical Indications for Handicrafts Deserve a Special Regime? Insights from Worldwide Law and Practice', in W. van Caenegem and J. Cleary (eds), *The Importance of Place: Geographical Indications as a Tool for Local and Regional Development* (2017).

this looms the phenomenon of climate change, which will affect all GIs globally. Climate change directly confronts arguments that physical geography is solely responsible for product quality. What if ideal growing conditions migrate to neighbouring regions due to changes in ambient temperature or patterns of rainfall? And to what extent should innovative technological interventions be permitted to counteract this and stabilize product quality for so-called traditional products?[61]

2 PDOs AND PGIs

In this section, we look at the scheme for the protection of designations of origin and geographical indications, which is governed by the Quality Schemes Regulation. *Designations of origin*, which are called 'protected designations of origin' (PDOs) once they are registered,[62] are defined as the name of a region, a specific place or, in exceptional cases, a country used to describe an agricultural product or foodstuff. To qualify for protection as a PDO, the named product must originate in the defined region, specific place, or country. It is also necessary to show that the quality or characteristics of the named product are essentially or exclusively the result of a particular geographical environment, with its inherent natural and human factors. It is also necessary to show that the production, processing, and preparation take place in the defined geographical area.[63] A number of different product names have been registered as PDOs in the United Kingdom, including Cornish clotted cream, West Country farmhouse Cheddar cheese, Jersey Royal potatoes, Shetland lamb, and White Stilton.[64] Some other well-known PDOs include Roquefort cheese (France), Gorgonzola (Italy), Feta (Greece), Camembert de Normandie (France), Kalamata olives (Greece), Chianti Classico olive oil (Italy), and Prosciutto de Parma (Italy).

The second type of designation protected by the Quality Schemes Regulation is known as *geographical indications*. Once a geographical indication is registered, it is known as a 'protected geographical indication' (PGI). Geographical indications are defined as the name of a region, specific place, or, in exceptional cases, a country, used to describe an agricultural product or foodstuff. To qualify for protection, a geographical indication must originate in that region, specific place, or country. The product or foodstuff needs to possess a specific quality, reputation, or other characteristic attributable to that geographical origin and the production. It is also necessary to show *either* that the production, processing, *or* preparation takes place in the defined geographical area.[65] A number of different geographical names have been registered as PGIs in the United Kingdom, including Cornish pasty, Rutland bitter, Whitstable oysters, Scottish beef, and Welsh lamb.[66]

---

[61] M. R. Mozelle and L. Thach, 'The Impact of Climate Change on the Global Wine Industry: Challenges and Solutions' (2014) 3(2) *Wine Economics and Policy* 81; L. F. Clark and W. A. Kerr, 'Climate Change and Terroir: The Challenge of Adapting Geographical Indications' (2017) 20 *JWIP* 88.

[62] This is the translation of *appellation d'origine contrôlée* (AOC).

[63] Quality Schemes Reg., Art. 5(1) (ex GI Reg. 2006, Art. 2(1); GI Reg. 1992, Art. 2(2)(a)).

[64] Other British PDOs include Orkney beef, Orkney lamb, Blue Stilton cheese, Beacon Fell Lancashire cheese, Swaledale cheese, Swaledale ewe's cheese, Bonchester cheese, Buxton cheese, Dovedale cheese, and Single Gloucester.

[65] Quality Schemes Reg., Art. 5(2) (ex GI Reg. 2006, Art. 2(1)).

[66] Other PGIs include Scottish lamb, Welsh beef, Teviotdale cheese, Dorset Blue cheese, Exmoor Blue cheese, Herefordshire cider, Herefordshire perry, Worcestershire cider, Worcestershire perry, Gloucestershire cider, Gloucestershire perry, Kentish ale, and Kentish strong ale.

As Lord Hoffmann said, 'a PGI is similar to a PDO except that the causal link between the place of origin and the quality of the product may be a matter of reputation rather than verifiable fact'.[67] Another difference is that while the production, processing, and preparation of a PDO *all* need to take place in the named geographic area, with a PGI it is only necessary for the production, processing, *or* preparation to take place in the named area.

The protection of designations of origin and geographical indications performs a number of different roles. On one level, the schemes aim to ensure that consumers are able to rely upon the names of goods as indicators of the quality of the items that they are purchasing. This enables them to purchase quality products with guarantees as to the methods of production and origin. The Quality Schemes Regulation also performs an educative role, insofar as it informs consumers about the origin and quality of agricultural products. Importantly, the Regulation aims to protect producers against piracy and unfair competition. In so doing, it aims to encourage investment in the production of quality local products. This is reflected in the fact that registered names are protected even where consumers are not misled about the origin of the goods. Another important and often overlooked feature of the Regulation is that it helps to promote and protect agricultural heritage in Europe. Indeed, as the European Parliament has said, designations of origin 'form part of a rich national heritage, which must be preserved'.[68] While the scheme has not been as popular in the United Kingdom as in some other member states,[69] it has generated interest in regional and traditional foods in the United Kingdom.[70] At a general level, the Regulation forms part of the EU's Agricultural Policy.[71] More specifically, it was designed to encourage the diversification of agricultural production and to promote products having certain characteristics to the benefit of the rural economy—particularly small farmers in disadvantaged, outlying, and upland areas.[72] The development of distinctive products is particularly important given the rapid market liberalization that is taking place in the agricultural sector.[73]

While the scheme has attracted a lot of support, it is not without its critics. In the early years, some were concerned that it might encourage protectionist tendencies, inhibit innovation within the context of regional products (by incorporating ossified authenticity requirements within the product specification) and stifle generic use by competitors (for example, German producers of Parmesan cheese).[74] While there is not much evidence that this has happened, there are nevertheless compelling reasons to be cautious about the extent to which the scheme can certify provenance or authenticity. If consumers are unaware of the significance of PDO or PGI logos, or the PGI permits a link that is so attenuated that the guarantee of origin becomes meaningless, the trustworthiness and effectiveness of public examination and registration are undermined.[75]

2.1 REGISTRATION

For a name to be protected as a designation of origin or as a geographical indication, it must be registered. Once a name is registered, it is automatically protected in all member

---

[67] *Consorzio Parma v. Asda* [2002] *FSR* 3, [8].

[68] This was a motivating factor in the early discussions. See *Motion for a Resolution on Protecting Community productions of cheeses with designations of origin* (28 April 1989) EEC Parliamentary Session Documents PE 128 390/Fin (withdrawn). See M. Kolia, 'Monopolising Names: EEC Proposals on the Protection of Trade Descriptions of Foodstuffs' [1992] *EIPR* 233, 234.

[69] Of the 1,429 or so names registered by May 2018 on DOOR, only 71 products originated from the United Kingdom.

states. It also enables parties who comply with the relevant rules to use the appropriate EU logo (see Fig. 43.1). Products designated as PDO or PGI on their labelling must accompany the designation with the appropriate logo.[76]

When EU laws to protect designations of origin and geographical indication were first introduced in 1993, a name could be registered using one of two routes: either the 'normal registration process'; or an 'accelerated (or simplified) process'.[77] The aim of the accelerated procedure was to ensure that names that had been protected in member states prior to the enactment of the 1992 GI Regulation were registered at the EU level. It was also meant to encourage the rapid harmonization of the national legal systems of the member states. The accelerated process was abolished in 2003,[78] primarily because it did not provide for a right of objection, which was said to be 'an essential requirement for protecting acquired rights and preventing injury on registration', and for legal security and transparency.[79] The abolition of the accelerated process did not affect the validity of the names that had previously been registered under the accelerated process, which continue to receive the same levels of protection as they received previously.[80]

2.1.1 Who can apply for registration?

Applications for registration may be made by groups of producers or processors. A 'group' is defined as 'any association, irrespective of its legal form, mainly composed of producers or processors working with the same product'.[81] Where a single individual or legal person is the only producer willing to submit an application and the defined geographical area possess 'characteristics which differ appreciably from those of neighbouring areas', the individual will be treated as a group.[82] Groups are only able to apply for registration in respect of agricultural products and foodstuffs that they 'produce or obtain'.[83]

Special provisions are made for the fact that geographical areas may not coincide with geopolitical borders. While the scheme envisages that applicants will ordinarily be from one member state, groups or individuals in different member states are able to lodge a

---

[70] L. Mason and C. Brown, *Traditional Foods of Britain: An Inventory* (1999)—part of a Europe-wide initiative to list foods and food products produced in one place for three generations or more.

[71] It is also part of a suite of laws regulating the naming of foods. See C. Lister, 'The Naming of Foods: The European Community's Rules for Non-brand Food Product Names' [1993] *ELR* 179.

[77] See *Opinion of the Committee of the Regions on the Protection of Geographical Indications and Designations of Origin for Agricultural Products and Foodstuffs* (14 November 2001) Opinion COR/2001/58. The romantic notion of the 'farmer' is evoked here in much the same way as the 'author' is used in copyright law.

[73] *Opinion of the Economic and Social Committee on the Proposal for a Council Regulation Amending Regulation No. 2081/92* (17 July 2002) COM(2002) 139 final, [2.10].

[74] Bently and Sherman (2014), 1120–1.

[75] D. Gangjee, 'Proving Provenance: Geographical Indications Certification and its Ambiguities' (2017) 98 *World Development* 12.

[76] Quality Schemes Reg., Art. 12(3). See also Commission Delegated Regulation (EU) No. 664/2014 of 18 December 2013 supplementing Regulation (EU) No. 1151/2012 (depicting the logos, referred to as symbols, in an Annex).

[77] See European Commission, *Communication to Traders Involved with Designations of Origin and Geographical Indications for Agricultural Products and Foodstuffs Concerning the Simplified Procedures as Laid Down in Art. 17 of Council Regulation (EEC) No. 2081/92* [1993] *OJ C* 273.

[78] Regulation (EC) No. 692/2003 of 8 April 2003 amending Regulation (EEC) No. 2081/92 on the protection of geographical indications and designations of origin for agricultural products and foodstuffs [2003] *OJ L* 99/1, Art. 1(15).

[79] Ibid., Recital 13.   [80] Ibid., Art. 1(15).   [81] Quality Schemes Reg., Art. 3(2).

[82] Quality Schemes Reg., Art. 49(1)(a)-(b). Notably, the provision does not mention processors. Applications can be made with another member state or with a third country that complies with the procedure set out in Art. 49.   [83] Quality Schemes Reg., Art. 49(1).

joint application where the geographical area extends beyond state borders.[84] Unless a decision was 'tainted by manifest error', it is for national courts, rather than the Court of Justice, to rule on the lawfulness of an application for a protected designation, such as the way in which geographical boundaries are drawn.[85]

2.1.2 The product specification

One of the central elements of the scheme regulated by the Quality Schemes Regulation is the 'product specification'. The specification performs a number of different roles. During the registration process, it sets out the information that is used to determine whether a name should be protected. Once a name is registered, the specification, which contains a detailed definition of the protected product, sets out the standards that producers and processors must meet if they wish to use the protected name. As a corollary, the specification also helps to delineate the scope of protection—that is, it provides the basis for ascertaining the scope of the intangible interest conferred by registration.[86]

Article 7(1) of the Regulation provides a non-exhaustive list of the information that needs to be included in a product specification.[87] This includes:

(a) the name to be protected as a designation of origin or geographical indication [of the agricultural product or foodstuff] as it is used, whether in trade or common language, and only in the languages which are or were historically used to describe the specific product in the defined geographical area;

(b) a description of the product, including the raw materials, if appropriate, as well as the principal physical, chemical, microbiological, or organoleptic characteristics of the product;

(c) the definition of the geographical area … ;

(d) evidence that the product originates in the defined geographical area … ;

(e) a description of the method of obtaining the product and, where appropriate, the authentic and unvarying local methods as well as information concerning packaging, if the applicant group so determines and gives sufficient product-specific justification as to why the packaging must take place in the limited geographical area to safeguard quality, to ensure the origin or ensure control … ;

(f) details establishing the following:

  (i) the link between the quality or characteristics of the product and the geographical environment … ; or

  (ii) … the link between a given quality, the reputation or other characteristics of the product and the geographical origin …

2.1.3 Registration

There are a number of steps that must be undertaken for a product name to gain protection (see Fig. 43.2). Applicants must submit an application form and a product

---

[84] Quality Schemes Reg., Art. 49(1).

[85] See *Carl Kuhne and ors v. Jutro Konservenfabrik*, Case C-269/99 [2001] *ECR* I–9517 (the decision as to where boundaries were to be drawn in relation to the PGI Spreewald gherkins was not a matter for the Court of Justice, but for the German courts). Geographical delimitation—especially where rivals are excluded from the zone of production—has proved controversial in the past. See *Northern Foods Plc v. Department for the Environment, Food and Rural Affairs* [2005] *EWHC* 2971 (Admin); M. J. Rippon, 'Traditional Foods, Territorial Boundaries and the TRIPS Agreement: The Case of the Melton Mowbray Pork Pie' (2013) 16 *JWIP* 262.

[86] *Consorzio del Prosciutto di Parma v. Asda*, Case C-108/01 [2003] *ECR* I–5121, [46]–[47].

[87] Additional guidance is provided in Commission Implementing Regulation (EU) No. 668/2014 of 13 June 2014 laying down rules for the application of Regulation (EU) No. 1151/2012 of the European Parliament and of the Council on quality schemes for agricultural products and foodstuffs [2014] *OJ L* 179/36.

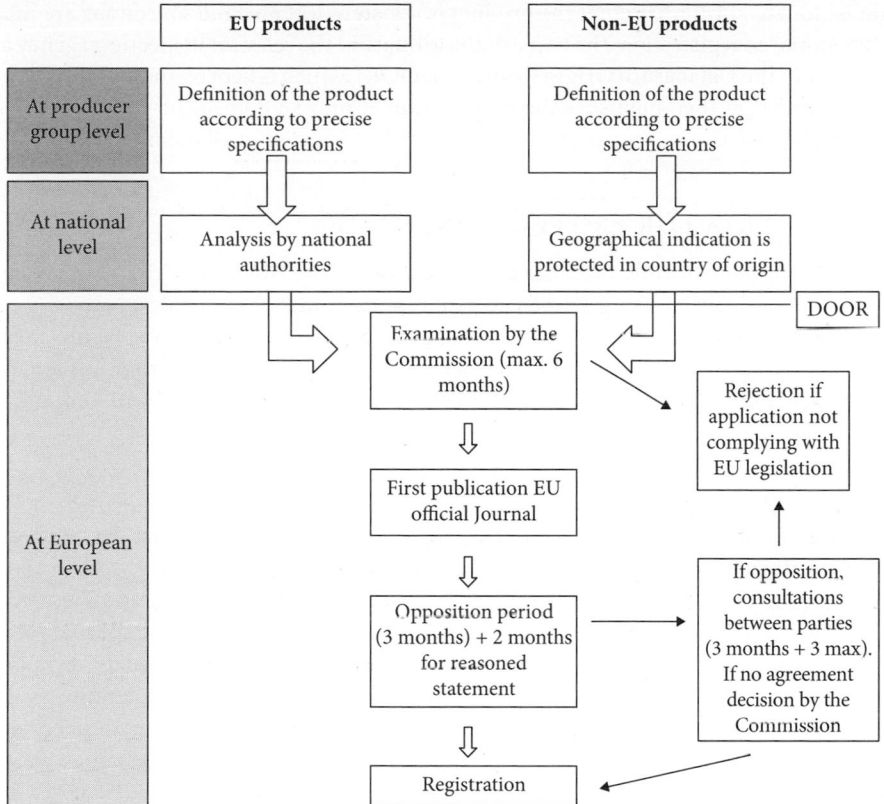

Fig. 43.2 Overview of the GI registration process

specification to the relevant national agency.[88] The application form is then examined by that national agency to see whether it is 'justified' in light of the criteria for protection.[89] If approved, the application and supporting documentation are submitted to the European Commission for final approval. The Commission then undertakes a formal examination of the application (for no more than six months) to determine whether it includes all of the particulars provided for in Article 7.[90] If the Commission decides that the name qualifies for protection, a summary sheet is published in the Official Journal of the European Communities.[91] Once the summary of the specification is published in the Official Journal, third parties have three months in which they are able to object to the registration on the basis that the name does not comply with criteria for protection in Article 5.[92] The Commission then invites the parties to try to reach a solution. If an acceptable solution is found, the 'summary sheet' for the product is republished in the

---

[88] Quality Schemes Reg., Art. 49(1)(2).   [89] Quality Schemes Reg., Art. 49(2).
[90] Quality Schemes Reg., Art. 50(1).
[91] This includes the name and address of the applicant, the name of the product, the main points of the application, references to the national provisions governing the preparation, production, or manufacture of the product, and, if necessary, the reasons for the decision: Quality Schemes Reg., Art. 50(2).
[92] Quality Schemes Reg., Art. 51(1) (previously the period was six months). Third parties are able to object to the registration on the basis that the name does not comply with conditions/criteria for protection in Quality Schemes Reg., Art. 49(1) (ex GI Reg. 2006, Art. 7(1)). On the 2006 provision, see *La Conqueste v. Commission*, T-215/00 [2001] *ECR* II-181 (CFI), [44]–[47].

Official Journal to confirm that the product is registered. If no valid objections are made to the proposed registration, the name of the group and the relevant inspection agency are entered into the Database of Origin Register (DOOR), which is kept by the Commission.[93] The Commission then publishes the names entered into DOOR in the Official Journal. Once registered, the product name is automatically protected in all member states.

2.2 CRITERIA FOR PROTECTION: NAMES

There are a number of different criteria that must be satisfied for a name of an agricultural product or foodstuff to be registered as a geographical indication or a designation of origin. When thinking about the threshold that must be passed for a name to be registered, it is helpful to distinguish between criteria relating to the 'name' and criteria that relate to the 'agricultural product or foodstuff' to which the name applies. We will look at each of these in turn.

2.2.1 Limitation on names

There are a number of restrictions that are placed on the types of name that are registrable under the Regulation.

(i) Geographic names The first point to note is that the Quality Schemes Regulation applies only to geographic names,[94] which are defined as names of regions, specific places, or, in exceptional cases, countries (the latter was introduced to accommodate very small countries, such as Luxembourg).[95] As such, it would not be possible to register the name of a member state (France), nor a fictitious or invented name. Similarly, where numbers were added to a geographical designation to distinguish mineral waters from the same area, the names were rejected on the basis that they were not 'geographical names'.[96] Article 5(3) creates an exception to the general rule that only geographic names are registrable (and, as we will see later, the rule that the name must identify a product that originates from a specific place). In particular, it provides that certain names shall be treated as designations of origin even though the raw materials for the product concerned come from a geographical area that is larger than or different from the geographical area. This is on condition that the production area of the raw material is defined, that special conditions exist for the production of the raw materials, that there are arrangements in place to control these conditions, and that the designations of origin were recognized as such prior to 1 May 2004.[97] For example, 'Feta', which is derived from the Latin and means 'to slice', does not designate a geographic place; nonetheless it was held to be registrable on its face under the 2006 Regulation.[98]

---

[93] Quality Schemes Reg., Art. 51(1).

[94] It has been suggested by the Commission that this refers to 'homogeneous areas': *Italian Republic v. Commission*, Case C-99/99 [2000] *ECR* I-11535, [24].

[95] *Commission v. Germany*, Case C-325/00 [2003] 1 *CMLR* 1 (AG Jacobs).

[96] The names were Dauner Quelle I, Dauner Quelle II, and Dauner Quelle III. See Regulation (EC) No. 1285/2001 or 28 June 2001 rejecting a list of applications for the registration of designations communicated under [GI Reg. 1992, Art. 17] [2001] *OJ L* 176/27 (29 June 2001), Recitals 1–4. Mineral waters have subsequently been removed from the ambit of the Quality Schemes Reg.

[97] Quality Schemes Reg., Art. 5(3)(a)–(d).

[98] Quality Schemes Reg., Art. 5(1)(a);. cf. Advocate-General La Pergola, *Denmark v. Community*, Joined Cases C-289/96, C-293/96 and C-299/96 [1999] *ECR* I-1541, [7] (arguing, on substantive grounds, that Feta should not have been registered). The question of the status of Feta was considered and held not to be generic in *Germany v. Commission of the European Communities*, Joined Cases C-465/02 and C-466/0 [2005] *ECR* I–09115. See generally D. Gangjee, 'Say Cheese: A Sharper Image of Generic Use through the Lens of *Feta*' [2007] *EIPR* 172.

(ii) Generic names A name will be not be registered as a protected designation where it is generic.[99] The name of a product is generic where it has 'become the common name of a product in the Union'.[100] That is, a name is generic where it designates the product *as such* without, in the view of the public, involving any reference to the geographic origin of the product.[101] This is the case even though the name originally related to the place or region where the product or foodstuff was originally produced or marketed. On this basis, names such as Cheddar, Brie, Camembert, Edam, Emmentaler, and Gouda would be generic and thus unregistrable.[102] While it is not possible to register names that are generic per se, it is possible to register a geographical name that incorporates a generic name. For example, Cheddar is a generic form of hard cheese and, as such, would not be eligible to be registered either as a PDO or PGI. Nonetheless, West Country farmhouse Cheddar cheese has been registered as a PDO.[103] To date, the courts have been very lenient when considering whether a name is generic. It seems that even in the face of overwhelming evidence that a name is widely used as the common name of a product in many countries throughout the Union, if it can be shown that the name is still able to evoke the place of production, it will not be excluded on the basis that it is generic.[104]

A range of factors will be taken into account when deciding the essentially evidential question of whether a name has become generic.[105] These include the situation in the member state in which the name originates and the areas in which the product is consumed,[106] and relevant national and EU laws, as well as how the product is viewed by consumers.[107] Once a name is registered, it cannot become generic.[108]

---

[99] Quality Schemes Reg., Arts 6(1), 13(2).

[100] Quality Schemes Reg., Art. 3(6). One issue that is unclear is *where* the name must be generic, 'in' the Union being non-specific. See generally *Denmark v. Commission*, Joined Cases C-289/96, C-293/96 and C-299/96 [1999] *ECR* I–1541. In relation to the marketing of a cheese in France labelled as 'parmesan', which did not comply with the specification for the PDO Parmigano Reggiano (registered by Italy under the accelerated Art. 17 process), the German government argued that 'parmesan' was generic insofar as it had become the common name for a foodstuff. The Court of Justice said that Germany had not provided sufficient evidence to conclude that parmesan was generic. See also *Canadane Cheese Trading v. Kouri*, Case C-317/95 [1997] *ECR* I–4681 (AG Ruiz-Jarabo Colomer).

[101] *Denmark v. Commission*, Joined Cases C-289/96, C-293/96, and C-299/96 [1999] *ECR* I–1541, [36].

[102] As was required by GI Reg. 1992, Art. 3(3), a non-exhaustive indicative list of the names of agricultural products and foodstuffs regarded as generic was presented by the Commission in 1996. However, it was not passed. See European Commission, *Proposal for a Council Decision Drawing up a Non-exhaustive, Indicative List of the Names of Agricultural Products and Foodstuffs Regarded as Being Generic, as Provided for in Article 3(3) Of Council Regulation No. 2081/92* (March 1996) COM(1996) 0038 final. This included Brie, Camembert, Cheddar, Edam, Emmentaler, and Gouda. See *Denmark v. Commission*, Joined Cases C-289/96, C-293/96 and C-299/96 [1999] *ECR* I–1541, [44].

[103] The registration of 'Feta', which had been to Greece under Regulation 1107/96, was annulled because the Commission had not taken account of all of the factors listed in Art. 3(1) when deciding whether the name should be registered: ibid., [103]. Feta was reinstated as a PDO by the Commission on 14 October 2002 by Regulation (EC) No. 1829/2002 amending the Annex to Regulation 2081/92 with regard to the name 'Feta' [2002] *OJ L* 277. This decision was upheld in *Germany v. Commission*, Joined Cases C-465/02 and C-466/0 [2005] *ECR* I–09115 (Feta was not generic).

[104] See *Feta* [2005] *ECR* I–9115; *Parmesan* [2008] *ECR* I–957; *Bavaria* [2009] *ECR* I–5491.

[105] For a comparative analysis of factors across jurisdictions, see D. Gangjee, 'Genericide: The Death of a Geographical Indication', in Gangjee (2016).

[106] Quality Schemes Reg., Art. 41(2). Art. 41(1) adds that the Regulation shall not affect the use of terms that are generic in the Union, even if the generic term is part of a name that is protected.

[107] For a consideration of the type of evidence that may be used, see *Consorzio per la tutela del formaggio Grana Padano v. OHIM*, T-291/03 [2008] *ETMR* 3; ('grana' was not generic); *Germany v. Commission*, Joined Cases C-465/02 and C-466/0 [2005] *ECR* I–09115.

[108] Quality Schemes Reg., Art. 41(1).

(iii) Homonymous names Special rules exist in relation to the registration of homonyms of names that are already registered[109]—that is, names that are spelled or pronounced in the same way. While there is no guidance as to the degree of similarity that is needed for these rules to apply, the Recitals to the 2003 amendments spoke of geographical names that are 'entirely or partially homonymous'.[110]

A homonymous name that meets the requirements of the Regulation can be registered, so long as there is a clear distinction (in practice) between the name on the register and the (subsequent) homonymous name. However, if a homonymous name misleads the public into believing that products come from another territory, it will not be registered. This is the case even if the name is used accurately for the territory in question.[111] In deciding whether a homonymous name will be registered, the Regulation says that it is necessary to take into account the need 'to ensure equitable treatment of the producers concerned', whether consumers will be misled, local and traditional usage, and finally the actual risk of confusion.[112]

(iv) Plant or animal names A name that conflicts with the name of a plant variety or an animal breed, which is likely to mislead consumers as to the 'true origin' of the product, may not be registered.[113]

(v) Trade marks As we will see, special rules were developed to prevent the dual protection of geographic names under both the Quality Schemes Regulation and as trade marks.[114] A designation of origin or geographical indication will not be registered where, in light of a trade mark's reputation, renown, and the length of time for which it has been used, registration is liable to mislead consumers as to the true identity of the product.[115]

2.3 CRITERIA FOR PROTECTION: AGRICULTURAL PRODUCTS AND FOODSTUFFS

There are also a number of restrictions placed on the types of agricultural product and foodstuff that can be protected as designations of origin and indication under the Quality Schemes Regulation.

2.3.1 Subject matter

The first and most general restriction is that the Quality Schemes Regulation only applies to certain agricultural products and foodstuffs. In order for a product to be protected as a designation of origin or indication, it must fall within one of the types of product listed in Annex I to the Quality Schemes Regulation.[116] These are: beer; chocolate and derived products; bread, pastry, cakes, confectionery, and other bakers' wares; beverages made from plant extracts; pasta; salt; natural gums and resins; mustard paste; hay; essential oils; cork; cochineal (a raw product of animal origin); flowers and ornamental plants; wool; wicker; scutched flax; leather; fur; and feather.

The Quality Schemes Regulation does not apply to wines (with the exception of wine vinegars), or to spirits (which are governed by specific legislation).[117] When the laws dealing

---

[109] Quality Schemes Reg., Art. 6(3).

[110] Regulation (EC) No. 692/2003 of 8 April 2003 amending Regulation (EEC) No. 2081/92 on the protection of geographical indications and designations of origin for agricultural products and foodstuffs [2003] *OJ L* 99/1, Recital 4.   [111] Quality Schemes Reg., Art. 6(3).

[112] Quality Schemes Reg., Art. 6(3).   [113] Quality Schemes Reg., Art. 6(2).

[114] See generally A. de Almeida, 'Key Differences between Trade Marks and Geographical Indications' (2008) 30 *EIPR* 406.   [115] Quality Schemes Reg., Art.6(4).

[116] Quality Schemes Reg., Art. 2(1).   [117] Quality Schemes Reg., Art. 2(2).

with designations of origin and indication were first enacted, they applied to the names of mineral and spring water. However, as a result of problems such as the use of identical names for different waters and the use of invented names,[118] the 1992 GI Regulation was amended to exclude mineral and spring waters from the types of product that are protectable.[119]

2.3.2 The product or foodstuff must originate from the named place

To qualify for protection as geographical indication or a designation of origin, the agricultural product or foodstuff must originate from the named geographical area, be it a region, specific place, or (exceptionally) a country[120]—that is, a name will not be protected where the product comes from outside the geographic area. In one decision, it was held that 'originating', 'originate', and 'origin' referred to the place where the product (in this case, Melton Mowbray pork pies) had their origin in the past, not where they come from now.[121]

As we have seen earlier, an exception is made to the requirement that the agricultural product or foodstuff must originate from the named geographic area in the case of 'raw materials' (which are defined as live animals, meat, and milk).[122] In particular, where the raw materials of a product originate from a geographic area that is larger than or different from the processing area, the product name may still be protected. For this to occur, the production area of the raw materials must be limited, there have to be special conditions for the production of the raw materials, and inspection arrangements need to be in place to ensure that these conditions are adhered to.[123] It is also necessary to show that the designation in question had been recognized as a designation of origin in the country of origin prior to 1 May 2004.[124]

2.3.3 Quality or character of the product or foodstuff

For a name to be protected as a geographical indication or a designation of origin under the Quality Schemes Regulation, it is necessary to show that the nominated geographic area imbues products from that region with certain characteristics or traits. The requirement that there must be a link between product and place means that abstract and general names that transcend geographic areas, such as 'mountain', would not qualify for protection, since there is no link between the quality or characteristics of the product and its specific geographical origin.[125] (As we will see, the term 'mountain product' is now protected as an optional quality term, which is able to protect geographically non-specific names.) Similarly, the fact that a product or foodstuff is closely linked to a country's traditional gastronomy, as distinct from a geographic area, would not, of itself, show the necessary connection to place.[126]

---

[118] See Regulation (EC) No. 1285/2001 or 28 June 2001 rejecting a list of applications for the registration of designations communicated under [GI Reg. 1992, Art. 17] [2001] *OJ L* 176/27 (29 June 2001), Recitals 1–4. Germany applied to have 314 names registered under the accelerated Art. 17 process: 125 of the names were not designations of origin and 15 names, which included 'numbers' to distinguish names of the same designation, were rejected because they were not geographic names.

[119] Regulation (EC) No. 692/2003 of 8 April 2003 amending Regulation (EEC) No. 2081/92 on the protection of geographical indications and designations of origin for agricultural products and foodstuffs [2003] *OJ L* 99/1.

[120] Quality Schemes Reg., Art. 5(1)(a) (for PDOs), (2)(a) (for PGIs) (ex GI Reg. 2006, Art. 2(1)).

[121] *Northern Foods v. Department for the Environment, Food and Rural Affairs* [2005] *EWHC* 2971 (Admin), [21]. See D. Gangjee, 'Melton Mowbray and the GI Pie in the Sky: Exploring Cartographies of Protection' [2006] *IPQ* 291. [122] Quality Schemes Reg., Art. 5(3).

[123] Quality Schemes Reg., Art. 5(3)(b)–(c). [124] Quality Schemes Reg., Art. 5(3)(d).

[125] *Jacques Pistre*, Cases C-321–324/94 [1977] *CMLR* 565 (ECJ), 587.

[126] *Consorzio per la Tutela del Formaggio Gorgonzola v. Kaserei Champiognon Hofmeister*, Case C-87/97 [1999] *ECR* I–1301, [9] (AG La Pergola).

The nature of the relationship between product and place necessary for a name to be registered is different for designations of origin (PDOs) from the nature that is necessary for geographic indications (PGIs). A *designation of origin* is defined as a name that identifies a product 'whose quality or characteristics are essentially or exclusively due to a particular geographical environment with its inherent natural and human factors'.[127] As Advocate-General La Pergola said:

> [T]he relationship between product and territory must be *exclusive*, in the sense that the product must have been conceived of, developed, and established exclusively in that area and nowhere else. Only this exclusive relationship justifies the grant of a collective monopoly: Precisely by virtue of the place where they are established.[128]

In contrast, for a name to qualify as a *geographical indication*, it is only necessary to show that the 'quality, reputation or other characteristics' of the named product is 'essentially attributable to its geographical origin'.[129] This definition differs from the 2006 GI Regulation in that it requires the product's attributes to be *essentially* attributable to its geographical origin. While Recital 22 of the 2012 Quality Schemes Regulation says that the changes to the definition of geographical indication (which were made to bring the EU scheme into line with TRIPS) were done 'without changing the concept of [the EU scheme]', it is possible that the 2012 Regulation may be interpreted as imposing a more rigorous threshold than had previously been the case.

2.3.4 Place of production, processing, or preparation

Another factor that must be satisfied for a name to be registered relates to the place where the named agricultural product or foodstuff is produced. Again, different standards apply depending on whether a name is to be registered as a PDO or a PGI. In relation to *designations of origin*, all of the 'production steps' must take place in the named geographic area.[130] (It is important to note that 'production step' is defined broadly to mean production, processing, or preparation.[131]) In contrast, to be protected as a *geographical indication*, it is necessary only for one of the production steps to take place in the defined geographic area.[132]

2.4 EXPLOITATION

One of the distinguishing features of the scheme established under the Quality Regulation is that it does not confer the right to use a registered name on either particular individuals or a specific group; rather, it confers the right to use the registered name and the relevant logo on *any* undertaking the products of which meet the prescribed geographic and qualitative requirements.[133] In other words, the right is not addressed to specific producers, but to an abstract group.[134] (While the group therefore remains open to anyone suitably qualified to join it, the initial group submitting the application does get to set the 'rules of the game' for belonging.) This means that producers who were not part of the original application are able to use a protected name, so long as their products conform to the

---

[127] Quality Schemes Reg., Art. 5(1)(b).
[128] *Consorzio Gorgonzola v. Hofmeister*, Case C-87/97 [1999] *ECR* I–1301, [7] (AG La Pergola).
[129] Quality Schemes Reg., Art. 5(2)(b).   [130] Quality Schemes Reg., Art. 5(1)(c).
[131] Quality Schemes Reg., Art. 3(7).   [132] Quality Schemes Reg., Art. 5(2)(c).
[133] *La Conqueste*, Case T-215/00 [2001] *ECR* II–181 (CFI), [32].
[134] Ibid., [32]–[33].

registered specification.[135] It also means that the interest in a protected name cannot be licensed or assigned to a third party (especially outside the nominated geographic area). While, in theory, the Quality Schemes Regulation might enable anyone to use a registered name if they comply with the specification, in practice, agricultural cooperatives, cartels of producers, or state interests may impose restrictions on the ability of third parties to produce or process agricultural products and foodstuffs.[136]

2.5 INFRINGEMENT

In this section, we look at the situations in which a registered name will be infringed (or misused). In particular, we consider who is entitled to sue in case of abuse, the scope of protection, and the situations in which the name will be infringed.

2.5.1 Who is entitled to sue?

One of the defining characteristics of the regime established under the Quality Schemes Regulation is that there is no 'owner' per se; rather, anyone who complies with the specification is eligible to use the name. It is clear that producers and processors using a registered name are able to sue to prevent abuses. Organizations formed to represent producers or processors working with the same product are also entitled to sue to protect a registered name.[137]

2.5.2 Scope of protection

The starting point for ascertaining the scope of protection available for a PDO or a PGI is the product specification. While the specification helps to delineate the scope of the intangible property protected by the Quality Schemes Regulation, the mere fact that something is included in a specification does not mean that it is automatically protected. This is because the only matters within a specification that are relevant are those that impact upon the quality of the product. This is important given, as Lord Hoffmann said, that the product specification is a 'discursive document', meaning that it contains information that is not intended to be enforceable.[138] For example, the 84-page specification submitted in support of the registration of Prosciutto di Parma as a PDO included information on the history of the pig in the Po Valley, and details about breeding and slaughtering, as well as how the ham was to be cured, stored, and sliced.

In other registration-based intellectual property regimes, such as patents and trade marks, one of the key issues in an infringement action is how the registered documents are to be interpreted. For example, in patent law, a lot of attention is given to whether the claims should be read literally, purposively, and so on. Less problematic, but equally important, is the question of the types of activity that fall within the owner's exclusive control. Although the focus is on protecting the name or designation, using the designation upon a product which deviates from the product specification (for example, violating certain packaging requirements or using impermissible ingredients) could lead to infringement, since it would constitute a misuse of the name. In relation to names registered under the Quality Schemes Regulation, such issues are dealt with by Article 13(1),

---

[135] To be eligible to use a PDO or a PGI, an agricultural product or foodstuff must comply with the specification: Quality Schemes Reg., Art. 7(1).

[136] See M. Kolia, 'Monopolising Names: EEC Proposals on the Protection of Trade Descriptions of Foodstuffs' [1992] *EIPR* 233.   [137] Quality Schemes Reg., Art. 45(1)(b).

[138] See *Consorzio Parma v. Asda* [2002] *FSR* 3 (HL), [29] (Lord Hoffmann).

which sets out both the types of activity that infringe and also how the underlying property interest is to be construed. While there will undoubtedly be situations in which the courts are called upon to decide how a name should be interpreted or whether products are the same, most of these issues are dealt with by Article 13(1).

Registered names are protected against any direct or indirect commercial use in respect of products not covered by the registration, including (but not limited to) situations in which the named product is used as an ingredient.[139] Where a supermarket sold 'Champagne sorbet', containing 12 per cent of genuine Champagne, the Comité Interprofessionnel du Vin de Champagne commenced proceedings on the basis that this would evoke and potentially take advantage of the reputation of the famous French sparkling wine. While referring the matter back to the national court for its final determination, the Court of Justice was inclined to permit a reasonable reference to a GI on product packaging, where it was genuinely used as an ingredient and provided certain criteria were satisfied. While there was clearly an *advantage* for the supermarket, this was not considered to be *unfair*.[140] This is subject to the proviso that the products are 'comparable' to the registered product or that using the name exploits the reputation of the protected name.[141] Registered names are also protected against any 'misuse, imitation, or evocation'.[142] This is the case even if the true origin of the product or service is indicated ('Cornish clotted cream' made in Spain), the name is translated, or the name is accompanied by an expression such as 'style', 'type', 'method', 'as produced in', 'imitation', or something similar. The provision not only applies to the named product as a product in its own right, but also applies where the named product is used as an ingredient in another product. A name is 'evoked' where the term used to designate a product incorporates part of a protected designation so that, 'when a consumer is confronted with the name of a product, the image triggered in his mind is that of the product whose designation is protected'.[143] As the Court of Justice has said, it 'is possible for a protected designation of origin to be evoked where there no likelihood of confusion between the products concerned'—and this was the case 'even where no Community protection extends to the parts of the designation which are echoed in the term or terms in issue'.[144] On this basis, the Court held that the name 'Gorgonzola' (which was a protected designation) was evoked, and thus infringed, where the phonetically and visually similar name 'Cambozola' was used in relation to a soft blue cheese that looked like Gorgonzola.[145] The Court of Justice has further clarified the admittedly objective but somewhat abstract

---

[139] Quality Schemes Reg., Art 13(1)(a).

[140] *Comité Interprofessionnel du Vin de Champagne v. Aldi Süd Dienstleistungs GmbH*, Case C-393/16, EU:C:2017:991. Criteria included the quantity of the GI product being used as an ingredient and whether the GI was incorporated within an essential characteristic of the product (here, the taste of the sorbet), as opposed to being prominently advertised despite being incidental to the product.

[141] The Court of Justice has considered the notion of 'comparable products' under comparable infringement provisions in the spirits Regulation No. 110/2008, Art. 16. A Finnish company sought to register two figurative marks containing a reference to 'Konjakit [Cognacs]' for spirit drinks. Spirit drinks was found to be a class comparable to Cognac: 'regardless of their various categories, ['spirit drinks'] have common objective characteristics and which are consumed, from the point of view of the relevant public, on occasions which are largely identical. Furthermore, they are frequently distributed through the same channels and subject to similar marketing rules'; *Bureau national interprofessionnel du Cognac v. Gust. Ranin Oy*, Joined Cases C-4 and 27/10 [2011] *ECR* I–6131, [54].   [142] Quality Schemes Reg., Art. 13(1)(b).

[143] *Consorzio Gorgonzola v. Hofmeister*, Case C-87/97 [1999] *ECR* I–1301, [25] (AG La Pergola).

[144] Ibid., [26].

[145] Ibid., [27]. In a similar vein, it was held that 'parmesan' would appear in principle to constitute an evocation of the PDO 'Parmigiano Reggiano': *Commission v. Germany*, Case C-132/05 [2008] *ECR* I-957 (Opinion of AG Mazák), [40].

and technical methodology of the evocation test, in a dispute between the producers of Calvados, protected as a spirit PGI for French apple brandy and Verlados, which was used for a Finnish cider spirit. While the familiar 'average consumer' standard would be applied when ascertaining whether there was evocation—and this hypothetical pan-European consumer continued to be reasonably observant and circumspect—the actual reaction of Finnish consumers and the conclusion that they would not be confused by the use of Verlados were not relevant. The phonetic and visual similarities between the two terms, coupled with the close similarity of goods, supported an objective finding of evocation.[146]

However the outer limits to evocation were identified in an appeal from the EUIPO, where the registration for 'Port Charlotte' whisky as a trade mark was opposed by the rights holders for the PDO Port. Interestingly, the Advocate-General (who found evocation to be established) and the Court of Justice parted ways on the issue of evocation.[147] The Court agreed with the lower tribunals reasoning: 'the sign PORT CHARLOTTE, read as a whole as a logical and conceptual unit, will be understood by the relevant public as designating a harbour named after a person called Charlotte, with no direct link being made with the designation of origin "[P]orto" or "[P]ort" or a port wine'.[148] The use of the trade mark would not evoke Port wine, since it had other connotations and referents, while the underlying products (whisky and fortified wine) were distinct enough to inhibit any mental association.

Article 13(1)(c), which focuses on the product to which the name attaches, provides that registered names are protected against:

> … any other false or misleading indication of the provenance, origin, nature or essential qualities of the product that is used on the inner or outer packaging, advertising material or documents relating to the product concerned, and the packaging of the product in a container liable to convey a false impression as to its origin.[149]

Finally, registered names are also protected against 'any other practice liable to mislead the consumer as to the true origin of the product'.[150]

In terms of classifying the categories of infringing uses identified in Article 13, the Court of Justice has indicated that the provisions 'refer to various situations in which the marketing of a product is accompanied by an explicit or implicit reference to a geographic indication in circumstances liable to mislead the public as to the origin of the product or, at the very least, to set in train in the mind of the public an association of ideas regarding that origin, or to enable the trader to take unfair advantage of the reputation of the geographical indication concerned'.[151] While misleading use and unfair advantage (or misappropriation) are familiar categories, the 'destination' of the forbidden train of association—identified as the third category—is less certain. If not a misleading or misappropriating use, one is left wondering why other associations may be prohibited (tarnishment or causing negative associations affecting the reputation of the product seems to be the only other possibility).

---

[146] *Viiniverla Oy v. Sosiaali-ja terveysalan lupa-ja valvontavirasto*, Case C-75/15, EU:C:2016:35 (Calvados PGI).

[147] *EUIPO v. Instituto dos Vinhos do Douro e do Porto, IP*, Case C-56/16P, EU:C:2017:394 (AG Campos Sánchez-Bordona); EU:C:2017:693 (ECJ).

[148] Ibid. (ECJ), [111]. The General Court's factual assessment on this point would therefore remain undisturbed.

[149] Quality Schemes Reg., Art. 13(1)(c).   [150] Quality Schemes Reg., Art. 13(1)(d).

[151] *Bureau national interprofessionnel du Cognac v. Gust. Ranin Oy*, Joined Cases C-4 and 27/10 [2011] *ECR* I-6131, [46] (considering the equivalent provisions in the Spirits Regulation).

As we saw earlier, it is possible to register a name where it includes terms that are deemed to be generic. However, as Article 41(1) says, the Regulation does not affect how generic terms are used. This principal is embodied in Article 13(1), which provides that use of a name of a product that is deemed to be generic does not fall within the scope of protection.

Secondary uses of agricultural products

One issue that has attracted a lot of attention is whether registration confers protection over what might be called 'secondary uses' of an agricultural product. While it might be acceptable for a specification to stipulate that a name can only be used if the product was grown and processed in the nominated geographic area, the question arises: is it also acceptable for the specification to stipulate that secondary activities—such as grating, slicing, bottling, or packaging of products—must also be carried out in the region? Is it acceptable, for example, for a specification to state that the name 'Parma ham' can only be used in relation to sliced ham, the slicing of which takes place in the nominated geographic area? What about the slicing of ham in a delicatessen, a restaurant, or at home in another location? Put differently, at what point in the food chain are the rights in a name exhausted?

The question of whether protection should extend to secondary uses was considered by the Court of Justice in the *Parma Ham*[152] and the *Ravil*[153] decisions. In both cases, the Court's starting point was to note that secondary activities carried out in relation to agricultural products have the potential to harm the quality and thus the reputation of the designation of origin.[154] That is, the Court accepted that the grating of cheese, and the slicing and packaging of ham, had the potential to impact upon the quality of the final product. The Court also added that if controls were not exercised over the way the particular activity was carried out, consumers would have no guarantee of the quality of the product other than the word of the retailer. It might also undermine the reputation of the protected name. Given this, the Court of Justice held that the requirement that secondary activities be carried out in the region was justifiable, so long as they were required to protect or preserve the quality of the agricultural product or foodstuff. In both cases, the Court found the requirement that the secondary activity (the slicing of the ham and the grating of the cheese) be carried out in the nominated geographic area to be necessary to ensure the quality of the products in question.

One situation in which quality is at issue is where the transportation of a product outside of a region creates risks to the quality and thus the reputation of the product. Where wine is transported in bulk, which is required if the wine is to be bottled outside the region, this increases the risk of oxidization.[155] The quality of the wine might also be affected by variations in temperature that arise during transportation. Similar problems might arise where delays between the picking and processing of a fruit undermine the quality of the end product (as with olive oil).[156]

---

[152] *Consorzio del Prosciutto di Parma v. Asda*, Case C-108/01 [2003] *ECR* I–5121.

[153] *Ravil*, Case C-469/00 [2003] *ECR* I–5053.

[154] Advocate-General Alber was not willing to extend the scope of protection to secondary factors such as packaging and grating, focusing instead on the 'uniqueness' of the product in relation to the environment in which it was produced.

[155] See *Belgium v. Spain*, Case C-388/95 [2000] *ECR* I–3123 (rebottling of Rioja wine).

[156] A more difficult situation arises, however, where it is technically feasible for the secondary activities to be carried on outside the nominated geographical area. The Court of Justice has consistently said that controls undertaken outside the geographical area provide fewer guarantees as to the quality and authenticity than those carried on within the nominated geographic area. They have also said that it was not reasonable to expect producers to have to monitor and supervise the way in which their products were prepared throughout the EU.

Any remaining doubts there might have been about whether registration covers secondary activities was resolved when the legislation was amended to state that producer groups were able to indicate in their specifications that packaging shall take place solely in the defined geographical area. This change is now reflected in Article 7(1)(e) of the 2012 Quality Schemes Regulation, which requires applicants to justify why the packaging needs to take place in the geographical area to safeguard quality.[157]

2.6 MONITORING AND ENFORCEMENT

One of the complaints that is made about the scheme to protect geographical indications and designations of origin is that the monitoring and enforcement of protected names is onerous and ineffectual. One of the goals of the Quality Schemes Regulation was to remedy these problems. To this end, Title V of the Regulation sets out what member states are required to do in order to monitor products and foodstuffs that are registered. This includes designating the competent authority (or authorities) that is (are) required to verify that named products comply with the corresponding specification and to monitor the use of registered names.[158] In the United Kingdom, the task of enforcement was delegated to the local Trading Standards Services under Article 10(1) of the 2006 GI Regulation,[159] and presumably also under Article 36 of the 2012 Quality Schemes Regulation. If an inspection body finds that a producer is not complying with the registered specification, it is obliged to ensure that the GI Regulation is complied with.[160] Member states are also required to take 'all necessary measures' in the event of a breach.[161] A recent review concludes that despite the overall harmonized framework, a wide diversity of implementing mechanisms exists. Since EU legislation stops short of the 'last mile', the methods of enforcement vary and data is limited on the extent to which judicial enforcement options exist across EU member states.[162]

2.7 AMENDMENT AND CANCELLATION

In certain situations, the European Commission is able to amend or cancel a registration. The Commission is given a general power to amend a specification to take account of matters such as scientific and technical developments, or to redefine a geographic

---

[157] 'Packaging' refers to the operations needed to prepare the product for sale, such as bottling or canning: *Opinion of the Economic and Social Committee on the Proposal for a Council Regulation Amending Regulation 2081/92* (17 July 2002) COM(2002) 139 final, [2.6]. See also GI Reg. 1992, Art. 4(2)(e). The later part of the Article dealing with packaging was introduced by Regulation (EC) No. 692/2003 of 8 April 2003 amending Regulation (EEC) No. 2081/92 on the protection of geographical indications and designations of origin for agricultural products and foodstuffs [2003] *OJ L* 99/1, Art. 1(2). In the *Parma Ham* decision, the House of Lords accepted that protection would not extend to the slicing of ham in restaurants and delicatessens, because this was not something that a specification ought to be able to control: see *Consorzio Parma v. Asda* [2002] FSR 3 (HL), [85] (Lord Scott of Foscote). [158] Quality Schemes Reg., Arts 36–40.

[159] *Consorzio del Prosciutto di Parma v. Asda* [1998] FSR 697, 709.

[160] Quality Schemes Reg., Art. 36(1); *Consorzio del Prosciutto di Parma v. Asda* [1998] FSR 697. An action for infringement might be brought under legislation such as of the Food Safety Act 1990, ss 14 and 15, the Food Labelling Regulations 1999 (SI 1996/1499), or the Consumer Protection from Unfair Trading Regulations 2008 (SI 2008/1277), regs 5(5)(p), 5(4)(b), 5(2)(a), 3(4)(a), 3(1). See *Consorzio del Prosciutto di Parma v. Asda* [1998] FSR 697, 709.

[161] Quality Schemes Reg., Art. 38. Article 13(3) requires member states to take appropriate administrative and judicial steps to prevent or stop the unlawful use of PDOs and PGOs.

[162] EUIPO, *Protection and Control of Geographical Indications for Agricultural Products in the EU Member States* (December 2017).

area.[163] The Commission is also given power to cancel a registration where 'compliance with the conditions of the specifications is not ensured' or where no product under the PDO or PGI has been placed on the market for at least seven years.[164]

2.8 REMEDIES

While other member states have implemented legislation setting out the penalties and remedies where a registered name is infringed, to date no such legislation has been introduced in the United Kingdom. In the absence of specific provisions, applicants need to rely on common law or equitable remedies.[165] This might include an injunction, an action for breach of statutory duty, or some equivalent order. An interesting development relates to the possibility of cross-border injunctions to enforce and protect names registered under the Regulation. In one decision, an Italian court (the Court of Bolzano) granted injunctive relief against defendants residing outside Italy (but within the European Union). This was done on the basis that the (then applicable) GI Regulation was directly and immediately applicable in all member states. The Court also said that because infringing acts would be sanctioned equally by courts in the defendant's country, this gives rise to rights directly enforceable against any EU citizen.[166]

2.9 RELATION WITH OTHER REGIMES

Member states are able to maintain national protection of communicated names until such time as a decision on registration has been taken.[167] Once a name has been registered at the EU level, national rules cease to apply.[168] In some situations, the Commission may allow an existing (unregistered) name to coexist with an identical registered name for a period not exceeding 15 years. For this to occur, it must be shown that the identical unregistered name has been used consistently and fairly for at least 25 years prior to the application for registration, that the unregistered name has never been used to profit from the reputation of the registered name, and that consumers have not been, nor could have been, misled as to the true origin of the product.[169] It is also necessary to show that the problems resulting from the use of the identical names were raised before the name was registered. The ongoing use of an identical unregistered name will be allowed only where the country of origin clearly and visibly appears on the labelling.[170] The Quality Schemes Regulation does not preclude member states from entering into

---

[163] Quality Schemes Reg., Art. 53.   [164] Quality Schemes Reg., Art. 53.

[165] Lord Hoffmann said that enforcement depends on the fact that of the GI Reg. 1992, Art. 8 [now Quality Schemes Reg., Art. 13(3)], lays down a clear rule and upon a general principle that the courts of the member states are obliged to provide remedies to enforce EU rights: *Consorzio Parma v. Asda* [2002] *FSR* 3 (HL), [25].

[166] *Consorzio per promozione dello Speck dell'Alto Adige* (28 April 1998) (unreported). See Societa Italiana Brevetti, 'Geographical Indications of Origin: Cross-Border Injunctions May Come in Handy' [2000] *EIPR* N 31.

[167] *Commission of the EC v. French Republic*, Case C-6/02 [2003] *ECR* I–2389.

[168] *Consorzio per la Tutela del Formaggio Gorgonzola v. Kaserei Champignon Hofmeister*, Case C-87/97 [1999] *ECR* I–1301. See also *Consorzio Parma v. Asda* [2002] *FSR* 3 (HL), [22]–[23] (Lord Hoffmann). *Assica v. Associazione fra produttori per la tutela del 'Salame Felino'*, Case C-35/13, EU:C:2014:306 [28]–[34]; pre-emption was affirmed in *Fage v. Chobani* [2014] *EWCA Civ* 5 [80]–[88] (however 'Greek yoghurt' did not qualify for protection under the Quality Schemes Reg., so the tort of passing off remained viable as an enforcement option in the United Kingdom).

[169] Quality Schemes Reg., Art. 15(1), (2).   [170] Quality Schemes Reg., Art. 15, Art. 15(3).

bilateral agreements with non-member countries,[171] or from protecting 'simple' or 'qualified' geographical indications of source under national laws.[172] The extent to which the unitary rights system for GIs has exhaustively harmonized protection at the EU level and consequently pre-empts any other forms of protection does not seem to have been fully thought through. For instance, one is left wondering whether (national or EUTM) trade mark registrations for designations also registered as EU GIs by the same rights holders are now invalid or unenforceable.[173]

A name cannot be registered as a PDO or a PGI if, in good faith, a similar trade mark already exists, has been applied for, or is established by use that, because of its reputation and renown or the length of time for which it has been used, might lead to confusion as to the true identity of the product.[174] Conversely, a name that has been registered as a PDO or a PGI under the Quality Schemes Regulation cannot subsequently be registered as a trade mark, so long as the product to which the name attaches is the same. It is also necessary to show that if the name were registered as a trade mark, it would fall within the scope of the protection offered to the PDO or PGI.[175]

3 TRADITIONAL SPECIALITIES GUARANTEED

The third type of designation recognized under the Quality Schemes Regulation is the so-called 'traditional specialities guaranteed' (TSG).[176] The aim of the TSG scheme is to safeguard traditional methods of production and recipes.[177] Unlike in the case of protected designations of origin and protected geographical indications, there is no need to establish a link between the named product and the nominated geographical area to qualify for protection as a certificate of specific character; instead, registration depends on a product having traditional features or characteristics. To date, the scheme has not proved to be very popular.[178] As the Quality Schemes Regulation notes, with 'only few names

---

[171] *Budejovicky Budvar v. Rudolf Ammersin*, Case C 216/01 [2005] *CMLR* 56 (ECJ).

[172] Where there is no link between provenance and quality or reputation: *Schutzverband gegen Unwesen in der Wirtschaft v. Warsteiner Brauerei Haus Cramer*, Case C-312/98 [2000] *ECR* I-9187, [10] [17]; *Schutzverband gegen Unwesen in der Wirtschaft v. Warsteiner Brauerei Haus Cramer*, Case C-312/98 [2000] *ECR* I-9187, [AG35] (AG Jacobs); *Jacques Pistre*, Cases C-321/94–C-324/94 [1977] *CMLR* 565.

[173] L. Bently and B. Sherman, 'The Impact of European Geographical Indications on National Rights in Member States' (2006) 96 *TMR* 850; N. Coppola, 'The CJEU Confirms the Exclusive Character of EU Competence in PDO/PGI Schemes' (2014) 9 *JIPLP* 718; C. Heath and D. Marie-Vivien, 'Geographical Indications and the Principles of Trade Mark Law—A Distinctly European Perspective' (2015) 46 *IIC* 819.

[174] TMA 1994, s. 3(1)(c), says that trade marks that consist exclusively of signs or designations that serve to indicate geographical origin should not be registered. See Chapter 37, section 3.3.10, pp. 1001–2.

[175] Quality Schemes Reg., Art. 14. The date at which conflict is judged is the date of submission of the application for registration (instead of the date of notice conferring the right as was initially the case: GI Reg. 2006, Art. 14(2)). On relationship with domain names, see WIPO Standing Committee on the Law of Trademarks, Industrial Designs and Geographical Indications, *Study Concerning the Use of Trademarks on the Internet* (April 1999) SCT/2(2)/9, [115]; M. Hopperger, 'International Protection of Geographical Indications: The Present Situation and Prospects for Future Developments' [1999] *WIPO Symposium: South Africa* 5, 17.

[176] This repealed and replaced Regulation (EC) No. 509/2006 of 20 March 2006 on agricultural products and foodstuffs as traditional specialities guaranteed [2006] *OJ L* 93/1 (the 'Traditional Specialties Reg. 2006'). In turn, the 2006 Regulation had replaced the earlier Traditional Specialties Reg. 1992, which came into force on 24 July 1993.   [177] Quality Schemes Reg., Art. 17.

[178] A. Tosato, 'The Protection of Traditional Foods in the EU: Traditional Specialities Guaranteed' (2013) 19(4) *European Law Journal* 545.

registered, the current scheme for traditional specialities guaranteed has failed to meet its potential'.[179] 'Traditional Farmfresh Turkey' and 'Traditionally Farmed Gloucestershire Old Spots Pork' are amongst the better known TSGs from the United Kingdom. Other products that have been protected as TSG include Mozzarella (cheese) and Jamon Serrano (meat). Names that are registered as certificates of special character are able to use the designation 'Traditional Speciality Guaranteed' (TSG) and the accompanying logo (see Fig. 43.1).

3.1 REGISTRATION

For a name to be protected as TSG, it must be registered. As with PGIs and PDOs, it is only possible for a group to apply to register a name as a TSG[180] (although, as was noted earlier, in certain situations, a single person may be treated as a group). As part of this process, the group must submit a product specification that contains: the name of the product; a description of the product showing the product's specific character (including its main physical, chemical, microbiological, or organoleptic characteristics); a description of the production method that producers must follow, including, where appropriate, the nature and characteristics of the raw material or ingredients used and the methods by which the product is prepared; and the key elements establishing the product's traditional character.[181] The application for registration is submitted to the competent authority in the member state.[182] After examination, the application is sent to the Commission who, in turn, sends a translation of the application to the other member states. The Commission also publishes the main points of the application in the Official Journal.[183] Third parties have three months from the date of publication in which to object to the proposed registration. If no one objects to the proposed registration, the name is entered into the Database of Origin Register (DOOR).[184] Once registered, a TSG can be amended or cancelled.[185] Where an objection is made, the Commission will invite the applicant and the party who opposed the application to engage in 'appropriate consultations' for no more than three months, following which, if no agreement is reached, the Commission will decide on the fate of the application. Provisions in the 2006 Traditional Foods Regulation that were designed to safeguard the established rights of third parties who are shown to be economically disadvantaged do not reappear in the 2012 Quality Scheme Regulation.[186]

3.2 CRITERIA FOR PROTECTION

The products or foodstuffs that are able to receive TSG protection are limited to: prepared meals; beer; chocolate and derived products; bread, pastry, cakes, confectionary, biscuits, and other baker wares; beverages made from plant extracts; pasta; and salt.[187] According to Article 18(1) of the Quality Schemes Regulation, to qualify for TSG registration, a name must describe a specific product or foodstuff that '(a) results from a mode of production, processing or composition corresponding to a traditional practice for that product or foodstuff; or (b) is produced from raw materials that are those traditionally

---

[179] Quality Schemes Reg., Recital 34.   [180] Quality Schemes Reg., Art. 49.
[181] Quality Schemes Reg., Art. 19(a)–(d).
[182] In the United Kingdom, this is the same as for PGIs and PDOs. See section 2.1, pp. 1194–8.
[183] Quality Schemes Reg., Art. 50.   [184] Quality Schemes Reg., Art. 22(1).
[185] Quality Schemes Reg., Arts 53, 54.
[186] See Traditional Specialties Reg. 2006, Art. 13(2) (repealed in 2013).
[187] Quality Schemes Reg., Art. 2(1).

used'.[188] It is also necessary for the name to have been 'traditionally used to refer to the specific product' or to 'identify the traditional character or specific character of the product'.[189] 'Traditional' is defined hereditarily as 'proven usage on the domestic market for period that allows transmission between generations' (which is deemed to require at least 30 years).[190] A name will not be registered if it only refers to claims of a general nature used for a set of products, or to claims provided by specific Union legislation.[191] To qualify for a certificate of special character, the product or foodstuff must comply with a product specification.[192] It is also necessary for inspection structures to be in place that ensure that products comply with the specification.[193]

3.3 SCOPE OF PROTECTION

Groups who comply with the product specification have the exclusive use of the name, the designation 'traditional speciality guaranteed' (TSG), and the accompanying logo. Registered names are protected against any misuse, imitation, or evocation, or against any other practice liable to mislead the consumer.[194]

4 OPTIONAL QUALITY TERMS

The fourth type of designation recognized in the Quality Schemes Regulation is the 'optional quality term'. The aim of the new scheme is to 'facilitate the communication within the internal market of the value adding characteristics of attributes of agricultural products'.[195] For a term to qualify as an optional quality term, it must relate either to a characteristic of one or more categories of products (but not a technical characteristic),[196] or to a farming or processing attribute that applies in specific areas. It is also necessary to show that use of the term adds value to the product as compared to products of a similar type and that the term has a 'European dimension' (whatever this may mean).[197] The Commission is empowered to reserve new terms and to amend the conditions of use of existing ones by delegated acts. An optional quality term may only be used to describe products that comply with the conditions of use that are attached to the term.[198]

'Mountain product' is the first optional quality term to be recognized by the Commission. As a result, in relation to the agricultural products listed in Annex 1 of the Quality Schemes Regulation, the term 'mountain product' can only be used to describe products in respect of which *both* the raw materials and the feedstuffs for farm animals come 'essentially' from mountain areas. In the case of processed products, the process must also take place in a mountain area.[199] A 'mountain area' is defined as an area

---

[188] Quality Schemes Reg., Art. 18(1).

[189] Quality Schemes Reg., Art. 18(2). 'Specific character' is defined in Art. 3(5) as 'the characteristic production attributes which distinguish a product in the Union'.

[190] Quality Schemes Reg., Art. 3(3).   [191] Quality Schemes Reg., Art. 18(4).

[192] Quality Schemes Reg., Art. 19(1).   [193] Quality Schemes Reg., Art. 37.

[194] Quality Schemes Reg., Art. 24.   [195] Quality Schemes Reg., Art. 27.

[196] Quality Schemes Reg., Art. 29(2).   [197] Quality Schemes Reg., Art. 29(1).

[198] Quality Schemes Reg., Art. 33(1).

[199] Quality Schemes Reg., Art. 31(1). See European Commission, *Report from the Commission to the European Parliament and the Council on the Case for an Optional Quality Term 'Product of Island Farming'* (December 2013) COM(2013) 888 final (setting out arguments for and against the adoption of the new term).

characterized by a considerable limitation of the possibilities for using the land and an appreciable increase in the cost of working it owing:

(i) to the existence, because of altitude, of very difficult climatic conditions, the effect of which is to shorten the growing season substantially;

(ii) at a lower altitude, to the presence over the greater part of the area in question of slopes too steep for the use of machinery or requiring the use of very expensive special equipment; or

(iii) to a combination of these two factors, where the handicap resulting from each taken separately is less acute, but the combination of the two gives rise to an equivalent handicap.[200]

While it is too early to determine whether this scheme will have any notable impact, it has added weight to the debate about the status of geographical indications as a form of intellectual property.[201]

---

[200] Quality Schemes Reg., Art. 31(2), referring to Regulation (EC) No. 1257/1999 of 17 May 1999 on support for rural development from the European Agricultural Guidance and Guarantee Fund (EAGGF) and amending and repealing certain Regulations [1999] *OJ L* 160/80 (26 June 1999), Art. 18(1).

[201] G. Evans, 'The Simplification of European Legislation for the Protection of Geographical Indications: The Proposed Regulation on Agricultural Product Quality Schemes' (2012) 34 *EIPR* 770, 772–3.

PART V

CONFIDENTIAL
INFORMATION

1 INTRODUCTION

Up until now, the law has refused to recognize a property right in ideas or information.[1] Nevertheless, people who generate ideas or have in their control previously undisclosed information will have the ability to prevent others from using or disclosing those ideas or that information if they can demonstrate that the latter are bound by an obligation. The law of breach of confidence determines when such obligations exist.[2] Because the action is largely concerned with the imposition of obligations, as long as the idea or information is (and remains) secret, there are few restrictions placed on the type of subject matter that can be protected. Accordingly, the action for breach of confidence is broad-ranging and has been used in relation to personal, commercial, and technical information, as well as trade secrets, know-how, and information about the government. What Keene LJ said remains true, 'breach of confidence is a developing area of the law, the boundaries of which are not immutable but may change to reflect changes in society, technology and business practice'.[3]

Because the action is so broad-ranging, it performs a number of different roles and protects a variety of interests.[4] Insofar as the action provides a space in which ideas can be tested and developed without fear of appropriation, it enables organizations to invest in and carry out research (and thus operates as an important supplement to the statutory intellectual property regimes).[5] In some cases, confidentiality encourages information to

---

[1] But cf. *Veolia ES Nottinghamshire Ltd and Nottinghamshire County Council v. Dowen* [2010] *EWCA Civ* 1214 (a decision that has already prompted criticism: see T. Aplin, 'Confidential information as property?' (2013) *King's LJ* 172); *Force India Formula One Team v. 1 Malaysian Racing Team* [2012] *RPC* (29) 757, [376].

[2] See Gurry (2012).　　[3] *Douglas v. Hello!* [2001] *QB* 967, 1011 (CA), [165].

[4] See D. Almeling, 'Seven Reasons Why Trade Secrets Are Increasingly Important' (2012) 27 *Berkeley Technology Law Journal* 1091.

[5] The action presents the possibility of a person gaining some limited protection as regards intellectual creations that, for some reason, are not covered by statutory regimes, e.g. business ideas: *Wheatley v. Bell* [1984] *FSR* 16. For empirical evidence of a growing use of secrecy as a means of protecting inventions, see the sources cited in Gurry (2012), 5–7, [1.09]–[1.15]. For an overview of the justifications for protecting trade secrets, see Gurry (2012), ch. 3. For a sceptical view, see R. Bone, 'A New Look at Trade Secret Law: Doctrine in Search of a Justification' (1998) 86 *Cal L Rev* 241.

be disclosed to a small circle of confidants. More often, however, the action operates to restrict disclosure[6] in order to protect individual autonomy, personality, and privacy.[7] By encouraging respect for agreements, it also promotes fair competition.[8] As such, breach of confidence has done some of the work that unfair competition law does in other legal systems.[9] Breach of confidence also performs many of the tasks performed by a general right of privacy; although it is now largely being superseded by the tort of misuse of private information.

The origins of the breach of confidence action are obscure.[10] Recent work has highlighted two possible genealogies. The first traces the action to a series of eighteenth-century decisions dealing with common law property rights (copyright) in unpublished works,[11] where rights over undisclosed information were first recognized.[12] A second history, espoused by Megarry J in *Coco v. Clark*,[13] traces the action back to the sixteenth century, when, in speaking about the general jurisdiction of the Court of Chancery (or conscience), Sir Thomas More said that 'three things are to be helped in conscience; Fraud, Accident and things of confidence'. Although the claim seems dubious as a matter of history, a number of modern commentators have adopted the corresponding view that the action for breach of confidence is an application of a broader notion of good faith.[14] While the origins of the action may be obscure, it is clear that, by the mid-nineteenth century, the courts had developed a series of principles that were relied upon to protect what we now call 'confidential information'. For example, in the 1849 decision in *Prince Albert v. Strange*,[15] Lord Cottenham LC ordered that publication of a catalogue describing Prince Albert's etchings be restrained, noting that 'this case by no means depends solely upon the question of property, for a breach of trust, confidence, or contract would itself entitle the plaintiff to an injunction'.

1.1 INTERNATIONAL INFLUENCES

Until recently,[16] it was not clear whether international treaties required protection of confidential information and trade secrets.[17] This situation changed, however, as a result of the fact that the 1994 Agreement on Trade-related Aspects of Intellectual Property Rights (TRIPS) requires members to afford protection to those who lawfully control 'undisclosed information'.[18] More specifically, Article 39 of TRIPS states that, in the course of

---

[6] E. Hettinger, 'Justifications for Intellectual Property' (1989) 19 *Philos Public Aff* 31.

[7] L. Paine, 'Trade Secrets and the Justifications of Intellectual Property: A Comment on Hettinger' (1991) 20 *Philos Public Aff* 247.   [8] *Interfirm Comparison v. Law Society of NSW* [1977] *RPC* 137.

[9] See J. Reichman, 'Legal Hybrids between Patent and Copyright Paradigms' (1994) 94 *Colum L Rev* 2432.

[10] See Gurry (2012), ch. 2; M. Richardson, M. Bryan, M. Vranken, and K. Barnett, *Breach of Confidence: Social Origins and Modern Developments* (2011); see also M. Richardson, *The Right to Privacy: Origins and Influences of a Nineteenth Century Idea* (2017).

[11] G. Hammond, 'The Origins of the Equitable Duty of Confidence' (1979) 8 *AALR* 71; S. Ricketson, 'Confidential Information: A New Proprietary Interest?' (1977–78) 11 *Melb U L Rev* 223, 233–5.

[12] But this was limited to unpublished ideas that were in recorded form, either in manuscript or otherwise: *Abernethy v. Hutchinson* (1824) 1 *H & Tw* 28; 47 *ER* 1313.

[13] [1969] *RPC* 41; *Fraser v. Evans* [1969] *QB* 349.   [14] *Seager v. Copydex (No. 1)* [1967] 2 *All ER* 415.

[15] (1849) 2 *De G & Sm* 652; 64 *ER* 293 (Knight Bruce LJ); (1849) 1 *Mac & G* 25; 41 *ER* 1171. See further L. Bently, '*Prince Albert v. Strange*', in C. Mitchell and P. Mitchell (eds), *Landmark Cases in Equity* (2012), ch. 8.

[16] See Gurry (2012), ch. 22.

[17] There were divergent views between countries whether Article 10bis of the Paris Convention required contracting parties to protect trade secrets.

[18] See R. Krasser, 'The Protection of Trade Secrets in the TRIPS Agreement', in Beier and Shricker, 216–25; S. Sandeen, 'The limits of trade secret law: Article 39 of the TRIPS Agreement and the Uniform Trade Secrets Act on which it is based', in R. Dreyfuss and K. Strandburg (eds), *The Law and Theory of Trade Secrecy: A Handbook of Contemporary Research* (2011), ch 20.

providing protection against unfair competition (as required by Article 10*bis* of the Paris Convention), members shall provide natural and legal persons with the possibility of preventing information lawfully within their control from being disclosed to, acquired by, or used by others without their consent in a manner contrary to honest commercial practice. Article 39 requires information to be protected if it is secret, has commercial value because it is secret, and has been subject to reasonable steps to keep it secret. There is now a clear relationship between TRIPS and the protection of trade secrets in the European Union as the definition of a trade secret in the Trade Secrets Directive[19] comes directly from Article 39(2).

1.2 DOCTRINAL BASIS OF THE ACTION

One issue that has preoccupied commentators over the last few decades is the doctrinal basis for the action. In particular, commentators have discussed whether breach of confidence has its roots in contract, tort, property, or equity.[20] While these debates may appear to be sterile, the decision as to the appropriate doctrinal basis of the action may have important consequences when it comes to matters such as conflicts of laws[21] and limitation periods. It has also been said that the failure to identify a single doctrinal or conceptual basis for the action is the reason why so many aspects of the action are unclear. In particular, the conceptual uncertainty is said to be the reason why there is confusion about the liability of third-party recipients (and accessories),[22] strangers, bona fide purchasers of information, and the remedies that are available to a confider.[23]

Instead of attempting to locate an assumed, but ever-elusive, doctrinal basis for breach of confidence, a preferable option is to treat breach of confidence as a separate cause of action in its own right.[24] This approach, which has found support in Canadian courts,[25] would mean that the action was not dependent upon a particular jurisdictional basis. The advantage of seeing breach of confidence as a *sui generis* action is that the courts would not be hidebound by particular conventions or models. As such, they could tailor rules to the circumstances as and when they present themselves. There is some evidence that courts are adopting precisely such an approach in relation to remedial responses and accessorial liability.

It may also be more fruitful to consider whether the existing law could be reorganized so as to make it more comprehensible, predictable, or just. One possibility would be to divide breach of confidence into several related actions. In so doing, the courts could better attune the rules to the interests involved and thereby provide greater clarity and certainty. Such an approach would recognize that different rules apply to different types

---

[19] Directive 2016/943 on the protection of undisclosed know-how and business information (trade secrets), Art. 2(1).

[20] Gurry (2012), ch. 4. The Supreme Court, in its most recent intervention in relation to trade secrets, seemed to favour equity: *Vestergaard Frandsens A/s v. Bestnet Europe Ltd* [2013] 1 *WLR* 1556, [22].

[21] See Chapter 45, section 10.2, pp. 1305–6. See also Gurry (2012), ch. 23; C. Wadlow, 'Bugs, Spies and Paparazzi: Jurisdiction over Actions for Breach of Confidence in Private International Law' [2008] *EIPR* 269.

[22] See *Vestergaard Frandsens A/s v. Bestnet Europe Ltd* [2013] 1 WLR 1556, discussed in Chapter 46, section 3, pp. 1225–31 (seeming to meld equitable principles drawn from 'knowing assistance' liability with other notions from joint tortfeasance).

[23] G. Jones, 'Restitution of Benefits Obtained in Breach of Another's Confidence' (1970) 86 *LQR* 463, 463; A. Weinrib, 'Information as Property' (1988) 28 *UTLJ* 117, 136.   [24] Gurry (2012), ch. 4.

[25] *LAC Minerals v. International Corona Presource* [1990] *FSR* 441 (SCC), 495 (Sopinka J); *Cadbury Schweppes v. FBI Foods* [2000] *FSR* 491 (SCC), 504–6.

of information—notably, personal,[26] commercial,[27] or government information. This could take place along lines similar to the changes that took place in the United States during the last century.[28] Indeed, this process that seems to have begun as a tort of misuse of private information is now the more appropriate cause of action in relation to protecting the confidentiality of personal information.

1.3 BREACH OF CONFIDENCE AND PRIVATE INFORMATION

While breach of confidence has performed many, but not all,[29] of the tasks that might otherwise be performed by a tort of privacy,[30] there have long been calls for the introduction of such a tort into British law.[31] The prospects of British law recognizing a general tort of privacy under the common law, at least one developed by the courts, received a serious setback in the House of Lords' decision in *Wainwright v. Home Office*,[32] in which, after speaking critically about a general right to privacy, Lord Hoffmann rejected 'the invitation to declare that since at the latest 1950 there has been a previously unknown tort of invasion of privacy'. As such, the question of whether there was a high-level principle of invasion of privacy 'would have to wait another day'.[33] Lord Hoffmann's comments in *Wainwright* were confirmed by the House of Lords in *Campbell v. MGN*.[34] While the Lords may not have agreed on how the law was to be applied, they were in agreement that there was 'no over-arching, all-embracing cause of action for "invasion of privacy"'.[35]

While there are still some areas of private life that the British courts are not willing to protect, it is clear that, since the turn of the millennium, there has been a remarkable change in the law protecting private information. This is largely as a result of developments following the coming into force of the Human Rights Act 1998, when the courts began to give effect to the requirement, contained in Article 8 of the European Convention on Human Rights (ECHR), that persons be afforded the 'right to respect for his private and family life, his home and his correspondence'.

There was a sustained period where developments relating to the protection of private information was shoe-horned into breach of confidence. Trying to protect private information under the law of confidence, according to Buxton LJ, created a 'feeling of discomfort'[36] amongst lawyers. In part, this is because the use of the label 'breach of confidence' is misleading. The reason for this is that the confidence label 'harks back to a time when the cause of action was based on improper use of information disclosed by one person to another in confidence';[37] now, however, the action applies where there is no 'disclosure' of confidential information or any relationship of trust or reliance. Another reason for the

---

[26] R. Wacks, *Personal Information* (1989), 131–2.

[27] J. Stedman, 'Trade Secrets' (1962) 23 *Ohio St LJ* 4, 26; R. Dreyfuss and K. Strandburg (eds), *The Law and Theory of Trade Secrecy: A Handbook of Contemporary Research* (2011).

[28] This followed from the famous article on privacy by S. Warren and L. Brandeis, 'The Right to Privacy' (1890) 4 *Harv L Rev* 193.

[29] *Peck v. UK* (2003) 36 *EHRR* (41) 719 (British law of confidence at that time did not provide adequate remedy where a party had been filmed using a CCTV camera); cf. *Earl Spencer v. UK* (1998) 25 *EHRR CD* 105 (law of confidence provided adequate remedy to restrain the publication of private information).

[30] See *Duchess of Argyll v. Duke of Argyll* [1967] 2 *Ch* 302; *Stephens v. Avery* [1988] *Ch* 499; cf. *Kaye v. Robertson* [1991] *FSR* 62.

[31] See generally G. Phillipson, 'Transforming Breach of Confidence? Towards a Common Law Right of Privacy under the Human Rights Act' [2003] *MLR* 726.

[32] [2003] *UKHL* 53, [2003] *All ER* 279, [35] (favouring specific legislative remedies rather than a general tort of privacy).   [33] Ibid., [30]. See also *McKennitt v. Ash* [2008] *QB* 73, [8].

[34] [2004] 2 *AC* 457.   [35] Ibid., 464, [11] (Lord Nicholls).   [36] *McKennitt v. Ash* [2008] *QB* 73, [8](iii).

[37] *Campbell v. MGN* [2004] 2 *AC* 457, [13]–[14] (Lord Nicholls).

discomfort is that information about an 'individual's private life would not, in ordinary usage, be called 'confidential'.

The issue of whether misuse of private information was a separate claim from breach of confidence was considered in *Google Inc v. Vidal-Hall*.[38] It was submitted to the Court of Appeal that the law of confidentiality had developed and adapted to protect against invasions of privacy.[39] The Court, however, rejected this argument, pointing out that misuse of private information protects different interests than confidence and, furthermore, that the courts had consistently emphasized that misuse was a developing area of law.[40] Accordingly, the court took the view there are now two separate and distinct causes of action: an action for breach of confidence and one for misuse of private information.[41] The existence of two causes of action appears to have subsequently been accepted by the Supreme Court in *PJS v. News Group Newspaper*[42] as Lord Mance, giving judgment for the majority included an entire section in his judgment to draw out distinctions between rights of confidence and rights of privacy in relation to the extent of disclosure that would defeat a claim.[43] Accordingly, it is now apparent that while breach of confidence can protect personal information, the more appropriate cause of action is misuse of private information. We therefore deal with these two causes of action separately.

1.4 DATA PROTECTION LEGISLATION

A discussion of the protection of personal confidential information cannot be seriously conducted without reference to data protection law,[44] which controls the way in which information about living identifiable persons is used. This became clear after *Campbell v. MGN*,[45] in which, as well as relying on the common law action for breach of confidence, Naomi Campbell also sought relief in relation to breaches of data protection law. While the action did not succeed in *Campbell*, it highlights an alternative cause of action that may be, and indeed has been, employed in other situations in which a person's image has been used without their permission.

From 25 May 2018, data protection has been governed[46] by the Data Protection Regulation[47] which contains seven[48] data protection principles. These state that data must be: processed fairly and lawfully; obtained and used for only specified and lawful purposes; adequate, relevant, and not excessive; accurate, and where necessary, kept up to date, kept for no longer than necessary; processed in accordance with individuals' rights (as defined); and kept secure.[49]

---

[38] [2015] FSR (25) 728.   [39] Ibid., [19]–[20].   [40] Ibid., [21].

[41] The two distinct torts approach was accepted without question by the Court of Appeal: *Representative Claimants v. MGN Ltd* [2016] FSR (13) 378, [88]; *PJS v. News Group Newspapers* [2016] EWCA Civ 393, [34]–[36].

[42] [2016] *AC 1081*.   [43] Ibid., [25]–[37].

[44] It is also recognized as a fundamental right under the Charter of Fundamental Rights of the European Union, Art. 8.

[45] [2003] 1 *All ER* 224, [72]–[138]. Also applied in *Douglas v. Hello! (No. 3)* [2003] 3 *All ER* 996, [230]–[239] (no defence to compensation). See generally M. Tugendhat, 'The Data Protection Act and the Media' [2000] *YC 8 ML* 135.

[46] Before that date, it is governed by the Data Protection Act 1998, which implemented Directive 95/46/EC on the protection of individuals with regard to the processing of personal data and on the free movement of such data.

[47] Regulation (EU) 2016/679 on the protection of natural persons with regard to the processing of personal data and on the free movement of such data, and repealing Directive 95/46/EC (General Data Protection Regulation).

[48] Under the Directive there were eight principles. The eighth related to the storage of data. This is now dealt with under Chapter V of the Regulation.

[49] See *Murray v. Express Newspapers* [2007] *EMLR* (22) 583, [69] *ff.*

2 ELEMENTS OF BREACH OF CONFIDENCE

According to the seminal case of *Coco v. Clark*,[50] in order to establish a claim for breach of confidence, the claimant must show that:

(i)   the information is capable of being protected;

(ii) the defendant owes the claimant an obligation to keep the information confidential; and

(iii) the defendant used the information in a way that breached that duty.

Once these three points have been proved, a defendant may raise a defence, the most significant being that the disclosure was justified in the public interest.

In the next three chapters, we will explore the elements of breach of confidence in more detail. Thus, in Chapter 44, we look at the type of information that is capable of being protected by the action. In Chapter 45, we look at the situations in which a duty of confidence arises between the parties. In Chapter 46, after looking at whether the duty of confidence has been breached, we examine the defences to breach. In Chapter 47, we consider the closely related tort of misuse of private information.

---

[50] [1969] *RPC* 41. It is important to note that there is a degree of fluidity in its application. For example, faced with similar facts, one court might justify its conclusion on the ground that the defendant is not under a duty, while another court would accept that the defendant was under a duty of confidentiality, but either limit the duty so as not to cover the defendant's conduct or provide a defence.

44

IS THE INFORMATION CAPABLE OF BEING PROTECTED?

1 INTRODUCTION

The first factor that must be shown in a breach of confidence action is that the information is capable of being protected. First, it is necessary to identify the information in issue. As O'Connor J said, 'it was essential that the claimant should make it absolutely clear and certain what it was that he alleged to be confidential [and] which he sought to protect'.[1] This is not an inquiry into the quality of the information per se, so much as it is a preliminary examination as to whether the information has been identified in such a way that the action can proceed. As such, it is akin to the question of what is a work in copyright law.

If a claimant does not identify the information in sufficient detail, their action may be struck out on the basis that it is speculative and an abuse of process.[2] Failure to identify the information may also lead the court to refuse to grant an injunction. For example, in *Suhner v. Transradio*,[3] the claimant gave the defendant 246 documents, saying that about 100 of the documents contained confidential designs and that part of the information in the other 146 documents was confidential. The court refused to grant an injunction primarily because 'it was very difficult to know precisely what information it is which the [claimants] say is confidential'.[4] Laddie J reiterated this position in the *Ocular Sciences* decision,[5] in which he said that the claimant should give full and proper particulars of all confidential information upon which they intend to rely. The reason for this is that unless the confidential information is properly identified, the injunction might be of uncertain

---

[1] *PA Thomas v. Mould* [1968] QB 913, 922. See also *Ocular Sciences v. Aspect Vision* [1997] RPC 289, 359–69; *CMI-Centers for Medical Innovation v. Phytopharm* [1999] FSR 235, 243; Gurry (2012), [5.73]–[5.77]. For consideration of whether there might be liability under professional disciplinary rules for disclosing a letter labelled 'private and confidential' even though it contained no confidential information, see *R v. The Chartered Institute of Management Accountants, ex parte May* [2013] EWHC 1574 (Admin) (no breach of the rules as formulated, nor at common law, without private or confidential information).

[2] *John Zinc v. Lloyds Bank* [1975] RPC 385; *Inline Logistics v. UCI Logistics* [2002] RPC 611, 620, [29]; *The Gadget Shop v. The Bug.Com* [2001] FSR 383, 405; *Devon and Cornwall Autistic Community Trust v. Pyrah and ors* [2012] EWPCC 46. [3] *Suhner v. Transradio* [1967] RPC 329.

[4] Ibid., 334. [5] *Ocular Sciences* [1997] RPC 289, 359.

scope and difficult to enforce. The absence of 'proper particulars of claim' could also compromise a defendant's ability to defend themselves. On this basis, Laddie J said that if the claimant fails to give proper particulars, it is open to the court to infer that the purpose of the litigation is harassment rather than the protection of the claimant's rights. On this basis, the action could be struck out as an abuse of process.[6]

With the exception of trivial or immoral information, no restrictions are placed on the *subject matter* that is protected by breach of confidence. As a result, the action has been used to protect a variety of subject matter: the idea for a new type of 'carpet grip';[7] the designs of Formula One cars,[8] a concept for a new television programme;[9] the genetic structure of a nectarine tree;[10] medical lectures;[11] marital secrets;[12] the cultural and religious secrets of an Aboriginal community;[13] and a report by the Department of Education on employment conditions.[14]

Information is protected irrespective of the *format* in which it appears. Thus the action applies equally to information when embodied in writing,[15] drawings,[16] photographs,[17] goods or products, or where it has been disclosed orally.[18] It is also clear that the information does not need to be fixed or in a permanent form. As such, the information may be written, oral, encrypted, embodied in physical objects (whether it be the genetic code of a tree or the design of a product), or take shape as a formula, a plan, or a sketch.

While there are very few restrictions placed on the subject matter that is capable of being protected and the format that the information needs to take, there are four limitations placed on the *type* of information that may be protected under the action. These are where the information is trivial, immoral, vague, or in the public domain. We will deal with each in turn.

2 TRIVIAL INFORMATION

The first limit placed on the type of information that is protected by breach of confidence is that the courts may not protect information that is trivial.[19] In *Coco v. Clark*,[20]

---

[6] Ibid. In some cases precision can cover what may seem quite a wide range of information, such as *all* photographic images of a wedding: *Douglas v. Hello!* [2008] 1 *AC* 1. Provided the defendant knows it is of the particular wedding the scope of any injunction or cause of action is clear.

[7] *Seager v. Copydex (No. 1)* [1967] 2 *All ER* 415.

[8] *Force India Formula One Team v. 1 Malaysia Racing Team* [2012] *EWHC* 616 (Ch), [2013] *EWCA Civ* 780.

[9] *Fraser v. Thames TV* [1983] 2 *All ER* 101; *Wade v. British Sky Broadcasting* [2016] *EWCA Civ* 1214.

[10] *Franklin v. Giddins* [1978] *Qd R* 72 (this involves taking a cutting from an orchard; today had the fruit sold from the tree had its genes sequenced—reversed engineered—it may have led to a different result; but not necessarily, as even with sequencing it may not be possible to reproduce the tree without the cutting).

[11] *Abernethy v. Hutchison* (1824) 1 *H & Tw* 28, 47 *ER* 1313.   [12] *Argyll v. Argyll* [1967] *Ch* 302.

[13] *Foster v. Mountford* [1978] *FSR* 582.

[14] *Director General of Education v. Public Services Association of New South Wales* (1985) 4 *IPR* 552.

[15] *Interfirm Comparison (Aust.) Pty v. Law Society of New South Wales* [1975] 2 *NSWLR* 104.

[16] *Saltman Engineering v. Campbell Engineering* (1948) 65 *RPC* 203; *Inline Logistics* [2002] *RPC* 611.

[17] *Hellewell v. Chief Constable of Derbyshire* [1995] 1 *WLR* 804; *Douglas v. Hello!* [2008] 1 *AC* 1; *Campbell v. MGN* [2004] 2 *AC* 457 (HL); *Theakston v. MGN* [2003] *EMLR* 398, [2002] *EWHC* 137 (QB).

[18] *Fraser v. Thames* [1983] 2 *All ER* 101.

[19] *Attorney-General v. Guardian* [1990] *AC* 109, 281–2; Gurry (2012), [5.57]–[5.60].

[20] [1969] *RPC* 41, 48. Where information is expressly protected through contract, the contract defines the coverage and can extend to trivial information: *Deloitte & Touche v. Dickson and ors* [2005] *EWHC* 721, [40] (Laddie J).

Megarry J said that he doubted 'whether equity would intervene unless the circumstances are of sufficient gravity; equity ought not to be invoked to protect trivial tittle-tattle, however confidential'. In the context of trade secrets, the courts have occasionally suggested that, to be protectable, an idea must be economically valuable or 'commercially attractive'.

The trivia exception has had little impact upon the information protected by breach of confidence. This is because the courts have been reluctant to label information as trivial. The potential scope of the exception is further restricted by the fact that it has been suggested that it would never apply to government information. The reason for this is that it is impossible for the court to determine whether such information is important or not.[21] As part of the new approach adopted in relation to personal information, in *Mills v. News Group Newspapers*,[22] the court held that the address of Heather Mills (model and then wife of Paul McCartney of Beatles fame) was protectable despite the 'relatively trivial character of the information'.

The reluctance of the courts to categorize information as trivial and thereby exclude it from the scope of protection can also be seen from the House of Lords' decision in *Douglas v. Hello!*.[23] While Lord Walker, in his dissenting speech, seems almost to have been prepared to dismiss the action on the ground that the information that the *Hello!* photographs revealed about the Douglas/Zeta-Jones wedding could not be said to be anything other than trivial,[24] the majority did not take the same view. Indeed, Baroness Hale, while emphasizing the importance of the triviality exception in restricting the scope of the breach of confidence action, said that she saw 'no principled reason' why photographic images of a wedding should not be protected.[25]

3 IMMORAL INFORMATION

It also seems that the courts will not enforce obligations of confidentiality relating to matters that are grossly immoral.[26] However, in the absence of a generally accepted code of morality, the courts have said that they should be extremely careful about castigating certain types of behaviour on the basis that it is immoral.[27] As such, as with the trivia exclusion, it seems that the exclusion of immoral information will have little impact upon the information protected by the action.

---

[21] *Attorney-General v. Guardian Newspapers* [1990] *AC* 109, 269 (Lord Griffiths); cf. ibid., 284 (Lord Goff) (recognizing exclusion, but limiting it to trivia of the most humdrum kind).

[22] [2001] *EMLR* 957 (when considering whether the information should be disclosed, the trivial nature of the information was weighed against the serious risk that stalkers would pose if the address were disclosed); cf. *M v. Secretary of State for Work and Pensions* [2006] *AC* 91, [83] (interference with private life had to be of some seriousness before Art. 8 ECHR was engaged).   [23] [2008] 1 *AC* 1.

[24] *Douglas v. Hello!* [2008] 1 *AC* 1, 81–3, [287]–[291] (clearly, Lord Walker also thought that *Creation Records v. News Group* [1997] *EMLR* 444 was wrongly decided and that the collection of objects around the swimming pool in that photograph was pure trivia) See Chapter 3, Fig. 3.1, p. 59.

[25] *Douglas v. Hello!* [2008] 1 *AC* 1, 87, [307] (Baroness Hale). For criticism of the majority on this point, see C. Michalos, '*Douglas v. Hello*: The Final Frontier' [2007] *Ent L Rev* 241.

[26] Following from decisions in copyright law: see Chapter 4, section 6, pp. 122–4.

[27] *Stevens v. Avery* [1988] 2 *All ER* 477, 480–1 (court rejects suggestion that a lesbian relationship is immoral); *Mosley v. News Group Newspapers* [2008] *EWHC* 687 (QB) (court rejected such an argument in relation to the hosting a sado-masochistic party).

4 INFORMATION THAT IS VAGUE

In many cases, the information protected by breach of confidence is detailed and specific. Information of this nature presents few problems. Thus detailed plans of a prototype engine shown by an inventor to a manufacturer or a detailed formula for a new pharmaceutical may be protected. However, breach of confidence also applies to more general ideas and concepts, such as a proposal for a new television series. The problem here is that if a claimant were able to impose confidentiality on very general ideas, this might enable them to impose unjustifiable burdens on anyone who received the information in confidence. To protect against this, the courts have said that the law will not protect information that is vague or general. More specifically, the courts have said that an aspiration or a desirable goal, the flavour of which can be captured in the phrase 'wouldn't it be great if . . . ?', will not be protected by the action.[28] Instead, such information is in the public domain, free to be used by all. It should be noted that the courts have been careful to stress that vagueness and simplicity are not the same thing.[29]

The exclusion of vague information can be seen in *De Maudsley v. Palumbo*.[30] The claimant in this case argued that the defendant, which ran the dance club the Ministry of Sound, had appropriated his ideas for a new type of dance club about which the claimant had told the defendant at a dinner party. The claimant's idea for the new dance club consisted of five features: the club would legally be open all night; it would be very large and fitted out in hi-tech industrial warehouse style; it would incorporate separate areas for drinking, dancing, and socializing; it would have an enclosed dance area in which the sound quality would be high; and it would employ top-quality DJs. Knox J held that all five features of the claimant's ideas were 'individually too vague' and thus not protectable. With the exception of the idea that the club would be legally open all night, he also said that the ideas were not novel. A similar approach was adopted in *Secton v. Delawood*.[31] In this case, the claimant company, which was involved in developing methods of separating oil and water, brought an action to prevent the defendants, who were former employees, from working in the same field. The Court refused to grant relief, holding that a bare goal, purpose, or possibility—a mere speculative idea—was not capable of being protected as a trade secret.

While general ideas may not be protected by breach of confidence, this does not mean that all ideas or concepts are therefore excluded. Indeed, one of the notable features of the action is that, unlike other areas of intellectual property such as copyright, breach of confidence provides protection over some of the more abstract aspects of the creative process. As with similar inquiries in other areas of intellectual property law, the difficult question is determining where and how the boundary is to be drawn between detailed information (which is clearly protectable) and very general ideas (which are not).

In thinking about where the dividing line is to be drawn, the courts have said that, to be protected, a concept or idea must be 'sufficiently developed to be capable of being realized'—that is, it is necessary to go beyond simply identifying a desirable goal and to show a 'considerable degree of particularity in a definitive product'.[32] This can be seen, for

---

[28] *De Maudsley v. Palumbo* [1996] *FSR* 447, 456.

[29] Ibid.; *Cranleigh Precision Engineering v. Bryant* [1965] 1 *WLR* 1293, 1309, 1310.

[30] [1996] *FSR* 447.

[31] *Secton Pty v. Delawood Pty* (1991) 21 *IPR* 136, 155 (Supreme Court of Victoria). See also *Intelsec Systems v. Grechi-Cini* [1999] 4 *All ER* 11, 31; cf. the simple idea developed into the finished business plan in *Wheatley v. Bell* [1984] *FSR* 16.

[32] *De Maudsley v. Palumbo* [1996] *FSR* 447; *Sales v. Stromberg* [2006] *FSR* (7) 89, 110 (designs of decorative pendants, although simple geometric shapes, were confidential).

example, in *Fraser v. Thames TV*,[33] which concerned an idea for a television series about the formation of a female rock group and the subsequent experiences of the members. Hirst J said that 'to be capable of protection the idea must be sufficiently developed, so that it would be seen to be a concept that has at least some attractiveness for a television programme and which is capable of being realized in actuality'.[34] Similarly, in *Talbot v. General Television*,[35] it was held that a new concept for a television series was protectable because it was 'capable of being realized in actuality'. The requirement that the idea must be capable of being realized 'as an actuality' has been taken to mean that the idea must be capable of being transformed into 'a finished product in the relevant medium'.[36]

So for example, a recipe for a jerk sauce was found to be too uncertain and vague to be protected on the basis it listed ingredients without any great precision along with the fatal suggestion that water should be added 'to gain the required thickness and strength' (without specifying the volume)[37] and so different chefs might produce different sauces based on the same 'recipe'.

Perhaps the best way in which to get a sense of the level of detail needed for an idea to be protected is to look at the way in which the issue has been construed in the cases. We have already seen earlier how, in *Palumbo*, the claimant's ideas for a new dance club were held to be too vague to be protected. In contrast, in *Talbot*, the court held that the proposal for a new television programme was sufficiently developed to be the subject of confidence. In this case, the claimant approached the defendant with an idea for a television series about real-life millionaires. While the claimant subsequently sent the defendant a more detailed outline, this did not add very much of substance to the initial idea.[38] As such, it seems that the general proposal for a new type of programme involving real-life millionaires would have been protected in its own right. In effect, this is what transpired in *Fraser v. Thames TV*, in which it was held that the claimant's concept for an idea for a television series about the formation of a female rock group was specific enough to be protected.

The level of detail required for an idea or concept to be protectable varies depending on the case in hand. Speaking about the level of detail needed for a proposal for a television programme to be protected, Hirst J said:

> I do not think that [the requirement of actuality] necessitates in every case a full synopsis. In some cases the nature of the idea may require extensive development of this kind in order to meet the criteria. But in others the criteria may be met by short unelaborated statement of an idea.[39]

One factor that will influence the level of specificity required is the way in which information is normally treated in the industry in question. Thus, in *Fraser v. Thames TV*, Hirst J said that the fact that it was normal practice in the theatre, television, and film industries to treat general proposals for new programmes as if they were protected was an important factor in his reaching the conclusion that the information was in fact protected.[40]

In some cases, the courts have suggested that the test for whether an idea or concept is sufficiently developed to be protectable is to consider whether the idea or concept

---

[33] *Fraser v. Thames* [1983] 2 *All ER* 101.   [34] Ibid., 122.   [35] [1981] *RPC* 1, 9.

[36] *De Maudsley v. Palumbo* [1996] *FSR* 447. Knox J distinguished between a 'mental product', which could be protected, and a mere 'aspiration', which could not.

[37] *Bailey v. Graham* [2011] *EWHC* 3098 (Ch), [104]–[110]; upheld on appeal [2012] *EWCA Civ* 1469 (Levi Roots' Reggae Reggae sauce).

[38] *Fraser v. Thames* [1983] 2 *All ER* 101, 121.

[39] Ibid. See further *Wade v. BBC* [2014] *EWHC* 634 (Ch), [55]–[56], [62] (Birss J) (pitch document for music talent show to be called *The Real Deal* was found to have the necessary quality of confidence); upheld on appeal [2016] *EWCA Civ* 1214.   [40] *Fraser v. Thames* [1983] 2 *All ER* 101, 121–2.

is 'attractive'.[41] However, as Knox J pointed out in *Palumbo*, this requirement 'doesn't advance things much because if the element is missing it is hardly likely to be appropriated'.[42] The flip side of this is that if a defendant uses the information, this would be proof of its attractiveness. As such, the relative attractiveness of the information adds little to the inquiry.

5 INFORMATION IN THE PUBLIC DOMAIN

One of the most important restrictions placed on the information that is protected by breach of confidence is that the action does not apply to material that is in the public domain. In contrast, the tort of misuse of private information may extend to information which is in the public domain because the further use of the information would harass the claimant.[43] As Laddie J said, '[p]rima facie, information that is in the public domain is not capable of being treated as confidential'.[44] The upshot of this is that, however confidential the circumstances of communication, 'there can be no breach of confidence in revealing to others something which is already common knowledge'.[45] In more positive terms, this means that, to be protected, the information must be relatively secret.

The notion of public domain has a different meaning in relation to breach of confidence than it has in other areas of intellectual property law. Before looking at what is meant by the 'public domain' in this context, it should be noted that the status of the information is a question of fact, not of intention. Consequently, information is still capable of being protected even though the confider intended the information to be published, but failed to do this.[46] Conversely, if material is in the public domain, it does not matter that the confider intended, but failed, to keep the information secret.[47]

5.1 'RELATIVE SECRECY'

In patent law, a single disclosure to one person is sufficient to place the information in the public domain and thus to destroy the novelty of an invention.[48] In contrast, breach of confidence is built around a notion of 'relative secrecy'. Accordingly, information may be available to the public and yet not sufficiently widely known for all confidentiality in it to be destroyed.[49] In essence, this means that it is possible for a number of people to know about the 'secret' and the information still not be in the public domain. The upshot of this is that the fact that information has been disclosed to a number of people does not necessarily mean that the information is incapable of being treated as confidential. For example, in *Prince Albert v. Strange*,[50] the court held that while Prince Albert had disclosed details of his engravings to friends and relatives, this did not destroy the confidentiality that existed in the information.

---

[41] *Talbot v. General TV* [1981] *RPC* 1, 9. [42] *De Maudsley v. Palumbo* [1996] *FSR* 447 (Knox J).

[43] See Chapter 47, section 2.2, pp. 1257–8.

[44] *CMI v. Phytopharm* [1999] *FSR* 235, 255. See also *A-G v. Guardian* [1990] *AC* 109, 282.

[45] *Coco v. Clark* [1969] *RPC* 41, 47.

[46] A mere intention to publish in due course should not deprive information of its confidential status: *Douglas v. Hello!* [2008] 1 *AC* 1; cf. *Times v. Mirror Group* [1993] *EMLR* 443.

[47] It is clear that if the confider publishes the information, the obligation comes to an end: *Mustad v. Allcock and Dosen* (1928) [1963] 3 *All ER* 416. [48] See Chapter 18, section 4, pp. 559–60.

[49] *R (on the application of Ingenious Media Holdings) v. Revenue and Customs* [2016] 1 *WLR* 4164, [25].

[50] (1849) 2 *De G & Sm* 652, 64 *ER* 293 (Knight Bruce LJ); (1849) 1 *Mac & G* 25, 41 *ER* 1171 (Cottenham LC).

The crucial question is: 'whether the information in question is so generally accessible that, in all the circumstances, it cannot be regarded as confidential'?[51] or, put another way, 'the protection of the law will not be withdrawn unless and until it is clear that a stage has been reached where there is no longer anything left to be protected'.[52] This difficulty is that, as Lord Toulson observed in *Ingenious Media Holdings*: 'Whether that stage has been reached may be a hard question on which reasonable people may disagree.'[53] The degree of publication required before secrecy is lost depends on a range of different factors.[54] These include: the type of information; the section of the public that has an interest in knowing about the information;[55] the domain in which the information was published; the location and extent of publication within that domain; the form in which the information is published; the length of time for which the publication is accessible;[56] and the vigour with which the information is likely to be pursued within that domain.[57]

In order to deprive information of its quality of confidence, a particular publication must reveal the substance of that information. Thus a partial disclosure deprives only that part of the information disclosed of its confidentiality.[58] The House of Lords in *Douglas v. Hello!* was divided over precisely the question of whether the information that had been confidential remained so after publication of the authorized photographs by *OK!*. According to Lord Nicholls, once the claimant had published its photos (an action that was expedited so as to limit the impact of *Hello!*'s revelation), there was nothing really left that was confidential in the defendant's different photographs of the same event. In contrast, the majority took a broader view. The content of the photographs was not equivalent to a verbal description of the event; each photograph was a separate piece of information. As Lord Brown explained, '[t]he secret consists no less of each and every visual image of the wedding than of the wedding as a whole'.[59] Disclosure of some photographs of the wedding therefore did not deprive other photographs of their 'quality of confidence'.

A publication will not 'reveal' information if it is merely speculative. In *BBC v. HarperCollins Publishers*,[60] the BBC sought an injunction to prevent publication of an autobiography of Ben Collins in which he revealed that he had played the part of 'The Stig' on the BBC show *Top Gear* between 2003 and 2010. In the show, 'The Stig' test drives motor cars dressed in a white suit and wearing a white helmet. His identity is deliberately concealed from the public. The BBC claimed that Collins was under an obligation to keep

---

[51] *Attorney-General v. Guardian Newspapers (No.2)* [1990] 1 *AC* 109, 282 (Lord Goff).

[52] *McKennitt v. Ash* [2006] *EMLR* 10, [81] (Eady J) cited with approval in *R (on the application of Ingenious Media Holdings) v. Revenue and Customs* [2016] 1 *WLR* 4164, [25].

[53] *R (on the application of Ingenious Media Holdings) v. Revenue and Customs* [2016] 1 *WLR* 4164, [25]. This presents difficulty for the knowledge/notice test as this is based on the reasonable person believing something to be confidential, but how does this work if reasonable persons can disagree? It is likely that this issue is only going to arise in the closest of cases.

[54] *BBC v. HarperCollins Publishers* [2011] *EMLR* 6, [53].

[55] In *Ryan v. Capital Leasing* (2 April 1993, High Court of Ireland) it was said that the public domain means that 'the information is well known to that section of the public which has an interest in knowing the information'. See P. Lavery, 'Secrecy, Springboards and the Public Domain' [1998] *EIPR* 93.

[56] Inclusion of formulae for cement in particulars of claim did not deprive the information of the quality of confidence despite the fact that, between the time the claim was lodged and trial, the public might have sought to inspect them: *Orr-Adams v. Bailey* [2013] *EWPCC* 30, [43]–[47] (Judge A. Michaels). See also *Burrows v. Emmett Smith* [2010] *EWHC* 22 (Ch), [34]–[35]; *G v. Day* [1982] 1 *NSWLR* 24 (ephemeral revelation on television did not deprive information of confidential status).   [57] Dean, 123–9.

[58] *House of Spring Gardens v. Point Blank* [1983] *FSR* 213, 255; *Attorney-General v. Times Newspapers* [2001] 1 *WLR* 885 (CA), 892–3.

[59] [2008] 1 *AC* 1, 73, [257] (Lord Nicholls); ibid., 48–9, [122] (Lord Hoffmann); ibid., 94, [329] (Lord Brown).   [60] [2011] *EMLR* 6.

his identity secret and Morgan J found that there was indeed an equitable duty of confidence.[61] Nevertheless, Morgan J rejected the application, finding that the fact that Collin's played 'The Stig' was, by that time, in the public domain. In so finding, he carefully distinguished between speculative claims that Collins was 'The Stig' and assertions of fact. In 13 newspaper articles reporting that the BBC was trying to restrain publication of an autobiography by a person playing 'The Stig', eight national newspapers 'made increasingly confident and increasingly clear statements that Mr Collins was The Stig'.[62] These statements would not be understood as speculation, but as statements of fact. The fact was thereafter generally accessible to all who had an interest in knowing it.[63]

The idea that information is in the public domain when it can be accessed by those with an interest in knowing has other implications. In *Franchi v. Franchi*,[64] the court was called upon to consider whether information was still confidential after it had been published in a patent specification in Belgium, but before it had been published in the United Kingdom. It was held that the fact that the information was in the public domain in another country might be relevant when considering whether the information was confidential in the United Kingdom. The court also held that, because patent agents were in the habit of inspecting foreign specifications, the information was in the public domain.[65]

The Internet provides a new challenge to some of these ideas. In one sense, where information is known in one place after publication on an open access website or social media platform it is known everywhere.[66] This is often a very simple view of the matter. There are many pages on websites, even well-known sites, where publication for a limited time might not be enough to affect its confidentiality.[67] Indeed, in relation to misuse of private information in *PJS v. News Group*[68] the Supreme Court had to consider whether an injunction should remain in place in relation to information about the sexual exploits of the spouse of a well-known celebrity, where that person's identity was widely available on the Internet and social media. It concluded the injunction had value because the alternative would be a media storm and much greater exposure to the information. While the considerations are different in confidence, the fact that the Internet is vast and continues to rapidly expand cannot be ignored. In this vast expanse, it may be that the information is little more than a needle or a handful of needles in a very big haystack. Accordingly, it is necessary to show more than the mere possibility of access before confidence is lost.

Another factor that may be useful in indicating whether information remains confidential is the extent to which further publication would harm the claimant.[69] In some cases, the requirement of harm and the finding that the information is confidential have operated as alternative grounds. This can be seen, for example, in the *Spycatcher* decision.[70] Peter Wright, who was under an obligation of confidentiality as a member of the Security Services, wrote a book called *Spycatcher*. The book was published in Australia, Ireland, and the United States. The *Sunday Times* began to serialize the book in England and *The Guardian/Observer* sought to repeat the story. The Attorney-General sought an injunction to prevent publication. Lord Keith said that the continued serialization of the

---

[61] As is common in the entertainment business, Collins acted through his service company, Collins Autosport Ltd, and it was the company that had contracted to provide Collins' services to the BBC.

[62] [2011] *EMLR* 6, [43].   [63] Ibid., [56].   [64] [1967] *RPC* 149.

[65] Now patent specifications are published online and accessed through a handful of databases with common classifications and so the facts of the *Franchi* case have long been overtaken.

[66] *Attorney-General v. Guardian Newspapers* [1987] 1 *WLR* 1248, 1269 (Browne-Wilkinson V-C).

[67] *Barclays Bank Plc v. Guardian News Media Ltd* [2009] *EWHC* 591 (QB).   [68] [2016] *AC* 1081.

[69] This is much more complicated in relation to misuse of private information as interests other than secrecy—such as harassment—come into play: see Chapter 47, section 2.2, p. 1258.

[70] *Attorney-General v. Guardian* [1990] *AC* 109.

book would not be a breach of confidence. This was because it would not have caused any further damage to the government.[71]

5.2 SPRINGBOARD DOCTRINE

One situation in which the breach of confidence action may provide protection over information that is in the public domain is where one party uses information that they have obtained in confidence to steal a march on competitors. This issue is dealt with by the so-called 'springboard' doctrine. In essence, the doctrine aims to ensure that a person who breaches a duty of confidence is not able to benefit from the breach. As Lord Denning said in *Seager v. Copydex*,[72] a person who obtained the information from a private source should not be in a better position than someone who went to the public source. The effect of the doctrine is to prevent a person who obtained the information from a private source from getting a head start without paying for it. As Roxburgh J said in *Terrapin v. Builders' Supply Co.*:

> [A] person who has obtained information in confidence is not allowed to use it as a spring-board for activities detrimental to the person who made the confidential communication, and a springboard it remains even when all the features have been published or can be ascertained by actual inspection by any member of the public.[73]

The claimant in this case manufactured prefabricated portable buildings. As part of a joint venture, the claimant gave the defendant detailed technical information about the prefabricated buildings. When the relationship broke down and the defendant continued to manufacture the buildings, the claimant sued for breach of confidence. The defendant claimed that the information was no longer capable of being protected by breach of confidence. This was because the claimant had sold buildings to members of the public (which could be dismantled to reveal the details) and also published a brochure that disclosed the technical details of the buildings. In short, the defendant argued that, because the information was now in the public domain, it was no longer capable of being protected. Roxburgh J held that, to obtain information equivalent to that initially given to the defendant, the defendant would have had to dismantle a portable building and construct tests. The initial information gave the confidant a head start over a member of the public. Under the springboard doctrine, the defendants were to be placed under a special disability to ensure that they did not get a head start over competitors.

The springboard doctrine was subject to a typically careful review[74] by Arnold J in *Vestergaard Frandsen v. Bestnet*[75] (a case concerned with mosquito nets that were developed to exude an insecticide). Arnold J found that the proper basis of the springboard doctrine lay in the notion of 'relative secrecy'—that is, 'that information may possess a limited degree of confidentiality even though it can be ascertained by reverse engineering

---

[71] Ibid., 260. Lord Keith said that, in relation to government secrets, it was necessary to show that there was a public interest in restraining disclosure and that, given that no harm would occur, this was absent.

[72] *Seager v. Copydex* [1967] 2 *All ER* 415, 417. See also *Schering Chemicals v. Falkman* [1982] *QB* 1, 15–16 (Denning MR dissenting).

[73] [1967] *RPC* 375, 391. See also *Saltman* (1948) 65 *RPC* 203 (the defendant could have taken the leather punch to pieces and constructed drawings, but had not done so and thus was liable). For criticism of the springboard doctrine on the basis of its inconsistency with the rule that, once in the public domain, the confidence ceases to exist, see Buxton LJ in *EPI Environmental Technologies v. Symphony Plastic Technologies* [2006] 1 *WLR* 495.

[74] There is a helpful summary of the principles in *QBE Management v. Dymoke* [2012] *EWHC* 80 (QB), [239] [247]. It was not a confidence case, but springboard relief is now granted more widely.

[75] *Vestergaard Frandsen A/S v. Bestnet* [2010] *FSR* 2, [42] *ff*.

or by a process of compilation from public domain source'.[76] Put another way, the issue is whether the past wrongdoing continues to confer a present (and future) benefit on the defendant[77] if they are allowed to use the information. In such a situation, he explained, a limited injunction would be appropriate. He rejected an alternative view that injunctive relief might be an appropriate remedy to prevent a person from continuing to benefit from past misuse (but other courts still persist with such thinking).[78]

The springboard doctrine thus attempts to prevent a person from using any special (relatively secret) information that they may have obtained in confidence to gain an advantage over others who would have had to obtain the information by other means (such as reverse engineering the publicly available embodiment of the information).[79] In so doing, the doctrine serves two goals: it promotes the integrity of confidential relations by minimizing any benefits that can be gained by a confidant utilizing information obtained in confidence; and it promotes fair relations between potential competitors.[80]

So far, we have focused on situations in which a person acquires information in confidence that could *later* be located from public sources. However, the springboard doctrine has also been extended to situations in which the confidential information was itself collated from public sources (rather than where private information has been disclosed to the public in a different form).[81] In *Roger Bullivant v. Ellis*,[82] the defendant had taken a copy of the list of customers from his employer during the course of his employment. While each of the names could have been acquired from public domain sources such as professional and trade directories, Falconer J granted an injunction to prevent the defendant from taking unfair advantage of the information. The Court of Appeal allowed the appeal and discharged the injunction, saying that such an injunction should not normally extend beyond the period for which the unfair advantage is expected to continue.[83]

The springboard doctrine has a number of important features. The first is that the restrictions imposed on private information do not last forever. In *Potters Ballotini v. Weston Baker*, Lord Denning explained that:

> Although a man must not use such information as a springboard to get a start over others, nevertheless the springboard does not last forever. If he does use it, a time may come when so much has happened that he can no longer be restrained.[84]

Accordingly, the appropriate remedy was to restrict the confidant from using the information for a limited time. The appropriate period is calculated by reference to the

---

[76] Ibid., [78].   [77] *Willis v. Jardine Lloyd Thompson* [2015] *EWCA Civ* 450, [22].

[78] Ibid., [93]. See also *Murray v. Yorkshire Fund Managers* [1998] 1 *WLR* 951, 960 (Nourse LJ) ('the springboard principle can have no application where, as here, the information has ceased to be confidential'); there is a conflict approach allowing springboard injunctions in such cases: see *Crowson v. Rider* [2007] *EWHC* 2942 (Ch); *First Conference Services v. Bracchi* [2009] *EWHC* 2176 (Ch); *Habro v. Hampton* [2014] *EWHC* 1781 (Ch); and it appears to be accepted in other Commonwealth jurisdictions: see Gurry (2012), [18.77] [18.79]. The English authorities are often tied up with fiduciary obligations.

[79] *Roger Bullivant v. Ellis* [1987] FSR 172, 183.

[80] *Aquaculture v. New Zealand Mussel Co.* (1985) 5 *IPR* 353, 383 ('a principle, founded on the concept of fairness'). Dean describes the springboard doctrine 'as close to a de facto doctrine of unfair competition as Anglo-American courts have come': Dean, 143.   [81] But cf. *Schering v. Falkman* [1982] *QB* 1.

[82] [1987] *FSR* 172.   [83] Ibid., 184.

[84] *Potters Ballotini v. Weston Baker* [1977] *RPC* 202; *Sun Valley Foods v. John Philip Vincent* [2002] *FSR* 82 (application for springboard relief rejected because the advantage that the defendant received from the misuse of the information was ephemeral and short term in nature).

time that it would take to discover the information from legitimate public sources;[85] that is, to return them to the position they would have been in but for the defendant's misconduct.[86]

The second feature of the action is that, because of the difficulties in calculating the duration of the confidant's head start and the problems of enforcing it by way of injunction, the courts have indicated that springboard relief should be avoided where monetary relief is adequate.[87]

5.3 ENCRYPTED INFORMATION

Another situation in which questions about the status of information arise is where information is encrypted. What is the effect of disclosing information in an encrypted form? If a person places encrypted information in the public domain, does this mean that the information is secret and potentially protectable? Or does it mean that the information is published and thus not protectable?

The question of whether the encrypted information that is in the public domain is capable of being protected by the law of confidentiality was considered in *Mars v. Teknowledge*.[88] The claimant in the case designed and manufactured coin-receiving and coin-changing mechanisms (which are used in vending machines). The mechanisms included 'discriminators' that function to determine the authenticity and denomination of a coin fed into the machine. One of the problems with the discriminators was that, whenever there was a change in the coinage, they had to be reprogrammed. The claimant developed a new discriminator (called the 'Cashflow'), which had the ability to be reprogrammed for new coin data. Cashflow consisted of 'a data layout, a serial communications protocol and an encryption system to make it difficult for third parties to find out by reverse engineering how to recalibrate (reprogram) the Cashflow discriminator'. Importantly, none of this information was published directly by the claimant. The defendant had broken the encryption system and reverse-engineered the Cashflow discriminator. The claimant brought an action arguing, among other things, that the defendant's activities by way of reverse engineering amounted to a breach of confidence.

Jacob J held that the encrypted information in the Cashflow machine did not have the necessary quality of confidence. After noting that the machine was freely available on the market,[89] Jacob J said that:

> Anyone with the necessary skill to de-crypt had access to the information. The fact that only a few have those skills is . . . neither here nor there. Anyone can acquire the skills and, anyway, a buyer is free to go to a man who has them.[90]

On this basis, Jacob J concluded that, because the information had been published, it was not capable of being protected.

The courts have adopted a similar approach in situations in which the information is embodied in an object in the public domain that can be accessed only through reverse

---

[85] If reverse engineering is not a possibility, the springboard metaphor is inappropriate: *Electro Cad Australia v. Mejati RCS SDN BHD* [1999] FSR 291, 307.

[86] *Universal Thermosensors v. Hibben* [1992] 1 WLR 840, 855.

[87] Ibid.; see also *Coco v. Clark* [1969] RPC 41, 47.   [88] [2000] FSR 138.

[89] For consideration of the situation in which the product has been hired rather than sold, so that the product is not 'freely available', see *K. S. Paul (Printing Machinery) v. Southern Instruments (Communications)* [1964] RPC 118.   [90] *Mars v. Teknowledge* [2000] FSR 138, 149.

engineering.[91] The cases have suggested that where information is embodied (or hidden) in a machine or a product that is in the public domain, the information is also in the public domain and thus not capable of being protected. The upshot of this is that information will be treated as having been published and thus in the public domain, even though it can be accessed only through a process of decryption or reverse engineering.

Accordingly, while we think that while the outcome of *Mars* and similar cases is correct, they are wrongly reasoned. In our view, the encrypted information in the *Mars* case was relatively secret.[92] Indeed, Jacob J acknowledged this when he indicated that a person who had received that information confidentially would be liable if they were to disclose it. The result in the cases is correct, however, because a person who legitimately reverse engineers a publicly available product should not be regarded as owing any duty of confidentiality.[93] This topic is dealt with in relation to the obligation of confidence in Chapter 45.

5.4 DISCLOSURE BY THE CONFIDANT

For some time, it was thought that, where information had entered the public domain as a result of a breach of confidence, this did not affect the status of the information. While the information may have been *public knowledge*, the fact that the information entered the public domain wrongfully meant that it was not *public property*.[94] This meant that the information remained confidential in spite of the fact that it was widely available. Others argued that once information was in the public domain, it was not capable of being protected by the action. This was the case even where disclosure arose through a breach of confidence.

Most of the confusion as to whether information disclosed through a breach of confidence is still capable of being protected by the action was resolved in *Spycatcher*.[95] In this decision, Lord Goff held that once information was widely available, there could be no obligation in the law of confidence respecting it.[96] This was because the subject matter of the obligation had vanished: once information is in the public domain, the courts cannot restrain further publication.[97]

Even though information that enters the public domain via a breach of confidence is not capable of being protected by the cause of action, this does not mean that the confidant is thereby absolved of liability. In these circumstances, the confidant has clearly committed a wrong and will be subject to the regular remedies for breach of confidence. Some cases have referred to the provision of remedies against the confidant in these circumstances as the 'springboard' doctrine,[98] the idea being that a person who obtained

---

[91] *Saltman* (1948) 65 *RPC* 203; more recently see *Volkswagen v. Garcia* [2014] *FSR* 12 where an interim injunction was granted to prevent the publication of an algorithm used by the car manufacture as part of the locking system for their cars. The algorithm had been decrypted by academics who wished to publish it in a paper. Birss J granted the injunction largely on the basis that the risk of mass car theft was sufficiently great to warrant it. He did not consider whether the information once decrypted remained confidential.

[92] But cf. *Ackroyds v. Islington Plastics* [1962] *RPC* 97, 104 (if what is in the public domain needs reverse engineering, that information ought to be treated as relatively secret).

[93] See Chapter 45, section 4.2.1, pp. 1229–30.

[94] *Cranleigh Precision Engineering v. Bryant* [1964] 3 *All ER* 289; *Speed Seal Products v. Paddington* [1986] *FSR* 309.

[95] *Attorney-General v. Guardian* [1990] *AC* 109. For commentary, see G. Jones, 'Breach of Confidence: After *Spycatcher*' (1990) 42 *CLP* 48.

[96] The law is different in relation to misuse of private information, see Chapter 47.

[97] Ibid.   [98] *Ocular Sciences* [1997] *RPC* 289, 399.

information in confidence is not allowed to use it as a springboard for activities detrimental to the person who made the confidential communication. We prefer to reserve the springboard metaphor for a different category of cases (which were discussed earlier). We will look at the remedies against an errant confidant when we look at remedies for breach of confidence later.

5.5 COMPILATIONS OF INFORMATION THAT IS IN THE PUBLIC DOMAIN

While information that is in the public domain will not be protected by the breach of confidence action, a distinction is drawn between such information (which is not protected) and information that builds upon such information (which may be protected). It is clear that where someone collects, arranges, or elaborates on elements that are already in the public domain, the resulting information is capable of being protected.[99] As Lord Greene MR said in *Saltman Engineering*,[100] 'it is perfectly possible to have a confidential document . . . which is the result of work done by the maker on materials which may be available for the use of anybody'. He added that 'what makes it confidential is the fact that the maker of the document has used his brain and thus produced a result which can only be produced by somebody who goes through the same process'.[101] In a similar vein, Megarry J said in *Coco v. Clark* that:

> [S]omething constructed solely from materials in the public domain may possess the necessary quality of confidentiality . . . But whether it is described as originality or novelty or ingenuity or otherwise, I think there must be some produce of the human brain which suffices to confer a confidential nature upon the information.[102]

It is clear that not all acts of compilation will produce results that are capable of being protected. Indeed, as Knox J has said, 'a combination of features which were not individually novel does not automatically become novel by being added together'.[103]

The status of compilations of information that is in the public domain was considered in *Ocular Sciences v. Aspect Vision*.[104] In this case, the claimant asserted that a booklet that contained a compendium of the detailed dimensions of the claimant's range of contact lenses was confidential. This was the case even though each of the lenses had been put on the market. The claimant argued that, to obtain even a small amount of the information contained in the booklet, a lens manufacturer would need to analyse thousands of lenses—a process that would take considerable time and effort. Laddie J said that he had great doubts as to whether 'a mere mechanical collection of data which is in the public domain' could be confidential.[105] He added that *Saltman* and *Coco* do not establish that the compilation of information in the public domain is always enough to confer confidentiality. While valuable and novel ideas could be produced by the judicious selection and combination of a number of items that are separately in the public domain, and such ideas would be capable of being the subject of an obligation of confidence, they would be such only if they were the 'product of the skill of the human brain'.[106] In contrast, Laddie J

---

[99] TRIPS, Art. 39(2).   [100] (1948) 65 *RPC* 203, 215.

[101] Ibid., 215.   [102] [1969] *RPC* 41, 47.

[103] *De Maudsley v. Palumbo* [1996] *FSR* 447, 459; cf. *Burrows v. Emmett Smith* [2010] *EWHC* 22 (Ch), [34] (the combination of elements in a proposed video game was original).

[104] [1997] *RPC* 289.   [105] Ibid., 374.

[106] Ibid., 375; also see Gurry (2012), [5.16] endorsed in *CF Partners (UK) v. Barclays Bank* [2014] *EWHC* 3049 (Ch), [125].

said that a 'mere non-selective list of publicly available information should not be treated as confidential even if putting it together involves some time and effort. No relevant skill is employed.'[107]

The difficult question is identifying the type and level of labour that needs to be exerted on material in the public domain for the resulting information to be capable of being protected. While this topic has attracted very little attention, it seems that the threshold for protection is low[108] and is certainly no more than some degree of skill, labour or judgement.[109] This can be seen in *Talbot*,[110] in which the court was called upon to decide whether a proposal for a television programme about real-life millionaires was capable of being protected by the law of confidence. While similar television programmes had already been made, the court held that the claimant's programme had a 'commercial twist' or a 'particular slant' that distinguished it from previous programmes. The unique feature of the proposal was that, as part of the programme, successful millionaires, such as Alan Bond[111] and Neil Diamond,[112] were to give the recipe for their success.

5.6 CONFIDENTIAL INFORMATION ABOUT PUBLIC INFORMATION?

The account so far has left at least one issue unexplained. This relates to the level of protection to be afforded to private information about public information. In *Cranleigh Precision Engineering v. Bryan*,[113] the defendant had been managing director of the claimant firm, which manufactured swimming pools made according to a patent owned by the company. In the course of his employment, the defendant learned of the previous grant of a patent (to a Bischoff) for similar swimming pools. Instead of informing the claimant, the defendant set up a rival business and purchased the Bischoff patent. The claimant sought an injunction to restrain the defendant from making use of information received in his capacity as managing director—in particular, 'the knowledge of the possible effect to and on the [claimant] of the existence and publication of the specification'. Roskill J granted an injunction preventing the defendant from making use of the patent.[114] In so doing, Roskill J rejected the defendant's argument that, because the information related to a patent that was in the public domain, the information in question was also in the public domain.

Although *Cranleigh* was initially interpreted as supporting the proposition that confiders could not be released from an obligation of confidentiality by their own acts,[115] subsequent case law has rejected this approach. The view taken of the case by Arnold J in *Vestergaard v. Bestnet*[116] was that the confidential information in the case 'was not the existence of the Bischoff patent, nor the information contained in it, but the relevance of the Bischoff patent to the [claimants'] business.' Accordingly, while information in the

---

[107] [1997] *RPC* 375.

[108] *International Scientific Communications v. Pattison* [1979] *FSR* 429, 434 (Goulding J).

[109] See Gurry (2012), [5.19]; i.e. the former test for originality in copyright law.

[110] *Talbot v. General TV* [1981] *RPC* 1, 9. See also *Fraser v. Thames* [1983] 2 *All ER* 101 and *Wade v. BBC* [2014] *EWHC* 634, upheld [2016] *EWCA Civ* 1214.

[111] A British/Australian businessman who subsequently went bankrupt and was convicted of fraud.

[112] The singer.   [113] [1965] 1 *WLR* 1293.

[114] More specifically, 'from overtly making use of their acquisition of [the patent] or any licence granted in respect thereof in support of or in connection with sales . . . etc. of above-ground swimming-pools in competition with the plaintiff's above-ground swimming-pools': ibid., 1296.

[115] *Speed Seal Products v. Paddington* [1986] *FSR* 309.   [116] [2010] *FSR* 2, [62],

public domain cannot be protected by the law of confidence, the context of that information or its relationship to something else can be separate and distinct information which is capable of protection under the law of confidence.

6 NOVEL AND ORIGINAL INFORMATION?

One of the key differences between breach of confidence and the statutory forms of intellectual property relates to the qualitative restrictions placed upon the intangible property that is protected. For example, novelty and non-obviousness play a key role in limiting the inventions that are patentable; similar restrictions exist in all of the other areas that we have covered in this book. With the exception of information that is vague, or in the public domain, there are few restrictions imposed on information that is protected. In a number of cases, however, the courts have begun to use language that suggests that they are working towards the imposition of some type of qualitative restriction upon the type of information protected by the action. For example, in *Coulthard v. Disco Mix*,[117] the High Court held that information relating to the techniques that the defendant used for creating mega-mixes was not confidential. The technique involved the defendant listing the recordings, identifying the beat and key of each song, and then mixing the songs together in an order that enabled them to be blended smoothly. Judge Sher QC doubted that information about the techniques used by the claimant in creating mega-mixes would be protected. The reason for this was that the techniques were 'pretty obvious once one is setting out to create a beat-mix'.[118] In other contexts, the courts have also spoken of the need for information to be *original* and *novel*. For example, in *De Maudsley v. Palumbo*,[119] Knox J said that, with the exception of the idea that the club would be legally open all night, the ideas were not novel.[120] More recently, in *Wade v. British Sky Broadcasting*,[121] Birss J suggested that ideas for a television programme which are too vague and unoriginal will not contain anything of the necessary quality of confidence to be protected. The courts have also used novelty and originality as a way of gauging whether information that builds upon material in the public domain is capable of being protected.

It is difficult to know what to make of these statements. A simple view of the remarks could be that they are an alternative way of setting out the rule that the law of confidence will not protect trivial information. While confidence will protect simple ideas in general[122] there are some ideas which are so simple and unimaginative that they become trivial or too vague to be protectable. Another view might be that ideas should not be protected where the receiver of the information would have already been aware of the ideas from their general knowledge of the world,[123] in other words the information was essentially in the public domain already—albeit in fragmentary form.

However, it is worth considering whether a requirement that the information be novel or some similar criteria would be desirable. To do so, it is helpful to ask: what purpose could they serve? In other words, what is to be gained from looking at breach of confidence in

---

[117] [1999] 2 *All ER* 457.

[118] Ibid., 474. (The claimant had not argued that the idea of a mega-mix was confidential.)

[119] *De Maudsley v. Palumbo* [1996] *FSR* 447.

[120] Ibid., 456 (idea 'must contain some significant element of originality').

[121] [2014] *EWHC* 634 (Ch), [56]; upheld on appeal [2016] *EWCA Civ* 1214.

[122] Ideas expressed as being very simple have been protected by the law of confidence: see *Cranleigh Precision Engineering v. Bryant* [1966] *RPC* 81, 89; *Coco v. Clark* [1969] *RPC* 41, 47.

[123] In a similar fashion to a patented invention lacking novelty over the common general knowledge.

this way? Unlike the situation with patents, the obligation of confidentiality applies only to those persons who are aware of the confidential nature of the information. As such, the consequence of protecting information that is not novel is much more limited than with patents. Having said that, problems could still arise if protection were to be given over information that was not novel. For example, in the absence of any restrictions as to the need for novelty (or obviousness), what would happen if a person were to approach a publisher and say, in confidence, 'I have an idea to write a textbook on intellectual property law'? In the absence of sort of requirement of novelty or the like, there is a possibility that the publisher could be prevented from commissioning other authors from working in the area.[124] A novelty or originality requirement would ensure that a rudimentary and unformed idea such as this would not be protected. A better view, we suggest, is that such an idea is essentially trivial and so does not warrant protection.

---

[124] Although the publisher would not be prevented from going ahead with an identical proposal independently put forward by another author.

45

OBLIGATION OF CONFIDENCE

1 INTRODUCTION

The second element that must be proved in a breach of confidence action is that the defendant was under a legal (as opposed merely to a moral) obligation of confidentiality.[1] While the rights recognized by copyright, patents, design right, and trade marks apply against anyone who deals with the intangible property within the relevant jurisdiction, traditionally the breach of confidence action applies only to those who receive information in confidence. The basic rule for when an obligation of confidence will arise is that a person owes an obligation where they have notice or knowledge that the material is confidential. In describing the situations in which an obligation of confidentiality will arise, it is common practice to focus on the nature of the relationship between the parties. In following this model, we look at the duties that arise where the parties are in a direct relationship, where there is an indirect relationship, and where there is no relationship between the parties. We then look at the duties that arise when the parties are in an employment relationship.[2]

2 DIRECT RELATIONSHIP

The first and most straightforward situation in which a duty of confidence may arise is where the parties are in a direct relationship with each other. In these circumstances, a duty of confidence may arise contractually, as a result of the type of relationship that exists between the parties, or because of the way in which the information is communicated. We will deal with each in turn.

2.1 CONTRACTUAL PROVISIONS AS TO CONFIDENTIALITY

A person may be under a contractual obligation not to use or disclose information. The contractual conditions of confidentiality may be express or implied.[3] Express obligations typically arise in employment contracts (at which we look later) and in the licensing of

---

[1] See *Attorney-General v. Jonathan Cape* [1976] *QB* 752; *Malone v. Metropolitan Police Commissioner* [1979] *Ch* 344.

[2] For considerations that arise in relation to disclosures to statutory bodies, see Gurry (2012), ch. 13.

[3] However, an express confidentiality agreement may be void. In the case of software, for example, a click-wrap restriction prohibiting decompilation may be void: see Chapter 9, sections 2.5, pp. 234–5, and Chapter 12, section 4, pp. 344–6.

know-how, and more generally in commercial 'non-disclosure agreements'. The relationship between banker and customer is an example of a situation in which an obligation of confidentiality will normally be implied into the contract.[4]

2.2 INTRINSIC NATURE OF THE RELATIONSHIP

In some cases, an obligation of confidentiality arises as a result of the type of the relationship that exists between parties. More specifically, an obligation of confidentiality might exist as part of a fiduciary relationship that exists between the parties. A 'fiduciary relationship' is an equitable relationship in which one party has a duty to act for the benefit of another,[5] and it arises, for example, between solicitor and client, or trustee and beneficiary.[6] Other relationships also attract obligations of confidentiality, for example between doctor and patient, priest and penitent, or between spouses.[7]

The manner in which the law of confidence and the law of fiduciaries interrelate is unclear.[8] Some courts and commentators have suggested that all confidential obligations are examples of fiduciary obligations.[9] However, such conflation seems inappropriate given that a number of persons normally subject to obligations of confidentiality (such as employees)[10] are not normally treated as fiduciaries.[11] It would seem preferable, at least for the sake of clarity, to keep the notions of 'fiduciaries' and 'confidences' distinct.

2.3 FROM THE MANNER OF COMMUNICATION

In some cases, an obligation of confidence may arise from the way in which the information is communicated between the parties.[12] In these circumstances, the test for whether there is a duty of confidence is to ask: would a reasonable recipient have realized that the information was given to them in confidence? As Megarry J said in *Coco v. Clark*:

> [I]t seems to me that if the circumstances are such that any reasonable man standing in the shoes of the recipient of the information would have realized that upon reasonable grounds the information was being given to him in confidence, then this should suffice to impose upon him the equitable obligation of confidence.[13]

This is an objective test, but assessed in the light of the knowledge of the recipient.[14] The question of whether a reasonable person would consider the information to have been

---

[4] *Tournier v. National & Provincial Bank* [1924] 1 *KB* 461; as to duties owned to bankers see Gurry (2012), [9.43]—[9.59].

[5] See *Bristol and West Building Society v. Mothew* [1998] *Ch* 1, 18.

[6] *Boardman v. Phipps* [1967] 2 *AC* 46.   [7] *Argyll v. Argyll* [1967] *Ch* 302.

[8] See Gurry (2012), [9.126]–[9.142] (confidentiality and fiduciary obligations are conceptually distinct, but may be overlapping or intertwined).

[9] *Schering v. Falkman* [1982] 1 *QB* 1, 27; *Attorney-General v. Blake* [1998] 1 *All ER* 833, 843 (not discussed by the House of Lords); *Ocular Sciences v. Aspect Vision* [1997] *RPC* 289, 413.

[10] *Balston v. Headline Filters* [1990] *FSR* 385; cf. *Attorney-General v. Blake* [1998] 1 *All ER* 833, 842.

[11] *Indata Equipment Supplies v. ACL* [1998] *FSR* 248, 256, 262, 264; *LAC Minerals v. International Corona Resources* [1990] *FSR* 441.

[12] *Vestergaard Frandsens A/s v. Bestnet Europe Ltd* [2013] 1 *WLR* 1556 (a person 'had agreed, or ought to have appreciated, that it was confidential'); Gurry (2012), [7.36]–[7.45].

[13] *Coco v. A. N. Clark (Engineers)* [1969] *RPC* 41, 48.

[14] Gurry (2012), [7.38]; *De Maudsley v. Palumbo* [1996] *FSR* 447, 458; cf. *Carflow Products v. Linwood Securities* [1996] *FSR* 424 (Jacob J) (leaving open whether the test might be subjective, because 'equity looks at the conscience of the individual'). See J. Phillips, 'Opportunity Knox' (1997) 1 *IPQ* 134 (preferring an objective test).

communicated to them in confidence always depends on the facts of the case. Perhaps the most straightforward situation is where a party makes an *express* statement that the information is confidential. In these circumstances, a defendant would find it very difficult to show that a reasonable confidant would not think themselves to be under an obligation of confidence.[15]

An obligation of confidence may also be *inferred* from the circumstances in question. When considering whether a reasonable person would infer that the information was confidential from the circumstances, the courts will take account of commonly held views, usages, and practices of the industry or trade in question. The way in which the parties understand their moral obligations may also be relevant.[16] While the question of whether the reasonable person would infer that the information is confidential always depends on the facts in hand, it may be helpful to outline some examples.

(i) *Normal conversation* Where a person blurts out information in public, no obligation of confidentiality would arise.[17] Equally, where information is disclosed in an informal, social setting, normally no obligation would arise.[18]

(ii) *Disclosures for a limited purpose* In most instances, where a person reveals information to someone for a limited purpose, this will give rise to an obligation that the information should be used only for that purpose.[19] This is because, where information is supplied for a specific purpose, the reasonable confidant would readily infer that the information should not be used for another purpose. This is sometimes referred to as the 'limited purpose' test.[20] There may be circumstances, however, under which information is transferred for a limited purpose, but it is not appropriate to infer an obligation of confidence.[21] This might be so outside the commercial field, particularly with respect to disclosures at social events or to public bodies.[22] Even in the commercial field, where the information could be protected by copyright, patent, or design right protection, a reasonable recipient might not assume that the information was given to them under an obligation of confidence.[23]

3 THIRD-PARTY RECIPIENTS

One of the most difficult issues that arises in this area of law concerns if and when parties outside an initial confider–confidant relationship will be bound by a duty of confidence.[24] More specifically, if a person owing an obligation of confidence discloses confidential information to a third party, what factors determine when that third party will be treated as being subject to an obligation not to use or disclose the information?[25]

---

[15] *Stephens v. Avery* [1988] 2 *All ER* 477; cf. *Dunsford and Elliott v. Johnson* [1978] *FSR* 143, 148; *Yates Circuit Foil Co. v. Electrofoils* [1976] *FSR* 345, 380.

[16] *Fraser v. Thames TV* [1983] 2 *All ER* 101, 121–2; *De Maudsley v. Palumbo* [1996] *FSR* 447, 457; cf. *Carflow Products (UK) v. Linwood Securities (Birmingham)* [1996] *FSR* 424.

[17] *Coco v. Clark* [1969] *RPC* 41, 48.

[18] *De Maudsley v. Palumbo* [1996] *FSR* 447, 458.

[19] *Ackroyds London v. Islington Plastics* [1962] *RPC* 97.

[20] See, for instance, *Kerry Ingredients v. Bakkavor Group* [2016] *EWHC* 2448 (Ch), [100].

[21] See *Re Baronetcy of Pringle of Stichill* [2016] *UKPC* 16 [65]–[68] (DNA evidence provided for one purpose can be used for inevitably related purpose).

[22] Gurry (2012), [7.05]–[7.35]; *De Maudsley v. Palumbo* [1996] *FSR* 447, 458.

[23] *Carflow v. Linwood* [1996] *FSR* 424.

The precise approach to the question of when a third party will come under an obligation has frequently been informed by assumptions about the proper jurisdictional basis for breach of confidence. If confidential information is property, should all recipients not be liable? Or is confidential information equitable property, binding all recipients other than bona fide purchasers without notice? Or is protection focused on the equitable obligation of confidence and third-party liability analogous to the liability of 'accessories' in a breach of trust? If the focus is on the obligation, where it is contractual, are the relevant standards those for inducing breach of contract? At different times, each of these approaches seems to have been taken. However, it is now possible to offer a few more concrete principles.

(i) An indirect recipient of the information who is aware of its confidential status will normally be bound by a duty of confidence. In *Spycatcher*,[26] Lord Keith said that '[i]t is a general rule of law that a third party who comes into possession of confidential information which he knows to be such, may come under a duty not to pass it on to anyone else'.

(ii) If a person receives information innocently, but subsequently discovers that the information is confidential, they will be bound by a duty of confidence.[27] For example, in *English & American v. Herbert Smith*,[28] the papers of the counsel acting for the claimants in an action pending in the Commercial Court were mistakenly sent to the solicitors for the other side, Herbert Smith. The solicitors, who were the first defendants in this case, realized the mistake, but were instructed by their client to inspect the papers. The claimant sought an interim injunction preventing the solicitors from using information derived from the privileged documents. Browne-Wilkinson V-C granted the injunction on the ground that it did not matter whether the defendants were innocent when they received the documents, given that later use of the information was unconscionable.

(iii) It is not yet completely clear what standard of 'knowledge' is required to establish the liability of a recipient of information. The critical distinction seems to be between so-called 'subjective knowledge'—that is, where a person knew or turned a blind eye to the realities (that the information was confidential)—and 'objective knowledge'—that is, where a person knew, or a reasonable person would have appreciated, that the information was confidential.[29] The House of Lords in *Campbell* seemed to recognize that 'constructive' notice was sufficient,[30] and in the

---

[24] Gurry (2012), [7.104]; J. Stuckey, 'The Liability of Innocent Third Parties Implicated in Another's Breach of Confidence' (1981) 4 *UNSWLJ* 73; S. Ricketson, 'Confidential Information: A New Proprietary Interest?' (1977–78) 11 *Melb U L Rev* 223, 244–5.

[25] If a third party has actively sought the information, it may be that they will have committed the tort of inducing breach of contract: see *British Industrial Plastics v. Ferguson* [1940] 1 *All ER* 479.

[26] *Attorney-General v. Guardian Newspapers (No. 2)* [1990] *AC* 109, 260 (Lord Keith), 268 (Lord Griffiths).

[27] *Stephenson Jordan & Harrison v. MacDonald & Evans* (1951) 68 *RPC* 190, (1952) 69 *RPC* 10; *Hoechst v. Chemiculture* [1993] *FSR* 270; *Cadbury Schweppes v. FBI Foods* [2000] *FSR* 491 (SCC), 504; *Vestergaard Frandsens A/s v. Bestnet Europe Ltd* [2013] 1 *WLR* 1556, [25]; cf. *Fractionated Cane Technology v. Ruiz-Avila* (1988) 7 *Qd R* 610.

[28] [1988] *FSR* 232.

[29] The Court of Appeal suggested a subjective (or dishonesty test) in *Thomas v. Pearce* [2000] *FSR* 718. Following developments in the law, this was said to be no longer good law by Arnold J in *Primary Group v. RBS* [2014] *RPC* 26, [223]–[224] which was followed in *Personal Management Solutions v. Brakes Bros* [2014] *EWHC* 3495 (QB), [176].

[30] *Campbell v. Mirror Group Newspapers* [2004] AC 457, [44] (Lord Hoffmann); P. Stanley, *The Law of Confidentiality: A Restatement* (2008), 27–30; Gurry (2012), [7.110].

Vestergaard v. Bestnet decision,[31] Lord Neuberger refers to the situation in which the recipient knew, or ought to have appreciated, that the information was confidential (the knowledge/notice test). Moreover, international standards require that liability exist where a person acquired or used information contrary to honest commercial practices, which includes where they knew 'or were grossly negligent in failing to know' that the information was revealed in breach of contract or confidence.[32]

(iv) It seems that the courts might grant an injunction, but not damages against a bona fide purchaser of confidential information.[33] In *Valeo Vision Société Anonyme v. Flexible Lamps*,[34] Valeo, which designed and manufactured lights for cars, disclosed details of the design to M. In turn, M revealed details of the lights to the defendant, which produced similar lights. Valeo sued the defendant for breach of confidence. Aldous J held that the information was confidential and that, despite being a bona fide purchaser, the defendant was subject to a duty of confidentiality. In so doing, Aldous J drew a distinction between a duty that will give rise to injunctive relief and one that would result in an award of damages. Aldous J indicated that while, when deciding whether to grant injunctive relief, the bona fide purchaser rule was too narrow, in order to get damages, the conscience of the defendant had to be affected. On the facts, the claimant failed to establish that the defendant knew that the information it used 'was the confidential property of the claimant nor did it know that it should not be used without the claimant's consent'.[35]

4 STRANGERS

A person may come by confidential information without having it imparted to them by the confidant or by a person owing an obligation of confidence,[36] for example a burglar might uncover confidential files, or a member of the public might find a confidential document in the street. In some cases, it is possible for a duty of confidence to arise even though there is no relationship between the parties.

Until recently, the case law dealing with the question as to whether (and if so, when) a stranger comes under an obligation of confidentiality was unclear. The House of Lords' decision in *Douglas v. Hello!*[37] clarified the matter. Prior to this, there were two competing views as to when a stranger receiving information was to be treated as owing a duty of confidence. The first focused on the conduct of the stranger in acquiring the information. Here, the courts looked at whether the stranger had *acted illegally*. The second line of cases focused on whether the stranger *knew* that the information was confidential. As we will see, the courts have been willing to impose an obligation of confidentiality on recipients

---

[31] [2013] 1 *WLR* 1556, [26] (Lord Neuberger) (referring to 'blind-eye knowledge' in defining the liability of an accessory who does not receive the information).

[32] See footnote to TRIPS, Art. 39.   [33] *Wheatley v. Bell* [1984] *FSR* 16.

[34] [1995] *RPC* 205.   [35] Ibid., 226.

[36] G. Wei, 'Surreptitious Takings of Confidential Information' (1992) 12 *Legal Studies* 302; M. Richardson, 'Breach of Confidence, Surreptitiously or Accidentally Obtained Information and Privacy: Theory Versus Law' (1994) 19 *Melb U L Rev* 673.

[37] [2008] 1 *AC* 1.

of information even where they were not in any relationship with the claimant and where the information was acquired legitimately. It is this latter approach, based on knowledge and conscionability, that was adopted by their Lordships in *Douglas v. Hello!*.

4.1 WAY IN WHICH THE INFORMATION WAS OBTAINED

In the early cases, the courts focused on the conduct of the person who acquired the information. More specifically, the courts looked at whether the stranger has acted illegally: if strangers acted illegally, they come under an obligation; if strangers acted legally, they do not. This distinction could be seen to explain the different outcomes in two cases of telephone tapping: *Malone v. Commissioner of Metropolitan Police*[38] and *Francome v. Mirror Group Newspapers*.[39] In the first case, the police tapped a telephone line and, as a result, prosecuted the claimant for handling stolen goods. The claimant sued the police for breach of confidence. The court held that the police did not come under an obligation of confidentiality.[40] In contrast, in *Francome*, it was a private investigator investigating breaches of Jockey Club rules (rather than the police) who illegally tapped the phone conversation of a jockey. The jockey concerned sought an interim injunction to prevent disclosure of the information. The Court of Appeal distinguished *Malone* and held that, in these circumstances, there was a serious question to be tried. Fox LJ noted that *Malone* was concerned with a case of authorized tapping rather than, as with the case in hand, with illegal tapping by private persons.

The different conclusions in *Francome* and *Malone* seem to depend on a distinction between a person who obtains information lawfully, who does not come under an obligation, and a person who obtains information unlawfully, who is subject to a duty of confidence.

4.2 KNOWLEDGE OF THE STRANGER

However, a second line of cases seemed to ground liability on a different basis: whether the stranger had *knowledge* that the information was confidential. In *Attorney-General v. Guardian (No. 2)*, Lord Goff said:

> I start with the broad general principle (which I do not intend in any way to be definitive) that a duty of confidence arises when confidential information comes to the knowledge of a person (the confidant) in circumstances where he has notice, or is held to have agreed, that the information is confidential, with the effect that it would be just in all the circumstances that he should be precluded from disclosing the information to others . . . I have expressed the circumstances in which the duty arises in broad terms, . . . to include certain situations, beloved of law teachers—where an obviously confidential document is wafted by an electric fan out of a window into a crowded street, or where an obviously confidential document, such as a private diary, is dropped in a public place, and is then picked up by a passer-by.[41]

According to Lord Goff, the key factor is not whether the stranger is acting illegally; rather, it is whether the stranger knows that the information is private or confidential. As such, the question is whether 'anything reasonably leads the observer to realize that what

---

[38] [1979] *Ch* 344.　　[39] [1984] 1 *WLR* 892.　　[40] *Malone v. MPC* [1979] *Ch* 344, 376.
[41] [1990] *AC* 109, 281–2. But cf. C. Hunt, 'Rethinking Surreptitious Takings in the Law of Confidence' [2011] *IPQ* 66 (arguing that knowledge should not be sufficient to give rise to equitable obligations).

he or she observes is confidential'.[42] In *Shelley Films v. Rex Features*,[43] Judge Mann QC held that there was a serious question to be tried that a person acted in breach of confidence by publishing photographs of the set of the film *Frankenstein*. The photographs had been taken without authority by a stranger during filming. But the judge thought it could be assumed that the photographer saw the signs at the entrance to the film studios that said 'Absolutely No Photography—All Films Will Be Confiscated' and 'No Admittance— Access to Authorized Persons Only'. These might have fixed the photographer with knowledge that the claimant regarded the information as confidential. Importantly, the judge seemed to regard knowledge, rather than illegality, as the touchstone.

The decision of the House of Lords in *Douglas v. Hello!* conclusively demonstrates that strangers can come under an obligation of confidence. In this case, *Hello!* had received the images of the Catherine Zeta-Jones/Michael Douglas wedding from a paparazzo photographer, Mr Thorpe, who had not been invited to the wedding. From various notices, however, it was clear that both he and *Hello!* must have been aware that the wedding was regarded as confidential (because photographs were to be published exclusively by *OK!*, the celebrity magazine). Affirming the analysis of Lindsay J at first instance, Lord Hoffmann (with whom Lords Brown and Baroness Hale agreed) had no doubt that Thorpe came under an obligation of confidentiality, which was binding upon *Hello!*. Douglas and Zeta-Jones had made it clear that there was to be no unauthorized photography, and had taken steps to exclude the uninvited and to preclude the taking of photographs. The rationale provided by Lindsay J—and seemingly adopted by their Lordships—was that Thorpe came under an obligation not because he was present illegally, but because he knew that the event was regarded as confidential. As for *Hello!*, Lindsay J explained that its 'conscience' was tainted and its actions lacked good faith, again because of its knowledge that the event was subject to an exclusive publication agreement with *OK!*.[44]

In *Tchenguiz v. Imerman*,[45] the logic was taken a step further. In this case, Tchenguiz accessed a server used by Mr Imerman to obtain his financial records. Tchenguiz wished to provide these to his sister, Mrs Imerman, to assist her in her divorce proceedings. Mr Imerman issued proceedings seeking to restrain use of the material. Having outlined the historical origins of the law of confidence, Lord Neuberger MR observed:

> If confidence applies to a defendant who adventitiously, but without authorisation, obtains information in respect of which he must have appreciated that the claimant had an expectation of privacy, it must, *a fortiori*, extend to a defendant who intentionally, and without authorisation, takes steps to obtain such information.[46]

4.2.1 Reverse engineering of encrypted information

These developments in the liability of strangers raise interesting questions with respect to potential liability for breach of confidence from acts of reverse engineering. If a person obtained information by dismantling a product (or decrypting a computer program), is that person to be taken to have appreciated that the information so acquired is confidential? The case law indicates that the answer is 'no'—at least where the product that is dismantled is freely available in the marketplace.

---

[42] M. Richardson, 'Breach of Confidence, Surreptitiously or Accidentally Obtained Information and Privacy: Theory Versus Law' (1994) 19 *Melb U L Rev* 673, 699.

[43] *Shelley Films v. Rex Features* [1994] *EMLR* 134.

[44] [2008] 1 *AC* 1, 46–7, [113]–[115] (Lord Hoffmann). See Gurry (2012), [7.94].

[45] [2011] *Fam* 116.   [46] Ibid., [67].

In *Mars v. Teknowledge*,[47] the claimant argued that a person buying a coin-operating machine that contained the encrypted information was under an implied duty of confidentiality in relation to the information. Applying the reasonable person test, Jacob J said that the information embodied in the machine was *not* obviously confidential. More specifically, Jacob J said:

> I cannot see why the mere fact of encryption makes that which is encrypted confidential or why anyone who de-crypts something in code, should necessarily be taken to be receiving information in confidence. He will appreciate that the source of the information did not want him to have access, but that is all.[48]

The decision in *Mars* should be contrasted with that in *Volkswagen v. Flavio Garcia*,[49] which concerned a threatened publication of an academic paper that would disclose the algorithms that were used by the claimant in its vehicle demobilizers. The defendants were cryptographers and had reverse engineered the algorithm from a chip, known as the 'Tango Programmer', which they had acquired from a Bulgarian website. The court, which was asked to grant an interim injunction, had to determine whether there was sufficient probability that the claimant would succeed at trial. They key question was whether the defendants were under an obligation of confidentiality. The court found that they were: the Tango Programmer, and thus the algorithm, had not been obtained from a legitimate source (such as one of the claimant's Porsche cars), but 'has a clearly murky origin'.[50] This was apparent to the judge from the website, which suggested that the vendor knew that the Tango Programmer was 'likely to facilitate crime'. Given that the defendants appreciated this, their 'consciences' were affected and they were under an obligation of confidence.

While it might be possible to distinguish these two cases by the differences in the origin of the information, in *Mars* the information was obtained lawfully from the owner of the information, whereas in *Volkswagen* it was received from a third party. This does not address the underlying difficulty with this approach, namely how it fits within the basic knowledge/notice test which is used to determine confidentiality. Put simply, the act of encryption gives notice that confidentiality is sought and this would be evident to anyone seeking to access the information.[51] Therefore, either encryption is an exception to the general rule or, we suggest a better approach, there is a positive right to reverse engineer a legitimately purchased product. The scope of that right might, however, be limited by contract or other means such as technical protection measures.[52] Indeed, the better approach we suggest is that provided for under the Trade Secrets Directive.[53]

4.3 TO WHOM IS THE OBLIGATION OWED?

Another question of significance that arose in *Douglas v. Hello!* was the question to whom the obligation was owed.[54] This question arose because the appeal was brought by *OK!* against *Hello!*, Douglas and Zeta-Jones having been satisfied by their victory, on Article 8 ECHR grounds, in the Court of Appeal. There, the Court had held that any obligation of

---

[47] [2000] *FSR* 138, discussed earlier.
[48] Ibid., 150. See T. Aplin, 'Reverse Engineering and Commercial Secrets' (2013) *CLP* 1.
[49] *Volkswagen Aktiengesellschaft v. Flavio D Garcia and ors* [2014] *FSR* 12.   [50] Ibid., [38].
[51] See T. Aplin 'Reverse Engineering and Commercial Secrets' (2013) 66 *CLP* 341, 358.
[52] See Chapter 13, section 4, pp. 374–81.
[53] The Trade Secrets Dir. (2016/943/EU), Art. 3(1)(b); Recital 16 states that reverse engineering of a lawfully acquired product should be permitted unless contractually restricted.
[54] For an extensive exploration, see Gurry (2012), ch. 8.

confidence was owed to Douglas and Zeta-Jones, and that the agreement into which they had entered with *OK!* had failed to transfer the benefit of any obligations to it. Indeed, Lord Phillips MR had gone so far as to say that the benefit of an obligation of confidence is not assignable. On appeal, the key issue was whether the obligations owed by Thorpe and *Hello!* were obligations owed to *OK!*. The majority held that they were, although Lord Hoffmann's reasoning is far from transparent. He explained that:

> [The point] of which one should never lose sight is that *OK!* had paid £1 million for the benefit of the obligation of confidence imposed upon all present at the wedding in respect of any photographs of the wedding . . . Unless there is some conceptual or policy reason why they should not have the benefit of that obligation, I cannot see why they were not entitled to enforce it.[55]

What is strange about Lord Hoffmann's reasoning is that it leaves unclear the precise legal mechanism by which an obligation came to be owed to *OK!*, as opposed to Douglas and Zeta-Jones. At one level, the implication is that any licensee of confidential information can bring an action against someone who uses that information in breach of confidence (at least if the latter person was aware that the licence or sharing arrangement existed). Lord Walker rightly observed, however, that, rather surprisingly, this would place a licensee of confidential information in a stronger legal position than licensees of other intellectual property rights.

5 EMPLOYEES

As we mentioned earlier, special considerations apply in relation to the application of the breach of confidence action between employer and employee. Because different obligations are imposed on an employee during employment from those that continue after the employment relationship has ended, we will deal with each separately.

5.1 DURING THE COURSE OF EMPLOYMENT

5.1.1 Express duties during employment

In many cases, the contract of employment will include express provisions dealing with the nature and scope of the duty of confidence owed by the employee to the employer. During the period of employment, the courts will enforce the express terms of the contract.[56] Any express terms imposing a duty of confidentiality upon the employee (it is rare for an employer to be under equivalent duty) are subject to the general rules of contract.

5.1.2 Implied duties during employment

While a contract might not contain express clauses imposing a duty of confidentiality upon an employee, this does not mean that employees will not be bound by a duty of confidence. As it was expressed by Lynskey J in *Bents Brewery v. Hogan*:[57]

---

[55] [2008] 1 *AC* 1, 47, [117].

[56] But note the Public Interest Disclosure Act 1998, s. 1, introducing the Employment Rights Act 1996, s. 43J (agreement void insofar as it purports to preclude a worker from making a protected disclosure). It has been suggested, however, that the effect of this protection has been 'incremental at best': see J. Ashton, '15 Years of Whistleblowing Protection under the Public Interest Disclosure Act 1998: Are We Still Shooting the Messenger' (2015) *ILJ* 29, 50. For other qualifications of such express obligations, see Gurry (2012), ch. 11.

[57] [1945] 2 *All ER* 570.

In my view, it is quite clear that an employee is under an obligation to his employers not to disclose confidential information obtained by him in the course of and as a result of his employment. Different judges, in various cases, have given different grounds for the existence of the obligation . . . Whatever the true ground may be, in my view, the obligation exists upon an employee not to disclose such confidential information. In my opinion, such obligation arises from an implied term in the contract of service.

Similarly, the courts have said that employees are under an implied duty of fidelity to their employers.[58] This duty of fidelity will prevent employees from disclosing information, from copying documents, and from competing with their employers.[59]

The courts have sometimes imposed more onerous obligations on more senior employees, primarily because of the fiduciary duty that they owe to their employer.[60] Fiduciary duties are automatically owed by directors and others in similar positions of trust.[61] The duty of a fiduciary is said to be one of 'single-minded or exclusive loyalty', to act in the employer's interests and not their own. The duty of fidelity is a less onerous obligation of loyalty, which is merely 'to take into consideration the interests of another'.[62]

5.2 AFTER EMPLOYMENT

Once the employment relationship has ended, different considerations apply.[63] On the one hand, employers have an interest in controlling the use that an employee is able to make of information that they acquired during the course of their employment. At the same time, this has been balanced against the fact that it would be unfair to enable employers to prohibit an employee from working in the same area again. This would effectively be the result if employers were able to control more generic skills that an employee might have gained during the course of their employment. If an employer repudiates the contract, it is unclear whether confidentiality obligations survive at all.[64]

5.2.1 Express obligations after employment: restraint of trade

An obligation specifically not to disclose trade secrets will rarely provide satisfactory protection to an ex-employer, since they would need to monitor carefully what every ex-employee is doing:[65] a near impossible challenge where an entire company's records can be carried on a single flash (USB) drive. In order to protect themselves, therefore, employers often include in their contracts of employment a clause—usually referred to as a 'restrictive covenant'—to the effect that the employee will not work in the same industry for a specified period after leaving employment. While acknowledging the importance of such clauses, the law also recognizes that employees should be free to make use of

---

[58] *Robb v. Green* [1895] 2 *QB* 315, 320; *Thomas Marshall v. Guinle* [1979] 1 *Ch* 227.

[59] *Hivac v. Park Royal Scientific Instruments* [1946] *Ch* 169.

[60] *Balston v. Headline Filters* [1990] *FSR* 385; *Helmut Integrated Systems Ltd v. Tunnard* [2007] *IRLR* 126; *Crowson Fabrics Ltd v. Rider* [2007] *FSR* 17 [77]–[85].

[61] *Item Software (UK) Ltd v. Fassahi* [200] 5] *ICR* 450, [41]; *Balston Ltd v. Headline Filters Ltd* [1990] *FSR* 385, [89] (Falconer J); *Tullett Prebon plc v. BGC Brokers LP and ors* [2010] *EWHC* 484 (QB), [66] (Jack J).

[62] *University of Nottingham v. Fishel* [2000] *ICR* 1462, 1492 (Elias J); *Helmet Integrated Systems Ltd v. Tunnard* [2007] *FSR* (16) 437, 448, [36] (Moses LJ).

[63] *Vestergaard Frandsens A/s v. Bestnet Europe Ltd* [2013] 1 *WLR* 1556, [44] (Lord Neuberger) (reiterating the social value of ex-employees engaging in honest competition with former employers).

[64] See *Campbell v. Frisbee* [2002] *EMLR* 31; *Rock Refrigerator Ltd v. Jones* [1977] 1 *All ER* 1; *General Billposting Co. Ltd v. Atkinson* [1909] *AC* 118.

[65] *Littlewoods Organisation v. Harris* [1978] 1 *All ER* 1026.

the personal skills, knowledge, experiences, and abilities gained in the course of their employment.[66] The courts have attempted to navigate these conflicting goals through the doctrine of restraint of trade.[67] In essence, this provides that a restrictive covenant will be struck down if the obligations go beyond what is reasonably necessary to protect the employer's interests.[68] More specifically, a restraint of trade clause will be enforceable only if it is appropriately limited as to time,[69] geographical coverage,[70] and the scope of activities (by reference to sector and roles).[71]

The operation of the doctrine can be seen from *Mont v. Mills*.[72] In this case, the defendant had been employed in the paper tissue industry for 20 years. He left the claimant company and signed a severance agreement, under which he received a large sum of money. The agreement also said that the defendant was required not to join another company in the tissue industry for one year. The defendant failed to honour this promise and became joint managing director of a competitor, whereupon the claimant sought an injunction. The Court of Appeal held that the severance agreement was unenforceable on the basis that it was an unjustifiable restraint of trade. This was because the undertaking was not limited as regards geographical area or the nature of the activities to which it applied. The Court declined to construe the clause restrictively—for to do so would provide employers with no incentive to impose restraints in appropriately limited terms.[73] Simon Brown LJ noted that the fact that the company had paid the ex-employee during the period of restraint did not prevent the agreement from being unenforceable. The law's concern was not merely that all persons should be able to earn a living. If that were the only policy, the law would permit an employer to buy such restraints. Rather, Simon Brown LJ argued, '[p]ublic policy clearly has regard to the public interest in competition and in the proper use of an employee's skills'.[74]

'Garden leave' The level of duty owed by employees to their employers differs markedly depending on whether or not they are employed.[75] If a company wishes to restrain an employee from entering into similar employment, the most effective mechanism is to retain them as an employee.[76] This is often done by placing employees on 'garden leave'. This occurs where an employee remains as a paid employee for a specified period of time, during which they are not required to attend work or carry out normal duties. In contrast with post-employment provisions, 'garden leave' agreements are not normally subject to the doctrine of restraint of trade; rather, they are enforceable. Even so, questions remain

---

[66] *Herbert Morris v. Saxelby* [1916] *AC* 688; *Attwood v. Lamont* [1920] 3 *KB* 571. On the potentially broader application of these principles, see *Force India Formula One Team v. 1 Malaysia Racing Team* [2012] *EWHC* 616 (Ch), but note that, on appeal, Lewison LJ did not regard any of this as relevant to the matters in hand: [2013] *RPC* 36, [61]; also see *PCCW-HKT Telephone v. Aiken* [2009] *HKCFA* 11 where Lord Hoffmann (sitting as a judge of the Hong Kong Court of Appeal) stated there is a 'public interest in allowing people to change jobs and make full use of their knowledge and skill'.

[67] See Chapter 12, section 2.2, pp. 329–31.

[68] The basic proposition stems from *Nordenfelt v. Maxim Nordenfelt* [1894] *AC* 535.

[69] *Herbert Morris* [1916] *AC* 688; cf. *Attorney-General v. Blake* [2000] 3 *WLR* 625, 647.

[70] *Commercial Plastics v. Vincent* [1964] 3 *All ER* 546; *Lansing Linde v. Kerr* [1991] 1 *All ER* 418, 426.

[71] *Technograph Printed Circuits Ltd v. Chalwyn* [1967] *FSR* 307; *Commercial Plastics Ltd v. Vincent* [1964] 3 *All ER* 546.

[72] [1993] *FSR* 577. See also *Thomas v. Farr* [2007] *ICR* 932.

[73] *Mont v. Mills* [1993] *FSR* 577, 585; *Lansing Linde* [1991] 1 *All ER* 418, 429.

[74] *Mont v. Mills* [1993] *FSR* 577, 587.

[75] In some cases, prompting an innocent employer to refuse to accept a repudiatory breach of contract by the employee: *Thomas Marshall* [1979] 1 *Ch* 227 (Megarry V-C).

[76] *Balston v. Headline Filters* [1990] *FSR* 385, 416.

as to what remedy is appropriate to enforce the contract.[77] In *GFI Group v. Egglestone*,[78] in which an employee was required to give 20 weeks' notice, the court granted an injunction to prevent the employee from working for a competitor for three months after he had given notice of resignation. Here, the court was influenced by the high pay that the employee received and the fact that the agreement had been negotiated between the parties (rather than imposed by the employer). Although the courts recognize employees' interest in exercising their skills, a 'garden leave' agreement will be enforced if failure to do so would harm the employer. The courts have suggested that an employer can utilize both a 'garden leave' agreement and a restrictive covenant, although the existence of the 'garden leave' agreement may be taken into account when determining the reasonableness of the restrictive covenant.[79]

5.2.2 Implied obligations after employment

In the absence of an express duty of confidence in the contract of employment, the courts may imply certain limited obligations on the use that ex-employees can make of information acquired during the course of their employment. In a normal business context,[80] the obligations imposed are primarily limited to the use that can be made of trade secrets.

The classic authority on the position of ex-employees is *Faccenda Chicken v. Fowler*.[81] In this case, the claimant, who sold fresh chickens from refrigerated vans, attempted to prevent a former employee from participating in a competing venture. The claimant argued that, in so doing, the ex-employee was utilizing confidential information concerning the customers, prices, products sold, and so forth. Because the ex-employee's contract contained no restrictive covenant, the Court of Appeal was called upon to decide the scope of implied post-employment obligations. The Court of Appeal held that an ex-employee's obligations were confined to 'trade secrets'. There is a difficulty in determining what a trade secret is, as identified by Straughton LJ in *Lansing Linde v. Kerr*:[82]

> It appears to me that the problem is one of definition: what are trade secrets, and how do they differ (if at all) from confidential information? [Counsel] suggested that a trade secret is information which, if disclosed to a competitor, would be liable to cause real (or significant) harm to the owner of the secret. I would add first, that it must be information used in a trade or business, and secondly that the owner must limit the dissemination of it or at least not encourage or permit widespread publication.

The sort of things which have been held to be trade secrets (rather than mere confidential information) include chemical formulae,[83] secret manufacturing processes,[84] designs and special methods of construction,[85] the names of customers and the products they buy,[86] and 'other information of a sufficiently high degree of confidentiality to amount to a trade secret'.[87]

In *Faccenda*, the Court of Appeal said that, in deciding whether information amounts to a trade secret, the court should consider four factors.

---

[77] *Credit Suisse Asset Management v. Armstrong* [1996] ICR 882, 892–4.   [78] [1994] *FSR* 535.
[79] *Credit Suisse v. Armstrong* [1996] ICR 882.
[80] But cf. *A-G v. Blake* [1998] 1 *All ER* 833 (in Secret Service context, duty of confidence survives as long as the information remains confidential).
[81] *Faccenda Chicken v. Fowler* [1987] 1 *Ch* 117.   [82] [1991] *1 WLR* 251, 260.
[83] *Amber Size & Chemical Co. v. Menzel* [1913] 2 *Ch* 239.   [84] *Herbert Morris* [1916] *AC* 688, 701.
[85] *Reid and Sigrist v. Moss and Mechanism* (1932) 49 *RPC* 461.
[86] *Lansing Linde v. Kerr* [1991] 1 *WLR* 251; also *Decorus v. Penfold* [2016] *EWHC* 1421 (QB), [93]–[94].
[87] *Printers & Finishers v. Holloway* [1965] *RPC* 239, 253; *Faccenda Chicken* [1987] 1 *Ch* 117, 136.

(i) *Nature of the employment* Under this heading, the court would consider things such as how near the employee is to the 'inner counsel' of the employer. This is because information made available only to trusted employees is more likely to constitute a trade secret than information disclosed to shop-floor workers.

(ii) *Nature of the information* To be capable of protection, the information must be defined with some degree of precision. Protection will not be available for general business methods and practices.[88] It has been said that just because the information is technical does not mean that it relates to trade secrets. If an employee is an expert or specialist, their general skill and knowledge might extend into the field of formulae, blends, or chemical processes.[89]

(iii) *Whether the employer impressed on the employee the confidentiality of the information* If information was specifically designated as a trade secret by the employer, it is more likely to be treated as such by the courts. However, the courts have noted that 'it would be unrealistic to expect a small and informal organization to adopt the same business disciplines as a larger and more bureaucratic concern'.[90] In the case of small businesses, the courts may treat information as a trade secret even though the employer did not identify it as such.

(iv) *Ease of isolation of the information* The final consideration taken into account when assessing whether information is a trade secret is whether the information can easily be isolated from other information (such as the employee's own stock of knowledge, skill, and expertise), which the employee is free to use or disclose.[91]

One issue that remains undecided is whether the obligations implied into an employment contract for the post-employment period change when an ex-employee intends to disclose, rather than use, the information. Because the policy considerations that restrict implied post-employment obligations to trade secrets aim to promote the mobility of labour and socially productive use of skills, it seems that the courts will be less generous to an ex-employee who sells information or exposes it gratuitously.[92]

---

[88] *Lancashire Fire v. S. & A. Lyons* [1996] *FSR* 629, 668; *Aveley/Cybervox v. Boman and Sign Electronic Signal* [1975] *FSR* 139; *Searle & Co. v. Celltech* [1982] *FSR* 92.

[89] *Ocular Sciences* [1997] *RPC* 289, 385 (Laddie J) (court should guard against imposing more stringent restraints on more technical employees).

[90] *Lancashire Fire* [1996] *FSR* 629, 668.

[91] *Printers and Finishers v. Holloway* [1965] *RPC* 239.

[92] *Faccenda Chicken v. Fowler* [1986] 3 *WLR* 288, 301; *United Indigo Chemical Co. Ltd v. Robinson* (1932) 49 *RPC* 178, 187; *Brooks v. Olysager Orms* [1998] *IRLR* 590.

46

BREACH AND DEFENCES

1 INTRODUCTION

In this chapter, we complete our examination of the breach of confidence action. After looking at the third factor that a claimant must show to sustain an action—namely, that the obligation of confidence has been breached, we look at the defences upon which a defendant may rely to escape liability. Finally, we consider the EU Trade Secrets Directive.

2 BREACH

The third and final factor that must be shown to establish breach of confidence is that the obligation of confidence has been breached.

2.1 SCOPE OF THE OBLIGATION

In order to determine whether the duty of confidence has been breached, it is first necessary to determine the scope of the obligation. At its most general, the duty of confidence prohibits the use and disclosure of the confidential information. While, logically, this would appear to mean that *acquisition* of information cannot be a breach of confidence (at least in cases in which no obligation arises until the information is acquired), the Court of Appeal has in fact held that the deliberate acquisition of information both gives rise to an obligation of confidence and involves the breach of that obligation.[1]

While the scope of the action *potentially* extends to any use or disclosure of the information, the scope of the obligations that are *actually* imposed upon an individual always depends on the facts of the case. In some circumstances, the obligation may provide that the confidential information should not be used or disclosed in any circumstances. In other situations, the confidant may use the information only for limited purposes, or for a certain period of time. Despite its importance, the question how the scope of the obligation is determined has received very little attention.

---

[1] *Tchenguiz v. Imerman* [2011] *Fam* 116 ('Intentionally obtaining such information, secretly and knowing that the claimant reasonably expects it to be private, is itself a breach of confidence'). Note that TRIPS, Art. 39, speaks of the disclosure, *acquisition*, or use of information as does the Trade Secrets Dir. (2016/943/EU), Art. 4(1).

Perhaps the most straightforward situation is where the obligation arises as a result of an *express* term in a contract or an express obligation in equity. In these situations, the scope of the obligation depends on the way in which the relevant provisions are interpreted. The task of determining the scope of the obligation becomes more difficult where the obligation is *implied* into a contract or imposed by equity. Presumably, in these cases, the scope of the obligation would depend on the views of the reasonable person in the circumstances.[2]

One area that warrants special attention is where the scope of the obligation arises via the so-called 'limited purpose test'.[3] As we saw earlier, where information is imparted for a limited purpose, this may give rise to an obligation of confidence. So one can readily infer that the information should not be used for another purpose and to do so breaches the obligation of confidence. In many cases, it will be clear from the circumstances that the confidant actually knew that the information being disclosed to them was to be used only for a restricted purpose. Thus, in *Kerry Ingredients v. Bakkavor Group*,[4] information was given by the claimant to the defendant to produce herb infused cooking oils for it to sell (such as basil olive oil) on its behalf. The defendant then used this information to make oil on its own account. This was held to be a breach of the obligation of confidentiality.

In other cases, the scope of the obligation is determined by the objective standard of what the confidant *ought* to have known. This can be seen from the Australian decision in *SmithKline & French v. Department of Community Health*.[5] In this case, the pharmaceutical company SK&F applied to the Australian Department of Community Services and Health for permission to market certain drugs. As part of the application process, SK&F supplied the Department with information concerning the drug. The Department of Community Services later proposed to use that information to decide whether it should authorize a different company to sell a related drug. SK&F argued that, in so doing, the Department had breached the duty of confidence owed to it. The reason for this was that SK&F had disclosed the information to the Department for only one specific purpose—namely, to enable its drug to be approved. The Federal Court refused the claimant's application for an injunction. The Court said that the scope of the obligation was not to be determined by the subjective views of the confider (here, SK&F); instead, it was to be decided by the objective standard of what the confidant knew or ought reasonably to have known in the circumstances. As such, the question to be considered was whether the relevant officers of the Department ought to have known that the data furnished by SK&F was disclosed for a limited purpose (thus excluding the Department's practice of using the data to evaluate other applications).

In so ruling, the Court suggested that a number of factors should be taken into account when determining the scope of the obligation. These include: whether the information was supplied gratuitously or for a consideration; whether there were any past practices that gave rise to an understanding that the use was limited; how sensitive the information was; whether the confider had any interest in the purpose for which the information was to be used; and whether the confider expressly warned the confidant against a particular disclosure or use of the information.

On the facts, the Federal Court held that the scope of the obligation did not restrict the Department's use of the information to the SK&F application. Two factors influenced

---

[2] Gurry (2012), [15.05].   [3] See Chapter 45, section 2.3(ii), p. 1237.

[4] [2016] *EWHC* 2448 (Ch).

[5] [1990] *FSR* 617, 647, 20 *IPR* 643. For the equivalent UK decision, see *R v. Licensing Authority, ex parte Smith-Kline & French Laboratories* [1989] *FSR* 440, 446 (obligation of confidence interpreted as of limited scope).

the Court in deciding that the equitable obligation had not been breached. The first was that previous practices (SK&F itself had submitted other applications in assessing which the Department relied upon information supplied earlier by SK&F) meant that 'it went without saying that the Department would look back at data that had already been submitted'.[6] The second factor that the Court stressed was that, in determining the scope of the obligation, it was necessary to 'have regard to the effect of the legal framework within which the parties were dealing', the Court adding that it would 'be slow to attribute to a regulatory authority knowledge that a party dealing with it expected it to act in a manner which would inhibit it in the exercise of its legal powers and obligations'.[7]

The question of the way in which the scope of the obligation should be determined was also considered by the Court of Appeal in *Source Informatics*.[8] In this case, Source collected information about doctors' prescribing habits and patterns, which it then sold to pharmaceutical companies, so that they could market their products more effectively. In return for a fee, pharmacists collated the relevant information from the prescription forms that had been completed by doctors and forwarded it to Source. Importantly, the information sent to Source did not include the name of the patients. The Department of Health issued a policy document that said that this process amounted to a breach of patient confidentiality. Source brought an action for judicial review, challenging the Department's policy. In particular, the company argued 'that disclosure by doctors or pharmacists to a third party of anonymous information (that is, information from which the identity of the patients may not be determined), does not constitute a breach of confidentiality'.[9] At first instance, the Department's policy had been upheld—but the Court of Appeal overturned the decision.

Simon Brown LJ began by noting that while the 'reasonable person' test is useful in determining whether there is a duty of confidence, it does not give guidance as to the scope of the obligation of confidentiality. In considering how the scope of the obligation was to be determined, Simon Brown LJ said that 'the touchstone by which to judge the scope of [the confidant's] duty and whether or not it has been fulfilled or breached is his own conscience, no more and no less'.[10] On the facts, this meant that it was necessary to ask 'would a reasonable pharmacist's conscience be troubled by the proposed use to be made of patients' prescriptions? Would he think that by entering Source's scheme he was breaking his customers' confidence, making unconscientious use of the information they provide?'[11] If the language used here is stripped bare, the test proposed is the same objective standard as that put forward in *SmithKline & French*.

Given this, it would be reasonable to assume that Simon Brown LJ would then have gone on to consider what the reasonable pharmacist knew or ought reasonably to have known in the circumstances.[12] Instead of adopting such an approach, Simon Brown LJ turned to focus on the type of information in question. In particular, he said that, in relation to personal information, 'the concern of the law is to protect the confider's personal privacy'.[13] Simon Brown LJ went on to say that the 'patient [has] no property in the information and no right to control its use provided only and always that his privacy is not put at risk'.[14] Using the language of rights, the Court held that the scope of the obligation was

---

[6] *SmithKline & French v. Department of Community Health* [1990] *FSR* 617, 646.   [7] Ibid., 647.
[8] *R v. Department of Health, ex parte Source Informatics* [2001] *QB* 424 (CA).   [9] Ibid., [5].
[10] Ibid., [31].   [11] Ibid.
[12] *SmithKline & French v. Department of Community Services and Health* (1991) 99 *ALR* 679, 691; followed in *ex parte Source Informatics* [2001] *QB* 424 (CA), 793.
[13] *R v. Department of Health, ex parte Source Informatics* [2001] *QB* 424 (CA), [34].   [14] Ibid.

limited to uses that would affect the confider's personal privacy. On the facts, the Court of Appeal held that, because the information had been used anonymously, the patient's privacy was safeguarded. The reasonable pharmacist's conscience ought not to have been troubled. As such, there was no breach of confidence. Despite the gesture towards the use of an objective standard of the reasonable pharmacist, the Court of Appeal relied more on the *a priori* language of rights (the patient's right of privacy) than on what a reasonable pharmacist would have concluded from the circumstances.[15]

One area in which problems may arise is where a number of people jointly generate information and one party later wants to develop it, but the others do not. For the most part, this question is decided in terms of the nature of the relationship between the parties. This can be seen in *Murray v. Yorkshire Fund Managers*.[16] In this case, a group of businessmen (including the claimant) developed a plan to take over an ailing business. While the financial backers were happy with the remainder of the team, they refused to work with the claimant. The claimant brought an action for breach of confidence, arguing that confidential information was disclosed to the defendant for the limited purpose of deciding whether the financier should invest in the venture disclosed in the business plan.[17] Rejecting this approach, Nourse LJ observed that there had never been a binding agreement that all of the members would continue to participate in the project, so that any of them could have withdrawn. He therefore concluded that the confidential information came into being for the purpose of facilitating the project and was best viewed as 'an adjunct of a relationship'. It followed that, when the claimant was excluded from the relationship, he lost the ability to control how the information was used.

The Court of Appeal decision should not be taken to be endorsing a view that one of several 'owners' of confidential information may use or exploit that information without the approval of the other 'co-owners'. Such a rule would raise complicated questions about who generated and contributed what information, and when such information came to be 'co-owned'. Rather, the Court of Appeal appears to have been attempting to produce a solution based on the expectations of the parties. This is also a sensible approach, in that if a different conclusion had been reached, it would have led to the unacceptable position in which one member of a team could prohibit the remaining members from using the information. If an individual member of a team has problems with the way in which jointly developed information is to be used, they should deal with it contractually at the outset of the arrangement.

2.2 HAS THE OBLIGATION BEEN BREACHED?

Once the scope of the obligation has been ascertained, it is then possible to consider whether the obligation has been breached. This is primarily a factual question. Before looking at this in more detail, it is important to note three things.

2.2.1 Derivation

The first is that, in order for a breach of confidence to occur, the information used by the defendant must have been *derived* from the confider's information and not from some other source. If the information has been independently generated, there is no breach. In

---

[15] The Court of Appeal might have reached the same conclusion had it looked at the conclusions that a reasonable pharmacist would have reached from the circumstances.

[16] [1998] 1 *WLR* 951.

CMI–Centers for Medical Innovation v. Phytopharm,[18] Laddie J noted that there are three ways of proving that a defendant has used the confidential information.

(i) The first is to show *direct evidence* of derivation. This would stem, for example, from an employee of the defendant who had seen the information being copied and then used.

(ii) The second way of proving derivation is *indirect*. For example, if the protected information were to contain a 'significant fingerprint'[19] and the defendant's use bore the same fingerprint, the court would infer that the defendant derived its product (etc.) from the claimant. For example, the defendant's product might have dimensions, a design, composition, or behaviour that is to be found only in the claimant's product, and which is consistent with use of the information and inconsistent with use of non-contaminated sources.[20] Laddie J also said that it might be possible to show that the defendant has gone to all of the same suppliers and customers as the claimant, and that it would be 'highly unlikely that the same group would have been approached had the defendant been working from uncontaminated sources'.[21]

(iii) Third, a claimant may be able to 'persuade the court that the defendant could not have got to the position they have with the speed he has had he simply started from legitimate sources and worked everything out for himself'.[22]

Even if an inference of derivation can be made from similarities, it is always open to the defendant to demonstrate independent creation. This is precisely what happened in the television format case, *Wade v. BBC*.[23] Here, the claimant had submitted a proposal for a music talent show, called *The Real Deal*, to the defendant. The proposed show was to feature singer-songwriters, with singer-songwriters as judges, and to have a 'whittle-down approach'. The defendant rejected the pitch, but went on to make a show entitled *Must Be the Music*. In contrast to the claimant's proposal, this was a Sunday night, rather than a prime-time, show, with an anti-music-industry tone (a cash prize rather than a record deal). However, the shows shared some features, including allowing downloads of the songs featured on the show, singer-songwriter contestants and judges, and the use of lapel badges (none of which was individually original). Without deciding that the shared features were sufficient in themselves to comprise confidential information,[24] Birss J considered whether the same features in the defendant's programme had been derived from the claimant's pitch. Given the evidence from those involved in developing *Must Be the Music*, he was persuaded that there was no derivation.[25] Only one person at the defendant company had seen the pitch and the ideas for *Must Be the Music* came from other people. A persuasive account was offered as to when and how the *Must Be the Music* format adopted each of the features that the two shows had in common.

2.2.2 The defendant's state of mind

The second general point to note is that the defendant's state of mind is not relevant when determining breach.[26] It is important to understand the distinction between knowledge

---

[17] Ibid., 960.   [18] [1999] *FSR* 235, 257–8.

[19] Ibid.; *Vestergaard Frandsen A/S v. Bestnet Europe Ltd* [2011] *EWCA Civ* 424, [19]–[20] (Jacob LJ); *Berkeley Administration v. McClelland* [1990] *FSR* 505, 528.

[20] Another example might be a customer list with 'fake' customers. If the list held by the defendant is the same as that held by the claimant—including the fake customers—it must have been copied. While the real names might have been generated honestly, this could not be said of the fake names.

of the confidential nature of the information creating the obligation; and the lack of any requirement to prove knowledge in relation to the breach. It essentially arises where the defendant was acting in good faith, but were guilty of unconscious copying leading them to breach the obligation of confidence.[27] Indeed, the Supreme Court has confirmed in *Vestergaard v. Bestnet*[28] that:

> once it was found that they had received the information in confidence, their state of mind when using the information was irrelevant to the question of whether they had abused the confidence.

2.2.3 Damage?

While there has been little discussion of whether, to be actionable, a breach of confidence must cause damage, it seems that it is necessary to show harm only in relation to government secrets. In fact, in the case of government secrets, it is now established that the Crown must demonstrate a public interest in restraining disclosure.[29] In *Attorney General v. Guardian (No. 2)*,[30] Lord Keith refused the government's claim to an injunction on the ground that it was necessary for the government to prove damage from the continued publication of *Spycatcher*, and it could prove none. In contrast, in the case of personal secrets, there is no need to prove damage. As the Court of Appeal said in *McKennitt v. Ash*,[31] in relation to an action for violation of private information, there was no need to show detriment beyond the fact that there had been an invasion of the claimant's private life. It also appears that, despite Megarry J's expression of doubt in *Coco v. Clark*,[32] there is also no reason for a claimant to prove harm in relation to commercial information. The Court of Appeal has said that if detriment is a requirement, the diversion of business opportunities could amount to a detriment to the person imparting the confidential information.[33]

2.2.4 Partial uses

A breach of confidence can occur even though the confidant does not use or disclose all of the confidential information that has been imparted or is subject to an obligation. Whether it will do so will vary with the circumstances of the case. If the claimant's confidential information is the product of a lot of work, a defendant might infringe if they use a part of the information.[34] However, if the confidential information was the product of very little effort, it is likely that there will be a breach of confidence only if all (or most) of the information was used. An approach of this nature was supported by the Court of

---

[21] *CMI–Centers for Medical Innovation v. Phytopharm* [1999] *FSR* 235, 258; *Talbot v. General Television Corp.* [1981] *RPC* 1, 17.

[22] *CMI–Centers for Medical Innovation v. Phytopharm* [1999] *FSR* 235, 257–8.

[23] [2014] *EWHC* 634 (Ch); upheld [2016] *EWCA Civ* 1214.

[24] [2014] *EWHC* 634 (Ch), [81], [122] (Birss J).   [25] Ibid., [121].

[26] But *mens rea* is often a component when establishing the defendant's obligation. See Chapter 45.

[27] *Seager v. Copydex* [1967] 1 *WLR* 923; *National Broach & Machine Co. v. Churchill Gear* [1965] *RPC* 61; *Terrapin Ltd v. Builders Supply Co. (Hayes)* [1967] *RPC* 375; *Talbot v. GTV* [1981] *RPC* 1, 17.

[28] [2013] 1 *WLR* 1556, [24].   [29] *Lord Advocate v. The Scotsman Publications Ltd* [1989] *FSR* 580.

[30] [1990] *AC* 109, 260 (Lord Keith).

[31] [2006] *EWCA Civ* 1714. See also *Bluck v. Information Commissioner* (2007) *WL* 4266,111, [2008] *WTLR* 1, [15]; *Attorney-General v. Guardian* [1990] *AC* 109, 256.

[32] [1969] *RPC* 41.

[33] *Federal Bank of the Middle East v. Hadkinson* [2000] 2 *All ER* 395, 413–14.

[34] *Amber Size v. Menzel* [1913] 2 *Ch* 239, 248 ('material part of the plaintiff's secret method').

Appeal in *Source Informatics* when Simon Brown LJ agreed with the comment that 'a confidant will be liable for breach of his duty if he misuses *only part* of the confidential information which has been disclosed to him, provided that the misuse relates to a *material* part of the information'.[35]

The question whether partial use of information could constitute a breach was considered in *De Maudsley v. Palumbo*.[36] As we saw earlier,[37] this was a breach of confidence action brought in relation to an idea for a nightclub (which was rejected because the information was too vague). The court suggested that, to breach, the defendant would have needed to have used substantially the same idea. The defendant had adopted only two of the five features of the claimant's idea for a nightclub (namely, that the club was to be open all night and to have separate dancing areas). Knox J held that (in these circumstances) partial use would not be sufficient to constitute an unauthorized use for the purposes of breach of confidence. The judge also took into account that the defendant had added a number of important features, such as the idea that the club would not sell alcohol and that admission would be limited to those over the age of 21.

2.2.5 Where the defendant alters the confidential information

Another situation in which questions about the nature of the breach arise is where the defendant adds to or alters the confidential information. In these cases, the information ultimately used or disclosed is different from the information that was originally disclosed by the claimant. In *Ocular Sciences*,[38] Laddie J took the view that it was a question of fact whether the use of a derived product should be treated as a use of the information employed in its creation. He said:

> It is not every derived product, process or business which should be treated as a camouflaged embodiment of the confidential information and not all ongoing exploitation of such products, processes or business should be treated as continued use of the information. It must be a matter of degree whether the extent and importance of the use of the confidential information is such that continued exploitation of the derived matter should be viewed as continued use of the information.[39]

It seems that similar reasoning would apply in other situations in which the information used by the defendant is different from the information that was originally disclosed by the claimant. Following similar logic, the courts held that information about etchings was replicated when it appeared in a catalogue containing descriptions of those etchings.[40] In another case, it was held that information about the processes for making sausage casings was used by the import of sausage casings that had been bought from a manufacturer who had wrongfully used that information.[41] However, it has been held that the use of a confidential computer program did not justify broader relief relating to the defendant's business, which had benefited from previous use of the program.[42] The problem here was that there was no evidence that the program made any significant contribution to the business.

---

[35] Gurry (1984), [15.10], quoted with approval in *ex parte Source Informatics* [2000] 1 *All ER* 786 (CA), 796.

[36] [1996] *FSR* 447.   [37] See Chapter 44, section 4, pp. 1210–12.

[38] [1997] *RPC* 289.   [39] Ibid., 404.

[40] *Prince Albert v. Strange* (1849) 2 *DeG & Sm* 652, 64 *ER* 293 (Knight Bruce LJ); (1849) 1 *Mac & G* 25, 41 *ER* 1171 (Cottenham LC).

[41] *Union Carbide Corp. v. Naturin Ltd* [1987] *FSR* 538, 547.

[42] *Ocular Sciences* [1997] *RPC* 289, 403.

3 ACCESSORY LIABILITY

As already observed, a third party who receives confidential information can come under an obligation of confidence. Such obligations are (almost certainly) treated in the same way as the primary obligations of a confidant. However, courts have been confronted also with issues of potential accessory liability. In cases of 'tort', the principles are well developed,[43] but the peculiar status of the action for breach of confidence has left doubts as to the way in which accessory liability should be assessed. In *Vestergaard Frandsens A/s v. Bestnet Europe Ltd*,[44] the Supreme Court was asked to consider precisely such a question. Here, Vestergaard had been involved in the manufacture of mosquito nets that were designed to leech insecticide slowly and thus protect users. Vestergaard had been assisted in developing its product by a consultant; in due course, the consultant established a competing firm (Bestnet) and, relying on information that originated with Vestergaard, produced a similar product. The liability of Bestnet and the consultant was established, but what was at issue before the Supreme Court was the liability of Ms Sig, an ex-employee of Vestergaard, who had worked as a sales and marketing assistant. Sig was, in fact, a key figure in setting up Bestnet, but had never received the confidential information, either while an employee of Vestergaard, or afterwards. Lord Neuberger, with whom the Supreme Court agreed, found that Sig was not liable under her employment contract, or under the standard rules of confidence. However, he acknowledged that 'a person who assists . . . in the misuse can be liable in a secondary sense'.[45] Drawing on the principles of the law of 'knowing assistance' in breach of trust, for such liability to exist, a person 'would normally have to know that the recipient was abusing confidential information. Knowledge in this context . . . would include what is sometimes called "blind-eye knowledge".'[46] Because Sig was unaware that the consultant was using Vestergaard's confidential information, such liability was not established. There was no 'blind-eye knowledge',[47] because there was no finding of dishonesty on Sig's part, and merely taking a risk in acting as she did was not sufficient to establish such dishonesty.[48] Although Lord Neuberger purported to adopt 'the approach of equity in this area', he later acknowledged that 'common design can, in principle, be invoked against a defendant in a claim based on misuse of confidential information'[49] (even though 'common design' is very much the language of joint tortfeasance). However, to be said to be a party to a common design, a person 'must share with the other party, or parties, to the design, each of the features of the design which make it wrongful'.[50] Although she was party to various activities that rendered the consultant and Bestnet liable, because Ms Sig did not know that confidential information was being misused, she was not herself party to any common design to commit a wrong.

4 DEFENCES

Once it is established that a defendant has breached an obligation of confidentiality, the only way in which they can escape liability is if they can show that they fall within one of the defences that are available to them. These include consent or authorization to use the

---

[43] See Chapter 48, Section 3.4, pp. 1287–96.   [44] [2013] *UKSC* 31.   [45] Ibid., [26].

[46] Citing *Royal Brunei Airlines Sdn Bhd v. Tan* [1995] 2 *AC* 378, 390–1 (Lord Nichols).

[47] Sometimes called 'Nelsonian knowledge' after the story of how Admiral Nelson put a telescope to his blind eye at the Battle of Copenhagen to avoid seeing a signal to retreat from his Commanding Officer.

[48] [2013] 1 *WLR* 1556, [40]–[43].

[49] Ibid., [33]. At first instance, Arnold J had found that 'common design' might be available to substantiate accessory liability for breach of confidence: [2010] *FSR* 2, [19].

[50] [2013] 1 *WLR* 1556, [34].

information and disclosure in the public interest, as well as a number of other equitable and statutory immunities. We examine these in turn.

4.1 CONSENT OR AUTHORIZATION

If a defendant is able to show that the claimant consented to or authorized the use of the information, they will be exempt from breach. Consent to the use or disclosure of information can arise through an express licence or from a release from liability. An express licence might be contractual in nature, as with a technology-licensing agreement, or gratuitous. Consent or authorization might also be implied from the circumstances.[51]

4.2 PUBLIC INTEREST DEFENCE

The most important defence available to a defendant is the public interest defence. This provides defendants with the opportunity to escape liability for breach if they can establish that the disclosure is justified in the public interest. As Lord Phillips said, 'the right of confidentiality, whether or not founded in contract, is not absolute. That right must give way where it is in the public interest that the confidential information shall be made public.'[52] The origin of the defence lies in the dicta of Wood V-C in the 1856 decision in *Gartside v. Outram*.[53] In that case, the claimant, who carried on business as a woolbroker, brought an action to restrain the defendant, an ex-employee, from communicating information about its business dealings. The defendant asserted that the claimant had been defrauding its customers using falsified business records. Wood V-C held that if the defendant were to make out the case pleaded by him, he would have 'a very good case for resisting this injunction'.[54] He said that:

> [T]here is no confidence as to the disclosure of iniquity. You cannot make me the confidant of a crime or a fraud, and be entitled to close up my lips upon any secret which you have the audacity to disclose to me relating to any fraudulent intention on your part: such a confidence cannot exist.[55]

Although Wood V-C's comments suggest that the public interest is not so much a defence as a reason why the court will not recognize an obligation of confidence in the first place, case law since the 1960s has treated public interest as a defence in its own right. For example, in *Initial Services v. Putterill*,[56] the defendant had been employed as a sales manager by the claimant company, a laundry firm. The defendant resigned and revealed documents to the *Daily Mail* exposing the claimant's price fixing. After the *Daily Mail* published articles about the price fixing, the claimant brought an action for breach of confidence. In response, the ex-employee argued that the disclosure was in the public interest because it revealed that the claimant was party to an unlawful price-fixing agreement. The claimant's action failed. Salmon and Winn LJJ applied the iniquity rule, but

---

[51] This was argued unsuccessfully in *Turner v. Royal Bank of Scotland* [1999] *Lloyd's Reports* 231 (bank customers consent to credit check by implication).

[52] *Campbell v. Frisbee* [2002] *EMLR* 31, [23]. See also *Douglas v. Hello!* [2008] 1 *AC* 1, [272] (Lord Walker), [307] (Baroness Hale) (contrasting public interest in disclosure with private interest in secrecy).

[53] (1856) 26 *LJ (NS) Ch* 113, 5 *WR* 35, 3 *Jur (NS)* 39, 28 *LTOS* 120. The judgment was delivered *extempore* and the reports vary. The judge was adopting a comment by Counsel, Serjeant Tisdall, in *Annesley v. Earl of Anglesea* (1743) 17 *State Trials* 1139, col. 1229.

[54] (1856) 26 *LJ (NS) Ch* 116, 5 *WR* 35, 3 *Jur (NS)* 39, 28 *LTOS* 120.

[55] Ibid., 114.   [56] [1968] 1 *QB* 396.

widened it to include improper trade practices. This was on the ground that 'what was iniquity in 1856 differed from what was iniquity in 1967'.[57] Lord Denning suggested a different test altogether: that the defence was not limited to crime or fraud, but rather covered any misconduct of such a nature that it is in the public interest to disclose.[58] Lord Denning reasserted this view in *Fraser v. Evans*,[59] in which he said that iniquity is merely an example of a 'just cause or excuse' for breaking a breach of confidence. More recently, the courts have incorporated the generalized public interest defence into a balancing process. For example, in *Spycatcher*, Lord Goff explained that, 'although the basis of the law's protection of confidence is a public interest that confidences should be preserved and protected by law, nevertheless that public interest may be outweighed by some other countervailing public interest which favours disclosure'.[60]

Indeed, in relation to personal information the approach taken by the court is usually to weigh two fundamental rights those of privacy and freedom of expression under Articles 8 and 10 of the European Convention of Human Rights. Indeed, most such claims are now framed as misuse of private information and so the balancing exercise in such cases will be considered in Chapter 47.

4.2.1 What is the public interest?

While it is impossible to delimit the types of circumstance in which a particular disclosure will be in the public interest, a number of different factors are taken into account when deciding whether the disclosure is in the public interest.[61]

(i) Nature of the information A key factor to be considered will be the nature of the information. If a disclosure relates to misdeeds of a serious nature and importance to the country, then it is likely to be justified as being 'in the public interest'.[62] Disclosure relating to a criminal offence, civil wrong,[63] non-compliance with a legal obligation, a miscarriage of justice, behaviour likely to endanger health or safety, or damage the environment are obvious examples of cases in which disclosure might be justified. Although the public interest defence is defined broadly, it does not permit the unauthorized disclosure of information that is merely 'interesting to the public'.[64] In this context, the law draws a distinction between matters that affect the moral, political, medical, or material welfare of the public (or a section thereof), *and* the public's entertainment, curiosity, or amusement.

Having said this, the courts have been willing in the past to permit the disclosure of confidential information in the public interest where it serves to correct a false image that a person has created about themselves. As the House of Lords made clear in *Campbell v. MGN*,[65] where a public figure makes untrue statements as to their private life, the press will normally be entitled to put the record straight—particularly where they have courted, rather than shunned, publicity. This can be seen, for example, in *Woodward v. Hutchins*,[66] in which the Court of Appeal held that disclosure by their former press agent of the private activities of a group of pop stars (including Tom Jones and Engelbert

---

[57] Ibid., 410.   [58] Ibid., 405.   [59] [1969] 1 *QB* 349.

[60] *Attorney-General v. Guardian* [1990] *AC* 109, 282. See also Lord Griffiths, ibid., 269.

[61] These factors are reflected in the provisions of the Public Interest Disclosure Act 1998, which protects employees from action by employers as regards 'protected disclosures'.

[62] *Beloff v. Pressdram* [1973] 1 *All ER* 241, 260; cf. *Bunn v. BBC* [1998] 3 *All ER* 552.

[63] *Frankson v. Home Office* [2003] 1 *WLR* 1952.

[64] *Lion Laboratories v. Evans* [1985] *QB* 526, 537.

[65] [2004] 2 *AC* 457, 467, [24] (Lord Nicholls); 474–5, [58] (Lord Hoffmann); 479, [82] (Lord Hope); 500, [151]–[152] (Baroness Hale).

[66] [1977] 1 *WLR* 760, 763.

Humperdink) was justifiable where they had falsely represented to the public that they were clean-living. According to Lord Denning, if the image that a public figure fostered was 'not a true image, it is in the public interest that it should be corrected', because, in these cases, 'it is a question of balancing the public interest in maintaining the confidence against the public interest in knowing the truth'.[67] While the application of *Woodward* as a defence to a confidence claim probably subsists,[68] it is not clear that merely correcting a false impression is not a sufficient defence to a claim for misuse of private information.[69] This effect of running such a defence in a confidence case is therefore nugatory.

(ii) Consequences of non-disclosure A disclosure may be justified as being in the public interest, even though it does not reveal wrongful behaviour or misconduct,[70] for example where the disclosure will protect public health or safety.[71] In *Lion Laboratories*,[72] the court held that it was legitimate for the press to disclose confidential internal papers that suggested that an alcohol-measuring machine was faulty. (The machine was used to test whether drivers were guilty of driving under the influence of alcohol.) The disclosure was justified because if the information had remained concealed, the life and liberty of an unascertainable number of persons might have been affected. Revelation in the press was justified because disclosure to the police might not have been adequate.[73]

(iii) Type of obligation Another factor that is likely to play a significant role in determining whether a disclosure is permissible is the type of obligation involved. It seems that the courts will treat some obligations as more absolute than others. For example, a disclosure by a priest or doctor could rarely be justified in the public interest.[74] In a rare case, the Court of Appeal held that a psychiatrist was justified in breaching the obligation of confidence that he owed to a patient who had been interned, by alerting the Home Office to the patient's interests in firearms and explosives.[75] This was vital information, directly relevant to public safety. The courts have also suggested that they will give more weight to obligations that arise through agreement than through other means. For example, in *Campbell v. Frisbee*, it was said that:

> [A] duty of confidentiality that has been expressly assumed under a contract [arguably] carries more weight, when balanced against the restriction of the right of freedom of expression, than a duty of confidentiality that is not buttressed by express agreement.[76]

(iv) Beliefs of the confidant Because the public interest defence covers any situation in which there is 'just cause or excuse' for breaking a confidence, the court is not confined to considering whether the information is *in fact* real misconduct. Instead, the court can also take into account whether the confidant believed on reasonable grounds that revelation was required in the public interest.[77] In other words, according to the broader 'just cause' characterization of the defence, a disclosure may be justified where the confidant

[67] Ibid., 764.   [68] *Campbell v. MGN* [2004] 2 *AC* 457

[69] See, for instance, *Mosley v. News Group Newspapers* [2008] *EWHC* 1777 (QB) (unsuccessfully argued that a public interest in exposing the crime of actual bodily harm taking place as part of sadomasochistic activities).

[70] *Malone v. Metropolitan Police Commissioner* [1979] *Ch* 344, 362 (Megarry V-C).

[71] *Hubbard v. Vosper* [1972] 2 *QB* 84.   [72] *Lion Laboratories v. Evans* [1985] *QB* 526.

[73] See also *W v. Egdell* [1990] 2 *WLR* 47; *Schering Chemicals v. Falkman* [1982] 1 *QB* 1.

[74] *X Health Authority v. Y* [1988] *RPC* 379, 395.   [75] *W v. Egdell* [1990] *Ch* 359.

[76] *Campbell v. Frisbee* [2002] *EMLR* 31, [22]. See R. Arnold, 'The Protection of Confidential Information in the Human Rights Era: Two Aspects' [2007] *JIPLP* 599 (questioning the significance of express contractual obligation).

[77] *Fraser v. Evans* [1969] 1 *All ER* 8.

reasonably believed that they were disclosing an iniquity, even if it turns out that they were wrong.[78] For example, in *Malone v. Metropolitan Police Commissioner*,[79] it was held that if the police owed a duty of confidentiality, nevertheless there was a reasonable suspicion of iniquity such as to justify the disclosure.

(v) Party to whom the information was disclosed Another factor that will influence whether a disclosure is justified is the party to whom the information is disclosed.[80] It may be legitimate to disclose information to one body, but not another. For example, while a disclosure is likely to be justified if it is made to a responsible body,[81] it is less likely to be justified if it is disclosed to the general public via a newspaper. As the Court of Appeal emphasized in *Lion Laboratories*,[82] newspapers must take special care not to confuse the public interest with their own interest in increasing circulation. Thus if the confidence relates to a crime, for a disclosure to be justified, it should normally be made to the police.[83] In *Francome v. Mirror Group Newspapers*,[84] an interim injunction was granted preventing disclosure in a newspaper of conversations that were alleged to reveal that Johnny Francome had breached Jockey Club regulations and possibly committed criminal offences. The main basis of the decision appears to have been that disclosure to the Jockey Club would have sufficed: there was no need for full newspaper disclosure.[85] Conversely, in *Jockey Club v. Buffham*,[86] the disclosure of confidential information regarding the Jockey Club in a current affairs television programme was permitted on the grounds that revealing wide-scale corruption is of legitimate interest to the wide section of the public who participate or follow racing. The reason why disclosure to the public at large might be considered acceptable in both *Lion Laboratories* and *Buffham*, in contrast to other cases, is that revelations could directly affect the behaviour of individuals. They may seek to challenge the reading on a breathalyser or cease betting on potentially corrupt races. Another situation where such a disclosure to the public might be acceptable is where the appropriate authorities are unlikely to act as they are complicit. Nevertheless, in general it remains the case that a disclosure to the public at large in a newspaper will usually not be justified.

(vi) Other factors A number of other factors may influence the court in determining whether disclosure is in the public interest. For example, in *Francome*, the court took account of the manner in which the information was acquired.[87] Another relevant factor is whether the person claiming the defence received remuneration for the disclosure.[88] While receipt of remuneration does not preclude the operation of the defence,[89] it may indicate that a defendant confused their own interests with those of the public.[90] Finally,

---

[78] Y. Cripps, *Disclosure in the Public Interest* (1994), 25–6. A difficulty can arise where the allegation, if untrue, is defamatory. It is not possible to obtain an injunction to prevent the publication of a libel, but it is to prevent the disclosure of information which is in breach of confidence.

[79] [1979] *Ch* 344, 377. See also *Woolgar v. Chief Constable of Sussex Police* [2000] 1 *WLR* 25, 36.

[80] The Employment Rights Act 1986 allows for disclosures to employers, prescribed bodies, and 'in other cases'. In the latter instance, the person to whom the information is revealed is a significant factor in assessing whether a disclosure is 'qualifying': ERA 1986, ss 43G(3)(a), 43H(2). See also *R v. Plymouth City Council* [2002] 1 *WLR* 2583, 2599, [50]; *Jockey Club v. Buffham* [2003] *QB* 462, 475–79.

[81] *Imutran v. Uncaged Campaigns* [2002] *FSR* 21, 28.   [82] [1985] *QB* 526.

[83] *Initial Services* [1968] 1 *QB* 396, 405–6.   [84] [1984] 1 *WLR* 892.

[85] Ibid., 899 (Lord Donaldson MR).   [86] [2003] *QB* 462.

[87] *Francome v. Mirror Group Newspapers* [1984] 1 *WLR* 892 (1949). See also ERA 1986, s. 43B(3) (not a qualifying disclosure if person commits an offence by making it).

[88] *Initial Services* [1968] 1 *QB* 396, 406.

[89] *Hubbard v. Vosper* [1972] 2 *QB* 84; *Church of Scientology v. Kaufman* [1973] *RPC* 627, 635; cf. ERA 1986, ss 43G(c), 43H(1)(c) (not a qualifying disclosure if person makes disclosure for personal gain).

[90] *Schering v. Falkman* [1982] 1 *QB* 1, 39.

it seems that the extent to which the information is already publicly available may impact on the operation of the public interest defence. If the information is not very confidential, disclosure may be justified even if there is only a low level of public interest.

(vii) Public and private interests Typically, the public interest defence is characterized as the balancing of one public interest against another. The idea that it might involve a balancing of public interest against a private interest was rejected in *W v. Egdell*,[91] in which the relevant private interest was that of the confider. It has yet to be seen, however, whether the courts might accept a defence of disclosure in the private interests of the person to whom the disclosure was made. For example, if a doctor who knew that a patient had a contagious disease were to disclose that information to a person in a sexual relationship with the patient, the court might be tempted to develop a defence of justified disclosure in the private interest.[92]

A related question is whether disclosure can be justified by reference to the confider's own interests. For example, is a doctor justified in revealing information about treatment of a child to the child's parents? While, in *Gillick*,[93] the majority of the House of Lords held that doctors did not have a duty to inform parents about the advice that the doctor had given to the children (here, in relation to contraception), the Lords did not express any view on whether, if doctors were to do so, they would be in breach. Lord Templeman, dissenting, was clear that 'confidentiality owed to an infant is not breached by disclosure to a parent responsible to that infant if the doctor considers that such disclosure is necessary in the interests of the infant'.[94]

4.3 FREEDOM OF EXPRESSION

One of the factors that the courts take into account in deciding whether to grant relief for breach of confidence is the right to freedom of expression provided for in Article 10 of the European Convention of Human Rights (ECHR). This right, which is directly applicable as between the parties to private litigation,[95] operates independently of the public interest defence. As the Court of Appeal said, interference with the right has to be justified 'even where there was no identifiable special public interest in the material in question being published, since the existence of a free press was desirable in itself'.[96] While freedom of expression is valuable as a counterforce to privacy, the courts have been at pains to point out that it is not an 'ace of trumps'[97]—that is, freedom of speech is not paramount and must be balanced against other interests.[98] The balancing exercise is considered in more detail as part of the discussion of misuse of private information.

4.4 MISCELLANEOUS IMMUNITIES

A defendant may also be immune from a breach of confidence action where they have revealed information pursuant to a statutory obligation or a court order. For instance,

---

[91] [1990] 2 *WLR* 47, 485.

[92] D. Caswell, 'Disclosure by a Physician of AIDS-related Patient Information: An Ethical and Legal Dilemma' (1989) 68 *Can BR* 225.

[93] *Gillick v. West Norfolk & Wisbech Health Authority* [1985] 3 *All ER* 402, 410–13.

[94] Ibid., 434.

[95] *Douglas v. Hello!* [2001] *QB* 967(CA), 1027, [133] (Sedley LJ); *Response Handling v. BBC* (2008) *SLT* 51 (OH).

[96] See *A v. B* [2003] *QB* 195 (CA), 205.   [97] *Douglas v. Hello! (No. 3)* [2003] 3 *All ER* 996, [185].

[98] *Imutran* [2002] *FSR* 21, 28, [17].

doctors have an obligation to report certain contagious diseases[99] and when they perform abortions.[100] There are also general obligations on many professionals to disclosure incidents of money laundering.[101]

Another way in which a defendant might be able to escape liability is via the equitable principle that, for a claimant to bring an action in equity, they must have 'clean hands'.[102] However, it is a principle which the courts see as having very limited application.[103]

5 THE EU DIRECTIVE

As will be clear, breach of confidence has a peculiarly common law heritage. However, in 2016 the European Union adopted a Directive on the protection of trade secrets.[104] The Directive must be implemented by Member States by 9 June 2018.[105] While this means that the UK government will have implemented the Directive, it only enacted legislation in relation to procedure and remedies and not the substantive provisions of the Directive.[106] The Directive is divided into two parts. The second part deals with remedies and largely reflects the provisions of the Enforcement Directive.[107] The first part deals with the substantive protection of trade secrets. This is the only part of the Directive which the United Kingdom believes needs implementing (notwithstanding many of the equivalent provisions were not made to implement the earlier Enforcement Directive).

The Directive provides only that Member States must provide certain redress to trade secret holders. It is a minimum standards Directive[108] and so member states are entitled to give more protection than that required by the Directive. This is significant in the context of English law as, in most respects, a breach of confidence action will go further than that required by the Directive.[109] Indeed, the government have taken the view that nothing further is required.[110]

The Directive does not dictate precisely how this is done. It does provide, however, that there should be no exclusive right in any trade secret.[111] Furthermore, as the Directive

---

[99] Under the Public Health (Control of Diseases) Act 1984 and the Public Health (Infectious Diseases) Regulations 1988 (SI 1988/1546).

[100] Abortion Act 1967; Abortion Regulations 1991 (SI 1991/499).

[101] Under the Proceeds of Crime Act 2002, Part 7.

[102] See *Hubbard v. Vosper* [1972] 2 *QB* 84, 101 (Megaw LJ); *Church of Scientology v. Kaufman* [1973] *RPC* 627.

[103] See *A-G v. Heinemann Publishers* [1989] 2 *FSR* 349, 506 (NSW).

[104] Trade Secrets Dir. (2016/943/EU). The European Commission commissioned a report on the role of trade secrets in encouraging innovation: Hogan Lovells International, *Study on Trade Secrets and Parasitic Copying (Look-alikes): Report on Trade Secrets for the European Commission* (September 2011) MARKT/2010/20/D; the Max Planck Institute have also undertaken a detailed assessment: see R. Knaak, A. Kur, and R Hilty, 'Comments of the Max Planck Institute for Innovation and Competition on the Proposal for a Directive on the protection of undisclosed know-how and business information (trade secrets) against their unlawful acquisition, use and disclosure' (2014) *IIC* 953.

[105] See generally, T. Aplin, 'A Critical Evaluation of the Proposed EU Trade Secrets Directive' (2014) *IPQ* 257.

[106] Trade Secrets (Enforcement, etc) Regulations 2018 (SI 2018/597)

[107] Dir. 2004/29/EC (although in cases of overlap the Trade Secrets Dir. takes precedence, Recital 39; see Dir. 2004/48/EC.

[108] Trade Secrets Dir., Art. 1(1).

[109] The substantive defences required by the Directive are probably more significant.

[110] IPO UK, *Consultation on Draft Regulations concerning trade secrets* (2018), 28.

[111] Trade Secrets Dir., Recital 16.

is based largely of the obligations under Article 39 of the Agreement on Trade Related Aspects of Intellectual Property Rights 1994 (TRIPS), which provides the protection of trade secrets is an act of unfair competition, it is likely that this is the view that will be taken by the Court of Justice.

The definition of 'subject matter'[112] applied in the Directive also comes from Article 39[113] and includes a condition—namely, that 'the information has been subject to reasonable steps under the circumstances, by the person lawfully in control of the information, to keep it secret'.[114] This appears to be a much stricter test than that applied under the law of confidence, which simply requires at least constructive knowledge that the person wants the information to be confidential.

The Directive also provides the circumstances under which acquisition, use, or disclosure is unlawful.[115] The *acquisition* of a trade secret is unlawful when it involves 'unauthorised access to, appropriation of, or copying of any documents, objects, materials, substances or electronic files, lawfully under the control of the trade secret holder, containing the trade secret or from which the trade secret can be deduced' or other conduct which is contrary to honest commercial practices.[116] The *use* or *disclosure* of the trade secret will be unlawful where the person using the information acquired it unlawfully, or used it in breach of confidentiality agreement or an agreement to limit the use of the trade secret (i.e. a limited purpose agreement).[117]

There are important safeguards for independent creation and reverse engineering. Under Article 3(1), the acquisition of trade secrets is said to be lawful when obtained by 'independent discovery or creation' or the 'observation, study, disassembly or test of a product or object that has been made available to the public or that it is lawfully in the possession of the acquirer of the information' (that is, reverse engineering).[118] However, a significant limitation has been imposed in that reverse engineering can be restricted by contractual agreement.[119] This may be a significant fetter as many trade secret holders would include such a restriction in their standard terms and conditions. This is why the Directive provides that the freedom to enter into such contracts can be restricted by law.

Moreover, the Directive explicitly deals with products made using trade secrets, which it designates 'infringing goods'.[120] It is provided that 'the production, offering or placing on the market of infringing goods, or the importation, export or storage of infringing goods' shall be considered an unlawful use of a trade secret where the person carrying out the activity knew, or ought to have known, that the trade secret was used unlawfully.[121] 'Infringing goods' are defined as goods whose 'design, quality, design, characteristics, functioning, production process or marketing of which significantly benefits from trade

---

[112] For an analysis of the uncertainties with this definition (and many other issues with the Directive), see S. Sandeen, 'Implementing the EU Trade Secret Directive: A View from the United States' [2017] *EIPR* 4, 5; also see N. Sousa e Silva, 'What Exactly is a Trade Secret under the Proposed Directive?' [2014] 9 *JIPLP* 923.

[113] See Trade Secrets Dir., Art. 2; see also Recital 14 (such definition should exclude trivial information, and should not extend to the knowledge and skills gained by employees in the normal course of their employment, and which are known among or accessible to persons within the circles that normally deal with the kind of information in question).

[114] Ibid., Art. 2(1)(c). The requirement can be traced back to the US Uniform Trade Secrets Act of 1979, as amended. On this aspect of US law, see especially B. Bone, 'Trade Secrecy, Innovation and the Requirement of Reasonable Secrecy Precautions', in R. Dreyfuss and K. Strandburg (eds), *The Law and Theory of Trade Secrecy: A Handbook of Contemporary Research* (2012). For signs of a similar requirement in English law, see *Cray Valley v. Deltech Europe* [2003] *EWHC* 728 (Ch).

[115] Trade Secrets Dir., Art. 4(2)–(4).   [116] Ibid., Art. 4(2).   [117] Ibid., Art. 4(3).

[118] There are other exceptions for information relating to workers and workers' representations.

[119] Trade Secrets Dir., Recital 16.   [120] Ibid., Art. 2(4).   [121] Ibid., Art. 4(5).

secrets unlawfully acquired, used or disclosed'.[122] The requirement of 'significance' will need elucidation in the context of specific cases and may prove difficult to apply in cases other than those of straightforward appropriation.

The Directive is general in its terms, and thus is applicable to trade secrets held by employees and ex-employees; and for this reason there is an exception relating to the provision of information to an employee.[123] It also appears that national doctrines, such as that relating to restraint of trade, will continue to apply and limitations on rules designed to protect ex-employees will remain applicable.[124] Furthermore, Recital 14 provides that the definition of trade secret does not extend to 'the experience and skills gained by employees in the normal course of their employment'. This appears to be a slight variation on the *Faccenda* criteria to an ex-employee,[125] but it is not clear whether it will be material.

The Directive contains safeguards that would correspond to the 'public interest' defence where the disclosure is for revealing misconduct, wrongdoing, or illegal activity.[126] This appears to be somewhat narrower than the current public interest defence in English law, and might be seen as a reversion to the older case law requiring an iniquity. However, this is counterbalanced somewhat by protection for 'exercising the right to freedom of expression and information as set out in the Charter'.[127] This is unlikely to go further than the courts currently do in the application of jurisprudence under Article 10 of the European Convention of Human Rights, but it may sweep up some aspects of the current public interest defence which fall outside that permitted by the Directive and would probably justify, for example, disclosures of the sort at issue in the *Lion Laboratories* case.[128] There is a final exception for protecting a legitimate interest recognized by Union or national law. It is not clear what such interests might be covered by this exemption. It is not the same as a use required by law (as that is provided for elsewhere[129]); it must be something less. It has been suggested that promoting competition and innovation may be a legitimate interest.[130] Notwithstanding the points of difference between the Directive and the English law identified, the government has suggested that all the required activities are permitted under existing employment and human rights enactments or the public interest defence.[131] This leaves it to the courts to model the breach of confidence action to be in accordance with the Directive.

---

[122] Ibid., Art. 2(4).   [123] Ibid., Art. 3(1)(c).   [124] See ibid., Art. 3(2).
[125] See Chapter 45, section 5.2.2, pp. 1234–5.   [126] Trade Secrets Dir., Art. 5(b).
[127] Ibid., Art. 5(a).
[128] *Lion Laboratories v. Evans* [1985] *QB* 526, discussed in section 4.2.1, pp. 1245–8.
[129] Trade Secrets Dir., Art., 3(2).
[130] T. Aplin, 'A Critical Evaluation of the Proposed EU Trade Secrets Directive' [2014] *IPQ* 257, 271.
[131] UK IPO, *Consultation on Draft Regulations concerning trade secrets* (2018), 28.

47

MISUSE OF PRIVATE INFORMATION

1 INTRODUCTION

The tort of misuse of private information originates from the action for breach of confidence, but it has mutated and evolved to become something quite different. The common law did not develop so as to create a free-standing right to privacy[1] rather the necessity to give effect to Article 8 of the European Convention on Human Rights (ECHR) under the Human Rights Act 1998 led to a need to protect privacy rights. It reads:

(1) Everyone has the right to respect for his private and family life, his home and his correspondence.
(2) There shall be no interference by a public authority with the exercise of this right except such as is in accordance with the law and is necessary in a democratic society in the interests of national security, public safety or the economic well-being of the country, for the prevention of disorder or crime, for the protection of health or morals, or for the protection of the rights and freedoms of others.

When the English courts were faced with the need to protect privacy, but without a common law action, they improvised,[2] and only recently have the courts completed the process by expressly recognizing a new tort of misuse of private information.[3] Yet it remains the case that many cases of misuse will also give rise to a confidence claim and, furthermore, that many principles from the law of confidence are equally applicable to misuse claims.[4]

The development of the tort of misuse of private information is therefore predicated on the fundamental rights in the Human Rights Act 1998 having 'horizontal effect'—that is between private parties—as well as 'vertical effect'—that is against the state. This possibility of such horizontal effect was first recognized by the Court of Appeal in *Douglas v.*

---

[1] *Wainwright v. Home Office* [2004] 2 *AC* 406.
[2] See *Google Inc v. Vidal-Hall* [2015] *FSR* (25) 728, [18].
[3] *PJS v. News Group Newspaper* [2016] *AC 1081*. A somewhat hidden factor in the evolution of the new tort is that most of the cases relating to misuse of private information have been against the media and so heard by the those expert in libel in the Queen's Bench Division and a few relating to family matters and so heard by family law judges in the Family Division; whereas trade secret cases, and only a few private information cases, have been heard in the Chancery Division usually by judges experienced in intellectual property matters.
[4] See *Imerman v. Tchenguiz* [2011] *Fam* 116, [65]–[67].

Hello![5] and gradually over the next 15 years the courts slowly broke the shackles of the law of confidence to create the new tort. A significant step along this way was *Campbell v. Mirror Group Newspapers*[6] where the House of Lords determined that information should be protected where the claimant has a 'reasonable expectation of privacy'. Their Lordships also held that there is no longer a need for an initial confidential relationship.[7] This expectation forms the first stage of the analysis of whether there has been an infringement of the right to privacy.

This test for whether there has been (or more often, would be, if no interim injunction granted) an infringement of the privacy right involves two stages. The first stage is whether the claimant has a reasonable expectation of privacy which must be respected under Article 8. Where such an expectation exists, the court moves onto the second stage to perform the so called 'ultimate' balancing test to see if there are other factors which would permit the disclosure of the information notwithstanding this right. We will examine each of these stages in turn.

2 'REASONABLE EXPECTATION OF PRIVACY'

Claimants can only have a reasonable expectation of privacy in information where it relates to them and not somebody else. This issue most commonly arises where there is an allegation that a 'jigsaw' identification could be made—that is where a combination of known facts can be combined so as to make the information relate to the claimant even where he or she is not expressly identified.[8] Once it is clear the information relates to a particular person there are two things to consider.[9] First, whether the information in question would usually be considered private; and secondly, whether the information in question remains sufficiently private or has entered the public realm.

2.1 PRIVATE INFORMATION

'[T]he touchstone of private life is whether in respect of the disclosed facts the person in question had a reasonable expectation of privacy'.[10] It is an objective assessment[11] and as Lord Hope stated:

> The mind that has to be examined is not [that] of the reader in general, but [that] of the person who is affected by the publicity . . . The question is what a reasonable person of

---

[5] [2001] *QB* 967, [110]; there had been earlier academic arguments suggesting this might be the case: see A. Lester and D. Pannick, 'The Impact of the Human Rights Act' (1998) 116 *LQR* 380; R. Buxton, 'The Human Rights Act and Private Law' (2000) 116 *LQR* 48; M. Hunt, 'The "Horizontal Effect" of the Human Rights Act' (1998) *Public Law* 423.

[6] [2004] 2 *AC* 457.

[7] A finding that has relevance for breach of confidence as well, as, in its modern form, this is not required: see Chapter 45.

[8] A similar example of this is where a child's address is provided but not their name: see *Green Corns Ltd v. CLA Verley Group* [2005] *EMLR (31)* 748, [61].

[9] There will be instances, of course, where there is a lot of speculation about who the person may be: see *CTB v. Newsgroup Newspapers* [2011] *EWHC* 1326, [14].

[10] *Campbell* [2004] 2 *AC* 457, 466, [21] (Lord Nicholls).

[11] *Murray v. Express Newspapers* [2009] *Ch* 481, [41].

ordinary sensibilities would feel if she was placed in the same position as the claimant and faced with the same publicity.[12]

In *In re JR 38*[13] the Supreme Court endorsed the comments of the Court of Appeal in *Murray v. MGN*:[14]

> . . . the question of whether there is a reasonable expectation of privacy is a broad one, which takes account of all the circumstances in the case. They include the attributes of the claimant, the nature of the activity in which the claimant was engaged, the place at which it was happening, the nature and purpose of the intrusion, the absence of consent and whether it was known or could be inferred, the effect on the claimant and the circumstances in which and the purpose for which the information came into the hands of the publisher.

There are many sorts of information which could be private. Importantly, the tort of misuse of private information goes further than the action for breach of confidence. So anything which could be confidential about a person would also prima facie be private. The information need not be true to be private and so a claim for misuse can be brought to prevent false private information being spread.[15]

The most obvious instances of private information would be that which relates to a person's health or well-being[16] or their emotional state at a time of grief.[17] There are many more cases, however, where the information sought to be kept private relates to relationships—whether extra marital and adulterous or transient and 'commercial' or heterosexual or homosexual—and the law has now reached the point where it is clear that the courts will treat all such information as private unless there is something manifestly criminal about the relationship.[18] Indeed, even a person's 'relationship status' (i.e. whether they are single or dating) is private information.[19] These are just some instances of what is private information, but there are many others examples: political views or religious commitments,[20] tax and financial affairs,[21] or naked pictures of the claimant.[22]

There are some areas of difficulty. For instance, whether a person's criminal convictions can be considered private information after sufficient time has passed. While there

---

[12] Ibid., 484, [99] (Lord Hope). In *Campbell*, this meant that, to determine whether the breach was objectionable, it was necessary to put oneself into the shoes of a reasonable person who is in need of that treatment: see ibid., 481–3 (Lord Hope).   [13] [2016] *AC* 1131, [88].

[14] [2009] *Ch* 481, [36].

[15] *AMM v. HXW* [2010] *EWHC* 2457 (QB), [14]. However, a difficult question arises where it could be a defamatory statement due to the rule in *Bonnard v. Perryman* [1891] 2 *Ch* 269, which usually prevents an injunction being granted to prevent an allegedly libellous publication: see *Ambrosidadou v. Coward* [2010] *EWHC* 1794 (QB).

[16] *Archer v. Williams* [2003] *EMLR* (38) 869, [34]–[35] (cosmetic surgery); *Campbell v. MGN* [2004] 2 *AC* 457 (drug addition); *Cornelius v. De Taranto* [2002] *EMLR* (6) 112 (mental health); *X Health Authority v. Y* [1988] 2 *All ER* 648 (doctor's HIV status); *W v. Egdell* [1990] *Ch* 359 (psychiatric report).

[17] *McKennit v. Ash* [2006] *EMLR* (10) 178 [80].

[18] See *BUQ v. HRE* [2012] *EWHC* 774 (QB), [61].

[19] *Applause Store Productions v. Raphael* [2008] *EWHC* 1781 (QB), [4]; *CC v. AB* [2007] *EMLR* (11) 312, [39].

[20] *Applause Store Productions v. Raphael* [2008] *EWHC* 1781 (QB), [8].

[21] *AB v. Barristers Benevolent Association* [2011] *EWHC* 3413 (QB); *Lord Browne of Madingley v. Associated Newspapers* [2007] *EMLR* (19) 515.

[22] *AMP v. Person Unknown* [2011] *EWHC* 3454 (TCC); *Rocknroll v. News Group Newspapers Ltd* [2013] *EWHC* 24 (Ch).

have been a number of cases considering the issue tangentially,[23] the Supreme Court has held that a caution, which involves an admission of being guilty of a criminal offence, is private after a reasonable period of time[24] and the High Court has held that (in some circumstances) a conviction can also after a reasonable time[25] become private again.[26] Another tricky area has been whether the identity of a person who has been arrested for an offence is private, particularly in relation to sexual offences.[27] One side of the argument is that it leads to witnesses and other complainants coming forward who might not otherwise do so. On the other hand, naming suspects may cause irreparable injury to their reputations even where they are actually innocent of the offence; and in relation to more serious crimes it might even lead to the person facing the risk of assaults or more serious injuries by vigilantes. In relation to both terrorist charges[28] and sexual offences[29] the Supreme Court has so far taken the view that disclosing the identity of the person arrested is acceptable as open justice trumps the rights of privacy. As we will see later, even if cases are found where such information may be private it may still be in the public interest to disclose it.

There is no protection, however, for trivial or anodyne information as Eady J put it: 'human rights are concerned with matters of substance . . . to publish that someone in the public eye has a bout of flu or a broken wrist is generally likely to do little harm'.[30] Similarly, details about a shopping trip for furniture[31] or visiting a friend's flat in Venice,[32] without more, are too mundane to warrant protection. Nevertheless, even mundane information obtained from phone tapping, reading private correspondence or emails, or photographing a private venue might attract an expectation of privacy.[33] This is because the method of obtaining the information is intrusive, rather than the information itself being private.

2.1.1 Photographs in a public place

A common issue is whether a person has a reasonable expectation of privacy in relation to the publication of a photograph of that person in a public place. Generally, a person engaged in mundane day-to-day activities will not have a reasonable expectation of

---

[23] Cases where the information has been said to be private include: *R (on the Application of L) (FC) v. Com of Police of the Metropolis* [2010] 1 *AC* 410; *A v. B* [2005] *EMLR* (36) 851, [33]; *R (on the application of Ellis) v Chief Constable of Essex Police* [2003] *EWHC* 1321 (Admin); *X (formerly Mary Bell) v. SO* [2003] *EMLR* (37) 850; but the contrary view was expressed in *KJO v. XIM* [2011] *EWHC* 1768 (QB), [16]; *CG v. Facebook Ireland* [2017] *EMLR* 12, [44]; *Elliott v. Chief Constable of Wiltshire* (*The Times*, 5 December 1996); *L v. Law Society* [2010] *EWCA Civ* 811, [24], [25] and [37]–[44].

[24] *R (T) v. Chief Constable of Greater Manchester* [2015] *AC* 49, [17].

[25] In *NT 1 & NT 2 v. Google LLC* [2018] *EWHC* 799 (QB), Warby J made much of the fact the convictions were spent under the Rehabilitation of Offenders Act 1974. It is probable that a conviction has to be spent before it could ever become private and where an offence attracted more than 48 months imprisonment it can never be spent.

[26] *NT 1 & NT 2 v. Google LLC* [2018] *EWHC* 799 (QB) at [171]–[172] and [224]–[226] (where it was misuse for one claimant and not the other due to the conduct of the claimant).

[27] Where the complainant has the right to anonymity: Sexual Offences (Amendment) Act 1992, s. 1.

[28] *Re Guardian News and Media* [2010] 2 *AC* 697; although where there is evidence they may face physical danger it may be the court orders they should not be identified: *Secretary of State of the Home Department v. AP (No. 2)* [2010] 1 *WLR* 1652.

[29] *PNM v. Times Newspapers* [2017] 3 *WLR 351*; albeit Lord Kerr and Lord Wilson dissented from a seven justice court.   [30] *A v. B* [2005] *EMLR* (36) 851, [33].

[31] *McKennitt v. Ash* [2006] *EMLR* (10) 178, [139].

[32] *Lord Browne of Madingley v. Associated Newspapers* [2007] *EMLR* (19) 515, [61].

[33] See generally, the phone hacking cases discussed in *Gulati v. Mirror Group Newspapers* [2016] *FSR* (12) 313; upheld on appeal [2016] FSR (13) 378.

privacy[34] as it was put in *Campbell v. Mirror Group Newspapers*:[35] 'the famous and even the not so famous who go out in public must accept that they may be photographed without their consent, just as they may be observed by others without their consent'.[36]

The situation where it involves children is more complex. In *Murray v. Express Newspapers*[37] a photograph was taken of J. K. Rowling (real name Joanne Murray) and her husband pushing their son in a pram down a public street in Edinburgh. The photograph, was taken using a long-range lens and showed the infant's face in profile. The action was brought by the parents on behalf of their infant son. The question arose whether routine acts, such as a visit to a shop or a ride on a bus, should not attract a reasonable expectation of privacy.

The Court of Appeal allowed Murray's appeal from the decision of Patten J (who had struck out Murray's claim).[38] The Court of Appeal took the view that there was an arguable case that her child had a reasonable expectation of privacy.[39] More recently, in *Weller v. Associated Newspapers*,[40] the Court of Appeal acknowledged that children do not have a greater right to privacy than adults, but there will be times when a child[41] might be entitled to privacy when an adult in the same situation would not.[42] Accordingly, a reasonable expectation of privacy depended on the facts of the particular case and, in *Murray*, Rowling had shielded the child from publicity and that was enough.

The approach of the European Court of Human Rights (ECtHR) in *von Hannover (No. 1)* shows the potential high-water mark for protection of public figures in public places.[43] It also appears to be a higher point than that which the English courts have yet reached and a point from which the ECtHR itself has stepped back. The German Federal Constitutional Court had said that, as a leading figure in contemporary society, Princess Caroline had to tolerate the publication of photographs of herself in a public place, even if they showed her in scenes of daily life, rather than in official duties. The ECtHR unanimously held that the publications had been a violation of Article 8. This was based on the fact that, in certain situations, a person has a legitimate expectation of protection for their private life—that is, 'there is a zone of interaction of a person with others, even in a public context, which may fall within the scope of private life'.[44] In reaching this decision, the Court drew a distinction between celebrities and people engaged in official public business. As the Court said:

> [A] fundamental distinction needs to be drawn between reporting facts—even controversial ones—capable of contributing to a debate in a democratic society relating to politicians in the exercise of their functions, for example, and reporting details of the private life of an individual who, as in this case, does not exercise official functions. While in the former case the press exercises its vital role of 'watchdog' in a democracy by contributing to imparting information and ideas on matters of public interest it does not do so in the latter case.[45]

The ECtHR said that the decisive factor in balancing the protection of private life against freedom of expression lies in the contribution that the published photographs and articles

---

[34] *John v. Associated Newspapers* [2006] *EMLR* (27) 772.   [35] [2004] 2 *AC* 457, [154].

[36] The Strasbourg Court has been more restrictive: see *Von Hannover v. Germany* (2005) 40 *EHRR* 1, [76]–[77]; *Sciacca v. Italy* (2006) 43 *EHRR* 20, [28]–[29].

[37] [2008] *EMLR* (12) 399.   [38] *Murray v. Express Newspapers Plc* [2007] *EMLR* (22) 583.

[39] [2008] *EMLR* (12) 399.   [40] [2016] 1 *WLR* 1541

[41] The differences will decrease as the child ages: *Spelman v. Express Newspapers* [2012] *EWHC* 355 (QB), [55].   [42] Ibid., [29]–[30].

[43] *Von Hannover (No. 1)*, App. No. 59320/00, (2005) 40 *EHRR* 1, [51].   [44] Ibid., [50].

[45] Ibid., [63].

make to a debate of general interest.[46] In this case, the Court said that the public does not have a legitimate interest in knowing where the applicant is and how she behaves in her private life. The Court also said that the photographs in question did not 'come within the sphere of any political or public debate because the published photos and accompanying commentaries relate exclusively to details of the applicant's private life'.[47] In two subsequent cases involving Princess Caroline, the ECtHR has found that although her Article 8 rights engaged they were not infringed by similar photographs.[48]

2.2 THE MODIFIED PUBLIC DOMAIN

While the law of confidence acknowledges that something can be relatively secret, the law of misuse of private information goes further. The starting point is the same, namely that there can be no reasonable expectation of privacy in relation to information in the public domain[49]—indeed where interim injunctions are obtained these are usually predicated on such injunctions lapsing if the information enters the public domain.[50]

While information may be quite widely known and still be private, there is always a tipping point, or a point where the 'dam bursts', and the information is incontrovertibly in the public domain. Thus, in *Mosley v. News Group Newspapers*,[51] a video recording of the claimant engaged in sadomasochistic practices had been viewed more than 1.5 million times and Eady J concluded that it was in the public domain and so any injunction would therefore be futile. Conversely, in another case, he suggested, that in principle the publication in a national newspaper may not always be enough to enter the public domain.[52] It is hardly surprising therefore, that in general the courts do not consider mere publication on the Internet to be enough in itself for such information to fall into the public domain. This is largely because there is a big difference between information being made available on the Internet and that information being known or known to be accessible to the general public. Put simply, the Internet is a very big haystack and unless there is reason for many people to sit on the needle it might never be found.[53] Furthermore, as the awareness of 'fake news' grows there is an increasing chance that even if a person came across information about a particular person they may not actually believe it to be true or reliable.[54]

The courts have also recognized that photographs convey more information that words. Lord Phillips MR in *Douglas v. Hello!* took the view that photographs are more than a means of conveying factual information as they can capture much more than words alone.[55] This means the courts sometimes take the view that each photograph is considered to be distinct and disclosing a photograph of a person doing something does not mean another photograph taken at about the same time with the person doing the same thing cannot be private.[56]

---

[46] Ibid., [76].   [47] Ibid., [64].

[48] *Von Hannover v. Germany (No. 2)* (2012) 55 *EHRR* 15; *Von Hannover v. Germany (No. 3)*, App. No. 8772/10, (2013); a similar result, not relating to Princess Caroline, was reached in *Lillo-Sternberg v. Norway* [2014] *ECHR* 59.

[49] See for instance, *McKennitt v. Ash* [2008] *QB* 73, [53]; *Douglas v. Hello!* [2006] *QB* 125, [105].

[50] See, e.g., *A v. B* [2005] *EMLR* (36) 851, [16]; *CTB v. News Group Newspapers* [2011] *EWHC* 1232 (QB), [27].

[51] [2008] *EWHC* 687 (QB), [33]–[35].   [52] *KGM v. News Group Newspapers* [2010] *EWHC* 3145, [22].

[53] As many websites monitor the number of views a particular item of information has received it can often be shown how many people have sat on the needle.

[54] There is also regularly speculation about who it might be so many wrong candidates put forward: see for instance *CTB v. News Group Newspapers Ltd* [2011] *EWHC* 1326 (QB), [14].

[55] [2006] *QB* 125, [106].   [56] See *Douglas v. Hello!* [2007] 1 *AC* 1.

In contrast to confidence, there is an additional factor which comes into play. The courts now recognize that the right to privacy includes the right to prevent intrusion and harassment into a person's private. This is demonstrated by the facts of *CTB v. News Group Newspapers*. The case related to a famous footballer having an extra-marital affair with a former contestant on the reality television show *Big Brother*. Eady J granted an injunction to prevent the naming of the footballer.[57]

Subsequently, his name was made available on a particular Twitter hashtag and it was argued by the newspaper that the injunction was ceasing to perform a useful purpose. The court disagreed, taking the view that, where an injunction had been already been granted, a court should be slow to remove the protection it had already granted if it would prevent harassment of the claimant.[58] Later the same day, a Member of Parliament named the footballer on the floor of the House of Commons[59] and, in turn, the newspapers returned to court once more saying surely now the injunction should be lifted.[60] Tugendhat J stated:

> It is obvious that if the purpose of the injunction were to preserve a secret, it would have failed in its purpose. But in so far as its purpose is to prevent intrusion or harassment, it has not failed. The fact that tens of thousands of people have named the claimant on the internet confirms that the claimant and his family need protection from intrusion into their private and family life.[61]

This reasoning was expanded in the Levenson Report:[62]

> There is a qualitative difference between photographs being available online and being displayed, or blazoned, on the front page of a newspaper such as the Sun. The fact of publication in a mass circulation newspaper multiplies and magnifies the intrusion, not simply because more people will be viewing the images, but also because more people will be talking about them. Thus, the fact of publication inflates the apparent newsworthiness of the photographs by placing them more firmly within the public domain and at the top of the news agenda.

The matter was considered in detail by the Supreme Court in *PJS v. News Group Newspapers*.[63] The cases revolved around the spouse of a famous person having a 'three-way' with two other people (neither of whom was the spouse). Some years after the incident, the two non-celebrity participants approached *The Sun* newspaper to sell their story. The High Court refused an injunction to stop *The Sun on Sunday* publishing the story but this was overturned by the Court of Appeal and an injunction was granted.[64] However, one of the two participants sold the story to an American magazine leading to an article naming everyone involved to be published. The story was not widely taken up in the United States although further stories appeared in Canada and Scotland. This led various newspapers[65] to ask the Court of Appeal to vacate the injunction on the grounds that

---

[57] [2011] *EWHC* 1232 (QB). It was a so-called 'Super Injunction', that is, an injunction where it is not even permitted to publish details that an injunction exists even if the person is not named. These are now very restricted: see Gurry (2012), [18–57]– [18.70].   [58] [2011] *EWHC* 1326 (QB).

[59] For a discussion of the reporting of this disclosure, see P. Johnson, 'What Can the Press Really Say? Contempt of Court and the Reporting of Parliamentary Proceedings' (2012) *Public Law* 491.

[60] [2011] *EWHC* 1326 (QB).   [61] [2011] *EWHC* 1326 (QB), [3].

[62] Leveson Inquiry, *Report into the Culture, Practices and Ethics of the Press* (2012 HC Papers 780-ii), 737, [3.4].   [63] [2016] *AC* 1081.

[64] [2016] *EMLR* (17) 322.

[65] All newspapers are bound by the injunction (even if not parties to the proceedings) when they are served with a copy of the injunction under the 'so-called' *Spycatcher principle*: see Gurry (2012), [18.45].

the story was available on the Internet.[66] The Court of Appeal did so and the Claimant appealed.[67] In the Supreme Court it was accepted that possibly as much as 25 per cent of the English population knew the identity of PJS and that secrecy had clearly been lost.[68] Yet the majority agreed with the reasoning and approach of Eady and Tugenhadt JJ in CTB[69] and confirmed the principle that even where there has been a significant loss of confidentiality the further dissemination of the information may be prevented where it would cause harassment and distress.[70] Accordingly, the current position is that only where there is no privacy left to be protected will an injunction be refused; but in making this decision the right of privacy extends well beyond confidentiality to harassment and intrusion. Furthermore, the courts will be very slow to allow an injunction to be vacated once it has been granted on the basis that the information has subsequently come into the public domain as otherwise injunctions could be undermined easily by international press organizations. Indeed, this is why one in four people knowing the identity of PJS (or PJS's partner) was not enough for the injunction to be lifted.

3 'ULTIMATE BALANCING TEST'

Once a claimant has a reasonable expectation of privacy in the information, the second stage requires the balancing of the countervailing interest of others, in particular the right to freedom of expression.[71] The starting point is that neither a claimant's Article 8 rights or the defendant's rights under Article 10 have a presumptive priority over the other,[72] rather whether a particular right takes priority over the other depends upon 'the intense focus on the individual circumstances'[73] as 'there are no hard and fast rules. It is a question of weighing the competing Convention rights and forming a judgment on the unique facts of the case'.[74] When making this intensely fact-based assessment there are certain facts the courts will take into account and to these we now turn.

3.1 HOW PRIVATE IS IT?

The claimant's expectation of privacy will vary from case to case so that some sorts of information will be more private than others.[75] Thus, at one end of the spectrum, medical information would be entitled to much greater protection than other less personal details. Essentially, the more intimate the aspect of the private life the greater the justification needed to publish the details.[76] It may also be that the expectation of privacy will be greater depending on how the particular information is communication. As already mentioned, a photograph or video may present a much greater intrusion than merely providing the details of the information in writing. As it was put by Eady J in *Mosley v. News Group Newspapers*:[77]

---

[66] [2016] *EWCA Civ* 393.

[67] The injunction remained in place during the appeal so that its purpose was not defeated.

[68] [2016] *AC* 1081, [57].   [69] Ibid., [32].

[70] Ibid., [59] (and the cases cited therein); in his dissent Lord Toulson took the view that preventing the publication of what is widely known leads to people not respecting the law as it suggests the courts are out of touch with reality: see ibid., [88].   [71] *Campbell* [2004] 2 *AC* 457, [137] (Baroness Hale).

[72] *Re S (a child)* [2005] 1 *AC* 593, [17].

[73] *Mosely v. News Group Newspapers* [2008] *EMLR* (20) 679, [12] (Eady J).

[74] *CDE v. MGN* [2010] *EWHC* 3308 (QB), [2].   [75] *Campbell v. MGN* [2004] 2 *AC* 457, [118].

[76] Ibid., [60]; also see *A v. B* [2003] *QB* 195, [11(vii)].   [77] [2008] *EMLR* (20) 679, [16].

Sometimes there may be a good case for revealing the fact of wrongdoing to the general public; it will not necessarily follow that photographs of 'every gory detail' also need to be published to achieve the public interest objective. Nor will it automatically justify clandestine recording, whether visual or audio.

Similar sentiments were expressed by Lord Hoffmann in *Campbell*:[78]

> ... there is a public interest in the disclosure of the existence of a sexual relationship (say, between a politician and someone whom she has appointed to public office) but the addition of salacious details or intimate photographs is disproportionate and unacceptable. The latter, even if accompanying a legitimate disclosure of the sexual relationship, would be too intrusive and demeaning.

3.1.1 Courting publicity

There are many people who attempt to achieve as much publicity as they can—often about aspects of their life which in the usual course of things would be considered private. The courts have accepted that a person, whether famous or not, cannot just turn off the tap of publicity when it suits them.[79] Conversely, where a person has taken steps to keep their private life private, the courts are more likely to grant protection than when they have not. The court approaches this issue by assuming that where a person has used personal information about their life to gain fame or notoriety, he or she is not particularly sensitive when it comes to invasions of their privacy.[80] Nevertheless, even those who have exposed the most personal things about themselves still have some expectation of privacy. Katie Price was originally a glamour model under the name Jordan, but she went on to become a reality television personality with her own television show and magazine column. On her show and in her column, she would disclose the most intimate details of her family life and relationships. Yet even she, who has courted the media par excellence, was found to have information which could possibly be protected under Article 8.[81]

3.2.2 Freedom of expression

The person trying to disclose the private information will usually rely on rights of freedom of expression under Article 10:

(1) Everyone has the right to freedom of expression. This right shall include freedom to hold opinions and to receive and impart information and ideas without interference by public authority and regardless of frontiers. This article shall not prevent States from requiring the licensing of broadcasting, television or cinema enterprises.

(2) The exercise of these freedoms, since it carries with it duties and responsibilities, may be subject to such formalities, conditions, restrictions or penalties as are prescribed by law and are necessary in a democratic society, in the interests of national security, territorial integrity or public safety, for the prevention of disorder or crime, for the protection of health or morals, for the protection of the reputation or the rights of others, for preventing the disclosure of information received in confidence, or for maintaining the authority and impartiality of the judiciary.

In balancing these competing interests under Articles 8 and 10, it has been held that the 'restrictions which the courts impose on the Article 10 right must be rational, fair and not

---

[78] [2004] 2 *AC* 457, [60].   [79] *A v. B* [2003] *QB* 195, [11(xii)].
[80] *Terry v. Persons Unknown* [2010] *EMLR* (16) 400, [127].
[81] See *Price v. Powel* [2012] *EWHC* 3527 (QB), [43] (this was a striking out application).

arbitrary, and they must impair the right no more than is necessary'.[82] The weight given to the expression rights engaged will vary[83] and there is special protection given to it at the interim stage.[84] While many cases involve simply the commercial interests of media organizations to sell news to the public, there will be instances where that process also involves a person 'setting the record straight'[85] or where the general public have an interest to know the information. The extent of the dissemination of the information is usually the key factor as it was put by Eady J in *CC v. AB*:[86]

> I recognise straight away that the Claimant is unlikely to obtain at trial a blanket restraint on any communication about the fact of the adulterous relationship. It would not be proportionate to any reasonable expectation on the Claimant's part to prevent the Defendant, for example, discussing his wife's adultery with a close friend, or with members of the family, or (if he needed to do so) with a family doctor, counsellor or social worker, or with his lawyers. What is in contention is the Defendant's desire, directly or indirectly, to put the relationship into the public domain through the press, and to support it with detail.

3.2.3 Free press

Accordingly, the expression rights of the media are not greater than those of individuals and in most cases—because of the effect of publication—will often be less. Nevertheless, the courts have recognized that there is a general public interest in retaining a 'free press'. At the simplest level, it means that the public are interested in salacious gossip about public figures and so newspapers will make more sales if they publish such information. Conversely, without providing such information sales will decline and the media organization would become unviable.[87] While this argument has received some support in the courts, it has now largely been rejected and privacy interests would outweigh this simple expression of the position.

Any argument based on the public interest in receiving the information therefore requires the relevant story itself to be the core of that argument. But the genuine existence of a public interest[88] is not enough in itself to permit publication, rather it goes into the scales of the ultimate balancing test. The public interest is most commonly expressed as part of the press' watchdog function.[89] However, what is in the public interest is an amorphous uncertain concept; it is neither merely 'newsworthy' nor as restrictive as something which the public 'needed to know'.[90] In *Reynolds v. Times Newspapers*[91] the Court of Appeal gave an indication of what it might mean:

---

[82] *Campbell* [2004] 2 *AC* 457, [115] (Lord Hope).

[83] It is not a trump card: see *Mosley v. News Group Newspapers* [2008] *EMLR* (20) 679, [10].

[84] Human Rights Act 1998, s. 12; see Chapter 49, section 1.1.1, pp. 1326–7.

[85] The *CTB* case was a good example of the court assisting in this process. Imogen Thomas had been accused by CTB of 'blackmailing' him by threatening publication. This was not true and a prepared statement was read in court: *CTB v. News Group Newspapers* [2011] *EWHC* 3099 (QB).

[86] [2007] *EMLR* (11) 312, [35].

[87] See, to this effect, *A v. B* [2003] *QB* 195, [11(xii)]; *Campbell v. Mirror Group Newspapers* [2004] 2 *AC* 257, [143].

[88] It needs to be established by evidence, not merely asserted: *Goodwin v. News Group Newspapers* [2011] *EWHC* 1309, [14]–[15].

[89] See for instance, *Reynolds v. Times Newspapers* [1999] 2 *AC* 127, 205 and 214; *Sunday Times v. UK* (1979–80) 2 *EHRR* 245, [65]; *Gaweda v. Poland* (2004) 39 *EHRR* 4, [34].

[90] *Jamel v. Wall Street Journal* [2007] 1 *AC* 359, [147] (a libel claim, but the principle is the same).

[91] [1998] 3 *WLR* 862, 909 (it was a libel case again, but the principles apply more generally).

We do not for an instant doubt that the common convenience and welfare of a modern plural democracy such as ours are best served by an ample flow of information to the public concerning, and by vigorous public discussion of, matters of public interest to the community. By that we mean matters relating to the public life of the community and those who take part in it, including within the expression 'public life' activities such as the conduct of government and political life, elections . . . and public administration, but we use the expression more widely than that, to embrace matters such as (for instance) the governance of public bodies, institutions and companies which give rise to a public interest in disclosure, but excluding matters which are personal and private, such that there is no public interest in their disclosure. Recognition that the common convenience and welfare of society are best served in this way is a modern democratic imperative which the law must accept.

There are many examples of things the disclosure of which has been found to be in the public interest: government and political conduct or misconduct;[92] the protection of public health;[93] school disciplinary practices;[94] police conduct or misconduct;[95] cheating and corruption in sport[96] or corporate malpractice.[97] These are just indicative of the sorts of things that might be relevant and are not a conclusive list, indeed such a list is almost impossible. Finally, there may be cases where the disclosure of private information is necessary to give added credence to the story or to otherwise support its credibility or simply that the story needs to be slightly shocking to engage the readership. Whether this is the case or not is largely editorial in nature and the courts accept that they cannot step into the shoes of a newspaper editor[98] but they do expect newspaper editors to act reasonably in this regard.[99]

3.2.4 Motivation for publication

Where the reason for publishing the information is to cause harm to the claimant then the right of free expression does not disappear, but rather the weight given to will be lowered. Accordingly, where a person wished to disclose the information to obtain revenge and did not care about the fall-out that would be caused to others, the court was firmly of the view that the balance fell in favour of restricting disclosure.[100] Where a person seeks to blackmail a celebrity unless they are paid off or otherwise rewarded it is unlikely that their Article 10 rights will be given much weight at all.[101] Nevertheless, where allegations of misconduct such as blackmail are made by a claimant they should be substantiated as it is a serious (even criminal) allegation against the person and so the strict requirements around civil allegations of fraud should apply—although in practice this does not always happen.

---

[92] See for instance, *A-G v. Jonathan Blake* [1976] QB 752; *Al Fagih v. HH Saudi Research and Marketing* [2002] *EMLR* (13) 215; *Galloway v. Telegraph Newspapers* [2005] *EMLR* (7) 115.

[93] *Hubbard v. Vosper* [1972] 2 QB 84; *McKeith v. News Group Newspapers* [2005] *EMLR* (32) 780.

[94] *Leeds City Council v. Channel Four Television* [2005] *EWHC* 3522 (Fam).

[95] *Flood v. Times Newspapers* [2012] 2 AC 273; *Hunt v. Times Newspapers* [2013] *EWHC* 1868 (QB).

[96] *Jockey Club v. Buffham* [2003] QB 462; *Grobbelaar v. News Group Newspapers* [2001] *EMLR* (18) 459; *Spelman v. Express Newspapers* [2012] *EWHC* 355 (QB), [22].

[97] *Cream Holdings v. Banerjee* [2005] 1 AC 253; *KGM v. News Group Newspapers* [2010] *EWHC* 3145 (QB), [39].

[98] *Campbell v. Mirror Group Newspapers* [2004] 2 AC 257, [59] (Lord Hoffmann) ('judges are not newspaper editors'); see also *AAA v. Associated Newspapers* [2013] *EMLR* (2) 54, [102]–[103]; *In re BBC* [2010] 1 AC 145, [25]–[26]; *Re Guardian News & Media* [2010] 2 AC 697, [63]; *Re S* [2005] 1 AC 593, [34].

[99] See *Terry v. Persons Unknown* [2010] *EMLR* (16) 400, [70]–[73].

[100] *CC v. AB* [2007] *EMLR* (11) 312.

[101] See *AMM v. HXW* [2010] *EWHC* 2457, [38]; *DFT v. TFD* [2010] *EWHC* 2335 (QB), [23].

3.2.5 The content, form, and potential for harm of the publication

Where the disclosure will do physical or psychological harm to the claimant this clearly will be a significant factor. In *Campbell*, while the House of Lords found that it was permissible to disclose information about Naomi Campbell's drug addiction to the public, so the question in *Campbell* was whether the disclosure of additional information relating to her attendance at Narcotics Anonymous could be protected by Article 8. The majority held that while the press was able to 'put the record straight' about Campbell's comments about her (lack of) drug use, information about the treatment which she was receiving ought to be treated differently.[102] While the minority downplayed the importance of the disclosure, the majority felt that the information about Campbell's treatment at Narcotics Anonymous was equivalent to the disclosure of treatment of a medical condition.[103] Importantly, the majority felt that there was a chance that the disclosure might undermine and disrupt Campbell's treatment. The Lords also noted that recovering addicts were particularly vulnerable and that an assurance of privacy was an essential part of the treatment.[104] On this basis, the Lords upheld Campbell's claims.[105]

A more extreme example would be where the publication of the information itself would lead to someone seeking to harm the claimant. At the age of 10, Jon Venables and Robert Thompson led away a 2 year-old child—James Bulger—from a shopping centre to brutally murder and mutilate him. When they were released from custody in their early twenties they were given new identities and the press were permanently prohibited from disclosing new photographs or any details of their new identities. The order was to protect them from the very clear and credible threats that they would be assaulted or even murdered (including such a threat from the father of the victim).[106] A much earlier child murderer –Mary Bell—was granted a similar order to protect not only her identity but also her child's.[107] Clearly, where there is a credible threat to a person's life—even if that person has committed the gravest criminal acts—the court is unlikely to allow their identity or personal information to be published.

3.2.6 Role models

There has been a view that where a person is a 'public figure' or even a 'role model' then the court should be more willing to allow disclosure of their misconduct. Indeed, the ECtHR has even indicated that a public figure may enjoy less protection than others.[108] It clearly makes sense that a public figure or a celebrity will inevitably expose their life to greater scrutiny than would be the case for 'ordinary folk'. Nevertheless, in *Campbell*, as Lord Phillips MR stated, just because a person has been elevated to the public sphere and others aspire to be like them should not enable the press to expose their 'feet of clay'.[109]

---

[102] The minority held that the additional information was of such an unremarkable and inconsequential nature that it could not be protected: *Campbell* [2004] 2 *AC* 457 (HL), 467, [26] (Lord Nicholls).

[103] Ibid., 479, [81] (Lord Hope).

[104] Ibid., 481, [90] (Lord Hope), 499, [146] (Baroness Hale).

[105] *The Mirror* challenged the conclusion, but the ECtHR thought that the decision was sound: *Mirror Group Newspapers v. UK*, App. No. 39401/04 [2011] *ECHR* 66, [151].

[106] *Venables v. News Group Newspapers* [2001] *Fam* 430; for a more recent example, see *A & B v. Persons Unknown* [2017] *EMLR* (11) 324.

[107] *X (formerly Mary Bell) v. O'Brien* [2003] *EMLR* (37) 850.

[108] *Ageyevy v. Russia*, App No. 7075/10 (18 April 2013), [221].

[109] *Campbell v. MGN* [2003] *QB* 633, [41].

Indeed, the number and range of potential role models is huge—and it is not necessarily something a person has chosen to be—some celebrities are famous because of the mess they have made of their lives or because of a particular public humiliation. In general, therefore, the courts have taken the view that 'role models' are entitled to private lives as much as anybody else.[110] Nevertheless this approach has not been uniform, in *Ferdinand v. MGN*,[111] a footballer was held to a higher standard because he was also captain of England and so was considered a role model. The contradiction between this case and others might be resolved by the particular facts in that case, namely that there appears to have been an implied obligation arising from being captain due to representations made by the FA and others about the standards expected in both the captain's public and private life.[112]

3.2.7 Hypocrisy etc.

Where a person has made a statement about their life that is untrue, the press may seek to correct that representation. Thus, in *Campbell*, Lord Phillips MR accepted the legitimacy of this: 'one principle . . . is that where a public figure chooses to make untrue pronouncements about his or her private life, the press will normally be entitled to put the record straight'.[113]

This clearly overstates the position. For example, a practising homosexual may not be ready to come out and so they continue to represent themselves as straight. The press would not be entitled to 'out' them simply based on the false statement alone. Similarly, someone with a serious disease such as cancer might not want the public to know about it.[114] In such cases, something more is needed to require disclosure, such as hypocrisy. The *Campbell* case presents an excellent example of this. Naomi Campbell had not only denied taking drugs but represented that she was one of the few models who did not take drugs at all—she was exceptional. The press was therefore entitled to correct this hypocrisy by demonstrating that she actually had drug addiction problems.

A more difficult example is *Ferdinand v. MGN*.[115] Rio Ferdinand had a wild reputation before 2006, but in that year he made various representations that he had changed his ways. Nevertheless, he had maintained contact with a former girlfriend and tried to meet up with her in hotel rooms after that date. The Court held that the press could publish the fact that, despite his protestations, Ferdinand had at least attempted to be unfaithful after stating he would mend his ways. As mentioned earlier, what seems to have been a significant factor in the determination of this case is his role as captain of the English football team which, the Court found, required him to keep up high standards off, as well as on, the pitch. Tugenhadt J felt it was acceptable for the press to report that he had not maintained the standards expected.

---

[110] *Mosley v. News Group Newspapers* [2008] *EMLR* (20) 679, [12]; *McKennit v. Ash* [2008] *QB* 73, [56], [62]–[64].   [111] [2011] *EWHC* 2454 (QB).

[112] This of course may arise in relation to other roles where it is made clear certain standards in a person's private life are expected as part of the job; the acceptability of imposing such standards in the first place is a different matter.

[113] [2003] *QB* 633, [43]; also see similar comments on appeal: [2004] *2 AC* 457, [58], [129].

[114] A famous example is Mo Mowlam who had a brain tumour and treatment whilst being Secretary of State for Northern Ireland. She tried to keep it secret but jibes about her appearance led her to disclose her condition.   [115] [2011] *EWHC* 2454 (QB).

4 CONCLUSION

The law of misuse of private information has evolved quickly and pervasively. It has broken free from its roots in breach of confidence. While it originates from rights granted by the European Convention of Human Rights, it seems to have stepped firmly out of the Strasbourg Court's shadow. In contrast to other areas of intellectual property, it is also largely unaffected by EU law and there is currently no proposal to change that fact. The greatest difficulty with this area of law is that decisions are usually made rapidly at the interim stage to prevent publication. Once prevented there is rarely, if ever, a desire for a defendant to continue to trial to have the matter considered substantively. This has led the higher courts (the Court of Appeal and the Supreme Court) to endorse the substantial case law developed at first instance (the High Court) in a way which is quite different from other areas of intellectual property.

PART VI

LITIGATION AND REMEDIES

It is sometimes said that intellectual property rights are only as good as the procedures and remedies by which they are enforced[1] and many legal disputes turn on procedure rather than the substantive law.[2] This highlights the importance of the so-called 'adjectival' aspects of intellectual property law—that is, the rules of evidence, procedure, litigation, and remedies. In the following two chapters, we intend to provide an introduction to these aspects of intellectual property law.

Until recently, the rules and practices that regulate litigation, procedure, and remedies have developed on a national basis, largely unaffected by international standards. There are, for example, only a few references in the Berne[3] and Paris[4] Conventions to matters of enforcement. As a result of recent changes in regional and international intellectual property law, the relative insularity of the adjectival aspects of British intellectual property law has ended.

Probably the most significant change at the international level is that matters relating to enforcement are comprehensively dealt with by Part III of the 1994 Agreement on Trade-related Aspects of Intellectual Property Rights (TRIPS).[5] This requires that members ensure that enforcement procedures are available so that intellectual-property right holders can take effective action against infringers. More specifically, the law of the member state must enable remedies to be obtained *expeditiously* so that imminent infringements can be prevented. Members are also required to provide remedies that are severe enough to deter further infringements. Procedures should be fair, equitable, and only as complicated, costly, or lengthy as is necessary.[6] TRIPS provides further details in relation to civil procedures, remedies, provisional measures, border measures, and criminal

---

[1] C. Greenhalgh, J. Phillips, R. Pitkethly, M. Rogers, and J. Tomalin, *Intellectual Property Enforcement in Smaller UK Firms* (2010), 3.

[2] R. Jacob, 'International Intellectual Property Litigation in the Next Millennium' (2000) 32 *Case Western Reserve Journal of International Law* 507, 507.

[3] Berne, Arts 16 (obligation to seize unlawful copies), 13(3).

[4] Paris, Arts 9 (seizure on import of goods unlawfully bearing a trade mark), 6*bis*(1), and 6*septies*(2) (injunctive relief for wrongful use of well-known mark).

[5] T. Dreier, 'TRIPS and the Enforcement of Intellectual Property Rights', in Beier and Shricker, 248.

[6] TRIPS, Art. 41.

liability. Because the standards required are expressed in terms of particular purposes or goals (such as that the procedures must not be unduly costly), it may be difficult to assess whether national procedures and remedies satisfy the international standards. Indeed, the vague manner in which the effects are enunciated means that they are unlikely to be enforced at the World Trade Organization (WTO).

Following the lead of TRIPS, the World Intellectual Property Organization (WIPO) Copyright Treaty (WCT), WIPO Performances and Phonograms Treaty (WPPT), and the Beijing Treaty on Audiovisual Performances[7] also require contracting parties to have enforcement procedures in place that provide effective action against acts of infringement covered by the treaties. These include expeditious remedies to prevent infringement and remedies that deter further infringement.[8] In addition, contracting states are required to provide 'effective legal remedies' for violation of Berne, TRIPS, and components of the WIPO treaties dealing with the digital agenda.[9]

While these changes mark an important shift in direction for international intellectual property law, for the most part they have had little impact upon British law. This has not been the case, however, with the changes that have taken place at the European level. In considering the impact of European initiatives on procedural and remedial matters, we need to distinguish between intellectual property rights at the EU level and EU rules relating to the enforcement of national rights. We deal with these in turn.

The development of EU intellectual property rights—currently European Union trade marks and Community plant varieties, registered and unregistered Community design rights—has brought with it a degree of EU regulation of the procedures by which rights are enforced. The most obvious impact is that member states must designate particular domestic courts as 'European/Community courts' (e.g. Community Design Courts[10]). These are courts in which actions to enforce European Union/Community rights and, in some circumstances, actions for declaration of invalidity are brought.[11] While matters of procedure and, with some exceptions, remedies are left to the law of the relevant member state,[12] the right to injunctions in relation to European/Community rights is governed by EU law: injunctive relief will be granted unless there are special reasons to the contrary.[13] Moreover, these courts have general jurisdiction to grant provisional measures (including protective ones, such as interim injunctions) that operate in all contracting states.[14]

The procedures and enforcement of *national* intellectual property rights has also been the focus of attention at the European level. Three matters are worth mentioning

---

[7] This Treaty is not yet in force. While the United Kingdom has signed the Treaty, it has yet to ratify it.

[8] WCT, Art. 14; WPPT, Art. 23; Beijing Treaty, Art. 20.

[9] Technological measures: WCT, Art. 11; WPPT, Art. 18; Beijing Treaty, Art 15; rights management information: WCT, Arts 12; WPPT, Art. 19; Beijing Treaty, Art. 16. Further standardization at international level has been proposed, most notably in the controversial Anti-Counterfeiting Trade Agreement (ACTA), which is unlikely ever to come into force. On 4 July 2012, the European Parliament rejected the ACTA 478 votes to 39, with 165 abstentions.

[10] See, for instance, the point made in *Samsung Electronics (UK) Ltd v. Apple Inc.* [2013] *FSR* (9) 135, [59].

[11] CDR, Arts 80 and 81; EUTMR, Arts 123 and 124.

[12] In the case of procedure, the forum, and in the case of remedies, those available in the country in which the infringement takes place: CDR, Art. 88; EUTMR, Arts 129, 130; *H. Gautzsch Großhandel GmbH & Co. KG v. Münchener Boulevard Mobel Joseph Duna GmbH,* Case C 479/12, EU:C:2014:75 (ECJ, Third Chamber).

[13] Protocol on Litigation, Art. 35(1); EUTMR, Art. 130; CDR, Art. 89; *Nokia Corp. v. Wardell,* Case C-316/05 [2007] 1 *CMLR* (37) 1167; *H. Gautzsch Großhandel,* Case C-479/12, EU:C:2014:75 (ECJ, Third Chamber), [48] ('special reasons' relates to factual circumstances specific to a given case).

[14] EUTMR, Art. 131; CDR, Art. 90; Protocol on Litigation, Art. 14.

at this stage.[15] First, the European Union has adopted a regulation governing jurisdiction and recognition and enforcement of judgments[16] as well as a regulation determining the applicable law to international intellectual property disputes.[17] These provisions are examined in more detail in Chapter 48.

Second, the European Union has also adopted measures that regulate the external borders of the Union. More specifically, it has put in place mechanisms that ensure that goods that infringe intellectual property rights can be retained by customs authorities when they are introduced into or exported from the EU.[18] These are discussed in Chapter 49.

The third matter that should be noted is the so-called Enforcement Directive.[19] In part, the Directive was motivated by a concern that different member states had different rules on enforcement, leading some to argue that some countries were softer on piracy than others. The Directive cherry-picked legal remedies and procedures from a host of different states, and directed member states to make the full panoply available to its judicial authorities. While much of the Directive sets out to harmonize[20] remedies that are familiar to a British lawyer (seizure orders,[21] disclosure orders,[22] interim injunctions,[23] final injunctions,[24] and the like), it is worth highlighting a few features of the Directive. It set out a general requirement of 'proportionality' to apply to all remedies covered by the Directive.[25] It introduced unfamiliar remedies,[26] such as publicity orders,[27] and used some unfamiliar terms in the assessment of monetary remedies. Indeed, some terms were so unfamiliar that the rule for damages was specifically enacted.[28]

Not long after the Enforcement Directive was adopted, a concerted attempt was made to introduce a directive requiring criminal remedies.[29] In the face of doubts over competence to legislate in relation to criminal matters, however, the proposal was abandoned.

[15] Another influence is the ECHR. In *Neij and Kolmisoppi (The Pirate Bay) v. Sweden*, App. No. 40,397/12 [2013] *ECDR* (7) 213 (ECtHR, Fifth Section), [38], a claim was made that Article 10 rights (freedom of expression) were infringed by imposing severe penalties on the defendants, the operators of the Pirate Bay file-sharing site. They had been sentenced to ten months and eight months in prison, plus joint liability of €5 million. The Court found no violation of their Article 10 rights. While, at [38], the Court acknowledged that the nature and severity of the penalties imposed are factors to be taken into account when assessing the proportionality of interference with the freedom of expression, on the facts of this case, the sanctions were not disproportionate. The Court noted that the defendants had not taken any action to remove the torrent files in question, despite having been urged to do so. That indifference meant the response of the national court was proportionate.

[16] Regulation (EU) No. 1215/2012, the Brussels Regulation (Recast); see Chapter 48, section 10, pp. 1312–21.   [17] Regulation (EC) No. 864/2007, Art. 8.

[18] Regulation (EU) No. 608/2013 of 12 June 2013 concerning customs enforcement of intellectual property rights and repealing Council Regulation (EC) No. 1383/2003 [2013] *OJ L* 81/15 (the 'Border Measures Regulation'). See Chapter 49, section 2, pp. 1331–4.

[19] Directive 2004/48/EC of the European Parliament and of the Council of 29 April 2004 on the enforcement of intellectual property rights [2004] *OJ L* 195/16.   [20] That is, impose minimum standards.

[21] Enforcement Dir., Art. 7.   [22] Enforcement Dir., Art. 8.   [23] Enforcement Dir., Art. 9.

[24] Enforcement Dir., Art. 11.   [25] Enforcement Dir., Art. 3. See Chapter 49, section 1.3.2, p. 1331.

[26] The English courts had applied a similar sort of remedy previously: see *Sony v. Saray* [1983] *FSR* 302, 307–8 (a requirement to fix corrective labels on goods). The courts have also found that the power exists to require publication of a statement that goods are not infringing (which is not required by the Directive): see *Apple v. Samsung* [2013] *FSR* (9) 135. So the jurisdiction to require publication must have existed previously.

[27] Enforcement Dir., Art. 15. See Chapter 49, section 7, pp. 1349–50.

[28] Intellectual Property (Enforcements) Regulations 2006, reg 3.

[29] See J. Gibson, 'The Directive Proposal on Criminal Sanctions', in *Criminal Enforcement: A Handbook of Contemporary Research* (Ed Geiger) (2012).

48

LITIGATION

1 INTRODUCTION

This chapter provides an overview of some of the more important aspects of intellectual property litigation.[1]

2 WHO CAN BRING PROCEEDINGS?

Most intellectual property proceedings are concerned with the infringement of rights. In some cases, however, would-be defendants might want reassurance that their proposed activities will not infringe. In these circumstances, a person may be able to apply to the court for a declaration that their activities are non-infringing.

2.1 CLAIM FOR INFRINGEMENT

Usually, it is the rights holder, as defined in the relevant legislation, who is able to bring an action for infringement.[2] In certain situations, however, other parties are able to litigate to protect their interests. For example, in some cases, equitable owners are able to bring an action where their intellectual property rights have been breached or infringed. To do so, they must join the legal owner before final judgment can be given.[3] A co-owner can also bring an action for infringement.[4] While exclusive licensees are usually able

---

[1] For an assessment, see C. Greenhalgh et al., *Intellectual Property Enforcement in Smaller UK Firms* (2010).

[2] This is not the same as the *registered* right holder: see *Xtralite (Rooflights) v. Harington Conway Ltd* [2004] *RPC* 7, [25].

[3] *Columbia Pictures Industries v. Robinson* [1988] *FSR* 531, 547; *Batjac Productions v. Simitar Entertainment* [1996] *FSR* 139, 149–52.

[4] PA 1977, s. 66(2); TMA 1994, s. 23(5) (but must join all other co-owners to proceedings, other than for interim relief); CDPA 1988, ss 173(2), 259; *Cescinsky v. Routledge* [1916] 2 *KB* 325. In the case of patents and trade marks, acts done or authorized by another co-owner may not amount to an infringement: PA 1977, s. 36; TMA 1994, s. 23(3).

to bring an action for infringement,[5] the question of whether a licensee of a sign is able to bring a passing off action depends on the circumstances.[6] In some cases, the courts have allowed representative actions to be brought, notably by trade associations such as the British Phonographic Industry.[7] Representative actions are allowed where there is a common interest and a common grievance, so that the remedy sought will be of benefit to all those who are represented. Despite a general prohibition on trading in litigation (so-called 'champerty'[8]), the courts have permitted copyright holders to delegate to third parties decisions about whether to bring litigation, in exchange for a percentage on returns.[9]

In cases of criminal infringement, the police and other relevant public authorities, such as the local weights and measures authority, may be empowered to take action,[10] while in many cases private prosecutions are also possible.[11]

2.2 DECLARATION OF NON-INFRINGEMENT

Given the cost and uncertainty of intellectual property litigation, it may be important for someone who plans to invest a lot of money in a particular activity to find out whether the proposed conduct is non-infringing[12] in advance of beginning.[13] One option is to seek legal advice[14] or, in some cases, an opinion from the Intellectual Property Office.[15] If greater assurance is needed, would-be defendants are able to apply to the High Court for a declaration that their activities are non-infringing.[16] A declaration of non-infringement can be made either under the court's general powers or (in relation to potential patent infringements) under the powers provided by the Patents Act 1977. We will look at each in turn.

---

[5] PA 1977, s. 67; RDA 1949, ss 15C, 24F; CDPA 1988, ss 101, 191L; TMA 1994, s. 31 (if the exclusive licence specifically grants the right to bring proceedings); CDR, Art. 32(3) (exclusive licensee can bring action if proprietor, having been given notice to do so); EUTMR, Art. 25(3). The position of a bare licensee is more varied: normally, a bare licensee cannot bring an action—but cf. TMA 1994, s. 30(3); CDPA 1988, s. 101A; *Douglas v. Hello!* [2008] 1 *AC* 1.

[6] *Scandecor Developments v. Scandecor Marketing* [1998] *FSR* 500 (CA).

[7] *CBS Songs v. Amstrad* [1988] *RPC* 567.

[8] A contract is void as contrary to public policy where it is for maintenance and champerty. They are no longer independent torts or crimes: see Criminal Law Act 1967, ss 13 and 14.

[9] *Golden Eye International Ltd v. Telefónica UK Ltd* [2012] *RPC* 28; [2013] *RPC* (14) 452. On the emergence of 'anti-piracy' businesses, see R. Lobato and J. Thomas, 'The Business of Anti-Piracy: New Zones of Enterprise in the Copyright Wars' (2012) 6 *Int J Comm* 606.

[10] The Consumer Protection (Unfair Commercial Practices) Regulations 2008 (SI 2008/127) also create certain offences, discussed in Chapter 49, section 10.3, p. 1343, which the trading standards offices enforce.

[11] In Scotland, private prosecutions are technically possible by way of bill of criminal letters. However, this has happened only a few times over the last century. On the other hand, in England and Wales, private prosecutions are routine.

[12] There are other sorts of declarations. For example, it is possible to get a declaration that a patent application is invalid (a so-called 'Arrow declaration'): see *Fujifilm Kyowa Kirin Biologics v. Abbvie Biotechnology* [2017] *RPC* (9) 295. These are important as there is no other mechanism, before grant, to challenge the patentability of an invention.

[13] *Research in Motion (UK) Ltd v. Visto Corp.* [2008] *FSR* (20) 499, [7]; *Actavis UK Ltd v. Eli Lilly & Co.* [2015] *RPC* (6) 73, [216] (albeit this case was overturned on different grounds).

[14] In the context of registered rights, would-be defendants may also apply to have the right revoked or declared invalid. We have dealt with this in the relevant chapters.　　[15] See section 11, pp. 1307–8.

[16] Confirmed by CPR 40.20; see also A. Bateson, 'The Positive Rise of the Negative Declaration' (2008) 3(10) *JIPLP* 633.

For a court to grant a declaration of non-infringement under its general powers, it must be satisfied that the possibility of infringement is real and not theoretical.[17] Traditionally, the court must also be satisfied that the applicant has a real interest in seeking the declaration and that there is a proper 'contradictor'—that is, a defendant who has a true interest in opposing the claim.[18] This means that declarations of non-infringement will be granted only where legal rights have been contested or, more specifically, where the right holder has already made a claim against the applicant for the declaration.[19] In recent years, however, there are instances where declarations have been granted where there is a real commercial advantages in doing so without any requirement for there to be a pre-existing claim.[20] This is particularly useful for setting technical standards. Where granted, the declarations will be in narrow terms—the courts being unwilling to make broad declarations.[21]

In addition to the general power that the courts have to make declarations of non-infringement, the Patents Act 1977 contains specific statutory provisions that enable declarations of non-infringement to be made in relation to potential uses of patented inventions.[22] In order to provide certainty to potential competitors and to facilitate investment, section 71 of the 1977 Act enables applicants to apply to the court or the Comptroller for a declaration that certain acts do not constitute an infringement of the patent. This is the case even though no claim has been made against the applicant.[23] Declarations will be made only where it can be shown that the person has applied in writing to the proprietor for a written acknowledgement that they are not infringing and the proprietor has refused or failed to provide such an acknowledgement.[24] The onus of proof lies on the party seeking the declaration.[25] The effect[26] of a declaration was explained by Pumfrey J in *Niche Generics v. Lundbeck*:[27]

> …The declaration merely tells the defendant that if the claimants can demonstrate that the manufacture is according to the process description which forms the subject matter of the declaration, then there is no infringement of the patent…. The question, infringement or

[17] In patent cases, it is not possible to put validity of a granted in issue when seeking a declaration: see PA 1977, s. 74(1). It has been the suggested that it was an accidental omission: *Organon Teknika v. Hoffmann-La Roche* [1996] FSR 383, 386 (although it appears the contrary was the case; see reference in Roughton, Johnson, and Cook (2014), [8.168]).

[18] *Point Solutions v. Focus Business Solution* [2006] FSR (31) 567.

[19] *Biogen v. Medeva* [1993] RPC 475, 489; *Coflexip v. Stolt Comex Seaway* [1999] FSR 473, 484.

[20] *Nokia Corp v. Interdigital Technology* [2007] FSR (23) 570, [19] and [20].

[21] This was raised in a different context in *Lever Fabergé Ltd v. Colgate Palmolive* [2006] FSR (19) 333, [7] where Lewinson J refused to make a declaration that 'patent is, and has at all times, been invalid' without the benefit of a full trial.

[22] PA 1977, s. 71. The section does not prevent a person applying under the inherent jurisdiction, but it appears that it is not possible to put the validity of the patent in issue when seeking a declaration under the inherent jurisdiction, because of PA 1977, s. 74. On the limits, see *Organon Teknika v. F. Hoffmann-La Roche AG* [1996] FSR 383.

[23] *Plastus Kreativ v. Minesota Mining and Manufacturing Co.* [1995] RPC 438, 442.

[24] *MMD Design & Consultancy* [1989] RPC 131, 135; *Wollard's Patent* [1989] RPC 141.

[25] *Rohm & Haas Co. v. Collag* [2001] FSR (28) 426. The court has a discretion: *Apotex v. Beecham* [2003] EWHC 1395 (Pat).

[26] In some European countries, the declaration of non-infringement has been used as a 'torpedo' by defendants to pre-empt a claimant's selection of a different jurisdiction. For example, a defendant who anticipates being sued in Germany might bring an action for a declaration of non-infringement in a more sympathetic country such as Italy: see, e.g., M. Franzosi, 'Comments to Novara High Court, 20 April 2000, *Novamont v. Biotec*' [2000] EIPR N142; *Research in Motion (UK) Ltd v. Visto Corp.* [2008] FSR (20) 499. On jurisdictional issues, see section 10.1, pp. 1299–305.   [27] [2004] FSR (20) 392, [24]–[25].

not, still has to be resolved according to the process used in relation to any particular batch of product supplied by the claimants to the market in the United Kingdom. Thus, if the patentee suspects infringement, an action for infringement can always be commenced. If the claimant in the action for the declaration of non-infringement succeeds in showing that the process used in manufacture is no different from that forming the subject matter of the declaration, then the action stops at that point.

3   WHO CAN BE SUED?

There are a number of parties who may be sued for infringement of intellectual property rights. In deciding who should be sued, claimants will be guided by a range of factors. These include pragmatic concerns such as the convenience of suing a central party rather than a range of disparate infringers (a manufacturer rather than a retailer, or an Internet service provider rather than a person who posts or receives information). In other cases, the relative financial robustness of the parties may determine who is sued.

3.1   PRIMARY INFRINGERS

The most obvious person to sue is the primary infringer—that is, the person directly responsible for the infringement or breach. We have dealt with the circumstances in which such persons will be liable in each of the infringement chapters.[28]

3.2   SECONDARY AND INDIRECT INFRINGERS

Most intellectual property regimes extend the scope of liability from immediate infringers such as manufacturers of infringing goods to include parties who provide means that enable infringement or engage in the marketing or distribution of infringing materials. Often, these are referred to as 'secondary infringers'. In most instances, to be liable, secondary or indirect infringers must have known, or it must have been obvious to a reasonable person, that they were enabling the infringement or dealing in infringing copies. As with primary infringers, the special provisions relating to secondary infringers have been considered in the earlier chapters on infringement.

3.3   EMPLOYERS

The general tortious rule that the employer will be vicariously liable when an employee commits an infringing act in the course of their employment applies as much to intellectual property rights as to other torts. Whether something is in the course of a person's employment is given a wide meaning and requires two questions to be asked. First, what 'field of activities' have been assigned to the employee. Second, whether there is a sufficient connection between the position in which the person was employed and the wrongful conduct to make it just for the employer to be liable.[29] This means conduct by an

---

[28] See Chapters 6, 8, 13, 22, 28, 30, 40, and 46.
[29] *Mohamud v. WM Morrison Supermarkets Plc* [2016] *AC* 677, [44]–[45].

employee, even if not specifically authorized or even if clearly unlawful, can be found to be sufficiently connected to the employment.[30]

3.4 JOINT TORTFEASORS

It is also possible to bring an action against a party where they are acting as a joint tortfeasor.[31] A person will be liable as a joint tortfeasor where they are connected, or somehow associated, with the infringement. It is important to note that not every connection is sufficient to render an associated person a joint tortfeasor.[32] In particular, mere assistance in the commission of a tort (knowing or otherwise) will not suffice to make a person civilly liable as a joint tortfeasor; rather, the test for a joint tortfeasor is that 'each person has made the infringing acts his own'.[33] The situations in which a party will be liable as a joint tortfeasor fall into two (overlapping) categories.[34] The first concerns the situation in which a person *procures* the commission of the tort; the second, the situation in which two or more persons joined in a *common design* pursuant to which the tort was committed. We deal with each in turn.

3.4.1 Procuring the tort

A person will be liable where they procure an infringement.[35] This might occur by way of inducement, incitement, or persuasion.[36] It is possible that a person procuring the commission of a tort by another is also party to a common design, but they are distinct.[37] A person procures something when they take the appropriate steps to see that something happens.[38] It does not require any form of discussion or agreement between the parties. Therefore, a person who sells an article in kit form with instructions, and that article, when constructed, infringes the claimant's intellectual property right, the seller will be a joint tortfeasor with the person who puts the kit together, because they have *procured* that infringement.[39] In contrast, while people who sell an article knowing that it is going to be used by some customers to infringe an intellectual property right may assist infringement, but they will not be treated as having induced the infringement. For example, in *CBS Songs v. Amstrad*,[40] the House of Lords was asked to consider whether, in selling a high-speed tape-to-tape recorder that the manufacturer and vendor knew was likely to be used to infringe copyright in sound recordings, the supplier was a joint tortfeasor. The

---

[30] *Mohamud v. WM Morrison Supermarkets Plc* [2016] *AC* 677 provides an extreme example. A shop worker assaulted a customer and the supermarket was found to be liable.

[31] P. Davies, 'Accessory Liability: Protecting Intellectual Property Rights' [2011] *IPQ* 390; J. Riordan, 'The Liability of Internet Intermediaries' (Unpublished PhD thesis, University of Oxford, 2013), 149–51; H. Carty, 'Passing off and Instruments of Deception: The Need for Clarity' [2003] *EIPR* 188.

[32] See *Crédit Lyonnaise v. Export Credit Guarantee Department* [1998] 1 *Lloyds LR* 19, 44, appealed on a different issue [1999] 2 *WLR* 540 (HL); *Lancashire Fires v. SA Lyons* [1996] *FSR* 629 (CA), 675 (breach of confidence); *Vestergaard Frandsen A/S v. Bestnet Europe Ltd* [2013] 1 *WLR* 1556, [32]–[39] (Lord Neuberger).

[33] *Crédit Lyonnaise v. Export Credit Guarantee Department* [1998] 1 *Lloyds LR* 19, 46; *SABAF SpA v. MFI Furniture* [2003] *RPC* (14) 264, [58]. In comparative law terms, this is 'a very high threshold': G. Dinwoodie, 'Secondary Liability for Online Trademark Infringement: The International Landscape' (2014) 36 *Colum JL & Arts* 463.

[34] *Unilever v. Gillette (UK)* [1989] *RPC* 583, 608; cf. *MCA Records Inc. v. Charly Records* [2002] *FSR* (26) 401, [51], [52].   [35] *CBS v. Amstrad* [1988] *AC* 1013, 1058 (Lord Templeman).

[36] Ibid.

[37] *Sea Shepherd v. Fish & Fish* [2015] *AC* 1229, [19]; *Unilever v. Gillette (UK)* [1989] *RPC* 583, 608.

[38] *AG Ref (No. 1 of 1975)* [1975] *QB* 773, 779.

[39] *Rotocrop International v. Genbourne* [1982] *FSR* 241, 259.   [40] [1988] *RPC* 500, 606.

House of Lords held that, because the supplier neither had control over how purchasers used the tape recorders nor had it asked purchasers to use the tape recorder in a particular way, the supplier did not procure the infringement.

Whether a person who makes available peer-to-peer software would be found to have procured an infringement is likely to turn on the facts.[41] This is because the provider will likely be unaware of any specific acts of infringement and 'absent the identification of such specific acts a finding of procurement would not in general be appropriate'.[42] That said, in a number of cases, the High Court has found there to have been procuring infringement through offering these sorts of services.[43] Furthermore, in *Sea Shepherd v. Fish & Fish*[44] Lord Sumption looked favourably on the US Supreme Court judgment in *Metro-Goldwyn-Mayer v. Grokster*,[45] which found the website liable as it had intended the website to be used for infringement so as to increase its use.[46] Furthermore, where a person makes material available online, it has been held by the Court of Appeal that they procure acts of infringement by those who access that material.[47]

3.4.2 Common design

Where two people combine to do or secure the doing of an act which constitutes a tort (a common design) they will be joint tortfeasors.[48] There are two elements. The accessory must have acted in a way which furthered the commission of the tort by the principal; and the accessory must have done so in pursuance of a common design to do so.[49] For parties to operate in a common design, it is not necessary for the secondary party to have mapped out a plan with the primary offender;[50] tacit agreement will suffice.[51] The common design need not be to infringe if the agreed action leads to an infringement.[52] Also, at least where liability is strict, it does not matter whether or not the parties knew they were infringing.[53] The fact that a parent company has financial control of a subsidiary is not enough of a connection to constitute a common design; the parent company must be shown to have 'taken part' in the primary act.[54] Equally, under this head, directors will be liable for acts

---

[41] But see P. S. Davies, 'Accessory Liability: Protecting Intellectual Property Rights' [2011] *IPQ* 390, 403

[42] *Twentieth Century Fox v. Newzbin* [2010] *FSR* (21) 512, [110] (Kitchin J).

[43] Ibid.; (finding joint tortfeasance through inducement, common design, authorization, and primary infringement by making available); *Dramatico Entertainment Ltd v. British Sky Broadcasting Ltd* [2012] *RPC* (27) 665, [83] (in which Arnold J concluded that the 'operators of [The Pirate Bay] induce, incite or persuade its users to commit infringements of copyright', but neither The Pirate Bay nor the defendant were represented); *EMI v. British Sky Broadcasting Ltd* [2013] *EWHC* 379 (Ch), [74] (finding that unrepresented websites KAT, H33T, and FENOPY had induced infringement, although this action was also undefended and there were alternative bases for liability); *Football Association Premier League v. British Sky Broadcasting Ltd* [2013] *EWHC* 2038 (Ch), [43]; *Twentieth Century Fox v. Sky* [2015] *EWHC* 1082 (Ch) (software provided to keep the indexes up to date to facilitate access is procuring), [55]; see also *1967 Limited v. British Sky Broadcasting* [2014] *EWHC* 3444 (Ch), [23].   [44] [2015] *AC* 1229.

[45] 545 *US* 913 (2005).   [46] *Sea Shepherd* [2015] *AC* 1229, [43].

[47] *Football Dataco Ltd v. Stan James Plc* [2013] *FSR* (30) 675, [96]–[100].

[48] *Sea Shepherd* [2015] *AC* 1229, [21].   [49] Ibid.

[50] *Puschner v. Tom Palmer (Scotland)* [1989] *RPC* 430. But mere supply does not amount to a common design: *SABAF v. MFI* [2003] *RPC* (14) 264, [59].

[51] *Unilever v. Gillette* [1989] *RPC* 583, 609. See also *Lubrizol v. Esso Petroleum (No. 1)* [1992] *RPC* 281.

[52] *Unilever v. Gillette* [1989] *RPC* 583, 609; *Ravenscroft v. Herbert* [1980] *RPC* 193, 210.

[53] *Morton-Norwich* [1978] *RPC* 501, 515; cf. *Vestergaard Frandsen A/S v. Bestnet Europe Ltd* [2013] 1 *WLR* 1556, [34], [37] (where knowledge is essential for the wrong, as in breach of confidence, the participant must also have knowledge).

[54] *Unilever v. Chefaro Proprietaries* [1994] *FSR* 135, 138; *Napp Pharmaceutical Group v. Asta Medica* [1999] *FSR* 370; *Coin Controls v. Suzo* [1997] *FSR* 660, 666; *The Mead Corp. v. Riverwood Multiple Packaging* [1997] *FSR* 484.

of the company only where they and the company 'joined together in concerted action to secure that [the infringing] acts were done'.[55]

3.5 LIABILITY OF INTERNET SERVICE PROVIDERS

As should be clear (from the discussion of 'communication' and 'authorization' in Chapter 6, and that of trade mark functions in Chapter 40) one issue that has caused particular concern to right holders is the position of those who provide services and facilities that facilitate infringement on the Internet.[56] These people, who effectively provide the hardware and infrastructure for the information society, include not just operators of peer-to-peer or streaming sites, but also multinational enterprises that provide the cables for communication, as well as others who provide access to the web through local 'servers', those who run websites on which others can post information, as well as those operating 'social networking' sites and providing browser and search services. It is frequently suggested that the difficulties with rights holders policing their own rights are so great that some of these service providers should incur liability (or responsibility) where infringing material was found on sites (or distributed through services) that they controlled. The argument is that these persons are in the best position to supervise and inspect their cyber premises, and that, like the owner of a place of entertainment or possibly the operators of markets, they should be liable for infringements that occur on their 'premises'.[57] Under UK law, such liability might arise by treating their acts as 'communications' of works or 'uses' of marks, or indirectly, by arguing their involvement amounts to 'authorization' of infringement (of copyright, at least),[58] or otherwise is so closely involved as to justify treatment of such providers as joint tortfeasors. In other countries, other principles, such as notions of 'duty of care' might ground liability.[59]

The European legislature decided to pre-empt the development of diverse national responses to these issues through a harmonizing directive, but took the view that, since service providers could incur liability in a range of different legal spheres (defamation, copyright, trade marks, obscenity, privacy, data protection, etc.), the issue fell outside the remit of the Information Society Directive, which was concerned only with copyright and related rights. Moreover, rather than intervene positively to define when a service provider would incur liability, the EU legislature decided instead to define the circumstances when Internet service providers would *not* be liable (in damages) for particular activities. The idea was to establish 'safe harbours', that is, types of activities which various national laws of differing scope should not reach.[60] This harmonization was provided for in Articles 12–15 of the EC Directive on Electronic Commerce (the e-Commerce Directive), which

---

[55] *MCA Records* [2002] *FSR* (26) 401, [53].

[56] C. Angelopoulos, *European Intermediary Liability in Copyright* (2017); J. Riordan, *The Liability of Internet Intermediaries* (2016); G. B. Dinwoodie (ed.), *Secondary Liability of Online Service Providers* (2017).

[57] Info. Soc. Dir., Recital 59.   [58] See Chapter 6.

[59] Angelopoulos, ch. 3 (comparing United Kingdom with France and Germany); G. B. Dinwoodie (ed.), *Secondary Liability of Online Service Providers* (2017).

[60] *Google France*, Cases 236/08–238/08 [2010] *ECR* I–2417, EU:C:2009:569, [AG142] (AG Poiares Maduro) ('The aim of Directive 2000/31 is to create a free and open public domain on the internet'). In *L'Oréal SA v. eBay International AG*, Case C-324/09, EU:C:2010;757, Advocate-General Jääskinen, at [AG136], suggests that because the immunities are based on 'lack of subjective fault', they should not be treated as if they are exceptions and 'narrowly interpreted'.

required member states to confer an immunity on such providers except in certain limited situations.[61]

These parallel, in large part, the so-called 'safe harbours' introduced into US law by the US Digital Millennium Copyright Act of 1998 (though in that case, only in relation to copyright). [62]

British implementation took the form of the Electronic Commerce (EC Directive) Regulations 2002.[63] For Internet and related service providers, this introduced three general immunities from liability, whether it be for the infringement of copyright or the violation of any other right.[64] The immunities apply to three categories of *activity*: 'mere conduits', 'caching', and 'hosting,' either alone or in combination.[65] The immunities in all cases excuse liability for damages, for any other monetary remedy, and for any criminal sanction, but they do not prohibit injunctive relief.[66] There is some suggestion that these immunities are only available to 'intermediaries', and therefore not as responses to a finding of primary liability.[67] However, as we have seen, the CJEU and UK courts have extended the ideas of 'communication' and 'authorization' to cover many acts of 'intermediaries', and there seems no good reason why these acts should not benefit from the immunities (if they otherwise can meet the relevant conditions).[68]

The beneficiaries of these immunities are so-called 'information society service providers'—that is, any service that is normally provided for remuneration, and which operates at a distance by electronic means and at the individual request of a recipient of the services.[69] Recognizing that 'free' is a complex idea, the notion of 'remuneration' has been interpreted broadly, so that the e-Commerce regime reaches a person who provides wireless access without charge.[70]

---

[61] e-Commerce Dir., 2000/31/EC. In respect of the question of the liability of internet intermediaries, the e-Commerce Dir. has been the subject of a 2007 Study, a public consultation on notice and takedown in 2012, and a further consultation from 2015–2016 on 'the regulatory environment for platforms, online intermediaries, data and cloud computing and the collaborative economy': G. Spindler et al., *Study on the Liability of Internet Intermediaries* (2007); https://ec.europa.eu/digital-single-market/en/news/results-public-consultation-regulatory-environment-platforms-online-intermediaries-data-and.

[62] Online Copyright Infringement Liability Limitation Act, Title II of the Digital Millennium Copyright Act, Pub. L. No. 105–304, amending Ch. 5 of Title 17 *USC*. In contrast with the US DMCA 1998, no provision is made for the benefit of information location tools. For commentaries, see A. Yen, 'Internet Service Provider Liability for Subscriber Copyright Infringement, Enterprise Liability and the First Amendment' (2000) 88 *Georgetown LJ* 1883. For comparisons, see V. McEvedy, 'The DMCA and the E-Commerce Directive' [2002] *EIPR* 65. [63] e-Commerce Regs, SI 2002/2013.

[64] e-Commerce Regs.

[65] *L'Oréal SA v. eBay International AG*, Case C-324/09, [2011] ECR I-06011[AG147]–[AG149] (AG Jääskinen).

[66] e-Commerce Regs, reg. 20(1)(b). In *Tobias Mc Fadden v. Sony Music Entertainment Germany GmbH*, Case C-484/14, EU:C:2016:689, [2016] *ECDR* 26, [79] the Court noted that while that the Directive precluded a copyright holder from claiming compensation (or associated costs) from a 'mere conduit' who provided access to a communication network that was then used by a third party to infringe copyright, the copyright holder could claim injunctive relief to prevent the continuation of that infringement (and would be entitled to the payment of the costs of giving formal notice and court costs).

[67] E. Rosati, 'The CJEU Pirate Bay Judgment and its Impact on the Liability of Online Platforms' (2017) *EIPR* 737. [68] J. Riordan, *The Liability of Internet Intermediaries* (2016), [12.01], [12.37].

[69] The concept includes the operator of an electronic marketplace: *L'Oréal SA v. eBay International AG*, Case C-324/09, [2011] ECR I-06011 [109].

[70] The condition was satisfied because the service is offered to users for free in order to advertise the provider's business: *Tobias McFadden v. Sony Music Entertainment Germany GmbH*, Case C-484/14, EU:C:2016:689, [2016] *ECDR* (26) 454, [43], [50], and [54]. For consideration of 'search services', see *Google France*, Cases 236/08–238/08 [2010] *ECR* I–2417, [AG131] (AG Poiares Maduro).

3.5.1 Mere Conduit

Where the service provided is the transmission in a communication network of information provided by a recipient of the service or is the provision of access to a communication network, the service provider is exempted from liability where it did not initiate the transmission or select the receiver of the transmission, and did not select or modify the information contained in the transmission.[71] The activities of most internet access providers would fall within this definition, whether they be cafes, hotels, or larger communications networks.

3.5.2 Caching

Where the service provided is the transmission in a communication network of information provided by a recipient of the service, the service provider shall not be liable if the information is the subject of 'automatic, immediate and temporary storage' and if the following conditions are satisfied:

(a) the information is the subject of automatic, intermediate and temporary storage where that storage is for the sole purpose of making more efficient onward transmission of the information to other recipients of the service upon their request, and
(b) the service provider—
  (i)   does not modify the information;
  (ii) complies with conditions on access to the information;
  (iii) complies with any rules regarding the updating of the information, specified in a manner widely recognised and used by industry;
  (iv) does not interfere with the lawful use of technology, widely recognised and used by industry, to obtain data on the use of the information; and
  (v)   acts expeditiously to remove or to disable access to the information he has stored upon obtaining actual knowledge of the fact that the information at the initial source of the transmission has been removed from the network, or access to it has been disabled, or that a court or an administrative authority has ordered such removal or disablement.[72]

3.5.3 Hosting

Where the service provided consists of storage of information provided by a recipient of the service, the service provider shall not be liable for storage where it has no actual knowledge of unlawful activity or information, and is not aware of facts or circumstances from which it would have been apparent to the service provider that the activity or information was unlawful; or, upon obtaining such knowledge or awareness, it acts expeditiously to remove or disable access to the information.[73] This immunity shields providers of server space, including cloud services, such as Microsoft's OneDrive, DropBox, iCloud, Mediafire, and potentially so-called 'cyberlockers', to which users upload infringing material.[74] There is

---

[71] e-Commerce Regs, reg. 17.   [72] e-Commerce Regs, reg. 18.

[73] e-Commerce Regs, reg. 19 (based on e-Commerce Dir., Art. 14). On the knowledge standard, see *L'Oréal SA v. eBay International AG*, Case C-324/09 [2011] *ECR* I–6011, [116] (Grand Chamber), [118]–[124] (awareness of facts or circumstances on the basis of which a diligent economic operator should have realized that [the activity was illegal]).

[74] Well-known 'cyberlockers' included Megaupload, RapidShare, and Hotfile. Magaupload, operated from New Zealand famously by Kim Dotcom, was closed down in 2012, as a result of action from the US Department of Justice. Rapidshare was subject to litigation in Germany brought by the CMO, GEMA, and eventually shut down in 2015. Hotfile stopped operating in 2013, after settlement of litigation brought by film copyright owners in the United States claiming that Hotfile was vicariously liable. See *Disney Enterprises v. Hotfile* (USDist Ct, Southern District of Florida, 28 August, 2013).

no liability prior to notice, but once notice is provided, the sites should take down the material (or forfeit the immunity). The immunity therefore facilitates the development of so-called 'notice-and-takedown' relationships,[75] according to which if a right holder provides notice the service provider will take the material down (or otherwise risk losing their immunity).

However, the scope of the hosting exemption is fiercely contested. In particular, the court has emphasized that the service provider must be both 'neutral', vis-à-vis the content, and 'passive'.[76] But how much activity, and what type of activity, turns a 'mere host' into a person actively involved? In one (trade mark) case, the Court indicated that setting the manner in which the material is displayed does not do so;[77] nor does providing general information; but something amounting to 'editorial control' of content would do.[78] In a second trade mark infringement case, the Court of Justice intimated that:

> Where an operator has provided assistance which entails, in particular, optimising the presentation of the offers for sale in question or promoting those offers, it must be considered not to have taken a neutral position between the customer-seller concerned and potential buyers but to have played an active role of such a kind as to give it knowledge of, or control over, the data relating to those offers for sale.[79]

In such cases, then, the immunity is forfeited. Subsequently, it has been suggested that the hosting exemption is not available to any operator which utilizes mechanisms that *actively* assist the user's presentation of content. Thus, if once a user of a video platform has selected one video, the system automatically offers that user another video (perhaps based on an algorithm derived from previous user choice), the system no longer operates merely as a hosting service (and should forfeit the immunity). In contrast, other commentators point out that the Court only considered 'optimization' to be relevant in so far as it indicated the operator had an active role that would give it *knowledge* or *control* of what was being offered.[80] As a result, an automated system that might promote particular works is compatible with hosting as long as the host remains unaware of the (infringing nature of the) content.[81] While it might be objected that this interpretation conflates the question of 'hosting' with the distinct condition (in Article 14(1)(a)) of 'knowledge,' it might be said that this latter interpretation is consistent with the spirit of the e-Commerce Directive.[82]

---

[75] *L'Oréal SA v. eBay International AG*, Case C-324/09, EU:C:2011:757, [AG155] (AG Jääskinen).

[76] *Google France*, Cases 236/08–238/08 [2010] *ECR* I–2417, [114], [AG143]. Despite the doubts expressed in *L'Oréal SA v. eBay International AG*, Case C-324/09, EU:C:2010:757, by Advocate-General Jääskinen, [AG140]–[AG141], the Court (Grand Chamber) reiterated the criteria at [113].

[77] *Google France*, Cases 236/08–238/08 [2010] *ECR* I–2417, [115].

[78] *Google France*, Cases 236/08–238/08 [2010] *ECR* I–2417, [118] (in a trade mark case, drafting the message or selecting the keyword).

[79] *L'Oréal SA v. eBay International AG*, Case C-324/09 [2011] *ECR* I–6011, EU:C:2011:474, [116] (Grand Chamber).

[80] Especially, ibid., [123] ('an active role allowing it to have knowledge or control of the data stored').

[81] See also *Google France*, Cases 236/08–238/08 [2010] *ECR* I–2417, [115].

[82] Controversially, proposed Recital 38 of the Commission Proposal for a Directive on Copyright in the Digital Single Market COM(2016) 593 final, tries to promote a particular interpretation, but without seeking to adjust the e-Commerce Directive itself. Paragraph 2 of that recital states: 'In respect of Article 14, it is necessary to verify whether the service provider plays an active role, including by optimising the presentation of the uploaded works or subject matter or promoting them, irrespective of the means used therefor.' Rather than identifying knowledge and control as the key factors, the recital purports to elevate a single consideration into a condition for the availability of the exemption.

3.5.4 The Prohibition on 'General Monitoring'

Although the e-Commerce Directive does not prevent injunctive relief being awarded to prevent infringement of copyright, it does, however, prohibit the imposition of any obligation to monitor.[83] Article 15(1) states that 'Member States shall not impose a general obligation on providers, when providing the services covered by Articles 12, 13 and 14, to monitor the information which they transmit or store, nor a general obligation actively to seek facts or circumstances indicating unlawful activity.'[84]

The scope of this prohibition is (like much else in this area) heatedly contested. Clearly, no 'general' obligation to monitor exists where a person complains to a service provider about a specific user posting particular material. But where a particular subscriber has repeatedly infringed, what about a requirement that the provider monitor all posts *by that person*? And if a platform has been required already to take down specific material, can it be required to ensure that no user uploads the same material again? [85]

In *Scarlet*, the Court of Justice considered whether the prohibition in Article 15 was breached by an order requiring an internet access provider (whose system had been used as a vehicle for infringing 'peer-to-peer' copying) to screen all content uploaded by all subscribers in order to identify and filter out the musical works for which the claimant held copyright.[86] The Court said the key question was whether the system would 'require an intermediary provider, such as an ISP, actively to monitor *all the data* of each of its customers in order to prevent any future infringement of intellectual-property rights.'[87] Given the character of the proposed system, the Court found that it would violate the prohibition of general monitoring obligations in Article 15 of the e-Commerce Directive.[88]

The question arises whether (on the assumption that they fall within the hosting exemption) the *Scarlet* holding would prohibit orders requiring filtering or content-recognition systems be installed on user-generated content platforms such as You Tube, or social media, such as Instagram. Such a filtering system would apply whenever a user uploaded content, and thus it might be argued that it monitors particular acts (rather than all acts). However, the overall effect would be inevitably to screen the content of all uploads, and at the very least to determine in relation to any given act, whether it involved 'upload'. It seems that, unless Article 15 is modified, such orders will not be possible.[89]

3.5.5 European Copyright Reform Proposals

In September 2016, the European Commission published a proposal for a new directive on Copyright in the Digital Single Market. Article 13 of the proposal seeks to impose

---

[83] For discussion, see C. Angelopoulos, *European Intermediary Liability in Copyright* (2017) 100–5; Art. 15. Recital 47 states: 'Member States are prevented from imposing a monitoring obligation on service providers only with respect to obligations of a general nature; this does not concern monitoring obligations in a specific case and, in particular, does not affect orders by national authorities in accordance with national legislation.'

[84] A derogation in Art. 15(2) allows member states to require information society service providers promptly to inform 'competent public authorities' of alleged unlawful activities.

[85] For application, see *Société des Producteurs de Phonogrammes en France v. Google*, No. 11–13.666 (French Supreme Court, 12 July 2012) (an obligation for providers of hosting services to prevent the reappearance of contents that they have already taken down—'notice and stay-down'—might amount to a general monitoring obligation prohibited by e-Commerce Dir., Art. 15).

[86] *Scarlet Extended v. SABAM*, Case C-70/10 [2011] *ECR* I–11959 (ECJ), [29] (describing 'the contested filtering system').

[87] Ibid., [36] (referring to *L'Oréal SA v. eBay International AG*, Case C-324/09 [2011] *ECR* I–6011, [139]).

[88] Ibid., [40].

[89] It would also need to be ascertained how far the 'no general monitoring' rule in fact rests upon fundamental rights (particularly personal data).

obligations on information service providers, seemingly including obligations to utilize content recognition technologies. The drafting quality of the provision, as introduced, was poor, but seemed to identify two sets of obligations on certain 'hosts', that is 'information society service providers that store and provide access to large amount of works or other subject-matter uploaded by their users'. The obligations were, first, to 'take measures to ensure the functioning of agreements concluded with rightholders' (an obligation which seems bizarrely to require contracts to be enforceable!) and, second, and more controversially, 'to prevent the availability on their services of works or other subject-matter identified by rightholders'. The proposed law adds that 'those measures, such as the use of effective content recognition technologies, shall be appropriate and proportionate.'

Critics of the proposal tend to make a number of objections. First, they observe that filtering mechanisms are intrinsically problematic as enforcement tools because it is not possible accurately to identify infringing, and only infringing, uses of copyright material. This is in part because copyright exceptions permit a range of uses of protected material, so merely identifying that corresponding material is being uploaded may catch permitted reuses (for example parodies or fair quotations).[90] Second, it is argued that requiring a service provider to utilize such mechanisms interferes with their right to do business (contrary, potentially to Article 16 of the Charter),[91] and, in any case, is likely to increase barriers to entry into the market for host services (and thus reinforce the dominance of existing operators, such as You Tube).[92] Third, it is noted that other aspects of the legality of such a prohibition are questionable, in particular, that they involve monitoring contrary to the prohibition in Article 15 of the e-Commerce Directive;[93] and the deployment of such 'censorship machines' impacts on freedom of speech and rights to personal data.[94] One commentator sums up the criticisms, saying that draft Article 13 is 'ill-conceived, badly-worded and incompatible with established law. It betrays a bewildering lack of understanding of European copyright law and an alarming disregard for the law of fundamental rights'.[95]

Some of these criticisms might well be accommodated by amending the proposal, for example, to require member states to impose obligations on hosts based on the 'duty of care' recognized in Recital 48 of the e-Commerce Directive.[96] Such duties could include

[90] The problems may be greater in some fields, such as photography, than others, such as perhaps recorded sound.

[91] *Scarlet Extended SA v. SABAM*, Case C-70/10 [2011] *ECR* I–11959, [46]–[49], [53] (ECJ); *SABAM v. Netlog NV*, Case C-360/10, EU:C:2012:85, [44]–[46], [52] (ECJ).

[92] ECS, *General Opinion on the EU Copyright Reform Package* (2017), 7. Quite how big a problem this is would depend on the expense of such technologies. Apart from Google's famous 'Content-ID' system, which is said to have cost many millions of dollars to develop, other commercial offerings, such as 'Audible Magic', appear to be much less costly.

[93] *Scarlet*, Case C-70/10, [2011] *ECR* I–11959, [34]–[40] (ECJ); *Netlog NV*, Case C-360/10, EU:C:2012:85, [33]–[38] (ECJ).

[94] EDRI, 'Deconstructing Article 13', available online at https://edri.org/files/copyright/copyright_proposal_article13.pdf; *Scarlet*, Case C-70/10 [2011] *ECR* I–11959, [50], [53] (ECJ); *Netlog NV*, Case C-360/10, EU:C:2012:85, [48]–[52].

[95] C. Angelopoulos, 'Outside the Safe Harbours, Intermediary Liability Capsizes into Incoherence' (6 October 2016) available online at http://copyrightblog.kluweriplaw.com/2016/10/06/eu-copyright-reform-outside-safe-harbours-intermediary-liability-capsizes-incoherence/.

[96] This specifies that the Directive 'does not affect the possibility for Member States of requiring service providers, who host information provided by recipients of their service, to apply duties of care, which can reasonably be expected from them and which are specified by national law, in order to detect and prevent certain types of illegal activities.' On the problems inherent in the idea of a duty of care in this context, see C. Angelopoulos, *European Intermediary Liability in Copyright: A Tort-Based Analysis* (2017), 94–6.

obligations on hosts to take action on being notified of infringements, and even to monitor the activities of particular persons. It is not out of the question that content recognition technologies could be improved, and their costs reduced, so that the objections grounded on freedom of expression and freedom to do business are rendered less significant.[97] Whether the objection to general monitoring grounded in the Charter, as opposed to Article 15 of the e-Commerce Directive can ever be surmounted is a different matter. In the *Scarlet* and *Netlog* decisions,[98] the Court of Justice held that orders against internet access providers and social networks that required the operators to filter all user communication were not compatible with user rights in personal data. The Court concluded that such orders did not respect the fair balance between these rights and those of the copyright holder. However, both decisions are so lacking in analysis that it is impossible to know how, if at all, such objections might be met.[99] The inevitable conclusion may be that it is never compatible with the Charter for a host to be obliged to install content recognition technologies.[100] At the time of writing,[101] the various committees of the European Parliament seem deeply divided, while the Council seems to be moving towards a softer version of Article 13 that does not mention 'content recognition technologies'.

That said, such technologies are already used in the context of private arrangements between right holders and hosts or platforms: the Charter and e-Commerce Directive being (assumed to be) irrelevant to agreements between private actors.[102] That is, it seems, users already face mechanisms that conflict with their rights to have their personal data and their freedom of expression. Pragmatically, then, there is some attraction to the idea of requiring that appropriate and proportionate mechanisms to prevent infringement of copyright be developed between stakeholders that include not just content owners and ISPs but also *user representatives and data protection supervisors*, and that these mechanisms include automated systems.[103] This is true not just in relation to hosting (or 'online

---

[97] *Scarlet*, Case C-70/10 [2011] *ECR* I–11959, [48] (explaining that the Art. 16 right was infringed because the order required the installation of 'a complicated, costly, permanent computer system at its own expense') and [52] (interference with free expression by blocking lawful content). The objections would, presumably, diminish if the filter was cheap and simple, and refined so that blocking of lawful content became *de minimis*.

[98] *Scarlet*, Case C-70/10 [2011] *ECR* I–11959, [50], [51], [53]; *Netlog NV*, Case C-360/10, EU:C:2012:85, [48], [49], [51].

[99] C. Angelopoulos, *European Intermediary Liability* (2017), 135, refers to the CJEU's reasoning as 'low on guidelines … inscrutable'. The more elaborate Opinion of Advocate-General Cruz-Villalón also offers no assistance. He regarded the proposed order as contrary to the Charter because it was not sufficiently grounded in 'law', an opinion which seems to suggest that the Commission would be advised to refine with even greater particularity when such orders to filter might be made. Other situations where interference with rights of personal data has been found unjustifiable, such as *Tele2 Sverige AB v. Post-och telestyreben*, Joined Cases 203/15 and C-698/15, EU:C:2016:970 (concerning indiscriminate retention of traffic data) seem rather far-removed from filtering copyright-protected content to offer much guidance.

[100] See C. Angelopoulos, *On Online Platforms and the Commission's New Proposal for a Directive on Copyright in the Digital Single Market* (January 2017) available online at https://juliareda.eu/wp-content/uploads/2017/03/angelopoulos_platforms_copyright_study.pdf. That said, the installation of such systems seems to be obligatory, at least in relation to some other wrongs, under the European Convention on Human Rights: *Delfi v. Estonia*, Application No. 64569/09 ([2015] *EMLR* (26) 563, ECHR, Grand Chamber).

[101] May 2018.

[102] In this respect, it is notable that the Court of Justice, in *UPC Telekabel Wien GmbH v. Constantin Film Verleih GmbH*, C-314/12, EU:C:2014:192, [52]–[54], required the ISP to 'ensure compliance with the fundamental right of internet users to freedom of information' when formulating the manner in which it implemented a 'blocking order.' It might be that this implies that all ISP behaviour that is designed to protect third party rights, but as a result affects users, must comply with fundamental rights.

[103] On such freedoms, see Chapter 9. For proposals relating to 'fair use by design', see Niva Elkin-Koren, 'Fair Use by Design' (2017) 64 *UCLA LR* 1082.

content sharing service providers') services (the focus of Article 13 of the proposed Directive), but other information services providers, such as search engines.

3.6 INJUNCTIVE RELIEF

Section 97A of the CDPA 1988 (which implements Article 8 of the Information Society Directive) imposes an important counterweight to those immunities.[104] This confers a power on the High Court to issue an injunction against a service provider where that person has actual knowledge of another person using their service to infringe copyright. In assessing whether the service provider has the appropriate knowledge, the Court is directed to take account of any notice received by the service provider under regulation 6(1)(c) of the e-Commerce Regulations 2002. Right holders are in a position to apply for an injunction against intermediaries whose services are used by a third party to infringe a copyright or related right. While the immunities given by the e-Commerce Directive prevent financial liability, if the service provider is informed of the illegal acts, thereafter it seems that it must take action to stop them from continuing or face injunctive relief. This power has been the legal basis for a series of blocking injunctions against ISPs, requiring them to block access to sites that are predominately involved in facilitating file-sharing.[105] As explained elsewhere, in formulating such injunctions, courts are required carefully to balance the various human rights at stake.

Under Article 11 of the Enforcement Directive,[106] member states are required to make provision for right holders 'to apply for an injunction against intermediaries whose services are used by third parties to infringe an intellectual property right'. While the term intermediaries includes those persons who provide facilities to market traders and the like,[107] it is most commonly considered in terms of intermediaries on the Internet. An additional provision, applicable to copyright and related rights can be found in Article 8(3) of the Information Society Directive.[108] The rationale is that such intermediaries are often 'best placed to bring such infringing activities to an end'.[109] There is no need to establish that the intermediary is liable either as a primary or secondary infringer.[110] Indeed, Article 11 offers the possibility of injunctive relief even when the intermediary is *within* the safe harbour and thus immune from monetary liability.[111] Member states are free to establish the 'conditions and modalities' of implementation,[112] and in the United Kingdom such action against intermediaries *in relation to copyright* is conditioned on the presence of actual knowledge of the infringing acts.[113] In relation to other intellectual

---

[104] Recital 45 of the e-Commerce Dir, states '[t]he limitations of the liability of intermediary service providers established in this Directive do not affect the possibility of injunctions of different kinds; such injunctions can in particular consist of orders by courts or administrative authorities requiring the termination or prevention of any infringement, including the removal of illegal information or the disabling of access to it.'

[105] See Chapter 49, section 3.2.1, p. 1336.

[106] Dir. 2004/48/EC; for some comparative views, see A. Roy, 'The Blocking Injunction: A Comparative and Critical Review of the EU, Singaporean and Australian Regimes' [2016] *EIPR* 92.

[107] *Tommy Hilfiger Licensing v. Delta Centres*, Case C-494/15, EU:C:2016:528.

[108] Dir. 2001/29/EC; Info. Soc. Dir. Art. 8(3); CDPA 1988, s. 97A.   [109] Info. Soc. Dir., Recital 59.

[110] Indeed, if they were liable as infringers there would be no need for a provision in the first place as a conventional cause of action would be available.

[111] *Twentieth Century Fox Film Corp. v. British Telecommunications Plc* [2011] *RPC* (28) 855, [113].

[112] Info. Soc. Dir., Recital 59.

[113] CDPA 1988, s. 97A. See further *Twentieth Century Fox Film Corp. v. British Telecommunications Plc* [2011] *RPC* (28) 855, [148] ('it is not essential to prove actual knowledge of a specific infringement of a specific copyright work by a specific individual').

property rights, there has been no express implementation, but it is clear that an injunction can be granted under the general jurisdiction of the court[114] with the same knowledge requirement.[115]

The power has proved particularly useful in the context of 'online intermediaries', where it has been used not only against service providers whose services support websites featuring infringing material, but also against those that offer their customers access to websites that themselves are infringing.[116] The power has been used to require service providers to block customer access to particular sites or servers[117] that facilitate infringement.[118] Because the intermediary is essentially innocent, it might seem appropriate that the costs incurred in executing such an order (as well as the costs of defending such an order) ought to be paid by the copyright owner that is seeking to enlist their assistance.[119] However, while the English courts have said that the costs of initiating proceedings should be borne by the rights holders,[120] if the Internet services provider (ISP) defends the proceedings, the costs of implementing the order should be paid by the ISP (as long as it is not 'excessive').[121] It seems conceivable that similar orders might be made against search engines that provide access to infringing sites, perhaps by requiring 'de-indexing'.[122] However, orders that require service providers to monitor the activities of their customers are precluded by the e-Commerce Directive,[123] and it has been held that this necessarily precludes systems designed to filter copyright material.[124]

---

[114] Senior Courts Act 1981, s. 37.

[115] *Cartier International AG v. British Sky Broadcasting* [2016] *ETMR* (43) 1306, [80]–[81].

[116] *LSG-Gesellschaft zur Wahrnehmung von Leistungsschutzrechten GmbH v. Tele2 Telecommunication GmbH*, Case C-557/07 [2009] *ECR* I–1227, [46]; *UPC Telekabel Wien GmbH v. Constantin Film Verleih GmbH, Wega Filmproduktionsgesellschaft mbH*, Case C-314/12, EU:C:2014:192 (ECJ, Fourth Chamber), [30]–[40] (it is not even necessary to show that any of the IAP's customers have accessed the site providing illegal material); *Twentieth Century Fox Film Corp. v. British Telecommunications Plc* [2011] *RPC* (28) 855, [108], [113].

[117] *Football Association Premier League v. British Telecommunications* [2017] *ECDR* (17) 346; as to the effectiveness of different techniques, see A. Roy and A. Marsoof, 'Blocking Injunctions and Collateral Damage' [2017] *EIPR* 74.

[118] See, e.g., *Football Association Premier League v. British Telecommunications* [2017] *ECDR* (17) 346; *Dramatico Entertainment Ltd v. British Sky Broadcasting Ltd* [2012] *RPC* (27) 665; *EMI Records Ltd v. British Sky Broadcasting Ltd* [2013] *EWHC* 379 (Ch).

[119] The injunction limits the freedom to conduct business that is protected under Art. 16 of the Charter. See *UPC Telekabel Wien GmbH v. Constantin Film Verleih GmbH, Wega Filmproduktionsgesellschaft mbH*, Case C-314/12 EU:C:2014:192 (ECJ, Fourth Chamber), [50]. In *Scarlet*, Case C-70/10 [2011] *ECR* I–11959 (ECJ, Third Chamber), [48], and *Netlog NV*, Case C-360/10 [2012] 2 *CMLR* 18 (ECJ, Third Chamber), [46], the Court said that it would be inappropriate to grant an injunction that would compel a social networking site to install a filtering system, because that 'would result in a serious infringement of the freedom of the hosting service provider to conduct its business since it would require that hosting service provider to install a complicated, costly, permanent computer system *at its own expense*' (emphasis added). Whether the objection still exists if the copyright holder pays is yet to be seen.

[120] *Twentieth Century Fox Film Corp. v. British Telecommunications Plc* [2011] *EWHC* 2714 (Ch), [53]–[55] (differentiating between various stages in proceedings).

[121] *Twentieth Century Fox Film Corp. v. British Telecommunications Plc* [2011] *RPC* (28) 855, [177]; *Twentieth Century Fox Film Corp. v. British Telecommunications Plc* [2011] *EWHC* 2714 (Ch), [32]–[33] (initial cost would be £5,000, plus £100 for each notification); *L'Oréal SA v. eBay International AG*, Case C-324/09 [2011] *ECR* I–6011, [139] (such measures 'must not be excessively costly').

[122] Similar to actions under the 'right to be forgotten': see *Google Spain SL v. Agencia Espanola de Proteccion de Datos*, Case C-131/12 [2014] *3 CMLR* 50.

[123] e-Commerce Dir., Art. 15; *Scarlet*, Case C-70/10 [2011] *ECR* I–11959, [35]; *Netlog NV*, Case C-360/10 [2012] 2 *CMLR* 18, [33].

[124] *Scarlet*, Case C-70/10 [2011] *ECR* I–11959, [39]–[40]; *Netlog NV*, Case C-360/10 [2012] 2 *CMLR* 18, [37]–[38].

4 OBTAINING AND PRESERVING EVIDENCE

Often, intellectual property right holders find out about infringement by chance. For example, a dissatisfied customer of a counterfeiter might complain to the right holder that the goods made by the infringer are faulty. Intellectual property rights owners also have more systematic ways of discovering infringements. In particular, collecting societies and trade associations such as the British Phonograph Industry's Anti-Piracy Unit, the Federation against Copyright Theft (FACT), which polices video piracy, and the Federation against Software Theft (FAST), which monitors software infringement, play an important role in identifying and policing infringement.

4.1 COLLECTING EVIDENCE

Once right holders discover that their rights are being infringed, it will usually be necessary for them to gather the relevant evidence. This might include evidence that an infringement has taken place, the details of the parties involved, and the extent of infringement. In some cases, evidence of infringement is obtained by ambushing or entrapping the defendant. For example, a legal practitioner might pose as a bona fide customer of a person selling infringing products or services. Such actions, which are called 'trap orders',[125] often involve a degree of deception by the person collecting the evidence.[126] Despite this, the courts have not objected to evidence obtained in this way, nor have claimants relying on such evidence been treated as lacking 'clean hands'.[127] Instead, the courts have left the probity of such techniques to be regulated by the appropriate professional bodies. Copyright owners and anyone whom they authorize are also given the power to seize and detain infringing copies without first obtaining a court order.[128] To protect the expectations of property owners and the public more generally, the availability of such self-help mechanisms is limited.

4.2 *NORWICH PHARMACAL* ORDERS

Another important source of evidence derives from the fact that intellectual property right holders are able to obtain a court order requiring a person to reveal information relevant to the action.[129] This may include the names and addresses of relevant parties, the dates and quantities imported, and the source of goods or materials.[130] Orders for discovery are particularly useful in that they enable right holders to trace the channels through which infringing goods are distributed. The so-called '*Norwich Pharmacal* order'[131] may require parties to identify, for example, persons serving as the source of goods in their possession

---

[125] Sometimes called the more neutral term 'test purchase'.

[126] As the purchaser is acting with the consent of the intellectual property right holder, there are risks where too much encouragement occurs. Compare *Kelly v. Batchelar* (1893) 10 *RPC* 289 (where a patentee's agent asked a person to make something in accordance with the a specific design: held to be consent); and *Dunlop Pneumatic Tyre Co. v. Neal* (1899) 16 *RPC* 247 (agent asks for machine to be repaired, and defendant elects to do it in an infringing way).   [127] *Marie Claire Album v. Hartstone Hosiery* [1993] *FSR* 692.

[128] CDPA 1988, ss 100, 196.

[129] CPR, r. 31. J. Riordan, 'The Liability of Internet Intermediaries' (2016), ch. 6, offers a useful account.

[130] This is provided for by the Enforcement Dir, Art. 8; it has been made clear that Art. 8 also entitles a person to an order for disclosure after a finding of infringement: *New Wave v. Alltoys*, Case C-427/15, EU:C:2017:18.

[131] These orders did not exist under Scottish law. Accordingly, provision was made by the Intellectual Property (Enforcement, etc) Regulation 2006 (SI 2006/1028), reg. 4.

or providing access to works online.[132] The order may even address third parties, who are not themselves named as a wrongdoer, if they are shown to have become involved in the transaction in question, and even where the wrongdoer is not in the United Kingdom.[133] The topic has taken on particular importance in relation to right holders' efforts to tackle file-sharing.[134] The most common scenario concerns an application to the court to force an Internet intermediary to reveal the identities of customers who appear to be infringing copyright. Here, a range of rights and freedoms need to be balanced: the right of the intellectual property owner; the right of the service provider to do business; and the rights of the user to their personal data. In *Promusicae*,[135] the Court of Justice held that the various directives did not require member states to provide for such orders in copyright proceedings, but merely that, when implementing the directives, member states ensure that 'a fair balance' is struck between the various fundamental rights protected by the European legal order.[136]

By placing the onus of balancing the 'various fundamental rights protected by the [EU] legal order' on national courts, the Court of Justice has adopted the rhetoric of balance (frustratingly) familiar in British intellectual property law. In *Golden Eye International Ltd v. Telefónica UK Ltd*,[137] the claimant involved in making pornographic films sought a *Norwich Pharmacal* order against O$_2$, a large ISP, to obtain disclosure of the names and addresses of more than 9,000 O$_2$ customers who were alleged to have committed infringements of copyright through peer-to-peer file-sharing. The ISP did not oppose the application, but the Court benefited from an intervention by the consumer rights organization Consumer Focus, putting the case for the 'real defendants'—that is, those whose names would be revealed. Arnold J observed that the key factor in determining whether to make an order was its proportionality, in relation to which a number of factors fell to be weighed.[138] On the one hand, the order sought to protect property rights,[139] but on the other revealing the identities of users of certain IP addresses implicates the right to privacy and the right to the protection of personal data under Article 8 of the European Convention on Human Rights (ECHR).[140] Because neither right automatically has precedence over the other, what is required to resolve the conflict is an intense focus on the comparative importance of the specific rights being claimed in the individual case and the justifications for interfering with or restricting each right. The proportionality test— or 'ultimate balancing test'—must be applied to each. For Arnold J, in the circumstances, it was necessary and proportionate to reveal the identities of those whose IP addresses appeared to be implicated in illegal file-sharing. As he explained, without the disclosure of this data, it would be impossible for the copyright owner to enforce its rights. The judge saw no reason to differentiate between owners of rights in non-pornographic material and those of rights in pornographic material. Nevertheless, the Court sought to safeguard

---

[132] *Norwich Pharmacal v. CCE* [1974] *AC* 133; *Ashworth Hospital* [2002] 1 *WLR* 2033; *Jade Engineering* [1996] *FSR* 461; *Wilko Retail v. Buyology* [2015] *FSR* (17) 432.

[133] See, e.g., *Norwich Pharmacal* [1974] *AC* 133; *Coca Cola. v. BT* [1999] *FSR* 518; *Eli Lilly v. Neopharma* [2008] *FSR* (25) 615; *Jade Engineering* [1996] *FSR* 461.   [134] *Polydor v. Brown* [2005] *EWHC* 319.

[135] *Productores de Música de España (Promusicae) v. Telefónica de España*, Case C-275/06 [2008] *ECR* I–271.

[136] Ibid., [71]. These were the e-Commerce Dir., the Information Society Dir., the Enforcement Dir., and the Directive on privacy and electronic communications.

[137] [2012] *RPC* (28) 698, [117] (Arnold J). Arnold J's decision not to award relief to two claimants who had outsourced their capacity to bring claims to Golden Eye was overturned on appeal: [2013] *RPC* (14) 452, although Arnold J's general approach was not questioned.

[138] See *Rugby Football Union v. Viagogo Ltd* [2012] 1 *WLR* 3333, [45] (Lord Kerr of Tonaghmore JSC).

[139] ECHR, First Protocol, Art. 1; Charter, Art. 17(2).   [140] ECHR, Art. 8(1); Charter, Art. 7.

the interests of the subscribers whose identities were disclosed by regulating the contents of the letters that the rights holders would subsequently send. In particular, the judge was conscious that any threat to publicize the identities of the subscribers was especially inappropriate given the potential embarrassment arising from the nature of the alleged infringement.[141] Moreover, the judge said that it would not be correct to demand a standard sum of £700 damages.[142]

One problem with an overly solicitous approach to the revelation of the identities of alleged infringers is the part that it has played in the practice of so-called 'speculative invoicing'. This problem, which became visible in litigation before the (then) Patents County Court,[143] involves an entity acting supposedly on behalf of copyright holders (under some sort of profit-sharing arrangement) to pursue small-scale infringers by sending letters before action to thousands of Internet subscribers, claiming a substantial sum in relation to alleged violations of copyright at the subscriber's Internet address.[144] The idea is to scare people into paying, not to ascertain whether there has been an actual infringement for which they were in some way legally responsible, nor actually to commence legal proceedings. In *Media CAT v. Adams*,[145] Judge Birss QC suggested that safeguards might be needed to prevent abuse of *Norwich Pharmacal* orders in this way.[146]

4.3 DIGITAL ECONOMY ACT 2010

Inspired by a French precedent known as the 'Hadopi' regime,[147] the Digital Economy Act 2010 was intended to establish the basis for a system of what has been variously termed 'graduated response' or 'three strikes and you're out' to deal with online copyright infringement by end-users.[148] The underlying idea is to impose obligations on ISPs to assist copyright holders in policing the activities of end-users by sending notices (so as to create a feeling that the activities are being watched) and, if necessary, limiting or terminating the service. The response is 'graduated' in the sense that it offers techniques of dealing with infringers that are less draconian than starting civil litigation (or criminal proceedings), as well as that the measures taken can be made proportionate to the severity or persistence of the activity. The regime faced an unsuccessful judicial review[149] and it appears that the government no longer intend to bring the legislation into force

---

[141] [2012] *RPC* (28) 698, [122] (commenting on the draft order, which would accompany the letter).

[142] Ibid., [133]–[138].   [143] *Media CAT v. Adams* [2011] *FSR* (28) 679, [112].

[144] There have been disciplinary findings made against solicitors who undertook this practice on various grounds, but usually because they became too interested in the outcome of the litigation (as they received the costs only from those who paid).   [145] [2011] *FSR* (28) 679, [112].

[146] Suggesting that a group litigation order under CPR, Pt 19, might be a potential safeguard. However, in *Golden Eye International Ltd v. Telefónica UK Ltd* [2012] *RPC* (28) 698, [142], Arnold J offers several reasons as to why such orders are unlikely to work.

[147] D. le Franc, 'The Metamorphosis of *Contrfaçon*', in L. Bently, J. Davis, and J. Ginsburg (eds), *Copyright and Piracy* (2010), ch. 4; C. Geiger, 'Honourable Attempt but (Ultimately) Disproportionately Offensive against Peer-to-peer on the Internet' [2011] *IIC* 457; J. de Beer and C. Clemmer, 'Global Trends in Online Copyright Enforcement: A Non-neutral Role for Network Intermediaries?' (2009) 49 *Jurimetrics J* 375; R. Giblin, 'Evaluating Graduated Response' (2014) 37 *Col JL & Arts* 147; C. Geiger, 'Challenges for the Enforcement of Copyright in the Online World: Time for a New Approach', in P. Torremans (ed.), *Research Handbook on Cross-Border Enforcement of Intellectual Property* (2015).

[148] For background, see BIS/DCMS, *Digital Britain: Final Report* (Cm. 7650, June 2009). For commentary, see A. Barron, '"Graduated Response" *à l'Anglaise*: Online Copyright Infringement and the Digital Economy Act 2010' (2011) 3 *J Media L* 305; J. Riordan, 'The Liability of Internet Intermediaries' (2016), ch. 5.

[149] *R (on the application of British Telecommunications Plc) v. Secretary of State for Business, Innovation and Skills* [2011] 3 *CMLR* (5) 98; partly overturned [2012] 2 *CMLR* (23) 667.

rather relying on a voluntary scheme called the Voluntary Copyright Alert Programme (or VCAP). The VCAO was negotiated between the music and film industry and four ISPs (BT, Virgin, Sky, and TalkTalk) and is modelled upon the 'copyright alert system' that was voluntarily adopted in the United States.[150]

4.4 SEARCH ORDERS

To enable intellectual property right owners to preserve evidence prior to trial, the English courts developed the so-called *'Anton Piller* order',[151] now renamed 'search order'.[152] In essence, a search order permits a claimant (and their solicitor) to inspect the defendant's premises and to seize or copy any information that is relevant to the alleged infringement. In intellectual property cases, applications for search orders are made either to a patents judge in the High Court or the Intellectual Property Enterprise Court, or to a Chancery judge.[153] Because the order aims to ensure that evidence is not destroyed, the application is made without giving notice to the other party. Given their potentially draconian nature,[154] search orders will be made only if the matter is urgent or otherwise desirable in the interests of justice.[155] Before an order will be granted, the courts require claimants to show that they have an extremely strong case of infringement on its face and that the potential damage to them is very serious. The claimant must also provide clear evidence that the defendant has incriminating material in their possession and that there is a real possibility that the evidence will be destroyed.[156] The search order is subject to procedural safeguards,[157] such as the need for a supervising solicitor (unconnected with the applicant) who is experienced in the operation of search orders.[158] The order may be served only on a weekday between 9.30 am and 5.30 pm (unless the court orders otherwise), and supervising solicitors must explain the terms of the order to the respondents in everyday language and advise them of their rights.[159] Failure to comply with an order is a contempt of court, resulting in imprisonment or a fine.[160]

The application for a search order may be combined with an interim injunction against infringement and a 'freezing order' (formerly known as a *'Mareva* injunction') ordering the retention of property pending the outcome of the litigation.[161] In addition, the search

---

[150] Similar schemes have been adopted or are being considered elsewhere, often facing substantial opposition: see, e.g., S. McVicar and C. Roche, 'Proposed Amendments to Australian Copyright Act to Tackle Online Piracy Will Increase Obligations on ISPs' [2015] *EIPR* 120.

[151] *Anton Piller v. Manufacturing Processes* [1976] *Ch* 55. See S. Gee, *Commercial Injunctions* (6th edn, 2016); M. Hoyle, *Freezing and Search Orders* (4th edn, 2017), ch. 8. For a Marxist interpretation of the development of the order, see F. Carrigan, 'The Political Economy of *Anton Piller* Orders' (1995) 11 *AJL & Soc* 33.

[152] CPA 1998, s. 7; CPR Practice Direction 25A.

[153] CPR Practice Direction 25A ('Interim Injunctions'), [1.1].

[154] *Universal Thermosensors v. Hibben* [1992] *FSR* 361; *Taylor Made Golf Company v. Rata and Rata* [1996] *FSR* 528, 535.   [155] CPR, r. 25.2(2)(b).

[156] The applicant should disclose all material facts: CPR Practice Direction 25A, [3.3].

[157] Ibid.

[158] Ibid., [7.2] (supervising solicitor must not be an employee or member of the applicant's firm of solicitors).

[159] Ibid., [7.4]. Where the supervising solicitor is a man and the respondent is likely to be an unaccompanied woman, at least one other person named in the order must be a woman and must accompany the supervising solicitor: ibid., [7.4(5)].

[160] *Taylor Made* [1996] *FSR* 528 (fine of £75,000). See the Notice to the Respondent in the sample order annexed to CPR Practice Direction 25A.

[161] CPR, r. 25(f) (sometimes called 'asset preservation orders').

order may require the defendant to provide information about the source of the infringing copies or their intended destination.[162]

5 PRESUMPTIONS

Normally, in civil actions, the obligation falls upon the claimant to prove their case on the balance of probabilities.[163] Therefore, where a party seeks the revocation or invalidity of a registered right it is for them to prove the right is not valid. There are however certain presumptions which mean something is presumed to be the case unless proved otherwise. Therefore, in relation to copyright, there is a presumption relating to the identity of the author,[164] publisher,[165] performer,[166] or (in the case of database right) the maker,[167] and the date on which a work (etc.) was published.[168] In copyright law, when an author is dead, it is presumed that the work was original and that it was first published where and when the claimant alleges.[169]

6 UNJUSTIFIED THREATS TO SUE

The cost and burden of intellectual property litigation means that the mere threat of litigation has the scope to act as a potent commercial weapon.[170] To ensure that the threat to sue is not misused, special provisions offer remedies against unjustified threats to litigate.[171] These exist in the case of patents, trade marks, registered designs, the unregistered design right, and Community designs, whether registered or unregistered.[172] There are no statutory provisions that protect against unjustified threats to sue in relation to copyright, passing off, or breach of confidence. In these cases, persons unjustifiably threatened with litigation have to resort to other means.[173]

[162] There is a statutory exception to the privilege against self-incrimination: Senior Courts Act 1981, s. 72; as to the scope of the statutory exemption see *Phillips v. Mulcaire* [2013] 1 *AC* 1.

[163] The burden of proof can be reversed under patent law in relation to the infringement of a process patent: PA 1977, s. 101.

[164] CDPA 1988, s. 104(2)–(4); *Waterlow Publishers v. Rose* [1995] FSR 207, 218. There is a separate presumption in relation to publication right: see Copyright and Related Rights Act 1996, reg. 17A.

[165] CDPA 1988, s. 105.   [166] CDPA 1988, s. 197A.   [167] See Database Regs, reg. 22(1).

[168] As regards copyright in sound recordings and computer programs, it is presumed that statements naming the copyright owner, or giving the date or place of first publication, are true: CDPA 1988, s. 105. See *Microsoft Corp. v. Electrowide* [1997] FSR 580, 594. Where copies of the database as published bear a label or a mark stating that the database was first published in a specified year, the label or mark shall be admissible as evidence of the facts stated and shall be presumed to be correct until the contrary is proved: Database Regs, reg. 22(3).   [169] CDPA 1988, s. 104(5).

[170] Another technique that is used to avoid unnecessary litigation is the issuing of certificates of contested validity. As well as acting as a victory trophy, the certificate may deter subsequent litigation: RDA 1949, s. 25; PA 1977, s. 65; TMA 1994, s. 73.

[171] See I. Davies and T. Scourfield, 'Threats: Is the Current Regime Still Justified?' [2007] *EIPR* 259; G. Schwartz and M. Gardner, 'Groundless Threats of Proceedings for IP Infringement' [2006] *Communications Law* 85.

[172] Community Designs Regulations 2005 (SI 2005/2339), [2].

[173] For a general discussion, see *Reckitt Benkiser UK v. Home Pairfum* [2004] FSR (37) 774.

6.1 THREATS TO SUE: PATENTS, TRADE MARKS, DESIGNS

Special statutory provisions exist in the case of patents,[174] trade marks,[175] registered designs,[176] and the unregistered design right[177] to protect parties against unjustified threats to sue. These statutory provisions 'ensure that threats of infringement proceedings are not made casually or recklessly, because of the potential damage and concern they can cause'.[178] The Intellectual Property (Unjustified Threats) Act 2017 applies to any threat made after 1 October 2017 whereas the old law applies to threats made before that date.[179] As a result, if owners threaten to sue, they must ensure that the threat can be justified.

In order to qualify for relief against a groundless threat, a claimant must establish that an actionable threat has been made and that, as a result, they have been aggrieved. If the defendant fails to justify the threat, the court will grant relief. We will deal with these factors in turn.

6.1.1 Actionable threats

In order for a claimant to be entitled to the relief provided, they must show that an actionable threat has been made. It should be noted that, in the case of patents, registered designs, and trade marks, special provisions limit the circumstances in which groundless threats are actionable.[180] In essence, these exclude threats made in relation to primary acts of infringement: rival manufacturers may threaten each other. The idea is that threats made to retailers are particularly likely to cause the retailer to stop stocking the goods because they have little to gain and much to lose from risking infringement. Thus, a threat to a retailer is particularly, likely to harm the supplier, without legal proceedings ever being commenced. However, problems have occurred where a threat relates both to primary and secondary acts. It is however a 'permitted communication' to communicate with a secondary infringer to discover who has infringed the right.[181]

Threats can take many different forms. Although actionable threats will usually be explicit, they may also be implicit[182] and may arise from a single letter[183] or communication.[184] It is necessary to show that a threat has been made against someone in particular; it is not enough for a claimant to show that a general threat has been made.[185] There is no need for an actionable threat to be communicated to the person threatened:

> If I threaten a man that I will bring an action against him, I threaten him none the less because I address that intimation to himself, and I threaten him none the less because I address the intimation to a third person.[186]

---

[174] PA 1977, s. 70.   [175] TMA 1994, s. 21.

[176] RDA 1949, s. 26; see, e.g., *Jaybeam v. Abru Aluminium* [1975] *FSR* 334.

[177] CDPA 1988, s. 253.   [178] *Prince v. Prince Sports Group* [1998] *FSR* 21, 33.

[179] See the Intellectual Property (Unjustified Threats) Act 2017 (Commencement and Transitional Provisions) Regulations 2017 (SI 2017/771) (C. 62).

[180] PA 1977, s. 70(4); RDA 1949, s. 26(2A); CDPA 1988, s. 253(3); TMA 1994, s. 21(1).

[181] PA 1977, s. 70B; TMA 1994, s. 21B; RDA 1949, s. 26B; CDPA 1988, s. 253B; there was already similar provision in relation to patents under old law: PA 1977, s. 70(6).

[182] *Bowden Controls v. Acco Cable Controls* [1990] *RPC* 427, 431; *Scandecor Development v. Scandecor Marketing* [1999] *FSR* 26, 47.

[183] When read in conjunction with other letters or circulars, the communication as a whole may be construed as giving rise to a threat of litigation: *Brain v. IBBG (No. 3)* [1997] *FSR* 511, 521–4. Later letters cannot nullify an earlier threat: *Prince v. Prince Sports* [1998] *FSR* 21, 33.

[184] The regime under the 2017 Act in respect of each right, refers to communications containing a 'threat of infringement proceedings'.   [185] *Speedycranes v. Thompson* [1978] *RPC* 221.

[186] *Skinner & Co. v. Perry* (1893) 10 *RPC* 1, 7; cited with approval in *Sudarshan Chemical Industries v. Clariant Produkte* [2014] *RPC* (6) 171, [120].

An interesting example of such an indirect threat occurs where a person complains to an online auction site that a third party is selling goods that infringe trade mark or design rights. One such case concerned a complaint to eBay about the advertisement of children's motor bikes in which the complainant claimed to hold a registered Community design right. When faced with such complaints, eBay takes what the court described as 'the line of least resistance'—that is, it will remove the listing; eBay does not, and could not be expected to, check the accuracy of the infringement claims. On the basis that 'unsupported and unchallengeable allegations of infringement are potentially an exceedingly damaging abuse of registered rights', the court held that there was 'arguably a threat in the notification to eBay'.[187] An injunction was granted to restrain the making of such complaints.

When considering whether a threat had been made, the document in question is looked at through the eyes of a reasonable person in the position of the recipient.[188] In so doing, the court will take into account matters such as the circumstances of the business or the background information available to a reasonable recipient.[189] The courts will pay particular attention to the initial impression that the communication makes on a reasonable addressee. There are certain 'permitted communications'. Accordingly, mere notification of the existence of a patent, trade mark, or other right will not constitute a threat of proceedings. It has been suggested, however, that notification of a patent (and presumably other statutory intellectual property rights) may constitute an actionable threat if it is 'given in such a context that a threat is seen to be intended'.[190] Certainly, it is not always easy to determine what may legitimately be said and when it becomes a threat.

6.1.2 Aggrieved

A person is able to bring an application for relief even though the threats have not been made against them. This means that right owners can bring an action where a shopkeeper who sells their products is threatened with litigation by a competitor. The availability of the action is limited by the requirement that claimants must show that they were 'aggrieved' by the threats. This excludes frivolous applications or applications by busybodies who have no real interest in the threats.[191] While a person can be aggrieved without having to prove actual damage at trial, they must show that something more than a merely fanciful or minimal commercial interest has been interfered with. The courts are more likely to infer an adverse effect where the threats are made directly against a party.[192] Where threats are made indirectly, claimants will need to demonstrate that they suffered actual or potential loss (which is not minimal).[193] This will be easier to prove where the threat was intended to scare off the claimant's customers.[194]

---

[187] *Quads 4 Kids v. Colin Campbell* [2006] *EWHC* 2482 (Ch), [31].

[188] PA 1977, s. 70(1); TMA 1944, s. 21(1); RDA 1949, s. 26(1); CDPA 1988, s. 253(1); see also *Brain v. IBBG (No. 3)* [1997] *FSR* 511, 521.

[189] *Brain v. Ingledew Brown Bennison & Garrett* [1996] *FSR* 341, 349. On whether 'without prejudice' discussions can be used as a basis for a threats claim, see *Unilever v. Procter & Gamble* [2000] *FSR* 344 (CA), 358; *Kooltrade v. XTS* [2001] *FSR* (13) 158; *ALM Manufacturing v. Black & Decker* [2003] *EWHC* 1646 (Ch).

[190] *Brain v. IBBG* [1997] *FSR* 511, 349; *Jaybeam* [1975] *FSR* 334, 340; *L'Oréal v. Johnson & Johnson* [2000] *ETMR* 691, 703.   [191] *Brain v. IBBG (No. 3)* [1997] *FSR* 511, 519.

[192] *John Summers & Sons v. Cold Metal Press Co.* (1948) 65 *RPC* 75; *Prince v. Prince Sports* [1998] *FSR* 21, 33–4.

[193] *Brain v. IBBG (No. 3)* [1997] *FSR* 511, 520; *John Summers & Sons v. Cold Metal Press Co.* (1948) 65 *RPC* 75.

[194] *Dimplex v. De'Longhi* [1996] *FSR* 622.

6.1.3 Groundless threats

Once a claimant has established that a threat has been made and that, as a result, they were aggrieved, the statutory provisions shift the onus onto the defendant to prove that the threats were justified.[195] To do this, the defendant will need to show that the right in question is valid[196] and that the acts in respect of which proceedings were threatened would constitute an infringement of the right. Where a threat was made after a patent application had been made, but before the patent had been granted, it is treated as a threat to bring proceedings after grant.[197]

6.1.4 Relief

If a claimant can show that they have been aggrieved as a result of an actionable threat and the defendant cannot establish that the threat was justified, the claimant is entitled to the relief provided in the relevant statutory provisions.[198] This includes a declaration that the threats are unjustifiable,[199] an injunction against the continuance of the threats,[200] and damages for any losses that were sustained as a result of the threats.[201] Under the old law, a legal adviser could be jointly liable for making threats as the agent of the right holder but advisers were granted immunity under the 2017 Act.[202]

6.2 THREATS TO SUE: COPYRIGHT, PASSING OFF, AND BREACH OF CONFIDENCE

There are no statutory provisions that protect against unjustified threats to sue in relation to copyright, passing off, or breach of confidence. In these circumstances, a person who suffers damage as a result of an unjustified threat will have to seek relief through alternative avenues.[203] In some cases, an aggrieved party may be able to bring an action for the tort of abuse of process.[204] A more important option is provided by the action for injurious falsehood. To succeed in an action for injurious falsehood, a claimant must prove that the statements were untrue and malicious. They must also show that they suffered special damage as a result of the statements. The notion of malice has proved difficult to define. It seems to require that the threat must be issued with a view to injuring the claimant rather than defending the defendant's rights. Moreover, it has been said that an honest belief in an unfounded claim is not malicious.[205]

---

[195] RDA 1949, s. 26(2); PA 1977, s. 70(2); CDPA 1988, s. 253(2); TMA 1994, s. 21(2).

[196] Prior to 2017, where a patent was believed to be valid but was not, and had the patent been valid it would have been infringed, then there was a defence: PA 1977, s. 70(2A).

[197] In relation to patents this was stated in *Brain v. Ingledew Brown Bennison & Garrett (No. 2)* [1997] *FSR* 271, 275; the 2017 Act makes provision so that it applies to all rights: PA 1977, s. 70E; TMA 1994, s. 21E; RDA 1949, s. 26E; CDPA 1988, s. 253E.

[198] PA 1977, s. 70C; TMA 1994, s. 21C; RDA 1949, s. 26C; CDPA 1988, s. 253C (previously, under the pre-2017 Act regime it was RDA 1949, s. 26(2); PA 1977, s. 70(3); CDPA 1988, s. 253(1); TMA 1994, s. 21(2)).

[199] See *L'Oréal v. Johnson & Johnson* [2000] *ETMR* 691.

[200] See *Prince v. Prince Sports* [1998] *FSR* 21, 36.

[201] See *Carflow Products v. Linwood Securities* [1998] *FSR* 691; *SDL Hair v. Next Row* [2014] *EWHC* 2084 (IPEC).   [202] See PA 1977, s. 70D; TMA 1994, s. 21D; RDA 1949, s. 26D; CDPA 1988, s. 253D.

[203] A person may also seek a declaration of non-infringement: see *Leco Instruments v. Land Pyrometers* [1982] *RPC* 133, 136.

[204] *Grainger v. Hill* (1838) 4 *Bing NC* 212. (132 *ER* 769). On the limits of the action, see *Pitman Training v. Nominet* [1997] *FSR* 797; *Essex Electric v. IPC Computer* [1991] *FSR* 690. On the distinction between the tort of abuse of process and malicious prosecution, see *Speed Seal Products v. Paddington* [1986] 1 *All ER* 91 (Fox LJ).   [205] *Greers v. Pearman and Corder* (1922) 39 *RPC* 406, 417; *Polydor v. Harlequin* [1980] *FSR* 26, 31.

7 COURTS AND TRIBUNALS

One of the methods that have been adopted to deal with the technical nature of intellectual property litigation has been to develop special courts and tribunals. In this section, we provide a brief overview of some of the courts and tribunals that operate in the United Kingdom.

7.1 VARIOUS TRIBUNALS

7.1.1 High Court

Disputes to do with all forms of intellectual property can be brought before the Chancery Division of the High Court. Proceedings under the Patents Act 1977 and Registered Designs Act 1949 are dealt with the by the Patents Court, which is a specialist court within the Chancery Division.[206] Proceedings before the Patents Court are heard before a specialist judge.[207] The Patents Court has a reputation for the quality of its decisions.[208] Despite this, it has been said that litigation before the Patents Court is time-consuming, laborious, long drawn-out, and, as a consequence, expensive.[209]

7.1.2 Intellectual Property Enterprise Court (formerly the Patents County Court)

The Patents County Court was established in 1990[210] with the aim of providing 'cheaper, speedier and more informal procedures to ensure that small and medium sized enterprises, and private individuals, were not deterred from innovation by the potential cost of litigation to safeguard their rights'.[211] After initial problems,[212] a series of changes were made to ensure its proceedings are cheap and quick.[213] In October 2013, the Patents County Court ceased to exist[214] and the work was transferred to the new Intellectual Property Enterprise Court (IPEC), another specialist list of the High Court.[215] The IPEC has jurisdiction to hear and determine any action or matter relating to intellectual

---

[206] CPR Practice Direction 63, r. 63.1(2)(e), defines 'patent' to include SPCs and r. 63.3 defines the business of the Patent Court to include proceedings under the RDA 1949, Community registered designs, and plant varieties.

[207] While a jury trial is technically possible, if the case is transferred to the Queen's Bench Division, the conditions allowing such a trial are so onerous that it has practically no application. Indeed, patent cases were exempted from jury trials long before other civil proceedings and the last patent jury was probably empaneled before the First World War.

[208] *Chaplin Patents Holding Co. v. Group Lotus, The Times*, 12 January 1994 (CA).

[209] R. Nott, 'Patent Litigation in England' [1994] *EIPR* 3.   [210] CDPA 1988, Pt VI—now repealed.

[211] See *Alk-Abello v. Meridian Medical Technologies* [2010] *EWPCC* 14, [32]; *Chaplin Patents Holding Co. v. Group Lotus, The Times*, 12 January 1994 (CA) (Sir Thomas Bingham MR); *Memminger-Iro v. Trip-Lite* [1992] *RPC* 210, 216 *per* Aldous J.

[212] *Composite Gutters v. Pre-Formed Components* [1993] *FSR* 305, 308; *Chaplin. v. Lotus, The Times*, 12 January 1994 (CA).

[213] These are a product of a number of initiatives, including: Intellectual Property Court User's Committee, *Final Report* (July 2009); Lord Justice Jackson, *Review of Civil Litigation Costs* (May 2009); and the Hargreaves Review. See generally, S. Thambisetty, 'Patent Litigation in the United Kingdom: Solutions in Search of a Problem' [2010] *EIPR* 238; J. Morton, 'Emerging Trends in the Patents Country Court' [2013] *EIPR* 181.

[214] This was part of the re-organization of the county court system so that there was a single county court (rather than various districts each with its own county court): see Crime and Courts Act 2013, Pt 2.

[215] CPR, Pt 63 ('Intellectual Property Claims'), rr 63.17 *ff.*

property rights.[216] The Court is equipped with a full range of remedies (such as interim and final injunctions, and search orders).[217]

The IPEC makes use of (very) active case management by the judge, as well as limitations on disclosure, use of expert evidence, and cross examination.[218] Most significant is a cost cap of £50,000,[219] along with scaled costs (so that, within that £50,000, only certain amounts can be claimed in relation to particular parts of the proceedings).[220] In these cases, there is a limit on damages of £500,000.[221] Finally, there is a small claims track available only for claims with value of up to £10,000 in relation to copyright, UK and Community registered trade marks, passing off, and UK and Community unregistered design right.[222] Decisions on the small claims track will be made by district judges, frequently on the basis of the papers.[223]

When deciding whether to transfer a (multi-track) matter to or from the IPEC, a number of factors fall to be considered.[224] First to be considered is the financial position of the parties: the IPEC is designed to offer access to the court system to those who could not otherwise afford it; thus a key factor is specified to be whether 'a party can only afford to bring or defend the claim in [the IPEC]'.[225] Second, the court should consider whether it would be more convenient or fair for the hearing to be held in another court, having regard especially to the value of the claim (including the value of an injunction), the relative complexity of the legal issues and the estimated length of trial,[226] the importance of the outcome to the public, and the facilities available at the court where the claim is being dealt with.[227]

7.1.3 County court

Occasionally, cases are heard in the regular county court. It has jurisdiction to hear cases on copyright,[228] unregistered design right, registered national and Community trade marks, passing off, and performances,[229] but not patents or registered designs.[230]

---

[216] CPR, r. 63.13 and Practice Direction 63, [16.1]. There were previously issues over the jurisdiction of the Patents County Court which no longer exist before the IPEC.

[217] CPA 1998, s. 7; CPR, r. 25; CPR Practice Direction 25A, [8.5].

[218] For a useful description, see *Caljan Rite-Hite v. Solvex* [2011] *FSR* (23) 621, [7] (Kitchin J).

[219] This was introduced in 2010.

[220] On deviation from the cap and scale, see *Henderson v. All around the World Recordings* [2013] *FSR* (42) 1021 (deviation from cap only in truly exceptional cases); *Brundle v. Perry* [2014] *EWHC* 979 (IPEC), [16] (deviation from scale will seldom happen, but likely to be more frequent than deviation from the cap). The cap is lifted where a claimant fails to accept a 'better' offer to settle under CPR, Pt 36: *Phonographic Performance Ltd v. Hagan* [2017] *FSR* (24) 511, but it is now the case that there is just a 25 per cent uplift on costs caps: *Martin v. Kogan* [2018] *FSR* (10) 258.   [221] CPR 63.17A(1).

[222] CPR Practice Direction 63 ('Intellectual Property Claims'), [16.1]; CPR, Pt 63, r. 63.2(1). The small claims track came into effect on 1 October 2012.

[223] An international trend is emerging of trying to improve 'access to justice' for creators and small enterprises. See, e.g., US Copyright Office, *Copyright Small Claims* (September 2013); Irish Copyright Committee, *Modernising Copyright* (2013), 10, 25–7.   [224] CPR, r. 63.18.

[225] CDPA 1988, s. 289(2); CPR Practice Direction 30, [9.1]; *Alk-Abello Ltd v. Meridian Medical Technologies* [2011] *FSR* (13) 351 [30] (providing guidance on transfers after the introduction of the costs cap). This is the 'decisive factor': ibid., [55]. But even so, if a small enterprise takes an aggressive and unfocused approach to litigation, the High Court may be the appropriate venue: *Comic Enterprises Ltd v. Twentieth Century Fox Film* [2012] *FSR* (30) 848; cf. *Destra Software Ltd v. Comada (UK) LLP* [2012] *EWPCC* 39.

[226] CPR Practice Direction 30, [9.1(2)]; *Comic Enterprises Ltd v. Twentieth Century Fox Film* [2012] *FSR* (30) 848, [18]; see also *Chaplin v. Lotus, The Times*, 12 January 1994 (CA).

[227] CPR, r. 30.3(e); CDPA 1988, s. 289(2).

[228] *PSM v. Specialised Fastener* [1993] *FSR* 113, 116; *McDonald v. Graham* [1994] *RPC* 407.

[229] See generally, High Court and County Courts Jurisdiction Order 1991; Community Trade Mark Regulations 2006 (SI 2006/1027), reg. 12.

[230] PA 1977, s. 130(1); RDA 1949, s. 27(1); TMA 1994, s. 75.

While certain forms of relief, such as search orders and delivery up,[231] are not available,[232] the county court can award interim injunctions, damages, and accounts of profits. Nevertheless, it is common to transfer proceedings from county courts to the IPEC.

7.1.4　Comptroller-General of Patents, Designs, and Trade Marks

The Comptroller (called the registrar in relation to registered designs and trade marks) has important powers to determine certain matters under various intellectual property statutes. In practice, these powers are delegated[233] to Hearing Officers who are officials within the Intellectual Property Office. The most significant relate to the validity and revocation of registered rights.[234] On being authorized by the parties, the Comptroller has the ability to hear infringement actions[235] and counterclaims for revocation of patents. The Comptroller also has jurisdiction over certain issues concerning unregistered design right.[236] The Comptroller provides litigants with a cheaper, quicker, and more specialized and informal forum than is offered by the Court.[237] Moreover, the courts have been extremely reluctant to stay court proceedings pending determination of the issues by the Comptroller. Hoffmann J said that these factors mean that the Comptroller and the UK IPO can be made to work as an alternative tribunal in infringement cases only by the giving of undertakings by the parties that will enable it to decide finally on those issues that are before it, and even then resort may still be had to the High Court in order to obtain injunctions.[238]

7.1.5　Community/EU courts

The various EU regimes, such as those relating to designs and trade marks, operate through national tribunals that are designated to function as Community/EU design and trade mark courts.[239] The High Court and IPEC have been designated as European Union trade mark and designs courts, while some county courts are also European Union trade mark courts.[240] Issues of validity can also be determined by European Union Intellectual Property Office.[241]

7.1.6　Unified patent court

As we saw earlier, one of the key components of the unitary patent package that has taken shape in the last couple of years is the establishment of a unified patent court.[242] The desire to establish a central Europe-wide patent court grew out of concerns about the current system—notably, legal uncertainty, forum shopping, duplication of costs, and

---

[231] County Courts Act 1994, s. 15, gives the court power to hear 'any action'.

[232] CPR Practice Direction 25A, [8.5].

[233] Under the Deregulation and Contracting Out Act 1994, s. 74.

[234] PA 1977, s. 75; RDA TMA 1994, s. 46 and 47; RDA 1949, s. 11ZB.

[235] PA 1977, s. 61(3). There have not been any such proceedings since 1977 and there were only three actions since it was introduced under the Patents Act 1949: see Banks Report (Cmnd 4407), [266].

[236] CDPA 1988, s. 246.　　　　　[237] But cf. *Ferro Corporation v. Escol Products* [1990] *RPC* 651.

[238] [1990] *RPC* 651, 652.

[239] CDR, Art. 80; EUTMR, Art. 123 (designation); *DHL Express France SAS v. Chronopost SA*, Case C-235/09 [2011] *ECR* I-2801, [AG20]–[AG27].

[240] Community Trade Mark Regulations 2006 (SI 2006/1027) (designating: for England, the High Court, and seven county courts; for Scotland, the Court of Session; and for Northern Ireland, the High Court); Community Designs (Designation of Community Design Courts) Regulations 2005 (SI 2005/696) (designating: for England, the High Court; for Scotland, the Court of Session; and for Northern Ireland, the High Court). See also Community Designs Regulations 2005 (SI 2005/2339).

[241] CDR, Art. 52.　　　　[242] See Chapter 14, section 4.5.1, pp. 409-16.

the resulting fragmentation of the internal market. To remedy these problems, on 19 February 2013 25 member states signed an international agreement to set up a unified patent court.[243] When established, the unified patent court will consist of a Court of First Instance, which, in turn, will consist of local, regional, and central divisions located in the Member States.[244] The central division of the Court of First Instance will be divided between London (responsible for chemical, pharmaceutical, and the life science patents), Munich (responsible for mechanical engineering patents), and Paris (responsible for all other patents).[245] There will also be a Court of Appeal, which will be based in Luxembourg.

8 PARALLEL PROCEEDINGS

Where rights are granted centrally (and can be challenged centrally)—as with European patents, EU trade marks, and Community designs—but are enforced locally, parallel proceedings can occur. Such proceedings raise at least two problems: first, which tribunal should stay proceedings—the central one, or the local one—and when? Second, what happens if the local proceedings reach a conclusion and the right on which they were based is then invalidated?

8.1 STAYS

The question of what to do in relation to parallel proceedings has existed for some time in relation to patents. Since issues of validity may be heard before the Comptroller, or opposition proceedings may be taking place at the European Patent Office (EPO),[246] a possibility exists that proceedings will be duplicated. These problems arise because the UK courts and the EPO have concurrent jurisdiction over questions of validity (infringement is heard only at the national level). The frequency of such parallel proceedings has increased by the introduction in the 2000 European Patents Convention (EPC 2000) of the possibility of central amendments at the EPO.[247] Such concurrent proceedings are potentially problematic, since while both decisions are *in rem* (meaning that they 'determine the validity of the patent not only as between the parties to the proceedings'), nonetheless the English court's jurisdiction over the question of validity is purely national.[248] A decision of an English court declaring a patent invalid or revoking it will have effect only in the United Kingdom. In contrast, a corresponding decision of the EPO will have effect in all of the states for which the patent is granted. This is particularly problematic as revocation has the effect of deeming the patent never having had effect. This gives rise to the problem of duplication of validity proceedings and conflicting decisions in the United Kingdom and at the EPO.

With domestic proceedings, some attempt is made to avoid such duplication by a provision that prohibits issues of validity from being raised before the Comptroller pending the outcome of a decision in the High Court. As between UK infringement (or invalidity) proceedings and oppositions at the EPO, the court has a discretion to order a stay, which

---

[243] *Agreement on a Unified Patent Court* [2013] *OJ C* 175/1 (20 June 2013).

[244] Ibid., Art. 7(1).

[245] The division is based on the International Patent Classification (IPC) system.

[246] EPC 2000, Art. 99; *Memminger-Iro* [1992] *RPC* 210.

[247] EPC 2000, Art. 105a; *Samsung Electronics Co. Ltd v. Apple Retail UK Ltd* [2015] *RPC* (3) 42, [18], [26].

[248] *Virgin Atlantic Airways v. Zodiac Seats* [2014] *AC* 160, [7].

it will exercise according to the facts of the case: often, the problem is how to balance the competing issues of (i) the costs of duplicating proceedings (perhaps unnecessarily) with (ii) the delays involved in staying local proceedings and awaiting the outcome of opposition at the EPO. In recent years, English courts have become frustrated with delays in the processes at the EPO and have tended to refuse stays where they could decide the issue more speedily.[249] However, that, in turn, exacerbated the problem as to what arises when a person has been found to infringe a patent in national proceedings, only for the patent to be revoked or amended (in a material manner) at the EPO. Following the decision of the Supreme Court in *Virgin v. Zodiac*,[250] dealing with the latter issue, the courts were asked to review the circumstances in which a stay will be ordered. The Court of Appeal did so in *IPCOM GmbH v. HTC Europe Co. Ltd*[251] Although the 'guidelines' have not changed radically, the Court reiterated that the default position should be to order a stay and that 'it is for the party opposing a stay to demonstrate why it should not be granted'.[252] Timing remains important (showing that the EPO proceedings will take considerably longer is a factor against a stay), as does the possibility that national proceedings will be concluded in a manner that deprives the party of the benefit of the EPO decision (although here undertakings to repay damages may remove this potential injustice).

The question of parallel proceedings also arises in EU trade mark and Community design litigation, in which invalidity proceedings are possible at the EUIPO and infringement proceedings (with potential counterclaim for invalidity) in national courts. The provisions of the EU trade marks Regulation (EUTMR) and Community Design Regulation (CDR) indicate that where invalidity proceedings have already commenced at the EUIPO, or validity is in issue before another EU trade mark or design court, a court hearing an action relating to a European Union trade mark or design shall stay the proceedings 'unless there are special grounds for continuing the hearing'.[253] This has led to the so-called 'EUIPO torpedo',[254] in which a defendant responds to letters before action by launching invalidity proceedings at the EUIPO (where, the cases tell us, it might take ten years before the issues are concluded).[255] In such cases, the issue of when a national court can decline a stay become critically important. When do such 'special reasons' exist to refuse a stay? The presumption of stay has been described as a 'strong one',[256] but even so, on a number of occasions, the English courts have been willing to refuse a stay.[257]

---

[249] *Unilin Beheer v. Berry Floor* [2007] *FSR* (25) 635, [25]; *Glaxo Group Ltd v. Genentech Inc.* [2008] *FSR* (18) 459 (stays were generally declined if the question of validity would be likely to be resolved quicker in the English court than in the EPO).   [250] *Virgin Atlantic Airways v. Zodiac Seats* [2014] *AC 160*.

[251] [2013] *EWCA Civ* 1496. See further *Samsung Electronics Co. Ltd v. Apple Retail UK Ltd* [2015] *RPC* (3) 42; *Actavis v. Pharmacia* [2014] *EWHC* 2265 (Pat).

[252] [2014] *RPC* (12) 397, [62], [68] (Guidelines 5 and 6).   [253] EUTMR, Art. 132; CDR, Art. 91.

[254] *Regent University v. Regent's University London* [2013] *EWPCC* 39, [34] (Wilson QC) (although at the time it was an 'OHIM torpedo').

[255] Ibid., [14]; *Starbucks (UK) Ltd v. British Sky Broadcasting Group Plc* [2012] *ETMR* (57) 1012, [56]. The length of time of the OHIM proceedings is 'irrelevant': ibid.,[110].

[256] Ibid., [112]; *Guccio Gucci Spa v. Shipton & Heneage Ltd* [2010] *EWHC* 1739 (Ch), [18] (Lewison J).

[257] *Samsung Electronics (UK) Ltd v. Apple Inc.* [2013] *FSR* (8) 119 (stay granted); *Starbucks (UK) Ltd v. British Sky Broadcasting Group Plc* [2012] *ETMR* (57) 102 (stay refused); *Hearst Holdings Inc. v. A.V.E.L.A. Inc.* [2014] *EWHC* 1553 (Ch), [38]–[43] (stay refused because both parties had allowed the English proceedings to take place in parallel with an Italian action and the English proceedings had been virtually completed); *Actavis Group PTC EHF v. Pharmacia LLC* [2014] *EWHC* 2611 (Pat) and [2014] *EWHC* 2265 (Pat) (granted on the basis of a very strict undertaking); *Fontem Holdings v. Ten Motives* [2015] *EWHC* 2752 (Pat) (refused due to other issues needing resolving); *Eli Lilly v. Janssen Sciences Ireland UC* [2016] *EWHC* 313 (Pat) (undertaking inadequate no stay).

They have declined to give much guidance as to when such refusal is appropriate, but it is clear that 'the nature and force of the special grounds' would have to be of sufficient importance and substance to justify the risk necessarily engendered by parallel and active proceedings of possible inconsistent decisions on the same point in different tribunals.[258] If there is no likelihood of conflicting judgments, because local proceedings relate only to infringement, this may justify continuation of local proceedings.[259] Equally, if the matter is very urgent and local proceedings would be expedited, there may be good grounds for refusal of a stay.[260] Otherwise, the norm should be to order a stay, but provide the local claimant with appropriate interim relief.[261]

8.2 EFFECT OF CENTRAL INVALIDATION ON A LOCAL JUDGMENT

If a stay is refused and litigation concludes in the United Kingdom, what happens if the EPO or the EUIPO holds that the patent, trade mark, or design is invalid? The Court of Appeal had held that the matter was closed once judgment was given.[262] However, in *Virgin Atlantic Airways Ltd v. Zodiac Seats*,[263] the Supreme Court indicated that this was not so. In this case, a damages award of a staggering £49 million was at stake, the award being made in English proceedings before the claimant amended the patent at the EPO (to avoid invalidity) so that the valid patent did not cover the defendant's previously infringing acts. A stay had been refused, but the money had not been paid over. Faced with the contention that the English decision was *res judicata*, the Supreme Court stated that, were this so, it would 'make the outcome dependent on the wholly adventitious question which of two concurrently competent jurisdictions completes its procedures first'.[264] Such a conclusion was indefensible. At least where the enquiry as to damages was not complete, the local judgment could be reviewed.

But what if damages had been paid over? Lord Sumption was doubtful whether anything could be done (in the absence of a pending appeal), but indicated that this was 'a question which will have to await a case in which it arises'.[265] Lord Neuberger was similarly vague indicating that, in such a case, 'a restitutionary claim' might be available, but declining to express 'a view on the strength of such a claim, which may well be highly dependent on the facts of the particular case'.[266] If the Court really thinks that the position should not depend on which procedure is completed first, such awards should be capable of being reopened. But such an approach would raise further questions, such as whether transactions entered into on the assumption that the patent is valid should be capable of being reopened. Once we move away from the simplest case, the issues surrounding the reopening of decisions and transactions become more problematic. No wonder the Court wanted the *Glaxo* principles, which had caused the English courts to refuse applications for stays, to be reviewed.[267]

---

[258] *Samsung Electronics (UK) Ltd v. Apple Inc.* [2013] FSR (8) 119, [49] (Lloyd J).

[259] Ibid., [19]–[24].

[260] *Starbucks (UK) Ltd v. British Sky Broadcasting Group Plc* [2013] FSR (16) 281.

[261] *Regent University v. Regent's University London* [2013] EWPCC 39.

[262] *Unilin Beheer BV v. Berry Floor NV* [2007] FSR (25) 635; *Coflexip SA v. Stolt Offshore MS Ltd (No. 2)* [2004] FSR (34) 708.   [263] [2014] AC 160, [34].

[264] Ibid., [36].   [265] Ibid., [36].

[266] Ibid., [67]; cf. *IPCOM GmbH v. HTC Europe Co. Ltd* [2014] RPC (12) 397, [49] (Floyd LJ).

[267] *Glaxo Group Ltd v. Genentech Inc.* [2008] FSR (18) 459.

9 EXPERTS AND SCIENTIFIC ADVISERS

Given the technical and novel nature of the subject matter of intellectual property law, it is not surprising that the courts frequently rely on experts for a range of different matters. While the court can,[268] and occasionally does,[269] rely on scientific advisers, it is more usual for the parties to lead expert evidence upon which the court makes its decision. Because the use of expert evidence increases the cost of intellectual property litigation, the permission of the court is required to call an expert or to put an expert's report in evidence. In practice, the courts strictly limit the use of experts to situations in which the cost is likely to be justified.[270] Thus expert evidence will likely be admitted in relation to the interpretation of scientific documents or as to the state of foreign law, but much less so on issues where a court feels itself able to decide (such as whether a substantial part of a copyright work has been reproduced, or whether two designs create the same overall impression or the likelihood of confusion in a passing off or trade mark action).[271] An expert's report should be addressed to the court and not to the party from whom the expert has received instructions. The courts have emphasized that experts should be impartial—that is, they should not assume the role of an advocate.[272]

10 JURISDICTIONAL ISSUES AND CONFLICTS OF LAW

Given the nature of intellectual property, it should come as no surprise that many intellectual property actions have a transnational dimension.[273] For example, the claimant may be domiciled in country A and the defendant in country B. In these circumstances, it is necessary to decide whether the action should be brought in country A or country B. More complex questions arise where the infringement occurs in a number of countries. This would be the case, for example, where the defendant manufactures infringing goods in country C and an importer sells them in country D. In these cases, a claimant may wish to sue both infringers in a single action. Even more complicated scenarios arise, for example, where copyright infringement takes place on the Internet.[274] Where disputes cross national boundaries, a number of questions arise. Here, we focus on whether a court has jurisdiction to hear a matter, the type of law that should be applied, and the situations in which foreign judgments will be recognized and enforced. A number of

---

[268] Senior Courts Act 1981, s. 70(3).   [269] See Roughton, Johnson, and Cook (2014), [15.138], [15.140].

[270] In *Interflora Inc. v. Marks & Spencer plc (No. 2)* [2013] *FSR* (26) 559, Lewison LJ noted that the growing cost of civil litigation has, as of 1 April 2013, led to the introduction of a reformulated 'overriding objective' into the CPR—namely, dealing with cases justly *and at proportionate cost.*

[271] On trade marks, see Chapter 38, section 2.3.4(i), p. 1042. On designs, see *Procter Gamble Co. v. Reckitt Benckiser (UK) Ltd* [2008] *FSR* (8) 208.

[272] The rules on experts are codified in CPR Practice Direction 35. On the duties and responsibilities of experts identified, see *The Ikarian Reefer* [1993] *FSR* 563.

[273] See Fawcett and Torremans; American Law Institute, *Intellectual Property: Principles Governing Jurisdiction, Choice of Law, and Judgments in Transnational Disputes* (2008); Max Planck Institute, *Conflicts of Law in Intellectual Property: The CLIP Principles and Commentary* (2013). The last has proved influential: see, e.g., *Lucasfilm v. Ainsworth* [2012] 1 *AC* 208, [94], [95], [109].

[274] Fawcett and Torremans, ch. 10.

considerations arise in answering these questions: the convenience and efficiency of litigation; the impact on national sovereignty; the desirability of allowing litigants to choose the jurisdiction most favourable to their claim (so-called 'forum shopping'); and national interests in attracting legal business.

10.1 JURISDICTION

The question of whether a court has jurisdiction to hear a matter where the infringement or breach of an intellectual property right crosses national boundaries depends on a number of factors.

10.1.1 Under the Brussels Regulation

The question of whether a British court has jurisdiction over a matter is largely governed by the Brussels Regulation (often also referred to as the 'Judgments Regulation').[275] The basic rule of the Regulation is that a person domiciled in a member state should be sued in the courts of that state.[276] Consequently, a British copyright owner must normally bring an action against a French infringer in French courts—the domicile of the claimant and the familiarity of the court with the relevant law being largely irrelevant. As Jacob J put it, in footballing terms, the claimant must 'play away'.[277] There are five qualifications to this basic rule that need to be noted, as follows.[278]

(i)   Where the matter involves a tort, a claimant *may* bring an action in the place where the harmful event occurred.[279]

(ii) Where there are a number of defendants, an action may be brought in the country in which any one of the defendants is domiciled.[280]

(iii) An action can be brought in a country other than that of the defendant's domicile if both parties agree.[281]

(iv) In proceedings concerned with the registration or validity of patents, trade mark, designs, or other similar rights required to be deposited or registered, the courts of that state have exclusive jurisdiction.[282]

(v)   Different rules apply in relation to preliminary measures.[283]

We consider each of these exceptions in turn. First, as regards 'tort', an action may be brought in the place in which the harmful event occurred. This exception to the defendant's domicile rule could be of wide application in the field of intellectual property, since most infringements of intellectual property are regarded as tortious. Doubts may exist,

---

[275] Regulation (EU) No. 1215/2012 of 12 December 2012 on jurisdiction and the recognition and enforcement of judgments in civil and commercial matters (recast) [2012] *OJ L* 351/1. This replaces the earlier Brussels Regulation (Regulation (EC) No 44/2001) which in turn replaced the 1968 Brussels Convention, which came into force in England on 1 January 1987.

[276] Brussels Reg., Art. 4. Domicile is determined under national law: Brussels Reg., Art. 62.

[277] *Mecklermedia v. DC Congress* [1997] *FSR* 627, 633.

[278] Which are to be narrowly construed: see *Athanasios Kalfelis v. Bankhaus Schroeder*, Case 189/87 [1988] *ECR* 5565.   [279] Brussels Reg., Art. 7(2).

[280] Brussels Reg., Art. 8(1).

[281] Brussels Reg., Art. 25. See, e.g., *Kitechnology v. Unicor Plastmaschinen* [1995] *FSR* 765, 774.

[282] Brussels Reg., Art. 24(4).   [283] Brussels Reg., Art. 35.

however, in relation to breach of confidence and the action relating to undisclosed private information.[284]

Where the action does relate to a tort, the key question will be where the harmful event occurred.[285] The Court of Justice has indicated that this embraces two distinct possibilities—the place of the event and the place of the harm—and the claimant may elect whichever they prefer.[286] One problem concerns whether, in the case of use on a website, it can be alleged that the infringement took place in many different jurisdictions (although the substantive question will limit it to the countries which are targeted[287]). The jurisprudence on this is in a state of development and, at present, it is somewhat convoluted. Advocate-General Jääskinen has stated that the case law reveals 'two lines of jurisprudence, one favouring an interpretation of that provision less extensive than the other'.[288]

Looking first at where the 'event' occurs, on one case, concerning database right, the Court held that the place where the event occurred was (at the very least) the place at which a communication of the database was targeted.[289] In a trade mark case, in contrast, the place where the event occurs (that is, from which an Internet communication, such as an advertisement, is made) is to be regarded as the place of establishment of the communicator rather than, for example, the place where the server is located.[290] This rule is likely to be applied in other cases as well. Thus, a person can be sued in the country from which they uploaded the infringing material.

In addition, a person can be sued where the damage occurred. As an intellectual property right can only be infringed where it is registered (or in the case of unregistered rights, protected), the damage can only take place where the alleged infringement occurred.[291] Importantly, it must be remembered that a court can have jurisdiction over an unmeritorious claim. This means that a person who *alleges* infringement of a French intellectual property right can sue in France even if *in fact* there is no actual infringement. This approach avoids mixing up the so called substantive law, and jurisdictional question. It does mean, however, that a person can be sued in a distant court in relation to a vexatious claim and having to rely on the rules for dismissing such claims (such as summary judgment in England), rather than contesting jurisdiction at the outset.

---

[284] On what is a 'tort', see *Athanasios Kalfelis v. Bankhaus Schroeder*, Case 189/87 [1988] *ECR* 5565. In matters of contract, jurisdiction is given to the courts of the place of performance of the obligation. On breach of confidence, see *Vidal-Hall v. Google Inc.* [2015] *FSR* (25) 728, [17]–[51] (not a tort, although misuse of private information might be); cf. *Rickshaw Investments and anor v. Nicolai Baron von Uexkull* [2006] *SGCA* 39; see also C. Wadlow, 'Bugs, Spies and Paparazzi: Jurisdiction over Actions for Breach of Confidence in Private International Law' (2008) *EIPR* 269 and Gurry (2012), [23.18]–[23.21].

[285] Brussels Reg., Art. 7(2).

[286] See *Bier v. Mines de Potasse d'Alsace*, Case 21/76 [1976] *ECR* 1735; *Shevill/Presse Alliance SA*, Case C-68/93 [1995] *ECR* I–415. There are disincentives in place to prevent a person from relying on the place of damage—in particular, that damages can be recovered only for that jurisdiction.

[287] See Chapter 6, section 6.4, pp. 173-4.

[288] *Coty Germany GmbH v. First Note Perfumes NV*, Case C-360/12, EU:C:2013:764 (AG Opinion), [4].

[289] *Football Dataco Ltd v. Sportradar GmbH*, Case C-173/11 [2013] 1 *CMLR* 29 (ECJ, Third Chamber). See also *SMI Group Ltd v. Levy* [2012] *EWHC* 3078 (Ch).

[290] *Wintersteiger AG v. Products 4U Sondermaschinenbau GmbH*, Case C-523/10, EU:C:2012:220 (ECJ, First Chamber). This venue is, of course, no different from the place of the defendant's domicile. AG Jääskinen, in *Pinckney v. KDG Mediatech AG*, Case C-170/12, EU:C:2013:400, [AG57], has argued that this criterion should also apply to copyright (and, in the case, would have been the United Kingdom). He viewed *Sportradar* as an example of the place of 'damage': ibid., [AG63].

[291] *Wintersteiger v. Products 4U Sondermaschinebau*, Case C-523/10, EU:C:2012:220, [25] and [28]; *Pinckney v. KDG Mediatech*, C-170/12 [2014] *FSR* (18) 354 (ECJ, Fourth Chamber).

In a personality rights case[292] (at least encompassing privacy), the Court has held that the place of the 'harmful event' also includes 'the centre of the claimant's interest'—that is, typically the place of domicile of the claimant—and that this court has jurisdiction to hear all alleged violations.[293] This latter approach, which is very 'claimant-friendly', seems likely to be strictly limited to personality torts and probably does not extend to copyright or other intellectual property rights.[294]

Second, the Regulation states that co-defendants may be sued in the country in which one of them is domiciled.[295] In practice, this seemingly straightforward provision has been construed rather inconsistently in the context of infringements of intellectual property rights. The Court of Justice has held that the provision is applicable only where a multiplicity of hearings based on the domicile of the defendant would present the possibility of contradictory judgments. In *Roche*,[296] in the context of a claim relating to infringement of a series of national patents brought against multiple defendants from the same corporate group (marketing the same product in Belgium, Germany, the United Kingdom, and elsewhere), the Court of Justice took an extremely narrow approach. It held that the Dutch court did not have jurisdiction to determine claims against non-Dutch co-defendants for infringements that took place outside the Netherlands because the co-defendants were alleged to infringe different national laws, so that there could be no possibility of contradictory judgments. However, in *Solvay v. Honeywell*,[297] *Roche* was distinguished where a number of the defendants from different countries were active in a single national market; then, joinder was necessary to avoid different conclusions.[298] An even more flexible approach still was taken in relation to copyright in the *Painer* case.[299] There, a photograph alleged to infringe the claimant's copyright was published in a number of independent papers in Germany and Austria. The claimant sued in Austria. The Court thought that proceedings in Germany and Austria might lead to irreconcilable judgments even though the laws operating in the two countries differed (possibly to a greater extent than the laws in the *Roche* case).[300] Thus the rules to prevent multiple cases might be justified. The Court hinted at an analysis based on a number of factors, of which the substantially identical nature of the laws was one,[301] whether the acts were 'substantially identical' another, and whether the co-defendants acted (or did not act) independently could be a third.[302] One cannot help but think that the Court was interested in providing flexibility for the personal claimant in the case, but we consequently seem once again to find ourselves faced with inconsistent, unpredictable, and ultimately incoherent guidance on to an important issue. *Roche* had attracted near universal criticism,[303] but the distinctions being drawn between the facts of it and *Solvay* do little to ameliorate the position, while the *Painer* decision seems to allow—perhaps surprisingly, in the copyright field—for the

---

[292] *eDate Advertising GmbH v. X*, Case C-509/09 [2011] *ECR* I–10269 (ECJ, Grand Chamber).

[293] Ibid.

[294] *Wintersteiger AG v. Products 4U Sondermaschinenbau GmbH*, Case C-523/10, EU:C:2012:220 (ECJ, First Chamber), [AG20].

[295] See *Kalfelis*, Case 189/87 [1988] *ECR* 5565.

[296] *Roche v. Primus*, Case C-539/03 [2006] *ECR* I–6535 (ECJ, First Chamber).

[297] *Solvay SA v. Honeywell Fluorine Products Europe BV*, Case C-616/10, EU:C:2012:445 (ECJ, Third Chamber).   [298] Ibid., [29].

[299] *Eva-Maria Painer v. Standard VerlagsGmbH and ors*, Case C-145/10 [2012] *ECDR* (6) 89, (ECJ, Third Chamber).   [300] Ibid., [76], [80].

[301] Ibid., [82].   [302] Ibid., [83].

[303] A. Briggs, 'Jurisdiction over Defences and Connected Claims' [2006] *LMCLQ* 447, 450, 451; P. Torremans, 'Exclusive Jurisdiction and Cross-Border IP (Patent) Infringement' [2007] *EIPR* 195, 201; A. Kur, 'A Farewell to Cross-Border Injunctions?' (2006) 37 *IIC* 844, 851.

joinder of wholly unconnected parties.[304] Where an action is brought against the coordinator of the infringements, joinder of foreign participants seems sensible in terms of 'procedural economy'.

The third and fourth exceptions concern the situation in which the parties have selected a forum (Article 25),[305] or the action concerns the registration or validity of patents, trade mark, designs, or other similar rights required to be deposited or registered (Article 24(4)). In these cases, the jurisdiction is *exclusive*: there is no question of alternative jurisdictions. If a court of a contracting state is presented with a *claim* that is 'principally concerned' with a matter over which the courts of another contracting state have exclusive jurisdiction, it should decline jurisdiction. While it should be relatively easy to determine whether the parties have a formal agreement governing the choice of jurisdiction (Article 25), it is more difficult to determine when Article 24(4) applies.[306]

Article 24(4) applies to the registration or validity of patents, trade marks, designs, or other similar rights required to be deposited or registered. The phrase 'other similar rights' refers to other registrable rights such as plant varieties, supplementary protection certificates (SPCs), and utility models. As such, it does not apply where the intellectual property right is unregistered, as with copyright, unregistered design right, or passing off.[307] Article 24(4) applies only to proceedings concerning the 'validity' of such rights.[308] Although, in certain circumstances, it is clear that an issue relating to a registered right does not concern validity (such as where the dispute is over ownership),[309] in many situations the matter is less clear. For example, in an action for infringement of a patent or design registration, one of the most common 'defences' is that the registration is invalid. The problem here is that while questions of validity and infringement are technically distinct, in British intellectual property law they are inextricably linked.

The question of whether an action is 'concerned with the registration or validity of patents, trade marks designs, or other similar rights' is a crucial one. In *GAT v. Luk Lamellen*,[310] the Court of Justice provided a very broad reading of the provision. The case concerned whether a German court had jurisdiction to hear an action between two German companies in which one alleged that the other had infringed its French patents. In effect, the Court of Justice held that the German court lacked jurisdiction (since issues of validity had been raised before the Düsseldorf court). The Court of Justice stated that Article 24(4) is applicable 'whatever the form of proceedings in which the issue of a patent's validity is raised, be it by way of an action or a plea in objection, at the time the case is brought or at a later stage in the proceedings'.[311] The decision seems to suggest that a court seised with jurisdiction must divest itself as soon as a defendant pleads a defence of invalidity.[312]

There are a number of problems with the *GAT v. LuK* ruling, the most obvious being that the same issues of patent validity might have to be simultaneously litigated in a number of countries, with a consequent negative impact on costs and convenience. The only positive thing that can be said for the decision is that it gave an impetus to negotiations over the unitary patent court.

---

[304] P. Torremans, 'Intellectual Property Puts Art 6(1) Brussels I Regulation to the Test' [2014] *IPQ* 1.

[305] The parties, however, cannot override the impact of Art. 24(4) by agreement. But note the possible impact of the Hague Convention on Choice of Court Agreements (2005), discussed in A. Kur, op. cit., 852.

[306] See, e.g., *Coin Controls* [1997] *FSR* 660.

[307] *Pearce v. Ove Arup* [1997] *FSR* 641.

[308] P. Torremans, 'Exclusive Jurisdiction and Cross-Border IP (Patent) Infringement' [2007] *EIPR* 195, 199.   [309] *Ferdinand Duijnstee v. Lodewijk Goderbauer*, Case 288/82 [1985] 1 *CMLR* 220.

[310] Case C-4/03 [2006] *ECR* I–6509 (ECJ, First Chamber).   [311] Ibid., [25].

[312] A. Briggs, 'Jurisdiction over Defences and Connected Claims' [2006] *LMCLQ* 447, 450, 451.

The fifth possible exception to the golden rule of the Brussels Regulation that a defendant should be sued in their state of domicile relates to 'provisional measures'. More specifically, Article 35 states that an application may be made to the courts of a contracting state for provisional measures (including protective measures that are available under the law of that state) even if, under the Brussels Regulation, the courts of another contracting state have jurisdiction over the substance of the matter. In appropriate circumstances, claimants can choose the forum in which they prefer to get an interim injunction even if that court could not grant final relief (because, for example, the case concerns a registered right in relation to which validity will be in issue).[313]

Because the first two exceptions to the rule that an action be brought in the domicile of the defendant give rise to *alternative* jurisdictions, they enable claimants to choose the forum. The possibility of alternative jurisdictions creates the problem that simultaneous proceedings might produce inconsistent judgments. Consequently, the Brussels Regulation contains provisions that deal with pending actions (*lis pendens*). These provide that, where a court of a contracting state is presented with a claim (for example on the basis of domicile) that has already been commenced elsewhere (for example on the basis of harm), the later action should be stayed. More specifically, Article 29 states that where a later court is presented with *the same cause of action* between the *same parties*, that court *must* decline jurisdiction.[314] In addition, a further provision gives the court a discretion to stay proceedings if it is presented with an action that is 'related' to one that is already being heard in the courts of another contracting state. This discretion arises only where the actions are 'related'—that is, where they are so closely connected that it is expedient that the actions be tried together to avoid the risk of irreconcilable judgments.[315] In exercising the discretion, the court will take into account the domicile of the defendant, the applicable law, and whether any UK action will need to be decided in any case.[316]

10.1.2 Where the Brussels Regulation is not applicable

The Brussels Regulation applies where a person is domiciled in the EU.[317] This is the case even if the claimant is domiciled outside the European Union,[318] the right is granted by a state outside the European Union, or the infringing acts took place outside of EU territories or member of the European Free Trade Association (EFTA). If the defendant is domiciled in the United Kingdom and a claim relates to infringement of American copyright by acts in the United States, the Regulation will apply and the UK court must accept jurisdiction. The Regulation will not necessarily apply where the defendant is not domiciled in a contracting state. Thus, if US citizen A were resident, but not domiciled, in the United Kingdom, and claimant B were to argue that the court should take jurisdiction

---

[313] *Solvay SA v. Honeywell Fluorine Products Europe BV*, Case C-616/10, EU:C:2012:445 (ECJ, Third Chamber), [49]–[50].

[314] An action for infringement of a trade mark is not the 'same action' as an action for passing off: *Mecklermedia* [1997] *FSR* 627, 637. While a wholly owned subsidiary might be regarded as the 'same party', a mere licensee will not: ibid. See also *Prudential v. Prudential of America* [2003] *ETMR* (69) 858, 867, [47].

[315] *Research in Motion (UK) Ltd v. Visto Corp.* [2008] *FSR* (20) 499; *Mecklermedia* [1997] *FSR* 627; *ABKCO Music Records v. Jodorowski* [2003] *ECDR* (3) 13.   [316] Ibid.

[317] The rule for Denmark is slightly different as the Regulation does not directly apply but similar rules apply under a separate agreement.

[318] *Société Group Josi Reinsurance Company SA v. Compagnie d'Assurances Universal General Insurance Company*, Case C-412/98 [2000] ECR I-5925 (an insurance case). But note the view in *Lucasfilm Ltd v. Ainsworth* [2010] *Ch* 503 that Art. 2 could not have abolished limits on subject matter jurisdiction, a view that the Supreme Court left unaddressed: [2012] 1 *AC* 208, [112]–[114].

over A for infringement of B's American copyright by acts in the United States, it seems that the traditional UK rules would apply.[319]

The traditional British rules on jurisdiction were long understood to preclude an action based on infringement of foreign intellectual property rights.[320] However, in *Lucasfilm v. Ainsworth*,[321] the Supreme Court has indicated that, at least in relation to cases for infringement of copyright, those objections no longer apply. Thus Lucasfilm could bring an action against Ainsworth, who was domiciled in England, for infringement of the claimant's US copyright. The Court reviewed the various grounds that had been raised to such action (such as the '*Mocambique* rule', the 'rule in *Phillips v. Eyre*', and the 'act of state' doctrine[322]), and found that the rationales for them had largely been undermined over the course of the twentieth century. The Court therefore held, quite narrowly, that:

[I]n the case of a claim for infringement of copyright *of the present kind*, the claim is one over which the English court has jurisdiction, provided that there is a basis for *in personam* jurisdiction over the defendant, or, to put it differently, the claim is justiciable.[323]

The position might well be different had the court been considering a copyright dispute over subsistence (as opposed to ownership and infringement) or other registered intellectual property rights, particularly if validity were in issue.[324] That said, in an action for a declaration of non-infringement of a patent owned by a US company in which validity was not in issue, Arnold J rejected a claim that the court should reject jurisdiction on the basis that it was '*non conveniens*'.[325]

10.1.3 EU/Community rights

Special rules exist on the allocation of jurisdiction in relation to ownership of European patents[326] and more generally for community rights (such as the European Union trade mark, design and plant variety rights). For example, Articles 94 and 97 of the European Union Trade Mark Regulation (EUTMR) incorporate principles similar to those in the Brussels Regulation.[327] The basic rule of the Brussels Regulation is maintained—namely, that a person should sue in the jurisdiction in which the defendant is domiciled. This is extended to those who are not domiciled, but who have an 'establishment', in the jurisdiction. The EUTMR also modifies the application of the Brussels Regulation by excluding Article 4, thereby conferring jurisdiction on the EU trade mark courts over defendants domiciled outside of contracting states (rather than applying national rules). If the defendant is not domiciled in the European Union, the action should be brought

---

[319] Similarly, if a British claimant were to want to bring an action against a US company alleging infringement of copyright in the United Kingdom, the UK court might give leave to serve a claim form outside the jurisdiction. See Fawcett and Torremans, chs 6 and 9; *Beecham Group v. Norton Healthcare* [1997] *FSR* 81; *Conductive Inkjet Technology Ltd v. Uni-Pixel Displays Inc.* [2014] *FSR* (22) 475; *Vidal-Hall v. Google Inc.* [2015] *FSR* (25) 728. For refusal of an application for a stay pending the outcome of parallel proceedings, see *Macdermid Offshore Solutions LLV v. Niche Products Ltd* [2014] *FSR* (21) 447.

[320] See Fawcett and Torremans, ch. 6.   [321] [2012] 1 *AC* 208.   [322] Ibid., [54]–[87].

[323] Ibid., [106] (emphasis added).

[324] Ibid. See P. Torremans, 'Star Wars Rids Us of Subject Matter Jurisdiction: The Supreme Court Does not Like Kafka either when it Comes to Copyright' [2011] *EIPR* 813, 817; G. Austin, 'The Concept of "Justiciability" in Foreign Copyright Infringement Cases' (2009) 40 *IIC* 393.

[325] *Actavis Group HF v. Eli Lilly & Co.* [2012] *EWHC* 3316 (Pat); upheld on appeal [2013] *RPC* (37) 985.

[326] Protocol on Jurisdiction and the Recognition of Decisions in respect to the Right to the Grant of a European Patent, 1973. Art. 4, allocates jurisdiction to the courts of the contracting state whose law determines the right. In EPC 2000, Art. 60, this is the law of the state in which the employee is mainly employed.

[327] EUTMR, Arts 122 and 125. The Community Design Regulation, Art. 82, applies very similar rules. Rather oddly, the CPVR bases its rules on the Lugano Convention. See Fawcett and Torremans, ch. 8.

where the claimant is domiciled. Where neither party is domiciled nor established in the European Union, the action should be brought in the place in which the European Union trade mark office is situated (that is, Alicante). These rules are mandatory and applied in strict sequence. As a result, there is a reduced possibility of there being competing alternative jurisdictions, and hence less scope for forum shopping. However, despite the strict scheme, Article 125(5) EUTMR also allocates jurisdiction based on the place of infringement.[328] If a claimant uses this forum, relief is territorially limited. Consequently, this route is less attractive than an action brought in the state of the defendant's domicile. Moreover, the rules relating to multiple defendants are maintained, so that an action can also be brought against a co-defendant in a court other than the court of the state in which they are domiciled. Because the applicable right is a EU one, the limitation imposed to the applicability of the Article by the Court of Justice in *Roche* is inapplicable.

Because the EU systems for registered trade marks and designs coexist beside harmonized national laws, provision is also made for dealing with simultaneous proceedings and successive actions.[329] These require the latter court to stay proceedings pending the determination of the earlier one, or, if judgment has been given, to follow suit. However, the rules apply only if the actions involve the same cause of action and the same parties. In *Prudential Assurance Co. v. Prudential Insurance Co. of America*,[330] the Court of Appeal held that the claimant was not prevented from bringing an infringement action in England based on infringement of its Community trade marks PRU or PRUDENTIAL by the defendant's use of PRUMERICA, merely because the claimant had been unsuccessful when opposing a national registration of PRUMERICA in opposition proceedings before the French Trade Marks Registry. While Article 136(2) EUTMR requires the court to reject an action for infringement 'if a final judgment on the merits has been given on the same cause of action and between the same parties on the basis of an identical national trade mark valid for identical goods or services', the Court of Appeal found that the English action did not concern an 'identical trade mark': the French action related to the validity of PRUMERICA, whereas the English one dealt with infringement of PRUDENTIAL.[331] This seems a rather formalistic way of applying Article 90.

10.2 APPLICABLE LAW

Once the court accepts that it has jurisdiction, the next issue to decide is the law that applies. The rules that apply to the infringement of all intellectual property rights are harmonized by the Rome II Regulation.[332] There is no distinction, as there is for jurisdiction,

---

[328] *Coty Germany GmbH v. First Note Perfumes NV*, Case C-360/12, EU:C:2014:1318 (ECJ, Fourth Chamber), (adopting a narrow construction distinct from that recognized in the jurisprudence under Brussels, Art. 5(3)).

[329] EUTMR, Art. 136; CDR, Art. 95. See section 8, pp. 1295–7.

[330] [2003] *ETMR* (69) 858. See further *Hearst Holdings Inc. v. A.V.E.L.A. Inc.* [2015] *FSR* (2) 17, [30], [33], finding that a prior Italian action did not relate to the same cause of action, even though it was based on the same mark, because it involved 'different defendants selling different goods with different images of Betty Boop'.   [331] [2003] *ETMR* (69) 858, [39] (Chadwick LJ).

[332] Regulation (EC) No. 864/2007 of 11 July 2007 on the law applicable to non-contractual obligations [2007] *OJ L* 199/40 (31 July 2007) ('Rome II'), Art. 8. The concept of intellectual property is defined, by example, in Recital 21. A different principle applies to cases of 'unfair competition': see Arts 6, 4. The Regulation does not regulate the rules on applicable law for violations of privacy and rights relating to personality, including defamation: Art. 1(2)(g). For consideration of breach of confidence, see C. Wadlow, 'Trade Secrets and the Rome II Regulation on the Law Applicable to Non-contractual Obligations' [2008] *EIPR* 309. For elaboration of the concept of unfair competition, see C. Wadlow, 'The Emergent European Law of Unfair Competition and Its Consumer Law Origins' [2012] *IPQ* 1.

based on the domicile of the parties. The Rome II Regulation adopts the 'universally acknowledged principle' that the *lex protectionis* is the applicable law in the case of non-contractual actions relating to intellectual property rights and, in contrast to other aspects of the regime, parties are not allowed to agree that a different law should apply.[333] For example, if a claimant brings an action in an English court against a defendant domiciled in the United Kingdom, alleging infringement of their Dutch copyright by acts in the Netherlands, the applicable law would be Dutch copyright law.[334] This is both the place where the act occurred and the law from which protection is claimed. Occasionally, these places will differ, as where a person in the Netherlands authorizes an infringement in the United Kingdom; in such circumstances, the governing law should be UK law.[335]

There are certain special rules,[336] relating to disputes about the ownership of European patents.[337] Where the right infringed is an EU right, such as a European Union trade mark, the relevant law is that of the regulation concerned. However, where the regulations do not apply, the relevant law is the law of the country in which the act of infringement took place.[338]

10.3 RECOGNITION OF JUDGMENTS

Where intellectual property matters cross jurisdictional boundaries, questions often arise about the recognition and enforcement of foreign judgments. This is largely governed by the Brussels Regulation. The general policy of the Regulation is that there should be free movement of judgments. This means that, once a court has assumed jurisdiction over a matter, any determinations that it makes should be recognized and, if necessary, enforced in other member states. So, for example, if a Dutch court holds that a British-domiciled co-defendant infringed the Dutch claimant's copyright, then the order of that court should be enforced by English courts. The procedure for recognition is straightforward: the judgment must first be registered and then notice is served on the person subject to it.[339]

The requirement that a court of a contracting state automatically recognizes judgments from other contracting states is qualified in a number of ways.[340] The most important is that, where the originating court assumed jurisdiction in breach of Article 24, then recognition must be refused. Thus, if a Dutch court were to order the revocation of a British patent, UK courts would not have to recognize the judgment, since it was made in respect of a claim principally concerned with validity. However, because the scope of Article 24(4) is unclear, it will be difficult to predict whether a British court would be able to refuse to recognize the Dutch judgment that a UK patent had been infringed. This is especially the case if the Dutch court were to form a conclusion as to the validity of the patent. A court can also refuse to enforce a judgment that is irreconcilable with a judgment given in a dispute between the same parties in the state in which recognition is sought.[341] In *Italian Leather SpA v. WECO Polstermobel GmbH*,[342] an Italian court ordered an interim

---

[333] Rome II, Art. 8(3) (excluding the operation of Art. 14).

[334] *Pearce v. Ove Arup* [1997] *FSR* 641, 542 (this was under the pre-Rome II regime, but the result would be the same).

[335] For systematic analysis, see G. B. Dinwoodie, R. C. Dreyfuss, and A. Kur, 'The Law Applicable to Secondary Liability in Intellectual Property Cases' (2010) 42 *NYU JILP* 201.

[336] Claims relating to privacy, and misuse of private information, are not harmonized under the Rome II Regulation. For a discussion, see Gurry (2012), [23.75]–[23.82].   [337] EPC 2000, Art. 60(1).

[338] Rome II, Art. 8(2); EUTMR, Art. 129; CDR, Art. 88.   [339] CJJA 1982, s. 4.

[340] Brussels, Arts 27(1) and 28. See also *Renault v. Maxicar*, Case C-38/98 [2000] *ECR* I–2973.

[341] Brussels, Art. 27(3).   [342] Case C-80/00 [2002] *ECR* I–4995.

injunction preventing the use of the claimant's mark longlife by a German defendant, whereas the German court had refused interim relief. When the German court was asked to enforce the Italian judgment in Germany, the German court sought the advice of the Court of Justice as to whether the judgments were irreconcilable, and if so, what the consequences were. The Court of Justice was clear that the judgments were irreconcilable and that the German court was obliged to enforce its own, rather than the Italian, decision.

11 ALTERNATIVE DISPUTE RESOLUTION

In many areas of law, the cost and hassle of litigation has encouraged the growth of mechanisms such as arbitration[343] and mediation for resolving disputes outside the court framework. For obvious reasons, it is difficult to know how widely such methods are used to resolve disputes concerning intellectual property.[344] The Civil Procedure Rules promote the use of alternative dispute resolution (ADR) by providing that proceedings may be stayed pending ADR[345] and by allowing courts to make early neutral evaluations of the merits of the case (thus prompting settlement).[346] Another reason is that ADR is becoming more widely used by international bodies. A notable example is the World Intellectual Property Organization (WIPO) Arbitration and Mediation Centre (established in 1994), which has more than 1,500 arbitrators and mediators.

Another mechanism that has been developed in the United Kingdom to minimize the costs of intellectual property litigation is the Intellectual Property Office's 'Opinion Service'.[347] The aim of the Opinion Service is to provide a 'quick, balanced, affordable and impartial assessment of issues relating to the validity or infringement of patents'.[348] Following a 2009 review, which found that opinions, although non-binding in nature, were helping to resolve disputes, the Intellectual Property Office conducted a further review, which recommended that the scope of the service should be extended.[349] These recommendations were taken up by the Intellectual Property Act 2014 and the scope of the Opinions Service extended to allow the UK IPO to give non-binding opinions on a wider range of issues concerning patent validity, and the validity and infringement of supplementary protection certificates.[350] At the same time, the Comptroller was given the

---

[343] There is a growing literature on the arbitration of intellectual property: see for instance, T. Cook and A. Garcia, *International Intellectual Property Arbitration* (2010); P. Chrocziel and B. Kasolowsky, *International Arbitration of Intellectual Property Disputes: A Practitioner's Guide* (2017).

[344] See W. Kingston, 'The Case for Compulsory Arbitration: Empirical Evidence' [2000] *EIPR* 154; W. Kingston, 'Reducing the Cost of Resolving Intellectual Property Disputes' [1995] *Eur J L Econ* 85. Research from the United States demonstrates that the likelihood of patent disputes being settled often depends on whether smaller or larger firms are involved: see J. Lanjouw and M. Schankerman, *Enforcing Intellectual Property Rights* (December 2001) NBER Working Paper No. 1656.

[345] CPR, r. 26.4. Note also the cooling-off period for friendly settlement of opposition proceedings in the OHIM and the UK TM Registry. See *Samuel Smith Old Brewery v. Lee* [2012] *FSR* (7) 263, [164] (Arnold J) (emphasizing that the case should have gone to mediation at an early stage); but compare *Uwug Ltd v. Ball* [2015] *EWHC* 74 (IPEC) [26] (the refusal to enter into mediation was reasonable as they were unlikely to be successful).

[346] Prior to the House of Lords' decision in *American Cyanamid v. Ethicon* [1975] *AC* 396 (see Chapter 49), litigants used to treat the grant of interlocutory relief as equivalent to such an early neutral evaluation.

[347] The Patent Opinion Service was introduced in 2005, PA 1977, ss 74A and 74B; Patents Rules 2007, r. 92–100.   [348] See UK IPO, *Review of the Opinions Service* (March 2010).

[349] UK IPO, *Consultation on the Patent Opinions Service* (2012); UK IPO, *Consultation on the Patents Opinions Service: Response Document* (2013).

[350] See Patents Rules 2007, r. 93(6) which prescribes the matters for PA 1977, s. 74A(1).

power to revoke a clearly invalid patent in certain cases:[351] essentially creating a limited right of re-examination. The 'Opinion Service' will also extend to provide voluntary, non-binding opinions on the validity and infringement of registered designs[352] and unregistered design right, in relation to how long the right will last, and who holds it.[353] The extension of the service to designs is dependent on delegated legislation being enacted, but, as yet, this has not happened.[354]

---

[351] See PA 1977, s. 73(1A) to (1C).   [352] RDA 1949, s. 28A.   [353] CDPA 1988, s. 249A.

[354] The draft regulations were published in UK IPO, *Consultation on the Implementation of a Design Opinions Service* (March 2015).

49

CIVIL AND CRIMINAL REMEDIES

In this chapter, we examine the civil and criminal remedies that a claimant may obtain for violation of intellectual property rights. We begin by considering the civil relief available before trial: interim injunctions; and prevention of imports. We then go on to look at the civil remedies available at full trial: final injunction; delivery up or destruction; damages; account of profits; and publicity orders. Finally, we turn to the various criminal remedies that may be available to an intellectual property right holder.

1 INTERIM INJUNCTIONS

Although, in appropriate cases, a tribunal will make an order for a speedy trial,[1] in many situations, there will be a significant delay between the time when a rights holder discovers that their rights are being infringed and the time when the matter is heard at trial. In order to ensure that the rights holder's interests are not undermined during this period, provision exists for interim orders, sometimes referred to as 'interlocutory', 'preliminary', 'provisional', or 'protective' relief.[2] The most important of these is the interim injunction.[3] This is a court order to stop the defendant's activities pending a final determination (or sometimes a requirement to do something—a so called mandatory injunction).[4] An

---

[1] The most important consideration is whether resolution of the dispute is so urgent as to justify the prejudice caused to other litigants. See *J. W. Spear & Sons v. Zynga Inc.* [2013] *FSR* (15) 270, [16]–[25] (Henderson J); *Starbucks (HK) Ltd v. British Sky Broadcasting Group plc and ors* [2012] *ETMR* (57) 1012, [66]–[78].

[2] TRIPS, Art. 50(2) and Enforcement Dir., Art. 9 (*ex parte* orders); TRIPS, Art. 50(6), Enforcement Dir., Art. 8, EUTMR, Art. 131, and CDR, Art. 90 (interim orders); *Hermès v. FHT*, Case C-53/96 [1998] *ECR* I–3603; *Dior and ors*, Joined Cases C-300/98 and C-392/98 [2000] *ECR* I–1130; *Schieving-Nijstad vof and ors v. Robert Groeneveld*, Case C-89/99 [2001] *ECR* I–5851.

[3] CPR, r. 25.1(a). *Ex parte* orders might be granted in appropriate cases and these include injunctions against persons unknown: *Bloomsbury Publishing Ltd v. News Group Newspapers Ltd* [2003] *FSR* 360.

[4] The rules are essentially the same for both types of injunction, and the classification has been called barren: *National Commercial Bank Jamaica v. Olint Corp.* [2009] 1 *WLR* 1405, [19] and [20]. However, where a person is required to do something it is more likely that the damage suffered can be said to be irreparable.

interim injunction can be granted before the issue of a claim form where the matter is urgent or this is otherwise desirable in the interests of justice.[5]

Applications for interim injunctions are usually decided on the basis of sworn written evidence which has not been subjected to cross-examination. Consequently, there is a risk that the tribunal's interim decision will differ from the result after matters are fully aired at trial. It is therefore important that, when a court grants interim relief, it does so in a way that minimizes the consequences to the parties that might arise from a hasty view of the merits of the case. In these circumstances, the courts must reconcile the conflicting demands of speed and correctness in decision making. On the one hand, there is a desire to examine the issues as fully as possible to ensure that the interim decision is accurate. On the other, since the evidence is necessarily inadequate, there is a desire to ignore the legal issues and focus instead on minimizing the injustices that will ensue from incorrect preliminary intervention.

Applications for interim injunctions in England and Wales are usually assessed according to the approach set out by the House of Lords in *American Cyanamid v. Ethicon*.[6] More recently the requirements have been modified to include issues of proportionality. It is important to note that some recent cases have been reluctant to follow these guidelines strictly and that questions have been raised as to whether the test might need to be reviewed in the light of European law.[7] It should also be noted that the Human Rights Act 1998 has modified the approach that must be taken in cases that concern freedom of expression.

In *American Cyanamid*, the claimant sought interim relief to restrain the defendant from infringing the claimant's patent. The defendant company planned to argue at trial either that it had not infringed or that the claimant's patent was invalid. When considering whether to grant interim relief, the High Court and the Court of Appeal said that the key question was whether the claimant had established a strong case on its face.[8] Overturning this approach, the House of Lords rejected previous suggestions to the effect that a case must be established on its face before a court could grant interim relief; instead, the Lords laid down a reduced threshold requirement:[9] for a court to be vested with the discretion to grant an interim injunction. First, it is necessary for a claimant to establish that there was 'a serious question to be tried'.[10] Second, the court should consider whether damages would be an adequate remedy for the party injured by the grant of, or refusal to grant, the injunction. Finally, the court should consider where the balance of convenience[11] lies.[12]

These requirements have been modified somewhat by the Enforcement Directive.[13] Article 3(2) provides that injunctions, and other remedies, must be effective, proportionate,

---

[5] CPR, r. 25.2(2)(b).

[6] [1975] *AC* 396. For the position in Scotland, see *Schuh Ltd v. Shhh . . . Ltd* [2011] *CSOH* 123, [12]–[13].

[7] On the implications of *Solvay SA v. Honeywell Fluorine Products Europe BV*, Case C-616/10, EU:C:2012:445 (ECJ, Third Chamber), see *Starbucks (HK) Ltd v. British Sky Broadcasting Group plc* [2013] *FSR* (16) 281, [110]; *Regents University v. Regent's University London* [2013] *EWPCC* 39, [34]–[37].

[8] [1974] *FSR* 312.

[9] The case sets down guidelines, rather than strict rules: *R. v. Secretary of State for Transport, ex parte Factortame Ltd (No. 2)* [1991] 1 *AC* 603, 671 (HL).

[10] *American Cyanamid v. Ethicon* [1975] *AC* 396, 407–9.

[11] This is sometimes said to be the balance of injustice: *Cayne v. Global Natural Resources* [1984] 1 *All ER* 225, 233.

[12] There were numerous criticisms of the judgment: A. Gore, 'Interlocutory Injunctions: A Final Judgment?' (1975) 38 *MLR* 672; P. Prescott, '*American Cyanamid v. Ethicon*' (1975) 91 *LQR* 168; for a more recent critique, see G. Mei, 'Interlocutory Injunctions in IP Infringement Actions in England and Wales and in Ireland: American Cyanamid Revisited' (2015) 46 *IIC* 175.

[13] In particular, Enforcement Dir., Art. 3(2).

and dissuasive and be applied in such a manner as to avoid the creation of barriers to legitimate trade and to provide safeguards against their abuse. This provision is directed to national courts and so should be considered when deciding whether to grant an injunction or not.[14]

1.1 SERIOUS QUESTION TO BE TRIED

The first task confronting a claimant seeking an interim injunction is that they must satisfy the threshold requirement that there is a serious question to be tried.[15] In other words, if the evidence reveals that the claimant does not have any real prospect of succeeding in their claim for a permanent injunction at trial, the court will not even consider the balance of convenience. According to Lord Diplock, when determining whether there is a serious question to be tried, the court should investigate only whether a known cause for action is revealed. In so doing, it should take account of points of law that necessarily arise on the facts that are revealed at the interlocutory stage. However, the courts should not embark upon mini-trials of disputed questions of fact or difficult questions of law.

A claimant might fail to demonstrate that there is a serious question to be tried for a number of reasons. In some cases, a claimant might fail to show a realistic cause for action. For example, if a straightforward reading of existing case law suggests that no cause of action exists, the application will be refused.[16] Moreover, if the claimant's case is dependent on overseas authorities,[17] or the extension of an existing action to new circumstances, the court might take the view that this falls before the threshold.[18] In contrast, where the existing authorities are merely unclear, the court will usually decline to resolve the dispute and treat the situation as raising a serious question to be tried.

More commonly, a court will find that there is no arguable case because the evidence is so insubstantial that it is clear that the case will fail.[19] In many situations, particularly in passing off and trade mark cases, the court will be able to make a fairly confident judgment on factual matters such as whether a name or get-up is not distinctive,[20] and whether there is a misrepresentation[21] or a likelihood of confusion.[22] The fact that a reasonable person could bring the action in good faith will not matter if it is so hopeless a case that no interim relief should be available.[23] Having said that, a case may be 'thin', but arguable.[24] Another reason why the court might hold that there is no serious question to be tried is because the defendant has a very strong prospect of a successful defence.[25] It should be noted that the question is not whether there is an arguable defence: if the defence is only arguable, there is a serious question to be tried.[26]

---

[14] *Tommy Hilfiger Licensing LLC v. Delta Center*, C-494/15, EU:C:2016:528, [31]–[37]; *Warner-Lambert Company v. Sandoz* [2016] *EWHC* 3317 (Pat), [74]–[76].

[15] It may be that the Directive requires a lower threshold than a serious issue to be tried: see Roughton, Johnson, and Cook, [8.13].

[16] *Mail Newspapers v. Insert Media* [1987] *RPC* 521, 529–30; *Schulke & Mayr v. Alkapharm* [1999] *FSR* 161, 166.   [17] *Lyngstad v. Anabas Products* [1977] *FSR* 62, 68 (Oliver LJ).

[18] *Times Newspapers v. MGN* [1993] *EMLR* 443; *Marcus Publishing v. Hutton Wild Communications* [1990] *RPC* 576, 584.

[19] On the nature of evidence, see CPR Practice Direction 25A, r. 3.

[20] *Marcus Publishing v. Hutton Wild Communications* [1990] *RPC* 576, 583; *County Sound* [1991] *FSR* 367, 372.   [21] *Consorzio Parma v. Marks & Spencer* [1991] *RPC* 351, 372.

[22] *Morning Star Co-operative Society v. Express Newspapers* [1979] *FSR* 113.

[23] *Mothercare v. Robson Books* [1979] *FSR* 466, 472–3.

[24] *Metric Resources Corporation v. Leasemetrix* [1979] *FSR* 571, 580.

[25] *News Group Newspapers v. Rocket Records* [1981] *FSR* 89, 102.

[26] But. cf. *Warner v. Channel Four* [1994] *EMLR* 1.

1.1.1 Freedom of expression

An important qualification to the threshold for injunctive relief set out in *American Cyanamid* was introduced by section 12(3) of the Human Rights Act 1998. This provides that, where a court is considering whether to grant relief that might affect the exercise of the Convention right to freedom of expression,[27] no relief should be granted that restrains publication prior to trial 'unless the court is satisfied that the applicant is likely to establish that publication should not be allowed'.[28] The court is further to take into consideration the extent to which the material has or is about to become available to the public. The courts also take account of whether it would be in the public interest for the material to be published.[29] The impact of section 12(3) was considered by the House of Lords in *Cream Holdings v. Banerjee*.[30] This case arose when Banerjee, a disgruntled ex-employee of Cream Holdings (a company that ran nightclubs, dance parties, and similar events), sent confidential information about corruption within Cream to Echo (which published the *Daily Post* and the *Liverpool Echo*). After some of the information was published, Cream sought injunctive relief to prevent further publication of the confidential information. The Court of Appeal, like the judge at first instance, granted an interlocutory injunction preventing the defendant from publishing the information until the matter could be heard at trial. The defendant appealed to the House of Lords, where the key question before the Lords was the meaning of 'likely' in section 12(3).

Delivering the judgment of the House, Lord Nicholls began by explaining that, when the Human Rights Act 1998 was still a Bill, concerns arose about the adverse impact that it might have on freedom of the press. In particular, the fear arose that:

> [A]pplying the conventional *American Cyanamid* approach, orders imposing prior restraint on newspapers might readily be granted by the courts to preserve the status quo until trial whenever applicants claimed that a threatened publication would infringe their rights under Article 8 [of the European Convention on Human Rights, or ECHR]. Section 12(3) was enacted to allay these fears.[31]

Confirming that the test to be applied under section 12(3) was more stringent than that under *American Cyanamid*, the Lords said that the principal purpose of section 12(3) was:

> . . . to buttress the protection afforded to freedom of speech at the interlocutory stage. It sought to do so by setting a higher threshold for the grant of interlocutory injunctions against the media than the *American Cyanamid* guideline of a 'serious question to be tried' or a 'real prospect' of success at the trial.[32]

Lord Nicholls then went on to consider whether, as Echo had argued, 'likely' in section 12(3) bears the meaning of 'more likely than not' or 'probably'. Rejecting this construction, Lord Nicholls said that such an interpretation would not be workable in practice, not

---

[27] Freedom of expression is most obviously at stake in cases of newspaper disclosure of private information, but there are plenty of other situations involving copyright, trade marks, and confidential information in which freedom of expression might be implicated. See, e.g., *Volkswagen Aktiengesellschaft v. Garcia* [2014] FSR (12) 232; *Unilever plc v. Griffin* [2010] FSR (33) 814. The approach in *Cream* has been held by the Court of Appeal to be applicable in all cases of comparative advertising: *Boehringer v. Vetplus* [2007] FSR (29) 737.

[28] This is in addition to the rule in *Bonnard v. Perryman* [1891] 2 Ch 269, which is a rule in libel cases that where a person is going to argue the truth of the allegation the court will not impose a prior restraint unless it is palpably untrue. The rule has some implications in cases where the information is private, but defamatory, and the claimant wants to sue in both libel and misuse of private information.

[29] Human Rights Act 1998, s. 12(4). The tribunal is also instructed to take into account 'any relevant privacy code'.   [30] [2005] AC 253.

[31] Ibid., [15].   [32] Ibid.

least because it would 'produce results Parliament cannot have intended'.[33] The reason for this is that if Echo's reading of section 12(3) were applied, it would mean that the courts would not be able to make a restraining order to prevent disclosure in the period during which the court was deciding whether the claim would succeed at trial—something that was very important in relation to confidential information, which cannot be protected once it is published. Another situation in which Lord Nicholls felt that the court should be able to exercise its discretion was where the consequences of the disclosure would be extremely serious, 'such as a grave risk of personal injury to a particular person'.[34] Practical considerations such as these led Lord Nicholls to say 'that "likely" in section 12(3) cannot have been intended to mean "more likely than not" in all situations'.[35] He went on to say that:

> There can be no single, rigid standard governing all applications for interim restraint orders. Rather, on its proper construction the effect of section 12(3) is that the court is not to make an interim restraint order unless satisfied the applicant's prospects of success at the trial are sufficiently favourable to justify such an order being made in the particular circumstances of the case.[36]

This in turn gave rise to a further question: what degree of likelihood makes the prospects of success 'sufficiently favourable'? In answering this, Lord Nicholls said that:

> [T]he general approach should be that courts will be exceedingly slow to make interim restraint orders where the applicant has not satisfied the court he will probably ('more likely than not') succeed at the trial. In general, that should be the threshold an applicant must cross before the court embarks on exercising its discretion, duly taking into account the relevant jurisprudence on Article 10 and any countervailing Convention rights. But there will be cases where it is necessary for a court to depart from this general approach and a lesser degree of likelihood will suffice as a prerequisite.[37]

This would include, for example, situations in which 'the potential adverse consequences of disclosure are particularly grave, or where a short-lived injunction is needed to enable the court to hear and give proper consideration to an application for interim relief pending the trial or any relevant appeal'.[38] On this basis, the Lords allowed the appeal and discharged the injunction.

1.2 ADEQUACY OF DAMAGES

Once a serious question has been found, the next matter to be considered is the adequacy of damages. In *American Cyanamid* it was stated that the 'governing principle'[39] in determining where the balance of convenience lies is the adequacy of compensation in damages to either party if an injunction is granted or refused. In *National Commercial Bank v. Olint Corp.*,[40] Lord Hoffmann explained what was being considered:

> that means that if damages will be an adequate remedy for the plaintiff, there are no grounds for interference with the defendant's freedom of action by the grant of an injunction. Likewise, if there is a serious issue to be tried and the plaintiff could be prejudiced by the acts or omissions of the defendant pending trial and the cross-undertaking in damages would provide the defendant with an adequate remedy if it turns out that his freedom of action should not have been restrained, then an injunction should ordinarily be granted.

---

[33] Ibid., [16]. [34] *Cream Holdings* [2005] *AC* 253, [18].
[35] Ibid., [20]. [36] Ibid., [22]. [37] Ibid. [38] Ibid., [22].
[39] *American Cyanamid v. Ethicon* [1975] *AC* 396, 408. [40] [2009] *UKPC* 16, [16].

This means that the 'basic principle is that the court should take whichever course seems likely to cause the least irremediable prejudice to one party or the other'.[41] Where the damage is to a non-financial interest, such as privacy or personal reputation or loss of goodwill, it is highly unlikely that the claimant would be compensated for the loss in question. As a result, interim injunctions are less likely to be awarded in patent cases, compared with confidentiality or copyright cases in which non-financial interests are often present.[42] In addition, if the claimant has been in the habit of licensing rights for royalties, it is likely that damages will be seen to be an adequate remedy.[43]

When assessing the inadequacy of damages, there are certain relevant factors which may be considered. This could arise where an injunction might cause job losses among the party's employees or a party might go out of business,[44] or where it might require price cuts (if they cannot return to pre-injunction levels if there is success).[45]

In general, the impact of this is that the smaller a defendant's business, the more likely it is that interim relief will be granted.[46] In some cases, in order to avoid unduly favouring rich claimants over poorer defendants, the courts have devised orders that allow a defendant to continue their allegedly infringing operations even where they cannot provide an undertaking. In these orders, the courts protect the claimant's rights by requiring the defendant to make payments into an account on a royalty-type basis.[47]

Where it is decided that there is irremediable prejudice to the claimant, the courts will consider whether it is possible to formulate a cross-undertaking to the court[48] that compensates the defendant for any harm caused in the period during which their activities were curtailed.[49] The court cannot compel a cross-undertaking to be given, but it can refuse the injunction if the claimant refuses.[50] If the cross-undertaking would be satisfactory, then an injunction will usually be granted. Usually, the question is merely one of the adequacy of damages, not of the claimant's ability to pay in the abstract. The reason for this is that if there were any doubt as to the reliability of the cross-undertaking, the court might require the claimant to provide security. If the claimant acted promptly, the chances are that the cross-undertaking will be satisfactory and that the interim relief will be granted. (This is because money spent in preparations for trade is usually quantifiable.)[51] Moreover, pending trial, the defendant can continue to trade in non-infringing ways (for example by selling non-infringing items or selling goods under a different trade mark) and so the businesses harm is not irremediable. This, however, will not be the case if timing is crucial to the defendant, for example where the defendant is satisfying a short-term fashion or seasonal demand,[52] where a third-party competitor of the defendant is about to launch,[53] or where the defendant's whole business is in allegedly infringing goods.[54] If the defendant is already selling the allegedly infringing goods on the market,

---

[41] Ibid., [17].   [42] *Catnic v. Stressline* [1976] FSR 157.

[43] *Smith & Nephew v. 3M United Kingdom* [1983] RPC 92, 102; cf. *Games Workshop v. Transworld Publishers* [1993] FSR 704, 714.

[44] *Artificial Solutions Germany GmbH v. Creative Virtual Ltd* [2007] EWHC 3185 (Ch), [51].

[45] *Chiron Corp. v. Organon Teknika Ltd* [1992] FSR 512, 514; *Warner Lambert v. Teva* [2011] EWHC 1691 (Pat), [14], [15].   [46] *Quantel v. Shima Seiki Europe* [1990] RPC 436.

[47] *Mirage v. Counter-feat* [1991] FSR 145, 154.   [48] And not the defendant.

[49] Enforcement Dir., Art. 9(7) requires compensation where an injunction is discharged.

[50] *Hoffmann-La Roche & Co. AG v. Secretary of State for Trade and Industry* [1975] AC 295.

[51] *Mothercare v. Robson Books* [1979] FSR 466, 475; cf. *Polaroid v. Eastman Kodak* [1977] FSR 25, 35.

[52] *Aljose Fashions v. Alfred Young & Co.* [1978] FSR 364; cf. *Monet of London v. Sybil Richards* [1978] FSR 368.   [53] *Silicon Graphics v. Indigo Graphic Systems* [1994] FSR 403, 418.

[54] *Mirage v. Counter-feat* [1991] FSR 145, 153.

the cross-undertaking is liable to be inadequate. This is because it will be very difficult to quantify losses incurred from withdrawing from a (usually expanding) market.[55]

1.3 BALANCE OF CONVENIENCE

In deciding whether to grant an interim injunction, the court will consider the balance of convenience.[56] This phrase is a little obtuse; it essentially means which side will suffer the least injustice if an injunction is granted (or not as the case may be). The inadequacy of damages is, properly, part of the consideration of the balance of convenience. However, where damages would be inadequate to both sides—as is so often the case—the final hurdle is a way of demonstrating which cause of action would cause the least overall suffering to the parties.

The factors that can be taken into account are long and varied. They have included the impact on the market which cannot be remedied[57] or whether the intellectual property right is due to expire soon.[58] Conversely the delay in seeking the interim injunction might suggest against an interim injunction being granted, particularly where the defendant suffered additional injustice due to the delay.[59] Similarly, where there can be an expedited trial, this might be an alternative to an interim injunction.[60] Where the defendant deliberately risked infringing, this might tip the balance of convenience in favour of an injunction.[61] A more extreme example would be where granting injunctive relief might prevent the public from having access to a life-saving drug, then such relief might be refused.[62]

Where the factors are evenly balanced, Lord Diplock suggested that the best course is to preserve the status quo. Subsequent cases have said that the status quo refers to the period preceding the issue of the 'statement of case' claiming a permanent injunction.[63] Thus if a defendant is doing something that they have not done before, all that the injunction does is to postpone their activities;[64] if the injunction would stop them from continuing to do something that they were already doing, this would cause greater inconvenience. The courts have been careful to prevent the desire to preserve the status quo from being used tactically. In particular, they have been careful to ensure that a defendant cannot alter the status quo, for example by embarking on a high-risk strategy.[65]

1.3.1 The merits of the case

The controversial factor that the court will consider in deciding whether an interim injunction should be granted is the relative strength, or merits, of the parties' cases. According to the traditional reading of *American Cyanamid*, the court should consider

---

[55] *Quantel v. Shima Seiki Europe* [1990] *RPC* 436.

[56] It has been said that the phrase is rather inept, and alternative phrases such as the 'balance of injustice' or 'prejudice' have sometimes been deployed.

[57] *Chiron Corp. v. Organon Teknika Ltd* [1992] *FSR* 512, 514; *Warner Lambert v. Teva* [2011] *EWHC* 1691 (Pat), [14]–[15].   [58] *Warner Lambert v. Teva* [2011] *EWHC* 1691 (Pat), [12].

[59] *Monsanto v. Stauffer Chemical Co. (NZ)* [1984] *FSR* 559, 572; see also *Silicon Graphics v. Indigo Graphic Systems* [1994] *FSR* 403.   [60] *Cephalon v. Orchid Europe* [2010] *EWHC* 2945 (Pat), [73]–[74].

[61] *News Group v. Rocket* [1981] *FSR* 89, 107; *Elanco Products v. Mandops (Agrochemical Specialists)* [1979] *FSR* 46; *SmithKline Beecham plc v. Apotex Europe* [2003] *FSR* (31) 544, [40].

[62] *Roussel-Uclaf* [1977] *FSR* 125, 131–2.

[63] *Garden Cottage Foods v. Milk Marketing Board* [1983] 2 *All ER* 770, 774. But not always: *Dunhill v. Sunoptic* [1979] *FSR* 337, 376 (date may well vary in different cases).

[64] *Elanco Products* [1979] *FSR* 46.

[65] *Jian Tools for Sales Inc. v. Roderick Manhattan Group Ltd* [1995] *FSR* 924, 943.

the merits of each party's case only in the last resort. Applying the approach strictly, the courts have often refused to indicate which of the parties' cases they consider to be stronger, for fear that it might prejudice the ultimate outcome.[66]

While *American Cyanamid* suggests that the strength of the parties' cases should not be considered until this final stage, nonetheless, in a number of cases, the courts have been influenced by the merits of the claimant's case when considering factors such as the adequacy of damages and the balance of convenience.[67] This generated a growing feeling of unease that judges were not following *American Cyanami*d.[68] In *Series 5 Software*, Laddie J criticized this trend, saying that he did 'not believe it is satisfactory to exercise the court's discretion to grant an interlocutory injunction by paying lip service to the guidance given in *American Cyanamid* while in practice applying different criteria'.[69] Laddie J took the opportunity in *Series 5 Software* 'to look again at *American Cyanamid* to see what it decided'.[70] His primary concern was to consider the extent to which Lord Diplock's judgment prevents a court from considering the legal and factual merits of the case. Laddie J argued that Lord Diplock could not have been intended the sea change attributed to him, given the fact that, in a subsequent decision, Lord Diplock himself said that to 'justify the grant of such a remedy the claimant must satisfy the court first that there is a strong prima-facie case'.[71] Laddie J argued that, when Lord Diplock said that the court should not consider the strength of the claimant's case, he was merely referring to the 'mandatory initial hurdle'. Indeed, a close analysis of the factors that Lord Diplock thought were relevant suggested that even he would consider the strength of the case.[72] Laddie J therefore argued that the prospect of success was still a relevant factor when considering the balance of convenience. However, he did accept that Lord Diplock had intended that this should be conducted so as to avoid a mini-trial.

Laddie J's reformulation has met with a mixed reception. In *Barnsley Brewery Company v. RBNB*,[73] Robert Walker J signalled his approval, stating that while *Series 5* 'is sometimes regarded as surprising or even heretical', it provided a valuable reminder of the background to and basic message contained in *American Cyanami*d. However, other judges have ignored *Series 5*, preferring to stick to *American Cyanamid* and the acknowledged exceptions to it.[74] In *Guardian Media Groups v. Associated Newspapers*,[75] the Court of Appeal said that the *American Cyanamid* principles had a degree of flexibility and:

> . . . do not prevent the court from giving proper weight to any clear view which the court can form at the time of the application for interim relief (and without the need for a mini-trial on copious affidavit evidence) as to the likely outcome at trial. That is particularly so

---

[66] *Sodastream v. Thorn Cascade* [1982] *RPC* 459, 467.

[67] *Dunhill v. Sunoptic* [1979] *FSR* 337, 374; *County Sound* [1991] *FSR* 367, 372.

[68] C. Gray, 'Interlocutory Injunctions since *American Cyanamid*' (1981) 40 *CLJ* 307, 338–9, refers to differences of appearance rather than substance.

[69] *Series 5 Software v. Clarke* [1996] 1 *All ER* 853, [1996] *FSR* 273, 277.

[70] Ibid. (the analysis appears to have been *obiter*).

[71] *Hoffmann-La Roche & Co. v. Secretary of State for Trade and Industry* [1975] *AC* 295, 360.

[72] For example, Lord Diplock stated that if damages would satisfy a claimant, no injunction should be granted, 'however strong the plaintiff's claim'—implying that if damages were not adequate, the strength of the claim was a relevant consideration: ibid., 408, as highlighted by Laddie J, in *Series 5 Software v. Clarke* [1996] 1 *All ER* 853, [1996] *FSR* 273, 284.

[73] [1997] *FSR* 462, 472 (refusing injunction largely because claimant's case in passing off, although not unarguable, was weak).

[74] *EMAP National Publications v. Security Publications* [1997] *FSR* 891; *Dyno-Rod v. Reeve* [1999] *FSR* 149, 151–2, 158–9.   [75] (20 January 2000) (*EWCA Civ*, unreported).

when the grant or withholding of interim relief may influence the ultimate commercial outcome.

The better view appears to be that the strength of each case is a relevant factor for the court to take into account when it exercises its discretion. However, strength should be considered only where there is no credible dispute as to the evidence and it is clear that one party's case is likely to succeed.[76]

1.3.2 Proportionality

The Enforcement Directive has led to the courts considering the proportionality of granting an injunction.[77] Thus, when granting an injunction it is necessary to balance the interests and rights[78] of the putative infringer and those of the patent proprietor, in particular the right to intellectual property under Article 17(2) of the EU Charter of Fundamental Freedoms and to property under Article 1, Protocol 1 of the European Convention of Human Rights.[79] One of the factors that can be taken into account when determining whether an injunction is proportionate is the cost of implementing it (compared to the benefit).[80] Nevertheless, in *Warner Lambert v. Sandoz*,[81] Arnold J summarized that the 'court's primary task remains that of taking the course which appears least likely to cause one party or another irremediable prejudice'. In other words, in most cases, the assessment of proportionality is simply part of the balance of convenience.

2 STOPPING IMPORTS

In many situations, the infringing products originate from other jurisdictions. In these circumstances, the claimant may try to prevent the infringement at its source. Alternatively, a claimant may try to intercept the infringing articles or materials at the point of import. There are two legal mechanisms for stopping articles that infringe intellectual property rights at their point of import to the United Kingdom.[82] The most important of these are the European procedures specified in the so-called 'Border Measures Regulation' of 2013.[83] In 2016 there were more than 77,705 interceptions of goods, said to have a value of some €672,899,102, and the bulk of which by value (72.2 per cent) came from China. The most frequently seized goods were cigarettes (24 per cent), but 16 per cent was for toys and 12 per cent for foodstuffs.[84] The other set of procedures, which are now of limited scope, derives from domestic legislation.[85]

---

[76] *Intelsec Systems v. Grech-Cini* [1999] 4 *All ER* 11, 26.

[77] *L'Oréal SA v. eBay International AG* (C-324/09) [2011] *RPC* 27, [139]–[144]; see also *Tommy Hilfiger Licensing LLC v. Delta Center*, C-494/15.   EU:C:2016:528.

[78] This would include: Charter of Fundamental Freedoms, Art. 16 (freedom to conduct a business), Art. 7 (private communications) and Art. 8 (privacy).

[79] *Golden Eye (International) Ltd and anor v. Telefonica UK Ltd* [2012] *RPC* 28, [116]–[147]; the general approach was endorsed by the Supreme Court in *Rugby Football Union v. Consolidated Information Services Ltd* [2012] 1 *WLR* 3333, [44]–[45].

[80] *Twentieth Century Fox Film Corporation and ors v. British Telecommunications Plc* [2011] *EWHC* 2714 (Ch), [32].   [81] [2016] *EWHC* 3317 (Pat), [75].

[82] TRIPS, Arts 51 and 52, require such measures.

[83] Regulation (EU) No. 608/2013 of 12 June 2013 concerning customs enforcement of intellectual property rights and repealing Council Regulation (EC) No 1383/2003 [2013] *OJ L* 181/15.

[84] European Commission, *Report of EU Customs Enforcement of Intellectual Property Rights: Results at the EU Border 2016* (2017).

[85] TMA 1994, s. 89; Trade Marks (Customs) Regulations 1994 (SI 1994/2625); CDPA 1988, s. 111.

2.1 EUROPEAN PROCEDURE

The European regulations[86] establish mechanisms that ensure that goods that infringe intellectual property rights, other than travellers' personal luggage,[87] can be retained by customs authorities when they are introduced into the European Union.[88] The Border Measures Regulation defines 'intellectual property rights' in Article 2(1) to cover goods infringing rights in trade marks, designs, copyright and related rights, geographical indications, patents, plant breeders' rights, and supplementary protection certificates, plus national laws of utility models and trade names.[89] The Regulation does not apply to parallel imports or overruns.[90]

Provisions are made in the Border Measures Regulation for a proactive intellectual property rights holder who gets wind of the fact that goods are going to be imported to make an 'application for Customs action'. That is, the right holder can apply to the relevant customs authorities designated by each member state (in the United Kingdom, HM Revenue and Customs, or HMRC, but the request can apply to authorities in other member states, too) to detain the goods, should they come into its hands.[91] As one would expect, right holders are required to describe the goods so that they can be 'readily' identified and to provide proof that they are entitled to submit the application.[92] The applicants must accept liability towards the persons involved in the event that action is discontinued or goods are found to be non-infringing.[93] The customs authorities must process the application by deciding whether the information is sufficient, determine the relevant 'action period', and forward details to the relevant offices.[94] If the customs office comes across goods that it suspects are infringing (within the decision), 'it shall suspend release of the goods or detain them'.[95] The office then informs the right holder and 'declarant or holder of the goods'. Right holders are given information necessary to assist them in establishing whether an intellectual property right has been infringed, including the opportunity to inspect the goods and to remove samples for analysis.[96]

Even if advance warning has not been given, but the relevant authority has sufficient grounds for suspecting that goods are infringing, the Regulation empowers the authority to prevent their transit temporarily.[97] The authority will attempt to contact the relevant intellectual property right holder, who must complete the standard application for customs action within four days. The customs office will not detain the goods indefinitely. Accordingly, there are three possible scenarios that might ensue.

First, the intellectual property right holder may take no further action. If so, the customs office should release the goods after ten days.[98]

---

[86] See generally, O. Vrins and M. Schneider (eds), *Enforcement of Intellectual Property Rights through Border Measures: Law and Practice in the EU* (2nd edn, 2012).

[87] BMR, Art. 1(4) (goods of a non-commercial nature contained in a traveller's personal luggage). But goods sent from outside the European Union to a personal address within are liable to seizure if they would be infringing within the Union: *Blomqvist v. Rolex SA*, Case C-98/13, EU:C:2014:55 (ECJ, Second Chamber).

[88] Goods 'in transit', where there is no evidence that the goods are to be directed at the European Union, are outside the scope of the Regulation: *Koninklijke Philips Electronics NV v. Lucheng Meijing Ind. Co.*, Joined Cases C-446/09 and C-495/09 [2012] *ETMR* (13) 248 (ECJ, First Chamber). The exclusive rights granted to EUTMs is different (see EUTMR, Art. 9(4)).

[89] BMR, Art. 2. See pp. 2–3, discussing the meaning of 'intellectual property right'.

[90] BMR, Art. 1(5).   [91] BMR, Art. 5.

[92] BMR, Art. 6(3). Persons entitled to submit an application are specified in Art. 3, and include not only rights holders, but also collective rights management organizations and 'professional defence bodies'.

[93] BMR, Art. 6(3)(n), (o).   [94] BMR, Arts 7–14.

[95] BMR, Art. 17(1). If it fails to detect them, the authority is not liable to the right holder: BMR, Art. 27.

[96] BMR, Arts 17(3), (4), 18(5), 19.   [97] BMR, Arts 18, 5(3).   [98] BMR, Art. 23.

Second, the intellectual property right holder (or other relevant third party) may commence an action for infringement in the relevant national tribunal (which could be a court or administrative body, depending of national provisions).[99] If this occurs, and the right holder informs the authority, detention of the goods can be continued pending the outcome of proceedings.[100] However, since that may not be for some time, the owner of the goods has an option of seeking the release of the goods on condition that they provide an appropriate security.[101] This option, it should be noted, is available only where the allegation is infringement of patent, design, plant breeders' right, utility model, or semi-conductor topography right (and thus not in cases of infringement of copyright, trade marks, or geographical indications). If the goods are found to be infringing at the substantive hearing, the competent authorities are empowered to destroy the goods and to take any measures that deprive the persons concerned of the economic benefits of the transaction.[102] Removing trade marks affixed to counterfeit goods is not normally regarded as sufficient.[103]

The third scenario is that the goods may be destroyed. Here, two procedures are available: a general one; and one concerned with small packages. First, the parties may agree to destruction of the goods without the need for proceedings.[104] This 'simplified procedure' for abandonment is to be used by the customs authorities only if three conditions are met:[105]

(i)   the right holder must inform the authority within ten working days that the goods infringe intellectual property rights;

(ii) the authorities must have the written agreement of the 'declarant or the holder of the goods', or their deemed consent;[106] and

(iii) the right holder must agree.

Before the goods are destroyed, samples may be taken for, among other things, educational purposes.[107]

The second procedure for destruction relates to 'small consignments' (that is, posted parcels comprising fewer than three items and weighing under 2 kilos), where the goods are counterfeit or pirated.[108] Here, the customs authority may give the declarant or holder notice of its intention to destroy the goods.[109] The 'declarant or holder' has ten days in which to respond to such a notice and may agree to destruction, or oppose it, or, in some cases, will 'be deemed to have agreed'.[110] Where there is agreement, or deemed agreement, the goods may be destroyed.[111]

---

[99] *Sintex Trading OÜ v. Maksu ja Tolliamet*, Case C-583/12, EU:C:2014:244 (ECJ, Second Chamber), [44] (customs authorities may themselves initiate proceedings), [49] (proceedings might be before customs authority).   [100] BMR, Art. 23.

[101] BMR, Art. 23.   [102] BMR, Art. 17.   [103] BMR, Art. 17.   [104] BMR, Art. 23.

[105] Until 1 January 2014, this procedure was optional for member states. It is now mandatory.

[106] BMR, Art. 23(1)(c). The declarant is the person making the customs declaration in their own name or the person in whose name a customs declaration is made. The holder is the owner or a person 'who has a similar right of disposal, or physical control, over the goods': BMR, Art. 2(14).

[107] BMR, Art. 23(2).

[108] BMR, Art. 26(6). For the definition of pirated or counterfeit goods, see Art. 2(5) and (6). This covers certain infringements of copyright, related rights, and designs, trade marks, and geographical indications.

[109] BMR, Art. 26(1).   [110] BMR, Art. 26(6).

[111] BMR, Art. 26(7). Otherwise, the right holder is informed and, if it takes no action, the goods will be released.

2.2 DOMESTIC PROCEDURE

A residual domestic procedure continues to coexist with the European Regulation, but does not apply to goods within the Regulation or goods that are already in free circulation within the European Economic Area (EEA). Under this procedure, copyright and trade mark owners may notify HMRC that infringing goods, materials, or articles are about to be imported, and request that this be prohibited.[112] Its impact in this sphere is thus restricted to parallel imports and overruns. The Commissioners may require an indemnity and security against any liability and expense that might accrue.[113] Once a notice is in force, import of the goods is prohibited. If HMRC finds such goods (other than for the private and domestic use of the person importing them), they will be seized and the owner informed.[114] The owner has one month in which to make a claim that the goods were not liable to seizure. If such notice is given, the Commissioners are obliged to bring proceedings for 'condemnation' of the goods (either in the magistrates' court or the High Court).[115] If successful, the goods will usually be destroyed.[116]

3 FINAL INJUNCTION

A final or perpetual injunction is usually granted to intellectual property right owners who prove at trial that their rights have been infringed by the defendant.[117] A final injunction will order the defendant not to carry on with certain activities. As such, it is directed at future conduct, whereas financial remedies operate in relation to past acts. The injunction, being equitable in origin, is a discretionary remedy.[118] This means that while final injunctions are normally awarded, they are not granted automatically. Although the law of injunctions is a topic with implications that extend well beyond intellectual property rights, here we consider four specific issues.

3.1 GENERAL APPROACH

An injunction is intended to prevent future infringement. Accordingly, the court needs to believe that the defendant will continue to infringe if there is no injunction. In practice, a finding that a person has infringed an intellectual property right is taken to imply an intention to continue to infringe;[119] unless it finished many years previously.[120] There are instances where, historically, the injunction might be refused and damages awarded instead, in accordance with *Shelfer v. City of London*.[121] These include situations in which the infringement is trivial, its value can be estimated in financial terms and adequately

---

[112] CDPA 1988, s. 111; Copyright (Customs) Regulations 1989 (SI 1989/1178), amended by Copyright (EC Measures Relating to Pirated Goods and Abolition of Restrictions on the Import of Goods) Regulations 1995 (SI 1995/1445); TMA 1994, ss 89, 112; Trade Marks (Customs) Regulations 1994 (SI 1994/2625). See HMRC, *Notice 34: Intellectual Property Rights* (January 2014).

[113] CDPA 1988, s. 112.   [114] Customs and Excise Management Act 1979, Sch. 3, para. 1(2).

[115] Customs and Excise Management Act 1979, Sch. 3, para. 8.

[116] CDPA 1988, s. 111(4); TMA 1994, s. 89(2).

[117] *Chiron v. Organon (No. 10)* [1995] *FSR* 325. It has not previously been the case that an injunction must be granted, but it has been suggested that the Enforcement Dir., Art. 12 might change this (based on its German origins): see P. Blok, 'A Harmonized Approach to Prohibitory Injunctions: Reconsidering Article 12 of the Enforcement Directive' (2016) 11 *JIPLP* 56.

[118] This is confirmed by Enforcement Dir., Recital 25.   [119] *Losh v. Hague* (1838) 1 *WPC* 200, 200–1.

[120] *Proctor v. Bayley & Sons* (1889) 6 *RPC* 538, 541.   [121] *Shelfer v. City of London* [1895] 1 Ch 287.

compensated, and an injunction would be oppressive on the defendant;[122] where a claimant is interested only in money; where the claimant's action is vexatious; or where the infringing act is old and there is no future threat.[123] Moreover, in circumstances under which licences of right are available to a defendant, injunctive relief will not normally be granted.[124] An injunction will not be refused simply because there is a public interest in widespread exploitation or dissemination of a particular product (such as a cure for HIV),[125] or because the infringing material comprises only a small portion of the defendant's products.[126]

Although the Court of Appeal has stated that 'the principles upon which the court will grant an injunction in intellectual property cases are exactly the same as those which apply in other cases',[127] the better view is that the conventional principles need to be considered in the light of the Enforcement Directive and specific EU legislation (where relevant).[128] In particular, Article 3(1) of the Enforcement Directive requires that 'measures, procedures and remedies shall be fair and equitable and shall not be unnecessarily complicated or costly, or entail unreasonable time-limits or unwarranted delays'. Moreover, Article 3(2) adds that they should be 'effective, proportionate and dissuasive and shall be applied in such a manner as to avoid the creation of barriers to legitimate trade and to provide for safeguards against their abuse'. Whether the conventional approach in all circumstances meets these standards—particularly that of 'proportionality'—is difficult to say. Nevertheless, we agree with Arnold J's statement in *HTC v. Nokia* that:

> ['T']he time has come to recognise that, in cases concerning infringements of intellectual property rights, the criteria to be applied when deciding whether or not to grant an injunction are those laid down by Article 3(2): efficacy, proportionality, dissuasiveness, the avoidance of creating barriers to legitimate trade and the provision of safeguards against abuse.[129]

Thus Arnold J proposed that the 'traditional approach' be abandoned at least for intellectual property rights within the meaning of the Directive (which probably would not include much of the law of confidentiality or passing off). Unfortunately, on the facts of the case, even taking this approach, Arnold J awarded an injunction (rendering his opinion on the Directive unnecessary for the decision).

---

[122] *Sterwin v. Brocades* [1979] *RPC* 481; *Navitaire Inc v. EasyJet Airline Co Ltd (No. 2)* [2006] *RPC* (4) 213, [104] (i.e. grossly disproportionate) (approved by Jacob LJ in *Virgin Atlantic Airways Ltd v. Premium Aircraft Interiors Group* [2009] *EWCA Civ* 1513, [2010] *FSR* 396, [23]–[25] (approving *Navitaire* as correct approach under the Enforcement Directive).

[123] *Raleigh v. Miller* (1949) 66 *RPC* 23; *Frayling Furniture v. Premier Upholstery* (unreported, 5 November 1999) (no injunction where infringement had taken place five years earlier apparently inadvertently and had not been repeated). Delay was an important consideration in the court's refusal of an injunction in *Banks v. EMI Songs Ltd (No. 2)* [1996] *EMLR* 452.

[124] RDA 1949, s. 11B(1)(a); PA 1977, s. 46(3)(c); CDPA 1988, ss 98(1)(a), 191K.

[125] *Chiron v. Organon (No. 10)* [1995] *FSR* 325; cf. *Roussel Uclaf* [1977] *FSR* 125, 131.

[126] *Macmillan v. Reed* [1993] *FSR* 455; *Mawman v. Tegg* (1826) 2 *Russ* 385, 38 ER 380. Some flexibility here is regarded by many as desirable to prevent 'hold-outs', particularly by patent owners who do not manufacture products themselves and thus seek to maximize licence fees: see M. Lemley and C. Shapiro, 'Patent Holdup and Royalty Stacking' (2007) 85 *Texas L Rev* 1991; S. Subramanian, 'Patent Trolls in Thickets' [2008] *EIPR* 182; *eBay Inc. v. MercExchange, LLC*, 547 US 388 (2006).

[127] *Specsavers International Healthcare Ltd v. Asda Stores Ltd* [2012] *FSR* (20) 616, [20].

[128] EUTMR, Art. 126; CDR, Art. 89 (indicating that the court should grant an injunction 'unless there are special reasons for not doing so'); *Nokia Corp. v. Joachim Wärdell*, Case C-316/05 [2006] *ECR* I–12,083 (ECJ, First Chamber) ('special reasons' given a very narrow construction).

[129] *HTC v. Nokia* [2014] *RPC* (30) 865, [26].

3.2 FORM OF INJUNCTION

It is normal practice to grant an injunction that corresponds to the rights that were infringed. For example, an injunction will usually be granted that restrains the defendant from infringing the patent in suit or restrains the defendant from passing off their goods as those of the claimant. Such broadly worded relief is appropriate because 'claimants cannot be adequately protected by orders which are cabined or confined'.[130] Despite criticism that such vaguely worded relief is unfair to a defendant,[131] it has been stated by the Court of Appeal in a patent case that the 'traditional form' of injunction sets out with as much clarity as the context admits what may not be done. This is because, while the wording of the order may look vague, the Patents Act 1977 and the claims form a context from which the specific meaning of the terms of the order can be understood.[132] Nevertheless, Aldous LJ has said that an order that simply restrains 'breach of confidence' will not be precise enough. Moreover, Aldous LJ reiterated that 'each case must be determined on its own facts and the discretion exercised accordingly'.[133] Consequently, although the traditional form of injunction will often be appropriate, in some cases more narrowly couched orders will be required, depending on the right involved, the honesty of the defendant, and all other circumstances.

3.2.1 Springboard injunctions

In the last few years, the courts have been asked to develop new forms of injunction on the grounds that it is 'just and convenient' to do so.[134] One such claim has been for injunctions that continue after the expiry of an intellectual property right (also known as 'springboard relief'). Although the idea of a post-expiry injunction may seem strange, given the policy of fixing the duration of many intellectual property rights, such orders have been thought to be desirable in cases in which infringing acts that have already taken place (during the term of the intellectual property right) have given a defendant a head start in the process of marketing legitimate goods in the post-expiry period. In *Dyson Appliances v. Hoover (No. 2)*,[135] Judge Fysh QC granted such an injunction against Hoover for a period of 12 months following expiry of Dyson's patent as it would be difficult to compensate Dyson in damages. It has been held in relation to breach of confidence cases, that an injunction should not be used as a punishment[136] and, it is suggested, that granting a post-expiry injunction such as that in *Dyson* is essentially a punishment. Nevertheless, in *Smith & Nephew v. Convatec Technologies*, a post-expiry injunction was held to be compatible with the Enforcement Directive and certain factors were set out as to when such an injunction is appropriate.[137]

3.2.2 Long-arm injunctions

The courts have proved less amenable to the idea of injunctions covering foreign territories (so-called 'long-arm relief'). In *Kirin-Amgen Inc. v. Transkaryotic Therapies Inc. (No. 2)*,[138] the claimant owned a patent relating to the production of erythropoietin (EPO) (using

---

[130] *Spectravest v. Aperknit* [1988] FSR 161, 174; *Aktiebolaget Volvo v. Heritage* [2000] FSR 253, 265–6.

[131] *Coflexip v. Stolt Comex Seaway* [1999] FSR 473, 476; *Microsoft v. Plato Technology* [1999] FSR 834; *Beautimatic v. Mitchell Pharmaceuticals* [2000] FSR 267, 284.

[132] *Coflexip v. Stolt Comex Seaway* [2001] RPC (9) 182, 188, [18] (Aldous LJ).   [133] Ibid.

[134] Senior Courts Act 1981, s. 37.   [135] [2001] RPC 544.

[136] *Vestergaard Frandsen v. Bestnet Europe* [2010] FSR 2, [92]–[93].

[137] [2014] RPC (22) 619, [130]–[131]; overturned on other grounds [2015] RPC (32) 928.

[138] [2002] RPC (3) 203, [54], [55].

genetic engineering), which the defendant had been held to infringe. Although appeals were pending, the claimant sought to amend the relief that it was seeking to include an order restraining the defendant from using outside the United Kingdom 'UK-derived cells', which could produce EPO. Refusing leave to amend in this way, Neuberger J held that the court could not 'at least in the absence of very exceptional circumstances, grant an injunction in a patent infringement case, restraining a person's activities abroad, even if those activities were only possible as a result of an infringement in this jurisdiction'.[139] This view was informed by the terms of the statutory tort defined in section 60 of the Patents Act 1977, as well as a clear sense that acts occurring abroad were matters for foreign law. In another case, the Court of Session refused to grant an injunction relating to infringement of unregistered design right that extended beyond Scotland to cover England and Wales.[140]

3.2.3 Blocking injunctions

In Chapter 48, we examined the possibility of an intellectual property right holder bringing an action against 'intermediaries'—in particular, Internet access providers (IAPs) or Internet service providers (ISPs).[141] This power has been used by the courts to order ISPs to block customer access to websites, such as Newzbin and the Pirate Bay, as well as servers which are used for streaming services[142] containing or giving access to copyright material without the permission of the relevant rights holder.[143] It has also been used to prevent websites being used to sell counterfeit goods[144] and it would apply to other intellectual property rights.[145] In exercising the power, the Court needs to consider the impact on fundamental rights, including private life and freedom of expression of the defendant, the website operator, and its users.[146] In particular, careful assessments need to be made as to the costs to the parties,[147] and the effectiveness and proportionality of such orders. The question is 'context-sensitive' and the Court should not make an order 'without thorough

---

[139] Ibid., [54].   [140] *UVG Ambulances v. Auto Conversions* [2000] *ECDR* 479.

[141] See Chapter 48, section 3.6, pp. 1296–7; CDPA 1988, ss 97A, 191JA, as inserted by the Copyright and Related Rights Regulations 2003 (SI 2003/2498). See generally, J. Riordan, 'The Liability of Internet Intermediaries' (2016).

[142] *Football Association Premier League v. British Telecommunications* [2017] *ECDR* (17) 346; *UEFA v. British Telecommunications* [2017] *EWHC* 3414 (Ch).

[143] *Twentieth Century Fox Film Corp. v. British Telecommunications Plc* [2011] *RPC* (28) 855; *Twentieth Century Fox Film Corp. v. British Telecommunications plc (No. 2)* [2011] *EWHC* 2714 (Ch); *Dramatico Entertainment Ltd v. British Sky Broadcasting Ltd* [2012] 3 *CMLR* (14) 328; *Dramatico Entertainment Ltd v. British Sky Broadcasting Ltd (No. 2)* [2012] *RPC* (27) 665; *EMI Records Ltd v. British Sky Broadcasting Ltd* [2013] *FSR* (31) 708; *Football Association Premier League Ltd v. British Sky Broadcasting Ltd* [2013] *ECDR* (14) 377; *Paramount Home Entertainment International v. British Sky Broadcasting Ltd* [2014] *ECDR* (7) 101. See also M. Husovec, 'Injunctions against Innocent Third Parties: The Case of Website Blocking' [2013] *JIPITEC* (arguing that these remedies signify a transformation in the nature of remedies from tortious to *in rem*).

[144] *Cartier International AG v. British Sky Broadcasting* [2016] *ETMR* (23) 518, [80]–[81].

[145] Where the court has jurisdiction over a person (so-called *in personam* jurisdiction), it is possible that the effect might be worldwide. The English courts have yet to expressly consider jurisdictions with extraterritorial effect, but those in Canada have done so: *Google Inc. v. Equustek Solutions Inc* (2017) *SCC* 34.

[146] *UPC Telekabel Wien GmbH v. Constantin Film Verleih GmbH, Wega Filmproduktionsgesellschaft mbH*, Case C-314/12, EU:C:2014:192 (ECJ, Fourth Chamber), [30]–[40]; *EMI Records Ltd v. British Sky Broadcasting Ltd* [2013] *ECDR* (8) 224, [94].

[147] No orders have yet been made that impose significant costs on the website operators; rather, the technical measures have so far already been available, and the cost of compliance is modest: *Twentieth Century Fox Film Corp. v. British Telecommunications Plc* [2011] *RPC* (28) 855, [177], [200]; *Twentieth Century Fox Film Corp. v. British Telecommunications Plc* [2011] *EWHC* 2714 (Ch), [32]–[33] (initial cost would be £5,000, plus £100 for each notification); *EMI Records Ltd v. British Sky Broadcasting Ltd* [2013] *ECDR* (8) 224, [101].

consideration of whether it is appropriate to make an order in the light of the specific facts of each case'.[148]

As to effectiveness, it is acknowledged that blocking injunctions can be circumvented, but nevertheless it has been said on a number of occasions that they are 'reasonably effective' to protect the rights of persons, the communication of whose works are facilitated or promoted from specific websites.[149] Indeed, the 'ranking' of 'The Pirate Bay' site fell considerably after the Court issued the blocking order.[150]

As to proportionality, courts must take special care that they are not unduly inhibiting freedom of expression and access to information. In cases in which the only contents of a site are infringing materials that comprise complete copies, proportionality favours protecting a copyright owner's (property) rights. If, however, a site contains parodic versions of copyright material, or quantities of non-infringing speech (for example the political positions of The Pirate Party) a blocking injunction is unlikely to be appropriate: it would go beyond what was required to protect the property rights of the intellectual property owners and prejudice the legitimate interests of the public.

3.3 EUROPEAN REMEDIES FOR INFRINGEMENT OF EUROPEAN RIGHTS

One of the most important attributes of EU rights (trade marks, designs, etc.) is that they result in a single action in a designated European Union (Community) court, which is given jurisdiction in respect of all of the member states.[151] That court can award Europe-wide relief.[152] The principles governing such relief were explained by the Court of Justice in *DHL v. Chronopost*,[153] a trade mark case in which Chronopost sought to enforce its trade mark, web-shipping for logistics services, against the defendant. The Paris Court of Appeal had limited the injunction to France, and the Cour de Cassation referred questions to the Court as to the approach to be taken. The Court indicated that, given the unitary nature of a Community (EU) right, 'as a rule' the court should grant Europe-wide relief.[154] That general approach might be departed from, for example, either where the claimant chooses not to seek Europe-wide relief or where use of a particular sign in some part of the Union had no damaging effect on any of the functions of the mark.[155] This second situation was considered in *Combit Software v. Commit Business Solutions*,[156] where it was found that German speaking consumers would find the two marks to be confusing, but English speaking consumers would not. The Court of Justice held that while confusion in only one part of the European Union would infringe a European trade mark, in such cases, an injunction should only extend to the areas where there would be confusion

---

[148] *EMI Records Ltd v. British Sky Broadcasting Ltd* [2013] *ECDR* (8) 224, [100].

[149] *Football Association Premier League Ltd v. British Sky Broadcasting Ltd* [2013] *ECDR* (14) 377, [55(v)]; *EMI Records Ltd v. British Sky Broadcasting Ltd* [2013] *ECDR* (8) 224, [104]. Arnold J said that he was of the view that 'a blocking order may be justified even if it only prevents access by a minority of users': *Twentieth Century Fox Film Corp. v. British Telecommunications Plc* [2011] *RPC* (28) 855, [192]–[198].

[150] In *EMI Records Ltd v. British Sky Broadcasting Ltd* [2013] *ECDR* (8) 224, [106], Arnold J noted that the ranking of The Pirate Bay site by the web analyst Alexa fell from 43 to 293.

[151] CDR, Arts 1(3), 83; EUTMR, Art. 126.   [152] EUTMR, Art. 130.

[153] *DHL Express France SAS v. Chronopost SA*, Case C-235/09 [2011] *ECR* I–2801 (ECJ, Grand Chamber). For the response of the French Court, see [2013] *ETMR* (8) 109. See V. Barresi, 'The Scope of CTM Injunctions: Constitutional and Practical Aspects' [2013] *IPQ* 344; L. Zelechowski, 'Infringement of a Community Trade Mark: Between EU-wide and non-EU-wide Scope of Prohibitive Injunctions' [2013] *EIPR* 287.

[154] Case C-235/09 [2011] *ECR* I–2801, [44].   [155] Ibid., [46]–[48].

[156] Case C-223/15, EU:C:2016:719.

and should exclude those areas where there would be no confusion. It is unlikely that such a carve-out would be justifiable in relation to enforcement of Community design right.

4 DELIVERY UP

As an adjunct to a final injunction, a court may order the delivery up or destruction of infringing articles.[157] While the defendant usually chooses which option to take,[158] if they have shown themselves to be unreliable, the court may demand delivery up.[159] The long-standing inherent equitable jurisdiction to make an order for delivery up aims to ensure that a defendant is not tempted to put the infringing copies into circulation in breach of the injunction.[160] If the infringement relates to a separable part of an article, the order will be for delivery up of that part.[161] In the case of trade marks and passing off, if a sign can be removed, the court will order that this be done rather than order delivery up of the goods.[162] Normally, such an order cannot be made once the right has expired.[163] Moreover, the order does not extend to third parties who have come into possession of infringing articles.[164]

In the case of patents and trade marks, there is an express statutory power to order delivery up and/or obliteration.[165] The statutory provisions, like the inherent jurisdiction, provide that, in cases in which it appears 'likely that such an order would not be complied with', the court can order delivery up to the claimant (or some other person) for erasure or destruction.

A more significant statutory extension has been made available in respect of the infringements of trade marks, performers' rights, unregistered design right, or copyright.[166] More specifically, a statutory procedure exists for the delivery up of infringing goods, illicit recordings, infringing articles, and infringing copies for the purposes of 'destruction' or 'forfeiture'. The new Intellectual Property Act 2014 has made changes in relation to registered designs to allow for the forfeiture of infringing products or articles.[167]

---

[157] Note CDR, Art. 89(1)(b)–(c) (on finding of infringement of Community design right, the court should order seizure of infringing products and materials used to manufacture infringing goods).

[158] *Lady Anne Tennant v. Associated Newspapers* [1979] FSR 298, 305.

[159] *Industrial Furnaces v. Reaves* [1970] RPC 605.

[160] *Mergethaler Linotype v. Intertype* (1926) 43 RPC 381. In *Chappell v. Columbia Gramophone Co.* [1914] 2 Ch 745, the Court of Appeal utilized the remedy to prevent the defendant from benefiting from its infringement by making it deliver up sound recordings derived from infringing acts, even though these were not infringing articles. For discussion of the case, see *Union Carbide v. BP* [1998] FSR 1. And note *Merck Canada v. Sigma (No. 2)* [2013] RPC (2) 33, [24]; [2013] RPC (35) 925 (CA) [94] ('retention of unlawfully imported stock would give it an unwarranted advantage when the SPC expires').

[161] *Mergethaler Linotype v. Intertype* (1926) 43 RPC 381; cf. *Industrial Furnaces* [1970] RPC 605.

[162] *Warwick Tyre v. New Motor and General Rubber* (1910) 27 RPC 161, 171.

[163] *Leggatt v. Hoods Darts Accessories* (1950) 67 RPC 134, 143; cf. *Merck Canada v. Sigma (No. 2)* [2013] RPC (2) 33, [24], [2013] RPC (35) 925, [94] (delivery up of imported goods that infringed a supplementary protection even though the defendant proposed to market them after the claimant's rights had expired).

[164] *Knowles v. John Bennett* (1895) 12 RPC 137, 148 (shipper).

[165] PA 1977, s. 61(1)(b); TMA 1994, s. 15; RDA, ss 24C and 24D; Community Design Regulations 2005, regs 1B and 1C (as amended by SI 2006/1208).

[166] Respectively: TMA 1994, s. 16; CDPA 1988, ss 195, 199 (criminal proceedings); CDPA 1988, ss 195, 199 (criminal proceedings); CDPA 1988, ss 204, 230, 231. For application to SPCs, see *Merck Canada v. Sigma Pharmaceuticals (No. 2)* [2013] RPC (2) 33, [19]–[21].

[167] IP Act 2014, s. 13, introducing RDA 1949, ss 35ZC, 35ZD.

In most cases, the power is available only where a person has infringing goods (etc.) in their possession, custody, or control in the course of business.[168] The power also applies where a person has in their possession anything specifically designed or adapted for making infringing goods (etc.), knowing or having reason to believe that it has been or is to be used to make infringing goods (etc.). The court may order delivery up to the right owner (or some other person), pending a further order either for destruction *or forfeiture* as the court thinks fit. The ability to order forfeiture goes well beyond the inherent power, which is confined to delivery for destruction.[169]

In considering whether the discretionary order for destruction or forfeiture is appropriate, the court is directed to take into account 'whether other remedies available in an action for infringement would be adequate to compensate the right owner and protect their interests'.[170] As yet, there is little indication as to when a forfeiture order will be made.[171] However, one obvious case in which the other remedies might be inadequate is where the defendant is bankrupt or unable to pay damages. Because the order might affect the rights of third parties having interests in the goods, third parties may appear in proceedings.[172]

5 DAMAGES

The most common financial remedy[173] for infringement of intellectual property rights is an award of damages.[174] The damages recoverable are the same as with other torts: the aim is to restore the victim to the position in which they would have been had no wrong been committed; the aim is not to punish the defendant.[175]

In some cases, damages will not be available where the defendant's infringement was innocent. More specifically, damages will not be awarded in an action for infringement of a registered design or a patent where the defendant proves that, at the date of infringement, they were not aware and had no reasonable grounds for supposing that the design was registered or the patent existed.[176] In either case, a person will not be deemed to have been aware or have had reasonable grounds for supposing that the design was registered or patent existed merely because the article is marked 'registered' or 'patented'.[177] This

---

[168] TMA 1994, s. 16; CDPA 1988, ss 99, 108 (criminal proceedings); CDPA 1988, ss 195, 199 (criminal proceedings); CDPA 1988, ss 204, 230, 231.

[169] But cf. TMA 1994, s. 97(6) (forfeiture of 'infringing goods, materials or articles' acquired in the course of investigating or prosecuting 'an offence' requires destruction).

[170] CDPA 1988, ss 204(2), 231(2).

[171] *Ocular Sciences v. Aspect Vision Care* [1997] *RPC* 289, 407 (Laddie J).

[172] TMA 1994, s. 19(3); *Miller Brewing Co. v. The Mersey Docks & Harbour Co.* [2004] *FSR* (5) 81.

[173] See C. Scott, 'Damages inquires and accounts of profits in the IPEC' (2016) *EIPR* 273.

[174] PA 1977, s. 61(1)(c); CDPA 1988, ss 96(2), 191(3), 229(2); RDA 1949, s. 24(2); TMA 1994, s. 14(2): PVA 1997, s. 13(2); CPVR, Art. 94. In relation to breach of confidence there is some doubt whether the remedy is damages or equitable compensation (see Gurry (2012), [19.23–19.24]). For a review of the differing approaches to damages across the European Union see N. Fox et al., 'Accounting for Differences: Damages and Profits in European Patent Infringement' (2015) *EIPR* 566.

[175] *General Tire & Rubber v. Firestone Tyre & Rubber* [1976] *RPC* 197, 214.

[176] RDA 1949, s. 24B; PA 1977, s. 62(1); CDPA 1988, ss 191J, 233.

[177] It is not enough to mark goods with the words 'patented'. In order to fix a defendant with knowledge or reasonable grounds, the 'patent number must be given': *Schenck Rotec v. Universal Balancing* [2012] *EWHC* 1920 (Pat), [209] (noting that PA 1977, s. 62(1), was compliant with Enforcement Dir., Art. 13).

does not apply, however, where the marking is accompanied by the registration, a patent number,[178] or a web address that provides relevant patent or registered design numbers.[179]

In the case of copyright, rights in performances, and unregistered design right, the legislation provides that damages will not be awarded in an action for infringement where it is shown that, at the time of the infringement, the defendant did not know, and had no reason to believe, that copyright (etc.) subsisted in the work to which the action relates.[180] In certain cases of infringement of performers' rights by a person who 'innocently acquired' an illicit recording, the only remedy available is damages 'not exceeding a reasonable royalty in respect of the act complained of'.[181] In contrast, in the case of trade mark infringement and passing off,[182] it seems that damages will be awarded even against an innocent defendant. It is difficult to conceive of any rational basis for such inconsistent approaches.

The financial remedies that are available in an intellectual property action (both damages and account of profits) need to be viewed in light of the Intellectual Property (Enforcement, etc.) Regulations 2006.[183] Regulation 3, which applies to cases of knowing infringement, explains that damages should reflect the 'actual prejudice' suffered by the claimant. Regulation 3(3) elaborates that 'all appropriate aspects shall be taken into account', including 'the negative economic consequences, including any lost profits,[184] which the claimant has suffered, and any unfair profits made by the defendant', as well as 'elements other than economic factors, including the moral prejudice caused to the claimant by the infringement'.[185] Alternatively, 'where appropriate', damages may be awarded 'on the basis of royalties or fees which would have been due had the defendant obtained a licence'. It has been suggested that this rule may create more flexibility in fashioning a remedy than might be the case under the common law and the rules of equity.[186] In any event, there are three ways in which damages can be calculated: (a) damages for 'lost sales'; (b) damages for 'lost licences' and (c) damages under the 'user principle'. Each of these methods of calculation will be considered in turn.

5.1 LOST SALES

The first way in which damages may be calculated is by reference to the sales that the claimant lost as a result of the competing sales of infringing goods (or services) made by the defendant. For example, if, prior to an infringement, the patentee of a widget was selling 200 widgets per year, but sold only 150 widgets after the infringement (the defendant selling 50 widgets), the damages are likely to be calculated as the profits that the patentee would have made on the 50 widgets. Clearly, this method of calculation[187] will be used only where the intellectual property right owner exploits the right by manufacturing

---

[178] *Lancer Boss v. Henley Forklift Co.* [1974] FSR 14; *Texas Iron Works Inc.'s Patent* [2000] RPC 207.

[179] PA 1977, s. 62(1A); RDA 1949, s 24B(2A) (inserted by the Digital Economy Act 2017, s. 36).

[180] CDPA 1988, ss 97(1), 191J, 233(1); *Nottinghamshire Healthcare v. News Group* [2002] RPC 962, [52] (a very limited defence); *Badge Sales* [2006] FSR 1; *Kohler Mira v. Bristan Group* [2015] FSR (9) 167, [18].

[181] CDPA 1988, s. 184(2).

[182] *Gillette UK v. Edenwest* [1994] RPC 279, 291–4; cf. *Marengo v. Daily Sketch* (1948) RPC 242 (leaving undecided whether there could be damages for innocent passing off); C. Best, 'Damages against the Innocent Infringer in Passing off and Trade Mark Infringement' (1985) 1 *IPJ* 205.

[183] SI 2006/1028 (effective for infringements occurring after 29 April 2006).

[184] As to the effect of this sort of provision, see P. Johnson, '"Damages" in European Law and the Traditional Accounts of Profit' (2013) 3 *QMJIP* 296.

[185] A claimant can recover for both economic harm and moral prejudice: *Christian Liffers v. Producciones Mandarina*, Case C-99/15, EU:C:2016:173. [186] *Aldi Stores v. Dunnes Stores* [2016] IEHC 256, [85].

[187] A summary of principles is set out in *Fabio v. LPC Group* [2012] RPC (30) 885, [69]–[70].

goods. Although the courts have indicated that proof of lost profits need not be minutely accurate, a claimant will often encounter difficulties.[188] In particular, problems may arise in relation to causation.[189] For example, where an infringer sells an infringing product at a cost that is less than that of the claimant's product, it will often be difficult to be certain that, absent infringement, sales that went to the defendant would have gone to the claimant.[190] Other difficulties may arise, including: discovering how many infringing items the defendant sold; establishing that the claimant's expected sales figures were justified; proving that the claimant would have had sufficient stock to cover the defendant's sales; or proving that the defendant's sales would not have gone to a competitor of the claimant (rather than the claimant).[191] In certain circumstances, the courts have got over these difficulties by presuming that the claimant would have made the sales.[192]

5.2 LOST LICENCES

Where a claimant usually exploits the intellectual property by way of granting licences, the court may make an award on a royalty basis—that is, the court can award the claimant a notional fee for each infringing act.[193] Here, the damages compensate for the misappropriation and represent the fee that the defendant would have paid for a licence for the use of the rights that they infringed. Such a royalty will be easy to determine where a claimant has been in the practice of granting licences: it will be the 'going rate'. In these cases, the claimant will need to show that the circumstances in which the going rate was being paid by others are the same or comparable with those in which the intellectual property right holder and infringer are assumed to strike their bargain.[194] Importantly, it is not necessary to actually show that a licence has been offered at the particular licence fee, rather that the fee is that which would have been charged if a licence had been sought. However, where *no* licence would ever have been granted then the user principle is more appropriate.

As the court is trying to work out what the licence fee would be on the market, the defendant's own financial position is not regarded as a relevant circumstance, and so it is not open to the defendant to argue that they could not have afforded to pay a reasonable rate.[195]

5.3 'USER PRINCIPLE'

Where the claimant was not in in the practice of granting licences, the court needs to find another way of assessing damages. It does this by the so called 'user principle'.[196] Essentially, this principle works on the basis of what licence fee would be charged had the

---

[188] *Watson Laidlaw* (1914) 31 *RPC* 104, 113.

[189] See *Coflexip SA v. Stolt Offshore MS* [2003] *FSR* (41) 728 (considering problems of causation in relation to defendant's acquisition of contracts, in execution of which it used claimant's patented process).

[190] *Columbia Pictures Industries v. Robinson* [1988] FSR 531, 535. See also *Prior v. Lansdowne Press* [1977] *RPC* 511.   [191] *Cow v. Cannon Rubber Manufacturers* [1961] RPC 236, 240.

[192] *Catnic Components v. Hill & Smith* [1983] FSR 512, 524; cf. *Blayney (t/a Aardvark Jewellery) v. Clogau St Davids Gold Mines* [2003] *FSR* (19) 360 (CA).

[193] Where the claimant has granted licences at a royalty rate, it is 'almost a rule of law' to assess damages as the amount that the defendant infringer would have had to pay for the number of infringing articles at the royalty rate had they had a licence: *Meters v. Metropolitan Gas Meters* (1910) 28 *RPC* 157, 164; *Catnic Components* [1983] *FSR* 512, 518. But the 'lost profits' approach is preferred in cases of trade marks and passing off: *Games Workshop* [1993] FSR 704, 713–14; *Dormeuil Frères v. Feraglow* [1990] *RPC* 449.

[194] *General Tire v. Firestone* [1976] RPC 197, 213.

[195] *Irvine v. TalkSport Ltd* [2003] *FSR* 619 (CA), [106] (Jonathan Parker LJ).

[196] It takes its name from Nicholas LJ in *Stoke-on-Trent City Council v. W & J Wass* [1988] 1 *WLR* 1406, 1416.

parties come to a deal (the so-called willing licensee/willing licensor).[197] This requires evidence to be led as to what the licence fee would be on the relevant market—that is, the goal is to establish what terms would have been reached between the actual licensor and the actual licensee, bearing in mind their strengths and weaknesses and the market as it exists, on the assumption that each was willing to negotiate with the other.[198] The process of calculation is 'intended to represent a robust and inexpensive cutting of a Gordian knot'.[199] In contrast to damages in relation to lost licences, the damages are based on the market price and so the availability of cheaper alternatives may be relevant evidence.[200] In other respects the two methods of assessing damages are very similar. It also does not matter that the intellectual property owner would not actually have granted a licence under any circumstances.[201]

Relationship between different methods of calculating damages Where more than one of the three avenues suggests itself as appropriate, the choice between the 'lost profits' and 'royalty' approaches to the calculation of damages is left to the claimant (even in 'licence of right cases').[202] In some circumstances, it may be appropriate to choose more than one avenue. For example, if a defendant sold 25 infringing works and the claimant would have made only 15 sales, then the claimant may claim for lost profits on those 15 sales plus a royalty in relation to the other 10 sales.[203]

5.4 DAMAGES IN BREACH OF CONFIDENCE CASES

It has been said that the measure of damages for breach of confidence should be tortious, reflecting loss to the claimant.[204] In *Seager v. Copydex (No. 2)*,[205] the Court of Appeal held that damages were to be assessed by reference to the market value of the information.[206] For some information, the sort of information which could be obtained by a competent consultant, the damages should be the fee a consultant would charge. Where the information is akin to an invention then it might be that a user-principle-based assessment is appropriate. In very rare cases it may be that a capitalized royalty is appropriate. Another possible way of assessing damages is the price a person would be willing to accept to loosen the obligation of confidence (so-called *Wrotham Park* damages[207]). In other words, the damages should take into account the profits made and use the information to determine

[197] See *Henderson v. All Around the World* [2014] *EWHC* 3087 (IPEC), [18]–[19]; *General Tire v. Firestone* [1976] *RPC* 197, 225; *Ludlow v. Williams* [2002] *FSR* (57) 868, 889–90 (court should err on side of generosity); cf. *SPE International v. Professional Preparation Contractors* [2002] *EWHC* 881 (Ch), [87] (Rimer J) (court should err on side of under-compensation).   [198] *General Tire v. Firestone* [1976] *RPC* 197, 221.

[199] *Douglas v. Hello! (No. 8)* [2004] *EMLR* 13, [61]; *Force India Formula One Team Ltd v. 1 Malaysia Racing Team Sdn Bhd* [2012] *RPC* (29) 757, [376] (Arnold J) (breach of confidence); *32 Red plc v. William Hill (International) Ltd* [2013] *EWHC* 815 (Ch) (award of £150,000 in trade mark case).

[200] See *Absolute Lofts South West London Ltd v. Artisan Home* [2015] *EWHC* 2608 (IPEC) (permission to appeal denied after oral hearing: [2016] *EWCA Civ* 1225).

[201] *32Red v. WHG* [2013] *EWHC* 815 (Ch), [29].

[202] *Gerber Garment Technology v. Lectra Systems* [1997] *RPC* 443 (CA), 486; *Douglas v. Hello! (No. 8)* [2004] *EMLR* (13) 223, [13].

[203] *Watson Laidlaw* (1914) 31 *RPC* 104; *Catnic v. Hill & Smith* [1983] *FSR* 512, 522; *Gerber Garment Technology v. Lectra Systems* [1997] *RPC* 443 (CA), 486; *Blayney* [2003] *FSR* (19) 360 (CA).

[204] *Indata Equipment Supplies v. ACL* [1998] *FSR* 248, 261, 264. See Gurry (2012), ch. 19.

[205] [1967] 2 *All ER* 415.

[206] *Talbot v. GTV* [1981] *RPC* 1, 22; *Aquaculture v. New Zealand Mussel* (1985) 5 *IPR* 353 (NZ High Court), [1990] 3 *NZLR* 299 (CANZ); *Gorne v. Scales* [2006] *EWCA Civ* 311, [74].

[207] Based on *Wrotham Park Estate v. Parkside Homes* [1974] 1 *WLR* 798.

what a person would be willing to accept.[208] Other techniques for the assessment of damages are by way of fair remuneration for a licence, loss of profit that the claimant would have gained,[209] or depreciation in the value of the right to have the information kept confidential.

5.5 DAMAGES IN MISUSE OF PRIVATE INFORMATION CASES

The assessment of damages in relation to the misuse of private information is different from that used for assessing other intellectual property matters (including breach of confidence) and the case law very limited.[210] The leading cases relate to phone hacking—the practice of unauthorized access to a famous person's mailbox—by journalists to obtain stories for newspapers. In *Gulati and ors v. MGN*,[211] Mann J set out the principles which were to be applied. He made it clear that the subject matter of the information is relevant to the damage suffered: medical and financial information may attract a higher degree of privacy than a photograph at a social meeting. Another relevant factor is the effect on the victim of the disclosure—is it transitory or life-changing—and finally it may be relevant that the victim is particularly sensitive to the disclosure of the information.[212] Furthermore, the Court of Appeal held that damages could be awarded to compensate a claimant for loss of control of the private information as well as for any distress caused.[213] In that case, damages were assessed for each article published (or where the hack was not used a payment for that as well) which ranged from £1,000 to £50,000. As the awards were cumulative[214] this meant that some claimants received very large awards.

5.6 SECONDARY LOSSES

Although the sum awarded is usually calculated on the basis of the loss to the value of the intellectual property right as a chose in action,[215] other secondary losses may also be recovered.[216] These are sometimes referred to as 'consequential' or 'parasitic' damages. The ability to claim such losses may be particularly important where goods incorporating intellectual property are marketed at low profit margins and the profits are largely made from the sale of associated goods or services (so called 'convoyed goods'). Such losses can be claimed if they are foreseeable, caused by the wrong,[217] and not excluded from recovery

---

[208] See *Vercoe v. Rutland Funds* [2010] *EWHC* 424; *Force India Formula One Team Limited v. 1 Malaysia Racing Team Sdn Bhd* [2012] *RPC* (29) 757, [386] and not dissented from by Court of Appeal: [2013] *RPC* (36) 947, [97].

[209] *Dawson & Mason Ltd v. Potter* [1986] 1 *All ER* 418; *Vestergaard v. Bestnet* [2013] *EWCA Civ* 428, [20]–[27] (Floyd LJ); *Flogas Britain Ltd v. Calor Gas Ltd* [2013] *EWHC* 3060 (Ch) (Proudman J); *Cadbury v. FBI* [2000] *FSR* 49 (SCC), 1, 513–14, 517; *Talbot v. GTV* [1981] *RPC* 1, 31–3.

[210] In *Mosley v. News Group Newspapers* [2008] *EMLR* (20) 679, a life-changing revelation was made about the claimant (namely that he had attended sadomasochistic sex parties) and he was awarded what was said to be the top of the scale for a single disclosure (£60,000). Comparisons were drawn with the damages for really serious psychiatric harm.   [211] [2017] *QB* 149.

[212] *Gulati v. MGN* [2012] *FSR* (12) 366, [229] approved by the Court of Appeal [2017] *QB* 149, [74] subject to a minor qualification.

[213] Ibid., [39]–[49]; The Australian Courts have also granted damages for non-economic loss in relation to a breach of confidence for personal information: see *Wilson v. Ferguson* [2015] *WASC* 15.

[214] The Court of Appeal took the view that the additional distress from repeated hacking might lessen rather than increase: [2017] *QB* 149, [75].

[215] *Sutherland Publishing Co. v. Caxton Publishing* [1936] 1 *All ER* 177, 180.

[216] But cf. *Catnic v. Hill & Smith* [1983] *FSR* 512, 534.

[217] *Work Model Enterprises v. Ecosystem & Clix Interiors* [1996] *FSR* 356, 362; see also *Alfrank Designs v. Exclusive (UK) Limited* [2015] *EWHC* 1372 (IPEC), [32] (statistical correlation is not enough).

by public policy.[218] A conceivable, but remote, result could not be deemed to be reasonably foreseeable. For example, where a seller loses the sale of a patented table they will also lose some sales of unpatented accompanying chairs.[219] Applying these principles, the courts have held, for example, that a copyright infringer would not be liable for cash-flow consequences for the copyright owner,[220] nor would an infringer be liable for losses on sales of the claimant's goods as a result of the defendant's distribution of an infringing catalogue.[221]

5.7 EXEMPLARY (PUNATIVE) DAMAGES

According to the House of Lords in *Rookes v. Barnard*,[222] a court may award exemplary damages where, in cynical disregard of a claimant's rights, a defendant infringed those rights, calculating that they would make a profit that would exceed the compensation payable to the claimant. The award is proper 'whenever it is necessary to teach a wrongdoer that a tort does not pay'.[223] The House of Lords made it clear in *Kuddus v. Chief Constable of Leicestershire Constabulary*[224] that the availability of exemplary damages is not confined (as had been previously thought) to causes of action in which the remedy had been recognized prior to *Rookes v. Barnard*.[225] In general, exemplary damages would be contrary to the principle that it is immaterial whether the infringement has been particularly advantageous (or useless in commercial terms)[226] and so such damages will rarely be awarded.[227] The situation in relation to breach of confidence is the same and exemplary damages are not available[228] (unlike, say, for libel claims).[229] There is an additional statutory regime for certain media claims, including misuse of private of private information, to award exemplary damages and aggravated damages[230] against relevant publishers[231] where the claim relates to news-related material.[232] The provision essentially covers claims against newspaper and magazine publishers (both print and online) who are not members of an approved regulator (and none of the major press organizations are members). As of 1 May 2018, no awards have been made under the statutory regime.

---

[218] *Gerber Garment Technology* [1997] *RPC* 443, 452. In *Kuwait Airways* [2002] 2 *AC* 833, [69]–[73], Lord Nicholls treated causation as encompassing two stages: a 'but for' test; and an enquiry into whether the loss was one for which the defendant 'ought fairly or reasonably or justly to be held liable'. The latter includes aspects of foreseeability and public policy, although normally evokes 'an immediate intuitive response'.

[219] *Alfrank Designs v. Exclusive (UK) Ltd* [2015] *EWHC* 1372 (IPEC), [34]–[35].

[220] *Claydon Architectural Metalwork v. Higgins & Sons* [1997] *FSR* 475.

[221] *Work Model Enterprises* [1996] *FSR* 396; *Paterson Zochonis v. Merfarken Packaging* [1983] *FSR* 273, 295; *Dyson v. Hoover* [2001] *RPC* (27) 544, 572.   [222] [1964] *AC* 1129, 1226–7.

[223] See Law Commission, *Aggravated, Exemplary and Restitutionary Damages* (1997) Law Com No. 247, [1.110].   [224] [2002] *AC* 122.

[225] The Court of Justice has also held that punitive damages are not contrary to the Enforcement Dir.: *Stowarzyszenie 'Oławska Telewizja Kablowa' v. Stowarzyszenie Filmowców Polskich*, Case C-367/15, EU:C:2017:36.   [226] *United Horse Shoe and Nail v. Stewart* (1888) 13 *App Cas* 401, 413 (HL).

[227] *Morton-Norwich Products v. Intercen (No. 2)* [1981] *FSR* 337, 353.

[228] This is not the case in other common law jurisdictions: see Gurry (2012), [19.35–19.40].

[229] *Mosley v. News Group Newspapers* [2008] *EMLR* (20) 679. The position in relation to misuse of private information has been clouded by Lord Toulson in his dissent in *PJS v. Newsgroup Newspapers* [2016] *AC* 1081, [92] suggesting the matter should be revisited.   [230] Crime and Courts Act 2013, ss 34, 36, and 39.

[231] See definition, Crime and Courts Act 2013, s. 41.

[232] See definition, Crime and Courts Act 2013, s. 42(7).

5.8 ADDITIONAL STATUTORY DAMAGES

In relation to copyright and rights in performances,[233] as well as publication right, database right, and unregistered design right,[234] a court may consider all of the circumstances—particularly the flagrancy of the infringement and any benefit accruing to the defendant[235]—and award such additional damages as the justice of the case requires.[236] The nature of additional damages is unclear. While it has been suggested that the purpose of additional damages is to be a deterrent[237] it is less clear whether there are other elements such as whether they are compensatory, exemplary, or restitutionary.[238] However, it has been held that their award is the exception rather than the rule, and a claimant needs to show special circumstances that would justify the imposition of an additional financial penalty.[239] Ideally, this should be done by full pleading, and the determination as to whether such damages should be awarded may be dealt with by the trial judge or the inquiry.[240] However, if there are issues on which evidence has not been given during the trial that might be relevant, the court will probably leave the assessment of additional damages to the inquiry stage.[241]

Factors that may be relevant in deciding to award additional damages include: (i) whether the defendant acted deliberately or 'couldn't care less';[242] (ii) whether the defendant was acting on legal advice;[243] (iii) whether the defendant was merely out to make money or had other motives;[244] (iv) whether the claimant and defendant were involved in negotiating a licence;[245] (v) the impact of the defendant's action on the claimant (such as disruption or upset);[246] (vi) whether there are any other mitigating circumstances;[247] and (vii) possibly the means of the defendant.[248] Additional damages are not available in addition to an account of profits.[249]

5.9 DAMAGES FOR 'MORAL PREJUDICE'

In addition to the economic harm caused by intellectual property infringement, it is also possible for a claimant to seek damages for so called 'moral prejudice'. The recovery of

---

[233] CDPA 1988, ss 97(2), 191J (i.e. the performers' property rights, but not for infringement of the non-property or recording rights).

[234] Copyright and Related Rights Regulations 1996 (SI 1996/2967), reg. 17(1); Copyright and Rights in Databases Regulations 1997 (SI 1997/3032), reg. 23; CDPA 1988, s. 229(3).

[235] *Ravenscroft v. Herbert* [1980] *RPC* 193, 208 (benefit implies a pecuniary advantage in excess of damages that they would otherwise have to pay).

[236] CDPA 1988, s. 97. This amended and replaced CA 1956, s. 17(3), which had confined such damages to circumstances under which 'effective relief would not otherwise be available'. As to the relationship between the Enforcement Dir. and additional damages, see *Absolute Lofts South West London Ltd v. Artisan Home Improvements Limited* [2015] *EWHC* 2608 (IPEC), [36]–[43].

[237] *Phonographic Performance v. Hagan* [2017] *FSR* (24) 511, [24]–[26].

[238] *Redrow Homes* [1998] 1 *All ER* 385, 391, 393; *Ludlow v. Williams* [2002] *FSR* (57) 868, 891–2; *Nottinghamshire Healthcare v. News Group Newspapers* [2002] *RPC* (49) 962 [48]–[51].

[239] *Pro Sieben, Media AG v. Carlton UK Television* [1998] *FSR* 43, 61 (Laddie J).

[240] *ZYX Music GmbH v. King* [1997] 2 *All ER* 129 (CA), 149.

[241] *O'Mara Books v. Express Newspapers* [1999] *FSR* 49, 57–8.

[242] *Ravenscroft* [1980] *RPC* 193, 208; *Fulton v. Totes Isotoner* [2003] *RPC* (16) 499, [116] (flagrancy implies something approaching premeditated commercial amorality); *Nottinghamshire Healthcare* [2002] *RPC* (49) 962, [52]–[53]; *Flogas Britain Ltd v. Calor Gas Ltd* [2014] *FSR* (34) 757, [136] ('scandalous and deceitful conduct').   [243] *Pro Sieben Media v. Carlton UK Television* [1998] *FSR* 43, 61–2.

[244] *ZYX Music GmbH v. King* [1995] *FSR* 566, 587, aff'd [1997] 2 *All ER* 129 (CA).

[245] *Ludlow v. Williams* [2002] *FSR* (57) 868.

[246] *Nottinghamshire Healthcare* [2002] *RPC* (49) 962, [55], [60].   [247] Such as an apology: ibid., [60].

[248] *O'Mara Books v. Express Newspapers* [1999] *FSR* 49, 57–8.

[249] *Redrow Homes* [1998] 1 *All ER* 385.

damages under this head originates from Article 13 of the Enforcement Directive[250] and while it is clear that moral prejudice is not an economic harm[251] it is not clear how such damages would be assessed. In *Henderson v. All Around the World*,[252] Judge Hacon took the view that moral prejudice entitled recovery in relation to mental distress, injury to feelings, and humiliation[253] and he went on to suggest such damages might be limited to situations where there was limited economic harm.[254] Since that decision, however, the Court of Justice has indicated that moral prejudice and economic harm are both recoverable. [255]

5.10 DAMAGES IN LIEU OF AN INJUNCTION

Where an injunction is refused,[256] damages may be awarded in lieu.[257] In contrast with the normal situation, where damages relate to past acts, this requires that the court must estimate damages prospectively. The conventional view is that this must be done once and for all.[258] The quantum is calculated by reference to the usual standard (what would be agreed by a willing licensor and licensee),[259] although there are clear problems with calculating not only the future value of a licence, but also precisely estimating what the defendant will do. The courts have contemplated the possibility of either a lump sum or an ongoing royalty.[260]

6 ACCOUNT OF PROFITS

In relation to most intellectual property rights,[261] a claimant may elect for an 'account of profits' instead of claiming damages.[262] An account of profits is an equitable remedy that deprives the defendant of any profits made as a result of their infringement. Because account of profits has its origins in the Court of Chancery, it has been treated as an alternative financial remedy to damages.[263] It cannot be claimed in addition to damages, even where the loss to the claimant and profit to the defendant are unrelated so that, when combined, the two remedies would not result

---

[250] It has been held that damages for moral prejudice might be available as part of the reasonable compensation owed in relation to published European trade mark applications under EUTMR, Art. 9(3): see *Nikolajeva*, Case C-280/15, EU:C:2016:467.

[251] *Kohler Mira Ltd v. Bristan Group Ltd* [2015] *FSR* (9) 167, [60].

[252] [2014] *EWHC* 3087 (IPEC), [85]–[95].   [253] Ibid., [94].

[254] Ibid., [94]; in some instances this has been awarded under additional damages in the past: see *Nichols Advanced Vehicle Systems Inc. v. Rees* [1979] *RPC* 127, 140.

[255] *Christian Liffers v. Producciones Mandarina*, Case C-99/15, EU:C:2016:173.

[256] See section 3, pp. 1334–9.

[257] For a discussion of the history, see R. Garcia Pérez, 'Injunctions in Intellectual Property Cases: What is the Power of the Courts?' (2016) 20 *IPQ* 87.

[258] *Jaggard v. Sawyer* [1995] 1 *WLR* 269, 280–1, 285–6; *HTC v. Nokia* [2014] *RPC* (30) 865 (Arnold J).

[259] These have been called 'negotiating damages': see *Force India Formula One Team Ltd v. 1 Malaysia Racing Team Sdn Bhd* [2012] *RPC* (29) 757, [383]–[386]. For discussion in the US context, see T. Gomez-Arostegui, 'Prospective Compensation in Lieu of a Final Injunction in Patent and Copyright Cases' (2010) 78 *Fordham L Rev* 1661.   [260] *HTC v. Nokia* [2014] *RPC* (30) 865, [14] (Arnold J).

[261] For registered design right, see RDA 1949, s. 24A.

[262] PA 1977, s. 61(1)(d); CDPA 1988, s. 96(2); TMA 1994, s. 14(2); *My Kinda Town v. Soll* [1982] *FSR* 147 (passing off); *Peter Pan v. Corsets Silhouette* [1963] 3 *All ER* 402 (breach of confidence); *Attorney-General v. Blake* [2000] 3 *WLR* 625, 641 (Lord Nicholls) (contractual breach of confidence).

[263] For the history, see L. Bently and C. Mitchell, 'Combining Money Awards for Patent Infringement: *Spring Form Inc. v. Toy Brokers Ltd*' [2003] *Restitution L Rev* 79.

in double liability.[264] Usually, election is solely a matter for the claimant, but because the remedy for account of profits is equitable (and therefore discretionary), the court may refuse it.[265] Where there is more than one claimant (for example a proprietor and exclusive licensee) or more than one defendant, it has been held that a single election must be made: as regards a single course of action, a claimant may not have an account against one defendant and damages against another.[266] The profits to be sought would be those actually made by the defendant through the infringement,[267] or if there are multiple defendants, the profit that each and every one of them has made.[268] If appropriate, the court will apportion a part of the total profit as that attributable to the infringement.[269]

In the case of patents, passing off, registered designs, and trade marks,[270] no order of an account will be made where a defendant acted innocently—that is, no order will be made if, at the date of infringement, the defendant was not aware and had no reasonable grounds for supposing that the intangible property right existed. For some time, it was thought that the decision to elect for an account of profits had to be made at the time of judgment. However, since a claimant would not necessarily have sufficient information on which to base the election, greater flexibility has been introduced so that the election should optimally take place only when the claimant can make an informed decision. Accordingly, the defendant may be ordered to undertake additional disclosure so as to facilitate this decision.[271]

6.1 CALCULATION OF PROFITS

The main difficulty raised by the remedy of an account concerns the way in which the profits are calculated. In part, this is because it will be very rare for the infringement of the intellectual property right to be the single cause of any profit. It is more likely that only part of the product sold by the defendant will have been infringing. In such cases, the court must try to determine what profits have been caused, in a legal sense, by those acts.[272] Under what is called the 'incremental approach', it has been suggested that, to determine the profits payable, the courts should compare the profit that the defendant made with that which they would have made had they not used the infringing material

---

[264] *Neilson v. Betts* (1871) *LR* 5 *HL* 1; *Redrow Homes* [1998] 1 *All ER* 385 (HL), 393 (explaining requirement on basis that the two remedies are inconsistent); *Hollister Inc. v. Medik Ostomy Supplies* [2013] *FSR* (24) 502, [56] (explaining election by reference to two very different 'bases' of remedies); PA 1977, s. 61(2). But cf. *Watson Laidlaw* (1914) 31 *RPC* 104, 119 (explaining the requirement of an election as a mechanism to prevent overlapping).

[265] *Hollister Inc. v. Medik Ostomy Supplies* [2013] *FSR* (24) 502, [55] (Kitchin LJ); *Van Zeller v. Mason* (1907) 25 *RPC* 37, 41; *Electrolux v. Electrix* (1953) 70 *RPC* 158.

[266] *Spring Form Inc. v. Toy Brokers* [2002] *FSR* (17) 276, 288, 290.

[267] CDPA 1988, s. 96(2). There is no defence of innocence: *Wienerworld Ltd v. Vision Video Ltd* [1998] *FSR* 832. If there are multiple claimants (such as a copyright owner and their licensee) or multiple defendants, the one election applies to all: *Spring Form Inc. v. Toy Brokers* [2002] *FSR* (17) 276 (a patent case).

[268] *Hotel Cipriani SRL v. Cipriani (Grosvenor Street) Ltd* [2010] *EWHC* 628 (Ch), [7].

[269] *Potton v. Yorkclose* [1990] *FSR* 11. See also *Cala Homes (South) v. Alfred McAlpine Homes East (No. 2)* [1996] *FSR* 36, 44; *Celanese International Corp. v. BP Chemicals Ltd* [1999] *RPC* 203, 225.

[270] PA 1977, s. 62(1); RDA 1949, s. 24B; *Conran v. Mean Fiddler* [1997] *FSR* 856, 861; *Gillette v. Edenwest* [1994] *RPC* 279, 290; *Edelsten v. Edelsten* (1863) 1 *De G & Sm* 18, 46 *ER* 72; *Spalding v. Gamage* (1915) 32 *RPC* 273, 283.

[271] *Island Records v. Tring International* [1995] *FSR* 560; *Brugger v. Medicaid* [1996] *FSR* 362, 364.

[272] *Celanese v. BP* [1999] *RPC* 203; *Union Carbide v. BP* [1998] *FSR* 1, 6. In a case of parallel importation in which the act would have been legitimate had notice been given to the trade mark proprietor, the same principles apply: *Hollister Inc. v. Medik Ostomy Supplies* [2013] *FSR* (24) 502, [73].

or process, the 'increment' being the profits attributable to the infringement.[273] However, this approach has been rejected on a number of occasions in favour of a less refined approach, under which the courts simply apportion the total net profits.[274]

With the 'apportionment approach', the court first ascertains the total net profits made by the defendant from the activity in question.[275] In calculating net profits, the court will deduct relevant expenses such as costs, overheads, and taxes[276] from the revenue received in relation to the infringing project. The court then attempts to locate a principled means for dividing up the profits, so as to define the portion attributable to the infringement. This is not a mathematical exercise,[277] but one of reasonable approximation.[278] So if the infringing process is one of five steps in the production of a particular product, in the absence of evidence suggesting otherwise, one fifth of the profits from the sale of the product would be attributed to the infringement. It has been said that the proportion of profits attributable to the infringing activity might best be determined by looking at the corresponding costs of the process of production.[279] In some—probably rare—circumstances, the court will ask itself what the importance is of the infringing activity or part to the ultimate profits.[280] As with damages, where there are secondary losses (i.e. lost profit on goods which would usually be conveyed with the infringing article) some of that profit can be apportioned towards the infringement.[281]

As with damages, where licences of right are made available, the amount to be rendered in an account of profits is not to exceed double the amount that would have been payable by the defendant as a licensee if such a licence on those terms had been granted before the earliest infringement.[282]

7 PUBLICITY ORDERS

It is very common for a successful party in litigation to advertise their victory, often as a warning to others who might be thinking of infringing. However, as a result of implementation of the Enforcement Directive,[283] an unsuccessful party can now be ordered to give notice of their opponent's success.[284] In *Samsung Electronics (UK) Ltd v. Apple Inc,,*[285] the

---

[273] *Siddell v. Vickers* (1888) 5 *RPC* 416; *My Kinda Town v. Soll* [1983] *RPC* 15.

[274] *Potton v. Yorkclose* [1990] *FSR* 11 (incremental approach is suitable only where the infringement was in the process of producing the work); *Cala Homes v. McAlpine* [1996] *FSR* 36, 44; *Celanese v. BP* [1999] *RPC* 203. See T. Moody-Stuart, 'Quantum in Accounts of Profits: The Acid Test' [1999] *EIPR* 147.

[275] *Potton v. Yorkclose* [1990] *FSR* 11.

[276] Overheads may be deducted if they can be shown to be properly attributable to the activity: *Hollister Inc. v. Medik Ostomy Supplies* [2012] *EWCA Civ* 1419, [2013] *FSR* (24) 502, 529, [85]; *Nigel Woolley and Timesource Ltd v. UP Global Sourcing UK Ltd* [2014] *EWHC* 493 (Ch).

[277] *Design & Display Ltd v. Ooo Abbott and anor* [2016] *EWCA Civ* 95, [53] (mathematic precision is impossible).   [278] *My Kinda Town v. Soll* [1993] *RPC* 15.

[279] *Potton v. Yorkclose* [1990] *FSR* 11, 18.

[280] *Celanese v. BP* [1999] *RPC* 203, 225; cf. *Potton v. Yorkclose* [1990] *FSR* 11, 18.

[281] *Design & Display Ltd v. Ooo Abbott and anor* [2016] *EWCA Civ* 95, [36].

[282] PA 1977, s. 46(3)(c); CDPA 1988, ss 98(1)(a), 191K, 239(1)(c).

[283] Stickers to inform purchasers had been ordered before this Directive: see *Sony v. Saray* [1983] *FSR* 302, 307–8.

[284] The Enforcement Dir. requires this only for a successful holder of an intellectual property right, but the general power under the Senior Courts Act 1981, s. 37, means that a parallel power is available for the benefit of a successful defendant: *Samsung Electronics (UK) Ltd v. Apple Inc.* [2013] *FSR* (9) 134, [75].

[285] Ibid., [69]. See further *ITV v. TV Catchup* [2013] *EWHC* 3638 (Ch), [5] (Floyd LJ); *Brundle v. Perry* [2014] *EWHC* 979 (IPEC), [18]–[24] (Judge Hacon).

Court of Appeal was faced with an application for an order for dissemination of judgment by Samsung, the successful defendant in design litigation over so-called 'tablet' designs of smartphones and other portable electronic devices. The Court indicated that an order was normally appropriate only where there was commercial uncertainty in the market-place that there is a 'real need to dispel' or to act as a 'supplementary deterrent to future infringers'.[286] Although Jacob LJ thought that such orders should not be granted as a matter of course, such an order was justified on the extraordinary facts of the *Samsung* case. What was extraordinary was that, after the finding of non-infringement in the English proceedings, Apple had secured Community-wide injunctive relief from a German court in proceedings that appeared to be a breach of the Community Design Regulation. Given the 'massive publicity' attendant on the German order, it was appropriate that Apple be required to dispel the 'real commercial uncertainty' surrounding the legitimacy of the Samsung product.[287] Apple was required within seven days to give notice of the judgment for one month on the home page of its website with a link to the judgment itself,[288] and to publish advertisements to similar effect in a number of national newspapers and relevant magazines. Apple's implementation of the order, however, was 'lackadaisical' and lacking 'in integrity', and after a further hearing the original order was replaced with one that was to be on the home page for longer (with Samsung being awarded its costs on an indemnity basis).[289]

8 CONSTRUCTIVE TRUSTS

In English law, a constructive trust cannot be imposed purely on the basis of unjust enrichment (a remedial constructive trust).[290] It has been considered on occasion whether a constructive trust can arise over property which results from infringement or over the profits of information disclosed in breach of confidence. In *Twentieth Century Fox v. Harris*,[291] it was unsuccessfully argued that a copyright owner has a proprietary claim over the fruits of copyright infringement by way of a constructive trust. In contrast, in relation to the fruits of the misuse of confidential information there have been numerous cases where such a trust has been said to be possible.[292] Importantly, such a constructive trust is not a remedy, but exists automatically by operation of law (an institutional constructive trust).

The first suggestion that a constructive trust may be available in relation to the activities of an errant confidant appeared in the *Spycatcher* case, in which various of the Law Lords suggested that Peter Wright held his copyright in the book on constructive trust for the Crown.[293] Although emanating from the House of Lords, these views were *obiter*, were expressed without the benefit of any argument from Wright, and might easily have been interpreted as being confined to the narrow situation in which the confidant was also a fiduciary. However, in *LAC Minerals*,[294] the majority in the Supreme Court of

---

[286] *Samsung Electronics (UK) Ltd v. Apple Inc.* [2012] *EWCA Civ* 1339, [2013] *FSR* (9) 134, [71].

[287] Ibid., [83].   [288] Ibid., [87].   [289] [2013] *FSR* (10) 166, [7], [32].

[290] *Westdeutsche Bank v. Islington LBC* [1996] *AC* 669.   [291] [2014] *FSR* (7) 128.

[292] See also Tang Hang Wu, 'Confidence and the Constructive Trust' (2003) 23 *Legal Studies* 135; M. Conaglen, 'Thinking about Proprietary Remedies for Breach of Confidence' [2008] *IPQ* 82.

[293] *Attorney General v. Guardian (No. 2)* [1990] *AC* 109, 139 (Scott J), 211 (Dillon LJ), 286 (Lord Goff).

[294] [1990] *FSR* 441, 445, 452. Sopinka J, dissenting, recognized that the remedy would be available in very special circumstances: ibid., 497.

Canada held that it was appropriate to impose a constructive trust over land that the defendant had bought after he had been told in confidence that it might be gold-bearing. In *Ocular Sciences v. Aspect Vision*,[295] Laddie J accepted that a constructive trust might be available where there was an existing fiduciary relationship and that there would usually be such a relationship where there existed a confidential obligation. The Vice Chancellor supported the principle of a constructive trust existing over the profits of misuse of confidential information in *A-G v. Blake*,[296] another case about spy memoirs, but the matter was not considered by the House of Lords on appeal.[297] It has been argued that there are advantages in constructive trusts coming into being over such profits as it will provide a mechanism to trace elicit profits as well as providing some sort of remedy where the information is no longer confidential.

9 TIME LIMITS

Delay in bringing proceedings may lead to an action for infringement being barred, under either statutory provisions or equitable principles. An action for infringement of copyright, patent, or trade mark must be commenced within six years of the wrongful act.[298]

Where a claimant expressly or impliedly represents that the defendant's conduct is non-infringing, they will thereafter be estopped from asserting their right. Where the claimant knows of their right against the defendant and that the defendant mistakenly believes that they are entitled to do what they are doing, yet the claimant stands by without asserting their right, they will be taken to have acquiesced in the wrong.[299]

10 CRIMINAL REMEDIES

Until recently, there has been little demand for criminal sanctions to protect intellectual property rights.[300] In part, this has been because the rights holders have preferred the lower standard of proof associated with the civil action. Recently, there has been increased interest in the use of criminal liabilities and sanctions, especially in the case of piracy and counterfeiting.[301] Criminal prosecution is attractive because of the publicity that a criminal trial can attract and the deterrent effect of the sanction.[302] There are four

---

[295] [1997] *RPC* 289, 413–14.   [296] [1997] *Ch* 84, 96.

[297] *A-G v. Blake* [2001] *AC* 268; although *Snepp v. United States*, 444 US 507 (1980), which had similar facts, was disapproved of (at 287–8).   [298] Limitation Act 1980, s. 2.

[299] See *Film Investors Overseas Services SA v. Home Video Channel* [1997] *EMLR* 347, 365; *Farmers Build v. Carrier Bulk Materials Handling* [1999] *RPC* 461, 486–9.

[300] For a useful collection of essays on the topic, see C. Geiger (ed.), *Criminal Enforcement of Intellectual Property* (2012).

[301] The government has funded the creation of the City of London Police Intellectual Property Crime Unit (PIPCU), dedicated to tackling serious organized intellectual property crime online. It has already targeted operators of websites that facilitate infringements. For surveys of activity, see IP Crime Group, *IP Crime Annual Report* 2011–12 (2013), available online at http://webarchive.nationalarchives.gov.uk/20140603094038/http://www.ipo.gov.uk/ipcreport11.pdf.

[302] In addition, criminal prosecutions are likely to be quicker than civil actions, and a losing prosecutor may avoid paying costs: Prosecution of Offences Act 1985, ss 16–18. TRIPS, Art. 61, requires members to provide for criminal procedures and penalties at least in cases of wilful trade mark counterfeiting and copyright piracy 'on a commercial scale'. On the international regime, see H. Grosse Ruse-Khan, 'Criminal Enforcement and International IP Law', in C. Geiger (ed.), *Criminal Enforcement of Intellectual Property* (2012), ch. 9.

categories of crime that concern us here: (i) crimes relating to copyright and trade mark infringements under the relevant statutes; (ii) the common law crime of conspiracy to defraud (and the statutory crime of obtaining services dishonestly); (iii) the crimes created by the Consumer Protection from Unfair Trading Regulations 2008; and (iv) finally, special crimes created by the intellectual property statutes that are intended to protect the integrity of intellectual property registers.

If a right owner chooses to pursue a criminal prosecution, they can do so by three routes. First, other than in Scotland,[303] the right owner or a representative[304] may commence criminal proceedings by 'laying an information' (or complaint) at a magistrates' court,[305] on the basis of which the court will issue a summons.[306] There is no requirement that a private prosecution is brought in the public interest.[307] Alternatively, the claimant may seek the assistance of the police or trading standards. There are particular advantages in involving the police as they may obtain a search warrant and police action carries a significant social stigma. However, if a charge is made by the police, the prosecution must be conducted by the Crown Prosecution Service (CPS);[308] it cannot then be handed back to the claimant.[309] This may be a dangerous tactic, because the CPS might decide not to prosecute.[310] The right holder may also enlist the help of administrative authorities, in particular trading standards departments. These authorities are obliged to enforce the Consumer Protection from Unfair Trading Regulations 2008, the criminal provisions of the Trade Marks Act 1994, and the Copyright, Designs and Patents Act 1988 (for copyright and performances);[311] there is no obligation in relation to the offences under the Registered Designs Act 1949.

10.1 STATUTORY INTELLECTUAL PROPERTY OFFENCES

In order to buttress the civil remedies and help to combat piracy, bootlegging, and counterfeiting, a number of statutory criminal offences have been introduced in relation to copyright, performers' rights, trade mark law, and registered designs. The number of people convicted of trade mark offences in England and Wales declined from 920 in 2006 to 490 in 2015; and for copyright offences the number has ranged from 249 in 2006, rising to 563 offences in 2009, before tailing off to 69 in 2015. There is no record of offences in relation to registered designs yet.[312]

---

[303] Private prosecutions are possible in Scotland through an application for a bill of criminal letters, but these are incredibly rare across all offences (a few times over the last hundred years).

[304] For example, a representative organization such as the Federation against Copyright Theft (FACT), the Federation against Software Theft (FAST), or a collecting society. See *Thames & Hudson v. Designs & Artists Copyright Society* [1995] *FSR* 153; *Scopelight Ltd v. Chief Constable of Northumbria* [2010] *QB* 438 (CA) (referring to role of FACT and determining that property seized by the Police under PACE 1984, s. 22, could be retained for use by FACT in a private prosecution).

[305] There should be separate 'information' for each individual copyright work: *R v. Ward* [1988] *Crim LR* 57.

[306] Any citizen may bring a private prosecution: Prosecution of Offences Act 1985, s. 6(1). See G. Harbottle, 'Criminal Remedies for Copyright and Performers' Rights Infringement under the Copyright, Designs and Patents Act 1988' [1994] *Ent L Rev* 12.

[307] *R (on the application of Ewing) v. Davis* [2007] 1 *WLR* 3223.

[308] In Scotland, by the Crown Office or by the Procurators Fiscal Service (PFS).

[309] See *R v. Ealing Justices, ex parte Dixon* [1989] 2 *All ER* 1050 (proceedings begun by police could not be prosecuted by FACT); cf. *R v. Croydon Justices, ex parte Holmberg* (1992) 157 *JP* 277.

[310] The Director of Public Prosecutions is under a duty to prosecute certain offences and may (in its discretion) prosecute others: Prosecution of Offences Act 1985, ss 3, 6(2).

[311] CDPA 1988, s. 107A, introduced by the Criminal Justice and Public Order Act 1994, s. 165 (effective 6 April 2007). In Northern Ireland, enforcement is the responsibility of the Department of Enterprise, Trade and Investment: CDPA 1988, s. 107A(3). A similar enforcement provision exists with respect to performances. No such duty or authority applies in relation to proceedings in Scotland.

[312] The figures are taken from the IP Crime Group, *IP Crime Report 2015/16* (2016), 12.

There are no criminal sanctions for the infringement of patents or for unregistered designs. On convicting a defendant for criminal copyright infringement, trade mark infringement, or registered design infringement the courts also have the power to order delivery up of infringing copies or goods, and to make certain compensation and confiscation orders.[313] Moreover, criminal proceedings on indictment is not subject to any statute of limitations.[314]

10.1.1 Offences in relation to copyright and performers rights

In relation to copyright, criminal liability is not confined to those normally considered to be pirates;[315] rather, criminal infringement covers most acts of primary and secondary infringement,[316] although in all cases criminal relief requires proof of knowledge or reason to know that copyright was being or would be infringed.[317] A successful criminal prosecution can result either in a fine or imprisonment, and the maximum penalty is ten years' imprisonment.[318] In sentencing, the courts have indicated that they consider copyright infringement to be an offence of 'real dishonesty' equivalent to cheating or stealing.[319] Conscious of the prevalence of such offences and the difficulties of detection,[320] the courts have emphasized that criminal copyright infringement is to be regarded as a very serious matter. The Court of Appeal gave some guidelines on sentencing in *R v. Evans*.[321] Of the

---

[313] Powers of Criminal Courts Act 1973, ss 35, 43 (property deprivation order); Magistrates' Courts Act 1980, s. 40 (power to award compensation up to £5,000); Criminal Justice Act 1988, as amended by the Proceeds of Crime Act 1995 and Criminal Justice Act 1988 (Confiscation Orders) Order 1995 (SI 1995/3145) (court may make confiscation order under Powers of Criminal Courts Act 1973, s. 43, in relation to offences under TMA 1994, s. 92, and CDPA 1988, s. 107); RDA 1949, ss 24C–D.

[314] In relation to summary only offences: see the Magistrates' Courts Act 1980, s. 127 (six month time limit).

[315] *Thames & Hudson v. DACS* [1995] *FSR* 153. On pirates, see D. Halbert, 'Intellectual Property Piracy: The Narrative Construction of Deviance' (1997) 10 *IJSL* 55; A. Johns, *Piracy: The Intellectual Property Wars from Gutenberg to Gates* (2009).

[316] CDPA 1988, ss 107–10. Note also CDPA 1988, ss 297 (fraudulently receiving programmes), 297A (making, etc. unauthorized decoders), 296ZB (circumventing technological measures), 198 (illicit recordings of performances); Rel. Rights Regs, reg. 17(1), (3) (applying offences to publication right but with modified penalties). There are no criminal offences in relation to the database right.

[317] CDPA 1988, ss 107–10. The presumptions of authorship, etc., do not apply, and problems of proving copyright ownership may arise: *Musa v. Le Maitre* [1987] *FSR* 272.

[318] CDPA 1988, s. 107(4), as amended by the Copyright and Trade Marks (Offences and Enforcement) Act 2002. Note that the maximum period for communicating the work to the public is two years: CDPA 1988, s. 107(2A), (4A) until 1 October 2017 when s. 32 of the Digital Economy Act 2017 increased it to ten years. A maximum of three months applies to many of the other offences, such as showing a film, or playing a sound recording in public: CDPA 1988, s. 107(3), (5), as amended by the Copyright, Designs and Patents Act 1988 (Amendment) Regulations 2010 (SI 2010/2694) (reducing the term from six months).

[319] *R v. Carter* [1983] *FSR* 303; *R v. Ian Dukett* [1998] 2 *Cr App R* (S) 59; *R v. Roy John Gibbons* (1995) 16 *Cr App R* (S) 398.

[320] *R v. Paul Godfrey Kemp* (1995) 16 *Cr App R* (S) 941; *R v. Roy John Gibbons* (1995) 16 *Cr App R* (S) 398.

[321] [2017] *1 Cr App R* (S) 56, [22] (12 months); also see *R v. Paul Godfrey Kemp* (1995) 16 *Cr App R* (S) 941 (six months). See also *R v. Lloyd* (1997) 2 *Cr App R* (S) 151 (six months); *R v. Gross* (1996) 2 *Cr App R* 189 (nine months); *R v. Roy John Gibbons* (1995) 16 *Cr App R* (S) 398 (seven months). But cf. *R v. Nimley* [2011] 1 *Cr App R* (S) 120 (six-month sentence inappropriate where defendant made recordings of four films in cinema and uploaded onto website for kudos, rather than money); *R v. Lewis* (1997) 1 *Cr App R* (S) 208 (sentence of 12 months for a person who ran a computer bulletin board for swapping more than 1,000 computer games); *R v. Kirkwood* (2006) 2 *Cr App R* (S) 39 (small-scale operation copying and distributing music, films, and video games, which developed from defendant's hobby, justified sentence of 21 months because infringement extended for three years); *R v. Alphor Holborough* [2002] *EWCA Crim* 2631 (CA) (three years' imprisonment for conspiracy to defraud based on sale of some 20,000 devices for over £400,000); *R v. Harold Christopher Carey* (1999) 1 *Cr App R* (S) 322 (four years for sale of some 650,000 smart cards); *R v. Maxwell King* (2001) 2 *Cr App R* (S) 28 (150 hours of community service for inciting the supply of 20 devices to enable unauthorized access to cable television contrary to the Computer Misuse Act 1990, s. 3).

seven points raised some are particularly worthy of note, namely that deterrent sentence is appropriate and, importantly, except in the case of amateur infringement, minor or short lived infringements, immediate custody is likely to be appropriate for the illegal distribution of infringing works.

Criminal offences also exist to protect performers.[322] These largely correspond to civil infringements and deal with the making, importing, and commercial dealing in illicit recordings, without sufficient consent. 'Sufficient consent' is defined, in relation to performers' rights, as the consent of the performers or owner of the performers' property rights, and in relation to recording rights, as the consent of the performer or the owner of the recording rights. Criminal liability is also imposed for infringement by making available a work, for example on the Internet, where the act took place in the course of business or 'to such an extent as to affect prejudicially the owner of the making available right'.[323] Liability depends on proof of knowledge or reason to believe that the recordings are 'illicit'.[324] The penalties are equivalent to those for infringement of copyright, so that a person convicted on indictment may receive a prison sentence of up to ten years.[325]

10.1.2 Offences in relation to trade marks

Special criminal provisions also exist to deal with trade mark infringement.[326] In particular, section 92 of the Trade Marks Act 1994 states that a person commits an offence if they apply to goods or their packaging a sign 'identical to, or likely to be mistaken for, a registered trade mark' without the consent of the proprietor and 'with a view to gain for himself or another, or with intent to cause loss to another'.[327] It is now clear that this requires a showing of trade mark use[328] and, furthermore, that it criminalizes parallel traded goods.[329] The section goes on to create further offences that capture parties who deal commercially in goods bearing such a sign or are otherwise involved in ancillary or preliminary acts that enable such exploitation.[330] The requirement that the sign be 'identical to, or likely to be mistaken for, a registered trade mark' uses language that differs from that used in civil infringement.[331] Moreover, it is an offence to apply the sign (etc.) to goods for which it is registered or to other goods only 'if the trade mark has a reputation in the UK, and the use of the sign takes . . . unfair advantage of; or is . . . detrimental to, the distinctive character or repute of the mark'.[332] It is a defence to a criminal prosecution to show that the accused 'believed on reasonable grounds that the use of the sign in the manner in which it was used . . . was not an infringement of the registered trade mark'.[333] As Lord Nicholls has explained, '[t]hose who act honestly and reasonably are not to be visited with criminal sanctions'.[334] Thus the defence applies equally to a situation in which a

---

[322] CDPA 1988, s. 198.   [323] CDPA 1988, s. 198(1A), (5A) (with a possible sentence of two years).

[324] On what is acceptable proof, see *Radford v. Kent County Council* (1998) 162 JP 697 (QBD).

[325] CDPA 1988, s. 198(5), for making, importing, and distributing illicit recordings (as amended by the Copyright, etc, and Trade Marks (Enforcement and Offences) Act 2002); other offences carry a maximum of six months' imprisonment.

[326] *S v. London Borough of Havering* [2003] 1 Cr App R 35, [10] (explaining rationale for criminal protection).

[327] On the meaning of 'with a view to' in TMA 1994, s. 92(1)(c), see *R v. Zaman* [2003] FSR (13) 230.

[328] *R v. Johnstone* [2003] FSR (42) 748.   [329] *R v. C and ors* [2017] 1 WLR 3006.

[330] But not importing: on which, see BMR, Art. 30, and section 2, pp. 1317–20.

[331] TMA 1994, s. 10(2). Note also BMR, Art. 2(5)a, referring to an identical sign or one 'which cannot be distinguished in its essential aspects from such trade mark' in the definition of counterfeit goods.

[332] TMA 1994, s. 92(4).   [333] TMA 1994, s. 92(5).

[334] *R v. Johnstone* [2003] FSR (42) 748, 763, [43].

defendant did not believe the mark was registered and that in which a defendant believed a mark was registered, but that the act was non-infringing.[335] This could be a belief that the use fell outside the scope of protection (for example that it was not in the course of trade), or that the use fell within an exception (for example of legitimate referential use). It is for the defendant to establish on the balance of probabilities an affirmative case of reasonable belief.[336]

The criminal penalties for infringement of trade marks are similar to those for criminal copyright infringement. A summary conviction can result in a custodial sentence of six months or a fine of up to £5,000; a conviction on indictment can result in a fine or imprisonment for up to ten years. The courts have not been swayed by pleas that counterfeiting has not misled anyone[337] and have repeatedly emphasized that trade mark infringement is 'properly a criminal offence' akin to stealing goodwill.[338] Consequently, it has been said that it is important that sentences be serious enough to operate as a deterrent.[339] The punishment will depend largely on the gravity and the scale of the infringement, and the persistence of the defendant.[340] As to gravity, the courts have treated the counterfeiting of pharmaceuticals as particularly heinous, because of the potential effects on public safety.[341] As to scale, the Court of Appeal has held that three years was an appropriate sentence for applying false trade marks to perfume such as Chanel no. 5, on a scale of 5,000–10,000 bottles per week.[342] With regard to persistence, an isolated lapse by a generally honest businessman will merely warrant a fine,[343] but even small-scale dealing in counterfeit watches has been held to warrant a prison sentence of three months.[344]

10.1.3 Offences in relation to registered designs

The introduction of criminal sanctions for registered[345] design infringement was very controversial. As is often the case, it is argued that criminal sanctions will increase the effectiveness of the law. The new provisions introduced criminal sanctions for the intentional copying of a registered design so as to make a product 'exactly to' or 'with features that differ only in immaterial details from' the design.[346] The new provisions are restricted to activities carried out in the course of business where the alleged infringer knew or had reason to believe that the design was registered, and they did not have the appropriate consent.[347] A defence applies where the alleged infringer reasonably believed that the design in question was invalid, for example if it was widely known in a design field.

---

[335] Ibid.

[336] Ibid., 764, [46]. This is a legal or persuasive burden, but was deemed by the House of Lords to be a justified derogation from the presumption of innocence contained in Art. 6(2) ECHR. Lord Nicholls found there to be 'compelling reasons' why the legislation should place the persuasive burden on the accused: ibid., 766, [52]–[53]. [337] *R v. Priestly* (1996) 2 *Cr App R* (S) 144.

[338] *R v. Bhad* (1999) 2 *Cr App R* (S) 139. [339] *R v. Adam* (1998) 2 *Cr App R* (S) 403.

[340] *R v. Kelly* (1996) 1 *Cr App R* (S) 61 (defendant's persistence in dishonest conduct justified imprisonment).

[341] *R v. Yanko* (1996) 1 *Cr App R* (S) 217 (four-five years for counterfeiting of medicinal products—steroids—under signs syntex and anapolon was not excessive).

[342] *R v. Priestly* (1996) 2 *Cr App R* (S) 144. See also *R v. Ansari, Horner, Ling & Ansari* (2000) 15 *Cr App R* (S) 94 (three years); *R v. Brayford* [2011] 1 *Cr App R* (S) 107 (two years not 'out of kilter' for importing 25,000 kilos of washing powder and 2,875 boxes bearing Persil marks, which would likely produce a profit of £20,000). [343] *R v. Bhad* (1999) 2 *Cr App R* (S) 139.

[344] *R v. Kelly* (1996) 1 *Cr App R* (S) 61 (possession of 30 watches).

[345] The criminal sanctions do not apply to unregistered designs.

[346] These are, for indictments, imprisonment for a term not exceeding ten years, a fine, or both: RDA 1949, s.35ZA(8). For summary convictions in England, Wales, and Northern Ireland, imprisonment up to six months, a fine, or both (in Scotland, imprisonment is up to 12 months, a fine, or both): RDA 1949, s. 35ZA(8)(b)–(c). [347] IP Act 2014, s. 13, introduces a new RDA 1949, s. 35ZA.

10.1.4 Confidential information

In English law, taking confidential information is not theft.[348] Section 1 of the Theft Act 1968 defines 'theft' as the 'dishonest appropriation of property belonging to another with the intention of permanently depriving the other of it'. While section 4 says that property includes 'other intangible property', it has been held in a number of cases that, for these purposes, information is not intangible property. In *Oxford v. Moss*,[349] an undergraduate at Liverpool University obtained the proofs of an examination paper before the exam. After reading the exam, the student returned the paper, but 'retained' the information. Smith J held that this did not amount to theft: information was not property and there was no intention to deprive the university of the information. While it might be possible in certain situations to treat specific breaches of confidence as carrying criminal liability on other grounds, these all carry limitations.[350]

A number of calls have been made for the criminalization of the act of misappropriating trade secrets[351] and, in the 1990s, the Law Commission issued a Consultation Paper.[352] The paper provisionally concluded that the case for criminal offences of trade secret misuse is a strong one, basing that view primarily on the close analogy between trade secrets and property 'in the strict sense', and on the economic importance of protecting business investment.[353] The paper reviewed the practical problems of legislating— in particular, difficulties associated with reaching a satisfactory definition of the concept of 'trade secrets'. The Law Commission said that it wanted to ensure that all misuses of trade secrets that were criminalized would be breaches of confidence at civil law, but made it clear that it did not wish to criminalize all acts that would incur civil liability under the present law. Views were sought, in particular, about the definition of 'trade secret', whether errant employees should be subject to criminal liability, and the appropriate scope of a public interest defence.[354] The consultation exercise has been abandoned and the Law Commission is no longer pursuing the question.

10.2 CONSPIRACY TO DEFRAUD

In some cases, the general common law crime of 'conspiracy to defraud' may be used to protect intellectual property rights.[355] This crime will be committed where someone dishonestly tries to obtain an economic advantage without the need to show that anyone was deceived.[356] It will be useful only in cases of organized piracy, in which there is some

---

[348] See A. Coleman, *The Legal Protection of Trade Secrets* (1992), ch. 7; it was made criminal in New Zealand with little engagement: A Kingsbury, 'Trade Secret Crime in New Zealand: What was the Problem and is Criminalization the Solution?' (2015) *EIPR* 147.   [349] (1979) 68 *Cr App R* 183.

[350] If two people steal a trade secret, this may constitute conspiracy to defraud: *R v. Lloyd* [1985] *QB* 29. Other criminal charges may be available under the Bribery Act 2010, s. 2, or the Computer Misuse Act 1990, which creates the offence of gaining unauthorized access to data held on a computer.

[351] A. Coleman, *The Legal Protection of Trade Secrets* (1992), 93; it is criminalized in the United States: US Economic Espionage Act of 1996.

[352] Law Commission, *Legislating the Criminal Code: Misuse of Trade Secrets* (November 1997) LCCP150. For a review, see J. Hull, 'Stealing Secrets: A Review of the Law Commission's Consultation Paper on the Misuse of Trade Secrets' (1998) 4 *IPQ* 422.   [353] Law Commission, op. cit., [3.1].

[354] For the Law Commission's provisional proposal, outlining specific purposes for disclosure that are in the public interest, but without prejudice to the generality of the defence, see ibid., [6.54].

[355] See *Attorney General's Guidelines for Prosecutors on the Use of the common law offence of conspiracy to defraud* (2007), Part B. However, generally prosecution is now under the Fraud Act 2006.

[356] *Scott v. Metropolitan Police Commissioner* [1975] *AC* 819; *R v. Bridgeman & Butt* [1996] *FSR* 538. In *Scott*, the defendant bribed cinema employees to hand over films so that they could be surreptitiously copied. The House of Lords held that this amounted to a conspiracy to defraud the owners of the copyright.

agreement between the parties. One advantage of bringing a charge of common law conspiracy to defraud is that the courts' discretion to imprison or fine an adult offender is unlimited.[357] Two statutory offences, carrying on a business for a fraudulent purpose and obtaining services dishonestly, introduced in sections 9 and 11 of the Fraud Act 2006, are also being used as a basis to prosecute persons involved in intellectual property infringement. The former provision was successfully invoked in *R v. Thornton* where the defendant made and sold counterfeit CDs and DVDs on a market stall. He was sentenced to two and a half years' imprisonment.[358]

10.3 CONSUMER PROTECTION

The Consumer Protection from Unfair Trading Regulations 2008,[359] which implement the 2005 EU Unfair Commercial Practices Directive,[360] impose criminal penalties where businesses mislead consumers (by act or omission), for example as to the main characteristics of a product (including the geographical or commercial origin of the product). These provisions thus apply to many cases of wrongful use of registered trade marks and passing off. Brand owners had hoped that the regulations, as proposed, would give private businesses the right to bring private civil actions (as Ireland has chosen to do), but the government declined to do so,[361] confining liability to criminal proceedings and leaving enforcement to the Competition and Markets Authority (CMA) and trading standards officers.[362] Trading standards officers are employed by local authorities (which are under a statutory duty to enforce the Act). The officers are empowered to make test purchases, enter premises, and inspect and seize goods. They do not have power to arrest offenders.[363] The authorities also bring proceedings, but if prosecution is not thought to be appropriate, they have power to issue 'formal cautions'. Offences under the 2008 Regulations carry a maximum of two years' imprisonment.[364]

---

[357] See Criminal Law Act 1977, s. 5. See *R v. Dowd* [2005] *EWCA Crim* 3582 (defendant, member of an Internet group that hacked into technologically protected copyright software, was not motivated by malice, but seriously damaged commercial interests; sentenced to 12 months). But see *R v. Holborough* [2002] *EWCA Crim* 2631 (taking into account the statutory limitation on sentencing of the specific offence—i.e. selling unauthorized decoders contrary to CDPA 1988, s. 297A, then subject to a maximum of two years' imprisonment—when reducing the defendant's sentence for conspiracy to defraud to three years).

[358] Noted in IP Crime Group, *IP Crime Report 2015/16* (2016), 60.

[359] SI 2008/1277 (repealing and replacing much of the Trade Descriptions Act 1968.) See further OFT, *Consumer Protection from Unfair Trading* (2008).

[360] Directive 2005/29/EC of 11 May 2005 concerning unfair business-to-consumer commercial practices in the internal market and amending Council Directive 84/450/EEC, Directives 97/7/EC, 98/27/EC and 2002/65/EC of the European Parliament and of the Council and Regulation (EC) No 2006/2004 of the European Parliament and of the Council [2005] *OJ L* 149/22.

[361] The Department of Business, Innovation and Skills issued a consultation to introduce such a right: *Consumer Protection: Review of the Enforcement Provisions of the Consumer Protection from Unfair Trading Regulations 2008 in respect of copycat packaging* (BIS/14/724). The government indicated that it would not be doing anything following this consultation: see Written Statement by Nick Boles, 13 October 2015 (HCWS232). [362] Consumer Protection from Unfair Trading Regulations 2008, reg. 19.

[363] Consumer Protection from Unfair Trading Regulations 2008, regs 20–22.

[364] Consumer Protection from Unfair Trading Regulations 2008, reg. 13(b). See *R v. Ahmadi* (1993) 15 *Cr App R* (S) 254 (six months for supplying recycled toner cartridges); *R v. Shekhar Kumar* (1992) 13 *Cr App R* (S) 498 (hirer of 26 counterfeit videos fined £5,000).

10.4 PROTECTING REGISTRATION

A number of criminal sanctions exist that aim to maintain the veracity of the registration regimes. In particular, it is an offence to make false entries on the register[365] and to make unauthorized claims to rights.[366] An interesting variation is contained in section 201 of the Copyright, Designs and Patents Act 1988, which makes it an offence for a person 'falsely to represent that he is authorised by another to give consent . . . in relation to a performance unless he believes on reasonable grounds that he is so authorised'. There is no criminal offence of wrongly representing that a work is protected by copyright, although a person who obtains benefits from such a false representation may well be guilty of an offence under section 2 of the Fraud Act 2006.

---

[365] PA 1977, s. 109; TMA 1994, s. 59; RDA 1949, s. 34.
[366] See, e.g., PA 1977, s. 110; TMA 1994, s. 60; Trade Marks (International Registration) Order 2008 (SI 2008/2206), art. 3; Community Trade Mark Regulations 2006 (SI 2006/1027), reg. 9; RDA 1949, s. 35; Community Design Regulations 2005 (SI 2005/2339), reg. 3.

INDEX